STATS™ Hockey Handbook 1999-2000

STATS, Inc.

Published by STATS Publishing
A division of Sports Team Analysis & Tracking Systems, Inc.

I dedicate this book to my nephew,
Michael Steven Janosi,
who, like the new millennium,
has no bounds on his future.

—Michael L. Janosi

Cover by Michael Parapetti

Cover photo by Layne Murdoch/Bruce Bennett Studios

First Edition: August, 1999

Printed in the United States of America

ISBN 1-884064-68-X

Acknowledgments

Numerous people contributed to the fourth edition of the STATS *Hockey Handbook*, and we'd like to thank them:

John Dewan, STATS' Chief Executive Officer, continues to make us the No. 1 source for sports statistics. Our President, Alan Leib, will help us grow in the years to come. John and Alan are assisted by Jennifer Manicki. Sue Dewan is in charge of Research & Development/Special Projects. Her team includes Bob Meyerhoff and Jim Osborne.

Vice President of Publishing Products Don Zminda oversees the department that produces this and all of our other sports titles. Don's department includes Jim Callis, Jim Henzler, Chuck Miller and yours truly. Jim Henzler handled all of the programming assignments for this book, while Chuck was responsible for design and layout. Thanks also to Thom Henninger, who assisted with stat-checking and also penned the introduction.

Spreading the word about this book and everything else in the world of STATS Publishing falls to Marc Elman and his team. Marc works with Mike Janosi, Antoinette Kelly, Michael Parapetti (who designed the cover) and Mike Sarkis.

The wonderful statistics in this book were gathered by the Data Collection Department headed by Allan Spear. His staff consists of Jeremy Alpert, Michelle Blanco, Jeff Chernow, Brian Cousins, Ryan Ellis, Mike Hammer, Robert Klein, Dan Matern, John Sasman, Jeff Schinski, Matt Senter, Bill Stephens and Joe Stillwell. Together, they oversee a vast reporter network. Robert oversees our NHL data collection, and he and Allan were invaluable in helping to resolve any questions we had along the way. Special thanks to Tanya Tyler, STATS' longtime hockey reporter, whose nimble fingers entered much of the 1998-99 NHL data.

The efforts of the Commercial Products, Fantasy, Interactive Products and Sales departments help pay most of our bills at STATS. Alan Leib oversees our Commercial Products division, which includes Ethan D. Cooperson, David Pinto, Joe Sclafani and Victor Zaslavsky. Steve Byrd is in charge of Fantasy, which also consists of Jim Corelis, Dan Ford, Stefan Kretschmann, Walter Lis, Marc Moeller, Mike Mooney, Oscar Palacios, Corey Roberts, Eric Robin, Jeff Smith, Yingmin Wang and Rick Wilton. Mike Canter runs Interactive and is assisted by Dave Carlson, Jacob Costello, Kevin Fullam, Will McCleskey, Tim Moriarty, Dean Peterson, Pat Quinn, Morris Srinivasan and Nick Stamm. Jim Capuano heads up the Sales Department comprising Greg Kirkorsky and Jacob Stein.

Our Financial/Administrative/Human Resources/Legal Department ensures that everything runs smoothly at our Morton Grove, Ill., headquarters. Sophia Barshak, Howard Lanin and Betty Moy handle all of the financial details. Susan Zamechek assists in finance and oversees the administrative aspects, assisted by Sherlinda Johnson and Diane Nguyen, while Tracy Lickton is in charge of human resources. Carol Savier aids with legal matters. Art Ashley provides programming support to all four groups.

Thanks again to the coolest team on earth.

—Tony Nistler

Acknowledgments

Table of Contents

Foreword

By Gary F. Thorne, ESPN

Standards by which to measure whatever the subject of discussion might be—we long for such measurement tools as part of our human nature. We may argue about how the numbers should be applied or what they really mean, but the standards need to be there to even begin the discussion.

In sports, the need for such numbers as yardsticks is especially necessary. They become the common path across the decades, and now even the millenniums. The import of the numbers in sports will be endlessly argued, but that is part of the joy of following sports.

What must exist for any of these discussions to even begin is a collection of the vital stats that are right. That's where the *STATS Hockey Handbook* takes its place on a sports fan's desk.

This is more than just a collection of the numbers, as necessary as those are to any comparison of players and teams. There are columns here that go behind the numbers. At what point in a game and a season were goals and points put on the board by a particular player? Did they come at crucial times in a game? Were they points in a winning cause or an accumulation of points in losses?

The arguments that can be made about any given player on these stats alone is endless, and best of all, fun. They are the numbers that help define the character of a player and his importance to a team. They are the kind of numbers that GMs and coaches crunch in deciding who they want on their teams and who they want on the ice when it's going to make a real difference.

Many like to play down the numbers. They want to talk about heart and desire and all those wonderfully unquantifiable attributes that are the magic of sports, and probably life in general. Yet don't those very attributes most often end up in the stat columns, the very result of having those qualities?

Also, like it or not, the numbers are about talent. At the NHL level you have the talent or you don't stay. That talent is reflected in the numbers. That talent combined with the unquantifiable attributes brings us the greatest numbers of all.

Some players parlay a career living off one or two years of good numbers and being with the right team at the right time. You'll look at their career numbers and say, "I thought he was better than that." Some players never get to the right team at the right time and you'll look at their numbers and say, "Man, I didn't know he was that good."

Then you'll look at Wayne Gretzky's numbers and you won't say anything, but you'll know *the* standard of greatness on the ice. Every structure must have a piece of earth on which to rest and grow. The stats of the NHL players are that piece of earth upon which fans can build their arguments for "keep 'em" or "trade 'em." Those stats provide the basis for day to day knowledgeable enjoyment of the games and the players.

For hockey fans, the *STATS Hockey Handbook* is a favorite chair friend, just sitting there with a wealth of information that's yours for the perusing. Enjoy the tales it has to tell.

Introduction

It's a time of staggering transition for the National Hockey League. The Stanley Cup left hockey's heartland for Texas, while the coolest game on ice returns to an old Southern friend, the city of Atlanta, where the Thrashers begin play this fall. On the ice, Jaromir Jagr of the Pittsburgh Penguins ascended the throne as the NHL's premier player, and The Great One, Wayne Gretzky, walked away from the game he dominated for two decades.

In the midst of these changing times, we return with the fourth edition of the *STATS Hockey Handbook*. It's our statistical recap of the 1998-99 NHL season, an exciting campaign that culminated in the Dallas Stars returning home with the Stanley Cup and Gretzky lacing up his skates for the last time as an active player. He took a lifetime of memories with him.

Luckily, we share many memories with hockey's greatest one, who departs with four Stanley Cup championships, nine Hart Trophies as the league's MVP and 3,321 career points in 21 seasons. Of course, the numbers don't say it all. While he holds or shares 61 NHL records, witnessing Gretzky on ice left one marveling at how he always seemed to have a view of the whole rink and could hit any teammate in that broad view with a pass of remarkable precision. Even more remarkable was his touch with the puck, which allowed him to shovel soft passes through defenders or dip and maneuver around them without losing the puck. In front of the net, he could undress goaltenders with a head fake, a tip-in, a quick shot or a no-look pass.

If he wasn't leaving defenders in his wake while heading up ice, he was setting up shop behind the net, delivering picture-perfect passes to teammates in the slot. Although Gretzky's passing set him apart as an offensive force, his shooting accuracy was just as legendary. It's why he holds the single-season goal-scoring record with 92 in the 1981-82 regular season. Two years later he became the only NHL player to score 100 goals in a season, as he netted 87 during the 80-game schedule and another 13 in the playoffs while leading the Edmonton Oilers to their first Stanley Cup championship.

Before Gretzky was finished making thousands of opponents look bad—converting impossible plays into goals with what appeared to be effortless moves—he scored seven assists in a game on three occasions, captured 10 NHL scoring titles (once by a 79-point margin), made 18 All-Star appearances and captained four Stanley Cup champions.

It's hard to comprehend hockey losing Gretzky, but as Bob McKenzie, associate editor of *The Hockey News*, noted in *THN*'s tribute issue, The Great One "isn't leaving the game. He's defining it, now and forever."

For Gretzky, the immediate future includes his induction into the Hall of Fame on November 22, and the arrival of his fourth child in January. It's a reminder that we all must look ahead.

As much as we hate to see Gretzky depart, a new season awaits us. The fourth edition of the *Handbook* not only digs deep into what happened during the 1998-99 season, it helps us prepare for what we will see during the 1999-2000 campaign.

We hope you'll find this fourth edition a useful tool as the new season approaches and unfolds. With the start of the post-Gretzky era, we'll be busy working on the *Handbook*'s fifth edition. But for now, enjoy the one that bears The Great One's final record.

—Thom Henninger

Career Statistics

The following section includes the records of all players who saw NHL action during the 1998-99 season.

Age is seasonal age through December 31, 1999, the approximate midpoint of the season.

Profiles: For many skaters and goalies, you will see a note just above the age, "(statistical profile on page 327)," for example. This directs you to the Profiles sections, where you'll find a detailed situational breakdown for the player's 1998-99 campaign.

Multi-Team Seasons: If a player saw action with more than one NHL team in a season, his stats for each team in the season(s) in question appear just above the career totals line at the bottom of each entry. The teams are listed in the order in which the player saw action.

Games Started/Times Pulled: Data for number of games started and times pulled (for goalies) is generally not available prior to the 1991-92 season. For players active before then, you'll see a dash (—) to indicate that this data is missing, both for the years in question and in the player's career total line.

Shots/Save Percentage: Data for shots against each goalie (and consequently, save percentage) was not kept by the NHL prior to the 1982-83 season. Since this only affects Grant Fuhr and John Vanbiesbrouck, you'll see career totals in these two categories for all goalies.

Miscellaneous: Other statistical categories that are not complete include outstanding efforts (OE) for goalies, power play and shorthanded goals allowed for goalies, power play assists for skaters, shorthanded goals for skaters, and number/nature of penalties for skaters. Players with missing data in any of these categories will have a dash in their career total line for that category. The (*) next to a season indicates the player appeared in that year's All-Star Game. For the 1986-87 season, we are including *Rendez-Vous '87* as that year's All-Star Game. And remember, there was no All-Star Game in the lockout-shortened 1994-95 campaign.

League Leaders: Throughout the career statistics, any stat which led the NHL in a given regular season will be in bold face.

An explanation of the categories and abbreviations used can be found on pages 538-540.

Antti Aalto

Pos: C **Shoots:** L **Ht:** 6'2" **Wt:** 190 **Born:** 3/4/75—Lappeenrana, Finland **Age:** 24

Overall											Power Play			Shorthand			Penalty							Misc	
Year	Tm	GP	G	A	Pts	+/–	GW	GT	S	SPct	G	A	Pts	G	A	Pts	Num	PIM	Maj	Mnr	Fgt	Rgh	HHT	Hat	P/G
97-98	Anh	3	0	0	0	-1	0	0	1	0.0	0	0	0	0	0	0	0	0	0	0	0	0	0	0	.00
98-99	Anh	73	3	5	8	-12	0	0	61	4.9	2	1	3	0	0	0	12	24	0	12	0	0	3	0	.11
2 Years		76	3	5	8	-13	0	0	62	4.8	2	1	3	0	0	0	12	24	0	12	0	0	3	0	.11
Postseason																									
Year	Tm	GP	G	A	Pts	+/–	GW	OT	S	SPct	G	A	Pts	G	A	Pts	Num	PIM	Maj	Mnr	Fgt	Rgh	HHT	Hat	P/G
98-99	Anh	4	0	0	0	0	0	0	0	–	0	0	0	0	0	0	1	2	0	1	0	0	0	0	.00

Greg Adams

(statistical profile on page 284)

Pos: LW **Shoots:** L **Ht:** 6'3" **Wt:** 195 **Born:** 8/1/63—Nelson, British Columbia **Age:** 36

Overall											Power Play			Shorthand			Penalty							Misc	
Year	Tm	GP	G	A	Pts	+/–	GW	GT	S	SPct	G	A	Pts	G	A	Pts	Num	PIM	Maj	Mnr	Fgt	Rgh	HHT	Hat	P/G
84-85	NJ	36	12	9	21	-14	0	0	63	19.0	5	–	–	0	–	–	–	14	–	–	–	–	–	0	.58
85-86	NJ	78	35	42	77	-7	2	0	202	17.3	10	–	–	0	–	–	–	30	–	–	–	–	–	0	.99
86-87	NJ	72	20	27	47	-16	1	0	143	14.0	6	–	–	0	–	–	–	19	–	–	–	–	–	0	.65
87-88	Van*	**80**	36	40	76	-24	3	0	227	15.9	12	–	–	0	–	–	–	30	–	–	–	–	–	1	.95
88-89	Van	61	19	14	33	-21	2	0	144	13.2	9	–	–	0	–	–	–	24	–	–	–	–	–	1	.54
89-90	Van	65	30	20	50	-8	1	1	181	16.6	13	–	–	0	–	–	–	18	–	–	–	–	–	0	.77
90-91	Van	55	21	24	45	-5	2	2	148	14.2	5	–	–	1	–	–	–	10	–	–	–	–	–	0	.82
91-92	Van	76	30	27	57	8	5	0	184	16.3	13	7	20	1	2	3	13	26	0	13	0	6	2	1	.75
92-93	Van	53	25	31	56	31	3	0	124	20.2	6	9	15	1	3	4	7	14	0	7	0	1	3	0	1.06
93-94	Van	68	13	24	37	-1	2	0	139	9.4	5	5	10	1	3	4	10	20	0	10	0	0	5	0	.54
94-95	2Tm	43	8	13	21	-3	0	0	72	11.1	3	4	7	2	0	2	8	16	0	8	0	0	5	0	.49
95-96	Dal	66	22	21	43	-21	1	0	140	15.7	11	9	20	1	1	2	11	33	1	9	0	1	4	0	.65
96-97	Dal	50	21	15	36	27	4	1	113	18.6	5	6	11	0	0	0	1	2	0	1	0	0	0	0	.72
97-98	Dal	49	14	18	32	11	1	0	75	18.7	7	7	14	0	0	0	10	20	0	10	0	2	4	0	.65
98-99	Pho	75	19	24	43	-1	3	0	176	10.8	5	6	11	0	1	1	13	26	0	13	0	1	2	0	.57
94-95	Van	31	5	10	15	1	0	0	56	8.9	2	1	3	2	0	2	6	12	0	6	0	0	4	0	.48
94-95	Dal	12	3	3	6	-4	0	0	16	18.8	1	3	4	0	0	0	2	4	0	2	0	0	1	0	.50
15 Years		927	325	349	674	-44	30	4	2131	15.3	115	–	–	7	–	–	–	302	–	–	–	–	–	3	.73
Postseason																									
Year	Tm	GP	G	A	Pts	+/–	GW	OT	S	SPct	G	A	Pts	G	A	Pts	Num	PIM	Maj	Mnr	Fgt	Rgh	HHT	Hat	P/G
88-89	Van	7	2	3	5	-1	0	0	18	11.1	0	–	–	0	–	–	1	2	0	1	0	–	–	0	.71
90-91	Van	5	0	0	0	-2	0	0	8	0.0	0	0	0	0	0	0	1	2	0	1	0	–	–	0	.00
91-92	Van	6	0	2	2	4	0	0	23	0.0	0	1	1	0	0	0	2	4	0	2	0	0	1	0	.33
92-93	Van	12	7	6	13	-1	1	1	42	16.7	5	3	8	0	0	0	3	6	0	3	0	0	1	0	1.08
93-94	Van	23	6	8	14	1	2	2	46	13.0	2	2	4	0	0	0	1	2	0	1	0	0	0	0	.61
94-95	Dal	5	2	0	2	1	0	0	14	14.3	0	0	0	0	0	0	0	0	0	0	0	0	0	0	.40
96-97	Dal	3	0	1	1	2	0	0	4	0.0	0	0	0	0	0	0	0	0	0	0	0	0	0	0	.33
97-98	Dal	12	2	2	4	4	2	0	14	14.3	0	0	0	0	0	0	0	0	0	0	0	0	0	0	.33
98-99	Pho	3	1	0	1	1	0	0	9	11.1	0	0	0	0	0	0	0	0	0	0	0	0	0	0	.33
9 Years		76	20	22	42	9	5	3	178	11.2	7	–	–	0	–	–	8	16	0	8	0	–	–	0	.55

Kevyn Adams

Pos: C **Shoots:** R **Ht:** 6'1" **Wt:** 182 **Born:** 10/8/74—Washington, DC **Age:** 25

Overall											Power Play			Shorthand			Penalty							Misc	
Year	Tm	GP	G	A	Pts	+/–	GW	GT	S	SPct	G	A	Pts	G	A	Pts	Num	PIM	Maj	Mnr	Fgt	Rgh	HHT	Hat	P/G
97-98	Tor	5	0	0	0	0	0	0	3	0.0	0	0	0	0	0	0	2	7	1	1	1	1	0	0	.00
98-99	Tor	1	0	0	0	0	0	0	1	0.0	0	0	0	0	0	0	0	0	0	0	0	0	0	0	.00
2 Years		6	0	0	0	0	0	0	4	0.0	0	0	0	0	0	0	2	7	1	1	1	1	0	0	.00
Postseason																									
Year	Tm	GP	G	A	Pts	+/–	GW	OT	S	SPct	G	A	Pts	G	A	Pts	Num	PIM	Maj	Mnr	Fgt	Rgh	HHT	Hat	P/G
98-99	Tor	7	0	2	2	-2	0	0	9	0.0	0	1	1	0	0	0	3	14	0	2	0	0	1	0	.29

Tommy Albelin

Pos: D **Shoots:** L **Ht:** 6'1" **Wt:** 190 **Born:** 5/21/64—Stockholm, Sweden **Age:** 35

Overall											Power Play			Shorthand			Penalty							Misc	
Year	Tm	GP	G	A	Pts	+/–	GW	GT	S	SPct	G	A	Pts	G	A	Pts	Num	PIM	Maj	Mnr	Fgt	Rgh	HHT	Hat	P/G
87-88	Que	60	3	23	26	-7	0	0	98	3.1	0	–	–	0	–	–	–	47	–	–	–	–	–	0	.43
88-89	2Tm	60	9	28	37	12	3	0	114	7.9	3	9	12	1	0	1	–	67	–	–	–	–	–	0	.62

Overall											Power Play			Shorthand			Penalty							Misc	
Year	Tm	GP	G	A	Pts	+/–	GW	GT	S	SPct	G	A	Pts	G	A	Pts	Num	PIM	Maj	Mnr	Fgt	Rgh	HHT	Hat	P/G
89-90	NJ	68	6	23	29	-1	0	0	125	4.8	4	9	13	0	0	0	–	63	–	–	–	–	–	0	.43
90-91	NJ	47	2	12	14	1	0	0	66	3.0	1	8	9	0	1	1	–	44	–	–	–	–	–	0	.30
91-92	NJ	19	0	4	4	7	0	0	18	0.0	0	0	0	0	0	0	2	4	0	2	0	0	1	0	.21
92-93	NJ	36	1	5	6	0	1	0	33	3.0	1	2	3	0	0	0	7	14	0	7	0	0	2	0	.17
93-94	NJ	62	2	17	19	20	1	0	62	3.2	1	8	9	0	0	0	14	36	0	13	0	5	3	0	.31
94-95	NJ	48	5	10	15	9	0	0	60	8.3	2	0	2	0	0	0	10	20	0	10	0	2	3	0	.31
95-96	2Tm	73	1	13	14	1	0	0	121	0.8	0	6	6	0	0	0	9	18	0	9	0	0	3	0	.19
96-97	Cgy	72	4	11	15	-8	0	0	103	3.9	2	7	9	0	0	0	7	14	0	7	0	1	0	0	.21
97-98	Cgy	69	2	17	19	9	2	0	88	2.3	1	3	4	0	3	3	16	32	0	16	0	3	8	0	.28
98-99	Cgy	60	1	5	6	-11	0	0	54	1.9	0	0	0	0	1	1	4	8	0	4	0	0	1	0	.10
88-89	Que	14	2	4	6	-6	1	0	16	12.5	1	2	3	0	0	0	–	27	–	–	–	–	–	0	.43
88-89	NJ	46	7	24	31	18	2	0	98	7.1	2	7	9	1	0	1	–	40	–	–	–	–	–	0	.67
95-96	NJ	53	1	12	13	0	0	0	90	1.1	0	5	5	0	0	0	7	14	0	7	0	0	2	0	.25
95-96	Cgy	20	0	1	1	1	0	0	31	0.0	0	1	1	0	0	0	2	4	0	2	0	0	1	0	.05
12 Years		674	36	168	204	32	7	0	942	3.8	15	–	–	1	–	–	–	367	–	–	–	–	–	0	.30

Postseason

Year	Tm	GP	G	A	Pts	+/–	GW	OT	S	SPct	G	A	Pts	G	A	Pts	Num	PIM	Maj	Mnr	Fgt	Rgh	HHT	Hat	P/G
90-91	NJ	3	0	1	1	1	0	0	6	0.0	0	–	–	0	–	–	1	2	0	1	0	–	–	0	.33
91-92	NJ	1	1	1	2	0	0	0	1	100.0	0	0	0	0	0	0	0	0	0	0	0	0	0	0	2.00
92-93	NJ	5	2	0	2	-1	1	0	9	22.2	1	0	1	0	0	0	0	0	0	0	0	0	0	0	.40
93-94	NJ	20	2	5	7	5	1	0	30	6.7	1	1	2	0	0	0	7	14	0	7	0	2	0	0	.35
94-95	NJ	20	1	7	8	5	0	0	17	5.9	0	4	4	0	0	0	1	2	0	1	0	0	0	0	.40
95-96	Cgy	4	0	0	0	-2	0	0	8	0.0	0	0	0	0	0	0	0	0	0	0	0	0	0	0	.00
6 Years		53	6	14	20	8	2	0	71	8.5	2	–	–	0	–	–	9	18	0	9	0	–	–	0	.38

Daniel Alfredsson

(statistical profile on page 284)

Pos: RW **Shoots:** R **Ht:** 5'11" **Wt:** 194 **Born:** 12/11/72—Goteberg, Sweden **Age:** 27

Overall											Power Play			Shorthand			Penalty							Misc	
Year	Tm	GP	G	A	Pts	+/–	GW	GT	S	SPct	G	A	Pts	G	A	Pts	Num	PIM	Maj	Mnr	Fgt	Rgh	HHT	Hat	P/G
95-96	Ott*	82	26	35	61	-18	3	1	212	12.3	8	18	26	2	0	2	14	28	0	14	0	1	5	1	.74
96-97	Ott*	76	24	47	71	5	1	2	247	9.7	11	20	31	1	2	3	15	30	0	15	0	1	7	0	.93
97-98	Ott*	55	17	28	45	7	7	0	149	11.4	7	9	16	0	0	0	9	18	0	9	0	0	4	0	.82
98-99	Ott	58	11	22	33	8	5	0	163	6.7	3	8	11	0	0	0	7	14	0	7	0	1	3	0	.57
4 Years		271	78	132	210	2	16	3	771	10.1	29	55	84	3	2	5	45	90	0	45	0	3	19	1	.77

Postseason

Year	Tm	GP	G	A	Pts	+/–	GW	OT	S	SPct	G	A	Pts	G	A	Pts	Num	PIM	Maj	Mnr	Fgt	Rgh	HHT	Hat	P/G
96-97	Ott	7	5	2	7	-1	2	1	23	21.7	3	2	5	0	0	0	3	6	0	3	0	0	1	0	1.00
97-98	Ott	11	7	2	9	-4	1	0	36	19.4	2	2	4	1	0	1	6	20	0	5	0	1	1	2	.82
98-99	Ott	4	1	2	3	-1	0	0	13	7.7	1	0	1	0	0	0	2	4	0	2	0	1	0	0	.75
3 Years		22	13	6	19	-6	3	1	72	18.1	6	4	10	1	0	1	11	30	0	10	0	2	2	2	.86

Chris Allen

Pos: D **Shoots:** R **Ht:** 6'2" **Wt:** 193 **Born:** 5/8/78—Chatham, Ontario **Age:** 21

Overall											Power Play			Shorthand			Penalty							Misc	
Year	Tm	GP	G	A	Pts	+/–	GW	GT	S	SPct	G	A	Pts	G	A	Pts	Num	PIM	Maj	Mnr	Fgt	Rgh	HHT	Hat	P/G
97-98	Fla	1	0	0	0	0	0	0	1	0.0	0	0	0	0	0	0	1	2	0	1	0	0	1	0	.00
98-99	Fla	1	0	0	0	1	0	0	0	–	0	0	0	0	0	0	0	0	0	0	0	0	0	0	.00
2 Years		2	0	0	0	1	0	0	1	0.0	0	0	0	0	0	0	1	2	0	1	0	0	1	0	.00

Jamie Allison

Pos: D **Shoots:** L **Ht:** 6'1" **Wt:** 190 **Born:** 5/13/75—Lindsay, Ontario **Age:** 24

Overall											Power Play			Shorthand			Penalty							Misc	
Year	Tm	GP	G	A	Pts	+/–	GW	GT	S	SPct	G	A	Pts	G	A	Pts	Num	PIM	Maj	Mnr	Fgt	Rgh	HHT	Hat	P/G
94-95	Cgy	1	0	0	0	0	0	0	0	–	0	0	0	0	0	0	0	0	0	0	0	0	0	0	.00
95-96		Did Not Play in NHL																							
96-97	Cgy	20	0	0	0	-4	0	0	8	0.0	0	0	0	0	0	0	13	35	3	10	3	3	5	0	.00
97-98	Cgy	43	3	8	11	3	1	0	27	11.1	0	0	0	0	2	2	27	104	6	17	6	8	3	0	.26
98-99	Chi	39	2	2	4	0	0	0	24	8.3	0	0	0	0	0	0	19	62	0	16	0	5	4	0	.10
4 Years		103	5	10	15	-1	1	0	59	8.5	0	0	0	0	2	2	59	201	9	43	9	16	12	0	.15

Jason Allison

(statistical profile on page 284)

Pos: C **Shoots:** R **Ht:** 6'3" **Wt:** 205 **Born:** 5/29/75—North York, Ontario **Age:** 24

Overall											Power Play			Shorthand			Penalty							Misc	
Year	Tm	GP	G	A	Pts	+/–	GW	GT	S	SPct	G	A	Pts	G	A	Pts	Num	PIM	Maj	Mnr	Fgt	Rgh	HHT	Hat	P/G
93-94	Was	2	0	1	1	1	0	0	5	0.0	0	0	0	0	0	0	0	0	0	0	0	0	0	0	.50
94-95	Was	12	2	1	3	-3	0	0	9	22.2	2	1	3	0	0	0	3	6	0	3	0	0	1	0	.25
95-96	Was	19	0	3	3	-3	0	0	18	0.0	0	1	1	0	0	0	1	2	0	1	0	1	0	0	.16
96-97	2Tm	72	8	26	34	-6	1	0	99	8.1	2	9	11	0	0	0	14	34	2	12	2	4	6	0	.47
97-98	Bos	81	33	50	83	33	8	2	158	20.9	5	20	25	0	2	2	19	60	2	15	2	1	6	2	1.02
98-99	Bos	82	23	53	76	5	3	0	158	14.6	5	25	30	1	0	1	27	68	2	24	1	5	10	1	.93
96-97	Was	53	5	17	22	-3	1	0	71	7.0	1	5	6	0	0	0	11	25	1	10	1	3	5	0	.42
96-97	Bos	19	3	9	12	-3	0	0	28	10.7	1	4	5	0	0	0	3	9	1	2	1	1	1	0	.63
6 Years		268	66	134	200	27	12	2	447	14.8	14	56	70	1	2	3	64	170	6	55	5	11	23	3	.75

Postseason

Year	Tm	GP	G	A	Pts	+/–	GW	OT	S	SPct	G	A	Pts	G	A	Pts	Num	PIM	Maj	Mnr	Fgt	Rgh	HHT	Hat	P/G
97-98	Bos	6	2	6	8	0	0	0	13	15.4	1	3	4	0	0	0	2	4	0	2	0	1	0	0	1.33
98-99	Bos	12	2	9	11	1	0	0	28	7.1	1	4	5	0	0	0	3	6	0	3	0	0	0	0	.92
2 Years		18	4	15	19	1	0	0	41	9.8	2	7	9	0	0	0	5	10	0	5	0	1	0	0	1.06

Tony Amonte

(statistical profile on page 284)

Pos: RW **Shoots:** L **Ht:** 6'0" **Wt:** 195 **Born:** 8/2/70—Hingham, Massachusetts **Age:** 29

Overall											Power Play			Shorthand			Penalty							Misc	
Year	Tm	GP	G	A	Pts	+/–	GW	GT	S	SPct	G	A	Pts	G	A	Pts	Num	PIM	Maj	Mnr	Fgt	Rgh	HHT	Hat	P/G
90-91										Did Not Play in Regular Season															
91-92	NYR	79	35	34	69	12	4	0	234	15.0	9	8	17	0	0	0	26	55	1	25	1	0	12	1	.87
92-93	NYR	83	33	43	76	0	4	1	270	12.2	13	11	24	0	0	0	19	49	1	17	1	3	6	0	.92
93-94	2Tm	79	17	25	42	0	4	0	195	8.7	4	9	13	0	0	0	17	37	1	16	1	5	4	0	.53
94-95	Chi	48	15	20	35	7	3	1	105	14.3	6	7	13	1	0	1	19	41	1	18	1	1	8	0	.73
95-96	Chi	81	31	32	63	10	5	0	216	14.4	5	13	18	4	0	4	31	62	0	31	0	7	9	1	.78
96-97	Chi*	81	41	36	77	35	4	2	266	15.4	9	6	15	2	1	3	28	64	0	27	0	5	10	2	.95
97-98	Chi*	82	31	42	73	21	5	0	296	10.5	7	12	19	3	3	6	29	66	0	28	0	1	12	0	.89
98-99	Chi	82	44	31	75	0	8	0	256	17.2	14	12	26	3	1	4	26	60	0	25	0	2	6	2	.91
93-94	NYR	72	16	22	38	5	4	0	179	8.9	3	7	10	0	0	0	14	31	1	13	1	2	4	0	.53
93-94	Chi	7	1	3	4	-5	0	0	16	6.3	1	2	3	0	0	0	3	6	0	3	0	3	0	0	.57
8 Years		615	247	263	510	85	37	4	1838	13.4	67	78	145	13	5	18	195	434	4	187	4	24	67	6	.83

Postseason

Year	Tm	GP	G	A	Pts	+/–	GW	OT	S	SPct	G	A	Pts	G	A	Pts	Num	PIM	Maj	Mnr	Fgt	Rgh	HHT	Hat	P/G
90-91	NYR	2	0	2	2	1	0	0	5	0.0	0	2	2	0	0	0	1	2	0	1	0	0	1	0	1.00
91-92	NYR	13	3	6	9	-7	0	0	36	8.3	2	3	5	0	0	0	1	2	0	1	0	0	1	0	.69
93-94	Chi	6	4	2	6	4	1	0	21	19.0	1	0	1	0	0	0	2	4	0	2	0	0	2	1	1.00
94-95	Chi	16	3	3	6	3	0	0	32	9.4	0	1	1	0	0	0	5	10	0	5	0	2	1	0	.38
95-96	Chi	7	2	4	6	2	0	0	14	14.3	1	2	3	0	0	0	3	6	0	3	0	1	1	0	.86
96-97	Chi	6	4	2	6	2	0	0	24	16.7	0	0	0	2	0	2	4	8	0	4	0	0	1	0	1.00
6 Years		50	16	19	35	5	1	0	132	12.1	4	8	12	2	0	2	16	32	0	16	0	3	7	1	.70

Mikael Andersson

Pos: RW **Shoots:** L **Ht:** 5'11" **Wt:** 184 **Born:** 5/10/66—Malmo, Sweden **Age:** 33

Overall											Power Play			Shorthand			Penalty							Misc	
Year	Tm	GP	G	A	Pts	+/–	GW	GT	S	SPct	G	A	Pts	G	A	Pts	Num	PIM	Maj	Mnr	Fgt	Rgh	HHT	Hat	P/G
85-86	Buf	32	1	9	10	0	0	0	13	7.7	0	–	–	0	–	–	2	4	0	2	0	–	–	0	.31
86-87	Buf	16	0	3	3	-2	0	0	6	0.0	0	–	–	0	–	–	0	0	0	0	0	0	0	0	.19
87-88	Buf	37	3	20	23	7	1	0	34	8.8	0	–	–	1	–	–	–	10	–	–	–	–	–	0	.62
88-89	Buf	14	0	1	1	-1	0	0	12	0.0	0	–	–	0	–	–	2	4	0	2	0	–	–	0	.07
89-90	Har	50	13	24	37	0	2	0	86	15.1	1	–	–	2	–	–	3	6	0	3	0	–	–	0	.74
90-91	Har	41	4	7	11	0	0	0	57	7.0	0	–	–	0	–	–	4	8	0	4	0	–	–	0	.27
91-92	Har	74	18	29	47	18	1	0	149	12.1	1	6	7	3	0	3	7	14	0	7	0	0	2	0	.64
92-93	TB	77	16	11	27	-14	4	0	169	9.5	3	1	4	2	2	4	7	14	0	7	0	0	4	1	.35
93-94	TB	76	13	12	25	8	2	1	136	9.6	1	0	1	1	1	2	6	23	1	4	0	0	2	0	.33
94-95	TB	36	4	7	11	-3	0	0	36	11.1	0	1	1	0	0	0	2	4	0	2	0	0	2	0	.31
95-96	TB	64	8	11	19	0	1	0	104	7.7	0	0	0	0	0	0	1	2	0	1	0	0	1	0	.30
96-97	TB	70	5	14	19	1	1	0	102	4.9	0	0	0	3	2	5	4	8	0	4	0	0	3	0	.27
97-98	TB	72	6	11	17	-4	1	0	105	5.7	0	0	0	1	2	3	9	29	1	7	1	0	6	0	.24
98-99	2Tm	47	2	4	6	-7	0	0	51	3.9	0	0	0	0	0	0	2	4	0	2	0	0	1	0	.13
98-99	TB	40	2	3	5	-8	0	0	40	5.0	0	0	0	0	0	0	2	4	0	2	0	0	1	0	.13
98-99	Phi	7	0	1	1	1	0	0	11	0.0	0	0	0	0	0	0	0	0	0	0	0	0	0	0	.14
14 Years		706	93	163	256	3	13	1	1060	8.8	6	–	–	13	–	–	–	130	–	–	–	–	–	1	.36

Postseason																									
Year	Tm	GP	G	A	Pts	+/–	GW	OT	S	SPct	G	A	Pts	G	A	Pts	Num	PIM	Maj	Mnr	Fgt	Rgh	HHT	Hat	P/G
87-88	Buf	1	1	0	1	0	0	0	1	100.0	0	0	0	0	0	0	0	0	0	0	0	0	0	0	1.00
89-90	Har	5	0	3	3	0	0	0	5	0.0	0	–	–	0	0	0	1	2	0	1	0	0	0	0	.60
91-92	Har	7	0	2	2	-2	0	0	10	0.0	0	0	0	0	1	1	3	6	0	3	0	0	3	0	.29
95-96	TB	6	1	1	2	0	0	0	4	25.0	0	0	0	0	1	1	0	0	0	0	0	0	0	0	.33
98-99	Phi	6	0	1	1	1	0	0	7	0.0	0	0	0	0	0	0	1	2	0	1	0	0	1	0	.17
5 Years		25	2	7	9	-1	0	0	27	7.4	0	–	–	0	2	2	5	10	0	5	0	0	4	0	.36

Dave Andreychuk

(statistical profile on page 285)

Pos: LW **Shoots:** R **Ht:** 6'4" **Wt:** 220 **Born:** 9/29/63—Hamilton, Ontario **Age:** 36

Overall											Power Play			Shorthand			Penalty							Misc	
Year	Tm	GP	G	A	Pts	+/–	GW	GT	S	SPct	G	A	Pts	G	A	Pts	Num	PIM	Maj	Mnr	Fgt	Rgh	HHT	Hat	P/G
82-83	Buf	43	14	23	37	6	1	0	66	21.2	3	–	–	0	–	–	–	16	–	–	–	–	–	0	.86
83-84	Buf	78	38	42	80	20	7	1	176	21.6	10	–	–	0	–	–	–	42	–	–	–	–	–	0	1.03
84-85	Buf	64	31	30	61	-4	2	1	153	20.3	14	–	–	0	–	–	–	54	–	–	–	–	–	0	.95
85-86	Buf	80	36	51	87	3	3	0	225	16.0	12	–	–	0	–	–	–	61	–	–	–	–	–	1	1.09
86-87	Buf	77	25	48	73	2	2	1	255	9.8	13	–	–	0	–	–	–	46	–	–	–	–	–	0	.95
87-88	Buf	**80**	30	48	78	1	5	0	253	11.9	15	–	–	0	–	–	–	112	–	–	–	–	–	3	.98
88-89	Buf	56	28	24	52	1	3	0	145	19.3	7	–	–	0	–	–	–	40	–	–	–	–	–	1	.93
89-90	Buf*	73	40	42	82	6	3	0	206	19.4	18	–	–	0	–	–	–	42	–	–	–	–	–	1	1.12
90-91	Buf	80	36	33	69	11	4	**3**	234	15.4	13	–	–	0	–	–	–	32	–	–	–	–	–	0	.86
91-92	Buf	80	41	50	91	-9	2	2	337	12.2	**28**	23	51	0	0	0	30	71	1	28	0	6	9	2	1.14
92-93	2Tm	83	54	45	99	4	4	1	310	17.4	**32**	22	54	0	0	0	28	56	0	28	0	5	11	1	1.19
93-94	Tor*	83	53	46	99	22	8	0	333	15.9	21	22	43	5	0	5	41	98	0	39	0	7	11	1	1.19
94-95	Tor	48	22	16	38	-7	2	2	168	13.1	8	6	14	0	0	0	13	34	0	12	0	1	7	0	.79
95-96	2Tm	76	28	29	57	-9	3	1	241	11.6	14	14	28	2	1	3	32	64	0	32	0	3	16	0	.75
96-97	NJ	**82**	27	34	61	38	2	1	233	11.6	4	5	9	1	0	1	20	48	0	19	0	2	8	0	.74
97-98	NJ	75	14	34	48	19	2	0	180	7.8	4	12	16	0	0	0	13	26	0	13	0	0	9	0	.64
98-99	NJ	52	15	13	28	1	3	1	110	13.6	4	4	8	0	0	0	10	20	0	10	0	3	3	0	.54
92-93	Buf	52	29	32	61	-8	2	0	171	17.0	20	17	37	0	0	0	24	48	0	24	0	5	9	1	1.17
92-93	Tor	31	25	13	38	12	2	1	139	18.0	12	5	17	0	0	0	4	8	0	4	0	0	2	0	1.23
95-96	Tor	61	20	24	44	-11	3	1	200	10.0	12	14	26	2	1	3	27	54	0	27	0	2	14	0	.72
95-96	NJ	15	8	5	13	2	0	0	41	19.5	2	0	2	0	0	0	5	10	0	5	0	1	2	0	.87
17 Years		1210	532	608	1140	105	56	14	3625	14.7	220	–	–	8	–	–	–	862	–	–	–	–	–	10	.94
Postseason																									
Year	Tm	GP	G	A	Pts	+/–	GW	OT	S	SPct	G	A	Pts	G	A	Pts	Num	PIM	Maj	Mnr	Fgt	Rgh	HHT	Hat	P/G
82-83	Buf	4	1	0	1	-2	0	0	3	33.3	0	0	0	0	0	0	2	4	0	2	0	–	–	0	.25
83-84	Buf	2	0	1	1	-2	0	0	5	0.0	0	0	0	0	0	0	1	2	0	1	0	–	–	0	.50
84-85	Buf	5	4	2	6	5	2	0	12	33.3	0	–	–	0	0	0	2	4	0	2	0	–	–	1	1.20
87-88	Buf	6	2	4	6	-2	0	0	15	13.3	1	–	–	0	0	0	0	0	0	0	0	0	0	0	1.00
88-89	Buf	5	0	3	3	0	0	0	15	0.0	0	–	–	0	–	–	0	0	0	0	0	0	0	0	.60
89-90	Buf	6	2	5	7	2	0	0	20	10.0	1	–	–	0	0	0	1	2	0	1	0	–	–	0	1.17
90-91	Buf	6	2	2	4	-2	0	0	21	9.5	1	–	–	0	–	–	4	8	0	4	0	–	–	0	.67
91-92	Buf	7	1	3	4	0	0	0	27	3.7	0	3	3	0	0	0	6	12	0	6	0	0	3	0	.57
92-93	Tor	21	12	7	19	6	3	0	72	16.7	4	4	8	0	0	0	12	35	1	10	0	1	0	0	.90
93-94	Tor	18	5	5	10	-3	0	0	50	10.0	3	5	8	1	0	1	8	16	0	8	0	3	2	0	.56
94-95	Tor	7	3	2	5	3	0	0	19	15.8	2	1	3	0	0	0	7	25	1	5	0	0	0	0	.71
96-97	NJ	1	0	0	0	0	0	0	5	0.0	0	0	0	0	0	0	0	0	0	0	0	0	0	0	.00
97-98	NJ	6	1	0	1	-2	0	0	17	5.9	1	0	1	0	0	0	2	4	0	2	0	0	1	0	.17
98-99	NJ	4	2	0	2	0	0	0	7	28.6	0	0	0	0	0	0	2	4	0	2	0	0	2	0	.50
14 Years		98	35	34	69	3	5	0	288	12.2	13	–	–	1	–	–	47	116	2	43	0	–	–	1	.70

Greg Andrusak

Pos: D **Shoots:** R **Ht:** 6'1" **Wt:** 195 **Born:** 11/14/69—Cranbrook, British Columbia **Age:** 30

Overall											Power Play			Shorthand			Penalty							Misc	
Year	Tm	GP	G	A	Pts	+/–	GW	GT	S	SPct	G	A	Pts	G	A	Pts	Num	PIM	Maj	Mnr	Fgt	Rgh	HHT	Hat	P/G
93-94	Pit	3	0	0	0	-1	0	0	4	0.0	0	0	0	0	0	0	1	2	0	1	0	0	1	0	.00
94-95	Pit	7	0	4	4	-1	0	0	7	0.0	0	3	3	0	0	0	3	6	0	3	0	0	1	0	.57
95-96	Pit	2	0	0	0	-1	0	0	1	0.0	0	0	0	0	0	0	0	0	0	0	0	0	0	0	.00
96-97											Did Not Play in NHL														
97-98											Did Not Play in NHL														
98-99	Pit	7	0	1	1	4	0	0	2	0.0	0	0	0	0	0	0	2	4	0	2	0	0	2	0	.14
4 Years		19	0	5	5	1	0	0	14	0.0	0	3	3	0	0	0	6	12	0	6	0	0	4	0	.26

									Postseason																
Year	Tm	GP	G	A	Pts	+/-	GW	OT	S	SPct	G	A	Pts	G	A	Pts	Num	PIM	Maj	Mnr	Fgt	Rgh	HHT	Hat	P/G
94-95	Pit	1	0	0	0	-1	0	0	1	0.0	0	0	0	0	0	0	0	0	0	0	0	0	0	0	.00
98-99	Pit	12	1	0	1	-1	1	0	9	11.1	0	0	0	0	0	0	3	6	0	3	0	0	3	0	.08
2 Years		13	1	0	1	-2	1	0	10	10.0	0	0	0	0	0	0	3	6	0	3	0	0	3	0	.08

Derek Armstrong

Pos: C **Shoots:** R **Ht:** 5'11" **Wt:** 180 **Born:** 4/23/73—Ottawa, Ontario **Age:** 26

			Overall								Power Play			Shorthand			Penalty							Misc	
Year	Tm	GP	G	A	Pts	+/-	GW	GT	S	SPct	G	A	Pts	G	A	Pts	Num	PIM	Maj	Mnr	Fgt	Rgh	HHT	Hat	P/G
93-94	NYI	1	0	0	0	0	0	0	2	0.0	0	0	0	0	0	0	0	0	0	0	0	0	0	0	.00
94-95											Did Not Play in NHL														
95-96	NYI	19	1	3	4	-6	0	0	23	4.3	0	1	1	0	0	0	7	14	0	7	0	0	3	0	.21
96-97	NYI	50	6	7	13	-8	2	0	36	16.7	0	1	1	0	0	0	12	33	3	9	3	2	5	0	.26
97-98	Ott	9	2	0	2	1	1	0	8	25.0	0	0	0	0	0	0	3	9	1	2	1	0	0	0	.22
98-99	NYR	3	0	0	0	0	0	0	1	0.0	0	0	0	0	0	0	0	0	0	0	0	0	0	0	.00
5 Years		82	9	10	19	-13	3	0	70	12.9	0	2	2	0	0	0	22	56	4	18	4	2	8	0	.23

Jason Arnott

(statistical profile on page 285)

Pos: C **Shoots:** R **Ht:** 6'3" **Wt:** 220 **Born:** 10/11/74—Collingworth, Ontario **Age:** 25

			Overall								Power Play			Shorthand			Penalty							Misc	
Year	Tm	GP	G	A	Pts	+/-	GW	GT	S	SPct	G	A	Pts	G	A	Pts	Num	PIM	Maj	Mnr	Fgt	Rgh	HHT	Hat	P/G
93-94	Edm	78	33	35	68	1	4	1	194	17.0	10	13	23	0	0	0	38	104	4	32	3	15	6	0	.87
94-95	Edm	42	15	22	37	-14	1	0	156	9.6	7	11	18	0	1	1	38	128	4	29	3	10	4	1	.88
95-96	Edm	64	28	31	59	-6	5	1	244	11.5	8	8	16	0	0	0	35	87	3	31	2	9	8	1	.92
96-97	Edm*	67	19	38	57	-21	2	1	248	7.7	10	22	32	1	0	1	35	92	2	31	2	4	7	0	.85
97-98	2Tm	70	10	23	33	-24	2	0	199	5.0	4	10	14	0	0	0	29	99	3	22	3	2	8	0	.47
98-99	NJ	74	27	27	54	10	3	1	200	13.5	8	12	20	0	0	0	34	79	1	32	1	5	11	0	.73
97-98	Edm	35	5	13	18	-16	0	0	100	5.0	1	6	7	0	0	0	20	78	2	14	2	1	4	0	.51
97-98	NJ	35	5	10	15	-8	2	0	99	5.1	3	4	7	0	0	0	9	21	1	8	1	1	4	0	.43
6 Years		395	132	176	308	-54	17	4	1241	10.6	47	76	123	1	1	2	209	589	17	177	14	45	44	2	.78
											Postseason														
Year	Tm	GP	G	A	Pts	+/-	GW	OT	S	SPct	G	A	Pts	G	A	Pts	Num	PIM	Maj	Mnr	Fgt	Rgh	HHT	Hat	P/G
96-97	Edm	12	3	6	9	-3	0	0	27	11.1	1	1	2	0	0	0	9	18	0	9	0	1	2	0	.75
97-98	NJ	5	0	2	2	1	0	0	6	0.0	0	1	1	0	0	0	0	0	0	0	0	0	0	0	.40
98-99	NJ	7	2	2	4	-3	0	0	12	16.7	1	1	2	0	0	0	2	4	0	2	0	0	0	0	.57
3 Years		24	5	10	15	-5	0	0	45	11.1	2	3	5	0	0	0	11	22	0	11	0	1	2	0	.63

Magnus Arvedson

(statistical profile on page 285)

Pos: LW **Shoots:** L **Ht:** 6'2" **Wt:** 198 **Born:** 11/25/71—Farjestad, Sweden **Age:** 28

			Overall								Power Play			Shorthand			Penalty							Misc	
Year	Tm	GP	G	A	Pts	+/-	GW	GT	S	SPct	G	A	Pts	G	A	Pts	Num	PIM	Maj	Mnr	Fgt	Rgh	HHT	Hat	P/G
97-98	Ott	61	11	15	26	2	0	1	90	12.2	0	1	1	1	0	1	18	36	0	18	0	2	6	0	.43
98-99	Ott	80	21	26	47	33	6	0	136	15.4	0	0	0	4	1	5	25	50	0	25	0	2	12	1	.59
2 Years		141	32	41	73	35	6	1	226	14.2	0	1	1	5	1	6	43	86	0	43	0	4	18	1	.52
											Postseason														
Year	Tm	GP	G	A	Pts	+/-	GW	OT	S	SPct	G	A	Pts	G	A	Pts	Num	PIM	Maj	Mnr	Fgt	Rgh	HHT	Hat	P/G
97-98	Ott	11	0	1	1	-6	0	0	21	0.0	0	0	0	0	0	0	3	6	0	3	0	0	2	0	.09
98-99	Ott	3	0	1	1	-1	0	0	8	0.0	0	0	0	0	0	0	1	2	0	1	0	0	0	0	.33
2 Years		14	0	2	2	-7	0	0	29	0.0	0	0	0	0	0	0	4	8	0	4	0	0	2	0	.14

Arron Asham

Pos: RW **Shoots:** R **Ht:** 5'11" **Wt:** 176 **Born:** 3/14/78—P.L. Prairie, Massachusetts **Age:** 21

			Overall								Power Play			Shorthand			Penalty							Misc	
Year	Tm	GP	G	A	Pts	+/-	GW	GT	S	SPct	G	A	Pts	G	A	Pts	Num	PIM	Maj	Mnr	Fgt	Rgh	HHT	Hat	P/G
98-99	Mon	7	0	0	0	-4	0	0	5	0.0	0	0	0	0	0	0	0	0	0	0	0	0	0	0	.00

Tom Askey

Pos: G **Catches:** L **Ht:** 6'2" **Wt:** 185 **Born:** 10/4/74—Kenmore, New York **Age:** 25

Overall																	Pen Shot		Offense		
Year	Tm	GP	GS	TP	W	L	T	Min	GA	GAA	Shots	SvPct	ShO	OE	PPGA	SHGA	Shots	GA	G	A	PIM
97-98	Anh	7	3	0	0	1	2	273	12	2.64	113	.894	0	1	1	0	0	0	0	0	0
98-99		Did Not Play in Regular Season																			

Postseason																					
Year	Tm	GP	GS	TP	W	L	Pct	Min	GA	GAA	Shots	SvPct	ShO	OE	PPGA	SHGA	Shots	GA	G	A	PIM
98-99	Anh	1	0	0	0	1	.000	30	2	4.00	11	.818	0	0	0	0	0	0	0	0	0

Blair Atcheynum

(statistical profile on page 285)

Pos: RW **Shoots:** R **Ht:** 6'1" **Wt:** 195 **Born:** 4/20/69—Estevan, Saskatchewan **Age:** 30

Overall										Power Play			Shorthand			Penalty							Misc	
Year	Tm	GP	G	A	Pts	+/-	GW	GT	S	SPct	G	A	Pts	G	A	Pts	Num	PIM	Maj	Mnr	Fgt	Rgh	HHT	Hat	P/G
92-93	Ott	4	0	1	1	-3	0	0	2	0.0	0	0	0	0	0	0	0	0	0	0	0	0	0	0	.25
93-94		Did Not Play in NHL																							
94-95		Did Not Play in NHL																							
95-96		Did Not Play in NHL																							
96-97		Did Not Play in NHL																							
97-98	StL	61	11	15	26	5	3	0	103	10.7	0	0	0	1	1	2	5	10	0	5	0	1	3	0	.43
98-99	2Tm	65	10	8	18	-8	2	0	93	10.8	2	0	2	0	2	2	5	18	0	4	0	1	3	0	.28
98-99	Nsh	53	8	6	14	-10	1	0	70	11.4	2	0	2	0	1	1	4	16	0	3	0	1	2	0	.26
98-99	StL	12	2	2	4	2	1	0	23	8.7	0	0	0	0	1	1	1	2	0	1	0	0	1	0	.33
3 Years		130	21	24	45	-6	5	0	198	10.6	2	0	2	1	3	4	10	28	0	9	0	2	6	0	.35

Postseason																								
Year	Tm	GP	G	A	Pts	+/-	GW	OT	S	SPct	G	A	Pts	G	A	Pts	Num	PIM	Maj	Mnr	Fgt	Rgh	HHT	Hat	P/G
97-98	StL	10	0	0	0	-2	0	0	13	0.0	0	0	0	0	0	0	1	2	0	1	0	0	0	0	.00
98-99	StL	13	1	3	4	2	0	0	19	5.3	0	0	0	0	0	0	3	6	0	3	0	1	0	0	.31
2 Years		23	1	3	4	0	0	0	32	3.1	0	0	0	0	0	0	4	8	0	4	0	1	0	0	.17

Jean-Sebastian Aubin

Pos: G **Catches:** R **Ht:** 5'11" **Wt:** 174 **Born:** 7/19/77—Montreal, Quebec **Age:** 22

Overall																	Pen Shot		Offense		
Year	Tm	GP	GS	TP	W	L	T	Min	GA	GAA	Shots	SvPct	ShO	OE	PPGA	SHGA	Shots	GA	G	A	PIM
98-99	Pit	17	11	6	4	3	6	756	28	2.22	304	.908	2	4	7	1	0	0	0	0	0

Serge Aubin

Pos: C **Shoots:** R **Ht:** 6'1" **Wt:** 176 **Born:** 2/15/75—Val D'or, Quebec **Age:** 24

Overall										Power Play			Shorthand			Penalty							Misc	
Year	Tm	GP	G	A	Pts	+/-	GW	GT	S	SPct	G	A	Pts	G	A	Pts	Num	PIM	Maj	Mnr	Fgt	Rgh	HHT	Hat	P/G
98-99	Col	1	0	0	0	0	0	0	1	0.0	0	0	0	0	0	0	0	0	0	0	0	0	0	0	.00

Adrian Aucoin

(statistical profile on page 286)

Pos: D **Shoots:** R **Ht:** 6'2" **Wt:** 210 **Born:** 7/3/73—Ottawa, Ontario **Age:** 26

Overall										Power Play			Shorthand			Penalty							Misc	
Year	Tm	GP	G	A	Pts	+/-	GW	GT	S	SPct	G	A	Pts	G	A	Pts	Num	PIM	Maj	Mnr	Fgt	Rgh	HHT	Hat	P/G
94-95	Van	1	1	0	1	1	0	0	2	50.0	0	0	0	0	0	0	0	0	0	0	0	0	0	0	1.00
95-96	Van	49	4	14	18	8	0	0	85	4.7	2	6	8	0	0	0	17	34	0	17	0	0	12	0	.37
96-97	Van	70	5	16	21	0	0	0	116	4.3	1	3	4	0	0	0	30	63	1	29	1	5	10	0	.30
97-98	Van	35	3	3	6	-4	1	0	44	6.8	1	0	1	0	0	0	9	21	1	8	0	0	5	0	.17
98-99	Van	82	23	11	34	-14	3	1	174	13.2	18	3	21	2	0	2	37	77	1	36	1	5	13	0	.41
5 Years		237	36	44	80	-9	4	1	421	8.6	22	12	34	2	0	2	93	195	3	90	2	10	40	0	.34

Postseason																								
Year	Tm	GP	G	A	Pts	+/-	GW	OT	S	SPct	G	A	Pts	G	A	Pts	Num	PIM	Maj	Mnr	Fgt	Rgh	HHT	Hat	P/G
94-95	Van	4	1	0	1	-1	0	0	2	50.0	1	0	1	0	0	0	0	0	0	0	0	0	0	0	.25
95-96	Van	6	0	0	0	-5	0	0	7	0.0	0	0	0	0	0	0	1	2	0	1	0	0	0	0	.00
2 Years		10	1	0	1	-6	0	0	9	11.1	1	0	1	0	0	0	1	2	0	1	0	0	0	0	.10

Phillipe Audet

Pos: LW **Shoots:** L **Ht:** 6'2" **Wt:** 175 **Born:** 6/4/77—Ottawa, Ontario **Age:** 22

Overall											Power Play			Shorthand			Penalty							Misc	
Year	Tm	GP	G	A	Pts	+/–	GW	GT	S	SPct	G	A	Pts	G	A	Pts	Num	PIM	Maj	Mnr	Fgt	Rgh	HHT	Hat	P/G
98-99	Det	4	0	0	0	-2	0	0	3	0.0	0	0	0	0	0	0	0	0	0	0	0	0	0	0	.00

Donald Audette

(statistical profile on page 286)

Pos: RW **Shoots:** R **Ht:** 5'8" **Wt:** 184 **Born:** 9/23/69—Laval, Quebec **Age:** 30

Overall											Power Play			Shorthand			Penalty							Misc	
Year	Tm	GP	G	A	Pts	+/–	GW	GT	S	SPct	G	A	Pts	G	A	Pts	Num	PIM	Maj	Mnr	Fgt	Rgh	HHT	Hat	P/G
89-90											Did Not Play in Regular Season														
90-91	Buf	8	4	3	7	-1	1	0	17	23.5	2	–	–	0	–	–	2	4	0	2	0	–	–	0	.88
91-92	Buf	63	31	17	48	-1	6	1	153	20.3	5	3	8	0	0	0	25	75	3	20	2	5	2	0	.76
92-93	Buf	44	12	7	19	-8	0	0	92	13.0	2	0	2	0	0	0	20	51	1	18	1	4	3	0	.43
93-94	Buf	77	29	30	59	2	4	0	207	14.0	16	12	28	1	0	1	19	41	1	18	1	2	4	0	.77
94-95	Buf	46	24	13	37	-3	7	0	124	19.4	13	10	23	0	0	0	12	27	1	11	1	2	4	1	.80
95-96	Buf	23	12	13	25	0	1	0	92	13.0	8	7	15	0	0	0	5	18	0	4	0	0	2	1	1.09
96-97	Buf	73	28	22	50	-6	5	1	182	15.4	8	6	14	0	0	0	24	48	0	24	0	2	11	0	.68
97-98	Buf	75	24	20	44	10	5	1	198	12.1	10	4	14	0	0	0	24	59	1	22	0	5	10	0	.59
98-99	LA	49	18	18	36	7	2	0	152	11.8	6	9	15	0	0	0	20	51	1	18	1	1	7	0	.73
9 Years		458	182	143	325	0	31	3	1217	15.0	70	–	–	1	–	–	151	374	8	137	6	–	–	2	.71

Postseason

Year	Tm	GP	G	A	Pts	+/–	GW	OT	S	SPct	G	A	Pts	G	A	Pts	Num	PIM	Maj	Mnr	Fgt	Rgh	HHT	Hat	P/G
89-90	Buf	2	0	0	0	-2	0	0	2	0.0	0	0	0	0	0	0	0	0	0	0	0	0	0	0	.00
92-93	Buf	8	2	2	4	1	0	0	18	11.1	0	1	1	0	0	0	3	6	0	3	0	2	0	0	.50
93-94	Buf	7	0	1	1	-1	0	0	8	0.0	0	0	0	0	0	0	3	6	0	3	0	2	1	0	.14
94-95	Buf	5	1	1	2	-2	0	0	12	8.3	1	1	2	0	0	0	2	4	0	2	0	0	1	0	.40
96-97	Buf	11	4	5	9	-3	0	0	33	12.1	3	2	5	0	0	0	3	6	0	3	0	0	1	0	.82
97-98	Buf	15	5	8	13	-4	2	0	31	16.1	3	3	6	0	0	0	5	10	0	5	0	0	3	0	.87
6 Years		48	12	17	29	-11	2	0	104	11.5	7	7	14	0	0	0	16	32	0	16	0	4	6	0	.60

Patrik Augusta

Pos: RW **Shoots:** L **Ht:** 5'10" **Wt:** 169 **Born:** 11/13/69—Jihlava, Czechoslovakia **Age:** 30

Overall											Power Play			Shorthand			Penalty							Misc	
Year	Tm	GP	G	A	Pts	+/–	GW	GT	S	SPct	G	A	Pts	G	A	Pts	Num	PIM	Maj	Mnr	Fgt	Rgh	HHT	Hat	P/G
93-94	Tor	2	0	0	0	0	0	0	3	0.0	0	0	0	0	0	0	0	0	0	0	0	0	0	0	.00
94-95											Did Not Play in NHL														
95-96											Did Not Play in NHL														
96-97											Did Not Play in NHL														
97-98											Did Not Play in NHL														
98-99	Was	2	0	0	0	0	0	0	4	0.0	0	0	0	0	0	0	0	0	0	0	0	0	0	0	.00
2 Years		4	0	0	0	0	0	0	7	0.0	0	0	0	0	0	0	0	0	0	0	0	0	0	0	.00

Per Axelsson

(statistical profile on page 286)

Pos: LW **Shoots:** R **Ht:** 6'1" **Wt:** 174 **Born:** 2/26/75—Kungalv, Sweden **Age:** 24

Overall											Power Play			Shorthand			Penalty							Misc	
Year	Tm	GP	G	A	Pts	+/–	GW	GT	S	SPct	G	A	Pts	G	A	Pts	Num	PIM	Maj	Mnr	Fgt	Rgh	HHT	Hat	P/G
97-98	Bos	82	8	19	27	-14	1	0	144	5.6	2	0	2	0	0	0	15	38	0	14	0	1	8	0	.33
98-99	Bos	77	7	10	17	-14	2	0	146	4.8	0	1	1	0	1	1	9	18	0	9	0	2	3	0	.22
2 Years		159	15	29	44	-28	3	0	290	5.2	2	1	3	0	1	1	24	56	0	23	0	3	11	0	.28

Postseason

Year	Tm	GP	G	A	Pts	+/–	GW	OT	S	SPct	G	A	Pts	G	A	Pts	Num	PIM	Maj	Mnr	Fgt	Rgh	HHT	Hat	P/G
97-98	Bos	6	1	0	1	-3	0	0	13	7.7	0	0	0	0	0	0	0	0	0	0	0	0	0	0	.17
98-99	Bos	12	1	1	2	-1	0	0	20	5.0	0	0	0	0	0	0	2	4	0	2	0	0	1	0	.17
2 Years		18	2	1	3	-4	0	0	33	6.1	0	0	0	0	0	0	2	4	0	2	0	0	1	0	.17

Dave Babych

Pos: D **Shoots:** L **Ht:** 6'2" **Wt:** 215 **Born:** 5/23/61—Edmonton, Alberta **Age:** 38

Overall											Power Play			Shorthand			Penalty							Misc	
Year	Tm	GP	G	A	Pts	+/–	GW	GT	S	SPct	G	A	Pts	G	A	Pts	Num	PIM	Maj	Mnr	Fgt	Rgh	HHT	Hat	P/G
80-81	Wpg	69	6	38	44	-61	0	0	209	2.9	3	–	–	0	–	–	–	90	–	–	–	–	–	0	.64
81-82	Wpg	79	19	49	68	-11	2	3	262	7.3	11	–	–	0	–	–	–	92	–	–	–	–	–	0	.86

		Overall									Power Play			Shorthand			Penalty							Misc	
Year	Tm	GP	G	A	Pts	+/–	GW	GT	S	SPct	G	A	Pts	G	A	Pts	Num	PIM	Maj	Mnr	Fgt	Rgh	HHT	Hat	P/G
82-83	Wpg*	79	13	61	74	-10	1	0	253	5.1	7	–	–	0	–	–	–	56	–	–	–	–	–	0	.94
83-84	Wpg*	66	18	39	57	-31	4	0	233	7.7	10	–	–	0	–	–	–	62	–	–	–	–	–	0	.86
84-85	Wpg	78	13	49	62	-16	1	0	239	5.4	6	–	–	0	–	–	–	78	–	–	–	–	–	0	.79
85-86	2Tm	81	14	55	69	1	2	0	205	6.8	9	–	–	1	–	–	–	50	–	–	–	–	–	0	.85
86-87	Har	66	8	33	41	-18	1	0	157	5.1	7	–	–	0	–	–	–	44	–	–	–	–	–	0	.62
87-88	Har	71	14	36	50	-25	2	1	233	6.0	10	–	–	0	–	–	–	54	–	–	–	–	–	0	.70
88-89	Har	70	6	41	47	-5	2	0	172	3.5	4	–	–	0	–	–	–	54	–	–	–	–	–	0	.67
89-90	Har	72	6	37	43	-16	1	0	164	3.7	4	–	–	0	–	–	–	62	–	–	–	–	–	0	.60
90-91	Har	8	0	6	6	-4	0	0	15	0.0	0	–	–	0	–	–	2	4	0	2	0	–	–	0	.75
91-92	Van	75	5	24	29	-2	1	0	148	3.4	4	12	16	0	0	0	26	63	1	24	1	2	19	1	.39
92-93	Van	43	3	16	19	6	0	0	78	3.8	3	6	9	0	0	0	22	44	0	22	0	1	10	0	.44
93-94	Van	73	4	28	32	0	2	0	96	4.2	0	8	8	0	0	0	26	52	0	26	0	2	13	0	.44
94-95	Van	40	3	11	14	-13	0	0	58	5.2	1	5	6	0	0	0	9	18	0	9	0	1	6	0	.35
95-96	Van	53	3	21	24	-5	0	0	69	4.3	3	6	9	0	1	1	19	38	0	19	0	0	13	0	.45
96-97	Van	78	5	22	27	-2	1	0	105	4.8	2	2	4	0	2	2	19	38	0	19	0	0	12	0	.35
97-98	2Tm	53	0	9	9	-9	0	0	46	0.0	0	1	1	0	0	0	19	49	1	17	1	0	10	0	.17
98-99	2Tm	41	2	6	8	-2	0	0	49	4.1	2	3	5	0	0	0	11	22	0	11	0	0	5	0	.20
85-86	Wpg	19	4	12	16	-1	0	0	53	7.5	2	–	–	0	–	–	–	14	–	–	–	–	–	0	.84
85-86	Har	62	10	43	53	2	2	0	152	6.6	7	–	–	1	–	–	–	36	–	–	–	–	–	0	.85
97-98	Van	47	0	9	9	-11	0	0	40	0.0	0	1	1	0	0	0	13	37	1	11	1	0	5	0	.19
97-98	Phi	6	0	0	0	2	0	0	6	0.0	0	0	0	0	0	0	6	12	0	6	0	0	5	0	.00
98-99	Phi	33	2	4	6	0	0	0	44	4.5	2	3	5	0	0	0	10	20	0	10	0	0	4	0	.18
98-99	LA	8	0	2	2	-2	0	0	5	0.0	0	0	0	0	0	0	1	2	0	1	0	0	1	0	.25
19 Years		1195	142	581	723	-223	20	4	2791	5.1	86	–	–	1	–	–	–	970	–	–	–	–	–	1	.61
											Postseason														
Year	Tm	GP	G	A	Pts	+/–	GW	OT	S	SPct	G	A	Pts	G	A	Pts	Num	PIM	Maj	Mnr	Fgt	Rgh	HHT	Hat	P/G
81-82	Wpg	4	1	2	3	–	0	0	–	–	1	–	–	0	0	0	–	29	–	–	–	–	–	0	.75
82-83	Wpg	3	0	0	0	-5	0	0	7	0.0	0	0	0	0	0	0	0	0	0	0	0	0	0	0	.00
83-84	Wpg	3	1	1	2	-6	0	0	13	7.7	1	–	–	0	–	–	0	0	0	0	0	0	0	0	.67
84-85	Wpg	8	2	7	9	-3	0	0	20	10.0	2	–	–	0	–	–	3	6	0	3	0	–	–	0	1.13
85-86	Har	8	1	3	4	0	0	0	18	5.6	0	–	–	0	–	–	–	14	–	–	–	–	–	0	.50
86-87	Har	6	1	1	2	-4	0	0	27	3.7	1	–	–	0	0	0	–	14	–	–	–	–	–	0	.33
87-88	Har	6	3	2	5	-1	0	0	23	13.0	0	–	–	0	0	0	1	2	0	1	0	–	–	0	.83
88-89	Har	4	1	5	6	1	0	0	16	6.3	0	–	–	0	–	–	1	2	0	1	0	–	–	0	1.50
89-90	Har	7	1	2	3	5	0	0	14	7.1	0	–	–	0	0	0	0	0	0	0	0	0	0	0	.43
91-92	Van	13	2	6	8	6	1	0	25	8.0	1	1	2	0	0	0	5	10	0	5	0	1	3	0	.62
92-93	Van	12	2	5	7	-2	0	0	25	8.0	1	2	3	0	0	0	3	6	0	3	0	0	2	0	.58
93-94	Van	24	3	5	8	4	1	0	26	11.5	0	1	1	0	0	0	6	12	0	6	0	0	4	0	.33
94-95	Van	11	2	2	4	-8	0	0	16	12.5	1	1	2	1	0	1	7	14	0	7	0	0	5	0	.36
97-98	Phi	5	1	0	1	2	0	0	12	8.3	1	0	1	0	0	0	2	4	0	2	0	0	1	0	.20
14 Years		114	21	41	62	-11	2	0	242	8.3	9	–	–	1	–	–	–	113	–	–	–	–	–	0	.54

Ryan Bach

Pos: G **Catches:** L **Ht:** 5'11" **Wt:** 179 **Born:** 10/21/73—Sherwood Park, Alberta **Age:** 26

		Overall															Pen Shot		Offense		
Year	Tm	GP	GS	TP	W	L	T	Min	GA	GAA	Shots	SvPct	ShO	OE	PPGA	SHGA	Shots	GA	G	A	PIM
98-99	LA	3	1	0	0	3	0	108	8	4.44	66	.879	0	0	0	0	0	0	0	0	0

Jamie Baker

Pos: C **Shoots:** L **Ht:** 5'11" **Wt:** 190 **Born:** 8/31/66—Nepean, Quebec **Age:** 33

		Overall									Power Play			Shorthand			Penalty							Misc	
Year	Tm	GP	G	A	Pts	+/–	GW	GT	S	SPct	G	A	Pts	G	A	Pts	Num	PIM	Maj	Mnr	Fgt	Rgh	HHT	Hat	P/G
89-90	Que	1	0	0	0	-1	0	0	0	–	0	0	0	0	0	0	0	0	0	0	0	0	0	0	.00
90-91	Que	18	2	0	2	-4	0	1	18	11.1	0	0	0	1	0	1	4	8	0	4	0	–	–	0	.11
91-92	Que	52	7	10	17	-5	1	0	77	9.1	3	2	5	0	0	0	16	32	0	16	0	2	13	0	.33
92-93	Ott	76	19	29	48	-20	2	0	160	11.9	10	14	24	0	0	0	27	54	0	27	0	5	14	0	.63
93-94	SJ	65	12	5	17	2	2	0	68	17.6	0	0	0	0	0	0	19	38	0	19	0	2	8	0	.26
94-95	SJ	43	7	4	11	-7	0	0	60	11.7	0	0	0	1	1	2	11	22	0	11	0	0	8	0	.26
95-96	SJ	77	16	17	33	-19	0	0	117	13.7	2	0	2	6	1	7	34	79	1	32	1	2	14	0	.43
96-97	Tor	58	8	8	16	2	3	0	69	11.6	1	1	2	0	1	1	14	28	0	14	0	1	8	0	.28
97-98	Tor	13	0	5	5	1	0	0	16	0.0	0	0	0	0	0	0	5	10	0	5	0	0	2	0	.38
98-99	SJ	1	0	1	1	1	0	0	1	0.0	0	0	0	0	0	0	0	0	0	0	0	0	0	0	1.00
10 Years		404	71	79	150	-50	8	1	586	12.1	16	17	33	8	3	11	130	271	1	128	1	–	–	0	.37

Postseason																									
Year	Tm	GP	G	A	Pts	+/–	GW	OT	S	SPct	G	A	Pts	G	A	Pts	Num	PIM	Maj	Mnr	Fgt	Rgh	HHT	Hat	P/G
93-94	SJ	14	3	2	5	-1	1	0	13	23.1	0	0	0	0	0	0	11	30	0	10	0	8	0	0	.36
94-95	SJ	11	2	2	4	-7	1	0	20	10.0	0	0	0	0	0	0	6	12	0	6	0	1	4	0	.36
2 Years		25	5	4	9	-8	2	0	33	15.2	0	0	0	0	0	0	17	42	0	16	0	9	4	0	.36

Drew Bannister

Pos: D **Shoots:** R **Ht:** 6'2" **Wt:** 200 **Born:** 9/4/74—Belleville, Ontario **Age:** 25

Overall											Power Play			Shorthand			Penalty							Misc	
Year	Tm	GP	G	A	Pts	+/–	GW	GT	S	SPct	G	A	Pts	G	A	Pts	Num	PIM	Maj	Mnr	Fgt	Rgh	HHT	Hat	P/G
95-96	TB	13	0	1	1	-1	0	0	10	0.0	0	0	0	0	0	0	2	4	0	2	0	0	1	0	.08
96-97	2Tm	65	4	14	18	-23	0	0	59	6.8	1	6	7	0	0	0	15	44	2	12	2	2	5	0	.28
97-98	2Tm	61	0	8	8	-9	0	0	50	0.0	0	1	1	0	0	0	32	89	3	27	1	6	8	0	.13
98-99	TB	21	1	2	3	-4	0	0	29	3.4	0	2	2	0	0	0	12	24	0	12	0	3	4	0	.14
96-97	TB	64	4	13	17	-21	0	0	57	7.0	1	6	7	0	0	0	15	44	2	12	2	2	5	0	.27
96-97	Edm	1	0	1	1	-2	0	0	2	0.0	0	0	0	0	0	0	0	0	0	0	0	0	0	0	1.00
97-98	Edm	34	0	2	2	-7	0	0	27	0.0	0	1	1	0	0	0	14	42	2	11	1	4	1	0	.06
97-98	Anh	27	0	6	6	-2	0	0	23	0.0	0	0	0	0	0	0	18	47	1	16	0	2	7	0	.22
4 Years		160	5	25	30	-37	0	0	148	3.4	1	9	10	0	0	0	61	161	5	53	3	11	18	0	.19
Postseason																									
Year	Tm	GP	G	A	Pts	+/–	GW	OT	S	SPct	G	A	Pts	G	A	Pts	Num	PIM	Maj	Mnr	Fgt	Rgh	HHT	Hat	P/G
96-97	Edm	12	0	0	0	-4	0	0	9	0.0	0	0	0	0	0	0	7	30	0	5	0	1	0	0	.00

Matthew Barnaby

(statistical profile on page 286)

Pos: RW **Shoots:** L **Ht:** 6'0" **Wt:** 188 **Born:** 5/4/73—Ottawa, Ontario **Age:** 26

Overall											Power Play			Shorthand			Penalty							Misc	
Year	Tm	GP	G	A	Pts	+/–	GW	GT	S	SPct	G	A	Pts	G	A	Pts	Num	PIM	Maj	Mnr	Fgt	Rgh	HHT	Hat	P/G
92-93	Buf	2	1	0	1	0	0	0	8	12.5	1	0	1	0	0	0	2	10	2	0	2	0	0	0	.50
93-94	Buf	35	2	4	6	-7	0	0	13	15.4	1	1	2	0	0	0	29	106	8	18	8	10	1	0	.17
94-95	Buf	23	1	1	2	-2	0	0	27	3.7	0	0	0	0	0	0	30	116	8	18	7	4	6	0	.09
95-96	Buf	73	15	16	31	-2	0	0	131	11.5	0	0	0	0	0	0	88	**335**	29	50	28	16	8	0	.42
96-97	Buf	68	19	24	43	16	1	0	121	15.7	2	2	4	0	0	0	63	249	17	37	16	18	3	0	.63
97-98	Buf	72	5	20	25	8	2	0	96	5.2	0	3	3	0	0	0	74	289	15	47	14	**31**	5	0	.35
98-99	2Tm	62	6	16	22	-12	3	0	79	7.6	1	5	6	0	0	0	55	177	9	41	9	**23**	5	0	.35
98-99	Buf	44	4	14	18	-2	3	0	52	7.7	0	5	5	0	0	0	41	143	7	29	7	15	4	0	.41
98-99	Pit	18	2	2	4	-10	0	0	27	7.4	1	0	1	0	0	0	14	34	2	12	2	8	1	0	.22
7 Years		335	49	81	130	1	6	0	475	10.3	5	11	16	0	0	0	341	1282	88	211	84	102	28	0	.39
Postseason																									
Year	Tm	GP	G	A	Pts	+/–	GW	OT	S	SPct	G	A	Pts	G	A	Pts	Num	PIM	Maj	Mnr	Fgt	Rgh	HHT	Hat	P/G
92-93	Buf	1	0	1	1	1	0	0	0	–	0	0	0	0	0	0	2	4	0	2	0	1	0	0	1.00
93-94	Buf	3	0	0	0	2	0	0	0	–	0	0	0	0	0	0	3	17	1	1	1	0	0	0	.00
96-97	Buf	8	0	4	4	2	0	0	12	0.0	0	0	0	0	0	0	10	36	0	8	0	2	1	0	.50
97-98	Buf	15	7	6	13	6	1	0	25	28.0	3	2	5	0	0	0	7	22	0	6	0	3	0	1	.87
98-99	Pit	13	0	0	0	-2	0	0	10	0.0	0	0	0	0	0	0	8	35	1	5	1	2	0	0	.00
5 Years		40	7	11	18	9	1	0	47	14.9	3	2	5	0	0	0	30	114	2	22	2	8	1	1	.45

Stu Barnes

(statistical profile on page 287)

Pos: C **Shoots:** R **Ht:** 5'11" **Wt:** 174 **Born:** 12/25/70—Edmonton, Alberta **Age:** 29

Overall											Power Play			Shorthand			Penalty							Misc	
Year	Tm	GP	G	A	Pts	+/–	GW	GT	S	SPct	G	A	Pts	G	A	Pts	Num	PIM	Maj	Mnr	Fgt	Rgh	HHT	Hat	P/G
91-92	Wpg	46	8	9	17	-2	0	0	75	10.7	4	2	6	0	0	0	13	26	0	13	0	0	7	1	.37
92-93	Wpg	38	12	10	22	-3	3	0	73	16.4	3	1	4	0	0	0	5	10	0	5	0	0	4	0	.58
93-94	2Tm	77	23	24	47	4	3	0	172	13.4	8	8	16	1	0	1	19	38	0	19	0	2	14	0	.61
94-95	Fla	41	10	19	29	7	2	0	93	10.8	1	5	6	0	1	1	4	8	0	4	0	1	1	0	.71
95-96	Fla	72	19	25	44	-12	5	2	158	12.0	8	13	21	0	0	0	19	46	0	18	0	1	9	0	.61
96-97	2Tm	81	19	30	49	-23	3	3	176	10.8	5	7	12	0	1	1	13	26	0	13	0	1	3	0	.60
97-98	Pit	78	30	35	65	15	5	0	196	15.3	15	13	28	1	1	2	15	30	0	15	0	3	11	1	.83
98-99	2Tm	81	20	16	36	-11	3	0	180	11.1	13	4	17	1	0	0	15	30	0	15	0	0	8	1	.44
93-94	Wpg	18	5	4	9	-1	0	0	24	20.8	2	1	3	0	0	0	4	8	0	4	0	1	3	0	.50
93-94	Fla	59	18	20	38	5	3	0	148	12.2	6	7	13	1	0	1	15	30	0	15	0	1	11	0	.64
96-97	Fla	19	2	8	10	-3	0	1	44	4.5	1	4	5	0	0	0	5	10	0	5	0	1	0	0	.53
96-97	Pit	62	17	22	39	-20	3	2	132	12.9	4	3	7	0	1	1	8	16	0	8	0	2	3	0	.63
98-99	Pit	64	20	12	32	-12	3	0	155	12.9	13	3	16	0	0	0	10	20	0	10	0	0	7	1	.50
98-99	Buf	17	0	4	4	1	0	0	25	0.0	0	1	1	0	0	0	5	10	0	5	0	0	1	0	.24
8 Years		514	141	168	309	-25	24	5	1123	12.6	57	53	110	2	3	5	103	214	0	102	0	7	57	3	.60

											Postseason														
Year	Tm	GP	G	A	Pts	+/–	GW	OT	S	SPct	G	A	Pts	G	A	Pts	Num	PIM	Maj	Mnr	Fgt	Rgh	HHT	Hat	P/G
92-93	Wpg	6	1	3	4	1	0	0	3	33.3	0	0	0	0	0	0	1	2	0	1	0	0	1	0	.67
95-96	Fla	22	6	10	16	10	2	0	57	10.5	2	4	6	0	0	0	2	4	0	2	0	1	0	0	.73
96-97	Pit	5	0	1	1	0	0	0	4	0.0	0	0	0	0	0	0	0	0	0	0	0	0	0	0	.20
97-98	Pit	6	3	3	6	2	1	0	12	25.0	0	2	2	0	0	0	1	2	0	1	0	0	0	0	1.00
98-99	Buf	21	7	3	10	-1	1	0	30	23.3	4	1	5	0	0	0	3	6	0	3	0	0	2	0	.48
5 Years		60	17	20	37	12	4	0	106	16.0	6	7	13	0	0	0	7	14	0	7	0	1	3	0	.62

Murray Baron

Pos: D **Shoots:** L **Ht:** 6'3" **Wt:** 215 **Born:** 6/1/67—Prince George, British Columbia **Age:** 32

				Overall							Power Play			Shorthand			Penalty							Misc	
Year	Tm	GP	G	A	Pts	+/–	GW	GT	S	SPct	G	A	Pts	G	A	Pts	Num	PIM	Maj	Mnr	Fgt	Rgh	HHT	Hat	P/G
89-90	Phi	16	2	2	4	-1	0	0	18	11.1	0	–	–	0	–	–	–	12	–	–	–	–	–	0	.25
90-91	Phi	67	8	8	16	-3	1	0	86	9.3	3	–	–	0	–	–	–	74	–	–	–	–	–	0	.24
91-92	StL	67	3	8	11	-3	0	0	55	5.5	0	0	0	0	0	0	36	94	2	32	1	2	22	0	.16
92-93	StL	53	2	2	4	-5	1	0	42	4.8	0	0	0	0	0	0	24	59	1	22	1	1	8	0	.08
93-94	StL	77	5	9	14	-14	0	0	73	6.8	0	0	0	0	1	1	41	123	3	34	2	7	9	0	.18
94-95	StL	39	0	5	5	9	0	0	28	0.0	0	0	0	0	1	1	34	93	3	29	3	3	12	0	.13
95-96	StL	82	2	9	11	3	0	0	86	2.3	0	0	0	0	0	0	67	190	8	55	6	6	17	0	.13
96-97	3Tm	79	1	7	8	-20	0	0	64	1.6	0	1	1	0	1	1	52	122	6	46	6	7	10	0	.10
97-98	Pho	45	1	5	6	-10	0	0	23	4.3	0	0	0	0	0	0	43	106	4	38	4	4	14	0	.13
98-99	Van	81	2	6	8	-23	0	0	53	3.8	0	0	0	0	0	0	49	115	3	45	3	6	9	0	.10
96-97	StL	11	0	2	2	-4	0	0	7	0.0	0	0	0	0	0	0	4	11	1	3	1	0	1	0	.18
96-97	Mon	60	1	5	6	-16	0	0	52	1.9	0	1	1	0	1	1	46	107	5	41	5	6	9	0	.10
96-97	Pho	8	0	0	0	0	0	0	5	0.0	0	0	0	0	0	0	2	4	0	2	0	1	0	0	.00
10 Years		606	26	61	87	-67	2	0	528	4.9	3	–	–	0	–	–	–	988	–	–	–	–	–	0	.14
											Postseason														
Year	Tm	GP	G	A	Pts	+/–	GW	OT	S	SPct	G	A	Pts	G	A	Pts	Num	PIM	Maj	Mnr	Fgt	Rgh	HHT	Hat	P/G
91-92	StL	2	0	0	0	-1	0	0	2	0.0	0	0	0	0	0	0	1	2	0	1	0	0	0	0	.00
92-93	StL	11	0	0	0	-5	0	0	8	0.0	0	0	0	0	0	0	6	12	0	6	0	1	3	0	.00
93-94	StL	4	0	0	0	-1	0	0	5	0.0	0	0	0	0	0	0	5	10	0	5	0	2	1	0	.00
94-95	StL	7	1	1	2	2	0	0	9	11.1	0	0	0	0	1	1	1	2	0	1	0	0	1	0	.29
95-96	StL	13	1	0	1	4	0	0	10	10.0	0	0	0	1	0	1	10	20	0	10	0	1	3	0	.08
96-97	Pho	1	0	0	0	0	0	0	0	–	0	0	0	0	0	0	0	0	0	0	0	0	0	0	.00
97-98	Pho	6	0	2	2	2	0	0	4	0.0	0	0	0	0	0	0	3	6	0	3	0	0	0	0	.33
7 Years		44	2	3	5	1	0	0	38	5.3	0	0	0	1	1	2	26	52	0	26	0	4	8	0	.11

Tom Barrasso

(statistical profile on page 396)

Pos: G **Catches:** R **Ht:** 6'3" **Wt:** 210 **Born:** 3/31/65—Boston, Massachusetts **Age:** 34

					Overall												Pen Shot		Offense		
Year	Tm	GP	GS	TP	W	L	T	Min	GA	GAA	Shots	SvPct	ShO	OE	PPGA	SHGA	Shots	GA	G	A	PIM
83-84	Buf	42	–	–	26	12	3	2475	117	2.84	1098	.893	2	–	–	–	1	1	0	2	20
84-85	Buf*	54	–	–	25	18	**10**	3248	144	**2.66**	1274	.887	**5**	–	–	–	1	0	0	6	41
85-86	Buf	60	–	–	29	24	5	**3561**	214	3.61	1778	.880	2	–	–	–	0	0	0	4	28
86-87	Buf	46	–	–	17	23	2	2501	152	3.65	1202	.874	2	–	–	–	0	0	0	1	22
87-88	Buf	54	–	–	25	18	8	3133	173	3.31	1658	.896	2	–	–	–	0	0	0	1	50
88-89	2Tm	54	–	–	20	22	7	2951	207	4.21	1730	.880	0	–	–	–	0	0	0	8	70
89-90	Pit	24	–	–	7	12	3	1294	101	4.68	748	.865	0	–	–	–	1	0	0	0	8
90-91	Pit	48	–	–	27	16	3	2754	165	3.59	1579	.896	1	–	–	–	1	1	0	5	40
91-92	Pit	57	57	5	25	22	9	3329	196	3.53	1702	.885	1	16	52	10	0	0	0	4	30
92-93	Pit	63	62	3	**43**	14	5	3702	186	3.01	1885	.901	4	22	48	**13**	0	0	0	8	24
93-94	Pit	44	44	6	22	15	5	2482	139	3.36	1304	.893	2	15	36	6	0	0	0	1	42
94-95	Pit	2	2	0	0	1	1	125	8	3.84	75	.893	0	1	3	0	0	0	0	0	0
95-96	Pit	49	48	3	29	16	2	2799	160	3.43	1626	.902	2	21	43	6	0	0	0	3	18
96-97	Pit	5	5	1	0	5	0	270	26	5.78	186	.860	0	0	7	2	1	1	0	0	0
97-98	Pit	63	61	**9**	31	14	13	3542	122	2.07	1556	.922	7	17	38	9	0	0	0	2	14
98-99	Pit	43	43	10	19	16	3	2306	98	2.55	993	.901	4	10	28	5	1	0	0	3	20
88-89	Buf	10	–	–	2	7	0	545	45	4.95	285	.842	0	–	–	–	0	0	0	3	21
88-89	Pit	44	–	–	18	15	7	2406	162	4.04	1445	.888	0	–	–	–	0	0	0	5	49
16 Years		708	–	–	345	248	79	40472	2208	3.27	20394	.892	34	–	–	–	6	3	0	48	427
									Postseason												
Year	Tm	GP	GS	TP	W	L	Pct	Min	GA	GAA	Shots	SvPct	ShO	OE	PPGA	SHGA	Shots	GA	G	A	PIM
83-84	Buf	3	–	–	0	2	.000	139	8	3.45	59	.864	0	–	–	–	0	0	0	0	7
84-85	Buf	5	–	–	2	3	.400	300	22	4.40	151	.854	0	–	–	–	0	0	0	0	2
87-88	Buf	4	–	–	1	3	.250	224	16	4.29	120	.867	0	–	–	–	0	0	0	0	0

Postseason																					
Year	Tm	GP	GS	TP	W	L	Pct	Min	GA	GAA	Shots	SvPct	ShO	OE	PPGA	SHGA	Shots	GA	G	A	PIM
88-89	Pit	11	–	–	7	4	.636	631	40	3.80	389	.897	0	–	–	–	0	0	0	1	8
90-91	Pit	20	–	–	12	7	.632	1175	51	2.60	629	.919	1	–	–	–	0	0	0	1	2
91-92	Pit	21	21	1	16	5	.762	1233	58	2.82	622	.907	1	9	13	3	0	0	0	2	4
92-93	Pit	12	12	0	7	5	.583	722	35	2.91	370	.905	2	7	9	5	0	0	0	3	4
93-94	Pit	6	6	0	2	4	.333	356	17	2.87	162	.895	0	2	3	2	0	0	0	0	4
94-95	Pit	2	1	0	0	1	.000	80	8	6.00	41	.805	0	0	1	0	1	0	0	0	2
95-96	Pit	10	10	1	4	5	.444	558	26	2.80	337	.923	1	4	7	0	0	0	0	0	8
97-98	Pit	6	6	0	2	4	.333	376	17	2.71	171	.901	0	2	5	0	0	0	0	0	2
98-99	Pit	13	13	0	6	7	.462	787	35	2.67	350	.900	1	3	6	1	0	0	0	0	4
12 Years		113	–	–	59	50	.541	6581	333	3.04	3401	.902	6	–	–	–	1	0	0	7	47

Lubos Bartecko

(statistical profile on page 287)

Pos: LW **Shoots:** L **Ht:** 6'1" **Wt:** 195 **Born:** 7/14/76—Kezmarok, Czechoslovakia **Age:** 23

Overall											Power Play			Shorthand			Penalty							Misc	
Year	Tm	GP	G	A	Pts	+/-	GW	GT	S	SPct	G	A	Pts	G	A	Pts	Num	PIM	Maj	Mnr	Fgt	Rgh	HHT	Hat	P/G
98-99	StL	32	5	11	16	4	1	0	37	13.5	0	4	4	0	0	0	3	6	0	3	0	0	0	0	.50
Postseason																									
Year	Tm	GP	G	A	Pts	+/-	GW	OT	S	SPct	G	A	Pts	G	A	Pts	Num	PIM	Maj	Mnr	Fgt	Rgh	HHT	Hat	P/G
98-99	StL	5	0	0	0	-3	0	0	8	0.0	0	0	0	0	0	0	1	2	0	1	0	0	0	0	.00

Andrei Bashkirov

Pos: LW **Shoots:** R **Ht:** 6'0" **Wt:** 198 **Born:** 6/22/70—Shelekhov, USSR **Age:** 29

Overall											Power Play			Shorthand			Penalty							Misc	
Year	Tm	GP	G	A	Pts	+/-	GW	GT	S	SPct	G	A	Pts	G	A	Pts	Num	PIM	Maj	Mnr	Fgt	Rgh	HHT	Hat	P/G
98-99	Mon	10	0	0	0	-3	0	0	4	0.0	0	0	0	0	0	0	0	0	0	0	0	0	0	0	.00

Bob Bassen

Pos: C **Shoots:** L **Ht:** 5'10" **Wt:** 185 **Born:** 5/6/65—Calgary, Alberta **Age:** 34

Overall											Power Play			Shorthand			Penalty							Misc	
Year	Tm	GP	G	A	Pts	+/–	GW	GT	S	SPct	G	A	Pts	G	A	Pts	Num	PIM	Maj	Mnr	Fgt	Rgh	HHT	Hat	P/G
85-86	NYI	11	2	1	3	0	0	0	5	40.0	0	–	–	0	–	–	3	6	0	3	0	–	–	0	.27
86-87	NYI	77	7	10	17	-17	1	0	59	11.9	0	–	–	0	–	–	–	89	–	–	–	–	–	0	.22
87-88	NYI	77	6	16	22	8	2	0	65	9.2	1	–	–	0	–	–	–	99	–	–	–	–	–	0	.29
88-89	2Tm	68	5	16	21	5	1	0	51	9.8	0	–	–	0	–	–	–	83	–	–	–	–	–	0	.31
89-90	Chi	6	1	1	2	1	0	0	7	14.3	0	–	–	0	–	–	4	8	0	4	0	–	–	0	.33
90-91	StL	79	16	18	34	17	1	0	117	13.7	0	–	–	2	–	–	–	183	–	–	–	–	–	0	.43
91-92	StL	79	7	25	32	12	1	0	101	6.9	0	1	1	0	2	2	55	167	11	41	11	8	12	0	.41
92-93	StL	53	9	10	19	0	0	0	61	14.8	0	0	0	1	2	3	27	63	3	24	3	5	4	0	.36
93-94	2Tm	83	13	15	28	-17	0	1	129	10.1	1	0	1	1	0	1	45	99	3	42	3	10	13	0	.34
94-95	Que	47	12	15	27	14	1	0	66	18.2	0	0	0	1	0	1	15	33	1	14	1	2	5	0	.57
95-96	Dal	13	0	1	1	-6	0	0	9	0.0	0	0	0	0	0	0	6	15	1	5	1	1	1	0	.08
96-97	Dal	46	5	7	12	5	2	0	50	10.0	0	0	0	0	0	0	16	41	3	13	3	4	4	0	.26
97-98	Dal	58	3	4	7	-4	1	0	40	7.5	0	0	0	0	0	0	21	57	5	16	5	5	6	0	.12
98-99	Cgy	41	1	2	3	-13	0	0	47	2.1	0	0	0	0	0	0	16	35	1	15	1	2	5	0	.07
88-89	NYI	19	1	4	5	0	0	0	14	7.1	0	–	–	0	–	–	–	21	–	–	–	–	–	0	.26
88-89	Chi	49	4	12	16	5	1	0	37	10.8	0	–	–	0	–	–	–	62	–	–	–	–	–	0	.33
93-94	StL	46	2	7	9	-14	0	0	73	2.7	0	0	0	1	0	1	22	44	0	22	0	0	11	0	.20
93-94	Que	37	11	8	19	-3	0	1	56	19.6	1	0	1	0	0	0	23	55	3	20	3	10	2	0	.51
14 Years		738	87	141	228	5	10	1	807	10.8	2	–	–	5	–	–	–	978	–	–	–	–	–	0	.31
Postseason																									
Year	Tm	GP	G	A	Pts	+/–	GW	OT	S	SPct	G	A	Pts	G	A	Pts	Num	PIM	Maj	Mnr	Fgt	Rgh	HHT	Hat	P/G
85-86	NYI	3	0	1	1	-1	0	0	1	0.0	0	–	–	0	0	0	0	0	0	0	0	0	0	0	.33
86-87	NYI	14	1	2	3	2	0	0	17	5.9	0	–	–	0	0	0	–	21	–	–	–	–	–	0	.21
87-88	NYI	6	0	1	1	2	0	0	4	0.0	0	–	–	0	–	–	–	23	–	–	–	–	–	0	.17
88-89	Chi	10	1	1	2	1	0	0	7	14.3	0	–	–	0	–	–	–	34	–	–	–	–	–	0	.20
89-90	Chi	1	0	0	0	-1	0	0	0	–	0	0	0	0	0	0	1	2	0	1	0	–	–	0	.00
90-91	StL	13	1	3	4	1	0	0	16	6.3	0	–	–	0	0	0	–	24	–	–	–	–	–	0	.31
91-92	StL	6	0	2	2	0	0	0	5	0.0	0	0	0	0	0	0	2	4	0	2	0	0	1	0	.33
92-93	StL	11	0	0	0	-7	0	0	6	0.0	0	0	0	0	0	0	5	10	0	5	0	1	3	0	.00
94-95	Que	5	2	4	6	2	0	0	10	20.0	0	0	0	0	0	0	0	0	0	0	0	0	0	0	1.20
96-97	Dal	7	3	1	4	3	0	0	12	25.0	0	0	0	0	0	0	2	4	0	2	0	0	0	0	.57
97-98	Dal	17	1	0	1	-3	0	0	13	7.7	0	0	0	0	0	0	6	12	0	6	0	0	2	0	.06
11 Years		93	9	15	24	-1	0	0	91	9.9	0	–	–	0	–	–	–	134	–	–	–	–	–	0	.26

Ryan Bast

Pos: D **Shoots:** R **Ht:** 6'2" **Wt:** 190 **Born:** 8/27/75—Spruce Grove, Alberta **Age:** 24

Overall											Power Play			Shorthand			Penalty							Misc	
Year	Tm	GP	G	A	Pts	+/–	GW	GT	S	SPct	G	A	Pts	G	A	Pts	Num	PIM	Maj	Mnr	Fgt	Rgh	HHT	Hat	P/G
98-99	Phi	2	0	1	1	0	0	0	1	0.0	0	0	0	0	0	0	0	0	0	0	0	0	0	0	.50

Shawn Bates

Pos: C **Shoots:** R **Ht:** 5'11" **Wt:** 205 **Born:** 4/3/75—Melrose, Massachusetts **Age:** 24

Overall											Power Play			Shorthand			Penalty							Misc	
Year	Tm	GP	G	A	Pts	+/–	GW	GT	S	SPct	G	A	Pts	G	A	Pts	Num	PIM	Maj	Mnr	Fgt	Rgh	HHT	Hat	P/G
97-98	Bos	13	2	0	2	-3	0	0	12	16.7	0	0	0	0	0	0	1	2	0	1	0	0	0	0	.15
98-99	Bos	33	5	4	9	3	0	0	30	16.7	0	0	0	0	0	0	1	2	0	1	0	0	1	0	.27
2 Years		46	7	4	11	0	0	0	42	16.7	0	0	0	0	0	0	2	4	0	2	0	0	1	0	.24

Postseason

Year	Tm	GP	G	A	Pts	+/–	GW	OT	S	SPct	G	A	Pts	G	A	Pts	Num	PIM	Maj	Mnr	Fgt	Rgh	HHT	Hat	P/G
98-99	Bos	12	0	0	0	-1	0	0	11	0.0	0	0	0	0	0	0	2	4	0	2	0	0	0	0	.00

Bates Battaglia

(statistical profile on page 287)

Pos: LW **Shoots:** L **Ht:** 6'2" **Wt:** 185 **Born:** 12/13/75—Chicago, Illinois **Age:** 24

Overall											Power Play			Shorthand			Penalty							Misc	
Year	Tm	GP	G	A	Pts	+/–	GW	GT	S	SPct	G	A	Pts	G	A	Pts	Num	PIM	Maj	Mnr	Fgt	Rgh	HHT	Hat	P/G
97-98	Car	33	2	4	6	-1	1	0	21	9.5	0	0	0	0	0	0	5	10	0	5	0	0	4	0	.18
98-99	Car	60	7	11	18	7	0	2	52	13.5	0	0	0	0	0	0	11	22	0	11	0	1	4	0	.30
2 Years		93	9	15	24	6	1	2	73	12.3	0	0	0	0	0	0	16	32	0	16	0	1	8	0	.26

Postseason

Year	Tm	GP	G	A	Pts	+/–	GW	OT	S	SPct	G	A	Pts	G	A	Pts	Num	PIM	Maj	Mnr	Fgt	Rgh	HHT	Hat	P/G
98-99	Car	6	0	3	3	3	0	0	7	0.0	0	0	0	0	0	0	4	8	0	4	0	0	2	0	.50

Ken Baumgartner

Pos: LW **Shoots:** L **Ht:** 6'1" **Wt:** 205 **Born:** 3/11/66—Flin Flon, Manitoba **Age:** 33

Overall											Power Play			Shorthand			Penalty							Misc	
Year	Tm	GP	G	A	Pts	+/–	GW	GT	S	SPct	G	A	Pts	G	A	Pts	Num	PIM	Maj	Mnr	Fgt	Rgh	HHT	Hat	P/G
87-88	LA	30	2	3	5	5	0	0	17	11.8	0	–	–	0	–	–	–	189	–	–	–	–	–	0	.17
88-89	LA	49	1	3	4	-9	0	0	15	6.7	0	–	–	0	–	–	–	288	–	–	–	–	–	0	.08
89-90	2Tm	65	1	5	6	-4	0	0	48	2.1	0	–	–	0	–	–	–	222	–	–	–	–	–	0	.09
90-91	NYI	78	1	6	7	-14	0	0	41	2.4	0	–	–	0	–	–	–	282	–	–	–	–	–	0	.09
91-92	2Tm	55	0	1	1	-9	0	0	16	0.0	0	0	0	0	0	0	56	225	19	30	18	11	9	0	.02
92-93	Tor	63	1	0	1	-11	0	0	23	4.3	0	0	0	0	0	0	45	155	11	30	11	10	3	0	.02
93-94	Tor	64	4	4	8	-6	0	0	34	11.8	0	0	0	0	0	0	52	185	19	30	18	16	0	0	.13
94-95	Tor	2	0	0	0	0	0	0	1	0.0	0	0	0	0	0	0	1	5	1	0	1	0	0	0	.00
95-96	2Tm	72	2	4	6	-5	1	0	32	6.3	0	0	0	0	0	0	52	193	19	29	19	14	3	0	.08
96-97	Anh	67	0	11	11	0	0	0	20	0.0	0	0	0	0	0	0	44	182	18	21	18	9	5	0	.16
97-98	Bos	82	0	1	1	-14	0	0	28	0.0	0	0	0	0	0	0	55	199	19	32	19	19	0	0	.01
98-99	Bos	69	1	3	4	-6	0	1	15	6.7	0	0	0	0	0	0	28	119	13	12	12	3	4	0	.06
89-90	LA	12	1	0	1	-10	0	0	7	14.3	0	0	0	0	0	0	–	28	–	–	–	–	–	0	.08
89-90	NYI	53	0	5	5	6	0	0	41	0.0	0	–	–	0	–	–	–	194	–	–	–	–	–	0	.09
91-92	NYI	44	0	1	1	-10	0	0	11	0.0	0	0	0	0	0	0	50	202	18	26	17	8	9	0	.02
91-92	Tor	11	0	0	0	1	0	0	5	0.0	0	0	0	0	0	0	6	23	1	4	1	3	0	0	.00
95-96	Tor	60	2	3	5	-5	1	0	27	7.4	0	0	0	0	0	0	40	152	16	21	16	9	3	0	.08
95-96	Anh	12	0	1	1	0	0	0	5	0.0	0	0	0	0	0	0	12	41	3	8	3	5	0	0	.08
12 Years		696	13	41	54	-73	1	1	290	4.5	0	–	–	0	–	–	–	2244	–	–	–	–	–	0	.08

Postseason

Year	Tm	GP	G	A	Pts	+/–	GW	OT	S	SPct	G	A	Pts	G	A	Pts	Num	PIM	Maj	Mnr	Fgt	Rgh	HHT	Hat	P/G
87-88	LA	5	0	1	1	-6	0	0	4	0.0	0	–	–	0	0	0	–	28	–	–	–	–	–	0	.20
88-89	LA	5	0	0	0	-2	0	0	1	0.0	0	0	0	0	0	0	4	8	0	4	0	–	–	0	.00
89-90	NYI	4	0	0	0	1	0	0	0	–	0	0	0	0	0	0	–	27	–	–	–	–	–	0	.00
92-93	Tor	7	1	0	1	1	0	0	2	50.0	0	0	0	0	0	0	0	0	0	0	0	0	0	0	.14
93-94	Tor	10	0	0	0	-1	0	0	3	0.0	0	0	0	0	0	0	5	18	0	4	0	1	1	0	.00
96-97	Anh	11	0	1	1	0	0	0	0	–	0	0	0	0	0	0	4	11	1	3	1	2	0	0	.09
97-98	Bos	6	0	0	0	0	0	0	1	0.0	0	0	0	0	0	0	4	14	2	2	2	1	0	0	.00
98-99	Bos	3	0	0	0	0	0	0	0	–	0	0	0	0	0	0	0	0	0	0	0	0	0	0	.00
8 Years		51	1	2	3	-7	0	0	11	9.1	0	–	–	0	0	0	–	106	–	–	–	–	–	0	.06

Nolan Baumgartner

Pos: D **Shoots:** R **Ht:** 6'1" **Wt:** 198 **Born:** 5/23/76—Calgary, Alberta **Age:** 23

Overall											Power Play			Shorthand			Penalty							Misc	
Year	Tm	GP	G	A	Pts	+/–	GW	GT	S	SPct	G	A	Pts	G	A	Pts	Num	PIM	Maj	Mnr	Fgt	Rgh	HHT	Hat	P/G
95-96	Was	1	0	0	0	-1	0	0	0	–	0	0	0	0	0	0	0	0	0	0	0	0	0	0	.00
96-97		Did Not Play in NHL																							
97-98	Was	4	0	1	1	0	0	0	4	0.0	0	1	1	0	0	0	0	0	0	0	0	0	0	0	.25
98-99	Was	5	0	0	0	-3	0	0	1	0.0	0	0	0	0	0	0	0	0	0	0	0	0	0	0	.00
3 Years		10	0	1	1	-4	0	0	5	0.0	0	1	1	0	0	0	0	0	0	0	0	0	0	0	.10
Postseason																									
Year	Tm	GP	G	A	Pts	+/–	GW	OT	S	SPct	G	A	Pts	G	A	Pts	Num	PIM	Maj	Mnr	Fgt	Rgh	HHT	Hat	P/G
95-96	Was	1	0	0	0	-1	0	0	0	–	0	0	0	0	0	0	1	10	0	0	0	0	0	0	.00

Wade Belak

Pos: D **Shoots:** R **Ht:** 6'5" **Wt:** 223 **Born:** 7/3/76—Saskatoon, Saskatchewan **Age:** 23

Overall											Power Play			Shorthand			Penalty							Misc	
Year	Tm	GP	G	A	Pts	+/–	GW	GT	S	SPct	G	A	Pts	G	A	Pts	Num	PIM	Maj	Mnr	Fgt	Rgh	HHT	Hat	P/G
96-97	Col	5	0	0	0	-1	0	0	1	0.0	0	0	0	0	0	0	4	11	1	3	1	1	2	0	.00
97-98	Col	8	1	1	2	-3	1	0	2	50.0	0	0	0	0	0	0	5	27	3	1	3	0	0	0	.25
98-99	2Tm	31	0	1	1	1	0	0	7	0.0	0	0	0	0	0	0	24	94	10	12	10	3	3	0	.03
98-99	Col	22	0	0	0	-2	0	0	5	0.0	0	0	0	0	0	0	17	71	7	8	7	0	3	0	.00
98-99	Cgy	9	0	1	1	3	0	0	2	0.0	0	0	0	0	0	0	7	23	3	4	3	3	0	0	.11
3 Years		44	1	2	3	-3	1	0	10	10.0	0	0	0	0	0	0	33	132	14	16	14	4	5	0	.07

Ken Belanger

Pos: LW **Shoots:** L **Ht:** 6'4" **Wt:** 225 **Born:** 5/14/74—Sault Ste. Marie, Ontario **Age:** 25

Overall											Power Play			Shorthand			Penalty							Misc	
Year	Tm	GP	G	A	Pts	+/–	GW	GT	S	SPct	G	A	Pts	G	A	Pts	Num	PIM	Maj	Mnr	Fgt	Rgh	HHT	Hat	P/G
94-95	Tor	3	0	0	0	0	0	0	1	0.0	0	0	0	0	0	0	3	9	1	2	1	1	0	0	.00
95-96	NYI	7	0	0	0	-2	0	0	0	–	0	0	0	0	0	0	8	27	1	6	1	5	0	0	.00
96-97	NYI	18	0	2	2	-1	0	0	5	0.0	0	0	0	0	0	0	21	102	12	6	12	1	0	0	.11
97-98	NYI	37	3	1	4	1	1	0	10	30.0	0	0	0	0	0	0	22	101	11	8	11	2	3	0	.11
98-99	2Tm	54	2	5	7	-1	0	0	19	10.5	0	0	0	0	0	0	45	182	12	26	11	11	5	0	.13
98-99	NYI	9	1	1	2	1	0	0	3	33.3	0	0	0	0	0	0	8	30	2	5	2	2	0	0	.22
98-99	Bos	45	1	4	5	-2	0	0	16	6.3	0	0	0	0	0	0	37	152	10	21	9	9	5	0	.11
5 Years		119	5	8	13	-3	1	0	35	14.3	0	0	0	0	0	0	99	421	37	48	36	20	8	0	.11
Postseason																									
Year	Tm	GP	G	A	Pts	+/–	GW	OT	S	SPct	G	A	Pts	G	A	Pts	Num	PIM	Maj	Mnr	Fgt	Rgh	HHT	Hat	P/G
98-99	Bos	12	1	0	1	2	0	0	7	14.3	0	0	0	0	0	0	8	16	0	8	0	3	0	0	.08

Ed Belfour

(statistical profile on page 396)

Pos: G **Catches:** L **Ht:** 5'11" **Wt:** 182 **Born:** 4/21/65—Carman, Manitoba **Age:** 34

Overall																	Pen Shot		Offense		
Year	Tm	GP	GS	TP	W	L	T	Min	GA	GAA	Shots	SvPct	ShO	OE	PPGA	SHGA	Shots	GA	G	A	PIM
88-89	Chi	23	–	–	4	12	3	1148	74	3.87	605	.878	0	–	–	–	0	0	0	1	6
89-90		Did Not Play in Regular Season																			
90-91	Chi	**74**	–	–	**43**	19	7	**4127**	170	**2.47**	**1883**	**.910**	4	–	–	–	0	0	0	3	34
91-92	Chi*	52	50	7	21	18	10	2928	132	2.70	1241	.894	**5**	10	40	8	0	0	0	2	38
92-93	Chi*	**71**	**70**	6	41	18	**11**	**4106**	177	2.59	1880	.906	**7**	20	65	7	2	1	0	3	28
93-94	Chi	70	70	8	37	24	6	3998	178	2.67	1892	.906	**7**	23	53	9	**3**	**1**	0	4	61
94-95	Chi	42	42	3	22	15	3	2450	93	2.28	990	.906	**5**	8	31	3	0	0	0	3	11
95-96	Chi*	50	49	2	22	17	10	2956	135	2.74	1373	.902	1	11	45	3	0	0	0	2	36
96-97	2Tm	46	45	1	14	24	6	2723	131	2.89	1317	.901	2	13	37	10	0	0	0	0	34
97-98	Dal*	61	60	3	37	12	10	3581	112	**1.88**	1335	.916	9	16	34	6	0	0	0	0	18
98-99	Dal	61	59	4	35	15	9	3536	117	1.99	1373	.915	5	11	34	3	0	0	0	0	26
96-97	Chi	33	32	0	11	15	6	1966	88	2.69	946	.907	1	11	24	6	0	0	0	0	26
96-97	SJ	13	13	1	3	9	0	757	43	3.41	371	.884	1	2	13	4	0	0	0	0	8
10 Years		550	–	–	276	174	75	31553	1319	2.51	13889	.905	45	–	–	–	5	2	0	18	292
Postseason																					
Year	Tm	GP	GS	TP	W	L	Pct	Min	GA	GAA	Shots	SvPct	ShO	OE	PPGA	SHGA	Shots	GA	G	A	PIM
89-90	Chi	9	–	–	4	2	.667	409	17	2.49	200	.915	0	–	–	–	0	0	0	1	6
90-91	Chi	6	–	–	2	4	.333	295	20	4.07	183	.891	0	–	–	–	1	1	0	0	6
91-92	Chi	18	17	3	12	4	.750	949	39	2.47	398	.902	1	3	11	2	0	0	0	0	0

Postseason																					
Year	Tm	GP	GS	TP	W	L	Pct	Min	GA	GAA	Shots	SvPct	ShO	OE	PPGA	SHGA	Shots	GA	G	A	PIM
92-93	Chi	4	4	0	0	4	.000	249	13	3.13	97	.866	0	0	7	1	0	0	0	0	2
93-94	Chi	6	6	0	2	4	.333	360	15	2.50	191	.921	0	3	9	1	0	0	0	0	2
94-95	Chi	16	16	2	9	7	.563	1014	37	2.19	479	.923	1	6	10	1	0	0	0	0	6
95-96	Chi	9	9	0	6	3	.667	666	23	2.07	323	.929	1	4	3	0	0	0	0	0	4
97-98	Dal	17	17	1	10	7	.588	1039	31	1.79	399	.922	1	3	11	2	0	0	0	0	18
98-99	Dal	23	23	0	16	7	.696	1544	43	1.67	617	.930	3	8	9	0	0	0	0	0	4
9 Years		108	–	–	61	42	.592	6525	238	2.19	2887	.918	7	–	–	–	1	1	0	1	48

Brian Bellows

(statistical profile on page 287)

Pos: LW **Shoots:** R **Ht:** 6'0" **Wt:** 190 **Born:** 9/1/64—St. Catharines, Ontario **Age:** 35

Overall											Power Play			Shorthand			Penalty							Misc	
Year	Tm	GP	G	A	Pts	+/-	GW	GT	S	SPct	G	A	Pts	G	A	Pts	Num	PIM	Maj	Mnr	Fgt	Rgh	HHT	Hat	P/G
82-83	Min	78	35	30	65	-12	3	1	184	19.0	15	–	–	1	–	–	–	27	–	–	–	–	–	0	.83
83-84	Min*	78	41	42	83	-2	5	1	236	17.4	14	–	–	5	–	–	–	66	–	–	–	–	–	0	1.06
84-85	Min	78	26	36	62	-18	3	1	211	12.3	8	–	–	1	–	–	–	72	–	–	–	–	–	0	.79
85-86	Min	77	31	48	79	16	2	**2**	256	12.1	11	–	–	2	–	–	–	46	–	–	–	–	–	1	1.03
86-87	Min	65	26	27	53	-13	2	0	200	13.0	8	–	–	1	–	–	–	34	–	–	–	–	–	0	.82
87-88	Min*	77	40	41	81	-8	4	0	283	14.1	21	–	–	1	–	–	–	81	–	–	–	–	–	1	1.05
88-89	Min	60	23	27	50	-14	4	1	196	11.7	7	–	–	0	–	–	–	55	–	–	–	–	–	1	.83
89-90	Min	**80**	55	44	99	-3	9	0	300	18.3	21	–	–	1	–	–	–	72	–	–	–	–	–	1	1.24
90-91	Min	80	35	40	75	-13	4	0	296	11.8	17	–	–	0	–	–	–	43	–	–	–	–	–	1	.94
91-92	Min*	80	30	45	75	-20	4	0	255	11.8	12	20	32	1	1	2	19	41	1	18	1	4	5	2	.94
92-93	Mon	82	40	48	88	4	5	0	260	15.4	16	19	35	0	0	0	22	44	0	22	0	5	5	1	1.07
93-94	Mon	77	33	38	71	9	2	1	251	13.1	13	14	27	0	0	0	18	36	0	18	0	4	6	0	.92
94-95	Mon	41	8	8	16	-7	1	0	110	7.3	1	4	5	0	0	0	4	8	0	4	0	0	1	0	.39
95-96	TB	79	23	26	49	-14	4	0	190	12.1	13	14	27	0	0	0	18	39	1	17	0	1	6	1	.62
96-97	2Tm	69	16	15	31	-15	1	0	168	9.5	8	3	11	0	0	0	11	22	0	11	0	0	7	0	.45
97-98	Was	11	6	3	9	-3	2	0	26	23.1	5	0	5	0	0	0	3	6	0	3	0	0	1	0	.82
98-99	Was	76	17	19	36	-12	3	0	166	10.2	8	3	11	0	0	0	13	26	0	13	0	0	3	0	.47
96-97	TB	7	1	2	3	-4	0	0	17	5.9	0	0	0	0	0	0	0	0	0	0	0	0	0	0	.43
96-97	Anh	62	15	13	28	-11	1	0	151	9.9	8	3	11	0	0	0	11	22	0	11	0	0	7	0	.45
17 Years		1188	485	537	1022	-125	58	7	3588	13.5	198	–	–	13	–	–	–	718	–	–	–	–	–	9	.86

Postseason																									
Year	Tm	GP	G	A	Pts	+/-	GW	OT	S	SPct	G	A	Pts	G	A	Pts	Num	PIM	Maj	Mnr	Fgt	Rgh	HHT	Hat	P/G
82-83	Min	9	5	4	9	-7	0	0	26	19.2	2	–	–	0	0	0	–	18	–	–	–	–	–	0	1.00
83-84	Min	16	2	12	14	-2	0	0	33	6.1	0	–	–	1	–	–	3	6	0	3	0	–	–	0	.88
84-85	Min	9	2	4	6	-2	0	0	26	7.7	0	–	–	1	–	–	3	9	1	2	–	–	–	0	.67
85-86	Min	5	5	0	5	1	0	0	16	31.3	3	0	3	0	0	0	–	16	–	–	–	–	–	0	1.00
88-89	Min	5	2	3	5	-5	0	0	15	13.3	2	–	–	0	–	–	4	8	0	4	0	–	–	0	1.00
89-90	Min	7	4	3	7	-4	1	0	28	14.3	3	–	–	0	0	0	–	10	–	–	–	–	–	0	1.00
90-91	Min	23	10	19	29	-6	1	0	68	14.7	6	–	–	0	–	–	–	30	–	–	–	–	–	0	1.26
91-92	Min	7	4	4	8	-4	1	0	14	28.6	2	3	5	0	0	0	7	14	0	7	0	1	3	0	1.14
92-93	Mon	18	6	9	15	6	0	0	72	8.3	2	3	5	0	0	0	9	18	0	9	0	3	2	0	.83
93-94	Mon	6	1	2	3	-2	0	0	16	6.3	0	2	2	0	0	0	1	2	0	1	0	0	0	0	.50
95-96	TB	6	2	0	2	-2	1	1	19	10.5	0	0	0	0	0	0	2	4	0	2	0	1	0	0	.33
96-97	Anh	11	2	4	6	-7	0	0	36	5.6	1	1	2	0	0	0	1	2	0	1	0	0	0	0	.55
97-98	Was	21	6	7	13	6	1	1	62	9.7	2	1	3	0	0	0	3	6	0	3	0	0	1	0	.62
13 Years		143	51	71	122	-28	5	2	431	11.8	23	–	–	2	–	–	–	143	–	–	–	–	–	0	.85

Josef Beranek

(statistical profile on page 288)

Pos: LW **Shoots:** L **Ht:** 6'2" **Wt:** 192 **Born:** 10/25/69—Litvinov, Czechoslovakia **Age:** 30

Overall											Power Play			Shorthand			Penalty							Misc	
Year	Tm	GP	G	A	Pts	+/-	GW	GT	S	SPct	G	A	Pts	G	A	Pts	Num	PIM	Maj	Mnr	Fgt	Rgh	HHT	Hat	P/G
91-92	Edm	58	12	16	28	-2	1	0	79	15.2	0	3	3	0	0	0	9	18	0	9	0	1	3	0	.48
92-93	2Tm	66	15	18	33	-8	0	0	130	11.5	1	4	5	0	0	0	29	78	4	24	4	10	4	0	.50
93-94	Phi	80	28	21	49	-2	2	0	182	15.4	6	3	9	0	0	0	30	85	3	25	2	6	5	0	.61
94-95	2Tm	**51**	13	18	31	-7	0	1	134	9.7	3	6	9	0	0	0	15	30	0	15	0	3	6	1	.61
95-96	Van	61	6	14	20	-11	1	0	131	4.6	0	1	1	0	0	0	30	60	0	30	0	7	9	0	.33
96-97	Pit	8	3	1	4	-1	0	0	15	20.0	1	0	1	0	0	0	2	4	0	2	0	1	1	0	.50
97-98		Did Not Play in NHL																							
98-99	Edm	66	19	30	49	6	2	0	160	11.9	7	10	17	0	0	0	10	23	1	9	1	2	1	0	.74
92-93	Edm	26	2	6	8	-7	0	0	44	4.5	0	2	2	0	0	0	11	28	2	9	2	2	1	0	.31
92-93	Phi	40	13	12	25	-1	0	0	86	15.1	1	2	3	0	0	0	18	50	2	15	2	8	3	0	.63
94-95	Phi	14	5	5	10	3	0	0	39	12.8	1	1	2	0	0	0	1	2	0	1	0	0	1	1	.71
94-95	Van	37	8	13	21	-10	0	1	95	8.4	2	5	7	0	0	0	14	28	0	14	0	3	5	0	.57
7 Years		390	96	118	214	-25	6	1	831	11.6	18	27	45	0	0	0	125	298	8	114	7	30	29	1	.55

Postseason																									
Year	Tm	GP	G	A	Pts	+/–	GW	OT	S	SPct	G	A	Pts	G	A	Pts	Num	PIM	Maj	Mnr	Fgt	Rgh	HHT	Hat	P/G
91-92	Edm	12	2	1	3	-6	1	0	17	11.8	1	1	2	0	0	0	0	0	0	0	0	0	0	0	.25
94-95	Van	11	1	1	2	-7	0	0	21	4.8	0	0	0	0	0	0	6	12	0	6	0	0	3	0	.18
95-96	Van	3	2	1	3	0	0	0	7	28.6	0	0	0	0	0	0	0	0	0	0	0	0	0	0	1.00
96-97	Pit	5	0	0	0	-4	0	0	17	0.0	0	0	0	0	0	0	1	2	0	1	0	0	0	0	.00
98-99	Edm	2	0	0	0	-1	0	0	0	–	0	0	0	0	0	0	2	4	0	2	0	1	0	0	.00
5 Years		33	5	3	8	-18	1	0	62	8.1	1	1	2	0	0	0	9	18	0	9	0	1	3	0	.24

Bryan Berard

(statistical profile on page 288)

Pos: D **Shoots:** L **Ht:** 6'1" **Wt:** 190 **Born:** 3/5/77—Woonsocket, Rhode Island **Age:** 22

Overall											Power Play			Shorthand			Penalty							Misc	
Year	Tm	GP	G	A	Pts	+/–	GW	GT	S	SPct	G	A	Pts	G	A	Pts	Num	PIM	Maj	Mnr	Fgt	Rgh	HHT	Hat	P/G
96-97	NYI	**82**	8	40	48	1	1	0	172	4.7	3	17	20	0	0	0	32	86	2	28	2	4	15	0	.59
97-98	NYI	75	14	32	46	-32	2	1	192	7.3	8	21	29	0	0	0	24	59	1	22	1	1	8	0	.61
98-99	2Tm	69	9	25	34	1	5	1	135	6.7	4	14	18	1	0	1	24	48	0	24	0	4	15	0	.49
98-99	NYI	31	4	11	15	-6	3	0	72	5.6	2	5	7	0	0	0	13	26	0	13	0	3	7	0	.48
98-99	Tor	38	5	14	19	7	2	1	63	7.9	2	9	11	0	0	0	11	22	0	11	0	1	8	0	.50
3 Years		226	31	97	128	-30	8	2	499	6.2	15	52	67	1	0	1	80	193	3	74	3	9	38	0	.57
Postseason																									
Year	Tm	GP	G	A	Pts	+/–	GW	OT	S	SPct	G	A	Pts	G	A	Pts	Num	PIM	Maj	Mnr	Fgt	Rgh	HHT	Hat	P/G
98-99	Tor	17	1	8	9	-10	0	0	29	3.4	1	7	8	0	0	0	4	8	0	4	0	2	1	0	.53

Drake Berehowsky

(statistical profile on page 288)

Pos: D **Shoots:** R **Ht:** 6'1" **Wt:** 211 **Born:** 1/3/72—Toronto, Ontario **Age:** 27

Overall											Power Play			Shorthand			Penalty							Misc	
Year	Tm	GP	G	A	Pts	+/–	GW	GT	S	SPct	G	A	Pts	G	A	Pts	Num	PIM	Maj	Mnr	Fgt	Rgh	HHT	Hat	P/G
90-91	Tor	8	0	1	1	-6	0	0	4	0.0	0	–	–	0	–	–	–	25	–	–	–	–	–	0	.13
91-92	Tor	1	0	0	0	0	0	0	0	–	0	0	0	0	0	0	0	0	0	0	0	0	0	0	.00
92-93	Tor	41	4	15	19	1	1	0	41	9.8	1	8	9	0	0	0	22	61	3	18	3	7	3	0	.46
93-94	Tor	49	2	8	10	-3	2	0	29	6.9	2	6	8	0	0	0	19	63	3	14	3	6	4	0	.20
94-95	2Tm	29	0	2	2	-9	0	0	14	0.0	0	0	0	0	0	0	11	28	2	9	2	7	1	0	.07
95-96	Pit	1	0	0	0	1	0	0	0	–	0	0	0	0	0	0	0	0	0	0	0	0	0	0	.00
96-97		Did Not Play in NHL																							
97-98	Edm	67	1	6	7	1	1	0	58	1.7	1	1	2	0	0	0	56	169	11	42	11	13	11	0	.10
98-99	Nsh	74	2	15	17	-9	0	0	79	2.5	0	4	4	0	1	1	53	140	6	45	4	7	**25**	0	.23
94-95	Tor	25	0	2	2	-10	0	0	12	0.0	0	0	0	0	0	0	6	15	1	5	1	4	1	0	.08
94-95	Pit	4	0	0	0	1	0	0	2	0.0	0	0	0	0	0	0	5	13	1	4	1	3	0	0	.00
8 Years		270	9	47	56	-24	4	0	225	4.0	4	–	–	0	–	–	–	486	–	–	–	–	–	0	.21
Postseason																									
Year	Tm	GP	G	A	Pts	+/–	GW	OT	S	SPct	G	A	Pts	G	A	Pts	Num	PIM	Maj	Mnr	Fgt	Rgh	HHT	Hat	P/G
94-95	Pit	1	0	0	0	-1	0	0	0	–	0	0	0	0	0	0	0	0	0	0	0	0	0	0	.00
95-96	Pit	1	0	0	0	0	0	0	0	–	0	0	0	0	0	0	0	0	0	0	0	0	0	0	.00
97-98	Edm	12	1	2	3	1	1	0	4	25.0	0	1	1	0	0	0	3	14	0	2	0	1	1	0	.25
3 Years		14	1	2	3	0	1	0	4	25.0	0	1	1	0	0	0	3	14	0	2	0	1	1	0	.21

Sergei Berezin

(statistical profile on page 288)

Pos: RW **Shoots:** R **Ht:** 5'10" **Wt:** 200 **Born:** 11/5/71—Voskresensk, USSR **Age:** 28

Overall											Power Play			Shorthand			Penalty							Misc	
Year	Tm	GP	G	A	Pts	+/–	GW	GT	S	SPct	G	A	Pts	G	A	Pts	Num	PIM	Maj	Mnr	Fgt	Rgh	HHT	Hat	P/G
96-97	Tor	73	25	16	41	-3	2	0	177	14.1	7	5	12	0	0	0	1	2	0	1	0	0	1	0	.56
97-98	Tor	68	16	15	31	-3	3	1	167	9.6	3	0	3	0	0	0	5	10	0	5	0	0	3	0	.46
98-99	Tor	76	37	22	59	16	4	0	263	14.1	9	3	12	1	1	2	6	12	0	6	0	1	2	2	.78
3 Years		217	78	53	131	10	9	1	607	12.9	19	8	27	1	1	2	12	24	0	12	0	1	6	2	.60
Postseason																									
Year	Tm	GP	G	A	Pts	+/–	GW	OT	S	SPct	G	A	Pts	G	A	Pts	Num	PIM	Maj	Mnr	Fgt	Rgh	HHT	Hat	P/G
98-99	Tor	17	6	6	12	0	2	1	65	9.2	2	2	4	0	0	0	2	4	0	2	0	0	1	0	.71

Bill Berg

Pos: LW **Shoots:** L **Ht:** 6'1" **Wt:** 205 **Born:** 10/21/67—St. Catharines, Ontario **Age:** 32

Overall											Power Play			Shorthand			Penalty							Misc	
Year Tm	GP	G	A	Pts	+/–	GW	GT	S	SPct		G	A	Pts	G	A	Pts	Num	PIM	Maj	Mnr	Fgt	Rgh	HHT	Hat	P/G
88-89 NYI	7	1	2	3	-2	0	0	10	10.0		1	–	–	0	–	–	–	10	–	–	–	–	–	0	.43
89-90											Did Not Play in NHL														
90-91 NYI	78	9	14	23	-3	0	0	95	9.5		0	–	–	0	–	–	–	67	–	–	–	–	–	0	.29
91-92 NYI	47	5	9	14	-18	1	0	60	8.3		1	0	1	0	2	2	14	28	0	14	0	1	8	0	.30
92-93 2Tm	80	13	11	24	3	2	0	113	11.5		0	0	0	3	0	3	32	103	5	24	4	8	5	0	.30
93-94 Tor	83	8	11	19	-3	1	0	99	8.1		0	0	0	0	0	0	37	93	1	34	1	13	8	0	.23
94-95 Tor	32	5	1	6	-11	2	0	57	8.8		0	0	0	0	0	0	9	26	0	8	0	4	1	0	.19
95-96 2Tm	41	3	2	5	-6	0	0	60	5.0		0	0	0	1	0	1	15	41	1	13	1	5	2	0	.12
96-97 NYR	67	8	6	14	2	3	0	84	9.5		0	0	0	2	0	2	17	37	1	16	1	6	4	0	.21
97-98 NYR	67	1	9	10	-15	0	0	74	1.4		0	0	0	0	0	0	14	55	1	10	1	1	6	0	.15
98-99 Ott	44	2	2	4	4	0	1	40	5.0		0	0	0	0	0	0	8	28	4	4	4	0	2	0	.09
92-93 NYI	22	6	3	9	4	0	0	30	20.0		0	0	0	2	0	2	12	49	3	7	2	1	2	0	.41
92-93 Tor	58	7	8	15	-1	2	0	83	8.4		0	0	0	1	0	1	20	54	2	17	2	7	3	0	.26
95-96 Tor	23	1	1	2	-6	0	0	33	3.0		0	0	0	0	0	0	11	33	1	9	1	4	2	0	.09
95-96 NYR	18	2	1	3	0	0	0	27	7.4		0	0	0	1	0	1	4	8	0	4	0	1	0	0	.17
10 Years	546	55	67	122	-49	9	1	692	7.9		2	–	–	6	–	–	–	488	–	–	–	–	–	0	.22

Postseason

Year Tm	GP	G	A	Pts	+/–	GW	OT	S	SPct	G	A	Pts	G	A	Pts	Num	PIM	Maj	Mnr	Fgt	Rgh	HHT	Hat	P/G
92-93 Tor	21	1	1	2	1	0	0	30	3.3	0	0	0	0	0	0	9	18	0	9	0	2	3	0	.10
93-94 Tor	18	1	2	3	-1	0	0	26	3.8	0	0	0	0	0	0	5	10	0	5	0	1	2	0	.17
94-95 Tor	7	0	1	1	-3	0	0	6	0.0	0	0	0	0	0	0	2	4	0	2	0	1	0	0	.14
95-96 NYR	10	1	0	1	-1	0	0	8	12.5	0	0	0	0	0	0	0	0	0	0	0	0	0	0	.10
96-97 NYR	3	0	0	0	-1	0	0	5	0.0	0	0	0	0	0	0	1	2	0	1	0	1	0	0	.00
98-99 Ott	2	0	0	0	0	0	0	0	–	0	0	0	0	0	0	0	0	0	0	0	0	0	0	.00
6 Years	61	3	4	7	-5	0	0	75	4.0	0	0	0	0	0	0	17	34	0	17	0	5	5	0	.11

Marc Bergevin

Pos: D **Shoots:** L **Ht:** 6'1" **Wt:** 213 **Born:** 8/11/65—Montreal, Quebec **Age:** 34

Overall										Power Play			Shorthand			Penalty							Misc	
Year Tm	GP	G	A	Pts	+/–	GW	GT	S	SPct	G	A	Pts	G	A	Pts	Num	PIM	Maj	Mnr	Fgt	Rgh	HHT	Hat	P/G
84-85 Chi	60	0	6	6	-9	0	0	41	0.0	0	–	–	0	–	–	–	54	–	–	–	–	–	0	.10
85-86 Chi	71	7	7	14	0	1	0	50	14.0	0	–	–	0	–	–	–	60	–	–	–	–	–	0	.20
86-87 Chi	66	4	10	14	4	0	1	56	7.1	0	–	–	0	–	–	–	66	–	–	–	–	–	0	.21
87-88 Chi	58	1	6	7	-19	0	0	51	2.0	0	–	–	0	–	–	–	85	–	–	–	–	–	0	.12
88-89 2Tm	69	2	13	15	-1	0	0	65	3.1	1	–	–	0	–	–	–	80	–	–	–	–	–	0	.22
89-90 NYI	18	0	4	4	-8	0	0	12	0.0	0	–	–	0	–	–	–	30	–	–	–	–	–	0	.22
90-91 Har	4	0	0	0	-3	0	0	2	0.0	0	0	0	0	0	0	2	4	0	2	0	–	–	0	.00
91-92 Har	75	7	17	24	-13	1	0	96	7.3	4	9	13	1	1	2	29	64	2	27	2	6	12	0	.32
92-93 TB	78	2	12	14	-16	0	0	69	2.9	0	0	0	0	0	0	26	66	2	23	2	4	11	0	.18
93-94 TB	83	1	15	16	-5	1	0	76	1.3	0	1	1	0	1	1	28	87	5	21	3	7	8	0	.19
94-95 TB	44	2	4	6	-6	0	0	32	6.3	0	0	0	1	0	1	13	51	3	8	3	1	2	0	.14
95-96 Det	70	1	9	10	7	0	0	26	3.8	0	0	0	0	1	1	15	33	1	14	1	1	9	0	.14
96-97 StL	**82**	0	4	4	-9	0	0	30	0.0	0	1	1	0	0	0	25	53	1	24	1	8	8	0	.05
97-98 StL	81	3	7	10	-2	0	0	40	7.5	0	0	0	0	1	1	32	90	6	25	6	7	5	0	.12
98-99 StL	52	1	1	2	-14	0	0	40	2.5	0	0	0	0	0	0	22	99	5	12	5	3	1	0	.04
88-89 Chi	11	0	0	0	-3	0	0	9	0.0	0	0	0	0	0	0	–	18	–	–	–	–	–	0	.00
88-89 NYI	58	2	13	15	2	0	0	56	3.6	1	–	–	0	–	–	–	62	–	–	–	–	–	0	.26
15 Years	911	31	115	146	-94	3	1	686	4.5	5	–	–	2	–	–	–	922	–	–	–	–	–	0	.16

Postseason

Year Tm	GP	G	A	Pts	+/–	GW	OT	S	SPct	G	A	Pts	G	A	Pts	Num	PIM	Maj	Mnr	Fgt	Rgh	HHT	Hat	P/G
84-85 Chi	6	0	3	3	-4	0	0	1	0.0	0	–	–	0	–	–	1	2	0	1	0	–	–	0	.50
85-86 Chi	3	0	0	0	-1	0	0	5	0.0	0	0	0	0	0	0	0	0	0	0	0	0	0	0	.00
86-87 Chi	3	1	0	1	-1	0	0	4	25.0	0	0	0	0	0	0	1	2	0	1	0	–	–	0	.33
89-90 NYI	1	0	0	0	0	0	0	1	0.0	0	0	0	0	0	0	1	2	0	1	0	–	–	0	.00
91-92 Har	5	0	0	0	1	0	0	7	0.0	0	0	0	0	0	0	1	2	0	1	0	0	1	0	.00
95-96 Det	17	1	0	1	-4	0	0	14	7.1	1	0	1	0	0	0	7	14	0	7	0	2	1	0	.06
96-97 StL	6	1	0	1	2	0	0	4	25.0	0	0	0	0	0	0	4	8	0	4	0	2	0	0	.17
97-98 StL	10	0	1	1	-1	0	0	6	0.0	0	0	0	0	0	0	4	8	0	4	0	1	3	0	.10
8 Years	51	3	4	7	-8	0	0	42	7.1	1	–	–	0	–	–	19	38	0	19	0	–	–	0	.14

Todd Bertuzzi

(statistical profile on page 289)

Pos: C **Shoots:** L **Ht:** 6'3" **Wt:** 224 **Born:** 2/2/75—Sudbury, Ontario **Age:** 24

Overall											Power Play			Shorthand			Penalty							Misc	
Year	Tm	GP	G	A	Pts	+/–	GW	GT	S	SPct	G	A	Pts	G	A	Pts	Num	PIM	Maj	Mnr	Fgt	Rgh	HHT	Hat	P/G
95-96	NYI	76	18	21	39	-14	2	0	127	14.2	4	3	7	0	0	0	28	83	1	24	1	5	8	0	.51
96-97	NYI	64	10	13	23	-3	1	0	79	12.7	3	2	5	0	0	0	26	68	0	24	0	4	12	0	.36
97-98	2Tm	74	13	20	33	-17	2	0	102	12.7	2	6	8	1	1	2	44	121	3	38	3	5	14	0	.45
98-99	Van	32	8	8	16	-6	3	0	72	11.1	1	3	4	0	0	0	22	44	0	22	0	5	6	0	.50
97-98	NYI	52	7	11	18	-19	1	0	63	11.1	1	3	4	0	0	0	25	58	0	24	0	3	10	0	.35
97-98	Van	22	6	9	15	2	1	0	39	15.4	1	3	4	1	1	2	19	63	3	14	3	2	4	0	.68
4 Years		246	49	62	111	-40	8	0	380	12.9	10	14	24	1	1	2	120	316	4	108	4	19	40	0	.45

Craig Berube

Pos: LW **Shoots:** L **Ht:** 6'2" **Wt:** 210 **Born:** 12/17/65—Calihoo, Alberta **Age:** 34

Overall											Power Play			Shorthand			Penalty							Misc	
Year	Tm	GP	G	A	Pts	+/–	GW	GT	S	SPct	G	A	Pts	G	A	Pts	Num	PIM	Maj	Mnr	Fgt	Rgh	HHT	Hat	P/G
86-87	Phi	7	0	0	0	2	0	0	4	0.0	0	0	0	0	0	0	–	57	–	–	–	–	–	0	.00
87-88	Phi	27	3	2	5	1	2	0	13	23.1	0	–	–	0	–	–	–	108	–	–	–	–	–	0	.19
88-89	Phi	53	1	1	2	-15	0	0	31	3.2	0	–	–	0	–	–	–	199	–	–	–	–	–	0	.04
89-90	Phi	74	4	14	18	-7	0	0	52	7.7	0	–	–	0	–	–	–	291	–	–	–	–	–	0	.24
90-91	Phi	74	8	9	17	-6	0	0	46	17.4	0	–	–	0	–	–	–	293	–	–	–	–	–	0	.23
91-92	2Tm	76	6	11	17	-5	1	0	69	8.7	1	1	2	0	0	0	79	264	22	52	20	10	4	0	.22
92-93	Cgy	77	4	8	12	-6	2	0	58	6.9	0	0	0	0	0	0	58	209	15	37	13	13	4	0	.16
93-94	Was	84	7	7	14	-4	0	0	48	14.6	0	0	0	0	0	0	78	305	23	45	23	10	3	0	.17
94-95	Was	43	2	4	6	-5	0	0	22	9.1	0	0	0	0	0	0	43	173	13	24	11	8	3	0	.14
95-96	Was	50	2	10	12	1	1	0	28	7.1	1	1	2	0	0	0	43	151	11	28	11	10	2	0	.24
96-97	Was	80	4	3	7	-11	1	0	55	7.3	0	0	0	0	0	0	66	218	18	44	17	21	3	0	.09
97-98	Was	74	6	9	15	-3	0	0	68	8.8	0	0	0	0	0	0	59	189	13	42	12	15	5	0	.20
98-99	2Tm	77	5	4	9	-10	0	0	52	9.6	0	0	0	0	0	0	48	194	14	27	14	7	4	0	.12
91-92	Tor	40	5	7	12	-2	1	0	42	11.9	1	1	2	0	0	0	38	109	11	27	11	6	2	0	.30
91-92	Cgy	36	1	4	5	-3	0	0	27	3.7	0	0	0	0	0	0	41	155	11	25	9	4	2	0	.14
98-99	Was	66	5	4	9	-7	0	0	45	11.1	0	0	0	0	0	0	41	166	12	23	12	6	4	0	.14
98-99	Phi	11	0	0	0	-3	0	0	7	0.0	0	0	0	0	0	0	7	28	2	4	2	1	0	0	.00
13 Years		796	52	82	134	-68	7	0	546	9.5	2	–	–	0	–	–	–	2651	–	–	–	–	–	0	.17

Postseason

Year	Tm	GP	G	A	Pts	+/–	GW	OT	S	SPct	G	A	Pts	G	A	Pts	Num	PIM	Maj	Mnr	Fgt	Rgh	HHT	Hat	P/G
86-87	Phi	5	0	0	0	0	0	0	2	0.0	0	0	0	0	0	0	–	17	–	–	–	–	–	0	.00
88-89	Phi	16	0	0	0	0	0	0	2	0.0	0	0	0	0	0	0	–	56	–	–	–	–	–	0	.00
92-93	Cgy	6	0	1	1	-2	0	0	3	0.0	0	0	0	0	0	0	5	21	1	3	1	0	0	0	.17
93-94	Was	8	0	0	0	-1	0	0	0	–	0	0	0	0	0	0	5	21	1	3	1	1	0	0	.00
94-95	Was	7	0	0	0	-3	0	0	4	0.0	0	0	0	0	0	0	9	29	1	7	1	3	0	0	.00
95-96	Was	2	0	0	0	-1	0	0	3	0.0	0	0	0	0	0	0	4	19	1	2	1	1	0	0	.00
97-98	Was	21	1	0	1	0	1	0	15	6.7	0	0	0	0	0	0	9	21	1	8	1	3	0	0	.05
98-99	Phi	6	1	0	1	1	0	0	7	14.3	0	0	0	0	0	0	2	4	0	2	0	2	0	0	.17
8 Years		71	2	1	3	-6	1	0	36	5.6	0	0	0	0	0	0	–	188	–	–	–	–	–	0	.04

Karel Betik

Pos: D **Shoots:** L **Ht:** 6'2" **Wt:** 208 **Born:** 10/28/78—Karvina, Czechoslovakia **Age:** 21

Overall											Power Play			Shorthand			Penalty							Misc	
Year	Tm	GP	G	A	Pts	+/–	GW	GT	S	SPct	G	A	Pts	G	A	Pts	Num	PIM	Maj	Mnr	Fgt	Rgh	HHT	Hat	P/G
98-99	TB	3	0	2	2	-3	0	0	2	0.0	0	0	0	0	0	0	1	2	0	1	0	0	1	0	.67

Jeff Beukeboom

Pos: D **Shoots:** R **Ht:** 6'5" **Wt:** 230 **Born:** 3/28/65—Ajax, Ontario **Age:** 34

Overall											Power Play			Shorthand			Penalty							Misc	
Year	Tm	GP	G	A	Pts	+/–	GW	GT	S	SPct	G	A	Pts	G	A	Pts	Num	PIM	Maj	Mnr	Fgt	Rgh	HHT	Hat	P/G
85-86		Did Not Play in Regular Season																							
86-87	Edm	44	3	8	11	7	1	0	24	12.5	1	–	–	0	–	–	–	124	–	–	–	–	–	0	.25
87-88	Edm	73	5	20	25	27	1	0	76	6.6	1	–	–	0	–	–	–	201	–	–	–	–	–	0	.34
88-89	Edm	36	0	5	5	2	0	0	26	0.0	0	0	0	0	1	1	–	94	–	–	–	–	–	0	.14
89-90	Edm	46	1	12	13	5	0	0	36	2.8	0	4	4	0	0	0	–	86	–	–	–	–	–	0	.28
90-91	Edm	67	3	7	10	6	0	0	48	6.3	0	0	0	0	2	2	–	150	–	–	–	–	–	0	.15
91-92	2Tm	74	1	15	16	23	0	0	48	2.1	0	0	0	0	2	2	68	200	8	55	8	10	20	0	.22
92-93	NYR	82	2	17	19	9	0	0	54	3.7	0	0	0	0	1	1	61	153	5	54	5	11	24	0	.23

Overall											Power Play			Shorthand			Penalty							Misc	
Year	Tm	GP	G	A	Pts	+/-	GW	GT	S	SPct	G	A	Pts	G	A	Pts	Num	PIM	Maj	Mnr	Fgt	Rgh	HHT	Hat	P/G
93-94	NYR	68	8	8	16	18	0	0	58	13.8	1	0	1	0	0	0	56	170	6	45	6	11	14	0	.24
94-95	NYR	44	1	3	4	3	0	0	29	3.4	0	0	0	0	1	1	28	70	2	25	2	9	7	0	.09
95-96	NYR	82	3	11	14	19	1	1	65	4.6	0	0	0	0	0	0	73	220	14	55	12	13	19	0	.17
96-97	NYR	80	3	9	12	22	0	0	55	5.5	0	0	0	0	1	1	63	167	11	51	11	15	16	0	.15
97-98	NYR	63	0	5	5	-25	0	0	23	0.0	0	0	0	0	0	0	53	195	11	35	10	6	13	0	.08
98-99	NYR	45	0	9	9	-2	0	0	8	0.0	0	0	0	0	2	2	20	60	4	15	4	2	5	0	.20
91-92	Edm	18	0	5	5	4	0	0	7	0.0	0	0	0	0	1	1	24	78	2	19	2	4	7	0	.28
91-92	NYR	56	1	10	11	19	0	0	41	2.4	0	0	0	0	1	1	44	122	6	36	6	6	13	0	.20
13 Years		804	30	129	159	114	3	1	550	5.5	3	–	–	0	–	–	–	1890	–	–	–	–	–	0	.20
Postseason																									
Year	Tm	GP	G	A	Pts	+/-	GW	OT	S	SPct	G	A	Pts	G	A	Pts	Num	PIM	Maj	Mnr	Fgt	Rgh	HHT	Hat	P/G
85-86	Edm	1	0	0	0	1	0	0	1	0.0	0	0	0	0	0	0	2	4	0	2	0	–	–	0	.00
87-88	Edm	7	0	0	0	1	0	0	2	0.0	0	0	0	0	0	0	–	16	–	–	–	–	–	0	.00
88-89	Edm	1	0	0	0	0	0	0	0	–	0	0	0	0	0	0	1	2	0	1	0	–	–	0	.00
89-90	Edm	2	0	0	0	2	0	0	0	–	0	0	0	0	0	0	0	0	0	0	0	0	0	0	.00
90-91	Edm	18	1	3	4	-5	0	0	15	6.7	0	–	–	0	0	0	–	28	–	–	–	–	–	0	.22
91-92	NYR	13	2	3	5	-2	0	0	10	20.0	0	0	0	0	0	0	14	47	1	11	0	5	2	0	.38
93-94	NYR	22	0	6	6	17	0	0	22	0.0	0	0	0	0	0	0	18	50	2	15	2	3	2	0	.27
94-95	NYR	9	0	0	0	1	0	0	11	0.0	0	0	0	0	0	0	5	10	0	5	0	0	2	0	.00
95-96	NYR	11	0	3	3	-1	0	0	12	0.0	0	0	0	0	0	0	3	6	0	3	0	0	3	0	.27
96-97	NYR	15	0	1	1	5	0	0	9	0.0	0	0	0	0	0	0	17	34	0	17	0	1	5	0	.07
10 Years		99	3	16	19	19	0	0	82	3.7	0	–	–	0	0	0	–	197	–	–	–	–	–	0	.19

Radim Bicanek

Pos: D **Shoots:** L **Ht:** 6'1" **Wt:** 210 **Born:** 1/18/75—Uherske Hradiste, Czechoslovakia **Age:** 24

Overall											Power Play			Shorthand			Penalty							Misc	
Year	Tm	GP	G	A	Pts	+/-	GW	GT	S	SPct	G	A	Pts	G	A	Pts	Num	PIM	Maj	Mnr	Fgt	Rgh	HHT	Hat	P/G
94-95	Ott	6	0	0	0	3	0	0	6	0.0	0	0	0	0	0	0	0	0	0	0	0	0	0	0	.00
95-96		Did Not Play in NHL																							
96-97	Ott	21	0	1	1	-4	0	0	27	0.0	0	0	0	0	0	0	4	8	0	4	0	0	2	0	.05
97-98	Ott	1	0	0	0	0	0	0	0	–	0	0	0	0	0	0	0	0	0	0	0	0	0	0	.00
98-99	2Tm	14	0	0	0	-4	0	0	13	0.0	0	0	0	0	0	0	5	10	0	5	0	0	4	0	.00
98-99	Ott	7	0	0	0	-1	0	0	6	0.0	0	0	0	0	0	0	2	4	0	2	0	0	1	0	.00
98-99	Chi	7	0	0	0	-3	0	0	7	0.0	0	0	0	0	0	0	3	6	0	3	0	0	3	0	.00
4 Years		42	0	1	1	-5	0	0	46	0.0	0	0	0	0	0	0	9	18	0	9	0	0	6	0	.02
Postseason																									
Year	Tm	GP	G	A	Pts	+/-	GW	OT	S	SPct	G	A	Pts	G	A	Pts	Num	PIM	Maj	Mnr	Fgt	Rgh	HHT	Hat	P/G
96-97	Ott	7	0	0	0	0	0	0	4	0.0	0	0	0	0	0	0	4	8	0	4	0	0	2	0	.00

Zac Bierk

Pos: G **Catches:** L **Ht:** 6'4" **Wt:** 205 **Born:** 9/17/76—Peterborough, Ontario **Age:** 23

Overall																Pen Shot		Offense		
Year	Tm	GP	GS	TP	W	L	T	Min	GA	GAA	Shots	SvPct	ShO	OE	PPGA	SHGA	Shots	GA	G	A	PIM
97-98	TB	13	5	4	1	4	1	433	30	4.16	210	.857	0	0	6	4	1	1	0	0	0
98-99	TB	1	1	0	0	1	0	59	2	2.03	21	.905	0	0	1	0	0	0	0	0	0
2 Years		14	6	4	1	5	1	492	32	3.90	231	.861	0	0	7	4	1	1	0	0	0

Craig Billington

(statistical profile on page 396)

Pos: G **Catches:** L **Ht:** 5'10" **Wt:** 170 **Born:** 9/11/66—London, Ontario **Age:** 33

Overall																Pen Shot		Offense		
Year	Tm	GP	GS	TP	W	L	T	Min	GA	GAA	Shots	SvPct	ShO	OE	PPGA	SHGA	Shots	GA	G	A	PIM
85-86	NJ	18	–	–	4	9	1	901	77	5.13	482	.840	0	–	–	–	0	0	0	1	0
86-87	NJ	22	–	–	4	13	2	1114	89	4.79	569	.844	0	–	–	–	1	0	0	0	12
87-88		Did Not Play in NHL																			
88-89	NJ	3	–	–	1	1	0	140	11	4.71	65	.831	0	–	–	–	0	0	0	0	0
89-90		Did Not Play in NHL																			
90-91		Did Not Play in NHL																			
91-92	NJ	26	23	2	13	7	1	1363	69	3.04	637	.892	2	7	23	1	0	0	0	1	2
92-93	NJ*	42	41	5	21	16	4	2389	146	3.67	1178	.876	2	11	41	8	0	0	0	1	8
93-94	Ott	63	56	**12**	11	**41**	4	3319	**254**	4.59	1801	.859	0	10	**70**	12	0	0	0	0	8
94-95	2Tm	17	13	3	5	7	2	845	51	3.62	380	.866	0	3	18	1	0	0	0	0	4
95-96	Bos	27	22	4	10	13	3	1380	79	3.43	594	.867	1	5	21	2	0	0	0	0	2

		Overall															Pen Shot		Offense		
Year	Tm	GP	GS	TP	W	L	T	Min	GA	GAA	Shots	SvPct	ShO	OE	PPGA	SHGA	Shots	GA	G	A	PIM
96-97	Col	23	19	2	11	8	2	1200	53	2.65	584	.909	1	9	9	3	0	0	0	2	2
97-98	Col	23	19	3	8	7	4	1162	45	2.32	588	.923	1	10	11	4	0	0	0	0	2
98-99	Col	21	18	2	11	8	1	1086	52	2.87	492	.894	0	5	11	5	0	0	0	0	2
94-95	Ott	9	7	1	0	6	2	472	32	4.07	240	.867	0	3	12	1	0	0	0	0	2
94-95	Bos	8	6	2	5	1	0	373	19	3.06	140	.864	0	0	6	0	0	0	0	0	2
11 Years		285	–	–	99	130	24	14899	926	3.73	7370	.874	7	–	–	–	1	0	0	5	42
		Postseason																			
Year	Tm	GP	GS	TP	W	L	Pct	Min	GA	GAA	Shots	SvPct	ShO	OE	PPGA	SHGA	Shots	GA	G	A	PIM
92-93	NJ	2	1	0	0	1	.000	78	5	3.85	39	.872	0	0	1	0	0	0	0	0	0
94-95	Bos	1	0	0	0	0	–	25	1	2.40	10	.900	0	0	1	0	0	0	0	0	0
95-96	Bos	1	1	0	0	1	.000	60	6	6.00	28	.786	0	0	1	0	0	0	0	0	2
96-97	Col	1	0	0	0	0	–	20	1	3.00	13	.923	0	0	0	0	0	0	0	0	0
97-98	Col	1	0	1	0	0	–	1	0	0.00	0	–	0	0	0	0	0	0	0	0	0
98-99	Col	1	0	0	0	0	–	9	1	6.67	6	.833	0	0	0	1	0	0	0	0	0
6 Years		7	2	1	0	2	.000	193	14	4.35	96	.854	0	0	3	1	0	0	0	0	2

Martin Biron

Pos: G **Catches:** L **Ht:** 6'1" **Wt:** 154 **Born:** 8/15/77—Lac St. Charles, Quebec **Age:** 22

		Overall															Pen Shot		Offense		
Year	Tm	GP	GS	TP	W	L	T	Min	GA	GAA	Shots	SvPct	ShO	OE	PPGA	SHGA	Shots	GA	G	A	PIM
95-96	Buf	3	2	2	0	2	0	118	10	5.08	64	.844	0	0	5	0	0	0	0	0	0
96-97		Did Not Play in NHL																			
97-98		Did Not Play in NHL																			
98-99	Buf	6	3	0	1	2	1	281	10	2.14	120	.917	0	1	2	0	0	0	0	0	0
2 Years		9	5	2	1	4	1	399	20	3.01	184	.891	0	1	7	0	0	0	0	0	0

James Black

(statistical profile on page 289)

Pos: C **Shoots:** L **Ht:** 6'0" **Wt:** 202 **Born:** 8/15/69—Regina, Saskatchewan **Age:** 30

		Overall								Power Play			Shorthand			Penalty							Misc	
Year	Tm	GP	G	A	Pts	+/-	GW	GT	S	SPct	G	A	Pts	G	A	Pts	Num	PIM	Maj	Mnr	Fgt	Rgh	HHT	Hat	P/G
89-90	Har	1	0	0	0	0	0	0	0	–	0	0	0	0	0	0	0	0	0	0	0	0	0	0	.00
90-91	Har	1	0	0	0	0	0	0	0	–	0	0	0	0	0	0	0	0	0	0	0	0	0	0	.00
91-92	Har	30	4	6	10	-4	1	0	54	7.4	1	1	2	0	0	0	5	10	0	5	0	0	2	0	.33
92-93	Min	10	2	1	3	0	0	0	10	20.0	0	0	0	0	0	0	2	4	0	2	0	0	1	0	.30
93-94	2Tm	15	2	3	5	-4	0	0	18	11.1	2	0	2	0	0	0	1	2	0	1	0	0	0	0	.33
94-95		Did Not Play in NHL																							
95-96	Chi	13	3	3	6	1	1	0	23	13.0	0	0	0	0	0	0	4	16	0	3	0	0	1	0	.46
96-97	Chi	64	12	11	23	6	3	0	122	9.8	0	1	1	0	0	0	10	20	0	10	0	1	3	0	.36
97-98	Chi	52	10	5	15	-8	3	1	90	11.1	2	2	4	1	1	2	4	8	0	4	0	0	1	0	.29
98-99	Was	75	16	14	30	5	3	0	135	11.9	1	3	4	1	0	1	7	14	0	7	0	0	1	0	.40
93-94	Dal	13	2	3	5	-4	0	0	16	12.5	2	0	2	0	0	0	1	2	0	1	0	0	0	0	.38
93-94	Buf	2	0	0	0	0	0	0	2	0.0	0	0	0	0	0	0	0	0	0	0	0	0	0	0	.00
9 Years		261	49	43	92	-4	11	1	452	10.8	6	7	13	2	1	3	33	74	0	32	0	1	9	0	.35
		Postseason																							
Year	Tm	GP	G	A	Pts	+/-	GW	OT	S	SPct	G	A	Pts	G	A	Pts	Num	PIM	Maj	Mnr	Fgt	Rgh	HHT	Hat	P/G
95-96	Chi	8	1	0	1	-1	0	0	6	16.7	0	0	0	0	0	0	1	2	0	1	0	0	0	0	.13
96-97	Chi	5	1	1	2	1	0	0	8	12.5	0	0	0	0	0	0	1	2	0	1	0	0	0	0	.40
2 Years		13	2	1	3	0	0	0	14	14.3	0	0	0	0	0	0	2	4	0	2	0	0	0	0	.23

Jason Blake

Pos: C **Shoots:** R **Ht:** 5'10" **Wt:** 180 **Born:** 9/2/73—Moorhead, Minnesota **Age:** 26

		Overall								Power Play			Shorthand			Penalty							Misc	
Year	Tm	GP	G	A	Pts	+/-	GW	GT	S	SPct	G	A	Pts	G	A	Pts	Num	PIM	Maj	Mnr	Fgt	Rgh	HHT	Hat	P/G
98-99	LA	1	1	0	1	1	0	0	5	20.0	0	0	0	0	0	0	0	0	0	0	0	0	0	0	1.00

Rob Blake

(statistical profile on page 289)

Pos: D **Shoots:** R **Ht:** 6'3" **Wt:** 222 **Born:** 12/10/69—Simcoe, Ontario **Age:** 30

		Overall								Power Play			Shorthand			Penalty							Misc	
Year	Tm	GP	G	A	Pts	+/-	GW	GT	S	SPct	G	A	Pts	G	A	Pts	Num	PIM	Maj	Mnr	Fgt	Rgh	HHT	Hat	P/G
89-90	LA	4	0	0	0	0	0	0	3	0.0	0	0	0	0	0	0	2	4	0	2	0	–	–	0	.00
90-91	LA	75	12	34	46	3	2	0	150	8.0	9	–	–	0	–	–	–	125	–	–	–	–	–	0	.61

		Overall									Power Play			Shorthand			Penalty							Misc	
Year	Tm	GP	G	A	Pts	+/–	GW	GT	S	SPct	G	A	Pts	G	A	Pts	Num	PIM	Maj	Mnr	Fgt	Rgh	HHT	Hat	P/G
91-92	LA	57	7	13	20	-5	0	0	131	5.3	5	6	11	0	0	0	40	102	2	36	1	8	17	0	.35
92-93	LA	76	16	43	59	18	4	1	243	6.6	10	22	32	0	2	2	66	152	4	61	3	9	**31**	0	.78
93-94	LA*	84	20	48	68	-7	6	0	304	6.6	7	26	33	0	3	3	56	137	3	51	3	11	21	0	.81
94-95	LA	24	4	7	11	-16	1	0	76	5.3	4	2	6	0	0	0	12	38	2	9	2	1	3	0	.46
95-96	LA	6	1	2	3	0	0	0	13	7.7	0	2	2	0	0	0	4	8	0	4	0	0	1	0	.50
96-97	LA*	62	8	23	31	-28	1	0	169	4.7	4	9	13	0	0	0	37	82	0	36	0	8	11	0	.50
97-98	LA	81	23	27	50	-3	4	0	261	8.8	11	11	22	0	1	1	40	94	2	37	2	4	12	0	.62
98-99	LA	62	12	23	35	-7	2	0	216	5.6	5	6	11	1	1	2	42	128	4	34	3	4	9	0	.56
10 Years		531	103	220	323	-45	20	1	1566	6.6	55	–	–	1	–	–	–	870	–	–	–	–	–	0	.61
Postseason																									
Year	Tm	GP	G	A	Pts	+/–	GW	OT	S	SPct	G	A	Pts	G	A	Pts	Num	PIM	Maj	Mnr	Fgt	Rgh	HHT	Hat	P/G
89-90	LA	8	1	3	4	-4	0	0	11	9.1	1	–	–	0	–	–	2	4	0	2	0	–	–	0	.50
90-91	LA	12	1	4	5	-1	0	0	19	5.3	1	–	–	0	–	–	–	26	–	–	–	–	–	0	.42
91-92	LA	6	2	1	3	2	0	0	12	16.7	0	1	1	0	0	0	6	12	0	6	0	1	2	0	.50
92-93	LA	23	4	6	10	3	0	0	60	6.7	1	2	3	1	0	1	19	46	0	18	0	8	5	0	.43
97-98	LA	4	0	0	0	-4	0	0	15	0.0	0	0	0	0	0	0	3	6	0	3	0	0	0	0	.00
5 Years		53	8	14	22	-4	0	0	117	6.8	3	–	–	1	–	–	–	94	–	–	–	–	–	0	.42

Sylvain Blouin

Pos: LW **Shoots:** L **Ht:** 6'3" **Wt:** 210 **Born:** 5/21/74—Montreal, Quebec **Age:** 25

		Overall									Power Play			Shorthand			Penalty							Misc	
Year	Tm	GP	G	A	Pts	+/–	GW	GT	S	SPct	G	A	Pts	G	A	Pts	Num	PIM	Maj	Mnr	Fgt	Rgh	HHT	Hat	P/G
96-97	NYR	6	0	0	0	-1	0	0	1	0.0	0	0	0	0	0	0	6	18	2	4	2	0	1	0	.00
97-98	NYR	1	0	0	0	0	0	0	0	–	0	0	0	0	0	0	1	5	1	0	1	0	0	0	.00
98-99	Mon	5	0	0	0	0	0	0	1	0.0	0	0	0	0	0	0	5	19	3	2	3	1	0	0	.00
3 Years		12	0	0	0	-1	0	0	2	0.0	0	0	0	0	0	0	12	42	6	6	6	1	1	0	.00

Doug Bodger

(statistical profile on page 289)

Pos: D **Shoots:** L **Ht:** 6'2" **Wt:** 215 **Born:** 6/18/66—Chemainus, British Columbia **Age:** 33

		Overall									Power Play			Shorthand			Penalty							Misc	
Year	Tm	GP	G	A	Pts	+/–	GW	GT	S	SPct	G	A	Pts	G	A	Pts	Num	PIM	Maj	Mnr	Fgt	Rgh	HHT	Hat	P/G
84-85	Pit	65	5	26	31	-24	1	0	119	4.2	3	10	13	0	–	–	–	67	–	–	–	–	–	0	.48
85-86	Pit	79	4	33	37	3	1	0	140	2.9	1	14	15	0	–	–	–	63	–	–	–	–	–	0	.47
86-87	Pit	76	11	38	49	6	1	0	176	6.3	5	15	20	0	–	–	–	52	–	–	–	–	–	0	.64
87-88	Pit	69	14	31	45	-3	1	0	184	7.6	13	20	33	0	–	–	–	103	–	–	–	–	–	0	.65
88-89	2Tm	71	8	44	52	15	1	0	156	5.1	6	–	–	0	–	–	–	59	–	–	–	–	–	0	.73
89-90	Buf	71	12	36	48	0	1	0	167	7.2	8	–	–	0	–	–	–	64	–	–	–	–	–	0	.68
90-91	Buf	58	5	23	28	-8	0	0	139	3.6	2	–	–	0	–	–	–	54	–	–	–	–	–	0	.48
91-92	Buf	73	11	35	46	1	1	0	180	6.1	4	28	32	0	0	0	46	108	0	44	0	11	18	0	.63
92-93	Buf	81	9	45	54	14	0	1	154	5.8	6	20	26	0	1	1	42	87	1	41	0	4	23	0	.67
93-94	Buf	75	7	32	39	8	1	0	144	4.9	5	19	24	1	1	2	38	76	0	38	0	5	19	0	.52
94-95	Buf	44	3	17	20	-3	0	0	87	3.4	2	10	12	0	3	3	22	47	1	21	1	4	7	0	.45
95-96	2Tm	73	4	24	28	-24	0	0	121	3.3	3	12	15	0	1	1	34	68	0	34	0	2	22	0	.38
96-97	SJ	81	1	15	16	-14	1	0	96	1.0	0	7	7	0	0	0	32	64	0	32	0	2	17	0	.20
97-98	2Tm	77	9	11	20	-1	1	0	96	9.4	3	7	10	0	0	0	27	57	1	26	1	1	15	0	.26
98-99	LA	65	3	11	14	1	0	0	67	4.5	0	5	5	0	1	1	17	34	0	17	0	0	11	0	.22
88-89	Pit	10	1	4	5	6	0	0	22	4.5	0	2	2	0	–	–	2	7	1	1	–	–	–	0	.50
88-89	Buf	61	7	40	47	9	1	0	134	5.2	6	–	–	0	–	–	–	52	–	–	–	–	–	0	.77
95-96	Buf	16	0	5	5	-6	0	0	27	0.0	0	3	3	0	0	0	9	18	0	9	0	1	6	0	.31
95-96	SJ	57	4	19	23	-18	0	0	94	4.3	3	9	12	0	1	1	25	50	0	25	0	1	16	0	.40
97-98	SJ	28	4	6	10	0	1	0	41	9.8	0	5	5	0	0	0	16	32	0	16	0	1	11	0	.36
97-98	NJ	49	5	5	10	-1	0	0	55	9.1	3	2	5	0	0	0	11	25	1	10	1	0	4	0	.20
15 Years		1058	106	421	527	-29	10	1	2026	5.2	61	–	–	1	–	–	–	1003	–	–	–	–	–	0	.50
Postseason																									
Year	Tm	GP	G	A	Pts	+/–	GW	OT	S	SPct	G	A	Pts	G	A	Pts	Num	PIM	Maj	Mnr	Fgt	Rgh	HHT	Hat	P/G
88-89	Buf	5	1	1	2	2	0	0	10	10.0	1	–	–	0	–	–	4	11	1	3	–	–	–	0	.40
89-90	Buf	6	1	5	6	-4	0	0	11	9.1	0	–	–	0	0	0	3	6	0	3	0	–	–	0	1.00
90-91	Buf	4	0	1	1	3	0	0	5	0.0	0	–	–	0	–	–	0	0	0	0	0	0	0	0	.25
91-92	Buf	7	2	1	3	1	1	0	11	18.2	2	1	3	0	0	0	1	2	0	1	0	0	1	0	.43
92-93	Buf	8	2	3	5	3	0	0	25	8.0	2	3	5	0	0	0	0	0	0	0	0	0	0	0	.63
93-94	Buf	7	0	3	3	0	0	0	15	0.0	0	1	1	0	0	0	3	6	0	3	0	0	3	0	.43
94-95	Buf	5	0	4	4	1	0	0	12	0.0	0	0	0	0	0	0	0	0	0	0	0	0	0	0	.80
97-98	NJ	5	0	0	0	-5	0	0	8	0.0	0	0	0	0	0	0	0	0	0	0	0	0	0	0	.00
8 Years		47	6	18	24	1	1	0	97	6.2	5	–	–	0	–	–	11	25	1	10	–	–	–	0	.51

Lonny Bohonos

Pos: RW **Shoots:** R **Ht:** 5'11" **Wt:** 190 **Born:** 5/20/73—Winnipeg, Manitoba **Age:** 26

Overall											Power Play			Shorthand			Penalty							Misc	
Year	Tm	GP	G	A	Pts	+/–	GW	GT	S	SPct	G	A	Pts	G	A	Pts	Num	PIM	Maj	Mnr	Fgt	Rgh	HHT	Hat	P/G
95-96	Van	3	0	1	1	1	0	0	3	0.0	0	0	0	0	0	0	0	0	0	0	0	0	0	0	.33
96-97	Van	36	11	11	22	-3	1	0	67	16.4	2	4	6	0	0	0	5	10	0	5	0	0	4	0	.61
97-98	2Tm	37	5	4	9	-8	0	0	50	10.0	0	0	0	0	0	0	4	8	0	4	0	0	3	0	.24
98-99	Tor	7	3	0	3	3	0	0	13	23.1	0	0	0	0	0	0	2	4	0	2	0	0	1	0	.43
97-98	Van	31	2	1	3	-9	0	0	37	5.4	0	0	0	0	0	0	2	4	0	2	0	0	1	0	.10
97-98	Tor	6	3	3	6	1	0	0	13	23.1	0	0	0	0	0	0	2	4	0	2	0	0	2	0	1.00
4 Years		83	19	16	35	-7	1	0	133	14.3	2	4	6	0	0	0	11	22	0	11	0	0	8	0	.42

Postseason																									
Year	Tm	GP	G	A	Pts	+/–	GW	OT	S	SPct	G	A	Pts	G	A	Pts	Num	PIM	Maj	Mnr	Fgt	Rgh	HHT	Hat	P/G
98-99	Tor	9	3	6	9	3	0	0	26	11.5	0	1	1	0	0	0	1	2	0	1	0	0	1	0	1.00

Patrick Boileau

Pos: D **Shoots:** R **Ht:** 6'0" **Wt:** 190 **Born:** 2/22/75—Montreal, Quebec **Age:** 24

Overall											Power Play			Shorthand			Penalty							Misc	
Year	Tm	GP	G	A	Pts	+/–	GW	GT	S	SPct	G	A	Pts	G	A	Pts	Num	PIM	Maj	Mnr	Fgt	Rgh	HHT	Hat	P/G
96-97	Was	1	0	0	0	0	0	0	0	–	0	0	0	0	0	0	0	0	0	0	0	0	0	0	.00
97-98		Did Not Play in NHL																							
98-99	Was	4	0	1	1	-4	0	0	7	0.0	0	1	1	0	0	0	1	2	0	1	0	0	0	0	.25
2 Years		5	0	1	1	-4	0	0	7	0.0	0	1	1	0	0	0	1	2	0	1	0	0	0	0	.20

Brad Bombardir

Pos: D **Shoots:** L **Ht:** 6'2" **Wt:** 205 **Born:** 5/5/72—Powell River, British Columbia **Age:** 27

Overall											Power Play			Shorthand			Penalty							Misc	
Year	Tm	GP	G	A	Pts	+/–	GW	GT	S	SPct	G	A	Pts	G	A	Pts	Num	PIM	Maj	Mnr	Fgt	Rgh	HHT	Hat	P/G
97-98	NJ	43	1	5	6	11	0	0	16	6.3	0	0	0	0	0	0	4	8	0	4	0	0	2	0	.14
98-99	NJ	56	1	7	8	-4	0	0	47	2.1	0	1	1	0	0	0	8	16	0	8	0	0	5	0	.14
2 Years		99	2	12	14	7	0	0	63	3.2	0	1	1	0	0	0	12	24	0	12	0	0	7	0	.14

Postseason																									
Year	Tm	GP	G	A	Pts	+/–	GW	OT	S	SPct	G	A	Pts	G	A	Pts	Num	PIM	Maj	Mnr	Fgt	Rgh	HHT	Hat	P/G
98-99	NJ	5	0	0	0	0	0	0	2	0.0	0	0	0	0	0	0	0	0	0	0	0	0	0	0	.00

Peter Bondra

(statistical profile on page 290)

Pos: RW **Shoots:** L **Ht:** 6'1" **Wt:** 200 **Born:** 2/7/68—Luck, USSR **Age:** 31

Overall											Power Play			Shorthand			Penalty							Misc	
Year	Tm	GP	G	A	Pts	+/–	GW	GT	S	SPct	G	A	Pts	G	A	Pts	Num	PIM	Maj	Mnr	Fgt	Rgh	HHT	Hat	P/G
90-91	Was	54	12	16	28	-10	1	0	95	12.6	4	–	–	0	–	–	–	47	–	–	–	–	–	1	.52
91-92	Was	71	28	28	56	16	3	0	158	17.7	4	3	7	0	0	0	21	42	0	21	0	2	9	0	.79
92-93	Was*	83	37	48	85	8	7	0	239	15.5	10	16	26	0	0	0	31	70	0	30	0	5	9	0	1.02
93-94	Was	69	24	19	43	22	2	0	200	12.0	4	6	10	0	0	0	20	40	0	20	0	4	9	1	.62
94-95	Was	47	**34**	9	43	9	3	1	177	19.2	12	6	18	**6**	0	**6**	8	24	0	7	0	1	4	1	.91
95-96	Was*	67	52	28	80	18	7	3	322	16.1	11	11	22	4	1	5	20	40	0	20	0	5	7	4	1.19
96-97	Was*	77	46	31	77	7	3	2	314	14.6	10	10	20	4	0	4	29	72	2	26	0	6	7	2	1.00
97-98	Was*	76	**52**	26	78	14	**13**	2	284	18.3	11	10	21	5	0	5	22	44	0	22	0	1	15	1	1.03
98-99	Was	66	31	24	55	-1	5	1	284	10.9	6	9	15	3	1	4	28	56	0	28	0	1	16	**3**	.83
9 Years		610	316	229	545	83	44	9	2073	15.2	72	–	–	22	–	–	–	435	–	–	–	–	–	13	.89

Postseason																									
Year	Tm	GP	G	A	Pts	+/–	GW	OT	S	SPct	G	A	Pts	G	A	Pts	Num	PIM	Maj	Mnr	Fgt	Rgh	HHT	Hat	P/G
90-91	Was	4	0	1	1	1	0	0	7	0.0	0	–	–	0	–	–	1	2	0	1	0	–	–	0	.25
91-92	Was	7	6	2	8	4	0	0	16	37.5	1	1	2	0	0	0	2	4	0	2	0	2	0	0	1.14
92-93	Was	6	0	6	6	2	0	0	16	0.0	0	2	2	0	0	0	0	0	0	0	0	0	0	0	1.00
93-94	Was	9	2	4	6	2	1	0	26	7.7	0	0	0	0	0	0	2	4	0	2	0	0	1	0	.67
94-95	Was	7	5	3	8	0	1	0	23	21.7	2	1	3	0	0	0	5	10	0	5	0	1	1	0	1.14
95-96	Was	6	3	2	5	0	1	0	36	8.3	2	0	2	0	0	0	4	8	0	4	0	1	1	0	.83
97-98	Was	17	7	5	12	4	2	1	48	14.6	3	2	5	0	0	0	6	12	0	6	0	1	2	0	.71
7 Years		56	23	23	46	13	5	1	172	13.4	8	–	–	0	–	–	20	40	0	20	0	–	–	0	.82

Brian Bonin

Pos: C **Shoots:** L **Ht:** 5'9" **Wt:** 189 **Born:** 11/28/73—St. Paul, Minnesota **Age:** 26

		Overall									Power Play			Shorthand			Penalty							Misc	
Year	Tm	GP	G	A	Pts	+/–	GW	GT	S	SPct	G	A	Pts	G	A	Pts	Num	PIM	Maj	Mnr	Fgt	Rgh	HHT	Hat	P/G
98-99	Pit	5	0	0	0	-2	0	0	2	0.0	0	0	0	0	0	0	0	0	0	0	0	0	0	0	.00

Postseason

Year	Tm	GP	G	A	Pts	+/–	GW	OT	S	SPct	G	A	Pts	G	A	Pts	Num	PIM	Maj	Mnr	Fgt	Rgh	HHT	Hat	P/G
98-99	Pit	3	0	0	0	-1	0	0	4	0.0	0	0	0	0	0	0	0	0	0	0	0	0	0	0	.00

Radek Bonk

(statistical profile on page 290)

Pos: C **Shoots:** L **Ht:** 6'3" **Wt:** 210 **Born:** 1/9/76—Krnov, Czechoslovakia **Age:** 23

		Overall									Power Play			Shorthand			Penalty							Misc	
Year	Tm	GP	G	A	Pts	+/–	GW	GT	S	SPct	G	A	Pts	G	A	Pts	Num	PIM	Maj	Mnr	Fgt	Rgh	HHT	Hat	P/G
94-95	Ott	42	3	8	11	-5	0	0	40	7.5	1	3	4	0	0	0	14	28	0	14	0	2	4	0	.26
95-96	Ott	76	16	19	35	-5	1	0	161	9.9	5	7	12	0	0	0	18	36	0	18	0	2	8	0	.46
96-97	Ott	53	5	13	18	-4	0	1	82	6.1	0	1	1	1	0	1	7	14	0	7	0	0	3	0	.34
97-98	Ott	65	7	9	16	-13	0	0	93	7.5	1	3	4	0	0	0	8	16	0	8	0	1	4	0	.25
98-99	Ott	81	16	16	32	15	6	0	110	14.5	0	0	0	1	1	2	24	48	0	24	0	3	9	0	.40
5 Years		317	47	65	112	-12	7	1	486	9.7	7	14	21	2	1	3	71	142	0	71	0	8	28	0	.35

Postseason

Year	Tm	GP	G	A	Pts	+/–	GW	OT	S	SPct	G	A	Pts	G	A	Pts	Num	PIM	Maj	Mnr	Fgt	Rgh	HHT	Hat	P/G
96-97	Ott	7	0	1	1	-1	0	0	4	0.0	0	0	0	0	0	0	2	4	0	2	0	0	1	0	.14
97-98	Ott	5	0	0	0	-3	0	0	6	0.0	0	0	0	0	0	0	1	2	0	1	0	1	0	0	.00
98-99	Ott	4	0	0	0	-1	0	0	8	0.0	0	0	0	0	0	0	3	6	0	3	0	0	1	0	.00
3 Years		16	0	1	1	-5	0	0	18	0.0	0	0	0	0	0	0	6	12	0	6	0	1	2	0	.06

Jason Bonsignore

Pos: C **Shoots:** R **Ht:** 6'4" **Wt:** 220 **Born:** 4/15/76—Rochester, New York **Age:** 23

		Overall									Power Play			Shorthand			Penalty							Misc	
Year	Tm	GP	G	A	Pts	+/–	GW	GT	S	SPct	G	A	Pts	G	A	Pts	Num	PIM	Maj	Mnr	Fgt	Rgh	HHT	Hat	P/G
94-95	Edm	1	1	0	1	-1	0	0	3	33.3	0	0	0	0	0	0	0	0	0	0	0	0	0	0	1.00
95-96	Edm	20	0	2	2	-6	0	0	13	0.0	0	0	0	0	0	0	2	4	0	2	0	0	2	0	.10
96-97		Did Not Play in NHL																							
97-98	TB	35	2	8	10	-11	0	0	29	6.9	0	1	1	0	0	0	11	22	0	11	0	0	8	0	.29
98-99	TB	23	0	3	3	-4	0	0	12	0.0	0	0	0	0	0	0	4	8	0	4	0	0	4	0	.13
4 Years		79	3	13	16	-22	0	0	57	5.3	0	1	1	0	0	0	17	34	0	17	0	0	14	0	.20

Dennis Bonvie

Pos: RW **Shoots:** R **Ht:** 5'11" **Wt:** 205 **Born:** 7/23/73—Antigonish, Nova Scotia **Age:** 26

		Overall									Power Play			Shorthand			Penalty							Misc	
Year	Tm	GP	G	A	Pts	+/–	GW	GT	S	SPct	G	A	Pts	G	A	Pts	Num	PIM	Maj	Mnr	Fgt	Rgh	HHT	Hat	P/G
94-95	Edm	2	0	0	0	0	0	0	0	–	0	0	0	0	0	0	0	0	0	0	0	0	0	0	.00
95-96	Edm	8	0	0	0	-3	0	0	0	–	0	0	0	0	0	0	9	47	7	1	7	0	1	0	.00
96-97		Did Not Play in NHL																							
97-98	Edm	4	0	0	0	0	0	0	0	–	0	0	0	0	0	0	5	27	3	1	3	0	1	0	.00
98-99	Chi	11	0	0	0	-4	0	0	1	0.0	0	0	0	0	0	0	9	44	6	2	6	1	0	0	.00
4 Years		25	0	0	0	-7	0	0	1	0.0	0	0	0	0	0	0	23	118	16	4	16	1	2	0	.00

Sebastien Bordeleau

(statistical profile on page 290)

Pos: C **Shoots:** R **Ht:** 5'11" **Wt:** 188 **Born:** 2/15/75—Vancouver, British Columbia **Age:** 24

		Overall									Power Play			Shorthand			Penalty							Misc	
Year	Tm	GP	G	A	Pts	+/–	GW	GT	S	SPct	G	A	Pts	G	A	Pts	Num	PIM	Maj	Mnr	Fgt	Rgh	HHT	Hat	P/G
95-96	Mon	4	0	0	0	-1	0	0	0	–	0	0	0	0	0	0	0	0	0	0	0	0	0	0	.00
96-97	Mon	28	2	9	11	-3	0	0	27	7.4	0	0	0	0	2	2	1	2	0	1	0	0	0	0	.39
97-98	Mon	53	6	8	14	5	0	1	55	10.9	2	3	5	1	0	1	18	36	0	18	0	2	7	0	.26
98-99	Nsh	72	16	24	40	-14	3	0	168	9.5	1	3	4	2	0	2	13	26	0	13	0	0	8	0	.56
4 Years		157	24	41	65	-13	3	1	250	9.6	3	6	9	3	2	5	32	64	0	32	0	2	15	0	.41

Postseason

Year	Tm	GP	G	A	Pts	+/–	GW	OT	S	SPct	G	A	Pts	G	A	Pts	Num	PIM	Maj	Mnr	Fgt	Rgh	HHT	Hat	P/G
97-98	Mon	5	0	0	0	-1	0	0	1	0.0	0	0	0	0	0	0	1	2	0	1	0	0	0	0	.00

Jason Botterill

Pos: LW **Shoots:** L **Ht:** 6'4" **Wt:** 217 **Born:** 5/19/76—Edmonton, Alberta **Age:** 23

		Overall									Power Play			Shorthand			Penalty							Misc	
Year	Tm	GP	G	A	Pts	+/–	GW	GT	S	SPct	G	A	Pts	G	A	Pts	Num	PIM	Maj	Mnr	Fgt	Rgh	HHT	Hat	P/G
97-98	Dal	4	0	0	0	-1	0	0	2	0.0	0	0	0	0	0	0	4	19	1	2	1	0	1	0	.00
98-99	Dal	17	0	0	0	-2	0	0	8	0.0	0	0	0	0	0	0	7	23	3	4	3	1	2	0	.00
2 Years		21	0	0	0	-3	0	0	10	0.0	0	0	0	0	0	0	11	42	4	6	4	1	3	0	.00

Joel Bouchard

(statistical profile on page 290)

Pos: D **Shoots:** L **Ht:** 6'0" **Wt:** 196 **Born:** 1/23/74—Montreal, Quebec **Age:** 25

		Overall									Power Play			Shorthand			Penalty							Misc	
Year	Tm	GP	G	A	Pts	+/–	GW	GT	S	SPct	G	A	Pts	G	A	Pts	Num	PIM	Maj	Mnr	Fgt	Rgh	HHT	Hat	P/G
94-95	Cgy	2	0	0	0	0	0	0	0	–	0	0	0	0	0	0	0	0	0	0	0	0	0	0	.00
95-96	Cgy	4	0	0	0	0	0	0	0	–	0	0	0	0	0	0	2	4	0	2	0	0	1	0	.00
96-97	Cgy	76	4	5	9	-23	0	0	61	6.6	0	1	1	1	0	1	23	49	1	22	1	0	13	0	.12
97-98	Cgy	44	5	7	12	0	1	0	51	9.8	0	1	1	1	1	2	23	57	1	21	1	5	12	0	.27
98-99	Nsh	64	4	11	15	-10	0	0	78	5.1	0	2	2	0	1	1	27	60	2	25	2	3	13	0	.23
5 Years		190	13	23	36	-33	1	0	190	6.8	0	4	4	2	2	4	75	170	4	70	4	8	39	0	.19

Philippe Boucher

Pos: D **Shoots:** R **Ht:** 6'3" **Wt:** 212 **Born:** 3/24/73—St. Appollinaire, Quebec **Age:** 26

		Overall									Power Play			Shorthand			Penalty							Misc	
Year	Tm	GP	G	A	Pts	+/–	GW	GT	S	SPct	G	A	Pts	G	A	Pts	Num	PIM	Maj	Mnr	Fgt	Rgh	HHT	Hat	P/G
92-93	Buf	18	0	4	4	1	0	0	28	0.0	0	1	1	0	0	0	7	14	0	7	0	0	2	0	.22
93-94	Buf	38	6	8	14	-1	1	0	67	9.0	4	4	8	0	0	0	13	29	1	12	1	0	6	0	.37
94-95	2Tm	15	2	4	6	3	0	0	30	6.7	0	2	2	0	0	0	2	4	0	2	0	0	2	0	.40
95-96	LA	53	7	16	23	-26	1	1	145	4.8	5	11	16	0	0	0	14	31	1	13	1	0	9	0	.43
96-97	LA	60	7	18	25	0	1	0	159	4.4	2	7	9	0	0	0	11	25	1	10	1	2	4	0	.42
97-98	LA	45	6	10	16	6	0	0	80	7.5	1	2	3	0	0	0	20	49	3	17	3	2	8	0	.36
98-99	LA	45	2	6	8	-12	0	0	87	2.3	1	3	4	0	0	0	13	32	2	11	2	2	6	0	.18
94-95	Buf	9	1	4	5	6	0	0	15	6.7	0	2	2	0	0	0	0	0	0	0	0	0	0	0	.56
94-95	LA	6	1	0	1	-3	0	0	15	6.7	0	0	0	0	0	0	2	4	0	2	0	0	2	0	.17
7 Years		274	30	66	96	-29	3	1	596	5.0	13	30	43	0	0	0	80	184	8	72	8	6	37	0	.35
											Postseason														
Year	Tm	GP	G	A	Pts	+/–	GW	OT	S	SPct	G	A	Pts	G	A	Pts	Num	PIM	Maj	Mnr	Fgt	Rgh	HHT	Hat	P/G
93-94	Buf	7	1	1	2	2	0	0	10	10.0	1	0	1	0	0	0	1	2	0	1	0	0	0	0	.29

Bob Boughner

(statistical profile on page 291)

Pos: D **Shoots:** R **Ht:** 6'0" **Wt:** 206 **Born:** 3/8/71—Windsor, Ontario **Age:** 28

		Overall									Power Play			Shorthand			Penalty							Misc	
Year	Tm	GP	G	A	Pts	+/–	GW	GT	S	SPct	G	A	Pts	G	A	Pts	Num	PIM	Maj	Mnr	Fgt	Rgh	HHT	Hat	P/G
95-96	Buf	31	0	1	1	3	0	0	14	0.0	0	0	0	0	0	0	29	104	10	17	10	8	5	0	.03
96-97	Buf	77	1	7	8	12	0	0	34	2.9	0	0	0	0	1	1	65	225	21	40	21	18	13	0	.10
97-98	Buf	69	1	3	4	5	0	0	26	3.8	0	0	0	0	0	0	51	165	13	35	13	16	4	0	.06
98-99	Nsh	79	3	10	13	-6	1	0	59	5.1	0	0	0	0	1	1	55	137	9	46	9	16	9	0	.16
4 Years		256	5	21	26	14	1	0	133	3.8	0	0	0	0	2	2	200	631	53	138	53	58	31	0	.10
											Postseason														
Year	Tm	GP	G	A	Pts	+/–	GW	OT	S	SPct	G	A	Pts	G	A	Pts	Num	PIM	Maj	Mnr	Fgt	Rgh	HHT	Hat	P/G
96-97	Buf	11	0	1	1	0	0	0	1	0.0	0	0	0	0	0	0	3	9	1	2	1	2	0	0	.09
97-98	Buf	14	0	4	4	9	0	0	7	0.0	0	0	0	0	0	0	6	15	1	5	1	1	1	0	.29
2 Years		25	0	5	5	9	0	0	8	0.0	0	0	0	0	0	0	9	24	2	7	2	3	1	0	.20

Ray Bourque

(statistical profile on page 291)

Pos: D **Shoots:** L **Ht:** 5'11" **Wt:** 219 **Born:** 12/28/60—Montreal, Quebec **Age:** 39

		Overall									Power Play			Shorthand			Penalty							Misc	
Year	Tm	GP	G	A	Pts	+/–	GW	GT	S	SPct	G	A	Pts	G	A	Pts	Num	PIM	Maj	Mnr	Fgt	Rgh	HHT	Hat	P/G
79-80	Bos	80	17	48	65	52	1	1	185	9.2	3	–	–	2	–	–	–	73	–	–	–	–	–	0	.81
80-81	Bos*	67	27	29	56	29	6	0	207	13.0	9	–	–	1	–	–	–	96	–	–	–	–	–	0	.84
81-82	Bos*	65	17	49	66	22	2	2	211	8.1	4	–	–	0	–	–	–	51	–	–	–	–	–	0	1.02
82-83	Bos*	65	22	51	73	49	5	2	205	10.7	7	–	–	0	–	–	–	20	–	–	–	–	–	1	1.12
83-84	Bos*	78	31	65	96	51	5	0	**340**	9.1	12	–	–	1	–	–	–	57	–	–	–	–	–	0	1.23
84-85	Bos*	73	20	66	86	30	1	0	333	6.0	10	–	–	1	–	–	–	53	–	–	–	–	–	0	1.18

Overall											Power Play			Shorthand			Penalty							Misc	
Year	Tm	GP	G	A	Pts	+/-	GW	GT	S	SPct	G	A	Pts	G	A	Pts	Num	PIM	Maj	Mnr	Fgt	Rgh	HHT	Hat	P/G
85-86	Bos*	74	19	58	77	17	3	0	289	6.6	11	–	–	0	–	–	–	68	–	–	–	–	–	0	1.04
86-87	Bos*	78	23	72	95	44	3	2	**334**	6.9	6	–	–	1	–	–	–	36	–	–	–	–	–	0	1.22
87-88	Bos*	78	17	64	81	34	5	0	344	4.9	7	–	–	1	–	–	–	72	–	–	–	–	–	0	1.04
88-89	Bos*	60	18	43	61	20	0	1	243	7.4	6	21	27	0	–	–	–	52	–	–	–	–	–	0	1.02
89-90	Bos*	76	19	65	84	31	3	0	310	6.1	8	39	47	0	–	–	–	50	–	–	–	–	–	0	1.11
90-91	Bos*	76	21	73	94	33	3	1	323	6.5	7	38	45	0	0	0	–	75	–	–	–	–	–	0	1.24
91-92	Bos*	80	21	60	81	11	2	0	334	6.3	7	28	35	1	0	1	28	56	0	28	0	8	11	0	1.01
92-93	Bos*	78	19	63	82	38	7	0	330	5.8	8	33	41	0	5	5	20	40	0	20	0	2	11	0	1.05
93-94	Bos*	72	20	71	91	26	1	1	386	5.2	10	42	52	3	2	5	29	58	0	29	0	6	14	0	1.26
94-95	Bos	46	12	31	43	3	2	0	**210**	5.7	9	20	29	0	0	0	10	20	0	10	0	0	5	0	.93
95-96	Bos*	82	20	62	82	31	2	1	390	5.1	9	29	38	2	0	2	29	58	0	29	0	3	19	0	1.00
96-97	Bos*	62	19	31	50	-11	3	1	230	8.3	8	9	17	1	5	6	9	18	0	9	0	1	5	0	.81
97-98	Bos*	82	13	35	48	2	3	1	264	4.9	9	21	30	0	2	2	29	80	2	25	1	3	9	0	.59
98-99	Bos	81	10	47	57	-7	3	0	262	3.8	8	31	39	0	1	1	17	34	0	17	0	0	6	0	.70
20 Years		1453	385	1083	1468	505	60	13	5730	6.7	158	–	–	14	–	–	–	1067	–	–	–	–	–	1	1.01
Postseason																									
Year	Tm	GP	G	A	Pts	+/-	GW	OT	S	SPct	G	A	Pts	G	A	Pts	Num	PIM	Maj	Mnr	Fgt	Rgh	HHT	Hat	P/G
79-80	Bos	10	2	9	11	–	0	0	–	–	0	–	–	0	–	–	–	27	–	–	–	–	–	0	1.10
80-81	Bos	3	0	1	1	–	0	0	–	–	0	–	–	0	–	–	1	2	0	1	0	–	–	0	.33
81-82	Bos	9	1	5	6	–	1	0	–	–	0	–	–	0	0	0	–	16	–	–	–	–	–	0	.67
82-83	Bos	17	8	15	23	15	1	0	79	10.1	2	–	–	0	–	–	–	10	–	–	–	–	–	0	1.35
83-84	Bos	3	0	2	2	-3	0	0	10	0.0	0	–	–	0	0	0	0	0	0	0	0	0	0	0	.67
84-85	Bos	5	0	3	3	1	0	0	15	0.0	0	–	–	0	0	0	2	4	0	2	0	–	–	0	.60
85-86	Bos	3	0	0	0	0	0	0	7	0.0	0	0	0	0	0	0	0	0	0	0	0	0	0	0	.00
86-87	Bos	4	1	2	3	-1	0	0	22	4.5	0	–	–	0	–	–	0	0	0	0	0	0	0	0	.75
87-88	Bos	23	3	18	21	16	1	0	65	4.6	0	–	–	0	–	–	–	26	–	–	–	–	–	0	.91
88-89	Bos	10	0	4	4	-1	0	0	40	0.0	0	–	–	0	–	–	3	6	0	3	0	–	–	0	.40
89-90	Bos	17	5	12	17	11	0	0	64	7.8	1	3	4	0	–	–	–	16	–	–	–	–	–	0	1.00
90-91	Bos	19	7	18	25	-4	0	0	84	8.3	3	14	17	0	0	0	–	12	–	–	–	–	–	0	1.32
91-92	Bos	12	3	6	9	-10	0	0	51	5.9	2	4	6	0	0	0	6	12	0	6	0	0	3	0	.75
92-93	Bos	4	1	0	1	-2	0	0	20	5.0	1	0	1	0	0	0	1	2	0	1	0	0	1	0	.25
93-94	Bos	13	2	8	10	-5	0	0	64	3.1	1	6	7	0	0	0	0	0	0	0	0	0	0	0	.77
94-95	Bos	5	0	3	3	-5	0	0	15	0.0	0	2	2	0	0	0	0	0	0	0	0	0	0	0	.60
95-96	Bos	5	1	6	7	-4	0	0	28	3.6	1	5	6	0	1	1	1	2	0	1	0	0	0	0	1.40
97-98	Bos	6	1	4	5	-2	0	0	42	2.4	1	3	4	0	0	0	1	2	0	1	0	0	0	0	.83
98-99	Bos	12	1	9	10	1	0	0	44	2.3	0	6	6	0	0	0	7	14	0	7	0	0	5	0	.83
19 Years		180	36	125	161	7	3	0	650	5.1	12	–	–	0	–	–	–	151	–	–	–	–	–	0	.89

Dan Boyle

Pos: D **Shoots:** R **Ht:** 5'11" **Wt:** 190 **Born:** 7/12/76—Ottawa, Ontario **Age:** 23

Overall											Power Play			Shorthand			Penalty							Misc	
Year	Tm	GP	G	A	Pts	+/-	GW	GT	S	SPct	G	A	Pts	G	A	Pts	Num	PIM	Maj	Mnr	Fgt	Rgh	HHT	Hat	P/G
98-99	Fla	22	3	5	8	0	1	0	31	9.7	1	2	3	0	0	0	3	6	0	3	0	0	2	0	.36

Donald Brashear

(statistical profile on page 291)

Pos: LW **Shoots:** L **Ht:** 6'2" **Wt:** 220 **Born:** 1/7/72—Bedford, Indiana **Age:** 27

Overall											Power Play			Shorthand			Penalty							Misc	
Year	Tm	GP	G	A	Pts	+/-	GW	GT	S	SPct	G	A	Pts	G	A	Pts	Num	PIM	Maj	Mnr	Fgt	Rgh	HHT	Hat	P/G
93-94	Mon	14	2	2	4	0	0	0	15	13.3	0	0	0	0	0	0	11	34	4	7	4	5	1	0	.29
94-95	Mon	20	1	1	2	-5	1	0	10	10.0	0	0	0	0	0	0	17	63	7	9	7	5	1	0	.10
95-96	Mon	67	0	4	4	-10	0	0	25	0.0	0	0	0	0	0	0	49	223	23	19	22	8	5	0	.06
96-97	2Tm	69	8	5	13	-8	2	0	61	13.1	0	0	0	0	0	0	55	245	21	25	21	9	6	0	.19
97-98	Van	77	9	9	18	-9	1	1	64	14.1	0	0	0	0	0	0	83	**372**	26	41	26	21	5	0	.23
98-99	Van	82	8	10	18	-25	1	0	112	7.1	2	1	3	0	0	0	63	209	17	42	17	15	13	0	.22
96-97	Mon	10	0	0	0	-2	0	0	6	0.0	0	0	0	0	0	0	10	38	6	4	6	2	0	0	.00
96-97	Van	59	8	5	13	-6	2	0	55	14.5	0	0	0	0	0	0	45	207	15	21	15	7	6	0	.22
6 Years		329	28	31	59	-57	5	1	287	9.8	2	1	3	0	0	0	278	1146	98	143	97	63	31	0	.18
Postseason																									
Year	Tm	GP	G	A	Pts	+/-	GW	OT	S	SPct	G	A	Pts	G	A	Pts	Num	PIM	Maj	Mnr	Fgt	Rgh	HHT	Hat	P/G
93-94	Mon	2	0	0	0	-1	0	0	2	0.0	0	0	0	0	0	0	0	0	0	0	0	0	0	0	.00
95-96	Mon	6	0	0	0	-1	0	0	0	–	0	0	0	0	0	0	1	2	0	1	0	0	0	0	.00
2 Years		8	0	0	0	-2	0	0	2	0.0	0	0	0	0	0	0	1	2	0	1	0	0	0	0	.00

Fred Brathwaite

(statistical profile on page 396)

Pos: G **Catches:** L **Ht:** 5'7" **Wt:** 170 **Born:** 11/24/72—Ottawa, Ontario **Age:** 27

Overall																	Pen Shot		Offense		
Year	Tm	GP	GS	TP	W	L	T	Min	GA	GAA	Shots	SvPct	ShO	OE	PPGA	SHGA	Shots	GA	G	A	PIM
93-94	Edm	19	14	1	3	10	3	982	58	3.54	523	.889	0	5	13	0	0	0	0	0	0
94-95	Edm	14	7	1	2	5	1	601	40	3.99	292	.863	0	0	11	1	0	0	0	0	0
95-96	Edm	7	2	0	0	2	0	293	12	2.46	140	.914	0	1	0	1	0	0	0	0	2
96-97										Did Not Play in NHL											
97-98										Did Not Play in NHL											
98-99	Cgy	28	28	1	11	9	7	1663	68	2.45	796	.915	1	12	20	3	0	0	0	2	2
4 Years		68	51	3	16	26	11	3539	178	3.02	1751	.898	1	18	44	5	0	0	0	2	4

Richard Brennan

Pos: D **Shoots:** R **Ht:** 6'2" **Wt:** 200 **Born:** 11/26/72—Schenectady, New York **Age:** 27

Overall											Power Play			Shorthand			Penalty							Misc	
Year	Tm	GP	G	A	Pts	+/–	GW	GT	S	SPct	G	A	Pts	G	A	Pts	Num	PIM	Maj	Mnr	Fgt	Rgh	HHT	Hat	P/G
96-97	Col	2	0	0	0	0	0	0	0	–	0	0	0	0	0	0	0	0	0	0	0	0	0	0	.00
97-98	SJ	11	1	2	3	-4	0	0	24	4.2	1	1	2	0	0	0	1	2	0	1	0	0	0	0	.27
98-99	NYR	24	1	3	4	-4	0	0	36	2.8	0	3	3	0	0	0	10	23	1	9	1	0	4	0	.17
3 Years		37	2	5	7	-8	0	0	60	3.3	1	4	5	0	0	0	11	25	1	10	1	0	4	0	.19

Eric Brewer

(statistical profile on page 291)

Pos: D **Shoots:** L **Ht:** 6'3" **Wt:** 191 **Born:** 4/17/79—Verona, British Columbia **Age:** 20

Overall											Power Play			Shorthand			Penalty							Misc	
Year	Tm	GP	G	A	Pts	+/–	GW	GT	S	SPct	G	A	Pts	G	A	Pts	Num	PIM	Maj	Mnr	Fgt	Rgh	HHT	Hat	P/G
98-99	NYI	63	5	6	11	-14	0	0	63	7.9	2	3	5	0	0	0	16	32	0	16	0	0	9	0	.17

Daniel Briere

(statistical profile on page 292)

Pos: C **Shoots:** R **Ht:** 5'9" **Wt:** 160 **Born:** 10/6/77—Gatineau, Quebec **Age:** 22

Overall											Power Play			Shorthand			Penalty							Misc	
Year	Tm	GP	G	A	Pts	+/–	GW	GT	S	SPct	G	A	Pts	G	A	Pts	Num	PIM	Maj	Mnr	Fgt	Rgh	HHT	Hat	P/G
97-98	Pho	5	1	0	1	1	0	0	4	25.0	0	0	0	0	0	0	1	2	0	1	0	0	1	0	.20
98-99	Pho	64	8	14	22	-3	2	0	90	8.9	2	2	4	0	0	0	11	30	0	10	0	0	2	0	.34
2 Years		69	9	14	23	-2	2	0	94	9.6	2	2	4	0	0	0	12	32	0	11	0	0	3	0	.33

Rod Brind'Amour

(statistical profile on page 292)

Pos: C **Shoots:** L **Ht:** 6'1" **Wt:** 200 **Born:** 8/9/70—Ottawa, Ontario **Age:** 29

Overall											Power Play			Shorthand			Penalty							Misc	
Year	Tm	GP	G	A	Pts	+/–	GW	GT	S	SPct	G	A	Pts	G	A	Pts	Num	PIM	Maj	Mnr	Fgt	Rgh	HHT	Hat	P/G
88-89										Did Not Play in Regular Season															
89-90	StL	79	26	35	61	23	1	1	160	16.3	10	–	–	0	–	–	–	46	–	–	–	–	–	0	.77
90-91	StL	78	17	32	49	2	3	0	169	10.1	4	–	–	0	–	–	–	93	–	–	–	–	–	0	.63
91-92	Phi*	80	33	44	77	-3	5	0	202	16.3	8	15	23	4	4	8	36	100	4	30	3	9	8	0	.96
92-93	Phi	81	37	49	86	-8	4	1	206	18.0	13	17	30	4	2	6	36	89	3	32	3	9	11	1	1.06
93-94	Phi	84	35	62	97	-9	4	0	230	15.2	14	17	31	1	3	4	34	85	3	30	3	9	11	0	1.15
94-95	Phi	48	12	27	39	-4	2	0	86	14.0	4	12	16	1	1	2	15	33	1	14	1	6	4	0	.81
95-96	Phi	82	26	61	87	20	5	**4**	213	12.2	4	22	26	4	2	6	34	110	6	25	5	6	11	0	1.06
96-97	Phi	**82**	27	32	59	2	3	2	205	13.2	8	5	13	2	2	4	19	41	1	18	1	4	9	0	.72
97-98	Phi	82	36	38	74	-2	8	0	205	17.6	10	13	23	2	2	4	23	54	0	22	0	3	10	0	.90
98-99	Phi	82	24	50	74	3	3	2	191	12.6	10	22	32	0	1	1	22	47	1	21	1	2	7	0	.90
10 Years		778	273	430	703	24	38	10	1867	14.6	85	–	–	18	–	–	–	698	–	–	–	–	–	1	.90

Postseason																									
Year	Tm	GP	G	A	Pts	+/–	GW	OT	S	SPct	G	A	Pts	G	A	Pts	Num	PIM	Maj	Mnr	Fgt	Rgh	HHT	Hat	P/G
88-89	StL	5	2	0	2	-2	0	0	4	50.0	0	0	0	0	0	0	2	4	0	2	0	–	–	0	.40
89-90	StL	12	5	8	13	0	0	0	29	17.2	1	–	–	0	–	–	3	6	0	3	0	–	–	0	1.08
90-91	StL	13	2	5	7	0	0	0	24	8.3	1	–	–	0	0	0	–	10	–	–	–	–	–	0	.54
94-95	Phi	15	6	9	15	5	1	0	28	21.4	2	0	2	1	2	3	4	8	0	4	0	0	1	0	1.00
95-96	Phi	12	2	5	7	-2	0	0	34	5.9	1	1	2	0	0	0	3	6	0	3	0	0	0	0	.58
96-97	Phi	19	13	8	21	9	1	0	65	20.0	4	2	6	2	0	2	5	10	0	5	0	1	0	0	1.11
97-98	Phi	5	2	2	4	2	0	0	15	13.3	0	1	1	0	0	0	2	7	1	1	1	0	1	0	.80
98-99	Phi	6	1	3	4	1	0	0	19	5.3	0	2	2	0	0	0	0	0	0	0	0	0	0	0	.67
8 Years		87	33	40	73	13	2	0	218	15.1	9	–	–	3	–	–	–	51	–	–	–	–	–	0	.84

Patrice Brisebois

(statistical profile on page 292)

Pos: D **Shoots:** R **Ht:** 6'2" **Wt:** 204 **Born:** 1/27/71—Montreal, Quebec **Age:** 28

		Overall									Power Play			Shorthand			Penalty							Misc	
Year	Tm	GP	G	A	Pts	+/–	GW	GT	S	SPct	G	A	Pts	G	A	Pts	Num	PIM	Maj	Mnr	Fgt	Rgh	HHT	Hat	P/G
90-91	Mon	10	0	2	2	1	0	0	11	0.0	0	–	–	0	–	–	2	4	0	2	0	–	–	0	.20
91-92	Mon	26	2	8	10	9	1	0	37	5.4	0	5	5	0	0	0	6	20	0	5	0	0	4	0	.38
92-93	Mon	70	10	21	31	6	2	0	123	8.1	4	8	12	0	0	0	30	79	1	27	0	6	11	0	.44
93-94	Mon	53	2	21	23	5	0	0	71	2.8	1	8	9	0	1	1	23	63	3	19	3	7	5	0	.43
94-95	Mon	35	4	8	12	-2	2	0	67	6.0	0	3	3	0	0	0	5	26	0	3	0	1	0	0	.34
95-96	Mon	69	9	27	36	10	1	0	127	7.1	3	16	19	0	0	0	20	65	3	15	2	0	3	0	.52
96-97	Mon	49	2	13	15	-7	1	0	72	2.8	0	5	5	0	0	0	12	24	0	12	0	2	4	0	.31
97-98	Mon	79	10	27	37	16	1	0	125	8.0	5	13	18	0	1	1	24	67	1	21	1	0	11	0	.47
98-99	Mon	54	3	9	12	-8	1	0	90	3.3	1	3	4	0	0	0	14	28	0	14	0	1	6	0	.22
9 Years		445	42	136	178	30	9	0	723	5.8	14	–	–	0	–	–	136	376	8	118	6	–	–	0	.40
Postseason																									
Year	Tm	GP	G	A	Pts	+/–	GW	OT	S	SPct	G	A	Pts	G	A	Pts	Num	PIM	Maj	Mnr	Fgt	Rgh	HHT	Hat	P/G
91-92	Mon	11	2	4	6	3	1	0	25	8.0	1	0	1	0	0	0	3	6	0	3	0	2	0	0	.55
92-93	Mon	20	0	4	4	5	0	0	35	0.0	0	0	0	0	0	0	9	18	0	9	0	3	2	0	.20
93-94	Mon	7	0	4	4	-3	0	0	11	0.0	0	1	1	0	0	0	3	6	0	3	0	1	1	0	.57
95-96	Mon	6	1	2	3	2	0	0	8	12.5	0	1	1	0	0	0	3	6	0	3	0	1	2	0	.50
96-97	Mon	3	1	1	2	3	1	1	3	33.3	0	0	0	0	0	0	4	24	0	2	0	1	0	0	.67
97-98	Mon	10	1	0	1	-5	0	0	26	3.8	0	0	0	0	0	0	0	0	0	0	0	0	0	0	.10
6 Years		57	5	15	20	5	2	1	108	4.6	1	2	3	0	0	0	22	60	0	20	0	8	5	0	.35

Martin Brochu

Pos: G **Catches:** L **Ht:** 5'11" **Wt:** 185 **Born:** 3/10/73—Anjou, Quebec **Age:** 26

		Overall															Pen Shot		Offense		
Year	Tm	GP	GS	TP	W	L	T	Min	GA	GAA	Shots	SvPct	ShO	OE	PPGA	SHGA	Shots	GA	G	A	PIM
98-99	Was	2	2	0	0	2	0	120	6	3.00	55	.891	0	0	3	0	0	0	0	0	2

Martin Brodeur

(statistical profile on page 396)

Pos: G **Catches:** L **Ht:** 6'1" **Wt:** 205 **Born:** 5/6/72—Montreal, Quebec **Age:** 27

		Overall															Pen Shot		Offense		
Year	Tm	GP	GS	TP	W	L	T	Min	GA	GAA	Shots	SvPct	ShO	OE	PPGA	SHGA	Shots	GA	G	A	PIM
91-92	NJ	4	2	0	2	1	0	179	10	3.35	85	.882	0	0	5	0	0	0	0	0	0
92-93		Did Not Play in NHL																			
93-94	NJ	47	46	7	27	11	8	2625	105	2.40	1238	.915	3	16	36	5	0	0	0	0	2
94-95	NJ	40	38	5	19	11	6	2184	89	2.45	908	.902	3	7	19	3	0	0	0	2	2
95-96	NJ*	77	75	7	34	**30**	12	**4433**	173	2.34	1954	.911	6	16	44	8	0	0	0	1	6
96-97	NJ*	67	64	**10**	37	14	13	3838	120	**1.88**	1633	.927	**10**	18	18	7	0	0	0	4	8
97-98	NJ*	70	69	3	**43**	17	8	4128	130	1.89	1569	.917	10	16	32	6	0	0	0	3	10
98-99	NJ	**70**	**70**	0	**39**	21	10	**4239**	162	2.29	1728	.906	4	10	40	5	0	0	0	4	4
7 Years		375	364	32	201	105	57	21626	789	2.19	9115	.913	36	83	194	34	0	0	0	14	32
Postseason																					
Year	Tm	GP	GS	TP	W	L	Pct	Min	GA	GAA	Shots	SvPct	ShO	OE	PPGA	SHGA	Shots	GA	G	A	PIM
91-92	NJ	1	0	0	0	1	.000	32	3	5.63	15	.800	0	0	0	0	0	0	0	0	0
93-94	NJ	17	17	1	8	9	.471	1171	38	1.95	531	.928	1	7	9	1	0	0	0	1	0
94-95	NJ	20	20	1	16	4	.800	1222	34	1.67	463	.927	3	6	10	2	0	0	0	1	6
96-97	NJ	10	10	0	5	5	.500	659	19	1.73	268	.929	2	4	3	2	0	0	1	0	0
97-98	NJ	6	6	0	2	4	.333	366	12	1.97	164	.927	0	2	4	0	0	0	0	1	0
98-99	NJ	7	7	0	3	4	.429	425	20	2.82	139	.856	0	0	4	0	0	0	0	2	2
6 Years		61	60	2	34	27	.557	3875	126	1.95	1580	.920	6	19	30	5	0	0	1	5	8

Brad Brown

Pos: D **Shoots:** R **Ht:** 6'3" **Wt:** 218 **Born:** 12/27/75—Baie Verte, Newfoundland **Age:** 24

		Overall									Power Play			Shorthand			Penalty							Misc	
Year	Tm	GP	G	A	Pts	+/–	GW	GT	S	SPct	G	A	Pts	G	A	Pts	Num	PIM	Maj	Mnr	Fgt	Rgh	HHT	Hat	P/G
96-97	Mon	8	0	0	0	-1	0	0	0	–	0	0	0	0	0	0	8	22	2	6	2	2	0	0	.00
97-98		Did Not Play in NHL																							
98-99	2Tm	66	1	7	8	-4	0	1	26	3.8	0	0	0	0	0	0	60	205	15	40	14	12	4	0	.12
98-99	Mon	5	0	0	0	0	0	0	0	–	0	0	0	0	0	0	5	21	1	3	1	0	0	0	.00
98-99	Chi	61	1	7	8	-4	0	1	26	3.8	0	0	0	0	0	0	55	184	14	37	13	12	4	0	.13
2 Years		74	1	7	8	-5	0	1	26	3.8	0	0	0	0	0	0	68	227	17	46	16	14	4	0	.11

Curtis Brown

(statistical profile on page 292)

Pos: C **Shoots:** L **Ht:** 6'0" **Wt:** 182 **Born:** 2/12/76—Unity, Saskatchewan **Age:** 23

Overall											Power Play			Shorthand			Penalty							Misc	
Year	Tm	GP	G	A	Pts	+/–	GW	GT	S	SPct	G	A	Pts	G	A	Pts	Num	PIM	Maj	Mnr	Fgt	Rgh	HHT	Hat	P/G
94-95	Buf	1	1	1	2	2	0	0	4	25.0	0	0	0	0	0	0	1	2	0	1	0	0	1	0	2.00
95-96	Buf	4	0	0	0	0	0	0	1	0.0	0	0	0	0	0	0	0	0	0	0	0	0	0	0	.00
96-97	Buf	28	4	3	7	4	1	0	31	12.9	0	0	0	0	0	0	9	18	0	9	0	0	8	0	.25
97-98	Buf	63	12	12	24	11	2	1	91	13.2	1	3	4	1	1	2	17	34	0	17	0	4	7	0	.38
98-99	Buf	78	16	31	47	23	3	**3**	128	12.5	5	5	10	1	1	2	24	56	0	23	0	2	13	0	.60
5 Years		174	33	47	80	40	6	4	255	12.9	6	8	14	2	2	4	51	110	0	50	0	6	29	0	.46
Postseason																									
Year	Tm	GP	G	A	Pts	+/–	GW	OT	S	SPct	G	A	Pts	G	A	Pts	Num	PIM	Maj	Mnr	Fgt	Rgh	HHT	Hat	P/G
97-98	Buf	13	1	2	3	6	0	0	23	4.3	1	0	1	0	0	0	5	10	0	5	0	0	0	0	.23
98-99	Buf	21	7	6	13	3	3	0	34	20.6	3	1	4	0	0	0	5	10	0	5	0	0	3	0	.62
2 Years		34	8	8	16	9	3	0	57	14.0	4	1	5	0	0	0	10	20	0	10	0	0	3	0	.47

Doug Brown

(statistical profile on page 293)

Pos: RW **Shoots:** R **Ht:** 5'10" **Wt:** 188 **Born:** 6/12/64—New Haven, Connecticut **Age:** 35

Overall											Power Play			Shorthand			Penalty							Misc	
Year	Tm	GP	G	A	Pts	+/–	GW	GT	S	SPct	G	A	Pts	G	A	Pts	Num	PIM	Maj	Mnr	Fgt	Rgh	HHT	Hat	P/G
86-87	NJ	4	0	1	1	-4	0	0	10	0.0	0	–	–	0	–	–	0	0	0	0	0	0	0	0	.25
87-88	NJ	70	14	11	25	7	2	0	112	12.5	1	–	–	4	–	–	–	20	–	–	–	–	–	0	.36
88-89	NJ	63	15	10	25	-7	2	0	110	13.6	4	1	5	0	2	2	–	15	–	–	–	–	–	0	.40
89-90	NJ	69	14	20	34	7	3	0	135	10.4	1	2	3	3	1	4	–	16	–	–	–	–	–	0	.49
90-91	NJ	58	14	16	30	18	2	1	122	11.5	0	0	0	2	0	2	2	4	0	2	0	–	–	0	.52
91-92	NJ	71	11	17	28	17	1	0	140	7.9	1	0	1	2	3	5	8	27	1	6	0	0	4	0	.39
92-93	NJ	15	0	5	5	3	0	0	17	0.0	0	0	0	0	0	0	1	2	0	1	0	0	1	0	.33
93-94	Pit	77	18	37	55	19	1	0	152	11.8	2	1	3	0	0	0	9	18	0	9	0	0	4	0	.71
94-95	Det	45	9	12	21	14	2	0	69	13.0	1	0	1	1	1	2	8	16	0	8	0	0	4	0	.47
95-96	Det	62	12	15	27	11	1	0	115	10.4	0	2	2	1	2	3	2	4	0	2	0	0	1	0	.44
96-97	Det	49	6	7	13	-3	0	0	69	8.7	1	1	2	0	1	1	4	8	0	4	0	1	2	0	.27
97-98	Det	80	19	23	42	17	5	0	145	13.1	6	7	13	1	0	1	6	12	0	6	0	0	4	1	.53
98-99	Det	80	9	19	28	5	1	0	180	5.0	3	1	4	1	2	3	17	42	0	16	0	1	11	0	.35
13 Years		743	141	193	334	104	20	1	1376	10.2	20	–	–	15	–	–	–	184	–	–	–	–	–	1	.45
Postseason																									
Year	Tm	GP	G	A	Pts	+/–	GW	OT	S	SPct	G	A	Pts	G	A	Pts	Num	PIM	Maj	Mnr	Fgt	Rgh	HHT	Hat	P/G
87-88	NJ	19	5	1	6	3	1	1	31	16.1	0	–	–	1	–	–	3	6	0	3	0	–	–	0	.32
89-90	NJ	6	0	1	1	-1	0	0	5	0.0	0	–	–	0	–	–	1	2	0	1	0	–	–	0	.17
90-91	NJ	7	2	2	4	1	0	0	14	14.3	0	–	–	1	–	–	1	2	0	1	0	–	–	0	.57
93-94	Pit	6	0	0	0	0	0	0	3	0.0	0	0	0	0	0	0	1	2	0	1	0	1	0	0	.00
94-95	Det	18	4	8	12	14	1	0	27	14.8	0	1	1	1	1	2	1	2	0	1	0	0	1	0	.67
95-96	Det	13	3	3	6	0	0	0	18	16.7	0	0	0	1	1	2	2	4	0	2	0	0	0	0	.46
96-97	Det	14	3	3	6	4	0	0	23	13.0	0	0	0	0	0	0	1	2	0	1	0	0	0	0	.43
97-98	Det	9	4	2	6	-1	1	0	19	21.1	3	0	3	0	0	0	0	0	0	0	0	0	0	0	.67
98-99	Det	10	2	2	4	0	1	0	15	13.3	1	1	2	0	0	0	2	4	0	2	0	0	0	0	.40
9 Years		102	23	22	45	20	4	1	155	14.8	4	–	–	4	–	–	12	24	0	12	0	–	–	0	.44

Kevin Brown

Pos: RW **Shoots:** R **Ht:** 6'1" **Wt:** 212 **Born:** 5/11/74—Birmingham, England **Age:** 25

Overall											Power Play			Shorthand			Penalty							Misc	
Year	Tm	GP	G	A	Pts	+/–	GW	GT	S	SPct	G	A	Pts	G	A	Pts	Num	PIM	Maj	Mnr	Fgt	Rgh	HHT	Hat	P/G
94-95	LA	23	2	3	5	-7	0	0	25	8.0	0	0	0	0	0	0	5	18	0	4	0	0	0	0	.22
95-96	LA	7	1	0	1	-2	0	0	9	11.1	0	0	0	0	0	0	2	4	0	2	0	1	0	0	.14
96-97	Har	11	0	4	4	-6	0	0	12	0.0	0	1	1	0	0	0	3	6	0	3	0	1	2	0	.36
97-98	Car	4	0	0	0	-2	0	0	0	–	0	0	0	0	0	0	0	0	0	0	0	0	0	0	.00
98-99	Edm	12	4	2	6	-2	0	0	13	30.8	2	1	3	0	0	0	0	0	0	0	0	0	0	0	.50
5 Years		57	7	9	16	-19	0	0	59	11.9	2	2	4	0	0	0	10	28	0	9	0	2	2	0	.28

Rob Brown

(statistical profile on page 293)

Pos: RW **Shoots:** L **Ht:** 5'11" **Wt:** 185 **Born:** 4/10/68—Kingston, Ontario **Age:** 31

Overall											Power Play			Shorthand			Penalty							Misc	
Year	Tm	GP	G	A	Pts	+/–	GW	GT	S	SPct	G	A	Pts	G	A	Pts	Num	PIM	Maj	Mnr	Fgt	Rgh	HHT	Hat	P/G
87-88	Pit	51	24	20	44	8	1	0	80	30.0	13	2	15	0	–	–	–	56	–	–	–	–	–	0	.86
88-89	Pit*	68	49	66	115	27	6	0	169	**29.0**	24	23	47	0	–	–	–	118	–	–	–	–	–	4	1.69

Overall											Power Play			Shorthand			Penalty							Misc	
Year	Tm	GP	G	A	Pts	+/-	GW	GT	S	SPct	G	A	Pts	G	A	Pts	Num	PIM	Maj	Mnr	Fgt	Rgh	HHT	Hat	P/G
89-90	Pit	**80**	33	47	80	-10	3	0	157	21.0	12	12	24	0	–	–	–	102	–	–	–	–	–	3	1.00
90-91	2Tm	69	24	34	58	-7	2	0	126	19.0	12	–	–	0	–	–	–	132	–	–	–	–	–	0	.84
91-92	2Tm	67	21	26	47	-15	3	2	106	19.8	16	14	30	0	0	0	31	73	1	29	1	3	7	0	.70
92-93	Chi	15	1	6	7	6	0	0	16	6.3	0	1	1	0	0	0	7	33	1	4	1	1	1	0	.47
93-94	Dal	1	0	0	0	-1	0	0	1	0.0	0	0	0	0	0	0	0	0	0	0	0	0	0	0	.00
94-95	LA	2	0	0	0	-2	0	0	1	0.0	0	0	0	0	0	0	0	0	0	0	0	0	0	0	.00
95-96											Did Not Play in NHL														
96-97											Did Not Play in NHL														
97-98	Pit	82	15	25	40	-1	4	0	172	8.7	4	11	15	0	0	0	24	59	1	22	1	2	8	0	.49
98-99	Pit	58	13	11	24	-15	1	0	78	16.7	9	6	15	0	0	0	8	16	0	8	0	0	2	0	.41
90-91	Pit	25	6	10	16	0	0	0	32	18.8	2	2	4	0	–	–	–	31	–	–	–	–	–	0	.64
90-91	Har	44	18	24	42	-7	2	0	94	19.1	10	–	–	0	–	–	–	101	–	–	–	–	–	0	.95
91-92	Har	42	16	15	31	-14	2	2	65	24.6	13	9	22	0	0	0	18	39	1	17	1	2	6	0	.74
91-92	Chi	25	5	11	16	-1	1	0	41	12.2	3	5	8	0	0	0	13	34	0	12	0	1	1	0	.64
10 Years		493	180	235	415	-10	20	2	906	19.9	90	–	–	0	–	–	–	589	–	–	–	–	–	7	.84
Postseason																									
Year	Tm	GP	G	A	Pts	+/-	GW	OT	S	SPct	G	A	Pts	G	A	Pts	Num	PIM	Maj	Mnr	Fgt	Rgh	HHT	Hat	P/G
88-89	Pit	11	5	3	8	-2	3	0	17	29.4	1	–	–	0	–	–	–	22	–	–	–	–	–	0	.73
90-91	Har	5	1	0	1	2	1	0	10	10.0	1	0	1	0	0	0	2	7	1	1	–	–	–	0	.20
91-92	Chi	8	2	4	6	1	0	0	8	25.0	1	2	3	0	0	0	2	4	0	2	0	0	0	0	.75
97-98	Pit	6	1	0	1	-4	0	0	10	10.0	1	0	1	0	0	0	2	4	0	2	0	1	1	0	.17
98-99	Pit	13	2	5	7	-2	0	0	14	14.3	2	4	6	0	0	0	4	8	0	4	0	1	0	0	.54
5 Years		43	11	12	23	-5	4	0	59	18.6	6	–	–	0	–	–	–	45	–	–	–	–	–	0	.53

Sean Brown

Pos: D **Shoots:** L **Ht:** 6'2" **Wt:** 205 **Born:** 11/5/76—Oshawa, Ontario **Age:** 23

Overall											Power Play			Shorthand			Penalty							Misc	
Year	Tm	GP	G	A	Pts	+/-	GW	GT	S	SPct	G	A	Pts	G	A	Pts	Num	PIM	Maj	Mnr	Fgt	Rgh	HHT	Hat	P/G
96-97	Edm	5	0	0	0	-1	0	0	2	0.0	0	0	0	0	0	0	2	4	0	2	0	0	1	0	.00
97-98	Edm	18	0	1	1	-1	0	0	9	0.0	0	0	0	0	0	0	14	43	5	9	5	2	3	0	.06
98-99	Edm	51	0	7	7	1	0	0	27	0.0	0	1	1	0	0	0	60	188	12	44	12	19	5	0	.14
3 Years		74	0	8	8	-1	0	0	38	0.0	0	1	1	0	0	0	76	235	17	55	17	21	9	0	.11
Postseason																									
Year	Tm	GP	G	A	Pts	+/-	GW	OT	S	SPct	G	A	Pts	G	A	Pts	Num	PIM	Maj	Mnr	Fgt	Rgh	HHT	Hat	P/G
98-99	Edm	1	0	0	0	0	0	0	0	–	0	0	0	0	0	0	1	10	0	0	0	0	0	0	.00

Benoit Brunet

(statistical profile on page 293)

Pos: LW **Shoots:** L **Ht:** 6'0" **Wt:** 194 **Born:** 8/24/68—Ste-Anne-de-Bellevue, Quebec **Age:** 31

Overall											Power Play			Shorthand			Penalty							Misc	
Year	Tm	GP	G	A	Pts	+/-	GW	GT	S	SPct	G	A	Pts	G	A	Pts	Num	PIM	Maj	Mnr	Fgt	Rgh	HHT	Hat	P/G
88-89	Mon	2	0	1	1	0	0	0	1	0.0	0	–	–	0	–	–	0	0	0	0	0	0	0	0	.50
89-90											Did Not Play in NHL														
90-91	Mon	17	1	3	4	-1	0	0	12	8.3	0	–	–	0	–	–	0	0	0	0	0	0	0	0	.24
91-92	Mon	18	4	6	10	4	0	0	37	10.8	0	3	3	0	0	0	7	14	0	7	0	0	3	0	.56
92-93	Mon	47	10	15	25	13	1	1	71	14.1	0	1	1	0	0	0	4	19	1	2	0	0	0	0	.53
93-94	Mon	71	10	20	30	14	1	0	92	10.9	0	0	0	3	1	4	10	20	0	10	0	1	3	0	.42
94-95	Mon	45	7	18	25	7	2	1	80	8.8	1	1	2	1	0	1	8	16	0	8	0	0	2	0	.56
95-96	Mon	26	7	8	15	-4	4	0	48	14.6	3	3	6	1	0	1	7	17	1	6	1	0	3	0	.58
96-97	Mon	39	10	13	23	6	2	1	63	15.9	2	1	3	0	1	1	7	14	0	7	0	1	3	0	.59
97-98	Mon	68	12	20	32	11	2	1	87	13.8	1	3	4	2	2	4	25	61	1	23	0	1	9	0	.47
98-99	Mon	60	14	17	31	-1	0	0	115	12.2	4	2	6	2	1	3	14	31	1	13	1	4	1	0	.52
10 Years		393	75	121	196	49	12	4	606	12.4	11	–	–	9	–	–	82	192	4	76	2	7	24	0	.50
Postseason																									
Year	Tm	GP	G	A	Pts	+/-	GW	OT	S	SPct	G	A	Pts	G	A	Pts	Num	PIM	Maj	Mnr	Fgt	Rgh	HHT	Hat	P/G
92-93	Mon	20	2	8	10	1	1	0	36	5.6	1	1	2	0	0	0	4	8	0	4	0	0	1	0	.50
93-94	Mon	7	1	4	5	1	0	0	13	7.7	0	0	0	0	0	0	4	16	0	3	0	1	1	0	.71
95-96	Mon	3	0	2	2	1	0	0	10	0.0	0	0	0	0	0	0	0	0	0	0	0	0	0	0	.67
96-97	Mon	4	1	3	4	4	0	0	8	12.5	0	0	0	1	0	1	2	4	0	2	0	1	0	0	1.00
97-98	Mon	8	1	0	1	1	1	1	5	20.0	0	0	0	0	0	0	2	4	0	2	0	1	0	0	.13
5 Years		42	5	17	22	8	2	1	72	6.9	1	1	2	1	0	1	12	32	0	11	0	3	2	0	.52

Andrew Brunette

(statistical profile on page 293)

Pos: LW **Shoots:** L **Ht:** 6'0" **Wt:** 212 **Born:** 8/24/73—Sudbury, Ontario **Age:** 26

Overall											Power Play			Shorthand			Penalty							Misc	
Year	Tm	GP	G	A	Pts	+/–	GW	GT	S	SPct	G	A	Pts	G	A	Pts	Num	PIM	Maj	Mnr	Fgt	Rgh	HHT	Hat	P/G
95-96	Was	11	3	3	6	5	1	0	16	18.8	0	0	0	0	0	0	0	0	0	0	0	0	0	0	.55
96-97	Was	23	4	7	11	-3	0	0	23	17.4	2	3	5	0	0	0	6	12	0	6	0	0	3	0	.48
97-98	Was	28	11	12	23	2	2	2	42	26.2	4	4	8	0	0	0	6	12	0	6	0	0	3	0	.82
98-99	Nsh	77	11	20	31	-10	1	0	65	16.9	7	6	13	0	0	0	13	26	0	13	0	1	7	0	.40
4 Years		139	29	42	71	-6	4	2	146	19.9	13	13	26	0	0	0	25	50	0	25	0	1	13	0	.51

Postseason

Year	Tm	GP	G	A	Pts	+/–	GW	OT	S	SPct	G	A	Pts	G	A	Pts	Num	PIM	Maj	Mnr	Fgt	Rgh	HHT	Hat	P/G
95-96	Was	6	1	3	4	-5	0	0	7	14.3	0	3	3	0	0	0	0	0	0	0	0	0	0	0	.67

Sergei Brylin

(statistical profile on page 294)

Pos: C **Shoots:** L **Ht:** 5'10" **Wt:** 190 **Born:** 1/13/74—Moscow, USSR **Age:** 25

Overall											Power Play			Shorthand			Penalty							Misc	
Year	Tm	GP	G	A	Pts	+/–	GW	GT	S	SPct	G	A	Pts	G	A	Pts	Num	PIM	Maj	Mnr	Fgt	Rgh	HHT	Hat	P/G
94-95	NJ	26	6	8	14	12	0	0	41	14.6	0	4	4	0	0	0	4	8	0	4	0	2	1	0	.54
95-96	NJ	50	4	5	9	-2	1	0	51	7.8	0	0	0	0	0	0	13	26	0	13	0	1	5	0	.18
96-97	NJ	29	2	2	4	-13	0	0	34	5.9	0	0	0	0	0	0	10	20	0	10	0	4	1	0	.14
97-98	NJ	18	2	3	5	4	0	1	20	10.0	0	0	0	0	0	0	0	0	0	0	0	0	0	0	.28
98-99	NJ	47	5	10	15	8	1	0	51	9.8	3	0	3	0	0	0	14	28	0	14	0	2	4	0	.32
5 Years		170	19	28	47	9	2	1	197	9.6	3	4	7	0	0	0	41	82	0	41	0	9	11	0	.28

Postseason

Year	Tm	GP	G	A	Pts	+/–	GW	OT	S	SPct	G	A	Pts	G	A	Pts	Num	PIM	Maj	Mnr	Fgt	Rgh	HHT	Hat	P/G
94-95	NJ	12	1	2	3	1	0	0	11	9.1	0	0	0	0	0	0	2	4	0	2	0	1	0	0	.25
98-99	NJ	5	3	1	4	2	1	0	12	25.0	1	0	1	0	0	0	2	4	0	2	0	1	1	0	.80
2 Years		17	4	3	7	3	1	0	23	17.4	1	0	1	0	0	0	4	8	0	4	0	2	1	0	.41

Jeff Buchanan

Pos: D **Shoots:** R **Ht:** 6'2" **Wt:** 200 **Born:** 5/23/71—Swift Current, Saskatchewan **Age:** 28

Overall											Power Play			Shorthand			Penalty							Misc	
Year	Tm	GP	G	A	Pts	+/–	GW	GT	S	SPct	G	A	Pts	G	A	Pts	Num	PIM	Maj	Mnr	Fgt	Rgh	HHT	Hat	P/G
98-99	Col	6	0	0	0	1	0	0	1	0.0	0	0	0	0	0	0	3	6	0	3	0	1	0	0	.00

Kelly Buchberger

Pos: RW **Shoots:** L **Ht:** 6'2" **Wt:** 200 **Born:** 12/2/66—Langenburg, Saskatchewan **Age:** 33

Overall											Power Play			Shorthand			Penalty							Misc	
Year	Tm	GP	G	A	Pts	+/–	GW	GT	S	SPct	G	A	Pts	G	A	Pts	Num	PIM	Maj	Mnr	Fgt	Rgh	HHT	Hat	P/G
86-87										Did Not Play in Regular Season															
87-88	Edm	19	1	0	1	-1	0	1	10	10.0	0	0	0	0	0	0	–	81	–	–	–	–	–	0	.05
88-89	Edm	66	5	9	14	-14	1	0	57	8.8	1	3	4	0	0	0	–	234	–	–	–	–	–	0	.21
89-90	Edm	55	2	6	8	-8	2	0	35	5.7	0	0	0	0	0	0	–	168	–	–	–	–	–	0	.15
90-91	Edm	64	3	1	4	-6	2	0	54	5.6	0	0	0	0	0	0	–	160	–	–	–	–	–	0	.06
91-92	Edm	79	20	24	44	9	3	1	90	22.2	0	1	1	4	1	5	46	157	11	31	11	10	9	0	.56
92-93	Edm	83	12	18	30	-27	3	0	92	13.0	1	0	1	2	5	7	40	133	7	29	6	9	8	1	.36
93-94	Edm	84	3	18	21	-20	0	0	93	3.2	0	0	0	0	0	0	66	199	17	47	16	8	12	0	.25
94-95	Edm	48	7	17	24	0	5	0	73	9.6	2	0	2	1	2	3	31	82	4	26	4	6	7	0	.50
95-96	Edm	82	11	14	25	-20	3	0	119	9.2	0	0	0	2	4	6	46	184	12	27	12	4	1	0	.30
96-97	Edm	81	8	30	38	4	3	0	78	10.3	0	0	0	0	4	4	43	159	11	27	11	5	7	0	.47
97-98	Edm	82	6	17	23	-10	1	0	86	7.0	1	0	1	1	0	1	41	122	8	31	8	6	11	0	.28
98-99	Edm	52	4	4	8	-6	1	0	29	13.8	0	0	0	2	0	2	18	68	8	9	8	2	3	0	.15
12 Years		795	82	158	240	-99	24	2	816	10.0	5	4	9	12	16	28	–	1747	–	–	–	–	–	1	.30

Postseason

Year	Tm	GP	G	A	Pts	+/–	GW	OT	S	SPct	G	A	Pts	G	A	Pts	Num	PIM	Maj	Mnr	Fgt	Rgh	HHT	Hat	P/G
86-87	Edm	3	0	0	0	0	0	0	1	0.0	0	0	0	0	0	0	1	5	1	0	–	0	0	0	.00
89-90	Edm	19	0	5	5	2	0	0	15	0.0	0	–	–	0	–	–	5	13	1	4	–	–	–	0	.26
90-91	Edm	12	2	1	3	-3	0	0	12	16.7	0	–	–	0	0	0	–	25	–	–	–	–	–	0	.25
91-92	Edm	16	1	4	5	2	0	0	12	8.3	0	0	0	0	0	0	12	32	0	11	0	4	1	0	.31
96-97	Edm	12	5	2	7	-1	1	1	19	26.3	0	0	0	0	0	0	8	16	0	8	0	0	0	0	.58
97-98	Edm	12	1	2	3	0	0	0	13	7.7	0	0	0	0	0	0	7	25	1	5	1	1	1	0	.25
98-99	Edm	4	0	0	0	-4	0	0	2	0.0	0	0	0	0	0	0	0	0	0	0	0	0	0	0	.00
7 Years		78	9	14	23	-4	1	1	74	12.2	0	–	–	0	–	–	–	116	–	–	–	–	–	0	.29

Jan Bulis

(statistical profile on page 294)

Pos: C **Shoots:** L **Ht:** 6'0" **Wt:** 208 **Born:** 3/18/78—Pardubice, Czechoslovakia **Age:** 21

Overall											Power Play			Shorthand			Penalty							Misc	
Year	Tm	GP	G	A	Pts	+/-	GW	GT	S	SPct	G	A	Pts	G	A	Pts	Num	PIM	Maj	Mnr	Fgt	Rgh	HHT	Hat	P/G
97-98	Was	48	5	11	16	-5	0	1	37	13.5	0	1	1	0	0	0	9	18	0	9	0	0	9	0	.33
98-99	Was	38	7	16	23	3	3	0	57	12.3	3	7	10	0	0	0	3	6	0	3	0	1	2	0	.61
2 Years		86	12	27	39	-2	3	1	94	12.8	3	8	11	0	0	0	12	24	0	12	0	1	11	0	.45

Pavel Bure

(statistical profile on page 294)

Pos: RW **Shoots:** L **Ht:** 5'10" **Wt:** 190 **Born:** 3/31/71—Moscow, USSR **Age:** 28

Overall											Power Play			Shorthand			Penalty							Misc	
Year	Tm	GP	G	A	Pts	+/-	GW	GT	S	SPct	G	A	Pts	G	A	Pts	Num	PIM	Maj	Mnr	Fgt	Rgh	HHT	Hat	P/G
91-92	Van	65	34	26	60	0	6	0	268	12.7	7	9	16	3	1	4	15	30	0	15	0	1	5	0	.92
92-93	Van*	83	60	50	110	35	9	0	**407**	14.7	13	20	33	**7**	2	**9**	29	69	1	27	0	2	10	2	1.33
93-94	Van*	76	**60**	47	107	1	9	0	374	16.0	**25**	18	43	4	2	6	39	86	0	38	0	5	10	3	1.41
94-95	Van	44	20	23	43	-8	2	0	198	10.1	6	7	13	2	**4**	**6**	18	47	1	16	0	3	3	1	.98
95-96	Van*	15	6	7	13	-2	0	0	78	7.7	1	4	5	1	0	1	4	8	0	4	0	1	1	0	.87
96-97	Van*	63	23	32	55	-14	2	0	265	8.7	4	8	12	1	2	3	20	40	0	20	0	3	7	0	.87
97-98	Van*	82	51	39	90	5	4	1	**329**	15.5	13	12	25	**6**	3	**9**	24	48	0	24	0	1	5	**3**	1.10
98-99	Fla	11	13	3	16	3	0	1	44	29.5	5	0	5	1	1	2	2	4	0	2	0	0	1	2	1.45
8 Years		439	267	227	494	20	32	2	1963	13.6	74	78	152	25	15	40	151	332	2	146	0	16	42	11	1.13
Postseason																									
Year	Tm	GP	G	A	Pts	+/-	GW	OT	S	SPct	G	A	Pts	G	A	Pts	Num	PIM	Maj	Mnr	Fgt	Rgh	HHT	Hat	P/G
91-92	Van	13	6	4	10	4	0	0	50	12.0	0	2	2	0	0	0	7	14	0	7	0	0	1	1	.77
92-93	Van	12	5	7	12	0	1	0	47	10.6	0	2	2	0	0	0	4	8	0	4	0	0	1	0	1.00
93-94	Van	24	16	15	31	8	2	1	101	15.8	3	7	10	0	0	0	13	40	2	10	0	0	1	0	1.29
94-95	Van	11	7	6	13	-1	0	0	39	17.9	2	3	5	2	2	4	5	10	0	5	0	0	2	0	1.18
4 Years		60	34	32	66	11	3	1	237	14.3	5	14	19	2	2	4	29	72	2	26	0	0	5	1	1.10

Valeri Bure

(statistical profile on page 294)

Pos: RW **Shoots:** R **Ht:** 5'11" **Wt:** 179 **Born:** 6/13/74—Moscow, USSR **Age:** 25

Overall											Power Play			Shorthand			Penalty							Misc	
Year	Tm	GP	G	A	Pts	+/-	GW	GT	S	SPct	G	A	Pts	G	A	Pts	Num	PIM	Maj	Mnr	Fgt	Rgh	HHT	Hat	P/G
94-95	Mon	24	3	1	4	-1	1	0	39	7.7	0	0	0	0	0	0	3	6	0	3	0	1	2	0	.17
95-96	Mon	77	22	20	42	10	1	2	143	15.4	5	8	13	0	0	0	14	28	0	14	0	0	8	0	.55
96-97	Mon	64	14	21	35	4	2	1	131	10.7	4	8	12	0	0	0	3	6	0	3	0	1	1	0	.55
97-98	2Tm	66	12	26	38	-5	2	0	179	6.7	2	11	13	0	0	0	12	35	1	10	0	0	5	1	.58
98-99	Cgy	80	26	27	53	0	4	0	260	10.0	7	13	20	0	0	0	11	22	0	11	0	2	0	0	.66
97-98	Mon	50	7	22	29	-5	1	0	134	5.2	2	10	12	0	0	0	11	33	1	9	0	0	4	0	.58
97-98	Cgy	16	5	4	9	0	1	0	45	11.1	0	1	1	0	0	0	1	2	0	1	0	0	1	1	.56
5 Years		311	77	95	172	8	10	3	752	10.2	18	40	58	0	0	0	43	97	1	41	0	4	16	1	.55
Postseason																									
Year	Tm	GP	G	A	Pts	+/-	GW	OT	S	SPct	G	A	Pts	G	A	Pts	Num	PIM	Maj	Mnr	Fgt	Rgh	HHT	Hat	P/G
95-96	Mon	6	0	1	1	-1	0	0	19	0.0	0	0	0	0	0	0	3	6	0	3	0	2	1	0	.17
96-97	Mon	5	0	1	1	-4	0	0	7	0.0	0	0	0	0	0	0	1	2	0	1	0	0	1	0	.20
2 Years		11	0	2	2	-5	0	0	26	0.0	0	0	0	0	0	0	4	8	0	4	0	2	2	0	.18

Marc Bureau

(statistical profile on page 295)

Pos: C **Shoots:** R **Ht:** 6'1" **Wt:** 202 **Born:** 5/19/66—Trois-Rivieres, Quebec **Age:** 33

Overall											Power Play			Shorthand			Penalty							Misc	
Year	Tm	GP	G	A	Pts	+/-	GW	GT	S	SPct	G	A	Pts	G	A	Pts	Num	PIM	Maj	Mnr	Fgt	Rgh	HHT	Hat	P/G
89-90	Cgy	5	0	0	0	-1	0	0	3	0.0	0	0	0	0	0	0	2	4	0	2	0	–	–	0	.00
90-91	2Tm	14	0	6	6	-7	0	0	12	0.0	0	–	–	0	–	–	3	6	0	3	0	–	–	0	.43
91-92	Min	46	6	4	10	-5	0	0	53	11.3	0	1	1	0	0	0	17	50	0	15	0	6	6	0	.22
92-93	TB	63	10	21	31	-12	1	0	132	7.6	1	5	6	2	1	3	28	111	5	18	3	1	4	0	.49
93-94	TB	75	8	7	15	-9	1	0	110	7.3	0	0	0	1	0	1	12	30	2	10	2	4	1	0	.20
94-95	TB	48	2	12	14	-8	0	1	72	2.8	0	1	1	1	1	2	15	30	0	15	0	6	3	0	.29
95-96	Mon	65	3	7	10	-3	1	0	43	7.0	0	1	1	0	1	1	20	46	2	18	1	4	6	0	.15
96-97	Mon	43	6	9	15	4	2	0	56	10.7	1	0	1	1	1	2	8	16	0	8	0	2	2	0	.35
97-98	Mon	74	13	6	19	0	2	0	82	15.9	0	0	0	0	2	2	6	12	0	6	0	0	3	0	.26
98-99	Phi	71	4	6	10	-2	0	0	52	7.7	0	0	0	0	0	0	5	10	0	5	0	0	4	0	.14
90-91	Cgy	5	0	0	0	-4	0	0	4	0.0	0	0	0	0	0	0	1	2	0	1	0	–	–	0	.00
90-91	Min	9	0	6	6	-3	0	0	8	0.0	0	–	–	0	–	–	2	4	0	2	0	–	–	0	.67
10 Years		504	52	78	130	-43	7	1	615	8.5	2	–	–	5	–	–	116	315	9	100	6	–	–	0	.26

											Postseason														
Year	Tm	GP	G	A	Pts	+/–	GW	OT	S	SPct	G	A	Pts	G	A	Pts	Num	PIM	Maj	Mnr	Fgt	Rgh	HHT	Hat	P/G
90-91	Min	23	3	2	5	-4	0	0	19	15.8	0	–	–	1	–	–	–	20	–	–	–	–	–	0	.22
91-92	Min	5	0	0	0	-3	0	0	1	0.0	0	0	0	0	0	0	3	14	0	2	0	2	0	0	.00
95-96	Mon	6	1	1	2	2	0	0	6	16.7	0	0	0	0	0	0	2	4	0	2	0	0	0	0	.33
97-98	Mon	10	1	2	3	-1	0	0	16	6.3	0	0	0	0	0	0	3	6	0	3	0	0	0	0	.30
98-99	Phi	6	0	2	2	2	0	0	3	0.0	0	0	0	0	0	0	1	2	0	1	0	1	0	0	.33
5 Years		50	5	7	12	-4	0	0	45	11.1	0	–	–	1	–	–	–	46	–	–	–	–	–	0	.24

Sean Burke

(statistical profile on page 397)

Pos: G **Catches:** L **Ht:** 6'4" **Wt:** 210 **Born:** 1/29/67—Windsor, Ontario **Age:** 32

					Overall												Pen Shot		Offense		
Year	Tm	GP	GS	TP	W	L	T	Min	GA	GAA	Shots	SvPct	ShO	OE	PPGA	SHGA	Shots	GA	G	A	PIM
87-88	NJ	13	–	–	10	1	0	689	35	3.05	300	.883	1	–	–	–	0	0	0	1	6
88-89	NJ*	62	–	–	22	**31**	9	3590	**230**	3.84	1823	.874	3	–	–	–	1	0	0	3	54
89-90	NJ	52	–	–	22	22	6	2914	175	3.60	1453	.880	0	–	–	–	0	0	0	1	38
90-91	NJ	35	–	–	8	12	8	1870	112	3.59	875	.872	0	–	–	–	0	0	0	0	18
91-92										Did Not Play in NHL											
92-93	Har	50	45	8	16	27	3	2656	184	4.16	1485	.876	0	14	58	5	0	0	0	2	25
93-94	Har	47	47	2	17	24	5	2750	137	2.99	1458	.906	2	22	43	3	0	0	0	0	16
94-95	Har	42	40	3	17	19	4	2418	108	2.68	1233	.912	0	18	30	5	1	0	0	1	8
95-96	Har	66	63	9	28	28	6	3669	190	3.11	2034	.907	4	26	67	6	**2**	0	0	6	16
96-97	Har	51	51	5	22	22	6	2985	134	2.69	1560	.914	4	19	29	6	0	0	0	2	14
97-98	3Tm	52	47	5	16	23	9	2885	142	2.95	1362	.896	2	15	35	5	2	0	0	2	20
98-99	Fla	59	58	6	21	24	14	3402	151	2.66	1624	.907	3	15	41	8	0	0	0	4	27
97-98	Car	25	23	1	7	11	5	1415	66	2.80	655	.899	1	8	19	2	0	0	0	1	6
97-98	Van	16	13	3	2	9	4	838	49	3.51	396	.876	0	2	11	0	0	0	0	1	14
97-98	Phi	11	11	1	7	3	0	632	27	2.56	311	.913	1	5	5	3	2	0	0	0	0
11 Years		529	–	–	199	233	70	29828	1598	3.21	15207	.895	19	–	–	–	6	0	0	22	242
									Postseason												
Year	Tm	GP	GS	TP	W	L	Pct	Min	GA	GAA	Shots	SvPct	ShO	OE	PPGA	SHGA	Shots	GA	G	A	PIM
87-88	NJ	17	–	–	9	8	.529	1001	57	3.42	515	.889	1	–	–	–	0	0	0	0	14
89-90	NJ	2	–	–	0	2	.000	125	8	3.84	57	.860	0	–	–	–	0	0	0	0	2
97-98	Phi	5	5	1	1	4	.200	283	17	3.60	121	.860	0	0	9	2	0	0	0	0	0
3 Years		24	–	–	10	14	.417	1409	82	3.49	693	.882	1	–	–	–	0	0	0	0	16

Shawn Burr

Pos: LW **Shoots:** L **Ht:** 6'1" **Wt:** 205 **Born:** 7/1/66—Sarnia, Ontario **Age:** 33

				Overall							Power Play			Shorthand					Penalty					Misc	
Year	Tm	GP	G	A	Pts	+/–	GW	GT	S	SPct	G	A	Pts	G	A	Pts	Num	PIM	Maj	Mnr	Fgt	Rgh	HHT	Hat	P/G
84-85	Det	9	0	0	0	-4	0	0	4	0.0	0	0	0	0	0	0	1	2	0	1	0	–	–	0	.00
85-86	Det	5	1	0	1	1	0	0	6	16.7	1	0	1	0	0	0	2	4	0	2	0	–	–	0	.20
86-87	Det	80	22	25	47	2	1	0	153	14.4	1	–	–	2	–	–	–	107	–	–	–	–	–	1	.59
87-88	Det	78	17	23	40	7	3	0	124	13.7	5	–	–	3	–	–	–	97	–	–	–	–	–	0	.51
88-89	Det	79	19	27	46	5	2	0	149	12.8	1	–	–	4	–	–	–	78	–	–	–	–	–	0	.58
89-90	Det	76	24	32	56	14	2	0	173	13.9	4	–	–	3	–	–	–	82	–	–	–	–	–	1	.74
90-91	Det	80	20	30	50	14	4	0	164	12.2	6	–	–	0	–	–	–	112	–	–	–	–	–	0	.63
91-92	Det	79	19	32	51	26	3	1	140	13.6	2	0	2	0	3	3	48	118	2	44	2	10	11	0	.65
92-93	Det	80	10	25	35	18	2	0	99	10.1	1	0	1	1	6	7	30	74	2	27	2	5	4	0	.44
93-94	Det	51	10	12	22	12	1	0	64	15.6	0	0	0	1	3	4	14	31	1	13	1	7	3	1	.43
94-95	Det	42	6	8	14	13	3	0	65	9.2	0	0	0	0	0	0	18	60	0	15	0	3	5	0	.33
95-96	TB	81	13	15	28	4	2	0	122	10.7	1	0	1	0	0	0	46	119	1	42	0	11	6	0	.35
96-97	TB	74	14	21	35	5	3	0	128	10.9	1	4	5	0	0	0	33	106	0	28	0	9	7	0	.47
97-98	SJ	42	6	6	12	2	0	0	63	9.5	0	0	0	0	0	0	21	50	0	20	0	3	5	0	.29
98-99	SJ	18	0	1	1	-3	0	0	22	0.0	0	1	1	0	0	0	9	29	1	7	0	2	1	0	.06
15 Years		874	181	257	438	116	26	1	1476	12.3	23	–	–	14	–	–	–	1069	–	–	–	–	–	3	.50
											Postseason														
Year	Tm	GP	G	A	Pts	+/–	GW	OT	S	SPct	G	A	Pts	G	A	Pts	Num	PIM	Maj	Mnr	Fgt	Rgh	HHT	Hat	P/G
86-87	Det	16	7	2	9	1	2	1	29	24.1	0	–	–	0	–	–	–	20	–	–	–	–	–	0	.56
87-88	Det	9	3	1	4	-3	1	0	17	17.6	0	–	–	0	–	–	–	14	–	–	–	–	–	0	.44
88-89	Det	6	1	2	3	2	0	0	8	12.5	0	–	–	0	0	0	3	6	0	3	0	–	–	0	.50
90-91	Det	7	0	4	4	-3	0	0	17	0.0	0	–	–	0	–	–	–	15	–	–	–	–	–	0	.57
91-92	Det	11	1	5	6	4	0	0	20	5.0	0	0	0	0	1	1	5	10	0	5	0	1	0	0	.55
92-93	Det	7	2	1	3	-2	0	0	8	25.0	0	0	0	1	1	2	1	2	0	1	0	0	1	0	.43
93-94	Det	7	2	0	2	3	2	0	13	15.4	0	0	0	0	0	0	3	6	0	3	0	0	0	0	.29
94-95	Det	16	0	2	2	-2	0	0	20	0.0	0	0	0	0	0	0	3	6	0	3	0	0	1	0	.13

Postseason																									
Year	Tm	GP	G	A	Pts	+/-	GW	OT	S	SPct	G	A	Pts	G	A	Pts	Num	PIM	Maj	Mnr	Fgt	Rgh	HHT	Hat	P/G
95-96	TB	6	0	2	2	0	0	0	5	0.0	0	0	0	0	1	1	4	8	0	4	0	0	0	0	.33
97-98	SJ	6	0	0	0	-1	0	0	4	0.0	0	0	0	0	0	0	4	8	0	4	0	1	0	0	.00
10 Years		91	16	19	35	-1	5	1	141	11.3	0	–	–	1	–	–	–	95	–	–	–	–	–	0	.38

Adam Burt

Pos: D **Shoots:** L **Ht:** 6'1" **Wt:** 208 **Born:** 1/15/69—Detroit, Michigan **Age:** 30

Overall											Power Play			Shorthand			Penalty							Misc	
Year	Tm	GP	G	A	Pts	+/-	GW	GT	S	SPct	G	A	Pts	G	A	Pts	Num	PIM	Maj	Mnr	Fgt	Rgh	HHT	Hat	P/G
88-89	Har	5	0	0	0	-1	0	0	1	0.0	0	0	0	0	0	0	3	6	0	3	0	–	–	0	.00
89-90	Har	63	4	8	12	3	0	1	83	4.8	1	–	–	0	–	–	–	105	–	–	–	–	–	0	.19
90-91	Har	42	2	7	9	-4	1	0	43	4.7	1	–	–	0	–	–	–	63	–	–	–	–	–	0	.21
91-92	Har	66	9	15	24	-16	1	0	89	10.1	4	6	10	0	0	0	36	93	7	29	7	7	12	0	.36
92-93	Har	65	6	14	20	-11	0	0	81	7.4	0	2	2	0	0	0	42	116	8	33	8	8	13	0	.31
93-94	Har	63	1	17	18	-4	0	0	91	1.1	0	3	3	0	0	0	29	75	3	25	3	6	9	0	.29
94-95	Har	46	7	11	18	0	1	0	73	9.6	3	4	7	0	0	0	25	65	5	20	5	9	5	0	.39
95-96	Har	78	4	9	13	-4	1	0	90	4.4	0	1	1	0	0	0	47	121	9	38	9	8	16	0	.17
96-97	Har	71	2	11	13	-13	0	0	85	2.4	0	3	3	0	2	2	32	79	5	27	5	6	14	0	.18
97-98	Car	76	1	11	12	-6	0	0	51	2.0	0	1	1	1	0	1	44	106	6	38	6	7	18	0	.16
98-99	2Tm	68	0	4	4	4	0	0	61	0.0	0	0	0	0	0	0	24	60	4	20	4	3	5	0	.06
98-99	Car	51	0	3	3	3	0	0	37	0.0	0	0	0	0	0	0	17	46	4	13	4	1	4	0	.06
98-99	Phi	17	0	1	1	1	0	0	24	0.0	0	0	0	0	0	0	7	14	0	7	0	2	1	0	.06
11 Years		643	36	107	143	-52	4	1	748	4.8	9	–	–	1	–	–	–	889	–	–	–	–	–	0	.22

Postseason																									
Year	Tm	GP	G	A	Pts	+/-	GW	OT	S	SPct	G	A	Pts	G	A	Pts	Num	PIM	Maj	Mnr	Fgt	Rgh	HHT	Hat	P/G
89-90	Har	2	0	0	0	-2	0	0	1	0.0	0	0	0	0	0	0	0	0	0	0	0	0	0	0	.00
91-92	Har	2	0	0	0	-1	0	0	0	–	0	0	0	0	0	0	0	0	0	0	0	0	0	0	.00
98-99	Phi	6	0	0	0	1	0	0	3	0.0	0	0	0	0	0	0	2	4	0	2	0	0	1	0	.00
3 Years		10	0	0	0	-2	0	0	4	0.0	0	0	0	0	0	0	2	4	0	2	0	0	1	0	.00

Sven Butenschon

Pos: D **Shoots:** L **Ht:** 6'5" **Wt:** 201 **Born:** 3/22/76—Itzehoe, West Germany **Age:** 23

Overall											Power Play			Shorthand			Penalty							Misc	
Year	Tm	GP	G	A	Pts	+/-	GW	GT	S	SPct	G	A	Pts	G	A	Pts	Num	PIM	Maj	Mnr	Fgt	Rgh	HHT	Hat	P/G
97-98	Pit	8	0	0	0	-1	0	0	4	0.0	0	0	0	0	0	0	3	6	0	3	0	0	3	0	.00
98-99	Pit	17	0	0	0	-7	0	0	8	0.0	0	0	0	0	0	0	3	6	0	3	0	1	1	0	.00
2 Years		25	0	0	0	-8	0	0	12	0.0	0	0	0	0	0	0	6	12	0	6	0	1	4	0	.00

Slava Butsayev

Pos: C **Shoots:** L **Ht:** 6'2" **Wt:** 200 **Born:** 6/13/70—Togliatti, USSR **Age:** 29

Overall											Power Play			Shorthand			Penalty							Misc	
Year	Tm	GP	G	A	Pts	+/-	GW	GT	S	SPct	G	A	Pts	G	A	Pts	Num	PIM	Maj	Mnr	Fgt	Rgh	HHT	Hat	P/G
92-93	Phi	52	2	14	16	3	0	0	58	3.4	0	0	0	0	0	0	25	61	1	23	0	7	8	0	.31
93-94	2Tm	59	12	11	23	0	3	0	85	14.1	2	3	5	0	0	0	23	68	2	19	0	3	6	1	.39
94-95	SJ	6	2	0	2	-2	0	0	6	33.3	0	0	0	0	0	0	0	0	0	0	0	0	0	0	.33
95-96	Anh	7	1	0	1	-4	0	0	9	11.1	0	0	0	0	0	0	0	0	0	0	0	0	0	0	.14
96-97		Did Not Play in NHL																							
97-98		Did Not Play in NHL																							
98-99	2Tm	3	0	1	1	-1	0	0	5	0.0	0	0	0	0	0	0	2	4	0	2	0	0	1	0	.33
93-94	Phi	47	12	9	21	2	3	0	79	15.2	2	2	4	0	0	0	18	58	2	14	0	3	4	1	.45
93-94	SJ	12	0	2	2	-2	0	0	6	0.0	0	1	1	0	0	0	5	10	0	5	0	0	2	0	.17
98-99	Fla	1	0	0	0	-1	0	0	0	–	0	0	0	0	0	0	1	2	0	1	0	0	1	0	.00
98-99	Ott	2	0	1	1	0	0	0	5	0.0	0	0	0	0	0	0	1	2	0	1	0	0	0	0	.50
5 Years		127	17	26	43	-4	3	0	163	10.4	2	3	5	0	0	0	50	133	3	44	0	10	15	1	.34

Petr Buzek

Pos: D **Shoots:** L **Ht:** 6'0" **Wt:** 205 **Born:** 4/26/77—Jihlava, Czechoslovakia **Age:** 22

Overall											Power Play			Shorthand			Penalty							Misc	
Year	Tm	GP	G	A	Pts	+/-	GW	GT	S	SPct	G	A	Pts	G	A	Pts	Num	PIM	Maj	Mnr	Fgt	Rgh	HHT	Hat	P/G
97-98	Dal	2	0	0	0	1	0	0	0	–	0	0	0	0	0	0	1	2	0	1	0	0	0	0	.00
98-99	Dal	2	0	0	0	0	0	0	0	–	0	0	0	0	0	0	1	2	0	1	0	0	1	0	.00
2 Years		4	0	0	0	1	0	0	0	–	0	0	0	0	0	0	2	4	0	2	0	0	1	0	.00

Dan Bylsma

Pos: RW **Shoots:** L **Ht:** 6'2" **Wt:** 215 **Born:** 9/19/70—Grand Haven, Michigan **Age:** 29

Overall											Power Play			Shorthand			Penalty							Misc	
Year	Tm	GP	G	A	Pts	+/–	GW	GT	S	SPct	G	A	Pts	G	A	Pts	Num	PIM	Maj	Mnr	Fgt	Rgh	HHT	Hat	P/G
95-96	LA	4	0	0	0	0	0	0	6	0.0	0	0	0	0	0	0	0	0	0	0	0	0	0	0	.00
96-97	LA	79	3	6	9	-15	0	0	86	3.5	0	1	1	0	0	0	9	32	2	6	2	0	3	0	.11
97-98	LA	65	3	9	12	9	0	1	57	5.3	0	0	0	0	1	1	11	33	1	9	1	3	4	0	.18
98-99	LA	8	0	0	0	-1	0	0	3	0.0	0	0	0	0	0	0	1	2	0	1	0	0	0	0	.00
4 Years		156	6	15	21	-7	0	1	152	3.9	0	1	1	0	1	1	21	67	3	16	3	3	7	0	.13

Postseason																									
Year	Tm	GP	G	A	Pts	+/–	GW	OT	S	SPct	G	A	Pts	G	A	Pts	Num	PIM	Maj	Mnr	Fgt	Rgh	HHT	Hat	P/G
97-98	LA	2	0	0	0	-3	0	0	1	0.0	0	0	0	0	0	0	0	0	0	0	0	0	0	0	.00

Eric Cairns

Pos: D **Shoots:** L **Ht:** 6'6" **Wt:** 230 **Born:** 6/27/74—Oakville, Ontario **Age:** 25

Overall											Power Play			Shorthand			Penalty							Misc	
Year	Tm	GP	G	A	Pts	+/–	GW	GT	S	SPct	G	A	Pts	G	A	Pts	Num	PIM	Maj	Mnr	Fgt	Rgh	HHT	Hat	P/G
96-97	NYR	40	0	1	1	-7	0	0	17	0.0	0	0	0	0	0	0	38	147	13	21	12	8	4	0	.03
97-98	NYR	39	0	3	3	-3	0	0	17	0.0	0	0	0	0	0	0	26	92	8	16	8	6	3	0	.08
98-99	NYI	9	0	3	3	1	0	0	2	0.0	0	0	0	0	0	0	6	23	1	4	1	1	1	0	.33
3 Years		88	0	7	7	-9	0	0	36	0.0	0	0	0	0	0	0	70	262	22	41	21	15	8	0	.08

Postseason																									
Year	Tm	GP	G	A	Pts	+/–	GW	OT	S	SPct	G	A	Pts	G	A	Pts	Num	PIM	Maj	Mnr	Fgt	Rgh	HHT	Hat	P/G
96-97	NYR	3	0	0	0	0	0	0	0	–	0	0	0	0	0	0	0	0	0	0	0	0	0	0	.00

Jim Campbell

(statistical profile on page 295)

Pos: RW **Shoots:** R **Ht:** 6'3" **Wt:** 205 **Born:** 4/3/73—Worcester, Massachusetts **Age:** 26

Overall											Power Play			Shorthand			Penalty							Misc	
Year	Tm	GP	G	A	Pts	+/–	GW	GT	S	SPct	G	A	Pts	G	A	Pts	Num	PIM	Maj	Mnr	Fgt	Rgh	HHT	Hat	P/G
95-96	Anh	16	2	3	5	0	0	0	25	8.0	1	1	2	0	0	0	7	36	2	3	1	0	1	0	.31
96-97	StL	68	23	20	43	3	6	1	169	13.6	5	5	10	0	2	2	27	68	2	24	1	5	6	0	.63
97-98	StL	76	22	19	41	0	6	1	147	15.0	7	8	15	0	0	0	22	55	1	20	1	2	5	0	.54
98-99	StL	55	4	21	25	-8	0	0	99	4.0	1	8	9	0	0	0	19	41	1	18	1	1	6	0	.45
4 Years		215	51	63	114	-5	12	2	440	11.6	14	22	36	0	2	2	75	200	6	65	4	8	18	0	.53

Postseason																									
Year	Tm	GP	G	A	Pts	+/–	GW	OT	S	SPct	G	A	Pts	G	A	Pts	Num	PIM	Maj	Mnr	Fgt	Rgh	HHT	Hat	P/G
96-97	StL	4	1	0	1	-1	0	0	6	16.7	1	0	1	0	0	0	3	6	0	3	0	0	0	0	.25
97-98	StL	10	7	3	10	-1	2	0	23	30.4	4	1	5	0	0	0	6	12	0	6	0	1	0	0	1.00
2 Years		14	8	3	11	-2	2	0	29	27.6	5	1	6	0	0	0	9	18	0	9	0	1	0	0	.79

Guy Carbonneau

(statistical profile on page 295)

Pos: C **Shoots:** R **Ht:** 5'11" **Wt:** 186 **Born:** 3/18/60—Sept-Iles, Quebec **Age:** 39

Overall											Power Play			Shorthand			Penalty							Misc	
Year	Tm	GP	G	A	Pts	+/–	GW	GT	S	SPct	G	A	Pts	G	A	Pts	Num	PIM	Maj	Mnr	Fgt	Rgh	HHT	Hat	P/G
80-81	Mon	2	0	1	1	0	0	0	1	0.0	0	–	–	0	–	–	0	0	0	0	0	0	0	0	.50
81-82											Did Not Play in NHL														
82-83	Mon	77	18	29	47	18	2	1	109	16.5	0	–	–	5	–	–	–	68	–	–	–	–	–	1	.61
83-84	Mon	78	24	30	54	5	2	1	166	14.5	3	–	–	7	–	–	–	75	–	–	–	–	–	0	.69
84-85	Mon	79	23	34	57	28	2	2	163	14.1	0	–	–	4	–	–	–	43	–	–	–	–	–	0	.72
85-86	Mon	80	20	36	56	18	3	0	147	13.6	1	–	–	2	–	–	–	57	–	–	–	–	–	0	.70
86-87	Mon	79	18	27	45	9	2	0	120	15.0	0	–	–	0	–	–	–	68	–	–	–	–	–	0	.57
87-88	Mon	**80**	17	21	38	14	1	0	109	15.6	0	–	–	3	–	–	–	61	–	–	–	–	–	0	.48
88-89	Mon	79	26	30	56	37	10	0	142	18.3	1	–	–	2	–	–	–	44	–	–	–	–	–	0	.71
89-90	Mon	68	19	36	55	21	3	0	125	15.2	1	–	–	1	–	–	–	37	–	–	–	–	–	0	.81
90-91	Mon	78	20	24	44	-1	3	1	131	15.3	4	–	–	1	–	–	–	63	–	–	–	–	–	0	.56
91-92	Mon	72	18	21	39	2	4	0	120	15.0	1	0	1	1	0	1	18	39	1	17	1	6	3	0	.54
92-93	Mon	61	4	13	17	-9	0	0	73	5.5	0	0	0	1	2	3	10	20	0	10	0	2	4	0	.28
93-94	Mon	79	14	24	38	16	1	0	120	11.7	0	3	3	0	2	2	24	48	0	24	0	8	7	1	.48
94-95	StL	42	5	11	16	11	1	0	33	15.2	1	0	1	0	0	0	4	16	0	3	0	3	0	0	.38
95-96	Dal	71	8	15	23	-2	1	0	54	14.8	0	0	0	2	1	3	15	38	0	14	0	2	5	0	.32
96-97	Dal	73	5	16	21	9	0	0	99	5.1	0	0	0	1	0	1	18	36	0	18	0	3	12	0	.29
97-98	Dal	77	7	17	24	3	1	0	81	8.6	0	0	0	1	0	1	16	40	0	15	0	4	3	0	.31
98-99	Dal	74	4	12	16	-3	2	0	60	6.7	0	1	1	0	0	0	14	31	1	13	1	1	6	0	.22
18 Years		1249	250	397	647	176	38	5	1853	13.5	12	–	–	31	–	–	–	784	–	–	–	–	–	2	.52

											Postseason														
Year	Tm	GP	G	A	Pts	+/–	GW	OT	S	SPct	G	A	Pts	G	A	Pts	Num	PIM	Maj	Mnr	Fgt	Rgh	HHT	Hat	P/G
82-83	Mon	3	0	1	1	-3	0	0	3	0.0	0	–	–	0	0	0	1	2	0	1	0	–	–	0	.33
83-84	Mon	15	4	3	7	3	1	0	17	23.5	0	–	–	0	–	–	–	12	–	–	–	–	–	0	.47
84-85	Mon	12	4	3	7	-4	1	0	24	16.7	0	–	–	1	–	–	4	8	0	4	0	–	–	0	.58
85-86	Mon	20	7	5	12	9	1	0	42	16.7	0	–	–	2	–	–	–	35	–	–	–	–	–	0	.60
86-87	Mon	17	3	8	11	1	0	0	25	12.0	0	–	–	0	–	–	–	20	–	–	–	–	–	0	.65
87-88	Mon	11	0	4	4	-3	0	0	13	0.0	0	–	–	0	–	–	1	2	0	1	0	–	–	0	.36
88-89	Mon	21	4	5	9	3	0	0	34	11.8	0	–	–	1	–	–	–	10	–	–	–	–	–	0	.43
89-90	Mon	11	2	3	5	-4	0	0	23	8.7	0	–	–	0	0	0	3	6	0	3	0	–	–	0	.45
90-91	Mon	13	1	5	6	-2	1	0	21	4.8	0	–	–	0	–	–	–	10	–	–	–	–	–	0	.46
91-92	Mon	11	1	1	2	-4	0	0	22	4.5	0	0	0	0	0	0	3	6	0	3	0	1	1	0	.18
92-93	Mon	20	3	3	6	3	2	2	35	8.6	0	0	0	1	0	1	5	10	0	5	0	1	1	0	.30
93-94	Mon	7	1	3	4	4	0	0	4	25.0	0	0	0	0	0	0	2	4	0	2	0	1	0	0	.57
94-95	StL	7	1	2	3	3	0	0	6	16.7	0	0	0	0	0	0	3	6	0	3	0	0	2	0	.43
96-97	Dal	7	0	1	1	-3	0	0	9	0.0	0	0	0	0	0	0	3	6	0	3	0	1	1	0	.14
97-98	Dal	16	3	1	4	0	0	0	19	15.8	0	0	0	0	0	0	3	6	0	3	0	1	1	0	.25
98-99	Dal	17	2	4	6	0	1	0	29	6.9	0	0	0	0	1	1	3	6	0	3	0	1	1	0	.35
16 Years		208	36	52	88	3	7	2	326	11.0	0	–	–	5	–	–	–	149	–	–	–	–	–	0	.42

Jim Carey

Pos: G **Catches:** L **Ht:** 6'2" **Wt:** 205 **Born:** 5/31/74—Dorchester, Massachusetts **Age:** 25

		Overall														Pen Shot		Offense		
Year	Tm	GP	GS	TP	W	L	T	Min	GA	GAA	Shots	SvPct	ShO	OE	PPGA	SHGA	Shots	GA	G	A	PIM
94-95	Was	28	28	3	18	6	3	1604	57	2.13	654	.913	4	6	16	1	0	0	0	0	0
95-96	Was	71	70	6	35	24	9	4069	153	2.26	1631	.906	**9**	15	47	5	1	**1**	0	1	6
96-97	2Tm	59	56	6	22	31	3	3297	169	3.08	1480	.886	1	8	34	6	2	1	0	0	2
97-98	Bos	10	7	1	3	2	1	496	24	2.90	225	.893	2	2	4	0	0	0	0	0	0
98-99	StL	4	3	1	1	2	0	202	13	3.86	76	.829	0	0	2	0	0	0	0	0	0
96-97	Was	40	39	2	17	18	3	2293	105	2.75	984	.893	1	6	22	5	1	0	0	0	2
96-97	Bos	19	17	4	5	13	0	1004	64	3.82	496	.871	0	2	12	1	1	1	0	0	0
5 Years		172	164	17	79	65	16	9668	416	2.58	4066	.898	16	31	103	12	3	2	0	1	8
									Postseason												
Year	Tm	GP	GS	TP	W	L	Pct	Min	GA	GAA	Shots	SvPct	ShO	OE	PPGA	SHGA	Shots	GA	G	A	PIM
94-95	Was	7	7	2	2	4	.333	358	25	4.19	151	.834	0	0	9	1	0	0	0	0	4
95-96	Was	3	3	2	0	1	.000	97	10	6.19	39	.744	0	0	4	0	0	0	0	0	0
2 Years		10	10	4	2	5	.286	455	35	4.62	190	.816	0	0	13	1	0	0	0	0	4

Terry Carkner

(statistical profile on page 295)

Pos: D **Shoots:** L **Ht:** 6'3" **Wt:** 210 **Born:** 3/7/66—Smiths Falls, Ontario **Age:** 33

		Overall									Power Play			Shorthand			Penalty							Misc	
Year	Tm	GP	G	A	Pts	+/-	GW	GT	S	SPct	G	A	Pts	G	A	Pts	Num	PIM	Maj	Mnr	Fgt	Rgh	HHT	Hat	P/G
86-87	NYR	52	2	13	15	-1	0	0	33	6.1	0	–	–	0	–	–	–	118	–	–	–	–	–	0	.29
87-88	Que	63	3	24	27	-8	1	0	54	5.6	2	–	–	0	–	–	–	159	–	–	–	–	–	0	.43
88-89	Phi	78	11	32	43	-6	1	0	84	13.1	2	–	–	1	–	–	–	149	–	–	–	–	–	0	.55
89-90	Phi	63	4	18	22	-8	1	0	60	6.7	1	–	–	0	–	–	–	169	–	–	–	–	–	0	.35
90-91	Phi	79	7	25	32	-15	1	0	97	7.2	6	–	–	0	–	–	–	204	–	–	–	–	–	0	.41
91-92	Phi	73	4	12	16	-14	0	0	70	5.7	0	2	2	1	0	1	64	195	9	50	6	21	7	0	.22
92-93	Phi	83	3	16	19	18	0	0	45	6.7	0	2	2	0	0	0	54	150	6	45	6	22	9	0	.23
93-94	Det	68	1	6	7	13	0	0	32	3.1	0	0	0	0	0	0	42	130	10	30	10	15	8	0	.10
94-95	Det	20	1	2	3	7	0	0	9	11.1	0	0	0	0	0	0	9	21	1	8	1	4	2	0	.15
95-96	Fla	73	3	10	13	10	0	0	42	7.1	1	2	3	0	0	0	30	80	4	25	3	16	4	0	.18
96-97	Fla	70	0	14	14	-4	0	0	38	0.0	0	1	1	0	0	0	37	96	2	33	2	9	9	0	.20
97-98	Fla	74	1	7	8	6	1	0	34	2.9	0	0	0	0	0	0	27	63	3	24	3	6	7	0	.11
98-99	Fla	62	2	9	11	0	0	0	25	8.0	0	0	0	0	1	1	20	54	2	17	2	1	4	0	.18
13 Years		858	42	188	230	-2	5	0	623	6.7	12	–	–	2	–	–	–	1588	–	–	–	–	–	0	.27
											Postseason														
Year	Tm	GP	G	A	Pts	+/–	GW	OT	S	SPct	G	A	Pts	G	A	Pts	Num	PIM	Maj	Mnr	Fgt	Rgh	HHT	Hat	P/G
86-87	NYR	1	0	0	0	0	0	0	1	0.0	0	0	0	0	0	0	0	0	0	0	0	0	0	0	.00
88-89	Phi	19	1	5	6	-1	0	0	21	4.8	0	–	–	1	–	–	–	28	–	–	–	–	–	0	.32
93-94	Det	7	0	0	0	-1	0	0	3	0.0	0	0	0	0	0	0	2	4	0	2	0	1	1	0	.00
95-96	Fla	22	0	4	4	8	0	0	15	0.0	0	0	0	0	0	0	5	10	0	5	0	1	0	0	.18
96-97	Fla	5	0	0	0	-3	0	0	7	0.0	0	0	0	0	0	0	3	6	0	3	0	0	0	0	.00
5 Years		54	1	9	10	3	0	0	47	2.1	0	–	–	1	–	–	–	48	–	–	–	–	–	0	.19

Keith Carney

(statistical profile on page 296)

Pos: D **Shoots:** L **Ht:** 6'2" **Wt:** 205 **Born:** 2/3/70—Providence, Rhode Island **Age:** 29

Overall											Power Play			Shorthand			Penalty							Misc	
Year	Tm	GP	G	A	Pts	+/–	GW	GT	S	SPct	G	A	Pts	G	A	Pts	Num	PIM	Maj	Mnr	Fgt	Rgh	HHT	Hat	P/G
91-92	Buf	14	1	2	3	-3	0	0	17	5.9	1	0	1	0	0	0	9	18	0	9	0	0	7	0	.21
92-93	Buf	30	2	4	6	3	1	0	26	7.7	0	1	1	0	0	0	19	55	3	15	2	0	11	0	.20
93-94	2Tm	37	4	8	12	14	0	0	37	10.8	0	3	3	0	0	0	18	39	1	17	1	2	10	0	.32
94-95	Chi	18	1	0	1	-1	1	0	14	7.1	0	0	0	0	0	0	4	11	1	3	1	0	1	0	.06
95-96	Chi	82	5	14	19	31	1	0	69	7.2	1	0	1	0	1	1	32	94	2	27	1	4	10	0	.23
96-97	Chi	81	3	15	18	26	1	0	77	3.9	0	3	3	0	0	0	23	62	0	21	0	4	7	0	.22
97-98	2Tm	80	3	19	22	-2	0	0	71	4.2	1	2	3	1	2	3	40	91	1	38	1	8	19	0	.28
98-99	Pho	82	2	14	16	15	0	0	62	3.2	0	0	0	2	1	3	31	62	0	31	0	1	12	0	.20
93-94	Buf	7	1	3	4	-1	0	0	6	16.7	0	1	1	0	0	0	2	4	0	2	0	0	0	0	.57
93-94	Chi	30	3	5	8	15	0	0	31	9.7	0	2	2	0	0	0	16	35	1	15	1	2	10	0	.27
97-98	Chi	60	2	13	15	-7	0	0	53	3.8	0	0	0	1	2	3	31	73	1	29	1	6	15	0	.25
97-98	Pho	20	1	6	7	5	0	0	18	5.6	1	2	3	0	0	0	9	18	0	9	0	2	4	0	.35
8 Years		424	21	76	97	83	4	0	373	5.6	3	9	12	3	4	7	176	432	8	161	6	19	77	0	.23

Postseason

Year	Tm	GP	G	A	Pts	+/–	GW	OT	S	SPct	G	A	Pts	G	A	Pts	Num	PIM	Maj	Mnr	Fgt	Rgh	HHT	Hat	P/G
91-92	Buf	7	0	3	3	0	0	0	6	0.0	0	2	2	0	0	0	0	0	0	0	0	0	0	0	.43
92-93	Buf	8	0	3	3	1	0	0	2	0.0	0	1	1	0	0	0	3	6	0	3	0	1	0	0	.38
93-94	Chi	6	0	1	1	2	0	0	3	0.0	0	0	0	0	0	0	2	4	0	2	0	0	0	0	.17
94-95	Chi	4	0	1	1	0	0	0	1	0.0	0	0	0	0	0	0	0	0	0	0	0	0	0	0	.25
95-96	Chi	10	0	3	3	-1	0	0	11	0.0	0	1	1	0	0	0	2	4	0	2	0	1	0	0	.30
96-97	Chi	6	1	1	2	-2	0	0	7	14.3	0	0	0	0	0	0	1	2	0	1	0	1	0	0	.33
97-98	Pho	6	0	0	0	-3	0	0	2	0.0	0	0	0	0	0	0	2	4	0	2	0	1	1	0	.00
98-99	Pho	7	1	2	3	5	0	0	5	20.0	0	0	0	0	0	0	5	10	0	5	0	2	1	0	.43
8 Years		54	2	14	16	2	0	0	37	5.4	0	4	4	0	0	0	15	30	0	15	0	6	2	0	.30

Bob Carpenter

(statistical profile on page 296)

Pos: C **Shoots:** L **Ht:** 6'0" **Wt:** 200 **Born:** 7/13/63—Beverly, Massachusetts **Age:** 36

Overall											Power Play			Shorthand			Penalty							Misc	
Year	Tm	GP	G	A	Pts	+/–	GW	GT	S	SPct	G	A	Pts	G	A	Pts	Num	PIM	Maj	Mnr	Fgt	Rgh	HHT	Hat	P/G
81-82	Was	80	32	35	67	-23	3	2	263	12.2	7	–	–	1	–	–	–	69	–	–	–	–	–	1	.84
82-83	Was	**80**	32	37	69	0	4	2	197	16.2	14	–	–	0	–	–	–	64	–	–	–	–	–	0	.86
83-84	Was	**80**	28	40	68	0	5	1	228	12.3	8	–	–	0	–	–	–	51	–	–	–	–	–	0	.85
84-85	Was*	**80**	53	42	95	20	7	1	260	20.4	12	–	–	0	–	–	–	87	–	–	–	–	–	0	1.19
85-86	Was	80	27	29	56	-12	3	0	205	13.2	7	–	–	0	–	–	–	105	–	–	–	–	–	0	.70
86-87	3Tm	60	9	18	27	-27	0	0	111	8.1	5	–	–	0	–	–	–	47	–	–	–	–	–	0	.45
87-88	LA	71	19	33	52	-21	2	0	176	10.8	10	–	–	0	–	–	–	84	–	–	–	–	–	1	.73
88-89	2Tm	57	16	24	40	7	3	0	137	11.7	4	–	–	0	–	–	–	26	–	–	–	–	–	0	.70
89-90	Bos	**80**	25	31	56	-3	5	0	220	11.4	5	12	17	0	–	–	–	97	–	–	–	–	–	1	.70
90-91	Bos	29	8	8	16	2	0	1	54	14.8	2	1	3	0	0	0	–	22	–	–	–	–	–	0	.55
91-92	Bos	60	25	23	48	-3	6	2	171	14.6	6	6	12	1	1	2	23	46	0	23	0	2	6	0	.80
92-93	Was	68	11	17	28	-16	0	0	141	7.8	2	2	4	0	1	1	27	65	1	25	0	3	9	0	.41
93-94	NJ	76	10	23	33	7	1	0	125	8.0	0	1	1	2	0	2	20	51	1	18	0	1	4	0	.43
94-95	NJ	41	5	11	16	-1	0	2	69	7.2	0	0	0	0	0	0	8	19	1	7	1	2	1	0	.39
95-96	NJ	52	5	5	10	-10	0	0	63	7.9	0	0	0	1	0	1	7	14	0	7	0	0	2	0	.19
96-97	NJ	62	4	15	19	6	0	0	76	5.3	0	0	0	1	0	1	7	14	0	7	0	0	4	0	.31
97-98	NJ	66	9	9	18	-4	1	0	81	11.1	0	1	1	1	2	3	11	22	0	11	0	1	5	0	.27
98-99	NJ	56	2	8	10	-3	0	0	69	2.9	0	1	1	0	0	0	14	36	0	13	0	0	5	0	.18
86-87	Was	22	5	7	12	-7	0	0	47	10.6	4	–	–	0	–	–	–	21	–	–	–	–	–	0	.55
86-87	NYR	28	2	8	10	-12	0	0	41	4.9	1	–	–	0	–	–	10	20	0	10	0	–	–	0	.36
86-87	LA	10	2	3	5	-8	0	0	23	8.7	0	–	–	0	–	–	3	6	0	3	0	–	–	0	.50
88-89	LA	39	11	15	26	3	1	0	91	12.1	3	–	–	0	–	–	–	16	–	–	–	–	–	0	.67
88-89	Bos	18	5	9	14	4	2	0	46	10.9	1	2	3	0	–	–	–	10	–	–	–	–	–	0	.78
18 Years		1178	320	408	728	-81	40	11	2646	12.1	82	–	–	7	–	–	–	919	–	–	–	–	–	3	.62

Postseason

Year	Tm	GP	G	A	Pts	+/–	GW	OT	S	SPct	G	A	Pts	G	A	Pts	Num	PIM	Maj	Mnr	Fgt	Rgh	HHT	Hat	P/G
82-83	Was	4	1	0	1	-4	0	0	11	9.1	0	0	0	0	0	0	1	2	0	1	0	–	–	0	.25
83-84	Was	8	2	1	3	-2	0	0	15	13.3	1	–	–	0	0	0	–	25	–	–	–	–	–	0	.38
84-85	Was	5	1	4	5	0	0	0	15	6.7	0	–	–	0	0	0	4	8	0	4	0	–	–	0	1.00
85-86	Was	9	5	4	9	4	1	0	24	20.8	2	–	–	0	–	–	–	12	–	–	–	–	–	0	1.00
86-87	LA	5	1	2	3	-4	0	0	4	25.0	0	–	–	0	0	0	1	2	0	1	0	–	–	0	.60
87-88	LA	5	1	1	2	-7	0	0	13	7.7	0	–	–	0	0	0	0	0	0	0	0	0	0	0	.40
88-89	Bos	8	1	1	2	-6	1	0	19	5.3	1	–	–	0	–	–	2	4	0	2	0	–	–	0	.25
89-90	Bos	21	4	6	10	-3	1	0	41	9.8	2	1	3	0	–	–	–	39	–	–	–	–	–	0	.48

										Postseason															
Year	Tm	GP	G	A	Pts	+/-	GW	OT	S	SPct	G	A	Pts	G	A	Pts	Num	PIM	Maj	Mnr	Fgt	Rgh	HHT	Hat	P/G
90-91	Bos	1	0	1	1	1	0	0	1	0.0	0	0	0	0	0	0	1	2	0	1	0	–	–	0	1.00
91-92	Bos	8	0	1	1	-1	0	0	13	0.0	0	0	0	0	0	0	3	6	0	3	0	0	1	0	.13
92-93	Was	6	1	4	5	2	0	0	13	7.7	0	1	1	0	0	0	3	6	0	3	0	0	0	0	.83
93-94	NJ	20	1	7	8	-1	0	0	39	2.6	0	0	0	0	0	0	10	20	0	10	0	4	3	0	.40
94-95	NJ	17	1	4	5	-1	0	0	21	4.8	1	0	1	0	0	0	3	6	0	3	0	0	1	0	.29
96-97	NJ	10	1	2	3	2	0	0	15	6.7	0	0	0	0	1	1	1	2	0	1	0	0	0	0	.30
97-98	NJ	6	1	0	1	0	0	0	3	33.3	0	0	0	0	0	0	0	0	0	0	0	0	0	0	.17
98-99	NJ	7	0	0	0	-1	0	0	7	0.0	0	0	0	0	0	0	1	2	0	1	0	0	0	0	.00
16 Years		140	21	38	59	-21	3	0	254	8.3	7	–	–	0	–	–	–	136	–	–	–	–	–	0	.42

Anson Carter

(statistical profile on page 296)

Pos: C **Shoots:** R **Ht:** 6'1" **Wt:** 175 **Born:** 6/6/74—Toronto, Ontario **Age:** 25

				Overall							Power Play			Shorthand			Penalty							Misc	
Year	Tm	GP	G	A	Pts	+/-	GW	GT	S	SPct	G	A	Pts	G	A	Pts	Num	PIM	Maj	Mnr	Fgt	Rgh	HHT	Hat	P/G
96-97	2Tm	38	11	7	18	-7	2	0	79	13.9	2	3	5	1	0	1	3	9	1	2	1	0	1	0	.47
97-98	Bos	78	16	27	43	7	4	0	179	8.9	6	6	12	0	0	0	10	31	1	8	1	0	4	0	.55
98-99	Bos	55	24	16	40	7	6	0	123	19.5	6	3	9	0	0	0	11	22	0	11	0	1	3	1	.73
96-97	Was	19	3	2	5	0	1	0	28	10.7	1	0	1	0	0	0	2	7	1	1	1	0	0	0	.26
96-97	Bos	19	8	5	13	-7	1	0	51	15.7	1	3	4	1	0	1	1	2	0	1	0	0	1	0	.68
3 Years		171	51	50	101	7	12	0	381	13.4	14	12	26	1	0	1	24	62	2	21	2	1	8	1	.59
										Postseason															
Year	Tm	GP	G	A	Pts	+/-	GW	OT	S	SPct	G	A	Pts	G	A	Pts	Num	PIM	Maj	Mnr	Fgt	Rgh	HHT	Hat	P/G
97-98	Bos	6	1	1	2	-3	0	0	19	5.3	0	0	0	0	0	0	0	0	0	0	0	0	0	0	.33
98-99	Bos	12	4	3	7	-3	1	1	27	14.8	1	1	2	0	0	0	0	0	0	0	0	0	0	0	.58
2 Years		18	5	4	9	-6	1	1	46	10.9	1	1	2	0	0	0	0	0	0	0	0	0	0	0	.50

Andrew Cassels

(statistical profile on page 296)

Pos: C **Shoots:** L **Ht:** 6'0" **Wt:** 192 **Born:** 7/23/69—Bramalea, Ontario **Age:** 30

				Overall							Power Play			Shorthand			Penalty							Misc	
Year	Tm	GP	G	A	Pts	+/-	GW	GT	S	SPct	G	A	Pts	G	A	Pts	Num	PIM	Maj	Mnr	Fgt	Rgh	HHT	Hat	P/G
89-90	Mon	6	2	0	2	1	1	0	5	40.0	0	0	0	0	0	0	1	2	0	1	0	–	–	0	.33
90-91	Mon	54	6	19	25	2	3	1	55	10.9	1	–	–	0	–	–	–	20	–	–	–	–	–	0	.46
91-92	Har	67	11	30	41	3	3	0	99	11.1	2	9	11	2	3	5	9	18	0	9	0	1	3	0	.61
92-93	Har	84	21	64	85	-11	1	0	134	15.7	8	30	38	3	4	7	24	62	2	21	2	5	4	0	1.01
93-94	Har	79	16	42	58	-21	3	0	126	12.7	8	18	26	1	3	4	17	37	1	16	1	2	4	0	.73
94-95	Har	46	7	30	37	-3	1	0	74	9.5	1	8	9	0	0	0	9	18	0	9	0	3	1	0	.80
95-96	Har	81	20	43	63	8	1	2	135	14.8	6	17	23	0	2	2	18	39	1	17	1	1	9	0	.78
96-97	Har	81	22	44	66	-16	2	0	142	15.5	8	14	22	0	2	2	11	46	0	8	0	1	2	0	.81
97-98	Cgy	81	17	27	44	-7	2	1	138	12.3	6	6	12	1	4	5	12	32	0	11	0	1	7	0	.54
98-99	Cgy	70	12	25	37	-12	3	0	97	12.4	4	11	15	1	3	4	9	18	0	9	0	1	2	0	.53
10 Years		649	134	324	458	-56	20	4	1005	13.3	44	–	–	8	–	–	–	292	–	–	–	–	–	0	.71
										Postseason															
Year	Tm	GP	G	A	Pts	+/-	GW	OT	S	SPct	G	A	Pts	G	A	Pts	Num	PIM	Maj	Mnr	Fgt	Rgh	HHT	Hat	P/G
90-91	Mon	8	0	2	2	-3	0	0	5	0.0	0	–	–	0	–	–	1	2	0	1	0	–	–	0	.25
91-92	Har	7	2	4	6	-1	0	0	10	20.0	1	1	2	0	1	1	3	6	0	3	0	0	1	0	.86
2 Years		15	2	6	8	-4	0	0	15	13.3	1	–	–	0	–	–	4	8	0	4	0	–	–	0	.53

Frederic Chabot

Pos: G **Catches:** R **Ht:** 5'11" **Wt:** 184 **Born:** 2/12/68—Hebertville, Quebec **Age:** 31

					Overall											Pen Shot		Offense		
Year	Tm	GP	GS	TP	W	L	T	Min	GA	GAA	Shots	SvPct	ShO	OE	PPGA	SHGA	Shots	GA	G	A	PIM
90-91	Mon	3	–	–	0	0	1	108	6	3.33	45	.867	0	–	–	–	0	0	0	0	0
91-92										Did Not Play in NHL											
92-93	Mon	1	0	0	0	0	0	40	1	1.50	19	.947	0	0	0	0	0	0	0	0	0
93-94	2Tm	5	1	2	0	2	1	130	10	4.62	64	.844	0	0	3	0	0	0	0	0	0
94-95										Did Not Play in NHL											
95-96										Did Not Play in NHL											
96-97										Did Not Play in NHL											
97-98	LA	12	9	3	3	3	2	554	29	3.14	267	.891	0	1	7	0	0	0	0	0	0
98-99	Mon	11	4	0	1	3	0	430	16	2.23	188	.915	0	3	1	0	0	0	0	0	2
93-94	Mon	1	1	0	0	1	0	60	5	5.00	24	.792	0	0	3	0	0	0	0	0	0
93-94	Phi	4	0	2	0	1	1	70	5	4.29	40	.875	0	0	0	0	0	0	0	0	0
5 Years		32	–	–	4	8	4	1262	62	2.95	583	.894	0	–	–	–	0	0	0	0	2

Shawn Chambers

(statistical profile on page 297)

Pos: D **Shoots:** L **Ht:** 6'2" **Wt:** 200 **Born:** 10/11/66—Sterling Heights, Michigan **Age:** 33

Overall											Power Play			Shorthand			Penalty							Misc	
Year	Tm	GP	G	A	Pts	+/–	GW	GT	S	SPct	G	A	Pts	G	A	Pts	Num	PIM	Maj	Mnr	Fgt	Rgh	HHT	Hat	P/G
87-88	Min	19	1	7	8	-6	0	0	28	3.6	1	–	–	0	–	–	–	21	–	–	–	–	–	0	.42
88-89	Min	72	5	19	24	-4	0	0	131	3.8	1	–	–	2	–	–	–	80	–	–	–	–	–	0	.33
89-90	Min	78	8	18	26	-2	2	0	116	6.9	0	–	–	1	–	–	–	81	–	–	–	–	–	0	.33
90-91	Min	29	1	3	4	2	0	0	55	1.8	0	–	–	0	–	–	–	24	–	–	–	–	–	0	.14
91-92	Was	2	0	0	0	-3	0	0	1	0.0	0	0	0	0	0	0	1	2	0	1	0	0	1	0	.00
92-93	TB	55	10	29	39	-21	1	0	152	6.6	5	18	23	0	1	1	18	36	0	18	0	4	12	0	.71
93-94	TB	66	11	23	34	-6	1	0	142	7.7	6	12	18	1	0	1	10	23	1	9	1	1	5	0	.52
94-95	2Tm	45	4	17	21	2	0	0	67	6.0	2	5	7	0	0	0	6	12	0	6	0	0	3	0	.47
95-96	NJ	64	2	21	23	1	1	0	112	1.8	2	13	15	0	0	0	9	18	0	9	0	1	5	0	.36
96-97	NJ	73	4	17	21	17	0	0	114	3.5	1	5	6	0	1	1	8	19	1	7	1	4	1	0	.29
97-98	Dal	57	2	22	24	11	0	0	73	2.7	1	12	13	1	1	2	9	26	0	8	0	2	4	0	.42
98-99	Dal	61	2	9	11	6	1	0	82	2.4	1	4	5	0	0	0	9	18	0	9	0	3	1	0	.18
94-95	TB	24	2	12	14	0	0	0	44	4.5	1	4	5	0	0	0	3	6	0	3	0	0	2	0	.58
94-95	NJ	21	2	5	7	2	0	0	23	8.7	1	1	2	0	0	0	3	6	0	3	0	0	1	0	.33
12 Years		621	50	185	235	-3	6	0	1073	4.7	20	–	–	5	–	–	–	360	–	–	–	–	–	0	.38
Postseason																									
Year	Tm	GP	G	A	Pts	+/–	GW	OT	S	SPct	G	A	Pts	G	A	Pts	Num	PIM	Maj	Mnr	Fgt	Rgh	HHT	Hat	P/G
88-89	Min	3	0	2	2	0	0	0	4	0.0	0	–	–	0	–	–	0	0	0	0	0	0	0	0	.67
89-90	Min	7	2	1	3	-5	0	0	13	15.4	1	–	–	0	0	0	–	10	–	–	–	–	–	0	.43
90-91	Min	23	0	7	7	-7	0	0	44	0.0	0	–	–	0	–	–	–	16	–	–	–	–	–	0	.30
94-95	NJ	20	4	5	9	2	0	0	36	11.1	2	1	3	0	0	0	1	2	0	1	0	1	0	0	.45
96-97	NJ	10	1	6	7	-2	0	0	17	5.9	1	5	6	0	1	1	3	6	0	3	0	0	2	0	.70
97-98	Dal	14	0	3	3	5	0	0	16	0.0	0	2	2	0	0	0	6	20	0	5	0	0	2	0	.21
98-99	Dal	17	0	2	2	-1	0	0	19	0.0	0	0	0	0	0	0	5	18	0	4	0	2	2	0	.12
7 Years		94	7	26	33	-8	0	0	149	4.7	4	–	–	0	–	–	–	72	–	–	–	–	–	0	.35

Zdeno Chara

Pos: D **Shoots:** L **Ht:** 6'8" **Wt:** 255 **Born:** 3/18/77—Trencin, USSR **Age:** 22

Overall											Power Play			Shorthand			Penalty							Misc	
Year	Tm	GP	G	A	Pts	+/–	GW	GT	S	SPct	G	A	Pts	G	A	Pts	Num	PIM	Maj	Mnr	Fgt	Rgh	HHT	Hat	P/G
97-98	NYI	25	0	1	1	1	0	0	10	0.0	0	0	0	0	0	0	15	50	4	10	4	2	1	0	.04
98-99	NYI	59	2	6	8	-8	0	0	56	3.6	0	0	0	1	0	1	33	83	3	29	3	6	8	0	.14
2 Years		84	2	7	9	-7	0	0	66	3.0	0	0	0	1	0	1	48	133	7	39	7	8	9	0	.11

Eric Charron

Pos: D **Shoots:** L **Ht:** 6'3" **Wt:** 192 **Born:** 1/14/70—Verdun, Quebec **Age:** 29

Overall											Power Play			Shorthand			Penalty							Misc	
Year	Tm	GP	G	A	Pts	+/–	GW	GT	S	SPct	G	A	Pts	G	A	Pts	Num	PIM	Maj	Mnr	Fgt	Rgh	HHT	Hat	P/G
92-93	Mon	3	0	0	0	0	0	0	0	–	0	0	0	0	0	0	1	2	0	1	0	0	0	0	.00
93-94	TB	4	0	0	0	0	0	0	1	0.0	0	0	0	0	0	0	1	2	0	1	0	0	0	0	.00
94-95	TB	45	1	4	5	1	0	0	33	3.0	0	1	1	0	1	1	13	26	0	13	0	0	5	0	.11
95-96	2Tm	18	0	1	1	-3	0	0	13	0.0	0	0	0	0	0	0	11	22	0	11	0	0	6	0	.06
96-97	Was	25	1	1	2	1	0	0	11	9.1	0	0	0	0	0	0	10	20	0	10	0	3	1	0	.08
97-98	Cgy	2	0	0	0	0	0	0	1	0.0	0	0	0	0	0	0	2	4	0	2	0	1	0	0	.00
98-99	Cgy	12	0	1	1	-6	0	0	9	0.0	0	0	0	0	0	0	7	14	0	7	0	0	5	0	.08
95-96	TB	14	0	0	0	-6	0	0	11	0.0	0	0	0	0	0	0	9	18	0	9	0	0	5	0	.00
95-96	Was	4	0	1	1	3	0	0	2	0.0	0	0	0	0	0	0	2	4	0	2	0	0	1	0	.25
7 Years		109	2	7	9	-7	0	0	68	2.9	0	1	1	0	1	1	45	90	0	45	0	4	17	0	.08
Postseason																									
Year	Tm	GP	G	A	Pts	+/–	GW	OT	S	SPct	G	A	Pts	G	A	Pts	Num	PIM	Maj	Mnr	Fgt	Rgh	HHT	Hat	P/G
95-96	Was	6	0	0	0	1	0	0	2	0.0	0	0	0	0	0	0	4	8	0	4	0	2	1	0	.00

Kelly Chase

(statistical profile on page 297)

Pos: RW **Shoots:** R **Ht:** 6'0" **Wt:** 199 **Born:** 10/25/67—Porcupine Plain, Saskatchewan **Age:** 32

Overall											Power Play			Shorthand			Penalty							Misc	
Year	Tm	GP	G	A	Pts	+/–	GW	GT	S	SPct	G	A	Pts	G	A	Pts	Num	PIM	Maj	Mnr	Fgt	Rgh	HHT	Hat	P/G
89-90	StL	43	1	3	4	-1	0	0	9	11.1	0	–	–	0	–	–	–	244	–	–	–	–	–	0	.09
90-91	StL	2	1	0	1	1	1	0	1	100.0	0	0	0	0	0	0	–	15	–	–	–	–	–	0	.50
91-92	StL	46	1	2	3	-6	0	0	29	3.4	0	0	0	0	0	0	63	264	22	32	20	17	1	0	.07
92-93	StL	49	2	5	7	-9	0	0	28	7.1	0	0	0	0	0	0	54	204	16	32	16	12	3	0	.14

		Overall									Power Play			Shorthand			Penalty							Misc	
Year	Tm	GP	G	A	Pts	+/–	GW	GT	S	SPct	G	A	Pts	G	A	Pts	Num	PIM	Maj	Mnr	Fgt	Rgh	HHT	Hat	P/G
93-94	StL	68	2	5	7	-5	0	0	57	3.5	0	0	0	0	0	0	77	278	20	49	20	30	3	0	.10
94-95	Har	28	0	4	4	1	0	0	15	0.0	0	0	0	0	0	0	30	141	11	13	11	5	0	0	.14
95-96	Har	55	2	4	6	-4	1	0	19	10.5	0	0	0	0	0	0	52	230	20	25	20	7	5	0	.11
96-97	2Tm	30	1	2	3	2	0	0	6	16.7	0	0	0	0	0	0	28	149	15	7	15	6	0	0	.10
97-98	StL	67	4	3	7	10	1	0	29	13.8	0	0	0	0	0	0	55	231	19	28	19	6	3	0	.10
98-99	StL	45	3	7	10	2	1	0	25	12.0	0	1	1	0	0	0	36	143	13	19	13	5	2	0	.22
96-97	Har	28	1	2	3	2	0	0	5	20.0	0	0	0	0	0	0	23	122	12	6	12	5	0	0	.11
96-97	Tor	2	0	0	0	0	0	0	1	0.0	0	0	0	0	0	0	5	27	3	1	3	1	0	0	.00
10 Years		433	17	35	52	-9	4	0	218	7.8	0	–	–	0	–	–	–	1899	–	–	–	–	–	0	.12
Postseason																									
Year	Tm	GP	G	A	Pts	+/–	GW	OT	S	SPct	G	A	Pts	G	A	Pts	Num	PIM	Maj	Mnr	Fgt	Rgh	HHT	Hat	P/G
89-90	StL	9	1	0	1	-1	0	0	4	25.0	0	0	0	0	0	0	–	46	–	–	–	–	–	0	.11
90-91	StL	6	0	0	0	-1	0	0	0	–	0	0	0	0	0	0	–	18	–	–	–	–	–	0	.00
91-92	StL	1	0	0	0	0	0	0	0	–	0	0	0	0	0	0	2	7	1	1	1	0	0	0	.00
93-94	StL	4	0	1	1	0	0	0	3	0.0	0	0	0	0	0	0	3	6	0	3	0	1	0	0	.25
97-98	StL	7	0	0	0	-2	0	0	0	–	0	0	0	0	0	0	6	23	1	4	1	1	1	0	.00
5 Years		27	1	1	2	-4	0	0	7	14.3	0	0	0	0	0	0	–	100	–	–	–	–	–	0	.07

Vladimir Chebaturkin

Pos: D **Shoots:** L **Ht:** 6'2" **Wt:** 213 **Born:** 4/23/75—Tyumen, USSR **Age:** 24

		Overall									Power Play			Shorthand			Penalty							Misc	
Year	Tm	GP	G	A	Pts	+/–	GW	GT	S	SPct	G	A	Pts	G	A	Pts	Num	PIM	Maj	Mnr	Fgt	Rgh	HHT	Hat	P/G
97-98	NYI	2	0	2	2	-1	0	0	0	–	0	0	0	0	0	0	0	0	0	0	0	0	0	0	1.00
98-99	NYI	8	0	0	0	6	0	0	4	0.0	0	0	0	0	0	0	6	12	0	6	0	0	2	0	.00
2 Years		10	0	2	2	5	0	0	4	0.0	0	0	0	0	0	0	6	12	0	6	0	0	2	0	.20

Chris Chelios

(statistical profile on page 297)

Pos: D **Shoots:** R **Ht:** 6'1" **Wt:** 190 **Born:** 1/25/62—Chicago, Illinois **Age:** 37

		Overall									Power Play			Shorthand			Penalty							Misc	
Year	Tm	GP	G	A	Pts	+/–	GW	GT	S	SPct	G	A	Pts	G	A	Pts	Num	PIM	Maj	Mnr	Fgt	Rgh	HHT	Hat	P/G
83-84	Mon	12	0	2	2	-5	0	0	23	0.0	0	–	–	0	–	–	–	12	–	–	–	–	–	0	.17
84-85	Mon*	74	9	55	64	11	0	0	199	4.5	2	–	–	1	–	–	–	87	–	–	–	–	–	0	.86
85-86	Mon	41	8	26	34	4	0	0	101	7.9	2	–	–	0	–	–	–	67	–	–	–	–	–	0	.83
86-87	Mon*	71	11	33	44	-5	2	0	141	7.8	6	–	–	0	–	–	–	124	–	–	–	–	–	0	.62
87-88	Mon	71	20	41	61	15	5	**3**	199	10.1	10	–	–	1	–	–	–	172	–	–	–	–	–	0	.86
88-89	Mon	**80**	15	58	73	35	6	0	206	7.3	8	–	–	0	–	–	–	185	–	–	–	–	–	0	.91
89-90	Mon*	53	9	22	31	20	1	0	123	7.3	1	–	–	2	–	–	–	136	–	–	–	–	–	0	.58
90-91	Chi*	77	12	52	64	23	2	0	187	6.4	5	–	–	2	–	–	–	192	–	–	–	–	–	0	.83
91-92	Chi*	80	9	47	56	24	2	1	239	3.8	2	22	24	2	1	3	79	245	5	65	4	23	11	0	.70
92-93	Chi*	84	15	58	73	14	2	0	290	5.2	8	39	47	0	4	4	83	282	4	66	3	21	11	0	.87
93-94	Chi*	76	16	44	60	12	2	0	219	7.3	7	26	33	1	3	4	72	212	4	61	4	20	8	0	.79
94-95	Chi	48	5	33	38	17	0	0	166	3.0	3	20	23	1	1	2	29	72	2	26	2	10	6	0	.79
95-96	Chi*	81	14	58	72	25	3	0	219	6.4	7	24	31	0	**6**	6	52	140	4	45	3	19	10	0	.89
96-97	Chi*	72	10	38	48	16	2	0	194	5.2	2	18	20	0	1	1	49	112	2	46	2	19	12	0	.67
97-98	Chi*	81	3	39	42	-7	0	0	205	1.5	1	22	23	0	0	0	51	151	3	43	3	11	9	0	.52
98-99	2Tm	75	9	27	36	1	1	1	187	4.8	3	11	14	1	1	2	37	93	1	34	1	15	4	0	.48
98-99	Chi	65	8	26	34	-4	0	1	172	4.7	2	10	12	1	1	2	35	89	1	32	1	14	4	0	.52
98-99	Det	10	1	1	2	5	1	0	15	6.7	1	1	2	0	0	0	2	4	0	2	0	1	0	0	.20
16 Years		1076	165	633	798	200	28	5	2898	5.7	67	–	–	11	–	–	–	2282	–	–	–	–	–	0	.74
Postseason																									
Year	Tm	GP	G	A	Pts	+/–	GW	OT	S	SPct	G	A	Pts	G	A	Pts	Num	PIM	Maj	Mnr	Fgt	Rgh	HHT	Hat	P/G
83-84	Mon	15	1	9	10	3	0	0	25	4.0	1	–	–	0	–	–	–	17	–	–	–	–	–	0	.67
84-85	Mon	9	2	8	10	2	0	0	19	10.5	2	–	–	0	–	–	–	17	–	–	–	–	–	0	1.11
85-86	Mon	20	2	9	11	3	0	0	57	3.5	1	–	–	0	–	–	–	49	–	–	–	–	–	0	.55
86-87	Mon	17	4	9	13	-1	0	0	49	8.2	2	–	–	1	–	–	–	38	–	–	–	–	–	0	.76
87-88	Mon	11	3	1	4	3	0	0	39	7.7	1	–	–	0	–	–	–	29	–	–	–	–	–	0	.36
88-89	Mon	21	4	15	19	2	2	0	53	7.5	1	–	–	0	–	–	–	28	–	–	–	–	–	0	.90
89-90	Mon	5	0	1	1	-4	0	0	6	0.0	0	–	–	0	0	0	4	8	0	4	0	–	–	0	.20
90-91	Chi	6	1	7	8	2	0	0	11	9.1	1	–	–	0	0	0	–	46	–	–	–	–	–	0	1.33
91-92	Chi	18	6	15	21	19	1	0	54	11.1	3	3	6	0	0	0	13	37	1	11	1	2	0	0	1.17
92-93	Chi	4	0	2	2	-1	0	0	18	0.0	0	1	1	0	0	0	3	14	0	2	0	1	0	0	.50
93-94	Chi	6	1	1	2	0	0	0	29	3.4	1	1	2	0	0	0	4	8	0	4	0	1	1	0	.33
94-95	Chi	16	4	7	11	6	3	2	49	8.2	0	3	3	1	0	1	6	12	0	6	0	0	3	0	.69
95-96	Chi	9	0	3	3	2	0	0	28	0.0	0	2	2	0	0	0	4	8	0	4	0	2	0	0	.33

Postseason																									
Year	Tm	GP	G	A	Pts	+/-	GW	OT	S	SPct	G	A	Pts	G	A	Pts	Num	PIM	Maj	Mnr	Fgt	Rgh	HHT	Hat	P/G
96-97	Chi	6	0	1	1	-2	0	0	18	0.0	0	0	0	0	0	0	4	8	0	4	0	2	1	0	.17
98-99	Det	10	0	4	4	-6	0	0	21	0.0	0	3	3	0	0	0	7	14	0	7	0	3	1	0	.40
15 Years		173	28	92	120	28	6	2	476	5.9	13	–	–	2	–	–	–	333	–	–	–	–	–	0	.69

In Memoriam

Steve Chiasson

Pos: D **Shoots:** L **Ht:** 6'1" **Wt:** 205 **Born:** 4/14/67—Barrie, Ontario **Died:** 5/3/99

Overall											Power Play			Shorthand			Penalty							Misc	
Year	Tm	GP	G	A	Pts	+/-	GW	GT	S	SPct	G	A	Pts	G	A	Pts	Num	PIM	Maj	Mnr	Fgt	Rgh	HHT	Hat	P/G
86-87	Det	45	1	4	5	-7	0	0	44	2.3	0	–	–	0	–	–	–	73	–	–	–	–	–	0	.11
87-88	Det	29	2	9	11	15	0	0	45	4.4	0	–	–	0	–	–	–	57	–	–	–	–	–	0	.38
88-89	Det	65	12	35	47	-6	0	0	187	6.4	5	–	–	2	–	–	–	149	–	–	–	–	–	0	.72
89-90	Det	67	14	28	42	-16	2	0	190	7.4	4	–	–	0	–	–	–	114	–	–	–	–	–	0	.63
90-91	Det	42	3	17	20	0	1	0	101	3.0	1	–	–	0	–	–	–	80	–	–	–	–	–	0	.48
91-92	Det	62	10	24	34	22	2	1	143	7.0	5	14	19	0	1	1	50	136	4	43	3	14	11	0	.55
92-93	Det*	79	12	50	62	14	1	0	227	5.3	6	27	33	0	2	2	57	155	3	50	3	10	26	0	.78
93-94	Det	82	13	33	46	17	2	0	238	5.5	4	13	17	1	4	5	53	122	0	51	0	11	15	0	.56
94-95	Cgy	45	2	23	25	10	0	0	110	1.8	1	11	12	0	0	0	18	39	1	17	1	3	12	0	.56
95-96	Cgy	76	8	25	33	3	2	0	175	4.6	5	11	16	0	1	1	27	62	0	26	0	3	12	0	.43
96-97	2Tm	65	8	22	30	-21	1	0	168	4.8	4	13	17	2	0	2	18	39	1	17	1	3	6	0	.46
97-98	Car	66	7	27	34	-2	0	0	173	4.0	6	13	19	0	0	0	23	65	1	20	1	3	8	0	.52
98-99	Car	28	1	8	9	7	0	0	74	1.4	1	4	5	0	0	0	8	16	0	8	0	0	4	0	.32
96-97	Cgy	47	5	11	16	-11	1	0	112	4.5	1	5	6	2	0	2	16	32	0	16	0	3	5	0	.34
96-97	Har	18	3	11	14	-10	0	0	56	5.4	3	8	11	0	0	0	2	7	1	1	1	0	1	0	.78
13 Years		751	93	305	398	36	11	1	1875	5.0	42	–	–	5	–	–	–	1107	–	–	–	–	–	0	.53
Postseason																									
Year	Tm	GP	G	A	Pts	+/-	GW	OT	S	SPct	G	A	Pts	G	A	Pts	Num	PIM	Maj	Mnr	Fgt	Rgh	HHT	Hat	P/G
86-87	Det	2	0	0	0	0	0	0	0	–	0	0	0	0	0	0	–	19	–	–	–	–	–	0	.00
87-88	Det	9	2	2	4	0	0	0	12	16.7	1	–	–	0	–	–	–	31	–	–	–	–	–	0	.44
88-89	Det	5	2	1	3	-3	0	0	18	11.1	1	–	–	0	0	0	3	6	0	3	0	–	–	0	.60
90-91	Det	5	3	1	4	-1	0	0	12	25.0	1	–	–	0	–	–	–	19	–	–	–	–	–	0	.80
91-92	Det	11	1	5	6	6	0	0	30	3.3	1	2	3	0	1	1	6	12	0	6	0	1	3	0	.55
92-93	Det	7	2	2	4	-3	1	0	21	9.5	1	2	3	0	0	0	4	19	1	2	0	0	0	0	.57
93-94	Det	7	2	3	5	3	1	0	13	15.4	2	1	3	0	0	0	1	2	0	1	0	0	0	0	.71
94-95	Cgy	7	1	2	3	9	0	0	16	6.3	1	0	1	0	0	0	3	9	1	2	1	0	0	0	.43
95-96	Cgy	4	2	1	3	0	0	0	20	10.0	0	0	0	0	0	0	0	0	0	0	0	0	0	0	.75
98-99	Car	6	1	2	3	1	0	0	17	5.9	1	1	2	0	0	0	1	2	0	1	0	0	0	0	.50
10 Years		63	16	19	35	12	2	0	159	10.1	9	–	–	0	–	–	–	119	–	–	–	–	–	0	.56

Tom Chorske

Pos: LW **Shoots:** R **Ht:** 6'1" **Wt:** 205 **Born:** 9/18/66—Minneapolis, Minnesota **Age:** 33

Overall											Power Play			Shorthand			Penalty							Misc	
Year	Tm	GP	G	A	Pts	+/-	GW	GT	S	SPct	G	A	Pts	G	A	Pts	Num	PIM	Maj	Mnr	Fgt	Rgh	HHT	Hat	P/G
89-90	Mon	14	3	1	4	2	0	0	19	15.8	0	–	–	0	–	–	1	2	0	1	0	–	–	0	.29
90-91	Mon	57	9	11	20	-8	1	0	82	11.0	3	–	–	0	–	–	–	32	–	–	–	–	–	0	.35
91-92	NJ	76	19	17	36	8	2	0	143	13.3	0	0	0	3	2	5	16	32	0	16	0	3	8	0	.47
92-93	NJ	50	7	12	19	-1	1	0	63	11.1	0	0	0	0	0	0	7	25	1	5	0	1	1	0	.38
93-94	NJ	76	21	20	41	14	4	0	131	16.0	1	0	1	1	2	3	12	32	0	11	0	2	4	0	.54
94-95	NJ	42	10	8	18	-4	2	0	59	16.9	0	0	0	0	1	1	8	16	0	8	0	1	0	0	.43
95-96	Ott	72	15	14	29	-9	1	0	118	12.7	0	1	1	2	0	2	9	21	1	8	0	1	3	0	.40
96-97	Ott	68	18	8	26	-1	1	0	116	15.5	1	1	2	1	1	2	8	16	0	8	0	1	3	0	.38
97-98	NYI	82	12	23	35	7	2	0	132	9.1	1	3	4	4	1	5	18	39	1	17	1	2	8	0	.43
98-99	3Tm	26	0	3	3	-8	0	0	44	0.0	0	0	0	0	0	0	4	8	0	4	0	1	2	0	.12
98-99	NYI	2	0	1	1	1	0	0	9	0.0	0	0	0	0	0	0	1	2	0	1	0	1	0	0	.50
98-99	Was	17	0	2	2	-4	0	0	22	0.0	0	0	0	0	0	0	2	4	0	2	0	0	1	0	.12
98-99	Cgy	7	0	0	0	-5	0	0	13	0.0	0	0	0	0	0	0	1	2	0	1	0	0	1	0	.00
10 Years		563	114	117	231	0	14	0	907	12.6	6	–	–	11	–	–	–	223	–	–	–	–	–	0	.41
Postseason																									
Year	Tm	GP	G	A	Pts	+/-	GW	OT	S	SPct	G	A	Pts	G	A	Pts	Num	PIM	Maj	Mnr	Fgt	Rgh	HHT	Hat	P/G
91-92	NJ	7	0	3	3	-2	0	0	16	0.0	0	0	0	0	0	0	2	4	0	2	0	1	0	0	.43
92-93	NJ	1	0	0	0	0	0	0	1	0.0	0	0	0	0	0	0	0	0	0	0	0	0	0	0	.00
93-94	NJ	20	4	3	7	0	1	0	32	12.5	0	0	0	0	0	0	0	0	0	0	0	0	0	0	.35
94-95	NJ	17	1	5	6	-2	0	0	21	4.8	0	0	0	0	0	0	2	4	0	2	0	0	0	0	.35
96-97	Ott	5	0	1	1	-1	0	0	3	0.0	0	0	0	0	0	0	1	2	0	1	0	0	0	0	.20
5 Years		50	5	12	17	-5	1	0	73	6.8	0	0	0	0	0	0	5	10	0	5	0	1	0	0	.34

Dino Ciccarelli

Pos: RW **Shoots:** R **Ht:** 5'10" **Wt:** 185 **Born:** 2/8/60—Sarnia, Ontario **Age:** 39

		Overall									Power Play			Shorthand			Penalty							Misc	
Year	**Tm**	**GP**	**G**	**A**	**Pts**	**+/–**	**GW**	**GT**	**S**	**SPct**	**G**	**A**	**Pts**	**G**	**A**	**Pts**	**Num**	**PIM**	**Maj**	**Mnr**	**Fgt**	**Rgh**	**HHT**	**Hat**	**P/G**
80-81	Min	32	18	12	30	2	0	1	126	14.3	8	–	–	0	–	–	–	29	–	–	–	–	–	1	.94
81-82	Min*	76	55	51	106	14	4	5	289	19.0	20	–	–	0	–	–	–	138	–	–	–	–	–	3	1.39
82-83	Min*	77	37	38	75	16	4	2	210	17.6	15	–	–	0	–	–	–	94	–	–	–	–	–	1	.97
83-84	Min	79	38	33	71	1	2	0	211	18.0	16	–	–	0	–	–	–	58	–	–	–	–	–	3	.90
84-85	Min	51	15	17	32	-10	0	1	133	11.3	5	–	–	0	–	–	–	41	–	–	–	–	–	0	.63
85-86	Min	75	44	45	89	12	5	0	262	16.8	19	–	–	0	–	–	–	51	–	–	–	–	–	3	1.19
86-87	Min	80	52	51	103	10	5	**3**	255	20.4	22	–	–	0	–	–	–	88	–	–	–	–	–	1	1.29
87-88	Min	67	41	45	86	-29	2	0	262	15.6	13	–	–	1	–	–	–	79	–	–	–	–	–	0	1.28
88-89	2Tm*	76	44	30	74	-6	8	1	247	17.8	16	–	–	0	–	–	–	76	–	–	–	–	–	3	.97
89-90	Was	**80**	41	38	79	-5	6	0	267	15.4	10	–	–	0	–	–	–	122	–	–	–	–	–	1	.99
90-91	Was	54	21	18	39	-17	2	**3**	186	11.3	2	–	–	0	–	–	–	66	–	–	–	–	–	1	.72
91-92	Was	78	38	38	76	-10	7	0	279	13.6	13	12	25	0	0	0	31	78	0	29	0	13	4	0	.97
92-93	Det	82	41	56	97	12	8	0	200	20.5	21	22	43	0	0	0	31	81	1	28	0	9	2	0	1.18
93-94	Det	66	28	29	57	10	1	2	153	18.3	12	8	20	0	0	0	31	73	1	29	0	12	6	1	.86
94-95	Det	42	16	27	43	12	3	0	106	15.1	6	11	17	0	0	0	18	39	1	17	1	4	4	0	1.02
95-96	Det	64	22	21	43	14	5	0	107	20.6	13	7	20	0	0	0	40	99	1	37	1	13	7	0	.67
96-97	TB*	77	35	25	60	-11	6	0	229	15.3	12	6	18	0	0	0	50	116	0	48	0	17	5	1	.78
97-98	2Tm	62	16	17	33	-16	4	2	161	9.9	5	5	10	0	0	0	35	70	0	35	0	22	4	0	.53
98-99	Fla	14	6	1	7	-1	1	0	23	26.1	5	1	6	0	0	0	8	27	1	6	0	2	1	0	.50
88-89	Min	65	32	27	59	-16	5	1	208	15.4	13	–	–	0	–	–	–	64	–	–	–	–	–	2	.91
88-89	Was	11	12	3	15	10	3	0	39	30.8	3	–	–	0	–	–	–	12	–	–	–	–	–	1	1.36
97-98	TB	34	11	6	17	-14	3	1	104	10.6	3	1	4	0	0	0	21	42	0	21	0	13	3	0	.50
97-98	Fla	28	5	11	16	-2	1	1	57	8.8	2	4	6	0	0	0	14	28	0	14	0	9	1	0	.57
19 Years		1232	608	592	1200	-2	73	20	3706	16.4	233	–	–	1	–	–	–	1425	–	–	–	–	–	19	.97

Postseason

Year	**Tm**	**GP**	**G**	**A**	**Pts**	**+/–**	**GW**	**OT**	**S**	**SPct**	**G**	**A**	**Pts**	**G**	**A**	**Pts**	**Num**	**PIM**	**Maj**	**Mnr**	**Fgt**	**Rgh**	**HHT**	**Hat**	**P/G**
80-81	Min	19	14	7	21	–	3	0	–	–	5	–	–	0	–	–	–	25	–	–	–	–	–	1	1.11
81-82	Min	4	3	1	4	–	1	0	–	–	2	–	–	0	0	0	1	2	0	1	0	–	–	1	1.00
82-83	Min	9	4	6	10	-1	2	1	22	18.2	1	–	–	0	0	0	4	11	1	3	–	–	–	0	1.11
83-84	Min	16	4	5	9	-6	1	0	38	10.5	1	–	–	0	–	–	–	27	–	–	–	–	–	0	.56
84-85	Min	9	3	3	6	-4	0	0	36	8.3	1	–	–	0	–	–	4	8	0	4	0	–	–	0	.67
85-86	Min	5	0	1	1	-6	0	0	8	0.0	0	–	–	0	–	–	3	6	0	3	0	–	–	0	.20
88-89	Was	6	3	3	6	-2	0	0	16	18.8	3	–	–	0	–	–	–	12	–	–	–	–	–	0	1.00
89-90	Was	8	8	3	11	0	1	1	28	28.6	1	–	–	0	–	–	3	6	0	3	0	–	–	1	1.38
90-91	Was	11	5	4	9	-3	2	1	44	11.4	3	–	–	0	–	–	–	22	–	–	–	–	–	0	.82
91-92	Was	7	5	4	9	-1	0	0	12	41.7	1	2	3	0	0	0	7	14	0	7	0	1	1	1	1.29
92-93	Det	7	4	2	6	-6	0	0	17	23.5	3	0	3	0	0	0	4	16	0	3	0	2	0	1	.86
93-94	Det	7	5	2	7	1	0	0	22	22.7	1	1	2	0	0	0	3	14	0	2	0	1	0	0	1.00
94-95	Det	16	9	2	11	-4	2	0	49	18.4	6	2	8	0	0	0	11	22	0	11	0	5	0	1	.69
95-96	Det	17	6	2	8	-6	1	0	36	16.7	6	1	7	0	0	0	13	26	0	13	0	0	0	0	.47
14 Years		141	73	45	118	-38	13	3	328	17.1	34	–	–	0	–	–	–	211	–	–	–	–	–	6	.84

Enrico Ciccone

Pos: D **Shoots:** L **Ht:** 6'5" **Wt:** 220 **Born:** 4/10/70—Montreal, Quebec **Age:** 29

		Overall									Power Play			Shorthand			Penalty							Misc	
Year	**Tm**	**GP**	**G**	**A**	**Pts**	**+/–**	**GW**	**GT**	**S**	**SPct**	**G**	**A**	**Pts**	**G**	**A**	**Pts**	**Num**	**PIM**	**Maj**	**Mnr**	**Fgt**	**Rgh**	**HHT**	**Hat**	**P/G**
91-92	Min	11	0	0	0	-2	0	0	2	0.0	0	0	0	0	0	0	14	48	4	9	4	0	0	0	.00
92-93	Min	31	0	1	1	2	0	0	13	0.0	0	0	0	0	0	0	39	115	7	30	6	8	4	0	.03
93-94	2Tm	57	1	2	3	-4	0	0	33	3.0	0	0	0	0	0	0	62	226	18	38	18	8	7	0	.05
94-95	TB	41	2	4	6	3	0	0	43	4.7	0	0	0	0	0	0	**61**	**225**	13	40	12	17	2	0	.15
95-96	2Tm	66	2	4	6	1	0	0	60	3.3	0	1	1	0	0	0	**94**	306	10	73	8	20	12	0	.09
96-97	Chi	67	2	2	4	-1	1	0	65	3.1	0	0	0	0	0	0	65	233	13	44	12	16	6	0	.06
97-98	3Tm	39	0	4	4	-2	0	0	22	0.0	0	1	1	0	0	0	42	175	9	25	9	10	2	0	.10
98-99	2Tm	59	3	1	4	-8	0	1	52	5.8	0	0	0	0	0	0	38	127	9	26	9	10	5	0	.07
93-94	Was	46	1	1	2	-2	0	0	23	4.3	0	0	0	0	0	0	46	174	14	27	14	5	5	0	.04
93-94	TB	11	0	1	1	-2	0	0	10	0.0	0	0	0	0	0	0	16	52	4	11	4	3	2	0	.09
95-96	TB	55	2	3	5	-4	0	0	48	4.2	0	1	1	0	0	0	78	258	10	59	8	14	11	0	.09
95-96	Chi	11	0	1	1	5	0	0	12	0.0	0	0	0	0	0	0	16	48	0	14	0	6	1	0	.09
97-98	Car	14	0	3	3	3	0	0	8	0.0	0	0	0	0	0	0	24	83	1	19	1	8	2	0	.21
97-98	Van	13	0	1	1	-2	0	0	7	0.0	0	1	1	0	0	0	8	47	5	1	5	0	0	0	.08
97-98	TB	12	0	0	0	-3	0	0	7	0.0	0	0	0	0	0	0	10	45	3	5	3	2	0	0	.00
98-99	TB	16	1	1	2	-1	0	0	9	11.1	0	0	0	0	0	0	9	24	2	7	2	1	2	0	.13
98-99	Was	43	2	0	2	-7	0	1	43	4.7	0	0	0	0	0	0	29	103	7	19	7	9	3	0	.05
8 Years		371	10	18	28	-11	1	1	290	3.4	0	2	2	0	0	0	415	1455	83	285	78	89	38	0	.08

Postseason																									
Year	Tm	GP	G	A	Pts	+/–	GW	OT	S	SPct	G	A	Pts	G	A	Pts	Num	PIM	Maj	Mnr	Fgt	Rgh	HHT	Hat	P/G
95-96	Chi	9	1	0	1	-1	0	0	4	25.0	0	0	0	0	0	0	7	30	0	5	0	1	0	0	.11
96-97	Chi	4	0	0	0	0	0	0	6	0.0	0	0	0	0	0	0	5	18	0	4	0	1	0	0	.00
2 Years		13	1	0	1	-1	0	0	10	10.0	0	0	0	0	0	0	12	48	0	9	0	2	0	0	.08

Brett Clark

Pos: D **Shoots:** L **Ht:** 6'0" **Wt:** 182 **Born:** 12/23/76—Moosomin, Saskatchewan **Age:** 23

Overall											Power Play			Shorthand			Penalty							Misc	
Year	Tm	GP	G	A	Pts	+/–	GW	GT	S	SPct	G	A	Pts	G	A	Pts	Num	PIM	Maj	Mnr	Fgt	Rgh	HHT	Hat	P/G
97-98	Mon	41	1	0	1	-3	0	0	26	3.8	0	0	0	0	0	0	6	20	0	5	0	1	1	0	.02
98-99	Mon	61	2	2	4	-3	0	0	36	5.6	0	0	0	0	0	0	8	16	0	8	0	0	4	0	.07
2 Years		102	3	2	5	-6	0	0	62	4.8	0	0	0	0	0	0	14	36	0	13	0	1	5	0	.05

Wendel Clark

(statistical profile on page 297)

Pos: LW **Shoots:** L **Ht:** 5'10" **Wt:** 194 **Born:** 10/25/66—Kelvington, Saskatchewan **Age:** 33

Overall											Power Play			Shorthand			Penalty							Misc	
Year	Tm	GP	G	A	Pts	+/–	GW	GT	S	SPct	G	A	Pts	G	A	Pts	Num	PIM	Maj	Mnr	Fgt	Rgh	HHT	Hat	P/G
85-86	Tor*	66	34	11	45	-27	3	0	164	20.7	4	–	–	0	–	–	–	227	–	–	–	–	–	1	.68
86-87	Tor	80	37	23	60	-23	1	2	246	15.0	15	–	–	0	–	–	–	271	–	–	–	–	–	1	.75
87-88	Tor	28	12	11	23	-13	1	1	93	12.9	4	–	–	0	–	–	–	80	–	–	–	–	–	0	.82
88-89	Tor	15	7	4	11	-3	1	0	30	23.3	3	–	–	0	–	–	–	66	–	–	–	–	–	0	.73
89-90	Tor	38	18	8	26	2	2	0	85	21.2	7	–	–	0	–	–	–	116	–	–	–	–	–	1	.68
90-91	Tor	63	18	16	34	-5	2	0	181	9.9	4	–	–	0	–	–	–	152	–	–	–	–	–	0	.54
91-92	Tor	43	19	21	40	-14	4	0	158	12.0	7	8	15	0	0	0	46	123	5	39	5	16	3	2	.93
92-93	Tor	66	17	22	39	2	5	1	146	11.6	2	7	9	0	0	0	68	193	11	54	10	24	4	0	.59
93-94	Tor	64	46	30	76	10	8	0	275	16.7	21	11	32	0	0	0	50	115	5	45	3	16	6	2	1.19
94-95	Que	37	12	18	30	-1	0	0	95	12.6	5	3	8	0	0	0	18	45	3	15	2	6	2	1	.81
95-96	2Tm	71	32	26	58	-5	3	1	237	13.5	8	10	18	0	0	0	32	76	4	28	4	9	3	0	.82
96-97	Tor	65	30	19	49	-2	6	0	212	14.2	6	6	12	0	0	0	29	75	3	25	3	15	0	1	.75
97-98	Tor	47	12	7	19	-21	3	0	140	8.6	4	3	7	0	0	0	30	80	4	25	4	11	4	0	.40
98-99	2Tm	77	32	16	48	-24	3	1	215	14.9	11	4	15	0	0	0	17	37	1	16	1	5	4	3	.62
95-96	NYI	58	24	19	43	-12	2	1	192	12.5	6	8	14	0	0	0	24	60	4	20	4	6	3	0	.74
95-96	Tor	13	8	7	15	7	1	0	45	17.8	2	2	4	0	0	0	8	16	0	8	0	3	0	0	1.15
98-99	TB	65	28	14	42	-25	2	1	171	16.4	11	4	15	0	0	0	16	35	1	15	1	5	4	3	.65
98-99	Det	12	4	2	6	1	1	0	44	9.1	0	0	0	0	0	0	1	2	0	1	0	0	0	0	.50
14 Years		760	326	232	558	-124	42	6	2277	14.3	101	–	–	0	–	–	–	1656	–	–	–	–	–	12	.73
Postseason																									
Year	Tm	GP	G	A	Pts	+/–	GW	OT	S	SPct	G	A	Pts	G	A	Pts	Num	PIM	Maj	Mnr	Fgt	Rgh	HHT	Hat	P/G
85-86	Tor	10	5	1	6	1	1	0	25	20.0	1	–	–	0	0	0	–	47	–	–	–	–	–	0	.60
86-87	Tor	13	6	5	11	6	1	0	61	9.8	3	–	–	0	0	0	–	38	–	–	–	–	–	0	.85
89-90	Tor	5	1	1	2	-2	0	0	14	7.1	0	–	–	0	–	–	–	19	–	–	–	–	–	0	.40
92-93	Tor	21	10	10	20	15	1	0	71	14.1	2	0	2	0	0	0	16	51	1	13	1	3	4	1	.95
93-94	Tor	18	9	7	16	0	1	0	72	12.5	2	3	5	0	0	0	12	24	0	12	0	6	1	0	.89
94-95	Que	6	1	2	3	-6	0	0	18	5.6	0	1	1	0	0	0	3	6	0	3	0	3	0	0	.50
95-96	Tor	6	2	2	4	-6	0	0	17	11.8	1	2	3	0	0	0	1	2	0	1	0	0	1	0	.67
98-99	Det	10	2	3	5	-1	0	0	29	6.9	1	1	2	0	0	0	5	10	0	5	0	1	0	0	.50
8 Years		89	36	31	67	7	4	0	307	11.7	10	–	–	0	–	–	–	197	–	–	–	–	–	1	.75

Daniel Cleary

Pos: LW **Shoots:** L **Ht:** 6'0" **Wt:** 203 **Born:** 12/18/78—Carbonear, Newfoundland **Age:** 21

Overall											Power Play			Shorthand			Penalty							Misc	
Year	Tm	GP	G	A	Pts	+/–	GW	GT	S	SPct	G	A	Pts	G	A	Pts	Num	PIM	Maj	Mnr	Fgt	Rgh	HHT	Hat	P/G
97-98	Chi	6	0	0	0	-2	0	0	4	0.0	0	0	0	0	0	0	0	0	0	0	0	0	0	0	.00
98-99	Chi	35	4	5	9	-1	0	0	49	8.2	0	0	0	0	0	0	8	24	0	7	0	2	2	0	.26
2 Years		41	4	5	9	-3	0	0	53	7.5	0	0	0	0	0	0	8	24	0	7	0	2	2	0	.22

Dan Cloutier

(statistical profile on page 397)

Pos: G **Catches:** L **Ht:** 6'1" **Wt:** 185 **Born:** 4/22/76—Mont-Laurier, Quebec **Age:** 23

Overall																	Pen Shot		Offense		
Year	Tm	GP	GS	TP	W	L	T	Min	GA	GAA	Shots	SvPct	ShO	OE	PPGA	SHGA	Shots	GA	G	A	PIM
97-98	NYR	12	9	3	4	5	1	551	23	2.50	248	.907	0	3	6	0	0	0	0	0	19
98-99	NYR	22	16	2	6	8	3	1097	49	2.68	570	.914	0	7	11	3	0	0	0	0	2
2 Years		34	25	5	10	13	4	1648	72	2.62	818	.912	0	10	17	3	0	0	0	0	21

Sylvain Cloutier

Pos: C **Shoots:** L **Ht:** 6'0" **Wt:** 191 **Born:** 2/13/74—Mont-Laurier, Quebec **Age:** 25

Overall											Power Play			Shorthand			Penalty							Misc	
Year	Tm	GP	G	A	Pts	+/–	GW	GT	S	SPct	G	A	Pts	G	A	Pts	Num	PIM	Maj	Mnr	Fgt	Rgh	HHT	Hat	P/G
98-99	Chi	7	0	0	0	-1	0	0	3	0.0	0	0	0	0	0	0	0	0	0	0	0	0	0	0	.00

Paul Coffey

(statistical profile on page 298)

Pos: D **Shoots:** L **Ht:** 6'0" **Wt:** 200 **Born:** 6/1/61—Weston, Ontario **Age:** 38

Overall											Power Play			Shorthand			Penalty							Misc	
Year	Tm	GP	G	A	Pts	+/–	GW	GT	S	SPct	G	A	Pts	G	A	Pts	Num	PIM	Maj	Mnr	Fgt	Rgh	HHT	Hat	P/G
80-81	Edm	74	9	23	32	4	0	0	113	8.0	2	–	–	0	–	–	–	130	–	–	–	–	–	0	.43
81-82	Edm*	80	29	60	89	35	1	0	234	12.4	13	–	–	0	–	–	–	106	–	–	–	–	–	0	1.11
82-83	Edm*	**80**	29	67	96	52	2	0	259	11.2	9	–	–	1	–	–	–	87	–	–	–	–	–	1	1.20
83-84	Edm*	**80**	40	86	126	52	4	1	258	15.5	14	–	–	1	–	–	–	104	–	–	–	–	–	0	1.58
84-85	Edm*	**80**	37	84	121	55	6	0	284	13.0	12	–	–	2	–	–	–	97	–	–	–	–	–	2	1.51
85-86	Edm*	79	48	90	138	61	3	1	307	15.6	9	–	–	**9**	–	–	–	120	–	–	–	–	–	1	1.75
86-87	Edm	59	17	50	67	12	3	0	165	10.3	10	–	–	2	–	–	–	49	–	–	–	–	–	0	1.14
87-88	Pit*	46	15	52	67	-1	2	0	193	7.8	6	36	42	2	–	–	–	93	–	–	–	–	–	1	1.46
88-89	Pit*	75	30	83	113	-10	2	0	342	8.8	11	53	64	0	–	–	–	195	–	–	–	–	–	0	1.51
89-90	Pit*	**80**	29	74	103	-25	3	1	324	9.0	10	38	48	0	–	–	–	95	–	–	–	–	–	0	1.29
90-91	Pit*	76	24	69	93	-18	3	0	240	10.0	8	33	41	0	–	–	–	128	–	–	–	–	–	0	1.22
91-92	2Tm*	64	11	58	69	1	1	0	232	4.7	5	26	31	0	2	2	26	87	1	21	1	7	8	0	1.08
92-93	2Tm*	80	12	75	87	16	0	0	254	4.7	5	46	51	0	0	0	37	77	1	36	1	7	10	0	1.09
93-94	Det*	80	14	63	77	28	3	0	278	5.0	5	31	36	0	2	2	42	106	2	38	2	8	17	0	.96
94-95	Det	45	14	44	58	18	2	0	181	7.7	4	**27**	**31**	1	0	1	24	72	0	21	0	7	5	0	1.29
95-96	Det*	76	14	60	74	19	3	0	234	6.0	3	30	33	1	0	1	41	90	0	40	0	9	20	0	.97
96-97	2Tm*	57	9	25	34	11	2	0	110	8.2	1	8	9	1	0	1	19	38	0	19	0	5	12	0	.60
97-98	Phi	57	2	27	29	3	1	0	107	1.9	1	19	20	0	0	0	15	30	0	15	0	2	10	0	.51
98-99	2Tm	54	2	12	14	-7	0	0	87	2.3	1	6	7	0	0	0	14	28	0	14	0	1	7	0	.26
91-92	Pit	54	10	54	64	4	1	0	207	4.8	5	24	29	0	2	2	19	62	0	16	0	5	8	0	1.19
91-92	LA	10	1	4	5	-3	0	0	25	4.0	0	2	2	0	0	0	7	25	1	5	1	2	0	0	.50
92-93	LA	50	8	49	57	9	0	0	182	4.4	2	28	30	0	0	0	25	50	0	25	0	6	8	0	1.14
92-93	Det	30	4	26	30	7	0	0	72	5.6	3	18	21	0	0	0	12	27	1	11	1	1	2	0	1.00
96-97	Har	20	3	5	8	0	1	0	39	7.7	1	2	3	0	0	0	9	18	0	9	0	2	6	0	.40
96-97	Phi	37	6	20	26	11	1	0	71	8.5	0	6	6	1	0	1	10	20	0	10	0	3	6	0	.70
98-99	Chi	10	0	4	4	-6	0	0	8	0.0	0	3	3	0	0	0	0	0	0	0	0	0	0	0	.40
98-99	Car	44	2	8	10	-1	0	0	79	2.5	1	3	4	0	0	0	14	28	0	14	0	1	7	0	.23
19 Years		1322	385	1102	1487	306	41	3	4202	9.2	129	–	–	20	–	–	–	1732	–	–	–	–	–	5	1.12

Postseason

Year	Tm	GP	G	A	Pts	+/–	GW	OT	S	SPct	G	A	Pts	G	A	Pts	Num	PIM	Maj	Mnr	Fgt	Rgh	HHT	Hat	P/G
80-81	Edm	9	4	3	7	–	0	0	–	–	1	–	–	0	–	–	–	22	–	–	–	–	–	0	.78
81-82	Edm	5	1	1	2	–	0	0	–	–	1	–	–	0	–	–	3	6	0	3	0	–	–	0	.40
82-83	Edm	16	7	7	14	15	0	0	42	16.7	2	–	–	2	–	–	–	15	–	–	–	–	–	0	.88
83-84	Edm	19	8	14	22	21	1	0	66	12.1	2	–	–	0	–	–	–	21	–	–	–	–	–	0	1.16
84-85	Edm	18	12	25	37	26	4	0	66	18.2	3	–	–	1	–	–	–	44	–	–	–	–	–	0	2.06
85-86	Edm	10	1	9	10	0	0	0	30	3.3	1	–	–	0	–	–	–	30	–	–	–	–	–	0	1.00
86-87	Edm	17	3	8	11	7	1	0	43	7.0	1	–	–	0	–	–	–	30	–	–	–	–	–	0	.65
88-89	Pit	11	2	13	15	-7	1	0	48	4.2	2	–	–	0	–	–	–	31	–	–	–	–	–	0	1.36
90-91	Pit	12	2	9	11	-1	0	0	37	5.4	0	–	–	0	–	–	3	6	0	3	0	–	–	0	.92
91-92	LA	6	4	3	7	-5	0	0	28	14.3	3	1	4	0	0	0	1	2	0	1	0	0	0	0	1.17
92-93	Det	7	2	9	11	-3	0	0	24	8.3	0	8	8	0	0	0	1	2	0	1	0	0	0	0	1.57
93-94	Det	7	1	6	7	6	0	0	23	4.3	0	2	2	0	1	1	4	8	0	4	0	1	1	0	1.00
94-95	Det	18	6	12	18	4	0	0	74	8.1	2	10	12	1	0	1	5	10	0	5	0	1	0	0	1.00
95-96	Det	17	5	9	14	-3	1	0	49	10.2	3	5	8	2	0	2	7	30	0	5	0	3	1	0	.82
96-97	Phi	17	1	8	9	-3	0	0	37	2.7	0	5	5	0	0	0	3	6	0	3	0	1	2	0	.53
98-99	Car	5	0	1	1	0	0	0	8	0.0	0	0	0	0	0	0	1	2	0	1	0	0	0	0	.20
16 Years		194	59	137	196	57	8	0	575	9.4	21	–	–	6	–	–	–	265	–	–	–	–	–	0	1.01

Craig Conroy

(statistical profile on page 298)

Pos: C **Shoots:** R **Ht:** 6'2" **Wt:** 190 **Born:** 9/4/71—Potsdam, New York **Age:** 28

Overall											Power Play			Shorthand			Penalty							Misc	
Year	Tm	GP	G	A	Pts	+/–	GW	GT	S	SPct	G	A	Pts	G	A	Pts	Num	PIM	Maj	Mnr	Fgt	Rgh	HHT	Hat	P/G
94-95	Mon	6	1	0	1	-1	0	0	4	25.0	0	0	0	0	0	0	0	0	0	0	0	0	0	0	.17
95-96	Mon	7	0	0	0	-4	0	0	1	0.0	0	0	0	0	0	0	1	2	0	1	0	0	0	0	.00
96-97	StL	61	6	11	17	0	1	0	74	8.1	0	0	0	0	2	2	12	43	1	9	0	0	8	0	.28

		Overall									Power Play			Shorthand			Penalty							Misc	
Year	Tm	GP	G	A	Pts	+/–	GW	GT	S	SPct	G	A	Pts	G	A	Pts	Num	PIM	Maj	Mnr	Fgt	Rgh	HHT	Hat	P/G
97-98	StL	81	14	29	43	20	1	0	118	11.9	0	1	1	3	1	4	19	46	0	18	0	0	11	0	.53
98-99	StL	69	14	25	39	14	1	0	134	10.4	0	0	0	1	2	3	19	38	0	19	0	0	14	1	.57
5 Years		224	35	65	100	29	3	0	331	10.6	0	1	1	4	5	9	51	129	1	47	0	0	33	1	.45
Postseason																									
Year	Tm	GP	G	A	Pts	+/–	GW	OT	S	SPct	G	A	Pts	G	A	Pts	Num	PIM	Maj	Mnr	Fgt	Rgh	HHT	Hat	P/G
96-97	StL	6	0	0	0	-1	0	0	4	0.0	0	0	0	0	0	0	4	8	0	4	0	1	0	0	.00
97-98	StL	10	1	2	3	-1	1	0	17	5.9	0	0	0	0	0	0	4	8	0	4	0	0	1	0	.30
98-99	StL	13	2	1	3	-3	0	0	20	10.0	0	0	0	0	0	0	3	6	0	3	0	1	1	0	.23
3 Years		29	3	3	6	-5	1	0	41	7.3	0	0	0	0	0	0	11	22	0	11	0	2	2	0	.21

Brandon Convery

Pos: C **Shoots:** R **Ht:** 6'1" **Wt:** 200 **Born:** 2/4/74—Kingston, Ontario **Age:** 25

		Overall									Power Play			Shorthand			Penalty							Misc	
Year	Tm	GP	G	A	Pts	+/–	GW	GT	S	SPct	G	A	Pts	G	A	Pts	Num	PIM	Maj	Mnr	Fgt	Rgh	HHT	Hat	P/G
95-96	Tor	11	5	2	7	-7	1	0	16	31.3	3	0	3	0	0	0	2	4	0	2	0	0	1	0	.64
96-97	Tor	39	2	8	10	-9	0	0	41	4.9	0	2	2	0	1	1	7	20	2	5	2	1	3	0	.26
97-98	Van	7	0	2	2	0	0	0	2	0.0	0	1	1	0	0	0	0	0	0	0	0	0	0	0	.29
98-99	2Tm	15	2	7	9	4	1	0	14	14.3	0	3	3	0	0	0	6	12	0	6	0	2	4	0	.60
98-99	Van	12	2	7	9	5	1	0	12	16.7	0	3	3	0	0	0	4	8	0	4	0	1	3	0	.75
98-99	LA	3	0	0	0	-1	0	0	2	0.0	0	0	0	0	0	0	2	4	0	2	0	1	1	0	.00
4 Years		72	9	19	28	-12	2	0	73	12.3	3	6	9	0	1	1	15	36	2	13	2	3	8	0	.39
Postseason																									
Year	Tm	GP	G	A	Pts	+/–	GW	OT	S	SPct	G	A	Pts	G	A	Pts	Num	PIM	Maj	Mnr	Fgt	Rgh	HHT	Hat	P/G
95-96	Tor	5	0	0	0	0	0	0	4	0.0	0	0	0	0	0	0	1	2	0	1	0	0	0	0	.00

Matt Cooke

Pos: LW **Shoots:** L **Ht:** 5'11" **Wt:** 192 **Born:** 9/7/78—Stirling, Ontario **Age:** 21

		Overall									Power Play			Shorthand			Penalty							Misc	
Year	Tm	GP	G	A	Pts	+/–	GW	GT	S	SPct	G	A	Pts	G	A	Pts	Num	PIM	Maj	Mnr	Fgt	Rgh	HHT	Hat	P/G
98-99	Van	30	0	2	2	-12	0	0	22	0.0	0	0	0	0	0	0	12	27	1	11	1	3	3	0	.07

Rene Corbet

(statistical profile on page 298)

Pos: LW **Shoots:** L **Ht:** 6'0" **Wt:** 190 **Born:** 6/25/73—Victoriaville, Quebec **Age:** 26

		Overall									Power Play			Shorthand			Penalty							Misc	
Year	Tm	GP	G	A	Pts	+/–	GW	GT	S	SPct	G	A	Pts	G	A	Pts	Num	PIM	Maj	Mnr	Fgt	Rgh	HHT	Hat	P/G
93-94	Que	9	1	1	2	1	0	0	14	7.1	0	1	1	0	0	0	0	0	0	0	0	0	0	0	.22
94-95	Que	8	0	3	3	3	0	0	4	0.0	0	0	0	0	0	0	1	2	0	1	0	0	1	0	.38
95-96	Col	33	3	6	9	10	0	0	35	8.6	0	0	0	0	0	0	11	33	1	9	1	4	4	0	.27
96-97	Col	76	12	15	27	14	3	1	128	9.4	1	2	3	0	0	0	26	67	5	21	5	7	6	0	.36
97-98	Col	68	16	12	28	8	4	2	117	13.7	4	5	9	0	0	0	43	133	13	29	13	12	6	0	.41
98-99	2Tm	73	13	18	31	1	1	0	127	10.2	3	7	10	0	0	0	24	68	4	19	4	5	4	0	.42
98-99	Col	53	8	14	22	3	1	0	82	9.8	2	6	8	0	0	0	19	58	4	14	4	5	3	0	.42
98-99	Cgy	20	5	4	9	-2	0	0	45	11.1	1	1	2	0	0	0	5	10	0	5	0	0	1	0	.45
6 Years		267	45	55	100	37	8	3	425	10.6	8	15	23	0	0	0	105	303	23	79	23	28	21	0	.37
Postseason																									
Year	Tm	GP	G	A	Pts	+/–	GW	OT	S	SPct	G	A	Pts	G	A	Pts	Num	PIM	Maj	Mnr	Fgt	Rgh	HHT	Hat	P/G
94-95	Que	2	0	1	1	1	0	0	0	–	0	0	0	0	1	1	0	0	0	0	0	0	0	0	.50
95-96	Col	8	3	2	5	3	1	0	9	33.3	1	0	1	0	0	0	1	2	0	1	0	0	0	0	.63
96-97	Col	17	2	2	4	0	0	0	31	6.5	0	1	1	0	0	0	8	27	1	6	1	3	0	0	.24
97-98	Col	2	0	0	0	0	0	0	5	0.0	0	0	0	0	0	0	1	2	0	1	0	0	0	0	.00
4 Years		29	5	5	10	4	1	0	45	11.1	1	1	2	0	1	1	10	31	1	8	1	3	0	0	.34

Bob Corkum

(statistical profile on page 298)

Pos: C **Shoots:** R **Ht:** 6'2" **Wt:** 216 **Born:** 12/18/67—Salisbury, Massachusetts **Age:** 32

		Overall									Power Play			Shorthand			Penalty							Misc	
Year	Tm	GP	G	A	Pts	+/–	GW	GT	S	SPct	G	A	Pts	G	A	Pts	Num	PIM	Maj	Mnr	Fgt	Rgh	HHT	Hat	P/G
89-90	Buf	8	2	0	2	2	1	0	6	33.3	0	0	0	0	0	0	2	4	0	2	0	–	–	0	.25
90-91		Did Not Play in NHL																							
91-92	Buf	20	2	4	6	-9	0	0	23	8.7	0	0	0	0	0	0	9	21	1	8	1	2	0	0	.30
92-93	Buf	68	6	4	10	-3	1	0	69	8.7	0	0	0	1	1	2	19	38	0	19	0	3	9	0	.15

Overall											Power Play			Shorthand			Penalty							Misc	
Year	Tm	GP	G	A	Pts	+/-	GW	GT	S	SPct	G	A	Pts	G	A	Pts	Num	PIM	Maj	Mnr	Fgt	Rgh	HHT	Hat	P/G
93-94	Anh	76	23	28	51	4	0	1	180	12.8	3	3	6	3	1	4	9	18	0	9	0	0	4	0	.67
94-95	Anh	44	10	9	19	-7	1	1	100	10.0	0	1	1	0	0	0	11	25	1	10	1	2	6	0	.43
95-96	2Tm	76	9	10	19	3	3	0	126	7.1	0	0	0	0	1	1	17	34	0	17	0	3	7	0	.25
96-97	Pho	80	9	11	20	-7	3	0	119	7.6	0	1	1	1	0	1	16	40	0	15	0	4	8	0	.25
97-98	Pho	76	12	9	21	-7	0	0	105	11.4	0	0	0	5	1	6	14	28	0	14	0	3	3	0	.28
98-99	Pho	77	9	10	19	-9	0	0	146	6.2	0	0	0	0	1	1	7	17	1	6	1	1	2	0	.25
95-96	Anh	48	5	7	12	0	1	0	88	5.7	0	0	0	0	1	1	13	26	0	13	0	3	4	0	.25
95-96	Phi	28	4	3	7	3	2	0	38	10.5	0	0	0	0	0	0	4	8	0	4	0	0	3	0	.25
9 Years		525	82	85	167	-33	9	2	874	9.4	3	5	8	10	5	15	104	225	3	100	3	–	–	0	.32
Postseason																									
Year	Tm	GP	G	A	Pts	+/-	GW	OT	S	SPct	G	A	Pts	G	A	Pts	Num	PIM	Maj	Mnr	Fgt	Rgh	HHT	Hat	P/G
89-90	Buf	5	1	0	1	0	0	0	4	25.0	0	0	0	0	0	0	2	4	0	2	0	–	–	0	.20
91-92	Buf	4	1	0	1	-1	0	0	9	11.1	1	0	1	0	0	0	0	0	0	0	0	0	0	0	.25
92-93	Buf	5	0	0	0	1	0	0	1	0.0	0	0	0	0	0	0	1	2	0	1	0	0	0	0	.00
95-96	Phi	12	1	2	3	-1	0	0	11	9.1	0	0	0	0	0	0	3	6	0	3	0	1	2	0	.25
96-97	Pho	7	2	2	4	-1	1	0	9	22.2	0	0	0	0	0	0	2	4	0	2	0	0	0	0	.57
97-98	Pho	6	1	0	1	-3	0	0	3	33.3	0	0	0	0	0	0	2	4	0	2	0	0	1	0	.17
98-99	Pho	7	0	1	1	1	0	0	6	0.0	0	0	0	0	0	0	2	4	0	2	0	0	1	0	.14
7 Years		46	6	5	11	-4	1	0	43	14.0	1	0	1	0	0	0	12	24	0	12	0	–	–	0	.24

Shayne Corson

(statistical profile on page 299)

Pos: LW **Shoots:** L **Ht:** 6'1" **Wt:** 199 **Born:** 8/13/66—Barrie, Ontario **Age:** 33

Overall											Power Play			Shorthand			Penalty							Misc	
Year	Tm	GP	G	A	Pts	+/-	GW	GT	S	SPct	G	A	Pts	G	A	Pts	Num	PIM	Maj	Mnr	Fgt	Rgh	HHT	Hat	P/G
85-86	Mon	3	0	0	0	-3	0	0	1	0.0	0	0	0	0	0	0	1	2	0	1	0	–	–	0	.00
86-87	Mon	55	12	11	23	10	3	0	69	17.4	0	–	–	1	–	–	–	144	–	–	–	–	–	0	.42
87-88	Mon	71	12	27	39	22	2	0	90	13.3	2	–	–	0	–	–	–	152	–	–	–	–	–	0	.55
88-89	Mon	**80**	26	24	50	-1	3	1	133	19.5	10	–	–	0	–	–	–	193	–	–	–	–	–	2	.63
89-90	Mon*	76	31	44	75	33	6	1	192	16.1	7	–	–	0	–	–	–	144	–	–	–	–	–	0	.99
90-91	Mon	71	23	24	47	9	2	1	164	14.0	7	–	–	0	–	–	–	138	–	–	–	–	–	0	.66
91-92	Mon	64	17	36	53	15	2	0	165	10.3	3	11	14	0	2	2	41	118	4	34	4	17	4	0	.83
92-93	Edm	80	16	31	47	-19	1	0	164	9.8	9	10	19	2	2	4	70	209	7	57	7	20	5	0	.59
93-94	Edm*	64	25	29	54	-8	3	1	171	14.6	11	10	21	0	0	0	41	118	4	34	3	13	6	1	.84
94-95	Edm	48	12	24	36	-17	1	0	131	9.2	2	9	11	0	1	1	21	86	4	13	4	3	0	0	.75
95-96	StL	77	18	28	46	3	0	2	150	12.0	13	9	22	0	1	1	67	192	6	56	5	15	11	0	.60
96-97	2Tm	58	8	16	24	-9	2	0	115	7.0	3	1	4	0	1	1	36	104	8	27	8	5	1	0	.41
97-98	Mon*	62	21	34	55	2	1	0	142	14.8	14	9	23	1	2	3	36	108	4	29	4	9	5	0	.89
98-99	Mon	63	12	20	32	-10	4	0	142	8.5	7	9	16	0	0	0	41	147	3	31	3	14	3	0	.51
96-97	StL	11	2	1	3	-4	0	0	19	10.5	1	0	1	0	0	0	9	24	2	7	2	1	0	0	.27
96-97	Mon	47	6	15	21	-5	2	0	96	6.3	2	1	3	0	1	1	27	80	6	20	6	4	1	0	.45
14 Years		872	233	348	581	27	30	6	1829	12.7	88	–	–	4	–	–	–	1855	–	–	–	–	–	3	.67
Postseason																									
Year	Tm	GP	G	A	Pts	+/-	GW	OT	S	SPct	G	A	Pts	G	A	Pts	Num	PIM	Maj	Mnr	Fgt	Rgh	HHT	Hat	P/G
86-87	Mon	17	6	5	11	4	1	0	30	20.0	1	–	–	1	–	–	–	30	–	–	–	–	–	0	.65
87-88	Mon	3	1	0	1	-3	0	0	9	11.1	0	0	0	0	0	0	–	12	–	–	–	–	–	0	.33
88-89	Mon	21	4	5	9	3	2	0	28	14.3	2	–	–	0	–	–	–	65	–	–	–	–	–	0	.43
89-90	Mon	11	2	8	10	8	0	0	29	6.9	0	–	–	0	0	0	–	20	–	–	–	–	–	0	.91
90-91	Mon	13	9	6	15	5	3	1	42	21.4	4	–	–	1	–	–	–	36	–	–	–	–	–	0	1.15
91-92	Mon	10	2	5	7	1	0	0	23	8.7	0	1	1	0	0	0	6	15	1	5	1	0	1	0	.70
95-96	StL	13	8	6	14	-1	1	0	37	21.6	6	3	9	1	0	1	11	22	0	11	0	7	2	0	1.08
96-97	Mon	5	1	0	1	-5	0	0	8	12.5	0	0	0	1	0	1	2	4	0	2	0	1	0	0	.20
97-98	Mon	10	3	6	9	3	1	0	33	9.1	1	2	3	0	0	0	9	26	0	8	0	2	1	0	.90
9 Years		103	36	41	77	15	8	1	239	15.1	14	–	–	4	–	–	–	230	–	–	–	–	–	0	.75

Patrick Cote

Pos: LW **Shoots:** L **Ht:** 6'3" **Wt:** 200 **Born:** 1/24/75—Lasalle, Quebec **Age:** 24

Overall											Power Play			Shorthand			Penalty							Misc	
Year	Tm	GP	G	A	Pts	+/-	GW	GT	S	SPct	G	A	Pts	G	A	Pts	Num	PIM	Maj	Mnr	Fgt	Rgh	HHT	Hat	P/G
95-96	Dal	2	0	0	0	-2	0	0	0	–	0	0	0	0	0	0	1	5	1	0	1	0	0	0	.00
96-97	Dal	3	0	0	0	0	0	0	1	0.0	0	0	0	0	0	0	5	27	3	1	3	0	0	0	.00
97-98	Dal	3	0	0	0	-1	0	0	3	0.0	0	0	0	0	0	0	3	15	3	0	3	0	0	0	.00
98-99	Nsh	70	1	2	3	-7	0	0	21	4.8	0	0	0	0	0	0	52	242	**30**	16	**30**	8	2	0	.04
4 Years		78	1	2	3	-10	0	0	25	4.0	0	0	0	0	0	0	61	289	37	17	37	8	2	0	.04

Sylvain Cote

(statistical profile on page 299)

Pos: D **Shoots:** R **Ht:** 6'0" **Wt:** 190 **Born:** 1/19/66—Quebec, Quebec **Age:** 33

Overall											Power Play			Shorthand			Penalty							Misc	
Year	Tm	GP	G	A	Pts	+/–	GW	GT	S	SPct	G	A	Pts	G	A	Pts	Num	PIM	Maj	Mnr	Fgt	Rgh	HHT	Hat	P/G
84-85	Har	67	3	9	12	-30	1	0	90	3.3	1	–	–	0	–	–	–	17	–	–	–	–	–	0	.18
85-86	Har	2	0	0	0	1	0	0	0	–	0	0	0	0	0	0	0	0	0	0	0	0	0	0	.00
86-87	Har	67	2	8	10	11	0	0	100	2.0	0	–	–	0	–	–	–	20	–	–	–	–	–	0	.15
87-88	Har	67	7	21	28	-8	0	0	142	4.9	0	–	–	1	–	–	–	30	–	–	–	–	–	0	.42
88-89	Har	78	8	9	17	-7	0	0	130	6.2	1	–	–	0	–	–	–	49	–	–	–	–	–	0	.22
89-90	Har	28	4	2	6	2	1	1	50	8.0	1	–	–	0	–	–	–	14	–	–	–	–	–	0	.21
90-91	Har	73	7	12	19	-17	0	0	154	4.5	1	–	–	0	–	–	–	17	–	–	–	–	–	0	.26
91-92	Was	78	11	29	40	7	2	0	151	7.3	6	14	20	0	1	1	14	31	1	13	1	0	9	0	.51
92-93	Was	77	21	29	50	28	3	0	206	10.2	8	9	17	2	1	3	17	34	0	17	0	2	7	0	.65
93-94	Was	84	16	35	51	30	2	0	212	7.5	3	11	14	2	0	2	33	66	0	33	0	1	19	0	.61
94-95	Was	47	5	14	19	2	2	0	124	4.0	1	6	7	0	3	3	17	53	1	14	0	0	10	0	.40
95-96	Was	81	5	33	38	5	2	0	212	2.4	3	11	14	0	2	2	20	40	0	20	0	2	13	0	.47
96-97	Was	57	6	18	24	11	0	0	131	4.6	2	7	9	0	0	0	14	28	0	14	0	6	6	0	.42
97-98	2Tm	71	4	21	25	-3	1	0	103	3.9	1	3	4	0	1	1	21	42	0	21	0	1	14	0	.35
98-99	Tor	79	5	24	29	22	1	0	119	4.2	0	9	9	0	0	0	14	28	0	14	0	2	7	0	.37
97-98	Was	59	1	15	16	-5	0	0	83	1.2	0	1	1	0	1	1	18	36	0	18	0	1	11	0	.27
97-98	Tor	12	3	6	9	2	1	0	20	15.0	1	2	3	0	0	0	3	6	0	3	0	0	3	0	.75
15 Years		956	104	264	368	54	15	1	1924	5.4	28	–	–	5	–	–	–	469	–	–	–	–	–	0	.38

Postseason																									
Year	Tm	GP	G	A	Pts	+/–	GW	OT	S	SPct	G	A	Pts	G	A	Pts	Num	PIM	Maj	Mnr	Fgt	Rgh	HHT	Hat	P/G
86-87	Har	2	0	2	2	4	0	0	2	0.0	0	–	–	0	0	0	1	2	0	1	0	–	–	0	1.00
87-88	Har	6	1	1	2	0	0	0	9	11.1	1	–	–	0	0	0	2	4	0	2	0	–	–	0	.33
88-89	Har	3	0	1	1	-3	0	0	2	0.0	0	–	–	0	–	–	2	4	0	2	0	–	–	0	.33
89-90	Har	5	0	0	0	0	0	0	10	0.0	0	0	0	0	0	0	1	2	0	1	0	–	–	0	.00
90-91	Har	6	0	2	2	2	0	0	10	0.0	0	–	–	0	–	–	1	2	0	1	0	–	–	0	.33
91-92	Was	7	1	2	3	4	0	0	13	7.7	0	0	0	0	0	0	2	4	0	2	0	0	1	0	.43
92-93	Was	6	1	1	2	-3	0	0	8	12.5	0	1	1	0	0	0	2	4	0	2	0	0	0	0	.33
93-94	Was	9	1	8	9	3	0	0	30	3.3	0	2	2	0	0	0	3	6	0	3	0	0	2	0	1.00
94-95	Was	7	1	3	4	-9	0	0	16	6.3	0	2	2	0	0	0	1	2	0	1	0	0	0	0	.57
95-96	Was	6	2	0	2	-3	0	0	25	8.0	1	0	1	0	0	0	6	12	0	6	0	0	3	0	.33
98-99	Tor	17	2	1	3	-3	0	0	19	10.5	0	0	0	0	0	0	5	10	0	5	0	0	4	0	.18
11 Years		74	9	21	30	-8	0	0	144	6.3	2	–	–	0	–	–	26	52	0	26	0	–	–	0	.41

Geoff Courtnall

(statistical profile on page 299)

Pos: LW **Shoots:** L **Ht:** 6'0" **Wt:** 195 **Born:** 8/18/62—Victoria, British Columbia **Age:** 37

Overall											Power Play			Shorthand			Penalty							Misc	
Year	Tm	GP	G	A	Pts	+/–	GW	GT	S	SPct	G	A	Pts	G	A	Pts	Num	PIM	Maj	Mnr	Fgt	Rgh	HHT	Hat	P/G
83-84	Bos	4	0	0	0	-1	0	0	1	0.0	0	0	0	0	0	0	0	0	0	0	0	0	0	0	.00
84-85	Bos	64	12	16	28	-3	1	0	91	13.2	0	–	–	0	–	–	–	82	–	–	–	–	–	0	.44
85-86	Bos	64	21	16	37	1	4	0	161	13.0	2	–	–	0	–	–	–	61	–	–	–	–	–	0	.58
86-87	Bos	65	13	23	36	-4	1	0	178	7.3	2	–	–	0	–	–	–	117	–	–	–	–	–	0	.55
87-88	2Tm	74	36	30	66	25	5	0	252	14.3	9	–	–	0	–	–	–	123	–	–	–	–	–	2	.89
88-89	Was	79	42	38	80	11	6	0	239	17.6	16	–	–	0	–	–	–	112	–	–	–	–	–	1	1.01
89-90	Was	**80**	35	39	74	27	2	1	307	11.4	9	–	–	0	–	–	–	104	–	–	–	–	–	1	.93
90-91	2Tm	77	33	32	65	16	8	0	263	12.5	12	–	–	0	–	–	–	64	–	–	–	–	–	0	.84
91-92	Van	70	23	34	57	-6	3	0	281	8.2	12	15	27	0	0	0	44	116	4	38	3	13	6	0	.81
92-93	Van	84	31	46	77	27	**11**	0	214	14.5	9	11	20	0	0	0	59	167	3	51	2	21	5	0	.92
93-94	Van	82	26	44	70	15	2	0	264	9.8	12	17	29	1	2	3	48	123	1	44	1	14	8	0	.85
94-95	Van	45	16	18	34	2	1	0	144	11.1	7	9	16	0	0	0	32	81	3	28	3	10	5	0	.76
95-96	StL	69	24	16	40	-9	1	2	228	10.5	7	7	14	1	0	1	41	101	1	38	1	8	6	1	.58
96-97	StL	**82**	17	40	57	3	2	0	203	8.4	4	10	14	0	0	0	36	86	2	33	2	5	9	0	.70
97-98	StL	79	31	31	62	12	5	0	189	16.4	6	8	14	0	0	0	41	94	4	37	4	8	5	1	.78
98-99	StL	24	5	7	12	2	2	0	60	8.3	1	2	3	0	0	0	14	28	0	14	0	3	6	0	.50
87-88	Bos	62	32	26	58	24	4	0	220	14.5	9	–	–	0	–	–	–	108	–	–	–	–	–	1	.94
87-88	Edm	12	4	4	8	1	1	0	32	12.5	0	–	–	0	–	–	–	15	–	–	–	–	–	1	.67
90-91	StL	66	27	30	57	19	6	0	216	12.5	9	–	–	0	–	–	–	56	–	–	–	–	–	0	.86
90-91	Van	11	6	2	8	-3	2	0	47	12.8	3	–	–	0	–	–	4	8	0	4	0	–	–	0	.73
16 Years		1042	365	430	795	118	54	3	3075	11.9	108	–	–	2	–	–	–	1459	–	–	–	–	–	6	.76

Postseason																									
Year	Tm	GP	G	A	Pts	+/–	GW	OT	S	SPct	G	A	Pts	G	A	Pts	Num	PIM	Maj	Mnr	Fgt	Rgh	HHT	Hat	P/G
84-85	Bos	5	0	2	2	-3	0	0	3	0.0	0	–	–	0	0	0	2	7	1	1	–	–	–	0	.40
85-86	Bos	3	0	0	0	-4	0	0	3	0.0	0	0	0	0	0	0	1	2	0	1	0	–	–	0	.00
86-87	Bos	1	0	0	0	0	0	0	2	0.0	0	0	0	0	0	0	0	0	0	0	0	0	0	0	.00

Postseason																										
Year	Tm	GP	G	A	Pts	+/–	GW	OT	S	SPct	G	A	Pts	G	A	Pts	Num	PIM	Maj	Mnr	Fgt	Rgh	HHT	Hat	P/G
87-88	Edm	19	0	3	3	2	0	0	33	0.0	0	–	–	0	–	–	–	67	–	–	–	–	–	0	.16
88-89	Was	6	2	5	7	2	0	0	19	10.5	1	–	–	0	–	–	–	12	–	–	–	–	–	0	1.17
89-90	Was	15	4	9	13	-3	2	0	49	8.2	1	–	–	0	–	–	–	32	–	–	–	–	–	0	.87
90-91	Van	6	3	5	8	2	0	0	26	11.5	0	–	–	0	–	–	2	4	0	2	0	–	–	1	1.33
91-92	Van	12	6	8	14	4	1	0	41	14.6	2	1	3	0	0	0	6	20	0	5	0	1	1	1	1.17
92-93	Van	12	4	10	14	7	1	0	43	9.3	1	2	3	0	0	0	6	12	0	6	0	2	1	0	1.17
93-94	Van	24	9	10	19	10	3	1	77	11.7	0	2	2	1	0	1	16	51	1	13	0	4	2	0	.79
94-95	Van	11	4	2	6	-8	1	0	31	12.9	3	1	4	1	0	1	13	34	0	12	0	3	0	0	.55
95-96	StL	13	0	3	3	2	0	0	26	0.0	0	0	0	0	0	0	7	14	0	7	0	0	1	0	.23
96-97	StL	6	3	1	4	0	2	0	11	27.3	1	1	2	0	0	0	6	23	1	4	0	0	2	0	.67
97-98	StL	10	2	8	10	-2	0	0	24	8.3	1	3	4	0	0	0	9	18	0	9	0	2	4	0	1.00
98-99	StL	13	2	4	6	-4	0	0	18	11.1	2	2	4	0	0	0	5	10	0	5	0	1	0	0	.46
15 Years		156	39	70	109	5	10	1	406	9.6	12	–	–	2	–	–	–	306	–	–	–	–	–	2	.70

Russ Courtnall

(statistical profile on page 299)

Pos: RW **Shoots:** R **Ht:** 5'11" **Wt:** 195 **Born:** 6/2/65—Duncan, British Columbia **Age:** 34

Overall											Power Play			Shorthand			Penalty							Misc	
Year	Tm	GP	G	A	Pts	+/–	GW	GT	S	SPct	G	A	Pts	G	A	Pts	Num	PIM	Maj	Mnr	Fgt	Rgh	HHT	Hat	P/G
83-84	Tor	14	3	9	12	0	0	0	29	10.3	1	–	–	0	–	–	3	6	0	3	0	–	–	0	.86
84-85	Tor	69	12	10	22	-23	1	0	130	9.2	0	–	–	2	–	–	–	44	–	–	–	–	–	0	.32
85-86	Tor	73	22	38	60	0	4	0	203	10.8	3	–	–	1	–	–	–	52	–	–	–	–	–	1	.82
86-87	Tor	79	29	44	73	-20	3	0	282	10.3	3	–	–	6	–	–	–	90	–	–	–	–	–	0	.92
87-88	Tor	65	23	26	49	-16	1	1	212	10.8	6	–	–	3	–	–	–	47	–	–	–	–	–	0	.75
88-89	2Tm	73	23	18	41	9	3	0	147	15.6	7	–	–	1	–	–	–	19	–	–	–	–	–	0	.56
89-90	Mon	**80**	27	32	59	14	2	2	294	9.2	3	–	–	0	–	–	–	27	–	–	–	–	–	1	.74
90-91	Mon	79	26	50	76	5	5	1	279	9.3	5	–	–	1	–	–	–	29	–	–	–	–	–	0	.96
91-92	Mon	27	7	14	21	6	1	1	63	11.1	0	2	2	1	0	1	3	6	0	3	0	0	1	0	.78
92-93	Min	84	36	43	79	1	3	2	294	12.2	14	14	28	2	1	3	15	49	1	12	1	0	6	1	.94
93-94	Dal*	84	23	57	80	6	4	0	231	10.0	5	16	21	0	0	0	20	59	1	17	1	4	7	0	.95
94-95	2Tm	45	11	24	35	2	2	0	132	8.3	2	10	12	2	1	3	7	17	1	6	1	1	4	1	.78
95-96	Van	81	26	39	65	25	4	2	205	12.7	6	4	10	4	5	**9**	16	40	0	15	0	2	6	1	.80
96-97	2Tm	61	11	24	35	1	2	0	125	8.8	2	7	9	1	1	2	10	26	2	8	2	3	1	0	.57
97-98	LA	58	12	6	18	-2	4	0	97	12.4	1	3	4	4	0	4	12	27	1	11	1	1	4	0	.31
98-99	LA	57	6	13	19	-9	1	0	77	7.8	0	0	0	1	1	2	8	19	1	7	1	0	1	0	.33
88-89	Tor	9	1	1	2	-2	0	0	11	9.1	0	–	–	1	–	–	2	4	0	2	0	–	–	0	.22
88-89	Mon	64	22	17	39	11	3	0	136	16.2	7	–	–	0	–	–	–	15	–	–	–	–	–	0	.61
94-95	Dal	32	7	10	17	-8	1	0	90	7.8	2	5	7	0	0	0	5	13	1	4	1	0	4	0	.53
94-95	Van	13	4	14	18	10	1	0	42	9.5	0	5	5	2	1	3	2	4	0	2	0	1	0	1	1.38
96-97	Van	47	9	19	28	4	1	0	101	8.9	1	5	6	0	1	1	9	24	2	7	2	2	1	0	.60
96-97	NYR	14	2	5	7	-3	1	0	24	8.3	1	2	3	1	0	1	1	2	0	1	0	1	0	0	.50
16 Years		1029	297	447	744	-1	40	9	2800	10.6	58	–	–	29	–	–	–	557	–	–	–	–	–	5	.72

Postseason																									
Year	Tm	GP	G	A	Pts	+/–	GW	OT	S	SPct	G	A	Pts	G	A	Pts	Num	PIM	Maj	Mnr	Fgt	Rgh	HHT	Hat	P/G
85-86	Tor	10	3	6	9	2	0	0	32	9.4	1	–	–	0	0	0	4	8	0	4	0	–	–	0	.90
86-87	Tor	13	3	4	7	1	0	0	31	9.7	1	–	–	0	0	0	4	11	1	3	–	–	–	0	.54
87-88	Tor	6	2	1	3	-5	0	0	10	20.0	0	–	–	0	–	–	0	0	0	0	0	0	0	0	.50
88-89	Mon	21	8	5	13	12	2	1	53	15.1	1	–	–	0	–	–	–	18	–	–	–	–	–	0	.62
89-90	Mon	11	5	1	6	1	0	0	38	13.2	0	–	–	0	0	0	–	10	–	–	–	–	–	0	.55
90-91	Mon	13	8	3	11	3	1	1	51	15.7	2	–	–	2	–	–	2	7	1	1	–	–	–	0	.85
91-92	Mon	10	1	1	2	-2	1	1	14	7.1	0	0	0	0	0	0	2	4	0	2	0	0	1	0	.20
93-94	Dal	9	1	8	9	-3	0	0	41	2.4	0	5	5	0	0	0	0	0	0	0	0	0	0	0	1.00
94-95	Van	11	4	8	12	1	1	0	27	14.8	0	2	2	2	2	4	5	21	1	3	1	0	1	0	1.09
95-96	Van	6	1	3	4	-4	0	0	8	12.5	0	1	1	0	0	0	1	2	0	1	0	0	1	0	.67
96-97	NYR	15	3	4	7	1	0	0	27	11.1	1	1	2	0	0	0	0	0	0	0	0	0	0	0	.47
97-98	LA	4	0	0	0	-2	0	0	7	0.0	0	0	0	0	0	0	1	2	0	1	0	0	0	0	.00
12 Years		129	39	44	83	5	5	3	339	11.5	6	–	–	4	–	–	–	83	–	–	–	–	–	0	.64

Marcel Cousineau

Pos: G **Catches:** L **Ht:** 5'9" **Wt:** 170 **Born:** 4/30/73—Delson, Quebec **Age:** 26

Overall															Pen Shot		Offense		
Year	Tm	GP	GS	TP	W	L	T	Min	GA	GAA	Shots	SvPct	ShO	OE	PPGA	SHGA	Shots	GA	G	A	PIM
96-97	Tor	13	8	2	3	5	1	566	31	3.29	317	.902	1	2	6	0	0	0	0	1	0
97-98	Tor	2	0	1	0	0	0	17	0	0.00	9	1.000	0	0	0	0	0	0	0	0	0
98-99	NYI	6	4	0	0	4	0	293	14	2.87	119	.882	0	0	4	1	0	0	0	0	0
3 Years		21	12	3	3	9	1	876	45	3.08	445	.899	1	2	10	1	0	0	0	1	0

Mike Craig

Pos: RW **Shoots:** R **Ht:** 6'1" **Wt:** 180 **Born:** 6/6/71—London, Ontario **Age:** 28

Overall											Power Play			Shorthand			Penalty							Misc	
Year	Tm	GP	G	A	Pts	+/-	GW	GT	S	SPct	G	A	Pts	G	A	Pts	Num	PIM	Maj	Mnr	Fgt	Rgh	HHT	Hat	P/G
90-91	Min	39	8	4	12	-11	2	0	59	13.6	1	–	–	0	–	–	–	32	–	–	–	–	–	0	.31
91-92	Min	67	15	16	31	-12	4	0	136	11.0	4	5	9	0	0	0	50	155	5	40	3	7	15	0	.46
92-93	Min	70	15	23	38	-11	0	0	131	11.5	7	11	18	0	0	0	41	106	0	38	0	9	6	0	.54
93-94	Dal	72	13	24	37	-14	2	0	150	8.7	3	8	11	0	0	0	49	139	3	42	2	10	7	0	.51
94-95	Tor	37	5	5	10	-21	1	0	61	8.2	1	0	1	0	0	0	6	12	0	6	0	1	2	0	.27
95-96	Tor	70	8	12	20	-8	1	0	108	7.4	1	0	1	0	0	0	21	42	0	21	0	6	4	0	.29
96-97	Tor	65	7	13	20	-20	0	0	128	5.5	1	2	3	0	0	0	27	62	0	26	0	3	7	0	.31
97-98											Did Not Play in NHL														
98-99	SJ	1	0	0	0	-1	0	0	1	0.0	0	0	0	0	0	0	0	0	0	0	0	0	0	0	.00
8 Years		421	71	97	168	-98	10	0	774	9.2	18	–	–	0	–	–	–	548	–	–	–	–	–	0	.40

Postseason																									
Year	Tm	GP	G	A	Pts	+/-	GW	OT	S	SPct	G	A	Pts	G	A	Pts	Num	PIM	Maj	Mnr	Fgt	Rgh	HHT	Hat	P/G
90-91	Min	10	1	1	2	-2	1	0	12	8.3	1	–	–	0	–	–	–	20	–	–	–	–	–	0	.20
91-92	Min	4	1	0	1	0	0	0	1	100.0	0	0	0	0	0	0	2	7	1	1	1	0	1	0	.25
93-94	Dal	4	0	0	0	-1	0	0	6	0.0	0	0	0	0	0	0	1	2	0	1	0	1	0	0	.00
94-95	Tor	2	0	1	1	0	0	0	7	0.0	0	0	0	0	0	0	1	2	0	1	0	1	0	0	.50
95-96	Tor	6	0	0	0	0	0	0	7	0.0	0	0	0	0	0	0	5	18	0	4	0	1	0	0	.00
5 Years		26	2	2	4	-3	1	0	33	6.1	1	–	–	0	–	–	–	49	–	–	–	–	–	0	.15

Murray Craven

(statistical profile on page 300)

Pos: LW **Shoots:** L **Ht:** 6'3" **Wt:** 190 **Born:** 7/20/64—Medicine Hat, Alberta **Age:** 35

Overall											Power Play			Shorthand			Penalty							Misc	
Year	Tm	GP	G	A	Pts	+/-	GW	GT	S	SPct	G	A	Pts	G	A	Pts	Num	PIM	Maj	Mnr	Fgt	Rgh	HHT	Hat	P/G
82-83	Det	31	4	7	11	4	1	0	21	19.0	0	–	–	0	–	–	3	6	0	3	0	–	–	0	.35
83-84	Det	15	0	4	4	2	0	0	8	0.0	0	–	–	0	–	–	3	6	0	3	0	–	–	0	.27
84-85	Phi	**80**	26	35	61	45	5	0	142	18.3	2	–	–	2	–	–	–	30	–	–	–	–	–	0	.76
85-86	Phi	78	21	33	54	24	6	0	182	11.5	2	–	–	0	–	–	–	34	–	–	–	–	–	0	.69
86-87	Phi	77	19	30	49	1	2	0	98	19.4	5	–	–	3	–	–	–	38	–	–	–	–	–	1	.64
87-88	Phi	72	30	46	76	25	2	1	184	16.3	6	–	–	2	–	–	–	58	–	–	–	–	–	1	1.06
88-89	Phi	51	9	28	37	4	2	0	89	10.1	0	–	–	0	–	–	–	52	–	–	–	–	–	0	.73
89-90	Phi	76	25	50	75	2	3	0	175	14.3	7	–	–	2	–	–	–	42	–	–	–	–	–	0	.99
90-91	Phi	77	19	47	66	-2	0	0	170	11.2	6	–	–	0	–	–	–	53	–	–	–	–	–	0	.86
91-92	2Tm	73	27	33	60	-2	1	1	152	17.8	9	6	15	4	2	6	20	46	2	18	2	0	12	1	.82
92-93	2Tm	77	25	52	77	-1	2	0	151	16.6	6	22	28	3	3	6	16	32	0	16	0	1	8	0	1.00
93-94	Van	78	15	40	55	5	3	0	115	13.0	2	12	14	1	3	4	15	30	0	15	0	1	8	0	.71
94-95	Chi	16	4	3	7	2	2	0	29	13.8	1	0	1	0	0	0	1	2	0	1	0	0	0	0	.44
95-96	Chi	66	18	29	47	20	7	0	86	20.9	5	1	6	1	1	2	18	36	0	18	0	0	11	0	.71
96-97	Chi	75	8	27	35	0	1	0	122	6.6	2	7	9	0	0	0	6	12	0	6	0	0	3	0	.47
97-98	SJ	67	12	17	29	4	3	0	107	11.2	2	3	5	3	0	3	11	25	1	10	1	2	4	0	.43
98-99	SJ	43	4	10	14	-3	1	0	55	7.3	0	3	3	1	0	1	9	18	0	9	0	1	3	0	.33
91-92	Phi	12	3	3	6	2	0	0	19	15.8	1	0	1	0	1	1	4	8	0	4	0	0	1	0	.50
91-92	Har	61	24	30	54	-4	1	1	133	18.0	8	6	14	4	1	5	16	38	2	14	2	0	11	1	.89
92-93	Har	67	25	42	67	-4	2	0	139	18.0	6	16	22	3	3	6	10	20	0	10	0	1	3	0	1.00
92-93	Van	10	0	10	10	3	0	0	12	0.0	0	6	6	0	0	0	6	12	0	6	0	0	5	0	1.00
17 Years		1052	266	491	757	130	41	2	1886	14.1	55	–	–	22	–	–	–	520	–	–	–	–	–	3	.72

Postseason																									
Year	Tm	GP	G	A	Pts	+/-	GW	OT	S	SPct	G	A	Pts	G	A	Pts	Num	PIM	Maj	Mnr	Fgt	Rgh	HHT	Hat	P/G
84-85	Phi	19	4	6	10	6	1	0	38	10.5	1	–	–	1	–	–	4	11	1	3	–	–	–	0	.53
85-86	Phi	5	0	3	3	0	0	0	10	0.0	0	–	–	0	0	0	2	4	0	2	0	–	–	0	.60
86-87	Phi	12	3	1	4	-4	0	0	15	20.0	2	–	–	0	–	–	3	9	1	2	–	–	–	0	.33
87-88	Phi	7	2	5	7	1	1	1	13	15.4	0	–	–	0	0	0	2	4	0	2	0	–	–	0	1.00
88-89	Phi	1	0	0	0	-1	0	0	2	0.0	0	0	0	0	0	0	1	2	0	1	0	–	–	0	.00
91-92	Har	7	3	3	6	0	0	0	20	15.0	0	2	2	1	0	1	3	6	0	3	0	0	1	0	.86
92-93	Van	12	4	6	10	0	1	0	27	14.8	1	3	4	0	0	0	2	4	0	2	0	0	0	0	.83
93-94	Van	22	4	9	13	10	1	0	38	10.5	0	0	0	0	0	0	9	18	0	9	0	0	5	0	.59
94-95	Chi	16	5	5	10	2	1	0	28	17.9	0	1	1	0	0	0	2	4	0	2	0	0	0	0	.63
95-96	Chi	9	1	4	5	-1	0	0	17	5.9	1	0	1	0	0	0	1	2	0	1	0	1	0	0	.56
96-97	Chi	2	0	0	0	-4	0	0	5	0.0	0	0	0	0	0	0	1	2	0	1	0	0	0	0	.00
97-98	SJ	6	1	1	2	-2	0	0	6	16.7	0	1	1	0	0	0	0	0	0	0	0	0	0	0	.33
12 Years		118	27	43	70	7	5	1	219	12.3	5	–	–	2	–	–	30	66	2	28	–	–	–	0	.59

Cory Cross

(statistical profile on page 300)

Pos: D **Shoots:** L **Ht:** 6'5" **Wt:** 227 **Born:** 1/3/71—Lloydminster, Alberta **Age:** 28

Overall											Power Play			Shorthand			Penalty							Misc	
Year	Tm	GP	G	A	Pts	+/-	GW	GT	S	SPct	G	A	Pts	G	A	Pts	Num	PIM	Maj	Mnr	Fgt	Rgh	HHT	Hat	P/G
93-94	TB	5	0	0	0	-3	0	0	5	0.0	0	0	0	0	0	0	3	6	0	3	0	0	2	0	.00
94-95	TB	43	1	5	6	-6	1	0	35	2.9	0	3	3	0	0	0	16	41	3	13	2	2	4	0	.14
95-96	TB	75	2	14	16	4	0	0	57	3.5	0	0	0	0	0	0	33	66	0	33	0	7	12	0	.21
96-97	TB	72	4	5	9	6	2	0	75	5.3	0	0	0	0	0	0	42	95	1	40	1	3	18	0	.13
97-98	TB	74	3	6	9	-24	0	0	72	4.2	0	1	1	1	0	1	37	77	1	36	1	4	12	0	.12
98-99	TB	67	2	16	18	-25	0	0	96	2.1	0	5	5	0	1	1	39	92	2	36	1	5	10	0	.27
6 Years		336	12	46	58	-48	3	0	340	3.5	0	9	9	1	1	2	170	377	7	161	5	21	58	0	.17
Postseason																									
Year	Tm	GP	G	A	Pts	+/-	GW	OT	S	SPct	G	A	Pts	G	A	Pts	Num	PIM	Maj	Mnr	Fgt	Rgh	HHT	Hat	P/G
95-96	TB	6	0	0	0	-4	0	0	6	0.0	0	0	0	0	0	0	7	22	0	6	0	4	1	0	.00

Philip Crowe

Pos: LW **Shoots:** L **Ht:** 6'2" **Wt:** 230 **Born:** 4/4/70—Nanton, Alberta **Age:** 29

Overall											Power Play			Shorthand			Penalty							Misc	
Year	Tm	GP	G	A	Pts	+/-	GW	GT	S	SPct	G	A	Pts	G	A	Pts	Num	PIM	Maj	Mnr	Fgt	Rgh	HHT	Hat	P/G
93-94	LA	31	0	2	2	4	0	0	5	0.0	0	0	0	0	0	0	18	77	11	6	11	1	0	0	.06
94-95											Did Not Play in NHL														
95-96	Phi	16	1	1	2	0	0	0	6	16.7	0	0	0	0	0	0	8	28	4	4	4	3	0	0	.13
96-97	Ott	26	0	1	1	0	0	0	8	0.0	0	0	0	0	0	0	6	30	6	0	6	0	0	0	.04
97-98	Ott	9	3	0	3	3	1	0	6	50.0	0	0	0	0	0	0	6	24	4	2	4	0	0	0	.33
98-99	Ott	8	0	1	1	1	0	0	2	0.0	0	0	0	0	0	0	2	4	0	2	0	0	1	0	.13
5 Years		90	4	5	9	8	1	0	27	14.8	0	0	0	0	0	0	40	163	25	14	25	4	1	0	.10
Postseason																									
Year	Tm	GP	G	A	Pts	+/-	GW	OT	S	SPct	G	A	Pts	G	A	Pts	Num	PIM	Maj	Mnr	Fgt	Rgh	HHT	Hat	P/G
96-97	Ott	3	0	0	0	0	0	0	1	0.0	0	0	0	0	0	0	4	16	0	3	0	1	0	0	.00

Mike Crowley

Pos: D **Shoots:** L **Ht:** 5'11" **Wt:** 190 **Born:** 7/4/75—Bloomington, Minnesota **Age:** 24

Overall											Power Play			Shorthand			Penalty							Misc	
Year	Tm	GP	G	A	Pts	+/-	GW	GT	S	SPct	G	A	Pts	G	A	Pts	Num	PIM	Maj	Mnr	Fgt	Rgh	HHT	Hat	P/G
97-98	Anh	8	2	2	4	0	1	0	17	11.8	0	0	0	0	0	0	4	8	0	4	0	0	2	0	.50
98-99	Anh	20	2	3	5	-10	1	0	41	4.9	1	2	3	0	0	0	8	16	0	8	0	1	4	0	.25
2 Years		28	4	5	9	-10	2	0	58	6.9	1	2	3	0	0	0	12	24	0	12	0	1	6	0	.32

Ted Crowley

Pos: D **Shoots:** R **Ht:** 6'2" **Wt:** 188 **Born:** 5/3/70—Concord, Massachusetts **Age:** 29

Overall											Power Play			Shorthand			Penalty							Misc	
Year	Tm	GP	G	A	Pts	+/-	GW	GT	S	SPct	G	A	Pts	G	A	Pts	Num	PIM	Maj	Mnr	Fgt	Rgh	HHT	Hat	P/G
93-94	Har	21	1	2	3	-1	0	0	28	3.6	1	0	1	0	0	0	5	10	0	5	0	0	3	0	.14
94-95											Did Not Play in NHL														
95-96											Did Not Play in NHL														
96-97											Did Not Play in NHL														
97-98											Did Not Play in NHL														
98-99	2Tm	13	1	2	3	-1	0	0	20	5.0	1	1	2	0	0	0	1	2	0	1	0	0	1	0	.23
98-99	Col	7	0	1	1	-1	0	0	10	0.0	0	1	1	0	0	0	1	2	0	1	0	0	1	0	.14
98-99	NYI	6	1	1	2	0	0	0	10	10.0	1	0	1	0	0	0	0	0	0	0	0	0	0	0	.33
2 Years		34	2	4	6	-2	0	0	48	4.2	2	1	3	0	0	0	6	12	0	6	0	0	4	0	.18

John Cullen

Pos: C **Shoots:** R **Ht:** 5'10" **Wt:** 182 **Born:** 8/2/64—Puslinch, Ontario **Age:** 35

Overall											Power Play			Shorthand			Penalty							Misc	
Year	Tm	GP	G	A	Pts	+/-	GW	GT	S	SPct	G	A	Pts	G	A	Pts	Num	PIM	Maj	Mnr	Fgt	Rgh	HHT	Hat	P/G
88-89	Pit	79	12	37	49	-25	0	0	121	9.9	8	–	–	0	–	–	–	112	–	–	–	–	–	0	.62
89-90	Pit	72	32	60	92	-13	4	0	197	16.2	9	20	29	0	–	–	–	138	–	–	–	–	–	1	1.28
90-91	2Tm*	78	39	71	110	-6	3	1	205	19.0	14	–	–	0	–	–	–	101	–	–	–	–	–	1	1.41
91-92	Har*	77	26	51	77	-28	4	0	172	15.1	10	26	36	0	0	0	39	141	5	28	4	13	6	1	1.00
92-93	2Tm	66	18	32	50	-23	1	0	124	14.5	13	17	30	0	0	0	32	111	5	23	3	6	6	0	.76
93-94	Tor	53	13	17	30	-2	4	1	80	16.3	2	4	6	0	0	0	25	67	3	21	3	11	3	0	.57

		Overall									Power Play			Shorthand			Penalty							Misc	
Year	Tm	GP	G	A	Pts	+/–	GW	GT	S	SPct	G	A	Pts	G	A	Pts	Num	PIM	Maj	Mnr	Fgt	Rgh	HHT	Hat	P/G
94-95	Pit	46	13	24	37	-4	1	0	88	14.8	2	7	9	0	0	0	22	66	2	18	1	6	5	0	.80
95-96	TB	76	16	34	50	1	3	0	152	10.5	8	12	20	0	0	0	31	65	1	30	0	10	10	0	.66
96-97	TB	70	18	37	55	-14	2	1	116	15.5	5	18	23	0	0	0	30	95	1	25	1	10	2	0	.79
97-98											Did Not Play in NHL														
98-99	TB	4	0	0	0	-2	0	0	3	0.0	0	0	0	0	0	0	1	2	0	1	0	0	1	0	.00
90-91	Pit	65	31	63	94	0	2	1	171	18.1	10	25	35	0	–	–	–	83	–	–	–	–	–	1	1.45
90-91	Har	13	8	8	16	-6	1	0	34	23.5	4	–	–	0	–	–	–	18	–	–	–	–	–	0	1.23
92-93	Har	19	5	4	9	-15	0	0	38	13.2	3	1	4	0	0	0	14	58	2	9	0	1	1	0	.47
92-93	Tor	47	13	28	41	-8	1	0	86	15.1	10	16	26	0	0	0	18	53	3	14	3	5	5	0	.87
10 Years		621	187	363	550	-116	22	3	1258	14.9	71	–	–	0	–	–	–	898	–	–	–	–	–	3	.89
Postseason																									
Year	Tm	GP	G	A	Pts	+/–	GW	OT	S	SPct	G	A	Pts	G	A	Pts	Num	PIM	Maj	Mnr	Fgt	Rgh	HHT	Hat	P/G
88-89	Pit	11	3	6	9	4	0	0	20	15.0	0	–	–	0	–	–	–	28	–	–	–	–	–	0	.82
90-91	Har	6	2	7	9	0	0	0	10	20.0	0	–	–	0	–	–	–	10	–	–	–	–	–	0	1.50
91-92	Har	7	2	1	3	-2	1	0	18	11.1	1	1	2	0	0	0	6	12	0	6	0	0	1	0	.43
92-93	Tor	12	2	3	5	-1	0	0	10	20.0	1	1	2	0	0	0	0	0	0	0	0	0	0	0	.42
93-94	Tor	3	0	0	0	0	0	0	3	0.0	0	0	0	0	0	0	0	0	0	0	0	0	0	0	.00
94-95	Pit	9	0	2	2	-4	0	0	7	0.0	0	1	1	0	0	0	4	8	0	4	0	3	1	0	.22
95-96	TB	5	3	3	6	4	0	0	6	50.0	0	1	1	1	0	1	0	0	0	0	0	0	0	0	1.20
7 Years		53	12	22	34	1	1	0	74	16.2	2	–	–	1	–	–	–	58	–	–	–	–	–	0	.64

Matt Cullen

(statistical profile on page 300)

Pos: C **Shoots:** L **Ht:** 6'1" **Wt:** 195 **Born:** 11/2/76—Virginia, Minnesota **Age:** 23

		Overall									Power Play			Shorthand			Penalty							Misc	
Year	Tm	GP	G	A	Pts	+/–	GW	GT	S	SPct	G	A	Pts	G	A	Pts	Num	PIM	Maj	Mnr	Fgt	Rgh	HHT	Hat	P/G
97-98	Anh	61	6	21	27	-4	0	0	75	8.0	2	4	6	0	0	0	10	23	1	9	1	0	6	0	.44
98-99	Anh	75	11	14	25	-12	1	1	112	9.8	5	2	7	1	0	1	22	47	1	21	1	2	9	0	.33
2 Years		136	17	35	52	-16	1	1	187	9.1	7	6	13	1	0	1	32	70	2	30	2	2	15	0	.38
Postseason																									
Year	Tm	GP	G	A	Pts	+/–	GW	OT	S	SPct	G	A	Pts	G	A	Pts	Num	PIM	Maj	Mnr	Fgt	Rgh	HHT	Hat	P/G
98-99	Anh	4	0	0	0	-2	0	0	6	0.0	0	0	0	0	0	0	0	0	0	0	0	0	0	0	.00

Jassen Cullimore

(statistical profile on page 300)

Pos: D **Shoots:** L **Ht:** 6'5" **Wt:** 234 **Born:** 12/4/72—Simcoe, Ontario **Age:** 27

		Overall									Power Play			Shorthand			Penalty							Misc	
Year	Tm	GP	G	A	Pts	+/–	GW	GT	S	SPct	G	A	Pts	G	A	Pts	Num	PIM	Maj	Mnr	Fgt	Rgh	HHT	Hat	P/G
94-95	Van	34	1	2	3	-2	0	0	30	3.3	0	0	0	0	1	1	11	39	3	7	2	0	5	0	.09
95-96	Van	27	1	1	2	4	1	0	12	8.3	0	0	0	0	0	0	9	21	1	8	1	1	3	0	.07
96-97	2Tm	52	2	6	8	2	1	0	54	3.7	0	3	3	1	0	1	22	44	0	22	0	3	4	0	.15
97-98	2Tm	28	1	2	3	-4	0	0	18	5.6	1	1	2	0	1	1	13	26	0	13	0	1	6	0	.11
98-99	TB	78	5	12	17	-22	1	0	73	6.8	1	3	4	1	0	1	39	81	1	38	1	3	20	0	.22
96-97	Van	3	0	0	0	-2	0	0	2	0.0	0	0	0	0	0	0	1	2	0	1	0	0	1	0	.00
96-97	Mon	49	2	6	8	4	1	0	52	3.8	0	3	3	1	0	1	21	42	0	21	0	3	3	0	.16
97-98	Mon	3	0	0	0	0	0	0	1	0.0	0	0	0	0	0	0	2	4	0	2	0	0	0	0	.00
97-98	TB	25	1	2	3	-4	0	0	17	5.9	1	1	2	0	1	1	11	22	0	11	0	1	6	0	.12
5 Years		219	10	23	33	-22	3	0	187	5.3	2	7	9	2	2	4	94	211	5	88	4	8	38	0	.15
Postseason																									
Year	Tm	GP	G	A	Pts	+/–	GW	OT	S	SPct	G	A	Pts	G	A	Pts	Num	PIM	Maj	Mnr	Fgt	Rgh	HHT	Hat	P/G
94-95	Van	11	0	0	0	-4	0	0	9	0.0	0	0	0	0	0	0	6	12	0	6	0	2	2	0	.00
96-97	Mon	2	0	0	0	-1	0	0	0	–	0	0	0	0	0	0	1	2	0	1	0	0	0	0	.00
2 Years		13	0	0	0	-5	0	0	9	0.0	0	0	0	0	0	0	7	14	0	7	0	2	2	0	.00

Jim Cummins

Pos: RW **Shoots:** R **Ht:** 6'2" **Wt:** 219 **Born:** 5/17/70—Dearborn, Michigan **Age:** 29

		Overall									Power Play			Shorthand			Penalty							Misc	
Year	Tm	GP	G	A	Pts	+/–	GW	GT	S	SPct	G	A	Pts	G	A	Pts	Num	PIM	Maj	Mnr	Fgt	Rgh	HHT	Hat	P/G
91-92	Det	1	0	0	0	0	0	0	0	–	0	0	0	0	0	0	2	7	1	1	1	1	0	0	.00
92-93	Det	7	1	1	2	0	0	0	5	20.0	0	0	0	0	0	0	11	58	4	4	4	1	0	0	.29
93-94	2Tm	26	1	2	3	-1	0	0	20	5.0	0	0	0	0	0	0	26	84	8	17	8	7	4	0	.12
94-95	2Tm	37	4	1	5	-6	1	0	23	17.4	0	0	0	0	0	0	32	158	18	9	16	0	3	0	.14
95-96	Chi	52	2	4	6	-1	2	0	34	5.9	0	0	0	0	0	0	46	180	16	25	15	9	5	0	.12
96-97	Chi	65	6	6	12	4	0	1	61	9.8	0	0	0	0	0	0	47	199	19	22	19	11	2	0	.18

		Overall									Power Play			Shorthand			Penalty							Misc	
Year	Tm	GP	G	A	Pts	+/–	GW	GT	S	SPct	G	A	Pts	G	A	Pts	Num	PIM	Maj	Mnr	Fgt	Rgh	HHT	Hat	P/G
97-98	2Tm	75	0	2	2	-16	0	0	43	0.0	0	0	0	0	0	0	60	225	19	35	19	6	6	0	.03
98-99	Pho	55	1	7	8	3	0	0	26	3.8	0	0	0	0	0	0	43	190	16	20	14	5	4	0	.15
93-94	Phi	22	1	2	3	0	0	0	17	5.9	0	0	0	0	0	0	21	71	7	13	7	6	3	0	.14
93-94	TB	4	0	0	0	-1	0	0	3	0.0	0	0	0	0	0	0	5	13	1	4	1	1	1	0	.00
94-95	TB	10	1	0	1	-3	1	0	3	33.3	0	0	0	0	0	0	9	41	5	3	5	0	0	0	.10
94-95	Chi	27	3	1	4	-3	0	0	20	15.0	0	0	0	0	0	0	23	117	13	6	11	0	3	0	.15
97-98	Chi	55	0	2	2	-9	0	0	33	0.0	0	0	0	0	0	0	45	178	16	24	16	3	5	0	.04
97-98	Pho	20	0	0	0	-7	0	0	10	0.0	0	0	0	0	0	0	15	47	3	11	3	3	1	0	.00
8 Years		318	15	23	38	-17	3	1	212	7.1	0	0	0	0	0	0	267	1101	101	133	96	40	24	0	.12
											Postseason														
Year	Tm	GP	G	A	Pts	+/–	GW	OT	S	SPct	G	A	Pts	G	A	Pts	Num	PIM	Maj	Mnr	Fgt	Rgh	HHT	Hat	P/G
94-95	Chi	14	1	1	2	3	1	0	8	12.5	0	0	0	0	0	0	2	4	0	2	0	0	1	0	.14
95-96	Chi	10	0	0	0	-1	0	0	3	0.0	0	0	0	0	0	0	1	2	0	1	0	0	0	0	.00
96-97	Chi	6	0	0	0	-5	0	0	3	0.0	0	0	0	0	0	0	8	24	0	7	0	2	0	0	.00
97-98	Pho	3	0	0	0	0	0	0	2	0.0	0	0	0	0	0	0	2	4	0	2	0	1	0	0	.00
98-99	Pho	3	0	1	1	1	0	0	0	–	0	0	0	0	0	0	0	0	0	0	0	0	0	0	.33
5 Years		36	1	2	3	-2	1	0	16	6.3	0	0	0	0	0	0	13	34	0	12	0	3	1	0	.08

Randy Cunneyworth

Pos: LW **Shoots:** L **Ht:** 6'0" **Wt:** 198 **Born:** 5/10/61—Etobicoke, Ontario **Age:** 38

		Overall									Power Play			Shorthand			Penalty							Misc	
Year	Tm	GP	G	A	Pts	+/–	GW	GT	S	SPct	G	A	Pts	G	A	Pts	Num	PIM	Maj	Mnr	Fgt	Rgh	HHT	Hat	P/G
80-81	Buf	1	0	0	0	0	0	0	1	0.0	0	0	0	0	0	0	1	2	0	1	0	–	–	0	.00
81-82	Buf	20	2	4	6	-3	0	0	33	6.1	0	–	–	0	–	–	–	47	–	–	–	–	–	0	.30
82-83											Did Not Play in NHL														
83-84											Did Not Play in NHL														
84-85											Did Not Play in NHL														
85-86	Pit	75	15	30	45	12	2	0	134	11.2	2	6	8	2	–	–	–	74	–	–	–	–	–	0	.60
86-87	Pit	79	26	27	53	14	5	0	169	15.4	3	2	5	2	–	–	–	142	–	–	–	–	–	2	.67
87-88	Pit	71	35	39	74	13	6	0	229	15.3	14	15	29	0	–	–	–	141	–	–	–	–	–	0	1.04
88-89	Pit	70	25	19	44	-22	1	0	163	15.3	10	5	15	0	–	–	–	156	–	–	–	–	–	0	.63
89-90	2Tm	71	14	15	29	-11	2	0	121	11.6	4	–	–	0	–	–	–	75	–	–	–	–	–	0	.41
90-91	Har	32	9	5	14	-6	1	0	56	16.1	0	–	–	0	–	–	–	49	–	–	–	–	–	0	.44
91-92	Har	39	7	10	17	-5	1	0	63	11.1	0	3	3	0	0	0	27	71	3	23	3	6	8	0	.44
92-93	Har	39	5	4	9	-1	1	0	47	10.6	0	0	0	0	0	0	26	63	1	24	1	7	6	0	.23
93-94	2Tm	79	13	11	24	-1	2	0	154	8.4	0	0	0	1	0	1	36	100	4	30	4	13	5	0	.30
94-95	Ott	48	5	5	10	-19	0	0	71	7.0	2	0	2	0	0	0	31	68	2	29	2	9	9	0	.21
95-96	Ott	81	17	19	36	-31	2	0	142	12.0	4	4	8	0	0	0	43	130	4	35	3	10	8	0	.44
96-97	Ott	76	12	24	36	-7	3	0	115	10.4	6	4	10	0	0	0	34	99	5	27	5	3	6	0	.47
97-98	Ott	71	2	11	13	-14	0	0	81	2.5	1	2	3	0	0	0	30	63	1	29	1	9	3	0	.18
98-99	Buf	14	2	2	4	1	1	0	12	16.7	0	0	0	0	0	0	0	0	0	0	0	0	0	0	.29
89-90	Wpg	28	5	6	11	-7	1	0	51	9.8	2	–	–	0	–	–	–	34	–	–	–	–	–	0	.39
89-90	Har	43	9	9	18	-4	1	0	70	12.9	2	–	–	0	–	–	–	41	–	–	–	–	–	0	.42
93-94	Har	63	9	8	17	-2	1	0	121	7.4	0	0	0	1	0	1	31	87	3	26	3	11	3	0	.27
93-94	Chi	16	4	3	7	1	1	0	33	12.1	0	0	0	0	0	0	5	13	1	4	1	2	2	0	.44
16 Years		866	189	225	414	-80	27	0	1591	11.9	46	–	–	5	–	–	–	1280	–	–	–	–	–	2	.48
											Postseason														
Year	Tm	GP	G	A	Pts	+/–	GW	OT	S	SPct	G	A	Pts	G	A	Pts	Num	PIM	Maj	Mnr	Fgt	Rgh	HHT	Hat	P/G
88-89	Pit	11	3	5	8	-1	1	0	20	15.0	1	–	–	0	–	–	–	26	–	–	–	–	–	0	.73
89-90	Har	4	0	0	0	-1	0	0	2	0.0	0	0	0	0	0	0	1	2	0	1	0	–	–	0	.00
90-91	Har	1	0	0	0	0	0	0	0	–	0	0	0	0	0	0	0	0	0	0	0	0	0	0	.00
91-92	Har	7	3	0	3	0	1	0	11	27.3	1	0	1	1	0	1	3	9	1	2	1	0	0	0	.43
93-94	Chi	6	0	0	0	-1	0	0	7	0.0	0	0	0	0	0	0	4	8	0	4	0	1	1	0	.00
96-97	Ott	7	1	1	2	-3	0	0	18	5.6	0	1	1	0	0	0	5	10	0	5	0	2	0	0	.29
97-98	Ott	6	0	1	1	0	0	0	2	0.0	0	0	0	0	0	0	3	6	0	3	0	2	0	0	.17
98-99	Buf	3	0	0	0	-1	0	0	2	0.0	0	0	0	0	0	0	0	0	0	0	0	0	0	0	.00
8 Years		45	7	7	14	-7	2	0	62	11.3	2	–	–	1	–	–	–	61	–	–	–	–	–	0	.31

Mariusz Czerkawski

(statistical profile on page 301)

Pos: RW **Shoots:** R **Ht:** 6'0" **Wt:** 195 **Born:** 4/13/72—Radomsko, Poland **Age:** 27

		Overall									Power Play			Shorthand			Penalty							Misc	
Year	Tm	GP	G	A	Pts	+/–	GW	GT	S	SPct	G	A	Pts	G	A	Pts	Num	PIM	Maj	Mnr	Fgt	Rgh	HHT	Hat	P/G
93-94	Bos	4	2	1	3	-2	0	0	11	18.2	1	0	1	0	0	0	0	0	0	0	0	0	0	0	.75
94-95	Bos	47	12	14	26	4	2	0	126	9.5	1	7	8	0	0	0	10	31	1	8	0	1	2	0	.55

Overall											Power Play			Shorthand			Penalty							Misc	
Year	Tm	GP	G	A	Pts	+/-	GW	GT	S	SPct	G	A	Pts	G	A	Pts	Num	PIM	Maj	Mnr	Fgt	Rgh	HHT	Hat	P/G
95-96	2Tm	70	17	23	40	-4	1	0	142	12.0	3	6	9	0	0	0	9	18	0	9	0	1	2	0	.57
96-97	Edm	76	26	21	47	0	3	0	182	14.3	4	5	9	0	0	0	8	16	0	8	0	0	2	2	.62
97-98	NYI	68	12	13	25	11	1	0	136	8.8	2	1	3	0	0	0	6	23	1	4	1	0	2	0	.37
98-99	NYI	78	21	17	38	-10	1	2	205	10.2	4	5	9	0	0	0	7	14	0	7	0	0	5	0	.49
95-96	Bos	33	5	6	11	-11	0	0	63	7.9	1	0	1	0	0	0	5	10	0	5	0	1	1	0	.33
95-96	Edm	37	12	17	29	7	1	0	79	15.2	2	6	8	0	0	0	4	8	0	4	0	0	1	0	.78
6 Years		343	90	89	179	-1	8	2	802	11.2	15	24	39	0	0	0	40	102	2	36	1	2	13	2	.52
Postseason																									
Year	Tm	GP	G	A	Pts	+/-	GW	OT	S	SPct	G	A	Pts	G	A	Pts	Num	PIM	Maj	Mnr	Fgt	Rgh	HHT	Hat	P/G
93-94	Bos	13	3	3	6	-1	0	0	22	13.6	1	2	3	0	0	0	2	4	0	2	0	1	1	0	.46
94-95	Bos	5	1	0	1	0	0	0	11	9.1	0	0	0	0	0	0	0	0	0	0	0	0	0	0	.20
96-97	Edm	12	2	1	3	-2	0	0	19	10.5	0	1	1	0	0	0	5	10	0	5	0	0	1	0	.25
3 Years		30	6	4	10	-3	0	0	52	11.5	1	3	4	0	0	0	7	14	0	7	0	1	2	0	.33

Andreas Dackell

(statistical profile on page 301)

Pos: RW **Shoots:** R **Ht:** 5'11" **Wt:** 191 **Born:** 12/29/72—Gavle, Sweden **Age:** 27

Overall											Power Play			Shorthand			Penalty							Misc	
Year	Tm	GP	G	A	Pts	+/-	GW	GT	S	SPct	G	A	Pts	G	A	Pts	Num	PIM	Maj	Mnr	Fgt	Rgh	HHT	Hat	P/G
96-97	Ott	79	12	19	31	-6	3	0	79	15.2	2	1	3	0	0	0	4	8	0	4	0	0	1	0	.39
97-98	Ott	82	15	18	33	-11	2	1	130	11.5	3	5	8	2	1	3	12	24	0	12	0	0	8	0	.40
98-99	Ott	77	15	35	50	9	3	0	107	14.0	6	10	16	0	0	0	15	30	0	15	0	1	6	0	.65
3 Years		238	42	72	114	-8	8	1	316	13.3	11	16	27	2	1	3	31	62	0	31	0	1	15	0	.48
Postseason																									
Year	Tm	GP	G	A	Pts	+/-	GW	OT	S	SPct	G	A	Pts	G	A	Pts	Num	PIM	Maj	Mnr	Fgt	Rgh	HHT	Hat	P/G
96-97	Ott	7	1	0	1	0	0	0	5	20.0	0	0	0	0	0	0	0	0	0	0	0	0	0	0	.14
97-98	Ott	11	1	1	2	-4	0	0	14	7.1	1	0	1	0	0	0	1	2	0	1	0	0	1	0	.18
98-99	Ott	4	0	1	1	-3	0	0	3	0.0	0	1	1	0	0	0	0	0	0	0	0	0	0	0	.25
3 Years		22	2	2	4	-7	0	0	22	9.1	1	1	2	0	0	0	1	2	0	1	0	0	1	0	.18

Byron Dafoe

(statistical profile on page 397)

Pos: G **Catches:** L **Ht:** 5'11" **Wt:** 190 **Born:** 2/25/71—Sussex, England **Age:** 28

Overall																Pen Shot		Offense		
Year	Tm	GP	GS	TP	W	L	T	Min	GA	GAA	Shots	SvPct	ShO	OE	PPGA	SHGA	Shots	GA	G	A	PIM
92-93	Was	1	0	1	0	0	0	1	0	0.00	0	–	0	0	0	0	0	0	0	0	0
93-94	Was	5	3	1	2	2	0	230	13	3.39	101	.871	0	1	6	0	0	0	0	0	0
94-95	Was	4	3	1	1	1	1	187	11	3.53	80	.863	0	0	2	0	0	0	0	0	0
95-96	LA	47	46	5	14	24	8	2666	172	3.87	1539	.888	1	17	50	9	1	**1**	0	0	6
96-97	LA	40	34	2	13	17	5	2162	112	3.11	1178	.905	0	14	22	8	0	0	0	0	0
97-98	Bos	65	63	5	30	25	9	3693	138	2.24	1602	.914	6	21	36	3	0	0	0	3	2
98-99	Bos	68	67	2	32	23	11	4001	133	1.99	1800	.926	**10**	24	25	4	0	0	0	2	25
7 Years		230	216	17	92	92	34	12940	579	2.68	6300	.908	17	77	141	24	1	1	0	5	33
Postseason																				
Year	Tm	GP	GS	TP	W	L	Pct	Min	GA	GAA	Shots	SvPct	ShO	OE	PPGA	SHGA	Shots	GA	G	A	PIM
93-94	Was	2	2	0	0	2	.000	118	5	2.54	39	.872	0	0	1	0	0	0	0	0	0
94-95	Was	1	0	0	0	0	–	20	1	3.00	3	.667	0	0	0	0	0	0	0	0	0
97-98	Bos	6	6	0	2	4	.333	422	14	1.99	159	.912	1	2	3	0	0	0	0	0	0
98-99	Bos	12	12	0	6	6	.500	768	26	2.03	330	.921	2	6	8	1	0	0	0	0	2
4 Years		21	20	0	8	12	.400	1328	46	2.08	531	.913	3	8	12	1	0	0	0	0	2

Kevin Dahl

Pos: D **Shoots:** R **Ht:** 5'11" **Wt:** 190 **Born:** 12/30/68—Regina, Saskatchewan **Age:** 31

Overall											Power Play			Shorthand			Penalty							Misc	
Year	Tm	GP	G	A	Pts	+/-	GW	GT	S	SPct	G	A	Pts	G	A	Pts	Num	PIM	Maj	Mnr	Fgt	Rgh	HHT	Hat	P/G
92-93	Cgy	61	2	9	11	9	0	0	40	5.0	1	0	1	0	0	0	28	56	0	28	0	5	13	0	.18
93-94	Cgy	33	0	3	3	-2	0	0	20	0.0	0	1	1	0	0	0	10	23	1	9	1	2	3	0	.09
94-95	Cgy	34	4	8	12	8	0	0	30	13.3	0	0	0	0	0	0	11	38	0	9	0	2	2	0	.35
95-96	Cgy	32	1	1	2	-2	1	0	17	5.9	0	0	0	0	0	0	13	26	0	13	0	2	4	0	.06
96-97	Pho	2	0	0	0	0	0	0	2	0.0	0	0	0	0	0	0	0	0	0	0	0	0	0	0	.00
97-98	Cgy	19	0	1	1	-3	0	0	17	0.0	0	0	0	0	0	0	3	6	0	3	0	0	1	0	.05
98-99	Tor	3	0	0	0	0	0	0	0	–	0	0	0	0	0	0	1	2	0	1	0	0	1	0	.00
7 Years		184	7	22	29	10	1	0	126	5.6	1	1	2	0	0	0	66	151	1	63	1	11	24	0	.16

												Postseason													
Year	Tm	GP	G	A	Pts	+/–	GW	OT	S	SPct	G	A	Pts	G	A	Pts	Num	PIM	Maj	Mnr	Fgt	Rgh	HHT	Hat	P/G
92-93	Cgy	6	0	2	2	-3	0	0	5	0.0	0	0	0	0	1	1	4	8	0	4	0	1	1	0	.33
93-94	Cgy	6	0	0	0	-3	0	0	4	0.0	0	0	0	0	0	0	2	4	0	2	0	1	1	0	.00
94-95	Cgy	3	0	0	0	-1	0	0	0	–	0	0	0	0	0	0	0	0	0	0	0	0	0	0	.00
95-96	Cgy	1	0	0	0	0	0	0	0	–	0	0	0	0	0	0	0	0	0	0	0	0	0	0	.00
4 Years		16	0	2	2	-7	0	0	9	0.0	0	0	0	0	1	1	6	12	0	6	0	2	2	0	.13

Ulf Dahlen

Pos: RW **Shoots:** L **Ht:** 6'4" **Wt:** 195 **Born:** 1/21/67—Ostersund, Sweden **Age:** 32

		Overall									Power Play			Shorthand			Penalty							Misc	
Year	Tm	GP	G	A	Pts	+/–	GW	GT	S	SPct	G	A	Pts	G	A	Pts	Num	PIM	Maj	Mnr	Fgt	Rgh	HHT	Hat	P/G
87-88	NYR	70	29	23	52	5	4	0	159	18.2	11	8	19	0	–	–	13	26	0	13	0	–	–	1	.74
88-89	NYR	56	24	19	43	-6	1	1	147	16.3	8	6	14	0	–	–	19	50	4	15	–	–	–	0	.77
89-90	2Tm	76	20	22	42	-3	4	0	135	14.8	13	–	–	0	–	–	–	30	–	–	–	–	–	0	.55
90-91	Min	66	21	18	39	7	3	0	133	15.8	4	–	–	0	–	–	3	6	0	3	0	–	–	1	.59
91-92	Min	79	36	30	66	-5	5	0	216	16.7	16	15	31	1	0	1	5	10	0	5	0	0	1	0	.84
92-93	Min	83	35	39	74	-20	6	0	223	15.7	13	21	34	0	0	0	3	6	0	3	0	0	2	1	.89
93-94	2Tm	78	25	44	69	-1	5	1	190	13.2	15	23	38	0	0	0	5	10	0	5	0	0	2	1	.88
94-95	SJ	46	11	23	34	-2	4	0	85	12.9	4	9	13	1	0	1	4	11	1	3	0	0	2	0	.74
95-96	SJ	59	16	12	28	-21	2	1	103	15.5	5	4	9	0	0	0	8	27	1	6	0	0	4	0	.47
96-97	2Tm	73	14	19	33	-2	4	0	131	10.7	4	4	8	0	0	0	9	18	0	9	0	0	2	0	.45
97-98		Did Not Play in NHL																							
98-99		Did Not Play in NHL																							
89-90	NYR	63	18	18	36	-4	4	0	111	16.2	13	–	–	0	–	–	–	30	–	–	–	–	–	0	.57
89-90	Min	13	2	4	6	1	0	0	24	8.3	0	–	–	0	–	–	0	0	0	0	0	0	0	0	.46
93-94	Dal	65	19	38	57	-1	3	1	147	12.9	12	20	32	0	0	0	5	10	0	5	0	0	2	0	.88
93-94	SJ	13	6	6	12	0	2	0	43	14.0	3	3	6	0	0	0	0	0	0	0	0	0	0	1	.92
96-97	SJ	43	8	11	19	-11	1	0	78	10.3	3	3	6	0	0	0	4	8	0	4	0	0	1	0	.44
96-97	Chi	30	6	8	14	9	3	0	53	11.3	1	1	2	0	0	0	5	10	0	5	0	0	1	0	.47
10 Years		686	231	249	480	-48	38	3	1522	15.2	93	–	–	2	–	–	–	194	–	–	–	–	–	4	.70
												Postseason													
Year	Tm	GP	G	A	Pts	+/–	GW	OT	S	SPct	G	A	Pts	G	A	Pts	Num	PIM	Maj	Mnr	Fgt	Rgh	HHT	Hat	P/G
88-89	NYR	4	0	0	0	-3	0	0	5	0.0	0	0	0	0	0	0	0	0	0	0	0	0	0	0	.00
89-90	Min	7	1	4	5	-2	0	0	19	5.3	0	–	–	0	0	0	1	2	0	1	0	0	0	0	.71
90-91	Min	15	2	6	8	-4	0	0	26	7.7	0	–	–	0	–	–	2	4	0	2	0	0	0	0	.53
91-92	Min	7	0	3	3	0	0	0	13	0.0	0	2	2	0	0	0	1	2	0	1	0	0	0	0	.43
93-94	SJ	14	6	2	8	-3	1	0	36	16.7	3	1	4	0	0	0	0	0	0	0	0	0	0	1	.57
94-95	SJ	11	5	4	9	-13	1	1	19	26.3	3	3	6	0	0	0	0	0	0	0	0	0	0	0	.82
96-97	Chi	5	0	1	1	0	0	0	2	0.0	0	0	0	0	0	0	0	0	0	0	0	0	0	0	.20
7 Years		63	14	20	34	-25	2	1	120	11.7	6	–	–	0	–	–	4	8	0	4	0	0	0	1	.54

Alexandre Daigle

(statistical profile on page 301)

Pos: C **Shoots:** L **Ht:** 6'0" **Wt:** 202 **Born:** 2/7/75—Montreal, Quebec **Age:** 24

		Overall									Power Play			Shorthand			Penalty							Misc	
Year	Tm	GP	G	A	Pts	+/–	GW	GT	S	SPct	G	A	Pts	G	A	Pts	Num	PIM	Maj	Mnr	Fgt	Rgh	HHT	Hat	P/G
93-94	Ott	84	20	31	51	-45	2	0	168	11.9	4	10	14	0	1	1	13	40	2	10	1	3	1	0	.61
94-95	Ott	47	16	21	37	-22	2	0	105	15.2	4	10	14	1	0	1	7	14	0	7	0	1	2	1	.79
95-96	Ott	50	5	12	17	-30	0	0	77	6.5	1	5	6	0	0	0	12	24	0	12	0	3	5	0	.34
96-97	Ott	**82**	26	25	51	-33	5	2	203	12.8	4	14	18	0	0	0	11	33	1	9	1	1	2	0	.62
97-98	2Tm	75	16	26	42	-8	5	1	146	11.0	8	7	15	0	0	0	7	14	0	7	0	1	3	1	.56
98-99	2Tm	63	9	8	17	-13	1	2	82	11.0	4	4	8	0	0	0	2	4	0	2	0	0	1	0	.27
97-98	Ott	38	7	9	16	-7	2	0	68	10.3	4	4	8	0	0	0	4	8	0	4	0	0	1	0	.42
97-98	Phi	37	9	17	26	-1	3	1	78	11.5	4	3	7	0	0	0	3	6	0	3	0	1	2	1	.70
98-99	Phi	31	3	2	5	-1	1	0	26	11.5	1	0	1	0	0	0	1	2	0	1	0	0	1	0	.16
98-99	TB	32	6	6	12	-12	0	2	56	10.7	3	4	7	0	0	0	1	2	0	1	0	0	0	0	.38
6 Years		401	92	123	215	-151	15	5	781	11.8	25	50	75	1	1	2	52	129	3	47	2	9	14	2	.54
												Postseason													
Year	Tm	GP	G	A	Pts	+/–	GW	OT	S	SPct	G	A	Pts	G	A	Pts	Num	PIM	Maj	Mnr	Fgt	Rgh	HHT	Hat	P/G
96-97	Ott	7	0	0	0	-5	0	0	16	0.0	0	0	0	0	0	0	1	2	0	1	0	0	1	0	.00
97-98	Phi	5	0	2	2	0	0	0	6	0.0	0	0	0	0	0	0	0	0	0	0	0	0	0	0	.40
2 Years		12	0	2	2	-5	0	0	22	0.0	0	0	0	0	0	0	1	2	0	1	0	0	1	0	.17

J.J. Daigneault

(statistical profile on page 301)

Pos: D **Shoots:** L **Ht:** 5'10" **Wt:** 186 **Born:** 10/12/65—Montreal, Quebec **Age:** 34

Overall											Power Play			Shorthand			Penalty							Misc	
Year	Tm	GP	G	A	Pts	+/–	GW	GT	S	SPct	G	A	Pts	G	A	Pts	Num	PIM	Maj	Mnr	Fgt	Rgh	HHT	Hat	P/G
84-85	Van	67	4	23	27	-14	0	0	93	4.3	2	–	–	0	–	–	–	69	–	–	–	–	–	0	.40
85-86	Van	64	5	23	28	-20	0	0	114	4.4	4	–	–	0	–	–	–	45	–	–	–	–	–	0	.44
86-87	Phi	77	6	16	22	12	1	0	82	7.3	0	–	–	0	–	–	–	56	–	–	–	–	–	0	.29
87-88	Phi	28	2	2	4	-8	0	0	20	10.0	2	–	–	0	–	–	–	12	–	–	–	–	–	0	.14
88-89		Did Not Play in NHL																							
89-90	Mon	36	2	10	12	11	1	0	40	5.0	0	–	–	0	–	–	–	14	–	–	–	–	–	0	.33
90-91	Mon	51	3	16	19	-2	0	0	68	4.4	2	–	–	0	–	–	–	31	–	–	–	–	–	0	.37
91-92	Mon	79	4	14	18	16	0	1	108	3.7	2	5	7	0	1	1	18	36	0	18	0	2	6	0	.23
92-93	Mon	66	8	10	18	25	1	0	68	11.8	0	3	3	0	0	0	23	57	1	21	1	2	10	0	.27
93-94	Mon	68	2	12	14	16	1	0	61	3.3	0	0	0	0	0	0	25	73	5	19	5	4	5	0	.21
94-95	Mon	45	3	5	8	2	0	0	36	8.3	0	0	0	0	1	1	16	40	0	15	0	3	6	0	.18
95-96	3Tm	57	4	7	11	-6	0	0	61	6.6	2	6	8	0	0	0	21	53	1	19	0	4	8	0	.19
96-97	2Tm	66	5	23	28	0	1	0	62	8.1	0	11	11	0	0	0	25	58	0	24	0	2	7	0	.42
97-98	2Tm	71	2	21	23	-9	1	0	92	2.2	1	10	11	0	0	0	19	49	1	17	1	1	3	0	.32
98-99	2Tm	70	2	9	11	-12	1	0	65	3.1	1	0	1	0	0	0	31	70	0	30	0	2	9	0	.16
95-96	Mon	7	0	1	1	0	0	0	3	0.0	0	0	0	0	0	0	3	6	0	3	0	1	1	0	.14
95-96	StL	37	1	3	4	-6	0	0	45	2.2	0	3	3	0	0	0	12	24	0	12	0	2	5	0	.11
95-96	Pit	13	3	3	6	0	0	0	13	23.1	2	3	5	0	0	0	6	23	1	4	0	1	2	0	.46
96-97	Pit	53	3	14	17	-5	1	0	49	6.1	0	5	5	0	0	0	18	36	0	18	0	2	4	0	.32
96-97	Anh	13	2	9	11	5	0	0	13	15.4	0	6	6	0	0	0	7	22	0	6	0	0	3	0	.85
97-98	Anh	53	2	15	17	-10	1	0	74	2.7	1	8	9	0	0	0	14	28	0	14	0	1	3	0	.32
97-98	NYI	18	0	6	6	1	0	0	18	0.0	0	2	2	0	0	0	5	21	1	3	1	0	0	0	.33
98-99	Nsh	35	2	2	4	-4	1	0	38	5.3	1	0	1	0	0	0	19	38	0	19	0	2	6	0	.11
98-99	Pho	35	0	7	7	-8	0	0	27	0.0	0	0	0	0	0	0	12	32	0	11	0	0	3	0	.20
14 Years		845	52	191	243	11	7	1	970	5.4	16	–	–	0	–	–	–	663	–	–	–	–	–	0	.29

Postseason

Year	Tm	GP	G	A	Pts	+/–	GW	OT	S	SPct	G	A	Pts	G	A	Pts	Num	PIM	Maj	Mnr	Fgt	Rgh	HHT	Hat	P/G
85-86	Van	3	0	2	2	-1	0	0	0	–	0	–	–	0	0	0	0	0	0	0	0	0	0	0	.67
86-87	Phi	9	1	0	1	-1	1	0	5	20.0	0	0	0	0	0	0	0	0	0	0	0	0	0	0	.11
89-90	Mon	9	0	0	0	4	0	0	13	0.0	0	0	0	0	0	0	1	2	0	1	0	0	0	0	.00
90-91	Mon	5	0	1	1	4	0	0	2	0.0	0	–	–	0	–	–	0	0	0	0	0	0	0	0	.20
91-92	Mon	11	0	3	3	-2	0	0	17	0.0	0	1	1	0	0	0	2	4	0	2	0	1	0	0	.27
92-93	Mon	20	1	3	4	2	0	0	33	3.0	0	0	0	0	0	0	11	22	0	11	0	4	1	0	.20
93-94	Mon	7	0	1	1	1	0	0	14	0.0	0	1	1	0	0	0	6	12	0	6	0	1	1	0	.14
95-96	Pit	17	1	9	10	4	1	0	30	3.3	1	2	3	0	0	0	11	36	2	8	2	0	2	0	.59
96-97	Anh	11	2	7	9	-6	1	0	24	8.3	1	6	7	0	0	0	8	16	0	8	0	1	2	0	.82
98-99	Pho	6	0	0	0	-1	0	0	4	0.0	0	0	0	0	0	0	4	8	0	4	0	0	3	0	.00
10 Years		98	5	26	31	4	3	0	142	3.5	2	–	–	0	–	–	43	100	2	40	2	7	9	0	.32

Vincent Damphousse

(statistical profile on page 302)

Pos: C **Shoots:** L **Ht:** 6'1" **Wt:** 191 **Born:** 12/17/67—Montreal, Quebec **Age:** 32

Overall											Power Play			Shorthand			Penalty							Misc	
Year	Tm	GP	G	A	Pts	+/–	GW	GT	S	SPct	G	A	Pts	G	A	Pts	Num	PIM	Maj	Mnr	Fgt	Rgh	HHT	Hat	P/G
86-87	Tor	80	21	25	46	-6	1	0	142	14.8	4	–	–	0	–	–	–	26	–	–	–	–	–	0	.58
87-88	Tor	75	12	36	48	2	2	0	111	10.8	1	–	–	0	–	–	–	40	–	–	–	–	–	0	.64
88-89	Tor	**80**	26	42	68	-8	4	0	190	13.7	6	–	–	0	–	–	–	75	–	–	–	–	–	1	.85
89-90	Tor	**80**	33	61	94	2	5	1	229	14.4	9	–	–	0	–	–	–	56	–	–	–	–	–	2	1.18
90-91	Tor*	79	26	47	73	-31	4	0	247	10.5	10	–	–	1	–	–	–	65	–	–	–	–	–	0	.92
91-92	Edm*	80	38	51	89	10	8	1	247	15.4	12	20	32	1	2	3	21	53	1	19	0	2	8	1	1.11
92-93	Mon	84	39	58	97	5	8	1	287	13.6	9	24	33	3	0	3	45	98	0	44	0	5	17	2	1.15
93-94	Mon	84	40	51	91	0	10	1	274	14.6	13	24	37	0	1	1	36	75	1	35	1	8	13	2	1.08
94-95	Mon	48	10	30	40	15	4	0	123	8.1	4	10	14	0	0	0	21	42	0	21	0	1	7	0	.83
95-96	Mon	80	38	56	94	5	3	0	254	15.0	11	24	35	4	1	5	65	158	4	59	2	4	18	0	1.18
96-97	Mon	**82**	27	54	81	-6	3	2	244	11.1	7	14	21	2	3	5	37	82	0	36	0	4	12	1	.99
97-98	Mon	76	18	41	59	14	5	0	164	11.0	2	13	15	1	2	3	29	58	0	29	0	3	11	2	.78
98-99	2Tm	77	19	30	49	-4	3	0	190	10.0	6	14	20	2	1	3	25	50	0	25	0	1	12	1	.64
98-99	Mon	65	12	24	36	-7	2	0	147	8.2	3	10	13	2	1	3	23	46	0	23	0	1	11	0	.55
98-99	SJ	12	7	6	13	3	1	0	43	16.3	3	4	7	0	0	0	2	4	0	2	0	0	1	1	1.08
13 Years		1005	347	582	929	-2	60	6	2702	12.8	94	–	–	14	–	–	–	878	–	–	–	–	–	12	.92

Postseason

Year	Tm	GP	G	A	Pts	+/–	GW	OT	S	SPct	G	A	Pts	G	A	Pts	Num	PIM	Maj	Mnr	Fgt	Rgh	HHT	Hat	P/G
86-87	Tor	12	1	5	6	-3	0	0	18	5.6	1	–	–	0	0	0	4	8	0	4	0	–	–	0	.50
87-88	Tor	6	0	1	1	-3	0	0	4	0.0	0	–	–	0	–	–	–	10	–	–	–	–	–	0	.17

											Postseason														
Year	Tm	GP	G	A	Pts	+/-	GW	OT	S	SPct	G	A	Pts	G	A	Pts	Num	PIM	Maj	Mnr	Fgt	Rgh	HHT	Hat	P/G
89-90	Tor	5	0	2	2	1	0	0	10	0.0	0	–	–	0	–	–	1	2	0	1	0	–	–	0	.40
91-92	Edm	16	6	8	14	5	0	0	45	13.3	1	2	3	0	0	0	4	8	0	4	0	1	0	0	.88
92-93	Mon	20	11	12	23	8	3	1	52	21.2	5	2	7	0	0	0	8	16	0	8	0	1	0	0	1.15
93-94	Mon	7	1	2	3	-1	0	0	14	7.1	0	0	0	0	0	0	4	8	0	4	0	0	1	0	.43
95-96	Mon	6	4	4	8	2	2	1	26	15.4	0	2	2	1	0	1	0	0	0	0	0	0	0	0	1.33
96-97	Mon	5	0	0	0	-5	0	0	7	0.0	0	0	0	0	0	0	1	2	0	1	0	0	0	0	.00
97-98	Mon	10	3	6	9	-4	0	0	42	7.1	1	3	4	0	0	0	11	22	0	11	0	0	3	0	.90
98-99	SJ	6	3	2	5	1	0	0	22	13.6	0	1	1	2	0	2	3	6	0	3	0	1	0	0	.83
10 Years		93	29	42	71	1	5	2	240	12.1	8	–	–	3	–	–	–	82	–	–	–	–	–	0	.76

Mathieu Dandenault

(statistical profile on page 302)

Pos: RW **Shoots:** R **Ht:** 6'1" **Wt:** 200 **Born:** 2/3/76—Sherbrooke, Quebec **Age:** 23

Overall											Power Play			Shorthand			Penalty							Misc	
Year	Tm	GP	G	A	Pts	+/-	GW	GT	S	SPct	G	A	Pts	G	A	Pts	Num	PIM	Maj	Mnr	Fgt	Rgh	HHT	Hat	P/G
95-96	Det	34	5	7	12	6	0	0	32	15.6	1	0	1	0	0	0	3	6	0	3	0	0	2	0	.35
96-97	Det	65	3	9	12	-10	0	0	81	3.7	0	0	0	0	0	0	10	28	0	9	0	0	4	0	.18
97-98	Det	68	5	12	17	5	0	0	75	6.7	0	0	0	0	0	0	16	43	1	14	0	0	6	0	.25
98-99	Det	75	4	10	14	17	0	0	94	4.3	0	1	1	0	0	0	28	59	1	27	1	2	12	0	.19
4 Years		242	17	38	55	18	0	0	282	6.0	1	1	2	0	0	0	57	136	2	53	1	2	24	0	.23
											Postseason														
Year	Tm	GP	G	A	Pts	+/-	GW	OT	S	SPct	G	A	Pts	G	A	Pts	Num	PIM	Maj	Mnr	Fgt	Rgh	HHT	Hat	P/G
97-98	Det	3	1	0	1	-2	0	0	4	25.0	1	0	1	0	0	0	0	0	0	0	0	0	0	0	.33
98-99	Det	10	0	1	1	0	0	0	15	0.0	0	1	1	0	0	0	0	0	0	0	0	0	0	0	.10
2 Years		13	1	1	2	-2	0	0	19	5.3	1	1	2	0	0	0	0	0	0	0	0	0	0	0	.15

Ken Daneyko

(statistical profile on page 302)

Pos: D **Shoots:** L **Ht:** 6'1" **Wt:** 215 **Born:** 4/17/64—Windsor, Ontario **Age:** 35

Overall											Power Play			Shorthand			Penalty							Misc	
Year	Tm	GP	G	A	Pts	+/-	GW	GT	S	SPct	G	A	Pts	G	A	Pts	Num	PIM	Maj	Mnr	Fgt	Rgh	HHT	Hat	P/G
83-84	NJ	11	1	4	5	-1	0	0	17	5.9	0	–	–	0	–	–	–	17	–	–	–	–	–	0	.45
84-85	NJ	1	0	0	0	-1	0	0	1	0.0	0	0	0	0	0	0	–	10	–	–	–	–	–	0	.00
85-86	NJ	44	0	10	10	0	0	0	48	0.0	0	–	–	0	–	–	–	100	–	–	–	–	–	0	.23
86-87	NJ	79	2	12	14	-13	0	0	113	1.8	0	–	–	0	–	–	–	183	–	–	–	–	–	0	.18
87-88	NJ	**80**	5	7	12	-3	0	0	82	6.1	1	–	–	0	–	–	–	239	–	–	–	–	–	0	.15
88-89	NJ	**80**	5	5	10	-22	0	0	108	4.6	1	1	2	0	0	0	–	283	–	–	–	–	–	0	.13
89-90	NJ	74	6	15	21	15	1	0	64	9.4	0	0	0	1	3	4	–	219	–	–	–	–	–	0	.28
90-91	NJ	80	4	16	20	-10	1	0	106	3.8	1	2	3	2	0	2	–	249	–	–	–	–	–	0	.25
91-92	NJ	80	1	7	8	7	0	0	57	1.8	0	0	0	0	0	0	61	170	8	50	8	6	17	0	.10
92-93	NJ	84	2	11	13	4	0	0	71	2.8	0	0	0	0	0	0	82	236	8	68	8	25	10	0	.15
93-94	NJ	78	1	9	10	27	1	0	60	1.7	0	0	0	0	0	0	63	176	6	53	6	23	12	0	.13
94-95	NJ	25	1	2	3	4	0	0	27	3.7	0	0	0	0	0	0	17	54	4	12	4	6	4	0	.12
95-96	NJ	80	2	4	6	-10	0	0	67	3.0	0	1	1	0	0	0	39	115	7	30	7	4	5	0	.08
96-97	NJ	77	2	7	9	24	0	1	63	3.2	0	0	0	0	1	1	28	70	2	25	2	9	6	0	.12
97-98	NJ	37	0	1	1	3	0	0	18	0.0	0	0	0	0	0	0	23	57	1	21	1	5	9	0	.03
98-99	NJ	82	2	9	11	27	0	0	63	3.2	0	0	0	0	0	0	30	63	1	29	1	8	6	0	.13
16 Years		992	34	119	153	51	3	1	965	3.5	3	–	–	3	–	–	–	2241	–	–	–	–	–	0	.15
											Postseason														
Year	Tm	GP	G	A	Pts	+/-	GW	OT	S	SPct	G	A	Pts	G	A	Pts	Num	PIM	Maj	Mnr	Fgt	Rgh	HHT	Hat	P/G
87-88	NJ	20	1	6	7	-3	0	0	27	3.7	0	–	–	0	–	–	–	49	–	–	–	–	–	0	.35
89-90	NJ	6	2	0	2	-4	0	0	3	66.7	0	0	0	0	0	0	–	21	–	–	–	–	–	0	.33
90-91	NJ	7	0	1	1	2	0	0	4	0.0	0	–	–	0	–	–	–	10	–	–	–	–	–	0	.14
91-92	NJ	7	0	3	3	3	0	0	6	0.0	0	0	0	0	1	1	4	16	0	3	0	1	2	0	.43
92-93	NJ	5	0	0	0	-1	0	0	4	0.0	0	0	0	0	0	0	4	8	0	4	0	3	0	0	.00
93-94	NJ	20	0	1	1	-6	0	0	8	0.0	0	0	0	0	0	0	17	45	1	15	1	3	2	0	.05
94-95	NJ	20	1	0	1	9	0	0	11	9.1	0	0	0	0	0	0	11	22	0	11	0	3	3	0	.05
96-97	NJ	10	0	0	0	1	0	0	8	0.0	0	0	0	0	0	0	10	28	0	9	0	3	1	0	.00
97-98	NJ	6	0	1	1	0	0	0	7	0.0	0	0	0	0	0	0	5	10	0	5	0	1	0	0	.17
98-99	NJ	7	0	0	0	3	0	0	5	0.0	0	0	0	0	0	0	4	8	0	4	0	2	1	0	.00
10 Years		108	4	12	16	4	0	0	83	4.8	0	–	–	0	–	–	–	217	–	–	–	–	–	0	.15

Jeff Daniels

Pos: LW **Shoots:** L **Ht:** 6'1" **Wt:** 200 **Born:** 6/24/68—Oshawa, Ontario **Age:** 31

		Overall									Power Play			Shorthand			Penalty							Misc	
Year	Tm	GP	G	A	Pts	+/-	GW	GT	S	SPct	G	A	Pts	G	A	Pts	Num	PIM	Maj	Mnr	Fgt	Rgh	HHT	Hat	P/G
90-91	Pit	11	0	2	2	0	0	0	6	0.0	0	–	–	0	–	–	1	2	0	1	0	–	–	0	.18
91-92	Pit	2	0	0	0	0	0	0	0	–	0	0	0	0	0	0	0	0	0	0	0	0	0	0	.00
92-93	Pit	58	5	4	9	-5	1	0	30	16.7	0	0	0	0	0	0	7	14	0	7	0	1	4	0	.16
93-94	2Tm	70	3	5	8	-1	1	0	52	5.8	0	0	0	0	0	0	6	20	0	5	0	1	1	0	.11
94-95	Fla	3	0	0	0	0	0	0	0	–	0	0	0	0	0	0	0	0	0	0	0	0	0	0	.00
95-96		Did Not Play in NHL																							
96-97	Har	10	0	2	2	2	0	0	6	0.0	0	0	0	0	0	0	0	0	0	0	0	0	0	0	.20
97-98	Car	2	0	0	0	0	0	0	1	0.0	0	0	0	0	0	0	0	0	0	0	0	0	0	0	.00
98-99	Nsh	9	1	3	4	-1	0	0	8	12.5	0	0	0	0	0	0	1	2	0	1	0	0	1	0	.44
93-94	Pit	63	3	5	8	-1	1	0	46	6.5	0	0	0	0	0	0	6	20	0	5	0	1	1	0	.13
93-94	Fla	7	0	0	0	0	0	0	6	0.0	0	0	0	0	0	0	0	0	0	0	0	0	0	0	.00
8 Years		165	9	16	25	-5	2	0	103	8.7	0	–	–	0	–	–	15	38	0	14	0	–	–	0	.15

Postseason																									
Year	Tm	GP	G	A	Pts	+/-	GW	OT	S	SPct	G	A	Pts	G	A	Pts	Num	PIM	Maj	Mnr	Fgt	Rgh	HHT	Hat	P/G
92-93	Pit	12	3	2	5	1	1	0	16	18.8	0	0	0	0	0	0	0	0	0	0	0	0	0	0	.42

Scott Daniels

Pos: LW **Shoots:** L **Ht:** 6'3" **Wt:** 214 **Born:** 9/19/69—Prince Albert, Saskatchewan **Age:** 30

		Overall									Power Play			Shorthand			Penalty							Misc	
Year	Tm	GP	G	A	Pts	+/-	GW	GT	S	SPct	G	A	Pts	G	A	Pts	Num	PIM	Maj	Mnr	Fgt	Rgh	HHT	Hat	P/G
92-93	Har	1	0	0	0	0	0	0	0	–	0	0	0	0	0	0	4	19	1	2	1	1	0	0	.00
93-94		Did Not Play in NHL																							
94-95	Har	12	0	2	2	1	0	0	7	0.0	0	0	0	0	0	0	13	55	7	5	7	1	2	0	.17
95-96	Har	53	3	4	7	-4	0	0	43	7.0	0	0	0	0	0	0	57	254	20	27	20	12	3	0	.13
96-97	Phi	56	5	3	8	2	2	0	48	10.4	0	0	0	0	0	0	63	237	21	36	21	11	4	0	.14
97-98	NJ	26	0	3	3	1	0	0	17	0.0	0	0	0	0	0	0	22	102	14	6	14	2	2	0	.12
98-99	NJ	1	0	0	0	0	0	0	0	–	0	0	0	0	0	0	0	0	0	0	0	0	0	0	.00
6 Years		149	8	12	20	0	2	0	115	7.0	0	0	0	0	0	0	159	667	63	76	63	27	11	0	.13

Postseason																									
Year	Tm	GP	G	A	Pts	+/-	GW	OT	S	SPct	G	A	Pts	G	A	Pts	Num	PIM	Maj	Mnr	Fgt	Rgh	HHT	Hat	P/G
97-98	NJ	1	0	0	0	0	0	0	0	–	0	0	0	0	0	0	0	0	0	0	0	0	0	0	.00

Johan Davidsson

Pos: C **Shoots:** R **Ht:** 6'1" **Wt:** 187 **Born:** 1/6/76—Jonkoping, Sweden **Age:** 23

		Overall									Power Play			Shorthand			Penalty							Misc	
Year	Tm	GP	G	A	Pts	+/-	GW	GT	S	SPct	G	A	Pts	G	A	Pts	Num	PIM	Maj	Mnr	Fgt	Rgh	HHT	Hat	P/G
98-99	Anh	64	3	5	8	-9	1	0	48	6.3	1	1	2	0	0	0	7	14	0	7	0	0	3	0	.13

Postseason																									
Year	Tm	GP	G	A	Pts	+/-	GW	OT	S	SPct	G	A	Pts	G	A	Pts	Num	PIM	Maj	Mnr	Fgt	Rgh	HHT	Hat	P/G
98-99	Anh	1	0	0	0	0	0	0	0	–	0	0	0	0	0	0	0	0	0	0	0	0	0	0	.00

Jason Dawe

(statistical profile on page 302)

Pos: RW **Shoots:** L **Ht:** 5'10" **Wt:** 189 **Born:** 5/29/73—North York, Ontario **Age:** 26

		Overall									Power Play			Shorthand			Penalty							Misc	
Year	Tm	GP	G	A	Pts	+/-	GW	GT	S	SPct	G	A	Pts	G	A	Pts	Num	PIM	Maj	Mnr	Fgt	Rgh	HHT	Hat	P/G
93-94	Buf	32	6	7	13	1	1	0	35	17.1	3	2	5	0	0	0	6	12	0	6	0	0	3	0	.41
94-95	Buf	42	7	4	11	-6	2	0	51	13.7	0	2	2	1	0	1	8	19	1	7	1	0	6	0	.26
95-96	Buf	67	25	25	50	-8	0	2	130	19.2	8	7	15	1	0	1	15	33	1	14	1	0	7	1	.75
96-97	Buf	81	22	26	48	14	3	0	136	16.2	4	8	12	1	1	2	16	32	0	16	0	2	6	0	.59
97-98	2Tm	81	20	19	39	8	3	1	134	14.9	4	6	10	1	0	1	17	42	0	16	0	1	8	1	.48
98-99	2Tm	59	6	8	14	0	1	0	81	7.4	1	1	2	0	0	0	11	22	0	11	0	2	4	0	.24
97-98	Buf	68	19	17	36	10	3	1	115	16.5	4	6	10	1	0	1	14	36	0	13	0	1	6	1	.53
97-98	NYI	13	1	2	3	-2	0	0	19	5.3	0	0	0	0	0	0	3	6	0	3	0	0	2	0	.23
98-99	NYI	22	2	3	5	0	0	0	29	6.9	0	1	1	0	0	0	4	8	0	4	0	1	1	0	.23
98-99	Mon	37	4	5	9	0	1	0	52	7.7	1	0	1	0	0	0	7	14	0	7	0	1	3	0	.24
6 Years		362	86	89	175	9	10	3	567	15.2	20	26	46	4	1	5	73	160	2	70	2	5	34	2	.48

Postseason																									
Year	Tm	GP	G	A	Pts	+/-	GW	OT	S	SPct	G	A	Pts	G	A	Pts	Num	PIM	Maj	Mnr	Fgt	Rgh	HHT	Hat	P/G
93-94	Buf	6	0	1	1	1	0	0	3	0.0	0	0	0	0	0	0	3	6	0	3	0	0	2	0	.17

											Postseason														
Year	Tm	GP	G	A	Pts	+/–	GW	OT	S	SPct	G	A	Pts	G	A	Pts	Num	PIM	Maj	Mnr	Fgt	Rgh	HHT	Hat	P/G
94-95	Buf	5	2	1	3	-2	0	0	10	20.0	0	0	0	0	0	0	3	6	0	3	0	0	1	0	.60
96-97	Buf	11	2	1	3	-2	0	0	19	10.5	0	0	0	0	0	0	3	6	0	3	0	1	1	0	.27
3 Years		22	4	3	7	-3	0	0	32	12.5	0	0	0	0	0	0	9	18	0	9	0	1	4	0	.32

Eric Daze

(statistical profile on page 303)

Pos: LW **Shoots:** L **Ht:** 6'6" **Wt:** 222 **Born:** 7/2/75—Montreal, Quebec **Age:** 24

				Overall							Power Play			Shorthand			Penalty							Misc	
Year	Tm	GP	G	A	Pts	+/–	GW	GT	S	SPct	G	A	Pts	G	A	Pts	Num	PIM	Maj	Mnr	Fgt	Rgh	HHT	Hat	P/G
94-95	Chi	4	1	1	2	2	0	0	1	100.0	0	0	0	0	0	0	1	2	0	1	0	0	0	0	.50
95-96	Chi	80	30	23	53	16	2	0	167	18.0	2	4	6	0	0	0	9	18	0	9	0	1	7	0	.66
96-97	Chi	71	22	19	41	-4	4	0	176	12.5	11	4	15	0	0	0	8	16	0	8	0	2	4	1	.58
97-98	Chi	80	31	11	42	4	7	1	216	14.4	10	2	12	0	0	0	11	22	0	11	0	1	5	1	.53
98-99	Chi	72	22	20	42	-13	2	**3**	189	11.6	8	9	17	0	0	0	7	22	0	6	0	2	1	0	.58
5 Years		307	106	74	180	5	15	4	749	14.2	31	19	50	0	0	0	36	80	0	35	0	6	17	2	.59
											Postseason														
Year	Tm	GP	G	A	Pts	+/–	GW	OT	S	SPct	G	A	Pts	G	A	Pts	Num	PIM	Maj	Mnr	Fgt	Rgh	HHT	Hat	P/G
94-95	Chi	16	0	1	1	-4	0	0	16	0.0	0	0	0	0	0	0	2	4	0	2	0	0	2	0	.06
95-96	Chi	10	3	5	8	4	1	0	32	9.4	0	2	2	0	0	0	0	0	0	0	0	0	0	0	.80
96-97	Chi	6	2	1	3	-1	0	0	15	13.3	0	0	0	0	0	0	1	2	0	1	0	0	1	0	.50
3 Years		32	5	7	12	-1	1	0	63	7.9	0	2	2	0	0	0	3	6	0	3	0	0	3	0	.38

Adam Deadmarsh

(statistical profile on page 303)

Pos: RW **Shoots:** R **Ht:** 6'0" **Wt:** 200 **Born:** 5/10/75—Trail, British Columbia **Age:** 24

				Overall							Power Play			Shorthand			Penalty							Misc	
Year	Tm	GP	G	A	Pts	+/–	GW	GT	S	SPct	G	A	Pts	G	A	Pts	Num	PIM	Maj	Mnr	Fgt	Rgh	HHT	Hat	P/G
94-95	Que	48	9	8	17	16	0	1	48	18.8	0	0	0	0	0	0	19	56	6	13	6	5	3	0	.35
95-96	Col	78	21	27	48	20	2	0	151	13.9	3	5	8	0	0	0	40	142	10	26	10	6	6	0	.62
96-97	Col	78	33	27	60	8	4	0	198	16.7	10	14	24	3	1	4	46	136	12	33	12	8	6	0	.77
97-98	Col	73	22	21	43	0	6	**3**	187	11.8	10	6	16	0	2	2	41	125	9	30	8	4	13	0	.59
98-99	Col	66	22	27	49	-2	3	1	152	14.5	10	10	20	0	1	1	35	99	7	27	7	2	8	0	.74
5 Years		343	107	110	217	42	15	5	736	14.5	33	35	68	3	4	7	181	558	44	129	43	25	36	0	.63
											Postseason														
Year	Tm	GP	G	A	Pts	+/–	GW	OT	S	SPct	G	A	Pts	G	A	Pts	Num	PIM	Maj	Mnr	Fgt	Rgh	HHT	Hat	P/G
94-95	Que	6	0	1	1	-3	0	0	6	0.0	0	0	0	0	0	0	0	0	0	0	0	0	0	0	.17
95-96	Col	22	5	12	17	8	0	0	40	12.5	1	5	6	0	0	0	7	25	1	5	0	2	1	0	.77
96-97	Col	17	3	6	9	-6	1	0	39	7.7	1	1	2	0	0	0	8	24	0	7	0	1	1	0	.53
97-98	Col	7	2	0	2	-1	0	0	14	14.3	1	0	1	0	0	0	2	4	0	2	0	0	0	0	.29
98-99	Col	19	8	4	12	2	0	0	44	18.2	3	1	4	0	1	1	10	20	0	10	0	1	0	0	.63
5 Years		71	18	23	41	0	1	0	143	12.6	6	7	13	0	1	1	27	73	1	24	0	4	2	0	.58

Kevin Dean

(statistical profile on page 303)

Pos: D **Shoots:** L **Ht:** 6'3" **Wt:** 205 **Born:** 4/1/69—Madison, Wisconsin **Age:** 30

				Overall							Power Play			Shorthand			Penalty							Misc	
Year	Tm	GP	G	A	Pts	+/–	GW	GT	S	SPct	G	A	Pts	G	A	Pts	Num	PIM	Maj	Mnr	Fgt	Rgh	HHT	Hat	P/G
94-95	NJ	17	0	1	1	6	0	0	11	0.0	0	0	0	0	0	0	2	4	0	2	0	0	1	0	.06
95-96	NJ	41	0	6	6	4	0	0	29	0.0	0	2	2	0	0	0	14	28	0	14	0	1	5	0	.15
96-97	NJ	28	2	4	6	2	0	0	21	9.5	0	1	1	0	0	0	3	6	0	3	0	0	1	0	.21
97-98	NJ	50	1	8	9	12	0	0	28	3.6	1	1	2	0	1	1	6	12	0	6	0	0	1	0	.18
98-99	NJ	62	1	10	11	4	0	0	51	2.0	1	1	2	0	0	0	11	22	0	11	0	0	4	0	.18
5 Years		198	4	29	33	28	0	0	140	2.9	2	5	7	0	1	1	36	72	0	36	0	1	12	0	.17
											Postseason														
Year	Tm	GP	G	A	Pts	+/–	GW	OT	S	SPct	G	A	Pts	G	A	Pts	Num	PIM	Maj	Mnr	Fgt	Rgh	HHT	Hat	P/G
94-95	NJ	3	0	2	2	0	0	0	4	0.0	0	2	2	0	0	0	0	0	0	0	0	0	0	0	.67
96-97	NJ	1	1	0	1	1	1	0	3	33.3	0	0	0	0	0	0	0	0	0	0	0	0	0	0	1.00
97-98	NJ	5	1	0	1	-1	0	0	4	25.0	0	0	0	0	0	0	1	2	0	1	0	0	0	0	.20
98-99	NJ	7	0	0	0	-4	0	0	7	0.0	0	0	0	0	0	0	0	0	0	0	0	0	0	0	.00
4 Years		16	2	2	4	-4	1	0	18	11.1	0	2	2	0	0	0	1	2	0	1	0	0	0	0	.25

Louie DeBrusk

Pos: LW **Shoots:** L **Ht:** 6'2" **Wt:** 215 **Born:** 3/19/71—Cambridge, Ontario **Age:** 28

Overall											Power Play			Shorthand			Penalty							Misc	
Year	Tm	GP	G	A	Pts	+/–	GW	GT	S	SPct	G	A	Pts	G	A	Pts	Num	PIM	Maj	Mnr	Fgt	Rgh	HHT	Hat	P/G
91-92	Edm	25	2	1	3	4	1	0	7	28.6	0	0	0	0	0	0	26	124	16	7	16	4	0	0	.12
92-93	Edm	51	8	2	10	-16	1	0	33	24.2	0	1	1	0	0	0	50	205	19	25	19	8	6	0	.20
93-94	Edm	48	4	6	10	-9	0	0	27	14.8	0	0	0	0	0	0	44	185	19	20	18	8	3	0	.21
94-95	Edm	34	2	0	2	-4	0	0	14	14.3	0	0	0	0	0	0	24	93	7	14	6	0	1	0	.06
95-96	Edm	38	1	3	4	-7	0	0	17	5.9	0	0	0	0	0	0	24	96	8	13	7	4	0	0	.11
96-97	Edm	32	2	0	2	-6	0	0	10	20.0	0	0	0	0	0	0	22	94	6	12	6	4	3	0	.06
97-98	TB	54	1	2	3	-2	0	0	14	7.1	0	0	0	0	0	0	44	166	18	23	18	6	4	0	.06
98-99	Pho	15	0	0	0	-2	0	0	6	0.0	0	0	0	0	0	0	8	34	6	2	6	0	0	0	.00
8 Years		297	20	14	34	-42	2	0	128	15.6	0	1	1	0	0	0	242	997	99	116	96	34	17	0	.11
Postseason																									
Year	Tm	GP	G	A	Pts	+/–	GW	OT	S	SPct	G	A	Pts	G	A	Pts	Num	PIM	Maj	Mnr	Fgt	Rgh	HHT	Hat	P/G
96-97	Edm	6	0	0	0	0	0	0	1	0.0	0	0	0	0	0	0	2	4	0	2	0	0	0	0	.00
98-99	Pho	6	2	0	2	-1	0	0	5	40.0	0	0	0	0	0	0	3	6	0	3	0	0	1	0	.33
2 Years		12	2	0	2	-1	0	0	6	33.3	0	0	0	0	0	0	5	10	0	5	0	0	1	0	.17

Jonathan Delisle

Pos: RW **Shoots:** R **Ht:** 5'10" **Wt:** 193 **Born:** 6/30/77—Ste-Anne des Plaines, Quebec **Age:** 22

Overall											Power Play			Shorthand			Penalty							Misc	
Year	Tm	GP	G	A	Pts	+/–	GW	GT	S	SPct	G	A	Pts	G	A	Pts	Num	PIM	Maj	Mnr	Fgt	Rgh	HHT	Hat	P/G
98-99	Mon	1	0	0	0	0	0	0	0	–	0	0	0	0	0	0	0	0	0	0	0	0	0	0	.00

Xavier Delisle

Pos: C **Shoots:** R **Ht:** 5'11" **Wt:** 184 **Born:** 5/24/77—Sillery, Quebec **Age:** 22

Overall											Power Play			Shorthand			Penalty							Misc	
Year	Tm	GP	G	A	Pts	+/–	GW	GT	S	SPct	G	A	Pts	G	A	Pts	Num	PIM	Maj	Mnr	Fgt	Rgh	HHT	Hat	P/G
98-99	TB	2	0	0	0	0	0	0	1	0.0	0	0	0	0	0	0	0	0	0	0	0	0	0	0	.00

Andy Delmore

Pos: D **Shoots:** R **Ht:** 6'1" **Wt:** 192 **Born:** 12/26/76—LaSalle, Ontario **Age:** 23

Overall											Power Play			Shorthand			Penalty							Misc	
Year	Tm	GP	G	A	Pts	+/–	GW	GT	S	SPct	G	A	Pts	G	A	Pts	Num	PIM	Maj	Mnr	Fgt	Rgh	HHT	Hat	P/G
98-99	Phi	2	0	1	1	-1	0	0	2	0.0	0	1	1	0	0	0	0	0	0	0	0	0	0	0	.50

Pavol Demitra

(statistical profile on page 303)

Pos: LW **Shoots:** L **Ht:** 5'11" **Wt:** 193 **Born:** 11/29/74—Dubnica, Czechoslovakia **Age:** 25

Overall											Power Play			Shorthand			Penalty							Misc	
Year	Tm	GP	G	A	Pts	+/–	GW	GT	S	SPct	G	A	Pts	G	A	Pts	Num	PIM	Maj	Mnr	Fgt	Rgh	HHT	Hat	P/G
93-94	Ott	12	1	1	2	-7	0	0	10	10.0	1	0	1	0	0	0	2	4	0	2	0	0	0	0	.17
94-95	Ott	16	4	3	7	-4	0	0	21	19.0	1	1	2	0	0	0	0	0	0	0	0	0	0	0	.44
95-96	Ott	31	7	10	17	-3	1	0	66	10.6	2	4	6	0	0	0	3	6	0	3	0	0	2	0	.55
96-97	StL	8	3	0	3	0	1	0	15	20.0	2	0	2	0	0	0	1	2	0	1	0	0	1	0	.38
97-98	StL	61	22	30	52	11	6	1	147	15.0	4	7	11	4	0	4	11	22	0	11	0	0	2	0	.85
98-99	StL	82	37	52	89	13	10	1	259	14.3	14	15	29	0	0	0	8	16	0	8	0	0	3	0	1.09
6 Years		210	74	96	170	10	18	2	518	14.3	24	27	51	4	0	4	25	50	0	25	0	0	8	0	.81
Postseason																									
Year	Tm	GP	G	A	Pts	+/–	GW	OT	S	SPct	G	A	Pts	G	A	Pts	Num	PIM	Maj	Mnr	Fgt	Rgh	HHT	Hat	P/G
96-97	StL	6	1	3	4	3	0	0	8	12.5	0	1	1	0	0	0	3	6	0	3	0	1	1	0	.67
97-98	StL	10	3	3	6	-3	0	0	32	9.4	0	1	1	0	0	0	1	2	0	1	0	0	0	0	.60
98-99	StL	13	5	4	9	-5	1	1	31	16.1	3	0	3	0	0	0	2	4	0	2	0	1	1	0	.69
3 Years		29	9	10	19	-5	1	1	71	12.7	3	2	5	0	0	0	6	12	0	6	0	2	2	0	.66

Marc Denis

Pos: G **Catches:** L **Ht:** 6'0" **Wt:** 188 **Born:** 8/1/77—Montreal, Quebec **Age:** 22

Overall															Pen Shot		Offense		
Year	Tm	GP	GS	TP	W	L	T	Min	GA	GAA	Shots	SvPct	ShO	OE	PPGA	SHGA	Shots	GA	G	A	PIM
96-97	Col	1	1	0	0	1	0	59	3	3.05	26	.885	0	0	0	0	0	0	0	0	0

Year	Tm	GP	GS	TP	W	L	T	Min	GA	GAA	Shots	SvPct	ShO	OE	PPGA	SHGA	Pen Shot Shots	Pen Shot GA	Offense G	Offense A	Offense PIM
97-98										Did Not Play in NHL											
98-99	Col	4	3	0	1	1	1	217	9	2.49	110	.918	0	3	3	0	0	0	0	0	0
2 Years		5	4	0	1	2	1	276	12	2.61	136	.912	0	3	3	0	0	0	0	0	0

Eric Desjardins

(statistical profile on page 304)

Pos: D **Shoots:** R **Ht:** 6'1" **Wt:** 205 **Born:** 6/14/69—Rouyn, Quebec **Age:** 30

		Overall									Power Play			Shorthand			Penalty							Misc	
Year	Tm	GP	G	A	Pts	+/-	GW	GT	S	SPct	G	A	Pts	G	A	Pts	Num	PIM	Maj	Mnr	Fgt	Rgh	HHT	Hat	P/G
88-89	Mon	36	2	12	14	9	0	0	39	5.1	1	–	–	0	–	–	–	26	–	–	–	–	–	0	.39
89-90	Mon	55	3	13	16	1	0	0	48	6.3	1	–	–	0	–	–	–	51	–	–	–	–	–	0	.29
90-91	Mon	62	7	18	25	7	1	0	114	6.1	0	–	–	0	–	–	–	27	–	–	–	–	–	0	.40
91-92	Mon*	77	6	32	38	17	2	0	141	4.3	4	9	13	0	0	0	25	50	0	25	0	6	11	0	.49
92-93	Mon	82	13	32	45	20	1	0	163	8.0	7	13	20	0	2	2	35	98	4	29	3	3	10	0	.55
93-94	Mon	84	12	23	35	-1	3	0	193	6.2	6	10	16	1	0	1	39	97	1	36	1	4	18	0	.42
94-95	2Tm	43	5	24	29	12	1	0	93	5.4	1	11	12	0	0	0	7	14	0	7	0	0	4	0	.67
95-96	Phi*	80	7	40	47	19	2	0	184	3.8	5	25	30	0	2	2	21	45	1	20	1	1	10	0	.59
96-97	Phi	**82**	12	34	46	25	1	0	183	6.6	5	11	16	1	1	2	25	50	0	25	0	0	11	0	.56
97-98	Phi	77	6	27	33	11	0	0	150	4.0	2	14	16	1	0	1	18	36	0	18	0	2	8	0	.43
98-99	Phi	68	15	36	51	18	2	0	190	7.9	6	18	24	0	1	1	19	38	0	19	0	1	11	0	.75
94-95	Mon	9	0	6	6	2	0	0	14	0.0	0	3	3	0	0	0	1	2	0	1	0	0	0	0	.67
94-95	Phi	34	5	18	23	10	1	0	79	6.3	1	8	9	0	0	0	6	12	0	6	0	0	4	0	.68
11 Years		746	88	291	379	138	13	0	1498	5.9	38	–	–	3	–	–	–	532	–	–	–	–	–	0	.51
											Postseason														
Year	Tm	GP	G	A	Pts	+/-	GW	OT	S	SPct	G	A	Pts	G	A	Pts	Num	PIM	Maj	Mnr	Fgt	Rgh	HHT	Hat	P/G
88-89	Mon	14	1	1	2	0	0	0	21	4.8	1	–	–	0	–	–	3	6	0	3	0	–	–	0	.14
89-90	Mon	6	0	0	0	0	0	0	15	0.0	0	0	0	0	0	0	–	10	–	–	–	–	–	0	.00
90-91	Mon	13	1	4	5	5	0	0	23	4.3	1	–	–	0	–	–	4	8	0	4	0	–	–	0	.38
91-92	Mon	11	3	3	6	0	0	0	28	10.7	1	1	2	0	1	1	2	4	0	2	0	0	1	0	.55
92-93	Mon	20	4	10	14	2	1	1	47	8.5	1	6	7	0	1	1	10	23	1	9	0	2	1	1	.70
93-94	Mon	7	0	2	2	-1	0	0	9	0.0	0	1	1	0	0	0	2	4	0	2	0	0	0	0	.29
94-95	Phi	15	4	4	8	13	2	1	35	11.4	1	1	2	0	0	0	5	10	0	5	0	0	4	0	.53
95-96	Phi	12	0	6	6	-5	0	0	26	0.0	0	5	5	0	0	0	1	2	0	1	0	0	1	0	.50
96-97	Phi	19	2	8	10	9	0	0	49	4.1	0	4	4	0	0	0	6	12	0	6	0	1	3	0	.53
97-98	Phi	5	0	1	1	-3	0	0	17	0.0	0	1	1	0	0	0	0	0	0	0	0	0	0	0	.20
98-99	Phi	6	2	2	4	1	1	0	21	9.5	1	1	2	0	0	0	2	4	0	2	0	0	0	0	.67
11 Years		128	17	41	58	21	4	2	291	5.8	6	–	–	0	–	–	–	83	–	–	–	–	–	1	.45

Boyd Devereaux

(statistical profile on page 304)

Pos: C **Shoots:** L **Ht:** 6'2" **Wt:** 195 **Born:** 4/16/78—Seaforth, Ontario **Age:** 21

		Overall									Power Play			Shorthand			Penalty							Misc	
Year	Tm	GP	G	A	Pts	+/-	GW	GT	S	SPct	G	A	Pts	G	A	Pts	Num	PIM	Maj	Mnr	Fgt	Rgh	HHT	Hat	P/G
97-98	Edm	38	1	4	5	-5	0	0	27	3.7	0	0	0	0	0	0	3	6	0	3	0	0	1	0	.13
98-99	Edm	61	6	8	14	2	4	1	39	15.4	0	0	0	1	0	1	10	23	1	9	1	3	0	0	.23
2 Years		99	7	12	19	-3	4	1	66	10.6	0	0	0	1	0	1	13	29	1	12	1	3	1	0	.19
											Postseason														
Year	Tm	GP	G	A	Pts	+/-	GW	OT	S	SPct	G	A	Pts	G	A	Pts	Num	PIM	Maj	Mnr	Fgt	Rgh	HHT	Hat	P/G
98-99	Edm	1	0	0	0	0	0	0	3	0.0	0	0	0	0	0	0	0	0	0	0	0	0	0	0	.00

Greg DeVries

Pos: D **Shoots:** L **Ht:** 6'3" **Wt:** 218 **Born:** 1/4/73—Sundridge, Ontario **Age:** 26

		Overall									Power Play			Shorthand			Penalty							Misc	
Year	Tm	GP	G	A	Pts	+/-	GW	GT	S	SPct	G	A	Pts	G	A	Pts	Num	PIM	Maj	Mnr	Fgt	Rgh	HHT	Hat	P/G
95-96	Edm	13	1	1	2	-2	0	0	8	12.5	0	0	0	0	0	0	6	12	0	6	0	2	3	0	.15
96-97	Edm	37	0	4	4	-2	0	0	31	0.0	0	0	0	0	0	0	17	52	6	11	6	3	1	0	.11
97-98	Edm	65	7	4	11	-17	0	0	53	13.2	1	0	1	0	1	1	27	80	6	20	6	4	9	0	.17
98-99	2Tm	73	1	3	4	-7	0	0	57	1.8	0	0	0	0	0	0	25	64	2	22	2	4	4	0	.05
98-99	Nsh	6	0	0	0	-4	0	0	1	0.0	0	0	0	0	0	0	2	4	0	2	0	1	1	0	.00
98-99	Col	67	1	3	4	-3	0	0	56	1.8	0	0	0	0	0	0	23	60	2	20	2	3	3	0	.06
4 Years		188	9	12	21	-28	0	0	149	6.0	1	0	1	0	1	1	75	208	14	59	14	13	17	0	.11
											Postseason														
Year	Tm	GP	G	A	Pts	+/-	GW	OT	S	SPct	G	A	Pts	G	A	Pts	Num	PIM	Maj	Mnr	Fgt	Rgh	HHT	Hat	P/G
96-97	Edm	12	0	1	1	4	0	0	16	0.0	0	0	0	0	0	0	4	8	0	4	0	3	1	0	.08

Postseason																									
Year	Tm	GP	G	A	Pts	+/–	GW	OT	S	SPct	G	A	Pts	G	A	Pts	Num	PIM	Maj	Mnr	Fgt	Rgh	HHT	Hat	P/G
97-98	Edm	7	0	0	0	-4	0	0	2	0.0	0	0	0	0	0	0	5	21	1	3	1	0	1	0	.00
98-99	Col	19	0	2	2	3	0	0	7	0.0	0	0	0	0	0	0	11	22	0	11	0	1	1	0	.11
3 Years		38	0	3	3	3	0	0	25	0.0	0	0	0	0	0	0	20	51	1	18	1	4	3	0	.08

Gerald Diduck

Pos: D **Shoots:** R **Ht:** 6'2" **Wt:** 217 **Born:** 4/6/65—Edmonton, Alberta **Age:** 34

Overall											Power Play			Shorthand			Penalty							Misc	
Year	Tm	GP	G	A	Pts	+/–	GW	GT	S	SPct	G	A	Pts	G	A	Pts	Num	PIM	Maj	Mnr	Fgt	Rgh	HHT	Hat	P/G
84-85	NYI	65	2	8	10	2	0	0	52	3.8	0	–	–	0	–	–	–	80	–	–	–	–	–	0	.15
85-86	NYI	10	1	2	3	5	0	0	6	16.7	0	–	–	0	–	–	1	2	0	1	0	–	–	0	.30
86-87	NYI	30	2	3	5	-3	0	0	54	3.7	0	–	–	0	–	–	–	67	–	–	–	–	–	0	.17
87-88	NYI	68	7	12	19	22	1	0	128	5.5	4	–	–	0	–	–	–	113	–	–	–	–	–	0	.28
88-89	NYI	65	11	21	32	9	0	0	132	8.3	6	–	–	0	–	–	–	155	–	–	–	–	–	0	.49
89-90	NYI	76	3	17	20	2	0	0	102	2.9	1	–	–	0	–	–	–	163	–	–	–	–	–	0	.26
90-91	2Tm	63	4	9	13	-5	1	0	100	4.0	0	–	–	0	–	–	–	105	–	–	–	–	–	0	.21
91-92	Van	77	6	21	27	-3	1	0	128	4.7	2	9	11	0	2	2	63	229	13	42	10	16	9	0	.35
92-93	Van	80	6	14	20	32	0	0	92	6.5	0	5	5	1	0	1	67	171	7	58	7	22	8	0	.25
93-94	Van	55	1	10	11	2	0	0	50	2.0	0	1	1	0	3	3	33	72	2	31	2	10	13	0	.20
94-95	2Tm	35	2	3	5	-5	0	0	42	4.8	1	1	2	0	0	0	20	63	5	14	4	8	2	0	.14
95-96	Har	79	1	9	10	7	0	0	93	1.1	0	0	0	0	1	1	41	88	2	39	2	4	15	0	.13
96-97	2Tm	67	2	12	14	-7	1	0	80	2.5	1	2	3	0	0	0	20	63	5	14	5	2	6	0	.21
97-98	Pho	78	8	10	18	14	4	0	104	7.7	1	0	1	0	1	1	45	118	4	39	4	3	12	0	.23
98-99	Pho	44	0	2	2	9	0	0	39	0.0	0	0	0	0	0	0	25	72	2	21	1	0	9	0	.05
90-91	Mon	32	1	2	3	3	0	0	34	2.9	0	–	–	0	–	–	–	39	–	–	–	–	–	0	.09
90-91	Van	31	3	7	10	-8	1	0	66	4.5	0	–	–	0	–	–	–	66	–	–	–	–	–	0	.32
94-95	Van	22	1	3	4	-8	0	0	25	4.0	1	1	2	0	0	0	6	15	1	5	1	3	1	0	.18
94-95	Chi	13	1	0	1	3	0	0	17	5.9	0	0	0	0	0	0	14	48	4	9	3	5	1	0	.08
96-97	Har	56	1	10	11	-9	1	0	59	1.7	0	2	2	0	0	0	14	40	4	10	4	2	5	0	.20
96-97	Pho	11	1	2	3	2	0	0	21	4.8	1	0	1	0	0	0	6	23	1	4	1	0	1	0	.27
15 Years		892	56	153	209	81	8	0	1202	4.7	16	–	–	1	–	–	–	1561	–	–	–	–	–	0	.23

Postseason																									
Year	Tm	GP	G	A	Pts	+/–	GW	OT	S	SPct	G	A	Pts	G	A	Pts	Num	PIM	Maj	Mnr	Fgt	Rgh	HHT	Hat	P/G
86-87	NYI	14	0	1	1	-7	0	0	18	0.0	0	–	–	0	0	0	–	35	–	–	–	–	–	0	.07
87-88	NYI	6	1	0	1	-1	0	0	12	8.3	1	0	1	0	0	0	–	42	–	–	–	–	–	0	.17
89-90	NYI	5	0	0	0	-5	0	0	12	0.0	0	0	0	0	0	0	–	12	–	–	–	–	–	0	.00
90-91	Van	6	1	0	1	-1	0	0	10	10.0	1	0	1	0	0	0	4	11	1	3	–	–	–	0	.17
91-92	Van	5	0	0	0	-3	0	0	7	0.0	0	0	0	0	0	0	5	10	0	5	0	5	0	0	.00
92-93	Van	12	4	2	6	1	0	0	17	23.5	0	0	0	0	0	0	6	12	0	6	0	1	2	0	.50
93-94	Van	24	1	7	8	1	0	0	32	3.1	0	1	1	0	1	1	11	22	0	11	0	3	4	0	.33
94-95	Chi	16	1	3	4	-4	0	0	21	4.8	0	1	1	0	0	0	11	22	0	11	0	3	4	0	.25
96-97	Pho	7	0	0	0	2	0	0	8	0.0	0	0	0	0	0	0	5	10	0	5	0	1	1	0	.00
97-98	Pho	6	0	2	2	-4	0	0	14	0.0	0	1	1	0	0	0	10	20	0	10	0	2	2	0	.33
98-99	Pho	3	0	0	0	-1	0	0	4	0.0	0	0	0	0	0	0	1	2	0	1	0	0	1	0	.00
11 Years		104	8	15	23	-22	0	0	155	5.2	2	–	–	0	1	1	–	198	–	–	–	–	–	0	.22

Rob DiMaio

(statistical profile on page 304)

Pos: C **Shoots:** R **Ht:** 5'10" **Wt:** 190 **Born:** 2/19/68—Calgary, Alberta **Age:** 31

Overall											Power Play			Shorthand			Penalty							Misc	
Year	Tm	GP	G	A	Pts	+/–	GW	GT	S	SPct	G	A	Pts	G	A	Pts	Num	PIM	Maj	Mnr	Fgt	Rgh	HHT	Hat	P/G
88-89	NYI	16	1	0	1	-6	1	0	16	6.3	0	0	0	0	0	0	–	30	–	–	–	–	–	0	.06
89-90	NYI	7	0	0	0	0	0	0	2	0.0	0	0	0	0	0	0	1	2	0	1	0	–	–	0	.00
90-91	NYI	1	0	0	0	0	0	0	0	–	0	0	0	0	0	0	0	0	0	0	0	0	0	0	.00
91-92	NYI	50	5	2	7	-23	0	0	43	11.6	0	0	0	2	0	2	17	43	3	14	3	7	2	0	.14
92-93	TB	54	9	15	24	0	0	0	75	12.0	2	1	3	0	0	0	25	62	4	21	4	6	4	0	.44
93-94	2Tm	53	11	12	23	-4	2	0	81	13.6	2	3	5	0	0	0	20	46	2	18	2	6	8	0	.43
94-95	Phi	36	3	1	4	8	0	1	34	8.8	0	0	0	0	0	0	17	53	1	14	1	7	1	0	.11
95-96	Phi	59	6	15	21	0	0	0	49	12.2	1	0	1	1	1	2	18	58	2	14	2	7	3	0	.36
96-97	Bos	72	13	15	28	-21	2	0	152	8.6	0	2	2	3	2	5	32	82	6	26	6	10	3	0	.39
97-98	Bos	79	10	17	27	-13	4	1	112	8.9	0	3	3	0	1	1	31	82	4	26	3	9	6	0	.34
98-99	Bos	71	7	14	21	-14	0	0	121	5.8	1	1	2	0	1	1	31	95	3	25	2	10	3	0	.30
93-94	TB	39	8	7	15	-5	1	0	51	15.7	2	3	5	0	0	0	17	40	2	15	2	5	6	0	.38
93-94	Phi	14	3	5	8	1	1	0	30	10.0	0	0	0	0	0	0	3	6	0	3	0	1	2	0	.57
11 Years		498	65	91	156	-73	9	2	685	9.5	6	10	16	6	5	11	–	553	–	–	–	–	–	0	.31

Postseason																									
Year	Tm	GP	G	A	Pts	+/–	GW	OT	S	SPct	G	A	Pts	G	A	Pts	Num	PIM	Maj	Mnr	Fgt	Rgh	HHT	Hat	P/G
89-90	NYI	1	1	0	1	2	0	0	4	25.0	0	0	0	0	0	0	2	4	0	2	0	–	–	0	1.00
94-95	Phi	15	2	4	6	3	1	0	8	25.0	0	0	0	1	0	1	2	4	0	2	0	2	0	0	.40
95-96	Phi	3	0	0	0	-1	0	0	1	0.0	0	0	0	0	0	0	0	0	0	0	0	0	0	0	.00
97-98	Bos	6	1	0	1	-3	0	0	14	7.1	0	0	0	0	0	0	4	8	0	4	0	2	0	0	.17
98-99	Bos	12	2	0	2	2	1	0	21	9.5	0	0	0	0	0	0	4	8	0	4	0	3	0	0	.17
5 Years		37	6	4	10	3	2	0	48	12.5	0	0	0	1	0	1	12	24	0	12	0	–	–	0	.27

Kevin Dineen

(statistical profile on page 304)

Pos: RW **Shoots:** R **Ht:** 5'11" **Wt:** 190 **Born:** 10/28/63—Quebec, Quebec **Age:** 36

Overall											Power Play			Shorthand			Penalty							Misc	
Year	Tm	GP	G	A	Pts	+/–	GW	GT	S	SPct	G	A	Pts	G	A	Pts	Num	PIM	Maj	Mnr	Fgt	Rgh	HHT	Hat	P/G
84-85	Har	57	25	16	41	-6	2	1	141	17.7	8	–	–	4	–	–	–	120	–	–	–	–	–	0	.72
85-86	Har	57	33	35	68	16	8	0	167	19.8	6	–	–	0	–	–	–	124	–	–	–	–	–	1	1.19
86-87	Har*	78	40	39	79	7	7	0	234	17.1	11	–	–	0	–	–	–	110	–	–	–	–	–	1	1.01
87-88	Har*	74	25	25	50	-14	4	1	223	11.2	5	–	–	0	–	–	–	217	–	–	–	–	–	0	.68
88-89	Har*	79	45	44	89	-6	4	0	294	15.3	20	–	–	1	–	–	–	167	–	–	–	–	–	1	1.13
89-90	Har	67	25	41	66	7	2	2	214	11.7	8	–	–	2	–	–	–	164	–	–	–	–	–	2	.99
90-91	Har	61	17	30	47	-15	2	0	161	10.6	4	–	–	0	–	–	–	104	–	–	–	–	–	0	.77
91-92	2Tm	80	30	32	62	-5	5	0	225	13.3	6	11	17	3	1	4	60	153	3	54	2	26	5	0	.78
92-93	Phi	83	35	28	63	14	7	1	241	14.5	6	6	12	3	4	7	69	201	5	58	3	22	16	3	.76
93-94	Phi	71	19	23	42	-9	2	1	156	12.2	5	4	9	1	0	1	52	113	3	49	3	15	8	2	.59
94-95	Phi	40	8	5	13	-1	2	0	55	14.5	4	0	4	0	1	1	15	39	3	12	3	3	1	0	.33
95-96	2Tm	46	2	9	11	-1	0	0	66	3.0	0	3	3	0	0	0	39	117	5	31	4	9	7	0	.24
96-97	Har	78	19	29	48	-6	5	2	185	10.3	8	7	15	0	1	1	50	141	3	43	2	12	5	0	.62
97-98	Car	54	7	16	23	-7	1	0	96	7.3	0	4	4	0	0	0	41	105	5	35	5	8	6	0	.43
98-99	Car	67	8	10	18	5	1	0	86	9.3	0	1	1	0	0	0	34	97	7	26	7	2	9	0	.27
91-92	Har	16	4	2	6	-6	1	0	28	14.3	1	1	2	0	0	0	10	23	1	9	1	3	1	0	.38
91-92	Phi	64	26	30	56	1	4	0	197	13.2	5	10	15	3	1	4	50	130	2	45	1	23	4	0	.88
95-96	Phi	26	0	2	2	-8	0	0	31	0.0	0	1	1	0	0	0	18	50	2	15	2	4	4	0	.08
95-96	Har	20	2	7	9	7	0	0	35	5.7	0	2	2	0	0	0	21	67	3	16	2	5	3	0	.45
15 Years		992	338	382	720	-21	52	8	2544	13.3	91	–	–	14	–	–	–	1972	–	–	–	–	–	10	.73

Postseason																									
Year	Tm	GP	G	A	Pts	+/–	GW	OT	S	SPct	G	A	Pts	G	A	Pts	Num	PIM	Maj	Mnr	Fgt	Rgh	HHT	Hat	P/G
85-86	Har	10	6	7	13	2	2	1	28	21.4	1	–	–	0	–	–	–	18	–	–	–	–	–	0	1.30
86-87	Har	6	2	1	3	-1	0	0	13	15.4	1	–	–	0	0	0	–	31	–	–	–	–	–	0	.50
87-88	Har	6	4	4	8	2	1	0	17	23.5	1	–	–	0	0	0	4	8	0	4	0	–	–	0	1.33
88-89	Har	4	1	0	1	0	0	0	10	10.0	0	0	0	0	0	0	–	10	–	–	–	–	–	0	.25
89-90	Har	6	3	2	5	4	1	1	15	20.0	0	–	–	0	0	0	–	18	–	–	–	–	–	0	.83
90-91	Har	6	1	0	1	-3	0	0	11	9.1	0	0	0	0	0	0	–	16	–	–	–	–	–	0	.17
94-95	Phi	15	6	4	10	2	1	0	24	25.0	1	0	1	0	0	0	9	18	0	9	0	4	0	0	.67
98-99	Car	6	0	0	0	0	0	0	4	0.0	0	0	0	0	0	0	4	8	0	4	0	2	0	0	.00
8 Years		59	23	18	41	6	5	2	122	18.9	4	–	–	0	–	–	–	127	–	–	–	–	–	0	.69

Chris Dingman

Pos: LW **Shoots:** L **Ht:** 6'4" **Wt:** 225 **Born:** 7/6/76—Edmonton, Alberta **Age:** 23

Overall											Power Play			Shorthand			Penalty							Misc	
Year	Tm	GP	G	A	Pts	+/–	GW	GT	S	SPct	G	A	Pts	G	A	Pts	Num	PIM	Maj	Mnr	Fgt	Rgh	HHT	Hat	P/G
97-98	Cgy	70	3	3	6	-11	0	0	47	6.4	1	0	1	0	0	0	43	149	13	27	13	14	8	0	.09
98-99	2Tm	3	0	0	0	-2	0	0	1	0.0	0	0	0	0	0	0	5	24	2	2	2	2	0	0	.00
98-99	Cgy	2	0	0	0	-2	0	0	1	0.0	0	0	0	0	0	0	3	17	1	1	1	1	0	0	.00
98-99	Col	1	0	0	0	0	0	0	0	–	0	0	0	0	0	0	2	7	1	1	1	1	0	0	.00
2 Years		73	3	3	6	-13	0	0	48	6.3	1	0	1	0	0	0	48	173	15	29	15	16	8	0	.08

Shane Doan

(statistical profile on page 305)

Pos: RW **Shoots:** R **Ht:** 6'1" **Wt:** 215 **Born:** 10/10/76—Halkirk, Saskatchewan **Age:** 23

Overall											Power Play			Shorthand			Penalty							Misc	
Year	Tm	GP	G	A	Pts	+/–	GW	GT	S	SPct	G	A	Pts	G	A	Pts	Num	PIM	Maj	Mnr	Fgt	Rgh	HHT	Hat	P/G
95-96	Wpg	74	7	10	17	-9	3	0	106	6.6	1	3	4	0	0	0	27	101	5	18	5	6	4	0	.23
96-97	Pho	63	4	8	12	-3	0	0	100	4.0	0	1	1	0	0	0	17	49	5	12	5	1	7	0	.19
97-98	Pho	33	5	6	11	-3	3	0	42	11.9	0	1	1	0	0	0	9	35	3	5	3	1	2	0	.33
98-99	Pho	79	6	16	22	-5	0	0	156	3.8	0	1	1	0	0	0	13	54	4	7	4	2	1	0	.28
4 Years		249	22	40	62	-20	6	0	404	5.4	1	6	7	0	0	0	66	239	17	42	17	10	14	0	.25

Postseason																									
Year	Tm	GP	G	A	Pts	+/–	GW	OT	S	SPct	G	A	Pts	G	A	Pts	Num	PIM	Maj	Mnr	Fgt	Rgh	HHT	Hat	P/G
95-96	Wpg	6	0	0	0	0	0	0	2	0.0	0	0	0	0	0	0	3	6	0	3	0	0	2	0	.00
96-97	Pho	4	0	0	0	-1	0	0	2	0.0	0	0	0	0	0	0	1	2	0	1	0	0	0	0	.00
97-98	Pho	6	1	0	1	-2	0	0	7	14.3	0	0	0	0	0	0	3	6	0	3	0	1	1	0	.17
98-99	Pho	7	2	2	4	4	2	1	17	11.8	0	0	0	0	0	0	3	6	0	3	0	2	1	0	.57
4 Years		23	3	2	5	1	2	1	28	10.7	0	0	0	0	0	0	10	20	0	10	0	3	4	0	.22

Jason Doig

Pos: D **Shoots:** R **Ht:** 6'3" **Wt:** 216 **Born:** 1/29/77—Montreal, Quebec **Age:** 22

Overall											Power Play			Shorthand			Penalty							Misc	
Year	Tm	GP	G	A	Pts	+/–	GW	GT	S	SPct	G	A	Pts	G	A	Pts	Num	PIM	Maj	Mnr	Fgt	Rgh	HHT	Hat	P/G
95-96	Wpg	15	1	1	2	-2	0	0	7	14.3	0	0	0	0	0	0	7	28	2	4	2	0	1	0	.13
96-97		Did Not Play in NHL																							
97-98	Pho	4	0	1	1	-4	0	0	1	0.0	0	0	0	0	0	0	6	12	0	6	0	0	5	0	.25
98-99	Pho	9	0	1	1	2	0	0	0	–	0	0	0	0	0	0	5	10	0	5	0	2	0	0	.11
3 Years		28	1	3	4	-4	0	0	8	12.5	0	0	0	0	0	0	18	50	2	15	2	2	6	0	.14

Bobby Dollas

(statistical profile on page 305)

Pos: D **Shoots:** L **Ht:** 6'2" **Wt:** 212 **Born:** 1/31/65—Montreal, Quebec **Age:** 34

Overall											Power Play			Shorthand			Penalty							Misc	
Year	Tm	GP	G	A	Pts	+/–	GW	GT	S	SPct	G	A	Pts	G	A	Pts	Num	PIM	Maj	Mnr	Fgt	Rgh	HHT	Hat	P/G
83-84	Wpg	1	0	0	0	-2	0	0	0	–	0	0	0	0	0	0	0	0	0	0	0	0	0	0	.00
84-85	Wpg	9	0	0	0	3	0	0	3	0.0	0	0	0	0	0	0	0	0	0	0	0	0	0	0	.00
85-86	Wpg	46	0	5	5	-3	0	0	50	0.0	0	–	–	0	–	–	–	66	–	–	–	–	–	0	.11
86-87		Did Not Play in NHL																							
87-88	Que	9	0	0	0	-4	0	0	5	0.0	0	0	0	0	0	0	1	2	0	1	0	–	–	0	.00
88-89	Que	16	0	3	3	-11	0	0	11	0.0	0	–	–	0	–	–	–	16	–	–	–	–	–	0	.19
89-90		Did Not Play in NHL																							
90-91	Det	56	3	5	8	6	1	0	59	5.1	0	–	–	0	–	–	–	20	–	–	–	–	–	0	.14
91-92	Det	27	3	1	4	4	0	0	26	11.5	0	0	0	1	0	1	10	20	0	10	0	0	4	0	.15
92-93	Det	6	0	0	0	-1	0	0	5	0.0	0	0	0	0	0	0	1	2	0	1	0	0	0	0	.00
93-94	Anh	77	9	11	20	20	1	0	121	7.4	1	5	6	0	0	0	26	55	1	25	1	3	9	0	.26
94-95	Anh	45	7	13	20	-3	1	0	70	10.0	3	3	6	1	0	1	6	12	0	6	0	0	3	0	.44
95-96	Anh	82	8	22	30	9	1	0	117	6.8	0	8	8	1	1	2	28	64	0	27	0	2	7	0	.37
96-97	Anh	79	4	14	18	17	1	1	96	4.2	1	3	4	0	0	0	22	55	1	20	1	3	9	0	.23
97-98	2Tm	52	2	6	8	-6	0	0	38	5.3	0	3	3	0	0	0	19	49	1	17	0	1	7	0	.15
98-99	Pit	70	2	8	10	-3	0	0	34	5.9	0	0	0	0	1	1	19	60	2	15	2	0	7	0	.14
97-98	Anh	22	0	1	1	-12	0	0	11	0.0	0	0	0	0	0	0	8	27	1	6	0	1	3	0	.05
97-98	Edm	30	2	5	7	6	0	0	27	7.4	0	3	3	0	0	0	11	22	0	11	0	0	4	0	.23
14 Years		575	38	88	126	26	5	1	635	6.0	5	–	–	3	–	–	–	421	–	–	–	–	–	0	.22

Postseason																									
Year	Tm	GP	G	A	Pts	+/–	GW	OT	S	SPct	G	A	Pts	G	A	Pts	Num	PIM	Maj	Mnr	Fgt	Rgh	HHT	Hat	P/G
85-86	Wpg	3	0	0	0	-2	0	0	0	–	0	0	0	0	0	0	1	2	0	1	0	–	–	0	.00
90-91	Det	7	1	0	1	-2	0	0	3	33.3	0	0	0	0	0	0	5	13	1	4	0	–	–	0	.14
91-92	Det	2	0	1	1	1	0	0	3	0.0	0	0	0	0	0	0	0	0	0	0	0	0	0	0	.50
96-97	Anh	11	0	0	0	-2	0	0	10	0.0	0	0	0	0	0	0	2	4	0	2	0	2	0	0	.00
97-98	Edm	11	0	0	0	2	0	0	10	0.0	0	0	0	0	0	0	4	16	0	3	0	0	1	0	.00
98-99	Pit	13	1	0	1	-4	0	0	6	16.7	0	0	0	0	0	0	3	6	0	3	0	1	1	0	.08
6 Years		47	2	1	3	-7	0	0	32	6.3	0	0	0	0	0	0	15	41	1	13	0	–	–	0	.06

Hnat Domenichelli

(statistical profile on page 305)

Pos: C **Shoots:** L **Ht:** 6'0" **Wt:** 185 **Born:** 2/17/76—Edmonton, Alberta **Age:** 23

Overall											Power Play			Shorthand			Penalty							Misc	
Year	Tm	GP	G	A	Pts	+/–	GW	GT	S	SPct	G	A	Pts	G	A	Pts	Num	PIM	Maj	Mnr	Fgt	Rgh	HHT	Hat	P/G
96-97	2Tm	23	3	3	6	-3	0	0	30	10.0	1	1	2	0	0	0	3	9	1	2	1	0	0	0	.26
97-98	Cgy	31	9	7	16	4	1	2	70	12.9	1	0	1	0	0	0	3	6	0	3	0	0	2	0	.52
98-99	Cgy	23	5	5	10	-4	0	0	45	11.1	3	1	4	0	0	0	4	11	1	3	1	0	0	0	.43
96-97	Har	13	2	1	3	-4	0	0	14	14.3	1	0	1	0	0	0	2	7	1	1	1	0	0	0	.23
96-97	Cgy	10	1	2	3	1	0	0	16	6.3	0	1	1	0	0	0	1	2	0	1	0	0	0	0	.30
3 Years		77	17	15	32	-3	1	2	145	11.7	5	2	7	0	0	0	10	26	2	8	2	0	2	0	.42

Tie Domi

(statistical profile on page 305)

Pos: RW **Shoots:** R **Ht:** 5'10" **Wt:** 200 **Born:** 11/1/69—Windsor, Ontario **Age:** 30

Overall											Power Play			Shorthand			Penalty							Misc	
Year	Tm	GP	G	A	Pts	+/–	GW	GT	S	SPct	G	A	Pts	G	A	Pts	Num	PIM	Maj	Mnr	Fgt	Rgh	HHT	Hat	P/G
89-90	Tor	2	0	0	0	0	0	0	0	–	0	0	0	0	0	0	–	42	–	–	–	–	–	0	.00
90-91	NYR	28	1	0	1	-5	0	0	5	20.0	0	0	0	0	0	0	–	185	–	–	–	–	–	0	.04
91-92	NYR	42	2	4	6	-4	1	0	20	10.0	0	0	0	0	0	0	55	246	16	28	16	20	1	0	.14
92-93	2Tm	61	5	10	15	1	0	0	40	12.5	0	0	0	0	0	0	78	344	20	42	20	14	5	0	.25
93-94	Wpg	81	8	11	19	-8	1	0	98	8.2	0	0	0	0	0	0	74	**347**	21	36	21	18	4	0	.23
94-95	2Tm	40	4	5	9	-5	0	0	46	8.7	0	0	0	0	0	0	40	159	13	22	13	11	2	0	.23
95-96	Tor	72	7	6	13	-3	1	0	61	11.5	0	0	0	0	0	0	71	297	25	36	24	19	4	0	.18
96-97	Tor	80	11	17	28	-17	1	0	98	11.2	2	1	3	0	0	0	69	275	27	35	26	13	8	0	.35
97-98	Tor	80	4	10	14	-5	0	1	72	5.6	0	0	0	0	0	0	**98**	365	27	60	26	23	8	0	.18
98-99	Tor	72	8	14	22	5	1	0	65	12.3	0	0	0	0	0	0	53	198	20	29	20	15	3	0	.31
92-93	NYR	12	2	0	2	-1	0	0	11	18.2	0	0	0	0	0	0	16	95	5	5	5	2	0	0	.17
92-93	Wpg	49	3	10	13	2	0	0	29	10.3	0	0	0	0	0	0	62	249	15	37	15	12	5	0	.27
94-95	Wpg	31	4	4	8	-6	0	0	34	11.8	0	0	0	0	0	0	32	128	8	19	8	9	1	0	.26
94-95	Tor	9	0	1	1	1	0	0	12	0.0	0	0	0	0	0	0	8	31	5	3	5	2	1	0	.11
10 Years		558	50	77	127	-41	5	1	505	9.9	2	1	3	0	0	0	–	2458	–	–	–	–	–	0	.23

Postseason

Year	Tm	GP	G	A	Pts	+/–	GW	OT	S	SPct	G	A	Pts	G	A	Pts	Num	PIM	Maj	Mnr	Fgt	Rgh	HHT	Hat	P/G
91-92	NYR	6	1	1	2	1	0	0	1	100.0	0	0	0	0	0	0	8	32	0	6	0	4	0	0	.33
92-93	Wpg	6	1	0	1	1	0	0	5	20.0	0	0	0	0	0	0	6	23	1	4	0	2	0	0	.17
94-95	Tor	7	1	0	1	-2	0	0	7	14.3	0	0	0	0	0	0	0	0	0	0	0	0	0	0	.14
95-96	Tor	6	0	2	2	0	0	0	4	0.0	0	0	0	0	0	0	2	4	0	2	0	1	0	0	.33
98-99	Tor	14	0	2	2	-1	0	0	7	0.0	0	1	1	0	0	0	8	24	0	7	0	4	1	0	.14
5 Years		39	3	5	8	-1	0	0	24	12.5	0	1	1	0	0	0	24	83	1	19	0	11	1	0	.21

Ted Donato

(statistical profile on page 306)

Pos: LW **Shoots:** L **Ht:** 5'10" **Wt:** 180 **Born:** 4/28/69—Boston, Massachusetts **Age:** 30

Overall											Power Play			Shorthand			Penalty							Misc	
Year	Tm	GP	G	A	Pts	+/–	GW	GT	S	SPct	G	A	Pts	G	A	Pts	Num	PIM	Maj	Mnr	Fgt	Rgh	HHT	Hat	P/G
91-92	Bos	10	1	2	3	-1	0	0	13	7.7	0	0	0	0	0	0	4	8	0	4	0	0	3	0	.30
92-93	Bos	82	15	20	35	2	5	0	118	12.7	3	11	14	2	0	2	21	61	1	18	0	3	8	0	.43
93-94	Bos	84	22	32	54	0	1	1	158	13.9	9	4	13	2	2	4	24	59	1	22	0	3	12	0	.64
94-95	Bos	47	10	10	20	3	1	0	71	14.1	1	2	3	0	1	1	5	10	0	5	0	0	4	0	.43
95-96	Bos	82	23	26	49	6	1	0	152	15.1	7	8	15	0	2	2	23	46	0	23	0	3	11	0	.60
96-97	Bos	67	25	26	51	-9	2	0	172	14.5	6	5	11	2	1	3	17	37	1	16	1	1	9	0	.76
97-98	Bos	79	16	23	39	6	5	1	129	12.4	3	7	10	0	0	0	23	54	0	22	0	1	8	0	.49
98-99	3Tm	82	11	16	27	-8	0	0	106	10.4	3	4	7	0	0	0	19	41	1	18	0	1	10	0	.33
98-99	Bos	14	1	3	4	0	0	0	22	4.5	0	1	1	0	0	0	2	4	0	2	0	0	1	0	.29
98-99	NYI	55	7	11	18	-10	0	0	68	10.3	2	3	5	0	0	0	12	27	1	11	0	1	5	0	.33
98-99	Ott	13	3	2	5	2	0	0	16	18.8	1	0	1	0	0	0	5	10	0	5	0	0	4	0	.38
8 Years		533	123	155	278	-1	15	2	919	13.4	32	41	73	6	6	12	136	316	4	128	1	12	65	0	.52

Postseason

Year	Tm	GP	G	A	Pts	+/–	GW	OT	S	SPct	G	A	Pts	G	A	Pts	Num	PIM	Maj	Mnr	Fgt	Rgh	HHT	Hat	P/G
91-92	Bos	15	3	4	7	0	1	1	20	15.0	0	2	2	0	0	0	2	4	0	2	0	0	1	0	.47
92-93	Bos	4	0	1	1	-7	0	0	9	0.0	0	1	1	0	0	0	0	0	0	0	0	0	0	0	.25
93-94	Bos	13	4	2	6	-1	1	0	18	22.2	2	2	4	0	0	0	5	10	0	5	0	0	1	0	.46
94-95	Bos	5	0	0	0	0	0	0	5	0.0	0	0	0	0	0	0	2	4	0	2	0	1	0	0	.00
95-96	Bos	5	1	2	3	-3	0	0	7	14.3	1	1	2	0	0	0	1	2	0	1	0	0	0	0	.60
97-98	Bos	5	0	0	0	-3	0	0	3	0.0	0	0	0	0	0	0	1	2	0	1	0	0	0	0	.00
98-99	Ott	1	0	0	0	0	0	0	0	–	0	0	0	0	0	0	0	0	0	0	0	0	0	0	.00
7 Years		48	8	9	17	-14	2	1	62	12.9	3	6	9	0	0	0	11	22	0	11	0	1	2	0	.35

Shean Donovan

(statistical profile on page 306)

Pos: RW **Shoots:** R **Ht:** 6'3" **Wt:** 210 **Born:** 1/22/75—Timmins, Ontario **Age:** 24

Overall											Power Play			Shorthand			Penalty							Misc	
Year	Tm	GP	G	A	Pts	+/–	GW	GT	S	SPct	G	A	Pts	G	A	Pts	Num	PIM	Maj	Mnr	Fgt	Rgh	HHT	Hat	P/G
94-95	SJ	14	0	0	0	-6	0	0	13	0.0	0	0	0	0	0	0	3	6	0	3	0	2	0	0	.00
95-96	SJ	74	13	8	21	-17	2	0	73	17.8	0	0	0	1	0	1	18	39	1	17	1	3	12	0	.28
96-97	SJ	73	9	6	15	-18	0	0	115	7.8	0	0	0	1	0	1	21	42	0	21	0	4	10	0	.21
97-98	2Tm	67	8	10	18	6	0	0	81	9.9	0	0	0	0	0	0	32	70	2	30	2	4	17	0	.27
98-99	Col	68	7	12	19	4	1	0	81	8.6	1	1	2	0	0	0	17	37	1	16	1	0	8	0	.28
97-98	SJ	20	3	3	6	3	0	0	24	12.5	0	0	0	0	0	0	11	22	0	11	0	1	6	0	.30
97-98	Col	47	5	7	12	3	0	0	57	8.8	0	0	0	0	0	0	21	48	2	19	2	3	11	0	.26
5 Years		296	37	36	73	-31	3	0	363	10.2	1	1	2	2	0	2	91	194	4	87	4	13	47	0	.25

Postseason																									
Year	Tm	GP	G	A	Pts	+/–	GW	OT	S	SPct	G	A	Pts	G	A	Pts	Num	PIM	Maj	Mnr	Fgt	Rgh	HHT	Hat	P/G
94-95	SJ	7	0	1	1	-1	0	0	7	0.0	0	0	0	0	0	0	3	6	0	3	0	1	2	0	.14
98-99	Col	5	0	0	0	0	0	0	1	0.0	0	0	0	0	0	0	1	2	0	1	0	0	0	0	.00
2 Years		12	0	1	1	-1	0	0	8	0.0	0	0	0	0	0	0	4	8	0	4	0	1	2	0	.08

Jim Dowd

Pos: C **Shoots:** R **Ht:** 6'1" **Wt:** 190 **Born:** 12/25/68—Brick, New Jersey **Age:** 31

Overall											Power Play			Shorthand			Penalty							Misc	
Year	Tm	GP	G	A	Pts	+/–	GW	GT	S	SPct	G	A	Pts	G	A	Pts	Num	PIM	Maj	Mnr	Fgt	Rgh	HHT	Hat	P/G
91-92	NJ	1	0	0	0	0	0	0	0	–	0	0	0	0	0	0	0	0	0	0	0	0	0	0	.00
92-93	NJ	1	0	0	0	-1	0	0	1	0.0	0	0	0	0	0	0	0	0	0	0	0	0	0	0	.00
93-94	NJ	15	5	10	15	8	0	0	26	19.2	2	5	7	0	0	0	0	0	0	0	0	0	0	0	1.00
94-95	NJ	10	1	4	5	-5	0	0	14	7.1	1	2	3	0	0	0	0	0	0	0	0	0	0	0	.50
95-96	2Tm	66	5	15	20	-9	0	0	76	6.6	0	0	0	0	2	2	10	23	1	9	1	0	5	0	.30
96-97	NYI	3	0	0	0	-1	0	0	0	–	0	0	0	0	0	0	0	0	0	0	0	0	0	0	.00
97-98	Cgy	48	6	8	14	10	0	0	58	10.3	0	1	1	1	0	1	6	12	0	6	0	0	4	0	.29
98-99	Edm	1	0	0	0	0	0	0	1	0.0	0	0	0	0	0	0	0	0	0	0	0	0	0	0	.00
95-96	NJ	28	4	9	13	-1	0	0	41	9.8	0	0	0	0	1	1	7	17	1	6	1	0	3	0	.46
95-96	Van	38	1	6	7	-8	0	0	35	2.9	0	0	0	0	1	1	3	6	0	3	0	0	2	0	.18
8 Years		145	17	37	54	2	0	0	176	9.7	3	8	11	1	2	3	16	35	1	15	1	0	9	0	.37
Postseason																									
Year	Tm	GP	G	A	Pts	+/–	GW	OT	S	SPct	G	A	Pts	G	A	Pts	Num	PIM	Maj	Mnr	Fgt	Rgh	HHT	Hat	P/G
93-94	NJ	19	2	6	8	-3	0	0	30	6.7	0	4	4	0	0	0	4	8	0	4	0	0	1	0	.42
94-95	NJ	11	2	1	3	3	1	0	12	16.7	0	0	0	0	0	0	4	8	0	4	0	1	1	0	.27
95-96	Van	1	0	0	0	-1	0	0	0	–	0	0	0	0	0	0	0	0	0	0	0	0	0	0	.00
3 Years		31	4	7	11	-1	1	0	42	9.5	0	4	4	0	0	0	8	16	0	8	0	1	2	0	.35

Dallas Drake

(statistical profile on page 306)

Pos: RW **Shoots:** L **Ht:** 6'0" **Wt:** 185 **Born:** 2/4/69—Trail, British Columbia **Age:** 30

Overall											Power Play			Shorthand			Penalty							Misc	
Year	Tm	GP	G	A	Pts	+/–	GW	GT	S	SPct	G	A	Pts	G	A	Pts	Num	PIM	Maj	Mnr	Fgt	Rgh	HHT	Hat	P/G
92-93	Det	72	18	26	44	15	5	0	89	20.2	3	4	7	2	0	2	34	93	3	29	2	3	5	0	.61
93-94	2Tm	62	13	27	40	-1	3	0	112	11.6	1	6	7	2	1	3	20	49	3	17	3	3	5	0	.65
94-95	Wpg	43	8	18	26	-6	1	0	66	12.1	0	3	3	0	0	0	15	30	0	15	0	1	7	0	.60
95-96	Wpg	69	19	20	39	-7	2	1	121	15.7	4	3	7	4	1	5	15	36	2	13	2	2	4	0	.57
96-97	Pho	63	17	19	36	-11	1	0	113	15.0	5	4	9	1	2	3	19	52	2	16	2	2	4	0	.57
97-98	Pho	60	11	29	40	17	2	0	112	9.8	3	1	4	0	1	1	23	71	3	18	3	3	6	0	.67
98-99	Pho	53	9	22	31	17	3	0	105	8.6	0	2	2	0	0	0	23	65	1	20	1	3	11	0	.58
93-94	Det	47	10	22	32	5	2	0	78	12.8	0	5	5	1	1	2	17	37	1	16	1	3	5	0	.68
93-94	Wpg	15	3	5	8	-6	1	0	34	8.8	1	1	2	1	0	1	3	12	2	1	2	0	0	0	.53
7 Years		422	95	161	256	24	17	1	718	13.2	16	23	39	9	5	14	149	396	14	128	13	17	42	0	.61
Postseason																									
Year	Tm	GP	G	A	Pts	+/–	GW	OT	S	SPct	G	A	Pts	G	A	Pts	Num	PIM	Maj	Mnr	Fgt	Rgh	HHT	Hat	P/G
92-93	Det	7	3	3	6	3	0	0	8	37.5	1	0	1	0	0	0	3	6	0	3	0	0	1	0	.86
95-96	Wpg	3	0	0	0	-2	0	0	3	0.0	0	0	0	0	0	0	0	0	0	0	0	0	0	0	.00
96-97	Pho	7	0	1	1	-2	0	0	12	0.0	0	0	0	0	0	0	1	2	0	1	0	0	0	0	.14
97-98	Pho	4	0	1	1	-4	0	0	4	0.0	0	0	0	0	0	0	1	2	0	1	0	0	0	0	.25
98-99	Pho	7	4	3	7	3	1	0	18	22.2	2	1	3	0	0	0	2	4	0	2	0	0	0	0	1.00
5 Years		28	7	8	15	-2	1	0	45	15.6	3	1	4	0	0	0	7	14	0	7	0	0	1	0	.54

Kris Draper

(statistical profile on page 306)

Pos: C **Shoots:** L **Ht:** 5'11" **Wt:** 190 **Born:** 5/24/71—Toronto, Ontario **Age:** 28

Overall											Power Play			Shorthand			Penalty							Misc	
Year	Tm	GP	G	A	Pts	+/–	GW	GT	S	SPct	G	A	Pts	G	A	Pts	Num	PIM	Maj	Mnr	Fgt	Rgh	HHT	Hat	P/G
90-91	Wpg	3	1	0	1	0	0	0	1	100.0	0	0	0	0	0	0	1	5	1	0	–	0	0	0	.33
91-92	Wpg	10	2	0	2	0	0	0	19	10.5	0	0	0	0	0	0	1	2	0	1	0	0	1	0	.20
92-93	Wpg	7	0	0	0	-6	0	0	5	0.0	0	0	0	0	0	0	1	2	0	1	0	0	0	0	.00
93-94	Det	39	5	8	13	11	0	0	55	9.1	0	0	0	1	1	2	10	31	1	8	0	1	4	0	.33
94-95	Det	36	2	6	8	1	0	0	44	4.5	0	0	0	0	1	1	11	22	0	11	0	2	3	0	.22
95-96	Det	52	7	9	16	2	0	0	51	13.7	0	0	0	1	2	3	16	32	0	16	0	3	2	0	.31
96-97	Det	76	8	5	13	-11	1	0	85	9.4	1	0	1	0	1	1	27	73	1	24	1	7	5	0	.17
97-98	Det	64	13	10	23	5	4	0	96	13.5	1	1	2	0	0	0	21	45	1	20	1	3	5	0	.36
98-99	Det	80	4	14	18	2	1	0	78	5.1	0	0	0	1	3	4	30	79	1	27	0	3	9	0	.23
9 Years		367	42	52	94	4	6	0	434	9.7	2	1	3	3	8	11	118	291	5	108	–	19	29	0	.26

Postseason																									
Year	Tm	GP	G	A	Pts	+/–	GW	OT	S	SPct	G	A	Pts	G	A	Pts	Num	PIM	Maj	Mnr	Fgt	Rgh	HHT	Hat	P/G
91-92	Wpg	2	0	0	0	-2	0	0	1	0.0	0	0	0	0	0	0	0	0	0	0	0	0	0	0	.00
93-94	Det	7	2	2	4	5	0	0	15	13.3	0	0	0	1	0	1	2	4	0	2	0	0	0	0	.57
94-95	Det	18	4	1	5	-2	1	0	22	18.2	0	0	0	1	0	1	6	12	0	6	0	1	0	0	.28
95-96	Det	18	4	2	6	2	0	0	25	16.0	0	0	0	1	0	1	9	18	0	9	0	3	3	0	.33
96-97	Det	20	2	4	6	5	0	0	30	6.7	0	0	0	1	1	2	6	12	0	6	0	1	0	0	.30
97-98	Det	19	1	3	4	4	1	1	20	5.0	0	0	0	0	1	1	6	12	0	6	0	2	1	0	.21
98-99	Det	10	0	1	1	-1	0	0	9	0.0	0	0	0	0	0	0	3	6	0	3	0	0	2	0	.10
7 Years		94	13	13	26	11	2	1	122	10.7	0	0	0	4	2	6	32	64	0	32	0	7	6	0	.28

Chris Drury

(statistical profile on page 307)

Pos: C **Shoots:** R **Ht:** 5'10" **Wt:** 180 **Born:** 8/20/76—Trumbull, Connecticut **Age:** 23

Overall											Power Play			Shorthand			Penalty							Misc	
Year	Tm	GP	G	A	Pts	+/–	GW	GT	S	SPct	G	A	Pts	G	A	Pts	Num	PIM	Maj	Mnr	Fgt	Rgh	HHT	Hat	P/G
98-99	Col	79	20	24	44	9	3	1	138	14.5	6	7	13	0	0	0	24	62	2	21	2	2	7	0	.56
Postseason																									
Year	Tm	GP	G	A	Pts	+/–	GW	OT	S	SPct	G	A	Pts	G	A	Pts	Num	PIM	Maj	Mnr	Fgt	Rgh	HHT	Hat	P/G
98-99	Col	19	6	2	8	2	4	1	40	15.0	0	0	0	0	0	0	2	4	0	2	0	0	0	0	.42

Ted Drury

(statistical profile on page 307)

Pos: C **Shoots:** L **Ht:** 6'0" **Wt:** 208 **Born:** 9/13/71—Boston, Massachusetts **Age:** 28

Overall											Power Play			Shorthand			Penalty							Misc	
Year	Tm	GP	G	A	Pts	+/–	GW	GT	S	SPct	G	A	Pts	G	A	Pts	Num	PIM	Maj	Mnr	Fgt	Rgh	HHT	Hat	P/G
93-94	2Tm	50	6	12	18	-15	1	1	80	7.5	0	1	1	1	0	1	14	36	0	13	0	4	6	0	.36
94-95	Har	34	3	6	9	-3	0	0	31	9.7	0	0	0	0	0	0	9	21	1	8	1	3	2	0	.26
95-96	Ott	42	9	7	16	-19	1	1	80	11.3	1	2	3	0	0	0	20	54	2	17	2	7	4	0	.38
96-97	Anh	73	9	9	18	-9	2	1	114	7.9	1	0	1	0	0	0	20	54	2	17	1	5	6	0	.25
97-98	Anh	73	6	10	16	-10	0	0	110	5.5	0	0	0	1	0	1	31	82	4	26	4	13	1	0	.22
98-99	Anh	75	5	6	11	2	0	0	79	6.3	0	0	0	0	0	0	28	83	1	24	1	7	5	0	.15
93-94	Cgy	34	5	7	12	-5	1	1	43	11.6	0	1	1	1	0	1	9	26	0	8	0	3	3	0	.35
93-94	Har	16	1	5	6	-10	0	0	37	2.7	0	0	0	0	0	0	5	10	0	5	0	1	3	0	.38
6 Years		347	38	50	88	-54	4	3	494	7.7	2	3	5	2	0	2	122	330	10	105	9	39	24	0	.25
Postseason																									
Year	Tm	GP	G	A	Pts	+/–	GW	OT	S	SPct	G	A	Pts	G	A	Pts	Num	PIM	Maj	Mnr	Fgt	Rgh	HHT	Hat	P/G
96-97	Anh	10	1	0	1	-2	0	0	17	5.9	0	0	0	0	0	0	2	4	0	2	0	1	0	0	.10
98-99	Anh	4	0	0	0	-6	0	0	4	0.0	0	0	0	0	0	0	0	0	0	0	0	0	0	0	.00
2 Years		14	1	0	1	-8	0	0	21	4.8	0	0	0	0	0	0	2	4	0	2	0	1	0	0	.07

Christian Dube

Pos: C **Shoots:** R **Ht:** 6'0" **Wt:** 190 **Born:** 4/25/77—Sherbrooke, Quebec **Age:** 22

Overall											Power Play			Shorthand			Penalty							Misc	
Year	Tm	GP	G	A	Pts	+/–	GW	GT	S	SPct	G	A	Pts	G	A	Pts	Num	PIM	Maj	Mnr	Fgt	Rgh	HHT	Hat	P/G
96-97	NYR	27	1	1	2	-4	0	0	14	7.1	1	1	2	0	0	0	2	4	0	2	0	1	1	0	.07
97-98		Did Not Play in NHL																							
98-99	NYR	6	0	0	0	0	0	0	0	–	0	0	0	0	0	0	0	0	0	0	0	0	0	0	.00
2 Years		33	1	1	2	-4	0	0	14	7.1	1	1	2	0	0	0	2	4	0	2	0	1	1	0	.06
Postseason																									
Year	Tm	GP	G	A	Pts	+/–	GW	OT	S	SPct	G	A	Pts	G	A	Pts	Num	PIM	Maj	Mnr	Fgt	Rgh	HHT	Hat	P/G
96-97	NYR	3	0	0	0	-2	0	0	0	–	0	0	0	0	0	0	0	0	0	0	0	0	0	0	.00

Steve Dubinsky

(statistical profile on page 307)

Pos: C **Shoots:** L **Ht:** 6'0" **Wt:** 190 **Born:** 7/9/70—Montreal, Quebec **Age:** 29

Overall											Power Play			Shorthand			Penalty							Misc	
Year	Tm	GP	G	A	Pts	+/–	GW	GT	S	SPct	G	A	Pts	G	A	Pts	Num	PIM	Maj	Mnr	Fgt	Rgh	HHT	Hat	P/G
93-94	Chi	27	2	6	8	1	0	0	20	10.0	0	1	1	0	0	0	8	16	0	8	0	2	0	0	.30
94-95	Chi	16	0	0	0	-5	0	0	16	0.0	0	0	0	0	0	0	4	8	0	4	0	2	0	0	.00
95-96	Chi	43	2	3	5	3	0	0	33	6.1	0	0	0	0	0	0	7	14	0	7	0	1	3	0	.12
96-97	Chi	5	0	0	0	2	0	0	4	0.0	0	0	0	0	0	0	0	0	0	0	0	0	0	0	.00
97-98	Chi	82	5	13	18	-6	0	0	112	4.5	0	0	0	1	3	4	19	57	1	16	1	6	5	0	.22
98-99	2Tm	63	4	10	14	-7	0	0	70	5.7	0	0	0	2	1	3	7	14	0	7	0	0	1	0	.22
98-99	Chi	2	0	0	0	0	0	0	1	0.0	0	0	0	0	0	0	0	0	0	0	0	0	0	0	.00
98-99	Cgy	61	4	10	14	-7	0	0	69	5.8	0	0	0	2	1	3	7	14	0	7	0	0	1	0	.23
6 Years		236	13	32	45	-12	0	0	255	5.1	0	1	1	3	4	7	45	109	1	42	1	11	9	0	.19

Postseason																									
Year	Tm	GP	G	A	Pts	+/–	GW	OT	S	SPct	G	A	Pts	G	A	Pts	Num	PIM	Maj	Mnr	Fgt	Rgh	HHT	Hat	P/G
93-94	Chi	6	0	0	0	-1	0	0	2	0.0	0	0	0	0	0	0	1	10	0	0	0	0	0	0	.00
96-97	Chi	4	1	0	1	0	0	0	6	16.7	0	0	0	0	0	0	2	4	0	2	0	0	0	0	.25
2 Years		10	1	0	1	-1	0	0	8	12.5	0	0	0	0	0	0	3	14	0	2	0	0	0	0	.10

Steve Duchesne

(statistical profile on page 307)

Pos: D **Shoots:** L **Ht:** 6'0" **Wt:** 198 **Born:** 6/30/65—Sept-Iles, Quebec **Age:** 34

Overall											Power Play			Shorthand			Penalty							Misc	
Year	Tm	GP	G	A	Pts	+/–	GW	GT	S	SPct	G	A	Pts	G	A	Pts	Num	PIM	Maj	Mnr	Fgt	Rgh	HHT	Hat	P/G
86-87	LA	75	13	25	38	8	2	1	113	11.5	5	–	–	0	–	–	–	74	–	–	–	–	–	0	.51
87-88	LA	71	16	39	55	0	4	0	190	8.4	5	–	–	0	–	–	–	109	–	–	–	–	–	0	.77
88-89	LA*	79	25	50	75	31	2	0	215	11.6	8	–	–	5	–	–	–	92	–	–	–	–	–	1	.95
89-90	LA*	79	20	42	62	-3	1	1	224	8.9	6	–	–	0	–	–	–	36	–	–	–	–	–	0	.78
90-91	LA	78	21	41	62	19	3	0	171	12.3	8	–	–	0	–	–	–	66	–	–	–	–	–	0	.79
91-92	Phi	78	18	38	56	-7	3	0	229	7.9	7	12	19	2	1	3	28	86	2	23	0	3	13	1	.72
92-93	Que*	82	20	62	82	15	2	1	227	8.8	8	37	45	0	0	0	23	57	1	21	0	1	10	0	1.00
93-94	StL	36	12	19	31	1	1	0	115	10.4	8	9	17	0	2	2	7	14	0	7	0	0	4	1	.86
94-95	StL	47	12	26	38	29	1	0	116	10.3	1	12	13	0	1	1	18	36	0	18	0	4	5	0	.81
95-96	Ott	62	12	24	36	-23	2	0	163	7.4	7	19	26	0	0	0	21	42	0	21	0	1	13	0	.58
96-97	Ott	78	19	28	47	-9	3	0	208	9.1	10	10	20	2	0	2	19	38	0	19	0	1	6	0	.60
97-98	StL	80	14	42	56	9	1	0	153	9.2	5	24	29	1	1	2	16	32	0	16	0	0	8	0	.70
98-99	2Tm	71	6	24	30	-6	2	0	118	5.1	2	16	18	0	0	0	12	24	0	12	0	0	9	0	.42
98-99	LA	60	4	19	23	-6	1	0	99	4.0	1	12	13	0	0	0	11	22	0	11	0	0	8	0	.38
98-99	Phi	11	2	5	7	0	1	0	19	10.5	1	4	5	0	0	0	1	2	0	1	0	0	1	0	.64
13 Years		916	208	460	668	64	27	3	2242	9.3	80	–	–	10	–	–	–	706	–	–	–	–	–	3	.73
Postseason																									
Year	Tm	GP	G	A	Pts	+/–	GW	OT	S	SPct	G	A	Pts	G	A	Pts	Num	PIM	Maj	Mnr	Fgt	Rgh	HHT	Hat	P/G
86-87	LA	5	2	2	4	-8	0	0	6	33.3	1	–	–	0	0	0	2	4	0	2	0	–	–	0	.80
87-88	LA	5	1	3	4	-5	0	0	11	9.1	1	–	–	0	0	0	–	14	–	–	–	–	–	0	.80
88-89	LA	11	4	4	8	-4	0	0	23	17.4	2	–	–	0	–	–	–	12	–	–	–	–	–	0	.73
89-90	LA	10	2	9	11	-2	0	0	32	6.3	1	–	–	0	–	–	3	6	0	3	0	–	–	0	1.10
90-91	LA	12	4	8	12	7	0	0	39	10.3	1	–	–	0	–	–	4	8	0	4	0	–	–	0	1.00
92-93	Que	6	0	5	5	0	0	0	14	0.0	0	1	1	0	0	0	3	6	0	3	0	0	1	0	.83
93-94	StL	4	0	2	2	-1	0	0	11	0.0	0	2	2	0	0	0	1	2	0	1	0	0	1	0	.50
94-95	StL	7	0	4	4	0	0	0	22	0.0	0	2	2	0	0	0	1	2	0	1	0	0	0	0	.57
96-97	Ott	7	1	4	5	-3	1	0	18	5.6	1	4	5	0	0	0	0	0	0	0	0	0	0	0	.71
97-98	StL	10	0	4	4	-8	0	0	28	0.0	0	3	3	0	0	0	3	6	0	3	0	0	2	0	.40
98-99	Phi	6	0	2	2	2	0	0	10	0.0	0	2	2	0	0	0	1	2	0	1	0	1	0	0	.33
11 Years		83	14	47	61	-22	1	0	214	6.5	7	–	–	0	–	–	–	62	–	–	–	–	–	0	.73

Jean-Pierre Dumont

(statistical profile on page 308)

Pos: RW **Shoots:** L **Ht:** 6'2" **Wt:** 200 **Born:** 4/1/78—Montreal, Quebec **Age:** 21

Overall											Power Play			Shorthand			Penalty							Misc	
Year	Tm	GP	G	A	Pts	+/–	GW	GT	S	SPct	G	A	Pts	G	A	Pts	Num	PIM	Maj	Mnr	Fgt	Rgh	HHT	Hat	P/G
98-99	Chi	25	9	6	15	7	2	0	42	21.4	0	1	1	0	0	0	5	10	0	5	0	1	1	1	.60

Mike Dunham

(statistical profile on page 397)

Pos: G **Catches:** L **Ht:** 6'3" **Wt:** 195 **Born:** 6/1/72—Johnson City, New York **Age:** 27

Overall																Pen Shot		Offense		
Year	Tm	GP	GS	TP	W	L	T	Min	GA	GAA	Shots	SvPct	ShO	OE	PPGA	SHGA	Shots	GA	G	A	PIM
96-97	NJ	26	16	4	8	7	1	1013	43	2.55	456	.906	2	6	6	2	0	0	0	0	2
97-98	NJ	15	12	2	5	5	3	773	29	2.25	332	.913	1	2	7	3	0	0	0	1	0
98-99	Nsh	44	43	5	16	23	3	2472	127	3.08	1387	.908	1	19	38	8	1	1	0	0	4
3 Years		85	71	11	29	35	7	4258	199	2.80	2175	.909	4	27	51	13	1	1	0	1	6

Radek Dvorak

(statistical profile on page 308)

Pos: RW **Shoots:** R **Ht:** 6'1" **Wt:** 185 **Born:** 3/9/77—Tabor, Czechoslovakia **Age:** 22

Overall											Power Play			Shorthand			Penalty							Misc	
Year	Tm	GP	G	A	Pts	+/–	GW	GT	S	SPct	G	A	Pts	G	A	Pts	Num	PIM	Maj	Mnr	Fgt	Rgh	HHT	Hat	P/G
95-96	Fla	77	13	14	27	5	4	0	126	10.3	0	1	1	0	0	0	10	20	0	10	0	0	3	0	.35
96-97	Fla	78	18	21	39	-2	1	0	139	12.9	2	5	7	0	0	0	15	30	0	15	0	4	2	0	.50
97-98	Fla	64	12	24	36	-1	0	1	112	10.7	2	2	4	3	2	5	11	33	1	9	1	0	7	0	.56

				Overall							Power Play			Shorthand					Penalty					Misc	
Year	Tm	GP	G	A	Pts	+/–	GW	GT	S	SPct	G	A	Pts	G	A	Pts	Num	PIM	Maj	Mnr	Fgt	Rgh	HHT	Hat	P/G
98-99	Fla	82	19	24	43	7	0	0	182	10.4	0	3	3	4	0	4	13	29	1	12	1	0	7	0	.52
4 Years		301	62	83	145	9	5	1	559	11.1	4	11	15	7	2	9	49	112	2	46	2	4	19	0	.48
											Postseason														
Year	Tm	GP	G	A	Pts	+/–	GW	OT	S	SPct	G	A	Pts	G	A	Pts	Num	PIM	Maj	Mnr	Fgt	Rgh	HHT	Hat	P/G
95-96	Fla	16	1	3	4	2	0	0	36	2.8	0	0	0	0	0	0	0	0	0	0	0	0	0	0	.25
96-97	Fla	3	0	0	0	0	0	0	1	0.0	0	0	0	0	0	0	0	0	0	0	0	0	0	0	.00
2 Years		19	1	3	4	2	0	0	37	2.7	0	0	0	0	0	0	0	0	0	0	0	0	0	0	.21

Karl Dykhuis

Pos: D **Shoots:** L **Ht:** 6'3" **Wt:** 214 **Born:** 7/8/72—Sept-Iles, Quebec **Age:** 27

				Overall							Power Play			Shorthand					Penalty					Misc	
Year	Tm	GP	G	A	Pts	+/–	GW	GT	S	SPct	G	A	Pts	G	A	Pts	Num	PIM	Maj	Mnr	Fgt	Rgh	HHT	Hat	P/G
91-92	Chi	6	1	3	4	-1	0	0	12	8.3	1	0	1	0	1	1	2	4	0	2	0	0	1	0	.67
92-93	Chi	12	0	5	5	2	0	0	10	0.0	0	1	1	0	0	0	0	0	0	0	0	0	0	0	.42
93-94											Did Not Play in NHL														
94-95	Phi	33	2	6	8	7	1	0	46	4.3	1	1	2	0	0	0	17	37	1	16	1	4	5	0	.24
95-96	Phi	82	5	15	20	12	0	0	104	4.8	1	7	8	0	0	0	46	101	3	43	3	8	15	0	.24
96-97	Phi	62	4	15	19	7	1	0	101	4.0	2	3	5	0	0	0	16	35	1	15	1	3	2	0	.31
97-98	TB	78	5	9	14	-8	0	0	91	5.5	0	1	1	1	0	1	40	110	2	35	1	3	10	0	.18
98-99	2Tm	78	4	5	9	-23	0	0	88	4.5	1	1	2	0	1	1	25	50	0	25	0	4	9	0	.12
98-99	TB	33	2	1	3	-21	0	0	27	7.4	0	0	0	0	1	1	9	18	0	9	0	3	2	0	.09
98-99	Phi	45	2	4	6	-2	0	0	61	3.3	1	1	2	0	0	0	16	32	0	16	0	1	7	0	.13
7 Years		351	21	58	79	-4	2	0	452	4.6	6	14	20	1	2	3	146	337	7	136	6	22	42	0	.23
											Postseason														
Year	Tm	GP	G	A	Pts	+/–	GW	OT	S	SPct	G	A	Pts	G	A	Pts	Num	PIM	Maj	Mnr	Fgt	Rgh	HHT	Hat	P/G
94-95	Phi	15	4	4	8	2	2	1	17	23.5	2	0	2	0	0	0	7	14	0	7	0	1	3	0	.53
95-96	Phi	12	2	2	4	6	0	0	18	11.1	1	1	2	0	0	0	7	22	0	6	0	1	1	0	.33
96-97	Phi	18	0	3	3	1	0	0	15	0.0	0	1	1	0	1	1	1	2	0	1	0	1	0	0	.17
98-99	Phi	5	1	0	1	1	0	0	12	8.3	0	0	0	0	0	0	2	4	0	2	0	2	0	0	.20
4 Years		50	7	9	16	10	2	1	62	11.3	3	2	5	0	1	1	17	42	0	16	0	5	4	0	.32

Joe Dziedzic

Pos: LW **Shoots:** L **Ht:** 6'3" **Wt:** 227 **Born:** 12/18/71—Minneapolis, Minnesota **Age:** 28

				Overall							Power Play			Shorthand					Penalty					Misc	
Year	Tm	GP	G	A	Pts	+/–	GW	GT	S	SPct	G	A	Pts	G	A	Pts	Num	PIM	Maj	Mnr	Fgt	Rgh	HHT	Hat	P/G
95-96	Pit	69	5	5	10	-5	3	0	44	11.4	0	0	0	0	0	0	24	68	4	19	4	3	6	0	.14
96-97	Pit	59	9	9	18	-4	1	0	85	10.6	0	0	0	0	0	0	23	63	3	19	3	6	2	0	.31
97-98											Did Not Play in NHL														
98-99	Pho	2	0	0	0	-2	0	0	1	0.0	0	0	0	0	0	0	0	0	0	0	0	0	0	0	.00
3 Years		130	14	14	28	-11	4	0	130	10.8	0	0	0	0	0	0	47	131	7	38	7	9	8	0	.22
											Postseason														
Year	Tm	GP	G	A	Pts	+/–	GW	OT	S	SPct	G	A	Pts	G	A	Pts	Num	PIM	Maj	Mnr	Fgt	Rgh	HHT	Hat	P/G
95-96	Pit	16	1	2	3	1	0	0	6	16.7	0	0	0	0	0	0	8	19	1	7	1	2	1	0	.19
96-97	Pit	5	0	1	1	-1	0	0	5	0.0	0	0	0	0	0	0	2	4	0	2	0	0	0	0	.20
2 Years		21	1	3	4	0	0	0	11	9.1	0	0	0	0	0	0	10	23	1	9	1	2	1	0	.19

Mike Eagles

Pos: C **Shoots:** L **Ht:** 5'10" **Wt:** 190 **Born:** 3/7/63—Sussex, New Brunswick **Age:** 36

				Overall							Power Play			Shorthand					Penalty					Misc	
Year	Tm	GP	G	A	Pts	+/–	GW	GT	S	SPct	G	A	Pts	G	A	Pts	Num	PIM	Maj	Mnr	Fgt	Rgh	HHT	Hat	P/G
82-83	Que	2	0	0	0	-1	0	0	1	0.0	0	0	0	0	0	0	1	2	0	1	0	–	–	0	.00
83-84											Did Not Play in NHL														
84-85											Did Not Play in NHL														
85-86	Que	73	11	12	23	3	1	1	68	16.2	1	–	–	0	–	–	17	49	5	12	–	–	–	0	.32
86-87	Que	73	13	19	32	-15	2	0	95	13.7	0	–	–	2	–	–	–	55	–	–	–	–	–	0	.44
87-88	Que	76	10	10	20	-18	2	0	89	11.2	1	–	–	2	–	–	–	74	–	–	–	–	–	0	.26
88-89	Chi	47	5	11	16	-8	0	0	39	12.8	0	–	–	0	–	–	–	44	–	–	–	–	–	0	.34
89-90	Chi	23	1	2	3	-4	0	0	23	4.3	0	–	–	0	–	–	–	34	–	–	–	–	–	0	.13
90-91	Wpg	44	0	9	9	-10	0	0	51	0.0	0	–	–	0	–	–	–	79	–	–	–	–	–	0	.20
91-92	Wpg	65	7	10	17	-17	0	0	60	11.7	0	0	0	1	2	3	38	118	6	29	4	6	8	0	.26
92-93	Wpg	84	8	18	26	-1	1	0	67	11.9	1	0	1	0	0	0	50	131	5	43	4	6	15	0	.31
93-94	Wpg	73	4	8	12	-20	0	0	53	7.5	0	0	0	1	1	2	34	96	4	28	3	7	5	0	.16

Year	Tm	GP	G	A	Pts	+/–	GW	GT	S	SPct	G	A	Pts	G	A	Pts	Num	PIM	Maj	Mnr	Fgt	Rgh	HHT	Hat	P/G
Overall											**Power Play**			**Shorthand**			**Penalty**							**Misc**	
94-95	2Tm	40	3	4	7	-11	0	0	28	10.7	0	1	1	0	1	1	14	48	4	9	3	0	5	0	.18
95-96	Was	70	4	7	11	-1	0	0	70	5.7	0	0	0	0	2	2	28	75	1	25	1	1	8	0	.16
96-97	Was	70	1	7	8	-4	0	0	38	2.6	0	0	0	0	1	1	18	42	2	16	2	3	8	0	.11
97-98	Was	36	1	3	4	-2	0	0	25	4.0	0	0	0	0	0	0	8	16	0	8	0	1	1	0	.11
98-99	Was	52	4	2	6	-5	0	0	41	9.8	0	0	0	0	0	0	15	50	4	10	4	5	2	0	.12
94-95	Wpg	27	2	1	3	-13	0	0	13	15.4	0	0	0	0	0	0	10	40	4	5	3	0	3	0	.11
94-95	Was	13	1	3	4	2	0	0	15	6.7	0	1	1	0	1	1	4	8	0	4	0	0	2	0	.31
15 Years		828	72	122	194	-114	6	1	748	9.6	3	–	–	6	–	–	–	913	–	–	–	–	–	0	.23

Postseason

Year	Tm	GP	G	A	Pts	+/–	GW	OT	S	SPct	G	A	Pts	G	A	Pts	Num	PIM	Maj	Mnr	Fgt	Rgh	HHT	Hat	P/G
85-86	Que	3	0	0	0	-1	0	0	4	0.0	0	0	0	0	0	0	1	2	0	1	0	–	–	0	.00
86-87	Que	4	1	0	1	-1	0	0	4	25.0	0	0	0	0	0	0	–	10	–	–	–	–	–	0	.25
91-92	Wpg	7	0	0	0	-5	0	0	5	0.0	0	0	0	0	0	0	4	8	0	4	0	1	0	0	.00
92-93	Wpg	5	0	1	1	-2	0	0	6	0.0	0	0	0	0	0	0	3	6	0	3	0	0	0	0	.20
94-95	Was	7	0	2	2	1	0	0	6	0.0	0	0	0	0	0	0	2	4	0	2	0	1	0	0	.29
95-96	Was	6	1	1	2	1	0	0	12	8.3	0	0	0	0	0	0	1	2	0	1	0	0	1	0	.33
97-98	Was	12	0	2	2	1	0	0	7	0.0	0	0	0	0	0	0	1	2	0	1	0	0	0	0	.17
7 Years		44	2	6	8	-6	0	0	44	4.5	0	0	0	0	0	0	–	34	–	–	–	–	–	0	.18

Dallas Eakins

Pos: D **Shoots:** L **Ht:** 6'2" **Wt:** 195 **Born:** 2/27/67—Dade City, Florida **Age:** 32

Year	Tm	GP	G	A	Pts	+/–	GW	GT	S	SPct	G	A	Pts	G	A	Pts	Num	PIM	Maj	Mnr	Fgt	Rgh	HHT	Hat	P/G
Overall											**Power Play**			**Shorthand**			**Penalty**							**Misc**	
92-93	Wpg	14	0	2	2	2	0	0	9	0.0	0	0	0	0	0	0	13	38	4	9	4	5	1	0	.14
93-94	Fla	1	0	0	0	0	0	0	2	0.0	0	0	0	0	0	0	0	0	0	0	0	0	0	0	.00
94-95	Fla	17	0	1	1	2	0	0	3	0.0	0	0	0	0	1	1	9	35	3	5	3	0	1	0	.06
95-96	2Tm	18	0	1	1	-1	0	0	6	0.0	0	0	0	0	0	0	14	34	2	12	2	1	3	0	.06
96-97	2Tm	7	0	0	0	-4	0	0	4	0.0	0	0	0	0	0	0	4	16	0	3	0	0	0	0	.00
97-98	Fla	23	0	1	1	1	0	0	16	0.0	0	0	0	0	0	0	12	44	4	7	4	1	3	0	.04
98-99	Tor	18	0	2	2	3	0	0	11	0.0	0	0	0	0	0	0	9	24	2	7	2	1	3	0	.11
95-96	StL	16	0	1	1	-2	0	0	6	0.0	0	0	0	0	0	0	14	34	2	12	2	1	3	0	.06
95-96	Wpg	2	0	0	0	1	0	0	0	–	0	0	0	0	0	0	0	0	0	0	0	0	0	0	.00
96-97	Pho	4	0	0	0	-3	0	0	2	0.0	0	0	0	0	0	0	1	10	0	0	0	0	0	0	.00
96-97	NYR	3	0	0	0	-1	0	0	2	0.0	0	0	0	0	0	0	3	6	0	3	0	0	0	0	.00
7 Years		98	0	7	7	3	0	0	51	0.0	0	0	0	0	1	1	61	191	15	43	15	8	11	0	.07

Postseason

Year	Tm	GP	G	A	Pts	+/–	GW	OT	S	SPct	G	A	Pts	G	A	Pts	Num	PIM	Maj	Mnr	Fgt	Rgh	HHT	Hat	P/G
96-97	NYR	4	0	0	0	-1	0	0	1	0.0	0	0	0	0	0	0	2	4	0	2	0	0	0	0	.00
98-99	Tor	1	0	0	0	0	0	0	0	–	0	0	0	0	0	0	0	0	0	0	0	0	0	0	.00
2 Years		5	0	0	0	-1	0	0	1	0.0	0	0	0	0	0	0	2	4	0	2	0	0	0	0	.00

Mike Eastwood

(statistical profile on page 308)

Pos: C **Shoots:** R **Ht:** 6'3" **Wt:** 205 **Born:** 7/1/67—Ottawa, Ontario **Age:** 32

Year	Tm	GP	G	A	Pts	+/–	GW	GT	S	SPct	G	A	Pts	G	A	Pts	Num	PIM	Maj	Mnr	Fgt	Rgh	HHT	Hat	P/G
Overall											**Power Play**			**Shorthand**			**Penalty**							**Misc**	
91-92	Tor	9	0	2	2	-4	0	0	6	0.0	0	1	1	0	0	0	2	4	0	2	0	0	1	0	.22
92-93	Tor	12	1	6	7	-2	0	0	11	9.1	0	1	1	0	0	0	5	21	1	3	0	0	2	0	.58
93-94	Tor	54	8	10	18	2	2	0	41	19.5	1	4	5	0	0	0	14	28	0	14	0	1	3	0	.33
94-95	2Tm	49	8	11	19	-9	0	0	55	14.5	0	1	1	0	1	1	18	36	0	18	0	5	5	0	.39
95-96	Wpg	80	14	14	28	-14	3	1	94	14.9	2	1	3	0	0	0	10	20	0	10	0	2	3	0	.35
96-97	2Tm	60	2	10	12	-1	0	0	44	4.5	0	0	0	0	1	1	3	14	0	2	0	0	1	0	.20
97-98	2Tm	58	6	5	11	-2	1	0	38	15.8	0	0	0	0	0	0	11	22	0	11	0	0	7	0	.19
98-99	StL	82	9	21	30	6	0	0	76	11.8	0	0	0	0	0	0	18	36	0	18	0	0	9	0	.37
94-95	Tor	36	5	5	10	-12	0	0	38	13.2	0	1	1	0	0	0	16	32	0	16	0	4	5	0	.28
94-95	Wpg	13	3	6	9	3	0	0	17	17.6	0	0	0	0	1	1	2	4	0	2	0	1	0	0	.69
96-97	Pho	33	1	3	4	-3	0	0	22	4.5	0	0	0	0	0	0	2	4	0	2	0	0	1	0	.12
96-97	NYR	27	1	7	8	2	0	0	22	4.5	0	0	0	0	1	1	1	10	0	0	0	0	0	0	.30
97-98	NYR	48	5	5	10	-2	0	0	34	14.7	0	0	0	0	0	0	8	16	0	8	0	0	5	0	.21
97-98	StL	10	1	0	1	0	1	0	4	25.0	0	0	0	0	0	0	3	6	0	3	0	0	2	0	.10
8 Years		404	48	79	127	-24	6	1	365	13.2	3	8	11	0	2	2	81	181	1	78	0	8	31	0	.31

Postseason

Year	Tm	GP	G	A	Pts	+/–	GW	OT	S	SPct	G	A	Pts	G	A	Pts	Num	PIM	Maj	Mnr	Fgt	Rgh	HHT	Hat	P/G
92-93	Tor	10	1	2	3	-1	0	0	6	16.7	0	0	0	0	0	0	4	8	0	4	0	0	2	0	.30

										Postseason															
Year	Tm	GP	G	A	Pts	+/–	GW	OT	S	SPct	G	A	Pts	G	A	Pts	Num	PIM	Maj	Mnr	Fgt	Rgh	HHT	Hat	P/G
93-94	Tor	18	3	2	5	-5	1	0	22	13.6	1	0	1	0	0	0	6	12	0	6	0	3	1	0	.28
95-96	Wpg	6	0	1	1	-1	0	0	2	0.0	0	0	0	0	0	0	1	2	0	1	0	1	0	0	.17
96-97	NYR	15	1	2	3	0	0	0	19	5.3	0	0	0	0	0	0	7	22	0	6	0	0	3	0	.20
97-98	StL	3	1	0	1	-1	1	0	4	25.0	0	0	0	0	0	0	0	0	0	0	0	0	0	0	.33
98-99	StL	13	1	1	2	2	0	0	8	12.5	0	0	0	0	0	0	3	6	0	3	0	0	2	0	.15
6 Years		65	7	8	15	-6	2	0	61	11.5	1	0	1	0	0	0	21	50	0	20	0	4	8	0	.23

Patrik Elias

(statistical profile on page 308)

Pos: LW **Shoots:** L **Ht:** 6'0" **Wt:** 195 **Born:** 4/13/76—Trebic, Czechoslovakia **Age:** 23

					Overall						Power Play			Shorthand						Penalty				Misc	
Year	Tm	GP	G	A	Pts	+/–	GW	GT	S	SPct	G	A	Pts	G	A	Pts	Num	PIM	Maj	Mnr	Fgt	Rgh	HHT	Hat	P/G
95-96	NJ	1	0	0	0	-1	0	0	2	0.0	0	0	0	0	0	0	0	0	0	0	0	0	0	0	.00
96-97	NJ	17	2	3	5	-4	0	0	23	8.7	0	0	0	0	0	0	1	2	0	1	0	0	0	0	.29
97-98	NJ	74	18	19	37	18	6	1	147	12.2	5	6	11	0	0	0	14	28	0	14	0	2	6	0	.50
98-99	NJ	74	17	33	50	19	2	0	157	10.8	3	10	13	0	0	0	13	34	0	12	0	4	3	0	.68
4 Years		166	37	55	92	32	8	1	329	11.2	8	16	24	0	0	0	28	64	0	27	0	6	9	0	.55
										Postseason															
Year	Tm	GP	G	A	Pts	+/–	GW	OT	S	SPct	G	A	Pts	G	A	Pts	Num	PIM	Maj	Mnr	Fgt	Rgh	HHT	Hat	P/G
96-97	NJ	8	2	3	5	0	0	0	18	11.1	1	2	3	0	0	0	2	4	0	2	0	0	1	0	.63
97-98	NJ	4	0	1	1	-2	0	0	9	0.0	0	0	0	0	0	0	0	0	0	0	0	0	0	0	.25
98-99	NJ	7	0	5	5	0	0	0	14	0.0	0	0	0	0	0	0	3	6	0	3	0	1	1	0	.71
3 Years		19	2	9	11	-2	0	0	41	4.9	1	2	3	0	0	0	5	10	0	5	0	1	2	0	.58

Dave Ellett

Pos: D **Shoots:** L **Ht:** 6'2" **Wt:** 205 **Born:** 3/30/64—Cleveland, Ohio **Age:** 35

					Overall						Power Play			Shorthand						Penalty				Misc	
Year	Tm	GP	G	A	Pts	+/–	GW	GT	S	SPct	G	A	Pts	G	A	Pts	Num	PIM	Maj	Mnr	Fgt	Rgh	HHT	Hat	P/G
84-85	Wpg	**80**	11	27	38	20	0	0	146	7.5	3	–	–	0	–	–	–	85	–	–	–	–	–	0	.48
85-86	Wpg	80	15	31	46	-38	1	0	168	8.9	2	–	–	0	–	–	–	96	–	–	–	–	–	0	.58
86-87	Wpg	78	13	31	44	19	2	2	159	8.2	5	–	–	0	–	–	–	53	–	–	–	–	–	0	.56
87-88	Wpg	68	13	45	58	-8	1	0	198	6.6	5	–	–	0	–	–	–	106	–	–	–	–	–	0	.85
88-89	Wpg*	75	22	34	56	-18	5	0	209	10.5	9	–	–	2	–	–	–	62	–	–	–	–	–	0	.75
89-90	Wpg	77	17	29	46	-15	1	0	205	8.3	8	–	–	0	–	–	–	96	–	–	–	–	–	0	.60
90-91	2Tm	77	12	37	49	-8	1	1	195	6.2	6	–	–	1	–	–	–	75	–	–	–	–	–	0	.64
91-92	Tor*	79	18	33	51	-13	4	0	225	8.0	9	20	29	1	1	2	30	95	1	25	0	3	10	0	.65
92-93	Tor	70	6	34	40	19	1	0	186	3.2	4	25	29	0	0	0	20	46	2	18	2	4	7	0	.57
93-94	Tor	68	7	36	43	6	1	1	146	4.8	5	24	29	0	0	0	21	42	0	21	0	3	11	0	.63
94-95	Tor	33	5	10	15	-6	1	0	84	6.0	3	6	9	0	0	0	9	26	0	8	0	2	2	0	.45
95-96	Tor	80	3	19	22	-10	0	0	153	2.0	1	6	7	1	1	2	24	59	1	22	0	6	8	0	.28
96-97	2Tm	76	6	15	21	-6	2	0	105	5.7	1	8	9	0	3	3	20	40	0	20	0	4	10	0	.28
97-98	Bos	82	3	20	23	3	1	0	129	2.3	2	8	10	0	1	1	28	67	1	26	1	4	10	0	.28
98-99	Bos	54	0	6	6	11	0	0	45	0.0	0	3	3	0	0	0	11	25	1	10	1	1	1	0	.11
90-91	Wpg	17	4	7	11	-4	0	0	41	9.8	1	–	–	1	–	–	3	6	0	3	0	–	–	0	.65
90-91	Tor	60	8	30	38	-4	1	1	154	5.2	5	–	–	0	–	–	–	69	–	–	–	–	–	0	.63
96-97	Tor	56	4	10	14	-8	1	0	83	4.8	0	3	3	0	3	3	17	34	0	17	0	2	10	0	.25
96-97	NJ	20	2	5	7	2	1	0	22	9.1	1	5	6	0	0	0	3	6	0	3	0	2	0	0	.35
15 Years		1077	151	407	558	-44	21	4	2353	6.4	63	–	–	5	–	–	–	973	–	–	–	–	–	0	.52
										Postseason															
Year	Tm	GP	G	A	Pts	+/–	GW	OT	S	SPct	G	A	Pts	G	A	Pts	Num	PIM	Maj	Mnr	Fgt	Rgh	HHT	Hat	P/G
84-85	Wpg	8	1	5	6	-3	0	0	20	5.0	1	–	–	0	–	–	2	4	0	2	0	–	–	0	.75
85-86	Wpg	3	0	1	1	-4	0	0	7	0.0	0	–	–	0	–	–	0	0	0	0	0	0	0	0	.33
86-87	Wpg	10	0	8	8	-1	0	0	22	0.0	0	–	–	0	–	–	1	2	0	1	0	–	–	0	.80
87-88	Wpg	5	1	2	3	-5	0	0	16	6.3	1	–	–	0	–	–	–	10	–	–	–	–	–	0	.60
89-90	Wpg	7	2	0	2	-6	1	1	22	9.1	2	0	2	0	0	0	3	6	0	3	0	–	–	0	.29
92-93	Tor	21	4	8	12	4	0	0	62	6.5	2	4	6	0	0	0	4	8	0	4	0	0	3	0	.57
93-94	Tor	18	3	15	18	1	0	0	33	9.1	3	11	14	0	0	0	10	31	1	8	1	3	3	0	1.00
94-95	Tor	7	0	2	2	-5	0	0	18	0.0	0	1	1	0	0	0	0	0	0	0	0	0	0	0	.29
95-96	Tor	6	0	0	0	-5	0	0	16	0.0	0	0	0	0	0	0	2	4	0	2	0	0	0	0	.00
96-97	NJ	10	0	3	3	-1	0	0	15	0.0	0	1	1	0	0	0	1	10	0	0	0	0	0	0	.30
97-98	Bos	6	0	1	1	-1	0	0	11	0.0	0	0	0	0	0	0	3	6	0	3	0	0	3	0	.17
98-99	Bos	8	0	0	0	0	0	0	4	0.0	0	0	0	0	0	0	2	4	0	2	0	0	1	0	.00
12 Years		109	11	45	56	-26	1	1	246	4.5	9	–	–	0	–	–	–	85	–	–	–	–	–	0	.51

Nelson Emerson

(statistical profile on page 309)

Pos: RW **Shoots:** R **Ht:** 5'11" **Wt:** 175 **Born:** 8/17/67—Waterford, Ontario **Age:** 32

Overall											Power Play			Shorthand			Penalty							Misc	
Year	Tm	GP	G	A	Pts	+/–	GW	GT	S	SPct	G	A	Pts	G	A	Pts	Num	PIM	Maj	Mnr	Fgt	Rgh	HHT	Hat	P/G
90-91	StL	4	0	3	3	-2	0	0	3	0.0	0	–	–	0	–	–	1	2	0	1	0	–	–	0	.75
91-92	StL	79	23	36	59	-5	2	0	143	16.1	3	18	21	0	0	0	22	66	2	18	0	3	6	0	.75
92-93	StL	82	22	51	73	2	4	0	196	11.2	5	34	39	2	0	2	27	62	0	26	0	5	11	0	.89
93-94	Wpg	83	33	41	74	-38	6	1	282	11.7	4	25	29	5	1	6	29	80	2	25	2	3	13	0	.89
94-95	Wpg	48	14	23	37	-12	1	0	122	11.5	4	10	14	1	2	3	13	26	0	13	0	3	3	1	.77
95-96	Har	81	29	29	58	-7	5	0	247	11.7	12	16	28	2	0	2	32	78	2	29	2	4	13	0	.72
96-97	Har	66	9	29	38	-21	2	0	194	4.6	2	15	17	1	0	1	17	34	0	17	0	3	5	0	.58
97-98	Car	81	21	24	45	-17	4	1	203	10.3	6	15	21	0	0	0	25	50	0	25	0	4	12	0	.56
98-99	3Tm	65	13	24	37	8	1	2	188	6.9	3	7	10	0	0	0	24	51	1	23	1	2	14	0	.57
98-99	Car	35	8	13	21	1	0	1	84	9.5	3	5	8	0	0	0	18	36	0	18	0	2	13	0	.60
98-99	Chi	27	4	10	14	8	1	1	94	4.3	0	1	1	0	0	0	5	13	1	4	1	0	1	0	.52
98-99	Ott	3	1	1	2	-1	0	0	10	10.0	0	1	1	0	0	0	1	2	0	1	0	0	0	0	.67
9 Years		589	164	260	424	-92	25	4	1578	10.4	39	–	–	11	–	–	190	449	7	177	5	–	–	1	.72

Postseason																									
Year	Tm	GP	G	A	Pts	+/–	GW	OT	S	SPct	G	A	Pts	G	A	Pts	Num	PIM	Maj	Mnr	Fgt	Rgh	HHT	Hat	P/G
91-92	StL	6	3	3	6	0	0	0	11	27.3	2	2	4	0	0	0	5	21	1	3	0	0	1	0	1.00
92-93	StL	11	1	6	7	3	0	0	43	2.3	0	3	3	0	0	0	3	6	0	3	0	0	3	0	.64
98-99	Ott	4	1	3	4	0	0	0	12	8.3	0	3	3	0	0	0	0	0	0	0	0	0	0	0	1.00
3 Years		21	5	12	17	3	0	0	66	7.6	2	8	10	0	0	0	8	27	1	6	0	0	4	0	.81

Anders Eriksson

(statistical profile on page 309)

Pos: D **Shoots:** L **Ht:** 6'3" **Wt:** 218 **Born:** 1/9/75—Bollnas, Sweden **Age:** 24

Overall											Power Play			Shorthand			Penalty							Misc	
Year	Tm	GP	G	A	Pts	+/–	GW	GT	S	SPct	G	A	Pts	G	A	Pts	Num	PIM	Maj	Mnr	Fgt	Rgh	HHT	Hat	P/G
95-96	Det	1	0	0	0	1	0	0	0	–	0	0	0	0	0	0	1	2	0	1	0	0	0	0	.00
96-97	Det	23	0	6	6	5	0	0	27	0.0	0	0	0	0	0	0	5	10	0	5	0	0	2	0	.26
97-98	Det	66	7	14	21	21	2	0	91	7.7	1	4	5	0	0	0	16	32	0	16	0	1	9	0	.32
98-99	2Tm	72	2	18	20	11	1	0	79	2.5	0	4	4	0	1	1	17	34	0	17	0	1	6	0	.28
98-99	Det	61	2	10	12	5	1	0	67	3.0	0	0	0	0	1	1	17	34	0	17	0	1	6	0	.20
98-99	Chi	11	0	8	8	6	0	0	12	0.0	0	4	4	0	0	0	0	0	0	0	0	0	0	0	.73
4 Years		162	9	38	47	38	3	0	197	4.6	1	8	9	0	1	1	39	78	0	39	0	2	17	0	.29

Postseason																									
Year	Tm	GP	G	A	Pts	+/–	GW	OT	S	SPct	G	A	Pts	G	A	Pts	Num	PIM	Maj	Mnr	Fgt	Rgh	HHT	Hat	P/G
95-96	Det	3	0	0	0	2	0	0	1	0.0	0	0	0	0	0	0	0	0	0	0	0	0	0	0	.00
97-98	Det	18	0	5	5	7	0	0	17	0.0	0	2	2	0	0	0	8	16	0	8	0	1	2	0	.28
2 Years		21	0	5	5	9	0	0	18	0.0	0	2	2	0	0	0	8	16	0	8	0	1	2	0	.24

Robert Esche

Pos: G **Catches:** R **Ht:** 6'1" **Wt:** 204 **Born:** 1/22/78—Utica, New York **Age:** 21

Overall																Pen Shot		Offense		
Year	Tm	GP	GS	TP	W	L	T	Min	GA	GAA	Shots	SvPct	ShO	OE	PPGA	SHGA	Shots	GA	G	A	PIM
98-99	Pho	3	1	0	0	1	0	130	7	3.23	50	.860	0	0	1	1	0	0	0	0	0

Bob Essensa

(statistical profile on page 397)

Pos: G **Catches:** L **Ht:** 6'0" **Wt:** 188 **Born:** 1/14/65—Toronto, Ontario **Age:** 34

Overall																Pen Shot		Offense		
Year	Tm	GP	GS	TP	W	L	T	Min	GA	GAA	Shots	SvPct	ShO	OE	PPGA	SHGA	Shots	GA	G	A	PIM
88-89	Wpg	20	–	–	6	8	3	1102	68	3.70	574	.882	1	–	–	–	1	**1**	0	0	0
89-90	Wpg	36	–	–	18	9	5	2035	107	3.15	988	.892	1	–	–	–	0	0	0	2	0
90-91	Wpg	55	–	–	19	24	6	2916	153	3.15	1496	.898	4	–	–	–	1	0	0	3	6
91-92	Wpg	47	46	7	21	17	6	2627	126	2.88	1407	.910	**5**	20	38	2	0	0	0	2	2
92-93	Wpg	67	65	5	33	26	6	3855	227	3.53	2119	.893	2	23	54	9	0	0	0	5	2
93-94	2Tm	69	66	**12**	23	37	8	3914	235	3.60	2051	.885	2	19	69	**14**	2	**1**	0	2	6
94-95										Did Not Play in NHL											
95-96										Did Not Play in NHL											
96-97	Edm	19	10	0	4	8	0	868	41	2.83	406	.899	1	4	7	3	0	0	0	0	4
97-98	Edm	16	11	0	6	6	1	825	35	2.55	404	.913	0	3	11	2	2	0	0	0	0
98-99	Edm	39	33	4	12	14	6	2091	96	2.75	974	.901	0	8	30	7	0	0	0	1	0
93-94	Wpg	56	54	12	19	30	6	3136	201	3.85	1714	.883	1	15	62	11	2	1	0	0	6
93-94	Det	13	12	0	4	7	2	778	34	2.62	337	.899	1	4	7	3	0	0	0	2	0
9 Years		368	–	–	142	149	41	20233	1088	3.23	10419	.896	16	–	–	–	6	2	0	15	20

Postseason																					
Year	Tm	GP	GS	TP	W	L	Pct	Min	GA	GAA	Shots	SvPct	ShO	OE	PPGA	SHGA	Shots	GA	G	A	PIM
89-90	Wpg	4	–	–	2	1	.667	206	12	3.50	100	.880	0	–	–	–	0	0	0	0	0
91-92	Wpg	1	0	0	0	0	–	33	3	5.45	17	.824	0	0	0	0	0	0	0	0	0
92-93	Wpg	6	6	0	2	4	.333	367	20	3.27	183	.891	0	1	4	0	0	0	0	0	2
93-94	Det	2	1	0	0	2	.000	109	9	4.95	43	.791	0	0	1	0	0	0	0	0	0
97-98	Edm	1	0	0	0	0	–	27	1	2.22	11	.909	0	0	0	0	0	0	0	0	0
5 Years		14	–	–	4	7	.364	742	45	3.64	354	.873	0	–	–	–	0	0	0	0	2

Kelly Fairchild

Pos: C **Shoots:** L **Ht:** 5'11" **Wt:** 180 **Born:** 4/9/73—Hibbing, Minnesota **Age:** 26

Overall											Power Play			Shorthand			Penalty							Misc	
Year	Tm	GP	G	A	Pts	+/–	GW	GT	S	SPct	G	A	Pts	G	A	Pts	Num	PIM	Maj	Mnr	Fgt	Rgh	HHT	Hat	P/G
95-96	Tor	1	0	1	1	1	0	0	1	0.0	0	0	0	0	0	0	1	2	0	1	0	0	1	0	1.00
96-97	Tor	22	0	2	2	-5	0	0	14	0.0	0	0	0	0	0	0	1	2	0	1	0	0	1	0	.09
97-98		Did Not Play in NHL																							
98-99	Dal	1	0	0	0	0	0	0	4	0.0	0	0	0	0	0	0	0	0	0	0	0	0	0	0	.00
3 Years		24	0	3	3	-4	0	0	19	0.0	0	0	0	0	0	0	2	4	0	2	0	0	2	0	.13

Pat Falloon

(statistical profile on page 309)

Pos: RW **Shoots:** R **Ht:** 5'11" **Wt:** 200 **Born:** 9/22/72—Foxwarren, Manitoba **Age:** 27

Overall											Power Play			Shorthand			Penalty							Misc	
Year	Tm	GP	G	A	Pts	+/–	GW	GT	S	SPct	G	A	Pts	G	A	Pts	Num	PIM	Maj	Mnr	Fgt	Rgh	HHT	Hat	P/G
91-92	SJ	79	25	34	59	-32	1	2	181	13.8	5	14	19	0	0	0	8	16	0	8	0	0	5	0	.75
92-93	SJ	41	14	14	28	-25	1	0	131	10.7	5	6	11	1	2	3	6	12	0	6	0	0	4	0	.68
93-94	SJ	83	22	31	53	-3	1	0	193	11.4	6	6	12	0	0	0	9	18	0	9	0	0	6	0	.64
94-95	SJ	46	12	7	19	-4	3	0	91	13.2	0	1	1	0	0	0	7	25	1	5	0	0	4	0	.41
95-96	2Tm	71	25	26	51	14	2	1	170	14.7	9	10	19	0	0	0	5	10	0	5	0	0	2	0	.72
96-97	Phi	52	11	12	23	-8	4	0	124	8.9	2	4	6	0	1	1	5	10	0	5	0	0	3	0	.44
97-98	2Tm	58	8	10	18	-8	0	0	136	5.9	3	4	7	0	0	0	8	16	0	8	0	0	3	0	.31
98-99	Edm	82	17	23	40	-4	2	0	152	11.2	8	7	15	0	0	0	10	20	0	10	0	0	6	0	.49
95-96	SJ	9	3	0	3	-1	0	1	18	16.7	0	0	0	0	0	0	2	4	0	2	0	0	1	0	.33
95-96	Phi	62	22	26	48	15	2	0	152	14.5	9	10	19	0	0	0	3	6	0	3	0	0	1	0	.77
97-98	Phi	30	5	7	12	3	0	0	63	7.9	1	3	4	0	0	0	4	8	0	4	0	0	2	0	.40
97-98	Ott	28	3	3	6	-11	0	0	73	4.1	2	1	3	0	0	0	4	8	0	4	0	0	1	0	.21
8 Years		512	134	157	291	-70	14	3	1178	11.4	38	52	90	1	3	4	58	127	1	56	0	0	33	0	.57
Postseason																									
Year	Tm	GP	G	A	Pts	+/–	GW	OT	S	SPct	G	A	Pts	G	A	Pts	Num	PIM	Maj	Mnr	Fgt	Rgh	HHT	Hat	P/G
93-94	SJ	14	1	2	3	-2	0	0	8	12.5	0	0	0	0	0	0	3	6	0	3	0	0	2	0	.21
94-95	SJ	11	3	1	4	-6	0	0	24	12.5	0	0	0	0	0	0	0	0	0	0	0	0	0	0	.36
95-96	Phi	12	3	2	5	-2	0	0	37	8.1	2	1	3	0	0	0	1	2	0	1	0	0	0	0	.42
96-97	Phi	14	3	1	4	-1	0	0	32	9.4	1	0	1	0	0	0	1	2	0	1	0	0	0	0	.29
97-98	Ott	1	0	0	0	0	0	0	2	0.0	0	0	0	0	0	0	0	0	0	0	0	0	0	0	.00
98-99	Edm	4	0	1	1	0	0	0	6	0.0	0	0	0	0	0	0	2	4	0	2	0	0	0	0	.25
6 Years		56	10	7	17	-11	0	0	109	9.2	3	1	4	0	0	0	7	14	0	7	0	0	2	0	.30

Rico Fata

Pos: C **Shoots:** L **Ht:** 5'11" **Wt:** 205 **Born:** 2/12/80—Sault Ste. Marie, Ontario **Age:** 19

Overall											Power Play			Shorthand			Penalty							Misc	
Year	Tm	GP	G	A	Pts	+/–	GW	GT	S	SPct	G	A	Pts	G	A	Pts	Num	PIM	Maj	Mnr	Fgt	Rgh	HHT	Hat	P/G
98-99	Cgy	20	0	1	1	0	0	0	13	0.0	0	0	0	0	0	0	2	4	0	2	0	0	0	0	.05

Sergei Fedorov

(statistical profile on page 309)

Pos: C **Shoots:** L **Ht:** 6'1" **Wt:** 200 **Born:** 12/13/69—Pskov, USSR **Age:** 30

Overall											Power Play			Shorthand			Penalty							Misc	
Year	Tm	GP	G	A	Pts	+/–	GW	GT	S	SPct	G	A	Pts	G	A	Pts	Num	PIM	Maj	Mnr	Fgt	Rgh	HHT	Hat	P/G
90-91	Det	77	31	48	79	11	5	1	259	12.0	11	15	26	3	1	4	26	66	2	23	1	2	10	0	1.03
91-92	Det*	80	32	54	86	26	5	0	249	12.9	7	20	27	2	3	5	33	72	2	31	2	12	8	0	1.08
92-93	Det	73	34	53	87	33	3	0	217	15.7	13	18	31	4	5	**9**	29	72	2	26	1	5	10	0	1.19
93-94	Det*	82	56	64	120	48	10	0	337	16.6	13	15	28	4	**7**	**11**	17	34	0	17	0	4	8	1	1.46
94-95	Det	42	20	30	50	6	5	0	147	13.6	7	9	16	3	0	3	12	24	0	12	0	4	4	1	1.19
95-96	Det*	78	39	68	107	49	11	1	306	12.7	11	26	37	3	2	5	17	48	2	14	0	2	3	0	1.37
96-97	Det	74	30	33	63	29	4	0	273	11.0	9	6	15	2	1	3	15	30	0	15	0	3	7	1	.85

Year	Tm	GP	G	A	Pts	+/–	GW	GT	S	SPct	G	A	Pts	G	A	Pts	Num	PIM	Maj	Mnr	Fgt	Rgh	HHT	Hat	P/G
		Overall									Power Play			Shorthand			Penalty							Misc	
97-98	Det	21	6	11	17	10	2	0	68	8.8	2	2	4	0	0	0	11	25	1	10	0	3	4	0	.81
98-99	Det	77	26	37	63	9	3	0	224	11.6	6	13	19	2	0	2	29	66	0	28	0	2	15	0	.82
9 Years		604	274	398	672	221	48	2	2080	13.2	79	124	203	23	19	42	189	437	9	176	4	37	69	3	1.11
Postseason																									
Year	Tm	GP	G	A	Pts	+/–	GW	OT	S	SPct	G	A	Pts	G	A	Pts	Num	PIM	Maj	Mnr	Fgt	Rgh	HHT	Hat	P/G
90-91	Det	7	1	5	6	-1	1	0	22	4.5	0	2	2	0	0	0	2	4	0	2	0	0	0	0	.86
91-92	Det	11	5	5	10	2	1	1	27	18.5	1	2	3	2	1	3	4	8	0	4	0	2	1	0	.91
92-93	Det	7	3	6	9	4	0	0	26	11.5	1	2	3	1	1	2	6	23	1	4	0	0	0	0	1.29
93-94	Det	7	1	7	8	-1	0	0	19	5.3	0	2	2	0	0	0	3	6	0	3	0	0	1	0	1.14
94-95	Det	17	7	17	24	13	0	0	53	13.2	3	7	10	0	2	2	3	6	0	3	0	0	3	0	1.41
95-96	Det	19	2	18	20	8	2	0	59	3.4	0	9	9	0	1	1	5	10	0	5	0	1	1	0	1.05
96-97	Det	20	8	12	20	5	4	0	79	10.1	3	5	8	0	0	0	6	12	0	6	0	1	2	0	1.00
97-98	Det	22	10	10	20	0	1	0	86	11.6	2	5	7	1	0	1	6	12	0	6	0	0	4	0	.91
98-99	Det	10	1	8	9	3	0	0	38	2.6	0	3	3	0	0	0	4	8	0	4	0	0	2	0	.90
9 Years		120	38	88	126	33	9	1	409	9.3	10	37	47	4	5	9	39	89	1	37	0	4	14	0	1.05

Brent Fedyk

(statistical profile on page 310)

Pos: LW **Shoots:** R **Ht:** 6'0" **Wt:** 194 **Born:** 3/8/67—Yorkton, Saskatchewan **Age:** 32

Year	Tm	GP	G	A	Pts	+/–	GW	GT	S	SPct	G	A	Pts	G	A	Pts	Num	PIM	Maj	Mnr	Fgt	Rgh	HHT	Hat	P/G
		Overall									Power Play			Shorthand			Penalty							Misc	
87-88	Det	2	0	1	1	-1	0	0	2	0.0	0	–	–	0	–	–	1	2	0	1	0	–	–	0	.50
88-89	Det	5	2	0	2	-1	0	0	6	33.3	1	0	1	0	0	0	0	0	0	0	0	0	0	0	.40
89-90	Det	27	1	4	5	-1	0	0	28	3.6	0	–	–	0	–	–	3	6	0	3	0	–	–	0	.19
90-91	Det	67	16	19	35	20	1	0	74	21.6	0	–	–	0	–	–	–	38	–	–	–	–	–	0	.52
91-92	Det	61	5	8	13	-5	1	0	60	8.3	0	0	0	0	0	0	17	42	0	16	0	1	8	0	.21
92-93	Phi	74	21	38	59	14	2	2	167	12.6	4	9	13	1	1	2	16	48	0	14	0	0	9	0	.80
93-94	Phi	72	20	18	38	-14	1	0	104	19.2	5	2	7	0	0	0	26	74	2	22	0	3	11	0	.53
94-95	Phi	30	8	4	12	-2	2	0	41	19.5	3	2	5	0	0	0	7	14	0	7	0	2	3	0	.40
95-96	2Tm	65	20	14	34	-16	0	0	113	17.7	8	4	12	0	1	1	23	54	0	22	0	0	15	0	.52
96-97											Did Not Play in NHL														
97-98											Did Not Play in NHL														
98-99	NYR	67	4	6	10	-11	0	0	47	8.5	0	0	0	1	1	2	15	30	0	15	0	0	7	0	.15
95-96	Phi	24	10	5	15	1	0	0	42	23.8	4	0	4	0	1	1	12	24	0	12	0	0	9	0	.63
95-96	Dal	41	10	9	19	-17	0	0	71	14.1	4	4	8	0	0	0	11	30	0	10	0	0	6	0	.46
10 Years		470	97	112	209	-17	7	2	642	15.1	21	–	–	2	–	–	–	308	–	–	–	–	–	0	.44
Postseason																									
Year	Tm	GP	G	A	Pts	+/–	GW	OT	S	SPct	G	A	Pts	G	A	Pts	Num	PIM	Maj	Mnr	Fgt	Rgh	HHT	Hat	P/G
90-91	Det	6	1	0	1	-3	1	0	3	33.3	0	0	0	0	0	0	1	2	0	1	0	–	–	0	.17
91-92	Det	1	0	0	0	0	0	0	0	–	0	0	0	0	0	0	1	2	0	1	0	0	0	0	.00
94-95	Phi	9	2	2	4	2	0	0	9	22.2	0	1	1	0	0	0	4	8	0	4	0	0	0	0	.44
3 Years		16	3	2	5	-1	1	0	12	25.0	0	1	1	0	0	0	6	12	0	6	0	–	–	0	.31

Scott Ferguson

Pos: D **Shoots:** L **Ht:** 6'1" **Wt:** 195 **Born:** 1/6/73—Camrose, Alberta **Age:** 26

Year	Tm	GP	G	A	Pts	+/–	GW	GT	S	SPct	G	A	Pts	G	A	Pts	Num	PIM	Maj	Mnr	Fgt	Rgh	HHT	Hat	P/G
		Overall									Power Play			Shorthand			Penalty							Misc	
97-98	Edm	1	0	0	0	1	0	0	0	–	0	0	0	0	0	0	0	0	0	0	0	0	0	0	.00
98-99	Anh	2	0	1	1	0	0	0	1	0.0	0	0	0	0	0	0	0	0	0	0	0	0	0	0	.50
2 Years		3	0	1	1	1	0	0	1	0.0	0	0	0	0	0	0	0	0	0	0	0	0	0	0	.33

Manny Fernandez

Pos: G **Catches:** L **Ht:** 6'0" **Wt:** 185 **Born:** 8/27/74—Etobicoke, Ontario **Age:** 25

Year	Tm	GP	GS	TP	W	L	T	Min	GA	GAA	Shots	SvPct	ShO	OE	PPGA	SHGA	Shots	GA	G	A	PIM
		Overall															Pen Shot		Offense		
94-95	Dal	1	1	0	0	1	0	59	3	3.05	27	.889	0	0	1	0	0	0	0	0	0
95-96	Dal	5	3	2	0	1	1	249	19	4.58	121	.843	0	0	7	1	0	0	0	0	0
96-97										Did Not Play in NHL											
97-98	Dal	2	1	1	1	0	0	69	2	1.74	35	.943	0	1	0	0	0	0	0	0	0
98-99	Dal	1	1	0	0	1	0	60	2	2.00	29	.931	0	0	0	0	0	0	0	0	0
4 Years		9	6	3	1	3	1	437	26	3.57	212	.877	0	1	8	1	0	0	0	0	0

Postseason																					
Year	Tm	GP	GS	TP	W	L	Pct	Min	GA	GAA	Shots	SvPct	ShO	OE	PPGA	SHGA	Shots	GA	G	A	PIM
97-98	Dal	1	0	0	0	0	–	2	0	0.00	0	–	0	0	0	0	0	0	0	0	0

Chris Ferraro

Pos: RW **Shoots:** R **Ht:** 5'10" **Wt:** 180 **Born:** 1/24/73—Port Jefferson, New York **Age:** 26

Overall											Power Play			Shorthand			Penalty							Misc	
Year	Tm	GP	G	A	Pts	+/–	GW	GT	S	SPct	G	A	Pts	G	A	Pts	Num	PIM	Maj	Mnr	Fgt	Rgh	HHT	Hat	P/G
95-96	NYR	2	1	0	1	-3	0	0	4	25.0	1	0	1	0	0	0	0	0	0	0	0	0	0	0	.50
96-97	NYR	12	1	1	2	1	0	0	23	4.3	0	1	1	0	0	0	3	6	0	3	0	0	3	0	.17
97-98	Pit	46	3	4	7	-2	0	0	42	7.1	0	1	1	0	0	0	16	43	1	14	0	2	5	0	.15
98-99	Edm	2	1	0	1	1	0	0	1	100.0	0	0	0	0	0	0	0	0	0	0	0	0	0	0	.50
4 Years		62	6	5	11	-3	0	0	70	8.6	1	2	3	0	0	0	19	49	1	17	0	2	8	0	.18

Peter Ferraro

(statistical profile on page 310)

Pos: C **Shoots:** R **Ht:** 5'10" **Wt:** 180 **Born:** 1/24/73—Port Jefferson, New York **Age:** 26

Overall											Power Play			Shorthand			Penalty							Misc	
Year	Tm	GP	G	A	Pts	+/–	GW	GT	S	SPct	G	A	Pts	G	A	Pts	Num	PIM	Maj	Mnr	Fgt	Rgh	HHT	Hat	P/G
95-96	NYR	5	0	1	1	-5	0	0	6	0.0	0	1	1	0	0	0	0	0	0	0	0	0	0	0	.20
96-97	NYR	2	0	0	0	0	0	0	3	0.0	0	0	0	0	0	0	0	0	0	0	0	0	0	0	.00
97-98	2Tm	30	3	4	7	-4	0	0	37	8.1	0	0	0	0	0	0	7	14	0	7	0	2	0	0	.23
98-99	Bos	46	6	8	14	10	1	0	61	9.8	1	1	2	0	0	0	14	44	0	12	0	1	7	0	.30
97-98	Pit	29	3	4	7	-2	0	0	34	8.8	0	0	0	0	0	0	6	12	0	6	0	2	0	0	.24
97-98	NYR	1	0	0	0	-2	0	0	3	0.0	0	0	0	0	0	0	1	2	0	1	0	0	0	0	.00
4 Years		83	9	13	22	1	1	0	107	8.4	1	2	3	0	0	0	21	58	0	19	0	3	7	0	.27
Postseason																									
Year	Tm	GP	G	A	Pts	+/–	GW	OT	S	SPct	G	A	Pts	G	A	Pts	Num	PIM	Maj	Mnr	Fgt	Rgh	HHT	Hat	P/G
96-97	NYR	2	0	0	0	0	0	0	2	0.0	0	0	0	0	0	0	0	0	0	0	0	0	0	0	.00

Ray Ferraro

(statistical profile on page 310)

Pos: C **Shoots:** L **Ht:** 5'10" **Wt:** 192 **Born:** 8/23/64—Trail, British Columbia **Age:** 35

Overall											Power Play			Shorthand			Penalty							Misc	
Year	Tm	GP	G	A	Pts	+/–	GW	GT	S	SPct	G	A	Pts	G	A	Pts	Num	PIM	Maj	Mnr	Fgt	Rgh	HHT	Hat	P/G
84-85	Har	44	11	17	28	-1	2	0	59	18.6	6	–	–	0	–	–	–	40	–	–	–	–	–	2	.64
85-86	Har	76	30	47	77	10	0	0	132	22.7	14	–	–	0	–	–	–	57	–	–	–	–	–	0	1.01
86-87	Har	80	27	32	59	-9	2	0	96	**28.1**	14	–	–	0	–	–	–	42	–	–	–	–	–	1	.74
87-88	Har	68	21	29	50	1	2	0	105	20.0	6	–	–	0	–	–	–	81	–	–	–	–	–	0	.74
88-89	Har	**80**	41	35	76	1	7	0	169	24.3	11	–	–	0	–	–	–	86	–	–	–	–	–	1	.95
89-90	Har	79	25	29	54	-15	4	1	138	18.1	7	–	–	0	–	–	–	109	–	–	–	–	–	1	.68
90-91	2Tm	76	21	21	42	-12	1	1	109	19.3	6	–	–	0	–	–	–	70	–	–	–	–	–	0	.55
91-92	NYI*	80	40	40	80	25	4	2	154	26.0	7	7	14	0	0	0	39	92	2	36	1	8	12	2	1.00
92-93	NYI	46	14	13	27	0	1	0	72	19.4	3	1	4	0	0	0	20	40	0	20	0	4	6	0	.59
93-94	NYI	82	21	32	53	1	3	**3**	136	15.4	5	7	12	0	0	0	40	83	1	39	1	8	12	0	.65
94-95	NYI	47	22	21	43	1	1	2	94	23.4	2	5	7	0	0	0	15	30	0	15	0	5	3	0	.91
95-96	2Tm	76	29	31	60	0	4	0	178	16.3	9	10	19	0	0	0	42	92	0	41	0	8	11	1	.79
96-97	LA	81	25	21	46	-22	2	1	152	16.4	11	6	17	0	0	0	44	112	0	41	0	3	14	0	.57
97-98	LA	40	6	9	15	-10	2	0	45	13.3	0	3	3	0	0	0	21	42	0	21	0	4	4	0	.38
98-99	LA	65	13	18	31	0	4	0	84	15.5	4	2	6	0	1	1	24	59	1	22	0	1	9	0	.48
90-91	Har	61	19	16	35	-11	1	1	91	20.9	5	–	–	0	–	–	–	52	–	–	–	–	–	0	.57
90-91	NYI	15	2	5	7	-1	0	0	18	11.1	1	–	–	0	–	–	–	18	–	–	–	–	–	0	.47
95-96	NYR	65	25	29	54	13	4	0	160	15.6	8	9	17	0	0	0	37	82	0	36	0	6	10	1	.83
95-96	LA	11	4	2	6	-13	0	0	18	22.2	1	1	2	0	0	0	5	10	0	5	0	2	1	0	.55
15 Years		1020	346	395	741	-30	39	10	1723	20.1	105	–	–	0	–	–	–	1035	–	–	–	–	–	8	.73
Postseason																									
Year	Tm	GP	G	A	Pts	+/–	GW	OT	S	SPct	G	A	Pts	G	A	Pts	Num	PIM	Maj	Mnr	Fgt	Rgh	HHT	Hat	P/G
85-86	Har	10	3	6	9	-1	0	0	14	21.4	3	–	–	0	–	–	2	4	0	2	0	–	–	0	.90
86-87	Har	6	1	1	2	-2	0	0	11	9.1	0	–	–	0	0	0	4	8	0	4	0	–	–	0	.33
87-88	Har	6	1	1	2	-5	0	0	6	16.7	1	–	–	0	0	0	3	6	0	3	0	–	–	0	.33
88-89	Har	4	2	0	2	-2	0	0	6	33.3	0	0	0	0	0	0	2	4	0	2	0	–	–	0	.50
89-90	Har	7	0	3	3	1	0	0	5	0.0	0	–	–	0	0	0	1	2	0	1	0	–	–	0	.43
92-93	NYI	18	13	7	20	5	2	2	47	27.7	4	0	4	1	0	1	9	18	0	9	0	1	3	1	1.11
93-94	NYI	4	1	0	1	-2	0	0	8	12.5	0	0	0	0	0	0	3	6	0	3	0	1	1	0	.25
97-98	LA	3	0	1	1	1	0	0	5	0.0	0	0	0	0	0	0	1	2	0	1	0	0	0	0	.33
8 Years		58	21	19	40	-5	2	2	102	20.6	8	–	–	1	–	–	25	50	0	25	0	–	–	1	.69

Eric Fichaud

Pos: G **Catches:** L **Ht:** 5'11" **Wt:** 171 **Born:** 11/4/75—Anjou, Quebec **Age:** 24

Overall																	Pen Shot		Offense		
Year	Tm	GP	GS	TP	W	L	T	Min	GA	GAA	Shots	SvPct	ShO	OE	PPGA	SHGA	Shots	GA	G	A	PIM
95-96	NYI	24	21	4	7	12	2	1234	68	3.31	659	.897	1	8	15	2	0	0	0	1	0
96-97	NYI	34	28	5	9	14	4	1759	91	3.10	897	.899	0	6	23	2	0	0	0	0	2
97-98	NYI	17	13	5	3	8	3	807	40	2.97	422	.905	0	4	11	2	0	0	0	0	0
98-99	Nsh	9	7	1	0	6	0	447	24	3.22	229	.895	0	1	8	0	1	0	0	0	0
4 Years		84	69	15	19	40	9	4247	223	3.15	2207	.899	1	19	57	6	1	0	0	1	2

Jeff Finley

Pos: D **Shoots:** L **Ht:** 6'2" **Wt:** 205 **Born:** 4/14/67—Edmonton, Alberta **Age:** 32

Overall											Power Play			Shorthand			Penalty							Misc	
Year	Tm	GP	G	A	Pts	+/–	GW	GT	S	SPct	G	A	Pts	G	A	Pts	Num	PIM	Maj	Mnr	Fgt	Rgh	HHT	Hat	P/G
87-88	NYI	10	0	5	5	5	0	0	9	0.0	0	–	–	0	–	–	–	15	–	–	–	–	–	0	.50
88-89	NYI	4	0	0	0	1	0	0	1	0.0	0	0	0	0	0	0	3	6	0	3	0	–	–	0	.00
89-90	NYI	11	0	1	1	0	0	0	7	0.0	0	–	–	0	–	–	0	0	0	0	0	0	0	0	.09
90-91	NYI	11	0	0	0	-1	0	0	0	–	0	0	0	0	0	0	2	4	0	2	0	–	–	0	.00
91-92	NYI	51	1	10	11	-6	0	0	25	4.0	0	3	3	0	1	1	13	26	0	13	0	2	9	0	.22
92-93		Did Not Play in NHL																							
93-94	Phi	55	1	8	9	16	0	0	43	2.3	0	0	0	0	0	0	12	24	0	12	0	4	4	0	.16
94-95		Did Not Play in NHL																							
95-96	Wpg	65	1	5	6	-2	0	0	27	3.7	0	0	0	0	0	0	35	81	1	33	1	4	17	0	.09
96-97	Pho	65	3	7	10	-8	1	0	38	7.9	1	0	1	0	1	1	20	40	0	20	0	3	10	0	.15
97-98	NYR	63	1	6	7	-3	0	0	32	3.1	0	1	1	0	0	0	26	55	1	25	1	0	8	0	.11
98-99	2Tm	32	1	2	3	11	0	0	16	6.3	0	0	0	0	0	0	10	20	0	10	0	0	7	0	.09
98-99	NYR	2	0	0	0	-1	0	0	0	–	0	0	0	0	0	0	0	0	0	0	0	0	0	0	.00
98-99	StL	30	1	2	3	12	0	0	16	6.3	0	0	0	0	0	0	10	20	0	10	0	0	7	0	.10
10 Years		367	8	44	52	13	1	0	198	4.0	1	–	–	0	–	–	–	271	–	–	–	–	–	0	.14
Postseason																									
Year	Tm	GP	G	A	Pts	+/–	GW	OT	S	SPct	G	A	Pts	G	A	Pts	Num	PIM	Maj	Mnr	Fgt	Rgh	HHT	Hat	P/G
87-88	NYI	1	0	0	0	-1	0	0	0	–	0	0	0	0	0	0	1	2	0	1	0	–	–	0	.00
89-90	NYI	5	0	2	2	-3	0	0	4	0.0	0	–	–	0	0	0	1	2	0	1	0	–	–	0	.40
95-96	Wpg	6	0	0	0	-4	0	0	3	0.0	0	0	0	0	0	0	2	4	0	2	0	0	1	0	.00
96-97	Pho	1	0	0	0	-1	0	0	1	0.0	0	0	0	0	0	0	1	2	0	1	0	0	1	0	.00
98-99	StL	13	1	2	3	-4	1	0	5	20.0	0	0	0	0	0	0	4	8	0	4	0	0	1	0	.23
5 Years		26	1	4	5	-13	1	0	13	7.7	0	–	–	0	0	0	9	18	0	9	0	–	–	0	.19

Stephane Fiset

(statistical profile on page 398)

Pos: G **Catches:** L **Ht:** 6'1" **Wt:** 197 **Born:** 6/17/70—Montreal, Quebec **Age:** 29

Overall																	Pen Shot		Offense		
Year	Tm	GP	GS	TP	W	L	T	Min	GA	GAA	Shots	SvPct	ShO	OE	PPGA	SHGA	Shots	GA	G	A	PIM
89-90	Que	6	–	–	0	5	1	342	34	5.96	199	.829	0	–	–	–	0	0	0	0	0
90-91	Que	3	–	–	0	2	1	186	12	3.87	123	.902	0	–	–	–	0	0	0	0	0
91-92	Que	23	20	4	7	10	2	1133	71	3.76	646	.890	1	7	23	5	2	0	0	0	6
92-93	Que	37	30	4	18	9	4	1939	110	3.40	945	.884	0	7	34	2	0	0	0	2	2
93-94	Que	50	49	6	20	25	4	2798	158	3.39	1434	.890	2	11	49	9	0	0	0	3	8
94-95	Que	32	30	2	17	10	3	1879	87	2.78	968	.910	2	12	26	3	0	0	0	3	2
95-96	Col	37	35	2	22	6	7	2107	103	2.93	1012	.898	1	12	35	5	1	**1**	0	1	2
96-97	LA	44	43	5	13	24	5	2482	132	3.19	1410	.906	4	19	22	6	0	0	0	0	2
97-98	LA	60	59	4	26	25	8	3497	158	2.71	1728	.909	2	22	47	7	2	0	0	1	8
98-99	LA	42	41	5	18	21	1	2403	104	2.60	1217	.915	3	16	21	4	**3**	**2**	0	0	2
10 Years		334	–	–	141	137	36	18766	969	3.10	9682	.900	15	–	–	–	8	3	0	10	32
Postseason																					
Year	Tm	GP	GS	TP	W	L	Pct	Min	GA	GAA	Shots	SvPct	ShO	OE	PPGA	SHGA	Shots	GA	G	A	PIM
92-93	Que	1	0	1	0	0	–	21	1	2.86	12	.917	0	0	1	0	0	0	0	0	0
94-95	Que	4	3	1	1	2	.333	209	16	4.59	115	.861	0	0	4	1	0	0	0	0	0
95-96	Col	1	0	1	0	0	–	1	0	0.00	0	–	0	0	0	0	0	0	0	0	0
97-98	LA	2	2	1	0	2	.000	93	7	4.52	61	.885	0	1	3	0	0	0	0	0	0
4 Years		8	5	4	1	4	.200	324	24	4.44	188	.872	0	1	8	1	0	0	0	0	0

Tom Fitzgerald

(statistical profile on page 310)

Pos: RW **Shoots:** R **Ht:** 6'0" **Wt:** 191 **Born:** 8/28/68—Billerica, Massachusetts **Age:** 31

		Overall									Power Play			Shorthand			Penalty							Misc	
Year	Tm	GP	G	A	Pts	+/–	GW	GT	S	SPct	G	A	Pts	G	A	Pts	Num	PIM	Maj	Mnr	Fgt	Rgh	HHT	Hat	P/G
88-89	NYI	23	3	5	8	1	1	0	24	12.5	0	–	–	0	–	–	–	10	–	–	–	–	–	0	.35
89-90	NYI	19	2	5	7	-3	1	0	24	8.3	0	–	–	0	–	–	2	4	0	2	0	–	–	0	.37
90-91	NYI	41	5	5	10	-9	2	0	60	8.3	0	–	–	0	–	–	–	24	–	–	–	–	–	0	.24
91-92	NYI	45	6	11	17	-3	2	0	71	8.5	0	0	0	2	1	3	14	28	0	14	0	2	5	0	.38
92-93	NYI	77	9	18	27	-2	1	0	83	10.8	0	1	1	3	2	5	14	34	2	12	2	1	5	0	.35
93-94	Fla	83	18	14	32	-3	1	0	144	12.5	0	3	3	3	1	4	19	54	0	17	0	2	8	0	.39
94-95	Fla	48	3	13	16	-3	0	0	78	3.8	0	0	0	0	0	0	14	31	1	13	1	3	2	0	.33
95-96	Fla	82	13	21	34	-3	2	0	141	9.2	1	1	2	6	0	6	28	75	1	25	0	5	8	0	.41
96-97	Fla	71	10	14	24	7	1	1	135	7.4	0	0	0	2	1	3	24	64	0	22	0	3	7	0	.34
97-98	2Tm	80	12	6	18	-4	1	0	119	10.1	0	0	0	2	0	2	26	79	1	22	1	2	9	0	.23
98-99	Nsh	80	13	19	32	-18	1	0	180	7.2	0	2	2	0	2	2	24	48	0	24	0	0	9	0	.40
97-98	Fla	69	10	5	15	-4	1	0	105	9.5	0	0	0	1	0	1	19	57	1	16	1	0	6	0	.22
97-98	Col	11	2	1	3	0	0	0	14	14.3	0	0	0	1	0	1	7	22	0	6	0	2	3	0	.27
11 Years		649	94	131	225	-40	13	1	1059	8.9	1	–	–	18	–	–	–	451	–	–	–	–	–	0	.35

Postseason

Year	Tm	GP	G	A	Pts	+/–	GW	OT	S	SPct	G	A	Pts	G	A	Pts	Num	PIM	Maj	Mnr	Fgt	Rgh	HHT	Hat	P/G
89-90	NYI	4	1	0	1	0	0	0	3	33.3	0	0	0	0	0	0	2	4	0	2	0	–	–	0	.25
92-93	NYI	18	2	5	7	2	0	0	21	9.5	0	0	0	2	2	4	5	18	0	4	0	1	0	0	.39
95-96	Fla	22	4	4	8	3	2	0	31	12.9	0	0	0	0	0	0	9	34	0	7	0	4	2	0	.36
96-97	Fla	5	0	1	1	-1	0	0	14	0.0	0	0	0	0	0	0	0	0	0	0	0	0	0	0	.20
97-98	Col	7	0	1	1	-2	0	0	8	0.0	0	0	0	0	0	0	6	20	0	5	0	2	1	0	.14
5 Years		56	7	11	18	2	2	0	77	9.1	0	0	0	2	2	4	22	76	0	18	0	–	–	0	.32

Mark Fitzpatrick

(statistical profile on page 398)

Pos: G **Catches:** L **Ht:** 6'2" **Wt:** 198 **Born:** 11/13/68—Toronto, Ontario **Age:** 31

		Overall																Pen Shot		Offense		
Year	Tm	GP	GS	TP	W	L	T	Min	GA	GAA	Shots	SvPct	ShO	OE	PPGA	SHGA	Shots	GA	G	A	PIM
88-89	2Tm	28	–	–	9	12	5	1584	105	3.98	879	.881	0	–	–	–	0	0	0	2	4
89-90	NYI	47	–	–	19	19	5	2653	150	3.39	1472	.898	3	–	–	–	1	0	0	2	18
90-91	NYI	2	–	–	1	1	0	120	6	3.00	60	.900	0	–	–	–	0	0	0	0	0
91-92	NYI	30	28	2	11	13	5	1743	93	3.20	949	.902	0	9	30	1	0	0	0	2	8
92-93	NYI	39	37	2	17	15	5	2253	130	3.46	1066	.878	0	6	32	2	0	0	0	1	2
93-94	Fla	28	26	1	12	8	6	1603	73	2.73	844	.914	1	15	23	6	0	0	0	2	4
94-95	Fla	15	13	2	6	7	2	819	36	2.64	361	.900	2	5	11	1	0	0	0	0	0
95-96	Fla	34	28	3	15	11	3	1786	88	2.96	810	.891	0	6	25	2	1	0	0	0	12
96-97	Fla	30	26	2	8	9	9	1680	66	2.36	771	.914	0	11	21	3	2	1	0	1	13
97-98	2Tm	46	43	6	9	31	3	2578	134	3.12	1240	.892	2	17	39	7	2	0	0	1	16
98-99	Chi	27	21	2	6	8	6	1403	64	2.74	682	.906	0	8	19	1	0	0	0	1	8
88-89	LA	17	–	–	6	7	3	957	64	4.01	566	.887	0	–	–	–	0	0	0	1	2
88-89	NYI	11	–	–	3	5	2	627	41	3.92	313	.869	0	–	–	–	0	0	0	1	2
97-98	Fla	12	10	1	2	7	2	640	32	3.00	265	.879	1	2	9	1	0	0	0	0	2
97-98	TB	34	33	5	7	24	1	1938	102	3.16	975	.895	1	15	30	6	2	0	0	1	14
11 Years		326	–	–	113	134	49	18222	945	3.11	9134	.897	8	–	–	–	6	1	0	12	85

Postseason

Year	Tm	GP	GS	TP	W	L	Pct	Min	GA	GAA	Shots	SvPct	ShO	OE	PPGA	SHGA	Shots	GA	G	A	PIM
89-90	NYI	4	–	–	0	2	.000	152	13	5.13	71	.817	0	–	–	–	0	0	0	0	19
92-93	NYI	3	0	0	0	1	.000	77	4	3.12	23	.826	0	0	1	0	0	0	0	0	2
95-96	Fla	2	0	0	0	0	–	60	6	6.00	30	.800	0	0	1	1	0	0	0	0	0
3 Years		9	–	–	0	3	.000	289	23	4.78	124	.815	0	–	–	–	0	0	0	0	21

Rory Fitzpatrick

Pos: D **Shoots:** R **Ht:** 6'2" **Wt:** 206 **Born:** 1/11/75—Rochester, New York **Age:** 24

		Overall									Power Play			Shorthand			Penalty							Misc	
Year	Tm	GP	G	A	Pts	+/–	GW	GT	S	SPct	G	A	Pts	G	A	Pts	Num	PIM	Maj	Mnr	Fgt	Rgh	HHT	Hat	P/G
95-96	Mon	42	0	2	2	-7	0	0	31	0.0	0	1	1	0	0	0	9	18	0	9	0	1	3	0	.05
96-97	2Tm	8	0	1	1	-4	0	0	6	0.0	0	0	0	0	0	0	4	8	0	4	0	1	2	0	.13
97-98		Did Not Play in NHL																							
98-99	StL	1	0	0	0	-3	0	0	0	–	0	0	0	0	0	0	1	2	0	1	0	0	0	0	.00
96-97	Mon	6	0	1	1	-2	0	0	5	0.0	0	0	0	0	0	0	3	6	0	3	0	1	2	0	.17
96-97	StL	2	0	0	0	-2	0	0	1	0.0	0	0	0	0	0	0	1	2	0	1	0	0	0	0	.00
3 Years		51	0	3	3	-14	0	0	37	0.0	0	1	1	0	0	0	14	28	0	14	0	2	5	0	.06

Postseason																									
Year	Tm	GP	G	A	Pts	+/-	GW	OT	S	SPct	G	A	Pts	G	A	Pts	Num	PIM	Maj	Mnr	Fgt	Rgh	HHT	Hat	P/G
95-96	Mon	6	1	1	2	-1	0	0	5	20.0	0	0	0	0	0	0	0	0	0	0	0	0	0	0	.33

Wade Flaherty

(statistical profile on page 398)

Pos: G **Catches:** R **Ht:** 6'0" **Wt:** 170 **Born:** 1/11/68—Terrace, British Columbia **Age:** 31

Overall																Pen Shot		Offense		
Year	Tm	GP	GS	TP	W	L	T	Min	GA	GAA	Shots	SvPct	ShO	OE	PPGA	SHGA	Shots	GA	G	A	PIM
91-92	SJ	3	3	0	0	3	0	178	13	4.38	120	.892	0	0	1	1	0	0	0	0	0
92-93	SJ	1	1	0	0	1	0	60	5	5.00	46	.891	0	0	0	0	0	0	0	0	0
93-94										Did Not Play in NHL											
94-95	SJ	18	13	3	5	6	1	852	44	3.10	455	.903	1	6	13	3	0	0	0	1	0
95-96	SJ	24	15	3	3	12	1	1137	92	4.85	689	.866	0	2	26	7	0	0	0	0	0
96-97	SJ	7	6	1	2	4	0	359	31	5.18	202	.847	0	1	9	3	0	0	0	0	0
97-98	NYI	16	11	2	4	4	3	694	23	1.99	309	.926	3	5	5	3	0	0	0	1	0
98-99	NYI	20	18	2	5	11	2	1048	53	3.03	491	.892	0	4	17	3	0	0	0	0	4
7 Years		89	67	11	19	41	7	4328	261	3.62	2312	.887	4	18	71	20	0	0	0	2	4
Postseason																					
Year	Tm	GP	GS	TP	W	L	Pct	Min	GA	GAA	Shots	SvPct	ShO	OE	PPGA	SHGA	Shots	GA	G	A	PIM
94-95	SJ	7	5	0	2	3	.400	377	31	4.93	195	.841	0	1	6	2	0	0	0	0	0

Theo Fleury

(statistical profile on page 311)

Pos: RW **Shoots:** R **Ht:** 5'6" **Wt:** 170 **Born:** 6/29/68—Oxbow, Saskatchewan **Age:** 31

Overall											Power Play			Shorthand			Penalty							Misc	
Year	Tm	GP	G	A	Pts	+/–	GW	GT	S	SPct	G	A	Pts	G	A	Pts	Num	PIM	Maj	Mnr	Fgt	Rgh	HHT	Hat	P/G
88-89	Cgy	36	14	20	34	5	3	0	89	15.7	5	–	–	0	–	–	19	46	0	18	0	–	–	0	.94
89-90	Cgy	**80**	31	35	66	22	6	**3**	200	15.5	9	–	–	3	–	–	54	157	3	46	–	–	–	0	.83
90-91	Cgy*	79	51	53	104	**48**	9	0	249	20.5	9	–	–	7	–	–	56	136	0	53	0	–	–	**5**	1.32
91-92	Cgy*	80	33	40	73	0	6	0	225	14.7	11	20	31	1	0	1	53	133	1	49	0	20	10	0	.91
92-93	Cgy	83	34	66	100	14	4	0	250	13.6	12	21	33	2	1	3	44	88	0	44	0	17	12	1	1.20
93-94	Cgy	83	40	45	85	30	6	0	278	14.4	16	12	28	1	2	3	66	186	2	58	0	12	13	1	1.02
94-95	Cgy	47	29	29	58	6	5	0	173	16.8	9	11	20	2	1	3	36	112	0	31	0	9	5	0	1.23
95-96	Cgy*	80	46	50	96	17	4	0	353	13.0	17	18	35	5	1	6	45	112	2	41	1	7	14	3	1.20
96-97	Cgy*	81	29	38	67	-12	3	3	336	8.6	9	15	24	2	1	3	48	104	0	47	0	8	6	1	.83
97-98	Cgy*	82	27	51	78	0	4	1	282	9.6	3	18	21	2	5	7	69	197	1	61	0	13	17	0	.95
98-99	2Tm	75	40	53	93	26	5	2	301	13.3	8	17	25	3	2	5	39	86	0	38	0	10	8	**3**	1.24
98-99	Cgy	60	30	39	69	18	3	1	250	12.0	7	13	20	3	2	5	30	68	0	29	0	9	6	2	1.15
98-99	Col	15	10	14	24	8	2	1	51	19.6	1	4	5	0	0	0	9	18	0	9	0	1	2	1	1.60
11 Years		806	374	480	854	156	55	9	2736	13.7	108	–	–	28	–	–	529	1357	9	486	–	–	–	14	1.06
Postseason																									
Year	Tm	GP	G	A	Pts	+/–	GW	OT	S	SPct	G	A	Pts	G	A	Pts	Num	PIM	Maj	Mnr	Fgt	Rgh	HHT	Hat	P/G
88-89	Cgy	22	5	6	11	-4	3	0	46	10.9	3	–	–	0	–	–	–	24	–	–	–	–	–	0	.50
89-90	Cgy	6	2	3	5	4	0	0	19	10.5	0	–	–	0	–	–	–	10	–	–	–	–	–	0	.83
90-91	Cgy	7	2	5	7	1	1	1	20	10.0	0	–	–	0	0	0	–	14	–	–	–	–	–	0	1.00
92-93	Cgy	6	5	7	12	-7	0	0	21	23.8	3	5	8	1	1	2	8	27	1	6	0	3	0	0	2.00
93-94	Cgy	7	6	4	10	1	2	0	23	26.1	1	3	4	0	0	0	1	5	1	0	0	0	0	0	1.43
94-95	Cgy	7	7	7	14	8	0	0	40	17.5	2	1	3	1	0	1	1	2	0	1	0	0	0	1	2.00
95-96	Cgy	4	2	1	3	1	0	0	28	7.1	0	0	0	0	0	0	3	14	0	2	0	0	1	0	.75
98-99	Col	18	5	12	17	-2	0	0	56	8.9	2	2	4	0	0	0	10	20	0	10	0	2	6	0	.94
8 Years		77	34	45	79	2	6	1	253	13.4	11	–	–	2	–	–	–	116	–	–	–	–	–	1	1.03

Adam Foote

(statistical profile on page 311)

Pos: D **Shoots:** R **Ht:** 6'2" **Wt:** 206 **Born:** 7/10/71—Toronto, Ontario **Age:** 28

Overall											Power Play			Shorthand			Penalty							Misc	
Year	Tm	GP	G	A	Pts	+/-	GW	GT	S	SPct	G	A	Pts	G	A	Pts	Num	PIM	Maj	Mnr	Fgt	Rgh	HHT	Hat	P/G
91-92	Que	46	2	5	7	-4	0	1	55	3.6	0	1	1	0	0	0	18	44	0	17	0	5	6	0	.15
92-93	Que	81	4	12	16	6	0	0	54	7.4	0	0	0	1	2	3	57	168	2	49	1	15	15	0	.20
93-94	Que	45	2	6	8	3	0	0	42	4.8	0	0	0	0	0	0	28	67	1	26	1	10	5	0	.18
94-95	Que	35	0	7	7	17	0	0	24	0.0	0	0	0	0	1	1	16	52	4	11	4	3	1	0	.20
95-96	Col	73	5	11	16	27	1	0	49	10.2	1	1	2	0	0	0	37	88	2	34	2	9	11	0	.22
96-97	Col	78	2	19	21	16	0	0	60	3.3	0	2	2	0	2	2	59	135	3	55	3	14	7	0	.27
97-98	Col	77	3	14	17	-3	1	0	64	4.7	0	1	1	0	1	1	48	124	4	42	4	11	6	0	.22
98-99	Col	64	5	16	21	20	0	0	83	6.0	3	5	8	0	0	0	39	92	2	36	2	12	5	0	.33
8 Years		499	23	90	113	82	2	1	431	5.3	4	10	14	1	6	7	302	770	18	270	17	79	56	0	.23

Postseason																									
Year	Tm	GP	G	A	Pts	+/-	GW	OT	S	SPct	G	A	Pts	G	A	Pts	Num	PIM	Maj	Mnr	Fgt	Rgh	HHT	Hat	P/G
92-93	Que	6	0	1	1	-3	0	0	6	0.0	0	0	0	0	0	0	1	2	0	1	0	0	0	0	.17
94-95	Que	6	0	1	1	-3	0	0	6	0.0	0	0	0	0	0	0	7	14	0	7	0	3	0	0	.17
95-96	Col	22	1	3	4	11	0	0	20	5.0	0	0	0	0	0	0	18	36	0	18	0	8	4	0	.18
96-97	Col	17	0	4	4	3	0	0	17	0.0	0	1	1	0	0	0	24	62	2	21	2	6	2	0	.24
97-98	Col	7	0	0	0	-1	0	0	12	0.0	0	0	0	0	0	0	6	23	1	4	1	0	0	0	.00
98-99	Col	19	2	3	5	3	0	0	28	7.1	1	0	1	0	0	0	12	24	0	12	0	5	2	0	.26
6 Years		77	3	12	15	10	0	0	89	3.4	1	1	2	0	0	0	68	161	3	63	3	22	8	0	.19

Colin Forbes

(statistical profile on page 311)

Pos: LW **Shoots:** L **Ht:** 6'3" **Wt:** 205 **Born:** 2/26/76—West Newminster, British Columbia **Age:** 23

Overall											Power Play			Shorthand			Penalty							Misc	
Year	Tm	GP	G	A	Pts	+/-	GW	GT	S	SPct	G	A	Pts	G	A	Pts	Num	PIM	Maj	Mnr	Fgt	Rgh	HHT	Hat	P/G
96-97	Phi	3	1	0	1	0	0	0	3	33.3	0	0	0	0	0	0	0	0	0	0	0	0	0	0	.33
97-98	Phi	63	12	7	19	2	2	0	93	12.9	2	0	2	0	1	1	17	59	3	12	3	1	3	0	.30
98-99	2Tm	80	12	8	20	-5	4	0	117	10.3	0	0	0	1	0	1	29	61	1	28	1	7	8	0	.25
98-99	Phi	66	9	7	16	0	4	0	92	9.8	0	0	0	0	0	0	24	51	1	23	1	5	6	0	.24
98-99	TB	14	3	1	4	-5	0	0	25	12.0	0	0	0	1	0	1	5	10	0	5	0	2	2	0	.29
3 Years		146	25	15	40	-3	6	0	213	11.7	2	0	2	1	1	2	46	120	4	40	4	8	11	0	.27
Postseason																									
Year	Tm	GP	G	A	Pts	+/-	GW	OT	S	SPct	G	A	Pts	G	A	Pts	Num	PIM	Maj	Mnr	Fgt	Rgh	HHT	Hat	P/G
96-97	Phi	3	0	0	0	0	0	0	3	0.0	0	0	0	0	0	0	0	0	0	0	0	0	0	0	.00
97-98	Phi	5	0	0	0	2	0	0	9	0.0	0	0	0	0	0	0	1	2	0	1	0	0	0	0	.00
2 Years		8	0	0	0	2	0	0	12	0.0	0	0	0	0	0	0	1	2	0	1	0	0	0	0	.00

Peter Forsberg

(statistical profile on page 311)

Pos: C **Shoots:** L **Ht:** 6'0" **Wt:** 190 **Born:** 7/20/73—Ornskoldsvik, Sweden **Age:** 26

Overall											Power Play			Shorthand			Penalty							Misc	
Year	Tm	GP	G	A	Pts	+/-	GW	GT	S	SPct	G	A	Pts	G	A	Pts	Num	PIM	Maj	Mnr	Fgt	Rgh	HHT	Hat	P/G
94-95	Que	47	15	35	50	17	3	0	86	17.4	3	12	15	0	1	1	8	16	0	8	0	0	4	0	1.06
95-96	Col*	82	30	86	116	26	3	0	217	13.8	7	32	39	3	4	7	22	47	1	21	0	3	8	2	1.41
96-97	Col*	65	28	58	86	31	4	0	188	14.9	5	21	26	4	3	7	35	73	1	34	1	9	12	1	1.32
97-98	Col*	72	25	66	91	6	7	1	202	12.4	7	30	37	3	0	3	43	94	0	42	0	7	8	0	1.26
98-99	Col	78	30	67	97	27	7	0	217	13.8	9	28	37	2	4	6	46	108	0	44	0	6	15	1	1.24
5 Years		344	128	312	440	107	24	1	910	14.1	31	123	154	12	12	24	154	338	2	149	1	25	47	4	1.28
Postseason																									
Year	Tm	GP	G	A	Pts	+/-	GW	OT	S	SPct	G	A	Pts	G	A	Pts	Num	PIM	Maj	Mnr	Fgt	Rgh	HHT	Hat	P/G
94-95	Que	6	2	4	6	2	0	0	13	15.4	1	0	1	0	0	0	2	4	0	2	0	0	1	0	1.00
95-96	Col	22	10	11	21	10	1	0	50	20.0	3	3	6	0	0	0	9	18	0	9	0	3	3	1	.95
96-97	Col	14	5	12	17	-6	0	0	35	14.3	3	5	8	0	0	0	5	10	0	5	0	1	1	0	1.21
97-98	Col	7	6	5	11	3	0	0	18	33.3	2	2	4	0	1	1	6	12	0	6	0	0	0	0	1.57
98-99	Col	19	8	16	24	7	0	0	54	14.8	1	8	9	1	0	1	10	31	1	8	0	0	1	0	1.26
5 Years		68	31	48	79	16	1	0	170	18.2	10	18	28	1	1	2	32	75	1	30	0	4	6	1	1.16

Ron Francis

(statistical profile on page 312)

Pos: C **Shoots:** L **Ht:** 6'3" **Wt:** 200 **Born:** 3/1/63—Sault Ste. Marie, Ontario **Age:** 36

Overall											Power Play			Shorthand			Penalty							Misc	
Year	Tm	GP	G	A	Pts	+/-	GW	GT	S	SPct	G	A	Pts	G	A	Pts	Num	PIM	Maj	Mnr	Fgt	Rgh	HHT	Hat	P/G
81-82	Har	59	25	43	68	-13	1	1	163	15.3	12	–	–	0	–	–	–	51	–	–	–	–	–	0	1.15
82-83	Har*	79	31	59	90	-25	4	0	212	14.6	4	–	–	2	–	–	–	60	–	–	–	–	–	1	1.14
83-84	Har	72	23	60	83	-10	5	2	202	11.4	5	–	–	0	–	–	–	45	–	–	–	–	–	1	1.15
84-85	Har*	**80**	24	57	81	-23	1	0	195	12.3	4	–	–	0	–	–	–	66	–	–	–	–	–	1	1.01
85-86	Har	53	24	53	77	8	4	1	120	20.0	7	–	–	1	–	–	–	24	–	–	–	–	–	2	1.45
86-87	Har	75	30	63	93	10	7	0	189	15.9	7	–	–	0	–	–	–	45	–	–	–	–	–	0	1.24
87-88	Har	**80**	25	50	75	-8	3	0	172	14.5	11	–	–	1	–	–	–	87	–	–	–	–	–	1	.94
88-89	Har	69	29	48	77	4	4	0	156	18.6	8	–	–	0	–	–	–	36	–	–	–	–	–	1	1.12
89-90	Har*	**80**	32	69	101	13	5	1	170	18.8	15	–	–	1	–	–	–	73	–	–	–	–	–	1	1.26
90-91	2Tm	81	23	64	87	-2	7	0	174	13.2	10	–	–	1	–	–	–	72	–	–	–	–	–	1	1.07
91-92	Pit	70	21	33	54	-7	2	1	121	17.4	5	9	14	1	3	4	15	30	0	15	0	7	4	0	.77
92-93	Pit	84	24	76	100	6	4	0	215	11.2	9	41	50	2	**7**	**9**	26	68	0	24	0	8	7	0	1.19
93-94	Pit	82	27	66	93	-3	2	1	216	12.5	8	33	41	0	3	3	27	62	0	26	0	8	6	0	1.13
94-95	Pit	44	11	**48**	59	**30**	1	0	94	11.7	3	18	21	0	1	1	9	18	0	9	0	0	2	0	1.34
95-96	Pit*	77	27	**92**	119	25	4	0	158	17.1	12	42	54	1	1	2	24	56	0	23	0	2	10	1	1.55

Overall											Power Play			Shorthand			Penalty							Misc	
Year	Tm	GP	G	A	Pts	+/–	GW	GT	S	SPct	G	A	Pts	G	A	Pts	Num	PIM	Maj	Mnr	Fgt	Rgh	HHT	Hat	P/G
96-97	Pit	81	27	63	90	7	2	0	183	14.8	10	24	34	1	1	2	10	20	0	10	0	1	3	0	1.11
97-98	Pit	81	25	62	87	12	5	2	189	13.2	7	25	32	0	0	0	10	20	0	10	0	2	6	1	1.07
98-99	Car	82	21	31	52	-2	2	1	133	15.8	8	10	18	0	0	0	17	34	0	17	0	2	6	0	.63
90-91	Har	67	21	55	76	-2	6	0	149	14.1	10	–	–	1	–	–	–	51	–	–	–	–	–	1	1.13
90-91	Pit	14	2	9	11	0	1	0	25	8.0	0	1	1	0	–	–	–	21	–	–	–	–	–	0	.79
18 Years		1329	449	1037	1486	22	63	10	3062	14.7	145	–	–	11	–	–	–	867	–	–	–	–	–	11	1.12
Postseason																									
Year	Tm	GP	G	A	Pts	+/–	GW	OT	S	SPct	G	A	Pts	G	A	Pts	Num	PIM	Maj	Mnr	Fgt	Rgh	HHT	Hat	P/G
85-86	Har	10	1	2	3	-1	0	0	27	3.7	0	–	–	0	–	–	2	4	0	2	0	–	–	0	.30
86-87	Har	6	2	2	4	-1	0	0	15	13.3	1	–	–	0	0	0	3	6	0	3	0	–	–	0	.67
87-88	Har	6	2	5	7	5	0	0	8	25.0	1	–	–	0	0	0	1	2	0	1	0	–	–	0	1.17
88-89	Har	4	0	2	2	-2	0	0	10	0.0	0	–	–	0	–	–	0	0	0	0	0	0	0	0	.50
89-90	Har	7	3	3	6	2	0	0	21	14.3	1	–	–	0	0	0	4	8	0	4	0	–	–	0	.86
90-91	Pit	24	7	10	17	13	4	0	48	14.6	0	–	–	0	–	–	–	24	–	–	–	–	–	0	.71
91-92	Pit	21	8	19	27	8	2	1	58	13.8	2	10	12	0	1	1	3	6	0	3	0	0	1	1	1.29
92-93	Pit	12	6	11	17	5	1	0	26	23.1	1	5	6	0	0	0	4	19	1	2	0	0	1	0	1.42
93-94	Pit	6	0	2	2	-2	0	0	9	0.0	0	1	1	0	0	0	3	6	0	3	0	0	2	0	.33
94-95	Pit	12	6	13	19	3	0	0	30	20.0	2	3	5	0	1	1	2	4	0	2	0	1	0	0	1.58
95-96	Pit	11	3	6	9	3	1	0	23	13.0	2	3	5	0	1	1	2	4	0	2	0	0	1	0	.82
96-97	Pit	5	1	2	3	-7	0	0	6	16.7	1	1	2	0	0	0	1	2	0	1	0	0	1	0	.60
97-98	Pit	6	1	5	6	5	0	0	19	5.3	0	3	3	0	0	0	1	2	0	1	0	0	0	0	1.00
98-99	Car	3	0	1	1	1	0	0	4	0.0	0	0	0	0	0	0	0	0	0	0	0	0	0	0	.33
14 Years		133	40	83	123	32	8	1	304	13.2	11	–	–	0	–	–	–	87	–	–	–	–	–	1	.92

Scott Fraser

Pos: RW **Shoots:** R **Ht:** 6'2" **Wt:** 206 **Born:** 5/3/72—Moncton, New Brunswick **Age:** 27

Overall											Power Play			Shorthand			Penalty							Misc	
Year	Tm	GP	G	A	Pts	+/–	GW	GT	S	SPct	G	A	Pts	G	A	Pts	Num	PIM	Maj	Mnr	Fgt	Rgh	HHT	Hat	P/G
95-96	Mon	15	2	0	2	-1	0	0	9	22.2	0	0	0	0	0	0	2	4	0	2	0	1	1	0	.13
96-97											Did Not Play in NHL														
97-98	Edm	29	12	11	23	6	2	0	61	19.7	6	7	13	0	0	0	3	6	0	3	0	0	1	0	.79
98-99	NYR	28	2	4	6	-12	0	0	35	5.7	1	1	2	0	0	0	7	14	0	7	0	0	1	0	.21
3 Years		72	16	15	31	-7	2	0	105	15.2	7	8	15	0	0	0	12	24	0	12	0	1	3	0	.43
Postseason																									
Year	Tm	GP	G	A	Pts	+/–	GW	OT	S	SPct	G	A	Pts	G	A	Pts	Num	PIM	Maj	Mnr	Fgt	Rgh	HHT	Hat	P/G
97-98	Edm	11	1	1	2	0	0	0	17	5.9	0	0	0	0	0	0	0	0	0	0	0	0	0	0	.18

Doug Friedman

Pos: LW **Shoots:** L **Ht:** 6'1" **Wt:** 195 **Born:** 9/1/71—Cape Elizabeth, Maine **Age:** 28

Overall											Power Play			Shorthand			Penalty							Misc	
Year	Tm	GP	G	A	Pts	+/–	GW	GT	S	SPct	G	A	Pts	G	A	Pts	Num	PIM	Maj	Mnr	Fgt	Rgh	HHT	Hat	P/G
97-98	Edm	16	0	0	0	0	0	0	8	0.0	0	0	0	0	0	0	7	20	2	5	2	2	0	0	.00
98-99	Nsh	2	0	1	1	0	0	0	3	0.0	0	0	0	0	0	0	4	14	2	2	2	1	0	0	.50
2 Years		18	0	1	1	0	0	0	11	0.0	0	0	0	0	0	0	11	34	4	7	4	3	0	0	.06

Jeff Friesen

(statistical profile on page 312)

Pos: LW **Shoots:** L **Ht:** 6'1" **Wt:** 200 **Born:** 8/5/76—Meadow Lake, Saskatchewan **Age:** 23

Overall											Power Play			Shorthand			Penalty							Misc	
Year	Tm	GP	G	A	Pts	+/–	GW	GT	S	SPct	G	A	Pts	G	A	Pts	Num	PIM	Maj	Mnr	Fgt	Rgh	HHT	Hat	P/G
94-95	SJ	48	15	10	25	-8	2	0	86	17.4	5	2	7	1	1	2	7	14	0	7	0	1	4	0	.52
95-96	SJ	79	15	31	46	-19	0	0	123	12.2	2	8	10	0	3	3	21	42	0	21	0	1	10	1	.58
96-97	SJ	**82**	28	34	62	-8	5	2	200	14.0	6	7	13	2	1	3	28	75	1	25	0	3	5	0	.76
97-98	SJ	79	31	32	63	8	7	0	186	16.7	7	14	21	**6**	1	7	20	40	0	20	0	0	6	0	.80
98-99	SJ	78	22	35	57	3	3	1	215	10.2	10	14	24	1	2	3	21	42	0	21	0	2	7	0	.73
5 Years		366	111	142	253	-24	17	3	810	13.7	30	45	75	10	8	18	97	213	1	94	0	7	32	1	.69
Postseason																									
Year	Tm	GP	G	A	Pts	+/–	GW	OT	S	SPct	G	A	Pts	G	A	Pts	Num	PIM	Maj	Mnr	Fgt	Rgh	HHT	Hat	P/G
94-95	SJ	11	1	5	6	-9	0	0	21	4.8	0	3	3	0	0	0	2	4	0	2	0	0	2	0	.55
97-98	SJ	6	0	1	1	-1	0	0	9	0.0	0	0	0	0	0	0	1	2	0	1	0	0	0	0	.17
98-99	SJ	6	2	2	4	-1	0	0	20	10.0	1	1	2	0	0	0	7	14	0	7	0	1	0	0	.67
3 Years		23	3	8	11	-11	0	0	50	6.0	1	4	5	0	0	0	10	20	0	10	0	1	2	0	.48

Grant Fuhr

(statistical profile on page 398)

Pos: G **Catches:** R **Ht:** 5'9" **Wt:** 190 **Born:** 9/28/62—Spruce Grove, Alberta **Age:** 37

Overall																		Pen Shot		Offense		
Year	Tm	GP	GS	TP	W	L	T	Min	GA	GAA	Shots	SvPct	ShO	OE	PPGA	SHGA		Shots	GA	G	A	PIM
81-82	Edm*	48	–	–	28	5	**14**	2847	157	3.31	–	–	0	–	–	–		0	0	0	6	6
82-83	Edm	32	–	–	13	12	5	1803	129	4.29	974	.868	0	–	–	–		0	0	0	0	6
83-84	Edm*	45	–	–	**30**	10	4	2625	171	3.91	1463	.883	1	–	–	–		**2**	0	0	14	6
84-85	Edm*	46	–	–	26	8	7	2559	165	3.87	1426	.884	1	–	–	–		0	0	0	3	6
85-86	Edm*	40	–	–	29	8	0	2184	143	3.93	1296	.890	0	–	–	–		0	0	0	2	0
86-87	Edm*	44	–	–	22	13	3	2388	137	3.44	1149	.881	0	–	–	–		0	0	0	2	6
87-88	Edm*	**75**	–	–	**40**	24	**9**	**4304**	**246**	3.43	**2066**	.881	**4**	–	–	–		0	0	0	8	16
88-89	Edm*	59	–	–	23	26	6	3341	213	3.83	1714	.876	1	–	–	–		0	0	0	1	6
89-90	Edm	21	–	–	9	7	3	1081	70	3.89	532	.868	1	–	–	–		0	0	0	0	2
90-91	Edm	13	–	–	6	4	3	778	39	3.01	380	.897	1	–	–	–		0	0	0	0	0
91-92	Tor	66	64	4	25	**33**	5	3774	**230**	3.66	1933	.881	2	10	57	5		1	1	0	1	4
92-93	2Tm	58	57	5	24	24	6	3359	185	3.30	1729	.893	1	21	42	12		2	1	0	0	10
93-94	Buf	32	31	6	13	12	3	1726	106	3.68	907	.883	2	10	31	4		0	0	0	4	16
94-95	2Tm	17	12	1	2	9	3	878	59	4.03	464	.873	0	3	21	2		0	0	0	0	2
95-96	StL	**79**	**79**	**17**	30	28	**16**	4365	209	2.87	**2157**	.903	3	26	**72**	7		1	0	0	1	8
96-97	StL	73	**73**	6	33	27	11	4261	193	2.72	1940	.901	3	19	48	8		1	0	0	2	6
97-98	StL	58	56	4	29	21	6	3274	138	2.53	1354	.898	3	10	32	4		0	0	0	2	6
98-99	StL	39	37	3	16	11	8	2193	89	2.44	827	.892	2	5	25	2		0	0	0	0	12
92-93	Tor	29	28	3	13	9	4	1665	87	3.14	826	.895	1	8	20	6		1	0	0	0	0
92-93	Buf	29	29	2	11	15	2	1694	98	3.47	903	.891	0	13	22	6		1	1	0	0	10
94-95	Buf	3	3	0	1	2	0	180	12	4.00	85	.859	0	1	4	0		0	0	0	0	0
94-95	LA	14	9	1	1	7	3	698	47	4.04	379	.876	0	2	17	2		0	0	0	0	2
18 Years		845	–	–	398	282	112	47740	2679	3.37	22311	.887	25	–	–	–		7	2	0	46	118

Postseason																					
Year	Tm	GP	GS	TP	W	L	Pct	Min	GA	GAA	Shots	SvPct	ShO	OE	PPGA	SHGA	Shots	GA	G	A	PIM
81-82	Edm	5	–	–	2	3	.400	309	26	5.05	–	–	0	–	–	–	0	0	0	1	0
82-83	Edm	1	–	–	0	0	–	11	0	0.00	–	–	0	–	–	–	0	0	0	0	0
83-84	Edm	16	–	–	11	4	.733	883	44	2.99	491	.910	1	–	–	–	0	0	0	3	4
84-85	Edm	18	–	–	15	3	.833	1064	55	3.10	522	.895	0	–	–	–	2	0	0	3	2
85-86	Edm	9	–	–	5	4	.556	541	28	3.11	273	.897	0	–	–	–	0	0	0	1	0
86-87	Edm	19	–	–	14	5	.737	1148	47	2.46	511	.908	0	–	–	–	0	0	0	1	0
87-88	Edm	19	–	–	16	2	.889	1136	55	2.90	471	.883	0	–	–	–	0	0	0	1	6
88-89	Edm	7	–	–	3	4	.429	417	24	3.45	227	.894	1	–	–	–	0	0	0	0	0
90-91	Edm	17	–	–	8	7	.533	1019	51	3.00	488	.895	0	–	–	–	0	0	0	2	2
92-93	Buf	8	8	1	3	4	.429	474	27	3.42	216	.875	1	2	10	1	0	0	0	0	2
95-96	StL	2	2	1	1	0	1.000	69	1	0.87	45	.978	0	1	1	0	0	0	0	0	0
96-97	StL	6	6	0	2	4	.333	357	13	2.18	183	.929	2	4	6	1	0	0	0	0	4
97-98	StL	10	10	1	6	4	.600	616	28	2.73	297	.906	0	3	6	3	0	0	0	1	2
98-99	StL	13	13	1	6	6	.500	790	31	2.35	305	.898	1	1	8	2	0	0	0	1	2
14 Years		150	–	–	92	50	.648	8834	430	2.92	4029	.900	6	–	–	–	2	0	0	14	24

Dave Gagner

(statistical profile on page 312)

Pos: C **Shoots:** L **Ht:** 5'10" **Wt:** 180 **Born:** 12/11/64—Chatham, Ontario **Age:** 35

Overall											Power Play			Shorthand			Penalty							Misc	
Year	Tm	GP	G	A	Pts	+/-	GW	GT	S	SPct	G	A	Pts	G	A	Pts	Num	PIM	Maj	Mnr	Fgt	Rgh	HHT	Hat	P/G
84-85	NYR	38	6	6	12	-16	0	0	52	11.5	0	–	–	1	–	–	5	16	2	3	–	–	–	0	.32
85-86	NYR	32	4	6	10	1	0	0	41	9.8	0	–	–	0	–	–	8	19	1	7	–	–	–	0	.31
86-87	NYR	10	1	4	5	-1	0	0	16	6.3	0	–	–	0	–	–	6	12	0	6	0	–	–	0	.50
87-88	Min	51	8	11	19	-14	0	0	87	9.2	0	–	–	2	–	–	–	55	–	–	–	–	–	0	.37
88-89	Min	75	35	43	78	13	3	2	183	19.1	11	–	–	3	–	–	–	104	–	–	–	–	–	2	1.04
89-90	Min	79	40	38	78	-1	3	0	238	16.8	10	–	–	0	–	–	–	54	–	–	–	–	–	0	.99
90-91	Min*	73	40	42	82	9	5	2	223	17.9	20	–	–	0	–	–	–	114	–	–	–	–	–	1	1.12
91-92	Min	78	31	40	71	-4	3	0	229	13.5	17	14	31	0	0	0	40	107	1	36	0	10	4	0	.91
92-93	Min	84	33	43	76	-13	5	1	230	14.3	17	21	38	0	0	0	55	143	3	49	1	10	14	0	.90
93-94	Dal	76	32	29	61	13	6	1	213	15.0	10	9	19	0	0	0	40	83	1	39	1	10	7	1	.80
94-95	Dal	48	14	28	42	2	2	1	138	10.1	7	12	19	0	1	1	18	42	2	16	1	7	5	0	.88
95-96	2Tm	73	21	28	49	-19	3	0	215	9.8	7	11	18	0	2	2	38	103	1	34	0	7	7	0	.67
96-97	Cgy	**82**	27	33	60	2	4	1	228	11.8	9	12	21	0	3	3	24	48	0	24	0	4	7	0	.73
97-98	Fla	78	20	28	48	-21	1	0	165	12.1	5	12	17	1	0	1	26	55	1	25	1	0	8	1	.62
98-99	2Tm	69	6	22	28	-16	1	1	100	6.0	2	10	12	0	0	0	22	63	1	19	1	0	11	0	.41
95-96	Dal	45	14	13	27	-17	2	0	145	9.7	6	9	15	0	0	0	18	44	0	17	0	4	2	0	.60
95-96	Tor	28	7	15	22	-2	1	0	70	10.0	1	2	3	0	2	2	20	59	1	17	0	3	5	0	.79
98-99	Fla	36	4	10	14	-7	0	1	50	8.0	2	5	7	0	0	0	14	39	1	12	1	0	7	0	.39
98-99	Van	33	2	12	14	-9	1	0	50	4.0	0	5	5	0	0	0	8	24	0	7	0	0	4	0	.42
15 Years		946	318	401	719	-65	36	9	2358	13.5	115	–	–	7	–	–	–	1018	–	–	–	–	–	5	.76

Postseason																									
Year	Tm	GP	G	A	Pts	+/-	GW	OT	S	SPct	G	A	Pts	G	A	Pts	Num	PIM	Maj	Mnr	Fgt	Rgh	HHT	Hat	P/G
89-90	Min	7	2	3	5	-3	0	0	28	7.1	1	–	–	0	0	0	–	16	–	–	–	–	–	0	.71
90-91	Min	23	12	15	27	-4	1	0	78	15.4	6	–	–	1	–	–	–	28	–	–	–	–	–	0	1.17
91-92	Min	7	2	4	6	-3	0	0	15	13.3	2	2	4	0	0	0	4	8	0	4	0	1	1	0	.86
93-94	Dal	9	5	1	6	-3	0	0	36	13.9	3	0	3	0	0	0	1	2	0	1	0	0	0	0	.67
94-95	Dal	5	1	1	2	0	0	0	10	10.0	1	1	2	0	0	0	2	4	0	2	0	0	0	0	.40
95-96	Tor	6	0	2	2	-5	0	0	8	0.0	0	1	1	0	0	0	3	6	0	3	0	0	0	0	.33
6 Years		57	22	26	48	-18	1	0	175	12.6	13	–	–	1	–	–	–	64	–	–	–	–	–	0	.84

Sean Gagnon

Pos: D **Shoots:** L **Ht:** 6'2" **Wt:** 210 **Born:** 9/11/73—Sault Ste. Marie, Ontario **Age:** 26

Overall											Power Play			Shorthand			Penalty							Misc	
Year	Tm	GP	G	A	Pts	+/-	GW	GT	S	SPct	G	A	Pts	G	A	Pts	Num	PIM	Maj	Mnr	Fgt	Rgh	HHT	Hat	P/G
97-98	Pho	5	0	1	1	1	0	0	3	0.0	0	0	0	0	0	0	4	14	2	2	2	0	1	0	.20
98-99	Pho	2	0	0	0	-2	0	0	1	0.0	0	0	0	0	0	0	2	7	1	1	1	0	0	0	.00
2 Years		7	0	1	1	-1	0	0	4	0.0	0	0	0	0	0	0	6	21	3	3	3	0	1	0	.14

Maxim Galanov

Pos: D **Shoots:** L **Ht:** 6'1" **Wt:** 200 **Born:** 3/13/74—Krasnoyarsk, USSR **Age:** 25

Overall											Power Play			Shorthand			Penalty							Misc	
Year	Tm	GP	G	A	Pts	+/–	GW	GT	S	SPct	G	A	Pts	G	A	Pts	Num	PIM	Maj	Mnr	Fgt	Rgh	HHT	Hat	P/G
97-98	NYR	6	0	1	1	1	0	0	5	0.0	0	0	0	0	0	0	1	2	0	1	0	0	1	0	.17
98-99	Pit	51	4	3	7	-8	0	1	44	9.1	2	1	3	0	0	0	7	14	0	7	0	0	2	0	.14
2 Years		57	4	4	8	-7	0	1	49	8.2	2	1	3	0	0	0	8	16	0	8	0	0	3	0	.14
Postseason																									
Year	Tm	GP	G	A	Pts	+/–	GW	OT	S	SPct	G	A	Pts	G	A	Pts	Num	PIM	Maj	Mnr	Fgt	Rgh	HHT	Hat	P/G
98-99	Pit	1	0	0	0	0	0	0	0	–	0	0	0	0	0	0	0	0	0	0	0	0	0	0	.00

Garry Galley

(statistical profile on page 312)

Pos: D **Shoots:** L **Ht:** 6'0" **Wt:** 205 **Born:** 4/16/63—Montreal, Quebec **Age:** 36

Overall											Power Play			Shorthand			Penalty							Misc	
Year	Tm	GP	G	A	Pts	+/–	GW	GT	S	SPct	G	A	Pts	G	A	Pts	Num	PIM	Maj	Mnr	Fgt	Rgh	HHT	Hat	P/G
84-85	LA	78	8	30	38	3	2	0	131	6.1	1	–	–	1	–	–	–	82	–	–	–	–	–	0	.49
85-86	LA	49	9	13	22	-9	1	0	57	15.8	1	–	–	0	–	–	–	46	–	–	–	–	–	0	.45
86-87	2Tm	48	6	21	27	-6	1	0	70	8.6	3	–	–	0	–	–	–	67	–	–	–	–	–	0	.56
87-88	Was	58	7	23	30	11	0	1	100	7.0	3	–	–	0	–	–	–	44	–	–	–	–	–	0	.52
88-89	Bos	78	8	22	30	-7	0	0	145	5.5	2	10	12	1	–	–	–	80	–	–	–	–	–	0	.38
89-90	Bos	71	8	27	35	2	0	0	142	5.6	1	4	5	0	–	–	–	75	–	–	–	–	–	0	.49
90-91	Bos*	70	6	21	27	0	0	0	128	4.7	1	7	8	0	0	0	–	84	–	–	–	–	–	0	.39
91-92	2Tm	77	5	27	32	-2	1	0	125	4.0	3	9	12	0	0	0	42	117	3	36	2	9	18	0	.42
92-93	Phi	83	13	49	62	18	3	1	231	5.6	4	21	25	1	3	4	40	115	1	35	0	9	15	0	.75
93-94	Phi*	81	10	60	70	-11	0	1	186	5.4	5	30	35	1	1	2	37	91	3	33	2	6	13	0	.86
94-95	2Tm	47	3	29	32	4	0	0	97	3.1	2	15	17	0	0	0	11	30	0	10	0	2	3	0	.68
95-96	Buf	78	10	44	54	-2	2	0	175	5.7	7	28	35	1	2	3	35	81	1	33	1	6	8	0	.69
96-97	Buf	71	4	34	38	10	1	0	84	4.8	1	13	14	1	0	1	32	102	2	26	2	7	7	0	.54
97-98	LA	74	9	28	37	-5	0	0	128	7.0	7	13	20	0	0	0	26	63	1	24	1	7	6	0	.50
98-99	LA	60	4	12	16	-9	0	0	77	5.2	3	4	7	0	2	2	15	30	0	15	0	0	8	0	.27
86-87	LA	30	5	11	16	-9	1	0	43	11.6	2	–	–	0	–	–	–	57	–	–	–	–	–	0	.53
86-87	Was	18	1	10	11	3	0	0	27	3.7	1	–	–	0	–	–	–	10	–	–	–	–	–	0	.61
91-92	Bos	38	2	12	14	-3	0	0	51	3.9	1	5	6	0	0	0	28	83	1	24	0	6	12	0	.37
91-92	Phi	39	3	15	18	1	1	0	74	4.1	2	4	6	0	0	0	14	34	2	12	2	3	6	0	.46
94-95	Phi	33	2	20	22	0	0	0	66	3.0	1	12	13	0	0	0	6	20	0	5	0	1	1	0	.67
94-95	Buf	14	1	9	10	4	0	0	31	3.2	1	3	4	0	0	0	5	10	0	5	0	1	2	0	.71
15 Years		1023	110	440	550	-3	11	3	1876	5.9	44	–	–	6	–	–	–	1107	–	–	–	–	–	0	.54
Postseason																									
Year	Tm	GP	G	A	Pts	+/–	GW	OT	S	SPct	G	A	Pts	G	A	Pts	Num	PIM	Maj	Mnr	Fgt	Rgh	HHT	Hat	P/G
84-85	LA	3	1	0	1	0	0	0	7	14.3	0	0	0	0	0	0	1	2	0	1	0	–	–	0	.33
86-87	Was	2	0	0	0	0	0	0	4	0.0	0	0	0	0	0	0	0	0	0	0	0	0	0	0	.00
87-88	Was	13	2	4	6	-1	0	0	21	9.5	0	–	–	0	–	–	5	13	1	4	–	–	–	0	.46
88-89	Bos	9	0	1	1	2	0	0	16	0.0	0	–	–	0	–	–	–	33	–	–	–	–	–	0	.11
89-90	Bos	21	3	3	6	-8	2	1	35	8.6	1	–	–	0	–	–	–	34	–	–	–	–	–	0	.29
90-91	Bos	16	1	5	6	-2	0	0	20	5.0	0	2	2	0	0	0	–	17	–	–	–	–	–	0	.38
94-95	Buf	5	0	3	3	-3	0	0	12	0.0	0	2	2	0	0	0	2	4	0	2	0	0	1	0	.60

Postseason																									
Year	Tm	GP	G	A	Pts	+/–	GW	OT	S	SPct	G	A	Pts	G	A	Pts	Num	PIM	Maj	Mnr	Fgt	Rgh	HHT	Hat	P/G
96-97	Buf	12	0	6	6	2	0	0	22	0.0	0	4	4	0	0	0	7	14	0	7	0	0	2	0	.50
97-98	LA	4	0	1	1	-2	0	0	6	0.0	0	0	0	0	0	0	1	2	0	1	0	1	0	0	.25
9 Years		85	7	23	30	-12	2	1	143	4.9	1	–	–	0	–	–	–	119	–	–	–	–	–	0	.35

Bruce Gardiner

(statistical profile on page 313)

Pos: C **Shoots:** R **Ht:** 6'1" **Wt:** 193 **Born:** 2/11/71—Barrie, Ontario **Age:** 28

Overall											Power Play			Shorthand			Penalty							Misc	
Year	Tm	GP	G	A	Pts	+/–	GW	GT	S	SPct	G	A	Pts	G	A	Pts	Num	PIM	Maj	Mnr	Fgt	Rgh	HHT	Hat	P/G
96-97	Ott	67	11	10	21	4	2	2	94	11.7	0	1	1	1	0	1	19	49	1	17	1	4	8	0	.31
97-98	Ott	55	7	11	18	2	0	0	64	10.9	0	0	0	0	0	0	22	50	2	20	2	2	11	0	.33
98-99	Ott	59	4	8	12	6	1	0	70	5.7	0	0	0	0	1	1	20	43	1	19	1	4	11	0	.20
3 Years		181	22	29	51	12	3	2	228	9.6	0	1	1	1	1	2	61	142	4	56	4	10	30	0	.28
Postseason																									
Year	Tm	GP	G	A	Pts	+/–	GW	OT	S	SPct	G	A	Pts	G	A	Pts	Num	PIM	Maj	Mnr	Fgt	Rgh	HHT	Hat	P/G
96-97	Ott	7	0	1	1	0	0	0	3	0.0	0	0	0	0	0	0	1	2	0	1	0	1	0	0	.14
97-98	Ott	11	1	3	4	-2	1	1	21	4.8	0	0	0	0	1	1	1	2	0	1	0	0	0	0	.36
98-99	Ott	3	0	0	0	0	0	0	4	0.0	0	0	0	0	0	0	2	4	0	2	0	1	0	0	.00
3 Years		21	1	4	5	-2	1	1	28	3.6	0	0	0	0	1	1	4	8	0	4	0	2	0	0	.24

Tyrone Garner

Pos: G **Catches:** L **Ht:** 6'1" **Wt:** 200 **Born:** 7/27/78—Stoney Creek, Ontario **Age:** 21

Overall																Pen Shot		Offense		
Year	Tm	GP	GS	TP	W	L	T	Min	GA	GAA	Shots	SvPct	ShO	OE	PPGA	SHGA	Shots	GA	G	A	PIM
98-99	Cgy	3	1	0	0	2	0	139	12	5.18	74	.838	0	0	2	1	0	0	0	0	0

Johan Garpenlov

(statistical profile on page 313)

Pos: LW **Shoots:** L **Ht:** 5'11" **Wt:** 185 **Born:** 3/21/68—Stockholm, Sweden **Age:** 31

Overall											Power Play			Shorthand			Penalty							Misc	
Year	Tm	GP	G	A	Pts	+/–	GW	GT	S	SPct	G	A	Pts	G	A	Pts	Num	PIM	Maj	Mnr	Fgt	Rgh	HHT	Hat	P/G
90-91	Det	71	18	22	40	-4	3	0	91	19.8	2	–	–	0	–	–	–	18	–	–	–	–	–	1	.56
91-92	2Tm	28	6	7	13	0	1	0	34	17.6	1	2	3	0	0	0	4	8	0	4	0	0	3	0	.46
92-93	SJ	79	22	44	66	-26	1	0	171	12.9	14	11	25	0	1	1	24	56	0	23	0	4	12	1	.84
93-94	SJ	80	18	35	53	9	3	0	125	14.4	7	8	15	0	0	0	14	28	0	14	0	1	7	0	.66
94-95	2Tm	40	4	10	14	1	0	0	44	9.1	0	3	3	0	0	0	1	2	0	1	0	0	0	0	.35
95-96	Fla	82	23	28	51	-10	7	1	130	17.7	8	14	22	0	0	0	18	36	0	18	0	0	9	1	.62
96-97	Fla	53	11	25	36	10	1	2	83	13.3	1	7	8	0	0	0	18	47	1	16	0	2	6	0	.68
97-98	Fla	39	2	3	5	-6	0	0	43	4.7	0	0	0	0	0	0	4	8	0	4	0	0	2	0	.13
98-99	Fla	64	8	9	17	-9	0	1	71	11.3	0	0	0	1	1	2	21	42	0	21	0	1	9	0	.27
91-92	Det	16	1	1	2	2	0	0	13	7.7	0	0	0	0	0	0	2	4	0	2	0	0	2	0	.13
91-92	SJ	12	5	6	11	-2	1	0	21	23.8	1	2	3	0	0	0	2	4	0	2	0	0	1	0	.92
94-95	SJ	13	1	1	2	-3	0	0	16	6.3	0	0	0	0	0	0	1	2	0	1	0	0	0	0	.15
94-95	Fla	27	3	9	12	4	0	0	28	10.7	0	3	3	0	0	0	0	0	0	0	0	0	0	0	.44
9 Years		536	112	183	295	-35	16	4	792	14.1	33	–	–	1	–	–	–	245	–	–	–	–	–	3	.55
Postseason																									
Year	Tm	GP	G	A	Pts	+/–	GW	OT	S	SPct	G	A	Pts	G	A	Pts	Num	PIM	Maj	Mnr	Fgt	Rgh	HHT	Hat	P/G
90-91	Det	6	0	1	1	-1	0	0	7	0.0	0	–	–	0	–	–	2	4	0	2	0	–	–	0	.17
93-94	SJ	14	4	6	10	0	2	0	23	17.4	0	1	1	0	0	0	3	6	0	3	0	0	1	0	.71
95-96	Fla	20	4	2	6	-2	0	0	35	11.4	0	0	0	0	0	0	4	8	0	4	0	1	1	0	.30
96-97	Fla	4	2	0	2	0	1	0	6	33.3	2	0	2	0	0	0	2	4	0	2	0	1	0	0	.50
4 Years		44	10	9	19	-3	3	0	71	14.1	2	–	–	0	–	–	11	22	0	11	0	–	–	0	.43

Mike Gaul

Pos: D **Shoots:** R **Ht:** 6'1" **Wt:** 200 **Born:** 4/22/73—Lachine, Quebec **Age:** 26

Overall											Power Play			Shorthand			Penalty							Misc	
Year	Tm	GP	G	A	Pts	+/–	GW	GT	S	SPct	G	A	Pts	G	A	Pts	Num	PIM	Maj	Mnr	Fgt	Rgh	HHT	Hat	P/G
98-99	Col	1	0	0	0	0	0	0	1	0.0	0	0	0	0	0	0	0	0	0	0	0	0	0	0	.00

Denis Gauthier

Pos: D **Shoots:** L **Ht:** 6'2" **Wt:** 195 **Born:** 10/1/76—Montreal, Quebec **Age:** 23

Overall											Power Play			Shorthand			Penalty							Misc	
Year	Tm	GP	G	A	Pts	+/–	GW	GT	S	SPct	G	A	Pts	G	A	Pts	Num	PIM	Maj	Mnr	Fgt	Rgh	HHT	Hat	P/G
97-98	Cgy	10	0	0	0	-5	0	0	3	0.0	0	0	0	0	0	0	8	16	0	8	0	0	1	0	.00
98-99	Cgy	55	3	4	7	3	0	0	40	7.5	0	0	0	0	1	1	27	68	2	24	2	2	6	0	.13
2 Years		65	3	4	7	-2	0	0	43	7.0	0	0	0	0	1	1	35	84	2	32	2	2	7	0	.11

Sean Gauthier

Pos: G **Catches:** L **Ht:** 5'11" **Wt:** 205 **Born:** 3/28/71—Sudbury, Ontario **Age:** 28

Overall																	Pen Shot		Offense		
Year	Tm	GP	GS	TP	W	L	T	Min	GA	GAA	Shots	SvPct	ShO	OE	PPGA	SHGA	Shots	GA	G	A	PIM
98-99	SJ	1	0	0	0	0	0	3	0	0.00	2	1.000	0	0	0	0	0	0	0	0	0

Aaron Gavey

Pos: C **Shoots:** L **Ht:** 6'2" **Wt:** 194 **Born:** 2/22/74—Sudbury, Ontario **Age:** 25

Overall											Power Play			Shorthand			Penalty							Misc	
Year	Tm	GP	G	A	Pts	+/–	GW	GT	S	SPct	G	A	Pts	G	A	Pts	Num	PIM	Maj	Mnr	Fgt	Rgh	HHT	Hat	P/G
95-96	TB	73	8	4	12	-6	2	0	65	12.3	1	2	3	1	0	1	21	56	2	18	2	0	8	0	.16
96-97	2Tm	57	8	11	19	-12	1	1	62	12.9	3	1	4	0	0	0	20	46	2	18	2	4	4	0	.33
97-98	Cgy	26	2	3	5	-5	1	0	27	7.4	0	0	0	0	0	0	5	24	2	2	2	0	0	0	.19
98-99	Dal	7	0	0	0	-1	0	0	4	0.0	0	0	0	0	0	0	5	10	0	5	0	4	0	0	.00
96-97	TB	16	1	2	3	-1	0	0	8	12.5	0	0	0	0	0	0	6	12	0	6	0	0	4	0	.19
96-97	Cgy	41	7	9	16	-11	1	1	54	13.0	3	1	4	0	0	0	14	34	2	12	2	4	0	0	.39
4 Years		163	18	18	36	-24	4	1	158	11.4	4	3	7	1	0	1	51	136	6	43	6	8	12	0	.22
Postseason																									
Year	Tm	GP	G	A	Pts	+/–	GW	OT	S	SPct	G	A	Pts	G	A	Pts	Num	PIM	Maj	Mnr	Fgt	Rgh	HHT	Hat	P/G
95-96	TB	6	0	0	0	-3	0	0	5	0.0	0	0	0	0	0	0	2	4	0	2	0	0	0	0	.00

Martin Gelinas

(statistical profile on page 313)

Pos: LW **Shoots:** L **Ht:** 5'11" **Wt:** 195 **Born:** 6/5/70—Shawinigan, Quebec **Age:** 29

Overall											Power Play			Shorthand			Penalty							Misc	
Year	Tm	GP	G	A	Pts	+/–	GW	GT	S	SPct	G	A	Pts	G	A	Pts	Num	PIM	Maj	Mnr	Fgt	Rgh	HHT	Hat	P/G
88-89	Edm	6	1	2	3	-1	0	0	14	7.1	0	0	0	0	0	0	0	0	0	0	0	0	0	0	.50
89-90	Edm	46	17	8	25	0	2	2	71	23.9	5	0	5	0	0	0	–	30	–	–	–	–	–	1	.54
90-91	Edm	73	20	20	40	-7	2	1	124	16.1	4	3	7	0	0	0	–	34	–	–	–	–	–	0	.55
91-92	Edm	68	11	18	29	14	0	0	94	11.7	1	2	3	0	0	0	20	62	2	16	0	3	5	0	.43
92-93	Edm	65	11	12	23	3	1	0	93	11.8	0	0	0	0	0	0	15	30	0	15	0	1	8	0	.35
93-94	2Tm	64	14	14	28	-8	1	2	107	13.1	3	2	5	0	0	0	17	34	0	17	0	5	7	0	.44
94-95	Van	46	13	10	23	8	4	0	75	17.3	1	0	1	0	1	1	14	36	0	13	0	4	2	0	.50
95-96	Van	81	30	26	56	8	5	1	181	16.6	3	4	7	4	1	5	28	59	1	27	1	3	7	0	.69
96-97	Van	74	35	33	68	6	3	1	177	19.8	6	5	11	1	1	2	18	42	2	16	2	3	7	2	.92
97-98	2Tm	64	16	18	34	-5	5	0	147	10.9	3	3	6	2	2	4	16	40	0	15	0	2	6	0	.53
98-99	Car	76	13	15	28	3	2	2	111	11.7	0	1	1	0	0	0	24	67	1	21	0	2	9	0	.37
93-94	Que	31	6	6	12	-2	0	1	53	11.3	0	0	0	0	0	0	4	8	0	4	0	2	0	0	.39
93-94	Van	33	8	8	16	-6	1	1	54	14.8	3	2	5	0	0	0	13	26	0	13	0	3	7	0	.48
97-98	Van	24	4	4	8	-6	1	0	49	8.2	1	1	2	1	1	2	5	10	0	5	0	1	2	0	.33
97-98	Car	40	12	14	26	1	4	0	98	12.2	2	2	4	1	1	2	11	30	0	10	0	1	4	0	.65
11 Years		663	181	176	357	21	25	9	1194	15.2	26	20	46	7	5	12	–	434	–	–	–	–	–	3	.54
Postseason																									
Year	Tm	GP	G	A	Pts	+/–	GW	OT	S	SPct	G	A	Pts	G	A	Pts	Num	PIM	Maj	Mnr	Fgt	Rgh	HHT	Hat	P/G
89-90	Edm	20	2	3	5	0	0	0	24	8.3	0	–	–	0	–	–	3	6	0	3	0	–	–	0	.25
90-91	Edm	18	3	6	9	4	1	0	29	10.3	0	–	–	0	0	0	–	25	–	–	–	–	–	0	.50
91-92	Edm	15	1	3	4	-3	0	0	15	6.7	0	1	1	0	0	0	5	10	0	5	0	1	0	0	.27
93-94	Van	24	5	4	9	-1	1	0	35	14.3	2	1	3	0	0	0	7	14	0	7	0	2	3	0	.38
94-95	Van	3	0	1	1	1	0	0	5	0.0	0	0	0	0	0	0	0	0	0	0	0	0	0	0	.33
95-96	Van	6	1	1	2	-1	0	0	8	12.5	1	0	1	0	0	0	6	12	0	6	0	1	4	0	.33
98-99	Car	6	0	3	3	-4	0	0	12	0.0	0	0	0	0	0	0	1	2	0	1	0	0	0	0	.50
7 Years		92	12	21	33	-4	2	0	128	9.4	3	–	–	0	–	–	–	69	–	–	–	–	–	0	.36

Jean-Sebastian Giguere

Pos: G **Catches:** L **Ht:** 6'0" **Wt:** 175 **Born:** 5/16/77—Montreal, Quebec **Age:** 22

		Overall															Pen Shot		Offense		
Year	Tm	GP	GS	TP	W	L	T	Min	GA	GAA	Shots	SvPct	ShO	OE	PPGA	SHGA	Shots	GA	G	A	PIM
96-97	Har	8	6	1	1	4	0	394	24	3.65	201	.881	0	2	3	2	0	0	0	0	0
97-98		Did Not Play in NHL																			
98-99	Cgy	15	14	1	6	7	1	860	46	3.21	447	.897	0	5	17	1	0	0	0	1	4
2 Years		23	20	2	7	11	1	1254	70	3.35	648	.892	0	7	20	3	0	0	0	1	4

Brent Gilchrist

Pos: LW **Shoots:** L **Ht:** 5'11" **Wt:** 180 **Born:** 4/3/67—Moose Jaw, Saskatchewan **Age:** 32

		Overall									Power Play			Shorthand			Penalty							Misc	
Year	Tm	GP	G	A	Pts	+/-	GW	GT	S	SPct	G	A	Pts	G	A	Pts	Num	PIM	Maj	Mnr	Fgt	Rgh	HHT	Hat	P/G
88-89	Mon	49	8	16	24	9	2	0	68	11.8	0	–	–	0	–	–	–	16	–	–	–	–	–	0	.49
89-90	Mon	57	9	15	24	3	0	0	80	11.3	1	–	–	0	–	–	–	28	–	–	–	–	–	0	.42
90-91	Mon	51	6	9	15	-3	1	0	81	7.4	1	–	–	0	–	–	–	10	–	–	–	–	–	0	.29
91-92	Mon	79	23	27	50	29	3	2	146	15.8	2	4	6	0	0	0	27	57	1	26	1	5	10	1	.63
92-93	2Tm	68	10	11	21	-12	0	0	106	9.4	2	2	4	0	2	2	19	49	1	17	1	1	9	0	.31
93-94	Dal	76	17	14	31	0	5	0	103	16.5	3	1	4	1	0	1	14	31	1	13	1	4	4	0	.41
94-95	Dal	32	9	4	13	-3	1	0	70	12.9	1	0	1	3	0	3	8	16	0	8	0	4	1	0	.41
95-96	Dal	77	20	22	42	-11	2	0	164	12.2	6	3	9	1	1	2	18	36	0	18	0	0	11	0	.55
96-97	Dal	67	10	20	30	6	2	0	116	8.6	2	3	5	0	0	0	12	24	0	12	0	0	5	0	.45
97-98	Det	61	13	14	27	4	3	1	124	10.5	5	1	6	0	0	0	20	40	0	20	0	1	9	0	.44
98-99	Det	5	1	0	1	-1	1	0	4	25.0	0	0	0	0	0	0	0	0	0	0	0	0	0	0	.20
92-93	Edm	60	10	10	20	-10	0	0	94	10.6	2	2	4	0	2	2	18	47	1	16	1	1	9	0	.33
92-93	Min	8	0	1	1	-2	0	0	12	0.0	0	0	0	0	0	0	1	2	0	1	0	0	0	0	.13
11 Years		622	126	152	278	21	20	3	1062	11.9	23	–	–	5	–	–	–	307	–	–	–	–	–	1	.45

Postseason

Year	Tm	GP	G	A	Pts	+/-	GW	OT	S	SPct	G	A	Pts	G	A	Pts	Num	PIM	Maj	Mnr	Fgt	Rgh	HHT	Hat	P/G
88-89	Mon	9	1	1	2	0	0	0	6	16.7	0	–	–	0	–	–	–	10	–	–	–	–	–	0	.22
89-90	Mon	8	2	0	2	2	0	0	9	22.2	0	0	0	0	0	0	1	2	0	1	0	–	–	0	.25
90-91	Mon	13	5	3	8	3	1	0	21	23.8	0	–	–	0	–	–	3	6	0	3	0	–	–	0	.62
91-92	Mon	11	2	4	6	-2	0	0	20	10.0	1	1	2	0	0	0	3	6	0	3	0	0	3	0	.55
93-94	Dal	9	3	1	4	-3	0	0	20	15.0	1	0	1	0	0	0	1	2	0	1	0	0	1	0	.44
94-95	Dal	5	0	1	1	-1	0	0	7	0.0	0	0	0	0	0	0	1	2	0	1	0	1	0	0	.20
96-97	Dal	6	2	2	4	0	0	0	20	10.0	0	0	0	0	0	0	1	2	0	1	0	0	1	0	.67
97-98	Det	15	2	1	3	2	0	0	17	11.8	0	0	0	0	0	0	6	12	0	6	0	1	1	0	.20
98-99	Det	3	0	0	0	-2	0	0	2	0.0	0	0	0	0	0	0	0	0	0	0	0	0	0	0	.00
9 Years		79	17	13	30	-1	1	0	122	13.9	2	–	–	0	–	–	–	42	–	–	–	–	–	0	.38

Hal Gill

(statistical profile on page 313)

Pos: D **Shoots:** L **Ht:** 6'6" **Wt:** 200 **Born:** 4/6/75—Concord, Massachusetts **Age:** 24

		Overall									Power Play			Shorthand			Penalty							Misc	
Year	Tm	GP	G	A	Pts	+/-	GW	GT	S	SPct	G	A	Pts	G	A	Pts	Num	PIM	Maj	Mnr	Fgt	Rgh	HHT	Hat	P/G
97-98	Bos	68	2	4	6	4	0	0	56	3.6	0	0	0	0	0	0	15	47	3	11	3	0	7	0	.09
98-99	Bos	80	3	7	10	-10	2	0	102	2.9	0	0	0	0	0	0	30	63	1	29	1	1	13	0	.13
2 Years		148	5	11	16	-6	2	0	158	3.2	0	0	0	0	0	0	45	110	4	40	4	1	20	0	.11

Postseason

Year	Tm	GP	G	A	Pts	+/-	GW	OT	S	SPct	G	A	Pts	G	A	Pts	Num	PIM	Maj	Mnr	Fgt	Rgh	HHT	Hat	P/G
97-98	Bos	6	0	0	0	-1	0	0	3	0.0	0	0	0	0	0	0	2	4	0	2	0	0	1	0	.00
98-99	Bos	12	0	0	0	-1	0	0	10	0.0	0	0	0	0	0	0	7	14	0	7	0	3	1	0	.00
2 Years		18	0	0	0	-2	0	0	13	0.0	0	0	0	0	0	0	9	18	0	9	0	3	2	0	.00

Todd Gill

Pos: D **Shoots:** L **Ht:** 6'0" **Wt:** 185 **Born:** 11/9/65—Brockville, Ontario **Age:** 34

		Overall									Power Play			Shorthand			Penalty							Misc	
Year	Tm	GP	G	A	Pts	+/-	GW	GT	S	SPct	G	A	Pts	G	A	Pts	Num	PIM	Maj	Mnr	Fgt	Rgh	HHT	Hat	P/G
84-85	Tor	10	1	0	1	-1	0	0	9	11.1	0	0	0	0	0	0	5	13	1	4	–	–	–	0	.10
85-86	Tor	15	1	2	3	0	0	0	9	11.1	0	–	–	0	–	–	–	28	–	–	–	–	–	0	.20
86-87	Tor	61	4	27	31	-3	0	0	51	7.8	1	–	–	0	–	–	–	92	–	–	–	–	–	0	.51
87-88	Tor	65	8	17	25	-20	3	0	109	7.3	1	–	–	0	–	–	–	131	–	–	–	–	–	0	.38
88-89	Tor	59	11	14	25	-3	1	0	92	12.0	0	–	–	0	–	–	–	72	–	–	–	–	–	0	.42
89-90	Tor	48	1	14	15	-8	0	0	44	2.3	0	–	–	0	–	–	–	92	–	–	–	–	–	0	.31

Overall											Power Play			Shorthand			Penalty							Misc	
Year	Tm	GP	G	A	Pts	+/–	GW	GT	S	SPct	G	A	Pts	G	A	Pts	Num	PIM	Maj	Mnr	Fgt	Rgh	HHT	Hat	P/G
90-91	Tor	72	2	22	24	-4	0	0	90	2.2	0	–	–	0	–	–	–	113	–	–	–	–	–	0	.33
91-92	Tor	74	2	15	17	-22	0	0	82	2.4	1	2	3	0	1	1	35	91	7	28	7	9	9	0	.23
92-93	Tor	69	11	32	43	4	2	0	113	9.7	5	18	23	0	0	0	30	66	2	28	2	11	4	0	.62
93-94	Tor	45	4	24	28	8	1	0	74	5.4	2	11	13	0	1	1	18	44	0	17	0	5	7	0	.62
94-95	Tor	47	7	25	32	-8	2	0	82	8.5	3	9	12	1	0	1	21	64	2	17	2	8	5	0	.68
95-96	Tor	74	7	18	25	-15	2	0	109	6.4	1	3	4	0	2	2	34	116	8	23	7	7	5	0	.34
96-97	SJ	79	0	21	21	-20	0	0	101	0.0	0	5	5	0	0	0	34	101	3	28	2	8	6	0	.27
97-98	2Tm	75	13	17	30	-11	2	0	122	10.7	7	9	16	0	0	0	19	41	1	18	1	2	7	0	.40
98-99	2Tm	51	4	5	9	-10	1	1	61	6.6	1	0	1	0	0	0	12	27	1	11	1	5	4	0	.18
97-98	SJ	64	8	13	21	-13	1	0	100	8.0	4	8	12	0	0	0	14	31	1	13	1	2	4	0	.33
97-98	StL	11	5	4	9	2	1	0	22	22.7	3	1	4	0	0	0	5	10	0	5	0	0	3	0	.82
98-99	StL	28	2	3	5	-6	0	1	36	5.6	1	0	1	0	0	0	8	16	0	8	0	2	4	0	.18
98-99	Det	23	2	2	4	-4	1	0	25	8.0	0	0	0	0	0	0	4	11	1	3	1	3	0	0	.17
15 Years		844	76	253	329	-113	14	1	1148	6.6	22	–	–	1	–	–	–	1091	–	–	–	–	–	0	.39
Postseason																									
Year	Tm	GP	G	A	Pts	+/–	GW	OT	S	SPct	G	A	Pts	G	A	Pts	Num	PIM	Maj	Mnr	Fgt	Rgh	HHT	Hat	P/G
85-86	Tor	1	0	0	0	0	0	0	1	0.0	0	0	0	0	0	0	0	0	0	0	0	0	0	0	.00
86-87	Tor	13	2	2	4	2	0	0	15	13.3	0	–	–	0	0	0	–	42	–	–	–	–	–	0	.31
87-88	Tor	6	1	3	4	1	0	0	9	11.1	1	–	–	0	–	–	–	20	–	–	–	–	–	0	.67
89-90	Tor	5	0	3	3	0	0	0	7	0.0	0	–	–	0	–	–	–	16	–	–	–	–	–	0	.60
92-93	Tor	21	1	10	11	1	0	0	41	2.4	0	5	5	0	0	0	6	26	2	3	2	1	2	0	.52
93-94	Tor	18	1	5	6	1	1	1	20	5.0	0	1	1	0	0	0	9	37	1	6	1	1	2	0	.33
94-95	Tor	7	0	3	3	-4	0	0	16	0.0	0	2	2	0	0	0	3	6	0	3	0	1	1	0	.43
95-96	Tor	6	0	0	0	-2	0	0	9	0.0	0	0	0	0	0	0	8	24	0	7	0	0	3	0	.00
97-98	StL	10	2	2	4	-3	0	0	16	12.5	1	2	3	1	0	1	5	10	0	5	0	2	1	0	.40
98-99	Det	2	0	1	1	0	0	0	3	0.0	0	0	0	0	0	0	0	0	0	0	0	0	0	0	.50
10 Years		89	7	29	36	-4	1	1	137	5.1	2	–	–	1	–	–	–	181	–	–	–	–	–	0	.40

Doug Gilmour

(statistical profile on page 314)

Pos: C **Shoots:** L **Ht:** 5'11" **Wt:** 175 **Born:** 6/25/63—Kingston, Ontario **Age:** 36

Overall											Power Play			Shorthand			Penalty							Misc	
Year	Tm	GP	G	A	Pts	+/–	GW	GT	S	SPct	G	A	Pts	G	A	Pts	Num	PIM	Maj	Mnr	Fgt	Rgh	HHT	Hat	P/G
83-84	StL	**80**	25	28	53	6	1	0	157	15.9	3	–	–	1	–	–	–	57	–	–	–	–	–	0	.66
84-85	StL	78	21	36	57	3	3	**3**	162	13.0	3	–	–	1	–	–	–	49	–	–	–	–	–	0	.73
85-86	StL	74	25	28	53	-3	5	0	183	13.7	2	–	–	1	–	–	–	41	–	–	–	–	–	1	.72
86-87	StL	80	42	63	105	-2	2	1	207	20.3	17	–	–	1	–	–	–	58	–	–	–	–	–	0	1.31
87-88	StL	72	36	50	86	-13	4	1	163	22.1	19	–	–	2	–	–	–	59	–	–	–	–	–	1	1.19
88-89	Cgy	72	26	59	85	45	5	1	161	16.1	11	–	–	0	–	–	22	44	0	22	0	–	–	0	1.18
89-90	Cgy	78	24	67	91	20	3	1	152	15.8	12	–	–	1	–	–	23	54	0	22	0	–	–	0	1.17
90-91	Cgy	78	20	61	81	27	5	0	135	14.8	2	–	–	2	–	–	45	144	2	37	–	–	–	0	1.04
91-92	2Tm	78	26	61	87	25	4	1	168	15.5	10	19	29	1	1	2	31	78	0	29	0	7	7	0	1.12
92-93	Tor*	83	32	95	127	32	2	2	211	15.2	15	44	59	3	2	5	38	100	0	35	0	14	8	0	1.53
93-94	Tor*	83	27	84	111	25	3	2	167	16.2	10	30	40	1	4	5	43	105	1	40	1	13	9	1	1.34
94-95	Tor	44	10	23	33	-5	1	1	73	13.7	3	12	15	0	0	0	13	26	0	13	0	6	3	0	.75
95-96	Tor	81	32	40	72	-5	3	0	180	17.8	10	19	29	2	2	4	37	77	1	36	1	10	4	0	.89
96-97	2Tm	81	22	60	82	2	1	1	143	15.4	4	18	22	1	0	1	30	68	0	29	0	7	9	0	1.01
97-98	NJ	63	13	40	53	10	5	0	94	13.8	3	20	23	0	1	1	22	68	0	19	0	8	6	0	.84
98-99	Chi	72	16	40	56	-16	4	0	110	14.5	7	13	20	1	0	1	25	56	2	23	2	6	6	0	.78
91-92	Cgy	38	11	27	38	12	1	0	64	17.2	4	10	14	1	0	1	19	46	0	18	0	6	6	0	1.00
91-92	Tor	40	15	34	49	13	3	1	104	14.4	6	9	15	0	1	1	12	32	0	11	0	1	1	0	1.23
96-97	Tor	61	15	45	60	-5	1	0	103	14.6	2	15	17	1	0	1	23	46	0	23	0	6	6	0	.98
96-97	NJ	20	7	15	22	7	0	1	40	17.5	2	3	5	0	0	0	7	22	0	6	0	1	3	0	1.10
16 Years		1197	397	835	1232	151	51	14	2466	16.1	131	–	–	18	–	–	–	1084	–	–	–	–	–	3	1.03
Postseason																									
Year	Tm	GP	G	A	Pts	+/–	GW	OT	S	SPct	G	A	Pts	G	A	Pts	Num	PIM	Maj	Mnr	Fgt	Rgh	HHT	Hat	P/G
83-84	StL	11	2	9	11	2	1	1	20	10.0	1	–	–	0	–	–	–	10	–	–	–	–	–	0	1.00
84-85	StL	3	1	1	2	-4	0	0	13	7.7	0	–	–	0	–	–	1	2	0	1	0	–	–	0	.67
85-86	StL	19	9	12	21	3	2	0	56	16.1	1	–	–	2	–	–	–	25	–	–	–	–	–	0	1.11
86-87	StL	6	2	2	4	1	1	0	14	14.3	1	–	–	0	0	0	–	16	–	–	–	–	–	0	.67
87-88	StL	10	3	14	17	3	0	0	18	16.7	1	–	–	0	–	–	–	18	–	–	–	–	–	0	1.70
88-89	Cgy	22	11	11	22	12	3	1	49	22.4	3	–	–	0	–	–	–	20	–	–	–	–	–	0	1.00
89-90	Cgy	6	3	1	4	-6	1	0	12	25.0	0	–	–	0	–	–	4	8	0	4	0	–	–	0	.67
90-91	Cgy	7	1	1	2	1	1	0	11	9.1	0	–	–	0	0	0	0	0	0	0	0	0	0	0	.29
92-93	Tor	21	10	25	35	16	1	1	51	19.6	4	8	12	0	0	0	7	30	0	5	0	2	1	0	1.67
93-94	Tor	18	6	22	28	3	1	0	31	19.4	5	11	16	0	2	2	9	42	0	6	0	3	1	0	1.56

Postseason																									
Year	Tm	GP	G	A	Pts	+/-	GW	OT	S	SPct	G	A	Pts	G	A	Pts	Num	PIM	Maj	Mnr	Fgt	Rgh	HHT	Hat	P/G
94-95	Tor	7	0	6	6	2	0	0	8	0.0	0	5	5	0	0	0	3	6	0	3	0	0	1	0	.86
95-96	Tor	6	1	7	8	-4	0	0	15	6.7	1	4	5	0	1	1	6	12	0	6	0	1	2	0	1.33
96-97	NJ	10	0	4	4	-2	0	0	21	0.0	0	2	2	0	1	1	7	14	0	7	0	2	1	0	.40
97-98	NJ	6	5	2	7	4	1	0	12	41.7	1	1	2	0	1	1	2	4	0	2	0	0	1	0	1.17
14 Years		152	54	117	171	31	12	3	331	16.3	18	–	–	2	–	–	–	207	–	–	–	–	–	0	1.13

Jonathan Girard

Pos: D **Shoots:** R **Ht:** 5'11" **Wt:** 192 **Born:** 5/27/80—Joliette, Quebec **Age:** 19

		Overall									Power Play			Shorthand			Penalty							Misc	
Year	Tm	GP	G	A	Pts	+/-	GW	GT	S	SPct	G	A	Pts	G	A	Pts	Num	PIM	Maj	Mnr	Fgt	Rgh	HHT	Hat	P/G
98-99	Bos	3	0	0	0	1	0	0	3	0.0	0	0	0	0	0	0	0	0	0	0	0	0	0	0	.00

Yan Golubovsky

Pos: D **Shoots:** R **Ht:** 6'4" **Wt:** 204 **Born:** 3/9/76—Novosibirsk, USSR **Age:** 23

		Overall									Power Play			Shorthand			Penalty							Misc	
Year	Tm	GP	G	A	Pts	+/-	GW	GT	S	SPct	G	A	Pts	G	A	Pts	Num	PIM	Maj	Mnr	Fgt	Rgh	HHT	Hat	P/G
97-98	Det	12	0	2	2	1	0	0	9	0.0	0	0	0	0	0	0	3	6	0	3	0	0	0	0	.17
98-99	Det	17	0	1	1	4	0	0	10	0.0	0	0	0	0	0	0	8	16	0	8	0	1	2	0	.06
2 Years		29	0	3	3	5	0	0	19	0.0	0	0	0	0	0	0	11	22	0	11	0	1	2	0	.10

Sergei Gonchar

(statistical profile on page 314)

Pos: D **Shoots:** L **Ht:** 6'2" **Wt:** 210 **Born:** 4/13/72—Chelyabinsk, USSR **Age:** 27

		Overall									Power Play			Shorthand			Penalty							Misc	
Year	Tm	GP	G	A	Pts	+/-	GW	GT	S	SPct	G	A	Pts	G	A	Pts	Num	PIM	Maj	Mnr	Fgt	Rgh	HHT	Hat	P/G
94-95	Was	31	2	5	7	4	0	0	38	5.3	0	0	0	0	0	0	11	22	0	11	0	2	4	0	.23
95-96	Was	78	15	26	41	25	4	0	139	10.8	4	10	14	0	0	0	30	60	0	30	0	9	14	0	.53
96-97	Was	57	13	17	30	-11	3	0	129	10.1	3	7	10	0	1	1	18	36	0	18	0	5	9	0	.53
97-98	Was	72	5	16	21	2	0	0	134	3.7	2	7	9	0	0	0	29	66	0	28	0	4	20	0	.29
98-99	Was	53	21	10	31	1	3	0	180	11.7	13	4	17	1	1	2	27	57	1	26	1	3	13	0	.58
5 Years		291	56	74	130	21	10	0	620	9.0	22	28	50	1	2	3	115	241	1	113	1	23	60	0	.45
Postseason																									
Year	Tm	GP	G	A	Pts	+/-	GW	OT	S	SPct	G	A	Pts	G	A	Pts	Num	PIM	Maj	Mnr	Fgt	Rgh	HHT	Hat	P/G
94-95	Was	7	2	2	4	8	1	0	15	13.3	0	0	0	0	0	0	1	2	0	1	0	2	0	0	.57
95-96	Was	6	2	4	6	-1	0	0	29	6.9	1	2	3	0	0	0	2	4	0	2	0	0	2	0	1.00
97-98	Was	21	7	4	11	2	2	0	37	18.9	3	2	5	1	0	1	15	30	0	15	0	4	6	0	.52
3 Years		34	11	10	21	9	3	0	81	13.6	4	4	8	1	0	1	18	36	0	18	0	6	8	0	.62

Robb Gordon

Pos: C **Shoots:** R **Ht:** 5'11" **Wt:** 190 **Born:** 1/13/76—Murrayville, British Columbia **Age:** 23

		Overall									Power Play			Shorthand			Penalty							Misc	
Year	Tm	GP	G	A	Pts	+/-	GW	GT	S	SPct	G	A	Pts	G	A	Pts	Num	PIM	Maj	Mnr	Fgt	Rgh	HHT	Hat	P/G
98-99	Van	4	0	0	0	0	0	0	1	0.0	0	0	0	0	0	0	1	2	0	1	0	0	0	0	.00

Tony Granato

(statistical profile on page 314)

Pos: RW **Shoots:** R **Ht:** 5'10" **Wt:** 185 **Born:** 7/25/64—Downers Grove, Illinois **Age:** 35

		Overall									Power Play			Shorthand			Penalty							Misc	
Year	Tm	GP	G	A	Pts	+/-	GW	GT	S	SPct	G	A	Pts	G	A	Pts	Num	PIM	Maj	Mnr	Fgt	Rgh	HHT	Hat	P/G
88-89	NYR	78	36	27	63	17	3	2	234	15.4	4	3	7	4	–	–	63	140	2	60	–	–	–	3	.81
89-90	2Tm	56	12	24	36	-1	0	0	120	10.0	2	–	–	0	–	–	–	122	–	–	–	–	–	0	.64
90-91	LA	68	30	34	64	22	3	0	197	15.2	11	–	–	1	–	–	–	154	–	–	–	–	–	0	.94
91-92	LA	80	39	29	68	4	8	1	223	17.5	7	8	15	2	2	4	76	187	1	71	0	13	12	1	.85
92-93	LA	81	37	45	82	-1	6	0	247	15.0	14	13	27	2	3	5	80	171	1	78	0	25	17	0	1.01
93-94	LA	50	7	14	21	-2	0	0	117	6.0	2	0	2	0	2	2	60	150	2	55	2	15	14	0	.42
94-95	LA	33	13	11	24	9	3	0	106	12.3	2	2	4	0	1	1	30	68	0	29	0	13	8	1	.73
95-96	LA	49	17	18	35	-5	1	2	156	10.9	5	4	9	0	1	1	23	46	0	23	0	4	7	0	.71
96-97	SJ*	76	25	15	40	-7	4	0	231	10.8	5	4	9	1	0	1	51	159	3	42	1	8	10	2	.53
97-98	SJ	59	16	9	25	3	2	0	119	13.4	3	1	4	0	0	0	27	70	0	25	0	4	9	0	.42
98-99	SJ	35	6	6	12	4	1	1	65	9.2	0	2	2	1	0	1	19	54	0	17	0	3	4	0	.34
89-90	NYR	37	7	18	25	1	0	0	79	8.9	1	–	–	0	–	–	–	77	–	–	–	–	–	0	.68
89-90	LA	19	5	6	11	-2	0	0	41	12.2	1	–	–	0	–	–	–	45	–	–	–	–	–	0	.58
11 Years		665	238	232	470	43	31	6	1815	13.1	55	–	–	11	–	–	–	1321	–	–	–	–	–	7	.71

Postseason																									
Year	Tm	GP	G	A	Pts	+/–	GW	OT	S	SPct	G	A	Pts	G	A	Pts	Num	PIM	Maj	Mnr	Fgt	Rgh	HHT	Hat	P/G
88-89	NYR	4	1	1	2	-1	0	0	16	6.3	0	–	–	0	0	0	–	21	–	–	–	–	–	0	.50
89-90	LA	10	5	4	9	-2	2	1	26	19.2	2	–	–	1	–	–	–	12	–	–	–	–	–	1	.90
90-91	LA	12	1	4	5	1	0	0	32	3.1	0	–	–	0	–	–	–	28	–	–	–	–	–	0	.42
91-92	LA	6	1	5	6	1	0	0	19	5.3	0	0	0	0	0	0	5	10	0	5	0	0	1	0	1.00
92-93	LA	24	6	11	17	3	1	0	77	7.8	1	1	2	0	0	0	25	50	0	25	0	5	9	0	.71
97-98	SJ	1	0	0	0	0	0	0	2	0.0	0	0	0	0	0	0	0	0	0	0	0	0	0	0	.00
98-99	SJ	6	1	1	2	-1	0	0	5	20.0	0	0	0	0	0	0	1	2	0	1	0	0	0	0	.33
7 Years		63	15	26	41	1	3	1	177	8.5	3	–	–	1	–	–	–	123	–	–	–	–	–	1	.65

Jean-Luc Grand Pierre

Pos: D **Shoots:** R **Ht:** 6'3" **Wt:** 207 **Born:** 2/2/77—Montreal, Quebec **Age:** 22

Overall											Power Play			Shorthand			Penalty							Misc	
Year	Tm	GP	G	A	Pts	+/–	GW	GT	S	SPct	G	A	Pts	G	A	Pts	Num	PIM	Maj	Mnr	Fgt	Rgh	HHT	Hat	P/G
98-99	Buf	16	0	1	1	0	0	0	11	0.0	0	0	0	0	0	0	7	17	1	6	1	0	3	0	.06

Benoit Gratton

Pos: LW **Shoots:** L **Ht:** 5'10" **Wt:** 163 **Born:** 12/28/76—Montreal, Quebec **Age:** 23

Overall											Power Play			Shorthand			Penalty							Misc	
Year	Tm	GP	G	A	Pts	+/–	GW	GT	S	SPct	G	A	Pts	G	A	Pts	Num	PIM	Maj	Mnr	Fgt	Rgh	HHT	Hat	P/G
97-98	Was	6	0	1	1	1	0	0	5	0.0	0	0	0	0	0	0	3	6	0	3	0	1	1	0	.17
98-99	Was	16	4	3	7	-1	0	0	24	16.7	0	1	1	0	0	0	8	16	0	8	0	3	3	0	.44
2 Years		22	4	4	8	0	0	0	29	13.8	0	1	1	0	0	0	11	22	0	11	0	4	4	0	.36

Chris Gratton

(statistical profile on page 314)

Pos: C **Shoots:** L **Ht:** 6'4" **Wt:** 218 **Born:** 7/5/75—Brantford, Ontario **Age:** 24

Overall											Power Play			Shorthand			Penalty							Misc	
Year	Tm	GP	G	A	Pts	+/–	GW	GT	S	SPct	G	A	Pts	G	A	Pts	Num	PIM	Maj	Mnr	Fgt	Rgh	HHT	Hat	P/G
93-94	TB	84	13	29	42	-25	2	1	161	8.1	5	11	16	1	0	1	43	123	7	34	7	10	5	0	.50
94-95	TB	46	7	20	27	-2	0	0	91	7.7	2	6	8	0	0	0	29	89	5	22	4	5	3	0	.59
95-96	TB	82	17	21	38	-13	3	0	183	9.3	7	7	14	0	0	0	40	105	3	35	3	8	10	0	.46
96-97	TB	**82**	30	32	62	-28	4	0	230	13.0	9	9	18	0	0	0	69	201	5	58	5	16	11	1	.76
97-98	Phi	82	22	40	62	11	2	0	182	12.1	5	8	13	0	0	0	53	159	7	42	7	11	9	0	.76
98-99	2Tm	78	8	26	34	-28	1	1	181	4.4	1	7	8	0	2	2	49	143	7	39	7	4	7	0	.44
98-99	Phi	26	1	7	8	-8	0	0	54	1.9	0	2	2	0	0	0	12	41	3	8	3	1	1	0	.31
98-99	TB	52	7	19	26	-20	1	1	127	5.5	1	5	6	0	2	2	37	102	4	31	4	3	6	0	.50
6 Years		454	97	168	265	-85	12	2	1028	9.4	29	48	77	1	2	3	283	820	34	230	33	54	45	1	.58

Postseason																									
Year	Tm	GP	G	A	Pts	+/–	GW	OT	S	SPct	G	A	Pts	G	A	Pts	Num	PIM	Maj	Mnr	Fgt	Rgh	HHT	Hat	P/G
95-96	TB	6	0	2	2	-3	0	0	4	0.0	0	1	1	0	0	0	8	27	1	6	1	1	1	0	.33
97-98	Phi	5	2	0	2	-1	0	0	16	12.5	0	0	0	0	0	0	5	10	0	5	0	1	0	0	.40
2 Years		11	2	2	4	-4	0	0	20	10.0	0	1	1	0	0	0	13	37	1	11	1	2	1	0	.36

Adam Graves

(statistical profile on page 315)

Pos: LW **Shoots:** L **Ht:** 6'0" **Wt:** 205 **Born:** 4/12/68—Toronto, Ontario **Age:** 31

Overall											Power Play			Shorthand			Penalty							Misc	
Year	Tm	GP	G	A	Pts	+/–	GW	GT	S	SPct	G	A	Pts	G	A	Pts	Num	PIM	Maj	Mnr	Fgt	Rgh	HHT	Hat	P/G
87-88	Det	9	0	1	1	-2	0	0	9	0.0	0	–	–	0	–	–	4	8	0	4	0	–	–	0	.11
88-89	Det	56	7	5	12	-5	1	0	60	11.7	0	–	–	0	–	–	–	60	–	–	–	–	–	0	.21
89-90	2Tm	76	9	13	22	0	1	0	94	9.6	1	–	–	0	–	–	–	136	–	–	–	–	–	1	.29
90-91	Edm	76	7	18	25	-21	1	0	126	5.6	2	5	7	0	0	0	–	127	–	–	–	–	–	0	.33
91-92	NYR	80	26	33	59	19	4	0	228	11.4	4	5	9	4	3	7	52	139	9	42	9	15	9	1	.74
92-93	NYR	84	36	29	65	-4	6	1	275	13.1	12	2	14	1	2	3	53	148	6	44	6	17	7	1	.77
93-94	NYR*	84	52	27	79	27	4	1	291	17.9	20	8	28	4	1	5	52	127	5	46	5	22	6	1	.94
94-95	NYR	47	17	14	31	9	3	0	185	9.2	9	6	15	0	1	1	21	51	3	18	3	5	1	1	.66
95-96	NYR	82	22	36	58	18	2	0	266	8.3	9	14	23	1	1	2	40	100	4	35	4	8	9	0	.71
96-97	NYR	**82**	33	28	61	10	3	**5**	269	12.3	10	6	16	4	2	6	30	66	2	28	2	14	5	1	.74
97-98	NYR	72	23	12	35	-30	2	1	226	10.2	10	5	15	0	0	0	19	41	1	18	1	5	6	0	.49
98-99	NYR	82	38	15	53	-12	7	0	239	15.9	14	6	20	2	1	3	18	47	1	16	1	3	7	0	.65
89-90	Det	13	0	1	1	-5	0	0	10	0.0	0	–	–	0	–	–	5	13	1	4	–	–	–	0	.08
89-90	Edm	63	9	12	21	5	1	0	84	10.7	1	1	2	0	0	0	–	123	–	–	–	–	–	1	.33
12 Years		830	270	231	501	9	34	8	2268	11.9	91	–	–	16	–	–	–	1050	–	–	–	–	–	6	.60

Postseason																									
Year	Tm	GP	G	A	Pts	+/–	GW	OT	S	SPct	G	A	Pts	G	A	Pts	Num	PIM	Maj	Mnr	Fgt	Rgh	HHT	Hat	P/G
88-89	Det	5	0	0	0	-1	0	0	6	0.0	0	0	0	0	0	0	2	4	0	2	0	–	–	0	.00
89-90	Edm	22	5	6	11	1	1	0	46	10.9	0	–	–	0	–	–	–	17	–	–	–	–	–	0	.50
90-91	Edm	18	2	4	6	7	0	0	48	4.2	0	–	–	0	0	0	–	22	–	–	–	–	–	0	.33
91-92	NYR	10	5	3	8	-6	1	0	33	15.2	1	0	1	0	0	0	7	22	0	6	0	3	0	0	.80
93-94	NYR	23	10	7	17	12	0	0	93	10.8	3	4	7	0	0	0	8	24	0	7	0	2	2	0	.74
94-95	NYR	10	4	4	8	-13	0	0	38	10.5	2	3	5	0	0	0	4	8	0	4	0	0	0	0	.80
95-96	NYR	10	7	1	8	-9	2	0	43	16.3	6	0	6	0	0	0	2	4	0	2	0	0	1	0	.80
96-97	NYR	15	2	1	3	1	2	1	39	5.1	1	1	2	0	0	0	6	12	0	6	0	2	1	0	.20
8 Years		113	35	26	61	-8	6	1	346	10.1	13	–	–	0	–	–	–	113	–	–	–	–	–	0	.54

Josh Green

Pos: LW **Shoots:** L **Ht:** 6'3" **Wt:** 210 **Born:** 11/16/77—Camrose, Alberta **Age:** 22

Overall											Power Play			Shorthand			Penalty							Misc	
Year	Tm	GP	G	A	Pts	+/–	GW	GT	S	SPct	G	A	Pts	G	A	Pts	Num	PIM	Maj	Mnr	Fgt	Rgh	HHT	Hat	P/G
98-99	LA	27	1	3	4	-5	0	0	35	2.9	1	0	1	0	0	0	4	8	0	4	0	1	1	0	.15

Travis Green

(statistical profile on page 315)

Pos: C **Shoots:** R **Ht:** 6'1" **Wt:** 193 **Born:** 12/20/70—Castlegar, British Columbia **Age:** 29

Overall											Power Play			Shorthand			Penalty							Misc	
Year	Tm	GP	G	A	Pts	+/–	GW	GT	S	SPct	G	A	Pts	G	A	Pts	Num	PIM	Maj	Mnr	Fgt	Rgh	HHT	Hat	P/G
92-93	NYI	61	7	18	25	4	0	0	115	6.1	1	1	2	0	0	0	16	43	1	14	1	0	2	0	.41
93-94	NYI	83	18	22	40	16	2	1	164	11.0	1	4	5	0	0	0	22	44	0	22	0	2	10	1	.48
94-95	NYI	42	5	7	12	-10	0	0	59	8.5	0	1	1	0	0	0	11	25	1	10	1	3	2	0	.29
95-96	NYI	69	25	45	70	-20	2	1	186	13.4	14	20	34	1	0	1	17	42	0	16	0	1	9	0	1.01
96-97	NYI	79	23	41	64	-5	3	0	177	13.0	10	9	19	0	0	0	19	38	0	19	0	3	11	0	.81
97-98	2Tm	76	19	23	42	-29	2	2	141	13.5	9	11	20	0	0	0	33	82	0	31	0	4	14	0	.55
98-99	Anh	79	13	17	30	-7	2	0	165	7.9	3	6	9	1	1	2	35	81	1	33	1	4	12	0	.38
97-98	NYI	54	14	12	26	-19	2	1	99	14.1	8	7	15	0	0	0	25	66	0	23	0	4	10	0	.48
97-98	Anh	22	5	11	16	-10	0	1	42	11.9	1	4	5	0	0	0	8	16	0	8	0	0	4	0	.73
7 Years		489	110	173	283	-51	11	4	1007	10.9	38	52	90	2	1	3	153	355	3	145	3	17	60	1	.58

Postseason																									
Year	Tm	GP	G	A	Pts	+/–	GW	OT	S	SPct	G	A	Pts	G	A	Pts	Num	PIM	Maj	Mnr	Fgt	Rgh	HHT	Hat	P/G
92-93	NYI	12	3	1	4	-3	1	0	27	11.1	0	0	0	0	0	0	3	6	0	3	0	2	1	0	.33
93-94	NYI	4	0	0	0	-5	0	0	7	0.0	0	0	0	0	0	0	1	2	0	1	0	0	1	0	.00
98-99	Anh	4	0	1	1	-4	0	0	12	0.0	0	1	1	0	0	0	2	4	0	2	0	0	0	0	.25
3 Years		20	3	2	5	-12	1	0	46	6.5	0	1	1	0	0	0	6	12	0	6	0	2	2	0	.25

Mark Greig

Pos: RW **Shoots:** R **Ht:** 5'11" **Wt:** 190 **Born:** 1/25/70—High River, Alberta **Age:** 29

Overall											Power Play			Shorthand			Penalty							Misc	
Year	Tm	GP	G	A	Pts	+/–	GW	GT	S	SPct	G	A	Pts	G	A	Pts	Num	PIM	Maj	Mnr	Fgt	Rgh	HHT	Hat	P/G
90-91	Har	4	0	0	0	-1	0	0	1	0.0	0	0	0	0	0	0	0	0	0	0	0	0	0	0	.00
91-92	Har	17	0	5	5	7	0	0	18	0.0	0	1	1	0	0	0	3	6	0	3	0	0	1	0	.29
92-93	Har	22	1	7	8	-11	0	0	16	6.3	0	2	2	0	0	0	12	27	1	11	1	4	3	0	.36
93-94	2Tm	44	6	7	13	-5	0	0	55	10.9	0	3	3	0	0	0	19	41	1	18	1	3	4	0	.30
94-95	Cgy	8	1	1	2	1	0	0	5	20.0	0	0	0	0	0	0	1	2	0	1	0	0	1	0	.25
95-96	Did Not Play in NHL																								
96-97	Did Not Play in NHL																								
97-98	Did Not Play in NHL																								
98-99	Phi	7	1	3	4	1	0	0	9	11.1	0	2	2	0	0	0	1	2	0	1	0	0	1	0	.57
93-94	Har	31	4	5	9	-6	0	0	41	9.8	0	3	3	0	0	0	14	31	1	13	1	2	3	0	.29
93-94	Tor	13	2	2	4	1	0	0	14	14.3	0	0	0	0	0	0	5	10	0	5	0	1	1	0	.31
6 Years		102	9	23	32	-8	0	0	104	8.7	0	8	8	0	0	0	36	78	2	34	2	7	10	0	.31

Postseason																									
Year	Tm	GP	G	A	Pts	+/–	GW	OT	S	SPct	G	A	Pts	G	A	Pts	Num	PIM	Maj	Mnr	Fgt	Rgh	HHT	Hat	P/G
98-99	Phi	2	0	1	1	1	0	0	3	0.0	0	0	0	0	0	0	0	0	0	0	0	0	0	0	.50

Wayne Gretzky

(statistical profile on page 315)

Pos: C **Shoots:** L **Ht:** 6'0" **Wt:** 180 **Born:** 1/26/61—Brantford, Ontario **Age:** 38

		Overall									Power Play			Shorthand			Penalty							Misc	
Year	**Tm**	**GP**	**G**	**A**	**Pts**	**+/–**	**GW**	**GT**	**S**	**SPct**	**G**	**A**	**Pts**	**G**	**A**	**Pts**	**Num**	**PIM**	**Maj**	**Mnr**	**Fgt**	**Rgh**	**HHT**	**Hat**	**P/G**
79-80	Edm*	79	51	**86**	**137**	15	6	4	284	18.0	13	–	–	1	–	–	–	21	–	–	–	–	–	2	**1.73**
80-81	Edm*	80	55	**109**	**164**	41	3	2	261	21.1	15	–	–	4	–	–	–	28	–	–	–	–	–	4	**2.05**
81-82	Edm*	80	**92**	**120**	**212**	**81**	**12**	4	**369**	24.9	18	–	–	**6**	–	–	–	26	–	–	–	–	–	**10**	**2.65**
82-83	Edm*	**80**	**71**	**125**	**196**	60	9	1	**348**	20.4	18	–	–	**6**	–	–	–	59	–	–	–	–	–	2	**2.45**
83-84	Edm*	74	**87**	**118**	**205**	**76**	11	0	324	**26.9**	**20**	–	–	**12**	–	–	–	39	–	–	–	–	–	**10**	**2.77**
84-85	Edm*	**80**	**73**	**135**	**208**	**98**	7	2	**358**	20.4	8	–	–	**11**	–	–	–	52	–	–	–	–	–	**6**	**2.60**
85-86	Edm*	80	52	**163**	**215**	71	6	1	**350**	14.9	11	–	–	3	–	–	–	46	–	–	–	–	–	3	**2.69**
86-87	Edm*	79	**62**	**121**	**183**	**70**	4	0	288	21.5	13	–	–	**7**	–	–	–	28	–	–	–	–	–	4	**2.32**
87-88	Edm*	64	40	**109**	149	39	3	0	211	19.0	9	–	–	5	–	–	–	24	–	–	–	–	–	2	**2.33**
88-89	LA*	78	54	**114**	168	15	5	2	303	17.8	11	–	–	5	–	–	–	26	–	–	–	–	–	2	2.15
89-90	LA*	73	40	**102**	**142**	8	4	1	236	16.9	10	–	–	4	–	–	–	42	–	–	–	–	–	1	1.95
90-91	LA*	78	41	**122**	**163**	30	5	2	212	19.3	8	–	–	0	–	–	–	16	–	–	–	–	–	2	**2.09**
91-92	LA*	74	31	**90**	121	-12	2	1	215	14.4	12	42	54	2	2	4	9	34	0	7	0	1	2	1	1.64
92-93	LA*	45	16	49	65	6	1	0	141	11.3	0	24	24	2	1	3	3	6	0	3	0	0	2	0	1.44
93-94	LA*	81	38	**92**	**130**	-25	0	1	233	16.3	14	**47**	**61**	4	3	7	10	20	0	10	0	0	2	0	**1.60**
94-95	LA	48	11	37	48	-20	1	0	142	7.7	3	19	22	0	3	3	3	6	0	3	0	0	0	0	1.00
95-96	2Tm*	80	23	79	102	-13	3	1	195	11.8	6	41	47	1	0	1	9	34	0	7	0	0	5	0	1.28
96-97	NYR*	**82**	25	**72**	97	12	2	1	286	8.7	6	25	31	0	1	1	10	28	0	9	0	4	5	0	1.18
97-98	NYR*	82	23	**67**	90	-11	4	2	201	11.4	6	24	30	0	0	0	10	28	0	9	0	0	4	1	1.10
98-99	NYR	70	9	53	62	-23	3	1	132	6.8	3	27	30	0	0	0	7	14	0	7	0	0	3	0	.89
95-96	LA	62	15	66	81	-7	2	1	144	10.4	5	32	37	0	0	0	8	32	0	6	0	0	4	0	1.31
95-96	StL	18	8	13	21	-6	1	0	51	15.7	1	9	10	1	0	1	1	2	0	1	0	0	1	0	1.17
20 Years		1487	894	1963	2857	518	91	26	5089	17.6	204	–	–	73	–	–	–	577	–	–	–	–	–	50	1.92
											Postseason														
Year	**Tm**	**GP**	**G**	**A**	**Pts**	**+/–**	**GW**	**OT**	**S**	**SPct**	**G**	**A**	**Pts**	**G**	**A**	**Pts**	**Num**	**PIM**	**Maj**	**Mnr**	**Fgt**	**Rgh**	**HHT**	**Hat**	**P/G**
79-80	Edm	3	2	1	3	–	0	0	–	–	0	–	–	0	–	–	0	0	0	0	0	0	0	0	1.00
80-81	Edm	9	7	14	21	–	1	0	–	–	2	–	–	1	–	–	2	4	0	2	0	–	–	2	2.33
81-82	Edm	5	5	7	12	–	1	1	–	–	1	–	–	1	–	–	4	8	0	4	0	–	–	0	2.40
82-83	Edm	16	12	26	38	19	3	0	76	15.8	2	–	–	3	–	–	2	4	0	2	0	–	–	2	2.38
83-84	Edm	19	13	22	35	18	3	0	86	15.1	2	–	–	0	–	–	–	12	–	–	–	–	–	0	1.84
84-85	Edm	18	17	30	47	28	3	0	67	25.4	4	–	–	2	–	–	2	4	0	2	0	–	–	2	2.61
85-86	Edm	10	8	11	19	0	2	0	42	19.0	4	–	–	1	–	–	1	2	0	1	0	–	–	1	1.90
86-87	Edm	21	5	29	34	10	0	0	55	9.1	2	–	–	0	–	–	3	6	0	3	0	–	–	0	1.62
87-88	Edm	19	12	31	43	9	3	1	62	19.4	5	–	–	1	–	–	–	16	–	–	–	–	–	0	2.26
88-89	LA	11	5	17	22	-4	0	0	42	11.9	1	–	–	1	–	–	0	0	0	0	0	0	0	0	2.00
89-90	LA	7	3	7	10	-4	0	0	13	23.1	1	–	–	0	–	–	0	0	0	0	0	0	0	0	1.43
90-91	LA	12	4	11	15	0	2	1	26	15.4	1	–	–	0	–	–	1	2	0	1	0	–	–	0	1.25
91-92	LA	6	2	5	7	-3	0	0	11	18.2	1	4	5	0	0	0	1	2	0	1	0	0	0	0	1.17
92-93	LA	24	15	25	40	6	3	1	76	19.7	4	9	13	1	2	3	2	4	0	2	0	0	2	1	1.67
95-96	StL	13	2	14	16	2	1	0	25	8.0	1	6	7	0	1	1	0	0	0	0	0	0	0	0	1.23
96-97	NYR	15	10	10	20	5	2	0	44	22.7	3	5	8	0	0	0	1	2	0	1	0	0	0	2	1.33
16 Years		208	122	260	382	86	24	4	625	17.3	34	–	–	11	–	–	–	66	–	–	–	–	–	10	1.84

Mike Grier

(statistical profile on page 315)

Pos: RW **Shoots:** R **Ht:** 6'1" **Wt:** 225 **Born:** 1/5/75—Detroit, Michigan **Age:** 24

		Overall									Power Play			Shorthand			Penalty							Misc	
Year	**Tm**	**GP**	**G**	**A**	**Pts**	**+/–**	**GW**	**GT**	**S**	**SPct**	**G**	**A**	**Pts**	**G**	**A**	**Pts**	**Num**	**PIM**	**Maj**	**Mnr**	**Fgt**	**Rgh**	**HHT**	**Hat**	**P/G**
96-97	Edm	79	15	17	32	7	2	0	89	16.9	4	1	5	0	0	0	15	45	5	10	5	4	0	0	.41
97-98	Edm	66	9	6	15	-3	1	0	90	10.0	1	0	1	0	0	0	21	73	5	14	5	6	2	0	.23
98-99	Edm	82	20	24	44	5	1	0	143	14.0	3	2	5	2	0	2	20	54	2	17	2	3	2	1	.54
3 Years		227	44	47	91	9	4	0	322	13.7	8	3	11	2	0	2	56	172	12	41	12	13	4	1	.40
											Postseason														
Year	**Tm**	**GP**	**G**	**A**	**Pts**	**+/–**	**GW**	**OT**	**S**	**SPct**	**G**	**A**	**Pts**	**G**	**A**	**Pts**	**Num**	**PIM**	**Maj**	**Mnr**	**Fgt**	**Rgh**	**HHT**	**Hat**	**P/G**
96-97	Edm	12	3	1	4	-2	1	0	21	14.3	1	1	2	0	0	0	2	4	0	2	0	0	0	0	.33
97-98	Edm	12	2	2	4	4	1	0	14	14.3	0	0	0	0	0	0	5	13	1	4	1	0	0	0	.33
98-99	Edm	4	1	1	2	3	0	0	9	11.1	0	0	0	0	0	0	3	6	0	3	0	1	0	0	.50
3 Years		28	6	4	10	5	2	0	44	13.6	1	1	2	0	0	0	10	23	1	9	1	1	0	0	.36

Stu Grimson

Pos: LW **Shoots:** L **Ht:** 6'6" **Wt:** 226 **Born:** 5/20/65—Kamloops, British Columbia **Age:** 34

Overall											Power Play			Shorthand			Penalty							Misc	
Year	Tm	GP	G	A	Pts	+/–	GW	GT	S	SPct	G	A	Pts	G	A	Pts	Num	PIM	Maj	Mnr	Fgt	Rgh	HHT	Hat	P/G
88-89	Cgy	1	0	0	0	0	0	0	0	–	0	0	0	0	0	0	1	5	1	0	–	0	0	0	.00
89-90	Cgy	3	0	0	0	-1	0	0	0	–	0	0	0	0	0	0	4	17	3	1	–	–	–	0	.00
90-91	Chi	35	0	1	1	-3	0	0	14	0.0	0	–	–	0	–	–	–	183	–	–	–	–	–	0	.03
91-92	Chi	54	2	2	4	-2	0	0	23	8.7	0	0	0	0	0	0	48	234	22	17	20	7	1	0	.07
92-93	Chi	78	1	1	2	2	0	0	14	7.1	1	0	1	0	0	0	54	193	23	29	23	9	2	0	.03
93-94	Anh	77	1	5	6	-6	0	0	34	2.9	0	0	0	0	0	0	63	199	19	42	18	15	3	0	.08
94-95	2Tm	42	0	1	1	-11	0	0	18	0.0	0	0	0	0	0	0	43	147	15	26	14	13	2	0	.02
95-96	Det	56	0	1	1	-10	0	0	19	0.0	0	0	0	0	0	0	36	128	16	19	15	4	0	0	.02
96-97	2Tm	76	2	2	4	-8	0	0	17	11.8	0	0	0	0	0	0	57	218	24	29	24	12	3	0	.05
97-98	Car	82	3	4	7	0	1	0	17	17.6	0	0	0	0	0	0	53	204	22	27	22	12	4	0	.09
98-99	Anh	73	3	0	3	0	1	0	10	30.0	0	0	0	0	0	0	49	158	20	29	20	9	3	0	.04
94-95	Anh	31	0	1	1	-7	0	0	14	0.0	0	0	0	0	0	0	29	110	12	15	11	7	2	0	.03
94-95	Det	11	0	0	0	-4	0	0	4	0.0	0	0	0	0	0	0	14	37	3	11	3	6	0	0	.00
96-97	Det	1	0	0	0	-1	0	0	0	–	0	0	0	0	0	0	0	0	0	0	0	0	0	0	.00
96-97	Har	75	2	2	4	-7	0	0	17	11.8	0	0	0	0	0	0	57	218	24	29	24	12	3	0	.05
11 Years		577	12	17	29	-39	2	0	166	7.2	1	–	–	0	–	–	–	1686	–	–	–	–	–	0	.05

Postseason

Year	Tm	GP	G	A	Pts	+/–	GW	OT	S	SPct	G	A	Pts	G	A	Pts	Num	PIM	Maj	Mnr	Fgt	Rgh	HHT	Hat	P/G
90-91	Chi	5	0	0	0	-1	0	0	2	0.0	0	0	0	0	0	0	–	46	–	–	–	–	–	0	.00
91-92	Chi	14	0	1	1	-1	0	0	2	0.0	0	0	0	0	0	0	1	10	0	0	0	0	0	0	.07
92-93	Chi	2	0	0	0	0	0	0	1	0.0	0	0	0	0	0	0	2	4	0	2	0	0	0	0	.00
94-95	Det	11	1	0	1	0	0	0	3	33.3	0	0	0	0	0	0	6	26	2	3	1	2	0	0	.09
95-96	Det	2	0	0	0	0	0	0	0	–	0	0	0	0	0	0	0	0	0	0	0	0	0	0	.00
98-99	Anh	3	0	0	0	0	0	0	0	–	0	0	0	0	0	0	7	30	0	5	0	5	0	0	.00
6 Years		37	1	1	2	-2	0	0	8	12.5	0	0	0	0	0	0	–	116	–	–	–	–	–	0	.05

Michal Grosek

(statistical profile on page 316)

Pos: LW **Shoots:** R **Ht:** 6'2" **Wt:** 207 **Born:** 6/1/75—Vyskov, Czechoslovakia **Age:** 24

Overall											Power Play			Shorthand			Penalty							Misc	
Year	Tm	GP	G	A	Pts	+/–	GW	GT	S	SPct	G	A	Pts	G	A	Pts	Num	PIM	Maj	Mnr	Fgt	Rgh	HHT	Hat	P/G
93-94	Wpg	3	1	0	1	-1	0	0	4	25.0	0	0	0	0	0	0	0	0	0	0	0	0	0	0	.33
94-95	Wpg	24	2	2	4	-3	1	0	27	7.4	0	0	0	0	0	0	5	21	1	3	1	1	1	0	.17
95-96	2Tm	23	6	4	10	-1	1	1	34	17.6	2	3	5	0	0	0	14	31	1	13	1	3	4	0	.43
96-97	Buf	**82**	15	21	36	25	2	1	117	12.8	1	4	5	0	0	0	23	71	3	18	3	6	4	1	.44
97-98	Buf	67	10	20	30	9	1	0	114	8.8	2	4	6	0	0	0	27	60	2	25	2	3	8	0	.45
98-99	Buf	76	20	30	50	21	3	1	140	14.3	4	8	12	0	0	0	36	102	2	31	1	4	8	0	.66
95-96	Wpg	1	0	0	0	-1	0	0	1	0.0	0	0	0	0	0	0	0	0	0	0	0	0	0	0	.00
95-96	Buf	22	6	4	10	0	1	1	33	18.2	2	3	5	0	0	0	14	31	1	13	1	3	4	0	.45
6 Years		275	54	77	131	50	8	3	436	12.4	9	19	28	0	0	0	105	285	9	90	8	17	25	1	.48

Postseason

Year	Tm	GP	G	A	Pts	+/–	GW	OT	S	SPct	G	A	Pts	G	A	Pts	Num	PIM	Maj	Mnr	Fgt	Rgh	HHT	Hat	P/G
96-97	Buf	12	3	3	6	3	0	0	18	16.7	0	0	0	0	0	0	4	8	0	4	0	0	0	0	.50
97-98	Buf	15	6	4	10	5	3	1	40	15.0	2	1	3	0	0	0	10	28	0	9	0	4	2	0	.67
98-99	Buf	13	0	4	4	1	0	0	20	0.0	0	3	3	0	0	0	10	28	0	9	0	3	2	0	.31
3 Years		40	9	11	20	9	3	1	78	11.5	2	4	6	0	0	0	24	64	0	22	0	7	4	0	.50

John Gruden

Pos: D **Shoots:** L **Ht:** 6'0" **Wt:** 190 **Born:** 4/6/70—Hastings, Minnesota **Age:** 29

Overall											Power Play			Shorthand			Penalty							Misc	
Year	Tm	GP	G	A	Pts	+/–	GW	GT	S	SPct	G	A	Pts	G	A	Pts	Num	PIM	Maj	Mnr	Fgt	Rgh	HHT	Hat	P/G
93-94	Bos	7	0	1	1	-3	0	0	8	0.0	0	0	0	0	0	0	1	2	0	1	0	0	1	0	.14
94-95	Bos	38	0	6	6	3	0	0	30	0.0	0	0	0	0	0	0	11	22	0	11	0	2	4	0	.16
95-96	Bos	14	0	0	0	-3	0	0	12	0.0	0	0	0	0	0	0	2	4	0	2	0	0	2	0	.00
96-97	Did Not Play in NHL																								
97-98	Did Not Play in NHL																								
98-99	Ott	13	0	1	1	0	0	0	10	0.0	0	0	0	0	0	0	4	8	0	4	0	0	0	0	.08
4 Years		72	0	8	8	-3	0	0	60	0.0	0	0	0	0	0	0	18	36	0	18	0	2	7	0	.11

Postseason

Year	Tm	GP	G	A	Pts	+/–	GW	OT	S	SPct	G	A	Pts	G	A	Pts	Num	PIM	Maj	Mnr	Fgt	Rgh	HHT	Hat	P/G
95-96	Bos	3	0	1	1	0	0	0	2	0.0	0	1	1	0	0	0	0	0	0	0	0	0	0	0	.33

Bill Guerin

(statistical profile on page 316)

Pos: RW **Shoots:** R **Ht:** 6'2" **Wt:** 210 **Born:** 11/9/70—Wilbraham, Massachusetts **Age:** 29

		Overall									Power Play			Shorthand			Penalty							Misc	
Year	Tm	GP	G	A	Pts	+/-	GW	GT	S	SPct	G	A	Pts	G	A	Pts	Num	PIM	Maj	Mnr	Fgt	Rgh	HHT	Hat	P/G
91-92	NJ	5	0	1	1	1	0	0	8	0.0	0	0	0	0	0	0	3	9	1	2	1	0	0	0	.20
92-93	NJ	65	14	20	34	14	2	0	123	11.4	0	1	1	0	0	0	24	63	5	19	5	6	5	0	.52
93-94	NJ	81	25	19	44	14	3	0	195	12.8	2	4	6	0	0	0	32	101	7	23	7	9	3	0	.54
94-95	NJ	48	12	13	25	6	3	0	96	12.5	4	2	6	0	0	0	19	72	6	11	6	5	1	0	.52
95-96	NJ	80	23	30	53	7	6	1	216	10.6	8	5	13	0	0	0	34	116	8	23	7	7	3	0	.66
96-97	NJ	**82**	29	18	47	-2	9	0	177	16.4	7	4	11	0	0	0	36	95	5	30	5	9	3	1	.57
97-98	2Tm	59	18	21	39	1	4	0	178	10.1	9	8	17	0	0	0	30	93	3	24	3	7	5	0	.66
98-99	Edm	80	30	34	64	7	2	1	261	11.5	13	9	22	0	0	0	41	133	9	29	9	4	8	0	.80
97-98	NJ	19	5	5	10	0	2	0	48	10.4	1	1	2	0	0	0	5	13	1	4	1	3	0	0	.53
97-98	Edm	40	13	16	29	1	2	0	130	10.0	8	7	15	0	0	0	25	80	2	20	2	4	5	0	.73
8 Years		500	151	156	307	48	29	2	1254	12.0	43	33	76	0	0	0	219	682	44	161	43	47	28	1	.61
										Postseason															
Year	Tm	GP	G	A	Pts	+/-	GW	OT	S	SPct	G	A	Pts	G	A	Pts	Num	PIM	Maj	Mnr	Fgt	Rgh	HHT	Hat	P/G
91-92	NJ	6	3	0	3	2	0	0	10	30.0	0	0	0	0	0	0	2	4	0	2	0	0	0	0	.50
92-93	NJ	5	1	1	2	-2	0	0	3	33.3	0	0	0	0	0	0	2	4	0	2	0	0	1	0	.40
93-94	NJ	17	2	1	3	1	1	0	49	4.1	0	0	0	0	0	0	12	35	1	10	1	3	0	0	.18
94-95	NJ	20	3	8	11	6	0	0	28	10.7	1	2	3	0	0	0	15	30	0	15	0	4	1	0	.55
96-97	NJ	8	2	1	3	-5	1	0	13	15.4	1	0	1	0	0	0	5	18	0	4	0	1	0	0	.38
97-98	Edm	12	7	1	8	-6	0	0	47	14.9	4	1	5	0	0	0	7	17	1	6	1	1	3	0	.67
98-99	Edm	3	0	2	2	-4	0	0	8	0.0	0	2	2	0	0	0	1	2	0	1	0	1	0	0	.67
7 Years		71	18	14	32	-8	2	0	158	11.4	6	5	11	0	0	0	44	110	2	40	2	10	5	0	.45

Steve Guolla

Pos: C **Shoots:** L **Ht:** 6'0" **Wt:** 190 **Born:** 3/15/73—Scarborough, Ontario **Age:** 26

		Overall									Power Play			Shorthand			Penalty							Misc	
Year	Tm	GP	G	A	Pts	+/-	GW	GT	S	SPct	G	A	Pts	G	A	Pts	Num	PIM	Maj	Mnr	Fgt	Rgh	HHT	Hat	P/G
96-97	SJ	43	13	8	21	-10	1	1	81	16.0	2	1	3	0	0	0	7	14	0	7	0	0	3	0	.49
97-98	SJ	7	1	1	2	-2	0	0	9	11.1	0	1	1	0	0	0	0	0	0	0	0	0	0	0	.29
98-99	SJ	14	2	2	4	3	1	0	22	9.1	0	0	0	0	0	0	3	6	0	3	0	0	1	0	.29
3 Years		64	16	11	27	-9	2	1	112	14.3	2	2	4	0	0	0	10	20	0	10	0	0	4	0	.42

Miloslav Guren

Pos: D **Shoots:** L **Ht:** 6'2" **Wt:** 209 **Born:** 9/24/76—Hradiste, Czechoslovakia **Age:** 23

		Overall									Power Play			Shorthand			Penalty							Misc	
Year	Tm	GP	G	A	Pts	+/-	GW	GT	S	SPct	G	A	Pts	G	A	Pts	Num	PIM	Maj	Mnr	Fgt	Rgh	HHT	Hat	P/G
98-99	Mon	12	0	1	1	-1	0	0	11	0.0	0	0	0	0	0	0	2	4	0	2	0	0	2	0	.08

Alexei Gusarov

(statistical profile on page 316)

Pos: D **Shoots:** L **Ht:** 6'3" **Wt:** 190 **Born:** 7/8/64—Leningrad, USSR **Age:** 35

		Overall									Power Play			Shorthand			Penalty							Misc	
Year	Tm	GP	G	A	Pts	+/-	GW	GT	S	SPct	G	A	Pts	G	A	Pts	Num	PIM	Maj	Mnr	Fgt	Rgh	HHT	Hat	P/G
90-91	Que	36	3	9	12	-4	0	0	36	8.3	1	–	–	0	–	–	–	12	–	–	–	–	–	0	.33
91-92	Que	68	5	18	23	-9	1	0	66	7.6	3	5	8	0	1	1	11	22	0	11	0	0	9	0	.34
92-93	Que	79	8	22	30	18	1	0	60	13.3	0	1	1	2	3	5	27	57	1	26	1	5	11	0	.38
93-94	Que	76	5	20	25	3	0	0	84	6.0	0	6	6	1	1	2	19	38	0	19	0	0	10	0	.33
94-95	Que	14	1	2	3	-1	1	0	7	14.3	0	0	0	0	0	0	3	6	0	3	0	0	2	0	.21
95-96	Col	65	5	15	20	29	0	0	42	11.9	0	4	4	0	0	0	28	56	0	28	0	1	16	0	.31
96-97	Col	58	2	12	14	4	0	0	33	6.1	0	1	1	0	0	0	10	28	0	9	0	1	4	0	.24
97-98	Col	72	4	10	14	9	1	0	47	8.5	0	1	1	1	1	2	21	42	0	21	0	0	14	0	.19
98-99	Col	54	3	10	13	12	0	0	28	10.7	1	3	4	0	0	0	12	24	0	12	0	1	9	0	.24
9 Years		522	36	118	154	61	4	0	403	8.9	5	–	–	4	–	–	–	285	–	–	–	–	–	0	.30
										Postseason															
Year	Tm	GP	G	A	Pts	+/-	GW	OT	S	SPct	G	A	Pts	G	A	Pts	Num	PIM	Maj	Mnr	Fgt	Rgh	HHT	Hat	P/G
92-93	Que	5	0	1	1	-3	0	0	7	0.0	0	0	0	0	0	0	0	0	0	0	0	0	0	0	.20
95-96	Col	21	0	9	9	13	0	0	15	0.0	0	1	1	0	0	0	6	12	0	6	0	0	5	0	.43
96-97	Col	17	0	3	3	3	0	0	9	0.0	0	0	0	0	0	0	7	14	0	7	0	5	2	0	.18
97-98	Col	7	0	1	1	1	0	0	3	0.0	0	0	0	0	0	0	3	6	0	3	0	1	2	0	.14
98-99	Col	5	0	0	0	1	0	0	2	0.0	0	0	0	0	0	0	1	2	0	1	0	0	0	0	.00
5 Years		55	0	14	14	15	0	0	36	0.0	0	1	1	0	0	0	17	34	0	17	0	6	9	0	.25

Sergey Gusev

Pos: D **Shoots:** L **Ht:** 6'1" **Wt:** 195 **Born:** 7/31/75—Neginy Tagel, USSR **Age:** 24

		Overall									Power Play			Shorthand			Penalty							Misc	
Year	Tm	GP	G	A	Pts	+/–	GW	GT	S	SPct	G	A	Pts	G	A	Pts	Num	PIM	Maj	Mnr	Fgt	Rgh	HHT	Hat	P/G
97-98	Dal	9	0	0	0	-5	0	0	5	0.0	0	0	0	0	0	0	1	2	0	1	0	0	1	0	.00
98-99	2Tm	36	1	7	8	-3	1	0	46	2.2	0	5	5	0	1	1	8	16	0	8	0	0	6	0	.22
98-99	Dal	22	1	4	5	5	1	0	30	3.3	0	3	3	0	0	0	3	6	0	3	0	0	2	0	.23
98-99	TB	14	0	3	3	-8	0	0	16	0.0	0	2	2	0	1	1	5	10	0	5	0	0	4	0	.21
2 Years		45	1	7	8	-8	1	0	51	2.0	0	5	5	0	1	1	9	18	0	9	0	0	7	0	.18

Jeff Hackett

(statistical profile on page 398)

Pos: G **Catches:** L **Ht:** 6'1" **Wt:** 195 **Born:** 6/1/68—London, Ontario **Age:** 31

		Overall															Pen Shot		Offense		
Year	Tm	GP	GS	TP	W	L	T	Min	GA	GAA	Shots	SvPct	ShO	OE	PPGA	SHGA	Shots	GA	G	A	PIM
88-89	NYI	13	–	–	4	7	0	662	39	3.53	329	.881	0	–	–	–	0	0	0	1	2
89-90		Did Not Play in NHL																			
90-91	NYI	30	–	–	5	18	1	1508	91	3.62	741	.877	0	–	–	–	0	0	0	0	4
91-92	SJ	42	40	6	11	27	1	2314	148	3.84	1366	.892	0	13	42	6	0	0	0	2	8
92-93	SJ	36	35	5	2	30	1	2000	176	5.28	1220	.856	0	5	44	9	0	0	0	1	4
93-94	Chi	22	14	2	2	12	3	1084	62	3.43	566	.890	0	6	18	1	1	**1**	0	1	2
94-95	Chi	7	4	1	1	3	2	328	13	2.38	150	.913	0	2	5	0	0	0	0	0	0
95-96	Chi	35	33	2	18	11	4	2000	80	2.40	948	.916	4	14	20	4	1	0	0	1	8
96-97	Chi	41	41	0	19	18	4	2473	89	2.16	1212	.927	2	18	29	3	**3**	**3**	0	1	6
97-98	Chi	58	58	3	21	25	11	3441	126	2.20	1520	.917	8	20	39	3	0	0	0	0	8
98-99	2Tm	63	62	8	26	26	10	3615	150	2.49	1616	.907	5	19	35	**11**	0	0	0	1	12
98-99	Chi	10	9	2	2	6	1	524	33	3.78	256	.871	0	2	11	4	0	0	0	0	6
98-99	Mon	53	53	6	24	20	9	3091	117	2.27	1360	.914	5	17	24	7	0	0	0	1	6
10 Years		347	–	–	109	177	37	19425	974	3.01	9668	.899	19	–	–	–	5	4	0	8	54
Postseason																					
Year	Tm	GP	GS	TP	W	L	Pct	Min	GA	GAA	Shots	SvPct	ShO	OE	PPGA	SHGA	Shots	GA	G	A	PIM
94-95	Chi	2	0	1	0	0	–	26	1	2.31	11	.909	0	0	1	0	0	0	0	0	0
95-96	Chi	1	1	0	0	1	.000	60	5	5.00	32	.844	0	0	2	0	0	0	0	0	0
96-97	Chi	6	6	2	2	4	.333	345	25	4.35	190	.868	0	3	9	0	0	0	0	0	0
3 Years		9	7	3	2	5	.286	431	31	4.32	233	.867	0	3	12	0	0	0	0	0	0

Steve Halko

Pos: D **Shoots:** R **Ht:** 6'1" **Wt:** 194 **Born:** 3/8/74—Etobicoke, Ontario **Age:** 25

		Overall									Power Play			Shorthand			Penalty							Misc	
Year	Tm	GP	G	A	Pts	+/–	GW	GT	S	SPct	G	A	Pts	G	A	Pts	Num	PIM	Maj	Mnr	Fgt	Rgh	HHT	Hat	P/G
97-98	Car	18	0	2	2	-1	0	0	7	0.0	0	0	0	0	0	0	5	10	0	5	0	0	2	0	.11
98-99	Car	20	0	3	3	5	0	0	6	0.0	0	0	0	0	0	0	9	24	2	7	2	0	3	0	.15
2 Years		38	0	5	5	4	0	0	13	0.0	0	0	0	0	0	0	14	34	2	12	2	0	5	0	.13
Postseason																									
Year	Tm	GP	G	A	Pts	+/–	GW	OT	S	SPct	G	A	Pts	G	A	Pts	Num	PIM	Maj	Mnr	Fgt	Rgh	HHT	Hat	P/G
98-99	Car	4	0	0	0	-2	0	0	2	0.0	0	0	0	0	0	0	1	2	0	1	0	0	0	0	.00

Kevin Haller

Pos: D **Shoots:** L **Ht:** 6'2" **Wt:** 192 **Born:** 12/5/70—Trochu, Alberta **Age:** 29

		Overall									Power Play			Shorthand			Penalty							Misc	
Year	Tm	GP	G	A	Pts	+/–	GW	GT	S	SPct	G	A	Pts	G	A	Pts	Num	PIM	Maj	Mnr	Fgt	Rgh	HHT	Hat	P/G
89-90	Buf	2	0	0	0	0	0	0	1	0.0	0	0	0	0	0	0	0	0	0	0	0	0	0	0	.00
90-91	Buf	21	1	8	9	9	0	0	42	2.4	1	–	–	0	–	–	–	20	–	–	–	–	–	0	.43
91-92	2Tm	66	8	17	25	-9	1	0	85	9.4	3	7	10	0	0	0	43	92	2	41	2	6	20	0	.38
92-93	Mon	73	11	14	25	7	1	0	126	8.7	6	8	14	0	0	0	49	117	1	46	1	5	19	0	.34
93-94	Mon	68	4	9	13	3	1	0	72	5.6	0	4	4	0	1	1	56	118	2	54	2	13	20	0	.19
94-95	Phi	36	2	8	10	16	0	0	26	7.7	0	1	1	0	0	0	17	48	2	14	2	1	8	0	.28
95-96	Phi	69	5	9	14	18	2	0	89	5.6	0	2	2	2	0	2	38	92	0	36	0	6	17	0	.20
96-97	2Tm	62	2	11	13	-12	0	0	77	2.6	0	2	2	0	0	0	41	85	1	40	1	10	14	0	.21
97-98	Car	65	3	5	8	-5	0	0	67	4.5	0	1	1	0	0	0	44	94	2	42	2	5	18	0	.12
98-99	Anh	82	1	6	7	-1	0	0	64	1.6	0	0	0	0	1	1	58	122	2	**56**	2	5	18	0	.09
91-92	Buf	58	6	15	21	-13	1	0	76	7.9	2	7	9	0	0	0	36	75	1	35	1	5	18	0	.36
91-92	Mon	8	2	2	4	4	0	0	9	22.2	1	0	1	0	0	0	7	17	1	6	1	1	2	0	.50
96-97	Phi	27	0	5	5	-1	0	0	34	0.0	0	0	0	0	0	0	17	37	1	16	1	2	4	0	.19
96-97	Har	35	2	6	8	-11	0	0	43	4.7	0	2	2	0	0	0	24	48	0	24	0	8	10	0	.23
10 Years		544	37	87	124	26	5	0	649	5.7	10	–	–	2	–	–	–	788	–	–	–	–	–	0	.23

Postseason																									
Year	Tm	GP	G	A	Pts	+/–	GW	OT	S	SPct	G	A	Pts	G	A	Pts	Num	PIM	Maj	Mnr	Fgt	Rgh	HHT	Hat	P/G
90-91	Buf	6	1	4	5	-1	0	0	13	7.7	0	–	–	0	–	–	–	10	–	–	–	–	–	0	.83
91-92	Mon	9	0	0	0	-3	0	0	12	0.0	0	0	0	0	0	0	3	6	0	3	0	1	1	0	.00
92-93	Mon	17	1	6	7	-1	0	0	24	4.2	1	5	6	0	0	0	8	16	0	8	0	1	4	0	.41
93-94	Mon	7	1	1	2	-3	0	0	8	12.5	0	1	1	0	0	0	4	19	1	2	0	0	0	0	.29
94-95	Phi	15	4	4	8	10	1	1	14	28.6	0	0	0	1	0	1	5	10	0	5	0	0	2	0	.53
95-96	Phi	6	0	1	1	0	0	0	6	0.0	0	0	0	0	0	0	4	8	0	4	0	0	2	0	.17
98-99	Anh	4	0	0	0	-1	0	0	7	0.0	0	0	0	0	0	0	1	2	0	1	0	0	0	0	.00
7 Years		64	7	16	23	1	1	1	84	8.3	1	–	–	1	–	–	–	71	–	–	–	–	–	0	.36

Trevor Halverson

Pos: LW **Shoots:** L **Ht:** 6'0" **Wt:** 194 **Born:** 4/6/71—White River, Ontario **Age:** 28

Overall											Power Play			Shorthand			Penalty							Misc	
Year	Tm	GP	G	A	Pts	+/–	GW	GT	S	SPct	G	A	Pts	G	A	Pts	Num	PIM	Maj	Mnr	Fgt	Rgh	HHT	Hat	P/G
98-99	Was	17	0	4	4	-5	0	0	16	0.0	0	0	0	0	0	0	8	28	4	4	4	0	1	0	.24

Roman Hamrlik

(statistical profile on page 316)

Pos: D **Shoots:** L **Ht:** 6'2" **Wt:** 200 **Born:** 4/12/74—Gottwaldov, Czechoslovakia **Age:** 25

Overall											Power Play			Shorthand			Penalty							Misc	
Year	Tm	GP	G	A	Pts	+/–	GW	GT	S	SPct	G	A	Pts	G	A	Pts	Num	PIM	Maj	Mnr	Fgt	Rgh	HHT	Hat	P/G
92-93	TB	67	6	15	21	-21	1	0	113	5.3	1	7	8	0	0	0	34	71	1	33	0	4	16	0	.31
93-94	TB	64	3	18	21	-14	0	0	158	1.9	0	5	5	0	0	0	58	135	1	55	1	18	14	0	.33
94-95	TB	48	12	11	23	-18	2	0	134	9.0	7	2	9	1	1	2	32	86	2	28	1	8	11	0	.48
95-96	TB*	82	16	49	65	-24	2	3	281	5.7	12	30	42	0	1	1	46	103	1	44	0	7	13	0	.79
96-97	TB	79	12	28	40	-29	0	1	238	5.0	6	16	22	0	1	1	23	57	1	21	1	4	11	0	.51
97-98	2Tm	78	9	32	41	-15	3	0	198	4.5	5	23	28	1	0	1	35	70	0	35	0	4	16	0	.53
98-99	Edm	75	8	24	32	9	0	0	172	4.7	3	14	17	0	0	0	35	70	0	35	0	4	15	0	.43
97-98	TB	37	3	12	15	-18	0	0	86	3.5	1	10	11	0	0	0	11	22	0	11	0	2	4	0	.41
97-98	Edm	41	6	20	26	3	3	0	112	5.4	4	13	17	1	0	1	24	48	0	24	0	2	12	0	.63
7 Years		493	66	177	243	-112	8	4	1294	5.1	34	97	131	2	3	5	263	592	6	251	3	49	96	0	.49
Postseason																									
Year	Tm	GP	G	A	Pts	+/–	GW	OT	S	SPct	G	A	Pts	G	A	Pts	Num	PIM	Maj	Mnr	Fgt	Rgh	HHT	Hat	P/G
95-96	TB	5	0	1	1	-1	0	0	10	0.0	0	0	0	0	0	0	2	4	0	2	0	1	1	0	.20
97-98	Edm	12	0	6	6	-4	0	0	19	0.0	0	6	6	0	0	0	6	12	0	6	0	2	1	0	.50
98-99	Edm	3	0	0	0	1	0	0	1	0.0	0	0	0	0	0	0	1	2	0	1	0	0	1	0	.00
3 Years		20	0	7	7	-4	0	0	30	0.0	0	6	6	0	0	0	9	18	0	9	0	3	3	0	.35

Michal Handzus

(statistical profile on page 317)

Pos: C **Shoots:** L **Ht:** 6'3" **Wt:** 191 **Born:** 3/11/77—Banska Bystrica, Czechoslovakia **Age:** 22

Overall											Power Play			Shorthand			Penalty							Misc	
Year	Tm	GP	G	A	Pts	+/–	GW	GT	S	SPct	G	A	Pts	G	A	Pts	Num	PIM	Maj	Mnr	Fgt	Rgh	HHT	Hat	P/G
98-99	StL	66	4	12	16	-9	0	0	78	5.1	0	1	1	0	0	0	15	30	0	15	0	0	6	0	.24
Postseason																									
Year	Tm	GP	G	A	Pts	+/–	GW	OT	S	SPct	G	A	Pts	G	A	Pts	Num	PIM	Maj	Mnr	Fgt	Rgh	HHT	Hat	P/G
98-99	StL	11	0	2	2	0	0	0	16	0.0	0	0	0	0	0	0	4	8	0	4	0	0	0	0	.18

Scott Hannan

Pos: D **Shoots:** L **Ht:** 6'2" **Wt:** 210 **Born:** 1/23/79—Richmond, British Columbia **Age:** 20

Overall											Power Play			Shorthand			Penalty							Misc	
Year	Tm	GP	G	A	Pts	+/–	GW	GT	S	SPct	G	A	Pts	G	A	Pts	Num	PIM	Maj	Mnr	Fgt	Rgh	HHT	Hat	P/G
98-99	SJ	5	0	2	2	0	0	0	4	0.0	0	1	1	0	0	0	3	6	0	3	0	0	1	0	.40

Tavis Hansen

Pos: C **Shoots:** R **Ht:** 6'1" **Wt:** 180 **Born:** 6/17/75—Prince Albert, Saskatchewan **Age:** 24

Overall											Power Play			Shorthand			Penalty							Misc	
Year	Tm	GP	G	A	Pts	+/–	GW	GT	S	SPct	G	A	Pts	G	A	Pts	Num	PIM	Maj	Mnr	Fgt	Rgh	HHT	Hat	P/G
94-95	Wpg	1	0	0	0	0	0	0	0	–	0	0	0	0	0	0	0	0	0	0	0	0	0	0	.00
95-96												Did Not Play in NHL													
96-97	Pho	1	0	0	0	0	0	0	0	–	0	0	0	0	0	0	0	0	0	0	0	0	0	0	.00
97-98												Did Not Play in NHL													

Overall											Power Play			Shorthand			Penalty							Misc	
Year	Tm	GP	G	A	Pts	+/-	GW	GT	S	SPct	G	A	Pts	G	A	Pts	Num	PIM	Maj	Mnr	Fgt	Rgh	HHT	Hat	P/G
98-99	Pho	20	2	1	3	-4	0	0	14	14.3	0	0	0	0	0	0	3	12	2	1	2	0	1	0	.15
3 Years		22	2	1	3	-4	0	0	14	14.3	0	0	0	0	0	0	3	12	2	1	2	0	1	0	.14
Postseason																									
Year	Tm	GP	G	A	Pts	+/-	GW	OT	S	SPct	G	A	Pts	G	A	Pts	Num	PIM	Maj	Mnr	Fgt	Rgh	HHT	Hat	P/G
98-99	Pho	2	0	0	0	1	0	0	1	0.0	0	0	0	0	0	0	0	0	0	0	0	0	0	0	.00

David Harlock

Pos: D **Shoots:** L **Ht:** 6'2" **Wt:** 195 **Born:** 3/16/71—Toronto, Ontario **Age:** 28

Overall											Power Play			Shorthand			Penalty							Misc	
Year	Tm	GP	G	A	Pts	+/-	GW	GT	S	SPct	G	A	Pts	G	A	Pts	Num	PIM	Maj	Mnr	Fgt	Rgh	HHT	Hat	P/G
93-94	Tor	6	0	0	0	-2	0	0	2	0.0	0	0	0	0	0	0	0	0	0	0	0	0	0	0	.00
94-95	Tor	1	0	0	0	-1	0	0	0	–	0	0	0	0	0	0	0	0	0	0	0	0	0	0	.00
95-96	Tor	1	0	0	0	0	0	0	0	–	0	0	0	0	0	0	0	0	0	0	0	0	0	0	.00
96-97		Did Not Play in NHL																							
97-98	Was	6	0	0	0	2	0	0	2	0.0	0	0	0	0	0	0	2	4	0	2	0	0	1	0	.00
98-99	NYI	70	2	6	8	-16	0	0	35	5.7	0	0	0	0	0	0	34	68	0	34	0	0	15	0	.11
5 Years		84	2	6	8	-17	0	0	39	5.1	0	0	0	0	0	0	36	72	0	36	0	0	16	0	.10

Todd Harvey

(statistical profile on page 317)

Pos: RW **Shoots:** R **Ht:** 6'0" **Wt:** 200 **Born:** 2/17/75—Hamilton, Ontario **Age:** 24

Overall											Power Play			Shorthand			Penalty							Misc	
Year	Tm	GP	G	A	Pts	+/-	GW	GT	S	SPct	G	A	Pts	G	A	Pts	Num	PIM	Maj	Mnr	Fgt	Rgh	HHT	Hat	P/G
94-95	Dal	40	11	9	20	-3	1	0	64	17.2	2	6	8	0	0	0	19	67	7	11	7	3	3	1	.50
95-96	Dal	69	9	20	29	-13	1	0	101	8.9	3	8	11	0	0	0	51	136	6	43	5	16	6	0	.42
96-97	Dal	71	9	22	31	19	2	0	99	9.1	1	1	2	0	0	0	43	142	16	26	14	11	6	0	.44
97-98	Dal	59	9	10	19	5	1	0	88	10.2	0	2	2	0	0	0	36	104	8	27	8	14	4	0	.32
98-99	NYR	37	11	17	28	-1	2	1	58	19.0	6	8	14	0	0	0	30	72	4	26	4	12	5	0	.76
5 Years		276	49	78	127	7	7	1	410	12.0	12	25	37	0	0	0	179	521	41	133	38	56	24	1	.46
Postseason																									
Year	Tm	GP	G	A	Pts	+/-	GW	OT	S	SPct	G	A	Pts	G	A	Pts	Num	PIM	Maj	Mnr	Fgt	Rgh	HHT	Hat	P/G
94-95	Dal	5	0	0	0	-1	0	0	7	0.0	0	0	0	0	0	0	4	8	0	4	0	0	1	0	.00
96-97	Dal	7	0	1	1	-2	0	0	15	0.0	0	1	1	0	0	0	5	10	0	5	0	1	2	0	.14
2 Years		12	0	1	1	-3	0	0	22	0.0	0	1	1	0	0	0	9	18	0	9	0	1	3	0	.08

Dominik Hasek

(statistical profile on page 399)

Pos: G **Catches:** L **Ht:** 5'11" **Wt:** 168 **Born:** 1/29/65—Pardubice, Czechoslovakia **Age:** 34

Overall																Pen Shot		Offense		
Year	Tm	GP	GS	TP	W	L	T	Min	GA	GAA	Shots	SvPct	ShO	OE	PPGA	SHGA	Shots	GA	G	A	PIM
90-91	Chi	5	3	1	3	0	1	195	8	2.46	93	.914	0	0	1	0	0	0	0	0	0
91-92	Chi	20	18	3	10	4	1	1014	44	2.60	413	.893	1	2	16	1	0	0	0	0	8
92-93	Buf	28	22	2	11	10	4	1429	75	3.15	720	.896	0	7	24	4	0	0	0	0	0
93-94	Buf	58	53	1	30	20	6	3358	109	**1.95**	1552	**.930**	**7**	23	27	4	0	0	0	3	6
94-95	Buf	41	41	2	19	14	7	2416	85	**2.11**	1221	**.930**	**5**	**19**	21	6	1	0	0	0	2
95-96	Buf*	59	58	5	22	**30**	6	3417	161	2.83	2011	**.920**	2	**32**	50	5	1	0	0	1	6
96-97	Buf*	67	66	0	37	20	10	4037	153	2.27	2177	**.930**	5	**36**	45	4	**3**	1	0	3	30
97-98	Buf*	**72**	**72**	6	33	23	13	**4220**	147	2.09	**2149**	**.932**	**13**	**37**	52	10	1	1	0	2	12
98-99	Buf	64	64	3	30	18	14	3817	119	1.87	1877	**.937**	9	**34**	38	7	0	0	0	0	14
9 Years		414	397	23	195	139	62	23903	901	2.26	12213	.926	42	190	274	41	6	2	0	9	78
Postseason																					
Year	Tm	GP	GS	TP	W	L	Pct	Min	GA	GAA	Shots	SvPct	ShO	OE	PPGA	SHGA	Shots	GA	G	A	PIM
90-91	Chi	3	0	0	0	0	–	69	3	2.61	39	.923	0	0	2	0	0	0	0	1	0
91-92	Chi	3	1	1	0	2	.000	158	8	3.04	70	.886	0	0	2	0	0	0	0	0	0
92-93	Buf	1	0	0	1	0	1.000	45	1	1.33	24	.958	0	0	0	1	0	0	0	0	0
93-94	Buf	7	7	0	3	4	.429	484	13	1.61	261	.950	2	4	6	0	0	0	0	0	2
94-95	Buf	5	5	0	1	4	.200	309	18	3.50	131	.863	0	0	3	1	0	0	0	0	0
96-97	Buf	3	3	1	1	1	.500	153	5	1.96	68	.926	0	0	4	0	0	0	0	0	2
97-98	Buf	15	15	0	10	5	.667	948	32	2.03	514	.938	1	10	9	1	0	0	0	0	4
98-99	Buf	19	19	2	13	6	.684	1217	36	1.77	587	.939	2	10	14	0	1	1	0	1	8
8 Years		56	50	4	29	22	.569	3383	116	2.06	1694	.932	5	24	40	3	1	1	0	2	16

Derian Hatcher

(statistical profile on page 317)

Pos: D **Shoots:** L **Ht:** 6'5" **Wt:** 225 **Born:** 6/4/72—Sterling Heights, Michigan **Age:** 27

Overall											Power Play			Shorthand			Penalty							Misc	
Year	Tm	GP	G	A	Pts	+/–	GW	GT	S	SPct	G	A	Pts	G	A	Pts	Num	PIM	Maj	Mnr	Fgt	Rgh	HHT	Hat	P/G
91-92	Min	43	8	4	12	7	2	0	51	15.7	0	0	0	0	0	0	26	88	4	19	4	3	9	0	.28
92-93	Min	67	4	15	19	-27	1	1	73	5.5	0	7	7	0	0	0	64	178	6	54	5	17	13	0	.28
93-94	Dal	83	12	19	31	19	2	0	132	9.1	2	5	7	1	0	1	72	211	9	58	9	15	15	0	.37
94-95	Dal	43	5	11	16	3	2	0	74	6.8	2	4	6	0	0	0	41	105	5	35	4	7	9	0	.37
95-96	Dal	79	8	23	31	-12	1	0	125	6.4	2	7	9	0	0	0	55	129	1	52	1	15	7	0	.39
96-97	Dal*	63	3	19	22	8	0	0	96	3.1	0	1	1	0	1	1	33	97	5	26	4	7	2	0	.35
97-98	Dal	70	6	25	31	9	2	0	74	8.1	3	9	12	0	0	0	45	132	6	36	6	6	7	0	.44
98-99	Dal	80	9	21	30	21	2	0	125	7.2	3	2	5	0	1	1	38	102	6	31	5	3	8	0	.38
8 Years		528	55	137	192	28	12	1	750	7.3	12	35	47	1	2	3	374	1042	42	311	38	73	70	0	.36
Postseason																									
Year	Tm	GP	G	A	Pts	+/–	GW	OT	S	SPct	G	A	Pts	G	A	Pts	Num	PIM	Maj	Mnr	Fgt	Rgh	HHT	Hat	P/G
91-92	Min	5	0	2	2	1	0	0	10	0.0	0	0	0	0	0	0	4	8	0	4	0	1	2	0	.40
93-94	Dal	9	0	2	2	-2	0	0	17	0.0	0	1	1	0	0	0	7	14	0	7	0	3	2	0	.22
96-97	Dal	7	0	2	2	1	0	0	7	0.0	0	0	0	0	0	0	10	20	0	10	0	6	2	0	.29
97-98	Dal	17	3	3	6	-1	0	0	22	13.6	2	1	3	0	0	0	14	39	1	12	0	2	3	0	.35
98-99	Dal	18	1	6	7	4	0	0	28	3.6	0	3	3	0	1	1	12	24	0	12	0	6	0	0	.39
5 Years		56	4	15	19	3	0	0	84	4.8	2	5	7	0	1	1	47	105	1	45	0	18	9	0	.34

Kevin Hatcher

(statistical profile on page 317)

Pos: D **Shoots:** R **Ht:** 6'3" **Wt:** 232 **Born:** 9/9/66—Detroit, Michigan **Age:** 33

Overall											Power Play			Shorthand			Penalty							Misc	
Year	Tm	GP	G	A	Pts	+/–	GW	GT	S	SPct	G	A	Pts	G	A	Pts	Num	PIM	Maj	Mnr	Fgt	Rgh	HHT	Hat	P/G
84-85	Was	2	1	0	1	1	0	0	3	33.3	0	0	0	1	0	1	0	0	0	0	0	0	0	0	.50
85-86	Was	79	9	10	19	6	1	0	132	6.8	1	–	–	0	–	–	–	119	–	–	–	–	–	0	.24
86-87	Was	78	8	16	24	-29	2	0	100	8.0	1	–	–	0	–	–	–	144	–	–	–	–	–	0	.31
87-88	Was	71	14	27	41	1	3	0	181	7.7	5	–	–	0	–	–	–	137	–	–	–	–	–	0	.58
88-89	Was	62	13	27	40	19	2	0	148	8.8	3	–	–	0	–	–	–	101	–	–	–	–	–	0	.65
89-90	Was*	**80**	13	41	54	4	2	0	240	5.4	4	–	–	0	–	–	–	102	–	–	–	–	–	0	.68
90-91	Was*	79	24	50	74	-10	3	0	267	9.0	9	–	–	2	–	–	–	69	–	–	–	–	–	0	.94
91-92	Was*	79	17	37	54	18	2	1	246	6.9	8	19	27	1	4	5	39	105	1	35	0	5	13	0	.68
92-93	Was	83	34	45	79	-7	6	0	329	10.3	13	20	33	1	0	1	46	114	2	42	0	5	14	1	.95
93-94	Was	72	16	24	40	-13	3	0	217	7.4	6	13	19	0	2	2	39	108	2	34	1	10	14	0	.56
94-95	Dal	47	10	19	29	-4	2	1	138	7.2	3	10	13	0	0	0	26	66	2	23	2	3	9	0	.62
95-96	Dal*	74	15	26	41	-24	3	2	237	6.3	7	15	22	0	0	0	29	58	0	29	0	3	10	1	.55
96-97	Pit*	80	15	39	54	11	1	0	199	7.5	9	16	25	0	1	1	38	103	1	34	1	3	14	0	.68
97-98	Pit	74	19	29	48	-3	3	1	169	11.2	13	11	24	1	2	3	25	66	0	23	0	1	9	0	.65
98-99	Pit	66	11	27	38	11	3	0	131	8.4	4	11	15	2	0	2	12	24	0	12	0	2	3	0	.58
15 Years		1026	219	417	636	-19	36	5	2737	8.0	86	–	–	8	–	–	–	1316	–	–	–	–	–	2	.62
Postseason																									
Year	Tm	GP	G	A	Pts	+/–	GW	OT	S	SPct	G	A	Pts	G	A	Pts	Num	PIM	Maj	Mnr	Fgt	Rgh	HHT	Hat	P/G
84-85	Was	1	0	0	0	1	0	0	1	0.0	0	0	0	0	0	0	0	0	0	0	0	0	0	0	.00
85-86	Was	9	1	1	2	5	0	0	11	9.1	0	–	–	0	–	–	–	19	–	–	–	–	–	0	.22
86-87	Was	7	1	0	1	-2	0	0	21	4.8	0	0	0	0	0	0	–	20	–	–	–	–	–	0	.14
87-88	Was	14	5	7	12	6	1	0	44	11.4	1	–	–	0	–	–	–	55	–	–	–	–	–	0	.86
88-89	Was	6	1	4	5	-3	0	0	19	5.3	1	–	–	0	–	–	–	20	–	–	–	–	–	0	.83
89-90	Was	11	0	8	8	4	0	0	37	0.0	0	–	–	0	–	–	–	32	–	–	–	–	–	0	.73
90-91	Was	11	3	3	6	-3	0	0	54	5.6	2	–	–	0	–	–	4	8	0	4	0	–	–	0	.55
91-92	Was	7	2	4	6	4	0	0	18	11.1	0	3	3	1	0	1	8	19	1	7	1	0	1	0	.86
92-93	Was	6	0	1	1	-5	0	0	18	0.0	0	1	1	0	0	0	7	14	0	7	0	3	0	0	.17
93-94	Was	11	3	4	7	-2	0	0	40	7.5	0	1	1	1	0	1	13	37	1	11	0	1	3	0	.64
94-95	Dal	5	2	1	3	-4	1	0	18	11.1	1	1	2	0	0	0	1	2	0	1	0	0	0	0	.60
96-97	Pit	5	1	1	2	-5	0	0	12	8.3	1	1	2	0	0	0	2	4	0	2	0	0	1	0	.40
97-98	Pit	6	1	0	1	1	0	0	15	6.7	1	0	1	0	0	0	6	12	0	6	0	1	3	0	.17
98-99	Pit	13	2	3	5	1	0	0	22	9.1	1	1	2	0	0	0	2	4	0	2	0	0	0	0	.38
14 Years		112	22	37	59	-2	2	0	330	6.7	8	–	–	2	–	–	–	246	–	–	–	–	–	0	.53

Dwayne Hay

Pos: LW **Shoots:** R **Ht:** 6'1" **Wt:** 183 **Born:** 2/11/77—London, Ontario **Age:** 22

Overall											Power Play			Shorthand			Penalty							Misc	
Year	Tm	GP	G	A	Pts	+/–	GW	GT	S	SPct	G	A	Pts	G	A	Pts	Num	PIM	Maj	Mnr	Fgt	Rgh	HHT	Hat	P/G
97-98	Was	2	0	0	0	0	0	0	1	0.0	0	0	0	0	0	0	1	2	0	1	0	0	0	0	.00

		Overall								Power Play			Shorthand			Penalty							Misc	
Year	Tm	GP	G	A	Pts	+/-	GW	GT	S	SPct	G	A	Pts	G	A	Pts	Num	PIM	Maj	Mnr	Fgt	Rgh	HHT	Hat	P/G
98-99	Fla	9	0	0	0	-1	0	0	3	0.0	0	0	0	0	0	0	0	0	0	0	0	0	0	0	.00
2 Years		11	0	0	0	-1	0	0	4	0.0	0	0	0	0	0	0	1	2	0	1	0	0	0	0	.00

Glenn Healy

Pos: G **Catches:** L **Ht:** 5'8" **Wt:** 194 **Born:** 8/23/62—Pickering, Ontario **Age:** 37

		Overall															Pen Shot		Offense		
Year	Tm	GP	GS	TP	W	L	T	Min	GA	GAA	Shots	SvPct	ShO	OE	PPGA	SHGA	Shots	GA	G	A	PIM
85-86	LA	1	–	–	0	0	0	51	6	7.06	35	.829	0	–	–	–	0	0	0	0	0
86-87		Did Not Play in NHL																			
87-88	LA	34	–	–	12	18	1	1869	135	4.33	1005	.866	1	–	–	–	0	0	0	2	6
88-89	LA	48	–	–	25	19	2	2699	192	4.27	1509	.873	0	–	–	–	0	0	0	1	28
89-90	NYI	39	–	–	12	19	6	2197	128	3.50	1210	.894	2	–	–	–	0	0	0	1	7
90-91	NYI	53	–	–	18	24	9	2999	166	3.32	1557	.893	0	–	–	–	0	0	0	2	0
91-92	NYI	37	31	4	14	16	4	1960	124	3.80	1045	.881	1	8	39	4	0	0	0	1	18
92-93	NYI	47	45	4	22	20	2	2655	146	3.30	1316	.889	1	13	43	6	1	0	0	2	2
93-94	NYR	29	17	4	10	12	2	1368	69	3.03	567	.878	2	3	26	1	0	0	0	2	2
94-95	NYR	17	13	0	8	6	1	888	35	2.36	377	.907	1	2	9	3	0	0	0	2	2
95-96	NYR	44	42	2	17	14	11	2564	124	2.90	1237	.900	2	12	55	6	0	0	0	1	8
96-97	NYR	23	21	0	5	12	4	1357	59	2.61	632	.907	1	7	20	0	0	0	0	0	4
97-98	Tor	21	17	3	4	10	2	1068	53	2.98	453	.883	0	2	15	1	0	0	0	0	0
98-99	Tor	9	9	0	6	3	0	546	27	2.97	257	.895	0	2	11	0	0	0	0	0	0
13 Years		402	–	–	153	173	44	22221	1264	3.41	11200	.887	11	–	–	–	1	0	0	14	77
		Postseason																			
Year	Tm	GP	GS	TP	W	L	Pct	Min	GA	GAA	Shots	SvPct	ShO	OE	PPGA	SHGA	Shots	GA	G	A	PIM
87-88	LA	4	–	–	1	3	.250	240	20	5.00	128	.844	0	–	–	–	0	0	0	0	0
88-89	LA	3	–	–	0	1	.000	97	6	3.71	59	.898	0	–	–	–	0	0	0	0	2
89-90	NYI	4	–	–	1	2	.333	166	9	3.25	79	.886	0	–	–	–	0	0	0	1	0
92-93	NYI	18	18	3	9	8	.529	1109	59	3.19	524	.887	0	3	14	2	0	0	0	3	0
93-94	NYR	2	0	0	0	0	–	68	1	0.88	17	.941	0	0	0	0	0	0	0	0	0
94-95	NYR	5	4	1	2	1	.667	230	13	3.39	93	.860	0	0	1	1	0	0	0	0	0
98-99	Tor	1	0	0	0	0	–	20	0	0.00	5	1.000	0	0	0	0	0	0	0	0	0
7 Years		37	–	–	13	15	.464	1930	108	3.36	905	.881	0	–	–	–	0	0	0	4	2

Guy Hebert

(statistical profile on page 399)

Pos: G **Catches:** L **Ht:** 5'11" **Wt:** 185 **Born:** 1/7/67—Troy, New York **Age:** 32

		Overall															Pen Shot		Offense		
Year	Tm	GP	GS	TP	W	L	T	Min	GA	GAA	Shots	SvPct	ShO	OE	PPGA	SHGA	Shots	GA	G	A	PIM
91-92	StL	13	11	0	5	5	1	738	36	2.93	393	.908	0	6	10	0	0	0	0	1	0
92-93	StL	24	17	1	8	8	2	1210	74	3.67	630	.883	1	3	22	9	0	0	0	0	2
93-94	Anh	52	49	3	20	27	3	2991	141	2.83	1513	.907	2	20	36	8	0	0	0	0	2
94-95	Anh	39	34	4	12	20	4	2092	109	3.13	1132	.904	2	13	28	6	0	0	0	0	2
95-96	Anh	59	58	6	28	23	5	3326	157	2.83	1820	.914	4	23	54	3	0	0	0	0	6
96-97	Anh*	67	66	8	29	25	12	3863	172	2.67	2133	.919	4	31	48	9	1	0	0	1	4
97-98	Anh	46	43	4	13	24	6	2660	130	2.93	1339	.903	3	13	29	5	**4**	0	0	1	4
98-99	Anh	69	67	3	31	29	9	4083	165	2.42	**2114**	.922	6	27	50	7	1	1	0	1	0
8 Years		369	345	29	146	161	42	20963	984	2.82	11074	.911	22	136	277	47	6	1	0	4	20
		Postseason																			
Year	Tm	GP	GS	TP	W	L	Pct	Min	GA	GAA	Shots	SvPct	ShO	OE	PPGA	SHGA	Shots	GA	G	A	PIM
92-93	StL	1	0	1	0	0	–	2	0	0.00	1	1.000	0	0	0	0	0	0	0	0	0
96-97	Anh	9	9	2	4	4	.500	534	18	2.02	255	.929	1	4	3	0	0	0	0	0	0
98-99	Anh	4	4	1	0	3	.000	208	15	4.33	124	.879	0	1	7	0	0	0	0	0	0
3 Years		14	13	4	4	7	.364	744	33	2.66	380	.913	1	5	10	0	0	0	0	0	0

Jochen Hecht

Pos: C **Shoots:** L **Ht:** 6'3" **Wt:** 196 **Born:** 6/21/77—Mannheim, West Germany **Age:** 22

		Overall								Power Play			Shorthand			Penalty							Misc	
Year	Tm	GP	G	A	Pts	+/-	GW	GT	S	SPct	G	A	Pts	G	A	Pts	Num	PIM	Maj	Mnr	Fgt	Rgh	HHT	Hat	P/G
98-99	StL	3	0	0	0	-2	0	0	4	0.0	0	0	0	0	0	0	0	0	0	0	0	0	0	0	.00
		Postseason																							
Year	Tm	GP	G	A	Pts	+/-	GW	OT	S	SPct	G	A	Pts	G	A	Pts	Num	PIM	Maj	Mnr	Fgt	Rgh	HHT	Hat	P/G
98-99	StL	5	2	0	2	4	0	0	20	10.0	0	0	0	0	0	0	0	0	0	0	0	0	0	0	.40

Bret Hedican

(statistical profile on page 318)

Pos: D **Shoots:** L **Ht:** 6'2" **Wt:** 205 **Born:** 8/10/70—St. Paul, Minnesota **Age:** 29

Overall											Power Play			Shorthand			Penalty							Misc	
Year	Tm	GP	G	A	Pts	+/–	GW	GT	S	SPct	G	A	Pts	G	A	Pts	Num	PIM	Maj	Mnr	Fgt	Rgh	HHT	Hat	P/G
91-92	StL	4	1	0	1	1	0	0	1	100.0	0	0	0	0	0	0	0	0	0	0	0	0	0	0	.25
92-93	StL	42	0	8	8	-2	0	0	40	0.0	0	1	1	0	0	0	15	30	0	15	0	0	10	0	.19
93-94	2Tm	69	0	12	12	-7	0	0	88	0.0	0	2	2	0	0	0	29	64	2	27	2	2	11	0	.17
94-95	Van	45	2	11	13	-3	0	0	56	3.6	0	3	3	0	2	2	17	34	0	17	0	6	7	0	.29
95-96	Van	77	6	23	29	8	0	0	113	5.3	1	7	8	0	4	4	40	83	1	39	1	4	13	0	.38
96-97	Van	67	4	15	19	-3	1	0	93	4.3	2	3	5	0	1	1	20	51	1	18	1	7	4	0	.28
97-98	Van	71	3	24	27	3	0	1	84	3.6	1	5	6	0	7	7	34	79	1	32	1	5	12	0	.38
98-99	2Tm	67	5	18	23	5	1	1	90	5.6	0	3	3	2	1	3	24	51	1	23	1	0	8	0	.34
93-94	StL	61	0	11	11	-8	0	0	78	0.0	0	1	1	0	0	0	29	64	2	27	2	2	11	0	.18
93-94	Van	8	0	1	1	1	0	0	10	0.0	0	1	1	0	0	0	0	0	0	0	0	0	0	0	.13
98-99	Van	42	2	11	13	7	0	1	52	3.8	0	3	3	2	0	2	17	34	0	17	0	0	7	0	.31
98-99	Fla	25	3	7	10	-2	1	0	38	7.9	0	0	0	0	1	1	7	17	1	6	1	0	1	0	.40
8 Years		442	21	111	132	2	2	2	565	3.7	4	24	28	2	15	17	179	392	6	171	6	24	65	0	.30
Postseason																									
Year	Tm	GP	G	A	Pts	+/–	GW	OT	S	SPct	G	A	Pts	G	A	Pts	Num	PIM	Maj	Mnr	Fgt	Rgh	HHT	Hat	P/G
91-92	StL	5	0	0	0	1	0	0	6	0.0	0	0	0	0	0	0	0	0	0	0	0	0	0	0	.00
92-93	StL	10	0	0	0	-4	0	0	5	0.0	0	0	0	0	0	0	7	14	0	7	0	0	5	0	.00
93-94	Van	24	1	6	7	13	0	0	22	4.5	0	1	1	0	0	0	8	16	0	8	0	4	3	0	.29
94-95	Van	11	0	2	2	-5	0	0	6	0.0	0	0	0	0	0	0	3	6	0	3	0	2	0	0	.18
95-96	Van	6	0	1	1	-2	0	0	2	0.0	0	0	0	0	0	0	5	10	0	5	0	1	2	0	.17
5 Years		56	1	9	10	3	0	0	41	2.4	0	1	1	0	0	0	23	46	0	23	0	7	10	0	.18

Shawn Heins

Pos: D **Shoots:** L **Ht:** 6'4" **Wt:** 220 **Born:** 12/24/73—Eganville, Ontario **Age:** 26

Overall											Power Play			Shorthand			Penalty							Misc	
Year	Tm	GP	G	A	Pts	+/–	GW	GT	S	SPct	G	A	Pts	G	A	Pts	Num	PIM	Maj	Mnr	Fgt	Rgh	HHT	Hat	P/G
98-99	SJ	5	0	0	0	0	0	0	4	0.0	0	0	0	0	0	0	5	13	1	4	1	0	1	0	.00

Steve Heinze

(statistical profile on page 318)

Pos: RW **Shoots:** R **Ht:** 6'0" **Wt:** 202 **Born:** 1/30/70—Lawrence, Massachusetts **Age:** 29

Overall											Power Play			Shorthand			Penalty							Misc	
Year	Tm	GP	G	A	Pts	+/–	GW	GT	S	SPct	G	A	Pts	G	A	Pts	Num	PIM	Maj	Mnr	Fgt	Rgh	HHT	Hat	P/G
91-92	Bos	14	3	4	7	-1	2	0	29	10.3	0	0	0	0	0	0	3	6	0	3	0	0	1	0	.50
92-93	Bos	73	18	13	31	20	4	0	146	12.3	0	0	0	2	2	4	12	24	0	12	0	2	8	1	.42
93-94	Bos	77	10	11	21	-2	1	0	183	5.5	0	0	0	2	1	3	13	32	2	11	2	1	4	0	.27
94-95	Bos	36	7	9	16	0	0	0	70	10.0	0	0	0	1	0	1	10	23	1	9	1	4	3	0	.44
95-96	Bos	76	16	12	28	-3	3	0	129	12.4	0	0	0	1	1	2	20	43	1	19	1	1	12	1	.37
96-97	Bos	30	17	8	25	-8	2	0	96	17.7	4	1	5	2	0	2	12	27	1	11	1	0	5	0	.83
97-98	Bos	61	26	20	46	8	6	0	160	16.3	9	7	16	0	0	0	19	54	0	17	0	0	10	2	.75
98-99	Bos	73	22	18	40	7	3	0	146	15.1	9	5	14	0	0	0	15	30	0	15	0	1	5	0	.55
8 Years		440	119	95	214	21	21	0	959	12.4	22	13	35	8	4	12	104	239	5	97	5	9	48	4	.49
Postseason																									
Year	Tm	GP	G	A	Pts	+/–	GW	OT	S	SPct	G	A	Pts	G	A	Pts	Num	PIM	Maj	Mnr	Fgt	Rgh	HHT	Hat	P/G
91-92	Bos	7	0	3	3	3	0	0	6	0.0	0	0	0	0	0	0	3	17	1	1	0	0	0	0	.43
92-93	Bos	4	1	1	2	-1	0	0	6	16.7	0	0	0	0	0	0	1	2	0	1	0	1	0	0	.50
93-94	Bos	13	2	3	5	6	0	0	16	12.5	0	0	0	0	0	0	2	7	1	1	1	1	0	0	.38
94-95	Bos	5	0	0	0	0	0	0	10	0.0	0	0	0	0	0	0	0	0	0	0	0	0	0	0	.00
95-96	Bos	5	1	1	2	1	0	0	20	5.0	0	0	0	1	0	1	2	4	0	2	0	0	1	0	.40
97-98	Bos	6	0	0	0	-4	0	0	15	0.0	0	0	0	0	0	0	3	6	0	3	0	0	3	0	.00
98-99	Bos	12	4	3	7	-1	0	0	23	17.4	2	1	3	0	0	0	0	0	0	0	0	0	0	0	.58
7 Years		52	8	11	19	4	0	0	96	8.3	2	1	3	1	0	1	11	36	2	8	1	2	4	0	.37

Milan Hejduk

(statistical profile on page 318)

Pos: RW **Shoots:** R **Ht:** 5'11" **Wt:** 165 **Born:** 2/14/76—Ssti-nad-Labem, Czechoslovakia **Age:** 23

Overall											Power Play			Shorthand			Penalty							Misc	
Year	Tm	GP	G	A	Pts	+/–	GW	GT	S	SPct	G	A	Pts	G	A	Pts	Num	PIM	Maj	Mnr	Fgt	Rgh	HHT	Hat	P/G
98-99	Col	82	14	34	48	8	5	0	178	7.9	4	7	11	0	0	0	13	26	0	13	0	0	5	0	.59

Postseason																									
Year	Tm	GP	G	A	Pts	+/–	GW	OT	S	SPct	G	A	Pts	G	A	Pts	Num	PIM	Maj	Mnr	Fgt	Rgh	HHT	Hat	P/G
98-99	Col	16	6	6	12	3	3	2	38	15.8	1	1	2	0	0	0	2	4	0	2	0	0	0	0	.75

Sami Helenius

Pos: D **Shoots:** L **Ht:** 6'5" **Wt:** 220 **Born:** 1/22/74—Helsinki, Finland **Age:** 25

Overall											Power Play			Shorthand			Penalty							Misc	
Year	Tm	GP	G	A	Pts	+/–	GW	GT	S	SPct	G	A	Pts	G	A	Pts	Num	PIM	Maj	Mnr	Fgt	Rgh	HHT	Hat	P/G
96-97	Cgy	3	0	1	1	1	0	0	1	0.0	0	0	0	0	0	0	0	0	0	0	0	0	0	0	.33
97-98		Did Not Play in NHL																							
98-99	2Tm	8	1	0	1	-5	0	0	4	25.0	0	0	0	1	0	1	10	23	1	9	1	1	1	0	.13
98-99	Cgy	4	0	0	0	-2	0	0	1	0.0	0	0	0	0	0	0	4	8	0	4	0	1	0	0	.00
98-99	TB	4	1	0	1	-3	0	0	3	33.3	0	0	0	1	0	1	6	15	1	5	1	0	1	0	.25
2 Years		11	1	1	2	-4	0	0	5	20.0	0	0	0	1	0	1	10	23	1	9	1	1	1	0	.18

Bryan Helmer

Pos: D **Shoots:** R **Ht:** 6'2" **Wt:** 209 **Born:** 7/15/72—Sault Ste. Marie, Ontario **Age:** 27

Overall											Power Play			Shorthand			Penalty							Misc	
Year	Tm	GP	G	A	Pts	+/–	GW	GT	S	SPct	G	A	Pts	G	A	Pts	Num	PIM	Maj	Mnr	Fgt	Rgh	HHT	Hat	P/G
98-99	2Tm	40	0	4	4	5	0	0	49	0.0	0	0	0	0	0	0	14	42	2	11	2	0	5	0	.10
98-99	Pho	11	0	0	0	2	0	0	11	0.0	0	0	0	0	0	0	6	23	1	4	1	0	3	0	.00
98-99	StL	29	0	4	4	3	0	0	38	0.0	0	0	0	0	0	0	8	19	1	7	1	0	2	0	.14

Jay Henderson

Pos: LW **Shoots:** L **Ht:** 5'11" **Wt:** 188 **Born:** 9/17/78—Edmonton, Alberta **Age:** 21

Overall											Power Play			Shorthand			Penalty							Misc	
Year	Tm	GP	G	A	Pts	+/–	GW	GT	S	SPct	G	A	Pts	G	A	Pts	Num	PIM	Maj	Mnr	Fgt	Rgh	HHT	Hat	P/G
98-99	Bos	4	0	0	0	-1	0	0	4	0.0	0	0	0	0	0	0	1	2	0	1	0	0	0	0	.00

Matt Henderson

Pos: RW **Shoots:** R **Ht:** 5'11" **Wt:** 188 **Born:** 6/22/74—White Bear Lake, Minnesota **Age:** 25

Overall											Power Play			Shorthand			Penalty							Misc	
Year	Tm	GP	G	A	Pts	+/–	GW	GT	S	SPct	G	A	Pts	G	A	Pts	Num	PIM	Maj	Mnr	Fgt	Rgh	HHT	Hat	P/G
98-99	Nsh	2	0	0	0	-1	0	0	0	–	0	0	0	0	0	0	1	2	0	1	0	0	1	0	.00

Darby Hendrickson

Pos: C **Shoots:** L **Ht:** 6'2" **Wt:** 195 **Born:** 8/28/72—Richfield, Minnesota **Age:** 27

Overall											Power Play			Shorthand			Penalty							Misc	
Year	Tm	GP	G	A	Pts	+/–	GW	GT	S	SPct	G	A	Pts	G	A	Pts	Num	PIM	Maj	Mnr	Fgt	Rgh	HHT	Hat	P/G
93-94		Did Not Play in Regular Season																							
94-95	Tor	8	0	1	1	0	0	0	4	0.0	0	0	0	0	0	0	2	4	0	2	0	0	1	0	.13
95-96	2Tm	62	7	10	17	-8	1	0	73	9.6	0	1	1	0	0	0	37	80	2	35	2	10	11	0	.27
96-97	Tor	64	11	6	17	-20	0	2	105	10.5	0	1	1	1	0	1	19	47	3	16	3	10	3	0	.27
97-98	Tor	80	8	4	12	-20	0	0	115	7.0	0	0	0	0	0	0	32	67	1	31	1	5	10	0	.15
98-99	2Tm	62	4	5	9	-19	0	0	70	5.7	1	0	1	0	0	0	23	52	2	21	2	3	9	0	.15
95-96	Tor	46	6	6	12	-2	0	0	43	14.0	0	1	1	0	0	0	22	47	1	21	1	4	8	0	.26
95-96	NYI	16	1	4	5	-6	1	0	30	3.3	0	0	0	0	0	0	15	33	1	14	1	6	3	0	.31
98-99	Tor	35	2	3	5	-4	0	0	34	5.9	0	0	0	0	0	0	12	30	2	10	2	2	4	0	.14
98-99	Van	27	2	2	4	-15	0	0	36	5.6	1	0	1	0	0	0	11	22	0	11	0	1	5	0	.15
5 Years		276	30	26	56	-67	1	2	367	8.2	1	2	3	1	0	1	113	250	8	105	8	28	34	0	.20

Postseason																									
Year	Tm	GP	G	A	Pts	+/–	GW	OT	S	SPct	G	A	Pts	G	A	Pts	Num	PIM	Maj	Mnr	Fgt	Rgh	HHT	Hat	P/G
93-94	Tor	2	0	0	0	-1	0	0	1	0.0	0	0	0	0	0	0	0	0	0	0	0	0	0	0	.00

Matt Herr

Pos: C **Shoots:** L **Ht:** 6'1" **Wt:** 205 **Born:** 5/26/76—Hackensack, New Jersey **Age:** 23

Overall											Power Play			Shorthand			Penalty							Misc	
Year	Tm	GP	G	A	Pts	+/–	GW	GT	S	SPct	G	A	Pts	G	A	Pts	Num	PIM	Maj	Mnr	Fgt	Rgh	HHT	Hat	P/G
98-99	Was	30	2	2	4	-7	0	0	40	5.0	1	1	2	0	0	0	4	8	0	4	0	0	1	0	.13

Jamie Heward

(statistical profile on page 318)

Pos: RW **Shoots:** R **Ht:** 6'2" **Wt:** 207 **Born:** 3/30/71—Regina, Saskatchewan **Age:** 28

		Overall									Power Play			Shorthand			Penalty							Misc	
Year	**Tm**	**GP**	**G**	**A**	**Pts**	**+/-**	**GW**	**GT**	**S**	**SPct**	**G**	**A**	**Pts**	**G**	**A**	**Pts**	**Num**	**PIM**	**Maj**	**Mnr**	**Fgt**	**Rgh**	**HHT**	**Hat**	**P/G**
95-96	Tor	5	0	0	0	-1	0	0	8	0.0	0	0	0	0	0	0	0	0	0	0	0	0	0	0	.00
96-97	Tor	20	1	4	5	-6	0	0	23	4.3	0	2	2	0	0	0	3	6	0	3	0	0	2	0	.25
97-98		Did Not Play in NHL																							
98-99	Nsh	63	6	12	18	-24	1	0	124	4.8	4	7	11	0	0	0	18	44	0	17	0	1	10	0	.29
3 Years		88	7	16	23	-31	1	0	155	4.5	4	9	13	0	0	0	21	50	0	20	0	1	12	0	.26

Ron Hextall

(statistical profile on page 399)

Pos: G **Catches:** L **Ht:** 6'3" **Wt:** 195 **Born:** 5/3/64—Winnipeg, Manitoba **Age:** 35

		Overall															Pen Shot		Offense		
Year	**Tm**	**GP**	**GS**	**TP**	**W**	**L**	**T**	**Min**	**GA**	**GAA**	**Shots**	**SvPct**	**ShO**	**OE**	**PPGA**	**SHGA**	**Shots**	**GA**	**G**	**A**	**PIM**
86-87	Phi	**66**	–	–	**37**	21	6	**3799**	190	3.00	**1933**	**.902**	1	–	–	–	0	0	0	6	104
87-88	Phi*	62	–	–	30	22	7	3561	208	3.50	1817	.886	0	–	–	–	2	**2**	1	6	104
88-89	Phi	64	–	–	30	28	6	3756	202	3.23	1860	.891	0	–	–	–	0	0	0	8	113
89-90	Phi	8	–	–	4	2	1	419	29	4.15	219	.868	0	–	–	–	0	0	0	0	14
90-91	Phi	36	–	–	13	16	5	2035	106	3.13	982	.892	0	–	–	–	0	0	0	1	10
91-92	Phi	45	43	1	16	21	6	2668	151	3.40	1294	.883	3	12	42	10	0	0	0	3	35
92-93	Que	54	52	8	29	16	5	2988	172	3.45	1529	.888	0	16	48	**13**	0	0	0	2	56
93-94	NYI	65	61	8	27	26	6	3581	184	3.08	1801	.898	5	19	57	6	1	**1**	0	3	52
94-95	Phi	31	31	2	17	9	4	1824	88	2.89	801	.890	1	5	23	**7**	1	**1**	0	0	13
95-96	Phi	53	51	3	31	13	7	3102	112	**2.17**	1292	.913	4	15	31	5	0	0	0	1	28
96-97	Phi	55	54	7	31	16	5	3094	132	2.56	1285	.897	5	11	27	4	0	0	0	0	43
97-98	Phi	46	44	2	21	17	7	2688	97	2.17	1089	.911	4	9	28	5	2	0	0	0	10
98-99	Phi	23	20	1	10	7	4	1235	52	2.53	464	.888	0	1	12	3	0	0	0	2	2
13 Years		608	–	–	296	214	69	34750	1723	2.97	16366	.895	23	–	–	–	6	4	1	32	584
		Postseason																			
Year	**Tm**	**GP**	**GS**	**TP**	**W**	**L**	**Pct**	**Min**	**GA**	**GAA**	**Shots**	**SvPct**	**ShO**	**OE**	**PPGA**	**SHGA**	**Shots**	**GA**	**G**	**A**	**PIM**
86-87	Phi	26	–	–	15	11	.577	1540	71	2.77	769	.908	2	–	–	–	0	0	0	1	43
87-88	Phi	7	–	–	2	4	.333	379	30	4.75	196	.847	0	–	–	–	0	0	0	2	30
88-89	Phi	15	–	–	8	7	.533	886	49	3.32	445	.890	0	–	–	–	0	0	1	0	28
92-93	Que	6	6	1	2	4	.333	372	18	2.90	211	.915	0	4	3	0	0	0	0	0	0
93-94	NYI	3	3	1	0	3	.000	158	16	6.08	80	.800	0	0	7	0	0	0	0	0	4
94-95	Phi	15	15	1	10	5	.667	897	42	2.81	437	.904	0	7	15	1	0	0	0	1	4
95-96	Phi	12	12	1	6	6	.500	760	27	2.13	319	.915	0	1	7	3	0	0	0	0	6
96-97	Phi	8	7	0	4	3	.571	444	22	2.97	203	.892	0	1	8	2	0	0	0	0	0
97-98	Phi	1	0	0	0	0	–	20	1	3.00	8	.875	0	0	0	0	0	0	0	0	0
9 Years		93	–	–	47	43	.522	5456	276	3.04	2668	.897	2	–	–	–	0	0	1	4	115

Alex Hicks

Pos: LW **Shoots:** L **Ht:** 6'0" **Wt:** 195 **Born:** 9/4/69—Calgary, Alberta **Age:** 30

		Overall									Power Play			Shorthand			Penalty							Misc	
Year	**Tm**	**GP**	**G**	**A**	**Pts**	**+/-**	**GW**	**GT**	**S**	**SPct**	**G**	**A**	**Pts**	**G**	**A**	**Pts**	**Num**	**PIM**	**Maj**	**Mnr**	**Fgt**	**Rgh**	**HHT**	**Hat**	**P/G**
95-96	Anh	64	10	11	21	11	2	1	83	12.0	0	0	0	0	0	0	14	37	3	11	3	1	3	0	.33
96-97	2Tm	73	7	21	28	-5	3	0	78	9.0	0	0	0	0	1	1	32	90	6	25	6	9	4	0	.38
97-98	Pit	58	7	13	20	4	1	1	78	9.0	0	1	1	0	1	1	16	54	2	12	2	5	2	0	.34
98-99	2Tm	55	0	7	7	-5	0	0	51	0.0	0	0	0	0	1	1	18	62	6	11	6	3	4	0	.13
96-97	Anh	18	2	6	8	1	0	0	21	9.5	0	0	0	0	0	0	7	14	0	7	0	3	1	0	.44
96-97	Pit	55	5	15	20	-6	3	0	57	8.8	0	0	0	0	1	1	25	76	6	18	6	6	3	0	.36
98-99	SJ	4	0	1	1	-1	0	0	4	0.0	0	0	0	0	0	0	2	4	0	2	0	0	1	0	.25
98-99	Fla	51	0	6	6	-4	0	0	47	0.0	0	0	0	0	1	1	16	58	6	9	6	3	3	0	.12
4 Years		250	24	52	76	5	6	2	290	8.3	0	1	1	0	3	3	80	243	17	59	17	18	13	0	.30
		Postseason																							
Year	**Tm**	**GP**	**G**	**A**	**Pts**	**+/-**	**GW**	**OT**	**S**	**SPct**	**G**	**A**	**Pts**	**G**	**A**	**Pts**	**Num**	**PIM**	**Maj**	**Mnr**	**Fgt**	**Rgh**	**HHT**	**Hat**	**P/G**
96-97	Pit	5	0	1	1	-1	0	0	2	0.0	0	0	0	0	0	0	1	2	0	1	0	0	0	0	.20
97-98	Pit	6	0	0	0	-5	0	0	6	0.0	0	0	0	0	0	0	1	2	0	1	0	0	0	0	.00
2 Years		11	0	1	1	-6	0	0	8	0.0	0	0	0	0	0	0	2	4	0	2	0	0	0	0	.09

Matt Higgins

Pos: C **Shoots:** L **Ht:** 6'2" **Wt:** 182 **Born:** 10/29/77—Calgary, Alberta **Age:** 22

Overall											Power Play			Shorthand			Penalty							Misc	
Year	Tm	GP	G	A	Pts	+/–	GW	GT	S	SPct	G	A	Pts	G	A	Pts	Num	PIM	Maj	Mnr	Fgt	Rgh	HHT	Hat	P/G
97-98	Mon	1	0	0	0	-1	0	0	1	0.0	0	0	0	0	0	0	0	0	0	0	0	0	0	0	.00
98-99	Mon	25	1	0	1	-2	0	0	12	8.3	0	0	0	0	0	0	0	0	0	0	0	0	0	0	.04
2 Years		26	1	0	1	-3	0	0	13	7.7	0	0	0	0	0	0	0	0	0	0	0	0	0	0	.04

Sean Hill

(statistical profile on page 319)

Pos: D **Shoots:** R **Ht:** 6'0" **Wt:** 203 **Born:** 2/14/70—Duluth, Minnesota **Age:** 29

Overall											Power Play			Shorthand			Penalty							Misc	
Year	Tm	GP	G	A	Pts	+/–	GW	GT	S	SPct	G	A	Pts	G	A	Pts	Num	PIM	Maj	Mnr	Fgt	Rgh	HHT	Hat	P/G
90-91		Did Not Play in Regular Season																							
91-92		Did Not Play in Regular Season																							
92-93	Mon	31	2	6	8	-5	1	0	37	5.4	1	2	3	0	0	0	24	54	2	22	2	3	11	0	.26
93-94	Anh	68	7	20	27	-12	1	0	165	4.2	2	12	14	1	1	2	35	78	0	34	0	7	10	0	.40
94-95	Ott	45	1	14	15	-11	0	0	107	0.9	0	6	6	0	0	0	15	30	0	15	0	2	7	0	.33
95-96	Ott	80	7	14	21	-26	2	0	157	4.5	2	2	4	0	2	2	39	94	0	37	0	6	16	0	.26
96-97	Ott	5	0	0	0	1	0	0	9	0.0	0	0	0	0	0	0	2	4	0	2	0	0	0	0	.00
97-98	2Tm	55	1	6	7	-5	0	0	53	1.9	0	1	1	0	0	0	23	54	0	22	0	2	8	0	.13
98-99	Car	54	0	10	10	9	0	0	44	0.0	0	0	0	0	0	0	24	48	0	24	0	3	5	0	.19
97-98	Ott	13	1	1	2	-3	0	0	16	6.3	0	0	0	0	0	0	3	6	0	3	0	1	2	0	.15
97-98	Car	42	0	5	5	-2	0	0	37	0.0	0	1	1	0	0	0	20	48	0	19	0	1	6	0	.12
7 Years		338	18	70	88	-49	4	0	572	3.1	5	23	28	1	3	4	162	362	2	156	2	23	57	0	.26

Postseason

Year	Tm	GP	G	A	Pts	+/–	GW	OT	S	SPct	G	A	Pts	G	A	Pts	Num	PIM	Maj	Mnr	Fgt	Rgh	HHT	Hat	P/G
90-91	Mon	1	0	0	0	1	0	0	0	–	0	0	0	0	0	0	0	0	0	0	0	0	0	0	.00
91-92	Mon	4	1	0	1	1	0	0	4	25.0	0	0	0	0	0	0	1	2	0	1	0	0	1	0	.25
92-93	Mon	3	0	0	0	1	0	0	2	0.0	0	0	0	0	0	0	2	4	0	2	0	2	0	0	.00
3 Years		8	1	0	1	3	0	0	6	16.7	0	0	0	0	0	0	3	6	0	3	0	2	1	0	.13

Corey Hirsch

Pos: G **Catches:** L **Ht:** 5'10" **Wt:** 160 **Born:** 7/1/72—Medicine Hat, Alberta **Age:** 27

Overall																Pen Shot		Offense		
Year	Tm	GP	GS	TP	W	L	T	Min	GA	GAA	Shots	SvPct	ShO	OE	PPGA	SHGA	Shots	GA	G	A	PIM
92-93	NYR	4	4	1	1	2	1	224	14	3.75	116	.879	0	2	4	3	0	0	0	0	0
93-94		Did Not Play in NHL																			
94-95		Did Not Play in NHL																			
95-96	Van	41	37	1	17	14	6	2338	114	2.93	1173	.903	1	15	39	7	0	0	0	2	2
96-97	Van	39	37	5	12	20	4	2127	116	3.27	1090	.894	2	11	33	3	1	0	0	1	6
97-98	Van	1	0	0	0	0	0	50	5	6.00	34	.853	0	0	3	0	0	0	0	0	0
98-99	Van	20	12	4	3	8	3	919	48	3.13	435	.890	1	4	11	2	2	1	0	0	0
5 Years		105	90	11	33	44	14	5658	297	3.15	2848	.896	4	32	90	15	3	1	0	3	8

Postseason

Year	Tm	GP	GS	TP	W	L	Pct	Min	GA	GAA	Shots	SvPct	ShO	OE	PPGA	SHGA	Shots	GA	G	A	PIM
95-96	Van	6	5	0	2	3	.400	338	21	3.73	166	.873	0	1	8	0	0	0	0	0	2

Todd Hlushko

Pos: LW **Shoots:** L **Ht:** 5'11" **Wt:** 200 **Born:** 2/7/70—Toronto, Ontario **Age:** 29

Overall											Power Play			Shorthand			Penalty							Misc	
Year	Tm	GP	G	A	Pts	+/–	GW	GT	S	SPct	G	A	Pts	G	A	Pts	Num	PIM	Maj	Mnr	Fgt	Rgh	HHT	Hat	P/G
93-94	Phi	2	1	0	1	1	0	0	2	50.0	0	0	0	0	0	0	0	0	0	0	0	0	0	0	.50
94-95	Cgy	2	0	1	1	1	0	0	3	0.0	0	0	0	0	0	0	1	2	0	1	0	0	0	0	.50
95-96	Cgy	4	0	0	0	0	0	0	6	0.0	0	0	0	0	0	0	3	6	0	3	0	2	0	0	.00
96-97	Cgy	58	7	11	18	-2	0	0	76	9.2	0	0	0	0	1	1	19	49	1	17	1	4	4	0	.31
97-98	Cgy	13	0	1	1	0	0	0	7	0.0	0	0	0	0	0	0	8	27	1	6	1	1	2	0	.08
98-99		Did Not Play in Regular Season																							
5 Years		79	8	13	21	0	0	0	94	8.5	0	0	0	0	1	1	31	84	2	27	2	7	6	0	.27

Postseason

Year	Tm	GP	G	A	Pts	+/–	GW	OT	S	SPct	G	A	Pts	G	A	Pts	Num	PIM	Maj	Mnr	Fgt	Rgh	HHT	Hat	P/G
94-95	Cgy	1	0	0	0	0	0	0	0	–	0	0	0	0	0	0	1	2	0	1	0	1	0	0	.00
98-99	Pit	2	0	0	0	0	0	0	1	0.0	0	0	0	0	0	0	0	0	0	0	0	0	0	0	.00
2 Years		3	0	0	0	0	0	0	1	0.0	0	0	0	0	0	0	1	2	0	1	0	1	0	0	.00

Kevin Hodson

Pos: G **Catches:** L **Ht:** 6'0" **Wt:** 182 **Born:** 3/27/72—Winnipeg, Manitoba **Age:** 27

Overall																	Pen Shot		Offense		
Year	Tm	GP	GS	TP	W	L	T	Min	GA	GAA	Shots	SvPct	ShO	OE	PPGA	SHGA	Shots	GA	G	A	PIM
95-96	Det	4	3	1	2	0	0	163	3	1.10	67	.955	1	1	2	0	0	0	0	0	0
96-97	Det	6	4	1	2	2	1	294	8	1.63	114	.930	1	1	4	0	0	0	0	1	0
97-98	Det	21	16	2	9	3	3	988	44	2.67	444	.901	2	4	11	1	0	0	0	0	2
98-99	2Tm	9	7	2	2	3	1	413	20	2.91	197	.898	0	3	3	1	0	0	0	0	0
98-99	Det	4	3	1	0	2	0	175	9	3.09	79	.886	0	1	2	0	0	0	0	0	0
98-99	TB	5	4	1	2	1	1	238	11	2.77	118	.907	0	2	1	1	0	0	0	0	0
4 Years		40	30	6	15	8	5	1858	75	2.42	822	.909	4	9	20	2	0	0	0	1	2
Postseason																					
Year	Tm	GP	GS	TP	W	L	Pct	Min	GA	GAA	Shots	SvPct	ShO	OE	PPGA	SHGA	Shots	GA	G	A	PIM
97-98	Det	1	0	0	0	0	–	1	0	0.00	0	–	0	0	0	0	0	0	0	0	0

Jonas Hoglund

(statistical profile on page 319)

Pos: RW **Shoots:** R **Ht:** 6'3" **Wt:** 213 **Born:** 8/29/72—Hammaro, Sweden **Age:** 27

Overall											Power Play			Shorthand			Penalty							Misc	
Year	Tm	GP	G	A	Pts	+/–	GW	GT	S	SPct	G	A	Pts	G	A	Pts	Num	PIM	Maj	Mnr	Fgt	Rgh	HHT	Hat	P/G
96-97	Cgy	68	19	16	35	-4	6	1	189	10.1	3	11	14	0	0	0	6	12	0	6	0	0	3	0	.51
97-98	2Tm	78	12	13	25	-7	0	0	186	6.5	4	2	6	0	0	0	11	22	0	11	0	1	4	0	.32
98-99	Mon	74	8	10	18	-5	0	1	122	6.6	1	1	2	0	0	0	8	16	0	8	0	0	6	0	.24
97-98	Cgy	50	6	8	14	-9	0	0	124	4.8	0	0	0	0	0	0	8	16	0	8	0	1	3	0	.28
97-98	Mon	28	6	5	11	2	0	0	62	9.7	4	2	6	0	0	0	3	6	0	3	0	0	1	0	.39
3 Years		220	39	39	78	-16	6	2	497	7.8	8	14	22	0	0	0	25	50	0	25	0	1	13	0	.35
Postseason																									
Year	Tm	GP	G	A	Pts	+/–	GW	OT	S	SPct	G	A	Pts	G	A	Pts	Num	PIM	Maj	Mnr	Fgt	Rgh	HHT	Hat	P/G
97-98	Mon	10	2	0	2	-1	0	0	7	28.6	0	0	0	0	0	0	0	0	0	0	0	0	0	0	.20

Benoit Hogue

(statistical profile on page 319)

Pos: C **Shoots:** L **Ht:** 5'10" **Wt:** 194 **Born:** 10/28/66—Repentigny, Quebec **Age:** 33

Overall											Power Play			Shorthand			Penalty							Misc	
Year	Tm	GP	G	A	Pts	+/–	GW	GT	S	SPct	G	A	Pts	G	A	Pts	Num	PIM	Maj	Mnr	Fgt	Rgh	HHT	Hat	P/G
87-88	Buf	3	1	1	2	3	1	0	3	33.3	0	–	–	0	–	–	0	0	0	0	0	0	0	0	.67
88-89	Buf	69	14	30	44	-4	0	0	114	12.3	1	–	–	2	–	–	–	120	–	–	–	–	–	0	.64
89-90	Buf	45	11	7	18	0	1	0	73	15.1	1	–	–	0	–	–	–	79	–	–	–	–	–	0	.40
90-91	Buf	76	19	28	47	-8	2	2	134	14.2	1	–	–	0	–	–	–	76	–	–	–	–	–	0	.62
91-92	2Tm	75	30	46	76	30	5	0	149	20.1	8	9	17	0	2	2	24	67	1	21	1	5	4	0	1.01
92-93	NYI	70	33	42	75	13	5	0	147	22.4	5	7	12	3	3	6	35	108	2	29	1	5	7	1	1.07
93-94	NYI	83	36	33	69	-7	3	0	218	16.5	9	9	18	5	0	5	31	73	1	29	1	5	8	0	.83
94-95	2Tm	45	9	7	16	0	2	1	66	13.6	2	1	3	0	0	0	13	34	0	12	0	1	4	0	.36
95-96	2Tm	78	19	45	64	10	5	0	155	12.3	5	15	20	0	1	1	37	104	2	32	2	7	6	0	.82
96-97	Dal	73	19	24	43	8	5	0	131	14.5	5	6	11	0	0	0	16	54	2	12	2	1	6	0	.59
97-98	Dal	53	6	16	22	7	1	0	55	10.9	3	3	6	0	0	0	16	35	1	15	1	3	4	0	.42
98-99	2Tm	74	12	17	29	-10	3	0	121	9.9	2	3	5	0	3	3	27	54	0	27	0	3	9	0	.39
91-92	Buf	3	0	1	1	0	0	0	6	0.0	0	0	0	0	0	0	0	0	0	0	0	0	0	0	.33
91-92	NYI	72	30	45	75	30	5	0	143	21.0	8	9	17	0	2	2	24	67	1	21	1	5	4	0	1.04
94-95	NYI	33	6	4	10	0	1	1	50	12.0	1	1	2	0	0	0	13	34	0	12	0	1	4	0	.30
94-95	Tor	12	3	3	6	0	1	0	16	18.8	1	0	1	0	0	0	0	0	0	0	0	0	0	0	.50
95-96	Tor	44	12	25	37	6	5	0	94	12.8	3	8	11	0	0	0	23	68	2	19	2	5	4	0	.84
95-96	Dal	34	7	20	27	4	0	0	61	11.5	2	7	9	0	1	1	14	36	0	13	0	2	2	0	.79
98-99	TB	62	11	14	25	-12	3	0	101	10.9	2	3	5	0	3	3	25	50	0	25	0	2	8	0	.40
98-99	Dal	12	1	3	4	2	0	0	20	5.0	0	0	0	0	0	0	2	4	0	2	0	1	1	0	.33
12 Years		744	209	296	505	42	33	3	1366	15.3	42	–	–	10	–	–	–	804	–	–	–	–	–	1	.68
Postseason																									
Year	Tm	GP	G	A	Pts	+/–	GW	OT	S	SPct	G	A	Pts	G	A	Pts	Num	PIM	Maj	Mnr	Fgt	Rgh	HHT	Hat	P/G
88-89	Buf	5	0	0	0	-1	0	0	4	0.0	0	0	0	0	0	0	–	17	–	–	–	–	–	0	.00
89-90	Buf	3	0	0	0	0	0	0	2	0.0	0	0	0	0	0	0	–	10	–	–	–	–	–	0	.00
90-91	Buf	5	3	1	4	-1	0	0	13	23.1	0	–	–	0	–	–	–	10	–	–	–	–	–	0	.80
92-93	NYI	18	6	6	12	7	1	0	37	16.2	0	1	1	2	0	2	10	31	1	8	1	4	1	0	.67
93-94	NYI	4	0	1	1	-3	0	0	5	0.0	0	1	1	0	0	0	2	4	0	2	0	1	0	0	.25
94-95	Tor	7	0	0	0	-4	0	0	6	0.0	0	0	0	0	0	0	3	6	0	3	0	0	2	0	.00
96-97	Dal	7	2	2	4	-1	0	0	16	12.5	1	1	2	0	0	0	3	6	0	3	0	1	1	0	.57
97-98	Dal	17	4	2	6	0	2	1	23	17.4	1	1	2	0	0	0	8	16	0	8	0	3	1	0	.35
98-99	Dal	14	0	2	2	-1	0	0	20	0.0	0	0	0	0	0	0	8	16	0	8	0	3	1	0	.14
9 Years		80	15	14	29	-4	3	1	126	11.9	2	–	–	2	–	–	–	116	–	–	–	–	–	0	.36

Josh Holden

Pos: C **Shoots:** L **Ht:** 5'11" **Wt:** 187 **Born:** 1/18/78—Calgary, Alberta **Age:** 21

Overall											Power Play			Shorthand			Penalty								Misc	
Year	Tm	GP	G	A	Pts	+/–	GW	GT	S	SPct	G	A	Pts	G	A	Pts	Num	PIM	Maj	Mnr	Fgt	Rgh	HHT	Hat	P/G
98-99	Van	30	2	4	6	-10	0	0	44	4.5	1	0	1	0	0	0	5	10	0	5	0	1	4	0	.20

Bobby Holik

(statistical profile on page 319)

Pos: LW **Shoots:** R **Ht:** 6'3" **Wt:** 225 **Born:** 1/1/71—Jihlava, Czechoslovakia **Age:** 28

Overall											Power Play			Shorthand			Penalty								Misc	
Year	Tm	GP	G	A	Pts	+/–	GW	GT	S	SPct	G	A	Pts	G	A	Pts	Num	PIM	Maj	Mnr	Fgt	Rgh	HHT	Hat	P/G
90-91	Har	78	21	22	43	-3	3	0	173	12.1	8	–	–	0	–	–	–	113	–	–	–	–	–	0	.55
91-92	Har	76	21	24	45	4	2	1	207	10.1	1	1	2	0	0	0	22	44	0	22	0	5	5	0	.59
92-93	NJ	61	20	19	39	-6	4	0	180	11.1	7	7	14	0	0	0	38	76	0	38	0	16	10	2	.64
93-94	NJ	70	13	20	33	28	3	0	130	10.0	2	1	3	0	0	0	30	72	4	26	3	4	10	0	.47
94-95	NJ	48	10	10	20	9	2	0	84	11.9	0	1	1	0	0	0	9	18	0	9	0	1	2	0	.42
95-96	NJ	63	13	17	30	9	1	1	157	8.3	1	3	4	0	0	0	29	58	0	29	0	8	6	0	.48
96-97	NJ	**82**	23	39	62	24	6	0	192	12.0	5	8	13	0	0	0	27	54	0	27	0	2	9	0	.76
97-98	NJ*	82	29	36	65	23	8	1	238	12.2	8	18	26	0	0	0	50	100	0	50	0	9	21	0	.79
98-99	NJ	78	27	37	64	16	8	0	253	10.7	5	9	14	0	0	0	54	119	1	52	0	12	13	1	.82
9 Years		638	177	224	401	104	37	3	1614	11.0	37	–	–	0	–	–	–	654	–	–	–	–	–	3	.63

Postseason

Year	Tm	GP	G	A	Pts	+/–	GW	OT	S	SPct	G	A	Pts	G	A	Pts	Num	PIM	Maj	Mnr	Fgt	Rgh	HHT	Hat	P/G
90-91	Har	6	0	0	0	-3	0	0	15	0.0	0	0	0	0	0	0	2	7	1	1	–	–	–	0	.00
91-92	Har	7	0	1	1	-2	0	0	18	0.0	0	0	0	0	0	0	3	6	0	3	0	0	2	0	.14
92-93	NJ	5	1	1	2	-1	0	0	10	10.0	0	0	0	0	0	0	3	6	0	3	0	0	0	0	.40
93-94	NJ	20	0	3	3	0	0	0	23	0.0	0	0	0	0	0	0	3	6	0	3	0	0	2	0	.15
94-95	NJ	20	4	4	8	7	1	0	33	12.1	2	0	2	0	0	0	11	22	0	11	0	1	3	0	.40
96-97	NJ	10	2	3	5	1	0	0	29	6.9	1	3	4	0	0	0	2	4	0	2	0	1	0	0	.50
97-98	NJ	5	0	0	0	-4	0	0	18	0.0	0	0	0	0	0	0	4	8	0	4	0	0	2	0	.00
98-99	NJ	7	0	7	7	-1	0	0	21	0.0	0	2	2	0	0	0	3	6	0	3	0	2	0	0	1.00
8 Years		80	7	19	26	-3	1	0	167	4.2	3	5	8	0	0	0	31	65	1	30	–	–	–	0	.33

Jason Holland

Pos: D **Shoots:** R **Ht:** 6'2" **Wt:** 193 **Born:** 4/30/76—Morinville, Alberta **Age:** 23

Overall											Power Play			Shorthand			Penalty								Misc	
Year	Tm	GP	G	A	Pts	+/–	GW	GT	S	SPct	G	A	Pts	G	A	Pts	Num	PIM	Maj	Mnr	Fgt	Rgh	HHT	Hat	P/G
96-97	NYI	4	1	0	1	1	0	0	3	33.3	0	0	0	0	0	0	0	0	0	0	0	0	0	0	.25
97-98	NYI	8	0	0	0	-4	0	0	6	0.0	0	0	0	0	0	0	2	4	0	2	0	0	0	0	.00
98-99	Buf	3	0	0	0	-1	0	0	2	0.0	0	0	0	0	0	0	4	8	0	4	0	0	2	0	.00
3 Years		15	1	0	1	-4	0	0	11	9.1	0	0	0	0	0	0	6	12	0	6	0	0	2	0	.07

Tomas Holmstrom

(statistical profile on page 320)

Pos: LW **Shoots:** L **Ht:** 6'0" **Wt:** 210 **Born:** 1/23/73—Pieta, Sweden **Age:** 26

Overall											Power Play			Shorthand			Penalty								Misc	
Year	Tm	GP	G	A	Pts	+/–	GW	GT	S	SPct	G	A	Pts	G	A	Pts	Num	PIM	Maj	Mnr	Fgt	Rgh	HHT	Hat	P/G
96-97	Det	47	6	3	9	-10	0	0	53	11.3	3	2	5	0	0	0	15	33	1	14	1	1	7	0	.19
97-98	Det	57	5	17	22	6	1	0	48	10.4	1	1	2	0	0	0	22	44	0	22	0	5	7	0	.39
98-99	Det	82	13	21	34	-11	4	0	100	13.0	5	9	14	0	0	0	33	69	1	32	1	9	3	0	.41
3 Years		186	24	41	65	-15	5	0	201	11.9	9	12	21	0	0	0	70	146	2	68	2	15	17	0	.35

Postseason

Year	Tm	GP	G	A	Pts	+/–	GW	OT	S	SPct	G	A	Pts	G	A	Pts	Num	PIM	Maj	Mnr	Fgt	Rgh	HHT	Hat	P/G
96-97	Det	1	0	0	0	-1	0	0	0	–	0	0	0	0	0	0	0	0	0	0	0	0	0	0	.00
97-98	Det	22	7	12	19	9	0	0	27	25.9	2	3	5	0	0	0	8	16	0	8	0	1	3	0	.86
98-99	Det	10	4	3	7	2	1	0	26	15.4	2	1	3	0	0	0	2	4	0	2	0	0	0	0	.70
3 Years		33	11	15	26	10	1	0	53	20.8	4	4	8	0	0	0	10	20	0	10	0	1	3	0	.79

Brian Holzinger

(statistical profile on page 320)

Pos: C **Shoots:** R **Ht:** 5'11" **Wt:** 190 **Born:** 10/10/72—Parma, Ohio **Age:** 27

Overall											Power Play			Shorthand			Penalty								Misc	
Year	Tm	GP	G	A	Pts	+/–	GW	GT	S	SPct	G	A	Pts	G	A	Pts	Num	PIM	Maj	Mnr	Fgt	Rgh	HHT	Hat	P/G
94-95	Buf	4	0	3	3	2	0	0	3	0.0	0	0	0	0	0	0	0	0	0	0	0	0	0	0	.75
95-96	Buf	58	10	10	20	-21	1	0	71	14.1	5	2	7	0	1	1	17	37	1	16	0	3	7	0	.34

Overall											Power Play			Shorthand			Penalty							Misc	
Year	Tm	GP	G	A	Pts	+/–	GW	GT	S	SPct	G	A	Pts	G	A	Pts	Num	PIM	Maj	Mnr	Fgt	Rgh	HHT	Hat	P/G
96-97	Buf	81	22	29	51	9	6	0	142	15.5	2	5	7	2	1	3	27	54	0	27	0	13	7	0	.63
97-98	Buf	69	14	21	35	-2	1	1	116	12.1	4	7	11	2	3	5	18	36	0	18	0	2	7	0	.51
98-99	Buf	81	17	17	34	2	2	0	143	11.9	5	5	10	0	1	1	21	45	1	20	1	2	8	0	.42
5 Years		293	63	80	143	-10	10	1	475	13.3	16	19	35	4	6	10	83	172	2	81	1	20	29	0	.49
Postseason																									
Year	Tm	GP	G	A	Pts	+/–	GW	OT	S	SPct	G	A	Pts	G	A	Pts	Num	PIM	Maj	Mnr	Fgt	Rgh	HHT	Hat	P/G
94-95	Buf	4	2	1	3	-3	0	0	6	33.3	1	0	1	0	0	0	1	2	0	1	0	0	1	0	.75
96-97	Buf	12	2	5	7	-3	1	0	20	10.0	0	3	3	1	0	1	4	8	0	4	0	1	0	0	.58
97-98	Buf	15	4	7	11	-2	0	0	24	16.7	1	4	5	1	0	1	9	18	0	9	0	3	1	0	.73
98-99	Buf	21	3	5	8	1	0	0	32	9.4	1	3	4	0	0	0	11	33	1	9	1	2	1	0	.38
4 Years		52	11	18	29	-7	1	0	82	13.4	3	10	13	2	0	2	25	61	1	23	1	6	3	0	.56

Marian Hossa

(statistical profile on page 320)

Pos: LW **Shoots:** L **Ht:** 6'1" **Wt:** 194 **Born:** 1/12/79—Stara Lubovna, Czechoslovakia **Age:** 20

Overall											Power Play			Shorthand			Penalty							Misc	
Year	Tm	GP	G	A	Pts	+/–	GW	GT	S	SPct	G	A	Pts	G	A	Pts	Num	PIM	Maj	Mnr	Fgt	Rgh	HHT	Hat	P/G
97-98	Ott	7	0	1	1	-1	0	0	10	0.0	0	1	1	0	0	0	0	0	0	0	0	0	0	0	.14
98-99	Ott	60	15	15	30	18	2	2	124	12.1	1	2	3	0	0	0	17	37	1	16	1	1	5	0	.50
2 Years		67	15	16	31	17	2	2	134	11.2	1	3	4	0	0	0	17	37	1	16	1	1	5	0	.46
Postseason																									
Year	Tm	GP	G	A	Pts	+/–	GW	OT	S	SPct	G	A	Pts	G	A	Pts	Num	PIM	Maj	Mnr	Fgt	Rgh	HHT	Hat	P/G
98-99	Ott	4	0	2	2	1	0	0	11	0.0	0	1	1	0	0	0	2	4	0	2	0	0	0	0	.50

Doug Houda

Pos: D **Shoots:** R **Ht:** 6'2" **Wt:** 190 **Born:** 6/3/66—Blairmore, Alberta **Age:** 33

Overall											Power Play			Shorthand			Penalty							Misc	
Year	Tm	GP	G	A	Pts	+/–	GW	GT	S	SPct	G	A	Pts	G	A	Pts	Num	PIM	Maj	Mnr	Fgt	Rgh	HHT	Hat	P/G
85-86	Det	6	0	0	0	-7	0	0	5	0.0	0	0	0	0	0	0	2	4	0	2	0	–	–	0	.00
86-87		Did Not Play in NHL																							
87-88	Det	11	1	1	2	0	0	0	10	10.0	0	–	–	0	–	–	–	10	–	–	–	–	–	0	.18
88-89	Det	57	2	11	13	17	0	0	38	5.3	0	–	–	0	–	–	–	67	–	–	–	–	–	0	.23
89-90	Det	73	2	9	11	-5	0	0	59	3.4	0	–	–	0	–	–	–	127	–	–	–	–	–	0	.15
90-91	2Tm	41	1	6	7	-5	0	1	42	2.4	0	–	–	0	–	–	–	84	–	–	–	–	–	0	.17
91-92	Har	56	3	6	9	-2	1	0	40	7.5	1	0	1	0	0	0	47	125	5	40	5	10	11	0	.16
92-93	Har	60	2	6	8	-19	0	0	43	4.7	0	0	0	0	0	0	57	167	7	46	7	5	12	0	.13
93-94	2Tm	61	2	6	8	-19	0	0	32	6.3	0	0	0	0	0	0	58	188	8	44	8	17	12	0	.13
94-95	Buf	28	1	2	3	1	0	0	21	4.8	0	0	0	0	1	1	17	68	6	9	6	4	2	0	.11
95-96	Buf	38	1	3	4	3	0	0	21	4.8	0	0	0	0	0	0	23	52	2	21	2	4	6	0	.11
96-97	NYI	70	2	8	10	1	0	0	29	6.9	0	2	2	0	0	0	31	99	7	22	7	9	6	0	.14
97-98	2Tm	55	2	4	6	-11	0	0	24	8.3	0	1	1	1	0	1	30	99	5	22	5	5	6	0	.11
98-99	Det	3	0	1	1	-2	0	0	1	0.0	0	0	0	0	0	0	0	0	0	0	0	0	0	0	.33
90-91	Det	22	0	4	4	-2	0	0	21	0.0	0	–	–	0	–	–	–	43	–	–	–	–	–	0	.18
90-91	Har	19	1	2	3	-3	0	1	21	4.8	0	–	–	0	–	–	–	41	–	–	–	–	–	0	.16
93-94	Har	7	0	0	0	-4	0	0	1	0.0	0	0	0	0	0	0	6	23	1	4	1	3	0	0	.00
93-94	LA	54	2	6	8	-15	0	0	31	6.5	0	0	0	0	0	0	52	165	7	40	7	14	12	0	.15
97-98	NYI	31	1	2	3	-6	0	0	15	6.7	0	1	1	0	0	0	15	47	3	11	3	4	2	0	.10
97-98	Anh	24	1	2	3	-5	0	0	9	11.1	0	0	0	1	0	1	15	52	2	11	2	1	4	0	.13
13 Years		559	19	63	82	-48	1	1	365	5.2	1	–	–	1	–	–	–	1090	–	–	–	–	–	0	.15
Postseason																									
Year	Tm	GP	G	A	Pts	+/–	GW	OT	S	SPct	G	A	Pts	G	A	Pts	Num	PIM	Maj	Mnr	Fgt	Rgh	HHT	Hat	P/G
88-89	Det	6	0	1	1	-1	0	0	3	0.0	0	–	–	0	0	0	0	0	0	0	0	0	0	0	.17
90-91	Har	6	0	0	0	-4	0	0	6	0.0	0	0	0	0	0	0	4	8	0	4	0	0	0	0	.00
91-92	Har	6	0	2	2	-2	0	0	4	0.0	0	0	0	0	1	1	5	13	1	4	1	1	1	0	.33
3 Years		18	0	3	3	-7	0	0	13	0.0	0	–	–	0	1	1	9	21	1	8	1	1	1	0	.17

Eric Houde

Pos: C **Shoots:** L **Ht:** 5'11" **Wt:** 191 **Born:** 12/19/76—Montreal, Quebec **Age:** 23

Overall											Power Play			Shorthand			Penalty							Misc	
Year	Tm	GP	G	A	Pts	+/–	GW	GT	S	SPct	G	A	Pts	G	A	Pts	Num	PIM	Maj	Mnr	Fgt	Rgh	HHT	Hat	P/G
96-97	Mon	13	0	2	2	1	0	0	1	0.0	0	0	0	0	0	0	1	2	0	1	0	0	0	0	.15
97-98	Mon	9	1	0	1	-3	1	0	4	25.0	0	0	0	0	0	0	0	0	0	0	0	0	0	0	.11
98-99	Mon	8	1	1	2	-2	1	0	4	25.0	0	0	0	0	0	0	1	2	0	1	0	0	0	0	.25
3 Years		30	2	3	5	-4	2	0	9	22.2	0	0	0	0	0	0	2	4	0	2	0	0	0	0	.17

													Postseason												
Year	Tm	GP	G	A	Pts	+/–	GW	OT	S	SPct	G	A	Pts	G	A	Pts	Num	PIM	Maj	Mnr	Fgt	Rgh	HHT	Hat	P/G
96-97	Mon	1	0	0	0	0	0	0	0	–	0	0	0	0	0	0	0	0	0	0	0	0	0	0	.00

Mike Hough

Pos: LW **Shoots:** L **Ht:** 6'1" **Wt:** 197 **Born:** 2/6/63—Montreal, Quebec **Age:** 36

Overall											Power Play			Shorthand			Penalty							Misc	
Year	Tm	GP	G	A	Pts	+/–	GW	GT	S	SPct	G	A	Pts	G	A	Pts	Num	PIM	Maj	Mnr	Fgt	Rgh	HHT	Hat	P/G
84-85											Did Not Play in Regular Season														
85-86											Did Not Play in NHL														
86-87	Que	56	6	8	14	-8	0	0	60	10.0	1	–	–	1	–	–	–	79	–	–	–	–	–	0	.25
87-88	Que	17	3	2	5	-8	1	0	23	13.0	0	–	–	0	–	–	1	2	0	1	0	–	–	0	.29
88-89	Que	46	9	10	19	-7	3	0	51	17.6	1	–	–	3	–	–	–	39	–	–	–	–	–	0	.41
89-90	Que	43	13	13	26	-24	0	0	93	14.0	3	–	–	1	–	–	–	84	–	–	–	–	–	0	.60
90-91	Que	63	13	20	33	-7	1	0	106	12.3	1	–	–	1	–	–	–	111	–	–	–	–	–	0	.52
91-92	Que	61	16	22	38	-1	1	0	92	17.4	6	6	12	2	1	3	33	77	1	31	1	5	11	0	.62
92-93	Que	77	8	22	30	-11	2	0	98	8.2	2	2	4	1	0	1	25	69	1	22	1	6	5	0	.39
93-94	Fla	78	6	23	29	3	1	0	106	5.7	0	0	0	1	2	3	20	62	2	16	1	1	5	0	.37
94-95	Fla	48	6	7	13	1	2	0	58	10.3	0	1	1	0	0	0	15	38	0	14	0	5	2	0	.27
95-96	Fla	64	7	16	23	4	1	0	66	10.6	0	0	0	1	0	1	13	37	1	11	0	5	0	0	.36
96-97	Fla	69	8	6	14	12	2	0	85	9.4	0	0	0	0	0	0	16	48	0	14	0	4	4	0	.20
97-98	NYI	74	5	7	12	-4	0	0	44	11.4	0	0	0	0	0	0	12	27	1	11	1	2	5	0	.16
98-99	NYI	11	0	0	0	-2	0	0	4	0.0	0	0	0	0	0	0	1	2	0	1	0	0	0	0	.00
13 Years		707	100	156	256	-52	14	0	886	11.3	14	–	–	11	–	–	–	675	–	–	–	–	–	0	.36

													Postseason												
Year	Tm	GP	G	A	Pts	+/–	GW	OT	S	SPct	G	A	Pts	G	A	Pts	Num	PIM	Maj	Mnr	Fgt	Rgh	HHT	Hat	P/G
84-85	Que	2	0	0	0	0	0	0	0	–	0	0	0	0	0	0	0	0	0	0	0	0	0	0	.00
86-87	Que	9	0	3	3	-1	0	0	6	0.0	0	–	–	0	–	–	–	26	–	–	–	–	–	0	.33
92-93	Que	6	0	1	1	0	0	0	18	0.0	0	0	0	0	0	0	1	2	0	1	0	0	0	0	.17
95-96	Fla	22	4	1	5	5	2	1	38	10.5	0	0	0	0	0	0	4	8	0	4	0	2	0	0	.23
96-97	Fla	5	1	0	1	-2	0	0	10	10.0	0	0	0	0	0	0	1	2	0	1	0	0	0	0	.20
5 Years		44	5	5	10	2	2	1	72	6.9	0	–	–	0	–	–	–	38	–	–	–	–	–	0	.23

Bill Houlder

(statistical profile on page 320)

Pos: D **Shoots:** L **Ht:** 6'2" **Wt:** 210 **Born:** 3/11/67—Thunder Bay, Ontario **Age:** 32

Overall											Power Play			Shorthand			Penalty							Misc	
Year	Tm	GP	G	A	Pts	+/–	GW	GT	S	SPct	G	A	Pts	G	A	Pts	Num	PIM	Maj	Mnr	Fgt	Rgh	HHT	Hat	P/G
87-88	Was	30	1	2	3	-2	0	0	20	5.0	0	–	–	0	–	–	–	10	–	–	–	–	–	0	.10
88-89	Was	8	0	3	3	7	0	0	5	0.0	0	–	–	0	–	–	2	4	0	2	0	–	–	0	.38
89-90	Was	41	1	11	12	8	0	1	49	2.0	0	–	–	0	–	–	–	28	–	–	–	–	–	0	.29
90-91	Buf	7	0	2	2	-2	0	0	7	0.0	0	–	–	0	–	–	2	4	0	2	0	–	–	0	.29
91-92	Buf	10	1	0	1	-2	0	0	18	5.6	0	0	0	0	0	0	4	8	0	4	0	1	2	0	.10
92-93	Buf	15	3	5	8	5	0	1	29	10.3	0	0	0	0	0	0	3	6	0	3	0	0	1	0	.53
93-94	Anh	80	14	25	39	-18	3	0	187	7.5	3	13	16	0	0	0	16	40	0	15	0	0	8	0	.49
94-95	StL	41	5	13	18	16	0	0	59	8.5	1	3	4	0	0	0	10	20	0	10	0	0	4	0	.44
95-96	TB	61	5	23	28	1	0	1	90	5.6	3	14	17	0	0	0	11	22	0	11	0	0	8	0	.46
96-97	TB	79	4	21	25	16	2	0	116	3.4	0	4	4	0	1	1	15	30	0	15	0	0	9	0	.32
97-98	SJ	82	7	25	32	13	2	0	102	6.9	4	12	16	0	1	1	24	48	0	24	0	0	11	0	.39
98-99	SJ	76	9	23	32	8	5	0	115	7.8	7	12	19	0	0	0	20	40	0	20	0	1	7	0	.42
12 Years		530	50	153	203	50	12	3	797	6.3	18	–	–	0	–	–	–	260	–	–	–	–	–	0	.38

													Postseason												
Year	Tm	GP	G	A	Pts	+/–	GW	OT	S	SPct	G	A	Pts	G	A	Pts	Num	PIM	Maj	Mnr	Fgt	Rgh	HHT	Hat	P/G
92-93	Buf	8	0	2	2	1	0	0	11	0.0	0	1	1	0	0	0	2	4	0	2	0	0	1	0	.25
94-95	StL	4	1	1	2	6	0	0	10	10.0	0	0	0	0	0	0	0	0	0	0	0	0	0	0	.50
95-96	TB	6	0	1	1	0	0	0	8	0.0	0	0	0	0	0	0	2	4	0	2	0	0	0	0	.17
97-98	SJ	6	1	2	3	0	0	0	8	12.5	0	2	2	0	0	0	1	2	0	1	0	0	1	0	.50
98-99	SJ	6	3	0	3	2	0	0	8	37.5	3	0	3	0	0	0	2	4	0	2	0	0	1	0	.50
5 Years		30	5	6	11	9	0	0	45	11.1	3	3	6	0	0	0	7	14	0	7	0	0	3	0	.37

Phil Housley

(statistical profile on page 321)

Pos: D **Shoots:** L **Ht:** 5'10" **Wt:** 190 **Born:** 3/9/64—St. Paul, Minnesota **Age:** 35

Overall											Power Play			Shorthand			Penalty							Misc	
Year	Tm	GP	G	A	Pts	+/–	GW	GT	S	SPct	G	A	Pts	G	A	Pts	Num	PIM	Maj	Mnr	Fgt	Rgh	HHT	Hat	P/G
82-83	Buf	77	19	47	66	-4	2	2	183	10.4	11	–	–	0	–	–	–	39	–	–	–	–	–	1	.86

		Overall									Power Play			Shorthand			Penalty							Misc	
Year	Tm	GP	G	A	Pts	+/–	GW	GT	S	SPct	G	A	Pts	G	A	Pts	Num	PIM	Maj	Mnr	Fgt	Rgh	HHT	Hat	P/G
83-84	Buf*	75	31	46	77	3	6	1	234	13.2	13	–	–	2	–	–	–	33	–	–	–	–	–	0	1.03
84-85	Buf	73	16	53	69	15	4	0	188	8.5	3	–	–	0	–	–	–	28	–	–	–	–	–	0	.95
85-86	Buf	79	15	47	62	-9	2	0	180	8.3	7	–	–	0	–	–	–	54	–	–	–	–	–	0	.78
86-87	Buf	78	21	46	67	-2	2	0	202	10.4	8	–	–	1	–	–	–	57	–	–	–	–	–	0	.86
87-88	Buf	74	29	37	66	-17	1	1	231	12.6	6	–	–	0	–	–	–	96	–	–	–	–	–	1	.89
88-89	Buf*	72	26	44	70	6	3	0	178	14.6	5	–	–	0	–	–	–	47	–	–	–	–	–	0	.97
89-90	Buf*	**80**	21	60	81	11	4	0	201	10.4	8	–	–	1	–	–	–	32	–	–	–	–	–	0	1.01
90-91	Wpg*	78	23	53	76	-13	3	0	206	11.2	12	–	–	1	–	–	–	24	–	–	–	–	–	0	.97
91-92	Wpg*	74	23	63	86	-5	4	1	234	9.8	11	46	57	0	0	0	35	92	2	31	0	4	17	0	1.16
92-93	Wpg*	80	18	79	97	-14	2	0	249	7.2	6	**50**	56	0	0	0	26	52	0	26	0	0	14	0	1.21
93-94	StL	26	7	15	22	-5	1	1	60	11.7	4	7	11	0	0	0	6	12	0	6	0	0	5	0	.85
94-95	Cgy	43	8	35	43	17	0	0	135	5.9	3	17	20	0	0	0	9	18	0	9	0	1	6	0	1.00
95-96	2Tm	81	17	51	68	-6	1	0	205	8.3	6	29	35	0	0	0	15	30	0	15	0	0	8	0	.84
96-97	Was	77	11	29	40	-10	2	0	167	6.6	3	17	20	1	0	1	12	24	0	12	0	2	7	0	.52
97-98	Was	64	6	25	31	-10	0	0	116	5.2	4	15	19	1	0	1	12	24	0	12	0	2	5	0	.48
98-99	Cgy	79	11	43	54	14	1	0	193	5.7	4	20	24	0	0	0	22	52	0	21	0	2	7	0	.68
95-96	Cgy	59	16	36	52	-2	1	0	155	10.3	6	21	27	0	0	0	11	22	0	11	0	0	7	0	.88
95-96	NJ	22	1	15	16	-4	0	0	50	2.0	0	8	8	0	0	0	4	8	0	4	0	0	1	0	.73
17 Years		1210	302	773	1075	-29	38	6	3162	9.6	114	–	–	7	–	–	–	714	–	–	–	–	–	2	.89

		Postseason																							
Year	Tm	GP	G	A	Pts	+/–	GW	OT	S	SPct	G	A	Pts	G	A	Pts	Num	PIM	Maj	Mnr	Fgt	Rgh	HHT	Hat	P/G
82-83	Buf	10	3	4	7	-5	0	0	31	9.7	1	–	–	0	0	0	1	2	0	1	0	–	–	0	.70
83-84	Buf	3	0	0	0	-1	0	0	11	0.0	0	0	0	0	0	0	3	6	0	3	0	–	–	0	.00
84-85	Buf	5	3	2	5	0	0	0	12	25.0	0	–	–	0	0	0	1	2	0	1	0	–	–	0	1.00
87-88	Buf	6	2	4	6	-5	0	0	20	10.0	1	–	–	0	0	0	3	6	0	3	0	–	–	0	1.00
88-89	Buf	5	1	3	4	0	0	0	10	10.0	0	–	–	0	–	–	1	2	0	1	0	–	–	0	.80
89-90	Buf	6	1	4	5	0	0	0	16	6.3	1	–	–	0	0	0	2	4	0	2	0	–	–	0	.83
91-92	Wpg	7	1	4	5	-6	1	0	31	3.2	1	4	5	0	0	0	0	0	0	0	0	0	0	0	.71
92-93	Wpg	6	0	7	7	-3	0	0	10	0.0	0	5	5	0	0	0	1	2	0	1	0	0	1	0	1.17
93-94	StL	4	2	1	3	-3	0	0	10	20.0	2	1	3	0	0	0	2	4	0	2	0	0	0	0	.75
94-95	Cgy	7	0	9	9	5	0	0	22	0.0	0	5	5	0	0	0	0	0	0	0	0	0	0	0	1.29
97-98	Was	18	0	4	4	-2	0	0	27	0.0	0	2	2	0	0	0	2	4	0	2	0	0	0	0	.22
11 Years		77	13	42	55	-20	1	0	200	6.5	6	–	–	0	–	–	16	32	0	16	0	–	–	0	.71

Jan Hrdina

(statistical profile on page 321)

Pos: C **Shoots:** R **Ht:** 6'0" **Wt:** 197 **Born:** 2/5/76—Hradec Kralove, Czechoslovakia **Age:** 23

		Overall									Power Play			Shorthand			Penalty							Misc	
Year	Tm	GP	G	A	Pts	+/–	GW	GT	S	SPct	G	A	Pts	G	A	Pts	Num	PIM	Maj	Mnr	Fgt	Rgh	HHT	Hat	P/G
98-99	Pit	82	13	29	42	-2	2	0	94	13.8	3	7	10	0	1	1	20	40	0	20	0	0	11	0	.51

		Postseason																							
Year	Tm	GP	G	A	Pts	+/–	GW	OT	S	SPct	G	A	Pts	G	A	Pts	Num	PIM	Maj	Mnr	Fgt	Rgh	HHT	Hat	P/G
98-99	Pit	13	4	1	5	-1	1	0	14	28.6	1	0	1	0	0	0	6	12	0	6	0	1	2	0	.38

Tony Hrkac

(statistical profile on page 321)

Pos: C **Shoots:** L **Ht:** 5'11" **Wt:** 170 **Born:** 7/7/66—Thunder Bay, Ontario **Age:** 33

		Overall									Power Play			Shorthand			Penalty							Misc	
Year	Tm	GP	G	A	Pts	+/–	GW	GT	S	SPct	G	A	Pts	G	A	Pts	Num	PIM	Maj	Mnr	Fgt	Rgh	HHT	Hat	P/G
86-87	Did Not Play in Regular Season																								
87-88	StL	67	11	37	48	5	3	0	86	12.8	2	–	–	1	–	–	–	22	–	–	–	–	–	0	.72
88-89	StL	70	17	28	45	-10	1	0	133	12.8	5	–	–	0	–	–	4	8	0	4	0	–	–	0	.64
89-90	2Tm	50	9	20	29	-4	0	1	70	12.9	3	–	–	0	–	–	5	10	0	5	0	–	–	0	.58
90-91	Que	70	16	32	48	-22	0	0	122	13.1	6	–	–	0	–	–	–	16	–	–	–	–	–	0	.69
91-92	2Tm	40	3	12	15	2	0	0	53	5.7	0	6	6	0	0	0	5	10	0	5	0	0	4	0	.38
92-93	Did Not Play in NHL																								
93-94	StL	36	6	5	11	-11	1	0	43	14.0	1	1	2	1	0	1	4	8	0	4	0	0	2	0	.31
94-95	Did Not Play in NHL																								
95-96	Did Not Play in NHL																								
96-97	Did Not Play in NHL																								
97-98	2Tm	49	13	14	27	3	1	0	57	22.8	7	5	12	0	0	0	5	10	0	5	0	0	4	0	.55
98-99	Dal	69	13	14	27	2	2	2	67	19.4	2	4	6	0	0	0	13	26	0	13	0	0	9	0	.39
89-90	StL	28	5	12	17	1	0	1	41	12.2	1	–	–	0	–	–	4	8	0	4	0	–	–	0	.61
89-90	Que	22	4	8	12	-5	0	0	29	13.8	2	–	–	0	–	–	1	2	0	1	0	–	–	0	.55
91-92	SJ	22	2	10	12	-2	0	0	31	6.5	0	5	5	0	0	0	2	4	0	2	0	0	2	0	.55
91-92	Chi	18	1	2	3	4	0	0	22	4.5	0	1	1	0	0	0	3	6	0	3	0	0	2	0	.17

Overall											Power Play			Shorthand			Penalty							Misc	
Year	Tm	GP	G	A	Pts	+/–	GW	GT	S	SPct	G	A	Pts	G	A	Pts	Num	PIM	Maj	Mnr	Fgt	Rgh	HHT	Hat	P/G
97-98	Dal	13	5	3	8	0	0	0	14	35.7	3	1	4	0	0	0	0	0	0	0	0	0	0	0	.62
97-98	Edm	36	8	11	19	3	1	0	43	18.6	4	4	8	0	0	0	5	10	0	5	0	0	4	0	.53
8 Years		451	88	162	250	-35	8	3	631	13.9	26	–	–	2	–	–	–	110	–	–	–	–	–	0	.55
Postseason																									
Year	Tm	GP	G	A	Pts	+/–	GW	OT	S	SPct	G	A	Pts	G	A	Pts	Num	PIM	Maj	Mnr	Fgt	Rgh	HHT	Hat	P/G
86-87	StL	3	0	0	0	0	0	0	6	0.0	0	0	0	0	0	0	0	0	0	0	0	0	0	0	.00
87-88	StL	10	6	1	7	1	1	0	21	28.6	3	–	–	1	–	–	2	4	0	2	0	0	0	1	.70
88-89	StL	4	1	1	2	-2	1	1	8	12.5	0	–	–	0	–	–	0	0	0	0	0	0	0	0	.50
91-92	Chi	3	0	0	0	0	0	0	2	0.0	0	0	0	0	0	0	1	2	0	1	0	0	1	0	.00
93-94	StL	4	0	0	0	-3	0	0	10	0.0	0	0	0	0	0	0	0	0	0	0	0	0	0	0	.00
97-98	Edm	12	0	3	3	2	0	0	11	0.0	0	0	0	0	0	0	1	2	0	1	0	0	1	0	.25
98-99	Dal	5	0	2	2	3	0	0	3	0.0	0	0	0	0	0	0	2	4	0	2	0	1	1	0	.40
7 Years		41	7	7	14	1	2	1	61	11.5	3	–	–	1	–	–	6	12	0	6	0	1	3	1	.34

Bill Huard

Pos: LW **Shoots:** R **Ht:** 6'1" **Wt:** 215 **Born:** 6/24/67—Welland, Ontario **Age:** 32

Overall											Power Play			Shorthand			Penalty							Misc	
Year	Tm	GP	G	A	Pts	+/–	GW	GT	S	SPct	G	A	Pts	G	A	Pts	Num	PIM	Maj	Mnr	Fgt	Rgh	HHT	Hat	P/G
92-93	Bos	2	0	0	0	0	0	0	0	–	0	0	0	0	0	0	0	0	0	0	0	0	0	0	.00
93-94	Ott	63	2	2	4	-19	0	0	24	8.3	0	0	0	0	0	0	37	162	16	16	16	5	2	0	.06
94-95	2Tm	33	3	3	6	0	0	1	21	14.3	0	0	0	0	0	0	21	77	9	11	9	1	2	0	.18
95-96	Dal	51	6	6	12	3	0	0	34	17.6	0	0	0	0	0	0	51	176	14	33	14	12	8	0	.24
96-97	Dal	40	5	6	11	5	0	0	34	14.7	0	0	0	0	0	0	30	105	7	20	7	12	2	0	.28
97-98	Edm	30	0	1	1	-5	0	0	12	0.0	0	0	0	0	0	0	19	72	6	11	6	6	1	0	.03
98-99	Edm	3	0	0	0	0	0	0	2	0.0	0	0	0	0	0	0	0	0	0	0	0	0	0	0	.00
94-95	Ott	26	1	1	2	-2	0	0	15	6.7	0	0	0	0	0	0	16	64	8	7	8	0	2	0	.08
94-95	Que	7	2	2	4	2	0	1	6	33.3	0	0	0	0	0	0	5	13	1	4	1	1	0	0	.57
7 Years		222	16	18	34	-16	0	1	127	12.6	0	0	0	0	0	0	158	592	52	91	52	36	15	0	.15
Postseason																									
Year	Tm	GP	G	A	Pts	+/–	GW	OT	S	SPct	G	A	Pts	G	A	Pts	Num	PIM	Maj	Mnr	Fgt	Rgh	HHT	Hat	P/G
94-95	Que	1	0	0	0	-1	0	0	0	–	0	0	0	0	0	0	0	0	0	0	0	0	0	0	.00
97-98	Edm	4	0	0	0	0	0	0	3	0.0	0	0	0	0	0	0	1	2	0	1	0	0	0	0	.00
2 Years		5	0	0	0	-1	0	0	3	0.0	0	0	0	0	0	0	1	2	0	1	0	0	0	0	.00

Joe Hulbig

Pos: LW **Shoots:** L **Ht:** 6'3" **Wt:** 215 **Born:** 9/29/73—Norwood, Massachusetts **Age:** 26

Overall											Power Play			Shorthand			Penalty							Misc	
Year	Tm	GP	G	A	Pts	+/–	GW	GT	S	SPct	G	A	Pts	G	A	Pts	Num	PIM	Maj	Mnr	Fgt	Rgh	HHT	Hat	P/G
96-97	Edm	6	0	0	0	-1	0	0	4	0.0	0	0	0	0	0	0	0	0	0	0	0	0	0	0	.00
97-98	Edm	17	2	2	4	-1	1	0	8	25.0	0	1	1	0	0	0	1	2	0	1	0	0	0	0	.24
98-99	Edm	1	0	0	0	1	0	0	2	0.0	0	0	0	0	0	0	1	2	0	1	0	0	1	0	.00
3 Years		24	2	2	4	-1	1	0	14	14.3	0	1	1	0	0	0	2	4	0	2	0	0	1	0	.17
Postseason																									
Year	Tm	GP	G	A	Pts	+/–	GW	OT	S	SPct	G	A	Pts	G	A	Pts	Num	PIM	Maj	Mnr	Fgt	Rgh	HHT	Hat	P/G
96-97	Edm	6	0	1	1	2	0	0	5	0.0	0	0	0	0	0	0	1	2	0	1	0	1	0	0	.17

Brett Hull

(statistical profile on page 321)

Pos: RW **Shoots:** R **Ht:** 5'11" **Wt:** 204 **Born:** 8/9/64—Belleville, Ontario **Age:** 35

Overall											Power Play			Shorthand			Penalty							Misc	
Year	Tm	GP	G	A	Pts	+/–	GW	GT	S	SPct	G	A	Pts	G	A	Pts	Num	PIM	Maj	Mnr	Fgt	Rgh	HHT	Hat	P/G
85-86		Did Not Play in Regular Season																							
86-87	Cgy	5	1	0	1	-1	1	0	5	20.0	0	0	0	0	0	0	0	0	0	0	0	0	0	0	.20
87-88	2Tm	65	32	32	64	14	3	0	211	15.2	6	–	–	0	–	–	8	16	0	8	0	–	–	1	.98
88-89	StL*	78	41	43	84	-17	6	1	305	13.4	16	–	–	0	–	–	–	33	–	–	–	–	–	0	1.08
89-90	StL*	**80**	**72**	41	113	-1	**12**	0	**385**	18.7	**27**	–	–	0	–	–	–	24	–	–	–	–	–	**5**	1.41
90-91	StL	78	**86**	45	131	23	**11**	1	**389**	22.1	**29**	–	–	0	–	–	–	22	–	–	–	–	–	4	1.68
91-92	StL*	73	**70**	39	109	-2	9	1	**408**	17.2	20	20	40	5	0	5	16	48	0	14	0	1	6	**8**	1.49
92-93	StL*	80	54	47	101	-27	2	1	390	13.8	29	29	58	0	0	0	15	41	1	13	0	0	5	0	1.26
93-94	StL*	81	57	40	97	-3	6	1	392	14.5	**25**	16	41	3	2	5	15	38	0	14	0	4	6	3	1.20
94-95	StL	48	29	21	50	13	6	0	200	14.5	9	7	16	3	3	**6**	5	10	0	5	0	0	1	2	1.04
95-96	StL*	70	43	40	83	4	6	0	327	13.1	16	17	33	5	1	6	11	30	0	10	0	2	5	2	1.19
96-97	StL*	77	42	40	82	-9	6	2	302	13.9	12	14	26	2	0	2	5	10	0	5	0	0	2	2	1.06

Overall											Power Play			Shorthand			Penalty							Misc	
Year	Tm	GP	G	A	Pts	+/–	GW	GT	S	SPct	G	A	Pts	G	A	Pts	Num	PIM	Maj	Mnr	Fgt	Rgh	HHT	Hat	P/G
97-98	StL	66	27	45	72	-1	6	0	211	12.8	10	12	22	0	1	1	9	26	0	8	0	0	4	1	1.09
98-99	Dal	60	32	26	58	19	**11**	0	192	16.7	15	6	21	0	0	0	15	30	0	15	0	0	9	0	.97
87-88	Cgy	52	26	24	50	10	3	0	153	17.0	4	–	–	0	–	–	6	12	0	6	0	–	–	1	.96
87-88	StL	13	6	8	14	4	0	0	58	10.3	2	–	–	0	–	–	2	4	0	2	0	–	–	0	1.08
13 Years		861	586	459	1045	12	85	7	3717	15.8	214	–	–	18	–	–	–	328	–	–	–	–	–	28	1.21
Postseason																									
Year	Tm	GP	G	A	Pts	+/–	GW	OT	S	SPct	G	A	Pts	G	A	Pts	Num	PIM	Maj	Mnr	Fgt	Rgh	HHT	Hat	P/G
85-86	Cgy	2	0	0	0	0	0	0	1	0.0	0	0	0	0	0	0	0	0	0	0	0	0	0	0	.00
86-87	Cgy	4	2	1	3	4	0	0	18	11.1	0	–	–	0	–	–	0	0	0	0	0	0	0	0	.75
87-88	StL	10	7	2	9	1	3	0	39	17.9	4	–	–	0	–	–	2	4	0	2	0	–	–	0	.90
88-89	StL	10	5	5	10	-4	2	1	43	11.6	1	–	–	0	–	–	3	6	0	3	0	–	–	0	1.00
89-90	StL	12	13	8	21	1	3	0	68	19.1	7	–	–	0	–	–	–	17	–	–	–	–	–	0	1.75
90-91	StL	13	11	8	19	5	2	0	58	19.0	3	–	–	0	0	0	2	4	0	2	0	–	–	0	1.46
91-92	StL	6	4	4	8	2	1	1	38	10.5	1	3	4	1	0	1	2	4	0	2	0	0	1	0	1.33
92-93	StL	11	8	5	13	-2	2	0	52	15.4	5	4	9	0	0	0	1	2	0	1	0	0	1	0	1.18
93-94	StL	4	2	1	3	1	0	0	22	9.1	1	0	1	0	0	0	0	0	0	0	0	0	0	0	.75
94-95	StL	7	6	2	8	0	0	0	34	17.6	2	1	3	0	0	0	0	0	0	0	0	0	0	0	1.14
95-96	StL	13	6	5	11	2	1	0	52	11.5	2	2	4	1	0	1	5	10	0	5	0	0	3	0	.85
96-97	StL	6	2	7	9	4	0	0	25	8.0	0	3	3	0	0	0	1	2	0	1	0	0	0	0	1.50
97-98	StL	10	3	3	6	-3	1	0	32	9.4	1	2	3	0	0	0	1	2	0	1	0	0	0	0	.60
98-99	Dal	22	8	7	15	3	2	1	86	9.3	3	1	4	0	0	0	2	4	0	2	0	0	1	0	.68
14 Years		130	77	58	135	14	17	3	568	13.6	30	–	–	2	–	–	–	55	–	–	–	–	–	0	1.04

Jody Hull

(statistical profile on page 322)

Pos: RW **Shoots:** R **Ht:** 6'2" **Wt:** 200 **Born:** 2/2/69—Petrolia, Ontario **Age:** 30

Overall											Power Play			Shorthand			Penalty							Misc	
Year	Tm	GP	G	A	Pts	+/–	GW	GT	S	SPct	G	A	Pts	G	A	Pts	Num	PIM	Maj	Mnr	Fgt	Rgh	HHT	Hat	P/G
88-89	Har	60	16	18	34	6	2	0	82	19.5	6	–	–	0	–	–	–	10	–	–	–	–	–	1	.57
89-90	Har	38	7	10	17	-6	0	0	46	15.2	2	–	–	0	–	–	–	21	–	–	–	–	–	0	.45
90-91	NYR	47	5	8	13	2	0	0	57	8.8	0	0	0	0	–	–	–	10	–	–	–	–	–	0	.28
91-92	NYR	3	0	0	0	-4	0	0	4	0.0	0	0	0	0	0	0	1	2	0	1	0	0	1	0	.00
92-93	Ott	69	13	21	34	-24	0	1	134	9.7	5	8	13	1	0	1	7	14	0	7	0	0	4	0	.49
93-94	Fla	69	13	13	26	6	5	1	100	13.0	0	0	0	1	2	3	4	8	0	4	0	0	4	0	.38
94-95	Fla	46	11	8	19	-1	4	0	63	17.5	0	1	1	0	0	0	4	8	0	4	0	1	1	0	.41
95-96	Fla	78	20	17	37	5	3	1	120	16.7	2	1	3	0	3	3	11	25	1	10	1	0	6	0	.47
96-97	Fla	67	10	6	16	1	2	1	92	10.9	0	2	2	1	0	1	2	4	0	2	0	0	1	0	.24
97-98	2Tm	49	4	4	8	3	2	0	51	7.8	0	0	0	1	1	2	4	8	0	4	0	1	2	0	.16
98-99	Phi	72	3	11	14	-2	1	1	73	4.1	0	0	0	0	1	1	6	12	0	6	0	0	2	0	.19
97-98	Fla	21	2	0	2	1	0	0	23	8.7	0	0	0	1	0	1	2	4	0	2	0	0	1	0	.10
97-98	TB	28	2	4	6	2	2	0	28	7.1	0	0	0	0	1	1	2	4	0	2	0	1	1	0	.21
11 Years		598	102	116	218	-14	19	5	822	12.4	15	–	–	4	–	–	–	122	–	–	–	–	–	1	.36
Postseason																									
Year	Tm	GP	G	A	Pts	+/–	GW	OT	S	SPct	G	A	Pts	G	A	Pts	Num	PIM	Maj	Mnr	Fgt	Rgh	HHT	Hat	P/G
88-89	Har	1	0	0	0	0	0	0	0	–	0	0	0	0	0	0	1	2	0	1	0	–	–	0	.00
89-90	Har	5	0	1	1	1	0	0	5	0.0	0	–	–	0	0	0	1	2	0	1	0	–	–	0	.20
95-96	Fla	14	3	2	5	4	0	0	18	16.7	0	0	0	0	0	0	0	0	0	0	0	0	0	0	.36
96-97	Fla	5	0	0	0	-1	0	0	12	0.0	0	0	0	0	0	0	0	0	0	0	0	0	0	0	.00
98-99	Phi	6	0	0	0	-1	0	0	6	0.0	0	0	0	0	0	0	2	4	0	2	0	0	1	0	.00
5 Years		31	3	3	6	3	0	0	41	7.3	0	–	–	0	0	0	4	8	0	4	0	–	–	0	.19

Cale Hulse

(statistical profile on page 322)

Pos: D **Shoots:** R **Ht:** 6'3" **Wt:** 215 **Born:** 11/10/73—Edmonton, Alberta **Age:** 26

Overall											Power Play			Shorthand			Penalty							Misc	
Year	Tm	GP	G	A	Pts	+/–	GW	GT	S	SPct	G	A	Pts	G	A	Pts	Num	PIM	Maj	Mnr	Fgt	Rgh	HHT	Hat	P/G
95-96	2Tm	11	0	0	0	1	0	0	9	0.0	0	0	0	0	0	0	7	20	2	5	2	1	1	0	.00
96-97	Cgy	63	1	6	7	-2	0	0	58	1.7	0	0	0	1	1	2	32	91	9	23	9	9	4	0	.11
97-98	Cgy	79	5	22	27	1	0	0	117	4.3	1	7	8	1	0	1	66	169	7	57	7	14	12	0	.34
98-99	Cgy	73	3	9	12	-8	0	0	83	3.6	0	1	1	0	0	0	48	117	7	41	7	6	13	0	.16
95-96	NJ	8	0	0	0	-2	0	0	5	0.0	0	0	0	0	0	0	6	15	1	5	1	1	1	0	.00
95-96	Cgy	3	0	0	0	3	0	0	4	0.0	0	0	0	0	0	0	1	5	1	0	1	0	0	0	.00
4 Years		226	9	37	46	-8	0	0	267	3.4	1	8	9	2	1	3	153	397	25	126	25	30	30	0	.20

							Postseason																		
Year	Tm	GP	G	A	Pts	+/–	GW	OT	S	SPct	G	A	Pts	G	A	Pts	Num	PIM	Maj	Mnr	Fgt	Rgh	HHT	Hat	P/G
95-96	Cgy	1	0	0	0	-2	0	0	2	0.0	0	0	0	0	0	0	0	0	0	0	0	0	0	0	.00

Dale Hunter

(statistical profile on page 322)

Pos: C **Shoots:** L **Ht:** 5'10" **Wt:** 200 **Born:** 7/31/60—Petrolia, Ontario **Age:** 39

		Overall									Power Play			Shorthand			Penalty							Misc	
Year	Tm	GP	G	A	Pts	+/–	GW	GT	S	SPct	G	A	Pts	G	A	Pts	Num	PIM	Maj	Mnr	Fgt	Rgh	HHT	Hat	P/G
80-81	Que	80	19	44	63	5	2	2	152	12.5	2	–	–	0	–	–	–	226	–	–	–	–	–	0	.79
81-82	Que	80	22	50	72	26	1	2	124	17.7	0	–	–	2	–	–	–	272	–	–	–	–	–	2	.90
82-83	Que	**80**	17	46	63	10	1	1	125	13.6	1	–	–	2	–	–	–	206	–	–	–	–	–	0	.79
83-84	Que	77	24	55	79	35	1	1	123	19.5	7	–	–	2	–	–	–	232	–	–	–	–	–	1	1.03
84-85	Que	**80**	20	52	72	23	3	0	115	17.4	3	–	–	3	–	–	77	209	13	62	–	–	–	0	.90
85-86	Que	80	28	42	70	6	4	0	152	18.4	7	–	–	0	–	–	111	265	9	100	–	–	–	0	.88
86-87	Que	46	10	29	39	4	0	0	53	18.9	0	–	–	0	–	–	–	135	–	–	–	–	–	0	.85
87-88	Was	79	22	37	59	7	1	2	126	17.5	11	–	–	0	–	–	–	240	–	–	–	–	–	0	.75
88-89	Was	**80**	20	37	57	-3	3	0	138	14.5	9	–	–	0	–	–	–	219	–	–	–	–	–	0	.71
89-90	Was	**80**	23	39	62	17	6	0	123	18.7	9	–	–	1	–	–	–	233	–	–	–	–	–	0	.78
90-91	Was	76	16	30	46	-22	2	0	106	15.1	9	–	–	0	–	–	–	234	–	–	–	–	–	0	.61
91-92	Was	80	28	50	78	-2	4	1	110	25.5	13	17	30	0	0	0	74	205	11	60	10	23	13	1	.98
92-93	Was	84	20	59	79	3	2	0	120	16.7	10	22	32	0	0	0	68	198	10	54	9	19	13	0	.94
93-94	Was	52	9	29	38	-4	1	0	61	14.8	1	6	7	0	0	0	53	131	3	48	3	23	5	0	.73
94-95	Was	45	8	15	23	-4	1	0	73	11.0	3	4	7	0	0	0	31	101	5	23	3	11	2	0	.51
95-96	Was	82	13	24	37	5	3	2	128	10.2	4	8	12	0	0	0	50	112	4	46	4	25	8	0	.45
96-97	Was*	**82**	14	32	46	-2	5	0	110	12.7	3	9	12	0	0	0	49	125	1	45	1	24	4	0	.56
97-98	Was	82	8	18	26	1	1	0	82	9.8	0	1	1	0	4	4	43	103	3	39	3	18	10	0	.32
98-99	2Tm	62	2	9	11	-7	0	0	24	8.3	0	1	1	0	1	1	37	119	7	27	7	15	3	0	.18
98-99	Was	50	0	5	5	-7	0	0	18	0.0	0	0	0	0	1	1	30	102	6	21	6	11	2	0	.10
98-99	Col	12	2	4	6	0	0	0	6	33.3	0	1	1	0	0	0	7	17	1	6	1	4	1	0	.50
19 Years		1407	323	697	1020	98	41	11	2045	15.8	92	–	–	10	–	–	–	3565	–	–	–	–	–	4	.72

							Postseason																		
Year	Tm	GP	G	A	Pts	+/–	GW	OT	S	SPct	G	A	Pts	G	A	Pts	Num	PIM	Maj	Mnr	Fgt	Rgh	HHT	Hat	P/G
80-81	Que	5	4	2	6	–	1	1	–	–	0	–	–	0	0	0	–	34	–	–	–	–	–	0	1.20
81-82	Que	16	3	7	10	–	2	1	–	–	1	–	–	0	–	–	–	52	–	–	–	–	–	0	.63
82-83	Que	4	2	1	3	0	0	0	7	28.6	0	–	–	0	0	0	–	24	–	–	–	–	–	0	.75
83-84	Que	9	2	3	5	-2	0	0	9	22.2	0	–	–	0	–	–	–	41	–	–	–	–	–	0	.56
84-85	Que	17	4	6	10	0	2	1	21	19.0	0	–	–	1	–	–	–	97	–	–	–	–	–	0	.59
85-86	Que	3	0	0	0	-1	0	0	9	0.0	0	0	0	0	0	0	–	15	–	–	–	–	–	0	.00
86-87	Que	13	1	7	8	-5	0	0	15	6.7	1	–	–	0	–	–	–	56	–	–	–	–	–	0	.62
87-88	Was	14	7	5	12	2	1	1	24	29.2	4	–	–	0	–	–	–	98	–	–	–	–	–	0	.86
88-89	Was	6	0	4	4	3	0	0	7	0.0	0	–	–	0	–	–	–	27	–	–	–	–	–	0	.67
89-90	Was	15	4	8	12	-1	0	0	13	30.8	1	–	–	0	–	–	–	61	–	–	–	–	–	0	.80
90-91	Was	11	1	9	10	2	0	0	16	6.3	0	–	–	0	–	–	–	41	–	–	–	–	–	0	.91
91-92	Was	7	1	4	5	-1	0	0	16	6.3	0	2	2	0	0	0	5	16	2	3	1	1	0	0	.71
92-93	Was	6	7	1	8	-7	1	0	18	38.9	4	0	4	0	0	0	12	35	1	10	0	4	1	1	1.33
93-94	Was	7	0	3	3	-2	0	0	7	0.0	0	1	1	0	0	0	7	14	0	7	0	3	1	0	.43
94-95	Was	7	4	4	8	0	0	0	13	30.8	2	1	3	0	0	0	8	24	0	7	0	5	0	0	1.14
95-96	Was	6	1	5	6	4	0	0	14	7.1	0	2	2	0	0	0	8	24	0	7	0	4	1	0	1.00
97-98	Was	21	0	4	4	-1	0	0	14	0.0	0	0	0	0	0	0	11	30	0	10	0	6	0	0	.19
98-99	Col	19	1	3	4	0	0	0	10	10.0	0	0	0	0	0	0	15	38	0	14	0	4	3	0	.21
18 Years		186	42	76	118	-9	7	4	213	16.4	13	–	–	1	–	–	–	727	–	–	–	–	–	1	.63

Mike Hurlbut

Pos: D **Shoots:** L **Ht:** 6'2" **Wt:** 200 **Born:** 10/7/66—Massena, New York **Age:** 33

		Overall									Power Play			Shorthand			Penalty							Misc	
Year	Tm	GP	G	A	Pts	+/–	GW	GT	S	SPct	G	A	Pts	G	A	Pts	Num	PIM	Maj	Mnr	Fgt	Rgh	HHT	Hat	P/G
92-93	NYR	23	1	8	9	4	0	0	26	3.8	1	3	4	0	0	0	8	16	0	8	0	1	3	0	.39
93-94	Que	1	0	0	0	-1	0	0	1	0.0	0	0	0	0	0	0	0	0	0	0	0	0	0	0	.00
94-95											Did Not Play in NHL														
95-96											Did Not Play in NHL														
96-97											Did Not Play in NHL														
97-98	Buf	3	0	0	0	-1	0	0	3	0.0	0	0	0	0	0	0	1	2	0	1	0	0	0	0	.00
98-99	Buf	1	0	0	0	2	0	0	2	0.0	0	0	0	0	0	0	0	0	0	0	0	0	0	0	.00
4 Years		28	1	8	9	4	0	0	32	3.1	1	3	4	0	0	0	9	18	0	9	0	1	3	0	.32

Jamie Huscroft

Pos: D **Shoots:** R **Ht:** 6'2" **Wt:** 200 **Born:** 1/9/67—Creston, British Columbia **Age:** 32

		Overall									Power Play			Shorthand			Penalty							Misc	
Year	**Tm**	**GP**	**G**	**A**	**Pts**	**+/–**	**GW**	**GT**	**S**	**SPct**	**G**	**A**	**Pts**	**G**	**A**	**Pts**	**Num**	**PIM**	**Maj**	**Mnr**	**Fgt**	**Rgh**	**HHT**	**Hat**	**P/G**
88-89	NJ	15	0	2	2	-3	0	0	9	0.0	0	0	0	0	0	0	–	51	–	–	–	–	–	0	.13
89-90	NJ	42	2	3	5	-2	0	0	19	10.5	0	0	0	0	0	0	–	149	–	–	–	–	–	0	.12
90-91	NJ	8	0	1	1	1	0	0	3	0.0	0	0	0	0	0	0	–	27	–	–	–	–	–	0	.13
91-92		Did Not Play in NHL																							
92-93		Did Not Play in NHL																							
93-94	Bos	36	0	1	1	-2	0	0	13	0.0	0	0	0	0	0	0	35	144	14	17	14	6	5	0	.03
94-95	Bos	34	0	6	6	-3	0	0	30	0.0	0	0	0	0	0	0	31	103	11	19	11	4	4	0	.18
95-96	Cgy	70	3	9	12	14	1	0	57	5.3	0	0	0	0	0	0	48	162	14	31	14	11	8	0	.17
96-97	2Tm	52	0	5	5	-2	0	0	40	0.0	0	0	0	0	0	0	48	151	13	33	13	13	10	0	.10
97-98	2Tm	51	0	4	4	-2	0	0	26	0.0	0	0	0	0	0	0	52	177	11	36	11	16	9	0	.08
98-99	2Tm	37	0	2	2	-4	0	0	27	0.0	0	0	0	0	0	0	35	90	4	30	4	9	9	0	.05
96-97	Cgy	39	0	4	4	2	0	0	33	0.0	0	0	0	0	0	0	38	117	11	26	11	10	9	0	.10
96-97	TB	13	0	1	1	-4	0	0	7	0.0	0	0	0	0	0	0	10	34	2	7	2	3	1	0	.08
97-98	TB	44	0	3	3	-4	0	0	21	0.0	0	0	0	0	0	0	37	122	8	26	8	13	8	0	.07
97-98	Van	7	0	1	1	2	0	0	5	0.0	0	0	0	0	0	0	15	55	3	10	3	3	1	0	.14
98-99	Van	26	0	1	1	-3	0	0	20	0.0	0	0	0	0	0	0	27	63	3	24	3	8	7	0	.04
98-99	Pho	11	0	1	1	-1	0	0	7	0.0	0	0	0	0	0	0	8	27	1	6	1	1	2	0	.09
9 Years		345	5	33	38	-3	1	0	224	2.2	0	0	0	0	0	0	–	1054	–	–	–	–	–	0	.11

Postseason

Year	**Tm**	**GP**	**G**	**A**	**Pts**	**+/–**	**GW**	**OT**	**S**	**SPct**	**G**	**A**	**Pts**	**G**	**A**	**Pts**	**Num**	**PIM**	**Maj**	**Mnr**	**Fgt**	**Rgh**	**HHT**	**Hat**	**P/G**
89-90	NJ	5	0	0	0	0	0	0	1	0.0	0	0	0	0	0	0	–	16	–	–	–	–	–	0	.00
90-91	NJ	3	0	0	0	0	0	0	0	–	0	0	0	0	0	0	3	6	0	3	0	–	–	0	.00
93-94	Bos	4	0	0	0	1	0	0	3	0.0	0	0	0	0	0	0	3	9	1	2	1	0	1	0	.00
94-95	Bos	5	0	0	0	0	0	0	0	–	0	0	0	0	0	0	4	11	1	3	1	2	0	0	.00
95-96	Cgy	4	0	1	1	-2	0	0	4	0.0	0	0	0	0	0	0	2	4	0	2	0	2	0	0	.25
5 Years		21	0	1	1	-1	0	0	8	0.0	0	0	0	0	0	0	–	46	–	–	–	–	–	0	.05

Jarome Iginla

(statistical profile on page 322)

Pos: RW **Shoots:** R **Ht:** 6'1" **Wt:** 202 **Born:** 7/1/77—Edmonton, Alberta **Age:** 22

		Overall									Power Play			Shorthand			Penalty							Misc	
Year	**Tm**	**GP**	**G**	**A**	**Pts**	**+/–**	**GW**	**GT**	**S**	**SPct**	**G**	**A**	**Pts**	**G**	**A**	**Pts**	**Num**	**PIM**	**Maj**	**Mnr**	**Fgt**	**Rgh**	**HHT**	**Hat**	**P/G**
95-96		Did Not Play in Regular Season																							
96-97	Cgy	**82**	21	29	50	-4	3	0	169	12.4	8	9	17	1	3	4	14	37	3	11	3	2	6	0	.61
97-98	Cgy	70	13	19	32	-10	1	0	154	8.4	0	5	5	2	1	3	10	29	3	7	3	2	2	0	.46
98-99	Cgy	82	28	23	51	1	4	1	211	13.3	7	9	16	0	0	0	23	58	4	19	4	9	2	0	.62
3 Years		234	62	71	133	-13	8	1	534	11.6	15	23	38	3	4	7	47	124	10	37	10	13	10	0	.57

Postseason

Year	**Tm**	**GP**	**G**	**A**	**Pts**	**+/–**	**GW**	**OT**	**S**	**SPct**	**G**	**A**	**Pts**	**G**	**A**	**Pts**	**Num**	**PIM**	**Maj**	**Mnr**	**Fgt**	**Rgh**	**HHT**	**Hat**	**P/G**
95-96	Cgy	2	1	1	2	2	0	0	6	16.7	0	0	0	0	0	0	0	0	0	0	0	0	0	0	1.00

Victor Ignatjev

Pos: D **Shoots:** L **Ht:** 6'3" **Wt:** 215 **Born:** 4/26/70—Riga, USSR **Age:** 29

		Overall									Power Play			Shorthand			Penalty							Misc	
Year	**Tm**	**GP**	**G**	**A**	**Pts**	**+/–**	**GW**	**GT**	**S**	**SPct**	**G**	**A**	**Pts**	**G**	**A**	**Pts**	**Num**	**PIM**	**Maj**	**Mnr**	**Fgt**	**Rgh**	**HHT**	**Hat**	**P/G**
98-99	Pit	11	0	1	1	-3	0	0	15	0.0	0	1	1	0	0	0	3	6	0	3	0	0	1	0	.09

Postseason

Year	**Tm**	**GP**	**G**	**A**	**Pts**	**+/–**	**GW**	**OT**	**S**	**SPct**	**G**	**A**	**Pts**	**G**	**A**	**Pts**	**Num**	**PIM**	**Maj**	**Mnr**	**Fgt**	**Rgh**	**HHT**	**Hat**	**P/G**
98-99	Pit	1	0	0	0	0	0	0	0	–	0	0	0	0	0	0	1	2	0	1	0	0	0	0	.00

Arturs Irbe

(statistical profile on page 399)

Pos: G **Catches:** L **Ht:** 5'8" **Wt:** 175 **Born:** 2/2/67—Riga, USSR **Age:** 32

		Overall														Pen Shot		Offense		
Year	**Tm**	**GP**	**GS**	**TP**	**W**	**L**	**T**	**Min**	**GA**	**GAA**	**Shots**	**SvPct**	**ShO**	**OE**	**PPGA**	**SHGA**	**Shots**	**GA**	**G**	**A**	**PIM**
91-92	SJ	13	11	3	2	6	3	645	48	4.47	365	.868	0	3	12	1	0	0	0	1	0
92-93	SJ	36	34	2	7	26	0	2074	142	4.11	1250	.886	1	10	34	2	0	0	0	0	10
93-94	SJ*	**74**	**73**	4	30	28	**16**	**4412**	209	2.84	2064	.899	3	25	63	10	0	0	0	2	16
94-95	SJ	38	35	5	14	19	3	2043	111	3.26	1056	.895	4	15	26	2	1	**1**	0	0	4
95-96	SJ	22	20	5	4	12	4	1112	85	4.59	607	.860	0	4	21	3	1	**1**	0	0	4
96-97	Dal	35	31	2	17	12	3	1965	88	2.69	825	.893	3	8	20	6	0	0	0	2	8

Year	Tm	Overall GP	GS	TP	W	L	T	Min	GA	GAA	Shots	SvPct	ShO	OE	PPGA	SHGA	Pen Shot Shots	GA	Offense G	A	PIM
97-98	Van	41	33	**9**	14	11	6	1999	91	2.73	982	.907	2	13	26	4	1	1	0	0	2
98-99	Car	62	61	4	27	20	12	3643	135	2.22	1753	.923	6	30	32	5	0	0	0	0	10
8 Years		321	298	34	115	134	47	17893	909	3.05	8902	.898	19	108	234	33	3	3	0	5	54
Postseason																					
Year	Tm	GP	GS	TP	W	L	Pct	Min	GA	GAA	Shots	SvPct	ShO	OE	PPGA	SHGA	Shots	GA	G	A	PIM
93-94	SJ	14	14	2	7	7	.500	806	50	3.72	399	.875	0	3	12	3	0	0	0	0	6
94-95	SJ	6	6	1	2	4	.333	316	27	5.13	210	.871	0	0	7	5	0	0	0	0	10
96-97	Dal	1	0	0	0	0	–	13	0	0.00	4	1.000	0	0	0	0	0	0	0	0	0
98-99	Car	6	6	0	2	4	.333	408	15	2.21	181	.917	0	0	4	0	0	0	0	0	0
4 Years		27	26	3	11	15	.423	1543	92	3.58	794	.884	0	3	23	8	0	0	0	0	16

Brad Isbister

Pos: RW **Shoots:** R **Ht:** 6'3" **Wt:** 222 **Born:** 5/7/77—Edmonton, Alberta **Age:** 22

Year	Tm	Overall GP	G	A	Pts	+/–	GW	GT	S	SPct	Power Play G	A	Pts	Shorthand G	A	Pts	Penalty Num	PIM	Maj	Mnr	Fgt	Rgh	HHT	Misc Hat	P/G
97-98	Pho	66	9	8	17	4	1	0	115	7.8	1	1	2	0	0	0	37	102	4	31	4	14	7	0	.26
98-99	Pho	32	4	4	8	1	2	0	48	8.3	0	0	0	0	0	0	13	46	4	8	4	2	0	0	.25
2 Years		98	13	12	25	5	3	0	163	8.0	1	1	2	0	0	0	50	148	8	39	8	16	7	0	.26
Postseason																									
Year	Tm	GP	G	A	Pts	+/–	GW	OT	S	SPct	G	A	Pts	G	A	Pts	Num	PIM	Maj	Mnr	Fgt	Rgh	HHT	Hat	P/G
97-98	Pho	5	0	0	0	-1	0	0	6	0.0	0	0	0	0	0	0	1	2	0	1	0	0	0	0	.00

Jaromir Jagr

(statistical profile on page 323)

Pos: RW **Shoots:** L **Ht:** 6'2" **Wt:** 228 **Born:** 2/15/72—Kladno, Czechoslovakia **Age:** 27

Year	Tm	Overall GP	G	A	Pts	+/–	GW	GT	S	SPct	Power Play G	A	Pts	Shorthand G	A	Pts	Penalty Num	PIM	Maj	Mnr	Fgt	Rgh	HHT	Misc Hat	P/G
90-91	Pit	80	27	30	57	-4	4	0	136	19.9	7	6	13	0	0	0	17	42	0	16	0	1	9	1	.71
91-92	Pit*	70	32	37	69	12	4	0	194	16.5	4	5	9	0	0	0	13	34	0	12	0	2	4	0	.99
92-93	Pit*	81	34	60	94	30	9	0	242	14.0	10	12	22	1	0	1	25	61	1	23	0	2	7	0	1.16
93-94	Pit	80	32	67	99	15	6	2	298	10.7	9	20	29	0	0	0	25	61	1	23	0	4	11	0	1.24
94-95	Pit	48	32	38	**70**	23	7	0	192	16.7	8	14	22	3	0	3	13	37	1	11	0	1	4	1	1.46
95-96	Pit*	82	62	87	149	31	**12**	1	**403**	15.4	20	31	51	1	2	3	48	96	0	48	0	8	19	0	1.82
96-97	Pit*	63	47	48	95	22	6	1	234	20.1	11	14	25	2	1	3	16	40	0	15	0	2	4	2	1.51
97-98	Pit*	77	35	**67**	**102**	17	8	2	262	13.4	7	**31**	**38**	0	0	0	32	64	0	32	0	6	12	0	**1.32**
98-99	Pit	81	44	**83**	**127**	17	7	2	343	12.8	10	**34**	44	1	0	1	33	66	0	33	0	5	16	0	**1.57**
9 Years		662	345	517	862	163	63	8	2304	15.0	86	167	253	8	3	11	222	501	3	213	0	31	86	4	1.30
Postseason																									
Year	Tm	GP	G	A	Pts	+/–	GW	OT	S	SPct	G	A	Pts	G	A	Pts	Num	PIM	Maj	Mnr	Fgt	Rgh	HHT	Hat	P/G
90-91	Pit	24	3	10	13	2	1	1	57	5.3	1	1	2	0	0	0	3	6	0	3	0	0	1	0	.54
91-92	Pit	21	11	13	24	4	4	1	59	18.6	2	3	5	0	0	0	3	6	0	3	0	2	1	0	1.14
92-93	Pit	12	5	4	9	3	1	0	47	10.6	1	0	1	0	0	0	6	23	1	4	0	0	2	0	.75
93-94	Pit	6	2	4	6	-3	1	0	16	12.5	0	0	0	0	0	0	4	16	0	3	0	0	1	0	1.00
94-95	Pit	12	10	5	15	3	1	0	55	18.2	2	2	4	1	0	1	3	6	0	3	0	2	0	0	1.25
95-96	Pit	18	11	12	23	7	1	0	74	14.9	5	4	9	1	0	1	9	18	0	9	0	5	2	1	1.28
96-97	Pit	5	4	4	8	-4	0	0	18	22.2	2	2	4	0	0	0	2	4	0	2	0	0	2	0	1.60
97-98	Pit	6	4	5	9	5	0	0	23	17.4	1	1	2	0	0	0	1	2	0	1	0	1	0	0	1.50
98-99	Pit	9	5	7	12	1	1	1	32	15.6	1	2	3	0	0	0	8	16	0	8	0	1	2	0	1.33
9 Years		113	55	64	119	18	10	3	381	14.4	15	15	30	2	0	2	39	97	1	36	0	11	11	1	1.05

John Jakopin

Pos: D **Shoots:** R **Ht:** 6'5" **Wt:** 220 **Born:** 5/16/75—Toronto, Ontario **Age:** 24

Year	Tm	Overall GP	G	A	Pts	+/–	GW	GT	S	SPct	Power Play G	A	Pts	Shorthand G	A	Pts	Penalty Num	PIM	Maj	Mnr	Fgt	Rgh	HHT	Misc Hat	P/G
97-98	Fla	2	0	0	0	-3	0	0	1	0.0	0	0	0	0	0	0	2	4	0	2	0	0	1	0	.00
98-99	Fla	3	0	0	0	-1	0	0	0	–	0	0	0	0	0	0	0	0	0	0	0	0	0	0	.00
2 Years		5	0	0	0	-4	0	0	1	0.0	0	0	0	0	0	0	2	4	0	2	0	0	1	0	.00

Craig Janney

(statistical profile on page 323)

Pos: C **Shoots:** L **Ht:** 6'1" **Wt:** 200 **Born:** 9/26/67—Hartford, Connecticut **Age:** 32

Overall											Power Play			Shorthand			Penalty							Misc	
Year	Tm	GP	G	A	Pts	+/–	GW	GT	S	SPct	G	A	Pts	G	A	Pts	Num	PIM	Maj	Mnr	Fgt	Rgh	HHT	Hat	P/G
87-88	Bos	15	7	9	16	6	1	0	29	24.1	1	–	–	0	–	–	0	0	0	0	0	0	0	1	1.07
88-89	Bos	62	16	46	62	20	2	0	95	16.8	2	18	20	0	–	–	–	12	–	–	–	–	–	0	1.00
89-90	Bos	55	24	38	62	3	5	2	105	22.9	11	23	34	0	–	–	2	4	0	2	0	–	–	0	1.13
90-91	Bos	77	26	66	92	15	5	0	133	19.5	9	24	33	1	0	1	4	8	0	4	0	–	–	0	1.19
91-92	2Tm	78	18	69	87	6	2	0	127	14.2	6	25	31	0	0	0	7	22	0	6	0	2	2	1	1.12
92-93	StL	84	24	82	106	-4	6	0	137	17.5	8	36	44	0	0	0	6	12	0	6	0	2	1	1	1.26
93-94	StL	69	16	68	84	-14	7	0	95	16.8	8	32	40	0	0	0	12	24	0	12	0	3	4	0	1.22
94-95	2Tm	35	7	20	27	-1	1	0	40	17.5	3	9	12	0	0	0	5	10	0	5	0	0	2	0	.77
95-96	2Tm	**84**	20	62	82	-33	2	0	91	22.0	7	28	35	0	0	0	9	26	0	8	0	0	5	0	.98
96-97	Pho	77	15	38	53	-1	1	0	88	17.0	5	8	13	0	0	0	9	26	0	8	0	1	3	0	.69
97-98	Pho	68	10	43	53	5	0	0	72	13.9	4	9	13	0	0	0	6	12	0	6	0	0	4	0	.78
98-99	2Tm	56	5	22	27	-15	0	1	45	11.1	2	11	13	0	0	0	7	14	0	7	0	1	3	0	.48
91-92	Bos	53	12	39	51	1	1	0	90	13.3	3	16	19	0	0	0	6	20	0	5	0	2	2	0	.96
91-92	StL	25	6	30	36	5	1	0	37	16.2	3	9	12	0	0	0	1	2	0	1	0	0	0	1	1.44
94-95	StL	8	2	5	7	3	0	0	9	22.2	1	2	3	0	0	0	0	0	0	0	0	0	0	0	.88
94-95	SJ	27	5	15	20	-4	1	0	31	16.1	2	7	9	0	0	0	5	10	0	5	0	0	2	0	.74
95-96	SJ	71	13	49	62	-35	1	0	78	16.7	5	20	25	0	0	0	9	26	0	8	0	0	5	0	.87
95-96	Wpg	13	7	13	20	2	1	0	13	53.8	2	8	10	0	0	0	0	0	0	0	0	0	0	0	1.54
98-99	TB	38	4	18	22	-13	0	1	36	11.1	2	9	11	0	0	0	5	10	0	5	0	1	1	0	.58
98-99	NYI	18	1	4	5	-2	0	0	9	11.1	0	2	2	0	0	0	2	4	0	2	0	0	2	0	.28
12 Years		760	188	563	751	-13	32	3	1057	17.8	66	–	–	1	–	–	–	170	–	–	–	–	–	3	.99

Postseason

Year	Tm	GP	G	A	Pts	+/–	GW	OT	S	SPct	G	A	Pts	G	A	Pts	Num	PIM	Maj	Mnr	Fgt	Rgh	HHT	Hat	P/G
87-88	Bos	23	6	10	16	-1	1	0	41	14.6	4	–	–	0	–	–	4	11	1	3	–	–	–	0	.70
88-89	Bos	10	4	9	13	1	0	0	23	17.4	0	–	–	0	–	–	–	21	–	–	–	–	–	0	1.30
89-90	Bos	18	3	19	22	3	2	0	27	11.1	1	6	7	0	–	–	1	2	0	1	0	–	–	0	1.22
90-91	Bos	18	4	18	22	-4	0	0	26	15.4	4	7	11	0	0	0	4	11	1	3	–	–	–	0	1.22
91-92	StL	6	0	6	6	-4	0	0	7	0.0	0	4	4	0	0	0	0	0	0	0	0	0	0	0	1.00
92-93	StL	11	2	9	11	4	2	1	11	18.2	1	3	4	0	0	0	0	0	0	0	0	0	0	0	1.00
93-94	StL	4	1	3	4	3	0	0	8	12.5	0	1	1	0	0	0	0	0	0	0	0	0	0	0	1.00
94-95	SJ	11	3	4	7	-13	1	0	17	17.6	0	0	0	0	0	0	2	4	0	2	0	0	1	0	.64
95-96	Wpg	6	1	2	3	0	0	0	6	16.7	0	0	0	0	0	0	0	0	0	0	0	0	0	0	.50
96-97	Pho	7	0	3	3	1	0	0	6	0.0	0	1	1	0	0	0	2	4	0	2	0	1	0	0	.43
97-98	Pho	6	0	3	3	-2	0	0	6	0.0	0	1	1	0	0	0	0	0	0	0	0	0	0	0	.50
11 Years		120	24	86	110	-12	6	1	178	13.5	10	–	–	0	–	–	–	53	–	–	–	–	–	0	.92

Mark Janssens

Pos: C **Shoots:** L **Ht:** 6'3" **Wt:** 212 **Born:** 5/19/68—Surrey, British Columbia **Age:** 31

Overall											Power Play			Shorthand			Penalty							Misc	
Year	Tm	GP	G	A	Pts	+/–	GW	GT	S	SPct	G	A	Pts	G	A	Pts	Num	PIM	Maj	Mnr	Fgt	Rgh	HHT	Hat	P/G
87-88	NYR	1	0	0	0	0	0	0	0	–	0	0	0	0	0	0	0	0	0	0	0	0	0	0	.00
88-89	NYR	5	0	0	0	-4	0	0	0	–	0	0	0	0	0	0	0	0	0	0	0	0	0	0	.00
89-90	NYR	**80**	5	8	13	-26	0	0	61	8.2	0	1	1	0	–	–	56	161	11	43	–	–	–	0	.16
90-91	NYR	67	9	7	16	-1	1	0	45	20.0	0	0	0	0	–	–	–	172	–	–	–	–	–	0	.24
91-92	2Tm	7	0	0	0	-2	0	0	1	0.0	0	0	0	0	0	0	1	5	1	0	1	0	0	0	.00
92-93	Har	76	12	17	29	-15	1	0	63	19.0	0	0	0	0	0	0	73	237	17	51	15	22	13	0	.38
93-94	Har	84	2	10	12	-13	0	0	52	3.8	0	1	1	0	0	0	49	137	13	36	13	15	9	0	.14
94-95	Har	46	2	5	7	-8	0	0	33	6.1	0	0	0	0	0	0	28	93	7	19	7	11	3	0	.15
95-96	Har	81	2	7	9	-13	0	0	63	3.2	0	0	0	0	0	0	46	155	13	30	13	7	6	0	.11
96-97	2Tm	66	2	6	8	-13	0	0	39	5.1	0	1	1	0	0	0	34	137	15	16	14	2	3	0	.12
97-98	3Tm	74	5	7	12	-21	1	0	53	9.4	0	0	0	0	0	0	52	154	14	37	14	8	10	0	.16
98-99	Chi	60	1	0	1	-11	0	0	27	3.7	0	0	0	0	0	0	17	65	5	10	5	3	2	0	.02
91-92	NYR	4	0	0	0	-1	0	0	0	–	0	0	0	0	0	0	1	5	1	0	1	0	0	0	.00
91-92	Min	3	0	0	0	-1	0	0	1	0.0	0	0	0	0	0	0	0	0	0	0	0	0	0	0	.00
96-97	Har	54	2	4	6	-10	0	0	30	6.7	0	1	1	0	0	0	23	90	12	10	12	2	1	0	.11
96-97	Anh	12	0	2	2	-3	0	0	9	0.0	0	0	0	0	0	0	11	47	3	6	2	0	2	0	.17
97-98	Anh	55	4	5	9	-22	1	0	43	9.3	0	0	0	0	0	0	39	116	10	28	10	6	7	0	.16
97-98	NYI	12	0	0	0	-3	0	0	4	0.0	0	0	0	0	0	0	11	34	4	7	4	1	2	0	.00
97-98	Pho	7	1	2	3	4	0	0	6	16.7	0	0	0	0	0	0	2	4	0	2	0	1	1	0	.43
12 Years		647	40	67	107	-127	3	0	437	9.2	0	3	3	0	–	–	–	1316	–	–	–	–	–	0	.17

Postseason

Year	Tm	GP	G	A	Pts	+/–	GW	OT	S	SPct	G	A	Pts	G	A	Pts	Num	PIM	Maj	Mnr	Fgt	Rgh	HHT	Hat	P/G
89-90	NYR	9	2	1	3	0	1	0	6	33.3	0	–	–	0	–	–	–	10	–	–	–	–	–	0	.33

Postseason																										
Year	Tm	GP	G	A	Pts	+/-	GW	OT	S	SPct	G	A	Pts	G	A	Pts	Num	PIM	Maj	Mnr	Fgt	Rgh	HHT	Hat	P/G
90-91	NYR	6	3	0	3	1	0	0	6	50.0	0	0	0	0	0	0	3	6	0	3	0	–	–	0	.50
96-97	Anh	11	0	0	0	-3	0	0	13	0.0	0	0	0	0	0	0	6	15	1	5	1	2	1	0	.00
97-98	Pho	1	0	0	0	0	0	0	0	–	0	0	0	0	0	0	1	2	0	1	0	1	0	0	.00
4 Years		27	5	1	6	-2	1	0	25	20.0	0	–	–	0	–	–	–	33	–	–	–	–	–	0	.22

Andreas Johansson

(statistical profile on page 323)

Pos: C **Shoots:** L **Ht:** 6'2" **Wt:** 209 **Born:** 5/19/73—Hofors, Sweden **Age:** 26

		Overall									Power Play			Shorthand			Penalty							Misc	
Year	Tm	GP	G	A	Pts	+/-	GW	GT	S	SPct	G	A	Pts	G	A	Pts	Num	PIM	Maj	Mnr	Fgt	Rgh	HHT	Hat	P/G
95-96	NYI	3	0	1	1	1	0	0	6	0.0	0	0	0	0	0	0	0	0	0	0	0	0	0	0	.33
96-97	2Tm	42	4	9	13	-12	0	0	59	6.8	1	1	2	0	0	0	10	20	0	10	0	1	2	0	.31
97-98	Pit	50	5	10	15	4	0	0	49	10.2	0	1	1	1	1	2	10	20	0	10	0	3	3	0	.30
98-99	Ott	69	21	16	37	1	6	0	144	14.6	7	8	15	0	0	0	13	34	0	12	0	2	2	0	.54
96-97	NYI	15	2	2	4	-6	0	0	21	9.5	1	1	2	0	0	0	0	0	0	0	0	0	0	0	.27
96-97	Pit	27	2	7	9	-6	0	0	38	5.3	0	0	0	0	0	0	10	20	0	10	0	1	2	0	.33
4 Years		164	30	36	66	-6	6	0	258	11.6	8	10	18	1	1	2	33	74	0	32	0	6	7	0	.40
Postseason																									
Year	Tm	GP	G	A	Pts	+/-	GW	OT	S	SPct	G	A	Pts	G	A	Pts	Num	PIM	Maj	Mnr	Fgt	Rgh	HHT	Hat	P/G
97-98	Pit	1	0	0	0	0	0	0	0	–	0	0	0	0	0	0	0	0	0	0	0	0	0	0	.00
98-99	Ott	2	0	0	0	-3	0	0	4	0.0	0	0	0	0	0	0	0	0	0	0	0	0	0	0	.00
2 Years		3	0	0	0	-3	0	0	4	0.0	0	0	0	0	0	0	0	0	0	0	0	0	0	0	.00

Calle Johansson

(statistical profile on page 323)

Pos: D **Shoots:** L **Ht:** 5'11" **Wt:** 200 **Born:** 2/14/67—Goteborg, Sweden **Age:** 32

		Overall									Power Play			Shorthand			Penalty							Misc	
Year	Tm	GP	G	A	Pts	+/-	GW	GT	S	SPct	G	A	Pts	G	A	Pts	Num	PIM	Maj	Mnr	Fgt	Rgh	HHT	Hat	P/G
87-88	Buf	71	4	38	42	12	0	0	93	4.3	2	–	–	0	–	–	–	37	–	–	–	–	–	0	.59
88-89	2Tm	59	3	18	21	-6	1	0	75	4.0	1	–	–	0	–	–	–	37	–	–	–	–	–	0	.36
89-90	Was	70	8	31	39	7	2	0	103	7.8	4	–	–	0	–	–	–	25	–	–	–	–	–	0	.56
90-91	Was	80	11	41	52	-2	2	0	128	8.6	2	–	–	1	–	–	–	23	–	–	–	–	–	0	.65
91-92	Was	80	14	42	56	2	2	0	119	11.8	5	26	31	2	1	3	23	49	1	22	0	4	10	0	.70
92-93	Was	77	7	38	45	3	0	1	133	5.3	6	20	26	0	0	0	28	56	0	28	0	5	5	0	.58
93-94	Was	84	9	33	42	3	1	0	141	6.4	4	12	16	0	0	0	20	59	1	17	0	6	4	0	.50
94-95	Was	46	5	26	31	-6	2	0	112	4.5	4	20	24	0	1	1	12	35	1	10	0	2	1	0	.67
95-96	Was	78	10	25	35	13	0	0	182	5.5	4	11	15	0	2	2	18	50	2	15	1	5	3	0	.45
96-97	Was	65	6	11	17	-2	0	0	133	4.5	2	4	6	0	0	0	8	16	0	8	0	2	1	0	.26
97-98	Was	73	15	20	35	-11	1	2	163	9.2	10	10	20	1	1	2	15	30	0	15	0	1	6	0	.48
98-99	Was	67	8	21	29	10	2	1	145	5.5	2	13	15	0	1	1	11	22	0	11	0	1	4	0	.43
88-89	Buf	47	2	11	13	-7	1	0	53	3.8	0	–	–	0	–	–	–	33	–	–	–	–	–	0	.28
88-89	Was	12	1	7	8	1	0	0	22	4.5	1	–	–	0	–	–	2	4	0	2	0	–	–	0	.67
12 Years		850	100	344	444	23	13	4	1527	6.5	46	–	–	4	–	–	–	439	–	–	–	–	–	0	.52
Postseason																									
Year	Tm	GP	G	A	Pts	+/-	GW	OT	S	SPct	G	A	Pts	G	A	Pts	Num	PIM	Maj	Mnr	Fgt	Rgh	HHT	Hat	P/G
87-88	Buf	6	0	1	1	-4	0	0	8	0.0	0	–	–	0	0	0	0	0	0	0	0	0	0	0	.17
88-89	Was	6	1	2	3	-2	0	0	13	7.7	1	–	–	0	–	–	0	0	0	0	0	0	0	0	.50
89-90	Was	15	1	6	7	2	0	0	17	5.9	0	–	–	0	–	–	2	4	0	2	0	0	0	0	.47
90-91	Was	10	2	7	9	-3	0	0	24	8.3	1	–	–	0	–	–	4	8	0	4	0	0	0	0	.90
91-92	Was	7	0	5	5	4	0	0	10	0.0	0	1	1	0	1	1	2	4	0	2	0	2	0	0	.71
92-93	Was	6	0	5	5	-4	0	0	4	0.0	0	4	4	0	0	0	2	4	0	2	0	0	0	0	.83
93-94	Was	6	1	3	4	4	1	0	12	8.3	0	1	1	0	1	1	2	4	0	2	0	0	2	0	.67
94-95	Was	7	3	1	4	6	0	0	21	14.3	1	0	1	0	1	1	0	0	0	0	0	0	0	0	.57
97-98	Was	21	2	8	10	9	0	0	42	4.8	0	4	4	0	0	0	8	16	0	8	0	1	4	0	.48
9 Years		84	10	38	48	12	1	0	151	6.6	3	–	–	0	–	–	20	40	0	20	0	3	6	0	.57

Brent Johnson

Pos: G **Catches:** L **Ht:** 6'1" **Wt:** 175 **Born:** 3/12/77—Farmington, Michigan **Age:** 22

		Overall															Pen Shot		Offense		
Year	Tm	GP	GS	TP	W	L	T	Min	GA	GAA	Shots	SvPct	ShO	OE	PPGA	SHGA	Shots	GA	G	A	PIM
98-99	StL	6	5	1	3	2	0	286	10	2.10	127	.921	0	1	0	0	0	0	0	0	0

Craig Johnson

(statistical profile on page 324)

Pos: LW **Shoots:** L **Ht:** 6'2" **Wt:** 198 **Born:** 3/8/72—St. Paul, Minnesota **Age:** 27

Overall											Power Play			Shorthand			Penalty							Misc	
Year	Tm	GP	G	A	Pts	+/–	GW	GT	S	SPct	G	A	Pts	G	A	Pts	Num	PIM	Maj	Mnr	Fgt	Rgh	HHT	Hat	P/G
94-95	StL	15	3	3	6	4	0	0	19	15.8	0	0	0	0	0	0	3	6	0	3	0	0	3	0	.40
95-96	2Tm	60	13	11	24	-8	0	0	97	13.4	4	0	4	0	0	0	18	36	0	18	0	4	6	0	.40
96-97	LA	31	4	3	7	-7	0	0	30	13.3	1	0	1	0	0	0	10	26	2	8	1	2	4	0	.23
97-98	LA	74	17	21	38	9	2	0	125	13.6	6	3	9	0	0	0	21	42	0	21	0	0	15	0	.51
98-99	LA	69	7	12	19	-12	2	0	94	7.4	2	0	2	0	0	0	16	32	0	16	0	3	11	0	.28
95-96	StL	49	8	7	15	-4	0	0	69	11.6	1	0	1	0	0	0	15	30	0	15	0	3	5	0	.31
95-96	LA	11	5	4	9	-4	0	0	28	17.9	3	0	3	0	0	0	3	6	0	3	0	1	1	0	.82
5 Years		249	44	50	94	-14	4	0	365	12.1	13	3	16	0	0	0	68	142	2	66	1	9	39	0	.38

Postseason

Year	Tm	GP	G	A	Pts	+/–	GW	OT	S	SPct	G	A	Pts	G	A	Pts	Num	PIM	Maj	Mnr	Fgt	Rgh	HHT	Hat	P/G
94-95	StL	1	0	0	0	0	0	0	0	–	0	0	0	0	0	0	1	2	0	1	0	0	1	0	.00
97-98	LA	4	1	0	1	0	0	0	3	33.3	0	0	0	0	0	0	2	4	0	2	0	0	1	0	.25
2 Years		5	1	0	1	0	0	0	3	33.3	0	0	0	0	0	0	3	6	0	3	0	0	2	0	.20

Greg Johnson

(statistical profile on page 324)

Pos: C **Shoots:** L **Ht:** 5'10" **Wt:** 194 **Born:** 3/16/71—Thunder Bay, Ontario **Age:** 28

Overall											Power Play			Shorthand			Penalty							Misc	
Year	Tm	GP	G	A	Pts	+/–	GW	GT	S	SPct	G	A	Pts	G	A	Pts	Num	PIM	Maj	Mnr	Fgt	Rgh	HHT	Hat	P/G
93-94	Det	52	6	11	17	-7	0	0	48	12.5	1	1	2	1	1	2	11	22	0	11	0	0	7	0	.33
94-95	Det	22	3	5	8	1	0	0	32	9.4	2	0	2	0	0	0	7	14	0	7	0	0	4	0	.36
95-96	Det	60	18	22	40	6	2	0	87	20.7	5	9	14	0	1	1	15	30	0	15	0	2	6	0	.67
96-97	2Tm	75	13	19	32	-18	0	0	108	12.0	1	4	5	0	2	2	13	26	0	13	0	0	9	0	.43
97-98	2Tm	74	12	22	34	-2	3	0	89	13.5	4	3	7	0	0	0	20	40	0	20	0	0	10	0	.46
98-99	Nsh	68	16	34	50	-8	0	0	120	13.3	2	11	13	3	1	4	12	24	0	12	0	0	9	0	.74
96-97	Det	43	6	10	16	-5	0	0	56	10.7	0	3	3	0	0	0	6	12	0	6	0	0	3	0	.37
96-97	Pit	32	7	9	16	-13	0	0	52	13.5	1	1	2	0	2	2	7	14	0	7	0	0	6	0	.50
97-98	Pit	5	1	0	1	0	0	0	4	25.0	0	0	0	0	0	0	1	2	0	1	0	0	0	0	.20
97-98	Chi	69	11	22	33	-2	3	0	85	12.9	4	3	7	0	0	0	19	38	0	19	0	0	10	0	.48
6 Years		351	68	113	181	-28	5	0	484	14.0	15	28	43	4	5	9	78	156	0	78	0	2	45	0	.52

Postseason

Year	Tm	GP	G	A	Pts	+/–	GW	OT	S	SPct	G	A	Pts	G	A	Pts	Num	PIM	Maj	Mnr	Fgt	Rgh	HHT	Hat	P/G
93-94	Det	7	2	2	4	-2	0	0	7	28.6	1	1	2	0	0	0	1	2	0	1	0	0	0	0	.57
94-95	Det	1	0	0	0	1	0	0	0	–	0	0	0	0	0	0	0	0	0	0	0	0	0	0	.00
95-96	Det	13	3	1	4	-3	0	0	11	27.3	0	0	0	0	0	0	4	8	0	4	0	0	1	0	.31
96-97	Pit	5	1	0	1	-1	0	0	2	50.0	0	0	0	0	0	0	1	2	0	1	0	0	1	0	.20
4 Years		26	6	3	9	-5	0	0	20	30.0	1	1	2	0	0	0	6	12	0	6	0	0	2	0	.35

Matt Johnson

Pos: LW **Shoots:** L **Ht:** 6'5" **Wt:** 230 **Born:** 11/23/75—Welland, Ontario **Age:** 24

Overall											Power Play			Shorthand			Penalty							Misc	
Year	Tm	GP	G	A	Pts	+/–	GW	GT	S	SPct	G	A	Pts	G	A	Pts	Num	PIM	Maj	Mnr	Fgt	Rgh	HHT	Hat	P/G
94-95	LA	14	1	0	1	0	0	0	4	25.0	0	0	0	0	0	0	15	102	8	1	6	0	0	0	.07
95-96	LA	1	0	0	0	0	0	0	1	0.0	0	0	0	0	0	0	1	5	1	0	1	0	0	0	.00
96-97	LA	52	1	3	4	-4	0	0	20	5.0	0	0	0	0	0	0	41	194	16	17	15	8	1	0	.08
97-98	LA	66	2	4	6	-8	0	0	18	11.1	0	0	0	0	0	0	66	249	23	37	23	18	2	0	.09
98-99	LA	49	2	1	3	-5	0	0	14	14.3	0	0	0	0	0	0	33	131	11	18	11	6	3	0	.06
5 Years		182	6	8	14	-17	0	0	57	10.5	0	0	0	0	0	0	156	681	59	73	56	32	6	0	.08

Postseason

Year	Tm	GP	G	A	Pts	+/–	GW	OT	S	SPct	G	A	Pts	G	A	Pts	Num	PIM	Maj	Mnr	Fgt	Rgh	HHT	Hat	P/G
97-98	LA	4	0	0	0	-1	0	0	0	–	0	0	0	0	0	0	3	6	0	3	0	3	0	0	.00

Mike Johnson

(statistical profile on page 324)

Pos: RW **Shoots:** R **Ht:** 6'3" **Wt:** 200 **Born:** 10/3/74—Scarborough, Ontario **Age:** 25

Overall											Power Play			Shorthand			Penalty							Misc	
Year	Tm	GP	G	A	Pts	+/–	GW	GT	S	SPct	G	A	Pts	G	A	Pts	Num	PIM	Maj	Mnr	Fgt	Rgh	HHT	Hat	P/G
96-97	Tor	13	2	2	4	-2	1	0	27	7.4	0	0	0	1	0	1	2	4	0	2	0	0	2	0	.31
97-98	Tor	82	15	32	47	-4	0	1	143	10.5	5	8	13	0	0	0	12	24	0	12	0	0	7	0	.57
98-99	Tor	79	20	24	44	13	2	0	149	13.4	5	4	9	3	0	3	16	35	1	15	0	1	6	0	.56
3 Years		174	37	58	95	7	3	1	319	11.6	10	12	22	4	0	4	30	63	1	29	0	1	15	0	.55

Postseason																									
Year	Tm	GP	G	A	Pts	+/–	GW	OT	S	SPct	G	A	Pts	G	A	Pts	Num	PIM	Maj	Mnr	Fgt	Rgh	HHT	Hat	P/G
98-99	Tor	17	3	2	5	-1	1	0	26	11.5	0	0	0	0	0	0	2	4	0	2	0	0	1	0	.29

Ryan Johnson

Pos: C **Shoots:** L **Ht:** 6'2" **Wt:** 185 **Born:** 6/14/76—Thunder Bay, Ontario **Age:** 23

Overall											Power Play			Shorthand			Penalty							Misc	
Year	Tm	GP	G	A	Pts	+/–	GW	GT	S	SPct	G	A	Pts	G	A	Pts	Num	PIM	Maj	Mnr	Fgt	Rgh	HHT	Hat	P/G
97-98	Fla	10	0	2	2	-4	0	0	6	0.0	0	0	0	0	0	0	0	0	0	0	0	0	0	0	.20
98-99	Fla	1	1	0	1	0	0	0	1	100.0	0	0	0	0	0	0	0	0	0	0	0	0	0	0	1.00
2 Years		11	1	2	3	-4	0	0	7	14.3	0	0	0	0	0	0	0	0	0	0	0	0	0	0	.27

Olli Jokinen

(statistical profile on page 324)

Pos: C **Shoots:** L **Ht:** 6'2" **Wt:** 210 **Born:** 12/5/78—Kuopio, Finland **Age:** 21

Overall											Power Play			Shorthand			Penalty							Misc	
Year	Tm	GP	G	A	Pts	+/–	GW	GT	S	SPct	G	A	Pts	G	A	Pts	Num	PIM	Maj	Mnr	Fgt	Rgh	HHT	Hat	P/G
97-98	LA	8	0	0	0	-5	0	0	12	0.0	0	0	0	0	0	0	3	6	0	3	0	0	1	0	.00
98-99	LA	66	9	12	21	-10	1	0	87	10.3	3	3	6	1	0	1	19	44	2	17	2	2	10	0	.32
2 Years		74	9	12	21	-15	1	0	99	9.1	3	3	6	1	0	1	22	50	2	20	2	2	11	0	.28

J.F. Jomphe

Pos: C **Shoots:** L **Ht:** 6'1" **Wt:** 195 **Born:** 12/28/72—Harve' St. Pierre, Quebec **Age:** 27

Overall											Power Play			Shorthand			Penalty							Misc	
Year	Tm	GP	G	A	Pts	+/–	GW	GT	S	SPct	G	A	Pts	G	A	Pts	Num	PIM	Maj	Mnr	Fgt	Rgh	HHT	Hat	P/G
95-96	Anh	31	2	12	14	7	0	0	46	4.3	2	1	3	0	0	0	18	39	1	17	1	5	7	0	.45
96-97	Anh	64	7	14	21	-9	0	0	81	8.6	0	2	2	1	1	2	22	53	3	19	3	6	9	0	.33
97-98	Anh	9	1	3	4	1	0	0	8	12.5	0	0	0	0	0	0	4	8	0	4	0	2	1	0	.44
98-99	2Tm	7	0	0	0	0	0	0	4	0.0	0	0	0	0	0	0	1	2	0	1	0	0	1	0	.00
98-99	Pho	1	0	0	0	0	0	0	0	–	0	0	0	0	0	0	1	2	0	1	0	0	1	0	.00
98-99	Mon	6	0	0	0	0	0	0	4	0.0	0	0	0	0	0	0	0	0	0	0	0	0	0	0	.00
4 Years		111	10	29	39	-1	0	0	139	7.2	2	3	5	1	1	2	45	102	4	41	4	13	18	0	.35

Keith Jones

(statistical profile on page 325)

Pos: RW **Shoots:** L **Ht:** 6'2" **Wt:** 200 **Born:** 11/8/68—Brantford, Ontario **Age:** 31

Overall											Power Play			Shorthand			Penalty							Misc	
Year	Tm	GP	G	A	Pts	+/–	GW	GT	S	SPct	G	A	Pts	G	A	Pts	Num	PIM	Maj	Mnr	Fgt	Rgh	HHT	Hat	P/G
92-93	Was	71	12	14	26	18	3	0	73	16.4	0	3	3	0	0	0	46	124	8	37	7	17	8	0	.37
93-94	Was	68	16	19	35	4	1	0	97	16.5	5	4	9	0	0	0	43	149	5	32	4	12	5	0	.51
94-95	Was	40	14	6	20	-2	4	0	85	16.5	1	2	3	0	0	0	27	65	1	25	0	7	4	0	.50
95-96	Was	68	18	23	41	8	2	0	155	11.6	5	9	14	0	0	0	43	103	3	39	2	11	6	0	.60
96-97	2Tm	78	25	23	48	3	7	0	170	14.7	14	6	20	1	0	1	41	118	4	34	3	10	7	0	.62
97-98	Col	23	3	7	10	-4	2	0	31	9.7	1	3	4	0	0	0	11	22	0	11	0	1	2	0	.43
98-99	2Tm	78	20	33	53	23	3	0	135	14.8	3	4	7	0	0	0	49	98	0	49	0	22	12	0	.68
96-97	Was	11	2	3	5	-2	0	0	12	16.7	1	0	1	0	0	0	5	13	1	4	1	1	1	0	.45
96-97	Col	67	23	20	43	5	7	0	158	14.6	13	6	19	1	0	1	36	105	3	30	2	9	6	0	.64
98-99	Col	12	2	2	4	-6	0	0	11	18.2	1	0	1	0	0	0	10	20	0	10	0	4	1	0	.33
98-99	Phi	66	18	31	49	29	3	0	124	14.5	2	4	6	0	0	0	39	78	0	39	0	18	11	0	.74
7 Years		426	108	125	233	50	22	0	746	14.5	29	31	60	1	0	1	260	679	21	227	16	80	44	0	.55

Postseason																									
Year	Tm	GP	G	A	Pts	+/–	GW	OT	S	SPct	G	A	Pts	G	A	Pts	Num	PIM	Maj	Mnr	Fgt	Rgh	HHT	Hat	P/G
92-93	Was	6	0	0	0	-3	0	0	2	0.0	0	0	0	0	0	0	2	10	2	0	2	0	0	0	.00
93-94	Was	11	0	1	1	1	0	0	14	0.0	0	0	0	0	0	0	14	36	0	13	0	6	2	0	.09
94-95	Was	7	4	4	8	-1	0	0	14	28.6	1	2	3	0	0	0	7	22	0	6	0	4	1	0	1.14
95-96	Was	2	0	0	0	-1	0	0	3	0.0	0	0	0	0	0	0	2	7	1	1	1	0	0	0	.00
96-97	Col	6	3	3	6	2	0	0	16	18.8	1	0	1	0	0	0	2	4	0	2	0	2	0	0	1.00
97-98	Col	7	0	0	0	-1	0	0	12	0.0	0	0	0	0	0	0	5	13	1	4	1	2	1	0	.00
98-99	Phi	6	2	1	3	4	0	0	11	18.2	0	0	0	0	0	0	7	14	0	7	0	2	1	0	.50
7 Years		45	9	9	18	1	0	0	72	12.5	2	2	4	0	0	0	39	106	4	33	4	16	5	0	.40

Ty Jones

Pos: RW **Shoots:** R **Ht:** 6'3" **Wt:** 218 **Born:** 2/22/79—Richland, Washington **Age:** 20

Overall											Power Play			Shorthand			Penalty							Misc	
Year	Tm	GP	G	A	Pts	+/–	GW	GT	S	SPct	G	A	Pts	G	A	Pts	Num	PIM	Maj	Mnr	Fgt	Rgh	HHT	Hat	P/G
98-99	Chi	8	0	0	0	-1	0	0	3	0.0	0	0	0	0	0	0	3	12	2	1	2	0	0	0	.00

Kenny Jonsson

(statistical profile on page 325)

Pos: D **Shoots:** L **Ht:** 6'3" **Wt:** 195 **Born:** 10/6/74—Angelholm, Sweden **Age:** 25

Overall											Power Play			Shorthand			Penalty							Misc	
Year	Tm	GP	G	A	Pts	+/–	GW	GT	S	SPct	G	A	Pts	G	A	Pts	Num	PIM	Maj	Mnr	Fgt	Rgh	HHT	Hat	P/G
94-95	Tor	39	2	7	9	-8	1	0	50	4.0	0	5	5	0	0	0	8	16	0	8	0	1	5	0	.23
95-96	2Tm	66	4	26	30	7	1	0	130	3.1	3	11	14	0	1	1	16	32	0	16	0	0	7	0	.45
96-97	NYI	81	3	18	21	10	0	0	92	3.3	1	4	5	0	0	0	12	24	0	12	0	2	4	0	.26
97-98	NYI	81	14	26	40	-2	2	0	108	13.0	6	12	18	0	2	2	29	58	0	29	0	3	11	0	.49
98-99	NYI	63	8	18	26	-18	0	0	91	8.8	6	11	17	0	1	1	17	34	0	17	0	1	7	0	.41
95-96	Tor	50	4	22	26	12	1	0	90	4.4	3	8	11	0	1	1	11	22	0	11	0	0	5	0	.52
95-96	NYI	16	0	4	4	-5	0	0	40	0.0	0	3	3	0	0	0	5	10	0	5	0	0	2	0	.25
5 Years		330	31	95	126	-11	4	0	471	6.6	16	43	59	0	4	4	82	164	0	82	0	7	34	0	.38
Postseason																									
Year	Tm	GP	G	A	Pts	+/–	GW	OT	S	SPct	G	A	Pts	G	A	Pts	Num	PIM	Maj	Mnr	Fgt	Rgh	HHT	Hat	P/G
94-95	Tor	4	0	0	0	-2	0	0	3	0.0	0	0	0	0	0	0	0	0	0	0	0	0	0	0	.00

Chris Joseph

Pos: D **Shoots:** R **Ht:** 6'2" **Wt:** 210 **Born:** 9/10/69—Burnaby, British Columbia **Age:** 30

Overall											Power Play			Shorthand			Penalty							Misc	
Year	Tm	GP	G	A	Pts	+/–	GW	GT	S	SPct	G	A	Pts	G	A	Pts	Num	PIM	Maj	Mnr	Fgt	Rgh	HHT	Hat	P/G
87-88	2Tm	24	0	8	8	-1	0	0	14	0.0	0	–	–	0	–	–	–	18	–	–	–	–	–	0	.33
88-89	Edm	44	4	5	9	-9	0	0	36	11.1	0	0	0	0	1	1	–	54	–	–	–	–	–	0	.20
89-90	Edm	4	0	2	2	-2	0	0	5	0.0	0	2	2	0	0	0	1	2	0	1	0	–	–	0	.50
90-91	Edm	49	5	17	22	3	0	0	74	6.8	2	6	8	0	0	0	–	59	–	–	–	–	–	0	.45
91-92	Edm	7	0	0	0	-1	0	0	5	0.0	0	0	0	0	0	0	4	8	0	4	0	1	2	0	.00
92-93	Edm	33	2	10	12	-9	0	0	49	4.1	1	5	6	0	0	0	24	48	0	24	0	6	9	0	.36
93-94	2Tm	76	11	20	31	-21	0	0	179	6.1	8	10	18	0	0	0	50	136	4	43	4	6	22	0	.41
94-95	Pit	33	5	10	15	3	0	0	73	6.8	3	2	5	0	0	0	15	46	0	13	0	2	6	0	.45
95-96	Pit	70	5	14	19	6	1	0	94	5.3	0	3	3	0	1	1	34	71	1	33	1	4	16	0	.27
96-97	Van	63	3	13	16	-21	1	0	99	3.0	2	8	10	0	0	0	28	62	2	26	2	6	10	0	.25
97-98	Phi	15	1	0	1	1	1	0	20	5.0	0	0	0	0	0	0	8	19	1	7	1	1	5	0	.07
98-99	Phi	2	0	0	0	0	0	0	1	0.0	0	0	0	0	0	0	1	2	0	1	0	0	1	0	.00
87-88	Pit	17	0	4	4	2	0	0	13	0.0	0	–	–	0	–	–	–	12	–	–	–	–	–	0	.24
87-88	Edm	7	0	4	4	-3	0	0	1	0.0	0	–	–	0	–	–	3	6	0	3	0	–	–	0	.57
93-94	Edm	10	1	1	2	-8	0	0	25	4.0	1	1	2	0	0	0	11	28	2	9	2	0	3	0	.20
93-94	TB	66	10	19	29	-13	0	0	154	6.5	7	9	16	0	0	0	39	108	2	34	2	6	19	0	.44
12 Years		420	36	99	135	-51	3	0	649	5.5	16	–	–	0	–	–	–	525	–	–	–	–	–	0	.32
Postseason																									
Year	Tm	GP	G	A	Pts	+/–	GW	OT	S	SPct	G	A	Pts	G	A	Pts	Num	PIM	Maj	Mnr	Fgt	Rgh	HHT	Hat	P/G
91-92	Edm	5	1	3	4	2	0	0	6	16.7	0	0	0	0	0	0	1	2	0	1	0	0	1	0	.80
94-95	Pit	10	1	1	2	-4	0	0	13	7.7	0	1	1	0	0	0	6	12	0	6	0	3	3	0	.20
95-96	Pit	15	1	0	1	1	0	0	15	6.7	0	0	0	0	0	0	4	8	0	4	0	1	0	0	.07
97-98	Phi	1	0	0	0	0	0	0	2	0.0	0	0	0	0	0	0	1	2	0	1	0	0	1	0	.00
4 Years		31	3	4	7	-1	0	0	36	8.3	0	1	1	0	0	0	12	24	0	12	0	4	5	0	.23

Curtis Joseph

(statistical profile on page 399)

Pos: G **Catches:** L **Ht:** 5'10" **Wt:** 182 **Born:** 4/29/67—Keswick, Ontario **Age:** 32

Overall																Pen Shot		Offense		
Year	Tm	GP	GS	TP	W	L	T	Min	GA	GAA	Shots	SvPct	ShO	OE	PPGA	SHGA	Shots	GA	G	A	PIM
89-90	StL	15	–	–	9	5	1	852	48	3.38	435	.890	0	–	–	–	0	0	0	1	0
90-91	StL	30	–	–	16	10	2	1710	89	3.12	874	.898	0	–	–	–	0	0	0	1	0
91-92	StL	60	58	4	27	20	10	3494	175	3.01	1953	.910	2	29	40	10	2	0	0	9	12
92-93	StL	68	67	7	29	28	9	3890	196	3.02	**2202**	**.911**	1	**28**	48	6	1	0	0	2	8
93-94	StL*	71	71	10	36	23	11	4127	213	3.10	**2382**	.911	1	**32**	53	10	1	0	0	3	4
94-95	StL	36	36	**8**	20	10	1	1914	89	2.79	904	.902	1	10	30	2	0	0	0	1	0
95-96	Edm	34	34	3	15	16	2	1936	111	3.44	971	.886	0	9	33	4	0	0	0	1	4
96-97	Edm	72	72	9	32	29	9	4100	200	2.93	2144	.907	6	28	**52**	10	1	1	0	2	20
97-98	Edm	71	71	5	29	31	9	4132	181	2.63	1901	.905	8	19	55	9	2	0	0	2	4

		Overall															Pen Shot		Offense		
Year	Tm	GP	GS	TP	W	L	T	Min	GA	GAA	Shots	SvPct	ShO	OE	PPGA	SHGA	Shots	GA	G	A	PIM
98-99	Tor	67	67	1	35	24	7	4001	**171**	2.56	1903	.910	3	25	48	5	2	1	0	5	6
10 Years		524	–	–	248	196	61	30156	1473	2.93	15669	.906	22	–	–	–	9	2	0	27	58
		Postseason																			
Year	Tm	GP	GS	TP	W	L	Pct	Min	GA	GAA	Shots	SvPct	ShO	OE	PPGA	SHGA	Shots	GA	G	A	PIM
89-90	StL	6	–	–	4	1	.800	327	18	3.30	167	.892	0	–	–	–	0	0	0	0	2
91-92	StL	6	6	0	2	4	.333	379	23	3.64	217	.894	0	2	9	1	0	0	0	1	0
92-93	StL	11	11	1	7	4	.636	715	27	2.27	438	.938	2	7	9	0	0	0	0	0	2
93-94	StL	4	4	0	0	4	.000	246	15	3.66	158	.905	0	2	6	0	0	0	0	0	0
94-95	StL	7	7	2	3	3	.500	392	24	3.67	178	.865	0	0	10	6	0	0	0	1	0
96-97	Edm	12	12	0	5	7	.417	767	36	2.82	405	.911	2	6	10	1	0	0	0	0	2
97-98	Edm	12	12	1	5	7	.417	716	23	1.93	319	.928	3	5	7	1	0	0	0	0	2
98-99	Tor	17	17	1	9	8	.529	1011	41	2.43	440	.907	1	4	13	3	0	0	0	0	2
8 Years		75	–	–	35	38	.479	4553	207	2.73	2322	.911	8	–	–	–	0	0	0	2	10

Ed Jovanovski

(statistical profile on page 325)

Pos: D **Shoots:** L **Ht:** 6'2" **Wt:** 210 **Born:** 6/26/76—Windsor, Ontario **Age:** 23

		Overall								Power Play			Shorthand			Penalty							Misc	
Year	Tm	GP	G	A	Pts	+/–	GW	GT	S	SPct	G	A	Pts	G	A	Pts	Num	PIM	Maj	Mnr	Fgt	Rgh	HHT	Hat	P/G
95-96	Fla	70	10	11	21	-3	2	0	116	8.6	2	3	5	0	0	0	49	137	5	41	5	16	11	0	.30
96-97	Fla	61	7	16	23	-1	1	0	80	8.8	3	5	8	0	0	0	63	172	10	51	10	19	3	0	.38
97-98	Fla	81	9	14	23	-12	3	1	142	6.3	2	5	7	1	0	1	59	158	8	49	7	19	11	0	.28
98-99	2Tm	72	5	22	27	-9	1	0	109	4.6	1	6	7	0	1	1	52	126	2	48	2	21	6	0	.38
98-99	Fla	41	3	13	16	-4	1	0	68	4.4	1	5	6	0	1	1	34	82	2	31	2	13	4	0	.39
98-99	Van	31	2	9	11	-5	0	0	41	4.9	0	1	1	0	0	0	18	44	0	17	0	8	2	0	.35
4 Years		284	31	63	94	-25	7	1	447	6.9	8	19	27	1	1	2	223	593	25	189	24	75	31	0	.33
		Postseason																							
Year	Tm	GP	G	A	Pts	+/–	GW	OT	S	SPct	G	A	Pts	G	A	Pts	Num	PIM	Maj	Mnr	Fgt	Rgh	HHT	Hat	P/G
95-96	Fla	22	1	8	9	2	0	0	51	2.0	0	3	3	0	0	0	19	52	2	16	2	8	4	0	.41
96-97	Fla	5	0	0	0	-4	0	0	7	0.0	0	0	0	0	0	0	2	4	0	2	0	2	0	0	.00
2 Years		27	1	8	9	-2	0	0	58	1.7	0	3	3	0	0	0	21	56	2	18	2	10	4	0	.33

Joe Juneau

(statistical profile on page 325)

Pos: LW **Shoots:** R **Ht:** 6'0" **Wt:** 195 **Born:** 1/5/68—Pont-Rouge, Quebec **Age:** 31

		Overall								Power Play			Shorthand			Penalty							Misc	
Year	Tm	GP	G	A	Pts	+/–	GW	GT	S	SPct	G	A	Pts	G	A	Pts	Num	PIM	Maj	Mnr	Fgt	Rgh	HHT	Hat	P/G
91-92	Bos	14	5	14	19	6	0	0	38	13.2	2	8	10	0	0	0	2	4	0	2	0	0	1	0	1.36
92-93	Bos	84	32	70	102	23	3	0	229	14.0	9	28	37	0	0	0	15	33	1	14	1	2	5	1	1.21
93-94	2Tm	74	19	66	85	11	2	1	164	11.6	6	28	34	0	0	0	15	41	1	13	0	0	7	0	1.15
94-95	Was	44	5	38	43	-1	0	1	70	7.1	3	22	25	0	1	1	4	8	0	4	0	0	2	0	.98
95-96	Was	80	14	50	64	-3	2	0	176	8.0	7	21	28	2	0	2	15	30	0	15	0	4	4	0	.80
96-97	Was	58	15	27	42	-11	3	0	124	12.1	9	9	18	1	0	1	4	8	0	4	0	0	1	1	.72
97-98	Was	56	9	22	31	-8	1	0	87	10.3	4	8	12	1	1	2	13	26	0	13	0	0	2	0	.55
98-99	2Tm	72	15	28	43	-4	3	0	150	10.0	2	12	14	1	0	1	11	22	0	11	0	0	7	0	.60
93-94	Bos	63	14	58	72	11	2	1	142	9.9	4	24	28	0	0	0	12	35	1	10	0	0	5	0	1.14
93-94	Was	11	5	8	13	0	0	0	22	22.7	2	4	6	0	0	0	3	6	0	3	0	0	2	0	1.18
98-99	Was	63	14	27	41	-3	3	0	142	9.9	2	11	13	1	0	1	10	20	0	10	0	0	7	0	.65
98-99	Buf	9	1	1	2	-1	0	0	8	12.5	0	1	1	0	0	0	1	2	0	1	0	0	0	0	.22
8 Years		482	114	315	429	13	14	2	1038	11.0	42	136	178	5	2	7	79	172	2	76	1	6	29	2	.89
		Postseason																							
Year	Tm	GP	G	A	Pts	+/–	GW	OT	S	SPct	G	A	Pts	G	A	Pts	Num	PIM	Maj	Mnr	Fgt	Rgh	HHT	Hat	P/G
91-92	Bos	15	4	8	12	-3	0	0	29	13.8	2	3	5	0	0	0	5	21	1	3	0	2	1	0	.80
92-93	Bos	4	2	4	6	-1	0	0	7	28.6	2	1	3	0	0	0	3	6	0	3	0	1	1	0	1.50
93-94	Was	11	4	5	9	-2	1	0	25	16.0	2	1	3	0	0	0	3	6	0	3	0	0	1	0	.82
94-95	Was	7	2	6	8	-2	0	0	16	12.5	0	3	3	0	0	0	1	2	0	1	0	1	0	0	1.14
95-96	Was	5	0	7	7	-4	0	0	20	0.0	0	4	4	0	0	0	3	6	0	3	0	1	0	0	1.40
97-98	Was	21	7	10	17	6	4	2	54	13.0	1	3	4	1	1	2	4	8	0	4	0	0	2	0	.81
98-99	Buf	20	3	8	11	-2	0	0	29	10.3	0	4	4	1	1	2	5	10	0	5	0	1	0	0	.55
7 Years		83	22	48	70	-8	5	2	180	12.2	7	19	26	2	2	4	24	59	1	22	0	6	5	0	.84

Tomas Kaberle

(statistical profile on page 326)

Pos: D **Shoots:** R **Ht:** 6'1" **Wt:** 186 **Born:** 3/2/78—Rakovnik, Czechoslovakia **Age:** 21

Overall											Power Play			Shorthand			Penalty							Misc	
Year	Tm	GP	G	A	Pts	+/–	GW	GT	S	SPct	G	A	Pts	G	A	Pts	Num	PIM	Maj	Mnr	Fgt	Rgh	HHT	Hat	P/G
98-99	Tor	57	4	18	22	3	2	0	71	5.6	0	5	5	0	1	1	6	12	0	6	0	0	1	0	.39
Postseason																									
Year	Tm	GP	G	A	Pts	+/–	GW	OT	S	SPct	G	A	Pts	G	A	Pts	Num	PIM	Maj	Mnr	Fgt	Rgh	HHT	Hat	P/G
98-99	Tor	14	0	3	3	0	0	0	14	0.0	0	0	0	0	0	0	1	2	0	1	0	0	1	0	.21

Valeri Kamensky

(statistical profile on page 326)

Pos: LW **Shoots:** R **Ht:** 6'2" **Wt:** 198 **Born:** 4/18/66—Voskresensk, USSR **Age:** 33

Overall											Power Play			Shorthand			Penalty							Misc	
Year	Tm	GP	G	A	Pts	+/–	GW	GT	S	SPct	G	A	Pts	G	A	Pts	Num	PIM	Maj	Mnr	Fgt	Rgh	HHT	Hat	P/G
91-92	Que	23	7	14	21	-1	1	0	42	16.7	2	7	9	0	0	0	7	14	0	7	0	0	4	0	.91
92-93	Que	32	15	22	37	13	0	1	94	16.0	2	5	7	3	2	5	7	14	0	7	0	0	3	0	1.16
93-94	Que	76	28	37	65	12	1	0	170	16.5	6	8	14	0	1	1	21	42	0	21	0	3	7	0	.86
94-95	Que	40	10	20	30	3	5	0	70	14.3	5	7	12	1	0	1	11	22	0	11	0	0	1	0	.75
95-96	Col	81	38	47	85	14	5	0	220	17.3	18	13	31	1	1	2	33	85	1	30	0	5	9	2	1.05
96-97	Col	68	28	38	66	5	4	1	165	17.0	8	18	26	0	0	0	19	38	0	19	0	6	7	1	.97
97-98	Col*	75	26	40	66	-2	4	0	173	15.0	8	19	27	0	0	0	26	60	0	25	0	3	7	1	.88
98-99	Col	65	14	30	44	1	2	0	123	11.4	2	10	12	0	0	0	14	28	0	14	0	2	2	1	.68
8 Years		460	166	248	414	45	22	2	1057	15.7	51	87	138	5	4	9	138	303	1	134	0	19	40	5	.90
Postseason																									
Year	Tm	GP	G	A	Pts	+/–	GW	OT	S	SPct	G	A	Pts	G	A	Pts	Num	PIM	Maj	Mnr	Fgt	Rgh	HHT	Hat	P/G
92-93	Que	6	0	1	1	-1	0	0	21	0.0	0	1	1	0	0	0	3	6	0	3	0	2	0	0	.17
94-95	Que	2	1	0	1	0	0	0	2	50.0	0	0	0	0	0	0	0	0	0	0	0	0	0	0	.50
95-96	Col	22	10	12	22	11	2	0	56	17.9	3	3	6	0	0	0	14	28	0	14	0	3	5	0	1.00
96-97	Col	17	8	14	22	-1	2	0	49	16.3	5	5	10	0	0	0	8	16	0	8	0	1	1	1	1.29
97-98	Col	7	2	3	5	1	0	0	17	11.8	1	1	2	0	0	0	5	18	0	4	0	0	1	0	.71
98-99	Col	10	4	5	9	5	1	0	18	22.2	1	1	2	0	0	0	2	4	0	2	0	0	0	0	.90
6 Years		64	25	35	60	15	5	0	163	15.3	10	11	21	0	0	0	32	72	0	31	0	6	7	1	.94

Sami Kapanen

(statistical profile on page 326)

Pos: LW **Shoots:** L **Ht:** 5'10" **Wt:** 173 **Born:** 6/14/73—Helsinki, Finland **Age:** 26

Overall											Power Play			Shorthand			Penalty							Misc	
Year	Tm	GP	G	A	Pts	+/–	GW	GT	S	SPct	G	A	Pts	G	A	Pts	Num	PIM	Maj	Mnr	Fgt	Rgh	HHT	Hat	P/G
95-96	Har	35	5	4	9	0	0	0	46	10.9	0	0	0	0	0	0	3	6	0	3	0	1	1	0	.26
96-97	Har	45	13	12	25	6	2	0	82	15.9	3	1	4	0	0	0	1	2	0	1	0	0	0	0	.56
97-98	Car	81	26	37	63	9	5	0	190	13.7	4	14	18	0	0	0	8	16	0	8	0	1	2	2	.78
98-99	Car	81	24	35	59	-1	7	0	254	9.4	5	12	17	0	0	0	5	10	0	5	0	1	1	0	.73
4 Years		242	68	88	156	14	14	0	572	11.9	12	27	39	0	0	0	17	34	0	17	0	3	4	2	.64
Postseason																									
Year	Tm	GP	G	A	Pts	+/–	GW	OT	S	SPct	G	A	Pts	G	A	Pts	Num	PIM	Maj	Mnr	Fgt	Rgh	HHT	Hat	P/G
98-99	Car	5	1	1	2	-2	0	0	8	12.5	0	0	0	0	0	0	0	0	0	0	0	0	0	0	.40

Paul Kariya

(statistical profile on page 326)

Pos: LW **Shoots:** L **Ht:** 5'11" **Wt:** 180 **Born:** 10/16/74—Vancouver, British Columbia **Age:** 25

Overall											Power Play			Shorthand			Penalty							Misc	
Year	Tm	GP	G	A	Pts	+/–	GW	GT	S	SPct	G	A	Pts	G	A	Pts	Num	PIM	Maj	Mnr	Fgt	Rgh	HHT	Hat	P/G
94-95	Anh	47	18	21	39	-17	3	1	134	13.4	7	8	15	1	0	1	2	4	0	2	0	0	0	0	.83
95-96	Anh*	82	50	58	108	9	9	0	349	14.3	20	21	41	3	3	6	10	20	0	10	0	0	9	0	1.32
96-97	Anh*	69	44	55	99	36	**10**	0	**340**	12.9	15	19	34	3	1	4	3	6	0	3	0	1	2	2	1.43
97-98	Anh	22	17	14	31	12	2	1	103	16.5	3	2	5	0	0	0	6	23	1	4	0	0	1	1	1.41
98-99	Anh	82	39	62	101	17	4	0	**429**	9.1	11	32	43	2	1	3	20	40	0	20	0	2	8	0	1.23
5 Years		302	168	210	378	57	28	2	1355	12.4	56	82	138	9	5	14	41	93	1	39	0	3	20	3	1.25
Postseason																									
Year	Tm	GP	G	A	Pts	+/–	GW	OT	S	SPct	G	A	Pts	G	A	Pts	Num	PIM	Maj	Mnr	Fgt	Rgh	HHT	Hat	P/G
96-97	Anh	11	7	6	13	-2	1	1	61	11.5	4	3	7	0	0	0	2	4	0	2	0	1	0	0	1.18
98-99	Anh	3	1	3	4	0	0	0	11	9.1	0	2	2	0	0	0	0	0	0	0	0	0	0	0	1.33
2 Years		14	8	9	17	-2	1	1	72	11.1	4	5	9	0	0	0	2	4	0	2	0	1	0	0	1.21

David Karpa

Pos: D **Shoots:** R **Ht:** 6'1" **Wt:** 210 **Born:** 5/7/71—Regina, Saskatchewan **Age:** 28

Overall											Power Play			Shorthand			Penalty							Misc	
Year	Tm	GP	G	A	Pts	+/–	GW	GT	S	SPct	G	A	Pts	G	A	Pts	Num	PIM	Maj	Mnr	Fgt	Rgh	HHT	Hat	P/G
91-92	Que	4	0	0	0	2	0	0	2	0.0	0	0	0	0	0	0	3	14	0	2	0	1	0	0	.00
92-93	Que	12	0	1	1	-6	0	0	2	0.0	0	0	0	0	0	0	5	13	1	4	1	1	1	0	.08
93-94	Que	60	5	12	17	0	0	0	48	10.4	2	4	6	0	0	0	44	148	12	29	12	9	2	0	.28
94-95	2Tm	28	1	5	6	-1	0	0	33	3.0	0	0	0	0	0	0	26	91	5	18	5	8	4	0	.21
95-96	Anh	72	3	16	19	-3	1	0	62	4.8	0	3	3	1	1	2	82	270	14	60	14	19	13	0	.26
96-97	Anh	69	2	11	13	11	1	0	90	2.2	0	1	1	0	0	0	67	210	12	50	11	15	13	0	.19
97-98	Anh	78	1	11	12	-3	0	0	64	1.6	0	1	1	0	1	1	74	217	7	61	7	20	12	0	.15
98-99	Car	33	0	2	2	1	0	0	21	0.0	0	1	1	0	0	0	18	55	1	15	1	4	2	0	.06
94-95	Que	2	0	0	0	-1	0	0	1	0.0	0	0	0	0	0	0	0	0	0	0	0	0	0	0	.00
94-95	Anh	26	1	5	6	0	0	0	32	3.1	0	0	0	0	0	0	26	91	5	18	5	8	4	0	.23
8 Years		356	12	58	70	1	2	0	322	3.7	2	10	12	1	2	3	319	1018	52	239	51	77	47	0	.20
Postseason																									
Year	Tm	GP	G	A	Pts	+/–	GW	OT	S	SPct	G	A	Pts	G	A	Pts	Num	PIM	Maj	Mnr	Fgt	Rgh	HHT	Hat	P/G
92-93	Que	3	0	0	0	0	0	0	3	0.0	0	0	0	0	0	0	0	0	0	0	0	0	0	0	.00
96-97	Anh	8	1	1	2	-2	1	0	13	7.7	0	0	0	0	0	0	6	20	0	5	0	3	1	0	.25
98-99	Car	2	0	0	0	-2	0	0	0	–	0	0	0	0	0	0	1	2	0	1	0	0	1	0	.00
3 Years		13	1	1	2	-4	1	0	16	6.3	0	0	0	0	0	0	7	22	0	6	0	3	2	0	.15

Alexander Karpovtsev

(statistical profile on page 327)

Pos: D **Shoots:** L **Ht:** 6'3" **Wt:** 215 **Born:** 4/7/70—Moscow, USSR **Age:** 29

Overall											Power Play			Shorthand			Penalty							Misc	
Year	Tm	GP	G	A	Pts	+/–	GW	GT	S	SPct	G	A	Pts	G	A	Pts	Num	PIM	Maj	Mnr	Fgt	Rgh	HHT	Hat	P/G
93-94	NYR	67	3	15	18	12	1	0	78	3.8	1	4	5	0	1	1	29	58	0	29	0	9	8	0	.27
94-95	NYR	47	4	8	12	-4	1	0	82	4.9	1	4	5	0	1	1	15	30	0	15	0	2	6	0	.26
95-96	NYR	40	2	16	18	12	1	0	71	2.8	1	7	8	0	0	0	13	26	0	13	0	1	5	0	.45
96-97	NYR	77	9	29	38	1	0	0	84	10.7	6	13	19	1	0	1	28	59	1	27	1	6	8	0	.49
97-98	NYR	47	3	7	10	-1	1	0	46	6.5	1	2	3	0	0	0	19	38	0	19	0	3	4	0	.21
98-99	2Tm	58	3	25	28	**39**	1	0	65	4.6	1	9	10	0	0	0	26	52	0	26	0	2	9	0	.48
98-99	NYR	2	1	0	1	1	0	0	4	25.0	0	0	0	0	0	0	0	0	0	0	0	0	0	0	.50
98-99	Tor	56	2	25	27	38	1	0	61	3.3	1	9	10	0	0	0	26	52	0	26	0	2	9	0	.48
6 Years		336	24	100	124	59	5	0	426	5.6	11	39	50	1	2	3	130	263	1	129	1	23	40	0	.37
Postseason																									
Year	Tm	GP	G	A	Pts	+/–	GW	OT	S	SPct	G	A	Pts	G	A	Pts	Num	PIM	Maj	Mnr	Fgt	Rgh	HHT	Hat	P/G
93-94	NYR	17	0	4	4	-6	0	0	14	0.0	0	1	1	0	0	0	6	12	0	6	0	0	3	0	.24
94-95	NYR	8	1	0	1	-1	0	0	8	12.5	0	0	0	0	0	0	0	0	0	0	0	0	0	0	.13
95-96	NYR	6	0	1	1	-2	0	0	5	0.0	0	0	0	0	0	0	2	4	0	2	0	1	0	0	.17
96-97	NYR	13	1	3	4	2	0	0	10	10.0	1	2	3	0	0	0	6	20	0	5	0	2	3	0	.31
98-99	Tor	14	1	3	4	-7	0	0	13	7.7	1	3	4	0	0	0	6	12	0	6	0	0	0	0	.29
5 Years		58	3	11	14	-14	0	0	50	6.0	2	6	8	0	0	0	20	48	0	19	0	3	6	0	.24

Darius Kasparaitis

Pos: D **Shoots:** L **Ht:** 5'11" **Wt:** 209 **Born:** 10/16/72—Elektrenai, USSR **Age:** 27

Overall											Power Play			Shorthand			Penalty							Misc	
Year	Tm	GP	G	A	Pts	+/–	GW	GT	S	SPct	G	A	Pts	G	A	Pts	Num	PIM	Maj	Mnr	Fgt	Rgh	HHT	Hat	P/G
92-93	NYI	79	4	17	21	15	0	0	92	4.3	0	0	0	0	1	1	57	166	4	48	2	12	5	0	.27
93-94	NYI	76	1	10	11	-6	0	0	81	1.2	0	1	1	0	2	2	56	142	2	51	2	13	4	0	.14
94-95	NYI	13	0	1	1	-11	0	0	8	0.0	0	0	0	0	0	0	7	22	0	6	0	2	0	0	.08
95-96	NYI	46	1	7	8	-12	0	0	34	2.9	0	0	0	0	1	1	34	93	3	29	2	7	8	0	.17
96-97	2Tm	75	2	21	23	17	0	0	58	3.4	0	1	1	0	2	2	38	100	0	35	0	13	7	0	.31
97-98	Pit	81	4	8	12	3	0	0	71	5.6	0	2	2	2	0	2	51	127	3	46	3	12	10	0	.15
98-99	Pit	48	1	4	5	12	0	0	32	3.1	0	0	0	0	0	0	35	70	0	35	0	7	7	0	.10
96-97	NYI	18	0	5	5	-7	0	0	12	0.0	0	0	0	0	1	1	8	16	0	8	0	2	3	0	.28
96-97	Pit	57	2	16	18	24	0	0	46	4.3	0	1	1	0	1	1	30	84	0	27	0	11	4	0	.32
7 Years		418	13	68	81	18	0	0	376	3.5	0	4	4	2	6	8	278	720	12	250	9	66	41	0	.19
Postseason																									
Year	Tm	GP	G	A	Pts	+/–	GW	OT	S	SPct	G	A	Pts	G	A	Pts	Num	PIM	Maj	Mnr	Fgt	Rgh	HHT	Hat	P/G
92-93	NYI	18	0	5	5	2	0	0	24	0.0	0	0	0	0	2	2	14	31	1	13	1	6	1	0	.28
93-94	NYI	4	0	0	0	-6	0	0	3	0.0	0	0	0	0	0	0	4	8	0	4	0	2	0	0	.00
96-97	Pit	5	0	0	0	-4	0	0	7	0.0	0	0	0	0	0	0	3	6	0	3	0	0	1	0	.00
97-98	Pit	5	0	0	0	-2	0	0	3	0.0	0	0	0	0	0	0	4	8	0	4	0	1	0	0	.00
4 Years		32	0	5	5	-10	0	0	37	0.0	0	0	0	0	2	2	25	53	1	24	1	9	2	0	.16

Mike Keane

(statistical profile on page 327)

Pos: RW **Shoots:** R **Ht:** 5'10" **Wt:** 185 **Born:** 5/29/67—Winnipeg, Manitoba **Age:** 32

			Overall								Power Play			Shorthand			Penalty							Misc	
Year	Tm	GP	G	A	Pts	+/–	GW	GT	S	SPct	G	A	Pts	G	A	Pts	Num	PIM	Maj	Mnr	Fgt	Rgh	HHT	Hat	P/G
88-89	Mon	69	16	19	35	9	1	0	90	17.8	5	–	–	0	–	–	–	69	–	–	–	–	–	0	.51
89-90	Mon	74	9	15	24	0	1	0	92	9.8	1	–	–	0	–	–	–	78	–	–	–	–	–	0	.32
90-91	Mon	73	13	23	36	6	2	0	109	11.9	2	–	–	1	–	–	–	50	–	–	–	–	–	0	.49
91-92	Mon	67	11	30	41	16	2	1	116	9.5	2	6	8	0	1	1	28	64	0	27	0	10	10	0	.61
92-93	Mon	77	15	45	60	29	1	0	120	12.5	0	2	2	0	1	1	38	95	1	35	1	7	10	0	.78
93-94	Mon	80	16	30	46	6	2	1	129	12.4	6	11	17	2	1	3	42	119	1	37	1	6	10	0	.58
94-95	Mon	48	10	10	20	5	0	0	75	13.3	1	1	2	0	0	0	6	15	1	5	1	0	3	0	.42
95-96	2Tm	73	10	17	27	-5	2	0	84	11.9	0	2	2	2	3	5	23	46	0	23	0	2	8	0	.37
96-97	Col	81	10	17	27	2	1	0	91	11.0	0	0	0	1	0	1	27	63	3	24	3	1	8	0	.33
97-98	2Tm	**83**	10	13	23	-12	1	0	128	7.8	2	2	4	0	0	0	23	52	2	21	2	4	6	0	.28
98-99	Dal	81	6	23	29	-2	1	0	106	5.7	1	3	4	1	0	1	28	62	2	26	2	3	10	0	.36
95-96	Mon	18	0	7	7	-6	0	0	17	0.0	0	2	2	0	1	1	3	6	0	3	0	0	3	0	.39
95-96	Col	55	10	10	20	1	2	0	67	14.9	0	0	0	2	2	4	20	40	0	20	0	2	5	0	.36
97-98	NYR	70	8	10	18	-12	0	0	113	7.1	2	2	4	0	0	0	22	47	1	21	1	4	6	0	.26
97-98	Dal	13	2	3	5	0	1	0	15	13.3	0	0	0	0	0	0	1	5	1	0	1	0	0	0	.38
11 Years		806	126	242	368	54	14	2	1140	11.1	20	–	–	7	–	–	–	713	–	–	–	–	–	0	.46
											Postseason														
Year	Tm	GP	G	A	Pts	+/–	GW	OT	S	SPct	G	A	Pts	G	A	Pts	Num	PIM	Maj	Mnr	Fgt	Rgh	HHT	Hat	P/G
88-89	Mon	21	4	3	7	4	0	0	21	19.0	2	–	–	0	–	–	–	17	–	–	–	–	–	0	.33
89-90	Mon	11	0	1	1	-3	0	0	13	0.0	0	–	–	0	0	0	4	8	0	4	0	–	–	0	.09
90-91	Mon	12	3	2	5	3	0	0	19	15.8	0	–	–	0	–	–	3	6	0	3	0	–	–	0	.42
91-92	Mon	8	1	1	2	1	0	0	7	14.3	0	1	1	0	0	0	4	16	0	3	0	0	1	0	.25
92-93	Mon	19	2	13	15	10	0	0	27	7.4	0	5	5	0	0	0	3	6	0	3	0	0	0	0	.79
93-94	Mon	6	3	1	4	1	0	0	8	37.5	0	0	0	0	0	0	2	4	0	2	0	0	1	0	.67
95-96	Col	22	3	2	5	2	1	1	22	13.6	0	0	0	0	0	0	8	16	0	8	0	0	3	0	.23
96-97	Col	17	3	1	4	2	1	0	17	17.6	0	0	0	0	0	0	8	24	0	7	0	1	3	0	.24
97-98	Dal	17	4	4	8	7	1	1	23	17.4	0	0	0	1	0	1	0	0	0	0	0	0	0	0	.47
98-99	Dal	23	5	2	7	-1	1	0	41	12.2	0	0	0	1	0	1	3	6	0	3	0	0	0	0	.26
10 Years		156	28	30	58	26	4	2	198	14.1	2	–	–	2	–	–	–	103	–	–	–	–	–	0	.37

Dan Keczmer

Pos: D **Shoots:** L **Ht:** 6'1" **Wt:** 190 **Born:** 5/25/68—Mt. Clemens, Michigan **Age:** 31

			Overall								Power Play			Shorthand			Penalty							Misc	
Year	Tm	GP	G	A	Pts	+/–	GW	GT	S	SPct	G	A	Pts	G	A	Pts	Num	PIM	Maj	Mnr	Fgt	Rgh	HHT	Hat	P/G
90-91	Min	9	0	1	1	0	0	0	6	0.0	0	–	–	0	–	–	3	6	0	3	0	–	–	0	.11
91-92	Har	1	0	0	0	-1	0	0	2	0.0	0	0	0	0	0	0	0	0	0	0	0	0	0	0	.00
92-93	Har	23	4	4	8	-3	1	0	38	10.5	2	1	3	0	0	0	14	28	0	14	0	1	8	0	.35
93-94	2Tm	69	1	21	22	-8	0	0	116	0.9	0	14	14	0	0	0	30	60	0	30	0	0	18	0	.32
94-95	Cgy	28	2	3	5	7	0	0	33	6.1	0	1	1	0	0	0	5	10	0	5	0	0	1	0	.18
95-96	Cgy	13	0	0	0	-6	0	0	13	0.0	0	0	0	0	0	0	7	14	0	7	0	0	4	0	.00
96-97	Dal	13	0	1	1	3	0	0	10	0.0	0	0	0	0	0	0	3	6	0	3	0	0	0	0	.08
97-98	Dal	17	1	2	3	5	0	0	9	11.1	0	0	0	0	0	0	13	26	0	13	0	1	4	0	.18
98-99	2Tm	38	0	1	1	-5	0	0	24	0.0	0	0	0	0	0	0	17	34	0	17	0	3	6	0	.03
93-94	Har	12	0	1	1	-6	0	0	12	0.0	0	1	1	0	0	0	6	12	0	6	0	0	3	0	.08
93-94	Cgy	57	1	20	21	-2	0	0	104	1.0	0	13	13	0	0	0	24	48	0	24	0	0	15	0	.37
98-99	Dal	22	0	1	1	-2	0	0	12	0.0	0	0	0	0	0	0	11	22	0	11	0	3	3	0	.05
98-99	Nsh	16	0	0	0	-3	0	0	12	0.0	0	0	0	0	0	0	6	12	0	6	0	0	3	0	.00
9 Years		211	8	33	41	-8	1	0	251	3.2	2	–	–	0	–	–	92	184	0	92	0	–	–	0	.19
											Postseason														
Year	Tm	GP	G	A	Pts	+/–	GW	OT	S	SPct	G	A	Pts	G	A	Pts	Num	PIM	Maj	Mnr	Fgt	Rgh	HHT	Hat	P/G
93-94	Cgy	3	0	0	0	0	0	0	6	0.0	0	0	0	0	0	0	2	4	0	2	0	0	0	0	.00
94-95	Cgy	7	0	1	1	0	0	0	6	0.0	0	0	0	0	0	0	1	2	0	1	0	0	0	0	.14
97-98	Dal	2	0	0	0	0	0	0	2	0.0	0	0	0	0	0	0	1	2	0	1	0	1	0	0	.00
3 Years		12	0	1	1	0	0	0	14	0.0	0	0	0	0	0	0	4	8	0	4	0	1	0	0	.08

Chris Kelleher

Pos: D **Shoots:** L **Ht:** 6'1" **Wt:** 210 **Born:** 3/23/75—Cambridge, Massachusetts **Age:** 24

			Overall								Power Play			Shorthand			Penalty							Misc	
Year	Tm	GP	G	A	Pts	+/–	GW	GT	S	SPct	G	A	Pts	G	A	Pts	Num	PIM	Maj	Mnr	Fgt	Rgh	HHT	Hat	P/G
98-99	Pit	1	0	0	0	0	0	0	0	–	0	0	0	0	0	0	0	0	0	0	0	0	0	0	.00

Steve Kelly

Pos: C **Shoots:** L **Ht:** 6'1" **Wt:** 190 **Born:** 10/26/76—Vancouver, British Columbia **Age:** 23

		Overall									Power Play			Shorthand			Penalty							Misc	
Year	Tm	GP	G	A	Pts	+/–	GW	GT	S	SPct	G	A	Pts	G	A	Pts	Num	PIM	Maj	Mnr	Fgt	Rgh	HHT	Hat	P/G
96-97	Edm	8	1	0	1	-1	1	0	6	16.7	0	0	0	0	0	0	3	6	0	3	0	1	0	0	.13
97-98	2Tm	43	2	3	5	-13	0	0	22	9.1	1	0	1	0	0	0	10	23	1	9	1	0	3	0	.12
98-99	TB	34	1	3	4	-15	1	0	15	6.7	0	0	0	0	0	0	12	27	1	11	1	2	4	0	.12
97-98	Edm	19	0	2	2	-4	0	0	5	0.0	0	0	0	0	0	0	4	8	0	4	0	0	1	0	.11
97-98	TB	24	2	1	3	-9	0	0	17	11.8	1	0	1	0	0	0	6	15	1	5	1	0	2	0	.13
3 Years		85	4	6	10	-29	2	0	43	9.3	1	0	1	0	0	0	25	56	2	23	2	3	7	0	.12
		Postseason																							
Year	Tm	GP	G	A	Pts	+/–	GW	OT	S	SPct	G	A	Pts	G	A	Pts	Num	PIM	Maj	Mnr	Fgt	Rgh	HHT	Hat	P/G
96-97	Edm	6	0	0	0	1	0	0	2	0.0	0	0	0	0	0	0	1	2	0	1	0	1	0	0	.00

Mike Kennedy

Pos: C **Shoots:** R **Ht:** 6'1" **Wt:** 204 **Born:** 4/13/72—Toronto, Ontario **Age:** 27

		Overall									Power Play			Shorthand			Penalty							Misc	
Year	Tm	GP	G	A	Pts	+/–	GW	GT	S	SPct	G	A	Pts	G	A	Pts	Num	PIM	Maj	Mnr	Fgt	Rgh	HHT	Hat	P/G
94-95	Dal	44	6	12	18	4	0	0	76	7.9	2	2	4	0	0	0	12	33	3	9	3	1	6	0	.41
95-96	Dal	61	9	17	26	-7	1	0	111	8.1	4	2	6	0	0	0	17	48	2	14	2	1	7	0	.43
96-97	Dal	24	1	6	7	3	1	0	26	3.8	0	0	0	0	0	0	5	13	1	4	1	1	2	0	.29
97-98	2Tm	15	0	1	1	-1	0	0	12	0.0	0	0	0	0	0	0	5	16	2	3	2	0	2	0	.07
98-99	NYI	1	0	0	0	0	0	0	0	–	0	0	0	0	0	0	1	2	0	1	0	0	0	0	.00
97-98	Tor	13	0	1	1	-2	0	0	12	0.0	0	0	0	0	0	0	4	14	2	2	2	0	1	0	.08
97-98	Dal	2	0	0	0	1	0	0	0	–	0	0	0	0	0	0	1	2	0	1	0	0	1	0	.00
5 Years		145	16	36	52	-1	2	0	225	7.1	6	4	10	0	0	0	40	112	8	31	8	3	17	0	.36
		Postseason																							
Year	Tm	GP	G	A	Pts	+/–	GW	OT	S	SPct	G	A	Pts	G	A	Pts	Num	PIM	Maj	Mnr	Fgt	Rgh	HHT	Hat	P/G
94-95	Dal	5	0	0	0	-1	0	0	3	0.0	0	0	0	0	0	0	3	9	1	2	1	0	1	0	.00

Dan Kesa

(statistical profile on page 327)

Pos: RW **Shoots:** R **Ht:** 6'0" **Wt:** 198 **Born:** 11/23/71—Vancouver, British Columbia **Age:** 28

		Overall									Power Play			Shorthand			Penalty							Misc	
Year	Tm	GP	G	A	Pts	+/–	GW	GT	S	SPct	G	A	Pts	G	A	Pts	Num	PIM	Maj	Mnr	Fgt	Rgh	HHT	Hat	P/G
93-94	Van	19	2	4	6	-3	1	0	18	11.1	1	0	1	0	0	0	5	18	0	4	0	2	1	0	.32
94-95		Did Not Play in NHL																							
95-96	Dal	3	0	0	0	-1	0	0	0	–	0	0	0	0	0	0	0	0	0	0	0	0	0	0	.00
96-97		Did Not Play in NHL																							
97-98		Did Not Play in NHL																							
98-99	Pit	67	2	8	10	-9	0	1	33	6.1	0	2	2	0	0	0	8	27	1	6	1	2	0	0	.15
3 Years		89	4	12	16	-13	1	1	51	7.8	1	2	3	0	0	0	13	45	1	10	1	4	1	0	.18
		Postseason																							
Year	Tm	GP	G	A	Pts	+/–	GW	OT	S	SPct	G	A	Pts	G	A	Pts	Num	PIM	Maj	Mnr	Fgt	Rgh	HHT	Hat	P/G
98-99	Pit	13	1	0	1	-2	1	0	5	20.0	1	0	1	0	0	0	0	0	0	0	0	0	0	0	.08

Nikolai Khabibulin

(statistical profile on page 400)

Pos: G **Catches:** L **Ht:** 6'1" **Wt:** 176 **Born:** 1/13/73—Sverdlovsk, USSR **Age:** 26

		Overall														Pen Shot		Offense		
Year	Tm	GP	GS	TP	W	L	T	Min	GA	GAA	Shots	SvPct	ShO	OE	PPGA	SHGA	Shots	GA	G	A	PIM
94-95	Wpg	26	22	5	8	9	4	1339	76	3.41	723	.895	0	7	17	1	1	0	0	1	4
95-96	Wpg	53	53	8	26	20	3	2914	152	3.13	1656	.908	2	26	48	8	1	0	0	0	12
96-97	Pho	72	69	6	30	33	6	4091	193	2.83	2094	.908	7	26	36	**13**	0	0	0	3	16
97-98	Pho*	70	70	8	30	28	10	4026	**184**	2.74	1835	.900	4	19	**56**	6	3	1	0	2	22
98-99	Pho	63	62	3	32	23	7	3657	130	2.13	1681	.923	8	24	34	3	0	0	0	0	8
5 Years		284	276	30	126	113	30	16027	735	2.75	7989	.908	21	102	191	31	5	1	0	6	62
		Postseason																		
Year	Tm	GP	GS	TP	W	L	Pct	Min	GA	GAA	Shots	SvPct	ShO	OE	PPGA	SHGA	Shots	GA	G	A	PIM
95-96	Wpg	6	6	0	2	4	.333	359	19	3.18	214	.911	0	2	8	2	0	0	0	0	0
96-97	Pho	7	7	0	3	4	.429	426	15	2.11	222	.932	1	5	6	0	0	0	0	0	6
97-98	Pho	4	3	1	2	1	.667	185	13	4.22	106	.877	0	0	3	0	0	0	0	1	0
98-99	Pho	7	7	0	3	4	.429	449	18	2.41	236	.924	0	3	9	0	0	0	0	0	2
4 Years		24	23	1	10	13	.435	1419	65	2.75	778	.916	1	10	26	2	0	0	0	1	8

Dimitri Khristich

(statistical profile on page 327)

Pos: LW **Shoots:** R **Ht:** 6'2" **Wt:** 190 **Born:** 7/23/69—Kiev, USSR **Age:** 30

Overall											Power Play			Shorthand			Penalty							Misc	
Year	Tm	GP	G	A	Pts	+/–	GW	GT	S	SPct	G	A	Pts	G	A	Pts	Num	PIM	Maj	Mnr	Fgt	Rgh	HHT	Hat	P/G
90-91	Was	40	13	14	27	-1	0	1	77	16.9	1	–	–	0	–	–	–	21	–	–	–	–	–	0	.68
91-92	Was	80	36	37	73	24	7	0	188	19.1	14	14	28	1	0	1	16	35	1	15	1	4	6	0	.91
92-93	Was	64	31	35	66	29	1	1	127	24.4	9	9	18	1	1	2	14	28	0	14	0	5	5	2	1.03
93-94	Was	83	29	29	58	-2	4	1	195	14.9	10	5	15	0	0	0	24	73	3	19	0	6	3	0	.70
94-95	Was	48	12	14	26	0	2	2	92	13.0	8	4	12	0	0	0	15	41	1	13	0	2	5	0	.54
95-96	LA	76	27	37	64	0	3	0	204	13.2	12	9	21	0	1	1	22	44	0	22	0	1	9	0	.84
96-97	LA*	75	19	37	56	8	2	0	135	14.1	3	6	9	0	2	2	15	38	0	14	0	2	5	0	.75
97-98	Bos	82	29	37	66	25	1	0	144	20.1	13	10	23	2	0	2	21	42	0	21	0	1	8	0	.80
98-99	Bos	79	29	42	71	11	6	1	144	**20.1**	13	7	20	1	0	1	24	48	0	24	0	1	10	1	.90
9 Years		627	225	282	507	94	26	6	1306	17.2	83	–	–	5	–	–	–	370	–	–	–	–	–	3	.81
Postseason																									
Year	Tm	GP	G	A	Pts	+/–	GW	OT	S	SPct	G	A	Pts	G	A	Pts	Num	PIM	Maj	Mnr	Fgt	Rgh	HHT	Hat	P/G
90-91	Was	11	1	3	4	-2	0	0	15	6.7	0	–	–	0	–	–	3	6	0	3	0	–	–	0	.36
91-92	Was	7	3	2	5	2	1	0	15	20.0	3	1	4	0	0	0	2	15	1	0	0	0	0	0	.71
92-93	Was	6	2	5	7	-2	0	0	15	13.3	1	2	3	0	1	1	1	2	0	1	0	0	0	0	1.17
93-94	Was	11	2	3	5	0	0	0	14	14.3	0	1	1	0	0	0	5	10	0	5	0	1	1	0	.45
94-95	Was	7	1	4	5	4	0	0	13	7.7	0	1	1	0	0	0	0	0	0	0	0	0	0	0	.71
97-98	Bos	6	2	2	4	1	0	0	15	13.3	2	0	2	0	0	0	1	2	0	1	0	0	0	0	.67
98-99	Bos	12	3	4	7	1	1	0	19	15.8	0	1	1	0	0	0	3	6	0	3	0	2	0	0	.58
7 Years		60	14	23	37	4	2	0	106	13.2	6	–	–	0	–	–	15	41	1	13	0	–	–	0	.62

Trevor Kidd

(statistical profile on page 400)

Pos: G **Catches:** L **Ht:** 6'2" **Wt:** 190 **Born:** 3/29/72—Dugald, Manitoba **Age:** 27

Overall																	Pen Shot		Offense		
Year	Tm	GP	GS	TP	W	L	T	Min	GA	GAA	Shots	SvPct	ShO	OE	PPGA	SHGA	Shots	GA	G	A	PIM
91-92	Cgy	2	2	0	1	1	0	120	8	4.00	56	.857	0	0	3	0	0	0	0	0	0
92-93										Did Not Play in NHL											
93-94	Cgy	31	26	2	13	7	6	1614	85	3.16	752	.887	0	6	32	4	1	**1**	0	4	4
94-95	Cgy	**43**	41	5	22	14	6	2463	107	2.61	1170	.909	3	15	31	3	1	0	0	1	2
95-96	Cgy	47	44	6	15	21	8	2570	119	2.78	1130	.895	3	6	40	7	1	**1**	0	2	4
96-97	Cgy	55	52	9	21	23	6	2979	141	2.84	1416	.900	4	16	38	**13**	0	0	0	2	16
97-98	Car	47	47	5	21	21	3	2685	97	2.17	1237	.922	3	16	24	3	2	0	0	0	2
98-99	Car	25	21	1	7	10	6	1358	61	2.70	640	.905	2	7	19	1	0	0	0	0	0
7 Years		250	233	28	100	97	35	13789	618	2.69	6401	.903	15	66	187	31	5	2	0	9	28
Postseason																					
Year	Tm	GP	GS	TP	W	L	Pct	Min	GA	GAA	Shots	SvPct	ShO	OE	PPGA	SHGA	Shots	GA	G	A	PIM
94-95	Cgy	7	7	1	3	4	.429	434	26	3.59	181	.856	1	1	6	0	0	0	0	0	0
95-96	Cgy	2	2	1	0	1	.000	83	9	6.51	40	.775	0	0	3	0	0	0	0	0	0
2 Years		9	9	2	3	5	.375	517	35	4.06	221	.842	1	1	9	0	0	0	0	0	0

Chad Kilger

(statistical profile on page 328)

Pos: C **Shoots:** L **Ht:** 6'4" **Wt:** 215 **Born:** 11/27/76—Cornwall, Ontario **Age:** 23

Overall											Power Play			Shorthand			Penalty							Misc	
Year	Tm	GP	G	A	Pts	+/–	GW	GT	S	SPct	G	A	Pts	G	A	Pts	Num	PIM	Maj	Mnr	Fgt	Rgh	HHT	Hat	P/G
95-96	2Tm	74	7	10	17	-4	1	0	57	12.3	0	0	0	0	0	0	17	34	0	17	0	1	6	0	.23
96-97	Pho	24	4	3	7	-5	0	0	30	13.3	1	0	1	0	0	0	5	13	1	4	1	0	1	0	.29
97-98	2Tm	32	3	9	12	0	1	0	32	9.4	2	2	4	0	0	0	5	10	0	5	0	0	2	0	.38
98-99	2Tm	77	15	12	27	-4	1	1	81	18.5	2	1	3	1	1	2	17	34	0	17	0	2	7	0	.35
95-96	Anh	45	5	7	12	-2	1	0	38	13.2	0	0	0	0	0	0	11	22	0	11	0	0	5	0	.27
95-96	Wpg	29	2	3	5	-2	0	0	19	10.5	0	0	0	0	0	0	6	12	0	6	0	1	1	0	.17
97-98	Pho	10	0	1	1	-2	0	0	9	0.0	0	0	0	0	0	0	2	4	0	2	0	0	2	0	.10
97-98	Chi	22	3	8	11	2	1	0	23	13.0	2	2	4	0	0	0	3	6	0	3	0	0	0	0	.50
98-99	Chi	64	14	11	25	-1	1	1	68	20.6	2	0	2	1	1	2	15	30	0	15	0	2	7	0	.39
98-99	Edm	13	1	1	2	-3	0	0	13	7.7	0	1	1	0	0	0	2	4	0	2	0	0	0	0	.15
4 Years		207	29	34	63	-13	3	1	200	14.5	5	3	8	1	1	2	44	91	1	43	1	3	16	0	.30
Postseason																									
Year	Tm	GP	G	A	Pts	+/–	GW	OT	S	SPct	G	A	Pts	G	A	Pts	Num	PIM	Maj	Mnr	Fgt	Rgh	HHT	Hat	P/G
95-96	Wpg	4	1	0	1	0	1	0	2	50.0	0	0	0	0	0	0	0	0	0	0	0	0	0	0	.25
98-99	Edm	4	0	0	0	-2	0	0	1	0.0	0	0	0	0	0	0	2	4	0	2	0	1	0	0	.00
2 Years		8	1	0	1	-2	1	0	3	33.3	0	0	0	0	0	0	2	4	0	2	0	1	0	0	.13

Derek King

(statistical profile on page 328)

Pos: LW **Shoots:** L **Ht:** 6'0" **Wt:** 210 **Born:** 2/11/67—Hamilton, Ontario **Age:** 32

Overall											Power Play			Shorthand			Penalty							Misc	
Year	Tm	GP	G	A	Pts	+/-	GW	GT	S	SPct	G	A	Pts	G	A	Pts	Num	PIM	Maj	Mnr	Fgt	Rgh	HHT	Hat	P/G
86-87	NYI	2	0	0	0	0	0	0	5	0.0	0	0	0	0	0	0	0	0	0	0	0	0	0	0	.00
87-88	NYI	55	12	24	36	7	4	0	94	12.8	1	–	–	0	–	–	–	30	–	–	–	–	–	0	.65
88-89	NYI	60	14	29	43	10	0	0	103	13.6	4	–	–	0	–	–	–	14	–	–	–	–	–	0	.72
89-90	NYI	46	13	27	40	2	1	0	91	14.3	5	–	–	0	–	–	–	20	–	–	–	–	–	1	.87
90-91	NYI	66	19	26	45	1	2	0	130	14.6	2	–	–	0	–	–	–	44	–	–	–	–	–	1	.68
91-92	NYI	80	40	38	78	-10	6	2	189	21.2	21	14	35	0	0	0	23	46	0	23	0	6	5	2	.98
92-93	NYI	77	38	38	76	-4	7	0	201	18.9	21	22	43	0	0	0	18	47	1	16	0	3	6	0	.99
93-94	NYI	78	30	40	70	18	7	1	171	17.5	10	16	26	0	0	0	24	59	1	22	1	7	8	1	.90
94-95	NYI	43	10	16	26	-5	0	0	118	8.5	7	4	11	0	0	0	15	41	1	13	1	3	2	0	.60
95-96	NYI	61	12	20	32	-10	0	1	154	7.8	5	1	6	1	0	1	10	23	1	9	1	1	5	0	.52
96-97	2Tm	**82**	26	33	59	-6	3	0	181	14.4	6	6	12	0	0	0	11	22	0	11	0	2	3	1	.72
97-98	Tor	77	21	25	46	-7	3	0	166	12.7	4	10	14	0	0	0	16	43	1	14	1	2	6	1	.60
98-99	Tor	81	24	28	52	15	4	0	150	16.0	8	8	16	0	0	0	10	20	0	10	0	1	3	0	.64
96-97	NYI	70	23	30	53	-6	3	0	153	15.0	5	6	11	0	0	0	10	20	0	10	0	2	2	1	.76
96-97	Har	12	3	3	6	0	0	0	28	10.7	1	0	1	0	0	0	1	2	0	1	0	0	1	0	.50
13 Years		808	259	344	603	11	37	4	1753	14.8	94	–	–	1	–	–	–	409	–	–	–	–	–	7	.75

Postseason

Year	Tm	GP	G	A	Pts	+/-	GW	OT	S	SPct	G	A	Pts	G	A	Pts	Num	PIM	Maj	Mnr	Fgt	Rgh	HHT	Hat	P/G
87-88	NYI	5	0	2	2	2	0	0	6	0.0	0	–	–	0	–	–	1	2	0	1	0	–	–	0	.40
89-90	NYI	4	0	0	0	-3	0	0	7	0.0	0	0	0	0	0	0	2	4	0	2	0	–	–	0	.00
92-93	NYI	18	3	11	14	3	1	0	48	6.3	0	3	3	0	0	0	7	14	0	7	0	1	1	0	.78
93-94	NYI	4	0	1	1	-3	0	0	6	0.0	0	0	0	0	0	0	0	0	0	0	0	0	0	0	.25
98-99	Tor	16	1	3	4	0	0	0	26	3.8	0	1	1	0	0	0	2	4	0	2	0	0	0	0	.25
5 Years		47	4	17	21	-1	1	0	93	4.3	0	–	–	0	–	–	12	24	0	12	0	–	–	0	.45

Kris King

Pos: LW **Shoots:** L **Ht:** 5'11" **Wt:** 205 **Born:** 2/18/66—Bracebridge, Ontario **Age:** 33

Overall											Power Play			Shorthand			Penalty							Misc	
Year	Tm	GP	G	A	Pts	+/-	GW	GT	S	SPct	G	A	Pts	G	A	Pts	Num	PIM	Maj	Mnr	Fgt	Rgh	HHT	Hat	P/G
87-88	Det	3	1	0	1	1	0	0	3	33.3	0	0	0	0	0	0	1	2	0	1	0	–	–	0	.33
88-89	Det	55	2	3	5	-7	0	0	34	5.9	0	–	–	0	–	–	–	168	–	–	–	–	–	0	.09
89-90	NYR	68	6	7	13	2	0	0	49	12.2	0	0	0	0	–	–	84	286	18	58	–	–	–	0	.19
90-91	NYR	72	11	14	25	-1	0	1	107	10.3	0	0	0	0	–	–	–	154	–	–	–	–	–	0	.35
91-92	NYR	79	10	9	19	13	2	0	97	10.3	0	0	0	0	0	0	77	224	18	57	17	25	11	0	.24
92-93	2Tm	78	8	11	19	4	1	0	74	10.8	0	0	0	0	0	0	62	203	13	44	12	14	11	0	.24
93-94	Wpg	83	4	8	12	-22	1	0	86	4.7	0	0	0	0	0	0	63	205	21	40	19	18	5	0	.14
94-95	Wpg	48	4	2	6	0	0	0	58	6.9	0	0	0	0	0	0	25	85	9	15	8	4	3	0	.13
95-96	Wpg	81	9	11	20	-7	2	0	89	10.1	0	0	0	1	2	3	56	151	13	43	13	13	11	0	.25
96-97	Pho	81	3	11	14	-7	0	0	57	5.3	0	1	1	0	0	0	51	185	25	25	24	5	4	0	.17
97-98	Tor	82	3	3	6	-13	2	0	53	5.7	0	0	0	0	0	0	60	199	21	37	20	10	10	0	.07
98-99	Tor	67	2	2	4	-16	1	0	34	5.9	0	0	0	1	0	1	32	105	11	20	11	9	3	0	.06
92-93	NYR	30	0	3	3	-1	0	0	23	0.0	0	0	0	0	0	0	25	67	3	21	3	6	5	0	.10
92-93	Wpg	48	8	8	16	5	1	0	51	15.7	0	0	0	0	0	0	37	136	10	23	9	8	6	0	.33
12 Years		797	63	81	144	-53	9	1	741	8.5	0	–	–	2	–	–	–	1967	–	–	–	–	–	0	.18

Postseason

Year	Tm	GP	G	A	Pts	+/-	GW	OT	S	SPct	G	A	Pts	G	A	Pts	Num	PIM	Maj	Mnr	Fgt	Rgh	HHT	Hat	P/G
88-89	Det	2	0	0	0	0	0	0	0	–	0	0	0	0	0	0	1	2	0	1	0	–	–	0	.00
89-90	NYR	10	0	1	1	1	0	0	4	0.0	0	–	–	0	–	–	–	30	–	–	–	–	–	0	.10
90-91	NYR	6	2	0	2	2	1	0	15	13.3	0	0	0	0	0	0	–	36	–	–	–	–	–	0	.33
91-92	NYR	13	4	1	5	4	3	1	15	26.7	0	0	0	0	0	0	7	14	0	7	0	4	2	0	.38
92-93	Wpg	6	1	1	2	-1	0	0	12	8.3	0	0	0	0	0	0	2	4	0	2	0	1	0	0	.33
95-96	Wpg	5	0	1	1	1	0	0	3	0.0	0	0	0	0	0	0	2	4	0	2	0	1	0	0	.20
96-97	Pho	7	0	0	0	-1	0	0	2	0.0	0	0	0	0	0	0	3	17	1	1	1	1	0	0	.00
98-99	Tor	17	1	1	2	-1	0	0	15	6.7	0	0	0	0	0	0	7	25	1	5	1	1	0	0	.12
8 Years		66	8	5	13	5	4	1	66	12.1	0	–	–	0	–	–	–	132	–	–	–	–	–	0	.20

Patrik Kjellberg

(statistical profile on page 328)

Pos: RW **Shoots:** L **Ht:** 6'2" **Wt:** 196 **Born:** 6/17/69—Falun, Sweden **Age:** 30

Overall											Power Play			Shorthand			Penalty							Misc	
Year	Tm	GP	G	A	Pts	+/-	GW	GT	S	SPct	G	A	Pts	G	A	Pts	Num	PIM	Maj	Mnr	Fgt	Rgh	HHT	Hat	P/G
92-93	Mon	7	0	0	0	-3	0	0	7	0.0	0	0	0	0	0	0	1	2	0	1	0	0	1	0	.00

Overall											Power Play			Shorthand			Penalty							Misc	
Year	Tm	GP	G	A	Pts	+/–	GW	GT	S	SPct	G	A	Pts	G	A	Pts	Num	PIM	Maj	Mnr	Fgt	Rgh	HHT	Hat	P/G
93-94											Did Not Play in NHL														
94-95											Did Not Play in NHL														
95-96											Did Not Play in NHL														
96-97											Did Not Play in NHL														
97-98											Did Not Play in NHL														
98-99	Nsh	71	11	20	31	-13	2	0	103	10.7	2	8	10	0	0	0	12	24	0	12	0	1	4	0	.44
2 Years		78	11	20	31	-16	2	0	110	10.0	2	8	10	0	0	0	13	26	0	13	0	1	5	0	.40

Trent Klatt

(statistical profile on page 328)

Pos: RW **Shoots:** R **Ht:** 6'1" **Wt:** 210 **Born:** 1/30/71—Robbinsdale, Minnesota **Age:** 28

Overall											Power Play			Shorthand			Penalty							Misc	
Year	Tm	GP	G	A	Pts	+/–	GW	GT	S	SPct	G	A	Pts	G	A	Pts	Num	PIM	Maj	Mnr	Fgt	Rgh	HHT	Hat	P/G
91-92	Min	1	0	0	0	0	0	0	1	0.0	0	0	0	0	0	0	0	0	0	0	0	0	0	0	.00
92-93	Min	47	4	19	23	2	0	0	69	5.8	1	1	2	0	0	0	15	38	0	14	0	4	3	0	.49
93-94	Dal	61	14	24	38	13	2	0	86	16.3	3	6	9	0	0	0	15	30	0	15	0	4	4	0	.62
94-95	Dal	47	12	10	22	-2	3	0	91	13.2	5	3	8	0	0	0	9	26	0	8	0	2	1	0	.47
95-96	2Tm	71	7	12	19	2	2	0	101	6.9	0	3	3	0	1	1	11	44	2	7	1	0	1	0	.27
96-97	Phi	76	24	21	45	9	5	0	131	18.3	5	3	8	5	0	5	10	20	0	10	0	3	4	1	.59
97-98	Phi	82	14	28	42	2	3	0	143	9.8	5	6	11	0	1	1	8	16	0	8	0	0	5	0	.51
98-99	2Tm	75	4	10	14	-3	0	0	60	6.7	0	0	0	0	1	1	6	12	0	6	0	0	3	0	.19
95-96	Dal	22	4	4	8	0	1	0	37	10.8	0	2	2	0	0	0	6	23	1	4	0	0	1	0	.36
95-96	Phi	49	3	8	11	2	1	0	64	4.7	0	1	1	0	1	1	5	21	1	3	1	0	0	0	.22
98-99	Phi	2	0	0	0	0	0	0	2	0.0	0	0	0	0	0	0	0	0	0	0	0	0	0	0	.00
98-99	Van	73	4	10	14	-3	0	0	58	6.9	0	0	0	0	1	1	6	12	0	6	0	0	3	0	.19
8 Years		460	79	124	203	23	15	0	682	11.6	19	22	41	5	3	8	74	186	2	68	1	13	21	1	.44
Postseason																									
Year	Tm	GP	G	A	Pts	+/–	GW	OT	S	SPct	G	A	Pts	G	A	Pts	Num	PIM	Maj	Mnr	Fgt	Rgh	HHT	Hat	P/G
91-92	Min	6	0	0	0	-4	0	0	7	0.0	0	0	0	0	0	0	1	2	0	1	0	0	0	0	.00
93-94	Dal	9	2	1	3	-1	0	0	14	14.3	1	0	1	0	0	0	2	4	0	2	0	1	0	0	.33
94-95	Dal	5	1	0	1	0	0	0	4	25.0	1	0	1	0	0	0	0	0	0	0	0	0	0	0	.20
95-96	Phi	12	4	1	5	1	0	0	16	25.0	0	0	0	0	0	0	0	0	0	0	0	0	0	0	.42
96-97	Phi	19	4	3	7	1	2	0	26	15.4	0	0	0	0	0	0	6	12	0	6	0	0	2	0	.37
97-98	Phi	5	0	0	0	-6	0	0	6	0.0	0	0	0	0	0	0	0	0	0	0	0	0	0	0	.00
6 Years		56	11	5	16	-9	2	0	73	15.1	2	0	2	0	0	0	9	18	0	9	0	1	2	0	.29

Ken Klee

(statistical profile on page 329)

Pos: RW **Shoots:** R **Ht:** 6'1" **Wt:** 205 **Born:** 4/24/71—Indianapolis, Indiana **Age:** 28

Overall											Power Play			Shorthand			Penalty							Misc	
Year	Tm	GP	G	A	Pts	+/–	GW	GT	S	SPct	G	A	Pts	G	A	Pts	Num	PIM	Maj	Mnr	Fgt	Rgh	HHT	Hat	P/G
94-95	Was	23	3	1	4	2	0	0	18	16.7	0	0	0	0	0	0	15	41	1	13	1	1	7	0	.17
95-96	Was	66	8	3	11	-1	2	0	76	10.5	0	0	0	1	0	1	30	60	0	30	0	2	14	0	.17
96-97	Was	80	3	8	11	-5	2	0	108	2.8	0	0	0	0	1	1	45	115	3	40	3	2	21	0	.14
97-98	Was	51	4	2	6	-3	1	0	44	9.1	0	0	0	0	0	0	19	46	0	18	0	0	11	0	.12
98-99	Was	78	7	13	20	-9	1	0	132	5.3	0	3	3	0	0	0	32	80	0	30	0	0	18	0	.26
5 Years		298	25	27	52	-16	6	0	378	6.6	0	3	3	1	1	2	141	342	4	131	4	5	71	0	.17
Postseason																									
Year	Tm	GP	G	A	Pts	+/–	GW	OT	S	SPct	G	A	Pts	G	A	Pts	Num	PIM	Maj	Mnr	Fgt	Rgh	HHT	Hat	P/G
94-95	Was	7	0	0	0	1	0	0	10	0.0	0	0	0	0	0	0	2	4	0	2	0	0	1	0	.00
95-96	Was	1	0	0	0	0	0	0	2	0.0	0	0	0	0	0	0	0	0	0	0	0	0	0	0	.00
97-98	Was	9	1	0	1	2	0	0	6	16.7	0	0	0	0	0	0	5	10	0	5	0	0	4	0	.11
3 Years		17	1	0	1	3	0	0	18	5.6	0	0	0	0	0	0	7	14	0	7	0	0	5	0	.06

Jon Klemm

Pos: D **Shoots:** R **Ht:** 6'3" **Wt:** 200 **Born:** 1/8/70—Cranbrook, British Columbia **Age:** 29

Overall											Power Play			Shorthand			Penalty							Misc	
Year	Tm	GP	G	A	Pts	+/–	GW	GT	S	SPct	G	A	Pts	G	A	Pts	Num	PIM	Maj	Mnr	Fgt	Rgh	HHT	Hat	P/G
91-92	Que	4	0	1	1	2	0	0	2	0.0	0	0	0	0	0	0	0	0	0	0	0	0	0	0	.25
92-93											Did Not Play in NHL														
93-94	Que	7	0	0	0	-1	0	0	11	0.0	0	0	0	0	0	0	2	4	0	2	0	0	0	0	.00
94-95	Que	4	1	0	1	3	0	0	5	20.0	0	0	0	0	0	0	1	2	0	1	0	1	0	0	.25
95-96	Col	56	3	12	15	12	1	0	61	4.9	0	1	1	1	1	2	10	20	0	10	0	0	6	0	.27
96-97	Col	80	9	15	24	12	1	0	103	8.7	1	2	3	2	0	2	17	37	1	16	1	0	9	0	.30

Overall											Power Play			Shorthand			Penalty							Misc	
Year	Tm	GP	G	A	Pts	+/–	GW	GT	S	SPct	G	A	Pts	G	A	Pts	Num	PIM	Maj	Mnr	Fgt	Rgh	HHT	Hat	P/G
97-98	Col	67	6	8	14	-3	0	1	60	10.0	0	0	0	0	0	0	15	30	0	15	0	0	8	0	.21
98-99	Col	39	1	2	3	4	0	0	28	3.6	0	0	0	0	0	0	14	31	1	13	1	0	4	0	.08
7 Years		257	20	38	58	29	2	1	270	7.4	1	3	4	3	1	4	59	124	2	57	2	1	27	0	.23
Postseason																									
Year	Tm	GP	G	A	Pts	+/–	GW	OT	S	SPct	G	A	Pts	G	A	Pts	Num	PIM	Maj	Mnr	Fgt	Rgh	HHT	Hat	P/G
95-96	Col	15	2	1	3	6	0	0	11	18.2	1	0	1	0	0	0	0	0	0	0	0	0	0	0	.20
96-97	Col	17	1	1	2	-1	0	0	20	5.0	0	0	0	0	0	0	3	6	0	3	0	0	2	0	.12
97-98	Col	4	0	0	0	1	0	0	1	0.0	0	0	0	0	0	0	0	0	0	0	0	0	0	0	.00
98-99	Col	19	0	1	1	1	0	0	11	0.0	0	0	0	0	0	0	5	10	0	5	0	1	1	0	.05
4 Years		55	3	3	6	7	0	0	43	7.0	1	0	1	0	0	0	8	16	0	8	0	1	3	0	.11

Petr Klima

Pos: LW **Shoots:** R **Ht:** 6'0" **Wt:** 188 **Born:** 12/23/64—Chaomutov, Czechoslovakia **Age:** 35

Overall											Power Play			Shorthand			Penalty							Misc	
Year	Tm	GP	G	A	Pts	+/–	GW	GT	S	SPct	G	A	Pts	G	A	Pts	Num	PIM	Maj	Mnr	Fgt	Rgh	HHT	Hat	P/G
85-86	Det	74	32	24	56	-39	4	0	174	18.4	8	–	–	0	–	–	–	16	–	–	–	–	–	2	.76
86-87	Det	77	30	23	53	-9	5	0	209	14.4	6	–	–	0	–	–	–	42	–	–	–	–	–	1	.69
87-88	Det	78	37	25	62	4	5	0	174	21.3	6	–	–	5	–	–	–	46	–	–	–	–	–	0	.79
88-89	Det	51	25	16	41	5	3	0	145	17.2	1	–	–	0	–	–	–	44	–	–	–	–	–	0	.80
89-90	2Tm	76	30	33	63	-9	3	0	186	16.1	9	–	–	0	–	–	–	72	–	–	–	–	–	0	.83
90-91	Edm	70	40	28	68	24	5	0	204	19.6	7	8	15	1	0	1	–	113	–	–	–	–	–	3	.97
91-92	Edm	57	21	13	34	-18	0	0	107	19.6	5	7	12	0	0	0	18	52	0	16	0	3	5	0	.60
92-93	Edm	68	32	16	48	-15	2	0	175	18.3	13	9	22	0	0	0	30	100	0	25	0	2	7	0	.71
93-94	TB	75	28	27	55	-15	2	0	167	16.8	10	12	22	0	0	0	23	76	2	18	0	3	4	0	.73
94-95	TB	47	13	13	26	-13	3	0	75	17.3	4	4	8	0	0	0	9	26	0	8	0	0	1	0	.55
95-96	TB	67	22	30	52	-25	3	2	164	13.4	8	20	28	0	0	0	26	68	0	24	0	3	7	0	.78
96-97	3Tm	33	2	12	14	-12	0	0	55	3.6	0	9	9	0	0	0	6	12	0	6	0	0	3	0	.42
97-98		Did Not Play in NHL																							
98-99	Det	13	1	0	1	-3	1	0	12	8.3	0	0	0	0	0	0	2	4	0	2	0	0	1	0	.08
89-90	Det	13	5	5	10	-8	0	0	37	13.5	2	–	–	0	–	–	3	6	0	3	0	–	–	0	.77
89-90	Edm	63	25	28	53	-1	3	0	149	16.8	7	9	16	0	0	0	–	66	–	–	–	–	–	0	.84
96-97	LA	8	0	4	4	-7	0	0	12	0.0	0	4	4	0	0	0	1	2	0	1	0	0	1	0	.50
96-97	Pit	9	1	3	4	-4	0	0	21	4.8	0	3	3	0	0	0	2	4	0	2	0	0	1	0	.44
96-97	Edm	16	1	5	6	-1	0	0	22	4.5	0	2	2	0	0	0	3	6	0	3	0	0	1	0	.38
13 Years		786	313	260	573	-125	36	2	1847	16.9	77	–	–	6	–	–	–	671	–	–	–	–	–	6	.73
Postseason																									
Year	Tm	GP	G	A	Pts	+/–	GW	OT	S	SPct	G	A	Pts	G	A	Pts	Num	PIM	Maj	Mnr	Fgt	Rgh	HHT	Hat	P/G
86-87	Det	13	1	2	3	0	0	0	45	2.2	0	–	–	0	–	–	2	4	0	2	0	–	–	0	.23
87-88	Det	12	10	8	18	9	4	0	38	26.3	2	–	–	1	–	–	–	10	–	–	–	–	–	2	1.50
88-89	Det	6	2	4	6	0	0	0	19	10.5	1	–	–	0	0	0	–	19	–	–	–	–	–	0	1.00
89-90	Edm	21	5	0	5	-2	1	1	25	20.0	1	0	1	0	0	0	4	8	0	4	0	–	–	0	.24
90-91	Edm	18	7	6	13	-1	3	1	51	13.7	1	–	–	0	0	0	–	16	–	–	–	–	–	1	.72
91-92	Edm	15	1	4	5	-1	0	0	22	4.5	0	1	1	0	0	0	4	8	0	4	0	2	1	0	.33
95-96	TB	4	2	0	2	0	0	0	9	22.2	2	0	2	0	0	0	3	14	0	2	0	0	0	0	.50
96-97	Edm	6	0	0	0	0	0	0	2	0.0	0	0	0	0	0	0	2	4	0	2	0	1	0	0	.00
8 Years		95	28	24	52	5	8	2	211	13.3	7	–	–	1	–	–	–	83	–	–	–	–	–	3	.55

Michael Knuble

(statistical profile on page 329)

Pos: RW **Shoots:** R **Ht:** 6'3" **Wt:** 225 **Born:** 7/4/72—Toronto, Ontario **Age:** 27

Overall											Power Play			Shorthand			Penalty							Misc	
Year	Tm	GP	G	A	Pts	+/–	GW	GT	S	SPct	G	A	Pts	G	A	Pts	Num	PIM	Maj	Mnr	Fgt	Rgh	HHT	Hat	P/G
96-97	Det	9	1	0	1	-1	0	0	10	10.0	0	0	0	0	0	0	0	0	0	0	0	0	0	0	.11
97-98	Det	53	7	6	13	2	0	0	54	13.0	0	0	0	0	0	0	8	16	0	8	0	1	5	0	.25
98-99	NYR	82	15	20	35	-7	1	0	113	13.3	3	6	9	0	0	0	13	26	0	13	0	1	8	0	.43
3 Years		144	23	26	49	-6	1	0	177	13.0	3	6	9	0	0	0	21	42	0	21	0	2	13	0	.34
Postseason																									
Year	Tm	GP	G	A	Pts	+/–	GW	OT	S	SPct	G	A	Pts	G	A	Pts	Num	PIM	Maj	Mnr	Fgt	Rgh	HHT	Hat	P/G
97-98	Det	3	0	1	1	0	0	0	1	0.0	0	0	0	0	0	0	0	0	0	0	0	0	0	0	.33

Joey Kocur

Pos: RW **Shoots:** R **Ht:** 6'0" **Wt:** 220 **Born:** 12/21/64—Calgary, Alberta **Age:** 35

		Overall									Power Play			Shorthand			Penalty							Misc	
Year	Tm	GP	G	A	Pts	+/-	GW	GT	S	SPct	G	A	Pts	G	A	Pts	Num	PIM	Maj	Mnr	Fgt	Rgh	HHT	Hat	P/G
84-85	Det	17	1	0	1	-4	0	0	7	14.3	0	0	0	0	0	0	–	64	–	–	–	–	–	0	.06
85-86	Det	59	9	6	15	-24	0	0	65	13.8	2	–	–	0	–	–	–	**377**	–	–	–	–	–	0	.25
86-87	Det	77	9	9	18	-10	2	0	81	11.1	2	–	–	0	–	–	–	276	–	–	–	–	–	0	.23
87-88	Det	63	7	7	14	-11	1	0	41	17.1	0	–	–	0	–	–	–	263	–	–	–	–	–	0	.22
88-89	Det	60	9	9	18	-4	1	0	76	11.8	1	–	–	0	–	–	–	213	–	–	–	–	–	0	.30
89-90	Det	71	16	20	36	-4	5	0	128	12.5	1	–	–	0	–	–	–	268	–	–	–	–	–	0	.51
90-91	2Tm	57	5	4	9	-7	0	0	73	6.8	0	–	–	0	–	–	–	289	–	–	–	–	–	0	.16
91-92	NYR	51	7	4	11	-4	2	0	72	9.7	0	0	0	0	0	0	39	121	9	28	9	11	2	0	.22
92-93	NYR	65	3	6	9	-9	0	0	43	7.0	2	1	3	0	0	0	40	131	9	28	9	14	2	0	.14
93-94	NYR	71	2	1	3	-9	0	0	43	4.7	0	0	0	0	0	0	44	129	11	32	10	16	3	0	.04
94-95	NYR	48	1	2	3	-4	0	0	25	4.0	0	0	0	0	0	0	20	71	5	13	4	8	0	0	.06
95-96	2Tm	45	1	3	4	-7	0	0	20	5.0	0	0	0	0	0	0	21	68	6	14	6	7	0	0	.09
96-97	Det	34	2	1	3	-7	1	0	38	5.3	0	0	0	0	0	0	25	70	4	20	4	11	2	0	.09
97-98	Det	63	6	5	11	7	2	0	53	11.3	0	1	1	0	0	0	28	92	4	21	4	9	1	0	.17
98-99	Det	39	2	5	7	0	0	0	20	10.0	0	0	0	0	0	0	24	87	5	16	5	9	3	0	.18
90-91	Det	52	5	4	9	-6	0	0	67	7.5	0	–	–	0	–	–	–	253	–	–	–	–	–	0	.17
90-91	NYR	5	0	0	0	-1	0	0	6	0.0	0	0	0	0	0	0	–	36	–	–	–	–	–	0	.00
95-96	NYR	38	1	2	3	-4	0	0	19	5.3	0	0	0	0	0	0	17	49	5	12	5	7	0	0	.08
95-96	Van	7	0	1	1	-3	0	0	1	0.0	0	0	0	0	0	0	4	19	1	2	1	0	0	0	.14
15 Years		820	80	82	162	-97	14	0	785	10.2	8	–	–	0	–	–	–	2519	–	–	–	–	–	0	.20

Postseason

Year	Tm	GP	G	A	Pts	+/-	GW	OT	S	SPct	G	A	Pts	G	A	Pts	Num	PIM	Maj	Mnr	Fgt	Rgh	HHT	Hat	P/G
84-85	Det	3	1	0	1	-2	0	0	1	100.0	0	0	0	0	0	0	1	5	1	0	–	0	0	0	.33
86-87	Det	16	2	3	5	-1	2	0	17	11.8	1	–	–	0	–	–	–	71	–	–	–	–	–	0	.31
87-88	Det	10	0	1	1	1	0	0	7	0.0	0	–	–	0	–	–	5	13	1	4	–	–	–	0	.10
88-89	Det	3	0	1	1	0	0	0	4	0.0	0	–	–	0	0	0	3	6	0	3	0	–	–	0	.33
90-91	NYR	6	0	2	2	-3	0	0	6	0.0	0	–	–	0	0	0	–	21	–	–	–	–	–	0	.33
91-92	NYR	12	1	1	2	-3	0	0	9	11.1	0	0	0	0	0	0	11	38	0	9	0	8	1	0	.17
93-94	NYR	20	1	1	2	-1	0	0	16	6.3	0	0	0	0	0	0	7	17	1	6	1	3	0	0	.10
94-95	NYR	10	0	0	0	0	0	0	1	0.0	0	0	0	0	0	0	4	8	0	4	0	1	0	0	.00
95-96	Van	1	0	0	0	0	0	0	0	–	0	0	0	0	0	0	0	0	0	0	0	0	0	0	.00
96-97	Det	19	1	3	4	5	0	0	16	6.3	0	0	0	0	0	0	7	22	0	6	0	3	0	0	.21
97-98	Det	18	4	0	4	-3	0	0	13	30.8	0	0	0	0	0	0	11	30	0	10	0	4	1	0	.22
11 Years		118	10	12	22	-7	2	0	90	11.1	1	–	–	0	–	–	–	231	–	–	–	–	–	0	.19

Ladislav Kohn

Pos: RW **Shoots:** L **Ht:** 5'10" **Wt:** 180 **Born:** 3/4/75—Uherske Hradiste, Czechoslovakia **Age:** 24

		Overall									Power Play			Shorthand			Penalty							Misc	
Year	Tm	GP	G	A	Pts	+/-	GW	GT	S	SPct	G	A	Pts	G	A	Pts	Num	PIM	Maj	Mnr	Fgt	Rgh	HHT	Hat	P/G
95-96	Cgy	5	1	0	1	-1	0	0	8	12.5	0	0	0	0	0	0	1	2	0	1	0	0	0	0	.20
96-97		Did Not Play in NHL																							
97-98	Cgy	4	0	1	1	2	0	0	2	0.0	0	0	0	0	0	0	0	0	0	0	0	0	0	0	.25
98-99	Tor	16	1	3	4	1	0	0	23	4.3	0	0	0	0	0	0	2	4	0	2	0	0	0	0	.25
3 Years		25	2	4	6	2	0	0	33	6.1	0	0	0	0	0	0	3	6	0	3	0	0	0	0	.24

Postseason

Year	Tm	GP	G	A	Pts	+/-	GW	OT	S	SPct	G	A	Pts	G	A	Pts	Num	PIM	Maj	Mnr	Fgt	Rgh	HHT	Hat	P/G
98-99	Tor	2	0	0	0	0	0	0	0	–	0	0	0	0	0	0	1	5	1	0	1	0	0	0	.00

Saku Koivu

(statistical profile on page 329)

Pos: C **Shoots:** L **Ht:** 5'10" **Wt:** 183 **Born:** 11/23/74—Turku, Finland **Age:** 25

		Overall									Power Play			Shorthand			Penalty							Misc	
Year	Tm	GP	G	A	Pts	+/-	GW	GT	S	SPct	G	A	Pts	G	A	Pts	Num	PIM	Maj	Mnr	Fgt	Rgh	HHT	Hat	P/G
95-96	Mon	82	20	25	45	-7	2	1	136	14.7	8	6	14	3	1	4	20	40	0	20	0	3	9	0	.55
96-97	Mon	50	17	39	56	7	3	0	135	12.6	5	12	17	0	1	1	19	38	0	19	0	6	3	0	1.12
97-98	Mon*	69	14	43	57	8	3	0	145	9.7	2	19	21	2	1	3	24	48	0	24	0	1	12	0	.83
98-99	Mon	65	14	30	44	-7	0	0	145	9.7	4	15	19	2	1	3	19	38	0	19	0	2	9	0	.68
4 Years		266	65	137	202	1	8	1	561	11.6	19	52	71	7	4	11	82	164	0	82	0	12	33	0	.76

Postseason

Year	Tm	GP	G	A	Pts	+/-	GW	OT	S	SPct	G	A	Pts	G	A	Pts	Num	PIM	Maj	Mnr	Fgt	Rgh	HHT	Hat	P/G
95-96	Mon	6	3	1	4	2	0	0	13	23.1	0	0	0	0	1	1	4	8	0	4	0	0	1	0	.67
96-97	Mon	5	1	3	4	1	0	0	10	10.0	0	0	0	0	0	0	5	10	0	5	0	0	2	0	.80

Postseason																									
Year	Tm	GP	G	A	Pts	+/-	GW	OT	S	SPct	G	A	Pts	G	A	Pts	Num	PIM	Maj	Mnr	Fgt	Rgh	HHT	Hat	P/G
97-98	Mon	6	2	3	5	4	0	0	14	14.3	1	0	1	0	0	0	1	2	0	1	0	0	1	0	.83
3 Years		17	6	7	13	7	0	0	37	16.2	1	0	1	0	1	1	10	20	0	10	0	0	4	0	.76

Olaf Kolzig

(statistical profile on page 400)

Pos: G **Catches:** L **Ht:** 6'3" **Wt:** 225 **Born:** 4/6/70—Johannesburg, South Africa **Age:** 29

		Overall																Pen Shot		Offense		
Year	Tm	GP	GS	TP	W	L	T	Min	GA	GAA	Shots	SvPct	ShO	OE	PPGA	SHGA	Shots	GA	G	A	PIM
89-90	Was	2	2	0	0	2	0	120	12	6.00	63	.810	0	0	2	1	0	0	0	0	0
90-91										Did Not Play in NHL											
91-92										Did Not Play in NHL											
92-93	Was	1	0	0	0	0	0	20	2	6.00	7	.714	0	0	1	0	0	0	0	0	0
93-94	Was	7	4	3	0	3	0	224	20	5.36	128	.844	0	0	4	0	0	0	0	0	0
94-95	Was	14	10	1	2	8	2	724	30	2.49	305	.902	0	1	8	0	0	0	0	0	4
95-96	Was	18	12	2	4	8	2	897	46	3.08	406	.887	0	4	20	2	1	0	0	0	2
96-97	Was	29	25	1	8	15	4	1645	71	2.59	758	.906	2	7	19	4	1	0	0	0	4
97-98	Was*	64	63	3	33	18	10	3788	139	2.20	1729	.920	5	23	26	3	0	0	0	1	12
98-99	Was	64	64	8	26	**31**	3	3586	154	2.58	1538	.900	4	11	37	4	0	0	0	2	19
8 Years		199	180	18	73	85	21	11004	474	2.58	4934	.904	11	46	117	14	2	0	0	3	41

Postseason																				
Year	Tm	GP	GS	TP	W	L	Pct	Min	GA	GAA	Shots	SvPct	ShO	OE	PPGA	SHGA	Shots	GA	G	A	PIM
94-95	Was	2	0	1	1	0	1.000	44	1	1.36	21	.952	0	0	0	0	0	0	0	0	0
95-96	Was	5	3	0	2	3	.400	341	11	1.94	167	.934	0	2	3	1	0	0	0	0	4
97-98	Was	21	21	0	12	9	.571	1351	44	1.95	740	.941	4	13	15	2	0	0	0	0	4
3 Years		28	24	1	15	12	.556	1736	56	1.94	928	.940	4	15	18	3	0	0	0	0	8

Steve Konowalchuk

(statistical profile on page 329)

Pos: C **Shoots:** L **Ht:** 6'1" **Wt:** 205 **Born:** 11/11/72—Salt Lake City, Utah **Age:** 27

		Overall									Power Play			Shorthand			Penalty							Misc	
Year	Tm	GP	G	A	Pts	+/-	GW	GT	S	SPct	G	A	Pts	G	A	Pts	Num	PIM	Maj	Mnr	Fgt	Rgh	HHT	Hat	P/G
91-92	Was	1	0	0	0	0	0	0	1	0.0	0	0	0	0	0	0	0	0	0	0	0	0	0	0	.00
92-93	Was	36	4	7	11	4	1	0	34	11.8	1	0	1	0	0	0	8	16	0	8	0	1	2	0	.31
93-94	Was	62	12	14	26	9	0	0	63	19.0	0	4	4	0	0	0	15	33	1	14	1	2	9	0	.42
94-95	Was	46	11	14	25	7	3	0	88	12.5	3	0	3	3	2	5	18	44	0	17	0	10	3	0	.54
95-96	Was	70	23	22	45	13	3	0	197	11.7	7	6	13	1	2	3	39	92	2	36	2	11	8	2	.64
96-97	Was	78	17	25	42	-3	3	1	155	11.0	2	5	7	1	1	2	24	67	1	21	0	5	5	0	.54
97-98	Was	80	10	24	34	9	2	0	131	7.6	2	1	3	0	0	0	33	80	2	30	2	12	7	0	.43
98-99	Was	45	12	12	24	0	2	0	98	12.2	4	5	9	1	0	1	13	26	0	13	0	4	5	0	.53
8 Years		418	89	118	207	39	14	1	767	11.6	19	21	40	6	5	11	150	358	6	139	5	45	39	2	.50

Postseason																									
Year	Tm	GP	G	A	Pts	+/-	GW	OT	S	SPct	G	A	Pts	G	A	Pts	Num	PIM	Maj	Mnr	Fgt	Rgh	HHT	Hat	P/G
92-93	Was	2	0	1	1	1	0	0	0	–	0	0	0	0	0	0	0	0	0	0	0	0	0	0	.50
93-94	Was	11	0	1	1	-1	0	0	6	0.0	0	0	0	0	0	0	5	10	0	5	0	2	2	0	.09
94-95	Was	7	2	5	7	2	0	0	18	11.1	0	0	0	1	0	1	6	12	0	6	0	1	2	0	1.00
95-96	Was	2	0	2	2	1	0	0	1	0.0	0	0	0	0	0	0	0	0	0	0	0	0	0	0	1.00
4 Years		22	2	9	11	3	0	0	25	8.0	0	0	0	1	0	1	11	22	0	11	0	3	4	0	.50

Dan Kordic

Pos: LW **Shoots:** L **Ht:** 6'5" **Wt:** 230 **Born:** 4/18/71—Edmonton, Alberta **Age:** 28

		Overall									Power Play			Shorthand			Penalty							Misc	
Year	Tm	GP	G	A	Pts	+/-	GW	GT	S	SPct	G	A	Pts	G	A	Pts	Num	PIM	Maj	Mnr	Fgt	Rgh	HHT	Hat	P/G
91-92	Phi	46	1	3	4	1	0	0	27	3.7	0	0	0	0	0	0	36	126	10	23	9	7	11	0	.09
92-93											Did Not Play in NHL														
93-94	Phi	4	0	0	0	0	0	0	0	–	0	0	0	0	0	0	1	5	1	0	1	0	0	0	.00
94-95											Did Not Play in NHL														
95-96	Phi	9	1	0	1	1	0	0	2	50.0	0	0	0	0	0	0	7	31	3	3	3	0	0	0	.11
96-97	Phi	75	1	4	5	-1	0	0	21	4.8	0	0	0	0	0	0	45	210	24	15	24	9	0	0	.07
97-98	Phi	61	1	1	2	-4	0	0	12	8.3	0	0	0	0	0	0	46	210	18	20	18	7	4	0	.03
98-99	Phi	2	0	0	0	-1	0	0	0	–	0	0	0	0	0	0	1	2	0	1	0	0	1	0	.00
6 Years		197	4	8	12	-4	0	0	62	6.5	0	0	0	0	0	0	136	584	56	62	55	23	16	0	.06

Postseason																									
Year	Tm	GP	G	A	Pts	+/-	GW	OT	S	SPct	G	A	Pts	G	A	Pts	Num	PIM	Maj	Mnr	Fgt	Rgh	HHT	Hat	P/G
96-97	Phi	12	1	0	1	1	0	0	3	33.3	0	0	0	0	0	0	7	22	0	6	0	2	0	0	.08

Igor Korolev

(statistical profile on page 330)

Pos: RW **Shoots:** L **Ht:** 6'1" **Wt:** 190 **Born:** 9/6/70—Moscow, USSR **Age:** 29

Overall											Power Play			Shorthand			Penalty							Misc	
Year	Tm	GP	G	A	Pts	+/-	GW	GT	S	SPct	G	A	Pts	G	A	Pts	Num	PIM	Maj	Mnr	Fgt	Rgh	HHT	Hat	P/G
92-93	StL	74	4	23	27	-1	0	0	76	5.3	2	3	5	0	0	0	10	20	0	10	0	0	7	0	.36
93-94	StL	73	6	10	16	-12	1	0	93	6.5	0	0	0	0	0	0	20	40	0	20	0	1	11	0	.22
94-95	Wpg	45	8	22	30	1	1	0	85	9.4	1	4	5	0	0	0	5	10	0	5	0	1	1	0	.67
95-96	Wpg	73	22	29	51	1	5	1	165	13.3	8	7	15	0	0	0	21	42	0	21	0	1	9	1	.70
96-97	Pho	41	3	7	10	-5	0	0	41	7.3	2	1	3	0	0	0	10	28	0	9	0	1	5	0	.24
97-98	Tor	78	17	22	39	-18	5	0	97	17.5	6	6	12	3	0	3	11	22	0	11	0	0	7	0	.50
98-99	Tor	66	13	34	47	11	2	0	99	13.1	1	9	10	0	0	0	23	46	0	23	0	2	15	0	.71
7 Years		450	73	147	220	-23	14	1	656	11.1	20	30	50	3	0	3	100	208	0	99	0	6	55	1	.49

Postseason																									
Year	Tm	GP	G	A	Pts	+/-	GW	OT	S	SPct	G	A	Pts	G	A	Pts	Num	PIM	Maj	Mnr	Fgt	Rgh	HHT	Hat	P/G
92-93	StL	3	0	0	0	-1	0	0	0	-	0	0	0	0	0	0	0	0	0	0	0	0	0	0	.00
93-94	StL	2	0	0	0	-2	0	0	4	0.0	0	0	0	0	0	0	0	0	0	0	0	0	0	0	.00
95-96	Wpg	6	0	3	3	-2	0	0	4	0.0	0	0	0	0	0	0	0	0	0	0	0	0	0	0	.50
96-97	Pho	1	0	0	0	0	0	0	1	0.0	0	0	0	0	0	0	0	0	0	0	0	0	0	0	.00
98-99	Tor	1	0	0	0	0	0	0	0	-	0	0	0	0	0	0	0	0	0	0	0	0	0	0	.00
5 Years		13	0	3	3	-5	0	0	9	0.0	0	0	0	0	0	0	0	0	0	0	0	0	0	0	.23

Alexander Korolyuk

(statistical profile on page 330)

Pos: RW **Shoots:** L **Ht:** 5'9" **Wt:** 190 **Born:** 1/15/76—Moscow, USSR **Age:** 23

Overall											Power Play			Shorthand			Penalty							Misc	
Year	Tm	GP	G	A	Pts	+/-	GW	GT	S	SPct	G	A	Pts	G	A	Pts	Num	PIM	Maj	Mnr	Fgt	Rgh	HHT	Hat	P/G
97-98	SJ	19	2	3	5	-5	0	0	23	8.7	1	0	1	0	0	0	3	6	0	3	0	0	2	0	.26
98-99	SJ	55	12	18	30	3	0	1	96	12.5	2	5	7	0	0	0	13	26	0	13	0	2	3	0	.55
2 Years		74	14	21	35	-2	0	1	119	11.8	3	5	8	0	0	0	16	32	0	16	0	2	5	0	.47

Postseason																									
Year	Tm	GP	G	A	Pts	+/-	GW	OT	S	SPct	G	A	Pts	G	A	Pts	Num	PIM	Maj	Mnr	Fgt	Rgh	HHT	Hat	P/G
98-99	SJ	6	1	3	4	-3	1	0	7	14.3	0	2	2	0	0	0	1	2	0	1	0	0	0	0	.67

Andrei Kovalenko

(statistical profile on page 330)

Pos: RW **Shoots:** L **Ht:** 5'10" **Wt:** 215 **Born:** 6/7/70—Balakovo, USSR **Age:** 29

Overall											Power Play			Shorthand			Penalty							Misc	
Year	Tm	GP	G	A	Pts	+/-	GW	GT	S	SPct	G	A	Pts	G	A	Pts	Num	PIM	Maj	Mnr	Fgt	Rgh	HHT	Hat	P/G
92-93	Que	81	27	41	68	13	4	0	153	17.6	8	6	14	1	1	2	27	57	1	26	1	2	11	1	.84
93-94	Que	58	16	17	33	-5	4	0	92	17.4	5	6	11	0	0	0	19	46	0	18	0	2	5	0	.57
94-95	Que	45	14	10	24	-4	3	0	63	22.2	1	3	4	0	0	0	10	31	1	8	0	0	4	0	.53
95-96	2Tm	77	28	28	56	20	6	1	131	21.4	6	8	14	0	0	0	19	49	1	17	0	2	7	0	.73
96-97	Edm	74	32	27	59	-5	2	0	163	19.6	14	11	25	0	0	0	31	81	1	28	0	10	9	0	.80
97-98	Edm	59	6	17	23	-14	2	1	89	6.7	1	9	10	0	0	0	14	28	0	14	0	5	5	0	.39
98-99	3Tm	74	19	21	40	-6	4	1	104	18.3	3	10	13	0	0	0	16	32	0	16	0	4	4	0	.54
95-96	Col	26	11	11	22	11	3	0	46	23.9	3	3	6	0	0	0	8	16	0	8	0	1	1	0	.85
95-96	Mon	51	17	17	34	9	3	1	85	20.0	3	5	8	0	0	0	11	33	1	9	0	1	6	0	.67
98-99	Edm	43	13	14	27	-4	3	1	75	17.3	2	8	10	0	0	0	15	30	0	15	0	3	4	0	.63
98-99	Phi	13	0	1	1	-5	0	0	8	0.0	0	1	1	0	0	0	1	2	0	1	0	1	0	0	.08
98-99	Car	18	6	6	12	3	1	0	21	28.6	1	1	2	0	0	0	0	0	0	0	0	0	0	0	.67
7 Years		468	142	161	303	-1	25	3	795	17.9	38	53	91	1	1	2	136	324	4	127	1	25	45	1	.65

Postseason																									
Year	Tm	GP	G	A	Pts	+/-	GW	OT	S	SPct	G	A	Pts	G	A	Pts	Num	PIM	Maj	Mnr	Fgt	Rgh	HHT	Hat	P/G
92-93	Que	4	1	0	1	-5	0	0	8	12.5	0	0	0	0	0	0	1	2	0	1	0	0	0	0	.25
94-95	Que	6	0	1	1	-3	0	0	6	0.0	0	0	0	0	0	0	1	2	0	1	0	0	1	0	.17
95-96	Mon	6	0	0	0	-2	0	0	9	0.0	0	0	0	0	0	0	3	6	0	3	0	1	0	0	.00
96-97	Edm	12	4	3	7	1	0	0	35	11.4	3	1	4	0	0	0	3	6	0	3	0	0	0	0	.58
97-98	Edm	1	0	0	0	0	0	0	2	0.0	0	0	0	0	0	0	1	2	0	1	0	0	0	0	.00
98-99	Car	4	0	2	2	1	0	0	3	0.0	0	0	0	0	0	0	1	2	0	1	0	0	1	0	.50
6 Years		33	5	6	11	-8	0	0	63	7.9	3	1	4	0	0	0	10	20	0	10	0	1	2	0	.33

Alexei Kovalev

(statistical profile on page 330)

Pos: RW **Shoots:** L **Ht:** 6'2" **Wt:** 210 **Born:** 2/24/73—Togliatti, USSR **Age:** 26

Overall											Power Play			Shorthand			Penalty							Misc	
Year	Tm	GP	G	A	Pts	+/–	GW	GT	S	SPct	G	A	Pts	G	A	Pts	Num	PIM	Maj	Mnr	Fgt	Rgh	HHT	Hat	P/G
92-93	NYR	65	20	18	38	-10	3	1	134	14.9	3	5	8	0	0	0	34	79	1	32	0	2	10	1	.58
93-94	NYR	76	23	33	56	18	3	0	184	12.5	7	6	13	0	0	0	52	154	6	42	1	7	15	0	.74
94-95	NYR	48	13	15	28	-6	1	0	103	12.6	1	5	6	1	0	1	15	30	0	15	0	2	3	0	.58
95-96	NYR	81	24	34	58	5	7	0	206	11.7	8	10	18	1	0	1	42	98	2	39	0	7	15	0	.72
96-97	NYR	45	13	22	35	11	0	0	110	11.8	1	8	9	0	0	0	21	42	0	21	0	1	13	1	.78
97-98	NYR	73	23	30	53	-22	3	1	173	13.3	8	14	22	0	0	0	22	44	0	22	0	1	14	0	.73
98-99	2Tm	77	23	30	53	2	5	0	191	12.0	6	9	15	1	0	1	23	49	1	22	1	2	14	0	.69
98-99	NYR	14	3	4	7	-6	1	0	35	8.6	1	2	3	0	0	0	6	12	0	6	0	1	3	0	.50
98-99	Pit	63	20	26	46	8	4	0	156	12.8	5	7	12	1	0	1	17	37	1	16	1	1	11	0	.73
7 Years		465	139	182	321	-2	22	2	1101	12.6	34	57	91	3	0	3	209	496	10	193	2	22	84	2	.69
Postseason																									
Year	Tm	GP	G	A	Pts	+/–	GW	OT	S	SPct	G	A	Pts	G	A	Pts	Num	PIM	Maj	Mnr	Fgt	Rgh	HHT	Hat	P/G
93-94	NYR	23	9	12	21	5	2	0	71	12.7	5	4	9	0	0	0	9	18	0	9	0	2	1	0	.91
94-95	NYR	10	4	7	11	2	0	0	23	17.4	0	2	2	0	0	0	5	10	0	5	0	1	3	0	1.10
95-96	NYR	11	3	4	7	0	1	0	31	9.7	0	2	2	0	0	0	7	14	0	7	0	1	2	0	.64
98-99	Pit	10	5	7	12	0	1	0	24	20.8	0	2	2	0	0	0	7	14	0	7	0	0	3	0	1.20
4 Years		54	21	30	51	7	4	0	149	14.1	5	10	15	0	0	0	28	56	0	28	0	4	9	0	.94

Slava Kozlov

(statistical profile on page 331)

Pos: C **Shoots:** L **Ht:** 5'10" **Wt:** 185 **Born:** 5/3/72—Voskresensk, USSR **Age:** 27

Overall											Power Play			Shorthand			Penalty							Misc	
Year	Tm	GP	G	A	Pts	+/–	GW	GT	S	SPct	G	A	Pts	G	A	Pts	Num	PIM	Maj	Mnr	Fgt	Rgh	HHT	Hat	P/G
91-92	Det	7	0	2	2	-2	0	0	9	0.0	0	0	0	0	0	0	1	2	0	1	0	0	1	0	.29
92-93	Det	17	4	1	5	-1	0	0	26	15.4	0	0	0	0	0	0	7	14	0	7	0	0	2	0	.29
93-94	Det	77	34	39	73	27	6	0	202	16.8	8	11	19	2	1	3	25	50	0	25	0	7	8	1	.95
94-95	Det	46	13	20	33	12	3	0	97	13.4	5	7	12	0	0	0	17	45	1	15	0	2	4	0	.72
95-96	Det	82	36	37	73	33	7	0	237	15.2	9	11	20	0	0	0	35	70	0	35	0	8	8	1	.89
96-97	Det	75	23	22	45	21	6	0	211	10.9	3	6	9	0	0	0	23	46	0	23	0	3	3	0	.60
97-98	Det	80	25	27	52	14	1	0	221	11.3	6	11	17	0	0	0	19	46	0	18	0	4	5	0	.65
98-99	Det	79	29	29	58	10	4	2	209	13.9	6	14	20	1	2	3	17	45	1	15	0	3	3	1	.73
8 Years		463	164	177	341	114	27	2	1212	13.5	37	60	97	3	3	6	144	318	2	139	0	27	34	3	.74
Postseason																									
Year	Tm	GP	G	A	Pts	+/–	GW	OT	S	SPct	G	A	Pts	G	A	Pts	Num	PIM	Maj	Mnr	Fgt	Rgh	HHT	Hat	P/G
92-93	Det	4	0	2	2	1	0	0	5	0.0	0	0	0	0	0	0	1	2	0	1	0	0	1	0	.50
93-94	Det	7	2	5	7	3	0	0	16	12.5	0	0	0	0	0	0	6	12	0	6	0	0	2	0	1.00
94-95	Det	18	9	7	16	12	4	1	45	20.0	1	3	4	0	0	0	5	10	0	5	0	1	1	0	.89
95-96	Det	19	5	7	12	3	1	0	38	13.2	2	1	3	0	0	0	5	10	0	5	0	1	2	0	.63
96-97	Det	20	8	5	13	3	2	1	58	13.8	4	4	8	0	0	0	7	14	0	7	0	1	1	0	.65
97-98	Det	22	6	8	14	4	4	0	47	12.8	1	2	3	0	0	0	5	10	0	5	0	1	1	0	.64
98-99	Det	10	6	1	7	-3	0	0	28	21.4	3	1	4	0	0	0	2	4	0	2	0	1	0	0	.70
7 Years		100	36	35	71	23	11	2	237	15.2	11	11	22	0	0	0	31	62	0	31	0	5	8	0	.71

Viktor Kozlov

(statistical profile on page 331)

Pos: C **Shoots:** R **Ht:** 6'5" **Wt:** 225 **Born:** 2/19/75—Togliatti, USSR **Age:** 24

Overall											Power Play			Shorthand			Penalty							Misc	
Year	Tm	GP	G	A	Pts	+/–	GW	GT	S	SPct	G	A	Pts	G	A	Pts	Num	PIM	Maj	Mnr	Fgt	Rgh	HHT	Hat	P/G
94-95	SJ	16	2	0	2	-5	0	0	23	8.7	0	0	0	0	0	0	1	2	0	1	0	0	1	0	.13
95-96	SJ	62	6	13	19	-15	0	0	107	5.6	1	4	5	0	0	0	3	6	0	3	0	0	2	0	.31
96-97	SJ	78	16	25	41	-16	4	0	184	8.7	4	8	12	0	0	0	16	40	0	15	0	1	8	0	.53
97-98	2Tm	64	17	13	30	-3	0	0	165	10.3	5	1	6	2	0	2	8	16	0	8	0	2	2	0	.47
98-99	Fla	65	16	35	51	13	1	0	209	7.7	5	10	15	1	1	2	12	24	0	12	0	0	9	0	.78
97-98	SJ	18	5	2	7	-2	0	0	51	9.8	2	0	2	0	0	0	1	2	0	1	0	0	1	0	.39
97-98	Fla	46	12	11	23	-1	0	0	114	10.5	3	1	4	2	0	2	7	14	0	7	0	2	1	0	.50
5 Years		285	57	86	143	-26	5	0	688	8.3	15	23	38	3	1	4	40	88	0	39	0	3	22	0	.50

Igor Kravchuk

(statistical profile on page 331)

Pos: D **Shoots:** L **Ht:** 6'1" **Wt:** 200 **Born:** 9/13/66—Ufa, USSR **Age:** 33

Overall											Power Play			Shorthand			Penalty							Misc	
Year	Tm	GP	G	A	Pts	+/–	GW	GT	S	SPct	G	A	Pts	G	A	Pts	Num	PIM	Maj	Mnr	Fgt	Rgh	HHT	Hat	P/G
91-92	Chi	18	1	8	9	-3	1	0	40	2.5	0	5	5	0	0	0	2	4	0	2	0	0	1	0	.50

Overall											Power Play			Shorthand			Penalty							Misc	
Year	Tm	GP	G	A	Pts	+/–	GW	GT	S	SPct	G	A	Pts	G	A	Pts	Num	PIM	Maj	Mnr	Fgt	Rgh	HHT	Hat	P/G
92-93	2Tm	55	10	17	27	3	0	0	143	7.0	4	5	9	0	1	1	16	32	0	16	0	0	8	0	.49
93-94	Edm	81	12	38	50	-12	2	0	197	6.1	5	19	24	0	0	0	8	16	0	8	0	2	2	0	.62
94-95	Edm	36	7	11	18	-15	0	0	93	7.5	3	5	8	1	0	1	9	29	1	7	0	2	2	0	.50
95-96	2Tm	66	7	16	23	-19	1	0	173	4.0	3	10	13	0	0	0	17	34	0	17	0	1	4	0	.35
96-97	StL	**82**	4	24	28	7	0	0	142	2.8	1	10	11	0	0	0	16	35	1	15	1	0	8	0	.34
97-98	Ott*	81	8	27	35	-19	1	1	191	4.2	3	13	16	1	0	1	4	8	0	4	0	0	2	0	.43
98-99	Ott	79	4	21	25	14	0	0	171	2.3	3	14	17	0	0	0	16	32	0	16	0	2	8	0	.32
92-93	Chi	38	6	9	15	11	0	0	101	5.9	3	2	5	0	1	1	15	30	0	15	0	0	7	0	.39
92-93	Edm	17	4	8	12	-8	0	0	42	9.5	1	3	4	0	0	0	1	2	0	1	0	0	1	0	.71
95-96	Edm	26	4	4	8	-13	0	0	59	6.8	3	3	6	0	0	0	5	10	0	5	0	1	2	0	.31
95-96	StL	40	3	12	15	-6	1	0	114	2.6	0	7	7	0	0	0	12	24	0	12	0	0	2	0	.38
8 Years		498	53	162	215	-44	5	1	1150	4.6	22	81	103	2	1	3	88	190	2	85	1	7	35	0	.43
Postseason																									
Year	Tm	GP	G	A	Pts	+/–	GW	OT	S	SPct	G	A	Pts	G	A	Pts	Num	PIM	Maj	Mnr	Fgt	Rgh	HHT	Hat	P/G
91-92	Chi	18	2	6	8	-2	0	0	48	4.2	1	3	4	0	0	0	4	8	0	4	0	0	4	0	.44
95-96	StL	10	1	5	6	0	1	1	14	7.1	0	2	2	0	0	0	2	4	0	2	0	0	1	0	.60
96-97	StL	2	0	0	0	-1	0	0	6	0.0	0	0	0	0	0	0	1	2	0	1	0	1	0	0	.00
97-98	Ott	11	2	3	5	-2	0	0	24	8.3	0	3	3	0	0	0	2	4	0	2	0	0	2	0	.45
98-99	Ott	4	0	0	0	-5	0	0	12	0.0	0	0	0	0	0	0	0	0	0	0	0	0	0	0	.00
5 Years		45	5	14	19	-10	1	1	104	4.8	1	8	9	0	0	0	9	18	0	9	0	1	7	0	.42

Sergei Krivokrasov

(statistical profile on page 331)

Pos: RW **Shoots:** L **Ht:** 5'10" **Wt:** 185 **Born:** 4/15/74—Angarsk, USSR **Age:** 25

Overall											Power Play			Shorthand			Penalty							Misc	
Year	Tm	GP	G	A	Pts	+/–	GW	GT	S	SPct	G	A	Pts	G	A	Pts	Num	PIM	Maj	Mnr	Fgt	Rgh	HHT	Hat	P/G
92-93	Chi	4	0	0	0	-2	0	0	0	–	0	0	0	0	0	0	1	2	0	1	0	0	0	0	.00
93-94	Chi	9	1	0	1	-2	0	0	7	14.3	0	0	0	0	0	0	2	4	0	2	0	0	0	0	.11
94-95	Chi	41	12	7	19	9	2	1	72	16.7	6	0	6	0	0	0	11	33	1	9	0	2	5	0	.46
95-96	Chi	46	6	10	16	10	1	0	52	11.5	0	0	0	0	0	0	16	32	0	16	0	1	6	0	.35
96-97	Chi	67	13	11	24	-1	3	0	104	12.5	2	1	3	0	0	0	21	42	0	21	0	4	7	0	.36
97-98	Chi	58	10	13	23	-1	2	0	127	7.9	1	0	1	0	0	0	15	33	1	14	1	3	7	0	.40
98-99	Nsh	70	25	23	48	-5	6	1	208	12.0	10	7	17	0	0	0	17	42	0	16	0	1	7	0	.69
7 Years		295	67	64	131	8	14	2	570	11.8	19	8	27	0	0	0	83	188	2	79	1	11	32	0	.44
Postseason																									
Year	Tm	GP	G	A	Pts	+/–	GW	OT	S	SPct	G	A	Pts	G	A	Pts	Num	PIM	Maj	Mnr	Fgt	Rgh	HHT	Hat	P/G
94-95	Chi	10	0	0	0	0	0	0	4	0.0	0	0	0	0	0	0	4	8	0	4	0	0	2	0	.00
95-96	Chi	5	1	0	1	-4	1	1	6	16.7	0	0	0	0	0	0	1	2	0	1	0	0	0	0	.20
96-97	Chi	6	1	0	1	-2	1	1	11	9.1	0	0	0	0	0	0	2	4	0	2	0	0	0	0	.17
3 Years		21	2	0	2	-6	2	2	21	9.5	0	0	0	0	0	0	7	14	0	7	0	0	2	0	.10

Robert Kron

(statistical profile on page 332)

Pos: LW **Shoots:** L **Ht:** 5'10" **Wt:** 182 **Born:** 2/27/67—Brno, Czechoslovakia **Age:** 32

Overall											Power Play			Shorthand			Penalty							Misc	
Year	Tm	GP	G	A	Pts	+/–	GW	GT	S	SPct	G	A	Pts	G	A	Pts	Num	PIM	Maj	Mnr	Fgt	Rgh	HHT	Hat	P/G
90-91	Van	76	12	20	32	-11	0	0	124	9.7	2	–	–	3	–	–	–	21	–	–	–	–	–	0	.42
91-92	Van	36	2	2	4	-9	0	0	49	4.1	0	1	1	0	0	0	1	2	0	1	0	0	1	0	.11
92-93	2Tm	45	14	13	27	5	2	1	97	14.4	4	0	4	2	0	2	5	18	0	4	0	0	2	0	.60
93-94	Har	77	24	26	50	0	3	0	194	12.4	2	5	7	1	1	2	4	8	0	4	0	0	2	0	.65
94-95	Har	37	10	8	18	-3	1	0	88	11.4	3	3	6	1	1	2	5	10	0	5	0	0	2	0	.49
95-96	Har	77	22	28	50	-1	3	0	203	10.8	8	9	17	1	2	3	3	6	0	3	0	0	2	0	.65
96-97	Har	68	10	12	22	-18	4	1	182	5.5	2	4	6	0	0	0	5	10	0	5	0	0	1	0	.32
97-98	Car	81	16	20	36	-8	2	1	175	9.1	4	3	7	0	1	1	6	12	0	6	0	0	2	0	.44
98-99	Car	75	9	16	25	-13	2	0	134	6.7	3	4	7	1	0	1	5	10	0	5	0	0	2	0	.33
92-93	Van	32	10	11	21	10	2	1	60	16.7	2	0	2	2	0	2	3	14	0	2	0	0	1	0	.66
92-93	Har	13	4	2	6	-5	0	0	37	10.8	2	0	2	0	0	0	2	4	0	2	0	0	1	0	.46
9 Years		572	119	145	264	-58	17	3	1246	9.6	28	–	–	9	–	–	–	97	–	–	–	–	–	0	.46
Postseason																									
Year	Tm	GP	G	A	Pts	+/–	GW	OT	S	SPct	G	A	Pts	G	A	Pts	Num	PIM	Maj	Mnr	Fgt	Rgh	HHT	Hat	P/G
91-92	Van	11	1	2	3	0	0	0	9	11.1	0	0	0	1	0	1	1	2	0	1	0	0	0	0	.27
98-99	Car	5	2	0	2	2	1	0	10	20.0	0	0	0	0	0	0	0	0	0	0	0	0	0	0	.40
2 Years		16	3	2	5	2	1	0	19	15.8	0	0	0	1	0	1	1	2	0	1	0	0	0	0	.31

Uwe Krupp

Pos: D **Shoots:** R **Ht:** 6'6" **Wt:** 235 **Born:** 6/24/65—Cologne, West Germany **Age:** 34

Overall											Power Play			Shorthand			Penalty							Misc	
Year	Tm	GP	G	A	Pts	+/-	GW	GT	S	SPct	G	A	Pts	G	A	Pts	Num	PIM	Maj	Mnr	Fgt	Rgh	HHT	Hat	P/G
86-87	Buf	26	1	4	5	-9	0	0	34	2.9	0	–	–	0	–	–	–	23	–	–	–	–	–	0	.19
87-88	Buf	75	2	9	11	-1	0	0	84	2.4	0	–	–	0	–	–	–	151	–	–	–	–	–	0	.15
88-89	Buf	70	5	13	18	0	0	0	51	9.8	0	–	–	1	–	–	–	55	–	–	–	–	–	0	.26
89-90	Buf	74	3	20	23	15	1	0	69	4.3	0	–	–	1	–	–	–	85	–	–	–	–	–	0	.31
90-91	Buf*	74	12	32	44	14	0	2	138	8.7	6	–	–	0	–	–	–	66	–	–	–	–	–	0	.59
91-92	2Tm	67	8	29	37	13	0	0	128	6.3	2	11	13	0	0	0	23	49	1	22	1	1	13	0	.55
92-93	NYI	80	9	29	38	6	2	0	116	7.8	2	15	17	0	1	1	28	67	1	26	1	3	12	0	.48
93-94	NYI	41	7	14	21	11	0	0	82	8.5	3	4	7	0	1	1	15	30	0	15	0	3	2	0	.51
94-95	Que	44	6	17	23	14	1	1	102	5.9	3	9	12	0	0	0	10	20	0	10	0	3	3	1	.52
95-96	Col	6	0	3	3	4	0	0	9	0.0	0	2	2	0	0	0	2	4	0	2	0	0	0	0	.50
96-97	Col	60	4	17	21	12	1	0	107	3.7	2	3	5	0	2	2	17	48	2	14	2	2	6	0	.35
97-98	Col	78	9	22	31	21	2	0	149	6.0	5	8	13	0	1	1	19	38	0	19	0	0	6	0	.40
98-99	Det	22	3	2	5	0	0	0	32	9.4	0	1	1	0	0	0	3	6	0	3	0	0	1	0	.23
91-92	Buf	8	2	0	2	0	0	0	13	15.4	0	0	0	0	0	0	3	6	0	3	0	0	0	0	.25
91-92	NYI	59	6	29	35	13	0	0	115	5.2	2	11	13	0	0	0	20	43	1	19	1	1	13	0	.59
13 Years		717	69	211	280	100	7	3	1101	6.3	23	–	–	2	–	–	–	642	–	–	–	–	–	1	.39

Postseason

Year	Tm	GP	G	A	Pts	+/-	GW	OT	S	SPct	G	A	Pts	G	A	Pts	Num	PIM	Maj	Mnr	Fgt	Rgh	HHT	Hat	P/G
87-88	Buf	6	0	0	0	-5	0	0	3	0.0	0	0	0	0	0	0	–	15	–	–	–	–	–	0	.00
88-89	Buf	5	0	1	1	-4	0	0	3	0.0	0	–	–	0	–	–	2	4	0	2	0	–	–	0	.20
89-90	Buf	6	0	0	0	-4	0	0	4	0.0	0	0	0	0	0	0	2	4	0	2	0	–	–	0	.00
90-91	Buf	6	1	1	2	-2	0	0	13	7.7	1	–	–	0	–	–	3	6	0	3	0	–	–	0	.33
92-93	NYI	18	1	5	6	2	0	0	28	3.6	0	0	0	0	0	0	6	12	0	6	0	1	1	0	.33
93-94	NYI	4	0	1	1	-3	0	0	4	0.0	0	1	1	0	0	0	2	4	0	2	0	0	1	0	.25
94-95	Que	5	0	2	2	-2	0	0	13	0.0	0	0	0	0	0	0	1	2	0	1	0	0	0	0	.40
95-96	Col	22	4	12	16	5	2	1	38	10.5	1	4	5	0	0	0	11	33	1	9	1	1	3	0	.73
97-98	Col	7	0	1	1	2	0	0	18	0.0	0	0	0	0	0	0	2	4	0	2	0	2	0	0	.14
9 Years		79	6	23	29	-11	2	1	124	4.8	2	–	–	0	–	–	–	84	–	–	–	–	–	0	.37

Paul Kruse

Pos: LW **Shoots:** L **Ht:** 6'0" **Wt:** 202 **Born:** 3/25/70—Merritt, British Columbia **Age:** 29

Overall											Power Play			Shorthand			Penalty							Misc	
Year	Tm	GP	G	A	Pts	+/-	GW	GT	S	SPct	G	A	Pts	G	A	Pts	Num	PIM	Maj	Mnr	Fgt	Rgh	HHT	Hat	P/G
90-91	Cgy	1	0	0	0	-1	0	0	0	–	0	0	0	0	0	0	2	7	1	1	–	–	–	0	.00
91-92	Cgy	16	3	1	4	1	0	0	12	25.0	0	0	0	0	0	0	18	65	7	10	7	3	3	0	.25
92-93	Cgy	27	2	3	5	2	0	0	17	11.8	0	0	0	0	0	0	12	41	3	8	3	1	2	0	.19
93-94	Cgy	68	3	8	11	-6	0	0	52	5.8	0	0	0	0	0	0	52	185	19	30	19	9	8	0	.16
94-95	Cgy	45	11	5	16	13	2	0	52	21.2	0	0	0	0	0	0	38	141	11	23	11	6	3	0	.36
95-96	Cgy	75	3	12	15	-5	0	0	83	3.6	0	0	0	0	0	0	51	145	9	40	9	9	9	0	.20
96-97	2Tm	62	6	2	8	-9	1	0	49	12.2	0	0	0	0	0	0	39	141	13	23	13	6	7	0	.13
97-98	2Tm	74	7	2	9	-11	2	1	52	13.5	0	0	0	0	0	0	50	187	13	31	13	11	9	0	.12
98-99	Buf	43	3	0	3	0	0	0	33	9.1	0	0	0	0	0	0	30	114	10	17	10	5	4	0	.07
96-97	Cgy	14	2	0	2	-4	1	0	10	20.0	0	0	0	0	0	0	8	30	2	5	2	0	2	0	.14
96-97	NYI	48	4	2	6	-5	0	0	39	10.3	0	0	0	0	0	0	31	111	11	18	11	6	5	0	.13
97-98	NYI	62	6	1	7	-12	2	1	44	13.6	0	0	0	0	0	0	38	138	10	24	10	9	8	0	.11
97-98	Buf	12	1	1	2	1	0	0	8	12.5	0	0	0	0	0	0	12	49	3	7	3	2	1	0	.17
9 Years		411	38	33	71	-16	5	1	350	10.9	0	0	0	0	0	0	292	1026	86	183	–	–	–	0	.17

Postseason

Year	Tm	GP	G	A	Pts	+/-	GW	OT	S	SPct	G	A	Pts	G	A	Pts	Num	PIM	Maj	Mnr	Fgt	Rgh	HHT	Hat	P/G
93-94	Cgy	7	0	0	0	-3	0	0	11	0.0	0	0	0	0	0	0	3	14	0	2	0	1	1	0	.00
94-95	Cgy	7	4	2	6	2	0	0	18	22.2	0	0	0	1	0	1	5	10	0	5	0	2	2	0	.86
95-96	Cgy	3	0	0	0	-1	0	0	3	0.0	0	0	0	0	0	0	2	4	0	2	0	1	0	0	.00
97-98	Buf	1	1	0	1	1	0	0	2	50.0	0	0	0	0	0	0	2	4	0	2	0	2	0	0	1.00
98-99	Buf	10	0	0	0	0	0	0	0	–	0	0	0	0	0	0	2	4	0	2	0	1	0	0	.00
5 Years		28	5	2	7	-1	0	0	34	14.7	0	0	0	1	0	1	14	36	0	13	0	7	3	0	.25

Filip Kuba

Pos: D **Shoots:** L **Ht:** 6'3" **Wt:** 202 **Born:** 12/29/76—Ostrava, Czechoslovakia **Age:** 23

Overall											Power Play			Shorthand			Penalty							Misc	
Year	Tm	GP	G	A	Pts	+/-	GW	GT	S	SPct	G	A	Pts	G	A	Pts	Num	PIM	Maj	Mnr	Fgt	Rgh	HHT	Hat	P/G
98-99	Fla	5	0	1	1	2	0	0	5	0.0	0	0	0	0	0	0	0	0	0	0	0	0	0	0	.20

Pavel Kubina

(statistical profile on page 332)

Pos: D **Shoots:** R **Ht:** 6'3" **Wt:** 213 **Born:** 2/3/68—Celadna, Czechoslovakia **Age:** 31

Overall											Power Play			Shorthand			Penalty							Misc	
Year	Tm	GP	G	A	Pts	+/–	GW	GT	S	SPct	G	A	Pts	G	A	Pts	Num	PIM	Maj	Mnr	Fgt	Rgh	HHT	Hat	P/G
97-98	TB	10	1	2	3	-1	0	0	8	12.5	0	0	0	0	0	0	7	22	0	6	0	0	4	0	.30
98-99	TB	68	9	12	21	-33	1	1	119	7.6	3	3	6	1	0	1	29	80	2	25	1	3	8	0	.31
2 Years		78	10	14	24	-34	1	1	127	7.9	3	3	6	1	0	1	36	102	2	31	1	3	12	0	.31

Oleg Kvasha

(statistical profile on page 332)

Pos: LW **Shoots:** R **Ht:** 6'5" **Wt:** 205 **Born:** 7/26/78—Moscow, USSR **Age:** 21

Overall											Power Play			Shorthand			Penalty							Misc	
Year	Tm	GP	G	A	Pts	+/–	GW	GT	S	SPct	G	A	Pts	G	A	Pts	Num	PIM	Maj	Mnr	Fgt	Rgh	HHT	Hat	P/G
98-99	Fla	68	12	13	25	5	2	1	138	8.7	4	5	9	0	0	0	17	45	1	15	1	0	4	0	.37

Antti Laaksonen

Pos: LW **Shoots:** L **Ht:** 6'0" **Wt:** 180 **Born:** 10/3/73—Tammela, Finland **Age:** 26

Overall											Power Play			Shorthand			Penalty							Misc	
Year	Tm	GP	G	A	Pts	+/–	GW	GT	S	SPct	G	A	Pts	G	A	Pts	Num	PIM	Maj	Mnr	Fgt	Rgh	HHT	Hat	P/G
98-99	Bos	11	1	2	3	-1	0	0	8	12.5	0	1	1	0	0	0	1	2	0	1	0	0	0	0	.27

Scott Lachance

(statistical profile on page 332)

Pos: D **Shoots:** L **Ht:** 6'1" **Wt:** 196 **Born:** 10/22/72—Charlottesville, Virginia **Age:** 27

Overall											Power Play			Shorthand			Penalty							Misc	
Year	Tm	GP	G	A	Pts	+/–	GW	GT	S	SPct	G	A	Pts	G	A	Pts	Num	PIM	Maj	Mnr	Fgt	Rgh	HHT	Hat	P/G
91-92	NYI	17	1	4	5	13	0	1	20	5.0	0	1	1	0	0	0	3	9	1	2	1	2	0	0	.29
92-93	NYI	75	7	17	24	-1	2	0	62	11.3	0	2	2	1	2	3	32	67	1	31	1	11	9	0	.32
93-94	NYI	74	3	11	14	-5	1	0	59	5.1	0	4	4	0	2	2	28	70	2	25	2	11	5	0	.19
94-95	NYI	26	6	7	13	2	0	0	56	10.7	3	3	6	0	0	0	10	26	2	8	2	2	3	0	.50
95-96	NYI	55	3	10	13	-19	0	0	81	3.7	1	5	6	0	0	0	24	54	2	22	2	1	4	0	.24
96-97	NYI*	81	3	11	14	-7	0	0	97	3.1	1	2	3	0	0	0	22	47	1	21	1	2	6	0	.17
97-98	NYI	63	2	11	13	-11	0	0	62	3.2	1	2	3	0	0	0	17	45	1	15	1	1	5	0	.21
98-99	2Tm	76	2	9	11	-21	0	0	59	3.4	1	2	3	0	0	0	19	41	1	18	1	2	7	0	.14
98-99	NYI	59	1	8	9	-19	0	0	37	2.7	1	1	2	0	0	0	15	30	0	15	0	2	5	0	.15
98-99	Mon	17	1	1	2	-2	0	0	22	4.5	0	1	1	0	0	0	4	11	1	3	1	0	2	0	.12
8 Years		467	27	80	107	-49	3	1	496	5.4	7	21	28	1	4	5	155	359	11	142	11	32	39	0	.23
Postseason																									
Year	Tm	GP	G	A	Pts	+/–	GW	OT	S	SPct	G	A	Pts	G	A	Pts	Num	PIM	Maj	Mnr	Fgt	Rgh	HHT	Hat	P/G
93-94	NYI	3	0	0	0	-5	0	0	3	0.0	0	0	0	0	0	0	0	0	0	0	0	0	0	0	.00

Dan LaCouture

Pos: LW **Shoots:** L **Ht:** 6'3" **Wt:** 210 **Born:** 4/18/77—Hyannis, Massachusetts **Age:** 22

Overall											Power Play			Shorthand			Penalty							Misc	
Year	Tm	GP	G	A	Pts	+/–	GW	GT	S	SPct	G	A	Pts	G	A	Pts	Num	PIM	Maj	Mnr	Fgt	Rgh	HHT	Hat	P/G
98-99	Edm	3	0	0	0	1	0	0	0	–	0	0	0	0	0	0	0	0	0	0	0	0	0	0	.00

Daniel Lacroix

Pos: LW **Shoots:** L **Ht:** 6'2" **Wt:** 205 **Born:** 3/11/69—Montreal, Quebec **Age:** 30

Overall											Power Play			Shorthand			Penalty							Misc	
Year	Tm	GP	G	A	Pts	+/–	GW	GT	S	SPct	G	A	Pts	G	A	Pts	Num	PIM	Maj	Mnr	Fgt	Rgh	HHT	Hat	P/G
93-94	NYR	4	0	0	0	0	0	0	0	–	0	0	0	0	0	0	0	0	0	0	0	0	0	0	.00
94-95	2Tm	24	1	0	1	-2	0	0	14	7.1	0	0	0	0	0	0	13	38	4	9	4	3	1	0	.04
95-96	NYR	25	2	2	4	-1	0	0	14	14.3	0	0	0	0	0	0	15	30	0	15	0	3	2	0	.16
96-97	Phi	74	7	1	8	-1	0	0	54	13.0	1	0	1	0	0	0	43	163	15	24	15	9	0	0	.11
97-98	Phi	56	1	4	5	0	0	0	28	3.6	0	0	0	0	0	0	40	135	13	25	12	10	3	0	.09
98-99	Edm	4	0	0	0	0	0	0	5	0.0	0	0	0	0	0	0	5	13	1	4	1	2	0	0	.00
94-95	Bos	23	1	0	1	-2	0	0	14	7.1	0	0	0	0	0	0	13	38	4	9	4	3	1	0	.04
94-95	NYR	1	0	0	0	0	0	0	0	–	0	0	0	0	0	0	0	0	0	0	0	0	0	0	.00
6 Years		187	11	7	18	-4	0	0	115	9.6	1	0	1	0	0	0	116	379	33	77	32	27	6	0	.10

Postseason																									
Year	Tm	GP	G	A	Pts	+/–	GW	OT	S	SPct	G	A	Pts	G	A	Pts	Num	PIM	Maj	Mnr	Fgt	Rgh	HHT	Hat	P/G
96-97	Phi	12	0	1	1	0	0	0	4	0.0	0	0	0	0	0	0	7	22	0	6	0	3	0	0	.08
97-98	Phi	4	0	0	0	0	0	0	0	–	0	0	0	0	0	0	2	4	0	2	0	1	0	0	.00
2 Years		16	0	1	1	0	0	0	4	0.0	0	0	0	0	0	0	9	26	0	8	0	4	0	0	.06

Eric Lacroix

Pos: LW **Shoots:** L **Ht:** 6'2" **Wt:** 210 **Born:** 7/15/71—Montreal, Quebec **Age:** 28

Overall											Power Play			Shorthand			Penalty							Misc	
Year	Tm	GP	G	A	Pts	+/–	GW	GT	S	SPct	G	A	Pts	G	A	Pts	Num	PIM	Maj	Mnr	Fgt	Rgh	HHT	Hat	P/G
93-94	Tor	3	0	0	0	0	0	0	3	0.0	0	0	0	0	0	0	1	2	0	1	0	0	1	0	.00
94-95	LA	45	9	7	16	2	1	0	64	14.1	2	1	3	1	0	1	27	54	0	27	0	6	4	0	.36
95-96	LA	72	16	16	32	-11	1	0	107	15.0	3	3	6	0	0	0	40	110	2	35	0	9	6	0	.44
96-97	Col	81	18	18	36	16	4	0	141	12.8	2	1	3	0	0	0	13	26	0	13	0	1	2	1	.44
97-98	Col	82	16	15	31	0	6	0	126	12.7	5	3	8	0	0	0	35	84	2	32	2	6	8	0	.38
98-99	3Tm	64	2	2	4	-12	1	0	38	5.3	0	1	1	0	0	0	9	18	0	9	0	3	1	0	.06
98-99	Col	7	0	0	0	-2	0	0	4	0.0	0	0	0	0	0	0	1	2	0	1	0	1	0	0	.00
98-99	LA	27	0	1	1	-5	0	0	17	0.0	0	0	0	0	0	0	6	12	0	6	0	2	1	0	.04
98-99	NYR	30	2	1	3	-5	1	0	17	11.8	0	1	1	0	0	0	2	4	0	2	0	0	0	0	.10
6 Years		347	61	58	119	-5	13	0	479	12.7	12	9	21	1	0	1	125	294	4	117	2	25	22	1	.34
Postseason																									
Year	Tm	GP	G	A	Pts	+/–	GW	OT	S	SPct	G	A	Pts	G	A	Pts	Num	PIM	Maj	Mnr	Fgt	Rgh	HHT	Hat	P/G
93-94	Tor	2	0	0	0	-1	0	0	0	–	0	0	0	0	0	0	0	0	0	0	0	0	0	0	.00
96-97	Col	17	1	4	5	2	0	0	15	6.7	0	0	0	0	0	0	4	19	1	2	1	1	0	0	.29
97-98	Col	7	0	0	0	-2	0	0	5	0.0	0	0	0	0	0	0	3	6	0	3	0	1	0	0	.00
3 Years		26	1	4	5	-1	0	0	20	5.0	0	0	0	0	0	0	7	25	1	5	1	2	0	0	.19

Nathan LaFayette

Pos: RW **Shoots:** R **Ht:** 6'1" **Wt:** 200 **Born:** 2/17/73—New Westminster, British Columbia **Age:** 26

Overall											Power Play			Shorthand			Penalty							Misc	
Year	Tm	GP	G	A	Pts	+/–	GW	GT	S	SPct	G	A	Pts	G	A	Pts	Num	PIM	Maj	Mnr	Fgt	Rgh	HHT	Hat	P/G
93-94	2Tm	49	3	4	7	-7	0	0	34	8.8	0	1	1	0	0	0	9	18	0	9	0	1	5	0	.14
94-95	2Tm	39	4	4	8	3	0	0	35	11.4	0	0	0	1	0	1	1	2	0	1	0	0	0	0	.21
95-96	2Tm	17	2	4	6	-4	0	0	28	7.1	1	0	1	0	0	0	4	8	0	4	0	0	1	0	.35
96-97	LA	15	1	3	4	-8	1	0	26	3.8	0	0	0	1	0	1	4	8	0	4	0	0	1	0	.27
97-98	LA	34	5	3	8	2	1	0	60	8.3	1	0	1	0	0	0	12	32	0	11	0	1	6	0	.24
98-99	LA	33	2	2	4	0	1	0	42	4.8	0	1	1	1	0	1	8	35	1	5	0	0	1	0	.12
93-94	StL	38	2	3	5	-9	0	0	23	8.7	0	0	0	0	0	0	7	14	0	7	0	0	5	0	.13
93-94	Van	11	1	1	2	2	0	0	11	9.1	0	1	1	0	0	0	2	4	0	2	0	1	0	0	.18
94-95	Van	27	4	4	8	2	0	0	30	13.3	0	0	0	1	0	1	1	2	0	1	0	0	0	0	.30
94-95	NYR	12	0	0	0	1	0	0	5	0.0	0	0	0	0	0	0	0	0	0	0	0	0	0	0	.00
95-96	NYR	5	0	0	0	-1	0	0	5	0.0	0	0	0	0	0	0	1	2	0	1	0	0	0	0	.00
95-96	LA	12	2	4	6	-3	0	0	23	8.7	1	0	1	0	0	0	3	6	0	3	0	0	1	0	.50
6 Years		187	17	20	37	-14	3	0	225	7.6	2	2	4	3	0	3	38	103	1	34	0	2	14	0	.20
Postseason																									
Year	Tm	GP	G	A	Pts	+/–	GW	OT	S	SPct	G	A	Pts	G	A	Pts	Num	PIM	Maj	Mnr	Fgt	Rgh	HHT	Hat	P/G
93-94	Van	20	2	7	9	13	0	0	24	8.3	0	0	0	0	0	0	2	4	0	2	0	1	1	0	.45
94-95	NYR	8	0	0	0	-1	0	0	1	0.0	0	0	0	0	0	0	1	2	0	1	0	0	0	0	.00
97-98	LA	4	0	0	0	-2	0	0	4	0.0	0	0	0	0	0	0	1	2	0	1	0	0	0	0	.00
3 Years		32	2	7	9	10	0	0	29	6.9	0	0	0	0	0	0	4	8	0	4	0	1	1	0	.28

Christian Laflamme

(statistical profile on page 333)

Pos: D **Shoots:** R **Ht:** 6'1" **Wt:** 202 **Born:** 11/24/76—St. Charles, Quebec **Age:** 23

Overall											Power Play			Shorthand			Penalty							Misc	
Year	Tm	GP	G	A	Pts	+/–	GW	GT	S	SPct	G	A	Pts	G	A	Pts	Num	PIM	Maj	Mnr	Fgt	Rgh	HHT	Hat	P/G
96-97	Chi	4	0	1	1	3	0	0	3	0.0	0	0	0	0	0	0	1	2	0	1	0	0	1	0	.25
97-98	Chi	72	0	11	11	14	0	0	75	0.0	0	1	1	0	1	1	28	59	1	27	1	5	4	0	.15
98-99	2Tm	73	2	12	14	-3	0	0	68	2.9	0	4	4	0	0	0	35	70	0	35	0	7	6	0	.19
98-99	Chi	62	2	11	13	0	0	0	53	3.8	0	4	4	0	0	0	35	70	0	35	0	7	6	0	.21
98-99	Edm	11	0	1	1	-3	0	0	15	0.0	0	0	0	0	0	0	0	0	0	0	0	0	0	0	.09
3 Years		149	2	24	26	14	0	0	146	1.4	0	5	5	0	1	1	64	131	1	63	1	12	11	0	.17
Postseason																									
Year	Tm	GP	G	A	Pts	+/–	GW	OT	S	SPct	G	A	Pts	G	A	Pts	Num	PIM	Maj	Mnr	Fgt	Rgh	HHT	Hat	P/G
98-99	Edm	4	0	1	1	-4	0	0	5	0.0	0	0	0	0	0	0	1	2	0	1	0	0	1	0	.25

Sasha Lakovic

Pos: LW **Shoots:** L **Ht:** 6'1" **Wt:** 205 **Born:** 9/7/71—Vancouver, British Columbia **Age:** 28

		Overall									Power Play			Shorthand			Penalty							Misc	
Year	Tm	GP	G	A	Pts	+/–	GW	GT	S	SPct	G	A	Pts	G	A	Pts	Num	PIM	Maj	Mnr	Fgt	Rgh	HHT	Hat	P/G
96-97	Cgy	19	0	1	1	-1	0	0	10	0.0	0	0	0	0	0	0	14	54	6	7	6	4	0	0	.05
97-98	NJ	2	0	0	0	0	0	0	2	0.0	0	0	0	0	0	0	1	5	1	0	1	0	0	0	.00
98-99	NJ	16	0	3	3	0	0	0	10	0.0	0	0	0	0	0	0	14	59	5	7	5	1	0	0	.19
3 Years		37	0	4	4	-1	0	0	22	0.0	0	0	0	0	0	0	29	118	12	14	12	5	0	0	.11

Denny Lambert

(statistical profile on page 333)

Pos: LW **Shoots:** L **Ht:** 5'11" **Wt:** 200 **Born:** 1/7/70—Wawa, Ontario **Age:** 29

		Overall									Power Play			Shorthand			Penalty							Misc	
Year	Tm	GP	G	A	Pts	+/–	GW	GT	S	SPct	G	A	Pts	G	A	Pts	Num	PIM	Maj	Mnr	Fgt	Rgh	HHT	Hat	P/G
94-95	Anh	13	1	3	4	3	0	0	14	7.1	0	0	0	0	0	0	2	4	0	2	0	1	1	0	.31
95-96	Anh	33	0	8	8	-2	0	0	28	0.0	0	0	0	0	0	0	16	55	5	10	5	5	3	0	.24
96-97	Ott	80	4	16	20	-4	1	0	58	6.9	0	0	0	0	0	0	62	217	23	36	23	17	6	0	.25
97-98	Ott	72	9	10	19	4	1	1	76	11.8	0	0	0	0	0	0	78	250	18	55	18	22	9	0	.26
98-99	Nsh	76	5	11	16	-3	0	0	66	7.6	1	0	1	0	0	0	62	218	18	39	18	19	3	0	.21
5 Years		274	19	48	67	-2	2	1	242	7.9	1	0	1	0	0	0	220	744	64	142	64	64	22	0	.24
											Postseason														
Year	Tm	GP	G	A	Pts	+/–	GW	OT	S	SPct	G	A	Pts	G	A	Pts	Num	PIM	Maj	Mnr	Fgt	Rgh	HHT	Hat	P/G
96-97	Ott	6	0	1	1	0	0	0	5	0.0	0	0	0	0	0	0	3	9	1	2	1	0	0	0	.17
97-98	Ott	11	0	0	0	2	0	0	5	0.0	0	0	0	0	0	0	8	19	1	7	1	3	0	0	.00
2 Years		17	0	1	1	2	0	0	10	0.0	0	0	0	0	0	0	11	28	2	9	2	3	0	0	.06

Eric Landry

Pos: C **Shoots:** L **Ht:** 5'11" **Wt:** 185 **Born:** 1/20/75—Gatineau, Quebec **Age:** 24

		Overall									Power Play			Shorthand			Penalty							Misc	
Year	Tm	GP	G	A	Pts	+/–	GW	GT	S	SPct	G	A	Pts	G	A	Pts	Num	PIM	Maj	Mnr	Fgt	Rgh	HHT	Hat	P/G
97-98	Cgy	12	1	0	1	-2	0	0	7	14.3	0	0	0	0	0	0	2	4	0	2	0	2	0	0	.08
98-99	Cgy	3	0	1	1	1	0	0	1	0.0	0	0	0	0	0	0	0	0	0	0	0	0	0	0	.33
2 Years		15	1	1	2	-1	0	0	8	12.5	0	0	0	0	0	0	2	4	0	2	0	2	0	0	.13

Robert Lang

(statistical profile on page 333)

Pos: C **Shoots:** R **Ht:** 6'2" **Wt:** 216 **Born:** 12/19/70—Teplice, Czechoslovakia **Age:** 29

		Overall									Power Play			Shorthand			Penalty							Misc	
Year	Tm	GP	G	A	Pts	+/–	GW	GT	S	SPct	G	A	Pts	G	A	Pts	Num	PIM	Maj	Mnr	Fgt	Rgh	HHT	Hat	P/G
92-93	LA	11	0	5	5	-3	0	0	3	0.0	0	0	0	0	0	0	1	2	0	1	0	0	0	0	.45
93-94	LA	32	9	10	19	7	0	0	41	22.0	0	2	2	0	0	0	5	10	0	5	0	0	2	0	.59
94-95	LA	36	4	8	12	-7	0	0	38	10.5	0	1	1	0	0	0	2	4	0	2	0	0	0	0	.33
95-96	LA	68	6	16	22	-15	0	1	71	8.5	0	0	0	2	2	4	5	10	0	5	0	1	2	0	.32
96-97		Did Not Play in NHL																							
97-98	2Tm	54	9	13	22	7	2	0	66	13.6	1	3	4	1	0	1	8	16	0	8	0	0	3	0	.41
98-99	Pit	72	21	23	44	-10	3	**3**	137	15.3	7	5	12	0	0	0	12	24	0	12	0	3	4	0	.61
97-98	Bos	3	0	0	0	1	0	0	2	0.0	0	0	0	0	0	0	1	2	0	1	0	0	1	0	.00
97-98	Pit	51	9	13	22	6	2	0	64	14.1	1	3	4	1	0	1	7	14	0	7	0	0	2	0	.43
6 Years		273	49	75	124	-21	5	4	356	13.8	8	11	19	3	2	5	33	66	0	33	0	4	11	0	.45
											Postseason														
Year	Tm	GP	G	A	Pts	+/–	GW	OT	S	SPct	G	A	Pts	G	A	Pts	Num	PIM	Maj	Mnr	Fgt	Rgh	HHT	Hat	P/G
97-98	Pit	6	0	3	3	-4	0	0	6	0.0	0	1	1	0	0	0	1	2	0	1	0	0	1	0	.50
98-99	Pit	12	0	2	2	-3	0	0	9	0.0	0	0	0	0	0	0	0	0	0	0	0	0	0	0	.17
2 Years		18	0	5	5	-7	0	0	15	0.0	0	1	1	0	0	0	1	2	0	1	0	0	1	0	.28

Darren Langdon

Pos: LW **Shoots:** L **Ht:** 6'1" **Wt:** 205 **Born:** 1/8/71—Deer Lake, Newfoundland **Age:** 28

		Overall									Power Play			Shorthand			Penalty							Misc	
Year	Tm	GP	G	A	Pts	+/–	GW	GT	S	SPct	G	A	Pts	G	A	Pts	Num	PIM	Maj	Mnr	Fgt	Rgh	HHT	Hat	P/G
94-95	NYR	18	1	1	2	0	0	0	6	16.7	0	0	0	0	0	0	18	62	6	11	6	3	2	0	.11
95-96	NYR	64	7	4	11	2	1	1	29	24.1	0	0	0	0	0	0	48	175	13	30	13	13	8	0	.17
96-97	NYR	60	3	6	9	-1	1	0	24	12.5	0	0	0	0	0	0	55	195	23	30	23	10	2	0	.15
97-98	NYR	70	3	3	6	0	0	0	15	20.0	0	0	0	0	0	0	51	197	21	26	21	8	7	0	.09
98-99	NYR	45	0	0	0	-3	0	0	8	0.0	0	0	0	0	0	0	20	80	8	10	8	3	4	0	.00
5 Years		257	14	14	28	-2	2	1	82	17.1	0	0	0	0	0	0	192	709	71	107	71	37	23	0	.11

Postseason																									
Year	Tm	GP	G	A	Pts	+/–	GW	OT	S	SPct	G	A	Pts	G	A	Pts	Num	PIM	Maj	Mnr	Fgt	Rgh	HHT	Hat	P/G
95-96	NYR	2	0	0	0	0	0	0	0	–	0	0	0	0	0	0	0	0	0	0	0	0	0	0	.00
96-97	NYR	10	0	0	0	-1	0	0	1	0.0	0	0	0	0	0	0	1	2	0	1	0	1	0	0	.00
2 Years		12	0	0	0	-1	0	0	1	0.0	0	0	0	0	0	0	1	2	0	1	0	1	0	0	.00

Jamie Langenbrunner

(statistical profile on page 333)

Pos: C **Shoots:** R **Ht:** 6'1" **Wt:** 208 **Born:** 7/24/75—Duluth, Minnesota **Age:** 24

Overall											Power Play			Shorthand			Penalty							Misc	
Year	Tm	GP	G	A	Pts	+/–	GW	GT	S	SPct	G	A	Pts	G	A	Pts	Num	PIM	Maj	Mnr	Fgt	Rgh	HHT	Hat	P/G
94-95	Dal	2	0	0	0	0	0	0	1	0.0	0	0	0	0	0	0	1	2	0	1	0	0	0	0	.00
95-96	Dal	12	2	2	4	-2	0	0	15	13.3	1	0	1	0	0	0	3	6	0	3	0	0	1	0	.33
96-97	Dal	76	13	26	39	-2	3	0	112	11.6	3	6	9	0	0	0	24	51	1	23	1	9	7	0	.51
97-98	Dal	81	23	29	52	9	6	1	159	14.5	8	11	19	0	0	0	29	61	1	28	1	14	6	0	.64
98-99	Dal	75	12	33	45	10	1	0	145	8.3	4	12	16	0	0	0	27	62	0	26	0	5	12	0	.60
5 Years		246	50	90	140	15	10	1	432	11.6	16	29	45	0	0	0	84	182	2	81	2	28	26	0	.57
Postseason																									
Year	Tm	GP	G	A	Pts	+/–	GW	OT	S	SPct	G	A	Pts	G	A	Pts	Num	PIM	Maj	Mnr	Fgt	Rgh	HHT	Hat	P/G
96-97	Dal	5	1	1	2	1	1	0	15	6.7	0	0	0	0	0	0	3	14	0	2	0	1	1	0	.40
97-98	Dal	16	1	4	5	-5	1	1	35	2.9	0	1	1	0	0	0	7	14	0	7	0	3	3	0	.31
98-99	Dal	23	10	7	17	7	3	0	46	21.7	4	1	5	0	0	0	8	16	0	8	0	2	2	0	.74
3 Years		44	12	12	24	3	5	1	96	12.5	4	2	6	0	0	0	18	44	0	17	0	6	6	0	.55

Daymond Langkow

(statistical profile on page 334)

Pos: C **Shoots:** L **Ht:** 5'11" **Wt:** 183 **Born:** 9/27/76—Edmonton, Alberta **Age:** 23

Overall											Power Play			Shorthand			Penalty							Misc	
Year	Tm	GP	G	A	Pts	+/–	GW	GT	S	SPct	G	A	Pts	G	A	Pts	Num	PIM	Maj	Mnr	Fgt	Rgh	HHT	Hat	P/G
95-96	TB	4	0	1	1	-1	0	0	4	0.0	0	0	0	0	0	0	0	0	0	0	0	0	0	0	.25
96-97	TB	79	15	13	28	1	1	1	170	8.8	3	3	6	1	0	1	13	35	3	10	3	5	5	0	.35
97-98	TB	68	8	14	22	-9	1	0	156	5.1	2	2	4	0	0	0	24	62	2	21	2	4	5	0	.32
98-99	2Tm	78	14	19	33	-8	2	0	149	9.4	4	5	9	1	0	1	15	39	3	12	3	5	5	0	.42
98-99	TB	22	4	6	10	0	1	0	40	10.0	1	1	2	0	0	0	6	15	1	5	1	2	3	0	.45
98-99	Phi	56	10	13	23	-8	1	0	109	9.2	3	4	7	1	0	1	9	24	2	7	2	3	2	0	.41
4 Years		229	37	47	84	-17	4	1	479	7.7	9	10	19	2	0	2	52	136	8	43	8	14	15	0	.37
Postseason																									
Year	Tm	GP	G	A	Pts	+/–	GW	OT	S	SPct	G	A	Pts	G	A	Pts	Num	PIM	Maj	Mnr	Fgt	Rgh	HHT	Hat	P/G
98-99	Phi	6	0	2	2	3	0	0	4	0.0	0	0	0	0	0	0	1	2	0	1	0	1	0	0	.33

Scott Langkow

Pos: G **Catches:** L **Ht:** 5'11" **Wt:** 190 **Born:** 4/21/75—Edmonton, Alberta **Age:** 24

Overall																	Pen Shot		Offense		
Year	Tm	GP	GS	TP	W	L	T	Min	GA	GAA	Shots	SvPct	ShO	OE	PPGA	SHGA	Shots	GA	G	A	PIM
95-96	Wpg	1	0	1	0	0	0	6	0	0.00	2	1.000	0	0	0	0	0	0	0	0	0
96-97		Did Not Play in NHL																			
97-98	Pho	3	2	0	0	1	1	137	10	4.38	60	.833	0	0	1	0	0	0	0	0	0
98-99	Pho	1	0	0	0	0	0	35	3	5.14	17	.824	0	0	0	0	0	0	0	0	0
3 Years		5	2	1	0	1	1	178	13	4.38	79	.835	0	0	1	0	0	0	0	0	0

Ian Laperriere

(statistical profile on page 334)

Pos: C **Shoots:** R **Ht:** 6'1" **Wt:** 195 **Born:** 1/19/74—Montreal, Quebec **Age:** 25

Overall											Power Play			Shorthand			Penalty							Misc	
Year	Tm	GP	G	A	Pts	+/–	GW	GT	S	SPct	G	A	Pts	G	A	Pts	Num	PIM	Maj	Mnr	Fgt	Rgh	HHT	Hat	P/G
93-94	StL	1	0	0	0	0	0	0	1	0.0	0	0	0	0	0	0	0	0	0	0	0	0	0	0	.00
94-95	StL	37	13	14	27	12	1	0	53	**24.5**	1	2	3	0	0	0	28	85	7	20	7	8	6	0	.73
95-96	3Tm	71	6	11	17	-11	1	1	70	8.6	1	1	2	0	1	1	47	155	7	35	6	9	11	0	.24
96-97	LA	62	8	15	23	-25	2	0	84	9.5	0	1	1	1	0	1	33	102	4	26	4	8	5	0	.37
97-98	LA	77	6	15	21	0	1	0	74	8.1	0	2	2	1	1	2	47	131	7	38	7	14	6	0	.27
98-99	LA	72	3	10	13	-5	1	0	62	4.8	0	1	1	0	1	1	36	138	14	19	14	8	4	0	.18
95-96	StL	33	3	6	9	-4	1	0	31	9.7	1	0	1	0	0	0	27	87	3	21	3	6	4	0	.27
95-96	NYR	28	1	2	3	-5	0	0	21	4.8	0	0	0	0	0	0	14	53	3	9	2	2	4	0	.11
95-96	LA	10	2	3	5	-2	0	1	18	11.1	0	1	1	0	1	1	6	15	1	5	1	1	3	0	.50
6 Years		320	36	65	101	-29	6	1	344	10.5	2	7	9	2	3	5	191	611	39	138	38	47	32	0	.32

Postseason																									
Year	Tm	GP	G	A	Pts	+/–	GW	OT	S	SPct	G	A	Pts	G	A	Pts	Num	PIM	Maj	Mnr	Fgt	Rgh	HHT	Hat	P/G
94-95	StL	7	0	4	4	3	0	0	10	0.0	0	0	0	0	0	0	5	21	1	3	0	1	0	0	.57
97-98	LA	4	1	0	1	0	0	0	6	16.7	0	0	0	0	0	0	3	6	0	3	0	1	1	0	.25
2 Years		11	1	4	5	3	0	0	16	6.3	0	0	0	0	0	0	8	27	1	6	0	2	1	0	.45

Darryl Laplante

Pos: C **Shoots:** L **Ht:** 6'0" **Wt:** 185 **Born:** 3/28/77—Calgary, Alberta **Age:** 22

Overall											Power Play			Shorthand			Penalty							Misc	
Year	Tm	GP	G	A	Pts	+/–	GW	GT	S	SPct	G	A	Pts	G	A	Pts	Num	PIM	Maj	Mnr	Fgt	Rgh	HHT	Hat	P/G
97-98	Det	2	0	0	0	0	0	0	2	0.0	0	0	0	0	0	0	0	0	0	0	0	0	0	0	.00
98-99	Det	3	0	0	0	0	0	0	0	–	0	0	0	0	0	0	0	0	0	0	0	0	0	0	.00
2 Years		5	0	0	0	0	0	0	2	0.0	0	0	0	0	0	0	0	0	0	0	0	0	0	0	.00

Claude Lapointe

(statistical profile on page 334)

Pos: C **Shoots:** L **Ht:** 5'9" **Wt:** 181 **Born:** 10/11/68—Lachine, Quebec **Age:** 31

Overall											Power Play			Shorthand			Penalty							Misc	
Year	Tm	GP	G	A	Pts	+/–	GW	GT	S	SPct	G	A	Pts	G	A	Pts	Num	PIM	Maj	Mnr	Fgt	Rgh	HHT	Hat	P/G
90-91	Que	13	2	2	4	3	0	0	7	28.6	0	–	–	0	–	–	2	4	0	2	0	–	–	0	.31
91-92	Que	78	13	20	33	-8	2	0	95	13.7	0	1	1	2	1	3	36	86	2	33	1	9	7	0	.42
92-93	Que	74	10	26	36	5	1	0	91	11.0	0	1	1	0	0	0	41	98	0	39	0	16	8	0	.49
93-94	Que	59	11	17	28	2	1	0	73	15.1	1	0	1	1	0	1	35	70	0	35	0	8	15	0	.47
94-95	Que	29	4	8	12	5	0	0	40	10.0	0	0	0	0	1	1	15	41	1	13	0	5	1	0	.41
95-96	2Tm	35	4	5	9	1	1	0	44	9.1	0	0	0	2	0	2	10	20	0	10	0	1	6	0	.26
96-97	NYI	73	13	5	18	-11	3	1	80	16.3	0	0	0	3	0	3	23	49	1	22	1	4	7	0	.25
97-98	NYI	78	10	10	20	-9	3	0	82	12.2	0	0	0	1	1	2	22	47	1	21	0	6	6	0	.26
98-99	NYI	82	14	23	37	-19	1	0	134	10.4	2	2	4	2	2	4	24	62	2	21	1	3	8	0	.45
95-96	Col	3	0	0	0	-1	0	0	0	–	0	0	0	0	0	0	0	0	0	0	0	0	0	0	.00
95-96	Cgy	32	4	5	9	2	1	0	44	9.1	0	0	0	2	0	2	10	20	0	10	0	1	6	0	.28
9 Years		521	81	116	197	-31	12	1	646	12.5	3	–	–	11	–	–	208	477	7	196	3	–	–	0	.38
Postseason																									
Year	Tm	GP	G	A	Pts	+/–	GW	OT	S	SPct	G	A	Pts	G	A	Pts	Num	PIM	Maj	Mnr	Fgt	Rgh	HHT	Hat	P/G
92-93	Que	6	2	4	6	4	0	0	9	22.2	0	1	1	0	0	0	4	8	0	4	0	4	0	0	1.00
94-95	Que	5	0	0	0	-1	0	0	0	–	0	0	0	0	0	0	4	8	0	4	0	3	0	0	.00
95-96	Cgy	2	0	0	0	-2	0	0	3	0.0	0	0	0	0	0	0	0	0	0	0	0	0	0	0	.00
3 Years		13	2	4	6	1	0	0	12	16.7	0	1	1	0	0	0	8	16	0	8	0	7	0	0	.46

Martin Lapointe

(statistical profile on page 334)

Pos: RW **Shoots:** R **Ht:** 5'11" **Wt:** 215 **Born:** 9/12/73—Ville Ste-Pierre, Quebec **Age:** 26

Overall											Power Play			Shorthand			Penalty							Misc	
Year	Tm	GP	G	A	Pts	+/–	GW	GT	S	SPct	G	A	Pts	G	A	Pts	Num	PIM	Maj	Mnr	Fgt	Rgh	HHT	Hat	P/G
91-92	Det	4	0	1	1	2	0	0	2	0.0	0	0	0	0	0	0	1	5	1	0	1	0	0	0	.25
92-93	Det	3	0	0	0	-2	0	0	2	0.0	0	0	0	0	0	0	0	0	0	0	0	0	0	0	.00
93-94	Det	50	8	8	16	7	0	0	45	17.8	2	0	2	0	0	0	18	55	1	15	1	4	5	0	.32
94-95	Det	39	4	6	10	1	1	0	46	8.7	0	0	0	0	0	0	23	73	1	19	1	3	5	0	.26
95-96	Det	58	6	3	9	0	0	0	76	7.9	1	0	1	0	0	0	27	93	5	19	4	3	8	0	.16
96-97	Det	78	16	17	33	-14	1	0	149	10.7	5	5	10	1	0	1	50	167	9	36	8	7	12	0	.42
97-98	Det	79	15	19	34	0	3	2	154	9.7	4	4	8	0	0	0	38	106	2	33	2	12	8	0	.43
98-99	Det	77	16	13	29	7	4	0	153	10.5	7	1	8	1	0	1	47	141	5	38	5	7	10	0	.38
8 Years		388	65	67	132	1	9	2	627	10.4	19	10	29	2	0	2	204	640	24	160	22	36	48	0	.34
Postseason																									
Year	Tm	GP	G	A	Pts	+/–	GW	OT	S	SPct	G	A	Pts	G	A	Pts	Num	PIM	Maj	Mnr	Fgt	Rgh	HHT	Hat	P/G
91-92	Det	3	0	1	1	0	0	0	4	0.0	0	0	0	0	0	0	2	4	0	2	0	1	1	0	.33
93-94	Det	4	0	0	0	0	0	0	2	0.0	0	0	0	0	0	0	3	6	0	3	0	1	0	0	.00
94-95	Det	2	0	1	1	1	0	0	0	–	0	0	0	0	0	0	4	8	0	4	0	3	0	0	.50
95-96	Det	11	1	2	3	2	0	0	15	6.7	0	0	0	0	0	0	6	12	0	6	0	1	1	0	.27
96-97	Det	20	4	8	12	8	1	1	37	10.8	1	2	3	0	0	0	19	60	2	15	2	3	4	0	.60
97-98	Det	21	9	6	15	6	1	0	55	16.4	2	1	3	1	0	1	10	20	0	10	0	5	1	0	.71
98-99	Det	10	0	2	2	0	0	0	14	0.0	0	0	0	0	0	0	10	20	0	10	0	4	4	0	.20
7 Years		71	14	20	34	17	2	1	127	11.0	3	3	6	1	0	1	54	130	2	50	2	18	11	0	.48

Georges Laraque

Pos: RW **Shoots:** R **Ht:** 6'3" **Wt:** 225 **Born:** 12/7/76—Montreal, Quebec **Age:** 23

Overall											Power Play			Shorthand			Penalty							Misc	
Year	Tm	GP	G	A	Pts	+/-	GW	GT	S	SPct	G	A	Pts	G	A	Pts	Num	PIM	Maj	Mnr	Fgt	Rgh	HHT	Hat	P/G
97-98	Edm	11	0	0	0	-4	0	0	4	0.0	0	0	0	0	0	0	10	59	5	2	5	1	0	0	.00
98-99	Edm	39	3	2	5	-1	0	0	17	17.6	0	0	0	0	0	0	15	57	9	6	9	3	0	0	.13
2 Years		50	3	2	5	-5	0	0	21	14.3	0	0	0	0	0	0	25	116	14	8	14	4	0	0	.10
Postseason																									
Year	Tm	GP	G	A	Pts	+/-	GW	OT	S	SPct	G	A	Pts	G	A	Pts	Num	PIM	Maj	Mnr	Fgt	Rgh	HHT	Hat	P/G
98-99	Edm	4	0	0	0	-2	0	0	1	0.0	0	0	0	0	0	0	1	2	0	1	0	0	0	0	.00

Igor Larionov

(statistical profile on page 335)

Pos: C **Shoots:** L **Ht:** 5'9" **Wt:** 170 **Born:** 12/3/60—Voskresensk, USSR **Age:** 39

Overall											Power Play			Shorthand			Penalty							Misc	
Year	Tm	GP	G	A	Pts	+/-	GW	GT	S	SPct	G	A	Pts	G	A	Pts	Num	PIM	Maj	Mnr	Fgt	Rgh	HHT	Hat	P/G
89-90	Van	74	17	27	44	-5	2	1	118	14.4	8	–	–	0	–	–	–	20	–	–	–	–	–	0	.59
90-91	Van	64	13	21	34	-3	0	0	66	19.7	1	–	–	1	–	–	–	14	–	–	–	–	–	0	.53
91-92	Van	72	21	44	65	7	4	0	97	21.6	10	11	21	3	3	6	19	54	0	17	0	0	16	2	.90
92-93		Did Not Play in NHL																							
93-94	SJ	60	18	38	56	20	2	1	72	25.0	3	13	16	2	0	2	20	40	0	20	0	1	8	2	.93
94-95	SJ	33	4	20	24	-3	1	0	69	5.8	0	2	2	0	2	2	7	14	0	7	0	0	3	0	.73
95-96	2Tm	73	22	51	73	31	5	0	113	19.5	10	16	26	1	2	3	17	34	0	17	0	0	12	0	1.00
96-97	Det	64	12	42	54	31	4	0	95	12.6	2	15	17	1	1	2	13	26	0	13	0	2	5	0	.84
97-98	Det*	69	8	39	47	14	2	1	93	8.6	3	13	16	0	1	1	20	40	0	20	0	0	12	0	.68
98-99	Det	75	14	49	63	13	2	1	83	16.9	4	18	22	2	2	4	24	48	0	24	0	0	19	0	.84
95-96	SJ	4	1	1	2	-6	0	0	5	20.0	1	0	1	0	0	0	0	0	0	0	0	0	0	0	.50
95-96	Det	69	21	50	71	37	5	0	108	19.4	9	16	25	1	2	3	17	34	0	17	0	0	12	0	1.03
9 Years		584	129	331	460	105	22	4	806	16.0	41	–	–	10	–	–	–	290	–	–	–	–	–	4	.79
Postseason																									
Year	Tm	GP	G	A	Pts	+/-	GW	OT	S	SPct	G	A	Pts	G	A	Pts	Num	PIM	Maj	Mnr	Fgt	Rgh	HHT	Hat	P/G
90-91	Van	6	1	0	1	-5	0	0	8	12.5	0	0	0	0	0	0	3	6	0	3	0	–	–	0	.17
91-92	Van	13	3	7	10	1	0	0	12	25.0	1	1	2	0	0	0	2	4	0	2	0	1	0	0	.77
93-94	SJ	14	5	13	18	-1	0	0	27	18.5	0	4	4	0	1	1	5	10	0	5	0	0	2	0	1.29
94-95	SJ	11	1	8	9	-4	0	0	19	5.3	0	2	2	0	0	0	1	2	0	1	0	0	1	0	.82
95-96	Det	19	6	7	13	5	2	0	46	13.0	3	1	4	0	2	2	3	6	0	3	0	0	3	0	.68
96-97	Det	20	4	8	12	8	1	0	29	13.8	3	4	7	0	0	0	4	8	0	4	0	0	3	0	.60
97-98	Det	22	3	10	13	5	0	0	27	11.1	0	4	4	0	0	0	6	12	0	6	0	0	6	0	.59
98-99	Det	7	0	2	2	-1	0	0	3	0.0	0	0	0	0	0	0	0	0	0	0	0	0	0	0	.29
8 Years		112	23	55	78	8	3	0	171	13.5	7	16	23	0	3	3	24	48	0	24	0	–	–	0	.70

Mario Larocque

Pos: D **Shoots:** R **Ht:** 6'2" **Wt:** 195 **Born:** 4/4/78—Montreal, Quebec **Age:** 21

Overall											Power Play			Shorthand			Penalty							Misc	
Year	Tm	GP	G	A	Pts	+/-	GW	GT	S	SPct	G	A	Pts	G	A	Pts	Num	PIM	Maj	Mnr	Fgt	Rgh	HHT	Hat	P/G
98-99	TB	5	0	0	0	-4	0	0	3	0.0	0	0	0	0	0	0	8	16	0	8	0	3	2	0	.00

Janne Laukkanen

(statistical profile on page 335)

Pos: D **Shoots:** L **Ht:** 6'0" **Wt:** 180 **Born:** 3/19/70—Lahti, Finland **Age:** 29

Overall											Power Play			Shorthand			Penalty							Misc	
Year	Tm	GP	G	A	Pts	+/-	GW	GT	S	SPct	G	A	Pts	G	A	Pts	Num	PIM	Maj	Mnr	Fgt	Rgh	HHT	Hat	P/G
94-95	Que	11	0	3	3	3	0	0	12	0.0	0	2	2	0	0	0	2	4	0	2	0	0	1	0	.27
95-96	2Tm	23	1	2	3	-1	0	0	35	2.9	1	0	1	0	0	0	7	14	0	7	0	0	5	0	.13
96-97	Ott	76	3	18	21	-14	0	0	109	2.8	2	7	9	0	1	1	38	76	0	38	0	1	18	0	.28
97-98	Ott	60	4	17	21	-15	2	0	69	5.8	2	6	8	0	1	1	32	64	0	32	0	1	18	0	.35
98-99	Ott	50	1	11	12	18	0	0	46	2.2	0	1	1	0	0	0	16	40	0	15	0	2	9	0	.24
95-96	Col	3	1	0	1	-1	0	0	4	25.0	1	0	1	0	0	0	0	0	0	0	0	0	0	0	.33
95-96	Ott	20	0	2	2	0	0	0	31	0.0	0	0	0	0	0	0	7	14	0	7	0	0	5	0	.10
5 Years		220	9	51	60	-9	2	0	271	3.3	5	16	21	0	2	2	95	198	0	94	0	4	51	0	.27
Postseason																									
Year	Tm	GP	G	A	Pts	+/-	GW	OT	S	SPct	G	A	Pts	G	A	Pts	Num	PIM	Maj	Mnr	Fgt	Rgh	HHT	Hat	P/G
94-95	Que	6	1	0	1	-2	0	0	11	9.1	0	0	0	0	0	0	1	2	0	1	0	0	1	0	.17
96-97	Ott	7	0	1	1	-1	0	0	7	0.0	0	1	1	0	0	0	3	6	0	3	0	1	0	0	.14
97-98	Ott	11	2	2	4	-3	1	0	14	14.3	1	1	2	0	0	0	4	8	0	4	0	0	3	0	.36

																		Postseason							
Year	Tm	GP	G	A	Pts	+/-	GW	OT	S	SPct	G	A	Pts	G	A	Pts	Num	PIM	Maj	Mnr	Fgt	Rgh	HHT	Hat	P/G
98-99	Ott	4	0	0	0	1	0	0	8	0.0	0	0	0	0	0	0	2	4	0	2	0	0	1	0	.00
4 Years		28	3	3	6	-5	1	0	40	7.5	1	2	3	0	0	0	10	20	0	10	0	1	5	0	.21

Paul Laus

(statistical profile on page 335)

Pos: D **Shoots:** R **Ht:** 6'1" **Wt:** 216 **Born:** 9/26/70—Beamsville, Ontario **Age:** 29

			Overall								Power Play			Shorthand			Penalty							Misc	
Year	Tm	GP	G	A	Pts	+/-	GW	GT	S	SPct	G	A	Pts	G	A	Pts	Num	PIM	Maj	Mnr	Fgt	Rgh	HHT	Hat	P/G
93-94	Fla	39	2	0	2	9	1	0	15	13.3	0	0	0	0	0	0	30	109	11	17	11	7	3	0	.05
94-95	Fla	37	0	7	7	12	0	0	18	0.0	0	0	0	0	0	0	39	138	12	24	12	8	5	0	.19
95-96	Fla	78	3	6	9	-2	0	0	45	6.7	0	0	0	0	0	0	71	236	26	43	26	12	9	0	.12
96-97	Fla	77	0	12	12	13	0	0	63	0.0	0	1	1	0	1	1	86	313	**39**	44	**39**	23	3	0	.16
97-98	Fla	77	0	11	11	-5	0	0	64	0.0	0	2	2	0	1	1	85	293	25	54	25	13	10	0	.14
98-99	Fla	75	1	9	10	-1	0	0	54	1.9	0	0	0	0	0	0	67	218	20	44	20	12	13	0	.13
6 Years		383	6	45	51	26	1	0	259	2.3	0	3	3	0	2	2	378	1307	133	226	133	75	43	0	.13
												Postseason													
Year	Tm	GP	G	A	Pts	+/-	GW	OT	S	SPct	G	A	Pts	G	A	Pts	Num	PIM	Maj	Mnr	Fgt	Rgh	HHT	Hat	P/G
95-96	Fla	21	2	6	8	3	0	0	18	11.1	0	2	2	0	0	0	20	62	2	16	1	5	2	0	.38
96-97	Fla	5	0	1	1	-3	0	0	6	0.0	0	0	0	0	0	0	2	4	0	2	0	2	0	0	.20
2 Years		26	2	7	9	0	0	0	24	8.3	0	2	2	0	0	0	22	66	2	18	1	7	2	0	.35

Mark Lawrence

(statistical profile on page 335)

Pos: RW **Shoots:** R **Ht:** 6'4" **Wt:** 212 **Born:** 5/27/72—Burlington, Ontario **Age:** 27

			Overall								Power Play			Shorthand			Penalty							Misc	
Year	Tm	GP	G	A	Pts	+/-	GW	GT	S	SPct	G	A	Pts	G	A	Pts	Num	PIM	Maj	Mnr	Fgt	Rgh	HHT	Hat	P/G
94-95	Dal	2	0	0	0	0	0	0	3	0.0	0	0	0	0	0	0	0	0	0	0	0	0	0	0	.00
95-96	Dal	13	0	1	1	0	0	0	13	0.0	0	0	0	0	0	0	7	17	1	6	1	0	3	0	.08
96-97											Did Not Play in NHL														
97-98	NYI	2	0	0	0	0	0	0	4	0.0	0	0	0	0	0	0	1	2	0	1	0	0	0	0	.00
98-99	NYI	60	14	16	30	-8	2	1	88	15.9	4	5	9	0	0	0	19	38	0	19	0	1	12	0	.50
4 Years		77	14	17	31	-8	2	1	108	13.0	4	5	9	0	0	0	27	57	1	26	1	1	15	0	.40

Steve Leach

Pos: RW **Shoots:** R **Ht:** 5'11" **Wt:** 194 **Born:** 1/16/66—Cambridge, Massachusetts **Age:** 33

			Overall								Power Play			Shorthand			Penalty							Misc	
Year	Tm	GP	G	A	Pts	+/-	GW	GT	S	SPct	G	A	Pts	G	A	Pts	Num	PIM	Maj	Mnr	Fgt	Rgh	HHT	Hat	P/G
85-86	Was	11	1	1	2	0	0	0	4	25.0	0	–	–	0	–	–	1	2	0	1	0	–	–	0	.18
86-87	Was	15	1	0	1	-4	0	0	17	5.9	0	0	0	0	0	0	3	6	0	3	0	–	–	0	.07
87-88	Was	8	1	1	2	2	1	0	5	20.0	0	–	–	0	–	–	–	17	–	–	–	–	–	0	.25
88-89	Was	74	11	19	30	-4	0	0	145	7.6	4	–	–	0	–	–	–	94	–	–	–	–	–	0	.41
89-90	Was	70	18	14	32	10	2	0	122	14.8	0	–	–	0	–	–	–	104	–	–	–	–	–	0	.46
90-91	Was	68	11	19	30	-9	1	0	134	8.2	4	–	–	0	–	–	–	99	–	–	–	–	–	0	.44
91-92	Bos	78	31	29	60	-8	4	0	243	12.8	12	12	24	0	1	1	53	147	11	41	10	18	10	0	.77
92-93	Bos	79	26	25	51	-6	4	1	256	10.2	9	8	17	0	0	0	54	126	6	48	6	11	10	0	.65
93-94	Bos	42	5	10	15	-10	1	1	89	5.6	1	2	3	0	0	0	24	74	6	17	6	6	5	0	.36
94-95	Bos	35	5	6	11	-3	1	0	82	6.1	1	2	3	0	0	0	24	68	4	19	4	7	5	0	.31
95-96	2Tm	73	11	17	28	-7	2	0	157	7.0	1	2	3	0	0	0	35	108	10	24	10	8	6	0	.38
96-97	StL	17	2	1	3	-2	0	0	33	6.1	0	0	0	0	0	0	6	24	4	2	4	0	1	0	.18
97-98	Car	45	4	5	9	-19	2	0	60	6.7	1	0	1	1	0	1	15	42	4	11	4	4	2	0	.20
98-99	2Tm	31	1	3	4	-7	0	0	27	3.7	0	0	0	0	0	0	13	43	3	9	3	2	0	0	.13
95-96	Bos	59	9	13	22	-4	2	0	124	7.3	1	0	1	0	0	0	27	86	8	18	8	6	5	0	.37
95-96	StL	14	2	4	6	-3	0	0	33	6.1	0	2	2	0	0	0	8	22	2	6	2	2	1	0	.43
98-99	Ott	9	0	2	2	-1	0	0	4	0.0	0	0	0	0	0	0	3	6	0	3	0	0	0	0	.22
98-99	Pho	22	1	1	2	-6	0	0	23	4.3	0	0	0	0	0	0	10	37	3	6	3	2	0	0	.09
14 Years		646	128	150	278	-67	18	2	1374	9.3	33	–	–	1	–	–	–	954	–	–	–	–	–	0	.43
												Postseason													
Year	Tm	GP	G	A	Pts	+/-	GW	OT	S	SPct	G	A	Pts	G	A	Pts	Num	PIM	Maj	Mnr	Fgt	Rgh	HHT	Hat	P/G
85-86	Was	6	0	1	1	0	0	0	6	0.0	0	–	–	0	–	–	0	0	0	0	0	0	0	0	.17
87-88	Was	9	2	1	3	1	1	0	6	33.3	0	–	–	0	–	–	0	0	0	0	0	0	0	0	.33
88-89	Was	6	1	0	1	-1	0	0	9	11.1	1	0	1	0	0	0	–	12	–	–	–	–	–	0	.17
89-90	Was	14	2	2	4	4	0	0	22	9.1	0	–	–	0	–	–	4	8	0	4	0	–	–	0	.29
90-91	Was	9	1	2	3	3	0	0	17	5.9	0	–	–	0	–	–	4	8	0	4	0	–	–	0	.33
91-92	Bos	15	4	0	4	-2	1	0	30	13.3	0	0	0	0	0	0	5	10	0	5	0	2	1	0	.27

Postseason																									
Year	Tm	GP	G	A	Pts	+/-	GW	OT	S	SPct	G	A	Pts	G	A	Pts	Num	PIM	Maj	Mnr	Fgt	Rgh	HHT	Hat	P/G
92-93	Bos	4	1	1	2	0	0	0	18	5.6	0	1	1	0	0	0	1	2	0	1	0	0	0	0	.50
93-94	Bos	5	0	1	1	-2	0	0	3	0.0	0	0	0	0	0	0	1	2	0	1	0	1	0	0	.20
95-96	StL	11	3	2	5	4	1	0	11	27.3	1	0	1	0	0	0	5	10	0	5	0	2	1	0	.45
96-97	StL	6	0	0	0	-2	0	0	8	0.0	0	0	0	0	0	0	7	33	1	4	1	3	0	0	.00
98-99	Pho	7	1	1	2	0	0	0	4	25.0	0	0	0	0	0	0	1	2	0	1	0	0	0	0	.29
11 Years		92	15	11	26	5	3	0	134	11.2	2	–	–	0	–	–	–	87	–	–	–	–	–	0	.28

Patrick Lebeau

Pos: LW **Shoots:** L **Ht:** 5'10" **Wt:** 173 **Born:** 3/17/70—St.Jerome, Quebec **Age:** 29

Overall											Power Play			Shorthand			Penalty							Misc	
Year	Tm	GP	G	A	Pts	+/-	GW	GT	S	SPct	G	A	Pts	G	A	Pts	Num	PIM	Maj	Mnr	Fgt	Rgh	HHT	Hat	P/G
90-91	Mon	2	1	1	2	0	0	0	3	33.3	0	–	–	0	–	–	0	0	0	0	0	0	0	0	1.00
91-92	Did Not Play in NHL																								
92-93	Cgy	1	0	0	0	0	0	0	0	–	0	0	0	0	0	0	0	0	0	0	0	0	0	0	.00
93-94	Fla	4	1	1	2	0	0	0	4	25.0	1	1	2	0	0	0	2	4	0	2	0	0	1	0	.50
94-95	Did Not Play in NHL																								
95-96	Did Not Play in NHL																								
96-97	Did Not Play in NHL																								
97-98	Did Not Play in NHL																								
98-99	Pit	8	1	0	1	-2	0	0	4	25.0	0	0	0	0	0	0	1	2	0	1	0	0	0	0	.13
4 Years		15	3	2	5	-2	0	0	11	27.3	1	–	–	0	–	–	3	6	0	3	0	0	1	0	.33

Vincent Lecavalier

(statistical profile on page 336)

Pos: C **Shoots:** L **Ht:** 6'4" **Wt:** 180 **Born:** 4/21/80—Ile-Bizard, Quebec **Age:** 19

Overall											Power Play			Shorthand			Penalty							Misc	
Year	Tm	GP	G	A	Pts	+/-	GW	GT	S	SPct	G	A	Pts	G	A	Pts	Num	PIM	Maj	Mnr	Fgt	Rgh	HHT	Hat	P/G
98-99	TB	82	13	15	28	-19	2	1	125	10.4	2	4	6	0	1	1	10	23	1	9	1	2	5	0	.34

John LeClair

(statistical profile on page 336)

Pos: LW **Shoots:** L **Ht:** 6'3" **Wt:** 226 **Born:** 7/5/69—St. Albans, Vermont **Age:** 30

Overall											Power Play			Shorthand			Penalty							Misc	
Year	Tm	GP	G	A	Pts	+/-	GW	GT	S	SPct	G	A	Pts	G	A	Pts	Num	PIM	Maj	Mnr	Fgt	Rgh	HHT	Hat	P/G
90-91	Mon	10	2	5	7	1	1	0	12	16.7	0	0	0	0	0	0	1	2	0	1	0	0	1	0	.70
91-92	Mon	59	8	11	19	5	0	0	73	11.0	3	1	4	0	0	0	7	14	0	7	0	1	3	0	.32
92-93	Mon	72	19	25	44	11	2	0	139	13.7	2	1	3	0	0	0	15	33	1	14	1	3	3	0	.61
93-94	Mon	74	19	24	43	17	1	0	153	12.4	1	3	4	0	0	0	16	32	0	16	0	3	4	0	.58
94-95	2Tm	46	26	28	54	20	7	0	131	19.8	6	11	17	0	0	0	15	30	0	15	0	1	9	2	1.17
95-96	Phi*	82	51	46	97	21	10	2	270	18.9	19	18	37	0	0	0	28	64	0	27	0	2	15	2	1.18
96-97	Phi*	**82**	50	47	97	**44**	5	2	324	15.4	10	6	16	0	0	0	29	58	0	29	0	6	7	2	1.18
97-98	Phi*	82	51	36	87	30	9	1	303	16.8	16	12	28	0	0	0	16	32	0	16	0	5	4	1	1.06
98-99	Phi	76	43	47	90	36	7	**3**	246	17.5	16	9	25	0	0	0	15	30	0	15	0	1	9	2	1.18
94-95	Mon	9	1	4	5	-1	0	0	18	5.6	1	1	2	0	0	0	5	10	0	5	0	0	4	0	.56
94-95	Phi	37	25	24	49	21	7	0	113	22.1	5	10	15	0	0	0	10	20	0	10	0	1	5	2	1.32
9 Years		583	269	269	538	185	42	8	1651	16.3	73	61	134	0	0	0	142	295	1	140	1	22	55	9	.92

Postseason																									
Year	Tm	GP	G	A	Pts	+/-	GW	OT	S	SPct	G	A	Pts	G	A	Pts	Num	PIM	Maj	Mnr	Fgt	Rgh	HHT	Hat	P/G
90-91	Mon	3	0	0	0	2	0	0	3	0.0	0	0	0	0	0	0	0	0	0	0	0	0	0	0	.00
91-92	Mon	8	1	1	2	-2	0	0	10	10.0	0	0	0	0	0	0	2	4	0	2	0	0	0	0	.25
92-93	Mon	20	4	6	10	2	3	2	44	9.1	0	1	1	0	0	0	7	14	0	7	0	1	2	0	.50
93-94	Mon	7	2	1	3	-1	0	0	13	15.4	1	1	2	0	0	0	4	8	0	4	0	1	0	0	.43
94-95	Phi	15	5	7	12	8	1	0	37	13.5	1	2	3	0	0	0	2	4	0	2	0	2	0	1	.80
95-96	Phi	11	6	5	11	3	1	0	25	24.0	4	1	5	0	0	0	3	6	0	3	0	2	0	0	1.00
96-97	Phi	19	9	12	21	5	3	0	79	11.4	4	4	8	0	0	0	5	10	0	5	0	2	1	0	1.11
97-98	Phi	5	1	1	2	-4	1	0	19	5.3	1	0	1	0	0	0	4	8	0	4	0	1	1	0	.40
98-99	Phi	6	3	0	3	0	0	0	15	20.0	2	0	2	0	0	0	6	12	0	6	0	2	1	0	.50
9 Years		94	31	33	64	13	9	2	245	12.7	13	9	22	0	0	0	33	66	0	33	0	11	5	1	.68

Mike LeClerc

Pos: LW **Shoots:** L **Ht:** 6'1" **Wt:** 205 **Born:** 11/30/76—Winnipeg, Manitoba **Age:** 23

Overall											Power Play			Shorthand			Penalty							Misc	
Year	Tm	GP	G	A	Pts	+/-	GW	GT	S	SPct	G	A	Pts	G	A	Pts	Num	PIM	Maj	Mnr	Fgt	Rgh	HHT	Hat	P/G
96-97	Anh	5	1	1	2	2	1	0	3	33.3	0	0	0	0	0	0	0	0	0	0	0	0	0	0	.40
97-98	Anh	7	0	0	0	-6	0	0	11	0.0	0	0	0	0	0	0	3	6	0	3	0	2	0	0	.00
98-99	Anh	7	0	0	0	-2	0	0	1	0.0	0	0	0	0	0	0	2	4	0	2	0	0	2	0	.00
3 Years		19	1	1	2	-6	1	0	15	6.7	0	0	0	0	0	0	5	10	0	5	0	2	2	0	.11

Postseason

Year	Tm	GP	G	A	Pts	+/-	GW	OT	S	SPct	G	A	Pts	G	A	Pts	Num	PIM	Maj	Mnr	Fgt	Rgh	HHT	Hat	P/G
96-97	Anh	1	0	0	0	0	0	0	0	–	0	0	0	0	0	0	0	0	0	0	0	0	0	0	.00
98-99	Anh	1	0	0	0	0	0	0	1	0.0	0	0	0	0	0	0	0	0	0	0	0	0	0	0	.00
2 Years		2	0	0	0	0	0	0	1	0.0	0	0	0	0	0	0	0	0	0	0	0	0	0	0	.00

Grant Ledyard

(statistical profile on page 336)

Pos: D **Shoots:** L **Ht:** 6'2" **Wt:** 195 **Born:** 11/19/61—Winnipeg, Manitoba **Age:** 38

Overall											Power Play			Shorthand			Penalty							Misc	
Year	Tm	GP	G	A	Pts	+/-	GW	GT	S	SPct	G	A	Pts	G	A	Pts	Num	PIM	Maj	Mnr	Fgt	Rgh	HHT	Hat	P/G
84-85	NYR	42	8	12	20	8	1	0	91	8.8	1	–	–	0	–	–	21	53	1	19	–	–	–	0	.48
85-86	2Tm	79	9	27	36	-29	2	0	170	5.3	4	–	–	0	–	–	–	98	–	–	–	–	–	0	.46
86-87	LA	67	14	23	37	-40	1	0	144	9.7	5	–	–	0	–	–	–	93	–	–	–	–	–	0	.55
87-88	2Tm	44	5	10	15	-11	1	0	81	6.2	2	–	–	0	–	–	–	66	–	–	–	–	–	0	.34
88-89	2Tm	74	4	16	20	2	2	0	106	3.8	1	–	–	0	–	–	–	51	–	–	–	–	–	0	.27
89-90	Buf	67	2	13	15	2	1	0	91	2.2	0	–	–	0	–	–	–	37	–	–	–	–	–	0	.22
90-91	Buf	60	8	23	31	13	1	1	118	6.8	2	–	–	1	–	–	–	46	–	–	–	–	–	0	.52
91-92	Buf	50	5	16	21	-4	0	0	87	5.7	0	4	4	0	0	0	17	45	1	15	1	3	5	0	.42
92-93	Buf	50	2	14	16	-2	0	0	79	2.5	1	2	3	0	0	0	17	45	1	15	1	3	9	0	.32
93-94	Dal	84	9	37	46	7	1	0	177	5.1	6	20	26	0	0	0	21	42	0	21	0	8	2	0	.55
94-95	Dal	38	5	13	18	6	0	1	79	6.3	4	6	10	0	1	1	10	20	0	10	0	2	3	0	.47
95-96	Dal	73	5	19	24	-15	1	0	123	4.1	2	8	10	0	1	1	10	20	0	10	0	0	6	0	.33
96-97	Dal	67	1	15	16	31	0	0	99	1.0	0	4	4	0	0	0	21	61	1	18	1	1	13	0	.24
97-98	2Tm	71	4	20	24	-4	0	0	90	4.4	2	8	10	0	1	1	10	20	0	10	0	1	3	0	.34
98-99	Bos	47	4	8	12	-8	2	0	47	8.5	1	4	5	0	0	0	11	33	1	9	1	0	4	0	.26
85-86	NYR	27	2	9	11	-7	0	0	57	3.5	0	–	–	0	–	–	–	20	–	–	–	–	–	0	.41
85-86	LA	52	7	18	25	-22	2	0	113	6.2	4	–	–	0	–	–	–	78	–	–	–	–	–	0	.48
87-88	LA	23	1	7	8	-7	0	0	40	2.5	1	–	–	0	–	–	–	52	–	–	–	–	–	0	.35
87-88	Was	21	4	3	7	-4	1	0	41	9.8	1	–	–	0	–	–	–	14	–	–	–	–	–	0	.33
88-89	Was	61	3	11	14	1	1	0	81	3.7	1	–	–	0	–	–	–	43	–	–	–	–	–	0	.23
88-89	Buf	13	1	5	6	1	1	0	25	4.0	0	–	–	0	–	–	4	8	0	4	0	–	–	0	.46
97-98	Van	49	2	13	15	-2	0	0	57	3.5	1	1	2	0	1	1	7	14	0	7	0	1	2	0	.31
97-98	Bos	22	2	7	9	-2	0	0	33	6.1	1	7	8	0	0	0	3	6	0	3	0	0	1	0	.41
15 Years		913	85	266	351	-44	13	2	1582	5.4	31	–	–	1	–	–	–	730	–	–	–	–	–	0	.38

Postseason

Year	Tm	GP	G	A	Pts	+/-	GW	OT	S	SPct	G	A	Pts	G	A	Pts	Num	PIM	Maj	Mnr	Fgt	Rgh	HHT	Hat	P/G
84-85	NYR	3	0	2	2	-2	0	0	12	0.0	0	–	–	0	0	0	2	4	0	2	0	–	–	0	.67
86-87	LA	5	0	0	0	-2	0	0	8	0.0	0	0	0	0	0	0	–	10	–	–	–	–	–	0	.00
87-88	Was	14	1	0	1	1	0	0	17	5.9	0	0	0	0	0	0	–	30	–	–	–	–	–	0	.07
88-89	Buf	5	1	2	3	-1	0	0	13	7.7	0	–	–	0	–	–	1	2	0	1	0	–	–	0	.60
90-91	Buf	6	3	3	6	-1	0	0	11	27.3	0	–	–	0	–	–	–	10	–	–	–	–	–	0	1.00
92-93	Buf	8	0	0	0	-5	0	0	12	0.0	0	0	0	0	0	0	4	8	0	4	0	1	2	0	.00
93-94	Dal	9	1	2	3	0	1	0	23	4.3	0	2	2	0	0	0	3	6	0	3	0	1	0	0	.33
94-95	Dal	3	0	0	0	-2	0	0	4	0.0	0	0	0	0	0	0	1	2	0	1	0	1	0	0	.00
96-97	Dal	7	0	2	2	-3	0	0	8	0.0	0	0	0	0	0	0	0	0	0	0	0	0	0	0	.29
97-98	Bos	6	0	0	0	-3	0	0	8	0.0	0	0	0	0	0	0	1	2	0	1	0	0	1	0	.00
98-99	Bos	2	0	0	0	-1	0	0	4	0.0	0	0	0	0	0	0	1	2	0	1	0	1	0	0	.00
11 Years		68	6	11	17	-19	1	0	120	5.0	0	–	–	0	–	–	–	76	–	–	–	–	–	0	.25

Brian Leetch

(statistical profile on page 336)

Pos: D **Shoots:** L **Ht:** 6'1" **Wt:** 190 **Born:** 3/3/68—Corpus Christi, Texas **Age:** 31

Overall											Power Play			Shorthand			Penalty							Misc	
Year	Tm	GP	G	A	Pts	+/-	GW	GT	S	SPct	G	A	Pts	G	A	Pts	Num	PIM	Maj	Mnr	Fgt	Rgh	HHT	Hat	P/G
87-88	NYR	17	2	12	14	5	1	0	40	5.0	1	7	8	0	–	–	0	0	0	0	0	0	0	0	.82
88-89	NYR	68	23	48	71	8	1	1	268	8.6	8	23	31	3	–	–	22	50	2	20	–	–	–	0	1.04
89-90	NYR*	72	11	45	56	-18	2	1	222	5.0	5	29	34	0	–	–	13	26	0	13	0	–	–	0	.78
90-91	NYR*	80	16	72	88	2	4	1	206	7.8	6	45	51	0	–	–	–	42	–	–	–	–	–	0	1.10

Overall											Power Play			Shorthand			Penalty							Misc	
Year	Tm	GP	G	A	Pts	+/–	GW	GT	S	SPct	G	A	Pts	G	A	Pts	Num	PIM	Maj	Mnr	Fgt	Rgh	HHT	Hat	P/G
91-92	NYR*	80	22	80	102	25	3	1	245	9.0	10	36	46	1	0	1	13	26	0	13	0	1	7	0	1.28
92-93	NYR	36	6	30	36	2	1	0	150	4.0	2	22	24	1	0	1	9	26	0	8	0	1	5	0	1.00
93-94	NYR*	84	23	56	79	28	4	0	328	7.0	17	36	53	1	2	3	28	67	1	26	0	0	15	0	.94
94-95	NYR	48	9	32	41	0	2	0	182	4.9	3	18	21	0	1	1	9	18	0	9	0	1	3	0	.85
95-96	NYR*	82	15	70	85	12	3	0	276	5.4	7	37	44	0	0	0	15	30	0	15	0	1	5	0	1.04
96-97	NYR*	**82**	20	58	78	31	2	0	256	7.8	9	21	30	0	2	2	20	40	0	20	0	1	9	0	.95
97-98	NYR*	76	17	33	50	-36	2	2	230	7.4	11	23	34	0	0	0	16	32	0	16	0	2	11	0	.66
98-99	NYR	82	13	42	55	-7	1	0	184	7.1	4	25	29	0	0	0	21	42	0	21	0	1	15	0	.67
12 Years		807	177	578	755	52	26	6	2587	6.8	83	322	405	6	–	–	–	399	–	–	–	–	–	0	.94
Postseason																									
Year	Tm	GP	G	A	Pts	+/–	GW	OT	S	SPct	G	A	Pts	G	A	Pts	Num	PIM	Maj	Mnr	Fgt	Rgh	HHT	Hat	P/G
88-89	NYR	4	3	2	5	-4	0	0	25	12.0	2	–	–	0	0	0	1	2	0	1	0	–	–	0	1.25
90-91	NYR	6	1	3	4	-2	0	0	13	7.7	0	–	–	0	0	0	0	0	0	0	0	0	0	0	.67
91-92	NYR	13	4	11	15	-5	0	0	67	6.0	1	9	10	1	1	2	2	4	0	2	0	0	2	0	1.15
93-94	NYR	23	11	23	34	19	4	0	88	12.5	4	10	14	0	0	0	3	6	0	3	0	0	2	0	1.48
94-95	NYR	10	6	8	14	-1	1	0	46	13.0	3	3	6	0	0	0	4	8	0	4	0	0	2	1	1.40
95-96	NYR	11	1	6	7	-11	0	0	34	2.9	1	5	6	0	0	0	2	4	0	2	0	0	1	0	.64
96-97	NYR	15	2	8	10	5	1	0	56	3.6	1	3	4	0	0	0	3	6	0	3	0	0	1	0	.67
7 Years		82	28	61	89	1	6	0	329	8.5	12	–	–	1	1	2	15	30	0	15	0	–	–	1	1.09

Patrice Lefebvre

Pos: RW **Shoots:** L **Ht:** 5'6" **Wt:** 160 **Born:** 6/28/67—Montreal, Quebec **Age:** 32

Overall											Power Play			Shorthand			Penalty							Misc	
Year	Tm	GP	G	A	Pts	+/–	GW	GT	S	SPct	G	A	Pts	G	A	Pts	Num	PIM	Maj	Mnr	Fgt	Rgh	HHT	Hat	P/G
98-99	Was	3	0	0	0	-2	0	0	2	0.0	0	0	0	0	0	0	1	2	0	1	0	0	1	0	.00

Sylvain Lefebvre

(statistical profile on page 337)

Pos: D **Shoots:** L **Ht:** 6'2" **Wt:** 205 **Born:** 10/14/67—Richmond, Quebec **Age:** 32

Overall											Power Play			Shorthand			Penalty							Misc	
Year	Tm	GP	G	A	Pts	+/–	GW	GT	S	SPct	G	A	Pts	G	A	Pts	Num	PIM	Maj	Mnr	Fgt	Rgh	HHT	Hat	P/G
89-90	Mon	68	3	10	13	18	0	0	89	3.4	0	–	–	0	–	–	–	61	–	–	–	–	–	0	.19
90-91	Mon	63	5	18	23	-11	1	0	76	6.6	1	–	–	0	–	–	–	30	–	–	–	–	–	0	.37
91-92	Mon	69	3	14	17	9	0	0	85	3.5	0	3	3	0	0	0	27	91	7	18	7	3	5	0	.25
92-93	Tor	81	2	12	14	8	0	0	81	2.5	0	1	1	0	0	0	30	90	2	25	2	4	12	0	.17
93-94	Tor	84	2	9	11	33	0	1	96	2.1	0	1	1	0	1	1	28	79	5	22	5	10	4	0	.13
94-95	Que	48	2	11	13	13	0	0	81	2.5	0	3	3	0	0	0	7	17	1	6	1	0	4	0	.27
95-96	Col	75	5	11	16	26	0	0	115	4.3	2	2	4	0	2	2	20	49	3	17	2	1	9	0	.21
96-97	Col	71	2	11	13	12	0	0	77	2.6	1	1	2	0	2	2	12	30	2	10	2	3	2	0	.18
97-98	Col	81	0	10	10	2	0	0	66	0.0	0	2	2	0	1	1	20	48	0	19	0	3	8	0	.12
98-99	Col	76	2	18	20	18	0	0	64	3.1	0	0	0	0	1	1	21	48	2	19	2	2	8	0	.26
10 Years		716	26	124	150	128	1	1	830	3.1	4	–	–	0	–	–	–	543	–	–	–	–	–	0	.21
Postseason																									
Year	Tm	GP	G	A	Pts	+/–	GW	OT	S	SPct	G	A	Pts	G	A	Pts	Num	PIM	Maj	Mnr	Fgt	Rgh	HHT	Hat	P/G
89-90	Mon	6	0	0	0	-1	0	0	6	0.0	0	0	0	0	0	0	1	2	0	1	0	–	–	0	.00
90-91	Mon	11	1	0	1	-6	0	0	8	12.5	0	0	0	0	0	0	3	6	0	3	0	–	–	0	.09
91-92	Mon	2	0	0	0	2	0	0	2	0.0	0	0	0	0	0	0	1	2	0	1	0	0	0	0	.00
92-93	Tor	21	3	3	6	9	0	0	27	11.1	0	0	0	0	0	0	6	20	0	5	0	0	3	0	.29
93-94	Tor	18	0	3	3	-3	0	0	26	0.0	0	0	0	0	1	1	8	16	0	8	0	1	1	0	.17
94-95	Que	6	0	2	2	5	0	0	7	0.0	0	0	0	0	0	0	1	2	0	1	0	1	0	0	.33
95-96	Col	22	0	5	5	6	0	0	22	0.0	0	0	0	0	0	0	6	12	0	6	0	2	3	0	.23
96-97	Col	17	0	0	0	-1	0	0	15	0.0	0	0	0	0	0	0	7	25	1	5	1	1	3	0	.00
97-98	Col	7	0	0	0	-1	0	0	4	0.0	0	0	0	0	0	0	2	4	0	2	0	0	0	0	.00
98-99	Col	19	0	1	1	6	0	0	16	0.0	0	0	0	0	0	0	6	12	0	6	0	1	3	0	.05
10 Years		129	4	14	18	16	0	0	133	3.0	0	0	0	0	1	1	41	101	1	38	1	–	–	0	.14

Manny LeGace

Pos: G **Catches:** L **Ht:** 5'9" **Wt:** 162 **Born:** 2/4/73—Toronto, Ontario **Age:** 26

Overall																Pen Shot		Offense		
Year	Tm	GP	GS	TP	W	L	T	Min	GA	GAA	Shots	SvPct	ShO	OE	PPGA	SHGA	Shots	GA	G	A	PIM
98-99	LA	17	14	1	2	9	2	899	39	2.60	439	.911	0	3	12	5	0	0	0	1	0

David Legwand

Pos: C **Shoots:** L **Ht:** 6'2" **Wt:** 180 **Born:** 8/17/80—Grosse Pte. Woods, Michigan **Age:** 19

		Overall									Power Play			Shorthand			Penalty							Misc	
Year	Tm	GP	G	A	Pts	+/-	GW	GT	S	SPct	G	A	Pts	G	A	Pts	Num	PIM	Maj	Mnr	Fgt	Rgh	HHT	Hat	P/G
98-99	Nsh	1	0	0	0	0	0	0	2	0.0	0	0	0	0	0	0	0	0	0	0	0	0	0	0	.00

Jere Lehtinen

(statistical profile on page 337)

Pos: RW **Shoots:** R **Ht:** 6'0" **Wt:** 192 **Born:** 6/24/73—Espoo, Finland **Age:** 26

		Overall									Power Play			Shorthand			Penalty							Misc	
Year	Tm	GP	G	A	Pts	+/-	GW	GT	S	SPct	G	A	Pts	G	A	Pts	Num	PIM	Maj	Mnr	Fgt	Rgh	HHT	Hat	P/G
95-96	Dal	57	6	22	28	5	1	0	109	5.5	0	5	5	0	0	0	8	16	0	8	0	0	2	0	.49
96-97	Dal	63	16	27	43	26	2	0	134	11.9	3	3	6	1	3	4	1	2	0	1	0	0	0	0	.68
97-98	Dal*	72	23	19	42	19	6	1	201	11.4	7	3	10	2	3	5	10	20	0	10	0	0	5	0	.58
98-99	Dal	74	20	32	52	29	2	0	173	11.6	7	10	17	1	1	2	9	18	0	9	0	0	5	0	.70
4 Years		266	65	100	165	79	11	1	617	10.5	17	21	38	4	7	11	28	56	0	28	0	0	12	0	.62
											Postseason														
Year	Tm	GP	G	A	Pts	+/-	GW	OT	S	SPct	G	A	Pts	G	A	Pts	Num	PIM	Maj	Mnr	Fgt	Rgh	HHT	Hat	P/G
96-97	Dal	7	2	2	4	1	0	0	15	13.3	0	0	0	0	0	0	0	0	0	0	0	0	0	0	.57
97-98	Dal	12	3	5	8	0	0	0	31	9.7	1	2	3	0	0	0	1	2	0	1	0	0	0	0	.67
98-99	Dal	23	10	3	13	8	0	0	55	18.2	1	1	2	1	0	1	1	2	0	1	0	0	0	0	.57
3 Years		42	15	10	25	9	0	0	101	14.9	2	3	5	1	0	1	2	4	0	2	0	0	0	0	.60

Claude Lemieux

(statistical profile on page 337)

Pos: RW **Shoots:** R **Ht:** 6'1" **Wt:** 225 **Born:** 7/16/65—Buckingham, Quebec **Age:** 34

		Overall									Power Play			Shorthand			Penalty							Misc	
Year	Tm	GP	G	A	Pts	+/-	GW	GT	S	SPct	G	A	Pts	G	A	Pts	Num	PIM	Maj	Mnr	Fgt	Rgh	HHT	Hat	P/G
83-84	Mon	8	1	1	2	-2	0	0	7	14.3	0	–	–	0	–	–	–	12	–	–	–	–	–	0	.25
84-85	Mon	1	0	1	1	1	0	0	0	–	0	–	–	0	–	–	2	7	1	1	–	–	–	0	1.00
85-86	Mon	10	1	2	3	-6	0	0	16	6.3	1	–	–	0	–	–	–	22	–	–	–	–	–	0	.30
86-87	Mon*	76	27	26	53	0	1	0	184	14.7	5	–	–	0	–	–	–	156	–	–	–	–	–	0	.70
87-88	Mon	78	31	30	61	16	3	1	241	12.9	6	–	–	0	–	–	–	137	–	–	–	–	–	0	.78
88-89	Mon	69	29	22	51	14	3	0	220	13.2	7	–	–	0	–	–	–	136	–	–	–	–	–	1	.74
89-90	Mon	39	8	10	18	-8	1	0	104	7.7	3	–	–	0	–	–	–	106	–	–	–	–	–	0	.46
90-91	NJ	78	30	17	47	-8	2	0	271	11.1	10	1	11	0	0	0	–	105	–	–	–	–	–	2	.60
91-92	NJ	74	41	27	68	9	8	**3**	296	13.9	13	9	22	1	1	2	37	109	1	32	1	7	7	0	.92
92-93	NJ	77	30	51	81	3	3	2	311	9.6	13	22	35	0	0	0	60	155	1	55	1	15	7	1	1.05
93-94	NJ	79	18	26	44	13	5	0	181	9.9	5	7	12	0	1	1	35	86	0	33	0	8	5	0	.56
94-95	NJ	45	6	13	19	2	1	0	117	5.1	1	0	1	0	1	1	20	86	2	13	2	6	1	0	.42
95-96	Col	79	39	32	71	14	10	0	315	12.4	9	6	15	2	1	3	46	117	3	41	1	11	7	2	.90
96-97	Col	45	11	17	28	-4	4	0	168	6.5	5	8	13	0	0	0	16	43	1	14	1	7	2	0	.62
97-98	Col	78	26	27	53	-7	1	1	261	10.0	11	7	18	1	0	1	33	115	3	25	3	9	2	1	.68
98-99	Col	82	27	24	51	0	8	1	292	9.2	11	14	25	0	1	1	39	102	0	36	0	7	6	0	.62
16 Years		918	325	326	651	37	50	8	2984	10.9	100	–	–	4	–	–	–	1494	–	–	–	–	–	7	.71
											Postseason														
Year	Tm	GP	G	A	Pts	+/-	GW	OT	S	SPct	G	A	Pts	G	A	Pts	Num	PIM	Maj	Mnr	Fgt	Rgh	HHT	Hat	P/G
85-86	Mon	20	10	5	15	1	4	2	51	19.6	4	–	–	0	–	–	–	68	–	–	–	–	–	0	.75
86-87	Mon	17	4	9	13	7	0	0	44	9.1	2	–	–	0	–	–	–	41	–	–	–	–	–	0	.76
87-88	Mon	11	3	2	5	-2	2	0	28	10.7	0	–	–	0	–	–	–	20	–	–	–	–	–	0	.45
88-89	Mon	18	4	3	7	0	1	0	46	8.7	1	–	–	0	–	–	–	58	–	–	–	–	–	0	.39
89-90	Mon	11	1	3	4	2	1	0	24	4.2	0	–	–	0	0	0	–	38	–	–	–	–	–	0	.36
90-91	NJ	7	4	0	4	-3	1	0	24	16.7	2	0	2	0	0	0	–	34	–	–	–	–	–	0	.57
91-92	NJ	7	4	3	7	1	0	0	33	12.1	1	1	2	0	0	0	9	26	0	8	0	2	3	0	1.00
92-93	NJ	5	2	0	2	-3	0	0	15	13.3	1	0	1	0	0	0	4	19	1	2	0	0	0	0	.40
93-94	NJ	20	7	11	18	4	2	0	50	14.0	0	2	2	0	1	1	14	44	0	12	0	1	1	0	.90
94-95	NJ	20	13	3	16	12	3	0	65	20.0	0	1	1	0	0	0	10	20	0	10	0	2	3	0	.80
95-96	Col	19	5	7	12	5	0	0	81	6.2	3	2	5	0	0	0	22	55	1	20	0	9	1	0	.63
96-97	Col	17	13	10	23	7	4	1	73	17.8	4	5	9	0	0	0	8	32	0	6	0	0	2	0	1.35
97-98	Col	7	3	3	6	2	1	0	29	10.3	1	1	2	0	0	0	4	8	0	4	0	2	1	0	.86
98-99	Col	19	3	11	14	5	0	0	69	4.3	1	5	6	0	1	1	9	26	0	8	0	0	1	0	.74
14 Years		198	76	70	146	38	19	3	632	12.0	20	–	–	0	–	–	–	489	–	–	–	–	–	0	.74

Jean-Yves Leroux

Pos: LW **Shoots:** L **Ht:** 6'2" **Wt:** 211 **Born:** 6/24/76—Montreal, Quebec **Age:** 23

Overall											Power Play			Shorthand			Penalty							Misc	
Year	Tm	GP	G	A	Pts	+/–	GW	GT	S	SPct	G	A	Pts	G	A	Pts	Num	PIM	Maj	Mnr	Fgt	Rgh	HHT	Hat	P/G
96-97	Chi	1	0	1	1	1	0	0	0	–	0	0	0	0	0	0	1	5	1	0	1	0	0	0	1.00
97-98	Chi	66	6	7	13	-2	0	0	57	10.5	0	0	0	0	0	0	17	55	7	10	7	7	1	0	.20
98-99	Chi	40	3	5	8	-7	0	0	47	6.4	0	1	1	0	0	0	9	21	1	8	1	1	2	0	.20
3 Years		107	9	13	22	-8	0	0	104	8.7	0	1	1	0	0	0	27	81	9	18	9	8	3	0	.21

Curtis Leschyshyn

Pos: D **Shoots:** L **Ht:** 6'1" **Wt:** 205 **Born:** 9/29/69—Thompson, Manitoba **Age:** 30

Overall											Power Play			Shorthand			Penalty							Misc	
Year	Tm	GP	G	A	Pts	+/–	GW	GT	S	SPct	G	A	Pts	G	A	Pts	Num	PIM	Maj	Mnr	Fgt	Rgh	HHT	Hat	P/G
88-89	Que	71	4	9	13	-32	0	0	58	6.9	1	–	–	1	–	–	–	71	–	–	–	–	–	0	.18
89-90	Que	68	2	6	8	-41	0	0	42	4.8	1	–	–	0	–	–	–	44	–	–	–	–	–	0	.12
90-91	Que	55	3	7	10	-19	1	0	57	5.3	2	–	–	0	–	–	–	49	–	–	–	–	–	0	.18
91-92	Que	42	5	12	17	-28	1	0	61	8.2	3	7	10	0	0	0	17	42	0	16	0	4	4	0	.40
92-93	Que	82	9	23	32	25	2	0	73	12.3	4	4	8	0	0	0	29	61	1	28	1	7	12	0	.39
93-94	Que	72	5	17	22	-2	2	0	97	5.2	3	8	11	0	0	0	23	65	1	20	0	5	10	0	.31
94-95	Que	44	2	13	15	29	0	0	43	4.7	0	4	4	0	2	2	10	20	0	10	0	1	5	0	.34
95-96	Col	77	4	15	19	32	1	0	76	5.3	0	2	2	0	2	2	35	73	1	34	1	5	17	0	.25
96-97	3Tm	77	4	18	22	-18	1	0	102	3.9	1	5	6	1	0	1	19	38	0	19	0	4	7	0	.29
97-98	Car	73	2	10	12	-2	1	0	53	3.8	1	1	2	0	0	0	21	45	1	20	1	1	7	0	.16
98-99	Car	65	2	7	9	-1	0	0	35	5.7	0	1	1	0	1	1	21	50	0	20	0	1	7	0	.14
96-97	Col	11	0	5	5	1	0	0	8	0.0	0	0	0	0	0	0	3	6	0	3	0	0	1	0	.45
96-97	Was	2	0	0	0	0	0	0	0	–	0	0	0	0	0	0	1	2	0	1	0	0	1	0	.00
96-97	Har	64	4	13	17	-19	1	0	94	4.3	1	5	6	1	0	1	15	30	0	15	0	4	5	0	.27
11 Years		726	42	137	179	-57	9	0	697	6.0	16	–	–	2	–	–	–	558	–	–	–	–	–	0	.25
Postseason																									
Year	Tm	GP	G	A	Pts	+/–	GW	OT	S	SPct	G	A	Pts	G	A	Pts	Num	PIM	Maj	Mnr	Fgt	Rgh	HHT	Hat	P/G
92-93	Que	6	1	1	2	3	0	0	5	20.0	1	0	1	0	0	0	3	6	0	3	0	1	0	0	.33
94-95	Que	3	0	1	1	-1	0	0	3	0.0	0	0	0	0	1	1	2	4	0	2	0	1	0	0	.33
95-96	Col	17	1	2	3	4	0	0	9	11.1	0	0	0	0	0	0	4	8	0	4	0	1	2	0	.18
98-99	Car	6	0	0	0	-3	0	0	4	0.0	0	0	0	0	0	0	3	6	0	3	0	0	1	0	.00
4 Years		32	2	4	6	3	0	0	21	9.5	1	0	1	0	1	1	12	24	0	12	0	3	3	0	.19

Trevor Letowski

Pos: C **Shoots:** R **Ht:** 5'10" **Wt:** 173 **Born:** 4/5/77—Thunder Bay, Ontario **Age:** 22

Overall											Power Play			Shorthand			Penalty							Misc	
Year	Tm	GP	G	A	Pts	+/–	GW	GT	S	SPct	G	A	Pts	G	A	Pts	Num	PIM	Maj	Mnr	Fgt	Rgh	HHT	Hat	P/G
98-99	Pho	14	2	2	4	1	0	0	8	25.0	0	0	0	0	0	0	1	2	0	1	0	0	0	0	.29

Doug Lidster

Pos: D **Shoots:** R **Ht:** 6'1" **Wt:** 195 **Born:** 10/18/60—Kamloops, British Columbia **Age:** 39

Overall											Power Play			Shorthand			Penalty							Misc	
Year	Tm	GP	G	A	Pts	+/–	GW	GT	S	SPct	G	A	Pts	G	A	Pts	Num	PIM	Maj	Mnr	Fgt	Rgh	HHT	Hat	P/G
83-84	Van	8	0	0	0	-7	0	0	7	0.0	0	0	0	0	0	0	2	4	0	2	0	–	–	0	.00
84-85	Van	78	6	24	30	-11	0	0	125	4.8	2	–	–	0	–	–	–	55	–	–	–	–	–	0	.38
85-86	Van	78	12	16	28	-12	0	0	151	7.9	1	–	–	1	–	–	–	56	–	–	–	–	–	0	.36
86-87	Van	80	12	51	63	-35	0	1	176	6.8	3	–	–	0	–	–	–	40	–	–	–	–	–	0	.79
87-88	Van	64	4	32	36	-19	0	0	133	3.0	2	–	–	1	–	–	–	105	–	–	–	–	–	0	.56
88-89	Van	63	5	17	22	-4	0	0	16	31.3	3	–	–	0	–	–	–	78	–	–	–	–	–	0	.35
89-90	Van	**80**	8	28	36	-16	0	1	143	5.6	1	–	–	0	–	–	–	36	–	–	–	–	–	0	.45
90-91	Van	78	6	32	38	-6	1	0	157	3.8	4	–	–	0	–	–	–	77	–	–	–	–	–	0	.49
91-92	Van	66	6	23	29	9	2	0	89	6.7	3	9	12	0	3	3	18	39	1	17	1	5	7	0	.44
92-93	Van	71	6	19	25	9	0	0	76	7.9	3	3	6	0	0	0	15	36	2	13	2	6	3	0	.35
93-94	NYR	34	0	2	2	-12	0	0	25	0.0	0	0	0	0	0	0	15	33	1	14	1	3	6	0	.06
94-95	StL	37	2	7	9	9	0	0	37	5.4	1	0	1	0	0	0	6	12	0	6	0	1	1	0	.24
95-96	NYR	59	5	9	14	11	0	0	73	6.8	0	2	2	0	2	2	25	50	0	25	0	1	11	0	.24
96-97	NYR	48	3	4	7	10	0	0	42	7.1	0	0	0	0	1	1	8	24	0	7	0	0	3	0	.15
97-98	NYR	36	0	4	4	2	0	0	25	0.0	0	0	0	0	0	0	12	24	0	12	0	1	6	0	.11
98-99	Dal	17	0	0	0	0	0	0	7	0.0	0	0	0	0	0	0	5	10	0	5	0	0	2	0	.00
16 Years		897	75	268	343	-72	3	2	1282	5.9	23	–	–	2	–	–	–	679	–	–	–	–	–	0	.38

Postseason																									
Year	Tm	GP	G	A	Pts	+/–	GW	OT	S	SPct	G	A	Pts	G	A	Pts	Num	PIM	Maj	Mnr	Fgt	Rgh	HHT	Hat	P/G
83-84	Van	2	0	1	1	0	0	0	5	0.0	0	–	–	0	0	0	0	0	0	0	0	0	0	0	.50
85-86	Van	3	0	1	1	-4	0	0	1	0.0	0	–	–	0	0	0	1	2	0	1	0	0	0	0	.33
88-89	Van	7	1	1	2	1	0	0	13	7.7	0	–	–	0	–	–	3	9	1	2	0	0	0	0	.29
90-91	Van	6	0	2	2	-3	0	0	9	0.0	0	–	–	0	–	–	3	6	0	3	0	0	0	0	.33
91-92	Van	11	1	2	3	3	0	0	6	16.7	0	1	1	0	0	0	4	11	1	3	1	0	3	0	.27
92-93	Van	12	0	3	3	3	0	0	8	0.0	0	0	0	0	0	0	4	8	0	4	0	0	2	0	.25
93-94	NYR	9	2	0	2	-4	0	0	9	22.2	0	0	0	0	0	0	5	10	0	5	0	0	3	0	.22
94-95	StL	4	0	0	0	6	0	0	1	0.0	0	0	0	0	0	0	1	2	0	1	0	0	0	0	.00
95-96	NYR	7	1	0	1	-4	0	0	5	20.0	1	0	1	0	0	0	3	6	0	3	0	2	0	0	.14
96-97	NYR	15	1	5	6	-2	0	0	20	5.0	0	0	0	0	1	1	4	8	0	4	0	0	3	0	.40
98-99	Dal	4	0	0	0	0	0	0	1	0.0	0	0	0	0	0	0	1	2	0	1	0	0	1	0	.00
11 Years		80	6	15	21	-4	0	0	78	7.7	1	–	–	0	–	–	29	64	2	27	1	2	12	0	.26

Nicklas Lidstrom

(statistical profile on page 337)

Pos: D **Shoots:** L **Ht:** 6'2" **Wt:** 190 **Born:** 4/28/70—Vasteras, Sweden **Age:** 29

Overall											Power Play			Shorthand			Penalty							Misc	
Year	Tm	GP	G	A	Pts	+/–	GW	GT	S	SPct	G	A	Pts	G	A	Pts	Num	PIM	Maj	Mnr	Fgt	Rgh	HHT	Hat	P/G
91-92	Det	80	11	49	60	36	1	1	168	6.5	5	26	31	0	1	1	11	22	0	11	0	0	6	0	.75
92-93	Det	84	7	34	41	7	2	0	156	4.5	3	17	20	0	4	4	14	28	0	14	0	0	14	0	.49
93-94	Det	84	10	46	56	43	3	0	200	5.0	4	14	18	0	2	2	13	26	0	13	0	0	6	0	.67
94-95	Det	43	10	16	26	15	0	0	90	11.1	7	4	11	0	0	0	3	6	0	3	0	0	1	0	.60
95-96	Det*	81	17	50	67	29	1	1	211	8.1	8	29	37	1	4	5	10	20	0	10	0	1	5	0	.83
96-97	Det	79	15	42	57	11	1	0	214	7.0	8	22	30	0	1	1	11	30	0	10	0	0	8	0	.72
97-98	Det*	80	17	42	59	22	1	1	205	8.3	7	26	33	1	2	3	9	18	0	9	0	0	6	0	.74
98-99	Det	81	14	43	57	14	3	0	205	6.8	6	23	29	2	2	4	7	14	0	7	0	0	2	0	.70
8 Years		612	101	322	423	177	12	3	1449	7.0	48	161	209	4	16	20	78	164	0	77	0	1	48	0	.69
Postseason																									
Year	Tm	GP	G	A	Pts	+/–	GW	OT	S	SPct	G	A	Pts	G	A	Pts	Num	PIM	Maj	Mnr	Fgt	Rgh	HHT	Hat	P/G
91-92	Det	11	1	2	3	-5	0	0	16	6.3	1	1	2	0	0	0	0	0	0	0	0	0	0	0	.27
92-93	Det	7	1	0	1	-2	0	0	8	12.5	1	0	1	0	0	0	0	0	0	0	0	0	0	0	.14
93-94	Det	7	3	2	5	4	0	0	20	15.0	1	1	2	1	0	1	0	0	0	0	0	0	0	0	.71
94-95	Det	18	4	12	16	4	2	1	37	10.8	3	8	11	0	0	0	4	8	0	4	0	0	3	0	.89
95-96	Det	19	5	9	14	2	0	0	50	10.0	1	7	8	0	0	0	5	10	0	5	0	0	3	0	.74
96-97	Det	20	2	6	8	12	0	0	79	2.5	0	4	4	0	0	0	1	2	0	1	0	0	0	0	.40
97-98	Det	22	6	13	19	12	2	0	59	10.2	2	6	8	0	0	0	4	8	0	4	0	0	1	0	.86
98-99	Det	10	2	9	11	0	0	0	29	6.9	2	8	10	0	0	0	2	4	0	2	0	0	0	0	1.10
8 Years		114	24	53	77	27	4	1	298	8.1	11	35	46	1	0	1	16	32	0	16	0	0	7	0	.68

Trevor Linden

(statistical profile on page 338)

Pos: C **Shoots:** R **Ht:** 6'4" **Wt:** 210 **Born:** 4/11/70—Medicine Hat, Alberta **Age:** 29

Overall											Power Play			Shorthand			Penalty							Misc	
Year	Tm	GP	G	A	Pts	+/–	GW	GT	S	SPct	G	A	Pts	G	A	Pts	Num	PIM	Maj	Mnr	Fgt	Rgh	HHT	Hat	P/G
88-89	Van	**80**	30	29	59	-10	2	0	186	16.1	10	–	–	1	–	–	–	41	–	–	–	–	–	2	.74
89-90	Van	73	21	30	51	-17	3	0	171	12.3	6	–	–	2	–	–	–	43	–	–	–	–	–	0	.70
90-91	Van*	80	33	37	70	-25	4	1	229	14.4	16	–	–	2	–	–	–	65	–	–	–	–	–	1	.88
91-92	Van*	80	31	44	75	3	6	1	201	15.4	6	20	26	1	3	4	34	101	3	28	3	7	5	0	.94
92-93	Van	84	33	39	72	19	3	0	209	15.8	8	7	15	0	0	0	32	64	0	32	0	4	7	0	.86
93-94	Van	84	32	29	61	6	3	0	234	13.7	10	10	20	2	0	2	27	73	1	24	1	6	4	0	.73
94-95	Van	48	18	22	40	-5	1	**3**	129	14.0	9	14	23	0	0	0	13	40	2	10	1	2	4	0	.83
95-96	Van	82	33	47	80	6	2	0	202	16.3	12	18	30	1	3	4	21	42	0	21	0	1	9	1	.98
96-97	Van	49	9	31	40	5	2	0	84	10.7	2	6	8	2	1	3	12	27	1	11	1	4	2	0	.82
97-98	2Tm	67	17	21	38	-14	2	0	133	12.8	5	9	14	2	2	4	23	82	4	16	4	0	9	0	.57
98-99	NYI	82	18	29	47	-14	1	0	167	10.8	8	12	20	1	2	3	16	32	0	16	0	3	10	0	.57
97-98	Van	42	7	14	21	-13	1	0	74	9.5	2	6	8	0	1	1	12	49	3	7	3	0	5	0	.50
97-98	NYI	25	10	7	17	-1	1	0	59	16.9	3	3	6	2	1	3	11	33	1	9	1	0	4	0	.68
11 Years		809	275	358	633	-46	29	5	1945	14.1	92	–	–	14	–	–	–	610	–	–	–	–	–	4	.78
Postseason																									
Year	Tm	GP	G	A	Pts	+/–	GW	OT	S	SPct	G	A	Pts	G	A	Pts	Num	PIM	Maj	Mnr	Fgt	Rgh	HHT	Hat	P/G
88-89	Van	7	3	4	7	-1	0	0	11	27.3	2	–	–	1	–	–	4	8	0	4	0	–	–	0	1.00
90-91	Van	6	0	7	7	3	0	0	12	0.0	0	–	–	0	–	–	1	2	0	1	0	–	–	0	1.17
91-92	Van	13	4	8	12	5	1	0	37	10.8	2	3	5	0	0	0	3	6	0	3	0	0	1	0	.92
92-93	Van	12	5	8	13	4	1	0	22	22.7	2	3	5	0	0	0	8	16	0	8	0	2	1	0	1.08
93-94	Van	24	12	13	25	3	1	1	67	17.9	5	6	11	1	0	1	9	18	0	9	0	1	2	0	1.04
94-95	Van	11	2	6	8	-1	0	0	19	10.5	1	3	4	0	0	0	6	12	0	6	0	2	2	0	.73

Postseason																									
Year	**Tm**	**GP**	**G**	**A**	**Pts**	**+/–**	**GW**	**OT**	**S**	**SPct**	**G**	**A**	**Pts**	**G**	**A**	**Pts**	**Num**	**PIM**	**Maj**	**Mnr**	**Fgt**	**Rgh**	**HHT**	**Hat**	**P/G**
95-96	Van	6	4	4	8	-1	0	0	14	28.6	2	3	5	0	0	0	3	6	0	3	0	0	1	1	1.33
7 Years		79	30	50	80	12	3	1	182	16.5	14	–	–	2	–	–	34	68	0	34	0	–	–	1	1.01

Mats Lindgren

(statistical profile on page 338)

Pos: C **Shoots:** L **Ht:** 6'2" **Wt:** 200 **Born:** 10/1/74—Skelleftea, Sweden **Age:** 25

Overall											**Power Play**			**Shorthand**			**Penalty**							**Misc**	
Year	**Tm**	**GP**	**G**	**A**	**Pts**	**+/–**	**GW**	**GT**	**S**	**SPct**	**G**	**A**	**Pts**	**G**	**A**	**Pts**	**Num**	**PIM**	**Maj**	**Mnr**	**Fgt**	**Rgh**	**HHT**	**Hat**	**P/G**
96-97	Edm	69	11	14	25	-7	1	0	71	15.5	2	1	3	3	0	3	6	12	0	6	0	0	3	0	.36
97-98	Edm	82	13	13	26	0	3	0	131	9.9	1	3	4	3	1	4	21	42	0	21	0	0	17	0	.32
98-99	2Tm	60	10	15	25	6	1	0	83	12.0	3	1	4	1	1	2	12	24	0	12	0	0	5	0	.42
98-99	Edm	48	5	12	17	4	0	0	53	9.4	0	0	0	1	1	2	11	22	0	11	0	0	5	0	.35
98-99	NYI	12	5	3	8	2	1	0	30	16.7	3	1	4	0	0	0	1	2	0	1	0	0	0	0	.67
3 Years		211	34	42	76	-1	5	0	285	11.9	6	5	11	7	2	9	39	78	0	39	0	0	25	0	.36
Postseason																									
Year	**Tm**	**GP**	**G**	**A**	**Pts**	**+/–**	**GW**	**OT**	**S**	**SPct**	**G**	**A**	**Pts**	**G**	**A**	**Pts**	**Num**	**PIM**	**Maj**	**Mnr**	**Fgt**	**Rgh**	**HHT**	**Hat**	**P/G**
96-97	Edm	12	0	4	4	-2	0	0	22	0.0	0	0	0	0	0	0	0	0	0	0	0	0	0	0	.33
97-98	Edm	12	1	1	2	0	0	0	16	6.3	0	0	0	0	0	0	5	10	0	5	0	1	0	0	.17
2 Years		24	1	5	6	-2	0	0	38	2.6	0	0	0	0	0	0	5	10	0	5	0	1	0	0	.25

Fredrik Lindquist

Pos: C **Shoots:** L **Ht:** 5'11" **Wt:** 176 **Born:** 6/21/73—Sodertalje, Sweden **Age:** 26

Overall											**Power Play**			**Shorthand**			**Penalty**							**Misc**	
Year	**Tm**	**GP**	**G**	**A**	**Pts**	**+/–**	**GW**	**GT**	**S**	**SPct**	**G**	**A**	**Pts**	**G**	**A**	**Pts**	**Num**	**PIM**	**Maj**	**Mnr**	**Fgt**	**Rgh**	**HHT**	**Hat**	**P/G**
98-99	Edm	8	0	0	0	-2	0	0	6	0.0	0	0	0	0	0	0	1	2	0	1	0	0	0	0	.00

Eric Lindros

(statistical profile on page 338)

Pos: C **Shoots:** R **Ht:** 6'4" **Wt:** 236 **Born:** 2/28/73—London, Ontario **Age:** 26

Overall											**Power Play**			**Shorthand**			**Penalty**							**Misc**	
Year	**Tm**	**GP**	**G**	**A**	**Pts**	**+/–**	**GW**	**GT**	**S**	**SPct**	**G**	**A**	**Pts**	**G**	**A**	**Pts**	**Num**	**PIM**	**Maj**	**Mnr**	**Fgt**	**Rgh**	**HHT**	**Hat**	**P/G**
92-93	Phi	61	41	34	75	28	5	1	180	22.8	8	10	18	1	0	1	58	147	5	51	4	16	8	3	1.23
93-94	Phi*	65	44	53	97	16	9	1	197	22.3	13	14	27	2	1	3	43	103	3	39	3	14	7	1	1.49
94-95	Phi	46	29	41	**70**	27	4	1	144	20.1	7	17	24	0	0	0	27	60	2	25	2	6	8	**3**	**1.52**
95-96	Phi*	73	47	68	115	26	4	0	294	16.0	15	24	39	0	1	1	70	163	5	64	5	13	15	1	1.58
96-97	Phi*	52	32	47	79	31	7	2	198	16.2	9	14	23	0	0	0	54	136	4	48	4	11	6	1	1.52
97-98	Phi*	63	30	41	71	14	4	0	202	14.9	10	14	24	1	0	1	57	134	4	52	4	12	12	1	1.13
98-99	Phi	71	40	53	93	35	2	**3**	242	16.5	10	17	27	1	0	1	50	120	4	45	2	4	16	0	1.31
7 Years		431	263	337	600	177	35	8	1457	18.1	72	110	182	5	2	7	359	863	27	324	24	76	72	10	1.39
Postseason																									
Year	**Tm**	**GP**	**G**	**A**	**Pts**	**+/–**	**GW**	**OT**	**S**	**SPct**	**G**	**A**	**Pts**	**G**	**A**	**Pts**	**Num**	**PIM**	**Maj**	**Mnr**	**Fgt**	**Rgh**	**HHT**	**Hat**	**P/G**
94-95	Phi	12	4	11	15	7	1	1	28	14.3	0	4	4	0	0	0	9	18	0	9	0	0	2	0	1.25
95-96	Phi	12	6	6	12	-1	2	0	46	13.0	3	3	6	0	0	0	16	43	1	14	1	3	3	0	1.00
96-97	Phi	19	12	14	26	7	1	0	71	16.9	4	3	7	0	0	0	20	40	0	20	0	3	3	1	1.37
97-98	Phi	5	1	2	3	-3	0	0	13	7.7	0	1	1	0	0	0	7	17	1	6	1	2	1	0	.60
4 Years		48	23	33	56	10	4	1	158	14.6	7	11	18	0	0	0	52	118	2	49	2	8	9	1	1.17

Bill Lindsay

(statistical profile on page 338)

Pos: LW **Shoots:** L **Ht:** 6'0" **Wt:** 190 **Born:** 5/17/71—Big Fork, Montana **Age:** 28

Overall											**Power Play**			**Shorthand**			**Penalty**							**Misc**	
Year	**Tm**	**GP**	**G**	**A**	**Pts**	**+/–**	**GW**	**GT**	**S**	**SPct**	**G**	**A**	**Pts**	**G**	**A**	**Pts**	**Num**	**PIM**	**Maj**	**Mnr**	**Fgt**	**Rgh**	**HHT**	**Hat**	**P/G**
91-92	Que	23	2	4	6	-6	1	0	35	5.7	0	0	0	0	0	0	7	14	0	7	0	0	4	0	.26
92-93	Que	44	4	9	13	0	0	0	58	6.9	0	0	0	0	0	0	8	16	0	8	0	2	3	0	.30
93-94	Fla	84	6	6	12	-2	0	0	90	6.7	0	0	0	0	0	0	36	97	3	31	2	6	7	0	.14
94-95	Fla	48	10	9	19	1	0	0	63	15.9	0	1	1	1	0	1	20	46	2	18	2	4	4	0	.40
95-96	Fla	73	12	22	34	13	2	0	118	10.2	0	0	0	3	3	6	20	57	3	16	3	3	2	0	.47
96-97	Fla	81	11	23	34	1	3	0	168	6.5	0	0	0	1	3	4	47	120	6	40	6	6	3	0	.42
97-98	Fla	82	12	16	28	-2	5	0	150	8.0	0	0	0	2	1	3	33	80	2	30	1	5	7	0	.34
98-99	Fla	75	12	15	27	-1	2	0	135	8.9	0	0	0	1	0	1	36	92	4	31	4	7	4	0	.36
8 Years		510	69	104	173	4	13	0	817	8.4	0	1	1	8	7	15	207	522	20	181	18	33	34	0	.34

Postseason																									
Year	Tm	GP	G	A	Pts	+/-	GW	OT	S	SPct	G	A	Pts	G	A	Pts	Num	PIM	Maj	Mnr	Fgt	Rgh	HHT	Hat	P/G
95-96	Fla	22	5	5	10	6	1	0	33	15.2	0	0	0	1	0	1	9	18	0	9	0	3	0	0	.45
96-97	Fla	3	0	1	1	0	0	0	4	0.0	0	0	0	0	0	0	4	8	0	4	0	0	0	0	.33
2 Years		25	5	6	11	6	1	0	37	13.5	0	0	0	1	0	1	13	26	0	13	0	3	0	0	.44

Dave Lowry

(statistical profile on page 339)

Pos: LW **Shoots:** L **Ht:** 6'1" **Wt:** 200 **Born:** 2/14/65—Sudbury, Ontario **Age:** 34

Overall											Power Play			Shorthand			Penalty							Misc	
Year	Tm	GP	G	A	Pts	+/-	GW	GT	S	SPct	G	A	Pts	G	A	Pts	Num	PIM	Maj	Mnr	Fgt	Rgh	HHT	Hat	P/G
85-86	Van	73	10	8	18	-21	1	0	66	15.2	1	–	–	0	–	–	–	143	–	–	–	–	–	0	.25
86-87	Van	70	8	10	18	-23	1	0	74	10.8	0	–	–	0	–	–	–	176	–	–	–	–	–	0	.26
87-88	Van	22	1	3	4	-2	0	0	14	7.1	0	–	–	0	–	–	–	38	–	–	–	–	–	0	.18
88-89	StL	21	3	3	6	1	0	0	22	13.6	0	–	–	1	–	–	4	11	1	3	–	–	–	0	.29
89-90	StL	78	19	6	25	1	1	1	98	19.4	0	–	–	2	–	–	–	75	–	–	–	–	–	0	.32
90-91	StL	79	19	21	40	19	5	0	123	15.4	0	–	–	2	–	–	–	168	–	–	–	–	–	0	.51
91-92	StL	75	7	13	20	-11	1	0	85	8.2	0	0	0	0	1	1	27	77	5	21	5	5	6	0	.27
92-93	StL	58	5	8	13	-18	0	0	59	8.5	0	0	0	0	0	0	34	101	3	28	2	12	5	0	.22
93-94	Fla	80	15	22	37	-4	3	1	122	12.3	3	6	9	0	0	0	28	64	0	27	0	10	9	0	.46
94-95	Fla	45	10	10	20	-3	3	0	70	14.3	2	5	7	0	0	0	11	25	1	10	1	1	4	0	.44
95-96	Fla	63	10	14	24	-2	1	0	83	12.0	0	5	5	0	0	0	15	36	2	13	2	3	6	0	.38
96-97	Fla	77	15	14	29	2	2	1	96	15.6	2	3	5	0	0	0	20	51	1	18	1	6	5	0	.38
97-98	2Tm	57	4	4	8	-1	1	0	51	7.8	0	0	0	0	0	0	18	53	3	14	3	1	8	0	.14
98-99	SJ	61	6	9	15	-5	0	1	58	10.3	2	1	3	0	0	0	12	24	0	12	0	3	3	0	.25
97-98	Fla	7	0	0	0	-1	0	0	4	0.0	0	0	0	0	0	0	1	2	0	1	0	0	1	0	.00
97-98	SJ	50	4	4	8	0	1	0	47	8.5	0	0	0	0	0	0	17	51	3	13	3	1	7	0	.16
14 Years		859	132	145	277	-67	19	4	1021	12.9	10	–	–	5	–	–	–	1042	–	–	–	–	–	0	.32

Postseason																									
Year	Tm	GP	G	A	Pts	+/-	GW	OT	S	SPct	G	A	Pts	G	A	Pts	Num	PIM	Maj	Mnr	Fgt	Rgh	HHT	Hat	P/G
85-86	Van	3	0	0	0	-2	0	0	1	0.0	0	0	0	0	0	0	0	0	0	0	0	0	0	0	.00
88-89	StL	10	0	5	5	0	0	0	18	0.0	0	–	–	0	–	–	2	4	0	2	0	–	–	0	.50
89-90	StL	12	2	1	3	-7	0	0	20	10.0	0	–	–	0	–	–	–	39	–	–	–	–	–	0	.25
90-91	StL	13	1	4	5	-6	0	0	21	4.8	0	–	–	0	0	0	–	35	–	–	–	–	–	0	.38
91-92	StL	6	0	1	1	0	0	0	6	0.0	0	0	0	0	0	0	6	20	0	5	0	1	0	0	.17
92-93	StL	11	2	0	2	-1	0	0	15	13.3	0	0	0	1	0	1	7	14	0	7	0	2	1	0	.18
95-96	Fla	22	10	7	17	8	2	1	45	22.2	4	2	6	0	0	0	14	39	1	12	1	5	4	0	.77
96-97	Fla	5	0	0	0	-3	0	0	8	0.0	0	0	0	0	0	0	0	0	0	0	0	0	0	0	.00
97-98	SJ	6	0	0	0	0	0	0	3	0.0	0	0	0	0	0	0	5	18	0	4	0	0	2	0	.00
98-99	SJ	1	0	0	0	0	0	0	0	–	0	0	0	0	0	0	0	0	0	0	0	0	0	0	.00
10 Years		89	15	18	33	-11	2	1	137	10.9	4	–	–	1	–	–	–	169	–	–	–	–	–	0	.37

Craig Ludwig

Pos: D **Shoots:** L **Ht:** 6'3" **Wt:** 220 **Born:** 3/15/61—Rhinelander, Wisconsin **Age:** 38

Overall											Power Play			Shorthand			Penalty							Misc	
Year	Tm	GP	G	A	Pts	+/-	GW	GT	S	SPct	G	A	Pts	G	A	Pts	Num	PIM	Maj	Mnr	Fgt	Rgh	HHT	Hat	P/G
82-83	Mon	**80**	0	25	25	4	0	0	81	0.0	0	–	–	0	–	–	–	59	–	–	–	–	–	0	.31
83-84	Mon	**80**	7	18	25	-10	1	0	116	6.0	0	–	–	0	–	–	–	52	–	–	–	–	–	0	.31
84-85	Mon	72	5	14	19	5	0	0	73	6.8	1	–	–	0	–	–	–	90	–	–	–	–	–	0	.26
85-86	Mon	69	2	4	6	7	0	0	58	3.4	0	–	–	0	–	–	–	63	–	–	–	–	–	0	.09
86-87	Mon	75	4	12	16	3	0	1	55	7.3	0	–	–	0	–	–	–	105	–	–	–	–	–	0	.21
87-88	Mon	74	4	10	14	17	0	0	81	4.9	0	–	–	0	–	–	–	69	–	–	–	–	–	0	.19
88-89	Mon	74	3	13	16	33	1	1	83	3.6	0	–	–	1	–	–	–	73	–	–	–	–	–	0	.22
89-90	Mon	73	1	15	16	24	0	0	49	2.0	0	–	–	0	–	–	–	108	–	–	–	–	–	0	.22
90-91	NYI	75	1	8	9	-24	0	0	46	2.2	0	–	–	0	–	–	–	77	–	–	–	–	–	0	.12
91-92	Min	73	2	9	11	0	0	0	51	3.9	0	0	0	0	0	0	23	54	0	22	0	2	3	0	.15
92-93	Min	78	1	10	11	1	0	0	66	1.5	0	0	0	0	1	1	60	153	3	54	2	5	8	0	.14
93-94	Dal	84	1	13	14	-1	0	0	65	1.5	1	0	1	0	1	1	52	123	1	49	0	14	11	0	.17
94-95	Dal	47	2	7	9	-6	0	0	55	3.6	0	0	0	0	0	0	21	61	1	18	1	3	6	0	.19
95-96	Dal	65	1	2	3	-17	0	0	47	2.1	0	0	0	0	0	0	35	70	0	35	0	9	10	0	.05
96-97	Dal	77	2	11	13	17	1	0	59	3.4	0	0	0	0	1	1	31	62	0	31	0	4	6	0	.17
97-98	Dal	80	0	7	7	21	0	0	46	0.0	0	0	0	0	1	1	56	131	1	53	0	8	18	0	.09
98-99	Dal	80	2	6	8	5	0	0	39	5.1	0	0	0	0	2	2	34	87	1	31	1	3	9	0	.10
17 Years		1256	38	184	222	79	3	2	1070	3.6	2	–	–	1	–	–	–	1437	–	–	–	–	–	0	.18

Postseason																									
Year	Tm	GP	G	A	Pts	+/-	GW	OT	S	SPct	G	A	Pts	G	A	Pts	Num	PIM	Maj	Mnr	Fgt	Rgh	HHT	Hat	P/G
82-83	Mon	3	0	0	0	0	0	0	4	0.0	0	0	0	0	0	0	1	2	0	1	0	–	–	0	.00

Postseason																										
Year	Tm	GP	G	A	Pts	+/–	GW	OT	S	SPct	G	A	Pts	G	A	Pts	Num	PIM	Maj	Mnr	Fgt	Rgh	HHT	Hat	P/G
83-84	Mon	15	0	3	3	5	0	0	14	0.0	0	–	–	0	–	–	–	23	–	–	–	–	–	0	.20
84-85	Mon	12	0	1	1	-7	0	0	13	0.0	0	–	–	0	–	–	3	6	0	3	0	–	–	0	.08
85-86	Mon	20	0	1	1	3	0	0	13	0.0	0	–	–	0	–	–	–	48	–	–	–	–	–	0	.05
86-87	Mon	17	2	3	5	2	1	0	14	14.3	0	–	–	0	–	–	–	30	–	–	–	–	–	0	.29
87-88	Mon	11	1	1	2	1	0	0	7	14.3	0	–	–	0	–	–	3	6	0	3	0	–	–	0	.18
88-89	Mon	21	0	2	2	10	0	0	18	0.0	0	–	–	0	–	–	–	24	–	–	–	–	–	0	.10
89-90	Mon	11	0	1	1	5	0	0	9	0.0	0	–	–	0	0	0	–	16	–	–	–	–	–	0	.09
91-92	Min	7	0	1	1	1	0	0	2	0.0	0	0	0	0	0	0	4	19	1	2	0	0	1	0	.14
93-94	Dal	9	0	3	3	3	0	0	15	0.0	0	0	0	0	0	0	4	8	0	4	0	2	0	0	.33
94-95	Dal	4	0	1	1	5	0	0	2	0.0	0	0	0	0	0	0	1	2	0	1	0	0	0	0	.25
96-97	Dal	7	0	2	2	1	0	0	5	0.0	0	0	0	0	0	0	5	18	0	4	0	0	2	0	.29
97-98	Dal	17	0	1	1	0	0	0	10	0.0	0	0	0	0	0	0	11	22	0	11	0	6	2	0	.06
98-99	Dal	23	1	4	5	2	0	0	6	16.7	0	0	0	0	0	0	10	20	0	10	0	1	2	0	.22
14 Years		177	4	24	28	31	1	0	132	3.0	0	–	–	0	–	–	–	244	–	–	–	–	–	0	.16

Warren Luhning

Pos: RW **Shoots:** R **Ht:** 6'2" **Wt:** 185 **Born:** 7/3/75—Edmonton, Alberta **Age:** 24

		Overall									Power Play			Shorthand			Penalty							Misc	
Year	Tm	GP	G	A	Pts	+/–	GW	GT	S	SPct	G	A	Pts	G	A	Pts	Num	PIM	Maj	Mnr	Fgt	Rgh	HHT	Hat	P/G
97-98	NYI	8	0	0	0	-4	0	0	6	0.0	0	0	0	0	0	0	0	0	0	0	0	0	0	0	.00
98-99	NYI	11	0	0	0	-4	0	0	11	0.0	0	0	0	0	0	0	4	8	0	4	0	2	1	0	.00
2 Years		19	0	0	0	-8	0	0	17	0.0	0	0	0	0	0	0	4	8	0	4	0	2	1	0	.00

Brad Lukowich

Pos: D **Shoots:** R **Ht:** 6'1" **Wt:** 170 **Born:** 8/12/76—Cranbrook, British Columbia **Age:** 23

		Overall									Power Play			Shorthand			Penalty							Misc	
Year	Tm	GP	G	A	Pts	+/–	GW	GT	S	SPct	G	A	Pts	G	A	Pts	Num	PIM	Maj	Mnr	Fgt	Rgh	HHT	Hat	P/G
97-98	Dal	4	0	1	1	-2	0	0	2	0.0	0	0	0	0	0	0	1	2	0	1	0	0	0	0	.25
98-99	Dal	14	1	2	3	3	0	0	8	12.5	0	0	0	0	0	0	4	19	1	2	1	1	0	0	.21
2 Years		18	1	3	4	1	0	0	10	10.0	0	0	0	0	0	0	5	21	1	3	1	1	0	0	.22
Postseason																									
Year	Tm	GP	G	A	Pts	+/–	GW	OT	S	SPct	G	A	Pts	G	A	Pts	Num	PIM	Maj	Mnr	Fgt	Rgh	HHT	Hat	P/G
98-99	Dal	8	0	1	1	3	0	0	6	0.0	0	0	0	0	0	0	2	4	0	2	0	0	1	0	.13

Jyrki Lumme

(statistical profile on page 339)

Pos: D **Shoots:** L **Ht:** 6'1" **Wt:** 207 **Born:** 7/16/67—Tampere, Finland **Age:** 32

		Overall									Power Play			Shorthand			Penalty							Misc	
Year	Tm	GP	G	A	Pts	+/–	GW	GT	S	SPct	G	A	Pts	G	A	Pts	Num	PIM	Maj	Mnr	Fgt	Rgh	HHT	Hat	P/G
88-89	Mon	21	1	3	4	3	0	0	18	5.6	1	–	–	0	–	–	–	10	–	–	–	–	–	0	.19
89-90	2Tm	65	4	26	30	17	1	0	109	3.7	0	–	–	0	–	–	–	49	–	–	–	–	–	0	.46
90-91	Van	80	5	27	32	-15	0	0	157	3.2	1	–	–	0	–	–	–	59	–	–	–	–	–	0	.40
91-92	Van	75	12	32	44	25	1	0	106	11.3	3	17	20	1	1	2	27	65	1	25	1	0	8	0	.59
92-93	Van	74	8	36	44	30	1	0	123	6.5	3	12	15	2	1	3	22	55	1	20	1	4	10	0	.59
93-94	Van	83	13	42	55	3	3	0	161	8.1	1	15	16	3	4	7	25	50	0	25	0	5	13	0	.66
94-95	Van	36	5	12	17	4	1	0	78	6.4	3	3	6	0	2	2	13	26	0	13	0	2	6	0	.47
95-96	Van	80	17	37	54	-9	2	2	192	8.9	8	17	25	0	2	2	25	50	0	25	0	1	14	0	.68
96-97	Van	66	11	24	35	8	2	0	107	10.3	5	10	15	0	1	1	16	32	0	16	0	0	10	0	.53
97-98	Van	74	9	21	30	-25	1	1	117	7.7	4	8	12	0	0	0	17	34	0	17	0	0	10	0	.41
98-99	Pho	60	7	21	28	5	4	0	121	5.8	1	9	10	0	1	1	17	34	0	17	0	0	12	0	.47
89-90	Mon	54	1	19	20	17	0	0	79	1.3	0	–	–	0	–	–	–	41	–	–	–	–	–	0	.37
89-90	Van	11	3	7	10	0	1	0	30	10.0	0	–	–	0	–	–	4	8	0	4	0	–	–	0	.91
11 Years		714	92	281	373	46	16	3	1289	7.1	30	–	–	6	–	–	–	464	–	–	–	–	–	0	.52
Postseason																									
Year	Tm	GP	G	A	Pts	+/–	GW	OT	S	SPct	G	A	Pts	G	A	Pts	Num	PIM	Maj	Mnr	Fgt	Rgh	HHT	Hat	P/G
90-91	Van	6	2	3	5	-4	0	0	7	28.6	1	–	–	1	–	–	0	0	0	0	0	0	0	0	.83
91-92	Van	13	2	3	5	3	1	0	20	10.0	1	2	3	0	0	0	2	4	0	2	0	1	1	0	.38
92-93	Van	12	0	5	5	4	0	0	25	0.0	0	3	3	0	0	0	3	6	0	3	0	1	1	0	.42
93-94	Van	24	2	11	13	8	1	0	53	3.8	2	5	7	0	0	0	8	16	0	8	0	2	3	0	.54
94-95	Van	11	2	6	8	0	0	0	23	8.7	1	2	3	0	2	2	4	8	0	4	0	0	1	0	.73
95-96	Van	6	1	3	4	-1	0	0	13	7.7	1	1	2	0	0	0	1	2	0	1	0	1	0	0	.67
98-99	Pho	7	0	1	1	-2	0	0	8	0.0	0	1	1	0	0	0	3	6	0	3	0	1	1	0	.14
7 Years		79	9	32	41	8	2	0	149	6.0	6	–	–	1	–	–	21	42	0	21	0	6	7	0	.52

Craig MacDonald

Pos: C **Shoots:** L **Ht:** 6'1" **Wt:** 183 **Born:** 4/7/77—Antigonish, Nova Scotia **Age:** 22

Overall											Power Play			Shorthand			Penalty							Misc	
Year	Tm	GP	G	A	Pts	+/-	GW	GT	S	SPct	G	A	Pts	G	A	Pts	Num	PIM	Maj	Mnr	Fgt	Rgh	HHT	Hat	P/G
98-99	Car	11	0	0	0	0	0	0	5	0.0	0	0	0	0	0	0	0	0	0	0	0	0	0	0	.00
Postseason																									
Year	Tm	GP	G	A	Pts	+/-	GW	OT	S	SPct	G	A	Pts	G	A	Pts	Num	PIM	Maj	Mnr	Fgt	Rgh	HHT	Hat	P/G
98-99	Car	1	0	0	0	0	0	0	0	–	0	0	0	0	0	0	0	0	0	0	0	0	0	0	.00

Al MacInnis

(statistical profile on page 339)

Pos: D **Shoots:** R **Ht:** 6'1" **Wt:** 202 **Born:** 7/11/63—Inverness, Nova Scotia **Age:** 36

Overall											Power Play			Shorthand			Penalty							Misc	
Year	Tm	GP	G	A	Pts	+/-	GW	GT	S	SPct	G	A	Pts	G	A	Pts	Num	PIM	Maj	Mnr	Fgt	Rgh	HHT	Hat	P/G
81-82	Cgy	2	0	0	0	0	0	0	2	0.0	0	0	0	0	0	0	0	0	0	0	0	0	0	0	.00
82-83	Cgy	14	1	3	4	0	0	0	7	14.3	0	–	–	0	–	–	3	9	1	2	–	–	–	0	.29
83-84	Cgy	51	11	34	45	0	2	1	160	6.9	7	–	–	0	–	–	21	42	0	21	0	–	–	0	.88
84-85	Cgy*	67	14	52	66	7	0	0	259	5.4	8	–	–	0	–	–	36	75	1	35	–	–	–	0	.99
85-86	Cgy	77	11	57	68	39	0	0	241	4.6	4	–	–	0	–	–	38	76	0	38	0	–	–	0	.88
86-87	Cgy	79	20	56	76	20	2	0	262	7.6	7	–	–	0	–	–	47	97	1	46	–	–	–	0	.96
87-88	Cgy*	**80**	25	58	83	13	2	0	245	10.2	7	–	–	2	–	–	50	114	2	47	–	–	–	0	1.04
88-89	Cgy	79	16	58	74	38	3	0	277	5.8	8	–	–	0	–	–	59	126	0	58	0	–	–	0	.94
89-90	Cgy*	79	28	62	90	20	3	0	304	9.2	14	–	–	1	–	–	41	82	0	41	0	–	–	0	1.14
90-91	Cgy*	78	28	75	103	42	1	1	305	9.2	17	–	–	0	–	–	41	90	0	40	0	–	–	0	1.32
91-92	Cgy*	72	20	57	77	13	0	1	304	6.6	11	37	48	0	1	1	36	83	1	34	1	3	15	1	1.07
92-93	Cgy	50	11	43	54	15	4	0	201	5.5	7	27	34	0	2	2	29	61	1	28	1	2	11	0	1.08
93-94	Cgy*	75	28	54	82	35	5	0	324	8.6	12	34	46	1	2	3	38	95	1	35	0	1	18	0	1.09
94-95	StL	32	8	20	28	19	0	0	110	7.3	2	10	12	0	1	1	16	43	1	14	0	4	4	0	.88
95-96	StL*	82	17	44	61	5	1	1	317	5.4	9	25	34	1	1	2	44	88	0	44	0	1	22	0	.74
96-97	StL*	72	13	30	43	2	1	0	296	4.4	6	11	17	1	2	3	31	65	1	30	1	6	19	1	.60
97-98	StL*	71	19	30	49	6	2	0	227	8.4	9	17	26	1	1	2	40	80	0	40	0	3	18	0	.69
98-99	StL	82	20	42	62	33	2	2	314	6.4	11	26	37	1	2	3	35	70	0	35	0	1	14	1	.76
18 Years		1142	290	775	1065	307	28	6	4155	7.0	139	–	–	8	–	–	605	1296	10	588	–	–	–	3	.93
Postseason																									
Year	Tm	GP	G	A	Pts	+/-	GW	OT	S	SPct	G	A	Pts	G	A	Pts	Num	PIM	Maj	Mnr	Fgt	Rgh	HHT	Hat	P/G
83-84	Cgy	11	2	12	14	-1	1	0	39	5.1	2	–	–	0	–	–	5	13	1	4	–	–	–	0	1.27
84-85	Cgy	4	1	2	3	-1	0	0	13	7.7	1	–	–	0	–	–	4	8	0	4	0	–	–	0	.75
85-86	Cgy	21	4	15	19	11	0	0	79	5.1	2	–	–	0	–	–	–	30	–	–	–	–	–	0	.90
86-87	Cgy	4	1	0	1	-1	0	0	10	10.0	1	0	1	0	0	0	0	0	0	0	0	0	0	0	.25
87-88	Cgy	7	3	6	9	0	0	0	28	10.7	2	–	–	0	–	–	–	18	–	–	–	–	–	0	1.29
88-89	Cgy	22	7	24	31	6	4	1	69	10.1	5	–	–	0	–	–	–	46	–	–	–	–	–	0	1.41
89-90	Cgy	6	2	3	5	1	0	0	19	10.5	1	–	–	0	–	–	4	8	0	4	0	–	–	0	.83
90-91	Cgy	7	2	3	5	-5	0	0	25	8.0	2	–	–	0	0	0	4	8	0	4	0	–	–	0	.71
92-93	Cgy	6	1	6	7	-4	0	0	25	4.0	1	4	5	0	0	0	5	10	0	5	0	2	2	0	1.17
93-94	Cgy	7	2	6	8	5	0	0	32	6.3	1	2	3	0	0	0	6	12	0	6	0	1	3	0	1.14
94-95	StL	7	1	5	6	-3	0	0	22	4.5	0	5	5	0	0	0	5	10	0	5	0	0	1	0	.86
95-96	StL	13	3	4	7	2	0	0	48	6.3	1	4	5	0	0	0	10	20	0	10	0	1	3	0	.54
96-97	StL	6	1	2	3	-1	0	0	22	4.5	1	2	3	0	0	0	2	4	0	2	0	0	1	0	.50
97-98	StL	8	2	6	8	1	0	0	27	7.4	1	3	4	0	0	0	6	12	0	6	0	0	1	0	1.00
98-99	StL	13	4	8	12	-2	0	0	66	6.1	2	6	8	0	0	0	10	20	0	10	0	0	7	0	.92
15 Years		142	36	102	138	8	5	1	524	6.9	23	–	–	0	–	–	–	219	–	–	–	–	–	0	.97

John MacLean

(statistical profile on page 339)

Pos: RW **Shoots:** R **Ht:** 6'0" **Wt:** 200 **Born:** 11/20/64—Oshawa, Ontario **Age:** 35

Overall											Power Play			Shorthand			Penalty							Misc	
Year	Tm	GP	G	A	Pts	+/-	GW	GT	S	SPct	G	A	Pts	G	A	Pts	Num	PIM	Maj	Mnr	Fgt	Rgh	HHT	Hat	P/G
83-84	NJ	23	1	0	1	-7	0	0	22	4.5	0	0	0	0	0	0	–	10	–	–	–	–	–	0	.04
84-85	NJ	61	13	20	33	-11	4	1	92	14.1	1	–	–	0	–	–	–	44	–	–	–	–	–	0	.54
85-86	NJ	74	21	36	57	-3	4	0	139	15.1	1	–	–	0	–	–	–	112	–	–	–	–	–	0	.77
86-87	NJ	80	31	36	67	-23	4	0	197	15.7	9	–	–	0	–	–	–	120	–	–	–	–	–	0	.84
87-88	NJ	76	23	16	39	-10	4	0	204	11.3	12	–	–	0	–	–	–	147	–	–	–	–	–	1	.51
88-89	NJ*	74	42	45	87	26	4	2	266	15.8	14	16	30	0	0	0	–	122	–	–	–	–	–	3	1.18
89-90	NJ	**80**	41	38	79	17	11	0	322	12.7	10	10	20	3	1	4	–	80	–	–	–	–	–	0	.99
90-91	NJ*	78	45	33	78	8	7	2	292	15.4	19	7	26	2	2	4	–	150	–	–	–	–	–	2	1.00
91-92	Did Not Play in NHL																								
92-93	NJ	80	24	24	48	-6	3	0	195	12.3	7	5	12	1	0	1	44	102	2	41	2	6	11	0	.60

Overall											Power Play			Shorthand			Penalty							Misc	
Year	Tm	GP	G	A	Pts	+/–	GW	GT	S	SPct	G	A	Pts	G	A	Pts	Num	PIM	Maj	Mnr	Fgt	Rgh	HHT	Hat	P/G
93-94	NJ	80	37	33	70	30	4	0	277	13.4	8	11	19	0	1	1	38	95	1	35	1	6	11	0	.88
94-95	NJ	46	17	12	29	13	0	0	139	12.2	2	6	8	1	0	1	12	32	0	11	0	3	3	0	.63
95-96	NJ	76	20	28	48	3	3	0	237	8.4	3	12	15	3	1	4	36	91	1	33	1	7	12	0	.63
96-97	NJ	80	29	25	54	11	6	0	254	11.4	5	3	8	0	0	0	23	49	1	22	1	6	4	0	.68
97-98	2Tm	77	16	27	43	-6	3	1	213	7.5	6	9	15	0	1	1	21	42	0	21	0	4	12	0	.56
98-99	NYR	82	28	27	55	5	2	0	231	12.1	11	7	18	1	2	3	19	46	0	18	0	0	10	0	.67
97-98	NJ	26	3	8	11	-6	1	0	74	4.1	1	3	4	0	0	0	7	14	0	7	0	2	2	0	.42
97-98	SJ	51	13	19	32	0	2	1	139	9.4	5	6	11	0	1	1	14	28	0	14	0	2	10	0	.63
15 Years		1067	388	400	788	47	59	6	3080	12.6	108	–	–	11	–	–	–	1242	–	–	–	–	–	6	.74
Postseason																									
Year	Tm	GP	G	A	Pts	+/–	GW	OT	S	SPct	G	A	Pts	G	A	Pts	Num	PIM	Maj	Mnr	Fgt	Rgh	HHT	Hat	P/G
87-88	NJ	20	7	11	18	2	2	0	50	14.0	2	–	–	0	–	–	–	60	–	–	–	–	–	0	.90
89-90	NJ	6	4	1	5	-1	0	0	22	18.2	2	–	–	1	–	–	–	12	–	–	–	–	–	0	.83
90-91	NJ	7	5	3	8	2	0	0	31	16.1	1	–	–	0	–	–	–	20	–	–	–	–	–	0	1.14
92-93	NJ	5	0	1	1	-5	0	0	9	0.0	0	0	0	0	0	0	5	10	0	5	0	0	0	0	.20
93-94	NJ	20	6	10	16	-2	1	0	65	9.2	2	5	7	0	0	0	7	22	0	6	0	1	2	0	.80
94-95	NJ	20	5	13	18	8	0	0	57	8.8	2	3	5	0	0	0	7	14	0	7	0	0	1	0	.90
96-97	NJ	10	4	5	9	1	1	0	32	12.5	2	1	3	1	0	1	2	4	0	2	0	0	1	0	.90
97-98	SJ	6	2	3	5	1	0	0	18	11.1	1	2	3	0	0	0	2	4	0	2	0	0	1	0	.83
8 Years		94	33	47	80	6	4	0	284	11.6	12	–	–	2	–	–	–	146	–	–	–	–	–	0	.85

Jamie Macoun

(statistical profile on page 340)

Pos: D **Shoots:** L **Ht:** 6'2" **Wt:** 196 **Born:** 8/17/61—Newmarket, Ontario **Age:** 38

Overall											Power Play			Shorthand			Penalty							Misc	
Year	Tm	GP	G	A	Pts	+/–	GW	GT	S	SPct	G	A	Pts	G	A	Pts	Num	PIM	Maj	Mnr	Fgt	Rgh	HHT	Hat	P/G
82-83	Cgy	22	1	4	5	3	0	0	18	5.6	0	–	–	0	–	–	7	25	1	5	–	–	–	0	.23
83-84	Cgy	72	9	23	32	3	0	2	165	5.5	0	–	–	1	–	–	32	97	3	26	–	–	–	0	.44
84-85	Cgy	70	9	30	39	44	2	0	129	7.0	0	–	–	0	–	–	28	67	1	26	–	–	–	0	.56
85-86	Cgy	77	11	21	32	14	1	0	133	8.3	0	–	–	2	–	–	39	81	1	38	–	–	–	0	.42
86-87	Cgy	79	7	33	40	33	0	0	137	5.1	1	–	–	0	–	–	47	111	3	43	–	–	–	0	.51
87-88												Did Not Play in NHL													
88-89	Cgy	72	8	19	27	40	2	0	89	9.0	0	–	–	0	–	–	27	76	2	23	–	–	–	0	.38
89-90	Cgy	78	8	27	35	34	1	0	120	6.7	1	–	–	0	–	–	35	70	0	35	0	–	–	0	.45
90-91	Cgy	79	7	15	22	29	0	0	117	6.0	1	–	–	1	–	–	38	84	0	37	0	–	–	0	.28
91-92	2Tm	76	5	25	30	10	0	0	129	3.9	3	5	8	0	0	0	27	71	3	23	2	0	8	0	.39
92-93	Tor	77	4	15	19	3	1	0	114	3.5	2	3	5	0	0	0	26	55	1	25	1	3	7	0	.25
93-94	Tor	82	3	27	30	-5	1	0	122	2.5	1	5	6	0	1	1	37	115	3	30	1	7	4	0	.37
94-95	Tor	46	2	8	10	-6	0	0	84	2.4	1	0	1	0	0	0	28	75	1	25	1	4	8	0	.22
95-96	Tor	82	0	8	8	2	0	0	74	0.0	0	0	0	0	1	1	38	87	1	36	0	9	6	0	.10
96-97	Tor	73	1	10	11	-14	1	0	64	1.6	0	0	0	0	1	1	29	93	1	24	1	3	9	0	.15
97-98	2Tm	74	0	7	7	-17	0	0	78	0.0	0	0	0	0	0	0	27	65	1	25	1	1	6	0	.09
98-99	Det	69	1	10	11	-1	0	0	62	1.6	0	0	0	0	0	0	18	36	0	18	0	2	7	0	.16
91-92	Cgy	37	2	12	14	10	0	0	58	3.4	1	0	1	0	0	0	18	53	3	14	2	0	4	0	.38
91-92	Tor	39	3	13	16	0	0	0	71	4.2	2	5	7	0	0	0	9	18	0	9	0	0	4	0	.41
97-98	Tor	67	0	7	7	-17	0	0	67	0.0	0	0	0	0	0	0	26	63	1	24	1	1	6	0	.10
97-98	Det	7	0	0	0	0	0	0	11	0.0	0	0	0	0	0	0	1	2	0	1	0	0	0	0	.00
16 Years		1128	76	282	358	172	9	2	1635	4.6	10	–	–	4	–	–	483	1208	22	439	–	–	–	0	.32
Postseason																									
Year	Tm	GP	G	A	Pts	+/–	GW	OT	S	SPct	G	A	Pts	G	A	Pts	Num	PIM	Maj	Mnr	Fgt	Rgh	HHT	Hat	P/G
82-83	Cgy	9	0	2	2	-6	0	0	5	0.0	0	–	–	0	–	–	4	8	0	4	0	–	–	0	.22
83-84	Cgy	11	1	0	1	-3	0	0	32	3.1	1	0	1	0	0	0	0	0	0	0	0	0	0	0	.09
84-85	Cgy	4	1	0	1	-2	0	0	12	8.3	0	0	0	0	0	0	2	4	0	2	0	–	–	0	.25
85-86	Cgy	22	1	6	7	8	0	0	42	2.4	0	–	–	0	–	–	–	23	–	–	–	–	–	0	.32
86-87	Cgy	3	0	1	1	-2	0	0	5	0.0	0	–	–	0	–	–	4	8	0	4	0	–	–	0	.33
88-89	Cgy	22	3	6	9	11	1	0	27	11.1	0	–	–	0	–	–	–	30	–	–	–	–	–	0	.41
89-90	Cgy	6	0	3	3	2	0	0	5	0.0	0	–	–	0	–	–	–	10	–	–	–	–	–	0	.50
90-91	Cgy	7	0	1	1	1	0	0	8	0.0	0	–	–	0	0	0	2	4	0	2	0	–	–	0	.14
92-93	Tor	21	0	6	6	7	0	0	43	0.0	0	1	1	0	0	0	18	36	0	18	0	3	1	0	.29
93-94	Tor	18	1	1	2	-4	0	0	35	2.9	0	1	1	0	0	0	6	12	0	6	0	1	1	0	.11
94-95	Tor	7	1	2	3	0	0	0	15	6.7	0	1	1	0	0	0	4	8	0	4	0	1	1	0	.43
95-96	Tor	6	0	2	2	3	0	0	10	0.0	0	0	0	0	0	0	4	8	0	4	0	1	1	0	.33
97-98	Det	22	2	2	4	3	2	0	21	9.5	0	0	0	0	0	0	9	18	0	9	0	0	1	0	.18
98-99	Det	1	0	0	0	-1	0	0	1	0.0	0	0	0	0	0	0	0	0	0	0	0	0	0	0	.00
14 Years		159	10	32	42	17	3	0	261	3.8	1	–	–	0	–	–	–	169	–	–	–	–	–	0	.26

John Madden

Pos: LW **Shoots:** L **Ht:** 5'11" **Wt:** 185 **Born:** 5/4/75—Barrie, Ontario **Age:** 24

Overall											Power Play			Shorthand			Penalty							Misc	
Year	Tm	GP	G	A	Pts	+/–	GW	GT	S	SPct	G	A	Pts	G	A	Pts	Num	PIM	Maj	Mnr	Fgt	Rgh	HHT	Hat	P/G
98-99	NJ	4	0	1	1	-2	0	0	4	0.0	0	1	1	0	0	0	0	0	0	0	0	0	0	0	.25

Adam Mair

Pos: C **Shoots:** R **Ht:** 6'0" **Wt:** 189 **Born:** 2/15/79—Hamilton, Ontario **Age:** 20

Overall											Power Play			Shorthand			Penalty							Misc	
Year	Tm	GP	G	A	Pts	+/–	GW	GT	S	SPct	G	A	Pts	G	A	Pts	Num	PIM	Maj	Mnr	Fgt	Rgh	HHT	Hat	P/G
98-99	Did Not Play in Regular Season																								
Postseason																									
Year	Tm	GP	G	A	Pts	+/–	GW	OT	S	SPct	G	A	Pts	G	A	Pts	Num	PIM	Maj	Mnr	Fgt	Rgh	HHT	Hat	P/G
98-99	Tor	5	1	0	1	-1	0	0	3	33.3	0	0	0	0	0	0	3	14	0	2	0	1	0	0	.20

Vladimir Malakhov

(statistical profile on page 340)

Pos: D **Shoots:** R **Ht:** 6'4" **Wt:** 227 **Born:** 8/30/68—Ekaterinburg, USSR **Age:** 31

Overall											Power Play			Shorthand			Penalty							Misc	
Year	Tm	GP	G	A	Pts	+/–	GW	GT	S	SPct	G	A	Pts	G	A	Pts	Num	PIM	Maj	Mnr	Fgt	Rgh	HHT	Hat	P/G
92-93	NYI	64	14	38	52	14	0	0	178	7.9	7	15	22	0	0	0	28	59	1	27	1	6	12	0	.81
93-94	NYI	76	10	47	57	29	2	0	235	4.3	4	23	27	0	0	0	33	80	2	30	2	2	12	0	.75
94-95	2Tm	40	4	17	21	-3	0	0	91	4.4	1	10	11	0	0	0	16	46	2	13	1	0	7	0	.53
95-96	Mon	61	5	23	28	7	0	0	122	4.1	2	12	14	0	1	1	24	79	5	17	4	0	8	0	.46
96-97	Mon	65	10	20	30	3	1	0	177	5.6	5	9	14	0	1	1	16	43	1	14	1	2	6	0	.46
97-98	Mon	74	13	31	44	16	2	0	166	7.8	8	17	25	0	1	1	35	70	0	35	0	9	8	1	.59
98-99	Mon	62	13	21	34	-7	3	0	143	9.1	8	8	16	0	1	1	33	77	1	31	1	3	8	0	.55
94-95	NYI	26	3	13	16	-1	0	0	61	4.9	1	7	8	0	0	0	9	32	2	6	1	0	5	0	.62
94-95	Mon	14	1	4	5	-2	0	0	30	3.3	0	3	3	0	0	0	7	14	0	7	0	0	2	0	.36
7 Years		442	69	197	266	59	8	0	1112	6.2	35	94	129	0	4	4	185	454	12	167	10	22	61	1	.60
Postseason																									
Year	Tm	GP	G	A	Pts	+/–	GW	OT	S	SPct	G	A	Pts	G	A	Pts	Num	PIM	Maj	Mnr	Fgt	Rgh	HHT	Hat	P/G
92-93	NYI	17	3	6	9	-3	0	0	53	5.7	1	4	5	0	0	0	6	12	0	6	0	2	3	0	.53
93-94	NYI	4	0	0	0	-5	0	0	7	0.0	0	0	0	0	0	0	3	6	0	3	0	0	3	0	.00
96-97	Mon	5	0	0	0	-3	0	0	12	0.0	0	0	0	0	0	0	3	6	0	3	0	0	0	0	.00
97-98	Mon	9	3	4	7	-3	0	0	19	15.8	2	1	3	0	0	0	5	10	0	5	0	0	1	0	.78
4 Years		35	6	10	16	-14	0	0	91	6.6	3	5	8	0	0	0	17	34	0	17	0	2	7	0	.46

Stewart Malgunas

Pos: D **Shoots:** L **Ht:** 6'0" **Wt:** 200 **Born:** 4/21/70—Prince George, British Columbia **Age:** 29

Overall											Power Play			Shorthand			Penalty							Misc	
Year	Tm	GP	G	A	Pts	+/–	GW	GT	S	SPct	G	A	Pts	G	A	Pts	Num	PIM	Maj	Mnr	Fgt	Rgh	HHT	Hat	P/G
93-94	Phi	67	1	3	4	2	0	0	54	1.9	0	0	0	0	0	0	36	86	2	33	2	1	16	0	.06
94-95	Phi	4	0	0	0	-1	0	0	1	0.0	0	0	0	0	0	0	2	4	0	2	0	0	2	0	.00
95-96	2Tm	30	0	1	1	-10	0	0	13	0.0	0	0	0	0	0	0	16	32	0	16	0	2	7	0	.03
96-97	Was	6	0	0	0	2	0	0	3	0.0	0	0	0	0	0	0	1	2	0	1	0	0	0	0	.00
97-98	Was	8	0	0	0	1	0	0	5	0.0	0	0	0	0	0	0	6	12	0	6	0	0	2	0	.00
98-99	Was	10	0	0	0	-5	0	0	2	0.0	0	0	0	0	0	0	3	6	0	3	0	0	1	0	.00
95-96	Wpg	29	0	1	1	-10	0	0	13	0.0	0	0	0	0	0	0	16	32	0	16	0	2	7	0	.03
95-96	Was	1	0	0	0	0	0	0	0	–	0	0	0	0	0	0	0	0	0	0	0	0	0	0	.00
6 Years		125	1	4	5	-11	0	0	78	1.3	0	0	0	0	0	0	64	142	2	61	2	3	28	0	.04

Manny Malhotra

(statistical profile on page 340)

Pos: C **Shoots:** L **Ht:** 6'1" **Wt:** 210 **Born:** 5/18/80—Mississauga, Ontario **Age:** 19

Overall											Power Play			Shorthand			Penalty							Misc	
Year	Tm	GP	G	A	Pts	+/–	GW	GT	S	SPct	G	A	Pts	G	A	Pts	Num	PIM	Maj	Mnr	Fgt	Rgh	HHT	Hat	P/G
98-99	NYR	73	8	8	16	-2	2	0	61	13.1	1	0	1	0	0	0	5	13	1	4	1	0	2	0	.22

Marek Malik

(statistical profile on page 340)

Pos: D **Shoots:** L **Ht:** 6'5" **Wt:** 190 **Born:** 6/24/75—Ostrava, Czechoslovakia **Age:** 24

Overall											Power Play			Shorthand			Penalty							Misc	
Year	Tm	GP	G	A	Pts	+/-	GW	GT	S	SPct	G	A	Pts	G	A	Pts	Num	PIM	Maj	Mnr	Fgt	Rgh	HHT	Hat	P/G
94-95	Har	1	0	1	1	1	0	0	0	–	0	0	0	0	0	0	0	0	0	0	0	0	0	0	1.00
95-96	Har	7	0	0	0	-3	0	0	2	0.0	0	0	0	0	0	0	2	4	0	2	0	0	2	0	.00
96-97	Har	47	1	5	6	5	1	0	33	3.0	0	0	0	0	0	0	25	50	0	25	0	1	12	0	.13
97-98											Did Not Play in NHL														
98-99	Car	52	2	9	11	-6	0	0	36	5.6	1	1	2	0	1	1	18	36	0	18	0	2	2	0	.21
4 Years		107	3	15	18	-3	1	0	71	4.2	1	1	2	0	1	1	45	90	0	45	0	3	16	0	.17

Postseason

Year	Tm	GP	G	A	Pts	+/-	GW	OT	S	SPct	G	A	Pts	G	A	Pts	Num	PIM	Maj	Mnr	Fgt	Rgh	HHT	Hat	P/G
98-99	Car	4	0	0	0	-2	0	0	0	–	0	0	0	0	0	0	2	4	0	2	0	2	0	0	.00

Dean Malkoc

Pos: D **Shoots:** L **Ht:** 6'3" **Wt:** 200 **Born:** 1/26/70—Vancouver, British Columbia **Age:** 29

Overall											Power Play			Shorthand			Penalty							Misc	
Year	Tm	GP	G	A	Pts	+/-	GW	GT	S	SPct	G	A	Pts	G	A	Pts	Num	PIM	Maj	Mnr	Fgt	Rgh	HHT	Hat	P/G
95-96	Van	41	0	2	2	-10	0	0	8	0.0	0	0	0	0	0	0	45	136	10	33	10	6	8	0	.05
96-97	Bos	33	0	0	0	-14	0	0	7	0.0	0	0	0	0	0	0	22	70	6	15	6	8	1	0	.00
97-98	Bos	40	1	0	1	-12	0	0	15	6.7	0	0	0	0	0	0	30	86	6	23	6	6	6	0	.03
98-99	NYI	2	0	1	1	3	0	0	1	0.0	0	0	0	0	0	0	2	7	1	1	1	0	0	0	.50
4 Years		116	1	3	4	-33	0	0	31	3.2	0	0	0	0	0	0	99	299	23	72	23	20	15	0	.03

Kirk Maltby

(statistical profile on page 341)

Pos: RW **Shoots:** R **Ht:** 6'0" **Wt:** 200 **Born:** 12/22/72—Guelph, Ontario **Age:** 27

Overall											Power Play			Shorthand			Penalty							Misc	
Year	Tm	GP	G	A	Pts	+/-	GW	GT	S	SPct	G	A	Pts	G	A	Pts	Num	PIM	Maj	Mnr	Fgt	Rgh	HHT	Hat	P/G
93-94	Edm	68	11	8	19	-2	1	0	89	12.4	0	0	0	1	0	1	34	74	2	32	2	14	5	0	.28
94-95	Edm	47	8	3	11	-11	1	1	73	11.0	0	1	1	2	0	2	23	49	1	22	1	10	4	0	.23
95-96	2Tm	55	3	6	9	-16	1	0	55	5.5	0	2	2	0	0	0	24	67	1	21	1	5	5	0	.16
96-97	Det	66	3	5	8	3	0	0	62	4.8	0	0	0	0	1	1	25	75	3	20	2	7	1	0	.12
97-98	Det	65	14	9	23	11	3	0	106	13.2	2	0	2	1	0	1	32	89	3	27	3	12	3	1	.35
98-99	Det	53	8	6	14	-6	2	0	76	10.5	0	1	1	1	0	1	17	34	0	17	0	6	3	0	.26
95-96	Edm	49	2	6	8	-16	1	0	51	3.9	0	2	2	0	0	0	21	61	1	18	1	4	5	0	.16
95-96	Det	6	1	0	1	0	0	0	4	25.0	0	0	0	0	0	0	3	6	0	3	0	1	0	0	.17
6 Years		354	47	37	84	-21	8	1	461	10.2	2	4	6	5	1	6	155	388	10	139	9	54	21	1	.24

Postseason

Year	Tm	GP	G	A	Pts	+/-	GW	OT	S	SPct	G	A	Pts	G	A	Pts	Num	PIM	Maj	Mnr	Fgt	Rgh	HHT	Hat	P/G
95-96	Det	8	0	1	1	0	0	0	5	0.0	0	0	0	0	0	0	2	4	0	2	0	1	0	0	.13
96-97	Det	20	5	2	7	6	1	0	35	14.3	0	0	0	1	0	1	12	24	0	12	0	4	1	0	.35
97-98	Det	22	3	1	4	2	0	0	31	9.7	0	0	0	1	1	2	15	30	0	15	0	4	2	0	.18
98-99	Det	10	1	0	1	-2	1	1	13	7.7	0	0	0	0	0	0	4	8	0	4	0	2	1	0	.10
4 Years		60	9	4	13	6	2	1	84	10.7	0	0	0	2	1	3	33	66	0	33	0	11	4	0	.22

Kent Manderville

(statistical profile on page 341)

Pos: LW **Shoots:** L **Ht:** 6'3" **Wt:** 200 **Born:** 4/12/71—Edmonton, Alberta **Age:** 28

Overall											Power Play			Shorthand			Penalty							Misc	
Year	Tm	GP	G	A	Pts	+/-	GW	GT	S	SPct	G	A	Pts	G	A	Pts	Num	PIM	Maj	Mnr	Fgt	Rgh	HHT	Hat	P/G
91-92	Tor	15	0	4	4	1	0	0	14	0.0	0	0	0	0	0	0	0	0	0	0	0	0	0	0	.27
92-93	Tor	18	1	1	2	-9	1	0	15	6.7	0	0	0	0	0	0	3	17	1	1	0	0	0	0	.11
93-94	Tor	67	7	9	16	5	1	0	81	8.6	0	0	0	0	0	0	22	63	1	19	0	8	6	0	.24
94-95	Tor	36	0	1	1	-2	0	0	43	0.0	0	0	0	0	0	0	11	22	0	11	0	3	5	0	.03
95-96	Edm	37	3	5	8	-5	0	0	63	4.8	0	0	0	2	2	4	12	38	2	9	1	0	5	0	.22
96-97	Har	44	6	5	11	3	1	0	51	11.8	0	0	0	0	1	1	9	18	0	9	0	3	2	1	.25
97-98	Car	77	4	4	8	-6	0	0	80	5.0	0	0	0	0	1	1	14	31	1	13	1	1	6	0	.10
98-99	Car	81	5	11	16	9	0	0	71	7.0	0	0	0	0	0	0	19	38	0	19	0	3	8	0	.20
8 Years		375	26	40	66	-4	3	0	418	6.2	0	0	0	2	4	6	90	227	5	81	2	18	32	1	.18

Postseason

Year	Tm	GP	G	A	Pts	+/-	GW	OT	S	SPct	G	A	Pts	G	A	Pts	Num	PIM	Maj	Mnr	Fgt	Rgh	HHT	Hat	P/G
92-93	Tor	18	1	0	1	-1	0	0	17	5.9	0	0	0	0	0	0	4	8	0	4	0	2	1	0	.06
93-94	Tor	12	1	0	1	-1	0	0	13	7.7	0	0	0	1	0	1	2	4	0	2	0	0	1	0	.08
94-95	Tor	7	0	0	0	-3	0	0	6	0.0	0	0	0	0	0	0	3	6	0	3	0	0	1	0	.00

Postseason																									
Year	Tm	GP	G	A	Pts	+/-	GW	OT	S	SPct	G	A	Pts	G	A	Pts	Num	PIM	Maj	Mnr	Fgt	Rgh	HHT	Hat	P/G
98-99	Car	6	0	0	0	0	0	0	6	0.0	0	0	0	0	0	0	1	2	0	1	0	1	0	0	.00
4 Years		43	2	0	2	-5	0	0	42	4.8	0	0	0	1	0	1	10	20	0	10	0	3	3	0	.05

Mike Maneluk

(statistical profile on page 341)

Pos: RW **Shoots:** R **Ht:** 5'11" **Wt:** 190 **Born:** 10/1/73—Winnipeg, Manitoba **Age:** 26

Overall											Power Play			Shorthand			Penalty							Misc	
Year	Tm	GP	G	A	Pts	+/-	GW	GT	S	SPct	G	A	Pts	G	A	Pts	Num	PIM	Maj	Mnr	Fgt	Rgh	HHT	Hat	P/G
98-99	3Tm	45	6	9	15	5	1	0	55	10.9	1	1	2	0	0	0	10	20	0	10	0	3	2	0	.33
98-99	Phi	13	2	6	8	4	0	0	23	8.7	0	1	1	0	0	0	4	8	0	4	0	1	1	0	.62
98-99	Chi	28	4	3	7	2	1	0	29	13.8	1	0	1	0	0	0	4	8	0	4	0	2	0	0	.25
98-99	NYR	4	0	0	0	-1	0	0	3	0.0	0	0	0	0	0	0	2	4	0	2	0	0	1	0	.00

Cameron Mann

Pos: RW **Shoots:** R **Ht:** 6'0" **Wt:** 194 **Born:** 4/20/77—Thompson, Manitoba **Age:** 22

Overall											Power Play			Shorthand			Penalty							Misc	
Year	Tm	GP	G	A	Pts	+/-	GW	GT	S	SPct	G	A	Pts	G	A	Pts	Num	PIM	Maj	Mnr	Fgt	Rgh	HHT	Hat	P/G
97-98	Bos	9	0	1	1	1	0	0	6	0.0	0	1	1	0	0	0	2	4	0	2	0	1	1	0	.11
98-99	Bos	33	5	2	7	0	1	1	42	11.9	1	0	1	0	0	0	7	17	1	6	1	4	2	0	.21
2 Years		42	5	3	8	1	1	1	48	10.4	1	1	2	0	0	0	9	21	1	8	1	5	3	0	.19
Postseason																									
Year	Tm	GP	G	A	Pts	+/-	GW	OT	S	SPct	G	A	Pts	G	A	Pts	Num	PIM	Maj	Mnr	Fgt	Rgh	HHT	Hat	P/G
98-99	Bos	1	0	0	0	0	0	0	0	–	0	0	0	0	0	0	0	0	0	0	0	0	0	0	.00

Dave Manson

(statistical profile on page 341)

Pos: D **Shoots:** L **Ht:** 6'2" **Wt:** 219 **Born:** 1/27/67—Prince Albert, Saskatchewan **Age:** 32

Overall											Power Play			Shorthand			Penalty							Misc	
Year	Tm	GP	G	A	Pts	+/-	GW	GT	S	SPct	G	A	Pts	G	A	Pts	Num	PIM	Maj	Mnr	Fgt	Rgh	HHT	Hat	P/G
86-87	Chi	63	1	8	9	-2	0	0	42	2.4	0	–	–	0	–	–	–	146	–	–	–	–	–	0	.14
87-88	Chi	54	1	6	7	-12	0	0	47	2.1	0	–	–	0	–	–	–	185	–	–	–	–	–	0	.13
88-89	Chi*	79	18	36	54	5	0	1	224	8.0	8	–	–	1	–	–	–	352	–	–	–	–	–	0	.68
89-90	Chi	59	5	23	28	4	1	0	126	4.0	1	–	–	0	–	–	–	301	–	–	–	–	–	0	.47
90-91	Chi	75	14	15	29	20	2	0	154	9.1	6	–	–	1	–	–	–	191	–	–	–	–	–	0	.39
91-92	Edm	79	15	32	47	9	2	0	206	7.3	7	13	20	0	1	1	82	220	8	70	5	15	16	0	.59
92-93	Edm*	83	15	30	45	-28	1	1	244	6.1	9	20	29	1	1	2	86	210	2	**80**	2	15	22	0	.54
93-94	2Tm	70	4	17	21	-13	0	0	180	2.2	1	5	6	0	0	0	75	191	3	68	1	17	18	0	.30
94-95	Wpg	44	3	15	18	-20	1	0	104	2.9	2	6	8	0	1	1	49	139	3	42	2	14	9	0	.41
95-96	Wpg	82	7	23	30	8	0	0	189	3.7	3	6	9	0	0	0	81	205	1	**75**	1	17	25	0	.37
96-97	2Tm	75	4	18	22	-26	0	0	175	2.3	2	8	10	0	1	1	58	187	5	46	5	13	11	0	.29
97-98	Mon	81	4	30	34	22	0	0	148	2.7	2	8	10	0	0	0	45	122	0	41	0	10	14	0	.42
98-99	2Tm	75	6	17	23	1	0	0	145	4.1	2	6	8	0	0	0	51	155	7	40	6	9	10	0	.31
93-94	Edm	57	3	13	16	-4	0	0	144	2.1	0	3	3	0	0	0	59	140	2	55	1	13	15	0	.28
93-94	Wpg	13	1	4	5	-9	0	0	36	2.8	1	2	3	0	0	0	16	51	1	13	0	4	3	0	.38
96-97	Pho	66	3	17	20	-25	0	0	153	2.0	2	7	9	0	1	1	52	164	4	42	4	11	11	0	.30
96-97	Mon	9	1	1	2	-1	0	0	22	4.5	0	1	1	0	0	0	6	23	1	4	1	2	0	0	.22
98-99	Mon	11	0	2	2	-3	0	0	11	0.0	0	1	1	0	0	0	9	48	2	4	1	0	1	0	.18
98-99	Chi	64	6	15	21	4	0	0	134	4.5	2	5	7	0	0	0	42	107	5	36	5	9	9	0	.33
13 Years		919	97	270	367	-32	7	2	1984	4.9	43	–	–	3	–	–	–	2604	–	–	–	–	–	0	.40
Postseason																									
Year	Tm	GP	G	A	Pts	+/-	GW	OT	S	SPct	G	A	Pts	G	A	Pts	Num	PIM	Maj	Mnr	Fgt	Rgh	HHT	Hat	P/G
86-87	Chi	3	0	0	0	-2	0	0	2	0.0	0	0	0	0	0	0	–	10	–	–	–	–	–	0	.00
87-88	Chi	5	0	0	0	1	0	0	7	0.0	0	0	0	0	0	0	–	27	–	–	–	–	–	0	.00
88-89	Chi	16	0	8	8	-2	0	0	39	0.0	0	–	–	0	–	–	–	84	–	–	–	–	–	0	.50
89-90	Chi	20	2	4	6	-5	0	0	36	5.6	1	–	–	0	–	–	–	46	–	–	–	–	–	0	.30
90-91	Chi	6	0	1	1	2	0	0	11	0.0	0	–	–	0	–	–	–	36	–	–	–	–	–	0	.17
91-92	Edm	16	3	9	12	-2	0	0	47	6.4	1	5	6	0	0	0	18	44	0	17	0	4	5	0	.75
95-96	Wpg	6	2	1	3	3	1	0	12	16.7	0	0	0	0	0	0	11	30	0	10	0	4	1	0	.50
96-97	Mon	5	0	0	0	6	0	0	10	0.0	0	0	0	0	0	0	7	17	1	6	1	1	1	0	.00
97-98	Mon	10	0	1	1	0	0	0	25	0.0	0	0	0	0	0	0	7	14	0	7	0	4	1	0	.10
9 Years		87	7	24	31	1	1	0	189	3.7	2	–	–	0	–	–	–	308	–	–	–	–	–	0	.36

Paul Mara

Pos: D **Shoots:** L **Ht:** 6'3" **Wt:** 185 **Born:** 9/7/79—Ridgewood, New Jersey **Age:** 20

Overall											Power Play			Shorthand			Penalty							Misc	
Year	Tm	GP	G	A	Pts	+/–	GW	GT	S	SPct	G	A	Pts	G	A	Pts	Num	PIM	Maj	Mnr	Fgt	Rgh	HHT	Hat	P/G
98-99	TB	1	1	1	2	-3	0	0	1	100.0	1	1	2	0	0	0	0	0	0	0	0	0	0	0	2.00

Norm Maracle

Pos: G **Catches:** L **Ht:** 5'9" **Wt:** 175 **Born:** 10/2/74—Belleville, Ontario **Age:** 25

Overall																Pen Shot		Offense		
Year	Tm	GP	GS	TP	W	L	T	Min	GA	GAA	Shots	SvPct	ShO	OE	PPGA	SHGA	Shots	GA	G	A	PIM
97-98	Det	4	2	0	2	0	1	178	6	2.02	63	.905	0	1	4	0	0	0	0	0	0
98-99	Det	16	12	1	6	5	2	821	31	2.27	379	.918	0	5	6	2	0	0	0	0	0
2 Years		20	14	1	8	5	3	999	37	2.22	442	.916	0	6	10	2	0	0	0	0	0
Postseason																					
Year	Tm	GP	GS	TP	W	L	Pct	Min	GA	GAA	Shots	SvPct	ShO	OE	PPGA	SHGA	Shots	GA	G	A	PIM
98-99	Det	2	0	0	0	0	–	58	3	3.10	22	.864	0	0	1	0	0	0	0	0	0

Todd Marchant

(statistical profile on page 342)

Pos: C **Shoots:** L **Ht:** 5'10" **Wt:** 175 **Born:** 8/12/73—Buffalo, New York **Age:** 26

Overall											Power Play			Shorthand			Penalty							Misc	
Year	Tm	GP	G	A	Pts	+/–	GW	GT	S	SPct	G	A	Pts	G	A	Pts	Num	PIM	Maj	Mnr	Fgt	Rgh	HHT	Hat	P/G
93-94	2Tm	4	0	1	1	-2	0	0	6	0.0	0	0	0	0	0	0	1	2	0	1	0	0	1	0	.25
94-95	Edm	45	13	14	27	-3	2	0	95	13.7	3	4	7	2	0	2	16	32	0	16	0	0	6	0	.60
95-96	Edm	81	19	19	38	-19	2	1	221	8.6	2	1	3	3	2	5	26	66	2	23	0	2	13	0	.47
96-97	Edm	79	14	19	33	11	3	0	202	6.9	0	3	3	4	0	4	18	44	0	17	0	6	6	0	.42
97-98	Edm	76	14	21	35	9	3	0	194	7.2	2	4	6	1	3	4	30	71	1	28	1	9	6	0	.46
98-99	Edm	82	14	22	36	3	2	0	183	7.7	3	2	5	1	0	1	23	65	1	20	0	3	6	0	.44
93-94	NYR	1	0	0	0	-1	0	0	1	0.0	0	0	0	0	0	0	0	0	0	0	0	0	0	0	.00
93-94	Edm	3	0	1	1	-1	0	0	5	0.0	0	0	0	0	0	0	1	2	0	1	0	0	1	0	.33
6 Years		367	74	96	170	-1	12	1	901	8.2	10	14	24	11	5	16	114	280	4	105	1	20	38	0	.46
Postseason																									
Year	Tm	GP	G	A	Pts	+/–	GW	OT	S	SPct	G	A	Pts	G	A	Pts	Num	PIM	Maj	Mnr	Fgt	Rgh	HHT	Hat	P/G
96-97	Edm	12	4	2	6	2	1	1	40	10.0	0	1	1	3	0	3	6	12	0	6	0	3	1	0	.50
97-98	Edm	12	1	1	2	0	0	0	17	5.9	0	0	0	0	0	0	5	10	0	5	0	0	3	0	.17
98-99	Edm	4	1	1	2	2	0	0	10	10.0	0	0	0	0	0	0	2	12	0	1	0	1	0	0	.50
3 Years		28	6	4	10	4	1	1	67	9.0	0	1	1	3	0	3	13	34	0	12	0	4	4	0	.36

Bryan Marchment

Pos: D **Shoots:** L **Ht:** 6'1" **Wt:** 205 **Born:** 5/1/69—Scarborough, Ontario **Age:** 30

Overall											Power Play			Shorthand			Penalty							Misc	
Year	Tm	GP	G	A	Pts	+/–	GW	GT	S	SPct	G	A	Pts	G	A	Pts	Num	PIM	Maj	Mnr	Fgt	Rgh	HHT	Hat	P/G
88-89	Wpg	2	0	0	0	0	0	0	1	0.0	0	0	0	0	0	0	1	2	0	1	0	–	–	0	.00
89-90	Wpg	7	0	2	2	0	0	0	5	0.0	0	–	–	0	–	–	–	28	–	–	–	–	–	0	.29
90-91	Wpg	28	2	2	4	-5	0	0	24	8.3	0	–	–	0	–	–	–	91	–	–	–	–	–	0	.14
91-92	Chi	58	5	10	15	-4	0	0	55	9.1	2	3	5	0	0	0	59	168	6	49	5	10	11	0	.26
92-93	Chi	78	5	15	20	15	1	0	75	6.7	1	2	3	0	0	0	97	313	13	74	10	16	17	0	.26
93-94	2Tm	55	4	11	15	-14	1	0	92	4.3	0	0	0	1	0	1	56	166	10	43	9	11	5	0	.27
94-95	Edm	40	1	5	6	-11	0	0	57	1.8	0	0	0	0	1	1	49	184	10	32	8	8	4	0	.15
95-96	Edm	78	3	15	18	-7	0	0	96	3.1	0	5	5	0	0	0	68	202	6	56	5	8	9	0	.23
96-97	Edm	71	3	13	16	13	0	0	89	3.4	1	0	1	0	1	1	48	132	4	41	2	8	13	0	.23
97-98	3Tm	61	2	11	13	-3	0	0	56	3.6	0	4	4	0	2	2	53	144	2	47	2	9	8	0	.21
98-99	SJ	59	2	6	8	-7	0	0	49	4.1	0	0	0	0	0	0	38	101	3	33	2	8	4	0	.14
93-94	Chi	13	1	4	5	-2	0	0	18	5.6	0	0	0	0	0	0	14	42	2	11	2	4	0	0	.38
93-94	Har	42	3	7	10	-12	1	0	74	4.1	0	0	0	1	0	1	42	124	8	32	7	7	5	0	.24
97-98	Edm	27	0	4	4	-2	0	0	23	0.0	0	2	2	0	0	0	21	58	0	19	0	1	3	0	.15
97-98	TB	22	2	4	6	-3	0	0	20	10.0	0	1	1	0	2	2	16	43	1	14	1	3	4	0	.27
97-98	SJ	12	0	3	3	2	0	0	13	0.0	0	1	1	0	0	0	16	43	1	14	1	5	1	0	.25
11 Years		537	27	90	117	-23	2	0	599	4.5	4	–	–	1	–	–	–	1531	–	–	–	–	–	0	.22
Postseason																									
Year	Tm	GP	G	A	Pts	+/–	GW	OT	S	SPct	G	A	Pts	G	A	Pts	Num	PIM	Maj	Mnr	Fgt	Rgh	HHT	Hat	P/G
91-92	Chi	16	1	0	1	0	0	0	11	9.1	0	0	0	0	0	0	15	36	2	13	2	2	5	0	.06
92-93	Chi	4	0	0	0	1	0	0	6	0.0	0	0	0	0	0	0	6	12	0	6	0	2	0	0	.00
96-97	Edm	3	0	0	0	-3	0	0	2	0.0	0	0	0	0	0	0	2	4	0	2	0	0	2	0	.00

Postseason																											
Year	Tm	GP	G	A	Pts	+/-	GW	OT	S	SPct	G	A	Pts	G	A	Pts	Num	PIM	Maj	Mnr	Fgt	Rgh	HHT	Hat	P/G
97-98	SJ	6	0	0	0	1	0	0	5	0.0	0	0	0	0	0	0	5	10	0	5	0	3	1	0	.00
98-99	SJ	6	0	0	0	0	0	0	7	0.0	0	0	0	0	0	0	2	4	0	2	0	2	0	0	.00
5 Years		35	1	0	1	-1	0	0	31	3.2	0	0	0	0	0	0	30	66	2	28	2	9	8	0	.03

Josef Marha

Pos: C **Shoots:** L **Ht:** 6'0" **Wt:** 176 **Born:** 6/2/76—Havlickuv Brod, Czechoslovakia **Age:** 23

Overall											Power Play			Shorthand			Penalty							Misc	
Year	Tm	GP	G	A	Pts	+/-	GW	GT	S	SPct	G	A	Pts	G	A	Pts	Num	PIM	Maj	Mnr	Fgt	Rgh	HHT	Hat	P/G
95-96	Col	2	0	1	1	1	0	0	2	0.0	0	0	0	0	0	0	0	0	0	0	0	0	0	0	.50
96-97	Col	6	0	1	1	0	0	0	6	0.0	0	0	0	0	0	0	0	0	0	0	0	0	0	0	.17
97-98	2Tm	23	9	9	18	4	0	0	31	29.0	3	4	7	0	0	0	2	4	0	2	0	0	2	0	.78
98-99	2Tm	32	2	6	8	1	1	0	45	4.4	1	0	1	0	0	0	2	4	0	2	0	0	1	0	.25
97-98	Col	11	2	5	7	0	0	0	10	20.0	0	3	3	0	0	0	2	4	0	2	0	0	2	0	.64
97-98	Anh	12	7	4	11	4	0	0	21	33.3	3	1	4	0	0	0	0	0	0	0	0	0	0	0	.92
98-99	Anh	10	0	1	1	-4	0	0	13	0.0	0	0	0	0	0	0	0	0	0	0	0	0	0	0	.10
98-99	Chi	22	2	5	7	5	1	0	32	6.3	1	0	1	0	0	0	2	4	0	2	0	0	1	0	.32
4 Years		63	11	17	28	6	1	0	84	13.1	4	4	8	0	0	0	4	8	0	4	0	0	3	0	.44

Daniil Markov

(statistical profile on page 342)

Pos: D **Shoots:** L **Ht:** 5'11" **Wt:** 176 **Born:** 7/11/76—Moscow, USSR **Age:** 23

Overall											Power Play			Shorthand			Penalty							Misc	
Year	Tm	GP	G	A	Pts	+/-	GW	GT	S	SPct	G	A	Pts	G	A	Pts	Num	PIM	Maj	Mnr	Fgt	Rgh	HHT	Hat	P/G
97-98	Tor	25	2	5	7	0	0	0	15	13.3	1	1	2	0	0	0	10	28	0	9	0	3	2	0	.28
98-99	Tor	57	4	8	12	5	0	1	34	11.8	0	0	0	0	1	1	18	47	1	16	1	1	4	0	.21
2 Years		82	6	13	19	5	0	1	49	12.2	1	1	2	0	1	1	28	75	1	25	1	4	6	0	.23
Postseason																									
Year	Tm	GP	G	A	Pts	+/-	GW	OT	S	SPct	G	A	Pts	G	A	Pts	Num	PIM	Maj	Mnr	Fgt	Rgh	HHT	Hat	P/G
98-99	Tor	17	0	6	6	9	0	0	11	0.0	0	0	0	0	0	0	5	18	0	4	0	1	1	0	.35

Patrick Marleau

(statistical profile on page 342)

Pos: C **Shoots:** L **Ht:** 6'2" **Wt:** 200 **Born:** 9/15/79—Aneroid, Saskatchewan **Age:** 20

Overall											Power Play			Shorthand			Penalty							Misc	
Year	Tm	GP	G	A	Pts	+/-	GW	GT	S	SPct	G	A	Pts	G	A	Pts	Num	PIM	Maj	Mnr	Fgt	Rgh	HHT	Hat	P/G
97-98	SJ	74	13	19	32	5	2	0	90	14.4	1	6	7	0	0	0	7	14	0	7	0	0	3	0	.43
98-99	SJ	81	21	24	45	10	4	1	134	15.7	4	6	10	0	0	0	12	24	0	12	0	1	4	0	.56
2 Years		155	34	43	77	15	6	1	224	15.2	5	12	17	0	0	0	19	38	0	19	0	1	7	0	.50
Postseason																									
Year	Tm	GP	G	A	Pts	+/-	GW	OT	S	SPct	G	A	Pts	G	A	Pts	Num	PIM	Maj	Mnr	Fgt	Rgh	HHT	Hat	P/G
97-98	SJ	5	0	1	1	-1	0	0	2	0.0	0	1	1	0	0	0	0	0	0	0	0	0	0	0	.20
98-99	SJ	6	2	1	3	-1	0	0	7	28.6	2	0	2	0	0	0	2	4	0	2	0	0	1	0	.50
2 Years		11	2	2	4	-2	0	0	9	22.2	2	1	3	0	0	0	2	4	0	2	0	0	1	0	.36

Grant Marshall

(statistical profile on page 342)

Pos: RW **Shoots:** R **Ht:** 6'1" **Wt:** 193 **Born:** 6/9/73—Mississauga, Ontario **Age:** 26

Overall											Power Play			Shorthand			Penalty							Misc	
Year	Tm	GP	G	A	Pts	+/-	GW	GT	S	SPct	G	A	Pts	G	A	Pts	Num	PIM	Maj	Mnr	Fgt	Rgh	HHT	Hat	P/G
94-95	Dal	2	0	1	1	1	0	0	0	–	0	0	0	0	0	0	0	0	0	0	0	0	0	0	.50
95-96	Dal	70	9	19	28	0	0	1	62	14.5	0	2	2	0	0	0	36	111	13	23	13	7	4	0	.40
96-97	Dal	56	6	4	10	5	0	0	62	9.7	0	0	0	0	0	0	27	98	12	14	12	6	1	0	.18
97-98	Dal	72	9	10	19	-2	1	0	91	9.9	3	3	6	0	0	0	30	96	12	18	12	6	5	0	.26
98-99	Dal	82	13	18	31	1	4	0	112	11.6	2	3	5	0	0	0	25	85	9	15	9	4	5	0	.38
5 Years		282	37	52	89	5	5	1	327	11.3	5	8	13	0	0	0	118	390	46	70	46	23	15	0	.32
Postseason																									
Year	Tm	GP	G	A	Pts	+/-	GW	OT	S	SPct	G	A	Pts	G	A	Pts	Num	PIM	Maj	Mnr	Fgt	Rgh	HHT	Hat	P/G
96-97	Dal	5	0	2	2	2	0	0	4	0.0	0	0	0	0	0	0	4	8	0	4	0	2	0	0	.40
97-98	Dal	17	0	2	2	0	0	0	8	0.0	0	0	0	0	0	0	10	47	1	6	0	4	1	0	.12
98-99	Dal	14	0	3	3	1	0	0	23	0.0	0	0	0	0	0	0	6	20	0	5	0	2	1	0	.21
3 Years		36	0	7	7	3	0	0	35	0.0	0	0	0	0	0	0	20	75	1	15	0	8	2	0	.19

Jason Marshall

Pos: D **Shoots:** R **Ht:** 6'2" **Wt:** 205 **Born:** 2/22/71—Cranbrook, British Columbia **Age:** 28

Overall											Power Play			Shorthand			Penalty							Misc	
Year	Tm	GP	G	A	Pts	+/–	GW	GT	S	SPct	G	A	Pts	G	A	Pts	Num	PIM	Maj	Mnr	Fgt	Rgh	HHT	Hat	P/G
91-92	StL	2	1	0	1	0	0	0	2	50.0	0	0	0	0	0	0	2	4	0	2	0	0	1	0	.50
92-93											Did Not Play in NHL														
93-94											Did Not Play in NHL														
94-95	Anh	1	0	0	0	-2	0	0	1	0.0	0	0	0	0	0	0	0	0	0	0	0	0	0	0	.00
95-96	Anh	24	0	1	1	3	0	0	9	0.0	0	0	0	0	0	0	15	42	4	11	4	2	4	0	.04
96-97	Anh	73	1	9	10	6	0	0	34	2.9	0	1	1	0	0	0	50	140	8	40	8	10	8	0	.14
97-98	Anh	72	3	6	9	-8	0	0	68	4.4	1	3	4	0	0	0	65	189	9	52	9	11	18	0	.13
98-99	Anh	72	1	7	8	-5	0	0	63	1.6	0	0	0	0	0	0	56	142	2	51	2	19	13	0	.11
6 Years		244	6	23	29	-6	0	0	177	3.4	1	4	5	0	0	0	188	517	23	156	23	42	44	0	.12

Postseason																									
Year	Tm	GP	G	A	Pts	+/–	GW	OT	S	SPct	G	A	Pts	G	A	Pts	Num	PIM	Maj	Mnr	Fgt	Rgh	HHT	Hat	P/G
96-97	Anh	7	0	1	1	1	0	0	3	0.0	0	0	0	0	0	0	2	4	0	2	0	2	0	0	.14
98-99	Anh	4	1	0	1	-1	0	0	5	20.0	1	0	1	0	0	0	5	10	0	5	0	0	2	0	.25
2 Years		11	1	1	2	0	0	0	8	12.5	1	0	1	0	0	0	7	14	0	7	0	2	2	0	.18

Steve Martins

Pos: C **Shoots:** L **Ht:** 5'9" **Wt:** 175 **Born:** 4/13/72—Gatineau, Quebec **Age:** 27

Overall											Power Play			Shorthand			Penalty							Misc	
Year	Tm	GP	G	A	Pts	+/–	GW	GT	S	SPct	G	A	Pts	G	A	Pts	Num	PIM	Maj	Mnr	Fgt	Rgh	HHT	Hat	P/G
95-96	Har	23	1	3	4	-3	0	0	27	3.7	0	0	0	0	0	0	4	8	0	4	0	1	2	0	.17
96-97	Har	2	0	1	1	0	0	0	2	0.0	0	0	0	0	0	0	0	0	0	0	0	0	0	0	.50
97-98	Car	3	0	0	0	0	0	0	0	–	0	0	0	0	0	0	0	0	0	0	0	0	0	0	.00
98-99	Ott	36	4	3	7	4	1	0	27	14.8	1	0	1	0	0	0	5	10	0	5	0	0	1	0	.19
4 Years		64	5	7	12	1	1	0	56	8.9	1	0	1	0	0	0	9	18	0	9	0	1	3	0	.19

Chris Mason

Pos: G **Catches:** R **Ht:** 6'0" **Wt:** 200 **Born:** 4/20/76—Red Deer, Alberta **Age:** 23

Overall																Pen Shot		Offense		
Year	Tm	GP	GS	TP	W	L	T	Min	GA	GAA	Shots	SvPct	ShO	OE	PPGA	SHGA	Shots	GA	G	A	PIM
98-99	Nsh	3	0	0	0	0	0	69	6	5.22	44	.864	0	0	0	0	0	0	0	0	0

Marquis Mathieu

Pos: C **Shoots:** R **Ht:** 5'11" **Wt:** 190 **Born:** 5/31/73—Hartford, Connecticut **Age:** 26

Overall											Power Play			Shorthand			Penalty							Misc	
Year	Tm	GP	G	A	Pts	+/–	GW	GT	S	SPct	G	A	Pts	G	A	Pts	Num	PIM	Maj	Mnr	Fgt	Rgh	HHT	Hat	P/G
98-99	Bos	9	0	0	0	-1	0	0	4	0.0	0	0	0	0	0	0	4	8	0	4	0	2	0	0	.00

Christian Matte

Pos: RW **Shoots:** R **Ht:** 6'0" **Wt:** 180 **Born:** 1/20/75—Hull, Quebec **Age:** 24

Overall											Power Play			Shorthand			Penalty							Misc	
Year	Tm	GP	G	A	Pts	+/–	GW	GT	S	SPct	G	A	Pts	G	A	Pts	Num	PIM	Maj	Mnr	Fgt	Rgh	HHT	Hat	P/G
96-97	Col	5	1	1	2	1	0	0	6	16.7	0	0	0	0	0	0	0	0	0	0	0	0	0	0	.40
97-98	Col	5	0	0	0	0	0	0	5	0.0	0	0	0	0	0	0	3	6	0	3	0	0	2	0	.00
98-99	Col	7	1	1	2	-2	0	0	9	11.1	0	0	0	0	0	0	0	0	0	0	0	0	0	0	.29
3 Years		17	2	2	4	-1	0	0	20	10.0	0	0	0	0	0	0	3	6	0	3	0	0	2	0	.24

Stephane Matteau

(statistical profile on page 343)

Pos: LW **Shoots:** L **Ht:** 6'4" **Wt:** 220 **Born:** 9/2/69—Rouyn, Quebec **Age:** 30

Overall											Power Play			Shorthand			Penalty							Misc	
Year	Tm	GP	G	A	Pts	+/–	GW	GT	S	SPct	G	A	Pts	G	A	Pts	Num	PIM	Maj	Mnr	Fgt	Rgh	HHT	Hat	P/G
90-91	Cgy	78	15	19	34	17	1	0	114	13.2	0	–	–	1	–	–	31	93	5	24	–	–	–	0	.44
91-92	2Tm	24	6	8	14	5	0	0	38	15.8	1	0	1	0	0	0	17	64	2	12	2	5	4	0	.58
92-93	Chi	79	15	18	33	6	4	0	95	15.8	2	2	4	0	1	1	31	98	4	24	3	9	7	0	.42
93-94	2Tm	77	19	19	38	15	2	1	135	14.1	3	1	4	0	3	3	24	57	3	21	3	7	8	0	.49
94-95	NYR	41	3	5	8	-8	0	0	37	8.1	0	0	0	0	0	0	11	25	1	10	1	3	2	0	.20
95-96	2Tm	78	11	15	26	-8	2	1	109	10.1	4	4	8	0	0	0	32	87	5	26	5	5	10	0	.33
96-97	StL	74	16	20	36	11	2	0	98	16.3	1	0	1	2	1	3	19	50	4	15	4	3	5	0	.49

Overall											Power Play			Shorthand			Penalty									Misc	
Year	Tm	GP	G	A	Pts	+/–	GW	GT	S	SPct	G	A	Pts	G	A	Pts	Num	PIM	Maj	Mnr	Fgt	Rgh	HHT	Hat	P/G
97-98	SJ	73	15	14	29	4	2	2	79	19.0	1	0	1	0	0	0	24	60	4	20	4	5	14	0	.40
98-99	SJ	68	8	15	23	2	0	0	72	11.1	0	1	1	0	1	1	25	73	5	19	5	3	8	0	.34
91-92	Cgy	4	1	0	1	2	0	0	7	14.3	0	0	0	0	0	0	4	19	1	2	1	2	0	0	.25
91-92	Chi	20	5	8	13	3	0	0	31	16.1	1	0	1	0	0	0	13	45	1	10	1	3	4	0	.65
93-94	Chi	65	15	16	31	10	2	0	113	13.3	2	1	3	0	3	3	23	55	3	20	3	6	8	0	.48
93-94	NYR	12	4	3	7	5	0	1	22	18.2	1	0	1	0	0	0	1	2	0	1	0	1	0	0	.58
95-96	NYR	32	4	2	6	-4	0	0	39	10.3	1	0	1	0	0	0	8	22	2	6	2	2	2	0	.19
95-96	StL	46	7	13	20	-4	2	1	70	10.0	3	4	7	0	0	0	24	65	3	20	3	3	8	0	.43
9 Years		592	108	133	241	44	13	4	777	13.9	12	–	–	3	–	–	214	607	33	171	–	–	–	0	.41
Postseason																									
Year	Tm	GP	G	A	Pts	+/–	GW	OT	S	SPct	G	A	Pts	G	A	Pts	Num	PIM	Maj	Mnr	Fgt	Rgh	HHT	Hat	P/G
90-91	Cgy	5	0	1	1	0	0	0	8	0.0	0	–	–	0	0	0	0	0	0	0	0	0	0	0	.20
91-92	Chi	18	4	6	10	5	0	0	32	12.5	1	3	4	1	0	1	8	24	0	7	0	3	3	0	.56
92-93	Chi	3	0	1	1	-1	0	0	2	0.0	0	0	0	0	0	0	1	2	0	1	0	0	0	0	.33
93-94	NYR	23	6	3	9	5	2	2	36	16.7	1	1	2	0	0	0	10	20	0	10	0	3	2	0	.39
94-95	NYR	9	0	1	1	-1	0	0	9	0.0	0	0	0	0	0	0	5	10	0	5	0	2	0	0	.11
95-96	StL	11	0	2	2	-2	0	0	13	0.0	0	0	0	0	0	0	4	8	0	4	0	1	1	0	.18
96-97	StL	5	0	0	0	0	0	0	2	0.0	0	0	0	0	0	0	0	0	0	0	0	0	0	0	.00
97-98	SJ	4	0	1	1	1	0	0	2	0.0	0	0	0	0	0	0	0	0	0	0	0	0	0	0	.25
98-99	SJ	5	0	0	0	-3	0	0	4	0.0	0	0	0	0	0	0	3	6	0	3	0	0	1	0	.00
9 Years		83	10	15	25	4	2	2	108	9.3	2	–	–	1	0	1	31	70	0	30	0	9	7	0	.30

Richard Matvichuk

(statistical profile on page 343)

Pos: D **Shoots:** L **Ht:** 6'2" **Wt:** 200 **Born:** 2/5/73—Edmonton, Alberta **Age:** 26

Overall											Power Play			Shorthand			Penalty									Misc	
Year	Tm	GP	G	A	Pts	+/–	GW	GT	S	SPct	G	A	Pts	G	A	Pts	Num	PIM	Maj	Mnr	Fgt	Rgh	HHT	Hat	P/G
92-93	Min	53	2	3	5	-8	0	0	51	3.9	1	0	1	0	0	0	13	26	0	13	0	4	5	0	.09
93-94	Dal	25	0	3	3	1	0	0	18	0.0	0	1	1	0	0	0	11	22	0	11	0	0	9	0	.12
94-95	Dal	14	0	2	2	-7	0	0	21	0.0	0	1	1	0	0	0	7	14	0	7	0	2	3	0	.14
95-96	Dal	73	6	16	22	4	1	0	81	7.4	0	3	3	0	0	0	30	71	1	28	1	8	5	0	.30
96-97	Dal	57	5	7	12	1	0	0	83	6.0	0	1	1	2	0	2	38	87	1	36	1	12	6	0	.21
97-98	Dal	74	3	15	18	7	0	0	71	4.2	0	2	2	0	0	0	30	63	1	29	0	9	7	0	.24
98-99	Dal	64	3	9	12	23	0	0	54	5.6	1	1	2	0	1	1	20	51	1	18	0	2	8	0	.19
7 Years		360	19	55	74	21	1	0	379	5.0	2	9	11	2	1	3	149	334	4	142	2	37	43	0	.21
Postseason																									
Year	Tm	GP	G	A	Pts	+/–	GW	OT	S	SPct	G	A	Pts	G	A	Pts	Num	PIM	Maj	Mnr	Fgt	Rgh	HHT	Hat	P/G
93-94	Dal	7	1	1	2	-2	0	0	14	7.1	1	1	2	0	0	0	6	12	0	6	0	0	2	0	.29
94-95	Dal	5	0	2	2	-3	0	0	6	0.0	0	2	2	0	0	0	2	4	0	2	0	2	0	0	.40
96-97	Dal	7	0	1	1	-1	0	0	8	0.0	0	0	0	0	0	0	6	20	0	5	0	3	0	0	.14
97-98	Dal	16	1	1	2	2	0	0	20	5.0	0	0	0	0	0	0	7	14	0	7	0	0	3	0	.13
98-99	Dal	22	1	5	6	4	0	0	26	3.8	0	0	0	0	0	0	10	20	0	10	0	3	1	0	.27
5 Years		57	3	10	13	0	0	0	74	4.1	1	3	4	0	0	0	31	70	0	30	0	8	6	0	.23

Brad May

(statistical profile on page 343)

Pos: LW **Shoots:** L **Ht:** 6'1" **Wt:** 206 **Born:** 11/29/71—Toronto, Ontario **Age:** 28

Overall											Power Play			Shorthand			Penalty									Misc	
Year	Tm	GP	G	A	Pts	+/–	GW	GT	S	SPct	G	A	Pts	G	A	Pts	Num	PIM	Maj	Mnr	Fgt	Rgh	HHT	Hat	P/G
91-92	Buf	69	11	6	17	-12	3	0	82	13.4	1	0	1	0	0	0	78	309	19	47	15	19	7	0	.25
92-93	Buf	82	13	13	26	3	1	0	114	11.4	0	1	1	0	0	0	69	242	16	46	16	15	6	0	.32
93-94	Buf	84	18	27	45	-6	3	0	166	10.8	3	9	12	0	0	0	61	171	11	48	11	14	6	0	.54
94-95	Buf	33	3	3	6	5	0	0	42	7.1	1	0	1	0	0	0	28	87	5	21	5	12	4	0	.18
95-96	Buf	79	15	29	44	6	4	0	168	8.9	3	5	8	0	0	0	**94**	295	17	70	17	**30**	5	0	.56
96-97	Buf	42	3	4	7	-8	1	0	75	4.0	1	2	3	0	0	0	39	106	4	33	4	10	4	0	.17
97-98	2Tm	63	13	10	23	2	2	0	97	13.4	4	1	5	0	0	0	47	154	4	37	4	19	6	0	.37
98-99	Van	66	6	11	17	-14	1	0	91	6.6	1	4	5	0	1	1	29	102	4	21	4	6	3	0	.26
97-98	Buf	36	4	7	11	2	0	0	41	9.8	0	0	0	0	0	0	32	113	3	24	3	13	2	0	.31
97-98	Van	27	9	3	12	0	2	0	56	16.1	4	1	5	0	0	0	15	41	1	13	1	6	4	0	.44
8 Years		518	82	103	185	-24	15	0	835	9.8	14	22	36	0	1	1	445	1466	80	323	76	125	41	0	.36
Postseason																									
Year	Tm	GP	G	A	Pts	+/–	GW	OT	S	SPct	G	A	Pts	G	A	Pts	Num	PIM	Maj	Mnr	Fgt	Rgh	HHT	Hat	P/G
91-92	Buf	7	1	4	5	3	1	0	18	5.6	0	0	0	0	0	0	1	2	0	1	0	0	0	0	.71
92-93	Buf	8	1	1	2	0	1	1	8	12.5	0	0	0	0	0	0	7	14	0	7	0	0	0	0	.25
93-94	Buf	7	0	2	2	2	0	0	11	0.0	0	0	0	0	0	0	3	9	1	2	1	1	0	0	.29

Postseason																									
Year	Tm	GP	G	A	Pts	+/–	GW	OT	S	SPct	G	A	Pts	G	A	Pts	Num	PIM	Maj	Mnr	Fgt	Rgh	HHT	Hat	P/G
94-95	Buf	4	0	0	0	0	0	0	4	0.0	0	0	0	0	0	0	1	2	0	1	0	1	0	0	.00
96-97	Buf	10	1	1	2	-2	0	0	7	14.3	0	0	0	0	0	0	8	32	0	6	0	4	0	0	.20
5 Years		36	3	8	11	3	2	1	48	6.3	0	0	0	0	0	0	20	59	1	17	1	6	0	0	.31

Jamal Mayers

Pos: C **Shoots:** R **Ht:** 6'1" **Wt:** 207 **Born:** 10/24/74—Toronto, Ontario **Age:** 25

Overall											Power Play			Shorthand			Penalty							Misc	
Year	Tm	GP	G	A	Pts	+/–	GW	GT	S	SPct	G	A	Pts	G	A	Pts	Num	PIM	Maj	Mnr	Fgt	Rgh	HHT	Hat	P/G
96-97	StL	6	0	1	1	-3	0	0	7	0.0	0	1	1	0	0	0	1	2	0	1	0	1	0	0	.17
97-98	Did Not Play in NHL																								
98-99	StL	34	4	5	9	-3	0	0	48	8.3	0	0	0	0	0	0	10	40	4	5	4	2	0	0	.26
2 Years		40	4	6	10	-6	0	0	55	7.3	0	1	1	0	0	0	11	42	4	6	4	3	0	0	.25
Postseason																									
Year	Tm	GP	G	A	Pts	+/–	GW	OT	S	SPct	G	A	Pts	G	A	Pts	Num	PIM	Maj	Mnr	Fgt	Rgh	HHT	Hat	P/G
98-99	StL	11	0	1	1	-2	0	0	9	0.0	0	0	0	0	0	0	4	8	0	4	0	1	1	0	.09

Chris McAllister

Pos: D **Shoots:** L **Ht:** 6'6" **Wt:** 236 **Born:** 6/16/75—Saskatoon, Saskatchewan **Age:** 24

Overall											Power Play			Shorthand			Penalty							Misc	
Year	Tm	GP	G	A	Pts	+/–	GW	GT	S	SPct	G	A	Pts	G	A	Pts	Num	PIM	Maj	Mnr	Fgt	Rgh	HHT	Hat	P/G
97-98	Van	36	1	2	3	-12	0	0	15	6.7	0	0	0	0	0	0	27	106	12	13	12	1	3	0	.08
98-99	2Tm	48	1	3	4	-3	0	1	18	5.6	0	0	0	0	0	0	28	102	10	16	10	6	1	0	.08
98-99	Van	28	1	1	2	-7	0	1	6	16.7	0	0	0	0	0	0	17	63	7	9	7	3	0	0	.07
98-99	Tor	20	0	2	2	4	0	0	12	0.0	0	0	0	0	0	0	11	39	3	7	3	3	1	0	.10
2 Years		84	2	5	7	-15	0	1	33	6.1	0	0	0	0	0	0	55	208	22	29	22	7	4	0	.08
Postseason																									
Year	Tm	GP	G	A	Pts	+/–	GW	OT	S	SPct	G	A	Pts	G	A	Pts	Num	PIM	Maj	Mnr	Fgt	Rgh	HHT	Hat	P/G
98-99	Tor	6	0	1	1	-1	0	0	2	0.0	0	0	0	0	0	0	2	4	0	2	0	2	0	0	.17

Chris McAlpine

Pos: D **Shoots:** R **Ht:** 6'0" **Wt:** 204 **Born:** 12/1/71—Roseville, Minnesota **Age:** 28

Overall											Power Play			Shorthand			Penalty							Misc	
Year	Tm	GP	G	A	Pts	+/–	GW	GT	S	SPct	G	A	Pts	G	A	Pts	Num	PIM	Maj	Mnr	Fgt	Rgh	HHT	Hat	P/G
94-95	NJ	24	0	3	3	4	0	0	19	0.0	0	0	0	0	0	0	7	17	1	6	0	0	2	0	.13
95-96	Did Not Play in NHL																								
96-97	StL	15	0	0	0	-2	0	0	3	0.0	0	0	0	0	0	0	8	24	0	7	0	1	2	0	.00
97-98	StL	54	3	7	10	14	0	0	35	8.6	0	0	0	0	0	0	18	36	0	18	0	4	9	0	.19
98-99	StL	51	1	1	2	-10	0	0	56	1.8	0	0	0	0	0	0	22	50	2	20	2	4	11	0	.04
4 Years		144	4	11	15	6	0	0	113	3.5	0	0	0	0	0	0	55	127	3	51	2	9	24	0	.10
Postseason																									
Year	Tm	GP	G	A	Pts	+/–	GW	OT	S	SPct	G	A	Pts	G	A	Pts	Num	PIM	Maj	Mnr	Fgt	Rgh	HHT	Hat	P/G
96-97	StL	4	0	1	1	1	0	0	6	0.0	0	0	0	0	0	0	0	0	0	0	0	0	0	0	.25
97-98	StL	10	0	0	0	-1	0	0	5	0.0	0	0	0	0	0	0	8	16	0	8	0	1	3	0	.00
98-99	StL	13	0	0	0	0	0	0	7	0.0	0	0	0	0	0	0	1	2	0	1	0	1	0	0	.00
3 Years		27	0	1	1	0	0	0	18	0.0	0	0	0	0	0	0	9	18	0	9	0	2	3	0	.04

Dean McAmmond

(statistical profile on page 343)

Pos: C **Shoots:** L **Ht:** 5'11" **Wt:** 185 **Born:** 6/15/73—Grand Cache, Alberta **Age:** 26

Overall											Power Play			Shorthand			Penalty							Misc	
Year	Tm	GP	G	A	Pts	+/–	GW	GT	S	SPct	G	A	Pts	G	A	Pts	Num	PIM	Maj	Mnr	Fgt	Rgh	HHT	Hat	P/G
91-92	Chi	5	0	2	2	-2	0	0	4	0.0	0	2	2	0	0	0	0	0	0	0	0	0	0	0	.40
92-93	Did Not Play in NHL																								
93-94	Edm	45	6	21	27	12	0	0	52	11.5	2	4	6	0	0	0	8	16	0	8	0	2	4	0	.60
94-95	Edm	6	0	0	0	-1	0	0	3	0.0	0	0	0	0	0	0	0	0	0	0	0	0	0	0	.00
95-96	Edm	53	15	15	30	6	0	0	79	19.0	4	4	8	0	0	0	10	23	1	9	1	2	4	0	.57
96-97	Edm	57	12	17	29	-15	6	0	106	11.3	4	5	9	0	0	0	11	28	2	9	2	3	3	0	.51
97-98	Edm	77	19	31	50	9	3	0	128	14.8	8	12	20	0	0	0	16	46	2	13	2	2	4	0	.65
98-99	2Tm	77	10	20	30	8	1	0	138	7.2	1	4	5	0	0	0	19	38	0	19	0	1	7	0	.39
98-99	Edm	65	9	16	25	5	0	0	122	7.4	1	4	5	0	0	0	18	36	0	18	0	1	6	0	.38
98-99	Chi	12	1	4	5	3	1	0	16	6.3	0	0	0	0	0	0	1	2	0	1	0	0	1	0	.42
7 Years		320	62	106	168	17	10	0	510	12.2	19	31	50	0	0	0	64	151	5	58	5	10	22	0	.53

Year	Tm	GP	G	A	Pts	+/-	GW	OT	S	SPct	G	A	Pts	G	A	Pts	Num	PIM	Maj	Mnr	Fgt	Rgh	HHT	Hat	P/G
Postseason																									
91-92	Chi	3	0	0	0	1	0	0	1	0.0	0	0	0	0	0	0	1	2	0	1	0	0	1	0	.00
97-98	Edm	12	1	4	5	0	0	0	22	4.5	0	0	0	0	0	0	6	12	0	6	0	2	1	0	.42
2 Years		15	1	4	5	1	0	0	23	4.3	0	0	0	0	0	0	7	14	0	7	0	2	2	0	.33

Mike McBain

Pos: D **Shoots:** L **Ht:** 6'2" **Wt:** 195 **Born:** 1/12/77—Kimberley, British Columbia **Age:** 22

		Overall									Power Play			Shorthand			Penalty							Misc	
Year	Tm	GP	G	A	Pts	+/-	GW	GT	S	SPct	G	A	Pts	G	A	Pts	Num	PIM	Maj	Mnr	Fgt	Rgh	HHT	Hat	P/G
97-98	TB	27	0	1	1	-10	0	0	17	0.0	0	0	0	0	0	0	4	8	0	4	0	0	4	0	.04
98-99	TB	37	0	6	6	-11	0	0	22	0.0	0	0	0	0	0	0	7	14	0	7	0	0	4	0	.16
2 Years		64	0	7	7	-21	0	0	39	0.0	0	0	0	0	0	0	11	22	0	11	0	0	8	0	.11

Bryan McCabe

(statistical profile on page 344)

Pos: D **Shoots:** L **Ht:** 6'1" **Wt:** 204 **Born:** 6/8/75—St. Catharines, Ontario **Age:** 24

		Overall									Power Play			Shorthand			Penalty							Misc	
Year	Tm	GP	G	A	Pts	+/-	GW	GT	S	SPct	G	A	Pts	G	A	Pts	Num	PIM	Maj	Mnr	Fgt	Rgh	HHT	Hat	P/G
95-96	NYI	82	7	16	23	-24	1	0	130	5.4	3	8	11	0	0	0	62	156	8	53	8	3	**29**	0	.28
96-97	NYI	**82**	8	20	28	-2	2	0	117	6.8	2	4	6	1	0	1	57	165	9	45	9	10	22	0	.34
97-98	2Tm	82	4	20	24	19	0	0	123	3.3	1	8	9	1	1	2	73	209	13	57	13	11	24	0	.29
98-99	Van	69	7	14	21	-11	0	0	98	7.1	1	6	7	2	1	3	47	120	6	40	6	8	9	0	.30
97-98	NYI	56	3	9	12	9	0	0	81	3.7	1	3	4	0	0	0	51	145	9	40	9	10	16	0	.21
97-98	Van	26	1	11	12	10	0	0	42	2.4	0	5	5	1	1	2	22	64	4	17	4	1	8	0	.46
4 Years		315	26	70	96	-18	3	0	468	5.6	7	26	33	4	2	6	239	650	36	195	36	32	84	0	.30

Sandy McCarthy

(statistical profile on page 344)

Pos: RW **Shoots:** R **Ht:** 6'3" **Wt:** 225 **Born:** 6/15/72—Toronto, Ontario **Age:** 27

		Overall									Power Play			Shorthand			Penalty							Misc	
Year	Tm	GP	G	A	Pts	+/-	GW	GT	S	SPct	G	A	Pts	G	A	Pts	Num	PIM	Maj	Mnr	Fgt	Rgh	HHT	Hat	P/G
93-94	Cgy	79	5	5	10	-3	0	0	39	12.8	0	0	0	0	0	0	42	173	19	19	19	6	7	0	.13
94-95	Cgy	37	5	3	8	1	2	0	29	17.2	0	1	1	0	0	0	31	101	13	18	13	6	4	0	.22
95-96	Cgy	75	9	7	16	-8	1	0	98	9.2	3	1	4	0	0	0	44	173	15	24	15	5	5	0	.21
96-97	Cgy	33	3	5	8	-8	1	0	38	7.9	1	0	1	0	0	0	22	113	7	9	7	2	1	0	.24
97-98	2Tm	66	8	10	18	-19	1	0	94	8.5	1	4	5	0	0	0	55	241	17	28	17	14	5	0	.27
98-99	2Tm	80	5	8	13	-24	0	0	107	4.7	1	0	1	0	0	0	42	160	12	25	12	10	3	0	.16
97-98	Cgy	52	8	5	13	-18	1	0	68	11.8	1	3	4	0	0	0	39	170	12	20	12	10	5	0	.25
97-98	TB	14	0	5	5	-1	0	0	26	0.0	0	1	1	0	0	0	16	71	5	8	5	4	0	0	.36
98-99	TB	67	5	7	12	-22	0	0	89	5.6	1	0	1	0	0	0	34	135	9	20	9	7	3	0	.18
98-99	Phi	13	0	1	1	-2	0	0	18	0.0	0	0	0	0	0	0	8	25	3	5	3	3	0	0	.08
6 Years		370	35	38	73	-61	5	0	405	8.6	6	6	12	0	0	0	236	961	83	123	83	43	25	0	.20
Postseason																									
Year	Tm	GP	G	A	Pts	+/-	GW	OT	S	SPct	G	A	Pts	G	A	Pts	Num	PIM	Maj	Mnr	Fgt	Rgh	HHT	Hat	P/G
93-94	Cgy	7	0	0	0	-2	0	0	3	0.0	0	0	0	0	0	0	5	34	0	2	0	2	0	0	.00
94-95	Cgy	6	0	1	1	-2	0	0	0	–	0	0	0	0	0	0	3	17	1	1	1	1	0	0	.17
95-96	Cgy	4	0	0	0	-3	0	0	4	0.0	0	0	0	0	0	0	5	10	0	5	0	1	1	0	.00
98-99	Phi	6	0	1	1	1	0	0	7	0.0	0	0	0	0	0	0	0	0	0	0	0	0	0	0	.17
4 Years		23	0	2	2	-6	0	0	14	0.0	0	0	0	0	0	0	13	61	1	8	1	4	1	0	.09

Darren McCarty

(statistical profile on page 344)

Pos: RW **Shoots:** R **Ht:** 6'1" **Wt:** 215 **Born:** 4/1/72—Burnaby, British Columbia **Age:** 27

		Overall									Power Play			Shorthand			Penalty							Misc	
Year	Tm	GP	G	A	Pts	+/-	GW	GT	S	SPct	G	A	Pts	G	A	Pts	Num	PIM	Maj	Mnr	Fgt	Rgh	HHT	Hat	P/G
93-94	Det	67	9	17	26	12	2	0	81	11.1	0	2	2	0	0	0	48	181	23	23	23	11	4	0	.39
94-95	Det	31	5	8	13	5	2	0	27	18.5	1	1	2	0	0	0	25	88	10	14	10	9	3	0	.42
95-96	Det	63	15	14	29	14	1	1	102	14.7	8	2	10	0	0	0	53	158	12	39	12	12	14	0	.46
96-97	Det	68	19	30	49	14	6	1	171	11.1	5	11	16	0	0	0	40	126	10	28	10	20	3	0	.72
97-98	Det	71	15	22	37	0	2	0	166	9.0	5	8	13	1	0	1	46	157	11	31	11	11	7	0	.52
98-99	Det	69	14	26	40	10	1	1	140	10.0	6	3	9	0	1	1	42	108	8	34	8	14	3	0	.58
6 Years		369	77	117	194	55	14	3	687	11.2	25	27	52	1	1	2	254	818	74	169	74	77	34	0	.53
Postseason																									
Year	Tm	GP	G	A	Pts	+/-	GW	OT	S	SPct	G	A	Pts	G	A	Pts	Num	PIM	Maj	Mnr	Fgt	Rgh	HHT	Hat	P/G
93-94	Det	7	2	2	4	3	0	0	6	33.3	0	0	0	0	0	0	4	8	0	4	0	0	3	0	.57

Postseason																									
Year	Tm	GP	G	A	Pts	+/–	GW	OT	S	SPct	G	A	Pts	G	A	Pts	Num	PIM	Maj	Mnr	Fgt	Rgh	HHT	Hat	P/G
94-95	Det	18	3	2	5	3	0	0	31	9.7	0	0	0	0	0	0	7	14	0	7	0	4	1	0	.28
95-96	Det	19	3	2	5	-2	1	0	30	10.0	0	0	0	0	0	0	10	20	0	10	0	6	4	0	.26
96-97	Det	20	3	4	7	1	2	0	34	8.8	0	0	0	0	0	0	13	34	0	12	0	3	2	0	.35
97-98	Det	22	3	8	11	9	1	0	46	6.5	0	2	2	0	2	2	17	34	0	17	0	4	10	0	.50
98-99	Det	10	1	1	2	-1	0	0	15	6.7	0	0	0	0	0	0	10	23	1	9	0	3	1	0	.20
6 Years		96	15	19	34	13	4	0	162	9.3	0	2	2	0	2	2	61	133	1	59	0	20	21	0	.35

Alyn McCauley

(statistical profile on page 344)

Pos: C **Shoots:** L **Ht:** 5'11" **Wt:** 185 **Born:** 5/29/77—Brockville, Ontario **Age:** 22

Overall											Power Play			Shorthand			Penalty							Misc	
Year	Tm	GP	G	A	Pts	+/–	GW	GT	S	SPct	G	A	Pts	G	A	Pts	Num	PIM	Maj	Mnr	Fgt	Rgh	HHT	Hat	P/G
97-98	Tor	60	6	10	16	-7	1	0	77	7.8	0	2	2	0	0	0	3	6	0	3	0	1	0	0	.27
98-99	Tor	39	9	15	24	7	1	1	76	11.8	1	4	5	0	0	0	1	2	0	1	0	0	0	0	.62
2 Years		99	15	25	40	0	2	1	153	9.8	1	6	7	0	0	0	4	8	0	4	0	1	0	0	.40

Trent McCleary

Pos: RW **Shoots:** R **Ht:** 6'0" **Wt:** 180 **Born:** 9/8/72—Swift Current, Saskatchewan **Age:** 27

Overall											Power Play			Shorthand			Penalty							Misc	
Year	Tm	GP	G	A	Pts	+/–	GW	GT	S	SPct	G	A	Pts	G	A	Pts	Num	PIM	Maj	Mnr	Fgt	Rgh	HHT	Hat	P/G
95-96	Ott	75	4	10	14	-15	0	0	58	6.9	0	0	0	1	1	2	31	68	2	29	1	6	6	0	.19
96-97	Bos	59	3	5	8	-16	1	0	41	7.3	0	0	0	0	1	1	11	33	1	9	0	2	4	0	.14
97-98		Did Not Play in NHL																							
98-99	Mon	46	0	0	0	-1	0	0	18	0.0	0	0	0	0	0	0	13	29	1	12	1	1	4	0	.00
3 Years		180	7	15	22	-32	1	0	117	6.0	0	0	0	1	2	3	55	130	4	50	2	9	14	0	.12

Shawn McEachern

(statistical profile on page 345)

Pos: LW **Shoots:** L **Ht:** 5'11" **Wt:** 195 **Born:** 2/28/69—Waltham, Massachusetts **Age:** 30

Overall											Power Play			Shorthand			Penalty							Misc	
Year	Tm	GP	G	A	Pts	+/–	GW	GT	S	SPct	G	A	Pts	G	A	Pts	Num	PIM	Maj	Mnr	Fgt	Rgh	HHT	Hat	P/G
91-92	Pit	15	0	4	4	1	0	0	14	0.0	0	1	1	0	0	0	0	0	0	0	0	0	0	0	.27
92-93	Pit	84	28	33	61	21	6	0	196	14.3	7	7	14	0	1	1	19	46	0	18	0	1	7	0	.73
93-94	2Tm	76	20	22	42	15	1	0	159	12.6	0	3	3	5	1	6	17	34	0	17	0	1	12	0	.55
94-95	Pit	44	13	13	26	4	1	0	97	13.4	1	1	2	2	0	2	11	22	0	11	0	0	6	0	.59
95-96	Bos	82	24	29	53	-5	3	0	238	10.1	3	3	6	2	1	3	17	34	0	17	0	0	8	0	.65
96-97	Ott	65	11	20	31	-5	2	0	150	7.3	0	3	3	1	1	2	9	18	0	9	0	0	5	0	.48
97-98	Ott	81	24	24	48	1	4	2	229	10.5	8	6	14	2	2	4	21	42	0	21	0	1	9	1	.59
98-99	Ott	77	31	25	56	8	4	1	223	13.9	7	6	13	0	0	0	19	46	0	18	0	3	11	0	.73
93-94	LA	49	8	13	21	2	0	0	81	9.9	0	1	1	3	1	4	12	24	0	12	0	1	8	0	.43
93-94	Pit	27	12	9	21	13	1	0	78	15.4	0	2	2	2	0	2	5	10	0	5	0	0	4	0	.78
8 Years		524	151	170	321	40	21	3	1306	11.6	26	30	56	12	6	18	113	242	0	111	0	6	58	1	.61
Postseason																									
Year	Tm	GP	G	A	Pts	+/–	GW	OT	S	SPct	G	A	Pts	G	A	Pts	Num	PIM	Maj	Mnr	Fgt	Rgh	HHT	Hat	P/G
91-92	Pit	19	2	7	9	6	0	0	36	5.6	0	0	0	0	0	0	2	4	0	2	0	0	1	0	.47
92-93	Pit	12	3	2	5	0	1	0	21	14.3	0	0	0	0	0	0	5	10	0	5	0	0	2	0	.42
93-94	Pit	6	1	0	1	-2	0	0	10	10.0	0	0	0	0	0	0	1	2	0	1	0	0	1	0	.17
94-95	Pit	11	0	2	2	-2	0	0	12	0.0	0	0	0	0	0	0	4	8	0	4	0	1	1	0	.18
95-96	Bos	5	2	1	3	-2	0	0	7	28.6	0	0	0	0	0	0	4	8	0	4	0	0	1	0	.60
96-97	Ott	7	2	0	2	-1	0	0	21	9.5	1	0	1	0	0	0	4	8	0	4	0	0	2	0	.29
97-98	Ott	11	0	4	4	-6	0	0	27	0.0	0	0	0	0	0	0	4	8	0	4	0	1	0	0	.36
98-99	Ott	4	2	0	2	1	0	0	11	18.2	1	0	1	0	0	0	3	6	0	3	0	1	0	0	.50
8 Years		75	12	16	28	-6	1	0	145	8.3	2	0	2	0	0	0	27	54	0	27	0	3	8	0	.37

Daniel McGillis

(statistical profile on page 345)

Pos: D **Shoots:** L **Ht:** 6'2" **Wt:** 225 **Born:** 7/1/72—Hawkesbury, Ontario **Age:** 27

Overall											Power Play			Shorthand			Penalty							Misc	
Year	Tm	GP	G	A	Pts	+/–	GW	GT	S	SPct	G	A	Pts	G	A	Pts	Num	PIM	Maj	Mnr	Fgt	Rgh	HHT	Hat	P/G
96-97	Edm	73	6	16	22	2	2	0	139	4.3	2	5	7	1	0	1	26	52	0	26	0	4	16	0	.30
97-98	2Tm	80	11	20	31	-21	3	1	137	8.0	6	9	15	0	1	1	49	109	1	47	0	6	18	0	.39
98-99	Phi	78	8	37	45	16	4	0	164	4.9	6	21	27	0	0	0	29	61	1	28	1	5	11	0	.58
97-98	Edm	67	10	15	25	-17	3	1	119	8.4	5	7	12	0	0	0	37	74	0	37	0	5	12	0	.37
97-98	Phi	13	1	5	6	-4	0	0	18	5.6	1	2	3	0	1	1	12	35	1	10	0	1	6	0	.46
3 Years		231	25	73	98	-3	9	1	440	5.7	14	35	49	1	1	2	104	222	2	101	1	15	45	0	.42

Postseason																									
Year	Tm	GP	G	A	Pts	+/–	GW	OT	S	SPct	G	A	Pts	G	A	Pts	Num	PIM	Maj	Mnr	Fgt	Rgh	HHT	Hat	P/G
96-97	Edm	12	0	5	5	8	0	0	20	0.0	0	1	1	0	0	0	8	24	0	7	0	2	1	0	.42
97-98	Phi	5	1	2	3	0	0	0	14	7.1	1	0	1	0	0	0	5	10	0	5	0	2	2	0	.60
98-99	Phi	6	0	1	1	2	0	0	15	0.0	0	0	0	0	0	0	6	12	0	6	0	2	1	0	.17
3 Years		23	1	8	9	10	0	0	49	2.0	1	1	2	0	0	0	19	46	0	18	0	6	4	0	.39

Marty McInnis

(statistical profile on page 345)

Pos: C **Shoots:** R **Ht:** 5'11" **Wt:** 183 **Born:** 6/2/70—Weymouth, Massachusetts **Age:** 29

Overall											Power Play			Shorthand			Penalty							Misc	
Year	Tm	GP	G	A	Pts	+/–	GW	GT	S	SPct	G	A	Pts	G	A	Pts	Num	PIM	Maj	Mnr	Fgt	Rgh	HHT	Hat	P/G
91-92	NYI	15	3	5	8	6	0	0	24	12.5	0	1	1	0	1	1	0	0	0	0	0	0	0	0	.53
92-93	NYI	56	10	20	30	7	0	0	60	16.7	0	2	2	1	0	1	12	24	0	12	0	1	7	0	.54
93-94	NYI	81	25	31	56	31	3	1	136	18.4	3	5	8	5	1	6	12	24	0	12	0	1	9	0	.69
94-95	NYI	41	9	7	16	-1	1	0	68	13.2	0	2	2	0	0	0	4	8	0	4	0	1	2	0	.39
95-96	NYI	74	12	34	46	-11	1	0	167	7.2	2	13	15	0	1	1	14	39	1	12	1	0	9	0	.62
96-97	2Tm	80	23	26	49	-8	4	1	182	12.6	5	7	12	1	2	3	11	22	0	11	0	0	8	0	.61
97-98	Cgy	75	19	25	44	1	0	0	128	14.8	5	5	10	4	1	5	17	34	0	17	0	0	13	1	.59
98-99	2Tm	81	19	35	54	-15	5	0	146	13.0	11	17	28	1	1	2	21	42	0	21	0	0	13	0	.67
96-97	NYI	70	20	22	42	-7	4	1	163	12.3	4	6	10	1	2	3	10	20	0	10	0	0	8	0	.60
96-97	Cgy	10	3	4	7	-1	0	0	19	15.8	1	1	2	0	0	0	1	2	0	1	0	0	0	0	.70
98-99	Cgy	6	1	1	2	-1	0	0	7	14.3	0	0	0	0	0	0	3	6	0	3	0	0	2	0	.33
98-99	Anh	75	18	34	52	-14	5	0	139	12.9	11	17	28	1	1	2	18	36	0	18	0	0	11	0	.69
8 Years		503	120	183	303	10	14	2	911	13.2	26	52	78	12	7	19	91	193	1	89	1	3	61	1	.60
Postseason																									
Year	Tm	GP	G	A	Pts	+/–	GW	OT	S	SPct	G	A	Pts	G	A	Pts	Num	PIM	Maj	Mnr	Fgt	Rgh	HHT	Hat	P/G
92-93	NYI	3	0	1	1	-1	0	0	1	0.0	0	0	0	0	0	0	0	0	0	0	0	0	0	0	.33
93-94	NYI	4	0	0	0	-5	0	0	7	0.0	0	0	0	0	0	0	0	0	0	0	0	0	0	0	.00
98-99	Anh	4	2	0	2	-1	0	0	12	16.7	2	0	2	0	0	0	1	2	0	1	0	0	0	0	.50
3 Years		11	2	1	3	-7	0	0	20	10.0	2	0	2	0	0	0	1	2	0	1	0	0	0	0	.27

Randy McKay

(statistical profile on page 345)

Pos: RW **Shoots:** R **Ht:** 6'2" **Wt:** 210 **Born:** 1/25/67—Montreal, Quebec **Age:** 32

Overall											Power Play			Shorthand			Penalty							Misc	
Year	Tm	GP	G	A	Pts	+/–	GW	GT	S	SPct	G	A	Pts	G	A	Pts	Num	PIM	Maj	Mnr	Fgt	Rgh	HHT	Hat	P/G
88-89	Det	3	0	0	0	-1	0	0	2	0.0	0	0	0	0	0	0	0	0	0	0	0	0	0	0	.00
89-90	Det	33	3	6	9	1	0	0	33	9.1	0	–	–	0	–	–	–	51	–	–	–	–	–	0	.27
90-91	Det	47	1	7	8	-15	0	0	22	4.5	0	–	–	0	–	–	–	183	–	–	–	–	–	0	.17
91-92	NJ	80	17	16	33	6	1	0	111	15.3	2	1	3	0	2	2	73	246	28	43	28	23	6	0	.41
92-93	NJ	73	11	11	22	0	2	0	94	11.7	1	0	1	0	0	0	56	206	18	33	18	17	1	0	.30
93-94	NJ	78	12	15	27	24	1	1	77	15.6	0	0	0	0	0	0	64	244	28	32	27	19	5	0	.35
94-95	NJ	33	5	7	12	10	0	0	44	11.4	0	1	1	0	0	0	13	44	6	7	6	3	1	0	.36
95-96	NJ	76	11	10	21	7	3	1	97	11.3	3	0	3	0	0	0	38	145	15	20	15	12	2	0	.28
96-97	NJ	77	9	18	27	15	2	0	92	9.8	0	2	2	0	0	0	27	109	13	12	13	8	1	1	.35
97-98	NJ	74	24	24	48	30	5	0	141	17.0	8	3	11	0	0	0	27	86	8	18	8	9	3	1	.65
98-99	NJ	70	17	20	37	10	5	0	136	12.5	3	4	7	0	0	0	37	143	7	24	7	5	5	0	.53
11 Years		644	110	134	244	87	19	2	849	13.0	17	–	–	0	–	–	–	1457	–	–	–	–	–	2	.38
Postseason																									
Year	Tm	GP	G	A	Pts	+/–	GW	OT	S	SPct	G	A	Pts	G	A	Pts	Num	PIM	Maj	Mnr	Fgt	Rgh	HHT	Hat	P/G
88-89	Det	2	0	0	0	-2	0	0	2	0.0	0	0	0	0	0	0	1	2	0	1	0	–	–	0	.00
90-91	Det	5	0	1	1	0	0	0	4	0.0	0	–	–	0	–	–	–	41	–	–	–	–	–	0	.20
91-92	NJ	7	1	3	4	1	0	0	12	8.3	1	1	2	0	0	0	5	10	0	5	0	3	1	0	.57
92-93	NJ	5	0	0	0	1	0	0	1	0.0	0	0	0	0	0	0	4	16	0	3	0	1	1	0	.00
93-94	NJ	20	1	2	3	-1	0	0	15	6.7	0	0	0	0	0	0	5	24	2	2	2	0	0	0	.15
94-95	NJ	19	8	4	12	5	2	1	30	26.7	2	1	3	0	0	0	4	11	1	3	1	1	1	0	.63
96-97	NJ	10	1	1	2	1	0	0	15	6.7	0	0	0	0	0	0	0	0	0	0	0	0	0	0	.20
97-98	NJ	6	0	1	1	-1	0	0	7	0.0	0	1	1	0	0	0	0	0	0	0	0	0	0	0	.17
98-99	NJ	7	3	2	5	1	1	0	16	18.8	0	2	2	0	0	0	1	2	0	1	0	0	1	0	.71
9 Years		81	14	14	28	5	3	1	102	13.7	3	–	–	0	–	–	–	106	–	–	–	–	–	0	.35

Jay McKee

Pos: D **Shoots:** L **Ht:** 6'3" **Wt:** 195 **Born:** 9/8/77—Kingston, Ontario **Age:** 22

Overall											Power Play			Shorthand			Penalty							Misc	
Year	Tm	GP	G	A	Pts	+/-	GW	GT	S	SPct	G	A	Pts	G	A	Pts	Num	PIM	Maj	Mnr	Fgt	Rgh	HHT	Hat	P/G
95-96	Buf	1	0	1	1	1	0	0	2	0.0	0	0	0	0	0	0	1	2	0	1	0	0	1	0	1.00
96-97	Buf	43	1	9	10	3	0	0	29	3.4	0	3	3	0	0	0	16	35	1	15	1	1	6	0	.23
97-98	Buf	56	1	13	14	-1	0	0	55	1.8	0	6	6	0	2	2	21	42	0	21	0	3	12	0	.25
98-99	Buf	72	0	6	6	20	0	0	57	0.0	0	0	0	0	1	1	29	75	3	25	3	9	5	0	.08
4 Years		172	2	29	31	23	0	0	143	1.4	0	9	9	0	3	3	67	154	4	62	4	13	24	0	.18

Postseason

Year	Tm	GP	G	A	Pts	+/-	GW	OT	S	SPct	G	A	Pts	G	A	Pts	Num	PIM	Maj	Mnr	Fgt	Rgh	HHT	Hat	P/G
96-97	Buf	3	0	0	0	0	0	0	1	0.0	0	0	0	0	0	0	0	0	0	0	0	0	0	0	.00
97-98	Buf	1	0	0	0	-1	0	0	0	–	0	0	0	0	0	0	0	0	0	0	0	0	0	0	.00
98-99	Buf	21	0	3	3	13	0	0	13	0.0	0	0	0	0	1	1	8	24	0	7	0	3	1	0	.14
3 Years		25	0	3	3	12	0	0	14	0.0	0	0	0	0	1	1	8	24	0	7	0	3	1	0	.12

Steve McKenna

Pos: LW **Shoots:** L **Ht:** 6'8" **Wt:** 247 **Born:** 8/21/73—Toronto, Ontario **Age:** 26

Overall											Power Play			Shorthand			Penalty							Misc	
Year	Tm	GP	G	A	Pts	+/-	GW	GT	S	SPct	G	A	Pts	G	A	Pts	Num	PIM	Maj	Mnr	Fgt	Rgh	HHT	Hat	P/G
96-97	LA	9	0	0	0	1	0	0	6	0.0	0	0	0	0	0	0	7	37	5	1	5	0	0	0	.00
97-98	LA	62	4	4	8	-9	0	1	42	9.5	1	0	1	0	0	0	41	150	12	25	12	10	3	0	.13
98-99	LA	20	1	0	1	-3	0	0	12	8.3	0	0	0	0	0	0	9	36	6	3	6	1	1	0	.05
3 Years		91	5	4	9	-11	0	1	60	8.3	1	0	1	0	0	0	57	223	23	29	23	11	4	0	.10

Postseason

Year	Tm	GP	G	A	Pts	+/-	GW	OT	S	SPct	G	A	Pts	G	A	Pts	Num	PIM	Maj	Mnr	Fgt	Rgh	HHT	Hat	P/G
97-98	LA	3	0	1	1	1	0	0	3	0.0	0	0	0	0	0	0	4	8	0	4	0	0	0	0	.33

Jim McKenzie

Pos: LW **Shoots:** L **Ht:** 6'4" **Wt:** 205 **Born:** 11/3/69—Gull Lake, Saskatchewan **Age:** 30

Overall											Power Play			Shorthand			Penalty							Misc	
Year	Tm	GP	G	A	Pts	+/-	GW	GT	S	SPct	G	A	Pts	G	A	Pts	Num	PIM	Maj	Mnr	Fgt	Rgh	HHT	Hat	P/G
89-90	Har	5	0	0	0	0	0	0	0	–	0	0	0	0	0	0	2	4	0	2	0	–	–	0	.00
90-91	Har	41	4	3	7	-7	0	0	16	25.0	0	–	–	0	–	–	–	108	–	–	–	–	–	0	.17
91-92	Har	67	5	1	6	-6	0	1	34	14.7	0	0	0	0	0	0	26	87	9	16	9	5	5	0	.09
92-93	Har	64	3	6	9	-10	0	0	36	8.3	0	0	0	0	0	0	54	202	10	36	10	26	3	0	.14
93-94	3Tm	71	3	5	8	-7	1	0	33	9.1	0	1	1	0	0	0	39	146	12	23	12	14	1	0	.11
94-95	Pit	39	2	1	3	-7	1	0	16	12.5	0	0	0	0	0	0	19	63	3	14	3	5	3	0	.08
95-96	Wpg	73	4	2	6	-4	0	0	28	14.3	0	0	0	0	0	0	46	202	18	21	16	5	7	0	.08
96-97	Pho	65	5	3	8	-5	1	0	38	13.2	0	0	0	0	0	0	47	200	22	20	22	11	2	1	.12
97-98	Pho	64	3	4	7	-7	0	0	35	8.6	0	0	0	0	0	0	41	146	16	23	16	7	6	0	.11
98-99	Anh	73	5	4	9	-18	1	0	59	8.5	1	0	1	0	0	0	27	99	7	17	7	4	2	0	.12
93-94	Har	26	1	2	3	-6	0	0	9	11.1	0	1	1	0	0	0	18	67	5	11	5	6	0	0	.12
93-94	Dal	34	2	3	5	4	1	0	18	11.1	0	0	0	0	0	0	16	63	5	9	5	7	0	0	.15
93-94	Pit	11	0	0	0	-5	0	0	6	0.0	0	0	0	0	0	0	5	16	2	3	2	1	1	0	.00
10 Years		562	34	29	63	-71	4	1	295	11.5	1	–	–	0	–	–	–	1257	–	–	–	–	–	1	.11

Postseason

Year	Tm	GP	G	A	Pts	+/-	GW	OT	S	SPct	G	A	Pts	G	A	Pts	Num	PIM	Maj	Mnr	Fgt	Rgh	HHT	Hat	P/G
90-91	Har	6	0	0	0	-2	0	0	2	0.0	0	0	0	0	0	0	4	8	0	4	0	–	–	0	.00
93-94	Pit	3	0	0	0	0	0	0	0	–	0	0	0	0	0	0	0	0	0	0	0	0	0	0	.00
94-95	Pit	5	0	0	0	0	0	0	0	–	0	0	0	0	0	0	2	4	0	2	0	1	0	0	.00
95-96	Wpg	1	0	0	0	0	0	0	0	–	0	0	0	0	0	0	1	2	0	1	0	0	0	0	.00
96-97	Pho	7	0	0	0	0	0	0	7	0.0	0	0	0	0	0	0	1	2	0	1	0	0	1	0	.00
97-98	Pho	1	0	0	0	0	0	0	0	–	0	0	0	0	0	0	0	0	0	0	0	0	0	0	.00
98-99	Anh	4	0	0	0	-2	0	0	5	0.0	0	0	0	0	0	0	2	4	0	2	0	1	0	0	.00
7 Years		27	0	0	0	-4	0	0	14	0.0	0	0	0	0	0	0	10	20	0	10	0	–	–	0	.00

Kyle McLaren

(statistical profile on page 346)

Pos: D **Shoots:** L **Ht:** 6'4" **Wt:** 219 **Born:** 6/18/77—Humboldt, Saskatchewan **Age:** 22

Overall											Power Play			Shorthand			Penalty							Misc	
Year	Tm	GP	G	A	Pts	+/-	GW	GT	S	SPct	G	A	Pts	G	A	Pts	Num	PIM	Maj	Mnr	Fgt	Rgh	HHT	Hat	P/G
95-96	Bos	74	5	12	17	16	0	0	74	6.8	0	0	0	0	1	1	28	73	3	24	3	4	7	0	.23
96-97	Bos	58	5	9	14	-9	1	0	68	7.4	0	0	0	0	1	1	21	54	4	17	4	5	8	0	.24

		Overall									Power Play			Shorthand			Penalty							Misc	
Year	Tm	GP	G	A	Pts	+/–	GW	GT	S	SPct	G	A	Pts	G	A	Pts	Num	PIM	Maj	Mnr	Fgt	Rgh	HHT	Hat	P/G
97-98	Bos	66	5	20	25	13	0	0	101	5.0	2	6	8	0	0	0	22	56	4	18	4	2	4	0	.38
98-99	Bos	52	6	18	24	1	0	0	97	6.2	3	8	11	0	0	0	17	48	2	14	2	3	3	0	.46
4 Years		250	21	59	80	21	1	0	340	6.2	5	14	19	0	2	2	88	231	13	73	13	14	22	0	.32
											Postseason														
Year	Tm	GP	G	A	Pts	+/–	GW	OT	S	SPct	G	A	Pts	G	A	Pts	Num	PIM	Maj	Mnr	Fgt	Rgh	HHT	Hat	P/G
95-96	Bos	5	0	0	0	-3	0	0	13	0.0	0	0	0	0	0	0	7	14	0	7	0	3	2	0	.00
97-98	Bos	6	1	0	1	-3	0	0	21	4.8	1	0	1	0	0	0	2	4	0	2	0	1	1	0	.17
98-99	Bos	12	0	3	3	4	0	0	21	0.0	0	0	0	0	0	0	5	10	0	5	0	0	1	0	.25
3 Years		23	1	3	4	-2	0	0	55	1.8	1	0	1	0	0	0	14	28	0	14	0	4	4	0	.17

Kirk McLean

(statistical profile on page 400)

Pos: G **Catches:** L **Ht:** 6'0" **Wt:** 182 **Born:** 6/26/66—Willowdale, Ontario **Age:** 33

		Overall															Pen Shot		Offense		
Year	Tm	GP	GS	TP	W	L	T	Min	GA	GAA	Shots	SvPct	ShO	OE	PPGA	SHGA	Shots	GA	G	A	PIM
85-86	NJ	2	–	–	1	1	0	111	11	5.95	59	.814	0	–	–	–	0	0	0	0	0
86-87	NJ	4	–	–	1	1	0	160	10	3.75	73	.863	0	–	–	–	0	0	0	0	0
87-88	Van	41	–	–	11	27	3	2380	147	3.71	1178	.875	1	–	–	–	0	0	0	2	8
88-89	Van	42	–	–	20	17	3	2477	127	3.08	1169	.891	4	–	–	–	1	**1**	0	1	6
89-90	Van*	**63**	–	–	21	**30**	**10**	**3739**	**216**	3.47	**1804**	.880	0	–	–	–	0	0	0	3	6
90-91	Van	41	–	–	10	22	3	1969	131	3.99	983	.867	0	–	–	–	0	0	0	0	4
91-92	Van*	65	63	2	**38**	17	9	3852	176	2.74	1780	.901	**5**	24	56	4	0	0	0	5	0
92-93	Van	54	54	1	28	21	5	3261	184	3.39	1615	.886	3	16	66	9	1	1	0	1	16
93-94	Van	52	52	0	23	26	3	3128	156	2.99	1430	.891	3	16	49	6	2	**1**	0	4	2
94-95	Van	40	40	3	18	12	**10**	2374	109	2.75	1140	.904	1	12	27	**7**	0	0	0	1	4
95-96	Van	45	45	4	15	21	9	2645	156	3.54	1292	.879	2	8	39	6	0	0	0	2	6
96-97	Van	44	41	1	21	18	3	2581	138	3.21	1247	.889	0	11	29	5	0	0	0	2	2
97-98	3Tm	44	41	6	14	21	5	2390	141	3.54	1188	.881	1	12	43	8	0	0	0	1	0
98-99	Fla	30	24	1	9	10	4	1597	73	2.74	727	.900	2	5	26	3	1	0	0	0	2
97-98	Van	29	28	4	6	17	4	1583	97	3.68	800	.879	1	9	29	5	0	0	0	0	0
97-98	Car	8	6	1	4	2	0	401	22	3.29	181	.878	0	1	5	2	0	0	0	1	0
97-98	Fla	7	7	1	4	2	1	406	22	3.25	207	.894	0	2	9	1	0	0	0	0	0
14 Years		567	–	–	230	244	67	32664	1775	3.26	15685	.887	22	–	–	–	5	3	0	22	56
								Postseason													
Year	Tm	GP	GS	TP	W	L	Pct	Min	GA	GAA	Shots	SvPct	ShO	OE	PPGA	SHGA	Shots	GA	G	A	PIM
88-89	Van	5	–	–	2	3	.400	302	18	3.58	167	.892	0	–	–	–	0	0	0	0	0
90-91	Van	2	–	–	1	1	.500	123	7	3.41	66	.894	0	–	–	–	1	1	0	0	0
91-92	Van	13	13	0	6	7	.462	785	33	2.52	364	.909	2	4	11	1	0	0	0	1	0
92-93	Van	12	12	0	6	6	.500	754	42	3.34	369	.886	0	2	12	2	0	0	0	3	0
93-94	Van	24	24	0	15	9	.625	1544	59	2.29	820	.928	4	15	20	2	0	0	0	1	0
94-95	Van	11	11	1	4	7	.364	660	36	3.27	336	.893	0	4	7	1	0	0	0	1	0
95-96	Van	1	1	1	0	1	.000	21	3	8.57	12	.750	0	0	0	0	0	0	0	0	0
7 Years		68	–	–	34	34	.500	4189	198	2.84	2134	.907	6	–	–	–	1	1	0	6	0

Jamie McLennan

(statistical profile on page 400)

Pos: G **Catches:** L **Ht:** 6'1" **Wt:** 192 **Born:** 6/30/71—Edmonton, Alberta **Age:** 28

		Overall															Pen Shot		Offense		
Year	Tm	GP	GS	TP	W	L	T	Min	GA	GAA	Shots	SvPct	ShO	OE	PPGA	SHGA	Shots	GA	G	A	PIM
93-94	NYI	22	19	2	8	7	6	1287	61	2.84	639	.905	0	5	18	3	0	0	0	1	6
94-95	NYI	21	18	2	6	11	2	1185	67	3.39	539	.876	0	2	20	6	0	0	0	0	2
95-96	NYI	13	12	4	3	9	1	636	39	3.68	342	.886	0	3	11	1	0	0	0	0	2
96-97		Did Not Play in NHL																			
97-98	StL	30	26	3	16	8	2	1658	60	2.17	618	.903	2	3	17	0	0	0	0	0	4
98-99	StL	33	30	5	13	14	4	1763	70	2.38	640	.891	3	7	16	1	0	0	0	0	0
5 Years		119	105	16	46	49	15	6529	297	2.73	2778	.893	5	20	82	11	0	0	0	1	14
								Postseason													
Year	Tm	GP	GS	TP	W	L	Pct	Min	GA	GAA	Shots	SvPct	ShO	OE	PPGA	SHGA	Shots	GA	G	A	PIM
93-94	NYI	2	1	0	0	1	.000	82	6	4.39	47	.872	0	0	1	0	0	0	0	0	0
97-98	StL	1	0	0	0	0	–	14	1	4.29	4	.750	0	0	1	0	0	0	0	0	0
98-99	StL	1	0	0	0	1	.000	37	0	0.00	7	1.000	0	0	0	0	0	0	0	0	6
3 Years		4	1	0	0	2	.000	133	7	3.16	58	.879	0	0	2	0	0	0	0	0	6

Marty McSorley

Pos: D **Shoots:** R **Ht:** 6'2" **Wt:** 230 **Born:** 5/18/63—Hamilton, Ontario **Age:** 36

Overall											Power Play			Shorthand			Penalty							Misc	
Year	Tm	GP	G	A	Pts	+/–	GW	GT	S	SPct	G	A	Pts	G	A	Pts	Num	PIM	Maj	Mnr	Fgt	Rgh	HHT	Hat	P/G
83-84	Pit	72	2	7	9	-39	0	0	75	2.7	0	–	–	0	–	–	–	224	–	–	–	–	–	0	.13
84-85	Pit	15	0	0	0	-3	0	0	11	0.0	0	0	0	0	0	0	–	15	–	–	–	–	–	0	.00
85-86	Edm	59	11	12	23	9	2	0	72	15.3	0	–	–	0	–	–	–	265	–	–	–	–	–	0	.39
86-87	Edm	41	2	4	6	-4	0	0	32	6.3	0	–	–	0	–	–	–	159	–	–	–	–	–	0	.15
87-88	Edm	60	9	17	26	23	1	0	66	13.6	0	–	–	0	–	–	–	223	–	–	–	–	–	0	.43
88-89	LA	66	10	17	27	3	1	0	87	11.5	2	–	–	0	–	–	–	350	–	–	–	–	–	0	.41
89-90	LA	75	15	21	36	2	0	1	127	11.8	2	–	–	1	–	–	–	322	–	–	–	–	–	0	.48
90-91	LA	61	7	32	39	**48**	1	0	100	7.0	1	–	–	1	–	–	–	221	–	–	–	–	–	0	.64
91-92	LA	71	7	22	29	-13	0	0	119	5.9	2	8	10	1	0	1	87	268	18	64	17	16	15	0	.41
92-93	LA	81	15	26	41	1	0	0	197	7.6	3	9	12	3	2	5	**107**	**399**	19	72	16	**34**	16	0	.51
93-94	2Tm	65	7	24	31	-12	1	1	160	4.4	1	12	13	0	2	2	60	194	14	42	14	17	12	0	.48
94-95	LA	41	3	18	21	-14	0	1	75	4.0	1	6	7	0	3	3	30	83	5	24	4	8	6	0	.51
95-96	2Tm	68	10	23	33	-20	1	0	130	7.7	1	8	9	1	2	3	53	169	13	37	13	15	9	0	.49
96-97	SJ	57	4	12	16	-6	1	1	74	5.4	0	1	1	1	0	1	55	186	12	38	12	21	3	0	.28
97-98	SJ	56	2	10	12	10	0	0	46	4.3	0	0	0	0	1	1	36	140	12	20	12	6	4	0	.21
98-99	Edm	46	2	3	5	-5	0	0	29	6.9	0	0	0	0	0	0	32	101	7	23	7	7	7	0	.11
93-94	Pit	47	3	18	21	-9	0	1	122	2.5	0	8	8	0	1	1	44	139	9	32	9	10	11	0	.45
93-94	LA	18	4	6	10	-3	1	0	38	10.5	1	4	5	0	1	1	16	55	5	10	5	7	1	0	.56
95-96	LA	59	10	21	31	-14	1	0	118	8.5	1	8	9	1	2	3	44	148	12	29	12	12	6	0	.53
95-96	NYR	9	0	2	2	-6	0	0	12	0.0	0	0	0	0	0	0	9	21	1	8	1	3	3	0	.22
16 Years		934	106	248	354	-20	8	4	1400	7.6	13	–	–	8	–	–	–	3319	–	–	–	–	–	0	.38

Postseason

Year	Tm	GP	G	A	Pts	+/–	GW	OT	S	SPct	G	A	Pts	G	A	Pts	Num	PIM	Maj	Mnr	Fgt	Rgh	HHT	Hat	P/G
85-86	Edm	8	0	2	2	3	0	0	4	0.0	0	–	–	0	–	–	–	50	–	–	–	–	–	0	.25
86-87	Edm	21	4	3	7	8	1	0	21	19.0	0	–	–	0	–	–	–	65	–	–	–	–	–	0	.33
87-88	Edm	16	0	3	3	2	0	0	15	0.0	0	–	–	0	–	–	–	67	–	–	–	–	–	0	.19
88-89	LA	11	0	2	2	-6	0	0	16	0.0	0	–	–	0	–	–	–	33	–	–	–	–	–	0	.18
89-90	LA	10	1	3	4	-8	0	0	26	3.8	1	–	–	0	–	–	–	18	–	–	–	–	–	0	.40
90-91	LA	12	0	0	0	-1	0	0	30	0.0	0	0	0	0	0	0	–	58	–	–	–	–	–	0	.00
91-92	LA	6	1	0	1	1	0	0	10	10.0	0	0	0	0	0	0	5	21	1	3	1	1	0	0	.17
92-93	LA	24	4	6	10	-2	1	0	42	9.5	2	1	3	0	2	2	19	60	2	15	1	5	6	0	.42
95-96	NYR	4	0	0	0	-1	0	0	3	0.0	0	0	0	0	0	0	0	0	0	0	0	0	0	0	.00
98-99	Edm	3	0	0	0	1	0	0	3	0.0	0	0	0	0	0	0	1	2	0	1	0	0	0	0	.00
10 Years		115	10	19	29	-3	2	0	170	5.9	3	–	–	0	–	–	–	374	–	–	–	–	–	0	.25

Scott Mellanby

(statistical profile on page 346)

Pos: RW **Shoots:** R **Ht:** 6'1" **Wt:** 199 **Born:** 6/11/66—Montreal, Quebec **Age:** 33

Overall											Power Play			Shorthand			Penalty							Misc	
Year	Tm	GP	G	A	Pts	+/–	GW	GT	S	SPct	G	A	Pts	G	A	Pts	Num	PIM	Maj	Mnr	Fgt	Rgh	HHT	Hat	P/G
85-86	Phi	2	0	0	0	-1	0	0	0	–	0	0	0	0	0	0	0	0	0	0	0	0	0	0	.00
86-87	Phi	71	11	21	32	8	0	2	118	9.3	1	–	–	0	–	–	–	94	–	–	–	–	–	0	.45
87-88	Phi	75	25	26	51	-7	2	0	190	13.2	7	–	–	0	–	–	–	185	–	–	–	–	–	0	.68
88-89	Phi	76	21	29	50	-13	3	0	202	10.4	11	–	–	0	–	–	–	183	–	–	–	–	–	0	.66
89-90	Phi	57	6	17	23	-4	1	0	104	5.8	0	–	–	0	–	–	–	77	–	–	–	–	–	0	.40
90-91	Phi	74	20	21	41	8	6	0	165	12.1	5	–	–	0	–	–	–	155	–	–	–	–	–	0	.55
91-92	Edm	80	23	27	50	5	5	0	159	14.5	7	3	10	0	0	0	67	197	13	51	12	15	11	0	.63
92-93	Edm	69	15	17	32	-4	3	1	114	13.2	6	3	9	0	0	0	56	147	9	46	8	12	14	0	.46
93-94	Fla	80	30	30	60	0	4	1	204	14.7	17	7	24	0	0	0	56	149	7	47	7	14	13	0	.75
94-95	Fla	48	13	12	25	-16	5	0	130	10.0	4	6	10	0	0	0	35	90	4	30	4	8	8	0	.52
95-96	Fla*	79	32	38	70	4	3	1	225	14.2	19	16	35	0	0	0	67	160	6	60	6	13	13	0	.89
96-97	Fla	**82**	27	29	56	7	4	0	221	12.2	9	6	15	1	0	1	56	170	6	45	6	11	8	0	.68
97-98	Fla	79	15	24	39	-14	1	0	188	8.0	6	6	12	0	0	0	44	127	5	36	5	6	12	0	.49
98-99	Fla	67	18	27	45	5	3	**3**	136	13.2	4	7	11	0	0	0	29	85	1	25	1	7	5	0	.67
14 Years		939	256	318	574	-22	40	8	2156	11.9	96	–	–	1	–	–	–	1819	–	–	–	–	–	0	.61

Postseason

Year	Tm	GP	G	A	Pts	+/–	GW	OT	S	SPct	G	A	Pts	G	A	Pts	Num	PIM	Maj	Mnr	Fgt	Rgh	HHT	Hat	P/G
86-87	Phi	24	5	5	10	7	1	0	43	11.6	0	–	–	0	–	–	–	46	–	–	–	–	–	0	.42
87-88	Phi	7	0	1	1	-6	0	0	14	0.0	0	–	–	0	0	0	–	16	–	–	–	–	–	0	.14
88-89	Phi	19	4	5	9	2	0	0	45	8.9	0	–	–	0	–	–	–	28	–	–	–	–	–	0	.47
91-92	Edm	16	2	1	3	-3	1	0	26	7.7	1	0	1	0	0	0	9	29	1	7	0	1	0	0	.19
95-96	Fla	22	3	6	9	-10	0	0	57	5.3	2	1	3	0	0	0	15	44	2	12	2	5	1	0	.41
96-97	Fla	5	0	2	2	-1	0	0	6	0.0	0	1	1	0	0	0	2	4	0	2	0	0	0	0	.40
6 Years		93	14	20	34	-11	2	0	191	7.3	3	–	–	0	–	–	–	167	–	–	–	–	–	0	.37

Jan Mertzig

Pos: D **Shoots:** R **Ht:** 6'4" **Wt:** 215 **Born:** 7/18/70—Stockholm, Sweden **Age:** 29

Overall											Power Play			Shorthand			Penalty							Misc	
Year	Tm	GP	G	A	Pts	+/-	GW	GT	S	SPct	G	A	Pts	G	A	Pts	Num	PIM	Maj	Mnr	Fgt	Rgh	HHT	Hat	P/G
98-99	NYR	23	0	2	2	-5	0	0	10	0.0	0	1	1	0	0	0	4	8	0	4	0	0	1	0	.09

Eric Messier

Pos: D **Shoots:** L **Ht:** 6'2" **Wt:** 200 **Born:** 10/29/73—Drummondville, Quebec **Age:** 26

Overall											Power Play			Shorthand			Penalty							Misc	
Year	Tm	GP	G	A	Pts	+/-	GW	GT	S	SPct	G	A	Pts	G	A	Pts	Num	PIM	Maj	Mnr	Fgt	Rgh	HHT	Hat	P/G
96-97	Col	21	0	0	0	7	0	0	11	0.0	0	0	0	0	0	0	2	4	0	2	0	1	1	0	.00
97-98	Col	62	4	12	16	4	0	0	66	6.1	0	6	6	0	0	0	10	20	0	10	0	0	6	0	.26
98-99	Col	31	4	2	6	0	1	0	30	13.3	1	0	1	0	0	0	7	14	0	7	0	0	2	0	.19
3 Years		114	8	14	22	11	1	0	107	7.5	1	6	7	0	0	0	19	38	0	19	0	1	9	0	.19
Postseason																									
Year	Tm	GP	G	A	Pts	+/-	GW	OT	S	SPct	G	A	Pts	G	A	Pts	Num	PIM	Maj	Mnr	Fgt	Rgh	HHT	Hat	P/G
96-97	Col	6	0	0	0	0	0	0	1	0.0	0	0	0	0	0	0	2	4	0	2	0	0	0	0	.00
98-99	Col	3	0	0	0	-1	0	0	1	0.0	0	0	0	0	0	0	0	0	0	0	0	0	0	0	.00
2 Years		9	0	0	0	-1	0	0	2	0.0	0	0	0	0	0	0	2	4	0	2	0	0	0	0	.00

Mark Messier

(statistical profile on page 346)

Pos: C **Shoots:** L **Ht:** 6'1" **Wt:** 205 **Born:** 1/18/61—Edmonton, Alberta **Age:** 38

Overall											Power Play			Shorthand			Penalty							Misc	
Year	Tm	GP	G	A	Pts	+/-	GW	GT	S	SPct	G	A	Pts	G	A	Pts	Num	PIM	Maj	Mnr	Fgt	Rgh	HHT	Hat	P/G
79-80	Edm	75	12	21	33	-10	1	1	113	10.6	1	–	–	1	–	–	–	120	–	–	–	–	–	0	.44
80-81	Edm	72	23	40	63	-12	1	1	179	12.8	4	–	–	0	–	–	–	102	–	–	–	–	–	1	.88
81-82	Edm*	78	50	38	88	21	3	2	235	21.3	10	–	–	0	–	–	–	119	–	–	–	–	–	2	1.13
82-83	Edm*	77	48	58	106	19	2	5	237	20.3	12	–	–	1	–	–	–	72	–	–	–	–	–	2	1.38
83-84	Edm*	73	37	64	101	40	7	0	219	16.9	7	–	–	4	–	–	–	165	–	–	–	–	–	2	1.38
84-85	Edm	55	23	31	54	8	1	0	136	16.9	4	–	–	5	–	–	–	57	–	–	–	–	–	0	.98
85-86	Edm*	63	35	49	84	36	7	0	201	17.4	10	–	–	5	–	–	–	68	–	–	–	–	–	1	1.33
86-87	Edm*	77	37	70	107	21	5	0	208	17.8	7	–	–	4	–	–	–	73	–	–	–	–	–	0	1.39
87-88	Edm*	77	37	74	111	21	7	2	182	20.3	12	–	–	3	–	–	–	103	–	–	–	–	–	1	1.44
88-89	Edm*	72	33	61	94	-5	4	1	164	20.1	6	28	34	6	6	12	–	130	–	–	–	–	–	1	1.31
89-90	Edm*	79	45	84	129	19	3	2	211	21.3	13	34	47	6	5	11	–	79	–	–	–	–	–	3	1.63
90-91	Edm*	53	12	52	64	15	2	0	109	11.0	3	18	21	1	0	1	–	34	–	–	–	–	–	0	1.21
91-92	NYR*	79	35	72	107	31	6	0	212	16.5	12	21	33	4	5	9	34	76	0	33	0	4	12	3	1.35
92-93	NYR	75	25	66	91	-6	2	0	215	11.6	7	23	30	2	2	4	32	72	0	31	0	10	8	0	1.21
93-94	NYR*	76	26	58	84	25	5	0	216	12.0	6	30	36	2	**7**	9	31	76	2	28	2	3	9	0	1.11
94-95	NYR	46	14	39	53	8	2	0	126	11.1	3	17	20	3	0	3	17	40	2	15	2	3	2	0	1.15
95-96	NYR*	74	47	52	99	29	5	1	241	19.5	14	23	37	1	3	4	46	122	2	41	2	8	10	1	1.34
96-97	NYR*	71	36	48	84	12	9	1	227	15.9	7	11	18	5	**6**	**11**	29	88	2	24	1	3	8	2	1.18
97-98	Van*	82	22	38	60	-10	2	0	139	15.8	8	17	25	2	2	4	29	58	0	29	0	6	10	0	.73
98-99	Van	59	13	35	48	-12	2	0	97	13.4	4	18	22	2	**5**	**7**	15	33	1	14	1	0	4	0	.81
20 Years		1413	610	1050	1660	250	76	16	3667	16.6	150	–	–	57	–	–	–	1687	–	–	–	–	–	19	1.17
Postseason																									
Year	Tm	GP	G	A	Pts	+/-	GW	OT	S	SPct	G	A	Pts	G	A	Pts	Num	PIM	Maj	Mnr	Fgt	Rgh	HHT	Hat	P/G
79-80	Edm	3	1	2	3	–	0	0	–	–	0	–	–	1	–	–	1	2	0	1	0	–	–	0	1.00
80-81	Edm	9	2	5	7	–	0	0	–	–	0	–	–	0	–	–	5	13	1	4	–	–	–	0	.78
81-82	Edm	5	1	2	3	–	0	0	–	–	0	–	–	0	–	–	4	8	0	4	0	–	–	0	.60
82-83	Edm	15	15	6	21	10	2	0	50	30.0	4	–	–	2	–	–	–	14	–	–	–	–	–	3	1.40
83-84	Edm	19	8	18	26	9	2	0	63	12.7	1	–	–	1	–	–	–	19	–	–	–	–	–	0	1.37
84-85	Edm	18	12	13	25	13	1	0	56	21.4	1	–	–	1	–	–	–	12	–	–	–	–	–	0	1.39
85-86	Edm	10	4	6	10	1	0	0	23	17.4	0	–	–	2	–	–	–	18	–	–	–	–	–	0	1.00
86-87	Edm	21	12	16	28	13	1	0	62	19.4	1	–	–	2	–	–	–	16	–	–	–	–	–	0	1.33
87-88	Edm	19	11	23	34	9	0	0	42	26.2	7	–	–	1	–	–	–	29	–	–	–	–	–	0	1.79
88-89	Edm	7	1	11	12	-1	0	0	23	4.3	0	–	–	0	–	–	4	8	0	4	0	–	–	0	1.71
89-90	Edm	22	9	22	31	5	1	0	47	19.1	1	–	–	1	–	–	–	20	–	–	–	–	–	0	1.41
90-91	Edm	18	4	11	15	2	0	0	41	9.8	1	–	–	0	0	0	–	16	–	–	–	–	–	0	.83
91-92	NYR	11	7	7	14	-4	0	0	27	25.9	2	1	3	2	0	2	3	6	0	3	0	0	0	0	1.27
93-94	NYR	23	12	18	30	14	4	0	75	16.0	2	8	10	1	1	2	15	33	1	14	0	2	7	1	1.30
94-95	NYR	10	3	10	13	-11	1	0	26	11.5	2	6	8	0	1	1	4	8	0	4	0	1	1	0	1.30
95-96	NYR	11	4	7	11	-10	1	0	41	9.8	2	4	6	0	0	0	8	16	0	8	0	1	0	0	1.00
96-97	NYR	15	3	9	12	2	1	0	43	7.0	0	3	3	0	0	0	3	6	0	3	0	0	2	0	.80
17 Years		236	109	186	295	52	14	0	619	17.0	24	–	–	14	–	–	–	244	–	–	–	–	–	4	1.25

Craig Millar

Pos: D **Shoots:** L **Ht:** 6'2" **Wt:** 200 **Born:** 5/10/77—Lachute, Quebec **Age:** 22

Overall											Power Play			Shorthand			Penalty							Misc	
Year	Tm	GP	G	A	Pts	+/–	GW	GT	S	SPct	G	A	Pts	G	A	Pts	Num	PIM	Maj	Mnr	Fgt	Rgh	HHT	Hat	P/G
96-97	Edm	1	0	0	0	0	0	0	1	0.0	0	0	0	0	0	0	1	2	0	1	0	1	0	0	.00
97-98	Edm	11	4	0	4	-3	0	0	10	40.0	1	0	1	0	0	0	4	8	0	4	0	0	1	0	.36
98-99	Edm	24	0	2	2	-6	0	0	18	0.0	0	0	0	0	0	0	8	19	1	7	0	0	2	0	.08
3 Years		36	4	2	6	-9	0	0	29	13.8	1	0	1	0	0	0	13	29	1	12	0	1	3	0	.17

Aaron Miller

(statistical profile on page 346)

Pos: D **Shoots:** R **Ht:** 6'3" **Wt:** 197 **Born:** 8/11/71—Buffalo, New York **Age:** 28

Overall											Power Play			Shorthand			Penalty							Misc	
Year	Tm	GP	G	A	Pts	+/–	GW	GT	S	SPct	G	A	Pts	G	A	Pts	Num	PIM	Maj	Mnr	Fgt	Rgh	HHT	Hat	P/G
93-94	Que	1	0	0	0	-1	0	0	0	–	0	0	0	0	0	0	0	0	0	0	0	0	0	0	.00
94-95	Que	9	0	3	3	2	0	0	12	0.0	0	0	0	0	0	0	3	6	0	3	0	0	0	0	.33
95-96	Col	5	0	0	0	0	0	0	2	0.0	0	0	0	0	0	0	0	0	0	0	0	0	0	0	.00
96-97	Col	56	5	12	17	15	3	0	47	10.6	0	1	1	0	0	0	6	15	1	5	1	0	4	0	.30
97-98	Col	55	2	2	4	0	0	0	29	6.9	0	0	0	0	0	0	16	51	1	13	1	6	5	0	.07
98-99	Col	76	5	13	18	3	2	0	87	5.7	1	1	2	0	0	0	21	42	0	21	0	6	5	0	.24
6 Years		202	12	30	42	19	5	0	177	6.8	1	2	3	0	0	0	46	114	2	42	2	12	14	0	.21
Postseason																									
Year	Tm	GP	G	A	Pts	+/–	GW	OT	S	SPct	G	A	Pts	G	A	Pts	Num	PIM	Maj	Mnr	Fgt	Rgh	HHT	Hat	P/G
96-97	Col	17	1	2	3	3	0	0	8	12.5	0	1	1	0	0	0	5	10	0	5	0	2	2	0	.18
97-98	Col	7	0	0	0	0	0	0	6	0.0	0	0	0	0	0	0	4	8	0	4	0	0	2	0	.00
98-99	Col	19	1	5	6	8	0	0	22	4.5	0	2	2	0	0	0	5	10	0	5	0	0	0	0	.32
3 Years		43	2	7	9	11	0	0	36	5.6	0	3	3	0	0	0	14	28	0	14	0	2	4	0	.21

Kelly Miller

Pos: LW **Shoots:** L **Ht:** 5'11" **Wt:** 200 **Born:** 3/3/63—Lansing, Michigan **Age:** 36

Overall											Power Play			Shorthand			Penalty							Misc	
Year	Tm	GP	G	A	Pts	+/–	GW	GT	S	SPct	G	A	Pts	G	A	Pts	Num	PIM	Maj	Mnr	Fgt	Rgh	HHT	Hat	P/G
84-85	NYR	5	0	2	2	-2	0	0	5	0.0	0	–	–	0	–	–	1	2	0	1	0	–	–	0	.40
85-86	NYR	74	13	20	33	3	3	0	112	11.6	0	–	–	1	–	–	17	52	6	11	–	–	–	0	.45
86-87	2Tm	77	16	26	42	5	1	0	108	14.8	5	–	–	1	–	–	–	48	–	–	–	–	–	0	.55
87-88	Was	**80**	9	23	32	9	3	0	96	9.4	0	–	–	1	–	–	–	35	–	–	–	–	–	0	.40
88-89	Was	78	19	21	40	13	3	0	121	15.7	2	–	–	1	–	–	–	45	–	–	–	–	–	0	.51
89-90	Was	**80**	18	22	40	-2	2	0	107	16.8	3	–	–	2	–	–	–	49	–	–	–	–	–	0	.50
90-91	Was	80	24	26	50	10	3	1	155	15.5	4	–	–	2	–	–	–	29	–	–	–	–	–	0	.63
91-92	Was	78	14	38	52	20	3	0	144	9.7	0	2	2	1	4	5	19	49	1	17	0	1	12	0	.67
92-93	Was	84	18	27	45	-2	3	0	144	12.5	3	1	4	0	3	3	16	32	0	16	0	1	9	0	.54
93-94	Was	84	14	25	39	8	3	0	138	10.1	0	1	1	1	3	4	16	32	0	16	0	1	9	0	.46
94-95	Was	48	10	13	23	5	1	0	70	14.3	2	3	5	0	1	1	3	6	0	3	0	0	1	0	.48
95-96	Was	74	7	13	20	7	1	0	93	7.5	0	1	1	2	1	3	15	30	0	15	0	1	7	0	.27
96-97	Was	77	10	14	24	4	3	0	95	10.5	0	0	0	1	1	2	15	33	1	14	1	3	7	0	.31
97-98	Was	76	7	7	14	-2	3	1	68	10.3	0	0	0	3	0	3	16	41	3	13	3	0	6	0	.18
98-99	Was	62	2	5	7	-5	1	0	49	4.1	0	0	0	0	0	0	9	29	1	7	1	1	3	0	.11
86-87	NYR	38	6	14	20	-5	1	0	58	10.3	2	–	–	0	–	–	11	22	0	11	0	–	–	0	.53
86-87	Was	39	10	12	22	10	0	0	50	20.0	3	–	–	1	–	–	–	26	–	–	–	–	–	0	.56
15 Years		1057	181	282	463	71	33	2	1505	12.0	19	–	–	16	–	–	–	512	–	–	–	–	–	0	.44
Postseason																									
Year	Tm	GP	G	A	Pts	+/–	GW	OT	S	SPct	G	A	Pts	G	A	Pts	Num	PIM	Maj	Mnr	Fgt	Rgh	HHT	Hat	P/G
84-85	NYR	3	0	0	0	-1	0	0	4	0.0	0	0	0	0	0	0	1	2	0	1	0	–	–	0	.00
85-86	NYR	16	3	4	7	-1	0	0	17	17.6	0	–	–	1	–	–	2	4	0	2	0	–	–	0	.44
86-87	Was	7	2	2	4	2	0	0	12	16.7	0	–	–	0	0	0	0	0	0	0	0	0	0	0	.57
87-88	Was	14	4	4	8	6	1	0	13	30.8	0	–	–	1	–	–	–	10	–	–	–	–	–	0	.57
88-89	Was	6	1	0	1	-6	1	1	14	7.1	0	0	0	0	0	0	1	2	0	1	0	–	–	0	.17
89-90	Was	15	3	5	8	3	0	0	26	11.5	0	–	–	1	–	–	–	23	–	–	–	–	–	0	.53
90-91	Was	11	4	2	6	0	0	0	27	14.8	0	–	–	1	–	–	3	6	0	3	0	–	–	0	.55
91-92	Was	7	1	2	3	2	0	0	9	11.1	0	0	0	0	0	0	2	4	0	2	0	0	0	0	.43
92-93	Was	6	0	3	3	-7	0	0	11	0.0	0	2	2	0	0	0	1	2	0	1	0	0	0	0	.50
93-94	Was	11	2	7	9	3	0	0	11	18.2	1	0	1	1	1	2	0	0	0	0	0	0	0	0	.82
94-95	Was	7	0	3	3	-2	0	0	5	0.0	0	0	0	0	0	0	2	4	0	2	0	0	2	0	.43
95-96	Was	6	0	1	1	-1	0	0	11	0.0	0	0	0	0	0	0	2	4	0	2	0	0	1	0	.17
97-98	Was	10	0	1	1	2	0	0	8	0.0	0	0	0	0	0	0	2	4	0	2	0	0	0	0	.10
13 Years		119	20	34	54	0	2	1	168	11.9	1	–	–	5	–	–	–	65	–	–	–	–	–	0	.45

Kevin Miller

Pos: C **Shoots:** R **Ht:** 5'11" **Wt:** 190 **Born:** 9/2/65—Lansing, Michigan **Age:** 34

		Overall									Power Play			Shorthand			Penalty							Misc	
Year	Tm	GP	G	A	Pts	+/-	GW	GT	S	SPct	G	A	Pts	G	A	Pts	Num	PIM	Maj	Mnr	Fgt	Rgh	HHT	Hat	P/G
88-89	NYR	24	3	5	8	-1	1	0	40	7.5	0	0	0	0	–	–	1	2	0	1	0	–	–	0	.33
89-90	NYR	16	0	5	5	-1	0	0	9	0.0	0	0	0	0	–	–	1	2	0	1	0	–	–	0	.31
90-91	2Tm	74	22	29	51	-3	3	0	136	16.2	1	–	–	3	–	–	–	67	–	–	–	–	–	0	.69
91-92	Det	80	20	26	46	6	4	0	130	15.4	3	4	7	1	2	3	17	53	1	14	1	0	6	1	.58
92-93	2Tm	82	24	25	49	2	4	2	163	14.7	8	3	11	3	2	5	31	100	2	25	0	1	8	1	.60
93-94	StL	75	23	25	48	6	5	0	154	14.9	6	7	13	3	2	5	21	83	3	14	1	0	4	1	.64
94-95	2Tm	36	8	12	20	4	2	0	60	13.3	1	1	2	1	0	1	5	13	1	4	1	1	1	0	.56
95-96	2Tm	81	28	25	53	-4	2	2	179	15.6	3	10	13	2	3	5	17	45	1	15	0	0	5	1	.65
96-97	Chi	69	14	17	31	-10	2	0	139	10.1	5	4	9	1	0	1	11	41	1	8	1	0	2	0	.45
97-98	Chi	37	4	7	11	-4	1	0	37	10.8	0	0	0	0	0	0	4	8	0	4	0	0	2	0	.30
98-99	NYI	33	1	5	6	-5	0	0	37	2.7	0	0	0	0	0	0	5	13	1	4	1	0	0	0	.18
90-91	NYR	63	17	27	44	1	3	0	113	15.0	1	–	–	2	–	–	–	63	–	–	–	–	–	0	.70
90-91	Det	11	5	2	7	-4	0	0	23	21.7	0	–	–	1	–	–	2	4	0	2	0	–	–	0	.64
92-93	Was	10	0	3	3	-4	0	0	10	0.0	0	0	0	0	0	0	8	35	1	5	0	0	0	0	.30
92-93	StL	72	24	22	46	6	4	2	153	15.7	8	3	11	3	2	5	23	65	1	20	0	1	8	1	.64
94-95	StL	15	2	5	7	4	0	0	19	10.5	0	0	0	0	0	0	0	0	0	0	0	0	0	0	.47
94-95	SJ	21	6	7	13	0	2	0	41	14.6	1	1	2	1	0	1	5	13	1	4	1	1	1	0	.62
95-96	SJ	68	22	20	42	-8	2	2	146	15.1	2	9	11	2	3	5	15	41	1	13	0	0	5	1	.62
95-96	Pit	13	6	5	11	4	0	0	33	18.2	1	1	2	0	0	0	2	4	0	2	0	0	0	0	.85
11 Years		607	147	181	328	-10	24	4	1084	13.6	27	–	–	14	–	–	–	427	–	–	–	–	–	4	.54

Postseason

Year	Tm	GP	G	A	Pts	+/-	GW	OT	S	SPct	G	A	Pts	G	A	Pts	Num	PIM	Maj	Mnr	Fgt	Rgh	HHT	Hat	P/G
89-90	NYR	1	0	0	0	-1	0	0	0	–	0	0	0	0	0	0	0	0	0	0	0	0	0	0	.00
90-91	Det	7	3	2	5	0	0	0	11	27.3	0	–	–	1	–	–	–	20	–	–	–	–	–	0	.71
91-92	Det	9	0	2	2	-4	0	0	13	0.0	0	2	2	0	0	0	2	4	0	2	0	0	0	0	.22
92-93	StL	10	0	3	3	-5	0	0	21	0.0	0	1	1	0	0	0	4	11	1	3	1	1	1	0	.30
93-94	StL	3	1	0	1	0	0	0	5	20.0	0	0	0	1	0	1	2	4	0	2	0	1	1	0	.33
94-95	SJ	6	0	0	0	-3	0	0	7	0.0	0	0	0	0	0	0	1	2	0	1	0	0	1	0	.00
95-96	Pit	18	3	2	5	-6	0	0	36	8.3	0	0	0	0	0	0	4	8	0	4	0	0	1	0	.28
96-97	Chi	6	0	1	1	0	0	0	10	0.0	0	0	0	0	1	1	0	0	0	0	0	0	0	0	.17
8 Years		60	7	10	17	-19	0	0	103	6.8	0	–	–	2	–	–	–	49	–	–	–	–	–	0	.28

Kip Miller

(statistical profile on page 347)

Pos: C **Shoots:** L **Ht:** 5'10" **Wt:** 190 **Born:** 6/11/69—Lansing, Michigan **Age:** 30

		Overall									Power Play			Shorthand			Penalty							Misc	
Year	Tm	GP	G	A	Pts	+/-	GW	GT	S	SPct	G	A	Pts	G	A	Pts	Num	PIM	Maj	Mnr	Fgt	Rgh	HHT	Hat	P/G
90-91	Que	13	4	3	7	-1	0	1	16	25.0	0	–	–	0	–	–	2	7	1	1	–	–	–	0	.54
91-92	2Tm	39	6	12	18	-22	2	0	49	12.2	2	2	4	0	0	0	7	14	0	7	0	0	4	0	.46
92-93		Did Not Play in NHL																							
93-94	SJ	11	2	2	4	-1	0	0	21	9.5	0	1	1	0	0	0	3	6	0	3	0	0	3	0	.36
94-95	NYI	8	0	1	1	1	0	0	11	0.0	0	0	0	0	0	0	0	0	0	0	0	0	0	0	.13
95-96	Chi	10	1	4	5	1	0	1	12	8.3	0	3	3	0	0	0	1	2	0	1	0	0	1	0	.50
96-97		Did Not Play in NHL																							
97-98	NYI	9	1	3	4	-2	0	0	11	9.1	0	1	1	0	0	0	1	2	0	1	0	0	0	0	.44
98-99	Pit	77	19	23	42	1	4	0	125	15.2	1	5	6	0	0	0	11	22	0	11	0	1	6	0	.55
91-92	Que	36	5	10	15	-21	2	0	46	10.9	1	1	2	0	0	0	6	12	0	6	0	0	3	0	.42
91-92	Min	3	1	2	3	-1	0	0	3	33.3	1	1	2	0	0	0	1	2	0	1	0	0	1	0	1.00
7 Years		167	33	48	81	-23	6	2	245	13.5	3	–	–	0	–	–	25	53	1	24	–	–	–	0	.49

Postseason

Year	Tm	GP	G	A	Pts	+/-	GW	OT	S	SPct	G	A	Pts	G	A	Pts	Num	PIM	Maj	Mnr	Fgt	Rgh	HHT	Hat	P/G
98-99	Pit	13	2	7	9	-1	0	0	18	11.1	1	1	2	0	0	0	4	19	1	2	0	0	1	0	.69

Craig Mills

Pos: RW **Shoots:** R **Ht:** 6'0" **Wt:** 190 **Born:** 8/27/76—Toronto, Ontario **Age:** 23

		Overall									Power Play			Shorthand			Penalty							Misc	
Year	Tm	GP	G	A	Pts	+/-	GW	GT	S	SPct	G	A	Pts	G	A	Pts	Num	PIM	Maj	Mnr	Fgt	Rgh	HHT	Hat	P/G
95-96	Wpg	4	0	2	2	0	0	0	0	–	0	0	0	0	0	0	0	0	0	0	0	0	0	0	.50
96-97		Did Not Play in NHL																							
97-98	Chi	20	0	3	3	1	0	0	5	0.0	0	0	0	0	0	0	10	34	2	7	2	3	0	0	.15
98-99	Chi	7	0	0	0	-2	0	0	1	0.0	0	0	0	0	0	0	1	2	0	1	0	1	0	0	.00
3 Years		31	0	5	5	-1	0	0	6	0.0	0	0	0	0	0	0	11	36	2	8	2	4	0	0	.16

Year	Tm	GP	G	A	Pts	+/–	GW	OT	S	SPct	G	A	Pts	G	A	Pts	Num	PIM	Maj	Mnr	Fgt	Rgh	HHT	Hat	P/G
									Postseason																
95-96	Wpg	1	0	0	0	0	0	0	0	–	0	0	0	0	0	0	0	0	0	0	0	0	0	0	.00

Boris Mironov

(statistical profile on page 347)

Pos: D **Shoots:** R **Ht:** 6'3" **Wt:** 220 **Born:** 3/21/72—Moscow, USSR **Age:** 27

			Overall								Power Play			Shorthand			Penalty							Misc	
Year	Tm	GP	G	A	Pts	+/–	GW	GT	S	SPct	G	A	Pts	G	A	Pts	Num	PIM	Maj	Mnr	Fgt	Rgh	HHT	Hat	P/G
93-94	2Tm	79	7	24	31	-33	0	1	145	4.8	5	15	20	0	0	0	55	110	0	55	0	11	11	0	.39
94-95	Edm	29	1	7	8	-9	0	0	48	2.1	0	5	5	0	0	0	16	40	0	15	0	6	5	0	.28
95-96	Edm	78	8	24	32	-23	1	0	158	5.1	7	10	17	0	0	0	45	101	1	43	1	12	13	0	.41
96-97	Edm	55	6	26	32	2	1	0	147	4.1	2	16	18	0	0	0	33	85	1	30	1	5	15	0	.58
97-98	Edm	81	16	30	46	-8	1	1	203	7.9	10	19	29	1	0	1	50	100	0	50	0	9	22	0	.57
98-99	2Tm	75	11	38	49	13	4	1	173	6.4	5	20	25	0	0	0	48	131	1	43	1	9	16	0	.65
93-94	Wpg	65	7	22	29	-29	0	1	122	5.7	5	14	19	0	0	0	48	96	0	48	0	9	8	0	.45
93-94	Edm	14	0	2	2	-4	0	0	23	0.0	0	1	1	0	0	0	7	14	0	7	0	2	3	0	.14
98-99	Edm	63	11	29	40	6	4	1	138	8.0	5	16	21	0	0	0	40	104	0	37	0	8	14	0	.63
98-99	Chi	12	0	9	9	7	0	0	35	0.0	0	4	4	0	0	0	8	27	1	6	1	1	2	0	.75
6 Years		397	49	149	198	-58	7	3	874	5.6	29	85	114	1	0	1	247	567	3	236	3	52	82	0	.50
									Postseason																
Year	Tm	GP	G	A	Pts	+/–	GW	OT	S	SPct	G	A	Pts	G	A	Pts	Num	PIM	Maj	Mnr	Fgt	Rgh	HHT	Hat	P/G
96-97	Edm	12	2	8	10	-6	0	0	31	6.5	2	3	5	0	2	2	8	16	0	8	0	3	2	0	.83
97-98	Edm	12	3	3	6	-3	1	0	26	11.5	1	3	4	0	0	0	12	27	1	11	1	2	4	0	.50
2 Years		24	5	11	16	-9	1	0	57	8.8	3	6	9	0	2	2	20	43	1	19	1	5	6	0	.67

Dmitri Mironov

(statistical profile on page 347)

Pos: D **Shoots:** R **Ht:** 6'3" **Wt:** 215 **Born:** 12/25/65—Moscow, USSR **Age:** 34

			Overall								Power Play			Shorthand			Penalty							Misc	
Year	Tm	GP	G	A	Pts	+/–	GW	GT	S	SPct	G	A	Pts	G	A	Pts	Num	PIM	Maj	Mnr	Fgt	Rgh	HHT	Hat	P/G
91-92	Tor	7	1	0	1	-4	1	0	7	14.3	0	0	0	0	0	0	0	0	0	0	0	0	0	0	.14
92-93	Tor	59	7	24	31	-1	1	1	105	6.7	4	10	14	0	0	0	20	40	0	20	0	0	10	0	.53
93-94	Tor	76	9	27	36	5	0	2	147	6.1	3	15	18	0	0	0	39	78	0	39	0	5	17	0	.47
94-95	Tor	33	5	12	17	6	0	0	68	7.4	2	8	10	0	0	0	14	28	0	14	0	0	9	0	.52
95-96	Pit	72	3	31	34	19	1	1	86	3.5	1	6	7	0	2	2	28	88	0	24	0	2	8	0	.47
96-97	2Tm	77	13	39	52	16	2	0	177	7.3	3	21	24	1	0	1	29	101	1	23	0	1	8	0	.68
97-98	2Tm*	77	8	35	43	-7	1	0	170	4.7	3	19	22	0	1	1	34	119	1	27	1	2	17	0	.56
98-99	Was	46	2	14	16	-5	0	0	86	2.3	2	5	7	0	1	1	24	80	0	20	0	0	9	0	.35
96-97	Pit	15	1	5	6	-4	1	0	19	5.3	0	2	2	0	0	0	8	24	0	7	0	1	0	0	.40
96-97	Anh	62	12	34	46	20	1	0	158	7.6	3	19	22	1	0	1	21	77	1	16	0	0	8	0	.74
97-98	Anh	66	6	30	36	-7	1	0	142	4.2	2	16	18	0	1	1	32	115	1	25	1	2	15	0	.55
97-98	Det	11	2	5	7	0	0	0	28	7.1	1	3	4	0	0	0	2	4	0	2	0	0	2	0	.64
8 Years		447	48	182	230	29	6	4	846	5.7	18	84	102	1	4	5	188	534	2	167	1	10	78	0	.51
									Postseason																
Year	Tm	GP	G	A	Pts	+/–	GW	OT	S	SPct	G	A	Pts	G	A	Pts	Num	PIM	Maj	Mnr	Fgt	Rgh	HHT	Hat	P/G
92-93	Tor	14	1	2	3	-4	0	0	11	9.1	1	1	2	0	0	0	1	2	0	1	0	0	0	0	.21
93-94	Tor	18	6	9	15	-3	0	0	29	20.7	6	8	14	0	0	0	3	6	0	3	0	0	1	0	.83
94-95	Tor	6	2	1	3	-1	0	0	11	18.2	1	1	2	0	0	0	1	2	0	1	0	1	0	0	.50
95-96	Pit	15	0	1	1	-6	0	0	10	0.0	0	0	0	0	0	0	5	10	0	5	0	0	1	0	.07
96-97	Anh	11	1	10	11	0	0	0	36	2.8	1	6	7	0	0	0	5	10	0	5	0	1	3	0	1.00
97-98	Det	7	0	3	3	1	0	0	15	0.0	0	1	1	0	0	0	3	14	0	2	0	0	0	0	.43
6 Years		71	10	26	36	-13	0	0	112	8.9	9	17	26	0	0	0	18	44	0	17	0	2	5	0	.51

Mike Modano

(statistical profile on page 347)

Pos: C **Shoots:** L **Ht:** 6'3" **Wt:** 200 **Born:** 6/7/70—Livonia, Michigan **Age:** 29

			Overall								Power Play			Shorthand			Penalty							Misc	
Year	Tm	GP	G	A	Pts	+/–	GW	GT	S	SPct	G	A	Pts	G	A	Pts	Num	PIM	Maj	Mnr	Fgt	Rgh	HHT	Hat	P/G
88-89										Did Not Play in Regular Season															
89-90	Min	**80**	29	46	75	-7	2	0	172	16.9	12	–	–	0	–	–	–	63	–	–	–	–	–	1	.94
90-91	Min	79	28	36	64	2	2	2	232	12.1	9	–	–	0	–	–	–	65	–	–	–	–	–	0	.81
91-92	Min	76	33	44	77	-9	8	2	256	12.9	5	20	25	0	0	0	23	46	0	23	0	0	10	0	1.01
92-93	Min*	82	33	60	93	-7	7	0	307	10.7	9	27	36	0	0	0	32	83	1	29	0	2	9	0	1.13
93-94	Dal	76	50	43	93	-8	4	2	281	17.8	18	21	39	0	0	0	23	54	0	22	0	1	10	1	1.22
94-95	Dal	30	12	17	29	7	0	0	100	12.0	4	7	11	1	0	1	4	8	0	4	0	1	1	0	.97
95-96	Dal	78	36	45	81	-12	4	1	320	11.3	8	21	29	4	1	5	22	63	1	19	0	1	10	1	1.04

Overall											Power Play			Shorthand			Penalty							Misc	
Year	Tm	GP	G	A	Pts	+/–	GW	GT	S	SPct	G	A	Pts	G	A	Pts	Num	PIM	Maj	Mnr	Fgt	Rgh	HHT	Hat	P/G
96-97	Dal*	80	35	48	83	43	9	2	291	12.0	9	8	17	5	2	7	17	42	0	16	0	2	9	0	1.04
97-98	Dal*	52	21	38	59	25	2	1	191	11.0	7	12	19	5	2	7	16	32	0	16	0	0	9	1	1.13
98-99	Dal	77	34	47	81	29	7	1	224	15.2	6	21	27	4	1	5	22	44	0	22	0	1	11	**3**	1.05
10 Years		710	311	424	735	63	45	11	2374	13.1	87	–	–	19	–	–	–	500	–	–	–	–	–	7	1.04
Postseason																									
Year	Tm	GP	G	A	Pts	+/–	GW	OT	S	SPct	G	A	Pts	G	A	Pts	Num	PIM	Maj	Mnr	Fgt	Rgh	HHT	Hat	P/G
88-89	Min	2	0	0	0	-2	0	0	0	–	0	0	0	0	0	0	0	0	0	0	0	0	0	0	.00
89-90	Min	7	1	1	2	-3	0	0	17	5.9	0	–	–	0	0	0	–	12	–	–	–	–	–	0	.29
90-91	Min	23	8	12	20	-3	1	0	59	13.6	3	–	–	0	–	–	–	16	–	–	–	–	–	0	.87
91-92	Min	7	3	2	5	-2	0	0	19	15.8	1	1	2	0	0	0	2	4	0	2	0	0	0	0	.71
93-94	Dal	9	7	3	10	-2	2	0	48	14.6	2	1	3	0	0	0	8	16	0	8	0	0	3	0	1.11
96-97	Dal	7	4	1	5	2	2	0	27	14.8	1	0	1	1	0	1	0	0	0	0	0	0	0	0	.71
97-98	Dal	17	4	10	14	4	1	0	49	8.2	1	3	4	0	1	1	6	12	0	6	0	0	5	0	.82
98-99	Dal	23	5	18	23	6	1	1	83	6.0	1	6	7	1	1	2	8	16	0	8	0	0	3	0	1.00
8 Years		95	32	47	79	0	7	1	302	10.6	9	–	–	2	–	–	–	76	–	–	–	–	–	0	.83

Fredrik Modin

(statistical profile on page 348)

Pos: LW **Shoots:** L **Ht:** 6'3" **Wt:** 222 **Born:** 10/8/74—Sundsvall, Sweden **Age:** 25

Overall											Power Play			Shorthand			Penalty							Misc	
Year	Tm	GP	G	A	Pts	+/–	GW	GT	S	SPct	G	A	Pts	G	A	Pts	Num	PIM	Maj	Mnr	Fgt	Rgh	HHT	Hat	P/G
96-97	Tor	76	6	7	13	-14	0	0	85	7.1	0	0	0	0	0	0	12	24	0	12	0	0	5	0	.17
97-98	Tor	74	16	16	32	-5	4	0	137	11.7	1	1	2	0	0	0	16	32	0	16	0	2	8	0	.43
98-99	Tor	67	16	15	31	14	3	1	108	14.8	1	1	2	0	0	0	16	35	1	15	1	0	11	0	.46
3 Years		217	38	38	76	-5	7	1	330	11.5	2	2	4	0	0	0	44	91	1	43	1	2	24	0	.35
Postseason																									
Year	Tm	GP	G	A	Pts	+/–	GW	OT	S	SPct	G	A	Pts	G	A	Pts	Num	PIM	Maj	Mnr	Fgt	Rgh	HHT	Hat	P/G
98-99	Tor	8	0	0	0	-2	0	0	11	0.0	0	0	0	0	0	0	3	6	0	3	0	1	1	0	.00

Jaroslav Modry

Pos: D **Shoots:** L **Ht:** 6'2" **Wt:** 218 **Born:** 2/27/71—Ceske-Budejovice, Czechoslovakia **Age:** 28

Overall											Power Play			Shorthand			Penalty							Misc	
Year	Tm	GP	G	A	Pts	+/–	GW	GT	S	SPct	G	A	Pts	G	A	Pts	Num	PIM	Maj	Mnr	Fgt	Rgh	HHT	Hat	P/G
93-94	NJ	41	2	15	17	10	0	0	35	5.7	2	2	4	0	0	0	9	18	0	9	0	1	6	0	.41
94-95	NJ	11	0	0	0	-1	0	0	10	0.0	0	0	0	0	0	0	0	0	0	0	0	0	0	0	.00
95-96	2Tm	73	4	17	21	-21	1	0	106	3.8	1	4	5	0	0	0	22	44	0	22	0	0	16	0	.29
96-97	LA	30	3	3	6	-13	0	0	32	9.4	1	0	1	1	0	1	11	25	1	10	1	3	4	0	.20
97-98		Did Not Play in NHL																							
98-99	LA	5	0	1	1	1	0	0	11	0.0	0	1	1	0	0	0	0	0	0	0	0	0	0	0	.20
95-96	Ott	64	4	14	18	-17	1	0	89	4.5	1	4	5	0	0	0	19	38	0	19	0	0	13	0	.28
95-96	LA	9	0	3	3	-4	0	0	17	0.0	0	0	0	0	0	0	3	6	0	3	0	0	3	0	.33
5 Years		160	9	36	45	-24	1	0	194	4.6	4	7	11	1	0	1	42	87	1	41	1	4	26	0	.28

Sandy Moger

Pos: C **Shoots:** R **Ht:** 6'3" **Wt:** 218 **Born:** 3/21/69—100 Mile House, British Columbia **Age:** 30

Overall											Power Play			Shorthand			Penalty							Misc	
Year	Tm	GP	G	A	Pts	+/–	GW	GT	S	SPct	G	A	Pts	G	A	Pts	Num	PIM	Maj	Mnr	Fgt	Rgh	HHT	Hat	P/G
94-95	Bos	18	2	6	8	-1	0	0	32	6.3	2	2	4	0	0	0	3	6	0	3	0	1	0	0	.44
95-96	Bos	80	15	14	29	-9	6	0	103	14.6	4	1	5	0	0	0	28	65	3	25	3	7	7	0	.36
96-97	Bos	34	10	3	13	-12	0	0	54	18.5	3	0	3	0	0	0	18	45	3	15	3	0	2	0	.38
97-98	LA	62	11	13	24	4	2	0	89	12.4	1	3	4	0	0	0	24	70	2	20	1	6	6	0	.39
98-99	LA	42	3	2	5	-9	2	0	28	10.7	0	1	1	0	0	0	13	26	0	13	0	0	2	0	.12
5 Years		236	41	38	79	-27	10	0	306	13.4	10	7	17	0	0	0	86	212	8	76	7	14	17	0	.33
Postseason																									
Year	Tm	GP	G	A	Pts	+/–	GW	OT	S	SPct	G	A	Pts	G	A	Pts	Num	PIM	Maj	Mnr	Fgt	Rgh	HHT	Hat	P/G
95-96	Bos	5	2	2	4	-1	0	0	12	16.7	1	1	2	0	0	0	6	12	0	6	0	2	1	0	.80

Alexander Mogilny

(statistical profile on page 348)

Pos: RW **Shoots:** L **Ht:** 5'11" **Wt:** 190 **Born:** 2/18/69—Khabarovsk, USSR **Age:** 30

Overall											Power Play			Shorthand			Penalty							Misc	
Year	Tm	GP	G	A	Pts	+/–	GW	GT	S	SPct	G	A	Pts	G	A	Pts	Num	PIM	Maj	Mnr	Fgt	Rgh	HHT	Hat	P/G
89-90	Buf	65	15	28	43	8	2	1	130	11.5	4	–	–	0	–	–	–	16	–	–	–	–	–	0	.66
90-91	Buf	62	30	34	64	14	5	0	201	14.9	3	–	–	3	–	–	–	16	–	–	–	–	–	1	1.03
91-92	Buf*	67	39	45	84	7	2	0	236	16.5	15	18	33	0	0	0	16	73	3	9	1	2	2	1	1.25
92-93	Buf*	77	**76**	51	127	7	**11**	0	360	21.1	27	21	48	0	1	1	16	40	0	15	0	2	7	**7**	1.65
93-94	Buf*	66	32	47	79	8	7	1	258	12.4	17	22	39	0	0	0	11	22	0	11	0	1	2	1	1.20
94-95	Buf	44	19	28	47	0	2	1	148	12.8	12	14	26	0	1	1	14	36	0	13	0	2	4	0	1.07
95-96	Van*	79	55	52	107	14	6	3	292	18.8	10	19	29	5	2	7	8	16	0	8	0	0	3	3	1.35
96-97	Van	76	31	42	73	9	4	1	174	17.8	7	9	16	1	1	2	9	18	0	9	0	1	3	1	.96
97-98	Van	51	18	27	45	-6	1	1	118	15.3	5	12	17	4	2	6	14	36	0	13	0	2	4	0	.88
98-99	Van	59	14	31	45	0	1	1	110	12.7	3	12	15	2	3	5	13	58	0	9	0	0	4	0	.76
10 Years		646	329	385	714	61	41	9	2027	16.2	103	–	–	15	–	–	–	331	–	–	–	–	–	14	1.11

Postseason

Year	Tm	GP	G	A	Pts	+/–	GW	OT	S	SPct	G	A	Pts	G	A	Pts	Num	PIM	Maj	Mnr	Fgt	Rgh	HHT	Hat	P/G
89-90	Buf	4	0	1	1	-2	0	0	8	0.0	0	–	–	0	0	0	1	2	0	1	0	–	–	0	.25
90-91	Buf	6	0	6	6	-1	0	0	20	0.0	0	–	–	0	–	–	1	2	0	1	0	–	–	0	1.00
91-92	Buf	2	0	2	2	-1	0	0	4	0.0	0	2	2	0	0	0	0	0	0	0	0	0	0	0	1.00
92-93	Buf	7	7	3	10	2	0	0	35	20.0	2	2	4	0	0	0	3	6	0	3	0	0	1	0	1.43
93-94	Buf	7	4	2	6	1	0	0	22	18.2	1	1	2	0	0	0	3	6	0	3	0	1	1	0	.86
94-95	Buf	5	3	2	5	-6	0	0	18	16.7	0	1	1	0	0	0	1	2	0	1	0	0	0	0	1.00
95-96	Van	6	1	8	9	-1	0	0	18	5.6	0	6	6	0	0	0	4	8	0	4	0	1	2	0	1.50
7 Years		37	15	24	39	-8	0	0	125	12.0	3	–	–	0	–	–	13	26	0	13	0	–	–	0	1.05

Ian Moran

Pos: RW **Shoots:** R **Ht:** 6'0" **Wt:** 206 **Born:** 8/24/72—Cleveland, Ohio **Age:** 27

Overall											Power Play			Shorthand			Penalty							Misc	
Year	Tm	GP	G	A	Pts	+/–	GW	GT	S	SPct	G	A	Pts	G	A	Pts	Num	PIM	Maj	Mnr	Fgt	Rgh	HHT	Hat	P/G
94-95		Did Not Play in Regular Season																							
95-96	Pit	51	1	1	2	-1	0	0	44	2.3	0	0	0	0	0	0	19	47	3	16	3	2	6	0	.04
96-97	Pit	36	4	5	9	-11	0	0	50	8.0	0	2	2	0	0	0	11	22	0	11	0	3	6	0	.25
97-98	Pit	37	1	6	7	0	1	0	33	3.0	0	0	0	0	0	0	8	19	1	7	1	1	3	0	.19
98-99	Pit	62	4	5	9	1	0	0	65	6.2	0	0	0	1	0	1	13	37	1	11	1	2	3	0	.15
4 Years		186	10	17	27	-11	1	0	192	5.2	0	2	2	1	0	1	51	125	5	45	5	8	18	0	.15

Postseason

Year	Tm	GP	G	A	Pts	+/–	GW	OT	S	SPct	G	A	Pts	G	A	Pts	Num	PIM	Maj	Mnr	Fgt	Rgh	HHT	Hat	P/G
94-95	Pit	8	0	0	0	0	0	0	1	0.0	0	0	0	0	0	0	0	0	0	0	0	0	0	0	.00
96-97	Pit	5	1	2	3	1	0	0	8	12.5	0	0	0	0	0	0	2	4	0	2	0	1	0	0	.60
97-98	Pit	6	0	0	0	-1	0	0	0	–	0	0	0	0	0	0	1	2	0	1	0	0	1	0	.00
98-99	Pit	13	0	2	2	-3	0	0	12	0.0	0	0	0	0	0	0	4	8	0	4	0	0	2	0	.15
4 Years		32	1	4	5	-3	0	0	21	4.8	0	0	0	0	0	0	7	14	0	7	0	1	3	0	.16

Jay More

Pos: D **Shoots:** R **Ht:** 6'3" **Wt:** 215 **Born:** 1/12/69—Souris, Manitoba **Age:** 30

Overall											Power Play			Shorthand			Penalty							Misc	
Year	Tm	GP	G	A	Pts	+/–	GW	GT	S	SPct	G	A	Pts	G	A	Pts	Num	PIM	Maj	Mnr	Fgt	Rgh	HHT	Hat	P/G
88-89	NYR	1	0	0	0	-1	0	0	0	–	0	0	0	0	0	0	0	0	0	0	0	0	0	0	.00
89-90	Min	5	0	0	0	1	0	0	4	0.0	0	0	0	0	0	0	–	16	–	–	–	–	–	0	.00
90-91		Did Not Play in NHL																							
91-92	SJ	46	4	13	17	-32	1	0	60	6.7	1	5	6	0	0	0	33	85	1	30	0	7	9	0	.37
92-93	SJ	73	5	6	11	-35	0	0	107	4.7	0	0	0	1	0	1	66	179	5	57	5	14	16	0	.15
93-94	SJ	49	1	6	7	-5	0	0	38	2.6	0	0	0	0	1	1	30	63	1	29	1	9	11	0	.14
94-95	SJ	45	0	6	6	7	0	0	25	0.0	0	0	0	0	0	0	27	71	3	23	3	6	7	0	.13
95-96	SJ	74	2	7	9	-32	0	0	67	3.0	0	0	0	0	0	0	54	147	5	46	5	9	18	0	.12
96-97	2Tm	37	1	7	8	10	1	0	28	3.6	0	0	0	0	1	1	24	62	2	21	2	7	3	0	.22
97-98	2Tm	58	5	7	12	7	0	0	57	8.8	0	1	1	1	0	1	29	61	1	28	1	4	12	0	.21
98-99	Nsh	18	0	2	2	2	0	0	24	0.0	0	0	0	0	0	0	9	18	0	9	0	0	2	0	.11
96-97	NYR	14	0	1	1	0	0	0	10	0.0	0	0	0	0	0	0	7	25	1	5	1	0	0	0	.07
96-97	Pho	23	1	6	7	10	1	0	18	5.6	0	0	0	0	1	1	17	37	1	16	1	7	3	0	.30
97-98	Pho	41	5	5	10	0	0	0	40	12.5	0	1	1	1	0	1	25	53	1	24	1	4	11	0	.24
97-98	Chi	17	0	2	2	7	0	0	17	0.0	0	0	0	0	0	0	4	8	0	4	0	0	1	0	.12
10 Years		406	18	54	72	-78	2	0	410	4.4	1	6	7	2	2	4	–	702	–	–	–	–	–	0	.18

Postseason																													
Year	Tm	GP	G	A	Pts	+/–	GW	OT	S	SPct	G	A	Pts	G	A	Pts	Num	PIM	Maj	Mnr	Fgt	Rgh	HHT	Hat	P/G
93-94	SJ	13	0	2	2	-3	0	0	5	0.0	0	0	0	0	0	0	12	32	0	11	0	2	4	0	.15
94-95	SJ	11	0	5	5	-2	0	0	11	0.0	0	2	2	0	0	0	3	6	0	3	0	0	0	0	.45
96-97	Pho	7	0	0	0	1	0	0	6	0.0	0	0	0	0	0	0	2	7	1	1	1	0	0	0	.00
3 Years		31	0	7	7	-4	0	0	22	0.0	0	2	2	0	0	0	17	45	1	15	1	2	4	0	.23

Ethan Moreau

(statistical profile on page 348)

Pos: LW **Shoots:** L **Ht:** 6'2" **Wt:** 205 **Born:** 9/22/75—Huntsville, Ontario **Age:** 24

Overall											Power Play			Shorthand			Penalty							Misc	
Year	Tm	GP	G	A	Pts	+/–	GW	GT	S	SPct	G	A	Pts	G	A	Pts	Num	PIM	Maj	Mnr	Fgt	Rgh	HHT	Hat	P/G
95-96	Chi	8	0	1	1	1	0	0	1	0.0	0	0	0	0	0	0	2	4	0	2	0	1	0	0	.13
96-97	Chi	**82**	15	16	31	13	1	1	114	13.2	0	0	0	0	0	0	43	123	7	34	7	10	13	0	.38
97-98	Chi	54	9	9	18	0	0	0	87	10.3	2	0	2	0	0	0	32	73	3	29	3	6	12	0	.33
98-99	2Tm	80	10	11	21	-3	2	0	96	10.4	0	2	2	0	0	0	39	92	2	36	2	9	11	0	.26
98-99	Chi	66	9	6	15	-5	1	0	80	11.3	0	1	1	0	0	0	35	84	2	32	2	7	10	0	.23
98-99	Edm	14	1	5	6	2	1	0	16	6.3	0	1	1	0	0	0	4	8	0	4	0	2	1	0	.43
4 Years		224	34	37	71	11	3	1	298	11.4	2	2	4	0	0	0	116	292	12	101	12	26	36	0	.32

Postseason																									
Year	Tm	GP	G	A	Pts	+/–	GW	OT	S	SPct	G	A	Pts	G	A	Pts	Num	PIM	Maj	Mnr	Fgt	Rgh	HHT	Hat	P/G
96-97	Chi	6	1	0	1	3	0	0	10	10.0	0	0	0	0	0	0	3	9	1	2	1	1	1	0	.17
98-99	Edm	4	0	3	3	3	0	0	6	0.0	0	0	0	0	0	0	3	6	0	3	0	0	0	0	.75
2 Years		10	1	3	4	6	0	0	16	6.3	0	0	0	0	0	0	6	15	1	5	1	1	1	0	.40

Alexei Morozov

(statistical profile on page 348)

Pos: RW **Shoots:** L **Ht:** 6'1" **Wt:** 180 **Born:** 2/16/77—Moscow, USSR **Age:** 22

Overall											Power Play			Shorthand			Penalty							Misc	
Year	Tm	GP	G	A	Pts	+/–	GW	GT	S	SPct	G	A	Pts	G	A	Pts	Num	PIM	Maj	Mnr	Fgt	Rgh	HHT	Hat	P/G
97-98	Pit	76	13	13	26	-4	3	0	80	16.3	2	0	2	0	0	0	4	8	0	4	0	0	1	0	.34
98-99	Pit	67	9	10	19	5	0	0	75	12.0	0	0	0	0	0	0	7	14	0	7	0	0	3	0	.28
2 Years		143	22	23	45	1	3	0	155	14.2	2	0	2	0	0	0	11	22	0	11	0	0	4	0	.31

Postseason																									
Year	Tm	GP	G	A	Pts	+/–	GW	OT	S	SPct	G	A	Pts	G	A	Pts	Num	PIM	Maj	Mnr	Fgt	Rgh	HHT	Hat	P/G
97-98	Pit	6	0	1	1	-3	0	0	10	0.0	0	0	0	0	0	0	1	2	0	1	0	0	0	0	.17
98-99	Pit	10	1	1	2	1	0	0	13	7.7	0	0	0	0	0	0	0	0	0	0	0	0	0	0	.20
2 Years		16	1	2	3	-2	0	0	23	4.3	0	0	0	0	0	0	1	2	0	1	0	0	0	0	.19

Derek Morris

(statistical profile on page 349)

Pos: D **Shoots:** R **Ht:** 5'11" **Wt:** 180 **Born:** 8/24/78—Edmonton, Alberta **Age:** 21

Overall											Power Play			Shorthand			Penalty							Misc	
Year	Tm	GP	G	A	Pts	+/–	GW	GT	S	SPct	G	A	Pts	G	A	Pts	Num	PIM	Maj	Mnr	Fgt	Rgh	HHT	Hat	P/G
97-98	Cgy	82	9	20	29	1	1	1	120	7.5	5	7	12	1	2	3	41	88	2	39	2	3	20	0	.35
98-99	Cgy	71	7	27	34	4	2	2	150	4.7	3	7	10	0	0	0	25	73	5	19	5	5	5	0	.48
2 Years		153	16	47	63	5	3	3	270	5.9	8	14	22	1	2	3	66	161	7	58	7	8	25	0	.41

Dave Morrisette

Pos: LW **Shoots:** L **Ht:** 6'1" **Wt:** 224 **Born:** 12/24/71—Quebec City, Quebec **Age:** 28

Overall											Power Play			Shorthand			Penalty							Misc	
Year	Tm	GP	G	A	Pts	+/–	GW	GT	S	SPct	G	A	Pts	G	A	Pts	Num	PIM	Maj	Mnr	Fgt	Rgh	HHT	Hat	P/G
98-99	Mon	10	0	0	0	1	0	0	2	0.0	0	0	0	0	0	0	9	52	6	1	6	1	0	0	.00

Brendan Morrison

(statistical profile on page 349)

Pos: C **Shoots:** L **Ht:** 5'11" **Wt:** 180 **Born:** 8/12/75—Vancouver, British Columbia **Age:** 24

Overall											Power Play			Shorthand			Penalty							Misc	
Year	Tm	GP	G	A	Pts	+/–	GW	GT	S	SPct	G	A	Pts	G	A	Pts	Num	PIM	Maj	Mnr	Fgt	Rgh	HHT	Hat	P/G
97-98	NJ	11	5	4	9	3	1	1	19	26.3	0	1	1	0	0	0	0	0	0	0	0	0	0	0	.82
98-99	NJ	76	13	33	46	-4	2	0	111	11.7	5	15	20	0	1	1	5	18	0	4	0	0	2	0	.61
2 Years		87	18	37	55	-1	3	1	130	13.8	5	16	21	0	1	1	5	18	0	4	0	0	2	0	.63

Postseason																									
Year	Tm	GP	G	A	Pts	+/–	GW	OT	S	SPct	G	A	Pts	G	A	Pts	Num	PIM	Maj	Mnr	Fgt	Rgh	HHT	Hat	P/G
97-98	NJ	3	0	1	1	-1	0	0	4	0.0	0	1	1	0	0	0	0	0	0	0	0	0	0	0	.33

Postseason																									
Year	Tm	GP	G	A	Pts	+/-	GW	OT	S	SPct	G	A	Pts	G	A	Pts	Num	PIM	Maj	Mnr	Fgt	Rgh	HHT	Hat	P/G
98-99	NJ	7	0	2	2	-1	0	0	10	0.0	0	1	1	0	0	0	0	0	0	0	0	0	0	0	.29
2 Years		10	0	3	3	-2	0	0	14	0.0	0	2	2	0	0	0	0	0	0	0	0	0	0	0	.30

Tyler Moss

Pos: G **Catches:** R **Ht:** 6'0" **Wt:** 184 **Born:** 7/29/75—Ottawa, Ontario **Age:** 24

Overall																Pen Shot		Offense		
Year	Tm	GP	GS	TP	W	L	T	Min	GA	GAA	Shots	SvPct	ShO	OE	PPGA	SHGA	Shots	GA	G	A	PIM
97-98	Cgy	6	6	0	2	3	1	367	20	3.27	186	.892	0	2	1	1	1	1	0	0	0
98-99	Cgy	11	9	1	3	7	0	550	23	2.51	295	.922	0	5	9	0	1	0	0	1	0
2 Years		17	15	1	5	10	1	917	43	2.81	481	.911	0	7	10	1	2	1	0	1	0

Mark Mowers

Pos: C **Shoots:** R **Ht:** 5'11" **Wt:** 190 **Born:** 2/16/74—Whitesboro, New York **Age:** 25

Overall											Power Play			Shorthand			Penalty							Misc	
Year	Tm	GP	G	A	Pts	+/-	GW	GT	S	SPct	G	A	Pts	G	A	Pts	Num	PIM	Maj	Mnr	Fgt	Rgh	HHT	Hat	P/G
98-99	Nsh	30	0	6	6	-4	0	0	24	0.0	0	0	0	0	0	0	2	4	0	2	0	0	2	0	.20

Bill Muckalt

(statistical profile on page 349)

Pos: RW **Shoots:** R **Ht:** 6'0" **Wt:** 190 **Born:** 7/15/74—Williams Lake, British Columbia **Age:** 25

Overall											Power Play			Shorthand			Penalty							Misc	
Year	Tm	GP	G	A	Pts	+/-	GW	GT	S	SPct	G	A	Pts	G	A	Pts	Num	PIM	Maj	Mnr	Fgt	Rgh	HHT	Hat	P/G
98-99	Van	73	16	20	36	-9	1	0	119	13.4	4	7	11	2	0	2	28	98	6	19	6	2	6	0	.49

Bryan Muir

Pos: D **Shoots:** L **Ht:** 6'4" **Wt:** 220 **Born:** 6/8/73—Winnipeg, Manitoba **Age:** 26

Overall											Power Play			Shorthand			Penalty							Misc	
Year	Tm	GP	G	A	Pts	+/-	GW	GT	S	SPct	G	A	Pts	G	A	Pts	Num	PIM	Maj	Mnr	Fgt	Rgh	HHT	Hat	P/G
95-96	Edm	5	0	0	0	-4	0	0	4	0.0	0	0	0	0	0	0	3	6	0	3	0	0	2	0	.00
96-97		Did Not Play in Regular Season																							
97-98	Edm	7	0	0	0	0	0	0	6	0.0	0	0	0	0	0	0	3	17	1	1	1	0	1	0	.00
98-99	2Tm	54	1	4	5	1	0	0	82	1.2	0	0	0	0	0	0	25	50	0	25	0	3	6	0	.09
98-99	NJ	1	0	0	0	0	0	0	4	0.0	0	0	0	0	0	0	0	0	0	0	0	0	0	0	.00
98-99	Chi	53	1	4	5	1	0	0	78	1.3	0	0	0	0	0	0	25	50	0	25	0	3	6	0	.09
3 Years		66	1	4	5	-3	0	0	92	1.1	0	0	0	0	0	0	31	73	1	29	1	3	9	0	.08
Postseason																									
Year	Tm	GP	G	A	Pts	+/-	GW	OT	S	SPct	G	A	Pts	G	A	Pts	Num	PIM	Maj	Mnr	Fgt	Rgh	HHT	Hat	P/G
96-97	Edm	5	0	0	0	-2	0	0	7	0.0	0	0	0	0	0	0	2	4	0	2	0	2	0	0	.00

Kirk Muller

(statistical profile on page 349)

Pos: LW **Shoots:** L **Ht:** 6'0" **Wt:** 205 **Born:** 2/8/66—Kingston, Ontario **Age:** 33

Overall											Power Play			Shorthand			Penalty							Misc	
Year	Tm	GP	G	A	Pts	+/-	GW	GT	S	SPct	G	A	Pts	G	A	Pts	Num	PIM	Maj	Mnr	Fgt	Rgh	HHT	Hat	P/G
84-85	NJ*	**80**	17	37	54	-31	0	0	157	10.8	9	–	–	1	–	–	–	69	–	–	–	–	–	0	.68
85-86	NJ*	77	25	41	66	-20	1	0	168	14.9	5	–	–	1	–	–	–	45	–	–	–	–	–	0	.86
86-87	NJ*	79	26	50	76	-7	4	0	193	13.5	10	–	–	1	–	–	–	75	–	–	–	–	–	1	.96
87-88	NJ*	**80**	37	57	94	19	1	1	215	17.2	17	–	–	2	–	–	–	114	–	–	–	–	–	3	1.18
88-89	NJ	**80**	31	43	74	-23	4	0	182	17.0	12	10	22	1	1	2	–	119	–	–	–	–	–	0	.93
89-90	NJ*	**80**	30	56	86	-1	6	1	200	15.0	9	12	21	0	0	0	–	74	–	–	–	–	–	0	1.08
90-91	NJ	80	19	51	70	1	3	1	221	8.6	7	19	26	0	5	5	–	76	–	–	–	–	–	0	.88
91-92	Mon*	78	36	41	77	15	7	1	191	18.8	15	15	30	1	0	1	40	86	2	38	2	10	12	2	.99
92-93	Mon*	80	37	57	94	8	4	0	231	16.0	12	21	33	0	1	1	37	77	1	36	1	9	6	0	1.18
93-94	Mon	76	23	34	57	-1	3	0	168	13.7	9	14	23	2	0	2	41	96	2	38	2	5	15	0	.75
94-95	2Tm	45	11	16	27	-18	2	1	97	11.3	4	3	7	1	0	1	22	47	1	21	1	4	5	0	.60
95-96	2Tm	51	13	19	32	-13	1	0	102	12.7	7	4	11	0	1	1	21	57	5	16	5	2	6	1	.63
96-97	2Tm	76	21	19	40	-25	4	0	174	12.1	10	5	15	1	0	1	36	89	3	32	3	7	11	0	.53
97-98	Fla	70	8	21	29	-14	3	1	115	7.0	1	3	4	0	1	1	27	54	0	27	0	6	12	0	.41
98-99	Fla	82	4	11	15	-11	1	0	107	3.7	0	1	1	0	0	0	20	49	3	17	3	3	5	0	.18
94-95	Mon	33	8	11	19	-21	1	1	81	9.9	3	2	5	0	0	0	15	33	1	14	1	4	2	0	.58
94-95	NYI	12	3	5	8	3	1	0	16	18.8	1	1	2	1	0	1	7	14	0	7	0	0	3	0	.67

		Overall									Power Play			Shorthand			Penalty							Misc	
Year	Tm	GP	G	A	Pts	+/–	GW	GT	S	SPct	G	A	Pts	G	A	Pts	Num	PIM	Maj	Mnr	Fgt	Rgh	HHT	Hat	P/G
95-96	NYI	15	4	3	7	-10	0	0	23	17.4	0	1	1	0	0	0	6	15	1	5	1	1	1	0	.47
95-96	Tor	36	9	16	25	-3	1	0	79	11.4	7	3	10	0	1	1	15	42	4	11	4	1	5	1	.69
96-97	Tor	66	20	17	37	-23	3	0	153	13.1	9	4	13	1	0	1	34	85	3	30	3	7	11	0	.56
96-97	Fla	10	1	2	3	-2	1	0	21	4.8	1	1	2	0	0	0	2	4	0	2	0	0	0	0	.30
15 Years		1114	338	553	891	-121	44	6	2521	13.4	127	–	–	11	–	–	–	1127	–	–	–	–	–	7	.80
											Postseason														
Year	Tm	GP	G	A	Pts	+/–	GW	OT	S	SPct	G	A	Pts	G	A	Pts	Num	PIM	Maj	Mnr	Fgt	Rgh	HHT	Hat	P/G
87-88	NJ	20	4	8	12	-10	0	0	35	11.4	0	–	–	0	–	–	–	37	–	–	–	–	–	0	.60
89-90	NJ	6	1	3	4	-2	0	0	12	8.3	0	–	–	0	–	–	4	11	1	3	–	–	–	0	.67
90-91	NJ	7	0	2	2	-3	0	0	16	0.0	0	–	–	0	–	–	–	10	–	–	–	–	–	0	.29
91-92	Mon	11	4	3	7	-1	1	0	23	17.4	2	1	3	1	0	1	6	31	1	3	0	0	2	0	.64
92-93	Mon	20	10	7	17	4	3	2	54	18.5	3	1	4	0	0	0	9	18	0	9	0	1	4	0	.85
93-94	Mon	7	6	2	8	0	2	1	16	37.5	3	1	4	0	0	0	2	4	0	2	0	0	1	0	1.14
95-96	Tor	6	3	2	5	-1	0	0	12	25.0	2	0	2	0	0	0	0	0	0	0	0	0	0	0	.83
96-97	Fla	5	1	2	3	-3	0	0	20	5.0	1	1	2	0	0	0	2	4	0	2	0	1	0	0	.60
8 Years		82	29	29	58	-16	6	3	188	15.4	11	–	–	1	–	–	–	115	–	–	–	–	–	0	.71

Gord Murphy

Pos: D **Shoots:** R **Ht:** 6'2" **Wt:** 195 **Born:** 2/23/67—Willowdale, Ontario **Age:** 32

		Overall									Power Play			Shorthand			Penalty							Misc	
Year	Tm	GP	G	A	Pts	+/–	GW	GT	S	SPct	G	A	Pts	G	A	Pts	Num	PIM	Maj	Mnr	Fgt	Rgh	HHT	Hat	P/G
88-89	Phi	75	4	31	35	-7	1	0	116	3.4	3	–	–	0	–	–	–	68	–	–	–	–	–	0	.47
89-90	Phi	75	14	27	41	-7	1	0	160	8.8	4	–	–	0	–	–	–	95	–	–	–	–	–	0	.55
90-91	Phi	80	11	31	42	-7	2	0	203	5.4	6	–	–	0	–	–	–	58	–	–	–	–	–	0	.53
91-92	2Tm	73	5	14	19	-2	0	1	132	3.8	0	4	4	0	0	0	31	84	2	27	1	4	13	0	.26
92-93	Bos	49	5	12	17	-13	2	0	68	7.4	3	4	7	0	0	0	28	62	2	26	2	3	12	0	.35
93-94	Fla	84	14	29	43	-11	2	**3**	172	8.1	9	19	28	0	0	0	30	71	1	28	1	7	10	0	.51
94-95	Fla	46	6	16	22	-14	0	0	94	6.4	5	6	11	0	0	0	8	24	0	7	0	1	2	0	.48
95-96	Fla	70	8	22	30	5	0	0	125	6.4	4	11	15	0	2	2	15	30	0	15	0	2	5	0	.43
96-97	Fla	80	8	15	23	3	0	0	137	5.8	2	4	6	0	2	2	20	51	1	18	1	9	6	0	.29
97-98	Fla	79	6	11	17	-3	0	0	123	4.9	3	1	4	0	2	2	23	46	0	23	0	4	8	0	.22
98-99	Fla	51	0	7	7	4	0	0	56	0.0	0	2	2	0	0	0	8	16	0	8	0	0	2	0	.14
91-92	Phi	31	2	8	10	-4	0	0	50	4.0	0	4	4	0	0	0	11	33	1	9	0	2	3	0	.32
91-92	Bos	42	3	6	9	2	0	1	82	3.7	0	0	0	0	0	0	20	51	1	18	1	2	10	0	.21
11 Years		762	81	215	296	-52	8	4	1386	5.8	39	–	–	0	–	–	–	605	–	–	–	–	–	0	.39
											Postseason														
Year	Tm	GP	G	A	Pts	+/–	GW	OT	S	SPct	G	A	Pts	G	A	Pts	Num	PIM	Maj	Mnr	Fgt	Rgh	HHT	Hat	P/G
88-89	Phi	19	2	7	9	0	1	0	32	6.3	1	–	–	0	–	–	5	13	1	4	–	–	–	0	.47
91-92	Bos	15	1	0	1	-1	0	0	28	3.6	0	0	0	0	0	0	6	12	0	6	0	0	3	0	.07
95-96	Fla	14	0	4	4	1	0	0	53	0.0	0	1	1	0	0	0	3	6	0	3	0	0	3	0	.29
96-97	Fla	5	0	5	5	0	0	0	18	0.0	0	4	4	0	0	0	2	4	0	2	0	0	1	0	1.00
4 Years		53	3	16	19	0	1	0	131	2.3	1	–	–	0	–	–	16	35	1	15	–	–	–	0	.36

Joe Murphy

(statistical profile on page 350)

Pos: RW **Shoots:** L **Ht:** 6'0" **Wt:** 194 **Born:** 10/16/67—London, Ontario **Age:** 32

		Overall									Power Play			Shorthand			Penalty							Misc	
Year	Tm	GP	G	A	Pts	+/–	GW	GT	S	SPct	G	A	Pts	G	A	Pts	Num	PIM	Maj	Mnr	Fgt	Rgh	HHT	Hat	P/G
86-87	Det	5	0	1	1	0	0	0	3	0.0	0	–	–	0	–	–	1	2	0	1	0	–	–	0	.20
87-88	Det	50	10	9	19	-4	2	0	82	12.2	1	–	–	0	–	–	–	37	–	–	–	–	–	0	.38
88-89	Det	26	1	7	8	-7	0	0	29	3.4	0	–	–	0	–	–	–	28	–	–	–	–	–	0	.31
89-90	2Tm	71	10	19	29	5	1	0	117	8.5	2	–	–	0	–	–	–	60	–	–	–	–	–	0	.41
90-91	Edm	80	27	35	62	2	4	1	141	19.1	4	11	15	1	2	3	–	35	–	–	–	–	–	0	.78
91-92	Edm	80	35	47	82	17	2	2	193	18.1	10	11	21	2	1	3	18	52	0	16	0	1	2	1	1.03
92-93	Chi	19	7	10	17	-3	1	0	43	16.3	5	6	11	0	0	0	9	18	0	9	0	1	2	0	.89
93-94	Chi	81	31	39	70	1	4	0	222	14.0	7	19	26	4	1	5	43	111	3	38	1	8	10	0	.86
94-95	Chi	40	23	18	41	7	3	0	120	19.2	7	8	15	0	1	1	32	89	3	27	3	5	4	0	1.03
95-96	Chi	70	22	29	51	-3	3	0	212	10.4	8	7	15	0	0	0	35	86	0	33	0	9	11	0	.73
96-97	StL	75	20	25	45	-1	2	1	151	13.2	4	7	11	1	1	2	26	69	3	22	3	7	3	0	.60
97-98	2Tm	37	9	13	22	9	0	0	81	11.1	4	3	7	0	0	0	15	36	2	13	0	3	4	0	.59
98-99	SJ	76	25	23	48	10	2	1	176	14.2	7	8	15	0	0	0	27	73	1	24	1	1	13	0	.63
89-90	Det	9	3	1	4	4	1	0	16	18.8	0	–	–	0	–	–	2	4	0	2	0	–	–	0	.44
89-90	Edm	62	7	18	25	1	0	0	101	6.9	2	0	2	0	0	0	–	56	–	–	–	–	–	0	.40
97-98	StL	27	4	9	13	8	0	0	52	7.7	2	1	3	0	0	0	11	22	0	11	0	3	3	0	.48
97-98	SJ	10	5	4	9	1	0	0	29	17.2	2	2	4	0	0	0	4	14	2	2	0	0	1	0	.90
13 Years		710	220	275	495	33	24	5	1570	14.0	59	–	–	8	–	–	–	696	–	–	–	–	–	1	.70

											Postseason														
Year	Tm	GP	G	A	Pts	+/-	GW	OT	S	SPct	G	A	Pts	G	A	Pts	Num	PIM	Maj	Mnr	Fgt	Rgh	HHT	Hat	P/G
87-88	Det	8	0	1	1	-2	0	0	5	0.0	0	–	–	0	–	–	3	6	0	3	0	–	–	0	.13
89-90	Edm	22	6	8	14	1	2	1	29	20.7	0	–	–	0	–	–	–	16	–	–	–	–	–	0	.64
90-91	Edm	15	2	5	7	3	1	0	22	9.1	1	–	–	0	0	0	–	14	–	–	–	–	–	0	.47
91-92	Edm	16	8	16	24	2	2	1	32	25.0	4	6	10	0	0	0	6	12	0	6	0	1	1	1	1.50
92-93	Chi	4	0	0	0	-2	0	0	8	0.0	0	0	0	0	0	0	4	8	0	4	0	0	1	0	.00
93-94	Chi	6	1	3	4	2	0	0	12	8.3	0	2	2	0	0	0	7	25	1	5	0	1	1	0	.67
94-95	Chi	16	9	3	12	-1	3	1	69	13.0	3	0	3	0	0	0	9	29	1	7	0	1	1	0	.75
95-96	Chi	10	6	2	8	1	2	1	38	15.8	0	1	1	0	0	0	11	33	1	9	0	1	2	0	.80
96-97	StL	6	1	1	2	-2	0	0	8	12.5	1	1	2	0	0	0	5	10	0	5	0	1	0	0	.33
97-98	SJ	6	1	1	2	-1	0	0	10	10.0	1	0	1	0	0	0	6	20	0	5	0	1	1	0	.33
98-99	SJ	6	0	3	3	0	0	0	21	0.0	0	2	2	0	0	0	2	4	0	2	0	0	0	0	.50
11 Years		115	34	43	77	1	10	4	254	13.4	10	–	–	0	–	–	–	177	–	–	–	–	–	1	.67

Larry Murphy

(statistical profile on page 350)

Pos: D **Shoots:** R **Ht:** 6'2" **Wt:** 218 **Born:** 3/8/61—Scarborough, Ontario **Age:** 38

		Overall									Power Play			Shorthand			Penalty							Misc	
Year	Tm	GP	G	A	Pts	+/-	GW	GT	S	SPct	G	A	Pts	G	A	Pts	Num	PIM	Maj	Mnr	Fgt	Rgh	HHT	Hat	P/G
80-81	LA	80	16	60	76	17	1	1	153	10.5	5	–	–	1	–	–	–	79	–	–	–	–	–	0	.95
81-82	LA	79	22	44	66	-13	2	4	191	11.5	8	–	–	1	–	–	–	95	–	–	–	–	–	0	.84
82-83	LA	77	14	48	62	2	2	0	172	8.1	9	–	–	0	–	–	–	81	–	–	–	–	–	0	.81
83-84	2Tm	78	13	36	49	8	2	0	149	8.7	2	–	–	0	–	–	–	50	–	–	–	–	–	0	.63
84-85	Was	79	13	42	55	21	0	0	153	8.5	3	–	–	0	–	–	–	51	–	–	–	–	–	0	.70
85-86	Was	78	21	44	65	2	2	1	180	11.7	8	–	–	1	–	–	–	50	–	–	–	–	–	0	.83
86-87	Was	80	23	58	81	25	4	2	226	10.2	8	–	–	0	–	–	–	39	–	–	–	–	–	0	1.01
87-88	Was	79	8	53	61	2	1	0	201	4.0	7	–	–	0	–	–	–	72	–	–	–	–	–	0	.77
88-89	2Tm	78	11	35	46	0	1	1	160	6.9	6	–	–	0	–	–	–	82	–	–	–	–	–	0	.59
89-90	Min	77	10	58	68	-13	1	1	173	5.8	4	–	–	0	–	–	–	44	–	–	–	–	–	0	.88
90-91	2Tm	75	9	34	43	-6	2	0	188	4.8	3	–	–	0	–	–	–	68	–	–	–	–	–	0	.57
91-92	Pit	77	21	56	77	33	3	0	206	10.2	7	25	32	2	0	2	24	48	0	24	0	3	15	0	1.00
92-93	Pit	83	22	63	85	45	2	0	230	9.6	6	36	42	2	0	2	31	73	1	29	0	5	11	0	1.02
93-94	Pit*	84	17	56	73	10	4	0	236	7.2	7	24	31	0	1	1	18	44	0	17	0	1	6	0	.87
94-95	Pit	48	13	25	38	12	3	0	124	10.5	4	7	11	0	3	3	9	18	0	9	0	0	6	0	.79
95-96	Tor*	82	12	49	61	-2	1	2	182	6.6	8	31	39	0	0	0	17	34	0	17	0	1	10	0	.74
96-97	2Tm	81	9	36	45	3	1	1	158	5.7	5	18	23	0	0	0	6	20	0	5	0	0	3	0	.56
97-98	Det	82	11	41	52	35	2	0	129	8.5	2	12	14	1	2	3	13	37	1	11	0	0	4	0	.63
98-99	Det	80	10	42	52	21	2	0	168	6.0	5	21	26	1	1	2	17	42	0	16	0	2	9	0	.65
83-84	LA	6	0	3	3	-4	0	0	11	0.0	0	–	–	0	–	–	0	0	0	0	0	0	0	0	.50
83-84	Was	72	13	33	46	12	2	0	138	9.4	2	–	–	0	–	–	–	50	–	–	–	–	–	0	.64
88-89	Was	65	7	29	36	-5	0	0	129	5.4	3	–	–	0	–	–	–	70	–	–	–	–	–	0	.55
88-89	Min	13	4	6	10	5	1	1	31	12.9	3	–	–	0	–	–	–	12	–	–	–	–	–	0	.77
90-91	Min	31	4	11	15	-8	2	0	103	3.9	1	–	–	0	–	–	–	38	–	–	–	–	–	0	.48
90-91	Pit	44	5	23	28	2	0	0	85	5.9	2	12	14	0	–	–	–	30	–	–	–	–	–	0	.64
96-97	Tor	69	7	32	39	1	0	1	137	5.1	4	16	20	0	0	0	6	20	0	5	0	0	3	0	.57
96-97	Det	12	2	4	6	2	1	0	21	9.5	1	2	3	0	0	0	0	0	0	0	0	0	0	0	.50
19 Years		1477	275	880	1155	202	36	13	3379	8.1	107	–	–	9	–	–	–	1027	–	–	–	–	–	0	.78

											Postseason														
Year	Tm	GP	G	A	Pts	+/-	GW	OT	S	SPct	G	A	Pts	G	A	Pts	Num	PIM	Maj	Mnr	Fgt	Rgh	HHT	Hat	P/G
80-81	LA	4	3	0	3	–	0	0	–	–	1	0	1	0	0	0	1	2	0	1	0	–	–	0	.75
81-82	LA	10	2	8	10	–	1	0	–	–	1	–	–	0	0	0	–	12	–	–	–	–	–	0	1.00
83-84	Was	8	0	3	3	1	0	0	20	0.0	0	–	–	0	0	0	3	6	0	3	0	–	–	0	.38
84-85	Was	5	2	3	5	-4	0	0	17	11.8	2	–	–	0	0	0	0	0	0	0	0	0	0	0	1.00
85-86	Was	9	1	5	6	1	0	0	21	4.8	1	–	–	0	–	–	3	6	0	3	0	–	–	0	.67
86-87	Was	7	2	2	4	3	1	0	25	8.0	0	–	–	0	0	0	3	6	0	3	0	–	–	0	.57
87-88	Was	13	4	4	8	0	1	0	21	19.0	2	–	–	0	–	–	–	33	–	–	–	–	–	0	.62
88-89	Min	5	0	2	2	-5	0	0	9	0.0	0	–	–	0	–	–	4	8	0	4	0	–	–	0	.40
89-90	Min	7	1	2	3	-4	1	0	16	6.3	0	–	–	0	0	0	–	31	–	–	–	–	–	0	.43
90-91	Pit	23	5	18	23	17	0	0	66	7.6	4	–	–	0	–	–	–	44	–	–	–	–	–	0	1.00
91-92	Pit	21	6	10	16	-4	1	0	59	10.2	3	7	10	0	1	1	8	19	1	7	1	2	3	0	.76
92-93	Pit	12	2	11	13	2	1	0	26	7.7	2	6	8	0	0	0	5	10	0	5	0	3	0	0	1.08
93-94	Pit	6	0	5	5	-6	0	0	13	0.0	0	2	2	0	0	0	0	0	0	0	0	0	0	0	.83
94-95	Pit	12	2	13	15	3	0	0	35	5.7	1	5	6	0	0	0	0	0	0	0	0	0	0	0	1.25
95-96	Tor	6	0	2	2	-8	0	0	16	0.0	0	2	2	0	0	0	2	4	0	2	0	0	1	0	.33
96-97	Det	20	2	9	11	16	1	0	51	3.9	1	3	4	0	0	0	4	8	0	4	0	1	0	0	.55
97-98	Det	22	3	12	15	12	1	0	36	8.3	1	4	5	2	1	3	1	2	0	1	0	0	0	0	.68
98-99	Det	10	0	2	2	2	0	0	14	0.0	0	1	1	0	0	0	4	8	0	4	0	0	2	0	.20
18 Years		200	35	111	146	26	8	0	445	6.7	19	–	–	2	–	–	–	199	–	–	–	–	–	0	.73

Chris Murray

Pos: RW **Shoots:** R **Ht:** 6'2" **Wt:** 209 **Born:** 10/25/74—Port Hardy, British Columbia **Age:** 25

Overall											Power Play			Shorthand			Penalty							Misc	
Year	Tm	GP	G	A	Pts	+/–	GW	GT	S	SPct	G	A	Pts	G	A	Pts	Num	PIM	Maj	Mnr	Fgt	Rgh	HHT	Hat	P/G
94-95	Mon	3	0	0	0	0	0	0	0	–	0	0	0	0	0	0	2	4	0	2	0	0	1	0	.00
95-96	Mon	48	3	4	7	5	1	0	32	9.4	0	0	0	0	0	0	35	163	15	14	13	9	1	0	.15
96-97	2Tm	64	5	3	8	-7	0	0	41	12.2	0	0	0	0	0	0	35	124	10	22	10	8	2	0	.13
97-98	2Tm	53	5	4	9	3	2	0	51	9.8	0	0	0	0	0	0	29	118	12	14	12	7	0	0	.17
98-99	2Tm	42	1	6	7	-2	0	0	37	2.7	0	0	0	0	0	0	21	79	7	12	7	6	0	0	.17
96-97	Mon	56	4	2	6	-8	0	0	32	12.5	0	0	0	0	0	0	30	114	10	17	10	5	1	0	.11
96-97	Har	8	1	1	2	1	0	0	9	11.1	0	0	0	0	0	0	5	10	0	5	0	3	1	0	.25
97-98	Car	7	0	1	1	2	0	0	3	0.0	0	0	0	0	0	0	4	22	2	1	2	0	0	0	.14
97-98	Ott	46	5	3	8	1	2	0	48	10.4	0	0	0	0	0	0	25	96	10	13	10	7	0	0	.17
98-99	Ott	38	1	6	7	-2	0	0	33	3.0	0	0	0	0	0	0	17	65	5	10	5	4	0	0	.18
98-99	Chi	4	0	0	0	0	0	0	4	0.0	0	0	0	0	0	0	4	14	2	2	2	2	0	0	.00
5 Years		210	14	17	31	-1	3	0	161	8.7	0	0	0	0	0	0	122	488	44	64	42	30	4	0	.15

Postseason

Year	Tm	GP	G	A	Pts	+/–	GW	OT	S	SPct	G	A	Pts	G	A	Pts	Num	PIM	Maj	Mnr	Fgt	Rgh	HHT	Hat	P/G
95-96	Mon	4	0	0	0	0	0	0	1	0.0	0	0	0	0	0	0	2	4	0	2	0	0	0	0	.00
97-98	Ott	11	1	0	1	-2	0	0	12	8.3	0	0	0	0	0	0	4	8	0	4	0	0	0	0	.09
2 Years		15	1	0	1	-2	0	0	13	7.7	0	0	0	0	0	0	6	12	0	6	0	0	0	0	.07

Glen Murray

(statistical profile on page 350)

Pos: RW **Shoots:** R **Ht:** 6'2" **Wt:** 221 **Born:** 11/1/72—Halifax, Nova Scotia **Age:** 27

Overall											Power Play			Shorthand			Penalty							Misc	
Year	Tm	GP	G	A	Pts	+/–	GW	GT	S	SPct	G	A	Pts	G	A	Pts	Num	PIM	Maj	Mnr	Fgt	Rgh	HHT	Hat	P/G
91-92	Bos	5	3	1	4	2	0	0	20	15.0	1	0	1	0	0	0	0	0	0	0	0	0	0	0	.80
92-93	Bos	27	3	4	7	-6	1	0	28	10.7	2	0	2	0	0	0	4	8	0	4	0	1	2	0	.26
93-94	Bos	81	18	13	31	-1	4	2	114	15.8	0	0	0	0	0	0	24	48	0	24	0	2	10	0	.38
94-95	Bos	35	5	2	7	-11	2	0	64	7.8	0	0	0	0	0	0	16	46	2	13	1	1	8	0	.20
95-96	Pit	69	14	15	29	4	2	0	100	14.0	0	0	0	0	0	0	23	57	1	21	0	1	15	0	.42
96-97	2Tm	77	16	14	30	-21	1	0	153	10.5	3	2	5	0	0	0	16	32	0	16	0	0	12	0	.39
97-98	LA	81	29	31	60	6	7	0	193	15.0	7	8	15	3	0	3	27	54	0	27	0	0	15	1	.74
98-99	LA	61	16	15	31	-14	3	0	173	9.2	3	3	6	3	0	3	18	36	0	18	0	1	11	0	.51
96-97	Pit	66	11	11	22	-19	1	0	127	8.7	3	1	4	0	0	0	12	24	0	12	0	0	8	0	.33
96-97	LA	11	5	3	8	-2	0	0	26	19.2	0	1	1	0	0	0	4	8	0	4	0	0	4	0	.73
8 Years		436	104	95	199	-41	20	2	845	12.3	16	13	29	6	0	6	128	281	3	123	1	6	73	1	.46

Postseason

Year	Tm	GP	G	A	Pts	+/–	GW	OT	S	SPct	G	A	Pts	G	A	Pts	Num	PIM	Maj	Mnr	Fgt	Rgh	HHT	Hat	P/G
91-92	Bos	15	4	2	6	-1	0	0	19	21.1	1	1	2	0	0	0	5	10	0	5	0	1	2	0	.40
93-94	Bos	13	4	5	9	-2	0	0	28	14.3	0	0	0	0	0	0	7	14	0	7	0	2	1	0	.69
94-95	Bos	2	0	0	0	-1	0	0	2	0.0	0	0	0	0	0	0	1	2	0	1	0	0	1	0	.00
95-96	Pit	18	2	6	8	2	1	0	21	9.5	0	0	0	0	0	0	5	10	0	5	0	1	3	0	.44
97-98	LA	4	2	0	2	2	0	0	13	15.4	0	0	0	0	0	0	3	6	0	3	0	1	0	0	.50
5 Years		52	12	13	25	0	1	0	83	14.5	1	1	2	0	0	0	21	42	0	21	0	5	7	0	.48

Rem Murray

(statistical profile on page 350)

Pos: LW **Shoots:** L **Ht:** 6'2" **Wt:** 195 **Born:** 10/9/72—Stratford, Ontario **Age:** 27

Overall											Power Play			Shorthand			Penalty							Misc	
Year	Tm	GP	G	A	Pts	+/–	GW	GT	S	SPct	G	A	Pts	G	A	Pts	Num	PIM	Maj	Mnr	Fgt	Rgh	HHT	Hat	P/G
96-97	Edm	**82**	11	20	31	9	2	0	85	12.9	1	3	4	0	1	1	8	16	0	8	0	2	1	1	.38
97-98	Edm	61	9	9	18	-9	0	0	59	15.3	2	3	5	2	0	2	14	39	1	12	1	4	4	0	.30
98-99	Edm	78	21	18	39	4	4	1	116	18.1	4	5	9	1	1	2	10	20	0	10	0	0	7	0	.50
3 Years		221	41	47	88	4	6	1	260	15.8	7	11	18	3	2	5	32	75	1	30	1	6	12	1	.40

Postseason

Year	Tm	GP	G	A	Pts	+/–	GW	OT	S	SPct	G	A	Pts	G	A	Pts	Num	PIM	Maj	Mnr	Fgt	Rgh	HHT	Hat	P/G
96-97	Edm	12	1	2	3	-1	0	0	7	14.3	0	0	0	0	2	2	2	4	0	2	0	0	0	0	.25
97-98	Edm	11	1	4	5	-1	0	0	15	6.7	0	0	0	0	0	0	1	2	0	1	0	0	1	0	.45
98-99	Edm	4	1	1	2	-1	0	0	6	16.7	0	0	0	0	0	0	1	2	0	1	0	0	0	0	.50
3 Years		27	3	7	10	-3	0	0	28	10.7	0	0	0	0	2	2	4	8	0	4	0	0	1	0	.37

Rob Murray

Pos: RW **Shoots:** R **Ht:** 6'1" **Wt:** 180 **Born:** 4/4/67—Toronto, Ontario **Age:** 32

Overall											Power Play			Shorthand			Penalty							Misc	
Year	Tm	GP	G	A	Pts	+/-	GW	GT	S	SPct	G	A	Pts	G	A	Pts	Num	PIM	Maj	Mnr	Fgt	Rgh	HHT	Hat	P/G
89-90	Was	41	2	7	9	-10	0	0	29	6.9	0	–	–	0	–	–	–	58	–	–	–	–	–	0	.22
90-91	Was	17	0	3	3	0	0	0	8	0.0	0	–	–	0	–	–	–	19	–	–	–	–	–	0	.18
91-92	Wpg	9	0	1	1	-2	0	0	2	0.0	0	0	0	0	0	0	6	18	2	4	2	0	3	0	.11
92-93	Wpg	10	1	0	1	0	1	0	4	25.0	0	0	0	0	0	0	3	6	0	3	0	0	0	0	.10
93-94	Wpg	6	0	0	0	0	0	0	1	0.0	0	0	0	0	0	0	1	2	0	1	0	1	0	0	.00
94-95	Wpg	10	0	2	2	1	0	0	5	0.0	0	0	0	0	0	0	1	2	0	1	0	0	0	0	.20
95-96	Wpg	1	0	0	0	-1	0	0	1	0.0	0	0	0	0	0	0	1	2	0	1	0	0	1	0	.00
96-97											Did Not Play in NHL														
97-98											Did Not Play in NHL														
98-99	Pho	13	1	2	3	2	0	0	11	9.1	0	0	0	0	0	0	2	4	0	2	0	0	1	0	.23
8 Years		107	4	15	19	-10	1	0	61	6.6	0	–	–	0	–	–	–	111	–	–	–	–	–	0	.18

Postseason

Year	Tm	GP	G	A	Pts	+/-	GW	OT	S	SPct	G	A	Pts	G	A	Pts	Num	PIM	Maj	Mnr	Fgt	Rgh	HHT	Hat	P/G
89-90	Was	9	0	0	0	-1	0	0	4	0.0	0	0	0	0	0	0	–	18	–	–	–	–	–	0	.00

Dana Murzyn

Pos: D **Shoots:** L **Ht:** 6'2" **Wt:** 208 **Born:** 12/9/66—Regina, Saskatchewan **Age:** 33

Overall											Power Play			Shorthand			Penalty							Misc	
Year	Tm	GP	G	A	Pts	+/-	GW	GT	S	SPct	G	A	Pts	G	A	Pts	Num	PIM	Maj	Mnr	Fgt	Rgh	HHT	Hat	P/G
85-86	Har	78	3	23	26	1	1	1	79	3.8	0	–	–	0	–	–	–	125	–	–	–	–	–	0	.33
86-87	Har	74	9	19	28	17	0	0	135	6.7	1	–	–	0	–	–	–	95	–	–	–	–	–	0	.38
87-88	2Tm	74	7	11	18	1	1	0	107	6.5	1	–	–	0	–	–	–	139	–	–	–	–	–	0	.24
88-89	Cgy	63	3	19	22	26	1	0	91	3.3	0	–	–	1	–	–	50	142	6	41	–	–	–	0	.35
89-90	Cgy	78	7	13	20	19	0	0	97	7.2	1	–	–	0	–	–	54	140	8	45	–	–	–	1	.26
90-91	2Tm	29	1	2	3	-7	0	0	40	2.5	0	–	–	0	–	–	19	38	0	19	0	–	–	0	.10
91-92	Van	70	3	11	14	15	0	0	99	3.0	0	1	1	1	1	2	48	147	9	36	8	11	9	0	.20
92-93	Van	79	5	11	16	34	2	0	82	6.1	0	0	0	0	2	2	62	196	8	48	8	15	8	0	.20
93-94	Van	80	6	14	20	4	0	0	79	7.6	0	0	0	1	0	1	40	109	7	32	6	10	10	0	.25
94-95	Van	40	0	8	8	14	0	0	29	0.0	0	0	0	0	0	0	34	129	7	22	6	8	4	0	.20
95-96	Van	69	2	10	12	9	0	0	68	2.9	0	0	0	0	2	2	51	130	4	45	3	6	14	0	.17
96-97	Van	61	1	7	8	7	0	0	70	1.4	0	0	0	0	0	0	37	118	4	29	4	5	9	0	.13
97-98	Van	31	5	2	7	-3	2	0	29	17.2	0	0	0	0	0	0	18	42	2	16	2	4	1	0	.23
98-99	Van	12	0	2	2	1	0	0	7	0.0	0	0	0	0	0	0	5	21	1	3	1	0	2	0	.17
87-88	Har	33	1	6	7	-8	0	0	49	2.0	1	–	–	0	–	–	–	45	–	–	–	–	–	0	.21
87-88	Cgy	41	6	5	11	9	1	0	58	10.3	0	–	–	0	–	–	33	94	4	27	–	–	–	0	.27
90-91	Cgy	19	0	2	2	-4	0	0	25	0.0	0	–	–	0	–	–	15	30	0	15	0	–	–	0	.11
90-91	Van	10	1	0	1	-3	0	0	15	6.7	0	0	0	0	0	0	4	8	0	4	0	–	–	0	.10
14 Years		838	52	152	204	138	7	1	1012	5.1	3	–	–	3	–	–	–	1571	–	–	–	–	–	1	.24

Postseason

Year	Tm	GP	G	A	Pts	+/-	GW	OT	S	SPct	G	A	Pts	G	A	Pts	Num	PIM	Maj	Mnr	Fgt	Rgh	HHT	Hat	P/G
85-86	Har	4	0	0	0	2	0	0	2	0.0	0	0	0	0	0	0	–	10	–	–	–	–	–	0	.00
86-87	Har	6	2	1	3	-2	1	0	19	10.5	1	–	–	0	0	0	–	29	–	–	–	–	–	0	.50
87-88	Cgy	5	2	0	2	2	0	0	6	33.3	0	0	0	0	0	0	5	13	1	4	–	–	–	0	.40
88-89	Cgy	21	0	3	3	2	0	0	33	0.0	0	–	–	0	–	–	–	20	–	–	–	–	–	0	.14
89-90	Cgy	6	2	2	4	2	0	0	14	14.3	0	–	–	1	–	–	1	2	0	1	0	–	–	0	.67
90-91	Van	6	0	1	1	-1	0	0	8	0.0	0	–	–	0	–	–	4	8	0	4	0	–	–	0	.17
91-92	Van	1	0	0	0	0	0	0	0	–	0	0	0	0	0	0	2	15	1	0	0	0	0	0	.00
92-93	Van	12	3	2	5	4	0	0	16	18.8	0	0	0	0	0	0	9	18	0	9	0	1	0	0	.42
93-94	Van	7	0	0	0	-4	0	0	7	0.0	0	0	0	0	0	0	2	4	0	2	0	0	1	0	.00
94-95	Van	8	0	1	1	-1	0	0	9	0.0	0	0	0	0	1	1	7	22	0	6	0	3	1	0	.13
95-96	Van	6	0	0	0	0	0	0	2	0.0	0	0	0	0	0	0	7	25	1	5	1	2	1	0	.00
11 Years		82	9	10	19	4	1	0	116	7.8	1	–	–	1	–	–	–	166	–	–	–	–	–	0	.23

Frank Musil

Pos: D **Shoots:** L **Ht:** 6'3" **Wt:** 215 **Born:** 12/17/64—Pardubice, Czechoslovakia **Age:** 35

Overall											Power Play			Shorthand			Penalty							Misc	
Year	Tm	GP	G	A	Pts	+/-	GW	GT	S	SPct	G	A	Pts	G	A	Pts	Num	PIM	Maj	Mnr	Fgt	Rgh	HHT	Hat	P/G
86-87	Min	72	2	9	11	0	0	0	83	2.4	0	–	–	0	–	–	–	148	–	–	–	–	–	0	.15
87-88	Min	**80**	9	8	17	-2	0	1	78	11.5	1	–	–	1	–	–	–	213	–	–	–	–	–	0	.21
88-89	Min	55	1	19	20	-4	1	0	78	1.3	0	–	–	0	–	–	–	54	–	–	–	–	–	0	.36
89-90	Min	56	2	8	10	0	1	0	78	2.6	0	–	–	0	–	–	–	109	–	–	–	–	–	0	.18

Overall											Power Play			Shorthand			Penalty							Misc	
Year	Tm	GP	G	A	Pts	+/–	GW	GT	S	SPct	G	A	Pts	G	A	Pts	Num	PIM	Maj	Mnr	Fgt	Rgh	HHT	Hat	P/G
90-91	2Tm	75	7	16	23	12	1	0	73	9.6	2	–	–	0	–	–	–	183	–	–	–	–	–	0	.31
91-92	Cgy	78	4	8	12	12	0	0	71	5.6	1	0	1	1	0	1	46	103	1	44	0	11	12	0	.15
92-93	Cgy	80	6	10	16	28	1	0	87	6.9	0	1	1	0	1	1	56	131	1	53	1	13	16	0	.20
93-94	Cgy	75	1	8	9	38	0	0	65	1.5	0	0	0	0	0	0	25	50	0	25	0	1	11	0	.12
94-95	Cgy	35	0	5	5	6	0	0	18	0.0	0	0	0	0	0	0	21	61	1	18	1	2	8	0	.14
95-96	Ott	65	1	3	4	-10	0	0	37	2.7	0	0	0	0	0	0	41	85	1	40	1	8	18	0	.06
96-97	Ott	57	0	5	5	6	0	0	24	0.0	0	0	0	0	0	0	29	58	0	29	0	3	13	0	.09
97-98	Edm	17	1	2	3	1	1	0	8	12.5	0	0	0	1	0	1	4	8	0	4	0	0	4	0	.18
98-99	Edm	39	0	3	3	0	0	0	9	0.0	0	0	0	0	0	0	17	34	0	17	0	4	11	0	.08
90-91	Min	8	0	2	2	0	0	0	5	0.0	0	–	–	0	–	–	–	23	–	–	–	–	–	0	.25
90-91	Cgy	67	7	14	21	12	1	0	68	10.3	2	–	–	0	–	–	63	160	6	55	–	–	–	0	.31
13 Years		784	34	104	138	87	5	1	709	4.8	4	–	–	3	–	–	–	1237	–	–	–	–	–	0	.18
Postseason																									
Year	Tm	GP	G	A	Pts	+/–	GW	OT	S	SPct	G	A	Pts	G	A	Pts	Num	PIM	Maj	Mnr	Fgt	Rgh	HHT	Hat	P/G
88-89	Min	5	1	1	2	0	0	0	9	11.1	0	–	–	0	–	–	2	4	0	2	0	–	–	0	.40
89-90	Min	4	0	0	0	-2	0	0	5	0.0	0	0	0	0	0	0	–	14	–	–	–	–	–	0	.00
90-91	Cgy	7	0	0	0	-6	0	0	4	0.0	0	0	0	0	0	0	–	10	–	–	–	–	–	0	.00
92-93	Cgy	6	1	1	2	2	0	0	10	10.0	0	0	0	0	0	0	2	7	1	1	1	0	0	0	.33
93-94	Cgy	7	0	1	1	2	0	0	6	0.0	0	0	0	0	0	0	2	4	0	2	0	0	1	0	.14
94-95	Cgy	5	0	1	1	0	0	0	3	0.0	0	0	0	0	1	1	0	0	0	0	0	0	0	0	.20
97-98	Edm	7	0	0	0	1	0	0	0	–	0	0	0	0	0	0	3	6	0	3	0	0	3	0	.00
98-99	Edm	1	0	0	0	-1	0	0	2	0.0	0	0	0	0	0	0	1	2	0	1	0	0	1	0	.00
8 Years		42	2	4	6	-4	0	0	39	5.1	0	–	–	0	–	–	–	47	–	–	–	–	–	0	.14

Brantt Myhres

Pos: RW **Shoots:** R **Ht:** 6'4" **Wt:** 222 **Born:** 3/18/74—Edmonton, Alberta **Age:** 25

Overall											Power Play			Shorthand			Penalty							Misc	
Year	Tm	GP	G	A	Pts	+/–	GW	GT	S	SPct	G	A	Pts	G	A	Pts	Num	PIM	Maj	Mnr	Fgt	Rgh	HHT	Hat	P/G
94-95	TB	15	2	0	2	-2	1	0	4	50.0	0	0	0	0	0	0	18	81	7	8	7	3	2	0	.13
95-96											Did Not Play in NHL														
96-97	TB	47	3	1	4	1	1	0	13	23.1	0	0	0	0	0	0	29	136	10	13	9	8	2	0	.09
97-98	Phi	23	0	0	0	-1	0	0	0	–	0	0	0	0	0	0	32	169	11	12	10	4	2	0	.00
98-99	SJ	30	1	0	1	-2	0	0	7	14.3	0	0	0	0	0	0	25	116	14	8	14	4	2	0	.03
4 Years		115	6	1	7	-4	2	0	24	25.0	0	0	0	0	0	0	104	502	42	41	40	19	8	0	.06

Dmitri Nabokov

Pos: C **Shoots:** R **Ht:** 6'2" **Wt:** 209 **Born:** 1/4/77—Novosibirsk, USSR **Age:** 22

Overall											Power Play			Shorthand			Penalty							Misc	
Year	Tm	GP	G	A	Pts	+/–	GW	GT	S	SPct	G	A	Pts	G	A	Pts	Num	PIM	Maj	Mnr	Fgt	Rgh	HHT	Hat	P/G
97-98	Chi	25	7	4	11	-1	2	0	34	20.6	3	2	5	0	0	0	5	10	0	5	0	1	3	0	.44
98-99	NYI	4	0	2	2	4	0	0	4	0.0	0	0	0	0	0	0	1	2	0	1	0	0	1	0	.50
2 Years		29	7	6	13	3	2	0	38	18.4	3	2	5	0	0	0	6	12	0	6	0	1	4	0	.45

Tyson Nash

Pos: LW **Shoots:** L **Ht:** 5'11" **Wt:** 189 **Born:** 3/11/75—Edmonton, Alberta **Age:** 24

Overall											Power Play			Shorthand			Penalty							Misc	
Year	Tm	GP	G	A	Pts	+/–	GW	GT	S	SPct	G	A	Pts	G	A	Pts	Num	PIM	Maj	Mnr	Fgt	Rgh	HHT	Hat	P/G
98-99	StL	2	0	0	0	-1	0	0	1	0.0	0	0	0	0	0	0	1	5	1	0	1	0	0	0	.00
Postseason																									
Year	Tm	GP	G	A	Pts	+/–	GW	OT	S	SPct	G	A	Pts	G	A	Pts	Num	PIM	Maj	Mnr	Fgt	Rgh	HHT	Hat	P/G
98-99	StL	1	0	0	0	-3	0	0	0	–	0	0	0	0	0	0	1	2	0	1	0	0	0	0	.00

Markus Naslund

(statistical profile on page 351)

Pos: RW **Shoots:** L **Ht:** 5'11" **Wt:** 185 **Born:** 7/30/73—Bonassund, Sweden **Age:** 26

Overall											Power Play			Shorthand			Penalty							Misc	
Year	Tm	GP	G	A	Pts	+/–	GW	GT	S	SPct	G	A	Pts	G	A	Pts	Num	PIM	Maj	Mnr	Fgt	Rgh	HHT	Hat	P/G
93-94	Pit	71	4	7	11	-3	0	0	80	5.0	1	0	1	0	0	0	12	27	1	11	1	1	7	0	.15
94-95	Pit	14	2	2	4	0	0	0	13	15.4	0	1	1	0	0	0	1	2	0	1	0	0	0	0	.29
95-96	2Tm	76	22	33	55	20	5	0	144	15.3	4	4	8	0	0	0	21	42	0	21	0	0	11	2	.72
96-97	Van	78	21	20	41	-15	4	0	120	17.5	4	5	9	0	0	0	15	30	0	15	0	0	7	0	.53
97-98	Van	76	14	20	34	5	0	0	106	13.2	2	3	5	1	0	1	28	56	0	28	0	3	11	0	.45

		Overall									Power Play			Shorthand			Penalty							Misc	
Year	Tm	GP	G	A	Pts	+/–	GW	GT	S	SPct	G	A	Pts	G	A	Pts	Num	PIM	Maj	Mnr	Fgt	Rgh	HHT	Hat	P/G
98-99	Van	80	36	30	66	-13	3	1	205	17.6	15	13	28	2	1	3	33	74	0	32	0	4	11	1	.83
95-96	Pit	66	19	33	52	17	4	0	125	15.2	3	4	7	0	0	0	18	36	0	18	0	0	11	1	.79
95-96	Van	10	3	0	3	3	1	0	19	15.8	1	0	1	0	0	0	3	6	0	3	0	0	0	1	.30
6 Years		395	99	112	211	-6	12	1	668	14.8	26	26	52	3	1	4	110	231	1	108	1	8	47	3	.53
											Postseason														
Year	Tm	GP	G	A	Pts	+/–	GW	OT	S	SPct	G	A	Pts	G	A	Pts	Num	PIM	Maj	Mnr	Fgt	Rgh	HHT	Hat	P/G
95-96	Van	6	1	2	3	-2	0	0	16	6.3	1	0	1	0	0	0	4	8	0	4	0	0	3	0	.50

Alain Nasreddine

Pos: D **Shoots:** R **Ht:** 6'1" **Wt:** 201 **Born:** 7/10/75—Montreal, Quebec **Age:** 24

		Overall									Power Play			Shorthand			Penalty							Misc	
Year	Tm	GP	G	A	Pts	+/–	GW	GT	S	SPct	G	A	Pts	G	A	Pts	Num	PIM	Maj	Mnr	Fgt	Rgh	HHT	Hat	P/G
98-99	2Tm	15	0	0	0	-1	0	0	3	0.0	0	0	0	0	0	0	15	52	2	11	2	5	3	0	.00
98-99	Chi	7	0	0	0	-2	0	0	2	0.0	0	0	0	0	0	0	8	19	1	7	1	3	2	0	.00
98-99	Mon	8	0	0	0	1	0	0	1	0.0	0	0	0	0	0	0	7	33	1	4	1	2	1	0	.00

Andrei Nazarov

(statistical profile on page 351)

Pos: LW **Shoots:** R **Ht:** 6'5" **Wt:** 230 **Born:** 5/22/74—Chelyabinsk, USSR **Age:** 25

		Overall									Power Play			Shorthand			Penalty							Misc	
Year	Tm	GP	G	A	Pts	+/–	GW	GT	S	SPct	G	A	Pts	G	A	Pts	Num	PIM	Maj	Mnr	Fgt	Rgh	HHT	Hat	P/G
93-94	SJ	1	0	0	0	0	0	0	0	–	0	0	0	0	0	0	0	0	0	0	0	0	0	0	.00
94-95	SJ	26	3	5	8	-1	0	0	19	15.8	0	1	1	0	0	0	18	94	6	7	5	3	2	0	.31
95-96	SJ	42	7	7	14	-15	1	0	55	12.7	2	2	4	0	0	0	20	62	2	16	2	4	3	0	.33
96-97	SJ	60	12	15	27	-4	1	0	116	10.3	1	2	3	0	0	0	53	222	12	31	11	9	6	0	.45
97-98	2Tm	54	2	2	4	-13	0	0	50	4.0	0	0	0	0	0	0	47	170	12	30	12	10	6	0	.07
98-99	2Tm	62	7	9	16	-4	2	1	71	9.9	0	3	3	0	0	0	22	73	7	14	5	2	3	0	.26
97-98	SJ	40	1	1	2	-4	0	0	31	3.2	0	0	0	0	0	0	33	112	10	21	10	7	5	0	.05
97-98	TB	14	1	1	2	-9	0	0	19	5.3	0	0	0	0	0	0	14	58	2	9	2	3	1	0	.14
98-99	TB	26	2	0	2	-5	0	0	18	11.1	0	0	0	0	0	0	11	43	7	4	5	0	2	0	.08
98-99	Cgy	36	5	9	14	1	2	1	53	9.4	0	3	3	0	0	0	11	30	0	10	0	2	1	0	.39
6 Years		245	31	38	69	-37	4	1	311	10.0	3	8	11	0	0	0	160	621	39	98	35	28	20	0	.28
											Postseason														
Year	Tm	GP	G	A	Pts	+/–	GW	OT	S	SPct	G	A	Pts	G	A	Pts	Num	PIM	Maj	Mnr	Fgt	Rgh	HHT	Hat	P/G
94-95	SJ	6	0	0	0	0	0	0	3	0.0	0	0	0	0	0	0	1	2	0	1	0	0	1	0	.00

Rumun Ndur

Pos: D **Shoots:** L **Ht:** 6'2" **Wt:** 200 **Born:** 7/7/75—Zaria, Nigeria **Age:** 24

		Overall									Power Play			Shorthand			Penalty							Misc	
Year	Tm	GP	G	A	Pts	+/–	GW	GT	S	SPct	G	A	Pts	G	A	Pts	Num	PIM	Maj	Mnr	Fgt	Rgh	HHT	Hat	P/G
96-97	Buf	2	0	0	0	1	0	0	0	–	0	0	0	0	0	0	1	2	0	1	0	0	0	0	.00
97-98	Buf	1	0	0	0	-1	0	0	0	–	0	0	0	0	0	0	1	2	0	1	0	0	1	0	.00
98-99	2Tm	39	1	3	4	-1	0	0	22	4.5	0	0	0	0	0	0	22	62	6	16	6	7	4	0	.10
98-99	Buf	8	0	0	0	1	0	0	1	0.0	0	0	0	0	0	0	5	16	2	3	2	2	0	0	.00
98-99	NYR	31	1	3	4	-2	0	0	21	4.8	0	0	0	0	0	0	17	46	4	13	4	5	4	0	.13
3 Years		42	1	3	4	-1	0	0	22	4.5	0	0	0	0	0	0	24	66	6	18	6	7	5	0	.10

Stanislav Neckar

Pos: D **Shoots:** L **Ht:** 6'1" **Wt:** 212 **Born:** 12/22/75—Ceske-Budejovice, Czechoslovakia **Age:** 24

		Overall									Power Play			Shorthand			Penalty							Misc	
Year	Tm	GP	G	A	Pts	+/–	GW	GT	S	SPct	G	A	Pts	G	A	Pts	Num	PIM	Maj	Mnr	Fgt	Rgh	HHT	Hat	P/G
94-95	Ott	48	1	3	4	-20	0	0	34	2.9	0	1	1	0	0	0	17	37	1	16	1	6	6	0	.08
95-96	Ott	82	3	9	12	-16	0	0	57	5.3	1	0	1	0	1	1	27	54	0	27	0	1	11	0	.15
96-97	Ott	5	0	0	0	2	0	0	3	0.0	0	0	0	0	0	0	1	2	0	1	0	0	1	0	.00
97-98	Ott	60	2	2	4	-14	0	0	43	4.7	0	0	0	0	0	0	14	31	1	13	1	1	3	0	.07
98-99	3Tm	32	0	3	3	1	0	0	16	0.0	0	0	0	0	0	0	9	18	0	9	0	1	1	0	.09
98-99	Ott	3	0	2	2	-1	0	0	2	0.0	0	0	0	0	0	0	0	0	0	0	0	0	0	0	.67
98-99	NYR	18	0	0	0	-1	0	0	8	0.0	0	0	0	0	0	0	4	8	0	4	0	0	1	0	.00
98-99	Pho	11	0	1	1	3	0	0	6	0.0	0	0	0	0	0	0	5	10	0	5	0	1	0	0	.09
5 Years		227	6	17	23	-47	0	0	153	3.9	1	1	2	0	1	1	68	142	2	66	2	9	22	0	.10

Postseason																									
Year	Tm	GP	G	A	Pts	+/–	GW	OT	S	SPct	G	A	Pts	G	A	Pts	Num	PIM	Maj	Mnr	Fgt	Rgh	HHT	Hat	P/G
97-98	Ott	9	0	0	0	-4	0	0	4	0.0	0	0	0	0	0	0	1	2	0	1	0	0	0	0	.00
98-99	Pho	6	0	1	1	3	0	0	0	–	0	0	0	0	0	0	2	4	0	2	0	0	0	0	.17
2 Years		15	0	1	1	-1	0	0	4	0.0	0	0	0	0	0	0	3	6	0	3	0	0	0	0	.07

Petr Nedved

(statistical profile on page 351)

Pos: C **Shoots:** L **Ht:** 6'3" **Wt:** 195 **Born:** 12/9/71—Liberec, Czechoslovakia **Age:** 28

Overall											Power Play			Shorthand			Penalty							Misc	
Year	Tm	GP	G	A	Pts	+/–	GW	GT	S	SPct	G	A	Pts	G	A	Pts	Num	PIM	Maj	Mnr	Fgt	Rgh	HHT	Hat	P/G
90-91	Van	61	10	6	16	-21	0	0	97	10.3	1	–	–	0	–	–	–	20	–	–	–	–	–	0	.26
91-92	Van	77	15	22	37	-3	1	1	99	15.2	5	6	11	0	0	0	18	36	0	18	0	1	11	0	.48
92-93	Van	84	38	33	71	20	3	0	149	25.5	2	13	15	1	0	1	37	96	2	33	1	6	10	0	.85
93-94	StL	19	6	14	20	2	0	1	63	9.5	2	5	7	0	0	0	4	8	0	4	0	0	3	0	1.05
94-95	NYR	46	11	12	23	-1	3	0	123	8.9	1	3	4	0	0	0	13	26	0	13	0	1	7	0	.50
95-96	Pit	80	45	54	99	37	5	1	204	22.1	8	12	20	1	2	3	34	68	0	34	0	2	16	1	1.24
96-97	Pit	74	33	38	71	-2	4	0	189	17.5	12	14	26	3	0	3	33	66	0	33	0	5	15	0	.96
97-98											Did Not Play in NHL														
98-99	NYR	56	20	27	47	-6	3	0	153	13.1	9	7	16	1	0	1	25	50	0	25	0	0	14	1	.84
8 Years		497	178	206	384	26	19	3	1077	16.5	40	–	–	6	–	–	–	370	–	–	–	–	–	2	.77
Postseason																									
Year	Tm	GP	G	A	Pts	+/–	GW	OT	S	SPct	G	A	Pts	G	A	Pts	Num	PIM	Maj	Mnr	Fgt	Rgh	HHT	Hat	P/G
90-91	Van	6	0	1	1	-5	0	0	9	0.0	0	–	–	0	–	–	0	0	0	0	0	0	0	0	.17
91-92	Van	10	1	4	5	3	0	0	19	5.3	0	1	1	0	0	0	4	16	0	3	0	0	3	0	.50
92-93	Van	12	2	3	5	-2	0	0	14	14.3	0	0	0	0	0	0	1	2	0	1	0	0	0	0	.42
93-94	StL	4	0	1	1	-2	0	0	13	0.0	0	0	0	0	0	0	2	4	0	2	0	0	1	0	.25
94-95	NYR	10	3	2	5	-4	0	0	28	10.7	2	0	2	0	0	0	3	6	0	3	0	1	1	0	.50
95-96	Pit	18	10	10	20	3	2	1	54	18.5	4	2	6	0	0	0	8	16	0	8	0	1	3	0	1.11
96-97	Pit	5	1	2	3	-2	0	0	10	10.0	0	0	0	1	0	1	6	12	0	6	0	1	2	0	.60
7 Years		65	17	23	40	-9	2	1	147	11.6	6	–	–	1	–	–	24	56	0	23	0	3	10	0	.62

Jeff Nelson

Pos: C **Shoots:** L **Ht:** 6'0" **Wt:** 190 **Born:** 12/18/72—Prince Albert, Saskatchewan **Age:** 27

Overall											Power Play			Shorthand			Penalty							Misc	
Year	Tm	GP	G	A	Pts	+/–	GW	GT	S	SPct	G	A	Pts	G	A	Pts	Num	PIM	Maj	Mnr	Fgt	Rgh	HHT	Hat	P/G
94-95	Was	10	1	0	1	-2	0	0	4	25.0	0	0	0	0	0	0	1	2	0	1	0	1	0	0	.10
95-96	Was	33	0	7	7	3	0	0	21	0.0	0	0	0	0	0	0	8	16	0	8	0	1	6	0	.21
96-97											Did Not Play in NHL														
97-98											Did Not Play in NHL														
98-99	Nsh	9	2	1	3	-1	0	0	8	25.0	0	0	0	0	0	0	1	2	0	1	0	0	0	0	.33
3 Years		52	3	8	11	0	0	0	33	9.1	0	0	0	0	0	0	10	20	0	10	0	2	6	0	.21
Postseason																									
Year	Tm	GP	G	A	Pts	+/–	GW	OT	S	SPct	G	A	Pts	G	A	Pts	Num	PIM	Maj	Mnr	Fgt	Rgh	HHT	Hat	P/G
95-96	Was	3	0	0	0	0	0	0	2	0.0	0	0	0	0	0	0	2	4	0	2	0	0	2	0	.00

Sergei Nemchinov

(statistical profile on page 351)

Pos: C **Shoots:** L **Ht:** 6'0" **Wt:** 201 **Born:** 1/14/64—Moscow, USSR **Age:** 35

Overall											Power Play			Shorthand			Penalty							Misc	
Year	Tm	GP	G	A	Pts	+/–	GW	GT	S	SPct	G	A	Pts	G	A	Pts	Num	PIM	Maj	Mnr	Fgt	Rgh	HHT	Hat	P/G
91-92	NYR	73	30	28	58	19	5	0	124	24.2	2	6	8	0	1	1	6	15	1	5	1	0	3	0	.79
92-93	NYR	81	23	31	54	15	3	0	144	16.0	0	2	2	1	1	2	13	34	0	12	0	1	7	1	.67
93-94	NYR	76	22	27	49	13	6	0	144	15.3	4	3	7	0	3	3	18	36	0	18	0	0	9	0	.64
94-95	NYR	47	7	6	13	-6	3	0	67	10.4	0	0	0	0	0	0	8	16	0	8	0	0	4	0	.28
95-96	NYR	78	17	15	32	9	2	0	118	14.4	0	1	1	0	0	0	19	38	0	19	0	1	12	0	.41
96-97	2Tm	69	8	16	24	9	2	0	97	8.2	1	1	2	0	0	0	8	16	0	8	0	0	4	0	.35
97-98	NYI	74	10	19	29	3	1	0	94	10.6	2	1	3	1	0	1	12	24	0	12	0	1	6	0	.39
98-99	2Tm	77	12	8	20	-13	1	0	74	16.2	2	0	2	0	0	0	14	28	0	14	0	0	8	0	.26
96-97	NYR	63	6	13	19	5	1	0	90	6.7	1	1	2	0	0	0	6	12	0	6	0	0	2	0	.30
96-97	Van	6	2	3	5	4	1	0	7	28.6	0	0	0	0	0	0	2	4	0	2	0	0	2	0	.83
98-99	NYI	67	8	8	16	-17	0	0	61	13.1	1	0	1	0	0	0	11	22	0	11	0	0	7	0	.24
98-99	NJ	10	4	0	4	4	1	0	13	30.8	1	0	1	0	0	0	3	6	0	3	0	0	1	0	.40
8 Years		575	129	150	279	49	23	0	862	15.0	11	14	25	2	5	7	98	207	1	96	1	3	53	1	.49

Postseason																									
Year	Tm	GP	G	A	Pts	+/–	GW	OT	S	SPct	G	A	Pts	G	A	Pts	Num	PIM	Maj	Mnr	Fgt	Rgh	HHT	Hat	P/G
91-92	NYR	13	1	4	5	-3	0	0	22	4.5	0	1	1	0	2	2	4	8	0	4	0	0	2	0	.38
93-94	NYR	23	2	5	7	1	0	0	33	6.1	0	0	0	0	0	0	3	6	0	3	0	1	0	0	.30
94-95	NYR	10	4	5	9	6	1	0	16	25.0	0	0	0	0	0	0	1	2	0	1	0	0	1	0	.90
95-96	NYR	6	0	1	1	2	0	0	5	0.0	0	0	0	0	0	0	1	2	0	1	0	1	0	0	.17
98-99	NJ	4	0	0	0	-2	0	0	2	0.0	0	0	0	0	0	0	0	0	0	0	0	0	0	0	.00
5 Years		56	7	15	22	4	1	0	78	9.0	0	1	1	0	2	2	9	18	0	9	0	2	3	0	.39

Jan Nemecek

Pos: D **Shoots:** R **Ht:** 6'1" **Wt:** 215 **Born:** 2/14/76—Pisek, Czechoslovakia **Age:** 23

Overall											Power Play			Shorthand			Penalty							Misc	
Year	Tm	GP	G	A	Pts	+/–	GW	GT	S	SPct	G	A	Pts	G	A	Pts	Num	PIM	Maj	Mnr	Fgt	Rgh	HHT	Hat	P/G
98-99	LA	6	1	0	1	-1	1	0	8	12.5	0	0	0	0	0	0	2	4	0	2	0	0	2	0	.17

David Nemirovsky

Pos: RW **Shoots:** R **Ht:** 6'1" **Wt:** 192 **Born:** 8/1/76—Toronto, Ontario **Age:** 23

Overall											Power Play			Shorthand			Penalty							Misc	
Year	Tm	GP	G	A	Pts	+/–	GW	GT	S	SPct	G	A	Pts	G	A	Pts	Num	PIM	Maj	Mnr	Fgt	Rgh	HHT	Hat	P/G
95-96	Fla	9	0	2	2	-1	0	0	6	0.0	0	0	0	0	0	0	1	2	0	1	0	0	0	0	.22
96-97	Fla	39	7	7	14	1	0	1	53	13.2	1	1	2	0	0	0	8	32	0	6	0	2	1	0	.36
97-98	Fla	41	9	12	21	-3	1	0	62	14.5	2	5	7	0	0	0	4	8	0	4	0	0	2	0	.51
98-99	Fla	2	0	1	1	1	0	0	2	0.0	0	0	0	0	0	0	0	0	0	0	0	0	0	0	.50
4 Years		91	16	22	38	-2	1	1	123	13.0	3	6	9	0	0	0	13	42	0	11	0	2	3	0	.42
Postseason																									
Year	Tm	GP	G	A	Pts	+/–	GW	OT	S	SPct	G	A	Pts	G	A	Pts	Num	PIM	Maj	Mnr	Fgt	Rgh	HHT	Hat	P/G
96-97	Fla	3	1	0	1	-2	0	0	4	25.0	0	0	0	0	0	0	0	0	0	0	0	0	0	0	.33

Bernie Nicholls

Pos: C **Shoots:** R **Ht:** 6'0" **Wt:** 190 **Born:** 6/24/61—Haliburton, Ontario **Age:** 38

Overall											Power Play			Shorthand			Penalty							Misc	
Year	Tm	GP	G	A	Pts	+/–	GW	GT	S	SPct	G	A	Pts	G	A	Pts	Num	PIM	Maj	Mnr	Fgt	Rgh	HHT	Hat	P/G
81-82	LA	22	14	18	32	2	1	0	63	22.2	8	–	–	1	–	–	–	27	–	–	–	–	–	3	1.45
82-83	LA	71	28	22	50	-23	3	1	171	16.4	12	–	–	0	–	–	–	124	–	–	–	–	–	0	.70
83-84	LA*	78	41	54	95	-21	2	1	255	16.1	8	–	–	4	–	–	–	83	–	–	–	–	–	2	1.22
84-85	LA	**80**	46	54	100	-4	6	**3**	329	14.0	15	–	–	0	–	–	–	76	–	–	–	–	–	2	1.25
85-86	LA	80	36	61	97	-5	0	0	281	12.8	10	–	–	4	–	–	–	78	–	–	–	–	–	1	1.21
86-87	LA	80	33	48	81	-16	2	1	227	14.5	10	–	–	1	–	–	–	101	–	–	–	–	–	1	1.01
87-88	LA	65	32	46	78	2	1	1	236	13.6	8	–	–	7	–	–	–	114	–	–	–	–	–	1	1.20
88-89	LA*	79	70	80	150	30	6	0	385	18.2	21	–	–	8	–	–	–	96	–	–	–	–	–	4	1.90
89-90	2Tm*	79	39	73	112	-9	1	0	287	13.6	15	–	–	0	–	–	–	86	–	–	–	–	–	0	1.42
90-91	NYR	71	25	48	73	5	2	0	163	15.3	8	22	30	0	–	–	–	96	–	–	–	–	–	0	1.03
91-92	2Tm	50	20	29	49	4	2	0	117	17.1	7	11	18	0	0	0	15	60	2	10	0	2	4	0	.98
92-93	2Tm	69	13	47	60	-13	1	0	132	9.8	5	21	26	0	0	0	28	80	0	25	0	6	3	0	.87
93-94	NJ	61	19	27	46	24	1	1	142	13.4	3	8	11	0	2	2	31	86	0	28	0	4	7	1	.75
94-95	Chi	48	22	29	51	4	5	0	114	19.3	11	16	27	2	0	2	16	32	0	16	0	4	3	**3**	1.06
95-96	Chi	59	19	41	60	11	2	2	100	19.0	6	16	22	0	1	1	22	60	0	20	0	4	6	0	1.02
96-97	SJ*	65	12	33	45	-21	0	1	137	8.8	2	12	14	1	3	4	18	63	1	14	0	3	3	0	.69
97-98	SJ	60	6	22	28	-4	0	0	81	7.4	3	6	9	0	0	0	9	26	0	8	0	1	3	0	.47
98-99	SJ	10	0	2	2	-4	0	0	11	0.0	0	2	2	0	0	0	2	4	0	2	0	0	0	0	.20
89-90	LA	47	27	48	75	-6	1	0	172	15.7	8	–	–	0	–	–	–	66	–	–	–	–	–	0	1.60
89-90	NYR	32	12	25	37	-3	0	0	115	10.4	7	–	–	0	–	–	6	20	0	5	0	–	–	0	1.16
91-92	NYR	1	0	0	0	-1	0	0	2	0.0	0	0	0	0	0	0	0	0	0	0	0	0	0	0	.00
91-92	Edm	49	20	29	49	5	2	0	115	17.4	7	11	18	0	0	0	15	60	2	10	0	2	4	0	1.00
92-93	Edm	46	8	32	40	-16	1	0	86	9.3	4	15	19	0	0	0	16	40	0	15	0	5	1	0	.87
92-93	NJ	23	5	15	20	3	0	0	46	10.9	1	6	7	0	0	0	12	40	0	10	0	1	2	0	.87
18 Years		1127	475	734	1209	-38	35	11	3231	14.7	152	–	–	28	–	–	–	1292	–	–	–	–	–	18	1.07
Postseason																									
Year	Tm	GP	G	A	Pts	+/–	GW	OT	S	SPct	G	A	Pts	G	A	Pts	Num	PIM	Maj	Mnr	Fgt	Rgh	HHT	Hat	P/G
81-82	LA	10	4	0	4	–	1	0	–	–	0	0	0	0	0	0	–	23	–	–	–	–	–	0	.40
84-85	LA	3	1	1	2	-2	0	0	15	6.7	0	–	–	0	0	0	3	9	1	2	–	–	–	0	.67
86-87	LA	5	2	5	7	1	0	0	16	12.5	1	–	–	0	0	0	3	6	0	3	0	–	–	0	1.40
87-88	LA	5	2	6	8	-3	0	0	22	9.1	1	–	–	0	0	0	4	11	1	3	–	–	–	0	1.60
88-89	LA	11	7	9	16	-2	1	0	50	14.0	3	–	–	0	–	–	–	12	–	–	–	–	–	0	1.45

Postseason																									
Year	Tm	GP	G	A	Pts	+/–	GW	OT	S	SPct	G	A	Pts	G	A	Pts	Num	PIM	Maj	Mnr	Fgt	Rgh	HHT	Hat	P/G
89-90	NYR	10	7	5	12	1	0	0	30	23.3	3	–	–	0	–	–	–	16	–	–	–	–	–	1	1.20
90-91	NYR	5	4	3	7	0	1	0	24	16.7	0	–	–	0	0	0	4	8	0	4	0	–	–	0	1.40
91-92	Edm	16	8	11	19	2	1	0	32	25.0	4	5	9	0	0	0	11	25	1	10	0	2	2	0	1.19
92-93	NJ	5	0	0	0	-5	0	0	3	0.0	0	0	0	0	0	0	3	6	0	3	0	2	0	0	.00
93-94	NJ	16	4	9	13	3	0	0	37	10.8	2	2	4	1	0	1	10	28	0	9	0	2	3	0	.81
94-95	Chi	16	1	11	12	0	0	0	28	3.6	1	3	4	0	1	1	4	8	0	4	0	0	2	0	.75
95-96	Chi	10	2	7	9	3	0	0	11	18.2	1	2	3	0	0	0	2	4	0	2	0	0	0	0	.90
97-98	SJ	6	0	5	5	-2	0	0	6	0.0	0	3	3	0	0	0	4	8	0	4	0	0	3	0	.83
13 Years		118	42	72	114	-4	4	0	274	13.9	16	–	–	1	–	–	–	164	–	–	–	–	–	1	.97

Eric Nickulas

Pos: C **Shoots:** R **Ht:** 5'11" **Wt:** 190 **Born:** 3/25/75—Cape Cod, Massachusetts **Age:** 24

Overall											Power Play			Shorthand			Penalty							Misc	
Year	Tm	GP	G	A	Pts	+/–	GW	GT	S	SPct	G	A	Pts	G	A	Pts	Num	PIM	Maj	Mnr	Fgt	Rgh	HHT	Hat	P/G
98-99	Bos	2	0	0	0	0	0	0	0	–	0	0	0	0	0	0	0	0	0	0	0	0	0	0	.00
Postseason																									
Year	Tm	GP	G	A	Pts	+/–	GW	OT	S	SPct	G	A	Pts	G	A	Pts	Num	PIM	Maj	Mnr	Fgt	Rgh	HHT	Hat	P/G
98-99	Bos	1	0	0	0	0	0	0	0	–	0	0	0	0	0	0	1	2	0	1	0	0	1	0	.00

Rob Niedermayer

(statistical profile on page 352)

Pos: C **Shoots:** L **Ht:** 6'2" **Wt:** 201 **Born:** 12/28/74—Cassiar, British Columbia **Age:** 25

Overall											Power Play			Shorthand			Penalty							Misc	
Year	Tm	GP	G	A	Pts	+/–	GW	GT	S	SPct	G	A	Pts	G	A	Pts	Num	PIM	Maj	Mnr	Fgt	Rgh	HHT	Hat	P/G
93-94	Fla	65	9	17	26	-11	2	0	67	13.4	3	9	12	0	0	0	17	51	3	13	2	2	7	0	.40
94-95	Fla	48	4	6	10	-13	0	0	58	6.9	1	2	3	0	0	0	15	36	2	13	2	3	2	0	.21
95-96	Fla	82	26	35	61	1	6	0	155	16.8	11	12	23	0	0	0	31	107	7	21	7	5	7	0	.74
96-97	Fla	60	14	24	38	4	2	0	136	10.3	3	7	10	0	1	1	21	54	4	17	4	2	8	0	.63
97-98	Fla	33	8	7	15	-9	2	0	64	12.5	5	1	6	0	0	0	15	41	1	13	1	1	1	0	.45
98-99	Fla	82	18	33	51	-13	3	2	142	12.7	6	10	16	1	0	1	25	50	0	25	0	3	14	0	.62
6 Years		370	79	122	201	-41	15	2	622	12.7	29	41	70	1	1	2	124	339	17	102	16	16	39	0	.54
Postseason																									
Year	Tm	GP	G	A	Pts	+/–	GW	OT	S	SPct	G	A	Pts	G	A	Pts	Num	PIM	Maj	Mnr	Fgt	Rgh	HHT	Hat	P/G
95-96	Fla	22	5	3	8	-8	2	0	48	10.4	2	1	3	0	0	0	6	12	0	6	0	1	0	0	.36
96-97	Fla	5	2	1	3	-1	0	0	5	40.0	1	1	2	0	0	0	3	6	0	3	0	1	2	0	.60
2 Years		27	7	4	11	-9	2	0	53	13.2	3	2	5	0	0	0	9	18	0	9	0	2	2	0	.41

Scott Niedermayer

(statistical profile on page 352)

Pos: D **Shoots:** L **Ht:** 6'0" **Wt:** 205 **Born:** 8/31/73—Edmonton, Alberta **Age:** 26

Overall											Power Play			Shorthand			Penalty							Misc	
Year	Tm	GP	G	A	Pts	+/–	GW	GT	S	SPct	G	A	Pts	G	A	Pts	Num	PIM	Maj	Mnr	Fgt	Rgh	HHT	Hat	P/G
91-92	NJ	4	0	1	1	1	0	0	4	0.0	0	0	0	0	0	0	1	2	0	1	0	0	0	0	.25
92-93	NJ	80	11	29	40	8	0	1	131	8.4	5	14	19	0	0	0	18	47	1	16	0	2	4	0	.50
93-94	NJ	81	10	36	46	34	2	1	135	7.4	5	9	14	0	1	1	21	42	0	21	0	0	11	0	.57
94-95	NJ	48	4	15	19	19	0	0	52	7.7	4	4	8	0	1	1	9	18	0	9	0	3	3	0	.40
95-96	NJ	79	8	25	33	5	0	0	179	4.5	6	10	16	0	3	3	23	46	0	23	0	5	9	0	.42
96-97	NJ	81	5	30	35	-4	3	0	159	3.1	3	15	18	0	0	0	21	64	2	17	2	2	6	0	.43
97-98	NJ*	81	14	43	57	5	1	0	175	8.0	11	18	29	0	0	0	12	27	1	11	1	3	5	0	.70
98-99	NJ	72	11	35	46	16	3	0	161	6.8	1	20	21	1	0	1	13	26	0	13	0	3	3	0	.64
8 Years		526	63	214	277	84	9	2	996	6.3	35	90	125	1	5	6	118	272	4	111	3	18	41	0	.53
Postseason																									
Year	Tm	GP	G	A	Pts	+/–	GW	OT	S	SPct	G	A	Pts	G	A	Pts	Num	PIM	Maj	Mnr	Fgt	Rgh	HHT	Hat	P/G
92-93	NJ	5	0	3	3	-3	0	0	11	0.0	0	2	2	0	0	0	1	2	0	1	0	0	0	0	.60
93-94	NJ	20	2	2	4	-1	0	0	29	6.9	1	0	1	0	0	0	4	8	0	4	0	1	2	0	.20
94-95	NJ	20	4	7	11	11	1	0	53	7.5	2	1	3	0	0	0	5	10	0	5	0	3	2	0	.55
96-97	NJ	10	2	4	6	0	1	0	34	5.9	2	3	5	0	0	0	3	6	0	3	0	1	1	0	.60
97-98	NJ	6	0	2	2	0	0	0	15	0.0	0	0	0	0	1	1	2	4	0	2	0	0	0	0	.33
98-99	NJ	7	1	3	4	-5	0	0	13	7.7	1	0	1	0	0	0	5	18	0	4	0	2	0	0	.57
6 Years		68	9	21	30	2	2	0	155	5.8	6	6	12	0	1	1	20	48	0	19	0	7	5	0	.44

Jeff Nielsen

Pos: RW **Shoots:** R **Ht:** 6'0" **Wt:** 200 **Born:** 9/20/71—Grand Rapids, Minnesota **Age:** 28

Overall											Power Play			Shorthand			Penalty							Misc	
Year	Tm	GP	G	A	Pts	+/-	GW	GT	S	SPct	G	A	Pts	G	A	Pts	Num	PIM	Maj	Mnr	Fgt	Rgh	HHT	Hat	P/G
96-97	NYR	2	0	0	0	-1	0	0	1	0.0	0	0	0	0	0	0	1	2	0	1	0	0	0	0	.00
97-98	Anh	32	4	5	9	-1	0	0	36	11.1	0	0	0	0	0	0	8	16	0	8	0	1	1	0	.28
98-99	Anh	80	5	4	9	-12	2	0	94	5.3	0	0	0	0	0	0	14	34	2	12	2	3	2	0	.11
3 Years		114	9	9	18	-14	2	0	131	6.9	0	0	0	0	0	0	23	52	2	21	2	4	3	0	.16
Postseason																									
Year	Tm	GP	G	A	Pts	+/-	GW	OT	S	SPct	G	A	Pts	G	A	Pts	Num	PIM	Maj	Mnr	Fgt	Rgh	HHT	Hat	P/G
98-99	Anh	4	0	0	0	-6	0	0	7	0.0	0	0	0	0	0	0	1	2	0	1	0	0	1	0	.00

Joe Nieuwendyk

(statistical profile on page 352)

Pos: C **Shoots:** L **Ht:** 6'1" **Wt:** 195 **Born:** 9/10/66—Oshawa, Ontario **Age:** 33

Overall											Power Play			Shorthand			Penalty							Misc	
Year	Tm	GP	G	A	Pts	+/-	GW	GT	S	SPct	G	A	Pts	G	A	Pts	Num	PIM	Maj	Mnr	Fgt	Rgh	HHT	Hat	P/G
86-87	Cgy	9	5	1	6	0	1	0	16	31.3	2	–	–	0	–	–	0	0	0	0	0	0	0	0	.67
87-88	Cgy*	75	51	41	92	20	8	0	212	24.1	**31**	–	–	3	–	–	10	23	1	9	–	–	–	4	1.23
88-89	Cgy*	77	51	31	82	26	**11**	2	215	23.7	19	–	–	3	–	–	20	40	0	20	0	–	–	2	1.06
89-90	Cgy*	79	45	50	95	32	3	0	226	19.9	18	–	–	0	–	–	16	40	0	15	0	–	–	1	1.20
90-91	Cgy	79	45	40	85	19	1	0	222	20.3	22	–	–	4	–	–	18	36	0	18	0	–	–	0	1.08
91-92	Cgy	69	22	34	56	-1	2	1	137	16.1	7	12	19	0	0	0	22	55	1	20	1	5	8	0	.81
92-93	Cgy	79	38	37	75	9	6	0	208	18.3	14	13	27	0	0	0	26	52	0	26	0	2	13	1	.95
93-94	Cgy*	64	36	39	75	19	7	1	191	18.8	14	14	28	1	0	1	24	51	1	23	0	6	3	1	1.17
94-95	Cgy	46	21	29	50	11	4	0	122	17.2	3	12	15	0	0	0	11	33	1	9	0	1	2	1	1.09
95-96	Dal	52	14	18	32	-17	3	0	138	10.1	8	8	16	0	0	0	15	41	1	13	0	0	10	0	.62
96-97	Dal	66	30	21	51	-5	2	2	173	17.3	8	10	18	0	0	0	16	32	0	16	0	2	8	0	.77
97-98	Dal	73	39	30	69	16	11	0	203	19.2	14	15	29	0	0	0	15	30	0	15	0	2	5	2	.95
98-99	Dal	67	28	27	55	11	8	1	157	17.8	8	10	18	0	0	0	17	34	0	17	0	3	9	0	.82
13 Years		835	425	398	823	140	67	7	2220	19.1	168	–	–	11	–	–	210	467	5	201	–	–	–	12	.99
Postseason																									
Year	Tm	GP	G	A	Pts	+/-	GW	OT	S	SPct	G	A	Pts	G	A	Pts	Num	PIM	Maj	Mnr	Fgt	Rgh	HHT	Hat	P/G
86-87	Cgy	6	2	2	4	-2	0	0	8	25.0	0	–	–	0	–	–	0	0	0	0	0	0	0	0	.67
87-88	Cgy	8	3	4	7	0	0	0	21	14.3	1	–	–	0	–	–	1	2	0	1	0	–	–	0	.88
88-89	Cgy	22	10	4	14	0	1	0	57	17.5	6	–	–	0	–	–	–	10	–	–	–	–	–	0	.64
89-90	Cgy	6	4	6	10	6	1	0	19	21.1	1	–	–	0	–	–	2	4	0	2	0	–	–	0	1.67
90-91	Cgy	7	4	1	5	-4	0	0	27	14.8	2	–	–	0	0	0	–	10	–	–	–	–	–	0	.71
92-93	Cgy	6	3	6	9	-4	0	0	21	14.3	1	3	4	0	0	0	5	10	0	5	0	2	3	0	1.50
93-94	Cgy	6	2	2	4	0	0	0	8	25.0	1	0	1	0	0	0	0	0	0	0	0	0	0	0	.67
94-95	Cgy	5	4	3	7	0	1	0	21	19.0	2	0	2	0	0	0	0	0	0	0	0	0	0	0	1.40
96-97	Dal	7	2	2	4	-1	0	0	21	9.5	0	1	1	0	0	0	3	6	0	3	0	1	1	0	.57
97-98	Dal	1	1	0	1	1	0	0	1	100.0	0	0	0	0	0	0	0	0	0	0	0	0	0	0	1.00
98-99	Dal	23	11	10	21	7	6	2	72	15.3	3	2	5	0	0	0	8	19	1	7	1	1	4	0	.91
11 Years		97	46	40	86	3	9	2	276	16.7	17	–	–	0	–	–	–	61	–	–	–	–	–	0	.89

Janne Niinimaa

(statistical profile on page 352)

Pos: D **Shoots:** L **Ht:** 6'1" **Wt:** 220 **Born:** 5/22/75—Raahe, Finland **Age:** 24

Overall											Power Play			Shorthand			Penalty							Misc	
Year	Tm	GP	G	A	Pts	+/-	GW	GT	S	SPct	G	A	Pts	G	A	Pts	Num	PIM	Maj	Mnr	Fgt	Rgh	HHT	Hat	P/G
96-97	Phi	77	4	40	44	12	2	0	141	2.8	1	23	24	0	0	0	25	58	0	24	0	3	13	0	.57
97-98	2Tm	77	4	39	43	13	1	0	134	3.0	3	21	24	0	1	1	31	62	0	31	0	1	20	0	.56
98-99	Edm	81	4	24	28	7	1	0	142	2.8	2	8	10	0	1	1	40	88	0	39	0	4	16	0	.35
97-98	Phi	66	3	31	34	6	1	0	115	2.6	2	17	19	0	0	0	28	56	0	28	0	1	18	0	.52
97-98	Edm	11	1	8	9	7	0	0	19	5.3	1	4	5	0	1	1	3	6	0	3	0	0	2	0	.82
3 Years		235	12	103	115	32	4	0	417	2.9	6	52	58	0	2	2	96	208	0	94	0	8	49	0	.49
Postseason																									
Year	Tm	GP	G	A	Pts	+/-	GW	OT	S	SPct	G	A	Pts	G	A	Pts	Num	PIM	Maj	Mnr	Fgt	Rgh	HHT	Hat	P/G
96-97	Phi	19	1	12	13	3	1	0	56	1.8	1	7	8	0	0	0	8	16	0	8	0	2	1	0	.68
97-98	Edm	11	1	1	2	3	1	0	20	5.0	0	0	0	0	0	0	6	12	0	6	0	1	4	0	.18
98-99	Edm	4	0	0	0	-2	0	0	5	0.0	0	0	0	0	0	0	1	2	0	1	0	0	1	0	.00
3 Years		34	2	13	15	4	2	0	81	2.5	1	7	8	0	0	0	15	30	0	15	0	3	6	0	.44

Andrei Nikolishin

(statistical profile on page 353)

Pos: LW **Shoots:** L **Ht:** 5'11" **Wt:** 200 **Born:** 3/25/73—Vorkuta, USSR **Age:** 26

Overall											Power Play			Shorthand			Penalty							Misc	
Year	Tm	GP	G	A	Pts	+/-	GW	GT	S	SPct	G	A	Pts	G	A	Pts	Num	PIM	Maj	Mnr	Fgt	Rgh	HHT	Hat	P/G
94-95	Har	39	8	10	18	7	0	0	57	14.0	1	3	4	1	0	1	5	10	0	5	0	0	4	0	.46
95-96	Har	61	14	37	51	-2	3	0	83	16.9	4	12	16	1	1	2	17	34	0	17	0	1	9	0	.84
96-97	2Tm	71	9	19	28	3	0	0	98	9.2	1	5	6	0	0	0	16	32	0	16	0	3	8	0	.39
97-98	Was	38	6	10	16	1	1	0	40	15.0	1	2	3	0	0	0	7	14	0	7	0	3	3	0	.42
98-99	Was	73	8	27	35	0	1	0	121	6.6	0	7	7	1	1	2	14	28	0	14	0	0	5	0	.48
96-97	Har	12	2	5	7	-2	0	0	25	8.0	0	2	2	0	0	0	1	2	0	1	0	1	0	0	.58
96-97	Was	59	7	14	21	5	0	0	73	9.6	1	3	4	0	0	0	15	30	0	15	0	2	8	0	.36
5 Years		282	45	103	148	9	5	0	399	11.3	7	29	36	3	2	5	59	118	0	59	0	7	29	0	.52
Postseason																									
Year	Tm	GP	G	A	Pts	+/-	GW	OT	S	SPct	G	A	Pts	G	A	Pts	Num	PIM	Maj	Mnr	Fgt	Rgh	HHT	Hat	P/G
97-98	Was	21	1	13	14	4	0	0	29	3.4	1	6	7	0	1	1	6	12	0	6	0	0	2	0	.67

Marcus Nilson

Pos: RW **Shoots:** R **Ht:** 6'2" **Wt:** 193 **Born:** 3/1/78—Balsta, Sweden **Age:** 21

Overall											Power Play			Shorthand			Penalty							Misc	
Year	Tm	GP	G	A	Pts	+/-	GW	GT	S	SPct	G	A	Pts	G	A	Pts	Num	PIM	Maj	Mnr	Fgt	Rgh	HHT	Hat	P/G
98-99	Fla	8	1	1	2	2	1	0	7	14.3	0	0	0	0	0	0	1	5	1	0	1	0	0	0	.25

Owen Nolan

(statistical profile on page 353)

Pos: RW **Shoots:** R **Ht:** 6'1" **Wt:** 215 **Born:** 2/12/72—Belfast, Northern Ireland **Age:** 27

Overall											Power Play			Shorthand			Penalty							Misc	
Year	Tm	GP	G	A	Pts	+/-	GW	GT	S	SPct	G	A	Pts	G	A	Pts	Num	PIM	Maj	Mnr	Fgt	Rgh	HHT	Hat	P/G
90-91	Que	59	3	10	13	-19	0	0	54	5.6	0	0	0	0	0	0	34	109	11	22	11	9	3	0	.22
91-92	Que*	75	42	31	73	-9	0	1	190	22.1	17	7	24	0	0	0	63	183	11	49	8	18	6	2	.97
92-93	Que	73	36	41	77	-1	4	1	241	14.9	15	15	30	0	0	0	61	185	5	50	5	20	4	2	1.05
93-94	Que	6	2	2	4	2	0	0	15	13.3	0	0	0	0	0	0	4	8	0	4	0	1	1	0	.67
94-95	Que	46	30	19	49	21	**8**	0	137	21.9	13	4	17	2	0	2	17	46	4	13	4	7	0	**3**	1.07
95-96	2Tm*	81	33	36	69	-33	2	0	207	15.9	16	13	29	1	2	3	46	146	10	33	9	12	6	1	.85
96-97	SJ*	72	31	32	63	-19	3	1	225	13.8	10	10	20	0	0	0	58	155	5	50	5	27	6	1	.88
97-98	SJ	75	14	27	41	-2	1	0	192	7.3	3	10	13	1	4	5	48	144	8	37	5	17	7	0	.55
98-99	SJ	78	19	26	45	16	3	1	207	9.2	6	8	14	2	0	2	48	129	3	42	3	17	4	0	.58
95-96	Col	9	4	4	8	-3	0	0	23	17.4	4	1	5	0	0	0	3	9	1	2	1	0	1	0	.89
95-96	SJ	72	29	32	61	-30	2	0	184	15.8	12	12	24	1	2	3	43	137	9	31	8	12	5	1	.85
9 Years		565	210	224	434	-44	21	4	1468	14.3	80	67	147	6	6	12	379	1105	57	300	50	128	37	9	.77
Postseason																									
Year	Tm	GP	G	A	Pts	+/-	GW	OT	S	SPct	G	A	Pts	G	A	Pts	Num	PIM	Maj	Mnr	Fgt	Rgh	HHT	Hat	P/G
92-93	Que	5	1	0	1	-2	0	0	12	8.3	0	0	0	0	0	0	1	2	0	1	0	1	0	0	.20
94-95	Que	6	2	3	5	2	0	0	12	16.7	0	0	0	0	0	0	3	6	0	3	0	1	0	0	.83
97-98	SJ	6	2	2	4	-1	1	0	16	12.5	2	1	3	0	0	0	6	26	2	3	0	0	0	0	.67
98-99	SJ	6	1	1	2	0	0	0	26	3.8	0	0	0	0	0	0	3	6	0	3	0	0	0	0	.33
4 Years		23	6	6	12	-1	1	0	66	9.1	2	1	3	0	0	0	13	40	2	10	0	2	0	0	.52

Brian Noonan

Pos: RW **Shoots:** R **Ht:** 6'1" **Wt:** 205 **Born:** 5/29/65—Boston, Massachusetts **Age:** 34

Overall											Power Play			Shorthand			Penalty							Misc	
Year	Tm	GP	G	A	Pts	+/-	GW	GT	S	SPct	G	A	Pts	G	A	Pts	Num	PIM	Maj	Mnr	Fgt	Rgh	HHT	Hat	P/G
87-88	Chi	77	10	20	30	-27	2	0	87	11.5	3	–	–	0	–	–	–	44	–	–	–	–	–	0	.39
88-89	Chi	45	4	12	16	-2	0	1	84	4.8	2	–	–	0	–	–	–	28	–	–	–	–	–	0	.36
89-90	Chi	8	0	2	2	0	0	0	13	0.0	0	–	–	0	–	–	3	6	0	3	0	–	–	0	.25
90-91	Chi	7	0	4	4	-1	0	0	12	0.0	0	–	–	0	–	–	1	2	0	1	0	–	–	0	.57
91-92	Chi	65	19	12	31	9	0	2	154	12.3	4	4	8	0	0	0	24	81	3	18	1	3	4	3	.48
92-93	Chi	63	16	14	30	3	3	0	129	12.4	5	4	9	0	0	0	26	82	2	21	0	3	5	0	.48
93-94	2Tm	76	18	23	41	7	6	1	160	11.3	10	9	19	0	0	0	29	69	1	27	1	6	10	0	.54
94-95	NYR	45	14	13	27	-3	1	0	95	14.7	7	3	10	0	1	1	9	26	0	8	0	1	1	1	.60
95-96	StL	81	13	22	35	2	6	0	131	9.9	3	5	8	1	1	2	31	84	2	27	2	5	5	0	.43
96-97	3Tm	73	12	22	34	-3	1	1	100	12.0	3	5	8	1	1	2	13	34	0	12	0	2	3	0	.47
97-98	Van	82	10	15	25	-19	2	2	87	11.5	1	0	1	0	0	0	20	62	2	16	2	5	6	0	.30
98-99	Pho	7	0	0	0	-3	0	0	1	0.0	0	0	0	0	0	0	0	0	0	0	0	0	0	0	.00
93-94	Chi	64	14	21	35	2	3	1	134	10.4	8	9	17	0	0	0	23	57	1	21	1	5	8	0	.55
93-94	NYR	12	4	2	6	5	3	0	26	15.4	2	0	2	0	0	0	6	12	0	6	0	1	2	0	.50

		Overall									Power Play			Shorthand			Penalty							Misc	
Year	Tm	GP	G	A	Pts	+/–	GW	GT	S	SPct	G	A	Pts	G	A	Pts	Num	PIM	Maj	Mnr	Fgt	Rgh	HHT	Hat	P/G
96-97	StL	13	2	5	7	2	0	0	13	15.4	0	0	0	0	0	0	0	0	0	0	0	0	0	0	.54
96-97	NYR	44	6	9	15	-7	1	1	62	9.7	3	3	6	0	0	0	10	28	0	9	0	1	3	0	.34
96-97	Van	16	4	8	12	2	0	0	25	16.0	0	2	2	1	1	2	3	6	0	3	0	1	0	0	.75
12 Years		629	116	159	275	-37	21	7	1053	11.0	38	–	–	2	–	–	–	518	–	–	–	–	–	4	.44

		Postseason																							
Year	Tm	GP	G	A	Pts	+/–	GW	OT	S	SPct	G	A	Pts	G	A	Pts	Num	PIM	Maj	Mnr	Fgt	Rgh	HHT	Hat	P/G
87-88	Chi	3	0	0	0	-1	0	0	0	–	0	0	0	0	0	0	2	4	0	2	0	–	–	0	.00
88-89	Chi	1	0	0	0	0	0	0	3	0.0	0	0	0	0	0	0	0	0	0	0	0	0	0	0	.00
91-92	Chi	18	6	9	15	-3	1	0	37	16.2	3	4	7	0	0	0	11	30	0	10	0	1	2	0	.83
92-93	Chi	4	3	0	3	0	0	0	13	23.1	1	0	1	0	0	0	2	4	0	2	0	1	0	1	.75
93-94	NYR	22	4	7	11	2	1	0	45	8.9	2	2	4	0	0	0	7	17	1	6	1	5	0	0	.50
94-95	NYR	5	0	0	0	0	0	0	5	0.0	0	0	0	0	0	0	4	8	0	4	0	1	0	0	.00
95-96	StL	13	4	1	5	-5	0	0	21	19.0	0	0	0	0	1	1	5	10	0	5	0	0	2	0	.38
98-99	Pho	5	0	2	2	2	0	0	10	0.0	0	0	0	0	0	0	2	4	0	2	0	1	1	0	.40
8 Years		71	17	19	36	-5	2	0	134	12.7	6	6	12	0	1	1	33	77	1	31	1	–	–	1	.51

Peter Nordstrom

Pos: C **Shoots:** R **Ht:** 6'1" **Wt:** 200 **Born:** 7/26/74—Munkfors, Sweden **Age:** 25

		Overall									Power Play			Shorthand			Penalty							Misc	
Year	Tm	GP	G	A	Pts	+/–	GW	GT	S	SPct	G	A	Pts	G	A	Pts	Num	PIM	Maj	Mnr	Fgt	Rgh	HHT	Hat	P/G
98-99	Bos	2	0	0	0	-1	0	0	0	–	0	0	0	0	0	0	0	0	0	0	0	0	0	0	.00

Mattias Norstrom

Pos: D **Shoots:** L **Ht:** 6'1" **Wt:** 205 **Born:** 1/2/72—Stockholm, Sweden **Age:** 27

		Overall									Power Play			Shorthand			Penalty							Misc	
Year	Tm	GP	G	A	Pts	+/–	GW	GT	S	SPct	G	A	Pts	G	A	Pts	Num	PIM	Maj	Mnr	Fgt	Rgh	HHT	Hat	P/G
93-94	NYR	9	0	2	2	0	0	0	3	0.0	0	0	0	0	0	0	3	6	0	3	0	0	1	0	.22
94-95	NYR	9	0	3	3	2	0	0	4	0.0	0	0	0	0	0	0	1	2	0	1	0	0	0	0	.33
95-96	2Tm	36	2	2	4	-3	0	0	34	5.9	0	1	1	0	0	0	20	40	0	20	0	3	7	0	.11
96-97	LA	80	1	21	22	-4	0	0	106	0.9	0	5	5	0	1	1	31	84	2	27	2	7	11	0	.28
97-98	LA	73	1	12	13	14	0	0	61	1.6	0	4	4	0	0	0	34	90	2	30	1	6	11	0	.18
98-99	LA	78	2	5	7	-10	0	0	61	3.3	0	0	0	1	0	1	18	36	0	18	0	3	7	0	.09
95-96	NYR	25	2	1	3	5	0	0	17	11.8	0	0	0	0	0	0	11	22	0	11	0	2	5	0	.12
95-96	LA	11	0	1	1	-8	0	0	17	0.0	0	1	1	0	0	0	9	18	0	9	0	1	2	0	.09
6 Years		285	6	45	51	-1	0	0	269	2.2	0	10	10	1	1	2	107	258	4	99	3	19	37	0	.18

		Postseason																							
Year	Tm	GP	G	A	Pts	+/–	GW	OT	S	SPct	G	A	Pts	G	A	Pts	Num	PIM	Maj	Mnr	Fgt	Rgh	HHT	Hat	P/G
94-95	NYR	3	0	0	0	-1	0	0	1	0.0	0	0	0	0	0	0	0	0	0	0	0	0	0	0	.00
97-98	LA	4	0	0	0	-1	0	0	3	0.0	0	0	0	0	0	0	1	2	0	1	0	0	1	0	.00
2 Years		7	0	0	0	-2	0	0	4	0.0	0	0	0	0	0	0	1	2	0	1	0	0	1	0	.00

Jeff Norton

(statistical profile on page 353)

Pos: D **Shoots:** L **Ht:** 6'2" **Wt:** 200 **Born:** 11/25/65—Cambridge, Massachusetts **Age:** 34

		Overall									Power Play			Shorthand			Penalty							Misc	
Year	Tm	GP	G	A	Pts	+/–	GW	GT	S	SPct	G	A	Pts	G	A	Pts	Num	PIM	Maj	Mnr	Fgt	Rgh	HHT	Hat	P/G
87-88	NYI	15	1	6	7	3	1	0	18	5.6	1	–	–	0	–	–	–	14	–	–	–	–	–	0	.47
88-89	NYI	69	1	30	31	-24	0	0	126	0.8	1	–	–	0	–	–	–	74	–	–	–	–	–	0	.45
89-90	NYI	60	4	49	53	-9	0	0	104	3.8	4	–	–	0	–	–	–	65	–	–	–	–	–	0	.88
90-91	NYI	44	3	25	28	-13	0	0	87	3.4	2	–	–	1	–	–	–	16	–	–	–	–	–	0	.64
91-92	NYI	28	1	18	19	2	0	0	34	2.9	0	8	8	1	1	2	9	18	0	9	0	0	4	0	.68
92-93	NYI	66	12	38	50	-3	0	0	127	9.4	5	19	24	0	0	0	21	45	1	20	1	6	6	0	.76
93-94	SJ	64	7	33	40	16	0	0	92	7.6	1	10	11	0	0	0	14	36	0	13	0	1	7	0	.63
94-95	2Tm	48	3	27	30	22	1	0	48	6.3	0	6	6	0	0	0	21	72	2	16	1	2	5	0	.63
95-96	2Tm	66	8	23	31	9	2	0	85	9.4	1	12	13	0	1	1	21	42	0	21	0	2	5	0	.47
96-97	2Tm	75	2	16	18	-7	0	0	81	2.5	0	6	6	0	1	1	22	58	2	19	2	4	7	0	.24
97-98	2Tm	56	4	13	17	-32	0	1	61	6.6	4	3	7	0	0	0	18	44	0	17	0	3	4	0	.30
98-99	2Tm	72	4	18	22	2	1	0	70	5.7	2	10	12	0	1	1	18	44	0	17	0	4	6	0	.31
94-95	SJ	20	1	9	10	1	0	0	21	4.8	0	1	1	0	0	0	10	39	1	7	0	0	2	0	.50
94-95	StL	28	2	18	20	21	1	0	27	7.4	0	5	5	0	0	0	11	33	1	9	1	2	3	0	.71
95-96	StL	36	4	7	11	4	1	0	33	12.1	0	4	4	0	0	0	13	26	0	13	0	1	2	0	.31
95-96	Edm	30	4	16	20	5	1	0	52	7.7	1	8	9	0	1	1	8	16	0	8	0	1	3	0	.67
96-97	Edm	62	2	11	13	-7	0	0	68	2.9	0	4	4	0	0	0	17	42	0	16	0	3	7	0	.21
96-97	TB	13	0	5	5	0	0	0	13	0.0	0	2	2	0	1	1	5	16	2	3	2	1	0	0	.38

Overall											Power Play			Shorthand			Penalty							Misc	
Year	Tm	GP	G	A	Pts	+/-	GW	GT	S	SPct	G	A	Pts	G	A	Pts	Num	PIM	Maj	Mnr	Fgt	Rgh	HHT	Hat	P/G
97-98	TB	37	4	6	10	-25	0	1	41	9.8	4	1	5	0	0	0	9	26	0	8	0	2	1	0	.27
97-98	Fla	19	0	7	7	-7	0	0	20	0.0	0	2	2	0	0	0	9	18	0	9	0	1	3	0	.37
98-99	Fla	3	0	0	0	0	0	0	2	0.0	0	0	0	0	0	0	1	2	0	1	0	0	1	0	.00
98-99	SJ	69	4	18	22	2	1	0	68	5.9	2	10	12	0	1	1	17	42	0	16	0	4	5	0	.32
12 Years		663	50	296	346	-34	5	1	933	5.4	21	–	–	2	–	–	–	528	–	–	–	–	–	0	.52
Postseason																									
Year	Tm	GP	G	A	Pts	+/-	GW	OT	S	SPct	G	A	Pts	G	A	Pts	Num	PIM	Maj	Mnr	Fgt	Rgh	HHT	Hat	P/G
87-88	NYI	3	0	2	2	-1	0	0	6	0.0	0	–	–	0	–	–	5	13	1	4	–	–	–	0	.67
89-90	NYI	4	1	3	4	0	0	0	7	14.3	0	–	–	0	0	0	–	17	–	–	–	–	–	0	1.00
92-93	NYI	10	1	1	2	-5	0	0	19	5.3	1	0	1	0	0	0	2	4	0	2	0	0	1	0	.20
93-94	SJ	14	1	5	6	4	0	0	24	4.2	0	1	1	0	0	0	10	20	0	10	0	4	3	0	.43
94-95	StL	7	1	1	2	1	0	0	13	7.7	0	1	1	0	0	0	4	11	1	3	1	1	0	0	.29
98-99	SJ	6	0	7	7	5	0	0	3	0.0	0	5	5	0	0	0	5	10	0	5	0	3	1	0	1.17
6 Years		44	4	19	23	4	0	0	72	5.6	1	–	–	0	–	–	–	75	–	–	–	–	–	0	.52

Teppo Numminen

(statistical profile on page 353)

Pos: D **Shoots:** R **Ht:** 6'1" **Wt:** 190 **Born:** 7/3/68—Tampere, Finland **Age:** 31

Overall											Power Play			Shorthand			Penalty							Misc	
Year	Tm	GP	G	A	Pts	+/-	GW	GT	S	SPct	G	A	Pts	G	A	Pts	Num	PIM	Maj	Mnr	Fgt	Rgh	HHT	Hat	P/G
88-89	Wpg	69	1	14	15	-11	0	1	85	1.2	0	–	–	1	–	–	–	36	–	–	–	–	–	0	.22
89-90	Wpg	79	11	32	43	-4	1	0	105	10.5	1	–	–	0	–	–	–	20	–	–	–	–	–	0	.54
90-91	Wpg	80	8	25	33	-15	0	0	151	5.3	3	–	–	0	–	–	–	28	–	–	–	–	–	0	.41
91-92	Wpg	80	5	34	39	15	1	0	143	3.5	4	15	19	0	1	1	16	32	0	16	0	1	10	0	.49
92-93	Wpg	66	7	30	37	4	0	0	103	6.8	3	7	10	1	0	1	15	33	1	14	1	0	9	0	.56
93-94	Wpg	57	5	18	23	-23	1	0	89	5.6	4	9	13	0	2	2	14	28	0	14	0	1	9	0	.40
94-95	Wpg	42	5	16	21	12	0	0	86	5.8	2	6	8	0	0	0	8	16	0	8	0	0	7	0	.50
95-96	Wpg	74	11	43	54	-4	3	0	165	6.7	6	22	28	0	1	1	11	22	0	11	0	1	6	0	.73
96-97	Pho	**82**	2	25	27	-3	0	0	135	1.5	0	9	9	0	0	0	14	28	0	14	0	0	9	0	.33
97-98	Pho	82	11	40	51	25	2	0	126	8.7	6	16	22	0	2	2	15	30	0	15	0	0	9	0	.62
98-99	Pho	82	10	30	40	3	0	2	156	6.4	1	15	16	0	2	2	15	30	0	15	0	0	8	0	.49
11 Years		793	76	307	383	-1	8	3	1344	5.7	30	–	–	2	–	–	–	303	–	–	–	–	–	0	.48
Postseason																									
Year	Tm	GP	G	A	Pts	+/-	GW	OT	S	SPct	G	A	Pts	G	A	Pts	Num	PIM	Maj	Mnr	Fgt	Rgh	HHT	Hat	P/G
89-90	Wpg	7	1	2	3	1	0	0	10	10.0	0	–	–	0	0	0	–	10	–	–	–	–	–	0	.43
91-92	Wpg	7	0	0	0	-3	0	0	9	0.0	0	0	0	0	0	0	0	0	0	0	0	0	0	0	.00
92-93	Wpg	6	1	1	2	-4	0	0	9	11.1	1	0	1	0	0	0	1	2	0	1	0	0	0	0	.33
95-96	Wpg	6	0	0	0	-3	0	0	6	0.0	0	0	0	0	0	0	1	2	0	1	0	0	1	0	.00
96-97	Pho	7	3	3	6	3	1	0	19	15.8	1	1	2	0	0	0	0	0	0	0	0	0	0	0	.86
97-98	Pho	1	0	0	0	0	0	0	0	–	0	0	0	0	0	0	0	0	0	0	0	0	0	0	.00
98-99	Pho	7	2	1	3	-5	0	0	18	11.1	2	1	3	0	0	0	2	4	0	2	0	0	0	0	.43
7 Years		41	7	7	14	-11	1	0	71	9.9	4	–	–	0	0	0	–	18	–	–	–	–	–	0	.34

Michael Nylander

(statistical profile on page 354)

Pos: C **Shoots:** L **Ht:** 5'11" **Wt:** 190 **Born:** 10/3/72—Stockholm, Sweden **Age:** 27

Overall											Power Play			Shorthand			Penalty							Misc	
Year	Tm	GP	G	A	Pts	+/-	GW	GT	S	SPct	G	A	Pts	G	A	Pts	Num	PIM	Maj	Mnr	Fgt	Rgh	HHT	Hat	P/G
92-93	Har	59	11	22	33	-7	1	0	85	12.9	3	4	7	0	0	0	14	36	0	13	0	3	1	1	.56
93-94	2Tm	73	13	42	55	8	1	2	95	13.7	4	7	11	0	0	0	15	30	0	15	0	1	2	0	.75
94-95	Cgy	6	0	1	1	1	0	0	2	0.0	0	0	0	0	0	0	1	2	0	1	0	0	1	0	.17
95-96	Cgy	73	17	38	55	0	6	0	163	10.4	4	15	19	0	0	0	10	20	0	10	0	0	3	0	.75
96-97		Did Not Play in NHL																							
97-98	Cgy	65	13	23	36	10	2	0	117	11.1	0	5	5	0	0	0	12	24	0	12	0	2	4	0	.55
98-99	2Tm	33	4	10	14	-9	0	0	33	12.1	1	4	5	0	0	0	4	8	0	4	0	0	1	0	.42
93-94	Har	58	11	33	44	-2	1	2	74	14.9	4	7	11	0	0	0	12	24	0	12	0	1	2	0	.76
93-94	Cgy	15	2	9	11	10	0	0	21	9.5	0	0	0	0	0	0	3	6	0	3	0	0	0	0	.73
98-99	Cgy	9	2	3	5	1	0	0	7	28.6	1	1	2	0	0	0	1	2	0	1	0	0	0	0	.56
98-99	TB	24	2	7	9	-10	0	0	26	7.7	0	3	3	0	0	0	3	6	0	3	0	0	1	0	.38
6 Years		309	58	136	194	3	10	2	495	11.7	12	35	47	0	0	0	56	120	0	55	0	6	12	1	.63
Postseason																									
Year	Tm	GP	G	A	Pts	+/-	GW	OT	S	SPct	G	A	Pts	G	A	Pts	Num	PIM	Maj	Mnr	Fgt	Rgh	HHT	Hat	P/G
93-94	Cgy	3	0	0	0	-1	0	0	3	0.0	0	0	0	0	0	0	0	0	0	0	0	0	0	0	.00
94-95	Cgy	6	0	6	6	-3	0	0	13	0.0	0	5	5	0	0	0	1	2	0	1	0	0	1	0	1.00
95-96	Cgy	4	0	0	0	-4	0	0	9	0.0	0	0	0	0	0	0	0	0	0	0	0	0	0	0	.00
3 Years		13	0	6	6	-8	0	0	25	0.0	0	5	5	0	0	0	1	2	0	1	0	0	1	0	.46

Sean O'Donnell

(statistical profile on page 354)

Pos: D **Shoots:** L **Ht:** 6'3" **Wt:** 228 **Born:** 10/13/71—Ottawa, Ontario **Age:** 28

Overall											Power Play			Shorthand			Penalty							Misc	
Year	**Tm**	**GP**	**G**	**A**	**Pts**	**+/–**	**GW**	**GT**	**S**	**SPct**	**G**	**A**	**Pts**	**G**	**A**	**Pts**	**Num**	**PIM**	**Maj**	**Mnr**	**Fgt**	**Rgh**	**HHT**	**Hat**	**P/G**
94-95	LA	15	0	2	2	-2	0	0	12	0.0	0	0	0	0	0	0	13	49	5	7	5	2	2	0	.13
95-96	LA	71	2	5	7	3	0	0	65	3.1	0	0	0	0	1	1	49	127	7	41	7	12	13	0	.10
96-97	LA	55	5	12	17	-13	0	0	68	7.4	2	4	6	0	1	1	45	144	10	32	9	12	9	0	.31
97-98	LA	80	2	15	17	7	1	0	71	2.8	0	3	3	0	2	2	67	179	7	57	7	17	17	0	.21
98-99	LA	80	1	13	14	1	0	0	64	1.6	0	4	4	0	1	1	52	186	14	33	14	9	4	0	.18
5 Years		301	10	47	57	-4	1	0	280	3.6	2	11	13	0	5	5	226	685	43	170	42	52	45	0	.19

Postseason

Year	**Tm**	**GP**	**G**	**A**	**Pts**	**+/–**	**GW**	**OT**	**S**	**SPct**	**G**	**A**	**Pts**	**G**	**A**	**Pts**	**Num**	**PIM**	**Maj**	**Mnr**	**Fgt**	**Rgh**	**HHT**	**Hat**	**P/G**
97-98	LA	4	1	0	1	1	0	0	7	14.3	0	0	0	0	0	0	7	36	2	3	2	0	0	0	.25

Jeff O'Neill

(statistical profile on page 354)

Pos: C **Shoots:** R **Ht:** 6'1" **Wt:** 183 **Born:** 2/23/76—King City, Ontario **Age:** 23

Overall											Power Play			Shorthand			Penalty							Misc	
Year	**Tm**	**GP**	**G**	**A**	**Pts**	**+/–**	**GW**	**GT**	**S**	**SPct**	**G**	**A**	**Pts**	**G**	**A**	**Pts**	**Num**	**PIM**	**Maj**	**Mnr**	**Fgt**	**Rgh**	**HHT**	**Hat**	**P/G**
95-96	Har	65	8	19	27	-3	1	0	65	12.3	1	3	4	0	0	0	20	40	0	20	0	3	7	0	.42
96-97	Har	72	14	16	30	-24	2	0	101	13.9	2	4	6	1	0	1	20	40	0	20	0	2	9	1	.42
97-98	Car	74	19	20	39	-8	4	1	114	16.7	7	4	11	1	1	2	32	67	1	31	1	4	17	0	.53
98-99	Car	75	16	15	31	3	2	0	121	13.2	4	6	10	0	0	0	22	66	2	18	1	1	7	0	.41
4 Years		286	57	70	127	-32	9	1	401	14.2	14	17	31	2	1	3	94	213	3	89	2	10	40	1	.44

Postseason

Year	**Tm**	**GP**	**G**	**A**	**Pts**	**+/–**	**GW**	**OT**	**S**	**SPct**	**G**	**A**	**Pts**	**G**	**A**	**Pts**	**Num**	**PIM**	**Maj**	**Mnr**	**Fgt**	**Rgh**	**HHT**	**Hat**	**P/G**
98-99	Car	6	0	1	1	-5	0	0	11	0.0	0	0	0	0	0	0	0	0	0	0	0	0	0	0	.17

Chris O'Sullivan

Pos: D **Shoots:** L **Ht:** 6'2" **Wt:** 185 **Born:** 5/15/74—Dorchester, Massachusetts **Age:** 25

Overall											Power Play			Shorthand			Penalty							Misc	
Year	**Tm**	**GP**	**G**	**A**	**Pts**	**+/–**	**GW**	**GT**	**S**	**SPct**	**G**	**A**	**Pts**	**G**	**A**	**Pts**	**Num**	**PIM**	**Maj**	**Mnr**	**Fgt**	**Rgh**	**HHT**	**Hat**	**P/G**
96-97	Cgy	27	2	8	10	0	1	0	41	4.9	1	6	7	0	0	0	1	2	0	1	0	0	1	0	.37
97-98	Cgy	12	0	2	2	4	0	0	12	0.0	0	1	1	0	0	0	5	10	0	5	0	2	1	0	.17
98-99	Cgy	10	0	1	1	-1	0	0	10	0.0	0	0	0	0	0	0	1	2	0	1	0	0	1	0	.10
3 Years		49	2	11	13	3	1	0	63	3.2	1	7	8	0	0	0	7	14	0	7	0	2	3	0	.27

Adam Oates

(statistical profile on page 354)

Pos: C **Shoots:** R **Ht:** 5'11" **Wt:** 185 **Born:** 8/27/62—Weston, Ontario **Age:** 37

Overall											Power Play			Shorthand			Penalty							Misc	
Year	**Tm**	**GP**	**G**	**A**	**Pts**	**+/–**	**GW**	**GT**	**S**	**SPct**	**G**	**A**	**Pts**	**G**	**A**	**Pts**	**Num**	**PIM**	**Maj**	**Mnr**	**Fgt**	**Rgh**	**HHT**	**Hat**	**P/G**
85-86	Det	38	9	11	20	-24	1	0	49	18.4	1	–	–	0	–	–	–	10	–	–	–	–	–	0	.53
86-87	Det	76	15	32	47	0	1	2	138	10.9	4	–	–	0	–	–	–	21	–	–	–	–	–	0	.62
87-88	Det	63	14	40	54	16	3	0	111	12.6	3	–	–	0	–	–	–	20	–	–	–	–	–	0	.86
88-89	Det	69	16	62	78	-1	1	1	127	12.6	2	–	–	0	–	–	–	14	–	–	–	–	–	0	1.13
89-90	StL	**80**	23	79	102	9	3	1	168	13.7	6	–	–	2	–	–	–	30	–	–	–	–	–	0	1.28
90-91	StL*	61	25	90	115	15	3	0	139	18.0	3	–	–	1	–	–	–	29	–	–	–	–	–	0	1.89
91-92	2Tm*	80	20	79	99	-9	4	2	191	10.5	6	30	36	0	2	2	11	22	0	11	0	0	5	0	1.24
92-93	Bos*	84	45	**97**	142	15	**11**	0	254	17.7	24	38	62	1	1	2	16	32	0	16	0	3	6	3	1.69
93-94	Bos*	77	32	80	112	10	3	0	197	16.2	16	29	45	2	3	5	17	45	1	15	0	3	6	2	1.45
94-95	Bos	48	12	41	53	-11	2	0	109	11.0	4	19	23	1	0	1	4	8	0	4	0	1	1	0	1.10
95-96	Bos	70	25	67	92	16	2	0	183	13.7	7	24	31	1	2	3	9	18	0	9	0	0	5	1	1.31
96-97	2Tm*	80	22	60	82	-5	5	0	160	13.8	3	16	19	2	4	6	7	14	0	7	0	0	4	0	1.03
97-98	Was	82	18	58	76	6	3	0	121	14.9	3	22	25	2	4	6	14	36	0	13	0	0	3	1	.93
98-99	Was	59	12	41	53	-1	0	0	79	15.2	3	18	21	0	3	3	11	22	0	11	0	0	4	0	.90
91-92	StL	54	10	59	69	-4	3	1	118	8.5	3	19	22	0	1	1	6	12	0	6	0	0	1	0	1.28
91-92	Bos	26	10	20	30	-5	1	1	73	13.7	3	11	14	0	1	1	5	10	0	5	0	0	4	0	1.15
96-97	Bos	63	18	52	70	-3	4	0	138	13.0	2	16	18	2	4	6	5	10	0	5	0	0	2	0	1.11
96-97	Was	17	4	8	12	-2	1	0	22	18.2	1	0	1	0	0	0	2	4	0	2	0	0	2	0	.71
14 Years		967	288	837	1125	36	42	6	2026	14.2	85	–	–	12	–	–	–	321	–	–	–	–	–	7	1.16

Postseason

Year	**Tm**	**GP**	**G**	**A**	**Pts**	**+/–**	**GW**	**OT**	**S**	**SPct**	**G**	**A**	**Pts**	**G**	**A**	**Pts**	**Num**	**PIM**	**Maj**	**Mnr**	**Fgt**	**Rgh**	**HHT**	**Hat**	**P/G**
86-87	Det	16	4	7	11	7	1	0	32	12.5	0	–	–	0	–	–	3	6	0	3	0	–	–	0	.69
87-88	Det	16	8	12	20	-2	1	0	33	24.2	4	–	–	0	–	–	3	6	0	3	0	–	–	0	1.25

											Postseason														
Year	Tm	GP	G	A	Pts	+/–	GW	OT	S	SPct	G	A	Pts	G	A	Pts	Num	PIM	Maj	Mnr	Fgt	Rgh	HHT	Hat	P/G
88-89	Det	6	0	8	8	-1	0	0	11	0.0	0	–	–	0	0	0	1	2	0	1	0	–	–	0	1.33
89-90	StL	12	2	12	14	-10	0	0	27	7.4	1	–	–	0	–	–	2	4	0	2	0	–	–	0	1.17
90-91	StL	13	7	13	20	7	1	0	39	17.9	2	–	–	0	0	0	–	10	–	–	–	–	–	1	1.54
91-92	Bos	15	5	14	19	-6	2	1	35	14.3	3	4	7	0	0	0	2	4	0	2	0	1	1	0	1.27
92-93	Bos	4	0	9	9	0	0	0	11	0.0	0	4	4	0	0	0	2	4	0	2	0	2	0	0	2.25
93-94	Bos	13	3	9	12	-3	0	0	42	7.1	2	4	6	0	0	0	4	8	0	4	0	0	2	0	.92
94-95	Bos	5	1	0	1	-6	0	0	7	14.3	1	0	1	0	0	0	1	2	0	1	0	0	1	0	.20
95-96	Bos	5	2	5	7	-3	0	0	13	15.4	0	3	3	1	1	2	1	2	0	1	0	0	1	0	1.40
97-98	Was	21	6	11	17	8	1	0	31	19.4	1	3	4	1	1	2	4	8	0	4	0	2	1	0	.81
11 Years		126	38	100	138	-9	6	1	281	13.5	14	–	–	2	–	–	–	56	–	–	–	–	–	1	1.10

Lyle Odelein

(statistical profile on page 355)

Pos: D **Shoots:** R **Ht:** 5'11" **Wt:** 210 **Born:** 7/21/68—Quill Lake, Saskatchewan **Age:** 31

		Overall									Power Play			Shorthand			Penalty							Misc	
Year	Tm	GP	G	A	Pts	+/–	GW	GT	S	SPct	G	A	Pts	G	A	Pts	Num	PIM	Maj	Mnr	Fgt	Rgh	HHT	Hat	P/G
89-90	Mon	8	0	2	2	-1	0	0	1	0.0	0	–	–	0	–	–	–	33	–	–	–	–	–	0	.25
90-91	Mon	52	0	2	2	7	0	0	25	0.0	0	–	–	0	–	–	–	259	–	–	–	–	–	0	.04
91-92	Mon	71	1	7	8	15	0	0	43	2.3	0	0	0	0	0	0	56	212	12	36	11	12	5	0	.11
92-93	Mon	83	2	14	16	35	0	0	79	2.5	0	0	0	0	0	0	60	205	15	40	15	9	7	0	.19
93-94	Mon	79	11	29	40	8	2	0	116	9.5	6	13	19	0	1	1	83	276	18	58	17	19	11	1	.51
94-95	Mon	48	3	7	10	-13	0	0	74	4.1	0	2	2	0	0	0	44	152	8	31	8	16	8	0	.21
95-96	Mon	79	3	14	17	8	0	0	74	4.1	0	2	2	1	0	1	57	230	12	35	12	13	8	0	.22
96-97	NJ	79	3	13	16	16	2	0	93	3.2	1	4	5	0	0	0	36	110	10	25	10	8	5	0	.20
97-98	NJ	79	4	19	23	11	0	0	76	5.3	1	6	7	0	1	1	59	171	7	48	7	7	10	0	.29
98-99	NJ	70	5	26	31	6	0	1	101	5.0	1	11	12	0	0	0	29	114	8	17	8	5	2	0	.44
10 Years		648	32	133	165	92	4	1	682	4.7	9	–	–	1	–	–	–	1762	–	–	–	–	–	1	.25
											Postseason														
Year	Tm	GP	G	A	Pts	+/–	GW	OT	S	SPct	G	A	Pts	G	A	Pts	Num	PIM	Maj	Mnr	Fgt	Rgh	HHT	Hat	P/G
90-91	Mon	12	0	0	0	-5	0	0	4	0.0	0	0	0	0	0	0	–	54	–	–	–	–	–	0	.00
91-92	Mon	7	0	0	0	-4	0	0	1	0.0	0	0	0	0	0	0	4	11	1	3	1	1	0	0	.00
92-93	Mon	20	1	5	6	9	0	0	20	5.0	0	0	0	0	0	0	11	30	0	10	0	6	1	0	.30
93-94	Mon	7	0	0	0	3	0	0	7	0.0	0	0	0	0	0	0	7	17	1	6	1	2	0	0	.00
95-96	Mon	6	1	1	2	1	0	0	5	20.0	0	0	0	1	0	1	3	6	0	3	0	1	0	0	.33
96-97	NJ	10	2	2	4	-3	0	0	27	7.4	1	2	3	0	0	0	4	19	1	2	1	1	1	0	.40
97-98	NJ	6	1	1	2	2	1	0	7	14.3	1	0	1	0	0	0	5	21	1	3	1	0	1	0	.33
98-99	NJ	7	0	3	3	-1	0	0	12	0.0	0	1	1	0	0	0	5	10	0	5	0	0	2	0	.43
8 Years		75	5	12	17	2	1	0	83	6.0	2	3	5	1	0	1	–	168	–	–	–	–	–	0	.23

Jeff Odgers

Pos: RW **Shoots:** R **Ht:** 6'0" **Wt:** 200 **Born:** 5/31/69—Spy Hill, Saskatchewan **Age:** 30

		Overall									Power Play			Shorthand			Penalty							Misc	
Year	Tm	GP	G	A	Pts	+/–	GW	GT	S	SPct	G	A	Pts	G	A	Pts	Num	PIM	Maj	Mnr	Fgt	Rgh	HHT	Hat	P/G
91-92	SJ	61	7	4	11	-21	0	0	64	10.9	0	1	1	0	0	0	58	217	23	31	23	12	5	0	.18
92-93	SJ	66	12	15	27	-26	0	0	100	12.0	6	3	9	0	0	0	67	253	21	39	19	12	11	0	.41
93-94	SJ	81	13	8	21	-13	0	1	73	17.8	7	4	11	0	0	0	59	222	24	31	23	11	9	0	.26
94-95	SJ	48	4	3	7	-8	1	0	47	8.5	0	0	0	0	0	0	31	117	13	16	13	7	1	0	.15
95-96	SJ	78	12	4	16	-4	1	1	84	14.3	0	0	0	0	0	0	53	192	18	31	17	14	9	0	.21
96-97	Bos	80	7	8	15	-15	1	0	84	8.3	1	1	2	0	0	0	56	197	23	31	23	14	5	0	.19
97-98	Col	68	5	8	13	5	0	0	47	10.6	0	0	0	0	0	0	58	213	27	29	27	11	8	0	.19
98-99	Col	75	2	3	5	-3	0	0	39	5.1	1	0	1	0	0	0	62	259	29	27	29	13	5	0	.07
8 Years		557	62	53	115	-85	3	2	538	11.5	15	9	24	0	0	0	444	1670	178	235	174	94	53	0	.21
											Postseason														
Year	Tm	GP	G	A	Pts	+/–	GW	OT	S	SPct	G	A	Pts	G	A	Pts	Num	PIM	Maj	Mnr	Fgt	Rgh	HHT	Hat	P/G
93-94	SJ	11	0	0	0	-2	0	0	6	0.0	0	0	0	0	0	0	4	11	1	3	1	0	1	0	.00
94-95	SJ	11	1	1	2	0	0	0	5	20.0	0	0	0	0	0	0	4	19	1	2	1	0	0	0	.18
97-98	Col	6	0	0	0	-1	0	0	4	0.0	0	0	0	0	0	0	7	25	1	5	1	3	0	0	.00
98-99	Col	15	1	0	1	0	1	0	3	33.3	0	0	0	0	0	0	7	14	0	7	0	5	1	0	.07
4 Years		43	2	1	3	-3	1	0	18	11.1	0	0	0	0	0	0	22	69	3	17	3	8	2	0	.07

Gino Odjick

Pos: LW **Shoots:** L **Ht:** 6'3" **Wt:** 210 **Born:** 9/7/70—Maniwaki, Quebec **Age:** 29

Overall											Power Play			Shorthand			Penalty							Misc	
Year	Tm	GP	G	A	Pts	+/–	GW	GT	S	SPct	G	A	Pts	G	A	Pts	Num	PIM	Maj	Mnr	Fgt	Rgh	HHT	Hat	P/G
90-91	Van	45	7	1	8	-6	0	1	39	17.9	0	0	0	0	0	0	67	296	22	33	22	11	3	0	.18
91-92	Van	65	4	6	10	-1	0	0	68	5.9	0	0	0	0	0	0	86	348	32	44	31	17	2	0	.15
92-93	Van	75	4	13	17	3	1	0	79	5.1	0	1	1	0	0	0	89	370	24	50	21	20	5	0	.23
93-94	Van	76	16	13	29	13	5	0	121	13.2	4	1	5	0	0	0	88	271	13	68	11	31	0	0	.38
94-95	Van	23	4	5	9	-3	0	0	35	11.4	0	1	1	0	0	0	33	109	9	22	7	7	5	0	.39
95-96	Van	55	3	4	7	-16	0	0	59	5.1	0	0	0	0	0	0	61	181	9	48	9	17	4	0	.13
96-97	Van	70	5	8	13	-5	0	0	85	5.9	1	0	1	0	0	0	85	**371**	19	48	19	15	4	0	.19
97-98	2Tm	48	3	2	5	-2	1	0	52	5.8	0	0	0	0	0	0	45	212	14	21	13	9	3	0	.10
98-99	NYI	23	4	3	7	-2	2	0	28	14.3	1	1	2	0	0	0	31	133	5	19	5	5	2	0	.30
97-98	Van	35	3	2	5	-3	1	0	36	8.3	0	0	0	0	0	0	37	181	9	18	8	7	2	0	.14
97-98	NYI	13	0	0	0	1	0	0	16	0.0	0	0	0	0	0	0	8	31	5	3	5	2	1	0	.00
9 Years		480	50	55	105	-19	9	1	566	8.8	6	4	10	0	0	0	585	2291	147	353	138	132	28	0	.22

Postseason

Year	Tm	GP	G	A	Pts	+/–	GW	OT	S	SPct	G	A	Pts	G	A	Pts	Num	PIM	Maj	Mnr	Fgt	Rgh	HHT	Hat	P/G
90-91	Van	6	0	0	0	-2	0	0	1	0.0	0	0	0	0	0	0	6	18	2	4	2	2	0	0	.00
91-92	Van	4	0	0	0	0	0	0	1	0.0	0	0	0	0	0	0	3	6	0	3	0	2	1	0	.00
92-93	Van	1	0	0	0	0	0	0	2	0.0	0	0	0	0	0	0	0	0	0	0	0	0	0	0	.00
93-94	Van	10	0	0	0	0	0	0	3	0.0	0	0	0	0	0	0	5	18	0	4	0	2	1	0	.00
94-95	Van	5	0	0	0	-2	0	0	7	0.0	0	0	0	0	0	0	10	47	1	6	1	3	0	0	.00
95-96	Van	6	3	1	4	2	2	0	6	50.0	0	0	0	0	0	0	3	6	0	3	0	0	2	0	.67
6 Years		32	3	1	4	-2	2	0	20	15.0	0	0	0	0	0	0	27	95	3	20	3	9	4	0	.13

Mattias Ohlund

(statistical profile on page 355)

Pos: D **Shoots:** L **Ht:** 6'2" **Wt:** 207 **Born:** 9/9/76—Pitea, Sweden **Age:** 23

Overall											Power Play			Shorthand			Penalty							Misc	
Year	Tm	GP	G	A	Pts	+/–	GW	GT	S	SPct	G	A	Pts	G	A	Pts	Num	PIM	Maj	Mnr	Fgt	Rgh	HHT	Hat	P/G
97-98	Van	77	7	23	30	3	0	0	172	4.1	1	8	9	0	4	4	34	76	0	33	0	3	11	0	.39
98-99	Van	74	9	26	35	-19	1	0	129	7.0	2	15	17	1	0	1	32	83	1	29	1	5	9	0	.47
2 Years		151	16	49	65	-16	1	0	301	5.3	3	23	26	1	4	5	66	159	1	62	1	8	20	0	.43

Fredrik Olausson

(statistical profile on page 355)

Pos: D **Shoots:** R **Ht:** 6'0" **Wt:** 198 **Born:** 10/5/66—Dadsejo, Sweden **Age:** 33

Overall											Power Play			Shorthand			Penalty							Misc	
Year	Tm	GP	G	A	Pts	+/–	GW	GT	S	SPct	G	A	Pts	G	A	Pts	Num	PIM	Maj	Mnr	Fgt	Rgh	HHT	Hat	P/G
86-87	Wpg	72	7	29	36	-3	2	0	119	5.9	1	–	–	0	–	–	–	24	–	–	–	–	–	0	.50
87-88	Wpg	38	5	10	15	3	2	0	65	7.7	2	–	–	0	–	–	–	18	–	–	–	–	–	0	.39
88-89	Wpg	75	15	47	62	6	1	0	178	8.4	4	–	–	0	–	–	–	32	–	–	–	–	–	0	.83
89-90	Wpg	77	9	46	55	-1	0	0	147	6.1	3	–	–	0	–	–	–	32	–	–	–	–	–	0	.71
90-91	Wpg	71	12	29	41	-22	0	0	168	7.1	5	–	–	0	–	–	–	24	–	–	–	–	–	0	.58
91-92	Wpg	77	20	42	62	-31	2	0	227	8.8	13	33	46	1	0	1	17	34	0	17	0	1	11	0	.81
92-93	Wpg	68	16	41	57	-4	3	0	165	9.7	11	27	38	0	0	0	11	22	0	11	0	0	6	0	.84
93-94	2Tm	73	11	24	35	-7	1	0	126	8.7	7	14	21	0	0	0	15	30	0	15	0	0	10	0	.48
94-95	Edm	33	0	10	10	-4	0	0	52	0.0	0	1	1	0	0	0	10	20	0	10	0	0	9	0	.30
95-96	2Tm	56	2	22	24	-7	0	0	83	2.4	1	15	16	0	0	0	19	38	0	19	0	1	10	0	.43
96-97	2Tm	71	9	29	38	16	3	0	110	8.2	3	13	16	0	0	0	16	32	0	16	0	0	9	0	.54
97-98	Pit	76	6	27	33	13	1	0	89	6.7	2	14	16	0	1	1	17	42	0	16	0	1	5	0	.43
98-99	Anh	74	16	40	56	17	2	0	121	13.2	10	33	43	0	0	0	15	30	0	15	0	1	12	0	.76
93-94	Wpg	18	2	5	7	-3	0	0	41	4.9	1	4	5	0	0	0	5	10	0	5	0	0	4	0	.39
93-94	Edm	55	9	19	28	-4	1	0	85	10.6	6	10	16	0	0	0	10	20	0	10	0	0	6	0	.51
95-96	Edm	20	0	6	6	-14	0	0	20	0.0	0	3	3	0	0	0	7	14	0	7	0	1	1	0	.30
95-96	Anh	36	2	16	18	7	0	0	63	3.2	1	12	13	0	0	0	12	24	0	12	0	0	9	0	.50
96-97	Anh	20	2	9	11	-4	0	0	35	5.7	1	4	5	0	0	0	4	8	0	4	0	0	3	0	.55
96-97	Pit	51	7	20	27	20	3	0	75	9.3	2	9	11	0	0	0	12	24	0	12	0	0	6	0	.53
13 Years		861	128	396	524	-24	17	0	1650	7.8	62	–	–	1	–	–	–	378	–	–	–	–	–	0	.61

Postseason

Year	Tm	GP	G	A	Pts	+/–	GW	OT	S	SPct	G	A	Pts	G	A	Pts	Num	PIM	Maj	Mnr	Fgt	Rgh	HHT	Hat	P/G
86-87	Wpg	10	2	3	5	0	0	0	23	8.7	1	–	–	0	–	–	2	4	0	2	0	–	–	0	.50
87-88	Wpg	5	1	1	2	-1	0	0	6	16.7	0	–	–	0	–	–	0	0	0	0	0	0	0	0	.40
89-90	Wpg	7	0	2	2	-5	0	0	9	0.0	0	–	–	0	0	0	1	2	0	1	0	–	–	0	.29
91-92	Wpg	7	1	5	6	-7	0	0	18	5.6	1	3	4	0	0	0	2	4	0	2	0	0	2	0	.86
92-93	Wpg	6	0	2	2	0	0	0	5	0.0	0	1	1	0	0	0	1	2	0	1	0	0	0	0	.33

Postseason																									
Year	Tm	GP	G	A	Pts	+/–	GW	OT	S	SPct	G	A	Pts	G	A	Pts	Num	PIM	Maj	Mnr	Fgt	Rgh	HHT	Hat	P/G
96-97	Pit	4	0	1	1	-1	0	0	5	0.0	0	1	1	0	0	0	0	0	0	0	0	0	0	0	.25
97-98	Pit	6	0	3	3	0	0	0	17	0.0	0	0	0	0	0	0	1	2	0	1	0	0	0	0	.50
98-99	Anh	4	0	2	2	-4	0	0	6	0.0	0	2	2	0	0	0	2	4	0	2	0	0	0	0	.50
8 Years		49	4	19	23	-18	0	0	89	4.5	2	–	–	0	–	–	9	18	0	9	0	–	–	0	.47

Ed Olczyk

(statistical profile on page 355)

Pos: C **Shoots:** L **Ht:** 6'1" **Wt:** 207 **Born:** 8/16/66—Chicago, Illinois **Age:** 33

Overall											Power Play			Shorthand			Penalty							Misc	
Year	Tm	GP	G	A	Pts	+/–	GW	GT	S	SPct	G	A	Pts	G	A	Pts	Num	PIM	Maj	Mnr	Fgt	Rgh	HHT	Hat	P/G
84-85	Chi	70	20	30	50	11	2	0	136	14.7	1	–	–	1	–	–	–	67	–	–	–	–	–	0	.71
85-86	Chi	79	29	50	79	2	2	0	218	13.3	8	–	–	1	–	–	–	47	–	–	–	–	–	0	1.00
86-87	Chi	79	16	35	51	-4	2	0	181	8.8	2	–	–	1	–	–	–	119	–	–	–	–	–	0	.65
87-88	Tor	**80**	42	33	75	-22	3	1	243	17.3	14	–	–	4	–	–	–	55	–	–	–	–	–	0	.94
88-89	Tor	**80**	38	52	90	0	4	1	249	15.3	11	–	–	2	–	–	–	75	–	–	–	–	–	1	1.13
89-90	Tor	79	32	56	88	0	4	0	208	15.4	6	–	–	0	–	–	–	78	–	–	–	–	–	1	1.11
90-91	2Tm	79	30	41	71	-27	2	2	226	13.3	14	–	–	0	–	–	–	82	–	–	–	–	–	0	.90
91-92	Wpg	64	32	33	65	11	7	1	245	13.1	12	18	30	0	0	0	24	67	1	21	0	4	12	0	1.02
92-93	2Tm	71	21	28	49	-2	1	1	190	11.1	2	12	14	0	0	0	22	52	0	21	0	5	5	1	.69
93-94	NYR	37	3	5	8	-1	1	0	40	7.5	0	0	0	0	0	0	10	28	0	9	0	3	4	0	.22
94-95	2Tm	33	4	9	13	-1	0	0	56	7.1	2	4	6	0	0	0	6	12	0	6	0	0	2	0	.39
95-96	Wpg	51	27	22	49	0	1	0	147	18.4	16	2	18	0	0	0	23	65	1	20	0	5	5	1	.96
96-97	2Tm	79	25	30	55	-14	6	0	195	12.8	5	13	18	1	0	1	24	51	1	23	1	0	12	1	.70
97-98	Pit	56	11	11	22	-9	1	0	123	8.9	5	2	7	1	2	3	16	35	1	15	1	2	7	0	.39
98-99	Chi	61	10	15	25	-3	2	0	88	11.4	2	2	4	1	0	1	13	29	1	12	1	1	6	0	.41
90-91	Tor	18	4	10	14	-7	0	0	45	8.9	0	–	–	0	–	–	5	13	1	4	–	–	–	0	.78
90-91	Wpg	61	26	31	57	-20	2	2	181	14.4	14	–	–	0	–	–	–	69	–	–	–	–	–	0	.93
92-93	Wpg	25	8	12	20	-11	0	1	81	9.9	2	6	8	0	0	0	9	26	0	8	0	2	0	0	.80
92-93	NYR	46	13	16	29	9	1	0	109	11.9	0	6	6	0	0	0	13	26	0	13	0	3	5	1	.63
94-95	NYR	20	2	1	3	-2	0	0	29	6.9	1	0	1	0	0	0	2	4	0	2	0	0	0	0	.15
94-95	Wpg	13	2	8	10	1	0	0	27	7.4	1	4	5	0	0	0	4	8	0	4	0	0	2	0	.77
96-97	LA	67	21	23	44	-22	5	0	166	12.7	5	11	16	1	0	1	21	45	1	20	1	0	10	1	.66
96-97	Pit	12	4	7	11	8	1	0	29	13.8	0	2	2	0	0	0	3	6	0	3	0	0	2	0	.92
15 Years		998	340	450	790	-59	38	6	2545	13.4	100	–	–	12	–	–	–	862	–	–	–	–	–	5	.79

Postseason																									
Year	Tm	GP	G	A	Pts	+/–	GW	OT	S	SPct	G	A	Pts	G	A	Pts	Num	PIM	Maj	Mnr	Fgt	Rgh	HHT	Hat	P/G
84-85	Chi	15	6	5	11	-4	0	0	35	17.1	1	–	–	1	–	–	4	11	1	3	–	–	–	0	.73
85-86	Chi	3	0	0	0	-6	0	0	10	0.0	0	0	0	0	0	0	0	0	0	0	0	0	0	0	.00
86-87	Chi	4	1	1	2	1	0	0	10	10.0	0	0	0	0	0	0	2	4	0	2	0	–	–	0	.50
87-88	Tor	6	5	4	9	1	1	1	17	29.4	1	–	–	1	–	–	1	2	0	1	0	–	–	1	1.50
89-90	Tor	5	1	2	3	3	0	0	15	6.7	0	–	–	0	–	–	–	14	–	–	–	–	–	0	.60
91-92	Wpg	6	2	1	3	0	1	0	16	12.5	0	1	1	0	0	0	2	4	0	2	0	0	1	0	.50
93-94	NYR	1	0	0	0	-1	0	0	1	0.0	0	0	0	0	0	0	0	0	0	0	0	0	0	0	.00
95-96	Wpg	6	1	2	3	0	0	0	15	6.7	0	0	0	0	0	0	3	6	0	3	0	1	1	0	.50
96-97	Pit	5	1	0	1	-2	1	0	11	9.1	0	0	0	1	0	1	6	12	0	6	0	0	0	0	.20
97-98	Pit	6	2	0	2	-3	1	0	6	33.3	1	0	1	1	0	1	2	4	0	2	0	0	1	0	.33
10 Years		57	19	15	34	-11	4	1	136	14.0	3	–	–	4	–	–	–	57	–	–	–	–	–	1	.60

David Oliver

Pos: RW **Shoots:** R **Ht:** 6'0" **Wt:** 190 **Born:** 4/17/71—Sechelt, British Columbia **Age:** 28

Overall											Power Play			Shorthand			Penalty							Misc	
Year	Tm	GP	G	A	Pts	+/–	GW	GT	S	SPct	G	A	Pts	G	A	Pts	Num	PIM	Maj	Mnr	Fgt	Rgh	HHT	Hat	P/G
94-95	Edm	44	16	14	30	-11	0	1	79	20.3	10	6	16	0	0	0	10	20	0	10	0	0	5	1	.68
95-96	Edm	80	20	19	39	-22	0	0	131	15.3	14	7	21	0	0	0	17	34	0	17	0	1	6	0	.49
96-97	2Tm	31	3	3	6	-5	0	0	35	8.6	0	1	1	0	0	0	4	8	0	4	0	0	2	0	.19
97-98		Did Not Play in NHL																							
98-99	Ott	17	2	5	7	1	0	0	18	11.1	0	0	0	0	0	0	2	4	0	2	0	0	1	0	.41
96-97	Edm	17	1	2	3	-8	0	0	22	4.5	0	1	1	0	0	0	2	4	0	2	0	0	1	0	.18
96-97	NYR	14	2	1	3	3	0	0	13	15.4	0	0	0	0	0	0	2	4	0	2	0	0	1	0	.21
4 Years		172	41	41	82	-37	0	1	263	15.6	24	14	38	0	0	0	33	66	0	33	0	1	14	1	.48

Postseason																									
Year	Tm	GP	G	A	Pts	+/–	GW	OT	S	SPct	G	A	Pts	G	A	Pts	Num	PIM	Maj	Mnr	Fgt	Rgh	HHT	Hat	P/G
96-97	NYR	3	0	0	0	0	0	0	0	–	0	0	0	0	0	0	0	0	0	0	0	0	0	0	.00

Krzysztof Oliwa

(statistical profile on page 356)

Pos: LW **Shoots:** L **Ht:** 6'5" **Wt:** 235 **Born:** 4/12/73—Tychy, Poland **Age:** 26

	Overall									Power Play			Shorthand			Penalty							Misc	
Year Tm	GP	G	A	Pts	+/–	GW	GT	S	SPct	G	A	Pts	G	A	Pts	Num	PIM	Maj	Mnr	Fgt	Rgh	HHT	Hat	P/G
96-97 NJ	1	0	0	0	-1	0	0	0	–	0	0	0	0	0	0	1	5	1	0	1	0	0	0	.00
97-98 NJ	73	2	3	5	3	2	0	53	3.8	0	0	0	0	0	0	78	295	**33**	40	**33**	21	0	0	.07
98-99 NJ	64	5	7	12	4	1	0	59	8.5	0	0	0	0	0	0	62	240	28	30	28	7	2	0	.19
3 Years	138	7	10	17	6	3	0	112	6.3	0	0	0	0	0	0	141	540	62	70	62	28	2	0	.12
	Postseason																							
Year Tm	GP	G	A	Pts	+/–	GW	OT	S	SPct	G	A	Pts	G	A	Pts	Num	PIM	Maj	Mnr	Fgt	Rgh	HHT	Hat	P/G
97-98 NJ	6	0	0	0	0	0	0	5	0.0	0	0	0	0	0	0	6	23	1	4	1	0	1	0	.00
98-99 NJ	1	0	0	0	0	0	0	0	–	0	0	0	0	0	0	1	2	0	1	0	0	0	0	.00
2 Years	7	0	0	0	0	0	0	5	0.0	0	0	0	0	0	0	7	25	1	5	1	0	1	0	.00

Vladimir Orszagh

Pos: RW **Shoots:** L **Ht:** 5'11" **Wt:** 173 **Born:** 5/24/77—Banska Bystrica, USSR **Age:** 22

	Overall									Power Play			Shorthand			Penalty							Misc	
Year Tm	GP	G	A	Pts	+/–	GW	GT	S	SPct	G	A	Pts	G	A	Pts	Num	PIM	Maj	Mnr	Fgt	Rgh	HHT	Hat	P/G
97-98 NYI	11	0	1	1	-3	0	0	9	0.0	0	0	0	0	0	0	1	2	0	1	0	1	0	0	.09
98-99 NYI	12	1	0	1	2	0	0	5	20.0	0	0	0	0	0	0	3	6	0	3	0	0	2	0	.08
2 Years	23	1	1	2	-1	0	0	14	7.1	0	0	0	0	0	0	4	8	0	4	0	1	2	0	.09

Chris Osgood

(statistical profile on page 401)

Pos: G **Catches:** L **Ht:** 5'10" **Wt:** 178 **Born:** 11/26/72—Peace River, Alberta **Age:** 27

	Overall														Pen Shot		Offense		
Year Tm	GP	GS	TP	W	L	T	Min	GA	GAA	Shots	SvPct	ShO	OE	PPGA	SHGA	Shots	GA	G	A	PIM
93-94 Det	41	37	5	23	8	5	2206	105	2.86	999	.895	2	10	28	5	1	0	0	0	2
94-95 Det	19	19	1	14	5	0	1087	41	2.26	496	.917	1	6	8	4	1	0	0	0	2
95-96 Det*	50	47	1	**39**	6	5	2933	106	2.17	1190	.911	5	11	26	5	0	0	1	2	4
96-97 Det*	47	45	1	23	13	9	2769	106	2.30	1175	.910	6	15	28	6	1	0	0	2	6
97-98 Det	64	64	6	33	20	11	3807	140	2.21	1605	.913	6	13	36	6	1	1	0	0	31
98-99 Det	63	63	4	34	25	4	3691	149	2.42	1654	.910	3	18	33	5	2	**2**	0	3	8
6 Years	284	275	18	166	77	34	16493	647	2.35	7119	.909	23	73	159	31	6	3	1	7	53
	Postseason																			
Year Tm	GP	GS	TP	W	L	Pct	Min	GA	GAA	Shots	SvPct	ShO	OE	PPGA	SHGA	Shots	GA	G	A	PIM
93-94 Det	6	6	1	3	2	.600	307	12	2.35	110	.891	1	1	5	1	0	0	0	0	0
94-95 Det	2	0	0	0	0	–	68	2	1.76	25	.920	0	0	2	0	0	0	0	0	0
95-96 Det	15	15	0	8	7	.533	936	33	2.12	322	.898	2	4	12	1	0	0	0	0	4
96-97 Det	2	0	0	0	0	–	47	2	2.55	21	.905	0	0	0	0	0	0	0	0	2
97-98 Det	22	22	1	16	6	.727	1361	48	2.12	588	.918	2	10	14	3	0	0	0	1	12
98-99 Det	6	6	0	4	2	.667	358	14	2.35	172	.919	1	2	5	1	0	0	0	0	0
6 Years	53	49	2	31	17	.646	3077	111	2.16	1238	.910	6	17	38	6	0	0	0	1	18

Sandis Ozolinsh

(statistical profile on page 356)

Pos: D **Shoots:** L **Ht:** 6'3" **Wt:** 205 **Born:** 8/3/72—Riga, USSR **Age:** 27

	Overall									Power Play			Shorthand			Penalty							Misc	
Year Tm	GP	G	A	Pts	+/–	GW	GT	S	SPct	G	A	Pts	G	A	Pts	Num	PIM	Maj	Mnr	Fgt	Rgh	HHT	Hat	P/G
92-93 SJ	37	7	16	23	-9	0	0	83	8.4	2	8	10	0	0	0	20	40	0	20	0	3	11	0	.62
93-94 SJ*	81	26	38	64	16	3	0	157	16.6	4	13	17	0	1	1	12	24	0	12	0	0	5	0	.79
94-95 SJ	48	9	16	25	-6	2	0	83	10.8	3	2	5	1	0	1	15	30	0	15	0	1	8	0	.52
95-96 2Tm	73	14	40	54	2	1	1	166	8.4	8	24	32	1	0	1	27	54	0	27	0	0	16	0	.74
96-97 Col*	80	23	45	68	4	4	1	232	9.9	13	29	**42**	0	1	1	40	88	0	39	0	5	22	0	.85
97-98 Col*	66	13	38	51	-12	2	1	135	9.6	9	26	35	0	0	0	23	65	1	20	1	1	9	0	.77
98-99 Col	39	7	25	32	10	3	0	81	8.6	4	17	21	0	0	0	11	22	0	11	0	0	6	0	.82
95-96 SJ	7	1	3	4	2	0	0	21	4.8	1	2	3	0	0	0	2	4	0	2	0	0	1	0	.57
95-96 Col	66	13	37	50	0	1	1	145	9.0	7	22	29	1	0	1	25	50	0	25	0	0	15	0	.76
7 Years	424	99	218	317	5	15	3	937	10.6	43	119	162	2	2	4	148	323	1	144	1	10	77	0	.75
	Postseason																							
Year Tm	GP	G	A	Pts	+/–	GW	OT	S	SPct	G	A	Pts	G	A	Pts	Num	PIM	Maj	Mnr	Fgt	Rgh	HHT	Hat	P/G
93-94 SJ	14	0	10	10	3	0	0	23	0.0	0	0	0	0	1	1	4	8	0	4	0	1	2	0	.71
94-95 SJ	11	3	2	5	-13	0	0	15	20.0	1	0	1	0	0	0	2	4	0	2	0	0	1	0	.45
95-96 Col	22	5	14	19	5	1	1	52	9.6	2	8	10	0	0	0	8	16	0	8	0	2	3	0	.86
96-97 Col	17	4	13	17	-1	1	0	39	10.3	2	10	12	0	0	0	12	24	0	12	0	0	4	0	1.00

									Postseason																
Year	Tm	GP	G	A	Pts	+/–	GW	OT	S	SPct	G	A	Pts	G	A	Pts	Num	PIM	Maj	Mnr	Fgt	Rgh	HHT	Hat	P/G
97-98	Col	7	0	7	7	-3	0	0	19	0.0	0	4	4	0	0	0	7	14	0	7	0	2	1	0	1.00
98-99	Col	19	4	8	12	-5	1	0	56	7.1	3	3	6	0	0	0	11	22	0	11	0	1	3	0	.63
6 Years		90	16	54	70	-14	3	1	204	7.8	8	25	33	0	1	1	44	88	0	44	0	6	14	0	.78

Zigmund Palffy

(statistical profile on page 356)

Pos: RW **Shoots:** L **Ht:** 5'10" **Wt:** 183 **Born:** 5/5/72—Skalica, Czechoslovakia **Age:** 27

			Overall								Power Play			Shorthand			Penalty							Misc	
Year	Tm	GP	G	A	Pts	+/–	GW	GT	S	SPct	G	A	Pts	G	A	Pts	Num	PIM	Maj	Mnr	Fgt	Rgh	HHT	Hat	P/G
93-94	NYI	5	0	0	0	-6	0	0	5	0.0	0	0	0	0	0	0	0	0	0	0	0	0	0	0	.00
94-95	NYI	33	10	7	17	3	1	0	75	13.3	1	2	3	0	0	0	3	6	0	3	0	1	2	0	.52
95-96	NYI	81	43	44	87	-17	6	0	257	16.7	17	22	39	1	1	2	24	56	0	23	0	1	8	2	1.07
96-97	NYI*	80	48	42	90	21	6	1	292	16.4	6	15	21	4	2	6	16	43	1	14	0	4	3	1	1.13
97-98	NYI*	82	45	42	87	-2	5	1	277	16.2	**17**	18	35	2	2	4	17	34	0	17	0	1	5	2	1.06
98-99	NYI	50	22	28	50	-6	1	0	168	13.1	5	10	15	2	0	2	17	34	0	17	0	0	5	1	1.00
6 Years		331	168	163	331	-7	19	2	1074	15.6	46	67	113	9	5	14	77	173	1	74	0	7	23	6	1.00

Jay Pandolfo

(statistical profile on page 356)

Pos: LW **Shoots:** L **Ht:** 6'1" **Wt:** 195 **Born:** 12/27/74—Winchester, Massachusetts **Age:** 25

			Overall								Power Play			Shorthand			Penalty							Misc	
Year	Tm	GP	G	A	Pts	+/–	GW	GT	S	SPct	G	A	Pts	G	A	Pts	Num	PIM	Maj	Mnr	Fgt	Rgh	HHT	Hat	P/G
96-97	NJ	46	6	8	14	-1	1	2	61	9.8	0	0	0	0	0	0	3	6	0	3	0	0	1	0	.30
97-98	NJ	23	1	3	4	-4	0	0	23	4.3	0	0	0	0	0	0	2	4	0	2	0	0	2	0	.17
98-99	NJ	70	14	13	27	3	4	0	100	14.0	1	1	2	1	0	1	5	10	0	5	0	0	1	0	.39
3 Years		139	21	24	45	-2	5	2	184	11.4	1	1	2	1	0	1	10	20	0	10	0	0	4	0	.32
									Postseason																
Year	Tm	GP	G	A	Pts	+/–	GW	OT	S	SPct	G	A	Pts	G	A	Pts	Num	PIM	Maj	Mnr	Fgt	Rgh	HHT	Hat	P/G
96-97	NJ	6	0	1	1	-2	0	0	11	0.0	0	0	0	0	0	0	0	0	0	0	0	0	0	0	.17
97-98	NJ	3	0	2	2	0	0	0	1	0.0	0	0	0	0	0	0	0	0	0	0	0	0	0	0	.67
98-99	NJ	7	1	0	1	-5	0	0	10	10.0	0	0	0	0	0	0	0	0	0	0	0	0	0	0	.14
3 Years		16	1	3	4	-7	0	0	22	4.5	0	0	0	0	0	0	0	0	0	0	0	0	0	0	.25

Greg Pankewicz

Pos: RW **Shoots:** R **Ht:** 6'0" **Wt:** 185 **Born:** 11/6/70—Drayton Valley, Alberta **Age:** 29

			Overall								Power Play			Shorthand			Penalty							Misc	
Year	Tm	GP	G	A	Pts	+/–	GW	GT	S	SPct	G	A	Pts	G	A	Pts	Num	PIM	Maj	Mnr	Fgt	Rgh	HHT	Hat	P/G
93-94	Ott	3	0	0	0	-1	0	0	3	0.0	0	0	0	0	0	0	1	2	0	1	0	1	0	0	.00
94-95											Did Not Play in NHL														
95-96											Did Not Play in NHL														
96-97											Did Not Play in NHL														
97-98											Did Not Play in NHL														
98-99	Cgy	18	0	3	3	0	0	0	10	0.0	0	0	0	0	0	0	6	20	0	5	0	1	2	0	.17
2 Years		21	0	3	3	-1	0	0	13	0.0	0	0	0	0	0	0	7	22	0	6	0	2	2	0	.14

Rich Parent

Pos: G **Catches:** L **Ht:** 6'2" **Wt:** 202 **Born:** 1/12/73—Montreal, Quebec **Age:** 26

						Overall										Pen Shot		Offense		
Year	Tm	GP	GS	TP	W	L	T	Min	GA	GAA	Shots	SvPct	ShO	OE	PPGA	SHGA	Shots	GA	G	A	PIM
97-98	StL	1	0	0	0	0	0	12	0	0.00	1	1.000	0	0	0	0	0	0	0	0	0
98-99	StL	10	7	0	4	3	1	519	22	2.54	193	.886	1	2	4	1	0	0	0	0	2
2 Years		11	7	0	4	3	1	531	22	2.49	194	.887	1	2	4	1	0	0	0	0	2

Richard Park

Pos: C **Shoots:** R **Ht:** 5'11" **Wt:** 190 **Born:** 5/27/76—Seoul, South Korea **Age:** 23

			Overall								Power Play			Shorthand			Penalty							Misc	
Year	Tm	GP	G	A	Pts	+/–	GW	GT	S	SPct	G	A	Pts	G	A	Pts	Num	PIM	Maj	Mnr	Fgt	Rgh	HHT	Hat	P/G
94-95	Pit	1	0	1	1	1	0	0	4	0.0	0	0	0	0	0	0	1	2	0	1	0	0	1	0	1.00
95-96	Pit	56	4	6	10	3	1	0	62	6.5	0	0	0	1	1	2	14	36	0	13	0	0	7	0	.18
96-97	2Tm	12	1	1	2	-1	0	0	10	10.0	0	0	0	0	0	0	5	10	0	5	0	1	4	0	.17
97-98	Anh	15	0	2	2	-3	0	0	14	0.0	0	0	0	0	0	0	4	8	0	4	0	0	3	0	.13

Overall											Power Play			Shorthand			Penalty							Misc	
Year	Tm	GP	G	A	Pts	+/–	GW	GT	S	SPct	G	A	Pts	G	A	Pts	Num	PIM	Maj	Mnr	Fgt	Rgh	HHT	Hat	P/G
98-99	Phi	7	0	0	0	-1	0	0	5	0.0	0	0	0	0	0	0	0	0	0	0	0	0	0	0	.00
96-97	Pit	1	0	0	0	-1	0	0	1	0.0	0	0	0	0	0	0	0	0	0	0	0	0	0	0	.00
96-97	Anh	11	1	1	2	0	0	0	9	11.1	0	0	0	0	0	0	5	10	0	5	0	1	4	0	.18
5 Years		91	5	10	15	-1	1	0	95	5.3	0	0	0	1	1	2	24	56	0	23	0	1	15	0	.16
Postseason																									
Year	Tm	GP	G	A	Pts	+/–	GW	OT	S	SPct	G	A	Pts	G	A	Pts	Num	PIM	Maj	Mnr	Fgt	Rgh	HHT	Hat	P/G
94-95	Pit	3	0	0	0	-1	0	0	5	0.0	0	0	0	0	0	0	1	2	0	1	0	0	0	0	.00
95-96	Pit	1	0	0	0	0	0	0	0	–	0	0	0	0	0	0	0	0	0	0	0	0	0	0	.00
96-97	Anh	11	0	1	1	-2	0	0	10	0.0	0	0	0	0	0	0	1	2	0	1	0	0	1	0	.09
3 Years		15	0	1	1	-3	0	0	15	0.0	0	0	0	0	0	0	2	4	0	2	0	0	1	0	.07

Scott Parker

Pos: RW **Shoots:** R **Ht:** 6'4" **Wt:** 220 **Born:** 1/29/78—Hanford, California **Age:** 21

Overall											Power Play			Shorthand			Penalty							Misc	
Year	Tm	GP	G	A	Pts	+/–	GW	GT	S	SPct	G	A	Pts	G	A	Pts	Num	PIM	Maj	Mnr	Fgt	Rgh	HHT	Hat	P/G
98-99	Col	27	0	0	0	-3	0	0	3	0.0	0	0	0	0	0	0	17	71	7	8	7	3	1	0	.00

Mark Parrish

(statistical profile on page 357)

Pos: LW **Shoots:** R **Ht:** 5'11" **Wt:** 191 **Born:** 2/2/77—Edina, Minnesota **Age:** 22

Overall											Power Play			Shorthand			Penalty							Misc	
Year	Tm	GP	G	A	Pts	+/–	GW	GT	S	SPct	G	A	Pts	G	A	Pts	Num	PIM	Maj	Mnr	Fgt	Rgh	HHT	Hat	P/G
98-99	Fla	73	24	13	37	-6	5	1	129	18.6	5	4	9	0	0	0	11	25	1	10	1	2	1	1	.51

Steve Passmore

Pos: G **Catches:** L **Ht:** 5'9" **Wt:** 165 **Born:** 1/29/73—Thunder Bay, Ontario **Age:** 26

Overall																Pen Shot		Offense		
Year	Tm	GP	GS	TP	W	L	T	Min	GA	GAA	Shots	SvPct	ShO	OE	PPGA	SHGA	Shots	GA	G	A	PIM
98-99	Edm	6	6	0	1	4	1	362	17	2.82	183	.907	0	2	4	0	0	0	0	1	2

James Patrick

Pos: D **Shoots:** R **Ht:** 6'2" **Wt:** 200 **Born:** 6/14/63—Winnipeg, Manitoba **Age:** 36

Overall											Power Play			Shorthand			Penalty							Misc	
Year	Tm	GP	G	A	Pts	+/–	GW	GT	S	SPct	G	A	Pts	G	A	Pts	Num	PIM	Maj	Mnr	Fgt	Rgh	HHT	Hat	P/G
83-84	NYR	12	1	7	8	6	0	0	15	6.7	0	–	–	0	–	–	1	2	0	1	0	–	–	0	.67
84-85	NYR	75	8	28	36	-17	1	0	101	7.9	4	–	–	1	–	–	27	71	3	23	–	–	–	0	.48
85-86	NYR	75	14	29	43	14	1	1	131	10.7	2	–	–	1	–	–	34	88	4	29	–	–	–	0	.57
86-87	NYR	78	10	45	55	13	0	0	143	7.0	5	–	–	0	–	–	25	62	4	21	–	–	–	0	.71
87-88	NYR	70	17	45	62	16	1	0	187	9.1	9	26	35	0	–	–	26	52	0	26	0	–	–	0	.89
88-89	NYR	68	11	36	47	3	2	1	147	7.5	6	23	29	0	–	–	15	41	1	13	–	–	–	0	.69
89-90	NYR	73	14	43	57	4	0	0	136	10.3	9	26	35	0	–	–	21	50	0	20	0	–	–	0	.78
90-91	NYR	74	10	49	59	-5	2	0	138	7.2	6	31	37	0	–	–	–	58	–	–	–	–	–	0	.80
91-92	NYR	80	14	57	71	34	1	0	148	9.5	6	28	34	0	2	2	27	54	0	27	0	3	11	0	.89
92-93	NYR	60	5	21	26	1	0	0	99	5.1	3	12	15	0	0	0	21	61	1	18	0	1	9	0	.43
93-94	3Tm	68	10	25	35	-5	2	1	91	11.0	5	13	18	1	0	1	16	40	0	15	0	5	4	0	.51
94-95	Cgy	43	0	10	10	-3	0	0	43	0.0	0	1	1	0	1	1	7	14	0	7	0	0	3	0	.23
95-96	Cgy	80	3	32	35	3	0	0	116	2.6	1	16	17	0	1	1	15	30	0	15	0	2	6	0	.44
96-97	Cgy	19	3	1	4	2	0	0	22	13.6	1	0	1	0	1	1	3	6	0	3	0	0	2	0	.21
97-98	Cgy	60	6	11	17	-2	1	0	57	10.5	1	3	4	0	2	2	13	26	0	13	0	0	5	0	.28
98-99	Buf	45	1	7	8	12	0	0	31	3.2	0	0	0	0	0	0	8	16	0	8	0	2	5	0	.18
93-94	NYR	6	0	3	3	1	0	0	6	0.0	0	1	1	0	0	0	1	2	0	1	0	0	0	0	.50
93-94	Har	47	8	20	28	-12	2	1	65	12.3	4	12	16	1	0	1	12	32	0	11	0	5	3	0	.60
93-94	Cgy	15	2	2	4	6	0	0	20	10.0	1	0	1	0	0	0	3	6	0	3	0	0	1	0	.27
16 Years		980	127	446	573	76	11	3	1605	7.9	58	–	–	3	–	–	–	671	–	–	–	–	–	0	.58
Postseason																									
Year	Tm	GP	G	A	Pts	+/–	GW	OT	S	SPct	G	A	Pts	G	A	Pts	Num	PIM	Maj	Mnr	Fgt	Rgh	HHT	Hat	P/G
83-84	NYR	5	0	3	3	1	0	0	4	0.0	0	–	–	0	–	–	1	2	0	1	0	–	–	0	.60
84-85	NYR	3	0	0	0	0	0	0	3	0.0	0	0	0	0	0	0	2	4	0	2	0	–	–	0	.00
85-86	NYR	16	1	5	6	1	0	0	16	6.3	0	–	–	0	–	–	–	34	–	–	–	–	–	0	.38
86-87	NYR	6	1	2	3	-5	1	0	10	10.0	1	–	–	0	0	0	1	2	0	1	0	–	–	0	.50
88-89	NYR	4	0	1	1	-1	0	0	6	0.0	0	–	–	0	0	0	1	2	0	1	0	–	–	0	.25
89-90	NYR	10	3	8	11	-2	1	0	25	12.0	2	–	–	0	–	–	0	0	0	0	0	0	0	0	1.10

											Postseason															
Year	Tm	GP	G	A	Pts	+/-	GW	OT	S	SPct	G	A	Pts	G	A	Pts	Num	PIM	Maj	Mnr	Fgt	Rgh	HHT	Hat	P/G
90-91	NYR	6	0	0	0	-1	0	0	7	0.0	0	0	0	0	0	0	3	6	0	3	0	–	–	0	.00
91-92	NYR	13	0	7	7	-4	0	0	21	0.0	0	5	5	0	0	0	6	12	0	6	0	0	4	0	.54
93-94	Cgy	7	0	1	1	-1	0	0	4	0.0	0	0	0	0	0	0	3	6	0	3	0	1	1	0	.14
94-95	Cgy	5	0	1	1	-2	0	0	4	0.0	0	0	0	0	0	0	0	0	0	0	0	0	0	0	.20
95-96	Cgy	4	0	0	0	-3	0	0	3	0.0	0	0	0	0	0	0	1	2	0	1	0	0	1	0	.00
98-99	Buf	20	0	1	1	6	0	0	11	0.0	0	0	0	0	0	0	6	12	0	6	0	1	2	0	.05
12 Years		99	5	29	34	-11	2	0	114	4.4	3	–	–	0	–	–	–	82	–	–	–	–	–	0	.34

Mike Peca

(statistical profile on page 357)

Pos: C **Shoots:** R **Ht:** 5'11" **Wt:** 181 **Born:** 3/26/74—Toronto, Ontario **Age:** 25

		Overall									Power Play			Shorthand			Penalty							Misc	
Year	Tm	GP	G	A	Pts	+/-	GW	GT	S	SPct	G	A	Pts	G	A	Pts	Num	PIM	Maj	Mnr	Fgt	Rgh	HHT	Hat	P/G
93-94	Van	4	0	0	0	-1	0	0	5	0.0	0	0	0	0	0	0	1	2	0	1	0	0	0	0	.00
94-95	Van	33	6	6	12	-6	1	1	46	13.0	2	2	4	0	0	0	11	30	0	10	0	3	1	0	.36
95-96	Buf	68	11	20	31	-1	1	0	109	10.1	4	4	8	3	1	4	28	67	1	26	0	3	9	0	.46
96-97	Buf	79	20	29	49	26	4	0	137	14.6	5	4	9	**6**	3	9	29	80	2	25	2	9	1	0	.62
97-98	Buf	61	18	22	40	12	1	1	132	13.6	6	7	13	5	4	**9**	27	57	1	26	0	5	10	0	.66
98-99	Buf	82	27	29	56	7	8	1	199	13.6	10	9	19	0	1	1	31	81	1	28	1	6	6	0	.68
6 Years		327	82	106	188	37	15	3	628	13.1	27	26	53	14	9	23	127	317	5	116	3	26	27	0	.57
											Postseason														
Year	Tm	GP	G	A	Pts	+/-	GW	OT	S	SPct	G	A	Pts	G	A	Pts	Num	PIM	Maj	Mnr	Fgt	Rgh	HHT	Hat	P/G
94-95	Van	5	0	1	1	0	0	0	7	0.0	0	0	0	0	0	0	4	8	0	4	0	1	1	0	.20
96-97	Buf	10	0	2	2	-3	0	0	20	0.0	0	1	1	0	0	0	4	8	0	4	0	0	1	0	.20
97-98	Buf	13	3	2	5	4	1	1	24	12.5	0	1	1	0	0	0	4	8	0	4	0	0	2	0	.38
98-99	Buf	21	5	8	13	1	0	0	37	13.5	2	2	4	1	1	2	9	18	0	9	0	3	2	0	.62
4 Years		49	8	13	21	2	1	1	88	9.1	2	4	6	1	1	2	21	42	0	21	0	4	6	0	.43

Denis Pederson

(statistical profile on page 357)

Pos: C **Shoots:** R **Ht:** 6'2" **Wt:** 205 **Born:** 9/10/75—Prince Albert, Saskatchewan **Age:** 24

		Overall									Power Play			Shorthand			Penalty							Misc	
Year	Tm	GP	G	A	Pts	+/-	GW	GT	S	SPct	G	A	Pts	G	A	Pts	Num	PIM	Maj	Mnr	Fgt	Rgh	HHT	Hat	P/G
95-96	NJ	10	3	1	4	-1	2	0	6	50.0	1	0	1	0	0	0	0	0	0	0	0	0	0	0	.40
96-97	NJ	70	12	20	32	7	3	0	106	11.3	3	1	4	0	0	0	22	62	6	16	6	9	2	0	.46
97-98	NJ	80	15	13	28	-6	1	1	135	11.1	7	4	11	0	0	0	32	97	11	21	11	10	2	0	.35
98-99	NJ	76	11	12	23	-10	1	0	145	7.6	3	2	5	0	0	0	24	66	6	18	6	7	4	0	.30
4 Years		236	41	46	87	-10	7	1	392	10.5	14	7	21	0	0	0	78	225	23	55	23	26	8	0	.37
											Postseason														
Year	Tm	GP	G	A	Pts	+/-	GW	OT	S	SPct	G	A	Pts	G	A	Pts	Num	PIM	Maj	Mnr	Fgt	Rgh	HHT	Hat	P/G
96-97	NJ	9	0	0	0	-2	0	0	6	0.0	0	0	0	0	0	0	1	2	0	1	0	0	0	0	.00
97-98	NJ	6	1	1	2	0	0	0	8	12.5	0	0	0	1	0	1	1	2	0	1	0	0	0	0	.33
98-99	NJ	3	0	1	1	0	0	0	3	0.0	0	0	0	0	0	0	0	0	0	0	0	0	0	0	.33
3 Years		18	1	2	3	-2	0	0	17	5.9	0	0	0	1	0	1	2	4	0	2	0	0	0	0	.17

Scott Pellerin

(statistical profile on page 357)

Pos: LW **Shoots:** L **Ht:** 5'10" **Wt:** 193 **Born:** 1/9/70—Shediac, New Brunswick **Age:** 29

		Overall									Power Play			Shorthand			Penalty							Misc	
Year	Tm	GP	G	A	Pts	+/-	GW	GT	S	SPct	G	A	Pts	G	A	Pts	Num	PIM	Maj	Mnr	Fgt	Rgh	HHT	Hat	P/G
92-93	NJ	45	10	11	21	-1	0	0	60	16.7	1	0	1	2	0	2	15	41	1	13	1	3	1	0	.47
93-94	NJ	1	0	0	0	0	0	0	0	–	0	0	0	0	0	0	1	2	0	1	0	0	0	0	.00
94-95		Did Not Play in NHL																							
95-96	NJ	6	2	1	3	1	0	0	9	22.2	0	0	0	0	0	0	0	0	0	0	0	0	0	0	.50
96-97	StL	54	8	10	18	12	2	0	76	10.5	0	0	0	2	0	2	12	35	1	10	1	3	4	0	.33
97-98	StL	80	8	21	29	14	0	0	96	8.3	1	0	1	1	2	3	24	62	2	21	2	4	6	0	.36
98-99	StL	80	20	21	41	1	4	0	138	14.5	0	2	2	**5**	1	6	21	42	0	21	0	3	10	0	.51
6 Years		266	48	64	112	27	6	0	379	12.7	2	2	4	10	3	13	73	182	4	66	4	13	21	0	.42
											Postseason														
Year	Tm	GP	G	A	Pts	+/-	GW	OT	S	SPct	G	A	Pts	G	A	Pts	Num	PIM	Maj	Mnr	Fgt	Rgh	HHT	Hat	P/G
96-97	StL	6	0	0	0	-1	0	0	7	0.0	0	0	0	0	0	0	3	6	0	3	0	0	0	0	.00
97-98	StL	10	0	2	2	1	0	0	10	0.0	0	0	0	0	1	1	5	10	0	5	0	1	1	0	.20
98-99	StL	8	1	0	1	-2	0	0	11	9.1	0	0	0	0	0	0	2	4	0	2	0	0	0	0	.13
3 Years		24	1	2	3	-2	0	0	28	3.6	0	0	0	0	1	1	10	20	0	10	0	1	1	0	.13

Jean-Marc Pelletier

Pos: G **Catches:** R **Ht:** 6'3" **Wt:** 200 **Born:** 3/4/78—Atlanta, Georgia **Age:** 21

Overall																	Pen Shot		Offense		
Year	Tm	GP	GS	TP	W	L	T	Min	GA	GAA	Shots	SvPct	ShO	OE	PPGA	SHGA	Shots	GA	G	A	PIM
98-99	Phi	1	1	0	0	1	0	60	5	5.00	29	.828	0	0	1	0	0	0	0	0	0

Ville Peltonen

(statistical profile on page 358)

Pos: LW **Shoots:** L **Ht:** 5'10" **Wt:** 180 **Born:** 5/24/73—Vantaa, Finland **Age:** 26

Overall											Power Play			Shorthand			Penalty							Misc	
Year	Tm	GP	G	A	Pts	+/-	GW	GT	S	SPct	G	A	Pts	G	A	Pts	Num	PIM	Maj	Mnr	Fgt	Rgh	HHT	Hat	P/G
95-96	SJ	31	2	11	13	-7	0	0	58	3.4	0	1	1	0	0	0	7	14	0	7	0	1	5	0	.42
96-97	SJ	28	2	3	5	-8	0	0	35	5.7	1	0	1	0	0	0	0	0	0	0	0	0	0	0	.18
97-98		Did Not Play in NHL																							
98-99	Nsh	14	5	5	10	1	0	0	31	16.1	1	2	3	0	0	0	1	2	0	1	0	0	0	0	.71
3 Years		73	9	19	28	-14	0	0	124	7.3	2	3	5	0	0	0	8	16	0	8	0	1	5	0	.38

Yanic Perreault

(statistical profile on page 358)

Pos: C **Shoots:** L **Ht:** 5'11" **Wt:** 189 **Born:** 4/4/71—Sherbrooke, Quebec **Age:** 28

Overall											Power Play			Shorthand			Penalty							Misc	
Year	Tm	GP	G	A	Pts	+/-	GW	GT	S	SPct	G	A	Pts	G	A	Pts	Num	PIM	Maj	Mnr	Fgt	Rgh	HHT	Hat	P/G
93-94	Tor	13	3	3	6	1	0	0	24	12.5	2	0	2	0	0	0	0	0	0	0	0	0	0	0	.46
94-95	LA	26	2	5	7	3	1	0	43	4.7	0	1	1	0	0	0	10	20	0	10	0	0	7	0	.27
95-96	LA	78	25	24	49	-11	7	0	175	14.3	8	9	17	3	1	4	8	16	0	8	0	1	3	0	.63
96-97	LA	41	11	14	25	0	0	0	98	11.2	1	3	4	1	1	2	10	20	0	10	0	1	5	0	.61
97-98	LA	79	28	20	48	6	3	0	206	13.6	3	3	6	2	0	2	16	32	0	16	0	2	5	2	.61
98-99	2Tm	76	17	25	42	7	3	0	141	12.1	4	4	8	3	2	5	21	42	0	21	0	4	9	1	.55
98-99	LA	64	10	17	27	-3	1	0	113	8.8	2	4	6	2	2	4	15	30	0	15	0	2	8	0	.42
98-99	Tor	12	7	8	15	10	2	0	28	25.0	2	0	2	1	0	1	6	12	0	6	0	2	1	1	1.25
6 Years		313	86	91	177	6	14	0	687	12.5	18	20	38	9	4	13	65	130	0	65	0	8	29	3	.57
Postseason																									
Year	Tm	GP	G	A	Pts	+/-	GW	OT	S	SPct	G	A	Pts	G	A	Pts	Num	PIM	Maj	Mnr	Fgt	Rgh	HHT	Hat	P/G
97-98	LA	4	1	2	3	-1	0	0	7	14.3	1	0	1	0	0	0	3	6	0	3	0	1	2	0	.75
98-99	Tor	17	3	6	9	-6	2	1	15	20.0	0	1	1	0	0	0	3	6	0	3	0	2	0	0	.53
2 Years		21	4	8	12	-7	2	1	22	18.2	1	1	2	0	0	0	6	12	0	6	0	3	2	0	.57

Ricard Persson

(statistical profile on page 358)

Pos: D **Shoots:** L **Ht:** 6'1" **Wt:** 203 **Born:** 8/24/69—Ostersund, Sweden **Age:** 30

Overall											Power Play			Shorthand			Penalty							Misc	
Year	Tm	GP	G	A	Pts	+/-	GW	GT	S	SPct	G	A	Pts	G	A	Pts	Num	PIM	Maj	Mnr	Fgt	Rgh	HHT	Hat	P/G
95-96	NJ	12	2	1	3	5	0	0	41	4.9	1	1	2	0	0	0	4	8	0	4	0	0	3	0	.25
96-97	2Tm	54	4	8	12	-2	0	0	70	5.7	1	1	2	0	0	0	21	45	1	20	1	4	5	0	.22
97-98	StL	1	0	0	0	0	0	0	0	–	0	0	0	0	0	0	0	0	0	0	0	0	0	0	.00
98-99	StL	54	1	12	13	4	0	0	52	1.9	0	1	1	0	0	0	41	94	4	37	4	4	19	0	.24
96-97	NJ	1	0	0	0	0	0	0	2	0.0	0	0	0	0	0	0	0	0	0	0	0	0	0	0	.00
96-97	StL	53	4	8	12	-2	0	0	68	5.9	1	1	2	0	0	0	21	45	1	20	1	4	5	0	.23
4 Years		121	7	21	28	7	0	0	163	4.3	2	3	5	0	0	0	66	147	5	61	5	8	27	0	.23
Postseason																									
Year	Tm	GP	G	A	Pts	+/-	GW	OT	S	SPct	G	A	Pts	G	A	Pts	Num	PIM	Maj	Mnr	Fgt	Rgh	HHT	Hat	P/G
96-97	StL	6	0	0	0	-1	0	0	1	0.0	0	0	0	0	0	0	4	27	1	1	1	0	0	0	.00
98-99	StL	13	0	3	3	-1	0	0	12	0.0	0	0	0	0	0	0	7	17	1	6	1	1	2	0	.23
2 Years		19	0	3	3	-2	0	0	13	0.0	0	0	0	0	0	0	11	44	2	7	2	1	2	0	.16

Brent Peterson

Pos: LW **Shoots:** L **Ht:** 6'3" **Wt:** 206 **Born:** 7/20/72—Calgary, Alberta **Age:** 27

Overall											Power Play			Shorthand			Penalty							Misc	
Year	Tm	GP	G	A	Pts	+/-	GW	GT	S	SPct	G	A	Pts	G	A	Pts	Num	PIM	Maj	Mnr	Fgt	Rgh	HHT	Hat	P/G
96-97	TB	17	2	0	2	-4	0	0	11	18.2	0	0	0	0	0	0	2	4	0	2	0	0	1	0	.12
97-98	TB	19	5	0	5	-2	0	0	15	33.3	0	0	0	0	0	0	1	2	0	1	0	0	0	0	.26
98-99	TB	20	2	1	3	-2	0	0	16	12.5	0	0	0	0	0	0	0	0	0	0	0	0	0	0	.15
3 Years		56	9	1	10	-8	0	0	42	21.4	0	0	0	0	0	0	3	6	0	3	0	0	1	0	.18

Robert Petrovicky

Pos: C **Shoots:** L **Ht:** 6'0" **Wt:** 183 **Born:** 10/26/73—Kosice, Czechoslovakia **Age:** 26

		Overall									Power Play			Shorthand			Penalty							Misc	
Year	Tm	GP	G	A	Pts	+/–	GW	GT	S	SPct	G	A	Pts	G	A	Pts	Num	PIM	Maj	Mnr	Fgt	Rgh	HHT	Hat	P/G
92-93	Har	42	3	6	9	-10	0	0	41	7.3	0	1	1	0	0	0	17	45	1	15	0	2	5	0	.21
93-94	Har	33	6	5	11	-1	0	0	33	18.2	1	1	2	0	0	0	14	39	1	12	0	0	2	0	.33
94-95	Har	2	0	0	0	0	0	0	1	0.0	0	0	0	0	0	0	0	0	0	0	0	0	0	0	.00
95-96	Dal	5	1	1	2	1	1	0	3	33.3	1	1	2	0	0	0	0	0	0	0	0	0	0	0	.40
96-97	StL	44	7	12	19	2	1	0	54	13.0	0	1	1	0	0	0	5	10	0	5	0	2	2	0	.43
97-98		Did Not Play in NHL																							
98-99	TB	28	3	4	7	-8	0	0	32	9.4	0	0	0	0	0	0	3	6	0	3	0	0	1	0	.25
6 Years		154	20	28	48	-16	2	0	164	12.2	2	4	6	0	0	0	39	100	2	35	0	4	10	0	.31
		Postseason																							
Year	Tm	GP	G	A	Pts	+/–	GW	OT	S	SPct	G	A	Pts	G	A	Pts	Num	PIM	Maj	Mnr	Fgt	Rgh	HHT	Hat	P/G
96-97	StL	2	0	0	0	1	0	0	1	0.0	0	0	0	0	0	0	0	0	0	0	0	0	0	0	.00

Chris Phillips

Pos: D **Shoots:** L **Ht:** 6'2" **Wt:** 213 **Born:** 3/9/72—Fort McMurray, Alberta **Age:** 27

		Overall									Power Play			Shorthand			Penalty							Misc	
Year	Tm	GP	G	A	Pts	+/–	GW	GT	S	SPct	G	A	Pts	G	A	Pts	Num	PIM	Maj	Mnr	Fgt	Rgh	HHT	Hat	P/G
97-98	Ott	72	5	11	16	2	2	0	107	4.7	2	6	8	0	0	0	19	38	0	19	0	1	11	0	.22
98-99	Ott	34	3	3	6	-5	0	0	51	5.9	2	1	3	0	0	0	16	32	0	16	0	5	4	0	.18
2 Years		106	8	14	22	-3	2	0	158	5.1	4	7	11	0	0	0	35	70	0	35	0	6	15	0	.21
		Postseason																							
Year	Tm	GP	G	A	Pts	+/–	GW	OT	S	SPct	G	A	Pts	G	A	Pts	Num	PIM	Maj	Mnr	Fgt	Rgh	HHT	Hat	P/G
97-98	Ott	11	0	2	2	-2	0	0	24	0.0	0	1	1	0	0	0	1	2	0	1	0	1	0	0	.18
98-99	Ott	3	0	0	0	-1	0	0	1	0.0	0	0	0	0	0	0	0	0	0	0	0	0	0	0	.00
2 Years		14	0	2	2	-3	0	0	25	0.0	0	1	1	0	0	0	1	2	0	1	0	1	0	0	.14

Michel Picard

(statistical profile on page 358)

Pos: LW **Shoots:** L **Ht:** 5'11" **Wt:** 198 **Born:** 11/7/69—Beauport, Ontario **Age:** 30

		Overall									Power Play			Shorthand			Penalty							Misc	
Year	Tm	GP	G	A	Pts	+/–	GW	GT	S	SPct	G	A	Pts	G	A	Pts	Num	PIM	Maj	Mnr	Fgt	Rgh	HHT	Hat	P/G
90-91	Har	5	1	0	1	-2	0	0	7	14.3	0	0	0	0	0	0	1	2	0	1	0	–	–	0	.20
91-92	Har	25	3	5	8	-2	0	0	41	7.3	1	1	2	0	0	0	3	6	0	3	0	0	2	0	.32
92-93	SJ	25	4	0	4	-17	0	0	32	12.5	2	0	2	0	0	0	8	24	0	7	0	1	2	0	.16
93-94		Did Not Play in NHL																							
94-95	Ott	24	5	8	13	-1	0	0	33	15.2	1	4	5	0	0	0	7	14	0	7	0	1	3	0	.54
95-96	Ott	17	2	6	8	-1	1	0	21	9.5	0	2	2	0	0	0	5	10	0	5	0	2	1	0	.47
96-97		Did Not Play in NHL																							
97-98	StL	16	1	8	9	3	0	0	19	5.3	0	0	0	0	0	0	9	29	1	7	1	3	3	0	.56
98-99	StL	45	11	11	22	5	2	0	69	15.9	0	1	1	0	0	0	8	16	0	8	0	4	1	0	.49
7 Years		157	27	38	65	-15	3	0	222	12.2	4	8	12	0	0	0	41	101	1	38	1	–	–	0	.41
		Postseason																							
Year	Tm	GP	G	A	Pts	+/–	GW	OT	S	SPct	G	A	Pts	G	A	Pts	Num	PIM	Maj	Mnr	Fgt	Rgh	HHT	Hat	P/G
98-99	StL	5	0	0	0	-3	0	0	7	0.0	0	0	0	0	0	0	1	2	0	1	0	0	0	0	.00

Rich Pilon

Pos: D **Shoots:** L **Ht:** 6'0" **Wt:** 205 **Born:** 4/30/68—Saskatoon, Saskatchewan **Age:** 31

		Overall									Power Play			Shorthand			Penalty							Misc	
Year	Tm	GP	G	A	Pts	+/–	GW	GT	S	SPct	G	A	Pts	G	A	Pts	Num	PIM	Maj	Mnr	Fgt	Rgh	HHT	Hat	P/G
88-89	NYI	62	0	14	14	-9	0	0	47	0.0	0	–	–	0	–	–	–	242	–	–	–	–	–	0	.23
89-90	NYI	14	0	2	2	2	0	0	5	0.0	0	–	–	0	–	–	–	31	–	–	–	–	–	0	.14
90-91	NYI	60	1	4	5	-12	0	0	33	3.0	0	–	–	0	–	–	–	126	–	–	–	–	–	0	.08
91-92	NYI	65	1	6	7	-1	0	0	27	3.7	0	0	0	0	0	0	57	183	7	44	5	18	13	0	.11
92-93	NYI	44	1	3	4	-4	0	0	20	5.0	0	0	0	0	0	0	50	164	8	37	8	15	7	0	.09
93-94	NYI	28	1	4	5	-4	0	0	20	5.0	0	0	0	0	0	0	26	75	5	20	4	5	1	0	.18
94-95	NYI	20	1	1	2	-3	0	0	11	9.1	0	0	0	0	0	0	17	40	2	15	2	8	3	0	.10
95-96	NYI	27	0	3	3	-9	0	0	7	0.0	0	0	0	0	0	0	33	72	2	31	2	13	5	0	.11
96-97	NYI	52	1	4	5	4	0	0	17	5.9	0	0	0	0	0	0	55	179	7	42	6	20	7	0	.10
97-98	NYI	76	0	7	7	1	0	0	37	0.0	0	0	0	0	0	0	94	291	13	**73**	11	28	11	0	.09
98-99	NYI	52	0	4	4	-8	0	0	27	0.0	0	0	0	0	0	0	38	88	4	34	4	7	7	0	.08
11 Years		500	6	52	58	-43	0	0	251	2.4	0	–	–	0	–	–	–	1491	–	–	–	–	–	0	.12

Postseason																									
Year	Tm	GP	G	A	Pts	+/-	GW	OT	S	SPct	G	A	Pts	G	A	Pts	Num	PIM	Maj	Mnr	Fgt	Rgh	HHT	Hat	P/G
92-93	NYI	15	0	0	0	5	0	0	7	0.0	0	0	0	0	0	0	10	50	2	5	1	3	1	0	.00

Lance Pitlick

Pos: D **Shoots:** R **Ht:** 6'0" **Wt:** 210 **Born:** 11/5/67—Minneapolis, Minnesota **Age:** 32

Overall											Power Play			Shorthand			Penalty							Misc	
Year	Tm	GP	G	A	Pts	+/-	GW	GT	S	SPct	G	A	Pts	G	A	Pts	Num	PIM	Maj	Mnr	Fgt	Rgh	HHT	Hat	P/G
94-95	Ott	15	0	1	1	-5	0	0	11	0.0	0	0	0	0	0	0	3	6	0	3	0	0	0	0	.07
95-96	Ott	28	1	6	7	-8	0	0	13	7.7	0	0	0	0	0	0	6	20	0	5	0	1	1	0	.25
96-97	Ott	66	5	5	10	2	1	0	54	9.3	0	0	0	0	0	0	34	91	5	28	5	11	5	0	.15
97-98	Ott	69	2	7	9	8	0	0	66	3.0	0	0	0	0	0	0	22	50	2	20	2	4	8	0	.13
98-99	Ott	50	3	6	9	7	0	0	34	8.8	0	0	0	0	0	0	15	33	1	14	1	2	3	0	.18
5 Years		228	11	25	36	4	1	0	178	6.2	0	0	0	0	0	0	80	200	8	70	8	18	17	0	.16
Postseason																									
Year	Tm	GP	G	A	Pts	+/-	GW	OT	S	SPct	G	A	Pts	G	A	Pts	Num	PIM	Maj	Mnr	Fgt	Rgh	HHT	Hat	P/G
96-97	Ott	7	0	0	0	-1	0	0	2	0.0	0	0	0	0	0	0	2	4	0	2	0	2	0	0	.00
97-98	Ott	11	0	1	1	-3	0	0	6	0.0	0	0	0	0	0	0	3	17	1	1	1	0	1	0	.09
98-99	Ott	2	0	0	0	-1	0	0	2	0.0	0	0	0	0	0	0	0	0	0	0	0	0	0	0	.00
3 Years		20	0	1	1	-5	0	0	10	0.0	0	0	0	0	0	0	5	21	1	3	1	2	1	0	.05

Domenic Pittis

Pos: C **Shoots:** L **Ht:** 5'11" **Wt:** 185 **Born:** 10/1/74—Calgary, Alberta **Age:** 25

Overall											Power Play			Shorthand			Penalty							Misc	
Year	Tm	GP	G	A	Pts	+/-	GW	GT	S	SPct	G	A	Pts	G	A	Pts	Num	PIM	Maj	Mnr	Fgt	Rgh	HHT	Hat	P/G
96-97	Pit	1	0	0	0	-1	0	0	0	–	0	0	0	0	0	0	0	0	0	0	0	0	0	0	.00
97-98											Did Not Play in NHL														
98-99	Buf	3	0	0	0	0	0	0	1	0.0	0	0	0	0	0	0	1	2	0	1	0	0	0	0	.00
2 Years		4	0	0	0	-1	0	0	1	0.0	0	0	0	0	0	0	1	2	0	1	0	0	0	0	.00

Michal Pivonka

(statistical profile on page 359)

Pos: C **Shoots:** L **Ht:** 6'2" **Wt:** 200 **Born:** 1/28/66—Kladno, Czechoslovakia **Age:** 33

Overall											Power Play			Shorthand			Penalty							Misc	
Year	Tm	GP	G	A	Pts	+/-	GW	GT	S	SPct	G	A	Pts	G	A	Pts	Num	PIM	Maj	Mnr	Fgt	Rgh	HHT	Hat	P/G
86-87	Was	73	18	25	43	-19	2	0	117	15.4	4	–	–	0	–	–	–	41	–	–	–	–	–	0	.59
87-88	Was	71	11	23	34	1	0	0	96	11.5	3	–	–	0	–	–	–	28	–	–	–	–	–	0	.48
88-89	Was	52	8	19	27	9	1	0	73	11.0	1	–	–	0	–	–	–	30	–	–	–	–	–	0	.52
89-90	Was	77	25	39	64	-7	0	0	149	16.8	10	–	–	3	–	–	–	54	–	–	–	–	–	0	.83
90-91	Was	79	20	50	70	3	4	0	172	11.6	6	–	–	0	–	–	–	34	–	–	–	–	–	0	.89
91-92	Was	80	23	57	80	10	2	1	177	13.0	7	16	23	4	1	5	22	47	1	21	1	2	9	1	1.00
92-93	Was	69	21	53	74	14	5	0	147	14.3	6	24	30	1	0	1	26	66	2	23	1	3	11	0	1.07
93-94	Was	82	14	36	50	2	4	0	138	10.1	5	10	15	0	0	0	19	38	0	19	0	6	6	0	.61
94-95	Was	46	10	23	33	3	2	0	80	12.5	4	9	13	2	2	4	18	50	2	15	1	4	4	0	.72
95-96	Was	73	16	65	81	18	5	0	168	9.5	6	18	24	2	2	4	18	36	0	18	0	0	12	0	1.11
96-97	Was	54	7	16	23	-15	1	0	83	8.4	2	4	6	0	2	2	11	22	0	11	0	0	3	0	.43
97-98	Was	33	3	6	9	5	1	0	38	7.9	0	1	1	0	0	0	10	20	0	10	0	1	6	0	.27
98-99	Was	36	5	6	11	-6	0	0	30	16.7	2	1	3	0	0	0	6	12	0	6	0	0	2	0	.31
13 Years		825	181	418	599	18	27	1	1468	12.3	56	–	–	12	–	–	–	478	–	–	–	–	–	1	.73
Postseason																									
Year	Tm	GP	G	A	Pts	+/-	GW	OT	S	SPct	G	A	Pts	G	A	Pts	Num	PIM	Maj	Mnr	Fgt	Rgh	HHT	Hat	P/G
86-87	Was	7	1	1	2	2	0	0	15	6.7	0	–	–	0	0	0	1	2	0	1	0	–	–	0	.29
87-88	Was	14	4	9	13	7	0	0	28	14.3	2	–	–	0	–	–	2	4	0	2	0	–	–	0	.93
88-89	Was	6	3	1	4	0	0	0	17	17.6	0	–	–	1	–	–	–	10	–	–	–	–	–	0	.67
89-90	Was	11	0	2	2	1	0	0	16	0.0	0	–	–	0	–	–	3	6	0	3	0	–	–	0	.18
90-91	Was	11	2	3	5	-6	0	0	26	7.7	0	–	–	0	–	–	4	8	0	4	0	–	–	0	.45
91-92	Was	7	1	5	6	4	1	0	19	5.3	1	1	2	0	0	0	5	13	1	4	1	2	1	0	.86
92-93	Was	6	0	2	2	-3	0	0	12	0.0	0	1	1	0	0	0	0	0	0	0	0	0	0	0	.33
93-94	Was	7	4	4	8	0	0	0	16	25.0	1	2	3	0	0	0	2	4	0	2	0	0	1	0	1.14
94-95	Was	7	1	4	5	2	0	0	9	11.1	0	1	1	0	0	0	5	21	1	3	0	0	3	0	.71
95-96	Was	6	3	2	5	1	0	0	17	17.6	1	1	2	0	0	0	5	18	0	4	0	1	0	0	.83
97-98	Was	13	0	3	3	5	0	0	16	0.0	0	0	0	0	0	0	0	0	0	0	0	0	0	0	.23
11 Years		95	19	36	55	13	1	0	191	9.9	5	–	–	1	–	–	–	86	–	–	–	–	–	0	.58

Derek Plante

(statistical profile on page 359)

Pos: C **Shoots:** L **Ht:** 5'11" **Wt:** 181 **Born:** 1/17/71—Cloquet, Minnesota **Age:** 28

Overall											Power Play			Shorthand			Penalty							Misc	
Year	Tm	GP	G	A	Pts	+/-	GW	GT	S	SPct	G	A	Pts	G	A	Pts	Num	PIM	Maj	Mnr	Fgt	Rgh	HHT	Hat	P/G
93-94	Buf	77	21	35	56	4	2	0	147	14.3	8	18	26	1	0	1	12	24	0	12	0	1	7	1	.73
94-95	Buf	47	3	19	22	-4	0	0	94	3.2	2	8	10	0	1	1	6	12	0	6	0	1	2	0	.47
95-96	Buf	76	23	33	56	-4	5	0	203	11.3	4	10	14	0	1	1	14	28	0	14	0	1	6	0	.74
96-97	Buf	**82**	27	26	53	14	6	1	191	14.1	5	5	10	0	1	1	12	24	0	12	0	0	4	0	.65
97-98	Buf	72	13	21	34	8	1	0	150	8.7	5	9	14	0	1	1	13	26	0	13	0	1	5	0	.47
98-99	2Tm	51	6	14	20	4	0	0	90	6.7	1	3	4	0	1	1	8	16	0	8	0	0	6	0	.39
98-99	Buf	41	4	11	15	3	0	0	66	6.1	0	2	2	0	1	1	6	12	0	6	0	0	4	0	.37
98-99	Dal	10	2	3	5	1	0	0	24	8.3	1	1	2	0	0	0	2	4	0	2	0	0	2	0	.50
6 Years		405	93	148	241	22	14	1	875	10.6	25	53	78	1	5	6	65	130	0	65	0	4	30	1	.60
Postseason																									
Year	Tm	GP	G	A	Pts	+/-	GW	OT	S	SPct	G	A	Pts	G	A	Pts	Num	PIM	Maj	Mnr	Fgt	Rgh	HHT	Hat	P/G
93-94	Buf	7	1	0	1	1	0	0	14	7.1	0	0	0	0	0	0	0	0	0	0	0	0	0	0	.14
96-97	Buf	12	4	6	10	4	2	1	26	15.4	1	2	3	0	1	1	2	4	0	2	0	0	0	0	.83
97-98	Buf	11	0	3	3	1	0	0	13	0.0	0	2	2	0	0	0	5	10	0	5	0	1	1	0	.27
98-99	Dal	6	1	0	1	0	0	0	8	12.5	0	0	0	0	0	0	2	4	0	2	0	0	0	0	.17
4 Years		36	6	9	15	6	2	1	61	9.8	1	4	5	0	1	1	9	18	0	9	0	1	1	0	.42

Steve Poapst

Pos: D **Shoots:** L **Ht:** 6'0" **Wt:** 180 **Born:** 1/3/69—Cornwall, Ontario **Age:** 30

Overall											Power Play			Shorthand			Penalty							Misc	
Year	Tm	GP	G	A	Pts	+/-	GW	GT	S	SPct	G	A	Pts	G	A	Pts	Num	PIM	Maj	Mnr	Fgt	Rgh	HHT	Hat	P/G
95-96	Was	3	1	0	1	-1	1	0	2	50.0	0	0	0	0	0	0	0	0	0	0	0	0	0	0	.33
96-97		Did Not Play in NHL																							
97-98		Did Not Play in NHL																							
98-99	Was	22	0	0	0	-8	0	0	11	0.0	0	0	0	0	0	0	4	8	0	4	0	0	2	0	.00
2 Years		25	1	0	1	-9	1	0	13	7.7	0	0	0	0	0	0	4	8	0	4	0	0	2	0	.04
Postseason																									
Year	Tm	GP	G	A	Pts	+/-	GW	OT	S	SPct	G	A	Pts	G	A	Pts	Num	PIM	Maj	Mnr	Fgt	Rgh	HHT	Hat	P/G
95-96	Was	6	0	0	0	0	0	0	6	0.0	0	0	0	0	0	0	0	0	0	0	0	0	0	0	.00

Shjon Podein

Pos: LW **Shoots:** L **Ht:** 6'2" **Wt:** 200 **Born:** 3/5/68—Rochester, Minnesota **Age:** 31

Overall											Power Play			Shorthand			Penalty							Misc	
Year	Tm	GP	G	A	Pts	+/-	GW	GT	S	SPct	G	A	Pts	G	A	Pts	Num	PIM	Maj	Mnr	Fgt	Rgh	HHT	Hat	P/G
92-93	Edm	40	13	6	19	-2	1	0	64	20.3	2	1	3	1	0	1	11	25	1	10	1	1	5	0	.48
93-94	Edm	28	3	5	8	3	0	0	26	11.5	0	0	0	0	0	0	4	8	0	4	0	1	2	0	.29
94-95	Phi	44	3	7	10	-2	1	0	48	6.3	0	0	0	0	1	1	15	33	1	14	1	4	3	0	.23
95-96	Phi	79	15	10	25	25	4	0	115	13.0	0	1	1	4	1	5	33	89	5	27	4	5	9	0	.32
96-97	Phi	**82**	14	18	32	7	4	0	153	9.2	0	1	1	0	1	1	16	41	3	13	3	6	4	0	.39
97-98	Phi	82	11	13	24	8	2	0	126	8.7	1	2	3	1	0	1	21	53	1	19	1	3	6	0	.29
98-99	2Tm	55	3	6	9	-5	0	0	75	4.0	0	0	0	0	0	0	12	24	0	12	0	1	4	0	.16
98-99	Phi	14	1	0	1	-2	0	0	26	3.8	0	0	0	0	0	0	0	0	0	0	0	0	0	0	.07
98-99	Col	41	2	6	8	-3	0	0	49	4.1	0	0	0	0	0	0	12	24	0	12	0	1	4	0	.20
7 Years		410	62	65	127	34	12	0	607	10.2	3	5	8	6	3	9	112	273	11	99	10	21	33	0	.31
Postseason																									
Year	Tm	GP	G	A	Pts	+/-	GW	OT	S	SPct	G	A	Pts	G	A	Pts	Num	PIM	Maj	Mnr	Fgt	Rgh	HHT	Hat	P/G
94-95	Phi	15	1	3	4	2	0	0	10	10.0	0	0	0	0	0	0	5	10	0	5	0	1	1	0	.27
95-96	Phi	12	1	2	3	2	1	0	19	5.3	0	0	0	0	0	0	10	50	2	5	1	1	2	0	.25
96-97	Phi	19	4	3	7	4	1	0	52	7.7	0	0	0	0	0	0	8	16	0	8	0	3	2	0	.37
97-98	Phi	5	0	0	0	-1	0	0	5	0.0	0	0	0	0	0	0	5	10	0	5	0	3	0	0	.00
98-99	Col	19	1	1	2	-1	0	0	33	3.0	0	0	0	0	0	0	6	12	0	6	0	3	1	0	.11
5 Years		70	7	9	16	6	2	0	119	5.9	0	0	0	0	0	0	34	98	2	29	1	11	6	0	.23

Jason Podollan

Pos: RW **Shoots:** R **Ht:** 6'2" **Wt:** 205 **Born:** 2/18/76—Vernon, British Columbia **Age:** 23

Overall											Power Play			Shorthand			Penalty							Misc	
Year	Tm	GP	G	A	Pts	+/-	GW	GT	S	SPct	G	A	Pts	G	A	Pts	Num	PIM	Maj	Mnr	Fgt	Rgh	HHT	Hat	P/G
96-97	2Tm	29	1	4	5	-5	0	0	30	3.3	1	0	1	0	0	0	5	10	0	5	0	2	2	0	.17
97-98		Did Not Play in NHL																							

					Overall						Power Play			Shorthand					Penalty					Misc	
Year	Tm	GP	G	A	Pts	+/–	GW	GT	S	SPct	G	A	Pts	G	A	Pts	Num	PIM	Maj	Mnr	Fgt	Rgh	HHT	Hat	P/G
98-99	2Tm	10	0	0	0	-3	0	0	9	0.0	0	0	0	0	0	0	1	5	1	0	1	0	0	0	.00
96-97	Fla	19	1	1	2	-3	0	0	20	5.0	1	0	1	0	0	0	2	4	0	2	0	0	1	0	.11
96-97	Tor	10	0	3	3	-2	0	0	10	0.0	0	0	0	0	0	0	3	6	0	3	0	2	1	0	.30
98-99	Tor	4	0	0	0	0	0	0	2	0.0	0	0	0	0	0	0	0	0	0	0	0	0	0	0	.00
98-99	LA	6	0	0	0	-3	0	0	7	0.0	0	0	0	0	0	0	1	5	1	0	1	0	0	0	.00
2 Years		39	1	4	5	-8	0	0	39	2.6	1	0	1	0	0	0	6	15	1	5	1	2	2	0	.13

Rudy Poeschek

Pos: D **Shoots:** R **Ht:** 6'2" **Wt:** 219 **Born:** 9/29/66—Kamloops, British Columbia **Age:** 33

					Overall						Power Play			Shorthand					Penalty					Misc	
Year	Tm	GP	G	A	Pts	+/–	GW	GT	S	SPct	G	A	Pts	G	A	Pts	Num	PIM	Maj	Mnr	Fgt	Rgh	HHT	Hat	P/G
87-88	NYR	1	0	0	0	0	0	0	1	0.0	0	0	0	0	0	0	1	2	0	1	0	–	–	0	.00
88-89	NYR	52	0	2	2	-8	0	0	17	0.0	0	0	0	0	–	–	42	199	25	12	–	–	–	0	.04
89-90	NYR	15	0	0	0	-1	0	0	1	0.0	0	0	0	0	0	0	13	55	7	5	–	–	–	0	.00
90-91	Wpg	1	0	0	0	0	0	0	0	–	0	0	0	0	0	0	1	5	1	0	–	0	0	0	.00
91-92	Wpg	4	0	0	0	-5	0	0	1	0.0	0	0	0	0	0	0	7	17	1	6	1	3	0	0	.00
92-93											Did Not Play in NHL														
93-94	TB	71	3	6	9	3	1	1	46	6.5	0	0	0	0	0	0	35	118	16	19	16	7	3	0	.13
94-95	TB	25	1	1	2	0	0	0	14	7.1	0	0	0	0	0	0	22	92	8	11	8	4	2	0	.08
95-96	TB	57	1	3	4	-2	0	0	36	2.8	0	0	0	0	0	0	25	88	10	14	10	5	1	0	.07
96-97	TB	60	0	6	6	-3	0	0	30	0.0	0	0	0	0	0	0	37	120	10	25	10	6	4	0	.10
97-98	StL	50	1	7	8	-5	0	0	29	3.4	0	0	0	0	0	0	16	64	8	7	8	3	2	0	.16
98-99	StL	16	0	0	0	0	0	0	8	0.0	0	0	0	0	0	0	9	33	5	4	5	1	0	0	.00
11 Years		352	6	25	31	-21	1	1	183	3.3	0	0	0	0	–	–	208	793	91	104	–	–	–	0	.09

Postseason

Year	Tm	GP	G	A	Pts	+/–	GW	OT	S	SPct	G	A	Pts	G	A	Pts	Num	PIM	Maj	Mnr	Fgt	Rgh	HHT	Hat	P/G
95-96	TB	3	0	0	0	0	0	0	2	0.0	0	0	0	0	0	0	6	12	0	6	0	1	0	0	.00
97-98	StL	2	0	0	0	-2	0	0	0	–	0	0	0	0	0	0	3	6	0	3	0	1	2	0	.00
2 Years		5	0	0	0	-2	0	0	2	0.0	0	0	0	0	0	0	9	18	0	9	0	2	2	0	.00

Peter Popovic

Pos: D **Shoots:** R **Ht:** 6'6" **Wt:** 239 **Born:** 2/10/68—Koping, Sweden **Age:** 31

					Overall						Power Play			Shorthand					Penalty					Misc	
Year	Tm	GP	G	A	Pts	+/–	GW	GT	S	SPct	G	A	Pts	G	A	Pts	Num	PIM	Maj	Mnr	Fgt	Rgh	HHT	Hat	P/G
93-94	Mon	47	2	12	14	10	0	0	58	3.4	1	5	6	0	0	0	13	26	0	13	0	1	6	0	.30
94-95	Mon	33	0	5	5	-10	0	0	23	0.0	0	0	0	0	0	0	4	8	0	4	0	2	0	0	.15
95-96	Mon	76	2	12	14	21	0	0	59	3.4	0	2	2	0	0	0	29	69	1	27	0	1	16	0	.18
96-97	Mon	78	1	13	14	9	0	0	82	1.2	0	0	0	0	1	1	16	32	0	16	0	0	8	0	.18
97-98	Mon	69	2	6	8	-6	0	0	40	5.0	0	0	0	0	0	0	19	38	0	19	0	0	10	0	.12
98-99	NYR	68	1	4	5	-12	0	0	64	1.6	0	0	0	0	0	0	20	40	0	20	0	0	13	0	.07
6 Years		371	8	52	60	12	0	0	326	2.5	1	7	8	0	1	1	101	213	1	99	0	4	53	0	.16

Postseason

Year	Tm	GP	G	A	Pts	+/–	GW	OT	S	SPct	G	A	Pts	G	A	Pts	Num	PIM	Maj	Mnr	Fgt	Rgh	HHT	Hat	P/G
93-94	Mon	6	0	1	1	3	0	0	5	0.0	0	1	1	0	0	0	0	0	0	0	0	0	0	0	.17
95-96	Mon	6	0	2	2	3	0	0	2	0.0	0	0	0	0	0	0	2	4	0	2	0	0	1	0	.33
96-97	Mon	3	0	0	0	-3	0	0	1	0.0	0	0	0	0	0	0	1	2	0	1	0	0	0	0	.00
97-98	Mon	10	1	1	2	2	0	0	3	33.3	0	0	0	0	0	0	1	2	0	1	0	0	1	0	.20
4 Years		25	1	4	5	5	0	0	11	9.1	0	1	1	0	0	0	4	8	0	4	0	0	2	0	.20

Tom Poti

(statistical profile on page 359)

Pos: D **Shoots:** L **Ht:** 6'3" **Wt:** 215 **Born:** 3/22/77—Worcester, Massachusetts **Age:** 22

					Overall						Power Play			Shorthand					Penalty					Misc	
Year	Tm	GP	G	A	Pts	+/–	GW	GT	S	SPct	G	A	Pts	G	A	Pts	Num	PIM	Maj	Mnr	Fgt	Rgh	HHT	Hat	P/G
98-99	Edm	73	5	16	21	10	3	0	94	5.3	2	7	9	0	0	0	21	42	0	21	0	0	14	0	.29

Postseason

Year	Tm	GP	G	A	Pts	+/–	GW	OT	S	SPct	G	A	Pts	G	A	Pts	Num	PIM	Maj	Mnr	Fgt	Rgh	HHT	Hat	P/G
98-99	Edm	4	0	1	1	-3	0	0	9	0.0	0	1	1	0	0	0	1	2	0	1	0	1	0	0	.25

Felix Potvin

Pos: G **Catches:** L **Ht:** 6'1" **Wt:** 191 **Born:** 6/23/71—Anjou, Quebec **Age:** 28

Overall																	Pen Shot		Offense		
Year	Tm	GP	GS	TP	W	L	T	Min	GA	GAA	Shots	SvPct	ShO	OE	PPGA	SHGA	Shots	GA	G	A	PIM
91-92	Tor	4	3	0	0	2	1	210	8	2.29	120	.933	0	3	4	0	0	0	0	0	0
92-93	Tor	48	46	1	25	15	7	2781	116	**2.50**	1286	.910	2	16	37	2	1	0	0	1	4
93-94	Tor*	66	66	4	34	22	9	3883	187	2.89	2010	.907	3	28	59	7	0	0	0	4	4
94-95	Tor	36	36	1	15	13	7	2144	104	2.91	1120	.907	0	15	20	5	0	0	0	0	4
95-96	Tor*	69	66	3	30	26	11	4009	192	2.87	2135	.910	2	27	58	7	0	0	0	0	4
96-97	Tor	**74**	72	6	27	**36**	7	**4271**	**224**	3.15	**2438**	.908	0	33	**52**	7	1	0	0	3	19
97-98	Tor	67	65	5	26	**33**	7	3864	176	2.73	1882	.906	5	20	35	**12**	0	0	0	0	8
98-99	2Tm	16	15	1	5	9	1	905	56	3.71	487	.885	0	4	12	1	0	0	0	0	0
98-99	Tor	5	5	0	3	2	0	299	19	3.81	142	.866	0	1	4	0	0	0	0	0	0
98-99	NYI	11	10	1	2	7	1	606	37	3.66	345	.893	0	3	8	1	0	0	0	0	0
8 Years		380	369	21	162	156	50	22067	1063	2.89	11478	.907	12	146	277	41	2	0	0	8	43
Postseason																					
Year	Tm	GP	GS	TP	W	L	Pct	Min	GA	GAA	Shots	SvPct	ShO	OE	PPGA	SHGA	Shots	GA	G	A	PIM
92-93	Tor	21	21	1	11	10	.524	1308	62	2.84	636	.903	1	5	20	7	0	0	0	0	6
93-94	Tor	18	18	1	9	9	.500	1124	46	2.46	520	.912	3	6	13	1	0	0	0	0	4
94-95	Tor	7	7	0	3	4	.429	424	20	2.83	253	.921	1	3	2	1	1	0	0	0	0
95-96	Tor	6	6	2	2	4	.333	350	19	3.26	198	.904	0	1	5	4	0	0	0	0	2
4 Years		52	52	4	25	27	.481	3206	147	2.75	1607	.909	5	15	40	13	1	0	0	0	12

Patrick Poulin

(statistical profile on page 359)

Pos: LW **Shoots:** L **Ht:** 6'1" **Wt:** 208 **Born:** 4/23/73—Vanier, Quebec **Age:** 26

Overall											Power Play			Shorthand			Penalty							Misc	
Year	Tm	GP	G	A	Pts	+/–	GW	GT	S	SPct	G	A	Pts	G	A	Pts	Num	PIM	Maj	Mnr	Fgt	Rgh	HHT	Hat	P/G
91-92	Har	1	0	0	0	-1	0	0	0	–	0	0	0	0	0	0	1	2	0	1	0	0	1	0	.00
92-93	Har	81	20	31	51	-19	2	0	160	12.5	4	6	10	0	0	0	17	37	1	16	1	3	7	0	.63
93-94	2Tm	67	14	14	28	-8	3	0	96	14.6	2	1	3	0	0	0	18	51	5	13	5	1	4	0	.42
94-95	Chi	45	15	15	30	13	2	0	77	19.5	4	2	6	0	0	0	15	53	5	9	4	0	7	0	.67
95-96	2Tm	46	7	9	16	7	0	1	51	13.7	1	0	1	0	0	0	8	16	0	8	0	0	4	0	.35
96-97	TB	73	12	14	26	-16	1	0	124	9.7	2	2	4	3	1	4	18	56	4	13	4	0	5	0	.36
97-98	2Tm	78	6	13	19	-4	1	0	88	6.8	0	2	2	1	2	3	12	27	1	11	1	1	6	0	.24
98-99	Mon	81	8	17	25	6	1	0	87	9.2	0	0	0	1	0	1	9	21	1	8	1	0	2	0	.31
93-94	Har	9	2	1	3	-8	0	0	13	15.4	1	0	1	0	0	0	4	11	1	3	1	0	0	0	.33
93-94	Chi	58	12	13	25	0	3	0	83	14.5	1	1	2	0	0	0	14	40	4	10	4	1	4	0	.43
95-96	Chi	38	7	8	15	7	0	1	40	17.5	1	0	1	0	0	0	8	16	0	8	0	0	4	0	.39
95-96	TB	8	0	1	1	0	0	0	11	0.0	0	0	0	0	0	0	0	0	0	0	0	0	0	0	.13
97-98	TB	44	2	7	9	-3	0	0	49	4.1	0	0	0	0	2	2	8	19	1	7	1	0	3	0	.20
97-98	Mon	34	4	6	10	-1	1	0	39	10.3	0	2	2	1	0	1	4	8	0	4	0	1	3	0	.29
8 Years		472	82	113	195	-22	10	1	683	12.0	13	13	26	5	3	8	98	263	17	79	16	5	36	0	.41
Postseason																									
Year	Tm	GP	G	A	Pts	+/–	GW	OT	S	SPct	G	A	Pts	G	A	Pts	Num	PIM	Maj	Mnr	Fgt	Rgh	HHT	Hat	P/G
91-92	Har	7	2	1	3	2	0	0	3	66.7	1	0	1	0	0	0	0	0	0	0	0	0	0	0	.43
93-94	Chi	4	0	0	0	0	0	0	3	0.0	0	0	0	0	0	0	0	0	0	0	0	0	0	0	.00
94-95	Chi	16	4	1	5	1	0	0	30	13.3	1	1	2	0	0	0	4	8	0	4	0	0	2	0	.31
95-96	TB	2	0	0	0	0	0	0	0	–	0	0	0	0	0	0	0	0	0	0	0	0	0	0	.00
97-98	Mon	3	0	0	0	-1	0	0	1	0.0	0	0	0	0	0	0	0	0	0	0	0	0	0	0	.00
5 Years		32	6	2	8	2	0	0	37	16.2	2	1	3	0	0	0	4	8	0	4	0	0	2	0	.25

Nolan Pratt

(statistical profile on page 360)

Pos: D **Shoots:** L **Ht:** 6'1" **Wt:** 210 **Born:** 8/14/75—Fort McMurray, Alberta **Age:** 24

Overall											Power Play			Shorthand			Penalty							Misc	
Year	Tm	GP	G	A	Pts	+/–	GW	GT	S	SPct	G	A	Pts	G	A	Pts	Num	PIM	Maj	Mnr	Fgt	Rgh	HHT	Hat	P/G
96-97	Har	9	0	2	2	0	0	0	4	0.0	0	0	0	0	0	0	3	6	0	3	0	0	1	0	.22
97-98	Car	23	0	2	2	-2	0	0	11	0.0	0	0	0	0	0	0	15	44	2	12	1	4	3	0	.09
98-99	Car	61	1	14	15	15	1	0	46	2.2	0	1	1	0	0	0	28	95	5	20	5	4	4	0	.25
3 Years		93	1	18	19	13	1	0	61	1.6	0	1	1	0	0	0	46	145	7	35	6	8	8	0	.20
Postseason																									
Year	Tm	GP	G	A	Pts	+/–	GW	OT	S	SPct	G	A	Pts	G	A	Pts	Num	PIM	Maj	Mnr	Fgt	Rgh	HHT	Hat	P/G
98-99	Car	3	0	0	0	0	0	0	3	0.0	0	0	0	0	0	0	1	2	0	1	0	1	0	0	.00

Keith Primeau

(statistical profile on page 360)

Pos: C **Shoots:** L **Ht:** 6'5" **Wt:** 220 **Born:** 11/24/71—Toronto, Ontario **Age:** 28

Overall											Power Play			Shorthand			Penalty							Misc	
Year	Tm	GP	G	A	Pts	+/–	GW	GT	S	SPct	G	A	Pts	G	A	Pts	Num	PIM	Maj	Mnr	Fgt	Rgh	HHT	Hat	P/G
90-91	Det	58	3	12	15	-12	1	0	33	9.1	0	–	–	0	–	–	–	106	–	–	–	–	–	0	.26
91-92	Det	35	6	10	16	9	0	0	27	22.2	0	0	0	0	0	0	26	83	5	19	4	8	1	0	.46
92-93	Det	73	15	17	32	-6	2	1	75	20.0	4	4	8	1	0	1	41	152	10	26	10	11	2	0	.44
93-94	Det	78	31	42	73	34	4	2	155	20.0	7	7	14	3	3	6	47	173	13	29	12	7	3	0	.94
94-95	Det	45	15	27	42	17	3	0	96	15.6	1	8	9	0	1	1	30	99	5	22	4	4	4	0	.93
95-96	Det	74	27	25	52	19	7	0	150	18.0	6	9	15	2	2	4	49	168	10	34	9	11	8	0	.70
96-97	Har	75	26	25	51	-3	2	2	169	15.4	6	4	10	3	2	5	55	161	9	43	8	9	14	0	.68
97-98	Car	81	26	37	63	19	2	0	180	14.4	7	11	18	3	1	4	46	110	6	40	6	13	8	0	.78
98-99	Car	78	30	32	62	8	5	1	178	16.9	9	6	15	1	0	1	33	75	3	30	3	7	10	0	.79
9 Years		597	179	227	406	85	26	6	1063	16.8	40	–	–	13	–	–	–	1127	–	–	–	–	–	0	.68

Postseason																									
Year	Tm	GP	G	A	Pts	+/–	GW	OT	S	SPct	G	A	Pts	G	A	Pts	Num	PIM	Maj	Mnr	Fgt	Rgh	HHT	Hat	P/G
90-91	Det	5	1	1	2	3	0	0	2	50.0	0	–	–	0	–	–	–	25	–	–	–	–	–	0	.40
91-92	Det	11	0	0	0	-1	0	0	11	0.0	0	0	0	0	0	0	3	14	0	2	0	0	0	0	.00
92-93	Det	7	0	2	2	1	0	0	7	0.0	0	0	0	0	0	0	9	26	0	8	0	2	0	0	.29
93-94	Det	7	0	2	2	0	0	0	12	0.0	0	0	0	0	0	0	3	6	0	3	0	1	0	0	.29
94-95	Det	17	4	5	9	-2	0	0	34	11.8	2	1	3	0	0	0	17	45	1	15	0	3	1	0	.53
95-96	Det	17	1	4	5	-1	0	0	40	2.5	0	2	2	0	1	1	10	28	0	9	0	2	1	0	.29
98-99	Car	6	0	3	3	-3	0	0	9	0.0	0	2	2	0	0	0	3	6	0	3	0	0	3	0	.50
7 Years		70	6	17	23	-3	0	0	115	5.2	2	–	–	0	–	–	–	150	–	–	–	–	–	0	.33

Wayne Primeau

(statistical profile on page 360)

Pos: C **Shoots:** L **Ht:** 6'3" **Wt:** 193 **Born:** 6/4/76—Scarborough, Ontario **Age:** 23

Overall											Power Play			Shorthand			Penalty							Misc	
Year	Tm	GP	G	A	Pts	+/–	GW	GT	S	SPct	G	A	Pts	G	A	Pts	Num	PIM	Maj	Mnr	Fgt	Rgh	HHT	Hat	P/G
94-95	Buf	1	1	0	1	-2	1	0	2	50.0	0	0	0	0	0	0	0	0	0	0	0	0	0	0	1.00
95-96	Buf	2	0	0	0	0	0	0	0	–	0	0	0	0	0	0	0	0	0	0	0	0	0	0	.00
96-97	Buf	45	2	4	6	-2	0	0	25	8.0	1	0	1	0	0	0	12	64	8	2	8	1	0	0	.13
97-98	Buf	69	6	6	12	9	1	0	51	11.8	2	1	3	0	0	0	21	87	7	11	7	2	6	0	.17
98-99	Buf	67	5	8	13	-6	0	1	55	9.1	0	1	1	0	0	0	12	38	2	9	2	3	4	0	.19
5 Years		184	14	18	32	-1	2	1	133	10.5	3	2	5	0	0	0	45	189	17	22	17	6	10	0	.17

Postseason																									
Year	Tm	GP	G	A	Pts	+/–	GW	OT	S	SPct	G	A	Pts	G	A	Pts	Num	PIM	Maj	Mnr	Fgt	Rgh	HHT	Hat	P/G
96-97	Buf	9	0	0	0	-2	0	0	4	0.0	0	0	0	0	0	0	3	6	0	3	0	0	0	0	.00
97-98	Buf	14	1	3	4	-1	0	0	10	10.0	0	1	1	0	1	1	3	6	0	3	0	2	0	0	.29
98-99	Buf	19	3	4	7	0	0	0	22	13.6	1	2	3	0	0	0	3	6	0	3	0	1	1	0	.37
3 Years		42	4	7	11	-3	0	0	36	11.1	1	3	4	0	1	1	9	18	0	9	0	3	1	0	.26

Bob Probert

(statistical profile on page 360)

Pos: LW **Shoots:** L **Ht:** 6'3" **Wt:** 225 **Born:** 6/5/65—Windsor, Ontario **Age:** 34

Overall											Power Play			Shorthand			Penalty							Misc	
Year	Tm	GP	G	A	Pts	+/–	GW	GT	S	SPct	G	A	Pts	G	A	Pts	Num	PIM	Maj	Mnr	Fgt	Rgh	HHT	Hat	P/G
85-86	Det	44	8	13	21	-14	0	0	46	17.4	3	–	–	0	–	–	–	186	–	–	–	–	–	0	.48
86-87	Det	63	13	11	24	-6	0	0	56	23.2	2	–	–	0	–	–	–	221	–	–	–	–	–	0	.38
87-88	Det*	74	29	33	62	16	5	1	126	23.0	15	–	–	0	–	–	–	**398**	–	–	–	–	–	1	.84
88-89	Det	25	4	2	6	-11	0	0	23	17.4	1	–	–	0	–	–	–	106	–	–	–	–	–	0	.24
89-90	Det	4	3	0	3	0	1	0	12	25.0	0	0	0	0	0	0	–	21	–	–	–	–	–	0	.75
90-91	Det	55	16	23	39	-3	3	0	88	18.2	4	–	–	0	–	–	–	315	–	–	–	–	–	0	.71
91-92	Det	63	20	24	44	16	1	0	96	20.8	8	5	13	0	0	0	79	276	18	53	18	20	1	0	.70
92-93	Det	80	14	29	43	-9	3	0	128	10.9	6	8	14	0	0	0	94	292	16	71	15	27	10	0	.54
93-94	Det	66	7	10	17	-1	0	0	105	6.7	1	1	2	0	0	0	74	275	21	45	20	25	1	0	.26
94-95		Did Not Play in NHL																							
95-96	Chi	78	19	21	40	15	3	0	97	19.6	1	4	5	0	0	0	78	237	19	56	19	21	6	0	.51
96-97	Chi	**82**	9	14	23	-3	3	0	111	8.1	1	0	1	0	0	0	**88**	326	18	58	17	27	6	0	.28
97-98	Chi	14	2	1	3	-7	0	0	18	11.1	2	0	2	0	0	0	10	48	4	4	4	4	0	0	.21
98-99	Chi	78	7	14	21	-11	3	0	87	8.0	0	2	2	0	0	0	57	206	20	33	20	12	2	0	.27
13 Years		726	151	195	346	-18	22	1	993	15.2	44	–	–	0	–	–	–	2907	–	–	–	–	–	1	.48

Postseason																									
Year	Tm	GP	G	A	Pts	+/–	GW	OT	S	SPct	G	A	Pts	G	A	Pts	Num	PIM	Maj	Mnr	Fgt	Rgh	HHT	Hat	P/G
86-87	Det	16	3	4	7	2	1	0	18	16.7	1	–	–	0	–	–	–	63	–	–	–	–	–	0	.44
87-88	Det	16	8	13	21	8	1	0	26	30.8	5	–	–	0	–	–	–	51	–	–	–	–	–	0	1.31

Postseason																									
Year	Tm	GP	G	A	Pts	+/–	GW	OT	S	SPct	G	A	Pts	G	A	Pts	Num	PIM	Maj	Mnr	Fgt	Rgh	HHT	Hat	P/G
90-91	Det	6	1	2	3	-2	0	0	4	25.0	0	–	–	0	–	–	–	50	–	–	–	–	–	0	.50
91-92	Det	11	1	6	7	2	0	0	13	7.7	0	1	1	0	0	0	14	28	0	14	0	6	0	0	.64
92-93	Det	7	0	3	3	-1	0	0	14	0.0	0	2	2	0	0	0	5	10	0	5	0	3	0	0	.43
93-94	Det	7	1	1	2	1	0	0	10	10.0	0	0	0	0	0	0	4	8	0	4	0	1	0	0	.29
95-96	Chi	10	0	2	2	-1	0	0	20	0.0	0	0	0	0	0	0	10	23	1	9	1	3	0	0	.20
96-97	Chi	6	2	1	3	-4	1	0	10	20.0	1	0	1	0	0	0	11	41	1	8	1	3	0	0	.50
8 Years		79	16	32	48	5	3	0	115	13.9	7	–	–	0	–	–	–	274	–	–	–	–	–	0	.61

Chris Pronger

(statistical profile on page 361)

Pos: D **Shoots:** L **Ht:** 6'5" **Wt:** 207 **Born:** 10/10/74—Dryden, Ontario **Age:** 25

		Overall									Power Play			Shorthand			Penalty							Misc	
Year	Tm	GP	G	A	Pts	+/–	GW	GT	S	SPct	G	A	Pts	G	A	Pts	Num	PIM	Maj	Mnr	Fgt	Rgh	HHT	Hat	P/G
93-94	Har	81	5	25	30	-3	0	0	174	2.9	2	11	13	0	1	1	51	113	1	49	1	9	14	0	.37
94-95	Har	43	5	9	14	-12	1	0	94	5.3	3	2	5	0	0	0	17	54	4	12	4	4	2	0	.33
95-96	StL	78	7	18	25	-18	1	0	138	5.1	3	8	11	1	0	1	48	110	2	45	2	9	16	0	.32
96-97	StL	79	11	24	35	15	0	0	147	7.5	4	11	15	0	0	0	54	143	1	49	1	9	11	0	.44
97-98	StL	81	9	27	36	**47**	2	0	145	6.2	1	8	9	0	2	2	72	180	4	65	4	11	12	0	.44
98-99	StL	67	13	33	46	3	0	0	172	7.6	8	17	25	0	1	1	51	113	1	49	1	5	11	0	.69
6 Years		429	50	136	186	32	4	0	870	5.7	21	57	78	1	4	5	293	713	13	269	13	47	66	0	.43
		Postseason																							
Year	Tm	GP	G	A	Pts	+/–	GW	OT	S	SPct	G	A	Pts	G	A	Pts	Num	PIM	Maj	Mnr	Fgt	Rgh	HHT	Hat	P/G
95-96	StL	13	1	5	6	0	0	0	20	5.0	0	2	2	0	1	1	8	16	0	8	0	2	2	0	.46
96-97	StL	6	1	1	2	0	0	0	19	5.3	0	1	1	0	0	0	7	22	0	6	0	2	1	0	.33
97-98	StL	10	1	9	10	-2	0	0	24	4.2	0	6	6	0	0	0	13	26	0	13	0	1	5	0	1.00
98-99	StL	13	1	4	5	-2	0	0	43	2.3	1	2	3	0	0	0	14	28	0	14	0	1	2	0	.38
4 Years		42	4	19	23	-4	0	0	106	3.8	1	11	12	0	1	1	42	92	0	41	0	6	10	0	.55

Sean Pronger

Pos: C **Shoots:** L **Ht:** 6'2" **Wt:** 205 **Born:** 11/30/72—Dryden, Ontario **Age:** 27

		Overall									Power Play			Shorthand			Penalty							Misc	
Year	Tm	GP	G	A	Pts	+/–	GW	GT	S	SPct	G	A	Pts	G	A	Pts	Num	PIM	Maj	Mnr	Fgt	Rgh	HHT	Hat	P/G
95-96	Anh	7	0	1	1	0	0	0	3	0.0	0	0	0	0	0	0	3	6	0	3	0	1	2	0	.14
96-97	Anh	39	7	7	14	6	1	1	43	16.3	1	1	2	0	0	0	10	20	0	10	0	1	5	0	.36
97-98	2Tm	67	6	15	21	-10	3	0	73	8.2	1	5	6	0	0	0	16	32	0	16	0	2	6	0	.31
98-99	3Tm	29	0	4	4	-1	0	0	14	0.0	0	0	0	0	0	0	4	8	0	4	0	2	1	0	.14
97-98	Anh	62	5	15	20	-9	2	0	68	7.4	1	5	6	0	0	0	15	30	0	15	0	2	6	0	.32
97-98	Pit	5	1	0	1	-1	1	0	5	20.0	0	0	0	0	0	0	1	2	0	1	0	0	0	0	.20
98-99	Pit	2	0	0	0	0	0	0	3	0.0	0	0	0	0	0	0	0	0	0	0	0	0	0	0	.00
98-99	NYR	14	0	3	3	-3	0	0	3	0.0	0	0	0	0	0	0	2	4	0	2	0	1	1	0	.21
98-99	LA	13	0	1	1	2	0	0	8	0.0	0	0	0	0	0	0	2	4	0	2	0	1	0	0	.08
4 Years		142	13	27	40	-5	4	1	133	9.8	2	6	8	0	0	0	33	66	0	33	0	6	14	0	.28
		Postseason																							
Year	Tm	GP	G	A	Pts	+/–	GW	OT	S	SPct	G	A	Pts	G	A	Pts	Num	PIM	Maj	Mnr	Fgt	Rgh	HHT	Hat	P/G
96-97	Anh	9	0	2	2	0	0	0	7	0.0	0	0	0	0	0	0	2	4	0	2	0	0	1	0	.22
97-98	Pit	5	0	0	0	-1	0	0	4	0.0	0	0	0	0	0	0	2	4	0	2	0	1	0	0	.00
2 Years		14	0	2	2	-1	0	0	11	0.0	0	0	0	0	0	0	4	8	0	4	0	1	1	0	.14

Vaclav Prospal

(statistical profile on page 361)

Pos: C **Shoots:** L **Ht:** 6'2" **Wt:** 190 **Born:** 2/17/75—Ceske-Budejovice, Czechoslovakia **Age:** 24

		Overall									Power Play			Shorthand			Penalty							Misc	
Year	Tm	GP	G	A	Pts	+/–	GW	GT	S	SPct	G	A	Pts	G	A	Pts	Num	PIM	Maj	Mnr	Fgt	Rgh	HHT	Hat	P/G
96-97	Phi	18	5	10	15	3	0	0	35	14.3	0	6	6	0	0	0	2	4	0	2	0	0	0	0	.83
97-98	2Tm	56	6	19	25	-11	0	0	88	6.8	4	8	12	0	0	0	9	21	1	8	1	3	4	0	.45
98-99	Ott	79	10	26	36	8	3	0	114	8.8	2	8	10	0	0	0	22	58	2	19	1	3	5	0	.46
97-98	Phi	41	5	13	18	-10	0	0	60	8.3	4	5	9	0	0	0	7	17	1	6	1	3	3	0	.44
97-98	Ott	15	1	6	7	-1	0	0	28	3.6	0	3	3	0	0	0	2	4	0	2	0	0	1	0	.47
3 Years		153	21	55	76	0	3	0	237	8.9	6	22	28	0	0	0	33	83	3	29	2	6	9	0	.50
		Postseason																							
Year	Tm	GP	G	A	Pts	+/–	GW	OT	S	SPct	G	A	Pts	G	A	Pts	Num	PIM	Maj	Mnr	Fgt	Rgh	HHT	Hat	P/G
96-97	Phi	5	1	3	4	0	0	0	10	10.0	0	2	2	0	0	0	2	4	0	2	0	0	0	0	.80
97-98	Ott	6	0	0	0	-2	0	0	7	0.0	0	0	0	0	0	0	0	0	0	0	0	0	0	0	.00
98-99	Ott	4	0	0	0	-2	0	0	6	0.0	0	0	0	0	0	0	0	0	0	0	0	0	0	0	.00
3 Years		15	1	3	4	-4	0	0	23	4.3	0	2	2	0	0	0	2	4	0	2	0	0	0	0	.27

Daren Puppa

Pos: G **Catches:** R **Ht:** 6'4" **Wt:** 205 **Born:** 3/23/65—Kirkland Lake, Ontario **Age:** 34

Overall																	Pen Shot		Offense		
Year	Tm	GP	GS	TP	W	L	T	Min	GA	GAA	Shots	SvPct	ShO	OE	PPGA	SHGA	Shots	GA	G	A	PIM
85-86	Buf	7	–	–	3	4	0	401	21	3.14	184	.886	1	–	–	–	0	0	0	0	0
86-87	Buf	3	–	–	0	2	1	185	13	4.22	80	.838	0	–	–	–	0	0	0	0	0
87-88	Buf	17	–	–	8	6	1	874	61	4.19	469	.870	0	–	–	–	0	0	0	1	4
88-89	Buf	37	–	–	17	10	6	1908	107	3.36	961	.889	1	–	–	–	0	0	0	4	12
89-90	Buf*	56	–	–	**31**	16	6	3241	156	2.89	1610	.903	1	–	–	–	0	0	0	4	4
90-91	Buf	38	–	–	15	11	6	2092	118	3.38	1029	.885	2	–	–	–	0	0	0	4	6
91-92	Buf	33	29	3	11	14	4	1757	114	3.89	932	.878	0	8	35	8	2	1	0	0	2
92-93	2Tm	32	30	4	17	7	4	1785	96	3.23	938	.898	2	12	25	5	0	0	0	1	0
93-94	TB	63	62	4	22	33	6	3653	165	2.71	1637	.899	4	14	42	12	0	0	0	1	2
94-95	TB	36	36	5	14	19	2	2013	90	2.68	946	.905	1	10	21	2	0	0	0	1	2
95-96	TB	57	55	7	29	16	9	3189	131	2.46	1605	.918	5	22	36	8	**2**	0	0	1	4
96-97	TB	6	6	2	1	1	2	325	14	2.58	150	.907	0	1	5	0	0	0	0	0	2
97-98	TB	26	25	3	5	14	6	1456	66	2.72	660	.900	0	6	20	2	0	0	0	0	6
98-99	TB	13	11	1	5	6	1	691	33	2.87	350	.906	2	4	11	2	0	0	0	1	0
92-93	Buf	24	22	4	11	5	4	1306	78	3.58	706	.890	0	8	19	4	0	0	0	1	0
92-93	Tor	8	8	0	6	2	0	479	18	2.25	232	.922	2	4	6	1	0	0	0	0	0
14 Years		424	–	–	178	159	54	23570	1185	3.02	11551	.897	19	–	–	–	4	1	0	18	44

Postseason																					
Year	Tm	GP	GS	TP	W	L	Pct	Min	GA	GAA	Shots	SvPct	ShO	OE	PPGA	SHGA	Shots	GA	G	A	PIM
87-88	Buf	3	–	–	1	1	.500	142	11	4.65	67	.836	0	–	–	–	0	0	0	0	0
89-90	Buf	6	–	–	2	4	.333	370	15	2.43	192	.922	0	–	–	–	0	0	0	0	0
90-91	Buf	2	–	–	0	1	.000	81	10	7.41	46	.783	0	–	–	–	0	0	0	0	0
92-93	Tor	1	0	0	0	0	–	20	1	3.00	7	.857	0	0	1	0	0	0	0	0	2
95-96	TB	4	4	3	1	3	.250	173	14	4.86	86	.837	0	0	6	0	0	0	0	0	0
5 Years		16	–	–	4	9	.308	786	51	3.89	398	.872	0	–	–	–	0	0	0	0	2

Jamie Pushor

Pos: D **Shoots:** R **Ht:** 6'3" **Wt:** 225 **Born:** 2/11/73—Lethbridge, Alberta **Age:** 26

Overall											Power Play			Shorthand			Penalty							Misc	
Year	Tm	GP	G	A	Pts	+/-	GW	GT	S	SPct	G	A	Pts	G	A	Pts	Num	PIM	Maj	Mnr	Fgt	Rgh	HHT	Hat	P/G
95-96	Det	5	0	1	1	2	0	0	6	0.0	0	0	0	0	0	0	3	17	1	1	1	0	0	0	.20
96-97	Det	75	4	7	11	1	0	0	63	6.3	0	0	0	0	0	0	41	129	13	27	12	6	9	0	.15
97-98	2Tm	64	2	7	9	3	0	0	51	3.9	0	0	0	0	0	0	33	81	5	28	5	9	6	0	.14
98-99	Anh	70	1	2	3	-20	0	0	75	1.3	0	0	0	0	0	0	31	112	6	21	6	2	8	0	.04
97-98	Det	54	2	5	7	2	0	0	43	4.7	0	0	0	0	0	0	28	71	5	23	5	7	5	0	.13
97-98	Anh	10	0	2	2	1	0	0	8	0.0	0	0	0	0	0	0	5	10	0	5	0	2	1	0	.20
4 Years		214	7	17	24	-14	0	0	195	3.6	0	0	0	0	0	0	108	339	25	77	24	17	23	0	.11

Postseason																									
Year	Tm	GP	G	A	Pts	+/-	GW	OT	S	SPct	G	A	Pts	G	A	Pts	Num	PIM	Maj	Mnr	Fgt	Rgh	HHT	Hat	P/G
96-97	Det	5	0	1	1	-1	0	0	3	0.0	0	0	0	0	1	1	1	5	1	0	1	0	0	0	.20
98-99	Anh	4	0	0	0	-3	0	0	6	0.0	0	0	0	0	0	0	3	6	0	3	0	1	1	0	.00
2 Years		9	0	1	1	-4	0	0	9	0.0	0	0	0	0	1	1	4	11	1	3	1	1	1	0	.11

Deron Quint

(statistical profile on page 361)

Pos: D **Shoots:** L **Ht:** 6'1" **Wt:** 182 **Born:** 3/12/76—Dover, New Hampshire **Age:** 23

Overall											Power Play			Shorthand			Penalty							Misc	
Year	Tm	GP	G	A	Pts	+/-	GW	GT	S	SPct	G	A	Pts	G	A	Pts	Num	PIM	Maj	Mnr	Fgt	Rgh	HHT	Hat	P/G
95-96	Wpg	51	5	13	18	-2	0	0	97	5.2	2	5	7	0	0	0	11	22	0	11	0	0	7	0	.35
96-97	Pho	27	3	11	14	-4	0	0	63	4.8	1	7	8	0	0	0	2	4	0	2	0	0	2	0	.52
97-98	Pho	32	4	7	11	-6	1	0	61	6.6	1	5	6	0	0	0	8	16	0	8	0	1	5	0	.34
98-99	Pho	60	5	8	13	-10	0	0	94	5.3	2	4	6	0	0	0	10	20	0	10	0	0	5	0	.22
4 Years		170	17	39	56	-22	1	0	315	5.4	6	21	27	0	0	0	31	62	0	31	0	1	19	0	.33

Postseason																									
Year	Tm	GP	G	A	Pts	+/-	GW	OT	S	SPct	G	A	Pts	G	A	Pts	Num	PIM	Maj	Mnr	Fgt	Rgh	HHT	Hat	P/G
96-97	Pho	7	0	2	2	2	0	0	13	0.0	0	1	1	0	0	0	0	0	0	0	0	0	0	0	.29

Stephane Quintal

(statistical profile on page 361)

Pos: D **Shoots:** R **Ht:** 6'3" **Wt:** 230 **Born:** 10/22/68—Boucherville, Quebec **Age:** 31

Overall											Power Play			Shorthand			Penalty							Misc	
Year	Tm	GP	G	A	Pts	+/–	GW	GT	S	SPct	G	A	Pts	G	A	Pts	Num	PIM	Maj	Mnr	Fgt	Rgh	HHT	Hat	P/G
88-89	Bos	26	0	1	1	-5	0	0	23	0.0	0	1	1	0	0	0	–	29	–	–	–	–	–	0	.04
89-90	Bos	38	2	2	4	-11	0	0	43	4.7	0	0	0	0	–	–	–	22	–	–	–	–	–	0	.11
90-91	Bos	45	2	6	8	2	0	0	54	3.7	1	1	2	0	1	1	–	89	–	–	–	–	–	0	.18
91-92	2Tm	75	4	16	20	-11	0	0	71	5.6	0	3	3	0	0	0	34	109	11	22	11	7	7	0	.27
92-93	StL	75	1	10	11	-6	0	0	81	1.2	0	0	0	1	2	3	34	100	8	25	8	5	7	0	.15
93-94	Wpg	81	8	18	26	-25	1	0	154	5.2	1	5	6	1	1	2	38	119	9	27	9	7	6	0	.32
94-95	Wpg	43	6	17	23	0	2	0	107	5.6	3	6	9	0	1	1	22	78	6	14	6	5	4	0	.53
95-96	Mon	68	2	14	16	-4	1	1	104	1.9	0	6	6	1	1	2	34	117	11	21	10	4	5	0	.24
96-97	Mon	71	7	15	22	1	0	0	139	5.0	1	5	6	0	1	1	27	100	10	15	9	5	1	0	.31
97-98	Mon	71	6	10	16	13	0	0	88	6.8	0	0	0	0	0	0	26	97	7	16	7	4	6	0	.23
98-99	Mon	82	8	19	27	-23	4	0	159	5.0	1	2	3	1	2	3	25	84	6	17	6	3	5	0	.33
91-92	Bos	49	4	10	14	-8	0	0	52	7.7	0	2	2	0	0	0	24	77	7	16	7	6	3	0	.29
91-92	StL	26	0	6	6	-3	0	0	19	0.0	0	1	1	0	0	0	10	32	4	6	4	1	4	0	.23
11 Years		675	46	128	174	-69	8	1	1023	4.5	7	29	36	4	–	–	–	944	–	–	–	–	–	0	.26
Postseason																									
Year	Tm	GP	G	A	Pts	+/–	GW	OT	S	SPct	G	A	Pts	G	A	Pts	Num	PIM	Maj	Mnr	Fgt	Rgh	HHT	Hat	P/G
90-91	Bos	3	0	1	1	0	0	0	1	0.0	0	0	0	0	0	0	2	7	1	1	–	–	–	0	.33
91-92	StL	4	1	2	3	0	0	0	5	20.0	1	1	2	0	0	0	3	6	0	3	0	1	1	0	.75
92-93	StL	9	0	0	0	0	0	0	10	0.0	0	0	0	0	0	0	4	8	0	4	0	1	1	0	.00
95-96	Mon	6	0	1	1	1	0	0	3	0.0	0	0	0	0	0	0	3	6	0	3	0	1	1	0	.17
96-97	Mon	5	0	1	1	-1	0	0	6	0.0	0	0	0	0	1	1	3	6	0	3	0	0	0	0	.20
97-98	Mon	9	0	2	2	2	0	0	12	0.0	0	0	0	0	0	0	2	4	0	2	0	0	2	0	.22
6 Years		36	1	7	8	2	0	0	37	2.7	1	1	2	0	1	1	17	37	1	16	–	–	–	0	.22

Marcus Ragnarsson

(statistical profile on page 362)

Pos: D **Shoots:** L **Ht:** 6'1" **Wt:** 220 **Born:** 8/13/71—Ostervala, Sweden **Age:** 28

Overall											Power Play			Shorthand			Penalty							Misc	
Year	Tm	GP	G	A	Pts	+/–	GW	GT	S	SPct	G	A	Pts	G	A	Pts	Num	PIM	Maj	Mnr	Fgt	Rgh	HHT	Hat	P/G
95-96	SJ	71	8	31	39	-24	0	0	94	8.5	4	13	17	0	0	0	21	42	0	21	0	1	6	0	.55
96-97	SJ	69	3	14	17	-18	0	0	57	5.3	2	4	6	0	0	0	26	63	1	24	0	1	10	0	.25
97-98	SJ	79	5	20	25	-11	2	0	91	5.5	3	7	10	0	1	1	27	65	1	25	0	0	9	0	.32
98-99	SJ	74	0	13	13	7	0	0	87	0.0	0	3	3	0	1	1	33	66	0	33	0	1	8	0	.18
4 Years		293	16	78	94	-46	2	0	329	4.9	9	27	36	0	2	2	107	236	2	103	0	3	33	0	.32
Postseason																									
Year	Tm	GP	G	A	Pts	+/–	GW	OT	S	SPct	G	A	Pts	G	A	Pts	Num	PIM	Maj	Mnr	Fgt	Rgh	HHT	Hat	P/G
97-98	SJ	6	0	0	0	2	0	0	4	0.0	0	0	0	0	0	0	2	4	0	2	0	0	1	0	.00
98-99	SJ	6	0	1	1	-4	0	0	9	0.0	0	1	1	0	0	0	3	6	0	3	0	1	1	0	.17
2 Years		12	0	1	1	-2	0	0	13	0.0	0	1	1	0	0	0	5	10	0	5	0	1	2	0	.08

Bill Ranford

(statistical profile on page 401)

Pos: G **Catches:** L **Ht:** 5'11" **Wt:** 189 **Born:** 12/14/66—Brandon, Manitoba **Age:** 33

Overall																	Pen Shot		Offense		
Year	Tm	GP	GS	TP	W	L	T	Min	GA	GAA	Shots	SvPct	ShO	OE	PPGA	SHGA	Shots	GA	G	A	PIM
85-86	Bos	4	–	–	3	1	0	240	10	2.50	106	.906	0	–	–	–	0	0	0	0	0
86-87	Bos	41	–	–	16	20	2	2234	124	3.33	1137	.891	3	–	–	–	0	0	0	1	8
87-88	Edm	6	–	–	3	0	2	325	16	2.95	159	.899	0	–	–	–	0	0	0	2	0
88-89	Edm	29	–	–	15	8	2	1509	88	3.50	718	.877	1	–	–	–	0	0	0	0	2
89-90	Edm	56	–	–	24	16	9	3107	165	3.19	1463	.887	1	–	–	–	**2**	0	0	2	18
90-91	Edm*	60	–	–	27	27	3	3415	182	3.20	1705	.893	0	–	–	–	0	0	0	4	6
91-92	Edm	67	65	8	27	26	10	3822	228	3.58	1971	.884	1	16	75	12	**3**	0	0	3	4
92-93	Edm	67	62	4	17	38	6	3753	240	3.84	2065	.884	1	15	**78**	7	2	0	0	3	10
93-94	Edm	71	70	7	22	34	11	4070	236	3.48	2325	.898	1	25	64	9	1	**1**	0	2	2
94-95	Edm	40	40	7	15	20	3	2203	**133**	3.62	1134	.883	2	10	**39**	**7**	1	0	0	2	2
95-96	2Tm	77	76	10	34	**30**	9	4322	**237**	3.29	2054	.885	2	23	71	7	1	0	0	3	2
96-97	2Tm	55	55	9	20	23	10	3156	171	3.25	1514	.887	2	12	33	4	0	0	0	1	7
97-98	Was	22	19	1	7	12	2	1183	55	2.79	555	.901	0	7	13	1	0	0	0	1	0
98-99	2Tm	36	30	4	6	18	4	1812	110	3.64	956	.885	1	9	32	1	1	1	0	0	2
95-96	Edm	37	37	7	13	18	5	2015	128	3.81	1024	.875	1	12	38	5	0	0	0	1	2
95-96	Bos	40	39	3	21	12	4	2307	109	2.83	1030	.894	1	11	33	2	1	0	0	2	0
96-97	Bos	37	37	7	12	16	8	2147	125	3.49	1102	.887	2	10	20	3	0	0	0	0	0
96-97	Was	18	18	2	8	7	2	1009	46	2.74	412	.888	0	2	13	1	0	0	0	1	7

Overall																	Pen Shot		Offense		
Year	Tm	GP	GS	TP	W	L	T	Min	GA	GAA	Shots	SvPct	ShO	OE	PPGA	SHGA	Shots	GA	G	A	PIM
98-99	TB	32	26	4	3	18	3	1568	102	3.90	858	.881	1	8	28	1	1	1	0	0	2
98-99	Det	4	4	0	3	0	1	244	8	1.97	98	.918	0	1	4	0	0	0	0	0	0
14 Years		631	–	–	236	273	73	35151	1995	3.41	17862	.888	15	–	–	–	11	2	0	24	63
Postseason																					
Year	Tm	GP	GS	TP	W	L	Pct	Min	GA	GAA	Shots	SvPct	ShO	OE	PPGA	SHGA	Shots	GA	G	A	PIM
85-86	Bos	2	–	–	0	2	.000	120	7	3.50	44	.841	0	–	–	–	0	0	0	0	0
86-87	Bos	2	–	–	0	2	.000	123	8	3.90	55	.855	0	–	–	–	0	0	0	0	0
89-90	Edm	22	–	–	16	6	.727	1401	59	2.53	672	.912	1	–	–	–	0	0	0	2	4
90-91	Edm	3	–	–	1	2	.333	135	8	3.56	78	.897	0	–	–	–	0	0	0	0	0
91-92	Edm	16	16	2	8	8	.500	909	51	3.37	484	.895	2	5	16	0	0	0	0	0	0
95-96	Bos	4	4	0	1	3	.250	239	16	4.02	112	.857	0	0	4	0	0	0	0	0	0
98-99	Det	4	4	2	2	2	.500	183	10	3.28	105	.905	1	2	3	0	0	0	0	0	0
7 Years		53	–	–	28	25	.528	3110	159	3.07	1550	.897	4	–	–	–	0	0	0	2	4

Paul Ranheim

(statistical profile on page 362)

Pos: LW **Shoots:** R **Ht:** 6'1" **Wt:** 210 **Born:** 1/25/66—St. Louis, Missouri **Age:** 33

Overall											Power Play			Shorthand			Penalty							Misc	
Year	Tm	GP	G	A	Pts	+/–	GW	GT	S	SPct	G	A	Pts	G	A	Pts	Num	PIM	Maj	Mnr	Fgt	Rgh	HHT	Hat	P/G
88-89	Cgy	5	0	0	0	-3	0	0	4	0.0	0	0	0	0	0	0	0	0	0	0	0	0	0	0	.00
89-90	Cgy	**80**	26	28	54	27	4	2	197	13.2	1	–	–	3	–	–	10	23	1	9	–	–	–	0	.68
90-91	Cgy	39	14	16	30	20	2	0	108	13.0	2	–	–	0	–	–	2	4	0	2	0	–	–	0	.77
91-92	Cgy	80	23	20	43	16	3	0	159	14.5	1	0	1	3	0	3	16	32	0	16	0	4	5	1	.54
92-93	Cgy	83	21	22	43	-4	1	0	179	11.7	3	1	4	4	2	6	13	26	0	13	0	1	4	0	.52
93-94	2Tm	82	10	17	27	-18	2	0	131	7.6	0	0	0	2	2	4	11	22	0	11	0	0	6	0	.33
94-95	Har	47	6	14	20	-3	1	0	73	8.2	0	1	1	0	0	0	5	10	0	5	0	0	2	0	.43
95-96	Har	73	10	20	30	-2	1	0	126	7.9	0	2	2	1	2	3	7	14	0	7	0	0	2	0	.41
96-97	Har	67	10	11	21	-13	1	0	96	10.4	0	1	1	3	1	4	9	18	0	9	0	0	2	0	.31
97-98	Car	73	5	9	14	-11	2	0	77	6.5	0	0	0	1	0	1	14	28	0	14	0	3	4	0	.19
98-99	Car	78	9	10	19	4	1	0	67	13.4	0	0	0	2	0	2	10	39	1	7	0	0	2	0	.24
93-94	Cgy	67	10	14	24	-7	2	0	110	9.1	0	0	0	2	2	4	10	20	0	10	0	0	6	0	.36
93-94	Har	15	0	3	3	-11	0	0	21	0.0	0	0	0	0	0	0	1	2	0	1	0	0	0	0	.20
11 Years		707	134	167	301	13	18	2	1217	11.0	7	–	–	19	–	–	97	216	2	93	–	–	–	1	.43
Postseason																									
Year	Tm	GP	G	A	Pts	+/–	GW	OT	S	SPct	G	A	Pts	G	A	Pts	Num	PIM	Maj	Mnr	Fgt	Rgh	HHT	Hat	P/G
89-90	Cgy	6	1	3	4	2	0	0	11	9.1	0	–	–	0	–	–	1	2	0	1	0	–	–	0	.67
90-91	Cgy	7	2	2	4	0	0	0	16	12.5	0	–	–	0	0	0	0	0	0	0	0	0	0	0	.57
92-93	Cgy	6	0	1	1	-1	0	0	7	0.0	0	0	0	0	0	0	0	0	0	0	0	0	0	0	.17
98-99	Car	6	0	0	0	0	0	0	5	0.0	0	0	0	0	0	0	1	2	0	1	0	1	0	0	.00
4 Years		25	3	6	9	1	0	0	39	7.7	0	–	–	0	–	–	2	4	0	2	0	–	–	0	.36

Erik Rasmussen

(statistical profile on page 362)

Pos: C **Shoots:** L **Ht:** 6'2" **Wt:** 205 **Born:** 3/28/77—Minneapolis, Minnesota **Age:** 22

Overall											Power Play			Shorthand			Penalty							Misc	
Year	Tm	GP	G	A	Pts	+/–	GW	GT	S	SPct	G	A	Pts	G	A	Pts	Num	PIM	Maj	Mnr	Fgt	Rgh	HHT	Hat	P/G
97-98	Buf	21	2	3	5	2	0	0	28	7.1	0	0	0	0	0	0	7	14	0	7	0	0	1	0	.24
98-99	Buf	42	3	7	10	6	0	0	40	7.5	0	0	0	0	0	0	9	37	1	6	0	1	4	0	.24
2 Years		63	5	10	15	8	0	0	68	7.4	0	0	0	0	0	0	16	51	1	13	0	1	5	0	.24
Postseason																									
Year	Tm	GP	G	A	Pts	+/–	GW	OT	S	SPct	G	A	Pts	G	A	Pts	Num	PIM	Maj	Mnr	Fgt	Rgh	HHT	Hat	P/G
98-99	Buf	21	2	4	6	2	1	0	23	8.7	0	0	0	0	0	0	5	18	0	4	0	1	0	0	.29

Peter Ratchuk

Pos: D **Shoots:** L **Ht:** 6'1" **Wt:** 180 **Born:** 9/10/77—Buffalo, New York **Age:** 22

Overall											Power Play			Shorthand			Penalty							Misc	
Year	Tm	GP	G	A	Pts	+/–	GW	GT	S	SPct	G	A	Pts	G	A	Pts	Num	PIM	Maj	Mnr	Fgt	Rgh	HHT	Hat	P/G
98-99	Fla	24	1	1	2	-1	0	0	34	2.9	0	0	0	0	0	0	5	10	0	5	0	0	2	0	.08

Mike Rathje

(statistical profile on page 362)

Pos: D **Shoots:** L **Ht:** 6'5" **Wt:** 230 **Born:** 5/11/74—Manville, Alberta **Age:** 25

		Overall									Power Play			Shorthand			Penalty							Misc	
Year	Tm	GP	G	A	Pts	+/–	GW	GT	S	SPct	G	A	Pts	G	A	Pts	Num	PIM	Maj	Mnr	Fgt	Rgh	HHT	Hat	P/G
93-94	SJ	47	1	9	10	-9	0	0	30	3.3	1	1	2	0	0	0	24	59	1	22	0	1	15	0	.21
94-95	SJ	42	2	7	9	-1	0	0	38	5.3	0	2	2	0	0	0	13	29	1	12	1	1	7	0	.21
95-96	SJ	27	0	7	7	-16	0	0	26	0.0	0	4	4	0	0	0	7	14	0	7	0	1	3	0	.26
96-97	SJ	31	0	8	8	-1	0	0	22	0.0	0	1	1	0	0	0	9	21	1	8	1	1	3	0	.26
97-98	SJ	81	3	12	15	-4	0	0	61	4.9	1	1	2	0	0	0	28	59	1	27	1	0	17	0	.19
98-99	SJ	82	5	9	14	15	1	0	67	7.5	2	2	4	0	2	2	18	36	0	18	0	0	12	0	.17
6 Years		310	11	52	63	-16	1	0	244	4.5	4	11	15	0	2	2	99	218	4	94	3	4	57	0	.20

Postseason

Year	Tm	GP	G	A	Pts	+/–	GW	OT	S	SPct	G	A	Pts	G	A	Pts	Num	PIM	Maj	Mnr	Fgt	Rgh	HHT	Hat	P/G
93-94	SJ	1	0	0	0	1	0	0	0	–	0	0	0	0	0	0	0	0	0	0	0	0	0	0	.00
94-95	SJ	11	5	2	7	-15	0	0	18	27.8	5	0	5	0	0	0	2	4	0	2	0	1	1	0	.64
97-98	SJ	6	1	0	1	-3	0	0	2	50.0	1	0	1	0	0	0	3	6	0	3	0	0	1	0	.17
98-99	SJ	6	0	0	0	-6	0	0	4	0.0	0	0	0	0	0	0	2	4	0	2	0	0	1	0	.00
4 Years		24	6	2	8	-23	0	0	24	25.0	6	0	6	0	0	0	7	14	0	7	0	1	3	0	.33

Rob Ray

Pos: RW **Shoots:** L **Ht:** 6'0" **Wt:** 203 **Born:** 6/8/68—Belleville, Ontario **Age:** 31

		Overall									Power Play			Shorthand			Penalty							Misc	
Year	Tm	GP	G	A	Pts	+/–	GW	GT	S	SPct	G	A	Pts	G	A	Pts	Num	PIM	Maj	Mnr	Fgt	Rgh	HHT	Hat	P/G
89-90	Buf	27	2	1	3	-2	0	0	20	10.0	0	–	–	0	–	–	–	99	–	–	–	–	–	0	.11
90-91	Buf	66	8	8	16	-11	1	0	54	14.8	0	–	–	0	–	–	–	**350**	–	–	–	–	–	0	.24
91-92	Buf	63	5	3	8	-9	0	0	29	17.2	0	0	0	0	0	0	71	354	20	32	19	11	1	0	.13
92-93	Buf	68	3	2	5	-3	0	0	28	10.7	1	0	1	0	0	0	53	211	19	28	18	10	0	0	.07
93-94	Buf	82	3	4	7	2	0	0	34	8.8	0	0	0	0	0	0	76	274	22	47	22	20	3	0	.09
94-95	Buf	47	0	3	3	-4	0	0	7	0.0	0	0	0	0	0	0	41	173	17	19	17	13	1	0	.06
95-96	Buf	71	3	6	9	-8	0	1	21	14.3	0	0	0	0	0	0	67	287	27	31	27	13	1	0	.13
96-97	Buf	**82**	7	3	10	3	1	0	45	15.6	0	0	0	0	0	0	77	286	20	48	20	**28**	1	0	.12
97-98	Buf	63	2	4	6	2	1	0	19	10.5	1	0	1	0	0	0	49	234	16	22	15	9	1	0	.10
98-99	Buf	76	0	4	4	-2	0	0	23	0.0	0	0	0	0	0	0	54	**261**	19	23	19	17	2	0	.05
10 Years		645	33	38	71	-32	3	1	280	11.8	2	–	–	0	–	–	–	2529	–	–	–	–	–	0	.11

Postseason

Year	Tm	GP	G	A	Pts	+/–	GW	OT	S	SPct	G	A	Pts	G	A	Pts	Num	PIM	Maj	Mnr	Fgt	Rgh	HHT	Hat	P/G
90-91	Buf	6	1	1	2	1	1	0	6	16.7	0	–	–	0	–	–	–	56	–	–	–	–	–	0	.33
91-92	Buf	7	0	0	0	-2	0	0	0	–	0	0	0	0	0	0	1	2	0	1	0	0	0	0	.00
93-94	Buf	7	1	0	1	1	0	0	4	25.0	0	0	0	0	0	0	9	43	3	4	3	1	0	0	.14
94-95	Buf	5	0	0	0	0	0	0	0	–	0	0	0	0	0	0	3	14	0	2	0	1	1	0	.00
96-97	Buf	12	0	1	1	-3	0	0	4	0.0	0	0	0	0	0	0	6	28	0	4	0	1	0	0	.08
97-98	Buf	10	0	0	0	-2	0	0	2	0.0	0	0	0	0	0	0	4	24	0	2	0	0	0	0	.00
98-99	Buf	5	1	0	1	1	1	0	1	100.0	0	0	0	0	0	0	0	0	0	0	0	0	0	0	.20
7 Years		52	3	2	5	-4	2	0	17	17.6	0	–	–	0	–	–	–	167	–	–	–	–	–	0	.10

Marty Reasoner

(statistical profile on page 363)

Pos: C **Shoots:** R **Ht:** 6'1" **Wt:** 185 **Born:** 2/26/77—Rochester, New York **Age:** 22

		Overall									Power Play			Shorthand			Penalty							Misc	
Year	Tm	GP	G	A	Pts	+/–	GW	GT	S	SPct	G	A	Pts	G	A	Pts	Num	PIM	Maj	Mnr	Fgt	Rgh	HHT	Hat	P/G
98-99	StL	22	3	7	10	2	0	0	33	9.1	1	4	5	0	0	0	4	8	0	4	0	0	2	0	.45

Mark Recchi

(statistical profile on page 363)

Pos: RW **Shoots:** L **Ht:** 5'10" **Wt:** 185 **Born:** 2/1/68—Kamloops, British Columbia **Age:** 31

		Overall									Power Play			Shorthand			Penalty							Misc	
Year	Tm	GP	G	A	Pts	+/–	GW	GT	S	SPct	G	A	Pts	G	A	Pts	Num	PIM	Maj	Mnr	Fgt	Rgh	HHT	Hat	P/G
88-89	Pit	15	1	1	2	-2	0	0	11	9.1	0	0	0	0	–	–	0	0	0	0	0	0	0	0	.13
89-90	Pit	74	30	37	67	6	4	1	143	21.0	6	4	10	2	–	–	–	44	–	–	–	–	–	0	.91
90-91	Pit*	78	40	73	113	0	9	0	184	21.7	12	27	39	0	–	–	–	48	–	–	–	–	–	0	1.45
91-92	2Tm	80	43	54	97	-21	5	1	210	20.5	20	28	48	1	0	1	36	96	0	33	0	8	7	1	1.21
92-93	Phi*	84	53	70	123	1	6	0	274	19.3	15	27	42	4	1	5	30	95	1	25	0	8	4	0	1.46
93-94	Phi*	84	40	67	107	-2	5	0	217	18.4	11	25	36	0	2	2	23	46	0	23	0	2	2	0	1.27
94-95	2Tm	49	16	32	48	-9	3	0	121	13.2	9	7	16	0	0	0	14	28	0	14	0	4	4	0	.98
95-96	Mon	82	28	50	78	20	6	0	191	14.7	11	19	30	2	0	2	26	69	3	22	2	1	8	0	.95
96-97	Mon*	**82**	34	46	80	-1	3	0	202	16.8	7	13	20	2	1	3	22	58	2	19	2	3	8	1	.98

Overall											Power Play			Shorthand			Penalty							Misc	
Year	Tm	GP	G	A	Pts	+/–	GW	GT	S	SPct	G	A	Pts	G	A	Pts	Num	PIM	Maj	Mnr	Fgt	Rgh	HHT	Hat	P/G
97-98	Mon*	82	32	42	74	11	6	0	216	14.8	9	20	29	1	0	1	20	51	1	18	1	3	5	1	.90
98-99	2Tm	71	16	37	53	-7	2	0	171	9.4	3	20	23	0	1	1	17	34	0	17	0	5	6	0	.75
91-92	Pit	58	33	37	70	-16	4	1	156	21.2	16	18	34	1	0	1	31	78	0	29	0	7	7	1	1.21
91-92	Phi	22	10	17	27	-5	1	0	54	18.5	4	10	14	0	0	0	5	18	0	4	0	1	0	0	1.23
94-95	Phi	10	2	3	5	-6	2	0	17	11.8	1	2	3	0	0	0	6	12	0	6	0	3	0	0	.50
94-95	Mon	39	14	29	43	-3	1	0	104	13.5	8	5	13	0	0	0	8	16	0	8	0	1	4	0	1.10
98-99	Mon	61	12	35	47	-4	2	0	152	7.9	3	19	22	0	1	1	14	28	0	14	0	5	4	0	.77
98-99	Phi	10	4	2	6	-3	0	0	19	21.1	0	1	1	0	0	0	3	6	0	3	0	0	2	0	.60
11 Years		781	333	509	842	-4	49	2	1940	17.2	103	190	293	12	–	–	–	569	–	–	–	–	–	3	1.08
Postseason																									
Year	Tm	GP	G	A	Pts	+/–	GW	OT	S	SPct	G	A	Pts	G	A	Pts	Num	PIM	Maj	Mnr	Fgt	Rgh	HHT	Hat	P/G
90-91	Pit	24	10	24	34	6	2	0	60	16.7	5	–	–	0	–	–	–	33	–	–	–	–	–	0	1.42
95-96	Mon	6	3	3	6	1	0	0	13	23.1	3	0	3	0	0	0	0	0	0	0	0	0	0	0	1.00
96-97	Mon	5	4	2	6	2	0	0	18	22.2	0	0	0	0	1	1	1	2	0	1	0	0	0	0	1.20
97-98	Mon	10	4	8	12	2	2	0	22	18.2	0	4	4	0	0	0	3	6	0	3	0	0	1	0	1.20
98-99	Phi	6	0	1	1	-1	0	0	18	0.0	0	1	1	0	0	0	1	2	0	1	0	1	0	0	.17
5 Years		51	21	38	59	10	4	0	131	16.0	8	–	–	0	–	–	–	43	–	–	–	–	–	0	1.16

Wade Redden

(statistical profile on page 363)

Pos: D **Shoots:** L **Ht:** 6'2" **Wt:** 205 **Born:** 6/12/77—Lloydminster, Saskatchewan **Age:** 22

Overall											Power Play			Shorthand			Penalty							Misc	
Year	Tm	GP	G	A	Pts	+/–	GW	GT	S	SPct	G	A	Pts	G	A	Pts	Num	PIM	Maj	Mnr	Fgt	Rgh	HHT	Hat	P/G
96-97	Ott	**82**	6	24	30	1	1	0	102	5.9	2	8	10	0	1	1	12	41	3	8	3	1	5	0	.37
97-98	Ott	80	8	14	22	17	2	0	103	7.8	3	3	6	0	0	0	12	27	1	11	1	0	4	0	.28
98-99	Ott	72	8	21	29	7	1	1	127	6.3	3	10	13	0	1	1	20	54	2	17	1	1	8	0	.40
3 Years		234	22	59	81	25	4	1	332	6.6	8	21	29	0	2	2	44	122	6	36	5	2	17	0	.35
Postseason																									
Year	Tm	GP	G	A	Pts	+/–	GW	OT	S	SPct	G	A	Pts	G	A	Pts	Num	PIM	Maj	Mnr	Fgt	Rgh	HHT	Hat	P/G
96-97	Ott	7	1	3	4	-4	0	0	11	9.1	0	1	1	0	0	0	1	2	0	1	0	1	0	0	.57
97-98	Ott	9	0	2	2	-5	0	0	11	0.0	0	2	2	0	0	0	1	2	0	1	0	0	0	0	.22
98-99	Ott	4	1	2	3	-1	0	0	11	9.1	1	1	2	0	0	0	1	2	0	1	0	0	1	0	.75
3 Years		20	2	7	9	-10	0	0	33	6.1	1	4	5	0	0	0	3	6	0	3	0	1	1	0	.45

Joe Reekie

(statistical profile on page 363)

Pos: D **Shoots:** L **Ht:** 6'3" **Wt:** 220 **Born:** 2/22/65—Victoria, British Columbia **Age:** 34

Overall											Power Play			Shorthand			Penalty							Misc	
Year	Tm	GP	G	A	Pts	+/–	GW	GT	S	SPct	G	A	Pts	G	A	Pts	Num	PIM	Maj	Mnr	Fgt	Rgh	HHT	Hat	P/G
85-86	Buf	3	0	0	0	-2	0	0	1	0.0	0	0	0	0	0	0	–	14	–	–	–	–	–	0	.00
86-87	Buf	56	1	8	9	6	0	0	56	1.8	0	–	–	0	–	–	–	82	–	–	–	–	–	0	.16
87-88	Buf	30	1	4	5	-3	0	0	23	4.3	0	–	–	0	–	–	–	68	–	–	–	–	–	0	.17
88-89	Buf	15	1	3	4	6	0	0	14	7.1	1	–	–	0	–	–	–	26	–	–	–	–	–	0	.27
89-90	NYI	31	1	8	9	13	1	0	22	4.5	0	–	–	0	–	–	–	43	–	–	–	–	–	0	.29
90-91	NYI	66	3	16	19	17	2	0	70	4.3	0	–	–	0	–	–	–	96	–	–	–	–	–	0	.29
91-92	NYI	54	4	12	16	15	0	1	59	6.8	0	1	1	0	0	0	34	85	3	30	3	8	6	0	.30
92-93	TB	42	2	11	13	2	0	0	53	3.8	0	2	2	0	0	0	25	69	1	22	1	2	14	0	.31
93-94	2Tm	85	1	16	17	15	0	0	98	1.0	0	0	0	0	1	1	54	156	8	43	7	10	19	0	.20
94-95	Was	48	1	6	7	10	0	0	52	1.9	0	0	0	0	2	2	44	97	3	41	3	13	11	0	.15
95-96	Was	78	3	7	10	7	0	0	52	5.8	0	0	0	0	0	0	58	149	3	52	3	16	17	0	.13
96-97	Was	65	1	8	9	8	0	0	65	1.5	0	0	0	0	1	1	44	107	1	41	1	12	12	0	.14
97-98	Was	68	2	8	10	15	1	0	59	3.4	0	0	0	0	1	1	35	70	0	35	0	7	8	0	.15
98-99	Was	73	0	10	10	12	0	0	81	0.0	0	0	0	0	0	0	34	68	0	34	0	2	15	0	.14
93-94	TB	73	1	11	12	8	0	0	88	1.1	0	0	0	0	1	1	44	127	5	36	4	9	16	0	.16
93-94	Was	12	0	5	5	7	0	0	10	0.0	0	0	0	0	0	0	10	29	3	7	3	1	3	0	.42
14 Years		714	21	117	138	121	4	1	705	3.0	1	–	–	0	–	–	–	1130	–	–	–	–	–	0	.19
Postseason																									
Year	Tm	GP	G	A	Pts	+/–	GW	OT	S	SPct	G	A	Pts	G	A	Pts	Num	PIM	Maj	Mnr	Fgt	Rgh	HHT	Hat	P/G
87-88	Buf	2	0	0	0	-3	0	0	1	0.0	0	0	0	0	0	0	2	4	0	2	0	–	–	0	.00
93-94	Was	11	2	1	3	1	1	0	11	18.2	0	0	0	1	0	1	9	29	1	7	1	0	5	0	.27
94-95	Was	7	0	0	0	-4	0	0	3	0.0	0	0	0	0	0	0	1	2	0	1	0	0	0	0	.00
97-98	Was	21	1	2	3	4	0	0	16	6.3	0	0	0	0	0	0	10	20	0	10	0	0	7	0	.14
4 Years		41	3	3	6	-2	1	0	31	9.7	0	0	0	1	0	1	22	55	1	20	1	–	–	0	.15

Jeff Reese

Pos: G **Catches:** L **Ht:** 5'9" **Wt:** 175 **Born:** 3/24/66—Brantford, Ontario **Age:** 33

Overall																	Pen Shot		Offense		
Year	Tm	GP	GS	TP	W	L	T	Min	GA	GAA	Shots	SvPct	ShO	OE	PPGA	SHGA	Shots	GA	G	A	PIM
87-88	Tor	5	–	–	1	2	1	249	17	4.10	128	.867	0	–	–	–	0	0	0	0	0
88-89	Tor	10	–	–	2	6	1	486	40	4.94	286	.860	0	–	–	–	0	0	0	0	4
89-90	Tor	21	–	–	9	6	3	1101	81	4.41	630	.871	0	–	–	–	2	0	0	0	4
90-91	Tor	30	–	–	6	13	3	1430	92	3.86	695	.868	1	–	–	–	0	0	0	1	10
91-92	2Tm	20	14	2	4	7	3	1000	57	3.42	500	.886	1	3	18	0	0	0	0	1	0
92-93	Cgy	26	21	2	14	4	1	1311	70	3.20	629	.889	1	6	26	2	0	0	0	1	12
93-94	2Tm	20	18	2	5	9	3	1099	57	3.11	529	.892	1	3	21	4	0	0	0	4	4
94-95	Har	11	8	3	2	5	1	477	26	3.27	234	.889	0	2	7	1	0	0	0	1	0
95-96	2Tm	26	22	5	9	10	1	1267	68	3.22	634	.893	1	3	22	0	0	0	0	0	0
96-97	NJ	3	2	1	0	2	0	138	13	5.65	65	.800	0	0	4	0	0	0	0	0	0
97-98										Did Not Play in NHL											
98-99	Tor	2	1	0	1	1	0	106	8	4.53	51	.843	0	0	1	1	0	0	0	0	0
91-92	Tor	8	6	1	1	5	1	413	20	2.91	210	.905	1	2	4	0	0	0	0	0	0
91-92	Cgy	12	8	1	3	2	2	587	37	3.78	290	.872	0	1	14	0	0	0	0	1	12
93-94	Cgy	1	1	1	0	0	0	13	1	4.62	5	.800	0	0	0	0	0	0	0	0	0
93-94	Har	19	17	1	5	9	3	1086	56	3.09	524	.893	1	3	21	4	0	0	0	1	0
95-96	Har	7	5	2	2	3	0	274	14	3.07	170	.918	1	2	5	0	0	0	0	0	0
95-96	TB	19	17	3	7	7	1	993	54	3.26	464	.884	0	1	17	0	0	0	0	0	0
11 Years		174	–	–	53	65	17	8664	529	3.66	4381	.879	5	–	–	–	2	0	0	8	30

Postseason																					
Year	Tm	GP	GS	TP	W	L	Pct	Min	GA	GAA	Shots	SvPct	ShO	OE	PPGA	SHGA	Shots	GA	G	A	PIM
89-90	Tor	2	–	–	1	1	.500	108	6	3.33	50	.880	0	–	–	–	0	0	0	0	0
92-93	Cgy	4	4	2	1	3	.250	209	17	4.88	91	.813	0	0	2	1	0	0	0	0	0
95-96	TB	5	2	0	1	1	.500	198	12	3.64	100	.880	0	0	4	0	0	0	0	0	0
3 Years		11	–	–	3	5	.375	515	35	4.08	241	.855	0	–	–	–	0	0	0	0	0

Robert Reichel

(statistical profile on page 364)

Pos: C **Shoots:** L **Ht:** 5'10" **Wt:** 185 **Born:** 6/25/71—Litvinov, Czechoslovakia **Age:** 28

Overall											Power Play			Shorthand			Penalty							Misc	
Year	Tm	GP	G	A	Pts	+/-	GW	GT	S	SPct	G	A	Pts	G	A	Pts	Num	PIM	Maj	Mnr	Fgt	Rgh	HHT	Hat	P/G
90-91	Cgy	66	19	22	41	17	3	0	131	14.5	3	–	–	0	–	–	11	22	0	11	0	–	–	0	.62
91-92	Cgy	77	20	34	54	1	3	0	181	11.0	8	16	24	0	0	0	12	32	0	11	0	1	6	0	.70
92-93	Cgy	80	40	48	88	25	5	0	238	16.8	12	16	28	0	0	0	23	54	0	22	0	4	6	2	1.10
93-94	Cgy	84	40	53	93	20	6	0	249	16.1	14	21	35	0	0	0	25	58	0	24	0	4	12	2	1.11
94-95	Cgy	48	18	17	35	-2	2	0	160	11.3	5	8	13	0	0	0	14	28	0	14	0	2	8	0	.73
95-96											Did Not Play in NHL														
96-97	2Tm	**82**	21	41	62	5	3	0	214	9.8	6	14	20	1	0	1	13	26	0	13	0	1	7	0	.76
97-98	NYI	82	25	40	65	-11	2	2	201	12.4	8	24	32	0	0	0	16	32	0	16	0	0	16	1	.79
98-99	2Tm	**83**	26	43	69	-13	4	1	236	11.0	8	24	32	1	0	1	23	54	0	22	0	0	11	0	.83
96-97	Cgy	70	16	27	43	-2	3	0	181	8.8	6	11	17	0	0	0	11	22	0	11	0	0	7	0	.61
96-97	NYI	12	5	14	19	7	0	0	33	15.2	0	3	3	1	0	1	2	4	0	2	0	1	0	0	1.58
98-99	NYI	70	19	37	56	-15	1	1	186	10.2	5	23	28	1	0	1	21	50	0	20	0	0	9	0	.80
98-99	Pho	13	7	6	13	2	3	0	50	14.0	3	1	4	0	0	0	2	4	0	2	0	0	2	0	1.00
8 Years		602	209	298	507	42	28	3	1610	13.0	64	–	–	2	–	–	137	306	0	133	0	–	–	5	.84

Postseason																									
Year	Tm	GP	G	A	Pts	+/-	GW	OT	S	SPct	G	A	Pts	G	A	Pts	Num	PIM	Maj	Mnr	Fgt	Rgh	HHT	Hat	P/G
90-91	Cgy	6	1	1	2	0	0	0	15	6.7	1	–	–	0	0	0	0	0	0	0	0	0	0	0	.33
92-93	Cgy	6	2	4	6	-6	0	0	18	11.1	2	3	5	0	0	0	1	2	0	1	0	0	0	0	1.00
93-94	Cgy	7	0	5	5	3	0	0	24	0.0	0	1	1	0	0	0	0	0	0	0	0	0	0	0	.71
94-95	Cgy	7	2	4	6	1	1	0	20	10.0	0	1	1	0	0	0	2	4	0	2	0	0	1	0	.86
98-99	Pho	7	1	3	4	-2	0	0	16	6.3	0	2	2	0	0	0	1	2	0	1	0	1	0	0	.57
5 Years		33	6	17	23	-4	1	0	93	6.5	3	–	–	0	0	0	4	8	0	4	0	1	1	0	.70

Dave Reid

(statistical profile on page 364)

Pos: LW **Shoots:** L **Ht:** 6'1" **Wt:** 217 **Born:** 5/15/64—Toronto, Ontario **Age:** 35

Overall											Power Play			Shorthand			Penalty							Misc	
Year	Tm	GP	G	A	Pts	+/-	GW	GT	S	SPct	G	A	Pts	G	A	Pts	Num	PIM	Maj	Mnr	Fgt	Rgh	HHT	Hat	P/G
83-84	Bos	8	1	0	1	1	0	0	4	25.0	0	0	0	0	0	0	1	2	0	1	0	–	–	0	.13
84-85	Bos	35	14	13	27	-1	5	0	52	26.9	2	–	–	0	–	–	–	27	–	–	–	–	–	0	.77
85-86	Bos	37	10	10	20	2	1	1	53	18.9	4	–	–	0	–	–	–	10	–	–	–	–	–	0	.54
86-87	Bos	12	3	3	6	-1	0	0	19	15.8	0	–	–	0	–	–	0	0	0	0	0	0	0	0	.50

Overall											Power Play			Shorthand			Penalty							Misc	
Year	Tm	GP	G	A	Pts	+/–	GW	GT	S	SPct	G	A	Pts	G	A	Pts	Num	PIM	Maj	Mnr	Fgt	Rgh	HHT	Hat	P/G
87-88	Bos	3	0	0	0	0	0	0	2	0.0	0	0	0	0	0	0	0	0	0	0	0	0	0	0	.00
88-89	Tor	77	9	21	30	12	0	0	87	10.3	1	–	–	1	–	–	–	22	–	–	–	–	–	0	.39
89-90	Tor	70	9	19	28	-8	1	0	97	9.3	0	–	–	4	–	–	3	9	1	2	–	–	–	0	.40
90-91	Tor	69	15	13	28	-10	0	0	110	13.6	1	–	–	**8**	–	–	–	18	–	–	–	–	–	0	.41
91-92	Bos	43	7	7	14	5	0	0	70	10.0	2	1	3	1	0	1	8	27	1	6	1	3	3	0	.33
92-93	Bos	65	20	16	36	12	2	0	116	17.2	1	1	2	5	3	8	5	10	0	5	0	1	2	0	.55
93-94	Bos	83	6	17	23	10	1	0	145	4.1	0	0	0	2	4	6	11	25	1	10	1	1	5	0	.28
94-95	Bos	38	5	5	10	8	0	1	47	10.6	0	0	0	0	0	0	1	10	0	0	0	0	0	0	.26
95-96	Bos	63	23	21	44	14	3	1	160	14.4	1	0	1	6	1	7	2	4	0	2	0	0	1	1	.70
96-97	Dal	**82**	19	20	39	12	4	0	135	14.1	1	1	2	1	2	3	5	10	0	5	0	0	3	1	.48
97-98	Dal	65	6	12	18	-15	1	0	90	6.7	3	3	6	0	0	0	7	14	0	7	0	0	2	0	.28
98-99	Dal	73	6	11	17	0	1	0	81	7.4	1	0	1	0	0	0	8	16	0	8	0	1	3	0	.23
16 Years		823	153	188	341	41	19	3	1268	12.1	17	–	–	28	–	–	–	204	–	–	–	–	–	2	.41
Postseason																									
Year	Tm	GP	G	A	Pts	+/–	GW	OT	S	SPct	G	A	Pts	G	A	Pts	Num	PIM	Maj	Mnr	Fgt	Rgh	HHT	Hat	P/G
84-85	Bos	5	1	0	1	0	0	0	11	9.1	0	0	0	0	0	0	0	0	0	0	0	0	0	0	.20
86-87	Bos	2	0	0	0	-1	0	0	1	0.0	0	0	0	0	0	0	0	0	0	0	0	0	0	0	.00
89-90	Tor	3	0	0	0	-2	0	0	1	0.0	0	0	0	0	0	0	0	0	0	0	0	0	0	0	.00
91-92	Bos	15	2	5	7	2	1	0	17	11.8	0	1	1	0	0	0	2	4	0	2	0	0	1	0	.47
93-94	Bos	13	2	1	3	-1	0	0	23	8.7	0	0	0	1	0	1	1	2	0	1	0	0	1	0	.23
94-95	Bos	5	0	0	0	1	0	0	2	0.0	0	0	0	0	0	0	0	0	0	0	0	0	0	0	.00
95-96	Bos	5	0	2	2	-3	0	0	4	0.0	0	1	1	0	0	0	1	2	0	1	0	0	1	0	.40
96-97	Dal	7	1	0	1	-2	0	0	10	10.0	0	0	0	0	0	0	2	4	0	2	0	1	1	0	.14
97-98	Dal	5	0	3	3	-2	0	0	8	0.0	0	3	3	0	0	0	1	2	0	1	0	0	0	0	.60
98-99	Dal	23	2	8	10	4	0	0	30	6.7	0	1	1	0	0	0	3	14	0	2	0	1	1	0	.43
10 Years		83	8	19	27	-4	1	0	107	7.5	0	6	6	1	0	1	10	28	0	9	0	2	5	0	.33

Todd Reirden

Pos: D **Shoots:** L **Ht:** 6'5" **Wt:** 220 **Born:** 6/25/71—Deerfield, Illinois **Age:** 28

Overall											Power Play			Shorthand			Penalty							Misc	
Year	Tm	GP	G	A	Pts	+/–	GW	GT	S	SPct	G	A	Pts	G	A	Pts	Num	PIM	Maj	Mnr	Fgt	Rgh	HHT	Hat	P/G
98-99	Edm	17	2	3	5	-1	0	0	26	7.7	0	1	1	0	0	0	10	20	0	10	0	1	2	0	.29

Mikael Renberg

(statistical profile on page 364)

Pos: RW **Shoots:** L **Ht:** 6'2" **Wt:** 218 **Born:** 5/5/72—Pitea, Sweden **Age:** 27

Overall											Power Play			Shorthand			Penalty							Misc	
Year	Tm	GP	G	A	Pts	+/–	GW	GT	S	SPct	G	A	Pts	G	A	Pts	Num	PIM	Maj	Mnr	Fgt	Rgh	HHT	Hat	P/G
93-94	Phi	83	38	44	82	8	1	0	195	19.5	9	14	23	0	0	0	18	36	0	18	0	8	2	1	.99
94-95	Phi	47	26	31	57	20	4	0	143	18.2	8	4	12	0	0	0	10	20	0	10	0	3	1	0	1.21
95-96	Phi	51	23	20	43	8	4	0	198	11.6	9	8	17	0	0	0	21	45	1	20	1	2	7	0	.84
96-97	Phi	77	22	37	59	36	4	1	249	8.8	1	8	9	0	0	0	27	65	1	25	1	7	8	0	.77
97-98	TB	68	16	22	38	-37	0	1	175	9.1	6	8	14	3	0	3	17	34	0	17	0	2	8	1	.56
98-99	2Tm	66	15	23	38	5	2	0	154	9.7	6	4	10	0	0	0	9	18	0	9	0	3	1	0	.58
98-99	TB	20	4	8	12	-2	0	0	42	9.5	2	2	4	0	0	0	2	4	0	2	0	1	0	0	.60
98-99	Phi	46	11	15	26	7	2	0	112	9.8	4	2	6	0	0	0	7	14	0	7	0	2	1	0	.57
6 Years		392	140	177	317	40	15	2	1114	12.6	39	46	85	3	0	3	102	218	2	99	2	25	27	2	.81
Postseason																									
Year	Tm	GP	G	A	Pts	+/–	GW	OT	S	SPct	G	A	Pts	G	A	Pts	Num	PIM	Maj	Mnr	Fgt	Rgh	HHT	Hat	P/G
94-95	Phi	15	6	7	13	5	0	0	45	13.3	2	3	5	0	0	0	3	6	0	3	0	0	1	0	.87
95-96	Phi	11	3	6	9	1	0	0	22	13.6	1	2	3	0	0	0	3	14	0	2	0	1	1	0	.82
96-97	Phi	18	5	6	11	1	0	0	35	14.3	2	1	3	0	0	0	2	4	0	2	0	0	0	0	.61
98-99	Phi	6	0	1	1	-1	0	0	18	0.0	0	0	0	0	0	0	0	0	0	0	0	0	0	0	.17
4 Years		50	14	20	34	6	0	0	120	11.7	5	6	11	0	0	0	8	24	0	7	0	1	2	0	.68

Pascal Rheaume

(statistical profile on page 364)

Pos: C **Shoots:** L **Ht:** 6'1" **Wt:** 200 **Born:** 6/21/73—Quebec, Quebec **Age:** 26

Overall											Power Play			Shorthand			Penalty							Misc	
Year	Tm	GP	G	A	Pts	+/–	GW	GT	S	SPct	G	A	Pts	G	A	Pts	Num	PIM	Maj	Mnr	Fgt	Rgh	HHT	Hat	P/G
96-97	NJ	2	1	0	1	1	0	0	5	20.0	0	0	0	0	0	0	0	0	0	0	0	0	0	0	.50
97-98	StL	48	6	9	15	4	0	0	45	13.3	1	2	3	0	0	0	13	35	3	10	3	3	4	0	.31
98-99	StL	60	9	18	27	10	0	0	85	10.6	2	0	2	0	0	0	9	24	2	7	2	2	5	0	.45
3 Years		110	16	27	43	15	0	0	135	11.9	3	2	5	0	0	0	22	59	5	17	5	5	9	0	.39

Postseason																									
Year	Tm	GP	G	A	Pts	+/-	GW	OT	S	SPct	G	A	Pts	G	A	Pts	Num	PIM	Maj	Mnr	Fgt	Rgh	HHT	Hat	P/G
97-98	StL	10	1	3	4	0	0	0	10	10.0	1	0	1	0	0	0	4	8	0	4	0	1	1	0	.40
98-99	StL	5	1	0	1	1	0	0	10	10.0	0	0	0	0	0	0	2	4	0	2	0	0	1	0	.20
2 Years		15	2	3	5	1	0	0	20	10.0	1	0	1	0	0	0	6	12	0	6	0	1	2	0	.33

Damian Rhodes

(statistical profile on page 401)

Pos: G **Catches:** L **Ht:** 6'0" **Wt:** 190 **Born:** 5/28/69—St. Paul, Minnesota **Age:** 30

Overall																Pen Shot		Offense		
Year	Tm	GP	GS	TP	W	L	T	Min	GA	GAA	Shots	SvPct	ShO	OE	PPGA	SHGA	Shots	GA	G	A	PIM
90-91	Tor	1	1	0	1	0	0	60	1	1.00	26	.962	0	0	0	0	0	0	0	0	0
91-92										Did Not Play in NHL											
92-93										Did Not Play in NHL											
93-94	Tor	22	18	0	9	7	3	1213	53	2.62	541	.902	0	3	15	2	1	0	0	0	2
94-95	Tor	13	12	0	6	6	1	760	34	2.68	404	.916	0	8	8	0	1	0	0	0	4
95-96	2Tm	47	46	3	14	27	5	2747	127	2.77	1342	.905	2	17	33	6	1	0	0	2	4
96-97	Ott	50	49	4	14	20	**14**	2934	133	2.72	1213	.890	1	6	30	5	1	0	0	2	2
97-98	Ott	50	46	6	19	19	7	2743	107	2.34	1148	.907	5	8	26	4	2	**2**	0	1	0
98-99	Ott	45	43	4	22	13	7	2480	101	2.44	1060	.905	3	8	23	8	0	0	1	1	4
95-96	Tor	11	10	1	4	5	1	624	29	2.79	301	.904	0	4	5	2	0	0	0	0	0
95-96	Ott	36	36	2	10	22	4	2123	98	2.77	1041	.906	2	13	28	4	1	0	0	2	4
7 Years		228	215	17	85	92	37	12937	556	2.58	5734	.903	11	50	135	25	6	2	1	6	16
Postseason																					
Year	Tm	GP	GS	TP	W	L	Pct	Min	GA	GAA	Shots	SvPct	ShO	OE	PPGA	SHGA	Shots	GA	G	A	PIM
93-94	Tor	1	0	0	0	0	–	1	0	0.00	0	–	0	0	0	0	0	0	0	0	0
97-98	Ott	10	10	1	5	5	.500	590	21	2.14	236	.911	0	3	6	3	0	0	0	0	0
98-99	Ott	2	2	0	0	2	.000	150	6	2.40	65	.908	0	1	2	0	0	0	0	0	0
3 Years		13	12	1	5	7	.417	741	27	2.19	301	.910	0	4	8	3	0	0	0	0	0

Mike Ricci

(statistical profile on page 365)

Pos: C **Shoots:** L **Ht:** 6'0" **Wt:** 190 **Born:** 10/27/71—Scarborough, Ontario **Age:** 28

Overall											Power Play			Shorthand			Penalty							Misc	
Year	Tm	GP	G	A	Pts	+/-	GW	GT	S	SPct	G	A	Pts	G	A	Pts	Num	PIM	Maj	Mnr	Fgt	Rgh	HHT	Hat	P/G
90-91	Phi	68	21	20	41	-8	4	0	121	17.4	9	–	–	0	–	–	–	64	–	–	–	–	–	0	.60
91-92	Phi	78	20	36	56	-10	0	0	149	13.4	11	10	21	2	1	3	37	93	1	34	1	7	12	0	.72
92-93	Que	77	27	51	78	8	10	1	142	19.0	12	23	35	1	3	4	56	123	1	54	1	13	9	0	1.01
93-94	Que	83	30	21	51	-9	6	1	138	21.7	13	5	18	3	0	3	47	113	1	44	1	11	11	1	.61
94-95	Que	48	15	21	36	5	1	1	73	20.5	9	7	16	0	1	1	20	40	0	20	0	7	4	0	.75
95-96	Col	62	6	21	27	1	1	0	73	8.2	3	7	10	0	0	0	26	52	0	26	0	1	13	0	.44
96-97	Col	63	13	19	32	-3	3	0	74	17.6	5	8	13	0	0	0	24	59	1	22	0	3	7	0	.51
97-98	2Tm	65	9	18	27	-4	2	0	91	9.9	5	5	10	0	0	0	16	32	0	16	0	4	7	0	.42
98-99	SJ	82	13	26	39	1	2	1	98	13.3	2	5	7	1	0	1	26	68	0	24	0	4	8	0	.48
97-98	Col	6	0	4	4	0	0	0	5	0.0	0	0	0	0	0	0	1	2	0	1	0	0	0	0	.67
97-98	SJ	59	9	14	23	-4	2	0	86	10.5	5	5	10	0	0	0	15	30	0	15	0	4	7	0	.39
9 Years		626	154	233	387	-19	29	4	959	16.1	69	–	–	7	–	–	–	644	–	–	–	–	–	1	.62
Postseason																									
Year	Tm	GP	G	A	Pts	+/-	GW	OT	S	SPct	G	A	Pts	G	A	Pts	Num	PIM	Maj	Mnr	Fgt	Rgh	HHT	Hat	P/G
92-93	Que	6	0	6	6	5	0	0	7	0.0	0	2	2	0	0	0	4	8	0	4	0	3	0	0	1.00
94-95	Que	6	1	3	4	4	0	0	9	11.1	0	0	0	0	0	0	4	8	0	4	0	1	0	0	.67
95-96	Col	22	6	11	17	-1	1	0	31	19.4	3	4	7	0	0	0	9	18	0	9	0	4	1	0	.77
96-97	Col	17	2	4	6	1	1	0	21	9.5	0	1	1	0	0	0	7	17	1	6	1	2	2	0	.35
97-98	SJ	6	1	3	4	0	0	0	8	12.5	0	2	2	0	0	0	3	6	0	3	0	0	1	0	.67
98-99	SJ	6	2	3	5	1	0	0	9	22.2	1	0	1	0	0	0	5	10	0	5	0	1	1	0	.83
6 Years		63	12	30	42	10	2	0	85	14.1	4	9	13	0	0	0	32	67	1	31	1	11	5	0	.67

Luke Richardson

Pos: D **Shoots:** L **Ht:** 6'3" **Wt:** 210 **Born:** 3/26/69—Ottawa, Ontario **Age:** 30

Overall											Power Play			Shorthand			Penalty							Misc	
Year	Tm	GP	G	A	Pts	+/-	GW	GT	S	SPct	G	A	Pts	G	A	Pts	Num	PIM	Maj	Mnr	Fgt	Rgh	HHT	Hat	P/G
87-88	Tor	78	4	6	10	-25	0	0	49	8.2	0	–	–	0	–	–	–	90	–	–	–	–	–	0	.13
88-89	Tor	55	2	7	9	-15	0	0	59	3.4	0	–	–	0	–	–	–	106	–	–	–	–	–	0	.16
89-90	Tor	67	4	14	18	-1	0	0	80	5.0	0	–	–	0	–	–	–	122	–	–	–	–	–	0	.27
90-91	Tor	78	1	9	10	-28	0	0	68	1.5	0	–	–	0	–	–	–	238	–	–	–	–	–	0	.13
91-92	Edm	75	2	19	21	-9	0	0	85	2.4	0	4	4	0	1	1	42	118	6	34	5	12	4	0	.28

			Overall								Power Play			Shorthand			Penalty							Misc	
Year	Tm	GP	G	A	Pts	+/–	GW	GT	S	SPct	G	A	Pts	G	A	Pts	Num	PIM	Maj	Mnr	Fgt	Rgh	HHT	Hat	P/G
92-93	Edm	82	3	10	13	-18	0	0	78	3.8	0	1	1	2	2	4	51	142	8	41	8	16	7	0	.16
93-94	Edm	69	2	6	8	-13	0	0	92	2.2	0	0	0	0	0	0	47	131	7	38	7	12	11	0	.12
94-95	Edm	46	3	10	13	-6	1	0	51	5.9	1	1	2	1	1	2	17	40	2	15	2	5	7	0	.28
95-96	Edm	82	2	9	11	-27	0	0	61	3.3	0	0	0	0	2	2	41	108	6	34	6	9	7	0	.13
96-97	Edm	**82**	1	11	12	9	0	0	67	1.5	0	2	2	0	1	1	34	91	5	28	4	10	9	0	.15
97-98	Phi	81	2	3	5	7	0	0	57	3.5	2	0	2	0	0	0	43	139	7	32	7	6	6	0	.06
98-99	Phi	78	0	6	6	-3	0	0	49	0.0	0	0	0	0	0	0	35	106	12	23	12	9	6	0	.08
12 Years		873	26	110	136	-129	1	0	796	3.3	3	–	–	3	–	–	–	1431	–	–	–	–	–	0	.16
											Postseason														
Year	Tm	GP	G	A	Pts	+/–	GW	OT	S	SPct	G	A	Pts	G	A	Pts	Num	PIM	Maj	Mnr	Fgt	Rgh	HHT	Hat	P/G
87-88	Tor	2	0	0	0	-4	0	0	1	0.0	0	0	0	0	0	0	0	0	0	0	0	0	0	0	.00
89-90	Tor	5	0	0	0	-1	0	0	5	0.0	0	0	0	0	0	0	–	22	–	–	–	–	–	0	.00
91-92	Edm	16	0	5	5	-2	0	0	11	0.0	0	0	0	0	0	0	13	45	1	10	1	4	2	0	.31
96-97	Edm	12	0	2	2	-4	0	0	6	0.0	0	0	0	0	0	0	7	14	0	7	0	1	1	0	.17
97-98	Phi	5	0	0	0	-3	0	0	2	0.0	0	0	0	0	0	0	0	0	0	0	0	0	0	0	.00
5 Years		40	0	7	7	-14	0	0	25	0.0	0	0	0	0	0	0	–	81	–	–	–	–	–	0	.18

Stephane Richer

(statistical profile on page 365)

Pos: RW **Shoots:** R **Ht:** 6'3" **Wt:** 226 **Born:** 6/7/66—Ripon, Quebec **Age:** 33

			Overall								Power Play			Shorthand			Penalty							Misc	
Year	Tm	GP	G	A	Pts	+/–	GW	GT	S	SPct	G	A	Pts	G	A	Pts	Num	PIM	Maj	Mnr	Fgt	Rgh	HHT	Hat	P/G
84-85	Mon	1	0	0	0	0	0	0	0	–	0	0	0	0	0	0	0	0	0	0	0	0	0	0	.00
85-86	Mon	65	21	16	37	1	2	1	112	18.8	5	–	–	0	–	–	–	50	–	–	–	–	–	1	.57
86-87	Mon	57	20	19	39	11	3	0	109	18.3	4	–	–	0	–	–	–	80	–	–	–	–	–	0	.68
87-88	Mon	72	50	28	78	12	**11**	1	263	19.0	16	–	–	0	–	–	–	72	–	–	–	–	–	2	1.08
88-89	Mon	68	25	35	60	4	6	0	214	11.7	11	–	–	0	–	–	–	61	–	–	–	–	–	0	.88
89-90	Mon*	75	51	40	91	35	8	0	269	19.0	9	–	–	0	–	–	–	46	–	–	–	–	–	2	1.21
90-91	Mon	75	31	30	61	0	4	1	221	14.0	9	–	–	0	–	–	–	53	–	–	–	–	–	1	.81
91-92	NJ	74	29	35	64	-1	6	1	240	12.1	5	11	16	1	0	1	11	25	1	10	1	2	4	1	.86
92-93	NJ	78	38	35	73	-1	7	1	286	13.3	7	12	19	1	0	1	14	44	0	12	0	3	4	1	.94
93-94	NJ	80	36	36	72	31	9	**3**	217	16.6	7	5	12	3	0	3	8	16	0	8	0	2	1	0	.90
94-95	NJ	45	23	16	39	8	5	1	133	17.3	1	2	3	2	0	2	5	10	0	5	0	3	0	0	.87
95-96	NJ	73	20	12	32	-8	3	0	192	10.4	3	1	4	4	1	5	11	30	0	10	0	2	2	1	.44
96-97	Mon	63	22	24	46	0	2	1	126	17.5	2	4	6	0	0	0	16	32	0	16	0	1	9	0	.73
97-98	2Tm	40	14	15	29	-6	2	0	95	14.7	5	3	8	0	3	3	11	41	1	8	1	2	3	0	.73
98-99	TB	64	12	21	33	-10	1	0	139	8.6	3	2	5	2	1	3	11	22	0	11	0	1	8	0	.52
97-98	Mon	14	5	4	9	1	0	0	24	20.8	2	1	3	0	0	0	1	5	1	0	1	0	0	0	.64
97-98	TB	26	9	11	20	-7	2	0	71	12.7	3	2	5	0	3	3	10	36	0	8	0	2	3	0	.77
15 Years		930	392	362	754	76	69	10	2616	15.0	87	–	–	13	–	–	–	582	–	–	–	–	–	9	.81
											Postseason														
Year	Tm	GP	G	A	Pts	+/–	GW	OT	S	SPct	G	A	Pts	G	A	Pts	Num	PIM	Maj	Mnr	Fgt	Rgh	HHT	Hat	P/G
85-86	Mon	16	4	1	5	-3	1	0	22	18.2	3	–	–	0	–	–	–	23	–	–	–	–	–	0	.31
86-87	Mon	5	3	2	5	3	1	0	12	25.0	0	–	–	0	–	–	0	0	0	0	0	0	0	0	1.00
87-88	Mon	8	7	5	12	1	2	0	31	22.6	1	–	–	0	–	–	3	6	0	3	0	–	–	0	1.50
88-89	Mon	21	6	5	11	-5	3	1	47	12.8	2	–	–	0	–	–	–	14	–	–	–	–	–	0	.52
89-90	Mon	9	7	3	10	8	1	0	22	31.8	1	–	–	0	0	0	1	2	0	1	0	–	–	0	1.11
90-91	Mon	13	9	5	14	0	1	1	44	20.5	1	–	–	0	–	–	3	6	0	3	0	–	–	0	1.08
91-92	NJ	7	1	2	3	-5	0	0	18	5.6	0	1	1	0	0	0	0	0	0	0	0	0	0	0	.43
92-93	NJ	5	2	2	4	-4	0	0	13	15.4	1	2	3	0	0	0	1	2	0	1	0	0	0	0	.80
93-94	NJ	20	7	5	12	2	2	2	72	9.7	3	2	5	0	0	0	3	6	0	3	0	3	0	0	.60
94-95	NJ	19	6	15	21	9	2	0	55	10.9	3	7	10	1	0	1	1	2	0	1	0	0	1	0	1.11
96-97	Mon	5	0	0	0	-3	0	0	9	0.0	0	0	0	0	0	0	0	0	0	0	0	0	0	0	.00
11 Years		128	52	45	97	3	13	4	345	15.1	15	–	–	1	–	–	–	61	–	–	–	–	–	0	.76

Barry Richter

(statistical profile on page 365)

Pos: D **Shoots:** L **Ht:** 6'2" **Wt:** 205 **Born:** 9/11/70—Madison, Wisconsin **Age:** 29

			Overall								Power Play			Shorthand			Penalty							Misc	
Year	Tm	GP	G	A	Pts	+/–	GW	GT	S	SPct	G	A	Pts	G	A	Pts	Num	PIM	Maj	Mnr	Fgt	Rgh	HHT	Hat	P/G
95-96	NYR	4	0	1	1	2	0	0	3	0.0	0	0	0	0	0	0	0	0	0	0	0	0	0	0	.25
96-97	Bos	50	5	13	18	-7	0	0	79	6.3	1	6	7	0	0	0	16	32	0	16	0	0	10	0	.36
97-98		Did Not Play in NHL																							
98-99	NYI	72	6	18	24	-4	2	0	111	5.4	0	8	8	0	0	0	17	34	0	17	0	0	9	0	.33
3 Years		126	11	32	43	-9	2	0	193	5.7	1	14	15	0	0	0	33	66	0	33	0	0	19	0	.34

Mike Richter

(statistical profile on page 401)

Pos: G **Catches:** L **Ht:** 5'11" **Wt:** 185 **Born:** 9/22/66—Abington, Pennsylvania **Age:** 33

Overall																	Pen Shot		Offense		
Year	Tm	GP	GS	TP	W	L	T	Min	GA	GAA	Shots	SvPct	ShO	OE	PPGA	SHGA	Shots	GA	G	A	PIM
88-89		Did Not Play in Regular Season																			
89-90	NYR	23	–	–	12	5	5	1320	66	3.00	686	.904	0	–	–	–	**2**	0	0	3	0
90-91	NYR	45	–	–	21	13	7	2596	135	3.12	1392	.903	0	–	–	–	0	0	0	1	4
91-92	NYR*	41	39	4	23	12	2	2298	119	3.11	1205	.901	3	14	29	5	1	0	0	0	6
92-93	NYR	38	35	3	13	19	3	2105	134	3.82	1180	.886	1	12	31	5	0	0	0	5	2
93-94	NYR*	68	67	**12**	**42**	12	6	3710	159	2.57	1758	.910	5	23	41	4	0	0	0	0	2
94-95	NYR	35	35	4	14	17	2	1993	97	2.92	884	.890	2	8	25	0	1	0	0	0	2
95-96	NYR	41	40	2	24	13	3	2396	107	2.68	1221	.912	3	13	34	5	0	0	0	1	4
96-97	NYR	61	61	2	33	22	6	3598	161	2.68	1945	.917	4	29	49	5	1	0	0	0	4
97-98	NYR	**72**	69	6	21	31	**15**	4143	**184**	2.66	1888	.903	0	15	47	**12**	3	1	0	1	2
98-99	NYR	68	66	6	27	30	8	3878	170	2.63	1898	.910	4	27	37	6	1	0	0	0	0
10 Years		492	–	–	230	174	57	28037	1332	2.85	14057	.905	22	–	–	–	9	1	0	11	26

Postseason																					
Year	Tm	GP	GS	TP	W	L	Pct	Min	GA	GAA	Shots	SvPct	ShO	OE	PPGA	SHGA	Shots	GA	G	A	PIM
88-89	NYR	1	–	–	0	1	.000	58	4	4.14	30	.867	0	–	–	–	0	0	0	0	0
89-90	NYR	6	–	–	3	2	.600	330	19	3.45	182	.896	0	–	–	–	1	0	0	0	0
90-91	NYR	6	–	–	2	4	.333	313	14	2.68	182	.923	1	–	–	–	0	0	0	0	0
91-92	NYR	7	7	1	4	2	.667	412	24	3.50	226	.894	1	1	5	0	0	0	0	0	0
93-94	NYR	23	23	2	16	7	.696	1417	49	2.07	623	.921	4	12	9	3	1	0	0	0	2
94-95	NYR	7	6	1	2	5	.286	384	23	3.59	189	.878	0	0	4	2	0	0	0	0	0
95-96	NYR	11	11	0	5	6	.455	661	36	3.27	308	.883	0	5	8	3	0	0	0	0	0
96-97	NYR	15	15	0	9	6	.600	939	33	2.11	488	.932	3	9	14	1	0	0	0	1	0
8 Years		76	–	–	41	33	.554	4514	202	2.68	2228	.909	9	–	–	–	2	0	0	1	2

Byron Ritchie

Pos: C **Shoots:** L **Ht:** 5'10" **Wt:** 188 **Born:** 4/24/77—Burnaby, British Columbia **Age:** 22

Overall										Power Play			Shorthand			Penalty							Misc	
Year	Tm	GP	G	A	Pts	+/-	GW	GT	S	SPct	G	A	Pts	G	A	Pts	Num	PIM	Maj	Mnr	Fgt	Rgh	HHT	Hat	P/G
98-99	Car	3	0	0	0	0	0	0	0	–	0	0	0	0	0	0	0	0	0	0	0	0	0	0	.00

Jamie Rivers

Pos: D **Shoots:** L **Ht:** 6'0" **Wt:** 200 **Born:** 3/16/75—Ottawa, Ontario **Age:** 24

Overall										Power Play			Shorthand			Penalty							Misc	
Year	Tm	GP	G	A	Pts	+/-	GW	GT	S	SPct	G	A	Pts	G	A	Pts	Num	PIM	Maj	Mnr	Fgt	Rgh	HHT	Hat	P/G
95-96	StL	3	0	0	0	-1	0	0	5	0.0	0	0	0	0	0	0	1	2	0	1	0	0	0	0	.00
96-97	StL	15	2	5	7	-4	0	0	9	22.2	1	2	3	0	0	0	3	6	0	3	0	0	1	0	.47
97-98	StL	59	2	4	6	5	1	0	53	3.8	1	1	2	0	0	0	18	36	0	18	0	0	5	0	.10
98-99	StL	76	2	5	7	-3	0	0	78	2.6	1	2	3	0	0	0	22	47	1	21	1	1	4	0	.09
4 Years		153	6	14	20	-3	1	0	145	4.1	3	5	8	0	0	0	44	91	1	43	1	1	10	0	.13

Postseason																								
Year	Tm	GP	G	A	Pts	+/-	GW	OT	S	SPct	G	A	Pts	G	A	Pts	Num	PIM	Maj	Mnr	Fgt	Rgh	HHT	Hat	P/G
98-99	StL	9	1	1	2	-2	1	0	4	25.0	1	0	1	0	0	0	1	2	0	1	0	0	0	0	.22

Craig Rivet

(statistical profile on page 365)

Pos: D **Shoots:** R **Ht:** 6'2" **Wt:** 195 **Born:** 9/13/74—North Bay, Ontario **Age:** 25

Overall										Power Play			Shorthand			Penalty							Misc	
Year	Tm	GP	G	A	Pts	+/-	GW	GT	S	SPct	G	A	Pts	G	A	Pts	Num	PIM	Maj	Mnr	Fgt	Rgh	HHT	Hat	P/G
94-95	Mon	5	0	1	1	2	0	0	2	0.0	0	0	0	0	0	0	1	5	1	0	1	0	0	0	.20
95-96	Mon	19	1	4	5	4	0	0	9	11.1	0	0	0	0	0	0	13	54	4	7	4	0	2	0	.26
96-97	Mon	35	0	4	4	7	0	0	24	0.0	0	0	0	0	0	0	16	54	2	12	2	4	3	0	.11
97-98	Mon	61	0	2	2	-3	0	0	26	0.0	0	0	0	0	0	0	28	93	7	19	7	3	4	0	.03
98-99	Mon	66	2	8	10	-3	0	0	39	5.1	0	0	0	0	0	0	23	66	4	18	4	5	6	0	.15
5 Years		186	3	19	22	7	0	0	100	3.0	0	0	0	0	0	0	81	272	18	56	18	12	15	0	.12

Postseason																								
Year	Tm	GP	G	A	Pts	+/-	GW	OT	S	SPct	G	A	Pts	G	A	Pts	Num	PIM	Maj	Mnr	Fgt	Rgh	HHT	Hat	P/G
96-97	Mon	5	0	1	1	-2	0	0	6	0.0	0	0	0	0	0	0	3	14	0	2	0	1	0	0	.20
97-98	Mon	5	0	0	0	-2	0	0	5	0.0	0	0	0	0	0	0	1	2	0	1	0	0	0	0	.00
2 Years		10	0	1	1	-4	0	0	11	0.0	0	0	0	0	0	0	4	16	0	3	0	1	0	0	.10

Gary Roberts

(statistical profile on page 366)

Pos: LW **Shoots:** L **Ht:** 6'1" **Wt:** 200 **Born:** 5/23/66—North York, Ontario **Age:** 33

		Overall									Power Play			Shorthand			Penalty							Misc	
Year	Tm	GP	G	A	Pts	+/-	GW	GT	S	SPct	G	A	Pts	G	A	Pts	Num	PIM	Maj	Mnr	Fgt	Rgh	HHT	Hat	P/G
86-87	Cgy	32	5	10	15	6	0	0	38	13.2	0	–	–	0	–	–	24	85	7	15	–	–	–	0	.47
87-88	Cgy	74	13	15	28	24	1	0	118	11.0	0	–	–	0	–	–	81	282	16	56	–	–	–	0	.38
88-89	Cgy	71	22	16	38	32	2	0	123	17.9	0	–	–	1	–	–	75	250	12	55	–	–	–	0	.54
89-90	Cgy	78	39	33	72	31	5	0	175	22.3	5	–	–	0	–	–	65	222	4	51	–	–	–	1	.92
90-91	Cgy	80	22	31	53	15	3	0	132	16.7	0	–	–	0	–	–	78	252	8	61	–	–	–	0	.66
91-92	Cgy*	76	53	37	90	32	2	**3**	196	**27.0**	15	7	22	0	1	1	66	207	9	51	5	11	10	2	1.18
92-93	Cgy*	58	38	41	79	32	4	2	166	22.9	8	9	17	3	0	3	48	172	4	36	4	10	6	2	1.36
93-94	Cgy	73	41	43	84	37	5	1	202	20.3	12	17	29	3	1	4	52	145	3	45	2	11	7	2	1.15
94-95	Cgy	8	2	2	4	1	0	0	20	10.0	2	1	3	0	0	0	12	43	1	9	1	4	0	0	.50
95-96	Cgy	35	22	20	42	15	5	1	84	**26.2**	9	7	16	0	0	0	24	78	2	19	2	9	2	3	1.20
96-97											Did Not Play in NHL														
97-98	Car	61	20	29	49	3	2	1	106	18.9	4	9	13	0	1	1	35	103	3	29	3	16	3	1	.80
98-99	Car	77	14	28	42	2	4	0	138	10.1	1	4	5	1	0	1	65	178	8	54	8	13	7	0	.55
12 Years		723	291	305	596	230	33	8	1498	19.4	56	–	–	8	–	–	625	2017	77	481	–	–	–	11	.82

Postseason

Year	Tm	GP	G	A	Pts	+/-	GW	OT	S	SPct	G	A	Pts	G	A	Pts	Num	PIM	Maj	Mnr	Fgt	Rgh	HHT	Hat	P/G
86-87	Cgy	2	0	0	0	-1	0	0	2	0.0	0	0	0	0	0	0	2	4	0	2	0	–	–	0	.00
87-88	Cgy	9	2	3	5	4	0	0	10	20.0	0	–	–	0	–	–	–	29	–	–	–	–	–	0	.56
88-89	Cgy	22	5	7	12	9	0	0	29	17.2	0	–	–	0	–	–	–	57	–	–	–	–	–	0	.55
89-90	Cgy	6	2	5	7	5	0	0	10	20.0	0	–	–	0	–	–	–	41	–	–	–	–	–	0	1.17
90-91	Cgy	7	1	3	4	-1	0	0	9	11.1	0	–	–	0	0	0	–	18	–	–	–	–	–	0	.57
92-93	Cgy	5	1	6	7	-2	0	0	4	25.0	1	0	1	0	0	0	8	43	1	4	0	2	0	0	1.40
93-94	Cgy	7	2	6	8	3	1	0	18	11.1	1	1	2	0	0	0	8	24	0	7	0	2	1	0	1.14
98-99	Car	6	1	1	2	-3	0	0	13	7.7	0	0	0	0	0	0	4	8	0	4	0	1	0	0	.33
8 Years		64	14	31	45	14	1	0	95	14.7	2	–	–	0	–	–	–	224	–	–	–	–	–	0	.70

Bert Robertsson

Pos: D **Shoots:** L **Ht:** 6'3" **Wt:** 205 **Born:** 6/30/74—Sodertalje, Sweden **Age:** 25

		Overall									Power Play			Shorthand			Penalty							Misc	
Year	Tm	GP	G	A	Pts	+/-	GW	GT	S	SPct	G	A	Pts	G	A	Pts	Num	PIM	Maj	Mnr	Fgt	Rgh	HHT	Hat	P/G
97-98	Van	30	2	4	6	2	0	0	19	10.5	0	0	0	0	0	0	12	24	0	12	0	3	4	0	.20
98-99	Van	39	2	2	4	-7	0	0	13	15.4	0	0	0	0	0	0	5	13	1	4	1	0	1	0	.10
2 Years		69	4	6	10	-5	0	0	32	12.5	0	0	0	0	0	0	17	37	1	16	1	3	5	0	.14

Luc Robitaille

(statistical profile on page 366)

Pos: LW **Shoots:** L **Ht:** 6'1" **Wt:** 204 **Born:** 2/17/66—Montreal, Quebec **Age:** 33

		Overall									Power Play			Shorthand			Penalty							Misc	
Year	Tm	GP	G	A	Pts	+/-	GW	GT	S	SPct	G	A	Pts	G	A	Pts	Num	PIM	Maj	Mnr	Fgt	Rgh	HHT	Hat	P/G
86-87	LA	79	45	39	84	-18	3	1	199	22.6	18	–	–	0	–	–	–	28	–	–	–	–	–	1	1.06
87-88	LA*	**80**	53	58	111	-9	6	1	220	24.1	17	–	–	0	–	–	–	82	–	–	–	–	–	3	1.39
88-89	LA*	78	46	52	98	5	4	0	237	19.4	10	–	–	0	–	–	–	65	–	–	–	–	–	1	1.26
89-90	LA*	**80**	52	49	101	8	7	0	210	**24.8**	20	–	–	0	–	–	–	38	–	–	–	–	–	2	1.26
90-91	LA*	76	45	46	91	28	5	1	229	19.7	11	–	–	0	–	–	–	68	–	–	–	–	–	0	1.20
91-92	LA*	80	44	63	107	-4	6	1	240	18.3	26	21	47	0	0	0	38	95	1	35	0	7	11	1	1.34
92-93	LA*	84	63	62	125	18	8	1	265	23.8	24	21	45	2	2	4	42	100	0	40	0	3	16	2	1.49
93-94	LA	83	44	42	86	-20	3	0	267	16.5	24	16	40	0	0	0	35	86	0	33	0	8	6	1	1.04
94-95	Pit	46	23	19	42	10	3	1	109	21.1	5	3	8	0	0	0	17	37	1	16	0	0	8	1	.91
95-96	NYR	77	23	46	69	13	4	2	223	10.3	11	15	26	0	0	0	36	80	0	35	0	6	13	0	.90
96-97	NYR	69	24	24	48	16	4	0	200	12.0	5	9	14	0	0	0	24	48	0	24	0	2	13	0	.70
97-98	LA	57	16	24	40	5	7	0	130	12.3	5	11	16	0	0	0	26	66	2	23	1	2	8	0	.70
98-99	LA	82	39	35	74	-1	7	0	292	13.4	11	10	21	0	0	0	27	54	0	27	0	5	5	1	.90
13 Years		971	517	559	1076	51	67	8	2821	18.3	187	–	–	2	–	–	–	847	–	–	–	–	–	13	1.11

Postseason

Year	Tm	GP	G	A	Pts	+/-	GW	OT	S	SPct	G	A	Pts	G	A	Pts	Num	PIM	Maj	Mnr	Fgt	Rgh	HHT	Hat	P/G
86-87	LA	5	1	4	5	-7	0	0	5	20.0	0	–	–	0	0	0	1	2	0	1	0	–	–	0	1.00
87-88	LA	5	2	5	7	-8	1	0	6	33.3	2	–	–	0	0	0	–	18	–	–	–	–	–	0	1.40
88-89	LA	11	2	6	8	0	1	0	24	8.3	0	–	–	0	–	–	–	10	–	–	–	–	–	0	.73
89-90	LA	10	5	5	10	-5	1	0	28	17.9	1	–	–	0	–	–	–	12	–	–	–	–	–	0	1.00
90-91	LA	12	12	4	16	-2	2	1	44	27.3	5	–	–	0	–	–	–	22	–	–	–	–	–	1	1.33
91-92	LA	6	3	4	7	-1	1	0	28	10.7	1	1	2	0	0	0	6	12	0	6	0	2	3	0	1.17
92-93	LA	24	9	13	22	-13	2	0	71	12.7	4	6	10	0	0	0	14	28	0	14	0	4	2	0	.92

Postseason																									
Year	Tm	GP	G	A	Pts	+/–	GW	OT	S	SPct	G	A	Pts	G	A	Pts	Num	PIM	Maj	Mnr	Fgt	Rgh	HHT	Hat	P/G
94-95	Pit	12	7	4	11	5	2	1	33	21.2	0	1	1	0	0	0	9	26	0	8	0	0	3	0	.92
95-96	NYR	11	1	5	6	1	0	0	36	2.8	0	1	1	0	0	0	4	8	0	4	0	0	2	0	.55
96-97	NYR	15	4	7	11	7	0	0	43	9.3	0	2	2	0	0	0	2	4	0	2	0	0	1	0	.73
97-98	LA	4	1	2	3	1	0	0	13	7.7	0	1	1	0	0	0	3	6	0	3	0	0	1	0	.75
11 Years		115	47	59	106	-22	10	2	331	14.2	13	–	–	0	–	–	–	148	–	–	–	–	–	1	.92

Randy Robitaille

Pos: C **Shoots:** L **Ht:** 5'11" **Wt:** 190 **Born:** 10/12/75—Ottawa, Ontario **Age:** 24

		Overall									Power Play			Shorthand			Penalty							Misc	
Year	Tm	GP	G	A	Pts	+/–	GW	GT	S	SPct	G	A	Pts	G	A	Pts	Num	PIM	Maj	Mnr	Fgt	Rgh	HHT	Hat	P/G
96-97	Bos	1	0	0	0	0	0	0	0	–	0	0	0	0	0	0	0	0	0	0	0	0	0	0	.00
97-98	Bos	4	0	0	0	-2	0	0	5	0.0	0	0	0	0	0	0	0	0	0	0	0	0	0	0	.00
98-99	Bos	4	0	2	2	-1	0	0	5	0.0	0	2	2	0	0	0	0	0	0	0	0	0	0	0	.50
3 Years		9	0	2	2	-3	0	0	10	0.0	0	2	2	0	0	0	0	0	0	0	0	0	0	0	.22
Postseason																									
Year	Tm	GP	G	A	Pts	+/–	GW	OT	S	SPct	G	A	Pts	G	A	Pts	Num	PIM	Maj	Mnr	Fgt	Rgh	HHT	Hat	P/G
98-99	Bos	1	0	0	0	0	0	0	0	–	0	0	0	0	0	0	0	0	0	0	0	0	0	0	.00

David Roche

Pos: C **Shoots:** L **Ht:** 6'4" **Wt:** 234 **Born:** 6/13/75—Lindsay, Ontario **Age:** 24

		Overall									Power Play			Shorthand			Penalty							Misc	
Year	Tm	GP	G	A	Pts	+/–	GW	GT	S	SPct	G	A	Pts	G	A	Pts	Num	PIM	Maj	Mnr	Fgt	Rgh	HHT	Hat	P/G
95-96	Pit	71	7	7	14	-5	1	0	65	10.8	0	0	0	0	0	0	38	130	18	20	17	10	4	0	.20
96-97	Pit	61	5	5	10	-13	0	0	53	9.4	2	1	3	0	0	0	37	155	11	20	11	12	2	0	.16
97-98		Did Not Play in NHL																							
98-99	Cgy	36	3	3	6	-1	2	0	30	10.0	1	0	1	0	0	0	19	44	2	17	2	10	3	0	.17
3 Years		168	15	15	30	-19	3	0	148	10.1	3	1	4	0	0	0	94	329	31	57	30	32	9	0	.18
Postseason																									
Year	Tm	GP	G	A	Pts	+/–	GW	OT	S	SPct	G	A	Pts	G	A	Pts	Num	PIM	Maj	Mnr	Fgt	Rgh	HHT	Hat	P/G
95-96	Pit	16	2	7	9	1	0	0	18	11.1	0	1	1	0	0	0	9	26	0	8	0	3	0	0	.56

Jeremy Roenick

(statistical profile on page 366)

Pos: C **Shoots:** R **Ht:** 6'0" **Wt:** 170 **Born:** 1/17/70—Boston, Massachusetts **Age:** 29

		Overall									Power Play			Shorthand			Penalty							Misc	
Year	Tm	GP	G	A	Pts	+/–	GW	GT	S	SPct	G	A	Pts	G	A	Pts	Num	PIM	Maj	Mnr	Fgt	Rgh	HHT	Hat	P/G
88-89	Chi	20	9	9	18	4	0	0	52	17.3	2	–	–	0	–	–	2	4	0	2	0	–	–	0	.90
89-90	Chi	78	26	40	66	2	4	0	173	15.0	6	–	–	0	–	–	–	54	–	–	–	–	–	1	.85
90-91	Chi*	79	41	53	94	38	10	1	194	21.1	15	–	–	4	–	–	–	80	–	–	–	–	–	2	1.19
91-92	Chi*	80	53	50	103	23	**13**	0	234	22.6	22	22	44	3	0	3	38	98	2	34	2	12	7	1	1.29
92-93	Chi*	84	50	57	107	15	3	**3**	255	19.6	22	29	51	3	0	3	37	86	4	33	3	10	9	1	1.27
93-94	Chi*	84	46	61	107	21	5	1	281	16.4	24	17	41	5	2	7	40	125	7	30	6	15	6	1	1.27
94-95	Chi	33	10	24	34	5	1	0	93	10.8	5	13	18	0	1	1	7	14	0	7	0	2	3	0	1.03
95-96	Chi	66	32	35	67	9	2	2	171	18.7	12	7	19	4	3	7	34	109	3	27	3	12	5	0	1.02
96-97	Pho	72	29	40	69	-7	7	0	228	12.7	10	11	21	3	3	6	41	115	3	35	3	12	5	0	.96
97-98	Pho	79	24	32	56	5	3	1	182	13.2	6	14	20	1	2	3	35	103	3	29	3	12	7	0	.71
98-99	Pho	78	24	48	72	7	3	0	203	11.8	4	19	23	0	2	2	51	130	4	45	3	16	10	0	.92
11 Years		753	344	449	793	122	51	8	2066	16.7	128	–	–	23	–	–	–	918	–	–	–	–	–	6	1.05
Postseason																									
Year	Tm	GP	G	A	Pts	+/–	GW	OT	S	SPct	G	A	Pts	G	A	Pts	Num	PIM	Maj	Mnr	Fgt	Rgh	HHT	Hat	P/G
88-89	Chi	10	1	3	4	0	1	0	12	8.3	1	–	–	0	–	–	2	7	1	1	–	–	–	0	.40
89-90	Chi	20	11	7	18	-1	1	0	47	23.4	4	–	–	0	–	–	4	8	0	4	0	–	–	0	.90
90-91	Chi	6	3	5	8	2	1	0	13	23.1	1	–	–	0	0	0	2	4	0	2	0	–	–	0	1.33
91-92	Chi	18	12	10	22	11	3	1	56	21.4	4	4	8	0	0	0	6	12	0	6	0	1	2	0	1.22
92-93	Chi	4	1	2	3	0	0	0	16	6.3	0	1	1	0	0	0	1	2	0	1	0	0	1	0	.75
93-94	Chi	6	1	6	7	4	1	1	15	6.7	0	2	2	0	0	0	1	2	0	1	0	0	0	0	1.17
94-95	Chi	8	1	2	3	-2	0	0	13	7.7	0	1	1	0	0	0	8	16	0	8	0	3	1	0	.38
95-96	Chi	10	5	7	12	6	1	1	21	23.8	1	2	3	0	0	0	1	2	0	1	0	1	0	0	1.20
96-97	Pho	6	2	4	6	6	0	0	16	12.5	0	1	1	0	0	0	2	4	0	2	0	0	2	0	1.00
97-98	Pho	6	5	3	8	-1	2	0	20	25.0	2	0	2	2	0	2	2	4	0	2	0	0	1	0	1.33
98-99	Pho	1	0	0	0	-1	0	0	2	0.0	0	0	0	0	0	0	0	0	0	0	0	0	0	0	.00
11 Years		95	42	49	91	24	10	3	231	18.2	13	–	–	2	–	–	29	61	1	28	–	–	–	0	.96

Stacy Roest

(statistical profile on page 366)

Pos: C **Shoots:** R **Ht:** 5'9" **Wt:** 192 **Born:** 3/15/74—Lethbridge, Alberta **Age:** 25

Overall											Power Play			Shorthand			Penalty							Misc	
Year	Tm	GP	G	A	Pts	+/–	GW	GT	S	SPct	G	A	Pts	G	A	Pts	Num	PIM	Maj	Mnr	Fgt	Rgh	HHT	Hat	P/G
98-99	Det	59	4	8	12	-7	1	0	50	8.0	0	1	1	0	0	0	7	14	0	7	0	0	5	0	.20

Dwayne Roloson

Pos: G **Catches:** L **Ht:** 6'1" **Wt:** 180 **Born:** 10/12/69—Simcoe, Ontario **Age:** 30

Overall																Pen Shot		Offense		
Year	Tm	GP	GS	TP	W	L	T	Min	GA	GAA	Shots	SvPct	ShO	OE	PPGA	SHGA	Shots	GA	G	A	PIM
96-97	Cgy	31	24	3	9	14	3	1618	78	2.89	760	.897	1	10	19	3	0	0	0	0	2
97-98	Cgy	39	34	1	11	16	8	2205	110	2.99	997	.890	0	6	31	7	2	0	0	4	10
98-99	Buf	18	15	3	6	8	2	911	42	2.77	460	.909	1	8	15	0	0	0	0	0	4
3 Years		88	73	7	26	38	13	4734	230	2.92	2217	.896	2	24	65	10	2	0	0	4	16
Postseason																					
Year	Tm	GP	GS	TP	W	L	Pct	Min	GA	GAA	Shots	SvPct	ShO	OE	PPGA	SHGA	Shots	GA	G	A	PIM
98-99	Buf	4	2	0	1	1	.500	139	10	4.32	67	.851	0	0	3	0	0	0	0	0	0

Brian Rolston

(statistical profile on page 367)

Pos: C **Shoots:** L **Ht:** 6'2" **Wt:** 200 **Born:** 2/21/73—Flint, Michigan **Age:** 26

Overall											Power Play			Shorthand			Penalty							Misc	
Year	Tm	GP	G	A	Pts	+/–	GW	GT	S	SPct	G	A	Pts	G	A	Pts	Num	PIM	Maj	Mnr	Fgt	Rgh	HHT	Hat	P/G
94-95	NJ	40	7	11	18	5	3	0	92	7.6	2	1	3	0	0	0	7	17	1	6	1	0	1	0	.45
95-96	NJ	58	13	11	24	9	4	1	139	9.4	3	4	7	1	0	1	4	8	0	4	0	0	2	0	.41
96-97	NJ	81	18	27	45	6	3	0	237	7.6	2	7	9	2	0	2	10	20	0	10	0	0	8	1	.56
97-98	NJ	76	16	14	30	7	1	0	185	8.6	0	3	3	2	0	2	8	16	0	8	0	0	6	0	.39
98-99	NJ	82	24	33	57	11	3	0	210	11.4	5	9	14	**5**	0	5	7	14	0	7	0	0	2	0	.70
5 Years		337	78	96	174	38	14	1	863	9.0	12	24	36	10	0	10	36	75	1	35	1	0	19	1	.52
Postseason																									
Year	Tm	GP	G	A	Pts	+/–	GW	OT	S	SPct	G	A	Pts	G	A	Pts	Num	PIM	Maj	Mnr	Fgt	Rgh	HHT	Hat	P/G
94-95	NJ	6	2	1	3	6	0	0	12	16.7	1	0	1	0	0	0	2	4	0	2	0	0	0	0	.50
96-97	NJ	10	4	1	5	0	0	0	45	8.9	1	0	1	2	0	2	3	6	0	3	0	1	1	0	.50
97-98	NJ	6	1	0	1	2	0	0	14	7.1	0	0	0	1	0	1	1	2	0	1	0	0	0	0	.17
98-99	NJ	7	1	0	1	-1	0	0	15	6.7	0	0	0	1	0	1	1	2	0	1	0	0	1	0	.14
4 Years		29	8	2	10	7	0	0	86	9.3	2	0	2	4	0	4	7	14	0	7	0	1	2	0	.34

Cliff Ronning

(statistical profile on page 367)

Pos: C **Shoots:** L **Ht:** 5'8" **Wt:** 165 **Born:** 10/1/65—Vancouver, British Columbia **Age:** 34

Overall											Power Play			Shorthand			Penalty							Misc	
Year	Tm	GP	G	A	Pts	+/–	GW	GT	S	SPct	G	A	Pts	G	A	Pts	Num	PIM	Maj	Mnr	Fgt	Rgh	HHT	Hat	P/G
85-86		Did Not Play in Regular Season																							
86-87	StL	42	11	14	25	-1	2	0	68	16.2	2	–	–	0	–	–	3	6	0	3	0	–	–	1	.60
87-88	StL	26	5	8	13	6	1	0	38	13.2	1	–	–	0	–	–	–	12	–	–	–	–	–	0	.50
88-89	StL	64	24	31	55	3	1	0	150	16.0	16	–	–	0	–	–	–	18	–	–	–	–	–	0	.86
89-90		Did Not Play in NHL																							
90-91	2Tm	59	20	24	44	0	2	0	113	17.7	7	–	–	0	–	–	–	10	–	–	–	–	–	0	.75
91-92	Van	80	24	47	71	18	2	1	216	11.1	6	17	23	0	0	0	21	42	0	21	0	4	7	0	.89
92-93	Van	79	29	56	85	19	2	0	209	13.9	10	18	28	0	0	0	15	30	0	15	0	4	3	1	1.08
93-94	Van	76	25	43	68	7	4	1	197	12.7	10	18	28	0	0	0	21	42	0	21	0	4	7	0	.89
94-95	Van	41	6	19	25	-4	2	0	93	6.5	3	9	12	0	0	0	8	27	1	6	0	1	1	0	.61
95-96	Van	79	22	45	67	16	1	1	187	11.8	5	10	15	0	0	0	21	42	0	21	0	0	10	1	.85
96-97	Pho	69	19	32	51	-9	2	0	171	11.1	8	15	23	0	0	0	9	26	0	8	0	0	4	0	.74
97-98	Pho	80	11	44	55	5	0	1	197	5.6	3	18	21	0	0	0	18	36	0	18	0	2	9	0	.69
98-99	2Tm	79	20	40	60	-3	4	0	257	7.8	10	13	23	0	0	0	17	42	0	16	0	0	10	0	.76
90-91	StL	48	14	18	32	2	2	0	81	17.3	5	–	–	0	–	–	–	10	–	–	–	–	–	0	.67
90-91	Van	11	6	6	12	-2	0	0	32	18.8	2	–	–	0	–	–	0	0	0	0	0	0	0	0	1.09
98-99	Pho	7	2	5	7	3	1	0	18	11.1	2	1	3	0	0	0	1	2	0	1	0	0	0	0	1.00
98-99	Nsh	72	18	35	53	-6	3	0	239	7.5	8	12	20	0	0	0	16	40	0	15	0	0	10	0	.74
12 Years		774	216	403	619	57	23	4	1896	11.4	81	–	–	0	–	–	–	333	–	–	–	–	–	3	.80
Postseason																									
Year	Tm	GP	G	A	Pts	+/–	GW	OT	S	SPct	G	A	Pts	G	A	Pts	Num	PIM	Maj	Mnr	Fgt	Rgh	HHT	Hat	P/G
85-86	StL	5	1	1	2	0	0	0	11	9.1	1	–	–	0	–	–	1	2	0	1	0	–	–	0	.40
86-87	StL	4	0	1	1	-1	0	0	8	0.0	0	–	–	0	0	0	0	0	0	0	0	0	0	0	.25

Postseason																										
Year	Tm	GP	G	A	Pts	+/–	GW	OT	S	SPct	G	A	Pts	G	A	Pts	Num	PIM	Maj	Mnr	Fgt	Rgh	HHT	Hat	P/G
88-89	StL	7	1	3	4	0	0	0	15	6.7	1	–	–	0	–	–	0	0	0	0	0	0	0	0	.57
90-91	Van	6	6	3	9	1	2	1	22	27.3	2	–	–	0	–	–	–	12	–	–	–	–	–	0	1.50
91-92	Van	13	8	5	13	5	1	0	49	16.3	1	1	2	0	0	0	3	6	0	3	0	2	0	0	1.00
92-93	Van	12	2	9	11	8	0	0	35	5.7	0	2	2	0	0	0	3	6	0	3	0	0	0	0	.92
93-94	Van	24	5	10	15	-2	2	0	69	7.2	2	3	5	0	0	0	8	16	0	8	0	1	4	0	.63
94-95	Van	11	3	5	8	-5	2	1	20	15.0	1	5	6	0	0	0	1	2	0	1	0	0	0	0	.73
95-96	Van	6	0	2	2	0	0	0	12	0.0	0	1	1	0	0	0	3	6	0	3	0	0	1	0	.33
96-97	Pho	7	0	7	7	2	0	0	11	0.0	0	2	2	0	0	0	2	12	0	1	0	0	1	0	1.00
97-98	Pho	6	1	3	4	-1	0	0	17	5.9	0	1	1	0	0	0	2	4	0	2	0	1	1	0	.67
11 Years		101	27	49	76	7	7	2	269	10.0	8	–	–	0	–	–	–	66	–	–	–	–	–	0	.75

Pavel Rosa

(statistical profile on page 367)

Pos: RW **Shoots:** R **Ht:** 5'11" **Wt:** 182 **Born:** 6/7/77—Most, Czechoslovakia **Age:** 22

Overall											Power Play			Shorthand			Penalty							Misc	
Year	Tm	GP	G	A	Pts	+/–	GW	GT	S	SPct	G	A	Pts	G	A	Pts	Num	PIM	Maj	Mnr	Fgt	Rgh	HHT	Hat	P/G
98-99	LA	29	4	12	16	0	0	0	61	6.6	0	3	3	0	0	0	3	6	0	3	0	0	1	0	.55

Mike Rosati

Pos: G **Catches:** R **Ht:** 5'10" **Wt:** 170 **Born:** 1/7/68—Toronto, Ontario **Age:** 31

Overall																Pen Shot		Offense		
Year	Tm	GP	GS	TP	W	L	T	Min	GA	GAA	Shots	SvPct	ShO	OE	PPGA	SHGA	Shots	GA	G	A	PIM
98-99	Was	1	0	0	1	0	0	28	0	0.00	12	1.000	0	0	0	0	0	0	0	0	0

Bob Rouse

(statistical profile on page 367)

Pos: D **Shoots:** R **Ht:** 6'2" **Wt:** 220 **Born:** 6/18/64—Surrey, British Columbia **Age:** 35

Overall											Power Play			Shorthand			Penalty							Misc	
Year	Tm	GP	G	A	Pts	+/–	GW	GT	S	SPct	G	A	Pts	G	A	Pts	Num	PIM	Maj	Mnr	Fgt	Rgh	HHT	Hat	P/G
83-84	Min	1	0	0	0	0	0	0	0	–	0	0	0	0	0	0	0	0	0	0	0	0	0	0	.00
84-85	Min	63	2	9	11	-14	0	0	80	2.5	0	–	–	0	–	–	–	113	–	–	–	–	–	0	.17
85-86	Min	75	1	14	15	15	1	0	91	1.1	0	–	–	0	–	–	–	151	–	–	–	–	–	0	.20
86-87	Min	72	2	10	12	6	0	0	71	2.8	0	–	–	0	–	–	–	179	–	–	–	–	–	0	.17
87-88	Min	74	0	12	12	-30	0	0	62	0.0	0	–	–	0	–	–	–	168	–	–	–	–	–	0	.16
88-89	2Tm	79	4	15	19	-3	0	0	85	4.7	0	–	–	1	–	–	–	160	–	–	–	–	–	0	.24
89-90	Was	70	4	16	20	-2	2	0	72	5.6	0	–	–	0	–	–	–	123	–	–	–	–	–	0	.29
90-91	2Tm	60	7	19	26	-18	0	0	65	10.8	2	–	–	0	–	–	–	75	–	–	–	–	–	0	.43
91-92	Tor	79	3	19	22	-20	0	0	115	2.6	1	4	5	0	0	0	44	97	3	41	3	14	15	0	.28
92-93	Tor	82	3	11	14	7	1	0	78	3.8	0	1	1	1	1	2	47	130	4	40	4	8	12	0	.17
93-94	Tor	63	5	11	16	8	0	0	77	6.5	1	1	2	1	2	3	35	101	5	28	5	7	13	0	.25
94-95	Det	48	1	7	8	14	1	0	51	2.0	0	1	1	0	0	0	15	36	2	13	2	3	6	0	.17
95-96	Det	58	0	6	6	5	0	0	49	0.0	0	0	0	0	0	0	21	48	2	19	2	0	7	0	.10
96-97	Det	70	4	9	13	8	0	0	70	5.7	0	0	0	2	1	3	25	58	0	24	0	8	7	0	.19
97-98	Det	71	1	11	12	-9	0	0	54	1.9	0	0	0	0	0	0	23	57	1	21	1	0	11	0	.17
98-99	SJ	70	0	11	11	0	0	0	75	0.0	0	2	2	0	0	0	22	44	0	22	0	0	13	0	.16
88-89	Min	66	4	13	17	-5	0	0	66	6.1	0	–	–	1	–	–	–	124	–	–	–	–	–	0	.26
88-89	Was	13	0	2	2	2	0	0	19	0.0	0	–	–	0	–	–	–	36	–	–	–	–	–	0	.15
90-91	Was	47	5	15	20	-7	0	0	50	10.0	1	–	–	0	–	–	–	65	–	–	–	–	–	0	.43
90-91	Tor	13	2	4	6	-11	0	0	15	13.3	1	–	–	0	–	–	–	10	–	–	–	–	–	0	.46
16 Years		1035	37	180	217	-33	5	0	1095	3.4	4	–	–	5	–	–	–	1540	–	–	–	–	–	0	.21
Postseason																									
Year	Tm	GP	G	A	Pts	+/–	GW	OT	S	SPct	G	A	Pts	G	A	Pts	Num	PIM	Maj	Mnr	Fgt	Rgh	HHT	Hat	P/G
85-86	Min	3	0	0	0	1	0	0	3	0.0	0	0	0	0	0	0	1	2	0	1	0	–	–	0	.00
88-89	Was	6	2	0	2	3	0	0	9	22.2	0	0	0	0	0	0	2	4	0	2	0	–	–	0	.33
89-90	Was	15	2	3	5	-4	0	0	18	11.1	1	–	–	0	–	–	–	47	–	–	–	–	–	0	.33
92-93	Tor	21	3	8	11	3	1	0	33	9.1	1	1	2	0	0	0	13	29	1	12	1	6	4	0	.52
93-94	Tor	18	0	3	3	-4	0	0	30	0.0	0	0	0	0	1	1	9	29	1	7	1	2	2	0	.17
94-95	Det	18	0	3	3	2	0	0	16	0.0	0	1	1	0	0	0	4	8	0	4	0	0	2	0	.17
95-96	Det	7	0	1	1	4	0	0	11	0.0	0	0	0	0	0	0	2	4	0	2	0	2	0	0	.14
96-97	Det	20	0	0	0	8	0	0	14	0.0	0	0	0	0	0	0	14	55	1	10	1	1	4	0	.00
97-98	Det	22	0	3	3	2	0	0	22	0.0	0	0	0	0	0	0	8	16	0	8	0	0	0	0	.14
98-99	SJ	6	0	0	0	-1	0	0	4	0.0	0	0	0	0	0	0	3	6	0	3	0	2	0	0	.00
10 Years		136	7	21	28	14	1	0	160	4.4	2	–	–	0	–	–	–	200	–	–	–	–	–	0	.21

Dominic Roussel

Pos: G **Catches:** L **Ht:** 6'1" **Wt:** 190 **Born:** 2/22/70—Hull, Quebec **Age:** 29

Overall																	Pen Shot		Offense		
Year	Tm	GP	GS	TP	W	L	T	Min	GA	GAA	Shots	SvPct	ShO	OE	PPGA	SHGA	Shots	GA	G	A	PIM
91-92	Phi	17	14	1	7	8	2	922	40	2.60	437	.908	1	4	12	1	0	0	0	1	2
92-93	Phi	34	29	5	13	11	5	1769	111	3.76	933	.881	1	9	32	4	0	0	0	2	11
93-94	Phi	60	55	8	29	20	5	3285	183	3.34	1762	.896	1	17	52	5	0	0	0	1	4
94-95	Phi	19	17	0	11	7	0	1075	42	2.34	486	.914	1	5	14	2	0	0	0	0	6
95-96	2Tm	16	11	1	4	5	2	741	38	3.08	312	.878	1	1	11	2	0	0	0	0	2
96-97		Did Not Play in NHL																			
97-98		Did Not Play in NHL																			
98-99	Anh	18	15	2	4	5	4	884	37	2.51	478	.923	1	7	10	0	0	0	0	0	0
95-96	Phi	9	8	1	2	3	2	456	22	2.89	178	.876	1	1	5	1	0	0	0	0	0
95-96	Wpg	7	3	0	2	2	0	285	16	3.37	134	.881	0	0	6	1	0	0	0	0	2
6 Years		164	141	17	68	56	18	8676	451	3.12	4408	.898	6	43	131	14	0	0	0	4	25

Postseason																					
Year	Tm	GP	GS	TP	W	L	Pct	Min	GA	GAA	Shots	SvPct	ShO	OE	PPGA	SHGA	Shots	GA	G	A	PIM
94-95	Phi	1	0	0	0	0	–	23	0	0.00	8	1.000	0	0	0	0	0	0	0	0	0

Patrick Roy

(statistical profile on page 401)

Pos: G **Catches:** L **Ht:** 6'0" **Wt:** 192 **Born:** 10/5/65—Quebec, Quebec **Age:** 34

Overall																	Pen Shot		Offense		
Year	Tm	GP	GS	TP	W	L	T	Min	GA	GAA	Shots	SvPct	ShO	OE	PPGA	SHGA	Shots	GA	G	A	PIM
84-85	Mon	1	–	–	1	0	0	20	0	0.00	2	1.000	0	–	–	–	0	0	0	0	0
85-86	Mon	47	–	–	23	18	3	2651	148	3.35	1185	.875	1	–	–	–	1	0	0	3	4
86-87	Mon	46	–	–	22	16	6	2686	131	2.93	1210	.892	1	–	–	–	1	1	0	1	8
87-88	Mon*	45	–	–	23	12	**9**	2586	125	2.90	1248	**.900**	3	–	–	–	0	0	0	2	14
88-89	Mon	48	–	–	33	5	6	2744	113	**2.47**	1228	**.908**	4	–	–	–	1	**1**	0	6	2
89-90	Mon*	54	–	–	**31**	16	5	3173	134	2.53	1524	**.912**	3	–	–	–	0	0	0	5	0
90-91	Mon*	48	–	–	25	15	6	2835	128	2.71	1362	.906	1	–	–	–	1	1	0	2	6
91-92	Mon*	67	66	4	36	22	8	3935	155	**2.36**	1806	**.914**	**5**	19	48	5	1	1	0	5	4
92-93	Mon*	62	62	4	31	25	5	3595	192	3.20	1814	.894	2	19	59	10	0	0	0	2	16
93-94	Mon*	68	65	6	35	17	11	3867	161	2.50	1956	.918	**7**	30	48	5	0	0	0	1	30
94-95	Mon	**43**	**43**	2	17	20	6	**2566**	127	2.97	**1357**	.906	1	16	33	2	0	0	0	1	20
95-96	2Tm	61	60	3	34	24	2	3565	165	2.78	1797	.908	2	29	38	**18**	**2**	0	0	0	10
96-97	Col*	62	62	4	**38**	15	7	3698	143	2.32	1861	.923	7	26	33	9	1	1	0	1	15
97-98	Col*	65	63	5	31	19	13	3835	153	2.39	1825	.916	4	25	42	8	1	1	0	3	39
98-99	Col	61	61	3	32	19	8	3648	139	2.29	1673	.917	5	17	49	7	0	0	0	2	28
95-96	Mon	22	22	2	12	9	1	1260	62	2.95	667	.907	1	15	15	3	0	0	0	0	6
95-96	Col	39	38	1	22	15	1	2305	103	2.68	1130	.909	1	14	23	15	2	0	0	0	4
15 Years		778	–	–	412	243	95	45404	2014	2.66	21848	.908	46	–	–	–	9	6	0	34	196

Postseason																					
Year	Tm	GP	GS	TP	W	L	Pct	Min	GA	GAA	Shots	SvPct	ShO	OE	PPGA	SHGA	Shots	GA	G	A	PIM
85-86	Mon	20	–	–	15	5	.750	1218	39	1.92	506	.923	1	–	–	–	0	0	0	0	10
86-87	Mon	6	–	–	4	2	.667	330	22	4.00	173	.873	0	–	–	–	0	0	0	0	0
87-88	Mon	8	–	–	3	4	.429	430	24	3.35	218	.890	0	–	–	–	0	0	0	0	0
88-89	Mon	19	–	–	13	6	.684	1206	42	2.09	528	.920	2	–	–	–	0	0	0	2	16
89-90	Mon	11	–	–	5	6	.455	641	26	2.43	292	.911	1	–	–	–	0	0	0	1	0
90-91	Mon	13	–	–	7	5	.583	785	40	3.06	394	.898	0	–	–	–	0	0	0	0	2
91-92	Mon	11	11	1	4	7	.364	686	30	2.62	312	.904	1	4	10	2	0	0	0	0	2
92-93	Mon	20	20	1	16	4	.800	1293	46	2.13	647	.929	0	13	12	1	0	0	0	1	4
93-94	Mon	6	6	0	3	3	.500	375	16	2.56	228	.930	0	3	6	0	0	0	0	0	0
95-96	Col	22	22	1	16	6	.727	1454	51	2.10	649	.921	3	10	17	2	0	0	0	0	0
96-97	Col	17	17	1	10	7	.588	1034	38	2.21	559	.932	3	7	7	4	0	0	0	0	12
97-98	Col	7	7	1	3	4	.429	430	18	2.51	191	.906	0	2	7	0	0	0	0	1	0
98-99	Col	19	19	1	11	8	.579	1173	52	2.66	650	.920	1	10	19	2	0	0	0	2	4
13 Years		179	–	–	110	67	.621	11055	444	2.41	5347	.917	12	–	–	–	0	0	0	7	50

Remi Royer

Pos: D **Shoots:** R **Ht:** 6'1" **Wt:** 193 **Born:** 2/12/78—Donnacona, Quebec **Age:** 21

Overall										Power Play			Shorthand			Penalty							Misc	
Year	Tm	GP	G	A	Pts	+/-	GW	GT	S	SPct	G	A	Pts	G	A	Pts	Num	PIM	Maj	Mnr	Fgt	Rgh	HHT	Hat	P/G
98-99	Chi	18	0	0	0	-10	0	0	24	0.0	0	0	0	0	0	0	21	67	3	16	3	9	1	0	.00

Steve Rucchin

(statistical profile on page 368)

Pos: C **Shoots:** L **Ht:** 6'3" **Wt:** 215 **Born:** 7/4/71—Thunder Bay, Ontario **Age:** 28

Overall											Power Play			Shorthand			Penalty							Misc	
Year	**Tm**	**GP**	**G**	**A**	**Pts**	**+/–**	**GW**	**GT**	**S**	**SPct**	**G**	**A**	**Pts**	**G**	**A**	**Pts**	**Num**	**PIM**	**Maj**	**Mnr**	**Fgt**	**Rgh**	**HHT**	**Hat**	**P/G**
94-95	Anh	43	6	11	17	7	1	0	59	10.2	0	0	0	0	0	0	6	23	1	4	0	0	3	0	.40
95-96	Anh	64	19	25	44	3	4	0	113	16.8	8	11	19	1	0	1	6	12	0	6	0	3	1	0	.69
96-97	Anh	79	19	48	67	26	2	1	153	12.4	6	10	16	1	2	3	12	24	0	12	0	2	4	0	.85
97-98	Anh	72	17	36	53	8	3	0	131	13.0	8	8	16	1	4	5	5	13	1	4	1	0	3	0	.74
98-99	Anh	69	23	39	62	11	5	1	145	15.9	5	17	22	1	0	1	11	22	0	11	0	0	4	0	.90
5 Years		327	84	159	243	55	15	2	601	14.0	27	46	73	4	6	10	40	94	2	37	1	5	15	0	.74
Postseason																									
Year	**Tm**	**GP**	**G**	**A**	**Pts**	**+/–**	**GW**	**OT**	**S**	**SPct**	**G**	**A**	**Pts**	**G**	**A**	**Pts**	**Num**	**PIM**	**Maj**	**Mnr**	**Fgt**	**Rgh**	**HHT**	**Hat**	**P/G**
96-97	Anh	8	1	2	3	-2	0	0	8	12.5	0	0	0	0	0	0	1	10	0	0	0	0	0	0	.38
98-99	Anh	4	0	3	3	0	0	0	10	0.0	0	1	1	0	0	0	0	0	0	0	0	0	0	0	.75
2 Years		12	1	5	6	-2	0	0	18	5.6	0	1	1	0	0	0	1	10	0	0	0	0	0	0	.50

Mike Rucinski

Pos: D **Shoots:** L **Ht:** 5'11" **Wt:** 188 **Born:** 3/30/75—Trenton, Michigan **Age:** 24

Overall											Power Play			Shorthand			Penalty							Misc	
Year	**Tm**	**GP**	**G**	**A**	**Pts**	**+/–**	**GW**	**GT**	**S**	**SPct**	**G**	**A**	**Pts**	**G**	**A**	**Pts**	**Num**	**PIM**	**Maj**	**Mnr**	**Fgt**	**Rgh**	**HHT**	**Hat**	**P/G**
97-98	Car	9	0	1	1	0	0	0	3	0.0	0	0	0	0	0	0	1	2	0	1	0	0	0	0	.11
98-99	Car	15	0	1	1	1	0	0	8	0.0	0	0	0	0	0	0	4	8	0	4	0	0	3	0	.07
2 Years		24	0	2	2	1	0	0	11	0.0	0	0	0	0	0	0	5	10	0	5	0	0	3	0	.08

Martin Rucinsky

(statistical profile on page 368)

Pos: LW **Shoots:** L **Ht:** 6'1" **Wt:** 205 **Born:** 3/11/71—Most, Czechoslovakia **Age:** 28

Overall											Power Play			Shorthand			Penalty							Misc	
Year	**Tm**	**GP**	**G**	**A**	**Pts**	**+/–**	**GW**	**GT**	**S**	**SPct**	**G**	**A**	**Pts**	**G**	**A**	**Pts**	**Num**	**PIM**	**Maj**	**Mnr**	**Fgt**	**Rgh**	**HHT**	**Hat**	**P/G**
91-92	2Tm	6	1	1	2	-2	0	0	5	20.0	0	0	0	0	0	0	1	2	0	1	0	0	1	0	.33
92-93	Que	77	18	30	48	16	1	**3**	133	13.5	4	9	13	0	0	0	24	51	1	23	1	4	5	0	.62
93-94	Que	60	9	23	32	4	1	0	96	9.4	4	5	9	0	0	0	29	58	0	29	0	6	10	0	.53
94-95	Que	20	3	6	9	5	0	0	32	9.4	0	0	0	0	0	0	7	14	0	7	0	0	1	0	.45
95-96	2Tm	78	29	46	75	18	4	0	181	16.0	9	14	23	2	2	4	30	68	0	29	0	7	7	1	.96
96-97	Mon	70	28	27	55	1	3	1	172	16.3	6	9	15	3	0	3	27	62	0	26	0	4	8	1	.79
97-98	Mon	78	21	32	53	13	3	0	192	10.9	5	9	14	3	2	5	38	84	0	37	0	1	17	0	.68
98-99	Mon	73	17	17	34	-25	1	0	180	9.4	5	6	11	0	1	1	21	50	0	20	0	2	10	0	.47
91-92	Edm	2	0	0	0	-3	0	0	1	0.0	0	0	0	0	0	0	0	0	0	0	0	0	0	0	.00
91-92	Que	4	1	1	2	1	0	0	4	25.0	0	0	0	0	0	0	1	2	0	1	0	0	1	0	.50
95-96	Col	22	4	11	15	10	1	0	39	10.3	0	2	2	0	0	0	7	14	0	7	0	3	4	0	.68
95-96	Mon	56	25	35	60	8	3	0	142	17.6	9	12	21	2	2	4	23	54	0	22	0	4	3	1	1.07
8 Years		462	126	182	308	30	13	4	991	12.7	33	52	85	8	5	13	177	389	1	172	1	24	59	2	.67
Postseason																									
Year	**Tm**	**GP**	**G**	**A**	**Pts**	**+/–**	**GW**	**OT**	**S**	**SPct**	**G**	**A**	**Pts**	**G**	**A**	**Pts**	**Num**	**PIM**	**Maj**	**Mnr**	**Fgt**	**Rgh**	**HHT**	**Hat**	**P/G**
92-93	Que	6	1	1	2	-3	0	0	10	10.0	1	0	1	0	0	0	2	4	0	2	0	0	1	0	.33
96-97	Mon	5	0	0	0	-5	0	0	10	0.0	0	0	0	0	0	0	2	4	0	2	0	1	1	0	.00
97-98	Mon	10	3	0	3	-2	0	0	35	8.6	1	0	1	0	0	0	2	4	0	2	0	0	1	0	.30
3 Years		21	4	1	5	-10	0	0	55	7.3	2	0	2	0	0	0	6	12	0	6	0	1	3	0	.24

Cam Russell

Pos: D **Shoots:** L **Ht:** 6'4" **Wt:** 200 **Born:** 1/12/69—Halifax, Nova Scotia **Age:** 30

Overall											Power Play			Shorthand			Penalty							Misc	
Year	**Tm**	**GP**	**G**	**A**	**Pts**	**+/–**	**GW**	**GT**	**S**	**SPct**	**G**	**A**	**Pts**	**G**	**A**	**Pts**	**Num**	**PIM**	**Maj**	**Mnr**	**Fgt**	**Rgh**	**HHT**	**Hat**	**P/G**
89-90	Chi	19	0	1	1	-3	0	0	10	0.0	0	–	–	0	–	–	–	27	–	–	–	–	–	0	.05
90-91	Chi	3	0	0	0	1	0	0	0	–	0	0	0	0	0	0	1	5	1	0	–	0	0	0	.00
91-92	Chi	19	0	0	0	-8	0	0	9	0.0	0	0	0	0	0	0	11	34	4	7	4	1	3	0	.00
92-93	Chi	67	2	4	6	5	0	0	49	4.1	0	0	0	0	0	0	37	151	15	18	15	2	8	0	.09
93-94	Chi	67	1	7	8	10	0	0	41	2.4	0	0	0	0	0	0	59	200	22	35	22	10	6	0	.12
94-95	Chi	33	1	3	4	4	0	0	18	5.6	0	0	0	0	0	0	26	88	12	14	12	6	0	0	.12
95-96	Chi	61	2	2	4	8	0	0	22	9.1	0	0	0	0	0	0	32	129	11	17	11	5	4	0	.07
96-97	Chi	44	1	1	2	-8	0	0	19	5.3	0	0	0	0	0	0	19	65	9	10	9	3	3	0	.05
97-98	Chi	41	1	1	2	3	1	0	18	5.6	0	0	0	0	0	0	26	79	9	17	9	7	3	0	.05
98-99	2Tm	42	1	2	3	-4	0	0	15	6.7	0	0	0	0	0	0	22	94	6	12	6	3	5	0	.07
98-99	Chi	7	0	0	0	1	0	0	1	0.0	0	0	0	0	0	0	2	10	2	0	2	0	0	0	.00
98-99	Col	35	1	2	3	-5	0	0	14	7.1	0	0	0	0	0	0	20	84	4	12	4	3	5	0	.09
10 Years		396	9	21	30	8	1	0	201	4.5	0	–	–	0	–	–	–	872	–	–	–	–	–	0	.08

											Postseason														
Year	Tm	GP	G	A	Pts	+/–	GW	OT	S	SPct	G	A	Pts	G	A	Pts	Num	PIM	Maj	Mnr	Fgt	Rgh	HHT	Hat	P/G
89-90	Chi	1	0	0	0	-1	0	0	0	–	0	0	0	0	0	0	0	0	0	0	0	0	0	0	.00
90-91	Chi	1	0	0	0	-1	0	0	0	–	0	0	0	0	0	0	0	0	0	0	0	0	0	0	.00
91-92	Chi	12	0	2	2	2	0	0	7	0.0	0	0	0	0	0	0	1	2	0	1	0	1	0	0	.17
92-93	Chi	4	0	0	0	0	0	0	3	0.0	0	0	0	0	0	0	0	0	0	0	0	0	0	0	.00
94-95	Chi	16	0	3	3	2	0	0	5	0.0	0	0	0	0	0	0	4	8	0	4	0	2	1	0	.19
95-96	Chi	6	0	0	0	-1	0	0	4	0.0	0	0	0	0	0	0	1	2	0	1	0	0	1	0	.00
96-97	Chi	4	0	0	0	0	0	0	1	0.0	0	0	0	0	0	0	2	4	0	2	0	2	0	0	.00
7 Years		44	0	5	5	1	0	0	20	0.0	0	0	0	0	0	0	8	16	0	8	0	5	2	0	.11

Terry Ryan

Pos: LW **Shoots:** L **Ht:** 6'1" **Wt:** 201 **Born:** 1/14/77—St. John's, Newfoundland **Age:** 22

				Overall							Power Play			Shorthand			Penalty							Misc	
Year	Tm	GP	G	A	Pts	+/–	GW	GT	S	SPct	G	A	Pts	G	A	Pts	Num	PIM	Maj	Mnr	Fgt	Rgh	HHT	Hat	P/G
96-97	Mon	3	0	0	0	0	0	0	0	–	0	0	0	0	0	0	0	0	0	0	0	0	0	0	.00
97-98	Mon	4	0	0	0	0	0	0	0	–	0	0	0	0	0	0	7	31	3	3	3	1	0	0	.00
98-99	Mon	1	0	0	0	0	0	0	0	–	0	0	0	0	0	0	1	5	1	0	1	0	0	0	.00
3 Years		8	0	0	0	0	0	0	0	–	0	0	0	0	0	0	8	36	4	3	4	1	0	0	.00

Warren Rychel

Pos: LW **Shoots:** L **Ht:** 6'0" **Wt:** 205 **Born:** 5/12/67—Tecumseh, Ontario **Age:** 32

				Overall							Power Play			Shorthand			Penalty							Misc	
Year	Tm	GP	G	A	Pts	+/–	GW	GT	S	SPct	G	A	Pts	G	A	Pts	Num	PIM	Maj	Mnr	Fgt	Rgh	HHT	Hat	P/G
88-89	Chi	2	0	0	0	-1	0	0	3	0.0	0	0	0	0	0	0	4	17	3	1	–	–	–	0	.00
89-90	Did Not Play in NHL																								
90-91	Did Not Play in Regular Season																								
91-92	Did Not Play in NHL																								
92-93	LA	70	6	7	13	-15	1	0	67	9.0	0	0	0	0	0	0	72	314	**30**	32	**29**	13	3	0	.19
93-94	LA	80	10	9	19	-19	3	0	105	9.5	0	1	1	0	0	0	91	322	28	56	28	17	6	0	.24
94-95	2Tm	33	1	6	7	-4	0	0	41	2.4	0	0	0	0	0	0	30	120	12	15	11	6	2	0	.21
95-96	Col	52	6	2	8	6	1	0	45	13.3	0	0	0	0	0	0	39	147	15	21	13	5	1	0	.15
96-97	Anh	70	10	7	17	6	1	0	59	16.9	1	0	1	1	0	1	56	218	14	34	13	6	4	0	.24
97-98	2Tm	71	5	6	11	-11	0	0	66	7.6	1	1	2	0	0	0	64	221	15	43	15	10	6	0	.15
98-99	Col	28	0	2	2	3	0	0	15	0.0	0	0	0	0	0	0	20	63	5	14	5	5	2	0	.07
94-95	LA	7	0	0	0	-5	0	0	7	0.0	0	0	0	0	0	0	5	19	3	2	3	1	1	0	.00
94-95	Tor	26	1	6	7	1	0	0	34	2.9	0	0	0	0	0	0	25	101	9	13	8	5	1	0	.27
97-98	Anh	63	5	6	11	-10	0	0	62	8.1	1	1	2	0	0	0	58	198	14	39	14	8	6	0	.17
97-98	Col	8	0	0	0	-1	0	0	4	0.0	0	0	0	0	0	0	6	23	1	4	1	2	0	0	.00
8 Years		406	38	39	77	-35	6	0	401	9.5	2	2	4	1	0	1	376	1422	122	216	–	–	–	0	.19

											Postseason														
Year	Tm	GP	G	A	Pts	+/–	GW	OT	S	SPct	G	A	Pts	G	A	Pts	Num	PIM	Maj	Mnr	Fgt	Rgh	HHT	Hat	P/G
90-91	Chi	3	1	3	4	1	1	0	7	14.3	1	–	–	0	0	0	1	2	0	1	0	–	–	0	1.33
92-93	LA	23	6	7	13	4	2	0	27	22.2	0	1	1	0	0	0	14	39	1	12	1	1	3	0	.57
94-95	Tor	3	0	0	0	-2	0	0	2	0.0	0	0	0	0	0	0	0	0	0	0	0	0	0	0	.00
95-96	Col	12	1	0	1	4	0	0	4	25.0	0	0	0	0	0	0	6	23	1	4	1	1	0	0	.08
96-97	Anh	11	0	2	2	-2	0	0	16	0.0	0	0	0	0	0	0	8	19	1	7	1	1	2	0	.18
97-98	Col	6	0	0	0	-2	0	0	4	0.0	0	0	0	0	0	0	5	24	2	2	2	2	0	0	.00
98-99	Col	12	0	1	1	-1	0	0	6	0.0	0	0	0	0	0	0	3	14	0	2	0	1	0	0	.08
7 Years		70	8	13	21	2	3	0	66	12.1	1	–	–	0	0	0	37	121	5	28	5	–	–	0	.30

Joe Sacco

Pos: RW **Shoots:** L **Ht:** 6'1" **Wt:** 195 **Born:** 2/4/69—Medford, Massachusetts **Age:** 30

				Overall							Power Play			Shorthand			Penalty							Misc	
Year	Tm	GP	G	A	Pts	+/–	GW	GT	S	SPct	G	A	Pts	G	A	Pts	Num	PIM	Maj	Mnr	Fgt	Rgh	HHT	Hat	P/G
90-91	Tor	20	0	5	5	-5	0	0	20	0.0	0	3	3	0	0	0	1	2	0	1	0	1	0	0	.25
91-92	Tor	17	7	4	11	8	1	0	40	17.5	0	0	0	0	0	0	2	4	0	2	0	0	2	0	.65
92-93	Tor	23	4	4	8	-4	0	0	38	10.5	0	1	1	0	0	0	4	8	0	4	0	0	0	0	.35
93-94	Anh	84	19	18	37	-11	2	1	206	9.2	3	5	8	1	1	2	25	61	1	23	0	4	10	0	.44
94-95	Anh	41	10	8	18	-8	0	0	77	13.0	2	2	4	0	0	0	10	23	1	9	1	3	4	0	.44
95-96	Anh	76	13	14	27	1	2	1	132	9.8	1	1	2	2	1	3	17	40	2	15	2	1	7	0	.36
96-97	Anh	77	12	17	29	1	2	0	131	9.2	1	1	2	1	1	2	12	35	1	10	1	1	5	0	.38
97-98	2Tm	80	11	14	25	0	2	0	122	9.0	0	0	0	2	0	2	17	34	0	17	0	2	5	0	.31
98-99	NYI	73	3	0	3	-24	2	0	84	3.6	0	0	0	1	0	1	17	45	1	15	1	1	2	0	.04

Overall											Power Play			Shorthand			Penalty							Misc	
Year	Tm	GP	G	A	Pts	+/–	GW	GT	S	SPct	G	A	Pts	G	A	Pts	Num	PIM	Maj	Mnr	Fgt	Rgh	HHT	Hat	P/G
97-98	Anh	55	8	11	19	-1	2	0	90	8.9	0	0	0	2	0	2	12	24	0	12	0	2	2	0	.35
97-98	NYI	25	3	3	6	1	0	0	32	9.4	0	0	0	0	0	0	5	10	0	5	0	0	3	0	.24
9 Years		491	79	84	163	-42	11	2	850	9.3	7	13	20	7	3	10	105	252	6	96	5	13	35	0	.33
Postseason																									
Year	Tm	GP	G	A	Pts	+/–	GW	OT	S	SPct	G	A	Pts	G	A	Pts	Num	PIM	Maj	Mnr	Fgt	Rgh	HHT	Hat	P/G
96-97	Anh	11	2	0	2	-4	0	0	20	10.0	0	0	0	0	0	0	1	2	0	1	0	0	1	0	.18

Joe Sakic

(statistical profile on page 368)

Pos: C **Shoots:** L **Ht:** 5'11" **Wt:** 185 **Born:** 7/7/69—Burnaby, British Columbia **Age:** 30

Overall											Power Play			Shorthand			Penalty							Misc	
Year	Tm	GP	G	A	Pts	+/–	GW	GT	S	SPct	G	A	Pts	G	A	Pts	Num	PIM	Maj	Mnr	Fgt	Rgh	HHT	Hat	P/G
88-89	Que	70	23	39	62	-36	2	1	148	15.5	10	–	–	0	–	–	–	24	–	–	–	–	–	2	.89
89-90	Que*	**80**	39	63	102	-40	2	1	234	16.7	8	–	–	1	–	–	–	27	–	–	–	–	–	1	1.28
90-91	Que*	80	48	61	109	-26	7	1	245	19.6	12	–	–	3	–	–	–	24	–	–	–	–	–	1	1.36
91-92	Que*	69	29	65	94	5	1	1	217	13.4	6	25	31	3	4	7	10	20	0	10	0	1	9	1	1.36
92-93	Que*	78	48	57	105	-3	4	1	264	18.2	20	27	47	2	1	3	20	40	0	20	0	2	7	0	1.35
93-94	Que*	84	28	64	92	-8	9	1	279	10.0	10	23	33	1	1	2	9	18	0	9	0	0	7	0	1.10
94-95	Que	47	19	43	62	7	5	0	157	12.1	3	19	22	2	1	3	11	30	0	10	0	1	5	0	1.32
95-96	Col*	82	51	69	120	14	7	1	339	15.0	17	33	50	6	2	8	22	44	0	22	0	5	10	0	1.46
96-97	Col*	65	22	52	74	-10	5	0	261	8.4	10	26	36	2	1	3	17	34	0	17	0	0	6	1	1.14
97-98	Col*	64	27	36	63	0	2	1	254	10.6	12	16	28	1	0	1	25	50	0	25	0	0	17	0	.98
98-99	Col	73	41	55	96	23	6	1	255	16.1	12	22	34	**5**	1	6	13	29	1	12	1	0	10	1	1.32
11 Years		792	375	604	979	-74	50	9	2653	14.1	120	–	–	26	–	–	–	340	–	–	–	–	–	7	1.24
Postseason																									
Year	Tm	GP	G	A	Pts	+/–	GW	OT	S	SPct	G	A	Pts	G	A	Pts	Num	PIM	Maj	Mnr	Fgt	Rgh	HHT	Hat	P/G
92-93	Que	6	3	3	6	-3	0	0	24	12.5	1	1	2	0	0	0	1	2	0	1	0	0	0	0	1.00
94-95	Que	6	4	1	5	-4	1	0	15	26.7	1	1	2	1	0	1	0	0	0	0	0	0	0	1	.83
95-96	Col	22	18	16	34	10	6	2	98	18.4	6	10	16	0	0	0	7	14	0	7	0	1	4	1	1.55
96-97	Col	17	8	17	25	5	0	0	50	16.0	3	9	12	0	0	0	7	14	0	7	0	0	4	0	1.47
97-98	Col	6	2	3	5	0	2	1	24	8.3	0	2	2	1	0	1	3	6	0	3	0	0	2	0	.83
98-99	Col	19	6	13	19	-2	1	0	56	10.7	1	5	6	1	0	1	4	8	0	4	0	0	3	0	1.00
6 Years		76	41	53	94	6	10	3	267	15.4	12	28	40	3	0	3	22	44	0	22	0	1	13	2	1.24

Ruslan Salei

(statistical profile on page 368)

Pos: D **Shoots:** L **Ht:** 6'2" **Wt:** 205 **Born:** 11/2/74—Minsk, USSR **Age:** 25

Overall											Power Play			Shorthand			Penalty							Misc	
Year	Tm	GP	G	A	Pts	+/–	GW	GT	S	SPct	G	A	Pts	G	A	Pts	Num	PIM	Maj	Mnr	Fgt	Rgh	HHT	Hat	P/G
96-97	Anh	30	0	1	1	-8	0	0	14	0.0	0	0	0	0	0	0	17	37	1	16	1	2	7	0	.03
97-98	Anh	66	5	10	15	7	0	1	104	4.8	1	4	5	0	0	0	32	70	2	30	2	0	11	0	.23
98-99	Anh	74	2	14	16	1	0	0	123	1.6	1	8	9	0	0	0	27	65	1	25	1	3	8	0	.22
3 Years		170	7	25	32	0	0	1	241	2.9	2	12	14	0	0	0	76	172	4	71	4	5	26	0	.19
Postseason																									
Year	Tm	GP	G	A	Pts	+/–	GW	OT	S	SPct	G	A	Pts	G	A	Pts	Num	PIM	Maj	Mnr	Fgt	Rgh	HHT	Hat	P/G
98-99	Anh	3	0	0	0	-4	0	0	5	0.0	0	0	0	0	0	0	2	4	0	2	0	0	1	0	.00

Sami Salo

(statistical profile on page 369)

Pos: D **Shoots:** L **Ht:** 6'3" **Wt:** 210 **Born:** 9/2/74—Turku, Finland **Age:** 25

Overall											Power Play			Shorthand			Penalty							Misc	
Year	Tm	GP	G	A	Pts	+/–	GW	GT	S	SPct	G	A	Pts	G	A	Pts	Num	PIM	Maj	Mnr	Fgt	Rgh	HHT	Hat	P/G
98-99	Ott	61	7	12	19	20	1	0	106	6.6	2	6	8	0	0	0	12	24	0	12	0	1	3	1	.31
Postseason																									
Year	Tm	GP	G	A	Pts	+/–	GW	OT	S	SPct	G	A	Pts	G	A	Pts	Num	PIM	Maj	Mnr	Fgt	Rgh	HHT	Hat	P/G
98-99	Ott	4	0	0	0	-3	0	0	10	0.0	0	0	0	0	0	0	0	0	0	0	0	0	0	0	.00

Tommy Salo

(statistical profile on page 402)

Pos: G **Catches:** L **Ht:** 5'11" **Wt:** 173 **Born:** 2/1/71—Surahammar, Sweden **Age:** 28

Overall																	Pen Shot		Offense		
Year	Tm	GP	GS	TP	W	L	T	Min	GA	GAA	Shots	SvPct	ShO	OE	PPGA	SHGA	Shots	GA	G	A	PIM
94-95	NYI	6	6	0	1	5	0	358	18	3.02	189	.905	0	2	3	2	0	0	0	1	0
95-96	NYI	10	8	3	1	7	1	523	35	4.02	250	.860	0	1	16	0	0	0	0	0	0

Year	Tm	GP	GS	TP	W	L	T	Min	GA	GAA	Shots	SvPct	ShO	OE	PPGA	SHGA	Pen Shot Shots	Pen Shot GA	Offense G	Offense A	Offense PIM
								Overall													
96-97	NYI	58	54	8	20	27	8	3208	151	2.82	1576	.904	5	18	30	7	1	1	0	1	4
97-98	NYI	62	58	**9**	23	29	5	3461	152	2.64	1617	.906	4	21	38	11	0	0	0	1	31
98-99	2Tm	64	63	5	25	28	9	3718	159	2.57	1647	.903	5	17	41	2	0	0	0	0	12
98-99	NYI	51	50	3	17	26	7	3018	132	2.62	1368	.904	5	15	31	2	0	0	0	0	12
98-99	Edm	13	13	2	8	2	2	700	27	2.31	279	.903	0	2	10	0	0	0	0	0	0
5 Years		200	189	25	70	96	23	11268	515	2.74	5279	.902	14	59	128	22	1	1	0	3	47
								Postseason													
Year	Tm	GP	GS	TP	W	L	Pct	Min	GA	GAA	Shots	SvPct	ShO	OE	PPGA	SHGA	Shots	GA	G	A	PIM
98-99	Edm	4	4	0	0	4	.000	296	11	2.23	149	.926	0	3	2	0	0	0	0	0	0

Sergei Samsonov

(statistical profile on page 369)

Pos: LW **Shoots:** L **Ht:** 5'8" **Wt:** 184 **Born:** 10/27/78—Moscow, USSR **Age:** 21

Year	Tm	GP	G	A	Pts	+/-	GW	GT	S	SPct	PP G	PP A	PP Pts	SH G	SH A	SH Pts	Num	PIM	Maj	Mnr	Fgt	Rgh	HHT	Hat	P/G
					Overall																				
97-98	Bos	81	22	25	47	9	3	0	159	13.8	7	8	15	0	0	0	4	8	0	4	0	0	3	1	.58
98-99	Bos	79	25	26	51	-6	8	1	160	15.6	6	10	16	0	0	0	9	18	0	9	0	0	4	0	.65
2 Years		160	47	51	98	3	11	1	319	14.7	13	18	31	0	0	0	13	26	0	13	0	0	7	1	.61
											Postseason														
Year	Tm	GP	G	A	Pts	+/-	GW	OT	S	SPct	G	A	Pts	G	A	Pts	Num	PIM	Maj	Mnr	Fgt	Rgh	HHT	Hat	P/G
97-98	Bos	6	2	5	7	1	1	0	18	11.1	0	4	4	0	0	0	0	0	0	0	0	0	0	0	1.17
98-99	Bos	11	3	1	4	3	0	0	21	14.3	0	0	0	0	0	0	0	0	0	0	0	0	0	0	.36
2 Years		17	5	6	11	4	1	0	39	12.8	0	4	4	0	0	0	0	0	0	0	0	0	0	0	.65

Kjell Samuelsson

Pos: D **Shoots:** R **Ht:** 6'6" **Wt:** 233 **Born:** 10/18/58—Tyngsryd, Sweden **Age:** 41

Year	Tm	GP	G	A	Pts	+/-	GW	GT	S	SPct	PP G	PP A	PP Pts	SH G	SH A	SH Pts	Num	PIM	Maj	Mnr	Fgt	Rgh	HHT	Hat	P/G
					Overall																				
85-86	NYR	9	0	0	0	-1	0	0	7	0.0	0	0	0	0	0	0	5	10	0	5	0	–	–	0	.00
86-87	2Tm	76	3	12	15	-11	0	0	48	6.3	0	–	–	0	–	–	–	136	–	–	–	–	–	0	.20
87-88	Phi*	74	6	24	30	28	0	0	118	5.1	3	–	–	0	–	–	–	184	–	–	–	–	–	0	.41
88-89	Phi	69	3	14	17	13	0	0	60	5.0	0	–	–	1	–	–	–	140	–	–	–	–	–	0	.25
89-90	Phi	66	5	17	22	20	1	0	88	5.7	0	–	–	0	–	–	–	91	–	–	–	–	–	0	.33
90-91	Phi	78	9	19	28	4	3	1	101	8.9	1	–	–	0	–	–	–	82	–	–	–	–	–	0	.36
91-92	2Tm	74	5	11	16	1	1	0	91	5.5	0	1	1	0	0	0	47	110	0	45	0	4	16	0	.22
92-93	Pit	63	3	6	9	25	1	0	63	4.8	0	1	1	0	1	1	45	106	0	43	0	6	12	0	.14
93-94	Pit	59	5	8	13	18	0	0	57	8.8	1	2	3	0	0	0	40	118	2	34	0	3	11	0	.22
94-95	Pit	41	1	6	7	8	0	0	37	2.7	0	0	0	0	0	0	23	54	0	22	0	4	5	0	.17
95-96	Phi	75	3	11	14	20	1	1	62	4.8	0	0	0	0	0	0	35	81	1	33	1	1	12	0	.19
96-97	Phi	34	4	3	7	17	0	0	36	11.1	0	0	0	0	0	0	14	47	1	11	0	1	1	0	.21
97-98	Phi	49	0	3	3	9	0	0	23	0.0	0	0	0	0	0	0	14	28	0	14	0	0	8	0	.06
98-99	TB	46	1	4	5	-6	0	0	22	4.5	0	0	0	0	1	1	15	38	0	14	0	1	5	0	.11
86-87	NYR	30	2	6	8	-2	0	0	20	10.0	0	–	–	0	–	–	25	50	0	25	0	–	–	0	.27
86-87	Phi	46	1	6	7	-9	0	0	28	3.6	0	–	–	0	–	–	–	86	–	–	–	–	–	0	.15
91-92	Phi	54	4	9	13	1	0	0	63	6.3	0	1	1	0	0	0	34	76	0	33	0	4	11	0	.24
91-92	Pit	20	1	2	3	0	1	0	28	3.6	0	0	0	0	0	0	13	34	0	12	0	0	5	0	.15
14 Years		813	48	138	186	145	7	2	813	5.9	5	–	–	1	–	–	–	1225	–	–	–	–	–	0	.23
											Postseason														
Year	Tm	GP	G	A	Pts	+/-	GW	OT	S	SPct	G	A	Pts	G	A	Pts	Num	PIM	Maj	Mnr	Fgt	Rgh	HHT	Hat	P/G
85-86	NYR	9	0	1	1	-2	0	0	9	0.0	0	–	–	0	–	–	4	8	0	4	0	–	–	0	.11
86-87	Phi	26	0	4	4	4	0	0	27	0.0	0	–	–	0	–	–	–	25	–	–	–	–	–	0	.15
87-88	Phi	7	2	5	7	8	1	0	11	18.2	0	–	–	0	0	0	–	23	–	–	–	–	–	0	1.00
88-89	Phi	19	1	3	4	13	0	0	16	6.3	0	–	–	0	–	–	–	24	–	–	–	–	–	0	.21
91-92	Pit	15	0	3	3	6	0	0	7	0.0	0	1	1	0	0	0	6	12	0	6	0	1	2	0	.20
92-93	Pit	12	0	3	3	4	0	0	15	0.0	0	1	1	0	0	0	1	2	0	1	0	0	1	0	.25
93-94	Pit	6	0	0	0	0	0	0	3	0.0	0	0	0	0	0	0	9	26	0	8	0	1	3	0	.00
94-95	Pit	11	0	1	1	-4	0	0	5	0.0	0	0	0	0	1	1	12	32	0	11	0	2	3	0	.09
95-96	Phi	12	1	0	1	0	0	0	7	14.3	0	0	0	0	0	0	8	24	0	7	0	0	5	0	.08
96-97	Phi	5	0	0	0	-3	0	0	4	0.0	0	0	0	0	0	0	1	2	0	1	0	0	0	0	.00
97-98	Phi	1	0	0	0	1	0	0	0	–	0	0	0	0	0	0	0	0	0	0	0	0	0	0	.00
11 Years		123	4	20	24	27	1	0	104	3.8	0	–	–	0	–	–	–	178	–	–	–	–	–	0	.20

Ulf Samuelsson

(statistical profile on page 369)

Pos: D **Shoots:** L **Ht:** 6'1" **Wt:** 200 **Born:** 3/16/64—Fagersta, Sweden **Age:** 35

Overall											Power Play			Shorthand			Penalty							Misc	
Year	Tm	GP	G	A	Pts	+/-	GW	GT	S	SPct	G	A	Pts	G	A	Pts	Num	PIM	Maj	Mnr	Fgt	Rgh	HHT	Hat	P/G
84-85	Har	41	2	6	8	-6	0	0	32	6.3	0	–	–	0	–	–	–	83	–	–	–	–	–	0	.20
85-86	Har	80	5	19	24	7	1	0	72	6.9	0	–	–	1	–	–	–	174	–	–	–	–	–	0	.30
86-87	Har*	78	2	31	33	28	0	0	104	1.9	0	–	–	0	–	–	–	162	–	–	–	–	–	0	.42
87-88	Har	76	8	33	41	-9	0	0	156	5.1	3	–	–	0	–	–	–	159	–	–	–	–	–	0	.54
88-89	Har	71	9	26	35	23	2	0	122	7.4	3	–	–	0	–	–	–	181	–	–	–	–	–	0	.49
89-90	Har	55	2	11	13	15	0	0	57	3.5	0	–	–	0	–	–	–	177	–	–	–	–	–	0	.24
90-91	2Tm	76	4	22	26	17	0	0	125	3.2	0	–	–	0	–	–	–	211	–	–	–	–	–	0	.34
91-92	Pit	62	1	14	15	2	1	0	75	1.3	1	4	5	0	1	1	69	206	4	58	4	23	14	0	.24
92-93	Pit	77	3	26	29	36	1	0	96	3.1	0	7	7	0	2	2	85	249	5	72	5	16	16	0	.38
93-94	Pit	80	5	24	29	23	0	1	106	4.7	1	4	5	0	1	1	86	199	1	82	1	21	20	0	.36
94-95	Pit	44	1	15	16	11	0	0	47	2.1	0	4	4	0	1	1	39	113	1	34	0	11	4	0	.36
95-96	NYR	74	1	18	19	9	0	0	66	1.5	0	3	3	0	0	0	54	122	2	51	1	12	20	0	.26
96-97	NYR	73	6	11	17	3	1	0	77	7.8	1	0	1	0	1	1	58	138	2	54	2	22	11	0	.23
97-98	NYR	73	3	9	12	1	2	0	59	5.1	0	1	1	0	0	0	54	122	2	51	2	9	14	0	.16
98-99	2Tm	71	4	8	12	5	0	0	39	10.3	0	2	2	0	0	0	48	99	1	47	1	17	11	0	.17
90-91	Har	62	3	18	21	13	0	0	110	2.7	0	–	–	0	–	–	–	174	–	–	–	–	–	0	.34
90-91	Pit	14	1	4	5	4	0	0	15	6.7	0	0	0	0	–	–	–	37	–	–	–	–	–	0	.36
98-99	NYR	67	4	8	12	6	0	0	37	10.8	0	2	2	0	0	0	45	93	1	44	1	15	10	0	.18
98-99	Det	4	0	0	0	-1	0	0	2	0.0	0	0	0	0	0	0	3	6	0	3	0	2	1	0	.00
15 Years		1031	56	273	329	165	8	1	1233	4.5	9	–	–	1	–	–	–	2395	–	–	–	–	–	0	.32

Postseason

Year	Tm	GP	G	A	Pts	+/-	GW	OT	S	SPct	G	A	Pts	G	A	Pts	Num	PIM	Maj	Mnr	Fgt	Rgh	HHT	Hat	P/G
85-86	Har	10	1	2	3	5	1	0	13	7.7	0	–	–	0	–	–	–	38	–	–	–	–	–	0	.30
86-87	Har	5	0	1	1	-2	0	0	4	0.0	0	–	–	0	0	0	–	41	–	–	–	–	–	0	.20
87-88	Har	5	0	0	0	-2	0	0	11	0.0	0	0	0	0	0	0	4	8	0	4	0	–	–	0	.00
88-89	Har	4	0	2	2	0	0	0	8	0.0	0	–	–	0	–	–	2	4	0	2	0	–	–	0	.50
89-90	Har	7	1	0	1	2	0	0	5	20.0	0	0	0	0	0	0	–	18	–	–	–	–	–	0	.14
90-91	Pit	20	3	2	5	7	1	0	21	14.3	1	–	–	0	–	–	–	34	–	–	–	–	–	0	.25
91-92	Pit	21	0	2	2	7	0	0	12	0.0	0	1	1	0	0	0	14	39	1	12	0	3	3	0	.10
92-93	Pit	12	1	5	6	5	0	0	14	7.1	0	0	0	0	1	1	12	24	0	12	0	4	1	0	.50
93-94	Pit	6	0	1	1	-3	0	0	6	0.0	0	0	0	0	0	0	5	18	0	4	0	1	2	0	.17
94-95	Pit	7	0	2	2	2	0	0	5	0.0	0	2	2	0	0	0	4	8	0	4	0	1	2	0	.29
95-96	NYR	11	1	5	6	-1	0	0	6	16.7	0	0	0	0	0	0	8	16	0	8	0	2	3	0	.55
96-97	NYR	15	0	2	2	1	0	0	11	0.0	0	0	0	0	0	0	11	30	0	10	0	3	3	0	.13
98-99	Det	9	0	3	3	1	0	0	6	0.0	0	0	0	0	0	0	5	10	0	5	0	1	0	0	.33
13 Years		132	7	27	34	22	2	0	122	5.7	1	–	–	0	–	–	–	288	–	–	–	–	–	0	.26

Geoff Sanderson

(statistical profile on page 369)

Pos: LW **Shoots:** L **Ht:** 6'0" **Wt:** 185 **Born:** 2/1/72—Hay River, NW Territories **Age:** 27

Overall											Power Play			Shorthand			Penalty							Misc	
Year	Tm	GP	G	A	Pts	+/-	GW	GT	S	SPct	G	A	Pts	G	A	Pts	Num	PIM	Maj	Mnr	Fgt	Rgh	HHT	Hat	P/G
90-91	Har	2	1	0	1	-2	0	0	2	50.0	0	0	0	0	0	0	0	0	0	0	0	0	0	0	.50
91-92	Har	64	13	18	31	5	1	0	98	13.3	2	1	3	0	0	0	9	18	0	9	0	0	5	0	.48
92-93	Har	82	46	43	89	-21	4	0	271	17.0	21	20	41	2	1	3	14	28	0	14	0	3	5	2	1.09
93-94	Har*	82	41	26	67	-13	6	2	266	15.4	15	9	24	1	0	1	21	42	0	21	0	4	8	0	.82
94-95	Har	46	18	14	32	-10	4	0	170	10.6	4	5	9	0	0	0	12	24	0	12	0	1	5	1	.70
95-96	Har	81	34	31	65	0	7	0	314	10.8	6	15	21	0	0	0	20	40	0	20	0	2	11	2	.80
96-97	Har*	**82**	36	31	67	-9	4	1	297	12.1	12	11	23	1	0	1	13	29	1	12	1	1	4	0	.82
97-98	3Tm	75	11	18	29	1	2	1	197	5.6	2	4	6	0	0	0	19	38	0	19	0	0	10	0	.39
98-99	Buf	75	12	18	30	8	1	0	155	7.7	1	5	6	0	0	0	11	22	0	11	0	0	6	1	.40
97-98	Car	40	7	10	17	-4	0	1	96	7.3	2	2	4	0	0	0	7	14	0	7	0	0	3	0	.43
97-98	Van	9	0	3	3	-1	0	0	29	0.0	0	0	0	0	0	0	2	4	0	2	0	0	1	0	.33
97-98	Buf	26	4	5	9	6	2	0	72	5.6	0	2	2	0	0	0	10	20	0	10	0	0	6	0	.35
9 Years		589	212	199	411	-41	29	4	1770	12.0	63	70	133	4	1	5	119	241	1	118	1	11	54	6	.70

Postseason

Year	Tm	GP	G	A	Pts	+/-	GW	OT	S	SPct	G	A	Pts	G	A	Pts	Num	PIM	Maj	Mnr	Fgt	Rgh	HHT	Hat	P/G
90-91	Har	3	0	0	0	0	0	0	4	0.0	0	0	0	0	0	0	0	0	0	0	0	0	0	0	.00
91-92	Har	7	1	0	1	-1	0	0	9	11.1	0	0	0	0	0	0	1	2	0	1	0	0	0	0	.14
97-98	Buf	14	3	1	4	0	1	1	25	12.0	1	0	1	0	0	0	2	4	0	2	0	0	0	0	.29
98-99	Buf	19	4	6	10	5	1	0	53	7.5	0	1	1	0	0	0	7	14	0	7	0	0	2	0	.53
4 Years		43	8	7	15	4	2	1	91	8.8	1	1	2	0	0	0	10	20	0	10	0	0	2	0	.35

Tomas Sandstrom

(statistical profile on page 370)

Pos: RW **Shoots:** L **Ht:** 6'2" **Wt:** 205 **Born:** 9/4/64—Jakobstad, Finland **Age:** 35

Overall											Power Play			Shorthand			Penalty							Misc	
Year	Tm	GP	G	A	Pts	+/–	GW	GT	S	SPct	G	A	Pts	G	A	Pts	Num	PIM	Maj	Mnr	Fgt	Rgh	HHT	Hat	P/G
84-85	NYR	74	29	29	58	3	3	1	190	15.3	5	–	–	0	–	–	21	51	3	18	–	–	–	0	.78
85-86	NYR	73	25	29	54	-4	1	0	238	10.5	8	–	–	2	–	–	50	109	3	47	–	–	–	0	.74
86-87	NYR*	64	40	34	74	8	5	0	240	16.7	13	–	–	0	–	–	26	60	0	25	0	–	–	4	1.16
87-88	NYR*	69	28	40	68	-6	3	0	204	13.7	11	20	31	0	–	–	38	95	1	35	–	–	–	0	.99
88-89	NYR	79	32	56	88	5	4	0	240	13.3	11	21	32	2	–	–	51	148	2	44	–	–	–	0	1.11
89-90	2Tm	76	32	39	71	-11	3	1	249	12.9	7	–	–	1	–	–	–	128	–	–	–	–	–	0	.93
90-91	LA*	68	45	44	89	27	6	1	221	20.4	16	–	–	0	–	–	–	106	–	–	–	–	–	3	1.31
91-92	LA	49	17	22	39	-2	4	0	147	11.6	5	5	10	0	0	0	28	70	2	25	0	13	4	0	.80
92-93	LA	39	25	27	52	12	3	1	134	18.7	8	8	16	0	0	0	23	57	1	21	0	8	5	1	1.33
93-94	2Tm	78	23	35	58	-7	3	1	193	11.9	4	10	14	0	0	0	36	83	1	34	0	12	11	0	.74
94-95	Pit	47	21	23	44	1	3	1	116	18.1	4	5	9	1	2	3	21	42	0	21	0	9	4	0	.94
95-96	Pit	58	35	35	70	4	2	0	187	18.7	17	13	30	1	3	4	29	69	1	27	0	9	7	0	1.21
96-97	2Tm	74	18	24	42	6	2	1	139	12.9	1	7	8	2	0	2	25	69	1	22	0	4	7	0	.57
97-98	Anh	77	9	8	17	-25	0	1	136	6.6	2	2	4	1	0	1	32	64	0	32	0	7	9	0	.22
98-99	Anh	58	15	17	32	-5	2	0	107	14.0	7	5	12	0	0	0	21	42	0	21	0	4	6	0	.55
89-90	NYR	48	19	19	38	-10	3	0	166	11.4	6	–	–	0	–	–	–	100	–	–	–	–	–	0	.79
89-90	LA	28	13	20	33	-1	0	1	83	15.7	1	–	–	1	–	–	–	28	–	–	–	–	–	0	1.18
93-94	LA	51	17	24	41	-12	2	1	121	14.0	4	10	14	0	0	0	24	59	1	22	0	6	7	0	.80
93-94	Pit	27	6	11	17	5	1	0	72	8.3	0	0	0	0	0	0	12	24	0	12	0	6	4	0	.63
96-97	Pit	40	9	15	24	4	0	0	73	12.3	1	4	5	1	0	1	11	33	1	9	0	2	3	0	.60
96-97	Det	34	9	9	18	2	2	1	66	13.6	0	3	3	1	0	1	14	36	0	13	0	2	4	0	.53
15 Years		983	394	462	856	6	44	8	2741	14.4	119	–	–	10	–	–	–	1193	–	–	–	–	–	8	.87
Postseason																									
Year	Tm	GP	G	A	Pts	+/–	GW	OT	S	SPct	G	A	Pts	G	A	Pts	Num	PIM	Maj	Mnr	Fgt	Rgh	HHT	Hat	P/G
84-85	NYR	3	0	2	2	-3	0	0	6	0.0	0	–	–	0	0	0	0	0	0	0	0	0	0	0	.67
85-86	NYR	16	4	6	10	-3	1	0	52	7.7	0	–	–	0	–	–	–	20	–	–	–	–	–	0	.63
86-87	NYR	6	1	2	3	-8	0	0	22	4.5	0	–	–	0	0	0	–	20	–	–	–	–	–	0	.50
88-89	NYR	4	3	2	5	-3	0	0	12	25.0	2	–	–	0	0	0	–	12	–	–	–	–	–	0	1.25
89-90	LA	10	5	4	9	-5	0	0	26	19.2	0	–	–	0	–	–	–	19	–	–	–	–	–	1	.90
90-91	LA	10	4	4	8	1	0	0	32	12.5	3	–	–	0	–	–	–	14	–	–	–	–	–	0	.80
91-92	LA	6	0	3	3	-2	0	0	13	0.0	0	1	1	0	0	0	4	8	0	4	0	0	1	0	.50
92-93	LA	24	8	17	25	-2	2	0	61	13.1	2	5	7	0	0	0	6	12	0	6	0	3	1	0	1.04
93-94	Pit	6	0	0	0	-4	0	0	10	0.0	0	0	0	0	0	0	2	4	0	2	0	1	0	0	.00
94-95	Pit	12	3	3	6	-5	0	0	22	13.6	2	1	3	0	0	0	4	16	0	3	0	3	0	0	.50
95-96	Pit	18	4	2	6	-6	1	0	44	9.1	0	0	0	0	1	1	7	30	0	5	0	3	0	0	.33
96-97	Det	20	0	4	4	-3	0	0	36	0.0	0	1	1	0	0	0	8	24	0	7	0	3	2	0	.20
98-99	Anh	4	0	0	0	-2	0	0	9	0.0	0	0	0	0	0	0	2	4	0	2	0	1	0	0	.00
13 Years		139	32	49	81	-45	4	0	345	9.3	9	–	–	0	–	–	–	183	–	–	–	–	–	1	.58

Yves Sarault

Pos: LW **Shoots:** L **Ht:** 6'1" **Wt:** 183 **Born:** 12/23/72—Valleyfield, Quebec **Age:** 27

Overall											Power Play			Shorthand			Penalty							Misc	
Year	Tm	GP	G	A	Pts	+/–	GW	GT	S	SPct	G	A	Pts	G	A	Pts	Num	PIM	Maj	Mnr	Fgt	Rgh	HHT	Hat	P/G
94-95	Mon	8	0	1	1	-1	0	0	9	0.0	0	0	0	0	0	0	0	0	0	0	0	0	0	0	.13
95-96	2Tm	25	2	1	3	-9	1	0	26	7.7	0	0	0	0	0	0	4	8	0	4	0	2	0	0	.12
96-97	Col	28	2	1	3	0	0	0	41	4.9	0	0	0	0	0	0	3	6	0	3	0	0	1	0	.11
97-98	Col	2	1	0	1	1	0	0	1	100.0	0	0	0	0	0	0	0	0	0	0	0	0	0	0	.50
98-99	Ott	11	0	1	1	1	0	0	7	0.0	0	0	0	0	0	0	2	4	0	2	0	0	1	0	.09
95-96	Mon	14	0	0	0	-7	0	0	14	0.0	0	0	0	0	0	0	2	4	0	2	0	2	0	0	.00
95-96	Cgy	11	2	1	3	-2	1	0	12	16.7	0	0	0	0	0	0	2	4	0	2	0	0	0	0	.27
5 Years		74	5	4	9	-8	1	0	84	6.0	0	0	0	0	0	0	9	18	0	9	0	2	2	0	.12
Postseason																									
Year	Tm	GP	G	A	Pts	+/–	GW	OT	S	SPct	G	A	Pts	G	A	Pts	Num	PIM	Maj	Mnr	Fgt	Rgh	HHT	Hat	P/G
96-97	Col	5	0	0	0	0	0	0	2	0.0	0	0	0	0	0	0	1	2	0	1	0	1	0	0	.00

Cory Sarich

Pos: D **Shoots:** R **Ht:** 6'3" **Wt:** 175 **Born:** 8/16/78—Saskatoon, Saskatchewan **Age:** 21

Overall											Power Play			Shorthand			Penalty							Misc	
Year	Tm	GP	G	A	Pts	+/–	GW	GT	S	SPct	G	A	Pts	G	A	Pts	Num	PIM	Maj	Mnr	Fgt	Rgh	HHT	Hat	P/G
98-99	Buf	4	0	0	0	3	0	0	2	0.0	0	0	0	0	0	0	0	0	0	0	0	0	0	0	.00

Miroslav Satan

(statistical profile on page 370)

Pos: LW **Shoots:** L **Ht:** 6'1" **Wt:** 185 **Born:** 10/22/74—Topolcany, Czechoslovakia **Age:** 25

Overall											Power Play			Shorthand			Penalty							Misc	
Year	Tm	GP	G	A	Pts	+/–	GW	GT	S	SPct	G	A	Pts	G	A	Pts	Num	PIM	Maj	Mnr	Fgt	Rgh	HHT	Hat	P/G
95-96	Edm	62	18	17	35	0	4	0	113	15.9	6	5	11	0	0	0	11	22	0	11	0	3	2	0	.56
96-97	2Tm	76	25	13	38	-3	3	0	119	**21.0**	7	4	11	0	0	0	13	26	0	13	0	1	7	1	.50
97-98	Buf	79	22	24	46	2	4	0	139	15.8	9	4	13	0	0	0	17	34	0	17	0	0	4	1	.58
98-99	Buf	81	40	26	66	24	6	1	208	19.2	13	8	21	3	0	3	18	44	0	17	0	1	10	0	.81
96-97	Edm	64	17	11	28	-4	2	0	90	18.9	5	4	9	0	0	0	11	22	0	11	0	1	6	0	.44
96-97	Buf	12	8	2	10	1	1	0	29	27.6	2	0	2	0	0	0	2	4	0	2	0	0	1	1	.83
4 Years		298	105	80	185	23	17	1	579	18.1	35	21	56	3	0	3	59	126	0	58	0	5	23	2	.62
Postseason																									
Year	Tm	GP	G	A	Pts	+/–	GW	OT	S	SPct	G	A	Pts	G	A	Pts	Num	PIM	Maj	Mnr	Fgt	Rgh	HHT	Hat	P/G
96-97	Buf	7	0	0	0	-1	0	0	5	0.0	0	0	0	0	0	0	0	0	0	0	0	0	0	0	.00
97-98	Buf	14	5	4	9	-9	1	0	20	25.0	4	3	7	0	0	0	2	4	0	2	0	0	0	0	.64
98-99	Buf	12	3	5	8	3	1	1	25	12.0	1	1	2	0	0	0	1	2	0	1	0	0	0	0	.67
3 Years		33	8	9	17	-7	2	1	50	16.0	5	4	9	0	0	0	3	6	0	3	0	0	0	0	.52

Andre Savage

Pos: C **Shoots:** R **Ht:** 6'0" **Wt:** 195 **Born:** 5/27/75—Ottawa, Ontario **Age:** 24

Overall											Power Play			Shorthand			Penalty							Misc	
Year	Tm	GP	G	A	Pts	+/–	GW	GT	S	SPct	G	A	Pts	G	A	Pts	Num	PIM	Maj	Mnr	Fgt	Rgh	HHT	Hat	P/G
98-99	Bos	6	1	0	1	2	0	0	8	12.5	0	0	0	0	0	0	0	0	0	0	0	0	0	0	.17

Brian Savage

(statistical profile on page 370)

Pos: LW **Shoots:** L **Ht:** 6'2" **Wt:** 192 **Born:** 2/24/71—Sudbury, Ontario **Age:** 28

Overall											Power Play			Shorthand			Penalty							Misc	
Year	Tm	GP	G	A	Pts	+/–	GW	GT	S	SPct	G	A	Pts	G	A	Pts	Num	PIM	Maj	Mnr	Fgt	Rgh	HHT	Hat	P/G
93-94	Mon	3	1	0	1	0	0	0	3	33.3	0	0	0	0	0	0	0	0	0	0	0	0	0	0	.33
94-95	Mon	37	12	7	19	5	0	0	64	18.8	0	0	0	0	0	0	12	27	1	11	1	3	4	0	.51
95-96	Mon	75	25	8	33	-8	4	0	150	16.7	4	3	7	0	0	0	14	28	0	14	0	5	4	1	.44
96-97	Mon	81	23	37	60	-14	2	0	219	10.5	5	7	12	0	0	0	18	39	1	17	1	4	4	1	.74
97-98	Mon	64	26	17	43	11	7	2	152	17.1	8	3	11	0	0	0	18	36	0	18	0	0	9	1	.67
98-99	Mon	54	16	10	26	-14	4	1	124	12.9	5	3	8	0	0	0	10	20	0	10	0	0	2	0	.48
6 Years		314	103	79	182	-20	17	3	712	14.5	22	16	38	0	0	0	72	150	2	70	2	12	23	3	.58
Postseason																									
Year	Tm	GP	G	A	Pts	+/–	GW	OT	S	SPct	G	A	Pts	G	A	Pts	Num	PIM	Maj	Mnr	Fgt	Rgh	HHT	Hat	P/G
93-94	Mon	3	0	2	2	0	0	0	6	0.0	0	1	1	0	0	0	0	0	0	0	0	0	0	0	.67
95-96	Mon	6	0	2	2	2	0	0	9	0.0	0	0	0	0	0	0	1	2	0	1	0	0	1	0	.33
96-97	Mon	5	1	1	2	1	0	0	6	16.7	0	0	0	0	0	0	0	0	0	0	0	0	0	0	.40
97-98	Mon	9	0	2	2	-2	0	0	24	0.0	0	0	0	0	0	0	3	6	0	3	0	0	0	0	.22
4 Years		23	1	7	8	1	0	0	45	2.2	0	1	1	0	0	0	4	8	0	4	0	0	1	0	.35

Marc Savard

(statistical profile on page 370)

Pos: C **Shoots:** L **Ht:** 5'11" **Wt:** 185 **Born:** 7/17/77—Ottawa, Ontario **Age:** 22

Overall											Power Play			Shorthand			Penalty							Misc	
Year	Tm	GP	G	A	Pts	+/–	GW	GT	S	SPct	G	A	Pts	G	A	Pts	Num	PIM	Maj	Mnr	Fgt	Rgh	HHT	Hat	P/G
97-98	NYR	28	1	5	6	-4	0	0	32	3.1	0	3	3	0	0	0	2	4	0	2	0	0	1	0	.21
98-99	NYR	70	9	36	45	-7	1	0	116	7.8	4	15	19	0	0	0	19	38	0	19	0	3	4	0	.64
2 Years		98	10	41	51	-11	1	0	148	6.8	4	18	22	0	0	0	21	42	0	21	0	3	5	0	.52

Ryan Savoia

Pos: C **Shoots:** R **Ht:** 6'0" **Wt:** 206 **Born:** 5/6/73—St. Catharines, Ontario **Age:** 26

Overall											Power Play			Shorthand			Penalty							Misc	
Year	Tm	GP	G	A	Pts	+/–	GW	GT	S	SPct	G	A	Pts	G	A	Pts	Num	PIM	Maj	Mnr	Fgt	Rgh	HHT	Hat	P/G
98-99	Pit	3	0	0	0	-1	0	0	0	–	0	0	0	0	0	0	0	0	0	0	0	0	0	0	.00

Dave Scatchard

(statistical profile on page 371)

Pos: C **Shoots:** R **Ht:** 6'2" **Wt:** 185 **Born:** 2/20/76—Hinton, Alberta **Age:** 23

Overall											Power Play			Shorthand			Penalty							Misc	
Year	Tm	GP	G	A	Pts	+/-	GW	GT	S	SPct	G	A	Pts	G	A	Pts	Num	PIM	Maj	Mnr	Fgt	Rgh	HHT	Hat	P/G
97-98	Van	76	13	11	24	-4	1	1	85	15.3	0	1	1	0	0	0	53	165	9	40	9	7	16	0	.32
98-99	Van	82	13	13	26	-12	2	0	130	10.0	0	1	1	2	3	5	58	140	8	50	7	12	14	0	.32
2 Years		158	26	24	50	-16	3	1	215	12.1	0	2	2	2	3	5	111	305	17	90	16	19	30	0	.32

Peter Schaefer

Pos: LW **Shoots:** L **Ht:** 5'11" **Wt:** 190 **Born:** 7/12/77—Yellow Grass, Saskatchewan **Age:** 22

Overall											Power Play			Shorthand			Penalty							Misc	
Year	Tm	GP	G	A	Pts	+/-	GW	GT	S	SPct	G	A	Pts	G	A	Pts	Num	PIM	Maj	Mnr	Fgt	Rgh	HHT	Hat	P/G
98-99	Van	25	4	4	8	-1	1	0	24	16.7	1	1	2	0	0	0	4	8	0	4	0	1	0	0	.32

Mathieu Schneider

(statistical profile on page 371)

Pos: D **Shoots:** L **Ht:** 5'10" **Wt:** 192 **Born:** 6/12/69—New York, New York **Age:** 30

Overall											Power Play			Shorthand			Penalty							Misc	
Year	Tm	GP	G	A	Pts	+/-	GW	GT	S	SPct	G	A	Pts	G	A	Pts	Num	PIM	Maj	Mnr	Fgt	Rgh	HHT	Hat	P/G
87-88	Mon	4	0	0	0	-2	0	0	2	0.0	0	0	0	0	0	0	1	2	0	1	0	–	–	0	.00
88-89											Did Not Play in NHL														
89-90	Mon	44	7	14	21	2	1	0	84	8.3	5	–	–	0	–	–	–	25	–	–	–	–	–	0	.48
90-91	Mon	69	10	20	30	7	3	0	164	6.1	5	–	–	0	–	–	–	63	–	–	–	–	–	0	.43
91-92	Mon	78	8	24	32	10	1	0	194	4.1	2	14	16	0	0	0	32	72	0	31	0	7	9	0	.41
92-93	Mon	60	13	31	44	8	2	0	169	7.7	3	13	16	0	0	0	36	91	1	33	0	8	6	0	.73
93-94	Mon	75	20	32	52	15	4	0	193	10.4	11	16	27	0	1	1	31	62	0	31	0	4	8	0	.69
94-95	2Tm	43	8	21	29	-8	2	0	118	6.8	3	10	13	0	0	0	34	79	1	32	1	8	8	0	.67
95-96	2Tm*	78	13	41	54	-20	1	0	191	6.8	7	33	40	0	0	0	42	103	1	39	0	5	7	0	.69
96-97	Tor	26	5	7	12	3	1	0	63	7.9	1	4	5	0	0	0	10	20	0	10	0	2	5	0	.46
97-98	Tor	76	11	26	37	-12	1	0	181	6.1	4	14	18	1	0	1	22	44	0	22	0	2	6	0	.49
98-99	NYR	75	10	24	34	-19	2	0	159	6.3	5	15	20	0	0	0	30	71	1	28	1	4	8	0	.45
94-95	Mon	30	5	15	20	-3	0	0	82	6.1	2	8	10	0	0	0	23	49	1	22	1	7	6	0	.67
94-95	NYI	13	3	6	9	-5	2	0	36	8.3	1	2	3	0	0	0	11	30	0	10	0	1	2	0	.69
95-96	NYI	65	11	36	47	-18	1	0	155	7.1	7	28	35	0	0	0	37	93	1	34	0	4	6	0	.72
95-96	Tor	13	2	5	7	-2	0	0	36	5.6	0	5	5	0	0	0	5	10	0	5	0	1	1	0	.54
11 Years		628	105	240	345	-16	18	0	1518	6.9	46	–	–	1	–	–	–	632	–	–	–	–	–	0	.55
Postseason																									
Year	Tm	GP	G	A	Pts	+/-	GW	OT	S	SPct	G	A	Pts	G	A	Pts	Num	PIM	Maj	Mnr	Fgt	Rgh	HHT	Hat	P/G
89-90	Mon	9	1	3	4	-3	0	0	14	7.1	1	–	–	0	0	0	–	31	–	–	–	–	–	0	.44
90-91	Mon	13	2	7	9	2	0	0	33	6.1	1	–	–	0	–	–	–	18	–	–	–	–	–	0	.69
91-92	Mon	10	1	4	5	-2	0	0	27	3.7	1	2	3	0	0	0	3	6	0	3	0	0	2	0	.50
92-93	Mon	11	1	2	3	10	0	0	24	4.2	0	1	1	0	0	0	8	16	0	8	0	2	1	0	.27
93-94	Mon	1	0	0	0	0	0	0	1	0.0	0	0	0	0	0	0	0	0	0	0	0	0	0	0	.00
95-96	Tor	6	0	4	4	-7	0	0	13	0.0	0	4	4	0	0	0	4	8	0	4	0	1	1	0	.67
6 Years		50	5	20	25	0	0	0	112	4.5	3	–	–	0	–	–	–	79	–	–	–	–	–	0	.50

Ray Schultz

Pos: D **Shoots:** L **Ht:** 6'2" **Wt:** 200 **Born:** 11/14/76—Red Deer, Alberta **Age:** 23

Overall											Power Play			Shorthand			Penalty							Misc	
Year	Tm	GP	G	A	Pts	+/-	GW	GT	S	SPct	G	A	Pts	G	A	Pts	Num	PIM	Maj	Mnr	Fgt	Rgh	HHT	Hat	P/G
97-98	NYI	13	0	1	1	3	0	0	4	0.0	0	0	0	0	0	0	11	45	5	5	5	0	2	0	.08
98-99	NYI	4	0	0	0	-2	0	0	2	0.0	0	0	0	0	0	0	2	7	1	1	1	0	0	0	.00
2 Years		17	0	1	1	1	0	0	6	0.0	0	0	0	0	0	0	13	52	6	6	6	0	2	0	.06

Corey Schwab

(statistical profile on page 402)

Pos: G **Catches:** L **Ht:** 6'0" **Wt:** 180 **Born:** 11/4/70—North Battleford, Saskatchewan **Age:** 29

Overall																Pen Shot		Offense		
Year	Tm	GP	GS	TP	W	L	T	Min	GA	GAA	Shots	SvPct	ShO	OE	PPGA	SHGA	Shots	GA	G	A	PIM
95-96	NJ	10	4	2	0	3	0	331	12	2.18	119	.899	0	0	4	0	0	0	0	0	31
96-97	TB	31	23	7	11	12	1	1462	74	3.04	719	.897	2	8	19	3	0	0	0	1	10
97-98	TB	16	13	2	2	9	1	821	40	2.92	370	.892	1	2	11	3	3	1	0	0	2
98-99	TB	40	35	7	8	25	3	2146	126	3.52	1153	.891	0	11	26	6	0	0	0	4	4
4 Years		97	75	18	21	49	5	4760	252	3.18	2361	.893	3	21	60	12	3	1	0	5	47

Teemu Selanne

(statistical profile on page 371)

Pos: RW **Shoots:** R **Ht:** 6'0" **Wt:** 200 **Born:** 7/3/70—Helsinki, Finland **Age:** 29

Overall											Power Play			Shorthand			Penalty							Misc	
Year	Tm	GP	G	A	Pts	+/–	GW	GT	S	SPct	G	A	Pts	G	A	Pts	Num	PIM	Maj	Mnr	Fgt	Rgh	HHT	Hat	P/G
92-93	Wpg*	84	**76**	56	132	8	7	0	387	19.6	24	25	49	0	0	0	17	45	1	15	0	3	4	5	1.57
93-94	Wpg*	51	25	29	54	-23	2	0	191	13.1	11	12	23	0	0	0	11	22	0	11	0	0	1	2	1.06
94-95	Wpg	45	22	26	48	1	1	1	167	13.2	8	10	18	2	0	2	1	2	0	1	0	0	0	0	1.07
95-96	2Tm*	79	40	68	108	5	5	0	267	15.0	9	39	48	1	0	1	11	22	0	11	0	1	7	3	1.37
96-97	Anh*	78	51	58	109	28	8	2	273	18.7	11	21	32	1	0	1	17	34	0	17	0	6	1	1	1.40
97-98	Anh*	73	**52**	34	86	12	10	**3**	268	19.4	10	7	17	1	1	2	15	30	0	15	0	2	5	**3**	1.18
98-99	Anh	75	**47**	60	107	18	7	1	281	16.7	**25**	29	**54**	0	0	0	15	30	0	15	0	2	6	1	1.43
95-96	Wpg	51	24	48	72	3	4	0	163	14.7	6	25	31	1	0	1	9	18	0	9	0	1	6	1	1.41
95-96	Anh	28	16	20	36	2	1	0	104	15.4	3	14	17	0	0	0	2	4	0	2	0	0	1	2	1.29
7 Years		485	313	331	644	49	40	7	1834	17.1	98	143	241	5	1	6	87	185	1	85	0	14	24	15	1.33
Postseason																									
Year	Tm	GP	G	A	Pts	+/–	GW	OT	S	SPct	G	A	Pts	G	A	Pts	Num	PIM	Maj	Mnr	Fgt	Rgh	HHT	Hat	P/G
92-93	Wpg	6	4	2	6	-3	2	1	27	14.8	2	2	4	0	0	0	1	2	0	1	0	0	0	1	1.00
96-97	Anh	11	7	3	10	-3	1	0	38	18.4	3	1	4	0	0	0	2	4	0	2	0	0	1	0	.91
98-99	Anh	4	2	2	4	-1	0	0	7	28.6	1	1	2	0	0	0	1	2	0	1	0	0	0	0	1.00
3 Years		21	13	7	20	-7	3	1	72	18.1	6	4	10	0	0	0	4	8	0	4	0	0	1	1	.95

Alexander Selivanov

(statistical profile on page 371)

Pos: RW **Shoots:** L **Ht:** 6'0" **Wt:** 206 **Born:** 3/23/71—Moscow, USSR **Age:** 28

Overall											Power Play			Shorthand			Penalty							Misc	
Year	Tm	GP	G	A	Pts	+/–	GW	GT	S	SPct	G	A	Pts	G	A	Pts	Num	PIM	Maj	Mnr	Fgt	Rgh	HHT	Hat	P/G
94-95	TB	43	10	6	16	-2	3	0	94	10.6	4	1	5	0	0	0	7	14	0	7	0	1	2	0	.37
95-96	TB	79	31	21	52	3	5	2	215	14.4	13	5	18	0	0	0	41	93	1	39	1	4	13	0	.66
96-97	TB	69	15	18	33	-3	4	0	187	8.0	3	5	8	0	0	0	25	61	1	23	1	9	9	0	.48
97-98	TB	70	16	19	35	-38	3	1	206	7.8	4	8	12	0	0	0	30	85	3	25	3	5	10	0	.50
98-99	2Tm	72	14	19	33	-8	1	0	177	7.9	2	9	11	0	0	0	21	42	0	21	0	1	11	1	.46
98-99	TB	43	6	13	19	-8	0	0	120	5.0	1	6	7	0	0	0	9	18	0	9	0	0	7	0	.44
98-99	Edm	29	8	6	14	0	1	0	57	14.0	1	3	4	0	0	0	12	24	0	12	0	1	4	1	.48
5 Years		333	86	83	169	-48	16	3	879	9.8	26	28	54	0	0	0	124	295	5	115	5	20	45	1	.51
Postseason																									
Year	Tm	GP	G	A	Pts	+/–	GW	OT	S	SPct	G	A	Pts	G	A	Pts	Num	PIM	Maj	Mnr	Fgt	Rgh	HHT	Hat	P/G
95-96	TB	6	2	2	4	2	1	1	22	9.1	0	0	0	0	0	0	3	6	0	3	0	0	0	0	.67
98-99	Edm	2	0	1	1	0	0	0	3	0.0	0	0	0	0	0	0	1	2	0	1	0	0	0	0	.50
2 Years		8	2	3	5	2	1	1	25	8.0	0	0	0	0	0	0	4	8	0	4	0	0	0	0	.63

Jeff Serowik

Pos: D **Shoots:** R **Ht:** 6'1" **Wt:** 210 **Born:** 1/10/67—Manchester, New Hampshire **Age:** 32

Overall											Power Play			Shorthand			Penalty							Misc	
Year	Tm	GP	G	A	Pts	+/–	GW	GT	S	SPct	G	A	Pts	G	A	Pts	Num	PIM	Maj	Mnr	Fgt	Rgh	HHT	Hat	P/G
90-91	Tor	1	0	0	0	0	0	0	1	0.0	0	0	0	0	0	0	0	0	0	0	0	0	0	0	.00
91-92											Did Not Play in NHL														
92-93											Did Not Play in NHL														
93-94											Did Not Play in NHL														
94-95	Bos	1	0	0	0	1	0	0	0	–	0	0	0	0	0	0	0	0	0	0	0	0	0	0	.00
95-96											Did Not Play in NHL														
96-97											Did Not Play in NHL														
97-98											Did Not Play in NHL														
98-99	Pit	26	0	6	6	-4	0	0	26	0.0	0	3	3	0	0	0	8	16	0	8	0	0	2	0	.23
3 Years		28	0	6	6	-3	0	0	27	0.0	0	3	3	0	0	0	8	16	0	8	0	0	2	0	.21

Brent Severyn

Pos: LW **Shoots:** R **Ht:** 6'2" **Wt:** 211 **Born:** 2/22/66—Vegreville, Alberta **Age:** 33

Overall											Power Play			Shorthand			Penalty							Misc	
Year	Tm	GP	G	A	Pts	+/–	GW	GT	S	SPct	G	A	Pts	G	A	Pts	Num	PIM	Maj	Mnr	Fgt	Rgh	HHT	Hat	P/G
89-90	Que	35	0	2	2	-19	0	0	28	0.0	0	–	–	0	–	–	–	42	–	–	–	–	–	0	.06
90-91											Did Not Play in NHL														
91-92											Did Not Play in NHL														
92-93											Did Not Play in NHL														
93-94	Fla	67	4	7	11	-1	1	0	93	4.3	1	1	2	0	1	1	44	156	12	28	12	11	11	0	.16

Overall											Power Play			Shorthand			Penalty							Misc	
Year	Tm	GP	G	A	Pts	+/–	GW	GT	S	SPct	G	A	Pts	G	A	Pts	Num	PIM	Maj	Mnr	Fgt	Rgh	HHT	Hat	P/G
94-95	2Tm	28	2	4	6	-2	0	0	32	6.3	1	1	2	0	0	0	24	71	5	18	5	5	5	0	.21
95-96	NYI	65	1	8	9	3	0	0	40	2.5	0	0	0	0	0	0	47	180	10	30	10	9	8	0	.14
96-97	Col	66	1	4	5	-6	0	0	55	1.8	0	0	0	0	0	0	42	193	23	14	23	7	2	0	.08
97-98	Anh	37	1	3	4	-3	0	0	27	3.7	0	0	0	0	0	0	28	133	7	14	7	5	3	0	.11
98-99	Dal	30	1	2	3	-2	0	0	22	4.5	0	0	0	0	0	0	16	50	6	10	6	4	3	0	.10
94-95	Fla	9	1	1	2	-3	0	0	10	10.0	1	1	2	0	0	0	10	37	3	6	3	3	1	0	.22
94-95	NYI	19	1	3	4	1	0	0	22	4.5	0	0	0	0	0	0	14	34	2	12	2	2	4	0	.21
7 Years		328	10	30	40	-30	1	0	297	3.4	2	–	–	0	–	–	–	825	–	–	–	–	–	0	.12

Postseason

Year	Tm	GP	G	A	Pts	+/–	GW	OT	S	SPct	G	A	Pts	G	A	Pts	Num	PIM	Maj	Mnr	Fgt	Rgh	HHT	Hat	P/G
96-97	Col	8	0	0	0	1	0	0	3	0.0	0	0	0	0	0	0	2	12	0	1	0	0	1	0	.00

Brendan Shanahan

(statistical profile on page 372)

Pos: LW **Shoots:** R **Ht:** 6'3" **Wt:** 220 **Born:** 1/23/69—Mimico, Ontario **Age:** 30

Overall											Power Play			Shorthand			Penalty							Misc	
Year	Tm	GP	G	A	Pts	+/–	GW	GT	S	SPct	G	A	Pts	G	A	Pts	Num	PIM	Maj	Mnr	Fgt	Rgh	HHT	Hat	P/G
87-88	NJ	65	7	19	26	-20	2	0	72	9.7	2	–	–	0	–	–	–	131	–	–	–	–	–	0	.40
88-89	NJ	68	22	28	50	2	0	1	152	14.5	9	8	17	0	0	0	–	115	–	–	–	–	–	1	.74
89-90	NJ	73	30	42	72	15	5	0	196	15.3	8	13	21	0	0	0	–	137	–	–	–	–	–	0	.99
90-91	NJ	75	29	37	66	4	2	**3**	195	14.9	7	12	19	0	0	0	–	141	–	–	–	–	–	0	.88
91-92	StL	80	33	36	69	-3	2	2	215	15.3	13	15	28	0	0	0	61	171	11	48	10	16	12	0	.86
92-93	StL	71	51	43	94	10	8	0	232	22.0	18	19	37	0	0	0	57	174	4	47	1	20	13	1	1.32
93-94	StL*	81	52	50	102	-9	8	1	**397**	13.1	15	27	42	**7**	1	8	75	211	7	63	7	18	15	**4**	1.26
94-95	StL	45	20	21	41	7	6	0	153	13.1	6	5	11	2	1	3	43	136	6	33	5	**19**	6	0	.91
95-96	Har*	74	44	34	78	2	6	0	280	15.7	17	14	31	2	1	3	42	125	3	35	3	13	10	1	1.05
96-97	2Tm*	81	47	41	88	32	7	2	336	14.0	**20**	15	35	3	2	5	43	131	7	33	6	7	10	**3**	1.09
97-98	Det*	75	28	29	57	6	9	1	266	10.5	15	9	24	1	0	1	51	154	4	42	4	9	17	0	.76
98-99	Det	81	31	27	58	2	5	0	288	10.8	5	11	16	0	2	2	46	123	5	39	4	6	15	2	.72
96-97	Har	2	1	0	1	1	0	0	13	7.7	0	0	0	1	0	1	0	0	0	0	0	0	0	0	.50
96-97	Det	79	46	41	87	31	7	2	323	14.2	20	15	35	2	2	4	43	131	7	33	6	7	10	3	1.10
12 Years		869	394	407	801	48	60	10	2782	14.2	135	–	–	15	–	–	–	1749	–	–	–	–	–	12	.92

Postseason

Year	Tm	GP	G	A	Pts	+/–	GW	OT	S	SPct	G	A	Pts	G	A	Pts	Num	PIM	Maj	Mnr	Fgt	Rgh	HHT	Hat	P/G
87-88	NJ	12	2	1	3	0	0	0	11	18.2	1	–	–	0	–	–	–	44	–	–	–	–	–	0	.25
89-90	NJ	6	3	3	6	0	1	0	16	18.8	1	–	–	0	–	–	–	20	–	–	–	–	–	0	1.00
90-91	NJ	7	3	5	8	3	0	0	20	15.0	2	–	–	0	–	–	–	12	–	–	–	–	–	0	1.14
91-92	StL	6	2	3	5	0	0	0	17	11.8	1	2	3	0	0	0	7	14	0	7	0	5	1	0	.83
92-93	StL	11	4	3	7	0	0	0	36	11.1	2	1	3	0	0	0	9	18	0	9	0	4	1	0	.64
93-94	StL	4	2	5	7	6	0	0	20	10.0	0	2	2	0	1	1	2	4	0	2	0	1	1	0	1.75
94-95	StL	5	4	5	9	2	1	0	23	17.4	1	3	4	0	0	0	7	14	0	7	0	1	1	1	1.80
96-97	Det	20	9	8	17	8	2	1	82	11.0	2	2	4	0	1	1	12	43	1	9	1	6	2	0	.85
97-98	Det	20	5	4	9	5	2	1	60	8.3	3	1	4	0	0	0	7	22	0	6	0	0	1	0	.45
98-99	Det	10	3	7	10	2	1	0	31	9.7	1	2	3	0	0	0	3	6	0	3	0	1	2	0	1.00
10 Years		101	37	44	81	26	7	2	316	11.7	14	–	–	0	–	–	–	197	–	–	–	–	–	1	.80

Darryl Shannon

(statistical profile on page 372)

Pos: D **Shoots:** L **Ht:** 6'2" **Wt:** 208 **Born:** 6/21/68—Barrie, Ontario **Age:** 31

Overall											Power Play			Shorthand			Penalty							Misc	
Year	Tm	GP	G	A	Pts	+/–	GW	GT	S	SPct	G	A	Pts	G	A	Pts	Num	PIM	Maj	Mnr	Fgt	Rgh	HHT	Hat	P/G
88-89	Tor	14	1	3	4	5	0	0	16	6.3	0	–	–	0	–	–	3	6	0	3	0	–	–	0	.29
89-90	Tor	10	0	1	1	-10	0	0	16	0.0	0	–	–	0	–	–	–	12	–	–	–	–	–	0	.10
90-91	Tor	10	0	1	1	1	0	0	3	0.0	0	–	–	0	–	–	0	0	0	0	0	0	0	0	.10
91-92	Tor	48	2	8	10	-17	0	0	50	4.0	1	2	3	0	0	0	10	23	1	9	1	2	4	0	.21
92-93	Tor	16	0	0	0	-5	0	0	10	0.0	0	0	0	0	0	0	4	11	1	3	1	2	0	0	.00
93-94	Wpg	20	0	4	4	-6	0	0	14	0.0	0	0	0	0	0	0	9	18	0	9	0	1	5	0	.20
94-95	Wpg	40	5	9	14	1	0	0	42	11.9	0	0	0	1	1	2	17	48	2	14	2	0	10	0	.35
95-96	2Tm	74	4	13	17	15	0	0	59	6.8	0	1	1	0	2	2	35	92	2	31	2	1	15	0	.23
96-97	Buf	**82**	4	19	23	23	1	0	94	4.3	1	2	3	0	1	1	47	112	6	41	5	3	**23**	0	.28
97-98	Buf	76	3	19	22	26	1	0	85	3.5	1	3	4	0	0	0	24	56	0	23	0	5	5	0	.29
98-99	Buf	71	3	12	15	28	0	1	80	3.8	1	2	3	0	0	0	26	52	0	26	0	2	15	0	.21
95-96	Wpg	48	2	7	9	5	0	0	34	5.9	0	0	0	0	2	2	25	72	2	21	2	1	7	0	.19
95-96	Buf	26	2	6	8	10	0	0	25	8.0	0	1	1	0	0	0	10	20	0	10	0	0	8	0	.31
11 Years		461	22	89	111	61	2	1	469	4.7	4	–	–	1	–	–	–	430	–	–	–	–	–	0	.24

Postseason																									
Year	Tm	GP	G	A	Pts	+/–	GW	OT	S	SPct	G	A	Pts	G	A	Pts	Num	PIM	Maj	Mnr	Fgt	Rgh	HHT	Hat	P/G
96-97	Buf	12	2	3	5	-1	0	0	8	25.0	1	0	1	0	0	0	4	8	0	4	0	0	2	0	.42
97-98	Buf	15	2	4	6	0	0	0	15	13.3	0	4	4	1	0	1	4	8	0	4	0	0	3	0	.40
98-99	Buf	2	0	0	0	-1	0	0	7	0.0	0	0	0	0	0	0	0	0	0	0	0	0	0	0	.00
3 Years		29	4	7	11	-2	0	0	30	13.3	1	4	5	1	0	1	8	16	0	8	0	0	5	0	.38

Jeff Shantz

(statistical profile on page 372)

Pos: C **Shoots:** R **Ht:** 6'0" **Wt:** 185 **Born:** 10/10/73—Duchess, Alberta **Age:** 26

Overall											Power Play			Shorthand			Penalty							Misc	
Year	Tm	GP	G	A	Pts	+/–	GW	GT	S	SPct	G	A	Pts	G	A	Pts	Num	PIM	Maj	Mnr	Fgt	Rgh	HHT	Hat	P/G
93-94	Chi	52	3	13	16	-14	0	0	56	5.4	0	1	1	0	0	0	15	30	0	15	0	2	8	0	.31
94-95	Chi	45	6	12	18	11	0	0	58	10.3	0	2	2	2	1	3	11	33	1	9	0	0	4	0	.40
95-96	Chi	78	6	14	20	12	0	0	72	8.3	1	0	1	2	1	3	12	24	0	12	0	1	2	0	.26
96-97	Chi	69	9	21	30	11	1	0	86	10.5	0	2	2	1	1	2	14	28	0	14	0	0	8	0	.43
97-98	Chi	61	11	20	31	0	2	0	69	15.9	1	4	5	2	2	4	18	36	0	18	0	1	7	0	.51
98-99	2Tm	76	13	17	30	14	3	0	82	15.9	1	0	1	1	1	2	22	44	0	22	0	1	9	0	.39
98-99	Chi	7	1	0	1	-1	0	0	5	20.0	0	0	0	0	0	0	2	4	0	2	0	1	1	0	.14
98-99	Cgy	69	12	17	29	15	3	0	77	15.6	1	0	1	1	1	2	20	40	0	20	0	0	8	0	.42
6 Years		381	48	97	145	34	6	0	423	11.3	3	9	12	8	6	14	92	195	1	90	0	5	38	0	.38
Postseason																									
Year	Tm	GP	G	A	Pts	+/–	GW	OT	S	SPct	G	A	Pts	G	A	Pts	Num	PIM	Maj	Mnr	Fgt	Rgh	HHT	Hat	P/G
93-94	Chi	6	0	0	0	-2	0	0	3	0.0	0	0	0	0	0	0	3	6	0	3	0	0	2	0	.00
94-95	Chi	16	3	1	4	0	0	0	16	18.8	0	0	0	0	0	0	1	2	0	1	0	0	0	0	.25
95-96	Chi	10	2	3	5	-2	0	0	9	22.2	0	1	1	0	0	0	3	6	0	3	0	1	0	0	.50
96-97	Chi	6	0	4	4	4	0	0	7	0.0	0	1	1	0	0	0	3	6	0	3	0	0	1	0	.67
4 Years		38	5	8	13	0	0	0	35	14.3	0	2	2	0	0	0	10	20	0	10	0	1	3	0	.34

Vadim Sharifijanov

(statistical profile on page 372)

Pos: RW **Shoots:** L **Ht:** 5'11" **Wt:** 210 **Born:** 12/23/75—Ufa, USSR **Age:** 24

Overall											Power Play			Shorthand			Penalty							Misc	
Year	Tm	GP	G	A	Pts	+/–	GW	GT	S	SPct	G	A	Pts	G	A	Pts	Num	PIM	Maj	Mnr	Fgt	Rgh	HHT	Hat	P/G
96-97	NJ	2	0	0	0	0	0	0	4	0.0	0	0	0	0	0	0	0	0	0	0	0	0	0	0	.00
97-98	Did Not Play in NHL																								
98-99	NJ	53	11	16	27	11	2	0	71	15.5	1	4	5	0	2	2	14	28	0	14	0	0	7	0	.51
2 Years		55	11	16	27	11	2	0	75	14.7	1	4	5	0	2	2	14	28	0	14	0	0	7	0	.49
Postseason																									
Year	Tm	GP	G	A	Pts	+/–	GW	OT	S	SPct	G	A	Pts	G	A	Pts	Num	PIM	Maj	Mnr	Fgt	Rgh	HHT	Hat	P/G
98-99	NJ	4	0	0	0	0	0	0	3	0.0	0	0	0	0	0	0	0	0	0	0	0	0	0	0	.00

Brad Shaw

Pos: D **Shoots:** R **Ht:** 6'0" **Wt:** 187 **Born:** 4/28/64—Cambridge, Ontario **Age:** 35

Overall											Power Play			Shorthand			Penalty							Misc	
Year	Tm	GP	G	A	Pts	+/–	GW	GT	S	SPct	G	A	Pts	G	A	Pts	Num	PIM	Maj	Mnr	Fgt	Rgh	HHT	Hat	P/G
85-86	Har	8	0	2	2	-1	0	0	17	0.0	0	–	–	0	–	–	2	4	0	2	0	–	–	0	.25
86-87	Har	2	0	0	0	0	0	0	2	0.0	0	0	0	0	0	0	0	0	0	0	0	0	0	0	.00
87-88	Har	1	0	0	0	-1	0	0	1	0.0	0	0	0	0	0	0	0	0	0	0	0	0	0	0	.00
88-89	Har	3	1	0	1	1	0	0	2	50.0	1	0	1	0	0	0	0	0	0	0	0	0	0	0	.33
89-90	Har	64	3	32	35	2	0	0	65	4.6	3	–	–	0	–	–	–	30	–	–	–	–	–	0	.55
90-91	Har	72	4	28	32	-10	1	0	129	3.1	2	–	–	0	–	–	–	29	–	–	–	–	–	0	.44
91-92	Har	62	3	22	25	1	0	0	101	3.0	0	15	15	0	0	0	22	44	0	22	0	4	13	0	.40
92-93	Ott	81	7	34	41	-47	0	0	166	4.2	4	22	26	0	1	1	17	34	0	17	0	0	9	0	.51
93-94	Ott	66	4	19	23	-41	0	0	113	3.5	1	9	10	0	0	0	28	59	1	27	1	0	21	0	.35
94-95	Ott	2	0	0	0	3	0	0	3	0.0	0	0	0	0	0	0	0	0	0	0	0	0	0	0	.00
95-96	Did Not Play in NHL																								
96-97	Did Not Play in NHL																								
97-98	Did Not Play in NHL																								
98-99	2Tm	16	0	0	0	0	0	0	15	0.0	0	0	0	0	0	0	4	8	0	4	0	0	3	0	.00
98-99	Was	4	0	0	0	0	0	0	5	0.0	0	0	0	0	0	0	2	4	0	2	0	0	1	0	.00
98-99	StL	12	0	0	0	0	0	0	10	0.0	0	0	0	0	0	0	2	4	0	2	0	0	2	0	.00
11 Years		377	22	137	159	-93	1	0	614	3.6	11	–	–	0	–	–	–	208	–	–	–	–	–	0	.42
Postseason																									
Year	Tm	GP	G	A	Pts	+/–	GW	OT	S	SPct	G	A	Pts	G	A	Pts	Num	PIM	Maj	Mnr	Fgt	Rgh	HHT	Hat	P/G
88-89	Har	3	1	0	1	0	0	0	7	14.3	0	0	0	0	0	0	0	0	0	0	0	0	0	0	.33

Postseason																									
Year	Tm	GP	G	A	Pts	+/-	GW	OT	S	SPct	G	A	Pts	G	A	Pts	Num	PIM	Maj	Mnr	Fgt	Rgh	HHT	Hat	P/G
89-90	Har	7	2	5	7	1	0	0	7	28.6	1	–	–	0	0	0	0	0	0	0	0	0	0	0	1.00
90-91	Har	6	1	2	3	-4	0	0	5	20.0	0	–	–	0	–	–	1	2	0	1	0	0	0	0	.50
91-92	Har	3	0	1	1	-2	0	0	9	0.0	0	1	1	0	0	0	2	4	0	2	0	0	2	0	.33
98-99	StL	4	0	0	0	2	0	0	3	0.0	0	0	0	0	0	0	0	0	0	0	0	0	0	0	.00
5 Years		23	4	8	12	-3	0	0	31	12.9	1	–	–	0	–	–	3	6	0	3	0	0	2	0	.52

Ray Sheppard

(statistical profile on page 373)

Pos: RW **Shoots:** R **Ht:** 6'1" **Wt:** 195 **Born:** 5/27/66—Pembroke, Ontario **Age:** 33

Overall											Power Play			Shorthand			Penalty							Misc	
Year	Tm	GP	G	A	Pts	+/-	GW	GT	S	SPct	G	A	Pts	G	A	Pts	Num	PIM	Maj	Mnr	Fgt	Rgh	HHT	Hat	P/G
87-88	Buf	74	38	27	65	-6	5	2	173	22.0	15	–	–	0	–	–	–	14	–	–	–	–	–	2	.88
88-89	Buf	67	22	21	43	-7	4	1	147	15.0	7	–	–	0	–	–	–	15	–	–	–	–	–	0	.64
89-90	Buf	18	4	2	6	3	1	0	31	12.9	1	–	–	0	–	–	0	0	0	0	0	0	0	0	.33
90-91	NYR	59	24	23	47	8	5	0	129	18.6	7	8	15	0	–	–	–	21	–	–	–	–	–	0	.80
91-92	Det	74	36	26	62	7	4	1	178	20.2	11	6	17	1	0	1	12	27	1	11	1	2	4	1	.84
92-93	Det	70	32	34	66	7	1	0	183	17.5	10	18	28	0	0	0	9	29	1	7	1	1	2	0	.94
93-94	Det	82	52	41	93	13	5	0	260	20.0	19	15	34	0	2	2	13	26	0	13	0	2	5	2	1.13
94-95	Det	43	30	10	40	11	5	1	125	24.0	11	2	13	0	0	0	7	17	1	6	1	1	2	1	.93
95-96	3Tm	70	37	23	60	-19	7	0	231	16.0	14	9	23	0	0	0	8	16	0	8	0	2	2	2	.86
96-97	Fla	68	29	31	60	4	7	0	226	12.8	13	9	22	0	0	0	2	4	0	2	0	0	0	**3**	.88
97-98	2Tm	71	18	19	37	-12	2	0	169	10.7	7	9	16	0	0	0	6	23	1	4	1	0	1	1	.52
98-99	Car	74	25	33	58	4	4	1	188	13.3	5	8	13	0	0	0	8	16	0	8	0	0	1	0	.78
95-96	Det	5	2	2	4	0	1	0	9	22.2	0	2	2	0	0	0	1	2	0	1	0	1	0	0	.80
95-96	SJ	51	27	19	46	-19	4	0	170	15.9	12	6	18	0	0	0	5	10	0	5	0	1	2	1	.90
95-96	Fla	14	8	2	10	0	2	0	52	15.4	2	1	3	0	0	0	2	4	0	2	0	0	0	1	.71
97-98	Fla	61	14	17	31	-14	1	0	136	10.3	5	8	13	0	0	0	5	21	1	3	1	0	1	1	.51
97-98	Car	10	4	2	6	2	1	0	33	12.1	2	1	3	0	0	0	1	2	0	1	0	0	0	0	.60
12 Years		770	347	290	637	13	50	6	2040	17.0	120	–	–	1	–	–	–	208	–	–	–	–	–	12	.83
Postseason																									
Year	Tm	GP	G	A	Pts	+/-	GW	OT	S	SPct	G	A	Pts	G	A	Pts	Num	PIM	Maj	Mnr	Fgt	Rgh	HHT	Hat	P/G
87-88	Buf	6	1	1	2	-7	0	0	9	11.1	1	–	–	0	0	0	1	2	0	1	0	–	–	0	.33
88-89	Buf	1	0	1	1	0	0	0	2	0.0	0	–	–	0	–	–	0	0	0	0	0	0	0	0	1.00
91-92	Det	11	6	2	8	1	0	0	27	22.2	3	1	4	0	0	0	2	4	0	2	0	0	0	1	.73
92-93	Det	7	2	3	5	2	0	0	8	25.0	2	2	4	0	0	0	0	0	0	0	0	0	0	0	.71
93-94	Det	7	2	1	3	0	0	0	15	13.3	0	0	0	0	0	0	2	4	0	2	0	1	0	0	.43
94-95	Det	17	4	3	7	-6	0	0	41	9.8	2	1	3	0	0	0	1	5	1	0	1	0	0	0	.41
95-96	Fla	21	8	8	16	4	0	0	47	17.0	3	2	5	0	0	0	0	0	0	0	0	0	0	0	.76
96-97	Fla	5	2	0	2	-4	0	0	12	16.7	1	0	1	0	0	0	0	0	0	0	0	0	0	0	.40
98-99	Car	6	5	1	6	-2	1	1	23	21.7	1	1	2	0	0	0	1	2	0	1	0	1	0	0	1.00
9 Years		81	30	20	50	-12	1	1	184	16.3	13	–	–	0	–	–	7	17	1	6	1	–	–	1	.62

Steve Shields

(statistical profile on page 402)

Pos: G **Catches:** L **Ht:** 6'3" **Wt:** 210 **Born:** 7/19/72—Toronto, Ontario **Age:** 27

Overall																Pen Shot		Offense		
Year	Tm	GP	GS	TP	W	L	T	Min	GA	GAA	Shots	SvPct	ShO	OE	PPGA	SHGA	Shots	GA	G	A	PIM
95-96	Buf	2	0	0	1	0	0	75	4	3.20	32	.875	0	0	0	0	0	0	0	0	2
96-97	Buf	13	13	0	3	8	2	789	39	2.97	447	.913	0	7	10	0	0	0	0	0	4
97-98	Buf	16	10	0	3	6	4	785	37	2.83	408	.909	0	5	13	2	0	0	0	0	17
98-99	SJ	37	34	2	15	11	8	2162	80	2.22	1011	.921	4	17	32	0	1	0	0	1	6
4 Years		68	57	2	22	25	14	3811	160	2.52	1898	.916	4	29	55	2	1	0	0	1	29
Postseason																				
Year	Tm	GP	GS	TP	W	L	Pct	Min	GA	GAA	Shots	SvPct	ShO	OE	PPGA	SHGA	Shots	GA	G	A	PIM
96-97	Buf	10	9	1	4	6	.400	570	26	2.74	334	.922	1	4	7	0	1	1	0	0	9
98-99	SJ	1	1	0	0	1	.000	60	6	6.00	36	.833	0	0	2	1	0	0	0	0	0
2 Years		11	10	1	4	7	.364	630	32	3.05	370	.914	1	4	9	1	1	1	0	0	9

Mikhail Shtalenkov

(statistical profile on page 402)

Pos: G **Catches:** L **Ht:** 6'2" **Wt:** 185 **Born:** 10/20/65—Moscow, USSR **Age:** 34

Overall																Pen Shot		Offense		
Year	Tm	GP	GS	TP	W	L	T	Min	GA	GAA	Shots	SvPct	ShO	OE	PPGA	SHGA	Shots	GA	G	A	PIM
93-94	Anh	10	9	1	3	4	1	543	24	2.65	265	.909	0	3	7	2	0	0	0	0	0
94-95	Anh	18	14	5	4	7	1	810	49	3.63	448	.891	0	5	19	2	1	**1**	0	0	2

Overall																	Pen Shot		Offense		
Year	Tm	GP	GS	TP	W	L	T	Min	GA	GAA	Shots	SvPct	ShO	OE	PPGA	SHGA	Shots	GA	G	A	PIM
95-96	Anh	30	24	1	7	16	3	1637	85	3.12	814	.896	0	5	27	2	0	0	0	2	2
96-97	Anh	24	16	2	7	8	1	1079	52	2.89	539	.904	2	3	14	2	1	0	0	0	4
97-98	Anh	40	36	8	13	18	5	2049	110	3.22	1031	.893	1	11	42	5	0	0	0	1	0
98-99	2Tm	38	34	4	13	19	4	2062	90	2.62	886	.898	3	11	25	3	0	0	0	0	2
98-99	Edm	34	30	4	12	17	3	1819	81	2.67	782	.896	3	9	23	3	0	0	0	0	2
98-99	Pho	4	4	0	1	2	1	243	9	2.22	104	.913	0	2	2	0	0	0	0	0	0
6 Years		160	133	21	47	72	15	8180	410	3.01	3983	.897	6	38	134	16	2	1	0	3	10
Postseason																					
Year	Tm	GP	GS	TP	W	L	Pct	Min	GA	GAA	Shots	SvPct	ShO	OE	PPGA	SHGA	Shots	GA	G	A	PIM
96-97	Anh	4	2	0	0	3	.000	211	10	2.84	162	.938	0	1	3	0	0	0	0	0	2

Mike Sillinger

(statistical profile on page 373)

Pos: C **Shoots:** R **Ht:** 5'10" **Wt:** 194 **Born:** 6/29/71—Regina, Saskatchewan **Age:** 28

Overall										Power Play			Shorthand			Penalty							Misc	
Year	Tm	GP	G	A	Pts	+/-	GW	GT	S	SPct	G	A	Pts	G	A	Pts	Num	PIM	Maj	Mnr	Fgt	Rgh	HHT	Hat	P/G
90-91	Det	3	0	1	1	-2	0	0	6	0.0	0	0	0	0	0	0	0	0	0	0	0	0	0	0	.33
91-92		Did Not Play in Regular Season																							
92-93	Det	51	4	17	21	0	0	0	47	8.5	0	0	0	0	0	0	8	16	0	8	0	1	4	0	.41
93-94	Det	62	8	21	29	2	1	0	91	8.8	0	4	4	1	0	1	5	10	0	5	0	0	3	0	.47
94-95	2Tm	28	4	11	15	4	0	0	39	10.3	2	2	4	0	0	0	4	8	0	4	0	1	3	0	.54
95-96	2Tm	74	14	24	38	-18	2	0	159	8.8	7	9	16	1	0	1	19	38	0	19	0	3	10	0	.51
96-97	Van	78	17	20	37	-3	2	0	112	15.2	3	1	4	3	1	4	11	25	1	10	1	2	5	0	.47
97-98	2Tm	75	21	20	41	-11	1	0	96	**21.9**	2	5	7	4	1	5	21	50	0	20	0	2	12	0	.55
98-99	2Tm	79	8	5	13	-29	0	0	92	8.7	0	0	0	2	0	2	18	36	0	18	0	4	9	0	.16
94-95	Det	13	2	6	8	3	0	0	11	18.2	0	1	1	0	0	0	1	2	0	1	0	0	1	0	.62
94-95	Anh	15	2	5	7	1	0	0	28	7.1	2	1	3	0	0	0	3	6	0	3	0	1	2	0	.47
95-96	Anh	62	13	21	34	-20	2	0	143	9.1	7	9	16	0	0	0	16	32	0	16	0	3	8	0	.55
95-96	Van	12	1	3	4	2	0	0	16	6.3	0	0	0	1	0	1	3	6	0	3	0	0	2	0	.33
97-98	Van	48	10	9	19	-14	1	0	56	17.9	1	1	2	2	1	3	13	34	0	12	0	1	7	0	.40
97-98	Phi	27	11	11	22	3	0	0	40	27.5	1	4	5	2	0	2	8	16	0	8	0	1	5	0	.81
98-99	Phi	25	0	3	3	-9	0	0	23	0.0	0	0	0	0	0	0	4	8	0	4	0	0	1	0	.12
98-99	TB	54	8	2	10	-20	0	0	69	11.6	0	0	0	2	0	2	14	28	0	14	0	4	8	0	.19
8 Years		450	76	119	195	-57	6	0	642	11.8	14	21	35	11	2	13	86	183	1	84	1	13	46	0	.43
Postseason																									
Year	Tm	GP	G	A	Pts	+/-	GW	OT	S	SPct	G	A	Pts	G	A	Pts	Num	PIM	Maj	Mnr	Fgt	Rgh	HHT	Hat	P/G
90-91	Det	3	0	1	1	0	0	0	3	0.0	0	–	–	0	–	–	0	0	0	0	0	0	0	0	.33
91-92	Det	8	2	2	4	4	0	0	7	28.6	0	0	0	0	0	0	1	2	0	1	0	0	0	0	.50
95-96	Van	6	0	0	0	-5	0	0	5	0.0	0	0	0	0	0	0	1	2	0	1	0	0	0	0	.00
97-98	Phi	3	1	0	1	1	0	0	7	14.3	0	0	0	0	0	0	0	0	0	0	0	0	0	0	.33
4 Years		20	3	3	6	0	0	0	22	13.6	0	–	–	0	–	–	2	4	0	2	0	0	0	0	.30

Jon Sim

Pos: C **Shoots:** L **Ht:** 5'9" **Wt:** 175 **Born:** 9/29/77—New Glasgow, Nova Scotia **Age:** 22

Overall										Power Play			Shorthand			Penalty							Misc	
Year	Tm	GP	G	A	Pts	+/-	GW	GT	S	SPct	G	A	Pts	G	A	Pts	Num	PIM	Maj	Mnr	Fgt	Rgh	HHT	Hat	P/G
98-99	Dal	7	1	0	1	1	0	0	8	12.5	0	0	0	0	0	0	6	12	0	6	0	2	1	0	.14
Postseason																									
Year	Tm	GP	G	A	Pts	+/-	GW	OT	S	SPct	G	A	Pts	G	A	Pts	Num	PIM	Maj	Mnr	Fgt	Rgh	HHT	Hat	P/G
98-99	Dal	4	0	0	0	-1	0	0	1	0.0	0	0	0	0	0	0	0	0	0	0	0	0	0	0	.00

Chris Simon

(statistical profile on page 373)

Pos: LW **Shoots:** L **Ht:** 6'3" **Wt:** 225 **Born:** 1/30/72—Wawa, Ontario **Age:** 27

Overall										Power Play			Shorthand			Penalty							Misc	
Year	Tm	GP	G	A	Pts	+/-	GW	GT	S	SPct	G	A	Pts	G	A	Pts	Num	PIM	Maj	Mnr	Fgt	Rgh	HHT	Hat	P/G
92-93	Que	16	1	1	2	-2	1	0	15	6.7	0	0	0	0	0	0	16	67	1	11	1	4	2	0	.13
93-94	Que	37	4	4	8	-2	1	0	39	10.3	0	0	0	0	0	0	40	132	12	26	11	12	1	0	.22
94-95	Que	29	3	9	12	14	0	0	33	9.1	0	0	0	0	0	0	30	106	10	18	10	3	3	0	.41
95-96	Col	64	16	18	34	10	1	0	105	15.2	4	3	7	0	0	0	72	250	14	50	12	20	8	0	.53
96-97	Was	42	9	13	22	-1	1	0	89	10.1	3	0	3	0	0	0	53	165	9	40	9	15	6	0	.52
97-98	Was	28	7	10	17	-1	1	0	71	9.9	4	4	8	0	0	0	11	38	0	9	0	2	0	0	.61
98-99	Was	23	3	7	10	-4	0	0	29	10.3	0	0	0	0	0	0	20	48	0	19	0	6	0	0	.43
7 Years		239	43	62	105	14	5	0	381	11.3	11	7	18	0	0	0	242	806	46	173	43	62	20	0	.44

Postseason																									
Year	Tm	GP	G	A	Pts	+/–	GW	OT	S	SPct	G	A	Pts	G	A	Pts	Num	PIM	Maj	Mnr	Fgt	Rgh	HHT	Hat	P/G
92-93	Que	5	0	0	0	-2	0	0	8	0.0	0	0	0	0	0	0	5	26	0	3	0	2	1	0	.00
94-95	Que	6	1	1	2	-1	1	0	9	11.1	0	0	0	0	0	0	4	19	1	2	0	0	0	0	.33
95-96	Col	12	1	2	3	-2	0	0	9	11.1	0	1	1	0	0	0	4	11	1	3	1	0	0	0	.25
97-98	Was	18	1	0	1	-3	0	0	17	5.9	0	0	0	0	0	0	13	26	0	13	0	3	1	0	.06
4 Years		41	3	3	6	-8	1	0	43	7.0	0	1	1	0	0	0	26	82	2	21	1	5	2	0	.15

Reid Simpson

Pos: LW **Shoots:** L **Ht:** 6'2" **Wt:** 220 **Born:** 5/21/69—Flin Flon, Manitoba **Age:** 30

Overall											Power Play			Shorthand			Penalty							Misc	
Year	Tm	GP	G	A	Pts	+/–	GW	GT	S	SPct	G	A	Pts	G	A	Pts	Num	PIM	Maj	Mnr	Fgt	Rgh	HHT	Hat	P/G
91-92	Phi	1	0	0	0	0	0	0	0	–	0	0	0	0	0	0	0	0	0	0	0	0	0	0	.00
92-93	Min	1	0	0	0	0	0	0	0	–	0	0	0	0	0	0	1	5	1	0	1	0	0	0	.00
93-94		Did Not Play in NHL																							
94-95	NJ	9	0	0	0	-1	0	0	5	0.0	0	0	0	0	0	0	6	27	5	1	5	1	0	0	.00
95-96	NJ	23	1	5	6	2	0	0	8	12.5	0	0	0	0	0	0	20	79	13	7	13	3	0	0	.26
96-97	NJ	27	0	4	4	0	0	0	17	0.0	0	0	0	0	0	0	15	60	10	5	10	3	1	0	.15
97-98	2Tm	44	3	2	5	-3	0	0	24	12.5	1	0	1	0	0	0	31	118	16	14	16	6	2	0	.11
98-99	Chi	53	5	4	9	2	0	0	23	21.7	1	0	1	0	0	0	38	145	15	20	15	10	1	0	.17
97-98	NJ	6	0	0	0	-2	0	0	5	0.0	0	0	0	0	0	0	5	16	2	3	2	2	1	0	.00
97-98	Chi	38	3	2	5	-1	0	0	19	15.8	1	0	1	0	0	0	26	102	14	11	14	4	1	0	.13
7 Years		158	9	15	24	0	0	0	77	11.7	2	0	2	0	0	0	111	434	60	47	60	23	4	0	.15
Postseason																									
Year	Tm	GP	G	A	Pts	+/–	GW	OT	S	SPct	G	A	Pts	G	A	Pts	Num	PIM	Maj	Mnr	Fgt	Rgh	HHT	Hat	P/G
96-97	NJ	5	0	0	0	-1	0	0	0	–	0	0	0	0	0	0	5	29	1	2	1	0	0	0	.00

Todd Simpson

(statistical profile on page 373)

Pos: D **Shoots:** L **Ht:** 6'3" **Wt:** 215 **Born:** 5/28/73—Edmonton, Alberta **Age:** 26

Overall											Power Play			Shorthand			Penalty							Misc	
Year	Tm	GP	G	A	Pts	+/–	GW	GT	S	SPct	G	A	Pts	G	A	Pts	Num	PIM	Maj	Mnr	Fgt	Rgh	HHT	Hat	P/G
95-96	Cgy	6	0	0	0	0	0	0	3	0.0	0	0	0	0	0	0	10	32	4	6	4	4	0	0	.00
96-97	Cgy	**82**	1	13	14	-14	0	1	85	1.2	0	0	0	0	0	0	65	208	18	44	17	12	12	0	.17
97-98	Cgy	53	1	5	6	-10	1	0	51	2.0	0	0	0	0	1	1	40	109	7	32	7	8	15	0	.11
98-99	Cgy	73	2	8	10	18	0	0	52	3.8	0	0	0	0	1	1	51	151	11	38	11	10	3	0	.14
4 Years		214	4	26	30	-6	1	1	191	2.1	0	0	0	0	2	2	166	500	40	120	39	34	30	0	.14

Jarrod Skalde

Pos: C **Shoots:** L **Ht:** 6'0" **Wt:** 190 **Born:** 2/26/71—Niagara Falls, Ontario **Age:** 28

Overall											Power Play			Shorthand			Penalty							Misc	
Year	Tm	GP	G	A	Pts	+/–	GW	GT	S	SPct	G	A	Pts	G	A	Pts	Num	PIM	Maj	Mnr	Fgt	Rgh	HHT	Hat	P/G
90-91	NJ	1	0	1	1	0	0	0	2	0.0	0	0	0	0	0	0	0	0	0	0	0	0	0	0	1.00
91-92	NJ	15	2	4	6	-1	2	0	25	8.0	0	0	0	0	0	0	2	4	0	2	0	0	1	0	.40
92-93	NJ	11	0	2	2	-3	0	0	11	0.0	0	0	0	0	0	0	2	4	0	2	0	0	0	0	.18
93-94	Anh	20	5	4	9	-3	2	0	25	20.0	2	1	3	0	0	0	5	10	0	5	0	1	1	0	.45
94-95		Did Not Play in NHL																							
95-96	Cgy	1	0	0	0	0	0	0	0	–	0	0	0	0	0	0	0	0	0	0	0	0	0	0	.00
96-97		Did Not Play in NHL																							
97-98	3Tm	30	4	7	11	-2	0	0	34	11.8	0	1	1	0	0	0	9	18	0	9	0	4	4	0	.37
98-99	SJ	17	1	1	2	-6	0	1	17	5.9	0	0	0	0	0	0	2	4	0	2	0	0	0	0	.12
97-98	SJ	22	4	6	10	-2	0	0	30	13.3	0	1	1	0	0	0	7	14	0	7	0	4	2	0	.45
97-98	Chi	7	0	1	1	0	0	0	4	0.0	0	0	0	0	0	0	2	4	0	2	0	0	2	0	.14
97-98	Dal	1	0	0	0	0	0	0	0	–	0	0	0	0	0	0	0	0	0	0	0	0	0	0	.00
7 Years		95	12	19	31	-15	4	1	114	10.5	2	2	4	0	0	0	20	40	0	20	0	5	6	0	.33

Andrei Skopintsev

Pos: D **Shoots:** R **Ht:** 6'0" **Wt:** 185 **Born:** 9/28/71—Elekrostal, USSR **Age:** 28

Overall											Power Play			Shorthand			Penalty							Misc	
Year	Tm	GP	G	A	Pts	+/–	GW	GT	S	SPct	G	A	Pts	G	A	Pts	Num	PIM	Maj	Mnr	Fgt	Rgh	HHT	Hat	P/G
98-99	TB	19	1	1	2	1	0	0	17	5.9	0	0	0	0	0	0	5	10	0	5	0	1	3	0	.11

Karlis Skrastinsh

Pos: D **Shoots:** L **Ht:** 6'1" **Wt:** 196 **Born:** 7/9/74—Riga, USSR **Age:** 25

			Overall								Power Play			Shorthand			Penalty							Misc	
Year	Tm	GP	G	A	Pts	+/–	GW	GT	S	SPct	G	A	Pts	G	A	Pts	Num	PIM	Maj	Mnr	Fgt	Rgh	HHT	Hat	P/G
98-99	Nsh	2	0	1	1	0	0	0	0	–	0	0	0	0	0	0	0	0	0	0	0	0	0	0	.50

Pavel Skrbek

Pos: D **Shoots:** L **Ht:** 6'3" **Wt:** 212 **Born:** 8/8/78—Kladno, Czechoslovakia **Age:** 21

			Overall								Power Play			Shorthand			Penalty							Misc	
Year	Tm	GP	G	A	Pts	+/–	GW	GT	S	SPct	G	A	Pts	G	A	Pts	Num	PIM	Maj	Mnr	Fgt	Rgh	HHT	Hat	P/G
98-99	Pit	4	0	0	0	2	0	0	1	0.0	0	0	0	0	0	0	1	2	0	1	0	0	1	0	.00

Brian Skrudland

Pos: C **Shoots:** L **Ht:** 6'0" **Wt:** 200 **Born:** 7/31/63—Peace River, Alberta **Age:** 36

			Overall								Power Play			Shorthand			Penalty							Misc	
Year	Tm	GP	G	A	Pts	+/–	GW	GT	S	SPct	G	A	Pts	G	A	Pts	Num	PIM	Maj	Mnr	Fgt	Rgh	HHT	Hat	P/G
85-86	Mon	65	9	13	22	3	0	0	62	14.5	0	–	–	2	–	–	–	57	–	–	–	–	–	0	.34
86-87	Mon	79	11	17	28	18	0	0	72	15.3	0	–	–	1	–	–	–	107	–	–	–	–	–	0	.35
87-88	Mon	79	12	24	36	14	3	0	96	12.5	0	–	–	1	–	–	–	112	–	–	–	–	–	0	.46
88-89	Mon	71	12	29	41	22	5	0	98	12.2	1	–	–	1	–	–	–	84	–	–	–	–	–	0	.58
89-90	Mon	59	11	31	42	21	1	0	70	15.7	4	–	–	0	–	–	–	56	–	–	–	–	–	0	.71
90-91	Mon	57	15	19	34	12	2	0	71	21.1	1	–	–	1	–	–	–	85	–	–	–	–	–	0	.60
91-92	Mon	42	3	3	6	-4	1	0	51	5.9	0	0	0	0	0	0	14	36	0	13	0	1	4	0	.14
92-93	2Tm	39	7	7	14	4	1	0	51	13.7	0	0	0	2	1	3	23	65	1	20	0	4	4	0	.36
93-94	Fla	79	15	25	40	13	1	0	110	13.6	0	0	0	2	1	3	52	136	0	48	0	5	25	0	.51
94-95	Fla	47	5	9	14	0	0	0	44	11.4	1	0	1	0	0	0	33	88	2	29	1	9	12	0	.30
95-96	Fla	79	7	20	27	6	1	0	90	7.8	0	1	1	1	1	2	48	129	3	42	2	6	15	0	.34
96-97	Fla	51	5	13	18	4	2	0	57	8.8	0	0	0	0	0	0	20	48	0	19	0	4	7	0	.35
97-98	2Tm	72	7	6	13	-6	1	0	55	12.7	0	0	0	0	0	0	23	49	1	22	1	2	12	0	.18
98-99	Dal	40	4	1	5	2	1	0	33	12.1	0	0	0	0	1	1	15	33	1	14	1	2	5	0	.13
92-93	Mon	23	5	3	8	1	1	0	29	17.2	0	0	0	2	0	2	18	55	1	15	0	4	3	0	.35
92-93	Cgy	16	2	4	6	3	0	0	22	9.1	0	0	0	0	1	1	5	10	0	5	0	0	1	0	.38
97-98	NYR	59	5	6	11	-4	1	0	42	11.9	0	0	0	0	0	0	18	39	1	17	1	2	8	0	.19
97-98	Dal	13	2	0	2	-2	0	0	13	15.4	0	0	0	0	0	0	5	10	0	5	0	0	4	0	.15
14 Years		859	123	217	340	109	19	0	960	12.8	7	–	–	11	–	–	–	1085	–	–	–	–	–	0	.40
											Postseason														
Year	Tm	GP	G	A	Pts	+/–	GW	OT	S	SPct	G	A	Pts	G	A	Pts	Num	PIM	Maj	Mnr	Fgt	Rgh	HHT	Hat	P/G
85-86	Mon	20	2	4	6	8	1	1	21	9.5	0	–	–	0	–	–	–	76	–	–	–	–	–	0	.30
86-87	Mon	14	1	5	6	2	0	0	11	9.1	0	–	–	0	–	–	–	29	–	–	–	–	–	0	.43
87-88	Mon	11	1	5	6	5	0	0	14	7.1	0	–	–	0	–	–	–	24	–	–	–	–	–	0	.55
88-89	Mon	21	3	7	10	3	0	0	24	12.5	0	–	–	0	–	–	–	40	–	–	–	–	–	0	.48
89-90	Mon	11	3	5	8	5	1	1	18	16.7	0	–	–	0	0	0	–	30	–	–	–	–	–	0	.73
90-91	Mon	13	3	10	13	7	0	0	15	20.0	1	–	–	0	–	–	–	42	–	–	–	–	–	0	1.00
91-92	Mon	11	1	1	2	-1	0	0	15	6.7	0	0	0	0	0	0	10	20	0	10	0	1	3	0	.18
92-93	Cgy	6	0	3	3	0	0	0	5	0.0	0	0	0	0	0	0	6	12	0	6	0	2	0	0	.50
95-96	Fla	21	1	3	4	6	0	0	27	3.7	0	0	0	0	0	0	9	18	0	9	0	4	2	0	.19
97-98	Dal	17	0	1	1	0	0	0	14	0.0	0	0	0	0	0	0	8	16	0	8	0	3	0	0	.06
98-99	Dal	19	0	2	2	0	0	0	10	0.0	0	0	0	0	0	0	8	16	0	8	0	2	3	0	.11
11 Years		164	15	46	61	35	2	2	174	8.6	1	–	–	0	–	–	–	323	–	–	–	–	–	0	.37

Peter Skudra

(statistical profile on page 402)

Pos: G **Catches:** L **Ht:** 6'1" **Wt:** 182 **Born:** 4/24/73—Riga, USSR **Age:** 26

					Overall												Pen Shot		Offense		
Year	Tm	GP	GS	TP	W	L	T	Min	GA	GAA	Shots	SvPct	ShO	OE	PPGA	SHGA	Shots	GA	G	A	PIM
97-98	Pit	17	11	3	6	4	3	851	26	1.83	341	.924	0	1	4	2	0	0	0	1	2
98-99	Pit	37	28	5	15	11	5	1914	89	2.79	822	.892	3	10	21	8	0	0	0	0	2
2 Years		54	39	8	21	15	8	2765	115	2.50	1163	.901	3	11	25	10	0	0	0	1	4

John Slaney

(statistical profile on page 374)

Pos: D **Shoots:** L **Ht:** 6'0" **Wt:** 185 **Born:** 2/2/72—St. John's, Newfoundland **Age:** 27

Overall											Power Play			Shorthand			Penalty							Misc	
Year	Tm	GP	G	A	Pts	+/-	GW	GT	S	SPct	G	A	Pts	G	A	Pts	Num	PIM	Maj	Mnr	Fgt	Rgh	HHT	Hat	P/G
93-94	Was	47	7	9	16	3	1	0	70	10.0	3	4	7	0	0	0	8	27	1	6	0	0	5	0	.34
94-95	Was	16	0	3	3	-3	0	0	21	0.0	0	3	3	0	0	0	3	6	0	3	0	1	1	0	.19
95-96	2Tm	38	6	14	20	7	0	0	75	8.0	3	5	8	1	2	3	7	14	0	7	0	0	2	0	.53
96-97	LA	32	3	11	14	-10	1	0	60	5.0	1	3	4	0	0	0	2	4	0	2	0	0	2	0	.44
97-98	Pho	55	3	14	17	-3	1	0	74	4.1	1	6	7	0	0	0	12	24	0	12	0	2	2	0	.31
98-99	Nsh	46	2	12	14	-12	1	0	84	2.4	0	6	6	0	1	1	7	14	0	7	0	0	5	0	.30
95-96	Col	7	0	3	3	2	0	0	12	0.0	0	1	1	0	0	0	2	4	0	2	0	0	1	0	.43
95-96	LA	31	6	11	17	5	0	0	63	9.5	3	4	7	1	2	3	5	10	0	5	0	0	1	0	.55
6 Years		234	21	63	84	-18	4	0	384	5.5	8	27	35	1	3	4	39	89	1	37	0	3	17	0	.36

Postseason

Year	Tm	GP	G	A	Pts	+/-	GW	OT	S	SPct	G	A	Pts	G	A	Pts	Num	PIM	Maj	Mnr	Fgt	Rgh	HHT	Hat	P/G
93-94	Was	11	1	1	2	-1	0	0	16	6.3	1	0	1	0	0	0	1	2	0	1	0	0	1	0	.18

Jiri Slegr

(statistical profile on page 374)

Pos: D **Shoots:** L **Ht:** 6'0" **Wt:** 217 **Born:** 5/30/71—Jihlava, Czechoslovakia **Age:** 28

Overall											Power Play			Shorthand			Penalty							Misc	
Year	Tm	GP	G	A	Pts	+/-	GW	GT	S	SPct	G	A	Pts	G	A	Pts	Num	PIM	Maj	Mnr	Fgt	Rgh	HHT	Hat	P/G
92-93	Van	41	4	22	26	16	0	0	89	4.5	2	8	10	0	0	0	38	109	3	32	3	3	13	0	.63
93-94	Van	78	5	33	38	0	0	0	160	3.1	1	19	20	0	0	0	32	86	2	28	1	6	13	0	.49
94-95	2Tm	31	2	10	12	-5	1	0	69	2.9	1	2	3	0	1	1	23	46	0	23	0	8	7	0	.39
95-96	Edm	57	4	13	17	-1	1	0	91	4.4	0	5	5	1	0	1	30	74	2	27	2	4	16	0	.30
96-97											Did Not Play in NHL														
97-98	Pit	73	5	12	17	10	0	0	131	3.8	1	4	5	1	1	2	39	109	5	32	5	2	17	0	.23
98-99	Pit	63	3	20	23	13	0	0	91	3.3	1	0	1	0	2	2	33	86	4	28	4	6	5	0	.37
94-95	Van	19	1	5	6	0	1	0	42	2.4	0	1	1	0	0	0	16	32	0	16	0	4	6	0	.32
94-95	Edm	12	1	5	6	-5	0	0	27	3.7	1	1	2	0	1	1	7	14	0	7	0	4	1	0	.50
6 Years		343	23	110	133	33	2	0	631	3.6	6	38	44	2	4	6	195	510	16	170	15	29	71	0	.39

Postseason

Year	Tm	GP	G	A	Pts	+/-	GW	OT	S	SPct	G	A	Pts	G	A	Pts	Num	PIM	Maj	Mnr	Fgt	Rgh	HHT	Hat	P/G
92-93	Van	5	0	3	3	0	0	0	5	0.0	0	2	2	0	0	0	2	4	0	2	0	0	1	0	.60
97-98	Pit	6	0	4	4	3	0	0	10	0.0	0	1	1	0	1	1	1	2	0	1	0	0	1	0	.67
98-99	Pit	13	1	3	4	1	1	0	17	5.9	0	0	0	0	0	0	6	12	0	6	0	1	3	0	.31
3 Years		24	1	10	11	4	1	0	32	3.1	0	3	3	0	1	1	9	18	0	9	0	1	5	0	.46

Blake Sloan

Pos: RW **Shoots:** R **Ht:** 5'10" **Wt:** 193 **Born:** 7/27/75—Park Ridge, Illinois **Age:** 24

Overall											Power Play			Shorthand			Penalty							Misc	
Year	Tm	GP	G	A	Pts	+/-	GW	GT	S	SPct	G	A	Pts	G	A	Pts	Num	PIM	Maj	Mnr	Fgt	Rgh	HHT	Hat	P/G
98-99	Dal	14	0	0	0	-1	0	0	7	0.0	0	0	0	0	0	0	5	10	0	5	0	1	4	0	.00

Postseason

Year	Tm	GP	G	A	Pts	+/-	GW	OT	S	SPct	G	A	Pts	G	A	Pts	Num	PIM	Maj	Mnr	Fgt	Rgh	HHT	Hat	P/G
98-99	Dal	19	0	2	2	-1	0	0	7	0.0	0	0	0	0	0	0	4	8	0	4	0	1	0	0	.11

Richard Smehlik

(statistical profile on page 374)

Pos: D **Shoots:** L **Ht:** 6'3" **Wt:** 222 **Born:** 1/23/70—Ostrava, Czechoslovakia **Age:** 29

Overall											Power Play			Shorthand			Penalty							Misc	
Year	Tm	GP	G	A	Pts	+/-	GW	GT	S	SPct	G	A	Pts	G	A	Pts	Num	PIM	Maj	Mnr	Fgt	Rgh	HHT	Hat	P/G
92-93	Buf	80	4	27	31	9	0	0	82	4.9	0	1	1	0	2	2	28	59	1	27	1	1	15	0	.39
93-94	Buf	84	14	27	41	22	1	1	106	13.2	3	7	10	3	3	6	29	69	1	27	0	3	16	0	.49
94-95	Buf	39	4	7	11	5	1	0	49	8.2	0	2	2	1	0	1	20	46	2	18	2	1	8	0	.28
95-96											Did Not Play in NHL														
96-97	Buf	62	11	19	30	19	1	0	100	11.0	2	4	6	0	0	0	20	43	1	19	1	2	11	0	.48
97-98	Buf	72	3	17	20	11	0	0	90	3.3	0	4	4	1	2	3	27	62	0	26	0	4	12	0	.28
98-99	Buf	72	3	11	14	-9	0	0	61	4.9	0	1	1	0	0	0	22	44	0	22	0	0	11	0	.19
6 Years		409	39	108	147	57	3	1	488	8.0	5	19	24	5	7	12	146	323	5	139	4	11	73	0	.36

Postseason

Year	Tm	GP	G	A	Pts	+/-	GW	OT	S	SPct	G	A	Pts	G	A	Pts	Num	PIM	Maj	Mnr	Fgt	Rgh	HHT	Hat	P/G
92-93	Buf	8	0	4	4	3	0	0	11	0.0	0	1	1	0	0	0	1	2	0	1	0	0	0	0	.50
93-94	Buf	7	0	2	2	-1	0	0	2	0.0	0	0	0	0	0	0	5	10	0	5	0	1	1	0	.29

Postseason																										
Year	Tm	GP	G	A	Pts	+/-	GW	OT	S	SPct	G	A	Pts	G	A	Pts	Num	PIM	Maj	Mnr	Fgt	Rgh	HHT	Hat	P/G
94-95	Buf	5	0	0	0	-1	0	0	3	0.0	0	0	0	0	0	0	1	2	0	1	0	0	1	0	.00
96-97	Buf	12	0	2	2	0	0	0	17	0.0	0	1	1	0	0	0	2	4	0	2	0	0	1	0	.17
97-98	Buf	15	0	2	2	3	0	0	12	0.0	0	1	1	0	0	0	3	6	0	3	0	0	1	0	.13
98-99	Buf	21	0	3	3	-4	0	0	20	0.0	0	1	1	0	0	0	5	10	0	5	0	1	1	0	.14
6 Years		68	0	13	13	0	0	0	65	0.0	0	4	4	0	0	0	17	34	0	17	0	2	5	0	.19

Brandon Smith

Pos: D **Shoots:** L **Ht:** 6'1" **Wt:** 196 **Born:** 2/25/73—Hazelton, British Columbia **Age:** 26

Overall											Power Play			Shorthand			Penalty							Misc	
Year	Tm	GP	G	A	Pts	+/-	GW	GT	S	SPct	G	A	Pts	G	A	Pts	Num	PIM	Maj	Mnr	Fgt	Rgh	HHT	Hat	P/G
98-99	Bos	5	0	0	0	2	0	0	2	0.0	0	0	0	0	0	0	0	0	0	0	0	0	0	0	.00

Dan Smith

Pos: D **Shoots:** L **Ht:** 6'2" **Wt:** 195 **Born:** 10/19/76—Fernie, British Columbia **Age:** 23

Overall											Power Play			Shorthand			Penalty							Misc	
Year	Tm	GP	G	A	Pts	+/-	GW	GT	S	SPct	G	A	Pts	G	A	Pts	Num	PIM	Maj	Mnr	Fgt	Rgh	HHT	Hat	P/G
98-99	Col	12	0	0	0	5	0	0	6	0.0	0	0	0	0	0	0	3	9	1	2	1	0	2	0	.00

Geoff Smith

Pos: D **Shoots:** L **Ht:** 6'3" **Wt:** 195 **Born:** 3/7/69—Edmonton, Alberta **Age:** 30

Overall											Power Play			Shorthand			Penalty							Misc	
Year	Tm	GP	G	A	Pts	+/-	GW	GT	S	SPct	G	A	Pts	G	A	Pts	Num	PIM	Maj	Mnr	Fgt	Rgh	HHT	Hat	P/G
89-90	Edm	74	4	11	15	13	0	0	66	6.1	1	1	2	0	0	0	–	52	–	–	–	–	–	0	.20
90-91	Edm	59	1	12	13	13	0	0	66	1.5	0	4	4	0	0	0	–	55	–	–	–	–	–	0	.22
91-92	Edm	74	2	16	18	-5	0	0	61	3.3	0	5	5	0	0	0	16	43	1	14	1	0	9	0	.24
92-93	Edm	78	4	14	18	-11	0	0	67	6.0	0	2	2	1	1	2	11	30	0	10	0	0	5	0	.23
93-94	2Tm	77	1	8	9	-13	0	0	67	1.5	0	0	0	0	0	0	25	50	0	25	0	2	11	0	.12
94-95	Fla	47	2	4	6	-5	0	0	40	5.0	0	1	1	0	0	0	11	22	0	11	0	2	7	0	.13
95-96	Fla	31	3	7	10	-4	0	0	34	8.8	2	0	2	0	0	0	10	20	0	10	0	1	4	0	.32
96-97	Fla	3	0	0	0	1	0	0	2	0.0	0	0	0	0	0	0	1	2	0	1	0	0	1	0	.00
97-98	NYR	15	1	1	2	-4	0	0	11	9.1	1	0	1	0	0	0	3	6	0	3	0	0	1	0	.13
98-99	NYR	4	0	0	0	-5	0	0	0	–	0	0	0	0	0	0	1	2	0	1	0	0	0	0	.00
93-94	Edm	21	0	3	3	-10	0	0	23	0.0	0	0	0	0	0	0	6	12	0	6	0	1	4	0	.14
93-94	Fla	56	1	5	6	-3	0	0	44	2.3	0	0	0	0	0	0	19	38	0	19	0	1	7	0	.11
10 Years		462	18	73	91	-20	0	0	414	4.3	4	13	17	1	1	2	–	282	–	–	–	–	–	0	.20
Postseason																									
Year	Tm	GP	G	A	Pts	+/-	GW	OT	S	SPct	G	A	Pts	G	A	Pts	Num	PIM	Maj	Mnr	Fgt	Rgh	HHT	Hat	P/G
89-90	Edm	3	0	0	0	0	0	0	1	0.0	0	0	0	0	0	0	0	0	0	0	0	0	0	0	.00
90-91	Edm	4	0	0	0	5	0	0	5	0.0	0	0	0	0	0	0	0	0	0	0	0	0	0	0	.00
91-92	Edm	5	0	1	1	2	0	0	5	0.0	0	0	0	0	0	0	3	6	0	3	0	1	1	0	.20
95-96	Fla	1	0	0	0	-1	0	0	0	–	0	0	0	0	0	0	1	2	0	1	0	0	0	0	.00
4 Years		13	0	1	1	6	0	0	11	0.0	0	0	0	0	0	0	4	8	0	4	0	1	1	0	.08

Jason Smith

(statistical profile on page 374)

Pos: D **Shoots:** R **Ht:** 6'3" **Wt:** 205 **Born:** 11/2/73—Calgary, Alberta **Age:** 26

Overall											Power Play			Shorthand			Penalty							Misc	
Year	Tm	GP	G	A	Pts	+/-	GW	GT	S	SPct	G	A	Pts	G	A	Pts	Num	PIM	Maj	Mnr	Fgt	Rgh	HHT	Hat	P/G
93-94	NJ	41	0	5	5	7	0	0	47	0.0	0	0	0	0	0	0	13	43	3	9	3	8	1	0	.12
94-95	NJ	2	0	0	0	-3	0	0	5	0.0	0	0	0	0	0	0	0	0	0	0	0	0	0	0	.00
95-96	NJ	64	2	1	3	5	0	0	52	3.8	0	0	0	0	0	0	31	86	8	23	7	8	7	0	.05
96-97	2Tm	78	1	7	8	-12	0	0	74	1.4	0	0	0	0	0	0	17	54	4	12	4	5	2	0	.10
97-98	Tor	81	3	13	16	-5	0	0	97	3.1	0	0	0	0	0	0	26	100	8	15	8	8	2	0	.20
98-99	2Tm	72	3	12	15	-9	0	0	68	4.4	0	0	0	0	0	0	14	51	5	8	5	3	2	0	.21
96-97	NJ	57	1	2	3	-8	0	0	48	2.1	0	0	0	0	0	0	9	38	4	4	4	2	0	0	.05
96-97	Tor	21	0	5	5	-4	0	0	26	0.0	0	0	0	0	0	0	8	16	0	8	0	3	2	0	.24
98-99	Tor	60	2	11	13	-9	0	0	53	3.8	0	0	0	0	0	0	10	40	4	5	4	2	2	0	.22
98-99	Edm	12	1	1	2	0	0	0	15	6.7	0	0	0	0	0	0	4	11	1	3	1	1	0	0	.17
6 Years		338	9	38	47	-17	0	0	343	2.6	0	0	0	0	0	0	101	334	28	67	27	32	14	0	.14
Postseason																									
Year	Tm	GP	G	A	Pts	+/-	GW	OT	S	SPct	G	A	Pts	G	A	Pts	Num	PIM	Maj	Mnr	Fgt	Rgh	HHT	Hat	P/G
93-94	NJ	6	0	0	0	-1	0	0	2	0.0	0	0	0	0	0	0	2	7	1	1	1	1	0	0	.00

Year	Tm	GP	G	A	Pts	+/–	GW	OT	S	SPct	G	A	Pts	G	A	Pts	Num	PIM	Maj	Mnr	Fgt	Rgh	HHT	Hat	P/G
Postseason																									
98-99	Edm	4	0	1	1	0	0	0	1	0.0	0	0	0	0	0	0	2	4	0	2	0	1	0	0	.25
2 Years		10	0	1	1	-1	0	0	3	0.0	0	0	0	0	0	0	4	11	1	3	1	2	0	0	.10

Steve Smith

(statistical profile on page 375)

Pos: D **Shoots:** L **Ht:** 6'4" **Wt:** 215 **Born:** 4/30/63—Glasgow, Scotland **Age:** 36

Overall											Power Play			Shorthand			Penalty							Misc	
Year	Tm	GP	G	A	Pts	+/–	GW	GT	S	SPct	G	A	Pts	G	A	Pts	Num	PIM	Maj	Mnr	Fgt	Rgh	HHT	Hat	P/G
84-85	Edm	2	0	0	0	-2	0	0	3	0.0	0	0	0	0	0	0	1	2	0	1	0	–	–	0	.00
85-86	Edm	55	4	20	24	30	1	0	74	5.4	1	–	–	0	–	–	–	166	–	–	–	–	–	0	.44
86-87	Edm	62	7	15	22	11	1	0	71	9.9	2	–	–	0	–	–	–	165	–	–	–	–	–	0	.35
87-88	Edm	79	12	43	55	40	1	0	116	10.3	5	–	–	0	–	–	–	286	–	–	–	–	–	0	.70
88-89	Edm	35	3	19	22	5	0	0	47	6.4	0	5	5	0	2	2	–	97	–	–	–	–	–	0	.63
89-90	Edm	75	7	34	41	6	1	0	125	5.6	3	18	21	0	1	1	–	171	–	–	–	–	–	0	.55
90-91	Edm*	77	13	41	54	14	2	0	114	11.4	4	15	19	0	2	2	–	193	–	–	–	–	–	0	.70
91-92	Chi	76	9	21	30	23	1	0	153	5.9	3	12	15	0	1	1	93	304	10	72	9	17	15	0	.39
92-93	Chi	78	10	47	57	12	2	0	212	4.7	7	31	38	1	1	2	71	214	8	57	6	15	16	0	.73
93-94	Chi	57	5	22	27	-5	1	0	89	5.6	1	11	12	0	0	0	62	174	6	52	5	16	14	0	.47
94-95	Chi	48	1	12	13	6	0	0	43	2.3	0	3	3	0	0	0	47	128	6	39	5	10	13	0	.27
95-96	Chi	37	0	9	9	12	0	0	17	0.0	0	2	2	0	0	0	27	71	3	23	3	11	5	0	.24
96-97	Chi	21	0	0	0	4	0	0	7	0.0	0	0	0	0	0	0	13	29	1	12	1	2	4	0	.00
97-98		Did Not Play in NHL																							
98-99	Cgy	69	1	14	15	3	0	0	42	2.4	0	2	2	0	0	0	40	80	0	40	0	1	14	0	.22
14 Years		771	72	297	369	159	10	0	1113	6.5	26	–	–	1	–	–	–	2080	–	–	–	–	–	0	.48
Postseason																									
Year	Tm	GP	G	A	Pts	+/–	GW	OT	S	SPct	G	A	Pts	G	A	Pts	Num	PIM	Maj	Mnr	Fgt	Rgh	HHT	Hat	P/G
85-86	Edm	6	0	1	1	4	0	0	5	0.0	0	–	–	0	–	–	–	14	–	–	–	–	–	0	.17
86-87	Edm	15	1	3	4	9	0	0	19	5.3	0	–	–	0	–	–	–	45	–	–	–	–	–	0	.27
87-88	Edm	19	1	11	12	16	0	0	26	3.8	1	–	–	0	–	–	–	55	–	–	–	–	–	0	.63
88-89	Edm	7	2	2	4	3	1	0	6	33.3	0	–	–	0	–	–	–	20	–	–	–	–	–	0	.57
89-90	Edm	22	5	10	15	15	1	0	35	14.3	0	–	–	1	–	–	–	37	–	–	–	–	–	0	.68
90-91	Edm	18	1	2	3	-8	0	0	30	3.3	1	–	–	0	0	0	–	45	–	–	–	–	–	0	.17
91-92	Chi	18	1	11	12	12	0	0	37	2.7	1	2	3	0	0	0	8	16	0	8	0	1	4	0	.67
92-93	Chi	4	0	0	0	-2	0	0	9	0.0	0	0	0	0	0	0	5	10	0	5	0	1	0	0	.00
94-95	Chi	16	0	1	1	2	0	0	11	0.0	0	0	0	0	0	0	13	26	0	13	0	1	6	0	.06
95-96	Chi	6	0	0	0	-2	0	0	3	0.0	0	0	0	0	0	0	4	16	0	3	0	0	0	0	.00
96-97	Chi	3	0	0	0	0	0	0	3	0.0	0	0	0	0	0	0	2	4	0	2	0	0	0	0	.00
11 Years		134	11	41	52	49	2	0	184	6.0	3	–	–	1	–	–	–	288	–	–	–	–	–	0	.39

Bryan Smolinski

(statistical profile on page 375)

Pos: C **Shoots:** R **Ht:** 6'1" **Wt:** 202 **Born:** 12/27/71—Toledo, Ohio **Age:** 28

Overall											Power Play			Shorthand			Penalty							Misc	
Year	Tm	GP	G	A	Pts	+/–	GW	GT	S	SPct	G	A	Pts	G	A	Pts	Num	PIM	Maj	Mnr	Fgt	Rgh	HHT	Hat	P/G
92-93	Bos	9	1	3	4	3	0	0	10	10.0	0	0	0	0	0	0	0	0	0	0	0	0	0	0	.44
93-94	Bos	83	31	20	51	4	5	0	179	17.3	4	4	8	3	1	4	31	82	4	26	3	6	7	0	.61
94-95	Bos	44	18	13	31	-3	5	0	121	14.9	6	3	9	0	0	0	14	31	1	13	1	5	5	1	.70
95-96	Pit	81	24	40	64	6	1	0	229	10.5	8	10	18	2	0	2	33	69	1	32	1	6	9	0	.79
96-97	NYI	64	28	28	56	8	1	1	183	15.3	9	9	18	0	0	0	11	25	1	10	1	1	1	0	.88
97-98	NYI	81	13	30	43	-16	4	0	203	6.4	3	7	10	0	1	1	17	34	0	17	0	3	10	0	.53
98-99	NYI	82	16	24	40	-7	3	0	223	7.2	7	8	15	0	0	0	23	49	1	22	1	4	6	0	.49
7 Years		444	131	158	289	-5	19	1	1148	11.4	37	41	78	5	2	7	129	290	8	120	7	25	38	1	.65
Postseason																									
Year	Tm	GP	G	A	Pts	+/–	GW	OT	S	SPct	G	A	Pts	G	A	Pts	Num	PIM	Maj	Mnr	Fgt	Rgh	HHT	Hat	P/G
92-93	Bos	4	1	0	1	-1	0	0	3	33.3	0	0	0	0	0	0	1	2	0	1	0	0	0	0	.25
93-94	Bos	13	5	4	9	-1	0	0	30	16.7	2	1	3	0	0	0	2	4	0	2	0	1	0	0	.69
94-95	Bos	5	0	1	1	-2	0	0	12	0.0	0	1	1	0	0	0	2	4	0	2	0	0	1	0	.20
95-96	Pit	18	5	4	9	-4	1	0	46	10.9	0	0	0	0	0	0	5	10	0	5	0	1	2	0	.50
4 Years		40	11	9	20	-8	1	0	91	12.1	2	2	4	0	0	0	10	20	0	10	0	2	3	0	.50

Brad Smyth

Pos: RW **Shoots:** R **Ht:** 6'0" **Wt:** 200 **Born:** 3/13/73—Ottawa, Ontario **Age:** 26

Overall											Power Play			Shorthand			Penalty							Misc	
Year	Tm	GP	G	A	Pts	+/-	GW	GT	S	SPct	G	A	Pts	G	A	Pts	Num	PIM	Maj	Mnr	Fgt	Rgh	HHT	Hat	P/G
95-96	Fla	7	1	1	2	-3	0	0	12	8.3	1	1	2	0	0	0	2	4	0	2	0	1	0	0	.29
96-97	2Tm	52	9	8	17	-10	1	1	84	10.7	0	2	2	0	0	0	18	76	8	8	8	1	6	0	.33
97-98	2Tm	10	1	3	4	-1	0	0	13	7.7	0	2	2	0	0	0	2	4	0	2	0	0	2	0	.40
98-99	Nsh	3	0	0	0	-1	0	0	5	0.0	0	0	0	0	0	0	3	6	0	3	0	0	1	0	.00
96-97	Fla	8	1	0	1	-3	0	0	10	10.0	0	0	0	0	0	0	1	2	0	1	0	0	1	0	.13
96-97	LA	44	8	8	16	-7	1	1	74	10.8	0	2	2	0	0	0	17	74	8	7	8	1	5	0	.36
97-98	LA	9	1	3	4	-1	0	0	12	8.3	0	2	2	0	0	0	2	4	0	2	0	0	2	0	.44
97-98	NYR	1	0	0	0	0	0	0	1	0.0	0	0	0	0	0	0	0	0	0	0	0	0	0	0	.00
4 Years		72	11	12	23	-15	1	1	114	9.6	1	5	6	0	0	0	25	90	8	15	8	2	9	0	.32

Ryan Smyth

(statistical profile on page 375)

Pos: LW **Shoots:** L **Ht:** 6'1" **Wt:** 195 **Born:** 2/21/76—Banff, Alberta **Age:** 23

Overall											Power Play			Shorthand			Penalty							Misc	
Year	Tm	GP	G	A	Pts	+/-	GW	GT	S	SPct	G	A	Pts	G	A	Pts	Num	PIM	Maj	Mnr	Fgt	Rgh	HHT	Hat	P/G
94-95	Edm	3	0	0	0	-1	0	0	2	0.0	0	0	0	0	0	0	0	0	0	0	0	0	0	0	.00
95-96	Edm	48	2	9	11	-10	0	0	65	3.1	1	0	1	0	0	0	14	28	0	14	0	2	5	0	.23
96-97	Edm	**82**	39	22	61	-7	4	0	265	14.7	**20**	4	24	0	0	0	31	76	2	28	2	6	4	1	.74
97-98	Edm	65	20	13	33	-24	2	2	205	9.8	10	7	17	0	0	0	22	44	0	22	0	2	8	0	.51
98-99	Edm	71	13	18	31	0	2	2	161	8.1	6	6	12	0	0	0	27	62	0	26	0	1	9	0	.44
5 Years		269	74	62	136	-42	8	4	698	10.6	37	17	54	0	0	0	94	210	2	90	2	11	26	1	.51

Postseason

Year	Tm	GP	G	A	Pts	+/-	GW	OT	S	SPct	G	A	Pts	G	A	Pts	Num	PIM	Maj	Mnr	Fgt	Rgh	HHT	Hat	P/G
96-97	Edm	12	5	5	10	-4	2	1	48	10.4	1	3	4	0	0	0	6	12	0	6	0	2	1	0	.83
97-98	Edm	12	1	3	4	-2	0	0	24	4.2	1	1	2	0	0	0	4	16	0	3	0	0	1	0	.33
98-99	Edm	3	3	0	3	-1	0	0	7	42.9	2	0	2	0	0	0	0	0	0	0	0	0	0	0	1.00
3 Years		27	9	8	17	-7	2	1	79	11.4	4	4	8	0	0	0	10	28	0	9	0	2	2	0	.63

Garth Snow

(statistical profile on page 403)

Pos: G **Catches:** L **Ht:** 6'3" **Wt:** 200 **Born:** 7/28/69—Wrentham, Massachusetts **Age:** 30

Overall																	Pen Shot		Offense		
Year	Tm	GP	GS	TP	W	L	T	Min	GA	GAA	Shots	SvPct	ShO	OE	PPGA	SHGA	Shots	GA	G	A	PIM
93-94	Que	5	5	1	3	2	0	279	16	3.44	127	.874	0	1	5	1	0	0	0	0	2
94-95	Que	2	2	0	1	1	0	119	11	5.55	63	.825	0	0	3	0	0	0	0	0	0
95-96	Phi	26	23	3	12	8	4	1437	69	2.88	648	.894	0	4	26	1	0	0	0	0	18
96-97	Phi	35	28	2	14	8	8	1884	79	2.52	816	.903	2	9	22	4	0	0	0	1	30
97-98	2Tm	41	35	3	17	15	4	2155	93	2.59	944	.901	1	8	26	4	0	0	0	0	22
98-99	Van	65	62	**13**	20	**31**	8	3501	**171**	2.93	1715	.900	6	16	53	7	1	0	0	1	34
97-98	Phi	29	27	1	14	9	4	1651	67	2.43	682	.902	1	5	18	1	0	0	0	0	18
97-98	Van	12	8	2	3	6	0	504	26	3.10	262	.901	0	3	8	3	0	0	0	0	4
6 Years		174	155	22	67	65	24	9375	439	2.81	4313	.898	9	38	135	17	1	0	0	2	106

Postseason

Year	Tm	GP	GS	TP	W	L	Pct	Min	GA	GAA	Shots	SvPct	ShO	OE	PPGA	SHGA	Shots	GA	G	A	PIM
94-95	Que	1	0	0	0	0	–	9	1	6.67	3	.667	0	0	0	0	0	0	0	0	0
95-96	Phi	1	0	1	0	0	–	1	0	0.00	0	–	0	0	0	0	0	0	0	0	0
96-97	Phi	12	12	1	8	4	.667	699	33	2.83	305	.892	0	4	11	3	0	0	0	2	11
3 Years		14	12	2	8	4	.667	709	34	2.88	308	.890	0	4	11	3	0	0	0	2	11

Martin Sonnenberg

Pos: LW **Shoots:** R **Ht:** 6'0" **Wt:** 200 **Born:** 1/23/78—Wetaskiwin, Alberta **Age:** 21

Overall											Power Play			Shorthand			Penalty							Misc	
Year	Tm	GP	G	A	Pts	+/-	GW	GT	S	SPct	G	A	Pts	G	A	Pts	Num	PIM	Maj	Mnr	Fgt	Rgh	HHT	Hat	P/G
98-99	Pit	44	1	1	2	-2	0	0	12	8.3	0	0	0	0	0	0	4	19	1	2	1	0	0	0	.05

Postseason

Year	Tm	GP	G	A	Pts	+/-	GW	OT	S	SPct	G	A	Pts	G	A	Pts	Num	PIM	Maj	Mnr	Fgt	Rgh	HHT	Hat	P/G
98-99	Pit	7	0	0	0	-2	0	0	0	–	0	0	0	0	0	0	0	0	0	0	0	0	0	0	.00

Brent Sopel

Pos: D **Shoots:** R **Ht:** 6'1" **Wt:** 190 **Born:** 1/7/77—Calgary, Alberta **Age:** 22

Overall											Power Play			Shorthand			Penalty							Misc	
Year	Tm	GP	G	A	Pts	+/–	GW	GT	S	SPct	G	A	Pts	G	A	Pts	Num	PIM	Maj	Mnr	Fgt	Rgh	HHT	Hat	P/G
98-99	Van	5	1	0	1	-1	0	0	5	20.0	1	0	1	0	0	0	2	4	0	2	0	0	1	0	.20

Lee Sorochan

Pos: D **Shoots:** L **Ht:** 5'11" **Wt:** 210 **Born:** 9/9/75—Edmonton, Alberta **Age:** 24

Overall											Power Play			Shorthand			Penalty							Misc	
Year	Tm	GP	G	A	Pts	+/–	GW	GT	S	SPct	G	A	Pts	G	A	Pts	Num	PIM	Maj	Mnr	Fgt	Rgh	HHT	Hat	P/G
98-99	Cgy	2	0	0	0	-3	0	0	5	0.0	0	0	0	0	0	0	0	0	0	0	0	0	0	0	.00

Sheldon Souray

Pos: D **Shoots:** L **Ht:** 6'4" **Wt:** 235 **Born:** 7/13/76—Elk Point, Alberta **Age:** 23

Overall											Power Play			Shorthand			Penalty							Misc	
Year	Tm	GP	G	A	Pts	+/–	GW	GT	S	SPct	G	A	Pts	G	A	Pts	Num	PIM	Maj	Mnr	Fgt	Rgh	HHT	Hat	P/G
97-98	NJ	60	3	7	10	18	1	0	74	4.1	0	0	0	0	0	0	28	85	7	20	7	9	1	0	.17
98-99	NJ	70	1	7	8	5	0	0	101	1.0	0	0	0	0	0	0	43	110	8	35	8	15	5	0	.11
2 Years		130	4	14	18	23	1	0	175	2.3	0	0	0	0	0	0	71	195	15	55	15	24	6	0	.14
Postseason																									
Year	Tm	GP	G	A	Pts	+/–	GW	OT	S	SPct	G	A	Pts	G	A	Pts	Num	PIM	Maj	Mnr	Fgt	Rgh	HHT	Hat	P/G
97-98	NJ	3	0	1	1	0	0	0	1	0.0	0	1	1	0	0	0	1	2	0	1	0	0	0	0	.33
98-99	NJ	2	0	1	1	1	0	0	0	–	0	0	0	0	0	0	0	0	0	0	0	0	0	0	.50
2 Years		5	0	2	2	1	0	0	1	0.0	0	1	1	0	0	0	1	2	0	1	0	0	0	0	.40

Jaroslav Spacek

(statistical profile on page 375)

Pos: D **Shoots:** L **Ht:** 5'11" **Wt:** 198 **Born:** 2/11/74—Rokycany, Czechoslovakia **Age:** 25

Overall											Power Play			Shorthand			Penalty							Misc	
Year	Tm	GP	G	A	Pts	+/–	GW	GT	S	SPct	G	A	Pts	G	A	Pts	Num	PIM	Maj	Mnr	Fgt	Rgh	HHT	Hat	P/G
98-99	Fla	63	3	12	15	15	0	0	92	3.3	2	2	4	1	1	2	14	28	0	14	0	2	8	0	.24

Corey Spring

Pos: RW **Shoots:** R **Ht:** 6'4" **Wt:** 214 **Born:** 5/31/71—Cranbrook, British Columbia **Age:** 28

Overall											Power Play			Shorthand			Penalty							Misc	
Year	Tm	GP	G	A	Pts	+/–	GW	GT	S	SPct	G	A	Pts	G	A	Pts	Num	PIM	Maj	Mnr	Fgt	Rgh	HHT	Hat	P/G
97-98	TB	8	1	0	1	-1	0	0	12	8.3	0	0	0	0	0	0	2	10	2	0	2	0	0	0	.13
98-99	TB	8	0	1	1	0	0	0	6	0.0	0	0	0	0	0	0	1	2	0	1	0	1	0	0	.13
2 Years		16	1	1	2	-1	0	0	18	5.6	0	0	0	0	0	0	3	12	2	1	2	1	0	0	.13

Martin St. Louis

Pos: C **Shoots:** L **Ht:** 5'9" **Wt:** 180 **Born:** 8/9/71—Laval, Quebec **Age:** 28

Overall											Power Play			Shorthand			Penalty							Misc	
Year	Tm	GP	G	A	Pts	+/–	GW	GT	S	SPct	G	A	Pts	G	A	Pts	Num	PIM	Maj	Mnr	Fgt	Rgh	HHT	Hat	P/G
98-99	Cgy	13	1	1	2	-2	0	0	14	7.1	0	1	1	0	0	0	5	10	0	5	0	1	3	0	.15

Steve Staios

Pos: RW **Shoots:** R **Ht:** 6'0" **Wt:** 190 **Born:** 7/28/73—Hamilton, Ontario **Age:** 26

Overall											Power Play			Shorthand			Penalty							Misc	
Year	Tm	GP	G	A	Pts	+/–	GW	GT	S	SPct	G	A	Pts	G	A	Pts	Num	PIM	Maj	Mnr	Fgt	Rgh	HHT	Hat	P/G
95-96	Bos	12	0	0	0	-5	0	0	4	0.0	0	0	0	0	0	0	2	4	0	2	0	1	0	0	.00
96-97	2Tm	63	3	14	17	-24	0	1	66	4.5	0	1	1	0	1	1	35	91	7	28	7	3	11	0	.27
97-98	Van	77	3	4	7	-3	1	0	45	6.7	0	0	0	0	0	0	43	134	8	32	8	4	14	0	.09
98-99	Van	57	0	2	2	-12	0	0	33	0.0	0	0	0	0	0	0	13	54	4	7	4	3	0	0	.04
96-97	Bos	54	3	8	11	-26	0	1	56	5.4	0	1	1	0	1	1	28	71	5	23	5	3	10	0	.20
96-97	Van	9	0	6	6	2	0	0	10	0.0	0	0	0	0	0	0	7	20	2	5	2	0	1	0	.67
4 Years		209	6	20	26	-44	1	1	148	4.1	0	1	1	0	1	1	93	283	19	69	19	11	25	0	.12
Postseason																									
Year	Tm	GP	G	A	Pts	+/–	GW	OT	S	SPct	G	A	Pts	G	A	Pts	Num	PIM	Maj	Mnr	Fgt	Rgh	HHT	Hat	P/G
95-96	Bos	3	0	0	0	-1	0	0	5	0.0	0	0	0	0	0	0	0	0	0	0	0	0	0	0	.00

Mike Stapleton

(statistical profile on page 376)

Pos: C **Shoots:** R **Ht:** 5'10" **Wt:** 183 **Born:** 5/5/66—Sarnia, Ontario **Age:** 33

Overall											Power Play			Shorthand			Penalty							Misc	
Year	Tm	GP	G	A	Pts	+/-	GW	GT	S	SPct	G	A	Pts	G	A	Pts	Num	PIM	Maj	Mnr	Fgt	Rgh	HHT	Hat	P/G
86-87	Chi	39	3	6	9	-9	0	0	54	5.6	0	–	–	0	–	–	3	6	0	3	0	–	–	0	.23
87-88	Chi	53	2	9	11	-10	1	0	50	4.0	0	–	–	0	–	–	–	59	–	–	–	–	–	0	.21
88-89	Chi	7	0	1	1	-1	0	0	6	0.0	0	–	–	0	–	–	2	7	1	1	0	–	–	0	.14
89-90		Did Not Play in NHL																							
90-91	Chi	7	0	1	1	0	0	0	6	0.0	0	–	–	0	–	–	1	2	0	1	0	–	–	0	.14
91-92	Chi	19	4	4	8	0	0	0	32	12.5	1	1	2	0	0	0	4	8	0	4	0	3	1	0	.42
92-93	Pit	78	4	9	13	-8	1	0	78	5.1	0	3	3	1	0	1	5	10	0	5	0	2	1	0	.17
93-94	2Tm	81	12	13	25	-5	0	1	102	11.8	4	5	9	0	0	0	15	46	0	13	0	4	6	0	.31
94-95	Edm	46	6	11	17	-12	2	0	59	10.2	3	4	7	0	0	0	9	21	1	8	1	1	4	0	.37
95-96	Wpg	58	10	14	24	-4	0	0	91	11.0	3	0	3	1	0	1	17	37	1	16	1	0	4	0	.41
96-97	Pho	55	4	11	15	-4	1	0	74	5.4	2	3	5	0	0	0	10	36	0	8	0	3	2	0	.27
97-98	Pho	64	5	5	10	-4	1	0	69	7.2	1	2	3	1	0	1	14	36	0	13	0	1	4	0	.16
98-99	Pho	76	9	9	18	-6	2	0	106	8.5	0	2	2	2	0	2	13	34	0	12	0	1	4	0	.24
93-94	Pit	58	7	4	11	-4	0	0	59	11.9	3	3	6	0	0	0	5	18	0	4	0	1	2	0	.19
93-94	Edm	23	5	9	14	-1	0	1	43	11.6	1	2	3	0	0	0	10	28	0	9	0	3	4	0	.61
12 Years		583	59	93	152	-63	8	1	727	8.1	14	–	–	5	–	–	–	302	–	–	–	–	–	0	.26

Postseason

Year	Tm	GP	G	A	Pts	+/-	GW	OT	S	SPct	G	A	Pts	G	A	Pts	Num	PIM	Maj	Mnr	Fgt	Rgh	HHT	Hat	P/G
86-87	Chi	4	0	0	0	0	0	0	7	0.0	0	0	0	0	0	0	1	2	0	1	0	–	–	0	.00
92-93	Pit	4	0	0	0	1	0	0	1	0.0	0	0	0	0	0	0	0	0	0	0	0	0	0	0	.00
95-96	Wpg	6	0	0	0	-1	0	0	1	0.0	0	0	0	0	0	0	5	21	1	3	0	1	1	0	.00
96-97	Pho	7	0	0	0	-1	0	0	5	0.0	0	0	0	0	0	0	3	14	0	2	0	0	0	0	.00
97-98	Pho	6	0	0	0	0	0	0	5	0.0	0	0	0	0	0	0	1	2	0	1	0	0	0	0	.00
98-99	Pho	7	1	0	1	-1	0	0	3	33.3	0	0	0	0	0	0	0	0	0	0	0	0	0	0	.14
6 Years		34	1	0	1	-2	0	0	22	4.5	0	0	0	0	0	0	10	39	1	7	0	–	–	0	.03

Ronnie Stern

(statistical profile on page 376)

Pos: RW **Shoots:** R **Ht:** 6'0" **Wt:** 195 **Born:** 1/11/67—Ste. Agatha Des Mont, Quebec **Age:** 32

Overall											Power Play			Shorthand			Penalty							Misc	
Year	Tm	GP	G	A	Pts	+/-	GW	GT	S	SPct	G	A	Pts	G	A	Pts	Num	PIM	Maj	Mnr	Fgt	Rgh	HHT	Hat	P/G
87-88	Van	15	0	0	0	-7	0	0	7	0.0	0	0	0	0	0	0	–	52	–	–	–	–	–	0	.00
88-89	Van	17	1	0	1	-4	0	0	13	7.7	0	0	0	0	0	0	–	49	–	–	–	–	–	0	.06
89-90	Van	34	2	3	5	-17	0	0	27	7.4	0	–	–	0	–	–	–	208	–	–	–	–	–	0	.15
90-91	2Tm	44	3	6	9	-14	0	0	45	6.7	0	–	–	0	–	–	–	240	–	–	–	–	–	0	.20
91-92	Cgy	72	13	9	22	0	1	0	96	13.5	0	0	0	1	1	2	90	338	18	59	15	28	6	1	.31
92-93	Cgy	70	10	15	25	4	1	0	82	12.2	0	0	0	0	0	0	74	207	9	61	7	19	6	1	.36
93-94	Cgy	71	9	20	29	6	3	0	105	8.6	0	0	0	1	0	1	78	243	13	59	10	19	5	0	.41
94-95	Cgy	39	9	4	13	4	0	0	69	13.0	1	0	1	0	0	0	47	163	7	34	7	14	2	1	.33
95-96	Cgy	52	10	5	15	2	1	1	64	15.6	0	1	1	0	0	0	40	111	5	33	4	6	2	0	.29
96-97	Cgy	79	7	10	17	-4	1	0	98	7.1	0	0	0	1	1	2	52	157	7	41	7	12	9	0	.22
97-98		Did Not Play in NHL																							
98-99	SJ	78	7	9	16	-3	2	0	94	7.4	1	0	1	0	0	0	60	158	10	49	10	12	6	0	.21
90-91	Van	31	2	3	5	-14	0	0	30	6.7	0	–	–	0	–	–	–	171	–	–	–	–	–	0	.16
90-91	Cgy	13	1	3	4	0	0	0	15	6.7	0	–	–	0	–	–	16	69	7	7	–	–	–	0	.31
11 Years		571	71	81	152	-33	9	1	700	10.1	2	–	–	3	–	–	–	1926	–	–	–	–	–	3	.27

Postseason

Year	Tm	GP	G	A	Pts	+/-	GW	OT	S	SPct	G	A	Pts	G	A	Pts	Num	PIM	Maj	Mnr	Fgt	Rgh	HHT	Hat	P/G
88-89	Van	3	0	1	1	0	0	0	6	0.0	0	–	–	0	–	–	–	17	–	–	–	–	–	0	.33
90-91	Cgy	7	1	3	4	0	0	0	12	8.3	0	–	–	0	0	0	–	14	–	–	–	–	–	0	.57
92-93	Cgy	6	0	0	0	-5	0	0	6	0.0	0	0	0	0	0	0	8	43	1	4	0	2	0	0	.00
93-94	Cgy	7	2	0	2	-1	0	0	11	18.2	0	0	0	0	0	0	2	12	0	1	0	0	0	0	.29
94-95	Cgy	7	3	1	4	4	0	0	19	15.8	1	0	1	1	1	2	4	8	0	4	0	2	0	0	.57
95-96	Cgy	4	0	2	2	2	0	0	7	0.0	0	0	0	0	0	0	4	8	0	4	0	2	0	0	.50
98-99	SJ	6	0	0	0	-1	0	0	10	0.0	0	0	0	0	0	0	3	6	0	3	0	1	1	0	.00
7 Years		40	6	7	13	-1	0	0	71	8.5	1	–	–	1	–	–	–	108	–	–	–	–	–	0	.33

Kevin Stevens

(statistical profile on page 376)

Pos: LW **Shoots:** L **Ht:** 6'3" **Wt:** 230 **Born:** 4/15/65—Brockton, Massachusetts **Age:** 34

Overall											Power Play			Shorthand			Penalty							Misc	
Year	Tm	GP	G	A	Pts	+/-	GW	GT	S	SPct	G	A	Pts	G	A	Pts	Num	PIM	Maj	Mnr	Fgt	Rgh	HHT	Hat	P/G
87-88	Pit	16	5	2	7	-6	0	0	22	22.7	2	1	3	0	–	–	4	8	0	4	0	–	–	0	.44

Overall											Power Play			Shorthand			Penalty							Misc	
Year	Tm	GP	G	A	Pts	+/–	GW	GT	S	SPct	G	A	Pts	G	A	Pts	Num	PIM	Maj	Mnr	Fgt	Rgh	HHT	Hat	P/G
88-89	Pit	24	12	3	15	-8	3	0	52	23.1	4	0	4	0	–	–	–	19	–	–	–	–	–	0	.63
89-90	Pit	76	29	41	70	-13	1	0	179	16.2	12	–	–	0	–	–	–	171	–	–	–	–	–	1	.92
90-91	Pit*	80	40	46	86	-1	6	2	253	15.8	18	20	38	0	–	–	–	133	–	–	–	–	–	1	1.08
91-92	Pit*	80	54	69	123	8	4	0	325	16.6	19	23	42	0	0	0	88	254	2	77	1	21	23	4	1.54
92-93	Pit*	72	55	56	111	17	5	1	326	16.9	26	18	44	0	0	0	64	177	3	56	2	17	10	3	1.54
93-94	Pit	83	41	47	88	-24	4	0	284	14.4	21	20	41	0	0	0	58	155	5	50	5	18	10	1	1.06
94-95	Pit	27	15	12	27	0	4	0	80	18.8	6	4	10	0	0	0	20	51	1	18	1	8	2	0	1.00
95-96	2Tm	61	13	23	36	-10	1	0	170	7.6	6	5	11	0	0	0	26	71	1	23	0	2	10	0	.59
96-97	LA	69	14	20	34	-27	1	1	175	8.0	4	2	6	0	0	0	41	96	2	38	2	14	7	0	.49
97-98	NYR	80	14	27	41	-7	3	1	144	9.7	5	7	12	0	0	0	43	130	4	35	4	13	5	0	.51
98-99	NYR	81	23	20	43	-10	3	0	136	16.9	8	6	14	0	0	0	32	64	0	32	0	6	7	1	.53
95-96	Bos	41	10	13	23	1	1	0	101	9.9	3	2	5	0	0	0	19	49	1	17	0	2	6	0	.56
95-96	LA	20	3	10	13	-11	0	0	69	4.3	3	3	6	0	0	0	7	22	0	6	0	0	4	0	.65
12 Years		749	315	366	681	-81	35	5	2146	14.7	131	–	–	0	–	–	–	1329	–	–	–	–	–	11	.91
Postseason																									
Year	Tm	GP	G	A	Pts	+/–	GW	OT	S	SPct	G	A	Pts	G	A	Pts	Num	PIM	Maj	Mnr	Fgt	Rgh	HHT	Hat	P/G
88-89	Pit	11	3	7	10	-1	0	0	21	14.3	0	–	–	0	–	–	–	16	–	–	–	–	–	0	.91
90-91	Pit	24	17	16	33	14	4	1	83	20.5	7	–	–	0	–	–	–	53	–	–	–	–	–	0	1.38
91-92	Pit	21	13	15	28	2	3	0	86	15.1	4	9	13	0	0	0	10	28	0	9	0	3	1	1	1.33
92-93	Pit	12	5	11	16	2	0	0	35	14.3	4	3	7	0	0	0	11	22	0	11	0	2	4	0	1.33
93-94	Pit	6	1	1	2	-5	0	0	20	5.0	0	0	0	0	0	0	5	10	0	5	0	3	0	0	.33
94-95	Pit	12	4	7	11	-5	1	0	32	12.5	3	2	5	0	0	0	9	21	1	8	1	4	1	0	.92
6 Years		86	43	57	100	7	8	1	277	15.5	18	–	–	0	–	–	–	150	–	–	–	–	–	1	1.16

Scott Stevens

(statistical profile on page 376)

Pos: D **Shoots:** L **Ht:** 6'1" **Wt:** 215 **Born:** 4/1/64—Kitchener, Ontario **Age:** 35

Overall											Power Play			Shorthand			Penalty							Misc	
Year	Tm	GP	G	A	Pts	+/–	GW	GT	S	SPct	G	A	Pts	G	A	Pts	Num	PIM	Maj	Mnr	Fgt	Rgh	HHT	Hat	P/G
82-83	Was	77	9	16	25	14	0	0	121	7.4	0	–	–	0	–	–	–	195	–	–	–	–	–	0	.32
83-84	Was	78	13	32	45	26	2	0	155	8.4	7	–	–	0	–	–	–	201	–	–	–	–	–	0	.58
84-85	Was*	**80**	21	44	65	19	5	0	170	12.4	16	–	–	0	–	–	–	221	–	–	–	–	–	0	.81
85-86	Was	73	15	38	53	0	2	0	121	12.4	3	–	–	0	–	–	–	165	–	–	–	–	–	0	.73
86-87	Was	77	10	51	61	13	0	0	165	6.1	2	–	–	0	–	–	–	283	–	–	–	–	–	0	.79
87-88	Was	**80**	12	60	72	14	2	0	231	5.2	5	–	–	1	–	–	–	184	–	–	–	–	–	0	.90
88-89	Was*	**80**	7	61	68	1	3	0	195	3.6	6	–	–	0	–	–	–	225	–	–	–	–	–	0	.85
89-90	Was	56	11	29	40	1	0	0	143	7.7	7	–	–	0	–	–	–	154	–	–	–	–	–	0	.71
90-91	StL*	78	5	44	49	23	1	0	160	3.1	1	–	–	0	–	–	–	150	–	–	–	–	–	0	.63
91-92	NJ*	68	17	42	59	24	2	0	156	10.9	7	12	19	1	3	4	48	124	4	42	4	14	6	0	.87
92-93	NJ*	81	12	45	57	14	1	0	146	8.2	8	13	21	0	0	0	53	120	2	50	2	15	11	0	.70
93-94	NJ*	83	18	60	78	**53**	4	0	215	8.4	5	21	26	1	1	2	45	112	2	41	2	17	9	0	.94
94-95	NJ	48	2	20	22	4	1	0	111	1.8	1	5	6	0	0	0	20	56	0	18	0	11	1	0	.46
95-96	NJ*	82	5	23	28	7	1	0	174	2.9	2	8	10	1	0	1	43	100	2	40	2	10	8	0	.34
96-97	NJ*	79	5	19	24	26	1	0	166	3.0	0	6	6	0	0	0	32	70	2	30	2	6	6	0	.30
97-98	NJ*	80	4	22	26	19	1	0	94	4.3	1	1	2	0	1	1	29	80	2	25	2	10	5	0	.33
98-99	NJ	75	5	22	27	29	1	0	111	4.5	0	0	0	0	3	3	32	64	0	32	0	12	2	0	.36
17 Years		1275	171	628	799	287	27	0	2634	6.5	71	–	–	4	–	–	–	2504	–	–	–	–	–	0	.63
Postseason																									
Year	Tm	GP	G	A	Pts	+/–	GW	OT	S	SPct	G	A	Pts	G	A	Pts	Num	PIM	Maj	Mnr	Fgt	Rgh	HHT	Hat	P/G
82-83	Was	4	1	0	1	-2	0	0	8	12.5	0	0	0	0	0	0	–	26	–	–	–	–	–	0	.25
83-84	Was	8	1	8	9	2	0	0	21	4.8	1	–	–	0	0	0	–	21	–	–	–	–	–	0	1.13
84-85	Was	5	0	1	1	-4	0	0	11	0.0	0	–	–	0	0	0	–	20	–	–	–	–	–	0	.20
85-86	Was	9	3	8	11	9	2	0	17	17.6	2	–	–	0	–	–	–	12	–	–	–	–	–	0	1.22
86-87	Was	7	0	5	5	4	0	0	19	0.0	0	–	–	0	0	0	–	19	–	–	–	–	–	0	.71
87-88	Was	13	1	11	12	-1	0	0	42	2.4	0	–	–	0	–	–	–	46	–	–	–	–	–	0	.92
88-89	Was	6	1	4	5	-2	0	0	16	6.3	0	–	–	0	–	–	4	11	1	3	–	–	–	0	.83
89-90	Was	15	2	7	9	-1	0	0	35	5.7	1	–	–	0	–	–	–	25	–	–	–	–	–	0	.60
90-91	StL	13	0	3	3	8	0	0	17	0.0	0	–	–	0	0	0	–	36	–	–	–	–	–	0	.23
91-92	NJ	7	2	1	3	-5	1	0	9	22.2	2	0	2	0	0	0	9	29	1	7	1	4	0	0	.43
92-93	NJ	5	2	2	4	-2	0	0	21	9.5	1	0	1	0	1	1	5	10	0	5	0	3	1	0	.80
93-94	NJ	20	2	9	11	-1	1	0	56	3.6	2	4	6	0	0	0	9	42	0	6	0	4	1	0	.55
94-95	NJ	20	1	7	8	10	1	0	54	1.9	0	3	3	0	0	0	8	24	0	7	0	4	2	0	.40
96-97	NJ	10	0	4	4	-2	0	0	27	0.0	0	0	0	0	0	0	1	2	0	1	0	0	0	0	.40
97-98	NJ	6	1	0	1	4	0	0	11	9.1	0	0	0	0	0	0	4	8	0	4	0	0	0	0	.17
98-99	NJ	7	2	1	3	-2	0	0	14	14.3	2	0	2	0	0	0	5	10	0	5	0	2	0	0	.43
16 Years		155	19	71	90	15	5	0	378	5.0	11	–	–	0	–	–	–	341	–	–	–	–	–	0	.58

Turner Stevenson

(statistical profile on page 377)

Pos: RW **Shoots:** R **Ht:** 6'3" **Wt:** 220 **Born:** 5/18/72—Port Alberni, British Columbia **Age:** 27

Overall											Power Play			Shorthand			Penalty							Misc	
Year	Tm	GP	G	A	Pts	+/-	GW	GT	S	SPct	G	A	Pts	G	A	Pts	Num	PIM	Maj	Mnr	Fgt	Rgh	HHT	Hat	P/G
92-93	Mon	1	0	0	0	-1	0	0	1	0.0	0	0	0	0	0	0	0	0	0	0	0	0	0	0	.00
93-94	Mon	2	0	0	0	-2	0	0	0	–	0	0	0	0	0	0	1	2	0	1	0	0	0	0	.00
94-95	Mon	41	6	1	7	0	1	0	35	17.1	0	0	0	0	0	0	21	86	12	8	12	2	1	0	.17
95-96	Mon	80	9	16	25	-2	2	0	101	8.9	0	2	2	0	0	0	49	167	15	31	14	11	9	0	.31
96-97	Mon	65	8	13	21	-14	0	0	76	10.5	1	1	2	0	0	0	31	97	9	21	9	2	7	0	.32
97-98	Mon	63	4	6	10	-8	0	0	43	9.3	1	0	1	0	0	0	37	110	12	25	12	4	9	0	.16
98-99	Mon	69	10	17	27	6	2	1	102	9.8	0	1	1	0	0	0	31	88	6	24	5	4	7	0	.39
7 Years		321	37	53	90	-21	5	1	358	10.3	2	4	6	0	0	0	170	550	54	110	52	23	33	0	.28
Postseason																									
Year	Tm	GP	G	A	Pts	+/-	GW	OT	S	SPct	G	A	Pts	G	A	Pts	Num	PIM	Maj	Mnr	Fgt	Rgh	HHT	Hat	P/G
93-94	Mon	3	0	2	2	1	0	0	2	0.0	0	0	0	0	0	0	0	0	0	0	0	0	0	0	.67
95-96	Mon	6	0	1	1	-1	0	0	7	0.0	0	0	0	0	0	0	1	2	0	1	0	0	0	0	.17
96-97	Mon	5	1	1	2	1	0	0	5	20.0	0	0	0	0	0	0	1	2	0	1	0	0	0	0	.40
97-98	Mon	10	3	4	7	1	0	0	21	14.3	0	0	0	0	0	0	6	12	0	6	0	1	1	0	.70
4 Years		24	4	8	12	2	0	0	35	11.4	0	0	0	0	0	0	8	16	0	8	0	1	1	0	.50

Cory Stillman

(statistical profile on page 377)

Pos: C **Shoots:** L **Ht:** 6'0" **Wt:** 185 **Born:** 12/20/73—Peterborough, Ontario **Age:** 26

Overall											Power Play			Shorthand			Penalty							Misc	
Year	Tm	GP	G	A	Pts	+/-	GW	GT	S	SPct	G	A	Pts	G	A	Pts	Num	PIM	Maj	Mnr	Fgt	Rgh	HHT	Hat	P/G
94-95	Cgy	10	0	2	2	1	0	0	7	0.0	0	1	1	0	0	0	1	2	0	1	0	0	0	0	.20
95-96	Cgy	74	16	19	35	-5	3	0	132	12.1	4	13	17	1	0	1	12	41	3	8	1	1	2	0	.47
96-97	Cgy	58	6	20	26	-6	0	0	112	5.4	2	8	10	0	0	0	7	14	0	7	0	0	1	0	.45
97-98	Cgy	72	27	22	49	-9	1	1	178	15.2	9	6	15	4	1	5	20	40	0	20	0	4	5	1	.68
98-99	Cgy	76	27	30	57	7	5	1	175	15.4	9	10	19	3	0	3	19	38	0	19	0	5	5	0	.75
5 Years		290	76	93	169	-12	9	2	604	12.6	24	38	62	8	1	9	59	135	3	55	1	10	13	1	.58
Postseason																									
Year	Tm	GP	G	A	Pts	+/-	GW	OT	S	SPct	G	A	Pts	G	A	Pts	Num	PIM	Maj	Mnr	Fgt	Rgh	HHT	Hat	P/G
95-96	Cgy	2	1	1	2	-2	0	0	5	20.0	0	0	0	0	0	0	0	0	0	0	0	0	0	0	1.00

P.J. Stock

Pos: LW **Shoots:** L **Ht:** 5'10" **Wt:** 190 **Born:** 5/26/75—Victoriaville, Quebec **Age:** 24

Overall											Power Play			Shorthand			Penalty							Misc	
Year	Tm	GP	G	A	Pts	+/-	GW	GT	S	SPct	G	A	Pts	G	A	Pts	Num	PIM	Maj	Mnr	Fgt	Rgh	HHT	Hat	P/G
97-98	NYR	38	2	3	5	4	1	0	9	22.2	0	0	0	0	0	0	26	114	10	12	10	6	2	0	.13
98-99	NYR	5	0	0	0	-1	0	0	0	–	0	0	0	0	0	0	3	6	0	3	0	2	0	0	.00
2 Years		43	2	3	5	3	1	0	9	22.2	0	0	0	0	0	0	29	120	10	15	10	8	2	0	.12

Jamie Storr

(statistical profile on page 403)

Pos: G **Catches:** L **Ht:** 6'1" **Wt:** 197 **Born:** 12/28/75—Brampton, Ontario **Age:** 24

Overall																	Pen Shot		Offense		
Year	Tm	GP	GS	TP	W	L	T	Min	GA	GAA	Shots	SvPct	ShO	OE	PPGA	SHGA	Shots	GA	G	A	PIM
94-95	LA	5	5	1	1	3	1	263	17	3.88	152	.888	0	2	3	0	0	0	0	0	0
95-96	LA	5	5	1	3	1	0	262	12	2.75	147	.918	0	3	1	1	0	0	0	0	0
96-97	LA	5	4	0	2	1	1	265	11	2.49	147	.925	0	2	1	0	0	0	0	0	0
97-98	LA	17	14	0	9	5	1	920	34	2.22	482	.929	2	6	9	5	0	0	0	0	0
98-99	LA	28	26	2	12	12	2	1525	61	2.40	724	.916	4	13	14	2	1	0	0	1	6
5 Years		60	54	4	27	22	5	3235	135	2.50	1652	.918	6	26	28	8	1	0	0	1	6
Postseason																					
Year	Tm	GP	GS	TP	W	L	Pct	Min	GA	GAA	Shots	SvPct	ShO	OE	PPGA	SHGA	Shots	GA	G	A	PIM
97-98	LA	3	2	0	0	2	.000	145	9	3.72	77	.883	0	0	5	0	0	0	0	0	0

Martin Straka

(statistical profile on page 377)

Pos: C **Shoots:** L **Ht:** 5'10" **Wt:** 175 **Born:** 9/3/72—Plzen, Czechoslovakia **Age:** 27

Overall											Power Play			Shorthand			Penalty							Misc	
Year	Tm	GP	G	A	Pts	+/-	GW	GT	S	SPct	G	A	Pts	G	A	Pts	Num	PIM	Maj	Mnr	Fgt	Rgh	HHT	Hat	P/G
92-93	Pit	42	3	13	16	2	1	0	28	10.7	0	2	2	0	0	0	9	29	1	7	0	0	1	0	.38
93-94	Pit	84	30	34	64	24	6	1	130	23.1	2	2	4	0	0	0	12	24	0	12	0	0	6	1	.76

Year	Tm	Overall GP	G	A	Pts	+/–	GW	GT	S	SPct	Power Play G	A	Pts	Shorthand G	A	Pts	Penalty Num	PIM	Maj	Mnr	Fgt	Rgh	HHT	Misc Hat	P/G
94-95	2Tm	37	5	13	18	-1	0	0	49	10.2	0	4	4	0	0	0	8	16	0	8	0	0	6	0	.49
95-96	3Tm	77	13	30	43	-19	1	0	98	13.3	6	9	15	0	0	0	15	41	1	13	0	2	7	0	.56
96-97	Fla	55	7	22	29	9	1	0	94	7.4	2	5	7	0	0	0	6	12	0	6	0	0	4	0	.53
97-98	Pit	75	19	23	42	-1	4	1	117	16.2	4	6	10	3	3	6	14	28	0	14	0	0	7	1	.56
98-99	Pit	80	35	48	83	12	4	1	177	19.8	5	17	22	4	2	6	13	26	0	13	0	0	8	1	1.04
94-95	Pit	31	4	12	16	0	0	0	36	11.1	0	3	3	0	0	0	8	16	0	8	0	0	6	0	.52
94-95	Ott	6	1	1	2	-1	0	0	13	7.7	0	1	1	0	0	0	0	0	0	0	0	0	0	0	.33
95-96	Ott	43	9	16	25	-13	1	0	63	14.3	5	4	9	0	0	0	9	29	1	7	0	2	2	0	.58
95-96	NYI	22	2	10	12	-7	0	0	18	11.1	0	4	4	0	0	0	3	6	0	3	0	0	2	0	.55
95-96	Fla	12	2	4	6	1	0	0	17	11.8	1	1	2	0	0	0	3	6	0	3	0	0	3	0	.50
7 Years		450	112	183	295	26	17	3	693	16.2	19	45	64	7	5	12	77	176	2	73	0	2	39	3	.66

Postseason

Year	Tm	GP	G	A	Pts	+/–	GW	OT	S	SPct	PP G	PP A	PP Pts	SH G	SH A	SH Pts	Num	PIM	Maj	Mnr	Fgt	Rgh	HHT	Hat	P/G
92-93	Pit	11	2	1	3	2	0	0	7	28.6	0	0	0	0	0	0	1	2	0	1	0	0	0	0	.27
93-94	Pit	6	1	0	1	-3	0	0	3	33.3	0	0	0	0	0	0	1	2	0	1	0	0	0	0	.17
95-96	Fla	13	2	2	4	-2	0	0	20	10.0	0	2	2	0	0	0	1	2	0	1	0	0	0	0	.31
96-97	Fla	4	0	0	0	-2	0	0	2	0.0	0	0	0	0	0	0	0	0	0	0	0	0	0	0	.00
97-98	Pit	6	2	0	2	-3	0	0	10	20.0	0	0	0	1	0	1	1	2	0	1	0	0	1	0	.33
98-99	Pit	13	6	9	15	0	0	0	27	22.2	1	3	4	0	0	0	3	6	0	3	0	1	2	1	1.15
6 Years		53	13	12	25	-8	0	0	69	18.8	1	5	6	1	0	1	7	14	0	7	0	1	3	1	.47

Jason Strudwick

Pos: D **Shoots:** L **Ht:** 6'3" **Wt:** 207 **Born:** 7/17/75—Edmonton, Alberta **Age:** 24

Year	Tm	Overall GP	G	A	Pts	+/–	GW	GT	S	SPct	Power Play G	A	Pts	Shorthand G	A	Pts	Penalty Num	PIM	Maj	Mnr	Fgt	Rgh	HHT	Misc Hat	P/G
95-96	NYI	1	0	0	0	0	0	0	0	–	0	0	0	0	0	0	2	7	1	1	1	1	0	0	.00
96-97		Did Not Play in NHL																							
97-98	2Tm	28	0	2	2	-2	0	0	8	0.0	0	0	0	0	0	0	14	65	7	5	7	1	1	0	.07
98-99	Van	65	0	3	3	-19	0	0	25	0.0	0	0	0	0	1	1	32	114	14	17	14	7	6	0	.05
97-98	NYI	17	0	1	1	1	0	0	3	0.0	0	0	0	0	0	0	8	36	4	3	4	0	1	0	.06
97-98	Van	11	0	1	1	-3	0	0	5	0.0	0	0	0	0	0	0	6	29	3	2	3	1	0	0	.09
3 Years		94	0	5	5	-21	0	0	33	0.0	0	0	0	0	1	1	48	186	22	23	22	9	7	0	.05

Jozef Stumpel

(statistical profile on page 377)

Pos: C **Shoots:** R **Ht:** 6'3" **Wt:** 216 **Born:** 6/20/72—Nitra, Czechoslovakia **Age:** 27

Year	Tm	Overall GP	G	A	Pts	+/–	GW	GT	S	SPct	Power Play G	A	Pts	Shorthand G	A	Pts	Penalty Num	PIM	Maj	Mnr	Fgt	Rgh	HHT	Misc Hat	P/G
91-92	Bos	4	1	0	1	1	0	0	3	33.3	0	0	0	0	0	0	0	0	0	0	0	0	0	0	.25
92-93	Bos	13	1	3	4	-3	0	0	8	12.5	0	0	0	0	0	0	2	4	0	2	0	0	1	0	.31
93-94	Bos	59	8	15	23	4	1	0	62	12.9	0	3	3	0	0	0	7	14	0	7	0	0	2	0	.39
94-95	Bos	44	5	13	18	4	2	0	46	10.9	1	2	3	0	0	0	4	8	0	4	0	0	0	0	.41
95-96	Bos	76	18	36	54	-8	2	0	158	11.4	5	15	20	0	0	0	7	14	0	7	0	0	5	1	.71
96-97	Bos	78	21	55	76	-22	1	0	168	12.5	6	18	24	0	0	0	7	14	0	7	0	0	2	0	.97
97-98	LA	77	21	58	79	17	2	1	162	13.0	4	17	21	0	2	2	21	53	1	19	1	8	6	1	1.03
98-99	LA	64	13	21	34	-18	1	0	131	9.9	1	5	6	0	2	2	5	10	0	5	0	0	1	0	.53
8 Years		415	88	201	289	-25	9	1	738	11.9	17	60	77	0	4	4	53	117	1	51	1	8	17	2	.70

Postseason

Year	Tm	GP	G	A	Pts	+/–	GW	OT	S	SPct	PP G	PP A	PP Pts	SH G	SH A	SH Pts	Num	PIM	Maj	Mnr	Fgt	Rgh	HHT	Hat	P/G
93-94	Bos	13	1	7	8	0	0	0	22	4.5	0	1	1	0	0	0	2	4	0	2	0	0	1	0	.62
94-95	Bos	5	0	0	0	-1	0	0	8	0.0	0	0	0	0	0	0	0	0	0	0	0	0	0	0	.00
95-96	Bos	5	1	2	3	-2	0	0	7	14.3	0	2	2	0	0	0	0	0	0	0	0	0	0	0	.60
97-98	LA	4	1	2	3	2	0	0	7	14.3	0	0	0	0	0	0	1	2	0	1	0	0	0	0	.75
4 Years		27	3	11	14	-1	0	0	44	6.8	0	3	3	0	0	0	3	6	0	3	0	0	1	0	.52

Marco Sturm

(statistical profile on page 378)

Pos: C **Shoots:** L **Ht:** 6'0" **Wt:** 190 **Born:** 9/8/78—Dingolfing, West Germany **Age:** 21

Year	Tm	Overall GP	G	A	Pts	+/–	GW	GT	S	SPct	Power Play G	A	Pts	Shorthand G	A	Pts	Penalty Num	PIM	Maj	Mnr	Fgt	Rgh	HHT	Misc Hat	P/G
97-98	SJ	74	10	20	30	-2	3	0	118	8.5	2	4	6	0	0	0	20	40	0	20	0	0	7	0	.41
98-99	SJ	78	16	22	38	7	3	2	140	11.4	3	8	11	2	2	4	26	52	0	26	0	1	10	1	.49
2 Years		152	26	42	68	5	6	2	258	10.1	5	12	17	2	2	4	46	92	0	46	0	1	17	1	.45

Postseason																									
Year	Tm	GP	G	A	Pts	+/-	GW	OT	S	SPct	G	A	Pts	G	A	Pts	Num	PIM	Maj	Mnr	Fgt	Rgh	HHT	Hat	P/G
97-98	SJ	2	0	0	0	-2	0	0	3	0.0	0	0	0	0	0	0	0	0	0	0	0	0	0	0	.00
98-99	SJ	6	2	2	4	1	1	0	15	13.3	0	1	1	0	0	0	2	4	0	2	0	0	0	0	.67
2 Years		8	2	2	4	-1	1	0	18	11.1	0	1	1	0	0	0	2	4	0	2	0	0	0	0	.50

Mike Sullivan

Pos: C **Shoots:** L **Ht:** 6'2" **Wt:** 190 **Born:** 2/27/68—Marshfield, Massachusetts **Age:** 31

Overall											Power Play			Shorthand			Penalty							Misc	
Year	Tm	GP	G	A	Pts	+/–	GW	GT	S	SPct	G	A	Pts	G	A	Pts	Num	PIM	Maj	Mnr	Fgt	Rgh	HHT	Hat	P/G
91-92	SJ	64	8	11	19	-18	1	0	72	11.1	1	2	3	0	1	1	6	15	1	5	1	1	4	0	.30
92-93	SJ	81	6	8	14	-42	0	0	95	6.3	0	0	0	2	3	5	15	30	0	15	0	0	7	0	.17
93-94	2Tm	45	4	5	9	-1	1	0	48	8.3	0	0	0	2	1	3	5	10	0	5	0	0	5	0	.20
94-95	Cgy	38	4	7	11	-2	2	0	31	12.9	0	0	0	0	0	0	7	14	0	7	0	0	5	0	.29
95-96	Cgy	81	9	12	21	-6	1	1	106	8.5	0	0	0	1	2	3	12	24	0	12	0	0	8	0	.26
96-97	Cgy	67	5	6	11	-11	2	0	64	7.8	0	0	0	3	0	3	5	10	0	5	0	0	1	0	.16
97-98	Bos	77	5	13	18	-1	2	0	83	6.0	0	1	1	0	0	0	17	34	0	17	0	1	10	0	.23
98-99	Pho	63	2	4	6	-11	1	0	66	3.0	0	0	0	1	1	2	12	24	0	12	0	1	2	0	.10
93-94	SJ	26	2	2	4	-3	1	0	21	9.5	0	0	0	2	0	2	2	4	0	2	0	0	2	0	.15
93-94	Cgy	19	2	3	5	2	0	0	27	7.4	0	0	0	0	1	1	3	6	0	3	0	0	3	0	.26
8 Years		516	43	66	109	-92	10	1	565	7.6	1	3	4	9	8	17	79	161	1	78	1	3	42	0	.21
Postseason																									
Year	Tm	GP	G	A	Pts	+/–	GW	OT	S	SPct	G	A	Pts	G	A	Pts	Num	PIM	Maj	Mnr	Fgt	Rgh	HHT	Hat	P/G
93-94	Cgy	7	1	1	2	0	0	0	7	14.3	0	0	0	1	0	1	4	8	0	4	0	0	2	0	.29
94-95	Cgy	7	3	5	8	5	1	0	12	25.0	0	0	0	0	2	2	1	2	0	1	0	0	1	1	1.14
95-96	Cgy	4	0	0	0	-1	0	0	5	0.0	0	0	0	0	0	0	0	0	0	0	0	0	0	0	.00
97-98	Bos	6	0	1	1	0	0	0	10	0.0	0	1	1	0	0	0	1	2	0	1	0	0	0	0	.17
98-99	Pho	5	0	0	0	0	0	0	2	0.0	0	0	0	0	0	0	1	2	0	1	0	0	0	0	.00
5 Years		29	4	7	11	4	1	0	36	11.1	0	1	1	1	2	3	7	14	0	7	0	0	3	1	.38

Steve Sullivan

(statistical profile on page 378)

Pos: C **Shoots:** R **Ht:** 5'9" **Wt:** 155 **Born:** 7/6/74—Timmins, Ontario **Age:** 25

Overall											Power Play			Shorthand			Penalty							Misc	
Year	Tm	GP	G	A	Pts	+/–	GW	GT	S	SPct	G	A	Pts	G	A	Pts	Num	PIM	Maj	Mnr	Fgt	Rgh	HHT	Hat	P/G
95-96	NJ	16	5	4	9	3	1	0	23	21.7	2	2	4	0	0	0	4	8	0	4	0	1	3	0	.56
96-97	2Tm	54	13	25	38	14	3	1	108	12.0	3	5	8	0	1	1	17	37	1	16	1	2	4	0	.70
97-98	Tor	63	10	18	28	-8	1	0	112	8.9	1	1	2	0	0	0	20	40	0	20	0	6	3	0	.44
98-99	Tor	63	20	20	40	12	5	0	110	18.2	4	7	11	0	0	0	14	28	0	14	0	4	5	1	.63
96-97	NJ	33	8	14	22	9	2	1	63	12.7	2	3	5	0	0	0	7	14	0	7	0	2	1	0	.67
96-97	Tor	21	5	11	16	5	1	0	45	11.1	1	2	3	0	1	1	10	23	1	9	1	0	3	0	.76
4 Years		196	48	67	115	21	10	1	353	13.6	10	15	25	0	1	1	55	113	1	54	1	13	15	1	.59
Postseason																									
Year	Tm	GP	G	A	Pts	+/–	GW	OT	S	SPct	G	A	Pts	G	A	Pts	Num	PIM	Maj	Mnr	Fgt	Rgh	HHT	Hat	P/G
98-99	Tor	13	3	3	6	-3	0	0	21	14.3	2	1	3	0	0	0	7	14	0	7	0	2	1	0	.46

Mats Sundin

(statistical profile on page 378)

Pos: C **Shoots:** R **Ht:** 6'4" **Wt:** 225 **Born:** 2/13/71—Bromma, Sweden **Age:** 28

Overall											Power Play			Shorthand			Penalty							Misc	
Year	Tm	GP	G	A	Pts	+/–	GW	GT	S	SPct	G	A	Pts	G	A	Pts	Num	PIM	Maj	Mnr	Fgt	Rgh	HHT	Hat	P/G
90-91	Que	80	23	36	59	-24	0	1	155	14.8	4	8	12	0	0	0	29	58	0	29	0	4	5	2	.74
91-92	Que	80	33	43	76	-19	2	1	231	14.3	8	12	20	2	0	2	42	103	1	39	1	7	11	1	.95
92-93	Que	80	47	67	114	21	9	1	215	21.9	13	34	47	4	5	**9**	37	96	2	33	0	3	9	1	1.43
93-94	Que	84	32	53	85	1	4	0	226	14.2	6	21	27	2	3	5	26	60	0	25	0	1	12	0	1.01
94-95	Tor	47	23	24	47	-5	4	1	173	13.3	9	10	19	0	0	0	7	14	0	7	0	1	2	0	1.00
95-96	Tor*	76	33	50	83	8	7	1	301	11.0	7	23	30	6	0	6	23	46	0	23	0	4	7	0	1.09
96-97	Tor*	**82**	41	53	94	6	8	1	281	14.6	7	13	20	4	3	7	24	59	1	22	0	2	14	1	1.15
97-98	Tor*	82	33	41	74	-3	5	1	219	15.1	9	12	21	1	3	4	23	49	1	22	1	2	13	0	.90
98-99	Tor	82	31	52	83	22	6	0	209	14.8	4	11	15	0	1	1	29	58	0	29	0	2	14	1	1.01
9 Years		693	296	419	715	7	45	7	2010	14.7	67	144	211	19	15	34	240	543	5	229	2	26	87	6	1.03
Postseason																									
Year	Tm	GP	G	A	Pts	+/–	GW	OT	S	SPct	G	A	Pts	G	A	Pts	Num	PIM	Maj	Mnr	Fgt	Rgh	HHT	Hat	P/G
92-93	Que	6	3	1	4	-4	0	0	19	15.8	1	1	2	0	0	0	3	6	0	3	0	1	1	0	.67
94-95	Tor	7	5	4	9	-2	1	0	27	18.5	2	2	4	0	0	0	2	4	0	2	0	0	0	0	1.29
95-96	Tor	6	3	1	4	-8	1	1	23	13.0	2	1	3	0	0	0	2	4	0	2	0	1	0	0	.67

Postseason																									
Year	Tm	GP	G	A	Pts	+/–	GW	OT	S	SPct	G	A	Pts	G	A	Pts	Num	PIM	Maj	Mnr	Fgt	Rgh	HHT	Hat	P/G
98-99	Tor	17	8	8	16	2	2	0	44	18.2	3	2	5	0	0	0	8	16	0	8	0	1	5	0	.94
4 Years		36	19	14	33	-12	4	1	113	16.8	8	6	14	0	0	0	15	30	0	15	0	3	6	0	.92

Niklas Sundstrom

(statistical profile on page 378)

Pos: LW **Shoots:** R **Ht:** 6'0" **Wt:** 195 **Born:** 6/6/75—Ornskoldsvik, Sweden **Age:** 24

Overall											Power Play			Shorthand			Penalty							Misc	
Year	Tm	GP	G	A	Pts	+/–	GW	GT	S	SPct	G	A	Pts	G	A	Pts	Num	PIM	Maj	Mnr	Fgt	Rgh	HHT	Hat	P/G
95-96	NYR	82	9	12	21	2	2	0	90	10.0	1	0	1	1	0	1	7	14	0	7	0	0	6	0	.26
96-97	NYR	**82**	24	28	52	23	4	0	132	18.2	5	2	7	1	2	3	10	20	0	10	0	0	3	0	.63
97-98	NYR	70	19	28	47	0	1	0	115	16.5	4	3	7	0	0	0	12	24	0	12	0	0	6	0	.67
98-99	NYR	81	13	30	43	-2	3	0	89	14.6	1	3	4	2	0	2	10	20	0	10	0	1	3	0	.53
4 Years		315	65	98	163	23	10	0	426	15.3	11	8	19	4	2	6	39	78	0	39	0	1	18	0	.52
Postseason																									
Year	Tm	GP	G	A	Pts	+/–	GW	OT	S	SPct	G	A	Pts	G	A	Pts	Num	PIM	Maj	Mnr	Fgt	Rgh	HHT	Hat	P/G
95-96	NYR	11	4	3	7	1	0	0	27	14.8	1	0	1	0	0	0	2	4	0	2	0	0	0	0	.64
96-97	NYR	9	0	5	5	3	0	0	18	0.0	0	0	0	0	0	0	1	2	0	1	0	0	1	0	.56
2 Years		20	4	8	12	4	0	0	45	8.9	1	0	1	0	0	0	3	6	0	3	0	0	1	0	.60

Gary Suter

Pos: D **Shoots:** L **Ht:** 6'0" **Wt:** 205 **Born:** 6/24/64—Madison, Wisconsin **Age:** 35

Overall											Power Play			Shorthand			Penalty							Misc	
Year	Tm	GP	G	A	Pts	+/–	GW	GT	S	SPct	G	A	Pts	G	A	Pts	Num	PIM	Maj	Mnr	Fgt	Rgh	HHT	Hat	P/G
85-86	Cgy*	80	18	50	68	11	4	0	195	9.2	9	–	–	0	–	–	62	141	3	58	–	–	–	0	.85
86-87	Cgy	68	9	40	49	-10	0	0	152	5.9	4	–	–	0	–	–	32	70	2	30	–	–	–	0	.72
87-88	Cgy*	75	21	70	91	39	3	0	204	10.3	6	–	–	1	–	–	59	124	2	57	–	–	–	0	1.21
88-89	Cgy*	63	13	49	62	26	1	0	216	6.0	8	–	–	0	–	–	39	78	0	39	0	–	–	0	.98
89-90	Cgy	76	16	60	76	4	1	0	211	7.6	5	–	–	0	–	–	43	97	1	41	–	–	–	0	1.00
90-91	Cgy*	79	12	58	70	26	1	0	258	4.7	6	–	–	0	–	–	51	102	0	51	0	–	–	0	.89
91-92	Cgy	70	12	43	55	1	0	0	189	6.3	4	25	29	0	0	0	49	128	2	44	1	1	22	0	.79
92-93	Cgy	81	23	58	81	-1	2	1	263	8.7	10	34	44	1	1	2	56	112	0	56	0	2	24	0	1.00
93-94	2Tm	41	6	12	18	-12	0	0	86	7.0	4	9	13	1	0	1	19	38	0	19	0	0	6	0	.44
94-95	Chi	48	10	27	37	14	0	0	144	6.9	5	19	24	0	1	1	18	42	2	16	0	1	9	0	.77
95-96	Chi*	82	20	47	67	3	4	0	242	8.3	12	29	41	2	3	5	40	80	0	40	0	1	20	0	.82
96-97	Chi	**82**	7	21	28	-4	0	1	225	3.1	3	11	14	0	0	0	35	70	0	35	0	3	17	0	.34
97-98	Chi	73	14	28	42	1	0	0	199	7.0	5	18	23	2	2	4	37	74	0	37	0	2	22	0	.58
98-99	SJ	1	0	0	0	0	0	0	1	0.0	0	0	0	0	0	0	0	0	0	0	0	0	0	0	.00
93-94	Cgy	25	4	9	13	-3	0	0	51	7.8	2	6	8	1	0	1	10	20	0	10	0	0	4	0	.52
93-94	Chi	16	2	3	5	-9	0	0	35	5.7	2	3	5	0	0	0	9	18	0	9	0	0	2	0	.31
14 Years		919	181	563	744	98	16	2	2585	7.0	81	–	–	7	–	–	540	1156	12	523	–	–	–	0	.81
Postseason																									
Year	Tm	GP	G	A	Pts	+/–	GW	OT	S	SPct	G	A	Pts	G	A	Pts	Num	PIM	Maj	Mnr	Fgt	Rgh	HHT	Hat	P/G
85-86	Cgy	10	2	8	10	1	1	0	17	11.8	0	–	–	0	–	–	4	8	0	4	0	–	–	0	1.00
86-87	Cgy	6	0	3	3	1	0	0	8	0.0	0	–	–	0	–	–	–	10	–	–	–	–	–	0	.50
87-88	Cgy	9	1	9	10	4	0	0	30	3.3	0	–	–	1	–	–	3	6	0	3	0	–	–	0	1.11
88-89	Cgy	5	0	3	3	3	0	0	16	0.0	0	–	–	0	–	–	–	10	–	–	–	–	–	0	.60
89-90	Cgy	6	0	1	1	0	0	0	20	0.0	0	–	–	0	–	–	–	14	–	–	–	–	–	0	.17
90-91	Cgy	7	1	6	7	0	0	0	11	9.1	1	–	–	0	0	0	–	12	–	–	–	–	–	0	1.00
92-93	Cgy	6	2	3	5	-9	0	0	13	15.4	0	1	1	1	1	2	4	8	0	4	0	0	1	0	.83
93-94	Chi	6	3	2	5	0	0	0	16	18.8	2	2	4	0	0	0	3	6	0	3	0	0	2	1	.83
94-95	Chi	12	2	5	7	-1	0	0	43	4.7	1	3	4	0	0	0	5	10	0	5	0	0	1	0	.58
95-96	Chi	10	3	3	6	1	1	0	27	11.1	2	1	3	0	0	0	4	8	0	4	0	0	2	0	.60
96-97	Chi	6	1	4	5	1	0	0	12	8.3	0	1	1	0	0	0	4	8	0	4	0	0	1	0	.83
11 Years		83	15	47	62	1	2	0	213	7.0	6	–	–	2	–	–	–	100	–	–	–	–	–	1	.75

Ron Sutter

Pos: C **Shoots:** R **Ht:** 6'0" **Wt:** 180 **Born:** 12/2/63—Viking, Alberta **Age:** 36

Overall											Power Play			Shorthand			Penalty							Misc	
Year	Tm	GP	G	A	Pts	+/–	GW	GT	S	SPct	G	A	Pts	G	A	Pts	Num	PIM	Maj	Mnr	Fgt	Rgh	HHT	Hat	P/G
82-83	Phi	10	1	1	2	0	0	0	1	100.0	0	–	–	0	–	–	3	9	1	2	–	–	–	0	.20
83-84	Phi	79	19	32	51	4	3	1	145	13.1	5	–	–	3	–	–	–	101	–	–	–	–	–	0	.65
84-85	Phi	73	16	29	45	13	5	0	140	11.4	2	–	–	0	–	–	–	94	–	–	–	–	–	0	.62
85-86	Phi	75	18	42	60	26	4	0	145	12.4	0	–	–	0	–	–	–	159	–	–	–	–	–	0	.80

Overall											Power Play			Shorthand			Penalty							Misc	
Year	Tm	GP	G	A	Pts	+/–	GW	GT	S	SPct	G	A	Pts	G	A	Pts	Num	PIM	Maj	Mnr	Fgt	Rgh	HHT	Hat	P/G
86-87	Phi	39	10	17	27	10	0	0	68	14.7	0	–	–	0	–	–	–	69	–	–	–	–	–	0	.69
87-88	Phi	69	8	25	33	-9	0	0	107	7.5	1	–	–	0	–	–	–	146	–	–	–	–	–	0	.48
88-89	Phi	55	26	22	48	25	2	0	106	24.5	4	–	–	1	–	–	–	80	–	–	–	–	–	0	.87
89-90	Phi	75	22	26	48	2	6	0	157	14.0	0	–	–	2	–	–	–	104	–	–	–	–	–	0	.64
90-91	Phi	80	17	28	45	2	1	0	149	11.4	2	–	–	0	–	–	–	92	–	–	–	–	–	0	.56
91-92	StL	68	19	27	46	9	1	1	106	17.9	5	7	12	4	2	6	40	91	1	38	0	6	10	0	.68
92-93	StL	59	12	15	27	-11	3	0	90	13.3	4	5	9	0	0	0	36	99	1	32	1	8	8	0	.46
93-94	2Tm	73	15	25	40	2	2	0	108	13.9	5	2	7	0	0	0	37	90	0	35	0	4	9	0	.55
94-95	NYI	27	1	4	5	-8	1	0	29	3.4	0	0	0	0	0	0	5	21	1	3	0	0	1	0	.19
95-96	Bos	18	5	7	12	10	0	0	34	14.7	0	0	0	1	1	2	12	24	0	12	0	1	4	0	.67
96-97	SJ	78	5	7	12	-8	1	0	78	6.4	1	0	1	2	2	4	23	65	1	20	0	3	4	0	.15
97-98	SJ	57	2	7	9	-2	1	0	57	3.5	0	0	0	0	0	0	11	22	0	11	0	0	7	0	.16
98-99	SJ	50	3	6	9	-8	1	0	67	4.5	0	0	0	0	0	0	13	40	2	10	1	0	2	0	.15
93-94	StL	36	6	12	18	-1	2	0	42	14.3	1	1	2	0	0	0	19	46	0	18	0	3	6	0	.50
93-94	Que	37	9	13	22	3	0	0	66	13.6	4	1	5	0	0	0	18	44	0	17	0	1	3	0	.59
17 Years		994	199	320	519	57	31	2	1587	12.5	29	–	–	13	–	–	–	1306	–	–	–	–	–	0	.52
Postseason																									
Year	Tm	GP	G	A	Pts	+/–	GW	OT	S	SPct	G	A	Pts	G	A	Pts	Num	PIM	Maj	Mnr	Fgt	Rgh	HHT	Hat	P/G
83-84	Phi	3	0	0	0	0	0	0	3	0.0	0	0	0	0	0	0	–	22	–	–	–	–	–	0	.00
84-85	Phi	19	4	8	12	-1	1	0	43	9.3	0	–	–	0	–	–	–	28	–	–	–	–	–	0	.63
85-86	Phi	5	0	2	2	2	0	0	11	0.0	0	–	–	0	0	0	–	10	–	–	–	–	–	0	.40
86-87	Phi	16	1	7	8	-3	0	0	22	4.5	0	–	–	0	–	–	–	12	–	–	–	–	–	0	.50
87-88	Phi	7	0	1	1	-7	0	0	3	0.0	0	–	–	0	0	0	–	26	–	–	–	–	–	0	.14
88-89	Phi	19	1	9	10	5	0	0	39	2.6	0	–	–	0	–	–	–	51	–	–	–	–	–	0	.53
91-92	StL	6	1	3	4	-1	0	0	9	11.1	1	1	2	0	0	0	4	8	0	4	0	2	1	0	.67
95-96	Bos	5	0	0	0	-2	0	0	4	0.0	0	0	0	0	0	0	4	8	0	4	0	2	0	0	.00
97-98	SJ	6	1	0	1	-1	0	0	7	14.3	0	0	0	0	0	0	3	14	0	2	0	1	1	0	.17
98-99	SJ	6	0	0	0	-1	0	0	10	0.0	0	0	0	0	0	0	2	4	0	2	0	0	1	0	.00
10 Years		92	8	30	38	-9	1	0	151	5.3	1	–	–	0	–	–	–	183	–	–	–	–	–	0	.41

Andy Sutton

Pos: D **Shoots:** R **Ht:** 6'6" **Wt:** 240 **Born:** 10/24/77—Edmonton, Alberta **Age:** 22

Overall											Power Play			Shorthand			Penalty							Misc	
Year	Tm	GP	G	A	Pts	+/–	GW	GT	S	SPct	G	A	Pts	G	A	Pts	Num	PIM	Maj	Mnr	Fgt	Rgh	HHT	Hat	P/G
98-99	SJ	31	0	3	3	-4	0	0	24	0.0	0	1	1	0	0	0	20	65	3	15	3	6	4	0	.10

Ken Sutton

Pos: D **Shoots:** L **Ht:** 6'0" **Wt:** 200 **Born:** 11/5/69—Edmonton, Alberta **Age:** 30

Overall											Power Play			Shorthand			Penalty							Misc	
Year	Tm	GP	G	A	Pts	+/–	GW	GT	S	SPct	G	A	Pts	G	A	Pts	Num	PIM	Maj	Mnr	Fgt	Rgh	HHT	Hat	P/G
90-91	Buf	15	3	6	9	2	0	0	26	11.5	2	–	–	0	–	–	5	13	1	4	–	–	–	0	.60
91-92	Buf	64	2	18	20	5	0	0	81	2.5	0	3	3	0	0	0	30	71	1	28	1	7	8	0	.31
92-93	Buf	63	8	14	22	-3	2	1	77	10.4	1	0	1	0	0	0	15	30	0	15	0	4	2	0	.35
93-94	Buf	78	4	20	24	-6	0	0	95	4.2	1	9	10	0	0	0	24	71	5	18	5	4	6	0	.31
94-95	2Tm	24	4	3	7	-3	1	0	40	10.0	0	2	2	0	1	1	14	42	2	11	2	6	1	0	.29
95-96	2Tm	38	0	8	8	-13	0	0	41	0.0	0	4	4	0	0	0	20	43	1	19	1	4	3	0	.21
96-97	Did Not Play in NHL																								
97-98	2Tm	21	0	0	0	-3	0	0	12	0.0	0	0	0	0	0	0	9	21	1	8	1	1	3	0	.00
98-99	NJ	5	1	0	1	1	0	0	5	20.0	0	0	0	0	0	0	0	0	0	0	0	0	0	0	.20
94-95	Buf	12	1	2	3	-2	1	0	12	8.3	0	1	1	0	1	1	8	30	2	5	2	3	0	0	.25
94-95	Edm	12	3	1	4	-1	0	0	28	10.7	0	1	1	0	0	0	6	12	0	6	0	3	1	0	.33
95-96	Edm	32	0	8	8	-12	0	0	38	0.0	0	4	4	0	0	0	18	39	1	17	1	4	2	0	.25
95-96	StL	6	0	0	0	-1	0	0	3	0.0	0	0	0	0	0	0	2	4	0	2	0	0	1	0	.00
97-98	NJ	13	0	0	0	1	0	0	5	0.0	0	0	0	0	0	0	3	6	0	3	0	1	0	0	.00
97-98	SJ	8	0	0	0	-4	0	0	7	0.0	0	0	0	0	0	0	6	15	1	5	1	0	3	0	.00
8 Years		308	22	69	91	-20	3	1	377	5.8	4	–	–	0	–	–	117	291	11	103	–	–	–	0	.30
Postseason																									
Year	Tm	GP	G	A	Pts	+/–	GW	OT	S	SPct	G	A	Pts	G	A	Pts	Num	PIM	Maj	Mnr	Fgt	Rgh	HHT	Hat	P/G
90-91	Buf	6	0	1	1	-4	0	0	13	0.0	0	–	–	0	–	–	1	2	0	1	0	–	–	0	.17
91-92	Buf	7	0	2	2	0	0	0	5	0.0	0	1	1	0	0	0	2	4	0	2	0	0	1	0	.29
92-93	Buf	8	3	1	4	3	0	0	16	18.8	0	0	0	0	0	0	4	8	0	4	0	3	1	0	.50
93-94	Buf	4	0	0	0	2	0	0	8	0.0	0	0	0	0	0	0	1	2	0	1	0	0	0	0	.00
95-96	StL	1	0	0	0	0	0	0	1	0.0	0	0	0	0	0	0	0	0	0	0	0	0	0	0	.00
5 Years		26	3	4	7	1	0	0	43	7.0	0	–	–	0	–	–	8	16	0	8	0	–	–	0	.27

Robert Svehla

(statistical profile on page 379)

Pos: D **Shoots:** L **Ht:** 6'1" **Wt:** 190 **Born:** 1/2/69—Martin, Czechoslovakia **Age:** 30

Overall											Power Play			Shorthand			Penalty							Misc	
Year	Tm	GP	G	A	Pts	+/–	GW	GT	S	SPct	G	A	Pts	G	A	Pts	Num	PIM	Maj	Mnr	Fgt	Rgh	HHT	Hat	P/G
94-95	Fla	5	1	1	2	3	0	0	6	16.7	1	0	1	0	0	0	0	0	0	0	0	0	0	0	.40
95-96	Fla	81	8	49	57	-3	0	0	146	5.5	7	27	34	0	2	2	43	94	0	42	0	4	18	0	.70
96-97	Fla*	**82**	13	32	45	2	3	0	159	8.2	5	14	19	0	0	0	43	86	0	43	0	8	20	0	.55
97-98	Fla	79	9	34	43	-3	0	0	144	6.3	3	23	26	0	1	1	39	113	1	34	0	4	14	0	.54
98-99	Fla	80	8	29	37	-13	0	1	157	5.1	4	12	16	0	3	3	40	83	1	39	1	4	17	0	.46
5 Years		327	39	145	184	-14	3	1	612	6.4	20	76	96	0	6	6	165	376	2	158	1	20	69	0	.56

Postseason

Year	Tm	GP	G	A	Pts	+/–	GW	OT	S	SPct	G	A	Pts	G	A	Pts	Num	PIM	Maj	Mnr	Fgt	Rgh	HHT	Hat	P/G
95-96	Fla	22	0	6	6	3	0	0	38	0.0	0	2	2	0	0	0	16	32	0	16	0	5	4	0	.27
96-97	Fla	5	1	4	5	-4	0	0	13	7.7	1	3	4	0	0	0	2	4	0	2	0	1	1	0	1.00
2 Years		27	1	10	11	-1	0	0	51	2.0	1	5	6	0	0	0	18	36	0	18	0	6	5	0	.41

Jaroslav Svejkovsky

(statistical profile on page 379)

Pos: RW **Shoots:** R **Ht:** 6'0" **Wt:** 195 **Born:** 10/1/76—Plzen, Czechoslovakia **Age:** 23

Overall											Power Play			Shorthand			Penalty							Misc	
Year	Tm	GP	G	A	Pts	+/–	GW	GT	S	SPct	G	A	Pts	G	A	Pts	Num	PIM	Maj	Mnr	Fgt	Rgh	HHT	Hat	P/G
96-97	Was	19	7	3	10	-1	1	0	30	23.3	2	1	3	0	0	0	2	4	0	2	0	0	2	1	.53
97-98	Was	17	4	1	5	-5	1	0	29	13.8	2	1	3	0	0	0	5	10	0	5	0	2	2	0	.29
98-99	Was	25	6	8	14	-2	2	0	50	12.0	4	3	7	0	0	0	6	12	0	6	0	1	4	0	.56
3 Years		61	17	12	29	-8	4	0	109	15.6	8	5	13	0	0	0	13	26	0	13	0	3	8	1	.48

Postseason

Year	Tm	GP	G	A	Pts	+/–	GW	OT	S	SPct	G	A	Pts	G	A	Pts	Num	PIM	Maj	Mnr	Fgt	Rgh	HHT	Hat	P/G
97-98	Was	1	0	0	0	0	0	0	0	–	0	0	0	0	0	0	1	2	0	1	0	0	0	0	.00

Petr Svoboda

(statistical profile on page 379)

Pos: D **Shoots:** L **Ht:** 6'1" **Wt:** 195 **Born:** 2/14/66—Most, Czechoslovakia **Age:** 33

Overall											Power Play			Shorthand			Penalty							Misc	
Year	Tm	GP	G	A	Pts	+/–	GW	GT	S	SPct	G	A	Pts	G	A	Pts	Num	PIM	Maj	Mnr	Fgt	Rgh	HHT	Hat	P/G
84-85	Mon	73	4	27	31	16	1	0	81	4.9	0	–	–	0	–	–	–	65	–	–	–	–	–	0	.42
85-86	Mon	73	1	18	19	24	0	0	63	1.6	0	–	–	0	–	–	–	93	–	–	–	–	–	0	.26
86-87	Mon	70	5	17	22	14	1	0	80	6.3	1	–	–	0	–	–	–	63	–	–	–	–	–	0	.31
87-88	Mon	69	7	22	29	46	1	0	138	5.1	2	–	–	0	–	–	–	149	–	–	–	–	–	0	.42
88-89	Mon	71	8	37	45	28	1	0	131	6.1	4	–	–	0	–	–	–	147	–	–	–	–	–	0	.63
89-90	Mon	60	5	31	36	20	2	0	90	5.6	2	–	–	0	–	–	–	98	–	–	–	–	–	0	.60
90-91	Mon	60	4	22	26	5	1	0	67	6.0	3	–	–	0	–	–	–	52	–	–	–	–	–	0	.43
91-92	2Tm	71	6	22	28	1	3	0	111	5.4	1	15	16	0	0	0	42	146	2	33	2	3	15	0	.39
92-93	Buf	40	2	24	26	3	1	0	61	3.3	1	14	15	0	1	1	24	59	1	22	0	3	6	0	.65
93-94	Buf	60	2	14	16	11	0	0	80	2.5	1	9	10	0	1	1	35	89	1	32	0	5	11	0	.27
94-95	2Tm	37	0	8	8	-5	0	0	39	0.0	0	5	5	0	0	0	27	70	0	25	0	5	7	0	.22
95-96	Phi	73	1	28	29	28	0	0	91	1.1	0	13	13	0	0	0	48	105	3	45	2	9	11	0	.40
96-97	Phi	67	2	12	14	10	0	0	36	5.6	1	1	2	0	0	0	32	94	2	27	1	1	13	0	.21
97-98	Phi	56	3	15	18	19	0	0	44	6.8	2	6	8	0	0	0	28	83	1	24	1	9	5	0	.32
98-99	2Tm	59	5	18	23	1	1	0	83	6.0	1	9	10	1	1	2	39	81	1	38	1	3	18	0	.39
91-92	Mon	58	5	16	21	9	3	0	88	5.7	1	10	11	0	0	0	28	94	2	22	2	2	11	0	.36
91-92	Buf	13	1	6	7	-8	0	0	23	4.3	0	5	5	0	0	0	14	52	0	11	0	1	4	0	.54
94-95	Buf	26	0	5	5	-5	0	0	22	0.0	0	3	3	0	0	0	22	60	0	20	0	4	6	0	.19
94-95	Phi	11	0	3	3	0	0	0	17	0.0	0	2	2	0	0	0	5	10	0	5	0	1	1	0	.27
98-99	Phi	25	4	2	6	5	1	0	37	10.8	1	0	1	1	0	1	14	28	0	14	0	1	5	0	.24
98-99	TB	34	1	16	17	-4	0	0	46	2.2	0	9	9	0	1	1	25	53	1	24	1	2	13	0	.50
15 Years		939	55	315	370	221	12	0	1195	4.6	19	–	–	1	–	–	–	1394	–	–	–	–	–	0	.39

Postseason

Year	Tm	GP	G	A	Pts	+/–	GW	OT	S	SPct	G	A	Pts	G	A	Pts	Num	PIM	Maj	Mnr	Fgt	Rgh	HHT	Hat	P/G
84-85	Mon	7	1	1	2	0	0	0	8	12.5	0	–	–	0	–	–	–	12	–	–	–	–	–	0	.29
85-86	Mon	8	0	0	0	2	0	0	3	0.0	0	0	0	0	0	0	–	21	–	–	–	–	–	0	.00
86-87	Mon	14	0	5	5	-1	0	0	15	0.0	0	–	–	0	–	–	–	10	–	–	–	–	–	0	.36
87-88	Mon	10	0	5	5	1	0	0	19	0.0	0	–	–	0	–	–	–	12	–	–	–	–	–	0	.50
88-89	Mon	21	1	11	12	-3	0	0	23	4.3	0	–	–	0	–	–	–	16	–	–	–	–	–	0	.57
89-90	Mon	10	0	5	5	7	0	0	12	0.0	0	–	–	0	0	0	1	2	0	1	0	–	–	0	.50
90-91	Mon	2	0	1	1	-1	0	0	5	0.0	0	–	–	0	–	–	1	2	0	1	0	–	–	0	.50
91-92	Buf	7	1	4	5	0	0	0	12	8.3	0	3	3	1	0	1	3	6	0	3	0	0	1	0	.71
93-94	Buf	3	0	0	0	-1	0	0	2	0.0	0	0	0	0	0	0	2	4	0	2	0	0	0	0	.00

Postseason																									
Year	Tm	GP	G	A	Pts	+/–	GW	OT	S	SPct	G	A	Pts	G	A	Pts	Num	PIM	Maj	Mnr	Fgt	Rgh	HHT	Hat	P/G
94-95	Phi	14	0	4	4	5	0	0	15	0.0	0	0	0	0	0	0	4	8	0	4	0	1	1	0	.29
95-96	Phi	12	0	6	6	6	0	0	17	0.0	0	4	4	0	0	0	7	22	0	6	0	1	2	0	.50
96-97	Phi	16	1	2	3	4	0	0	9	11.1	0	0	0	0	0	0	8	16	0	8	0	0	2	0	.19
97-98	Phi	3	0	1	1	-1	0	0	1	0.0	0	1	1	0	0	0	2	4	0	2	0	0	0	0	.33
13 Years		127	4	45	49	18	0	0	141	2.8	0	–	–	1	–	–	–	135	–	–	–	–	–	0	.39

Don Sweeney

(statistical profile on page 379)

Pos: D **Shoots:** L **Ht:** 5'10" **Wt:** 184 **Born:** 8/17/66—St. Stephen, New Brunswick **Age:** 33

Overall											Power Play			Shorthand			Penalty							Misc	
Year	Tm	GP	G	A	Pts	+/–	GW	GT	S	SPct	G	A	Pts	G	A	Pts	Num	PIM	Maj	Mnr	Fgt	Rgh	HHT	Hat	P/G
88-89	Bos	36	3	5	8	-6	0	0	35	8.6	0	1	1	0	–	–	–	20	–	–	–	–	–	0	.22
89-90	Bos	58	3	5	8	11	0	0	49	6.1	0	0	0	0	–	–	–	58	–	–	–	–	–	0	.14
90-91	Bos	77	8	13	21	2	3	0	102	7.8	0	1	1	1	0	1	–	67	–	–	–	–	–	0	.27
91-92	Bos	75	3	11	14	-9	1	0	92	3.3	0	0	0	0	1	1	26	74	2	22	1	5	5	0	.19
92-93	Bos	84	7	27	34	34	0	0	107	6.5	0	0	0	1	0	1	27	68	2	24	1	7	9	0	.40
93-94	Bos	75	6	15	21	29	2	0	136	4.4	1	0	1	2	0	2	25	50	0	25	0	6	10	0	.28
94-95	Bos	47	3	19	22	6	2	0	102	2.9	1	6	7	0	0	0	12	24	0	12	0	2	5	0	.47
95-96	Bos	77	4	24	28	-4	3	0	142	2.8	2	6	8	0	2	2	21	42	0	21	0	2	10	0	.36
96-97	Bos	**82**	3	23	26	-5	0	0	113	2.7	0	3	3	0	1	1	18	39	1	17	1	1	11	0	.32
97-98	Bos	59	1	15	16	12	0	0	55	1.8	0	1	1	0	0	0	12	24	0	12	0	1	2	0	.27
98-99	Bos	81	2	10	12	14	0	0	79	2.5	0	2	2	0	1	1	24	64	0	22	0	2	11	0	.15
11 Years		751	43	167	210	84	11	0	1012	4.2	4	20	24	4	–	–	–	530	–	–	–	–	–	0	.28
Postseason																									
Year	Tm	GP	G	A	Pts	+/–	GW	OT	S	SPct	G	A	Pts	G	A	Pts	Num	PIM	Maj	Mnr	Fgt	Rgh	HHT	Hat	P/G
89-90	Bos	21	1	5	6	-10	0	0	27	3.7	1	0	1	0	–	–	–	18	–	–	–	–	–	0	.29
90-91	Bos	19	3	0	3	-3	0	0	31	9.7	0	0	0	0	0	0	–	25	–	–	–	–	–	0	.16
91-92	Bos	15	0	0	0	-3	0	0	13	0.0	0	0	0	0	0	0	5	10	0	5	0	1	2	0	.00
92-93	Bos	4	0	0	0	-1	0	0	5	0.0	0	0	0	0	0	0	2	4	0	2	0	1	1	0	.00
93-94	Bos	12	2	1	3	-2	1	1	11	18.2	0	0	0	0	0	0	2	4	0	2	0	1	0	0	.25
94-95	Bos	5	0	0	0	-4	0	0	8	0.0	0	0	0	0	0	0	2	4	0	2	0	0	0	0	.00
95-96	Bos	5	0	2	2	-3	0	0	12	0.0	0	0	0	0	1	1	3	6	0	3	0	1	1	0	.40
98-99	Bos	11	3	0	3	2	0	0	16	18.8	1	0	1	0	0	0	3	6	0	3	0	0	1	0	.27
8 Years		92	9	8	17	-24	1	1	123	7.3	2	0	2	0	–	–	–	77	–	–	–	–	–	0	.18

Darryl Sydor

(statistical profile on page 380)

Pos: D **Shoots:** L **Ht:** 6'0" **Wt:** 195 **Born:** 5/13/72—Edmonton, Alberta **Age:** 27

Overall											Power Play			Shorthand			Penalty							Misc	
Year	Tm	GP	G	A	Pts	+/–	GW	GT	S	SPct	G	A	Pts	G	A	Pts	Num	PIM	Maj	Mnr	Fgt	Rgh	HHT	Hat	P/G
91-92	LA	18	1	5	6	-3	0	0	18	5.6	0	3	3	0	0	0	11	22	0	11	0	1	6	0	.33
92-93	LA	80	6	23	29	-2	1	0	112	5.4	0	7	7	0	1	1	27	63	3	24	3	3	12	0	.36
93-94	LA	84	8	27	35	-9	0	0	146	5.5	1	9	10	0	1	1	40	94	2	37	2	7	17	0	.42
94-95	LA	48	4	19	23	-2	0	1	96	4.2	3	1	4	0	1	1	18	36	0	18	0	6	9	0	.48
95-96	2Tm	**84**	3	17	20	-12	0	0	117	2.6	2	8	10	0	0	0	32	75	1	30	1	3	12	0	.24
96-97	Dal	**82**	8	40	48	37	2	0	142	5.6	2	21	23	0	0	0	24	51	1	23	1	8	5	0	.59
97-98	Dal*	79	11	35	46	17	1	0	166	6.6	4	24	28	1	0	1	21	51	3	18	3	5	3	1	.58
98-99	Dal	74	14	34	48	-1	2	1	163	8.6	9	26	35	0	0	0	18	50	2	15	2	3	6	0	.65
95-96	LA	58	1	11	12	-11	0	0	84	1.2	1	4	5	0	0	0	17	34	0	17	0	2	7	0	.21
95-96	Dal	26	2	6	8	-1	0	0	33	6.1	1	4	5	0	0	0	15	41	1	13	1	1	5	0	.31
8 Years		549	55	200	255	25	6	2	960	5.7	21	99	120	1	3	4	191	442	12	176	12	36	70	1	.46
Postseason																									
Year	Tm	GP	G	A	Pts	+/–	GW	OT	S	SPct	G	A	Pts	G	A	Pts	Num	PIM	Maj	Mnr	Fgt	Rgh	HHT	Hat	P/G
92-93	LA	24	3	8	11	4	0	0	29	10.3	2	3	5	0	0	0	8	16	0	8	0	1	4	0	.46
96-97	Dal	7	0	2	2	-2	0	0	24	0.0	0	2	2	0	0	0	0	0	0	0	0	0	0	0	.29
97-98	Dal	17	0	5	5	5	0	0	38	0.0	0	2	2	0	0	0	7	14	0	7	0	1	1	0	.29
98-99	Dal	23	3	9	12	8	1	0	49	6.1	1	6	7	0	0	0	8	16	0	8	0	1	4	0	.52
4 Years		71	6	24	30	15	1	0	140	4.3	3	13	16	0	0	0	23	46	0	23	0	3	9	0	.42

Michal Sykora

Pos: D **Shoots:** L **Ht:** 6'4" **Wt:** 230 **Born:** 7/5/73—Pardubice, Czechoslovakia **Age:** 26

Overall											Power Play			Shorthand			Penalty							Misc	
Year	Tm	GP	G	A	Pts	+/–	GW	GT	S	SPct	G	A	Pts	G	A	Pts	Num	PIM	Maj	Mnr	Fgt	Rgh	HHT	Hat	P/G
93-94	SJ	22	1	4	5	-4	0	0	22	4.5	0	1	1	0	0	0	7	14	0	7	0	0	5	0	.23

		Overall									Power Play			Shorthand			Penalty							Misc	
Year	Tm	GP	G	A	Pts	+/–	GW	GT	S	SPct	G	A	Pts	G	A	Pts	Num	PIM	Maj	Mnr	Fgt	Rgh	HHT	Hat	P/G
94-95	SJ	16	0	4	4	6	0	0	6	0.0	0	0	0	0	1	1	5	10	0	5	0	0	4	0	.25
95-96	SJ	79	4	16	20	-14	0	0	80	5.0	1	0	1	0	0	0	27	54	0	27	0	4	17	0	.25
96-97	2Tm	63	3	14	17	4	0	0	77	3.9	1	2	3	0	0	0	25	69	1	22	0	3	11	0	.27
97-98	Chi	28	1	3	4	-10	0	0	35	2.9	0	2	2	0	0	0	6	12	0	6	0	2	3	0	.14
98-99	TB	10	1	2	3	-7	1	0	24	4.2	0	2	2	0	0	0	0	0	0	0	0	0	0	0	.30
96-97	SJ	35	2	5	7	0	0	0	39	5.1	1	1	2	0	0	0	20	59	1	17	0	3	8	0	.20
96-97	Chi	28	1	9	10	4	0	0	38	2.6	0	1	1	0	0	0	5	10	0	5	0	0	3	0	.36
6 Years		218	10	43	53	-25	1	0	244	4.1	2	7	9	0	1	1	70	159	1	67	0	9	40	0	.24

Postseason

Year	Tm	GP	G	A	Pts	+/–	GW	OT	S	SPct	G	A	Pts	G	A	Pts	Num	PIM	Maj	Mnr	Fgt	Rgh	HHT	Hat	P/G
96-97	Chi	1	0	0	0	-2	0	0	1	0.0	0	0	0	0	0	0	0	0	0	0	0	0	0	0	.00

Petr Sykora

(statistical profile on page 380)

Pos: C **Shoots:** L **Ht:** 5'11" **Wt:** 185 **Born:** 11/19/76—Plzen, Czechoslovakia **Age:** 23

		Overall									Power Play			Shorthand			Penalty							Misc	
Year	Tm	GP	G	A	Pts	+/–	GW	GT	S	SPct	G	A	Pts	G	A	Pts	Num	PIM	Maj	Mnr	Fgt	Rgh	HHT	Hat	P/G
95-96	NJ	63	18	24	42	7	3	0	128	14.1	8	11	19	0	0	0	16	32	0	16	0	0	9	0	.67
96-97	NJ	19	1	2	3	-8	0	0	26	3.8	0	1	1	0	0	0	2	4	0	2	0	0	1	0	.16
97-98	NJ	58	16	20	36	0	4	0	130	12.3	3	10	13	1	0	1	11	22	0	11	0	2	1	0	.62
98-99	NJ	80	29	43	72	16	7	0	222	13.1	15	11	26	0	0	0	11	22	0	11	0	2	4	0	.90
4 Years		220	64	89	153	15	14	0	506	12.6	26	33	59	1	0	1	40	80	0	40	0	4	15	0	.70

Postseason

Year	Tm	GP	G	A	Pts	+/–	GW	OT	S	SPct	G	A	Pts	G	A	Pts	Num	PIM	Maj	Mnr	Fgt	Rgh	HHT	Hat	P/G
96-97	NJ	2	0	0	0	1	0	0	10	0.0	0	0	0	0	0	0	1	2	0	1	0	0	0	0	.00
97-98	NJ	2	0	0	0	0	0	0	5	0.0	0	0	0	0	0	0	0	0	0	0	0	0	0	0	.00
98-99	NJ	7	3	3	6	-3	1	0	12	25.0	0	2	2	0	0	0	2	4	0	2	0	0	0	0	.86
3 Years		11	3	3	6	-2	1	0	27	11.1	0	2	2	0	0	0	3	6	0	3	0	0	0	0	.55

Petr Sykora

Pos: C **Shoots:** R **Ht:** 6'2" **Wt:** 180 **Born:** 12/21/78—Parduvush, Czechoslovakia **Age:** 21

		Overall									Power Play			Shorthand			Penalty							Misc	
Year	Tm	GP	G	A	Pts	+/–	GW	GT	S	SPct	G	A	Pts	G	A	Pts	Num	PIM	Maj	Mnr	Fgt	Rgh	HHT	Hat	P/G
98-99	Nsh	2	0	0	0	-1	0	0	2	0.0	0	0	0	0	0	0	0	0	0	0	0	0	0	0	.00

Dean Sylvester

Pos: RW **Shoots:** R **Ht:** 6'2" **Wt:** 185 **Born:** 10/30/72—Hanson, Massachusetts **Age:** 27

		Overall									Power Play			Shorthand			Penalty							Misc	
Year	Tm	GP	G	A	Pts	+/–	GW	GT	S	SPct	G	A	Pts	G	A	Pts	Num	PIM	Maj	Mnr	Fgt	Rgh	HHT	Hat	P/G
98-99	Buf	1	0	0	0	-1	0	0	1	0.0	0	0	0	0	0	0	0	0	0	0	0	0	0	0	.00

Postseason

Year	Tm	GP	G	A	Pts	+/–	GW	OT	S	SPct	G	A	Pts	G	A	Pts	Num	PIM	Maj	Mnr	Fgt	Rgh	HHT	Hat	P/G
98-99	Buf	4	0	0	0	-1	0	0	2	0.0	0	0	0	0	0	0	1	2	0	1	0	0	0	0	.00

Rick Tabaracci

(statistical profile on page 403)

Pos: G **Catches:** L **Ht:** 5'11" **Wt:** 180 **Born:** 1/2/69—Toronto, Ontario **Age:** 30

		Overall															Pen Shot		Offense		
Year	Tm	GP	GS	TP	W	L	T	Min	GA	GAA	Shots	SvPct	ShO	OE	PPGA	SHGA	Shots	GA	G	A	PIM
88-89	Pit	1	–	–	0	0	0	33	4	7.27	21	.810	0	–	–	–	0	0	0	0	2
89-90		Did Not Play in NHL																			
90-91	Wpg	24	–	–	4	9	4	1093	71	3.90	570	.875	1	–	–	–	1	0	0	1	8
91-92	Wpg	18	17	3	6	7	3	966	52	3.23	470	.889	0	5	16	1	1	1	0	1	4
92-93	2Tm	25	20	1	8	12	0	1302	80	3.69	658	.878	2	8	22	4	0	0	0	0	14
93-94	Was	32	31	5	13	14	2	1770	91	3.08	817	.889	2	7	21	4	0	0	0	0	6
94-95	2Tm	13	10	2	3	3	3	596	21	2.11	240	.913	0	1	9	1	0	0	0	2	2
95-96	Cgy	43	38	3	19	16	3	2391	117	2.94	1087	.892	3	8	40	2	0	0	0	2	8
96-97	2Tm	62	57	7	22	29	6	3373	152	2.70	1570	.903	5	16	29	9	0	0	0	1	12
97-98	Cgy	42	42	5	13	22	6	2419	116	2.88	1087	.893	0	11	37	5	2	0	0	1	14
98-99	Was	23	16	0	4	12	3	1193	50	2.51	530	.906	2	6	15	3	**3**	0	0	0	2
92-93	Wpg	19	15	1	5	10	0	959	70	4.38	496	.859	0	4	19	4	0	0	0	0	10
92-93	Was	6	5	0	3	2	0	343	10	1.75	162	.938	2	4	3	0	0	0	0	0	4

							Overall									Pen Shot		Offense		
Year	Tm	GP	GS	TP	W	L	T	Min	GA	GAA	Shots	SvPct	ShO	OE	PPGA	SHGA	Shots	GA	G	A	PIM
94-95	Was	8	7	2	1	3	2	394	16	2.44	147	.891	0	0	8	1	0	0	0	1	2
94-95	Cgy	5	3	0	2	0	1	202	5	1.49	93	.946	0	1	1	0	0	0	0	1	0
96-97	Cgy	7	6	0	2	4	0	361	14	2.33	155	.910	1	2	1	3	0	0	0	0	0
96-97	TB	55	51	7	20	25	6	3012	138	2.75	1415	.902	4	14	28	6	0	0	0	1	12
10 Years		283	–	–	92	124	30	15136	754	2.99	7050	.893	15	–	–	–	7	1	0	8	72
							Postseason													
Year	Tm	GP	GS	TP	W	L	Pct	Min	GA	GAA	Shots	SvPct	ShO	OE	PPGA	SHGA	Shots	GA	G	A	PIM
91-92	Wpg	7	7	1	3	4	.429	387	26	4.03	212	.877	0	2	5	1	0	0	0	0	0
92-93	Was	4	4	0	1	3	.250	304	14	2.76	160	.913	0	0	1	0	0	0	0	0	4
93-94	Was	2	1	0	0	2	.000	111	6	3.24	50	.880	0	0	0	0	0	0	0	0	0
94-95	Cgy	1	0	0	0	0	–	19	0	0.00	9	1.000	0	0	0	0	0	0	0	0	0
95-96	Cgy	3	2	0	0	3	.000	204	7	2.06	84	.917	0	2	1	0	0	0	0	0	0
5 Years		17	14	1	4	12	.250	1025	53	3.10	515	.897	0	4	7	1	0	0	0	0	4

Robbie Tallas

Pos: G **Catches:** L **Ht:** 6'0" **Wt:** 163 **Born:** 3/20/73—Edmonton, Alberta **Age:** 26

							Overall									Pen Shot		Offense		
Year	Tm	GP	GS	TP	W	L	T	Min	GA	GAA	Shots	SvPct	ShO	OE	PPGA	SHGA	Shots	GA	G	A	PIM
95-96	Bos	1	1	0	1	0	0	60	3	3.00	29	.897	0	0	1	0	0	0	0	0	0
96-97	Bos	28	22	4	8	12	1	1244	69	3.33	587	.882	1	5	17	0	0	0	0	0	0
97-98	Bos	14	12	1	6	3	3	788	24	1.83	326	.926	1	5	4	0	0	0	0	0	0
98-99	Bos	17	15	1	7	7	2	987	43	2.61	421	.898	1	3	8	5	1	0	0	0	0
4 Years		60	50	6	22	22	6	3079	139	2.71	1363	.898	3	13	30	5	1	0	0	0	0

Chris Tamer

Pos: D **Shoots:** L **Ht:** 6'1" **Wt:** 207 **Born:** 11/17/70—Dearborn, Michigan **Age:** 29

			Overall							Power Play			Shorthand			Penalty							Misc	
Year	Tm	GP	G	A	Pts	+/–	GW	GT	S	SPct	G	A	Pts	G	A	Pts	Num	PIM	Maj	Mnr	Fgt	Rgh	HHT	Hat	P/G
93-94	Pit	12	0	0	0	3	0	0	10	0.0	0	0	0	0	0	0	3	9	1	2	1	1	1	0	.00
94-95	Pit	36	2	0	2	0	0	0	26	7.7	0	0	0	0	0	0	19	82	12	6	11	1	3	0	.06
95-96	Pit	70	4	10	14	20	1	0	75	5.3	0	1	1	0	1	1	56	153	11	44	11	17	9	0	.20
96-97	Pit	45	2	4	6	-25	0	0	56	3.6	0	0	0	1	0	1	40	131	9	28	9	12	4	0	.13
97-98	Pit	79	0	7	7	4	0	0	55	0.0	0	1	1	0	0	0	52	181	15	33	15	12	2	0	.09
98-99	2Tm	63	1	5	6	-14	1	0	48	2.1	0	0	0	0	0	0	36	124	12	22	12	4	7	0	.10
98-99	Pit	11	0	0	0	-2	0	0	2	0.0	0	0	0	0	0	0	6	32	4	1	4	0	0	0	.00
98-99	NYR	52	1	5	6	-12	1	0	46	2.2	0	0	0	0	0	0	30	92	8	21	8	4	7	0	.12
6 Years		305	9	26	35	-12	2	0	270	3.3	0	2	2	1	1	2	206	680	60	135	59	47	26	0	.11
											Postseason													
Year	Tm	GP	G	A	Pts	+/–	GW	OT	S	SPct	G	A	Pts	G	A	Pts	Num	PIM	Maj	Mnr	Fgt	Rgh	HHT	Hat	P/G
93-94	Pit	5	0	0	0	1	0	0	2	0.0	0	0	0	0	0	0	1	2	0	1	0	0	0	0	.00
94-95	Pit	4	0	0	0	-4	0	0	0	–	0	0	0	0	0	0	5	18	0	4	0	2	0	0	.00
95-96	Pit	18	0	7	7	0	0	0	23	0.0	0	0	0	0	1	1	12	24	0	12	0	3	2	0	.39
96-97	Pit	4	0	0	0	-1	0	0	3	0.0	0	0	0	0	0	0	2	4	0	2	0	0	0	0	.00
97-98	Pit	6	0	1	1	-1	0	0	2	0.0	0	0	0	0	1	1	2	4	0	2	0	0	0	0	.17
5 Years		37	0	8	8	-5	0	0	30	0.0	0	0	0	0	2	2	22	52	0	21	0	5	2	0	.22

Chris Taylor

Pos: C **Shoots:** L **Ht:** 6'0" **Wt:** 189 **Born:** 3/6/72—Stratford, Ontario **Age:** 27

			Overall							Power Play			Shorthand			Penalty							Misc	
Year	Tm	GP	G	A	Pts	+/–	GW	GT	S	SPct	G	A	Pts	G	A	Pts	Num	PIM	Maj	Mnr	Fgt	Rgh	HHT	Hat	P/G
94-95	NYI	10	0	3	3	1	0	0	13	0.0	0	2	2	0	0	0	1	2	0	1	0	0	1	0	.30
95-96	NYI	11	0	1	1	1	0	0	4	0.0	0	0	0	0	0	0	1	2	0	1	0	0	1	0	.09
96-97	NYI	1	0	0	0	0	0	0	1	0.0	0	0	0	0	0	0	0	0	0	0	0	0	0	0	.00
97-98											Did Not Play in NHL														
98-99	Bos	37	3	5	8	-3	0	0	60	5.0	0	0	0	1	0	1	6	12	0	6	0	0	3	0	.22
4 Years		59	3	9	12	-1	0	0	78	3.8	0	2	2	1	0	1	8	16	0	8	0	0	5	0	.20

Tim Taylor

(statistical profile on page 380)

Pos: C **Shoots:** L **Ht:** 6'1" **Wt:** 190 **Born:** 2/6/69—Stratford, Ontario **Age:** 30

Overall											Power Play			Shorthand			Penalty							Misc	
Year	Tm	GP	G	A	Pts	+/-	GW	GT	S	SPct	G	A	Pts	G	A	Pts	Num	PIM	Maj	Mnr	Fgt	Rgh	HHT	Hat	P/G
93-94	Det	1	1	0	1	-1	0	0	4	25.0	0	0	0	0	0	0	0	0	0	0	0	0	0	0	1.00
94-95	Det	22	0	4	4	3	0	0	21	0.0	0	2	2	0	0	0	8	16	0	8	0	5	2	0	.18
95-96	Det	72	11	14	25	11	4	0	81	13.6	1	0	1	1	0	1	14	39	1	12	1	4	5	0	.35
96-97	Det	44	3	4	7	-6	0	2	44	6.8	0	1	1	1	0	1	15	52	2	11	2	6	2	0	.16
97-98	Bos	79	20	11	31	-16	0	1	127	15.7	1	2	3	3	0	3	24	57	3	21	3	5	9	0	.39
98-99	Bos	49	4	7	11	-10	1	0	76	5.3	0	2	2	0	0	0	18	55	1	15	0	4	5	0	.22
6 Years		267	39	40	79	-19	5	3	353	11.0	2	7	9	5	0	5	79	219	7	67	6	24	23	0	.30

Postseason

Year	Tm	GP	G	A	Pts	+/-	GW	OT	S	SPct	G	A	Pts	G	A	Pts	Num	PIM	Maj	Mnr	Fgt	Rgh	HHT	Hat	P/G
94-95	Det	6	0	1	1	-4	0	0	11	0.0	0	0	0	0	0	0	2	12	0	1	0	1	0	0	.17
95-96	Det	18	0	4	4	0	0	0	10	0.0	0	1	1	0	0	0	2	4	0	2	0	1	0	0	.22
96-97	Det	2	0	0	0	-1	0	0	0	–	0	0	0	0	0	0	0	0	0	0	0	0	0	0	.00
97-98	Bos	6	0	0	0	-2	0	0	10	0.0	0	0	0	0	0	0	5	10	0	5	0	2	1	0	.00
98-99	Bos	12	0	3	3	1	0	0	11	0.0	0	1	1	0	0	0	4	8	0	4	0	3	0	0	.25
5 Years		44	0	8	8	-6	0	0	42	0.0	0	2	2	0	0	0	13	34	0	12	0	7	1	0	.18

Chris Terreri

Pos: G **Catches:** L **Ht:** 5'8" **Wt:** 160 **Born:** 11/15/64—Warwick, Rhode Island **Age:** 35

Overall																	Pen Shot		Offense		
Year	Tm	GP	GS	TP	W	L	T	Min	GA	GAA	Shots	SvPct	ShO	OE	PPGA	SHGA	Shots	GA	G	A	PIM
86-87	NJ	7	–	–	0	3	1	286	21	4.41	173	.879	0	–	–	–	0	0	0	0	0
87-88		Did Not Play in NHL																			
88-89	NJ	8	–	–	0	4	2	402	18	2.69	170	.894	0	–	–	–	1	1	0	0	2
89-90	NJ	35	–	–	15	12	3	1931	110	3.42	1004	.890	0	–	–	–	0	0	0	0	0
90-91	NJ	53	–	–	24	21	7	2970	144	2.91	1348	.893	1	–	–	–	2	1	0	3	2
91-92	NJ	54	53	4	22	22	10	3186	169	3.18	1511	.888	1	12	36	9	1	0	0	1	13
92-93	NJ	48	43	1	19	21	3	2672	151	3.39	1324	.886	2	13	38	11	0	0	0	0	6
93-94	NJ	44	38	3	20	11	4	2340	106	2.72	1141	.907	2	16	31	3	1	1	0	2	4
94-95	NJ	15	10	2	3	7	2	734	31	2.53	309	.900	0	2	9	0	0	0	0	0	0
95-96	2Tm	50	48	7	16	29	1	2726	164	3.61	1414	.884	0	10	42	10	0	0	0	5	4
96-97	2Tm	29	25	1	10	11	5	1629	74	2.73	745	.901	0	8	17	1	0	0	0	0	0
97-98	Chi	21	20	0	8	10	2	1222	49	2.41	519	.906	2	3	17	1	2	0	0	1	2
98-99	NJ	12	12	0	8	3	1	726	30	2.48	294	.898	1	1	7	0	0	0	0	1	0
95-96	NJ	4	3	0	3	0	0	210	9	2.57	92	.902	0	1	1	1	0	0	0	0	0
95-96	SJ	46	45	7	13	29	1	2516	155	3.70	1322	.883	0	9	41	9	0	0	0	5	4
96-97	SJ	22	18	1	6	10	3	1200	55	2.75	553	.901	0	6	12	1	0	0	0	0	0
96-97	Chi	7	7	0	4	1	2	429	19	2.66	192	.901	0	2	5	0	0	0	0	0	0
12 Years		376	–	–	145	154	41	20824	1067	3.07	9952	.893	9	–	–	–	7	3	0	13	33

Postseason

Year	Tm	GP	GS	TP	W	L	Pct	Min	GA	GAA	Shots	SvPct	ShO	OE	PPGA	SHGA	Shots	GA	G	A	PIM
89-90	NJ	4	–	–	2	2	.500	238	13	3.28	103	.874	0	–	–	–	0	0	0	0	0
90-91	NJ	7	–	–	3	4	.429	428	21	2.94	216	.903	0	–	–	–	0	0	0	0	2
91-92	NJ	7	7	1	3	3	.500	386	23	3.58	203	.887	0	3	9	4	0	0	0	0	0
92-93	NJ	4	4	1	1	3	.250	219	17	4.66	118	.856	0	1	6	1	0	0	0	0	0
93-94	NJ	4	3	0	3	0	1.000	200	9	2.70	111	.919	0	1	2	0	0	0	0	0	4
94-95	NJ	1	0	0	0	0	–	8	0	0.00	2	1.000	0	0	0	0	0	0	0	0	0
96-97	Chi	2	0	0	0	0	–	44	3	4.09	28	.893	0	0	3	0	0	0	0	0	2
7 Years		29	–	–	12	12	.500	1523	86	3.39	781	.890	0	–	–	–	0	0	0	0	8

In Memoriam

Dmitri Tertyshny

(statistical profile on page 380)

Pos: D **Shoots:** L **Ht:** 6'1" **Wt:** 178 **Born:** 12/26/76—Chelyabinsk, USSR **Died:** 7/23/99

Overall											Power Play			Shorthand			Penalty							Misc	
Year	Tm	GP	G	A	Pts	+/-	GW	GT	S	SPct	G	A	Pts	G	A	Pts	Num	PIM	Maj	Mnr	Fgt	Rgh	HHT	Hat	P/G
98-99	Phi	62	2	8	10	-1	0	0	68	2.9	1	3	4	0	0	0	15	30	0	15	0	1	8	0	.16

Postseason

Year	Tm	GP	G	A	Pts	+/-	GW	OT	S	SPct	G	A	Pts	G	A	Pts	Num	PIM	Maj	Mnr	Fgt	Rgh	HHT	Hat	P/G
98-99	Phi	1	0	0	0	0	0	0	1	0.0	0	0	0	0	0	0	1	2	0	1	0	0	0	0	.00

Alexei Tezikov

Pos: D **Shoots:** L **Ht:** 6'1" **Wt:** 198 **Born:** 6/22/78—Togliatti, USSR **Age:** 21

		Overall									Power Play			Shorthand			Penalty							Misc	
Year	Tm	GP	G	A	Pts	+/–	GW	GT	S	SPct	G	A	Pts	G	A	Pts	Num	PIM	Maj	Mnr	Fgt	Rgh	HHT	Hat	P/G
98-99	Was	5	0	0	0	-1	0	0	4	0.0	0	0	0	0	0	0	0	0	0	0	0	0	0	0	.00

Jose Theodore

Pos: G **Catches:** R **Ht:** 5'11" **Wt:** 179 **Born:** 9/13/76—Laval, Quebec **Age:** 23

		Overall															Pen Shot		Offense		
Year	Tm	GP	GS	TP	W	L	T	Min	GA	GAA	Shots	SvPct	ShO	OE	PPGA	SHGA	Shots	GA	G	A	PIM
95-96	Mon	1	0	0	0	0	0	8	1	7.50	2	.500	0	0	0	0	0	0	0	0	0
96-97	Mon	16	14	3	5	6	2	820	53	3.88	508	.896	0	4	15	0	0	0	0	0	0
97-98		Did Not Play in Regular Season																			
98-99	Mon	18	16	3	4	12	0	913	50	3.29	406	.877	1	5	10	3	1	1	0	0	0
3 Years		35	30	6	9	18	2	1741	104	3.58	916	.886	1	9	25	3	1	1	0	0	0
		Postseason																			
Year	Tm	GP	GS	TP	W	L	Pct	Min	GA	GAA	Shots	SvPct	ShO	OE	PPGA	SHGA	Shots	GA	G	A	PIM
96-97	Mon	2	2	0	1	1	.500	168	7	2.50	108	.935	0	1	3	1	0	0	0	0	0
97-98	Mon	3	0	0	0	1	.000	120	1	0.50	35	.971	0	0	0	0	0	0	0	0	0
2 Years		5	2	0	1	2	.333	288	8	1.67	143	.944	0	1	3	1	0	0	0	0	0

Chris Therien

(statistical profile on page 381)

Pos: D **Shoots:** L **Ht:** 6'3" **Wt:** 235 **Born:** 12/14/71—Ottawa, Ontario **Age:** 28

		Overall									Power Play			Shorthand			Penalty							Misc	
Year	Tm	GP	G	A	Pts	+/–	GW	GT	S	SPct	G	A	Pts	G	A	Pts	Num	PIM	Maj	Mnr	Fgt	Rgh	HHT	Hat	P/G
94-95	Phi	48	3	10	13	8	0	0	53	5.7	1	2	3	0	0	0	15	38	0	14	0	1	6	0	.27
95-96	Phi	82	6	17	23	16	1	0	123	4.9	3	1	4	0	0	0	39	89	1	37	1	5	14	0	.28
96-97	Phi	71	2	22	24	26	0	0	107	1.9	0	3	3	0	2	2	21	64	2	17	1	1	10	0	.34
97-98	Phi	78	3	16	19	5	1	0	102	2.9	1	2	3	0	1	1	29	80	2	25	2	1	11	0	.24
98-99	Phi	74	3	15	18	16	0	0	115	2.6	1	0	1	0	1	1	20	48	0	19	0	2	8	0	.24
5 Years		353	17	80	97	71	2	0	500	3.4	6	8	14	0	4	4	124	319	5	112	4	10	49	0	.27
		Postseason																							
Year	Tm	GP	G	A	Pts	+/–	GW	OT	S	SPct	G	A	Pts	G	A	Pts	Num	PIM	Maj	Mnr	Fgt	Rgh	HHT	Hat	P/G
94-95	Phi	15	0	0	0	-2	0	0	24	0.0	0	0	0	0	0	0	5	10	0	5	0	0	2	0	.00
95-96	Phi	12	0	0	0	-5	0	0	17	0.0	0	0	0	0	0	0	9	18	0	9	0	1	0	0	.00
96-97	Phi	19	1	6	7	14	1	0	36	2.8	0	0	0	0	0	0	3	6	0	3	0	1	0	0	.37
97-98	Phi	5	0	1	1	-1	0	0	15	0.0	0	0	0	0	0	0	2	4	0	2	0	0	1	0	.20
98-99	Phi	6	0	0	0	1	0	0	6	0.0	0	0	0	0	0	0	3	6	0	3	0	0	0	0	.00
5 Years		57	1	7	8	7	1	0	98	1.0	0	0	0	0	0	0	22	44	0	22	0	2	3	0	.14

Jocelyn Thibault

(statistical profile on page 403)

Pos: G **Catches:** L **Ht:** 5'11" **Wt:** 170 **Born:** 1/12/75—Montreal, Quebec **Age:** 24

		Overall															Pen Shot		Offense		
Year	Tm	GP	GS	TP	W	L	T	Min	GA	GAA	Shots	SvPct	ShO	OE	PPGA	SHGA	Shots	GA	G	A	PIM
93-94	Que	29	26	7	8	13	3	1504	83	3.31	768	.892	0	3	24	5	1	0	0	0	2
94-95	Que	18	16	3	12	2	2	898	35	2.34	423	.917	1	5	9	0	1	0	0	0	0
95-96	2Tm	50	49	4	26	17	5	2892	138	2.86	1480	.907	3	15	49	6	0	0	0	0	2
96-97	Mon	61	54	6	22	24	11	3397	164	2.90	1815	.910	1	25	40	8	0	0	0	0	0
97-98	Mon	47	42	2	19	15	8	2652	109	2.47	1109	.902	2	8	37	4	2	**2**	0	2	0
98-99	2Tm	62	60	4	24	30	7	3543	159	2.69	1685	.906	5	16	**58**	5	0	0	0	1	2
95-96	Col	10	9	1	3	4	2	558	28	3.01	222	.874	0	1	13	2	0	0	0	0	0
95-96	Mon	40	40	3	23	13	3	2334	110	2.83	1258	.913	3	14	36	4	0	0	0	0	2
98-99	Mon	10	9	1	3	4	2	529	23	2.61	250	.908	1	3	9	0	0	0	0	0	0
98-99	Chi	52	51	3	21	26	5	3014	136	2.71	1435	.905	4	13	49	5	0	0	0	1	2
6 Years		267	247	26	111	101	36	14886	688	2.77	7280	.905	12	72	217	28	4	2	0	3	6
		Postseason																			
Year	Tm	GP	GS	TP	W	L	Pct	Min	GA	GAA	Shots	SvPct	ShO	OE	PPGA	SHGA	Shots	GA	G	A	PIM
94-95	Que	3	3	1	1	2	.333	148	8	3.24	76	.895	0	1	3	0	0	0	0	0	0
95-96	Mon	6	6	1	2	4	.333	311	18	3.47	188	.904	0	4	7	1	0	0	0	0	0
96-97	Mon	3	3	0	0	3	.000	179	13	4.36	101	.871	0	0	6	2	0	0	0	0	0
97-98	Mon	2	1	1	0	0	–	43	4	5.58	16	.750	0	0	1	0	0	0	0	1	0
4 Years		14	13	3	3	9	.250	681	43	3.79	381	.887	0	5	17	3	0	0	0	1	0

Steve Thomas

(statistical profile on page 381)

Pos: LW **Shoots:** R **Ht:** 5'11" **Wt:** 185 **Born:** 7/15/63—Stockport, England **Age:** 36

Overall											Power Play			Shorthand			Penalty							Misc	
Year	**Tm**	**GP**	**G**	**A**	**Pts**	**+/–**	**GW**	**GT**	**S**	**SPct**	**G**	**A**	**Pts**	**G**	**A**	**Pts**	**Num**	**PIM**	**Maj**	**Mnr**	**Fgt**	**Rgh**	**HHT**	**Hat**	**P/G**
84-85	Tor	18	1	1	2	-13	0	0	26	3.8	0	–	–	0	–	–	1	2	0	1	0	–	–	0	.11
85-86	Tor	65	20	37	57	-15	5	0	197	10.2	5	–	–	0	–	–	–	36	–	–	–	–	–	0	.88
86-87	Tor	78	35	27	62	-3	7	1	245	14.3	3	–	–	0	–	–	–	114	–	–	–	–	–	0	.79
87-88	Chi	30	13	13	26	1	3	1	69	18.8	5	–	–	0	–	–	–	40	–	–	–	–	–	1	.87
88-89	Chi	45	21	19	40	-2	0	0	124	16.9	8	–	–	0	–	–	–	69	–	–	–	–	–	0	.89
89-90	Chi	76	40	30	70	-3	7	0	235	17.0	13	–	–	0	–	–	–	91	–	–	–	–	–	2	.92
90-91	Chi	69	19	35	54	8	3	0	192	9.9	2	–	–	0	–	–	–	129	–	–	–	–	–	1	.78
91-92	2Tm	**82**	30	48	78	8	3	1	245	12.2	3	18	21	0	0	0	30	97	7	21	5	4	7	1	.95
92-93	NYI	79	37	50	87	3	7	0	264	14.0	12	26	38	0	0	0	40	111	5	33	4	9	9	0	1.10
93-94	NYI	78	42	33	75	-9	5	2	249	16.9	17	13	30	0	0	0	46	139	5	37	5	7	12	1	.96
94-95	NYI	47	11	15	26	-14	2	0	133	8.3	3	6	9	0	0	0	20	60	4	15	4	4	1	0	.55
95-96	NJ	81	26	35	61	-2	6	1	192	13.5	6	11	17	0	0	0	32	98	6	24	5	1	7	0	.75
96-97	NJ	57	15	19	34	9	2	0	124	12.1	1	2	3	0	0	0	17	46	4	13	4	0	4	0	.60
97-98	NJ	55	14	10	24	4	4	1	111	12.6	3	1	4	0	0	0	12	32	0	11	0	3	4	0	.44
98-99	Tor	78	28	45	73	26	7	0	209	13.4	11	7	18	0	0	0	15	33	1	14	1	3	4	0	.94
91-92	Chi	11	2	6	8	-3	1	0	35	5.7	0	0	0	0	0	0	6	26	2	3	1	1	1	0	.73
91-92	NYI	71	28	42	70	11	2	1	210	13.3	3	18	21	0	0	0	24	71	5	18	4	3	6	1	.99
15 Years		938	352	417	769	-2	61	7	2615	13.5	92	–	–	0	–	–	–	1097	–	–	–	–	–	6	.82

Postseason

Year	**Tm**	**GP**	**G**	**A**	**Pts**	**+/–**	**GW**	**OT**	**S**	**SPct**	**G**	**A**	**Pts**	**G**	**A**	**Pts**	**Num**	**PIM**	**Maj**	**Mnr**	**Fgt**	**Rgh**	**HHT**	**Hat**	**P/G**
85-86	Tor	10	6	8	14	2	0	0	36	16.7	3	–	–	0	0	0	3	9	1	2	–	–	–	0	1.40
86-87	Tor	13	2	3	5	-4	0	0	31	6.5	1	–	–	0	0	0	5	13	1	4	–	–	–	0	.38
87-88	Chi	3	1	2	3	1	0	0	7	14.3	0	–	–	0	–	–	3	6	0	3	0	–	–	0	1.00
88-89	Chi	12	3	5	8	-2	2	0	23	13.0	1	–	–	0	–	–	–	10	–	–	–	–	–	0	.67
89-90	Chi	20	7	6	13	2	3	0	60	11.7	1	–	–	0	–	–	–	33	–	–	–	–	–	0	.65
90-91	Chi	6	1	2	3	3	0	0	17	5.9	0	–	–	0	0	0	–	15	–	–	–	–	–	0	.50
92-93	NYI	18	9	8	17	-1	1	0	66	13.6	1	2	3	0	0	0	13	37	1	11	0	6	0	0	.94
93-94	NYI	4	1	0	1	-5	0	0	9	11.1	1	0	1	0	0	0	4	8	0	4	0	1	1	0	.25
96-97	NJ	10	1	1	2	-6	0	0	25	4.0	0	1	1	0	0	0	5	18	0	4	0	0	1	0	.20
97-98	NJ	6	0	3	3	1	0	0	12	0.0	0	0	0	0	0	0	1	2	0	1	0	0	1	0	.50
98-99	Tor	17	6	3	9	-1	1	0	41	14.6	2	0	2	0	0	0	6	12	0	6	0	2	2	0	.53
11 Years		119	37	41	78	-10	7	0	327	11.3	10	–	–	0	–	–	–	163	–	–	–	–	–	0	.66

Rocky Thompson

Pos: RW **Shoots:** R **Ht:** 6'2" **Wt:** 195 **Born:** 8/8/77—Calgary, Alberta **Age:** 22

Overall											Power Play			Shorthand			Penalty							Misc	
Year	**Tm**	**GP**	**G**	**A**	**Pts**	**+/–**	**GW**	**GT**	**S**	**SPct**	**G**	**A**	**Pts**	**G**	**A**	**Pts**	**Num**	**PIM**	**Maj**	**Mnr**	**Fgt**	**Rgh**	**HHT**	**Hat**	**P/G**
97-98	Cgy	12	0	0	0	0	0	0	3	0.0	0	0	0	0	0	0	13	61	9	3	9	2	0	0	.00
98-99	Cgy	3	0	0	0	0	0	0	0	–	0	0	0	0	0	0	4	25	3	0	3	0	0	0	.00
2 Years		15	0	0	0	0	0	0	3	0.0	0	0	0	0	0	0	17	86	12	3	12	2	0	0	.00

Joe Thornton

(statistical profile on page 381)

Pos: C **Shoots:** L **Ht:** 6'4" **Wt:** 198 **Born:** 7/2/79—London, Ontario **Age:** 20

Overall											Power Play			Shorthand			Penalty							Misc	
Year	**Tm**	**GP**	**G**	**A**	**Pts**	**+/–**	**GW**	**GT**	**S**	**SPct**	**G**	**A**	**Pts**	**G**	**A**	**Pts**	**Num**	**PIM**	**Maj**	**Mnr**	**Fgt**	**Rgh**	**HHT**	**Hat**	**P/G**
97-98	Bos	55	3	4	7	-6	1	0	33	9.1	0	1	1	0	0	0	8	19	1	7	1	3	2	0	.13
98-99	Bos	81	16	25	41	3	1	0	128	12.5	7	8	15	0	0	0	26	69	3	22	2	6	5	0	.51
2 Years		136	19	29	48	-3	2	0	161	11.8	7	9	16	0	0	0	34	88	4	29	3	9	7	0	.35

Postseason

Year	**Tm**	**GP**	**G**	**A**	**Pts**	**+/–**	**GW**	**OT**	**S**	**SPct**	**G**	**A**	**Pts**	**G**	**A**	**Pts**	**Num**	**PIM**	**Maj**	**Mnr**	**Fgt**	**Rgh**	**HHT**	**Hat**	**P/G**
97-98	Bos	6	0	0	0	0	0	0	3	0.0	0	0	0	0	0	0	3	9	1	2	1	0	1	0	.00
98-99	Bos	11	3	6	9	1	2	0	15	20.0	2	2	4	0	0	0	2	4	0	2	0	0	1	0	.82
2 Years		17	3	6	9	1	2	0	18	16.7	2	2	4	0	0	0	5	13	1	4	1	0	2	0	.53

Scott Thornton

(statistical profile on page 381)

Pos: C **Shoots:** L **Ht:** 6'3" **Wt:** 219 **Born:** 1/9/71—London, Ontario **Age:** 28

Overall											Power Play			Shorthand			Penalty							Misc	
Year	**Tm**	**GP**	**G**	**A**	**Pts**	**+/–**	**GW**	**GT**	**S**	**SPct**	**G**	**A**	**Pts**	**G**	**A**	**Pts**	**Num**	**PIM**	**Maj**	**Mnr**	**Fgt**	**Rgh**	**HHT**	**Hat**	**P/G**
90-91	Tor	33	1	3	4	-15	0	0	31	3.2	0	–	–	0	–	–	–	30	–	–	–	–	–	0	.12
91-92	Edm	15	0	1	1	-6	0	0	11	0.0	0	0	0	0	0	0	13	43	3	9	3	1	3	0	.07

Overall											Power Play			Shorthand			Penalty							Misc	
Year	Tm	GP	G	A	Pts	+/–	GW	GT	S	SPct	G	A	Pts	G	A	Pts	Num	PIM	Maj	Mnr	Fgt	Rgh	HHT	Hat	P/G
92-93	Edm	9	0	1	1	-4	0	0	7	0.0	0	0	0	0	0	0	0	0	0	0	0	0	0	0	.11
93-94	Edm	61	4	7	11	-15	0	0	65	6.2	0	1	1	0	0	0	28	104	8	17	7	2	5	0	.18
94-95	Edm	47	10	12	22	-4	1	0	69	14.5	0	3	3	1	0	1	25	89	5	17	5	2	5	0	.47
95-96	Edm	77	9	9	18	-25	3	0	95	9.5	0	2	2	2	0	2	47	149	5	37	5	9	5	0	.23
96-97	Mon	73	10	10	20	-19	1	0	110	9.1	1	1	2	1	0	1	45	128	10	34	10	8	8	0	.27
97-98	Mon	67	6	9	15	0	1	2	51	11.8	1	1	2	0	0	0	48	158	10	34	10	11	6	0	.22
98-99	Mon	47	7	4	11	-2	1	1	56	12.5	1	0	1	0	0	0	31	87	3	26	3	5	8	0	.23
9 Years		429	47	56	103	-90	7	3	495	9.5	3	–	–	4	–	–	–	788	–	–	–	–	–	0	.24
Postseason																									
Year	Tm	GP	G	A	Pts	+/–	GW	OT	S	SPct	G	A	Pts	G	A	Pts	Num	PIM	Maj	Mnr	Fgt	Rgh	HHT	Hat	P/G
91-92	Edm	1	0	0	0	-1	0	0	1	0.0	0	0	0	0	0	0	0	0	0	0	0	0	0	0	.00
96-97	Mon	5	1	0	1	1	0	0	11	9.1	0	0	0	0	0	0	1	2	0	1	0	1	0	0	.20
97-98	Mon	9	0	2	2	0	0	0	13	0.0	0	0	0	0	0	0	5	10	0	5	0	0	2	0	.22
3 Years		15	1	2	3	0	0	0	25	4.0	0	0	0	0	0	0	6	12	0	6	0	1	2	0	.20

Esa Tikkanen

Pos: LW **Shoots:** L **Ht:** 6'1" **Wt:** 200 **Born:** 1/25/65—Helsinki, Finland **Age:** 34

Overall											Power Play			Shorthand			Penalty							Misc	
Year	Tm	GP	G	A	Pts	+/–	GW	GT	S	SPct	G	A	Pts	G	A	Pts	Num	PIM	Maj	Mnr	Fgt	Rgh	HHT	Hat	P/G
84-85		Did Not Play in Regular Season																							
85-86	Edm	35	7	6	13	5	2	0	44	15.9	0	–	–	0	–	–	–	28	–	–	–	–	–	0	.37
86-87	Edm*	76	34	44	78	44	6	1	126	27.0	7	–	–	0	–	–	–	120	–	–	–	–	–	2	1.03
87-88	Edm	**80**	23	51	74	21	2	0	142	16.2	6	–	–	1	–	–	–	153	–	–	–	–	–	1	.93
88-89	Edm	67	31	47	78	10	4	0	151	20.5	6	16	22	8	3	11	–	92	–	–	–	–	–	1	1.16
89-90	Edm	79	30	33	63	17	6	0	199	15.1	6	16	22	4	0	4	–	161	–	–	–	–	–	0	.80
90-91	Edm	79	27	42	69	22	6	0	235	11.5	3	12	15	2	2	4	–	85	–	–	–	–	–	1	.87
91-92	Edm	40	12	16	28	-8	1	0	117	10.3	6	7	13	2	1	3	22	44	0	22	0	3	8	0	.70
92-93	2Tm	81	16	24	40	-24	3	0	202	7.9	2	5	7	4	1	5	43	94	0	42	0	11	9	0	.49
93-94	NYR	83	22	32	54	5	4	0	257	8.6	5	16	21	3	1	4	49	114	0	47	0	12	16	0	.65
94-95	StL	43	12	23	35	13	1	1	107	11.2	5	8	13	2	1	3	11	22	0	11	0	3	3	0	.81
95-96	3Tm	58	14	30	44	1	2	0	95	14.7	8	14	22	1	0	1	18	36	0	18	0	2	3	0	.76
96-97	2Tm	76	13	17	30	-9	2	2	133	9.8	4	8	12	2	1	3	24	72	0	21	0	5	5	0	.39
97-98	2Tm	48	3	18	21	-11	2	0	67	4.5	1	8	9	0	0	0	9	18	0	9	0	0	7	0	.44
98-99	NYR	32	0	3	3	-5	0	0	25	0.0	0	0	0	0	0	0	11	38	0	9	0	2	2	0	.09
92-93	Edm	66	14	19	33	-11	3	0	162	8.6	2	5	7	4	1	5	34	76	0	33	0	9	7	0	.50
92-93	NYR	15	2	5	7	-13	0	0	40	5.0	0	0	0	0	0	0	9	18	0	9	0	2	2	0	.47
95-96	StL	11	1	4	5	1	0	0	19	5.3	0	2	2	1	0	1	9	18	0	9	0	0	2	0	.45
95-96	NJ	9	0	2	2	-6	0	0	15	0.0	0	1	1	0	0	0	2	4	0	2	0	0	1	0	.22
95-96	Van	38	13	24	37	6	2	0	61	21.3	8	11	19	0	0	0	7	14	0	7	0	2	0	0	.97
96-97	Van	62	12	15	27	-9	2	1	103	11.7	4	7	11	1	1	2	21	66	0	18	0	5	4	0	.44
96-97	NYR	14	1	2	3	0	0	1	30	3.3	0	1	1	1	0	1	3	6	0	3	0	0	1	0	.21
97-98	Fla	28	1	8	9	-7	0	0	34	2.9	0	4	4	0	0	0	8	16	0	8	0	0	6	0	.32
97-98	Was	20	2	10	12	-4	2	0	33	6.1	1	4	5	0	0	0	1	2	0	1	0	0	1	0	.60
14 Years		877	244	386	630	81	41	4	1900	12.8	59	–	–	29	–	–	–	1077	–	–	–	–	–	5	.72
Postseason																									
Year	Tm	GP	G	A	Pts	+/–	GW	OT	S	SPct	G	A	Pts	G	A	Pts	Num	PIM	Maj	Mnr	Fgt	Rgh	HHT	Hat	P/G
84-85	Edm	3	0	0	0	-1	0	0	3	0.0	0	0	0	0	0	0	1	2	0	1	0	–	–	0	.00
85-86	Edm	8	3	2	5	1	0	0	19	15.8	0	–	–	0	–	–	2	7	1	1	–	–	–	0	.63
86-87	Edm	21	7	2	9	1	1	0	39	17.9	1	–	–	0	–	–	–	22	–	–	–	–	–	0	.43
87-88	Edm	19	10	17	27	2	1	0	42	23.8	5	–	–	0	–	–	–	72	–	–	–	–	–	1	1.42
88-89	Edm	7	1	3	4	-1	0	0	17	5.9	0	–	–	0	–	–	–	12	–	–	–	–	–	0	.57
89-90	Edm	22	13	11	24	12	0	0	54	24.1	2	–	–	2	–	–	–	26	–	–	–	–	–	0	1.09
90-91	Edm	18	12	8	20	3	3	2	76	15.8	3	–	–	0	0	0	–	24	–	–	–	–	–	1	1.11
91-92	Edm	16	5	3	8	-1	1	0	37	13.5	1	2	3	0	0	0	4	8	0	4	0	1	2	1	.50
93-94	NYR	23	4	4	8	1	1	0	56	7.1	0	0	0	0	0	0	17	34	0	17	0	7	4	0	.35
94-95	StL	7	2	2	4	-1	1	0	19	10.5	1	0	1	0	0	0	6	20	0	5	0	2	1	0	.57
95-96	Van	6	3	2	5	-3	0	0	13	23.1	2	2	4	0	0	0	1	2	0	1	0	0	1	0	.83
96-97	NYR	15	9	3	12	2	3	2	45	20.0	3	2	5	1	0	1	13	26	0	13	0	2	3	0	.80
97-98	Was	21	3	3	6	-2	0	0	23	13.0	1	0	1	0	1	1	10	20	0	10	0	2	3	0	.29
13 Years		186	72	60	132	13	11	4	443	16.3	19	–	–	3	–	–	–	275	–	–	–	–	–	3	.71

Brad Tiley

Pos: D **Shoots:** L **Ht:** 6'1" **Wt:** 185 **Born:** 7/5/71—Markdale, Ontario **Age:** 28

Overall											Power Play			Shorthand			Penalty							Misc	
Year	Tm	GP	G	A	Pts	+/–	GW	GT	S	SPct	G	A	Pts	G	A	Pts	Num	PIM	Maj	Mnr	Fgt	Rgh	HHT	Hat	P/G
97-98	Pho	1	0	0	0	1	0	0	0	–	0	0	0	0	0	0	0	0	0	0	0	0	0	0	.00
98-99	Pho	8	0	0	0	-1	0	0	1	0.0	0	0	0	0	0	0	0	0	0	0	0	0	0	0	.00
2 Years		9	0	0	0	0	0	0	1	0.0	0	0	0	0	0	0	0	0	0	0	0	0	0	0	.00

Postseason

Year	Tm	GP	G	A	Pts	+/–	GW	OT	S	SPct	G	A	Pts	G	A	Pts	Num	PIM	Maj	Mnr	Fgt	Rgh	HHT	Hat	P/G
98-99	Pho	1	0	0	0	0	0	0	0	–	0	0	0	0	0	0	0	0	0	0	0	0	0	0	.00

Mattias Timander

Pos: D **Shoots:** L **Ht:** 6'3" **Wt:** 210 **Born:** 4/16/74—Solleftea, Sweden **Age:** 25

Overall											Power Play			Shorthand			Penalty							Misc	
Year	Tm	GP	G	A	Pts	+/–	GW	GT	S	SPct	G	A	Pts	G	A	Pts	Num	PIM	Maj	Mnr	Fgt	Rgh	HHT	Hat	P/G
96-97	Bos	41	1	8	9	-9	0	1	62	1.6	0	3	3	0	0	0	7	14	0	7	0	1	2	0	.22
97-98	Bos	23	1	1	2	-9	0	0	17	5.9	0	0	0	0	0	0	3	6	0	3	0	0	1	0	.09
98-99	Bos	22	0	6	6	4	0	0	22	0.0	0	2	2	0	0	0	5	10	0	5	0	0	3	0	.27
3 Years		86	2	15	17	-14	0	1	101	2.0	0	5	5	0	0	0	15	30	0	15	0	1	6	0	.20

Postseason

Year	Tm	GP	G	A	Pts	+/–	GW	OT	S	SPct	G	A	Pts	G	A	Pts	Num	PIM	Maj	Mnr	Fgt	Rgh	HHT	Hat	P/G
98-99	Bos	4	1	1	2	3	0	0	3	33.3	0	0	0	0	0	0	1	2	0	1	0	0	0	0	.50

Kimmo Timonen

(statistical profile on page 382)

Pos: D **Shoots:** L **Ht:** 5'9" **Wt:** 180 **Born:** 3/18/75—Kuopio, Finland **Age:** 24

Overall											Power Play			Shorthand			Penalty							Misc	
Year	Tm	GP	G	A	Pts	+/–	GW	GT	S	SPct	G	A	Pts	G	A	Pts	Num	PIM	Maj	Mnr	Fgt	Rgh	HHT	Hat	P/G
98-99	Nsh	50	4	8	12	-4	0	0	75	5.3	1	5	6	0	0	0	15	30	0	15	0	0	8	0	.24

Mark Tinordi

Pos: D **Shoots:** L **Ht:** 6'4" **Wt:** 218 **Born:** 5/9/66—Red Deer, Alberta **Age:** 33

Overall											Power Play			Shorthand			Penalty							Misc	
Year	Tm	GP	G	A	Pts	+/–	GW	GT	S	SPct	G	A	Pts	G	A	Pts	Num	PIM	Maj	Mnr	Fgt	Rgh	HHT	Hat	P/G
87-88	NYR	24	1	2	3	-5	0	0	13	7.7	0	0	0	0	–	–	15	50	4	10	–	–	–	0	.13
88-89	Min	47	2	3	5	-9	0	0	39	5.1	0	–	–	0	–	–	–	107	–	–	–	–	–	0	.11
89-90	Min	66	3	7	10	0	0	0	50	6.0	1	–	–	0	–	–	–	240	–	–	–	–	–	0	.15
90-91	Min	69	5	27	32	1	2	0	92	5.4	1	–	–	0	–	–	–	189	–	–	–	–	–	0	.46
91-92	Min*	63	4	24	28	-13	0	0	93	4.3	4	12	16	0	2	2	55	179	7	42	6	15	5	0	.44
92-93	Min	69	15	27	42	-1	2	0	122	12.3	7	10	17	0	0	0	61	157	1	56	1	25	3	0	.61
93-94	Dal	61	6	18	24	6	0	0	112	5.4	1	9	10	0	1	1	51	143	11	39	11	19	6	0	.39
94-95	Was	42	3	9	12	-5	1	0	71	4.2	2	1	3	0	1	1	23	71	3	18	3	4	3	0	.29
95-96	Was	71	3	10	13	26	0	0	82	3.7	2	3	5	0	0	0	37	113	5	29	4	12	3	0	.18
96-97	Was	56	2	6	8	3	0	1	53	3.8	0	0	0	0	1	1	34	118	6	24	5	13	1	0	.14
97-98	Was	47	8	9	17	9	0	0	57	14.0	0	0	0	1	1	2	18	39	1	17	1	5	5	0	.36
98-99	Was	48	0	6	6	-6	0	0	32	0.0	0	0	0	0	2	2	33	108	6	24	6	6	4	0	.13
12 Years		663	52	148	200	6	5	1	816	6.4	18	–	–	1	–	–	–	1514	–	–	–	–	–	0	.30

Postseason

Year	Tm	GP	G	A	Pts	+/–	GW	OT	S	SPct	G	A	Pts	G	A	Pts	Num	PIM	Maj	Mnr	Fgt	Rgh	HHT	Hat	P/G
88-89	Min	5	0	0	0	-4	0	0	8	0.0	0	0	0	0	0	0	0	0	0	0	0	0	0	0	.00
89-90	Min	7	0	1	1	1	0	0	5	0.0	0	–	–	0	0	0	–	16	–	–	–	–	–	0	.14
90-91	Min	23	5	6	11	-1	0	0	54	9.3	4	–	–	0	–	–	–	78	–	–	–	–	–	0	.48
91-92	Min	7	1	2	3	-6	0	0	15	6.7	0	2	2	0	0	0	4	11	1	3	0	0	0	0	.43
94-95	Was	1	0	0	0	-2	0	0	2	0.0	0	0	0	0	0	0	1	2	0	1	0	0	0	0	.00
95-96	Was	6	0	0	0	-2	0	0	9	0.0	0	0	0	0	0	0	5	16	2	3	2	2	0	0	.00
97-98	Was	21	1	2	3	6	0	0	14	7.1	0	0	0	0	0	0	14	42	2	11	2	3	3	0	.14
7 Years		70	7	11	18	-8	0	0	107	6.5	4	–	–	0	–	–	–	165	–	–	–	–	–	0	.26

German Titov

(statistical profile on page 382)

Pos: C **Shoots:** L **Ht:** 6'1" **Wt:** 190 **Born:** 10/16/65—Moscow, USSR **Age:** 34

Overall											Power Play			Shorthand			Penalty							Misc	
Year	Tm	GP	G	A	Pts	+/–	GW	GT	S	SPct	G	A	Pts	G	A	Pts	Num	PIM	Maj	Mnr	Fgt	Rgh	HHT	Hat	P/G
93-94	Cgy	76	27	18	45	20	2	0	153	17.6	8	2	10	3	1	4	14	28	0	14	0	0	7	0	.59

Overall											Power Play			Shorthand			Penalty							Misc	
Year	Tm	GP	G	A	Pts	+/–	GW	GT	S	SPct	G	A	Pts	G	A	Pts	Num	PIM	Maj	Mnr	Fgt	Rgh	HHT	Hat	P/G
94-95	Cgy	40	12	12	24	6	3	0	88	13.6	3	2	5	2	1	3	8	16	0	8	0	0	5	1	.60
95-96	Cgy	82	28	39	67	9	2	2	214	13.1	13	13	26	2	4	6	12	24	0	12	0	1	5	0	.82
96-97	Cgy	79	22	30	52	-12	4	0	192	11.5	12	13	25	0	0	0	18	36	0	18	0	2	9	1	.66
97-98	Cgy	68	18	22	40	-1	2	0	133	13.5	6	3	9	1	1	2	19	38	0	19	0	1	11	0	.59
98-99	Pit	72	11	45	56	18	3	1	113	9.7	3	16	19	1	0	1	17	34	0	17	0	1	9	0	.78
6 Years		417	118	166	284	40	16	3	893	13.2	45	49	94	9	7	16	88	176	0	88	0	5	46	2	.68
Postseason																									
Year	Tm	GP	G	A	Pts	+/–	GW	OT	S	SPct	G	A	Pts	G	A	Pts	Num	PIM	Maj	Mnr	Fgt	Rgh	HHT	Hat	P/G
93-94	Cgy	7	2	1	3	-4	0	0	16	12.5	1	0	1	0	0	0	2	4	0	2	0	1	0	0	.43
94-95	Cgy	7	5	3	8	1	0	0	14	35.7	0	0	0	1	0	1	3	6	0	3	0	0	2	0	1.14
95-96	Cgy	4	0	2	2	0	0	0	13	0.0	0	0	0	0	0	0	0	0	0	0	0	0	0	0	.50
98-99	Pit	11	3	5	8	4	0	0	15	20.0	0	1	1	0	0	0	2	4	0	2	0	1	0	0	.73
4 Years		29	10	11	21	1	0	0	58	17.2	1	1	2	1	0	1	7	14	0	7	0	2	2	0	.72

Keith Tkachuk

(statistical profile on page 382)

Pos: LW **Shoots:** L **Ht:** 6'2" **Wt:** 210 **Born:** 3/28/72—Melrose, Massachusetts **Age:** 27

Overall											Power Play			Shorthand			Penalty							Misc	
Year	Tm	GP	G	A	Pts	+/–	GW	GT	S	SPct	G	A	Pts	G	A	Pts	Num	PIM	Maj	Mnr	Fgt	Rgh	HHT	Hat	P/G
91-92	Wpg	17	3	5	8	0	0	0	22	13.6	2	2	4	0	0	0	8	28	4	4	4	2	1	0	.47
92-93	Wpg	83	28	23	51	-13	2	1	199	14.1	12	6	18	0	0	0	74	201	7	63	7	22	9	0	.61
93-94	Wpg	84	41	40	81	-12	3	1	218	18.8	22	16	38	3	1	4	**96**	255	5	**85**	3	25	10	1	.96
94-95	Wpg	48	22	29	51	-4	2	1	129	17.1	7	10	17	2	3	5	58	152	4	**51**	4	18	6	0	1.06
95-96	Wpg	76	50	48	98	11	6	0	249	20.1	20	21	41	2	1	3	61	156	6	53	5	12	10	1	1.29
96-97	Pho*	81	**52**	34	86	-1	7	1	296	17.6	9	10	19	2	0	2	80	228	4	**69**	4	22	11	2	1.06
97-98	Pho*	69	40	26	66	9	8	1	232	17.2	11	10	21	0	1	1	65	147	3	61	3	18	7	**3**	.96
98-99	Pho	68	36	32	68	22	7	1	258	14.0	11	6	17	2	2	4	52	151	5	43	5	7	5	1	1.00
8 Years		526	272	237	509	12	35	6	1603	17.0	94	81	175	11	8	19	494	1318	38	429	35	126	59	8	.97
Postseason																									
Year	Tm	GP	G	A	Pts	+/–	GW	OT	S	SPct	G	A	Pts	G	A	Pts	Num	PIM	Maj	Mnr	Fgt	Rgh	HHT	Hat	P/G
91-92	Wpg	7	3	0	3	-3	0	0	14	21.4	0	0	0	0	0	0	7	30	0	5	0	2	1	0	.43
92-93	Wpg	6	4	0	4	-5	0	0	17	23.5	1	0	1	0	0	0	7	14	0	7	0	2	1	0	.67
95-96	Wpg	6	1	2	3	0	0	0	16	6.3	0	0	0	0	0	0	11	22	0	11	0	2	1	0	.50
96-97	Pho	7	6	0	6	2	0	0	37	16.2	2	0	2	0	0	0	2	7	1	1	1	0	0	0	.86
97-98	Pho	6	3	3	6	-1	0	0	24	12.5	0	2	2	0	0	0	5	10	0	5	0	1	0	0	1.00
98-99	Pho	7	1	3	4	-4	0	0	22	4.5	1	2	3	0	0	0	5	13	1	4	1	1	2	0	.57
6 Years		39	18	8	26	-11	0	0	130	13.8	4	4	8	0	0	0	37	96	2	33	2	8	5	0	.67

Rick Tocchet

(statistical profile on page 382)

Pos: RW **Shoots:** R **Ht:** 6'0" **Wt:** 205 **Born:** 4/9/64—Scarborough, Ontario **Age:** 35

Overall											Power Play			Shorthand			Penalty							Misc	
Year	Tm	GP	G	A	Pts	+/–	GW	GT	S	SPct	G	A	Pts	G	A	Pts	Num	PIM	Maj	Mnr	Fgt	Rgh	HHT	Hat	P/G
84-85	Phi	75	14	25	39	6	0	0	112	12.5	0	–	–	0	–	–	–	181	–	–	–	–	–	0	.52
85-86	Phi	69	14	21	35	12	1	0	107	13.1	3	–	–	0	–	–	–	284	–	–	–	–	–	0	.51
86-87	Phi	69	21	26	47	16	5	0	147	14.3	1	–	–	1	–	–	–	288	–	–	–	–	–	0	.68
87-88	Phi	65	31	33	64	3	3	0	182	17.0	10	–	–	2	–	–	–	301	–	–	–	–	–	3	.98
88-89	Phi*	66	45	36	81	-1	5	3	220	20.5	16	–	–	1	–	–	–	183	–	–	–	–	–	2	1.23
89-90	Phi*	75	37	59	96	4	0	0	269	13.8	15	–	–	1	–	–	–	196	–	–	–	–	–	2	1.28
90-91	Phi*	70	40	31	71	2	5	1	217	18.4	8	–	–	0	–	–	–	150	–	–	–	–	–	1	1.01
91-92	2Tm	61	27	32	59	15	2	1	166	16.3	8	8	16	1	0	1	56	151	5	48	5	20	8	1	.97
92-93	Pit*	80	48	61	109	28	5	0	240	20.0	20	20	40	4	0	4	90	252	8	76	8	29	18	2	1.36
93-94	Pit	51	14	26	40	-15	2	1	150	9.3	5	11	16	1	1	2	46	134	6	37	6	23	8	0	.78
94-95	LA	36	18	17	35	-8	3	0	95	18.9	7	5	12	1	0	1	25	70	4	20	4	8	3	1	.97
95-96	2Tm	71	29	31	60	10	3	1	185	15.7	10	10	20	0	0	0	57	181	9	43	8	16	10	2	.85
96-97	2Tm	53	21	19	40	-3	2	1	157	13.4	4	2	6	0	0	0	36	98	6	29	6	9	3	0	.75
97-98	Pho	68	26	19	45	1	6	0	161	16.1	8	6	14	0	0	0	58	157	11	46	9	18	10	0	.66
98-99	Pho	81	26	30	56	5	5	0	178	14.6	6	9	15	1	0	1	51	147	7	41	7	10	8	0	.69
91-92	Phi	42	13	16	29	3	1	1	107	12.1	4	5	9	0	0	0	37	102	4	31	4	14	3	0	.69
91-92	Pit	19	14	16	30	12	1	0	59	23.7	4	3	7	1	0	1	19	49	1	17	1	6	5	1	1.58
95-96	LA	44	13	23	36	3	0	1	100	13.0	4	6	10	0	0	0	32	117	7	21	6	8	5	0	.82
95-96	Bos	27	16	8	24	7	3	0	85	18.8	6	4	10	0	0	0	25	64	2	22	2	8	5	2	.89
96-97	Bos	40	16	14	30	-3	1	1	120	13.3	3	2	5	0	0	0	26	67	5	21	5	8	0	0	.75
96-97	Was	13	5	5	10	0	1	0	37	13.5	1	0	1	0	0	0	10	31	1	8	1	1	3	0	.77
15 Years		990	411	466	877	75	47	8	2586	15.9	121	–	–	13	–	–	–	2773	–	–	–	–	–	14	.89

Postseason																									
Year	Tm	GP	G	A	Pts	+/-	GW	OT	S	SPct	G	A	Pts	G	A	Pts	Num	PIM	Maj	Mnr	Fgt	Rgh	HHT	Hat	P/G
84-85	Phi	19	3	4	7	-1	2	0	41	7.3	0	–	–	0	–	–	–	72	–	–	–	–	–	0	.37
85-86	Phi	5	1	2	3	1	0	0	10	10.0	0	–	–	0	0	0	–	26	–	–	–	–	–	0	.60
86-87	Phi	26	11	10	21	7	2	0	61	18.0	0	–	–	1	–	–	–	72	–	–	–	–	–	0	.81
87-88	Phi	5	1	4	5	-1	0	0	7	14.3	1	–	–	0	0	0	–	55	–	–	–	–	–	0	1.00
88-89	Phi	16	6	6	12	0	1	0	58	10.3	2	–	–	0	–	–	–	69	–	–	–	–	–	0	.75
91-92	Pit	14	6	13	19	0	1	0	30	20.0	3	5	8	0	0	0	9	24	2	7	2	0	1	0	1.36
92-93	Pit	12	7	6	13	2	0	0	45	15.6	1	3	4	0	0	0	12	24	0	12	0	3	4	0	1.08
93-94	Pit	6	2	3	5	-2	1	0	14	14.3	1	0	1	0	0	0	6	20	0	5	0	3	1	0	.83
95-96	Bos	5	4	0	4	-7	1	0	20	20.0	3	0	3	0	0	0	9	21	1	8	1	3	1	0	.80
97-98	Pho	6	6	2	8	0	0	0	12	50.0	3	1	4	0	0	0	7	25	1	5	1	2	0	0	1.33
98-99	Pho	7	0	3	3	-3	0	0	14	0.0	0	2	2	0	0	0	4	8	0	4	0	0	0	0	.43
11 Years		121	47	53	100	-4	8	0	312	15.1	14	–	–	1	–	–	–	416	–	–	–	–	–	0	.83

Jeff Toms

Pos: LW **Shoots:** L **Ht:** 6'5" **Wt:** 200 **Born:** 6/4/74—Swift Current, Saskatchewan **Age:** 25

Overall											Power Play			Shorthand			Penalty							Misc	
Year	Tm	GP	G	A	Pts	+/-	GW	GT	S	SPct	G	A	Pts	G	A	Pts	Num	PIM	Maj	Mnr	Fgt	Rgh	HHT	Hat	P/G
95-96	TB	1	0	0	0	0	0	0	1	0.0	0	0	0	0	0	0	0	0	0	0	0	0	0	0	.00
96-97	TB	34	2	8	10	2	1	0	53	3.8	0	0	0	0	0	0	1	10	0	0	0	0	0	0	.29
97-98	2Tm	46	4	6	10	-17	1	0	69	5.8	0	0	0	0	1	1	6	15	1	5	1	1	3	0	.22
98-99	Was	21	1	5	6	0	0	0	30	3.3	0	0	0	0	1	1	1	2	0	1	0	0	0	0	.29
97-98	TB	13	1	2	3	-6	0	0	14	7.1	0	0	0	0	0	0	2	7	1	1	1	1	0	0	.23
97-98	Was	33	3	4	7	-11	1	0	55	5.5	0	0	0	0	1	1	4	8	0	4	0	0	3	0	.21
4 Years		102	7	19	26	-15	2	0	153	4.6	0	0	0	0	2	2	8	27	1	6	1	1	3	0	.25
Postseason																									
Year	Tm	GP	G	A	Pts	+/-	GW	OT	S	SPct	G	A	Pts	G	A	Pts	Num	PIM	Maj	Mnr	Fgt	Rgh	HHT	Hat	P/G
97-98	Was	1	0	0	0	-1	0	0	0	–	0	0	0	0	0	0	0	0	0	0	0	0	0	0	.00

Patrick Traverse

(statistical profile on page 383)

Pos: D **Shoots:** L **Ht:** 6'3" **Wt:** 190 **Born:** 3/14/74—Montreal, Quebec **Age:** 25

Overall											Power Play			Shorthand			Penalty							Misc	
Year	Tm	GP	G	A	Pts	+/-	GW	GT	S	SPct	G	A	Pts	G	A	Pts	Num	PIM	Maj	Mnr	Fgt	Rgh	HHT	Hat	P/G
95-96	Ott	5	0	0	0	-1	0	0	2	0.0	0	0	0	0	0	0	1	2	0	1	0	0	1	0	.00
96-97		Did Not Play in NHL																							
97-98		Did Not Play in NHL																							
98-99	Ott	46	1	9	10	12	0	0	35	2.9	0	2	2	0	1	1	11	22	0	11	0	1	6	0	.22
2 Years		51	1	9	10	11	0	0	37	2.7	0	2	2	0	1	1	12	24	0	12	0	1	7	0	.20

Dan Trebil

Pos: D **Shoots:** R **Ht:** 6'3" **Wt:** 210 **Born:** 4/10/74—Bloomington, Minnesota **Age:** 25

Overall											Power Play			Shorthand			Penalty							Misc	
Year	Tm	GP	G	A	Pts	+/-	GW	GT	S	SPct	G	A	Pts	G	A	Pts	Num	PIM	Maj	Mnr	Fgt	Rgh	HHT	Hat	P/G
96-97	Anh	29	3	3	6	5	0	0	30	10.0	0	0	0	0	1	1	6	23	1	4	1	1	0	0	.21
97-98	Anh	21	0	1	1	-8	0	0	11	0.0	0	0	0	0	0	0	1	2	0	1	0	0	0	0	.05
98-99	Anh	6	0	0	0	-2	0	0	1	0.0	0	0	0	0	0	0	0	0	0	0	0	0	0	0	.00
3 Years		56	3	4	7	-5	0	0	42	7.1	0	0	0	0	1	1	7	25	1	5	1	1	0	0	.13
Postseason																									
Year	Tm	GP	G	A	Pts	+/-	GW	OT	S	SPct	G	A	Pts	G	A	Pts	Num	PIM	Maj	Mnr	Fgt	Rgh	HHT	Hat	P/G
96-97	Anh	9	0	1	1	-6	0	0	10	0.0	0	0	0	0	0	0	3	6	0	3	0	0	0	0	.11
98-99	Anh	1	0	0	0	0	0	0	0	–	0	0	0	0	0	0	1	2	0	1	0	1	0	0	.00
2 Years		10	0	1	1	-6	0	0	10	0.0	0	0	0	0	0	0	4	8	0	4	0	1	0	0	.10

Andrei Trefilov

Pos: G **Catches:** L **Ht:** 6'0" **Wt:** 190 **Born:** 8/31/69—Kirovo-Chepetsk, USSR **Age:** 30

Overall																Pen Shot		Offense		
Year	Tm	GP	GS	TP	W	L	T	Min	GA	GAA	Shots	SvPct	ShO	OE	PPGA	SHGA	Shots	GA	G	A	PIM
92-93	Cgy	1	1	0	0	0	1	65	5	4.62	39	.872	0	0	1	0	0	0	0	0	2
93-94	Cgy	11	10	1	3	4	2	623	26	2.50	305	.915	2	4	8	1	0	0	0	0	4
94-95	Cgy	6	4	2	0	3	0	236	16	4.07	130	.877	0	0	5	0	1	0	0	0	0
95-96	Buf	22	18	2	8	8	1	1094	64	3.51	660	.903	0	6	13	6	0	0	0	0	4
96-97	Buf	3	3	1	0	2	0	159	10	3.77	98	.898	0	1	4	0	0	0	0	0	0

Overall																	Pen Shot		Offense		
Year	Tm	GP	GS	TP	W	L	T	Min	GA	GAA	Shots	SvPct	ShO	OE	PPGA	SHGA	Shots	GA	G	A	PIM
97-98	Chi	6	4	0	1	4	0	299	17	3.41	145	.883	0	3	2	1	2	0	0	0	0
98-99	2Tm	5	5	3	0	4	0	187	15	4.81	104	.856	0	0	5	1	0	0	0	0	0
98-99	Chi	1	1	1	0	1	0	25	4	9.60	20	.800	0	0	1	0	0	0	0	0	0
98-99	Cgy	4	4	2	0	3	0	162	11	4.07	84	.869	0	0	4	1	0	0	0	0	0
7 Years		54	45	9	12	25	4	2663	153	3.45	1481	.897	2	14	38	9	3	0	0	0	10
Postseason																					
Year	Tm	GP	GS	TP	W	L	Pct	Min	GA	GAA	Shots	SvPct	ShO	OE	PPGA	SHGA	Shots	GA	G	A	PIM
96-97	Buf	1	0	0	0	0	–	5	0	0.00	4	1.000	0	0	0	0	0	0	0	0	0

Yanick Tremblay

Pos: D **Shoots:** R **Ht:** 6'2" **Wt:** 185 **Born:** 11/15/75—Pointe-aux-Trembles, Quebec **Age:** 24

Overall										Power Play			Shorthand			Penalty							Misc	
Year	Tm	GP	G	A	Pts	+/–	GW	GT	S	SPct	G	A	Pts	G	A	Pts	Num	PIM	Maj	Mnr	Fgt	Rgh	HHT	Hat	P/G
96-97	Tor	5	0	0	0	-4	0	0	2	0.0	0	0	0	0	0	0	0	0	0	0	0	0	0	0	.00
97-98	Tor	38	2	4	6	-6	0	0	45	4.4	1	2	3	0	0	0	3	6	0	3	0	0	0	0	.16
98-99	Tor	35	2	7	9	0	0	0	37	5.4	0	3	3	0	0	0	8	16	0	8	0	1	6	0	.26
3 Years		78	4	11	15	-10	0	0	84	4.8	1	5	6	0	0	0	11	22	0	11	0	1	6	0	.19

Pascal Trepanier

Pos: D **Shoots:** R **Ht:** 6'0" **Wt:** 205 **Born:** 4/9/73—Gaspe, Quebec **Age:** 26

Overall										Power Play			Shorthand			Penalty							Misc	
Year	Tm	GP	G	A	Pts	+/–	GW	GT	S	SPct	G	A	Pts	G	A	Pts	Num	PIM	Maj	Mnr	Fgt	Rgh	HHT	Hat	P/G
97-98	Col	15	0	1	1	-2	0	0	9	0.0	0	0	0	0	0	0	9	18	0	9	0	3	0	0	.07
98-99	Anh	45	2	4	6	0	1	0	49	4.1	0	2	2	0	0	0	20	48	0	19	0	7	2	0	.13
2 Years		60	2	5	7	-2	1	0	58	3.4	0	2	2	0	0	0	29	66	0	28	0	10	2	0	.12

Pavel Trnka

Pos: D **Shoots:** L **Ht:** 6'3" **Wt:** 200 **Born:** 7/27/76—Plzen, Czechoslovakia **Age:** 23

Overall										Power Play			Shorthand			Penalty							Misc	
Year	Tm	GP	G	A	Pts	+/–	GW	GT	S	SPct	G	A	Pts	G	A	Pts	Num	PIM	Maj	Mnr	Fgt	Rgh	HHT	Hat	P/G
97-98	Anh	48	3	4	7	-4	0	1	46	6.5	1	3	4	0	0	0	20	40	0	20	0	4	12	0	.15
98-99	Anh	63	0	4	4	-6	0	0	50	0.0	0	1	1	0	0	0	30	60	0	30	0	3	13	0	.06
2 Years		111	3	8	11	-10	0	1	96	3.1	1	4	5	0	0	0	50	100	0	50	0	7	25	0	.10
Postseason																									
Year	Tm	GP	G	A	Pts	+/–	GW	OT	S	SPct	G	A	Pts	G	A	Pts	Num	PIM	Maj	Mnr	Fgt	Rgh	HHT	Hat	P/G
98-99	Anh	4	0	1	1	-3	0	0	2	0.0	0	1	1	0	0	0	1	2	0	1	0	0	0	0	.25

Vladimir Tsyplakov

(statistical profile on page 383)

Pos: LW **Shoots:** L **Ht:** 6'1" **Wt:** 200 **Born:** 4/17/69—Inta, USSR **Age:** 30

Overall										Power Play			Shorthand			Penalty							Misc	
Year	Tm	GP	G	A	Pts	+/–	GW	GT	S	SPct	G	A	Pts	G	A	Pts	Num	PIM	Maj	Mnr	Fgt	Rgh	HHT	Hat	P/G
95-96	LA	23	5	5	10	1	0	0	40	12.5	0	2	2	0	0	0	2	4	0	2	0	0	0	0	.43
96-97	LA	67	16	23	39	8	2	0	118	13.6	1	5	6	0	0	0	6	12	0	6	0	0	0	0	.58
97-98	LA	73	18	34	52	15	1	0	113	15.9	2	4	6	0	0	0	9	18	0	9	0	3	3	0	.71
98-99	LA	69	11	12	23	-7	2	0	111	9.9	0	2	2	2	1	3	16	32	0	16	0	1	7	0	.33
4 Years		232	50	74	124	17	5	0	382	13.1	3	13	16	2	1	3	33	66	0	33	0	4	10	0	.53
Postseason																									
Year	Tm	GP	G	A	Pts	+/–	GW	OT	S	SPct	G	A	Pts	G	A	Pts	Num	PIM	Maj	Mnr	Fgt	Rgh	HHT	Hat	P/G
97-98	LA	4	0	1	1	-1	0	0	4	0.0	0	0	0	0	0	0	4	8	0	4	0	1	2	0	.25

Darcy Tucker

(statistical profile on page 383)

Pos: C **Shoots:** L **Ht:** 5'11" **Wt:** 182 **Born:** 3/15/75—Castor, Alberta **Age:** 24

Overall										Power Play			Shorthand			Penalty							Misc	
Year	Tm	GP	G	A	Pts	+/–	GW	GT	S	SPct	G	A	Pts	G	A	Pts	Num	PIM	Maj	Mnr	Fgt	Rgh	HHT	Hat	P/G
95-96	Mon	3	0	0	0	-1	0	0	1	0.0	0	0	0	0	0	0	0	0	0	0	0	0	0	0	.00
96-97	Mon	73	7	13	20	-5	3	1	62	11.3	1	1	2	0	0	0	28	110	10	15	10	5	3	0	.27
97-98	2Tm	74	7	13	20	-14	0	0	63	11.1	1	0	1	1	1	2	39	146	12	23	12	8	2	0	.27
98-99	TB	82	21	22	43	-34	3	0	178	11.8	8	7	15	2	0	2	48	176	8	33	8	10	7	0	.52
97-98	Mon	39	1	5	6	-6	0	0	19	5.3	0	0	0	0	0	0	17	57	5	11	5	5	1	0	.15
97-98	TB	35	6	8	14	-8	0	0	44	13.6	1	0	1	1	1	2	22	89	7	12	7	3	1	0	.40
4 Years		232	35	48	83	-54	6	1	304	11.5	10	8	18	3	1	4	115	432	30	71	30	23	12	0	.36

Postseason																									
Year	Tm	GP	G	A	Pts	+/–	GW	OT	S	SPct	G	A	Pts	G	A	Pts	Num	PIM	Maj	Mnr	Fgt	Rgh	HHT	Hat	P/G
96-97	Mon	4	0	0	0	0	0	0	4	0.0	0	0	0	0	0	0	0	0	0	0	0	0	0	0	.00

Ron Tugnutt

(statistical profile on page 403)

Pos: G **Catches:** L **Ht:** 5'11" **Wt:** 165 **Born:** 10/22/67—Scarborough, Ontario **Age:** 32

Overall																Pen Shot		Offense		
Year	Tm	GP	GS	TP	W	L	T	Min	GA	GAA	Shots	SvPct	ShO	OE	PPGA	SHGA	Shots	GA	G	A	PIM
87-88	Que	6	–	–	2	3	0	284	16	3.38	123	.870	0	–	–	–	0	0	0	1	0
88-89	Que	26	–	–	10	10	3	1367	82	3.60	756	.892	0	–	–	–	0	0	0	3	2
89-90	Que	35	–	–	5	24	3	1978	152	4.61	1080	.859	0	–	–	–	0	0	0	0	2
90-91	Que	56	–	–	12	**29**	10	3144	212	4.05	1851	.885	0	–	–	–	0	0	0	0	0
91-92	2Tm	33	30	7	7	18	3	1707	116	4.08	855	.864	1	3	39	4	1	0	0	0	2
92-93	Edm	26	22	5	9	12	2	1338	93	4.17	767	.879	0	7	28	3	1	1	0	0	2
93-94	2Tm	36	31	3	12	18	2	1898	100	3.16	1000	.900	1	11	28	4	1	0	0	0	2
94-95	Mon	7	5	0	1	3	1	346	18	3.12	172	.895	0	1	4	1	0	0	0	0	0
95-96										Did Not Play in NHL											
96-97	Ott	37	33	2	17	15	1	1991	93	2.80	882	.895	3	11	17	7	1	0	0	1	0
97-98	Ott	42	36	4	15	14	8	2236	84	2.25	882	.905	3	4	21	5	0	0	0	0	0
98-99	Ott	43	39	2	22	10	8	2508	75	**1.79**	1005	.925	3	9	21	5	2	1	0	0	0
91-92	Que	30	28	6	6	17	3	1583	106	4.02	782	.864	1	3	35	4	1	0	0	0	0
91-92	Edm	3	2	1	1	1	0	124	10	4.84	73	.863	0	0	4	0	0	0	0	0	2
93-94	Anh	28	26	2	10	15	1	1520	76	3.00	828	.908	1	11	24	3	1	0	0	0	2
93-94	Mon	8	5	1	2	3	1	378	24	3.81	172	.860	0	0	4	1	0	0	0	0	0
11 Years		347	–	–	112	156	41	18797	1041	3.32	9373	.889	11	–	–	–	6	2	0	5	10

Postseason																				
Year	Tm	GP	GS	TP	W	L	Pct	Min	GA	GAA	Shots	SvPct	ShO	OE	PPGA	SHGA	Shots	GA	G	A	PIM
91-92	Edm	2	0	0	0	0	–	60	3	3.00	34	.912	0	0	1	0	0	0	0	0	0
93-94	Mon	1	1	0	0	1	.000	59	5	5.08	25	.800	0	0	1	1	0	0	0	0	0
96-97	Ott	7	7	0	3	4	.429	425	14	1.98	169	.917	1	2	2	1	0	0	0	0	0
97-98	Ott	2	1	0	0	1	.000	74	6	4.86	25	.760	0	0	1	1	0	0	0	0	0
98-99	Ott	2	2	0	0	2	.000	118	6	3.05	41	.854	0	0	2	0	0	0	0	0	0
5 Years		14	11	0	3	8	.273	736	34	2.77	294	.884	1	2	7	3	0	0	0	0	0

Darren Turcotte

Pos: C **Shoots:** L **Ht:** 6'0" **Wt:** 182 **Born:** 3/2/68—Boston, Massachusetts **Age:** 31

Overall										Power Play			Shorthand			Penalty							Misc	
Year	Tm	GP	G	A	Pts	+/–	GW	GT	S	SPct	G	A	Pts	G	A	Pts	Num	PIM	Maj	Mnr	Fgt	Rgh	HHT	Hat	P/G
88-89	NYR	20	7	3	10	0	2	0	49	14.3	2	1	3	0	–	–	2	4	0	2	0	–	–	1	.50
89-90	NYR	76	32	34	66	3	4	0	205	15.6	10	18	28	1	–	–	16	32	0	16	0	–	–	1	.87
90-91	NYR*	74	26	41	67	-5	3	1	212	12.3	15	19	34	2	–	–	–	37	–	–	–	–	–	1	.91
91-92	NYR	71	30	23	53	11	4	1	216	13.9	13	12	25	1	2	3	23	57	1	21	0	2	10	1	.75
92-93	NYR	71	25	28	53	-3	3	1	213	11.7	7	14	21	3	0	3	16	40	0	15	0	0	5	0	.75
93-94	2Tm	32	4	15	19	-13	0	0	60	6.7	0	5	5	0	0	0	7	17	1	6	0	1	2	0	.59
94-95	Har	47	17	18	35	-1	3	0	121	14.0	3	7	10	1	0	1	11	22	0	11	0	0	4	0	.74
95-96	2Tm	68	22	21	43	5	4	0	167	13.2	2	6	8	1	1	2	15	30	0	15	0	0	7	0	.63
96-97	SJ	65	16	21	37	-8	4	0	126	12.7	3	8	11	1	0	1	8	16	0	8	0	0	4	0	.57
97-98	StL	62	12	6	18	6	1	0	75	16.0	3	1	4	0	1	1	9	26	0	8	0	3	3	0	.29
98-99	Nsh	40	4	5	9	-11	1	0	73	5.5	0	0	0	0	0	0	8	16	0	8	0	1	1	0	.23
93-94	NYR	13	2	4	6	-2	0	0	17	11.8	0	3	3	0	0	0	5	13	1	4	0	1	1	0	.46
93-94	Har	19	2	11	13	-11	0	0	43	4.7	0	2	2	0	0	0	2	4	0	2	0	0	1	0	.68
95-96	Wpg	59	16	16	32	-3	2	0	134	11.9	2	5	7	0	1	1	13	26	0	13	0	0	5	0	.54
95-96	SJ	9	6	5	11	8	2	0	33	18.2	0	1	1	1	0	1	2	4	0	2	0	0	2	0	1.22
11 Years		626	195	215	410	-16	29	3	1517	12.9	58	91	149	10	–	–	–	297	–	–	–	–	–	4	.65

Postseason																								
Year	Tm	GP	G	A	Pts	+/–	GW	OT	S	SPct	G	A	Pts	G	A	Pts	Num	PIM	Maj	Mnr	Fgt	Rgh	HHT	Hat	P/G
88-89	NYR	1	0	0	0	-1	0	0	0	–	0	0	0	0	0	0	0	0	0	0	0	0	0	0	.00
89-90	NYR	10	1	6	7	-3	1	0	25	4.0	0	–	–	0	–	–	2	4	0	2	0	0	0	0	.70
90-91	NYR	6	1	2	3	-2	0	0	19	5.3	1	–	–	0	0	0	0	0	0	0	0	0	0	0	.50
91-92	NYR	8	4	0	4	1	0	0	22	18.2	2	0	2	1	0	1	3	6	0	3	0	0	3	0	.50
97-98	StL	10	0	0	0	-4	0	0	5	0.0	0	0	0	0	0	0	1	2	0	1	0	0	1	0	.00
5 Years		35	6	8	14	-9	1	0	71	8.5	3	–	–	1	–	–	6	12	0	6	0	0	4	0	.40

Roman Turek

(statistical profile on page 404)

Pos: G **Catches:** R **Ht:** 6'3" **Wt:** 200 **Born:** 5/21/70—Pisek, Czechoslovakia **Age:** 29

Overall																	Pen Shot		Offense		
Year	Tm	GP	GS	TP	W	L	T	Min	GA	GAA	Shots	SvPct	ShO	OE	PPGA	SHGA	Shots	GA	G	A	PIM
96-97	Dal	6	5	2	3	1	0	263	9	2.05	129	.930	0	1	1	1	0	0	0	0	0
97-98	Dal	23	21	1	11	10	1	1324	49	2.22	496	.901	1	2	8	3	0	0	0	0	2
98-99	Dal	26	22	3	16	3	3	1382	48	2.08	562	.915	1	6	9	1	0	0	0	0	0
3 Years		55	48	6	30	14	4	2969	106	2.14	1187	.911	2	9	18	5	0	0	0	0	2

Pierre Turgeon

(statistical profile on page 383)

Pos: C **Shoots:** L **Ht:** 6'1" **Wt:** 195 **Born:** 8/29/69—Rouyn, Quebec **Age:** 30

Overall											Power Play			Shorthand			Penalty							Misc	
Year	Tm	GP	G	A	Pts	+/-	GW	GT	S	SPct	G	A	Pts	G	A	Pts	Num	PIM	Maj	Mnr	Fgt	Rgh	HHT	Hat	P/G
87-88	Buf	76	14	28	42	-8	3	0	101	13.9	8	–	–	0	–	–	–	34	–	–	–	–	–	0	.55
88-89	Buf	**80**	34	54	88	-3	5	0	182	18.7	19	–	–	0	–	–	–	26	–	–	–	–	–	0	1.10
89-90	Buf*	**80**	40	66	106	10	10	1	193	20.7	17	–	–	1	–	–	–	29	–	–	–	–	–	1	1.33
90-91	Buf	78	32	47	79	14	3	0	174	18.4	13	–	–	2	–	–	–	26	–	–	–	–	–	1	1.01
91-92	2Tm	77	40	55	95	7	6	0	207	19.3	13	20	33	0	0	0	10	20	0	10	0	1	4	2	1.23
92-93	NYI*	83	58	74	132	-1	10	2	301	19.3	24	30	54	0	1	1	13	26	0	13	0	3	5	4	1.59
93-94	NYI*	69	38	56	94	14	6	0	254	15.0	10	22	32	4	3	7	9	18	0	9	0	0	3	2	1.36
94-95	2Tm	49	24	23	47	0	4	0	160	15.0	5	12	17	2	0	2	7	14	0	7	0	1	1	1	.96
95-96	Mon*	80	38	58	96	19	6	0	297	12.8	17	18	35	1	1	2	22	44	0	22	0	3	13	1	1.20
96-97	2Tm	78	26	59	85	8	7	1	216	12.0	5	22	27	0	0	0	7	14	0	7	0	1	3	0	1.09
97-98	StL	60	22	46	68	13	4	0	140	15.7	6	17	23	0	1	1	12	24	0	12	0	3	3	0	1.13
98-99	StL	67	31	34	65	4	5	2	193	16.1	10	9	19	0	0	0	18	36	0	18	0	1	9	1	.97
91-92	Buf	8	2	6	8	-1	0	0	14	14.3	0	4	4	0	0	0	2	4	0	2	0	0	0	0	1.00
91-92	NYI	69	38	49	87	8	6	0	193	19.7	13	16	29	0	0	0	8	16	0	8	0	1	4	2	1.26
94-95	NYI	34	13	14	27	-12	2	0	93	14.0	3	8	11	2	0	2	5	10	0	5	0	1	1	0	.79
94-95	Mon	15	11	9	20	12	2	0	67	16.4	2	4	6	0	0	0	2	4	0	2	0	0	0	1	1.33
96-97	Mon	9	1	10	11	4	0	0	22	4.5	0	4	4	0	0	0	1	2	0	1	0	0	1	0	1.22
96-97	StL	69	25	49	74	4	7	1	194	12.9	5	18	23	0	0	0	6	12	0	6	0	1	2	0	1.07
12 Years		877	397	600	997	77	69	6	2418	16.4	147	–	–	10	–	–	–	311	–	–	–	–	–	13	1.14
Postseason																									
Year	Tm	GP	G	A	Pts	+/-	GW	OT	S	SPct	G	A	Pts	G	A	Pts	Num	PIM	Maj	Mnr	Fgt	Rgh	HHT	Hat	P/G
87-88	Buf	6	4	3	7	-6	0	0	8	50.0	3	–	–	0	0	0	2	4	0	2	0	–	–	0	1.17
88-89	Buf	5	3	5	8	0	0	0	7	42.9	1	–	–	0	–	–	1	2	0	1	0	–	–	0	1.60
89-90	Buf	6	2	4	6	2	1	0	13	15.4	0	–	–	0	0	0	1	2	0	1	0	–	–	0	1.00
90-91	Buf	6	3	1	4	-1	0	0	13	23.1	1	–	–	0	–	–	3	6	0	3	0	–	–	0	.67
92-93	NYI	11	6	7	13	2	0	0	45	13.3	1	1	2	0	0	0	0	0	0	0	0	0	0	0	1.18
93-94	NYI	4	0	1	1	-4	0	0	7	0.0	0	0	0	0	0	0	0	0	0	0	0	0	0	0	.25
95-96	Mon	6	2	4	6	1	0	0	18	11.1	0	2	2	0	0	0	1	2	0	1	0	0	0	0	1.00
96-97	StL	5	1	1	2	0	0	0	8	12.5	1	0	1	0	0	0	1	2	0	1	0	0	0	0	.40
97-98	StL	10	4	4	8	-5	0	0	27	14.8	2	2	4	0	0	0	1	2	0	1	0	0	0	0	.80
98-99	StL	13	4	9	13	3	2	2	42	9.5	0	4	4	0	0	0	3	6	0	3	0	0	1	0	1.00
10 Years		72	29	39	68	-8	3	2	188	15.4	9	–	–	0	–	–	13	26	0	13	0	–	–	0	.94

Oleg Tverdovsky

(statistical profile on page 384)

Pos: D **Shoots:** L **Ht:** 6'0" **Wt:** 185 **Born:** 5/8/76—Donetsk, USSR **Age:** 23

Overall											Power Play			Shorthand			Penalty							Misc	
Year	Tm	GP	G	A	Pts	+/-	GW	GT	S	SPct	G	A	Pts	G	A	Pts	Num	PIM	Maj	Mnr	Fgt	Rgh	HHT	Hat	P/G
94-95	Anh	36	3	9	12	-6	0	0	26	11.5	1	2	3	1	0	1	7	14	0	7	0	1	3	0	.33
95-96	2Tm	82	7	23	30	-7	0	0	119	5.9	2	6	8	0	0	0	15	41	1	13	0	1	5	0	.37
96-97	Pho*	**82**	10	45	55	-5	2	0	144	6.9	3	27	30	1	0	1	15	30	0	15	0	2	7	0	.67
97-98	Pho	46	7	12	19	1	1	1	83	8.4	4	7	11	0	0	0	6	12	0	6	0	0	2	0	.41
98-99	Pho	82	7	18	25	11	2	0	117	6.0	2	4	6	0	0	0	16	32	0	16	0	0	7	0	.30
95-96	Anh	51	7	15	22	0	0	0	84	8.3	2	2	4	0	0	0	12	35	1	10	0	1	3	0	.43
95-96	Wpg	31	0	8	8	-7	0	0	35	0.0	0	4	4	0	0	0	3	6	0	3	0	0	2	0	.26
5 Years		328	34	107	141	-6	5	1	489	7.0	12	46	58	2	0	2	59	129	1	57	0	4	24	0	.43
Postseason																									
Year	Tm	GP	G	A	Pts	+/-	GW	OT	S	SPct	G	A	Pts	G	A	Pts	Num	PIM	Maj	Mnr	Fgt	Rgh	HHT	Hat	P/G
95-96	Wpg	6	0	1	1	-2	0	0	8	0.0	0	0	0	0	0	0	0	0	0	0	0	0	0	0	.17
96-97	Pho	7	0	1	1	0	0	0	10	0.0	0	0	0	0	0	0	0	0	0	0	0	0	0	0	.14
97-98	Pho	6	0	7	7	-2	0	0	7	0.0	0	4	4	0	0	0	0	0	0	0	0	0	0	0	1.17
98-99	Pho	6	0	2	2	3	0	0	6	0.0	0	1	1	0	0	0	3	6	0	3	0	0	0	0	.33
4 Years		25	0	11	11	-1	0	0	31	0.0	0	5	5	0	0	0	3	6	0	3	0	0	0	0	.44

Tony Twist

Pos: LW **Shoots:** L **Ht:** 6'1" **Wt:** 224 **Born:** 5/9/68—Sherwood Park, Alberta **Age:** 31

Overall											Power Play			Shorthand			Penalty							Misc	
Year	Tm	GP	G	A	Pts	+/–	GW	GT	S	SPct	G	A	Pts	G	A	Pts	Num	PIM	Maj	Mnr	Fgt	Rgh	HHT	Hat	P/G
89-90	StL	28	0	0	0	-2	0	0	2	0.0	0	0	0	0	0	0	–	124	–	–	–	–	–	0	.00
90-91	Que	24	0	0	0	-4	0	0	2	0.0	0	0	0	0	0	0	–	104	–	–	–	–	–	0	.00
91-92	Que	44	0	1	1	-3	0	0	9	0.0	0	0	0	0	0	0	38	164	16	17	15	8	0	0	.02
92-93	Que	34	0	2	2	0	0	0	14	0.0	0	0	0	0	0	0	14	64	4	7	3	4	1	0	.06
93-94	Que	49	0	4	4	-1	0	0	15	0.0	0	0	0	0	0	0	30	101	11	18	11	8	1	0	.08
94-95	StL	28	3	0	3	0	1	0	8	37.5	0	0	0	0	0	0	23	89	9	12	9	7	1	0	.11
95-96	StL	51	3	2	5	-1	1	0	12	25.0	0	0	0	0	0	0	25	100	14	10	14	5	3	0	.10
96-97	StL	64	1	2	3	-8	0	0	21	4.8	0	0	0	0	0	0	36	121	11	23	11	16	1	0	.05
97-98	StL	60	1	1	2	-4	0	0	17	5.9	0	0	0	0	0	0	27	105	9	15	9	5	5	0	.03
98-99	StL	63	2	6	8	0	0	0	23	8.7	0	0	0	0	0	0	41	149	9	27	9	12	2	0	.13
10 Years		445	10	18	28	-23	2	0	123	8.1	0	0	0	0	0	0	–	1121	–	–	–	–	–	0	.06
Postseason																									
Year	Tm	GP	G	A	Pts	+/–	GW	OT	S	SPct	G	A	Pts	G	A	Pts	Num	PIM	Maj	Mnr	Fgt	Rgh	HHT	Hat	P/G
94-95	StL	1	0	0	0	0	0	0	1	0.0	0	0	0	0	0	0	3	6	0	3	0	1	0	0	.00
95-96	StL	10	1	1	2	0	0	0	1	100.0	0	0	0	0	0	0	8	16	0	8	0	2	1	0	.20
96-97	StL	6	0	0	0	0	0	0	0	–	0	0	0	0	0	0	0	0	0	0	0	0	0	0	.00
98-99	StL	1	0	0	0	-1	0	0	0	–	0	0	0	0	0	0	0	0	0	0	0	0	0	0	.00
4 Years		18	1	1	2	-1	0	0	2	50.0	0	0	0	0	0	0	11	22	0	11	0	3	1	0	.11

Igor Ulanov

(statistical profile on page 384)

Pos: D **Shoots:** R **Ht:** 6'2" **Wt:** 205 **Born:** 10/1/69—Kraskokamsk, USSR **Age:** 30

Overall											Power Play			Shorthand			Penalty							Misc	
Year	Tm	GP	G	A	Pts	+/–	GW	GT	S	SPct	G	A	Pts	G	A	Pts	Num	PIM	Maj	Mnr	Fgt	Rgh	HHT	Hat	P/G
91-92	Wpg	27	2	9	11	5	0	0	23	8.7	0	0	0	0	0	0	24	67	1	21	0	6	8	0	.41
92-93	Wpg	56	2	14	16	6	0	0	26	7.7	0	0	0	0	1	1	49	124	6	42	6	17	5	0	.29
93-94	Wpg	74	0	17	17	-11	0	0	46	0.0	0	1	1	0	2	2	64	165	7	55	6	20	13	0	.23
94-95	2Tm	22	1	4	5	1	0	0	13	7.7	0	0	0	0	0	0	9	29	1	7	1	1	2	0	.23
95-96	2Tm	64	3	9	12	11	1	0	37	8.1	0	0	0	0	0	0	29	116	6	18	3	0	5	0	.19
96-97	TB	59	1	7	8	2	0	1	56	1.8	0	1	1	0	0	0	40	108	4	34	4	13	6	0	.14
97-98	2Tm	49	2	8	10	-7	0	0	36	5.6	1	0	1	0	0	0	31	97	1	26	1	7	4	0	.20
98-99	Mon	76	3	9	12	-3	0	0	55	5.5	0	1	1	0	0	0	46	109	3	42	3	4	22	0	.16
94-95	Wpg	19	1	3	4	-2	0	0	13	7.7	0	0	0	0	0	0	8	27	1	6	1	1	2	0	.21
94-95	Was	3	0	1	1	3	0	0	0	–	0	0	0	0	0	0	1	2	0	1	0	0	0	0	.33
95-96	Chi	53	1	8	9	12	0	0	24	4.2	0	0	0	0	0	0	20	92	4	11	1	0	5	0	.17
95-96	TB	11	2	1	3	-1	1	0	13	15.4	0	0	0	0	0	0	9	24	2	7	2	0	0	0	.27
97-98	TB	45	2	7	9	-5	0	0	32	6.3	1	0	1	0	0	0	25	85	1	20	1	5	1	0	.20
97-98	Mon	4	0	1	1	-2	0	0	4	0.0	0	0	0	0	0	0	6	12	0	6	0	2	3	0	.25
8 Years		427	14	77	91	4	1	1	292	4.8	1	3	4	0	3	3	292	815	29	245	24	68	65	0	.21
Postseason																									
Year	Tm	GP	G	A	Pts	+/–	GW	OT	S	SPct	G	A	Pts	G	A	Pts	Num	PIM	Maj	Mnr	Fgt	Rgh	HHT	Hat	P/G
91-92	Wpg	7	0	0	0	-4	0	0	11	0.0	0	0	0	0	0	0	10	39	1	7	0	1	1	0	.00
92-93	Wpg	4	0	0	0	-1	0	0	1	0.0	0	0	0	0	0	0	2	4	0	2	0	1	1	0	.00
94-95	Was	2	0	0	0	0	0	0	1	0.0	0	0	0	0	0	0	2	4	0	2	0	1	0	0	.00
95-96	TB	5	0	0	0	-1	0	0	2	0.0	0	0	0	0	0	0	6	15	1	5	1	3	0	0	.00
97-98	Mon	10	1	4	5	3	0	0	6	16.7	0	1	1	0	0	0	6	12	0	6	0	2	0	0	.50
5 Years		28	1	4	5	-3	0	0	21	4.8	0	1	1	0	0	0	26	74	2	22	1	8	2	0	.18

Robert Valicevic

Pos: RW **Shoots:** R **Ht:** 6'2" **Wt:** 197 **Born:** 1/6/71—Detroit, Michigan **Age:** 28

Overall											Power Play			Shorthand			Penalty							Misc	
Year	Tm	GP	G	A	Pts	+/–	GW	GT	S	SPct	G	A	Pts	G	A	Pts	Num	PIM	Maj	Mnr	Fgt	Rgh	HHT	Hat	P/G
98-99	Nsh	19	4	2	6	4	2	0	23	17.4	0	0	0	0	0	0	1	2	0	1	0	0	0	0	.32

Garry Valk

(statistical profile on page 384)

Pos: LW **Shoots:** L **Ht:** 6'1" **Wt:** 205 **Born:** 11/27/67—Edmonton, Alberta **Age:** 32

Overall											Power Play			Shorthand			Penalty							Misc	
Year	Tm	GP	G	A	Pts	+/–	GW	GT	S	SPct	G	A	Pts	G	A	Pts	Num	PIM	Maj	Mnr	Fgt	Rgh	HHT	Hat	P/G
90-91	Van	59	10	11	21	-23	1	0	90	11.1	1	–	–	0	–	–	–	67	–	–	–	–	–	0	.36
91-92	Van	65	8	17	25	3	2	0	93	8.6	2	2	4	1	0	1	17	56	2	13	1	2	7	0	.38
92-93	Van	48	6	7	13	6	2	1	46	13.0	0	0	0	0	1	1	18	77	3	11	2	3	4	0	.27

Overall											Power Play			Shorthand			Penalty							Misc	
Year	Tm	GP	G	A	Pts	+/-	GW	GT	S	SPct	G	A	Pts	G	A	Pts	Num	PIM	Maj	Mnr	Fgt	Rgh	HHT	Hat	P/G
93-94	Anh	78	18	27	45	8	5	0	165	10.9	4	5	9	1	2	3	43	100	2	40	1	7	14	0	.58
94-95	Anh	36	3	6	9	-4	0	0	53	5.7	0	0	0	0	0	0	17	34	0	17	0	6	5	0	.25
95-96	Anh	79	12	12	24	8	2	0	108	11.1	1	2	3	1	0	1	47	125	5	40	2	9	18	1	.30
96-97	2Tm	70	10	11	21	-8	1	0	100	10.0	0	0	0	0	1	1	32	78	2	29	1	6	7	0	.30
97-98	Pit	39	2	1	3	-3	0	1	32	6.3	0	0	0	0	1	1	15	33	1	14	1	3	4	0	.08
98-99	Tor	77	8	21	29	8	0	1	93	8.6	1	3	4	0	0	0	25	53	1	24	1	1	5	0	.38
96-97	Anh	53	7	7	14	-2	1	0	68	10.3	0	0	0	0	0	0	25	53	1	24	1	5	5	0	.26
96-97	Pit	17	3	4	7	-6	0	0	32	9.4	0	0	0	0	1	1	7	25	1	5	0	1	2	0	.41
9 Years		551	77	113	190	-5	13	3	780	9.9	9	–	–	3	–	–	–	623	–	–	–	–	–	1	.34
Postseason																									
Year	Tm	GP	G	A	Pts	+/-	GW	OT	S	SPct	G	A	Pts	G	A	Pts	Num	PIM	Maj	Mnr	Fgt	Rgh	HHT	Hat	P/G
90-91	Van	5	0	0	0	-4	0	0	4	0.0	0	0	0	0	0	0	–	20	–	–	–	–	–	0	.00
91-92	Van	4	0	0	0	-2	0	0	3	0.0	0	0	0	0	0	0	1	5	1	0	1	0	0	0	.00
92-93	Van	7	0	1	1	-3	0	0	6	0.0	0	0	0	0	0	0	6	12	0	6	0	0	0	0	.14
98-99	Tor	17	3	4	7	-1	1	1	14	21.4	0	0	0	0	0	0	11	22	0	11	0	2	3	0	.41
4 Years		33	3	5	8	-10	1	1	27	11.1	0	0	0	0	0	0	–	59	–	–	–	–	–	0	.24

Shaun Van Allen

(statistical profile on page 384)

Pos: C **Shoots:** L **Ht:** 6'1" **Wt:** 200 **Born:** 8/29/67—Calgary, Alberta **Age:** 32

Overall											Power Play			Shorthand			Penalty							Misc	
Year	Tm	GP	G	A	Pts	+/-	GW	GT	S	SPct	G	A	Pts	G	A	Pts	Num	PIM	Maj	Mnr	Fgt	Rgh	HHT	Hat	P/G
90-91	Edm	2	0	0	0	0	0	0	0	–	0	0	0	0	0	0	0	0	0	0	0	0	0	0	.00
91-92											Did Not Play in NHL														
92-93	Edm	21	1	4	5	-2	0	0	19	5.3	0	1	1	0	0	0	3	6	0	3	0	0	1	0	.24
93-94	Anh	80	8	25	33	0	1	0	104	7.7	2	6	8	2	1	3	32	64	0	32	0	6	15	0	.41
94-95	Anh	45	8	21	29	-4	1	0	68	11.8	1	7	8	1	1	2	16	32	0	16	0	4	11	0	.64
95-96	Anh	49	8	17	25	13	2	0	78	10.3	0	2	2	0	1	1	19	41	1	18	1	0	7	0	.51
96-97	Ott	80	11	14	25	-8	2	0	123	8.9	1	1	2	1	1	2	16	35	1	15	1	1	9	0	.31
97-98	Ott	80	4	15	19	4	0	0	104	3.8	0	1	1	0	1	1	20	48	0	19	0	5	3	0	.24
98-99	Ott	79	6	11	17	3	0	0	47	12.8	0	0	0	1	0	1	15	30	0	15	0	5	4	0	.22
8 Years		436	46	107	153	6	6	0	543	8.5	4	18	22	5	5	10	121	256	2	118	2	21	50	0	.35
Postseason																									
Year	Tm	GP	G	A	Pts	+/-	GW	OT	S	SPct	G	A	Pts	G	A	Pts	Num	PIM	Maj	Mnr	Fgt	Rgh	HHT	Hat	P/G
96-97	Ott	7	0	1	1	-3	0	0	8	0.0	0	0	0	0	0	0	2	4	0	2	0	2	0	0	.14
97-98	Ott	11	0	1	1	-3	0	0	16	0.0	0	0	0	0	0	0	5	10	0	5	0	0	1	0	.09
98-99	Ott	4	0	0	0	-1	0	0	2	0.0	0	0	0	0	0	0	0	0	0	0	0	0	0	0	.00
3 Years		22	0	2	2	-7	0	0	26	0.0	0	0	0	0	0	0	7	14	0	7	0	2	1	0	.09

Darren Van Impe

(statistical profile on page 385)

Pos: D **Shoots:** L **Ht:** 6'1" **Wt:** 205 **Born:** 5/18/73—Saskatoon, Saskatchewan **Age:** 26

Overall											Power Play			Shorthand			Penalty							Misc	
Year	Tm	GP	G	A	Pts	+/-	GW	GT	S	SPct	G	A	Pts	G	A	Pts	Num	PIM	Maj	Mnr	Fgt	Rgh	HHT	Hat	P/G
94-95	Anh	1	0	1	1	0	0	0	0	–	0	0	0	0	0	0	2	4	0	2	0	0	2	0	1.00
95-96	Anh	16	1	2	3	8	1	0	13	7.7	0	0	0	0	0	0	3	14	0	2	0	0	0	0	.19
96-97	Anh	74	4	19	23	3	0	0	107	3.7	2	8	10	0	1	1	31	90	4	25	4	2	13	0	.31
97-98	2Tm	69	3	11	14	-6	0	0	71	4.2	2	5	7	0	1	1	17	40	2	15	2	2	4	0	.20
98-99	Bos	60	5	15	20	-5	0	0	92	5.4	4	8	12	0	0	0	24	66	6	18	6	2	7	0	.33
97-98	Anh	19	1	3	4	-10	0	0	21	4.8	0	1	1	0	0	0	2	4	0	2	0	0	0	0	.21
97-98	Bos	50	2	8	10	4	0	0	50	4.0	2	4	6	0	1	1	15	36	2	13	2	2	4	0	.20
5 Years		220	13	48	61	0	1	0	283	4.6	8	21	29	0	2	2	77	214	12	62	12	6	26	0	.28
Postseason																									
Year	Tm	GP	G	A	Pts	+/-	GW	OT	S	SPct	G	A	Pts	G	A	Pts	Num	PIM	Maj	Mnr	Fgt	Rgh	HHT	Hat	P/G
96-97	Anh	9	0	2	2	-3	0	0	11	0.0	0	1	1	0	0	0	4	16	0	3	0	2	0	0	.22
97-98	Bos	6	2	1	3	0	1	1	19	10.5	1	1	2	0	0	0	0	0	0	0	0	0	0	0	.50
98-99	Bos	11	1	2	3	-3	0	0	18	5.6	1	2	3	0	0	0	2	4	0	2	0	1	1	0	.27
3 Years		26	3	5	8	-6	1	1	48	6.3	2	4	6	0	0	0	6	20	0	5	0	3	1	0	.31

John Vanbiesbrouck

(statistical profile on page 404)

Pos: G **Catches:** L **Ht:** 5'8" **Wt:** 176 **Born:** 9/4/63—Detroit, Michigan **Age:** 36

Overall																Pen Shot		Offense		
Year	Tm	GP	GS	TP	W	L	T	Min	GA	GAA	Shots	SvPct	ShO	OE	PPGA	SHGA	Shots	GA	G	A	PIM
81-82	NYR	1	–	–	1	0	0	60	1	1.00	30	.967	0	–	–	–	0	0	0	0	0

Overall																	Pen Shot		Offense		
Year	Tm	GP	GS	TP	W	L	T	Min	GA	GAA	Shots	SvPct	ShO	OE	PPGA	SHGA	Shots	GA	G	A	PIM
82-83										Did Not Play in NHL											
83-84	NYR	3	–	–	2	1	0	180	10	3.33	85	.882	0	–	–	–	0	0	0	0	2
84-85	NYR	42	–	–	12	24	3	2358	166	4.22	1346	.877	1	–	–	–	0	0	0	5	17
85-86	NYR	61	–	–	**31**	21	5	3326	184	3.32	1625	.887	3	–	–	–	0	0	0	3	16
86-87	NYR	50	–	–	18	20	5	2656	161	3.64	1369	.882	0	–	–	–	1	0	0	1	18
87-88	NYR	56	–	–	27	22	7	3319	187	3.38	1700	.890	2	–	–	–	1	1	0	5	46
88-89	NYR	56	–	–	28	21	4	3207	197	3.69	1666	.882	0	–	–	–	1	0	0	2	30
89-90	NYR	47	–	–	19	19	7	2734	154	3.38	1362	.887	1	–	–	–	1	**1**	0	2	24
90-91	NYR	40	–	–	15	18	6	2257	126	3.35	1154	.891	3	–	–	–	0	0	0	3	18
91-92	NYR	45	41	4	27	13	3	2526	120	2.85	1331	.910	2	18	31	7	1	0	0	3	23
92-93	NYR	48	45	2	20	18	7	2757	152	3.31	1525	.900	4	12	49	10	0	0	0	1	18
93-94	Fla*	57	57	2	21	25	11	3440	145	2.53	1912	.924	1	30	42	8	1	0	0	0	38
94-95	Fla	37	35	2	14	15	4	2087	86	2.47	1000	.914	4	14	21	5	0	0	0	1	6
95-96	Fla*	57	54	6	26	20	7	3178	142	2.68	1473	.904	2	16	38	10	0	0	0	2	10
96-97	Fla*	57	56	4	27	19	10	3347	128	2.29	1582	.919	2	19	29	**13**	1	1	0	2	8
97-98	Fla	60	58	4	18	29	11	3451	165	2.87	1638	.899	4	18	53	10	3	1	0	3	6
98-99	Phi	62	61	3	27	18	**15**	3712	135	2.18	1380	.902	6	10	40	4	0	0	0	1	12
17 Years		779	–	–	333	303	105	44595	2259	3.04	22178	.898	35	–	–	–	10	4	0	34	292

Postseason																					
Year	Tm	GP	GS	TP	W	L	Pct	Min	GA	GAA	Shots	SvPct	ShO	OE	PPGA	SHGA	Shots	GA	G	A	PIM
83-84	NYR	1	–	–	0	0	–	1	0	0.00	0	–	0	–	–	–	0	0	0	0	0
84-85	NYR	1	–	–	0	0	–	20	0	0.00	12	1.000	0	–	–	–	0	0	0	0	0
85-86	NYR	16	–	–	8	8	.500	899	49	3.27	477	.897	1	–	–	–	0	0	0	2	2
86-87	NYR	4	–	–	1	3	.250	195	11	3.38	110	.900	1	–	–	–	0	0	0	0	2
88-89	NYR	2	–	–	0	1	.000	107	6	3.36	55	.891	0	–	–	–	0	0	0	0	0
89-90	NYR	6	–	–	2	3	.400	298	15	3.02	153	.902	0	–	–	–	0	0	0	0	4
90-91	NYR	1	–	–	0	0	–	52	1	1.15	22	.955	0	–	–	–	0	0	0	0	0
91-92	NYR	7	6	0	2	5	.286	368	23	3.75	179	.872	0	0	6	1	2	1	0	0	2
95-96	Fla	22	22	2	12	10	.545	1332	50	2.25	735	.932	1	15	19	1	0	0	0	1	20
96-97	Fla	5	5	0	1	4	.200	328	13	2.38	184	.929	1	3	2	0	0	0	0	0	0
98-99	Phi	6	6	0	2	4	.333	369	9	1.46	146	.938	1	2	5	0	1	0	0	0	2
11 Years		71	–	–	28	38	.424	3969	177	2.68	2073	.915	5	–	–	–	3	1	0	3	32

Ryan VandenBussche

Pos: RW **Shoots:** R **Ht:** 6'0" **Wt:** 200 **Born:** 2/28/73—Simcoe, Ontario **Age:** 26

Overall											Power Play			Shorthand			Penalty							Misc	
Year	Tm	GP	G	A	Pts	+/-	GW	GT	S	SPct	G	A	Pts	G	A	Pts	Num	PIM	Maj	Mnr	Fgt	Rgh	HHT	Hat	P/G
96-97	NYR	11	1	0	1	-2	0	0	4	25.0	0	0	0	0	0	0	9	30	4	5	4	1	0	0	.09
97-98	2Tm	20	1	1	2	-2	0	0	2	50.0	0	0	0	0	0	0	10	43	5	4	5	1	0	0	.10
98-99	Chi	6	0	0	0	0	0	0	3	0.0	0	0	0	0	0	0	3	17	1	1	1	0	0	0	.00
97-98	NYR	16	1	0	1	-2	0	0	2	50.0	0	0	0	0	0	0	9	38	4	4	4	1	0	0	.06
97-98	Chi	4	0	1	1	0	0	0	0	–	0	0	0	0	0	0	1	5	1	0	1	0	0	0	.25
3 Years		37	2	1	3	-4	0	0	9	22.2	0	0	0	0	0	0	22	90	10	10	10	2	0	0	.08

Vaclav Varada

(statistical profile on page 385)

Pos: RW **Shoots:** L **Ht:** 6'0" **Wt:** 200 **Born:** 4/26/76—Vsetin, Czechoslovakia **Age:** 23

Overall											Power Play			Shorthand			Penalty							Misc	
Year	Tm	GP	G	A	Pts	+/-	GW	GT	S	SPct	G	A	Pts	G	A	Pts	Num	PIM	Maj	Mnr	Fgt	Rgh	HHT	Hat	P/G
95-96	Buf	1	0	0	0	0	0	0	2	0.0	0	0	0	0	0	0	0	0	0	0	0	0	0	0	.00
96-97	Buf	5	0	0	0	0	0	0	2	0.0	0	0	0	0	0	0	1	2	0	1	0	0	1	0	.00
97-98	Buf	27	5	6	11	0	1	1	27	18.5	0	0	0	0	0	0	6	15	1	5	1	1	3	0	.41
98-99	Buf	72	7	24	31	11	1	0	123	5.7	1	3	4	0	0	0	29	61	1	28	1	4	10	0	.43
4 Years		105	12	30	42	11	2	1	154	7.8	1	3	4	0	0	0	36	78	2	34	2	5	14	0	.40

Postseason																									
Year	Tm	GP	G	A	Pts	+/-	GW	OT	S	SPct	G	A	Pts	G	A	Pts	Num	PIM	Maj	Mnr	Fgt	Rgh	HHT	Hat	P/G
97-98	Buf	15	3	4	7	3	0	0	24	12.5	0	0	0	0	0	0	9	18	0	9	0	0	1	0	.47
98-99	Buf	21	5	4	9	2	0	0	38	13.2	1	0	1	0	0	0	7	14	0	7	0	2	1	0	.43
2 Years		36	8	8	16	5	0	0	62	12.9	1	0	1	0	0	0	16	32	0	16	0	2	2	0	.44

Herbert Vasiljevs

Pos: C **Shoots:** R **Ht:** 5'11" **Wt:** 170 **Born:** 5/27/76—Riga, USSR **Age:** 23

Overall											Power Play			Shorthand			Penalty							Misc	
Year	Tm	GP	G	A	Pts	+/–	GW	GT	S	SPct	G	A	Pts	G	A	Pts	Num	PIM	Maj	Mnr	Fgt	Rgh	HHT	Hat	P/G
98-99	Fla	5	0	0	0	-1	0	0	6	0.0	0	0	0	0	0	0	1	2	0	1	0	0	1	0	.00

Andrey Vasilyev

Pos: LW **Shoots:** R **Ht:** 5'8" **Wt:** 183 **Born:** 3/30/72—Voskresensk, USSR **Age:** 27

Overall											Power Play			Shorthand			Penalty							Misc	
Year	Tm	GP	G	A	Pts	+/–	GW	GT	S	SPct	G	A	Pts	G	A	Pts	Num	PIM	Maj	Mnr	Fgt	Rgh	HHT	Hat	P/G
94-95	NYI	2	0	0	0	0	0	0	2	0.0	0	0	0	0	0	0	1	2	0	1	0	1	0	0	.00
95-96	NYI	10	2	5	7	4	1	0	12	16.7	0	0	0	0	0	0	1	2	0	1	0	0	0	0	.70
96-97	NYI	3	0	0	0	-3	0	0	1	0.0	0	0	0	0	0	0	1	2	0	1	0	0	0	0	.00
97-98		Did Not Play in NHL																							
98-99	Pho	1	0	0	0	-2	0	0	0	–	0	0	0	0	0	0	0	0	0	0	0	0	0	0	.00
4 Years		16	2	5	7	-1	1	0	15	13.3	0	0	0	0	0	0	3	6	0	3	0	1	0	0	.44

Dennis Vaske

Pos: D **Shoots:** L **Ht:** 6'2" **Wt:** 210 **Born:** 10/11/67—Rockford, Illinois **Age:** 32

Overall											Power Play			Shorthand			Penalty							Misc	
Year	Tm	GP	G	A	Pts	+/–	GW	GT	S	SPct	G	A	Pts	G	A	Pts	Num	PIM	Maj	Mnr	Fgt	Rgh	HHT	Hat	P/G
90-91	NYI	5	0	0	0	4	0	0	3	0.0	0	0	0	0	0	0	1	2	0	1	0	0	1	0	.00
91-92	NYI	39	0	1	1	5	0	0	26	0.0	0	0	0	0	0	0	18	39	1	17	1	1	13	0	.03
92-93	NYI	27	1	5	6	9	0	0	15	6.7	0	0	0	0	0	0	16	32	0	16	0	0	8	0	.22
93-94	NYI	65	2	11	13	21	0	0	71	2.8	0	1	1	0	1	1	38	76	0	38	0	2	13	0	.20
94-95	NYI	41	1	11	12	3	0	0	48	2.1	0	2	2	0	0	0	21	53	1	19	0	2	8	0	.29
95-96	NYI	19	1	6	7	-13	1	0	19	5.3	1	5	6	0	0	0	5	21	1	3	0	0	0	0	.37
96-97	NYI	17	0	4	4	3	0	0	19	0.0	0	0	0	0	0	0	6	12	0	6	0	0	4	0	.24
97-98	NYI	19	0	3	3	2	0	0	16	0.0	0	0	0	0	0	0	6	12	0	6	0	0	1	0	.16
98-99	Bos	3	0	0	0	-3	0	0	0	–	0	0	0	0	0	0	3	6	0	3	0	0	1	0	.00
9 Years		235	5	41	46	31	1	0	217	2.3	1	8	9	0	1	1	114	253	3	109	1	5	49	0	.20
Postseason																									
Year	Tm	GP	G	A	Pts	+/–	GW	OT	S	SPct	G	A	Pts	G	A	Pts	Num	PIM	Maj	Mnr	Fgt	Rgh	HHT	Hat	P/G
92-93	NYI	18	0	6	6	-3	0	0	23	0.0	0	0	0	0	0	0	7	14	0	7	0	1	1	0	.33
93-94	NYI	4	0	1	1	-1	0	0	0	–	0	0	0	0	0	0	1	2	0	1	0	0	0	0	.25
2 Years		22	0	7	7	-4	0	0	23	0.0	0	0	0	0	0	0	8	16	0	8	0	1	1	0	.32

Pat Verbeek

(statistical profile on page 385)

Pos: RW **Shoots:** R **Ht:** 5'9" **Wt:** 190 **Born:** 5/24/64—Sarnia, Ontario **Age:** 35

Overall											Power Play			Shorthand			Penalty							Misc	
Year	Tm	GP	G	A	Pts	+/–	GW	GT	S	SPct	G	A	Pts	G	A	Pts	Num	PIM	Maj	Mnr	Fgt	Rgh	HHT	Hat	P/G
82-83	NJ	6	3	2	5	-2	0	1	12	25.0	0	–	–	0	–	–	4	8	0	4	0	–	–	0	.83
83-84	NJ	79	20	27	47	-19	2	0	167	12.0	5	–	–	1	–	–	–	158	–	–	–	–	–	0	.59
84-85	NJ	78	15	18	33	-24	1	1	147	10.2	5	–	–	1	–	–	–	162	–	–	–	–	–	0	.42
85-86	NJ	76	25	28	53	-24	0	0	159	15.7	4	–	–	1	–	–	–	79	–	–	–	–	–	1	.70
86-87	NJ	74	35	24	59	-23	5	0	143	24.5	17	–	–	0	–	–	–	120	–	–	–	–	–	1	.80
87-88	NJ	73	46	31	77	29	8	0	179	25.7	13	–	–	0	–	–	–	227	–	–	–	–	–	2	1.05
88-89	NJ	77	26	21	47	-18	1	0	175	14.9	9	6	15	0	0	0	–	189	–	–	–	–	–	1	.61
89-90	Har	**80**	44	45	89	1	5	1	219	20.1	14	–	–	0	–	–	–	228	–	–	–	–	–	0	1.11
90-91	Har*	80	43	39	82	0	5	1	247	17.4	15	–	–	0	–	–	–	246	–	–	–	–	–	0	1.03
91-92	Har	76	22	35	57	-16	3	0	163	13.5	10	14	24	0	0	0	90	243	5	79	2	26	16	0	.75
92-93	Har	84	39	43	82	-7	6	2	235	16.6	16	15	31	0	0	0	66	197	3	56	1	15	16	2	.98
93-94	Har	84	37	38	75	-15	3	1	226	16.4	15	10	25	1	1	2	64	177	3	56	2	17	20	2	.89
94-95	2Tm	48	17	16	33	-2	2	1	131	13.0	7	4	11	0	0	0	34	71	1	33	1	11	7	0	.69
95-96	NYR*	69	41	41	82	29	6	2	252	16.3	17	16	33	0	0	0	55	129	1	52	0	12	16	2	1.19
96-97	Dal	81	17	36	53	3	4	0	172	9.9	5	9	14	0	0	0	60	128	0	59	0	14	13	0	.65
97-98	Dal	82	31	26	57	15	8	1	190	16.3	9	9	18	0	0	0	66	170	2	60	1	25	12	1	.70
98-99	Dal	78	17	17	34	11	2	1	134	12.7	8	6	14	0	0	0	50	133	3	44	3	14	4	0	.44
94-95	Har	29	7	11	18	0	0	1	75	9.3	3	3	6	0	0	0	25	53	1	24	1	8	6	0	.62
94-95	NYR	19	10	5	15	-2	2	0	56	17.9	4	1	5	0	0	0	9	18	0	9	0	3	1	0	.79
17 Years		1225	478	487	965	-62	61	12	2951	16.2	169	–	–	4	–	–	–	2665	–	–	–	–	–	12	.79

Year	Tm	GP	G	A	Pts	+/–	GW	OT	S	SPct	G	A	Pts	G	A	Pts	Num	PIM	Maj	Mnr	Fgt	Rgh	HHT	Hat	P/G
Postseason																									
87-88	NJ	20	4	8	12	-11	1	0	44	9.1	2	–	–	0	–	–	–	51	–	–	–	–	–	0	.60
89-90	Har	7	2	2	4	1	1	0	19	10.5	1	–	–	0	0	0	–	26	–	–	–	–	–	0	.57
90-91	Har	6	3	2	5	0	0	0	15	20.0	2	–	–	0	–	–	–	40	–	–	–	–	–	0	.83
91-92	Har	7	0	2	2	1	0	0	15	0.0	0	1	1	0	0	0	6	12	0	6	0	2	1	0	.29
94-95	NYR	10	4	6	10	-8	0	0	29	13.8	3	2	5	0	0	0	10	20	0	10	0	3	1	0	1.00
95-96	NYR	11	3	6	9	-8	0	0	38	7.9	1	4	5	0	0	0	6	12	0	6	0	0	5	0	.82
96-97	Dal	7	1	3	4	-2	0	0	19	5.3	1	0	1	0	0	0	4	16	0	3	0	0	0	0	.57
97-98	Dal	17	3	2	5	-3	1	0	25	12.0	2	2	4	0	0	0	13	26	0	13	0	2	4	0	.29
98-99	Dal	18	3	4	7	4	1	0	33	9.1	0	1	1	0	0	0	7	14	0	7	0	1	2	0	.39
9 Years		103	23	35	58	-26	4	0	237	9.7	12	–	–	0	–	–	–	217	–	–	–	–	–	0	.56

Mike Vernon

(statistical profile on page 404)

Pos: G **Catches:** L **Ht:** 5'9" **Wt:** 170 **Born:** 2/24/63—Calgary, Alberta **Age:** 36

Year	Tm	GP	GS	TP	W	L	T	Min	GA	GAA	Shots	SvPct	ShO	OE	PPGA	SHGA	Shots	GA	G	A	PIM
Overall																	Pen Shot		Offense		
82-83	Cgy	2	–	–	0	2	0	100	11	6.60	46	.761	0	–	–	–	0	0	0	0	0
83-84	Cgy	1	–	–	0	1	0	11	4	21.82	6	.333	0	–	–	–	0	0	0	0	0
84-85		Did Not Play in NHL																			
85-86	Cgy	18	–	–	9	3	3	921	52	3.39	417	.875	1	–	–	–	0	0	0	1	4
86-87	Cgy	54	–	–	30	21	1	2957	178	3.61	1528	.884	1	–	–	–	1	1	0	2	14
87-88	Cgy*	64	–	–	39	16	7	3565	210	3.53	1708	.877	1	–	–	–	0	0	0	7	47
88-89	Cgy*	52	–	–	**37**	6	5	2938	130	2.65	1263	.897	0	–	–	–	2	**1**	0	4	18
89-90	Cgy*	47	–	–	23	14	9	2795	146	3.13	1122	.870	0	–	–	–	0	0	0	3	21
90-91	Cgy*	54	–	–	31	19	3	3121	172	3.31	1406	.878	1	–	–	–	0	0	0	4	8
91-92	Cgy	63	62	7	24	30	9	3640	217	3.58	1853	.883	0	18	76	8	2	**2**	0	7	8
92-93	Cgy*	64	62	5	29	26	9	3732	203	3.26	1804	.887	2	17	56	7	0	0	0	2	42
93-94	Cgy	48	46	4	26	17	5	2798	131	2.81	1209	.892	3	10	49	3	1	0	0	0	14
94-95	Det	30	29	0	19	6	4	1807	76	2.52	710	.893	1	3	20	3	0	0	0	0	8
95-96	Det	32	32	2	21	7	2	1855	70	2.26	723	.903	3	7	16	4	1	0	0	0	2
96-97	Det	33	33	3	13	11	8	1952	79	2.43	782	.899	0	4	14	2	0	0	0	0	35
97-98	SJ	62	59	5	30	22	8	3564	146	2.46	1401	.896	5	10	42	3	1	1	0	2	24
98-99	SJ	49	48	3	16	22	10	2831	107	2.27	1200	.911	4	16	29	4	0	0	0	0	8
16 Years		673	–	–	347	223	83	38587	1932	3.00	17178	.888	22	–	–	–	8	5	0	32	253

Year	Tm	GP	GS	TP	W	L	Pct	Min	GA	GAA	Shots	SvPct	ShO	OE	PPGA	SHGA	Shots	GA	G	A	PIM
Postseason																					
85-86	Cgy	21	–	–	12	9	.571	1229	60	2.93	583	.897	0	–	–	–	0	0	0	1	0
86-87	Cgy	5	–	–	2	3	.400	263	16	3.65	136	.882	0	–	–	–	0	0	0	0	0
87-88	Cgy	9	–	–	4	4	.500	515	34	3.96	210	.838	0	–	–	–	0	0	0	2	2
88-89	Cgy	22	–	–	16	5	.762	1381	52	2.26	550	.905	3	–	–	–	0	0	0	0	14
89-90	Cgy	6	–	–	2	3	.400	342	19	3.33	150	.873	0	–	–	–	0	0	0	0	0
90-91	Cgy	7	–	–	3	4	.429	427	21	2.95	204	.897	0	–	–	–	0	0	0	0	2
92-93	Cgy	4	2	0	1	1	.500	150	15	6.00	81	.815	0	0	3	0	0	0	0	0	2
93-94	Cgy	7	7	0	3	4	.429	466	23	2.96	220	.895	0	2	6	1	0	0	0	0	2
94-95	Det	18	18	2	12	6	.667	1063	41	2.31	370	.889	1	1	12	1	0	0	0	0	0
95-96	Det	4	4	0	2	2	.500	243	11	2.72	81	.864	0	0	1	0	0	0	0	0	2
96-97	Det	20	20	2	16	4	.800	1229	36	1.76	494	.927	1	4	15	0	0	0	0	1	12
97-98	SJ	6	6	1	2	4	.333	348	14	2.41	138	.899	1	2	6	1	0	0	0	0	0
98-99	SJ	5	5	0	2	3	.400	321	13	2.43	172	.924	0	5	5	0	0	0	0	1	0
13 Years		134	–	–	77	52	.597	7977	355	2.67	3389	.895	6	–	–	–	0	0	0	5	36

Terry Virtue

Pos: D **Shoots:** R **Ht:** 6'0" **Wt:** 200 **Born:** 8/12/70—Scarborough, Ontario **Age:** 29

Year	Tm	GP	G	A	Pts	+/–	GW	GT	S	SPct	G	A	Pts	G	A	Pts	Num	PIM	Maj	Mnr	Fgt	Rgh	HHT	Hat	P/G
Overall											Power Play			Shorthand			Penalty							Misc	
98-99	Bos	4	0	0	0	2	0	0	2	0.0	0	0	0	0	0	0	0	0	0	0	0	0	0	0	.00

Mark Visheau

Pos: D **Shoots:** R **Ht:** 6'6" **Wt:** 235 **Born:** 6/27/73—Burlington, Ontario **Age:** 26

Year	Tm	GP	G	A	Pts	+/–	GW	GT	S	SPct	G	A	Pts	G	A	Pts	Num	PIM	Maj	Mnr	Fgt	Rgh	HHT	Hat	P/G
Overall											Power Play			Shorthand			Penalty							Misc	
93-94	Wpg	1	0	0	0	0	0	0	1	0.0	0	0	0	0	0	0	0	0	0	0	0	0	0	0	.00
94-95		Did Not Play in NHL																							

Year	Tm	GP	G	A	Pts	+/–	GW	GT	S	SPct	PP G	PP A	PP Pts	SH G	SH A	SH Pts	Num	PIM	Maj	Mnr	Fgt	Rgh	HHT	Hat	P/G
		Overall									Power Play			Shorthand			Penalty							Misc	
95-96											Did Not Play in NHL														
96-97											Did Not Play in NHL														
97-98											Did Not Play in NHL														
98-99	LA	28	1	3	4	-7	0	0	10	10.0	0	0	0	0	1	1	26	107	13	11	13	2	1	0	.14
2 Years		29	1	3	4	-7	0	0	11	9.1	0	0	0	0	1	1	26	107	13	11	13	2	1	0	.14

Tomas Vokoun

(statistical profile on page 404)

Pos: G **Catches:** R **Ht:** 6'0" **Wt:** 212 **Born:** 7/2/76—Karlovy Vary, Czechoslovakia **Age:** 23

Year	Tm	GP	GS	TP	W	L	T	Min	GA	GAA	Shots	SvPct	ShO	OE	PPGA	SHGA	Pen Shot Shots	Pen Shot GA	Offense G	Offense A	Offense PIM
96-97	Mon	1	1	1	0	0	0	20	4	12.00	14	.714	0	0	1	0	0	0	0	0	0
97-98										Did Not Play in NHL											
98-99	Nsh	37	32	5	12	18	4	1954	96	2.95	1041	.908	1	14	29	2	0	0	0	1	6
2 Years		38	33	6	12	18	4	1974	100	3.04	1055	.905	1	14	30	2	0	0	0	1	6

Jan Vopat

(statistical profile on page 385)

Pos: D **Shoots:** L **Ht:** 6'0" **Wt:** 207 **Born:** 3/22/73—Most, Czechoslovakia **Age:** 26

Year	Tm	GP	G	A	Pts	+/–	GW	GT	S	SPct	PP G	PP A	PP Pts	SH G	SH A	SH Pts	Num	PIM	Maj	Mnr	Fgt	Rgh	HHT	Hat	P/G
95-96	LA	11	1	4	5	3	0	0	13	7.7	0	3	3	0	0	0	2	4	0	2	0	0	1	0	.45
96-97	LA	33	4	5	9	3	1	1	44	9.1	0	1	1	0	0	0	7	22	0	6	0	1	2	0	.27
97-98	LA	21	1	5	6	8	1	0	13	7.7	0	1	1	0	0	0	5	10	0	5	0	0	2	0	.29
98-99	Nsh	55	5	6	11	0	0	0	46	10.9	0	1	1	0	1	1	14	28	0	14	0	0	4	0	.20
4 Years		120	11	20	31	14	2	1	116	9.5	0	6	6	0	1	1	28	64	0	27	0	1	9	0	.26

Postseason

Year	Tm	GP	G	A	Pts	+/–	GW	OT	S	SPct	G	A	Pts	G	A	Pts	Num	PIM	Maj	Mnr	Fgt	Rgh	HHT	Hat	P/G
97-98	LA	2	0	1	1	1	0	0	1	0.0	0	0	0	0	0	0	1	2	0	1	0	0	1	0	.50

Roman Vopat

Pos: C **Shoots:** L **Ht:** 6'3" **Wt:** 221 **Born:** 4/21/76—Litvinov, Czechoslovakia **Age:** 23

Year	Tm	GP	G	A	Pts	+/–	GW	GT	S	SPct	PP G	PP A	PP Pts	SH G	SH A	SH Pts	Num	PIM	Maj	Mnr	Fgt	Rgh	HHT	Hat	P/G
95-96	StL	25	2	3	5	-8	1	0	33	6.1	1	0	1	0	0	0	17	48	2	14	2	1	4	0	.20
96-97	LA	29	4	5	9	-7	2	0	54	7.4	1	0	1	0	0	0	17	60	6	10	6	3	3	0	.31
97-98	LA	25	0	3	3	-7	0	0	36	0.0	0	0	0	0	0	0	17	55	7	10	7	5	3	0	.12
98-99	3Tm	54	0	3	3	-7	0	0	27	0.0	0	0	0	0	0	0	29	90	8	20	8	7	1	0	.06
98-99	LA	3	0	0	0	0	0	0	2	0.0	0	0	0	0	0	0	3	6	0	3	0	0	1	0	.00
98-99	Chi	3	0	0	0	-4	0	0	0	–	0	0	0	0	0	0	2	4	0	2	0	0	0	0	.00
98-99	Phi	48	0	3	3	-3	0	0	25	0.0	0	0	0	0	0	0	24	80	8	15	8	7	0	0	.06
4 Years		133	6	14	20	-29	3	0	150	4.0	2	0	2	0	0	0	80	253	23	54	23	16	11	0	.15

Vladimir Vorobiev

Pos: RW **Shoots:** R **Ht:** 6'3" **Wt:** 205 **Born:** 10/2/72—Cherepovets, USSR **Age:** 27

Year	Tm	GP	G	A	Pts	+/–	GW	GT	S	SPct	PP G	PP A	PP Pts	SH G	SH A	SH Pts	Num	PIM	Maj	Mnr	Fgt	Rgh	HHT	Hat	P/G
96-97	NYR	16	5	5	10	4	0	0	42	11.9	2	1	3	0	0	0	3	6	0	3	0	0	2	0	.63
97-98	NYR	15	2	2	4	-10	1	0	27	7.4	0	2	2	0	0	0	3	6	0	3	0	0	0	0	.27
98-99	Edm	2	2	0	2	1	0	0	5	40.0	0	0	0	0	0	0	1	2	0	1	0	0	1	0	1.00
3 Years		33	9	7	16	-5	1	0	74	12.2	2	3	5	0	0	0	7	14	0	7	0	0	3	0	.48

Postseason

Year	Tm	GP	G	A	Pts	+/–	GW	OT	S	SPct	G	A	Pts	G	A	Pts	Num	PIM	Maj	Mnr	Fgt	Rgh	HHT	Hat	P/G
98-99	Edm	1	0	0	0	-1	0	0	1	0.0	0	0	0	0	0	0	0	0	0	0	0	0	0	0	.00

Jimmy Waite

Pos: G **Catches:** L **Ht:** 6'1" **Wt:** 180 **Born:** 4/15/69—Sherbrooke, Quebec **Age:** 30

Year	Tm	GP	GS	TP	W	L	T	Min	GA	GAA	Shots	SvPct	ShO	OE	PPGA	SHGA	Pen Shot Shots	Pen Shot GA	Offense G	Offense A	Offense PIM
88-89	Chi	11	–	–	0	7	1	494	43	5.22	253	.830	0	–	–	–	0	0	0	0	0
89-90	Chi	4	–	–	2	0	0	183	14	4.59	92	.848	0	–	–	–	0	0	0	0	0

Overall																	Pen Shot		Offense		
Year	Tm	GP	GS	TP	W	L	T	Min	GA	GAA	Shots	SvPct	ShO	OE	PPGA	SHGA	Shots	GA	G	A	PIM
90-91	Chi	1	–	–	1	0	0	60	2	2.00	28	.929	0	–	–	–	0	0	0	0	0
91-92	Chi	17	11	0	4	7	4	877	54	3.69	347	.844	0	1	20	1	0	0	0	1	0
92-93	Chi	20	14	2	6	7	1	996	49	2.95	411	.881	2	2	16	3	0	0	0	0	0
93-94	SJ	15	11	1	3	7	0	697	50	4.30	319	.843	0	2	14	3	0	0	0	0	6
94-95	Chi	2	2	0	1	1	0	119	5	2.52	51	.902	0	1	0	0	0	0	0	0	0
95-96	Chi	1	0	0	0	0	0	31	0	0.00	8	1.000	0	0	0	0	0	0	0	0	0
96-97	Chi	2	2	1	0	1	1	105	7	4.00	58	.879	0	1	1	0	0	0	0	0	0
97-98	Pho	17	10	0	5	6	1	793	28	2.12	322	.913	1	3	9	0	0	0	0	0	2
98-99	Pho	16	15	2	6	5	4	898	41	2.74	390	.895	1	2	8	1	0	0	0	0	2
11 Years		106	–	–	28	41	12	5253	293	3.35	2279	.871	4	–	–	–	0	0	0	1	10
Postseason																					
Year	Tm	GP	GS	TP	W	L	Pct	Min	GA	GAA	Shots	SvPct	ShO	OE	PPGA	SHGA	Shots	GA	G	A	PIM
93-94	SJ	2	0	0	0	0	–	40	3	4.50	17	.824	0	0	1	2	0	0	0	0	0
97-98	Pho	4	3	1	0	3	.000	171	11	3.86	97	.887	0	0	4	0	0	0	0	0	0
2 Years		6	3	1	0	3	.000	211	14	3.98	114	.877	0	0	5	2	0	0	0	0	0

Scott Walker

(statistical profile on page 386)

Pos: RW **Shoots:** R **Ht:** 5'9" **Wt:** 180 **Born:** 7/19/73—Montreal, Quebec **Age:** 26

Overall											Power Play			Shorthand			Penalty							Misc	
Year	Tm	GP	G	A	Pts	+/–	GW	GT	S	SPct	G	A	Pts	G	A	Pts	Num	PIM	Maj	Mnr	Fgt	Rgh	HHT	Hat	P/G
94-95	Van	11	0	1	1	0	0	0	8	0.0	0	0	0	0	0	0	8	33	3	4	3	3	0	0	.09
95-96	Van	63	4	8	12	-7	1	0	45	8.9	0	0	0	1	1	2	34	137	7	21	7	7	3	0	.19
96-97	Van	64	3	15	18	2	0	0	55	5.5	0	0	0	0	0	0	35	132	10	21	10	9	3	0	.28
97-98	Van	59	3	10	13	-8	1	0	40	7.5	0	0	0	1	0	1	36	164	12	17	11	8	3	0	.22
98-99	Nsh	71	15	25	40	0	2	0	96	15.6	0	2	2	1	1	2	35	103	3	29	3	10	9	0	.56
5 Years		268	25	59	84	-13	4	0	244	10.2	0	2	2	3	2	5	148	569	35	92	34	37	18	0	.31

Aaron Ward

(statistical profile on page 386)

Pos: D **Shoots:** R **Ht:** 6'2" **Wt:** 225 **Born:** 1/17/73—Windsor, Ontario **Age:** 26

Overall											Power Play			Shorthand			Penalty							Misc	
Year	Tm	GP	G	A	Pts	+/–	GW	GT	S	SPct	G	A	Pts	G	A	Pts	Num	PIM	Maj	Mnr	Fgt	Rgh	HHT	Hat	P/G
93-94	Det	5	1	0	1	2	0	0	3	33.3	0	0	0	0	0	0	2	4	0	2	0	0	2	0	.20
94-95	Det	1	0	1	1	1	0	0	0	–	0	0	0	0	0	0	1	2	0	1	0	0	0	0	1.00
95-96		Did Not Play in NHL																							
96-97	Det	49	2	5	7	-9	0	0	40	5.0	0	1	1	0	1	1	19	52	2	16	2	2	4	0	.14
97-98	Det	52	5	5	10	-1	1	0	47	10.6	0	0	0	0	0	0	18	47	1	16	1	2	8	0	.19
98-99	Det	60	3	8	11	-5	0	0	46	6.5	0	0	0	0	1	1	19	52	2	16	1	6	6	0	.18
5 Years		167	11	19	30	-12	1	0	136	8.1	0	1	1	0	2	2	59	157	5	51	4	10	20	0	.18
Postseason																									
Year	Tm	GP	G	A	Pts	+/–	GW	OT	S	SPct	G	A	Pts	G	A	Pts	Num	PIM	Maj	Mnr	Fgt	Rgh	HHT	Hat	P/G
96-97	Det	19	0	0	0	1	0	0	9	0.0	0	0	0	0	0	0	3	17	1	1	1	0	0	0	.00
98-99	Det	8	0	1	1	2	0	0	6	0.0	0	0	0	0	0	0	4	8	0	4	0	2	0	0	.13
2 Years		27	0	1	1	3	0	0	15	0.0	0	0	0	0	0	0	7	25	1	5	1	2	0	0	.04

Dixon Ward

(statistical profile on page 386)

Pos: RW **Shoots:** R **Ht:** 6'0" **Wt:** 200 **Born:** 9/23/68—Leduc, Alberta **Age:** 31

Overall											Power Play			Shorthand			Penalty							Misc	
Year	Tm	GP	G	A	Pts	+/–	GW	GT	S	SPct	G	A	Pts	G	A	Pts	Num	PIM	Maj	Mnr	Fgt	Rgh	HHT	Hat	P/G
92-93	Van	70	22	30	52	34	0	1	111	19.8	4	5	9	1	2	3	27	82	4	21	2	2	5	0	.74
93-94	2Tm	67	12	3	15	-22	1	0	90	13.3	4	0	4	0	0	0	27	82	4	21	3	11	2	0	.22
94-95	Tor	22	0	3	3	-4	0	0	15	0.0	0	0	0	0	0	0	11	31	3	8	3	2	2	0	.14
95-96	Buf	8	2	2	4	1	1	0	12	16.7	0	0	0	0	0	0	3	6	0	3	0	0	0	0	.50
96-97	Buf	79	13	32	45	17	4	0	93	14.0	1	3	4	2	2	4	11	36	2	8	2	1	6	0	.57
97-98	Buf	71	10	13	23	9	3	1	99	10.1	0	1	1	2	1	3	17	42	0	16	0	3	7	0	.32
98-99	Buf	78	20	24	44	10	4	1	101	19.8	2	6	8	1	0	1	18	44	0	17	0	4	3	1	.56
93-94	Van	33	6	1	7	-14	1	0	46	13.0	2	0	2	0	0	0	13	37	1	11	1	5	1	0	.21
93-94	LA	34	6	2	8	-8	0	0	44	13.6	2	0	2	0	0	0	14	45	3	10	2	6	1	0	.24
7 Years		395	79	107	186	45	13	3	521	15.2	11	15	26	6	5	11	114	323	13	94	10	23	25	1	.47
Postseason																									
Year	Tm	GP	G	A	Pts	+/–	GW	OT	S	SPct	G	A	Pts	G	A	Pts	Num	PIM	Maj	Mnr	Fgt	Rgh	HHT	Hat	P/G
92-93	Van	9	2	3	5	1	0	0	12	16.7	2	0	2	0	0	0	0	0	0	0	0	0	0	0	.56
96-97	Buf	12	2	3	5	2	1	0	23	8.7	0	0	0	1	1	2	3	6	0	3	0	1	0	0	.42

Postseason																									
Year	Tm	GP	G	A	Pts	+/–	GW	OT	S	SPct	G	A	Pts	G	A	Pts	Num	PIM	Maj	Mnr	Fgt	Rgh	HHT	Hat	P/G
97-98	Buf	15	3	8	11	8	0	0	29	10.3	0	0	0	0	1	1	3	6	0	3	0	1	2	0	.73
98-99	Buf	21	7	5	12	6	3	0	38	18.4	0	0	0	2	0	2	16	32	0	16	0	5	5	0	.57
4 Years		57	14	19	33	17	4	0	102	13.7	2	0	2	3	2	5	22	44	0	22	0	7	7	0	.58

Ed Ward

Pos: RW **Shoots:** R **Ht:** 6'3" **Wt:** 205 **Born:** 11/10/69—Edmonton, Alberta **Age:** 30

Overall											Power Play			Shorthand			Penalty							Misc	
Year	Tm	GP	G	A	Pts	+/–	GW	GT	S	SPct	G	A	Pts	G	A	Pts	Num	PIM	Maj	Mnr	Fgt	Rgh	HHT	Hat	P/G
93-94	Que	7	1	0	1	0	0	0	3	33.3	0	0	0	0	0	0	1	5	1	0	1	0	0	0	.14
94-95	Cgy	2	1	1	2	-2	0	0	1	100.0	0	0	0	0	0	0	1	2	0	1	0	1	0	0	1.00
95-96	Cgy	41	3	5	8	-2	0	0	33	9.1	0	0	0	0	0	0	15	44	2	12	1	3	1	0	.20
96-97	Cgy	40	5	8	13	-3	1	0	33	15.2	0	0	0	0	0	0	16	49	3	12	3	1	3	0	.33
97-98	Cgy	64	4	5	9	-1	0	1	52	7.7	0	0	0	0	0	0	39	122	4	31	4	7	4	0	.14
98-99	Cgy	68	3	5	8	-4	0	0	56	5.4	0	0	0	0	0	0	25	67	3	21	3	5	4	0	.12
6 Years		222	17	24	41	-12	1	1	178	9.6	0	0	0	0	0	0	97	289	13	77	12	17	12	0	.18

Jeff Ware

Pos: D **Shoots:** L **Ht:** 6'4" **Wt:** 220 **Born:** 5/19/77—Toronto, Ontario **Age:** 22

Overall											Power Play			Shorthand			Penalty							Misc	
Year	Tm	GP	G	A	Pts	+/–	GW	GT	S	SPct	G	A	Pts	G	A	Pts	Num	PIM	Maj	Mnr	Fgt	Rgh	HHT	Hat	P/G
96-97	Tor	13	0	0	0	2	0	0	4	0.0	0	0	0	0	0	0	3	6	0	3	0	0	2	0	.00
97-98	Tor	2	0	0	0	1	0	0	0	–	0	0	0	0	0	0	0	0	0	0	0	0	0	0	.00
98-99	Fla	6	0	1	1	-6	0	0	1	0.0	0	0	0	0	0	0	3	6	0	3	0	0	2	0	.17
3 Years		21	0	1	1	-3	0	0	5	0.0	0	0	0	0	0	0	6	12	0	6	0	0	4	0	.05

Rhett Warrener

Pos: D **Shoots:** R **Ht:** 6'1" **Wt:** 209 **Born:** 1/27/76—Shaunavon, Saskatchewan **Age:** 23

Overall											Power Play			Shorthand			Penalty							Misc	
Year	Tm	GP	G	A	Pts	+/–	GW	GT	S	SPct	G	A	Pts	G	A	Pts	Num	PIM	Maj	Mnr	Fgt	Rgh	HHT	Hat	P/G
95-96	Fla	28	0	3	3	4	0	0	19	0.0	0	0	0	0	0	0	16	46	2	13	2	1	6	0	.11
96-97	Fla	62	4	9	13	20	1	0	58	6.9	1	2	3	0	0	0	28	88	8	19	8	0	10	0	.21
97-98	Fla	79	0	4	4	-16	0	0	66	0.0	0	0	0	0	0	0	33	99	11	22	11	4	6	0	.05
98-99	2Tm	61	1	7	8	2	0	0	44	2.3	0	3	3	0	0	0	29	84	6	22	6	6	10	0	.13
98-99	Fla	48	0	7	7	-1	0	0	33	0.0	0	3	3	0	0	0	22	64	4	17	4	4	7	0	.15
98-99	Buf	13	1	0	1	3	0	0	11	9.1	0	0	0	0	0	0	7	20	2	5	2	2	3	0	.08
4 Years		230	5	23	28	10	1	0	187	2.7	1	5	6	0	0	0	106	317	27	76	27	11	32	0	.12
Postseason																									
Year	Tm	GP	G	A	Pts	+/–	GW	OT	S	SPct	G	A	Pts	G	A	Pts	Num	PIM	Maj	Mnr	Fgt	Rgh	HHT	Hat	P/G
95-96	Fla	21	0	3	3	3	0	0	14	0.0	0	0	0	0	0	0	5	10	0	5	0	0	5	0	.14
96-97	Fla	5	0	0	0	0	0	0	5	0.0	0	0	0	0	0	0	0	0	0	0	0	0	0	0	.00
98-99	Buf	20	1	3	4	12	0	0	21	4.8	0	0	0	0	1	1	12	32	0	11	0	2	7	0	.20
3 Years		46	1	6	7	15	0	0	40	2.5	0	0	0	0	1	1	17	42	0	16	0	2	12	0	.15

Todd Warriner

(statistical profile on page 386)

Pos: LW **Shoots:** L **Ht:** 6'1" **Wt:** 188 **Born:** 1/3/74—Blenheim, Ontario **Age:** 25

Overall											Power Play			Shorthand			Penalty							Misc	
Year	Tm	GP	G	A	Pts	+/–	GW	GT	S	SPct	G	A	Pts	G	A	Pts	Num	PIM	Maj	Mnr	Fgt	Rgh	HHT	Hat	P/G
94-95	Tor	5	0	0	0	-3	0	0	1	0.0	0	0	0	0	0	0	0	0	0	0	0	0	0	0	.00
95-96	Tor	57	7	8	15	-11	0	0	79	8.9	1	0	1	0	0	0	13	26	0	13	0	2	7	0	.26
96-97	Tor	75	12	21	33	-3	0	1	146	8.2	2	5	7	2	0	2	15	41	1	13	0	0	3	0	.44
97-98	Tor	45	5	8	13	5	1	0	73	6.8	0	0	0	0	0	0	10	20	0	10	0	3	5	0	.29
98-99	Tor	53	9	10	19	-6	1	0	96	9.4	1	2	3	0	0	0	14	28	0	14	0	0	7	0	.36
5 Years		235	33	47	80	-18	2	1	395	8.4	4	7	11	2	0	2	52	115	1	50	0	5	22	0	.34
Postseason																									
Year	Tm	GP	G	A	Pts	+/–	GW	OT	S	SPct	G	A	Pts	G	A	Pts	Num	PIM	Maj	Mnr	Fgt	Rgh	HHT	Hat	P/G
95-96	Tor	6	1	1	2	0	0	0	13	7.7	0	0	0	0	0	0	1	2	0	1	0	0	1	0	.33
98-99	Tor	9	0	0	0	0	0	0	12	0.0	0	0	0	0	0	0	1	2	0	1	0	0	0	0	.00
2 Years		15	1	1	2	0	0	0	25	4.0	0	0	0	0	0	0	2	4	0	2	0	0	1	0	.13

Steve Washburn

Pos: C **Shoots:** L **Ht:** 6'2" **Wt:** 191 **Born:** 4/10/75—Ottawa, Ontario **Age:** 24

Overall											Power Play			Shorthand			Penalty							Misc	
Year	Tm	GP	G	A	Pts	+/-	GW	GT	S	SPct	G	A	Pts	G	A	Pts	Num	PIM	Maj	Mnr	Fgt	Rgh	HHT	Hat	P/G
95-96	Fla	1	0	1	1	1	0	0	1	0.0	0	0	0	0	0	0	0	0	0	0	0	0	0	0	1.00
96-97	Fla	18	3	6	9	2	0	0	21	14.3	1	0	1	0	0	0	2	4	0	2	0	0	2	0	.50
97-98	Fla	58	11	8	19	-6	2	0	61	18.0	4	2	6	0	1	1	16	32	0	16	0	1	9	0	.33
98-99	2Tm	12	0	0	0	-1	0	0	6	0.0	0	0	0	0	0	0	3	6	0	3	0	0	0	0	.00
98-99	Fla	4	0	0	0	-1	0	0	0	–	0	0	0	0	0	0	2	4	0	2	0	0	0	0	.00
98-99	Van	8	0	0	0	0	0	0	6	0.0	0	0	0	0	0	0	1	2	0	1	0	0	0	0	.00
4 Years		89	14	15	29	-4	2	0	89	15.7	5	2	7	0	1	1	21	42	0	21	0	1	11	0	.33

Postseason

Year	Tm	GP	G	A	Pts	+/-	GW	OT	S	SPct	G	A	Pts	G	A	Pts	Num	PIM	Maj	Mnr	Fgt	Rgh	HHT	Hat	P/G
95-96	Fla	1	0	1	1	0	0	0	0	–	0	0	0	0	0	0	0	0	0	0	0	0	0	0	1.00

Mike Watt

(statistical profile on page 387)

Pos: LW **Shoots:** L **Ht:** 6'2" **Wt:** 210 **Born:** 3/31/76—Seaforth, Ontario **Age:** 23

Overall											Power Play			Shorthand			Penalty							Misc	
Year	Tm	GP	G	A	Pts	+/-	GW	GT	S	SPct	G	A	Pts	G	A	Pts	Num	PIM	Maj	Mnr	Fgt	Rgh	HHT	Hat	P/G
97-98	Edm	14	1	2	3	-4	1	0	14	7.1	0	1	1	0	0	0	2	4	0	2	0	0	0	0	.21
98-99	NYI	75	8	17	25	-2	4	0	75	10.7	0	1	1	0	0	0	6	12	0	6	0	2	3	0	.33
2 Years		89	9	19	28	-6	5	0	89	10.1	0	2	2	0	0	0	8	16	0	8	0	2	3	0	.31

Steve Webb

Pos: RW **Shoots:** L **Ht:** 6'0" **Wt:** 195 **Born:** 4/30/75—Peterborough, Ontario **Age:** 24

Overall											Power Play			Shorthand			Penalty							Misc	
Year	Tm	GP	G	A	Pts	+/-	GW	GT	S	SPct	G	A	Pts	G	A	Pts	Num	PIM	Maj	Mnr	Fgt	Rgh	HHT	Hat	P/G
96-97	NYI	41	1	4	5	-10	0	0	21	4.8	1	1	2	0	0	0	38	144	20	17	20	4	6	0	.12
97-98	NYI	20	0	0	0	-2	0	0	6	0.0	0	0	0	0	0	0	10	35	5	5	5	2	1	0	.00
98-99	NYI	45	0	0	0	-10	0	0	18	0.0	0	0	0	0	0	0	9	32	2	6	2	0	0	0	.00
3 Years		106	1	4	5	-22	0	0	45	2.2	1	1	2	0	0	0	57	211	27	28	27	6	7	0	.05

Kevin Weekes

Pos: G **Catches:** R **Ht:** 6'0" **Wt:** 175 **Born:** 4/4/75—Toronto, Ontario **Age:** 24

Overall																	Pen Shot		Offense		
Year	Tm	GP	GS	TP	W	L	T	Min	GA	GAA	Shots	SvPct	ShO	OE	PPGA	SHGA	Shots	GA	G	A	PIM
97-98	Fla	11	7	2	0	5	1	485	32	3.96	247	.870	0	1	11	4	1	1	0	0	0
98-99	Van	11	8	1	0	8	1	532	34	3.83	257	.868	0	2	13	0	0	0	0	0	0
2 Years		22	15	3	0	13	2	1017	66	3.89	504	.869	0	3	24	4	1	1	0	0	0

Doug Weight

(statistical profile on page 387)

Pos: C **Shoots:** L **Ht:** 5'11" **Wt:** 200 **Born:** 1/21/71—Warren, Michigan **Age:** 28

Overall											Power Play			Shorthand			Penalty							Misc	
Year	Tm	GP	G	A	Pts	+/-	GW	GT	S	SPct	G	A	Pts	G	A	Pts	Num	PIM	Maj	Mnr	Fgt	Rgh	HHT	Hat	P/G
90-91		Did Not Play in Regular Season																							
91-92	NYR	53	8	22	30	-3	2	0	72	11.1	0	8	8	0	0	0	10	23	1	9	1	1	4	0	.57
92-93	2Tm	78	17	31	48	2	1	0	125	13.6	3	11	14	0	0	0	19	65	1	15	0	3	2	0	.62
93-94	Edm	84	24	50	74	-22	1	0	188	12.8	4	24	28	1	0	1	18	47	1	16	1	3	8	0	.88
94-95	Edm	48	7	33	40	-17	1	0	104	6.7	1	20	21	0	0	0	21	69	1	17	1	4	7	0	.83
95-96	Edm*	82	25	79	104	-19	2	1	204	12.3	9	37	46	0	0	0	38	95	1	35	1	8	8	1	1.27
96-97	Edm	80	21	61	82	1	2	0	235	8.9	4	**35**	39	0	0	0	28	80	0	25	0	3	6	0	1.03
97-98	Edm*	79	26	44	70	1	4	0	205	12.7	9	20	29	0	1	1	29	69	1	27	1	4	9	0	.89
98-99	Edm	43	6	31	37	-8	0	1	79	7.6	1	15	16	0	0	0	6	12	0	6	0	1	0	0	.86
92-93	NYR	65	15	25	40	4	1	0	90	16.7	3	9	12	0	0	0	14	55	1	10	0	1	0	0	.62
92-93	Edm	13	2	6	8	-2	0	0	35	5.7	0	2	2	0	0	0	5	10	0	5	0	2	2	0	.62
8 Years		547	134	351	485	-65	13	2	1212	11.1	31	170	201	1	1	2	169	460	6	150	5	27	44	1	.89

Postseason

Year	Tm	GP	G	A	Pts	+/-	GW	OT	S	SPct	G	A	Pts	G	A	Pts	Num	PIM	Maj	Mnr	Fgt	Rgh	HHT	Hat	P/G
90-91	NYR	1	0	0	0	0	0	0	0	–	0	0	0	0	0	0	0	0	0	0	0	0	0	0	.00
91-92	NYR	7	2	2	4	3	0	0	4	50.0	1	0	1	0	0	0	0	0	0	0	0	0	0	0	.57
96-97	Edm	12	3	8	11	0	0	0	54	5.6	0	4	4	0	0	0	4	8	0	4	0	1	1	0	.92
97-98	Edm	12	2	7	9	-4	1	0	26	7.7	2	4	6	0	0	0	7	14	0	7	0	2	0	0	.75

Year	Tm	GP	G	A	Pts	+/-	GW	OT	S	SPct	G	A	Pts	G	A	Pts	Num	PIM	Maj	Mnr	Fgt	Rgh	HHT	Hat	P/G
Postseason																									
98-99	Edm	4	1	1	2	-3	0	0	4	25.0	0	1	1	0	0	0	2	15	1	0	0	0	0	0	.50
5 Years		36	8	18	26	-4	1	0	88	9.1	3	9	12	0	0	0	13	37	1	11	0	3	1	0	.72

Eric Weinrich

(statistical profile on page 387)

Pos: D **Shoots:** L **Ht:** 6'1" **Wt:** 210 **Born:** 12/19/66—Roanoke, Virginia **Age:** 33

		Overall									Power Play			Shorthand			Penalty							Misc	
Year	Tm	GP	G	A	Pts	+/-	GW	GT	S	SPct	G	A	Pts	G	A	Pts	Num	PIM	Maj	Mnr	Fgt	Rgh	HHT	Hat	P/G
88-89	NJ	2	0	0	0	-1	0	0	3	0.0	0	0	0	0	0	0	0	0	0	0	0	0	0	0	.00
89-90	NJ	19	2	7	9	1	1	0	16	12.5	1	5	6	0	0	0	4	11	1	3	–	–	–	0	.47
90-91	NJ	76	4	34	38	10	0	0	96	4.2	1	13	14	0	1	1	–	48	–	–	–	–	–	0	.50
91-92	NJ	76	7	25	32	10	0	0	97	7.2	5	12	17	0	0	0	26	55	1	25	1	9	8	0	.42
92-93	Har	79	7	29	36	-11	2	0	104	6.7	0	8	8	2	1	3	27	76	2	23	2	5	9	0	.46
93-94	2Tm	62	4	24	28	1	2	0	115	3.5	2	13	15	0	1	1	15	33	1	14	1	4	6	0	.45
94-95	Chi	48	3	10	13	1	2	0	50	6.0	1	3	4	0	0	0	15	33	1	14	1	6	3	0	.27
95-96	Chi	77	5	10	15	14	0	0	76	6.6	0	1	1	0	0	0	27	65	1	25	1	2	12	0	.19
96-97	Chi	81	7	25	32	19	0	1	115	6.1	1	6	7	0	0	0	23	62	0	21	0	8	7	0	.40
97-98	Chi	82	2	21	23	10	0	0	85	2.4	0	7	7	0	1	1	37	106	0	33	0	10	10	0	.28
98-99	2Tm	80	7	15	22	-25	1	1	119	5.9	4	10	14	0	0	0	32	89	3	27	3	1	13	0	.28
93-94	Har	8	1	1	2	-5	0	0	10	10.0	1	1	2	0	0	0	1	2	0	1	0	1	0	0	.25
93-94	Chi	54	3	23	26	6	2	0	105	2.9	1	12	13	0	1	1	14	31	1	13	1	3	6	0	.48
98-99	Chi	14	1	3	4	-13	0	0	24	4.2	0	2	2	0	0	0	6	12	0	6	0	0	2	0	.29
98-99	Mon	66	6	12	18	-12	1	1	95	6.3	4	8	12	0	0	0	26	77	3	21	3	1	11	0	.27
11 Years		682	48	200	248	29	8	2	876	5.5	15	78	93	2	4	6	–	578	–	–	–	–	–	0	.36
Postseason																									
Year	Tm	GP	G	A	Pts	+/-	GW	OT	S	SPct	G	A	Pts	G	A	Pts	Num	PIM	Maj	Mnr	Fgt	Rgh	HHT	Hat	P/G
89-90	NJ	6	1	3	4	3	0	0	11	9.1	0	–	–	0	–	–	–	17	–	–	–	–	–	0	.67
90-91	NJ	7	1	2	3	-2	0	0	12	8.3	1	–	–	0	–	–	3	6	0	3	0	–	–	0	.43
91-92	NJ	7	0	2	2	-4	0	0	4	0.0	0	1	1	0	0	0	2	4	0	2	0	1	0	0	.29
93-94	Chi	6	0	2	2	2	0	0	4	0.0	0	0	0	0	0	0	3	6	0	3	0	0	2	0	.33
94-95	Chi	16	1	5	6	8	0	0	14	7.1	0	1	1	0	0	0	2	4	0	2	0	1	1	0	.38
95-96	Chi	10	1	4	5	2	0	0	13	7.7	1	0	1	0	0	0	5	10	0	5	0	1	3	0	.50
96-97	Chi	6	0	1	1	-1	0	0	8	0.0	0	0	0	0	0	0	2	4	0	2	0	1	1	0	.17
7 Years		58	4	19	23	8	0	0	66	6.1	2	–	–	0	–	–	–	51	–	–	–	–	–	0	.40

Chris Wells

Pos: C **Shoots:** L **Ht:** 6'6" **Wt:** 223 **Born:** 11/12/75—Calgary, Alberta **Age:** 24

		Overall									Power Play			Shorthand			Penalty							Misc	
Year	Tm	GP	G	A	Pts	+/-	GW	GT	S	SPct	G	A	Pts	G	A	Pts	Num	PIM	Maj	Mnr	Fgt	Rgh	HHT	Hat	P/G
95-96	Pit	54	2	2	4	-6	0	0	25	8.0	0	0	0	1	0	1	20	59	1	17	0	2	7	0	.07
96-97	Fla	47	2	6	8	5	0	0	29	6.9	0	0	0	0	0	0	14	42	2	11	1	2	3	0	.17
97-98	Fla	61	5	10	15	4	0	0	57	8.8	0	1	1	1	3	4	22	47	1	21	1	4	8	0	.25
98-99	Fla	20	0	2	2	-4	0	0	28	0.0	0	0	0	0	0	0	14	31	1	13	1	3	5	0	.10
4 Years		182	9	20	29	-1	0	0	139	6.5	0	1	1	2	3	5	70	179	5	62	3	11	23	0	.16
Postseason																									
Year	Tm	GP	G	A	Pts	+/-	GW	OT	S	SPct	G	A	Pts	G	A	Pts	Num	PIM	Maj	Mnr	Fgt	Rgh	HHT	Hat	P/G
96-97	Fla	3	0	0	0	-1	0	0	1	0.0	0	0	0	0	0	0	0	0	0	0	0	0	0	0	.00

Brad Werenka

(statistical profile on page 387)

Pos: D **Shoots:** L **Ht:** 6'1" **Wt:** 221 **Born:** 2/12/69—Two Hills, Alberta **Age:** 30

		Overall									Power Play			Shorthand			Penalty							Misc	
Year	Tm	GP	G	A	Pts	+/-	GW	GT	S	SPct	G	A	Pts	G	A	Pts	Num	PIM	Maj	Mnr	Fgt	Rgh	HHT	Hat	P/G
92-93	Edm	27	5	4	9	1	1	0	38	13.2	0	1	1	1	1	2	12	24	0	12	0	1	2	0	.33
93-94	2Tm	26	0	11	11	3	0	0	28	0.0	0	2	2	0	0	0	11	22	0	11	0	3	5	0	.42
94-95		Did Not Play in NHL																							
95-96	Chi	9	0	0	0	-2	0	0	2	0.0	0	0	0	0	0	0	4	8	0	4	0	1	2	0	.00
96-97		Did Not Play in NHL																							
97-98	Pit	71	3	15	18	15	0	0	50	6.0	2	4	6	0	2	2	23	46	0	23	0	6	7	0	.25
98-99	Pit	81	6	18	24	17	4	0	77	7.8	1	1	2	0	2	2	38	93	3	34	3	3	12	0	.30
93-94	Edm	15	0	4	4	-1	0	0	11	0.0	0	1	1	0	0	0	7	14	0	7	0	1	3	0	.27
93-94	Que	11	0	7	7	4	0	0	17	0.0	0	1	1	0	0	0	4	8	0	4	0	2	2	0	.64
5 Years		214	14	48	62	34	5	0	195	7.2	3	8	11	1	5	6	88	193	3	84	3	14	28	0	.29

Postseason																									
Year	Tm	GP	G	A	Pts	+/–	GW	OT	S	SPct	G	A	Pts	G	A	Pts	Num	PIM	Maj	Mnr	Fgt	Rgh	HHT	Hat	P/G
97-98	Pit	6	1	0	1	-3	0	0	3	33.3	0	0	0	1	0	1	4	8	0	4	0	0	0	0	.17
98-99	Pit	13	1	1	2	0	0	0	10	10.0	0	0	0	0	0	0	3	6	0	3	0	0	1	0	.15
2 Years		19	2	1	3	-3	0	0	13	15.4	0	0	0	1	0	1	7	14	0	7	0	0	1	0	.16

Brian Wesenberg

Pos: RW **Shoots:** R **Ht:** 6'3" **Wt:** 182 **Born:** 5/9/77—Peterborough, Ontario **Age:** 22

Overall											Power Play			Shorthand			Penalty							Misc	
Year	Tm	GP	G	A	Pts	+/–	GW	GT	S	SPct	G	A	Pts	G	A	Pts	Num	PIM	Maj	Mnr	Fgt	Rgh	HHT	Hat	P/G
98-99	Phi	1	0	0	0	1	0	0	0	–	0	0	0	0	0	0	1	5	1	0	1	0	0	0	.00

Glen Wesley

(statistical profile on page 388)

Pos: D **Shoots:** L **Ht:** 6'1" **Wt:** 201 **Born:** 10/2/68—Red Deer, Alberta **Age:** 31

Overall											Power Play			Shorthand			Penalty							Misc	
Year	Tm	GP	G	A	Pts	+/–	GW	GT	S	SPct	G	A	Pts	G	A	Pts	Num	PIM	Maj	Mnr	Fgt	Rgh	HHT	Hat	P/G
87-88	Bos	79	7	30	37	21	0	0	158	4.4	1	–	–	2	–	–	–	69	–	–	–	–	–	0	.47
88-89	Bos*	77	19	35	54	23	1	1	181	10.5	8	17	25	1	–	–	–	61	–	–	–	–	–	0	.70
89-90	Bos	78	9	27	36	6	4	0	166	5.4	5	18	23	0	–	–	–	48	–	–	–	–	–	0	.46
90-91	Bos	80	11	32	43	0	1	0	199	5.5	5	21	26	1	1	2	–	78	–	–	–	–	–	0	.54
91-92	Bos	78	9	37	46	-9	1	0	211	4.3	4	21	25	0	0	0	27	54	0	27	0	5	9	0	.59
92-93	Bos	64	8	25	33	-2	0	0	183	4.4	4	16	20	1	1	2	22	47	1	21	1	0	8	0	.52
93-94	Bos	81	14	44	58	1	1	1	265	5.3	6	33	39	1	0	1	32	64	0	32	0	3	21	1	.72
94-95	Har	48	2	14	16	-6	1	0	125	1.6	1	10	11	0	0	0	21	50	0	20	0	3	12	0	.33
95-96	Har	68	8	16	24	-9	1	0	129	6.2	6	9	15	0	0	0	36	88	0	34	0	4	16	0	.35
96-97	Har	68	6	26	32	0	0	0	126	4.8	3	11	14	1	0	1	20	40	0	20	0	3	10	0	.47
97-98	Car	82	6	19	25	7	1	0	121	5.0	1	7	8	0	1	1	18	36	0	18	0	1	8	0	.30
98-99	Car	74	7	17	24	14	2	1	112	6.3	0	5	5	0	0	0	22	44	0	22	0	0	11	0	.32
12 Years		877	106	322	428	46	13	3	1976	5.4	44	–	–	7	–	–	–	679	–	–	–	–	–	1	.49
Postseason																									
Year	Tm	GP	G	A	Pts	+/–	GW	OT	S	SPct	G	A	Pts	G	A	Pts	Num	PIM	Maj	Mnr	Fgt	Rgh	HHT	Hat	P/G
87-88	Bos	23	6	8	14	5	0	0	42	14.3	4	–	–	1	–	–	–	22	–	–	–	–	–	0	.61
88-89	Bos	10	0	2	2	0	0	0	14	0.0	0	–	–	0	–	–	2	4	0	2	0	–	–	0	.20
89-90	Bos	21	2	6	8	6	1	0	30	6.7	0	3	3	0	–	–	–	36	–	–	–	–	–	0	.38
90-91	Bos	19	2	9	11	-8	0	0	47	4.3	2	7	9	0	0	0	–	19	–	–	–	–	–	0	.58
91-92	Bos	15	2	4	6	3	0	0	35	5.7	0	2	2	0	0	0	8	16	0	8	0	1	3	0	.40
92-93	Bos	4	0	0	0	-2	0	0	12	0.0	0	0	0	0	0	0	0	0	0	0	0	0	0	0	.00
93-94	Bos	13	3	3	6	0	0	0	35	8.6	1	2	3	0	0	0	6	12	0	6	0	0	4	0	.46
98-99	Car	6	0	0	0	0	0	0	15	0.0	0	0	0	0	0	0	1	2	0	1	0	0	0	0	.00
8 Years		111	15	32	47	4	1	0	230	6.5	7	–	–	1	–	–	–	111	–	–	–	–	–	0	.42

Brian White

Pos: D **Shoots:** R **Ht:** 6'1" **Wt:** 180 **Born:** 2/7/76—Winchester, Massachusetts **Age:** 23

Overall											Power Play			Shorthand			Penalty							Misc	
Year	Tm	GP	G	A	Pts	+/–	GW	GT	S	SPct	G	A	Pts	G	A	Pts	Num	PIM	Maj	Mnr	Fgt	Rgh	HHT	Hat	P/G
98-99	Col	2	0	0	0	0	0	0	0	–	0	0	0	0	0	0	0	0	0	0	0	0	0	0	.00

Peter White

Pos: C **Shoots:** L **Ht:** 5'11" **Wt:** 200 **Born:** 3/15/69—Montreal, Quebec **Age:** 30

Overall											Power Play			Shorthand			Penalty							Misc	
Year	Tm	GP	G	A	Pts	+/–	GW	GT	S	SPct	G	A	Pts	G	A	Pts	Num	PIM	Maj	Mnr	Fgt	Rgh	HHT	Hat	P/G
93-94	Edm	26	3	5	8	1	0	0	17	17.6	0	0	0	0	0	0	1	2	0	1	0	0	0	0	.31
94-95	Edm	9	2	4	6	1	0	0	13	15.4	2	0	2	0	0	0	0	0	0	0	0	0	0	0	.67
95-96	2Tm	27	5	3	8	-14	0	0	34	14.7	1	1	2	0	0	0	0	0	0	0	0	0	0	0	.30
96-97											Did Not Play in NHL														
97-98											Did Not Play in NHL														
98-99	Phi	3	0	0	0	0	0	0	0	–	0	0	0	0	0	0	0	0	0	0	0	0	0	0	.00
95-96	Edm	26	5	3	8	-14	0	0	34	14.7	1	1	2	0	0	0	0	0	0	0	0	0	0	0	.31
95-96	Tor	1	0	0	0	0	0	0	0	–	0	0	0	0	0	0	0	0	0	0	0	0	0	0	.00
4 Years		65	10	12	22	-12	0	0	64	15.6	3	1	4	0	0	0	1	2	0	1	0	0	0	0	.34

Todd White

(statistical profile on page 388)

Pos: C **Shoots:** L **Ht:** 5'10" **Wt:** 180 **Born:** 5/21/75—Kanata, Ontario **Age:** 24

Overall											Power Play			Shorthand			Penalty							Misc	
Year	Tm	GP	G	A	Pts	+/-	GW	GT	S	SPct	G	A	Pts	G	A	Pts	Num	PIM	Maj	Mnr	Fgt	Rgh	HHT	Hat	P/G
97-98	Chi	7	1	0	1	0	0	0	3	33.3	0	0	0	0	0	0	1	2	0	1	0	0	0	0	.14
98-99	Chi	35	5	8	13	-1	0	0	43	11.6	2	2	4	0	0	0	10	20	0	10	0	2	2	0	.37
2 Years		42	6	8	14	-1	0	0	46	13.0	2	2	4	0	0	0	11	22	0	11	0	2	2	0	.33

Ray Whitney

(statistical profile on page 388)

Pos: C **Shoots:** R **Ht:** 5'10" **Wt:** 175 **Born:** 5/8/72—Edmonton, Alberta **Age:** 27

Overall											Power Play			Shorthand			Penalty							Misc	
Year	Tm	GP	G	A	Pts	+/-	GW	GT	S	SPct	G	A	Pts	G	A	Pts	Num	PIM	Maj	Mnr	Fgt	Rgh	HHT	Hat	P/G
91-92	SJ	2	0	3	3	-1	0	0	4	0.0	0	2	2	0	0	0	0	0	0	0	0	0	0	0	1.50
92-93	SJ	26	4	6	10	-14	0	0	24	16.7	1	2	3	0	0	0	2	4	0	2	0	0	1	0	.38
93-94	SJ	61	14	26	40	2	0	1	82	17.1	1	8	9	0	0	0	7	14	0	7	0	0	2	0	.66
94-95	SJ	39	13	12	25	-7	1	0	67	19.4	4	4	8	0	0	0	7	14	0	7	0	2	2	0	.64
95-96	SJ	60	17	24	41	-23	2	0	106	16.0	4	8	12	2	1	3	8	16	0	8	0	1	6	0	.68
96-97	SJ	12	0	2	2	-6	0	0	24	0.0	0	0	0	0	0	0	2	4	0	2	0	0	2	0	.17
97-98	2Tm	77	33	32	65	9	2	0	175	18.9	12	17	29	0	0	0	10	28	0	9	0	1	6	0	.84
98-99	Fla	81	26	38	64	-3	6	1	193	13.5	7	17	24	0	0	0	9	18	0	9	0	1	3	0	.79
97-98	Edm	9	1	3	4	-1	0	0	19	5.3	0	2	2	0	0	0	0	0	0	0	0	0	0	0	.44
97-98	Fla	68	32	29	61	10	2	0	156	20.5	12	15	27	0	0	0	10	28	0	9	0	1	6	0	.90
8 Years		358	107	143	250	-43	11	2	675	15.9	29	58	87	2	1	3	45	98	0	44	0	5	22	0	.70
Postseason																									
Year	Tm	GP	G	A	Pts	+/-	GW	OT	S	SPct	G	A	Pts	G	A	Pts	Num	PIM	Maj	Mnr	Fgt	Rgh	HHT	Hat	P/G
93-94	SJ	14	0	4	4	-4	0	0	16	0.0	0	1	1	0	0	0	4	8	0	4	0	1	1	0	.29
94-95	SJ	11	4	4	8	-3	1	1	15	26.7	0	2	2	0	0	0	1	2	0	1	0	0	1	0	.73
2 Years		25	4	8	12	-7	1	1	31	12.9	0	3	3	0	0	0	5	10	0	5	0	1	2	0	.48

Jason Wiemer

(statistical profile on page 388)

Pos: C **Shoots:** L **Ht:** 6'2" **Wt:** 219 **Born:** 4/14/76—Kimberley, British Columbia **Age:** 23

Overall											Power Play			Shorthand			Penalty							Misc	
Year	Tm	GP	G	A	Pts	+/-	GW	GT	S	SPct	G	A	Pts	G	A	Pts	Num	PIM	Maj	Mnr	Fgt	Rgh	HHT	Hat	P/G
94-95	TB	36	1	4	5	-2	0	0	10	10.0	0	0	0	0	0	0	15	44	2	12	2	4	2	0	.14
95-96	TB	66	9	9	18	-9	1	0	89	10.1	4	3	7	0	0	0	32	81	3	28	3	11	6	1	.27
96-97	TB	63	9	5	14	-13	0	0	103	8.7	2	0	2	0	1	1	43	134	8	32	8	9	6	0	.22
97-98	2Tm	79	12	10	22	-10	2	0	122	9.8	3	0	3	0	0	0	55	160	6	45	5	12	11	0	.28
98-99	Cgy	78	8	13	21	-12	1	0	128	6.3	1	3	4	0	0	0	59	177	9	46	8	9	11	0	.27
97-98	TB	67	8	9	17	-9	0	0	106	7.5	2	0	2	0	0	0	45	132	6	36	5	6	8	0	.25
97-98	Cgy	12	4	1	5	-1	2	0	16	25.0	1	0	1	0	0	0	10	28	0	9	0	6	3	0	.42
5 Years		322	39	41	80	-46	4	0	452	8.6	10	6	16	0	1	1	204	596	28	163	26	45	36	1	.25
Postseason																									
Year	Tm	GP	G	A	Pts	+/-	GW	OT	S	SPct	G	A	Pts	G	A	Pts	Num	PIM	Maj	Mnr	Fgt	Rgh	HHT	Hat	P/G
95-96	TB	6	1	0	1	-3	0	0	11	9.1	1	0	1	0	0	0	6	28	0	4	0	1	2	0	.17

David Wilkie

Pos: D **Shoots:** R **Ht:** 6'2" **Wt:** 207 **Born:** 5/30/74—Ellensburgh, Washington **Age:** 25

Overall											Power Play			Shorthand			Penalty							Misc	
Year	Tm	GP	G	A	Pts	+/-	GW	GT	S	SPct	G	A	Pts	G	A	Pts	Num	PIM	Maj	Mnr	Fgt	Rgh	HHT	Hat	P/G
94-95	Mon	1	0	0	0	0	0	0	0	–	0	0	0	0	0	0	0	0	0	0	0	0	0	0	.00
95-96	Mon	24	1	5	6	-10	0	0	39	2.6	1	2	3	0	0	0	5	10	0	5	0	0	2	0	.25
96-97	Mon	61	6	9	15	-9	0	0	65	9.2	3	2	5	0	0	0	23	63	3	19	3	1	6	0	.25
97-98	2Tm	34	2	5	7	-22	1	0	48	4.2	0	3	3	0	0	0	9	21	1	8	1	0	0	0	.21
98-99	TB	46	1	7	8	-19	0	0	35	2.9	0	3	3	0	0	0	23	69	5	17	5	1	6	0	.17
97-98	Mon	5	1	0	1	-1	1	0	2	50.0	0	0	0	0	0	0	2	4	0	2	0	0	0	0	.20
97-98	TB	29	1	5	6	-21	0	0	46	2.2	0	3	3	0	0	0	7	17	1	6	1	0	0	0	.21
5 Years		166	10	26	36	-60	1	0	187	5.3	4	10	14	0	0	0	60	163	9	49	9	2	14	0	.22
Postseason																									
Year	Tm	GP	G	A	Pts	+/-	GW	OT	S	SPct	G	A	Pts	G	A	Pts	Num	PIM	Maj	Mnr	Fgt	Rgh	HHT	Hat	P/G
95-96	Mon	6	1	2	3	1	0	0	11	9.1	0	1	1	0	0	0	6	12	0	6	0	1	3	0	.50
96-97	Mon	2	0	0	0	0	0	0	1	0.0	0	0	0	0	0	0	1	2	0	1	0	0	0	0	.00
2 Years		8	1	2	3	1	0	0	12	8.3	0	1	1	0	0	0	7	14	0	7	0	1	3	0	.38

Derek Wilkinson

Pos: G **Catches:** L **Ht:** 6'0" **Wt:** 178 **Born:** 7/29/74—Lasalle, Ontario **Age:** 25

Overall																	Pen Shot		Offense		
Year	Tm	GP	GS	TP	W	L	T	Min	GA	GAA	Shots	SvPct	ShO	OE	PPGA	SHGA	Shots	GA	G	A	PIM
95-96	TB	4	3	0	0	3	0	200	15	4.50	105	.857	0	0	2	1	0	0	0	0	2
96-97	TB	5	2	1	0	2	1	169	12	4.26	72	.833	0	0	3	0	0	0	0	0	0
97-98	TB	8	6	3	2	4	1	311	17	3.28	148	.885	0	1	5	1	0	0	0	0	0
98-99	TB	5	5	2	1	3	1	253	13	3.08	128	.898	0	1	2	0	0	0	0	0	0
4 Years		22	16	6	3	12	3	933	57	3.67	453	.874	0	2	12	2	0	0	0	0	2

Neil Wilkinson

Pos: D **Shoots:** R **Ht:** 6'3" **Wt:** 194 **Born:** 8/15/67—Selkirk, Manitoba **Age:** 32

Overall										Power Play			Shorthand			Penalty							Misc	
Year	Tm	GP	G	A	Pts	+/-	GW	GT	S	SPct	G	A	Pts	G	A	Pts	Num	PIM	Maj	Mnr	Fgt	Rgh	HHT	Hat	P/G
89-90	Min	36	0	5	5	-1	0	0	36	0.0	0	–	–	0	–	–	–	100	–	–	–	–	–	0	.14
90-91	Min	50	2	9	11	-5	0	0	55	3.6	0	–	–	0	–	–	–	117	–	–	–	–	–	0	.22
91-92	SJ	60	4	15	19	-11	0	0	95	4.2	1	4	5	0	0	0	37	107	3	31	3	6	14	0	.32
92-93	SJ	59	1	7	8	-50	0	0	51	2.0	0	2	2	1	1	2	31	96	6	23	5	3	10	0	.14
93-94	Chi	72	3	9	12	2	0	0	72	4.2	1	1	2	0	1	1	42	116	8	33	8	11	11	0	.17
94-95	Wpg	40	1	4	5	-26	0	0	25	4.0	0	0	0	0	0	0	22	75	5	15	4	2	9	0	.13
95-96	2Tm	62	3	14	17	12	1	0	59	5.1	0	0	0	1	0	1	46	120	4	40	3	10	12	0	.27
96-97	Pit	23	0	0	0	-12	0	0	16	0.0	0	0	0	0	0	0	12	36	4	8	4	2	1	0	.00
97-98	Pit	34	2	4	6	0	0	0	19	10.5	1	1	2	0	1	1	9	24	2	7	2	2	2	0	.18
98-99	Pit	24	0	0	0	-2	0	0	11	0.0	0	0	0	0	0	0	8	22	2	6	2	2	1	0	.00
95-96	Wpg	21	1	4	5	1	1	0	17	5.9	0	0	0	1	0	1	15	33	1	14	1	3	6	0	.24
95-96	Pit	41	2	10	12	11	0	0	42	4.8	0	0	0	0	0	0	31	87	3	26	2	7	6	0	.29
10 Years		460	16	67	83	-93	1	0	439	3.6	3	–	–	2	–	–	–	813	–	–	–	–	–	0	.18

Postseason																								
Year	Tm	GP	G	A	Pts	+/-	GW	OT	S	SPct	G	A	Pts	G	A	Pts	Num	PIM	Maj	Mnr	Fgt	Rgh	HHT	Hat	P/G
89-90	Min	7	0	2	2	1	0	0	8	0.0	0	–	–	0	0	0	4	11	1	3	–	–	–	0	.29
90-91	Min	22	3	3	6	1	0	0	31	9.7	1	–	–	0	–	–	–	12	–	–	–	–	–	0	.27
93-94	Chi	4	0	0	0	-1	0	0	1	0.0	0	0	0	0	0	0	0	0	0	0	0	0	0	0	.00
95-96	Pit	15	0	1	1	-2	0	0	20	0.0	0	0	0	0	0	0	7	14	0	7	0	2	1	0	.07
96-97	Pit	5	0	0	0	-2	0	0	1	0.0	0	0	0	0	0	0	2	4	0	2	0	1	0	0	.00
5 Years		53	3	6	9	-3	0	0	61	4.9	1	–	–	0	–	–	–	41	–	–	–	–	–	0	.17

Shane Willis

Pos: RW **Shoots:** R **Ht:** 6'0" **Wt:** 176 **Born:** 6/13/77—Edmonton, Alberta **Age:** 22

Overall										Power Play			Shorthand			Penalty							Misc	
Year	Tm	GP	G	A	Pts	+/-	GW	GT	S	SPct	G	A	Pts	G	A	Pts	Num	PIM	Maj	Mnr	Fgt	Rgh	HHT	Hat	P/G
98-99	Car	7	0	0	0	-2	0	0	1	0.0	0	0	0	0	0	0	0	0	0	0	0	0	0	0	.00

Clarke Wilm

(statistical profile on page 389)

Pos: C **Shoots:** L **Ht:** 6'0" **Wt:** 195 **Born:** 10/24/76—Central Butte, Saskatchewan **Age:** 23

Overall										Power Play			Shorthand			Penalty							Misc	
Year	Tm	GP	G	A	Pts	+/-	GW	GT	S	SPct	G	A	Pts	G	A	Pts	Num	PIM	Maj	Mnr	Fgt	Rgh	HHT	Hat	P/G
98-99	Cgy	78	10	8	18	11	0	0	94	10.6	2	0	2	2	0	2	22	53	3	19	3	1	6	0	.23

Landon Wilson

Pos: RW **Shoots:** R **Ht:** 6'2" **Wt:** 216 **Born:** 3/13/71—St. Louis, Missouri **Age:** 28

Overall										Power Play			Shorthand			Penalty							Misc	
Year	Tm	GP	G	A	Pts	+/-	GW	GT	S	SPct	G	A	Pts	G	A	Pts	Num	PIM	Maj	Mnr	Fgt	Rgh	HHT	Hat	P/G
95-96	Col	7	1	0	1	3	0	0	6	16.7	0	0	0	0	0	0	3	6	0	3	0	1	1	0	.14
96-97	2Tm	49	8	12	20	-5	0	0	83	9.6	0	1	1	0	0	0	23	72	6	16	6	8	5	0	.41
97-98	Bos	28	1	5	6	3	0	0	26	3.8	0	2	2	0	0	0	2	7	1	1	1	0	0	0	.21
98-99	Bos	22	3	3	6	0	0	0	32	9.4	0	0	0	0	0	0	7	17	1	6	1	2	1	0	.27
96-97	Col	9	1	2	3	1	0	0	7	14.3	0	0	0	0	0	0	6	23	1	4	1	3	1	0	.33
96-97	Bos	40	7	10	17	-6	0	0	76	9.2	0	1	1	0	0	0	17	49	5	12	5	5	4	0	.43
4 Years		106	13	20	33	1	0	0	147	8.8	0	3	3	0	0	0	35	102	8	26	8	11	7	0	.31

Postseason																								
Year	Tm	GP	G	A	Pts	+/-	GW	OT	S	SPct	G	A	Pts	G	A	Pts	Num	PIM	Maj	Mnr	Fgt	Rgh	HHT	Hat	P/G
97-98	Bos	1	0	0	0	0	0	0	1	0.0	0	0	0	0	0	0	0	0	0	0	0	0	0	0	.00

Postseason																									
Year	Tm	GP	G	A	Pts	+/–	GW	OT	S	SPct	G	A	Pts	G	A	Pts	Num	PIM	Maj	Mnr	Fgt	Rgh	HHT	Hat	P/G
98-99	Bos	8	1	1	2	-2	1	0	14	7.1	1	0	1	0	0	0	4	8	0	4	0	0	2	0	.25
2 Years		9	1	1	2	-2	1	0	15	6.7	1	0	1	0	0	0	4	8	0	4	0	0	2	0	.22

Mike Wilson

Pos: D **Shoots:** L **Ht:** 6'6" **Wt:** 212 **Born:** 2/26/75—Brampton, Ontario **Age:** 24

Overall											Power Play			Shorthand			Penalty							Misc	
Year	Tm	GP	G	A	Pts	+/–	GW	GT	S	SPct	G	A	Pts	G	A	Pts	Num	PIM	Maj	Mnr	Fgt	Rgh	HHT	Hat	P/G
95-96	Buf	58	4	8	12	13	1	0	52	7.7	1	0	1	0	1	1	19	41	1	18	1	3	5	0	.21
96-97	Buf	77	2	9	11	13	1	0	57	3.5	0	0	0	0	0	0	21	51	3	18	3	3	5	0	.14
97-98	Buf	66	4	4	8	13	1	0	52	7.7	0	0	0	0	0	0	24	48	0	24	0	3	10	0	.12
98-99	2Tm	34	1	2	3	12	1	0	48	2.1	0	0	0	0	0	0	14	47	1	11	1	0	5	0	.09
98-99	Buf	30	1	2	3	10	1	0	40	2.5	0	0	0	0	0	0	14	47	1	11	1	0	5	0	.10
98-99	Fla	4	0	0	0	2	0	0	8	0.0	0	0	0	0	0	0	0	0	0	0	0	0	0	0	.00
4 Years		235	11	23	34	51	4	0	209	5.3	1	0	1	0	1	1	78	187	5	71	5	9	25	0	.14
Postseason																									
Year	Tm	GP	G	A	Pts	+/–	GW	OT	S	SPct	G	A	Pts	G	A	Pts	Num	PIM	Maj	Mnr	Fgt	Rgh	HHT	Hat	P/G
96-97	Buf	10	0	1	1	3	0	0	8	0.0	0	0	0	0	0	0	1	2	0	1	0	0	1	0	.10
97-98	Buf	15	0	1	1	-4	0	0	16	0.0	0	0	0	0	0	0	5	13	1	4	1	1	1	0	.07
2 Years		25	0	2	2	-1	0	0	24	0.0	0	0	0	0	0	0	6	15	1	5	1	1	2	0	.08

Johan Witehall

Pos: LW **Shoots:** L **Ht:** 6'1" **Wt:** 198 **Born:** 1/7/72—Goteborg, Sweden **Age:** 27

Overall											Power Play			Shorthand			Penalty							Misc	
Year	Tm	GP	G	A	Pts	+/–	GW	GT	S	SPct	G	A	Pts	G	A	Pts	Num	PIM	Maj	Mnr	Fgt	Rgh	HHT	Hat	P/G
98-99	NYR	4	0	0	0	0	0	0	1	0.0	0	0	0	0	0	0	0	0	0	0	0	0	0	0	.00

Brendan Witt

Pos: D **Shoots:** L **Ht:** 6'2" **Wt:** 215 **Born:** 2/20/75—Humboldt, Saskatchewan **Age:** 24

Overall											Power Play			Shorthand			Penalty							Misc	
Year	Tm	GP	G	A	Pts	+/–	GW	GT	S	SPct	G	A	Pts	G	A	Pts	Num	PIM	Maj	Mnr	Fgt	Rgh	HHT	Hat	P/G
95-96	Was	48	2	3	5	-4	1	0	44	4.5	0	0	0	0	0	0	31	85	5	25	5	10	6	0	.10
96-97	Was	44	3	2	5	-20	0	0	41	7.3	0	0	0	0	0	0	25	88	10	14	10	7	0	0	.11
97-98	Was	64	1	7	8	-11	0	0	68	1.5	0	1	1	0	1	1	40	112	8	31	8	13	6	0	.13
98-99	Was	54	2	5	7	-6	0	0	51	3.9	0	0	0	0	0	0	29	87	7	21	7	3	6	0	.13
4 Years		210	8	17	25	-41	1	0	204	3.9	0	1	1	0	1	1	125	372	30	91	30	33	18	0	.12
Postseason																									
Year	Tm	GP	G	A	Pts	+/–	GW	OT	S	SPct	G	A	Pts	G	A	Pts	Num	PIM	Maj	Mnr	Fgt	Rgh	HHT	Hat	P/G
97-98	Was	16	1	0	1	-1	0	0	9	11.1	0	0	0	0	0	0	7	14	0	7	0	3	0	0	.06

Jason Woolley

(statistical profile on page 389)

Pos: D **Shoots:** L **Ht:** 6'1" **Wt:** 188 **Born:** 7/27/69—Toronto, Ontario **Age:** 30

Overall											Power Play			Shorthand			Penalty							Misc	
Year	Tm	GP	G	A	Pts	+/–	GW	GT	S	SPct	G	A	Pts	G	A	Pts	Num	PIM	Maj	Mnr	Fgt	Rgh	HHT	Hat	P/G
91-92	Was	1	0	0	0	1	0	0	2	0.0	0	0	0	0	0	0	0	0	0	0	0	0	0	0	.00
92-93	Was	26	0	2	2	3	0	0	11	0.0	0	1	1	0	0	0	5	10	0	5	0	0	1	0	.08
93-94	Was	10	1	2	3	2	0	0	15	6.7	0	1	1	0	0	0	2	4	0	2	0	0	2	0	.30
94-95	Fla	34	4	9	13	-1	0	1	76	5.3	1	6	7	0	0	0	9	18	0	9	0	1	4	0	.38
95-96	Fla	52	6	28	34	-9	0	0	98	6.1	3	19	22	0	0	0	16	32	0	16	0	1	7	0	.65
96-97	2Tm	60	6	30	36	4	1	0	86	7.0	2	13	15	0	0	0	15	30	0	15	0	2	9	0	.60
97-98	Buf	71	9	26	35	8	2	1	129	7.0	3	18	21	0	0	0	16	35	1	15	1	4	6	0	.49
98-99	Buf	80	10	33	43	16	2	1	154	6.5	4	16	20	0	0	0	31	62	0	31	0	2	16	0	.54
96-97	Fla	3	0	0	0	1	0	0	7	0.0	0	0	0	0	0	0	1	2	0	1	0	0	1	0	.00
96-97	Pit	57	6	30	36	3	1	0	79	7.6	2	13	15	0	0	0	14	28	0	14	0	2	8	0	.63
8 Years		334	36	130	166	24	5	3	571	6.3	13	74	87	0	0	0	94	191	1	93	1	10	45	0	.50
Postseason																									
Year	Tm	GP	G	A	Pts	+/–	GW	OT	S	SPct	G	A	Pts	G	A	Pts	Num	PIM	Maj	Mnr	Fgt	Rgh	HHT	Hat	P/G
93-94	Was	4	1	0	1	0	1	0	2	50.0	0	0	0	0	0	0	2	4	0	2	0	0	2	0	.25
95-96	Fla	13	2	6	8	3	1	0	27	7.4	1	4	5	0	0	0	7	14	0	7	0	0	5	0	.62
96-97	Pit	5	0	3	3	-1	0	0	9	0.0	0	1	1	0	0	0	0	0	0	0	0	0	0	0	.60
97-98	Buf	15	2	9	11	8	1	0	32	6.3	1	6	7	0	0	0	6	12	0	6	0	2	1	0	.73

Postseason																										
Year	Tm	GP	G	A	Pts	+/-	GW	OT	S	SPct	G	A	Pts	G	A	Pts	Num	PIM	Maj	Mnr	Fgt	Rgh	HHT	Hat	P/G
98-99	Buf	21	4	11	15	0	1	1	43	9.3	2	7	9	0	0	0	5	10	0	5	0	0	2	0	.71
5 Years		58	9	29	38	10	4	1	113	8.0	4	18	22	0	0	0	20	40	0	20	0	2	10	0	.66

Peter Worrell

Pos: LW **Shoots:** L **Ht:** 6'6" **Wt:** 225 **Born:** 8/18/77—Pierrefonds, Quebec **Age:** 22

Overall											Power Play			Shorthand			Penalty							Misc	
Year	Tm	GP	G	A	Pts	+/-	GW	GT	S	SPct	G	A	Pts	G	A	Pts	Num	PIM	Maj	Mnr	Fgt	Rgh	HHT	Hat	P/G
97-98	Fla	19	0	0	0	-4	0	0	15	0.0	0	0	0	0	0	0	35	153	9	19	9	7	2	0	.00
98-99	Fla	62	4	5	9	0	2	0	50	8.0	0	0	0	0	0	0	**69**	258	24	39	21	22	5	0	.15
2 Years		81	4	5	9	-4	2	0	65	6.2	0	0	0	0	0	0	104	411	33	58	30	29	7	0	.11

Ken Wregget

(statistical profile on page 404)

Pos: G **Catches:** L **Ht:** 6'1" **Wt:** 205 **Born:** 3/25/64—Brandon, Manitoba **Age:** 35

Overall																	Pen Shot		Offense		
Year	Tm	GP	GS	TP	W	L	T	Min	GA	GAA	Shots	SvPct	ShO	OE	PPGA	SHGA	Shots	GA	G	A	PIM
83-84	Tor	3	–	–	1	1	1	165	14	5.09	128	.891	0	–	–	–	0	0	0	0	0
84-85	Tor	23	–	–	2	15	3	1278	103	4.84	752	.863	0	–	–	–	0	0	0	1	10
85-86	Tor	30	–	–	9	13	4	1566	113	4.33	901	.875	0	–	–	–	0	0	0	0	16
86-87	Tor	56	–	–	22	**28**	3	3026	200	3.97	1598	.875	0	–	–	–	1	1	0	4	20
87-88	Tor	56	–	–	12	**35**	4	3000	222	4.44	1712	.870	2	–	–	–	2	0	0	5	40
88-89	2Tm	35	–	–	10	21	2	2018	152	4.52	1110	.863	0	–	–	–	0	0	0	3	20
89-90	Phi	51	–	–	22	24	3	2961	169	3.42	1560	.892	0	–	–	–	1	**1**	0	2	12
90-91	Phi	30	–	–	10	14	3	1484	88	3.56	660	.867	0	–	–	–	0	0	0	0	6
91-92	2Tm	32	30	4	14	11	3	1707	106	3.73	759	.860	0	4	30	2	1	1	0	2	2
92-93	Pit	25	22	1	13	7	2	1368	78	3.42	692	.887	0	5	24	6	1	0	0	1	6
93-94	Pit	42	38	0	21	12	7	2456	138	3.37	1291	.893	1	15	36	5	0	0	0	1	8
94-95	Pit	38	38	3	**25**	9	2	2208	118	3.21	1219	.903	0	16	35	2	0	0	0	0	14
95-96	Pit	37	34	1	20	13	2	2132	115	3.24	1205	.905	3	13	35	6	1	0	0	2	8
96-97	Pit	46	43	7	17	17	6	2514	136	3.25	1383	.902	2	16	33	4	0	0	0	1	6
97-98	Pit	15	10	4	3	6	2	611	28	2.75	293	.904	0	2	4	5	0	0	0	0	6
98-99	Cgy	27	26	1	10	12	4	1590	67	2.53	712	.906	1	5	26	0	0	0	0	1	8
88-89	Phi	3	–	–	1	1	0	130	13	6.00	73	.822	0	–	–	–	0	0	0	0	0
88-89	Tor	32	–	–	9	20	2	1888	139	4.42	1037	.866	0	–	–	–	0	0	0	3	20
91-92	Phi	23	23	3	9	8	3	1259	75	3.57	557	.865	0	1	22	1	1	1	0	2	0
91-92	Pit	9	7	1	5	3	0	448	31	4.15	202	.847	0	3	8	1	0	0	0	0	2
16 Years		546	–	–	211	238	51	30084	1847	3.68	15975	.884	9	–	–	–	7	3	0	23	182

Postseason																					
Year	Tm	GP	GS	TP	W	L	Pct	Min	GA	GAA	Shots	SvPct	ShO	OE	PPGA	SHGA	Shots	GA	G	A	PIM
85-86	Tor	10	–	–	6	4	.600	607	32	3.16	323	.901	1	–	–	–	0	0	0	0	4
86-87	Tor	13	–	–	7	6	.538	761	29	2.29	368	.921	1	–	–	–	0	0	0	1	4
87-88	Tor	2	–	–	0	1	.000	108	11	6.11	62	.823	0	–	–	–	0	0	0	0	2
88-89	Phi	5	–	–	2	2	.500	268	10	2.24	139	.928	0	–	–	–	0	0	0	0	16
91-92	Pit	1	0	0	0	0	–	40	4	6.00	16	.750	0	0	0	0	0	0	0	0	0
94-95	Pit	11	11	1	5	6	.455	661	33	3.00	349	.905	1	4	9	1	0	0	0	0	7
95-96	Pit	9	8	0	7	2	.778	599	23	2.30	328	.930	0	5	7	0	1	0	0	1	0
96-97	Pit	5	5	0	1	4	.200	297	18	3.64	211	.915	0	2	4	2	0	0	0	0	2
8 Years		56	–	–	28	25	.528	3341	160	2.87	1796	.911	3	–	–	–	1	0	0	2	35

Jamie Wright

Pos: LW **Shoots:** L **Ht:** 6'0" **Wt:** 172 **Born:** 5/13/76—Kitchener, Ontario **Age:** 23

Overall											Power Play			Shorthand			Penalty							Misc	
Year	Tm	GP	G	A	Pts	+/-	GW	GT	S	SPct	G	A	Pts	G	A	Pts	Num	PIM	Maj	Mnr	Fgt	Rgh	HHT	Hat	P/G
97-98	Dal	21	4	2	6	8	2	0	15	26.7	0	0	0	0	0	0	1	2	0	1	0	0	1	0	.29
98-99	Dal	11	0	0	0	-3	0	0	10	0.0	0	0	0	0	0	0	0	0	0	0	0	0	0	0	.00
2 Years		32	4	2	6	5	2	0	25	16.0	0	0	0	0	0	0	1	2	0	1	0	0	1	0	.19

Postseason																									
Year	Tm	GP	G	A	Pts	+/-	GW	OT	S	SPct	G	A	Pts	G	A	Pts	Num	PIM	Maj	Mnr	Fgt	Rgh	HHT	Hat	P/G
97-98	Dal	5	0	0	0	3	0	0	6	0.0	0	0	0	0	0	0	0	0	0	0	0	0	0	0	.00

Tyler Wright

Pos: C **Shoots:** R **Ht:** 5'11" **Wt:** 185 **Born:** 4/6/73—Canora, Saskatchewan **Age:** 26

Overall											Power Play			Shorthand			Penalty							Misc	
Year	Tm	GP	G	A	Pts	+/–	GW	GT	S	SPct	G	A	Pts	G	A	Pts	Num	PIM	Maj	Mnr	Fgt	Rgh	HHT	Hat	P/G
92-93	Edm	7	1	1	2	-4	0	0	7	14.3	0	0	0	0	0	0	4	19	1	2	1	0	0	0	.29
93-94	Edm	5	0	0	0	-3	0	0	2	0.0	0	0	0	0	0	0	2	4	0	2	0	2	0	0	.00
94-95	Edm	6	1	0	1	1	0	0	6	16.7	0	0	0	0	0	0	3	14	0	2	0	1	0	0	.17
95-96	Edm	23	1	0	1	-7	0	0	18	5.6	0	0	0	0	0	0	11	33	1	9	1	3	0	0	.04
96-97	Pit	45	2	2	4	-7	2	0	30	6.7	0	0	0	0	0	0	21	70	4	15	3	3	3	0	.09
97-98	Pit	82	3	4	7	-3	0	0	46	6.5	1	0	1	0	0	0	34	112	4	26	4	8	2	0	.09
98-99	Pit	61	0	0	0	-2	0	0	16	0.0	0	0	0	0	0	0	23	90	4	15	4	7	1	0	.00
7 Years		229	8	7	15	-25	2	0	125	6.4	1	0	1	0	0	0	98	342	14	71	13	24	6	0	.07
Postseason																									
Year	Tm	GP	G	A	Pts	+/–	GW	OT	S	SPct	G	A	Pts	G	A	Pts	Num	PIM	Maj	Mnr	Fgt	Rgh	HHT	Hat	P/G
97-98	Pit	6	0	1	1	0	0	0	3	0.0	0	0	0	0	1	1	2	4	0	2	0	1	0	0	.17
98-99	Pit	13	0	0	0	-2	0	0	3	0.0	0	0	0	0	0	0	4	19	1	2	1	1	0	0	.00
2 Years		19	0	1	1	-2	0	0	6	0.0	0	0	0	0	1	1	6	23	1	4	1	2	0	0	.05

Vitali Yachmenev

(statistical profile on page 389)

Pos: RW **Shoots:** L **Ht:** 5'9" **Wt:** 191 **Born:** 1/5/75—Chelyabinsk, USSR **Age:** 24

Overall											Power Play			Shorthand			Penalty							Misc	
Year	Tm	GP	G	A	Pts	+/–	GW	GT	S	SPct	G	A	Pts	G	A	Pts	Num	PIM	Maj	Mnr	Fgt	Rgh	HHT	Hat	P/G
95-96	LA	80	19	34	53	-3	2	0	133	14.3	6	18	24	1	1	2	8	16	0	8	0	0	6	1	.66
96-97	LA	65	10	22	32	-9	2	1	97	10.3	2	3	5	0	0	0	5	10	0	5	0	0	2	0	.49
97-98	LA	4	0	1	1	1	0	0	4	0.0	0	0	0	0	0	0	2	4	0	2	0	0	0	0	.25
98-99	Nsh	55	7	10	17	-10	2	0	83	8.4	0	0	0	1	0	1	5	10	0	5	0	0	2	0	.31
4 Years		204	36	67	103	-21	6	1	317	11.4	8	21	29	2	1	3	20	40	0	20	0	0	10	1	.50

Terry Yake

(statistical profile on page 389)

Pos: RW **Shoots:** R **Ht:** 5'11" **Wt:** 185 **Born:** 10/22/68—New Westminster, British Columbia **Age:** 31

Overall											Power Play			Shorthand			Penalty							Misc	
Year	Tm	GP	G	A	Pts	+/–	GW	GT	S	SPct	G	A	Pts	G	A	Pts	Num	PIM	Maj	Mnr	Fgt	Rgh	HHT	Hat	P/G
88-89	Har	2	0	0	0	1	0	0	0	–	0	0	0	0	0	0	0	0	0	0	0	0	0	0	.00
89-90	Har	2	0	1	1	-1	0	0	2	0.0	0	–	–	0	–	–	0	0	0	0	0	0	0	0	.50
90-91	Har	19	1	4	5	-3	1	0	19	5.3	0	–	–	0	–	–	–	10	–	–	–	–	–	0	.26
91-92	Har	15	1	1	2	-2	0	0	12	8.3	0	0	0	0	0	0	2	4	0	2	0	0	1	0	.13
92-93	Har	66	22	31	53	3	2	0	98	22.4	4	10	14	1	2	3	23	46	0	23	0	3	8	0	.80
93-94	Anh	82	21	31	52	2	2	0	188	11.2	5	10	15	0	1	1	22	44	0	22	0	3	11	1	.63
94-95	Tor	19	3	2	5	1	2	0	26	11.5	1	1	2	0	0	0	1	2	0	1	0	0	1	0	.26
95-96		Did Not Play in NHL																							
96-97		Did Not Play in NHL																							
97-98	StL	65	10	15	25	1	4	0	60	16.7	3	3	6	1	0	1	19	38	0	19	0	3	8	0	.38
98-99	StL	60	9	18	27	-9	4	0	59	15.3	3	11	14	0	0	0	17	34	0	17	0	2	5	0	.45
9 Years		330	67	103	170	-7	15	0	464	14.4	16	–	–	2	–	–	–	178	–	–	–	–	–	1	.52
Postseason																									
Year	Tm	GP	G	A	Pts	+/–	GW	OT	S	SPct	G	A	Pts	G	A	Pts	Num	PIM	Maj	Mnr	Fgt	Rgh	HHT	Hat	P/G
90-91	Har	6	1	1	2	0	0	0	5	20.0	0	–	–	1	–	–	–	16	–	–	–	–	–	0	.33
97-98	StL	10	2	1	3	-3	1	0	6	33.3	2	0	2	0	0	0	3	6	0	3	0	0	1	0	.30
98-99	StL	13	1	2	3	-3	0	0	13	7.7	1	2	3	0	0	0	7	14	0	7	0	1	4	0	.23
3 Years		29	4	4	8	-6	1	0	24	16.7	3	–	–	1	–	–	–	36	–	–	–	–	–	0	.28

Alexei Yashin

(statistical profile on page 390)

Pos: C **Shoots:** R **Ht:** 6'3" **Wt:** 225 **Born:** 11/5/73—Sverdlovsk, USSR **Age:** 26

Overall											Power Play			Shorthand			Penalty							Misc	
Year	Tm	GP	G	A	Pts	+/–	GW	GT	S	SPct	G	A	Pts	G	A	Pts	Num	PIM	Maj	Mnr	Fgt	Rgh	HHT	Hat	P/G
93-94	Ott*	83	30	49	79	-49	3	0	232	12.9	11	16	27	2	1	3	11	22	0	11	0	0	5	1	.95
94-95	Ott	47	21	23	44	-20	1	0	154	13.6	11	10	21	0	0	0	10	20	0	10	0	3	0	1	.94
95-96	Ott	46	15	24	39	-15	1	0	143	10.5	8	7	15	0	0	0	14	28	0	14	0	3	7	1	.85
96-97	Ott	**82**	35	40	75	-7	5	1	291	12.0	10	17	27	0	1	1	18	44	0	17	0	8	2	0	.91
97-98	Ott	82	33	39	72	6	6	0	291	11.3	5	13	18	0	0	0	12	24	0	12	0	1	5	1	.88
98-99	Ott	82	44	50	94	16	5	1	337	13.1	19	23	42	0	1	1	27	54	0	27	0	3	11	1	1.15
6 Years		422	178	225	403	-69	21	2	1448	12.3	64	86	150	2	3	5	92	192	0	91	0	18	30	5	.95

Postseason																									
Year	Tm	GP	G	A	Pts	+/–	GW	OT	S	SPct	G	A	Pts	G	A	Pts	Num	PIM	Maj	Mnr	Fgt	Rgh	HHT	Hat	P/G
96-97	Ott	7	1	5	6	-2	0	0	21	4.8	1	4	5	0	0	0	1	2	0	1	0	0	0	0	.86
97-98	Ott	11	5	3	8	-6	2	1	42	11.9	3	1	4	0	0	0	4	8	0	4	0	1	1	0	.73
98-99	Ott	4	0	0	0	-4	0	0	24	0.0	0	0	0	0	0	0	5	10	0	5	0	1	2	0	.00
3 Years		22	6	8	14	-12	2	1	87	6.9	4	5	9	0	0	0	10	20	0	10	0	2	3	0	.64

Trent Yawney

Pos: D **Shoots:** L **Ht:** 6'3" **Wt:** 195 **Born:** 9/29/65—Hudson Bay, Saskatchewan **Age:** 34

Overall											Power Play			Shorthand			Penalty							Misc	
Year	Tm	GP	G	A	Pts	+/–	GW	GT	S	SPct	G	A	Pts	G	A	Pts	Num	PIM	Maj	Mnr	Fgt	Rgh	HHT	Hat	P/G
87-88	Chi	15	2	8	10	1	0	0	26	7.7	2	–	–	0	–	–	–	15	–	–	–	–	–	0	.67
88-89	Chi	69	5	19	24	-5	0	0	75	6.7	3	–	–	1	–	–	–	116	–	–	–	–	–	0	.35
89-90	Chi	70	5	15	20	-6	1	0	58	8.6	1	–	–	0	–	–	–	82	–	–	–	–	–	0	.29
90-91	Chi	61	3	13	16	6	0	0	52	5.8	3	–	–	0	–	–	–	77	–	–	–	–	–	0	.26
91-92	Cgy	47	4	9	13	-5	0	0	33	12.1	1	4	5	0	1	1	17	45	1	15	0	4	10	0	.28
92-93	Cgy	63	1	16	17	9	0	0	61	1.6	0	6	6	0	1	1	32	67	1	31	1	4	9	0	.27
93-94	Cgy	58	6	15	21	21	1	1	62	9.7	1	5	6	1	0	1	27	60	2	25	2	6	10	0	.36
94-95	Cgy	37	0	2	2	-4	0	0	20	0.0	0	0	0	0	0	0	37	108	6	29	5	7	8	0	.05
95-96	Cgy	69	0	3	3	-1	0	0	51	0.0	0	1	1	0	0	0	34	88	4	29	4	3	11	0	.04
96-97	StL	39	0	2	2	2	0	0	8	0.0	0	0	0	0	1	1	7	17	1	6	1	1	0	0	.05
97-98	Chi	45	1	0	1	-5	0	0	19	5.3	0	0	0	0	0	0	24	76	4	18	3	5	4	0	.02
98-99	Chi	20	0	0	0	-6	0	0	11	0.0	0	0	0	0	0	0	9	32	2	6	2	1	1	0	.00
12 Years		593	27	102	129	7	2	1	476	5.7	11	–	–	2	–	–	–	783	–	–	–	–	–	0	.22
Postseason																									
Year	Tm	GP	G	A	Pts	+/–	GW	OT	S	SPct	G	A	Pts	G	A	Pts	Num	PIM	Maj	Mnr	Fgt	Rgh	HHT	Hat	P/G
87-88	Chi	5	0	4	4	1	0	0	3	0.0	0	–	–	0	–	–	4	8	0	4	0	–	–	0	.80
88-89	Chi	15	3	6	9	9	0	0	17	17.6	0	–	–	1	–	–	–	20	–	–	–	–	–	0	.60
89-90	Chi	20	3	5	8	-1	1	0	27	11.1	3	–	–	0	–	–	–	27	–	–	–	–	–	0	.40
90-91	Chi	1	0	0	0	0	0	0	1	0.0	0	0	0	0	0	0	0	0	0	0	0	0	0	0	.00
92-93	Cgy	6	3	2	5	-3	0	0	16	18.8	1	1	2	0	0	0	3	6	0	3	0	2	1	0	.83
93-94	Cgy	7	0	0	0	-5	0	0	11	0.0	0	0	0	0	0	0	8	16	0	8	0	2	3	0	.00
94-95	Cgy	2	0	0	0	-4	0	0	1	0.0	0	0	0	0	0	0	1	2	0	1	0	0	0	0	.00
95-96	Cgy	4	0	0	0	-3	0	0	1	0.0	0	0	0	0	0	0	1	2	0	1	0	1	0	0	.00
8 Years		60	9	17	26	-6	1	0	77	11.7	4	–	–	1	–	–	–	81	–	–	–	–	–	0	.43

Stephane Yelle

(statistical profile on page 390)

Pos: C **Shoots:** L **Ht:** 6'1" **Wt:** 192 **Born:** 5/9/74—Ottawa, Ontario **Age:** 25

Overall											Power Play			Shorthand			Penalty							Misc	
Year	Tm	GP	G	A	Pts	+/–	GW	GT	S	SPct	G	A	Pts	G	A	Pts	Num	PIM	Maj	Mnr	Fgt	Rgh	HHT	Hat	P/G
95-96	Col	71	13	14	27	15	1	0	93	14.0	0	1	1	2	2	4	11	30	0	10	0	1	5	0	.38
96-97	Col	79	9	17	26	1	1	0	89	10.1	0	0	0	1	2	3	19	38	0	19	0	0	11	0	.33
97-98	Col	81	7	15	22	-10	0	0	93	7.5	0	0	0	1	0	1	24	48	0	24	0	1	17	0	.27
98-99	Col	72	8	7	15	-8	0	0	99	8.1	1	0	1	0	0	0	20	40	0	20	0	1	12	0	.21
4 Years		303	37	53	90	-2	2	0	374	9.9	1	1	2	4	4	8	74	156	0	73	0	3	45	0	.30
Postseason																									
Year	Tm	GP	G	A	Pts	+/–	GW	OT	S	SPct	G	A	Pts	G	A	Pts	Num	PIM	Maj	Mnr	Fgt	Rgh	HHT	Hat	P/G
95-96	Col	22	1	4	5	2	0	0	24	4.2	0	0	0	1	0	1	4	8	0	4	0	0	1	0	.23
96-97	Col	12	1	6	7	5	0	0	19	5.3	0	0	0	0	0	0	1	2	0	1	0	0	0	0	.58
97-98	Col	7	1	0	1	-3	0	0	7	14.3	0	0	0	0	0	0	2	12	0	1	0	0	0	0	.14
98-99	Col	10	0	1	1	-1	0	0	18	0.0	0	0	0	0	0	0	3	6	0	3	0	0	2	0	.10
4 Years		51	3	11	14	3	0	0	68	4.4	0	0	0	1	0	1	10	28	0	9	0	0	3	0	.27

Juha Ylonen

(statistical profile on page 390)

Pos: C **Shoots:** L **Ht:** 6'0" **Wt:** 185 **Born:** 2/13/72—Helsinki, Finland **Age:** 27

Overall											Power Play			Shorthand			Penalty							Misc	
Year	Tm	GP	G	A	Pts	+/–	GW	GT	S	SPct	G	A	Pts	G	A	Pts	Num	PIM	Maj	Mnr	Fgt	Rgh	HHT	Hat	P/G
96-97	Pho	2	0	0	0	0	0	0	2	0.0	0	0	0	0	0	0	0	0	0	0	0	0	0	0	.00
97-98	Pho	55	1	11	12	-3	0	0	60	1.7	0	1	1	1	1	2	5	10	0	5	0	0	2	0	.22
98-99	Pho	59	6	17	23	18	1	0	66	9.1	2	0	2	0	0	0	10	20	0	10	0	0	4	0	.39
3 Years		116	7	28	35	15	1	0	128	5.5	2	1	3	1	1	2	15	30	0	15	0	0	6	0	.30
Postseason																									
Year	Tm	GP	G	A	Pts	+/–	GW	OT	S	SPct	G	A	Pts	G	A	Pts	Num	PIM	Maj	Mnr	Fgt	Rgh	HHT	Hat	P/G
98-99	Pho	2	0	2	2	2	0	0	2	0.0	0	0	0	0	0	0	1	2	0	1	0	0	1	0	1.00

Harry York

(statistical profile on page 390)

Pos: C **Shoots:** L **Ht:** 6'2" **Wt:** 220 **Born:** 4/16/74—Ponoka, Alberta **Age:** 25

Overall											Power Play			Shorthand			Penalty							Misc	
Year	Tm	GP	G	A	Pts	+/–	GW	GT	S	SPct	G	A	Pts	G	A	Pts	Num	PIM	Maj	Mnr	Fgt	Rgh	HHT	Hat	P/G
96-97	StL	74	14	18	32	1	3	0	86	16.3	3	2	5	1	0	1	12	24	0	12	0	1	5	0	.43
97-98	2Tm	60	4	6	10	-1	0	0	44	9.1	0	0	0	0	0	0	14	31	1	13	1	0	6	0	.17
98-99	3Tm	56	7	9	16	-3	0	1	60	11.7	1	2	3	0	0	0	12	24	0	12	0	1	3	0	.29
97-98	StL	58	4	6	10	0	0	0	42	9.5	0	0	0	0	0	0	14	31	1	13	1	0	6	0	.17
97-98	NYR	2	0	0	0	-1	0	0	2	0.0	0	0	0	0	0	0	0	0	0	0	0	0	0	0	.00
98-99	NYR	5	0	0	0	-1	0	0	5	0.0	0	0	0	0	0	0	2	4	0	2	0	0	1	0	.00
98-99	Pit	2	0	0	0	0	0	0	0	–	0	0	0	0	0	0	0	0	0	0	0	0	0	0	.00
98-99	Van	49	7	9	16	-2	0	1	55	12.7	1	2	3	0	0	0	10	20	0	10	0	1	2	0	.33
3 Years		190	25	33	58	-3	3	1	190	13.2	4	4	8	1	0	1	38	79	1	37	1	2	14	0	.31

Postseason

Year	Tm	GP	G	A	Pts	+/–	GW	OT	S	SPct	G	A	Pts	G	A	Pts	Num	PIM	Maj	Mnr	Fgt	Rgh	HHT	Hat	P/G
96-97	StL	5	0	0	0	-1	0	0	2	0.0	0	0	0	0	0	0	1	2	0	1	0	0	0	0	.00

Jason York

(statistical profile on page 391)

Pos: D **Shoots:** R **Ht:** 6'3" **Wt:** 216 **Born:** 5/20/70—Nepean, Ontario **Age:** 29

Overall											Power Play			Shorthand			Penalty							Misc	
Year	Tm	GP	G	A	Pts	+/–	GW	GT	S	SPct	G	A	Pts	G	A	Pts	Num	PIM	Maj	Mnr	Fgt	Rgh	HHT	Hat	P/G
92-93	Det	2	0	0	0	0	0	0	1	0.0	0	0	0	0	0	0	0	0	0	0	0	0	0	0	.00
93-94	Det	7	1	2	3	0	0	0	9	11.1	0	2	2	0	0	0	1	2	0	1	0	0	1	0	.43
94-95	2Tm	25	1	10	11	4	0	0	28	3.6	0	5	5	0	0	0	7	14	0	7	0	1	3	0	.44
95-96	Anh	79	3	21	24	-7	0	0	106	2.8	0	6	6	0	0	0	44	88	0	44	0	7	19	0	.30
96-97	Ott	75	4	17	21	-8	0	0	121	3.3	1	6	7	0	0	0	32	67	1	31	1	4	13	0	.28
97-98	Ott	73	3	13	16	8	0	0	109	2.8	0	5	5	0	0	0	31	62	0	31	0	5	11	0	.22
98-99	Ott	79	4	31	35	17	0	1	177	2.3	2	14	16	0	1	1	24	48	0	24	0	0	14	0	.44
94-95	Det	10	1	2	3	0	0	0	6	16.7	0	1	1	0	0	0	1	2	0	1	0	0	1	0	.30
94-95	Anh	15	0	8	8	4	0	0	22	0.0	0	4	4	0	0	0	6	12	0	6	0	1	2	0	.53
7 Years		340	16	94	110	14	0	1	551	2.9	3	38	41	0	1	1	139	281	1	138	1	17	61	0	.32

Postseason

Year	Tm	GP	G	A	Pts	+/–	GW	OT	S	SPct	G	A	Pts	G	A	Pts	Num	PIM	Maj	Mnr	Fgt	Rgh	HHT	Hat	P/G
96-97	Ott	7	0	0	0	-3	0	0	18	0.0	0	0	0	0	0	0	2	4	0	2	0	1	0	0	.00
97-98	Ott	7	1	1	2	-2	0	0	13	7.7	1	0	1	0	0	0	2	7	1	1	1	0	1	0	.29
98-99	Ott	4	1	1	2	-1	0	0	12	8.3	0	0	0	0	0	0	2	4	0	2	0	0	0	0	.50
3 Years		18	2	2	4	-6	0	0	43	4.7	1	0	1	0	0	0	6	15	1	5	1	1	1	0	.22

Scott Young

(statistical profile on page 391)

Pos: RW **Shoots:** R **Ht:** 6'0" **Wt:** 190 **Born:** 10/1/67—Clinton, Massachusetts **Age:** 32

Overall											Power Play			Shorthand			Penalty							Misc	
Year	Tm	GP	G	A	Pts	+/–	GW	GT	S	SPct	G	A	Pts	G	A	Pts	Num	PIM	Maj	Mnr	Fgt	Rgh	HHT	Hat	P/G
87-88	Har	7	0	0	0	-6	0	0	6	0.0	0	0	0	0	0	0	1	2	0	1	0	–	–	0	.00
88-89	Har	76	19	40	59	-21	2	0	203	9.4	6	–	–	0	–	–	–	27	–	–	–	–	–	0	.78
89-90	Har	**80**	24	40	64	-24	5	0	239	10.0	10	–	–	2	–	–	–	47	–	–	–	–	–	0	.80
90-91	2Tm	77	17	25	42	-6	5	0	210	8.1	6	–	–	2	–	–	–	41	–	–	–	–	–	0	.55
91-92		Did Not Play in NHL																							
92-93	Que	82	30	30	60	5	5	0	225	13.3	9	17	26	6	0	6	10	20	0	10	0	0	6	1	.73
93-94	Que	76	26	25	51	-4	1	0	236	11.0	6	11	17	1	0	1	7	14	0	7	0	0	5	1	.67
94-95	Que	48	18	21	39	9	0	0	167	10.8	3	9	12	3	0	3	7	14	0	7	0	3	3	1	.81
95-96	Col	81	21	39	60	2	5	0	229	9.2	7	11	18	0	1	1	21	50	0	20	0	1	9	0	.74
96-97	Col	72	18	19	37	-5	0	0	164	11.0	7	13	20	0	0	0	7	14	0	7	0	1	4	1	.51
97-98	Anh	73	13	20	33	-13	1	0	187	7.0	4	9	13	2	1	3	11	22	0	11	0	1	5	0	.45
98-99	StL	75	24	28	52	8	4	0	205	11.7	8	11	19	0	0	0	12	27	1	11	1	0	5	0	.69
90-91	Har	34	6	9	15	-9	2	0	94	6.4	3	–	–	1	–	–	4	8	0	4	0	–	–	0	.44
90-91	Pit	43	11	16	27	3	3	0	116	9.5	3	6	9	1	–	–	–	33	–	–	–	–	–	0	.63
11 Years		747	210	287	497	-55	28	0	2071	10.1	66	–	–	16	–	–	–	278	–	–	–	–	–	4	.67

Postseason

Year	Tm	GP	G	A	Pts	+/–	GW	OT	S	SPct	G	A	Pts	G	A	Pts	Num	PIM	Maj	Mnr	Fgt	Rgh	HHT	Hat	P/G
87-88	Har	4	1	0	1	2	0	0	8	12.5	0	0	0	0	0	0	0	0	0	0	0	0	0	0	.25
88-89	Har	4	2	0	2	-4	0	0	16	12.5	0	0	0	0	0	0	2	4	0	2	0	0	0	0	.50
89-90	Har	7	2	0	2	-2	0	0	15	13.3	0	0	0	0	0	0	1	2	0	1	0	0	0	0	.29
90-91	Pit	17	1	6	7	1	0	0	21	4.8	1	–	–	0	–	–	1	2	0	1	0	0	0	0	.41
92-93	Que	6	4	1	5	5	2	1	23	17.4	0	1	1	0	0	0	0	0	0	0	0	0	0	0	.83
94-95	Que	6	3	3	6	3	0	0	12	25.0	0	1	1	1	0	1	1	2	0	1	0	0	1	0	1.00

Postseason																									
Year	Tm	GP	G	A	Pts	+/–	GW	OT	S	SPct	G	A	Pts	G	A	Pts	Num	PIM	Maj	Mnr	Fgt	Rgh	HHT	Hat	P/G
95-96	Col	22	3	12	15	6	0	0	61	4.9	0	6	6	0	0	0	5	10	0	5	0	1	3	0	.68
96-97	Col	17	4	2	6	-1	0	0	21	19.0	2	1	3	0	0	0	3	14	0	2	0	1	0	0	.35
98-99	StL	13	4	7	11	2	1	1	40	10.0	1	5	6	0	0	0	5	10	0	5	0	1	2	0	.85
9 Years		96	24	31	55	12	3	2	217	11.1	4	–	–	1	–	–	18	44	0	17	0	3	6	0	.57

Paul Ysebaert

Pos: C **Shoots:** L **Ht:** 6'1" **Wt:** 194 **Born:** 5/15/66—Corunna, Ontario **Age:** 33

Overall											Power Play			Shorthand			Penalty							Misc	
Year	Tm	GP	G	A	Pts	+/–	GW	GT	S	SPct	G	A	Pts	G	A	Pts	Num	PIM	Maj	Mnr	Fgt	Rgh	HHT	Hat	P/G
88-89	NJ	5	0	4	4	2	0	0	4	0.0	0	2	2	0	0	0	0	0	0	0	0	0	0	0	.80
89-90	NJ	5	1	2	3	0	0	0	6	16.7	0	0	0	0	0	0	0	0	0	0	0	0	0	0	.60
90-91	2Tm	62	19	21	40	-7	1	0	128	14.8	6	–	–	0	–	–	–	22	–	–	–	–	–	0	.65
91-92	Det	79	35	40	75	**44**	3	1	211	16.6	3	14	17	4	2	6	22	55	1	20	0	3	7	1	.95
92-93	Det	80	34	28	62	19	8	1	186	18.3	3	5	8	3	1	4	21	42	0	21	0	3	6	0	.78
93-94	2Tm	71	14	21	35	-7	1	0	151	9.3	3	9	12	0	0	0	13	26	0	13	0	2	5	0	.49
94-95	2Tm	44	12	16	28	3	1	0	93	12.9	0	2	2	0	0	0	9	18	0	9	0	0	2	0	.64
95-96	TB	55	16	15	31	-19	1	0	135	11.9	4	6	10	1	0	1	8	16	0	8	0	2	1	0	.56
96-97	TB	39	5	12	17	1	0	0	91	5.5	2	2	4	0	0	0	2	4	0	2	0	0	1	0	.44
97-98	TB	82	13	27	40	-43	0	0	145	9.0	2	13	15	1	2	3	16	32	0	16	0	1	7	0	.49
98-99	TB	10	0	1	1	-5	0	0	10	0.0	0	0	0	0	0	0	1	2	0	1	0	0	0	0	.10
90-91	NJ	11	4	3	7	1	0	0	14	28.6	1	0	1	0	0	0	3	6	0	3	0	–	–	0	.64
90-91	Det	51	15	18	33	-8	1	0	114	13.2	5	–	–	0	–	–	–	16	–	–	–	–	–	0	.65
93-94	Wpg	60	9	18	27	-8	0	0	120	7.5	1	7	8	0	0	0	9	18	0	9	0	1	3	0	.45
93-94	Chi	11	5	3	8	1	1	0	31	16.1	2	2	4	0	0	0	4	8	0	4	0	1	2	0	.73
94-95	Chi	15	4	5	9	4	1	0	23	17.4	0	0	0	0	0	0	3	6	0	3	0	0	0	0	.60
94-95	TB	29	8	11	19	-1	0	0	70	11.4	0	2	2	0	0	0	6	12	0	6	0	0	2	0	.66
11 Years		532	149	187	336	-12	15	2	1160	12.8	23	–	–	9	–	–	–	217	–	–	–	–	–	1	.63
Postseason																									
Year	Tm	GP	G	A	Pts	+/–	GW	OT	S	SPct	G	A	Pts	G	A	Pts	Num	PIM	Maj	Mnr	Fgt	Rgh	HHT	Hat	P/G
90-91	Det	2	0	2	2	2	0	0	5	0.0	0	–	–	0	–	–	0	0	0	0	0	0	0	0	1.00
91-92	Det	10	1	0	1	-1	0	0	24	4.2	0	0	0	0	0	0	5	10	0	5	0	2	2	0	.10
92-93	Det	7	3	1	4	2	1	0	11	27.3	0	0	0	1	0	1	1	2	0	1	0	0	0	0	.57
93-94	Chi	6	0	0	0	-2	0	0	9	0.0	0	0	0	0	0	0	4	8	0	4	0	1	2	0	.00
95-96	TB	5	0	0	0	-6	0	0	4	0.0	0	0	0	0	0	0	0	0	0	0	0	0	0	0	.00
5 Years		30	4	3	7	-5	1	0	53	7.5	0	–	–	1	–	–	10	20	0	10	0	3	4	0	.23

Dimitri Yushkevich

(statistical profile on page 391)

Pos: D **Shoots:** L **Ht:** 5'11" **Wt:** 208 **Born:** 11/19/71—Cherepovec, USSR **Age:** 28

Overall											Power Play			Shorthand			Penalty							Misc	
Year	Tm	GP	G	A	Pts	+/–	GW	GT	S	SPct	G	A	Pts	G	A	Pts	Num	PIM	Maj	Mnr	Fgt	Rgh	HHT	Hat	P/G
92-93	Phi	82	5	27	32	12	1	0	155	3.2	1	1	2	0	0	0	34	71	1	33	1	1	13	0	.39
93-94	Phi	75	5	25	30	-8	2	0	136	3.7	1	3	4	0	2	2	35	86	0	33	0	6	13	0	.40
94-95	Phi	40	5	9	14	-4	1	0	80	6.3	3	0	3	1	0	1	18	47	1	16	0	5	4	0	.35
95-96	Tor	69	1	10	11	-14	0	0	96	1.0	1	2	3	0	1	1	27	54	0	27	0	2	9	0	.16
96-97	Tor	74	4	10	14	-24	1	0	99	4.0	1	1	2	1	0	1	24	56	0	23	0	6	9	0	.19
97-98	Tor	72	0	12	12	-13	0	0	92	0.0	0	4	4	0	0	0	39	78	0	39	0	7	17	0	.17
98-99	Tor	78	6	22	28	25	0	0	95	6.3	2	7	9	1	1	2	36	88	0	34	0	4	19	0	.36
7 Years		490	26	115	141	-26	5	0	753	3.5	9	18	27	3	4	7	213	480	2	205	1	31	84	0	.29
Postseason																									
Year	Tm	GP	G	A	Pts	+/–	GW	OT	S	SPct	G	A	Pts	G	A	Pts	Num	PIM	Maj	Mnr	Fgt	Rgh	HHT	Hat	P/G
94-95	Phi	15	1	5	6	-2	0	0	25	4.0	0	3	3	0	1	1	6	12	0	6	0	2	0	0	.40
95-96	Tor	4	0	0	0	1	0	0	3	0.0	0	0	0	0	0	0	0	0	0	0	0	0	0	0	.00
98-99	Tor	17	1	5	6	7	0	0	17	5.9	1	2	3	0	0	0	7	22	0	6	0	3	0	0	.35
3 Years		36	2	10	12	6	0	0	45	4.4	1	5	6	0	1	1	13	34	0	12	0	5	0	0	.33

Steve Yzerman

(statistical profile on page 391)

Pos: C **Shoots:** R **Ht:** 5'11" **Wt:** 185 **Born:** 5/9/65—Cranbrook, British Columbia **Age:** 34

Overall											Power Play			Shorthand			Penalty							Misc	
Year	Tm	GP	G	A	Pts	+/–	GW	GT	S	SPct	G	A	Pts	G	A	Pts	Num	PIM	Maj	Mnr	Fgt	Rgh	HHT	Hat	P/G
83-84	Det*	**80**	39	48	87	-17	2	1	177	22.0	13	–	–	0	–	–	–	33	–	–	–	–	–	1	1.09
84-85	Det	**80**	30	59	89	-17	3	0	231	13.0	9	–	–	0	–	–	–	58	–	–	–	–	–	1	1.11
85-86	Det	51	14	28	42	-24	3	0	132	10.6	3	–	–	0	–	–	–	16	–	–	–	–	–	0	.82

Year	Tm	Overall GP	G	A	Pts	+/–	GW	GT	S	SPct	Power Play G	A	Pts	Shorthand G	A	Pts	Penalty Num	PIM	Maj	Mnr	Fgt	Rgh	HHT	Misc Hat	P/G
86-87	Det	80	31	59	90	-1	2	1	217	14.3	9	–	–	1	–	–	–	43	–	–	–	–	–	0	1.13
87-88	Det*	64	50	52	102	30	6	0	242	20.7	10	–	–	6	–	–	–	44	–	–	–	–	–	2	1.59
88-89	Det*	**80**	65	90	155	17	7	2	**388**	16.8	17	–	–	3	–	–	–	61	–	–	–	–	–	2	1.94
89-90	Det*	79	62	65	127	-6	8	2	332	18.7	16	–	–	**7**	–	–	–	79	–	–	–	–	–	3	1.61
90-91	Det*	80	51	57	108	-2	4	1	326	15.6	12	–	–	6	–	–	–	34	–	–	–	–	–	3	1.35
91-92	Det*	79	45	58	103	26	9	0	295	15.3	9	18	27	**8**	2	10	24	64	0	22	0	3	5	3	1.30
92-93	Det*	84	58	79	137	33	6	0	307	18.9	13	28	41	**7**	2	**9**	19	44	2	17	2	2	7	3	1.63
93-94	Det	58	24	58	82	11	3	1	217	11.1	7	17	24	3	3	6	18	36	0	18	0	2	5	0	1.41
94-95	Det	47	12	26	38	6	1	0	134	9.0	4	15	19	0	0	0	13	40	2	10	1	0	2	0	.81
95-96	Det	80	36	59	95	29	8	0	220	16.4	16	22	38	2	5	7	20	64	0	17	0	5	8	0	1.19
96-97	Det*	81	22	63	85	22	3	0	232	9.5	8	18	26	0	2	2	23	78	0	19	0	2	9	0	1.05
97-98	Det	75	24	45	69	3	0	2	188	12.8	6	21	27	2	1	3	23	46	0	23	0	0	11	0	.92
98-99	Det	80	29	45	74	8	4	0	231	12.6	13	11	24	2	1	3	13	42	0	11	0	3	5	0	.93
16 Years		1178	592	891	1483	118	69	10	3869	15.3	165	–	–	47	–	–	–	782	–	–	–	–	–	18	1.26

Postseason

Year	Tm	GP	G	A	Pts	+/–	GW	OT	S	SPct	PP G	A	Pts	SH G	A	Pts	Num	PIM	Maj	Mnr	Fgt	Rgh	HHT	Hat	P/G
83-84	Det	4	3	3	6	1	1	0	9	33.3	1	–	–	0	–	–	0	0	0	0	0	0	0	0	1.50
84-85	Det	3	2	1	3	-5	0	0	11	18.2	0	–	–	0	0	0	1	2	0	1	0	–	–	0	1.00
86-87	Det	16	5	13	18	-2	0	0	41	12.2	1	–	–	0	–	–	4	8	0	4	0	–	–	0	1.13
87-88	Det	3	1	3	4	-3	0	0	12	8.3	0	–	–	0	–	–	3	6	0	3	0	–	–	0	1.33
88-89	Det	6	5	5	10	-7	0	0	35	14.3	2	–	–	0	0	0	1	2	0	1	0	–	–	1	1.67
90-91	Det	7	3	3	6	-1	0	0	27	11.1	1	–	–	0	–	–	2	4	0	2	0	–	–	1	.86
91-92	Det	11	3	5	8	-3	1	0	48	6.3	0	3	3	1	1	2	6	12	0	6	0	1	0	0	.73
92-93	Det	7	4	3	7	-4	1	0	24	16.7	1	2	3	1	0	1	2	4	0	2	0	0	1	0	1.00
93-94	Det	3	1	3	4	4	0	0	8	12.5	0	0	0	0	1	1	0	0	0	0	0	0	0	0	1.33
94-95	Det	15	4	8	12	-2	1	0	37	10.8	2	4	6	0	0	0	0	0	0	0	0	0	0	0	.80
95-96	Det	18	8	12	20	-1	1	1	52	15.4	4	7	11	0	0	0	2	4	0	2	0	0	1	1	1.11
96-97	Det	20	7	6	13	3	2	0	65	10.8	3	2	5	0	0	0	2	4	0	2	0	0	1	0	.65
97-98	Det	22	6	18	24	10	0	0	65	9.2	3	5	8	1	2	3	7	22	0	6	0	0	1	0	1.09
98-99	Det	10	9	4	13	2	2	0	41	22.0	4	1	5	0	0	0	0	0	0	0	0	0	0	1	1.30
14 Years		145	61	87	148	-8	9	1	475	12.8	22	–	–	3	–	–	30	68	0	29	0	–	–	4	1.02

Rob Zamuner

(statistical profile on page 392)

Pos: LW **Shoots:** L **Ht:** 6'2" **Wt:** 206 **Born:** 9/17/69—Oakville, Ontario **Age:** 30

Year	Tm	Overall GP	G	A	Pts	+/–	GW	GT	S	SPct	Power Play G	A	Pts	Shorthand G	A	Pts	Penalty Num	PIM	Maj	Mnr	Fgt	Rgh	HHT	Misc Hat	P/G
91-92	NYR	9	1	2	3	0	0	0	11	9.1	0	0	0	0	0	0	1	2	0	1	0	0	0	0	.33
92-93	TB	84	15	28	43	-25	0	2	183	8.2	1	11	12	0	0	0	30	74	2	27	2	5	10	0	.51
93-94	TB	59	6	6	12	-9	1	0	109	5.5	0	0	0	0	0	0	21	42	0	21	0	2	12	0	.20
94-95	TB	43	9	6	15	-3	1	0	74	12.2	0	1	1	3	2	5	9	24	2	7	2	1	4	0	.35
95-96	TB	72	15	20	35	11	4	0	152	9.9	0	2	2	3	1	4	27	62	0	26	0	3	16	0	.49
96-97	TB	**82**	17	33	50	3	3	0	216	7.9	0	0	0	4	4	8	28	56	0	28	0	4	18	0	.61
97-98	TB	77	14	12	26	-31	4	1	126	11.1	0	2	2	3	1	4	19	41	1	18	1	5	7	1	.34
98-99	TB	58	8	11	19	-15	2	0	89	9.0	1	1	2	1	2	3	12	24	0	12	0	0	7	0	.33
8 Years		484	85	118	203	-69	15	3	960	8.9	2	17	19	14	10	24	147	325	5	140	5	20	74	1	.42

Postseason

Year	Tm	GP	G	A	Pts	+/–	GW	OT	S	SPct	PP G	A	Pts	SH G	A	Pts	Num	PIM	Maj	Mnr	Fgt	Rgh	HHT	Hat	P/G
95-96	TB	6	2	3	5	-1	0	0	10	20.0	0	0	0	1	0	1	5	10	0	5	0	0	1	0	.83

Richard Zednik

(statistical profile on page 392)

Pos: LW **Shoots:** L **Ht:** 5'10" **Wt:** 190 **Born:** 1/6/76—Bystrica, Czechoslovakia **Age:** 23

Year	Tm	Overall GP	G	A	Pts	+/–	GW	GT	S	SPct	Power Play G	A	Pts	Shorthand G	A	Pts	Penalty Num	PIM	Maj	Mnr	Fgt	Rgh	HHT	Misc Hat	P/G
95-96	Was	1	0	0	0	0	0	0	0	–	0	0	0	0	0	0	0	0	0	0	0	0	0	0	.00
96-97	Was	11	2	1	3	-5	0	0	21	9.5	1	0	1	0	0	0	2	4	0	2	0	0	2	0	.27
97-98	Was	65	17	9	26	-2	2	0	148	11.5	2	0	2	0	0	0	14	28	0	14	0	2	7	0	.40
98-99	Was	49	9	8	17	-6	2	0	115	7.8	1	1	2	0	0	0	21	50	0	20	0	4	9	0	.35
4 Years		126	28	18	46	-13	4	0	284	9.9	4	1	5	0	0	0	37	82	0	36	0	6	18	0	.37

Postseason

Year	Tm	GP	G	A	Pts	+/–	GW	OT	S	SPct	PP G	A	Pts	SH G	A	Pts	Num	PIM	Maj	Mnr	Fgt	Rgh	HHT	Hat	P/G
97-98	Was	17	7	3	10	0	0	0	40	17.5	2	2	4	0	0	0	8	16	0	8	0	3	3	0	.59

Valeri Zelepukin

(statistical profile on page 392)

Pos: LW **Shoots:** L **Ht:** 6'1" **Wt:** 195 **Born:** 9/17/68—Voskresensk, USSR **Age:** 31

Overall											Power Play			Shorthand			Penalty							Misc	
Year	Tm	GP	G	A	Pts	+/–	GW	GT	S	SPct	G	A	Pts	G	A	Pts	Num	PIM	Maj	Mnr	Fgt	Rgh	HHT	Hat	P/G
91-92	NJ	44	13	18	31	11	3	0	94	13.8	3	2	5	0	0	0	14	28	0	14	0	4	5	0	.70
92-93	NJ	78	23	41	64	19	2	0	174	13.2	5	8	13	1	0	1	24	70	2	20	0	0	9	0	.82
93-94	NJ	82	26	31	57	36	0	0	155	16.8	8	4	12	0	0	0	32	70	2	30	2	7	9	0	.70
94-95	NJ	4	1	2	3	3	0	0	6	16.7	0	0	0	0	0	0	3	6	0	3	0	0	1	0	.75
95-96	NJ	61	6	9	15	-10	1	1	86	7.0	3	2	5	0	0	0	29	107	3	21	2	3	7	0	.25
96-97	NJ	71	14	24	38	-10	2	0	111	12.6	3	3	6	0	0	0	18	36	0	18	0	5	6	0	.54
97-98	2Tm	68	4	18	22	-2	0	0	101	4.0	0	5	5	0	0	0	31	89	1	27	1	5	5	0	.32
98-99	Phi	74	16	9	25	0	5	0	129	12.4	0	2	2	0	0	0	21	48	2	19	2	2	3	0	.34
97-98	NJ	35	2	8	10	0	0	0	54	3.7	0	1	1	0	0	0	12	32	0	11	0	2	4	0	.29
97-98	Edm	33	2	10	12	-2	0	0	47	4.3	0	4	4	0	0	0	19	57	1	16	1	3	1	0	.36
8 Years		482	103	152	255	47	13	1	856	12.0	22	26	48	1	0	1	172	454	10	152	7	26	45	0	.53

Postseason

Year	Tm	GP	G	A	Pts	+/–	GW	OT	S	SPct	G	A	Pts	G	A	Pts	Num	PIM	Maj	Mnr	Fgt	Rgh	HHT	Hat	P/G
91-92	NJ	4	1	1	2	0	0	0	8	12.5	0	0	0	0	0	0	1	2	0	1	0	0	0	0	.50
92-93	NJ	5	0	2	2	-1	0	0	7	0.0	0	0	0	0	0	0	0	0	0	0	0	0	0	0	.40
93-94	NJ	20	5	2	7	1	0	0	40	12.5	1	1	2	0	0	0	7	14	0	7	0	2	2	0	.35
94-95	NJ	18	1	2	3	1	1	0	12	8.3	0	1	1	0	0	0	6	12	0	6	0	3	1	0	.17
96-97	NJ	8	3	2	5	3	1	0	13	23.1	1	0	1	0	0	0	2	12	0	1	0	1	0	1	.63
97-98	Edm	8	1	2	3	3	0	0	8	12.5	0	0	0	0	0	0	1	2	0	1	0	0	1	0	.38
98-99	Phi	4	1	0	1	1	1	0	5	20.0	0	0	0	0	0	0	2	4	0	2	0	0	1	0	.25
7 Years		67	12	11	23	8	3	0	93	12.9	2	2	4	0	0	0	19	46	0	18	0	6	5	1	.34

Jason Zent

Pos: LW **Shoots:** L **Ht:** 5'11" **Wt:** 216 **Born:** 4/15/71—Buffalo, New York **Age:** 28

Overall											Power Play			Shorthand			Penalty							Misc	
Year	Tm	GP	G	A	Pts	+/–	GW	GT	S	SPct	G	A	Pts	G	A	Pts	Num	PIM	Maj	Mnr	Fgt	Rgh	HHT	Hat	P/G
96-97	Ott	22	3	3	6	5	0	0	20	15.0	0	0	0	0	0	0	3	9	1	2	1	0	0	0	.27
97-98	Ott	3	0	0	0	0	0	0	1	0.0	0	0	0	0	0	0	2	4	0	2	0	0	1	0	.00
98-99	Phi	2	0	0	0	0	0	0	1	0.0	0	0	0	0	0	0	0	0	0	0	0	0	0	0	.00
3 Years		27	3	3	6	5	0	0	22	13.6	0	0	0	0	0	0	5	13	1	4	1	0	1	0	.22

Rob Zettler

Pos: D **Shoots:** L **Ht:** 6'2" **Wt:** 202 **Born:** 3/8/68—Sept-Iles, Quebec **Age:** 31

Overall											Power Play			Shorthand			Penalty							Misc	
Year	Tm	GP	G	A	Pts	+/–	GW	GT	S	SPct	G	A	Pts	G	A	Pts	Num	PIM	Maj	Mnr	Fgt	Rgh	HHT	Hat	P/G
88-89	Min	2	0	0	0	-1	0	0	0	–	0	0	0	0	0	0	0	0	0	0	0	0	0	0	.00
89-90	Min	31	0	8	8	-7	0	0	21	0.0	0	–	–	0	–	–	–	45	–	–	–	–	–	0	.26
90-91	Min	47	1	4	5	-10	0	0	30	3.3	0	–	–	0	–	–	–	119	–	–	–	–	–	0	.11
91-92	SJ	74	1	8	9	-23	0	0	72	1.4	0	1	1	0	3	3	40	99	1	37	0	11	9	0	.12
92-93	SJ	80	0	7	7	-50	0	0	60	0.0	0	0	0	0	1	1	62	150	6	55	5	14	17	0	.09
93-94	2Tm	75	0	7	7	-26	0	0	55	0.0	0	0	0	0	0	0	46	134	6	37	6	5	15	0	.09
94-95	Phi	32	0	1	1	-3	0	0	17	0.0	0	0	0	0	0	0	11	34	4	7	4	1	2	0	.03
95-96	Tor	29	0	1	1	-1	0	0	11	0.0	0	0	0	0	0	0	17	48	2	14	1	4	5	0	.03
96-97	Tor	48	2	12	14	8	0	0	31	6.5	0	0	0	0	0	0	21	51	3	18	3	5	6	0	.29
97-98	Tor	59	0	7	7	-8	0	0	28	0.0	0	2	2	0	0	0	47	108	2	44	2	13	12	0	.12
98-99	Nsh	2	0	0	0	-2	0	0	0	–	0	0	0	0	0	0	1	2	0	1	0	0	1	0	.00
93-94	SJ	42	0	3	3	-7	0	0	28	0.0	0	0	0	0	0	0	24	65	3	20	3	3	7	0	.07
93-94	Phi	33	0	4	4	-19	0	0	27	0.0	0	0	0	0	0	0	22	69	3	17	3	2	8	0	.12
11 Years		479	4	55	59	-123	0	0	325	1.2	0	–	–	0	–	–	–	790	–	–	–	–	–	0	.12

Postseason

Year	Tm	GP	G	A	Pts	+/–	GW	OT	S	SPct	G	A	Pts	G	A	Pts	Num	PIM	Maj	Mnr	Fgt	Rgh	HHT	Hat	P/G
94-95	Phi	1	0	0	0	1	0	0	1	0.0	0	0	0	0	0	0	1	2	0	1	0	0	0	0	.00
95-96	Tor	2	0	0	0	0	0	0	1	0.0	0	0	0	0	0	0	0	0	0	0	0	0	0	0	.00
2 Years		3	0	0	0	1	0	0	2	0.0	0	0	0	0	0	0	1	2	0	1	0	0	0	0	.00

Peter Zezel

(statistical profile on page 392)

Pos: C **Shoots:** L **Ht:** 5'11" **Wt:** 220 **Born:** 4/22/65—Toronto, Ontario **Age:** 34

Overall											Power Play			Shorthand			Penalty							Misc	
Year	Tm	GP	G	A	Pts	+/–	GW	GT	S	SPct	G	A	Pts	G	A	Pts	Num	PIM	Maj	Mnr	Fgt	Rgh	HHT	Hat	P/G
84-85	Phi	65	15	46	61	22	2	1	91	16.5	8	–	–	0	–	–	–	26	–	–	–	–	–	0	.94

		Overall									Power Play			Shorthand			Penalty							Misc	
Year	Tm	GP	G	A	Pts	+/–	GW	GT	S	SPct	G	A	Pts	G	A	Pts	Num	PIM	Maj	Mnr	Fgt	Rgh	HHT	Hat	P/G
85-86	Phi	79	17	37	54	27	4	0	144	11.8	4	–	–	0	–	–	–	76	–	–	–	–	–	0	.68
86-87	Phi	71	33	39	72	21	7	0	181	18.2	6	–	–	2	–	–	–	71	–	–	–	–	–	1	1.01
87-88	Phi	69	22	35	57	7	1	0	133	16.5	14	–	–	0	–	–	–	42	–	–	–	–	–	0	.83
88-89	2Tm	78	21	49	70	-14	4	0	149	14.1	5	–	–	1	–	–	–	42	–	–	–	–	–	0	.90
89-90	StL	73	25	47	72	-9	3	0	158	15.8	7	–	–	0	–	–	–	30	–	–	–	–	–	0	.99
90-91	2Tm	52	21	19	40	-20	5	0	90	23.3	12	–	–	0	–	–	–	14	–	–	–	–	–	0	.77
91-92	Tor	64	16	33	49	-22	1	0	125	12.8	4	14	18	0	0	0	13	26	0	13	0	1	4	0	.77
92-93	Tor	70	12	23	35	0	4	0	102	11.8	0	3	3	0	0	0	12	24	0	12	0	1	5	0	.50
93-94	Tor	41	8	8	16	5	0	0	47	17.0	0	0	0	0	0	0	4	19	1	2	0	1	1	0	.39
94-95	Dal	30	6	5	11	-6	1	0	47	12.8	0	1	1	0	1	1	4	19	1	2	0	0	2	0	.37
95-96	StL	57	8	13	21	-2	1	0	87	9.2	2	7	9	0	1	1	6	12	0	6	0	0	4	0	.37
96-97	2Tm	53	4	12	16	10	1	0	62	6.5	0	1	1	0	0	0	8	16	0	8	0	0	4	0	.30
97-98	2Tm	30	5	15	20	15	1	0	40	12.5	2	1	3	0	1	1	1	2	0	1	0	0	0	0	.67
98-99	Van	41	6	8	14	5	2	0	45	13.3	1	1	2	0	0	0	8	16	0	8	0	0	6	0	.34
88-89	Phi	26	4	13	17	-13	0	0	34	11.8	0	–	–	0	–	–	–	15	–	–	–	–	–	0	.65
88-89	StL	52	17	36	53	-1	4	0	115	14.8	5	–	–	1	–	–	–	27	–	–	–	–	–	0	1.02
90-91	Was	20	7	5	12	-13	0	0	21	33.3	6	–	–	0	–	–	–	10	–	–	–	–	–	0	.60
90-91	Tor	32	14	14	28	-7	5	0	69	20.3	6	–	–	0	–	–	2	4	0	2	0	–	–	0	.88
96-97	StL	35	4	9	13	6	1	0	49	8.2	0	1	1	0	0	0	6	12	0	6	0	0	3	0	.37
96-97	NJ	18	0	3	3	4	0	0	13	0.0	0	0	0	0	0	0	2	4	0	2	0	0	1	0	.17
97-98	NJ	5	0	3	3	2	0	0	3	0.0	0	0	0	0	0	0	0	0	0	0	0	0	0	0	.60
97-98	Van	25	5	12	17	13	1	0	37	13.5	2	1	3	0	1	1	1	2	0	1	0	0	0	0	.68
15 Years		873	219	389	608	39	37	1	1501	14.6	65	–	–	3	–	–	–	435	–	–	–	–	–	1	.70

Postseason																									
Year	Tm	GP	G	A	Pts	+/–	GW	OT	S	SPct	G	A	Pts	G	A	Pts	Num	PIM	Maj	Mnr	Fgt	Rgh	HHT	Hat	P/G
84-85	Phi	19	1	8	9	-5	0	0	24	4.2	1	–	–	0	–	–	–	28	–	–	–	–	–	0	.47
85-86	Phi	5	3	1	4	-2	1	0	11	27.3	1	–	–	0	0	0	2	4	0	2	0	–	–	1	.80
86-87	Phi	25	3	10	13	6	1	0	36	8.3	1	–	–	1	–	–	–	10	–	–	–	–	–	0	.52
87-88	Phi	7	3	2	5	0	0	0	15	20.0	0	–	–	0	0	0	2	7	1	1	–	–	–	0	.71
88-89	StL	10	6	6	12	-2	1	0	31	19.4	1	–	–	1	–	–	2	4	0	2	0	–	–	1	1.20
89-90	StL	12	1	7	8	3	0	0	28	3.6	1	–	–	0	–	–	2	4	0	2	0	–	–	0	.67
92-93	Tor	20	2	1	3	-6	0	0	40	5.0	0	0	0	0	0	0	3	6	0	3	0	1	1	0	.15
93-94	Tor	18	2	4	6	-2	1	1	32	6.3	0	0	0	0	1	1	4	8	0	4	0	0	0	0	.33
94-95	Dal	3	1	0	1	0	0	0	3	33.3	0	0	0	0	0	0	0	0	0	0	0	0	0	0	.33
95-96	StL	10	3	0	3	4	0	0	17	17.6	0	0	0	1	0	1	1	2	0	1	0	0	0	0	.30
96-97	NJ	2	0	0	0	0	0	0	4	0.0	0	0	0	0	0	0	0	0	0	0	0	0	0	0	.00
11 Years		131	25	39	64	-4	4	1	241	10.4	5	–	–	3	–	–	–	73	–	–	–	–	–	2	.49

Alexei Zhamnov

(statistical profile on page 393)

Pos: C **Shoots:** L **Ht:** 6'1" **Wt:** 195 **Born:** 10/1/70—Moscow, USSR **Age:** 29

		Overall									Power Play			Shorthand			Penalty							Misc	
Year	Tm	GP	G	A	Pts	+/–	GW	GT	S	SPct	G	A	Pts	G	A	Pts	Num	PIM	Maj	Mnr	Fgt	Rgh	HHT	Hat	P/G
92-93	Wpg	68	25	47	72	7	4	1	163	15.3	6	16	22	1	0	1	18	58	2	14	0	1	7	0	1.06
93-94	Wpg	61	26	45	71	-20	1	1	196	13.3	7	22	29	0	0	0	19	62	0	16	0	4	5	2	1.16
94-95	Wpg	48	30	35	65	5	4	0	155	19.4	9	16	25	0	0	0	10	20	0	10	0	2	4	2	1.35
95-96	Wpg	58	22	37	59	-4	2	0	199	11.1	5	23	28	0	0	0	27	65	1	25	0	3	10	1	1.02
96-97	Chi	74	20	42	62	18	2	0	208	9.6	6	16	22	1	2	3	24	56	0	23	0	4	10	1	.84
97-98	Chi	70	21	28	49	16	3	1	193	10.9	6	8	14	2	1	3	25	61	1	23	0	7	12	0	.70
98-99	Chi	76	20	41	61	-10	2	1	200	10.0	8	17	25	1	1	2	21	50	0	20	0	3	7	0	.80
7 Years		455	164	275	439	12	18	4	1314	12.5	47	118	165	5	4	9	144	372	4	131	0	24	55	6	.96

Postseason																									
Year	Tm	GP	G	A	Pts	+/–	GW	OT	S	SPct	G	A	Pts	G	A	Pts	Num	PIM	Maj	Mnr	Fgt	Rgh	HHT	Hat	P/G
92-93	Wpg	6	0	2	2	-4	0	0	13	0.0	0	1	1	0	0	0	1	2	0	1	0	0	1	0	.33
95-96	Wpg	6	2	1	3	0	0	0	11	18.2	0	0	0	0	0	0	4	8	0	4	0	1	1	0	.50
2 Years		12	2	3	5	-4	0	0	24	8.3	0	1	1	0	0	0	5	10	0	5	0	1	2	0	.42

Alexei Zhitnik

(statistical profile on page 393)

Pos: D **Shoots:** L **Ht:** 5'11" **Wt:** 202 **Born:** 10/10/72—Kiev, USSR **Age:** 27

		Overall									Power Play			Shorthand			Penalty							Misc	
Year	Tm	GP	G	A	Pts	+/–	GW	GT	S	SPct	G	A	Pts	G	A	Pts	Num	PIM	Maj	Mnr	Fgt	Rgh	HHT	Hat	P/G
92-93	LA	78	12	36	48	-3	2	0	136	8.8	5	14	19	0	0	0	40	80	0	40	0	2	18	0	.62
93-94	LA	81	12	40	52	-11	1	1	227	5.3	11	18	29	0	0	0	45	101	1	43	0	2	23	0	.64
94-95	2Tm	32	4	10	14	-6	0	0	66	6.1	3	5	8	0	0	0	25	61	1	23	0	0	10	0	.44
95-96	Buf	80	6	30	36	-25	0	0	193	3.1	5	18	23	0	2	2	29	58	0	29	0	0	15	0	.45

Overall											Power Play			Shorthand			Penalty							Misc	
Year	Tm	GP	G	A	Pts	+/–	GW	GT	S	SPct	G	A	Pts	G	A	Pts	Num	PIM	Maj	Mnr	Fgt	Rgh	HHT	Hat	P/G
96-97	Buf	80	7	28	35	10	0	1	170	4.1	3	11	14	1	2	3	38	95	1	35	0	1	19	0	.44
97-98	Buf	78	15	30	45	19	3	2	191	7.9	2	15	17	3	2	5	51	102	0	51	0	1	**32**	0	.58
98-99	Buf	81	7	26	33	-6	2	0	185	3.8	3	13	16	1	0	1	48	96	0	48	0	4	23	0	.41
94-95	LA	11	2	5	7	-3	0	0	33	6.1	2	1	3	0	0	0	8	27	1	6	0	0	2	0	.64
94-95	Buf	21	2	5	7	-3	0	0	33	6.1	1	4	5	0	0	0	17	34	0	17	0	0	8	0	.33
7 Years		510	63	200	263	-22	8	4	1168	5.4	32	94	126	5	6	11	276	593	3	269	0	10	140	0	.52
Postseason																									
Year	Tm	GP	G	A	Pts	+/–	GW	OT	S	SPct	G	A	Pts	G	A	Pts	Num	PIM	Maj	Mnr	Fgt	Rgh	HHT	Hat	P/G
92-93	LA	24	3	9	12	-4	1	0	42	7.1	2	5	7	0	0	0	13	26	0	13	0	2	8	0	.50
94-95	Buf	5	0	1	1	-7	0	0	12	0.0	0	1	1	0	0	0	7	14	0	7	0	1	4	0	.20
96-97	Buf	12	1	0	1	-9	0	0	16	6.3	0	0	0	0	0	0	8	16	0	8	0	1	2	0	.08
97-98	Buf	15	0	3	3	1	0	0	24	0.0	0	1	1	0	0	0	18	36	0	18	0	2	8	0	.20
98-99	Buf	21	4	11	15	-6	2	0	58	6.9	4	9	13	0	1	1	26	52	0	26	0	3	12	0	.71
5 Years		77	8	24	32	-25	3	0	152	5.3	6	16	22	0	1	1	72	144	0	72	0	9	34	0	.42

Sergei Zholtok

(statistical profile on page 393)

Pos: C **Shoots:** R **Ht:** 6'0" **Wt:** 195 **Born:** 12/2/72—Riga, USSR **Age:** 27

Overall											Power Play			Shorthand			Penalty							Misc	
Year	Tm	GP	G	A	Pts	+/–	GW	GT	S	SPct	G	A	Pts	G	A	Pts	Num	PIM	Maj	Mnr	Fgt	Rgh	HHT	Hat	P/G
92-93	Bos	1	0	1	1	1	0	0	2	0.0	0	0	0	0	0	0	0	0	0	0	0	0	0	0	1.00
93-94	Bos	24	2	1	3	-7	0	0	25	8.0	1	0	1	0	0	0	1	2	0	1	0	0	1	0	.13
94-95		Did Not Play in NHL																							
95-96		Did Not Play in NHL																							
96-97	Ott	57	12	16	28	2	0	0	96	12.5	5	4	9	0	0	0	4	19	1	2	1	1	0	0	.49
97-98	Ott	78	10	13	23	-7	1	1	127	7.9	7	7	14	0	0	0	8	16	0	8	0	2	3	0	.29
98-99	Mon	70	7	15	22	-12	3	0	102	6.9	2	4	6	0	0	0	3	6	0	3	0	0	2	0	.31
5 Years		230	31	46	77	-23	4	1	352	8.8	15	15	30	0	0	0	16	43	1	14	1	3	6	0	.33
Postseason																									
Year	Tm	GP	G	A	Pts	+/–	GW	OT	S	SPct	G	A	Pts	G	A	Pts	Num	PIM	Maj	Mnr	Fgt	Rgh	HHT	Hat	P/G
96-97	Ott	7	1	1	2	0	0	0	16	6.3	1	0	1	0	0	0	0	0	0	0	0	0	0	0	.29
97-98	Ott	11	0	2	2	-1	0	0	23	0.0	0	1	1	0	0	0	0	0	0	0	0	0	0	0	.18
2 Years		18	1	3	4	-1	0	0	39	2.6	1	1	2	0	0	0	0	0	0	0	0	0	0	0	.22

Doug Zmolek

(statistical profile on page 393)

Pos: D **Shoots:** L **Ht:** 6'2" **Wt:** 220 **Born:** 11/3/70—Rochester, Minnesota **Age:** 29

Overall											Power Play			Shorthand			Penalty							Misc	
Year	Tm	GP	G	A	Pts	+/–	GW	GT	S	SPct	G	A	Pts	G	A	Pts	Num	PIM	Maj	Mnr	Fgt	Rgh	HHT	Hat	P/G
92-93	SJ	84	5	10	15	-50	0	0	94	5.3	2	3	5	0	0	0	72	229	15	52	14	15	23	0	.18
93-94	2Tm	75	1	4	5	-7	0	0	32	3.1	0	0	0	0	0	0	44	133	15	29	15	7	12	0	.07
94-95	Dal	42	0	5	5	-6	0	0	28	0.0	0	1	1	0	0	0	20	67	9	11	9	3	4	0	.12
95-96	2Tm	58	2	5	7	-5	0	0	36	5.6	0	2	2	0	0	0	33	87	7	26	7	7	15	0	.12
96-97	LA	57	1	0	1	-22	0	0	28	3.6	0	0	0	0	0	0	32	116	12	18	12	6	4	0	.02
97-98	LA	46	0	8	8	0	0	0	23	0.0	0	0	0	0	1	1	28	111	13	13	12	6	3	0	.17
98-99	Chi	62	0	14	14	1	0	0	33	0.0	0	1	1	0	0	0	30	102	6	21	6	6	4	0	.23
93-94	SJ	68	0	4	4	-8	0	0	29	0.0	0	0	0	0	0	0	40	122	14	26	14	6	10	0	.06
93-94	Dal	7	1	0	1	1	0	0	3	33.3	0	0	0	0	0	0	4	11	1	3	1	1	2	0	.14
95-96	Dal	42	1	5	6	1	0	0	26	3.8	0	2	2	0	0	0	25	65	5	20	5	5	13	0	.14
95-96	LA	16	1	0	1	-6	0	0	10	10.0	0	0	0	0	0	0	8	22	2	6	2	2	2	0	.06
7 Years		424	9	46	55	-89	0	0	274	3.3	2	7	9	0	1	1	259	845	77	170	75	50	65	0	.13
Postseason																									
Year	Tm	GP	G	A	Pts	+/–	GW	OT	S	SPct	G	A	Pts	G	A	Pts	Num	PIM	Maj	Mnr	Fgt	Rgh	HHT	Hat	P/G
93-94	Dal	7	0	1	1	-2	0	0	2	0.0	0	0	0	0	0	0	2	4	0	2	0	1	0	0	.14
94-95	Dal	5	0	0	0	-2	0	0	3	0.0	0	0	0	0	0	0	5	10	0	5	0	2	0	0	.00
97-98	LA	2	0	0	0	0	0	0	0	–	0	0	0	0	0	0	1	2	0	1	0	0	1	0	.00
3 Years		14	0	1	1	-4	0	0	5	0.0	0	0	0	0	0	0	8	16	0	8	0	3	1	0	.07

Sergei Zubov

(statistical profile on page 394)

Pos: D **Shoots:** R **Ht:** 6'1" **Wt:** 200 **Born:** 7/22/70—Moscow, USSR **Age:** 29

Overall											Power Play			Shorthand			Penalty							Misc	
Year	Tm	GP	G	A	Pts	+/–	GW	GT	S	SPct	G	A	Pts	G	A	Pts	Num	PIM	Maj	Mnr	Fgt	Rgh	HHT	Hat	P/G
92-93	NYR	49	8	23	31	-1	0	0	93	8.6	3	9	12	0	0	0	2	4	0	2	0	0	1	0	.63
93-94	NYR	78	12	77	89	20	1	0	222	5.4	9	40	49	0	1	1	18	39	1	17	1	3	11	0	1.14

Overall											Power Play			Shorthand			Penalty							Misc	
Year	Tm	GP	G	A	Pts	+/–	GW	GT	S	SPct	G	A	Pts	G	A	Pts	Num	PIM	Maj	Mnr	Fgt	Rgh	HHT	Hat	P/G
94-95	NYR	38	10	26	36	-2	0	0	116	8.6	6	13	19	0	1	1	9	18	0	9	0	0	4	0	.95
95-96	Pit	64	11	55	66	28	1	0	141	7.8	3	29	32	2	2	4	11	22	0	11	0	0	6	0	1.03
96-97	Dal	78	13	30	43	19	3	0	133	9.8	1	9	10	0	2	2	12	24	0	12	0	0	7	0	.55
97-98	Dal*	73	10	47	57	16	2	1	148	6.8	5	29	34	1	1	2	8	16	0	8	0	1	5	0	.78
98-99	Dal	81	10	41	51	9	3	0	155	6.5	5	22	27	0	0	0	10	20	0	10	0	0	7	0	.63
7 Years		461	74	299	373	89	10	1	1008	7.3	32	151	183	3	7	10	70	143	1	69	1	4	41	0	.81
Postseason																									
Year	Tm	GP	G	A	Pts	+/–	GW	OT	S	SPct	G	A	Pts	G	A	Pts	Num	PIM	Maj	Mnr	Fgt	Rgh	HHT	Hat	P/G
93-94	NYR	22	5	14	19	10	0	0	60	8.3	2	7	9	0	0	0	0	0	0	0	0	0	0	0	.86
94-95	NYR	10	3	8	11	-9	0	0	34	8.8	1	6	7	0	0	0	1	2	0	1	0	0	0	0	1.10
95-96	Pit	18	1	14	15	9	0	0	53	1.9	1	8	9	0	0	0	6	26	2	3	1	0	1	0	.83
96-97	Dal	7	0	3	3	4	0	0	9	0.0	0	1	1	0	1	1	1	2	0	1	0	0	0	0	.43
97-98	Dal	17	4	5	9	3	1	0	34	11.8	3	2	5	0	0	0	1	2	0	1	0	0	1	0	.53
98-99	Dal	23	1	12	13	13	0	0	46	2.2	0	4	4	0	0	0	2	4	0	2	0	1	0	0	.57
6 Years		97	14	56	70	30	1	0	236	5.9	7	28	35	0	1	1	11	36	2	8	1	1	2	0	.72

Dainius Zubrus

(statistical profile on page 394)

Pos: RW **Shoots:** L **Ht:** 6'3" **Wt:** 215 **Born:** 6/16/78—Elektrenai, USSR **Age:** 21

Overall											Power Play			Shorthand			Penalty							Misc	
Year	Tm	GP	G	A	Pts	+/–	GW	GT	S	SPct	G	A	Pts	G	A	Pts	Num	PIM	Maj	Mnr	Fgt	Rgh	HHT	Hat	P/G
96-97	Phi	68	8	13	21	3	2	0	71	11.3	1	2	3	0	0	0	11	22	0	11	0	3	3	0	.31
97-98	Phi	69	8	25	33	29	5	0	101	7.9	1	3	4	0	0	0	14	42	2	11	2	4	4	0	.48
98-99	2Tm	80	6	10	16	-8	1	0	80	7.5	0	1	1	1	0	1	13	29	1	12	1	1	5	0	.20
98-99	Phi	63	3	5	8	-5	0	0	49	6.1	0	0	0	1	0	1	11	25	1	10	1	1	5	0	.13
98-99	Mon	17	3	5	8	-3	1	0	31	9.7	0	1	1	0	0	0	2	4	0	2	0	0	0	0	.47
3 Years		217	22	48	70	24	8	0	252	8.7	2	6	8	1	0	1	38	93	3	34	3	8	12	0	.32
Postseason																									
Year	Tm	GP	G	A	Pts	+/–	GW	OT	S	SPct	G	A	Pts	G	A	Pts	Num	PIM	Maj	Mnr	Fgt	Rgh	HHT	Hat	P/G
96-97	Phi	19	5	4	9	3	1	0	28	17.9	1	0	1	0	0	0	6	12	0	6	0	1	3	0	.47
97-98	Phi	5	0	1	1	2	0	0	6	0.0	0	0	0	0	0	0	1	2	0	1	0	0	1	0	.20
2 Years		24	5	5	10	5	1	0	34	14.7	1	0	1	0	0	0	7	14	0	7	0	1	4	0	.42

Andrei Zyuzin

Pos: D **Shoots:** L **Ht:** 6'1" **Wt:** 195 **Born:** 1/21/78—Ufa, USSR **Age:** 21

Overall											Power Play			Shorthand			Penalty							Misc	
Year	Tm	GP	G	A	Pts	+/–	GW	GT	S	SPct	G	A	Pts	G	A	Pts	Num	PIM	Maj	Mnr	Fgt	Rgh	HHT	Hat	P/G
97-98	SJ	56	6	7	13	8	2	0	72	8.3	2	2	4	0	0	0	33	66	0	33	0	4	16	0	.23
98-99	SJ	25	3	1	4	5	0	0	44	6.8	2	0	2	0	0	0	12	38	2	9	1	1	3	0	.16
2 Years		81	9	8	17	13	2	0	116	7.8	4	2	6	0	0	0	45	104	2	42	1	5	19	0	.21
Postseason																									
Year	Tm	GP	G	A	Pts	+/–	GW	OT	S	SPct	G	A	Pts	G	A	Pts	Num	PIM	Maj	Mnr	Fgt	Rgh	HHT	Hat	P/G
97-98	SJ	6	1	0	1	-2	1	1	6	16.7	0	0	0	0	0	0	3	14	0	2	0	0	1	0	.17

Skater Profiles

The following section provides statistical breakdowns for skaters who played in at least 10 games *and* scored at least 10 points in 1998-99.

For definitions of statistical categories, please consult the Glossary.

Greg Adams

Phoenix Coyotes — Left Wing

1998-99 Season

	GP	G	A	Pts	+/–	PIM	PP	SH	S	SPct	P/G
Overall	75	19	24	43	-1	26	5	0	176	10.8	.57
Home	40	12	14	26	0	22	3	0	106	11.3	.65
Away	35	7	10	17	-1	4	2	0	70	10.0	.49
vs. Division	24	5	6	11	-5	10	2	0	54	9.3	.46
vs. Conference	55	14	19	33	0	18	4	0	126	11.1	.60
vs. Playoff	43	7	14	21	-6	18	2	0	96	7.3	.49
vs. Non-Playoff	32	12	10	22	5	8	3	0	80	15.0	.69
Pre All-Star	42	10	12	22	0	14	3	0	92	10.9	.52
Post All-Star	33	9	12	21	-1	12	2	0	84	10.7	.64
Day	5	1	6	7	3	0	1	0	12	8.3	1.40
Night	70	18	18	36	-4	26	4	0	164	11.0	.51

	GP	G	A	Pts	+/–	PIM	PP	SH	S	SPct	P/G
National TV	14	4	2	6	5	12	0	0	31	12.9	.43
0 Days Rest	13	3	3	6	-4	6	1	0	33	9.1	.46
1 Days Rest	35	9	13	22	4	12	2	0	78	11.5	.63
2 Days Rest	15	5	5	10	1	6	2	0	37	13.5	.67
3+ Days Rest	12	2	3	5	-2	2	0	0	28	7.1	.42

	G	A	Pts	PIM
1st Period	7	6	13	6
2nd Period	3	13	16	14
3rd Period	9	5	14	6
Overtime	0	0	0	0
Last 5 Min	4	1	5	10

	G	A	Pts	PIM
Winning	8	9	17	10
Losing	3	7	10	14
Tied	8	8	16	2
Clutch	3	2	5	4
Blowouts	0	0	0	10

Daniel Alfredsson

Ottawa Senators — Right Wing

1998-99 Season

	GP	G	A	Pts	+/–	PIM	PP	SH	S	SPct	P/G
Overall	58	11	22	33	8	14	3	0	163	6.7	.57
Home	31	5	13	18	7	12	3	0	87	5.7	.58
Away	27	6	9	15	1	2	0	0	76	7.9	.56
vs. Division	14	3	4	7	3	0	1	0	38	7.9	.50
vs. Conference	45	9	14	23	6	6	3	0	121	7.4	.51
vs. Playoff	33	7	13	20	3	6	2	0	96	7.3	.61
vs. Non-Playoff	25	4	9	13	5	8	1	0	67	6.0	.52
Pre All-Star	31	6	9	15	4	8	2	0	97	6.2	.48
Post All-Star	27	5	13	18	4	6	1	0	66	7.6	.67
Day	3	1	3	4	-1	0	0	0	11	9.1	1.33
Night	55	10	19	29	9	14	3	0	152	6.6	.53

	GP	G	A	Pts	+/–	PIM	PP	SH	S	SPct	P/G
National TV	6	2	2	4	2	2	0	0	22	9.1	.67
0 Days Rest	6	3	2	5	4	2	2	0	15	20.0	.83
1 Days Rest	32	5	13	18	3	8	1	0	93	5.4	.56
2 Days Rest	13	3	4	7	2	2	0	0	38	7.9	.54
3+ Days Rest	7	0	3	3	-1	2	0	0	17	0.0	.43

	G	A	Pts	PIM
1st Period	2	9	11	2
2nd Period	4	9	13	6
3rd Period	5	4	9	6
Overtime	0	0	0	0
Last 5 Min	2	6	8	10

	G	A	Pts	PIM
Winning	6	8	14	8
Losing	0	10	10	0
Tied	5	4	9	6
Clutch	1	0	1	4
Blowouts	0	2	2	4

Jason Allison

Boston Bruins — Center

1998-99 Season

	GP	G	A	Pts	+/–	PIM	PP	SH	S	SPct	P/G
Overall	82	23	53	76	5	68	5	1	158	14.6	.93
Home	41	14	25	39	10	44	1	1	87	16.1	.95
Away	41	9	28	37	-5	24	4	0	71	12.7	.90
vs. Division	20	6	13	19	-1	8	2	1	40	15.0	.95
vs. Conference	58	18	39	57	2	45	3	1	114	15.8	.98
vs. Playoff	46	10	27	37	-1	42	1	0	77	13.0	.80
vs. Non-Playoff	36	13	26	39	6	26	4	1	81	16.0	1.08
Pre All-Star	43	9	29	38	-3	24	2	1	91	9.9	.88
Post All-Star	39	14	24	38	8	44	3	0	67	20.9	.97
Day	16	2	12	14	1	27	0	1	24	8.3	.88
Night	66	21	41	62	4	41	5	0	134	15.7	.94

	GP	G	A	Pts	+/–	PIM	PP	SH	S	SPct	P/G
National TV	10	2	10	12	1	6	0	0	9	22.2	1.20
0 Days Rest	17	2	9	11	-7	8	0	0	26	7.7	.65
1 Days Rest	39	13	24	37	6	35	1	1	80	16.3	.95
2 Days Rest	13	3	12	15	-1	13	2	0	26	11.5	1.15
3+ Days Rest	13	5	8	13	7	12	2	0	26	19.2	1.00

	G	A	Pts	PIM
1st Period	6	15	21	18
2nd Period	8	20	28	23
3rd Period	8	18	26	27
Overtime	1	0	1	0
Last 5 Min	11	14	25	29

	G	A	Pts	PIM
Winning	9	19	28	44
Losing	7	14	21	16
Tied	7	20	27	8
Clutch	4	4	8	2
Blowouts	2	1	3	6

Tony Amonte

Chicago Blackhawks — Right Wing

1998-99 Season

	GP	G	A	Pts	+/–	PIM	PP	SH	S	SPct	P/G
Overall	82	44	31	75	0	60	14	3	256	17.2	.91
Home	41	24	15	39	12	30	7	1	137	17.5	.95
Away	41	20	16	36	-12	30	7	2	119	16.8	.88
vs. Division	18	11	6	17	1	20	2	1	48	22.9	.94
vs. Conference	54	30	20	50	-2	32	10	3	165	18.2	.93
vs. Playoff	52	24	16	40	-5	40	7	2	151	15.9	.77
vs. Non-Playoff	30	20	15	35	5	20	7	1	105	19.0	1.17
Pre All-Star	45	24	15	39	-8	38	10	1	144	16.7	.87
Post All-Star	37	20	16	36	8	22	4	2	112	17.9	.97
Day	10	7	3	10	4	6	1	2	30	23.3	1.00
Night	72	37	28	65	-4	54	13	1	226	16.4	.90

	GP	G	A	Pts	+/–	PIM	PP	SH	S	SPct	P/G
National TV	17	11	7	18	5	12	4	1	55	20.0	1.06
0 Days Rest	14	8	8	16	3	14	3	1	44	18.2	1.14
1 Days Rest	42	17	13	30	-15	36	5	1	120	14.2	.71
2 Days Rest	14	11	4	15	9	6	1	1	54	20.4	1.07
3+ Days Rest	12	8	6	14	3	4	5	0	38	21.1	1.17

	G	A	Pts	PIM
1st Period	12	12	24	12
2nd Period	14	7	21	32
3rd Period	17	12	29	16
Overtime	1	0	1	0
Last 5 Min	19	10	29	22

	G	A	Pts	PIM
Winning	11	4	15	12
Losing	16	14	30	36
Tied	17	13	30	12
Clutch	9	3	12	6
Blowouts	2	2	4	8

Dave Andreychuk

New Jersey Devils — Left Wing

1998-99 Season

	GP	G	A	Pts	+/–	PIM	PP	SH	S	SPct	P/G
Overall	52	15	13	28	1	20	4	0	110	13.6	.54
Home	22	6	8	14	0	6	3	0	41	14.6	.64
Away	30	9	5	14	1	14	1	0	69	13.0	.47
vs. Division	17	6	5	11	2	6	0	0	41	14.6	.65
vs. Conference	39	13	9	22	-1	16	4	0	83	15.7	.56
vs. Playoff	28	9	7	16	-1	8	2	0	57	15.8	.57
vs. Non-Playoff	24	6	6	12	2	12	2	0	53	11.3	.50
Pre All-Star	29	11	11	22	1	16	3	0	71	15.5	.76
Post All-Star	23	4	2	6	0	4	1	0	39	10.3	.26
Day	6	3	0	3	1	0	0	0	17	17.6	.50
Night	46	12	13	25	0	20	4	0	93	12.9	.54

	GP	G	A	Pts	+/–	PIM	PP	SH	S	SPct	P/G
National TV	5	0	1	1	-2	0	0	0	5	0.0	.20
0 Days Rest	6	2	1	3	0	0	0	0	11	18.2	.50
1 Days Rest	21	6	6	12	1	14	4	0	41	14.6	.57
2 Days Rest	14	6	2	8	-1	4	0	0	32	18.8	.57
3+ Days Rest	11	1	4	5	1	2	0	0	26	3.8	.45

	G	A	Pts	PIM		G	A	Pts	PIM
1st Period	4	6	10	2	Winning	9	3	12	10
2nd Period	5	4	9	12	Losing	2	2	4	8
3rd Period	5	3	8	6	Tied	4	8	12	2
Overtime	1	0	1	0	Clutch	5	1	6	0
Last 5 Min	4	2	6	4	Blowouts	0	0	0	0

Jason Arnott

New Jersey Devils — Center

1998-99 Season

	GP	G	A	Pts	+/–	PIM	PP	SH	S	SPct	P/G
Overall	74	27	27	54	10	79	8	0	200	13.5	.73
Home	38	14	15	29	-3	45	5	0	98	14.3	.76
Away	36	13	12	25	13	34	3	0	102	12.7	.69
vs. Division	20	11	8	19	5	22	4	0	62	17.7	.95
vs. Conference	54	21	20	41	14	67	7	0	149	14.1	.76
vs. Playoff	43	19	17	36	2	46	6	0	111	17.1	.84
vs. Non-Playoff	31	8	10	18	8	33	2	0	89	9.0	.58
Pre All-Star	39	10	9	19	-4	37	5	0	96	10.4	.49
Post All-Star	35	17	18	35	14	42	3	0	104	16.3	1.00
Day	11	4	3	7	3	6	0	0	33	12.1	.64
Night	63	23	24	47	7	73	8	0	167	13.8	.75

	GP	G	A	Pts	+/–	PIM	PP	SH	S	SPct	P/G
National TV	6	1	3	4	-2	14	0	0	18	5.6	.67
0 Days Rest	15	2	7	9	-1	26	1	0	38	5.3	.60
1 Days Rest	29	12	12	24	4	30	5	0	78	15.4	.83
2 Days Rest	17	7	4	11	6	15	2	0	48	14.6	.65
3+ Days Rest	13	6	4	10	1	8	0	0	36	16.7	.77

	G	A	Pts	PIM		G	A	Pts	PIM
1st Period	8	10	18	30	Winning	10	11	21	39
2nd Period	8	7	15	18	Losing	7	7	14	24
3rd Period	11	10	21	29	Tied	10	9	19	16
Overtime	0	0	0	2	Clutch	2	4	6	2
Last 5 Min	5	10	15	25	Blowouts	0	2	2	2

Magnus Arvedson

Ottawa Senators — Left Wing

1998-99 Season

	GP	G	A	Pts	+/–	PIM	PP	SH	S	SPct	P/G
Overall	80	21	26	47	33	50	0	4	136	15.4	.59
Home	40	11	14	25	14	28	0	2	73	15.1	.63
Away	40	10	12	22	19	22	0	2	63	15.9	.55
vs. Division	19	3	3	6	5	6	0	0	32	9.4	.32
vs. Conference	56	14	23	37	29	36	0	3	94	14.9	.66
vs. Playoff	46	8	10	18	9	24	0	2	82	9.8	.39
vs. Non-Playoff	34	13	16	29	24	26	0	2	54	24.1	.85
Pre All-Star	43	10	11	21	15	26	0	2	82	12.2	.49
Post All-Star	37	11	15	26	18	24	0	2	54	20.4	.70
Day	3	1	1	2	1	0	0	0	4	25.0	.67
Night	77	20	25	45	32	50	0	4	132	15.2	.58

	GP	G	A	Pts	+/–	PIM	PP	SH	S	SPct	P/G
National TV	11	4	5	9	4	4	0	0	17	23.5	.82
0 Days Rest	12	4	8	12	14	0	0	1	21	19.0	1.00
1 Days Rest	42	9	13	22	8	24	0	1	61	14.8	.52
2 Days Rest	16	6	1	7	5	14	0	1	30	20.0	.44
3+ Days Rest	10	2	4	6	6	12	0	1	24	8.3	.60

	G	A	Pts	PIM		G	A	Pts	PIM
1st Period	4	4	8	18	Winning	10	13	23	26
2nd Period	7	10	17	18	Losing	4	7	11	16
3rd Period	10	12	22	14	Tied	7	6	13	8
Overtime	0	0	0	0	Clutch	3	5	8	2
Last 5 Min	8	10	18	14	Blowouts	0	3	3	4

Blair Atcheynum

St. Louis Blues — Right Wing

1998-99 Season

	GP	G	A	Pts	+/–	PIM	PP	SH	S	SPct	P/G
Overall	65	10	8	18	-8	18	2	0	93	10.8	.28
Home	30	5	6	11	-3	4	1	0	44	11.4	.37
Away	35	5	2	7	-5	14	1	0	49	10.2	.20
vs. Division	14	3	0	3	-6	12	0	0	26	11.5	.21
vs. Conference	46	9	5	14	-4	16	1	0	72	12.5	.30
vs. Playoff	42	5	4	9	-12	16	2	0	58	8.6	.21
vs. Non-Playoff	23	5	4	9	4	2	0	0	35	14.3	.39
Pre All-Star	29	5	4	9	-3	10	1	0	35	14.3	.31
Post All-Star	36	5	4	9	-5	8	1	0	58	8.6	.25
Day	11	2	1	3	-2	4	0	0	19	10.5	.27
Night	54	8	7	15	-6	14	2	0	74	10.8	.28

	GP	G	A	Pts	+/–	PIM	PP	SH	S	SPct	P/G
National TV	5	2	0	2	0	2	0	0	9	22.2	.40
0 Days Rest	13	3	2	5	0	0	0	0	22	13.6	.38
1 Days Rest	25	1	3	4	-6	10	1	0	36	2.8	.16
2 Days Rest	14	5	2	7	2	2	1	0	16	31.3	.50
3+ Days Rest	13	1	1	2	-4	6	0	0	19	5.3	.15

	G	A	Pts	PIM		G	A	Pts	PIM
1st Period	2	4	6	2	Winning	4	1	5	2
2nd Period	2	3	5	2	Losing	4	3	7	12
3rd Period	6	1	7	12	Tied	2	4	6	4
Overtime	0	0	0	2	Clutch	1	0	1	2
Last 5 Min	1	2	3	4	Blowouts	0	1	1	0

Adrian Aucoin

Vancouver Canucks — Defense

1998-99 Season

	GP	G	A	Pts	+/–	PIM	PP	SH	S	SPct	P/G
Overall	82	23	11	34	-14	77	18	2	174	13.2	.41
Home	41	9	5	14	-6	40	7	0	78	11.5	.34
Away	41	14	6	20	-8	37	11	2	96	14.6	.49
vs. Division	18	7	0	7	-2	12	6	1	33	21.2	.39
vs. Conference	55	14	7	21	-12	43	11	1	108	13.0	.38
vs. Playoff	53	12	7	19	-10	55	10	1	106	11.3	.36
vs. Non-Playoff	29	11	4	15	-4	22	8	1	68	16.2	.52
Pre All-Star	45	11	8	19	0	52	8	1	91	12.1	.42
Post All-Star	37	12	3	15	-14	25	10	1	83	14.5	.41
Day	3	0	1	1	-3	7	0	0	13	0.0	.33
Night	79	23	10	33	-11	70	18	2	161	14.3	.42

	GP	G	A	Pts	+/–	PIM	PP	SH	S	SPct	P/G
National TV	20	8	3	11	-6	16	7	0	48	16.7	.55
0 Days Rest	13	6	3	9	2	16	5	0	29	20.7	.69
1 Days Rest	46	10	5	15	-15	45	8	1	90	11.1	.33
2 Days Rest	16	5	2	7	-2	14	4	1	37	13.5	.44
3+ Days Rest	7	2	1	3	1	2	1	0	18	11.1	.43

	G	A	Pts	PIM		G	A	Pts	PIM
1st Period	4	2	6	31	Winning	5	3	8	24
2nd Period	11	5	16	26	Losing	11	6	17	45
3rd Period	8	4	12	20	Tied	7	2	9	8
Overtime	0	0	0	0	Clutch	1	0	1	6
Last 5 Min	8	2	10	27	Blowouts	2	0	2	19

Donald Audette

Los Angeles Kings — Right Wing

1998-99 Season

	GP	G	A	Pts	+/–	PIM	PP	SH	S	SPct	P/G
Overall	49	18	18	36	7	51	6	0	152	11.8	.73
Home	25	10	14	24	1	31	4	0	73	13.7	.96
Away	24	8	4	12	6	20	2	0	79	10.1	.50
vs. Division	17	2	6	8	-1	6	1	0	48	4.2	.47
vs. Conference	38	12	16	28	0	41	5	0	123	9.8	.74
vs. Playoff	37	10	11	21	0	33	3	0	119	8.4	.57
vs. Non-Playoff	12	8	7	15	7	18	3	0	33	24.2	1.25
Pre All-Star	14	4	7	11	3	23	2	0	42	9.5	.79
Post All-Star	35	14	11	25	4	28	4	0	110	12.7	.71
Day	2	0	0	0	0	2	0	0	8	0.0	.00
Night	47	18	18	36	7	49	6	0	144	12.5	.77

	GP	G	A	Pts	+/–	PIM	PP	SH	S	SPct	P/G
National TV	11	1	3	4	1	27	1	0	33	3.0	.36
0 Days Rest	6	3	3	6	1	4	0	0	18	16.7	1.00
1 Days Rest	23	7	8	15	5	29	2	0	61	11.5	.65
2 Days Rest	13	6	6	12	2	14	3	0	52	11.5	.92
3+ Days Rest	7	2	1	3	-1	4	1	0	21	9.5	.43

	G	A	Pts	PIM		G	A	Pts	PIM
1st Period	5	7	12	8	Winning	4	4	8	20
2nd Period	5	5	10	12	Losing	6	6	12	16
3rd Period	8	4	12	31	Tied	8	8	16	15
Overtime	0	2	2	0	Clutch	2	4	6	8
Last 5 Min	6	7	13	10	Blowouts	0	0	0	0

Per Axelsson

Boston Bruins — Left Wing

1998-99 Season

	GP	G	A	Pts	+/–	PIM	PP	SH	S	SPct	P/G
Overall	77	7	10	17	-14	18	0	0	146	4.8	.22
Home	38	5	6	11	-4	12	0	0	82	6.1	.29
Away	39	2	4	6	-10	6	0	0	64	3.1	.15
vs. Division	17	2	3	5	-5	6	0	0	33	6.1	.29
vs. Conference	53	4	3	7	-14	14	0	0	107	3.7	.13
vs. Playoff	42	5	5	10	-10	10	0	0	78	6.4	.24
vs. Non-Playoff	35	2	5	7	-4	8	0	0	68	2.9	.20
Pre All-Star	39	5	6	11	-3	6	0	0	65	7.7	.28
Post All-Star	38	2	4	6	-11	12	0	0	81	2.5	.16
Day	14	2	1	3	3	4	0	0	26	7.7	.21
Night	63	5	9	14	-17	14	0	0	120	4.2	.22

	GP	G	A	Pts	+/–	PIM	PP	SH	S	SPct	P/G
National TV	10	0	0	0	-4	2	0	0	17	0.0	.00
0 Days Rest	14	1	1	2	-5	2	0	0	19	5.3	.14
1 Days Rest	35	4	5	9	0	10	0	0	78	5.1	.26
2 Days Rest	15	1	2	3	-3	2	0	0	27	3.7	.20
3+ Days Rest	13	1	2	3	-6	4	0	0	22	4.5	.23

	G	A	Pts	PIM		G	A	Pts	PIM
1st Period	1	4	5	2	Winning	3	2	5	8
2nd Period	1	5	6	14	Losing	1	3	4	4
3rd Period	5	1	6	2	Tied	3	5	8	6
Overtime	0	0	0	0	Clutch	0	1	1	0
Last 5 Min	0	1	1	4	Blowouts	1	0	1	0

Matthew Barnaby

Pittsburgh Penguins — Right Wing

1998-99 Season

	GP	G	A	Pts	+/–	PIM	PP	SH	S	SPct	P/G
Overall	62	6	16	22	-12	177	1	0	79	7.6	.35
Home	30	3	8	11	-9	110	0	0	47	6.4	.37
Away	32	3	8	11	-3	67	1	0	32	9.4	.34
vs. Division	17	3	4	7	0	40	1	0	24	12.5	.41
vs. Conference	42	6	14	20	-4	102	1	0	60	10.0	.48
vs. Playoff	37	4	9	13	-11	94	1	0	42	9.5	.35
vs. Non-Playoff	25	2	7	9	-1	83	0	0	37	5.4	.36
Pre All-Star	36	4	14	18	4	106	0	0	49	8.2	.50
Post All-Star	26	2	2	4	-16	71	1	0	30	6.7	.15
Day	10	1	1	2	-3	17	0	0	18	5.6	.20
Night	52	5	15	20	-9	160	1	0	61	8.2	.38

	GP	G	A	Pts	+/–	PIM	PP	SH	S	SPct	P/G
National TV	13	0	2	2	-6	22	0	0	14	0.0	.15
0 Days Rest	15	1	5	6	1	46	0	0	19	5.3	.40
1 Days Rest	20	3	4	7	-7	66	1	0	32	9.4	.35
2 Days Rest	14	1	3	4	-4	59	0	0	15	6.7	.29
3+ Days Rest	13	1	4	5	-2	6	0	0	13	7.7	.38

	G	A	Pts	PIM		G	A	Pts	PIM
1st Period	4	5	9	81	Winning	3	8	11	90
2nd Period	2	4	6	49	Losing	0	4	4	66
3rd Period	0	7	7	45	Tied	3	4	7	21
Overtime	0	0	0	2	Clutch	0	0	0	2
Last 5 Min	2	6	8	54	Blowouts	0	2	2	23

Stu Barnes

Buffalo Sabres — Center

1998-99 Season

	GP	G	A	Pts	+/–	PIM	PP	SH	S	SPct	P/G
Overall	81	20	16	36	-11	30	13	0	180	11.1	.44
Home	40	8	9	17	-9	10	6	0	100	8.0	.43
Away	41	12	7	19	-2	20	7	0	80	15.0	.46
vs. Division	17	2	2	4	-7	12	0	0	32	6.3	.24
vs. Conference	59	13	11	24	-4	20	8	0	139	9.4	.41
vs. Playoff	43	7	6	13	-3	20	4	0	91	7.7	.30
vs. Non-Playoff	38	13	10	23	-8	10	9	0	89	14.6	.61
Pre All-Star	41	15	10	25	-7	14	10	0	95	15.8	.61
Post All-Star	40	5	6	11	-4	16	3	0	85	5.9	.28
Day	9	1	1	2	-3	0	1	0	12	8.3	.22
Night	72	19	15	34	-8	30	12	0	168	11.3	.47

	GP	G	A	Pts	+/–	PIM	PP	SH	S	SPct	P/G
National TV	16	4	2	6	-9	2	4	0	30	13.3	.38
0 Days Rest	17	5	1	6	-4	10	4	0	28	17.9	.35
1 Days Rest	30	5	4	9	-2	8	2	0	77	6.5	.30
2 Days Rest	22	4	8	12	-4	8	3	0	43	9.3	.55
3+ Days Rest	12	6	3	9	-1	4	4	0	32	18.8	.75

	G	A	Pts	PIM		G	A	Pts	PIM
1st Period	4	4	8	6	Winning	7	7	14	12
2nd Period	9	9	18	14	Losing	7	4	11	10
3rd Period	7	2	9	10	Tied	6	5	11	8
Overtime	0	1	1	0	Clutch	0	3	3	4
Last 5 Min	5	5	10	14	Blowouts	0	0	0	2

Lubos Bartecko

St. Louis Blues — Left Wing

1998-99 Season

	GP	G	A	Pts	+/–	PIM	PP	SH	S	SPct	P/G
Overall	32	5	11	16	4	6	0	0	37	13.5	.50
Home	18	3	6	9	5	2	0	0	23	13.0	.50
Away	14	2	5	7	-1	4	0	0	14	14.3	.50
vs. Division	7	1	2	3	-3	0	0	0	6	16.7	.43
vs. Conference	20	3	6	9	1	4	0	0	21	14.3	.45
vs. Playoff	16	3	9	12	5	4	0	0	21	14.3	.75
vs. Non-Playoff	16	2	2	4	-1	2	0	0	16	12.5	.25
Pre All-Star	13	2	5	7	-2	4	0	0	13	15.4	.54
Post All-Star	19	3	6	9	6	2	0	0	24	12.5	.47
Day	7	2	3	5	4	2	0	0	6	33.3	.71
Night	25	3	8	11	0	4	0	0	31	9.7	.44

	GP	G	A	Pts	+/–	PIM	PP	SH	S	SPct	P/G
National TV	8	0	3	3	-1	2	0	0	4	0.0	.38
0 Days Rest	4	0	4	4	1	0	0	0	1	0.0	1.00
1 Days Rest	16	4	6	10	6	2	0	0	20	20.0	.63
2 Days Rest	5	0	0	0	-1	0	0	0	8	0.0	.00
3+ Days Rest	7	1	1	2	-2	4	0	0	8	12.5	.29

	G	A	Pts	PIM		G	A	Pts	PIM
1st Period	1	7	8	4	Winning	2	2	4	2
2nd Period	2	1	3	2	Losing	1	5	6	4
3rd Period	2	3	5	0	Tied	2	4	6	0
Overtime	0	0	0	0	Clutch	0	1	1	0
Last 5 Min	0	4	4	2	Blowouts	0	0	0	2

Bates Battaglia

Carolina Hurricanes — Left Wing

1998-99 Season

	GP	G	A	Pts	+/–	PIM	PP	SH	S	SPct	P/G
Overall	60	7	11	18	7	22	0	0	52	13.5	.30
Home	28	4	6	10	6	10	0	0	23	17.4	.36
Away	32	3	5	8	1	12	0	0	29	10.3	.25
vs. Division	14	1	3	4	-1	8	0	0	12	8.3	.29
vs. Conference	45	6	7	13	7	16	0	0	48	12.5	.29
vs. Playoff	29	3	2	5	0	12	0	0	25	12.0	.17
vs. Non-Playoff	31	4	9	13	7	10	0	0	27	14.8	.42
Pre All-Star	28	1	4	5	4	8	0	0	17	5.9	.18
Post All-Star	32	6	7	13	3	14	0	0	35	17.1	.41
Day	5	0	0	0	0	0	0	0	2	0.0	.00
Night	55	7	11	18	7	22	0	0	50	14.0	.33

	GP	G	A	Pts	+/–	PIM	PP	SH	S	SPct	P/G
National TV	1	0	1	1	1	2	0	0	1	0.0	1.00
0 Days Rest	13	2	5	7	2	6	0	0	20	10.0	.54
1 Days Rest	20	3	2	5	3	8	0	0	19	15.8	.25
2 Days Rest	13	2	1	3	5	4	0	0	6	33.3	.23
3+ Days Rest	14	0	3	3	-3	4	0	0	7	0.0	.21

	G	A	Pts	PIM		G	A	Pts	PIM
1st Period	3	3	6	10	Winning	3	2	5	6
2nd Period	1	5	6	10	Losing	3	5	8	6
3rd Period	3	3	6	2	Tied	1	4	5	10
Overtime	0	0	0	0	Clutch	1	1	2	2
Last 5 Min	2	1	3	4	Blowouts	0	0	0	0

Brian Bellows

Washington Capitals — Left Wing

1998-99 Season

	GP	G	A	Pts	+/–	PIM	PP	SH	S	SPct	P/G
Overall	76	17	19	36	-12	26	8	0	166	10.2	.47
Home	37	7	10	17	-12	8	4	0	85	8.2	.46
Away	39	10	9	19	0	18	4	0	81	12.3	.49
vs. Division	15	9	7	16	4	12	6	0	37	24.3	1.07
vs. Conference	52	13	17	30	-1	20	7	0	111	11.7	.58
vs. Playoff	45	9	9	18	-6	16	3	0	88	10.2	.40
vs. Non-Playoff	31	8	10	18	-6	10	5	0	78	10.3	.58
Pre All-Star	43	8	8	16	-2	14	3	0	95	8.4	.37
Post All-Star	33	9	11	20	-10	12	5	0	71	12.7	.61
Day	1	0	1	1	0	0	0	0	4	0.0	1.00
Night	75	17	18	35	-12	26	8	0	162	10.5	.47

	GP	G	A	Pts	+/–	PIM	PP	SH	S	SPct	P/G
National TV	11	1	6	7	2	2	0	0	23	4.3	.64
0 Days Rest	13	4	6	10	6	4	1	0	27	14.8	.77
1 Days Rest	33	8	9	17	-13	14	5	0	76	10.5	.52
2 Days Rest	13	1	1	2	-7	8	0	0	26	3.8	.15
3+ Days Rest	17	4	3	7	2	0	2	0	37	10.8	.41

	G	A	Pts	PIM		G	A	Pts	PIM
1st Period	1	6	7	10	Winning	4	6	10	10
2nd Period	9	5	14	6	Losing	8	8	16	10
3rd Period	6	8	14	10	Tied	5	5	10	6
Overtime	1	0	1	0	Clutch	2	3	5	4
Last 5 Min	4	4	8	12	Blowouts	1	1	2	2

Josef Beranek

Edmonton Oilers — Left Wing

1998-99 Season

	GP	G	A	Pts	+/–	PIM	PP	SH	S	SPct	P/G
Overall	66	19	30	49	6	23	7	0	160	11.9	.74
Home	35	11	14	25	4	14	3	0	93	11.8	.71
Away	31	8	16	24	2	9	4	0	67	11.9	.77
vs. Division	12	5	7	12	6	12	1	0	36	13.9	1.00
vs. Conference	43	14	20	34	2	19	6	0	112	12.5	.79
vs. Playoff	38	7	17	24	0	13	1	0	83	8.4	.63
vs. Non-Playoff	28	12	13	25	6	10	6	0	77	15.6	.89
Pre All-Star	39	14	19	33	5	10	6	0	87	16.1	.85
Post All-Star	27	5	11	16	1	13	1	0	73	6.8	.59
Day	4	3	3	6	2	0	0	0	8	37.5	1.50
Night	62	16	27	43	4	23	7	0	152	10.5	.69

	GP	G	A	Pts	+/–	PIM	PP	SH	S	SPct	P/G
National TV	9	1	4	5	0	0	0	0	19	5.3	.56
0 Days Rest	8	2	4	6	2	0	1	0	20	10.0	.75
1 Days Rest	32	11	15	26	9	21	5	0	80	13.8	.81
2 Days Rest	13	2	7	9	2	0	1	0	31	6.5	.69
3+ Days Rest	13	4	4	8	-7	2	0	0	29	13.8	.62

	G	A	Pts	PIM		G	A	Pts	PIM
1st Period	7	14	21	15	Winning	4	9	13	6
2nd Period	7	7	14	4	Losing	7	12	19	15
3rd Period	4	9	13	4	Tied	8	9	17	2
Overtime	1	0	1	0	Clutch	2	2	4	0
Last 5 Min	3	12	15	8	Blowouts	0	3	3	2

Bryan Berard

Toronto Maple Leafs — Defense

1998-99 Season

	GP	G	A	Pts	+/–	PIM	PP	SH	S	SPct	P/G
Overall	69	9	25	34	1	48	4	0	135	6.7	.49
Home	33	3	16	19	2	20	1	0	60	5.0	.58
Away	36	6	9	15	-1	28	3	0	75	8.0	.42
vs. Division	17	1	9	10	-3	16	1	0	32	3.1	.59
vs. Conference	52	5	17	22	-1	40	2	0	102	4.9	.42
vs. Playoff	41	5	18	23	-5	32	3	0	72	6.9	.56
vs. Non-Playoff	28	4	7	11	6	16	1	0	63	6.3	.39
Pre All-Star	35	5	15	20	-4	26	3	0	77	6.5	.57
Post All-Star	34	4	10	14	5	22	1	0	58	6.9	.41
Day	2	0	0	0	-1	0	0	0	4	0.0	.00
Night	67	9	25	34	2	48	4	0	131	6.9	.51

	GP	G	A	Pts	+/–	PIM	PP	SH	S	SPct	P/G
National TV	15	1	3	4	9	14	0	0	19	5.3	.27
0 Days Rest	13	0	4	4	-4	10	0	0	27	0.0	.31
1 Days Rest	31	5	11	16	6	18	1	0	54	9.3	.52
2 Days Rest	13	2	2	4	0	6	2	0	28	7.1	.31
3+ Days Rest	12	2	8	10	-1	14	1	0	26	7.7	.83

	G	A	Pts	PIM		G	A	Pts	PIM
1st Period	1	5	6	22	Winning	1	8	9	14
2nd Period	3	11	14	14	Losing	2	13	15	28
3rd Period	3	9	12	10	Tied	6	4	10	6
Overtime	2	0	2	2	Clutch	3	1	4	4
Last 5 Min	3	6	9	16	Blowouts	0	2	2	2

Drake Berehowsky

Nashville Predators — Defense

1998-99 Season

	GP	G	A	Pts	+/–	PIM	PP	SH	S	SPct	P/G
Overall	74	2	15	17	-9	140	0	0	79	2.5	.23
Home	36	2	7	9	-4	69	0	0	46	4.3	.25
Away	38	0	8	8	-5	71	0	0	33	0.0	.21
vs. Division	15	0	2	2	-4	17	0	0	14	0.0	.13
vs. Conference	49	1	10	11	-3	76	0	0	47	2.1	.22
vs. Playoff	46	1	9	10	-16	80	0	0	39	2.6	.22
vs. Non-Playoff	28	1	6	7	7	60	0	0	40	2.5	.25
Pre All-Star	39	0	7	7	-3	97	0	0	45	0.0	.18
Post All-Star	35	2	8	10	-6	43	0	0	34	5.9	.29
Day	7	0	0	0	-5	6	0	0	5	0.0	.00
Night	67	2	15	17	-4	134	0	0	74	2.7	.25

	GP	G	A	Pts	+/–	PIM	PP	SH	S	SPct	P/G
National TV	2	0	1	1	1	17	0	0	2	0.0	.50
0 Days Rest	11	0	2	2	-4	8	0	0	14	0.0	.18
1 Days Rest	36	2	9	11	1	89	0	0	44	4.5	.31
2 Days Rest	14	0	2	2	-2	16	0	0	10	0.0	.14
3+ Days Rest	13	0	2	2	-4	27	0	0	11	0.0	.15

	G	A	Pts	PIM		G	A	Pts	PIM
1st Period	1	3	4	55	Winning	0	4	4	69
2nd Period	1	7	8	47	Losing	1	4	5	63
3rd Period	0	5	5	38	Tied	1	7	8	8
Overtime	0	0	0	0	Clutch	0	2	2	4
Last 5 Min	1	6	7	52	Blowouts	0	1	1	8

Sergei Berezin

Toronto Maple Leafs — Right Wing

1998-99 Season

	GP	G	A	Pts	+/–	PIM	PP	SH	S	SPct	P/G
Overall	76	37	22	59	16	12	9	1	263	14.1	.78
Home	37	18	9	27	5	8	5	0	127	14.2	.73
Away	39	19	13	32	11	4	4	1	136	14.0	.82
vs. Division	17	4	4	8	6	6	0	1	59	6.8	.47
vs. Conference	51	23	12	35	10	10	4	1	180	12.8	.69
vs. Playoff	42	20	14	34	5	4	6	1	148	13.5	.81
vs. Non-Playoff	34	17	8	25	11	8	3	0	115	14.8	.74
Pre All-Star	40	15	12	27	10	4	5	0	125	12.0	.68
Post All-Star	36	22	10	32	6	8	4	1	138	15.9	.89
Day	1	0	2	2	1	0	0	0	1	0.0	2.00
Night	75	37	20	57	15	12	9	1	262	14.1	.76

	GP	G	A	Pts	+/–	PIM	PP	SH	S	SPct	P/G
National TV	25	10	3	13	7	8	2	0	93	10.8	.52
0 Days Rest	16	9	1	10	4	2	2	1	57	15.8	.63
1 Days Rest	31	13	12	25	10	2	1	0	100	13.0	.81
2 Days Rest	14	5	3	8	0	4	2	0	48	10.4	.57
3+ Days Rest	15	10	6	16	2	4	4	0	58	17.2	1.07

	G	A	Pts	PIM		G	A	Pts	PIM
1st Period	20	3	23	6	Winning	16	9	25	8
2nd Period	11	12	23	2	Losing	10	8	18	4
3rd Period	6	7	13	4	Tied	11	5	16	0
Overtime	0	0	0	0	Clutch	2	1	3	0
Last 5 Min	14	3	17	2	Blowouts	1	1	2	0

Todd Bertuzzi

Vancouver Canucks — Center

1998-99 Season

	GP	G	A	Pts	+/-	PIM	PP	SH	S	SPct	P/G
Overall	32	8	8	16	-6	44	1	0	72	11.1	.50
Home	16	2	2	4	-4	26	0	0	24	8.3	.25
Away	16	6	6	12	-2	18	1	0	48	12.5	.75
vs. Division	4	0	1	1	-2	8	0	0	6	0.0	.25
vs. Conference	16	1	5	6	-7	30	0	0	30	3.3	.38
vs. Playoff	19	4	4	8	-6	32	0	0	34	11.8	.42
vs. Non-Playoff	13	4	4	8	0	12	1	0	38	10.5	.62
Pre All-Star	14	4	4	8	6	18	1	0	29	13.8	.57
Post All-Star	18	4	4	8	-12	26	0	0	43	9.3	.44
Day	3	0	2	2	-3	8	0	0	10	0.0	.67
Night	29	8	6	14	-3	36	1	0	62	12.9	.48

	GP	G	A	Pts	+/-	PIM	PP	SH	S	SPct	P/G
National TV	7	3	2	5	-2	16	0	0	16	18.8	.71
0 Days Rest	4	1	1	2	0	12	0	0	11	9.1	.50
1 Days Rest	18	6	3	9	-2	10	1	0	39	15.4	.50
2 Days Rest	7	1	3	4	-3	10	0	0	18	5.6	.57
3+ Days Rest	3	0	1	1	-1	12	0	0	4	0.0	.33

	G	A	Pts	PIM		G	A	Pts	PIM
1st Period	1	0	1	16	Winning	2	1	3	6
2nd Period	2	3	5	14	Losing	3	4	7	28
3rd Period	5	5	10	12	Tied	3	3	6	10
Overtime	0	0	0	2	Clutch	2	1	3	8
Last 5 Min	0	1	1	18	Blowouts	1	1	2	12

James Black

Washington Capitals — Center

1998-99 Season

	GP	G	A	Pts	+/-	PIM	PP	SH	S	SPct	P/G
Overall	75	16	14	30	5	14	1	1	135	11.9	.40
Home	37	8	6	14	8	4	0	0	73	11.0	.38
Away	38	8	8	16	-3	10	1	1	62	12.9	.42
vs. Division	12	5	3	8	5	2	1	0	26	19.2	.67
vs. Conference	53	12	12	24	13	10	1	1	97	12.4	.45
vs. Playoff	45	7	8	15	0	8	0	0	63	11.1	.33
vs. Non-Playoff	30	9	6	15	5	6	1	1	72	12.5	.50
Pre All-Star	37	5	9	14	3	2	0	0	56	8.9	.38
Post All-Star	38	11	5	16	2	12	1	1	79	13.9	.42
Day	3	2	1	3	1	0	0	0	8	25.0	1.00
Night	72	14	13	27	4	14	1	1	127	11.0	.38

	GP	G	A	Pts	+/-	PIM	PP	SH	S	SPct	P/G
National TV	10	3	2	5	2	2	0	1	17	17.6	.50
0 Days Rest	13	2	4	6	2	2	0	0	13	15.4	.46
1 Days Rest	38	10	8	18	1	8	1	0	78	12.8	.47
2 Days Rest	10	2	0	2	1	0	0	1	15	13.3	.20
3+ Days Rest	14	2	2	4	1	4	0	0	29	6.9	.29

	G	A	Pts	PIM		G	A	Pts	PIM
1st Period	3	4	7	2	Winning	11	3	14	2
2nd Period	7	5	12	8	Losing	3	7	10	10
3rd Period	6	5	11	4	Tied	2	4	6	2
Overtime	0	0	0	0	Clutch	2	1	3	0
Last 5 Min	5	4	9	4	Blowouts	3	0	3	0

Rob Blake

Los Angeles Kings — Defense

1998-99 Season

	GP	G	A	Pts	+/-	PIM	PP	SH	S	SPct	P/G
Overall	62	12	23	35	-7	128	5	1	216	5.6	.56
Home	32	5	14	19	-2	94	3	0	113	4.4	.59
Away	30	7	9	16	-5	34	2	1	103	6.8	.53
vs. Division	18	2	4	6	-6	45	1	0	60	3.3	.33
vs. Conference	44	7	13	20	-13	106	2	0	168	4.2	.45
vs. Playoff	45	9	14	23	-7	81	3	1	138	6.5	.51
vs. Non-Playoff	17	3	9	12	0	47	2	0	78	3.8	.71
Pre All-Star	27	3	12	15	1	53	1	1	88	3.4	.56
Post All-Star	35	9	11	20	-8	75	4	0	128	7.0	.57
Day	4	0	1	1	-4	0	0	0	7	0.0	.25
Night	58	12	22	34	-3	128	5	1	209	5.7	.59

	GP	G	A	Pts	+/-	PIM	PP	SH	S	SPct	P/G
National TV	14	3	2	5	-1	49	2	0	47	6.4	.36
0 Days Rest	7	2	1	3	-1	4	1	1	25	8.0	.43
1 Days Rest	31	8	13	21	0	74	4	0	99	8.1	.68
2 Days Rest	13	2	6	8	-3	14	0	0	50	4.0	.62
3+ Days Rest	11	0	3	3	-3	36	0	0	42	0.0	.27

	G	A	Pts	PIM		G	A	Pts	PIM
1st Period	4	9	13	35	Winning	5	10	15	73
2nd Period	6	6	12	33	Losing	2	5	7	49
3rd Period	2	7	9	60	Tied	5	8	13	6
Overtime	0	1	1	0	Clutch	0	2	2	2
Last 5 Min	0	8	8	26	Blowouts	0	0	0	14

Doug Bodger

Los Angeles Kings — Defense

1998-99 Season

	GP	G	A	Pts	+/-	PIM	PP	SH	S	SPct	P/G
Overall	65	3	11	14	1	34	0	0	67	4.5	.22
Home	31	3	6	9	-4	20	0	0	34	8.8	.29
Away	34	0	5	5	5	14	0	0	33	0.0	.15
vs. Division	19	1	2	3	-2	16	0	0	18	5.6	.16
vs. Conference	44	3	6	9	-3	24	0	0	51	5.9	.20
vs. Playoff	44	2	6	8	-6	24	0	0	43	4.7	.18
vs. Non-Playoff	21	1	5	6	7	10	0	0	24	4.2	.29
Pre All-Star	29	0	7	7	0	10	0	0	30	0.0	.24
Post All-Star	36	3	4	7	1	24	0	0	37	8.1	.19
Day	5	0	1	1	2	8	0	0	2	0.0	.20
Night	60	3	10	13	-1	26	0	0	65	4.6	.22

	GP	G	A	Pts	+/-	PIM	PP	SH	S	SPct	P/G
National TV	15	2	0	2	-1	14	0	0	18	11.1	.13
0 Days Rest	10	0	2	2	5	4	0	0	11	0.0	.20
1 Days Rest	30	1	5	6	-1	12	0	0	22	4.5	.20
2 Days Rest	14	2	2	4	1	14	0	0	23	8.7	.29
3+ Days Rest	11	0	2	2	-4	4	0	0	11	0.0	.18

	G	A	Pts	PIM		G	A	Pts	PIM
1st Period	1	6	7	10	Winning	1	2	3	10
2nd Period	1	1	2	16	Losing	2	3	5	22
3rd Period	1	4	5	8	Tied	0	6	6	2
Overtime	0	0	0	0	Clutch	0	1	1	4
Last 5 Min	2	2	4	4	Blowouts	0	0	0	6

Peter Bondra

Washington Capitals — Right Wing

1998-99 Season

	GP	G	A	Pts	+/-	PIM	PP	SH	S	SPct	P/G
Overall	66	31	24	55	-1	56	6	3	284	10.9	.83
Home	33	16	12	28	0	32	2	1	146	11.0	.85
Away	33	15	12	27	-1	24	4	2	138	10.9	.82
vs. Division	11	12	6	18	8	4	1	1	40	30.0	1.64
vs. Conference	47	27	21	48	5	38	4	3	202	13.4	1.02
vs. Playoff	39	16	15	31	-1	42	2	1	153	10.5	.79
vs. Non-Playoff	27	15	9	24	0	14	4	2	131	11.5	.89
Pre All-Star	42	15	10	25	-7	40	3	2	171	8.8	.60
Post All-Star	24	16	14	30	6	16	3	1	113	14.2	1.25
Day	3	0	1	1	-3	0	0	0	10	0.0	.33
Night	63	31	23	54	2	56	6	3	274	11.3	.86
National TV	9	5	6	11	1	16	0	0	44	11.4	1.22
0 Days Rest	11	6	2	8	-6	12	1	1	45	13.3	.73
1 Days Rest	33	18	12	30	3	24	4	1	139	12.9	.91
2 Days Rest	11	3	4	7	0	12	0	0	51	5.9	.64
3+ Days Rest	11	4	6	10	2	8	1	1	49	8.2	.91

	G	A	Pts	PIM		G	A	Pts	PIM
1st Period	6	9	15	22	Winning	13	9	22	34
2nd Period	14	8	22	26	Losing	10	6	16	22
3rd Period	11	7	18	8	Tied	8	9	17	0
Overtime	0	0	0	0	Clutch	4	1	5	4
Last 5 Min	8	5	13	22	Blowouts	4	2	6	2

Radek Bonk

Ottawa Senators — Center

1998-99 Season

	GP	G	A	Pts	+/-	PIM	PP	SH	S	SPct	P/G
Overall	81	16	16	32	15	48	0	1	110	14.5	.40
Home	41	9	12	21	11	20	0	1	59	15.3	.51
Away	40	7	4	11	4	28	0	0	51	13.7	.28
vs. Division	19	1	2	3	0	8	0	0	18	5.6	.16
vs. Conference	56	13	15	28	13	28	0	1	72	18.1	.50
vs. Playoff	46	7	5	12	3	24	0	0	67	10.4	.26
vs. Non-Playoff	35	9	11	20	12	24	0	1	43	20.9	.57
Pre All-Star	44	9	7	16	9	30	0	0	58	15.5	.36
Post All-Star	37	7	9	16	6	18	0	1	52	13.5	.43
Day	3	0	1	1	1	0	0	0	2	0.0	.33
Night	78	16	15	31	14	48	0	1	108	14.8	.40
National TV	11	2	3	5	2	4	0	1	13	15.4	.45
0 Days Rest	13	6	3	9	9	10	0	0	24	25.0	.69
1 Days Rest	42	6	10	16	2	30	0	0	54	11.1	.38
2 Days Rest	15	2	1	3	1	4	0	0	20	10.0	.20
3+ Days Rest	11	2	2	4	3	4	0	1	12	16.7	.36

	G	A	Pts	PIM		G	A	Pts	PIM
1st Period	5	2	7	14	Winning	9	10	19	28
2nd Period	6	7	13	24	Losing	1	2	3	10
3rd Period	5	7	12	10	Tied	6	4	10	10
Overtime	0	0	0	0	Clutch	3	3	6	2
Last 5 Min	6	4	10	12	Blowouts	1	1	2	10

Sebastien Bordeleau

Nashville Predators — Center

1998-99 Season

	GP	G	A	Pts	+/-	PIM	PP	SH	S	SPct	P/G
Overall	72	16	24	40	-14	26	1	2	168	9.5	.56
Home	36	10	10	20	-10	6	1	1	97	10.3	.56
Away	36	6	14	20	-4	20	0	1	71	8.5	.56
vs. Division	15	3	5	8	-7	10	0	1	26	11.5	.53
vs. Conference	49	13	19	32	-7	20	1	2	107	12.1	.65
vs. Playoff	45	7	14	21	-14	18	0	0	105	6.7	.47
vs. Non-Playoff	27	9	10	19	0	8	1	2	63	14.3	.70
Pre All-Star	38	6	10	16	-8	6	0	0	88	6.8	.42
Post All-Star	34	10	14	24	-6	20	1	2	80	12.5	.71
Day	7	4	0	4	-2	6	0	0	17	23.5	.57
Night	65	12	24	36	-12	20	1	2	151	7.9	.55
National TV	1	2	2	4	3	0	0	0	2	100.0	4.00
0 Days Rest	10	0	2	2	-7	6	0	0	21	0.0	.20
1 Days Rest	35	13	13	26	-2	4	1	2	88	14.8	.74
2 Days Rest	12	2	3	5	-3	12	0	0	26	7.7	.42
3+ Days Rest	15	1	6	7	-2	4	0	0	33	3.0	.47

	G	A	Pts	PIM		G	A	Pts	PIM
1st Period	2	6	8	18	Winning	7	5	12	6
2nd Period	7	8	15	2	Losing	6	11	17	20
3rd Period	6	10	16	6	Tied	3	8	11	0
Overtime	1	0	1	0	Clutch	4	4	8	0
Last 5 Min	6	9	15	10	Blowouts	2	1	3	2

Joel Bouchard

Nashville Predators — Defense

1998-99 Season

	GP	G	A	Pts	+/-	PIM	PP	SH	S	SPct	P/G
Overall	64	4	11	15	-10	60	0	0	78	5.1	.23
Home	32	2	8	10	-2	29	0	0	39	5.1	.31
Away	32	2	3	5	-8	31	0	0	39	5.1	.16
vs. Division	12	1	1	2	-9	13	0	0	15	6.7	.17
vs. Conference	41	3	9	12	-14	44	0	0	54	5.6	.29
vs. Playoff	39	1	6	7	-12	37	0	0	51	2.0	.18
vs. Non-Playoff	25	3	5	8	2	23	0	0	27	11.1	.32
Pre All-Star	27	2	4	6	-3	23	0	0	27	7.4	.22
Post All-Star	37	2	7	9	-7	37	0	0	51	3.9	.24
Day	6	0	0	0	0	4	0	0	5	0.0	.00
Night	58	4	11	15	-10	56	0	0	73	5.5	.26
National TV	1	0	0	0	-2	0	0	0	0	–	.00
0 Days Rest	11	1	0	1	-4	10	0	0	11	9.1	.09
1 Days Rest	30	2	4	6	-2	34	0	0	36	5.6	.20
2 Days Rest	11	0	4	4	1	2	0	0	13	0.0	.36
3+ Days Rest	12	1	3	4	-5	14	0	0	18	5.6	.33

	G	A	Pts	PIM		G	A	Pts	PIM
1st Period	1	5	6	20	Winning	0	1	1	21
2nd Period	1	4	5	26	Losing	4	5	9	22
3rd Period	2	2	4	14	Tied	0	5	5	17
Overtime	0	0	0	0	Clutch	0	2	2	6
Last 5 Min	0	3	3	16	Blowouts	0	0	0	6

Bob Boughner

Nashville Predators — Defense

1998-99 Season

	GP	G	A	Pts	+/–	PIM	PP	SH	S	SPct	P/G
Overall	79	3	10	13	-6	137	0	0	59	5.1	.16
Home	39	3	7	10	2	50	0	0	38	7.9	.26
Away	40	0	3	3	-8	87	0	0	21	0.0	.08
vs. Division	17	1	2	3	-8	29	0	0	15	6.7	.18
vs. Conference	52	1	7	8	-8	103	0	0	29	3.4	.15
vs. Playoff	49	1	5	6	-9	88	0	0	30	3.3	.12
vs. Non-Playoff	30	2	5	7	3	49	0	0	29	6.9	.23
Pre All-Star	42	1	5	6	-4	75	0	0	35	2.9	.14
Post All-Star	37	2	5	7	-2	62	0	0	24	8.3	.19
Day	8	0	2	2	1	11	0	0	4	0.0	.25
Night	71	3	8	11	-7	126	0	0	55	5.5	.15

	GP	G	A	Pts	+/–	PIM	PP	SH	S	SPct	P/G
National TV	2	0	1	1	-1	10	0	0	1	0.0	.50
0 Days Rest	13	1	0	1	1	29	0	0	9	11.1	.08
1 Days Rest	39	1	7	8	1	66	0	0	30	3.3	.21
2 Days Rest	13	1	1	2	-5	15	0	0	10	10.0	.15
3+ Days Rest	14	0	2	2	-3	27	0	0	10	0.0	.14

	G	A	Pts	PIM		G	A	Pts	PIM
1st Period	2	2	4	55	Winning	1	2	3	30
2nd Period	0	5	5	56	Losing	1	3	4	95
3rd Period	1	3	4	26	Tied	1	5	6	12
Overtime	0	0	0	0	Clutch	1	1	2	6
Last 5 Min	1	3	4	33	Blowouts	0	1	1	20

Ray Bourque

Boston Bruins — Defense

1998-99 Season

	GP	G	A	Pts	+/–	PIM	PP	SH	S	SPct	P/G
Overall	81	10	47	57	-7	34	8	0	262	3.8	.70
Home	41	5	23	28	2	18	3	0	144	3.5	.68
Away	40	5	24	29	-9	16	5	0	118	4.2	.73
vs. Division	19	2	12	14	1	6	1	0	55	3.6	.74
vs. Conference	57	5	31	36	-4	16	3	0	194	2.6	.63
vs. Playoff	45	5	16	21	-5	26	4	0	139	3.6	.47
vs. Non-Playoff	36	5	31	36	-2	8	4	0	123	4.1	1.00
Pre All-Star	42	4	24	28	4	22	3	0	138	2.9	.67
Post All-Star	39	6	23	29	-11	12	5	0	124	4.8	.74
Day	16	3	9	12	0	4	2	0	42	7.1	.75
Night	65	7	38	45	-7	30	6	0	220	3.2	.69

	GP	G	A	Pts	+/–	PIM	PP	SH	S	SPct	P/G
National TV	9	3	5	8	-4	6	3	0	33	9.1	.89
0 Days Rest	17	2	10	12	-14	14	2	0	53	3.8	.71
1 Days Rest	38	5	24	29	8	14	3	0	124	4.0	.76
2 Days Rest	13	3	8	11	0	4	3	0	36	8.3	.85
3+ Days Rest	13	0	5	5	-1	2	0	0	49	0.0	.38

	G	A	Pts	PIM		G	A	Pts	PIM
1st Period	4	13	17	6	Winning	1	18	19	16
2nd Period	2	16	18	10	Losing	3	12	15	10
3rd Period	4	17	21	18	Tied	6	17	23	8
Overtime	0	1	1	0	Clutch	1	6	7	0
Last 5 Min	1	19	20	8	Blowouts	0	3	3	0

Donald Brashear

Vancouver Canucks — Left Wing

1998-99 Season

	GP	G	A	Pts	+/–	PIM	PP	SH	S	SPct	P/G
Overall	82	8	10	18	-25	209	2	0	112	7.1	.22
Home	41	3	6	9	-12	102	0	0	39	7.7	.22
Away	41	5	4	9	-13	107	2	0	73	6.8	.22
vs. Division	18	2	0	2	0	63	1	0	23	8.7	.11
vs. Conference	55	7	6	13	-15	158	2	0	73	9.6	.24
vs. Playoff	53	5	6	11	-18	109	2	0	69	7.2	.21
vs. Non-Playoff	29	3	4	7	-7	100	0	0	43	7.0	.24
Pre All-Star	45	5	5	10	-11	123	0	0	65	7.7	.22
Post All-Star	37	3	5	8	-14	86	2	0	47	6.4	.22
Day	3	1	2	3	-3	2	1	0	7	14.3	1.00
Night	79	7	8	15	-22	207	1	0	105	6.7	.19

	GP	G	A	Pts	+/–	PIM	PP	SH	S	SPct	P/G
National TV	20	2	4	6	-9	51	1	0	28	7.1	.30
0 Days Rest	13	2	1	3	-1	36	1	0	13	15.4	.23
1 Days Rest	46	3	6	9	-20	131	1	0	64	4.7	.20
2 Days Rest	16	2	2	4	-3	21	0	0	29	6.9	.25
3+ Days Rest	7	1	1	2	-1	21	0	0	6	16.7	.29

	G	A	Pts	PIM		G	A	Pts	PIM
1st Period	2	1	3	80	Winning	3	2	5	60
2nd Period	2	1	3	64	Losing	4	4	8	132
3rd Period	4	8	12	63	Tied	1	4	5	17
Overtime	0	0	0	2	Clutch	0	2	2	6
Last 5 Min	1	1	2	47	Blowouts	1	0	1	52

Eric Brewer

New York Islanders — Defense

1998-99 Season

	GP	G	A	Pts	+/–	PIM	PP	SH	S	SPct	P/G
Overall	63	5	6	11	-14	32	2	0	63	7.9	.17
Home	31	2	2	4	2	12	1	0	28	7.1	.13
Away	32	3	4	7	-16	20	1	0	35	8.6	.22
vs. Division	14	0	1	1	-3	6	0	0	12	0.0	.07
vs. Conference	43	3	4	7	-16	24	2	0	37	8.1	.16
vs. Playoff	40	3	4	7	-14	18	1	0	42	7.1	.18
vs. Non-Playoff	23	2	2	4	0	14	1	0	21	9.5	.17
Pre All-Star	34	3	4	7	-11	14	0	0	31	9.7	.21
Post All-Star	29	2	2	4	-3	18	2	0	32	6.3	.14
Day	9	1	0	1	-3	6	0	0	10	10.0	.11
Night	54	4	6	10	-11	26	2	0	53	7.5	.19

	GP	G	A	Pts	+/–	PIM	PP	SH	S	SPct	P/G
National TV	5	0	0	0	-3	4	0	0	5	0.0	.00
0 Days Rest	10	0	5	5	-8	8	0	0	17	0.0	.50
1 Days Rest	20	2	0	2	0	4	1	0	17	11.8	.10
2 Days Rest	16	3	0	3	-3	4	1	0	20	15.0	.19
3+ Days Rest	17	0	1	1	-3	16	0	0	9	0.0	.06

	G	A	Pts	PIM		G	A	Pts	PIM
1st Period	3	0	3	12	Winning	0	3	3	8
2nd Period	0	2	2	6	Losing	2	3	5	18
3rd Period	2	4	6	14	Tied	3	0	3	6
Overtime	0	0	0	0	Clutch	0	0	0	2
Last 5 Min	0	0	0	8	Blowouts	0	1	1	6

Daniel Briere

Phoenix Coyotes — Center

1998-99 Season

	GP	G	A	Pts	+/–	PIM	PP	SH	S	SPct	P/G
Overall	64	8	14	22	-3	30	2	0	90	8.9	.34
Home	30	4	7	11	-3	16	0	0	51	7.8	.37
Away	34	4	7	11	0	14	2	0	39	10.3	.32
vs. Division	17	2	3	5	-2	14	1	0	18	11.1	.29
vs. Conference	41	4	6	10	-6	24	2	0	59	6.8	.24
vs. Playoff	36	0	5	5	-9	22	0	0	44	0.0	.14
vs. Non-Playoff	28	8	9	17	6	8	2	0	46	17.4	.61
Pre All-Star	38	6	4	10	0	12	2	0	55	10.9	.26
Post All-Star	26	2	10	12	-3	18	0	0	35	5.7	.46
Day	5	1	2	3	3	2	0	0	10	10.0	.60
Night	59	7	12	19	-6	28	2	0	80	8.8	.32

	GP	G	A	Pts	+/–	PIM	PP	SH	S	SPct	P/G
National TV	10	1	1	2	1	10	0	0	10	10.0	.20
0 Days Rest	10	1	1	2	-4	12	0	0	10	10.0	.20
1 Days Rest	35	6	8	14	4	10	2	0	51	11.8	.40
2 Days Rest	11	1	4	5	-1	4	0	0	17	5.9	.45
3+ Days Rest	8	0	1	1	-2	4	0	0	12	0.0	.13

	G	A	Pts	PIM		G	A	Pts	PIM
1st Period	1	4	5	4	Winning	3	6	9	8
2nd Period	4	4	8	20	Losing	1	6	7	18
3rd Period	3	6	9	6	Tied	4	2	6	4
Overtime	0	0	0	0	Clutch	2	1	3	0
Last 5 Min	1	4	5	6	Blowouts	0	2	2	14

Rod Brind'Amour

Philadelphia Flyers — Center

1998-99 Season

	GP	G	A	Pts	+/–	PIM	PP	SH	S	SPct	P/G
Overall	82	24	50	74	3	47	10	0	191	12.6	.90
Home	41	16	26	42	8	25	8	0	95	16.8	1.02
Away	41	8	24	32	-5	22	2	0	96	8.3	.78
vs. Division	20	6	11	17	3	8	2	0	46	13.0	.85
vs. Conference	57	17	31	48	-2	27	7	0	127	13.4	.84
vs. Playoff	46	14	29	43	2	33	5	0	100	14.0	.93
vs. Non-Playoff	36	10	21	31	1	14	5	0	91	11.0	.86
Pre All-Star	44	17	30	47	10	27	7	0	106	16.0	1.07
Post All-Star	38	7	20	27	-7	20	3	0	85	8.2	.71
Day	15	5	9	14	0	6	1	0	37	13.5	.93
Night	67	19	41	60	3	41	9	0	154	12.3	.90

	GP	G	A	Pts	+/–	PIM	PP	SH	S	SPct	P/G
National TV	18	4	14	18	3	18	1	0	43	9.3	1.00
0 Days Rest	12	3	8	11	0	12	2	0	22	13.6	.92
1 Days Rest	42	13	20	33	-5	23	6	0	100	13.0	.79
2 Days Rest	18	7	15	22	10	10	2	0	52	13.5	1.22
3+ Days Rest	10	1	7	8	-2	2	0	0	17	5.9	.80

	G	A	Pts	PIM		G	A	Pts	PIM
1st Period	10	13	23	20	Winning	7	22	29	23
2nd Period	10	17	27	21	Losing	5	19	24	14
3rd Period	4	20	24	6	Tied	12	9	21	10
Overtime	0	0	0	0	Clutch	1	4	5	2
Last 5 Min	7	20	27	25	Blowouts	0	2	2	6

Patrice Brisebois

Montreal Canadiens — Defense

1998-99 Season

	GP	G	A	Pts	+/–	PIM	PP	SH	S	SPct	P/G
Overall	54	3	9	12	-8	28	1	0	90	3.3	.22
Home	26	2	7	9	-4	10	1	0	43	4.7	.35
Away	28	1	2	3	-4	18	0	0	47	2.1	.11
vs. Division	12	0	1	1	-6	14	0	0	18	0.0	.08
vs. Conference	41	3	8	11	-6	24	1	0	69	4.3	.27
vs. Playoff	35	0	5	5	-10	26	0	0	55	0.0	.14
vs. Non-Playoff	19	3	4	7	2	2	1	0	35	8.6	.37
Pre All-Star	31	1	4	5	-12	20	1	0	60	1.7	.16
Post All-Star	23	2	5	7	4	8	0	0	30	6.7	.30
Day	3	0	2	2	-2	2	0	0	10	0.0	.67
Night	51	3	7	10	-6	26	1	0	80	3.8	.20

	GP	G	A	Pts	+/–	PIM	PP	SH	S	SPct	P/G
National TV	17	1	2	3	-7	10	1	0	29	3.4	.18
0 Days Rest	13	1	2	3	-2	10	0	0	28	3.6	.23
1 Days Rest	19	1	2	3	-5	10	0	0	27	3.7	.16
2 Days Rest	11	1	4	5	2	2	1	0	19	5.3	.45
3+ Days Rest	11	0	1	1	-3	6	0	0	16	0.0	.09

	G	A	Pts	PIM		G	A	Pts	PIM
1st Period	1	1	2	12	Winning	1	3	4	8
2nd Period	0	3	3	12	Losing	0	4	4	12
3rd Period	2	5	7	4	Tied	2	2	4	8
Overtime	0	0	0	0	Clutch	1	0	1	2
Last 5 Min	2	3	5	10	Blowouts	0	2	2	4

Curtis Brown

Buffalo Sabres — Center

1998-99 Season

	GP	G	A	Pts	+/–	PIM	PP	SH	S	SPct	P/G
Overall	78	16	31	47	23	56	5	1	128	12.5	.60
Home	38	11	17	28	20	26	3	1	65	16.9	.74
Away	40	5	14	19	3	30	2	0	63	7.9	.48
vs. Division	19	5	7	12	13	10	0	1	32	15.6	.63
vs. Conference	53	9	18	27	15	44	2	1	84	10.7	.51
vs. Playoff	44	12	20	32	13	24	4	1	78	15.4	.73
vs. Non-Playoff	34	4	11	15	10	32	1	0	50	8.0	.44
Pre All-Star	42	11	19	30	19	28	3	1	77	14.3	.71
Post All-Star	36	5	12	17	4	28	2	0	51	9.8	.47
Day	5	1	3	4	-2	0	1	0	8	12.5	.80
Night	73	15	28	43	25	56	4	1	120	12.5	.59

	GP	G	A	Pts	+/–	PIM	PP	SH	S	SPct	P/G
National TV	14	3	3	6	-4	4	2	0	19	15.8	.43
0 Days Rest	19	4	9	13	4	14	1	0	29	13.8	.68
1 Days Rest	27	4	16	20	15	14	2	0	47	8.5	.74
2 Days Rest	18	4	5	9	2	16	1	1	28	14.3	.50
3+ Days Rest	14	4	1	5	2	12	1	0	24	16.7	.36

	G	A	Pts	PIM		G	A	Pts	PIM
1st Period	4	11	15	14	Winning	3	11	14	22
2nd Period	3	12	15	12	Losing	9	8	17	30
3rd Period	9	8	17	28	Tied	4	12	16	4
Overtime	0	0	0	2	Clutch	2	4	6	2
Last 5 Min	7	7	14	12	Blowouts	1	0	1	16

Doug Brown

Detroit Red Wings — Right Wing

1998-99 Season

	GP	G	A	Pts	+/–	PIM	PP	SH	S	SPct	P/G
Overall	80	9	19	28	5	42	3	1	180	5.0	.35
Home	39	6	11	17	7	22	2	1	97	6.2	.44
Away	41	3	8	11	-2	20	1	0	83	3.6	.27
vs. Division	17	4	2	6	-1	6	2	0	46	8.7	.35
vs. Conference	53	6	12	18	3	30	3	0	120	5.0	.34
vs. Playoff	46	3	8	11	4	22	1	1	98	3.1	.24
vs. Non-Playoff	34	6	11	17	1	20	2	0	82	7.3	.50
Pre All-Star	45	7	7	14	-2	24	3	1	110	6.4	.31
Post All-Star	35	2	12	14	7	18	0	0	70	2.9	.40
Day	13	0	2	2	0	8	0	0	27	0.0	.15
Night	67	9	17	26	5	34	3	1	153	5.9	.39

	GP	G	A	Pts	+/–	PIM	PP	SH	S	SPct	P/G
National TV	30	3	6	9	0	14	1	0	53	5.7	.30
0 Days Rest	12	1	3	4	-2	4	1	0	30	3.3	.33
1 Days Rest	38	3	9	12	2	28	1	1	76	3.9	.32
2 Days Rest	21	4	5	9	2	4	1	0	52	7.7	.43
3+ Days Rest	9	1	2	3	3	6	0	0	22	4.5	.33

	G	A	Pts	PIM		G	A	Pts	PIM
1st Period	2	6	8	12	Winning	6	7	13	26
2nd Period	1	7	8	8	Losing	2	3	5	14
3rd Period	6	5	11	22	Tied	1	9	10	2
Overtime	0	1	1	0	Clutch	1	1	2	8
Last 5 Min	2	3	5	16	Blowouts	0	0	0	14

Rob Brown

Pittsburgh Penguins — Right Wing

1998-99 Season

	GP	G	A	Pts	+/–	PIM	PP	SH	S	SPct	P/G
Overall	58	13	11	24	-15	16	9	0	78	16.7	.41
Home	26	4	4	8	-8	4	3	0	30	13.3	.31
Away	32	9	7	16	-7	12	6	0	48	18.8	.50
vs. Division	17	3	2	5	-3	8	3	0	20	15.0	.29
vs. Conference	43	11	9	20	-10	16	7	0	63	17.5	.47
vs. Playoff	34	8	6	14	-15	12	7	0	51	15.7	.41
vs. Non-Playoff	24	5	5	10	0	4	2	0	27	18.5	.42
Pre All-Star	30	4	7	11	-1	8	2	0	39	10.3	.37
Post All-Star	28	9	4	13	-14	8	7	0	39	23.1	.46
Day	12	4	2	6	-6	2	4	0	23	17.4	.50
Night	46	9	9	18	-9	14	5	0	55	16.4	.39

	GP	G	A	Pts	+/–	PIM	PP	SH	S	SPct	P/G
National TV	14	3	1	4	-6	2	3	0	19	15.8	.29
0 Days Rest	13	4	2	6	0	2	2	0	19	21.1	.46
1 Days Rest	21	7	2	9	-9	4	5	0	36	19.4	.43
2 Days Rest	17	2	2	4	-2	8	2	0	18	11.1	.24
3+ Days Rest	7	0	5	5	-4	2	0	0	5	0.0	.71

	G	A	Pts	PIM		G	A	Pts	PIM
1st Period	3	5	8	6	Winning	4	4	8	2
2nd Period	7	3	10	6	Losing	6	5	11	12
3rd Period	3	3	6	4	Tied	3	2	5	2
Overtime	0	0	0	0	Clutch	1	0	1	0
Last 5 Min	2	5	7	2	Blowouts	0	0	0	2

Benoit Brunet

Montreal Canadiens — Left Wing

1998-99 Season

	GP	G	A	Pts	+/–	PIM	PP	SH	S	SPct	P/G
Overall	60	14	17	31	-1	31	4	2	115	12.2	.52
Home	31	9	10	19	2	19	3	2	62	14.5	.61
Away	29	5	7	12	-3	12	1	0	53	9.4	.41
vs. Division	16	5	2	7	-7	12	1	1	34	14.7	.44
vs. Conference	40	8	14	22	2	25	2	2	78	10.3	.55
vs. Playoff	38	11	8	19	-4	22	3	1	70	15.7	.50
vs. Non-Playoff	22	3	9	12	3	9	1	1	45	6.7	.55
Pre All-Star	41	10	11	21	2	29	2	2	78	12.8	.51
Post All-Star	19	4	6	10	-3	2	2	0	37	10.8	.53
Day	3	1	0	1	-2	0	1	0	2	50.0	.33
Night	57	13	17	30	1	31	3	2	113	11.5	.53

	GP	G	A	Pts	+/–	PIM	PP	SH	S	SPct	P/G
National TV	20	6	5	11	-2	10	2	2	41	14.6	.55
0 Days Rest	11	4	1	5	-4	6	1	1	19	21.1	.45
1 Days Rest	23	5	5	10	0	12	2	0	45	11.1	.43
2 Days Rest	13	0	2	2	-3	4	0	0	21	0.0	.15
3+ Days Rest	13	5	9	14	6	9	1	1	30	16.7	1.08

	G	A	Pts	PIM		G	A	Pts	PIM
1st Period	2	4	6	11	Winning	1	10	11	13
2nd Period	8	4	12	2	Losing	5	3	8	14
3rd Period	4	9	13	18	Tied	8	4	12	4
Overtime	0	0	0	0	Clutch	1	2	3	4
Last 5 Min	4	3	7	4	Blowouts	1	1	2	4

Andrew Brunette

Nashville Predators — Left Wing

1998-99 Season

	GP	G	A	Pts	+/–	PIM	PP	SH	S	SPct	P/G
Overall	77	11	20	31	-10	26	7	0	65	16.9	.40
Home	38	5	8	13	-1	10	3	0	34	14.7	.34
Away	39	6	12	18	-9	16	4	0	31	19.4	.46
vs. Division	16	2	7	9	-5	2	2	0	14	14.3	.56
vs. Conference	50	8	15	23	-6	16	5	0	38	21.1	.46
vs. Playoff	49	8	10	18	-12	14	5	0	39	20.5	.37
vs. Non-Playoff	28	3	10	13	2	12	2	0	26	11.5	.46
Pre All-Star	44	7	15	22	0	20	4	0	50	14.0	.50
Post All-Star	33	4	5	9	-10	6	3	0	15	26.7	.27
Day	7	0	1	1	-4	2	0	0	3	0.0	.14
Night	70	11	19	30	-6	24	7	0	62	17.7	.43

	GP	G	A	Pts	+/–	PIM	PP	SH	S	SPct	P/G
National TV	2	1	3	4	0	0	1	0	4	25.0	2.00
0 Days Rest	13	1	4	5	-7	4	1	0	9	11.1	.38
1 Days Rest	35	4	9	13	-4	8	4	0	26	15.4	.37
2 Days Rest	15	3	2	5	1	6	0	0	14	21.4	.33
3+ Days Rest	14	3	5	8	0	8	2	0	16	18.8	.57

	G	A	Pts	PIM		G	A	Pts	PIM
1st Period	3	8	11	10	Winning	1	5	6	12
2nd Period	6	8	14	8	Losing	7	9	16	14
3rd Period	2	4	6	8	Tied	3	6	9	0
Overtime	0	0	0	0	Clutch	0	1	1	0
Last 5 Min	5	6	11	6	Blowouts	0	1	1	2

Sergei Brylin

New Jersey Devils — Center

1998-99 Season

	GP	G	A	Pts	+/–	PIM	PP	SH	S	SPct	P/G
Overall	47	5	10	15	8	28	3	0	51	9.8	.32
Home	28	4	6	10	6	22	3	0	37	10.8	.36
Away	19	1	4	5	2	6	0	0	14	7.1	.26
vs. Division	10	0	1	1	0	4	0	0	5	0.0	.10
vs. Conference	32	3	7	10	9	24	2	0	30	10.0	.31
vs. Playoff	26	2	8	10	9	12	1	0	27	7.4	.38
vs. Non-Playoff	21	3	2	5	-1	16	2	0	24	12.5	.24
Pre All-Star	27	3	5	8	2	16	2	0	26	11.5	.30
Post All-Star	20	2	5	7	6	12	1	0	25	8.0	.35
Day	9	1	3	4	2	2	1	0	10	10.0	.44
Night	38	4	7	11	6	26	2	0	41	9.8	.29

	GP	G	A	Pts	+/–	PIM	PP	SH	S	SPct	P/G
National TV	3	0	0	0	-2	2	0	0	0	–	.00
0 Days Rest	8	0	1	1	0	4	0	0	5	0.0	.13
1 Days Rest	13	2	4	6	3	10	1	0	15	13.3	.46
2 Days Rest	9	2	3	5	4	6	1	0	12	16.7	.56
3+ Days Rest	17	1	2	3	1	8	1	0	19	5.3	.18

	G	A	Pts	PIM		G	A	Pts	PIM
1st Period	2	2	4	14	Winning	3	2	5	12
2nd Period	2	6	8	4	Losing	0	4	4	12
3rd Period	1	2	3	10	Tied	2	4	6	4
Overtime	0	0	0	0	Clutch	0	1	1	0
Last 5 Min	0	3	3	14	Blowouts	1	0	1	4

Jan Bulis

Washington Capitals — Center

1998-99 Season

	GP	G	A	Pts	+/–	PIM	PP	SH	S	SPct	P/G
Overall	38	7	16	23	3	6	3	0	57	12.3	.61
Home	22	5	10	15	1	6	1	0	28	17.9	.68
Away	16	2	6	8	2	0	2	0	29	6.9	.50
vs. Division	6	1	4	5	3	4	0	0	10	10.0	.83
vs. Conference	32	6	15	21	5	6	2	0	50	12.0	.66
vs. Playoff	24	5	8	13	0	4	2	0	33	15.2	.54
vs. Non-Playoff	14	2	8	10	3	2	1	0	24	8.3	.71
Pre All-Star	15	4	5	9	4	0	1	0	23	17.4	.60
Post All-Star	23	3	11	14	-1	6	2	0	34	8.8	.61
Day	3	0	1	1	0	0	0	0	4	0.0	.33
Night	35	7	15	22	3	6	3	0	53	13.2	.63

	GP	G	A	Pts	+/–	PIM	PP	SH	S	SPct	P/G
National TV	6	1	4	5	3	0	1	0	10	10.0	.83
0 Days Rest	6	1	0	1	-1	0	1	0	11	9.1	.17
1 Days Rest	21	1	12	13	4	6	0	0	31	3.2	.62
2 Days Rest	6	2	1	3	-3	0	2	0	9	22.2	.50
3+ Days Rest	5	3	3	6	3	0	0	0	6	50.0	1.20

	G	A	Pts	PIM		G	A	Pts	PIM
1st Period	1	4	5	0	Winning	2	7	9	4
2nd Period	5	11	16	6	Losing	1	5	6	2
3rd Period	1	1	2	0	Tied	4	4	8	0
Overtime	0	0	0	0	Clutch	0	0	0	0
Last 5 Min	3	3	6	2	Blowouts	1	2	3	0

Pavel Bure

Florida Panthers — Right Wing

1998-99 Season

	GP	G	A	Pts	+/–	PIM	PP	SH	S	SPct	P/G
Overall	11	13	3	16	3	4	5	1	44	29.5	1.45
Home	5	5	3	8	2	4	3	1	20	25.0	1.60
Away	6	8	0	8	1	0	2	0	24	33.3	1.33
vs. Division	0	0	0	0	0	0	0	0	0	–	–
vs. Conference	8	7	3	10	2	0	2	0	30	23.3	1.25
vs. Playoff	8	10	2	12	1	4	4	1	29	34.5	1.50
vs. Non-Playoff	3	3	1	4	2	0	1	0	15	20.0	1.33
Pre All-Star	2	3	0	3	2	0	1	0	9	33.3	1.50
Post All-Star	9	10	3	13	1	4	4	1	35	28.6	1.44
Day	0	0	0	0	0	0	0	0	0	–	–
Night	11	13	3	16	3	4	5	1	44	29.5	1.45

	GP	G	A	Pts	+/–	PIM	PP	SH	S	SPct	P/G
National TV	1	0	0	0	-2	0	0	0	3	0.0	.00
0 Days Rest	3	1	1	2	-1	0	0	0	14	7.1	.67
1 Days Rest	2	2	0	2	1	0	0	0	7	28.6	1.00
2 Days Rest	1	1	0	1	-1	2	1	0	5	20.0	1.00
3+ Days Rest	5	9	2	11	4	2	4	1	18	50.0	2.20

	G	A	Pts	PIM		G	A	Pts	PIM
1st Period	4	0	4	2	Winning	4	2	6	0
2nd Period	4	0	4	2	Losing	6	0	6	4
3rd Period	5	3	8	0	Tied	3	1	4	0
Overtime	0	0	0	0	Clutch	0	0	0	0
Last 5 Min	2	1	3	2	Blowouts	1	0	1	0

Valeri Bure

Calgary Flames — Right Wing

1998-99 Season

	GP	G	A	Pts	+/–	PIM	PP	SH	S	SPct	P/G
Overall	80	26	27	53	0	22	7	0	260	10.0	.66
Home	41	15	14	29	3	8	4	0	130	11.5	.71
Away	39	11	13	24	-3	14	3	0	130	8.5	.62
vs. Division	18	4	9	13	2	4	1	0	65	6.2	.72
vs. Conference	53	15	19	34	5	18	2	0	171	8.8	.64
vs. Playoff	50	15	13	28	-10	14	4	0	154	9.7	.56
vs. Non-Playoff	30	11	14	25	10	8	3	0	106	10.4	.83
Pre All-Star	44	9	17	26	-1	14	2	0	123	7.3	.59
Post All-Star	36	17	10	27	1	8	5	0	137	12.4	.75
Day	4	2	1	3	1	0	1	0	11	18.2	.75
Night	76	24	26	50	-1	22	6	0	249	9.6	.66

	GP	G	A	Pts	+/–	PIM	PP	SH	S	SPct	P/G
National TV	13	5	3	8	-2	2	2	0	41	12.2	.62
0 Days Rest	16	7	5	12	8	2	2	0	60	11.7	.75
1 Days Rest	38	9	9	18	-9	8	3	0	105	8.6	.47
2 Days Rest	13	5	5	10	0	8	1	0	49	10.2	.77
3+ Days Rest	13	5	8	13	1	4	1	0	46	10.9	1.00

	G	A	Pts	PIM		G	A	Pts	PIM
1st Period	8	10	18	2	Winning	5	6	11	12
2nd Period	8	11	19	10	Losing	10	11	21	10
3rd Period	9	6	15	10	Tied	11	10	21	0
Overtime	1	0	1	0	Clutch	3	3	6	0
Last 5 Min	6	7	13	6	Blowouts	2	1	3	4

Marc Bureau

Philadelphia Flyers — Center

1998-99 Season

	GP	G	A	Pts	+/–	PIM	PP	SH	S	SPct	P/G
Overall	71	4	6	10	-2	10	0	0	52	7.7	.14
Home	35	3	3	6	-3	6	0	0	21	14.3	.17
Away	36	1	3	4	1	4	0	0	31	3.2	.11
vs. Division	18	0	2	2	2	4	0	0	13	0.0	.11
vs. Conference	48	1	2	3	-3	10	0	0	27	3.7	.06
vs. Playoff	41	1	3	4	-2	4	0	0	30	3.3	.10
vs. Non-Playoff	30	3	3	6	0	6	0	0	22	13.6	.20
Pre All-Star	33	3	4	7	-2	4	0	0	27	11.1	.21
Post All-Star	38	1	2	3	0	6	0	0	25	4.0	.08
Day	15	1	0	1	-2	2	0	0	10	10.0	.07
Night	56	3	6	9	0	8	0	0	42	7.1	.16

	GP	G	A	Pts	+/–	PIM	PP	SH	S	SPct	P/G
National TV	17	0	0	0	-2	2	0	0	12	0.0	.00
0 Days Rest	11	1	0	1	-2	2	0	0	13	7.7	.09
1 Days Rest	37	1	4	5	-1	6	0	0	30	3.3	.14
2 Days Rest	15	1	2	3	0	2	0	0	5	20.0	.20
3+ Days Rest	8	1	0	1	1	0	0	0	4	25.0	.13

	G	A	Pts	PIM
1st Period	1	2	3	4
2nd Period	2	2	4	4
3rd Period	1	2	3	2
Overtime	0	0	0	0
Last 5 Min	0	0	0	0

	G	A	Pts	PIM
Winning	1	3	4	4
Losing	0	1	1	2
Tied	3	2	5	4
Clutch	0	0	0	0
Blowouts	0	0	0	0

Jim Campbell

St. Louis Blues — Right Wing

1998-99 Season

	GP	G	A	Pts	+/–	PIM	PP	SH	S	SPct	P/G
Overall	55	4	21	25	-8	41	1	0	99	4.0	.45
Home	26	1	7	8	-7	12	0	0	52	1.9	.31
Away	29	3	14	17	-1	29	1	0	47	6.4	.59
vs. Division	12	2	4	6	0	6	0	0	21	9.5	.50
vs. Conference	37	4	15	19	-3	24	1	0	60	6.7	.51
vs. Playoff	31	1	10	11	-10	18	0	0	61	1.6	.35
vs. Non-Playoff	24	3	11	14	2	23	1	0	38	7.9	.58
Pre All-Star	34	2	11	13	-9	25	0	0	66	3.0	.38
Post All-Star	21	2	10	12	1	16	1	0	33	6.1	.57
Day	6	0	2	2	0	2	0	0	9	0.0	.33
Night	49	4	19	23	-8	39	1	0	90	4.4	.47

	GP	G	A	Pts	+/–	PIM	PP	SH	S	SPct	P/G
National TV	12	1	6	7	2	10	0	0	17	5.9	.58
0 Days Rest	7	1	2	3	-1	8	0	0	16	6.3	.43
1 Days Rest	23	2	10	12	-7	10	1	0	42	4.8	.52
2 Days Rest	12	0	2	2	-4	15	0	0	18	0.0	.17
3+ Days Rest	13	1	7	8	4	8	0	0	23	4.3	.62

	G	A	Pts	PIM
1st Period	0	11	11	23
2nd Period	3	6	9	14
3rd Period	1	4	5	4
Overtime	0	0	0	0
Last 5 Min	1	6	7	6

	G	A	Pts	PIM
Winning	2	9	11	20
Losing	2	5	7	10
Tied	0	7	7	11
Clutch	0	0	0	0
Blowouts	1	0	1	0

Guy Carbonneau

Dallas Stars — Center

1998-99 Season

	GP	G	A	Pts	+/–	PIM	PP	SH	S	SPct	P/G
Overall	74	4	12	16	-3	31	0	0	60	6.7	.22
Home	38	3	8	11	0	17	0	0	31	9.7	.29
Away	36	1	4	5	-3	14	0	0	29	3.4	.14
vs. Division	22	2	1	3	1	14	0	0	24	8.3	.14
vs. Conference	51	4	7	11	-1	24	0	0	46	8.7	.22
vs. Playoff	43	2	6	8	-3	20	0	0	36	5.6	.19
vs. Non-Playoff	31	2	6	8	0	11	0	0	24	8.3	.26
Pre All-Star	42	1	11	12	-2	15	0	0	34	2.9	.29
Post All-Star	32	3	1	4	-1	16	0	0	26	11.5	.13
Day	7	0	0	0	-1	4	0	0	5	0.0	.00
Night	67	4	12	16	-2	27	0	0	55	7.3	.24

	GP	G	A	Pts	+/–	PIM	PP	SH	S	SPct	P/G
National TV	11	0	1	1	-1	2	0	0	11	0.0	.09
0 Days Rest	11	1	2	3	1	6	0	0	9	11.1	.27
1 Days Rest	37	0	6	6	-4	15	0	0	35	0.0	.16
2 Days Rest	12	2	3	5	3	2	0	0	6	33.3	.42
3+ Days Rest	14	1	1	2	-3	8	0	0	10	10.0	.14

	G	A	Pts	PIM
1st Period	1	3	4	8
2nd Period	2	6	8	10
3rd Period	1	3	4	13
Overtime	0	0	0	0
Last 5 Min	0	2	2	8

	G	A	Pts	PIM
Winning	2	4	6	21
Losing	0	1	1	4
Tied	2	7	9	6
Clutch	1	1	2	2
Blowouts	0	0	0	11

Terry Carkner

Florida Panthers — Defense

1998-99 Season

	GP	G	A	Pts	+/–	PIM	PP	SH	S	SPct	P/G
Overall	62	2	9	11	0	54	0	0	25	8.0	.18
Home	30	1	8	9	5	35	0	0	11	9.1	.30
Away	32	1	1	2	-5	19	0	0	14	7.1	.06
vs. Division	13	1	1	2	-1	10	0	0	4	25.0	.15
vs. Conference	48	2	7	9	3	46	0	0	20	10.0	.19
vs. Playoff	41	0	6	6	-1	31	0	0	14	0.0	.15
vs. Non-Playoff	21	2	3	5	1	23	0	0	11	18.2	.24
Pre All-Star	32	1	4	5	-3	33	0	0	13	7.7	.16
Post All-Star	30	1	5	6	3	21	0	0	12	8.3	.20
Day	4	0	1	1	-1	6	0	0	1	0.0	.25
Night	58	2	8	10	1	48	0	0	24	8.3	.17

	GP	G	A	Pts	+/–	PIM	PP	SH	S	SPct	P/G
National TV	4	0	1	1	-2	4	0	0	2	0.0	.25
0 Days Rest	12	0	0	0	-6	4	0	0	4	0.0	.00
1 Days Rest	23	1	5	6	2	23	0	0	14	7.1	.26
2 Days Rest	11	0	2	2	1	6	0	0	2	0.0	.18
3+ Days Rest	16	1	2	3	3	21	0	0	5	20.0	.19

	G	A	Pts	PIM
1st Period	1	3	4	14
2nd Period	0	2	2	10
3rd Period	1	4	5	30
Overtime	0	0	0	0
Last 5 Min	0	3	3	15

	G	A	Pts	PIM
Winning	0	4	4	29
Losing	1	3	4	19
Tied	1	2	3	6
Clutch	0	1	1	2
Blowouts	0	0	0	10

Keith Carney

Phoenix Coyotes — Defense

1998-99 Season

	GP	G	A	Pts	+/–	PIM	PP	SH	S	SPct	P/G
Overall	82	2	14	16	15	62	0	2	62	3.2	.20
Home	41	1	7	8	13	34	0	1	31	3.2	.20
Away	41	1	7	8	2	28	0	1	31	3.2	.20
vs. Division	24	0	6	6	4	22	0	0	17	0.0	.25
vs. Conference	56	1	12	13	14	40	0	1	42	2.4	.23
vs. Playoff	48	2	7	9	6	44	0	2	34	5.9	.19
vs. Non-Playoff	34	0	7	7	9	18	0	0	28	0.0	.21
Pre All-Star	42	0	8	8	10	36	0	0	30	0.0	.19
Post All-Star	40	2	6	8	5	26	0	2	32	6.3	.20
Day	6	0	1	1	4	4	0	0	3	0.0	.17
Night	76	2	13	15	11	58	0	2	59	3.4	.20

	GP	G	A	Pts	+/–	PIM	PP	SH	S	SPct	P/G
National TV	14	0	0	0	3	8	0	0	18	0.0	.00
0 Days Rest	13	1	3	4	-3	16	0	1	9	11.1	.31
1 Days Rest	42	1	9	10	11	26	0	1	34	2.9	.24
2 Days Rest	16	0	1	1	2	14	0	0	12	0.0	.06
3+ Days Rest	11	0	1	1	5	6	0	0	7	0.0	.09

	G	A	Pts	PIM		G	A	Pts	PIM
1st Period	0	3	3	16	Winning	2	7	9	24
2nd Period	1	4	5	24	Losing	0	7	7	28
3rd Period	1	7	8	20	Tied	0	0	0	10
Overtime	0	0	0	2	Clutch	0	3	3	4
Last 5 Min	0	2	2	14	Blowouts	1	0	1	4

Bob Carpenter

New Jersey Devils — Center

1998-99 Season

	GP	G	A	Pts	+/–	PIM	PP	SH	S	SPct	P/G
Overall	56	2	8	10	-3	36	0	0	69	2.9	.18
Home	25	0	4	4	0	10	0	0	38	0.0	.16
Away	31	2	4	6	-3	26	0	0	31	6.5	.19
vs. Division	14	0	4	4	-3	6	0	0	15	0.0	.29
vs. Conference	40	2	7	9	-3	20	0	0	51	3.9	.23
vs. Playoff	35	1	6	7	1	16	0	0	47	2.1	.20
vs. Non-Playoff	21	1	2	3	-4	20	0	0	22	4.5	.14
Pre All-Star	28	0	3	3	-2	16	0	0	31	0.0	.11
Post All-Star	28	2	5	7	-1	20	0	0	38	5.3	.25
Day	7	0	1	1	-4	2	0	0	6	0.0	.14
Night	49	2	7	9	1	34	0	0	63	3.2	.18

	GP	G	A	Pts	+/–	PIM	PP	SH	S	SPct	P/G
National TV	6	0	1	1	-1	4	0	0	9	0.0	.17
0 Days Rest	8	0	0	0	-3	6	0	0	9	0.0	.00
1 Days Rest	17	0	2	2	-4	8	0	0	20	0.0	.12
2 Days Rest	12	0	1	1	-6	4	0	0	8	0.0	.08
3+ Days Rest	19	2	5	7	10	18	0	0	32	6.3	.37

	G	A	Pts	PIM		G	A	Pts	PIM
1st Period	1	3	4	8	Winning	1	4	5	26
2nd Period	1	1	2	12	Losing	1	1	2	6
3rd Period	0	4	4	16	Tied	0	3	3	4
Overtime	0	0	0	0	Clutch	0	1	1	10
Last 5 Min	1	3	4	16	Blowouts	0	0	0	4

Anson Carter

Boston Bruins — Center

1998-99 Season

	GP	G	A	Pts	+/–	PIM	PP	SH	S	SPct	P/G
Overall	55	24	16	40	7	22	6	0	123	19.5	.73
Home	27	10	9	19	7	12	2	0	59	16.9	.70
Away	28	14	7	21	0	10	4	0	64	21.9	.75
vs. Division	13	4	5	9	7	4	0	0	33	12.1	.69
vs. Conference	40	19	12	31	10	14	3	0	88	21.6	.78
vs. Playoff	29	8	8	16	6	10	1	0	57	14.0	.55
vs. Non-Playoff	26	16	8	24	1	12	5	0	66	24.2	.92
Pre All-Star	24	6	7	13	1	10	2	0	40	15.0	.54
Post All-Star	31	18	9	27	6	12	4	0	83	21.7	.87
Day	10	2	4	6	3	4	1	0	25	8.0	.60
Night	45	22	12	34	4	18	5	0	98	22.4	.76

	GP	G	A	Pts	+/–	PIM	PP	SH	S	SPct	P/G
National TV	7	6	2	8	4	0	2	0	18	33.3	1.14
0 Days Rest	12	3	3	6	-6	8	1	0	22	13.6	.50
1 Days Rest	23	13	8	21	10	8	3	0	59	22.0	.91
2 Days Rest	9	2	3	5	-2	0	0	0	24	8.3	.56
3+ Days Rest	11	6	2	8	5	6	2	0	18	33.3	.73

	G	A	Pts	PIM		G	A	Pts	PIM
1st Period	3	6	9	4	Winning	16	6	22	12
2nd Period	7	5	12	12	Losing	4	3	7	6
3rd Period	14	4	18	6	Tied	4	7	11	4
Overtime	0	1	1	0	Clutch	4	2	6	4
Last 5 Min	11	4	15	4	Blowouts	0	0	0	0

Andrew Cassels

Calgary Flames — Center

1998-99 Season

	GP	G	A	Pts	+/–	PIM	PP	SH	S	SPct	P/G
Overall	70	12	25	37	-12	18	4	1	97	12.4	.53
Home	31	7	6	13	-7	4	1	0	53	13.2	.42
Away	39	5	19	24	-5	14	3	1	44	11.4	.62
vs. Division	16	3	4	7	-6	6	0	1	19	15.8	.44
vs. Conference	47	10	14	24	-8	14	2	1	68	14.7	.51
vs. Playoff	42	5	13	18	-16	12	2	0	52	9.6	.43
vs. Non-Playoff	28	7	12	19	4	6	2	1	45	15.6	.68
Pre All-Star	46	9	16	25	-4	14	4	0	63	14.3	.54
Post All-Star	24	3	9	12	-8	4	0	1	34	8.8	.50
Day	4	0	0	0	-1	2	0	0	5	0.0	.00
Night	66	12	25	37	-11	16	4	1	92	13.0	.56

	GP	G	A	Pts	+/–	PIM	PP	SH	S	SPct	P/G
National TV	12	3	2	5	-2	2	1	0	19	15.8	.42
0 Days Rest	14	2	7	9	2	4	0	0	20	10.0	.64
1 Days Rest	33	2	8	10	-12	10	1	0	38	5.3	.30
2 Days Rest	12	2	5	7	0	2	2	0	22	9.1	.58
3+ Days Rest	11	6	5	11	-2	2	1	1	17	35.3	1.00

	G	A	Pts	PIM		G	A	Pts	PIM
1st Period	3	5	8	4	Winning	4	9	13	4
2nd Period	5	10	15	4	Losing	2	9	11	14
3rd Period	3	10	13	10	Tied	6	7	13	0
Overtime	1	0	1	0	Clutch	1	3	4	2
Last 5 Min	4	5	9	8	Blowouts	0	2	2	0

Shawn Chambers

Dallas Stars — Defense

1998-99 Season

	GP	G	A	Pts	+/–	PIM	PP	SH	S	SPct	P/G
Overall	61	2	9	11	6	18	1	0	82	2.4	.18
Home	32	2	7	9	6	12	1	0	42	4.8	.28
Away	29	0	2	2	0	6	0	0	40	0.0	.07
vs. Division	19	0	2	2	4	4	0	0	27	0.0	.11
vs. Conference	42	1	8	9	5	10	0	0	56	1.8	.21
vs. Playoff	37	1	3	4	5	16	1	0	53	1.9	.11
vs. Non-Playoff	24	1	6	7	1	2	0	0	29	3.4	.29
Pre All-Star	36	2	2	4	2	14	1	0	46	4.3	.11
Post All-Star	25	0	7	7	4	4	0	0	36	0.0	.28
Day	7	0	0	0	-1	0	0	0	12	0.0	.00
Night	54	2	9	11	7	18	1	0	70	2.9	.20

	GP	G	A	Pts	+/–	PIM	PP	SH	S	SPct	P/G
National TV	11	0	0	0	-2	2	0	0	17	0.0	.00
0 Days Rest	9	0	0	0	-2	4	0	0	9	0.0	.00
1 Days Rest	30	2	4	6	4	8	1	0	43	4.7	.20
2 Days Rest	10	0	4	4	3	2	0	0	14	0.0	.40
3+ Days Rest	12	0	1	1	1	4	0	0	16	0.0	.08

	G	A	Pts	PIM
1st Period	0	3	3	4
2nd Period	1	5	6	6
3rd Period	1	1	2	8
Overtime	0	0	0	0
Last 5 Min	0	3	3	4

	G	A	Pts	PIM
Winning	0	6	6	12
Losing	1	1	2	0
Tied	1	2	3	6
Clutch	0	1	1	4
Blowouts	0	1	1	0

Kelly Chase

St. Louis Blues — Right Wing

1998-99 Season

	GP	G	A	Pts	+/–	PIM	PP	SH	S	SPct	P/G
Overall	45	3	7	10	2	143	0	0	25	12.0	.22
Home	28	0	4	4	3	91	0	0	16	0.0	.14
Away	17	3	3	6	-1	52	0	0	9	33.3	.35
vs. Division	10	2	3	5	3	12	0	0	7	28.6	.50
vs. Conference	31	2	6	8	2	91	0	0	16	12.5	.26
vs. Playoff	26	1	2	3	0	72	0	0	12	8.3	.12
vs. Non-Playoff	19	2	5	7	2	71	0	0	13	15.4	.37
Pre All-Star	26	1	4	5	4	95	0	0	12	8.3	.19
Post All-Star	19	2	3	5	-2	48	0	0	13	15.4	.26
Day	3	0	0	0	0	9	0	0	0	–	.00
Night	42	3	7	10	2	134	0	0	25	12.0	.24

	GP	G	A	Pts	+/–	PIM	PP	SH	S	SPct	P/G
National TV	11	0	2	2	-1	32	0	0	1	0.0	.18
0 Days Rest	2	0	0	0	-1	19	0	0	1	0.0	.00
1 Days Rest	18	2	2	4	-2	52	0	0	13	15.4	.22
2 Days Rest	8	0	1	1	2	33	0	0	1	0.0	.13
3+ Days Rest	17	1	4	5	3	39	0	0	10	10.0	.29

	G	A	Pts	PIM
1st Period	3	2	5	65
2nd Period	0	2	2	28
3rd Period	0	3	3	50
Overtime	0	0	0	0
Last 5 Min	2	1	3	38

	G	A	Pts	PIM
Winning	1	4	5	69
Losing	1	2	3	52
Tied	1	1	2	22
Clutch	0	0	0	0
Blowouts	0	1	1	37

Chris Chelios

Detroit Red Wings — Defense

1998-99 Season

	GP	G	A	Pts	+/–	PIM	PP	SH	S	SPct	P/G
Overall	75	9	27	36	1	93	3	1	187	4.8	.48
Home	41	4	17	21	7	66	1	1	94	4.3	.51
Away	34	5	10	15	-6	27	2	0	93	5.4	.44
vs. Division	16	2	9	11	0	8	1	0	38	5.3	.69
vs. Conference	53	5	22	27	-5	55	1	0	125	4.0	.51
vs. Playoff	45	6	18	24	2	41	1	1	107	5.6	.53
vs. Non-Playoff	30	3	9	12	-1	52	2	0	80	3.8	.40
Pre All-Star	40	5	16	21	-2	68	2	0	96	5.2	.53
Post All-Star	35	4	11	15	3	25	1	1	91	4.4	.43
Day	10	2	3	5	-3	4	1	1	24	8.3	.50
Night	65	7	24	31	4	89	2	0	163	4.3	.48

	GP	G	A	Pts	+/–	PIM	PP	SH	S	SPct	P/G
National TV	18	2	5	7	-2	10	0	1	48	4.2	.39
0 Days Rest	11	1	2	3	-1	6	0	0	28	3.6	.27
1 Days Rest	38	7	11	18	-8	47	3	1	97	7.2	.47
2 Days Rest	13	0	8	8	4	22	0	0	38	0.0	.62
3+ Days Rest	13	1	6	7	6	18	0	0	24	4.2	.54

	G	A	Pts	PIM
1st Period	3	9	12	18
2nd Period	2	8	10	33
3rd Period	4	10	14	42
Overtime	0	0	0	0
Last 5 Min	1	8	9	35

	G	A	Pts	PIM
Winning	1	5	6	16
Losing	7	9	16	73
Tied	1	13	14	4
Clutch	0	2	2	6
Blowouts	0	0	0	15

Wendel Clark

Detroit Red Wings — Left Wing

1998-99 Season

	GP	G	A	Pts	+/–	PIM	PP	SH	S	SPct	P/G
Overall	77	32	16	48	-24	37	11	0	215	14.9	.62
Home	41	14	10	24	-9	25	4	0	122	11.5	.59
Away	36	18	6	24	-15	12	7	0	93	19.4	.67
vs. Division	13	8	3	11	-9	4	4	0	45	17.8	.85
vs. Conference	52	20	13	33	-13	27	6	0	146	13.7	.63
vs. Playoff	47	23	9	32	-12	31	8	0	129	17.8	.68
vs. Non-Playoff	30	9	7	16	-12	6	3	0	86	10.5	.53
Pre All-Star	41	19	11	30	-5	22	7	0	115	16.5	.73
Post All-Star	36	13	5	18	-19	15	4	0	100	13.0	.50
Day	6	3	1	4	2	0	0	0	15	20.0	.67
Night	71	29	15	44	-26	37	11	0	200	14.5	.62

	GP	G	A	Pts	+/–	PIM	PP	SH	S	SPct	P/G
National TV	7	6	0	6	0	2	1	0	26	23.1	.86
0 Days Rest	13	6	1	7	-11	8	3	0	31	19.4	.54
1 Days Rest	33	17	4	21	-4	10	3	0	98	17.3	.64
2 Days Rest	17	4	4	8	-6	6	3	0	54	7.4	.47
3+ Days Rest	14	5	7	12	-3	13	2	0	32	15.6	.86

	G	A	Pts	PIM
1st Period	11	4	15	8
2nd Period	7	7	14	8
3rd Period	13	5	18	19
Overtime	1	0	1	2
Last 5 Min	8	2	10	19

	G	A	Pts	PIM
Winning	7	6	13	6
Losing	13	4	17	25
Tied	12	6	18	6
Clutch	4	0	4	4
Blowouts	1	0	1	8

Paul Coffey

Carolina Hurricanes — Defense

1998-99 Season

	GP	G	A	Pts	+/–	PIM	PP	SH	S	SPct	P/G
Overall	54	2	12	14	-7	28	1	0	87	2.3	.26
Home	24	0	6	6	-2	8	0	0	39	0.0	.25
Away	30	2	6	8	-5	20	1	0	48	4.2	.27
vs. Division	13	0	1	1	-1	4	0	0	17	0.0	.08
vs. Conference	39	2	9	11	2	14	1	0	56	3.6	.28
vs. Playoff	28	1	9	10	-6	20	0	0	48	2.1	.36
vs. Non-Playoff	26	1	3	4	-1	8	1	0	39	2.6	.15
Pre All-Star	20	0	7	7	-10	8	0	0	25	0.0	.35
Post All-Star	34	2	5	7	3	20	1	0	62	3.2	.21
Day	6	1	1	2	-3	2	1	0	15	6.7	.33
Night	48	1	11	12	-4	26	0	0	72	1.4	.25

	GP	G	A	Pts	+/–	PIM	PP	SH	S	SPct	P/G
National TV	3	0	0	0	1	2	0	0	4	0.0	.00
0 Days Rest	10	0	3	3	-7	6	0	0	24	0.0	.30
1 Days Rest	19	1	1	2	-1	6	1	0	30	3.3	.11
2 Days Rest	12	0	7	7	-1	8	0	0	15	0.0	.58
3+ Days Rest	13	1	1	2	2	8	0	0	18	5.6	.15

	G	A	Pts	PIM		G	A	Pts	PIM
1st Period	0	2	2	10	Winning	1	2	3	8
2nd Period	2	7	9	12	Losing	0	7	7	10
3rd Period	0	3	3	6	Tied	1	3	4	10
Overtime	0	0	0	0	Clutch	0	1	1	2
Last 5 Min	0	5	5	0	Blowouts	0	0	0	0

Craig Conroy

St. Louis Blues — Center

1998-99 Season

	GP	G	A	Pts	+/–	PIM	PP	SH	S	SPct	P/G
Overall	69	14	25	39	14	38	0	1	134	10.4	.57
Home	33	4	13	17	3	14	0	1	68	5.9	.52
Away	36	10	12	22	11	24	0	0	66	15.2	.61
vs. Division	15	2	7	9	9	10	0	0	36	5.6	.60
vs. Conference	47	11	20	31	17	28	0	1	88	12.5	.66
vs. Playoff	37	5	10	15	-3	16	0	1	65	7.7	.41
vs. Non-Playoff	32	9	15	24	17	22	0	0	69	13.0	.75
Pre All-Star	42	5	15	20	4	20	0	0	83	6.0	.48
Post All-Star	27	9	10	19	10	18	0	1	51	17.6	.70
Day	7	1	5	6	2	4	0	1	10	10.0	.86
Night	62	13	20	33	12	34	0	0	124	10.5	.53

	GP	G	A	Pts	+/–	PIM	PP	SH	S	SPct	P/G
National TV	14	2	7	9	6	8	0	0	27	7.4	.64
0 Days Rest	10	1	3	4	1	6	0	0	18	5.6	.40
1 Days Rest	33	10	14	24	9	22	0	1	68	14.7	.73
2 Days Rest	15	1	5	6	0	6	0	0	30	3.3	.40
3+ Days Rest	11	2	3	5	4	4	0	0	18	11.1	.45

	G	A	Pts	PIM		G	A	Pts	PIM
1st Period	4	10	14	16	Winning	6	11	17	12
2nd Period	6	6	12	18	Losing	4	7	11	22
3rd Period	4	9	13	4	Tied	4	7	11	4
Overtime	0	0	0	0	Clutch	2	3	5	2
Last 5 Min	8	8	16	6	Blowouts	0	1	1	4

Rene Corbet

Calgary Flames — Left Wing

1998-99 Season

	GP	G	A	Pts	+/–	PIM	PP	SH	S	SPct	P/G
Overall	73	13	18	31	1	68	3	0	127	10.2	.42
Home	30	3	6	9	-1	28	1	0	44	6.8	.30
Away	43	10	12	22	2	40	2	0	83	12.0	.51
vs. Division	19	3	2	5	-2	16	1	0	40	7.5	.26
vs. Conference	51	8	13	21	2	42	2	0	97	8.2	.41
vs. Playoff	43	9	11	20	1	50	3	0	66	13.6	.47
vs. Non-Playoff	30	4	7	11	0	18	0	0	61	6.6	.37
Pre All-Star	41	6	12	18	2	45	1	0	71	8.5	.44
Post All-Star	32	7	6	13	-1	23	2	0	56	12.5	.41
Day	8	1	2	3	-1	11	0	0	9	11.1	.38
Night	65	12	16	28	2	57	3	0	118	10.2	.43

	GP	G	A	Pts	+/–	PIM	PP	SH	S	SPct	P/G
National TV	16	2	3	5	1	17	0	0	23	8.7	.31
0 Days Rest	14	4	3	7	-2	8	2	0	33	12.1	.50
1 Days Rest	33	2	9	11	-3	38	0	0	46	4.3	.33
2 Days Rest	14	6	4	10	5	10	1	0	28	21.4	.71
3+ Days Rest	12	1	2	3	1	12	0	0	20	5.0	.25

	G	A	Pts	PIM		G	A	Pts	PIM
1st Period	5	6	11	17	Winning	4	4	8	22
2nd Period	3	8	11	36	Losing	3	9	12	36
3rd Period	5	4	9	15	Tied	6	5	11	10
Overtime	0	0	0	0	Clutch	3	1	4	2
Last 5 Min	4	7	11	13	Blowouts	0	1	1	4

Bob Corkum

Phoenix Coyotes — Center

1998-99 Season

	GP	G	A	Pts	+/–	PIM	PP	SH	S	SPct	P/G
Overall	77	9	10	19	-9	17	0	0	146	6.2	.25
Home	38	5	5	10	-5	11	0	0	79	6.3	.26
Away	39	4	5	9	-4	6	0	0	67	6.0	.23
vs. Division	23	1	3	4	-2	7	0	0	36	2.8	.17
vs. Conference	52	3	9	12	-4	7	0	0	93	3.2	.23
vs. Playoff	46	5	7	12	-5	8	0	0	88	5.7	.26
vs. Non-Playoff	31	4	3	7	-4	9	0	0	58	6.9	.23
Pre All-Star	41	4	5	9	5	9	0	0	82	4.9	.22
Post All-Star	36	5	5	10	-14	8	0	0	64	7.8	.28
Day	6	2	1	3	1	0	0	0	8	25.0	.50
Night	71	7	9	16	-10	17	0	0	138	5.1	.23

	GP	G	A	Pts	+/–	PIM	PP	SH	S	SPct	P/G
National TV	13	3	5	8	6	2	0	0	24	12.5	.62
0 Days Rest	12	3	1	4	-4	0	0	0	24	12.5	.33
1 Days Rest	37	4	4	8	-8	15	0	0	67	6.0	.22
2 Days Rest	16	1	3	4	-2	2	0	0	28	3.6	.25
3+ Days Rest	12	1	2	3	5	0	0	0	27	3.7	.25

	G	A	Pts	PIM		G	A	Pts	PIM
1st Period	3	2	5	6	Winning	6	5	11	8
2nd Period	1	3	4	2	Losing	2	2	4	7
3rd Period	5	4	9	9	Tied	1	3	4	2
Overtime	0	1	1	0	Clutch	2	1	3	0
Last 5 Min	5	6	11	5	Blowouts	1	0	1	0

Shayne Corson

Montreal Canadiens — Left Wing

1998-99 Season

	GP	G	A	Pts	+/–	PIM	PP	SH	S	SPct	P/G
Overall	63	12	20	32	-10	147	7	0	142	8.5	.51
Home	27	8	11	19	-2	43	6	0	59	13.6	.70
Away	36	4	9	13	-8	104	1	0	83	4.8	.36
vs. Division	11	1	3	4	-5	39	1	0	22	4.5	.36
vs. Conference	43	10	16	26	-6	90	5	0	102	9.8	.60
vs. Playoff	36	6	10	16	-6	82	4	0	87	6.9	.44
vs. Non-Playoff	27	6	10	16	-4	65	3	0	55	10.9	.59
Pre All-Star	36	8	10	18	-7	65	7	0	80	10.0	.50
Post All-Star	27	4	10	14	-3	82	0	0	62	6.5	.52
Day	2	0	0	0	-2	2	0	0	5	0.0	.00
Night	61	12	20	32	-8	145	7	0	137	8.8	.52

	GP	G	A	Pts	+/–	PIM	PP	SH	S	SPct	P/G
National TV	19	2	8	10	-1	55	2	0	36	5.6	.53
0 Days Rest	13	2	5	7	-6	4	1	0	21	9.5	.54
1 Days Rest	24	3	8	11	-2	82	2	0	58	5.2	.46
2 Days Rest	15	5	5	10	0	20	4	0	38	13.2	.67
3+ Days Rest	11	2	2	4	-2	41	0	0	25	8.0	.36

	G	A	Pts	PIM
1st Period	3	4	7	19
2nd Period	6	9	15	22
3rd Period	3	7	10	106
Overtime	0	0	0	0
Last 5 Min	4	5	9	48

	G	A	Pts	PIM
Winning	4	6	10	43
Losing	2	4	6	95
Tied	6	10	16	9
Clutch	0	1	1	25
Blowouts	1	0	1	26

Sylvain Cote

Toronto Maple Leafs — Defense

1998-99 Season

	GP	G	A	Pts	+/–	PIM	PP	SH	S	SPct	P/G
Overall	79	5	24	29	22	28	0	0	119	4.2	.37
Home	41	2	15	17	24	16	0	0	63	3.2	.41
Away	38	3	9	12	-2	12	0	0	56	5.4	.32
vs. Division	20	1	5	6	4	4	0	0	38	2.6	.30
vs. Conference	56	2	13	15	8	20	0	0	87	2.3	.27
vs. Playoff	45	0	14	14	5	16	0	0	62	0.0	.31
vs. Non-Playoff	34	5	10	15	17	12	0	0	57	8.8	.44
Pre All-Star	46	3	16	19	8	16	0	0	77	3.9	.41
Post All-Star	33	2	8	10	14	12	0	0	42	4.8	.30
Day	1	0	0	0	0	0	0	0	0	–	.00
Night	78	5	24	29	22	28	0	0	119	4.2	.37

	GP	G	A	Pts	+/–	PIM	PP	SH	S	SPct	P/G
National TV	27	3	7	10	15	16	0	0	44	6.8	.37
0 Days Rest	17	2	7	9	-1	8	0	0	32	6.3	.53
1 Days Rest	33	2	9	11	15	8	0	0	52	3.8	.33
2 Days Rest	14	1	4	5	8	10	0	0	19	5.3	.36
3+ Days Rest	15	0	4	4	0	2	0	0	16	0.0	.27

	G	A	Pts	PIM
1st Period	2	5	7	8
2nd Period	0	12	12	10
3rd Period	3	6	9	10
Overtime	0	1	1	0
Last 5 Min	1	4	5	14

	G	A	Pts	PIM
Winning	2	9	11	20
Losing	0	7	7	8
Tied	3	8	11	0
Clutch	0	3	3	2
Blowouts	2	3	5	6

Geoff Courtnall

St. Louis Blues — Left Wing

1998-99 Season

	GP	G	A	Pts	+/–	PIM	PP	SH	S	SPct	P/G
Overall	24	5	7	12	2	28	1	0	60	8.3	.50
Home	11	1	4	5	2	16	0	0	24	4.2	.45
Away	13	4	3	7	0	12	1	0	36	11.1	.54
vs. Division	6	2	2	4	0	4	0	0	17	11.8	.67
vs. Conference	18	4	6	10	0	16	1	0	47	8.5	.56
vs. Playoff	14	3	4	7	0	20	1	0	33	9.1	.50
vs. Non-Playoff	10	2	3	5	2	8	0	0	27	7.4	.50
Pre All-Star	21	3	7	10	1	26	0	0	54	5.6	.48
Post All-Star	3	2	0	2	1	2	1	0	6	33.3	.67
Day	2	0	0	0	-1	0	0	0	1	0.0	.00
Night	22	5	7	12	3	28	1	0	59	8.5	.55

	GP	G	A	Pts	+/–	PIM	PP	SH	S	SPct	P/G
National TV	2	1	0	1	1	0	0	0	3	33.3	.50
0 Days Rest	5	1	1	2	-3	8	1	0	9	11.1	.40
1 Days Rest	6	2	3	5	3	8	0	0	21	9.5	.83
2 Days Rest	6	0	2	2	2	2	0	0	13	0.0	.33
3+ Days Rest	7	2	1	3	0	10	0	0	17	11.8	.43

	G	A	Pts	PIM
1st Period	2	3	5	10
2nd Period	1	3	4	12
3rd Period	2	1	3	6
Overtime	0	0	0	0
Last 5 Min	1	0	1	8

	G	A	Pts	PIM
Winning	2	2	4	14
Losing	1	3	4	4
Tied	2	2	4	10
Clutch	1	0	1	4
Blowouts	0	0	0	2

Russ Courtnall

Los Angeles Kings — Right Wing

1998-99 Season

	GP	G	A	Pts	+/–	PIM	PP	SH	S	SPct	P/G
Overall	57	6	13	19	-9	19	0	1	77	7.8	.33
Home	26	4	7	11	3	13	0	1	32	12.5	.42
Away	31	2	6	8	-12	6	0	0	45	4.4	.26
vs. Division	17	1	3	4	-6	6	0	0	22	4.5	.24
vs. Conference	41	4	10	14	-13	17	0	0	62	6.5	.34
vs. Playoff	39	4	9	13	-7	10	0	0	53	7.5	.33
vs. Non-Playoff	18	2	4	6	-2	9	0	1	24	8.3	.33
Pre All-Star	21	2	3	5	-4	6	0	0	28	7.1	.24
Post All-Star	36	4	10	14	-5	13	0	1	49	8.2	.39
Day	5	1	3	4	-2	0	0	0	5	20.0	.80
Night	52	5	10	15	-7	19	0	1	72	6.9	.29

	GP	G	A	Pts	+/–	PIM	PP	SH	S	SPct	P/G
National TV	13	2	4	6	-5	11	0	0	18	11.1	.46
0 Days Rest	9	0	2	2	-2	2	0	0	16	0.0	.22
1 Days Rest	30	2	7	9	-3	6	0	1	37	5.4	.30
2 Days Rest	9	3	2	5	-3	4	0	0	11	27.3	.56
3+ Days Rest	9	1	2	3	-1	7	0	0	13	7.7	.33

	G	A	Pts	PIM
1st Period	1	5	6	8
2nd Period	3	5	8	6
3rd Period	2	3	5	5
Overtime	0	0	0	0
Last 5 Min	2	6	8	4

	G	A	Pts	PIM
Winning	2	5	7	11
Losing	3	5	8	8
Tied	1	3	4	0
Clutch	1	0	1	0
Blowouts	1	1	2	2

Murray Craven

San Jose Sharks — Left Wing

1998-99 Season

	GP	G	A	Pts	+/–	PIM	PP	SH	S	SPct	P/G
Overall	43	4	10	14	-3	18	0	1	55	7.3	.33
Home	19	1	2	3	-2	6	0	0	21	4.8	.16
Away	24	3	8	11	-1	12	0	1	34	8.8	.46
vs. Division	12	0	1	1	1	4	0	0	13	0.0	.08
vs. Conference	28	0	6	6	-3	12	0	0	34	0.0	.21
vs. Playoff	26	2	4	6	-2	6	0	1	31	6.5	.23
vs. Non-Playoff	17	2	6	8	-1	12	0	0	24	8.3	.47
Pre All-Star	29	1	6	7	-2	12	0	0	35	2.9	.24
Post All-Star	14	3	4	7	-1	6	0	1	20	15.0	.50
Day	3	0	2	2	2	2	0	0	4	0.0	.67
Night	40	4	8	12	-5	16	0	1	51	7.8	.30

	GP	G	A	Pts	+/–	PIM	PP	SH	S	SPct	P/G
National TV	5	0	0	0	0	4	0	0	5	0.0	.00
0 Days Rest	6	0	2	2	-4	2	0	0	8	0.0	.33
1 Days Rest	23	3	5	8	1	14	0	1	32	9.4	.35
2 Days Rest	6	1	2	3	-1	2	0	0	9	11.1	.50
3+ Days Rest	8	0	1	1	1	0	0	0	6	0.0	.13

	G	A	Pts	PIM		G	A	Pts	PIM
1st Period	2	3	5	2	Winning	1	5	6	8
2nd Period	0	2	2	8	Losing	0	2	2	6
3rd Period	2	5	7	8	Tied	3	3	6	4
Overtime	0	0	0	0	Clutch	0	1	1	2
Last 5 Min	0	3	3	4	Blowouts	0	0	0	2

Cory Cross

Tampa Bay Lightning — Defense

1998-99 Season

	GP	G	A	Pts	+/–	PIM	PP	SH	S	SPct	P/G
Overall	67	2	16	18	-25	92	0	0	96	2.1	.27
Home	32	0	7	7	-1	38	0	0	41	0.0	.22
Away	35	2	9	11	-24	54	0	0	55	3.6	.31
vs. Division	12	0	5	5	-4	10	0	0	22	0.0	.42
vs. Conference	46	0	12	12	-10	69	0	0	63	0.0	.26
vs. Playoff	41	1	9	10	-21	80	0	0	59	1.7	.24
vs. Non-Playoff	26	1	7	8	-4	12	0	0	37	2.7	.31
Pre All-Star	43	2	13	15	-14	63	0	0	62	3.2	.35
Post All-Star	24	0	3	3	-11	29	0	0	34	0.0	.13
Day	4	0	2	2	2	4	0	0	6	0.0	.50
Night	63	2	14	16	-27	88	0	0	90	2.2	.25

	GP	G	A	Pts	+/–	PIM	PP	SH	S	SPct	P/G
National TV	1	0	0	0	2	2	0	0	0	–	.00
0 Days Rest	12	0	4	4	-11	30	0	0	17	0.0	.33
1 Days Rest	27	1	6	7	-3	48	0	0	35	2.9	.26
2 Days Rest	18	1	5	6	-5	8	0	0	27	3.7	.33
3+ Days Rest	10	0	1	1	-6	6	0	0	17	0.0	.10

	G	A	Pts	PIM		G	A	Pts	PIM
1st Period	0	5	5	23	Winning	1	5	6	16
2nd Period	1	5	6	28	Losing	1	7	8	72
3rd Period	1	6	7	41	Tied	0	4	4	4
Overtime	0	0	0	0	Clutch	0	2	2	10
Last 5 Min	1	2	3	25	Blowouts	0	2	2	26

Matt Cullen

Anaheim Mighty Ducks — Center

1998-99 Season

	GP	G	A	Pts	+/–	PIM	PP	SH	S	SPct	P/G
Overall	75	11	14	25	-12	47	5	1	112	9.8	.33
Home	38	5	9	14	-2	24	1	1	53	9.4	.37
Away	37	6	5	11	-10	23	4	0	59	10.2	.30
vs. Division	23	3	2	5	1	13	1	0	30	10.0	.22
vs. Conference	53	8	9	17	-12	29	4	1	71	11.3	.32
vs. Playoff	45	7	9	16	-12	25	3	1	69	10.1	.36
vs. Non-Playoff	30	4	5	9	0	22	2	0	43	9.3	.30
Pre All-Star	38	2	7	9	-5	22	1	1	57	3.5	.24
Post All-Star	37	9	7	16	-7	25	4	0	55	16.4	.43
Day	1	0	0	0	0	0	0	0	2	0.0	.00
Night	74	11	14	25	-12	47	5	1	110	10.0	.34

	GP	G	A	Pts	+/–	PIM	PP	SH	S	SPct	P/G
National TV	13	3	3	6	2	17	2	0	21	14.3	.46
0 Days Rest	15	3	2	5	3	8	1	0	21	14.3	.33
1 Days Rest	34	3	4	7	-15	17	2	1	49	6.1	.21
2 Days Rest	10	1	2	3	0	10	1	0	12	8.3	.30
3+ Days Rest	16	4	6	10	0	12	1	0	30	13.3	.63

	G	A	Pts	PIM		G	A	Pts	PIM
1st Period	2	4	6	14	Winning	3	3	6	37
2nd Period	6	5	11	16	Losing	4	5	9	6
3rd Period	3	5	8	17	Tied	4	6	10	4
Overtime	0	0	0	0	Clutch	1	1	2	4
Last 5 Min	2	2	4	21	Blowouts	0	0	0	11

Jassen Cullimore

Tampa Bay Lightning — Defense

1998-99 Season

	GP	G	A	Pts	+/–	PIM	PP	SH	S	SPct	P/G
Overall	78	5	12	17	-22	81	1	1	73	6.8	.22
Home	38	3	5	8	-5	51	1	1	39	7.7	.21
Away	40	2	7	9	-17	30	0	0	34	5.9	.23
vs. Division	14	3	3	6	1	16	0	1	15	20.0	.43
vs. Conference	53	3	10	13	-11	46	0	1	42	7.1	.25
vs. Playoff	49	2	7	9	-18	59	0	0	48	4.2	.18
vs. Non-Playoff	29	3	5	8	-4	22	1	1	25	12.0	.28
Pre All-Star	41	3	7	10	-11	44	1	0	38	7.9	.24
Post All-Star	37	2	5	7	-11	37	0	1	35	5.7	.19
Day	5	0	1	1	-1	2	0	0	6	0.0	.20
Night	73	5	11	16	-21	79	1	1	67	7.5	.22

	GP	G	A	Pts	+/–	PIM	PP	SH	S	SPct	P/G
National TV	1	0	0	0	2	0	0	0	0	–	.00
0 Days Rest	15	1	4	5	-10	16	0	0	15	6.7	.33
1 Days Rest	32	2	4	6	-8	29	1	1	32	6.3	.19
2 Days Rest	18	1	0	1	-6	22	0	0	15	6.7	.06
3+ Days Rest	13	1	4	5	2	14	0	0	11	9.1	.38

	G	A	Pts	PIM		G	A	Pts	PIM
1st Period	1	3	4	24	Winning	0	2	2	20
2nd Period	1	5	6	35	Losing	3	8	11	53
3rd Period	3	4	7	22	Tied	2	2	4	8
Overtime	0	0	0	0	Clutch	0	1	1	0
Last 5 Min	2	6	8	15	Blowouts	0	3	3	10

Mariusz Czerkawski

New York Islanders — Right Wing

1998-99 Season

	GP	G	A	Pts	+/–	PIM	PP	SH	S	SPct	P/G
Overall	78	21	17	38	-10	14	4	0	205	10.2	.49
Home	39	10	10	20	-2	10	3	0	103	9.7	.51
Away	39	11	7	18	-8	4	1	0	102	10.8	.46
vs. Division	19	5	2	7	-6	2	1	0	42	11.9	.37
vs. Conference	55	14	12	26	-13	8	2	0	142	9.9	.47
vs. Playoff	48	12	10	22	-14	6	3	0	123	9.8	.46
vs. Non-Playoff	30	9	7	16	4	8	1	0	82	11.0	.53
Pre All-Star	45	11	10	21	-4	10	4	0	108	10.2	.47
Post All-Star	33	10	7	17	-6	4	0	0	97	10.3	.52
Day	10	3	0	3	-1	2	0	0	27	11.1	.30
Night	68	18	17	35	-9	12	4	0	178	10.1	.51

	GP	G	A	Pts	+/–	PIM	PP	SH	S	SPct	P/G
National TV	5	2	0	2	-2	0	0	0	21	9.5	.40
0 Days Rest	12	2	1	3	-9	0	0	0	39	5.1	.25
1 Days Rest	35	10	10	20	5	6	1	0	90	11.1	.57
2 Days Rest	19	8	4	12	0	6	2	0	54	14.8	.63
3+ Days Rest	12	1	2	3	-6	2	1	0	22	4.5	.25

	G	A	Pts	PIM		G	A	Pts	PIM
1st Period	6	5	11	6	Winning	6	4	10	4
2nd Period	10	6	16	2	Losing	10	8	18	8
3rd Period	5	5	10	6	Tied	5	5	10	2
Overtime	0	1	1	0	Clutch	3	1	4	2
Last 5 Min	4	6	10	2	Blowouts	0	0	0	2

Andreas Dackell

Ottawa Senators — Right Wing

1998-99 Season

	GP	G	A	Pts	+/–	PIM	PP	SH	S	SPct	P/G
Overall	77	15	35	50	9	30	6	0	107	14.0	.65
Home	37	3	16	19	-1	22	1	0	48	6.3	.51
Away	40	12	19	31	10	8	5	0	59	20.3	.78
vs. Division	18	2	9	11	0	8	0	0	23	8.7	.61
vs. Conference	52	10	30	40	9	20	4	0	72	13.9	.77
vs. Playoff	44	10	14	24	1	20	4	0	60	16.7	.55
vs. Non-Playoff	33	5	21	26	8	10	2	0	47	10.6	.79
Pre All-Star	40	10	14	24	9	10	4	0	64	15.6	.60
Post All-Star	37	5	21	26	0	20	2	0	43	11.6	.70
Day	3	1	2	3	3	0	0	0	3	33.3	1.00
Night	74	14	33	47	6	30	6	0	104	13.5	.64

	GP	G	A	Pts	+/–	PIM	PP	SH	S	SPct	P/G
National TV	9	1	5	6	2	4	0	0	10	10.0	.67
0 Days Rest	12	3	3	6	-2	6	2	0	23	13.0	.50
1 Days Rest	39	8	22	30	8	20	2	0	48	16.7	.77
2 Days Rest	15	1	7	8	2	2	0	0	23	4.3	.53
3+ Days Rest	11	3	3	6	1	2	2	0	13	23.1	.55

	G	A	Pts	PIM		G	A	Pts	PIM
1st Period	5	11	16	10	Winning	4	16	20	16
2nd Period	6	7	13	10	Losing	3	7	10	4
3rd Period	3	17	20	10	Tied	8	12	20	10
Overtime	1	0	1	0	Clutch	2	7	9	0
Last 5 Min	4	11	15	8	Blowouts	1	4	5	4

Alexandre Daigle

Tampa Bay Lightning — Center

1998-99 Season

	GP	G	A	Pts	+/–	PIM	PP	SH	S	SPct	P/G
Overall	63	9	8	17	-13	4	4	0	82	11.0	.27
Home	31	5	5	10	-5	2	2	0	46	10.9	.32
Away	32	4	3	7	-8	2	2	0	36	11.1	.22
vs. Division	13	5	2	7	-7	2	4	0	23	21.7	.54
vs. Conference	44	7	6	13	-10	4	4	0	64	10.9	.30
vs. Playoff	39	4	5	9	-6	2	2	0	52	7.7	.23
vs. Non-Playoff	24	5	3	8	-7	2	2	0	30	16.7	.33
Pre All-Star	31	3	2	5	-1	2	1	0	26	11.5	.16
Post All-Star	32	6	6	12	-12	2	3	0	56	10.7	.38
Day	6	1	1	2	2	0	1	0	10	10.0	.33
Night	57	8	7	15	-15	4	3	0	72	11.1	.26

	GP	G	A	Pts	+/–	PIM	PP	SH	S	SPct	P/G
National TV	5	0	1	1	1	0	0	0	1	0.0	.20
0 Days Rest	8	1	0	1	-6	2	1	0	11	9.1	.13
1 Days Rest	26	3	3	6	-3	2	1	0	31	9.7	.23
2 Days Rest	12	0	1	1	0	0	0	0	10	0.0	.08
3+ Days Rest	17	5	4	9	-4	0	2	0	30	16.7	.53

	G	A	Pts	PIM		G	A	Pts	PIM
1st Period	3	4	7	0	Winning	1	3	4	2
2nd Period	3	2	5	2	Losing	6	1	7	2
3rd Period	3	2	5	2	Tied	2	4	6	0
Overtime	0	0	0	0	Clutch	0	0	0	0
Last 5 Min	4	1	5	0	Blowouts	2	0	2	0

J.J. Daigneault

Phoenix Coyotes — Defense

1998-99 Season

	GP	G	A	Pts	+/–	PIM	PP	SH	S	SPct	P/G
Overall	70	2	9	11	-12	70	1	0	65	3.1	.16
Home	37	1	5	6	-6	38	1	0	36	2.8	.16
Away	33	1	4	5	-6	32	0	0	29	3.4	.15
vs. Division	18	0	3	3	-11	22	0	0	14	0.0	.17
vs. Conference	48	0	6	6	-6	48	0	0	39	0.0	.13
vs. Playoff	43	2	4	6	-12	52	1	0	41	4.9	.14
vs. Non-Playoff	27	0	5	5	0	18	0	0	24	0.0	.19
Pre All-Star	39	2	2	4	-8	40	1	0	41	4.9	.10
Post All-Star	31	0	7	7	-4	30	0	0	24	0.0	.23
Day	8	1	1	2	2	4	0	0	11	9.1	.25
Night	62	1	8	9	-14	66	1	0	54	1.9	.15

	GP	G	A	Pts	+/–	PIM	PP	SH	S	SPct	P/G
National TV	5	0	0	0	-4	14	0	0	2	0.0	.00
0 Days Rest	7	1	3	4	0	8	0	0	11	9.1	.57
1 Days Rest	39	0	3	3	-11	38	0	0	35	0.0	.08
2 Days Rest	11	1	1	2	3	8	1	0	10	10.0	.18
3+ Days Rest	13	0	2	2	-4	16	0	0	9	0.0	.15

	G	A	Pts	PIM		G	A	Pts	PIM
1st Period	1	2	3	44	Winning	1	5	6	32
2nd Period	1	2	3	14	Losing	1	3	4	32
3rd Period	0	5	5	12	Tied	0	1	1	6
Overtime	0	0	0	0	Clutch	0	1	1	2
Last 5 Min	0	3	3	22	Blowouts	0	0	0	4

Vincent Damphousse

San Jose Sharks — Center

1998-99 Season

	GP	G	A	Pts	+/–	PIM	PP	SH	S	SPct	P/G
Overall	77	19	30	49	-4	50	6	2	190	10.0	.64
Home	38	9	17	26	1	28	4	1	96	9.4	.68
Away	39	10	13	23	-5	22	2	1	94	10.6	.59
vs. Division	20	2	10	12	-5	12	0	2	47	4.3	.60
vs. Conference	53	14	25	39	-2	28	4	2	127	11.0	.74
vs. Playoff	48	8	18	26	-14	38	2	2	109	7.3	.54
vs. Non-Playoff	29	11	12	23	10	12	4	0	81	13.6	.79
Pre All-Star	41	8	17	25	-4	34	3	1	102	7.8	.61
Post All-Star	36	11	13	24	0	16	3	1	88	12.5	.67
Day	4	0	2	2	-4	2	0	0	7	0.0	.50
Night	73	19	28	47	0	48	6	2	183	10.4	.64

	GP	G	A	Pts	+/–	PIM	PP	SH	S	SPct	P/G
National TV	24	8	12	20	-9	20	3	2	59	13.6	.83
0 Days Rest	15	5	5	10	-1	10	2	1	34	14.7	.67
1 Days Rest	31	3	16	19	-7	14	1	1	71	4.2	.61
2 Days Rest	19	4	6	10	-1	14	1	0	50	8.0	.53
3+ Days Rest	12	7	3	10	5	12	2	0	35	20.0	.83

	G	A	Pts	PIM		G	A	Pts	PIM
1st Period	2	10	12	18	Winning	7	8	15	20
2nd Period	6	10	16	14	Losing	7	8	15	26
3rd Period	11	10	21	18	Tied	5	14	19	4
Overtime	0	0	0	0	Clutch	0	1	1	2
Last 5 Min	4	10	14	8	Blowouts	1	1	2	14

Mathieu Dandenault

Detroit Red Wings — Right Wing

1998-99 Season

	GP	G	A	Pts	+/–	PIM	PP	SH	S	SPct	P/G
Overall	75	4	10	14	17	59	0	0	94	4.3	.19
Home	37	2	7	9	13	21	0	0	56	3.6	.24
Away	38	2	3	5	4	38	0	0	38	5.3	.13
vs. Division	17	2	1	3	7	8	0	0	26	7.7	.18
vs. Conference	49	3	10	13	12	40	0	0	65	4.6	.27
vs. Playoff	43	3	7	10	5	51	0	0	42	7.1	.23
vs. Non-Playoff	32	1	3	4	12	8	0	0	52	1.9	.13
Pre All-Star	39	2	4	6	9	33	0	0	42	4.8	.15
Post All-Star	36	2	6	8	8	26	0	0	52	3.8	.22
Day	13	0	1	1	4	8	0	0	12	0.0	.08
Night	62	4	9	13	13	51	0	0	82	4.9	.21

	GP	G	A	Pts	+/–	PIM	PP	SH	S	SPct	P/G
National TV	28	0	1	1	-3	18	0	0	32	0.0	.04
0 Days Rest	10	0	2	2	1	12	0	0	6	0.0	.20
1 Days Rest	34	0	5	5	8	14	0	0	45	0.0	.15
2 Days Rest	22	2	2	4	2	19	0	0	30	6.7	.18
3+ Days Rest	9	2	1	3	6	14	0	0	13	15.4	.33

	G	A	Pts	PIM		G	A	Pts	PIM
1st Period	0	0	0	12	Winning	1	5	6	28
2nd Period	4	5	9	20	Losing	2	2	4	27
3rd Period	0	5	5	27	Tied	1	3	4	4
Overtime	0	0	0	0	Clutch	0	0	0	2
Last 5 Min	0	3	3	12	Blowouts	0	2	2	6

Ken Daneyko

New Jersey Devils — Defense

1998-99 Season

	GP	G	A	Pts	+/–	PIM	PP	SH	S	SPct	P/G
Overall	82	2	9	11	27	63	0	0	63	3.2	.13
Home	41	1	5	6	4	25	0	0	36	2.8	.15
Away	41	1	4	5	23	38	0	0	27	3.7	.12
vs. Division	20	0	2	2	10	16	0	0	11	0.0	.10
vs. Conference	58	1	7	8	23	43	0	0	40	2.5	.14
vs. Playoff	46	0	6	6	13	34	0	0	32	0.0	.13
vs. Non-Playoff	36	2	3	5	14	29	0	0	31	6.5	.14
Pre All-Star	44	1	4	5	17	39	0	0	32	3.1	.11
Post All-Star	38	1	5	6	10	24	0	0	31	3.2	.16
Day	12	1	0	1	1	17	0	0	18	5.6	.08
Night	70	1	9	10	26	46	0	0	45	2.2	.14

	GP	G	A	Pts	+/–	PIM	PP	SH	S	SPct	P/G
National TV	7	0	0	0	-1	6	0	0	4	0.0	.00
0 Days Rest	17	0	5	5	9	14	0	0	13	0.0	.29
1 Days Rest	34	0	3	3	0	27	0	0	19	0.0	.09
2 Days Rest	21	1	1	2	8	14	0	0	21	4.8	.10
3+ Days Rest	10	1	0	1	10	8	0	0	10	10.0	.10

	G	A	Pts	PIM		G	A	Pts	PIM
1st Period	1	5	6	27	Winning	0	2	2	28
2nd Period	1	1	2	20	Losing	1	2	3	22
3rd Period	0	3	3	14	Tied	1	5	6	13
Overtime	0	0	0	2	Clutch	0	0	0	8
Last 5 Min	0	1	1	27	Blowouts	0	1	1	4

Jason Dawe

Montreal Canadiens — Right Wing

1998-99 Season

	GP	G	A	Pts	+/–	PIM	PP	SH	S	SPct	P/G
Overall	59	6	8	14	0	22	1	0	81	7.4	.24
Home	29	6	3	9	4	10	1	0	36	16.7	.31
Away	30	0	5	5	-4	12	0	0	45	0.0	.17
vs. Division	14	3	0	3	-3	6	1	0	27	11.1	.21
vs. Conference	41	5	4	9	-1	14	1	0	56	8.9	.22
vs. Playoff	32	5	6	11	-1	12	1	0	42	11.9	.34
vs. Non-Playoff	27	1	2	3	1	10	0	0	39	2.6	.11
Pre All-Star	39	3	6	9	-3	16	0	0	56	5.4	.23
Post All-Star	20	3	2	5	3	6	1	0	25	12.0	.25
Day	3	0	0	0	0	2	0	0	4	0.0	.00
Night	56	6	8	14	0	20	1	0	77	7.8	.25

	GP	G	A	Pts	+/–	PIM	PP	SH	S	SPct	P/G
National TV	12	2	1	3	1	4	1	0	19	10.5	.25
0 Days Rest	10	0	1	1	-1	2	0	0	9	0.0	.10
1 Days Rest	21	3	3	6	0	8	0	0	24	12.5	.29
2 Days Rest	16	0	4	4	1	8	0	0	21	0.0	.25
3+ Days Rest	12	3	0	3	0	4	1	0	27	11.1	.25

	G	A	Pts	PIM		G	A	Pts	PIM
1st Period	2	4	6	8	Winning	3	2	5	10
2nd Period	2	2	4	6	Losing	2	2	4	12
3rd Period	2	2	4	8	Tied	1	4	5	0
Overtime	0	0	0	0	Clutch	0	0	0	0
Last 5 Min	1	1	2	2	Blowouts	0	0	0	0

Eric Daze

Chicago Blackhawks — Left Wing

1998-99 Season

	GP	G	A	Pts	+/–	PIM	PP	SH	S	SPct	P/G
Overall	72	22	20	42	-13	22	8	0	189	11.6	.58
Home	36	10	9	19	-9	16	5	0	96	10.4	.53
Away	36	12	11	23	-4	6	3	0	93	12.9	.64
vs. Division	16	3	5	8	-2	2	1	0	46	6.5	.50
vs. Conference	48	13	14	27	-2	8	4	0	124	10.5	.56
vs. Playoff	48	16	9	25	-8	22	7	0	122	13.1	.52
vs. Non-Playoff	24	6	11	17	-5	0	1	0	67	9.0	.71
Pre All-Star	36	10	5	15	-18	14	5	0	93	10.8	.42
Post All-Star	36	12	15	27	5	8	3	0	96	12.5	.75
Day	10	4	4	8	-1	8	2	0	32	12.5	.80
Night	62	18	16	34	-12	14	6	0	157	11.5	.55

	GP	G	A	Pts	+/–	PIM	PP	SH	S	SPct	P/G
National TV	17	3	5	8	-3	2	1	0	42	7.1	.47
0 Days Rest	12	7	4	11	-1	4	3	0	35	20.0	.92
1 Days Rest	35	10	6	16	-10	12	3	0	86	11.6	.46
2 Days Rest	14	2	7	9	0	4	1	0	40	5.0	.64
3+ Days Rest	11	3	3	6	-2	2	1	0	28	10.7	.55

	G	A	Pts	PIM		G	A	Pts	PIM
1st Period	2	8	10	0	Winning	3	5	8	4
2nd Period	8	7	15	6	Losing	12	5	17	14
3rd Period	12	5	17	16	Tied	7	10	17	4
Overtime	0	0	0	0	Clutch	3	0	3	2
Last 5 Min	6	3	9	0	Blowouts	3	1	4	14

Adam Deadmarsh

Colorado Avalanche — Right Wing

1998-99 Season

	GP	G	A	Pts	+/–	PIM	PP	SH	S	SPct	P/G
Overall	66	22	27	49	-2	99	10	0	152	14.5	.74
Home	30	10	13	23	-5	56	4	0	75	13.3	.77
Away	36	12	14	26	3	43	6	0	77	15.6	.72
vs. Division	15	6	5	11	-9	65	4	0	31	19.4	.73
vs. Conference	44	13	19	32	-2	77	7	0	102	12.7	.73
vs. Playoff	37	10	16	26	2	64	4	0	81	12.3	.70
vs. Non-Playoff	29	12	11	23	-4	35	6	0	71	16.9	.79
Pre All-Star	40	11	14	25	-4	65	4	0	94	11.7	.63
Post All-Star	26	11	13	24	2	34	6	0	58	19.0	.92
Day	11	1	6	7	1	2	0	0	25	4.0	.64
Night	55	21	21	42	-3	97	10	0	127	16.5	.76

	GP	G	A	Pts	+/–	PIM	PP	SH	S	SPct	P/G
National TV	19	6	8	14	3	37	3	0	50	12.0	.74
0 Days Rest	11	4	3	7	-7	10	4	0	26	15.4	.64
1 Days Rest	32	11	18	29	-6	37	5	0	75	14.7	.91
2 Days Rest	12	5	3	8	8	24	1	0	29	17.2	.67
3+ Days Rest	11	2	3	5	3	28	0	0	22	9.1	.45

	G	A	Pts	PIM		G	A	Pts	PIM
1st Period	10	7	17	28	Winning	8	9	17	78
2nd Period	5	9	14	52	Losing	5	5	10	17
3rd Period	7	11	18	19	Tied	9	13	22	4
Overtime	0	0	0	0	Clutch	1	7	8	4
Last 5 Min	3	9	12	43	Blowouts	0	2	2	7

Kevin Dean

New Jersey Devils — Defense

1998-99 Season

	GP	G	A	Pts	+/–	PIM	PP	SH	S	SPct	P/G
Overall	62	1	10	11	4	22	1	0	51	2.0	.18
Home	30	1	6	7	5	10	1	0	27	3.7	.23
Away	32	0	4	4	-1	12	0	0	24	0.0	.13
vs. Division	15	0	3	3	7	8	0	0	7	0.0	.20
vs. Conference	44	0	7	7	2	20	0	0	33	0.0	.16
vs. Playoff	34	1	3	4	0	16	1	0	30	3.3	.12
vs. Non-Playoff	28	0	7	7	4	6	0	0	21	0.0	.25
Pre All-Star	35	0	6	6	-2	14	0	0	26	0.0	.17
Post All-Star	27	1	4	5	6	8	1	0	25	4.0	.19
Day	11	0	3	3	5	2	0	0	9	0.0	.27
Night	51	1	7	8	-1	20	1	0	42	2.4	.16

	GP	G	A	Pts	+/–	PIM	PP	SH	S	SPct	P/G
National TV	5	0	0	0	3	0	0	0	2	0.0	.00
0 Days Rest	11	0	1	1	-1	6	0	0	12	0.0	.09
1 Days Rest	21	0	7	7	5	4	0	0	20	0.0	.33
2 Days Rest	16	1	1	2	0	2	1	0	13	7.7	.13
3+ Days Rest	14	0	1	1	0	10	0	0	6	0.0	.07

	G	A	Pts	PIM		G	A	Pts	PIM
1st Period	0	3	3	14	Winning	1	2	3	16
2nd Period	0	4	4	4	Losing	0	3	3	4
3rd Period	1	2	3	4	Tied	0	5	5	2
Overtime	0	1	1	0	Clutch	0	1	1	2
Last 5 Min	0	2	2	2	Blowouts	1	0	1	4

Pavol Demitra

St. Louis Blues — Left Wing

1998-99 Season

	GP	G	A	Pts	+/–	PIM	PP	SH	S	SPct	P/G
Overall	82	37	52	89	13	16	14	0	259	14.3	1.09
Home	41	23	29	52	5	6	9	0	132	17.4	1.27
Away	41	14	23	37	8	10	5	0	127	11.0	.90
vs. Division	18	9	14	23	-1	2	6	0	48	18.8	1.28
vs. Conference	55	23	40	63	6	8	10	0	166	13.9	1.15
vs. Playoff	46	19	26	45	-2	4	6	0	144	13.2	.98
vs. Non-Playoff	36	18	26	44	15	12	8	0	115	15.7	1.22
Pre All-Star	42	21	24	45	3	8	11	0	125	16.8	1.07
Post All-Star	40	16	28	44	10	8	3	0	134	11.9	1.10
Day	11	7	11	18	4	2	3	0	45	15.6	1.64
Night	71	30	41	71	9	14	11	0	214	14.0	1.00

	GP	G	A	Pts	+/–	PIM	PP	SH	S	SPct	P/G
National TV	17	9	9	18	2	6	3	0	60	15.0	1.06
0 Days Rest	12	5	4	9	-2	0	2	0	31	16.1	.75
1 Days Rest	43	18	32	50	12	16	4	0	140	12.9	1.16
2 Days Rest	17	9	9	18	2	0	6	0	61	14.8	1.06
3+ Days Rest	10	5	7	12	1	0	2	0	27	18.5	1.20

	G	A	Pts	PIM		G	A	Pts	PIM
1st Period	13	23	36	6	Winning	15	25	40	12
2nd Period	11	15	26	4	Losing	13	10	23	2
3rd Period	13	13	26	6	Tied	9	17	26	2
Overtime	0	1	1	0	Clutch	6	3	9	0
Last 5 Min	9	15	24	0	Blowouts	0	2	2	0

Eric Desjardins

Philadelphia Flyers — Defense

1998-99 Season

	GP	G	A	Pts	+/–	PIM	PP	SH	S	SPct	P/G
Overall	68	15	36	51	18	38	6	0	190	7.9	.75
Home	36	5	23	28	11	12	2	0	93	5.4	.78
Away	32	10	13	23	7	26	4	0	97	10.3	.72
vs. Division	14	2	9	11	0	12	2	0	36	5.6	.79
vs. Conference	45	9	20	29	6	26	5	0	122	7.4	.64
vs. Playoff	38	9	19	28	8	22	3	0	98	9.2	.74
vs. Non-Playoff	30	6	17	23	10	16	3	0	92	6.5	.77
Pre All-Star	40	8	23	31	19	24	3	0	101	7.9	.78
Post All-Star	28	7	13	20	-1	14	3	0	89	7.9	.71
Day	11	3	4	7	-2	6	1	0	34	8.8	.64
Night	57	12	32	44	20	32	5	0	156	7.7	.77

	GP	G	A	Pts	+/–	PIM	PP	SH	S	SPct	P/G
National TV	15	4	9	13	-1	10	3	0	38	10.5	.87
0 Days Rest	8	1	4	5	2	8	0	0	12	8.3	.63
1 Days Rest	32	7	18	25	13	16	3	0	92	7.6	.78
2 Days Rest	17	6	7	13	2	8	3	0	46	13.0	.76
3+ Days Rest	11	1	7	8	1	6	0	0	40	2.5	.73

	G	A	Pts	PIM		G	A	Pts	PIM
1st Period	5	14	19	8	Winning	5	16	21	16
2nd Period	1	12	13	18	Losing	3	13	16	12
3rd Period	9	10	19	12	Tied	7	7	14	10
Overtime	0	0	0	0	Clutch	2	3	5	4
Last 5 Min	5	15	20	8	Blowouts	2	1	3	2

Boyd Devereaux

Edmonton Oilers — Center

1998-99 Season

	GP	G	A	Pts	+/–	PIM	PP	SH	S	SPct	P/G
Overall	61	6	8	14	2	23	0	1	39	15.4	.23
Home	34	3	6	9	2	9	0	1	24	12.5	.26
Away	27	3	2	5	0	14	0	0	15	20.0	.19
vs. Division	15	0	1	1	-1	7	0	0	7	0.0	.07
vs. Conference	45	2	5	7	-2	15	0	0	23	8.7	.16
vs. Playoff	33	4	3	7	-1	14	0	1	21	19.0	.21
vs. Non-Playoff	28	2	5	7	3	9	0	0	18	11.1	.25
Pre All-Star	41	6	7	13	3	19	0	1	34	17.6	.32
Post All-Star	20	0	1	1	-1	4	0	0	5	0.0	.05
Day	2	1	0	1	2	0	0	0	3	33.3	.50
Night	59	5	8	13	0	23	0	1	36	13.9	.22

	GP	G	A	Pts	+/–	PIM	PP	SH	S	SPct	P/G
National TV	9	1	2	3	3	2	0	1	5	20.0	.33
0 Days Rest	8	2	0	2	1	4	0	0	6	33.3	.25
1 Days Rest	29	1	4	5	-2	8	0	0	12	8.3	.17
2 Days Rest	10	2	1	3	4	2	0	1	9	22.2	.30
3+ Days Rest	14	1	3	4	-1	9	0	0	12	8.3	.29

	G	A	Pts	PIM		G	A	Pts	PIM
1st Period	1	5	6	6	Winning	4	1	5	19
2nd Period	3	1	4	4	Losing	1	3	4	0
3rd Period	2	2	4	13	Tied	1	4	5	4
Overtime	0	0	0	0	Clutch	2	0	2	0
Last 5 Min	2	1	3	9	Blowouts	0	0	0	6

Rob DiMaio

Boston Bruins — Center

1998-99 Season

	GP	G	A	Pts	+/–	PIM	PP	SH	S	SPct	P/G
Overall	71	7	14	21	-14	95	1	0	121	5.8	.30
Home	37	5	9	14	-3	51	0	0	71	7.0	.38
Away	34	2	5	7	-11	44	1	0	50	4.0	.21
vs. Division	19	3	7	10	-2	44	1	0	37	8.1	.53
vs. Conference	51	5	11	16	-11	66	1	0	89	5.6	.31
vs. Playoff	40	3	6	9	-15	72	1	0	80	3.8	.23
vs. Non-Playoff	31	4	8	12	1	23	0	0	41	9.8	.39
Pre All-Star	35	3	11	14	-3	58	0	0	52	5.8	.40
Post All-Star	36	4	3	7	-11	37	1	0	69	5.8	.19
Day	14	0	6	6	4	12	0	0	24	0.0	.43
Night	57	7	8	15	-18	83	1	0	97	7.2	.26

	GP	G	A	Pts	+/–	PIM	PP	SH	S	SPct	P/G
National TV	10	1	2	3	-5	4	0	0	15	6.7	.30
0 Days Rest	15	2	2	4	-4	42	0	0	28	7.1	.27
1 Days Rest	29	1	8	9	-3	33	0	0	46	2.2	.31
2 Days Rest	11	1	1	2	-3	10	0	0	19	5.3	.18
3+ Days Rest	16	3	3	6	-4	10	1	0	28	10.7	.38

	G	A	Pts	PIM		G	A	Pts	PIM
1st Period	0	4	4	29	Winning	3	5	8	54
2nd Period	5	1	6	35	Losing	1	3	4	33
3rd Period	2	9	11	31	Tied	3	6	9	8
Overtime	0	0	0	0	Clutch	1	1	2	2
Last 5 Min	0	2	2	56	Blowouts	0	1	1	6

Kevin Dineen

Carolina Hurricanes — Right Wing

1998-99 Season

	GP	G	A	Pts	+/–	PIM	PP	SH	S	SPct	P/G
Overall	67	8	10	18	5	97	0	0	86	9.3	.27
Home	35	4	7	11	3	61	0	0	46	8.7	.31
Away	32	4	3	7	2	36	0	0	40	10.0	.22
vs. Division	14	3	4	7	5	23	0	0	22	13.6	.50
vs. Conference	51	7	9	16	5	75	0	0	70	10.0	.31
vs. Playoff	34	3	3	6	-3	29	0	0	42	7.1	.18
vs. Non-Playoff	33	5	7	12	8	68	0	0	44	11.4	.36
Pre All-Star	41	6	6	12	6	61	0	0	55	10.9	.29
Post All-Star	26	2	4	6	-1	36	0	0	31	6.5	.23
Day	7	1	0	1	0	12	0	0	9	11.1	.14
Night	60	7	10	17	5	85	0	0	77	9.1	.28

	GP	G	A	Pts	+/–	PIM	PP	SH	S	SPct	P/G
National TV	1	0	0	0	0	0	0	0	1	0.0	.00
0 Days Rest	12	3	0	3	2	11	0	0	19	15.8	.25
1 Days Rest	27	1	3	4	2	42	0	0	28	3.6	.15
2 Days Rest	16	2	4	6	0	36	0	0	21	9.5	.38
3+ Days Rest	12	2	3	5	1	8	0	0	18	11.1	.42

	G	A	Pts	PIM		G	A	Pts	PIM
1st Period	4	2	6	21	Winning	1	2	3	51
2nd Period	2	7	9	46	Losing	4	6	10	30
3rd Period	2	1	3	30	Tied	3	2	5	16
Overtime	0	0	0	0	Clutch	0	0	0	20
Last 5 Min	0	2	2	41	Blowouts	0	1	1	11

Shane Doan

Phoenix Coyotes — Right Wing

1998-99 Season

	GP	G	A	Pts	+/–	PIM	PP	SH	S	SPct	P/G
Overall	79	6	16	22	-5	54	0	0	156	3.8	.28
Home	41	2	6	8	-4	33	0	0	90	2.2	.20
Away	38	4	10	14	-1	21	0	0	66	6.1	.37
vs. Division	24	2	4	6	0	2	0	0	48	4.2	.25
vs. Conference	54	6	13	19	2	35	0	0	111	5.4	.35
vs. Playoff	45	6	8	14	-3	40	0	0	95	6.3	.31
vs. Non-Playoff	34	0	8	8	-2	14	0	0	61	0.0	.24
Pre All-Star	41	2	7	9	-2	33	0	0	78	2.6	.22
Post All-Star	38	4	9	13	-3	21	0	0	78	5.1	.34
Day	6	1	1	2	2	0	0	0	12	8.3	.33
Night	73	5	15	20	-7	54	0	0	144	3.5	.27

	GP	G	A	Pts	+/–	PIM	PP	SH	S	SPct	P/G
National TV	13	0	1	1	-1	2	0	0	16	0.0	.08
0 Days Rest	11	3	4	7	-2	26	0	0	28	10.7	.64
1 Days Rest	39	1	9	10	1	17	0	0	76	1.3	.26
2 Days Rest	16	2	3	5	0	4	0	0	35	5.7	.31
3+ Days Rest	13	0	0	0	-4	7	0	0	17	0.0	.00

	G	A	Pts	PIM		G	A	Pts	PIM
1st Period	1	4	5	6	Winning	2	8	10	24
2nd Period	2	6	8	46	Losing	4	4	8	18
3rd Period	3	6	9	2	Tied	0	4	4	12
Overtime	0	0	0	0	Clutch	0	2	2	0
Last 5 Min	3	7	10	27	Blowouts	0	1	1	4

Bobby Dollas

Pittsburgh Penguins — Defense

1998-99 Season

	GP	G	A	Pts	+/–	PIM	PP	SH	S	SPct	P/G
Overall	70	2	8	10	-3	60	0	0	34	5.9	.14
Home	35	1	3	4	2	41	0	0	20	5.0	.11
Away	35	1	5	6	-5	19	0	0	14	7.1	.17
vs. Division	18	1	1	2	2	8	0	0	5	20.0	.11
vs. Conference	51	2	6	8	-1	54	0	0	23	8.7	.16
vs. Playoff	41	1	6	7	-6	18	0	0	22	4.5	.17
vs. Non-Playoff	29	1	2	3	3	42	0	0	12	8.3	.10
Pre All-Star	36	1	4	5	-7	46	0	0	20	5.0	.14
Post All-Star	34	1	4	5	4	14	0	0	14	7.1	.15
Day	15	1	1	2	8	2	0	0	8	12.5	.13
Night	55	1	7	8	-11	58	0	0	26	3.8	.15

	GP	G	A	Pts	+/–	PIM	PP	SH	S	SPct	P/G
National TV	17	2	0	2	2	8	0	0	3	66.7	.12
0 Days Rest	13	1	1	2	2	27	0	0	9	11.1	.15
1 Days Rest	27	0	4	4	-5	17	0	0	10	0.0	.15
2 Days Rest	17	1	1	2	4	10	0	0	8	12.5	.12
3+ Days Rest	13	0	2	2	-4	6	0	0	7	0.0	.15

	G	A	Pts	PIM		G	A	Pts	PIM
1st Period	1	1	2	12	Winning	0	2	2	46
2nd Period	1	5	6	10	Losing	2	5	7	10
3rd Period	0	2	2	38	Tied	0	1	1	4
Overtime	0	0	0	0	Clutch	0	1	1	0
Last 5 Min	0	3	3	11	Blowouts	0	1	1	36

Hnat Domenichelli

Calgary Flames — Center

1998-99 Season

	GP	G	A	Pts	+/–	PIM	PP	SH	S	SPct	P/G
Overall	23	5	5	10	-4	11	3	0	45	11.1	.43
Home	6	2	1	3	1	2	1	0	16	12.5	.50
Away	17	3	4	7	-5	9	2	0	29	10.3	.41
vs. Division	6	1	5	6	3	5	0	0	10	10.0	1.00
vs. Conference	16	2	5	7	-2	5	1	0	29	6.9	.44
vs. Playoff	14	3	3	6	-5	4	1	0	24	12.5	.43
vs. Non-Playoff	9	2	2	4	1	7	2	0	21	9.5	.44
Pre All-Star	4	1	0	1	-1	2	0	0	8	12.5	.25
Post All-Star	19	4	5	9	-3	9	3	0	37	10.8	.47
Day	1	0	0	0	0	2	0	0	5	0.0	.00
Night	22	5	5	10	-4	9	3	0	40	12.5	.45

	GP	G	A	Pts	+/–	PIM	PP	SH	S	SPct	P/G
National TV	5	1	2	3	-1	2	1	0	11	9.1	.60
0 Days Rest	8	3	1	4	1	0	1	0	14	21.4	.50
1 Days Rest	5	1	2	3	-2	0	1	0	6	16.7	.60
2 Days Rest	4	1	0	1	-2	2	1	0	5	20.0	.25
3+ Days Rest	6	0	2	2	-1	9	0	0	20	0.0	.33

	G	A	Pts	PIM		G	A	Pts	PIM
1st Period	2	1	3	7	Winning	0	2	2	7
2nd Period	3	0	3	2	Losing	2	2	4	4
3rd Period	0	4	4	2	Tied	3	1	4	0
Overtime	0	0	0	0	Clutch	0	1	1	0
Last 5 Min	0	2	2	5	Blowouts	0	0	0	7

Tie Domi

Toronto Maple Leafs — Right Wing

1998-99 Season

	GP	G	A	Pts	+/–	PIM	PP	SH	S	SPct	P/G
Overall	72	8	14	22	5	198	0	0	65	12.3	.31
Home	39	3	10	13	5	131	0	0	33	9.1	.33
Away	33	5	4	9	0	67	0	0	32	15.6	.27
vs. Division	18	2	3	5	-1	58	0	0	16	12.5	.28
vs. Conference	48	6	8	14	-1	139	0	0	48	12.5	.29
vs. Playoff	39	3	7	10	-1	144	0	0	31	9.7	.26
vs. Non-Playoff	33	5	7	12	6	54	0	0	34	14.7	.36
Pre All-Star	38	4	8	12	0	97	0	0	35	11.4	.32
Post All-Star	34	4	6	10	5	101	0	0	30	13.3	.29
Day	1	0	0	0	-1	0	0	0	0	–	.00
Night	71	8	14	22	6	198	0	0	65	12.3	.31

	GP	G	A	Pts	+/–	PIM	PP	SH	S	SPct	P/G
National TV	25	2	6	8	-1	55	0	0	28	7.1	.32
0 Days Rest	16	2	4	6	3	41	0	0	15	13.3	.38
1 Days Rest	31	2	2	4	-7	80	0	0	22	9.1	.13
2 Days Rest	10	3	2	5	1	30	0	0	18	16.7	.50
3+ Days Rest	15	1	6	7	8	47	0	0	10	10.0	.47

	G	A	Pts	PIM		G	A	Pts	PIM
1st Period	4	2	6	63	Winning	5	8	13	78
2nd Period	3	8	11	71	Losing	1	4	5	111
3rd Period	1	4	5	64	Tied	2	2	4	9
Overtime	0	0	0	0	Clutch	1	0	1	0
Last 5 Min	2	2	4	65	Blowouts	1	3	4	43

Ted Donato

Ottawa Senators — Left Wing

1998-99 Season

	GP	G	A	Pts	+/–	PIM	PP	SH	S	SPct	P/G
Overall	82	11	16	27	-8	41	3	0	106	10.4	.33
Home	39	4	6	10	-11	12	1	0	47	8.5	.26
Away	43	7	10	17	3	29	2	0	59	11.9	.40
vs. Division	21	3	6	9	-2	11	0	0	28	10.7	.43
vs. Conference	56	9	12	21	-4	35	2	0	69	13.0	.38
vs. Playoff	51	5	7	12	-12	18	1	0	56	8.9	.24
vs. Non-Playoff	31	6	9	15	4	23	2	0	50	12.0	.48
Pre All-Star	46	6	11	17	-4	25	1	0	64	9.4	.37
Post All-Star	36	5	5	10	-4	16	2	0	42	11.9	.28
Day	9	0	2	2	-2	6	0	0	9	0.0	.22
Night	73	11	14	25	-6	35	3	0	97	11.3	.34

	GP	G	A	Pts	+/–	PIM	PP	SH	S	SPct	P/G
National TV	3	0	1	1	0	0	0	0	5	0.0	.33
0 Days Rest	16	4	7	11	2	12	0	0	17	23.5	.69
1 Days Rest	37	5	4	9	-4	19	2	0	40	12.5	.24
2 Days Rest	16	0	4	4	-5	8	0	0	20	0.0	.25
3+ Days Rest	13	2	1	3	-1	2	1	0	29	6.9	.23

	G	A	Pts	PIM		G	A	Pts	PIM
1st Period	2	8	10	19	Winning	0	4	4	14
2nd Period	6	5	11	16	Losing	8	7	15	21
3rd Period	3	3	6	6	Tied	3	5	8	6
Overtime	0	0	0	0	Clutch	0	1	1	0
Last 5 Min	2	3	5	11	Blowouts	0	1	1	6

Shean Donovan

Colorado Avalanche — Right Wing

1998-99 Season

	GP	G	A	Pts	+/–	PIM	PP	SH	S	SPct	P/G
Overall	68	7	12	19	4	37	1	0	81	8.6	.28
Home	33	2	5	7	0	25	0	0	44	4.5	.21
Away	35	5	7	12	4	12	1	0	37	13.5	.34
vs. Division	13	2	0	2	1	13	0	0	17	11.8	.15
vs. Conference	44	7	5	12	4	29	1	0	54	13.0	.27
vs. Playoff	38	3	7	10	5	29	0	0	45	6.7	.26
vs. Non-Playoff	30	4	5	9	-1	8	1	0	36	11.1	.30
Pre All-Star	38	5	6	11	1	25	1	0	46	10.9	.29
Post All-Star	30	2	6	8	3	12	0	0	35	5.7	.27
Day	12	0	3	3	-1	4	0	0	12	0.0	.25
Night	56	7	9	16	5	33	1	0	69	10.1	.29

	GP	G	A	Pts	+/–	PIM	PP	SH	S	SPct	P/G
National TV	17	0	3	3	0	17	0	0	17	0.0	.18
0 Days Rest	10	1	3	4	1	4	0	0	15	6.7	.40
1 Days Rest	32	4	5	9	4	14	1	0	40	10.0	.28
2 Days Rest	10	1	3	4	-2	4	0	0	9	11.1	.40
3+ Days Rest	16	1	1	2	1	15	0	0	17	5.9	.13

	G	A	Pts	PIM		G	A	Pts	PIM
1st Period	1	2	3	21	Winning	2	5	7	19
2nd Period	5	4	9	10	Losing	4	6	10	18
3rd Period	1	6	7	6	Tied	1	1	2	0
Overtime	0	0	0	0	Clutch	0	2	2	2
Last 5 Min	2	3	5	15	Blowouts	1	1	2	0

Dallas Drake

Phoenix Coyotes — Right Wing

1998-99 Season

	GP	G	A	Pts	+/–	PIM	PP	SH	S	SPct	P/G
Overall	53	9	22	31	17	65	0	0	105	8.6	.58
Home	26	4	13	17	12	41	0	0	50	8.0	.65
Away	27	5	9	14	5	24	0	0	55	9.1	.52
vs. Division	15	2	6	8	4	22	0	0	29	6.9	.53
vs. Conference	35	7	17	24	13	51	0	0	67	10.4	.69
vs. Playoff	32	7	12	19	10	20	0	0	63	11.1	.59
vs. Non-Playoff	21	2	10	12	7	45	0	0	42	4.8	.57
Pre All-Star	34	8	13	21	17	40	0	0	76	10.5	.62
Post All-Star	19	1	9	10	0	25	0	0	29	3.4	.53
Day	2	0	0	0	0	0	0	0	2	0.0	.00
Night	51	9	22	31	17	65	0	0	103	8.7	.61

	GP	G	A	Pts	+/–	PIM	PP	SH	S	SPct	P/G
National TV	9	2	5	7	2	4	0	0	23	8.7	.78
0 Days Rest	7	1	2	3	3	4	0	0	9	11.1	.43
1 Days Rest	23	3	10	13	5	42	0	0	42	7.1	.57
2 Days Rest	9	1	5	6	3	9	0	0	19	5.3	.67
3+ Days Rest	14	4	5	9	6	10	0	0	35	11.4	.64

	G	A	Pts	PIM		G	A	Pts	PIM
1st Period	1	10	11	22	Winning	2	12	14	20
2nd Period	4	5	9	25	Losing	2	5	7	39
3rd Period	3	7	10	18	Tied	5	5	10	6
Overtime	1	0	1	0	Clutch	1	1	2	2
Last 5 Min	3	4	7	30	Blowouts	0	2	2	2

Kris Draper

Detroit Red Wings — Center

1998-99 Season

	GP	G	A	Pts	+/–	PIM	PP	SH	S	SPct	P/G
Overall	80	4	14	18	2	79	0	1	78	5.1	.23
Home	40	3	7	10	-1	42	0	0	41	7.3	.25
Away	40	1	7	8	3	37	0	1	37	2.7	.20
vs. Division	18	3	3	6	4	21	0	0	17	17.6	.33
vs. Conference	54	3	9	12	-1	53	0	0	59	5.1	.22
vs. Playoff	46	3	4	7	-4	52	0	1	44	6.8	.15
vs. Non-Playoff	34	1	10	11	6	27	0	0	34	2.9	.32
Pre All-Star	46	3	7	10	-5	46	0	0	46	6.5	.22
Post All-Star	34	1	7	8	7	33	0	1	32	3.1	.24
Day	13	2	1	3	3	8	0	1	12	16.7	.23
Night	67	2	13	15	-1	71	0	0	66	3.0	.22

	GP	G	A	Pts	+/–	PIM	PP	SH	S	SPct	P/G
National TV	30	1	7	8	-1	10	0	1	31	3.2	.27
0 Days Rest	12	0	2	2	-3	16	0	0	12	0.0	.17
1 Days Rest	37	3	7	10	2	24	0	1	39	7.7	.27
2 Days Rest	24	1	3	4	-1	18	0	0	21	4.8	.17
3+ Days Rest	7	0	2	2	4	21	0	0	6	0.0	.29

	G	A	Pts	PIM		G	A	Pts	PIM
1st Period	1	4	5	18	Winning	3	7	10	49
2nd Period	1	7	8	33	Losing	1	3	4	30
3rd Period	2	3	5	28	Tied	0	4	4	0
Overtime	0	0	0	0	Clutch	0	0	0	2
Last 5 Min	3	5	8	21	Blowouts	0	0	0	8

Chris Drury

Colorado Avalanche — Center

1998-99 Season

	GP	G	A	Pts	+/–	PIM	PP	SH	S	SPct	P/G
Overall	79	20	24	44	9	62	6	0	138	14.5	.56
Home	40	8	13	21	3	27	2	0	79	10.1	.53
Away	39	12	11	23	6	35	4	0	59	20.3	.59
vs. Division	18	2	3	5	-2	12	2	0	34	5.9	.28
vs. Conference	55	13	17	30	4	41	4	0	101	12.9	.55
vs. Playoff	43	7	10	17	6	36	2	0	69	10.1	.40
vs. Non-Playoff	36	13	14	27	3	26	4	0	69	18.8	.75
Pre All-Star	42	10	12	22	2	35	3	0	67	14.9	.52
Post All-Star	37	10	12	22	7	27	3	0	71	14.1	.59
Day	15	5	2	7	-1	9	2	0	22	22.7	.47
Night	64	15	22	37	10	53	4	0	116	12.9	.58

	GP	G	A	Pts	+/–	PIM	PP	SH	S	SPct	P/G
National TV	22	7	3	10	5	15	1	0	44	15.9	.45
0 Days Rest	13	2	5	7	1	11	1	0	27	7.4	.54
1 Days Rest	38	14	14	28	7	33	4	0	64	21.9	.74
2 Days Rest	14	3	5	8	3	8	1	0	25	12.0	.57
3+ Days Rest	14	1	0	1	-2	10	0	0	22	4.5	.07

	G	A	Pts	PIM		G	A	Pts	PIM
1st Period	2	7	9	21	Winning	7	9	16	22
2nd Period	9	10	19	33	Losing	12	6	18	33
3rd Period	9	7	16	8	Tied	1	9	10	7
Overtime	0	0	0	0	Clutch	2	2	4	4
Last 5 Min	5	5	10	10	Blowouts	3	2	5	14

Ted Drury

Anaheim Mighty Ducks — Center

1998-99 Season

	GP	G	A	Pts	+/–	PIM	PP	SH	S	SPct	P/G
Overall	75	5	6	11	2	83	0	0	79	6.3	.15
Home	38	3	4	7	4	49	0	0	46	6.5	.18
Away	37	2	2	4	-2	34	0	0	33	6.1	.11
vs. Division	23	2	1	3	1	37	0	0	26	7.7	.13
vs. Conference	53	3	4	7	3	65	0	0	62	4.8	.13
vs. Playoff	47	3	3	6	0	67	0	0	44	6.8	.13
vs. Non-Playoff	28	2	3	5	2	16	0	0	35	5.7	.18
Pre All-Star	39	2	2	4	6	30	0	0	27	7.4	.10
Post All-Star	36	3	4	7	-4	53	0	0	52	5.8	.19
Day	1	0	0	0	0	2	0	0	1	0.0	.00
Night	74	5	6	11	2	81	0	0	78	6.4	.15

	GP	G	A	Pts	+/–	PIM	PP	SH	S	SPct	P/G
National TV	12	1	2	3	7	23	0	0	13	7.7	.25
0 Days Rest	13	1	1	2	1	10	0	0	14	7.1	.15
1 Days Rest	37	2	4	6	5	53	0	0	44	4.5	.16
2 Days Rest	12	2	0	2	-4	16	0	0	16	12.5	.17
3+ Days Rest	13	0	1	1	0	4	0	0	5	0.0	.08

	G	A	Pts	PIM		G	A	Pts	PIM
1st Period	2	1	3	36	Winning	1	3	4	29
2nd Period	0	1	1	28	Losing	2	0	2	46
3rd Period	3	4	7	17	Tied	2	3	5	8
Overtime	0	0	0	2	Clutch	0	0	0	2
Last 5 Min	1	1	2	35	Blowouts	1	0	1	22

Steve Dubinsky

Calgary Flames — Center

1998-99 Season

	GP	G	A	Pts	+/–	PIM	PP	SH	S	SPct	P/G
Overall	63	4	10	14	-7	14	0	2	70	5.7	.22
Home	38	1	6	7	-7	6	0	0	36	2.8	.18
Away	25	3	4	7	0	8	0	2	34	8.8	.28
vs. Division	15	0	2	2	0	0	0	0	21	0.0	.13
vs. Conference	43	3	6	9	-2	4	0	1	58	5.2	.21
vs. Playoff	38	3	8	11	-3	12	0	1	40	7.5	.29
vs. Non-Playoff	25	1	2	3	-4	2	0	1	30	3.3	.12
Pre All-Star	37	3	3	6	-7	10	0	2	35	8.6	.16
Post All-Star	26	1	7	8	0	4	0	0	35	2.9	.31
Day	2	0	0	0	-2	0	0	0	1	0.0	.00
Night	61	4	10	14	-5	14	0	2	69	5.8	.23

	GP	G	A	Pts	+/–	PIM	PP	SH	S	SPct	P/G
National TV	11	0	0	0	-6	8	0	0	3	0.0	.00
0 Days Rest	10	1	1	2	-3	4	0	1	11	9.1	.20
1 Days Rest	32	2	3	5	-9	8	0	1	34	5.9	.16
2 Days Rest	9	1	2	3	2	2	0	0	12	8.3	.33
3+ Days Rest	12	0	4	4	3	0	0	0	13	0.0	.33

	G	A	Pts	PIM		G	A	Pts	PIM
1st Period	1	1	2	4	Winning	3	2	5	2
2nd Period	0	6	6	6	Losing	1	5	6	10
3rd Period	3	3	6	4	Tied	0	3	3	2
Overtime	0	0	0	0	Clutch	1	1	2	0
Last 5 Min	1	3	4	6	Blowouts	0	0	0	6

Steve Duchesne

Philadelphia Flyers — Defense

1998-99 Season

	GP	G	A	Pts	+/–	PIM	PP	SH	S	SPct	P/G
Overall	71	6	24	30	-6	24	2	0	118	5.1	.42
Home	35	4	14	18	1	12	1	0	54	7.4	.51
Away	36	2	10	12	-7	12	1	0	64	3.1	.33
vs. Division	20	0	6	6	-5	4	0	0	30	0.0	.30
vs. Conference	50	4	19	23	-3	16	1	0	85	4.7	.46
vs. Playoff	46	3	12	15	-6	18	2	0	64	4.7	.33
vs. Non-Playoff	25	3	12	15	0	6	0	0	54	5.6	.60
Pre All-Star	42	2	12	14	-3	18	1	0	69	2.9	.33
Post All-Star	29	4	12	16	-3	6	1	0	49	8.2	.55
Day	6	0	3	3	-4	2	0	0	3	0.0	.50
Night	65	6	21	27	-2	22	2	0	115	5.2	.42

	GP	G	A	Pts	+/–	PIM	PP	SH	S	SPct	P/G
National TV	13	2	5	7	-1	2	1	0	23	8.7	.54
0 Days Rest	10	1	3	4	-3	2	1	0	19	5.3	.40
1 Days Rest	38	2	14	16	-7	12	1	0	67	3.0	.42
2 Days Rest	10	2	6	8	7	2	0	0	13	15.4	.80
3+ Days Rest	13	1	1	2	-3	8	0	0	19	5.3	.15

	G	A	Pts	PIM		G	A	Pts	PIM
1st Period	3	7	10	10	Winning	3	5	8	14
2nd Period	2	6	8	4	Losing	1	7	8	6
3rd Period	1	10	11	10	Tied	2	12	14	4
Overtime	0	1	1	0	Clutch	0	3	3	0
Last 5 Min	2	8	10	6	Blowouts	0	1	1	2

Jean-Pierre Dumont

Chicago Blackhawks — Right Wing

1998-99 Season

	GP	G	A	Pts	+/–	PIM	PP	SH	S	SPct	P/G
Overall	25	9	6	15	7	10	0	0	42	21.4	.60
Home	13	6	4	10	3	0	0	0	24	25.0	.77
Away	12	3	2	5	4	10	0	0	18	16.7	.42
vs. Division	7	3	0	3	1	8	0	0	8	37.5	.43
vs. Conference	14	6	3	9	6	8	0	0	19	31.6	.64
vs. Playoff	17	4	3	7	2	4	0	0	27	14.8	.41
vs. Non-Playoff	8	5	3	8	5	6	0	0	15	33.3	1.00
Pre All-Star	7	0	0	0	-2	4	0	0	6	0.0	.00
Post All-Star	18	9	6	15	9	6	0	0	36	25.0	.83
Day	7	2	2	4	2	0	0	0	9	22.2	.57
Night	18	7	4	11	5	10	0	0	33	21.2	.61

	GP	G	A	Pts	+/–	PIM	PP	SH	S	SPct	P/G
National TV	6	5	1	6	2	2	0	0	15	33.3	1.00
0 Days Rest	5	0	0	0	0	0	0	0	5	0.0	.00
1 Days Rest	10	1	3	4	2	10	0	0	11	9.1	.40
2 Days Rest	5	5	3	8	4	0	0	0	20	25.0	1.60
3+ Days Rest	5	3	0	3	1	0	0	0	6	50.0	.60

	G	A	Pts	PIM		G	A	Pts	PIM
1st Period	4	2	6	4	Winning	5	1	6	4
2nd Period	2	1	3	2	Losing	1	0	1	4
3rd Period	3	3	6	4	Tied	3	5	8	2
Overtime	0	0	0	0	Clutch	0	0	0	0
Last 5 Min	3	0	3	4	Blowouts	1	0	1	0

Radek Dvorak

Florida Panthers — Right Wing

1998-99 Season

	GP	G	A	Pts	+/–	PIM	PP	SH	S	SPct	P/G
Overall	82	19	24	43	7	29	0	4	182	10.4	.52
Home	41	8	14	22	1	6	0	1	90	8.9	.54
Away	41	11	10	21	6	23	0	3	92	12.0	.51
vs. Division	15	2	4	6	-1	6	0	1	38	5.3	.40
vs. Conference	58	11	19	30	3	18	0	3	125	8.8	.52
vs. Playoff	49	11	14	25	0	19	0	2	99	11.1	.51
vs. Non-Playoff	33	8	10	18	7	10	0	2	83	9.6	.55
Pre All-Star	44	7	10	17	-5	16	0	3	95	7.4	.39
Post All-Star	38	12	14	26	12	13	0	1	87	13.8	.68
Day	4	0	1	1	0	2	0	0	11	0.0	.25
Night	78	19	23	42	7	27	0	4	171	11.1	.54

	GP	G	A	Pts	+/–	PIM	PP	SH	S	SPct	P/G
National TV	4	1	2	3	-4	2	0	0	9	11.1	.75
0 Days Rest	19	4	7	11	0	11	0	2	39	10.3	.58
1 Days Rest	33	10	8	18	8	12	0	2	71	14.1	.55
2 Days Rest	16	2	7	9	5	2	0	0	37	5.4	.56
3+ Days Rest	14	3	2	5	-6	4	0	0	35	8.6	.36

	G	A	Pts	PIM		G	A	Pts	PIM
1st Period	6	10	16	2	Winning	7	8	15	4
2nd Period	5	7	12	16	Losing	7	9	16	16
3rd Period	8	7	15	6	Tied	5	7	12	9
Overtime	0	0	0	5	Clutch	0	1	1	5
Last 5 Min	5	6	11	15	Blowouts	3	1	4	6

Mike Eastwood

St. Louis Blues — Center

1998-99 Season

	GP	G	A	Pts	+/–	PIM	PP	SH	S	SPct	P/G
Overall	82	9	21	30	6	36	0	0	76	11.8	.37
Home	41	6	11	17	1	24	0	0	41	14.6	.41
Away	41	3	10	13	5	12	0	0	35	8.6	.32
vs. Division	18	1	10	11	5	14	0	0	16	6.3	.61
vs. Conference	55	7	16	23	6	28	0	0	46	15.2	.42
vs. Playoff	46	7	7	14	-1	22	0	0	43	16.3	.30
vs. Non-Playoff	36	2	14	16	7	14	0	0	33	6.1	.44
Pre All-Star	42	6	10	16	7	22	0	0	41	14.6	.38
Post All-Star	40	3	11	14	-1	14	0	0	35	8.6	.35
Day	11	1	6	7	1	8	0	0	8	12.5	.64
Night	71	8	15	23	5	28	0	0	68	11.8	.32

	GP	G	A	Pts	+/–	PIM	PP	SH	S	SPct	P/G
National TV	17	1	4	5	-4	12	0	0	15	6.7	.29
0 Days Rest	12	2	3	5	-2	6	0	0	16	12.5	.42
1 Days Rest	43	6	9	15	2	12	0	0	41	14.6	.35
2 Days Rest	17	0	5	5	2	12	0	0	15	0.0	.29
3+ Days Rest	10	1	4	5	4	6	0	0	4	25.0	.50

	G	A	Pts	PIM		G	A	Pts	PIM
1st Period	4	9	13	14	Winning	3	7	10	14
2nd Period	0	4	4	18	Losing	4	6	10	14
3rd Period	5	8	13	4	Tied	2	8	10	8
Overtime	0	0	0	0	Clutch	0	3	3	0
Last 5 Min	2	6	8	10	Blowouts	0	1	1	2

Patrik Elias

New Jersey Devils — Left Wing

1998-99 Season

	GP	G	A	Pts	+/–	PIM	PP	SH	S	SPct	P/G
Overall	74	17	33	50	19	34	3	0	157	10.8	.68
Home	38	4	14	18	7	22	0	0	82	4.9	.47
Away	36	13	19	32	12	12	3	0	75	17.3	.89
vs. Division	20	7	13	20	12	4	0	0	44	15.9	1.00
vs. Conference	54	12	25	37	16	28	0	0	109	11.0	.69
vs. Playoff	40	6	18	24	4	12	1	0	72	8.3	.60
vs. Non-Playoff	34	11	15	26	15	22	2	0	85	12.9	.76
Pre All-Star	38	7	14	21	-1	22	0	0	66	10.6	.55
Post All-Star	36	10	19	29	20	12	3	0	91	11.0	.81
Day	11	1	7	8	4	2	0	0	17	5.9	.73
Night	63	16	26	42	15	32	3	0	140	11.4	.67

	GP	G	A	Pts	+/–	PIM	PP	SH	S	SPct	P/G
National TV	6	0	2	2	0	4	0	0	16	0.0	.33
0 Days Rest	13	3	6	9	1	6	1	0	25	12.0	.69
1 Days Rest	30	8	12	20	16	10	1	0	79	10.1	.67
2 Days Rest	21	4	10	14	1	16	0	0	37	10.8	.67
3+ Days Rest	10	2	5	7	1	2	1	0	16	12.5	.70

	G	A	Pts	PIM		G	A	Pts	PIM
1st Period	6	12	18	6	Winning	8	13	21	24
2nd Period	3	11	14	6	Losing	1	6	7	8
3rd Period	8	10	18	22	Tied	8	14	22	2
Overtime	0	0	0	0	Clutch	4	3	7	0
Last 5 Min	6	6	12	18	Blowouts	1	0	1	2

Nelson Emerson

Ottawa Senators — Right Wing

1998-99 Season

	GP	G	A	Pts	+/–	PIM	PP	SH	S	SPct	P/G
Overall	65	13	24	37	8	51	3	0	188	6.9	.57
Home	33	9	12	21	4	33	2	0	90	10.0	.64
Away	32	4	12	16	4	18	1	0	98	4.1	.50
vs. Division	10	3	5	8	2	8	2	0	32	9.4	.80
vs. Conference	45	10	17	27	2	41	3	0	132	7.6	.60
vs. Playoff	38	7	9	16	0	37	0	0	98	7.1	.42
vs. Non-Playoff	27	6	15	21	8	14	3	0	90	6.7	.78
Pre All-Star	46	10	20	30	2	40	3	0	124	8.1	.65
Post All-Star	19	3	4	7	6	11	0	0	64	4.7	.37
Day	5	1	2	3	2	2	0	0	13	7.7	.60
Night	60	12	22	34	6	49	3	0	175	6.9	.57

	GP	G	A	Pts	+/–	PIM	PP	SH	S	SPct	P/G
National TV	8	1	2	3	1	11	0	0	19	5.3	.38
0 Days Rest	13	1	3	4	-3	16	1	0	44	2.3	.31
1 Days Rest	28	5	6	11	1	16	0	0	80	6.3	.39
2 Days Rest	15	3	12	15	6	10	1	0	32	9.4	1.00
3+ Days Rest	9	4	3	7	4	9	1	0	32	12.5	.78

	G	A	Pts	PIM
1st Period	4	9	13	12
2nd Period	3	10	13	29
3rd Period	6	4	10	10
Overtime	0	1	1	0
Last 5 Min	4	6	10	14

	G	A	Pts	PIM
Winning	2	2	4	16
Losing	8	9	17	27
Tied	3	13	16	8
Clutch	1	3	4	2
Blowouts	1	2	3	2

Anders Eriksson

Chicago Blackhawks — Defense

1998-99 Season

	GP	G	A	Pts	+/–	PIM	PP	SH	S	SPct	P/G
Overall	72	2	18	20	11	34	0	0	79	2.5	.28
Home	36	1	9	10	8	12	0	0	36	2.8	.28
Away	36	1	9	10	3	22	0	0	43	2.3	.28
vs. Division	17	0	6	6	8	8	0	0	10	0.0	.35
vs. Conference	45	2	12	14	10	22	0	0	50	4.0	.31
vs. Playoff	43	0	9	9	1	26	0	0	46	0.0	.21
vs. Non-Playoff	29	2	9	11	10	8	0	0	33	6.1	.38
Pre All-Star	46	2	9	11	4	28	0	0	49	4.1	.24
Post All-Star	26	0	9	9	7	6	0	0	30	0.0	.35
Day	10	0	4	4	3	2	0	0	10	0.0	.40
Night	62	2	14	16	8	32	0	0	69	2.9	.26

	GP	G	A	Pts	+/–	PIM	PP	SH	S	SPct	P/G
National TV	24	1	8	9	3	14	0	0	32	3.1	.38
0 Days Rest	12	0	5	5	3	4	0	0	10	0.0	.42
1 Days Rest	30	1	4	5	7	10	0	0	42	2.4	.17
2 Days Rest	20	1	5	6	-1	16	0	0	19	5.3	.30
3+ Days Rest	10	0	4	4	2	4	0	0	8	0.0	.40

	G	A	Pts	PIM
1st Period	0	7	7	8
2nd Period	1	7	8	8
3rd Period	1	4	5	18
Overtime	0	0	0	0
Last 5 Min	2	7	9	14

	G	A	Pts	PIM
Winning	2	8	10	16
Losing	0	2	2	18
Tied	0	8	8	0
Clutch	0	1	1	4
Blowouts	1	1	2	2

Pat Falloon

Edmonton Oilers — Right Wing

1998-99 Season

	GP	G	A	Pts	+/–	PIM	PP	SH	S	SPct	P/G
Overall	82	17	23	40	-4	20	8	0	152	11.2	.49
Home	41	9	14	23	1	14	4	0	74	12.2	.56
Away	41	8	9	17	-5	6	4	0	78	10.3	.41
vs. Division	18	4	5	9	-1	8	3	0	39	10.3	.50
vs. Conference	55	14	18	32	1	14	6	0	110	12.7	.58
vs. Playoff	47	8	14	22	-4	6	4	0	83	9.6	.47
vs. Non-Playoff	35	9	9	18	0	14	4	0	69	13.0	.51
Pre All-Star	44	11	10	21	2	12	5	0	92	12.0	.48
Post All-Star	38	6	13	19	-6	8	3	0	60	10.0	.50
Day	4	1	2	3	2	0	0	0	4	25.0	.75
Night	78	16	21	37	-6	20	8	0	148	10.8	.47

	GP	G	A	Pts	+/–	PIM	PP	SH	S	SPct	P/G
National TV	13	2	2	4	3	4	1	0	26	7.7	.31
0 Days Rest	14	2	3	5	-2	4	2	0	24	8.3	.36
1 Days Rest	40	7	14	21	0	10	3	0	79	8.9	.53
2 Days Rest	16	4	4	8	0	4	3	0	27	14.8	.50
3+ Days Rest	12	4	2	6	-2	2	0	0	22	18.2	.50

	G	A	Pts	PIM
1st Period	6	9	15	4
2nd Period	6	8	14	6
3rd Period	5	6	11	10
Overtime	0	0	0	0
Last 5 Min	6	5	11	4

	G	A	Pts	PIM
Winning	6	3	9	8
Losing	5	11	16	10
Tied	6	9	15	2
Clutch	1	1	2	0
Blowouts	0	1	1	2

Sergei Fedorov

Detroit Red Wings — Center

1998-99 Season

	GP	G	A	Pts	+/–	PIM	PP	SH	S	SPct	P/G
Overall	77	26	37	63	9	66	6	2	224	11.6	.82
Home	41	14	24	38	1	30	3	0	107	13.1	.93
Away	36	12	13	25	8	36	3	2	117	10.3	.69
vs. Division	18	6	9	15	-2	10	2	0	62	9.7	.83
vs. Conference	49	16	21	37	5	30	3	1	134	11.9	.76
vs. Playoff	43	9	16	25	-5	24	4	0	110	8.2	.58
vs. Non-Playoff	34	17	21	38	14	42	2	2	114	14.9	1.12
Pre All-Star	46	11	18	29	0	22	1	1	122	9.0	.63
Post All-Star	31	15	19	34	9	44	5	1	102	14.7	1.10
Day	12	3	6	9	1	10	1	0	31	9.7	.75
Night	65	23	31	54	8	56	5	2	193	11.9	.83

	GP	G	A	Pts	+/–	PIM	PP	SH	S	SPct	P/G
National TV	27	7	10	17	2	14	2	1	67	10.4	.63
0 Days Rest	12	1	6	7	3	18	0	1	33	3.0	.58
1 Days Rest	36	14	17	31	5	38	5	1	102	13.7	.86
2 Days Rest	22	8	11	19	0	6	1	0	68	11.8	.86
3+ Days Rest	7	3	3	6	1	4	0	0	21	14.3	.86

	G	A	Pts	PIM
1st Period	12	14	26	24
2nd Period	9	10	19	10
3rd Period	5	11	16	32
Overtime	0	2	2	0
Last 5 Min	6	9	15	14

	G	A	Pts	PIM
Winning	7	11	18	32
Losing	5	9	14	24
Tied	14	17	31	10
Clutch	0	6	6	2
Blowouts	1	2	3	6

Brent Fedyk

New York Rangers — Left Wing

1998-99 Season

	GP	G	A	Pts	+/–	PIM	PP	SH	S	SPct	P/G
Overall	67	4	6	10	-11	30	0	1	47	8.5	.15
Home	36	3	3	6	-1	14	0	1	33	9.1	.17
Away	31	1	3	4	-10	16	0	0	14	7.1	.13
vs. Division	16	0	1	1	-3	10	0	0	7	0.0	.06
vs. Conference	47	1	4	5	-9	20	0	0	32	3.1	.11
vs. Playoff	45	1	4	5	-7	20	0	0	22	4.5	.11
vs. Non-Playoff	22	3	2	5	-4	10	0	1	25	12.0	.23
Pre All-Star	30	0	1	1	-8	12	0	0	25	0.0	.03
Post All-Star	37	4	5	9	-3	18	0	1	22	18.2	.24
Day	11	1	4	5	3	8	0	0	3	33.3	.45
Night	56	3	2	5	-14	22	0	1	44	6.8	.09

	GP	G	A	Pts	+/–	PIM	PP	SH	S	SPct	P/G
National TV	21	3	4	7	0	10	0	1	15	20.0	.33
0 Days Rest	12	1	0	1	-4	6	0	0	8	12.5	.08
1 Days Rest	27	2	2	4	-3	16	0	0	19	10.5	.15
2 Days Rest	17	1	4	5	0	6	0	1	12	8.3	.29
3+ Days Rest	11	0	0	0	-4	2	0	0	8	0.0	.00

	G	A	Pts	PIM
1st Period	1	1	2	18
2nd Period	1	2	3	4
3rd Period	2	3	5	8
Overtime	0	0	0	0
Last 5 Min	0	1	1	6

	G	A	Pts	PIM
Winning	2	2	4	8
Losing	2	3	5	20
Tied	0	1	1	2
Clutch	0	0	0	0
Blowouts	1	1	2	6

Peter Ferraro

Boston Bruins — Center

1998-99 Season

	GP	G	A	Pts	+/–	PIM	PP	SH	S	SPct	P/G
Overall	46	6	8	14	10	44	1	0	61	9.8	.30
Home	21	0	4	4	3	34	0	0	20	0.0	.19
Away	25	6	4	10	7	10	1	0	41	14.6	.40
vs. Division	8	2	1	3	2	10	1	0	12	16.7	.38
vs. Conference	30	3	4	7	5	34	1	0	33	9.1	.23
vs. Playoff	25	3	1	4	2	12	0	0	29	10.3	.16
vs. Non-Playoff	21	3	7	10	8	32	1	0	32	9.4	.48
Pre All-Star	29	5	6	11	10	38	1	0	43	11.6	.38
Post All-Star	17	1	2	3	0	6	0	0	18	5.6	.18
Day	11	1	2	3	3	4	0	0	11	9.1	.27
Night	35	5	6	11	7	40	1	0	50	10.0	.31

	GP	G	A	Pts	+/–	PIM	PP	SH	S	SPct	P/G
National TV	4	0	0	0	0	2	0	0	2	0.0	.00
0 Days Rest	9	1	1	2	1	6	0	0	10	10.0	.22
1 Days Rest	19	3	4	7	5	8	0	0	30	10.0	.37
2 Days Rest	6	0	0	0	0	6	0	0	5	0.0	.00
3+ Days Rest	12	2	3	5	4	24	1	0	16	12.5	.42

	G	A	Pts	PIM
1st Period	2	3	5	26
2nd Period	3	4	7	10
3rd Period	1	1	2	8
Overtime	0	0	0	0
Last 5 Min	0	3	3	4

	G	A	Pts	PIM
Winning	3	3	6	26
Losing	1	3	4	14
Tied	2	2	4	4
Clutch	0	0	0	2
Blowouts	1	0	1	2

Ray Ferraro

Los Angeles Kings — Center

1998-99 Season

	GP	G	A	Pts	+/–	PIM	PP	SH	S	SPct	P/G
Overall	65	13	18	31	0	59	4	0	84	15.5	.48
Home	31	7	9	16	4	18	3	0	39	17.9	.52
Away	34	6	9	15	-4	41	1	0	45	13.3	.44
vs. Division	19	5	7	12	1	14	2	0	28	17.9	.63
vs. Conference	43	9	9	18	-7	28	4	0	57	15.8	.42
vs. Playoff	44	9	14	23	-2	30	3	0	58	15.5	.52
vs. Non-Playoff	21	4	4	8	2	29	1	0	26	15.4	.38
Pre All-Star	30	6	7	13	0	41	2	0	32	18.8	.43
Post All-Star	35	7	11	18	0	18	2	0	52	13.5	.51
Day	4	0	0	0	-9	0	0	0	8	0.0	.00
Night	61	13	18	31	9	59	4	0	76	17.1	.51

	GP	G	A	Pts	+/–	PIM	PP	SH	S	SPct	P/G
National TV	13	1	2	3	-12	2	0	0	21	4.8	.23
0 Days Rest	10	1	4	5	1	10	0	0	12	8.3	.50
1 Days Rest	28	6	6	12	2	33	2	0	35	17.1	.43
2 Days Rest	15	4	6	10	0	12	2	0	25	16.0	.67
3+ Days Rest	12	2	2	4	-3	4	0	0	12	16.7	.33

	G	A	Pts	PIM
1st Period	6	6	12	20
2nd Period	3	7	10	10
3rd Period	3	5	8	29
Overtime	1	0	1	0
Last 5 Min	4	5	9	25

	G	A	Pts	PIM
Winning	4	4	8	14
Losing	5	8	13	39
Tied	4	6	10	6
Clutch	1	0	1	15
Blowouts	1	1	2	6

Tom Fitzgerald

Nashville Predators — Right Wing

1998-99 Season

	GP	G	A	Pts	+/–	PIM	PP	SH	S	SPct	P/G
Overall	80	13	19	32	-18	48	0	0	180	7.2	.40
Home	40	6	11	17	-3	22	0	0	103	5.8	.43
Away	40	7	8	15	-15	26	0	0	77	9.1	.38
vs. Division	18	1	4	5	-5	12	0	0	30	3.3	.28
vs. Conference	53	9	15	24	-10	30	0	0	119	7.6	.45
vs. Playoff	49	4	11	15	-14	30	0	0	109	3.7	.31
vs. Non-Playoff	31	9	8	17	-4	18	0	0	71	12.7	.55
Pre All-Star	43	5	8	13	-15	22	0	0	93	5.4	.30
Post All-Star	37	8	11	19	-3	26	0	0	87	9.2	.51
Day	8	0	4	4	-2	8	0	0	10	0.0	.50
Night	72	13	15	28	-16	40	0	0	170	7.6	.39

	GP	G	A	Pts	+/–	PIM	PP	SH	S	SPct	P/G
National TV	2	1	0	1	-3	0	0	0	5	20.0	.50
0 Days Rest	14	4	0	4	-6	8	0	0	38	10.5	.29
1 Days Rest	35	5	14	19	1	22	0	0	70	7.1	.54
2 Days Rest	16	2	3	5	-4	8	0	0	42	4.8	.31
3+ Days Rest	15	2	2	4	-9	10	0	0	30	6.7	.27

	G	A	Pts	PIM
1st Period	1	5	6	26
2nd Period	5	5	10	12
3rd Period	7	8	15	10
Overtime	0	1	1	0
Last 5 Min	2	4	6	8

	G	A	Pts	PIM
Winning	2	5	7	16
Losing	8	8	16	26
Tied	3	6	9	6
Clutch	2	3	5	2
Blowouts	2	1	3	8

Theo Fleury

Colorado Avalanche — Right Wing

1998-99 Season

	GP	G	A	Pts	+/–	PIM	PP	SH	S	SPct	P/G
Overall	75	40	53	93	26	86	8	3	301	13.3	1.24
Home	43	23	34	57	26	40	3	1	164	14.0	1.33
Away	32	17	19	36	0	46	5	2	137	12.4	1.13
vs. Division	15	7	11	18	-2	20	1	0	57	12.3	1.20
vs. Conference	52	32	39	71	25	54	7	3	200	16.0	1.37
vs. Playoff	44	20	34	54	16	58	4	2	182	11.0	1.23
vs. Non-Playoff	31	20	19	39	10	28	4	1	119	16.8	1.26
Pre All-Star	46	21	26	47	5	52	6	2	200	10.5	1.02
Post All-Star	29	19	27	46	21	34	2	1	101	18.8	1.59
Day	8	8	5	13	5	12	0	0	35	22.9	1.63
Night	67	32	48	80	21	74	8	3	266	12.0	1.19

	GP	G	A	Pts	+/–	PIM	PP	SH	S	SPct	P/G
National TV	13	8	8	16	9	12	1	0	51	15.7	1.23
0 Days Rest	14	10	10	20	0	10	3	0	47	21.3	1.43
1 Days Rest	38	20	21	41	14	24	3	2	165	12.1	1.08
2 Days Rest	10	1	16	17	8	22	1	0	39	2.6	1.70
3+ Days Rest	13	9	6	15	4	30	1	1	50	18.0	1.15

	G	A	Pts	PIM		G	A	Pts	PIM
1st Period	16	17	33	34	Winning	14	12	26	30
2nd Period	12	20	32	30	Losing	13	22	35	40
3rd Period	12	15	27	22	Tied	13	19	32	16
Overtime	0	1	1	0	Clutch	4	7	11	12
Last 5 Min	12	16	28	36	Blowouts	2	1	3	16

Adam Foote

Colorado Avalanche — Defense

1998-99 Season

	GP	G	A	Pts	+/–	PIM	PP	SH	S	SPct	P/G
Overall	64	5	16	21	20	92	3	0	83	6.0	.33
Home	35	3	10	13	16	68	1	0	52	5.8	.37
Away	29	2	6	8	4	24	2	0	31	6.5	.28
vs. Division	13	1	1	2	2	21	1	0	17	5.9	.15
vs. Conference	47	3	15	18	18	45	3	0	67	4.5	.38
vs. Playoff	36	2	9	11	12	66	0	0	43	4.7	.31
vs. Non-Playoff	28	3	7	10	8	26	3	0	40	7.5	.36
Pre All-Star	27	2	6	8	3	41	2	0	42	4.8	.30
Post All-Star	37	3	10	13	17	51	1	0	41	7.3	.35
Day	13	1	6	7	5	12	0	0	10	10.0	.54
Night	51	4	10	14	15	80	3	0	73	5.5	.27

	GP	G	A	Pts	+/–	PIM	PP	SH	S	SPct	P/G
National TV	20	1	5	6	8	25	0	0	24	4.2	.30
0 Days Rest	12	1	0	1	-1	16	0	0	23	4.3	.08
1 Days Rest	31	3	8	11	12	32	3	0	42	7.1	.35
2 Days Rest	9	0	4	4	6	6	0	0	3	0.0	.44
3+ Days Rest	12	1	4	5	3	38	0	0	15	6.7	.42

	G	A	Pts	PIM		G	A	Pts	PIM
1st Period	1	4	5	49	Winning	1	4	5	58
2nd Period	2	7	9	22	Losing	3	5	8	22
3rd Period	2	5	7	21	Tied	1	7	8	12
Overtime	0	0	0	0	Clutch	1	1	2	0
Last 5 Min	1	3	4	24	Blowouts	0	0	0	4

Colin Forbes

Tampa Bay Lightning — Left Wing

1998-99 Season

	GP	G	A	Pts	+/–	PIM	PP	SH	S	SPct	P/G
Overall	80	12	8	20	-5	61	0	1	117	10.3	.25
Home	40	8	4	12	2	24	0	1	55	14.5	.30
Away	40	4	4	8	-7	37	0	0	62	6.5	.20
vs. Division	20	1	3	4	-4	12	0	0	32	3.1	.20
vs. Conference	54	6	5	11	-3	45	0	1	75	8.0	.20
vs. Playoff	44	4	6	10	-8	43	0	0	67	6.0	.23
vs. Non-Playoff	36	8	2	10	3	18	0	1	50	16.0	.28
Pre All-Star	42	9	7	16	4	33	0	0	60	15.0	.38
Post All-Star	38	3	1	4	-9	28	0	1	57	5.3	.11
Day	12	1	0	1	-2	8	0	0	14	7.1	.08
Night	68	11	8	19	-3	53	0	1	103	10.7	.28

	GP	G	A	Pts	+/–	PIM	PP	SH	S	SPct	P/G
National TV	11	1	1	2	-1	15	0	0	14	7.1	.18
0 Days Rest	13	1	1	2	-5	12	0	0	17	5.9	.15
1 Days Rest	38	2	2	4	-10	25	0	0	51	3.9	.11
2 Days Rest	17	4	4	8	6	16	0	0	26	15.4	.47
3+ Days Rest	12	5	1	6	4	8	0	1	23	21.7	.50

	G	A	Pts	PIM		G	A	Pts	PIM
1st Period	3	2	5	20	Winning	6	4	10	29
2nd Period	5	4	9	33	Losing	2	1	3	18
3rd Period	4	2	6	8	Tied	4	3	7	14
Overtime	0	0	0	0	Clutch	1	0	1	0
Last 5 Min	4	0	4	14	Blowouts	1	1	2	8

Peter Forsberg

Colorado Avalanche — Center

1998-99 Season

	GP	G	A	Pts	+/–	PIM	PP	SH	S	SPct	P/G
Overall	78	30	67	97	27	108	9	2	217	13.8	1.24
Home	40	16	27	43	4	36	6	2	105	15.2	1.08
Away	38	14	40	54	23	72	3	0	112	12.5	1.42
vs. Division	17	7	10	17	-1	34	3	0	48	14.6	1.00
vs. Conference	54	19	44	63	19	82	7	2	152	12.5	1.17
vs. Playoff	43	10	36	46	9	66	1	0	109	9.2	1.07
vs. Non-Playoff	35	20	31	51	18	42	8	2	108	18.5	1.46
Pre All-Star	44	13	39	52	16	60	2	1	121	10.7	1.18
Post All-Star	34	17	28	45	11	48	7	1	96	17.7	1.32
Day	14	4	7	11	-2	16	1	0	33	12.1	.79
Night	64	26	60	86	29	92	8	2	184	14.1	1.34

	GP	G	A	Pts	+/–	PIM	PP	SH	S	SPct	P/G
National TV	20	4	19	23	5	32	2	0	53	7.5	1.15
0 Days Rest	13	5	11	16	-1	22	3	0	34	14.7	1.23
1 Days Rest	39	16	31	47	10	60	4	2	116	13.8	1.21
2 Days Rest	11	7	10	17	11	8	2	0	32	21.9	1.55
3+ Days Rest	15	2	15	17	7	18	0	0	35	5.7	1.13

	G	A	Pts	PIM		G	A	Pts	PIM
1st Period	11	15	26	36	Winning	10	20	30	42
2nd Period	9	18	27	26	Losing	6	23	29	56
3rd Period	10	33	43	44	Tied	14	24	38	10
Overtime	0	1	1	2	Clutch	6	10	16	20
Last 5 Min	9	25	34	48	Blowouts	3	5	8	18

Ron Francis

Carolina Hurricanes — Center

1998-99 Season

	GP	G	A	Pts	+/–	PIM	PP	SH	S	SPct	P/G
Overall	82	21	31	52	-2	34	8	0	133	15.8	.63
Home	41	9	18	27	2	12	3	0	68	13.2	.66
Away	41	12	13	25	-4	22	5	0	65	18.5	.61
vs. Division	15	6	9	15	-4	2	3	0	36	16.7	1.00
vs. Conference	59	13	27	40	-2	24	4	0	100	13.0	.68
vs. Playoff	44	12	16	28	-6	20	5	0	63	19.0	.64
vs. Non-Playoff	38	9	15	24	4	14	3	0	70	12.9	.63
Pre All-Star	45	8	14	22	-9	14	3	0	56	14.3	.49
Post All-Star	37	13	17	30	7	20	5	0	77	16.9	.81
Day	7	1	2	3	-2	0	0	0	8	12.5	.43
Night	75	20	29	49	0	34	8	0	125	16.0	.65

	GP	G	A	Pts	+/–	PIM	PP	SH	S	SPct	P/G
National TV	2	1	1	2	3	0	0	0	3	33.3	1.00
0 Days Rest	17	5	4	9	0	8	3	0	28	17.9	.53
1 Days Rest	32	4	13	17	-3	12	0	0	57	7.0	.53
2 Days Rest	23	6	6	12	-2	12	3	0	30	20.0	.52
3+ Days Rest	10	6	8	14	3	2	2	0	18	33.3	1.40

	G	A	Pts	PIM		G	A	Pts	PIM
1st Period	9	10	19	8	Winning	7	7	14	14
2nd Period	6	12	18	14	Losing	6	8	14	18
3rd Period	6	9	15	12	Tied	8	16	24	2
Overtime	0	0	0	0	Clutch	4	4	8	2
Last 5 Min	4	12	16	12	Blowouts	0	0	0	2

Jeff Friesen

San Jose Sharks — Left Wing

1998-99 Season

	GP	G	A	Pts	+/–	PIM	PP	SH	S	SPct	P/G
Overall	78	22	35	57	3	42	10	1	215	10.2	.73
Home	39	10	20	30	4	28	5	0	108	9.3	.77
Away	39	12	15	27	-1	14	5	1	107	11.2	.69
vs. Division	23	6	7	13	-1	16	1	0	68	8.8	.57
vs. Conference	54	12	26	38	-2	32	3	1	144	8.3	.70
vs. Playoff	47	13	17	30	-5	18	5	1	120	10.8	.64
vs. Non-Playoff	31	9	18	27	8	24	5	0	95	9.5	.87
Pre All-Star	41	12	18	30	0	14	7	0	124	9.7	.73
Post All-Star	37	10	17	27	3	28	3	1	91	11.0	.73
Day	7	2	1	3	-3	2	2	0	12	16.7	.43
Night	71	20	34	54	6	40	8	1	203	9.9	.76

	GP	G	A	Pts	+/–	PIM	PP	SH	S	SPct	P/G
National TV	11	2	6	8	-2	12	1	0	26	7.7	.73
0 Days Rest	13	4	8	12	4	8	2	1	42	9.5	.92
1 Days Rest	40	14	17	31	4	18	7	0	116	12.1	.78
2 Days Rest	14	0	6	6	-2	8	0	0	25	0.0	.43
3+ Days Rest	11	4	4	8	-3	8	1	0	32	12.5	.73

	G	A	Pts	PIM		G	A	Pts	PIM
1st Period	4	7	11	12	Winning	9	12	21	24
2nd Period	14	12	26	20	Losing	5	9	14	10
3rd Period	4	16	20	10	Tied	8	14	22	8
Overtime	0	0	0	0	Clutch	1	5	6	4
Last 5 Min	6	10	16	12	Blowouts	1	1	2	8

Dave Gagner

Vancouver Canucks — Center

1998-99 Season

	GP	G	A	Pts	+/–	PIM	PP	SH	S	SPct	P/G
Overall	69	6	22	28	-16	63	2	0	100	6.0	.41
Home	34	1	8	9	-7	18	0	0	51	2.0	.26
Away	35	5	14	19	-9	45	2	0	49	10.2	.54
vs. Division	13	1	3	4	2	18	0	0	23	4.3	.31
vs. Conference	45	4	13	17	-9	44	2	0	62	6.5	.38
vs. Playoff	42	3	9	12	-15	39	1	0	64	4.7	.29
vs. Non-Playoff	27	3	13	16	-1	24	1	0	36	8.3	.59
Pre All-Star	38	4	12	16	-7	41	2	0	51	7.8	.42
Post All-Star	31	2	10	12	-9	22	0	0	49	4.1	.39
Day	6	1	1	2	-3	2	0	0	11	9.1	.33
Night	63	5	21	26	-13	61	2	0	89	5.6	.41

	GP	G	A	Pts	+/–	PIM	PP	SH	S	SPct	P/G
National TV	9	0	7	7	-1	4	0	0	17	0.0	.78
0 Days Rest	15	0	5	5	-4	15	0	0	19	0.0	.33
1 Days Rest	28	3	9	12	-9	24	0	0	39	7.7	.43
2 Days Rest	11	0	2	2	-5	18	0	0	14	0.0	.18
3+ Days Rest	15	3	6	9	2	6	2	0	28	10.7	.60

	G	A	Pts	PIM		G	A	Pts	PIM
1st Period	1	8	9	19	Winning	0	3	3	8
2nd Period	3	5	8	10	Losing	4	13	17	28
3rd Period	2	9	11	24	Tied	2	6	8	27
Overtime	0	0	0	10	Clutch	1	0	1	16
Last 5 Min	1	7	8	28	Blowouts	0	3	3	20

Garry Galley

Los Angeles Kings — Defense

1998-99 Season

	GP	G	A	Pts	+/–	PIM	PP	SH	S	SPct	P/G
Overall	60	4	12	16	-9	30	3	0	77	5.2	.27
Home	32	3	10	13	6	22	2	0	44	6.8	.41
Away	28	1	2	3	-15	8	1	0	33	3.0	.11
vs. Division	19	0	2	2	-6	10	0	0	29	0.0	.11
vs. Conference	42	2	5	7	-10	26	1	0	57	3.5	.17
vs. Playoff	42	2	8	10	-8	26	1	0	56	3.6	.24
vs. Non-Playoff	18	2	4	6	-1	4	2	0	21	9.5	.33
Pre All-Star	33	2	6	8	-2	18	1	0	39	5.1	.24
Post All-Star	27	2	6	8	-7	12	2	0	38	5.3	.30
Day	2	0	0	0	-2	0	0	0	5	0.0	.00
Night	58	4	12	16	-7	30	3	0	72	5.6	.28

	GP	G	A	Pts	+/–	PIM	PP	SH	S	SPct	P/G
National TV	11	0	1	1	-3	8	0	0	19	0.0	.09
0 Days Rest	7	1	0	1	-5	2	1	0	5	20.0	.14
1 Days Rest	24	2	8	10	-7	12	2	0	35	5.7	.42
2 Days Rest	12	1	2	3	1	10	0	0	16	6.3	.25
3+ Days Rest	17	0	2	2	2	6	0	0	21	0.0	.12

	G	A	Pts	PIM		G	A	Pts	PIM
1st Period	1	5	6	10	Winning	1	3	4	16
2nd Period	1	2	3	12	Losing	2	6	8	12
3rd Period	2	5	7	8	Tied	1	3	4	2
Overtime	0	0	0	0	Clutch	0	0	0	2
Last 5 Min	0	3	3	4	Blowouts	1	0	1	0

Bruce Gardiner

Ottawa Senators — Center

1998-99 Season

	GP	G	A	Pts	+/-	PIM	PP	SH	S	SPct	P/G
Overall	59	4	8	12	6	43	0	0	70	5.7	.20
Home	28	0	4	4	3	12	0	0	33	0.0	.14
Away	31	4	4	8	3	31	0	0	37	10.8	.26
vs. Division	16	1	2	3	1	12	0	0	16	6.3	.19
vs. Conference	42	3	5	8	3	30	0	0	46	6.5	.19
vs. Playoff	33	2	3	5	-3	23	0	0	45	4.4	.15
vs. Non-Playoff	26	2	5	7	9	20	0	0	25	8.0	.27
Pre All-Star	38	4	6	10	7	23	0	0	45	8.9	.26
Post All-Star	21	0	2	2	-1	20	0	0	25	0.0	.10
Day	3	0	0	0	0	0	0	0	3	0.0	.00
Night	56	4	8	12	6	43	0	0	67	6.0	.21

	GP	G	A	Pts	+/-	PIM	PP	SH	S	SPct	P/G
National TV	9	0	1	1	-2	10	0	0	4	0.0	.11
0 Days Rest	10	2	2	4	2	14	0	0	14	14.3	.40
1 Days Rest	27	1	2	3	1	10	0	0	31	3.2	.11
2 Days Rest	11	0	3	3	3	4	0	0	14	0.0	.27
3+ Days Rest	11	1	1	2	0	15	0	0	11	9.1	.18

	G	A	Pts	PIM		G	A	Pts	PIM
1st Period	1	0	1	16	Winning	2	3	5	29
2nd Period	3	4	7	8	Losing	1	2	3	8
3rd Period	0	4	4	17	Tied	1	3	4	6
Overtime	0	0	0	2	Clutch	0	2	2	2
Last 5 Min	2	3	5	10	Blowouts	0	0	0	6

Johan Garpenlov

Florida Panthers — Left Wing

1998-99 Season

	GP	G	A	Pts	+/-	PIM	PP	SH	S	SPct	P/G
Overall	64	8	9	17	-9	42	0	1	71	11.3	.27
Home	30	3	5	8	-8	12	0	0	31	9.7	.27
Away	34	5	4	9	-1	30	0	1	40	12.5	.26
vs. Division	13	0	3	3	-1	8	0	0	12	0.0	.23
vs. Conference	48	5	6	11	-9	40	0	1	48	10.4	.23
vs. Playoff	36	6	5	11	-4	26	0	1	41	14.6	.31
vs. Non-Playoff	28	2	4	6	-5	16	0	0	30	6.7	.21
Pre All-Star	39	4	3	7	-8	32	0	0	47	8.5	.18
Post All-Star	25	4	6	10	-1	10	0	1	24	16.7	.40
Day	4	0	0	0	-4	0	0	0	2	0.0	.00
Night	60	8	9	17	-5	42	0	1	69	11.6	.28

	GP	G	A	Pts	+/-	PIM	PP	SH	S	SPct	P/G
National TV	3	0	1	1	-2	0	0	0	2	0.0	.33
0 Days Rest	15	1	1	2	-2	18	0	0	12	8.3	.13
1 Days Rest	24	5	3	8	-9	14	0	1	25	20.0	.33
2 Days Rest	11	2	1	3	0	2	0	0	14	14.3	.27
3+ Days Rest	14	0	4	4	2	8	0	0	20	0.0	.29

	G	A	Pts	PIM		G	A	Pts	PIM
1st Period	3	4	7	10	Winning	1	2	3	12
2nd Period	1	2	3	14	Losing	5	1	6	20
3rd Period	4	3	7	18	Tied	2	6	8	10
Overtime	0	0	0	0	Clutch	0	0	0	4
Last 5 Min	3	0	3	6	Blowouts	0	0	0	8

Martin Gelinas

Carolina Hurricanes — Left Wing

1998-99 Season

	GP	G	A	Pts	+/-	PIM	PP	SH	S	SPct	P/G
Overall	76	13	15	28	3	67	0	0	111	11.7	.37
Home	38	5	11	16	-1	22	0	0	60	8.3	.42
Away	38	8	4	12	4	45	0	0	51	15.7	.32
vs. Division	14	1	4	5	4	4	0	0	18	5.6	.36
vs. Conference	54	11	14	25	5	53	0	0	76	14.5	.46
vs. Playoff	43	8	9	17	-2	34	0	0	66	12.1	.40
vs. Non-Playoff	33	5	6	11	5	33	0	0	45	11.1	.33
Pre All-Star	43	6	5	11	-2	24	0	0	53	11.3	.26
Post All-Star	33	7	10	17	5	43	0	0	58	12.1	.52
Day	7	0	2	2	1	23	0	0	6	0.0	.29
Night	69	13	13	26	2	44	0	0	105	12.4	.38

	GP	G	A	Pts	+/-	PIM	PP	SH	S	SPct	P/G
National TV	2	1	0	1	0	2	0	0	5	20.0	.50
0 Days Rest	15	0	1	1	-5	12	0	0	20	0.0	.07
1 Days Rest	30	5	10	15	2	29	0	0	43	11.6	.50
2 Days Rest	20	5	1	6	2	20	0	0	27	18.5	.30
3+ Days Rest	11	3	3	6	4	6	0	0	21	14.3	.55

	G	A	Pts	PIM		G	A	Pts	PIM
1st Period	4	6	10	20	Winning	0	3	3	33
2nd Period	5	4	9	27	Losing	10	8	18	18
3rd Period	4	5	9	20	Tied	3	4	7	16
Overtime	0	0	0	0	Clutch	3	0	3	12
Last 5 Min	2	2	4	35	Blowouts	0	0	0	0

Hal Gill

Boston Bruins — Defense

1998-99 Season

	GP	G	A	Pts	+/-	PIM	PP	SH	S	SPct	P/G
Overall	80	3	7	10	-10	63	0	0	102	2.9	.13
Home	40	2	4	6	1	33	0	0	57	3.5	.15
Away	40	1	3	4	-11	30	0	0	45	2.2	.10
vs. Division	20	2	1	3	-5	29	0	0	21	9.5	.15
vs. Conference	56	3	4	7	-7	53	0	0	75	4.0	.13
vs. Playoff	46	2	4	6	-8	43	0	0	62	3.2	.13
vs. Non-Playoff	34	1	3	4	-2	20	0	0	40	2.5	.12
Pre All-Star	43	2	4	6	-2	32	0	0	59	3.4	.14
Post All-Star	37	1	3	4	-8	31	0	0	43	2.3	.11
Day	15	1	2	3	2	14	0	0	18	5.6	.20
Night	65	2	5	7	-12	49	0	0	84	2.4	.11

	GP	G	A	Pts	+/-	PIM	PP	SH	S	SPct	P/G
National TV	10	0	0	0	-8	12	0	0	8	0.0	.00
0 Days Rest	16	0	1	1	-9	2	0	0	14	0.0	.06
1 Days Rest	38	2	3	5	-3	33	0	0	61	3.3	.13
2 Days Rest	13	1	2	3	1	16	0	0	14	7.1	.23
3+ Days Rest	13	0	1	1	1	12	0	0	13	0.0	.08

	G	A	Pts	PIM		G	A	Pts	PIM
1st Period	0	1	1	18	Winning	0	3	3	37
2nd Period	0	3	3	35	Losing	1	3	4	20
3rd Period	2	3	5	10	Tied	2	1	3	6
Overtime	1	0	1	0	Clutch	2	0	2	2
Last 5 Min	1	1	2	21	Blowouts	0	1	1	6

Doug Gilmour

Chicago Blackhawks — Center

1998-99 Season

	GP	G	A	Pts	+/–	PIM	PP	SH	S	SPct	P/G
Overall	72	16	40	56	-16	56	7	1	110	14.5	.78
Home	34	8	17	25	-9	26	5	1	58	13.8	.74
Away	38	8	23	31	-7	30	2	0	52	15.4	.82
vs. Division	14	4	7	11	-1	11	0	0	16	25.0	.79
vs. Conference	49	10	30	40	-9	46	3	1	65	15.4	.82
vs. Playoff	46	11	25	36	-9	35	4	1	75	14.7	.78
vs. Non-Playoff	26	5	15	20	-7	21	3	0	35	14.3	.77
Pre All-Star	45	10	23	33	-14	33	4	1	79	12.7	.73
Post All-Star	27	6	17	23	-2	23	3	0	31	19.4	.85
Day	8	0	4	4	-3	15	0	0	12	0.0	.50
Night	64	16	36	52	-13	41	7	1	98	16.3	.81

	GP	G	A	Pts	+/–	PIM	PP	SH	S	SPct	P/G
National TV	13	5	6	11	-5	6	2	0	23	21.7	.85
0 Days Rest	12	3	8	11	-5	6	2	0	21	14.3	.92
1 Days Rest	38	6	19	25	-15	25	3	0	52	11.5	.66
2 Days Rest	11	7	6	13	3	15	2	1	24	29.2	1.18
3+ Days Rest	11	0	7	7	1	10	0	0	13	0.0	.64

	G	A	Pts	PIM		G	A	Pts	PIM
1st Period	7	13	20	27	Winning	4	7	11	8
2nd Period	7	12	19	13	Losing	8	19	27	24
3rd Period	2	14	16	16	Tied	4	14	18	24
Overtime	0	1	1	0	Clutch	0	5	5	4
Last 5 Min	3	5	8	24	Blowouts	0	4	4	8

Sergei Gonchar

Washington Capitals — Defense

1998-99 Season

	GP	G	A	Pts	+/–	PIM	PP	SH	S	SPct	P/G
Overall	53	21	10	31	1	57	13	1	180	11.7	.58
Home	27	14	7	21	1	20	8	1	99	14.1	.78
Away	26	7	3	10	0	37	5	0	81	8.6	.38
vs. Division	9	5	3	8	8	18	2	1	38	13.2	.89
vs. Conference	35	14	8	22	4	40	8	1	116	12.1	.63
vs. Playoff	31	9	4	13	-1	27	8	0	105	8.6	.42
vs. Non-Playoff	22	12	6	18	2	30	5	1	75	16.0	.82
Pre All-Star	29	8	2	10	5	25	4	0	87	9.2	.34
Post All-Star	24	13	8	21	-4	32	9	1	93	14.0	.88
Day	3	2	1	3	-1	2	2	0	13	15.4	1.00
Night	50	19	9	28	2	55	11	1	167	11.4	.56

	GP	G	A	Pts	+/–	PIM	PP	SH	S	SPct	P/G
National TV	5	3	0	3	0	6	3	0	22	13.6	.60
0 Days Rest	9	3	2	5	-2	10	3	0	31	9.7	.56
1 Days Rest	24	13	7	20	8	31	7	1	87	14.9	.83
2 Days Rest	8	1	1	2	-6	2	1	0	31	3.2	.25
3+ Days Rest	12	4	0	4	1	14	2	0	31	12.9	.33

	G	A	Pts	PIM		G	A	Pts	PIM
1st Period	5	2	7	16	Winning	8	3	11	18
2nd Period	10	4	14	24	Losing	7	5	12	37
3rd Period	6	4	10	17	Tied	6	2	8	2
Overtime	0	0	0	0	Clutch	3	0	3	6
Last 5 Min	8	2	10	16	Blowouts	3	2	5	11

Tony Granato

San Jose Sharks — Right Wing

1998-99 Season

	GP	G	A	Pts	+/–	PIM	PP	SH	S	SPct	P/G
Overall	35	6	6	12	4	54	0	1	65	9.2	.34
Home	20	5	3	8	4	22	0	1	41	12.2	.40
Away	15	1	3	4	0	32	0	0	24	4.2	.27
vs. Division	15	3	2	5	3	14	0	1	30	10.0	.33
vs. Conference	27	6	4	10	4	48	0	1	51	11.8	.37
vs. Playoff	21	2	3	5	0	24	0	0	36	5.6	.24
vs. Non-Playoff	14	4	3	7	4	30	0	1	29	13.8	.50
Pre All-Star	30	6	5	11	3	50	0	1	55	10.9	.37
Post All-Star	5	0	1	1	1	4	0	0	10	0.0	.20
Day	3	0	0	0	-1	14	0	0	5	0.0	.00
Night	32	6	6	12	5	40	0	1	60	10.0	.38

	GP	G	A	Pts	+/–	PIM	PP	SH	S	SPct	P/G
National TV	3	0	1	1	2	6	0	0	6	0.0	.33
0 Days Rest	6	1	0	1	0	2	0	0	19	5.3	.17
1 Days Rest	12	1	3	4	-1	16	0	0	19	5.3	.33
2 Days Rest	7	1	2	3	4	16	0	0	10	10.0	.43
3+ Days Rest	10	3	1	4	1	20	0	1	17	17.6	.40

	G	A	Pts	PIM		G	A	Pts	PIM
1st Period	0	1	1	24	Winning	0	3	3	32
2nd Period	3	3	6	16	Losing	4	3	7	12
3rd Period	3	2	5	14	Tied	2	0	2	10
Overtime	0	0	0	0	Clutch	2	1	3	10
Last 5 Min	2	2	4	34	Blowouts	0	1	1	6

Chris Gratton

Tampa Bay Lightning — Center

1998-99 Season

	GP	G	A	Pts	+/–	PIM	PP	SH	S	SPct	P/G
Overall	78	8	26	34	-28	143	1	0	181	4.4	.44
Home	37	5	13	18	-6	69	1	0	95	5.3	.49
Away	41	3	13	16	-22	74	0	0	86	3.5	.39
vs. Division	18	1	8	9	-8	21	0	0	47	2.1	.50
vs. Conference	61	5	20	25	-21	133	1	0	141	3.5	.41
vs. Playoff	52	6	15	21	-19	94	0	0	116	5.2	.40
vs. Non-Playoff	26	2	11	13	-9	49	1	0	65	3.1	.50
Pre All-Star	41	2	13	15	-10	86	0	0	93	2.2	.37
Post All-Star	37	6	13	19	-18	57	1	0	88	6.8	.51
Day	7	2	0	2	-6	11	0	0	25	8.0	.29
Night	71	6	26	32	-22	132	1	0	156	3.8	.45

	GP	G	A	Pts	+/–	PIM	PP	SH	S	SPct	P/G
National TV	2	0	2	2	3	0	0	0	3	0.0	1.00
0 Days Rest	13	1	2	3	-11	17	0	0	27	3.7	.23
1 Days Rest	35	4	12	16	-6	71	0	0	87	4.6	.46
2 Days Rest	19	2	9	11	-3	39	1	0	46	4.3	.58
3+ Days Rest	11	1	3	4	-8	16	0	0	21	4.8	.36

	G	A	Pts	PIM		G	A	Pts	PIM
1st Period	2	8	10	33	Winning	3	9	12	24
2nd Period	2	11	13	48	Losing	2	6	8	104
3rd Period	4	7	11	62	Tied	3	11	14	15
Overtime	0	0	0	0	Clutch	2	2	4	28
Last 5 Min	3	10	13	76	Blowouts	0	1	1	6

Adam Graves

New York Rangers — Left Wing

1998-99 Season

	GP	G	A	Pts	+/–	PIM	PP	SH	S	SPct	P/G
Overall	82	38	15	53	-12	47	14	2	239	15.9	.65
Home	41	15	9	24	-11	18	6	0	125	12.0	.59
Away	41	23	6	29	-1	29	8	2	114	20.2	.71
vs. Division	20	9	3	12	-4	10	4	0	52	17.3	.60
vs. Conference	58	28	9	37	-3	43	9	2	171	16.4	.64
vs. Playoff	52	18	10	28	-6	16	8	2	137	13.1	.54
vs. Non-Playoff	30	20	5	25	-6	31	6	0	102	19.6	.83
Pre All-Star	45	19	6	25	-12	39	10	0	113	16.8	.56
Post All-Star	37	19	9	28	0	8	4	2	126	15.1	.76
Day	12	7	1	8	-2	2	3	1	43	16.3	.67
Night	70	31	14	45	-10	45	11	1	196	15.8	.64

	GP	G	A	Pts	+/–	PIM	PP	SH	S	SPct	P/G
National TV	23	13	4	17	0	4	5	1	76	17.1	.74
0 Days Rest	16	8	3	11	-5	6	3	0	46	17.4	.69
1 Days Rest	34	15	5	20	-7	12	6	0	99	15.2	.59
2 Days Rest	20	12	4	16	2	21	3	2	71	16.9	.80
3+ Days Rest	12	3	3	6	-2	8	2	0	23	13.0	.50

	G	A	Pts	PIM		G	A	Pts	PIM
1st Period	14	8	22	23	Winning	15	5	20	25
2nd Period	11	3	14	16	Losing	11	5	16	12
3rd Period	10	4	14	8	Tied	12	5	17	10
Overtime	3	0	3	0	Clutch	6	1	7	2
Last 5 Min	13	3	16	18	Blowouts	5	1	6	21

Travis Green

Anaheim Mighty Ducks — Center

1998-99 Season

	GP	G	A	Pts	+/–	PIM	PP	SH	S	SPct	P/G
Overall	79	13	17	30	-7	81	3	1	165	7.9	.38
Home	40	6	8	14	-3	36	2	1	88	6.8	.35
Away	39	7	9	16	-4	45	1	0	77	9.1	.41
vs. Division	24	3	4	7	-1	35	1	1	50	6.0	.29
vs. Conference	54	8	12	20	-6	57	3	1	108	7.4	.37
vs. Playoff	49	8	9	17	-6	53	1	0	91	8.8	.35
vs. Non-Playoff	30	5	8	13	-1	28	2	1	74	6.8	.43
Pre All-Star	42	9	8	17	-4	47	2	1	91	9.9	.40
Post All-Star	37	4	9	13	-3	34	1	0	74	5.4	.35
Day	1	1	0	1	0	0	0	0	1	100.0	1.00
Night	78	12	17	29	-7	81	3	1	164	7.3	.37

	GP	G	A	Pts	+/–	PIM	PP	SH	S	SPct	P/G
National TV	13	2	5	7	7	8	1	0	21	9.5	.54
0 Days Rest	15	2	3	5	2	33	1	0	30	6.7	.33
1 Days Rest	39	7	6	13	-7	26	0	1	77	9.1	.33
2 Days Rest	12	3	4	7	-5	8	2	0	32	9.4	.58
3+ Days Rest	13	1	4	5	3	14	0	0	26	3.8	.38

	G	A	Pts	PIM		G	A	Pts	PIM
1st Period	4	8	12	36	Winning	5	9	14	36
2nd Period	8	4	12	29	Losing	2	2	4	22
3rd Period	1	5	6	16	Tied	6	6	12	23
Overtime	0	0	0	0	Clutch	1	2	3	2
Last 5 Min	3	2	5	18	Blowouts	0	0	0	2

Wayne Gretzky

New York Rangers — Center

1998-99 Season

	GP	G	A	Pts	+/–	PIM	PP	SH	S	SPct	P/G
Overall	70	9	53	62	-23	14	3	0	132	6.8	.89
Home	32	5	25	30	-8	6	2	0	78	6.4	.94
Away	38	4	28	32	-15	8	1	0	54	7.4	.84
vs. Division	17	4	12	16	1	0	1	0	47	8.5	.94
vs. Conference	48	7	31	38	-17	8	3	0	96	7.3	.79
vs. Playoff	43	3	26	29	-17	12	1	0	80	3.8	.67
vs. Non-Playoff	27	6	27	33	-6	2	2	0	52	11.5	1.22
Pre All-Star	45	7	36	43	-15	6	3	0	84	8.3	.96
Post All-Star	25	2	17	19	-8	8	0	0	48	4.2	.76
Day	8	2	5	7	-4	0	1	0	20	10.0	.88
Night	62	7	48	55	-19	14	2	0	112	6.3	.89

	GP	G	A	Pts	+/–	PIM	PP	SH	S	SPct	P/G
National TV	18	3	10	13	-10	2	0	0	37	8.1	.72
0 Days Rest	13	2	14	16	-5	0	1	0	14	14.3	1.23
1 Days Rest	27	4	16	20	-8	4	1	0	63	6.3	.74
2 Days Rest	19	3	18	21	-5	2	1	0	38	7.9	1.11
3+ Days Rest	11	0	5	5	-5	8	0	0	17	0.0	.45

	G	A	Pts	PIM		G	A	Pts	PIM
1st Period	1	14	15	8	Winning	5	23	28	2
2nd Period	3	18	21	6	Losing	3	19	22	10
3rd Period	5	20	25	0	Tied	1	11	12	2
Overtime	0	1	1	0	Clutch	2	4	6	0
Last 5 Min	3	17	20	2	Blowouts	0	8	8	0

Mike Grier

Edmonton Oilers — Right Wing

1998-99 Season

	GP	G	A	Pts	+/–	PIM	PP	SH	S	SPct	P/G
Overall	82	20	24	44	5	54	3	2	143	14.0	.54
Home	41	14	12	26	5	21	2	2	71	19.7	.63
Away	41	6	12	18	0	33	1	0	72	8.3	.44
vs. Division	18	10	6	16	12	15	2	1	40	25.0	.89
vs. Conference	55	17	15	32	2	43	3	2	93	18.3	.58
vs. Playoff	47	9	19	28	6	38	1	1	83	10.8	.60
vs. Non-Playoff	35	11	5	16	-1	16	2	1	60	18.3	.46
Pre All-Star	44	7	14	21	-2	23	0	1	74	9.5	.48
Post All-Star	38	13	10	23	7	31	3	1	69	18.8	.61
Day	4	1	0	1	0	2	0	0	8	12.5	.25
Night	78	19	24	43	5	52	3	2	135	14.1	.55

	GP	G	A	Pts	+/–	PIM	PP	SH	S	SPct	P/G
National TV	13	9	4	13	9	17	1	1	27	33.3	1.00
0 Days Rest	14	3	3	6	-3	13	1	1	34	8.8	.43
1 Days Rest	40	9	11	20	0	28	2	1	62	14.5	.50
2 Days Rest	16	6	5	11	4	9	0	0	33	18.2	.69
3+ Days Rest	12	2	5	7	4	4	0	0	14	14.3	.58

	G	A	Pts	PIM		G	A	Pts	PIM
1st Period	4	5	9	21	Winning	10	9	19	4
2nd Period	8	8	16	23	Losing	6	6	12	42
3rd Period	8	11	19	8	Tied	4	9	13	8
Overtime	0	0	0	2	Clutch	1	6	7	4
Last 5 Min	6	6	12	34	Blowouts	3	0	3	2

Michal Grosek

Buffalo Sabres — Left Wing

1998-99 Season																							
	GP	G	A	Pts	+/–	PIM	PP	SH	S	SPct	P/G		GP	G	A	Pts	+/–	PIM	PP	SH	S	SPct	P/G
Overall	76	20	30	50	21	102	4	0	140	14.3	.66	National TV	13	3	3	6	-5	17	2	0	27	11.1	.46
Home	39	12	17	29	19	53	1	0	60	20.0	.74	0 Days Rest	18	3	8	11	-3	20	0	0	36	8.3	.61
Away	37	8	13	21	2	49	3	0	80	10.0	.57	1 Days Rest	30	6	12	18	11	24	0	0	48	12.5	.60
vs. Division	18	5	8	13	8	39	1	0	32	15.6	.72	2 Days Rest	16	7	8	15	14	38	1	0	30	23.3	.94
vs. Conference	52	12	20	32	13	90	3	0	94	12.8	.62	3+ Days Rest	12	4	2	6	-1	20	3	0	26	15.4	.50
vs. Playoff	43	8	18	26	14	56	1	0	75	10.7	.60		G	A	Pts	PIM		G	A	Pts	PIM		
vs. Non-Playoff	33	12	12	24	7	46	3	0	65	18.5	.73	1st Period	5	12	17	25	Winning	7	9	16	52		
Pre All-Star	43	11	19	30	12	75	2	0	86	12.8	.70	2nd Period	7	9	16	29	Losing	7	10	17	42		
Post All-Star	33	9	11	20	9	27	2	0	54	16.7	.61	3rd Period	8	9	17	48	Tied	6	11	17	8		
Day	5	2	2	4	2	7	0	0	9	22.2	.80	Overtime	0	0	0	0	Clutch	4	4	8	2		
Night	71	18	28	46	19	95	4	0	131	13.7	.65	Last 5 Min	3	9	12	20	Blowouts	1	0	1	26		

Bill Guerin

Edmonton Oilers — Right Wing

1998-99 Season																							
	GP	G	A	Pts	+/–	PIM	PP	SH	S	SPct	P/G		GP	G	A	Pts	+/–	PIM	PP	SH	S	SPct	P/G
Overall	80	30	34	64	7	133	13	0	261	11.5	.80	National TV	12	6	5	11	-1	33	4	0	44	13.6	.92
Home	39	10	12	22	-1	51	5	0	131	7.6	.56	0 Days Rest	13	3	4	7	-1	30	2	0	36	8.3	.54
Away	41	20	22	42	8	82	8	0	130	15.4	1.02	1 Days Rest	40	16	20	36	6	45	5	0	145	11.0	.90
vs. Division	16	3	12	15	4	35	2	0	56	5.4	.94	2 Days Rest	16	7	6	13	3	44	3	0	47	14.9	.81
vs. Conference	53	16	26	42	4	104	5	0	160	10.0	.79	3+ Days Rest	11	4	4	8	-1	14	3	0	33	12.1	.73
vs. Playoff	46	16	21	37	-1	83	5	0	148	10.8	.80		G	A	Pts	PIM		G	A	Pts	PIM		
vs. Non-Playoff	34	14	13	27	8	50	8	0	113	12.4	.79	1st Period	8	7	15	62	Winning	15	13	28	22		
Pre All-Star	44	20	17	37	12	68	10	0	136	14.7	.84	2nd Period	9	10	19	28	Losing	9	12	21	96		
Post All-Star	36	10	17	27	-5	65	3	0	125	8.0	.75	3rd Period	13	16	29	43	Tied	6	9	15	15		
Day	4	3	0	3	-3	2	1	0	14	21.4	.75	Overtime	0	1	1	0	Clutch	2	5	7	0		
Night	76	27	34	61	10	131	12	0	247	10.9	.80	Last 5 Min	10	10	20	63	Blowouts	3	2	5	6		

Alexei Gusarov

Colorado Avalanche — Defense

1998-99 Season																							
	GP	G	A	Pts	+/–	PIM	PP	SH	S	SPct	P/G		GP	G	A	Pts	+/–	PIM	PP	SH	S	SPct	P/G
Overall	54	3	10	13	12	24	1	0	28	10.7	.24	National TV	16	1	3	4	8	6	0	0	9	11.1	.25
Home	30	2	7	9	11	16	1	0	17	11.8	.30	0 Days Rest	6	0	0	0	-2	6	0	0	3	0.0	.00
Away	24	1	3	4	1	8	0	0	11	9.1	.17	1 Days Rest	30	1	3	4	5	14	1	0	13	7.7	.13
vs. Division	12	0	3	3	0	2	0	0	9	0.0	.25	2 Days Rest	8	1	4	5	2	2	0	0	4	25.0	.63
vs. Conference	36	2	5	7	7	18	1	0	19	10.5	.19	3+ Days Rest	10	1	3	4	7	2	0	0	8	12.5	.40
vs. Playoff	32	1	5	6	10	14	0	0	13	7.7	.19		G	A	Pts	PIM		G	A	Pts	PIM		
vs. Non-Playoff	22	2	5	7	2	10	1	0	15	13.3	.32	1st Period	1	3	4	14	Winning	3	4	7	10		
Pre All-Star	20	1	8	9	2	12	0	0	13	7.7	.45	2nd Period	1	4	5	6	Losing	0	1	1	8		
Post All-Star	34	2	2	4	10	12	1	0	15	13.3	.12	3rd Period	1	3	4	4	Tied	0	5	5	6		
Day	13	1	0	1	3	2	0	0	9	11.1	.08	Overtime	0	0	0	0	Clutch	1	1	2	2		
Night	41	2	10	12	9	22	1	0	19	10.5	.29	Last 5 Min	2	4	6	8	Blowouts	0	2	2	4		

Roman Hamrlik

Edmonton Oilers — Defense

1998-99 Season																							
	GP	G	A	Pts	+/–	PIM	PP	SH	S	SPct	P/G		GP	G	A	Pts	+/–	PIM	PP	SH	S	SPct	P/G
Overall	75	8	24	32	9	70	3	0	172	4.7	.43	National TV	11	0	4	4	8	16	0	0	20	0.0	.36
Home	38	3	10	13	2	32	2	0	99	3.0	.34	0 Days Rest	12	1	2	3	0	14	0	0	22	4.5	.25
Away	37	5	14	19	7	38	1	0	73	6.8	.51	1 Days Rest	36	3	11	14	5	34	1	0	81	3.7	.39
vs. Division	16	2	9	11	8	24	1	0	47	4.3	.69	2 Days Rest	15	2	5	7	6	14	1	0	45	4.4	.47
vs. Conference	48	5	20	25	3	50	2	0	112	4.5	.52	3+ Days Rest	12	2	6	8	-2	8	1	0	24	8.3	.67
vs. Playoff	43	5	12	17	2	40	2	0	87	5.7	.40		G	A	Pts	PIM		G	A	Pts	PIM		
vs. Non-Playoff	32	3	12	15	7	30	1	0	85	3.5	.47	1st Period	5	7	12	18	Winning	1	3	4	28		
Pre All-Star	38	4	16	20	1	30	1	0	82	4.9	.53	2nd Period	2	6	8	24	Losing	5	10	15	38		
Post All-Star	37	4	8	12	8	40	2	0	90	4.4	.32	3rd Period	1	10	11	28	Tied	2	11	13	4		
Day	4	3	1	4	0	8	2	0	13	23.1	1.00	Overtime	0	1	1	0	Clutch	0	4	4	0		
Night	71	5	23	28	9	62	1	0	159	3.1	.39	Last 5 Min	2	10	12	16	Blowouts	0	3	3	10		

Michal Handzus

St. Louis Blues — Center

1998-99 Season

	GP	G	A	Pts	+/–	PIM	PP	SH	S	SPct	P/G
Overall	66	4	12	16	-9	30	0	0	78	5.1	.24
Home	35	1	8	9	3	12	0	0	37	2.7	.26
Away	31	3	4	7	-12	18	0	0	41	7.3	.23
vs. Division	14	2	5	7	-5	10	0	0	22	9.1	.50
vs. Conference	43	3	9	12	-6	26	0	0	56	5.4	.28
vs. Playoff	37	2	6	8	-4	20	0	0	41	4.9	.22
vs. Non-Playoff	29	2	6	8	-5	10	0	0	37	5.4	.28
Pre All-Star	42	2	9	11	-9	20	0	0	51	3.9	.26
Post All-Star	24	2	3	5	0	10	0	0	27	7.4	.21
Day	6	1	3	4	3	2	0	0	8	12.5	.67
Night	60	3	9	12	-12	28	0	0	70	4.3	.20

	GP	G	A	Pts	+/–	PIM	PP	SH	S	SPct	P/G
National TV	12	1	4	5	2	8	0	0	14	7.1	.42
0 Days Rest	10	2	1	3	1	8	0	0	12	16.7	.30
1 Days Rest	32	2	7	9	-3	14	0	0	37	5.4	.28
2 Days Rest	14	0	1	1	-4	0	0	0	17	0.0	.07
3+ Days Rest	10	0	3	3	-3	8	0	0	12	0.0	.30

	G	A	Pts	PIM		G	A	Pts	PIM
1st Period	4	3	7	6	Winning	2	5	7	14
2nd Period	0	4	4	16	Losing	0	2	2	10
3rd Period	0	5	5	8	Tied	2	5	7	6
Overtime	0	0	0	0	Clutch	0	3	3	0
Last 5 Min	0	4	4	8	Blowouts	0	1	1	6

Todd Harvey

New York Rangers — Right Wing

1998-99 Season

	GP	G	A	Pts	+/–	PIM	PP	SH	S	SPct	P/G
Overall	37	11	17	28	-1	72	6	0	58	19.0	.76
Home	19	4	8	12	-4	45	2	0	31	12.9	.63
Away	18	7	9	16	3	27	4	0	27	25.9	.89
vs. Division	10	3	2	5	-2	25	2	0	13	23.1	.50
vs. Conference	26	9	11	20	3	60	5	0	41	22.0	.77
vs. Playoff	25	9	6	15	-5	45	5	0	45	20.0	.60
vs. Non-Playoff	12	2	11	13	4	27	1	0	13	15.4	1.08
Pre All-Star	33	10	14	24	2	59	5	0	50	20.0	.73
Post All-Star	4	1	3	4	-3	13	1	0	8	12.5	1.00
Day	4	0	2	2	-1	8	0	0	4	0.0	.50
Night	33	11	15	26	0	64	6	0	54	20.4	.79

	GP	G	A	Pts	+/–	PIM	PP	SH	S	SPct	P/G
National TV	7	2	1	3	0	8	1	0	11	18.2	.43
0 Days Rest	7	3	5	8	0	19	2	0	9	33.3	1.14
1 Days Rest	14	3	3	6	-1	26	1	0	19	15.8	.43
2 Days Rest	7	5	6	11	7	8	3	0	19	26.3	1.57
3+ Days Rest	9	0	3	3	-7	19	0	0	11	0.0	.33

	G	A	Pts	PIM		G	A	Pts	PIM
1st Period	6	3	9	31	Winning	2	11	13	21
2nd Period	2	7	9	27	Losing	4	3	7	43
3rd Period	3	6	9	14	Tied	5	3	8	8
Overtime	0	1	1	0	Clutch	1	2	3	4
Last 5 Min	3	4	7	17	Blowouts	1	4	5	6

Derian Hatcher

Dallas Stars — Defense

1998-99 Season

	GP	G	A	Pts	+/–	PIM	PP	SH	S	SPct	P/G
Overall	80	9	21	30	21	102	3	0	125	7.2	.38
Home	41	4	11	15	5	67	1	0	66	6.1	.37
Away	39	5	10	15	16	35	2	0	59	8.5	.38
vs. Division	23	3	2	5	7	33	2	0	26	11.5	.22
vs. Conference	54	5	11	16	7	89	2	0	81	6.2	.30
vs. Playoff	46	3	15	18	10	84	1	0	64	4.7	.39
vs. Non-Playoff	34	6	6	12	11	18	2	0	61	9.8	.35
Pre All-Star	43	6	9	15	12	51	1	0	60	10.0	.35
Post All-Star	37	3	12	15	9	51	2	0	65	4.6	.41
Day	8	0	3	3	-2	6	0	0	15	0.0	.38
Night	72	9	18	27	23	96	3	0	110	8.2	.38

	GP	G	A	Pts	+/–	PIM	PP	SH	S	SPct	P/G
National TV	13	0	2	2	0	27	0	0	18	0.0	.15
0 Days Rest	14	1	2	3	2	12	1	0	19	5.3	.21
1 Days Rest	44	7	12	19	15	52	1	0	75	9.3	.43
2 Days Rest	12	1	6	7	6	28	1	0	18	5.6	.58
3+ Days Rest	10	0	1	1	-2	10	0	0	13	0.0	.10

	G	A	Pts	PIM		G	A	Pts	PIM
1st Period	4	8	12	60	Winning	5	11	16	73
2nd Period	3	10	13	17	Losing	2	3	5	20
3rd Period	2	2	4	25	Tied	2	7	9	9
Overtime	0	1	1	0	Clutch	0	2	2	6
Last 5 Min	2	9	11	32	Blowouts	0	2	2	20

Kevin Hatcher

Pittsburgh Penguins — Defense

1998-99 Season

	GP	G	A	Pts	+/–	PIM	PP	SH	S	SPct	P/G
Overall	66	11	27	38	11	24	4	2	131	8.4	.58
Home	31	7	12	19	18	14	3	2	58	12.1	.61
Away	35	4	15	19	-7	10	1	0	73	5.5	.54
vs. Division	15	2	3	5	-3	6	1	0	26	7.7	.33
vs. Conference	47	7	19	26	7	18	2	0	88	8.0	.55
vs. Playoff	33	4	10	14	2	14	2	0	66	6.1	.42
vs. Non-Playoff	33	7	17	24	9	10	2	2	65	10.8	.73
Pre All-Star	41	7	21	28	8	14	3	1	86	8.1	.68
Post All-Star	25	4	6	10	3	10	1	1	45	8.9	.40
Day	8	1	2	3	2	8	0	0	10	10.0	.38
Night	58	10	25	35	9	16	4	2	121	8.3	.60

	GP	G	A	Pts	+/–	PIM	PP	SH	S	SPct	P/G
National TV	15	1	7	8	-5	4	0	0	33	3.0	.53
0 Days Rest	11	1	4	5	1	2	1	0	19	5.3	.45
1 Days Rest	26	5	10	15	4	16	1	1	63	7.9	.58
2 Days Rest	18	5	8	13	8	4	2	1	32	15.6	.72
3+ Days Rest	11	0	5	5	-2	2	0	0	17	0.0	.45

	G	A	Pts	PIM		G	A	Pts	PIM
1st Period	2	5	7	6	Winning	2	6	8	14
2nd Period	3	13	16	10	Losing	4	12	16	4
3rd Period	5	9	14	8	Tied	5	9	14	6
Overtime	1	0	1	0	Clutch	1	2	3	4
Last 5 Min	4	10	14	12	Blowouts	1	2	3	6

Bret Hedican

Florida Panthers — Defense

1998-99 Season

	GP	G	A	Pts	+/–	PIM	PP	SH	S	SPct	P/G
Overall	67	5	18	23	5	51	0	2	90	5.6	.34
Home	34	1	11	12	2	25	0	0	46	2.2	.35
Away	33	4	7	11	3	26	0	2	44	9.1	.33
vs. Division	16	3	6	9	9	17	0	1	21	14.3	.56
vs. Conference	46	5	14	19	6	39	0	2	67	7.5	.41
vs. Playoff	42	3	8	11	-9	34	0	2	56	5.4	.26
vs. Non-Playoff	25	2	10	12	14	17	0	0	34	5.9	.48
Pre All-Star	45	3	13	16	9	38	0	2	55	5.5	.36
Post All-Star	22	2	5	7	-4	13	0	0	35	5.7	.32
Day	0	0	0	0	0	0	0	0	0	–	–
Night	67	5	18	23	5	51	0	2	90	5.6	.34

	GP	G	A	Pts	+/–	PIM	PP	SH	S	SPct	P/G
National TV	11	0	3	3	-5	2	0	0	12	0.0	.27
0 Days Rest	11	3	3	6	10	12	0	1	24	12.5	.55
1 Days Rest	30	0	5	5	-2	20	0	0	31	0.0	.17
2 Days Rest	16	1	5	6	0	4	0	1	23	4.3	.38
3+ Days Rest	10	1	5	6	-3	15	0	0	12	8.3	.60

	G	A	Pts	PIM		G	A	Pts	PIM
1st Period	1	9	10	22	Winning	2	11	13	17
2nd Period	1	4	5	15	Losing	1	4	5	32
3rd Period	3	5	8	14	Tied	2	3	5	2
Overtime	0	0	0	0	Clutch	1	0	1	4
Last 5 Min	1	4	5	20	Blowouts	0	1	1	15

Steve Heinze

Boston Bruins — Right Wing

1998-99 Season

	GP	G	A	Pts	+/–	PIM	PP	SH	S	SPct	P/G
Overall	73	22	18	40	7	30	9	0	146	15.1	.55
Home	39	13	14	27	9	12	6	0	87	14.9	.69
Away	34	9	4	13	-2	18	3	0	59	15.3	.38
vs. Division	17	5	4	9	-2	10	4	0	35	14.3	.53
vs. Conference	53	13	14	27	4	20	5	0	104	12.5	.51
vs. Playoff	41	7	8	15	-8	22	3	0	82	8.5	.37
vs. Non-Playoff	32	15	10	25	15	8	6	0	64	23.4	.78
Pre All-Star	42	13	10	23	1	24	4	0	96	13.5	.55
Post All-Star	31	9	8	17	6	6	5	0	50	18.0	.55
Day	15	5	4	9	6	2	2	0	27	18.5	.60
Night	58	17	14	31	1	28	7	0	119	14.3	.53

	GP	G	A	Pts	+/–	PIM	PP	SH	S	SPct	P/G
National TV	8	0	3	3	2	2	0	0	14	0.0	.38
0 Days Rest	14	4	2	6	-4	2	3	0	35	11.4	.43
1 Days Rest	35	9	14	23	12	12	3	0	67	13.4	.66
2 Days Rest	10	5	0	5	1	6	1	0	18	27.8	.50
3+ Days Rest	14	4	2	6	-2	10	2	0	26	15.4	.43

	G	A	Pts	PIM		G	A	Pts	PIM
1st Period	9	4	13	4	Winning	7	2	9	12
2nd Period	8	7	15	16	Losing	8	8	16	14
3rd Period	5	5	10	10	Tied	7	8	15	4
Overtime	0	2	2	0	Clutch	2	3	5	2
Last 5 Min	6	12	18	8	Blowouts	0	2	2	0

Milan Hejduk

Colorado Avalanche — Right Wing

1998-99 Season

	GP	G	A	Pts	+/–	PIM	PP	SH	S	SPct	P/G
Overall	82	14	34	48	8	26	4	0	178	7.9	.59
Home	41	8	24	32	16	10	3	0	89	9.0	.78
Away	41	6	10	16	-8	16	1	0	89	6.7	.39
vs. Division	18	2	5	7	-4	0	1	0	45	4.4	.39
vs. Conference	56	6	25	31	1	20	2	0	108	5.6	.55
vs. Playoff	45	10	14	24	2	16	4	0	84	11.9	.53
vs. Non-Playoff	37	4	20	24	6	10	0	0	94	4.3	.65
Pre All-Star	45	5	16	21	-2	14	2	0	104	4.8	.47
Post All-Star	37	9	18	27	10	12	2	0	74	12.2	.73
Day	15	3	10	13	4	8	1	0	35	8.6	.87
Night	67	11	24	35	4	18	3	0	143	7.7	.52

	GP	G	A	Pts	+/–	PIM	PP	SH	S	SPct	P/G
National TV	22	7	8	15	6	10	2	0	48	14.6	.68
0 Days Rest	13	2	1	3	-7	4	1	0	31	6.5	.23
1 Days Rest	43	5	19	24	11	10	1	0	96	5.2	.56
2 Days Rest	14	3	9	12	2	8	0	0	30	10.0	.86
3+ Days Rest	12	4	5	9	2	4	2	0	21	19.0	.75

	G	A	Pts	PIM		G	A	Pts	PIM
1st Period	3	14	17	14	Winning	3	8	11	16
2nd Period	4	12	16	6	Losing	3	13	16	8
3rd Period	7	8	15	6	Tied	8	13	21	2
Overtime	0	0	0	0	Clutch	4	1	5	2
Last 5 Min	6	7	13	4	Blowouts	0	3	3	0

Jamie Heward

Nashville Predators — Right Wing

1998-99 Season

	GP	G	A	Pts	+/–	PIM	PP	SH	S	SPct	P/G
Overall	63	6	12	18	-24	44	4	0	124	4.8	.29
Home	35	2	8	10	-15	22	2	0	78	2.6	.29
Away	28	4	4	8	-9	22	2	0	46	8.7	.29
vs. Division	15	2	1	3	-7	12	1	0	26	7.7	.20
vs. Conference	41	5	8	13	-14	28	3	0	68	7.4	.32
vs. Playoff	41	5	7	12	-18	34	3	0	93	5.4	.29
vs. Non-Playoff	22	1	5	6	-6	10	1	0	31	3.2	.27
Pre All-Star	37	3	9	12	-18	38	2	0	78	3.8	.32
Post All-Star	26	3	3	6	-6	6	2	0	46	6.5	.23
Day	6	0	0	0	-4	14	0	0	10	0.0	.00
Night	57	6	12	18	-20	30	4	0	114	5.3	.32

	GP	G	A	Pts	+/–	PIM	PP	SH	S	SPct	P/G
National TV	1	0	0	0	0	0	0	0	0	–	.00
0 Days Rest	9	1	2	3	-4	4	1	0	17	5.9	.33
1 Days Rest	24	2	5	7	-6	8	2	0	48	4.2	.29
2 Days Rest	16	0	5	5	-7	20	0	0	28	0.0	.31
3+ Days Rest	14	3	0	3	-7	12	1	0	31	9.7	.21

	G	A	Pts	PIM		G	A	Pts	PIM
1st Period	3	2	5	12	Winning	0	4	4	18
2nd Period	2	5	7	26	Losing	3	6	9	24
3rd Period	1	5	6	6	Tied	3	2	5	2
Overtime	0	0	0	0	Clutch	0	1	1	6
Last 5 Min	2	4	6	8	Blowouts	0	1	1	12

Sean Hill

Carolina Hurricanes — Defense

1998-99 Season

	GP	G	A	Pts	+/–	PIM	PP	SH	S	SPct	P/G
Overall	54	0	10	10	9	48	0	0	44	0.0	.19
Home	27	0	7	7	5	16	0	0	27	0.0	.26
Away	27	0	3	3	4	32	0	0	17	0.0	.11
vs. Division	7	0	0	0	2	8	0	0	4	0.0	.00
vs. Conference	35	0	7	7	8	32	0	0	24	0.0	.20
vs. Playoff	30	0	7	7	-3	28	0	0	22	0.0	.23
vs. Non-Playoff	24	0	3	3	12	20	0	0	22	0.0	.13
Pre All-Star	32	0	3	3	2	22	0	0	26	0.0	.09
Post All-Star	22	0	7	7	7	26	0	0	18	0.0	.32
Day	2	0	0	0	-3	2	0	0	3	0.0	.00
Night	52	0	10	10	12	46	0	0	41	0.0	.19

	GP	G	A	Pts	+/–	PIM	PP	SH	S	SPct	P/G
National TV	2	0	0	0	1	4	0	0	0	–	.00
0 Days Rest	11	0	0	0	0	12	0	0	7	0.0	.00
1 Days Rest	15	0	3	3	1	12	0	0	13	0.0	.20
2 Days Rest	19	0	6	6	11	18	0	0	21	0.0	.32
3+ Days Rest	9	0	1	1	-3	6	0	0	3	0.0	.11

	G	A	Pts	PIM		G	A	Pts	PIM
1st Period	0	4	4	10	Winning	0	5	5	20
2nd Period	0	2	2	20	Losing	0	1	1	16
3rd Period	0	4	4	16	Tied	0	4	4	12
Overtime	0	0	0	2	Clutch	0	0	0	4
Last 5 Min	0	1	1	10	Blowouts	0	0	0	0

Jonas Hoglund

Montreal Canadiens — Right Wing

1998-99 Season

	GP	G	A	Pts	+/–	PIM	PP	SH	S	SPct	P/G
Overall	74	8	10	18	-5	16	1	0	122	6.6	.24
Home	34	3	7	10	-2	2	0	0	58	5.2	.29
Away	40	5	3	8	-3	14	1	0	64	7.8	.20
vs. Division	17	0	1	1	-4	2	0	0	31	0.0	.06
vs. Conference	50	3	6	9	-7	8	0	0	78	3.8	.18
vs. Playoff	45	4	8	12	-10	4	0	0	79	5.1	.27
vs. Non-Playoff	29	4	2	6	5	12	1	0	43	9.3	.21
Pre All-Star	42	6	6	12	-1	10	1	0	69	8.7	.29
Post All-Star	32	2	4	6	-4	6	0	0	53	3.8	.19
Day	3	0	1	1	-2	0	0	0	4	0.0	.33
Night	71	8	9	17	-3	16	1	0	118	6.8	.24

	GP	G	A	Pts	+/–	PIM	PP	SH	S	SPct	P/G
National TV	18	1	1	2	-2	4	0	0	34	2.9	.11
0 Days Rest	17	2	1	3	-4	4	0	0	22	9.1	.18
1 Days Rest	27	3	7	10	1	8	1	0	52	5.8	.37
2 Days Rest	14	1	2	3	1	2	0	0	21	4.8	.21
3+ Days Rest	16	2	0	2	-3	2	0	0	27	7.4	.13

	G	A	Pts	PIM		G	A	Pts	PIM
1st Period	2	2	4	8	Winning	2	1	3	6
2nd Period	2	5	7	4	Losing	6	4	10	8
3rd Period	4	3	7	4	Tied	0	5	5	2
Overtime	0	0	0	0	Clutch	0	1	1	4
Last 5 Min	2	1	3	4	Blowouts	0	0	0	2

Benoit Hogue

Dallas Stars — Center

1998-99 Season

	GP	G	A	Pts	+/–	PIM	PP	SH	S	SPct	P/G
Overall	74	12	17	29	-10	54	2	0	121	9.9	.39
Home	37	8	10	18	-7	28	2	0	61	13.1	.49
Away	37	4	7	11	-3	26	0	0	60	6.7	.30
vs. Division	16	1	5	6	-3	20	0	0	31	3.2	.38
vs. Conference	54	7	11	18	-13	48	2	0	88	8.0	.33
vs. Playoff	49	9	9	18	-8	30	2	0	78	11.5	.37
vs. Non-Playoff	25	3	8	11	-2	24	0	0	43	7.0	.44
Pre All-Star	39	3	5	8	-20	32	2	0	55	5.5	.21
Post All-Star	35	9	12	21	10	22	0	0	66	13.6	.60
Day	6	0	0	0	-1	2	0	0	9	0.0	.00
Night	68	12	17	29	-9	52	2	0	112	10.7	.43

	GP	G	A	Pts	+/–	PIM	PP	SH	S	SPct	P/G
National TV	3	0	2	2	2	2	0	0	6	0.0	.67
0 Days Rest	14	1	2	3	-3	12	0	0	18	5.6	.21
1 Days Rest	27	9	6	15	1	20	2	0	52	17.3	.56
2 Days Rest	20	0	3	3	-5	8	0	0	27	0.0	.15
3+ Days Rest	13	2	6	8	-3	14	0	0	24	8.3	.62

	G	A	Pts	PIM		G	A	Pts	PIM
1st Period	7	2	9	14	Winning	4	8	12	4
2nd Period	1	6	7	30	Losing	3	6	9	46
3rd Period	3	9	12	10	Tied	5	3	8	4
Overtime	1	0	1	0	Clutch	3	2	5	6
Last 5 Min	7	8	15	20	Blowouts	0	4	4	6

Bobby Holik

New Jersey Devils — Left Wing

1998-99 Season

	GP	G	A	Pts	+/–	PIM	PP	SH	S	SPct	P/G
Overall	78	27	37	64	16	119	5	0	253	10.7	.82
Home	38	15	18	33	0	28	3	0	134	11.2	.87
Away	40	12	19	31	16	91	2	0	119	10.1	.78
vs. Division	19	8	10	18	8	22	1	0	43	18.6	.95
vs. Conference	54	13	26	39	7	77	2	0	160	8.1	.72
vs. Playoff	44	17	19	36	6	79	2	0	142	12.0	.82
vs. Non-Playoff	34	10	18	28	10	40	3	0	111	9.0	.82
Pre All-Star	42	19	22	41	15	64	4	0	133	14.3	.98
Post All-Star	36	8	15	23	1	55	1	0	120	6.7	.64
Day	11	3	7	10	1	10	0	0	30	10.0	.91
Night	67	24	30	54	15	109	5	0	223	10.8	.81

	GP	G	A	Pts	+/–	PIM	PP	SH	S	SPct	P/G
National TV	7	1	3	4	0	23	1	0	24	4.2	.57
0 Days Rest	16	5	13	18	16	22	1	0	43	11.6	1.13
1 Days Rest	31	12	13	25	2	50	2	0	99	12.1	.81
2 Days Rest	19	6	6	12	-2	31	1	0	71	8.5	.63
3+ Days Rest	12	4	5	9	0	16	1	0	40	10.0	.75

	G	A	Pts	PIM		G	A	Pts	PIM
1st Period	10	14	24	24	Winning	7	12	19	74
2nd Period	8	15	23	34	Losing	6	9	15	33
3rd Period	8	8	16	61	Tied	14	16	30	12
Overtime	1	0	1	0	Clutch	4	3	7	8
Last 5 Min	9	10	19	34	Blowouts	0	2	2	10

Tomas Holmstrom

Detroit Red Wings — Left Wing

1998-99 Season

	GP	G	A	Pts	+/–	PIM	PP	SH	S	SPct	P/G
Overall	82	13	21	34	-11	69	5	0	100	13.0	.41
Home	41	5	14	19	4	37	2	0	51	9.8	.46
Away	41	8	7	15	-15	32	3	0	49	16.3	.37
vs. Division	18	2	3	5	-5	27	1	0	20	10.0	.28
vs. Conference	54	9	12	21	-6	57	3	0	70	12.9	.39
vs. Playoff	47	3	9	12	-16	30	1	0	48	6.3	.26
vs. Non-Playoff	35	10	12	22	5	39	4	0	52	19.2	.63
Pre All-Star	46	8	11	19	-14	38	5	0	63	12.7	.41
Post All-Star	36	5	10	15	3	31	0	0	37	13.5	.42
Day	13	3	4	7	-1	10	0	0	15	20.0	.54
Night	69	10	17	27	-10	59	5	0	85	11.8	.39

	GP	G	A	Pts	+/–	PIM	PP	SH	S	SPct	P/G
National TV	30	3	8	11	-5	33	1	0	35	8.6	.37
0 Days Rest	12	3	1	4	-9	6	1	0	17	17.6	.33
1 Days Rest	39	5	12	17	1	43	0	0	35	14.3	.44
2 Days Rest	24	1	6	7	-5	12	1	0	33	3.0	.29
3+ Days Rest	7	4	2	6	2	8	3	0	15	26.7	.86

	G	A	Pts	PIM		G	A	Pts	PIM
1st Period	4	6	10	25	Winning	5	11	16	37
2nd Period	6	8	14	28	Losing	5	4	9	28
3rd Period	3	7	10	16	Tied	3	6	9	4
Overtime	0	0	0	0	Clutch	1	0	1	2
Last 5 Min	7	5	12	21	Blowouts	0	1	1	10

Brian Holzinger

Buffalo Sabres — Center

1998-99 Season

	GP	G	A	Pts	+/–	PIM	PP	SH	S	SPct	P/G
Overall	81	17	17	34	2	45	5	0	143	11.9	.42
Home	41	10	11	21	-1	23	3	0	76	13.2	.51
Away	40	7	6	13	3	22	2	0	67	10.4	.33
vs. Division	20	7	3	10	3	6	2	0	36	19.4	.50
vs. Conference	57	13	8	21	-2	35	5	0	104	12.5	.37
vs. Playoff	47	7	8	15	3	31	2	0	75	9.3	.32
vs. Non-Playoff	34	10	9	19	-1	14	3	0	68	14.7	.56
Pre All-Star	42	13	9	22	10	21	5	0	71	18.3	.52
Post All-Star	39	4	8	12	-8	24	0	0	72	5.6	.31
Day	6	1	0	1	-3	2	0	0	10	10.0	.17
Night	75	16	17	33	5	43	5	0	133	12.0	.44

	GP	G	A	Pts	+/–	PIM	PP	SH	S	SPct	P/G
National TV	15	2	3	5	2	10	1	0	19	10.5	.33
0 Days Rest	20	5	5	10	2	8	1	0	34	14.7	.50
1 Days Rest	29	7	9	16	4	15	2	0	55	12.7	.55
2 Days Rest	21	3	1	4	-6	20	2	0	40	7.5	.19
3+ Days Rest	11	2	2	4	2	2	0	0	14	14.3	.36

	G	A	Pts	PIM		G	A	Pts	PIM
1st Period	5	4	9	14	Winning	5	9	14	19
2nd Period	7	4	11	4	Losing	6	6	12	16
3rd Period	5	9	14	27	Tied	6	2	8	10
Overtime	0	0	0	0	Clutch	1	0	1	6
Last 5 Min	6	4	10	6	Blowouts	2	3	5	0

Marian Hossa

Ottawa Senators — Left Wing

1998-99 Season

	GP	G	A	Pts	+/–	PIM	PP	SH	S	SPct	P/G
Overall	60	15	15	30	18	37	1	0	124	12.1	.50
Home	29	7	6	13	11	23	1	0	61	11.5	.45
Away	31	8	9	17	7	14	0	0	63	12.7	.55
vs. Division	15	2	3	5	2	8	0	0	41	4.9	.33
vs. Conference	45	13	15	28	18	29	1	0	91	14.3	.62
vs. Playoff	36	7	9	16	9	16	0	0	82	8.5	.44
vs. Non-Playoff	24	8	6	14	9	21	1	0	42	19.0	.58
Pre All-Star	23	4	7	11	8	6	0	0	42	9.5	.48
Post All-Star	37	11	8	19	10	31	1	0	82	13.4	.51
Day	3	1	0	1	1	2	0	0	4	25.0	.33
Night	57	14	15	29	17	35	1	0	120	11.7	.51

	GP	G	A	Pts	+/–	PIM	PP	SH	S	SPct	P/G
National TV	6	2	0	2	3	4	0	0	13	15.4	.33
0 Days Rest	8	5	6	11	13	4	0	0	10	50.0	1.38
1 Days Rest	34	8	6	14	7	23	0	0	75	10.7	.41
2 Days Rest	13	1	3	4	-1	8	1	0	29	3.4	.31
3+ Days Rest	5	1	0	1	-1	2	0	0	10	10.0	.20

	G	A	Pts	PIM		G	A	Pts	PIM
1st Period	1	1	2	16	Winning	6	5	11	19
2nd Period	6	6	12	4	Losing	6	5	11	12
3rd Period	8	8	16	17	Tied	3	5	8	6
Overtime	0	0	0	0	Clutch	4	3	7	2
Last 5 Min	3	3	6	12	Blowouts	1	1	2	11

Bill Houlder

San Jose Sharks — Defense

1998-99 Season

	GP	G	A	Pts	+/–	PIM	PP	SH	S	SPct	P/G
Overall	76	9	23	32	8	40	7	0	115	7.8	.42
Home	37	3	10	13	7	22	3	0	50	6.0	.35
Away	39	6	13	19	1	18	4	0	65	9.2	.49
vs. Division	23	4	6	10	1	8	4	0	43	9.3	.43
vs. Conference	55	9	15	24	7	34	7	0	92	9.8	.44
vs. Playoff	43	3	16	19	6	26	3	0	67	4.5	.44
vs. Non-Playoff	33	6	7	13	2	14	4	0	48	12.5	.39
Pre All-Star	44	4	16	20	9	28	4	0	64	6.3	.45
Post All-Star	32	5	7	12	-1	12	3	0	51	9.8	.38
Day	6	0	4	4	3	2	0	0	10	0.0	.67
Night	70	9	19	28	5	38	7	0	105	8.6	.40

	GP	G	A	Pts	+/–	PIM	PP	SH	S	SPct	P/G
National TV	11	1	2	3	-2	2	0	0	18	5.6	.27
0 Days Rest	12	1	1	2	2	4	1	0	14	7.1	.17
1 Days Rest	40	6	13	19	7	26	4	0	73	8.2	.48
2 Days Rest	13	1	7	8	2	6	1	0	19	5.3	.62
3+ Days Rest	11	1	2	3	-3	4	1	0	9	11.1	.27

	G	A	Pts	PIM		G	A	Pts	PIM
1st Period	5	6	11	12	Winning	1	5	6	14
2nd Period	1	10	11	16	Losing	0	7	7	18
3rd Period	3	6	9	12	Tied	8	11	19	8
Overtime	0	1	1	0	Clutch	1	3	4	4
Last 5 Min	2	6	8	14	Blowouts	0	0	0	2

Phil Housley

Calgary Flames — Defense

1998-99 Season

	GP	G	A	Pts	+/–	PIM	PP	SH	S	SPct	P/G
Overall	79	11	43	54	14	52	4	0	193	5.7	.68
Home	39	6	21	27	7	34	1	0	88	6.8	.69
Away	40	5	22	27	7	18	3	0	105	4.8	.68
vs. Division	17	4	10	14	0	6	2	0	44	9.1	.82
vs. Conference	53	9	29	38	20	46	4	0	126	7.1	.72
vs. Playoff	48	5	22	27	0	38	3	0	102	4.9	.56
vs. Non-Playoff	31	6	21	27	14	14	1	0	91	6.6	.87
Pre All-Star	46	2	25	27	0	26	1	0	109	1.8	.59
Post All-Star	33	9	18	27	14	26	3	0	84	10.7	.82
Day	4	0	1	1	-3	2	0	0	8	0.0	.25
Night	75	11	42	53	17	50	4	0	185	5.9	.71

	GP	G	A	Pts	+/–	PIM	PP	SH	S	SPct	P/G
National TV	12	0	6	6	1	6	0	0	26	0.0	.50
0 Days Rest	17	3	11	14	5	12	1	0	44	6.8	.82
1 Days Rest	36	4	14	18	3	18	1	0	91	4.4	.50
2 Days Rest	14	2	8	10	4	12	2	0	35	5.7	.71
3+ Days Rest	12	2	10	12	2	10	0	0	23	8.7	1.00

	G	A	Pts	PIM		G	A	Pts	PIM
1st Period	4	14	18	24	Winning	3	12	15	26
2nd Period	5	15	20	14	Losing	5	19	24	16
3rd Period	2	13	15	14	Tied	3	12	15	10
Overtime	0	1	1	0	Clutch	0	2	2	4
Last 5 Min	3	7	10	24	Blowouts	1	2	3	0

Jan Hrdina

Pittsburgh Penguins — Center

1998-99 Season

	GP	G	A	Pts	+/–	PIM	PP	SH	S	SPct	P/G
Overall	82	13	29	42	-2	40	3	0	94	13.8	.51
Home	41	6	19	25	3	22	3	0	55	10.9	.61
Away	41	7	10	17	-5	18	0	0	39	17.9	.41
vs. Division	20	1	6	7	-7	8	0	0	16	6.3	.35
vs. Conference	58	9	22	31	-3	20	3	0	70	12.9	.53
vs. Playoff	45	9	15	24	-8	24	2	0	56	16.1	.53
vs. Non-Playoff	37	4	14	18	6	16	1	0	38	10.5	.49
Pre All-Star	41	5	11	16	-5	16	2	0	41	12.2	.39
Post All-Star	41	8	18	26	3	24	1	0	53	15.1	.63
Day	15	1	5	6	-6	12	0	0	19	5.3	.40
Night	67	12	24	36	4	28	3	0	75	16.0	.54

	GP	G	A	Pts	+/–	PIM	PP	SH	S	SPct	P/G
National TV	18	1	4	5	-2	12	0	0	14	7.1	.28
0 Days Rest	15	2	6	8	3	6	0	0	13	15.4	.53
1 Days Rest	36	9	10	19	-5	20	3	0	53	17.0	.53
2 Days Rest	21	1	10	11	3	6	0	0	20	5.0	.52
3+ Days Rest	10	1	3	4	-3	8	0	0	8	12.5	.40

	G	A	Pts	PIM		G	A	Pts	PIM
1st Period	6	12	18	10	Winning	4	5	9	20
2nd Period	2	7	9	20	Losing	4	13	17	14
3rd Period	5	9	14	10	Tied	5	11	16	6
Overtime	0	1	1	0	Clutch	2	4	6	0
Last 5 Min	5	12	17	18	Blowouts	1	0	1	0

Tony Hrkac

Dallas Stars — Center

1998-99 Season

	GP	G	A	Pts	+/–	PIM	PP	SH	S	SPct	P/G
Overall	69	13	14	27	2	26	2	0	67	19.4	.39
Home	35	4	8	12	0	10	1	0	29	13.8	.34
Away	34	9	6	15	2	16	1	0	38	23.7	.44
vs. Division	19	6	3	9	1	4	1	0	19	31.6	.47
vs. Conference	48	7	13	20	1	20	1	0	42	16.7	.42
vs. Playoff	39	8	10	18	3	14	2	0	36	22.2	.46
vs. Non-Playoff	30	5	4	9	-1	12	0	0	31	16.1	.30
Pre All-Star	37	5	10	15	5	18	2	0	38	13.2	.41
Post All-Star	32	8	4	12	-3	8	0	0	29	27.6	.38
Day	9	3	1	4	-2	0	1	0	14	21.4	.44
Night	60	10	13	23	4	26	1	0	53	18.9	.38

	GP	G	A	Pts	+/–	PIM	PP	SH	S	SPct	P/G
National TV	12	2	5	7	3	4	0	0	11	18.2	.58
0 Days Rest	9	1	1	2	-1	4	0	0	6	16.7	.22
1 Days Rest	37	6	9	15	5	10	2	0	39	15.4	.41
2 Days Rest	10	2	4	6	-2	10	0	0	8	25.0	.60
3+ Days Rest	13	4	0	4	0	2	0	0	14	28.6	.31

	G	A	Pts	PIM		G	A	Pts	PIM
1st Period	4	6	10	12	Winning	5	8	13	16
2nd Period	5	7	12	10	Losing	3	1	4	4
3rd Period	4	1	5	4	Tied	5	5	10	6
Overtime	0	0	0	0	Clutch	1	0	1	0
Last 5 Min	3	4	7	4	Blowouts	0	0	0	4

Brett Hull

Dallas Stars — Right Wing

1998-99 Season

	GP	G	A	Pts	+/–	PIM	PP	SH	S	SPct	P/G
Overall	60	32	26	58	19	30	15	0	192	16.7	.97
Home	32	16	14	30	5	10	9	0	87	18.4	.94
Away	28	16	12	28	14	20	6	0	105	15.2	1.00
vs. Division	19	10	4	14	1	12	4	0	63	15.9	.74
vs. Conference	43	26	14	40	9	22	13	0	140	18.6	.93
vs. Playoff	35	20	12	32	11	20	9	0	113	17.7	.91
vs. Non-Playoff	25	12	14	26	8	10	6	0	79	15.2	1.04
Pre All-Star	33	16	16	32	10	18	9	0	115	13.9	.97
Post All-Star	27	16	10	26	9	12	6	0	77	20.8	.96
Day	7	3	1	4	0	0	2	0	22	13.6	.57
Night	53	29	25	54	19	30	13	0	170	17.1	1.02

	GP	G	A	Pts	+/–	PIM	PP	SH	S	SPct	P/G
National TV	10	5	2	7	-3	4	3	0	33	15.2	.70
0 Days Rest	9	8	1	9	7	4	0	0	36	22.2	1.00
1 Days Rest	25	11	14	25	12	14	8	0	69	15.9	1.00
2 Days Rest	12	8	8	16	1	2	5	0	39	20.5	1.33
3+ Days Rest	14	5	3	8	-1	10	2	0	48	10.4	.57

	G	A	Pts	PIM		G	A	Pts	PIM
1st Period	14	10	24	12	Winning	8	12	20	22
2nd Period	12	7	19	6	Losing	7	4	11	8
3rd Period	5	8	13	12	Tied	17	10	27	0
Overtime	1	1	2	0	Clutch	3	4	7	0
Last 5 Min	7	9	16	6	Blowouts	0	2	2	4

Jody Hull

Philadelphia Flyers — Right Wing

1998-99 Season

	GP	G	A	Pts	+/-	PIM	PP	SH	S	SPct	P/G
Overall	72	3	11	14	-2	12	0	0	73	4.1	.19
Home	39	1	8	9	5	4	0	0	50	2.0	.23
Away	33	2	3	5	-7	8	0	0	23	8.7	.15
vs. Division	19	1	3	4	-3	2	0	0	25	4.0	.21
vs. Conference	51	2	8	10	-4	10	0	0	53	3.8	.20
vs. Playoff	39	3	5	8	0	0	0	0	35	8.6	.21
vs. Non-Playoff	33	0	6	6	-2	12	0	0	38	0.0	.18
Pre All-Star	36	2	10	12	9	8	0	0	38	5.3	.33
Post All-Star	36	1	1	2	-11	4	0	0	35	2.9	.06
Day	14	0	3	3	-4	0	0	0	13	0.0	.21
Night	58	3	8	11	2	12	0	0	60	5.0	.19

	GP	G	A	Pts	+/-	PIM	PP	SH	S	SPct	P/G
National TV	15	1	1	2	-3	0	0	0	13	7.7	.13
0 Days Rest	9	1	0	1	0	4	0	0	9	11.1	.11
1 Days Rest	38	1	4	5	-4	2	0	0	38	2.6	.13
2 Days Rest	12	1	4	5	1	4	0	0	15	6.7	.42
3+ Days Rest	13	0	3	3	1	2	0	0	11	0.0	.23

	G	A	Pts	PIM		G	A	Pts	PIM
1st Period	2	4	6	4	Winning	1	6	7	4
2nd Period	1	2	3	6	Losing	1	2	3	8
3rd Period	0	5	5	2	Tied	1	3	4	0
Overtime	0	0	0	0	Clutch	0	1	1	0
Last 5 Min	1	3	4	0	Blowouts	0	0	0	2

Cale Hulse

Calgary Flames — Defense

1998-99 Season

	GP	G	A	Pts	+/-	PIM	PP	SH	S	SPct	P/G
Overall	73	3	9	12	-8	117	0	0	83	3.6	.16
Home	36	1	7	8	-3	49	0	0	54	1.9	.22
Away	37	2	2	4	-5	68	0	0	29	6.9	.11
vs. Division	13	0	1	1	-3	16	0	0	14	0.0	.08
vs. Conference	49	3	5	8	-5	71	0	0	64	4.7	.16
vs. Playoff	46	3	5	8	-5	80	0	0	54	5.6	.17
vs. Non-Playoff	27	0	4	4	-3	37	0	0	29	0.0	.15
Pre All-Star	44	1	5	6	-8	79	0	0	38	2.6	.14
Post All-Star	29	2	4	6	0	38	0	0	45	4.4	.21
Day	4	0	1	1	1	9	0	0	5	0.0	.25
Night	69	3	8	11	-9	108	0	0	78	3.8	.16

	GP	G	A	Pts	+/-	PIM	PP	SH	S	SPct	P/G
National TV	12	0	2	2	-3	16	0	0	15	0.0	.17
0 Days Rest	15	1	1	2	-5	16	0	0	15	6.7	.13
1 Days Rest	32	0	7	7	-9	55	0	0	39	0.0	.22
2 Days Rest	12	0	0	0	3	27	0	0	10	0.0	.00
3+ Days Rest	14	2	1	3	3	19	0	0	19	10.5	.21

	G	A	Pts	PIM		G	A	Pts	PIM
1st Period	0	4	4	49	Winning	1	0	1	35
2nd Period	1	4	5	41	Losing	2	4	6	67
3rd Period	2	1	3	27	Tied	0	5	5	15
Overtime	0	0	0	0	Clutch	0	0	0	6
Last 5 Min	1	3	4	18	Blowouts	0	0	0	8

Dale Hunter

Colorado Avalanche — Center

1998-99 Season

	GP	G	A	Pts	+/-	PIM	PP	SH	S	SPct	P/G
Overall	62	2	9	11	-7	119	0	0	24	8.3	.18
Home	35	1	8	9	0	28	0	0	12	8.3	.26
Away	27	1	1	2	-7	91	0	0	12	8.3	.07
vs. Division	12	0	2	2	-3	35	0	0	3	0.0	.17
vs. Conference	47	1	8	9	-4	99	0	0	17	5.9	.19
vs. Playoff	33	1	2	3	-8	90	0	0	13	7.7	.09
vs. Non-Playoff	29	1	7	8	1	29	0	0	11	9.1	.28
Pre All-Star	40	0	4	4	-5	92	0	0	15	0.0	.10
Post All-Star	22	2	5	7	-2	27	0	0	9	22.2	.32
Day	5	1	1	2	0	4	0	0	2	50.0	.40
Night	57	1	8	9	-7	115	0	0	22	4.5	.16

	GP	G	A	Pts	+/-	PIM	PP	SH	S	SPct	P/G
National TV	11	1	0	1	0	12	0	0	8	12.5	.09
0 Days Rest	11	0	0	0	-5	55	0	0	5	0.0	.00
1 Days Rest	25	1	5	6	4	32	0	0	7	14.3	.24
2 Days Rest	10	0	2	2	-1	17	0	0	6	0.0	.20
3+ Days Rest	16	1	2	3	-5	15	0	0	6	16.7	.19

	G	A	Pts	PIM		G	A	Pts	PIM
1st Period	0	3	3	60	Winning	1	4	5	38
2nd Period	1	3	4	14	Losing	0	1	1	69
3rd Period	1	3	4	43	Tied	1	4	5	12
Overtime	0	0	0	2	Clutch	1	0	1	4
Last 5 Min	1	2	3	26	Blowouts	0	0	0	30

Jarome Iginla

Calgary Flames — Right Wing

1998-99 Season

	GP	G	A	Pts	+/-	PIM	PP	SH	S	SPct	P/G
Overall	82	28	23	51	1	58	7	0	211	13.3	.62
Home	41	17	11	28	7	28	5	0	124	13.7	.68
Away	41	11	12	23	-6	30	2	0	87	12.6	.56
vs. Division	18	7	9	16	-6	4	2	0	52	13.5	.89
vs. Conference	55	18	20	38	7	41	5	0	151	11.9	.69
vs. Playoff	51	17	14	31	1	39	3	0	138	12.3	.61
vs. Non-Playoff	31	11	9	20	0	19	4	0	73	15.1	.65
Pre All-Star	46	18	9	27	-2	41	5	0	96	18.8	.59
Post All-Star	36	10	14	24	3	17	2	0	115	8.7	.67
Day	4	1	1	2	1	4	0	0	3	33.3	.50
Night	78	27	22	49	0	54	7	0	208	13.0	.63

	GP	G	A	Pts	+/-	PIM	PP	SH	S	SPct	P/G
National TV	13	7	4	11	2	13	2	0	32	21.9	.85
0 Days Rest	17	4	2	6	-3	13	2	0	30	13.3	.35
1 Days Rest	39	10	14	24	0	26	0	0	89	11.2	.62
2 Days Rest	14	7	3	10	4	11	2	0	50	14.0	.71
3+ Days Rest	12	7	4	11	0	8	3	0	42	16.7	.92

	G	A	Pts	PIM		G	A	Pts	PIM
1st Period	6	12	18	17	Winning	8	9	17	16
2nd Period	7	8	15	19	Losing	12	6	18	23
3rd Period	15	3	18	8	Tied	8	8	16	19
Overtime	0	0	0	14	Clutch	5	1	6	14
Last 5 Min	9	4	13	29	Blowouts	2	1	3	2

Jaromir Jagr

Pittsburgh Penguins — Right Wing

1998-99 Season

	GP	G	A	Pts	+/–	PIM	PP	SH	S	SPct	P/G
Overall	81	44	83	127	17	66	10	1	343	12.8	1.57
Home	41	25	49	74	23	34	3	1	190	13.2	1.80
Away	40	19	34	53	-6	32	7	0	153	12.4	1.33
vs. Division	19	9	18	27	-1	16	2	0	90	10.0	1.42
vs. Conference	57	31	63	94	14	46	8	1	241	12.9	1.65
vs. Playoff	44	24	41	65	1	24	5	1	172	14.0	1.48
vs. Non-Playoff	37	20	42	62	16	42	5	0	171	11.7	1.68
Pre All-Star	41	17	40	57	6	34	6	0	160	10.6	1.39
Post All-Star	40	27	43	70	11	32	4	1	183	14.8	1.75
Day	15	9	11	20	3	14	3	0	63	14.3	1.33
Night	66	35	72	107	14	52	7	1	280	12.5	1.62

	GP	G	A	Pts	+/–	PIM	PP	SH	S	SPct	P/G
National TV	18	6	14	20	5	20	0	0	76	7.9	1.11
0 Days Rest	15	7	9	16	-1	12	2	0	60	11.7	1.07
1 Days Rest	36	19	38	57	-2	26	5	1	152	12.5	1.58
2 Days Rest	19	12	24	36	18	16	0	0	92	13.0	1.89
3+ Days Rest	11	6	12	18	2	12	3	0	39	15.4	1.64

	G	A	Pts	PIM		G	A	Pts	PIM
1st Period	13	22	35	34	Winning	12	30	42	46
2nd Period	14	25	39	20	Losing	15	28	43	10
3rd Period	14	34	48	12	Tied	17	25	42	10
Overtime	3	2	5	0	Clutch	5	9	14	6
Last 5 Min	15	25	40	20	Blowouts	0	4	4	10

Craig Janney

New York Islanders — Center

1998-99 Season

	GP	G	A	Pts	+/–	PIM	PP	SH	S	SPct	P/G
Overall	56	5	22	27	-15	14	2	0	45	11.1	.48
Home	30	1	11	12	-6	4	0	0	19	5.3	.40
Away	26	4	11	15	-9	10	2	0	26	15.4	.58
vs. Division	11	1	7	8	-3	2	0	0	10	10.0	.73
vs. Conference	38	5	12	17	-9	6	2	0	28	17.9	.45
vs. Playoff	35	5	11	16	-8	8	2	0	31	16.1	.46
vs. Non-Playoff	21	0	11	11	-7	6	0	0	14	0.0	.52
Pre All-Star	40	4	18	22	-14	12	2	0	37	10.8	.55
Post All-Star	16	1	4	5	-1	2	0	0	8	12.5	.31
Day	4	0	1	1	1	0	0	0	1	0.0	.25
Night	52	5	21	26	-16	14	2	0	44	11.4	.50

	GP	G	A	Pts	+/–	PIM	PP	SH	S	SPct	P/G
National TV	2	0	0	0	-1	2	0	0	2	0.0	.00
0 Days Rest	10	2	4	6	-3	6	1	0	9	22.2	.60
1 Days Rest	18	0	8	8	-3	2	0	0	13	0.0	.44
2 Days Rest	16	1	5	6	-8	4	1	0	12	8.3	.38
3+ Days Rest	12	2	5	7	-1	2	0	0	11	18.2	.58

	G	A	Pts	PIM		G	A	Pts	PIM
1st Period	2	8	10	6	Winning	0	2	2	0
2nd Period	2	3	5	4	Losing	3	10	13	14
3rd Period	1	11	12	4	Tied	2	10	12	0
Overtime	0	0	0	0	Clutch	0	1	1	0
Last 5 Min	2	6	8	4	Blowouts	0	2	2	4

Andreas Johansson

Ottawa Senators — Center

1998-99 Season

	GP	G	A	Pts	+/–	PIM	PP	SH	S	SPct	P/G
Overall	69	21	16	37	1	34	7	0	144	14.6	.54
Home	39	16	11	27	11	28	6	0	93	17.2	.69
Away	30	5	5	10	-10	6	1	0	51	9.8	.33
vs. Division	16	4	3	7	-2	18	0	0	36	11.1	.44
vs. Conference	45	13	9	22	-7	30	3	0	92	14.1	.49
vs. Playoff	39	12	7	19	-2	26	4	0	81	14.8	.49
vs. Non-Playoff	30	9	9	18	3	8	3	0	63	14.3	.60
Pre All-Star	43	17	10	27	4	24	6	0	99	17.2	.63
Post All-Star	26	4	6	10	-3	10	1	0	45	8.9	.38
Day	3	1	0	1	-1	2	1	0	5	20.0	.33
Night	66	20	16	36	2	32	6	0	139	14.4	.55

	GP	G	A	Pts	+/–	PIM	PP	SH	S	SPct	P/G
National TV	10	2	3	5	3	6	0	0	20	10.0	.50
0 Days Rest	11	5	2	7	6	2	2	0	21	23.8	.64
1 Days Rest	31	9	9	18	1	12	2	0	71	12.7	.58
2 Days Rest	13	2	5	7	-2	16	0	0	20	10.0	.54
3+ Days Rest	14	5	0	5	-4	4	3	0	32	15.6	.36

	G	A	Pts	PIM		G	A	Pts	PIM
1st Period	11	7	18	4	Winning	4	8	12	10
2nd Period	5	6	11	26	Losing	5	3	8	12
3rd Period	5	3	8	4	Tied	12	5	17	12
Overtime	0	0	0	0	Clutch	3	0	3	2
Last 5 Min	7	2	9	10	Blowouts	1	0	1	0

Calle Johansson

Washington Capitals — Defense

1998-99 Season

	GP	G	A	Pts	+/–	PIM	PP	SH	S	SPct	P/G
Overall	67	8	21	29	10	22	2	0	145	5.5	.43
Home	34	6	8	14	4	8	1	0	75	8.0	.41
Away	33	2	13	15	6	14	1	0	70	2.9	.45
vs. Division	11	3	7	10	9	2	1	0	21	14.3	.91
vs. Conference	48	8	15	23	15	12	2	0	100	8.0	.48
vs. Playoff	40	2	9	11	1	18	0	0	83	2.4	.28
vs. Non-Playoff	27	6	12	18	9	4	2	0	62	9.7	.67
Pre All-Star	43	7	11	18	1	20	2	0	99	7.1	.42
Post All-Star	24	1	10	11	9	2	0	0	46	2.2	.46
Day	3	1	0	1	1	2	0	0	9	11.1	.33
Night	64	7	21	28	9	20	2	0	136	5.1	.44

	GP	G	A	Pts	+/–	PIM	PP	SH	S	SPct	P/G
National TV	9	1	1	2	5	4	0	0	22	4.5	.22
0 Days Rest	11	2	1	3	3	8	0	0	32	6.3	.27
1 Days Rest	33	3	12	15	2	8	1	0	59	5.1	.45
2 Days Rest	13	2	5	7	-1	0	0	0	25	8.0	.54
3+ Days Rest	10	1	3	4	6	6	1	0	29	3.4	.40

	G	A	Pts	PIM		G	A	Pts	PIM
1st Period	1	4	5	0	Winning	3	7	10	10
2nd Period	2	10	12	14	Losing	1	8	9	12
3rd Period	5	7	12	8	Tied	4	6	10	0
Overtime	0	0	0	0	Clutch	0	2	2	2
Last 5 Min	1	3	4	8	Blowouts	0	5	5	2

Craig Johnson

Los Angeles Kings — Left Wing

1998-99 Season

	GP	G	A	Pts	+/–	PIM	PP	SH	S	SPct	P/G
Overall	69	7	12	19	-12	32	2	0	94	7.4	.28
Home	34	4	5	9	-4	12	2	0	53	7.5	.26
Away	35	3	7	10	-8	20	0	0	41	7.3	.29
vs. Division	22	2	1	3	-13	2	0	0	28	7.1	.14
vs. Conference	49	6	6	12	-17	20	2	0	73	8.2	.24
vs. Playoff	45	4	6	10	-11	10	0	0	60	6.7	.22
vs. Non-Playoff	24	3	6	9	-1	22	2	0	34	8.8	.38
Pre All-Star	38	4	3	7	-10	16	1	0	56	7.1	.18
Post All-Star	31	3	9	12	-2	16	1	0	38	7.9	.39
Day	5	1	0	1	-4	0	0	0	8	12.5	.20
Night	64	6	12	18	-8	32	2	0	86	7.0	.28

	GP	G	A	Pts	+/–	PIM	PP	SH	S	SPct	P/G
National TV	13	2	2	4	-1	10	1	0	25	8.0	.31
0 Days Rest	11	2	3	5	0	6	1	0	16	12.5	.45
1 Days Rest	27	1	5	6	-8	8	0	0	32	3.1	.22
2 Days Rest	13	4	2	6	1	4	1	0	23	17.4	.46
3+ Days Rest	18	0	2	2	-5	14	0	0	23	0.0	.11

	G	A	Pts	PIM		G	A	Pts	PIM
1st Period	2	3	5	16	Winning	2	3	5	16
2nd Period	3	7	10	10	Losing	2	5	7	12
3rd Period	1	1	2	6	Tied	3	4	7	4
Overtime	1	1	2	0	Clutch	1	1	2	4
Last 5 Min	2	4	6	14	Blowouts	0	0	0	0

Greg Johnson

Nashville Predators — Center

1998-99 Season

	GP	G	A	Pts	+/–	PIM	PP	SH	S	SPct	P/G
Overall	68	16	34	50	-8	24	2	3	120	13.3	.74
Home	36	10	19	29	-1	6	0	3	76	13.2	.81
Away	32	6	15	21	-7	18	2	0	44	13.6	.66
vs. Division	15	4	9	13	-5	2	0	1	36	11.1	.87
vs. Conference	43	9	25	34	-7	8	2	2	85	10.6	.79
vs. Playoff	42	11	18	29	-11	14	1	3	70	15.7	.69
vs. Non-Playoff	26	5	16	21	3	10	1	0	50	10.0	.81
Pre All-Star	41	9	22	31	1	4	0	2	80	11.3	.76
Post All-Star	27	7	12	19	-9	20	2	1	40	17.5	.70
Day	8	4	2	6	-3	6	0	2	18	22.2	.75
Night	60	12	32	44	-5	18	2	1	102	11.8	.73

	GP	G	A	Pts	+/–	PIM	PP	SH	S	SPct	P/G
National TV	1	0	1	1	0	0	0	0	3	0.0	1.00
0 Days Rest	10	3	8	11	4	2	1	1	18	16.7	1.10
1 Days Rest	33	9	8	17	-8	18	0	2	56	16.1	.52
2 Days Rest	12	1	10	11	2	2	0	0	21	4.8	.92
3+ Days Rest	13	3	8	11	-6	2	1	0	25	12.0	.85

	G	A	Pts	PIM		G	A	Pts	PIM
1st Period	3	10	13	8	Winning	4	10	14	14
2nd Period	7	12	19	10	Losing	6	13	19	6
3rd Period	6	12	18	6	Tied	6	11	17	4
Overtime	0	0	0	0	Clutch	1	5	6	0
Last 5 Min	2	10	12	8	Blowouts	2	0	2	0

Mike Johnson

Toronto Maple Leafs — Right Wing

1998-99 Season

	GP	G	A	Pts	+/–	PIM	PP	SH	S	SPct	P/G
Overall	79	20	24	44	13	35	5	3	149	13.4	.56
Home	40	11	10	21	11	21	2	2	84	13.1	.53
Away	39	9	14	23	2	14	3	1	65	13.8	.59
vs. Division	19	5	6	11	-1	17	1	2	39	12.8	.58
vs. Conference	53	15	15	30	3	29	3	3	99	15.2	.57
vs. Playoff	44	7	12	19	7	23	2	3	73	9.6	.43
vs. Non-Playoff	35	13	12	25	6	12	3	0	76	17.1	.71
Pre All-Star	46	16	12	28	10	18	4	3	104	15.4	.61
Post All-Star	33	4	12	16	3	17	1	0	45	8.9	.48
Day	1	0	0	0	0	0	0	0	0	–	.00
Night	78	20	24	44	13	35	5	3	149	13.4	.56

	GP	G	A	Pts	+/–	PIM	PP	SH	S	SPct	P/G
National TV	27	8	8	16	9	12	2	1	54	14.8	.59
0 Days Rest	17	5	8	13	6	6	2	0	39	12.8	.76
1 Days Rest	32	9	9	18	8	19	2	2	67	13.4	.56
2 Days Rest	14	5	5	10	7	8	1	0	23	21.7	.71
3+ Days Rest	16	1	2	3	-8	2	0	1	20	5.0	.19

	G	A	Pts	PIM		G	A	Pts	PIM
1st Period	4	10	14	18	Winning	10	9	19	17
2nd Period	8	6	14	7	Losing	7	5	12	14
3rd Period	8	8	16	10	Tied	3	10	13	4
Overtime	0	0	0	0	Clutch	0	3	3	2
Last 5 Min	3	7	10	7	Blowouts	5	0	5	0

Olli Jokinen

Los Angeles Kings — Center

1998-99 Season

	GP	G	A	Pts	+/–	PIM	PP	SH	S	SPct	P/G
Overall	66	9	12	21	-10	44	3	1	87	10.3	.32
Home	34	3	6	9	-3	34	0	1	43	7.0	.26
Away	32	6	6	12	-7	10	3	0	44	13.6	.38
vs. Division	23	4	2	6	-5	17	2	1	37	10.8	.26
vs. Conference	52	8	11	19	-7	36	3	1	70	11.4	.37
vs. Playoff	48	5	3	8	-13	30	2	1	65	7.7	.17
vs. Non-Playoff	18	4	9	13	3	14	1	0	22	18.2	.72
Pre All-Star	31	5	4	9	-1	16	2	0	47	10.6	.29
Post All-Star	35	4	8	12	-9	28	1	1	40	10.0	.34
Day	4	0	0	0	-2	0	0	0	3	0.0	.00
Night	62	9	12	21	-8	44	3	1	84	10.7	.34

	GP	G	A	Pts	+/–	PIM	PP	SH	S	SPct	P/G
National TV	14	0	0	0	-4	14	0	0	13	0.0	.00
0 Days Rest	10	1	7	8	1	6	0	0	8	12.5	.80
1 Days Rest	31	6	3	9	-1	14	2	1	39	15.4	.29
2 Days Rest	14	1	1	2	-4	9	0	0	18	5.6	.14
3+ Days Rest	11	1	1	2	-6	15	1	0	22	4.5	.18

	G	A	Pts	PIM		G	A	Pts	PIM
1st Period	1	4	5	21	Winning	4	4	8	17
2nd Period	3	4	7	13	Losing	1	5	6	23
3rd Period	4	4	8	10	Tied	4	3	7	4
Overtime	1	0	1	0	Clutch	1	0	1	0
Last 5 Min	4	1	5	15	Blowouts	0	0	0	8

Keith Jones

Philadelphia Flyers — Right Wing

1998-99 Season

	GP	G	A	Pts	+/–	PIM	PP	SH	S	SPct	P/G
Overall	78	20	33	53	23	98	3	0	135	14.8	.68
Home	38	11	18	29	19	44	2	0	74	14.9	.76
Away	40	9	15	24	4	54	1	0	61	14.8	.60
vs. Division	17	6	6	12	4	26	0	0	22	27.3	.71
vs. Conference	52	11	18	29	6	70	1	0	77	14.3	.56
vs. Playoff	46	11	19	30	11	70	2	0	81	13.6	.65
vs. Non-Playoff	32	9	14	23	12	28	1	0	54	16.7	.72
Pre All-Star	40	10	17	27	19	52	1	0	70	14.3	.68
Post All-Star	38	10	16	26	4	46	2	0	65	15.4	.68
Day	14	6	8	14	7	14	1	0	26	23.1	1.00
Night	64	14	25	39	16	84	2	0	109	12.8	.61

	GP	G	A	Pts	+/–	PIM	PP	SH	S	SPct	P/G
National TV	19	7	7	14	7	28	1	0	37	18.9	.74
0 Days Rest	10	2	0	2	-3	20	1	0	20	10.0	.20
1 Days Rest	41	8	16	24	9	32	2	0	60	13.3	.59
2 Days Rest	15	4	9	13	10	22	0	0	28	14.3	.87
3+ Days Rest	12	6	8	14	7	24	0	0	27	22.2	1.17

	G	A	Pts	PIM		G	A	Pts	PIM
1st Period	7	9	16	28	Winning	9	15	24	32
2nd Period	6	11	17	34	Losing	4	8	12	40
3rd Period	6	13	19	36	Tied	7	10	17	26
Overtime	1	0	1	0	Clutch	4	2	6	8
Last 5 Min	8	6	14	26	Blowouts	2	1	3	8

Kenny Jonsson

New York Islanders — Defense

1998-99 Season

	GP	G	A	Pts	+/–	PIM	PP	SH	S	SPct	P/G
Overall	63	8	18	26	-18	34	6	0	91	8.8	.41
Home	32	6	12	18	-7	14	5	0	51	11.8	.56
Away	31	2	6	8	-11	20	1	0	40	5.0	.26
vs. Division	16	3	6	9	-12	24	2	0	20	15.0	.56
vs. Conference	46	5	15	20	-17	30	4	0	68	7.4	.43
vs. Playoff	38	5	11	16	-10	16	4	0	56	8.9	.42
vs. Non-Playoff	25	3	7	10	-8	18	2	0	35	8.6	.40
Pre All-Star	35	7	9	16	-5	18	6	0	38	18.4	.46
Post All-Star	28	1	9	10	-13	16	0	0	53	1.9	.36
Day	7	2	3	5	-4	8	1	0	10	20.0	.71
Night	56	6	15	21	-14	26	5	0	81	7.4	.38

	GP	G	A	Pts	+/–	PIM	PP	SH	S	SPct	P/G
National TV	4	1	1	2	-3	6	0	0	7	14.3	.50
0 Days Rest	8	0	3	3	-6	4	0	0	12	0.0	.38
1 Days Rest	32	4	10	14	-5	24	3	0	42	9.5	.44
2 Days Rest	14	1	1	2	-4	4	1	0	21	4.8	.14
3+ Days Rest	9	3	4	7	-3	2	2	0	16	18.8	.78

	G	A	Pts	PIM		G	A	Pts	PIM
1st Period	4	5	9	8	Winning	1	3	4	6
2nd Period	2	7	9	16	Losing	5	11	16	22
3rd Period	2	6	8	10	Tied	2	4	6	6
Overtime	0	0	0	0	Clutch	1	1	2	2
Last 5 Min	4	6	10	10	Blowouts	1	0	1	2

Ed Jovanovski

Vancouver Canucks — Defense

1998-99 Season

	GP	G	A	Pts	+/–	PIM	PP	SH	S	SPct	P/G
Overall	72	5	22	27	-9	126	1	0	109	4.6	.38
Home	36	3	10	13	-7	59	1	0	61	4.9	.36
Away	36	2	12	14	-2	67	0	0	48	4.2	.39
vs. Division	14	1	4	5	0	29	1	0	25	4.0	.36
vs. Conference	50	3	13	16	-7	75	1	0	72	4.2	.32
vs. Playoff	41	2	13	15	-14	60	1	0	56	3.6	.37
vs. Non-Playoff	31	3	9	12	5	66	0	0	53	5.7	.39
Pre All-Star	43	3	13	16	-2	82	1	0	69	4.3	.37
Post All-Star	29	2	9	11	-7	44	0	0	40	5.0	.38
Day	5	2	2	4	-2	6	1	0	10	20.0	.80
Night	67	3	20	23	-7	120	0	0	99	3.0	.34

	GP	G	A	Pts	+/–	PIM	PP	SH	S	SPct	P/G
National TV	8	2	1	3	0	24	0	0	10	20.0	.38
0 Days Rest	16	2	3	5	1	18	0	0	20	10.0	.31
1 Days Rest	30	1	12	13	-6	65	1	0	45	2.2	.43
2 Days Rest	12	1	2	3	1	16	0	0	16	6.3	.25
3+ Days Rest	14	1	5	6	-5	27	0	0	28	3.6	.43

	G	A	Pts	PIM		G	A	Pts	PIM
1st Period	2	5	7	24	Winning	0	6	6	60
2nd Period	1	7	8	40	Losing	3	7	10	38
3rd Period	2	10	12	60	Tied	2	9	11	28
Overtime	0	0	0	2	Clutch	0	2	2	8
Last 5 Min	2	3	5	44	Blowouts	1	1	2	35

Joe Juneau

Buffalo Sabres — Left Wing

1998-99 Season

	GP	G	A	Pts	+/–	PIM	PP	SH	S	SPct	P/G
Overall	72	15	28	43	-4	22	2	1	150	10.0	.60
Home	34	5	17	22	0	10	1	0	74	6.8	.65
Away	38	10	11	21	-4	12	1	1	76	13.2	.55
vs. Division	11	5	5	10	3	2	1	0	26	19.2	.91
vs. Conference	54	12	23	35	-2	16	2	0	112	10.7	.65
vs. Playoff	45	9	11	20	-6	16	1	1	94	9.6	.44
vs. Non-Playoff	27	6	17	23	2	6	1	0	56	10.7	.85
Pre All-Star	42	8	18	26	-4	16	2	1	108	7.4	.62
Post All-Star	30	7	10	17	0	6	0	0	42	16.7	.57
Day	3	0	3	3	0	0	0	0	2	0.0	1.00
Night	69	15	25	40	-4	22	2	1	148	10.1	.58

	GP	G	A	Pts	+/–	PIM	PP	SH	S	SPct	P/G
National TV	12	5	4	9	1	2	1	0	26	19.2	.75
0 Days Rest	15	4	4	8	-2	8	1	0	30	13.3	.53
1 Days Rest	28	8	10	18	5	10	0	0	51	15.7	.64
2 Days Rest	15	2	8	10	-3	0	1	0	35	5.7	.67
3+ Days Rest	14	1	6	7	-4	4	0	1	34	2.9	.50

	G	A	Pts	PIM		G	A	Pts	PIM
1st Period	4	5	9	12	Winning	3	9	12	12
2nd Period	8	15	23	6	Losing	6	10	16	8
3rd Period	3	8	11	4	Tied	6	9	15	2
Overtime	0	0	0	0	Clutch	0	2	2	0
Last 5 Min	3	7	10	2	Blowouts	2	2	4	0

Tomas Kaberle

Toronto Maple Leafs — Defense

1998-99 Season

	GP	G	A	Pts	+/–	PIM	PP	SH	S	SPct	P/G
Overall	57	4	18	22	3	12	0	0	71	5.6	.39
Home	29	0	9	9	3	6	0	0	37	0.0	.31
Away	28	4	9	13	0	6	0	0	34	11.8	.46
vs. Division	14	1	3	4	-1	4	0	0	22	4.5	.29
vs. Conference	35	3	8	11	-7	10	0	0	50	6.0	.31
vs. Playoff	32	2	7	9	-6	4	0	0	43	4.7	.28
vs. Non-Playoff	25	2	11	13	9	8	0	0	28	7.1	.52
Pre All-Star	42	3	14	17	-3	6	0	0	47	6.4	.40
Post All-Star	15	1	4	5	6	6	0	0	24	4.2	.33
Day	1	0	0	0	-1	0	0	0	1	0.0	.00
Night	56	4	18	22	4	12	0	0	70	5.7	.39

	GP	G	A	Pts	+/–	PIM	PP	SH	S	SPct	P/G
National TV	18	2	6	8	9	2	0	0	24	8.3	.44
0 Days Rest	14	2	3	5	3	2	0	0	16	12.5	.36
1 Days Rest	19	0	10	10	6	0	0	0	22	0.0	.53
2 Days Rest	7	1	1	2	-1	2	0	0	8	12.5	.29
3+ Days Rest	17	1	4	5	-5	8	0	0	25	4.0	.29

	G	A	Pts	PIM		G	A	Pts	PIM
1st Period	0	2	2	4	Winning	3	11	14	8
2nd Period	2	8	10	2	Losing	0	5	5	2
3rd Period	1	8	9	6	Tied	1	2	3	2
Overtime	1	0	1	0	Clutch	1	0	1	0
Last 5 Min	1	4	5	12	Blowouts	0	2	2	2

Valeri Kamensky

Colorado Avalanche — Left Wing

1998-99 Season

	GP	G	A	Pts	+/–	PIM	PP	SH	S	SPct	P/G
Overall	65	14	30	44	1	28	2	0	123	11.4	.68
Home	30	5	13	18	1	14	1	0	58	8.6	.60
Away	35	9	17	26	0	14	1	0	65	13.8	.74
vs. Division	13	5	7	12	-6	4	1	0	27	18.5	.92
vs. Conference	42	10	14	24	-2	22	1	0	77	13.0	.57
vs. Playoff	38	9	14	23	5	20	1	0	78	11.5	.61
vs. Non-Playoff	27	5	16	21	-4	8	1	0	45	11.1	.78
Pre All-Star	43	9	22	31	-3	18	2	0	83	10.8	.72
Post All-Star	22	5	8	13	4	10	0	0	40	12.5	.59
Day	10	2	4	6	6	8	0	0	21	9.5	.60
Night	55	12	26	38	-5	20	2	0	102	11.8	.69

	GP	G	A	Pts	+/–	PIM	PP	SH	S	SPct	P/G
National TV	17	2	7	9	5	4	0	0	28	7.1	.53
0 Days Rest	10	2	7	9	4	4	0	0	16	12.5	.90
1 Days Rest	34	9	20	29	2	14	2	0	71	12.7	.85
2 Days Rest	11	1	1	2	-2	4	0	0	16	6.3	.18
3+ Days Rest	10	2	2	4	-3	6	0	0	20	10.0	.40

	G	A	Pts	PIM		G	A	Pts	PIM
1st Period	2	10	12	8	Winning	5	8	13	12
2nd Period	4	7	11	12	Losing	5	8	13	8
3rd Period	8	12	20	6	Tied	4	14	18	8
Overtime	0	1	1	2	Clutch	1	9	10	2
Last 5 Min	4	6	10	8	Blowouts	0	0	0	2

Sami Kapanen

Carolina Hurricanes — Left Wing

1998-99 Season

	GP	G	A	Pts	+/–	PIM	PP	SH	S	SPct	P/G
Overall	81	24	35	59	-1	10	5	0	254	9.4	.73
Home	40	12	21	33	6	8	2	0	127	9.4	.83
Away	41	12	14	26	-7	2	3	0	127	9.4	.63
vs. Division	15	5	5	10	-6	2	1	0	56	8.9	.67
vs. Conference	59	18	23	41	-6	8	4	0	172	10.5	.69
vs. Playoff	44	11	19	30	1	8	3	0	119	9.2	.68
vs. Non-Playoff	37	13	16	29	-2	2	2	0	135	9.6	.78
Pre All-Star	44	13	19	32	0	2	3	0	106	12.3	.73
Post All-Star	37	11	16	27	-1	8	2	0	148	7.4	.73
Day	7	4	4	8	-2	0	1	0	27	14.8	1.14
Night	74	20	31	51	1	10	4	0	227	8.8	.69

	GP	G	A	Pts	+/–	PIM	PP	SH	S	SPct	P/G
National TV	2	0	1	1	0	0	0	0	7	0.0	.50
0 Days Rest	16	3	6	9	-2	0	1	0	50	6.0	.56
1 Days Rest	32	8	10	18	-2	2	1	0	96	8.3	.56
2 Days Rest	22	9	14	23	1	6	3	0	69	13.0	1.05
3+ Days Rest	11	4	5	9	2	2	0	0	39	10.3	.82

	G	A	Pts	PIM		G	A	Pts	PIM
1st Period	8	11	19	0	Winning	9	15	24	2
2nd Period	10	11	21	8	Losing	4	8	12	6
3rd Period	6	13	19	2	Tied	11	12	23	2
Overtime	0	0	0	0	Clutch	2	4	6	2
Last 5 Min	7	9	16	4	Blowouts	0	1	1	2

Paul Kariya

Anaheim Mighty Ducks — Left Wing

1998-99 Season

	GP	G	A	Pts	+/–	PIM	PP	SH	S	SPct	P/G
Overall	82	39	62	101	17	40	11	2	429	9.1	1.23
Home	41	20	35	55	12	18	4	0	227	8.8	1.34
Away	41	19	27	46	5	22	7	2	202	9.4	1.12
vs. Division	24	13	16	29	10	8	3	0	110	11.8	1.21
vs. Conference	57	28	43	71	8	30	7	2	285	9.8	1.25
vs. Playoff	50	22	33	55	10	16	6	0	260	8.5	1.10
vs. Non-Playoff	32	17	29	46	7	24	5	2	169	10.1	1.44
Pre All-Star	45	20	41	61	8	26	5	1	252	7.9	1.36
Post All-Star	37	19	21	40	9	14	6	1	177	10.7	1.08
Day	1	0	3	3	4	0	0	0	9	0.0	3.00
Night	81	39	59	98	13	40	11	2	420	9.3	1.21

	GP	G	A	Pts	+/–	PIM	PP	SH	S	SPct	P/G
National TV	13	5	7	12	6	6	0	1	59	8.5	.92
0 Days Rest	15	7	9	16	7	2	2	1	73	9.6	1.07
1 Days Rest	42	19	33	52	6	32	3	1	229	8.3	1.24
2 Days Rest	13	9	11	20	-3	2	5	0	71	12.7	1.54
3+ Days Rest	12	4	9	13	7	4	1	0	56	7.1	1.08

	G	A	Pts	PIM		G	A	Pts	PIM
1st Period	12	16	28	10	Winning	20	26	46	14
2nd Period	11	27	38	20	Losing	11	20	31	16
3rd Period	16	18	34	8	Tied	8	16	24	10
Overtime	0	1	1	2	Clutch	8	7	15	2
Last 5 Min	15	15	30	14	Blowouts	1	3	4	4

Alexander Karpovtsev

Toronto Maple Leafs — Defense

1998-99 Season

	GP	G	A	Pts	+/–	PIM	PP	SH	S	SPct	P/G
Overall	58	3	25	28	39	52	1	0	65	4.6	.48
Home	30	1	12	13	17	26	0	0	32	3.1	.43
Away	28	2	13	15	22	26	1	0	33	6.1	.54
vs. Division	14	0	2	2	-1	16	0	0	15	0.0	.14
vs. Conference	40	0	15	15	20	36	0	0	50	0.0	.38
vs. Playoff	34	2	13	15	16	30	1	0	39	5.1	.44
vs. Non-Playoff	24	1	12	13	23	22	0	0	26	3.8	.54
Pre All-Star	28	2	12	14	24	22	1	0	31	6.5	.50
Post All-Star	30	1	13	14	15	30	0	0	34	2.9	.47
Day	0	0	0	0	0	0	0	0	0	–	–
Night	58	3	25	28	39	52	1	0	65	4.6	.48

	GP	G	A	Pts	+/–	PIM	PP	SH	S	SPct	P/G
National TV	18	1	10	11	12	16	0	0	14	7.1	.61
0 Days Rest	12	1	5	6	11	16	1	0	12	8.3	.50
1 Days Rest	24	1	13	14	17	20	0	0	26	3.8	.58
2 Days Rest	7	1	3	4	4	0	0	0	7	14.3	.57
3+ Days Rest	15	0	4	4	7	16	0	0	20	0.0	.27

	G	A	Pts	PIM
1st Period	0	9	9	24
2nd Period	2	11	13	16
3rd Period	1	5	6	12
Overtime	0	0	0	0
Last 5 Min	1	6	7	18

	G	A	Pts	PIM
Winning	0	12	12	28
Losing	2	5	7	12
Tied	1	8	9	12
Clutch	0	2	2	2
Blowouts	0	0	0	10

Mike Keane

Dallas Stars — Right Wing

1998-99 Season

	GP	G	A	Pts	+/–	PIM	PP	SH	S	SPct	P/G
Overall	81	6	23	29	-2	62	1	1	106	5.7	.36
Home	41	4	11	15	2	23	0	0	54	7.4	.37
Away	40	2	12	14	-4	39	1	1	52	3.8	.35
vs. Division	23	3	4	7	0	23	1	0	33	9.1	.30
vs. Conference	55	3	15	18	-7	50	1	0	72	4.2	.33
vs. Playoff	48	4	12	16	-4	41	1	1	57	7.0	.33
vs. Non-Playoff	33	2	11	13	2	21	0	0	49	4.1	.39
Pre All-Star	43	3	12	15	-2	46	1	1	49	6.1	.35
Post All-Star	38	3	11	14	0	16	0	0	57	5.3	.37
Day	10	2	2	4	-4	6	0	1	14	14.3	.40
Night	71	4	21	25	2	56	1	0	92	4.3	.35

	GP	G	A	Pts	+/–	PIM	PP	SH	S	SPct	P/G
National TV	14	1	4	5	0	4	0	0	20	5.0	.36
0 Days Rest	14	0	2	2	-4	10	0	0	17	0.0	.14
1 Days Rest	43	4	13	17	3	31	1	1	62	6.5	.40
2 Days Rest	14	2	6	8	-3	14	0	0	18	11.1	.57
3+ Days Rest	10	0	2	2	2	7	0	0	9	0.0	.20

	G	A	Pts	PIM
1st Period	2	12	14	24
2nd Period	4	6	10	17
3rd Period	0	5	5	19
Overtime	0	0	0	2
Last 5 Min	1	5	6	19

	G	A	Pts	PIM
Winning	2	11	13	34
Losing	1	4	5	13
Tied	3	8	11	15
Clutch	0	2	2	9
Blowouts	0	0	0	4

Dan Kesa

Pittsburgh Penguins — Right Wing

1998-99 Season

	GP	G	A	Pts	+/–	PIM	PP	SH	S	SPct	P/G
Overall	67	2	8	10	-9	27	0	0	33	6.1	.15
Home	34	0	4	4	-7	8	0	0	18	0.0	.12
Away	33	2	4	6	-2	19	0	0	15	13.3	.18
vs. Division	15	0	0	0	-3	0	0	0	4	0.0	.00
vs. Conference	44	1	6	7	-5	8	0	0	17	5.9	.16
vs. Playoff	39	2	4	6	-8	6	0	0	21	9.5	.15
vs. Non-Playoff	28	0	4	4	-1	21	0	0	12	0.0	.14
Pre All-Star	31	1	2	3	-1	21	0	0	15	6.7	.10
Post All-Star	36	1	6	7	-8	6	0	0	18	5.6	.19
Day	13	1	2	3	-3	2	0	0	10	10.0	.23
Night	54	1	6	7	-6	25	0	0	23	4.3	.13

	GP	G	A	Pts	+/–	PIM	PP	SH	S	SPct	P/G
National TV	16	1	1	2	-2	12	0	0	8	12.5	.13
0 Days Rest	12	0	1	1	2	0	0	0	2	0.0	.08
1 Days Rest	32	0	6	6	-5	27	0	0	17	0.0	.19
2 Days Rest	16	2	1	3	-2	0	0	0	12	16.7	.19
3+ Days Rest	7	0	0	0	-4	0	0	0	2	0.0	.00

	G	A	Pts	PIM
1st Period	0	2	2	21
2nd Period	0	3	3	2
3rd Period	2	3	5	4
Overtime	0	0	0	0
Last 5 Min	1	4	5	0

	G	A	Pts	PIM
Winning	1	3	4	22
Losing	1	2	3	0
Tied	0	3	3	5
Clutch	0	0	0	0
Blowouts	0	0	0	0

Dimitri Khristich

Boston Bruins — Left Wing

1998-99 Season

	GP	G	A	Pts	+/–	PIM	PP	SH	S	SPct	P/G
Overall	79	29	42	71	11	48	13	1	144	20.1	.90
Home	39	12	24	36	8	22	6	1	61	19.7	.92
Away	40	17	18	35	3	26	7	0	83	20.5	.88
vs. Division	19	8	11	19	1	10	5	0	32	25.0	1.00
vs. Conference	57	23	31	54	7	36	12	1	106	21.7	.95
vs. Playoff	44	12	24	36	7	18	7	0	74	16.2	.82
vs. Non-Playoff	35	17	18	35	4	30	6	1	70	24.3	1.00
Pre All-Star	42	20	26	46	6	28	8	1	85	23.5	1.10
Post All-Star	37	9	16	25	5	20	5	0	59	15.3	.68
Day	16	8	9	17	2	4	3	0	28	28.6	1.06
Night	63	21	33	54	9	44	10	1	116	18.1	.86

	GP	G	A	Pts	+/–	PIM	PP	SH	S	SPct	P/G
National TV	9	5	3	8	-3	8	1	0	23	21.7	.89
0 Days Rest	16	4	5	9	-4	12	3	0	25	16.0	.56
1 Days Rest	37	8	23	31	4	22	6	0	66	12.1	.84
2 Days Rest	12	8	6	14	2	6	1	0	29	27.6	1.17
3+ Days Rest	14	9	8	17	9	8	3	1	24	37.5	1.21

	G	A	Pts	PIM
1st Period	6	13	19	16
2nd Period	12	11	23	14
3rd Period	11	18	29	18
Overtime	0	0	0	0
Last 5 Min	8	16	24	12

	G	A	Pts	PIM
Winning	14	16	30	24
Losing	8	8	16	16
Tied	7	18	25	8
Clutch	2	7	9	0
Blowouts	2	2	4	6

Chad Kilger

Edmonton Oilers — Center

1998-99 Season

	GP	G	A	Pts	+/-	PIM	PP	SH	S	SPct	P/G
Overall	77	15	12	27	-4	34	2	1	81	18.5	.35
Home	39	9	3	12	0	22	1	1	48	18.8	.31
Away	38	6	9	15	-4	12	1	0	33	18.2	.39
vs. Division	20	3	5	8	-2	8	1	0	26	11.5	.40
vs. Conference	55	13	10	23	0	18	2	1	61	21.3	.42
vs. Playoff	46	5	6	11	-10	18	0	1	47	10.6	.24
vs. Non-Playoff	31	10	6	16	6	16	2	0	34	29.4	.52
Pre All-Star	45	7	8	15	-3	24	1	1	47	14.9	.33
Post All-Star	32	8	4	12	-1	10	1	0	34	23.5	.38
Day	6	2	0	2	-1	0	0	0	5	40.0	.33
Night	71	13	12	25	-3	34	2	1	76	17.1	.35

	GP	G	A	Pts	+/-	PIM	PP	SH	S	SPct	P/G
National TV	15	1	1	2	-6	6	0	0	14	7.1	.13
0 Days Rest	12	3	4	7	2	4	1	0	13	23.1	.58
1 Days Rest	42	6	7	13	-9	18	1	0	41	14.6	.31
2 Days Rest	8	3	1	4	2	6	0	0	10	30.0	.50
3+ Days Rest	15	3	0	3	1	6	0	1	17	17.6	.20

	G	A	Pts	PIM		G	A	Pts	PIM
1st Period	6	5	11	18	Winning	6	1	7	12
2nd Period	4	3	7	8	Losing	4	7	11	20
3rd Period	5	4	9	8	Tied	5	4	9	2
Overtime	0	0	0	0	Clutch	2	1	3	4
Last 5 Min	5	2	7	6	Blowouts	0	1	1	8

Derek King

Toronto Maple Leafs — Left Wing

1998-99 Season

	GP	G	A	Pts	+/-	PIM	PP	SH	S	SPct	P/G
Overall	81	24	28	52	15	20	8	0	150	16.0	.64
Home	40	11	11	22	13	16	5	0	84	13.1	.55
Away	41	13	17	30	2	4	3	0	66	19.7	.73
vs. Division	20	5	4	9	-5	6	3	0	38	13.2	.45
vs. Conference	56	16	17	33	6	10	5	0	108	14.8	.59
vs. Playoff	46	13	14	27	6	10	6	0	77	16.9	.59
vs. Non-Playoff	35	11	14	25	9	10	2	0	73	15.1	.71
Pre All-Star	45	16	14	30	6	10	5	0	93	17.2	.67
Post All-Star	36	8	14	22	9	10	3	0	57	14.0	.61
Day	1	0	0	0	0	0	0	0	3	0.0	.00
Night	80	24	28	52	15	20	8	0	147	16.3	.65

	GP	G	A	Pts	+/-	PIM	PP	SH	S	SPct	P/G
National TV	28	11	9	20	10	8	2	0	60	18.3	.71
0 Days Rest	18	7	9	16	6	2	2	0	30	23.3	.89
1 Days Rest	34	11	8	19	10	10	5	0	65	16.9	.56
2 Days Rest	14	5	8	13	6	4	0	0	26	19.2	.93
3+ Days Rest	15	1	3	4	-7	4	1	0	29	3.4	.27

	G	A	Pts	PIM		G	A	Pts	PIM
1st Period	11	8	19	8	Winning	10	13	23	12
2nd Period	4	10	14	4	Losing	7	6	13	8
3rd Period	8	10	18	8	Tied	7	9	16	0
Overtime	1	0	1	0	Clutch	3	1	4	0
Last 5 Min	5	4	9	6	Blowouts	2	4	6	4

Patrik Kjellberg

Nashville Predators — Right Wing

1998-99 Season

	GP	G	A	Pts	+/-	PIM	PP	SH	S	SPct	P/G
Overall	71	11	20	31	-13	24	2	0	103	10.7	.44
Home	35	5	15	20	-6	16	1	0	62	8.1	.57
Away	36	6	5	11	-7	8	1	0	41	14.6	.31
vs. Division	16	3	3	6	-7	10	0	0	18	16.7	.38
vs. Conference	48	10	11	21	-10	20	2	0	77	13.0	.44
vs. Playoff	45	8	12	20	-10	12	1	0	69	11.6	.44
vs. Non-Playoff	26	3	8	11	-3	12	1	0	34	8.8	.42
Pre All-Star	43	9	16	25	-5	18	2	0	65	13.8	.58
Post All-Star	28	2	4	6	-8	6	0	0	38	5.3	.21
Day	8	1	3	4	-4	0	0	0	13	7.7	.50
Night	63	10	17	27	-9	24	2	0	90	11.1	.43

	GP	G	A	Pts	+/-	PIM	PP	SH	S	SPct	P/G
National TV	2	0	2	2	-1	0	0	0	4	0.0	1.00
0 Days Rest	12	2	3	5	-4	0	0	0	17	11.8	.42
1 Days Rest	32	6	10	16	1	6	2	0	52	11.5	.50
2 Days Rest	15	3	2	5	-8	16	0	0	19	15.8	.33
3+ Days Rest	12	0	5	5	-2	2	0	0	15	0.0	.42

	G	A	Pts	PIM		G	A	Pts	PIM
1st Period	6	4	10	4	Winning	3	4	7	10
2nd Period	4	10	14	12	Losing	4	11	15	10
3rd Period	1	6	7	8	Tied	4	5	9	4
Overtime	0	0	0	0	Clutch	0	1	1	0
Last 5 Min	7	2	9	6	Blowouts	0	1	1	2

Trent Klatt

Vancouver Canucks — Right Wing

1998-99 Season

	GP	G	A	Pts	+/-	PIM	PP	SH	S	SPct	P/G
Overall	75	4	10	14	-3	12	0	0	60	6.7	.19
Home	34	3	5	8	4	10	0	0	19	15.8	.24
Away	41	1	5	6	-7	2	0	0	41	2.4	.15
vs. Division	16	0	2	2	2	0	0	0	8	0.0	.13
vs. Conference	51	4	8	12	2	6	0	0	37	10.8	.24
vs. Playoff	47	4	7	11	-2	12	0	0	46	8.7	.23
vs. Non-Playoff	28	0	3	3	-1	0	0	0	14	0.0	.11
Pre All-Star	44	3	8	11	-1	4	0	0	43	7.0	.25
Post All-Star	31	1	2	3	-2	8	0	0	17	5.9	.10
Day	2	0	0	0	-4	0	0	0	1	0.0	.00
Night	73	4	10	14	1	12	0	0	59	6.8	.19

	GP	G	A	Pts	+/-	PIM	PP	SH	S	SPct	P/G
National TV	16	2	0	2	-3	4	0	0	10	20.0	.13
0 Days Rest	10	0	2	2	2	0	0	0	5	0.0	.20
1 Days Rest	41	3	6	9	-4	12	0	0	36	8.3	.22
2 Days Rest	12	0	2	2	2	0	0	0	13	0.0	.17
3+ Days Rest	12	1	0	1	-3	0	0	0	6	16.7	.08

	G	A	Pts	PIM		G	A	Pts	PIM
1st Period	1	1	2	6	Winning	0	2	2	4
2nd Period	1	4	5	4	Losing	2	6	8	8
3rd Period	2	5	7	2	Tied	2	2	4	0
Overtime	0	0	0	0	Clutch	0	1	1	0
Last 5 Min	1	1	2	0	Blowouts	0	0	0	2

Ken Klee

Washington Capitals — Right Wing

1998-99 Season

	GP	G	A	Pts	+/–	PIM	PP	SH	S	SPct	P/G
Overall	78	7	13	20	-9	80	0	0	132	5.3	.26
Home	40	3	7	10	-5	32	0	0	73	4.1	.25
Away	38	4	6	10	-4	48	0	0	59	6.8	.26
vs. Division	15	1	2	3	1	18	0	0	30	3.3	.20
vs. Conference	54	7	9	16	1	58	0	0	91	7.7	.30
vs. Playoff	45	3	10	13	-8	54	0	0	67	4.5	.29
vs. Non-Playoff	33	4	3	7	-1	26	0	0	65	6.2	.21
Pre All-Star	40	5	6	11	-1	42	0	0	49	10.2	.28
Post All-Star	38	2	7	9	-8	38	0	0	83	2.4	.24
Day	3	2	1	3	2	4	0	0	7	28.6	1.00
Night	75	5	12	17	-11	76	0	0	125	4.0	.23

	GP	G	A	Pts	+/–	PIM	PP	SH	S	SPct	P/G
National TV	11	0	4	4	1	4	0	0	17	0.0	.36
0 Days Rest	11	0	4	4	-2	6	0	0	16	0.0	.36
1 Days Rest	38	2	6	8	-8	34	0	0	68	2.9	.21
2 Days Rest	16	3	1	4	1	26	0	0	29	10.3	.25
3+ Days Rest	13	2	2	4	0	14	0	0	19	10.5	.31

	G	A	Pts	PIM		G	A	Pts	PIM
1st Period	3	2	5	40	Winning	3	7	10	26
2nd Period	3	5	8	30	Losing	3	2	5	52
3rd Period	1	5	6	10	Tied	1	4	5	2
Overtime	0	1	1	0	Clutch	0	2	2	0
Last 5 Min	3	2	5	14	Blowouts	0	1	1	10

Michael Knuble

New York Rangers — Right Wing

1998-99 Season

	GP	G	A	Pts	+/–	PIM	PP	SH	S	SPct	P/G
Overall	82	15	20	35	-7	26	3	0	113	13.3	.43
Home	41	8	6	14	-6	22	2	0	59	13.6	.34
Away	41	7	14	21	-1	4	1	0	54	13.0	.51
vs. Division	20	2	3	5	-9	6	0	0	26	7.7	.25
vs. Conference	58	11	13	24	-15	20	3	0	90	12.2	.41
vs. Playoff	52	7	10	17	-6	16	1	0	61	11.5	.33
vs. Non-Playoff	30	8	10	18	-1	10	2	0	52	15.4	.60
Pre All-Star	45	9	11	20	-1	14	1	0	63	14.3	.44
Post All-Star	37	6	9	15	-6	12	2	0	50	12.0	.41
Day	12	1	2	3	-5	2	0	0	17	5.9	.25
Night	70	14	18	32	-2	24	3	0	96	14.6	.46

	GP	G	A	Pts	+/–	PIM	PP	SH	S	SPct	P/G
National TV	23	1	4	5	-15	6	1	0	36	2.8	.22
0 Days Rest	16	3	5	8	-1	4	0	0	19	15.8	.50
1 Days Rest	34	8	9	17	-8	16	2	0	50	16.0	.50
2 Days Rest	20	3	4	7	0	4	1	0	34	8.8	.35
3+ Days Rest	12	1	2	3	2	2	0	0	10	10.0	.25

	G	A	Pts	PIM		G	A	Pts	PIM
1st Period	5	10	15	12	Winning	1	6	7	12
2nd Period	3	3	6	6	Losing	11	5	16	12
3rd Period	7	6	13	8	Tied	3	9	12	2
Overtime	0	1	1	0	Clutch	1	3	4	2
Last 5 Min	3	4	7	8	Blowouts	2	0	2	2

Saku Koivu

Montreal Canadiens — Center

1998-99 Season

	GP	G	A	Pts	+/–	PIM	PP	SH	S	SPct	P/G
Overall	65	14	30	44	-7	38	4	2	145	9.7	.68
Home	35	9	14	23	-6	24	4	1	85	10.6	.66
Away	30	5	16	21	-1	14	0	1	60	8.3	.70
vs. Division	17	4	5	9	-8	16	0	1	46	8.7	.53
vs. Conference	45	10	19	29	-9	30	3	2	103	9.7	.64
vs. Playoff	43	9	16	25	-8	28	1	2	101	8.9	.58
vs. Non-Playoff	22	5	14	19	1	10	3	0	44	11.4	.86
Pre All-Star	33	6	14	20	-5	14	1	1	67	9.0	.61
Post All-Star	32	8	16	24	-2	24	3	1	78	10.3	.75
Day	3	2	0	2	-3	6	1	0	9	22.2	.67
Night	62	12	30	42	-4	32	3	2	136	8.8	.68

	GP	G	A	Pts	+/–	PIM	PP	SH	S	SPct	P/G
National TV	20	6	7	13	0	20	1	1	47	12.8	.65
0 Days Rest	13	2	6	8	-3	14	1	1	26	7.7	.62
1 Days Rest	29	9	10	19	-6	18	3	1	72	12.5	.66
2 Days Rest	14	1	11	12	6	2	0	0	23	4.3	.86
3+ Days Rest	9	2	3	5	-4	4	0	0	24	8.3	.56

	G	A	Pts	PIM		G	A	Pts	PIM
1st Period	3	11	14	10	Winning	6	7	13	12
2nd Period	8	12	20	14	Losing	3	8	11	22
3rd Period	3	7	10	14	Tied	5	15	20	4
Overtime	0	0	0	0	Clutch	1	2	3	6
Last 5 Min	2	10	12	16	Blowouts	1	1	2	4

Steve Konowalchuk

Washington Capitals — Center

1998-99 Season

	GP	G	A	Pts	+/–	PIM	PP	SH	S	SPct	P/G
Overall	45	12	12	24	0	26	4	1	98	12.2	.53
Home	20	6	5	11	-1	8	1	1	49	12.2	.55
Away	25	6	7	13	1	18	3	0	49	12.2	.52
vs. Division	6	0	3	3	2	8	0	0	14	0.0	.50
vs. Conference	35	10	10	20	2	16	3	1	79	12.7	.57
vs. Playoff	30	7	7	14	-2	16	3	0	58	12.1	.47
vs. Non-Playoff	15	5	5	10	2	10	1	1	40	12.5	.67
Pre All-Star	28	7	5	12	1	12	1	1	64	10.9	.43
Post All-Star	17	5	7	12	-1	14	3	0	34	14.7	.71
Day	3	0	2	2	2	0	0	0	5	0.0	.67
Night	42	12	10	22	-2	26	4	1	93	12.9	.52

	GP	G	A	Pts	+/–	PIM	PP	SH	S	SPct	P/G
National TV	5	3	2	5	3	2	1	0	14	21.4	1.00
0 Days Rest	9	2	2	4	1	2	1	0	15	13.3	.44
1 Days Rest	20	5	5	10	0	10	1	0	52	9.6	.50
2 Days Rest	7	2	2	4	-5	10	1	1	15	13.3	.57
3+ Days Rest	9	3	3	6	4	4	1	0	16	18.8	.67

	G	A	Pts	PIM		G	A	Pts	PIM
1st Period	3	2	5	14	Winning	4	3	7	12
2nd Period	4	5	9	6	Losing	4	4	8	10
3rd Period	5	5	10	6	Tied	4	5	9	4
Overtime	0	0	0	0	Clutch	2	2	4	0
Last 5 Min	2	2	4	10	Blowouts	0	1	1	6

Igor Korolev

Toronto Maple Leafs — Right Wing

1998-99 Season

	GP	G	A	Pts	+/–	PIM	PP	SH	S	SPct	P/G
Overall	66	13	34	47	11	46	1	0	99	13.1	.71
Home	34	9	18	27	3	18	1	0	48	18.8	.79
Away	32	4	16	20	8	28	0	0	51	7.8	.63
vs. Division	16	4	3	7	0	12	0	0	25	16.0	.44
vs. Conference	45	9	22	31	4	30	0	0	73	12.3	.69
vs. Playoff	37	10	16	26	5	24	1	0	57	17.5	.70
vs. Non-Playoff	29	3	18	21	6	22	0	0	42	7.1	.72
Pre All-Star	43	11	21	32	10	28	1	0	58	19.0	.74
Post All-Star	23	2	13	15	1	18	0	0	41	4.9	.65
Day	1	1	1	2	1	0	0	0	1	100.0	2.00
Night	65	12	33	45	10	46	1	0	98	12.2	.69

	GP	G	A	Pts	+/–	PIM	PP	SH	S	SPct	P/G
National TV	23	7	7	14	-2	20	0	0	31	22.6	.61
0 Days Rest	14	4	6	10	-2	12	0	0	18	22.2	.71
1 Days Rest	27	6	16	22	14	20	0	0	36	16.7	.81
2 Days Rest	11	0	5	5	-3	10	0	0	19	0.0	.45
3+ Days Rest	14	3	7	10	2	4	1	0	26	11.5	.71

	G	A	Pts	PIM		G	A	Pts	PIM
1st Period	3	11	14	12	Winning	4	15	19	20
2nd Period	8	15	23	16	Losing	3	9	12	24
3rd Period	2	8	10	18	Tied	6	10	16	2
Overtime	0	0	0	0	Clutch	0	3	3	4
Last 5 Min	2	12	14	4	Blowouts	0	2	2	10

Alexander Korolyuk

San Jose Sharks — Right Wing

1998-99 Season

	GP	G	A	Pts	+/–	PIM	PP	SH	S	SPct	P/G
Overall	55	12	18	30	3	26	2	0	96	12.5	.55
Home	26	6	8	14	0	12	1	0	48	12.5	.54
Away	29	6	10	16	3	14	1	0	48	12.5	.55
vs. Division	14	4	3	7	0	10	1	0	34	11.8	.50
vs. Conference	37	11	13	24	0	20	2	0	69	15.9	.65
vs. Playoff	30	9	10	19	2	14	1	0	65	13.8	.63
vs. Non-Playoff	25	3	8	11	1	12	1	0	31	9.7	.44
Pre All-Star	18	2	5	7	-1	10	0	0	29	6.9	.39
Post All-Star	37	10	13	23	4	16	2	0	67	14.9	.62
Day	5	0	0	0	-2	2	0	0	8	0.0	.00
Night	50	12	18	30	5	24	2	0	88	13.6	.60

	GP	G	A	Pts	+/–	PIM	PP	SH	S	SPct	P/G
National TV	9	0	3	3	-4	6	0	0	17	0.0	.33
0 Days Rest	9	4	3	7	-1	4	1	0	13	30.8	.78
1 Days Rest	27	4	6	10	-1	14	0	0	48	8.3	.37
2 Days Rest	11	2	4	6	2	8	0	0	25	8.0	.55
3+ Days Rest	8	2	5	7	3	0	1	0	10	20.0	.88

	G	A	Pts	PIM		G	A	Pts	PIM
1st Period	4	7	11	4	Winning	4	8	12	14
2nd Period	4	5	9	18	Losing	4	3	7	6
3rd Period	4	6	10	2	Tied	4	7	11	6
Overtime	0	0	0	2	Clutch	1	2	3	2
Last 5 Min	5	5	10	4	Blowouts	1	0	1	2

Andrei Kovalenko

Carolina Hurricanes — Right Wing

1998-99 Season

	GP	G	A	Pts	+/–	PIM	PP	SH	S	SPct	P/G
Overall	74	19	21	40	-6	32	3	0	104	18.3	.54
Home	33	7	8	15	-3	12	1	0	42	16.7	.45
Away	41	12	13	25	-3	20	2	0	62	19.4	.61
vs. Division	13	3	5	8	4	8	1	0	28	10.7	.62
vs. Conference	49	13	12	25	-6	20	3	0	72	18.1	.51
vs. Playoff	38	12	9	21	-7	10	1	0	42	28.6	.55
vs. Non-Playoff	36	7	12	19	1	22	2	0	62	11.3	.53
Pre All-Star	42	13	14	27	-4	30	2	0	71	18.3	.64
Post All-Star	32	6	7	13	-2	2	1	0	33	18.2	.41
Day	5	0	2	2	-1	2	0	0	6	0.0	.40
Night	69	19	19	38	-5	30	3	0	98	19.4	.55

	GP	G	A	Pts	+/–	PIM	PP	SH	S	SPct	P/G
National TV	11	1	5	6	0	2	0	0	12	8.3	.55
0 Days Rest	12	1	2	3	-4	6	0	0	12	8.3	.25
1 Days Rest	31	12	7	19	-1	20	3	0	50	24.0	.61
2 Days Rest	16	5	7	12	2	4	0	0	20	25.0	.75
3+ Days Rest	15	1	5	6	-3	2	0	0	22	4.5	.40

	G	A	Pts	PIM		G	A	Pts	PIM
1st Period	4	7	11	10	Winning	5	6	11	12
2nd Period	6	4	10	6	Losing	8	12	20	14
3rd Period	8	10	18	16	Tied	6	3	9	6
Overtime	1	0	1	0	Clutch	3	3	6	6
Last 5 Min	6	4	10	14	Blowouts	0	3	3	0

Alexei Kovalev

Pittsburgh Penguins — Right Wing

1998-99 Season

	GP	G	A	Pts	+/–	PIM	PP	SH	S	SPct	P/G
Overall	77	23	30	53	2	49	6	1	191	12.0	.69
Home	40	9	17	26	6	27	2	1	91	9.9	.65
Away	37	14	13	27	-4	22	4	0	100	14.0	.73
vs. Division	18	3	6	9	-6	18	1	0	41	7.3	.50
vs. Conference	51	11	20	31	-5	39	3	0	117	9.4	.61
vs. Playoff	46	12	17	29	-3	24	2	1	111	10.8	.63
vs. Non-Playoff	31	11	13	24	5	25	4	0	80	13.8	.77
Pre All-Star	36	12	14	26	-7	25	4	0	82	14.6	.72
Post All-Star	41	11	16	27	9	24	2	1	109	10.1	.66
Day	15	5	6	11	7	8	0	1	39	12.8	.73
Night	62	18	24	42	-5	41	6	0	152	11.8	.68

	GP	G	A	Pts	+/–	PIM	PP	SH	S	SPct	P/G
National TV	16	4	7	11	1	4	1	1	46	8.7	.69
0 Days Rest	16	3	6	9	-3	8	1	0	35	8.6	.56
1 Days Rest	33	10	13	23	3	22	1	1	91	11.0	.70
2 Days Rest	17	6	7	13	3	6	2	0	38	15.8	.76
3+ Days Rest	11	4	4	8	-1	13	2	0	27	14.8	.73

	G	A	Pts	PIM		G	A	Pts	PIM
1st Period	11	5	16	14	Winning	9	7	16	9
2nd Period	6	12	18	23	Losing	4	14	18	24
3rd Period	5	12	17	12	Tied	10	9	19	16
Overtime	1	1	2	0	Clutch	2	5	7	6
Last 5 Min	5	10	15	21	Blowouts	1	0	1	4

Slava Kozlov

Detroit Red Wings — Center

1998-99 Season

	GP	G	A	Pts	+/–	PIM	PP	SH	S	SPct	P/G
Overall	79	29	29	58	10	45	6	1	209	13.9	.73
Home	40	19	13	32	8	33	4	1	105	18.1	.80
Away	39	10	16	26	2	12	2	0	104	9.6	.67
vs. Division	17	7	6	13	7	6	1	1	45	15.6	.76
vs. Conference	52	19	15	34	3	37	5	1	133	14.3	.65
vs. Playoff	45	20	15	35	0	29	4	0	116	17.2	.78
vs. Non-Playoff	34	9	14	23	10	16	2	1	93	9.7	.68
Pre All-Star	43	9	9	18	-5	31	2	0	110	8.2	.42
Post All-Star	36	20	20	40	15	14	4	1	99	20.2	1.11
Day	13	7	4	11	-2	6	2	0	33	21.2	.85
Night	66	22	25	47	12	39	4	1	176	12.5	.71

	GP	G	A	Pts	+/–	PIM	PP	SH	S	SPct	P/G
National TV	30	13	11	24	-4	31	4	0	82	15.9	.80
0 Days Rest	10	0	3	3	1	0	0	0	30	0.0	.30
1 Days Rest	39	21	17	38	13	43	5	0	99	21.2	.97
2 Days Rest	22	6	3	9	-9	0	1	1	52	11.5	.41
3+ Days Rest	8	2	6	8	5	2	0	0	28	7.1	1.00

	G	A	Pts	PIM		G	A	Pts	PIM
1st Period	12	10	22	8	Winning	9	11	20	14
2nd Period	7	11	18	8	Losing	5	11	16	29
3rd Period	9	8	17	29	Tied	15	7	22	2
Overtime	1	0	1	0	Clutch	3	2	5	4
Last 5 Min	6	4	10	25	Blowouts	1	1	2	8

Viktor Kozlov

Florida Panthers — Center

1998-99 Season

	GP	G	A	Pts	+/–	PIM	PP	SH	S	SPct	P/G
Overall	65	16	35	51	13	24	5	1	209	7.7	.78
Home	33	8	19	27	6	10	2	0	101	7.9	.82
Away	32	8	16	24	7	14	3	1	108	7.4	.75
vs. Division	13	4	7	11	0	8	0	0	47	8.5	.85
vs. Conference	43	10	21	31	11	18	3	1	142	7.0	.72
vs. Playoff	41	10	21	31	5	14	4	1	130	7.7	.76
vs. Non-Playoff	24	6	14	20	8	10	1	0	79	7.6	.83
Pre All-Star	36	7	21	28	9	8	2	1	122	5.7	.78
Post All-Star	29	9	14	23	4	16	3	0	87	10.3	.79
Day	2	0	0	0	-1	0	0	0	7	0.0	.00
Night	63	16	35	51	14	24	5	1	202	7.9	.81

	GP	G	A	Pts	+/–	PIM	PP	SH	S	SPct	P/G
National TV	2	2	0	2	0	0	0	0	7	28.6	1.00
0 Days Rest	14	3	7	10	3	4	0	0	56	5.4	.71
1 Days Rest	24	4	13	17	3	12	1	1	68	5.9	.71
2 Days Rest	12	3	7	10	4	2	2	0	36	8.3	.83
3+ Days Rest	15	6	8	14	3	6	2	0	49	12.2	.93

	G	A	Pts	PIM		G	A	Pts	PIM
1st Period	5	10	15	14	Winning	5	15	20	10
2nd Period	6	7	13	6	Losing	7	12	19	10
3rd Period	5	18	23	4	Tied	4	8	12	4
Overtime	0	0	0	0	Clutch	1	2	3	2
Last 5 Min	5	9	14	10	Blowouts	2	2	4	0

Igor Kravchuk

Ottawa Senators — Defense

1998-99 Season

	GP	G	A	Pts	+/–	PIM	PP	SH	S	SPct	P/G
Overall	79	4	21	25	14	32	3	0	171	2.3	.32
Home	39	2	12	14	4	20	2	0	81	2.5	.36
Away	40	2	9	11	10	12	1	0	90	2.2	.28
vs. Division	20	2	3	5	0	10	2	0	46	4.3	.25
vs. Conference	54	3	13	16	11	22	3	0	116	2.6	.30
vs. Playoff	46	4	10	14	-3	18	3	0	103	3.9	.30
vs. Non-Playoff	33	0	11	11	17	14	0	0	68	0.0	.33
Pre All-Star	44	2	10	12	3	16	1	0	103	1.9	.27
Post All-Star	35	2	11	13	11	16	2	0	68	2.9	.37
Day	3	0	1	1	2	2	0	0	6	0.0	.33
Night	76	4	20	24	12	30	3	0	165	2.4	.32

	GP	G	A	Pts	+/–	PIM	PP	SH	S	SPct	P/G
National TV	11	0	5	5	5	4	0	0	20	0.0	.45
0 Days Rest	13	0	5	5	1	4	0	0	29	0.0	.38
1 Days Rest	40	3	11	14	10	18	2	0	94	3.2	.35
2 Days Rest	13	1	0	1	1	6	1	0	29	3.4	.08
3+ Days Rest	13	0	5	5	2	4	0	0	19	0.0	.38

	G	A	Pts	PIM		G	A	Pts	PIM
1st Period	2	9	11	8	Winning	1	10	11	24
2nd Period	1	9	10	14	Losing	1	7	8	4
3rd Period	1	3	4	10	Tied	2	4	6	4
Overtime	0	0	0	0	Clutch	1	1	2	0
Last 5 Min	1	5	6	12	Blowouts	0	0	0	2

Sergei Krivokrasov

Nashville Predators — Right Wing

1998-99 Season

	GP	G	A	Pts	+/–	PIM	PP	SH	S	SPct	P/G
Overall	70	25	23	48	-5	42	10	0	208	12.0	.69
Home	33	11	10	21	-10	18	7	0	105	10.5	.64
Away	37	14	13	27	5	24	3	0	103	13.6	.73
vs. Division	15	4	4	8	-10	4	3	0	50	8.0	.53
vs. Conference	48	20	18	38	-1	18	10	0	150	13.3	.79
vs. Playoff	41	11	12	23	-14	22	4	0	111	9.9	.56
vs. Non-Playoff	29	14	11	25	9	20	6	0	97	14.4	.86
Pre All-Star	35	15	13	28	2	24	5	0	104	14.4	.80
Post All-Star	35	10	10	20	-7	18	5	0	104	9.6	.57
Day	4	1	1	2	-1	0	0	0	7	14.3	.50
Night	66	24	22	46	-4	42	10	0	201	11.9	.70

	GP	G	A	Pts	+/–	PIM	PP	SH	S	SPct	P/G
National TV	2	3	2	5	4	2	1	0	9	33.3	2.50
0 Days Rest	12	4	6	10	1	8	1	0	43	9.3	.83
1 Days Rest	32	12	9	21	-4	32	5	0	93	12.9	.66
2 Days Rest	13	5	3	8	-2	0	1	0	34	14.7	.62
3+ Days Rest	13	4	5	9	0	2	3	0	38	10.5	.69

	G	A	Pts	PIM		G	A	Pts	PIM
1st Period	7	7	14	6	Winning	6	5	11	8
2nd Period	8	5	13	12	Losing	9	13	22	20
3rd Period	10	11	21	12	Tied	10	5	15	14
Overtime	0	0	0	12	Clutch	4	4	8	16
Last 5 Min	7	6	13	20	Blowouts	1	1	2	2

Robert Kron

Carolina Hurricanes — Left Wing

1998-99 Season

	GP	G	A	Pts	+/–	PIM	PP	SH	S	SPct	P/G
Overall	75	9	16	25	-13	10	3	1	134	6.7	.33
Home	38	5	8	13	-5	6	1	1	64	7.8	.34
Away	37	4	8	12	-8	4	2	0	70	5.7	.32
vs. Division	14	1	5	6	6	0	1	0	28	3.6	.43
vs. Conference	55	7	14	21	-6	4	2	1	109	6.4	.38
vs. Playoff	39	3	9	12	-15	8	0	1	65	4.6	.31
vs. Non-Playoff	36	6	7	13	2	2	3	0	69	8.7	.36
Pre All-Star	44	6	5	11	-7	8	2	1	72	8.3	.27
Post All-Star	31	3	11	14	-6	2	1	0	62	4.8	.42
Day	7	2	3	5	0	0	1	0	10	20.0	.57
Night	68	7	13	20	-13	10	2	1	124	5.6	.31

	GP	G	A	Pts	+/–	PIM	PP	SH	S	SPct	P/G
National TV	1	0	0	0	0	0	0	0	2	0.0	.00
0 Days Rest	15	1	2	3	-3	0	0	0	27	3.7	.20
1 Days Rest	28	5	4	9	-5	8	1	1	49	10.2	.36
2 Days Rest	22	2	3	5	-7	2	1	0	40	5.0	.23
3+ Days Rest	10	1	7	8	2	0	1	0	18	5.6	.70

	G	A	Pts	PIM		G	A	Pts	PIM
1st Period	3	4	7	6	Winning	3	5	8	2
2nd Period	6	6	12	2	Losing	2	8	10	6
3rd Period	0	6	6	2	Tied	4	3	7	2
Overtime	0	0	0	0	Clutch	0	0	0	0
Last 5 Min	4	0	4	0	Blowouts	0	0	0	0

Pavel Kubina

Tampa Bay Lightning — Defense

1998-99 Season

	GP	G	A	Pts	+/–	PIM	PP	SH	S	SPct	P/G
Overall	68	9	12	21	-33	80	3	1	119	7.6	.31
Home	37	5	7	12	-14	40	2	0	76	6.6	.32
Away	31	4	5	9	-19	40	1	1	43	9.3	.29
vs. Division	14	1	2	3	-12	2	0	0	31	3.2	.21
vs. Conference	49	7	10	17	-18	66	2	1	80	8.8	.35
vs. Playoff	42	5	7	12	-24	58	2	0	63	7.9	.29
vs. Non-Playoff	26	4	5	9	-9	22	1	1	56	7.1	.35
Pre All-Star	33	3	7	10	-14	60	1	0	53	5.7	.30
Post All-Star	35	6	5	11	-19	20	2	1	66	9.1	.31
Day	5	2	1	3	0	8	1	0	5	40.0	.60
Night	63	7	11	18	-33	72	2	1	114	6.1	.29

	GP	G	A	Pts	+/–	PIM	PP	SH	S	SPct	P/G
National TV	1	1	0	1	3	0	0	1	2	50.0	1.00
0 Days Rest	11	3	3	6	-7	9	0	0	23	13.0	.55
1 Days Rest	29	4	5	9	-10	43	1	1	59	6.8	.31
2 Days Rest	13	0	3	3	-1	8	0	0	18	0.0	.23
3+ Days Rest	15	2	1	3	-15	20	2	0	19	10.5	.20

	G	A	Pts	PIM		G	A	Pts	PIM
1st Period	2	4	6	24	Winning	3	2	5	16
2nd Period	3	3	6	24	Losing	3	4	7	60
3rd Period	4	5	9	32	Tied	3	6	9	4
Overtime	0	0	0	0	Clutch	2	1	3	5
Last 5 Min	3	2	5	31	Blowouts	1	0	1	10

Oleg Kvasha

Florida Panthers — Left Wing

1998-99 Season

	GP	G	A	Pts	+/–	PIM	PP	SH	S	SPct	P/G
Overall	68	12	13	25	5	45	4	0	138	8.7	.37
Home	34	7	10	17	3	8	4	0	78	9.0	.50
Away	34	5	3	8	2	37	0	0	60	8.3	.24
vs. Division	12	0	4	4	7	4	0	0	28	0.0	.33
vs. Conference	48	8	9	17	9	33	3	0	96	8.3	.35
vs. Playoff	42	8	5	13	-1	25	3	0	79	10.1	.31
vs. Non-Playoff	26	4	8	12	6	20	1	0	59	6.8	.46
Pre All-Star	41	7	6	13	3	35	2	0	94	7.4	.32
Post All-Star	27	5	7	12	2	10	2	0	44	11.4	.44
Day	4	0	0	0	0	4	0	0	10	0.0	.00
Night	64	12	13	25	5	41	4	0	128	9.4	.39

	GP	G	A	Pts	+/–	PIM	PP	SH	S	SPct	P/G
National TV	1	1	0	1	1	0	0	0	2	50.0	1.00
0 Days Rest	14	2	2	4	1	6	1	0	23	8.7	.29
1 Days Rest	26	2	4	6	0	31	1	0	40	5.0	.23
2 Days Rest	13	2	3	5	0	4	0	0	29	6.9	.38
3+ Days Rest	15	6	4	10	4	4	2	0	46	13.0	.67

	G	A	Pts	PIM		G	A	Pts	PIM
1st Period	7	4	11	14	Winning	2	4	6	12
2nd Period	3	3	6	25	Losing	3	4	7	25
3rd Period	2	6	8	6	Tied	7	5	12	8
Overtime	0	0	0	0	Clutch	0	1	1	2
Last 5 Min	2	3	5	25	Blowouts	1	1	2	6

Scott Lachance

Montreal Canadiens — Defense

1998-99 Season

	GP	G	A	Pts	+/–	PIM	PP	SH	S	SPct	P/G
Overall	76	2	9	11	-21	41	1	0	59	3.4	.14
Home	39	0	7	7	-15	21	0	0	29	0.0	.18
Away	37	2	2	4	-6	20	1	0	30	6.7	.11
vs. Division	20	0	5	5	3	8	0	0	9	0.0	.25
vs. Conference	54	1	9	10	-14	30	1	0	44	2.3	.19
vs. Playoff	47	2	6	8	-7	29	1	0	26	7.7	.17
vs. Non-Playoff	29	0	3	3	-14	12	0	0	33	0.0	.10
Pre All-Star	40	1	7	8	-12	20	1	0	25	4.0	.20
Post All-Star	36	1	2	3	-9	21	0	0	34	2.9	.08
Day	8	0	1	1	-1	0	0	0	4	0.0	.13
Night	68	2	8	10	-20	41	1	0	55	3.6	.15

	GP	G	A	Pts	+/–	PIM	PP	SH	S	SPct	P/G
National TV	8	0	2	2	-1	4	0	0	8	0.0	.25
0 Days Rest	14	1	2	3	-2	16	1	0	10	10.0	.21
1 Days Rest	33	0	6	6	-5	17	0	0	26	0.0	.18
2 Days Rest	14	0	0	0	-7	4	0	0	13	0.0	.00
3+ Days Rest	15	1	1	2	-7	4	0	0	10	10.0	.13

	G	A	Pts	PIM		G	A	Pts	PIM
1st Period	0	1	1	11	Winning	1	6	7	4
2nd Period	1	5	6	20	Losing	1	2	3	32
3rd Period	1	3	4	10	Tied	0	1	1	5
Overtime	0	0	0	0	Clutch	0	1	1	2
Last 5 Min	0	2	2	15	Blowouts	0	0	0	2

Christian Laflamme

Edmonton Oilers — Defense

1998-99 Season

	GP	G	A	Pts	+/–	PIM	PP	SH	S	SPct	P/G
Overall	73	2	12	14	-3	70	0	0	68	2.9	.19
Home	38	2	7	9	6	24	0	0	33	6.1	.24
Away	35	0	5	5	-9	46	0	0	35	0.0	.14
vs. Division	20	2	1	3	8	16	0	0	25	8.0	.15
vs. Conference	53	2	7	9	3	50	0	0	51	3.9	.17
vs. Playoff	45	1	9	10	-2	48	0	0	43	2.3	.22
vs. Non-Playoff	28	1	3	4	-1	22	0	0	25	4.0	.14
Pre All-Star	40	1	3	4	-7	54	0	0	29	3.4	.10
Post All-Star	33	1	9	10	4	16	0	0	39	2.6	.30
Day	6	1	3	4	0	6	0	0	9	11.1	.67
Night	67	1	9	10	-3	64	0	0	59	1.7	.15

	GP	G	A	Pts	+/–	PIM	PP	SH	S	SPct	P/G
National TV	14	1	3	4	1	10	0	0	16	6.3	.29
0 Days Rest	9	0	2	2	3	14	0	0	7	0.0	.22
1 Days Rest	38	2	4	6	-5	36	0	0	43	4.7	.16
2 Days Rest	10	0	1	1	1	8	0	0	9	0.0	.10
3+ Days Rest	16	0	5	5	-2	12	0	0	9	0.0	.31

	G	A	Pts	PIM		G	A	Pts	PIM
1st Period	1	3	4	30	Winning	0	6	6	26
2nd Period	0	5	5	22	Losing	2	4	6	28
3rd Period	1	4	5	18	Tied	0	2	2	16
Overtime	0	0	0	0	Clutch	0	1	1	4
Last 5 Min	1	4	5	10	Blowouts	0	0	0	10

Denny Lambert

Nashville Predators — Left Wing

1998-99 Season

	GP	G	A	Pts	+/–	PIM	PP	SH	S	SPct	P/G
Overall	76	5	11	16	-3	218	1	0	66	7.6	.21
Home	38	2	8	10	-6	118	0	0	32	6.3	.26
Away	38	3	3	6	3	100	1	0	34	8.8	.16
vs. Division	17	1	2	3	-4	79	0	0	12	8.3	.18
vs. Conference	49	3	9	12	-2	162	1	0	41	7.3	.24
vs. Playoff	49	3	5	8	-9	137	0	0	33	9.1	.16
vs. Non-Playoff	27	2	6	8	6	81	1	0	33	6.1	.30
Pre All-Star	41	4	8	12	-2	128	1	0	34	11.8	.29
Post All-Star	35	1	3	4	-1	90	0	0	32	3.1	.11
Day	8	1	1	2	-6	17	0	0	6	16.7	.25
Night	68	4	10	14	3	201	1	0	60	6.7	.21

	GP	G	A	Pts	+/–	PIM	PP	SH	S	SPct	P/G
National TV	2	1	1	2	2	10	1	0	3	33.3	1.00
0 Days Rest	12	0	2	2	-3	28	0	0	11	0.0	.17
1 Days Rest	38	3	8	11	2	132	1	0	31	9.7	.29
2 Days Rest	15	1	1	2	-4	28	0	0	13	7.7	.13
3+ Days Rest	11	1	0	1	2	30	0	0	11	9.1	.09

	G	A	Pts	PIM		G	A	Pts	PIM
1st Period	2	2	4	123	Winning	1	4	5	70
2nd Period	2	4	6	59	Losing	2	4	6	124
3rd Period	1	5	6	36	Tied	2	3	5	24
Overtime	0	0	0	0	Clutch	0	2	2	9
Last 5 Min	2	5	7	67	Blowouts	1	1	2	16

Robert Lang

Pittsburgh Penguins — Center

1998-99 Season

	GP	G	A	Pts	+/–	PIM	PP	SH	S	SPct	P/G
Overall	72	21	23	44	-10	24	7	0	137	15.3	.61
Home	38	14	11	25	4	12	4	0	74	18.9	.66
Away	34	7	12	19	-14	12	3	0	63	11.1	.56
vs. Division	17	6	6	12	-1	4	0	0	31	19.4	.71
vs. Conference	49	15	16	31	-1	14	3	0	96	15.6	.63
vs. Playoff	35	8	12	20	-6	10	2	0	55	14.5	.57
vs. Non-Playoff	37	13	11	24	-4	14	5	0	82	15.9	.65
Pre All-Star	41	18	12	30	-11	14	5	0	92	19.6	.73
Post All-Star	31	3	11	14	1	10	2	0	45	6.7	.45
Day	11	1	5	6	3	0	1	0	15	6.7	.55
Night	61	20	18	38	-13	24	6	0	122	16.4	.62

	GP	G	A	Pts	+/–	PIM	PP	SH	S	SPct	P/G
National TV	16	2	3	5	-11	4	0	0	28	7.1	.31
0 Days Rest	14	2	6	8	-1	6	1	0	30	6.7	.57
1 Days Rest	29	7	7	14	-6	10	3	0	49	14.3	.48
2 Days Rest	19	9	5	14	-2	8	3	0	44	20.5	.74
3+ Days Rest	10	3	5	8	-1	0	0	0	14	21.4	.80

	G	A	Pts	PIM		G	A	Pts	PIM
1st Period	3	6	9	6	Winning	10	11	21	14
2nd Period	13	8	21	10	Losing	8	5	13	8
3rd Period	5	9	14	8	Tied	3	7	10	2
Overtime	0	0	0	0	Clutch	2	3	5	0
Last 5 Min	7	7	14	2	Blowouts	0	0	0	8

Jamie Langenbrunner

Dallas Stars — Center

1998-99 Season

	GP	G	A	Pts	+/–	PIM	PP	SH	S	SPct	P/G
Overall	75	12	33	45	10	62	4	0	145	8.3	.60
Home	40	8	21	29	5	32	3	0	75	10.7	.73
Away	35	4	12	16	5	30	1	0	70	5.7	.46
vs. Division	21	2	12	14	7	8	1	0	43	4.7	.67
vs. Conference	49	6	19	25	8	42	3	0	90	6.7	.51
vs. Playoff	45	7	23	30	3	38	3	0	88	8.0	.67
vs. Non-Playoff	30	5	10	15	7	24	1	0	57	8.8	.50
Pre All-Star	38	6	20	26	7	34	4	0	65	9.2	.68
Post All-Star	37	6	13	19	3	28	0	0	80	7.5	.51
Day	9	1	1	2	-4	8	0	0	21	4.8	.22
Night	66	11	32	43	14	54	4	0	124	8.9	.65

	GP	G	A	Pts	+/–	PIM	PP	SH	S	SPct	P/G
National TV	12	1	3	4	-4	10	0	0	28	3.6	.33
0 Days Rest	14	1	3	4	-5	8	1	0	30	3.3	.29
1 Days Rest	38	7	20	27	11	38	2	0	73	9.6	.71
2 Days Rest	10	2	4	6	1	12	1	0	13	15.4	.60
3+ Days Rest	13	2	6	8	3	4	0	0	29	6.9	.62

	G	A	Pts	PIM		G	A	Pts	PIM
1st Period	4	11	15	20	Winning	3	15	18	36
2nd Period	3	15	18	28	Losing	4	5	9	16
3rd Period	5	7	12	12	Tied	5	13	18	10
Overtime	0	0	0	2	Clutch	1	1	2	2
Last 5 Min	5	8	13	22	Blowouts	0	1	1	10

Daymond Langkow

Philadelphia Flyers — Center

1998-99 Season

	GP	G	A	Pts	+/–	PIM	PP	SH	S	SPct	P/G
Overall	78	14	19	33	-8	39	4	1	149	9.4	.42
Home	40	6	9	15	-9	22	2	0	70	8.6	.38
Away	38	8	10	18	1	17	2	1	79	10.1	.47
vs. Division	12	4	4	8	0	8	2	1	23	17.4	.67
vs. Conference	45	9	11	20	-4	35	3	1	82	11.0	.44
vs. Playoff	42	6	8	14	-13	24	2	0	72	8.3	.33
vs. Non-Playoff	36	8	11	19	5	15	2	1	77	10.4	.53
Pre All-Star	40	7	13	20	11	17	1	0	74	9.5	.50
Post All-Star	38	7	6	13	-19	22	3	1	75	9.3	.34
Day	13	2	1	3	-3	4	0	1	14	14.3	.23
Night	65	12	18	30	-5	35	4	0	135	8.9	.46

	GP	G	A	Pts	+/–	PIM	PP	SH	S	SPct	P/G
National TV	17	4	1	5	-9	8	1	1	34	11.8	.29
0 Days Rest	12	1	3	4	1	4	1	0	24	4.2	.33
1 Days Rest	39	8	8	16	-10	19	2	1	76	10.5	.41
2 Days Rest	16	2	3	5	-4	7	0	0	31	6.5	.31
3+ Days Rest	11	3	5	8	5	9	1	0	18	16.7	.73

	G	A	Pts	PIM		G	A	Pts	PIM
1st Period	3	5	8	6	Winning	4	7	11	8
2nd Period	5	10	15	14	Losing	5	4	9	29
3rd Period	6	4	10	19	Tied	5	8	13	2
Overtime	0	0	0	0	Clutch	0	0	0	2
Last 5 Min	3	3	6	22	Blowouts	1	1	2	14

Ian Laperriere

Los Angeles Kings — Center

1998-99 Season

	GP	G	A	Pts	+/–	PIM	PP	SH	S	SPct	P/G
Overall	72	3	10	13	-5	138	0	0	62	4.8	.18
Home	37	2	7	9	3	99	0	0	32	6.3	.24
Away	35	1	3	4	-8	39	0	0	30	3.3	.11
vs. Division	23	0	5	5	2	42	0	0	20	0.0	.22
vs. Conference	54	2	8	10	-4	96	0	0	48	4.2	.19
vs. Playoff	50	3	8	11	1	75	0	0	43	7.0	.22
vs. Non-Playoff	22	0	2	2	-6	63	0	0	19	0.0	.09
Pre All-Star	35	1	5	6	-4	87	0	0	31	3.2	.17
Post All-Star	37	2	5	7	-1	51	0	0	31	6.5	.19
Day	5	1	1	2	3	2	0	0	8	12.5	.40
Night	67	2	9	11	-8	136	0	0	54	3.7	.16

	GP	G	A	Pts	+/–	PIM	PP	SH	S	SPct	P/G
National TV	16	2	4	6	1	15	0	0	16	12.5	.38
0 Days Rest	12	0	1	1	-7	20	0	0	12	0.0	.08
1 Days Rest	35	1	4	5	-2	67	0	0	30	3.3	.14
2 Days Rest	14	2	3	5	4	29	0	0	15	13.3	.36
3+ Days Rest	11	0	2	2	0	22	0	0	5	0.0	.18

	G	A	Pts	PIM		G	A	Pts	PIM
1st Period	0	5	5	38	Winning	0	4	4	70
2nd Period	2	3	5	25	Losing	2	3	5	66
3rd Period	1	2	3	73	Tied	1	3	4	2
Overtime	0	0	0	2	Clutch	0	0	0	4
Last 5 Min	0	1	1	65	Blowouts	1	0	1	42

Claude Lapointe

New York Islanders — Center

1998-99 Season

	GP	G	A	Pts	+/–	PIM	PP	SH	S	SPct	P/G
Overall	82	14	23	37	-19	62	2	2	134	10.4	.45
Home	41	7	10	17	-17	22	2	1	68	10.3	.41
Away	41	7	13	20	-2	40	0	1	66	10.6	.49
vs. Division	20	4	8	12	-3	14	1	0	40	10.0	.60
vs. Conference	58	12	17	29	-15	43	2	2	102	11.8	.50
vs. Playoff	51	9	12	21	-15	29	0	1	93	9.7	.41
vs. Non-Playoff	31	5	11	16	-4	33	2	1	41	12.2	.52
Pre All-Star	46	11	13	24	-8	40	2	2	78	14.1	.52
Post All-Star	36	3	10	13	-11	22	0	0	56	5.4	.36
Day	11	1	3	4	-3	2	0	0	17	5.9	.36
Night	71	13	20	33	-16	60	2	2	117	11.1	.46

	GP	G	A	Pts	+/–	PIM	PP	SH	S	SPct	P/G
National TV	6	2	0	2	-1	6	0	0	4	50.0	.33
0 Days Rest	14	3	6	9	-4	28	0	0	30	10.0	.64
1 Days Rest	37	8	10	18	-10	20	1	1	63	12.7	.49
2 Days Rest	20	1	2	3	-2	10	0	0	28	3.6	.15
3+ Days Rest	11	2	5	7	-3	4	1	1	13	15.4	.64

	G	A	Pts	PIM		G	A	Pts	PIM
1st Period	3	3	6	17	Winning	7	7	14	14
2nd Period	1	9	10	37	Losing	4	9	13	37
3rd Period	10	11	21	8	Tied	3	7	10	11
Overtime	0	0	0	0	Clutch	5	3	8	0
Last 5 Min	4	6	10	17	Blowouts	0	1	1	6

Martin Lapointe

Detroit Red Wings — Right Wing

1998-99 Season

	GP	G	A	Pts	+/–	PIM	PP	SH	S	SPct	P/G
Overall	77	16	13	29	7	141	7	1	153	10.5	.38
Home	38	11	5	16	9	61	4	1	83	13.3	.42
Away	39	5	8	13	-2	80	3	0	70	7.1	.33
vs. Division	16	3	5	8	8	29	2	0	35	8.6	.50
vs. Conference	51	9	10	19	8	89	4	0	107	8.4	.37
vs. Playoff	45	8	8	16	-1	90	4	1	77	10.4	.36
vs. Non-Playoff	32	8	5	13	8	51	3	0	76	10.5	.41
Pre All-Star	45	9	10	19	4	100	2	1	91	9.9	.42
Post All-Star	32	7	3	10	3	41	5	0	62	11.3	.31
Day	12	3	3	6	4	12	2	0	21	14.3	.50
Night	65	13	10	23	3	129	5	1	132	9.8	.35

	GP	G	A	Pts	+/–	PIM	PP	SH	S	SPct	P/G
National TV	29	4	4	8	-8	63	1	0	54	7.4	.28
0 Days Rest	11	2	2	4	-2	48	1	0	17	11.8	.36
1 Days Rest	36	9	6	15	12	49	5	0	71	12.7	.42
2 Days Rest	20	3	3	6	-9	40	0	0	53	5.7	.30
3+ Days Rest	10	2	2	4	6	4	1	1	12	16.7	.40

	G	A	Pts	PIM		G	A	Pts	PIM
1st Period	4	6	10	39	Winning	8	3	11	56
2nd Period	6	6	12	36	Losing	7	5	12	83
3rd Period	6	1	7	66	Tied	1	5	6	2
Overtime	0	0	0	0	Clutch	1	1	2	0
Last 5 Min	6	3	9	61	Blowouts	0	0	0	18

Igor Larionov

Detroit Red Wings — Center

1998-99 Season

	GP	G	A	Pts	+/–	PIM	PP	SH	S	SPct	P/G
Overall	75	14	49	63	13	48	4	2	83	16.9	.84
Home	39	8	26	34	10	22	4	0	44	18.2	.87
Away	36	6	23	29	3	26	0	2	39	15.4	.81
vs. Division	17	2	13	15	9	8	0	0	16	12.5	.88
vs. Conference	50	9	32	41	11	30	2	2	51	17.6	.82
vs. Playoff	43	7	29	36	1	34	2	1	49	14.3	.84
vs. Non-Playoff	32	7	20	27	12	14	2	1	34	20.6	.84
Pre All-Star	45	7	22	29	0	36	2	0	52	13.5	.64
Post All-Star	30	7	27	34	13	12	2	2	31	22.6	1.13
Day	11	1	11	12	2	8	0	1	11	9.1	1.09
Night	64	13	38	51	11	40	4	1	72	18.1	.80

	GP	G	A	Pts	+/–	PIM	PP	SH	S	SPct	P/G
National TV	26	4	15	19	2	12	0	2	27	14.8	.73
0 Days Rest	11	0	6	6	0	12	0	0	11	0.0	.55
1 Days Rest	32	9	23	32	13	14	1	2	40	22.5	1.00
2 Days Rest	22	2	9	11	-6	16	1	0	21	9.5	.50
3+ Days Rest	10	3	11	14	6	6	2	0	11	27.3	1.40

	G	A	Pts	PIM		G	A	Pts	PIM
1st Period	5	17	22	14	Winning	4	18	22	14
2nd Period	2	17	19	26	Losing	5	12	17	32
3rd Period	7	15	22	6	Tied	5	19	24	2
Overtime	0	0	0	2	Clutch	2	5	7	4
Last 5 Min	3	9	12	16	Blowouts	0	1	1	2

Janne Laukkanen

Ottawa Senators — Defense

1998-99 Season

	GP	G	A	Pts	+/–	PIM	PP	SH	S	SPct	P/G
Overall	50	1	11	12	18	40	0	0	46	2.2	.24
Home	23	1	7	8	11	20	0	0	31	3.2	.35
Away	27	0	4	4	7	20	0	0	15	0.0	.15
vs. Division	13	0	3	3	1	22	0	0	12	0.0	.23
vs. Conference	37	1	8	9	12	34	0	0	30	3.3	.24
vs. Playoff	32	0	7	7	12	36	0	0	30	0.0	.22
vs. Non-Playoff	18	1	4	5	6	4	0	0	16	6.3	.28
Pre All-Star	22	0	3	3	10	10	0	0	19	0.0	.14
Post All-Star	28	1	8	9	8	30	0	0	27	3.7	.32
Day	3	0	0	0	1	0	0	0	2	0.0	.00
Night	47	1	11	12	17	40	0	0	44	2.3	.26

	GP	G	A	Pts	+/–	PIM	PP	SH	S	SPct	P/G
National TV	5	0	3	3	1	2	0	0	4	0.0	.60
0 Days Rest	7	0	0	0	4	4	0	0	4	0.0	.00
1 Days Rest	27	1	9	10	10	16	0	0	29	3.4	.37
2 Days Rest	10	0	1	1	0	16	0	0	11	0.0	.10
3+ Days Rest	6	0	1	1	4	4	0	0	2	0.0	.17

	G	A	Pts	PIM		G	A	Pts	PIM
1st Period	0	3	3	10	Winning	1	1	2	16
2nd Period	0	4	4	24	Losing	0	4	4	20
3rd Period	1	3	4	6	Tied	0	6	6	4
Overtime	0	1	1	0	Clutch	0	1	1	2
Last 5 Min	0	1	1	24	Blowouts	1	0	1	8

Paul Laus

Florida Panthers — Defense

1998-99 Season

	GP	G	A	Pts	+/–	PIM	PP	SH	S	SPct	P/G
Overall	75	1	9	10	-1	218	0	0	54	1.9	.13
Home	39	1	4	5	-4	106	0	0	30	3.3	.13
Away	36	0	5	5	3	112	0	0	24	0.0	.14
vs. Division	13	0	1	1	1	34	0	0	7	0.0	.08
vs. Conference	52	1	5	6	0	153	0	0	40	2.5	.12
vs. Playoff	46	0	9	9	-3	131	0	0	30	0.0	.20
vs. Non-Playoff	29	1	0	1	2	87	0	0	24	4.2	.03
Pre All-Star	43	1	6	7	1	158	0	0	31	3.2	.16
Post All-Star	32	0	3	3	-2	60	0	0	23	0.0	.09
Day	3	0	0	0	1	7	0	0	3	0.0	.00
Night	72	1	9	10	-2	211	0	0	51	2.0	.14

	GP	G	A	Pts	+/–	PIM	PP	SH	S	SPct	P/G
National TV	3	0	0	0	-2	0	0	0	3	0.0	.00
0 Days Rest	17	0	2	2	1	62	0	0	14	0.0	.12
1 Days Rest	28	1	1	2	0	89	0	0	18	5.6	.07
2 Days Rest	15	0	2	2	-1	30	0	0	10	0.0	.13
3+ Days Rest	15	0	4	4	-1	37	0	0	12	0.0	.27

	G	A	Pts	PIM		G	A	Pts	PIM
1st Period	0	2	2	81	Winning	1	2	3	94
2nd Period	1	3	4	78	Losing	0	4	4	90
3rd Period	0	4	4	59	Tied	0	3	3	34
Overtime	0	0	0	0	Clutch	0	0	0	2
Last 5 Min	0	1	1	46	Blowouts	0	0	0	56

Mark Lawrence

New York Islanders — Right Wing

1998-99 Season

	GP	G	A	Pts	+/–	PIM	PP	SH	S	SPct	P/G
Overall	60	14	16	30	-8	38	4	0	88	15.9	.50
Home	30	4	7	11	-8	22	3	0	54	7.4	.37
Away	30	10	9	19	0	16	1	0	34	29.4	.63
vs. Division	14	5	3	8	0	4	1	0	12	41.7	.57
vs. Conference	42	11	11	22	-3	16	2	0	52	21.2	.52
vs. Playoff	37	9	10	19	-5	32	3	0	60	15.0	.51
vs. Non-Playoff	23	5	6	11	-3	6	1	0	28	17.9	.48
Pre All-Star	24	5	5	10	-2	10	0	0	26	19.2	.42
Post All-Star	36	9	11	20	-6	28	4	0	62	14.5	.56
Day	9	2	4	6	-2	6	0	0	12	16.7	.67
Night	51	12	12	24	-6	32	4	0	76	15.8	.47

	GP	G	A	Pts	+/–	PIM	PP	SH	S	SPct	P/G
National TV	6	0	1	1	-2	2	0	0	8	0.0	.17
0 Days Rest	9	2	1	3	1	2	0	0	12	16.7	.33
1 Days Rest	29	9	10	19	-4	14	2	0	33	27.3	.66
2 Days Rest	14	2	4	6	-2	14	1	0	33	6.1	.43
3+ Days Rest	8	1	1	2	-3	8	1	0	10	10.0	.25

	G	A	Pts	PIM		G	A	Pts	PIM
1st Period	5	5	10	16	Winning	5	2	7	16
2nd Period	4	4	8	14	Losing	5	8	13	14
3rd Period	5	7	12	8	Tied	4	6	10	8
Overtime	0	0	0	0	Clutch	3	0	3	0
Last 5 Min	3	1	4	8	Blowouts	0	0	0	10

Vincent Lecavalier

Tampa Bay Lightning — Center

1998-99 Season

	GP	G	A	Pts	+/–	PIM	PP	SH	S	SPct	P/G
Overall	82	13	15	28	-19	23	2	0	125	10.4	.34
Home	41	9	10	19	2	10	1	0	65	13.8	.46
Away	41	4	5	9	-21	13	1	0	60	6.7	.22
vs. Division	15	0	2	2	-11	0	0	0	21	0.0	.13
vs. Conference	57	9	13	22	-13	19	0	0	88	10.2	.39
vs. Playoff	51	9	12	21	-7	15	1	0	81	11.1	.41
vs. Non-Playoff	31	4	3	7	-12	8	1	0	44	9.1	.23
Pre All-Star	45	7	5	12	-13	6	2	0	58	12.1	.27
Post All-Star	37	6	10	16	-6	17	0	0	67	9.0	.43
Day	5	1	1	2	2	2	0	0	7	14.3	.40
Night	77	12	14	26	-21	21	2	0	118	10.2	.34

	GP	G	A	Pts	+/–	PIM	PP	SH	S	SPct	P/G
National TV	1	0	1	1	2	0	0	0	3	0.0	1.00
0 Days Rest	16	2	2	4	-11	4	1	0	19	10.5	.25
1 Days Rest	35	8	8	16	-1	15	1	0	53	15.1	.46
2 Days Rest	20	2	3	5	-3	2	0	0	37	5.4	.25
3+ Days Rest	11	1	2	3	-4	2	0	0	16	6.3	.27

	G	A	Pts	PIM
1st Period	7	7	14	10
2nd Period	3	5	8	2
3rd Period	3	3	6	11
Overtime	0	0	0	0
Last 5 Min	3	4	7	6

	G	A	Pts	PIM
Winning	1	3	4	8
Losing	6	5	11	11
Tied	6	7	13	4
Clutch	1	0	1	0
Blowouts	1	1	2	9

John LeClair

Philadelphia Flyers — Left Wing

1998-99 Season

	GP	G	A	Pts	+/–	PIM	PP	SH	S	SPct	P/G
Overall	76	43	47	90	36	30	16	0	246	17.5	1.18
Home	38	28	29	57	25	12	12	0	133	21.1	1.50
Away	38	15	18	33	11	18	4	0	113	13.3	.87
vs. Division	18	8	10	18	5	4	5	0	58	13.8	1.00
vs. Conference	54	28	27	55	14	22	11	0	169	16.6	1.02
vs. Playoff	41	23	33	56	24	18	9	0	123	18.7	1.37
vs. Non-Playoff	35	20	14	34	12	12	7	0	123	16.3	.97
Pre All-Star	44	27	29	56	30	14	11	0	149	18.1	1.27
Post All-Star	32	16	18	34	6	16	5	0	97	16.5	1.06
Day	13	7	9	16	9	2	3	0	46	15.2	1.23
Night	63	36	38	74	27	28	13	0	200	18.0	1.17

	GP	G	A	Pts	+/–	PIM	PP	SH	S	SPct	P/G
National TV	15	9	9	18	11	4	4	0	45	20.0	1.20
0 Days Rest	11	3	7	10	5	10	1	0	30	10.0	.91
1 Days Rest	37	24	25	49	21	12	8	0	117	20.5	1.32
2 Days Rest	17	9	11	20	6	4	3	0	55	16.4	1.18
3+ Days Rest	11	7	4	11	4	4	4	0	44	15.9	1.00

	G	A	Pts	PIM
1st Period	10	17	27	10
2nd Period	12	17	29	6
3rd Period	21	13	34	12
Overtime	0	0	0	2
Last 5 Min	13	14	27	10

	G	A	Pts	PIM
Winning	18	21	39	14
Losing	12	10	22	6
Tied	13	16	29	10
Clutch	2	4	6	4
Blowouts	2	1	3	4

Grant Ledyard

Boston Bruins — Defense

1998-99 Season

	GP	G	A	Pts	+/–	PIM	PP	SH	S	SPct	P/G
Overall	47	4	8	12	-8	33	1	0	47	8.5	.26
Home	23	1	4	5	4	23	0	0	20	5.0	.22
Away	24	3	4	7	-12	10	1	0	27	11.1	.29
vs. Division	7	1	3	4	-1	4	1	0	11	9.1	.57
vs. Conference	31	4	7	11	-7	25	1	0	35	11.4	.35
vs. Playoff	26	1	2	3	-6	16	0	0	22	4.5	.12
vs. Non-Playoff	21	3	6	9	-2	17	1	0	25	12.0	.43
Pre All-Star	23	2	4	6	-1	23	1	0	27	7.4	.26
Post All-Star	24	2	4	6	-7	10	0	0	20	10.0	.25
Day	10	0	2	2	-4	2	0	0	4	0.0	.20
Night	37	4	6	10	-4	31	1	0	43	9.3	.27

	GP	G	A	Pts	+/–	PIM	PP	SH	S	SPct	P/G
National TV	6	0	1	1	0	4	0	0	2	0.0	.17
0 Days Rest	5	0	1	1	0	0	0	0	4	0.0	.20
1 Days Rest	20	0	3	3	-10	25	0	0	16	0.0	.15
2 Days Rest	5	0	0	0	-4	0	0	0	6	0.0	.00
3+ Days Rest	17	4	4	8	6	8	1	0	21	19.0	.47

	G	A	Pts	PIM
1st Period	2	2	4	23
2nd Period	1	4	5	4
3rd Period	1	2	3	6
Overtime	0	0	0	0
Last 5 Min	1	2	3	4

	G	A	Pts	PIM
Winning	4	5	9	29
Losing	0	0	0	2
Tied	0	3	3	2
Clutch	0	1	1	0
Blowouts	1	1	2	0

Brian Leetch

New York Rangers — Defense

1998-99 Season

	GP	G	A	Pts	+/–	PIM	PP	SH	S	SPct	P/G
Overall	82	13	42	55	-7	42	4	0	184	7.1	.67
Home	41	8	23	31	-2	26	3	0	109	7.3	.76
Away	41	5	19	24	-5	16	1	0	75	6.7	.59
vs. Division	20	4	11	15	-3	8	2	0	37	10.8	.75
vs. Conference	58	9	35	44	-7	32	2	0	136	6.6	.76
vs. Playoff	52	10	25	35	0	24	3	0	116	8.6	.67
vs. Non-Playoff	30	3	17	20	-7	18	1	0	68	4.4	.67
Pre All-Star	45	6	21	27	-5	20	2	0	98	6.1	.60
Post All-Star	37	7	21	28	-2	22	2	0	86	8.1	.76
Day	12	4	6	10	-5	2	2	0	22	18.2	.83
Night	70	9	36	45	-2	40	2	0	162	5.6	.64

	GP	G	A	Pts	+/–	PIM	PP	SH	S	SPct	P/G
National TV	23	5	11	16	-9	10	2	0	44	11.4	.70
0 Days Rest	16	1	8	9	-6	10	1	0	39	2.6	.56
1 Days Rest	34	6	17	23	3	16	1	0	70	8.6	.68
2 Days Rest	20	5	11	16	2	12	2	0	46	10.9	.80
3+ Days Rest	12	1	6	7	-6	4	0	0	29	3.4	.58

	G	A	Pts	PIM
1st Period	2	11	13	20
2nd Period	4	18	22	14
3rd Period	7	12	19	6
Overtime	0	1	1	2
Last 5 Min	5	11	16	12

	G	A	Pts	PIM
Winning	4	12	16	16
Losing	8	18	26	18
Tied	1	12	13	8
Clutch	1	5	6	6
Blowouts	1	4	5	6

Sylvain Lefebvre

Colorado Avalanche — Defense

1998-99 Season

	GP	G	A	Pts	+/–	PIM	PP	SH	S	SPct	P/G
Overall	76	2	18	20	18	48	0	0	64	3.1	.26
Home	38	0	11	11	11	25	0	0	34	0.0	.29
Away	38	2	7	9	7	23	0	0	30	6.7	.24
vs. Division	16	0	2	2	-4	8	0	0	11	0.0	.13
vs. Conference	53	1	13	14	11	38	0	0	43	2.3	.26
vs. Playoff	44	2	10	12	7	29	0	0	38	5.3	.27
vs. Non-Playoff	32	0	8	8	11	19	0	0	26	0.0	.25
Pre All-Star	39	0	9	9	6	20	0	0	34	0.0	.23
Post All-Star	37	2	9	11	12	28	0	0	30	6.7	.30
Day	15	0	5	5	5	24	0	0	9	0.0	.33
Night	61	2	13	15	13	24	0	0	55	3.6	.25

	GP	G	A	Pts	+/–	PIM	PP	SH	S	SPct	P/G
National TV	21	1	6	7	9	19	0	0	24	4.2	.33
0 Days Rest	13	1	2	3	3	11	0	0	16	6.3	.23
1 Days Rest	38	1	8	9	5	14	0	0	27	3.7	.24
2 Days Rest	13	0	3	3	7	14	0	0	10	0.0	.23
3+ Days Rest	12	0	5	5	3	9	0	0	11	0.0	.42

	G	A	Pts	PIM		G	A	Pts	PIM
1st Period	0	5	5	17	Winning	2	4	6	16
2nd Period	0	7	7	15	Losing	0	5	5	32
3rd Period	2	6	8	16	Tied	0	9	9	0
Overtime	0	0	0	0	Clutch	1	3	4	2
Last 5 Min	1	3	4	30	Blowouts	0	0	0	2

Jere Lehtinen

Dallas Stars — Right Wing

1998-99 Season

	GP	G	A	Pts	+/–	PIM	PP	SH	S	SPct	P/G
Overall	74	20	32	52	29	18	7	1	173	11.6	.70
Home	37	8	14	22	10	12	2	1	84	9.5	.59
Away	37	12	18	30	19	6	5	0	89	13.5	.81
vs. Division	21	5	9	14	4	2	2	0	54	9.3	.67
vs. Conference	51	16	20	36	11	16	6	1	122	13.1	.71
vs. Playoff	43	15	19	34	24	6	6	1	88	17.0	.79
vs. Non-Playoff	31	5	13	18	5	12	1	0	85	5.9	.58
Pre All-Star	38	15	11	26	14	6	6	1	94	16.0	.68
Post All-Star	36	5	21	26	15	12	1	0	79	6.3	.72
Day	9	1	2	3	0	4	0	0	16	6.3	.33
Night	65	19	30	49	29	14	7	1	157	12.1	.75

	GP	G	A	Pts	+/–	PIM	PP	SH	S	SPct	P/G
National TV	14	2	5	7	-1	4	1	0	25	8.0	.50
0 Days Rest	12	2	9	11	10	0	0	1	21	9.5	.92
1 Days Rest	40	11	17	28	17	14	3	0	105	10.5	.70
2 Days Rest	11	2	4	6	6	2	2	0	20	10.0	.55
3+ Days Rest	11	5	2	7	-4	2	2	0	27	18.5	.64

	G	A	Pts	PIM		G	A	Pts	PIM
1st Period	7	13	20	10	Winning	11	13	24	12
2nd Period	8	11	19	6	Losing	4	5	9	4
3rd Period	5	7	12	2	Tied	5	14	19	2
Overtime	0	1	1	0	Clutch	3	3	6	0
Last 5 Min	6	11	17	8	Blowouts	0	2	2	2

Claude Lemieux

Colorado Avalanche — Right Wing

1998-99 Season

	GP	G	A	Pts	+/–	PIM	PP	SH	S	SPct	P/G
Overall	82	27	24	51	0	102	11	0	292	9.2	.62
Home	41	15	12	27	-3	32	8	0	146	10.3	.66
Away	41	12	12	24	3	70	3	0	146	8.2	.59
vs. Division	18	5	4	9	-7	38	3	0	57	8.8	.50
vs. Conference	56	19	16	35	1	78	6	0	191	9.9	.63
vs. Playoff	45	14	9	23	4	60	6	0	160	8.8	.51
vs. Non-Playoff	37	13	15	28	-4	42	5	0	132	9.8	.76
Pre All-Star	45	17	6	23	-2	56	9	0	175	9.7	.51
Post All-Star	37	10	18	28	2	46	2	0	117	8.5	.76
Day	15	5	5	10	-1	14	1	0	46	10.9	.67
Night	67	22	19	41	1	88	10	0	246	8.9	.61

	GP	G	A	Pts	+/–	PIM	PP	SH	S	SPct	P/G
National TV	22	8	3	11	6	46	2	0	73	11.0	.50
0 Days Rest	13	5	3	8	-2	22	1	0	52	9.6	.62
1 Days Rest	43	14	13	27	2	36	6	0	155	9.0	.63
2 Days Rest	14	5	4	9	3	10	1	0	50	10.0	.64
3+ Days Rest	12	3	4	7	-3	34	3	0	35	8.6	.58

	G	A	Pts	PIM		G	A	Pts	PIM
1st Period	8	8	16	14	Winning	7	7	14	40
2nd Period	9	4	13	46	Losing	8	8	16	48
3rd Period	9	12	21	40	Tied	12	9	21	14
Overtime	1	0	1	2	Clutch	5	3	8	10
Last 5 Min	11	4	15	38	Blowouts	1	0	1	2

Nicklas Lidstrom

Detroit Red Wings — Defense

1998-99 Season

	GP	G	A	Pts	+/–	PIM	PP	SH	S	SPct	P/G
Overall	81	14	43	57	14	14	6	2	205	6.8	.70
Home	41	8	22	30	22	6	4	1	108	7.4	.73
Away	40	6	21	27	-8	8	2	1	97	6.2	.68
vs. Division	17	2	11	13	13	2	0	0	39	5.1	.76
vs. Conference	53	7	31	38	12	12	4	0	116	6.0	.72
vs. Playoff	47	7	17	24	-9	2	6	0	114	6.1	.51
vs. Non-Playoff	34	7	26	33	23	12	0	2	91	7.7	.97
Pre All-Star	46	8	22	30	13	10	5	1	112	7.1	.65
Post All-Star	35	6	21	27	1	4	1	1	93	6.5	.77
Day	13	2	2	4	-4	2	1	0	34	5.9	.31
Night	68	12	41	53	18	12	5	2	171	7.0	.78

	GP	G	A	Pts	+/–	PIM	PP	SH	S	SPct	P/G
National TV	29	4	11	15	-5	8	3	0	70	5.7	.52
0 Days Rest	12	1	5	6	-4	6	0	0	36	2.8	.50
1 Days Rest	39	6	21	27	4	6	1	2	110	5.5	.69
2 Days Rest	23	5	11	16	6	2	4	0	46	10.9	.70
3+ Days Rest	7	2	6	8	8	0	1	0	13	15.4	1.14

	G	A	Pts	PIM		G	A	Pts	PIM
1st Period	6	16	22	6	Winning	5	13	18	12
2nd Period	5	16	21	6	Losing	3	13	16	2
3rd Period	3	11	14	2	Tied	6	17	23	0
Overtime	0	0	0	0	Clutch	2	5	7	0
Last 5 Min	3	7	10	0	Blowouts	1	1	2	4

Trevor Linden

New York Islanders — Center

1998-99 Season

	GP	G	A	Pts	+/–	PIM	PP	SH	S	SPct	P/G
Overall	82	18	29	47	-14	32	8	1	167	10.8	.57
Home	41	13	20	33	-3	16	7	1	97	13.4	.80
Away	41	5	9	14	-11	16	1	0	70	7.1	.34
vs. Division	20	7	11	18	-1	4	3	0	31	22.6	.90
vs. Conference	58	13	24	37	-12	20	6	1	115	11.3	.64
vs. Playoff	51	11	21	32	-14	26	5	0	98	11.2	.63
vs. Non-Playoff	31	7	8	15	0	6	3	1	69	10.1	.48
Pre All-Star	46	11	15	26	-9	20	5	1	96	11.5	.57
Post All-Star	36	7	14	21	-5	12	3	0	71	9.9	.58
Day	11	2	4	6	0	4	0	0	15	13.3	.55
Night	71	16	25	41	-14	28	8	1	152	10.5	.58

	GP	G	A	Pts	+/–	PIM	PP	SH	S	SPct	P/G
National TV	6	0	2	2	1	4	0	0	8	0.0	.33
0 Days Rest	14	3	7	10	-6	6	1	0	29	10.3	.71
1 Days Rest	37	4	12	16	-7	12	2	0	66	6.1	.43
2 Days Rest	20	6	4	10	-2	4	2	0	44	13.6	.50
3+ Days Rest	11	5	6	11	1	10	3	1	28	17.9	1.00

	G	A	Pts	PIM		G	A	Pts	PIM
1st Period	4	12	16	12	Winning	6	8	14	10
2nd Period	8	9	17	6	Losing	10	13	23	18
3rd Period	6	8	14	14	Tied	2	8	10	4
Overtime	0	0	0	0	Clutch	0	4	4	4
Last 5 Min	6	5	11	6	Blowouts	0	1	1	4

Mats Lindgren

New York Islanders — Center

1998-99 Season

	GP	G	A	Pts	+/–	PIM	PP	SH	S	SPct	P/G
Overall	60	10	15	25	6	24	3	1	83	12.0	.42
Home	25	4	3	7	2	14	0	0	33	12.1	.28
Away	35	6	12	18	4	10	3	1	50	12.0	.51
vs. Division	10	4	1	5	3	2	2	0	22	18.2	.50
vs. Conference	42	9	11	20	8	20	3	1	62	14.5	.48
vs. Playoff	36	8	11	19	6	10	3	1	58	13.8	.53
vs. Non-Playoff	24	2	4	6	0	14	0	0	25	8.0	.25
Pre All-Star	33	2	10	12	5	18	0	0	43	4.7	.36
Post All-Star	27	8	5	13	1	6	3	1	40	20.0	.48
Day	5	1	1	2	0	2	1	0	10	10.0	.40
Night	55	9	14	23	6	22	2	1	73	12.3	.42

	GP	G	A	Pts	+/–	PIM	PP	SH	S	SPct	P/G
National TV	7	1	0	1	2	2	0	0	10	10.0	.14
0 Days Rest	7	0	0	0	-4	2	0	0	4	0.0	.00
1 Days Rest	28	5	7	12	4	10	2	1	38	13.2	.43
2 Days Rest	14	2	5	7	1	10	1	0	23	8.7	.50
3+ Days Rest	11	3	3	6	5	2	0	0	18	16.7	.55

	G	A	Pts	PIM		G	A	Pts	PIM
1st Period	5	3	8	8	Winning	5	6	11	12
2nd Period	3	6	9	8	Losing	2	4	6	12
3rd Period	2	6	8	8	Tied	3	5	8	0
Overtime	0	0	0	0	Clutch	0	2	2	2
Last 5 Min	5	6	11	2	Blowouts	2	2	4	4

Eric Lindros

Philadelphia Flyers — Center

1998-99 Season

	GP	G	A	Pts	+/–	PIM	PP	SH	S	SPct	P/G
Overall	71	40	53	93	35	120	10	1	242	16.5	1.31
Home	36	23	30	53	26	58	4	0	124	18.5	1.47
Away	35	17	23	40	9	62	6	1	118	14.4	1.14
vs. Division	17	12	13	25	6	30	2	0	56	21.4	1.47
vs. Conference	49	28	34	62	21	77	6	1	169	16.6	1.27
vs. Playoff	38	27	26	53	22	68	7	1	137	19.7	1.39
vs. Non-Playoff	33	13	27	40	13	52	3	0	105	12.4	1.21
Pre All-Star	42	26	33	59	28	77	5	1	137	19.0	1.40
Post All-Star	29	14	20	34	7	43	5	0	105	13.3	1.17
Day	11	5	8	13	8	8	1	0	32	15.6	1.18
Night	60	35	45	80	27	112	9	1	210	16.7	1.33

	GP	G	A	Pts	+/–	PIM	PP	SH	S	SPct	P/G
National TV	12	8	8	16	11	20	1	0	41	19.5	1.33
0 Days Rest	11	5	4	9	2	17	1	0	37	13.5	.82
1 Days Rest	35	22	31	53	21	42	4	1	127	17.3	1.51
2 Days Rest	14	8	10	18	6	23	3	0	41	19.5	1.29
3+ Days Rest	11	5	8	13	6	38	2	0	37	13.5	1.18

	G	A	Pts	PIM		G	A	Pts	PIM
1st Period	15	11	26	46	Winning	17	18	35	45
2nd Period	10	17	27	38	Losing	14	15	29	47
3rd Period	15	24	39	34	Tied	9	20	29	28
Overtime	0	1	1	2	Clutch	3	4	7	6
Last 5 Min	9	12	21	43	Blowouts	0	5	5	14

Bill Lindsay

Florida Panthers — Left Wing

1998-99 Season

	GP	G	A	Pts	+/–	PIM	PP	SH	S	SPct	P/G
Overall	75	12	15	27	-1	92	0	1	135	8.9	.36
Home	37	8	9	17	7	34	0	1	66	12.1	.46
Away	38	4	6	10	-8	58	0	0	69	5.8	.26
vs. Division	14	3	1	4	-1	13	0	1	33	9.1	.29
vs. Conference	51	9	8	17	-3	59	0	1	96	9.4	.33
vs. Playoff	44	6	10	16	-5	36	0	1	79	7.6	.36
vs. Non-Playoff	31	6	5	11	4	56	0	0	56	10.7	.35
Pre All-Star	44	8	8	16	-3	65	0	0	90	8.9	.36
Post All-Star	31	4	7	11	2	27	0	1	45	8.9	.35
Day	4	0	2	2	0	11	0	0	10	0.0	.50
Night	71	12	13	25	-1	81	0	1	125	9.6	.35

	GP	G	A	Pts	+/–	PIM	PP	SH	S	SPct	P/G
National TV	2	0	1	1	0	0	0	0	3	0.0	.50
0 Days Rest	18	1	2	3	-1	32	0	0	27	3.7	.17
1 Days Rest	28	6	5	11	-1	36	0	0	56	10.7	.39
2 Days Rest	14	3	5	8	4	12	0	1	26	11.5	.57
3+ Days Rest	15	2	3	5	-3	12	0	0	26	7.7	.33

	G	A	Pts	PIM		G	A	Pts	PIM
1st Period	3	6	9	34	Winning	8	2	10	46
2nd Period	3	7	10	24	Losing	0	4	4	22
3rd Period	6	2	8	34	Tied	4	9	13	24
Overtime	0	0	0	0	Clutch	2	0	2	2
Last 5 Min	5	3	8	32	Blowouts	1	1	2	15

Dave Lowry

San Jose Sharks — Left Wing

1998-99 Season

	GP	G	A	Pts	+/–	PIM	PP	SH	S	SPct	P/G
Overall	61	6	9	15	-5	24	2	0	58	10.3	.25
Home	32	3	7	10	-1	14	1	0	33	9.1	.31
Away	29	3	2	5	-4	10	1	0	25	12.0	.17
vs. Division	18	2	1	3	-1	10	1	0	19	10.5	.17
vs. Conference	45	5	6	11	-4	18	2	0	41	12.2	.24
vs. Playoff	35	5	4	9	-2	20	1	0	31	16.1	.26
vs. Non-Playoff	26	1	5	6	-3	4	1	0	27	3.7	.23
Pre All-Star	31	5	5	10	2	14	1	0	28	17.9	.32
Post All-Star	30	1	4	5	-7	10	1	0	30	3.3	.17
Day	4	0	1	1	-1	4	0	0	4	0.0	.25
Night	57	6	8	14	-4	20	2	0	54	11.1	.25

	GP	G	A	Pts	+/–	PIM	PP	SH	S	SPct	P/G
National TV	9	0	1	1	-4	2	0	0	11	0.0	.11
0 Days Rest	11	2	1	3	0	8	1	0	12	16.7	.27
1 Days Rest	23	3	6	9	2	4	1	0	23	13.0	.39
2 Days Rest	9	0	0	0	-3	6	0	0	6	0.0	.00
3+ Days Rest	18	1	2	3	-4	6	0	0	17	5.9	.17

	G	A	Pts	PIM		G	A	Pts	PIM
1st Period	2	2	4	8	Winning	2	2	4	2
2nd Period	0	4	4	8	Losing	3	3	6	14
3rd Period	4	3	7	8	Tied	1	4	5	8
Overtime	0	0	0	0	Clutch	2	1	3	0
Last 5 Min	3	2	5	12	Blowouts	0	0	0	0

Jyrki Lumme

Phoenix Coyotes — Defense

1998-99 Season

	GP	G	A	Pts	+/–	PIM	PP	SH	S	SPct	P/G
Overall	60	7	21	28	5	34	1	0	121	5.8	.47
Home	26	3	9	12	2	12	1	0	52	5.8	.46
Away	34	4	12	16	3	22	0	0	69	5.8	.47
vs. Division	16	3	7	10	7	6	0	0	28	10.7	.63
vs. Conference	37	6	16	22	4	24	1	0	88	6.8	.59
vs. Playoff	34	3	11	14	6	22	0	0	62	4.8	.41
vs. Non-Playoff	26	4	10	14	-1	12	1	0	59	6.8	.54
Pre All-Star	42	3	19	22	9	28	0	0	89	3.4	.52
Post All-Star	18	4	2	6	-4	6	1	0	32	12.5	.33
Day	4	3	1	4	0	0	1	0	11	27.3	1.00
Night	56	4	20	24	5	34	0	0	110	3.6	.43

	GP	G	A	Pts	+/–	PIM	PP	SH	S	SPct	P/G
National TV	10	1	2	3	1	2	0	0	16	6.3	.30
0 Days Rest	9	1	3	4	-1	4	0	0	26	3.8	.44
1 Days Rest	28	4	8	12	4	12	1	0	51	7.8	.43
2 Days Rest	11	1	5	6	4	8	0	0	20	5.0	.55
3+ Days Rest	12	1	5	6	-2	10	0	0	24	4.2	.50

	G	A	Pts	PIM		G	A	Pts	PIM
1st Period	1	8	9	12	Winning	2	5	7	8
2nd Period	6	10	16	16	Losing	0	3	3	8
3rd Period	0	3	3	6	Tied	5	13	18	18
Overtime	0	0	0	0	Clutch	0	0	0	4
Last 5 Min	0	5	5	2	Blowouts	0	0	0	2

Al MacInnis

St. Louis Blues — Defense

1998-99 Season

	GP	G	A	Pts	+/–	PIM	PP	SH	S	SPct	P/G
Overall	82	20	42	62	33	70	11	1	314	6.4	.76
Home	41	12	23	35	18	40	6	1	156	7.7	.85
Away	41	8	19	27	15	30	5	0	158	5.1	.66
vs. Division	18	5	11	16	9	12	3	0	77	6.5	.89
vs. Conference	55	16	30	46	20	48	10	1	227	7.0	.84
vs. Playoff	46	7	26	33	6	52	6	1	162	4.3	.72
vs. Non-Playoff	36	13	16	29	27	18	5	0	152	8.6	.81
Pre All-Star	42	12	17	29	9	42	7	0	145	8.3	.69
Post All-Star	40	8	25	33	24	28	4	1	169	4.7	.83
Day	11	3	5	8	-2	10	2	0	48	6.3	.73
Night	71	17	37	54	35	60	9	1	266	6.4	.76

	GP	G	A	Pts	+/–	PIM	PP	SH	S	SPct	P/G
National TV	17	5	5	10	6	16	3	1	86	5.8	.59
0 Days Rest	12	2	6	8	-2	8	2	0	35	5.7	.67
1 Days Rest	43	13	26	39	28	28	5	1	188	6.9	.91
2 Days Rest	17	4	6	10	5	24	3	0	55	7.3	.59
3+ Days Rest	10	1	4	5	2	10	1	0	36	2.8	.50

	G	A	Pts	PIM		G	A	Pts	PIM
1st Period	10	14	24	32	Winning	11	14	25	30
2nd Period	5	15	20	30	Losing	6	16	22	28
3rd Period	5	13	18	8	Tied	3	12	15	12
Overtime	0	0	0	0	Clutch	3	2	5	6
Last 5 Min	7	12	19	30	Blowouts	0	4	4	8

John MacLean

New York Rangers — Right Wing

1998-99 Season

	GP	G	A	Pts	+/–	PIM	PP	SH	S	SPct	P/G
Overall	82	28	27	55	5	46	11	1	231	12.1	.67
Home	41	18	17	35	6	38	7	1	115	15.7	.85
Away	41	10	10	20	-1	8	4	0	116	8.6	.49
vs. Division	20	6	9	15	12	18	2	0	63	9.5	.75
vs. Conference	58	18	17	35	12	36	6	1	162	11.1	.60
vs. Playoff	52	15	15	30	6	26	6	0	144	10.4	.58
vs. Non-Playoff	30	13	12	25	-1	20	5	1	87	14.9	.83
Pre All-Star	45	16	10	26	-3	28	7	1	121	13.2	.58
Post All-Star	37	12	17	29	8	18	4	0	110	10.9	.78
Day	12	3	8	11	5	6	0	1	36	8.3	.92
Night	70	25	19	44	0	40	11	0	195	12.8	.63

	GP	G	A	Pts	+/–	PIM	PP	SH	S	SPct	P/G
National TV	23	6	13	19	4	8	3	0	70	8.6	.83
0 Days Rest	16	4	4	8	1	0	1	0	46	8.7	.50
1 Days Rest	34	13	14	27	3	12	5	0	91	14.3	.79
2 Days Rest	20	9	7	16	0	26	4	1	56	16.1	.80
3+ Days Rest	12	2	2	4	1	8	1	0	38	5.3	.33

	G	A	Pts	PIM		G	A	Pts	PIM
1st Period	10	4	14	8	Winning	11	10	21	26
2nd Period	11	9	20	28	Losing	6	7	13	16
3rd Period	7	11	18	10	Tied	11	10	21	4
Overtime	0	3	3	0	Clutch	4	7	11	0
Last 5 Min	9	4	13	4	Blowouts	1	2	3	2

Jamie Macoun

Detroit Red Wings — Defense

1998-99 Season

	GP	G	A	Pts	+/–	PIM	PP	SH	S	SPct	P/G
Overall	69	1	10	11	-1	36	0	0	62	1.6	.16
Home	35	1	5	6	-5	18	0	0	39	2.6	.17
Away	34	0	5	5	4	18	0	0	23	0.0	.15
vs. Division	13	0	3	3	-2	10	0	0	16	0.0	.23
vs. Conference	46	0	6	6	-2	24	0	0	44	0.0	.13
vs. Playoff	39	0	3	3	-8	20	0	0	31	0.0	.08
vs. Non-Playoff	30	1	7	8	7	16	0	0	31	3.2	.27
Pre All-Star	43	1	5	6	-10	28	0	0	39	2.6	.14
Post All-Star	26	0	5	5	9	8	0	0	23	0.0	.19
Day	11	0	2	2	3	0	0	0	10	0.0	.18
Night	58	1	8	9	-4	36	0	0	52	1.9	.16

	GP	G	A	Pts	+/–	PIM	PP	SH	S	SPct	P/G
National TV	26	0	3	3	-2	10	0	0	21	0.0	.12
0 Days Rest	9	0	0	0	-6	10	0	0	5	0.0	.00
1 Days Rest	29	1	4	5	8	12	0	0	33	3.0	.17
2 Days Rest	19	0	2	2	-5	8	0	0	15	0.0	.11
3+ Days Rest	12	0	4	4	2	6	0	0	9	0.0	.33

	G	A	Pts	PIM		G	A	Pts	PIM
1st Period	0	3	3	10	Winning	1	5	6	28
2nd Period	1	1	2	18	Losing	0	3	3	8
3rd Period	0	6	6	8	Tied	0	2	2	0
Overtime	0	0	0	0	Clutch	0	1	1	2
Last 5 Min	0	2	2	12	Blowouts	0	4	4	12

Vladimir Malakhov

Montreal Canadiens — Defense

1998-99 Season

	GP	G	A	Pts	+/–	PIM	PP	SH	S	SPct	P/G
Overall	62	13	21	34	-7	77	8	0	143	9.1	.55
Home	33	9	15	24	-1	24	5	0	75	12.0	.73
Away	29	4	6	10	-6	53	3	0	68	5.9	.34
vs. Division	14	4	4	8	-8	20	2	0	31	12.9	.57
vs. Conference	42	9	19	28	-7	63	5	0	98	9.2	.67
vs. Playoff	38	9	11	20	-17	61	6	0	89	10.1	.53
vs. Non-Playoff	24	4	10	14	10	16	2	0	54	7.4	.58
Pre All-Star	38	8	12	20	0	55	4	0	82	9.8	.53
Post All-Star	24	5	9	14	-7	22	4	0	61	8.2	.58
Day	3	0	1	1	-6	0	0	0	6	0.0	.33
Night	59	13	20	33	-1	77	8	0	137	9.5	.56

	GP	G	A	Pts	+/–	PIM	PP	SH	S	SPct	P/G
National TV	20	5	9	14	-9	16	3	0	50	10.0	.70
0 Days Rest	11	3	5	8	-8	12	2	0	35	8.6	.73
1 Days Rest	25	7	6	13	-3	24	3	0	57	12.3	.52
2 Days Rest	14	1	7	8	8	35	1	0	29	3.4	.57
3+ Days Rest	12	2	3	5	-4	6	2	0	22	9.1	.42

	G	A	Pts	PIM		G	A	Pts	PIM
1st Period	5	4	9	12	Winning	2	7	9	20
2nd Period	6	11	17	30	Losing	4	8	12	45
3rd Period	2	6	8	35	Tied	7	6	13	12
Overtime	0	0	0	0	Clutch	0	0	0	17
Last 5 Min	8	7	15	25	Blowouts	0	2	2	8

Manny Malhotra

New York Rangers — Center

1998-99 Season

	GP	G	A	Pts	+/–	PIM	PP	SH	S	SPct	P/G
Overall	73	8	8	16	-2	13	1	0	61	13.1	.22
Home	37	2	2	4	-2	11	0	0	39	5.1	.11
Away	36	6	6	12	0	2	1	0	22	27.3	.33
vs. Division	15	1	4	5	0	2	1	0	11	9.1	.33
vs. Conference	50	4	8	12	0	4	1	0	42	9.5	.24
vs. Playoff	43	3	3	6	-5	6	0	0	31	9.7	.14
vs. Non-Playoff	30	5	5	10	3	7	1	0	30	16.7	.33
Pre All-Star	37	5	2	7	-2	9	0	0	26	19.2	.19
Post All-Star	36	3	6	9	0	4	1	0	35	8.6	.25
Day	10	1	1	2	-2	4	1	0	8	12.5	.20
Night	63	7	7	14	0	9	0	0	53	13.2	.22

	GP	G	A	Pts	+/–	PIM	PP	SH	S	SPct	P/G
National TV	19	2	3	5	0	2	1	0	21	9.5	.26
0 Days Rest	11	1	2	3	-1	0	0	0	10	10.0	.27
1 Days Rest	32	1	5	6	-4	4	1	0	27	3.7	.19
2 Days Rest	17	4	1	5	5	7	0	0	12	33.3	.29
3+ Days Rest	13	2	0	2	-2	2	0	0	12	16.7	.15

	G	A	Pts	PIM		G	A	Pts	PIM
1st Period	6	3	9	6	Winning	1	4	5	7
2nd Period	0	0	0	5	Losing	4	3	7	2
3rd Period	2	5	7	2	Tied	3	1	4	4
Overtime	0	0	0	0	Clutch	0	2	2	0
Last 5 Min	2	3	5	5	Blowouts	1	1	2	0

Marek Malik

Carolina Hurricanes — Defense

1998-99 Season

	GP	G	A	Pts	+/–	PIM	PP	SH	S	SPct	P/G
Overall	52	2	9	11	-6	36	1	0	36	5.6	.21
Home	26	1	5	6	-3	14	0	0	21	4.8	.23
Away	26	1	4	5	-3	22	1	0	15	6.7	.19
vs. Division	12	1	0	1	1	18	0	0	14	7.1	.08
vs. Conference	40	2	6	8	-5	32	1	0	29	6.9	.20
vs. Playoff	28	1	6	7	-4	12	1	0	18	5.6	.25
vs. Non-Playoff	24	1	3	4	-2	24	0	0	18	5.6	.17
Pre All-Star	16	0	3	3	-6	10	0	0	14	0.0	.19
Post All-Star	36	2	6	8	0	26	1	0	22	9.1	.22
Day	5	0	2	2	1	2	0	0	5	0.0	.40
Night	47	2	7	9	-7	34	1	0	31	6.5	.19

	GP	G	A	Pts	+/–	PIM	PP	SH	S	SPct	P/G
National TV	2	1	0	1	0	0	1	0	3	33.3	.50
0 Days Rest	9	1	3	4	-4	6	0	0	5	20.0	.44
1 Days Rest	22	1	4	5	-4	18	1	0	15	6.7	.23
2 Days Rest	12	0	1	1	-3	6	0	0	8	0.0	.08
3+ Days Rest	9	0	1	1	5	6	0	0	8	0.0	.11

	G	A	Pts	PIM		G	A	Pts	PIM
1st Period	0	3	3	14	Winning	0	3	3	20
2nd Period	1	4	5	18	Losing	2	2	4	8
3rd Period	1	2	3	4	Tied	0	4	4	8
Overtime	0	0	0	0	Clutch	0	0	0	4
Last 5 Min	0	2	2	10	Blowouts	0	0	0	0

Kirk Maltby

Detroit Red Wings — Right Wing

1998-99 Season

	GP	G	A	Pts	+/–	PIM	PP	SH	S	SPct	P/G
Overall	53	8	6	14	-6	34	0	1	76	10.5	.26
Home	26	3	4	7	-7	16	0	1	33	9.1	.27
Away	27	5	2	7	1	18	0	0	43	11.6	.26
vs. Division	11	3	3	6	4	8	0	0	11	27.3	.55
vs. Conference	33	5	5	10	-3	28	0	0	44	11.4	.30
vs. Playoff	28	2	4	6	-3	18	0	0	44	4.5	.21
vs. Non-Playoff	25	6	2	8	-3	16	0	1	32	18.8	.32
Pre All-Star	22	3	4	7	-2	16	0	0	25	12.0	.32
Post All-Star	31	5	2	7	-4	18	0	1	51	9.8	.23
Day	8	1	0	1	-1	8	0	0	15	6.7	.13
Night	45	7	6	13	-5	26	0	1	61	11.5	.29

	GP	G	A	Pts	+/–	PIM	PP	SH	S	SPct	P/G
National TV	20	2	1	3	-4	12	0	0	34	5.9	.15
0 Days Rest	6	0	0	0	0	4	0	0	11	0.0	.00
1 Days Rest	26	5	2	7	-8	16	0	1	44	11.4	.27
2 Days Rest	12	1	3	4	0	8	0	0	10	10.0	.33
3+ Days Rest	9	2	1	3	2	6	0	0	11	18.2	.33

	G	A	Pts	PIM		G	A	Pts	PIM
1st Period	4	4	8	10	Winning	2	4	6	18
2nd Period	3	2	5	8	Losing	1	0	1	12
3rd Period	1	0	1	16	Tied	5	2	7	4
Overtime	0	0	0	0	Clutch	0	0	0	6
Last 5 Min	3	1	4	12	Blowouts	1	0	1	2

Kent Manderville

Carolina Hurricanes — Left Wing

1998-99 Season

	GP	G	A	Pts	+/–	PIM	PP	SH	S	SPct	P/G
Overall	81	5	11	16	9	38	0	0	71	7.0	.20
Home	40	2	8	10	4	14	0	0	36	5.6	.25
Away	41	3	3	6	5	24	0	0	35	8.6	.15
vs. Division	15	1	0	1	1	12	0	0	13	7.7	.07
vs. Conference	59	3	8	11	8	30	0	0	52	5.8	.19
vs. Playoff	44	2	7	9	5	10	0	0	34	5.9	.20
vs. Non-Playoff	37	3	4	7	4	28	0	0	37	8.1	.19
Pre All-Star	44	3	7	10	8	20	0	0	38	7.9	.23
Post All-Star	37	2	4	6	1	18	0	0	33	6.1	.16
Day	7	0	0	0	-1	0	0	0	7	0.0	.00
Night	74	5	11	16	10	38	0	0	64	7.8	.22

	GP	G	A	Pts	+/–	PIM	PP	SH	S	SPct	P/G
National TV	2	1	0	1	1	0	0	0	4	25.0	.50
0 Days Rest	17	2	0	2	-1	4	0	0	14	14.3	.12
1 Days Rest	32	2	7	9	7	20	0	0	21	9.5	.28
2 Days Rest	22	1	4	5	2	10	0	0	29	3.4	.23
3+ Days Rest	10	0	0	0	1	4	0	0	7	0.0	.00

	G	A	Pts	PIM		G	A	Pts	PIM
1st Period	1	6	7	16	Winning	2	3	5	22
2nd Period	2	2	4	12	Losing	1	5	6	12
3rd Period	2	3	5	10	Tied	2	3	5	4
Overtime	0	0	0	0	Clutch	0	0	0	4
Last 5 Min	0	3	3	8	Blowouts	0	1	1	0

Mike Maneluk

New York Rangers — Right Wing

1998-99 Season

	GP	G	A	Pts	+/–	PIM	PP	SH	S	SPct	P/G
Overall	45	6	9	15	5	20	1	0	55	10.9	.33
Home	19	2	5	7	3	10	1	0	26	7.7	.37
Away	26	4	4	8	2	10	0	0	29	13.8	.31
vs. Division	12	3	3	6	-1	2	0	0	18	16.7	.50
vs. Conference	37	3	8	11	2	12	0	0	47	6.4	.30
vs. Playoff	25	2	6	8	4	6	0	0	30	6.7	.32
vs. Non-Playoff	20	4	3	7	1	14	1	0	25	16.0	.35
Pre All-Star	36	6	8	14	8	16	1	0	49	12.2	.39
Post All-Star	9	0	1	1	-3	4	0	0	6	0.0	.11
Day	5	0	1	1	0	4	0	0	5	0.0	.20
Night	40	6	8	14	5	16	1	0	50	12.0	.35

	GP	G	A	Pts	+/–	PIM	PP	SH	S	SPct	P/G
National TV	7	0	1	1	1	2	0	0	4	0.0	.14
0 Days Rest	7	0	3	3	1	4	0	0	7	0.0	.43
1 Days Rest	14	2	5	7	3	4	0	0	15	13.3	.50
2 Days Rest	5	2	0	2	2	0	0	0	5	40.0	.40
3+ Days Rest	19	2	1	3	-1	12	1	0	28	7.1	.16

	G	A	Pts	PIM		G	A	Pts	PIM
1st Period	2	1	3	14	Winning	2	2	4	6
2nd Period	1	2	3	0	Losing	2	6	8	8
3rd Period	3	6	9	6	Tied	2	1	3	6
Overtime	0	0	0	0	Clutch	0	1	1	0
Last 5 Min	1	1	2	14	Blowouts	0	0	0	0

Dave Manson

Chicago Blackhawks — Defense

1998-99 Season

	GP	G	A	Pts	+/–	PIM	PP	SH	S	SPct	P/G
Overall	75	6	17	23	1	155	2	0	145	4.1	.31
Home	39	4	10	14	10	85	1	0	66	6.1	.36
Away	36	2	7	9	-9	70	1	0	79	2.5	.25
vs. Division	18	0	5	5	-1	39	0	0	35	0.0	.28
vs. Conference	53	2	10	12	3	123	1	0	105	1.9	.23
vs. Playoff	47	4	10	14	-6	112	1	0	91	4.4	.30
vs. Non-Playoff	28	2	7	9	7	43	1	0	54	3.7	.32
Pre All-Star	39	2	11	13	-4	78	2	0	73	2.7	.33
Post All-Star	36	4	6	10	5	77	0	0	72	5.6	.28
Day	10	2	1	3	-5	30	0	0	25	8.0	.30
Night	65	4	16	20	6	125	2	0	120	3.3	.31

	GP	G	A	Pts	+/–	PIM	PP	SH	S	SPct	P/G
National TV	21	2	9	11	3	36	0	0	37	5.4	.52
0 Days Rest	14	2	2	4	3	36	1	0	29	6.9	.29
1 Days Rest	32	1	8	9	-6	59	0	0	61	1.6	.28
2 Days Rest	14	2	2	4	2	27	0	0	21	9.5	.29
3+ Days Rest	15	1	5	6	2	33	1	0	34	2.9	.40

	G	A	Pts	PIM		G	A	Pts	PIM
1st Period	3	4	7	56	Winning	1	4	5	65
2nd Period	2	6	8	61	Losing	1	8	9	73
3rd Period	1	7	8	38	Tied	4	5	9	17
Overtime	0	0	0	0	Clutch	0	0	0	6
Last 5 Min	2	4	6	36	Blowouts	0	1	1	38

Todd Marchant

Edmonton Oilers — Center

1998-99 Season

	GP	G	A	Pts	+/–	PIM	PP	SH	S	SPct	P/G
Overall	82	14	22	36	3	65	3	1	183	7.7	.44
Home	41	6	12	18	3	41	1	1	94	6.4	.44
Away	41	8	10	18	0	24	2	0	89	9.0	.44
vs. Division	18	3	7	10	7	10	1	0	39	7.7	.56
vs. Conference	55	9	16	25	2	38	2	0	115	7.8	.45
vs. Playoff	47	11	11	22	-2	35	2	1	103	10.7	.47
vs. Non-Playoff	35	3	11	14	5	30	1	0	80	3.8	.40
Pre All-Star	44	6	10	16	-1	18	1	0	97	6.2	.36
Post All-Star	38	8	12	20	4	47	2	1	86	9.3	.53
Day	4	0	1	1	0	0	0	0	0	–	.25
Night	78	14	21	35	3	65	3	1	183	7.7	.45

	GP	G	A	Pts	+/–	PIM	PP	SH	S	SPct	P/G
National TV	13	1	6	7	8	8	0	0	27	3.7	.54
0 Days Rest	14	2	4	6	2	4	1	0	35	5.7	.43
1 Days Rest	40	6	10	16	-5	24	1	0	88	6.8	.40
2 Days Rest	16	3	5	8	6	23	0	1	36	8.3	.50
3+ Days Rest	12	3	3	6	0	14	1	0	24	12.5	.50

	G	A	Pts	PIM		G	A	Pts	PIM
1st Period	4	5	9	16	Winning	6	7	13	16
2nd Period	5	7	12	39	Losing	5	7	12	41
3rd Period	5	10	15	10	Tied	3	8	11	8
Overtime	0	0	0	0	Clutch	3	4	7	6
Last 5 Min	6	6	12	25	Blowouts	1	1	2	2

Daniil Markov

Toronto Maple Leafs — Defense

1998-99 Season

	GP	G	A	Pts	+/–	PIM	PP	SH	S	SPct	P/G
Overall	57	4	8	12	5	47	0	0	34	11.8	.21
Home	25	2	5	7	5	8	0	0	23	8.7	.28
Away	32	2	3	5	0	39	0	0	11	18.2	.16
vs. Division	16	2	2	4	1	2	0	0	8	25.0	.25
vs. Conference	40	2	5	7	-1	29	0	0	23	8.7	.18
vs. Playoff	33	2	4	6	8	35	0	0	16	12.5	.18
vs. Non-Playoff	24	2	4	6	-3	12	0	0	18	11.1	.25
Pre All-Star	27	2	1	3	0	14	0	0	11	18.2	.11
Post All-Star	30	2	7	9	5	33	0	0	23	8.7	.30
Day	0	0	0	0	0	0	0	0	0	–	–
Night	57	4	8	12	5	47	0	0	34	11.8	.21

	GP	G	A	Pts	+/–	PIM	PP	SH	S	SPct	P/G
National TV	20	2	2	4	1	6	0	0	13	15.4	.20
0 Days Rest	10	1	2	3	0	8	0	0	8	12.5	.30
1 Days Rest	23	1	4	5	3	27	0	0	13	7.7	.22
2 Days Rest	9	1	1	2	1	4	0	0	3	33.3	.22
3+ Days Rest	15	1	1	2	1	8	0	0	10	10.0	.13

	G	A	Pts	PIM		G	A	Pts	PIM
1st Period	0	4	4	10	Winning	0	4	4	43
2nd Period	3	3	6	25	Losing	2	1	3	4
3rd Period	1	1	2	12	Tied	2	3	5	0
Overtime	0	0	0	0	Clutch	1	1	2	2
Last 5 Min	1	4	5	23	Blowouts	0	0	0	27

Patrick Marleau

San Jose Sharks — Center

1998-99 Season

	GP	G	A	Pts	+/–	PIM	PP	SH	S	SPct	P/G
Overall	81	21	24	45	10	24	4	0	134	15.7	.56
Home	41	15	9	24	9	16	3	0	75	20.0	.59
Away	40	6	15	21	1	8	1	0	59	10.2	.53
vs. Division	24	5	8	13	-2	6	3	0	38	13.2	.54
vs. Conference	57	16	16	32	2	18	4	0	100	16.0	.56
vs. Playoff	48	11	12	23	1	8	3	0	73	15.1	.48
vs. Non-Playoff	33	10	12	22	9	16	1	0	61	16.4	.67
Pre All-Star	45	11	11	22	3	14	3	0	62	17.7	.49
Post All-Star	36	10	13	23	7	10	1	0	72	13.9	.64
Day	7	1	0	1	-1	4	0	0	10	10.0	.14
Night	74	20	24	44	11	20	4	0	124	16.1	.59

	GP	G	A	Pts	+/–	PIM	PP	SH	S	SPct	P/G
National TV	11	4	2	6	-3	4	3	0	22	18.2	.55
0 Days Rest	13	4	4	8	4	6	1	0	23	17.4	.62
1 Days Rest	42	6	16	22	4	12	0	0	50	12.0	.52
2 Days Rest	15	8	3	11	5	6	2	0	34	23.5	.73
3+ Days Rest	11	3	1	4	-3	0	1	0	27	11.1	.36

	G	A	Pts	PIM		G	A	Pts	PIM
1st Period	9	7	16	8	Winning	7	6	13	10
2nd Period	7	8	15	8	Losing	4	7	11	12
3rd Period	5	9	14	8	Tied	10	11	21	2
Overtime	0	0	0	0	Clutch	1	2	3	0
Last 5 Min	3	4	7	4	Blowouts	1	1	2	4

Grant Marshall

Dallas Stars — Right Wing

1998-99 Season

	GP	G	A	Pts	+/–	PIM	PP	SH	S	SPct	P/G
Overall	82	13	18	31	1	85	2	0	112	11.6	.38
Home	41	8	12	20	3	33	1	0	53	15.1	.49
Away	41	5	6	11	-2	52	1	0	59	8.5	.27
vs. Division	24	3	6	9	1	33	0	0	32	9.4	.38
vs. Conference	56	9	12	21	-1	59	1	0	70	12.9	.38
vs. Playoff	48	8	11	19	0	58	1	0	55	14.5	.40
vs. Non-Playoff	34	5	7	12	1	27	1	0	57	8.8	.35
Pre All-Star	43	8	9	17	5	42	0	0	51	15.7	.40
Post All-Star	39	5	9	14	-4	43	2	0	61	8.2	.36
Day	10	1	1	2	-2	10	0	0	8	12.5	.20
Night	72	12	17	29	3	75	2	0	104	11.5	.40

	GP	G	A	Pts	+/–	PIM	PP	SH	S	SPct	P/G
National TV	14	2	3	5	-1	11	0	0	14	14.3	.36
0 Days Rest	15	2	2	4	-7	14	1	0	21	9.5	.27
1 Days Rest	44	7	7	14	2	43	1	0	64	10.9	.32
2 Days Rest	13	4	5	9	5	21	0	0	18	22.2	.69
3+ Days Rest	10	0	4	4	1	7	0	0	9	0.0	.40

	G	A	Pts	PIM		G	A	Pts	PIM
1st Period	7	5	12	28	Winning	10	10	20	61
2nd Period	4	7	11	31	Losing	0	2	2	12
3rd Period	2	6	8	26	Tied	3	6	9	12
Overtime	0	0	0	0	Clutch	0	2	2	2
Last 5 Min	4	3	7	25	Blowouts	1	0	1	14

Stephane Matteau

San Jose Sharks — Left Wing

1998-99 Season

	GP	G	A	Pts	+/–	PIM	PP	SH	S	SPct	P/G
Overall	68	8	15	23	2	73	0	0	72	11.1	.34
Home	31	4	7	11	5	34	0	0	32	12.5	.35
Away	37	4	8	12	-3	39	0	0	40	10.0	.32
vs. Division	21	2	7	9	0	10	0	0	27	7.4	.43
vs. Conference	48	5	12	17	2	40	0	0	55	9.1	.35
vs. Playoff	40	6	10	16	1	36	0	0	35	17.1	.40
vs. Non-Playoff	28	2	5	7	1	37	0	0	37	5.4	.25
Pre All-Star	36	4	10	14	4	45	0	0	33	12.1	.39
Post All-Star	32	4	5	9	-2	28	0	0	39	10.3	.28
Day	6	1	1	2	0	13	0	0	6	16.7	.33
Night	62	7	14	21	2	60	0	0	66	10.6	.34

	GP	G	A	Pts	+/–	PIM	PP	SH	S	SPct	P/G
National TV	11	1	1	2	2	27	0	0	12	8.3	.18
0 Days Rest	11	0	2	2	3	2	0	0	9	0.0	.18
1 Days Rest	32	7	5	12	2	44	0	0	42	16.7	.38
2 Days Rest	10	0	3	3	-2	17	0	0	7	0.0	.30
3+ Days Rest	15	1	5	6	-1	10	0	0	14	7.1	.40

	G	A	Pts	PIM		G	A	Pts	PIM
1st Period	2	5	7	33	Winning	3	5	8	37
2nd Period	0	4	4	23	Losing	4	5	9	21
3rd Period	6	6	12	17	Tied	1	5	6	15
Overtime	0	0	0	0	Clutch	1	5	6	4
Last 5 Min	2	6	8	40	Blowouts	0	0	0	11

Richard Matvichuk

Dallas Stars — Defense

1998-99 Season

	GP	G	A	Pts	+/–	PIM	PP	SH	S	SPct	P/G
Overall	64	3	9	12	23	51	1	0	54	5.6	.19
Home	34	2	8	10	8	35	1	0	29	6.9	.29
Away	30	1	1	2	15	16	0	0	25	4.0	.07
vs. Division	16	0	3	3	8	23	0	0	12	0.0	.19
vs. Conference	43	2	7	9	10	37	1	0	32	6.3	.21
vs. Playoff	37	1	5	6	16	20	0	0	28	3.6	.16
vs. Non-Playoff	27	2	4	6	7	31	1	0	26	7.7	.22
Pre All-Star	41	3	7	10	14	22	1	0	29	10.3	.24
Post All-Star	23	0	2	2	9	29	0	0	25	0.0	.09
Day	5	0	0	0	2	21	0	0	5	0.0	.00
Night	59	3	9	12	21	30	1	0	49	6.1	.20

	GP	G	A	Pts	+/–	PIM	PP	SH	S	SPct	P/G
National TV	10	0	1	1	2	21	0	0	6	0.0	.10
0 Days Rest	10	0	2	2	5	10	0	0	5	0.0	.20
1 Days Rest	34	1	4	5	13	33	0	0	36	2.8	.15
2 Days Rest	8	1	1	2	7	6	0	0	3	33.3	.25
3+ Days Rest	12	1	2	3	-2	2	1	0	10	10.0	.25

	G	A	Pts	PIM		G	A	Pts	PIM
1st Period	0	2	2	20	Winning	1	4	5	41
2nd Period	1	6	7	10	Losing	1	3	4	2
3rd Period	2	1	3	21	Tied	1	2	3	8
Overtime	0	0	0	0	Clutch	1	0	1	17
Last 5 Min	1	3	4	29	Blowouts	0	1	1	4

Brad May

Vancouver Canucks — Left Wing

1998-99 Season

	GP	G	A	Pts	+/–	PIM	PP	SH	S	SPct	P/G
Overall	66	6	11	17	-14	102	1	0	91	6.6	.26
Home	32	3	7	10	-6	52	1	0	38	7.9	.31
Away	34	3	4	7	-8	50	0	0	53	5.7	.21
vs. Division	12	0	4	4	-3	38	0	0	14	0.0	.33
vs. Conference	42	2	8	10	-11	81	0	0	58	3.4	.24
vs. Playoff	45	4	7	11	-11	55	1	0	68	5.9	.24
vs. Non-Playoff	21	2	4	6	-3	47	0	0	23	8.7	.29
Pre All-Star	39	2	11	13	-8	67	1	0	52	3.8	.33
Post All-Star	27	4	0	4	-6	35	0	0	39	10.3	.15
Day	3	1	1	2	-2	0	0	0	5	20.0	.67
Night	63	5	10	15	-12	102	1	0	86	5.8	.24

	GP	G	A	Pts	+/–	PIM	PP	SH	S	SPct	P/G
National TV	16	3	2	5	-3	35	1	0	21	14.3	.31
0 Days Rest	9	1	3	4	0	5	0	0	12	8.3	.44
1 Days Rest	35	3	2	5	-13	54	0	0	51	5.9	.14
2 Days Rest	15	2	5	7	3	24	1	0	19	10.5	.47
3+ Days Rest	7	0	1	1	-4	19	0	0	9	0.0	.14

	G	A	Pts	PIM		G	A	Pts	PIM
1st Period	3	4	7	14	Winning	2	2	4	22
2nd Period	0	5	5	42	Losing	1	3	4	74
3rd Period	3	2	5	46	Tied	3	6	9	6
Overtime	0	0	0	0	Clutch	0	1	1	12
Last 5 Min	2	4	6	27	Blowouts	0	1	1	41

Dean McAmmond

Chicago Blackhawks — Center

1998-99 Season

	GP	G	A	Pts	+/–	PIM	PP	SH	S	SPct	P/G
Overall	77	10	20	30	8	38	1	0	138	7.2	.39
Home	36	6	10	16	8	12	0	0	70	8.6	.44
Away	41	4	10	14	0	26	1	0	68	5.9	.34
vs. Division	13	1	4	5	1	2	0	0	22	4.5	.38
vs. Conference	47	7	14	21	4	28	1	0	83	8.4	.45
vs. Playoff	46	7	12	19	10	24	1	0	86	8.1	.41
vs. Non-Playoff	31	3	8	11	-2	14	0	0	52	5.8	.35
Pre All-Star	41	7	9	16	4	26	1	0	77	9.1	.39
Post All-Star	36	3	11	14	4	12	0	0	61	4.9	.39
Day	6	1	1	2	2	0	0	0	10	10.0	.33
Night	71	9	19	28	6	38	1	0	128	7.0	.39

	GP	G	A	Pts	+/–	PIM	PP	SH	S	SPct	P/G
National TV	14	2	3	5	2	6	0	0	23	8.7	.36
0 Days Rest	13	2	2	4	1	10	1	0	16	12.5	.31
1 Days Rest	31	4	8	12	8	14	0	0	61	6.6	.39
2 Days Rest	18	1	3	4	0	12	0	0	32	3.1	.22
3+ Days Rest	15	3	7	10	-1	2	0	0	29	10.3	.67

	G	A	Pts	PIM		G	A	Pts	PIM
1st Period	3	6	9	12	Winning	5	10	15	22
2nd Period	2	8	10	18	Losing	2	3	5	14
3rd Period	5	6	11	8	Tied	3	7	10	2
Overtime	0	0	0	0	Clutch	2	1	3	2
Last 5 Min	5	4	9	8	Blowouts	0	2	2	2

Bryan McCabe

Vancouver Canucks — Defense

1998-99 Season

	GP	G	A	Pts	+/–	PIM	PP	SH	S	SPct	P/G
Overall	69	7	14	21	-11	120	1	2	98	7.1	.30
Home	34	5	7	12	-2	66	0	1	44	11.4	.35
Away	35	2	7	9	-9	54	1	1	54	3.7	.26
vs. Division	16	2	2	4	-1	42	0	1	27	7.4	.25
vs. Conference	49	7	8	15	-12	97	1	2	71	9.9	.31
vs. Playoff	48	6	11	17	-3	78	1	1	65	9.2	.35
vs. Non-Playoff	21	1	3	4	-8	42	0	1	33	3.0	.19
Pre All-Star	32	4	6	10	-7	68	1	1	37	10.8	.31
Post All-Star	37	3	8	11	-4	52	0	1	61	4.9	.30
Day	2	0	1	1	-2	2	0	0	4	0.0	.50
Night	67	7	13	20	-9	118	1	2	94	7.4	.30

	GP	G	A	Pts	+/–	PIM	PP	SH	S	SPct	P/G
National TV	18	1	3	4	-4	19	0	1	25	4.0	.22
0 Days Rest	11	3	2	5	-1	36	0	1	18	16.7	.45
1 Days Rest	40	3	10	13	-10	57	1	1	47	6.4	.33
2 Days Rest	12	1	1	2	5	21	0	0	19	5.3	.17
3+ Days Rest	6	0	1	1	-5	6	0	0	14	0.0	.17

	G	A	Pts	PIM		G	A	Pts	PIM
1st Period	2	4	6	40	Winning	2	2	4	42
2nd Period	4	4	8	43	Losing	2	8	10	64
3rd Period	1	6	7	37	Tied	3	4	7	14
Overtime	0	0	0	0	Clutch	0	1	1	6
Last 5 Min	2	3	5	49	Blowouts	0	1	1	26

Sandy McCarthy

Philadelphia Flyers — Right Wing

1998-99 Season

	GP	G	A	Pts	+/–	PIM	PP	SH	S	SPct	P/G
Overall	80	5	8	13	-24	160	1	0	107	4.7	.16
Home	41	3	6	9	-7	101	1	0	63	4.8	.22
Away	39	2	2	4	-17	59	0	0	44	4.5	.10
vs. Division	15	0	1	1	-6	23	0	0	19	0.0	.07
vs. Conference	56	4	5	9	-19	110	1	0	80	5.0	.16
vs. Playoff	51	3	7	10	-13	112	0	0	72	4.2	.20
vs. Non-Playoff	29	2	1	3	-11	48	1	0	35	5.7	.10
Pre All-Star	44	4	4	8	-18	96	1	0	53	7.5	.18
Post All-Star	36	1	4	5	-6	64	0	0	54	1.9	.14
Day	8	0	1	1	-2	18	0	0	9	0.0	.13
Night	72	5	7	12	-22	142	1	0	98	5.1	.17

	GP	G	A	Pts	+/–	PIM	PP	SH	S	SPct	P/G
National TV	8	0	0	0	-2	7	0	0	12	0.0	.00
0 Days Rest	15	0	1	1	-7	31	0	0	18	0.0	.07
1 Days Rest	34	3	6	9	-4	58	0	0	60	5.0	.26
2 Days Rest	17	1	1	2	-5	32	1	0	20	5.0	.12
3+ Days Rest	14	1	0	1	-8	39	0	0	9	11.1	.07

	G	A	Pts	PIM		G	A	Pts	PIM
1st Period	2	4	6	56	Winning	2	0	2	28
2nd Period	2	1	3	40	Losing	2	4	6	130
3rd Period	1	3	4	64	Tied	1	4	5	2
Overtime	0	0	0	0	Clutch	0	1	1	21
Last 5 Min	1	3	4	54	Blowouts	0	0	0	52

Darren McCarty

Detroit Red Wings — Right Wing

1998-99 Season

	GP	G	A	Pts	+/–	PIM	PP	SH	S	SPct	P/G
Overall	69	14	26	40	10	108	6	0	140	10.0	.58
Home	33	10	16	26	9	68	4	0	63	15.9	.79
Away	36	4	10	14	1	40	2	0	77	5.2	.39
vs. Division	16	3	10	13	9	13	1	0	34	8.8	.81
vs. Conference	47	8	23	31	15	75	4	0	97	8.2	.66
vs. Playoff	39	6	14	20	-8	60	3	0	69	8.7	.51
vs. Non-Playoff	30	8	12	20	18	48	3	0	71	11.3	.67
Pre All-Star	46	12	23	35	9	71	5	0	96	12.5	.76
Post All-Star	23	2	3	5	1	37	1	0	44	4.5	.22
Day	8	1	3	4	0	8	1	0	11	9.1	.50
Night	61	13	23	36	10	100	5	0	129	10.1	.59

	GP	G	A	Pts	+/–	PIM	PP	SH	S	SPct	P/G
National TV	22	3	8	11	3	21	2	0	34	8.8	.50
0 Days Rest	11	0	1	1	-3	7	0	0	27	0.0	.09
1 Days Rest	29	6	9	15	6	70	4	0	55	10.9	.52
2 Days Rest	20	5	12	17	4	22	2	0	42	11.9	.85
3+ Days Rest	9	3	4	7	3	9	0	0	16	18.8	.78

	G	A	Pts	PIM		G	A	Pts	PIM
1st Period	4	6	10	32	Winning	7	12	19	58
2nd Period	5	13	18	25	Losing	3	5	8	44
3rd Period	5	7	12	51	Tied	4	9	13	6
Overtime	0	0	0	0	Clutch	1	2	3	11
Last 5 Min	1	8	9	40	Blowouts	2	2	4	21

Alyn McCauley

Toronto Maple Leafs — Center

1998-99 Season

	GP	G	A	Pts	+/–	PIM	PP	SH	S	SPct	P/G
Overall	39	9	15	24	7	2	1	0	76	11.8	.62
Home	24	7	9	16	8	2	1	0	48	14.6	.67
Away	15	2	6	8	-1	0	0	0	28	7.1	.53
vs. Division	9	0	2	2	-5	0	0	0	12	0.0	.22
vs. Conference	23	5	9	14	1	0	1	0	49	10.2	.61
vs. Playoff	22	4	4	8	-1	2	0	0	38	10.5	.36
vs. Non-Playoff	17	5	11	16	8	0	1	0	38	13.2	.94
Pre All-Star	35	7	15	22	4	2	1	0	64	10.9	.63
Post All-Star	4	2	0	2	3	0	0	0	12	16.7	.50
Day	1	0	0	0	0	0	0	0	1	0.0	.00
Night	38	9	15	24	7	2	1	0	75	12.0	.63

	GP	G	A	Pts	+/–	PIM	PP	SH	S	SPct	P/G
National TV	13	3	7	10	4	0	1	0	31	9.7	.77
0 Days Rest	9	0	5	5	1	0	0	0	15	0.0	.56
1 Days Rest	14	4	4	8	2	0	0	0	25	16.0	.57
2 Days Rest	5	2	5	7	5	0	1	0	12	16.7	1.40
3+ Days Rest	11	3	1	4	-1	2	0	0	24	12.5	.36

	G	A	Pts	PIM		G	A	Pts	PIM
1st Period	3	6	9	0	Winning	2	8	10	2
2nd Period	3	4	7	2	Losing	3	1	4	0
3rd Period	3	4	7	0	Tied	4	6	10	0
Overtime	0	1	1	0	Clutch	1	1	2	0
Last 5 Min	3	3	6	0	Blowouts	0	4	4	0

Shawn McEachern

Ottawa Senators — Left Wing

1998-99 Season

	GP	G	A	Pts	+/–	PIM	PP	SH	S	SPct	P/G
Overall	77	31	25	56	8	46	7	0	223	13.9	.73
Home	38	15	13	28	3	30	3	0	111	13.5	.74
Away	39	16	12	28	5	16	4	0	112	14.3	.72
vs. Division	19	9	4	13	1	12	1	0	52	17.3	.68
vs. Conference	52	24	19	43	11	24	5	0	145	16.6	.83
vs. Playoff	45	13	12	25	-3	32	3	0	118	11.0	.56
vs. Non-Playoff	32	18	13	31	11	14	4	0	105	17.1	.97
Pre All-Star	45	21	18	39	14	32	4	0	137	15.3	.87
Post All-Star	32	10	7	17	-6	14	3	0	86	11.6	.53
Day	3	1	1	2	2	4	0	0	9	11.1	.67
Night	74	30	24	54	6	42	7	0	214	14.0	.73

	GP	G	A	Pts	+/–	PIM	PP	SH	S	SPct	P/G
National TV	11	8	2	10	2	26	1	0	27	29.6	.91
0 Days Rest	13	5	4	9	-2	8	2	0	36	13.9	.69
1 Days Rest	38	17	10	27	9	32	4	0	110	15.5	.71
2 Days Rest	15	4	5	9	4	4	0	0	49	8.2	.60
3+ Days Rest	11	5	6	11	-3	2	1	0	28	17.9	1.00

	G	A	Pts	PIM		G	A	Pts	PIM
1st Period	12	5	17	16	Winning	10	12	22	14
2nd Period	10	10	20	12	Losing	11	3	14	14
3rd Period	9	10	19	6	Tied	10	10	20	18
Overtime	0	0	0	12	Clutch	5	4	9	14
Last 5 Min	10	8	18	26	Blowouts	3	2	5	4

Daniel McGillis

Philadelphia Flyers — Defense

1998-99 Season

	GP	G	A	Pts	+/–	PIM	PP	SH	S	SPct	P/G
Overall	78	8	37	45	16	61	6	0	164	4.9	.58
Home	40	4	25	29	13	23	4	0	91	4.4	.73
Away	38	4	12	16	3	38	2	0	73	5.5	.42
vs. Division	20	1	12	13	5	15	1	0	40	2.5	.65
vs. Conference	55	5	28	33	7	45	4	0	122	4.1	.60
vs. Playoff	45	3	19	22	9	37	2	0	89	3.4	.49
vs. Non-Playoff	33	5	18	23	7	24	4	0	75	6.7	.70
Pre All-Star	44	6	20	26	17	34	5	0	106	5.7	.59
Post All-Star	34	2	17	19	-1	27	1	0	58	3.4	.56
Day	15	1	9	10	4	12	1	0	27	3.7	.67
Night	63	7	28	35	12	49	5	0	137	5.1	.56

	GP	G	A	Pts	+/–	PIM	PP	SH	S	SPct	P/G
National TV	17	1	8	9	13	12	0	0	28	3.6	.53
0 Days Rest	11	2	5	7	4	6	0	0	27	7.4	.64
1 Days Rest	37	4	16	20	-3	30	4	0	75	5.3	.54
2 Days Rest	18	1	10	11	12	17	1	0	44	2.3	.61
3+ Days Rest	12	1	6	7	3	8	1	0	18	5.6	.58

	G	A	Pts	PIM		G	A	Pts	PIM
1st Period	3	14	17	20	Winning	4	8	12	31
2nd Period	4	10	14	33	Losing	1	15	16	16
3rd Period	1	13	14	4	Tied	3	14	17	14
Overtime	0	0	0	4	Clutch	0	2	2	4
Last 5 Min	2	6	8	12	Blowouts	0	0	0	4

Marty McInnis

Anaheim Mighty Ducks — Center

1998-99 Season

	GP	G	A	Pts	+/–	PIM	PP	SH	S	SPct	P/G
Overall	81	19	35	54	-15	42	11	1	146	13.0	.67
Home	40	11	23	34	-3	16	7	0	85	12.9	.85
Away	41	8	12	20	-12	26	4	1	61	13.1	.49
vs. Division	22	3	10	13	1	8	3	0	37	8.1	.59
vs. Conference	59	13	26	39	-6	34	8	0	102	12.7	.66
vs. Playoff	51	11	20	31	-15	30	7	1	94	11.7	.61
vs. Non-Playoff	30	8	15	23	0	12	4	0	52	15.4	.77
Pre All-Star	45	13	16	29	-11	26	7	1	84	15.5	.64
Post All-Star	36	6	19	25	-4	16	4	0	62	9.7	.69
Day	2	0	0	0	0	0	0	0	3	0.0	.00
Night	79	19	35	54	-15	42	11	1	143	13.3	.68

	GP	G	A	Pts	+/–	PIM	PP	SH	S	SPct	P/G
National TV	13	8	5	13	3	6	4	1	30	26.7	1.00
0 Days Rest	15	4	2	6	-1	12	3	0	19	21.1	.40
1 Days Rest	41	6	21	27	-9	18	5	0	67	9.0	.66
2 Days Rest	13	6	5	11	-4	6	2	0	32	18.8	.85
3+ Days Rest	12	3	7	10	-1	6	1	1	28	10.7	.83

	G	A	Pts	PIM		G	A	Pts	PIM
1st Period	6	14	20	14	Winning	6	15	21	14
2nd Period	6	6	12	16	Losing	5	10	15	24
3rd Period	7	15	22	12	Tied	8	10	18	4
Overtime	0	0	0	0	Clutch	1	5	6	2
Last 5 Min	3	10	13	8	Blowouts	0	2	2	0

Randy McKay

New Jersey Devils — Right Wing

1998-99 Season

	GP	G	A	Pts	+/–	PIM	PP	SH	S	SPct	P/G
Overall	70	17	20	37	10	143	3	0	136	12.5	.53
Home	36	8	10	18	1	92	2	0	64	12.5	.50
Away	34	9	10	19	9	51	1	0	72	12.5	.56
vs. Division	17	7	10	17	7	35	1	0	31	22.6	1.00
vs. Conference	50	12	15	27	4	117	1	0	99	12.1	.54
vs. Playoff	38	12	15	27	8	49	3	0	66	18.2	.71
vs. Non-Playoff	32	5	5	10	2	94	0	0	70	7.1	.31
Pre All-Star	34	12	12	24	13	88	3	0	80	15.0	.71
Post All-Star	36	5	8	13	-3	55	0	0	56	8.9	.36
Day	11	3	1	4	-2	29	1	0	17	17.6	.36
Night	59	14	19	33	12	114	2	0	119	11.8	.56

	GP	G	A	Pts	+/–	PIM	PP	SH	S	SPct	P/G
National TV	6	2	0	2	1	0	0	0	20	10.0	.33
0 Days Rest	14	4	4	8	9	17	0	0	32	12.5	.57
1 Days Rest	27	6	7	13	-1	37	2	0	43	14.0	.48
2 Days Rest	20	3	5	8	0	42	0	0	43	7.0	.40
3+ Days Rest	9	4	4	8	2	47	1	0	18	22.2	.89

	G	A	Pts	PIM		G	A	Pts	PIM
1st Period	8	7	15	13	Winning	7	5	12	101
2nd Period	4	10	14	39	Losing	3	7	10	15
3rd Period	5	1	6	77	Tied	7	8	15	27
Overtime	0	2	2	14	Clutch	2	3	5	16
Last 5 Min	3	8	11	50	Blowouts	0	0	0	10

Kyle McLaren

Boston Bruins — Defense

1998-99 Season

	GP	G	A	Pts	+/–	PIM	PP	SH	S	SPct	P/G
Overall	52	6	18	24	1	48	3	0	97	6.2	.46
Home	27	2	6	8	0	36	1	0	59	3.4	.30
Away	25	4	12	16	1	12	2	0	38	10.5	.64
vs. Division	15	1	6	7	2	2	1	0	28	3.6	.47
vs. Conference	39	6	11	17	4	33	3	0	69	8.7	.44
vs. Playoff	27	2	9	11	3	17	1	0	44	4.5	.41
vs. Non-Playoff	25	4	9	13	-2	31	2	0	53	7.5	.52
Pre All-Star	25	5	4	9	-5	32	3	0	54	9.3	.36
Post All-Star	27	1	14	15	6	16	0	0	43	2.3	.56
Day	9	0	3	3	3	4	0	0	16	0.0	.33
Night	43	6	15	21	-2	44	3	0	81	7.4	.49

	GP	G	A	Pts	+/–	PIM	PP	SH	S	SPct	P/G
National TV	6	1	3	4	1	6	1	0	9	11.1	.67
0 Days Rest	10	0	5	5	-4	6	0	0	19	0.0	.50
1 Days Rest	23	4	7	11	9	36	2	0	45	8.9	.48
2 Days Rest	9	1	4	5	-3	4	0	0	17	5.9	.56
3+ Days Rest	10	1	2	3	-1	2	1	0	16	6.3	.30

	G	A	Pts	PIM		G	A	Pts	PIM
1st Period	2	5	7	10	Winning	1	7	8	36
2nd Period	1	8	9	8	Losing	3	8	11	6
3rd Period	3	5	8	30	Tied	2	3	5	6
Overtime	0	0	0	0	Clutch	0	3	3	19
Last 5 Min	3	8	11	31	Blowouts	1	0	1	0

Scott Mellanby

Florida Panthers — Right Wing

1998-99 Season

	GP	G	A	Pts	+/–	PIM	PP	SH	S	SPct	P/G
Overall	67	18	27	45	5	85	4	0	136	13.2	.67
Home	33	9	16	25	7	46	2	0	69	13.0	.76
Away	34	9	11	20	-2	39	2	0	67	13.4	.59
vs. Division	12	5	8	13	6	10	2	0	27	18.5	1.08
vs. Conference	50	13	22	35	6	63	3	0	99	13.1	.70
vs. Playoff	42	12	17	29	0	55	2	0	90	13.3	.69
vs. Non-Playoff	25	6	10	16	5	30	2	0	46	13.0	.64
Pre All-Star	34	11	13	24	2	29	3	0	70	15.7	.71
Post All-Star	33	7	14	21	3	56	1	0	66	10.6	.64
Day	4	2	3	5	0	0	0	0	9	22.2	1.25
Night	63	16	24	40	5	85	4	0	127	12.6	.63

	GP	G	A	Pts	+/–	PIM	PP	SH	S	SPct	P/G
National TV	4	0	2	2	-1	2	0	0	10	0.0	.50
0 Days Rest	14	2	6	8	-2	12	1	0	31	6.5	.57
1 Days Rest	26	8	7	15	8	28	1	0	46	17.4	.58
2 Days Rest	14	3	10	13	-2	14	2	0	30	10.0	.93
3+ Days Rest	13	5	4	9	1	31	0	0	29	17.2	.69

	G	A	Pts	PIM		G	A	Pts	PIM
1st Period	5	5	10	27	Winning	5	9	14	34
2nd Period	6	10	16	10	Losing	7	12	19	38
3rd Period	7	12	19	48	Tied	6	6	12	13
Overtime	0	0	0	0	Clutch	1	1	2	16
Last 5 Min	4	5	9	53	Blowouts	1	2	3	8

Mark Messier

Vancouver Canucks — Center

1998-99 Season

	GP	G	A	Pts	+/–	PIM	PP	SH	S	SPct	P/G
Overall	59	13	35	48	-12	33	4	2	97	13.4	.81
Home	30	5	20	25	-7	14	2	2	43	11.6	.83
Away	29	8	15	23	-5	19	2	0	54	14.8	.79
vs. Division	13	5	4	9	-5	11	3	0	15	33.3	.69
vs. Conference	37	8	23	31	-13	25	3	1	58	13.8	.84
vs. Playoff	37	6	21	27	-19	27	3	0	55	10.9	.73
vs. Non-Playoff	22	7	14	21	7	6	1	2	42	16.7	.95
Pre All-Star	44	13	26	39	-10	25	4	2	73	17.8	.89
Post All-Star	15	0	9	9	-2	8	0	0	24	0.0	.60
Day	2	0	0	0	-2	2	0	0	1	0.0	.00
Night	57	13	35	48	-10	31	4	2	96	13.5	.84

	GP	G	A	Pts	+/–	PIM	PP	SH	S	SPct	P/G
National TV	15	2	10	12	-3	8	1	1	29	6.9	.80
0 Days Rest	7	2	3	5	-3	11	1	0	18	11.1	.71
1 Days Rest	34	7	22	29	-7	12	1	1	59	11.9	.85
2 Days Rest	10	3	6	9	2	4	2	0	9	33.3	.90
3+ Days Rest	8	1	4	5	-4	6	0	1	11	9.1	.63

	G	A	Pts	PIM		G	A	Pts	PIM
1st Period	4	11	15	12	Winning	5	7	12	12
2nd Period	4	11	15	15	Losing	3	13	16	15
3rd Period	5	13	18	6	Tied	5	15	20	6
Overtime	0	0	0	0	Clutch	0	4	4	2
Last 5 Min	4	9	13	14	Blowouts	2	1	3	2

Aaron Miller

Colorado Avalanche — Defense

1998-99 Season

	GP	G	A	Pts	+/–	PIM	PP	SH	S	SPct	P/G
Overall	76	5	13	18	3	42	1	0	87	5.7	.24
Home	38	5	7	12	1	32	1	0	48	10.4	.32
Away	38	0	6	6	2	10	0	0	39	0.0	.16
vs. Division	17	1	3	4	-13	8	0	0	21	4.8	.24
vs. Conference	51	3	11	14	-4	22	0	0	58	5.2	.27
vs. Playoff	41	3	7	10	6	24	0	0	44	6.8	.24
vs. Non-Playoff	35	2	6	8	-3	18	1	0	43	4.7	.23
Pre All-Star	43	3	4	7	-5	36	1	0	48	6.3	.16
Post All-Star	33	2	9	11	8	6	0	0	39	5.1	.33
Day	13	1	2	3	0	0	0	0	12	8.3	.23
Night	63	4	11	15	3	42	1	0	75	5.3	.24

	GP	G	A	Pts	+/–	PIM	PP	SH	S	SPct	P/G
National TV	21	0	3	3	4	12	0	0	21	0.0	.14
0 Days Rest	11	0	1	1	1	6	0	0	9	0.0	.09
1 Days Rest	39	4	9	13	3	22	1	0	49	8.2	.33
2 Days Rest	12	0	1	1	2	0	0	0	14	0.0	.08
3+ Days Rest	14	1	2	3	-3	14	0	0	15	6.7	.21

	G	A	Pts	PIM		G	A	Pts	PIM
1st Period	1	4	5	14	Winning	2	3	5	24
2nd Period	0	5	5	12	Losing	1	6	7	14
3rd Period	4	3	7	14	Tied	2	4	6	4
Overtime	0	1	1	2	Clutch	1	2	3	4
Last 5 Min	1	4	5	10	Blowouts	0	1	1	6

Kip Miller

Pittsburgh Penguins — Center

1998-99 Season

	GP	G	A	Pts	+/–	PIM	PP	SH	S	SPct	P/G
Overall	77	19	23	42	1	22	1	0	125	15.2	.55
Home	40	13	16	29	8	8	1	0	70	18.6	.73
Away	37	6	7	13	-7	14	0	0	55	10.9	.35
vs. Division	16	1	4	5	-5	4	0	0	23	4.3	.31
vs. Conference	53	15	12	27	0	14	1	0	82	18.3	.51
vs. Playoff	43	8	11	19	-5	10	0	0	75	10.7	.44
vs. Non-Playoff	34	11	12	23	6	12	1	0	50	22.0	.68
Pre All-Star	38	3	5	8	-6	20	0	0	51	5.9	.21
Post All-Star	39	16	18	34	7	2	1	0	74	21.6	.87
Day	13	2	3	5	0	2	0	0	26	7.7	.38
Night	64	17	20	37	1	20	1	0	99	17.2	.58

	GP	G	A	Pts	+/–	PIM	PP	SH	S	SPct	P/G
National TV	17	2	6	8	3	6	0	0	21	9.5	.47
0 Days Rest	13	5	3	8	4	6	0	0	20	25.0	.62
1 Days Rest	34	9	11	20	-7	12	1	0	64	14.1	.59
2 Days Rest	22	2	8	10	4	2	0	0	28	7.1	.45
3+ Days Rest	8	3	1	4	0	2	0	0	13	23.1	.50

	G	A	Pts	PIM		G	A	Pts	PIM
1st Period	5	7	12	4	Winning	6	11	17	6
2nd Period	5	7	12	12	Losing	6	7	13	10
3rd Period	7	8	15	6	Tied	7	5	12	6
Overtime	2	1	3	0	Clutch	5	3	8	4
Last 5 Min	8	8	16	8	Blowouts	1	1	2	0

Boris Mironov

Chicago Blackhawks — Defense

1998-99 Season

	GP	G	A	Pts	+/–	PIM	PP	SH	S	SPct	P/G
Overall	75	11	38	49	13	131	5	0	173	6.4	.65
Home	38	5	17	22	7	71	3	0	105	4.8	.58
Away	37	6	21	27	6	60	2	0	68	8.8	.73
vs. Division	12	4	7	11	5	40	1	0	31	12.9	.92
vs. Conference	46	4	23	27	-3	95	1	0	112	3.6	.59
vs. Playoff	47	7	18	25	3	73	4	0	97	7.2	.53
vs. Non-Playoff	28	4	20	24	10	58	1	0	76	5.3	.86
Pre All-Star	41	6	21	27	14	84	1	0	95	6.3	.66
Post All-Star	34	5	17	22	-1	47	4	0	78	6.4	.65
Day	5	0	5	5	0	21	0	0	16	0.0	1.00
Night	70	11	33	44	13	110	5	0	157	7.0	.63

	GP	G	A	Pts	+/–	PIM	PP	SH	S	SPct	P/G
National TV	13	1	8	9	10	39	1	0	30	3.3	.69
0 Days Rest	11	2	5	7	3	12	1	0	25	8.0	.64
1 Days Rest	35	7	19	26	0	64	3	0	82	8.5	.74
2 Days Rest	16	0	6	6	5	26	0	0	31	0.0	.38
3+ Days Rest	13	2	8	10	5	29	1	0	35	5.7	.77

	G	A	Pts	PIM		G	A	Pts	PIM
1st Period	3	13	16	30	Winning	6	14	20	79
2nd Period	5	9	14	27	Losing	2	16	18	40
3rd Period	3	15	18	74	Tied	3	8	11	12
Overtime	0	1	1	0	Clutch	1	7	8	8
Last 5 Min	3	8	11	56	Blowouts	1	2	3	4

Dmitri Mironov

Washington Capitals — Defense

1998-99 Season

	GP	G	A	Pts	+/–	PIM	PP	SH	S	SPct	P/G
Overall	46	2	14	16	-5	80	2	0	86	2.3	.35
Home	22	1	6	7	1	16	1	0	47	2.1	.32
Away	24	1	8	9	-6	64	1	0	39	2.6	.38
vs. Division	7	0	6	6	4	20	0	0	11	0.0	.86
vs. Conference	33	2	10	12	2	58	2	0	56	3.6	.36
vs. Playoff	28	1	7	8	1	56	1	0	54	1.9	.29
vs. Non-Playoff	18	1	7	8	-6	24	1	0	32	3.1	.44
Pre All-Star	42	2	13	15	-5	80	2	0	79	2.5	.36
Post All-Star	4	0	1	1	0	0	0	0	7	0.0	.25
Day	0	0	0	0	0	0	0	0	0	–	–
Night	46	2	14	16	-5	80	2	0	86	2.3	.35

	GP	G	A	Pts	+/–	PIM	PP	SH	S	SPct	P/G
National TV	6	1	5	6	6	4	1	0	9	11.1	1.00
0 Days Rest	7	1	1	2	3	36	1	0	17	5.9	.29
1 Days Rest	18	0	4	4	-6	24	0	0	35	0.0	.22
2 Days Rest	9	1	6	7	0	4	1	0	12	8.3	.78
3+ Days Rest	12	0	3	3	-2	16	0	0	22	0.0	.25

	G	A	Pts	PIM		G	A	Pts	PIM
1st Period	0	3	3	28	Winning	1	3	4	30
2nd Period	2	8	10	24	Losing	1	6	7	50
3rd Period	0	3	3	28	Tied	0	5	5	0
Overtime	0	0	0	0	Clutch	0	1	1	4
Last 5 Min	0	5	5	12	Blowouts	0	0	0	4

Mike Modano

Dallas Stars — Center

1998-99 Season

	GP	G	A	Pts	+/–	PIM	PP	SH	S	SPct	P/G
Overall	77	34	47	81	29	44	6	4	224	15.2	1.05
Home	38	16	24	40	16	24	3	2	103	15.5	1.05
Away	39	18	23	41	13	20	3	2	121	14.9	1.05
vs. Division	22	5	10	15	2	20	1	0	50	10.0	.68
vs. Conference	52	20	34	54	8	32	5	1	138	14.5	1.04
vs. Playoff	44	19	29	48	15	26	3	3	131	14.5	1.09
vs. Non-Playoff	33	15	18	33	14	18	3	1	93	16.1	1.00
Pre All-Star	43	15	31	46	14	30	4	1	115	13.0	1.07
Post All-Star	34	19	16	35	15	14	2	3	109	17.4	1.03
Day	7	1	2	3	-1	8	1	0	23	4.3	.43
Night	70	33	45	78	30	36	5	4	201	16.4	1.11

	GP	G	A	Pts	+/–	PIM	PP	SH	S	SPct	P/G
National TV	13	3	4	7	-3	10	1	0	38	7.9	.54
0 Days Rest	13	5	9	14	7	6	3	1	43	11.6	1.08
1 Days Rest	42	23	25	48	18	28	3	2	128	18.0	1.14
2 Days Rest	10	4	5	9	5	4	0	1	24	16.7	.90
3+ Days Rest	12	2	8	10	-1	6	0	0	29	6.9	.83

	G	A	Pts	PIM		G	A	Pts	PIM
1st Period	12	17	29	14	Winning	14	15	29	30
2nd Period	12	17	29	14	Losing	6	10	16	4
3rd Period	9	12	21	16	Tied	14	22	36	10
Overtime	1	1	2	0	Clutch	3	8	11	6
Last 5 Min	13	11	24	14	Blowouts	3	0	3	6

Fredrik Modin

Toronto Maple Leafs — Left Wing

1998-99 Season

	GP	G	A	Pts	+/–	PIM	PP	SH	S	SPct	P/G
Overall	67	16	15	31	14	35	1	0	108	14.8	.46
Home	35	9	9	18	4	14	1	0	57	15.8	.51
Away	32	7	6	13	10	21	0	0	51	13.7	.41
vs. Division	15	1	1	2	-3	6	0	0	22	4.5	.13
vs. Conference	42	8	6	14	2	16	0	0	62	12.9	.33
vs. Playoff	39	9	10	19	2	17	0	0	57	15.8	.49
vs. Non-Playoff	28	7	5	12	12	18	1	0	51	13.7	.43
Pre All-Star	46	12	11	23	8	25	1	0	78	15.4	.50
Post All-Star	21	4	4	8	6	10	0	0	30	13.3	.38
Day	1	0	0	0	-1	0	0	0	0	–	.00
Night	66	16	15	31	15	35	1	0	108	14.8	.47

	GP	G	A	Pts	+/–	PIM	PP	SH	S	SPct	P/G
National TV	23	3	4	7	4	10	0	0	28	10.7	.30
0 Days Rest	15	3	0	3	3	15	0	0	32	9.4	.20
1 Days Rest	26	10	9	19	6	6	1	0	34	29.4	.73
2 Days Rest	12	0	2	2	0	8	0	0	12	0.0	.17
3+ Days Rest	14	3	4	7	5	6	0	0	30	10.0	.50

	G	A	Pts	PIM		G	A	Pts	PIM
1st Period	2	3	5	8	Winning	7	5	12	31
2nd Period	6	6	12	19	Losing	5	3	8	2
3rd Period	7	6	13	8	Tied	4	7	11	2
Overtime	1	0	1	0	Clutch	1	0	1	0
Last 5 Min	2	2	4	10	Blowouts	3	2	5	6

Alexander Mogilny

Vancouver Canucks — Right Wing

1998-99 Season

	GP	G	A	Pts	+/–	PIM	PP	SH	S	SPct	P/G
Overall	59	14	31	45	0	58	3	2	110	12.7	.76
Home	31	9	14	23	0	8	2	1	62	14.5	.74
Away	28	5	17	22	0	50	1	1	48	10.4	.79
vs. Division	12	3	7	10	-1	22	1	0	25	12.0	.83
vs. Conference	40	8	18	26	-7	50	2	1	75	10.7	.65
vs. Playoff	35	8	13	21	-5	50	2	0	58	13.8	.60
vs. Non-Playoff	24	6	18	24	5	8	1	2	52	11.5	1.00
Pre All-Star	26	5	17	22	2	30	1	2	41	12.2	.85
Post All-Star	33	9	14	23	-2	28	2	0	69	13.0	.70
Day	3	1	1	2	-1	2	0	0	7	14.3	.67
Night	56	13	30	43	1	56	3	2	103	12.6	.77

	GP	G	A	Pts	+/–	PIM	PP	SH	S	SPct	P/G
National TV	16	1	8	9	-1	22	0	0	23	4.3	.56
0 Days Rest	10	1	5	6	-5	40	0	0	13	7.7	.60
1 Days Rest	31	10	16	26	-4	10	3	2	62	16.1	.84
2 Days Rest	9	1	3	4	3	6	0	0	16	6.3	.44
3+ Days Rest	9	2	7	9	6	2	0	0	19	10.5	1.00

	G	A	Pts	PIM		G	A	Pts	PIM
1st Period	3	9	12	44	Winning	5	8	13	4
2nd Period	5	6	11	12	Losing	6	13	19	48
3rd Period	6	16	22	2	Tied	3	10	13	6
Overtime	0	0	0	0	Clutch	2	3	5	2
Last 5 Min	3	8	11	28	Blowouts	1	5	6	0

Ethan Moreau

Edmonton Oilers — Left Wing

1998-99 Season

	GP	G	A	Pts	+/–	PIM	PP	SH	S	SPct	P/G
Overall	80	10	11	21	-3	92	0	0	96	10.4	.26
Home	43	3	7	10	-2	35	0	0	43	7.0	.23
Away	37	7	4	11	-1	57	0	0	53	13.2	.30
vs. Division	21	3	4	7	-2	16	0	0	27	11.1	.33
vs. Conference	58	10	9	19	4	67	0	0	72	13.9	.33
vs. Playoff	48	7	4	11	-6	62	0	0	55	12.7	.23
vs. Non-Playoff	32	3	7	10	3	30	0	0	41	7.3	.31
Pre All-Star	43	6	3	9	-5	58	0	0	46	13.0	.21
Post All-Star	37	4	8	12	2	34	0	0	50	8.0	.32
Day	7	0	2	2	-3	10	0	0	6	0.0	.29
Night	73	10	9	19	0	82	0	0	90	11.1	.26

	GP	G	A	Pts	+/–	PIM	PP	SH	S	SPct	P/G
National TV	15	1	5	6	1	22	0	0	17	5.9	.40
0 Days Rest	13	3	2	5	5	27	0	0	12	25.0	.38
1 Days Rest	42	7	5	12	-13	32	0	0	56	12.5	.29
2 Days Rest	10	0	1	1	4	8	0	0	14	0.0	.10
3+ Days Rest	15	0	3	3	1	25	0	0	14	0.0	.20

	G	A	Pts	PIM		G	A	Pts	PIM
1st Period	1	2	3	35	Winning	0	2	2	27
2nd Period	1	5	6	12	Losing	6	7	13	57
3rd Period	8	4	12	45	Tied	4	2	6	8
Overtime	0	0	0	0	Clutch	2	1	3	0
Last 5 Min	2	1	3	26	Blowouts	1	1	2	8

Alexei Morozov

Pittsburgh Penguins — Right Wing

1998-99 Season

	GP	G	A	Pts	+/–	PIM	PP	SH	S	SPct	P/G
Overall	67	9	10	19	5	14	0	0	75	12.0	.28
Home	32	6	1	7	2	6	0	0	28	21.4	.22
Away	35	3	9	12	3	8	0	0	47	6.4	.34
vs. Division	18	4	3	7	-3	4	0	0	22	18.2	.39
vs. Conference	50	7	9	16	5	10	0	0	61	11.5	.32
vs. Playoff	38	3	5	8	1	8	0	0	36	8.3	.21
vs. Non-Playoff	29	6	5	11	4	6	0	0	39	15.4	.38
Pre All-Star	26	5	5	10	6	8	0	0	40	12.5	.38
Post All-Star	41	4	5	9	-1	6	0	0	35	11.4	.22
Day	15	0	3	3	-1	4	0	0	12	0.0	.20
Night	52	9	7	16	6	10	0	0	63	14.3	.31

	GP	G	A	Pts	+/–	PIM	PP	SH	S	SPct	P/G
National TV	16	1	5	6	0	4	0	0	17	5.9	.38
0 Days Rest	13	1	4	5	2	2	0	0	13	7.7	.38
1 Days Rest	30	3	3	6	0	4	0	0	35	8.6	.20
2 Days Rest	17	4	1	5	-1	4	0	0	13	30.8	.29
3+ Days Rest	7	1	2	3	4	4	0	0	14	7.1	.43

	G	A	Pts	PIM		G	A	Pts	PIM
1st Period	5	0	5	4	Winning	3	2	5	8
2nd Period	2	6	8	10	Losing	2	5	7	6
3rd Period	2	3	5	0	Tied	4	3	7	0
Overtime	0	1	1	0	Clutch	0	2	2	0
Last 5 Min	2	3	5	2	Blowouts	0	0	0	4

Derek Morris

Calgary Flames — Defense

1998-99 Season

	GP	G	A	Pts	+/–	PIM	PP	SH	S	SPct	P/G
Overall	71	7	27	34	4	73	3	0	150	4.7	.48
Home	38	4	17	21	10	26	2	0	87	4.6	.55
Away	33	3	10	13	-6	47	1	0	63	4.8	.39
vs. Division	17	1	6	7	-2	15	1	0	32	3.1	.41
vs. Conference	48	6	19	25	6	46	2	0	94	6.4	.52
vs. Playoff	45	5	17	22	2	47	2	0	85	5.9	.49
vs. Non-Playoff	26	2	10	12	2	26	1	0	65	3.1	.46
Pre All-Star	45	5	17	22	2	65	2	0	104	4.8	.49
Post All-Star	26	2	10	12	2	8	1	0	46	4.3	.46
Day	4	0	1	1	1	0	0	0	9	0.0	.25
Night	67	7	26	33	3	73	3	0	141	5.0	.49

	GP	G	A	Pts	+/–	PIM	PP	SH	S	SPct	P/G
National TV	12	0	6	6	1	2	0	0	22	0.0	.50
0 Days Rest	14	1	5	6	-1	15	0	0	28	3.6	.43
1 Days Rest	35	5	12	17	-1	17	2	0	77	6.5	.49
2 Days Rest	10	0	5	5	3	29	0	0	21	0.0	.50
3+ Days Rest	12	1	5	6	3	12	1	0	24	4.2	.50

	G	A	Pts	PIM		G	A	Pts	PIM
1st Period	0	10	10	23	Winning	4	4	8	32
2nd Period	5	8	13	14	Losing	3	13	16	33
3rd Period	2	8	10	36	Tied	0	10	10	8
Overtime	0	1	1	0	Clutch	2	4	6	24
Last 5 Min	3	11	14	13	Blowouts	0	0	0	4

Brendan Morrison

New Jersey Devils — Center

1998-99 Season

	GP	G	A	Pts	+/–	PIM	PP	SH	S	SPct	P/G
Overall	76	13	33	46	-4	18	5	0	111	11.7	.61
Home	36	5	16	21	0	2	1	0	46	10.9	.58
Away	40	8	17	25	-4	16	4	0	65	12.3	.63
vs. Division	18	6	7	13	-2	0	3	0	30	20.0	.72
vs. Conference	54	11	23	34	-3	6	4	0	83	13.3	.63
vs. Playoff	44	7	16	23	-10	4	3	0	56	12.5	.52
vs. Non-Playoff	32	6	17	23	6	14	2	0	55	10.9	.72
Pre All-Star	39	5	17	22	-6	16	3	0	56	8.9	.56
Post All-Star	37	8	16	24	2	2	2	0	55	14.5	.65
Day	11	2	4	6	2	0	0	0	20	10.0	.55
Night	65	11	29	40	-6	18	5	0	91	12.1	.62

	GP	G	A	Pts	+/–	PIM	PP	SH	S	SPct	P/G
National TV	7	2	3	5	-1	12	2	0	9	22.2	.71
0 Days Rest	13	3	10	13	-1	10	1	0	23	13.0	1.00
1 Days Rest	30	6	12	18	-5	4	1	0	45	13.3	.60
2 Days Rest	23	2	8	10	2	4	2	0	33	6.1	.43
3+ Days Rest	10	2	3	5	0	0	1	0	10	20.0	.50

	G	A	Pts	PIM		G	A	Pts	PIM
1st Period	6	10	16	4	Winning	4	16	20	14
2nd Period	4	12	16	14	Losing	5	9	14	0
3rd Period	3	11	14	0	Tied	4	8	12	4
Overtime	0	0	0	0	Clutch	0	5	5	0
Last 5 Min	3	12	15	10	Blowouts	1	1	2	0

Bill Muckalt

Vancouver Canucks — Right Wing

1998-99 Season

	GP	G	A	Pts	+/–	PIM	PP	SH	S	SPct	P/G
Overall	73	16	20	36	-9	98	4	2	119	13.4	.49
Home	36	7	12	19	-1	56	2	1	55	12.7	.53
Away	37	9	8	17	-8	42	2	1	64	14.1	.46
vs. Division	15	3	2	5	-2	27	0	0	24	12.5	.33
vs. Conference	47	12	10	22	-6	59	3	2	88	13.6	.47
vs. Playoff	47	11	11	22	-3	45	2	2	81	13.6	.47
vs. Non-Playoff	26	5	9	14	-6	53	2	0	38	13.2	.54
Pre All-Star	45	14	13	27	3	40	3	2	71	19.7	.60
Post All-Star	28	2	7	9	-12	58	1	0	48	4.2	.32
Day	3	0	1	1	1	5	0	0	4	0.0	.33
Night	70	16	19	35	-10	93	4	2	115	13.9	.50

	GP	G	A	Pts	+/–	PIM	PP	SH	S	SPct	P/G
National TV	18	3	7	10	-4	36	1	1	34	8.8	.56
0 Days Rest	12	3	3	6	-2	26	0	0	20	15.0	.50
1 Days Rest	39	8	11	19	-9	60	3	2	65	12.3	.49
2 Days Rest	15	3	4	7	3	10	0	0	28	10.7	.47
3+ Days Rest	7	2	2	4	-1	2	1	0	6	33.3	.57

	G	A	Pts	PIM		G	A	Pts	PIM
1st Period	5	4	9	28	Winning	1	6	7	41
2nd Period	4	9	13	2	Losing	10	13	23	47
3rd Period	7	7	14	66	Tied	5	1	6	10
Overtime	0	0	0	2	Clutch	0	2	2	6
Last 5 Min	4	6	10	25	Blowouts	0	2	2	43

Kirk Muller

Florida Panthers — Left Wing

1998-99 Season

	GP	G	A	Pts	+/–	PIM	PP	SH	S	SPct	P/G
Overall	82	4	11	15	-11	49	0	0	107	3.7	.18
Home	41	4	3	7	-4	32	0	0	63	6.3	.17
Away	41	0	8	8	-7	17	0	0	44	0.0	.20
vs. Division	15	2	1	3	0	12	0	0	17	11.8	.20
vs. Conference	58	4	9	13	-10	30	0	0	75	5.3	.22
vs. Playoff	49	2	6	8	-11	28	0	0	52	3.8	.16
vs. Non-Playoff	33	2	5	7	0	21	0	0	55	3.6	.21
Pre All-Star	44	2	4	6	-7	36	0	0	61	3.3	.14
Post All-Star	38	2	7	9	-4	13	0	0	46	4.3	.24
Day	4	1	0	1	-1	0	0	0	10	10.0	.25
Night	78	3	11	14	-10	49	0	0	97	3.1	.18

	GP	G	A	Pts	+/–	PIM	PP	SH	S	SPct	P/G
National TV	4	0	1	1	-2	2	0	0	0	–	.25
0 Days Rest	19	0	1	1	-3	6	0	0	21	0.0	.05
1 Days Rest	33	0	6	6	-4	11	0	0	40	0.0	.18
2 Days Rest	16	3	3	6	2	12	0	0	27	11.1	.38
3+ Days Rest	14	1	1	2	-6	20	0	0	19	5.3	.14

	G	A	Pts	PIM		G	A	Pts	PIM
1st Period	1	2	3	21	Winning	3	4	7	10
2nd Period	3	5	8	15	Losing	1	3	4	21
3rd Period	0	4	4	13	Tied	0	4	4	18
Overtime	0	0	0	0	Clutch	0	0	0	2
Last 5 Min	2	1	3	12	Blowouts	0	1	1	6

Joe Murphy

San Jose Sharks — Right Wing

1998-99 Season

	GP	G	A	Pts	+/–	PIM	PP	SH	S	SPct	P/G
Overall	76	25	23	48	10	73	7	0	176	14.2	.63
Home	37	9	11	20	2	22	1	0	94	9.6	.54
Away	39	16	12	28	8	51	6	0	82	19.5	.72
vs. Division	21	5	6	11	-2	26	1	0	41	12.2	.52
vs. Conference	52	21	18	39	6	44	7	0	138	15.2	.75
vs. Playoff	43	10	14	24	5	40	1	0	76	13.2	.56
vs. Non-Playoff	33	15	9	24	5	33	6	0	100	15.0	.73
Pre All-Star	39	11	10	21	6	24	1	0	103	10.7	.54
Post All-Star	37	14	13	27	4	49	6	0	73	19.2	.73
Day	6	3	2	5	3	2	1	0	10	30.0	.83
Night	70	22	21	43	7	71	6	0	166	13.3	.61

	GP	G	A	Pts	+/–	PIM	PP	SH	S	SPct	P/G
National TV	10	4	3	7	-7	10	3	0	21	19.0	.70
0 Days Rest	12	5	6	11	6	8	0	0	33	15.2	.92
1 Days Rest	38	16	11	27	5	37	6	0	78	20.5	.71
2 Days Rest	14	2	2	4	0	4	0	0	27	7.4	.29
3+ Days Rest	12	2	4	6	-1	24	1	0	38	5.3	.50

	G	A	Pts	PIM		G	A	Pts	PIM
1st Period	9	11	20	18	Winning	10	6	16	41
2nd Period	7	7	14	33	Losing	7	6	13	22
3rd Period	9	5	14	22	Tied	8	11	19	10
Overtime	0	0	0	0	Clutch	1	1	2	0
Last 5 Min	4	4	8	18	Blowouts	0	0	0	4

Larry Murphy

Detroit Red Wings — Defense

1998-99 Season

	GP	G	A	Pts	+/–	PIM	PP	SH	S	SPct	P/G
Overall	80	10	42	52	21	42	5	1	168	6.0	.65
Home	40	4	23	27	22	14	2	0	82	4.9	.68
Away	40	6	19	25	-1	28	3	1	86	7.0	.63
vs. Division	17	6	11	17	14	6	3	1	52	11.5	1.00
vs. Conference	53	7	32	39	16	26	3	1	123	5.7	.74
vs. Playoff	47	3	25	28	-2	20	2	1	78	3.8	.60
vs. Non-Playoff	33	7	17	24	23	22	3	0	90	7.8	.73
Pre All-Star	46	7	25	32	14	36	3	1	98	7.1	.70
Post All-Star	34	3	17	20	7	6	2	0	70	4.3	.59
Day	13	1	9	10	2	4	0	0	22	4.5	.77
Night	67	9	33	42	19	38	5	1	146	6.2	.63

	GP	G	A	Pts	+/–	PIM	PP	SH	S	SPct	P/G
National TV	29	4	15	19	3	10	3	0	65	6.2	.66
0 Days Rest	12	3	3	6	-4	8	2	0	23	13.0	.50
1 Days Rest	37	3	20	23	11	22	1	0	78	3.8	.62
2 Days Rest	23	1	13	14	5	8	0	1	55	1.8	.61
3+ Days Rest	8	3	6	9	9	4	2	0	12	25.0	1.13

	G	A	Pts	PIM		G	A	Pts	PIM
1st Period	2	13	15	4	Winning	4	20	24	18
2nd Period	3	19	22	20	Losing	2	8	10	20
3rd Period	5	10	15	18	Tied	4	14	18	4
Overtime	0	0	0	0	Clutch	2	3	5	10
Last 5 Min	3	11	14	22	Blowouts	1	3	4	6

Glen Murray

Los Angeles Kings — Right Wing

1998-99 Season

	GP	G	A	Pts	+/–	PIM	PP	SH	S	SPct	P/G
Overall	61	16	15	31	-14	36	3	3	173	9.2	.51
Home	29	7	8	15	-9	18	2	1	84	8.3	.52
Away	32	9	7	16	-5	18	1	2	89	10.1	.50
vs. Division	18	4	2	6	-5	6	0	2	56	7.1	.33
vs. Conference	44	11	11	22	-16	24	3	3	119	9.2	.50
vs. Playoff	38	9	10	19	-5	28	1	2	110	8.2	.50
vs. Non-Playoff	23	7	5	12	-9	8	2	1	63	11.1	.52
Pre All-Star	37	15	13	28	-5	18	3	3	110	13.6	.76
Post All-Star	24	1	2	3	-9	18	0	0	63	1.6	.13
Day	5	0	0	0	-3	6	0	0	11	0.0	.00
Night	56	16	15	31	-11	30	3	3	162	9.9	.55

	GP	G	A	Pts	+/–	PIM	PP	SH	S	SPct	P/G
National TV	13	0	3	3	-2	10	0	0	31	0.0	.23
0 Days Rest	10	3	2	5	-4	2	1	0	34	8.8	.50
1 Days Rest	30	11	10	21	-11	20	2	3	86	12.8	.70
2 Days Rest	10	0	1	1	-2	8	0	0	20	0.0	.10
3+ Days Rest	11	2	2	4	3	6	0	0	33	6.1	.36

	G	A	Pts	PIM		G	A	Pts	PIM
1st Period	4	2	6	8	Winning	7	5	12	8
2nd Period	4	8	12	16	Losing	4	6	10	26
3rd Period	8	5	13	12	Tied	5	4	9	2
Overtime	0	0	0	0	Clutch	0	0	0	0
Last 5 Min	4	3	7	12	Blowouts	0	1	1	6

Rem Murray

Edmonton Oilers — Left Wing

1998-99 Season

	GP	G	A	Pts	+/–	PIM	PP	SH	S	SPct	P/G
Overall	78	21	18	39	4	20	4	1	116	18.1	.50
Home	37	13	8	21	5	8	2	1	52	25.0	.57
Away	41	8	10	18	-1	12	2	0	64	12.5	.44
vs. Division	17	6	4	10	4	6	2	1	27	22.2	.59
vs. Conference	53	16	12	28	5	10	4	1	81	19.8	.53
vs. Playoff	46	15	11	26	-1	12	3	1	70	21.4	.57
vs. Non-Playoff	32	6	7	13	5	8	1	0	46	13.0	.41
Pre All-Star	40	10	7	17	3	12	1	0	59	16.9	.43
Post All-Star	38	11	11	22	1	8	3	1	57	19.3	.58
Day	4	0	2	2	2	2	0	0	3	0.0	.50
Night	74	21	16	37	2	18	4	1	113	18.6	.50

	GP	G	A	Pts	+/–	PIM	PP	SH	S	SPct	P/G
National TV	12	3	2	5	0	0	0	0	20	15.0	.42
0 Days Rest	14	0	3	3	-4	6	0	0	14	0.0	.21
1 Days Rest	37	12	10	22	4	8	4	0	65	18.5	.59
2 Days Rest	15	5	2	7	1	2	0	0	22	22.7	.47
3+ Days Rest	12	4	3	7	3	4	0	1	15	26.7	.58

	G	A	Pts	PIM		G	A	Pts	PIM
1st Period	4	5	9	6	Winning	6	4	10	10
2nd Period	7	8	15	8	Losing	8	6	14	4
3rd Period	10	4	14	6	Tied	7	8	15	6
Overtime	0	1	1	0	Clutch	4	4	8	0
Last 5 Min	4	6	10	2	Blowouts	0	1	1	2

Markus Naslund

Vancouver Canucks — Right Wing

1998-99 Season

	GP	G	A	Pts	+/–	PIM	PP	SH	S	SPct	P/G
Overall	80	36	30	66	-13	74	15	2	205	17.6	.83
Home	40	20	10	30	1	44	8	0	98	20.4	.75
Away	40	16	20	36	-14	30	7	2	107	15.0	.90
vs. Division	18	6	10	16	-1	28	2	2	41	14.6	.89
vs. Conference	55	24	21	45	-13	50	10	2	145	16.6	.82
vs. Playoff	51	23	17	40	-11	56	10	2	140	16.4	.78
vs. Non-Playoff	29	13	13	26	-2	18	5	0	65	20.0	.90
Pre All-Star	43	23	16	39	-6	44	11	0	117	19.7	.91
Post All-Star	37	13	14	27	-7	30	4	2	88	14.8	.73
Day	3	1	1	2	-4	0	1	0	4	25.0	.67
Night	77	35	29	64	-9	74	14	2	201	17.4	.83

	GP	G	A	Pts	+/–	PIM	PP	SH	S	SPct	P/G
National TV	19	8	5	13	-6	18	5	0	54	14.8	.68
0 Days Rest	12	6	6	12	-1	10	1	0	37	16.2	1.00
1 Days Rest	46	16	15	31	-13	44	7	0	104	15.4	.67
2 Days Rest	14	10	6	16	4	4	3	2	47	21.3	1.14
3+ Days Rest	8	4	3	7	-3	16	4	0	17	23.5	.88

	G	A	Pts	PIM		G	A	Pts	PIM
1st Period	12	7	19	30	Winning	10	6	16	24
2nd Period	11	12	23	36	Losing	15	19	34	40
3rd Period	13	11	24	8	Tied	11	5	16	10
Overtime	0	0	0	0	Clutch	4	1	5	0
Last 5 Min	6	9	15	24	Blowouts	2	3	5	8

Andrei Nazarov

Calgary Flames — Left Wing

1998-99 Season

	GP	G	A	Pts	+/–	PIM	PP	SH	S	SPct	P/G
Overall	62	7	9	16	-4	73	0	0	71	9.9	.26
Home	29	2	3	5	0	31	0	0	32	6.3	.17
Away	33	5	6	11	-4	42	0	0	39	12.8	.33
vs. Division	16	2	2	4	0	12	0	0	18	11.1	.25
vs. Conference	44	6	8	14	-3	54	0	0	44	13.6	.32
vs. Playoff	39	4	5	9	-10	55	0	0	42	9.5	.23
vs. Non-Playoff	23	3	4	7	6	18	0	0	29	10.3	.30
Pre All-Star	27	2	0	2	-7	47	0	0	19	10.5	.07
Post All-Star	35	5	9	14	3	26	0	0	52	9.6	.40
Day	3	0	1	1	1	10	0	0	4	0.0	.33
Night	59	7	8	15	-5	63	0	0	67	10.4	.25

	GP	G	A	Pts	+/–	PIM	PP	SH	S	SPct	P/G
National TV	6	0	1	1	-2	4	0	0	6	0.0	.17
0 Days Rest	12	2	1	3	2	7	0	0	17	11.8	.25
1 Days Rest	22	3	2	5	-4	31	0	0	29	10.3	.23
2 Days Rest	11	1	4	5	1	12	0	0	11	9.1	.45
3+ Days Rest	17	1	2	3	-3	23	0	0	14	7.1	.18

	G	A	Pts	PIM		G	A	Pts	PIM
1st Period	3	3	6	32	Winning	1	3	4	20
2nd Period	1	3	4	15	Losing	4	2	6	48
3rd Period	3	3	6	26	Tied	2	4	6	5
Overtime	0	0	0	0	Clutch	0	0	0	2
Last 5 Min	1	1	2	14	Blowouts	0	1	1	14

Petr Nedved

New York Rangers — Center

1998-99 Season

	GP	G	A	Pts	+/–	PIM	PP	SH	S	SPct	P/G
Overall	56	20	27	47	-6	50	9	1	153	13.1	.84
Home	30	13	14	27	-2	26	6	1	88	14.8	.90
Away	26	7	13	20	-4	24	3	0	65	10.8	.77
vs. Division	11	7	3	10	-2	6	3	1	33	21.2	.91
vs. Conference	39	16	17	33	-6	34	7	1	114	14.0	.85
vs. Playoff	34	14	18	32	0	28	7	1	100	14.0	.94
vs. Non-Playoff	22	6	9	15	-6	22	2	0	53	11.3	.68
Pre All-Star	26	9	14	23	-4	28	3	0	71	12.7	.88
Post All-Star	30	11	13	24	-2	22	6	1	82	13.4	.80
Day	9	5	2	7	-1	8	3	0	30	16.7	.78
Night	47	15	25	40	-5	42	6	1	123	12.2	.85

	GP	G	A	Pts	+/–	PIM	PP	SH	S	SPct	P/G
National TV	15	8	6	14	-2	14	5	1	42	19.0	.93
0 Days Rest	9	4	2	6	-4	8	2	0	20	20.0	.67
1 Days Rest	28	10	14	24	-6	20	4	1	80	12.5	.86
2 Days Rest	11	5	8	13	4	20	2	0	31	16.1	1.18
3+ Days Rest	8	1	3	4	0	2	1	0	22	4.5	.50

	G	A	Pts	PIM		G	A	Pts	PIM
1st Period	4	9	13	18	Winning	8	10	18	22
2nd Period	8	10	18	18	Losing	6	6	12	24
3rd Period	7	7	14	14	Tied	6	11	17	4
Overtime	1	1	2	0	Clutch	3	4	7	2
Last 5 Min	3	11	14	8	Blowouts	1	1	2	6

Sergei Nemchinov

New Jersey Devils — Center

1998-99 Season

	GP	G	A	Pts	+/–	PIM	PP	SH	S	SPct	P/G
Overall	77	12	8	20	-13	28	2	0	74	16.2	.26
Home	39	5	3	8	-7	10	0	0	42	11.9	.21
Away	38	7	5	12	-6	18	2	0	32	21.9	.32
vs. Division	20	3	2	5	0	8	0	0	22	13.6	.25
vs. Conference	53	10	5	15	-9	24	1	0	56	17.9	.28
vs. Playoff	46	8	5	13	-8	16	1	0	53	15.1	.28
vs. Non-Playoff	31	4	3	7	-5	12	1	0	21	19.0	.23
Pre All-Star	44	5	3	8	-13	16	1	0	35	14.3	.18
Post All-Star	33	7	5	12	0	12	1	0	39	17.9	.36
Day	13	3	1	4	2	4	0	0	17	17.6	.31
Night	64	9	7	16	-15	24	2	0	57	15.8	.25

	GP	G	A	Pts	+/–	PIM	PP	SH	S	SPct	P/G
National TV	6	1	0	1	0	4	0	0	3	33.3	.17
0 Days Rest	15	5	2	7	-2	2	1	0	16	31.3	.47
1 Days Rest	31	4	3	7	-11	14	1	0	25	16.0	.23
2 Days Rest	17	0	2	2	-2	6	0	0	17	0.0	.12
3+ Days Rest	14	3	1	4	2	6	0	0	16	18.8	.29

	G	A	Pts	PIM		G	A	Pts	PIM
1st Period	2	1	3	14	Winning	4	2	6	10
2nd Period	4	3	7	10	Losing	5	4	9	12
3rd Period	6	4	10	4	Tied	3	2	5	6
Overtime	0	0	0	0	Clutch	2	2	4	2
Last 5 Min	3	0	3	4	Blowouts	1	0	1	0

Rob Niedermayer

Florida Panthers — Center

1998-99 Season

	GP	G	A	Pts	+/–	PIM	PP	SH	S	SPct	P/G
Overall	82	18	33	51	-13	50	6	1	142	12.7	.62
Home	41	11	18	29	-3	26	2	1	80	13.8	.71
Away	41	7	15	22	-10	24	4	0	62	11.3	.54
vs. Division	15	2	6	8	2	12	0	0	28	7.1	.53
vs. Conference	58	11	22	33	-13	20	5	1	95	11.6	.57
vs. Playoff	49	12	19	31	-15	22	3	1	81	14.8	.63
vs. Non-Playoff	33	6	14	20	2	28	3	0	61	9.8	.61
Pre All-Star	44	12	20	32	-5	28	5	0	84	14.3	.73
Post All-Star	38	6	13	19	-8	22	1	1	58	10.3	.50
Day	4	4	1	5	2	2	1	0	11	36.4	1.25
Night	78	14	32	46	-15	48	5	1	131	10.7	.59

	GP	G	A	Pts	+/–	PIM	PP	SH	S	SPct	P/G
National TV	4	1	0	1	-8	4	0	0	5	20.0	.25
0 Days Rest	19	3	6	9	-6	8	1	0	25	12.0	.47
1 Days Rest	33	9	14	23	-3	24	4	0	58	15.5	.70
2 Days Rest	16	4	6	10	1	4	0	0	36	11.1	.63
3+ Days Rest	14	2	7	9	-5	14	1	1	23	8.7	.64

	G	A	Pts	PIM		G	A	Pts	PIM
1st Period	7	12	19	10	Winning	5	7	12	26
2nd Period	4	9	13	18	Losing	6	12	18	10
3rd Period	7	12	19	22	Tied	7	14	21	14
Overtime	0	0	0	0	Clutch	1	2	3	4
Last 5 Min	3	9	12	12	Blowouts	1	2	3	6

Scott Niedermayer

New Jersey Devils — Defense

1998-99 Season

	GP	G	A	Pts	+/–	PIM	PP	SH	S	SPct	P/G
Overall	72	11	35	46	16	26	1	1	161	6.8	.64
Home	36	5	14	19	5	10	1	1	82	6.1	.53
Away	36	6	21	27	11	16	0	0	79	7.6	.75
vs. Division	16	1	8	9	2	2	0	0	38	2.6	.56
vs. Conference	51	9	25	34	11	18	0	1	107	8.4	.67
vs. Playoff	41	8	19	27	9	18	1	0	90	8.9	.66
vs. Non-Playoff	31	3	16	19	7	8	0	1	71	4.2	.61
Pre All-Star	34	5	16	21	1	12	1	1	74	6.8	.62
Post All-Star	38	6	19	25	15	14	0	0	87	6.9	.66
Day	12	1	6	7	2	4	0	0	25	4.0	.58
Night	60	10	29	39	14	22	1	1	136	7.4	.65

	GP	G	A	Pts	+/–	PIM	PP	SH	S	SPct	P/G
National TV	7	1	1	2	-3	4	0	0	21	4.8	.29
0 Days Rest	15	2	6	8	0	6	0	0	40	5.0	.53
1 Days Rest	29	3	17	20	4	10	0	0	61	4.9	.69
2 Days Rest	20	4	8	12	6	8	0	1	44	9.1	.60
3+ Days Rest	8	2	4	6	6	2	1	0	16	12.5	.75

	G	A	Pts	PIM		G	A	Pts	PIM
1st Period	2	11	13	10	Winning	4	16	20	14
2nd Period	6	14	20	6	Losing	3	4	7	8
3rd Period	3	10	13	10	Tied	4	15	19	4
Overtime	0	0	0	0	Clutch	1	3	4	2
Last 5 Min	3	9	12	14	Blowouts	1	2	3	2

Joe Nieuwendyk

Dallas Stars — Center

1998-99 Season

	GP	G	A	Pts	+/–	PIM	PP	SH	S	SPct	P/G
Overall	67	28	27	55	11	34	8	0	157	17.8	.82
Home	34	20	14	34	5	16	7	0	78	25.6	1.00
Away	33	8	13	21	6	18	1	0	79	10.1	.64
vs. Division	20	11	5	16	7	18	2	0	47	23.4	.80
vs. Conference	45	20	18	38	9	22	7	0	106	18.9	.84
vs. Playoff	40	19	17	36	6	26	6	0	84	22.6	.90
vs. Non-Playoff	27	9	10	19	5	8	2	0	73	12.3	.70
Pre All-Star	33	9	14	23	-2	18	4	0	65	13.8	.70
Post All-Star	34	19	13	32	13	16	4	0	92	20.7	.94
Day	7	3	2	5	1	2	1	0	13	23.1	.71
Night	60	25	25	50	10	32	7	0	144	17.4	.83

	GP	G	A	Pts	+/–	PIM	PP	SH	S	SPct	P/G
National TV	12	4	3	7	-3	6	2	0	31	12.9	.58
0 Days Rest	10	1	2	3	-1	8	0	0	26	3.8	.30
1 Days Rest	35	16	18	34	9	14	2	0	88	18.2	.97
2 Days Rest	9	3	6	9	4	2	2	0	16	18.8	1.00
3+ Days Rest	13	8	1	9	-1	10	4	0	27	29.6	.69

	G	A	Pts	PIM		G	A	Pts	PIM
1st Period	11	8	19	16	Winning	12	17	29	24
2nd Period	8	10	18	12	Losing	4	6	10	6
3rd Period	8	9	17	6	Tied	12	4	16	4
Overtime	1	0	1	0	Clutch	3	1	4	0
Last 5 Min	6	3	9	10	Blowouts	1	2	3	6

Janne Niinimaa

Edmonton Oilers — Defense

1998-99 Season

	GP	G	A	Pts	+/–	PIM	PP	SH	S	SPct	P/G
Overall	81	4	24	28	7	88	2	0	142	2.8	.35
Home	40	4	13	17	2	36	2	0	72	5.6	.43
Away	41	0	11	11	5	52	0	0	70	0.0	.27
vs. Division	18	0	7	7	2	30	0	0	32	0.0	.39
vs. Conference	54	3	17	20	7	64	1	0	98	3.1	.37
vs. Playoff	47	3	12	15	0	56	1	0	73	4.1	.32
vs. Non-Playoff	34	1	12	13	7	32	1	0	69	1.4	.38
Pre All-Star	43	0	13	13	8	46	0	0	72	0.0	.30
Post All-Star	38	4	11	15	-1	42	2	0	70	5.7	.39
Day	4	0	1	1	1	2	0	0	9	0.0	.25
Night	77	4	23	27	6	86	2	0	133	3.0	.35

	GP	G	A	Pts	+/–	PIM	PP	SH	S	SPct	P/G
National TV	13	0	3	3	4	8	0	0	17	0.0	.23
0 Days Rest	14	0	2	2	-5	16	0	0	21	0.0	.14
1 Days Rest	38	2	12	14	7	44	1	0	73	2.7	.37
2 Days Rest	16	1	1	2	3	16	0	0	23	4.3	.13
3+ Days Rest	13	1	9	10	2	12	1	0	25	4.0	.77

	G	A	Pts	PIM		G	A	Pts	PIM
1st Period	1	7	8	30	Winning	0	11	11	40
2nd Period	1	9	10	44	Losing	2	9	11	38
3rd Period	2	7	9	14	Tied	2	4	6	10
Overtime	0	1	1	0	Clutch	0	3	3	2
Last 5 Min	0	8	8	24	Blowouts	0	3	3	8

Andrei Nikolishin

Washington Capitals — Left Wing

1998-99 Season

	GP	G	A	Pts	+/–	PIM	PP	SH	S	SPct	P/G
Overall	73	8	27	35	0	28	0	1	121	6.6	.48
Home	36	4	12	16	-1	14	0	0	61	6.6	.44
Away	37	4	15	19	1	14	0	1	60	6.7	.51
vs. Division	13	2	7	9	7	0	0	1	22	9.1	.69
vs. Conference	53	6	19	25	7	12	0	1	95	6.3	.47
vs. Playoff	45	5	13	18	-1	18	0	0	75	6.7	.40
vs. Non-Playoff	28	3	14	17	1	10	0	1	46	6.5	.61
Pre All-Star	34	3	15	18	4	12	0	1	57	5.3	.53
Post All-Star	39	5	12	17	-4	16	0	0	64	7.8	.44
Day	3	1	1	2	0	2	0	0	6	16.7	.67
Night	70	7	26	33	0	26	0	1	115	6.1	.47

	GP	G	A	Pts	+/–	PIM	PP	SH	S	SPct	P/G
National TV	10	2	3	5	3	0	0	0	19	10.5	.50
0 Days Rest	13	2	8	10	5	4	0	0	18	11.1	.77
1 Days Rest	37	3	13	16	-2	10	0	0	68	4.4	.43
2 Days Rest	11	1	3	4	-3	8	0	0	19	5.3	.36
3+ Days Rest	12	2	3	5	0	6	0	1	16	12.5	.42

	G	A	Pts	PIM		G	A	Pts	PIM
1st Period	2	5	7	10	Winning	1	8	9	6
2nd Period	2	10	12	6	Losing	2	13	15	22
3rd Period	4	11	15	12	Tied	5	6	11	0
Overtime	0	1	1	0	Clutch	1	4	5	4
Last 5 Min	1	10	11	6	Blowouts	0	5	5	2

Owen Nolan

San Jose Sharks — Right Wing

1998-99 Season

	GP	G	A	Pts	+/–	PIM	PP	SH	S	SPct	P/G
Overall	78	19	26	45	16	129	6	2	207	9.2	.58
Home	40	9	16	25	11	71	3	2	114	7.9	.63
Away	38	10	10	20	5	58	3	0	93	10.8	.53
vs. Division	23	5	7	12	-1	15	2	0	57	8.8	.52
vs. Conference	53	10	16	26	4	95	3	1	137	7.3	.49
vs. Playoff	47	11	15	26	7	50	4	1	122	9.0	.55
vs. Non-Playoff	31	8	11	19	9	79	2	1	85	9.4	.61
Pre All-Star	43	10	14	24	2	64	2	1	113	8.8	.56
Post All-Star	35	9	12	21	14	65	4	1	94	9.6	.60
Day	7	1	1	2	1	23	0	0	10	10.0	.29
Night	71	18	25	43	15	106	6	2	197	9.1	.61

	GP	G	A	Pts	+/–	PIM	PP	SH	S	SPct	P/G
National TV	11	0	2	2	0	26	0	0	26	0.0	.18
0 Days Rest	13	5	5	10	8	41	1	0	36	13.9	.77
1 Days Rest	39	9	13	22	6	51	4	0	107	8.4	.56
2 Days Rest	15	4	4	8	3	33	1	1	44	9.1	.53
3+ Days Rest	11	1	4	5	-1	4	0	1	20	5.0	.45

	G	A	Pts	PIM		G	A	Pts	PIM
1st Period	8	6	14	31	Winning	8	9	17	62
2nd Period	6	11	17	46	Losing	3	6	9	55
3rd Period	5	9	14	48	Tied	8	11	19	12
Overtime	0	0	0	4	Clutch	2	1	3	10
Last 5 Min	3	5	8	47	Blowouts	0	3	3	26

Jeff Norton

San Jose Sharks — Defense

1998-99 Season

	GP	G	A	Pts	+/–	PIM	PP	SH	S	SPct	P/G
Overall	72	4	18	22	2	44	2	0	70	5.7	.31
Home	34	0	8	8	0	16	0	0	33	0.0	.24
Away	38	4	10	14	2	28	2	0	37	10.8	.37
vs. Division	21	1	6	7	-2	26	0	0	19	5.3	.33
vs. Conference	50	3	12	15	1	38	2	0	49	6.1	.30
vs. Playoff	41	1	9	10	0	36	1	0	41	2.4	.24
vs. Non-Playoff	31	3	9	12	2	8	1	0	29	10.3	.39
Pre All-Star	35	1	11	12	7	16	1	0	45	2.2	.34
Post All-Star	37	3	7	10	-5	28	1	0	25	12.0	.27
Day	7	1	4	5	2	4	1	0	6	16.7	.71
Night	65	3	14	17	0	40	1	0	64	4.7	.26

	GP	G	A	Pts	+/–	PIM	PP	SH	S	SPct	P/G
National TV	10	1	2	3	-2	4	1	0	10	10.0	.30
0 Days Rest	11	0	4	4	0	16	0	0	10	0.0	.36
1 Days Rest	37	4	6	10	1	8	2	0	40	10.0	.27
2 Days Rest	14	0	3	3	0	16	0	0	13	0.0	.21
3+ Days Rest	10	0	5	5	1	4	0	0	7	0.0	.50

	G	A	Pts	PIM		G	A	Pts	PIM
1st Period	1	11	12	10	Winning	0	3	3	20
2nd Period	0	1	1	24	Losing	1	2	3	18
3rd Period	3	5	8	10	Tied	3	13	16	6
Overtime	0	1	1	0	Clutch	2	3	5	0
Last 5 Min	1	6	7	10	Blowouts	0	1	1	6

Teppo Numminen

Phoenix Coyotes — Defense

1998-99 Season

	GP	G	A	Pts	+/–	PIM	PP	SH	S	SPct	P/G
Overall	82	10	30	40	3	30	1	0	156	6.4	.49
Home	41	3	10	13	1	16	0	0	82	3.7	.32
Away	41	7	20	27	2	14	1	0	74	9.5	.66
vs. Division	24	3	6	9	0	6	1	0	41	7.3	.38
vs. Conference	56	8	22	30	11	20	1	0	112	7.1	.54
vs. Playoff	48	7	18	25	8	18	1	0	79	8.9	.52
vs. Non-Playoff	34	3	12	15	-5	12	0	0	77	3.9	.44
Pre All-Star	42	8	17	25	15	18	0	0	87	9.2	.60
Post All-Star	40	2	13	15	-12	12	1	0	69	2.9	.38
Day	6	0	2	2	1	2	0	0	11	0.0	.33
Night	76	10	28	38	2	28	1	0	145	6.9	.50

	GP	G	A	Pts	+/–	PIM	PP	SH	S	SPct	P/G
National TV	14	2	3	5	9	10	0	0	24	8.3	.36
0 Days Rest	13	1	11	12	-3	4	0	0	31	3.2	.92
1 Days Rest	42	6	11	17	4	14	1	0	70	8.6	.40
2 Days Rest	16	1	5	6	-1	8	0	0	31	3.2	.38
3+ Days Rest	11	2	3	5	3	4	0	0	24	8.3	.45

	G	A	Pts	PIM		G	A	Pts	PIM
1st Period	2	12	14	6	Winning	3	5	8	18
2nd Period	3	11	14	6	Losing	6	8	14	10
3rd Period	5	7	12	18	Tied	1	17	18	2
Overtime	0	0	0	0	Clutch	3	1	4	10
Last 5 Min	4	5	9	6	Blowouts	0	1	1	0

Michael Nylander

Tampa Bay Lightning — Center

1998-99 Season

	GP	G	A	Pts	+/–	PIM	PP	SH	S	SPct	P/G
Overall	33	4	10	14	-9	8	1	0	33	12.1	.42
Home	19	3	4	7	-4	8	1	0	16	18.8	.37
Away	14	1	6	7	-5	0	0	0	17	5.9	.50
vs. Division	7	1	1	2	-3	4	1	0	7	14.3	.29
vs. Conference	18	3	3	6	-7	6	1	0	16	18.8	.33
vs. Playoff	23	0	8	8	-8	4	0	0	23	0.0	.35
vs. Non-Playoff	10	4	2	6	-1	4	1	0	10	40.0	.60
Pre All-Star	10	2	3	5	1	2	1	0	7	28.6	.50
Post All-Star	23	2	7	9	-10	6	0	0	26	7.7	.39
Day	2	1	1	2	2	0	0	0	5	20.0	1.00
Night	31	3	9	12	-11	8	1	0	28	10.7	.39

	GP	G	A	Pts	+/–	PIM	PP	SH	S	SPct	P/G
National TV	1	0	0	0	0	2	0	0	0	–	.00
0 Days Rest	5	0	0	0	-8	0	0	0	5	0.0	.00
1 Days Rest	12	2	2	4	-4	6	0	0	15	13.3	.33
2 Days Rest	6	0	4	4	0	0	0	0	6	0.0	.67
3+ Days Rest	10	2	4	6	3	2	1	0	7	28.6	.60

	G	A	Pts	PIM		G	A	Pts	PIM
1st Period	3	5	8	6	Winning	0	0	0	2
2nd Period	0	3	3	2	Losing	2	7	9	6
3rd Period	1	2	3	0	Tied	2	3	5	0
Overtime	0	0	0	0	Clutch	0	1	1	0
Last 5 Min	1	4	5	2	Blowouts	0	0	0	2

Sean O'Donnell

Los Angeles Kings — Defense

1998-99 Season

	GP	G	A	Pts	+/–	PIM	PP	SH	S	SPct	P/G
Overall	80	1	13	14	1	186	0	0	64	1.6	.18
Home	40	1	7	8	0	85	0	0	29	3.4	.20
Away	40	0	6	6	1	101	0	0	35	0.0	.15
vs. Division	22	0	2	2	0	52	0	0	17	0.0	.09
vs. Conference	55	1	9	10	2	129	0	0	45	2.2	.18
vs. Playoff	54	1	8	9	-1	118	0	0	46	2.2	.17
vs. Non-Playoff	26	0	5	5	2	68	0	0	18	0.0	.19
Pre All-Star	45	1	10	11	5	106	0	0	39	2.6	.24
Post All-Star	35	0	3	3	-4	80	0	0	25	0.0	.09
Day	5	0	2	2	-2	9	0	0	2	0.0	.40
Night	75	1	11	12	3	177	0	0	62	1.6	.16

	GP	G	A	Pts	+/–	PIM	PP	SH	S	SPct	P/G
National TV	15	1	1	2	-6	27	0	0	12	8.3	.13
0 Days Rest	12	0	1	1	-2	40	0	0	15	0.0	.08
1 Days Rest	41	1	6	7	2	103	0	0	32	3.1	.17
2 Days Rest	15	0	3	3	4	35	0	0	6	0.0	.20
3+ Days Rest	12	0	3	3	-3	8	0	0	11	0.0	.25

	G	A	Pts	PIM		G	A	Pts	PIM
1st Period	0	3	3	75	Winning	0	3	3	76
2nd Period	1	4	5	59	Losing	1	6	7	89
3rd Period	0	6	6	45	Tied	0	4	4	21
Overtime	0	0	0	7	Clutch	0	1	1	19
Last 5 Min	1	5	6	73	Blowouts	0	0	0	44

Jeff O'Neill

Carolina Hurricanes — Center

1998-99 Season

	GP	G	A	Pts	+/–	PIM	PP	SH	S	SPct	P/G
Overall	75	16	15	31	3	66	4	0	121	13.2	.41
Home	39	7	8	15	-1	25	3	0	59	11.9	.38
Away	36	9	7	16	4	41	1	0	62	14.5	.44
vs. Division	12	3	6	9	3	4	0	0	26	11.5	.75
vs. Conference	52	12	12	24	-3	48	4	0	76	15.8	.46
vs. Playoff	41	6	6	12	-3	52	3	0	62	9.7	.29
vs. Non-Playoff	34	10	9	19	6	14	1	0	59	16.9	.56
Pre All-Star	45	9	9	18	1	35	2	0	71	12.7	.40
Post All-Star	30	7	6	13	2	31	2	0	50	14.0	.43
Day	7	1	1	2	0	14	0	0	11	9.1	.29
Night	68	15	14	29	3	52	4	0	110	13.6	.43

	GP	G	A	Pts	+/–	PIM	PP	SH	S	SPct	P/G
National TV	2	0	1	1	1	2	0	0	3	0.0	.50
0 Days Rest	15	3	2	5	3	18	1	0	33	9.1	.33
1 Days Rest	28	3	4	7	-4	20	1	0	37	8.1	.25
2 Days Rest	22	7	5	12	3	24	1	0	35	20.0	.55
3+ Days Rest	10	3	4	7	1	4	1	0	16	18.8	.70

	G	A	Pts	PIM		G	A	Pts	PIM
1st Period	4	5	9	11	Winning	6	6	12	16
2nd Period	6	6	12	14	Losing	6	4	10	28
3rd Period	6	4	10	41	Tied	4	5	9	22
Overtime	0	0	0	0	Clutch	1	1	2	12
Last 5 Min	6	3	9	25	Blowouts	1	0	1	15

Adam Oates

Washington Capitals — Center

1998-99 Season

	GP	G	A	Pts	+/–	PIM	PP	SH	S	SPct	P/G
Overall	59	12	41	53	-1	22	3	0	79	15.2	.90
Home	32	7	22	29	-2	12	0	0	52	13.5	.91
Away	27	5	19	24	1	10	3	0	27	18.5	.89
vs. Division	13	0	15	15	8	8	0	0	9	0.0	1.15
vs. Conference	40	8	32	40	5	16	1	0	46	17.4	1.00
vs. Playoff	35	6	24	30	-3	12	1	0	43	14.0	.86
vs. Non-Playoff	24	6	17	23	2	10	2	0	36	16.7	.96
Pre All-Star	20	6	8	14	-1	6	3	0	34	17.6	.70
Post All-Star	39	6	33	39	0	16	0	0	45	13.3	1.00
Day	2	0	3	3	0	0	0	0	1	0.0	1.50
Night	57	12	38	50	-1	22	3	0	78	15.4	.88

	GP	G	A	Pts	+/–	PIM	PP	SH	S	SPct	P/G
National TV	11	1	13	14	2	6	0	0	20	5.0	1.27
0 Days Rest	9	0	6	6	-4	8	0	0	6	0.0	.67
1 Days Rest	31	7	24	31	2	8	2	0	40	17.5	1.00
2 Days Rest	10	1	7	8	-1	2	0	0	16	6.3	.80
3+ Days Rest	9	4	4	8	2	4	1	0	17	23.5	.89

	G	A	Pts	PIM		G	A	Pts	PIM
1st Period	4	5	9	6	Winning	2	16	18	8
2nd Period	3	19	22	8	Losing	5	13	18	12
3rd Period	5	16	21	8	Tied	5	12	17	2
Overtime	0	1	1	0	Clutch	1	6	7	0
Last 5 Min	3	9	12	4	Blowouts	0	6	6	2

Lyle Odelein

New Jersey Devils — Defense

1998-99 Season

	GP	G	A	Pts	+/–	PIM	PP	SH	S	SPct	P/G
Overall	70	5	26	31	6	114	1	0	101	5.0	.44
Home	34	3	11	14	-4	48	1	0	54	5.6	.41
Away	36	2	15	17	10	66	0	0	47	4.3	.47
vs. Division	17	0	5	5	3	14	0	0	22	0.0	.29
vs. Conference	49	3	18	21	6	102	0	0	72	4.2	.43
vs. Playoff	39	1	14	15	1	72	0	0	48	2.1	.38
vs. Non-Playoff	31	4	12	16	5	42	1	0	53	7.5	.52
Pre All-Star	41	0	15	15	2	69	0	0	51	0.0	.37
Post All-Star	29	5	11	16	4	45	1	0	50	10.0	.55
Day	9	1	3	4	3	14	1	0	9	11.1	.44
Night	61	4	23	27	3	100	0	0	92	4.3	.44

	GP	G	A	Pts	+/–	PIM	PP	SH	S	SPct	P/G
National TV	6	0	1	1	-4	14	0	0	10	0.0	.17
0 Days Rest	14	0	5	5	2	12	0	0	20	0.0	.36
1 Days Rest	28	3	14	17	4	30	1	0	38	7.9	.61
2 Days Rest	17	1	2	3	-4	68	0	0	30	3.3	.18
3+ Days Rest	11	1	5	6	4	4	0	0	13	7.7	.55

	G	A	Pts	PIM
1st Period	1	10	11	36
2nd Period	4	10	14	26
3rd Period	0	6	6	52
Overtime	0	0	0	0
Last 5 Min	2	5	7	35

	G	A	Pts	PIM
Winning	1	8	9	80
Losing	3	7	10	32
Tied	1	11	12	2
Clutch	0	0	0	4
Blowouts	0	1	1	2

Mattias Ohlund

Vancouver Canucks — Defense

1998-99 Season

	GP	G	A	Pts	+/–	PIM	PP	SH	S	SPct	P/G
Overall	74	9	26	35	-19	83	2	1	129	7.0	.47
Home	37	6	14	20	-2	34	2	1	65	9.2	.54
Away	37	3	12	15	-17	49	0	0	64	4.7	.41
vs. Division	15	1	6	7	-3	18	0	0	20	5.0	.47
vs. Conference	49	3	17	20	-19	65	1	0	72	4.2	.41
vs. Playoff	48	3	11	14	-18	67	1	0	74	4.1	.29
vs. Non-Playoff	26	6	15	21	-1	16	1	1	55	10.9	.81
Pre All-Star	45	6	16	22	-8	61	1	0	84	7.1	.49
Post All-Star	29	3	10	13	-11	22	1	1	45	6.7	.45
Day	3	0	2	2	-4	0	0	0	4	0.0	.67
Night	71	9	24	33	-15	83	2	1	125	7.2	.46

	GP	G	A	Pts	+/–	PIM	PP	SH	S	SPct	P/G
National TV	19	5	8	13	-8	12	2	1	40	12.5	.68
0 Days Rest	12	0	1	1	-8	2	0	0	19	0.0	.08
1 Days Rest	40	7	14	21	-9	61	1	1	74	9.5	.53
2 Days Rest	14	2	7	9	3	14	1	0	30	6.7	.64
3+ Days Rest	8	0	4	4	-5	6	0	0	6	0.0	.50

	G	A	Pts	PIM
1st Period	3	1	4	18
2nd Period	4	11	15	22
3rd Period	2	14	16	43
Overtime	0	0	0	0
Last 5 Min	1	3	4	16

	G	A	Pts	PIM
Winning	2	5	7	18
Losing	4	15	19	63
Tied	3	6	9	2
Clutch	0	3	3	0
Blowouts	1	2	3	49

Fredrik Olausson

Anaheim Mighty Ducks — Defense

1998-99 Season

	GP	G	A	Pts	+/–	PIM	PP	SH	S	SPct	P/G
Overall	74	16	40	56	17	30	10	0	121	13.2	.76
Home	36	9	24	33	19	10	6	0	65	13.8	.92
Away	38	7	16	23	-2	20	4	0	56	12.5	.61
vs. Division	22	3	12	15	7	10	2	0	38	7.9	.68
vs. Conference	52	7	28	35	4	26	5	0	79	8.9	.67
vs. Playoff	48	10	28	38	9	24	6	0	82	12.2	.79
vs. Non-Playoff	26	6	12	18	8	6	4	0	39	15.4	.69
Pre All-Star	39	10	19	29	11	14	8	0	70	14.3	.74
Post All-Star	35	6	21	27	6	16	2	0	51	11.8	.77
Day	1	0	4	4	4	0	0	0	4	0.0	4.00
Night	73	16	36	52	13	30	10	0	117	13.7	.71

	GP	G	A	Pts	+/–	PIM	PP	SH	S	SPct	P/G
National TV	12	3	6	9	2	8	1	0	15	20.0	.75
0 Days Rest	13	3	7	10	-2	8	1	0	17	17.6	.77
1 Days Rest	35	6	20	26	7	22	5	0	60	10.0	.74
2 Days Rest	11	2	8	10	5	0	2	0	18	11.1	.91
3+ Days Rest	15	5	5	10	7	0	2	0	26	19.2	.67

	G	A	Pts	PIM
1st Period	7	14	21	14
2nd Period	5	18	23	8
3rd Period	4	7	11	8
Overtime	0	1	1	0
Last 5 Min	4	10	14	10

	G	A	Pts	PIM
Winning	5	18	23	12
Losing	6	13	19	18
Tied	5	9	14	0
Clutch	0	2	2	2
Blowouts	0	2	2	8

Ed Olczyk

Chicago Blackhawks — Center

1998-99 Season

	GP	G	A	Pts	+/–	PIM	PP	SH	S	SPct	P/G
Overall	61	10	15	25	-3	29	2	1	88	11.4	.41
Home	31	7	8	15	7	19	1	0	47	14.9	.48
Away	30	3	7	10	-10	10	1	1	41	7.3	.33
vs. Division	14	3	5	8	3	6	1	0	21	14.3	.57
vs. Conference	41	7	9	16	-3	21	1	1	55	12.7	.39
vs. Playoff	40	6	6	12	-6	21	1	1	60	10.0	.30
vs. Non-Playoff	21	4	9	13	3	8	1	0	28	14.3	.62
Pre All-Star	27	3	4	7	-4	8	0	0	39	7.7	.26
Post All-Star	34	7	11	18	1	21	2	1	49	14.3	.53
Day	8	2	1	3	-2	9	1	0	11	18.2	.38
Night	53	8	14	22	-1	20	1	1	77	10.4	.42

	GP	G	A	Pts	+/–	PIM	PP	SH	S	SPct	P/G
National TV	15	2	2	4	2	9	0	0	19	10.5	.27
0 Days Rest	11	1	2	3	-3	9	0	0	15	6.7	.27
1 Days Rest	24	4	5	9	-4	10	1	0	36	11.1	.38
2 Days Rest	10	3	5	8	1	6	1	0	17	17.6	.80
3+ Days Rest	16	2	3	5	3	4	0	1	20	10.0	.31

	G	A	Pts	PIM
1st Period	2	6	8	8
2nd Period	5	2	7	11
3rd Period	3	7	10	10
Overtime	0	0	0	0
Last 5 Min	2	6	8	15

	G	A	Pts	PIM
Winning	3	5	8	11
Losing	3	3	6	16
Tied	4	7	11	2
Clutch	1	6	7	4
Blowouts	0	1	1	4

Krzysztof Oliwa

New Jersey Devils — Left Wing

1998-99 Season

	GP	G	A	Pts	+/–	PIM	PP	SH	S	SPct	P/G
Overall	64	5	7	12	4	240	0	0	59	8.5	.19
Home	35	2	6	8	3	131	0	0	39	5.1	.23
Away	29	3	1	4	1	109	0	0	20	15.0	.14
vs. Division	13	1	1	2	-1	33	0	0	14	7.1	.15
vs. Conference	43	5	3	8	5	153	0	0	41	12.2	.19
vs. Playoff	38	3	5	8	6	123	0	0	26	11.5	.21
vs. Non-Playoff	26	2	2	4	-2	117	0	0	33	6.1	.15
Pre All-Star	32	3	2	5	0	112	0	0	27	11.1	.16
Post All-Star	32	2	5	7	4	128	0	0	32	6.3	.22
Day	10	0	1	1	0	46	0	0	12	0.0	.10
Night	54	5	6	11	4	194	0	0	47	10.6	.20

	GP	G	A	Pts	+/–	PIM	PP	SH	S	SPct	P/G
National TV	5	0	0	0	-2	34	0	0	2	0.0	.00
0 Days Rest	9	1	1	2	0	29	0	0	6	16.7	.22
1 Days Rest	22	2	1	3	1	91	0	0	23	8.7	.14
2 Days Rest	16	1	2	3	-1	48	0	0	11	9.1	.19
3+ Days Rest	17	1	3	4	4	72	0	0	19	5.3	.24

	G	A	Pts	PIM
1st Period	3	4	7	86
2nd Period	1	1	2	78
3rd Period	1	2	3	76
Overtime	0	0	0	0
Last 5 Min	1	4	5	65

	G	A	Pts	PIM
Winning	1	3	4	121
Losing	1	3	4	103
Tied	3	1	4	16
Clutch	1	0	1	0
Blowouts	0	1	1	12

Sandis Ozolinsh

Colorado Avalanche — Defense

1998-99 Season

	GP	G	A	Pts	+/–	PIM	PP	SH	S	SPct	P/G
Overall	39	7	25	32	10	22	4	0	81	8.6	.82
Home	20	3	16	19	1	10	2	0	48	6.3	.95
Away	19	4	9	13	9	12	2	0	33	12.1	.68
vs. Division	9	2	10	12	-2	4	1	0	26	7.7	1.33
vs. Conference	29	4	23	27	7	20	3	0	62	6.5	.93
vs. Playoff	20	3	10	13	11	14	1	0	35	8.6	.65
vs. Non-Playoff	19	4	15	19	-1	8	3	0	46	8.7	1.00
Pre All-Star	5	0	2	2	2	2	0	0	9	0.0	.40
Post All-Star	34	7	23	30	8	20	4	0	72	9.7	.88
Day	9	0	4	4	2	8	0	0	10	0.0	.44
Night	30	7	21	28	8	14	4	0	71	9.9	.93

	GP	G	A	Pts	+/–	PIM	PP	SH	S	SPct	P/G
National TV	12	1	6	7	7	8	0	0	19	5.3	.58
0 Days Rest	6	0	4	4	3	6	0	0	7	0.0	.67
1 Days Rest	19	3	14	17	1	12	1	0	49	6.1	.89
2 Days Rest	6	2	3	5	2	2	1	0	15	13.3	.83
3+ Days Rest	8	2	4	6	4	2	2	0	10	20.0	.75

	G	A	Pts	PIM
1st Period	4	9	13	12
2nd Period	2	6	8	2
3rd Period	0	10	10	8
Overtime	1	0	1	0
Last 5 Min	2	4	6	4

	G	A	Pts	PIM
Winning	1	6	7	14
Losing	1	12	13	4
Tied	5	7	12	4
Clutch	1	2	3	2
Blowouts	0	1	1	6

Zigmund Palffy

New York Islanders — Right Wing

1998-99 Season

	GP	G	A	Pts	+/–	PIM	PP	SH	S	SPct	P/G
Overall	50	22	28	50	-6	34	5	2	168	13.1	1.00
Home	25	14	19	33	1	8	2	0	94	14.9	1.32
Away	25	8	9	17	-7	26	3	2	74	10.8	.68
vs. Division	12	7	7	14	0	2	2	2	38	18.4	1.17
vs. Conference	37	17	19	36	-11	28	3	2	120	14.2	.97
vs. Playoff	31	16	20	36	-6	26	5	2	101	15.8	1.16
vs. Non-Playoff	19	6	8	14	0	8	0	0	67	9.0	.74
Pre All-Star	14	3	7	10	-6	6	1	0	46	6.5	.71
Post All-Star	36	19	21	40	0	28	4	2	122	15.6	1.11
Day	8	10	4	14	5	0	3	2	30	33.3	1.75
Night	42	12	24	36	-11	34	2	0	138	8.7	.86

	GP	G	A	Pts	+/–	PIM	PP	SH	S	SPct	P/G
National TV	5	4	1	5	-1	4	1	0	17	23.5	1.00
0 Days Rest	8	3	2	5	-2	16	1	0	20	15.0	.63
1 Days Rest	22	10	13	23	-2	8	3	0	75	13.3	1.05
2 Days Rest	13	7	7	14	1	4	1	2	51	13.7	1.08
3+ Days Rest	7	2	6	8	-3	6	0	0	22	9.1	1.14

	G	A	Pts	PIM
1st Period	6	11	17	14
2nd Period	8	10	18	4
3rd Period	8	7	15	14
Overtime	0	0	0	2
Last 5 Min	5	8	13	8

	G	A	Pts	PIM
Winning	4	12	16	4
Losing	9	8	17	22
Tied	9	8	17	8
Clutch	1	4	5	4
Blowouts	2	1	3	12

Jay Pandolfo

New Jersey Devils — Left Wing

1998-99 Season

	GP	G	A	Pts	+/–	PIM	PP	SH	S	SPct	P/G
Overall	70	14	13	27	3	10	1	1	100	14.0	.39
Home	34	9	9	18	4	0	1	1	52	17.3	.53
Away	36	5	4	9	-1	10	0	0	48	10.4	.25
vs. Division	17	4	2	6	-1	4	0	1	24	16.7	.35
vs. Conference	48	13	10	23	5	4	1	1	68	19.1	.48
vs. Playoff	39	7	7	14	0	2	0	0	55	12.7	.36
vs. Non-Playoff	31	7	6	13	3	8	1	1	45	15.6	.42
Pre All-Star	42	10	7	17	-1	8	0	1	65	15.4	.40
Post All-Star	28	4	6	10	4	2	1	0	35	11.4	.36
Day	9	2	4	6	3	2	0	0	17	11.8	.67
Night	61	12	9	21	0	8	1	1	83	14.5	.34

	GP	G	A	Pts	+/–	PIM	PP	SH	S	SPct	P/G
National TV	5	1	0	1	0	0	0	0	13	7.7	.20
0 Days Rest	14	3	0	3	-4	0	0	0	21	14.3	.21
1 Days Rest	29	3	6	9	-4	4	1	0	40	7.5	.31
2 Days Rest	15	3	6	9	7	2	0	0	21	14.3	.60
3+ Days Rest	12	5	1	6	4	4	0	1	18	27.8	.50

	G	A	Pts	PIM
1st Period	5	6	11	0
2nd Period	3	2	5	8
3rd Period	5	5	10	2
Overtime	1	0	1	0
Last 5 Min	6	1	7	2

	G	A	Pts	PIM
Winning	6	4	10	6
Losing	3	3	6	4
Tied	5	6	11	0
Clutch	4	1	5	2
Blowouts	1	0	1	0

Mark Parrish

Florida Panthers — Left Wing

1998-99 Season

	GP	G	A	Pts	+/–	PIM	PP	SH	S	SPct	P/G
Overall	73	24	13	37	-6	25	5	0	129	18.6	.51
Home	38	10	8	18	-3	17	1	0	75	13.3	.47
Away	35	14	5	19	-3	8	4	0	54	25.9	.54
vs. Division	13	4	3	7	1	4	0	0	22	18.2	.54
vs. Conference	51	18	10	28	-2	10	3	0	85	21.2	.55
vs. Playoff	45	12	10	22	-11	13	3	0	71	16.9	.49
vs. Non-Playoff	28	12	3	15	5	12	2	0	58	20.7	.54
Pre All-Star	36	11	7	18	-1	12	4	0	73	15.1	.50
Post All-Star	37	13	6	19	-5	13	1	0	56	23.2	.51
Day	3	0	1	1	2	0	0	0	3	0.0	.33
Night	70	24	12	36	-8	25	5	0	126	19.0	.51

	GP	G	A	Pts	+/–	PIM	PP	SH	S	SPct	P/G
National TV	4	0	1	1	-6	9	0	0	4	0.0	.25
0 Days Rest	15	5	2	7	-4	2	1	0	35	14.3	.47
1 Days Rest	25	10	1	11	-5	11	3	0	49	20.4	.44
2 Days Rest	15	4	7	11	5	8	0	0	18	22.2	.73
3+ Days Rest	18	5	3	8	-2	4	1	0	27	18.5	.44

	G	A	Pts	PIM		G	A	Pts	PIM
1st Period	6	2	8	8	Winning	8	4	12	6
2nd Period	5	8	13	6	Losing	9	6	15	15
3rd Period	13	3	16	11	Tied	7	3	10	4
Overtime	0	0	0	0	Clutch	3	1	4	0
Last 5 Min	7	4	11	2	Blowouts	1	1	2	2

Mike Peca

Buffalo Sabres — Center

1998-99 Season

	GP	G	A	Pts	+/–	PIM	PP	SH	S	SPct	P/G
Overall	82	27	29	56	7	81	10	0	199	13.6	.68
Home	41	15	16	31	10	45	4	0	114	13.2	.76
Away	41	12	13	25	-3	36	6	0	85	14.1	.61
vs. Division	20	6	7	13	4	10	1	0	39	15.4	.65
vs. Conference	57	15	24	39	11	55	4	0	137	10.9	.68
vs. Playoff	47	16	12	28	0	42	6	0	117	13.7	.60
vs. Non-Playoff	35	11	17	28	7	39	4	0	82	13.4	.80
Pre All-Star	43	17	13	30	0	36	9	0	105	16.2	.70
Post All-Star	39	10	16	26	7	45	1	0	94	10.6	.67
Day	6	1	3	4	1	2	0	0	14	7.1	.67
Night	76	26	26	52	6	79	10	0	185	14.1	.68

	GP	G	A	Pts	+/–	PIM	PP	SH	S	SPct	P/G
National TV	15	5	4	9	0	8	1	0	26	19.2	.60
0 Days Rest	21	7	10	17	-3	20	3	0	44	15.9	.81
1 Days Rest	30	14	8	22	4	14	7	0	78	17.9	.73
2 Days Rest	20	5	6	11	2	25	0	0	53	9.4	.55
3+ Days Rest	11	1	5	6	4	22	0	0	24	4.2	.55

	G	A	Pts	PIM		G	A	Pts	PIM
1st Period	7	7	14	22	Winning	8	4	12	31
2nd Period	9	12	21	45	Losing	10	13	23	36
3rd Period	10	8	18	12	Tied	9	12	21	14
Overtime	1	2	3	2	Clutch	4	5	9	8
Last 5 Min	12	8	20	26	Blowouts	1	2	3	0

Denis Pederson

New Jersey Devils — Center

1998-99 Season

	GP	G	A	Pts	+/–	PIM	PP	SH	S	SPct	P/G
Overall	76	11	12	23	-10	66	3	0	145	7.6	.30
Home	37	8	6	14	-7	41	2	0	77	10.4	.38
Away	39	3	6	9	-3	25	1	0	68	4.4	.23
vs. Division	17	1	3	4	-2	10	1	0	21	4.8	.24
vs. Conference	53	8	9	17	-8	36	2	0	98	8.2	.32
vs. Playoff	42	3	9	12	-7	21	1	0	80	3.8	.29
vs. Non-Playoff	34	8	3	11	-3	45	2	0	65	12.3	.32
Pre All-Star	44	6	8	14	-1	48	2	0	94	6.4	.32
Post All-Star	32	5	4	9	-9	18	1	0	51	9.8	.28
Day	10	6	1	7	0	6	2	0	30	20.0	.70
Night	66	5	11	16	-10	60	1	0	115	4.3	.24

	GP	G	A	Pts	+/–	PIM	PP	SH	S	SPct	P/G
National TV	6	0	1	1	-4	10	0	0	10	0.0	.17
0 Days Rest	16	2	2	4	-9	25	1	0	40	5.0	.25
1 Days Rest	29	6	4	10	-5	15	2	0	53	11.3	.34
2 Days Rest	19	3	2	5	0	18	0	0	31	9.7	.26
3+ Days Rest	12	0	4	4	4	8	0	0	21	0.0	.33

	G	A	Pts	PIM		G	A	Pts	PIM
1st Period	5	5	10	36	Winning	6	2	8	46
2nd Period	5	3	8	15	Losing	3	3	6	11
3rd Period	1	3	4	15	Tied	2	7	9	9
Overtime	0	1	1	0	Clutch	1	2	3	5
Last 5 Min	2	3	5	37	Blowouts	0	0	0	0

Scott Pellerin

St. Louis Blues — Left Wing

1998-99 Season

	GP	G	A	Pts	+/–	PIM	PP	SH	S	SPct	P/G
Overall	80	20	21	41	1	42	0	5	138	14.5	.51
Home	40	13	9	22	5	24	0	2	74	17.6	.55
Away	40	7	12	19	-4	18	0	3	64	10.9	.48
vs. Division	18	6	3	9	6	12	0	1	30	20.0	.50
vs. Conference	54	15	15	30	4	34	0	3	89	16.9	.56
vs. Playoff	46	8	12	20	-7	30	0	1	74	10.8	.43
vs. Non-Playoff	34	12	9	21	8	12	0	4	64	18.8	.62
Pre All-Star	41	10	6	16	-4	22	0	2	69	14.5	.39
Post All-Star	39	10	15	25	5	20	0	3	69	14.5	.64
Day	10	2	6	8	1	12	0	0	17	11.8	.80
Night	70	18	15	33	0	30	0	5	121	14.9	.47

	GP	G	A	Pts	+/–	PIM	PP	SH	S	SPct	P/G
National TV	16	2	8	10	2	16	0	0	31	6.5	.63
0 Days Rest	11	1	2	3	-6	8	0	0	13	7.7	.27
1 Days Rest	43	12	11	23	4	30	0	2	79	15.2	.53
2 Days Rest	16	5	7	12	-1	2	0	2	29	17.2	.75
3+ Days Rest	10	2	1	3	4	2	0	1	17	11.8	.30

	G	A	Pts	PIM		G	A	Pts	PIM
1st Period	11	6	17	20	Winning	4	5	9	24
2nd Period	6	8	14	8	Losing	6	11	17	14
3rd Period	3	7	10	14	Tied	10	5	15	4
Overtime	0	0	0	0	Clutch	0	1	1	0
Last 5 Min	7	8	15	6	Blowouts	1	0	1	4

Ville Peltonen

Nashville Predators — Left Wing

1998-99 Season

	GP	G	A	Pts	+/–	PIM	PP	SH	S	SPct	P/G
Overall	14	5	5	10	1	2	1	0	31	16.1	.71
Home	7	3	1	4	0	2	1	0	15	20.0	.57
Away	7	2	4	6	1	0	0	0	16	12.5	.86
vs. Division	4	2	0	2	1	0	0	0	8	25.0	.50
vs. Conference	10	4	4	8	3	0	1	0	24	16.7	.80
vs. Playoff	7	2	2	4	1	0	0	0	14	14.3	.57
vs. Non-Playoff	7	3	3	6	0	2	1	0	17	17.6	.86
Pre All-Star	14	5	5	10	1	2	1	0	31	16.1	.71
Post All-Star	0	0	0	0	0	0	0	0	0	–	–
Day	1	0	0	0	0	0	0	0	3	0.0	.00
Night	13	5	5	10	1	2	1	0	28	17.9	.77

	GP	G	A	Pts	+/–	PIM	PP	SH	S	SPct	P/G
National TV	1	0	1	1	0	0	0	0	4	0.0	1.00
0 Days Rest	2	1	1	2	0	0	1	0	7	14.3	1.00
1 Days Rest	7	4	1	5	1	2	0	0	15	26.7	.71
2 Days Rest	3	0	1	1	1	0	0	0	3	0.0	.33
3+ Days Rest	2	0	2	2	-1	0	0	0	6	0.0	1.00

	G	A	Pts	PIM		G	A	Pts	PIM
1st Period	0	1	1	2	Winning	0	0	0	0
2nd Period	3	2	5	0	Losing	5	2	7	2
3rd Period	2	2	4	0	Tied	0	3	3	0
Overtime	0	0	0	0	Clutch	0	0	0	0
Last 5 Min	1	1	2	0	Blowouts	1	0	1	0

Yanic Perreault

Toronto Maple Leafs — Center

1998-99 Season

	GP	G	A	Pts	+/–	PIM	PP	SH	S	SPct	P/G
Overall	76	17	25	42	7	42	4	3	141	12.1	.55
Home	40	9	16	25	5	16	2	1	77	11.7	.63
Away	36	8	9	17	2	26	2	2	64	12.5	.47
vs. Division	20	5	4	9	1	12	2	1	33	15.2	.45
vs. Conference	49	12	16	28	7	20	3	3	78	15.4	.57
vs. Playoff	48	10	13	23	1	22	3	1	80	12.5	.48
vs. Non-Playoff	28	7	12	19	6	20	1	2	61	11.5	.68
Pre All-Star	42	8	13	21	-1	20	2	2	88	9.1	.50
Post All-Star	34	9	12	21	8	22	2	1	53	17.0	.62
Day	2	2	0	2	1	2	0	2	5	40.0	1.00
Night	74	15	25	40	6	40	4	1	136	11.0	.54

	GP	G	A	Pts	+/–	PIM	PP	SH	S	SPct	P/G
National TV	15	3	9	12	7	14	1	0	21	14.3	.80
0 Days Rest	10	0	3	3	0	8	0	0	16	0.0	.30
1 Days Rest	40	11	12	23	-3	12	2	3	84	13.1	.58
2 Days Rest	11	2	4	6	4	12	0	0	19	10.5	.55
3+ Days Rest	15	4	6	10	6	10	2	0	22	18.2	.67

	G	A	Pts	PIM		G	A	Pts	PIM
1st Period	3	9	12	10	Winning	10	8	18	20
2nd Period	7	8	15	18	Losing	3	6	9	18
3rd Period	7	8	15	14	Tied	4	11	15	4
Overtime	0	0	0	0	Clutch	3	1	4	6
Last 5 Min	4	8	12	16	Blowouts	2	0	2	4

Ricard Persson

St. Louis Blues — Defense

1998-99 Season

	GP	G	A	Pts	+/–	PIM	PP	SH	S	SPct	P/G
Overall	54	1	12	13	4	94	0	0	52	1.9	.24
Home	27	1	3	4	-1	55	0	0	34	2.9	.15
Away	27	0	9	9	5	39	0	0	18	0.0	.33
vs. Division	11	0	1	1	-3	12	0	0	8	0.0	.09
vs. Conference	35	1	8	9	2	47	0	0	33	3.0	.26
vs. Playoff	28	0	8	8	-4	58	0	0	29	0.0	.29
vs. Non-Playoff	26	1	4	5	8	36	0	0	23	4.3	.19
Pre All-Star	15	0	1	1	-1	23	0	0	12	0.0	.07
Post All-Star	39	1	11	12	5	71	0	0	40	2.5	.31
Day	9	1	4	5	9	12	0	0	8	12.5	.56
Night	45	0	8	8	-5	82	0	0	44	0.0	.18

	GP	G	A	Pts	+/–	PIM	PP	SH	S	SPct	P/G
National TV	12	0	3	3	-1	24	0	0	11	0.0	.25
0 Days Rest	6	0	2	2	-3	8	0	0	3	0.0	.33
1 Days Rest	34	1	6	7	5	68	0	0	34	2.9	.21
2 Days Rest	10	0	3	3	-3	12	0	0	12	0.0	.30
3+ Days Rest	4	0	1	1	5	6	0	0	3	0.0	.25

	G	A	Pts	PIM		G	A	Pts	PIM
1st Period	0	4	4	25	Winning	1	6	7	62
2nd Period	0	3	3	39	Losing	0	5	5	24
3rd Period	1	5	6	28	Tied	0	1	1	8
Overtime	0	0	0	2	Clutch	0	2	2	4
Last 5 Min	0	3	3	39	Blowouts	1	0	1	17

Michel Picard

St. Louis Blues — Left Wing

1998-99 Season

	GP	G	A	Pts	+/–	PIM	PP	SH	S	SPct	P/G
Overall	45	11	11	22	5	16	0	0	69	15.9	.49
Home	21	3	7	10	1	10	0	0	31	9.7	.48
Away	24	8	4	12	4	6	0	0	38	21.1	.50
vs. Division	11	2	1	3	-4	12	0	0	19	10.5	.27
vs. Conference	30	6	7	13	1	14	0	0	46	13.0	.43
vs. Playoff	27	7	8	15	8	6	0	0	47	14.9	.56
vs. Non-Playoff	18	4	3	7	-3	10	0	0	22	18.2	.39
Pre All-Star	22	4	4	8	-4	6	0	0	23	17.4	.36
Post All-Star	23	7	7	14	9	10	0	0	46	15.2	.61
Day	7	3	2	5	1	2	0	0	14	21.4	.71
Night	38	8	9	17	4	14	0	0	55	14.5	.45

	GP	G	A	Pts	+/–	PIM	PP	SH	S	SPct	P/G
National TV	10	2	2	4	-1	2	0	0	12	16.7	.40
0 Days Rest	8	1	2	3	3	4	0	0	12	8.3	.38
1 Days Rest	16	5	4	9	4	8	0	0	31	16.1	.56
2 Days Rest	7	2	1	3	0	2	0	0	9	22.2	.43
3+ Days Rest	14	3	4	7	-2	2	0	0	17	17.6	.50

	G	A	Pts	PIM		G	A	Pts	PIM
1st Period	3	3	6	10	Winning	6	4	10	4
2nd Period	5	3	8	4	Losing	1	2	3	6
3rd Period	3	5	8	2	Tied	4	5	9	6
Overtime	0	0	0	0	Clutch	1	2	3	2
Last 5 Min	5	2	7	6	Blowouts	0	1	1	0

Michal Pivonka

Washington Capitals — Center

1998-99 Season

	GP	G	A	Pts	+/–	PIM	PP	SH	S	SPct	P/G
Overall	36	5	6	11	-6	12	2	0	30	16.7	.31
Home	20	2	4	6	-2	6	1	0	12	16.7	.30
Away	16	3	2	5	-4	6	1	0	18	16.7	.31
vs. Division	8	0	1	1	-1	0	0	0	6	0.0	.13
vs. Conference	26	4	5	9	-5	8	2	0	23	17.4	.35
vs. Playoff	19	5	2	7	-4	12	2	0	17	29.4	.37
vs. Non-Playoff	17	0	4	4	-2	0	0	0	13	0.0	.24
Pre All-Star	14	4	3	7	-5	8	2	0	18	22.2	.50
Post All-Star	22	1	3	4	-1	4	0	0	12	8.3	.18
Day	2	0	0	0	-2	0	0	0	4	0.0	.00
Night	34	5	6	11	-4	12	2	0	26	19.2	.32

	GP	G	A	Pts	+/–	PIM	PP	SH	S	SPct	P/G
National TV	5	1	0	1	-3	2	1	0	3	33.3	.20
0 Days Rest	4	1	0	1	-1	4	1	0	4	25.0	.25
1 Days Rest	22	2	5	7	-4	6	1	0	14	14.3	.32
2 Days Rest	3	2	0	2	0	2	0	0	4	50.0	.67
3+ Days Rest	7	0	1	1	-1	0	0	0	8	0.0	.14

	G	A	Pts	PIM
1st Period	1	3	4	6
2nd Period	3	2	5	2
3rd Period	1	1	2	4
Overtime	0	0	0	0
Last 5 Min	0	0	0	4

	G	A	Pts	PIM
Winning	1	2	3	6
Losing	4	2	6	6
Tied	0	2	2	0
Clutch	0	1	1	0
Blowouts	1	0	1	4

Derek Plante

Dallas Stars — Center

1998-99 Season

	GP	G	A	Pts	+/–	PIM	PP	SH	S	SPct	P/G
Overall	51	6	14	20	4	16	1	0	90	6.7	.39
Home	28	2	11	13	3	12	1	0	52	3.8	.46
Away	23	4	3	7	1	4	0	0	38	10.5	.30
vs. Division	18	2	6	8	1	8	1	0	34	5.9	.44
vs. Conference	34	4	10	14	4	12	1	0	56	7.1	.41
vs. Playoff	32	3	8	11	-1	14	0	0	50	6.0	.34
vs. Non-Playoff	19	3	6	9	5	2	1	0	40	7.5	.47
Pre All-Star	22	1	5	6	1	6	0	0	37	2.7	.27
Post All-Star	29	5	9	14	3	10	1	0	53	9.4	.48
Day	6	1	2	3	-2	2	1	0	12	8.3	.50
Night	45	5	12	17	6	14	0	0	78	6.4	.38

	GP	G	A	Pts	+/–	PIM	PP	SH	S	SPct	P/G
National TV	9	2	4	6	1	0	1	0	15	13.3	.67
0 Days Rest	8	1	3	4	0	0	0	0	11	9.1	.50
1 Days Rest	16	3	3	6	0	4	1	0	32	9.4	.38
2 Days Rest	13	1	2	3	4	6	0	0	22	4.5	.23
3+ Days Rest	14	1	6	7	0	6	0	0	25	4.0	.50

	G	A	Pts	PIM
1st Period	1	5	6	12
2nd Period	3	4	7	2
3rd Period	2	5	7	2
Overtime	0	0	0	0
Last 5 Min	3	3	6	2

	G	A	Pts	PIM
Winning	3	4	7	10
Losing	3	4	7	4
Tied	0	6	6	2
Clutch	0	0	0	0
Blowouts	1	0	1	0

Tom Poti

Edmonton Oilers — Defense

1998-99 Season

	GP	G	A	Pts	+/–	PIM	PP	SH	S	SPct	P/G
Overall	73	5	16	21	10	42	2	0	94	5.3	.29
Home	37	3	11	14	0	10	2	0	42	7.1	.38
Away	36	2	5	7	10	32	0	0	52	3.8	.19
vs. Division	15	2	3	5	5	2	1	0	25	8.0	.33
vs. Conference	50	4	14	18	8	22	2	0	70	5.7	.36
vs. Playoff	41	2	13	15	4	30	1	0	47	4.3	.37
vs. Non-Playoff	32	3	3	6	6	12	1	0	47	6.4	.19
Pre All-Star	39	3	8	11	2	22	2	0	55	5.5	.28
Post All-Star	34	2	8	10	8	20	0	0	39	5.1	.29
Day	4	0	1	1	3	4	0	0	3	0.0	.25
Night	69	5	15	20	7	38	2	0	91	5.5	.29

	GP	G	A	Pts	+/–	PIM	PP	SH	S	SPct	P/G
National TV	12	1	2	3	3	0	1	0	17	5.9	.25
0 Days Rest	13	1	2	3	-2	8	0	0	14	7.1	.23
1 Days Rest	32	1	8	9	12	14	0	0	44	2.3	.28
2 Days Rest	12	0	3	3	3	10	0	0	12	0.0	.25
3+ Days Rest	16	3	3	6	-3	10	2	0	24	12.5	.38

	G	A	Pts	PIM
1st Period	1	3	4	12
2nd Period	1	9	10	14
3rd Period	2	4	6	16
Overtime	1	0	1	0
Last 5 Min	4	5	9	14

	G	A	Pts	PIM
Winning	0	8	8	10
Losing	2	5	7	24
Tied	3	3	6	8
Clutch	2	2	4	8
Blowouts	1	0	1	0

Patrick Poulin

Montreal Canadiens — Left Wing

1998-99 Season

	GP	G	A	Pts	+/–	PIM	PP	SH	S	SPct	P/G
Overall	81	8	17	25	6	21	0	1	87	9.2	.31
Home	40	6	10	16	4	13	0	1	49	12.2	.40
Away	41	2	7	9	2	8	0	0	38	5.3	.22
vs. Division	20	1	1	2	-4	2	0	1	23	4.3	.10
vs. Conference	56	5	11	16	-1	10	0	1	62	8.1	.29
vs. Playoff	50	5	8	13	-3	6	0	1	50	10.0	.26
vs. Non-Playoff	31	3	9	12	9	15	0	0	37	8.1	.39
Pre All-Star	45	7	9	16	2	15	0	1	48	14.6	.36
Post All-Star	36	1	8	9	4	6	0	0	39	2.6	.25
Day	3	0	1	1	-2	0	0	0	5	0.0	.33
Night	78	8	16	24	8	21	0	1	82	9.8	.31

	GP	G	A	Pts	+/–	PIM	PP	SH	S	SPct	P/G
National TV	24	4	5	9	2	8	0	1	35	11.4	.38
0 Days Rest	17	3	4	7	3	6	0	1	21	14.3	.41
1 Days Rest	35	4	4	8	-3	11	0	0	31	12.9	.23
2 Days Rest	18	1	4	5	3	2	0	0	26	3.8	.28
3+ Days Rest	11	0	5	5	3	2	0	0	9	0.0	.45

	G	A	Pts	PIM
1st Period	2	2	4	4
2nd Period	4	6	10	17
3rd Period	2	9	11	0
Overtime	0	0	0	0
Last 5 Min	1	7	8	9

	G	A	Pts	PIM
Winning	3	5	8	11
Losing	3	6	9	8
Tied	2	6	8	2
Clutch	0	3	3	0
Blowouts	0	1	1	6

Nolan Pratt

Carolina Hurricanes — Defense

1998-99 Season

	GP	G	A	Pts	+/–	PIM	PP	SH	S	SPct	P/G
Overall	61	1	14	15	15	95	0	0	46	2.2	.25
Home	32	1	6	7	8	47	0	0	26	3.8	.22
Away	29	0	8	8	7	48	0	0	20	0.0	.28
vs. Division	12	0	3	3	1	27	0	0	9	0.0	.25
vs. Conference	45	0	10	10	10	65	0	0	35	0.0	.22
vs. Playoff	36	1	8	9	11	45	0	0	24	4.2	.25
vs. Non-Playoff	25	0	6	6	4	50	0	0	22	0.0	.24
Pre All-Star	24	1	4	5	2	38	0	0	13	7.7	.21
Post All-Star	37	0	10	10	13	57	0	0	33	0.0	.27
Day	5	0	1	1	0	12	0	0	3	0.0	.20
Night	56	1	13	14	15	83	0	0	43	2.3	.25

	GP	G	A	Pts	+/–	PIM	PP	SH	S	SPct	P/G
National TV	2	0	1	1	1	4	0	0	3	0.0	.50
0 Days Rest	12	1	4	5	5	7	0	0	11	9.1	.42
1 Days Rest	22	0	5	5	6	57	0	0	19	0.0	.23
2 Days Rest	16	0	5	5	4	23	0	0	7	0.0	.31
3+ Days Rest	11	0	0	0	0	8	0	0	9	0.0	.00

	G	A	Pts	PIM		G	A	Pts	PIM
1st Period	0	4	4	50	Winning	0	5	5	33
2nd Period	0	4	4	27	Losing	0	8	8	35
3rd Period	1	6	7	18	Tied	1	1	2	27
Overtime	0	0	0	0	Clutch	0	1	1	2
Last 5 Min	0	4	4	16	Blowouts	0	0	0	0

Keith Primeau

Carolina Hurricanes — Center

1998-99 Season

	GP	G	A	Pts	+/–	PIM	PP	SH	S	SPct	P/G
Overall	78	30	32	62	8	75	9	1	178	16.9	.79
Home	39	17	17	34	9	36	5	1	95	17.9	.87
Away	39	13	15	28	-1	39	4	0	83	15.7	.72
vs. Division	13	4	7	11	2	13	2	0	34	11.8	.85
vs. Conference	55	17	23	40	6	61	7	0	120	14.2	.73
vs. Playoff	42	18	17	35	-1	41	4	0	98	18.4	.83
vs. Non-Playoff	36	12	15	27	9	34	5	1	80	15.0	.75
Pre All-Star	45	22	16	38	3	44	8	1	112	19.6	.84
Post All-Star	33	8	16	24	5	31	1	0	66	12.1	.73
Day	7	3	5	8	4	6	1	1	15	20.0	1.14
Night	71	27	27	54	4	69	8	0	163	16.6	.76

	GP	G	A	Pts	+/–	PIM	PP	SH	S	SPct	P/G
National TV	2	0	1	1	0	0	0	0	4	0.0	.50
0 Days Rest	15	4	5	9	6	10	0	1	34	11.8	.60
1 Days Rest	30	10	12	22	-2	31	3	0	66	15.2	.73
2 Days Rest	24	14	10	24	5	30	4	0	58	24.1	1.00
3+ Days Rest	9	2	5	7	-1	4	2	0	20	10.0	.78

	G	A	Pts	PIM		G	A	Pts	PIM
1st Period	14	9	23	14	Winning	12	9	21	31
2nd Period	7	15	22	29	Losing	8	9	17	38
3rd Period	9	7	16	32	Tied	10	14	24	6
Overtime	0	1	1	0	Clutch	2	5	7	6
Last 5 Min	10	8	18	28	Blowouts	0	0	0	10

Wayne Primeau

Buffalo Sabres — Center

1998-99 Season

	GP	G	A	Pts	+/–	PIM	PP	SH	S	SPct	P/G
Overall	67	5	8	13	-6	38	0	0	55	9.1	.19
Home	33	2	6	8	-5	30	0	0	31	6.5	.24
Away	34	3	2	5	-1	8	0	0	24	12.5	.15
vs. Division	15	1	1	2	0	8	0	0	11	9.1	.13
vs. Conference	47	4	6	10	-3	22	0	0	37	10.8	.21
vs. Playoff	37	2	3	5	-5	30	0	0	32	6.3	.14
vs. Non-Playoff	30	3	5	8	-1	8	0	0	23	13.0	.27
Pre All-Star	30	2	3	5	-2	28	0	0	27	7.4	.17
Post All-Star	37	3	5	8	-4	10	0	0	28	10.7	.22
Day	5	0	0	0	0	12	0	0	2	0.0	.00
Night	62	5	8	13	-6	26	0	0	53	9.4	.21

	GP	G	A	Pts	+/–	PIM	PP	SH	S	SPct	P/G
National TV	14	0	2	2	0	4	0	0	8	0.0	.14
0 Days Rest	15	2	3	5	2	6	0	0	14	14.3	.33
1 Days Rest	24	2	3	5	-4	30	0	0	24	8.3	.21
2 Days Rest	15	1	2	3	-1	2	0	0	7	14.3	.20
3+ Days Rest	13	0	0	0	-3	0	0	0	10	0.0	.00

	G	A	Pts	PIM		G	A	Pts	PIM
1st Period	1	4	5	6	Winning	0	5	5	17
2nd Period	3	2	5	9	Losing	2	1	3	19
3rd Period	1	2	3	23	Tied	3	2	5	2
Overtime	0	0	0	0	Clutch	0	1	1	2
Last 5 Min	1	3	4	16	Blowouts	0	1	1	12

Bob Probert

Chicago Blackhawks — Left Wing

1998-99 Season

	GP	G	A	Pts	+/–	PIM	PP	SH	S	SPct	P/G
Overall	78	7	14	21	-11	206	0	0	87	8.0	.27
Home	39	5	7	12	-5	96	0	0	41	12.2	.31
Away	39	2	7	9	-6	110	0	0	46	4.3	.23
vs. Division	18	1	0	1	-1	41	0	0	17	5.9	.06
vs. Conference	52	1	7	8	-10	156	0	0	48	2.1	.15
vs. Playoff	49	4	10	14	-2	120	0	0	43	9.3	.29
vs. Non-Playoff	29	3	4	7	-9	86	0	0	44	6.8	.24
Pre All-Star	41	2	6	8	-11	104	0	0	49	4.1	.20
Post All-Star	37	5	8	13	0	102	0	0	38	13.2	.35
Day	10	0	1	1	-3	31	0	0	11	0.0	.10
Night	68	7	13	20	-8	175	0	0	76	9.2	.29

	GP	G	A	Pts	+/–	PIM	PP	SH	S	SPct	P/G
National TV	17	1	5	6	-3	30	0	0	10	10.0	.35
0 Days Rest	12	2	6	8	2	31	0	0	12	16.7	.67
1 Days Rest	39	2	3	5	-13	86	0	0	48	4.2	.13
2 Days Rest	15	2	4	6	2	60	0	0	14	14.3	.40
3+ Days Rest	12	1	1	2	-2	29	0	0	13	7.7	.17

	G	A	Pts	PIM		G	A	Pts	PIM
1st Period	1	5	6	55	Winning	1	5	6	76
2nd Period	3	3	6	83	Losing	1	7	8	76
3rd Period	3	6	9	68	Tied	5	2	7	54
Overtime	0	0	0	0	Clutch	1	2	3	4
Last 5 Min	3	3	6	52	Blowouts	0	0	0	31

Chris Pronger

St. Louis Blues — Defense

1998-99 Season

	GP	G	A	Pts	+/–	PIM	PP	SH	S	SPct	P/G
Overall	67	13	33	46	3	113	8	0	172	7.6	.69
Home	32	8	17	25	2	63	4	0	90	8.9	.78
Away	35	5	16	21	1	50	4	0	82	6.1	.60
vs. Division	13	4	13	17	2	10	1	0	34	11.8	1.31
vs. Conference	44	11	24	35	0	66	6	0	109	10.1	.80
vs. Playoff	41	8	14	22	-2	91	6	0	101	7.9	.54
vs. Non-Playoff	26	5	19	24	5	22	2	0	71	7.0	.92
Pre All-Star	38	9	19	28	4	75	4	0	101	8.9	.74
Post All-Star	29	4	14	18	-1	38	4	0	71	5.6	.62
Day	9	3	6	9	-4	18	2	0	21	14.3	1.00
Night	58	10	27	37	7	95	6	0	151	6.6	.64

	GP	G	A	Pts	+/–	PIM	PP	SH	S	SPct	P/G
National TV	14	2	7	9	-3	14	0	0	33	6.1	.64
0 Days Rest	11	1	4	5	1	10	1	0	25	4.0	.45
1 Days Rest	31	6	13	19	1	59	5	0	77	7.8	.61
2 Days Rest	13	3	8	11	-5	20	0	0	33	9.1	.85
3+ Days Rest	12	3	8	11	6	24	2	0	37	8.1	.92

	G	A	Pts	PIM		G	A	Pts	PIM
1st Period	5	11	16	36	Winning	2	14	16	38
2nd Period	6	10	16	49	Losing	4	13	17	59
3rd Period	2	12	14	26	Tied	7	6	13	16
Overtime	0	0	0	2	Clutch	1	3	4	6
Last 5 Min	4	11	15	28	Blowouts	0	0	0	6

Vaclav Prospal

Ottawa Senators — Center

1998-99 Season

	GP	G	A	Pts	+/–	PIM	PP	SH	S	SPct	P/G
Overall	79	10	26	36	8	58	2	0	114	8.8	.46
Home	39	6	16	22	12	30	2	0	54	11.1	.56
Away	40	4	10	14	-4	28	0	0	60	6.7	.35
vs. Division	20	3	6	9	2	19	0	0	32	9.4	.45
vs. Conference	56	8	19	27	3	48	2	0	86	9.3	.48
vs. Playoff	46	7	16	23	6	27	1	0	73	9.6	.50
vs. Non-Playoff	33	3	10	13	2	31	1	0	41	7.3	.39
Pre All-Star	43	4	17	21	1	37	2	0	61	6.6	.49
Post All-Star	36	6	9	15	7	21	0	0	53	11.3	.42
Day	3	0	1	1	0	4	0	0	1	0.0	.33
Night	76	10	25	35	8	54	2	0	113	8.8	.46

	GP	G	A	Pts	+/–	PIM	PP	SH	S	SPct	P/G
National TV	10	1	4	5	2	2	0	0	9	11.1	.50
0 Days Rest	13	1	8	9	7	25	0	0	18	5.6	.69
1 Days Rest	38	3	10	13	-1	18	1	0	48	6.3	.34
2 Days Rest	15	4	4	8	3	13	1	0	30	13.3	.53
3+ Days Rest	13	2	4	6	-1	2	0	0	18	11.1	.46

	G	A	Pts	PIM		G	A	Pts	PIM
1st Period	3	10	13	27	Winning	5	4	9	16
2nd Period	6	8	14	15	Losing	3	4	7	34
3rd Period	1	8	9	16	Tied	2	18	20	8
Overtime	0	0	0	0	Clutch	0	3	3	4
Last 5 Min	2	4	6	17	Blowouts	0	0	0	4

Deron Quint

Phoenix Coyotes — Defense

1998-99 Season

	GP	G	A	Pts	+/–	PIM	PP	SH	S	SPct	P/G
Overall	60	5	8	13	-10	20	2	0	94	5.3	.22
Home	30	3	4	7	1	8	1	0	48	6.3	.23
Away	30	2	4	6	-11	12	1	0	46	4.3	.20
vs. Division	15	2	2	4	-1	4	0	0	25	8.0	.27
vs. Conference	37	3	6	9	-9	16	1	0	57	5.3	.24
vs. Playoff	33	4	2	6	-8	12	2	0	48	8.3	.18
vs. Non-Playoff	27	1	6	7	-2	8	0	0	46	2.2	.26
Pre All-Star	30	1	5	6	-3	12	0	0	30	3.3	.20
Post All-Star	30	4	3	7	-7	8	2	0	64	6.3	.23
Day	4	1	2	3	1	0	1	0	14	7.1	.75
Night	56	4	6	10	-11	20	1	0	80	5.0	.18

	GP	G	A	Pts	+/–	PIM	PP	SH	S	SPct	P/G
National TV	11	1	2	3	2	0	0	0	18	5.6	.27
0 Days Rest	11	0	1	1	-9	6	0	0	9	0.0	.09
1 Days Rest	30	3	3	6	3	6	1	0	55	5.5	.20
2 Days Rest	11	2	3	5	-2	2	1	0	22	9.1	.45
3+ Days Rest	8	0	1	1	-2	6	0	0	8	0.0	.13

	G	A	Pts	PIM		G	A	Pts	PIM
1st Period	0	3	3	8	Winning	2	1	3	6
2nd Period	3	1	4	8	Losing	3	3	6	6
3rd Period	2	4	6	4	Tied	0	4	4	8
Overtime	0	0	0	0	Clutch	1	1	2	0
Last 5 Min	1	0	1	2	Blowouts	0	0	0	2

Stephane Quintal

Montreal Canadiens — Defense

1998-99 Season

	GP	G	A	Pts	+/–	PIM	PP	SH	S	SPct	P/G
Overall	82	8	19	27	-23	84	1	1	159	5.0	.33
Home	41	4	11	15	-1	26	1	0	91	4.4	.37
Away	41	4	8	12	-22	58	0	1	68	5.9	.29
vs. Division	20	1	7	8	-7	15	0	0	30	3.3	.40
vs. Conference	56	7	14	21	-13	49	1	1	106	6.6	.38
vs. Playoff	51	3	14	17	-20	47	0	0	84	3.6	.33
vs. Non-Playoff	31	5	5	10	-3	37	1	1	75	6.7	.32
Pre All-Star	46	5	12	17	-3	54	1	0	81	6.2	.37
Post All-Star	36	3	7	10	-20	30	0	1	78	3.8	.28
Day	3	0	0	0	-4	7	0	0	4	0.0	.00
Night	79	8	19	27	-19	77	1	1	155	5.2	.34

	GP	G	A	Pts	+/–	PIM	PP	SH	S	SPct	P/G
National TV	25	1	7	8	-6	24	0	0	33	3.0	.32
0 Days Rest	17	0	3	3	-11	36	0	0	35	0.0	.18
1 Days Rest	36	4	7	11	-9	16	1	0	76	5.3	.31
2 Days Rest	18	3	4	7	-1	8	0	0	25	12.0	.39
3+ Days Rest	11	1	5	6	-2	24	0	1	23	4.3	.55

	G	A	Pts	PIM		G	A	Pts	PIM
1st Period	3	4	7	21	Winning	1	4	5	13
2nd Period	2	10	12	30	Losing	2	8	10	62
3rd Period	3	5	8	33	Tied	5	7	12	9
Overtime	0	0	0	0	Clutch	1	1	2	0
Last 5 Min	1	6	7	28	Blowouts	0	1	1	14

Marcus Ragnarsson

San Jose Sharks — Defense

1998-99 Season

	GP	G	A	Pts	+/–	PIM	PP	SH	S	SPct	P/G
Overall	74	0	13	13	7	66	0	0	87	0.0	.18
Home	38	0	8	8	10	36	0	0	41	0.0	.21
Away	36	0	5	5	-3	30	0	0	46	0.0	.14
vs. Division	22	0	4	4	2	30	0	0	30	0.0	.18
vs. Conference	51	0	9	9	-3	52	0	0	62	0.0	.18
vs. Playoff	43	0	9	9	5	34	0	0	46	0.0	.21
vs. Non-Playoff	31	0	4	4	2	32	0	0	41	0.0	.13
Pre All-Star	37	0	4	4	0	30	0	0	35	0.0	.11
Post All-Star	37	0	9	9	7	36	0	0	52	0.0	.24
Day	7	0	0	0	-5	2	0	0	8	0.0	.00
Night	67	0	13	13	12	64	0	0	79	0.0	.19

	GP	G	A	Pts	+/–	PIM	PP	SH	S	SPct	P/G
National TV	11	0	2	2	1	8	0	0	13	0.0	.18
0 Days Rest	12	0	4	4	8	14	0	0	21	0.0	.33
1 Days Rest	38	0	6	6	0	28	0	0	41	0.0	.16
2 Days Rest	15	0	1	1	-4	12	0	0	18	0.0	.07
3+ Days Rest	9	0	2	2	3	12	0	0	7	0.0	.22

	G	A	Pts	PIM		G	A	Pts	PIM
1st Period	0	6	6	26	Winning	0	6	6	24
2nd Period	0	4	4	20	Losing	0	1	1	20
3rd Period	0	3	3	20	Tied	0	6	6	22
Overtime	0	0	0	0	Clutch	0	0	0	4
Last 5 Min	0	2	2	22	Blowouts	0	1	1	6

Paul Ranheim

Carolina Hurricanes — Left Wing

1998-99 Season

	GP	G	A	Pts	+/–	PIM	PP	SH	S	SPct	P/G
Overall	78	9	10	19	4	39	0	2	67	13.4	.24
Home	40	3	5	8	-1	16	0	0	36	8.3	.20
Away	38	6	5	11	5	23	0	2	31	19.4	.29
vs. Division	15	1	2	3	0	12	0	1	21	4.8	.20
vs. Conference	57	9	7	16	4	20	0	2	56	16.1	.28
vs. Playoff	41	7	4	11	-1	10	0	1	32	21.9	.27
vs. Non-Playoff	37	2	6	8	5	29	0	1	35	5.7	.22
Pre All-Star	41	3	7	10	0	8	0	1	32	9.4	.24
Post All-Star	37	6	3	9	4	31	0	1	35	17.1	.24
Day	7	1	1	2	1	12	0	1	5	20.0	.29
Night	71	8	9	17	3	27	0	1	62	12.9	.24

	GP	G	A	Pts	+/–	PIM	PP	SH	S	SPct	P/G
National TV	2	0	1	1	1	0	0	0	4	0.0	.50
0 Days Rest	15	2	3	5	2	0	0	0	13	15.4	.33
1 Days Rest	30	4	4	8	1	33	0	1	27	14.8	.27
2 Days Rest	21	0	2	2	0	6	0	0	12	0.0	.10
3+ Days Rest	12	3	1	4	1	0	0	1	15	20.0	.33

	G	A	Pts	PIM		G	A	Pts	PIM
1st Period	2	6	8	6	Winning	4	2	6	4
2nd Period	2	3	5	4	Losing	4	3	7	21
3rd Period	5	1	6	29	Tied	1	5	6	14
Overtime	0	0	0	0	Clutch	1	0	1	2
Last 5 Min	3	1	4	4	Blowouts	1	0	1	0

Erik Rasmussen

Buffalo Sabres — Center

1998-99 Season

	GP	G	A	Pts	+/–	PIM	PP	SH	S	SPct	P/G
Overall	42	3	7	10	6	37	0	0	40	7.5	.24
Home	22	1	4	5	6	31	0	0	24	4.2	.23
Away	20	2	3	5	0	6	0	0	16	12.5	.25
vs. Division	8	0	1	1	-1	25	0	0	7	0.0	.13
vs. Conference	26	1	4	5	2	29	0	0	24	4.2	.19
vs. Playoff	25	1	4	5	2	35	0	0	25	4.0	.20
vs. Non-Playoff	17	2	3	5	4	2	0	0	15	13.3	.29
Pre All-Star	27	2	5	7	7	27	0	0	27	7.4	.26
Post All-Star	15	1	2	3	-1	10	0	0	13	7.7	.20
Day	4	0	0	0	1	4	0	0	3	0.0	.00
Night	38	3	7	10	5	33	0	0	37	8.1	.26

	GP	G	A	Pts	+/–	PIM	PP	SH	S	SPct	P/G
National TV	6	1	2	3	3	0	0	0	3	33.3	.50
0 Days Rest	7	2	1	3	1	2	0	0	7	28.6	.43
1 Days Rest	16	0	3	3	3	16	0	0	14	0.0	.19
2 Days Rest	8	1	2	3	0	15	0	0	8	12.5	.38
3+ Days Rest	11	0	1	1	2	4	0	0	11	0.0	.09

	G	A	Pts	PIM		G	A	Pts	PIM
1st Period	1	1	2	4	Winning	2	1	3	2
2nd Period	1	2	3	4	Losing	1	0	1	16
3rd Period	1	4	5	19	Tied	0	6	6	19
Overtime	0	0	0	10	Clutch	1	3	4	25
Last 5 Min	1	1	2	27	Blowouts	0	0	0	2

Mike Rathje

San Jose Sharks — Defense

1998-99 Season

	GP	G	A	Pts	+/–	PIM	PP	SH	S	SPct	P/G
Overall	82	5	9	14	15	36	2	0	67	7.5	.17
Home	41	2	4	6	12	14	1	0	40	5.0	.15
Away	41	3	5	8	3	22	1	0	27	11.1	.20
vs. Division	24	0	3	3	0	8	0	0	17	0.0	.13
vs. Conference	57	3	6	9	3	22	0	0	45	6.7	.16
vs. Playoff	48	2	6	8	4	24	1	0	40	5.0	.17
vs. Non-Playoff	34	3	3	6	11	12	1	0	27	11.1	.18
Pre All-Star	45	3	2	5	2	18	1	0	39	7.7	.11
Post All-Star	37	2	7	9	13	18	1	0	28	7.1	.24
Day	7	0	1	1	0	4	0	0	4	0.0	.14
Night	75	5	8	13	15	32	2	0	63	7.9	.17

	GP	G	A	Pts	+/–	PIM	PP	SH	S	SPct	P/G
National TV	11	0	2	2	-2	2	0	0	7	0.0	.18
0 Days Rest	14	1	4	5	8	6	0	0	7	14.3	.36
1 Days Rest	42	2	3	5	3	24	2	0	32	6.3	.12
2 Days Rest	15	1	2	3	5	2	0	0	17	5.9	.20
3+ Days Rest	11	1	0	1	-1	4	0	0	11	9.1	.09

	G	A	Pts	PIM		G	A	Pts	PIM
1st Period	1	3	4	10	Winning	3	4	7	20
2nd Period	1	1	2	16	Losing	2	1	3	4
3rd Period	3	5	8	10	Tied	0	4	4	12
Overtime	0	0	0	0	Clutch	0	2	2	4
Last 5 Min	3	3	6	6	Blowouts	1	0	1	6

Marty Reasoner

St. Louis Blues — Center

1998-99 Season

	GP	G	A	Pts	+/–	PIM	PP	SH	S	SPct	P/G
Overall	22	3	7	10	2	8	1	0	33	9.1	.45
Home	9	1	4	5	-2	2	1	0	15	6.7	.56
Away	13	2	3	5	4	6	0	0	18	11.1	.38
vs. Division	7	1	1	2	-1	0	0	0	12	8.3	.29
vs. Conference	14	2	5	7	-1	2	1	0	20	10.0	.50
vs. Playoff	13	2	3	5	1	6	1	0	18	11.1	.38
vs. Non-Playoff	9	1	4	5	1	2	0	0	15	6.7	.56
Pre All-Star	22	3	7	10	2	8	1	0	33	9.1	.45
Post All-Star	0	0	0	0	0	0	0	0	0	–	–
Day	1	0	0	0	0	0	0	0	2	0.0	.00
Night	21	3	7	10	2	8	1	0	31	9.7	.48

	GP	G	A	Pts	+/–	PIM	PP	SH	S	SPct	P/G
National TV	3	1	0	1	1	2	0	0	4	25.0	.33
0 Days Rest	5	0	1	1	0	4	0	0	4	0.0	.20
1 Days Rest	7	0	4	4	1	2	0	0	10	0.0	.57
2 Days Rest	4	1	1	2	0	0	0	0	9	11.1	.50
3+ Days Rest	6	2	1	3	1	2	1	0	10	20.0	.50

	G	A	Pts	PIM		G	A	Pts	PIM
1st Period	3	3	6	0	Winning	0	3	3	2
2nd Period	0	3	3	4	Losing	2	2	4	4
3rd Period	0	1	1	4	Tied	1	2	3	2
Overtime	0	0	0	0	Clutch	0	0	0	0
Last 5 Min	2	1	3	2	Blowouts	0	0	0	0

Mark Recchi

Philadelphia Flyers — Right Wing

1998-99 Season

	GP	G	A	Pts	+/–	PIM	PP	SH	S	SPct	P/G
Overall	71	16	37	53	-7	34	3	0	171	9.4	.75
Home	35	9	25	34	1	22	2	0	82	11.0	.97
Away	36	7	12	19	-8	12	1	0	89	7.9	.53
vs. Division	16	5	6	11	1	10	0	0	39	12.8	.69
vs. Conference	48	10	29	39	-2	16	3	0	115	8.7	.81
vs. Playoff	46	12	21	33	-7	22	0	0	112	10.7	.72
vs. Non-Playoff	25	4	16	20	0	12	3	0	59	6.8	.80
Pre All-Star	42	9	24	33	-7	16	3	0	94	9.6	.79
Post All-Star	29	7	13	20	0	18	0	0	77	9.1	.69
Day	5	1	3	4	-4	2	0	0	18	5.6	.80
Night	66	15	34	49	-3	32	3	0	153	9.8	.74

	GP	G	A	Pts	+/–	PIM	PP	SH	S	SPct	P/G
National TV	24	8	18	26	2	14	2	0	47	17.0	1.08
0 Days Rest	14	1	9	10	-9	0	0	0	26	3.8	.71
1 Days Rest	28	5	13	18	-2	18	0	0	67	7.5	.64
2 Days Rest	16	5	8	13	-2	12	2	0	39	12.8	.81
3+ Days Rest	13	5	7	12	6	4	1	0	39	12.8	.92

	G	A	Pts	PIM		G	A	Pts	PIM
1st Period	5	10	15	14	Winning	6	10	16	20
2nd Period	7	12	19	16	Losing	5	11	16	12
3rd Period	4	15	19	4	Tied	5	16	21	2
Overtime	0	0	0	0	Clutch	1	2	3	0
Last 5 Min	5	11	16	12	Blowouts	2	1	3	4

Wade Redden

Ottawa Senators — Defense

1998-99 Season

	GP	G	A	Pts	+/–	PIM	PP	SH	S	SPct	P/G
Overall	72	8	21	29	7	54	3	0	127	6.3	.40
Home	38	5	11	16	8	36	1	0	58	8.6	.42
Away	34	3	10	13	-1	18	2	0	69	4.3	.38
vs. Division	18	0	5	5	-6	16	0	0	30	0.0	.28
vs. Conference	52	2	17	19	2	26	1	0	87	2.3	.37
vs. Playoff	41	3	11	14	-4	14	0	0	66	4.5	.34
vs. Non-Playoff	31	5	10	15	11	40	3	0	61	8.2	.48
Pre All-Star	43	5	13	18	10	40	2	0	76	6.6	.42
Post All-Star	29	3	8	11	-3	14	1	0	51	5.9	.38
Day	3	1	0	1	-1	2	1	0	6	16.7	.33
Night	69	7	21	28	8	52	2	0	121	5.8	.41

	GP	G	A	Pts	+/–	PIM	PP	SH	S	SPct	P/G
National TV	10	0	4	4	0	2	0	0	12	0.0	.40
0 Days Rest	12	0	6	6	11	4	0	0	19	0.0	.50
1 Days Rest	36	4	6	10	-1	42	2	0	61	6.6	.28
2 Days Rest	13	2	5	7	-4	4	1	0	30	6.7	.54
3+ Days Rest	11	2	4	6	1	4	0	0	17	11.8	.55

	G	A	Pts	PIM		G	A	Pts	PIM
1st Period	3	7	10	36	Winning	4	8	12	42
2nd Period	0	6	6	12	Losing	2	6	8	6
3rd Period	5	8	13	6	Tied	2	7	9	6
Overtime	0	0	0	0	Clutch	3	1	4	0
Last 5 Min	4	8	12	28	Blowouts	0	1	1	2

Joe Reekie

Washington Capitals — Defense

1998-99 Season

	GP	G	A	Pts	+/–	PIM	PP	SH	S	SPct	P/G
Overall	73	0	10	10	12	68	0	0	81	0.0	.14
Home	37	0	9	9	13	24	0	0	46	0.0	.24
Away	36	0	1	1	-1	44	0	0	35	0.0	.03
vs. Division	12	0	4	4	13	16	0	0	17	0.0	.33
vs. Conference	52	0	6	6	14	54	0	0	58	0.0	.12
vs. Playoff	45	0	6	6	2	38	0	0	53	0.0	.13
vs. Non-Playoff	28	0	4	4	10	30	0	0	28	0.0	.14
Pre All-Star	34	0	3	3	4	32	0	0	35	0.0	.09
Post All-Star	39	0	7	7	8	36	0	0	46	0.0	.18
Day	3	0	0	0	0	6	0	0	3	0.0	.00
Night	70	0	10	10	12	62	0	0	78	0.0	.14

	GP	G	A	Pts	+/–	PIM	PP	SH	S	SPct	P/G
National TV	10	0	1	1	9	16	0	0	8	0.0	.10
0 Days Rest	12	0	1	1	-5	10	0	0	11	0.0	.08
1 Days Rest	37	0	7	7	22	36	0	0	45	0.0	.19
2 Days Rest	12	0	1	1	-5	8	0	0	14	0.0	.08
3+ Days Rest	12	0	1	1	0	14	0	0	11	0.0	.08

	G	A	Pts	PIM		G	A	Pts	PIM
1st Period	0	1	1	42	Winning	0	4	4	30
2nd Period	0	4	4	16	Losing	0	3	3	34
3rd Period	0	5	5	10	Tied	0	3	3	4
Overtime	0	0	0	0	Clutch	0	2	2	0
Last 5 Min	0	2	2	28	Blowouts	0	0	0	8

Robert Reichel

Phoenix Coyotes — Center

1998-99 Season

	GP	G	A	Pts	+/–	PIM	PP	SH	S	SPct	P/G
Overall	83	26	43	69	-13	54	8	1	236	11.0	.83
Home	44	18	26	44	-5	36	5	0	123	14.6	1.00
Away	39	8	17	25	-8	18	3	1	113	7.1	.64
vs. Division	23	7	11	18	-6	10	4	0	76	9.2	.78
vs. Conference	60	19	27	46	-12	40	6	1	169	11.2	.77
vs. Playoff	50	11	24	35	-13	32	4	1	140	7.9	.70
vs. Non-Playoff	33	15	19	34	0	22	4	0	96	15.6	1.03
Pre All-Star	46	11	26	37	-14	30	3	0	104	10.6	.80
Post All-Star	37	15	17	32	1	24	5	1	132	11.4	.86
Day	10	3	5	8	-2	4	2	0	38	7.9	.80
Night	73	23	38	61	-11	50	6	1	198	11.6	.84

	GP	G	A	Pts	+/–	PIM	PP	SH	S	SPct	P/G
National TV	7	3	4	7	-1	0	1	0	24	12.5	1.00
0 Days Rest	16	7	7	14	-5	6	3	1	52	13.5	.88
1 Days Rest	37	11	20	31	3	34	3	0	104	10.6	.84
2 Days Rest	17	3	7	10	-4	4	0	0	47	6.4	.59
3+ Days Rest	13	5	9	14	-7	10	2	0	33	15.2	1.08

	G	A	Pts	PIM		G	A	Pts	PIM
1st Period	8	16	24	12	Winning	9	7	16	18
2nd Period	12	11	23	16	Losing	5	17	22	34
3rd Period	6	15	21	26	Tied	12	19	31	2
Overtime	0	1	1	0	Clutch	2	6	8	10
Last 5 Min	5	14	19	10	Blowouts	0	4	4	8

Dave Reid

Dallas Stars — Left Wing

1998-99 Season

	GP	G	A	Pts	+/–	PIM	PP	SH	S	SPct	P/G
Overall	73	6	11	17	0	16	1	0	81	7.4	.23
Home	39	4	9	13	7	8	1	0	45	8.9	.33
Away	34	2	2	4	-7	8	0	0	36	5.6	.12
vs. Division	22	0	3	3	-1	2	0	0	20	0.0	.14
vs. Conference	49	1	8	9	-1	10	0	0	47	2.1	.18
vs. Playoff	43	3	6	9	-3	14	0	0	50	6.0	.21
vs. Non-Playoff	30	3	5	8	3	2	1	0	31	9.7	.27
Pre All-Star	40	3	6	9	-1	8	0	0	49	6.1	.23
Post All-Star	33	3	5	8	1	8	1	0	32	9.4	.24
Day	8	0	1	1	0	4	0	0	12	0.0	.13
Night	65	6	10	16	0	12	1	0	69	8.7	.25

	GP	G	A	Pts	+/–	PIM	PP	SH	S	SPct	P/G
National TV	11	0	2	2	-2	2	0	0	11	0.0	.18
0 Days Rest	11	0	1	1	-1	6	0	0	10	0.0	.09
1 Days Rest	39	6	6	12	4	8	1	0	53	11.3	.31
2 Days Rest	10	0	2	2	-1	2	0	0	9	0.0	.20
3+ Days Rest	13	0	2	2	-2	0	0	0	9	0.0	.15

	G	A	Pts	PIM		G	A	Pts	PIM
1st Period	4	2	6	10	Winning	3	5	8	8
2nd Period	2	4	6	4	Losing	0	0	0	4
3rd Period	0	5	5	2	Tied	3	6	9	4
Overtime	0	0	0	0	Clutch	0	1	1	0
Last 5 Min	0	1	1	2	Blowouts	1	1	2	4

Mikael Renberg

Philadelphia Flyers — Right Wing

1998-99 Season

	GP	G	A	Pts	+/–	PIM	PP	SH	S	SPct	P/G
Overall	66	15	23	38	5	18	6	0	154	9.7	.58
Home	36	8	12	20	2	10	3	0	82	9.8	.56
Away	30	7	11	18	3	8	3	0	72	9.7	.60
vs. Division	13	3	6	9	0	4	2	0	29	10.3	.69
vs. Conference	41	7	16	23	3	8	4	0	88	8.0	.56
vs. Playoff	34	6	11	17	7	14	3	0	76	7.9	.50
vs. Non-Playoff	32	9	12	21	-2	4	3	0	78	11.5	.66
Pre All-Star	28	6	10	16	2	4	3	0	57	10.5	.57
Post All-Star	38	9	13	22	3	14	3	0	97	9.3	.58
Day	12	3	4	7	3	4	1	0	31	9.7	.58
Night	54	12	19	31	2	14	5	0	123	9.8	.57

	GP	G	A	Pts	+/–	PIM	PP	SH	S	SPct	P/G
National TV	14	5	3	8	-2	4	3	0	39	12.8	.57
0 Days Rest	10	2	5	7	5	2	1	0	22	9.1	.70
1 Days Rest	34	7	11	18	-4	10	3	0	84	8.3	.53
2 Days Rest	11	4	2	6	1	2	2	0	23	17.4	.55
3+ Days Rest	11	2	5	7	3	4	0	0	25	8.0	.64

	G	A	Pts	PIM		G	A	Pts	PIM
1st Period	3	10	13	4	Winning	4	5	9	12
2nd Period	5	6	11	10	Losing	7	5	12	6
3rd Period	7	7	14	4	Tied	4	13	17	0
Overtime	0	0	0	0	Clutch	1	0	1	0
Last 5 Min	1	2	3	6	Blowouts	1	0	1	0

Pascal Rheaume

St. Louis Blues — Center

1998-99 Season

	GP	G	A	Pts	+/–	PIM	PP	SH	S	SPct	P/G
Overall	60	9	18	27	10	24	2	0	85	10.6	.45
Home	29	6	8	14	4	15	2	0	35	17.1	.48
Away	31	3	10	13	6	9	0	0	50	6.0	.42
vs. Division	13	5	4	9	7	16	1	0	18	27.8	.69
vs. Conference	40	9	14	23	11	18	2	0	56	16.1	.58
vs. Playoff	33	3	5	8	-8	6	1	0	42	7.1	.24
vs. Non-Playoff	27	6	13	19	18	18	1	0	43	14.0	.70
Pre All-Star	33	5	8	13	4	22	2	0	49	10.2	.39
Post All-Star	27	4	10	14	6	2	0	0	36	11.1	.52
Day	8	2	3	5	4	0	0	0	9	22.2	.63
Night	52	7	15	22	6	24	2	0	76	9.2	.42

	GP	G	A	Pts	+/–	PIM	PP	SH	S	SPct	P/G
National TV	14	3	3	6	4	0	1	0	18	16.7	.43
0 Days Rest	6	1	3	4	1	0	0	0	10	10.0	.67
1 Days Rest	29	5	7	12	2	4	1	0	41	12.2	.41
2 Days Rest	11	1	4	5	1	4	1	0	10	10.0	.45
3+ Days Rest	14	2	4	6	6	16	0	0	24	8.3	.43

	G	A	Pts	PIM		G	A	Pts	PIM
1st Period	2	7	9	7	Winning	4	8	12	13
2nd Period	5	4	9	11	Losing	4	5	9	9
3rd Period	2	6	8	6	Tied	1	5	6	2
Overtime	0	1	1	0	Clutch	0	3	3	2
Last 5 Min	2	6	8	9	Blowouts	1	0	1	7

Mike Ricci

San Jose Sharks — Center

1998-99 Season

	GP	G	A	Pts	+/–	PIM	PP	SH	S	SPct	P/G
Overall	82	13	26	39	1	68	2	1	98	13.3	.48
Home	41	6	12	18	6	40	0	0	56	10.7	.44
Away	41	7	14	21	-5	28	2	1	42	16.7	.51
vs. Division	24	4	6	10	0	18	1	0	35	11.4	.42
vs. Conference	57	9	17	26	-2	48	1	0	73	12.3	.46
vs. Playoff	48	8	15	23	-1	34	1	0	55	14.5	.48
vs. Non-Playoff	34	5	11	16	2	34	1	1	43	11.6	.47
Pre All-Star	45	9	16	25	3	30	1	1	57	15.8	.56
Post All-Star	37	4	10	14	-2	38	1	0	41	9.8	.38
Day	7	3	2	5	0	4	1	1	13	23.1	.71
Night	75	10	24	34	1	64	1	0	85	11.8	.45

	GP	G	A	Pts	+/–	PIM	PP	SH	S	SPct	P/G
National TV	11	3	1	4	0	16	0	0	15	20.0	.36
0 Days Rest	14	0	5	5	-2	6	0	0	11	0.0	.36
1 Days Rest	42	4	17	21	3	42	1	0	50	8.0	.50
2 Days Rest	15	7	2	9	1	12	1	1	19	36.8	.60
3+ Days Rest	11	2	2	4	-1	8	0	0	18	11.1	.36

	G	A	Pts	PIM		G	A	Pts	PIM
1st Period	4	5	9	12	Winning	4	5	9	26
2nd Period	1	9	10	22	Losing	4	12	16	26
3rd Period	8	12	20	30	Tied	5	9	14	16
Overtime	0	0	0	4	Clutch	4	4	8	18
Last 5 Min	8	5	13	20	Blowouts	1	0	1	4

Stephane Richer

Tampa Bay Lightning — Right Wing

1998-99 Season

	GP	G	A	Pts	+/–	PIM	PP	SH	S	SPct	P/G
Overall	64	12	21	33	-10	22	3	2	139	8.6	.52
Home	32	6	15	21	0	10	3	0	64	9.4	.66
Away	32	6	6	12	-10	12	0	2	75	8.0	.38
vs. Division	12	4	1	5	-7	6	3	0	33	12.1	.42
vs. Conference	47	10	15	25	-7	14	3	1	107	9.3	.53
vs. Playoff	41	8	16	24	-2	14	1	1	87	9.2	.59
vs. Non-Playoff	23	4	5	9	-8	8	2	1	52	7.7	.39
Pre All-Star	28	3	8	11	-11	10	1	1	55	5.5	.39
Post All-Star	36	9	13	22	1	12	2	1	84	10.7	.61
Day	4	2	0	2	1	0	0	1	8	25.0	.50
Night	60	10	21	31	-11	22	3	1	131	7.6	.52

	GP	G	A	Pts	+/–	PIM	PP	SH	S	SPct	P/G
National TV	1	1	1	2	3	0	0	0	4	25.0	2.00
0 Days Rest	13	0	2	2	-7	6	0	0	34	0.0	.15
1 Days Rest	25	6	11	17	2	10	1	1	54	11.1	.68
2 Days Rest	15	4	4	8	1	6	2	1	34	11.8	.53
3+ Days Rest	11	2	4	6	-6	0	0	0	17	11.8	.55

	G	A	Pts	PIM		G	A	Pts	PIM
1st Period	5	6	11	6	Winning	3	7	10	6
2nd Period	3	9	12	8	Losing	5	9	14	16
3rd Period	4	6	10	8	Tied	4	5	9	0
Overtime	0	0	0	0	Clutch	0	2	2	0
Last 5 Min	4	8	12	4	Blowouts	1	0	1	6

Barry Richter

New York Islanders — Defense

1998-99 Season

	GP	G	A	Pts	+/–	PIM	PP	SH	S	SPct	P/G
Overall	72	6	18	24	-4	34	0	0	111	5.4	.33
Home	36	4	11	15	0	14	0	0	64	6.3	.42
Away	36	2	7	9	-4	20	0	0	47	4.3	.25
vs. Division	17	2	2	4	0	12	0	0	28	7.1	.24
vs. Conference	51	3	15	18	-6	24	0	0	76	3.9	.35
vs. Playoff	43	4	12	16	-9	22	0	0	50	8.0	.37
vs. Non-Playoff	29	2	6	8	5	12	0	0	61	3.3	.28
Pre All-Star	40	3	5	8	-9	12	0	0	58	5.2	.20
Post All-Star	32	3	13	16	5	22	0	0	53	5.7	.50
Day	9	0	1	1	1	10	0	0	7	0.0	.11
Night	63	6	17	23	-5	24	0	0	104	5.8	.37

	GP	G	A	Pts	+/–	PIM	PP	SH	S	SPct	P/G
National TV	5	0	1	1	1	6	0	0	5	0.0	.20
0 Days Rest	11	1	1	2	-6	6	0	0	11	9.1	.18
1 Days Rest	30	3	5	8	-4	12	0	0	44	6.8	.27
2 Days Rest	18	2	8	10	7	12	0	0	34	5.9	.56
3+ Days Rest	13	0	4	4	-1	4	0	0	22	0.0	.31

	G	A	Pts	PIM		G	A	Pts	PIM
1st Period	2	7	9	16	Winning	1	7	8	10
2nd Period	3	9	12	12	Losing	4	7	11	22
3rd Period	1	2	3	6	Tied	1	4	5	2
Overtime	0	0	0	0	Clutch	0	1	1	0
Last 5 Min	1	3	4	2	Blowouts	0	0	0	4

Craig Rivet

Montreal Canadiens — Defense

1998-99 Season

	GP	G	A	Pts	+/–	PIM	PP	SH	S	SPct	P/G
Overall	66	2	8	10	-3	66	0	0	39	5.1	.15
Home	34	1	4	5	1	37	0	0	22	4.5	.15
Away	32	1	4	5	-4	29	0	0	17	5.9	.16
vs. Division	17	0	1	1	-6	18	0	0	10	0.0	.06
vs. Conference	46	2	6	8	-5	51	0	0	33	6.1	.17
vs. Playoff	43	1	5	6	-4	50	0	0	27	3.7	.14
vs. Non-Playoff	23	1	3	4	1	16	0	0	12	8.3	.17
Pre All-Star	40	2	6	8	1	51	0	0	20	10.0	.20
Post All-Star	26	0	2	2	-4	15	0	0	19	0.0	.08
Day	3	0	0	0	0	2	0	0	3	0.0	.00
Night	63	2	8	10	-3	64	0	0	36	5.6	.16

	GP	G	A	Pts	+/–	PIM	PP	SH	S	SPct	P/G
National TV	21	1	3	4	-6	29	0	0	7	14.3	.19
0 Days Rest	14	0	4	4	2	29	0	0	7	0.0	.29
1 Days Rest	25	1	1	2	-8	17	0	0	12	8.3	.08
2 Days Rest	15	0	1	1	-2	13	0	0	6	0.0	.07
3+ Days Rest	12	1	2	3	5	7	0	0	14	7.1	.25

	G	A	Pts	PIM		G	A	Pts	PIM
1st Period	0	3	3	30	Winning	1	2	3	20
2nd Period	1	2	3	29	Losing	1	5	6	38
3rd Period	1	3	4	7	Tied	0	1	1	8
Overtime	0	0	0	0	Clutch	0	2	2	2
Last 5 Min	0	1	1	2	Blowouts	0	0	0	0

Gary Roberts

Carolina Hurricanes — Left Wing

1998-99 Season

	GP	G	A	Pts	+/–	PIM	PP	SH	S	SPct	P/G
Overall	77	14	28	42	2	178	1	1	138	10.1	.55
Home	38	11	12	23	5	82	1	0	69	15.9	.61
Away	39	3	16	19	-3	96	0	1	69	4.3	.49
vs. Division	13	3	4	7	-3	26	1	0	24	12.5	.54
vs. Conference	54	11	17	28	-2	109	1	1	92	12.0	.52
vs. Playoff	42	6	15	21	-2	120	0	0	79	7.6	.50
vs. Non-Playoff	35	8	13	21	4	58	1	1	59	13.6	.60
Pre All-Star	41	9	20	29	-1	90	0	0	76	11.8	.71
Post All-Star	36	5	8	13	3	88	1	1	62	8.1	.36
Day	7	0	1	1	-4	9	0	0	10	0.0	.14
Night	70	14	27	41	6	169	1	1	128	10.9	.59

	GP	G	A	Pts	+/–	PIM	PP	SH	S	SPct	P/G
National TV	2	0	0	0	1	26	0	0	4	0.0	.00
0 Days Rest	15	2	7	9	0	61	0	0	26	7.7	.60
1 Days Rest	29	5	5	10	-7	60	0	0	49	10.2	.34
2 Days Rest	23	5	10	15	7	41	0	1	43	11.6	.65
3+ Days Rest	10	2	6	8	2	16	1	0	20	10.0	.80

	G	A	Pts	PIM		G	A	Pts	PIM
1st Period	3	10	13	50	Winning	3	11	14	44
2nd Period	4	9	13	60	Losing	2	7	9	94
3rd Period	6	9	15	66	Tied	9	10	19	40
Overtime	1	0	1	2	Clutch	2	3	5	37
Last 5 Min	4	9	13	66	Blowouts	1	0	1	9

Luc Robitaille

Los Angeles Kings — Left Wing

1998-99 Season

	GP	G	A	Pts	+/–	PIM	PP	SH	S	SPct	P/G
Overall	82	39	35	74	-1	54	11	0	292	13.4	.90
Home	41	18	21	39	3	24	7	0	137	13.1	.95
Away	41	21	14	35	-4	30	4	0	155	13.5	.85
vs. Division	24	11	7	18	-1	20	3	0	90	12.2	.75
vs. Conference	57	31	19	50	-1	34	9	0	213	14.6	.88
vs. Playoff	56	25	25	50	-2	36	7	0	205	12.2	.89
vs. Non-Playoff	26	14	10	24	1	18	4	0	87	16.1	.92
Pre All-Star	45	25	19	44	2	26	6	0	160	15.6	.98
Post All-Star	37	14	16	30	-3	28	5	0	132	10.6	.81
Day	5	0	0	0	-3	10	0	0	22	0.0	.00
Night	77	39	35	74	2	44	11	0	270	14.4	.96

	GP	G	A	Pts	+/–	PIM	PP	SH	S	SPct	P/G
National TV	16	5	6	11	-3	18	1	0	61	8.2	.69
0 Days Rest	13	8	5	13	-3	4	2	0	52	15.4	1.00
1 Days Rest	42	13	19	32	-3	32	5	0	147	8.8	.76
2 Days Rest	16	10	6	16	2	14	2	0	55	18.2	1.00
3+ Days Rest	11	8	5	13	3	4	2	0	38	21.1	1.18

	G	A	Pts	PIM		G	A	Pts	PIM
1st Period	17	8	25	18	Winning	8	12	20	18
2nd Period	9	16	25	26	Losing	14	14	28	34
3rd Period	11	11	22	10	Tied	17	9	26	2
Overtime	2	0	2	0	Clutch	6	3	9	0
Last 5 Min	13	6	19	20	Blowouts	0	2	2	10

Jeremy Roenick

Phoenix Coyotes — Center

1998-99 Season

	GP	G	A	Pts	+/–	PIM	PP	SH	S	SPct	P/G
Overall	78	24	48	72	7	130	4	0	203	11.8	.92
Home	37	9	24	33	2	85	0	0	97	9.3	.89
Away	41	15	24	39	5	45	4	0	106	14.2	.95
vs. Division	22	4	9	13	-1	62	0	0	60	6.7	.59
vs. Conference	53	16	33	49	8	102	4	0	138	11.6	.92
vs. Playoff	45	10	26	36	-4	84	1	0	99	10.1	.80
vs. Non-Playoff	33	14	22	36	11	46	3	0	104	13.5	1.09
Pre All-Star	40	16	26	42	12	61	4	0	103	15.5	1.05
Post All-Star	38	8	22	30	-5	69	0	0	100	8.0	.79
Day	5	2	3	5	2	12	0	0	13	15.4	1.00
Night	73	22	45	67	5	118	4	0	190	11.6	.92

	GP	G	A	Pts	+/–	PIM	PP	SH	S	SPct	P/G
National TV	13	2	10	12	1	26	0	0	32	6.3	.92
0 Days Rest	12	6	9	15	-2	19	4	0	31	19.4	1.25
1 Days Rest	39	10	16	26	-1	81	0	0	104	9.6	.67
2 Days Rest	16	5	13	18	6	16	0	0	41	12.2	1.13
3+ Days Rest	11	3	10	13	4	14	0	0	27	11.1	1.18

	G	A	Pts	PIM		G	A	Pts	PIM
1st Period	7	18	25	37	Winning	10	17	27	52
2nd Period	7	17	24	49	Losing	5	13	18	45
3rd Period	10	12	22	42	Tied	9	18	27	33
Overtime	0	1	1	2	Clutch	1	4	5	4
Last 5 Min	5	12	17	48	Blowouts	1	2	3	9

Stacy Roest

Detroit Red Wings — Center

1998-99 Season

	GP	G	A	Pts	+/–	PIM	PP	SH	S	SPct	P/G
Overall	59	4	8	12	-7	14	0	0	50	8.0	.20
Home	31	3	6	9	-1	10	0	0	31	9.7	.29
Away	28	1	2	3	-6	4	0	0	19	5.3	.11
vs. Division	13	1	3	4	3	0	0	0	11	9.1	.31
vs. Conference	37	3	5	8	-4	10	0	0	28	10.7	.22
vs. Playoff	32	2	1	3	-7	12	0	0	26	7.7	.09
vs. Non-Playoff	27	2	7	9	0	2	0	0	24	8.3	.33
Pre All-Star	30	2	6	8	-4	8	0	0	31	6.5	.27
Post All-Star	29	2	2	4	-3	6	0	0	19	10.5	.14
Day	11	2	1	3	1	2	0	0	12	16.7	.27
Night	48	2	7	9	-8	12	0	0	38	5.3	.19

	GP	G	A	Pts	+/–	PIM	PP	SH	S	SPct	P/G
National TV	17	1	0	1	-6	4	0	0	12	8.3	.06
0 Days Rest	9	0	0	0	-5	0	0	0	11	0.0	.00
1 Days Rest	23	3	6	9	1	2	0	0	23	13.0	.39
2 Days Rest	14	1	0	1	-1	4	0	0	10	10.0	.07
3+ Days Rest	13	0	2	2	-2	8	0	0	6	0.0	.15

	G	A	Pts	PIM		G	A	Pts	PIM
1st Period	1	1	2	2	Winning	3	3	6	8
2nd Period	2	2	4	8	Losing	0	4	4	4
3rd Period	1	5	6	4	Tied	1	1	2	2
Overtime	0	0	0	0	Clutch	0	1	1	0
Last 5 Min	0	3	3	2	Blowouts	0	1	1	4

Brian Rolston

New Jersey Devils — Center

1998-99 Season

	GP	G	A	Pts	+/–	PIM	PP	SH	S	SPct	P/G
Overall	82	24	33	57	11	14	5	5	210	11.4	.70
Home	41	10	20	30	7	4	2	1	102	9.8	.73
Away	41	14	13	27	4	10	3	4	108	13.0	.66
vs. Division	20	6	9	15	1	2	1	2	50	12.0	.75
vs. Conference	58	17	27	44	11	8	4	4	151	11.3	.76
vs. Playoff	46	16	14	30	4	6	2	3	120	13.3	.65
vs. Non-Playoff	36	8	19	27	7	8	3	2	90	8.9	.75
Pre All-Star	44	12	19	31	-1	8	3	3	112	10.7	.70
Post All-Star	38	12	14	26	12	6	2	2	98	12.2	.68
Day	12	3	4	7	1	2	1	0	21	14.3	.58
Night	70	21	29	50	10	12	4	5	189	11.1	.71

	GP	G	A	Pts	+/–	PIM	PP	SH	S	SPct	P/G
National TV	7	0	4	4	0	0	0	0	15	0.0	.57
0 Days Rest	17	4	7	11	-2	2	1	1	34	11.8	.65
1 Days Rest	34	13	12	25	1	4	3	2	95	13.7	.74
2 Days Rest	21	5	8	13	5	6	1	0	52	9.6	.62
3+ Days Rest	10	2	6	8	7	2	0	2	29	6.9	.80

	G	A	Pts	PIM		G	A	Pts	PIM
1st Period	6	10	16	6	Winning	8	12	20	6
2nd Period	13	10	23	6	Losing	6	7	13	8
3rd Period	5	12	17	2	Tied	10	14	24	0
Overtime	0	1	1	0	Clutch	3	4	7	0
Last 5 Min	10	12	22	12	Blowouts	1	1	2	2

Cliff Ronning

Nashville Predators — Center

1998-99 Season

	GP	G	A	Pts	+/–	PIM	PP	SH	S	SPct	P/G
Overall	79	20	40	60	-3	42	10	0	257	7.8	.76
Home	39	15	18	33	-8	16	8	0	140	10.7	.85
Away	40	5	22	27	5	26	2	0	117	4.3	.68
vs. Division	18	6	6	12	1	4	2	0	45	13.3	.67
vs. Conference	54	15	29	44	3	30	8	0	174	8.6	.81
vs. Playoff	53	16	23	39	-9	20	8	0	171	9.4	.74
vs. Non-Playoff	26	4	17	21	6	22	2	0	86	4.7	.81
Pre All-Star	43	11	24	35	3	28	6	0	134	8.2	.81
Post All-Star	36	9	16	25	-6	14	4	0	123	7.3	.69
Day	8	2	2	4	-5	4	2	0	25	8.0	.50
Night	71	18	38	56	2	38	8	0	232	7.8	.79

	GP	G	A	Pts	+/–	PIM	PP	SH	S	SPct	P/G
National TV	3	0	3	3	0	10	0	0	13	0.0	1.00
0 Days Rest	13	4	8	12	-3	24	3	0	39	10.3	.92
1 Days Rest	36	6	22	28	3	8	3	0	107	5.6	.78
2 Days Rest	17	4	8	12	0	6	1	0	61	6.6	.71
3+ Days Rest	13	6	2	8	-3	4	3	0	50	12.0	.62

	G	A	Pts	PIM		G	A	Pts	PIM
1st Period	7	12	19	6	Winning	4	5	9	8
2nd Period	5	20	25	16	Losing	10	21	31	32
3rd Period	8	8	16	20	Tied	6	14	20	2
Overtime	0	0	0	0	Clutch	3	0	3	4
Last 5 Min	6	12	18	12	Blowouts	0	0	0	6

Pavel Rosa

Los Angeles Kings — Right Wing

1998-99 Season

	GP	G	A	Pts	+/–	PIM	PP	SH	S	SPct	P/G
Overall	29	4	12	16	0	6	0	0	61	6.6	.55
Home	16	4	6	10	2	4	0	0	35	11.4	.63
Away	13	0	6	6	-2	2	0	0	26	0.0	.46
vs. Division	10	0	2	2	-1	2	0	0	17	0.0	.20
vs. Conference	23	0	11	11	1	2	0	0	45	0.0	.48
vs. Playoff	22	2	9	11	-1	6	0	0	45	4.4	.50
vs. Non-Playoff	7	2	3	5	1	0	0	0	16	12.5	.71
Pre All-Star	15	3	9	12	0	4	0	0	35	8.6	.80
Post All-Star	14	1	3	4	0	2	0	0	26	3.8	.29
Day	2	0	0	0	-2	0	0	0	4	0.0	.00
Night	27	4	12	16	2	6	0	0	57	7.0	.59

	GP	G	A	Pts	+/–	PIM	PP	SH	S	SPct	P/G
National TV	4	0	0	0	-2	2	0	0	7	0.0	.00
0 Days Rest	3	0	2	2	0	2	0	0	7	0.0	.67
1 Days Rest	12	1	3	4	-2	4	0	0	22	4.5	.33
2 Days Rest	7	0	5	5	2	0	0	0	14	0.0	.71
3+ Days Rest	7	3	2	5	0	0	0	0	18	16.7	.71

	G	A	Pts	PIM		G	A	Pts	PIM
1st Period	2	3	5	2	Winning	1	3	4	6
2nd Period	2	5	7	4	Losing	2	5	7	0
3rd Period	0	3	3	0	Tied	1	4	5	0
Overtime	0	1	1	0	Clutch	0	2	2	0
Last 5 Min	3	5	8	0	Blowouts	0	0	0	0

Bob Rouse

San Jose Sharks — Defense

1998-99 Season

	GP	G	A	Pts	+/–	PIM	PP	SH	S	SPct	P/G
Overall	70	0	11	11	0	44	0	0	75	0.0	.16
Home	36	0	7	7	5	22	0	0	41	0.0	.19
Away	34	0	4	4	-5	22	0	0	34	0.0	.12
vs. Division	18	0	2	2	-1	10	0	0	22	0.0	.11
vs. Conference	46	0	6	6	-4	38	0	0	49	0.0	.13
vs. Playoff	42	0	5	5	-1	30	0	0	40	0.0	.12
vs. Non-Playoff	28	0	6	6	1	14	0	0	35	0.0	.21
Pre All-Star	45	0	9	9	1	26	0	0	51	0.0	.20
Post All-Star	25	0	2	2	-1	18	0	0	24	0.0	.08
Day	7	0	0	0	0	6	0	0	5	0.0	.00
Night	63	0	11	11	0	38	0	0	70	0.0	.17

	GP	G	A	Pts	+/–	PIM	PP	SH	S	SPct	P/G
National TV	6	0	1	1	2	8	0	0	4	0.0	.17
0 Days Rest	8	0	3	3	-2	4	0	0	7	0.0	.38
1 Days Rest	35	0	5	5	2	24	0	0	39	0.0	.14
2 Days Rest	14	0	1	1	0	12	0	0	20	0.0	.07
3+ Days Rest	13	0	2	2	0	4	0	0	9	0.0	.15

	G	A	Pts	PIM		G	A	Pts	PIM
1st Period	0	2	2	20	Winning	0	5	5	12
2nd Period	0	0	0	20	Losing	0	6	6	22
3rd Period	0	9	9	4	Tied	0	0	0	10
Overtime	0	0	0	0	Clutch	0	2	2	2
Last 5 Min	0	3	3	10	Blowouts	0	0	0	4

Steve Rucchin

Anaheim Mighty Ducks — Center

1998-99 Season

	GP	G	A	Pts	+/–	PIM	PP	SH	S	SPct	P/G
Overall	69	23	39	62	11	22	5	1	145	15.9	.90
Home	33	15	18	33	8	8	4	1	81	18.5	1.00
Away	36	8	21	29	3	14	1	0	64	12.5	.81
vs. Division	18	6	8	14	6	6	1	0	47	12.8	.78
vs. Conference	47	14	26	40	6	18	3	1	102	13.7	.85
vs. Playoff	43	17	18	35	3	12	3	1	100	17.0	.81
vs. Non-Playoff	26	6	21	27	8	10	2	0	45	13.3	1.04
Pre All-Star	45	14	27	41	4	18	3	0	96	14.6	.91
Post All-Star	24	9	12	21	7	4	2	1	49	18.4	.88
Day	1	2	2	4	4	0	0	0	3	66.7	4.00
Night	68	21	37	58	7	22	5	1	142	14.8	.85

	GP	G	A	Pts	+/–	PIM	PP	SH	S	SPct	P/G
National TV	11	4	5	9	6	2	0	1	22	18.2	.82
0 Days Rest	12	0	6	6	1	6	0	0	20	0.0	.50
1 Days Rest	34	15	19	34	6	8	2	0	72	20.8	1.00
2 Days Rest	10	3	10	13	-2	8	2	0	25	12.0	1.30
3+ Days Rest	13	5	4	9	6	0	1	1	28	17.9	.69

	G	A	Pts	PIM		G	A	Pts	PIM
1st Period	7	13	20	6	Winning	8	15	23	12
2nd Period	6	11	17	12	Losing	7	11	18	6
3rd Period	9	15	24	4	Tied	8	13	21	4
Overtime	1	0	1	0	Clutch	2	7	9	0
Last 5 Min	6	14	20	4	Blowouts	2	2	4	0

Martin Rucinsky

Montreal Canadiens — Left Wing

1998-99 Season

	GP	G	A	Pts	+/–	PIM	PP	SH	S	SPct	P/G
Overall	73	17	17	34	-25	50	5	0	180	9.4	.47
Home	34	8	12	20	-3	24	2	0	75	10.7	.59
Away	39	9	5	14	-22	26	3	0	105	8.6	.36
vs. Division	17	3	4	7	-11	10	1	0	44	6.8	.41
vs. Conference	50	14	13	27	-17	32	5	0	125	11.2	.54
vs. Playoff	46	11	9	20	-23	34	5	0	117	9.4	.43
vs. Non-Playoff	27	6	8	14	-2	16	0	0	63	9.5	.52
Pre All-Star	40	9	13	22	-12	30	4	0	103	8.7	.55
Post All-Star	33	8	4	12	-13	20	1	0	77	10.4	.36
Day	3	1	0	1	-3	2	1	0	10	10.0	.33
Night	70	16	17	33	-22	48	4	0	170	9.4	.47

	GP	G	A	Pts	+/–	PIM	PP	SH	S	SPct	P/G
National TV	22	4	5	9	-14	16	1	0	51	7.8	.41
0 Days Rest	16	1	6	7	-10	2	1	0	36	2.8	.44
1 Days Rest	32	7	8	15	-7	28	1	0	89	7.9	.47
2 Days Rest	14	5	2	7	-6	12	3	0	29	17.2	.50
3+ Days Rest	11	4	1	5	-2	8	0	0	26	15.4	.45

	G	A	Pts	PIM		G	A	Pts	PIM
1st Period	5	4	9	14	Winning	5	6	11	14
2nd Period	5	7	12	18	Losing	4	6	10	32
3rd Period	7	6	13	18	Tied	8	5	13	4
Overtime	0	0	0	0	Clutch	2	2	4	2
Last 5 Min	5	9	14	22	Blowouts	0	1	1	8

Joe Sakic

Colorado Avalanche — Center

1998-99 Season

	GP	G	A	Pts	+/–	PIM	PP	SH	S	SPct	P/G
Overall	73	41	55	96	23	29	12	5	255	16.1	1.32
Home	37	25	35	60	17	9	10	2	137	18.2	1.62
Away	36	16	20	36	6	20	2	3	118	13.6	1.00
vs. Division	16	6	13	19	-3	6	4	1	55	10.9	1.19
vs. Conference	49	30	34	64	12	25	10	5	167	18.0	1.31
vs. Playoff	39	22	24	46	7	10	5	3	127	17.3	1.18
vs. Non-Playoff	34	19	31	50	16	19	7	2	128	14.8	1.47
Pre All-Star	36	20	26	46	8	16	4	5	138	14.5	1.28
Post All-Star	37	21	29	50	15	13	8	0	117	17.9	1.35
Day	14	7	8	15	2	9	3	0	47	14.9	1.07
Night	59	34	47	81	21	20	9	5	208	16.3	1.37

	GP	G	A	Pts	+/–	PIM	PP	SH	S	SPct	P/G
National TV	21	11	15	26	8	10	0	2	68	16.2	1.24
0 Days Rest	11	6	11	17	2	6	0	2	37	16.2	1.55
1 Days Rest	37	15	23	38	10	17	6	0	119	12.6	1.03
2 Days Rest	12	10	13	23	11	2	2	2	49	20.4	1.92
3+ Days Rest	13	10	8	18	0	4	4	1	50	20.0	1.38

	G	A	Pts	PIM		G	A	Pts	PIM
1st Period	11	13	24	13	Winning	9	17	26	14
2nd Period	18	21	39	6	Losing	16	16	32	10
3rd Period	12	20	32	10	Tied	16	22	38	5
Overtime	0	1	1	0	Clutch	3	7	10	2
Last 5 Min	9	22	31	0	Blowouts	0	3	3	2

Ruslan Salei

Anaheim Mighty Ducks — Defense

1998-99 Season

	GP	G	A	Pts	+/–	PIM	PP	SH	S	SPct	P/G
Overall	74	2	14	16	1	65	1	0	123	1.6	.22
Home	38	1	9	10	5	24	1	0	62	1.6	.26
Away	36	1	5	6	-4	41	0	0	61	1.6	.17
vs. Division	22	1	5	6	1	20	1	0	39	2.6	.27
vs. Conference	54	1	10	11	-8	38	1	0	85	1.2	.20
vs. Playoff	47	2	6	8	0	49	1	0	73	2.7	.17
vs. Non-Playoff	27	0	8	8	1	16	0	0	50	0.0	.30
Pre All-Star	39	2	7	9	-1	31	1	0	84	2.4	.23
Post All-Star	35	0	7	7	2	34	0	0	39	0.0	.20
Day	1	1	0	1	4	0	0	0	2	50.0	1.00
Night	73	1	14	15	-3	65	1	0	121	0.8	.21

	GP	G	A	Pts	+/–	PIM	PP	SH	S	SPct	P/G
National TV	13	0	4	4	1	20	0	0	11	0.0	.31
0 Days Rest	13	0	3	3	-2	8	0	0	12	0.0	.23
1 Days Rest	40	2	4	6	-2	45	1	0	88	2.3	.15
2 Days Rest	11	0	3	3	0	8	0	0	16	0.0	.27
3+ Days Rest	10	0	4	4	5	4	0	0	7	0.0	.40

	G	A	Pts	PIM		G	A	Pts	PIM
1st Period	1	3	4	25	Winning	1	4	5	34
2nd Period	1	5	6	18	Losing	0	6	6	19
3rd Period	0	6	6	22	Tied	1	4	5	12
Overtime	0	0	0	0	Clutch	0	2	2	0
Last 5 Min	0	2	2	10	Blowouts	0	0	0	16

Sami Salo

Ottawa Senators — Defense

1998-99 Season

	GP	G	A	Pts	+/–	PIM	PP	SH	S	SPct	P/G
Overall	61	7	12	19	20	24	2	0	106	6.6	.31
Home	29	2	6	8	9	10	1	0	47	4.3	.28
Away	32	5	6	11	11	14	1	0	59	8.5	.34
vs. Division	16	2	1	3	2	6	0	0	28	7.1	.19
vs. Conference	42	6	9	15	16	20	1	0	78	7.7	.36
vs. Playoff	36	5	5	10	10	8	0	0	68	7.4	.28
vs. Non-Playoff	25	2	7	9	10	16	2	0	38	5.3	.36
Pre All-Star	27	1	4	5	8	12	0	0	38	2.6	.19
Post All-Star	34	6	8	14	12	12	2	0	68	8.8	.41
Day	3	0	0	0	2	2	0	0	4	0.0	.00
Night	58	7	12	19	18	22	2	0	102	6.9	.33

	GP	G	A	Pts	+/–	PIM	PP	SH	S	SPct	P/G
National TV	8	1	1	2	6	8	1	0	16	6.3	.25
0 Days Rest	9	1	1	2	2	2	0	0	20	5.0	.22
1 Days Rest	34	2	8	10	12	10	1	0	55	3.6	.29
2 Days Rest	10	4	3	7	1	6	1	0	20	20.0	.70
3+ Days Rest	8	0	0	0	5	6	0	0	11	0.0	.00

	G	A	Pts	PIM		G	A	Pts	PIM
1st Period	0	6	6	0	Winning	2	5	7	22
2nd Period	4	3	7	16	Losing	3	2	5	0
3rd Period	3	3	6	8	Tied	2	5	7	2
Overtime	0	0	0	0	Clutch	1	2	3	0
Last 5 Min	1	3	4	8	Blowouts	0	0	0	6

Sergei Samsonov

Boston Bruins — Left Wing

1998-99 Season

	GP	G	A	Pts	+/–	PIM	PP	SH	S	SPct	P/G
Overall	79	25	26	51	-6	18	6	0	160	15.6	.65
Home	39	14	13	27	-2	8	4	0	88	15.9	.69
Away	40	11	13	24	-4	10	2	0	72	15.3	.60
vs. Division	19	7	7	14	-1	0	1	0	37	18.9	.74
vs. Conference	56	15	18	33	-6	14	4	0	111	13.5	.59
vs. Playoff	44	12	19	31	2	8	3	0	78	15.4	.70
vs. Non-Playoff	35	13	7	20	-8	10	3	0	82	15.9	.57
Pre All-Star	43	15	20	35	-8	8	4	0	80	18.8	.81
Post All-Star	36	10	6	16	2	10	2	0	80	12.5	.44
Day	16	8	3	11	3	6	1	0	35	22.9	.69
Night	63	17	23	40	-9	12	5	0	125	13.6	.63

	GP	G	A	Pts	+/–	PIM	PP	SH	S	SPct	P/G
National TV	9	3	3	6	-3	2	1	0	23	13.0	.67
0 Days Rest	16	4	2	6	-8	4	2	0	33	12.1	.38
1 Days Rest	36	13	11	24	-4	10	2	0	80	16.3	.67
2 Days Rest	13	5	5	10	0	2	1	0	20	25.0	.77
3+ Days Rest	14	3	8	11	6	2	1	0	27	11.1	.79

	G	A	Pts	PIM		G	A	Pts	PIM
1st Period	11	9	20	0	Winning	9	10	19	8
2nd Period	9	9	18	2	Losing	6	7	13	4
3rd Period	5	8	13	16	Tied	10	9	19	6
Overtime	0	0	0	0	Clutch	1	3	4	10
Last 5 Min	12	10	22	8	Blowouts	0	0	0	0

Ulf Samuelsson

Detroit Red Wings — Defense

1998-99 Season

	GP	G	A	Pts	+/–	PIM	PP	SH	S	SPct	P/G
Overall	71	4	8	12	5	99	0	0	39	10.3	.17
Home	37	2	6	8	3	64	0	0	23	8.7	.22
Away	34	2	2	4	2	35	0	0	16	12.5	.12
vs. Division	18	2	2	4	-1	26	0	0	9	22.2	.22
vs. Conference	49	4	4	8	2	65	0	0	26	15.4	.16
vs. Playoff	44	1	4	5	0	61	0	0	17	5.9	.11
vs. Non-Playoff	27	3	4	7	5	38	0	0	22	13.6	.26
Pre All-Star	44	3	4	7	0	69	0	0	27	11.1	.16
Post All-Star	27	1	4	5	5	30	0	0	12	8.3	.19
Day	10	0	2	2	0	10	0	0	4	0.0	.20
Night	61	4	6	10	5	89	0	0	35	11.4	.16

	GP	G	A	Pts	+/–	PIM	PP	SH	S	SPct	P/G
National TV	18	1	2	3	-6	22	0	0	5	20.0	.17
0 Days Rest	12	0	1	1	-2	16	0	0	6	0.0	.08
1 Days Rest	30	1	6	7	0	38	0	0	14	7.1	.23
2 Days Rest	15	1	1	2	5	25	0	0	8	12.5	.13
3+ Days Rest	14	2	0	2	2	20	0	0	11	18.2	.14

	G	A	Pts	PIM		G	A	Pts	PIM
1st Period	2	4	6	42	Winning	2	2	4	51
2nd Period	1	2	3	29	Losing	1	4	5	34
3rd Period	1	2	3	28	Tied	1	2	3	14
Overtime	0	0	0	0	Clutch	0	1	1	6
Last 5 Min	0	1	1	30	Blowouts	2	0	2	12

Geoff Sanderson

Buffalo Sabres — Left Wing

1998-99 Season

	GP	G	A	Pts	+/–	PIM	PP	SH	S	SPct	P/G
Overall	75	12	18	30	8	22	1	0	155	7.7	.40
Home	38	5	11	16	3	12	0	0	87	5.7	.42
Away	37	7	7	14	5	10	1	0	68	10.3	.38
vs. Division	17	4	3	7	3	0	0	0	28	14.3	.41
vs. Conference	53	9	10	19	6	16	0	0	103	8.7	.36
vs. Playoff	41	8	10	18	4	8	1	0	92	8.7	.44
vs. Non-Playoff	34	4	8	12	4	14	0	0	63	6.3	.35
Pre All-Star	40	9	9	18	4	12	1	0	73	12.3	.45
Post All-Star	35	3	9	12	4	10	0	0	82	3.7	.34
Day	5	2	2	4	1	0	0	0	14	14.3	.80
Night	70	10	16	26	7	22	1	0	141	7.1	.37

	GP	G	A	Pts	+/–	PIM	PP	SH	S	SPct	P/G
National TV	14	4	1	5	2	8	0	0	22	18.2	.36
0 Days Rest	18	4	2	6	7	4	0	0	40	10.0	.33
1 Days Rest	23	3	10	13	5	8	0	0	48	6.3	.57
2 Days Rest	17	1	3	4	-5	6	0	0	29	3.4	.24
3+ Days Rest	17	4	3	7	1	4	1	0	38	10.5	.41

	G	A	Pts	PIM		G	A	Pts	PIM
1st Period	5	3	8	12	Winning	5	7	12	6
2nd Period	4	5	9	4	Losing	4	8	12	12
3rd Period	3	10	13	6	Tied	3	3	6	4
Overtime	0	0	0	0	Clutch	1	1	2	2
Last 5 Min	2	3	5	4	Blowouts	0	3	3	2

Tomas Sandstrom

Anaheim Mighty Ducks — Right Wing

1998-99 Season

	GP	G	A	Pts	+/–	PIM	PP	SH	S	SPct	P/G
Overall	58	15	17	32	-5	42	7	0	107	14.0	.55
Home	30	8	9	17	-3	20	4	0	61	13.1	.57
Away	28	7	8	15	-2	22	3	0	46	15.2	.54
vs. Division	21	7	6	13	1	12	4	0	38	18.4	.62
vs. Conference	43	13	13	26	-5	24	7	0	74	17.6	.60
vs. Playoff	38	9	9	18	-7	28	5	0	69	13.0	.47
vs. Non-Playoff	20	6	8	14	2	14	2	0	38	15.8	.70
Pre All-Star	21	6	2	8	-2	24	3	0	48	12.5	.38
Post All-Star	37	9	15	24	-3	18	4	0	59	15.3	.65
Day	0	0	0	0	0	0	0	0	0	–	–
Night	58	15	17	32	-5	42	7	0	107	14.0	.55

	GP	G	A	Pts	+/–	PIM	PP	SH	S	SPct	P/G
National TV	10	2	7	9	6	10	0	0	16	12.5	.90
0 Days Rest	12	3	4	7	1	6	1	0	19	15.8	.58
1 Days Rest	27	9	7	16	-3	22	5	0	51	17.6	.59
2 Days Rest	7	2	2	4	-1	2	0	0	18	11.1	.57
3+ Days Rest	12	1	4	5	-2	12	1	0	19	5.3	.42

	G	A	Pts	PIM		G	A	Pts	PIM
1st Period	4	6	10	14	Winning	5	8	13	16
2nd Period	4	7	11	16	Losing	6	5	11	16
3rd Period	7	4	11	12	Tied	4	4	8	10
Overtime	0	0	0	0	Clutch	2	0	2	6
Last 5 Min	5	4	9	8	Blowouts	0	1	1	0

Miroslav Satan

Buffalo Sabres — Left Wing

1998-99 Season

	GP	G	A	Pts	+/–	PIM	PP	SH	S	SPct	P/G
Overall	81	40	26	66	24	44	13	3	208	19.2	.81
Home	41	22	17	39	24	28	6	2	130	16.9	.95
Away	40	18	9	27	0	16	7	1	78	23.1	.68
vs. Division	20	8	9	17	10	8	2	0	46	17.4	.85
vs. Conference	56	31	16	47	15	36	9	3	138	22.5	.84
vs. Playoff	47	26	18	44	19	22	8	1	125	20.8	.94
vs. Non-Playoff	34	14	8	22	5	22	5	2	83	16.9	.65
Pre All-Star	42	19	16	35	11	18	6	2	104	18.3	.83
Post All-Star	39	21	10	31	13	26	7	1	104	20.2	.79
Day	6	5	2	7	2	2	2	0	18	27.8	1.17
Night	75	35	24	59	22	42	11	3	190	18.4	.79

	GP	G	A	Pts	+/–	PIM	PP	SH	S	SPct	P/G
National TV	15	4	8	12	-4	4	2	0	35	11.4	.80
0 Days Rest	20	12	6	18	-3	4	7	1	56	21.4	.90
1 Days Rest	30	19	7	26	12	24	5	2	92	20.7	.87
2 Days Rest	19	6	9	15	14	12	0	0	38	15.8	.79
3+ Days Rest	12	3	4	7	1	4	1	0	22	13.6	.58

	G	A	Pts	PIM		G	A	Pts	PIM
1st Period	12	8	20	16	Winning	11	6	17	20
2nd Period	13	6	19	10	Losing	13	13	26	8
3rd Period	14	12	26	8	Tied	16	7	23	16
Overtime	1	0	1	10	Clutch	5	3	8	10
Last 5 Min	9	9	18	14	Blowouts	3	1	4	0

Brian Savage

Montreal Canadiens — Left Wing

1998-99 Season

	GP	G	A	Pts	+/–	PIM	PP	SH	S	SPct	P/G
Overall	54	16	10	26	-14	20	5	0	124	12.9	.48
Home	28	9	5	14	-5	10	3	0	70	12.9	.50
Away	26	7	5	12	-9	10	2	0	54	13.0	.46
vs. Division	14	5	2	7	-3	6	2	0	33	15.2	.50
vs. Conference	38	14	8	22	-7	12	5	0	92	15.2	.58
vs. Playoff	35	9	7	16	-6	12	2	0	77	11.7	.46
vs. Non-Playoff	19	7	3	10	-8	8	3	0	47	14.9	.53
Pre All-Star	29	10	7	17	-6	14	3	0	66	15.2	.59
Post All-Star	25	6	3	9	-8	6	2	0	58	10.3	.36
Day	1	0	1	1	-2	0	0	0	3	0.0	1.00
Night	53	16	9	25	-12	20	5	0	121	13.2	.47

	GP	G	A	Pts	+/–	PIM	PP	SH	S	SPct	P/G
National TV	16	3	1	4	-8	6	2	0	38	7.9	.25
0 Days Rest	10	5	1	6	-4	6	3	0	32	15.6	.60
1 Days Rest	23	3	2	5	-8	8	2	0	48	6.3	.22
2 Days Rest	10	4	2	6	-1	2	0	0	25	16.0	.60
3+ Days Rest	11	4	5	9	-1	4	0	0	19	21.1	.82

	G	A	Pts	PIM		G	A	Pts	PIM
1st Period	5	5	10	2	Winning	7	1	8	6
2nd Period	5	3	8	12	Losing	3	1	4	8
3rd Period	6	2	8	6	Tied	6	8	14	6
Overtime	0	0	0	0	Clutch	1	1	2	0
Last 5 Min	4	4	8	4	Blowouts	0	0	0	2

Marc Savard

New York Rangers — Center

1998-99 Season

	GP	G	A	Pts	+/–	PIM	PP	SH	S	SPct	P/G
Overall	70	9	36	45	-7	38	4	0	116	7.8	.64
Home	33	4	17	21	-5	16	2	0	54	7.4	.64
Away	37	5	19	24	-2	22	2	0	62	8.1	.65
vs. Division	14	0	10	10	-5	14	0	0	17	0.0	.71
vs. Conference	48	3	26	29	-6	34	2	0	82	3.7	.60
vs. Playoff	43	5	23	28	-4	30	1	0	68	7.4	.65
vs. Non-Playoff	27	4	13	17	-3	8	3	0	48	8.3	.63
Pre All-Star	33	6	15	21	2	14	4	0	53	11.3	.64
Post All-Star	37	3	21	24	-9	24	0	0	63	4.8	.65
Day	11	2	7	9	-1	12	1	0	16	12.5	.82
Night	59	7	29	36	-6	26	3	0	100	7.0	.61

	GP	G	A	Pts	+/–	PIM	PP	SH	S	SPct	P/G
National TV	20	1	18	19	-3	20	0	0	31	3.2	.95
0 Days Rest	13	1	7	8	-1	12	0	0	24	4.2	.62
1 Days Rest	31	5	16	21	-1	10	1	0	46	10.9	.68
2 Days Rest	16	3	8	11	-2	10	3	0	27	11.1	.69
3+ Days Rest	10	0	5	5	-3	6	0	0	19	0.0	.50

	G	A	Pts	PIM		G	A	Pts	PIM
1st Period	1	14	15	12	Winning	4	13	17	20
2nd Period	6	11	17	6	Losing	4	10	14	18
3rd Period	2	9	11	20	Tied	1	13	14	0
Overtime	0	2	2	0	Clutch	1	5	6	2
Last 5 Min	1	9	10	12	Blowouts	1	2	3	2

Dave Scatchard

Vancouver Canucks — Center

1998-99 Season

	GP	G	A	Pts	+/–	PIM	PP	SH	S	SPct	P/G
Overall	82	13	13	26	-12	140	0	2	130	10.0	.32
Home	41	6	5	11	-5	61	0	0	72	8.3	.27
Away	41	7	8	15	-7	79	0	2	58	12.1	.37
vs. Division	18	3	8	11	5	40	0	0	29	10.3	.61
vs. Conference	55	9	10	19	-4	111	0	1	92	9.8	.35
vs. Playoff	53	8	10	18	-1	84	0	1	92	8.7	.34
vs. Non-Playoff	29	5	3	8	-11	56	0	1	38	13.2	.28
Pre All-Star	45	8	6	14	-1	82	0	1	86	9.3	.31
Post All-Star	37	5	7	12	-11	58	0	1	44	11.4	.32
Day	3	1	0	1	-3	7	0	0	3	33.3	.33
Night	79	12	13	25	-9	133	0	2	127	9.4	.32

	GP	G	A	Pts	+/–	PIM	PP	SH	S	SPct	P/G
National TV	20	1	2	3	-9	48	0	0	33	3.0	.15
0 Days Rest	13	3	2	5	2	26	0	0	14	21.4	.38
1 Days Rest	46	7	7	14	-16	81	0	2	81	8.6	.30
2 Days Rest	16	2	4	6	3	20	0	0	25	8.0	.38
3+ Days Rest	7	1	0	1	-1	13	0	0	10	10.0	.14

	G	A	Pts	PIM		G	A	Pts	PIM
1st Period	5	5	10	43	Winning	4	5	9	40
2nd Period	3	4	7	52	Losing	4	5	9	84
3rd Period	5	4	9	45	Tied	5	3	8	16
Overtime	0	0	0	0	Clutch	1	1	2	6
Last 5 Min	2	1	3	17	Blowouts	0	1	1	31

Mathieu Schneider

New York Rangers — Defense

1998-99 Season

	GP	G	A	Pts	+/–	PIM	PP	SH	S	SPct	P/G
Overall	75	10	24	34	-19	71	5	0	159	6.3	.45
Home	36	5	11	16	-13	24	2	0	92	5.4	.44
Away	39	5	13	18	-6	47	3	0	67	7.5	.46
vs. Division	18	1	5	6	-3	16	0	0	44	2.3	.33
vs. Conference	52	5	16	21	-12	61	2	0	108	4.6	.40
vs. Playoff	50	6	13	19	-13	63	4	0	107	5.6	.38
vs. Non-Playoff	25	4	11	15	-6	8	1	0	52	7.7	.60
Pre All-Star	38	4	13	17	-9	20	2	0	82	4.9	.45
Post All-Star	37	6	11	17	-10	51	3	0	77	7.8	.46
Day	11	0	6	6	-1	12	0	0	17	0.0	.55
Night	64	10	18	28	-18	59	5	0	142	7.0	.44

	GP	G	A	Pts	+/–	PIM	PP	SH	S	SPct	P/G
National TV	21	1	7	8	-1	18	0	0	41	2.4	.38
0 Days Rest	14	3	5	8	-10	14	2	0	31	9.7	.57
1 Days Rest	31	2	9	11	-6	24	1	0	74	2.7	.35
2 Days Rest	17	3	9	12	3	27	1	0	25	12.0	.71
3+ Days Rest	13	2	1	3	-6	6	1	0	29	6.9	.23

	G	A	Pts	PIM		G	A	Pts	PIM
1st Period	2	11	13	12	Winning	3	7	10	26
2nd Period	3	6	9	28	Losing	3	9	12	20
3rd Period	5	7	12	31	Tied	4	8	12	25
Overtime	0	0	0	0	Clutch	1	4	5	23
Last 5 Min	2	6	8	39	Blowouts	0	2	2	2

Teemu Selanne

Anaheim Mighty Ducks — Right Wing

1998-99 Season

	GP	G	A	Pts	+/–	PIM	PP	SH	S	SPct	P/G
Overall	75	47	60	107	18	30	25	0	281	16.7	1.43
Home	37	26	30	56	5	14	17	0	151	17.2	1.51
Away	38	21	30	51	13	16	8	0	130	16.2	1.34
vs. Division	22	15	20	35	14	6	6	0	98	15.3	1.59
vs. Conference	51	33	39	72	8	18	17	0	208	15.9	1.41
vs. Playoff	48	25	44	69	14	22	13	0	175	14.3	1.44
vs. Non-Playoff	27	22	16	38	4	8	12	0	106	20.8	1.41
Pre All-Star	38	21	29	50	7	16	9	0	132	15.9	1.32
Post All-Star	37	26	31	57	11	14	16	0	149	17.4	1.54
Day	1	3	2	5	4	0	2	0	5	60.0	5.00
Night	74	44	58	102	14	30	23	0	276	15.9	1.38

	GP	G	A	Pts	+/–	PIM	PP	SH	S	SPct	P/G
National TV	12	6	12	18	9	6	2	0	42	14.3	1.50
0 Days Rest	14	8	11	19	9	6	4	0	51	15.7	1.36
1 Days Rest	37	24	33	57	3	16	12	0	142	16.9	1.54
2 Days Rest	10	7	6	13	0	6	4	0	41	17.1	1.30
3+ Days Rest	14	8	10	18	6	2	5	0	47	17.0	1.29

	G	A	Pts	PIM		G	A	Pts	PIM
1st Period	15	24	39	14	Winning	23	20	43	14
2nd Period	19	14	33	10	Losing	14	21	35	10
3rd Period	13	22	35	4	Tied	10	19	29	6
Overtime	0	0	0	2	Clutch	5	6	11	2
Last 5 Min	16	13	29	6	Blowouts	3	1	4	4

Alexander Selivanov

Edmonton Oilers — Right Wing

1998-99 Season

	GP	G	A	Pts	+/–	PIM	PP	SH	S	SPct	P/G
Overall	72	14	19	33	-8	42	2	0	177	7.9	.46
Home	34	5	7	12	-3	18	1	0	87	5.7	.35
Away	38	9	12	21	-5	24	1	0	90	10.0	.55
vs. Division	12	2	4	6	-2	14	0	0	26	7.7	.50
vs. Conference	49	12	15	27	2	36	2	0	110	10.9	.55
vs. Playoff	44	8	13	21	-9	26	1	0	101	7.9	.48
vs. Non-Playoff	28	6	6	12	1	16	1	0	76	7.9	.43
Pre All-Star	42	6	13	19	-8	18	1	0	116	5.2	.45
Post All-Star	30	8	6	14	0	24	1	0	61	13.1	.47
Day	4	0	0	0	-2	6	0	0	6	0.0	.00
Night	68	14	19	33	-6	36	2	0	171	8.2	.49

	GP	G	A	Pts	+/–	PIM	PP	SH	S	SPct	P/G
National TV	4	1	1	2	-1	4	0	0	11	9.1	.50
0 Days Rest	15	3	4	7	-4	10	0	0	39	7.7	.47
1 Days Rest	29	5	10	15	-6	14	1	0	61	8.2	.52
2 Days Rest	17	4	4	8	0	10	1	0	55	7.3	.47
3+ Days Rest	11	2	1	3	2	8	0	0	22	9.1	.27

	G	A	Pts	PIM		G	A	Pts	PIM
1st Period	3	6	9	16	Winning	7	4	11	18
2nd Period	5	6	11	12	Losing	7	9	16	22
3rd Period	6	7	13	14	Tied	0	6	6	2
Overtime	0	0	0	0	Clutch	0	2	2	2
Last 5 Min	3	7	10	10	Blowouts	1	2	3	6

Brendan Shanahan

Detroit Red Wings — Left Wing

1998-99 Season

	GP	G	A	Pts	+/–	PIM	PP	SH	S	SPct	P/G
Overall	81	31	27	58	2	123	5	0	288	10.8	.72
Home	41	18	10	28	10	27	2	0	141	12.8	.68
Away	40	13	17	30	-8	96	3	0	147	8.8	.75
vs. Division	18	8	5	13	4	28	1	0	63	12.7	.72
vs. Conference	53	23	14	37	4	85	3	0	193	11.9	.70
vs. Playoff	46	16	10	26	-17	70	3	0	155	10.3	.57
vs. Non-Playoff	35	15	17	32	19	53	2	0	133	11.3	.91
Pre All-Star	46	17	17	34	3	75	2	0	177	9.6	.74
Post All-Star	35	14	10	24	-1	48	3	0	111	12.6	.69
Day	12	3	4	7	-3	19	2	0	32	9.4	.58
Night	69	28	23	51	5	104	3	0	256	10.9	.74

	GP	G	A	Pts	+/–	PIM	PP	SH	S	SPct	P/G
National TV	29	9	7	16	-11	36	2	0	98	9.2	.55
0 Days Rest	11	3	3	6	-4	28	0	0	36	8.3	.55
1 Days Rest	38	12	15	27	2	64	3	0	136	8.8	.71
2 Days Rest	25	11	3	14	-1	22	1	0	89	12.4	.56
3+ Days Rest	7	5	6	11	5	9	1	0	27	18.5	1.57

	G	A	Pts	PIM		G	A	Pts	PIM
1st Period	6	11	17	31	Winning	19	12	31	61
2nd Period	17	7	24	43	Losing	3	5	8	50
3rd Period	8	9	17	47	Tied	9	10	19	12
Overtime	0	0	0	2	Clutch	2	2	4	30
Last 5 Min	8	5	13	47	Blowouts	2	0	2	0

Darryl Shannon

Buffalo Sabres — Defense

1998-99 Season

	GP	G	A	Pts	+/–	PIM	PP	SH	S	SPct	P/G
Overall	71	3	12	15	28	52	1	0	80	3.8	.21
Home	35	3	9	12	16	28	1	0	40	7.5	.34
Away	36	0	3	3	12	24	0	0	40	0.0	.08
vs. Division	19	0	3	3	14	12	0	0	16	0.0	.16
vs. Conference	51	3	7	10	21	38	1	0	55	5.5	.20
vs. Playoff	41	2	5	7	12	26	0	0	40	5.0	.17
vs. Non-Playoff	30	1	7	8	16	26	1	0	40	2.5	.27
Pre All-Star	42	2	11	13	24	38	1	0	50	4.0	.31
Post All-Star	29	1	1	2	4	14	0	0	30	3.3	.07
Day	4	0	0	0	1	0	0	0	4	0.0	.00
Night	67	3	12	15	27	52	1	0	76	3.9	.22

	GP	G	A	Pts	+/–	PIM	PP	SH	S	SPct	P/G
National TV	13	0	1	1	6	4	0	0	16	0.0	.08
0 Days Rest	17	0	5	5	10	8	0	0	19	0.0	.29
1 Days Rest	24	2	4	6	8	20	0	0	24	8.3	.25
2 Days Rest	15	0	1	1	4	12	0	0	19	0.0	.07
3+ Days Rest	15	1	2	3	6	12	1	0	18	5.6	.20

	G	A	Pts	PIM		G	A	Pts	PIM
1st Period	1	1	2	18	Winning	2	6	8	22
2nd Period	0	7	7	18	Losing	1	2	3	18
3rd Period	2	4	6	16	Tied	0	4	4	12
Overtime	0	0	0	0	Clutch	1	1	2	2
Last 5 Min	0	2	2	12	Blowouts	0	1	1	2

Jeff Shantz

Calgary Flames — Center

1998-99 Season

	GP	G	A	Pts	+/–	PIM	PP	SH	S	SPct	P/G
Overall	76	13	17	30	14	44	1	1	82	15.9	.39
Home	42	9	7	16	5	30	1	1	45	20.0	.38
Away	34	4	10	14	9	14	0	0	37	10.8	.41
vs. Division	18	4	4	8	3	14	1	0	19	21.1	.44
vs. Conference	49	9	12	21	17	30	1	0	58	15.5	.43
vs. Playoff	45	6	7	13	10	22	0	0	47	12.8	.29
vs. Non-Playoff	31	7	10	17	4	22	1	1	35	20.0	.55
Pre All-Star	44	9	8	17	3	26	1	1	43	20.9	.39
Post All-Star	32	4	9	13	11	18	0	0	39	10.3	.41
Day	3	2	0	2	3	8	0	1	4	50.0	.67
Night	73	11	17	28	11	36	1	0	78	14.1	.38

	GP	G	A	Pts	+/–	PIM	PP	SH	S	SPct	P/G
National TV	12	1	2	3	0	2	0	0	9	11.1	.25
0 Days Rest	14	2	6	8	0	4	0	0	19	10.5	.57
1 Days Rest	35	8	7	15	6	30	1	1	36	22.2	.43
2 Days Rest	14	2	1	3	4	8	0	0	15	13.3	.21
3+ Days Rest	13	1	3	4	4	2	0	0	12	8.3	.31

	G	A	Pts	PIM		G	A	Pts	PIM
1st Period	5	7	12	14	Winning	3	3	6	18
2nd Period	4	4	8	18	Losing	4	6	10	16
3rd Period	3	6	9	10	Tied	6	8	14	10
Overtime	1	0	1	2	Clutch	2	2	4	6
Last 5 Min	3	4	7	14	Blowouts	0	1	1	2

Vadim Sharifijanov

New Jersey Devils — Right Wing

1998-99 Season

	GP	G	A	Pts	+/–	PIM	PP	SH	S	SPct	P/G
Overall	53	11	16	27	11	28	1	0	71	15.5	.51
Home	29	6	8	14	3	16	1	0	43	14.0	.48
Away	24	5	8	13	8	12	0	0	28	17.9	.54
vs. Division	12	2	5	7	5	6	1	0	19	10.5	.58
vs. Conference	38	8	10	18	10	22	1	0	53	15.1	.47
vs. Playoff	30	7	8	15	4	14	0	0	44	15.9	.50
vs. Non-Playoff	23	4	8	12	7	14	1	0	27	14.8	.52
Pre All-Star	27	7	11	18	8	10	0	0	41	17.1	.67
Post All-Star	26	4	5	9	3	18	1	0	30	13.3	.35
Day	8	1	2	3	-1	6	1	0	10	10.0	.38
Night	45	10	14	24	12	22	0	0	61	16.4	.53

	GP	G	A	Pts	+/–	PIM	PP	SH	S	SPct	P/G
National TV	5	2	1	3	1	4	1	0	5	40.0	.60
0 Days Rest	8	2	2	4	4	10	1	0	9	22.2	.50
1 Days Rest	14	3	5	8	0	4	0	0	13	23.1	.57
2 Days Rest	14	4	3	7	3	12	0	0	27	14.8	.50
3+ Days Rest	17	2	6	8	4	2	0	0	22	9.1	.47

	G	A	Pts	PIM		G	A	Pts	PIM
1st Period	3	2	5	6	Winning	4	6	10	20
2nd Period	5	10	15	12	Losing	3	5	8	4
3rd Period	3	4	7	10	Tied	4	5	9	4
Overtime	0	0	0	0	Clutch	0	4	4	0
Last 5 Min	3	5	8	8	Blowouts	0	0	0	2

Ray Sheppard

Carolina Hurricanes — Right Wing

1998-99 Season

	GP	G	A	Pts	+/–	PIM	PP	SH	S	SPct	P/G
Overall	74	25	33	58	4	16	5	0	188	13.3	.78
Home	38	14	16	30	3	6	3	0	99	14.1	.79
Away	36	11	17	28	1	10	2	0	89	12.4	.78
vs. Division	13	3	8	11	4	0	0	0	32	9.4	.85
vs. Conference	52	19	21	40	3	8	4	0	140	13.6	.77
vs. Playoff	38	13	18	31	-8	8	2	0	103	12.6	.82
vs. Non-Playoff	36	12	15	27	12	8	3	0	85	14.1	.75
Pre All-Star	42	15	23	38	3	4	4	0	104	14.4	.90
Post All-Star	32	10	10	20	1	12	1	0	84	11.9	.63
Day	7	3	4	7	2	2	1	0	12	25.0	1.00
Night	67	22	29	51	2	14	4	0	176	12.5	.76

	GP	G	A	Pts	+/–	PIM	PP	SH	S	SPct	P/G
National TV	1	1	0	1	1	0	0	0	2	50.0	1.00
0 Days Rest	15	7	3	10	2	4	1	0	45	15.6	.67
1 Days Rest	27	6	12	18	-5	4	1	0	60	10.0	.67
2 Days Rest	21	7	15	22	4	4	2	0	55	12.7	1.05
3+ Days Rest	11	5	3	8	3	4	1	0	28	17.9	.73

	G	A	Pts	PIM		G	A	Pts	PIM
1st Period	5	14	19	6	Winning	11	8	19	8
2nd Period	12	9	21	4	Losing	5	10	15	8
3rd Period	8	10	18	6	Tied	9	15	24	0
Overtime	0	0	0	0	Clutch	2	2	4	0
Last 5 Min	7	8	15	6	Blowouts	0	0	0	0

Mike Sillinger

Tampa Bay Lightning — Center

1998-99 Season

	GP	G	A	Pts	+/–	PIM	PP	SH	S	SPct	P/G
Overall	79	8	5	13	-29	36	0	2	92	8.7	.16
Home	38	1	3	4	-11	18	0	0	42	2.4	.11
Away	41	7	2	9	-18	18	0	2	50	14.0	.22
vs. Division	19	1	2	3	-8	8	0	0	20	5.0	.16
vs. Conference	62	7	4	11	-22	26	0	1	70	10.0	.18
vs. Playoff	53	4	2	6	-23	24	0	0	63	6.3	.11
vs. Non-Playoff	26	4	3	7	-6	12	0	2	29	13.8	.27
Pre All-Star	42	2	3	5	-14	12	0	1	42	4.8	.12
Post All-Star	37	6	2	8	-15	24	0	1	50	12.0	.22
Day	6	0	0	0	-4	2	0	0	8	0.0	.00
Night	73	8	5	13	-25	34	0	2	84	9.5	.18

	GP	G	A	Pts	+/–	PIM	PP	SH	S	SPct	P/G
National TV	2	0	0	0	-1	2	0	0	2	0.0	.00
0 Days Rest	14	3	1	4	-3	2	0	0	18	16.7	.29
1 Days Rest	34	4	2	6	-15	20	0	2	36	11.1	.18
2 Days Rest	19	1	2	3	-4	10	0	0	24	4.2	.16
3+ Days Rest	12	0	0	0	-7	4	0	0	14	0.0	.00

	G	A	Pts	PIM		G	A	Pts	PIM
1st Period	4	0	4	10	Winning	2	1	3	10
2nd Period	3	2	5	14	Losing	3	2	5	20
3rd Period	1	3	4	12	Tied	3	2	5	6
Overtime	0	0	0	0	Clutch	0	1	1	4
Last 5 Min	1	0	1	14	Blowouts	1	0	1	8

Chris Simon

Washington Capitals — Left Wing

1998-99 Season

	GP	G	A	Pts	+/–	PIM	PP	SH	S	SPct	P/G
Overall	23	3	7	10	-4	48	0	0	29	10.3	.43
Home	12	2	3	5	1	34	0	0	20	10.0	.42
Away	11	1	4	5	-5	14	0	0	9	11.1	.45
vs. Division	4	1	0	1	-1	2	0	0	5	20.0	.25
vs. Conference	15	3	6	9	2	36	0	0	22	13.6	.60
vs. Playoff	15	3	6	9	-1	38	0	0	21	14.3	.60
vs. Non-Playoff	8	0	1	1	-3	10	0	0	8	0.0	.13
Pre All-Star	23	3	7	10	-4	48	0	0	29	10.3	.43
Post All-Star	0	0	0	0	0	0	0	0	0	–	–
Day	0	0	0	0	0	0	0	0	0	–	–
Night	23	3	7	10	-4	48	0	0	29	10.3	.43

	GP	G	A	Pts	+/–	PIM	PP	SH	S	SPct	P/G
National TV	3	0	2	2	0	4	0	0	3	0.0	.67
0 Days Rest	5	1	3	4	0	4	0	0	2	50.0	.80
1 Days Rest	7	1	2	3	0	28	0	0	14	7.1	.43
2 Days Rest	5	0	0	0	-3	8	0	0	8	0.0	.00
3+ Days Rest	6	1	2	3	-1	8	0	0	5	20.0	.50

	G	A	Pts	PIM		G	A	Pts	PIM
1st Period	1	0	1	10	Winning	0	2	2	10
2nd Period	2	3	5	16	Losing	1	2	3	34
3rd Period	0	4	4	22	Tied	2	3	5	4
Overtime	0	0	0	0	Clutch	0	2	2	4
Last 5 Min	0	3	3	22	Blowouts	0	0	0	10

Todd Simpson

Calgary Flames — Defense

1998-99 Season

	GP	G	A	Pts	+/–	PIM	PP	SH	S	SPct	P/G
Overall	73	2	8	10	18	151	0	0	52	3.8	.14
Home	37	0	4	4	6	45	0	0	26	0.0	.11
Away	36	2	4	6	12	106	0	0	26	7.7	.17
vs. Division	15	1	1	2	2	27	0	0	11	9.1	.13
vs. Conference	49	2	6	8	18	100	0	0	33	6.1	.16
vs. Playoff	44	0	4	4	7	90	0	0	27	0.0	.09
vs. Non-Playoff	29	2	4	6	11	61	0	0	25	8.0	.21
Pre All-Star	46	1	4	5	4	106	0	0	28	3.6	.11
Post All-Star	27	1	4	5	14	45	0	0	24	4.2	.19
Day	3	0	0	0	1	2	0	0	0	–	.00
Night	70	2	8	10	17	149	0	0	52	3.8	.14

	GP	G	A	Pts	+/–	PIM	PP	SH	S	SPct	P/G
National TV	10	0	1	1	1	4	0	0	8	0.0	.10
0 Days Rest	15	0	3	3	7	42	0	0	15	0.0	.20
1 Days Rest	34	1	2	3	3	56	0	0	17	5.9	.09
2 Days Rest	13	0	1	1	7	25	0	0	13	0.0	.08
3+ Days Rest	11	1	2	3	1	28	0	0	7	14.3	.27

	G	A	Pts	PIM		G	A	Pts	PIM
1st Period	2	1	3	86	Winning	1	6	7	55
2nd Period	0	2	2	30	Losing	0	1	1	77
3rd Period	0	5	5	35	Tied	1	1	2	19
Overtime	0	0	0	0	Clutch	0	0	0	4
Last 5 Min	1	2	3	35	Blowouts	0	0	0	27

John Slaney

Nashville Predators — Defense

1998-99 Season

	GP	G	A	Pts	+/-	PIM	PP	SH	S	SPct	P/G
Overall	46	2	12	14	-12	14	0	0	84	2.4	.30
Home	21	0	6	6	-10	8	0	0	44	0.0	.29
Away	25	2	6	8	-2	6	0	0	40	5.0	.32
vs. Division	11	1	4	5	-5	6	0	0	15	6.7	.45
vs. Conference	34	2	10	12	-9	10	0	0	57	3.5	.35
vs. Playoff	28	1	5	6	-11	4	0	0	44	2.3	.21
vs. Non-Playoff	18	1	7	8	-1	10	0	0	40	2.5	.44
Pre All-Star	23	0	4	4	-7	6	0	0	40	0.0	.17
Post All-Star	23	2	8	10	-5	8	0	0	44	4.5	.43
Day	4	0	1	1	-1	0	0	0	5	0.0	.25
Night	42	2	11	13	-11	14	0	0	79	2.5	.31

	GP	G	A	Pts	+/-	PIM	PP	SH	S	SPct	P/G
National TV	1	0	0	0	0	0	0	0	1	0.0	.00
0 Days Rest	7	1	2	3	-2	2	0	0	14	7.1	.43
1 Days Rest	19	1	6	7	-3	2	0	0	37	2.7	.37
2 Days Rest	5	0	1	1	0	0	0	0	5	0.0	.20
3+ Days Rest	15	0	3	3	-7	10	0	0	28	0.0	.20

	G	A	Pts	PIM
1st Period	1	4	5	2
2nd Period	0	4	4	6
3rd Period	1	4	5	6
Overtime	0	0	0	0
Last 5 Min	0	2	2	4

	G	A	Pts	PIM
Winning	1	3	4	10
Losing	0	6	6	2
Tied	1	3	4	2
Clutch	0	0	0	2
Blowouts	0	1	1	0

Jiri Slegr

Pittsburgh Penguins — Defense

1998-99 Season

	GP	G	A	Pts	+/-	PIM	PP	SH	S	SPct	P/G
Overall	63	3	20	23	13	86	1	0	91	3.3	.37
Home	32	3	14	17	22	50	1	0	53	5.7	.53
Away	31	0	6	6	-9	36	0	0	38	0.0	.19
vs. Division	14	1	2	3	-4	18	0	0	19	5.3	.21
vs. Conference	42	2	17	19	8	61	0	0	59	3.4	.45
vs. Playoff	36	1	10	11	2	32	1	0	49	2.0	.31
vs. Non-Playoff	27	2	10	12	11	54	0	0	42	4.8	.44
Pre All-Star	23	1	6	7	-2	52	0	0	33	3.0	.30
Post All-Star	40	2	14	16	15	34	1	0	58	3.4	.40
Day	13	0	5	5	7	2	0	0	18	0.0	.38
Night	50	3	15	18	6	84	1	0	73	4.1	.36

	GP	G	A	Pts	+/-	PIM	PP	SH	S	SPct	P/G
National TV	15	0	3	3	2	14	0	0	24	0.0	.20
0 Days Rest	11	0	5	5	6	12	0	0	13	0.0	.45
1 Days Rest	26	2	6	8	3	17	1	0	35	5.7	.31
2 Days Rest	14	1	5	6	9	24	0	0	26	3.8	.43
3+ Days Rest	12	0	4	4	-5	33	0	0	17	0.0	.33

	G	A	Pts	PIM
1st Period	3	7	10	22
2nd Period	0	5	5	21
3rd Period	0	5	5	43
Overtime	0	3	3	0
Last 5 Min	0	5	5	41

	G	A	Pts	PIM
Winning	0	7	7	56
Losing	1	4	5	16
Tied	2	9	11	14
Clutch	0	4	4	2
Blowouts	0	1	1	16

Richard Smehlik

Buffalo Sabres — Defense

1998-99 Season

	GP	G	A	Pts	+/-	PIM	PP	SH	S	SPct	P/G
Overall	72	3	11	14	-9	44	0	0	61	4.9	.19
Home	35	2	6	8	1	24	0	0	37	5.4	.23
Away	37	1	5	6	-10	20	0	0	24	4.2	.16
vs. Division	20	0	5	5	-1	18	0	0	13	0.0	.25
vs. Conference	50	2	9	11	-7	36	0	0	38	5.3	.22
vs. Playoff	44	2	9	11	-4	26	0	0	34	5.9	.25
vs. Non-Playoff	28	1	2	3	-5	18	0	0	27	3.7	.11
Pre All-Star	34	0	9	9	-6	30	0	0	29	0.0	.26
Post All-Star	38	3	2	5	-3	14	0	0	32	9.4	.13
Day	5	0	0	0	-2	2	0	0	5	0.0	.00
Night	67	3	11	14	-7	42	0	0	56	5.4	.21

	GP	G	A	Pts	+/-	PIM	PP	SH	S	SPct	P/G
National TV	14	1	3	4	-1	4	0	0	11	9.1	.29
0 Days Rest	17	0	4	4	-11	4	0	0	15	0.0	.24
1 Days Rest	26	2	4	6	2	16	0	0	22	9.1	.23
2 Days Rest	17	1	3	4	-1	2	0	0	15	6.7	.24
3+ Days Rest	12	0	0	0	1	22	0	0	9	0.0	.00

	G	A	Pts	PIM
1st Period	0	3	3	12
2nd Period	2	3	5	22
3rd Period	1	5	6	8
Overtime	0	0	0	2
Last 5 Min	1	7	8	18

	G	A	Pts	PIM
Winning	1	6	7	26
Losing	1	4	5	6
Tied	1	1	2	12
Clutch	1	0	1	4
Blowouts	0	0	0	0

Jason Smith

Edmonton Oilers — Defense

1998-99 Season

	GP	G	A	Pts	+/-	PIM	PP	SH	S	SPct	P/G
Overall	72	3	12	15	-9	51	0	0	68	4.4	.21
Home	39	3	3	6	-1	38	0	0	39	7.7	.15
Away	33	0	9	9	-8	13	0	0	29	0.0	.27
vs. Division	18	0	0	0	-7	11	0	0	17	0.0	.00
vs. Conference	50	1	7	8	-15	25	0	0	50	2.0	.16
vs. Playoff	41	3	5	8	-6	37	0	0	40	7.5	.20
vs. Non-Playoff	31	0	7	7	-3	14	0	0	28	0.0	.23
Pre All-Star	45	2	8	10	-8	35	0	0	45	4.4	.22
Post All-Star	27	1	4	5	-1	16	0	0	23	4.3	.19
Day	2	0	0	0	-1	2	0	0	1	0.0	.00
Night	70	3	12	15	-8	49	0	0	67	4.5	.21

	GP	G	A	Pts	+/-	PIM	PP	SH	S	SPct	P/G
National TV	23	0	3	3	1	14	0	0	19	0.0	.13
0 Days Rest	13	0	3	3	4	7	0	0	18	0.0	.23
1 Days Rest	30	2	1	3	-17	18	0	0	28	7.1	.10
2 Days Rest	12	0	6	6	4	2	0	0	9	0.0	.50
3+ Days Rest	17	1	2	3	0	24	0	0	13	7.7	.18

	G	A	Pts	PIM
1st Period	0	2	2	7
2nd Period	1	5	6	27
3rd Period	2	5	7	17
Overtime	0	0	0	0
Last 5 Min	0	3	3	9

	G	A	Pts	PIM
Winning	2	5	7	33
Losing	1	6	7	18
Tied	0	1	1	0
Clutch	0	1	1	0
Blowouts	1	2	3	4

Steve Smith

Calgary Flames — Defense

1998-99 Season

	GP	G	A	Pts	+/–	PIM	PP	SH	S	SPct	P/G
Overall	69	1	14	15	3	80	0	0	42	2.4	.22
Home	35	0	9	9	5	34	0	0	18	0.0	.26
Away	34	1	5	6	-2	46	0	0	24	4.2	.18
vs. Division	11	0	2	2	2	14	0	0	7	0.0	.18
vs. Conference	44	0	10	10	10	62	0	0	24	0.0	.23
vs. Playoff	42	0	5	5	0	46	0	0	26	0.0	.12
vs. Non-Playoff	27	1	9	10	3	34	0	0	16	6.3	.37
Pre All-Star	45	1	9	10	-1	50	0	0	25	4.0	.22
Post All-Star	24	0	5	5	4	30	0	0	17	0.0	.21
Day	3	0	0	0	0	4	0	0	0	–	.00
Night	66	1	14	15	3	76	0	0	42	2.4	.23

	GP	G	A	Pts	+/–	PIM	PP	SH	S	SPct	P/G
National TV	10	0	2	2	0	14	0	0	2	0.0	.20
0 Days Rest	13	0	2	2	1	14	0	0	11	0.0	.15
1 Days Rest	32	1	8	9	1	34	0	0	18	5.6	.28
2 Days Rest	12	0	2	2	-2	12	0	0	9	0.0	.17
3+ Days Rest	12	0	2	2	3	20	0	0	4	0.0	.17

	G	A	Pts	PIM		G	A	Pts	PIM
1st Period	0	8	8	34	Winning	0	5	5	28
2nd Period	1	3	4	22	Losing	1	3	4	36
3rd Period	0	3	3	22	Tied	0	6	6	16
Overtime	0	0	0	2	Clutch	0	1	1	4
Last 5 Min	0	5	5	18	Blowouts	0	1	1	6

Bryan Smolinski

New York Islanders — Center

1998-99 Season

	GP	G	A	Pts	+/–	PIM	PP	SH	S	SPct	P/G
Overall	82	16	24	40	-7	49	7	0	223	7.2	.49
Home	41	10	11	21	0	20	4	0	107	9.3	.51
Away	41	6	13	19	-7	29	3	0	116	5.2	.46
vs. Division	20	6	8	14	2	15	4	0	50	12.0	.70
vs. Conference	58	14	16	30	-3	35	7	0	151	9.3	.52
vs. Playoff	51	13	18	31	-3	30	5	0	123	10.6	.61
vs. Non-Playoff	31	3	6	9	-4	19	2	0	100	3.0	.29
Pre All-Star	46	8	14	22	-7	34	5	0	131	6.1	.48
Post All-Star	36	8	10	18	0	15	2	0	92	8.7	.50
Day	11	1	3	4	-1	4	0	0	34	2.9	.36
Night	71	15	21	36	-6	45	7	0	189	7.9	.51

	GP	G	A	Pts	+/–	PIM	PP	SH	S	SPct	P/G
National TV	6	0	3	3	0	9	0	0	21	0.0	.50
0 Days Rest	14	5	6	11	-5	8	4	0	51	9.8	.79
1 Days Rest	37	6	8	14	-2	25	2	0	92	6.5	.38
2 Days Rest	20	3	7	10	0	4	1	0	52	5.8	.50
3+ Days Rest	11	2	3	5	0	12	0	0	28	7.1	.45

	G	A	Pts	PIM		G	A	Pts	PIM
1st Period	6	6	12	14	Winning	6	3	9	14
2nd Period	5	11	16	19	Losing	6	15	21	35
3rd Period	5	7	12	16	Tied	4	6	10	0
Overtime	0	0	0	0	Clutch	2	1	3	4
Last 5 Min	2	8	10	9	Blowouts	0	1	1	4

Ryan Smyth

Edmonton Oilers — Left Wing

1998-99 Season

	GP	G	A	Pts	+/–	PIM	PP	SH	S	SPct	P/G
Overall	71	13	18	31	0	62	6	0	161	8.1	.44
Home	32	6	10	16	0	38	2	0	78	7.7	.50
Away	39	7	8	15	0	24	4	0	83	8.4	.38
vs. Division	16	3	5	8	0	6	3	0	35	8.6	.50
vs. Conference	49	11	14	25	0	42	6	0	112	9.8	.51
vs. Playoff	43	8	10	18	2	50	2	0	92	8.7	.42
vs. Non-Playoff	28	5	8	13	-2	12	4	0	69	7.2	.46
Pre All-Star	40	5	7	12	0	30	1	0	97	5.2	.30
Post All-Star	31	8	11	19	0	32	5	0	64	12.5	.61
Day	2	0	0	0	1	2	0	0	3	0.0	.00
Night	69	13	18	31	-1	60	6	0	158	8.2	.45

	GP	G	A	Pts	+/–	PIM	PP	SH	S	SPct	P/G
National TV	11	1	3	4	-4	16	1	0	23	4.3	.36
0 Days Rest	12	0	2	2	-2	8	0	0	25	0.0	.17
1 Days Rest	35	8	10	18	2	26	4	0	88	9.1	.51
2 Days Rest	11	3	2	5	4	14	0	0	19	15.8	.45
3+ Days Rest	13	2	4	6	-4	14	2	0	29	6.9	.46

	G	A	Pts	PIM		G	A	Pts	PIM
1st Period	2	3	5	30	Winning	3	6	9	34
2nd Period	6	8	14	18	Losing	5	8	13	14
3rd Period	5	7	12	14	Tied	5	4	9	14
Overtime	0	0	0	0	Clutch	4	2	6	2
Last 5 Min	3	4	7	8	Blowouts	1	2	3	6

Jaroslav Spacek

Florida Panthers — Defense

1998-99 Season

	GP	G	A	Pts	+/–	PIM	PP	SH	S	SPct	P/G
Overall	63	3	12	15	15	28	2	1	92	3.3	.24
Home	31	2	6	8	9	12	1	1	52	3.8	.26
Away	32	1	6	7	6	16	1	0	40	2.5	.22
vs. Division	10	1	2	3	1	0	1	0	21	4.8	.30
vs. Conference	44	1	9	10	8	18	1	0	65	1.5	.23
vs. Playoff	35	2	6	8	4	8	1	1	37	5.4	.23
vs. Non-Playoff	28	1	6	7	11	20	1	0	55	1.8	.25
Pre All-Star	28	2	3	5	0	18	2	0	37	5.4	.18
Post All-Star	35	1	9	10	15	10	0	1	55	1.8	.29
Day	2	0	0	0	0	0	0	0	1	0.0	.00
Night	61	3	12	15	15	28	2	1	91	3.3	.25

	GP	G	A	Pts	+/–	PIM	PP	SH	S	SPct	P/G
National TV	2	0	0	0	0	2	0	0	0	–	.00
0 Days Rest	15	1	1	2	-2	10	1	0	23	4.3	.13
1 Days Rest	24	1	5	6	9	12	0	1	31	3.2	.25
2 Days Rest	10	0	3	3	5	2	0	0	17	0.0	.30
3+ Days Rest	14	1	3	4	3	4	1	0	21	4.8	.29

	G	A	Pts	PIM		G	A	Pts	PIM
1st Period	1	3	4	8	Winning	1	2	3	14
2nd Period	0	3	3	8	Losing	1	7	8	10
3rd Period	2	6	8	12	Tied	1	3	4	4
Overtime	0	0	0	0	Clutch	0	1	1	0
Last 5 Min	0	5	5	4	Blowouts	2	1	3	6

Mike Stapleton

Phoenix Coyotes — Center

1998-99 Season

	GP	G	A	Pts	+/–	PIM	PP	SH	S	SPct	P/G
Overall	76	9	9	18	-6	34	0	2	106	8.5	.24
Home	39	6	3	9	-5	24	0	1	51	11.8	.23
Away	37	3	6	9	-1	10	0	1	55	5.5	.24
vs. Division	23	2	4	6	2	22	0	0	28	7.1	.26
vs. Conference	54	7	6	13	-5	32	0	1	80	8.8	.24
vs. Playoff	45	8	4	12	4	14	0	2	71	11.3	.27
vs. Non-Playoff	31	1	5	6	-10	20	0	0	35	2.9	.19
Pre All-Star	40	5	6	11	-5	24	0	2	49	10.2	.28
Post All-Star	36	4	3	7	-1	10	0	0	57	7.0	.19
Day	6	0	0	0	1	2	0	0	10	0.0	.00
Night	70	9	9	18	-7	32	0	2	96	9.4	.26

	GP	G	A	Pts	+/–	PIM	PP	SH	S	SPct	P/G
National TV	14	2	1	3	-1	2	0	0	16	12.5	.21
0 Days Rest	12	1	2	3	1	6	0	0	18	5.6	.25
1 Days Rest	37	5	5	10	-3	26	0	1	53	9.4	.27
2 Days Rest	15	0	0	0	-5	0	0	0	17	0.0	.00
3+ Days Rest	12	3	2	5	1	2	0	1	18	16.7	.42

	G	A	Pts	PIM		G	A	Pts	PIM
1st Period	3	1	4	12	Winning	2	5	7	14
2nd Period	2	4	6	2	Losing	4	3	7	16
3rd Period	4	4	8	20	Tied	3	1	4	4
Overtime	0	0	0	0	Clutch	1	2	3	2
Last 5 Min	1	3	4	12	Blowouts	1	0	1	2

Ronnie Stern

San Jose Sharks — Right Wing

1998-99 Season

	GP	G	A	Pts	+/–	PIM	PP	SH	S	SPct	P/G
Overall	78	7	9	16	-3	158	1	0	94	7.4	.21
Home	39	4	5	9	3	80	0	0	39	10.3	.23
Away	39	3	4	7	-6	78	1	0	55	5.5	.18
vs. Division	21	2	2	4	-2	46	1	0	29	6.9	.19
vs. Conference	53	4	5	9	-4	122	1	0	59	6.8	.17
vs. Playoff	45	4	4	8	-5	81	1	0	52	7.7	.18
vs. Non-Playoff	33	3	5	8	2	77	0	0	42	7.1	.24
Pre All-Star	43	5	5	10	2	90	1	0	55	9.1	.23
Post All-Star	35	2	4	6	-5	68	0	0	39	5.1	.17
Day	7	0	2	2	-1	15	0	0	10	0.0	.29
Night	71	7	7	14	-2	143	1	0	84	8.3	.20

	GP	G	A	Pts	+/–	PIM	PP	SH	S	SPct	P/G
National TV	11	0	1	1	0	19	0	0	6	0.0	.09
0 Days Rest	12	3	1	4	4	10	0	0	13	23.1	.33
1 Days Rest	39	4	4	8	-3	90	1	0	57	7.0	.21
2 Days Rest	15	0	1	1	-4	37	0	0	16	0.0	.07
3+ Days Rest	12	0	3	3	0	21	0	0	8	0.0	.25

	G	A	Pts	PIM		G	A	Pts	PIM
1st Period	3	3	6	69	Winning	2	5	7	79
2nd Period	2	3	5	38	Losing	3	3	6	55
3rd Period	2	3	5	49	Tied	2	1	3	24
Overtime	0	0	0	2	Clutch	0	1	1	6
Last 5 Min	1	4	5	54	Blowouts	0	0	0	43

Kevin Stevens

New York Rangers — Left Wing

1998-99 Season

	GP	G	A	Pts	+/–	PIM	PP	SH	S	SPct	P/G
Overall	81	23	20	43	-10	64	8	0	136	16.9	.53
Home	40	10	12	22	-1	32	2	0	65	15.4	.55
Away	41	13	8	21	-9	32	6	0	71	18.3	.51
vs. Division	20	9	8	17	6	16	3	0	39	23.1	.85
vs. Conference	58	17	14	31	-10	44	6	0	89	19.1	.53
vs. Playoff	51	12	13	25	-6	42	3	0	80	15.0	.49
vs. Non-Playoff	30	11	7	18	-4	22	5	0	56	19.6	.60
Pre All-Star	44	10	14	24	1	36	2	0	70	14.3	.55
Post All-Star	37	13	6	19	-11	28	6	0	66	19.7	.51
Day	12	5	5	10	0	18	1	0	23	21.7	.83
Night	69	18	15	33	-10	46	7	0	113	15.9	.48

	GP	G	A	Pts	+/–	PIM	PP	SH	S	SPct	P/G
National TV	23	9	6	15	-6	20	3	0	37	24.3	.65
0 Days Rest	16	5	3	8	-5	14	4	0	26	19.2	.50
1 Days Rest	33	9	14	23	2	26	3	0	60	15.0	.70
2 Days Rest	20	7	3	10	-3	18	1	0	34	20.6	.50
3+ Days Rest	12	2	0	2	-4	6	0	0	16	12.5	.17

	G	A	Pts	PIM		G	A	Pts	PIM
1st Period	8	7	15	26	Winning	9	7	16	32
2nd Period	8	10	18	18	Losing	7	5	12	32
3rd Period	7	3	10	20	Tied	7	8	15	0
Overtime	0	0	0	0	Clutch	2	0	2	2
Last 5 Min	0	2	2	22	Blowouts	3	1	4	12

Scott Stevens

New Jersey Devils — Defense

1998-99 Season

	GP	G	A	Pts	+/–	PIM	PP	SH	S	SPct	P/G
Overall	75	5	22	27	29	64	0	0	111	4.5	.36
Home	36	3	9	12	14	34	0	0	56	5.4	.33
Away	39	2	13	15	15	30	0	0	55	3.6	.38
vs. Division	18	1	9	10	11	20	0	0	29	3.4	.56
vs. Conference	54	2	19	21	25	52	0	0	86	2.3	.39
vs. Playoff	40	2	13	15	15	28	0	0	60	3.3	.38
vs. Non-Playoff	35	3	9	12	14	36	0	0	51	5.9	.34
Pre All-Star	42	4	13	17	15	38	0	0	67	6.0	.40
Post All-Star	33	1	9	10	14	26	0	0	44	2.3	.30
Day	11	1	4	5	7	14	0	0	20	5.0	.45
Night	64	4	18	22	22	50	0	0	91	4.4	.34

	GP	G	A	Pts	+/–	PIM	PP	SH	S	SPct	P/G
National TV	6	1	2	3	1	2	0	0	9	11.1	.50
0 Days Rest	16	1	3	4	1	16	0	0	25	4.0	.25
1 Days Rest	30	2	8	10	12	26	0	0	45	4.4	.33
2 Days Rest	17	2	6	8	11	12	0	0	22	9.1	.47
3+ Days Rest	12	0	5	5	5	10	0	0	19	0.0	.42

	G	A	Pts	PIM		G	A	Pts	PIM
1st Period	2	7	9	10	Winning	1	8	9	32
2nd Period	2	7	9	30	Losing	2	4	6	28
3rd Period	1	7	8	24	Tied	2	10	12	4
Overtime	0	1	1	0	Clutch	0	4	4	2
Last 5 Min	2	11	13	12	Blowouts	0	0	0	6

Turner Stevenson

Montreal Canadiens — Right Wing

1998-99 Season

	GP	G	A	Pts	+/–	PIM	PP	SH	S	SPct	P/G
Overall	69	10	17	27	6	88	0	0	102	9.8	.39
Home	34	7	10	17	9	38	0	0	52	13.5	.50
Away	35	3	7	10	-3	50	0	0	50	6.0	.29
vs. Division	19	1	4	5	-6	14	0	0	26	3.8	.26
vs. Conference	50	7	10	17	-4	68	0	0	72	9.7	.34
vs. Playoff	47	5	10	15	-4	39	0	0	61	8.2	.32
vs. Non-Playoff	22	5	7	12	10	49	0	0	41	12.2	.55
Pre All-Star	33	2	10	12	0	39	0	0	57	3.5	.36
Post All-Star	36	8	7	15	6	49	0	0	45	17.8	.42
Day	3	0	1	1	-1	2	0	0	4	0.0	.33
Night	66	10	16	26	7	86	0	0	98	10.2	.39

	GP	G	A	Pts	+/–	PIM	PP	SH	S	SPct	P/G
National TV	23	2	4	6	-3	19	0	0	31	6.5	.26
0 Days Rest	15	3	1	4	-2	8	0	0	21	14.3	.27
1 Days Rest	28	3	10	13	4	48	0	0	32	9.4	.46
2 Days Rest	14	3	3	6	1	8	0	0	29	10.3	.43
3+ Days Rest	12	1	3	4	3	24	0	0	20	5.0	.33

	G	A	Pts	PIM		G	A	Pts	PIM
1st Period	1	8	9	18	Winning	3	4	7	48
2nd Period	5	3	8	49	Losing	4	6	10	34
3rd Period	4	6	10	21	Tied	3	7	10	6
Overtime	0	0	0	0	Clutch	3	1	4	2
Last 5 Min	3	6	9	24	Blowouts	1	1	2	16

Cory Stillman

Calgary Flames — Center

1998-99 Season

	GP	G	A	Pts	+/–	PIM	PP	SH	S	SPct	P/G
Overall	76	27	30	57	7	38	9	3	175	15.4	.75
Home	38	9	19	28	6	10	2	1	88	10.2	.74
Away	38	18	11	29	1	28	7	2	87	20.7	.76
vs. Division	18	7	7	14	0	6	2	0	40	17.5	.78
vs. Conference	55	18	22	40	4	28	5	1	121	14.9	.73
vs. Playoff	46	13	19	32	-3	26	6	1	110	11.8	.70
vs. Non-Playoff	30	14	11	25	10	12	3	2	65	21.5	.83
Pre All-Star	40	13	13	26	0	22	5	0	88	14.8	.65
Post All-Star	36	14	17	31	7	16	4	3	87	16.1	.86
Day	4	0	1	1	0	4	0	0	9	0.0	.25
Night	72	27	29	56	7	34	9	3	166	16.3	.78

	GP	G	A	Pts	+/–	PIM	PP	SH	S	SPct	P/G
National TV	11	5	3	8	1	4	2	0	28	17.9	.73
0 Days Rest	16	4	8	12	0	10	2	0	27	14.8	.75
1 Days Rest	34	14	6	20	-1	20	3	1	87	16.1	.59
2 Days Rest	13	5	8	13	6	4	2	2	39	12.8	1.00
3+ Days Rest	13	4	8	12	2	4	2	0	22	18.2	.92

	G	A	Pts	PIM		G	A	Pts	PIM
1st Period	7	7	14	16	Winning	12	8	20	10
2nd Period	11	12	23	14	Losing	11	9	20	22
3rd Period	9	9	18	8	Tied	4	13	17	6
Overtime	0	2	2	0	Clutch	2	4	6	2
Last 5 Min	10	5	15	6	Blowouts	1	1	2	0

Martin Straka

Pittsburgh Penguins — Center

1998-99 Season

	GP	G	A	Pts	+/–	PIM	PP	SH	S	SPct	P/G
Overall	80	35	48	83	12	26	5	4	177	19.8	1.04
Home	40	18	27	45	16	14	1	2	90	20.0	1.13
Away	40	17	21	38	-4	12	4	2	87	19.5	.95
vs. Division	20	5	11	16	4	6	1	0	38	13.2	.80
vs. Conference	58	24	33	57	9	16	3	3	126	19.0	.98
vs. Playoff	43	19	23	42	1	12	3	2	80	23.8	.98
vs. Non-Playoff	37	16	25	41	11	14	2	2	97	16.5	1.11
Pre All-Star	41	21	26	47	8	16	4	2	105	20.0	1.15
Post All-Star	39	14	22	36	4	10	1	2	72	19.4	.92
Day	14	5	7	12	8	4	0	1	34	14.7	.86
Night	66	30	41	71	4	22	5	3	143	21.0	1.08

	GP	G	A	Pts	+/–	PIM	PP	SH	S	SPct	P/G
National TV	17	12	7	19	2	6	3	1	48	25.0	1.12
0 Days Rest	15	7	6	13	-1	4	1	2	38	18.4	.87
1 Days Rest	34	13	22	35	0	10	4	2	63	20.6	1.03
2 Days Rest	20	11	14	25	15	6	0	0	52	21.2	1.25
3+ Days Rest	11	4	6	10	-2	6	0	0	24	16.7	.91

	G	A	Pts	PIM		G	A	Pts	PIM
1st Period	9	18	27	10	Winning	12	13	25	4
2nd Period	11	15	26	12	Losing	15	14	29	16
3rd Period	15	15	30	4	Tied	8	21	29	6
Overtime	0	0	0	0	Clutch	5	3	8	0
Last 5 Min	13	11	24	2	Blowouts	1	2	3	2

Jozef Stumpel

Los Angeles Kings — Center

1998-99 Season

	GP	G	A	Pts	+/–	PIM	PP	SH	S	SPct	P/G
Overall	64	13	21	34	-18	10	1	0	131	9.9	.53
Home	33	8	9	17	-8	4	0	0	73	11.0	.52
Away	31	5	12	17	-10	6	1	0	58	8.6	.55
vs. Division	18	2	3	5	-9	4	1	0	42	4.8	.28
vs. Conference	46	9	16	25	-16	10	1	0	99	9.1	.54
vs. Playoff	46	10	14	24	-19	8	1	0	90	11.1	.52
vs. Non-Playoff	18	3	7	10	1	2	0	0	41	7.3	.56
Pre All-Star	32	8	10	18	-8	6	1	0	64	12.5	.56
Post All-Star	32	5	11	16	-10	4	0	0	67	7.5	.50
Day	3	0	0	0	-4	0	0	0	3	0.0	.00
Night	61	13	21	34	-14	10	1	0	128	10.2	.56

	GP	G	A	Pts	+/–	PIM	PP	SH	S	SPct	P/G
National TV	13	5	3	8	-2	4	0	0	32	15.6	.62
0 Days Rest	8	1	3	4	-6	0	0	0	10	10.0	.50
1 Days Rest	32	8	12	20	-6	8	1	0	63	12.7	.63
2 Days Rest	13	2	5	7	-2	0	0	0	28	7.1	.54
3+ Days Rest	11	2	1	3	-4	2	0	0	30	6.7	.27

	G	A	Pts	PIM		G	A	Pts	PIM
1st Period	2	9	11	2	Winning	4	6	10	0
2nd Period	3	5	8	6	Losing	6	8	14	4
3rd Period	8	6	14	2	Tied	3	7	10	6
Overtime	0	1	1	0	Clutch	3	2	5	2
Last 5 Min	5	7	12	4	Blowouts	1	0	1	2

Marco Sturm

San Jose Sharks — Center

1998-99 Season

	GP	G	A	Pts	+/–	PIM	PP	SH	S	SPct	P/G
Overall	78	16	22	38	7	52	3	2	140	11.4	.49
Home	37	7	10	17	3	18	2	1	74	9.5	.46
Away	41	9	12	21	4	34	1	1	66	13.6	.51
vs. Division	21	2	4	6	1	20	1	1	30	6.7	.29
vs. Conference	53	11	16	27	1	34	2	2	88	12.5	.51
vs. Playoff	46	9	10	19	-4	28	2	2	75	12.0	.41
vs. Non-Playoff	32	7	12	19	11	24	1	0	65	10.8	.59
Pre All-Star	45	11	11	22	4	32	3	2	75	14.7	.49
Post All-Star	33	5	11	16	3	20	0	0	65	7.7	.48
Day	6	3	2	5	-1	4	0	1	11	27.3	.83
Night	72	13	20	33	8	48	3	1	129	10.1	.46

	GP	G	A	Pts	+/–	PIM	PP	SH	S	SPct	P/G
National TV	10	2	3	5	-1	6	0	1	15	13.3	.50
0 Days Rest	13	2	2	4	1	10	0	0	26	7.7	.31
1 Days Rest	42	9	12	21	4	30	3	2	73	12.3	.50
2 Days Rest	12	2	1	3	0	4	0	0	16	12.5	.25
3+ Days Rest	11	3	7	10	2	8	0	0	25	12.0	.91

	G	A	Pts	PIM		G	A	Pts	PIM
1st Period	4	9	13	22	Winning	8	9	17	16
2nd Period	4	4	8	24	Losing	3	3	6	24
3rd Period	7	9	16	6	Tied	5	10	15	12
Overtime	1	0	1	0	Clutch	5	5	10	0
Last 5 Min	7	7	14	16	Blowouts	1	0	1	6

Steve Sullivan

Toronto Maple Leafs — Center

1998-99 Season

	GP	G	A	Pts	+/–	PIM	PP	SH	S	SPct	P/G
Overall	63	20	20	40	12	28	4	0	110	18.2	.63
Home	34	9	10	19	6	12	2	0	57	15.8	.56
Away	29	11	10	21	6	16	2	0	53	20.8	.72
vs. Division	17	2	3	5	-2	10	1	0	30	6.7	.29
vs. Conference	47	15	15	30	9	28	3	0	80	18.8	.64
vs. Playoff	35	12	10	22	8	12	1	0	58	20.7	.63
vs. Non-Playoff	28	8	10	18	4	16	3	0	52	15.4	.64
Pre All-Star	28	6	9	15	4	14	0	0	46	13.0	.54
Post All-Star	35	14	11	25	8	14	4	0	64	21.9	.71
Day	0	0	0	0	0	0	0	0	0	–	–
Night	63	20	20	40	12	28	4	0	110	18.2	.63

	GP	G	A	Pts	+/–	PIM	PP	SH	S	SPct	P/G
National TV	22	11	6	17	10	18	2	0	48	22.9	.77
0 Days Rest	11	4	6	10	6	2	0	0	18	22.2	.91
1 Days Rest	26	7	10	17	7	6	3	0	49	14.3	.65
2 Days Rest	10	5	2	7	3	12	0	0	25	20.0	.70
3+ Days Rest	16	4	2	6	-4	8	1	0	18	22.2	.38

	G	A	Pts	PIM		G	A	Pts	PIM
1st Period	4	7	11	2	Winning	10	9	19	16
2nd Period	10	9	19	18	Losing	7	7	14	12
3rd Period	6	4	10	8	Tied	3	4	7	0
Overtime	0	0	0	0	Clutch	2	1	3	4
Last 5 Min	5	6	11	2	Blowouts	2	2	4	0

Mats Sundin

Toronto Maple Leafs — Center

1998-99 Season

	GP	G	A	Pts	+/–	PIM	PP	SH	S	SPct	P/G
Overall	82	31	52	83	22	58	4	0	209	14.8	1.01
Home	41	15	31	46	14	26	0	0	113	13.3	1.12
Away	41	16	21	37	8	32	4	0	96	16.7	.90
vs. Division	20	2	7	9	-3	18	0	0	54	3.7	.45
vs. Conference	56	16	33	49	8	44	2	0	141	11.3	.88
vs. Playoff	46	17	21	38	4	40	2	0	124	13.7	.83
vs. Non-Playoff	36	14	31	45	18	18	2	0	85	16.5	1.25
Pre All-Star	46	16	31	47	7	28	4	0	134	11.9	1.02
Post All-Star	36	15	21	36	15	30	0	0	75	20.0	1.00
Day	1	0	0	0	-1	0	0	0	6	0.0	.00
Night	81	31	52	83	23	58	4	0	203	15.3	1.02

	GP	G	A	Pts	+/–	PIM	PP	SH	S	SPct	P/G
National TV	28	6	19	25	13	18	1	0	64	9.4	.89
0 Days Rest	18	7	12	19	10	8	2	0	47	14.9	1.06
1 Days Rest	35	14	24	38	10	38	0	0	102	13.7	1.09
2 Days Rest	14	4	8	12	3	6	2	0	30	13.3	.86
3+ Days Rest	15	6	8	14	-1	6	0	0	30	20.0	.93

	G	A	Pts	PIM		G	A	Pts	PIM
1st Period	9	16	25	22	Winning	12	19	31	32
2nd Period	13	17	30	16	Losing	7	11	18	24
3rd Period	8	16	24	20	Tied	12	22	34	2
Overtime	1	3	4	0	Clutch	5	7	12	2
Last 5 Min	8	14	22	10	Blowouts	3	2	5	12

Niklas Sundstrom

New York Rangers — Left Wing

1998-99 Season

	GP	G	A	Pts	+/–	PIM	PP	SH	S	SPct	P/G
Overall	81	13	30	43	-2	20	1	2	89	14.6	.53
Home	41	3	18	21	-2	6	1	0	49	6.1	.51
Away	40	10	12	22	0	14	0	2	40	25.0	.55
vs. Division	19	1	7	8	-7	6	0	0	16	6.3	.42
vs. Conference	57	10	17	27	-11	10	1	2	61	16.4	.47
vs. Playoff	52	9	18	27	-6	14	1	1	58	15.5	.52
vs. Non-Playoff	29	4	12	16	4	6	0	1	31	12.9	.55
Pre All-Star	44	8	19	27	-8	14	1	0	48	16.7	.61
Post All-Star	37	5	11	16	6	6	0	2	41	12.2	.43
Day	12	1	2	3	0	4	0	1	17	5.9	.25
Night	69	12	28	40	-2	16	1	1	72	16.7	.58

	GP	G	A	Pts	+/–	PIM	PP	SH	S	SPct	P/G
National TV	23	3	6	9	-2	4	0	1	21	14.3	.39
0 Days Rest	15	1	3	4	-5	6	0	0	9	11.1	.27
1 Days Rest	34	4	15	19	-6	8	1	0	39	10.3	.56
2 Days Rest	19	3	10	13	9	2	0	1	18	16.7	.68
3+ Days Rest	13	5	2	7	0	4	0	1	23	21.7	.54

	G	A	Pts	PIM		G	A	Pts	PIM
1st Period	4	8	12	12	Winning	6	11	17	10
2nd Period	3	8	11	6	Losing	4	14	18	4
3rd Period	6	14	20	2	Tied	3	5	8	6
Overtime	0	0	0	0	Clutch	3	4	7	0
Last 5 Min	4	7	11	4	Blowouts	2	2	4	4

Robert Svehla

Florida Panthers — Defense

1998-99 Season

	GP	G	A	Pts	+/–	PIM	PP	SH	S	SPct	P/G
Overall	80	8	29	37	-13	83	4	0	157	5.1	.46
Home	40	6	12	18	-10	36	4	0	94	6.4	.45
Away	40	2	17	19	-3	47	0	0	63	3.2	.48
vs. Division	14	1	4	5	0	12	0	0	30	3.3	.36
vs. Conference	57	7	22	29	-8	53	3	0	106	6.6	.51
vs. Playoff	48	7	18	25	-18	61	4	0	95	7.4	.52
vs. Non-Playoff	32	1	11	12	5	22	0	0	62	1.6	.38
Pre All-Star	42	5	17	22	-9	38	2	0	90	5.6	.52
Post All-Star	38	3	12	15	-4	45	2	0	67	4.5	.39
Day	4	0	0	0	-7	4	0	0	5	0.0	.00
Night	76	8	29	37	-6	79	4	0	152	5.3	.49

	GP	G	A	Pts	+/–	PIM	PP	SH	S	SPct	P/G
National TV	4	1	0	1	-5	0	1	0	4	25.0	.25
0 Days Rest	18	1	7	8	-5	12	1	0	30	3.3	.44
1 Days Rest	33	2	10	12	-7	41	2	0	55	3.6	.36
2 Days Rest	15	3	3	6	1	8	1	0	37	8.1	.40
3+ Days Rest	14	2	9	11	-2	22	0	0	35	5.7	.79

	G	A	Pts	PIM		G	A	Pts	PIM
1st Period	3	7	10	32	Winning	3	8	11	30
2nd Period	0	8	8	39	Losing	3	13	16	23
3rd Period	5	13	18	12	Tied	2	8	10	30
Overtime	0	1	1	0	Clutch	0	5	5	8
Last 5 Min	0	9	9	20	Blowouts	1	2	3	12

Jaroslav Svejkovsky

Washington Capitals — Right Wing

1998-99 Season

	GP	G	A	Pts	+/–	PIM	PP	SH	S	SPct	P/G
Overall	25	6	8	14	-2	12	4	0	50	12.0	.56
Home	16	2	6	8	-7	8	2	0	25	8.0	.50
Away	9	4	2	6	5	4	2	0	25	16.0	.67
vs. Division	6	3	0	3	2	4	2	0	10	30.0	.50
vs. Conference	16	6	5	11	-2	8	4	0	39	15.4	.69
vs. Playoff	13	3	5	8	-2	6	2	0	28	10.7	.62
vs. Non-Playoff	12	3	3	6	0	6	2	0	22	13.6	.50
Pre All-Star	7	2	0	2	2	4	0	0	15	13.3	.29
Post All-Star	18	4	8	12	-4	8	4	0	35	11.4	.67
Day	2	2	1	3	-2	0	2	0	8	25.0	1.50
Night	23	4	7	11	0	12	2	0	42	9.5	.48

	GP	G	A	Pts	+/–	PIM	PP	SH	S	SPct	P/G
National TV	6	2	2	4	-3	2	1	0	17	11.8	.67
0 Days Rest	3	1	1	2	-3	2	1	0	5	20.0	.67
1 Days Rest	13	4	6	10	1	10	2	0	28	14.3	.77
2 Days Rest	6	1	0	1	0	0	1	0	13	7.7	.17
3+ Days Rest	3	0	1	1	0	0	0	0	4	0.0	.33

	G	A	Pts	PIM		G	A	Pts	PIM
1st Period	2	2	4	6	Winning	3	2	5	8
2nd Period	1	4	5	2	Losing	1	3	4	2
3rd Period	3	2	5	4	Tied	2	3	5	2
Overtime	0	0	0	0	Clutch	0	0	0	0
Last 5 Min	2	1	3	2	Blowouts	1	0	1	2

Petr Svoboda

Tampa Bay Lightning — Defense

1998-99 Season

	GP	G	A	Pts	+/–	PIM	PP	SH	S	SPct	P/G
Overall	59	5	18	23	1	81	1	1	83	6.0	.39
Home	30	3	12	15	1	37	1	1	44	6.8	.50
Away	29	2	6	8	0	44	0	0	39	5.1	.28
vs. Division	14	1	4	5	-7	14	0	1	17	5.9	.36
vs. Conference	45	4	12	16	0	62	0	1	56	7.1	.36
vs. Playoff	35	2	13	15	1	47	0	1	49	4.1	.43
vs. Non-Playoff	24	3	5	8	0	34	1	0	34	8.8	.33
Pre All-Star	35	4	4	8	1	50	1	1	55	7.3	.23
Post All-Star	24	1	14	15	0	31	0	0	28	3.6	.63
Day	5	0	3	3	0	4	0	0	12	0.0	.60
Night	54	5	15	20	1	77	1	1	71	7.0	.37

	GP	G	A	Pts	+/–	PIM	PP	SH	S	SPct	P/G
National TV	2	1	1	2	2	4	0	0	1	100.0	1.00
0 Days Rest	7	0	0	0	-2	6	0	0	12	0.0	.00
1 Days Rest	25	2	9	11	-2	28	0	1	33	6.1	.44
2 Days Rest	13	2	4	6	4	18	0	0	17	11.8	.46
3+ Days Rest	14	1	5	6	1	29	1	0	21	4.8	.43

	G	A	Pts	PIM		G	A	Pts	PIM
1st Period	1	9	10	28	Winning	3	7	10	32
2nd Period	2	4	6	25	Losing	1	5	6	33
3rd Period	2	5	7	24	Tied	1	6	7	16
Overtime	0	0	0	4	Clutch	0	0	0	12
Last 5 Min	2	5	7	20	Blowouts	1	0	1	14

Don Sweeney

Boston Bruins — Defense

1998-99 Season

	GP	G	A	Pts	+/–	PIM	PP	SH	S	SPct	P/G
Overall	81	2	10	12	14	64	0	0	79	2.5	.15
Home	41	2	7	9	8	36	0	0	37	5.4	.22
Away	40	0	3	3	6	28	0	0	42	0.0	.08
vs. Division	20	1	4	5	6	8	0	0	16	6.3	.25
vs. Conference	57	1	7	8	13	48	0	0	52	1.9	.14
vs. Playoff	45	0	4	4	4	20	0	0	44	0.0	.09
vs. Non-Playoff	36	2	6	8	10	44	0	0	35	5.7	.22
Pre All-Star	43	2	8	10	4	40	0	0	40	5.0	.23
Post All-Star	38	0	2	2	10	24	0	0	39	0.0	.05
Day	15	2	1	3	11	8	0	0	14	14.3	.20
Night	66	0	9	9	3	56	0	0	65	0.0	.14

	GP	G	A	Pts	+/–	PIM	PP	SH	S	SPct	P/G
National TV	9	0	0	0	4	2	0	0	8	0.0	.00
0 Days Rest	16	0	2	2	-3	12	0	0	17	0.0	.13
1 Days Rest	39	2	6	8	20	40	0	0	35	5.7	.21
2 Days Rest	13	0	0	0	-2	8	0	0	14	0.0	.00
3+ Days Rest	13	0	2	2	-1	4	0	0	13	0.0	.15

	G	A	Pts	PIM		G	A	Pts	PIM
1st Period	0	4	4	36	Winning	2	4	6	46
2nd Period	1	4	5	16	Losing	0	2	2	16
3rd Period	1	2	3	12	Tied	0	4	4	2
Overtime	0	0	0	0	Clutch	0	1	1	2
Last 5 Min	1	4	5	10	Blowouts	0	1	1	4

Darryl Sydor

Dallas Stars — Defense

1998-99 Season

	GP	G	A	Pts	+/–	PIM	PP	SH	S	SPct	P/G
Overall	74	14	34	48	-1	50	9	0	163	8.6	.65
Home	37	10	23	33	8	18	7	0	95	10.5	.89
Away	37	4	11	15	-9	32	2	0	68	5.9	.41
vs. Division	23	3	8	11	-2	25	2	0	43	7.0	.48
vs. Conference	52	8	24	32	-6	40	6	0	115	7.0	.62
vs. Playoff	43	7	19	26	-4	35	5	0	99	7.1	.60
vs. Non-Playoff	31	7	15	22	3	15	4	0	64	10.9	.71
Pre All-Star	43	12	24	36	-7	17	7	0	100	12.0	.84
Post All-Star	31	2	10	12	6	33	2	0	63	3.2	.39
Day	10	1	3	4	-2	19	1	0	22	4.5	.40
Night	64	13	31	44	1	31	8	0	141	9.2	.69

	GP	G	A	Pts	+/–	PIM	PP	SH	S	SPct	P/G
National TV	12	1	5	6	-4	4	1	0	24	4.2	.50
0 Days Rest	13	1	2	3	-3	4	0	0	26	3.8	.23
1 Days Rest	37	6	19	25	4	19	5	0	74	8.1	.68
2 Days Rest	12	2	9	11	1	19	1	0	34	5.9	.92
3+ Days Rest	12	5	4	9	-3	8	3	0	29	17.2	.75

	G	A	Pts	PIM		G	A	Pts	PIM
1st Period	5	19	24	12	Winning	4	8	12	14
2nd Period	5	11	16	23	Losing	4	11	15	32
3rd Period	4	4	8	15	Tied	6	15	21	4
Overtime	0	0	0	0	Clutch	2	0	2	2
Last 5 Min	2	9	11	15	Blowouts	0	0	0	4

Petr Sykora

New Jersey Devils — Center

1998-99 Season

	GP	G	A	Pts	+/–	PIM	PP	SH	S	SPct	P/G
Overall	80	29	43	72	16	22	15	0	222	13.1	.90
Home	40	14	19	33	4	12	6	0	104	13.5	.83
Away	40	15	24	39	12	10	9	0	118	12.7	.98
vs. Division	19	7	14	21	7	4	4	0	38	18.4	1.11
vs. Conference	57	19	31	50	13	18	10	0	161	11.8	.88
vs. Playoff	45	17	21	38	4	10	9	0	127	13.4	.84
vs. Non-Playoff	35	12	22	34	12	12	6	0	95	12.6	.97
Pre All-Star	42	13	18	31	-1	16	8	0	99	13.1	.74
Post All-Star	38	16	25	41	17	6	7	0	123	13.0	1.08
Day	12	6	9	15	4	2	3	0	38	15.8	1.25
Night	68	23	34	57	12	20	12	0	184	12.5	.84

	GP	G	A	Pts	+/–	PIM	PP	SH	S	SPct	P/G
National TV	7	4	3	7	-1	2	2	0	26	15.4	1.00
0 Days Rest	16	12	8	20	-4	4	9	0	49	24.5	1.25
1 Days Rest	34	15	18	33	15	10	5	0	95	15.8	.97
2 Days Rest	19	2	12	14	2	6	1	0	56	3.6	.74
3+ Days Rest	11	0	5	5	3	2	0	0	22	0.0	.45

	G	A	Pts	PIM		G	A	Pts	PIM
1st Period	12	14	26	6	Winning	10	17	27	18
2nd Period	8	17	25	6	Losing	6	9	15	4
3rd Period	9	12	21	10	Tied	13	17	30	0
Overtime	0	0	0	0	Clutch	1	4	5	0
Last 5 Min	8	9	17	6	Blowouts	0	2	2	4

Tim Taylor

Boston Bruins — Center

1998-99 Season

	GP	G	A	Pts	+/–	PIM	PP	SH	S	SPct	P/G
Overall	49	4	7	11	-10	55	0	0	76	5.3	.22
Home	26	2	5	7	-3	29	0	0	43	4.7	.27
Away	23	2	2	4	-7	26	0	0	33	6.1	.17
vs. Division	11	1	0	1	-4	0	0	0	18	5.6	.09
vs. Conference	36	3	3	6	-9	51	0	0	64	4.7	.17
vs. Playoff	26	2	5	7	-4	12	0	0	48	4.2	.27
vs. Non-Playoff	23	2	2	4	-6	43	0	0	28	7.1	.17
Pre All-Star	11	2	0	2	-1	12	0	0	14	14.3	.18
Post All-Star	38	2	7	9	-9	43	0	0	62	3.2	.24
Day	13	1	1	2	2	27	0	0	25	4.0	.15
Night	36	3	6	9	-12	28	0	0	51	5.9	.25

	GP	G	A	Pts	+/–	PIM	PP	SH	S	SPct	P/G
National TV	8	0	0	0	-3	18	0	0	10	0.0	.00
0 Days Rest	9	0	1	1	-6	8	0	0	20	0.0	.11
1 Days Rest	22	2	5	7	3	45	0	0	30	6.7	.32
2 Days Rest	8	0	1	1	-1	0	0	0	10	0.0	.13
3+ Days Rest	10	2	0	2	-6	2	0	0	16	12.5	.20

	G	A	Pts	PIM		G	A	Pts	PIM
1st Period	2	1	3	18	Winning	0	0	0	45
2nd Period	1	3	4	12	Losing	1	3	4	8
3rd Period	1	3	4	23	Tied	3	4	7	2
Overtime	0	0	0	2	Clutch	1	0	1	2
Last 5 Min	2	1	3	8	Blowouts	1	0	1	2

Dmitri Tertyshny

Philadelphia Flyers — Defense

1998-99 Season

	GP	G	A	Pts	+/–	PIM	PP	SH	S	SPct	P/G
Overall	62	2	8	10	-1	30	1	0	68	2.9	.16
Home	31	0	6	6	2	10	0	0	29	0.0	.19
Away	31	2	2	4	-3	20	1	0	39	5.1	.13
vs. Division	10	1	2	3	3	8	1	0	11	9.1	.30
vs. Conference	40	1	6	7	-9	20	1	0	43	2.3	.18
vs. Playoff	33	1	2	3	-3	18	0	0	34	2.9	.09
vs. Non-Playoff	29	1	6	7	2	12	1	0	34	2.9	.24
Pre All-Star	33	0	6	6	3	18	0	0	32	0.0	.18
Post All-Star	29	2	2	4	-4	12	1	0	36	5.6	.14
Day	11	0	0	0	6	4	0	0	6	0.0	.00
Night	51	2	8	10	-7	26	1	0	62	3.2	.20

	GP	G	A	Pts	+/–	PIM	PP	SH	S	SPct	P/G
National TV	13	0	0	0	5	10	0	0	10	0.0	.00
0 Days Rest	9	0	2	2	-3	2	0	0	8	0.0	.22
1 Days Rest	26	2	2	4	-3	22	1	0	32	6.3	.15
2 Days Rest	10	0	0	0	4	2	0	0	15	0.0	.00
3+ Days Rest	17	0	4	4	1	4	0	0	13	0.0	.24

	G	A	Pts	PIM		G	A	Pts	PIM
1st Period	1	2	3	10	Winning	1	3	4	12
2nd Period	1	4	5	10	Losing	0	2	2	6
3rd Period	0	2	2	10	Tied	1	3	4	12
Overtime	0	0	0	0	Clutch	0	0	0	2
Last 5 Min	0	3	3	2	Blowouts	0	0	0	2

Chris Therien

Philadelphia Flyers — Defense

1998-99 Season

	GP	G	A	Pts	+/–	PIM	PP	SH	S	SPct	P/G
Overall	74	3	15	18	16	48	1	0	115	2.6	.24
Home	36	1	9	10	18	10	0	0	47	2.1	.28
Away	38	2	6	8	-2	38	1	0	68	2.9	.21
vs. Division	19	1	2	3	0	16	1	0	21	4.8	.16
vs. Conference	52	2	10	12	3	30	1	0	80	2.5	.23
vs. Playoff	43	2	9	11	9	38	1	0	66	3.0	.26
vs. Non-Playoff	31	1	6	7	7	10	0	0	49	2.0	.23
Pre All-Star	37	1	9	10	20	30	1	0	51	2.0	.27
Post All-Star	37	2	6	8	-4	18	0	0	64	3.1	.22
Day	14	1	1	2	0	10	0	0	20	5.0	.14
Night	60	2	14	16	16	38	1	0	95	2.1	.27

	GP	G	A	Pts	+/–	PIM	PP	SH	S	SPct	P/G
National TV	17	0	1	1	-1	4	0	0	28	0.0	.06
0 Days Rest	10	1	3	4	6	4	0	0	23	4.3	.40
1 Days Rest	37	2	10	12	6	34	1	0	56	3.6	.32
2 Days Rest	15	0	0	0	-1	8	0	0	26	0.0	.00
3+ Days Rest	12	0	2	2	5	2	0	0	10	0.0	.17

	G	A	Pts	PIM		G	A	Pts	PIM
1st Period	2	3	5	12	Winning	1	8	9	14
2nd Period	1	4	5	12	Losing	1	4	5	10
3rd Period	0	8	8	12	Tied	1	3	4	24
Overtime	0	0	0	12	Clutch	0	0	0	12
Last 5 Min	0	5	5	22	Blowouts	0	1	1	8

Steve Thomas

Toronto Maple Leafs — Left Wing

1998-99 Season

	GP	G	A	Pts	+/–	PIM	PP	SH	S	SPct	P/G
Overall	78	28	45	73	26	33	11	0	209	13.4	.94
Home	39	15	21	36	18	19	6	0	108	13.9	.92
Away	39	13	24	37	8	14	5	0	101	12.9	.95
vs. Division	18	4	4	8	-1	2	0	0	53	7.5	.44
vs. Conference	52	14	30	44	10	17	4	0	143	9.8	.85
vs. Playoff	44	12	30	42	10	12	6	0	121	9.9	.95
vs. Non-Playoff	34	16	15	31	16	21	5	0	88	18.2	.91
Pre All-Star	46	18	21	39	11	27	6	0	128	14.1	.85
Post All-Star	32	10	24	34	15	6	5	0	81	12.3	1.06
Day	1	0	0	0	-1	0	0	0	4	0.0	.00
Night	77	28	45	73	27	33	11	0	205	13.7	.95

	GP	G	A	Pts	+/–	PIM	PP	SH	S	SPct	P/G
National TV	27	10	12	22	12	6	3	0	70	14.3	.81
0 Days Rest	17	6	5	11	6	6	2	0	43	14.0	.65
1 Days Rest	33	13	25	38	10	19	8	0	87	14.9	1.15
2 Days Rest	13	5	5	10	5	4	1	0	35	14.3	.77
3+ Days Rest	15	4	10	14	5	4	0	0	44	9.1	.93

	G	A	Pts	PIM		G	A	Pts	PIM
1st Period	8	13	21	6	Winning	10	16	26	27
2nd Period	11	17	28	17	Losing	6	11	17	2
3rd Period	8	13	21	8	Tied	12	18	30	4
Overtime	1	2	3	2	Clutch	1	7	8	4
Last 5 Min	8	11	19	6	Blowouts	0	6	6	8

Joe Thornton

Boston Bruins — Center

1998-99 Season

	GP	G	A	Pts	+/–	PIM	PP	SH	S	SPct	P/G
Overall	81	16	25	41	3	69	7	0	128	12.5	.51
Home	41	9	13	22	4	46	4	0	79	11.4	.54
Away	40	7	12	19	-1	23	3	0	49	14.3	.48
vs. Division	20	4	9	13	0	27	2	0	35	11.4	.65
vs. Conference	57	10	20	30	0	50	5	0	94	10.6	.53
vs. Playoff	45	9	9	18	-2	27	5	0	67	13.4	.40
vs. Non-Playoff	36	7	16	23	5	42	2	0	61	11.5	.64
Pre All-Star	43	8	10	18	3	33	4	0	59	13.6	.42
Post All-Star	38	8	15	23	0	36	3	0	69	11.6	.61
Day	15	4	4	8	6	10	1	0	36	11.1	.53
Night	66	12	21	33	-3	59	6	0	92	13.0	.50

	GP	G	A	Pts	+/–	PIM	PP	SH	S	SPct	P/G
National TV	9	5	2	7	-2	8	3	0	11	45.5	.78
0 Days Rest	16	4	2	6	-3	12	2	0	24	16.7	.38
1 Days Rest	39	10	13	23	7	38	4	0	76	13.2	.59
2 Days Rest	13	1	5	6	0	13	0	0	13	7.7	.46
3+ Days Rest	13	1	5	6	-1	6	1	0	15	6.7	.46

	G	A	Pts	PIM		G	A	Pts	PIM
1st Period	6	6	12	34	Winning	3	12	15	36
2nd Period	6	10	16	10	Losing	5	8	13	23
3rd Period	4	9	13	25	Tied	8	5	13	10
Overtime	0	0	0	0	Clutch	2	3	5	2
Last 5 Min	6	7	13	25	Blowouts	1	0	1	6

Scott Thornton

Montreal Canadiens — Center

1998-99 Season

	GP	G	A	Pts	+/–	PIM	PP	SH	S	SPct	P/G
Overall	47	7	4	11	-2	87	1	0	56	12.5	.23
Home	27	4	3	7	2	60	1	0	37	10.8	.26
Away	20	3	1	4	-4	27	0	0	19	15.8	.20
vs. Division	11	1	0	1	-3	43	0	0	15	6.7	.09
vs. Conference	34	7	2	9	0	77	1	0	38	18.4	.26
vs. Playoff	25	4	1	5	-7	57	1	0	32	12.5	.20
vs. Non-Playoff	22	3	3	6	5	30	0	0	24	12.5	.27
Pre All-Star	15	2	1	3	4	34	0	0	17	11.8	.20
Post All-Star	32	5	3	8	-6	53	1	0	39	12.8	.25
Day	2	1	0	1	-1	2	0	0	4	25.0	.50
Night	45	6	4	10	-1	85	1	0	52	11.5	.22

	GP	G	A	Pts	+/–	PIM	PP	SH	S	SPct	P/G
National TV	15	3	0	3	-1	50	0	0	21	14.3	.20
0 Days Rest	9	1	0	1	-1	31	0	0	7	14.3	.11
1 Days Rest	19	3	3	6	-2	36	1	0	32	9.4	.32
2 Days Rest	10	1	1	2	0	8	0	0	10	10.0	.20
3+ Days Rest	9	2	0	2	1	12	0	0	7	28.6	.22

	G	A	Pts	PIM		G	A	Pts	PIM
1st Period	2	0	2	63	Winning	3	2	5	35
2nd Period	2	3	5	12	Losing	3	2	5	48
3rd Period	3	1	4	12	Tied	1	0	1	4
Overtime	0	0	0	0	Clutch	1	0	1	0
Last 5 Min	4	2	6	10	Blowouts	0	1	1	6

Kimmo Timonen

Nashville Predators — Defense

1998-99 Season

	GP	G	A	Pts	+/–	PIM	PP	SH	S	SPct	P/G
Overall	50	4	8	12	-4	30	1	0	75	5.3	.24
Home	24	2	6	8	-3	12	0	0	42	4.8	.33
Away	26	2	2	4	-1	18	1	0	33	6.1	.15
vs. Division	11	1	3	4	1	6	0	0	20	5.0	.36
vs. Conference	35	2	6	8	-4	20	0	0	50	4.0	.23
vs. Playoff	33	1	5	6	-12	26	0	0	44	2.3	.18
vs. Non-Playoff	17	3	3	6	8	4	1	0	31	9.7	.35
Pre All-Star	15	0	1	1	4	12	0	0	21	0.0	.07
Post All-Star	35	4	7	11	-8	18	1	0	54	7.4	.31
Day	7	0	1	1	-4	10	0	0	5	0.0	.14
Night	43	4	7	11	0	20	1	0	70	5.7	.26

	GP	G	A	Pts	+/–	PIM	PP	SH	S	SPct	P/G
National TV	1	0	0	0	0	0	0	0	1	0.0	.00
0 Days Rest	10	1	0	1	1	6	0	0	20	5.0	.10
1 Days Rest	20	2	4	6	-2	12	1	0	27	7.4	.30
2 Days Rest	9	1	0	1	-7	6	0	0	16	6.3	.11
3+ Days Rest	11	0	4	4	4	6	0	0	12	0.0	.36

	G	A	Pts	PIM		G	A	Pts	PIM
1st Period	0	2	2	14	Winning	0	2	2	10
2nd Period	1	2	3	8	Losing	3	3	6	18
3rd Period	3	4	7	8	Tied	1	3	4	2
Overtime	0	0	0	0	Clutch	0	1	1	2
Last 5 Min	0	3	3	10	Blowouts	1	1	2	2

German Titov

Pittsburgh Penguins — Center

1998-99 Season

	GP	G	A	Pts	+/–	PIM	PP	SH	S	SPct	P/G
Overall	72	11	45	56	18	34	3	1	113	9.7	.78
Home	37	5	24	29	13	18	0	1	58	8.6	.78
Away	35	6	21	27	5	16	3	0	55	10.9	.77
vs. Division	17	3	6	9	0	8	2	0	28	10.7	.53
vs. Conference	49	8	25	33	11	28	2	1	80	10.0	.67
vs. Playoff	39	6	25	31	10	24	1	0	65	9.2	.79
vs. Non-Playoff	33	5	20	25	8	10	2	1	48	10.4	.76
Pre All-Star	38	6	26	32	8	18	2	0	63	9.5	.84
Post All-Star	34	5	19	24	10	16	1	1	50	10.0	.71
Day	11	3	7	10	7	10	1	0	15	20.0	.91
Night	61	8	38	46	11	24	2	1	98	8.2	.75

	GP	G	A	Pts	+/–	PIM	PP	SH	S	SPct	P/G
National TV	14	4	9	13	-1	6	2	0	24	16.7	.93
0 Days Rest	12	2	4	6	0	4	1	0	15	13.3	.50
1 Days Rest	30	7	24	31	13	16	1	1	56	12.5	1.03
2 Days Rest	18	0	9	9	4	6	0	0	27	0.0	.50
3+ Days Rest	12	2	8	10	1	8	1	0	15	13.3	.83

	G	A	Pts	PIM		G	A	Pts	PIM
1st Period	1	17	18	8	Winning	7	11	18	16
2nd Period	3	9	12	12	Losing	2	16	18	14
3rd Period	7	16	23	14	Tied	2	18	20	4
Overtime	0	3	3	0	Clutch	2	7	9	0
Last 5 Min	4	16	20	6	Blowouts	1	0	1	8

Keith Tkachuk

Phoenix Coyotes — Left Wing

1998-99 Season

	GP	G	A	Pts	+/–	PIM	PP	SH	S	SPct	P/G
Overall	68	36	32	68	22	151	11	2	258	14.0	1.00
Home	33	21	13	34	12	68	7	1	139	15.1	1.03
Away	35	15	19	34	10	83	4	1	119	12.6	.97
vs. Division	20	6	4	10	4	57	1	0	78	7.7	.50
vs. Conference	47	27	25	52	22	109	8	0	184	14.7	1.11
vs. Playoff	40	20	18	38	11	99	6	1	154	13.0	.95
vs. Non-Playoff	28	16	14	30	11	52	5	1	104	15.4	1.07
Pre All-Star	30	17	16	33	20	45	6	0	91	18.7	1.10
Post All-Star	38	19	16	35	2	106	5	2	167	11.4	.92
Day	5	2	2	4	4	44	1	0	13	15.4	.80
Night	63	34	30	64	18	107	10	2	245	13.9	1.02

	GP	G	A	Pts	+/–	PIM	PP	SH	S	SPct	P/G
National TV	12	8	3	11	4	34	3	0	45	17.8	.92
0 Days Rest	10	5	9	14	4	14	1	0	37	13.5	1.40
1 Days Rest	31	15	11	26	8	79	2	2	125	12.0	.84
2 Days Rest	13	10	6	16	3	44	5	0	54	18.5	1.23
3+ Days Rest	14	6	6	12	7	14	3	0	42	14.3	.86

	G	A	Pts	PIM		G	A	Pts	PIM
1st Period	19	12	31	50	Winning	11	14	25	94
2nd Period	8	8	16	42	Losing	8	8	16	49
3rd Period	9	11	20	57	Tied	17	10	27	8
Overtime	0	1	1	2	Clutch	3	2	5	10
Last 5 Min	9	10	19	54	Blowouts	1	1	2	16

Rick Tocchet

Phoenix Coyotes — Right Wing

1998-99 Season

	GP	G	A	Pts	+/–	PIM	PP	SH	S	SPct	P/G
Overall	81	26	30	56	5	147	6	1	178	14.6	.69
Home	41	14	17	31	4	71	4	0	92	15.2	.76
Away	40	12	13	25	1	76	2	1	86	14.0	.63
vs. Division	24	6	7	13	4	80	1	1	49	12.2	.54
vs. Conference	55	16	19	35	10	127	3	1	111	14.4	.64
vs. Playoff	48	14	18	32	1	79	3	0	96	14.6	.67
vs. Non-Playoff	33	12	12	24	4	68	3	1	82	14.6	.73
Pre All-Star	41	14	16	30	12	81	2	1	86	16.3	.73
Post All-Star	40	12	14	26	-7	66	4	0	92	13.0	.65
Day	6	1	2	3	2	10	0	0	13	7.7	.50
Night	75	25	28	53	3	137	6	1	165	15.2	.71

	GP	G	A	Pts	+/–	PIM	PP	SH	S	SPct	P/G
National TV	14	3	6	9	8	32	0	0	19	15.8	.64
0 Days Rest	13	6	5	11	-2	10	2	0	36	16.7	.85
1 Days Rest	40	12	14	26	0	70	3	0	88	13.6	.65
2 Days Rest	16	4	7	11	3	45	0	0	26	15.4	.69
3+ Days Rest	12	4	4	8	4	22	1	1	28	14.3	.67

	G	A	Pts	PIM		G	A	Pts	PIM
1st Period	7	12	19	63	Winning	9	12	21	72
2nd Period	12	10	22	26	Losing	9	4	13	57
3rd Period	6	8	14	58	Tied	8	14	22	18
Overtime	1	0	1	0	Clutch	1	1	2	4
Last 5 Min	9	3	12	67	Blowouts	2	0	2	33

Patrick Traverse

Ottawa Senators — Defense

1998-99 Season

	GP	G	A	Pts	+/-	PIM	PP	SH	S	SPct	P/G
Overall	46	1	9	10	12	22	0	0	35	2.9	.22
Home	27	1	3	4	10	10	0	0	23	4.3	.15
Away	19	0	6	6	2	12	0	0	12	0.0	.32
vs. Division	10	0	2	2	2	4	0	0	9	0.0	.20
vs. Conference	37	1	9	10	11	14	0	0	31	3.2	.27
vs. Playoff	26	1	4	5	2	14	0	0	19	5.3	.19
vs. Non-Playoff	20	0	5	5	10	8	0	0	16	0.0	.25
Pre All-Star	31	1	7	8	8	12	0	0	22	4.5	.26
Post All-Star	15	0	2	2	4	10	0	0	13	0.0	.13
Day	1	0	0	0	0	0	0	0	1	0.0	.00
Night	45	1	9	10	12	22	0	0	34	2.9	.22

	GP	G	A	Pts	+/-	PIM	PP	SH	S	SPct	P/G
National TV	5	0	2	2	0	0	0	0	5	0.0	.40
0 Days Rest	6	0	3	3	2	0	0	0	1	0.0	.50
1 Days Rest	18	0	3	3	4	8	0	0	14	0.0	.17
2 Days Rest	7	0	0	0	4	6	0	0	8	0.0	.00
3+ Days Rest	15	1	3	4	2	8	0	0	12	8.3	.27

	G	A	Pts	PIM		G	A	Pts	PIM
1st Period	0	1	1	10	Winning	1	5	6	14
2nd Period	0	5	5	6	Losing	0	4	4	6
3rd Period	1	3	4	4	Tied	0	0	0	2
Overtime	0	0	0	2	Clutch	0	2	2	4
Last 5 Min	0	1	1	12	Blowouts	1	1	2	0

Vladimir Tsyplakov

Los Angeles Kings — Left Wing

1998-99 Season

	GP	G	A	Pts	+/-	PIM	PP	SH	S	SPct	P/G
Overall	69	11	12	23	-7	32	0	2	111	9.9	.33
Home	35	6	7	13	3	18	0	1	55	10.9	.37
Away	34	5	5	10	-10	14	0	1	56	8.9	.29
vs. Division	21	4	2	6	-10	12	0	0	36	11.1	.29
vs. Conference	45	8	9	17	-5	26	0	1	78	10.3	.38
vs. Playoff	49	8	3	11	-12	16	0	1	83	9.6	.22
vs. Non-Playoff	20	3	9	12	5	16	0	1	28	10.7	.60
Pre All-Star	45	8	11	19	2	20	0	2	72	11.1	.42
Post All-Star	24	3	1	4	-9	12	0	0	39	7.7	.17
Day	4	1	1	2	-3	4	0	0	5	20.0	.50
Night	65	10	11	21	-4	28	0	2	106	9.4	.32

	GP	G	A	Pts	+/-	PIM	PP	SH	S	SPct	P/G
National TV	11	1	3	4	1	2	0	0	18	5.6	.36
0 Days Rest	12	2	4	6	0	0	0	0	17	11.8	.50
1 Days Rest	33	6	5	11	-9	12	0	2	54	11.1	.33
2 Days Rest	12	2	2	4	3	12	0	0	20	10.0	.33
3+ Days Rest	12	1	1	2	-1	8	0	0	20	5.0	.17

	G	A	Pts	PIM		G	A	Pts	PIM
1st Period	5	5	10	4	Winning	3	5	8	12
2nd Period	2	2	4	14	Losing	3	3	6	14
3rd Period	4	5	9	14	Tied	5	4	9	6
Overtime	0	0	0	0	Clutch	1	0	1	2
Last 5 Min	4	4	8	12	Blowouts	0	0	0	2

Darcy Tucker

Tampa Bay Lightning — Center

1998-99 Season

	GP	G	A	Pts	+/-	PIM	PP	SH	S	SPct	P/G
Overall	82	21	22	43	-34	176	8	2	178	11.8	.52
Home	41	10	11	21	-21	42	5	1	97	10.3	.51
Away	41	11	11	22	-13	134	3	1	81	13.6	.54
vs. Division	15	1	7	8	-4	40	1	0	38	2.6	.53
vs. Conference	57	11	18	29	-14	130	6	0	122	9.0	.51
vs. Playoff	51	14	11	25	-29	83	6	1	116	12.1	.49
vs. Non-Playoff	31	7	11	18	-5	93	2	1	62	11.3	.58
Pre All-Star	45	12	12	24	-20	94	4	2	100	12.0	.53
Post All-Star	37	9	10	19	-14	82	4	0	78	11.5	.51
Day	5	2	2	4	2	26	0	0	15	13.3	.80
Night	77	19	20	39	-36	150	8	2	163	11.7	.51

	GP	G	A	Pts	+/-	PIM	PP	SH	S	SPct	P/G
National TV	1	0	1	1	0	2	0	0	1	0.0	1.00
0 Days Rest	16	2	3	5	-5	30	0	0	32	6.3	.31
1 Days Rest	35	10	12	22	-13	96	5	1	84	11.9	.63
2 Days Rest	20	6	5	11	-5	22	2	1	39	15.4	.55
3+ Days Rest	11	3	2	5	-11	28	1	0	23	13.0	.45

	G	A	Pts	PIM		G	A	Pts	PIM
1st Period	5	7	12	35	Winning	4	7	11	37
2nd Period	10	6	16	86	Losing	9	12	21	108
3rd Period	6	9	15	53	Tied	8	3	11	31
Overtime	0	0	0	2	Clutch	2	1	3	28
Last 5 Min	7	8	15	90	Blowouts	1	1	2	32

Pierre Turgeon

St. Louis Blues — Center

1998-99 Season

	GP	G	A	Pts	+/-	PIM	PP	SH	S	SPct	P/G
Overall	67	31	34	65	4	36	10	0	193	16.1	.97
Home	35	16	17	33	2	18	6	0	102	15.7	.94
Away	32	15	17	32	2	18	4	0	91	16.5	1.00
vs. Division	14	9	4	13	-3	8	5	0	37	24.3	.93
vs. Conference	46	23	20	43	0	26	7	0	128	18.0	.93
vs. Playoff	39	17	14	31	-11	16	5	0	121	14.0	.79
vs. Non-Playoff	28	14	20	34	15	20	5	0	72	19.4	1.21
Pre All-Star	28	11	11	22	-3	16	2	0	85	12.9	.79
Post All-Star	39	20	23	43	7	20	8	0	108	18.5	1.10
Day	9	4	7	11	2	4	1	0	19	21.1	1.22
Night	58	27	27	54	2	32	9	0	174	15.5	.93

	GP	G	A	Pts	+/-	PIM	PP	SH	S	SPct	P/G
National TV	12	8	6	14	3	6	4	0	40	20.0	1.17
0 Days Rest	9	1	0	1	-9	6	1	0	16	6.3	.11
1 Days Rest	36	19	21	40	10	16	8	0	106	17.9	1.11
2 Days Rest	12	7	8	15	3	12	1	0	34	20.6	1.25
3+ Days Rest	10	4	5	9	0	2	0	0	37	10.8	.90

	G	A	Pts	PIM		G	A	Pts	PIM
1st Period	14	15	29	18	Winning	15	13	28	20
2nd Period	6	11	17	12	Losing	8	8	16	10
3rd Period	10	8	18	6	Tied	8	13	21	6
Overtime	1	0	1	0	Clutch	2	2	4	2
Last 5 Min	8	11	19	14	Blowouts	1	0	1	10

Oleg Tverdovsky

Phoenix Coyotes — Defense

1998-99 Season

	GP	G	A	Pts	+/–	PIM	PP	SH	S	SPct	P/G
Overall	82	7	18	25	11	32	2	0	117	6.0	.30
Home	41	2	10	12	7	16	1	0	56	3.6	.29
Away	41	5	8	13	4	16	1	0	61	8.2	.32
vs. Division	24	4	4	8	1	12	1	0	49	8.2	.33
vs. Conference	56	6	10	16	10	28	2	0	89	6.7	.29
vs. Playoff	48	6	6	12	-7	20	2	0	70	8.6	.25
vs. Non-Playoff	34	1	12	13	18	12	0	0	47	2.1	.38
Pre All-Star	42	5	11	16	12	12	2	0	61	8.2	.38
Post All-Star	40	2	7	9	-1	20	0	0	56	3.6	.23
Day	6	0	1	1	2	4	0	0	8	0.0	.17
Night	76	7	17	24	9	28	2	0	109	6.4	.32

	GP	G	A	Pts	+/–	PIM	PP	SH	S	SPct	P/G
National TV	14	2	5	7	4	6	1	0	22	9.1	.50
0 Days Rest	13	1	2	3	1	10	0	0	15	6.7	.23
1 Days Rest	42	2	10	12	4	14	0	0	62	3.2	.29
2 Days Rest	16	3	3	6	1	6	1	0	28	10.7	.38
3+ Days Rest	11	1	3	4	5	2	1	0	12	8.3	.36

	G	A	Pts	PIM		G	A	Pts	PIM
1st Period	5	5	10	8	Winning	2	7	9	18
2nd Period	1	5	6	10	Losing	1	3	4	12
3rd Period	1	8	9	14	Tied	4	8	12	2
Overtime	0	0	0	0	Clutch	0	4	4	2
Last 5 Min	1	4	5	6	Blowouts	0	0	0	4

Igor Ulanov

Montreal Canadiens — Defense

1998-99 Season

	GP	G	A	Pts	+/–	PIM	PP	SH	S	SPct	P/G
Overall	76	3	9	12	-3	109	0	0	55	5.5	.16
Home	39	2	5	7	4	61	0	0	31	6.5	.18
Away	37	1	4	5	-7	48	0	0	24	4.2	.14
vs. Division	17	1	0	1	-3	37	0	0	14	7.1	.06
vs. Conference	50	3	4	7	-4	85	0	0	37	8.1	.14
vs. Playoff	46	1	5	6	-5	70	0	0	33	3.0	.13
vs. Non-Playoff	30	2	4	6	2	39	0	0	22	9.1	.20
Pre All-Star	44	2	3	5	-3	59	0	0	29	6.9	.11
Post All-Star	32	1	6	7	0	50	0	0	26	3.8	.22
Day	3	0	0	0	-1	6	0	0	2	0.0	.00
Night	73	3	9	12	-2	103	0	0	53	5.7	.16

	GP	G	A	Pts	+/–	PIM	PP	SH	S	SPct	P/G
National TV	22	1	0	1	0	38	0	0	15	6.7	.05
0 Days Rest	14	0	0	0	-6	24	0	0	7	0.0	.00
1 Days Rest	33	0	6	6	-2	41	0	0	30	0.0	.18
2 Days Rest	17	0	1	1	-2	31	0	0	10	0.0	.06
3+ Days Rest	12	3	2	5	7	13	0	0	8	37.5	.42

	G	A	Pts	PIM		G	A	Pts	PIM
1st Period	1	1	2	27	Winning	1	4	5	34
2nd Period	0	5	5	39	Losing	1	4	5	52
3rd Period	2	3	5	43	Tied	1	1	2	23
Overtime	0	0	0	0	Clutch	0	2	2	20
Last 5 Min	2	3	5	22	Blowouts	2	0	2	14

Garry Valk

Toronto Maple Leafs — Left Wing

1998-99 Season

	GP	G	A	Pts	+/–	PIM	PP	SH	S	SPct	P/G
Overall	77	8	21	29	8	53	1	0	93	8.6	.38
Home	39	3	10	13	-3	31	0	0	46	6.5	.33
Away	38	5	11	16	11	22	1	0	47	10.6	.42
vs. Division	19	1	3	4	1	20	0	0	20	5.0	.21
vs. Conference	53	5	15	20	6	34	0	0	60	8.3	.38
vs. Playoff	41	4	12	16	-4	23	1	0	47	8.5	.39
vs. Non-Playoff	36	4	9	13	12	30	0	0	46	8.7	.36
Pre All-Star	42	3	9	12	1	29	1	0	57	5.3	.29
Post All-Star	35	5	12	17	7	24	0	0	36	13.9	.49
Day	0	0	0	0	0	0	0	0	0	–	–
Night	77	8	21	29	8	53	1	0	93	8.6	.38

	GP	G	A	Pts	+/–	PIM	PP	SH	S	SPct	P/G
National TV	27	2	8	10	7	24	0	0	30	6.7	.37
0 Days Rest	16	2	5	7	1	8	0	0	20	10.0	.44
1 Days Rest	33	4	7	11	4	22	0	0	36	11.1	.33
2 Days Rest	13	1	5	6	2	12	1	0	19	5.3	.46
3+ Days Rest	15	1	4	5	1	11	0	0	18	5.6	.33

	G	A	Pts	PIM		G	A	Pts	PIM
1st Period	2	11	13	17	Winning	5	9	14	25
2nd Period	5	6	11	16	Losing	3	5	8	18
3rd Period	1	4	5	20	Tied	0	7	7	10
Overtime	0	0	0	0	Clutch	0	1	1	6
Last 5 Min	3	4	7	10	Blowouts	1	1	2	10

Shaun Van Allen

Ottawa Senators — Center

1998-99 Season

	GP	G	A	Pts	+/–	PIM	PP	SH	S	SPct	P/G
Overall	79	6	11	17	3	30	0	1	47	12.8	.22
Home	38	3	2	5	1	16	0	0	19	15.8	.13
Away	41	3	9	12	2	14	0	1	28	10.7	.29
vs. Division	19	0	1	1	-6	8	0	0	10	0.0	.05
vs. Conference	55	4	7	11	0	22	0	0	32	12.5	.20
vs. Playoff	45	2	6	8	-5	18	0	0	19	10.5	.18
vs. Non-Playoff	34	4	5	9	8	12	0	1	28	14.3	.26
Pre All-Star	42	4	3	7	-1	12	0	1	28	14.3	.17
Post All-Star	37	2	8	10	4	18	0	0	19	10.5	.27
Day	2	0	0	0	0	0	0	0	0	–	.00
Night	77	6	11	17	3	30	0	1	47	12.8	.22

	GP	G	A	Pts	+/–	PIM	PP	SH	S	SPct	P/G
National TV	11	1	2	3	1	4	0	0	9	11.1	.27
0 Days Rest	12	2	1	3	0	2	0	1	7	28.6	.25
1 Days Rest	42	2	3	5	-1	20	0	0	25	8.0	.12
2 Days Rest	14	1	4	5	1	2	0	0	6	16.7	.36
3+ Days Rest	11	1	3	4	3	6	0	0	9	11.1	.36

	G	A	Pts	PIM		G	A	Pts	PIM
1st Period	0	1	1	8	Winning	2	3	5	16
2nd Period	1	6	7	8	Losing	3	6	9	8
3rd Period	5	4	9	14	Tied	1	2	3	6
Overtime	0	0	0	0	Clutch	0	0	0	4
Last 5 Min	2	3	5	6	Blowouts	1	2	3	2

Darren Van Impe

Boston Bruins — Defense

1998-99 Season

	GP	G	A	Pts	+/–	PIM	PP	SH	S	SPct	P/G
Overall	60	5	15	20	-5	66	4	0	92	5.4	.33
Home	30	3	8	11	3	29	3	0	47	6.4	.37
Away	30	2	7	9	-8	37	1	0	45	4.4	.30
vs. Division	14	1	5	6	-1	2	1	0	24	4.2	.43
vs. Conference	43	4	11	15	-6	45	3	0	69	5.8	.35
vs. Playoff	33	4	6	10	-9	28	3	0	59	6.8	.30
vs. Non-Playoff	27	1	9	10	4	38	1	0	33	3.0	.37
Pre All-Star	39	5	12	17	-1	51	4	0	72	6.9	.44
Post All-Star	21	0	3	3	-4	15	0	0	20	0.0	.14
Day	12	0	3	3	-1	10	0	0	11	0.0	.25
Night	48	5	12	17	-4	56	4	0	81	6.2	.35

	GP	G	A	Pts	+/–	PIM	PP	SH	S	SPct	P/G
National TV	6	0	5	5	-1	9	0	0	8	0.0	.83
0 Days Rest	13	2	2	4	-1	10	1	0	14	14.3	.31
1 Days Rest	24	2	7	9	-7	36	2	0	41	4.9	.38
2 Days Rest	7	0	0	0	-2	4	0	0	13	0.0	.00
3+ Days Rest	16	1	6	7	5	16	1	0	24	4.2	.44

	G	A	Pts	PIM		G	A	Pts	PIM
1st Period	1	6	7	22	Winning	3	6	9	35
2nd Period	1	4	5	16	Losing	1	5	6	15
3rd Period	3	5	8	28	Tied	1	4	5	16
Overtime	0	0	0	0	Clutch	1	0	1	5
Last 5 Min	2	7	9	27	Blowouts	0	2	2	9

Vaclav Varada

Buffalo Sabres — Right Wing

1998-99 Season

	GP	G	A	Pts	+/–	PIM	PP	SH	S	SPct	P/G
Overall	72	7	24	31	11	61	1	0	123	5.7	.43
Home	34	3	15	18	12	29	1	0	60	5.0	.53
Away	38	4	9	13	-1	32	0	0	63	6.3	.34
vs. Division	18	2	6	8	4	16	0	0	26	7.7	.44
vs. Conference	53	4	18	22	9	51	1	0	89	4.5	.42
vs. Playoff	41	2	12	14	1	38	0	0	59	3.4	.34
vs. Non-Playoff	31	5	12	17	10	23	1	0	64	7.8	.55
Pre All-Star	43	7	12	19	4	41	1	0	65	10.8	.44
Post All-Star	29	0	12	12	7	20	0	0	58	0.0	.41
Day	5	0	1	1	-2	8	0	0	7	0.0	.20
Night	67	7	23	30	13	53	1	0	116	6.0	.45

	GP	G	A	Pts	+/–	PIM	PP	SH	S	SPct	P/G
National TV	13	2	5	7	4	8	0	0	30	6.7	.54
0 Days Rest	21	2	9	11	3	12	0	0	32	6.3	.52
1 Days Rest	21	2	6	8	6	21	0	0	26	7.7	.38
2 Days Rest	18	1	4	5	-2	16	1	0	38	2.6	.28
3+ Days Rest	12	2	5	7	4	12	0	0	27	7.4	.58

	G	A	Pts	PIM		G	A	Pts	PIM
1st Period	2	4	6	22	Winning	2	8	10	31
2nd Period	2	9	11	32	Losing	3	9	12	14
3rd Period	3	9	12	7	Tied	2	7	9	16
Overtime	0	2	2	0	Clutch	2	5	7	0
Last 5 Min	3	8	11	19	Blowouts	0	0	0	2

Pat Verbeek

Dallas Stars — Right Wing

1998-99 Season

	GP	G	A	Pts	+/–	PIM	PP	SH	S	SPct	P/G
Overall	78	17	17	34	11	133	8	0	134	12.7	.44
Home	40	12	13	25	8	90	7	0	70	17.1	.63
Away	38	5	4	9	3	43	1	0	64	7.8	.24
vs. Division	21	3	8	11	4	30	2	0	34	8.8	.52
vs. Conference	52	12	13	25	5	90	5	0	87	13.8	.48
vs. Playoff	44	11	12	23	4	81	4	0	81	13.6	.52
vs. Non-Playoff	34	6	5	11	7	52	4	0	53	11.3	.32
Pre All-Star	43	11	6	17	1	54	7	0	69	15.9	.40
Post All-Star	35	6	11	17	10	79	1	0	65	9.2	.49
Day	8	1	1	2	-1	21	0	0	14	7.1	.25
Night	70	16	16	32	12	112	8	0	120	13.3	.46

	GP	G	A	Pts	+/–	PIM	PP	SH	S	SPct	P/G
National TV	13	3	1	4	0	22	0	0	24	12.5	.31
0 Days Rest	14	1	2	3	1	30	0	0	21	4.8	.21
1 Days Rest	42	7	9	16	8	72	2	0	69	10.1	.38
2 Days Rest	11	7	3	10	3	17	4	0	29	24.1	.91
3+ Days Rest	11	2	3	5	-1	14	2	0	15	13.3	.45

	G	A	Pts	PIM		G	A	Pts	PIM
1st Period	8	7	15	47	Winning	9	6	15	92
2nd Period	6	5	11	41	Losing	3	3	6	33
3rd Period	3	5	8	43	Tied	5	8	13	8
Overtime	0	0	0	2	Clutch	1	1	2	8
Last 5 Min	5	2	7	71	Blowouts	0	0	0	11

Jan Vopat

Nashville Predators — Defense

1998-99 Season

	GP	G	A	Pts	+/–	PIM	PP	SH	S	SPct	P/G
Overall	55	5	6	11	0	28	0	0	46	10.9	.20
Home	24	3	2	5	4	12	0	0	17	17.6	.21
Away	31	2	4	6	-4	16	0	0	29	6.9	.19
vs. Division	12	1	2	3	-1	6	0	0	7	14.3	.25
vs. Conference	40	5	5	10	9	22	0	0	37	13.5	.25
vs. Playoff	33	2	3	5	-5	18	0	0	24	8.3	.15
vs. Non-Playoff	22	3	3	6	5	10	0	0	22	13.6	.27
Pre All-Star	33	5	3	8	5	14	0	0	34	14.7	.24
Post All-Star	22	0	3	3	-5	14	0	0	12	0.0	.14
Day	6	0	0	0	-2	2	0	0	5	0.0	.00
Night	49	5	6	11	2	26	0	0	41	12.2	.22

	GP	G	A	Pts	+/–	PIM	PP	SH	S	SPct	P/G
National TV	2	1	1	2	3	0	0	0	2	50.0	1.00
0 Days Rest	10	1	1	2	-3	0	0	0	10	10.0	.20
1 Days Rest	22	0	1	1	-4	16	0	0	9	0.0	.05
2 Days Rest	9	1	3	4	3	4	0	0	9	11.1	.44
3+ Days Rest	14	3	1	4	4	8	0	0	18	16.7	.29

	G	A	Pts	PIM		G	A	Pts	PIM
1st Period	1	0	1	16	Winning	0	0	0	12
2nd Period	3	0	3	4	Losing	2	6	8	8
3rd Period	1	6	7	8	Tied	3	0	3	8
Overtime	0	0	0	0	Clutch	1	0	1	0
Last 5 Min	0	1	1	4	Blowouts	0	3	3	0

Scott Walker

Nashville Predators — Right Wing

1998-99 Season

	GP	G	A	Pts	+/–	PIM	PP	SH	S	SPct	P/G
Overall	71	15	25	40	0	103	0	1	96	15.6	.56
Home	33	8	16	24	0	41	0	0	46	17.4	.73
Away	38	7	9	16	0	62	0	1	50	14.0	.42
vs. Division	16	5	5	10	-1	11	0	1	25	20.0	.63
vs. Conference	49	11	21	32	4	66	0	1	61	18.0	.65
vs. Playoff	43	9	13	22	0	51	0	0	60	15.0	.51
vs. Non-Playoff	28	6	12	18	0	52	0	1	36	16.7	.64
Pre All-Star	36	5	11	16	4	60	0	1	50	10.0	.44
Post All-Star	35	10	14	24	-4	43	0	0	46	21.7	.69
Day	7	1	4	5	3	8	0	0	8	12.5	.71
Night	64	14	21	35	-3	95	0	1	88	15.9	.55

	GP	G	A	Pts	+/–	PIM	PP	SH	S	SPct	P/G
National TV	2	0	1	1	1	6	0	0	1	0.0	.50
0 Days Rest	13	1	3	4	0	21	0	1	15	6.7	.31
1 Days Rest	31	6	11	17	-4	64	0	0	42	14.3	.55
2 Days Rest	14	4	6	10	1	6	0	0	22	18.2	.71
3+ Days Rest	13	4	5	9	3	12	0	0	17	23.5	.69

	G	A	Pts	PIM		G	A	Pts	PIM
1st Period	3	6	9	19	Winning	4	2	6	35
2nd Period	7	13	20	12	Losing	6	15	21	66
3rd Period	5	6	11	72	Tied	5	8	13	2
Overtime	0	0	0	0	Clutch	3	2	5	8
Last 5 Min	6	7	13	10	Blowouts	1	1	2	8

Aaron Ward

Detroit Red Wings — Defense

1998-99 Season

	GP	G	A	Pts	+/–	PIM	PP	SH	S	SPct	P/G
Overall	60	3	8	11	-5	52	0	0	46	6.5	.18
Home	26	0	4	4	-5	29	0	0	21	0.0	.15
Away	34	3	4	7	0	23	0	0	25	12.0	.21
vs. Division	12	0	2	2	-2	4	0	0	6	0.0	.17
vs. Conference	39	2	4	6	-5	38	0	0	27	7.4	.15
vs. Playoff	35	3	4	7	-1	20	0	0	26	11.5	.20
vs. Non-Playoff	25	0	4	4	-4	32	0	0	20	0.0	.16
Pre All-Star	24	2	1	3	-8	31	0	0	16	12.5	.13
Post All-Star	36	1	7	8	3	21	0	0	30	3.3	.22
Day	9	0	2	2	1	19	0	0	11	0.0	.22
Night	51	3	6	9	-6	33	0	0	35	8.6	.18

	GP	G	A	Pts	+/–	PIM	PP	SH	S	SPct	P/G
National TV	23	1	4	5	-3	15	0	0	17	5.9	.22
0 Days Rest	6	0	0	0	-2	2	0	0	4	0.0	.00
1 Days Rest	29	3	5	8	1	29	0	0	26	11.5	.28
2 Days Rest	15	0	3	3	-3	2	0	0	12	0.0	.20
3+ Days Rest	10	0	0	0	-1	19	0	0	4	0.0	.00

	G	A	Pts	PIM		G	A	Pts	PIM
1st Period	3	1	4	12	Winning	1	3	4	25
2nd Period	0	5	5	17	Losing	1	2	3	19
3rd Period	0	2	2	21	Tied	1	3	4	8
Overtime	0	0	0	2	Clutch	0	0	0	4
Last 5 Min	0	0	0	10	Blowouts	0	0	0	2

Dixon Ward

Buffalo Sabres — Right Wing

1998-99 Season

	GP	G	A	Pts	+/–	PIM	PP	SH	S	SPct	P/G
Overall	78	20	24	44	10	44	2	1	101	19.8	.56
Home	39	14	10	24	9	24	2	1	57	24.6	.62
Away	39	6	14	20	1	20	0	0	44	13.6	.51
vs. Division	19	6	11	17	9	8	0	1	21	28.6	.89
vs. Conference	53	15	18	33	14	30	0	1	68	22.1	.62
vs. Playoff	43	7	11	18	1	14	0	0	57	12.3	.42
vs. Non-Playoff	35	13	13	26	9	30	2	1	44	29.5	.74
Pre All-Star	42	13	16	29	7	24	2	1	50	26.0	.69
Post All-Star	36	7	8	15	3	20	0	0	51	13.7	.42
Day	6	1	1	2	-1	0	0	0	9	11.1	.33
Night	72	19	23	42	11	44	2	1	92	20.7	.58

	GP	G	A	Pts	+/–	PIM	PP	SH	S	SPct	P/G
National TV	14	1	6	7	3	12	0	0	10	10.0	.50
0 Days Rest	18	8	9	17	2	6	2	0	23	34.8	.94
1 Days Rest	30	4	6	10	4	14	0	0	37	10.8	.33
2 Days Rest	17	3	3	6	-1	2	0	0	27	11.1	.35
3+ Days Rest	13	5	6	11	5	22	0	1	14	35.7	.85

	G	A	Pts	PIM		G	A	Pts	PIM
1st Period	7	9	16	20	Winning	6	6	12	12
2nd Period	7	6	13	20	Losing	8	10	18	18
3rd Period	5	8	13	4	Tied	6	8	14	14
Overtime	1	1	2	0	Clutch	2	4	6	0
Last 5 Min	4	12	16	12	Blowouts	1	1	2	2

Todd Warriner

Toronto Maple Leafs — Left Wing

1998-99 Season

	GP	G	A	Pts	+/–	PIM	PP	SH	S	SPct	P/G
Overall	53	9	10	19	-6	28	1	0	96	9.4	.36
Home	26	3	3	6	-2	12	0	0	50	6.0	.23
Away	27	6	7	13	-4	16	1	0	46	13.0	.48
vs. Division	12	2	1	3	2	4	0	0	21	9.5	.25
vs. Conference	38	7	6	13	-10	14	1	0	70	10.0	.34
vs. Playoff	32	4	7	11	-3	20	0	0	54	7.4	.34
vs. Non-Playoff	21	5	3	8	-3	8	1	0	42	11.9	.38
Pre All-Star	21	5	7	12	2	10	1	0	46	10.9	.57
Post All-Star	32	4	3	7	-8	18	0	0	50	8.0	.22
Day	1	1	1	2	1	0	0	0	1	100.0	2.00
Night	52	8	9	17	-7	28	1	0	95	8.4	.33

	GP	G	A	Pts	+/–	PIM	PP	SH	S	SPct	P/G
National TV	17	3	3	6	-1	8	0	0	31	9.7	.35
0 Days Rest	12	2	2	4	-3	8	1	0	18	11.1	.33
1 Days Rest	19	1	3	4	-4	14	0	0	40	2.5	.21
2 Days Rest	9	4	3	7	2	2	0	0	19	21.1	.78
3+ Days Rest	13	2	2	4	-1	4	0	0	19	10.5	.31

	G	A	Pts	PIM		G	A	Pts	PIM
1st Period	4	2	6	14	Winning	5	2	7	14
2nd Period	3	5	8	6	Losing	1	4	5	8
3rd Period	2	3	5	8	Tied	3	4	7	6
Overtime	0	0	0	0	Clutch	0	1	1	0
Last 5 Min	2	1	3	8	Blowouts	0	0	0	4

Mike Watt

New York Islanders — Left Wing

1998-99 Season

	GP	G	A	Pts	+/–	PIM	PP	SH	S	SPct	P/G
Overall	75	8	17	25	-2	12	0	0	75	10.7	.33
Home	37	3	7	10	-7	6	0	0	36	8.3	.27
Away	38	5	10	15	5	6	0	0	39	12.8	.39
vs. Division	17	2	7	9	4	0	0	0	15	13.3	.53
vs. Conference	52	5	14	19	0	6	0	0	53	9.4	.37
vs. Playoff	46	5	9	14	-7	8	0	0	45	11.1	.30
vs. Non-Playoff	29	3	8	11	5	4	0	0	30	10.0	.38
Pre All-Star	42	5	11	16	1	6	0	0	41	12.2	.38
Post All-Star	33	3	6	9	-3	6	0	0	34	8.8	.27
Day	11	0	3	3	-1	2	0	0	3	0.0	.27
Night	64	8	14	22	-1	10	0	0	72	11.1	.34

	GP	G	A	Pts	+/–	PIM	PP	SH	S	SPct	P/G
National TV	5	0	0	0	1	2	0	0	4	0.0	.00
0 Days Rest	11	1	4	5	-2	0	0	0	11	9.1	.45
1 Days Rest	32	2	8	10	3	4	0	0	30	6.7	.31
2 Days Rest	19	2	3	5	-3	2	0	0	19	10.5	.26
3+ Days Rest	13	3	2	5	0	6	0	0	15	20.0	.38

	G	A	Pts	PIM		G	A	Pts	PIM
1st Period	2	0	2	0	Winning	3	6	9	4
2nd Period	4	11	15	6	Losing	0	8	8	8
3rd Period	2	6	8	6	Tied	5	3	8	0
Overtime	0	0	0	0	Clutch	0	1	1	0
Last 5 Min	0	1	1	6	Blowouts	0	0	0	2

Doug Weight

Edmonton Oilers — Center

1998-99 Season

	GP	G	A	Pts	+/–	PIM	PP	SH	S	SPct	P/G
Overall	43	6	31	37	-8	12	1	0	79	7.6	.86
Home	22	2	12	14	-5	4	1	0	42	4.8	.64
Away	21	4	19	23	-3	8	0	0	37	10.8	1.10
vs. Division	10	3	4	7	-1	2	1	0	27	11.1	.70
vs. Conference	29	6	20	26	-1	8	1	0	59	10.2	.90
vs. Playoff	26	3	24	27	-3	8	0	0	41	7.3	1.04
vs. Non-Playoff	17	3	7	10	-5	4	1	0	38	7.9	.59
Pre All-Star	6	0	7	7	-1	0	0	0	7	0.0	1.17
Post All-Star	37	6	24	30	-7	12	1	0	72	8.3	.81
Day	3	0	3	3	-3	0	0	0	4	0.0	1.00
Night	40	6	28	34	-5	12	1	0	75	8.0	.85

	GP	G	A	Pts	+/–	PIM	PP	SH	S	SPct	P/G
National TV	7	1	3	4	0	2	0	0	16	6.3	.57
0 Days Rest	7	1	3	4	-4	2	0	0	15	6.7	.57
1 Days Rest	20	3	19	22	0	10	0	0	30	10.0	1.10
2 Days Rest	8	1	3	4	-1	0	0	0	18	5.6	.50
3+ Days Rest	8	1	6	7	-3	0	1	0	16	6.3	.88

	G	A	Pts	PIM		G	A	Pts	PIM
1st Period	2	7	9	2	Winning	0	11	11	6
2nd Period	2	11	13	8	Losing	5	12	17	4
3rd Period	2	12	14	2	Tied	1	8	9	2
Overtime	0	1	1	0	Clutch	1	3	4	2
Last 5 Min	1	6	7	6	Blowouts	1	3	4	2

Eric Weinrich

Montreal Canadiens — Defense

1998-99 Season

	GP	G	A	Pts	+/–	PIM	PP	SH	S	SPct	P/G
Overall	80	7	15	22	-25	89	4	0	119	5.9	.28
Home	39	4	8	12	-9	39	2	0	61	6.6	.31
Away	41	3	7	10	-16	50	2	0	58	5.2	.24
vs. Division	17	2	1	3	-5	12	1	0	24	8.3	.18
vs. Conference	50	4	8	12	-10	52	1	0	75	5.3	.24
vs. Playoff	50	4	11	15	-20	51	2	0	68	5.9	.30
vs. Non-Playoff	30	3	4	7	-5	38	2	0	51	5.9	.23
Pre All-Star	44	4	9	13	-21	35	1	0	63	6.3	.30
Post All-Star	36	3	6	9	-4	54	3	0	56	5.4	.25
Day	3	0	1	1	-3	4	0	0	6	0.0	.33
Night	77	7	14	21	-22	85	4	0	113	6.2	.27

	GP	G	A	Pts	+/–	PIM	PP	SH	S	SPct	P/G
National TV	19	2	3	5	-2	33	1	0	23	8.7	.26
0 Days Rest	15	1	3	4	-5	26	1	0	20	5.0	.27
1 Days Rest	38	5	10	15	-11	44	3	0	60	8.3	.39
2 Days Rest	15	1	1	2	-4	8	0	0	20	5.0	.13
3+ Days Rest	12	0	1	1	-5	11	0	0	19	0.0	.08

	G	A	Pts	PIM		G	A	Pts	PIM
1st Period	4	4	8	26	Winning	1	1	2	23
2nd Period	3	8	11	24	Losing	3	9	12	60
3rd Period	0	3	3	39	Tied	3	5	8	6
Overtime	0	0	0	0	Clutch	0	0	0	9
Last 5 Min	3	5	8	18	Blowouts	0	2	2	30

Brad Werenka

Pittsburgh Penguins — Defense

1998-99 Season

	GP	G	A	Pts	+/–	PIM	PP	SH	S	SPct	P/G
Overall	81	6	18	24	17	93	1	0	77	7.8	.30
Home	41	3	15	18	12	43	0	0	41	7.3	.44
Away	40	3	3	6	5	50	1	0	36	8.3	.15
vs. Division	20	1	6	7	1	10	0	0	15	6.7	.35
vs. Conference	57	4	15	19	14	65	0	0	55	7.3	.33
vs. Playoff	44	3	7	10	4	39	0	0	37	8.1	.23
vs. Non-Playoff	37	3	11	14	13	54	1	0	40	7.5	.38
Pre All-Star	41	3	11	14	11	50	1	0	40	7.5	.34
Post All-Star	40	3	7	10	6	43	0	0	37	8.1	.25
Day	14	0	0	0	-1	20	0	0	14	0.0	.00
Night	67	6	18	24	18	73	1	0	63	9.5	.36

	GP	G	A	Pts	+/–	PIM	PP	SH	S	SPct	P/G
National TV	18	1	2	3	4	20	1	0	14	7.1	.17
0 Days Rest	14	1	3	4	-2	19	0	0	14	7.1	.29
1 Days Rest	35	3	8	11	12	48	1	0	31	9.7	.31
2 Days Rest	22	1	4	5	6	8	0	0	20	5.0	.23
3+ Days Rest	10	1	3	4	1	18	0	0	12	8.3	.40

	G	A	Pts	PIM		G	A	Pts	PIM
1st Period	3	5	8	24	Winning	2	8	10	63
2nd Period	1	7	8	32	Losing	1	5	6	16
3rd Period	2	6	8	37	Tied	3	5	8	14
Overtime	0	0	0	0	Clutch	0	3	3	0
Last 5 Min	2	8	10	36	Blowouts	0	0	0	17

Glen Wesley

Carolina Hurricanes — Defense

1998-99 Season

	GP	G	A	Pts	+/–	PIM	PP	SH	S	SPct	P/G
Overall	74	7	17	24	14	44	0	0	112	6.3	.32
Home	37	5	8	13	13	16	0	0	54	9.3	.35
Away	37	2	9	11	1	28	0	0	58	3.4	.30
vs. Division	13	4	0	4	3	14	0	0	21	19.0	.31
vs. Conference	52	5	11	16	9	36	0	0	80	6.3	.31
vs. Playoff	41	3	10	13	0	20	0	0	67	4.5	.32
vs. Non-Playoff	33	4	7	11	14	24	0	0	45	8.9	.33
Pre All-Star	45	4	10	14	12	20	0	0	69	5.8	.31
Post All-Star	29	3	7	10	2	24	0	0	43	7.0	.34
Day	6	0	2	2	4	4	0	0	8	0.0	.33
Night	68	7	15	22	10	40	0	0	104	6.7	.32

	GP	G	A	Pts	+/–	PIM	PP	SH	S	SPct	P/G
National TV	1	0	0	0	0	0	0	0	1	0.0	.00
0 Days Rest	16	0	4	4	4	8	0	0	27	0.0	.25
1 Days Rest	28	1	6	7	-1	18	0	0	42	2.4	.25
2 Days Rest	21	2	5	7	5	8	0	0	30	6.7	.33
3+ Days Rest	9	4	2	6	6	10	0	0	13	30.8	.67

	G	A	Pts	PIM
1st Period	3	8	11	20
2nd Period	1	5	6	16
3rd Period	3	3	6	8
Overtime	0	1	1	0
Last 5 Min	2	6	8	18

	G	A	Pts	PIM
Winning	0	3	3	24
Losing	2	3	5	14
Tied	5	11	16	6
Clutch	2	3	5	0
Blowouts	0	0	0	0

Todd White

Chicago Blackhawks — Center

1998-99 Season

	GP	G	A	Pts	+/–	PIM	PP	SH	S	SPct	P/G
Overall	35	5	8	13	-1	20	2	0	43	11.6	.37
Home	15	3	3	6	2	4	1	0	18	16.7	.40
Away	20	2	5	7	-3	16	1	0	25	8.0	.35
vs. Division	8	2	1	3	0	2	0	0	13	15.4	.38
vs. Conference	24	3	5	8	3	8	0	0	31	9.7	.33
vs. Playoff	22	4	3	7	-4	16	2	0	30	13.3	.32
vs. Non-Playoff	13	1	5	6	3	4	0	0	13	7.7	.46
Pre All-Star	18	4	3	7	0	10	1	0	21	19.0	.39
Post All-Star	17	1	5	6	-1	10	1	0	22	4.5	.35
Day	3	0	1	1	-2	2	0	0	8	0.0	.33
Night	32	5	7	12	1	18	2	0	35	14.3	.38

	GP	G	A	Pts	+/–	PIM	PP	SH	S	SPct	P/G
National TV	9	1	2	3	-3	12	0	0	13	7.7	.33
0 Days Rest	4	1	1	2	1	4	0	0	5	20.0	.50
1 Days Rest	22	3	4	7	-5	10	2	0	30	10.0	.32
2 Days Rest	3	0	0	0	-2	6	0	0	3	0.0	.00
3+ Days Rest	6	1	3	4	5	0	0	0	5	20.0	.67

	G	A	Pts	PIM
1st Period	0	2	2	8
2nd Period	4	3	7	4
3rd Period	1	3	4	8
Overtime	0	0	0	0
Last 5 Min	1	3	4	8

	G	A	Pts	PIM
Winning	0	0	0	4
Losing	4	7	11	14
Tied	1	1	2	2
Clutch	0	0	0	2
Blowouts	1	1	2	4

Ray Whitney

Florida Panthers — Center

1998-99 Season

	GP	G	A	Pts	+/–	PIM	PP	SH	S	SPct	P/G
Overall	81	26	38	64	-3	18	7	0	193	13.5	.79
Home	41	14	22	36	3	10	3	0	104	13.5	.88
Away	40	12	16	28	-6	8	4	0	89	13.5	.70
vs. Division	14	4	4	8	1	2	0	0	39	10.3	.57
vs. Conference	57	17	24	41	-4	10	3	0	129	13.2	.72
vs. Playoff	49	16	23	39	-7	10	4	0	116	13.8	.80
vs. Non-Playoff	32	10	15	25	4	8	3	0	77	13.0	.78
Pre All-Star	43	14	19	33	2	8	4	0	89	15.7	.77
Post All-Star	38	12	19	31	-5	10	3	0	104	11.5	.82
Day	4	2	2	4	1	0	0	0	7	28.6	1.00
Night	77	24	36	60	-4	18	7	0	186	12.9	.78

	GP	G	A	Pts	+/–	PIM	PP	SH	S	SPct	P/G
National TV	4	0	1	1	-7	0	0	0	11	0.0	.25
0 Days Rest	18	7	7	14	-4	6	2	0	44	15.9	.78
1 Days Rest	33	9	19	28	3	8	1	0	63	14.3	.85
2 Days Rest	16	5	5	10	1	2	1	0	54	9.3	.63
3+ Days Rest	14	5	7	12	-3	2	3	0	32	15.6	.86

	G	A	Pts	PIM
1st Period	2	13	15	6
2nd Period	6	13	19	6
3rd Period	18	12	30	6
Overtime	0	0	0	0
Last 5 Min	2	4	6	2

	G	A	Pts	PIM
Winning	12	14	26	10
Losing	9	12	21	4
Tied	5	12	17	4
Clutch	4	0	4	2
Blowouts	0	3	3	6

Jason Wiemer

Calgary Flames — Center

1998-99 Season

	GP	G	A	Pts	+/–	PIM	PP	SH	S	SPct	P/G
Overall	78	8	13	21	-12	177	1	0	128	6.3	.27
Home	38	4	9	13	-1	80	0	0	71	5.6	.34
Away	40	4	4	8	-11	97	1	0	57	7.0	.20
vs. Division	16	1	2	3	-2	20	1	0	21	4.8	.19
vs. Conference	52	6	11	17	-2	106	1	0	85	7.1	.33
vs. Playoff	47	6	9	15	-2	123	1	0	82	7.3	.32
vs. Non-Playoff	31	2	4	6	-10	54	0	0	46	4.3	.19
Pre All-Star	46	5	10	15	-6	133	0	0	75	6.7	.33
Post All-Star	32	3	3	6	-6	44	1	0	53	5.7	.19
Day	4	0	1	1	-2	16	0	0	3	0.0	.25
Night	74	8	12	20	-10	161	1	0	125	6.4	.27

	GP	G	A	Pts	+/–	PIM	PP	SH	S	SPct	P/G
National TV	11	0	2	2	-3	38	0	0	22	0.0	.18
0 Days Rest	16	0	2	2	-7	21	0	0	17	0.0	.13
1 Days Rest	36	3	7	10	-3	93	1	0	61	4.9	.28
2 Days Rest	14	3	1	4	-4	32	0	0	27	11.1	.29
3+ Days Rest	12	2	3	5	2	31	0	0	23	8.7	.42

	G	A	Pts	PIM
1st Period	4	6	10	39
2nd Period	2	3	5	63
3rd Period	2	4	6	73
Overtime	0	0	0	2
Last 5 Min	3	2	5	45

	G	A	Pts	PIM
Winning	2	5	7	48
Losing	3	2	5	121
Tied	3	6	9	8
Clutch	1	1	2	12
Blowouts	0	1	1	29

Clarke Wilm

Calgary Flames — Center

1998-99 Season

	GP	G	A	Pts	+/-	PIM	PP	SH	S	SPct	P/G
Overall	78	10	8	18	11	53	2	2	94	10.6	.23
Home	38	4	2	6	9	21	1	0	42	9.5	.16
Away	40	6	6	12	2	32	1	2	52	11.5	.30
vs. Division	18	5	3	8	9	13	1	1	24	20.8	.44
vs. Conference	53	6	6	12	13	39	1	1	64	9.4	.23
vs. Playoff	50	8	6	14	5	24	2	2	62	12.9	.28
vs. Non-Playoff	28	2	2	4	6	29	0	0	32	6.3	.14
Pre All-Star	43	6	4	10	4	38	1	2	49	12.2	.23
Post All-Star	35	4	4	8	7	15	1	0	45	8.9	.23
Day	4	0	1	1	1	4	0	0	6	0.0	.25
Night	74	10	7	17	10	49	2	2	88	11.4	.23

	GP	G	A	Pts	+/-	PIM	PP	SH	S	SPct	P/G
National TV	12	2	1	3	-3	7	2	0	9	22.2	.25
0 Days Rest	16	4	4	8	3	17	0	0	19	21.1	.50
1 Days Rest	35	4	3	7	2	16	2	1	49	8.2	.20
2 Days Rest	13	2	1	3	1	11	0	1	15	13.3	.23
3+ Days Rest	14	0	0	0	5	9	0	0	11	0.0	.00

	G	A	Pts	PIM		G	A	Pts	PIM
1st Period	2	3	5	23	Winning	3	2	5	20
2nd Period	3	2	5	10	Losing	4	3	7	25
3rd Period	5	3	8	18	Tied	3	3	6	8
Overtime	0	0	0	2	Clutch	0	0	0	2
Last 5 Min	0	1	1	19	Blowouts	0	0	0	0

Jason Woolley

Buffalo Sabres — Defense

1998-99 Season

	GP	G	A	Pts	+/-	PIM	PP	SH	S	SPct	P/G
Overall	80	10	33	43	16	62	4	0	154	6.5	.54
Home	40	5	19	24	12	28	1	0	74	6.8	.60
Away	40	5	14	19	4	34	3	0	80	6.3	.48
vs. Division	19	1	9	10	11	16	0	0	40	2.5	.53
vs. Conference	55	7	20	27	12	46	3	0	112	6.3	.49
vs. Playoff	45	6	18	24	8	42	2	0	86	7.0	.53
vs. Non-Playoff	35	4	15	19	8	20	2	0	68	5.9	.54
Pre All-Star	43	3	19	22	14	44	1	0	97	3.1	.51
Post All-Star	37	7	14	21	2	18	3	0	57	12.3	.57
Day	5	0	0	0	0	4	0	0	9	0.0	.00
Night	75	10	33	43	16	58	4	0	145	6.9	.57

	GP	G	A	Pts	+/-	PIM	PP	SH	S	SPct	P/G
National TV	15	1	6	7	3	16	0	0	28	3.6	.47
0 Days Rest	20	1	7	8	0	18	1	0	35	2.9	.40
1 Days Rest	28	3	12	15	7	12	1	0	58	5.2	.54
2 Days Rest	19	5	7	12	4	22	2	0	38	13.2	.63
3+ Days Rest	13	1	7	8	5	10	0	0	23	4.3	.62

	G	A	Pts	PIM		G	A	Pts	PIM
1st Period	4	14	18	24	Winning	4	9	13	24
2nd Period	4	11	15	20	Losing	4	12	16	14
3rd Period	2	8	10	14	Tied	2	12	14	24
Overtime	0	0	0	4	Clutch	1	4	5	6
Last 5 Min	5	8	13	22	Blowouts	0	2	2	2

Vitali Yachmenev

Nashville Predators — Right Wing

1998-99 Season

	GP	G	A	Pts	+/-	PIM	PP	SH	S	SPct	P/G
Overall	55	7	10	17	-10	10	0	1	83	8.4	.31
Home	29	6	5	11	-1	10	0	0	56	10.7	.38
Away	26	1	5	6	-9	0	0	1	27	3.7	.23
vs. Division	11	2	4	6	-1	2	0	0	14	14.3	.55
vs. Conference	35	5	8	13	-5	8	0	0	52	9.6	.37
vs. Playoff	34	3	5	8	-12	6	0	0	46	6.5	.24
vs. Non-Playoff	21	4	5	9	2	4	0	1	37	10.8	.43
Pre All-Star	28	5	7	12	-4	10	0	0	42	11.9	.43
Post All-Star	27	2	3	5	-6	0	0	1	41	4.9	.19
Day	8	0	2	2	-2	0	0	0	11	0.0	.25
Night	47	7	8	15	-8	10	0	1	72	9.7	.32

	GP	G	A	Pts	+/-	PIM	PP	SH	S	SPct	P/G
National TV	1	0	0	0	-2	0	0	0	1	0.0	.00
0 Days Rest	8	1	3	4	1	6	0	0	16	6.3	.50
1 Days Rest	30	3	5	8	-9	0	0	1	46	6.5	.27
2 Days Rest	8	2	2	4	1	0	0	0	12	16.7	.50
3+ Days Rest	9	1	0	1	-3	4	0	0	9	11.1	.11

	G	A	Pts	PIM		G	A	Pts	PIM
1st Period	1	1	2	6	Winning	2	3	5	8
2nd Period	3	5	8	2	Losing	2	4	6	2
3rd Period	3	4	7	2	Tied	3	3	6	0
Overtime	0	0	0	0	Clutch	1	1	2	0
Last 5 Min	1	0	1	4	Blowouts	1	0	1	0

Terry Yake

St. Louis Blues — Right Wing

1998-99 Season

	GP	G	A	Pts	+/-	PIM	PP	SH	S	SPct	P/G
Overall	60	9	18	27	-9	34	3	0	59	15.3	.45
Home	30	3	8	11	-3	10	1	0	27	11.1	.37
Away	30	6	10	16	-6	24	2	0	32	18.8	.53
vs. Division	11	1	3	4	-4	10	0	0	9	11.1	.36
vs. Conference	38	4	11	15	-5	26	1	0	35	11.4	.39
vs. Playoff	32	5	11	16	-9	18	3	0	33	15.2	.50
vs. Non-Playoff	28	4	7	11	0	16	0	0	26	15.4	.39
Pre All-Star	21	4	9	13	-4	12	3	0	21	19.0	.62
Post All-Star	39	5	9	14	-5	22	0	0	38	13.2	.36
Day	9	2	2	4	0	8	0	0	12	16.7	.44
Night	51	7	16	23	-9	26	3	0	47	14.9	.45

	GP	G	A	Pts	+/-	PIM	PP	SH	S	SPct	P/G
National TV	15	2	5	7	-3	10	1	0	18	11.1	.47
0 Days Rest	6	2	3	5	-2	2	1	0	10	20.0	.83
1 Days Rest	36	5	9	14	-7	24	1	0	29	17.2	.39
2 Days Rest	12	0	3	3	1	4	0	0	9	0.0	.25
3+ Days Rest	6	2	3	5	-1	4	1	0	11	18.2	.83

	G	A	Pts	PIM		G	A	Pts	PIM
1st Period	2	6	8	12	Winning	3	7	10	12
2nd Period	1	9	10	12	Losing	3	6	9	20
3rd Period	6	3	9	10	Tied	3	5	8	2
Overtime	0	0	0	0	Clutch	3	0	3	2
Last 5 Min	4	8	12	8	Blowouts	1	1	2	2

Alexei Yashin

Ottawa Senators — Center

1998-99 Season

	GP	G	A	Pts	+/–	PIM	PP	SH	S	SPct	P/G
Overall	82	44	50	94	16	54	19	0	337	13.1	1.15
Home	41	25	23	48	4	36	12	0	166	15.1	1.17
Away	41	19	27	46	12	18	7	0	171	11.1	1.12
vs. Division	20	10	6	16	3	12	5	0	85	11.8	.80
vs. Conference	57	35	37	72	16	30	14	0	235	14.9	1.26
vs. Playoff	47	18	24	42	0	30	10	0	187	9.6	.89
vs. Non-Playoff	35	26	26	52	16	24	9	0	150	17.3	1.49
Pre All-Star	45	20	33	53	21	26	6	0	184	10.9	1.18
Post All-Star	37	24	17	41	-5	28	13	0	153	15.7	1.11
Day	3	3	2	5	1	0	2	0	13	23.1	1.67
Night	79	41	48	89	15	54	17	0	324	12.7	1.13

	GP	G	A	Pts	+/–	PIM	PP	SH	S	SPct	P/G
National TV	11	10	4	14	5	4	6	0	47	21.3	1.27
0 Days Rest	13	7	12	19	5	2	2	0	50	14.0	1.46
1 Days Rest	43	27	25	52	10	28	11	0	186	14.5	1.21
2 Days Rest	16	7	7	14	4	16	4	0	61	11.5	.88
3+ Days Rest	10	3	6	9	-3	8	2	0	40	7.5	.90

	G	A	Pts	PIM
1st Period	15	18	33	12
2nd Period	12	17	29	22
3rd Period	17	14	31	20
Overtime	0	1	1	0
Last 5 Min	11	20	31	12

	G	A	Pts	PIM
Winning	23	17	40	32
Losing	9	14	23	12
Tied	12	19	31	10
Clutch	4	6	10	4
Blowouts	3	3	6	8

Stephane Yelle

Colorado Avalanche — Center

1998-99 Season

	GP	G	A	Pts	+/–	PIM	PP	SH	S	SPct	P/G
Overall	72	8	7	15	-8	40	1	0	99	8.1	.21
Home	38	5	2	7	-2	22	0	0	51	9.8	.18
Away	34	3	5	8	-6	18	1	0	48	6.3	.24
vs. Division	17	0	2	2	-4	0	0	0	32	0.0	.12
vs. Conference	49	5	2	7	-5	18	1	0	70	7.1	.14
vs. Playoff	39	3	4	7	-2	24	0	0	41	7.3	.18
vs. Non-Playoff	33	5	3	8	-6	16	1	0	58	8.6	.24
Pre All-Star	36	5	2	7	-6	22	1	0	62	8.1	.19
Post All-Star	36	3	5	8	-2	18	0	0	37	8.1	.22
Day	13	0	0	0	0	4	0	0	11	0.0	.00
Night	59	8	7	15	-8	36	1	0	88	9.1	.25

	GP	G	A	Pts	+/–	PIM	PP	SH	S	SPct	P/G
National TV	19	3	1	4	3	12	0	0	20	15.0	.21
0 Days Rest	10	3	3	6	-1	8	1	0	16	18.8	.60
1 Days Rest	39	3	2	5	-6	22	0	0	52	5.8	.13
2 Days Rest	10	2	2	4	1	2	0	0	12	16.7	.40
3+ Days Rest	13	0	0	0	-2	8	0	0	19	0.0	.00

	G	A	Pts	PIM
1st Period	1	2	3	10
2nd Period	5	2	7	16
3rd Period	2	3	5	14
Overtime	0	0	0	0
Last 5 Min	2	2	4	14

	G	A	Pts	PIM
Winning	4	4	8	16
Losing	2	2	4	14
Tied	2	1	3	10
Clutch	2	1	3	0
Blowouts	0	0	0	2

Juha Ylonen

Phoenix Coyotes — Center

1998-99 Season

	GP	G	A	Pts	+/–	PIM	PP	SH	S	SPct	P/G
Overall	59	6	17	23	18	20	2	0	66	9.1	.39
Home	32	1	13	14	16	8	0	0	28	3.6	.44
Away	27	5	4	9	2	12	2	0	38	13.2	.33
vs. Division	19	1	5	6	4	4	0	0	22	4.5	.32
vs. Conference	41	4	11	15	12	14	2	0	45	8.9	.37
vs. Playoff	35	3	12	15	11	12	1	0	35	8.6	.43
vs. Non-Playoff	24	3	5	8	7	8	1	0	31	9.7	.33
Pre All-Star	42	4	11	15	14	18	2	0	49	8.2	.36
Post All-Star	17	2	6	8	4	2	0	0	17	11.8	.47
Day	5	2	1	3	5	2	0	0	8	25.0	.60
Night	54	4	16	20	13	18	2	0	58	6.9	.37

	GP	G	A	Pts	+/–	PIM	PP	SH	S	SPct	P/G
National TV	11	0	7	7	8	6	0	0	13	0.0	.64
0 Days Rest	9	1	5	6	0	2	1	0	11	9.1	.67
1 Days Rest	26	3	6	9	10	12	1	0	29	10.3	.35
2 Days Rest	12	2	1	3	4	4	0	0	19	10.5	.25
3+ Days Rest	12	0	5	5	4	2	0	0	7	0.0	.42

	G	A	Pts	PIM
1st Period	2	5	7	4
2nd Period	3	4	7	10
3rd Period	1	7	8	6
Overtime	0	1	1	0
Last 5 Min	0	6	6	2

	G	A	Pts	PIM
Winning	2	8	10	10
Losing	1	4	5	6
Tied	3	5	8	4
Clutch	1	2	3	2
Blowouts	0	2	2	2

Harry York

Vancouver Canucks — Center

1998-99 Season

	GP	G	A	Pts	+/–	PIM	PP	SH	S	SPct	P/G
Overall	56	7	9	16	-3	24	1	0	60	11.7	.29
Home	28	4	3	7	0	12	1	0	30	13.3	.25
Away	28	3	6	9	-3	12	0	0	30	10.0	.32
vs. Division	14	2	2	4	1	0	1	0	18	11.1	.29
vs. Conference	42	6	5	11	-1	18	1	0	38	15.8	.26
vs. Playoff	34	5	6	11	-4	16	1	0	36	13.9	.32
vs. Non-Playoff	22	2	3	5	1	8	0	0	24	8.3	.23
Pre All-Star	26	5	5	10	1	8	1	0	27	18.5	.38
Post All-Star	30	2	4	6	-4	16	0	0	33	6.1	.20
Day	2	0	0	0	-1	2	0	0	1	0.0	.00
Night	54	7	9	16	-2	22	1	0	59	11.9	.30

	GP	G	A	Pts	+/–	PIM	PP	SH	S	SPct	P/G
National TV	18	1	2	3	-3	10	0	0	14	7.1	.17
0 Days Rest	9	0	1	1	-4	2	0	0	10	0.0	.11
1 Days Rest	28	4	6	10	-3	14	1	0	34	11.8	.36
2 Days Rest	8	2	2	4	3	4	0	0	8	25.0	.50
3+ Days Rest	11	1	0	1	1	4	0	0	8	12.5	.09

	G	A	Pts	PIM
1st Period	2	4	6	10
2nd Period	1	3	4	10
3rd Period	4	2	6	4
Overtime	0	0	0	0
Last 5 Min	4	0	4	4

	G	A	Pts	PIM
Winning	2	0	2	6
Losing	4	3	7	16
Tied	1	6	7	2
Clutch	2	0	2	2
Blowouts	0	1	1	8

Jason York

Ottawa Senators — Defense

1998-99 Season

	GP	G	A	Pts	+/-	PIM	PP	SH	S	SPct	P/G
Overall	79	4	31	35	17	48	2	0	177	2.3	.44
Home	40	1	19	20	13	28	1	0	100	1.0	.50
Away	39	3	12	15	4	20	1	0	77	3.9	.38
vs. Division	20	0	2	2	2	16	0	0	43	0.0	.10
vs. Conference	57	3	18	21	10	34	1	0	133	2.3	.37
vs. Playoff	45	2	15	17	-3	38	0	0	102	2.0	.38
vs. Non-Playoff	34	2	16	18	20	10	2	0	75	2.7	.53
Pre All-Star	42	4	18	22	13	18	2	0	82	4.9	.52
Post All-Star	37	0	13	13	4	30	0	0	95	0.0	.35
Day	3	0	2	2	0	0	0	0	6	0.0	.67
Night	76	4	29	33	17	48	2	0	171	2.3	.43

	GP	G	A	Pts	+/-	PIM	PP	SH	S	SPct	P/G
National TV	11	1	7	8	4	4	1	0	35	2.9	.73
0 Days Rest	12	3	6	9	13	12	2	0	22	13.6	.75
1 Days Rest	43	1	16	17	2	18	0	0	103	1.0	.40
2 Days Rest	16	0	6	6	2	14	0	0	28	0.0	.38
3+ Days Rest	8	0	3	3	0	4	0	0	24	0.0	.38

	G	A	Pts	PIM		G	A	Pts	PIM
1st Period	1	13	14	24	Winning	1	10	11	24
2nd Period	1	7	8	16	Losing	2	9	11	6
3rd Period	2	11	13	8	Tied	1	12	13	18
Overtime	0	0	0	0	Clutch	0	2	2	2
Last 5 Min	2	10	12	12	Blowouts	0	3	3	6

Scott Young

St. Louis Blues — Right Wing

1998-99 Season

	GP	G	A	Pts	+/-	PIM	PP	SH	S	SPct	P/G
Overall	75	24	28	52	8	27	8	0	205	11.7	.69
Home	38	10	14	24	4	23	3	0	96	10.4	.63
Away	37	14	14	28	4	4	5	0	109	12.8	.76
vs. Division	16	5	11	16	7	4	2	0	48	10.4	1.00
vs. Conference	52	19	22	41	3	19	7	0	148	12.8	.79
vs. Playoff	43	10	13	23	-2	12	5	0	109	9.2	.53
vs. Non-Playoff	32	14	15	29	10	15	3	0	96	14.6	.91
Pre All-Star	40	7	13	20	4	10	3	0	112	6.3	.50
Post All-Star	35	17	15	32	4	17	5	0	93	18.3	.91
Day	9	4	3	7	-4	11	0	0	30	13.3	.78
Night	66	20	25	45	12	16	8	0	175	11.4	.68

	GP	G	A	Pts	+/-	PIM	PP	SH	S	SPct	P/G
National TV	15	5	5	10	-3	4	2	0	38	13.2	.67
0 Days Rest	11	5	4	9	0	6	2	0	27	18.5	.82
1 Days Rest	36	10	16	26	6	17	3	0	95	10.5	.72
2 Days Rest	16	6	4	10	-2	4	2	0	52	11.5	.63
3+ Days Rest	12	3	4	7	4	0	1	0	31	9.7	.58

	G	A	Pts	PIM		G	A	Pts	PIM
1st Period	4	17	21	11	Winning	10	7	17	19
2nd Period	10	7	17	6	Losing	4	5	9	8
3rd Period	10	4	14	8	Tied	10	16	26	0
Overtime	0	0	0	2	Clutch	4	3	7	4
Last 5 Min	8	10	18	17	Blowouts	1	0	1	11

Dimitri Yushkevich

Toronto Maple Leafs — Defense

1998-99 Season

	GP	G	A	Pts	+/-	PIM	PP	SH	S	SPct	P/G
Overall	78	6	22	28	25	88	2	1	95	6.3	.36
Home	37	4	10	14	13	34	1	1	50	8.0	.38
Away	41	2	12	14	12	54	1	0	45	4.4	.34
vs. Division	19	1	1	2	2	12	1	0	31	3.2	.11
vs. Conference	53	4	14	18	16	32	1	0	70	5.7	.34
vs. Playoff	44	1	7	8	7	52	0	0	53	1.9	.18
vs. Non-Playoff	34	5	15	20	18	36	2	1	42	11.9	.59
Pre All-Star	42	5	14	19	14	68	2	1	61	8.2	.45
Post All-Star	36	1	8	9	11	20	0	0	34	2.9	.25
Day	1	1	0	1	0	2	0	0	1	100.0	1.00
Night	77	5	22	27	25	86	2	1	94	5.3	.35

	GP	G	A	Pts	+/-	PIM	PP	SH	S	SPct	P/G
National TV	25	3	4	7	9	18	1	0	32	9.4	.28
0 Days Rest	17	0	7	7	11	32	0	0	22	0.0	.41
1 Days Rest	34	4	9	13	12	34	0	1	42	9.5	.38
2 Days Rest	12	1	3	4	1	10	1	0	12	8.3	.33
3+ Days Rest	15	1	3	4	1	12	1	0	19	5.3	.27

	G	A	Pts	PIM		G	A	Pts	PIM
1st Period	0	7	7	16	Winning	3	10	13	78
2nd Period	2	8	10	46	Losing	1	5	6	8
3rd Period	4	6	10	26	Tied	2	7	9	2
Overtime	0	1	1	0	Clutch	2	3	5	0
Last 5 Min	1	8	9	16	Blowouts	1	4	5	20

Steve Yzerman

Detroit Red Wings — Center

1998-99 Season

	GP	G	A	Pts	+/-	PIM	PP	SH	S	SPct	P/G
Overall	80	29	45	74	8	42	13	2	231	12.6	.93
Home	41	12	31	43	15	14	6	0	104	11.5	1.05
Away	39	17	14	31	-7	28	7	2	127	13.4	.79
vs. Division	16	5	15	20	10	0	1	0	46	10.9	1.25
vs. Conference	52	22	30	52	14	8	9	1	160	13.8	1.00
vs. Playoff	47	17	21	38	-9	38	10	1	128	13.3	.81
vs. Non-Playoff	33	12	24	36	17	4	3	1	103	11.7	1.09
Pre All-Star	46	19	28	47	13	38	8	1	144	13.2	1.02
Post All-Star	34	10	17	27	-5	4	5	1	87	11.5	.79
Day	13	4	8	12	-2	0	2	1	34	11.8	.92
Night	67	25	37	62	10	42	11	1	197	12.7	.93

	GP	G	A	Pts	+/-	PIM	PP	SH	S	SPct	P/G
National TV	29	9	17	26	-4	2	4	1	81	11.1	.90
0 Days Rest	12	7	3	10	-1	24	2	1	38	18.4	.83
1 Days Rest	39	14	21	35	0	12	7	1	112	12.5	.90
2 Days Rest	23	6	18	24	4	2	3	0	66	9.1	1.04
3+ Days Rest	6	2	3	5	5	4	1	0	15	13.3	.83

	G	A	Pts	PIM		G	A	Pts	PIM
1st Period	11	18	29	6	Winning	12	21	33	6
2nd Period	10	13	23	4	Losing	8	9	17	34
3rd Period	8	13	21	32	Tied	9	15	24	2
Overtime	0	1	1	0	Clutch	3	5	8	0
Last 5 Min	8	15	23	36	Blowouts	2	2	4	8

Rob Zamuner

Tampa Bay Lightning — Left Wing

1998-99 Season

	GP	G	A	Pts	+/–	PIM	PP	SH	S	SPct	P/G
Overall	58	8	11	19	-15	24	1	1	89	9.0	.33
Home	30	5	5	10	-5	8	0	1	53	9.4	.33
Away	28	3	6	9	-10	16	1	0	36	8.3	.32
vs. Division	12	3	5	8	-4	6	1	0	18	16.7	.67
vs. Conference	43	7	7	14	-9	18	1	1	65	10.8	.33
vs. Playoff	37	5	4	9	-13	20	0	1	57	8.8	.24
vs. Non-Playoff	21	3	7	10	-2	4	1	0	32	9.4	.48
Pre All-Star	24	3	3	6	1	12	0	0	39	7.7	.25
Post All-Star	34	5	8	13	-16	12	1	1	50	10.0	.38
Day	5	0	2	2	-1	2	0	0	6	0.0	.40
Night	53	8	9	17	-14	22	1	1	83	9.6	.32

	GP	G	A	Pts	+/–	PIM	PP	SH	S	SPct	P/G
National TV	0	0	0	0	0	0	0	0	0	–	–
0 Days Rest	11	1	2	3	-8	6	1	0	21	4.8	.27
1 Days Rest	23	3	7	10	0	6	0	1	39	7.7	.43
2 Days Rest	14	3	1	4	-3	8	0	0	20	15.0	.29
3+ Days Rest	10	1	1	2	-4	4	0	0	9	11.1	.20

	G	A	Pts	PIM		G	A	Pts	PIM
1st Period	1	2	3	10	Winning	4	2	6	8
2nd Period	4	5	9	8	Losing	2	8	10	10
3rd Period	3	4	7	6	Tied	2	1	3	6
Overtime	0	0	0	0	Clutch	0	1	1	0
Last 5 Min	1	4	5	8	Blowouts	1	0	1	2

Richard Zednik

Washington Capitals — Left Wing

1998-99 Season

	GP	G	A	Pts	+/–	PIM	PP	SH	S	SPct	P/G
Overall	49	9	8	17	-6	50	1	0	115	7.8	.35
Home	25	6	2	8	2	30	1	0	51	11.8	.32
Away	24	3	6	9	-8	20	0	0	64	4.7	.38
vs. Division	9	2	4	6	3	10	0	0	27	7.4	.67
vs. Conference	30	6	6	12	-1	36	0	0	73	8.2	.40
vs. Playoff	31	7	5	12	-6	32	1	0	66	10.6	.39
vs. Non-Playoff	18	2	3	5	0	18	0	0	49	4.1	.28
Pre All-Star	15	3	2	5	-4	28	1	0	34	8.8	.33
Post All-Star	34	6	6	12	-2	22	0	0	81	7.4	.35
Day	2	0	1	1	1	2	0	0	3	0.0	.50
Night	47	9	7	16	-7	48	1	0	112	8.0	.34

	GP	G	A	Pts	+/–	PIM	PP	SH	S	SPct	P/G
National TV	7	2	0	2	3	4	0	0	14	14.3	.29
0 Days Rest	7	2	1	3	-2	2	0	0	18	11.1	.43
1 Days Rest	23	4	3	7	0	16	0	0	54	7.4	.30
2 Days Rest	10	0	1	1	-4	10	0	0	19	0.0	.10
3+ Days Rest	9	3	3	6	0	22	1	0	24	12.5	.67

	G	A	Pts	PIM		G	A	Pts	PIM
1st Period	2	4	6	16	Winning	1	3	4	34
2nd Period	3	3	6	16	Losing	5	1	6	14
3rd Period	4	1	5	18	Tied	3	4	7	2
Overtime	0	0	0	0	Clutch	0	0	0	0
Last 5 Min	1	7	8	8	Blowouts	1	1	2	4

Valeri Zelepukin

Philadelphia Flyers — Left Wing

1998-99 Season

	GP	G	A	Pts	+/–	PIM	PP	SH	S	SPct	P/G
Overall	74	16	9	25	0	48	0	0	129	12.4	.34
Home	39	7	6	13	-2	29	0	0	69	10.1	.33
Away	35	9	3	12	2	19	0	0	60	15.0	.34
vs. Division	17	4	2	6	2	6	0	0	31	12.9	.35
vs. Conference	49	9	7	16	1	28	0	0	83	10.8	.33
vs. Playoff	43	6	4	10	-8	25	0	0	65	9.2	.23
vs. Non-Playoff	31	10	5	15	8	23	0	0	64	15.6	.48
Pre All-Star	36	7	5	12	6	19	0	0	62	11.3	.33
Post All-Star	38	9	4	13	-6	29	0	0	67	13.4	.34
Day	15	3	2	5	-4	6	0	0	28	10.7	.33
Night	59	13	7	20	4	42	0	0	101	12.9	.34

	GP	G	A	Pts	+/–	PIM	PP	SH	S	SPct	P/G
National TV	18	3	2	5	-7	12	0	0	36	8.3	.28
0 Days Rest	11	2	1	3	2	15	0	0	20	10.0	.27
1 Days Rest	37	10	4	14	-4	14	0	0	71	14.1	.38
2 Days Rest	14	2	1	3	-1	19	0	0	18	11.1	.21
3+ Days Rest	12	2	3	5	3	0	0	0	20	10.0	.42

	G	A	Pts	PIM		G	A	Pts	PIM
1st Period	3	3	6	19	Winning	4	1	5	21
2nd Period	5	3	8	19	Losing	5	3	8	6
3rd Period	7	3	10	8	Tied	7	5	12	21
Overtime	1	0	1	2	Clutch	1	0	1	2
Last 5 Min	3	1	4	8	Blowouts	0	1	1	8

Peter Zezel

Vancouver Canucks — Center

1998-99 Season

	GP	G	A	Pts	+/–	PIM	PP	SH	S	SPct	P/G
Overall	41	6	8	14	5	16	1	0	45	13.3	.34
Home	20	4	4	8	6	10	1	0	20	20.0	.40
Away	21	2	4	6	-1	6	0	0	25	8.0	.29
vs. Division	11	2	1	3	3	6	0	0	13	15.4	.27
vs. Conference	28	6	5	11	8	16	1	0	33	18.2	.39
vs. Playoff	25	2	5	7	3	10	0	0	29	6.9	.28
vs. Non-Playoff	16	4	3	7	2	6	1	0	16	25.0	.44
Pre All-Star	35	6	7	13	4	16	1	0	43	14.0	.37
Post All-Star	6	0	1	1	1	0	0	0	2	0.0	.17
Day	1	2	1	3	1	2	1	0	5	40.0	3.00
Night	40	4	7	11	4	14	0	0	40	10.0	.28

	GP	G	A	Pts	+/–	PIM	PP	SH	S	SPct	P/G
National TV	10	0	2	2	0	2	0	0	6	0.0	.20
0 Days Rest	5	2	1	3	5	4	0	0	8	25.0	.60
1 Days Rest	19	1	3	4	-4	4	0	0	16	6.3	.21
2 Days Rest	12	1	2	3	2	4	0	0	15	6.7	.25
3+ Days Rest	5	2	2	4	2	4	1	0	6	33.3	.80

	G	A	Pts	PIM		G	A	Pts	PIM
1st Period	1	1	2	6	Winning	1	2	3	12
2nd Period	3	2	5	8	Losing	3	5	8	4
3rd Period	2	5	7	2	Tied	2	1	3	0
Overtime	0	0	0	0	Clutch	1	1	2	0
Last 5 Min	1	1	2	4	Blowouts	0	1	1	4

Alexei Zhamnov

Chicago Blackhawks — Center

1998-99 Season																						
	GP	G	A	Pts	+/–	PIM	PP	SH	S	SPct	P/G		GP	G	A	Pts	+/–	PIM	PP	SH	S	SPct	P/G
Overall	76	20	41	61	-10	50	8	1	200	10.0	.80	National TV	14	4	7	11	0	24	2	0	35	11.4	.79
Home	37	11	22	33	7	16	5	1	99	11.1	.89	0 Days Rest	13	3	5	8	0	4	1	0	36	8.3	.62
Away	39	9	19	28	-17	34	3	0	101	8.9	.72	1 Days Rest	37	6	20	26	-16	34	3	0	103	5.8	.70
vs. Division	17	5	11	16	-2	24	2	0	50	10.0	.94	2 Days Rest	13	7	12	19	6	8	3	0	34	20.6	1.46
vs. Conference	52	14	27	41	-8	44	5	1	143	9.8	.79	3+ Days Rest	13	4	4	8	0	4	1	1	27	14.8	.62
vs. Playoff	46	9	21	30	-14	38	4	1	109	8.3	.65		G	A	Pts	PIM		G	A	Pts	PIM			
vs. Non-Playoff	30	11	20	31	4	12	4	0	91	12.1	1.03	1st Period	7	11	18	10	Winning	4	4	8	12			
Pre All-Star	43	9	22	31	-12	20	4	1	119	7.6	.72	2nd Period	6	13	19	16	Losing	8	19	27	32			
Post All-Star	33	11	19	30	2	30	4	0	81	13.6	.91	3rd Period	7	17	24	24	Tied	8	18	26	6			
Day	10	3	10	13	3	8	1	0	27	11.1	1.30	Overtime	0	0	0	0	Clutch	4	5	9	2			
Night	66	17	31	48	-13	42	7	1	173	9.8	.73	Last 5 Min	5	16	21	8	Blowouts	2	1	3	4			

Alexei Zhitnik

Buffalo Sabres — Defense

1998-99 Season																						
	GP	G	A	Pts	+/–	PIM	PP	SH	S	SPct	P/G		GP	G	A	Pts	+/–	PIM	PP	SH	S	SPct	P/G
Overall	81	7	26	33	-6	96	3	1	185	3.8	.41	National TV	15	2	5	7	0	16	0	1	33	6.1	.47
Home	41	3	9	12	0	30	2	0	81	3.7	.29	0 Days Rest	20	4	6	10	-4	24	2	1	61	6.6	.50
Away	40	4	17	21	-6	66	1	1	104	3.8	.53	1 Days Rest	30	3	12	15	5	38	1	0	61	4.9	.50
vs. Division	20	3	5	8	-1	20	1	1	40	7.5	.40	2 Days Rest	19	0	5	5	-6	24	0	0	42	0.0	.26
vs. Conference	56	4	14	18	-4	66	2	1	118	3.4	.32	3+ Days Rest	12	0	3	3	-1	10	0	0	21	0.0	.25
vs. Playoff	47	5	16	21	-7	48	2	1	110	4.5	.45		G	A	Pts	PIM		G	A	Pts	PIM			
vs. Non-Playoff	34	2	10	12	1	48	1	0	75	2.7	.35	1st Period	3	8	11	28	Winning	3	6	9	46			
Pre All-Star	42	5	14	19	-11	60	2	1	102	4.9	.45	2nd Period	0	10	10	44	Losing	1	11	12	26			
Post All-Star	39	2	12	14	5	36	1	0	83	2.4	.36	3rd Period	4	8	12	22	Tied	3	9	12	24			
Day	6	1	2	3	-4	4	1	0	10	10.0	.50	Overtime	0	0	0	2	Clutch	0	3	3	8			
Night	75	6	24	30	-2	92	2	1	175	3.4	.40	Last 5 Min	2	6	8	22	Blowouts	0	2	2	12			

Sergei Zholtok

Montreal Canadiens — Center

1998-99 Season																						
	GP	G	A	Pts	+/–	PIM	PP	SH	S	SPct	P/G		GP	G	A	Pts	+/–	PIM	PP	SH	S	SPct	P/G
Overall	70	7	15	22	-12	6	2	0	102	6.9	.31	National TV	22	2	3	5	-6	2	2	0	28	7.1	.23
Home	35	2	6	8	-9	4	1	0	55	3.6	.23	0 Days Rest	13	2	3	5	-4	0	1	0	14	14.3	.38
Away	35	5	9	14	-3	2	1	0	47	10.6	.40	1 Days Rest	29	2	5	7	-8	4	1	0	41	4.9	.24
vs. Division	18	1	4	5	-4	0	1	0	21	4.8	.28	2 Days Rest	16	3	2	5	1	2	0	0	24	12.5	.31
vs. Conference	49	4	12	16	-7	4	2	0	59	6.8	.33	3+ Days Rest	12	0	5	5	-1	0	0	0	23	0.0	.42
vs. Playoff	41	6	7	13	-8	2	2	0	57	10.5	.32		G	A	Pts	PIM		G	A	Pts	PIM			
vs. Non-Playoff	29	1	8	9	-4	4	0	0	45	2.2	.31	1st Period	2	5	7	2	Winning	2	3	5	4			
Pre All-Star	37	3	4	7	-9	6	0	0	46	6.5	.19	2nd Period	4	6	10	2	Losing	1	6	7	2			
Post All-Star	33	4	11	15	-3	0	2	0	56	7.1	.45	3rd Period	1	4	5	2	Tied	4	6	10	0			
Day	2	0	0	0	0	0	0	0	1	0.0	.00	Overtime	0	0	0	0	Clutch	0	1	1	0			
Night	68	7	15	22	-12	6	2	0	101	6.9	.32	Last 5 Min	1	5	6	2	Blowouts	0	0	0	0			

Doug Zmolek

Chicago Blackhawks — Defense

1998-99 Season																						
	GP	G	A	Pts	+/–	PIM	PP	SH	S	SPct	P/G		GP	G	A	Pts	+/–	PIM	PP	SH	S	SPct	P/G
Overall	62	0	14	14	1	102	0	0	33	0.0	.23	National TV	10	0	2	2	-5	4	0	0	5	0.0	.20
Home	33	0	4	4	2	26	0	0	20	0.0	.12	0 Days Rest	11	0	1	1	0	21	0	0	3	0.0	.09
Away	29	0	10	10	-1	76	0	0	13	0.0	.34	1 Days Rest	24	0	10	10	0	34	0	0	19	0.0	.42
vs. Division	11	0	5	5	3	11	0	0	6	0.0	.45	2 Days Rest	10	0	1	1	0	7	0	0	3	0.0	.10
vs. Conference	37	0	10	10	5	57	0	0	17	0.0	.27	3+ Days Rest	17	0	2	2	1	40	0	0	8	0.0	.12
vs. Playoff	41	0	12	12	-1	82	0	0	25	0.0	.29		G	A	Pts	PIM		G	A	Pts	PIM			
vs. Non-Playoff	21	0	2	2	2	20	0	0	8	0.0	.10	1st Period	0	1	1	29	Winning	0	3	3	57			
Pre All-Star	36	0	9	9	3	61	0	0	20	0.0	.25	2nd Period	0	6	6	60	Losing	0	9	9	38			
Post All-Star	26	0	5	5	-2	41	0	0	13	0.0	.19	3rd Period	0	7	7	13	Tied	0	2	2	7			
Day	8	0	1	1	1	18	0	0	4	0.0	.13	Overtime	0	0	0	0	Clutch	0	2	2	0			
Night	54	0	13	13	0	84	0	0	29	0.0	.24	Last 5 Min	0	5	5	19	Blowouts	0	5	5	31			

Sergei Zubov

Dallas Stars — Defense

1998-99 Season

	GP	G	A	Pts	+/–	PIM	PP	SH	S	SPct	P/G
Overall	81	10	41	51	9	20	5	0	155	6.5	.63
Home	41	4	29	33	11	8	2	0	85	4.7	.80
Away	40	6	12	18	-2	12	3	0	70	8.6	.45
vs. Division	23	3	14	17	3	6	2	0	41	7.3	.74
vs. Conference	55	5	31	36	6	18	4	0	103	4.9	.65
vs. Playoff	47	7	30	37	4	12	4	0	85	8.2	.79
vs. Non-Playoff	34	3	11	14	5	8	1	0	70	4.3	.41
Pre All-Star	43	6	17	23	-2	10	3	0	82	7.3	.53
Post All-Star	38	4	24	28	11	10	2	0	73	5.5	.74
Day	9	0	6	6	-2	2	0	0	17	0.0	.67
Night	72	10	35	45	11	18	5	0	138	7.2	.63

	GP	G	A	Pts	+/–	PIM	PP	SH	S	SPct	P/G
National TV	14	2	5	7	-3	2	1	0	28	7.1	.50
0 Days Rest	14	3	2	5	3	6	1	0	29	10.3	.36
1 Days Rest	44	5	24	29	8	10	3	0	88	5.7	.66
2 Days Rest	12	2	9	11	1	0	1	0	21	9.5	.92
3+ Days Rest	11	0	6	6	-3	4	0	0	17	0.0	.55

	G	A	Pts	PIM
1st Period	0	14	14	4
2nd Period	9	17	26	12
3rd Period	1	9	10	4
Overtime	0	1	1	0
Last 5 Min	3	13	16	2

	G	A	Pts	PIM
Winning	6	16	22	14
Losing	3	8	11	4
Tied	1	17	18	2
Clutch	0	2	2	0
Blowouts	0	1	1	4

Dainius Zubrus

Montreal Canadiens — Right Wing

1998-99 Season

	GP	G	A	Pts	+/–	PIM	PP	SH	S	SPct	P/G
Overall	80	6	10	16	-8	29	0	1	80	7.5	.20
Home	41	1	4	5	-8	12	0	0	43	2.3	.12
Away	39	5	6	11	0	17	0	1	37	13.5	.28
vs. Division	19	3	2	5	2	10	0	0	15	20.0	.26
vs. Conference	56	3	6	9	-7	27	0	0	52	5.8	.16
vs. Playoff	43	3	4	7	-4	21	0	0	38	7.9	.16
vs. Non-Playoff	37	3	6	9	-4	8	0	1	42	7.1	.24
Pre All-Star	44	3	4	7	-3	23	0	1	36	8.3	.16
Post All-Star	36	3	6	9	-5	6	0	0	44	6.8	.25
Day	8	0	0	0	-4	2	0	0	8	0.0	.00
Night	72	6	10	16	-4	27	0	1	72	8.3	.22

	GP	G	A	Pts	+/–	PIM	PP	SH	S	SPct	P/G
National TV	13	2	2	4	2	2	0	1	9	22.2	.31
0 Days Rest	11	1	2	3	-1	2	0	1	8	12.5	.27
1 Days Rest	40	1	4	5	-5	12	0	0	35	2.9	.13
2 Days Rest	16	2	3	5	2	6	0	0	18	11.1	.31
3+ Days Rest	13	2	1	3	-4	9	0	0	19	10.5	.23

	G	A	Pts	PIM
1st Period	2	2	4	10
2nd Period	3	5	8	4
3rd Period	1	3	4	15
Overtime	0	0	0	0
Last 5 Min	1	1	2	6

	G	A	Pts	PIM
Winning	0	2	2	14
Losing	3	1	4	11
Tied	3	7	10	4
Clutch	0	1	1	2
Blowouts	0	0	0	0

Goalie Profiles

The following section provides statistical breakdowns for goaltenders who played a minimum of 1,000 minutes in 1998-99.

Explanations of the abbreviations used can be found in the Glossary.

Tom Barrasso

Pittsburgh Penguins — Goaltender

1998-99 Season																					
	G	Min	GAA	W	L	T	ShO	GA	SA	SvPct		G	Min	GAA	W	L	T	ShO	GA	SA	SvPct
Overall	43	2306	2.55	19	16	3	4	98	993	.901	National TV	11	652	2.67	5	6	0	1	29	292	.901
Home	19	914	1.97	9	3	2	3	30	394	.924	Day	5	279	2.15	3	2	0	1	10	138	.928
Away	24	1391	2.93	10	13	1	1	68	599	.886	Night	38	2026	2.61	16	14	3	3	88	855	.897
vs. Division	11	587	3.17	3	6	1	0	31	248	.875	Start	43	2306	2.55	19	16	3	4	98	993	.901
vs. Conference	30	1568	2.53	12	12	2	3	66	648	.898	Non Start	0	0	–	0	0	0	0	0	0	–
vs. Playoff	20	1115	2.69	7	10	2	1	50	487	.897	0 Days Rest	7	418	2.15	4	3	0	1	15	200	.925
vs. Non-Playoff	23	1191	2.42	12	6	1	3	48	506	.905	1 Days Rest	14	702	2.56	5	6	1	0	30	303	.901
Pre All-Star	28	1551	2.51	13	10	3	2	65	646	.899	2 Days Rest	9	451	2.53	3	2	2	1	19	181	.895
Post All-Star	15	754	2.63	6	6	0	2	33	347	.905	3+ Days Rest	13	733	2.78	7	5	0	2	34	309	.890

Ed Belfour

Dallas Stars — Goaltender

1998-99 Season																					
	G	Min	GAA	W	L	T	ShO	GA	SA	SvPct		G	Min	GAA	W	L	T	ShO	GA	SA	SvPct
Overall	61	3536	1.99	35	15	9	5	117	1373	.915	National TV	10	572	1.89	3	4	2	1	18	195	.908
Home	34	1959	1.96	23	7	3	4	64	686	.907	Day	6	357	1.68	1	3	1	1	10	118	.915
Away	27	1576	2.02	12	8	6	1	53	687	.923	Night	55	3178	2.02	34	12	8	4	107	1255	.915
vs. Division	18	1047	1.78	12	4	1	3	31	409	.924	Start	59	3490	1.96	35	14	9	5	114	1354	.916
vs. Conference	41	2402	2.02	24	10	5	4	81	924	.912	Non Start	2	45	4.00	0	1	0	0	3	19	.842
vs. Playoff	38	2145	2.01	22	10	5	2	72	836	.914	0 Days Rest	2	77	1.56	1	0	0	0	2	36	.944
vs. Non-Playoff	23	1390	1.94	13	5	4	3	45	537	.916	1 Days Rest	27	1554	1.85	14	6	6	3	48	618	.922
Pre All-Star	34	1904	2.05	20	8	5	3	65	720	.910	2 Days Rest	16	969	2.23	9	5	2	0	36	385	.906
Post All-Star	27	1630	1.91	15	7	4	2	52	653	.920	3+ Days Rest	16	933	1.99	11	4	1	2	31	334	.907

Craig Billington

Colorado Avalanche — Goaltender

1998-99 Season																					
	G	Min	GAA	W	L	T	ShO	GA	SA	SvPct		G	Min	GAA	W	L	T	ShO	GA	SA	SvPct
Overall	21	1086	2.87	11	8	1	0	52	492	.894	National TV	4	237	2.53	2	2	0	0	10	108	.907
Home	6	283	4.03	1	3	1	0	19	124	.847	Day	2	119	3.03	1	1	0	0	6	55	.891
Away	15	801	2.47	10	5	0	0	33	368	.910	Night	19	965	2.86	10	7	1	0	46	437	.895
vs. Division	5	304	3.36	2	2	1	0	17	132	.871	Start	18	1050	2.97	9	8	1	0	52	481	.892
vs. Conference	14	740	2.76	7	5	1	0	34	327	.896	Non Start	3	35	0.00	2	0	0	0	0	11	1.000
vs. Playoff	12	611	2.65	6	5	0	0	27	279	.903	0 Days Rest	1	60	1.00	1	0	0	0	1	31	.968
vs. Non-Playoff	9	474	3.16	5	3	1	0	25	213	.883	1 Days Rest	6	266	3.61	3	3	0	0	16	124	.871
Pre All-Star	14	702	2.99	7	6	0	0	35	308	.886	2 Days Rest	0	0	–	0	0	0	0	0	0	–
Post All-Star	7	383	2.66	4	2	1	0	17	184	.908	3+ Days Rest	14	759	2.77	7	5	1	0	35	337	.896

Fred Brathwaite

Calgary Flames — Goaltender

1998-99 Season																					
	G	Min	GAA	W	L	T	ShO	GA	SA	SvPct		G	Min	GAA	W	L	T	ShO	GA	SA	SvPct
Overall	28	1663	2.45	11	9	7	1	68	796	.915	National TV	4	238	1.76	2	2	0	0	7	110	.936
Home	14	859	2.10	6	4	4	1	30	406	.926	Day	1	58	2.07	0	1	0	0	2	35	.943
Away	14	803	2.84	5	5	3	0	38	390	.903	Night	27	1604	2.47	11	8	7	1	66	761	.913
vs. Division	6	355	2.37	3	3	0	0	14	163	.914	Start	28	1663	2.45	11	9	7	1	68	796	.915
vs. Conference	22	1296	2.45	8	7	6	1	53	624	.915	Non Start	0	0	–	0	0	0	0	0	0	–
vs. Playoff	16	928	2.46	6	5	4	1	38	437	.913	0 Days Rest	3	184	1.96	1	1	1	0	6	86	.930
vs. Non-Playoff	12	734	2.45	5	4	3	0	30	359	.916	1 Days Rest	12	739	2.44	4	4	4	0	30	352	.915
Pre All-Star	7	422	1.99	3	3	1	1	14	218	.936	2 Days Rest	4	188	2.55	2	1	0	0	8	103	.922
Post All-Star	21	1240	2.61	8	6	6	0	54	578	.907	3+ Days Rest	9	550	2.62	4	3	2	1	24	255	.906

Martin Brodeur

New Jersey Devils — Goaltender

1998-99 Season																					
	G	Min	GAA	W	L	T	ShO	GA	SA	SvPct		G	Min	GAA	W	L	T	ShO	GA	SA	SvPct
Overall	70	4239	2.29	39	21	10	4	162	1728	.906	National TV	7	420	2.00	3	3	1	0	14	166	.916
Home	33	2011	2.39	14	12	7	2	80	757	.894	Day	10	605	2.28	6	3	1	0	23	239	.904
Away	37	2227	2.21	25	9	3	2	82	971	.916	Night	60	3633	2.30	33	18	9	4	139	1489	.907
vs. Division	16	965	2.67	11	4	1	0	43	393	.891	Start	70	4238	2.29	39	21	10	4	162	1728	.906
vs. Conference	50	3032	2.28	28	14	8	4	115	1247	.908	Non Start	0	0	–	0	0	0	0	0	0	–
vs. Playoff	39	2362	2.64	20	13	6	1	104	1001	.896	0 Days Rest	9	537	2.35	6	3	0	0	21	232	.909
vs. Non-Playoff	31	1876	1.86	19	8	4	3	58	727	.920	1 Days Rest	24	1455	2.31	17	4	3	1	56	600	.907
Pre All-Star	38	2301	2.48	21	12	5	2	95	951	.900	2 Days Rest	23	1400	2.23	7	10	6	2	52	555	.906
Post All-Star	32	1936	2.08	18	9	5	2	67	777	.914	3+ Days Rest	14	845	2.34	9	4	1	1	33	341	.903

Sean Burke

Florida Panthers — Goaltender

1998-99 Season																					
	G	Min	GAA	W	L	T	ShO	GA	SA	SvPct		G	Min	GAA	W	L	T	ShO	GA	SA	SvPct
Overall	59	3402	2.66	21	24	14	3	151	1624	.907	National TV	3	149	5.64	0	3	0	0	14	81	.827
Home	31	1772	2.61	14	11	6	2	77	861	.911	Day	3	183	2.62	1	1	1	0	8	91	.912
Away	28	1629	2.73	7	13	8	1	74	763	.903	Night	56	3218	2.67	20	23	13	3	143	1533	.907
vs. Division	12	738	2.11	5	3	4	1	26	323	.920	Start	58	3353	2.68	21	23	14	3	150	1610	.907
vs. Conference	40	2349	2.81	14	17	9	2	110	1138	.903	Non Start	1	48	1.25	0	1	0	0	1	14	.929
vs. Playoff	34	1900	3.25	7	16	11	1	103	970	.894	0 Days Rest	7	392	2.91	2	4	1	1	19	199	.905
vs. Non-Playoff	25	1501	1.92	14	8	3	2	48	654	.927	1 Days Rest	15	874	1.92	9	4	2	2	28	435	.936
Pre All-Star	31	1826	2.50	13	9	9	1	76	831	.909	2 Days Rest	16	936	2.69	3	8	5	0	42	434	.903
Post All-Star	28	1574	2.86	8	15	5	2	75	793	.905	3+ Days Rest	21	1198	3.11	7	8	6	0	62	556	.888

Dan Cloutier

New York Rangers — Goaltender

1998-99 Season																					
	G	Min	GAA	W	L	T	ShO	GA	SA	SvPct		G	Min	GAA	W	L	T	ShO	GA	SA	SvPct
Overall	22	1097	2.68	6	8	3	0	49	570	.914	National TV	8	383	2.19	2	3	1	0	14	191	.927
Home	7	351	1.88	2	2	0	0	11	181	.939	Day	4	228	2.11	2	1	0	0	8	103	.922
Away	15	745	3.06	4	6	3	0	38	389	.902	Night	18	868	2.83	4	7	3	0	41	467	.912
vs. Division	5	276	2.39	2	2	0	0	11	137	.920	Start	16	887	2.77	6	7	2	0	41	454	.910
vs. Conference	14	703	2.82	4	6	2	0	33	360	.908	Non Start	6	208	2.31	0	1	1	0	8	116	.931
vs. Playoff	13	642	2.43	1	5	3	0	26	334	.922	0 Days Rest	1	60	4.00	1	0	0	0	4	33	.879
vs. Non-Playoff	9	454	3.04	5	3	0	0	23	236	.903	1 Days Rest	3	179	2.01	1	1	1	0	6	110	.945
Pre All-Star	12	591	2.34	3	4	2	0	23	300	.923	2 Days Rest	2	65	3.69	1	0	0	0	4	31	.871
Post All-Star	10	504	3.10	3	4	1	0	26	270	.904	3+ Days Rest	16	792	2.65	3	7	2	0	35	396	.912

Byron Dafoe

Boston Bruins — Goaltender

1998-99 Season																					
	G	Min	GAA	W	L	T	ShO	GA	SA	SvPct		G	Min	GAA	W	L	T	ShO	GA	SA	SvPct
Overall	68	4001	1.99	32	23	11	10	133	1800	.926	National TV	8	397	2.27	4	2	1	1	15	156	.904
Home	37	2214	1.76	19	9	8	5	65	991	.934	Day	12	698	1.12	7	1	3	4	13	278	.953
Away	31	1786	2.28	13	14	3	5	68	809	.916	Night	56	3302	2.18	25	22	8	6	120	1522	.921
vs. Division	20	1166	1.90	11	7	2	2	37	518	.929	Start	67	3981	2.00	32	23	11	10	133	1790	.926
vs. Conference	48	2818	2.02	25	15	7	8	95	1273	.925	Non Start	1	19	0.00	0	0	0	0	0	10	1.000
vs. Playoff	39	2319	1.86	18	15	6	6	72	1050	.931	0 Days Rest	8	487	1.97	3	3	2	0	16	201	.920
vs. Non-Playoff	29	1681	2.18	14	8	5	4	61	750	.919	1 Days Rest	29	1664	1.84	16	9	3	7	51	765	.933
Pre All-Star	35	2033	2.07	15	13	6	4	70	954	.927	2 Days Rest	14	812	2.00	6	5	2	2	27	361	.925
Post All-Star	33	1967	1.92	17	10	5	6	63	846	.926	3+ Days Rest	17	1036	2.26	7	6	4	1	39	473	.918

Mike Dunham

Nashville Predators — Goaltender

1998-99 Season																					
	G	Min	GAA	W	L	T	ShO	GA	SA	SvPct		G	Min	GAA	W	L	T	ShO	GA	SA	SvPct
Overall	44	2472	3.08	16	23	3	1	127	1387	.908	National TV	1	39	4.62	0	0	0	0	3	15	.800
Home	23	1284	3.27	9	12	1	0	70	708	.901	Day	3	142	2.54	2	1	0	0	6	67	.910
Away	21	1187	2.88	7	11	2	1	57	679	.916	Night	41	2329	3.12	14	22	3	1	121	1320	.908
vs. Division	10	556	4.10	2	8	0	0	38	349	.891	Start	43	2432	3.11	15	23	3	1	126	1373	.908
vs. Conference	31	1779	3.17	12	16	2	0	94	1003	.906	Non Start	1	40	1.50	1	0	0	0	1	14	.929
vs. Playoff	22	1286	3.22	7	13	2	0	69	765	.910	0 Days Rest	1	59	3.05	0	1	0	0	3	34	.912
vs. Non-Playoff	22	1185	2.94	9	10	1	1	58	622	.907	1 Days Rest	18	1021	3.17	7	10	1	0	54	570	.905
Pre All-Star	22	1220	2.90	10	10	1	0	59	665	.911	2 Days Rest	7	365	3.45	2	4	0	0	21	228	.908
Post All-Star	22	1251	3.26	6	13	2	1	68	722	.906	3+ Days Rest	18	1026	2.87	7	8	2	1	49	555	.912

Bob Essensa

Edmonton Oilers — Goaltender

1998-99 Season																					
	G	Min	GAA	W	L	T	ShO	GA	SA	SvPct		G	Min	GAA	W	L	T	ShO	GA	SA	SvPct
Overall	39	2091	2.75	12	14	6	0	96	974	.901	National TV	5	243	2.47	1	2	1	0	10	100	.900
Home	19	996	3.01	7	6	2	0	50	439	.886	Day	1	58	6.21	0	1	0	0	6	31	.806
Away	20	1094	2.52	5	8	4	0	46	535	.914	Night	38	2032	2.66	12	13	6	0	90	943	.905
vs. Division	7	395	2.89	3	4	0	0	19	177	.893	Start	33	1854	2.85	12	12	6	0	88	879	.900
vs. Conference	28	1463	3.16	8	12	3	0	77	683	.887	Non Start	6	236	2.03	0	2	0	0	8	95	.916
vs. Playoff	25	1327	3.26	6	10	5	0	72	659	.891	0 Days Rest	1	30	2.00	0	0	0	0	1	13	.923
vs. Non-Playoff	14	763	1.89	6	4	1	0	24	315	.924	1 Days Rest	11	647	2.60	5	3	2	0	28	269	.896
Pre All-Star	22	1155	2.44	8	6	4	0	47	503	.907	2 Days Rest	8	458	2.49	3	4	0	0	19	235	.919
Post All-Star	17	935	3.14	4	8	2	0	49	471	.896	3+ Days Rest	19	954	3.02	4	7	4	0	48	457	.895

Stephane Fiset

Los Angeles Kings — Goaltender

1998-99 Season	G	Min	GAA	W	L	T	ShO	GA	SA	SvPct		G	Min	GAA	W	L	T	ShO	GA	SA	SvPct
Overall	42	2403	2.60	18	21	1	3	104	1217	.915	National TV	14	776	2.47	5	7	1	2	32	421	.924
Home	22	1291	2.32	12	7	1	2	50	631	.921	Day	4	173	4.16	0	3	0	0	12	96	.875
Away	20	1111	2.92	6	14	0	1	54	586	.908	Night	38	2229	2.48	18	18	1	3	92	1121	.918
vs. Division	13	724	2.73	3	10	0	1	33	348	.905	Start	41	2347	2.53	18	20	1	3	99	1189	.917
vs. Conference	32	1828	2.76	11	18	1	2	84	933	.910	Non Start	1	54	5.56	0	1	0	0	5	28	.821
vs. Playoff	32	1805	2.69	11	18	1	2	81	900	.910	0 Days Rest	3	180	2.00	2	1	0	1	6	109	.945
vs. Non-Playoff	10	597	2.31	7	3	0	1	23	317	.927	1 Days Rest	11	626	2.88	4	5	0	1	30	335	.910
Pre All-Star	13	743	2.26	5	6	1	1	28	376	.926	2 Days Rest	15	851	2.89	6	9	0	1	41	394	.896
Post All-Star	29	1659	2.75	13	15	0	2	76	841	.910	3+ Days Rest	13	743	2.18	6	6	1	0	27	379	.929

Mark Fitzpatrick

Chicago Blackhawks — Goaltender

1998-99 Season	G	Min	GAA	W	L	T	ShO	GA	SA	SvPct		G	Min	GAA	W	L	T	ShO	GA	SA	SvPct
Overall	27	1403	2.74	6	8	6	0	64	682	.906	National TV	3	156	2.31	1	1	0	0	6	78	.923
Home	9	422	2.56	2	2	2	0	18	190	.905	Day	5	285	2.74	1	1	2	0	13	150	.913
Away	18	980	2.82	4	6	4	0	46	492	.907	Night	22	1117	2.74	5	7	4	0	51	532	.904
vs. Division	8	440	2.05	4	2	1	0	15	228	.934	Start	21	1224	2.75	5	8	6	0	56	612	.908
vs. Conference	15	809	2.82	4	5	3	0	38	398	.905	Non Start	6	178	2.70	1	0	0	0	8	70	.886
vs. Playoff	17	875	2.81	2	6	4	0	41	438	.906	0 Days Rest	2	124	1.45	1	0	1	0	3	68	.956
vs. Non-Playoff	10	527	2.62	4	2	2	0	23	244	.906	1 Days Rest	6	299	2.61	1	2	1	0	13	136	.904
Pre All-Star	16	847	2.62	3	6	4	0	37	421	.912	2 Days Rest	1	29	0.00	0	0	0	0	0	13	1.000
Post All-Star	11	555	2.92	3	2	2	0	27	261	.897	3+ Days Rest	18	949	3.03	4	6	4	0	48	465	.897

Wade Flaherty

New York Islanders — Goaltender

1998-99 Season	G	Min	GAA	W	L	T	ShO	GA	SA	SvPct		G	Min	GAA	W	L	T	ShO	GA	SA	SvPct
Overall	20	1048	3.03	5	11	2	0	53	491	.892	National TV	2	118	2.03	0	2	0	0	4	68	.941
Home	10	492	3.66	2	4	2	0	30	215	.860	Day	2	119	2.02	1	1	0	0	4	63	.937
Away	10	556	2.48	3	7	0	0	23	276	.917	Night	18	928	3.17	4	10	2	0	49	428	.886
vs. Division	4	179	3.35	1	2	0	0	10	102	.902	Start	18	1024	3.05	5	11	2	0	52	486	.893
vs. Conference	15	738	3.33	4	9	0	0	41	355	.885	Non Start	2	24	2.50	0	0	0	0	1	5	.800
vs. Playoff	13	706	3.48	2	8	2	0	41	327	.875	0 Days Rest	0	0	–	0	0	0	0	0	0	–
vs. Non-Playoff	7	342	2.11	3	3	0	0	12	164	.927	1 Days Rest	6	298	2.82	2	4	0	0	14	149	.906
Pre All-Star	8	348	3.62	1	4	1	0	21	169	.876	2 Days Rest	4	242	3.72	0	3	1	0	15	112	.866
Post All-Star	12	700	2.74	4	7	1	0	32	322	.901	3+ Days Rest	10	507	2.84	3	4	1	0	24	230	.896

Grant Fuhr

St. Louis Blues — Goaltender

1998-99 Season	G	Min	GAA	W	L	T	ShO	GA	SA	SvPct		G	Min	GAA	W	L	T	ShO	GA	SA	SvPct
Overall	39	2193	2.44	16	11	8	2	89	827	.892	National TV	6	318	3.21	1	4	0	0	17	112	.848
Home	17	1019	2.41	9	5	3	1	41	384	.893	Day	6	321	3.36	2	3	0	0	18	114	.842
Away	22	1173	2.46	7	6	5	1	48	443	.892	Night	33	1871	2.28	14	8	8	2	71	713	.900
vs. Division	7	392	3.06	2	2	2	0	20	152	.868	Start	37	2152	2.43	16	11	8	2	87	816	.893
vs. Conference	25	1352	2.40	10	6	5	1	54	523	.897	Non Start	2	40	3.00	0	0	0	0	2	11	.818
vs. Playoff	31	1745	2.48	11	10	7	1	72	664	.892	0 Days Rest	4	201	3.58	1	2	0	0	12	83	.855
vs. Non-Playoff	8	447	2.28	5	1	1	1	17	163	.896	1 Days Rest	16	975	2.22	6	4	6	1	36	346	.896
Pre All-Star	22	1164	2.63	7	6	5	1	51	425	.880	2 Days Rest	8	391	1.84	4	1	1	0	12	156	.923
Post All-Star	17	1028	2.22	9	5	3	1	38	402	.905	3+ Days Rest	11	625	2.78	5	4	1	1	29	242	.880

Jeff Hackett

Montreal Canadiens — Goaltender

1998-99 Season	G	Min	GAA	W	L	T	ShO	GA	SA	SvPct		G	Min	GAA	W	L	T	ShO	GA	SA	SvPct
Overall	63	3615	2.49	26	26	10	5	150	1616	.907	National TV	16	914	2.36	8	7	1	1	36	375	.904
Home	35	1982	2.54	16	12	6	2	84	832	.899	Day	3	158	4.94	0	3	0	0	13	60	.783
Away	28	1632	2.43	10	14	4	3	66	784	.916	Night	60	3457	2.38	26	23	10	5	137	1556	.912
vs. Division	13	706	2.80	5	7	0	0	33	327	.899	Start	62	3575	2.45	26	25	10	5	146	1599	.909
vs. Conference	40	2321	2.59	15	18	6	3	100	1006	.901	Non Start	1	40	6.00	0	1	0	0	4	17	.765
vs. Playoff	37	2120	2.63	13	17	7	2	93	981	.905	0 Days Rest	9	503	3.22	2	6	1	1	27	219	.877
vs. Non-Playoff	26	1495	2.29	13	9	3	3	57	635	.910	1 Days Rest	25	1424	2.57	9	10	5	1	61	612	.900
Pre All-Star	35	1992	2.59	13	14	7	2	86	903	.905	2 Days Rest	12	695	1.81	7	4	1	2	21	339	.938
Post All-Star	28	1622	2.37	13	12	3	3	64	713	.910	3+ Days Rest	17	992	2.48	8	6	3	1	41	446	.908

Dominik Hasek

Buffalo Sabres — Goaltender

1998-99 Season																				
	G	Min	GAA	W	L	T	ShO	GA	SA	SvPct		G	Min	GAA	W	L	T	ShO	GA	SA	SvPct
Overall	64	3817	1.87	30	18	14	9	119	1877	.937	National TV	13	792	1.74	5	5	3	2	23	394	.942
Home	31	1824	2.01	18	8	4	4	61	897	.932	Day	5	317	2.84	1	2	2	0	15	151	.901
Away	33	1991	1.75	12	10	10	5	58	980	.941	Night	59	3499	1.78	29	16	12	9	104	1726	.940
vs. Division	18	1109	1.79	9	5	4	0	33	595	.945	Start	64	3816	1.87	30	18	14	9	119	1877	.937
vs. Conference	49	2924	1.70	25	11	11	8	83	1449	.943	Non Start	0	0	–	0	0	0	0	0	0	–
vs. Playoff	37	2245	2.00	14	11	11	3	75	1114	.933	0 Days Rest	14	850	2.26	7	5	2	1	32	424	.925
vs. Non-Playoff	27	1571	1.68	16	7	3	6	44	763	.942	1 Days Rest	21	1214	1.88	12	6	2	5	38	601	.937
Pre All-Star	41	2393	1.86	22	10	7	8	74	1216	.939	2 Days Rest	14	822	1.61	5	3	5	3	22	387	.943
Post All-Star	23	1423	1.90	8	8	7	1	45	661	.932	3+ Days Rest	15	929	1.74	6	4	5	0	27	465	.942

Guy Hebert

Anaheim Mighty Ducks — Goaltender

1998-99 Season																				
	G	Min	GAA	W	L	T	ShO	GA	SA	SvPct		G	Min	GAA	W	L	T	ShO	GA	SA	SvPct
Overall	69	4083	2.42	31	29	9	6	165	2114	.922	National TV	11	660	1.73	9	2	0	3	19	356	.947
Home	38	2277	2.21	19	13	6	5	84	1226	.931	Day	1	59	2.03	1	0	0	0	2	33	.939
Away	31	1806	2.69	12	16	3	1	81	888	.909	Night	68	4023	2.43	30	29	9	6	163	2081	.922
vs. Division	20	1186	1.82	11	6	3	2	36	612	.941	Start	67	3992	2.40	30	28	9	6	160	2062	.922
vs. Conference	48	2842	2.32	21	21	6	4	110	1452	.924	Non Start	2	90	3.33	1	1	0	0	5	52	.904
vs. Playoff	43	2513	2.77	14	23	6	2	116	1326	.913	0 Days Rest	9	542	2.10	5	3	1	0	19	275	.931
vs. Non-Playoff	26	1569	1.87	17	6	3	4	49	788	.938	1 Days Rest	30	1774	2.37	12	14	4	3	70	855	.918
Pre All-Star	37	2232	2.26	15	15	7	4	84	1167	.928	2 Days Rest	15	874	3.23	6	7	2	1	47	490	.904
Post All-Star	32	1850	2.63	16	14	2	2	81	947	.914	3+ Days Rest	15	892	1.95	8	5	2	2	29	494	.941

Ron Hextall

Philadelphia Flyers — Goaltender

1998-99 Season																				
	G	Min	GAA	W	L	T	ShO	GA	SA	SvPct		G	Min	GAA	W	L	T	ShO	GA	SA	SvPct
Overall	23	1235	2.53	10	7	4	0	52	464	.888	National TV	4	246	2.93	2	1	1	0	12	94	.872
Home	14	776	2.32	7	3	3	0	30	295	.898	Day	2	125	2.88	0	1	1	0	6	48	.875
Away	9	459	2.88	3	4	1	0	22	169	.870	Night	21	1110	2.49	10	6	3	0	46	416	.889
vs. Division	6	325	3.14	2	3	1	0	17	125	.864	Start	20	1192	2.57	10	7	3	0	51	453	.887
vs. Conference	19	1040	2.48	8	6	4	0	43	387	.889	Non Start	3	43	1.40	0	0	1	0	1	11	.909
vs. Playoff	12	624	2.50	4	4	3	0	26	225	.884	0 Days Rest	1	60	4.00	0	1	0	0	4	25	.840
vs. Non-Playoff	11	611	2.55	6	3	1	0	26	239	.891	1 Days Rest	1	61	4.92	0	1	0	0	5	34	.853
Pre All-Star	13	727	2.23	8	3	2	0	27	280	.904	2 Days Rest	2	82	4.39	0	1	1	0	6	28	.786
Post All-Star	10	507	2.96	2	4	2	0	25	184	.864	3+ Days Rest	19	1031	2.15	10	4	3	0	37	377	.902

Arturs Irbe

Carolina Hurricanes — Goaltender

1998-99 Season																				
	G	Min	GAA	W	L	T	ShO	GA	SA	SvPct		G	Min	GAA	W	L	T	ShO	GA	SA	SvPct
Overall	62	3643	2.22	27	20	12	6	135	1753	.923	National TV	1	64	1.88	0	0	1	0	2	32	.938
Home	34	1999	2.13	17	8	8	4	71	922	.923	Day	4	249	2.65	1	1	2	0	11	151	.927
Away	28	1643	2.34	10	12	4	2	64	831	.923	Night	58	3393	2.19	26	19	10	6	124	1602	.923
vs. Division	11	684	2.19	5	1	5	1	25	321	.922	Start	61	3596	2.25	27	20	12	6	135	1731	.922
vs. Conference	44	2597	2.33	20	13	10	3	101	1283	.921	Non Start	1	46	0.00	0	0	0	0	0	22	1.000
vs. Playoff	34	1985	2.60	11	15	7	3	86	980	.912	0 Days Rest	6	363	1.98	2	3	1	1	12	179	.933
vs. Non-Playoff	28	1657	1.77	16	5	5	3	49	773	.937	1 Days Rest	22	1293	2.27	9	9	4	0	49	656	.925
Pre All-Star	32	1884	2.20	14	11	5	5	69	908	.924	2 Days Rest	15	856	2.73	4	3	6	1	39	417	.906
Post All-Star	30	1758	2.25	13	9	7	1	66	845	.922	3+ Days Rest	19	1129	1.86	12	5	1	4	35	501	.930

Curtis Joseph

Toronto Maple Leafs — Goaltender

1998-99 Season																				
	G	Min	GAA	W	L	T	ShO	GA	SA	SvPct		G	Min	GAA	W	L	T	ShO	GA	SA	SvPct
Overall	67	4001	2.56	35	24	7	3	171	1903	.910	National TV	23	1390	2.55	13	8	2	0	59	640	.908
Home	37	2245	2.38	21	11	5	1	89	1042	.915	Day	1	59	4.07	0	1	0	0	4	23	.826
Away	30	1755	2.80	14	13	2	2	82	861	.905	Night	66	3942	2.54	35	23	7	3	167	1880	.911
vs. Division	16	964	2.49	7	8	1	0	40	436	.908	Start	67	4001	2.56	35	24	7	3	171	1903	.910
vs. Conference	46	2777	2.79	20	21	5	1	129	1295	.900	Non Start	0	0	–	0	0	0	0	0	0	–
vs. Playoff	39	2306	2.42	21	13	4	2	93	1108	.916	0 Days Rest	9	501	2.40	3	3	2	1	20	260	.923
vs. Non-Playoff	28	1694	2.76	14	11	3	1	78	795	.902	1 Days Rest	23	1398	3.00	8	10	5	0	70	662	.894
Pre All-Star	38	2244	2.73	21	13	3	1	102	1058	.904	2 Days Rest	15	897	2.07	11	4	0	1	31	408	.924
Post All-Star	29	1756	2.36	14	11	4	2	69	845	.918	3+ Days Rest	20	1203	2.49	13	7	0	1	50	573	.913

Nikolai Khabibulin

Phoenix Coyotes — Goaltender

1998-99 Season

	G	Min	GAA	W	L	T	ShO	GA	SA	SvPct		G	Min	GAA	W	L	T	ShO	GA	SA	SvPct
Overall	63	3657	2.13	32	23	7	8	130	1681	.923	National TV	10	599	1.30	9	1	0	1	13	282	.954
Home	33	1997	2.04	19	10	4	5	68	912	.925	Day	6	359	1.34	5	1	0	2	8	148	.946
Away	30	1659	2.24	13	13	3	3	62	769	.919	Night	57	3297	2.22	27	22	7	6	122	1533	.920
vs. Division	21	1262	1.62	10	9	2	5	34	587	.942	Start	62	3637	2.14	32	23	7	8	130	1679	.923
vs. Conference	42	2486	1.86	24	14	3	6	77	1144	.933	Non Start	1	18	0.00	0	0	0	0	0	2	1.000
vs. Playoff	36	2107	2.39	16	16	4	4	84	981	.914	0 Days Rest	3	102	3.53	1	1	0	0	6	29	.793
vs. Non-Playoff	27	1549	1.78	16	7	3	4	46	700	.934	1 Days Rest	29	1684	2.21	12	13	4	4	62	807	.923
Pre All-Star	31	1803	1.93	18	8	4	4	58	802	.928	2 Days Rest	14	841	2.28	8	5	1	1	32	389	.918
Post All-Star	32	1852	2.33	14	15	3	4	72	879	.918	3+ Days Rest	17	1027	1.75	11	4	2	3	30	456	.934

Trevor Kidd

Carolina Hurricanes — Goaltender

1998-99 Season

	G	Min	GAA	W	L	T	ShO	GA	SA	SvPct		G	Min	GAA	W	L	T	ShO	GA	SA	SvPct
Overall	25	1358	2.70	7	10	6	2	61	640	.905	National TV	1	65	2.77	0	0	1	0	3	31	.903
Home	9	505	2.61	3	4	1	1	22	222	.901	Day	3	184	0.65	2	0	1	1	2	85	.976
Away	16	852	2.75	4	6	5	1	39	418	.907	Night	22	1173	3.02	5	10	5	1	59	555	.894
vs. Division	4	253	2.85	0	1	3	0	12	110	.891	Start	21	1230	2.59	7	9	5	2	53	580	.909
vs. Conference	18	1015	2.66	5	6	5	1	45	449	.900	Non Start	4	127	3.78	0	1	1	0	8	60	.867
vs. Playoff	13	700	2.83	2	6	3	2	33	367	.910	0 Days Rest	1	59	2.03	1	0	0	0	2	40	.950
vs. Non-Playoff	12	657	2.56	5	4	3	0	28	273	.897	1 Days Rest	1	58	3.10	0	1	0	0	3	32	.906
Pre All-Star	16	844	2.70	6	7	2	1	38	381	.900	2 Days Rest	4	196	3.06	1	2	1	0	10	90	.889
Post All-Star	9	514	2.68	1	3	4	1	23	259	.911	3+ Days Rest	19	1043	2.65	5	7	5	2	46	478	.904

Olaf Kolzig

Washington Capitals — Goaltender

1998-99 Season

	G	Min	GAA	W	L	T	ShO	GA	SA	SvPct		G	Min	GAA	W	L	T	ShO	GA	SA	SvPct
Overall	64	3586	2.58	26	31	3	4	154	1538	.900	National TV	9	509	2.36	6	2	0	1	20	229	.913
Home	32	1852	2.62	13	17	1	1	81	773	.895	Day	3	177	3.73	1	2	0	0	11	67	.836
Away	32	1733	2.53	13	14	2	3	73	765	.905	Night	61	3408	2.52	25	29	3	4	143	1471	.903
vs. Division	12	721	1.75	8	3	1	2	21	324	.935	Start	64	3585	2.58	26	31	3	4	154	1538	.900
vs. Conference	46	2630	2.49	22	18	3	3	109	1167	.907	Non Start	0	0	–	0	0	0	0	0	0	–
vs. Playoff	38	2123	2.71	14	21	1	2	96	920	.896	0 Days Rest	6	329	3.10	3	2	0	0	17	141	.879
vs. Non-Playoff	26	1462	2.38	12	10	2	2	58	618	.906	1 Days Rest	27	1530	2.35	13	11	1	1	60	648	.907
Pre All-Star	35	1939	2.72	13	18	1	3	88	844	.896	2 Days Rest	15	808	3.12	2	10	2	0	42	358	.883
Post All-Star	29	1646	2.41	13	13	2	1	66	694	.905	3+ Days Rest	16	916	2.29	8	8	0	3	35	391	.910

Kirk McLean

Florida Panthers — Goaltender

1998-99 Season

	G	Min	GAA	W	L	T	ShO	GA	SA	SvPct		G	Min	GAA	W	L	T	ShO	GA	SA	SvPct
Overall	30	1597	2.74	9	10	4	2	73	727	.900	National TV	2	89	6.07	0	1	0	0	9	36	.750
Home	13	717	2.85	3	6	1	0	34	299	.886	Day	1	65	2.77	0	0	1	0	3	27	.889
Away	17	878	2.67	6	4	3	2	39	428	.909	Night	29	1531	2.74	9	10	3	2	70	700	.900
vs. Division	3	184	1.96	1	1	1	0	6	73	.918	Start	24	1411	2.59	9	10	4	2	61	645	.905
vs. Conference	21	1181	2.44	8	8	2	1	48	524	.908	Non Start	6	184	3.91	0	0	0	0	12	82	.854
vs. Playoff	21	1102	2.78	4	7	4	1	51	502	.898	0 Days Rest	2	89	4.04	0	1	0	0	6	26	.769
vs. Non-Playoff	9	493	2.68	5	3	0	1	22	225	.902	1 Days Rest	6	331	2.18	4	1	0	1	12	149	.919
Pre All-Star	15	864	2.71	4	7	2	1	39	406	.904	2 Days Rest	5	249	2.65	2	2	0	0	11	105	.895
Post All-Star	15	732	2.79	5	3	2	1	34	321	.894	3+ Days Rest	17	926	2.85	3	6	4	1	44	447	.902

Jamie McLennan

St. Louis Blues — Goaltender

1998-99 Season

	G	Min	GAA	W	L	T	ShO	GA	SA	SvPct		G	Min	GAA	W	L	T	ShO	GA	SA	SvPct
Overall	33	1763	2.38	13	14	4	3	70	640	.891	National TV	7	400	1.95	4	2	1	1	13	138	.906
Home	20	1090	1.87	9	7	2	3	34	348	.902	Day	4	194	2.16	3	1	0	0	7	87	.920
Away	13	672	3.21	4	7	2	0	36	292	.877	Night	29	1568	2.41	10	13	4	3	63	553	.886
vs. Division	9	471	2.55	5	4	0	1	20	166	.880	Start	30	1660	2.39	12	14	3	3	66	601	.890
vs. Conference	24	1216	2.62	10	10	2	2	53	453	.883	Non Start	3	102	2.35	1	0	1	0	4	39	.897
vs. Playoff	12	592	3.45	1	8	2	0	34	212	.840	0 Days Rest	4	197	2.74	1	3	0	0	9	78	.885
vs. Non-Playoff	21	1170	1.85	12	6	2	3	36	428	.916	1 Days Rest	8	412	2.33	4	2	1	1	16	132	.879
Pre All-Star	24	1291	2.37	9	11	3	2	51	457	.888	2 Days Rest	9	546	1.65	4	3	2	2	15	164	.909
Post All-Star	9	471	2.42	4	3	1	1	19	183	.896	3+ Days Rest	12	606	2.97	4	6	1	0	30	266	.887

Chris Osgood

Detroit Red Wings — Goaltender

1998-99 Season	G	Min	GAA	W	L	T	ShO	GA	SA	SvPct		G	Min	GAA	W	L	T	ShO	GA	SA	SvPct
Overall	63	3691	2.42	34	25	4	3	149	1654	.910	National TV	24	1440	2.29	10	12	2	2	55	607	.909
Home	31	1824	2.30	20	10	1	1	70	803	.913	Day	11	664	2.35	6	4	1	2	26	312	.917
Away	32	1867	2.54	14	15	3	2	79	851	.907	Night	52	3027	2.44	28	21	3	1	123	1342	.908
vs. Division	14	819	2.05	10	4	0	0	28	342	.918	Start	63	3691	2.42	34	25	4	3	149	1654	.910
vs. Conference	39	2241	2.44	22	16	1	2	91	1044	.913	Non Start	0	0	–	0	0	0	0	0	0	–
vs. Playoff	35	2036	2.62	15	18	2	1	89	952	.907	0 Days Rest	7	378	3.02	2	5	0	0	19	185	.897
vs. Non-Playoff	28	1654	2.18	19	7	2	2	60	702	.915	1 Days Rest	23	1358	2.39	12	7	4	1	54	581	.907
Pre All-Star	36	2062	2.59	19	16	1	2	89	930	.904	2 Days Rest	18	1061	2.09	12	6	0	1	37	492	.925
Post All-Star	27	1629	2.21	15	9	3	1	60	724	.917	3+ Days Rest	15	892	2.62	8	7	0	1	39	396	.902

Bill Ranford

Detroit Red Wings — Goaltender

1998-99 Season	G	Min	GAA	W	L	T	ShO	GA	SA	SvPct		G	Min	GAA	W	L	T	ShO	GA	SA	SvPct
Overall	36	1812	3.64	6	18	4	1	110	956	.885	National TV	1	59	3.05	1	0	0	0	3	30	.900
Home	17	924	3.31	5	9	1	1	51	477	.893	Day	1	60	5.00	0	1	0	0	5	27	.815
Away	19	887	3.99	1	9	3	0	59	479	.877	Night	35	1752	3.60	6	17	4	1	105	929	.887
vs. Division	10	510	3.18	2	5	1	0	27	269	.900	Start	30	1662	3.36	6	18	4	1	93	871	.893
vs. Conference	27	1381	3.78	4	15	3	1	87	708	.877	Non Start	6	149	6.85	0	0	0	0	17	85	.800
vs. Playoff	21	1000	3.78	1	11	3	0	63	514	.877	0 Days Rest	3	137	4.82	0	3	0	0	11	90	.878
vs. Non-Playoff	15	811	3.48	5	7	1	1	47	442	.894	1 Days Rest	4	205	3.80	0	3	0	0	13	92	.859
Pre All-Star	24	1332	3.60	3	15	3	1	80	717	.888	2 Days Rest	8	458	3.28	2	5	0	1	25	229	.891
Post All-Star	12	479	3.76	3	3	1	0	30	239	.874	3+ Days Rest	21	1010	3.62	4	7	4	0	61	545	.888

Damian Rhodes

Ottawa Senators — Goaltender

1998-99 Season	G	Min	GAA	W	L	T	ShO	GA	SA	SvPct		G	Min	GAA	W	L	T	ShO	GA	SA	SvPct
Overall	45	2480	2.44	22	13	7	3	101	1060	.905	National TV	6	319	2.45	2	4	0	0	13	137	.905
Home	18	1002	1.98	9	5	4	1	33	414	.920	Day	1	60	3.00	1	0	0	0	3	27	.889
Away	27	1476	2.76	13	8	3	2	68	646	.895	Night	44	2419	2.43	21	13	7	3	98	1033	.905
vs. Division	12	715	2.43	2	6	3	0	29	293	.901	Start	43	2419	2.38	22	12	7	3	96	1033	.907
vs. Conference	35	1918	2.63	16	12	4	3	84	838	.900	Non Start	2	60	5.00	0	1	0	0	5	27	.815
vs. Playoff	27	1471	2.61	11	9	5	2	64	638	.900	0 Days Rest	4	244	0.98	3	0	1	1	4	102	.961
vs. Non-Playoff	18	1008	2.20	11	4	2	1	37	422	.912	1 Days Rest	9	455	2.51	5	3	0	1	19	211	.910
Pre All-Star	25	1329	2.75	12	9	2	1	61	572	.893	2 Days Rest	7	325	2.77	2	2	3	0	15	137	.891
Post All-Star	20	1150	2.09	10	4	5	2	40	488	.918	3+ Days Rest	25	1453	2.60	12	8	3	1	63	610	.897

Mike Richter

New York Rangers — Goaltender

1998-99 Season	G	Min	GAA	W	L	T	ShO	GA	SA	SvPct		G	Min	GAA	W	L	T	ShO	GA	SA	SvPct
Overall	68	3878	2.63	27	30	8	4	170	1898	.910	National TV	18	1014	3.20	7	8	2	2	54	490	.890
Home	38	2133	2.45	15	17	5	3	87	1002	.913	Day	9	503	2.62	3	4	2	0	22	245	.910
Away	30	1744	2.86	12	13	3	1	83	896	.907	Night	59	3373	2.63	24	26	6	4	148	1653	.910
vs. Division	16	947	2.53	6	6	4	0	40	447	.911	Start	66	3796	2.61	27	29	8	4	165	1854	.911
vs. Conference	49	2824	2.63	17	22	7	2	124	1367	.909	Non Start	2	81	3.70	0	1	0	0	5	44	.886
vs. Playoff	44	2524	2.50	15	21	7	4	105	1212	.913	0 Days Rest	7	385	3.74	2	4	0	0	24	191	.874
vs. Non-Playoff	24	1352	2.88	12	9	1	0	65	686	.905	1 Days Rest	27	1517	2.61	11	12	4	1	66	758	.913
Pre All-Star	37	2136	2.67	14	17	5	3	95	996	.905	2 Days Rest	16	881	2.79	8	4	2	2	41	445	.908
Post All-Star	31	1741	2.58	13	13	3	1	75	902	.917	3+ Days Rest	18	1093	2.14	6	10	2	1	39	504	.923

Patrick Roy

Colorado Avalanche — Goaltender

1998-99 Season	G	Min	GAA	W	L	T	ShO	GA	SA	SvPct		G	Min	GAA	W	L	T	ShO	GA	SA	SvPct
Overall	61	3648	2.29	32	19	8	5	139	1673	.917	National TV	18	1083	2.11	10	6	2	1	38	521	.927
Home	34	2036	2.15	19	11	4	4	73	924	.921	Day	12	731	2.13	5	4	3	2	26	333	.922
Away	27	1611	2.46	13	8	4	1	66	749	.912	Night	49	2917	2.32	27	15	5	3	113	1340	.916
vs. Division	13	780	2.54	6	6	1	0	33	362	.909	Start	61	3648	2.29	32	19	8	5	139	1673	.917
vs. Conference	43	2586	2.18	22	13	7	5	94	1194	.921	Non Start	0	0	–	0	0	0	0	0	0	–
vs. Playoff	34	2035	2.18	17	12	4	5	74	974	.924	0 Days Rest	7	421	2.42	3	3	1	0	17	200	.915
vs. Non-Playoff	27	1612	2.42	15	7	4	0	65	699	.907	1 Days Rest	23	1377	2.05	12	6	4	3	47	582	.919
Pre All-Star	30	1790	2.21	14	12	3	3	66	778	.915	2 Days Rest	8	475	2.15	5	3	0	0	17	219	.922
Post All-Star	31	1857	2.36	18	7	5	2	73	895	.918	3+ Days Rest	23	1373	2.53	12	7	3	2	58	672	.914

Tommy Salo

Edmonton Oilers — Goaltender

1998-99 Season																					
	G	Min	GAA	W	L	T	ShO	GA	SA	SvPct		G	Min	GAA	W	L	T	ShO	GA	SA	SvPct
Overall	64	3718	2.57	25	28	9	5	159	1647	.903	National TV	7	388	2.47	3	2	1	0	16	151	.894
Home	39	2248	2.51	15	18	5	2	94	978	.904	Day	8	491	2.93	1	5	2	0	24	192	.875
Away	25	1468	2.66	10	10	4	3	65	669	.903	Night	56	3226	2.51	24	23	7	5	135	1455	.907
vs. Division	22	1326	2.40	10	8	4	0	53	577	.908	Start	63	3697	2.55	25	28	9	5	157	1640	.904
vs. Conference	47	2719	2.60	19	20	6	2	118	1169	.899	Non Start	1	20	6.00	0	0	0	0	2	7	.714
vs. Playoff	41	2339	2.77	15	19	5	2	108	1062	.898	0 Days Rest	8	446	2.69	1	4	2	0	20	219	.909
vs. Non-Playoff	23	1378	2.22	10	9	4	3	51	585	.913	1 Days Rest	29	1635	2.61	13	11	4	2	71	714	.901
Pre All-Star	32	1889	2.60	13	17	2	5	82	846	.903	2 Days Rest	10	605	2.58	4	5	1	3	26	248	.895
Post All-Star	32	1827	2.53	12	11	7	0	77	801	.904	3+ Days Rest	17	1030	2.45	7	8	2	0	42	466	.910

Corey Schwab

Tampa Bay Lightning — Goaltender

1998-99 Season																					
	G	Min	GAA	W	L	T	ShO	GA	SA	SvPct		G	Min	GAA	W	L	T	ShO	GA	SA	SvPct
Overall	40	2146	3.52	8	25	3	0	126	1153	.891	National TV	1	60	1.00	1	0	0	0	1	30	.967
Home	19	1053	3.19	4	11	2	0	56	531	.895	Day	2	123	2.93	0	1	1	0	6	64	.906
Away	21	1092	3.85	4	14	1	0	70	622	.887	Night	38	2022	3.56	8	24	2	0	120	1089	.890
vs. Division	6	265	4.30	0	3	1	0	19	140	.864	Start	35	1970	3.41	8	24	3	0	112	1058	.894
vs. Conference	29	1536	3.28	6	16	3	0	84	829	.899	Non Start	5	175	4.80	0	1	0	0	14	95	.853
vs. Playoff	27	1457	3.62	5	18	2	0	88	810	.891	0 Days Rest	5	212	4.81	1	2	0	0	17	138	.877
vs. Non-Playoff	13	688	3.31	3	7	1	0	38	343	.889	1 Days Rest	13	689	3.66	3	10	0	0	42	376	.888
Pre All-Star	11	637	3.30	3	8	0	0	35	339	.897	2 Days Rest	7	385	3.12	1	5	0	0	20	205	.902
Post All-Star	29	1508	3.62	5	17	3	0	91	814	.888	3+ Days Rest	15	858	3.29	3	8	3	0	47	434	.892

Steve Shields

San Jose Sharks — Goaltender

1998-99 Season																					
	G	Min	GAA	W	L	T	ShO	GA	SA	SvPct		G	Min	GAA	W	L	T	ShO	GA	SA	SvPct
Overall	37	2162	2.22	15	11	8	4	80	1011	.921	National TV	5	299	2.01	2	3	0	1	10	139	.928
Home	19	1111	2.21	7	7	3	2	41	489	.916	Day	4	243	2.72	2	1	1	0	11	98	.888
Away	18	1050	2.23	8	4	5	2	39	522	.925	Night	33	1918	2.16	13	10	7	4	69	913	.924
vs. Division	11	619	2.23	3	5	2	1	23	283	.919	Start	34	2047	2.26	15	11	8	4	77	967	.920
vs. Conference	25	1442	2.08	10	9	4	4	50	659	.924	Non Start	3	115	1.57	0	0	0	0	3	44	.932
vs. Playoff	25	1430	2.31	9	8	5	2	55	662	.917	0 Days Rest	2	120	2.00	2	0	0	0	4	68	.941
vs. Non-Playoff	12	731	2.05	6	3	3	2	25	349	.928	1 Days Rest	5	308	2.73	1	2	2	0	14	154	.909
Pre All-Star	15	878	2.05	4	5	4	1	30	367	.918	2 Days Rest	7	425	1.98	4	2	1	2	14	193	.927
Post All-Star	22	1283	2.34	11	6	4	3	50	644	.922	3+ Days Rest	23	1308	2.20	8	7	5	2	48	596	.919

Mikhail Shtalenkov

Phoenix Coyotes — Goaltender

1998-99 Season																					
	G	Min	GAA	W	L	T	ShO	GA	SA	SvPct		G	Min	GAA	W	L	T	ShO	GA	SA	SvPct
Overall	38	2062	2.62	13	19	4	3	90	886	.898	National TV	5	239	2.26	3	1	0	1	9	119	.924
Home	15	794	2.34	4	9	1	3	31	341	.909	Day	1	65	2.77	0	0	1	0	3	26	.885
Away	23	1268	2.79	9	10	3	0	59	545	.892	Night	37	1997	2.61	13	19	3	3	87	860	.899
vs. Division	6	318	1.89	4	1	0	2	10	130	.923	Start	34	1911	2.61	13	16	4	3	83	836	.901
vs. Conference	26	1369	2.63	10	12	2	3	60	583	.897	Non Start	4	151	2.78	0	3	0	0	7	50	.860
vs. Playoff	22	1197	2.76	7	10	3	2	55	529	.896	0 Days Rest	5	266	2.71	1	3	1	0	12	113	.894
vs. Non-Playoff	16	864	2.43	6	9	1	1	35	357	.902	1 Days Rest	9	476	3.28	1	6	1	0	26	190	.863
Pre All-Star	28	1513	2.62	10	13	3	2	66	653	.899	2 Days Rest	6	318	3.02	3	2	0	0	16	171	.906
Post All-Star	10	549	2.62	3	6	1	1	24	233	.897	3+ Days Rest	18	1001	2.16	8	8	2	3	36	412	.913

Peter Skudra

Pittsburgh Penguins — Goaltender

1998-99 Season																					
	G	Min	GAA	W	L	T	ShO	GA	SA	SvPct		G	Min	GAA	W	L	T	ShO	GA	SA	SvPct
Overall	37	1914	2.79	15	11	5	3	89	822	.892	National TV	6	276	2.83	2	2	0	0	13	103	.874
Home	23	1217	2.86	10	6	4	2	58	520	.888	Day	6	276	2.39	3	1	0	1	11	112	.902
Away	14	696	2.67	5	5	1	1	31	302	.897	Night	31	1638	2.86	12	10	5	2	78	710	.890
vs. Division	9	443	3.12	1	4	2	1	23	205	.888	Start	28	1650	2.44	14	10	3	3	67	716	.906
vs. Conference	25	1339	3.09	10	9	3	3	69	605	.886	Non Start	9	264	5.00	1	1	2	0	22	106	.792
vs. Playoff	23	1152	2.66	8	8	2	3	51	494	.897	0 Days Rest	4	183	2.62	2	1	0	0	8	78	.897
vs. Non-Playoff	14	761	3.00	7	3	3	0	38	328	.884	1 Days Rest	14	846	2.13	7	5	2	2	30	366	.918
Pre All-Star	12	622	2.99	4	3	3	1	31	258	.880	2 Days Rest	5	272	2.87	1	2	1	1	13	120	.892
Post All-Star	25	1291	2.70	11	8	2	2	58	564	.897	3+ Days Rest	14	610	3.74	5	3	2	0	38	258	.853

Garth Snow

Vancouver Canucks — Goaltender

1998-99 Season	G	Min	GAA	W	L	T	ShO	GA	SA	SvPct		G	Min	GAA	W	L	T	ShO	GA	SA	SvPct
Overall	65	3501	2.93	20	31	8	6	171	1715	.900	National TV	16	844	2.77	5	7	2	0	39	401	.903
Home	32	1743	2.58	11	13	5	2	75	777	.903	Day	2	72	5.00	1	1	0	0	6	34	.824
Away	33	1756	3.28	9	18	3	4	96	938	.898	Night	63	3427	2.89	19	30	8	6	165	1681	.902
vs. Division	16	893	2.82	6	7	2	2	42	455	.908	Start	62	3461	2.95	20	31	8	6	170	1695	.900
vs. Conference	45	2385	3.14	13	21	6	4	125	1189	.895	Non Start	3	39	1.54	0	0	0	0	1	20	.950
vs. Playoff	44	2373	2.81	11	22	7	4	111	1171	.905	0 Days Rest	9	521	1.96	4	3	1	1	17	275	.938
vs. Non-Playoff	21	1126	3.20	9	9	1	2	60	544	.890	1 Days Rest	30	1601	3.04	7	18	3	4	81	736	.890
Pre All-Star	39	2087	2.99	12	19	4	2	104	1050	.901	2 Days Rest	11	611	3.24	4	5	1	0	33	324	.898
Post All-Star	26	1412	2.85	8	12	4	4	67	665	.899	3+ Days Rest	15	766	3.13	5	5	3	1	40	380	.895

Jamie Storr

Los Angeles Kings — Goaltender

1998-99 Season	G	Min	GAA	W	L	T	ShO	GA	SA	SvPct		G	Min	GAA	W	L	T	ShO	GA	SA	SvPct
Overall	28	1525	2.40	12	12	2	4	61	724	.916	National TV	3	123	3.90	0	2	0	0	8	87	.908
Home	13	736	2.45	6	6	1	3	30	329	.909	Day	2	64	4.69	0	1	0	0	5	28	.821
Away	15	788	2.36	6	6	1	1	31	395	.922	Night	26	1460	2.30	12	11	2	4	56	696	.920
vs. Division	8	429	2.10	3	4	0	1	15	237	.937	Start	26	1496	2.37	12	12	1	4	59	713	.917
vs. Conference	20	1040	2.25	9	7	2	3	39	511	.924	Non Start	2	28	4.29	0	0	1	0	2	11	.818
vs. Playoff	20	1039	2.60	8	9	1	2	45	525	.914	0 Days Rest	1	60	1.00	1	0	0	0	1	25	.960
vs. Non-Playoff	8	485	1.98	4	3	1	2	16	199	.920	1 Days Rest	7	408	2.21	5	2	0	1	15	179	.916
Pre All-Star	18	1022	2.47	9	8	1	3	42	472	.911	2 Days Rest	3	180	2.67	2	1	0	0	8	92	.913
Post All-Star	10	502	2.27	3	4	1	1	19	252	.925	3+ Days Rest	17	876	2.53	4	9	2	3	37	428	.914

Rick Tabaracci

Washington Capitals — Goaltender

1998-99 Season	G	Min	GAA	W	L	T	ShO	GA	SA	SvPct		G	Min	GAA	W	L	T	ShO	GA	SA	SvPct
Overall	23	1193	2.51	4	12	3	2	50	530	.906	National TV	2	118	2.03	1	1	0	1	4	51	.922
Home	11	605	2.48	3	6	1	0	25	270	.907	Day	0	0	–	0	0	0	0	0	0	–
Away	12	587	2.56	1	6	2	2	25	260	.904	Night	23	1193	2.51	4	12	3	2	50	530	.906
vs. Division	2	123	2.93	0	1	1	0	6	58	.897	Start	16	961	2.31	4	10	2	2	37	429	.914
vs. Conference	12	652	2.39	3	6	2	1	26	285	.909	Non Start	7	231	3.38	0	2	1	0	13	101	.871
vs. Playoff	12	660	3.00	2	8	0	0	33	307	.893	0 Days Rest	3	170	3.18	0	3	0	0	9	83	.892
vs. Non-Playoff	11	533	1.91	2	4	3	2	17	223	.924	1 Days Rest	3	184	1.30	1	1	1	1	4	68	.941
Pre All-Star	12	621	2.13	2	5	3	1	22	285	.923	2 Days Rest	1	60	0.00	1	0	0	1	0	29	1.000
Post All-Star	11	571	2.94	2	7	0	1	28	245	.886	3+ Days Rest	16	778	2.85	2	8	2	0	37	350	.894

Jocelyn Thibault

Chicago Blackhawks — Goaltender

1998-99 Season	G	Min	GAA	W	L	T	ShO	GA	SA	SvPct		G	Min	GAA	W	L	T	ShO	GA	SA	SvPct
Overall	62	3543	2.69	24	30	7	5	159	1685	.906	National TV	19	1043	3.34	5	14	0	0	58	474	.878
Home	34	1972	2.28	19	13	1	4	75	884	.915	Day	6	321	3.93	2	4	0	1	21	160	.869
Away	28	1570	3.21	5	17	6	1	84	801	.895	Night	56	3221	2.57	22	26	7	4	138	1525	.910
vs. Division	15	782	3.22	4	9	1	0	42	363	.884	Start	60	3488	2.68	24	30	6	5	156	1663	.906
vs. Conference	44	2486	2.78	15	23	5	2	115	1185	.903	Non Start	2	55	3.27	0	0	1	0	3	22	.864
vs. Playoff	39	2185	2.99	13	22	3	2	109	1028	.894	0 Days Rest	8	452	2.12	2	3	3	0	16	218	.927
vs. Non-Playoff	23	1358	2.21	11	8	4	3	50	657	.924	1 Days Rest	22	1193	3.52	3	16	3	1	70	573	.878
Pre All-Star	32	1856	2.59	11	16	4	3	80	924	.913	2 Days Rest	15	905	2.25	9	5	1	1	34	441	.923
Post All-Star	30	1686	2.81	13	14	3	2	79	761	.896	3+ Days Rest	17	991	2.36	10	6	0	3	39	453	.914

Ron Tugnutt

Ottawa Senators — Goaltender

1998-99 Season	G	Min	GAA	W	L	T	ShO	GA	SA	SvPct		G	Min	GAA	W	L	T	ShO	GA	SA	SvPct
Overall	43	2508	1.79	22	10	8	3	75	1005	.925	National TV	6	344	2.09	4	0	1	0	12	139	.914
Home	25	1490	1.77	13	6	4	1	44	617	.929	Day	2	119	2.02	1	1	0	0	4	51	.922
Away	18	1017	1.83	9	4	4	2	31	388	.920	Night	41	2388	1.78	21	9	8	3	71	954	.926
vs. Division	9	504	1.43	6	2	1	1	12	212	.943	Start	39	2312	1.84	22	9	7	3	71	941	.925
vs. Conference	27	1541	1.91	14	6	5	1	49	605	.919	Non Start	4	195	1.23	0	1	1	0	4	64	.938
vs. Playoff	24	1404	1.54	9	6	7	2	36	549	.934	0 Days Rest	1	39	3.08	0	1	0	0	2	13	.846
vs. Non-Playoff	19	1103	2.12	13	4	1	1	39	456	.914	1 Days Rest	12	722	1.41	7	2	2	2	17	294	.942
Pre All-Star	24	1397	1.63	13	5	4	1	38	571	.933	2 Days Rest	7	380	1.89	4	3	0	0	12	156	.923
Post All-Star	19	1110	2.00	9	5	4	2	37	434	.915	3+ Days Rest	23	1364	1.94	11	4	6	1	44	542	.919

Roman Turek

Dallas Stars — Goaltender

1998-99 Season	G	Min	GAA	W	L	T	ShO	GA	SA	SvPct		G	Min	GAA	W	L	T	ShO	GA	SA	SvPct
Overall	26	1382	2.08	16	3	3	1	48	562	.915	National TV	5	222	2.16	3	0	1	0	8	86	.907
Home	11	515	2.45	6	1	1	0	21	208	.899	Day	4	187	3.53	3	1	0	0	11	86	.872
Away	15	866	1.87	10	2	2	1	27	354	.924	Night	22	1194	1.86	13	2	3	1	37	476	.922
vs. Division	8	402	1.79	6	0	1	0	12	180	.933	Start	22	1291	2.09	15	3	3	1	45	538	.916
vs. Conference	17	929	2.07	11	3	2	1	32	385	.917	Non Start	4	89	2.02	1	0	0	0	3	24	.875
vs. Playoff	14	710	2.37	6	1	3	0	28	300	.907	0 Days Rest	0	0	–	0	0	0	0	0	0	–
vs. Non-Playoff	12	670	1.79	10	2	0	1	20	262	.924	1 Days Rest	0	0	–	0	0	0	0	0	0	–
Pre All-Star	13	705	1.96	7	1	2	0	23	289	.920	2 Days Rest	6	300	2.60	4	1	0	1	13	135	.904
Post All-Star	13	676	2.22	9	2	1	1	25	273	.908	3+ Days Rest	20	1081	1.94	12	2	3	0	35	427	.918

John Vanbiesbrouck

Philadelphia Flyers — Goaltender

1998-99 Season	G	Min	GAA	W	L	T	ShO	GA	SA	SvPct		G	Min	GAA	W	L	T	ShO	GA	SA	SvPct
Overall	62	3712	2.18	27	18	15	6	135	1380	.902	National TV	14	854	2.60	6	5	3	1	37	324	.886
Home	28	1671	1.97	14	5	8	2	55	602	.909	Day	13	804	2.69	5	3	5	0	36	293	.877
Away	34	2040	2.35	13	13	7	4	80	778	.897	Night	49	2907	2.04	22	15	10	6	99	1087	.909
vs. Division	15	899	2.40	5	5	4	2	36	309	.883	Start	61	3689	2.20	27	18	15	6	135	1373	.902
vs. Conference	40	2375	2.17	15	14	9	5	86	821	.895	Non Start	1	22	0.00	0	0	0	0	0	7	1.000
vs. Playoff	36	2137	2.22	14	10	10	2	79	815	.903	0 Days Rest	4	252	1.67	1	1	2	0	7	96	.927
vs. Non-Playoff	26	1574	2.13	13	8	5	4	56	565	.901	1 Days Rest	22	1290	2.09	10	8	3	3	45	471	.904
Pre All-Star	33	1958	1.81	16	7	8	6	59	729	.919	2 Days Rest	13	801	2.25	5	4	4	0	30	292	.897
Post All-Star	29	1753	2.60	11	11	7	0	76	651	.883	3+ Days Rest	23	1368	2.32	11	5	6	3	53	521	.898

Mike Vernon

San Jose Sharks — Goaltender

1998-99 Season	G	Min	GAA	W	L	T	ShO	GA	SA	SvPct		G	Min	GAA	W	L	T	ShO	GA	SA	SvPct
Overall	49	2831	2.27	16	22	10	4	107	1200	.911	National TV	6	357	2.18	2	4	0	1	13	140	.907
Home	24	1384	1.86	10	8	6	3	43	556	.923	Day	3	179	3.02	1	2	0	0	9	85	.894
Away	25	1446	2.66	6	14	4	1	64	644	.901	Night	46	2651	2.22	15	20	10	4	98	1115	.912
vs. Division	15	828	2.32	4	9	1	3	32	348	.908	Start	48	2803	2.29	16	22	10	4	107	1190	.910
vs. Conference	35	2012	2.53	11	17	6	3	85	837	.898	Non Start	1	28	0.00	0	0	0	0	0	10	1.000
vs. Playoff	27	1497	2.40	6	14	6	3	60	641	.906	0 Days Rest	1	60	5.00	0	1	0	0	5	32	.844
vs. Non-Playoff	22	1334	2.11	10	8	4	1	47	559	.916	1 Days Rest	17	1017	2.06	9	8	0	2	35	422	.917
Pre All-Star	32	1873	2.40	11	13	8	3	75	797	.906	2 Days Rest	13	724	2.07	3	5	4	0	25	293	.915
Post All-Star	17	957	2.01	5	9	2	1	32	403	.921	3+ Days Rest	18	1029	2.45	4	8	6	2	42	453	.907

Tomas Vokoun

Nashville Predators — Goaltender

1998-99 Season	G	Min	GAA	W	L	T	ShO	GA	SA	SvPct		G	Min	GAA	W	L	T	ShO	GA	SA	SvPct
Overall	37	1954	2.95	12	18	4	1	96	1041	.908	National TV	2	80	4.50	1	1	0	0	6	30	.800
Home	18	958	2.51	6	7	3	1	40	540	.926	Day	4	225	3.73	0	3	1	0	14	107	.869
Away	19	995	3.38	6	11	1	0	56	501	.888	Night	33	1727	2.85	12	15	3	1	82	934	.912
vs. Division	7	347	2.42	2	2	1	0	14	214	.935	Start	32	1794	2.94	11	17	3	1	88	956	.908
vs. Conference	24	1250	2.78	9	10	2	1	58	669	.913	Non Start	5	159	3.02	1	1	1	0	8	85	.906
vs. Playoff	26	1372	3.02	8	14	2	1	69	765	.910	0 Days Rest	3	138	1.30	1	1	0	1	3	63	.952
vs. Non-Playoff	11	581	2.79	4	4	2	0	27	276	.902	1 Days Rest	12	649	2.59	6	4	2	0	28	347	.919
Pre All-Star	20	976	3.20	6	9	3	1	52	527	.901	2 Days Rest	6	342	3.51	1	5	0	0	20	175	.886
Post All-Star	17	977	2.70	6	9	1	0	44	514	.914	3+ Days Rest	16	822	3.28	4	8	2	0	45	456	.901

Ken Wregget

Calgary Flames — Goaltender

1998-99 Season	G	Min	GAA	W	L	T	ShO	GA	SA	SvPct		G	Min	GAA	W	L	T	ShO	GA	SA	SvPct
Overall	27	1590	2.53	10	12	4	1	67	712	.906	National TV	4	238	3.03	1	3	0	0	12	80	.850
Home	12	728	2.88	4	6	2	1	35	291	.880	Day	2	119	1.51	1	1	0	0	3	40	.925
Away	15	861	2.23	6	6	2	0	32	421	.924	Night	25	1470	2.61	9	11	4	1	64	672	.905
vs. Division	6	369	2.28	2	2	2	0	14	164	.915	Start	26	1539	2.57	9	12	4	1	66	686	.904
vs. Conference	20	1166	2.42	8	8	3	0	47	547	.914	Non Start	1	50	1.20	1	0	0	0	1	26	.962
vs. Playoff	21	1224	2.89	5	12	3	0	59	559	.894	0 Days Rest	3	184	2.93	1	1	1	0	9	94	.904
vs. Non-Playoff	6	365	1.32	5	0	1	1	8	153	.948	1 Days Rest	9	507	2.49	1	6	1	1	21	232	.909
Pre All-Star	11	632	2.85	3	5	2	1	30	301	.900	2 Days Rest	4	244	2.21	2	1	1	0	9	103	.913
Post All-Star	16	957	2.32	7	7	2	0	37	411	.910	3+ Days Rest	11	653	2.57	6	4	1	0	28	283	.901

Team Section

Team Game Logs

Game scores marked with an asterisk (*) indicate overtime games. The team's "goalie of record" and Game Stars (if any) for each game are denoted in bold type. Team single-game highs and lows in scoring, shots and power plays are also denoted in bold. A dagger (†) in the opponent column indicates the game was played at a neutral site.

Standings & Team Statistics

For both regular-season and postseason statistics, "team highs" for each category are designated in bold type. A skater had to play in at least 41 team games in 1998-99 to be counted as that team's +/– leader. Players who spent the 1998-99 season with more than one team will be listed on multiple team pages and indicated by a dagger (†), with their statistics listed only on the team with which they were accumulated. Rookies are identified by an asterisk (*).

Team Highlights

This section includes team situational records, individual and team streaks, a team Game Star breakdown and miscellaneous statistics.

Mighty Ducks of Anaheim 1998-99 Game Log (35-34-13)

					Goalies		Shots		Power Plays		Game Stars		
Date	Opp	Score	W/L/T	Record	W/T	L/T	Anh	Opp	Anh	Opp	1st	2nd	3rd
10/10	@Was	0-1	L	0-1-0	Kolzig	**Roussel**	29	34	0-6	1-6	Juneau	Kolzig	**Roussel**
10/11	@Phi	1-4	L	0-2-0	Vanbiesbrouck	**Hebert**	22	32	1-7	2-8	Lindros	LeClair	McGillis
10/13	@Mon	0-1	L	0-3-0	Thibault	**Hebert**	30	24	0-3	1-3	Thibault	Malakhov	**Hebert**
10/15	@Chi	5-3	W	1-3-0	**Hebert**	Hackett	31	26	0-5	1-7	**Selanne**	**Kariya**	Gilmour
10/21	Bos	3-**0**	W	2-3-0	**Hebert**	Dafoe	30	26	2-4	0-6	**Crowley**	**Hebert**	**Kariya**
10/25	Pho	2-2*	T	2-3-1	**Hebert**	Khabibulin	34	36	0-5	0-5	**Hebert**	Khabibulin	**Kariya**
10/28	TB	5-3	W	3-3-1	**Hebert**	Puppa	31	45	1-5	2-9	**Grimson**	**Hebert**	**Sandstrom**
10/30	@Dal	3-3*	T	3-3-2	**Hebert**	Turek	34	27	0-5	1-3	**Rucchin**	Nieuwendyk	**Kariya**
10/31	@StL	2-2*	T	3-3-3	**Hebert**	Fuhr	27	45	0-5	1-5	**Hebert**	MacInnis	Young
11/04	StL	1-3	L	3-4-3	Fuhr	**Hebert**	29	36	1-5	0-2	Picard	**Davidsson**	Demitra
11/06	SJ	2-2*	T	3-4-4	**Hebert**	Shields	**47**	30	2-**9**	0-6	**Sandstrom**	Shields	**Salei**
11/08	Det	2-3	L	3-5-4	Osgood	**Hebert**	39	34	2-7	1-6	Osgood	Shanahan	**McInnis**
11/11	Car	5-4*	W	4-5-4	**Hebert**	Kidd	41	29	1-5	0-3	**Rucchin**	Primeau	**Kariya**
11/13	@Van	2-5	L	4-6-4	Snow	**Roussel**	26	25	0-5	0-4	Snow	McCabe	**Kariya**
11/14	@Cgy	1-**0**	W	5-6-4	**Hebert**	Moss	28	24	1-5	0-5	**Hebert**	Moss	**Crowley**
11/16	LA	3-1	W	6-6-4	**Hebert**	LeGace	28	39	1-3	1-6	**Hebert**	**Green**	**Davidsson**
11/18	NYR	3-1	W	7-6-4	**Hebert**	Richter	16	30	1-7	0-9	**Rucchin**	**Hebert**	**Haller**
11/20	Edm	2-3*	L	7-7-4	Shtalenkov	**Hebert**	21	23	1-5	1-5	Kovalenko	**Aalto**	Hamrlik
11/22	Chi	4-1	W	8-7-4	**Hebert**	Fitzpatrick	23	27	1-3	1-5	**McInnis**	**Kariya**	**Salei**
11/25	@Det	2-5	L	8-8-4	Maracle	**Hebert**	28	35	1-5	2-3	Fedorov	Murphy	Maracle
11/27	@Nsh	1-3	L	8-9-4	Dunham	**Roussel**	27	31	1-8	1-4	Kjellberg	Dunham	Bouchard
11/29	@Car	1-3	L	8-10-4	Irbe	**Hebert**	31	36	0-3	1-4	Pratt	Irbe	Francis
12/01	@Pit	4-4*	T	8-10-5	**Hebert**	Barrasso	35	36	2-2	1-4	Jagr	Straka	**Selanne**
12/03	@Chi	1-4	L	8-11-5	Thibault	**Hebert**	25	18	1-6	1-7	Zhamnov	Kilger	Thibault
12/06	@SJ	2-1	W	9-11-5	**Hebert**	Shields	23	24	2-6	1-6	**Kariya**	Nolan	**Haller**
12/09	Van	4-4*	T	9-11-6	**Hebert**	Hirsch	34	41	1-5	0-2	**Davidsson**	Messier	**Cullen**
12/11	Was	1-**0**	W	10-11-6	**Hebert**	Kolzig	24	31	1-4	0-2	**Hebert**	Nikolishin	**McInnis**
12/13	LA	3-**0**	W	11-11-6	**Hebert**	Fiset	34	35	1-2	0-4	**Hebert**	**Selanne**	**Kariya**
12/16	Nsh	6-1	W	12-11-6	**Hebert**	Vokoun	37	39	**4**-7	0-4	**Hebert**	**Selanne**	**Green**
12/18	NYI	2-2*	T	12-11-7	**Hebert**	Salo	41	32	1-3	0-4	**Olausson**	Linden	**Salei**
12/21	Col	2-4	L	12-12-7	Billington	**Hebert**	29	33	1-6	1-4	Kamensky	**Olausson**	Drury
12/22	@Col	1-**0**	W	13-12-7	**Roussel**	Roy	20	45	0-6	0-5	**Roussel**	Foote	**Nielsen**
12/28	@Ott	2-2*	T	13-12-8	**Roussel**	Tugnutt	16	39	0-3	0-6	**Roussel**	McEachern	**Salei**
12/30	@Tor	1-4	L	13-13-8	Joseph	**Hebert**	31	39	0-3	0-3	Modin	Smith	Joseph
1/01	@Buf	**7**-2	W	14-13-8	**Hebert**	Hasek	31	33	2-4	1-4	**Selanne**	**Rucchin**	**Kariya**
1/02	@Bos	1-2	L	14-14-8	Dafoe	**Hebert**	30	26	1-3	1-3	Bourque	**Rucchin**	McLaren
1/04	@Nsh	1-2	L	14-15-8	Vokoun	**Hebert**	29	20	1-4	1-4	Ronning	Vokoun	**Kariya**
1/06	Buf	2-3*	L	14-16-8	Hasek	**Hebert**	25	19	0-2	1-5	Peca	**Kariya**	Varada
1/08	Pho	4-1	W	15-16-8	**Roussel**	Khabibulin	30	22	1-3	0-4	**Kariya**	**Cullen**	**Salei**
1/10	Edm	6-4	W	16-16-8	**Hebert**	Shtalenkov	29	49	3-**9**	2-8	**Selanne**	**Olausson**	**Trepanier**
1/13	Cgy	1-2	L	16-17-8	Brathwaite	**Hebert**	32	29	1-6	0-5	Wiemer	**Olausson**	Brathwaite
1/15	Dal	1-3	L	16-18-8	Belfour	**Hebert**	28	29	1-2	1-2	Modano	**Trepanier**	Lehtinen
1/18	Pit	5-3	W	17-18-8	**Hebert**	Barrasso	29	47	2-7	1-7	**McInnis**	Straka	**Selanne**
1/20	NJ	3-4	L	17-19-8	Brodeur	**Roussel**	35	28	0-5	1-5	Stevens	**Rucchin**	Sharifijanov
1/21	@Pho	3-3*	T	17-19-9	**Roussel**	Khabibulin	24	44	1-6	1-6	Numminen	**Kariya**	Stapleton
1/27	Col	3-4	L	17-20-9	Roy	**Hebert**	34	22	1-5	1-3	Roy	**Selanne**	Sakic
1/28	@Col	2-6	L	17-21-9	Roy	**Hebert**	34	38	1-5	2-4	Yelle	Lemieux	Sakic
1/30	@Edm	0-1	L	17-22-9	Shtalenkov	**Hebert**	22	27	0-5	0-6	Niinimaa	Shtalenkov	**Salei**
2/03	Chi	3-**0**	W	18-22-9	**Hebert**	Thibault	23	35	1-3	0-2	**Hebert**	**Cullen**	**Salei**
2/05	@TB	5-3	W	19-22-9	**Hebert**	Ranford	33	31	2-4	1-4	**Kariya**	**Selanne**	Kubina
2/06	@StL	4-3	W	20-22-9	**Hebert**	Fuhr	19	26	1-5	2-4	MacInnis	**Cullen**	**Selanne**
2/10	Phi	5-4	W	21-22-9	**Hebert**	Vanbiesbrouck	24	32	3-6	3-9	**Selanne**	Lindros	**Olausson**
2/12	Dal	2-3	L	21-23-9	Belfour	**Hebert**	28	29	1-5	1-7	Belfour	Hatcher	**Selanne**
2/14	@Pho	5-1	W	22-23-9	**Hebert**	Waite	28	38	0-5	0-3	**Rucchin**	**Hebert**	Corkum
2/15	@LA	3-1	W	23-23-9	**Hebert**	Fiset	29	24	1-4	0-3	**Sandstrom**	**Hebert**	Jokinen

2/17	Edm	2-6	L	23-24-9	Shtalenkov	**Hebert**	32	31	1-7	0-3	Selivanov	Guerin	Shtalenkov
2/19	@Cgy	3-6	L	23-25-9	Wregget	**Hebert**	38	32	2-6	1-4	Fleury	**Kariya**	Bassen
2/20	@Van	5-1	W	24-25-9	**Hebert**	Hirsch	22	26	3-4	1-6	**McInnis**	**Selanne**	**Kariya**
2/24	@Edm	2-1	W	25-25-9	**Roussel**	Passmore	24	33	0-2	0-5	**Kariya**	Falloon	**Salei**
2/26	SJ	3-1	W	26-25-9	**Hebert**	Vernon	30	31	2-4	0-4	**Selanne**	**Hebert**	**Green**
2/27	@SJ	4-1	W	27-25-9	**Hebert**	Shields	30	29	1-6	1-9	**Selanne**	**Kariya**	**Haller**
3/03	LA	2-1	W	28-25-9	**Hebert**	Fiset	14	34	1-4	0-5	**Hebert**	Robitaille	**Selanne**
3/05	Nsh	3-2	W	29-25-9	**Roussel**	Dunham	34	24	1-4	1-4	**Nielsen**	**Drury**	**Salei**
3/07	Det	3-1	W	30-25-9	**Hebert**	Osgood	25	34	1-**9**	1-8	**Hebert**	Yzerman	**Haller**
3/10	Van	4-4*	T	30-25-10	**Hebert**	Weekes	45	28	3-5	2-6	**Kariya**	Naslund	**McInnis**
3/12	@Dal	0-4	L	30-26-10	Belfour	**Hebert**	27	34	0-6	0-5	Nieuwendyk	Belfour	Modano
3/13	@Pho	0-1	L	30-27-10	Khabibulin	**Hebert**	27	22	0-5	0-4	Khabibulin	**Selanne**	Stapleton
3/17	Ott	2-2*	T	30-27-11	**Hebert**	Rhodes	21	43	0-1	1-3	Hossa	**Hebert**	Yashin
3/18	@LA	4-2	W	31-27-11	**Hebert**	Fiset	24	39	2-3	1-6	**Kariya**	**Selanne**	**Hebert**
3/21	Fla	2-5	L	31-28-11	Burke	**Hebert**	27	41	1-2	1-4	Whitney	Kozlov	Lindsay
3/26	Dal	5-1	W	32-28-11	**Hebert**	Belfour	32	26	2-2	1-4	**Selanne**	**Kariya**	**Hebert**
3/28	Cgy	5-1	W	33-28-11	**Hebert**	Brathwaite	26	26	0-0	1-5	**Kariya**	**Selanne**	**Hebert**
3/31	@NJ	1-7	L	33-29-11	Brodeur	**Hebert**	14	36	1-3	2-3	Sharifijanov	Andreychuk	McKay
4/02	@NYR	4-1	W	34-29-11	**Hebert**	Richter	28	**13**	1-5	0-5	**Selanne**	**Kariya**	**Green**
4/03	@NYI	2-2*	T	34-29-12	**Roussel**	Flaherty	26	33	1-4	0-2	**Cullen**	Lindgren	Flaherty
4/05	@Det	2-3	L	34-30-12	Ranford	**Hebert**	18	33	1-2	0-6	Yzerman	Lidstrom	Dandenault
4/07	@Dal	1-5	L	34-31-12	Belfour	**Hebert**	23	26	1-2	2-5	Zubov	Hull	Belfour
4/09	SJ	1-4	L	34-32-12	Shields	**Hebert**	29	31	1-6	1-4	Shields	Murphy	Ragnarsson
4/11	Pho	3-**0**	W	35-32-12	**Hebert**	Khabibulin	31	40	0-7	0-6	**Hebert**	**Kariya**	**Nielsen**
4/14	StL	1-3	L	35-33-12	Fuhr	**Hebert**	32	24	0-3	0-**1**	Fuhr	MacInnis	**Kariya**
4/15	@LA	3-4*	L	35-34-12	Fiset	**Roussel**	25	44	0-3	2-5	Ferraro	**Selanne**	Robitaille
4/17	@SJ	3-3*	T	35-34-13	**Roussel**	Shields	30	29	2-7	0-5	Nolan	Korolyuk	**Kariya**
						Postseason							
4/21	@Det	**3**-5	L	0-1	Osgood	**Askey**	29	37	1-5	1-6	Yzerman	**Kariya**	Clark
4/23	@Det	1-5	L	0-2	Osgood	**Hebert**	**31**	36	1-5	3-9	Shanahan	Fedorov	Chelios
4/25	Det	2-4	L	0-3	Osgood	**Hebert**	24	**24**	**2-6**	2-6	Lidstrom	**Marshall**	Fedorov
4/27	Det	0-**3**	L	0-4	Osgood	**Hebert**	**31**	38	0-4	1-**2**	Osgood	Shanahan	Yzerman

Mighty Ducks of Anaheim 1998-99 Player Statistics

Skater	Ps	Regular Season GP	G	A	Pts	+/–	PIM	PP	SH	GW	GT	S	SPct	P/G	Postseason GP	G	A	Pts	+/–	PIM	PP	SH	GW	OT	S	SPct	P/G
Teemu Selanne	R	75	47	60	107	18	30	25	0	7	1	281	16.7	1.43	4	2	2	4	-1	2	1	0	0	0	7	28.6	1.00
Paul Kariya	L	82	39	62	101	17	40	11	2	4	0	429	9.1	1.23	3	1	3	4	0	0	0	0	0	0	11	9.1	1.33
Steve Rucchin	C	69	23	39	62	11	22	5	1	5	1	145	15.9	.90	4	0	3	3	0	0	0	0	0	0	10	0.0	.75
Fredrik Olausson	D	74	16	40	56	17	30	10	0	2	0	121	13.2	.76	4	0	2	2	-4	4	0	0	0	0	6	0.0	.50
Marty McInnis†	C	75	18	34	52	-14	36	11	1	5	0	139	12.9	.69	4	2	0	2	-1	2	2	0	0	0	12	16.7	.50
Tomas Sandstrom	R	58	15	17	32	-5	42	7	0	2	0	107	14.0	.55	4	0	0	0	-2	4	0	0	0	0	9	0.0	.00
Travis Green	C	79	13	17	30	-7	81	3	1	2	0	165	7.9	.38	4	0	1	1	-4	4	0	0	0	0	12	0.0	.25
Matt Cullen	C	75	11	14	25	-12	47	5	1	1	1	112	9.8	.33	4	0	0	0	-2	0	0	0	0	0	6	0.0	.00
Ruslan Salei	D	74	2	14	16	1	65	1	0	0	0	123	1.6	.22	3	0	0	0	-4	4	0	0	0	0	5	0.0	.00
Ted Drury	C	75	5	6	11	2	83	0	0	0	0	79	6.3	.15	4	0	0	0	-6	0	0	0	0	0	4	0.0	.00
Jim McKenzie	L	73	5	4	9	-18	99	1	0	1	0	59	8.5	.12	4	0	0	0	-2	4	0	0	0	0	5	0.0	.00
Jeff Nielsen	R	80	5	4	9	-12	34	0	0	2	0	94	5.3	.11	4	0	0	0	-6	2	0	0	0	0	7	0.0	.00
* Johan Davidsson	C	64	3	5	8	-9	14	1	0	1	0	48	6.3	.13	1	0	0	0	0	0	0	0	0	0	0	—	.00
* Antti Aalto	C	73	3	5	8	-12	24	2	0	0	0	61	4.9	.11	4	0	0	0	0	2	0	0	0	0	0	—	.00
Jason Marshall	D	72	1	7	8	-5	142	0	0	0	0	63	1.6	.11	4	1	0	1	-1	10	1	0	0	0	5	20.0	.25
Kevin Haller	D	82	1	6	7	-1	122	0	0	0	0	64	1.6	.09	4	0	0	0	-1	2	0	0	0	0	7	0.0	.00
* Pascal Trepanier	D	45	2	4	6	0	48	0	0	1	0	49	4.1	.13	—	—	—	—	—	—	—	—	—	—	—	—	—
* Mike Crowley	D	20	2	3	5	-10	16	1	0	1	0	41	4.9	.25	—	—	—	—	—	—	—	—	—	—	—	—	—
Pavel Trnka	D	63	0	4	4	-6	60	0	0	0	0	50	0.0	.06	4	0	1	1	-3	2	0	0	0	0	2	0.0	.25
Stu Grimson	L	73	3	0	3	0	158	0	0	1	0	10	30.0	.04	3	0	0	0	0	30	0	0	0	0	0	—	.00
Jamie Pushor	D	70	1	2	3	-20	112	0	0	0	0	75	1.3	.04	4	0	0	0	-3	6	0	0	0	0	6	0.0	.00
* Scott Ferguson	D	2	0	1	1	0	0	0	0	0	0	1	0.0	.50	—	—	—	—	—	—	—	—	—	—	—	—	—
Josef Marha†	C	10	0	1	1	-4	0	0	0	0	0	13	0.0	.10	—	—	—	—	—	—	—	—	—	—	—	—	—
Guy Hebert	G	69	0	1	1	—	0	0	0	0	0	0	—	.01	4	0	0	0	—	0	0	0	0	0	0	—	.00
Tom Askey	G	—	—	—	—	—	—	—	—	—	—	—	—	—	1	0	0	0	—	0	0	0	0	0	0	—	.00
Dan Trebil	D	6	0	0	0	-2	0	0	0	0	0	1	0.0	.00	1	0	0	0	0	2	0	0	0	0	0	—	.00
* Mike LeClerc	L	7	0	0	0	-2	4	0	0	0	0	1	0.0	.00	1	0	0	0	0	0	0	0	0	0	1	0.0	.00
Dominic Roussel	G	18	0	0	0	—	0	0	0	0	0	0	—	.00	—	—	—	—	—	—	—	—	—	—	—	—	—
Bench		—	—	—	—	—	0	—	—	—	—	—	—	—	—	—	—	—	—	0	—	—	—	—	—	—	—
TEAM TOTALS		82	215	350	565	-73	1309	83	6	35	3	2331	9.2	6.89	4	6	12	18	-40	80	4	0	0	0	115	5.2	4.50

Goaltender	Regular Season G	Min	GAA	W	L	T	ENG	ShO	GA	SA	SvPct	Postseason G	Min	GAA	W	L	ENG	ShO	GA	SA	SvPct
Guy Hebert	69	4083	2.42	31	29	9	3	6	165	2114	.922	4	208	4.33	0	3	0	0	15	124	.879
Dominic Roussel	18	884	2.51	4	5	4	1	1	37	478	.923	—	—	—	—	—	—	—	—	—	—
Tom Askey	—	—	—	—	—	—	—	—	—	—	—	1	30	4.00	0	1	0	0	2	11	.818
TEAM TOTALS	82	4990	2.49	35	34	13	4	7	206	2596	.921	4	240	4.25	0	4	0	0	17	135	.874

1998-99 Mighty Ducks of Anaheim

Record When:

Overtime games	1-3-13
In second game of back-to-back games	7-5-3
Vs playoff teams	17-24-9
Leading after two periods	28-3-7
Tied after two periods	5-10-2
Losing after two periods	2-21-4
Scoring first	27-6-9
More shots than opponents	11-14-5
Fewer shots than opponents	23-20-8
Team had at least one fighting major	14-16-4
Team had more PIM	13-12-5
Team had fewer PIM	15-15-6
Team had even PIM	7-7-2

Team

Longest winning streak	7	Feb. 20 — Mar. 7
Longest unbeaten streak	8	Feb. 20 — Mar. 10
Longest losing streak	3	5 times
Longest winless streak	5	3 times
Most shots, game	47	vs. SJ, Nov. 6
Most shots, period	22	1st, vs. Det, Nov. 8
Fewest shots, game	14	2 times
Fewest shots, period	2	2 times

Individual

Longest goal streak	8	Teemu Selanne
Longest point streak	17	Teemu Selanne
Most goals, game	3	Teemu Selanne
Most assists, game	4	3 times
Most points, game	5	Teemu Selanne
Highest +/–, game	5	Jason Marshall
Lowest +/–, game	-3	18 times
Most shots, game	12	Paul Kariya [2]

Did You Know?

Over the last three seasons, Anaheim has a winning percentage of .523 (77-69-27) in games Paul Kariya has played, compared to .356 (20-41-12) in games Kariya has not played.

Miscellaneous

		NHL Rank
PP Pct.	22.0 (83-378)	1
SH goals allowed	7	9t
PK Pct.	84.5 (327-387)	14
SH goals scored	6	21t
Special Team Index	106.2	3
Shots on goal	2,331 (28.4/G)	10
Shots against	2,596 (31.7/G)	25
Unassisted goals	18	2t
Unassisted goals allowed	8	2t
Team Average Weight	200.2	15
Game Star Points	380	15

Game Star Breakdown

Player	1st	2nd	3rd	Pts
Guy Hebert	11	7	4	80
Paul Kariya	7	9	11	73
Teemu Selanne	8	9	5	72
Steve Rucchin	4	3	0	29
Marty McInnis	3	0	3	18
Matt Cullen	1	3	1	15
Fredrik Olausson	1	3	1	15
Dominic Roussel	2	0	1	11
Tomas Sandstrom	2	0	1	11
Johan Davidsson	1	1	1	9
Ruslan Salei	0	0	9	9
Jeff Nielsen	1	0	2	7
Mike Crowley	1	0	1	6
Travis Green	0	1	3	6
Stu Grimson	1	0	0	5
Pascal Trepanier	0	1	1	4
Kevin Haller	0	0	4	4
Antti Aalto	0	1	0	3
Ted Drury	0	1	0	3

Boston Bruins 1998-99 Game Log (39-30-13)

Date	Opp	Score	W/L/T	Record	Goalies W/T	Goalies L/T	Shots Bos	Shots Opp	Power Plays Bos	Power Plays Opp	Game Stars 1st	Game Stars 2nd	Game Stars 3rd
10/10	StL	3-3*	T	0-0-1	**Dafoe**	Fuhr	24	32	2-8	1-3	**Baumgartner**	Demitra	**Samsonov**
10/12	NYI	3-**0**	W	1-0-1	**Dafoe**	Salo	17	28	1-5	0-4	**Dafoe**	Lapointe	**Samsonov**
10/14	@Col	3-**0**	W	2-0-1	**Dafoe**	Roy	23	34	2-6	0-6	**Dafoe**	**Bourque**	**Allison**
10/16	@LA	1-2*	L	2-1-1	Fiset	**Dafoe**	23	27	0-4	1-2	Robitaille	Fiset	**Dafoe**
10/18	@SJ	3-**0**	W	3-1-1	**Tallas**	Vernon	17	22	1-6	0-4	**Tallas**	Nolan	**Khristich**
10/19	@Pho	1-3	L	3-2-1	Khabibulin	**Dafoe**	14	26	0-5	1-6	Roenick	Corkum	Ylonen
10/21	@Anh	0-3	L	3-3-1	Hebert	**Dafoe**	26	30	0-6	2-4	Crowley	Hebert	Kariya
10/24	@NJ	1-3	L	3-4-1	Terreri	**Tallas**	21	31	1-4	1-3	Pandolfo	Terreri	Stevens
10/28	@Mon	**9**-2	W	4-4-1	**Dafoe**	Theodore	34	35	**5-9**	0-5	**Dafoe**	**Ferraro**	**Thornton**
10/29	Mon	1-1*	T	4-4-2	**Dafoe**	Thibault	31	23	**1-9**	1-5	Recchi	Thibault	**Dafoe**
10/31	Car	0-2	L	4-5-2	Irbe	**Tallas**	34	24	0-4	0-3	Irbe	**Tallas**	Chiasson
11/03	@Buf	2-4	L	4-6-2	Hasek	**Dafoe**	20	32	1-6	0-5	Satan	Grosek	Hasek
11/05	Tor	4-1	W	5-6-2	**Dafoe**	Joseph	30	35	2-6	1-7	**Samsonov**	**Khristich**	**Dafoe**
11/07	@Pit	0-**0***	T	5-6-3	**Dafoe**	Aubin	18	26	0-3	0-2	**Dafoe**	Aubin	Jagr
11/08	@Car	5-2	W	6-6-3	**Dafoe**	Irbe	31	31	3-8	0-7	**Khristich**	**Bourque**	**Van Impe**
11/13	@NYR	3-3*	T	6-6-4	**Dafoe**	Richter	27	25	1-5	2-4	MacLean	Kovalev	**Khristich**
11/14	Dal	1-3	L	6-7-4	Turek	**Dafoe**	28	29	0-4	0-4	Hull	Turek	**Dafoe**
11/19	Fla	5-5*	T	6-7-5	**Dafoe**	Burke	29	44	1-3	1-5	Laus	**Van Impe**	Kvasha
11/21	Was	5-4*	W	7-7-5	**Tallas**	Tabaracci	**45**	35	2-6	0-3	**Allison**	**Khristich**	Gonchar
11/24	@TB	4-1	W	8-7-5	**Tallas**	Ranford	33	16	1-4	0-4	**Khristich**	**Bourque**	**Heinze**
11/25	@Fla	1-**0**	W	9-7-5	**Dafoe**	McLean	19	23	1-1	0-3	**Samsonov**	**Dafoe**	McLean
11/27	Mon	5-1	W	10-7-5	**Dafoe**	Hackett	26	25	0-3	0-5	**Bourque**	**DiMaio**	**Samsonov**
12/01	Van	1-1*	T	10-7-6	**Dafoe**	Snow	27	21	0-6	0-2	**Samsonov**	Ohlund	**Carter**
12/05	Pit	2-1	W	11-7-6	**Dafoe**	Barrasso	22	34	0-2	0-2	**Dafoe**	Kovalev	Jagr
12/10	@Car	3-2	W	12-7-6	**Dafoe**	Kidd	16	28	0-1	1-**1**	**T.Taylor**	Gelinas	Emerson
12/12	Buf	1-4	L	12-8-6	Hasek	**Dafoe**	37	20	0-6	1-4	Hasek	Satan	Grosek
12/16	@Det	3-5	L	12-9-6	Osgood	**Dafoe**	26	25	0-6	2-3	Fedorov	**Allison**	Holmstrom
12/17	Ott	5-2	W	13-9-6	**Dafoe**	Rhodes	27	31	2-3	0-4	**Bourque**	**DiMaio**	**Axelsson**
12/19	Det	4-1	W	14-9-6	**Dafoe**	Maracle	32	24	2-5	0-5	**Dafoe**	**Gill**	**Bourque**
12/21	TB	3-2	W	15-9-6	**Tallas**	Ranford	34	26	1-6	1-4	**McLaren**	**Allison**	Gratton
12/23	Phi	1-2	L	15-10-6	Vanbiesbrouck	**Dafoe**	29	32	0-4	0-3	LeClair	**Thornton**	Lindros
12/26	@NYI	2-4	L	15-11-6	Flaherty	**Dafoe**	27	21	0-3	1-5	Linden	Watt	Chara
12/28	@Was	1-5	L	15-12-6	Tabaracci	**Dafoe**	22	37	0-4	0-3	Konowalchuk	Bondra	Gonchar
12/30	@Nsh	5-2	W	16-12-6	**Tallas**	Vokoun	38	29	1-4	0-3	**Carter**	**Heinze**	Bordeleau
12/31	@Dal	1-6	L	16-13-6	Belfour	**Tallas**	31	26	1-2	1-3	Verbeek	Zubov	Belfour
1/02	Anh	2-1	W	17-13-6	**Dafoe**	Hebert	26	30	1-3	1-3	**Bourque**	Rucchin	**McLaren**
1/04	Cgy	5-1	W	18-13-6	**Dafoe**	Garner	37	40	0-2	0-5	**Samsonov**	**DiMaio**	**McLaren**
1/07	Tor	2-1	W	19-13-6	**Dafoe**	Healy	27	28	0-3	0-3	**Dafoe**	**Allison**	Korolev
1/09	@Tor	3-6	L	19-14-6	Joseph	**Dafoe**	32	23	2-6	1-4	Johnson	Joseph	Valk
1/15	@Buf	1-2	L	19-15-6	Hasek	**Dafoe**	34	24	0-3	0-3	Holzinger	Hasek	**Khristich**
1/16	TB	2-2*	T	19-15-7	**Tallas**	Ranford	29	39	0-4	0-6	**Tallas**	Kubina	Ranford
1/18	Nsh	8-1	W	20-15-7	**Dafoe**	Vokoun	37	17	1-5	0-3	**Heinze**	**Ferraro**	**Sweeney**
1/21	Ott	1-3	L	20-16-7	Tugnutt	**Dafoe**	26	28	0-6	0-4	Salo	Tugnutt	**Dafoe**
1/26	@NYI	1-4	L	20-17-7	Salo	**Dafoe**	26	20	0-4	0-4	Reichel	Palffy	Richter
1/28	NJ	0-2	L	20-18-7	Brodeur	**Dafoe**	40	30	0-3	0-**1**	Brodeur	Arnott	**Thornton**
1/30	@Pit	2-5	L	20-19-7	Skudra	**Tallas**	27	28	0-6	0-4	Kovalev	Titov	Hatcher
1/31	Car	0-**0***	T	20-19-8	**Dafoe**	Kidd	36	24	0-4	0-3	**Sweeney**	Manderville	**Bourque**
2/02	Col	2-3	L	20-20-8	Roy	**Dafoe**	25	22	1-7	1-5	Drury	**Allison**	Forsberg
2/04	NYI	4-5	L	20-21-8	Potvin	**Dafoe**	41	38	0-4	0-2	**Allison**	Linden	Pilon
2/06	@Phi	2-2*	T	20-21-9	**Tallas**	Hextall	29	27	0-3	1-8	**Samsonov**	Lindros	**Bourque**
2/07	NYR	3-2	W	21-21-9	**Dafoe**	Richter	23	27	1-5	0-4	**Thornton**	Leetch	**Allison**
2/09	@Edm	2-**0**	W	22-21-9	**Dafoe**	Shtalenkov	27	31	1-5	0-7	**Dafoe**	**Gill**	Grier
2/12	@Cgy	3-4	L	22-22-9	Brathwaite	**Dafoe**	25	32	1-4	2-5	Stillman	**Bourque**	Fleury
2/13	@Van	1-3	L	22-23-9	Snow	**Tallas**	15	24	1-4	0-3	Bertuzzi	Mogilny	**Carter**
2/18	@Ott	0-2	L	22-24-9	Tugnutt	**Dafoe**	30	28	0-5	1-3	Tugnutt	Bonk	Prospal

2/21	@Chi	6-3	W	23-24-9	**Tallas**	Thibault	28	31	1-5	1-3	**Khristich**	**Samsonov**	**Allison**
2/23	Ott	5-2	W	24-24-9	**Dafoe**	Tugnutt	32	28	1-2	0-4	**Mann**	**Dafoe**	McEachern
2/25	NJ	3-3*	T	24-24-10	**Dafoe**	Brodeur	28	39	0-2	0-2	Arnott	**Thornton**	Sykora
2/27	Was	4-3	W	25-24-10	**Dafoe**	Kolzig	19	36	3-5	1-4	**Dafoe**	Klee	**Khristich**
3/02	Pho	3-2	W	26-24-10	**Dafoe**	Esche	22	30	0-4	0-3	**McLaren**	Roenick	**Axelsson**
3/03	@Car	1-2	L	26-25-10	Irbe	**Dafoe**	24	25	0-3	0-6	Gelinas	Wesley	Irbe
3/05	@NJ	4-1	W	27-25-10	**Dafoe**	Brodeur	21	25	0-4	1-2	**Thornton**	**Dafoe**	**McLaren**
3/07	NYR	1-3	L	27-26-10	Richter	**Dafoe**	38	18	0-6	0-6	Richter	Schneider	**Bourque**
3/09	Fla	2-**0**	W	28-26-10	**Dafoe**	Burke	41	19	1-5	0-5	**Bourque**	**Khristich**	**Dafoe**
3/12	@NYR	5-4	W	29-26-10	**Dafoe**	Richter	38	44	1-4	0-4	**Carter**	MacLean	Graves
3/13	@Buf	1-3	L	29-27-10	Roloson	**Dafoe**	32	22	1-4	0-2	Roloson	Grosek	**Heinze**
3/17	@Tor	4-1	W	30-27-10	**Dafoe**	Joseph	29	26	2-6	0-4	**Dafoe**	Korolev	**McLaren**
3/20	SJ	2-2*	T	30-27-11	**Dafoe**	Shields	31	20	1-3	0-3	**Allison**	Sturm	**Heinze**
3/21	@Was	4-1	W	31-27-11	**Dafoe**	Kolzig	34	19	1-6	0-**1**	**Allison**	**McLaren**	**Bourque**
3/24	@Ott	3-**0**	W	32-27-11	**Dafoe**	Tugnutt	17	28	1-2	0-5	**Dafoe**	**Gill**	**Bourque**
3/25	Chi	3-3*	T	32-27-12	**Dafoe**	Thibault	26	22	3-7	1-3	**Bourque**	**Heinze**	Mironov
3/27	@Tor	2-2*	T	32-27-13	**Dafoe**	Joseph	26	27	1-5	0-4	Markov	**McLaren**	Joseph
3/30	LA	1-2*	L	32-28-13	Storr	**Dafoe**	25	27	0-2	0-**1**	Jokinen	**Dafoe**	R.Blake
4/01	@Mon	3-2	W	33-28-13	**Dafoe**	Hackett	24	24	1-4	0-2	**Carter**	**Bourque**	**Thornton**
4/03	Phi	3-**0**	W	34-28-13	**Dafoe**	Vanbiesbrouck	20	24	0-3	0-3	**Bates**	**Samsonov**	**Dafoe**
4/05	Mon	3-**0**	W	35-28-13	**Dafoe**	Chabot	26	25	1-3	0-**1**	**Carter**	**Sweeney**	**Dafoe**
4/07	@Fla	5-2	W	36-28-13	**Dafoe**	McLean	26	18	2-6	1-4	**Carter**	**DiMaio**	Johnson
4/08	@TB	0-3	L	36-29-13	Hodson	**Tallas**	27	21	0-**9**	0-4	Richer	**Tallas**	Schwab
4/10	TB	3-2	W	37-29-13	**Tallas**	Schwab	33	21	2-8	0-4	**Thornton**	**Heinze**	Svoboda
4/15	Pit	4-2	W	38-29-13	**Dafoe**	Barrasso	25	**15**	1-2	1-2	**Allison**	**Gill**	Kovalev
4/17	Buf	2-1*	W	39-29-13	**Dafoe**	Hasek	29	23	0-2	0-2	**Gill**	**Samsonov**	Brown
4/18	@Phi	1-3	L	39-30-13	Vanbiesbrouck	**Tallas**	11	22	0-1	2-5	LeClair	Greig	Desjardins

Postseason

4/22	@Car	2-**0**	W	1-0	**Dafoe**	Irbe	29	**19**	0-4	0-4	**DiMaio**	**Dafoe**	**Belanger**
4/24	@Car	2-3*	L	1-1	Irbe	**Dafoe**	24	30	0-1	0-4	Sheppard	Gelinas	**Heinze**
4/26	Car	2-3	L	1-2	Irbe	**Dafoe**	26	21	1-5	1-4	Roberts	**Allison**	Battaglia
4/28	Car	4-1	W	2-2	**Dafoe**	Irbe	30	23	1-3	0-3	**Sweeney**	**Thornton**	**Axelsson**
4/30	@Car	4-3*	W	3-2	**Dafoe**	Irbe	**52**	40	1-6	1-**2**	**Carter**	**Axelsson**	**Bourque**
5/02	Car	2-**0**	W	4-2	**Dafoe**	Irbe	21	31	1-5	0-4	**Dafoe**	**Carter**	**Thornton**
5/06	Buf	4-2	W	1-0	**Dafoe**	Hasek	22	30	**2**-5	1-3	**Allison**	Woolley	**Heinze**
5/09	Buf	1-3	L	1-1	Hasek	**Dafoe**	29	29	1-**9**	1-6	Brown	Peca	**Sweeney**
5/12	@Buf	2-3	L	1-2	Hasek	**Dafoe**	21	25	1-4	1-5	Ward	Warrener	**Carter**
5/14	@Buf	0-3	L	1-3	Hasek	**Dafoe**	24	39	0-7	1-6	Hasek	Zhitnik	Peca
5/16	Buf	**5**-3	W	2-3	**Dafoe**	Hasek	34	23	0-5	1-3	**Samsonov**	**T.Taylor**	Primeau
5/18	@Buf	2-3	L	2-4	Hasek	**Dafoe**	25	21	1-5	1-3	Sanderson	Primeau	Peca

Boston Bruins 1998-99 Player Statistics

Skater	Ps	Regular Season GP	G	A	Pts	+/–	PIM	PP	SH	GW	GT	S	SPct	P/G	Postseason GP	G	A	Pts	+/–	PIM	PP	SH	GW	OT	S	SPct	P/G
Jason Allison	C	**82**	23	**53**	**76**	5	68	5	**1**	3	0	158	14.6	**.93**	**12**	2	**9**	**11**	1	6	1	0	0	0	28	7.1	**.92**
Dimitri Khristich	L	79	**29**	42	71	11	48	**13**	**1**	6	**1**	144	**20.1**	.90	**12**	3	4	7	1	6	0	0	1	0	19	15.8	.58
Ray Bourque	D	81	10	47	57	-7	34	8	0	3	0	**262**	3.8	.70	**12**	1	**9**	10	1	14	0	0	0	0	**44**	2.3	.83
Sergei Samsonov	L	79	25	26	51	-6	18	6	0	**8**	**1**	160	15.6	.65	11	3	1	4	3	0	0	0	0	0	21	14.3	.36
Joe Thornton	C	81	16	25	41	3	69	7	0	1	0	128	12.5	.51	11	3	6	9	1	4	**2**	0	**2**	0	15	**20.0**	.82
Anson Carter	C	55	24	16	40	7	22	6	0	6	0	123	19.5	.73	**12**	**4**	3	7	-3	0	1	0	1	**1**	27	14.8	.58
Steve Heinze	R	73	22	18	40	7	30	9	0	3	0	146	15.1	.55	**12**	**4**	3	7	-1	0	**2**	0	0	0	23	17.4	.58
Kyle McLaren	D	52	6	18	24	1	48	3	0	0	0	97	6.2	.46	**12**	0	3	3	**4**	10	0	0	0	0	21	0.0	.25
Rob DiMaio	C	71	7	14	21	-14	95	1	0	0	0	121	5.8	.30	**12**	2	0	2	2	8	0	0	1	0	21	9.5	.17
Darren Van Impe	D	60	5	15	20	-5	66	4	0	0	0	92	5.4	.33	11	1	2	3	-3	4	1	0	0	0	18	5.6	.27
Per Axelsson	L	77	7	10	17	-14	18	0	0	2	0	146	4.8	.22	**12**	1	1	2	-1	4	0	0	0	0	20	5.0	.17
Peter Ferraro	C	46	6	8	14	10	44	1	0	1	0	61	9.8	.30	—	—	—	—	—	—	—	—	—	—	—	—	—
Grant Ledyard	D	47	4	8	12	-8	33	1	0	2	0	47	8.5	.26	2	0	0	0	-1	2	0	0	0	0	4	0.0	.00
Don Sweeney	D	81	2	10	12	**14**	64	0	0	0	0	79	2.5	.15	11	3	0	3	2	6	1	0	0	0	16	18.8	.27
Tim Taylor	C	49	4	7	11	-10	55	0	0	1	0	76	5.3	.22	**12**	0	3	3	1	8	0	0	0	0	11	0.0	.25
Hal Gill	D	80	3	7	10	-10	63	0	0	2	0	102	2.9	.13	**12**	0	0	0	-1	14	0	0	0	0	10	0.0	.00
* Shawn Bates	C	33	5	4	9	3	2	0	0	0	0	30	16.7	.27	**12**	0	0	0	-1	4	0	0	0	0	11	0.0	.00
Chris Taylor	C	37	3	5	8	-3	12	0	**1**	0	0	60	5.0	.22	—	—	—	—	—	—	—	—	—	—	—	—	—
* Cameron Mann	R	33	5	2	7	0	17	1	0	1	**1**	42	11.9	.21	1	0	0	0	0	0	0	0	0	0	0	—	.00
Landon Wilson	R	22	3	3	6	0	17	0	0	0	0	32	9.4	.27	8	1	1	2	-2	8	1	0	1	0	14	7.1	.25
Mattias Timander	D	22	0	6	6	4	10	0	0	0	0	22	0.0	.27	4	1	1	2	3	2	0	0	0	0	3	33.3	.50
Dave Ellett	D	54	0	6	6	11	25	0	0	0	0	45	0.0	.11	8	0	0	0	0	4	0	0	0	0	4	0.0	.00
Ken Belanger†	L	45	1	4	5	-2	**152**	0	0	0	0	16	6.3	.11	**12**	1	0	1	2	**16**	0	0	0	0	7	14.3	.08
Ted Donato†	L	14	1	3	4	0	4	0	0	0	0	22	4.5	.29	—	—	—	—	—	—	—	—	—	—	—	—	—
Ken Baumgartner	L	69	1	3	4	-6	119	0	0	0	**1**	15	6.7	.06	3	0	0	0	0	0	0	0	0	0	0	—	.00
* Antti Laaksonen	L	11	1	2	3	-1	2	0	0	0	0	8	12.5	.27	—	—	—	—	—	—	—	—	—	—	—	—	—
* Randy Robitaille	C	4	0	2	2	-1	0	0	0	0	0	5	0.0	.50	1	0	0	0	0	0	0	0	0	0	0	—	.00
Byron Dafoe	G	68	0	2	2	—	25	0	0	0	0	0	—	.03	**12**	0	0	0	—	2	0	0	0	0	0	—	.00
* Andre Savage	C	6	1	0	1	2	0	0	0	0	0	8	12.5	.17	—	—	—	—	—	—	—	—	—	—	—	—	—
* Eric Nickulas	C	2	0	0	0	0	0	0	0	0	0	0	—	.00	1	0	0	0	0	2	0	0	0	0	0	—	.00
* Peter Nordstrom	C	2	0	0	0	-1	0	0	0	0	0	0	—	.00	—	—	—	—	—	—	—	—	—	—	—	—	—
* Jonathan Girard	D	3	0	0	0	1	0	0	0	0	0	3	0.0	.00	—	—	—	—	—	—	—	—	—	—	—	—	—
Dennis Vaske	D	3	0	0	0	-3	6	0	0	0	0	0	—	.00	—	—	—	—	—	—	—	—	—	—	—	—	—
* Jay Henderson	L	4	0	0	0	-1	2	0	0	0	0	4	0.0	.00	—	—	—	—	—	—	—	—	—	—	—	—	—
Terry Virtue	D	4	0	0	0	2	0	0	0	0	0	2	0.0	.00	—	—	—	—	—	—	—	—	—	—	—	—	—
* Brandon Smith	D	5	0	0	0	2	0	0	0	0	0	2	0.0	.00	—	—	—	—	—	—	—	—	—	—	—	—	—
* Marquis Mathieu	C	9	0	0	0	-1	8	0	0	0	0	4	0.0	.00	—	—	—	—	—	—	—	—	—	—	—	—	—
Robbie Tallas	G	17	0	0	0	—	0	0	0	0	0	0	—	.00	—	—	—	—	—	—	—	—	—	—	—	—	—
Bench		—	—	—	—	—	0	—	—	—	—	—	—	—	—	—	—	—	—	0	—	—	—	—	—	—	—
TEAM TOTALS		82	214	366	580	-10	1176	65	3	39	4	2262	9.5	7.07	12	30	46	76	8	124	9	0	6	1	337	8.9	6.33

Goaltender	Regular Season G	Min	GAA	W	L	T	ENG	ShO	GA	SA	SvPct	Postseason G	Min	GAA	W	L	ENG	ShO	GA	SA	SvPct
Byron Dafoe	**68**	**4001**	**1.99**	**32**	**23**	**11**	**3**	**10**	**133**	**1800**	**.926**	**12**	**768**	**2.03**	**6**	**6**	**1**	**2**	**26**	**330**	**.921**
Robbie Tallas	17	987	2.61	7	7	2	2	1	43	421	.898	—	—	—	—	—	—	—	—	—	—
TEAM TOTALS	82	5001	2.17	39	30	13	5	11	181	2226	.919	12	772	2.10	6	6	1	2	27	331	.918

1998-99 Boston Bruins

Record When:

Overtime games	2-2-13
In second game of back-to-back games	5-8-4
Vs playoff teams	19-20-7
Leading after two periods	27-1-3
Tied after two periods	9-9-8
Losing after two periods	3-20-2
Scoring first	28-5-6
More shots than opponents	16-15-7
Fewer shots than opponents	21-15-6
Team had at least one fighting major	19-6-4
Team had more PIM	11-7-3
Team had fewer PIM	19-20-8
Team had even PIM	9-3-2

Team

Longest winning streak	4	2 times
Longest unbeaten streak	8	Nov. 19 — Dec. 10
Longest losing streak	4	Jan. 21 — Jan. 30
Longest winless streak	8	Jan. 21 — Feb. 6
Most shots, game	45	vs. Was, Nov. 21
Most shots, period	21	2nd, vs. Buf, Dec. 12
Fewest shots, game	11	@Phi, Apr. 18
Fewest shots, period	2	2 times

Individual

Longest goal streak	3	4 times
Longest point streak	7	Sergei Samsonov
Most goals, game	3	3 times
Most assists, game	3	7 times
Most points, game	5	Dimitri Khristich
Highest +/–, game	3	9 times
Lowest +/–, game	-5	Darren Van Impe
Most shots, game	9	3 times

Did You Know?

Harry Sinden's 27-year tenure as general manager of the Bruins is the fourth-longest by any man with one team in NHL history. Sinden is the only GM to serve a team for more than 25 years without winning the Stanley Cup.

Miscellaneous

		NHL Rank
PP Pct.	17.7 (65-368)	8
SH goals allowed	9	15t
PK Pct.	89.2 (272-305)	1
SH goals scored	3	27
Special Team Index	105.4	7
Shots on goal	2,262 (27.6/G)	17
Shots against	2,226 (27.1/G)	12
Unassisted goals	15	6t
Unassisted goals allowed	12	13t
Team Average Weight	196.8	24
Game Star Points	400	10

Game Star Breakdown

Player	1st	2nd	3rd	Pts
Byron Dafoe	11	4	8	75
Ray Bourque	5	5	6	46
Jason Allison	5	4	3	40
Sergei Samsonov	5	3	3	37
Dimitri Khristich	3	3	4	28
Anson Carter	5	0	2	27
Joe Thornton	3	2	3	24
Kyle McLaren	2	2	4	20
Hal Gill	1	4	0	17
Steve Heinze	1	3	3	17
Robbie Tallas	2	2	0	16
Rob DiMaio	0	4	0	12
Don Sweeney	1	1	1	9
Peter Ferraro	0	2	0	6
Shawn Bates	1	0	0	5
Ken Baumgartner	1	0	0	5
Cameron Mann	1	0	0	5
Tim Taylor	1	0	0	5
Darren Van Impe	0	1	1	4
Per Axelsson	0	0	2	2

Buffalo Sabres 1998-99 Game Log (37-28-17)

Date	Opp	Score	W/L/T	Record	Goalies W/T	Goalies L/T	Shots Buf	Shots Opp	Power Plays Buf	Power Plays Opp	Game Stars 1st	Game Stars 2nd	Game Stars 3rd
10/10	@Dal	1-4	L	0-1-0	Belfour	**Hasek**	28	26	1-6	3-8	Modano	Zubov	Sydor
10/12	@Col	3-**0**	W	1-1-0	**Hasek**	Roy	27	32	2-10	0-8	**Peca**	**Ward**	**Hasek**
10/16	Fla	2-2*	T	1-1-1	**Hasek**	Burke	25	34	1-6	1-5	Kvasha	**Hasek**	**Sanderson**
10/17	@Mon	4-3	W	2-1-1	**Hasek**	Thibault	27	35	2-**11**	0-3	**Ward**	Damphousse	Brunet
10/23	Was	0-1	L	2-2-1	Kolzig	**Hasek**	30	36	0-7	0-5	Kolzig	**Hasek**	Bondra
10/24	@NYI	4-5	L	2-3-1	Salo	**Hasek**	36	28	1-6	1-4	Lapointe	Smolinski	**Sanderson**
10/27	@NYR	0-**0***	T	2-3-2	**Hasek**	Richter	24	16	0-5	0-6	Richter	**Hasek**	Samuelsson
10/30	Tor	4-1	W	3-3-2	**Hasek**	Joseph	23	37	1-3	0-6	**Plante**	**Hasek**	**Smehlik**
10/31	@Tor	6-3	W	4-3-2	**Hasek**	Potvin	25	33	1-3	0-5	**Sanderson**	**Peca**	K.King
11/03	Bos	4-2	W	5-3-2	**Hasek**	Dafoe	32	20	0-5	1-6	**Satan**	**Grosek**	**Hasek**
11/07	@Phi	2-2*	T	5-3-3	**Hasek**	Vanbiesbrouck	19	37	0-2	1-4	**Hasek**	Brind'Amour	**Sanderson**
11/10	Ott	2-2*	T	5-3-4	**Hasek**	Rhodes	23	40	0-5	1-8	**Hasek**	Rhodes	**Brown**
11/12	@Was	2-**0**	W	6-3-4	**Hasek**	Kolzig	25	23	0-2	0-6	**Hasek**	**Peca**	Reekie
11/14	Chi	6-1	W	7-3-4	**Hasek**	Trefilov	37	21	2-2	0-3	**Grosek**	**Holzinger**	**Sanderson**
11/20	Tor	4-1	W	8-3-4	**Hasek**	Potvin	26	33	0-4	0-5	**Brown**	**Ward**	**Holzinger**
11/21	@Tor	1-2	L	8-4-4	Joseph	**Hasek**	18	31	0-5	0-3	Domi	Sullivan	**Brown**
11/25	NYR	4-2	W	9-4-4	**Hasek**	Cloutier	30	26	1-2	1-3	**Ward**	**Peca**	**Varada**
11/28	@Fla	2-6	L	9-5-4	McLean	**Roloson**	23	47	1-5	3-9	Whitney	Svehla	McLean
11/29	@TB	6-3	W	10-5-4	**Hasek**	Schwab	33	33	0-3	1-3	**Peca**	Tucker	**Brown**
12/02	Fla	2-1	W	11-5-4	**Hasek**	McLean	28	28	0-4	0-4	**Hasek**	**Ward**	Whitney
12/04	Phi	3-**0**	W	12-5-4	**Hasek**	Vanbiesbrouck	15	31	1-5	0-7	**Hasek**	**Shannon**	**Sanderson**
12/05	@Nsh	3-1	W	13-5-4	**Hasek**	Fichaud	28	37	0-3	1-7	**Hasek**	Fichaud	**Holzinger**
12/08	@StL	2-2*	T	13-5-5	**Hasek**	McLennan	16	43	1-6	1-8	**Hasek**	Demitra	**Brown**
12/11	NYR	2-**0**	W	14-5-5	**Hasek**	Richter	32	16	1-6	0-4	**Peca**	**Hasek**	Richter
12/12	@Bos	4-1	W	15-5-5	**Hasek**	Dafoe	20	37	1-4	0-6	**Hasek**	**Satan**	**Grosek**
12/18	Mon	4-2	W	16-5-5	**Hasek**	Theodore	21	38	0-5	0-7	**Ward**	**Hasek**	**Brown**
12/19	Car	2-3	L	16-6-5	Kidd	**Hasek**	**40**	20	0-6	1-7	Kidd	Primeau	**Satan**
12/21	@Car	4-1	W	17-6-5	**Hasek**	Kidd	33	20	2-6	0-6	**Woolley**	**Satan**	**Peca**
12/23	TB	2-**0**	W	18-6-5	**Hasek**	Ranford	22	38	1-5	0-7	**Hasek**	**Holzinger**	**Satan**
12/26	@NJ	2-**0**	W	19-6-5	**Hasek**	Brodeur	24	34	0-3	0-4	**Hasek**	Brodeur	**Satan**
12/28	NJ	4-7	L	19-7-5	Brodeur	**Roloson**	**40**	18	2-6	2-5	Morrison	**Peca**	Lakovic
12/30	Ott	2-3*	L	19-8-5	Rhodes	**Hasek**	23	44	0-3	1-4	Dackell	McEachern	**Hasek**
1/01	Anh	2-7	L	19-9-5	Hebert	**Hasek**	33	31	1-4	2-4	Selanne	Rucchin	Kariya
1/02	Cgy	**7**-1	W	20-9-5	**Roloson**	Trefilov	35	32	**3**-4	0-3	**Ward**	**Roloson**	**Satan**
1/06	@Anh	3-2*	W	21-9-5	**Hasek**	Hebert	19	25	1-5	0-**2**	**Peca**	Kariya	**Varada**
1/07	@LA	2-4	L	21-10-5	Storr	**Roloson**	23	24	1-5	1-**2**	Robitaille	R.Blake	Storr
1/09	@SJ	2-2*	T	21-10-6	**Hasek**	Shields	31	26	2-7	1-5	Nolan	**Woolley**	Friesen
1/11	@Pho	0-1	L	21-11-6	Khabibulin	**Hasek**	23	22	0-3	0-3	Khabibulin	Drake	**Hasek**
1/13	StL	2-4	L	21-12-6	Fuhr	**Hasek**	25	30	1-10	3-7	Pronger	MacInnis	Fuhr
1/15	Bos	2-1	W	22-12-6	**Hasek**	Dafoe	24	34	0-3	0-3	**Holzinger**	**Hasek**	Khristich
1/16	@Ott	1-1*	T	22-12-7	**Hasek**	Tugnutt	15	39	1-7	0-4	**Hasek**	Arvedson	Laukkanen
1/18	@Fla	4-**0**	W	23-12-7	**Hasek**	Burke	39	33	1-4	0-5	**Zhitnik**	**Hasek**	**Peca**
1/19	@TB	1-2	L	23-13-7	Schwab	**Hasek**	15	32	0-3	0-6	Zamuner	Wilkie	Kubina
1/26	Pho	1-1*	T	23-13-8	**Hasek**	Khabibulin	27	25	1-4	1-4	Khabibulin	**Hasek**	**Brown**
1/28	Nsh	2-4	L	23-14-8	Vokoun	**Hasek**	32	31	0-2	1-5	Atcheynum	Ronning	**Peca**
1/30	LA	4-1	W	24-14-8	**Hasek**	Storr	31	26	0-2	0-5	**Sanderson**	**Peca**	**Zhitnik**
2/02	@Pit	3-5	L	24-15-8	Skudra	**Hasek**	34	29	1-3	2-6	Jagr	Miller	Hrdina
2/03	Col	3-5	L	24-16-8	Roy	**Hasek**	**40**	35	1-3	2-6	Corbet	**Satan**	Kamensky
2/06	@Mon	2-3	L	24-17-8	Hackett	**Roloson**	29	19	1-7	1-**2**	Weinrich	**Peca**	Chabot
2/07	@Was	1-3	L	24-18-8	Kolzig	**Hasek**	20	34	0-4	0-4	Konowalchuk	Kolzig	Johansson
2/09	@Ott	1-1*	T	24-18-9	**Hasek**	Rhodes	32	37	0-7	1-5	Martins	**Hasek**	Rhodes
2/11	Mon	5-2	W	25-18-9	**Hasek**	Theodore	17	37	0-4	0-6	**Cunneyworth**	**Hasek**	**Kruse**
2/13	NYI	2-2*	T	25-18-10	**Hasek**	Salo	26	18	0-4	0-3	Czerkawski	**Kruse**	**Satan**
2/15	Car	3-2	W	26-18-10	**Hasek**	Irbe	36	38	0-4	0-5	**Satan**	Gelinas	**Peca**
2/17	Tor	2-3*	L	26-19-10	Healy	**Hasek**	27	29	0-3	1-4	Sundin	**Satan**	Sullivan

2/19	SJ	4-2	W	27-19-10	**Roloson**	Shields	28	32	0-6	1-5	**Brown**	**Satan**	**Roloson**
2/21	Det	4-4*	T	27-19-11	**Roloson**	Osgood	25	38	1-1	1-**2**	Kozlov	**Satan**	**Grosek**
2/24	@Cgy	2-2*	T	27-19-12	**Roloson**	Brathwaite	28	35	0-4	0-4	Brathwaite	Wiemer	**Roloson**
2/26	@Edm	3-6	L	27-20-12	Essensa	**Biron**	30	39	0-3	3-7	Marchant	McAmmond	Grier
2/28	@Van	2-**0**	W	28-20-12	**Roloson**	Snow	18	**15**	0-3	0-4	**Shannon**	**Zhitnik**	Strudwick
3/03	Edm	3-5	L	28-21-12	Passmore	**Roloson**	32	26	0-5	1-4	Mironov	**Peca**	Passmore
3/05	Dal	2-1	W	29-21-12	**Biron**	Belfour	28	27	1-6	0-3	**Biron**	**Peca**	Belfour
3/07	Phi	1-1*	T	29-21-13	**Biron**	Vanbiesbrouck	22	31	0-5	0-3	**Biron**	**Shannon**	Zelepukin
3/08	@Car	1-4	L	29-22-13	Irbe	**Roloson**	32	34	1-4	0-3	Kovalenko	Irbe	Hill
3/11	TB	2-5	L	29-23-13	Schwab	**Biron**	37	21	0-6	1-4	Schwab	Petrovicky	**Grosek**
3/13	Bos	3-1	W	30-23-13	**Roloson**	Dafoe	22	32	0-2	1-4	**Roloson**	**Grosek**	Heinze
3/15	NYI	2-1	W	31-23-13	**Roloson**	Flaherty	22	24	1-5	1-8	**Satan**	**Barnes**	**Roloson**
3/19	@NYR	3-2*	W	32-23-13	**Hasek**	Richter	24	29	2-4	2-7	**Satan**	**Hasek**	Schneider
3/23	@NJ	1-1*	T	32-23-14	**Hasek**	Brodeur	19	32	0-2	0-**2**	**Satan**	Nemchinov	**Hasek**
3/24	@Det	1-2	L	32-24-14	Osgood	**Roloson**	25	30	0-3	0-3	Fedorov	Yzerman	Brown
3/27	@Pit	1-1*	T	32-24-15	**Hasek**	Aubin	25	32	0-6	0-8	Aubin	**Hasek**	Barnaby
3/28	Pit	4-3*	W	33-24-15	**Hasek**	Aubin	21	22	2-5	3-7	**Ward**	Jagr	**Satan**
3/31	@Chi	1-2	L	33-25-15	Thibault	**Hasek**	20	25	0-5	0-5	Thibault	Manson	Dumont
4/03	@Mon	1-2	L	33-26-15	Chabot	**Hasek**	32	24	0-3	1-5	Chabot	Koivu	**Peca**
4/05	Pit	3-1	W	34-26-15	**Hasek**	Skudra	22	26	0-4	0-4	**Hasek**	**Woolley**	Brown
4/06	@NYI	4-3	W	35-26-15	**Roloson**	Flaherty	21	41	2-3	2-5	**Woolley**	**Peca**	Brewer
4/09	Fla	3-1	W	36-26-15	**Hasek**	Burke	22	29	1-6	0-5	**Woolley**	**Hasek**	**Satan**
4/10	@Ott	1-1*	T	36-26-16	**Hasek**	Rhodes	12	18	0-5	1-8	**Hasek**	Yashin	**Woolley**
4/13	@Phi	2-2*	T	36-26-17	**Hasek**	Vanbiesbrouck	15	33	0-3	1-5	LeClair	**Hasek**	Desjardins
4/14	NJ	1-2	L	36-27-17	Brodeur	**Roloson**	30	34	0-5	1-3	**Roloson**	Brodeur	Niedermayer
4/17	@Bos	1-2*	L	36-28-17	Dafoe	**Hasek**	23	29	0-2	0-**2**	Gill	Samsonov	**Brown**
4/18	Was	3-**0**	W	37-28-17	**Hasek**	Brochu	29	25	1-3	0-**2**	**Hasek**	**Satan**	**Warrener**

Postseason

4/21	@Ott	2-1	W	1-0	**Hasek**	Tugnutt	15	41	1-3	1-9	**Hasek**	**Peca**	Emerson
4/23	@Ott	3-2*	W	2-0	**Hasek**	Rhodes	39	47	1-7	2-9	**Satan**	**Hasek**	McEachern
4/25	Ott	3-**0**	W	3-0	**Hasek**	Rhodes	26	31	1-5	0-4	**Hasek**	**Holzinger**	**Varada**
4/27	Ott	4-3	W	4-0	**Hasek**	Tugnutt	26	43	1-3	0-5	**Varada**	**Hasek**	Alfredsson
5/06	@Bos	2-4	L	0-1	Dafoe	**Hasek**	30	22	1-3	2-5	Allison	**Woolley**	Heinze
5/09	@Bos	3-1	W	1-1	**Hasek**	Dafoe	29	29	1-6	1-9	**Brown**	**Peca**	Sweeney
5/12	Bos	3-2	W	2-1	**Hasek**	Dafoe	25	**21**	1-5	1-4	**Ward**	**Warrener**	Carter
5/14	Bos	3-**0**	W	3-1	**Hasek**	Dafoe	39	24	1-6	0-7	**Hasek**	**Zhitnik**	**Peca**
5/16	@Bos	3-5	L	3-2	Dafoe	**Hasek**	23	34	1-3	0-5	Samsonov	T.Taylor	**Primeau**
5/18	Bos	3-2	W	4-2	**Hasek**	Dafoe	21	25	1-3	1-5	**Sanderson**	**Primeau**	**Peca**
5/23	@Tor	**5**-4	W	1-0	**Roloson**	Joseph	21	32	1-4	3-9	**Sanderson**	Sundin	**Rasmussen**
5/25	@Tor	3-6	L	1-1	Joseph	**Roloson**	33	28	**3**-5	0-5	Joseph	**Barnes**	Perreault
5/27	Tor	4-2	W	2-1	**Hasek**	Joseph	24	26	1-**8**	1-4	**Satan**	**Hasek**	Sullivan
5/29	Tor	**5**-2	W	3-1	**Hasek**	Joseph	32	33	0-4	1-5	**Sanderson**	**Satan**	**Ray**
5/31	@Tor	4-2	W	4-1	**Hasek**	Joseph	24	22	1-4	1-7	**Rasmussen**	K.King	**Varada**
6/08	@Dal	3-2*	W	1-0	**Hasek**	Belfour	24	37	1-4	1-10	**Woolley**	**Hasek**	Lehtinen
6/10	@Dal	2-4	L	1-1	Belfour	**Hasek**	21	31	2-4	0-6	Hull	Nieuwendyk	**Primeau**
6/12	Dal	1-2	L	1-2	Belfour	**Hasek**	12	29	0-**8**	0-**2**	Nieuwendyk	Langenbrunner	**Barnes**
6/15	Dal	2-1	W	2-2	**Hasek**	Belfour	18	31	0-5	1-3	**Hasek**	**Ward**	Belfour
6/17	@Dal	0-2	L	2-3	Belfour	**Hasek**	23	**21**	0-3	1-3	Belfour	Hatcher	Verbeek
6/19	Dal	1-2*	L	2-4	Belfour	**Hasek**	**54**	50	0-2	0-**2**	Hull	Belfour	**Barnes**

Buffalo Sabres 1998-99 Player Statistics

Skater	Ps	Regular Season GP	G	A	Pts	+/–	PIM	PP	SH	GW	GT	S	SPct	P/G	Postseason GP	G	A	Pts	+/–	PIM	PP	SH	GW	OT	S	SPct	P/G
Miroslav Satan	L	81	**40**	26	**66**	24	44	**13**	**3**	6	1	**208**	19.2	**.81**	12	3	5	8	3	2	1	0	1	**1**	25	12.0	.67
Mike Peca	C	**82**	27	29	56	7	81	10	0	**8**	1	199	13.6	.68	**21**	5	8	13	1	18	2	1	0	0	37	13.5	.62
Michal Grosek	L	76	20	30	50	21	102	4	0	3	1	140	14.3	.66	13	0	4	4	1	28	0	0	0	0	20	0.0	.31
Curtis Brown	C	78	16	31	47	23	56	5	1	3	**3**	128	12.5	.60	**21**	**7**	6	13	3	10	3	0	**3**	0	34	20.6	.62
Dixon Ward	R	78	20	24	44	10	44	2	1	4	1	101	**19.8**	.56	**21**	**7**	5	12	6	32	0	**2**	**3**	0	38	18.4	.57
Jason Woolley	D	80	10	**33**	43	16	62	4	0	2	1	154	6.5	.54	**21**	4	**11**	**15**	0	10	2	0	1	**1**	43	9.3	**.71**
Brian Holzinger	C	81	17	17	34	2	45	5	0	2	0	143	11.9	.42	**21**	3	5	8	1	33	1	0	0	0	32	9.4	.38
Alexei Zhitnik	D	81	7	26	33	-6	96	3	1	2	0	185	3.8	.41	**21**	4	**11**	**15**	-6	**52**	**4**	0	2	0	**58**	6.9	**.71**
Vaclav Varada	R	72	7	24	31	11	61	1	0	1	0	123	5.7	.43	**21**	5	4	9	2	14	1	0	0	0	38	13.2	.43
Geoff Sanderson	L	75	12	18	30	8	22	1	0	1	0	155	7.7	.40	19	4	6	10	5	14	0	0	1	0	53	7.5	.53
Matthew Barnaby†	R	44	4	14	18	-2	143	0	0	3	0	52	7.7	.41	—	—	—	—	—	—	—	—	—	—	—	—	—
Derek Plante†	C	41	4	11	15	3	12	0	0	0	0	66	6.1	.37	—	—	—	—	—	—	—	—	—	—	—	—	—
Darryl Shannon	D	71	3	12	15	**28**	52	1	0	0	1	80	3.8	.21	2	0	0	0	-1	0	0	0	0	0	7	0.0	.00
Richard Smehlik	D	72	3	11	14	-9	44	0	0	0	0	61	4.9	.19	**21**	0	3	3	-4	10	0	0	0	0	20	0.0	.14
Wayne Primeau	C	67	5	8	13	-6	38	0	0	0	1	55	9.1	.19	19	3	4	7	0	6	1	0	0	0	22	13.6	.37
* Erik Rasmussen	C	42	3	7	10	6	37	0	0	0	0	40	7.5	.24	**21**	2	4	6	2	18	0	0	1	0	23	8.7	.29
James Patrick	D	45	1	7	8	12	16	0	0	0	0	31	3.2	.18	20	0	1	1	6	12	0	0	0	0	11	0.0	.05
Jay McKee	D	72	0	6	6	20	75	0	0	0	0	57	0.0	.08	**21**	0	3	3	**13**	24	0	0	0	0	13	0.0	.14
Randy Cunneyworth	L	14	2	2	4	1	0	0	0	1	0	12	16.7	.29	3	0	0	0	-1	0	0	0	0	0	2	0.0	.00
Stu Barnes†	C	17	0	4	4	1	10	0	0	0	0	25	0.0	.24	**21**	**7**	3	10	-1	6	**4**	0	1	0	30	**23.3**	.48
Rob Ray	R	76	0	4	4	-2	**261**	0	0	0	0	23	0.0	.05	5	1	0	1	1	0	0	0	1	0	1	100.0	.20
Paul Kruse	L	43	3	0	3	0	114	0	0	0	0	33	9.1	.07	10	0	0	0	0	4	0	0	0	0	0	—	.00
Mike Wilson†	D	30	1	2	3	10	47	0	0	1	0	40	2.5	.10	—	—	—	—	—	—	—	—	—	—	—	—	—
Joe Juneau†	L	9	1	1	2	-1	2	0	0	0	0	8	12.5	.22	20	3	8	11	-2	10	0	1	0	0	29	10.3	.55
Rhett Warrener†	D	13	1	0	1	3	20	0	0	0	0	11	9.1	.08	20	1	3	4	12	32	0	0	0	0	21	4.8	.20
* J. Grand Pierre	D	16	0	1	1	0	17	0	0	0	0	11	0.0	.06	—	—	—	—	—	—	—	—	—	—	—	—	—
Mike Hurlbut	D	1	0	0	0	2	0	0	0	0	0	2	0.0	.00	—	—	—	—	—	—	—	—	—	—	—	—	—
* Dean Sylvester	R	1	0	0	0	-1	0	0	0	0	0	1	0.0	.00	4	0	0	0	-1	2	0	0	0	0	2	0.0	.00
* Jason Holland	D	3	0	0	0	-1	8	0	0	0	0	2	0.0	.00	—	—	—	—	—	—	—	—	—	—	—	—	—
* Domenic Pittis	C	3	0	0	0	0	2	0	0	0	0	1	0.0	.00	—	—	—	—	—	—	—	—	—	—	—	—	—
* Cory Sarich	D	4	0	0	0	3	0	0	0	0	0	2	0.0	.00	—	—	—	—	—	—	—	—	—	—	—	—	—
* Martin Biron	G	6	0	0	0	—	0	0	0	0	0	0	—	.00	—	—	—	—	—	—	—	—	—	—	—	—	—
* Rumun Ndur†	D	8	0	0	0	1	16	0	0	0	0	1	0.0	.00	—	—	—	—	—	—	—	—	—	—	—	—	—
Dwayne Roloson	G	18	0	0	0	—	4	0	0	0	0	0	—	.00	4	0	0	0	—	0	0	0	0	0	0	—	.00
Dominik Hasek	G	64	0	0	0	—	14	0	0	0	0	0	—	.00	19	0	1	1	—	8	0	0	0	0	0	—	.05
Bench		—	—	—	—	—	0	—	—	—	—	—	—	—	—	—	—	—	—	0	—	—	—	—	—	—	—
TEAM TOTALS		82	207	348	555	184	1545	49	6	37	10	2150	9.6	6.77	21	59	95	154	40	345	19	4	14	2	559	10.6	7.33

Goaltender	Regular Season G	Min	GAA	W	L	T	ENG	ShO	GA	SA	SvPct	Postseason G	Min	GAA	W	L	ENG	ShO	GA	SA	SvPct
Dominik Hasek	**64**	**3817**	**1.87**	**30**	**18**	**14**	**2**	**9**	**119**	**1877**	**.937**	**19**	**1217**	**1.77**	**13**	**6**	**2**	**2**	**36**	**587**	**.939**
* Martin Biron	6	281	2.14	1	2	1	1	0	10	120	.917	—	—	—	—	—	—	—	—	—	—
Dwayne Roloson	18	911	2.77	6	8	2	1	1	42	460	.909	4	139	4.32	1	1	1	0	10	67	.851
TEAM TOTALS	82	5020	2.09	37	28	17	4	10	175	2461	.929	21	1361	2.16	14	7	3	2	49	657	.925

1998-99 Buffalo Sabres

Record When:

Overtime games	3-3-17
In second game of back-to-back games	9-10-2
Vs playoff teams	17-17-13
Leading after two periods	28-1-3
Tied after two periods	4-6-9
Losing after two periods	5-21-5
Scoring first	31-4-4
More shots than opponents	12-13-4
Fewer shots than opponents	23-15-13
Team had at least one fighting major	14-13-5
Team had more PIM	20-13-11
Team had fewer PIM	13-9-3
Team had even PIM	4-6-3

Team

Longest winning streak	4	Nov. 29 — Dec. 5
Longest unbeaten streak	9	Oct. 27 — Nov. 20
Longest losing streak	4	Feb. 2 — Feb. 7
Longest winless streak	5	Feb. 2 — Feb. 9
Most shots, game	40	3 times
Most shots, period	20	3rd, vs. Col, Feb. 3
Fewest shots, game	12	@Ott, Apr. 10
Fewest shots, period	0	3rd, @Ott, Jan. 16

Individual

Longest goal streak	8	Miroslav Satan
Longest point streak	9	Miroslav Satan
Most goals, game	3	2 times
Most assists, game	3	Geoff Sanderson
Most points, game	3	17 times
Highest +/–, game	4	3 times
Lowest +/–, game	-4	Alexei Zhitnik
Most shots, game	7	3 times

Did You Know?

Rob Ray's league-high 261 penalty minutes last season were the fewest by the league leader in a full season since 1972-73, when Philadelphia's Dave Schultz topped the NHL with 259 penalty minutes.

Miscellaneous

		NHL Rank
PP Pct.	13.5 (49-363)	21
SH goals allowed	7	9t
PK Pct.	86.2 (344-399)	7
SH goals scored	6	21t
Special Team Index	99.3	16
Shots on goal	2,150 (26.2/G)	20
Shots against	2,461 (30.0/G)	23
Unassisted goals	15	6t
Unassisted goals allowed	11	12
Team Average Weight	196.0	25
Game Star Points	407	8

Game Star Breakdown

Player	1st	2nd	3rd	Pts
Dominik Hasek	14	15	5	120
Miroslav Satan	5	7	7	53
Mike Peca	4	9	5	52
Dixon Ward	5	3	0	34
Jason Woolley	3	2	1	22
Curtis Brown	2	0	7	17
Dwayne Roloson	2	1	3	16
Geoff Sanderson	2	0	5	15
Michal Grosek	1	2	3	14
Brian Holzinger	1	2	2	13
Darryl Shannon	1	2	0	11
Martin Biron	2	0	0	10
Alexei Zhitnik	1	1	1	9
Randy Cunneyworth	1	0	0	5
Derek Plante	1	0	0	5
Paul Kruse	0	1	1	4
Stu Barnes	0	1	0	3
Vaclav Varada	0	0	2	2
Richard Smehlik	0	0	1	1
Rhett Warrener	0	0	1	1

Calgary Flames 1998-99 Game Log (30-40-12)

					Goalies		Shots		Power Plays		Game Stars		
Date	Opp	Score	W/L/T	Record	W/T	L/T	Cgy	Opp	Cgy	Opp	1st	2nd	3rd
10/09	SJ†	3-3*	T	0-0-1	**Wregget**	Vernon	30	25	0-4	1-7	**Wregget**	Ricci	Murphy
10/10	@SJ†	5-3	W	1-0-1	**Wregget**	Vernon	32	26	2-**8**	1-8	**Fleury**	Marleau	**Morris**
10/16	Tor	3-7	L	1-1-1	Potvin	**Wregget**	33	31	1-5	0-6	Sundin	McCauley	**Iginla**
10/18	@Det	0-2	L	1-2-1	Osgood	**Wregget**	32	28	0-**8**	0-4	Osgood	Shanahan	**Fleury**
10/20	@Dal	1-3	L	1-3-1	Turek	**Wregget**	14	37	0-6	2-11	Sydor	Zubov	Carbonneau
10/23	@Nsh	4-3	W	2-3-1	**Wregget**	Dunham	24	27	2-6	1-8	**Iginla**	Johnson	**Housley**
10/24	@StL	3-4	L	2-4-1	McLennan	**Wregget**	19	36	0-4	2-8	MacInnis	Pronger	**Fleury**
10/28	Pit	2-5	L	2-5-1	Skudra	**Wregget**	16	21	1-6	5-9	Jagr	Barnes	**Iginla**
10/30	Was	0-**0***	T	2-5-2	**Wregget**	Tabaracci	20	27	0-3	0-2	**Wregget**	Tabaracci	**Housley**
11/01	@Chi	4-1	W	3-5-2	**Wregget**	Hackett	19	25	1-3	1-6	**Wregget**	**Fleury**	**Simpson**
11/03	@Det	5-2	W	4-5-2	**Moss**	Osgood	26	47	**3**-5	1-10	**Fleury**	**Housley**	**Moss**
11/06	Nsh	1-2	L	4-6-2	Dunham	**Moss**	32	27	1-5	1-3	Dunham	**Iginla**	Fitzgerald
11/08	Col	3-1	W	5-6-2	**Giguere**	Roy	20	40	0-2	1-7	**Giguere**	**Smith**	Sakic
11/10	LA	5-4*	W	6-6-2	**Giguere**	Bach	37	26	0-2	0-4	**Cassels**	Murray	Jokinen
11/12	Van	3-4	L	6-7-2	Snow	**Moss**	29	24	1-5	2-4	Ohlund	**Shantz**	Messier
11/14	Anh	0-1	L	6-8-2	Hebert	**Moss**	24	28	0-5	1-5	Hebert	**Moss**	Crowley
11/16	Det	5-3	W	7-8-2	**Moss**	Osgood	34	34	1-3	0-3	**Morris**	**Moss**	Krupp
11/19	@Mon	3-4	L	7-9-2	Hackett	**Giguere**	19	36	1-5	1-6	Stevenson	Damphousse	**Giguere**
11/21	@Ott	1-4	L	7-10-2	Rhodes	**Moss**	24	27	0-5	2-7	Yashin	York	Van Allen
11/23	@Tor	2-3	L	7-11-2	Joseph	**Giguere**	29	33	2-3	2-6	Korolev	Joseph	**Morris**
11/25	@Nsh	3-4	L	7-12-2	Dunham	**Giguere**	22	33	0-3	1-6	Yachmenev	Bouchard	**Iginla**
11/27	Edm	2-3	L	7-13-2	Shtalenkov	**Moss**	31	36	0-2	0-3	Kovalenko	**Moss**	Hamrlik
11/28	Chi	5-4	W	8-13-2	**Giguere**	Thibault	37	21	2-4	3-4	**Cassels**	Amonte	**Fleury**
12/03	TB	4-1	W	9-13-2	**Moss**	Schwab	24	30	1-5	1-4	**Moss**	**Morris**	**Fleury**
12/05	Pho	2-3	L	9-14-2	Khabibulin	**Moss**	18	37	0-3	1-3	Carney	Isbister	**Moss**
12/07	Dal	2-3	L	9-15-2	Turek	**Moss**	25	32	0-6	2-6	Modano	**Morris**	Carbonneau
12/11	@TB	2-1	W	10-15-2	**Giguere**	Bierk	21	25	1-1	0-3	**Stillman**	**Cassels**	Renberg
12/12	@Fla	4-2	W	11-15-2	**Giguere**	McLean	35	38	1-3	0-2	**Fleury**	Kozlov	**Giguere**
12/14	@NYR	2-5	L	11-16-2	Richter	**Giguere**	37	29	0-6	3-5	Richter	Savard	Knuble
12/17	@Phi	3-3*	T	11-16-3	**Giguere**	Vanbiesbrouck	35	42	1-7	1-3	**Fleury**	Renberg	**Giguere**
12/18	@NJ	5-2	W	12-16-3	**Giguere**	Terreri	25	38	1-6	1-5	**Giguere**	**Wilm**	**Fleury**
12/22	Van	3-5	L	12-17-3	Snow	**Giguere**	26	27	2-7	1-5	York	Scatchard	**Gauthier**
12/23	@Van	2-5	L	12-18-3	Snow	**Giguere**	20	25	1-4	0-1	Naslund	Zezel	Muckalt
12/27	Col	1-2	L	12-19-3	Billington	**Giguere**	31	28	0-4	1-2	Billington	Foote	**Cassels**
12/29	Phi	3-4*	L	12-20-3	Hextall	**Trefilov**	27	37	1-4	0-5	**Trefilov**	Zubrus	Zelepukin
12/31	Mon	1-2	L	12-21-3	Hackett	**Trefilov**	26	24	0-4	2-3	Hackett	**Trefilov**	Koivu
1/02	@Buf	1-7	L	12-22-3	Roloson	**Trefilov**	32	35	0-3	3-4	Ward	Roloson	Satan
1/04	@Bos	1-5	L	12-23-3	Dafoe	**Garner**	40	37	0-5	0-2	Samsonov	DiMaio	McLaren
1/05	@Pit	1-5	L	12-24-3	Barrasso	**Garner**	29	25	0-7	1-6	Barrasso	Hatcher	Straka
1/08	Dal	1-**0**	W	13-24-3	**Brathwaite**	Belfour	27	21	0-2	0-3	**Brathwaite**	**Shantz**	**Bassen**
1/10	Fla	1-2	L	13-25-3	Burke	**Brathwaite**	25	35	0-6	0-5	Whitney	Jovanovski	**Brathwaite**
1/13	@Anh	2-1	W	14-25-3	**Brathwaite**	Hebert	29	32	0-5	1-6	**Wiemer**	Olausson	**Brathwaite**
1/14	@LA	0-3	L	14-26-3	Storr	**Brathwaite**	22	30	0-6	1-5	Audette	Robitaille	Storr
1/16	@SJ	3-3*	T	14-26-4	**Brathwaite**	Vernon	22	33	1-5	1-6	Nolan	Marleau	**Fleury**
1/19	Det	3-1	W	15-26-4	**Brathwaite**	Maracle	33	37	1-3	1-4	**Brathwaite**	**Iginla**	Yzerman
1/21	@Col	2-4	L	15-27-4	Roy	**Brathwaite**	24	30	0-7	2-9	Corbet	Sakic	Forsberg
1/28	Chi	6-6*	T	15-27-5	**Brathwaite**	Thibault	40	37	0-4	2-4	**Fleury**	Gilmour	**Housley**
1/30	StL	4-3*	W	16-27-5	**Brathwaite**	Parent	19	23	0-6	1-2	Pronger	**Fleury**	**Shantz**
2/01	@Dal	2-2*	T	16-27-6	**Brathwaite**	Belfour	29	33	0-3	1-5	**Brathwaite**	Belfour	**Fleury**
2/02	@Pho	2-2*	T	16-27-7	**Brathwaite**	Khabibulin	36	28	0-5	1-4	Tkachuk	**Simpson**	Khabibulin
2/04	Nsh	2-2*	T	16-27-8	**Brathwaite**	Dunham	36	27	0-4	1-4	**Albelin**	Fitzgerald	**Nazarov**
2/06	Ott	1-2	L	16-28-8	Rhodes	**Brathwaite**	20	18	1-5	1-3	Arvedson	**Brathwaite**	Yashin
2/08	Edm	2-1	W	17-28-8	**Brathwaite**	Essensa	26	36	1-5	0-8	**Brathwaite**	Essensa	**Housley**
2/09	@Col	2-1	W	18-28-8	**Wregget**	Roy	29	29	0-5	0-5	**Wregget**	**Nazarov**	**Fleury**
2/12	Bos	4-3	W	19-28-8	**Brathwaite**	Dafoe	32	25	2-5	1-4	**Stillman**	Bourque	**Fleury**

2/19	Anh	6-3	W	20-28-8	**Wregget**	Hebert	32	38	1-4	2-6	**Fleury**	Kariya	**Bassen**
2/20	LA	2-2*	T	20-28-9	**Brathwaite**	Storr	27	33	0-3	1-5	R.Blake	**Brathwaite**	**Fleury**
2/22	NYR	6-2	W	21-28-9	**Brathwaite**	Richter	38	31	1-2	1-6	**Fleury**	**Stillman**	**Housley**
2/24	Buf	2-2*	T	21-28-10	**Brathwaite**	Roloson	35	28	0-4	0-4	**Brathwaite**	**Wiemer**	Roloson
2/26	StL	2-4	L	21-29-10	Johnson	**Brathwaite**	29	34	0-4	0-3	Conroy	**Hulse**	MacInnis
3/01	SJ	1-2	L	21-30-10	Vernon	**Wregget**	30	14	0-4	1-3	Houlder	Vernon	**Stillman**
3/05	@Van	5-1	W	22-30-10	**Brathwaite**	Snow	30	23	2-6	1-6	**Stillman**	**Iginla**	**Brathwaite**
3/06	@LA	4-1	W	23-30-10	**Brathwaite**	Fiset	28	28	1-6	0-6	**Brathwaite**	**Stillman**	Norstrom
3/09	@StL	**7**-4	W	24-30-10	**Wregget**	Carey	34	33	1-**8**	2-5	**Iginla**	**Corbet**	**Stillman**
3/12	@Car	1-2	L	24-31-10	Irbe	**Wregget**	31	24	0-7	0-5	Kovalenko	Battaglia	Hill
3/13	@Was	5-4*	W	25-31-10	**Brathwaite**	Tabaracci	27	35	1-2	0-1	**Bure**	**Housley**	Oates
3/16	@Nsh	4-2	W	26-31-10	**Wregget**	Dunham	34	34	1-2	2-4	**Bure**	**Stillman**	Keczmer
3/17	@Chi	1-3	L	26-32-10	Thibault	**Brathwaite**	25	34	0-3	0-4	Amonte	**Brathwaite**	Olczyk
3/21	NYI	2-1	W	27-32-10	**Wregget**	Flaherty	34	**12**	1-7	0-5	**Bure**	Flaherty	**Cassels**
3/22	@Edm	2-2*	T	27-32-11	**Wregget**	Salo	31	32	2-5	1-7	**Housley**	Hamrlik	**Wregget**
3/25	Mon	2-1	W	28-32-11	**Wregget**	Hackett	36	28	0-5	1-5	**Wregget**	Hackett	**Bure**
3/27	@Pho	1-2	L	28-33-11	Khabibulin	**Wregget**	35	25	1-2	0-2	Khabibulin	Tverdovsky	Reichel
3/28	@Anh	1-5	L	28-34-11	Hebert	**Brathwaite**	26	26	1-5	0-**0**	Kariya	Selanne	Hebert
3/30	@Col	3-3*	T	28-34-12	**Wregget**	Roy	34	24	2-4	1-4	**Morris**	Fleury	**Bure**
4/01	Pho	1-4	L	28-35-12	Khabibulin	**Wregget**	34	23	0-6	0-3	Tkachuk	Adams	Tocchet
4/03	Tor	1-5	L	28-36-12	Joseph	**Wregget**	28	23	1-2	0-4	Sundin	Karpovtsev	**Cassels**
4/07	@Edm	2-4	L	28-37-12	Salo	**Wregget**	25	30	0-2	2-4	Weight	Marchant	Poti
4/09	Edm	1-4	L	28-38-12	Salo	**Wregget**	27	25	0-4	2-6	Niinimaa	**Cassels**	Guerin
4/12	Van	0-2	L	28-39-12	Snow	**Brathwaite**	**41**	23	0-4	0-1	Snow	**Brathwaite**	Aucoin
4/14	@Van	5-4	W	29-39-12	**Brathwaite**	Snow	33	25	0-2	1-3	Naslund	**Iginla**	Scatchard
4/15	Col	5-1	W	30-39-12	**Wregget**	Roy	24	25	1-2	0-2	**Stillman**	**Wilm**	**Domenichelli**
4/17	@Edm	2-3	L	30-40-12	Salo	**Brathwaite**	33	27	1-4	1-4	Grier	**Wilm**	Weight

† game played in Japan

Calgary Flames 1998-99 Player Statistics

Regular Season

Skater	Ps	GP	G	A	Pts	+/–	PIM	PP	SH	GW	GT	S	SPct	P/G
Theo Fleury†	R	60	**30**	39	**69**	**18**	68	7	**3**	3	1	250	12.0	**1.15**
Cory Stillman	C	76	27	30	57	7	38	**9**	**3**	**5**	1	175	**15.4**	.75
Phil Housley	D	79	11	**43**	54	14	52	4	0	1	0	193	5.7	.68
Valeri Bure	R	80	26	27	53	0	22	7	0	4	0	**260**	10.0	.66
Jarome Iginla	R	**82**	28	23	51	1	58	7	0	4	1	211	13.3	.62
Andrew Cassels	C	70	12	25	37	-12	18	4	1	3	0	97	12.4	.53
Derek Morris	D	71	7	27	34	4	73	3	0	2	**2**	150	4.7	.48
Jeff Shantz†	C	69	12	17	29	15	40	1	1	3	0	77	15.6	.42
Jason Wiemer	C	78	8	13	21	-12	**177**	1	0	1	0	128	6.3	.27
* Clarke Wilm	C	78	10	8	18	11	53	2	2	0	0	94	10.6	.23
Steve Smith	D	69	1	14	15	3	80	0	0	0	0	42	2.4	.22
Andrei Nazarov†	L	36	5	9	14	1	30	0	0	2	1	53	9.4	.39
Steve Dubinsky†	C	61	4	10	14	-7	14	0	2	0	0	69	5.8	.23
Cale Hulse	D	73	3	9	12	-8	117	0	0	0	0	83	3.6	.16
Hnat Domenichelli	C	23	5	5	10	-4	11	3	0	0	0	45	11.1	.43
Todd Simpson	D	73	2	8	10	**18**	151	0	0	0	0	52	3.8	.14
Rene Corbet†	L	20	5	4	9	-2	10	1	0	0	0	45	11.1	.45
Ed Ward	R	68	3	5	8	-4	67	0	0	0	0	56	5.4	.12
* Denis Gauthier	D	55	3	4	7	3	68	0	0	0	0	40	7.5	.13
David Roche	C	36	3	3	6	-1	44	1	0	2	0	30	10.0	.17
Tommy Albelin	D	60	1	5	6	-11	8	0	0	0	0	54	1.9	.10
Michael Nylander†	C	9	2	3	5	1	2	1	0	0	0	7	28.6	.56
Bob Bassen	C	41	1	2	3	-13	35	0	0	0	0	47	2.1	.07
Greg Pankewicz	R	18	0	3	3	0	20	0	0	0	0	10	0.0	.17
Marty McInnis†	C	6	1	1	2	-1	6	0	0	0	0	7	14.3	.33
* Martin St. Louis	C	13	1	1	2	-2	10	0	0	0	0	14	7.1	.15
Fred Brathwaite	G	28	0	2	2	—	2	0	0	0	0	0	—	.07
* Eric Landry	C	3	0	1	1	1	0	0	0	0	0	1	0.0	.33
* Wade Belak†	D	9	0	1	1	3	23	0	0	0	0	2	0.0	.11
Chris O'Sullivan	D	10	0	1	1	-1	2	0	0	0	0	10	0.0	.10
* Tyler Moss	G	11	0	1	1	—	0	0	0	0	0	0	—	.09
Eric Charron	D	12	0	1	1	-6	14	0	0	0	0	9	0.0	.08
* J. Giguere	G	15	0	1	1	—	4	0	0	0	0	0	—	.07
* Rico Fata	C	20	0	1	1	0	4	0	0	0	0	13	0.0	.05
Ken Wregget	G	27	0	1	1	—	8	0	0	0	0	0	—	.04
Chris Dingman†	L	2	0	0	0	-2	17	0	0	0	0	1	0.0	.00
* Lee Sorochan	D	2	0	0	0	-3	0	0	0	0	0	5	0.0	.00
* Tyrone Garner	G	3	0	0	0	—	0	0	0	0	0	0	—	.00
* Rocky Thompson	R	3	0	0	0	0	25	0	0	0	0	0	—	.00
* Sami Helenius†	D	4	0	0	0	-2	8	0	0	0	0	1	0.0	.00
Andrei Trefilov†	G	4	0	0	0	—	0	0	0	0	0	0	—	.00
Tom Chorske†	L	7	0	0	0	-5	2	0	0	0	0	13	0.0	.00
Bench		—	—	—	—	—	0	—	—	—	—	—	—	—
TEAM TOTALS		82	211	348	559	4	1381	51	12	30	6	2344	9.0	6.82

Postseason

GP	G	A	Pts	+/–	PIM	PP	SH	GW	OT	S	SPct	P/G

Team Did Not Qualify for Postseason Play

Regular Season

Goaltender	G	Min	GAA	W	L	T	ENG	ShO	GA	SA	SvPct
Fred Brathwaite	**28**	**1663**	**2.45**	**11**	9	**7**	**3**	**1**	**68**	**796**	**.915**
* Tyler Moss	11	550	2.51	3	7	0	0	0	23	295	.922
Ken Wregget	27	1590	2.53	10	**12**	4	2	**1**	67	712	.906
* J. Giguere	15	860	3.21	6	7	1	2	0	46	447	.897
Andrei Trefilov†	4	162	4.07	0	3	0	0	0	11	84	.869
* Tyrone Garner	3	139	5.18	0	2	0	0	0	12	74	.838
TEAM TOTALS	82	4990	2.81	30	40	12	7	2	234	2415	.903

Postseason

G	Min	GAA	W	L	ENG	ShO	GA	SA	SvPct

1998-99 Calgary Flames

Record When:

Overtime games	3-1-12
In second game of back-to-back games	8-6-3
Vs playoff teams	15-28-8
Leading after two periods	21-5-2
Tied after two periods	7-12-5
Losing after two periods	2-23-5
Scoring first	22-10-4
More shots than opponents	11-18-6
Fewer shots than opponents	15-21-6
Team had at least one fighting major	13-19-4
Team had more PIM	13-20-6
Team had fewer PIM	13-18-2
Team had even PIM	4-2-4

Team

Longest winning streak	4	Feb. 8 — Feb. 19
Longest unbeaten streak	7	Feb. 8 — Feb. 24
Longest losing streak	8	Dec. 22 — Jan. 5
Longest winless streak	8	2 times
Most shots, game	41	vs. Van, Apr. 12
Most shots, period	19	2 times
Fewest shots, game	14	@Dal, Oct. 20
Fewest shots, period	1	3rd, @TB, Dec. 11

Individual

Longest goal streak	3	Theo Fleury [2]
Longest point streak	8	2 times
Most goals, game	3	Theo Fleury [2]
Most assists, game	3	3 times
Most points, game	5	Theo Fleury
Highest +/–, game	4	2 times
Lowest +/–, game	-4	Tommy Albelin
Most shots, game	9	Theo Fleury [2]

Did You Know?

The Flames were the only NHL team whose roster at the end of the 1998-99 season did not include a single forward who had ever recorded a 30-goal season in the NHL.

Miscellaneous

		NHL Rank
PP Pct.	14.3 (51-357)	19
SH goals allowed	6	6t
PK Pct.	79.8 (308-386)	26
SH goals scored	12	3t
Special Team Index	95.5	23
Shots on goal	2,344 (28.6/G)	9
Shots against	2,415 (29.5/G)	21
Unassisted goals	13	14t
Unassisted goals allowed	14	16
Team Average Weight	197.0	22
Game Star Points	335	20

Game Star Breakdown

Player	1st	2nd	3rd	Pts
Theo Fleury	7	2	10	51
Fred Brathwaite	6	4	3	45
Cory Stillman	4	3	2	31
Ken Wregget	5	0	1	26
Jarome Iginla	2	4	3	25
Andrew Cassels	2	2	3	19
Derek Morris	2	2	2	18
Valeri Bure	3	0	2	17
Tyler Moss	1	3	2	16
Phil Housley	1	2	5	16
J. Giguere	2	0	3	13
Clarke Wilm	0	3	0	9
Andrei Trefilov	1	1	0	8
Jason Wiemer	1	1	0	8
Jeff Shantz	0	2	1	7
Tommy Albelin	1	0	0	5
Andrei Nazarov	0	1	1	4
Todd Simpson	0	1	1	4
Rene Corbet	0	1	0	3
Cale Hulse	0	1	0	3
Steve Smith	0	1	0	3
Bob Bassen	0	0	2	2
Hnat Domenichelli	0	0	1	1
Denis Gauthier	0	0	1	1

Carolina Hurricanes 1998-99 Game Log (34-30-18)

Date	Opp	Score	W/L/T	Record	Goalies W/T	Goalies L/T	Shots Car	Shots Opp	Power Plays Car	Power Plays Opp	Game Stars 1st	Game Stars 2nd	Game Stars 3rd
10/10	TB	4-4*	T	0-0-1	**Kidd**	Puppa	34	25	3-9	1-5	**Francis**	Janney	**Chiasson**
10/13	@Nsh	2-3	L	0-1-1	Dunham	**Kidd**	36	30	0-8	1-3	Dunham	Brunette	Johnson
10/15	Dal	2-2*	T	0-1-2	**Irbe**	Belfour	22	38	0-3	0-3	**Roberts**	**Irbe**	Modano
10/17	Phi	1-1*	T	0-1-3	**Irbe**	Vanbiesbrouck	19	19	1-6	0-5	**Wesley**	Lindros	**Irbe**
10/20	Van	3-1	W	1-1-3	**Irbe**	Snow	27	17	1-8	0-4	**Primeau**	**Irbe**	**Roberts**
10/24	@Ott	3-1	W	2-1-3	**Irbe**	Rhodes	26	28	1-5	1-8	**Primeau**	Prospal	**Irbe**
10/25	LA	2-3	L	2-2-3	LeGace	**Kidd**	31	25	0-4	0-1	Robitaille	**Primeau**	LeGace
10/28	Chi	2-0	W	3-2-3	**Irbe**	Fitzpatrick	23	21	0-2	0-2	**Kapanen**	**Irbe**	Fitzpatrick
10/30	@NYR	0-1	L	3-3-3	Richter	**Irbe**	30	24	0-7	1-5	Richter	Harvey	Gretzky
10/31	@Bos	2-0	W	4-3-3	**Irbe**	Tallas	24	34	0-3	0-4	**Irbe**	Tallas	**Chiasson**
11/02	Col	2-3	L	4-4-3	Billington	**Irbe**	21	23	0-3	0-3	Forsberg	Billington	Kamensky
11/05	@NYI	6-3	W	5-4-3	**Kidd**	Salo	31	19	0-4	1-3	**O'Neill**	**Manderville**	**Ranheim**
11/06	@Was	3-2	W	6-4-3	**Irbe**	Kolzig	31	34	0-3	1-6	**O'Neill**	Juneau	**Manderville**
11/08	Bos	2-5	L	6-5-3	Dafoe	**Irbe**	31	31	0-7	3-8	Khristich	Bourque	Van Impe
11/11	@Anh	4-5*	L	6-6-3	Hebert	**Kidd**	29	41	0-3	1-5	Rucchin	**Primeau**	Kariya
11/12	@SJ	0-3	L	6-7-3	Vernon	**Irbe**	20	18	0-5	1-4	Vernon	Friesen	Ricci
11/14	@LA	5-3	W	7-7-3	**Irbe**	LeGace	29	40	2-7	0-7	**Primeau**	**Sheppard**	Robitaille
11/17	Mon	5-4	W	8-7-3	**Irbe**	Theodore	26	31	1-4	3-7	**Dineen**	**Sheppard**	**Roberts**
11/19	@NJ	2-3*	L	8-8-3	Brodeur	**Irbe**	20	41	2-4	0-7	Pandolfo	**Irbe**	**Sheppard**
11/20	Phi	1-3	L	8-9-3	Hextall	**Irbe**	19	27	0-5	1-5	Hextall	**Sheppard**	Lindros
11/22	NJ	2-5	L	8-10-3	Brodeur	**Irbe**	28	40	0-4	0-4	McKay	Pederson	Pandolfo
11/25	SJ	3-0	W	9-10-3	**Kidd**	Vernon	24	36	0-3	0-4	**Primeau**	**Kidd**	**Sheppard**
11/28	@NYI	3-1	W	10-10-3	**Kidd**	Salo	23	22	1-5	0-3	**Primeau**	**Kapanen**	**Dineen**
11/29	Anh	3-1	W	11-10-3	**Irbe**	Hebert	36	31	1-4	0-3	**Pratt**	**Irbe**	**Francis**
12/02	Mon	4-1	W	12-10-3	**Kidd**	Hackett	20	25	1-2	0-2	**Sheppard**	**Wesley**	**Kidd**
12/04	Pit	3-3*	T	12-10-4	**Irbe**	Barrasso	14	25	1-2	0-3	**Kron**	Kesa	**Emerson**
12/05	@Fla	3-3*	T	12-10-5	**Kidd**	Burke	27	26	1-5	2-5	Ciccarelli	**Sheppard**	Parrish
12/10	Bos	2-3	L	12-11-5	Dafoe	**Kidd**	28	16	1-1	0-1	T.Taylor	**Gelinas**	**Emerson**
12/12	Det	3-0	W	13-11-5	**Irbe**	Osgood	26	35	0-9	0-6	**Primeau**	**Irbe**	**Wesley**
12/15	Edm	3-0	W	14-11-5	**Irbe**	Shtalenkov	24	29	0-3	0-2	**Irbe**	**Wesley**	**Roberts**
12/18	@Ott	1-5	L	14-12-5	Tugnutt	**Irbe**	24	34	1-4	2-4	Yashin	McEachern	Tugnutt
12/19	@Buf	3-2	W	15-12-5	**Kidd**	Hasek	20	40	1-7	0-6	**Kidd**	**Primeau**	Satan
12/21	Buf	1-4	L	15-13-5	Hasek	**Kidd**	20	33	0-6	2-6	Woolley	Satan	Peca
12/23	@NYR	1-0	W	16-13-5	**Irbe**	Richter	25	29	0-5	0-3	**Sheppard**	**Irbe**	Richter
12/26	NYR	3-6	L	16-14-5	Richter	**Kidd**	22	20	1-5	0-2	Nedved	Graves	Pronger
12/30	TB	4-3	W	17-14-5	**Irbe**	Ranford	38	27	2-5	2-5	**Roberts**	Clark	**Dineen**
1/01	@Fla	3-3*	T	17-14-6	**Irbe**	Burke	28	33	0-4	1-4	Niedermayer	**Primeau**	**Ranheim**
1/02	Nsh	4-1	W	18-14-6	**Kidd**	Vokoun	22	27	2-7	0-4	**Kapanen**	**Kidd**	**Wesley**
1/04	Ott	4-4*	T	18-14-7	**Irbe**	Tugnutt	24	35	0-1	0-2	**Ranheim**	**Manderville**	York
1/07	@Pit	2-4	L	18-15-7	Barrasso	**Kidd**	25	24	1-3	3-5	Jagr	Barrasso	Straka
1/09	@Phi	0-2	L	18-16-7	Hextall	**Irbe**	20	30	0-4	0-4	Lindros	Brind'Amour	Hextall
1/14	Fla	3-2	W	19-16-7	**Irbe**	Burke	23	16	1-5	0-3	**Francis**	**Wesley**	Ratchuk
1/16	Was	2-3*	L	19-17-7	Kolzig	**Irbe**	21	38	1-7	0-2	Miller	**Primeau**	**Irbe**
1/18	Tor	4-2	W	20-17-7	**Irbe**	Joseph	26	31	0-2	1-4	**Roberts**	**Francis**	**Irbe**
1/21	@Det	1-4	L	20-18-7	Osgood	**Irbe**	26	26	0-5	1-4	Osgood	Lidstrom	**Primeau**
1/26	@Pit	5-3	W	21-18-7	**Irbe**	Skudra	22	35	0-2	0-3	**Sheppard**	**Kron**	**Irbe**
1/28	NYR	3-2*	W	22-18-7	**Irbe**	Richter	30	26	0-3	1-5	**Roberts**	**Manderville**	Schneider
1/30	@Mon	3-1	W	23-18-7	**Irbe**	Hackett	10	45	2-5	1-7	**Irbe**	**Kron**	Rucinsky
1/31	@Bos	0-0*	T	23-18-8	**Kidd**	Dafoe	24	36	0-3	0-4	Sweeney	**Manderville**	Bourque
2/03	NJ	1-4	L	23-19-8	Brodeur	**Irbe**	30	35	1-6	1-5	Sykora	**Primeau**	Brodeur
2/05	@Was	1-4	L	23-20-8	Kolzig	**Kidd**	24	28	0-6	1-4	Bondra	Kolzig	Tinordi
2/06	Fla	3-3*	T	23-20-9	**Irbe**	Burke	41	33	0-5	0-3	Parrish	**Sheppard**	**Primeau**
2/10	@Tor	6-5	W	24-20-9	**Irbe**	Joseph	25	29	1-4	0-2	**Francis**	Berezin	**Roberts**
2/12	@NYR	3-1	W	25-20-9	**Irbe**	Richter	26	31	0-4	0-5	**Irbe**	**Kapanen**	Leetch
2/13	@NJ	4-6	L	25-21-9	Brodeur	**Kidd**	30	30	0-5	1-6	Morrison	Sykora	Daneyko

2/15	@Buf	2-3	L	25-22-9	Hasek	**Irbe**	38	36	0-5	0-4	Satan	**Gelinas**	Peca
2/18	Was	2-2*	T	25-22-10	**Irbe**	Kolzig	39	22	0-8	1-4	**Battaglia**	Kolzig	Juneau
2/20	@TB	3-2	W	26-22-10	**Irbe**	Schwab	30	30	0-6	1-5	**Kapanen**	Samuelsson	**Roberts**
2/21	NYI	4-1	W	27-22-10	**Irbe**	Salo	37	29	1-3	0-3	**O'Neill**	**Irbe**	**Primeau**
2/24	@Tor	2-2*	T	27-22-11	**Irbe**	Joseph	31	31	1-3	0-4	**Primeau**	McCauley	Sundin
2/26	@Van	0-1	L	27-23-11	Snow	**Irbe**	23	**16**	0-**10**	0-9	Snow	**Primeau**	Aucoin
2/27	@Edm	2-2*	T	27-23-12	**Irbe**	Passmore	36	32	0-5	1-5	Passmore	McAmmond	**Primeau**
3/03	Bos	2-1	W	28-23-12	**Irbe**	Dafoe	25	24	0-6	0-3	**Gelinas**	**Wesley**	**Irbe**
3/06	@Fla	2-2*	T	28-23-13	**Irbe**	McLean	15	35	2-3	1-6	**Irbe**	Mellanby	**Primeau**
3/08	Buf	4-1	W	29-23-13	**Irbe**	Roloson	34	32	0-3	1-4	**Kovalenko**	**Irbe**	**Hill**
3/10	Pit	2-3*	L	29-24-13	Skudra	**Irbe**	21	26	0-3	0-**1**	Miller	**Kapanen**	Straka
3/12	Cgy	2-1	W	30-24-13	**Irbe**	Wregget	24	31	0-5	0-7	**Kovalenko**	**Battaglia**	**Hill**
3/15	@Pho	5-5*	T	30-24-14	**Kidd**	Khabibulin	29	42	1-5	1-2	Tkachuk	**Francis**	Roenick
3/18	@Col	2-3	L	30-25-14	Roy	**Kidd**	29	34	1-6	1-6	Sakic	Foote	**Primeau**
3/21	@Dal	2-3*	L	30-26-14	Belfour	**Irbe**	28	17	0-4	0-3	Modano	Hatcher	**Kapanen**
3/22	@StL	2-5	L	30-27-14	Fuhr	**Irbe**	22	27	1-6	1-5	Picard	Demitra	Turgeon
3/24	NYI	2-1	W	31-27-14	**Irbe**	Flaherty	29	25	0-6	0-4	**Kovalenko**	**Irbe**	**Kron**
3/26	Tor	2-7	L	31-28-14	Joseph	**Irbe**	25	27	0-7	1-6	Thomas	Modin	Sundin
3/28	TB	3-3*	T	31-28-15	**Irbe**	Hodson	33	34	0-3	1-2	**Francis**	**Kapanen**	Daigle
3/30	@Phi	3-3*	T	31-28-16	**Kidd**	Hextall	21	31	1-4	3-6	Brind'Amour	**Halko**	Renberg
4/03	@Chi	1-2	L	31-29-16	Thibault	**Irbe**	25	26	0-5	1-6	Thibault	**Irbe**	Leroux
4/06	NJ	4-2	W	32-29-16	**Irbe**	Brodeur	15	32	1-6	1-4	**Irbe**	**Primeau**	**Hill**
4/07	@Mon	0-2	L	32-30-16	Theodore	**Irbe**	27	31	0-3	0-2	Theodore	Thornton	Rivet
4/10	@NYI	**6**-1	W	33-30-16	**Kidd**	Flaherty	24	25	0-3	0-3	**Kapanen**	**Roberts**	**Kidd**
4/14	Was	3-**0**	W	34-30-16	**Irbe**	Brochu	26	19	2-5	0-5	**Francis**	**Irbe**	**Kron**
4/16	@TB	2-2*	T	34-30-17	**Kidd**	Schwab	26	32	1-4	1-3	**Kidd**	Richer	Samuelsson
4/17	Ott	1-1*	T	34-30-18	**Irbe**	Tugnutt	25	31	0-2	1-4	**Battaglia**	Tugnutt	**Irbe**

Postseason

4/22	Bos	0-**2**	L	0-1	Dafoe	**Irbe**	19	29	0-**4**	0-4	DiMaio	Dafoe	Belanger
4/24	Bos	**3-2***	W	1-1	**Irbe**	Dafoe	30	24	0-**4**	0-**1**	**Sheppard**	**Gelinas**	Heinze
4/26	@Bos	**3-2**	W	2-1	**Irbe**	Dafoe	21	26	**1-4**	1-5	**Roberts**	Allison	**Battaglia**
4/28	@Bos	1-4	L	2-2	Dafoe	**Irbe**	23	30	0-3	1-3	Sweeney	Thornton	Axelsson
4/30	Bos	**3**-4*	L	2-3	Dafoe	**Irbe**	**40**	52	**1**-2	1-6	Carter	Axelsson	Bourque
5/02	@Bos	0-**2**	L	2-4	Dafoe	**Irbe**	31	**21**	0-**4**	1-5	Dafoe	Carter	Thornton

Carolina Hurricanes 1998-99 Player Statistics

		Regular Season													Postseason												
Skater	**Ps**	**GP**	**G**	**A**	**Pts**	**+/–**	**PIM**	**PP**	**SH**	**GW**	**GT**	**S**	**SPct**	**P/G**	**GP**	**G**	**A**	**Pts**	**+/–**	**PIM**	**PP**	**SH**	**GW**	**OT**	**S**	**SPct**	**P/G**
Keith Primeau	C	78	**30**	32	**62**	8	75	**9**	1	5	1	178	**16.9**	**.79**	**6**	0	**3**	3	-3	6	0	0	0	0	9	0.0	.50
Sami Kapanen	L	81	24	**35**	59	-1	10	5	0	**7**	0	**254**	9.4	.73	5	1	1	2	-2	0	0	0	0	0	8	12.5	.40
Ray Sheppard	R	74	25	33	58	4	16	5	0	4	1	188	13.3	.78	**6**	**5**	1	**6**	-2	2	**1**	0	**1**	**1**	**23**	**21.7**	**1.00**
Ron Francis	C	**82**	21	31	52	-2	34	8	0	2	1	133	15.8	.63	3	0	1	1	1	0	0	0	0	0	4	0.0	.33
Gary Roberts	L	77	14	28	42	2	**178**	1	1	4	0	138	10.1	.55	**6**	1	1	2	-3	**8**	0	0	0	0	13	7.7	.33
Jeff O'Neill	C	75	16	15	31	3	66	4	0	2	0	121	13.2	.41	**6**	0	1	1	-5	0	0	0	0	0	11	0.0	.17
Martin Gelinas	L	76	13	15	28	3	67	0	0	2	**2**	111	11.7	.37	**6**	0	**3**	3	-4	2	0	0	0	0	12	0.0	.50
Robert Kron	L	75	9	16	25	-13	10	3	1	2	0	134	6.7	.33	5	2	0	2	2	0	0	0	**1**	0	10	20.0	.40
Glen Wesley	D	74	7	17	24	14	44	0	0	2	1	112	6.3	.32	**6**	0	0	0	0	2	0	0	0	0	15	0.0	.00
Nelson Emerson†	R	35	8	13	21	1	36	3	0	0	1	84	9.5	.60	—	—	—	—	—	—	—	—	—	—	—	—	—
Paul Ranheim	L	78	9	10	19	4	39	0	**2**	1	0	67	13.4	.24	**6**	0	0	0	0	2	0	0	0	0	5	0.0	.00
Kevin Dineen	R	67	8	10	18	5	97	0	0	1	0	86	9.3	.27	**6**	0	0	0	0	**8**	0	0	0	0	4	0.0	.00
Bates Battaglia	L	60	7	11	18	7	22	0	0	0	**2**	52	13.5	.30	**6**	0	**3**	3	**3**	**8**	0	0	0	0	7	0.0	.50
Kent Manderville	L	81	5	11	16	9	38	0	0	0	0	71	7.0	.20	**6**	0	0	0	0	2	0	0	0	0	6	0.0	.00
Nolan Pratt	D	61	1	14	15	**15**	95	0	0	1	0	46	2.2	.25	3	0	0	0	0	2	0	0	0	0	3	0.0	.00
Andrei Kovalenko†	R	18	6	6	12	3	0	1	0	1	0	21	28.6	.67	4	0	2	2	1	2	0	0	0	0	3	0.0	.50
Marek Malik	D	52	2	9	11	-6	36	1	0	0	0	36	5.6	.21	4	0	0	0	-2	4	0	0	0	0	0	—	.00
Paul Coffey†	D	44	2	8	10	-1	28	1	0	0	0	79	2.5	.23	5	0	1	1	0	2	0	0	0	0	8	0.0	.20
Sean Hill	D	54	0	10	10	9	48	0	0	0	0	44	0.0	.19	—	—	—	—	—	—	—	—	—	—	—	—	—
Curtis Leschyshyn	D	65	2	7	9	-1	50	0	0	0	0	35	5.7	.14	**6**	0	0	0	-3	6	0	0	0	0	4	0.0	.00
Steve Chiasson	D	28	1	8	9	7	16	1	0	0	0	74	1.4	.32	**6**	1	2	3	1	2	**1**	0	0	0	17	5.9	.50
* Steve Halko	D	20	0	3	3	5	24	0	0	0	0	6	0.0	.15	4	0	0	0	-2	2	0	0	0	0	2	0.0	.00
Adam Burt†	D	51	0	3	3	3	46	0	0	0	0	37	0.0	.06	—	—	—	—	—	—	—	—	—	—	—	—	—
David Karpa	D	33	0	2	2	1	55	0	0	0	0	21	0.0	.06	2	0	0	0	-2	2	0	0	0	0	0	—	.00
* Mike Rucinski	D	15	0	1	1	1	8	0	0	0	0	8	0.0	.07	—	—	—	—	—	—	—	—	—	—	—	—	—
* Byron Ritchie	C	3	0	0	0	0	0	0	0	0	0	0	—	.00	—	—	—	—	—	—	—	—	—	—	—	—	—
* Shane Willis	R	7	0	0	0	-2	0	0	0	0	0	1	0.0	.00	—	—	—	—	—	—	—	—	—	—	—	—	—
* Craig MacDonald	C	11	0	0	0	0	0	0	0	0	0	5	0.0	.00	1	0	0	0	0	0	0	0	0	0	0	—	.00
Trevor Kidd	G	25	0	0	0	—	0	0	0	0	0	0	—	.00	—	—	—	—	—	—	—	—	—	—	—	—	—
Arturs Irbe	G	62	0	0	0	—	10	0	0	0	0	0	—	.00	**6**	0	0	0	—	0	0	0	0	0	0	—	.00
Bench		—	—	—	—	—	0	—	—	—	—	—	—	—	—	—	—	—	—	0	—	—	—	—	—	—	—
TEAM TOTALS		82	210	348	558	78	1148	42	5	34	9	2142	9.8	6.80	6	10	19	29	-20	62	2	0	2	1	164	6.1	4.83

	Regular Season										Postseason									
Goaltender	**G**	**Min**	**GAA**	**W**	**L**	**T**	**ENG**	**ShO**	**GA**	**SA**	**SvPct**	**G**	**Min**	**GAA**	**W**	**L**	**ENG**	**ShO**	**GA**	**SA**	**SvPct**
Arturs Irbe	**62**	**3643**	**2.22**	**27**	**20**	**12**	**3**	**6**	**135**	**1753**	**.923**	**6**	**408**	**2.21**	**2**	**4**	**1**	0	**15**	**181**	**.917**
Trevor Kidd	25	1358	2.70	7	10	6	**3**	2	61	640	.905	—	—	—	—	—	—	—	—	—	—
TEAM TOTALS	82	5022	2.41	34	30	18	6	8	202	2399	.916	6	412	2.33	2	4	1	0	16	182	.912

1998-99 Carolina Hurricanes

Record When:

Overtime games	1-5-18
In second game of back-to-back games	6-6-5
Vs playoff teams	13-21-10
Leading after two periods	25-2-6
Tied after two periods	6-6-6
Losing after two periods	3-22-6
Scoring first	29-11-6
More shots than opponents	13-10-5
Fewer shots than opponents	20-17-11
Team had at least one fighting major	9-11-4
Team had more PIM	12-8-10
Team had fewer PIM	18-15-5
Team had even PIM	4-7-3

Team

Longest winning streak	4	Nov. 25 — Dec. 2
Longest unbeaten streak	6	Nov. 25 — Dec. 5
Longest losing streak	3	3 times
Longest winless streak	4	4 times
Most shots, game	41	vs. Fla, Feb. 6
Most shots, period	19	2nd, vs. Fla, Feb. 6
Fewest shots, game	10	@Mon, Jan. 30
Fewest shots, period	0	3rd, @Mon, Jan. 30

Individual

Longest goal streak	6	Ray Sheppard
Longest point streak	11	Ray Sheppard
Most goals, game	2	16 times
Most assists, game	3	4 times
Most points, game	5	Ron Francis
Highest +/–, game	4	4 times
Lowest +/–, game	-4	Marek Malik
Most shots, game	8	3 times

Did You Know?

Carolina's winning percentage of .524 in 1998-99 was the worst by an NHL division-winner since the 1988-89 Detroit Red Wings won the Norris Division with a winning percentage of .500.

Miscellaneous

		NHL Rank
PP Pct.	11.0 (42-382)	27
SH goals allowed	6	6t
PK Pct.	85.3 (295-346)	12
SH goals scored	5	25
Special Team Index	96.1	21
Shots on goal	2,142 (26.1/G)	23
Shots against	2,399 (29.3/G)	18
Unassisted goals	14	8t
Unassisted goals allowed	9	4t
Team Average Weight	196.9	23
Game Star Points	409	7

Game Star Breakdown

Player	1st	2nd	3rd	Pts
Arturs Irbe	6	12	7	73
Keith Primeau	7	8	6	65
Sami Kapanen	4	4	1	33
Ron Francis	5	2	1	32
Ray Sheppard	3	5	2	32
Gary Roberts	4	1	5	28
Glen Wesley	1	4	2	19
Trevor Kidd	2	2	2	18
Andrei Kovalenko	3	0	0	15
Jeff O'Neill	3	0	0	15
Bates Battaglia	2	1	0	13
Robert Kron	1	2	2	13
Kent Manderville	0	4	1	13
Martin Gelinas	1	2	0	11
Kevin Dineen	1	0	2	7
Paul Ranheim	1	0	2	7
Nolan Pratt	1	0	0	5
Steve Halko	0	1	0	3
Sean Hill	0	0	3	3
Steve Chiasson	0	0	2	2
Nelson Emerson	0	0	2	2

Chicago Blackhawks 1998-99 Game Log (29-41-12)

					Goalies		Shots		Power Plays		Game Stars		
Date	Opp	Score	W/L/T	Record	W/T	L/T	Chi	Opp	Chi	Opp	1st	2nd	3rd
10/10	NJ	2-1	W	1-0-0	**Hackett**	Brodeur	15	36	1-5	0-3	**Hackett**	**Gilmour**	**Amonte**
10/13	@Dal	1-3	L	1-1-0	Belfour	**Hackett**	14	31	0-5	1-9	**Hackett**	Modano	Belfour
10/15	Anh	3-5	L	1-2-0	Hebert	**Hackett**	26	31	1-7	0-5	Selanne	Kariya	**Gilmour**
10/17	Dal	4-3	W	2-2-0	**Hackett**	Belfour	36	29	1-5	3-7	**Chelios**	Hull	**Moreau**
10/19	@Mon	2-1	W	3-2-0	**Fitzpatrick**	Theodore	20	27	0-3	1-6	**Fitzpatrick**	**Daze**	Damphousse
10/22	SJ	2-2*	T	3-2-1	**Hackett**	Shields	33	25	1-**8**	0-7	**Amonte**	Nolan	**Chelios**
10/24	Nsh	5-4	W	4-2-1	**Fitzpatrick**	Fichaud	25	23	1-4	1-3	**Amonte**	**Kilger**	**Zhamnov**
10/28	@Car	0-2	L	4-3-1	Irbe	**Fitzpatrick**	21	23	0-2	0-2	Kapanen	Irbe	**Fitzpatrick**
10/30	Fla	3-7	L	4-4-1	Burke	**Hackett**	33	25	1-**8**	3-11	Parrish	Niedermayer	Whitney
11/01	Cgy	1-4	L	4-5-1	Wregget	**Hackett**	25	19	1-6	1-3	Wregget	Fleury	Simpson
11/04	@Fla	1-2	L	4-6-1	Burke	**Fitzpatrick**	34	32	0-5	1-6	Ciccarelli	Lindsay	Burke
11/06	@TB	2-2*	T	4-6-2	**Fitzpatrick**	Ranford	37	24	2-4	1-5	Ranford	**Chelios**	Kubina
11/08	Edm	2-3*	L	4-7-2	Shtalenkov	**Fitzpatrick**	24	32	0-4	1-5	Beranek	Shtalenkov	**Chelios**
11/10	@StL	2-5	L	4-8-2	McLennan	**Hackett**	14	41	0-3	3-6	Turgeon	Demitra	Twist
11/12	Tor	3-10	L	4-9-2	Potvin	**Hackett**	25	30	1-7	2-8	Sundin	Yushkevich	D.King
11/14	@Buf	1-6	L	4-10-2	Hasek	**Trefilov**	21	37	0-3	2-2	Grosek	Holzinger	Sanderson
11/15	Ott	2-2*	T	4-10-3	**Fitzpatrick**	Rhodes	25	31	2-4	0-7	**Fitzpatrick**	Rhodes	**Amonte**
11/17	@Nsh	2-1	W	5-10-3	**Fitzpatrick**	Dunham	32	38	1-4	1-6	**Amonte**	**Gilmour**	Ronning
11/21	@LA	0-5	L	5-11-3	Storr	**Thibault**	21	32	0-2	2-7	Storr	LaFayette	Duchesne
11/22	@Anh	1-4	L	5-12-3	Hebert	**Fitzpatrick**	27	23	1-5	1-3	McInnis	Kariya	Salei
11/24	@Pho	2-3	L	5-13-3	Khabibulin	**Thibault**	32	23	0-3	1-2	Tkachuk	Roenick	Drake
11/28	@Cgy	4-5	L	5-14-3	Giguere	**Thibault**	21	37	**3**-4	2-4	Cassels	**Amonte**	Fleury
11/29	@Edm	3-2	W	6-14-3	**Thibault**	Shtalenkov	18	38	1-1	2-8	**Chelios**	**Thibault**	Smyth
12/03	Anh	4-1	W	7-14-3	**Thibault**	Hebert	18	25	1-7	1-6	**Zhamnov**	**Kilger**	**Thibault**
12/06	TB	**7**-5	W	8-14-3	**Thibault**	Schwab	30	36	1-3	0-3	**Zhamnov**	**Kilger**	**Amonte**
12/08	@Det	2-3	L	8-15-3	Osgood	**Fitzpatrick**	33	45	0-2	0-3	Yzerman	Osgood	**Fitzpatrick**
12/09	Edm	3-1	W	9-15-3	**Thibault**	Shtalenkov	18	25	0-5	0-4	**Daze**	**Thibault**	**Chelios**
12/11	Tor	2-3	L	9-16-3	Healy	**Thibault**	30	19	1-4	0-4	Healy	Yushkevich	Johnson
12/13	Dal	2-2*	T	9-16-4	**Fitzpatrick**	Belfour	30	32	1-2	1-2	Belfour	**Fitzpatrick**	**Amonte**
12/17	Was	1-3	L	9-17-4	Kolzig	**Thibault**	19	29	1-3	2-8	Konowalchuk	Johansson	**Manson**
12/19	@Phi	1-3	L	9-18-4	Vanbiesbrouck	**Fitzpatrick**	24	40	0-4	1-6	Bureau	Vanbiesbrouck	McGillis
12/20	LA	1-4	L	9-19-4	Storr	**Thibault**	25	34	0-2	1-4	Murray	Storr	**Zhamnov**
12/23	Pho	4-3	W	10-19-4	**Thibault**	Waite	17	35	2-5	3-8	**Gilmour**	Roenick	**Thibault**
12/26	Phi	2-3	L	10-20-4	Vanbiesbrouck	**Thibault**	20	28	1-5	1-8	Lindros	Desjardins	**Gilmour**
12/31	NYI	1-**0**	W	11-20-4	**Thibault**	Cousineau	21	28	0-2	0-3	**Thibault**	Cousineau	Palffy
1/02	@Det	2-5	L	11-21-4	Osgood	**Thibault**	35	35	2-5	0-6	Yzerman	Murphy	McCarty
1/03	Det	1-3	L	11-22-4	Osgood	**Thibault**	27	26	0-3	2-6	Lidstrom	Osgood	Murphy
1/05	@NYI	1-1*	T	11-22-5	**Thibault**	Salo	23	41	0-4	0-8	**Thibault**	Salo	Reichel
1/07	@StL	2-4	L	11-23-5	McLennan	**Thibault**	15	32	0-5	1-5	Pronger	Demitra	**Gilmour**
1/09	@Nsh	3-3*	T	11-23-6	**Fitzpatrick**	Vokoun	34	27	0-3	0-4	Johnson	Yachmenev	Berehowsky
1/10	Col	2-3*	L	11-24-6	Billington	**Thibault**	26	37	0-5	1-3	Sakic	**Thibault**	Lemieux
1/12	@Col	1-4	L	11-25-6	Roy	**Thibault**	24	30	1-5	0-3	Forsberg	Sakic	Roy
1/15	@NYR	3-1	W	12-25-6	**Thibault**	Richter	26	33	0-2	0-4	**Thibault**	**Maneluk**	Sundstrom
1/17	Pho	1-1*	T	12-25-7	**Thibault**	Waite	22	21	0-6	1-5	**Brown**	Waite	**Thibault**
1/21	Mon	3-**0**	W	13-25-7	**Thibault**	Hackett	37	33	1-4	0-2	**Thibault**	Hackett	**Gilmour**
1/27	@Edm	4-3*	W	14-25-7	**Thibault**	Essensa	33	38	0-2	2-6	Niinimaa	**Gilmour**	**Amonte**
1/28	@Cgy	6-6*	T	14-25-8	**Thibault**	Brathwaite	37	40	2-4	0-4	Fleury	**Gilmour**	Housley
1/30	@Van	2-3	L	14-26-8	Snow	**Thibault**	20	26	0-6	1-6	Naslund	**Amonte**	Mogilny
2/01	@SJ	1-5	L	14-27-8	Vernon	**Thibault**	23	33	0-3	1-5	Friesen	Nolan	Ragnarsson
2/03	@Anh	0-3	L	14-28-8	Hebert	**Thibault**	35	23	0-2	1-3	Hebert	Cullen	Salei
2/04	@LA	2-3	L	14-29-8	Fiset	**Thibault**	37	33	1-6	0-4	Audette	Duchesne	**Kilger**
2/06	@Pho	0-3	L	14-30-8	Khabibulin	**Thibault**	28	35	0-2	1-7	Khabibulin	Lumme	Ylonen
2/10	SJ	2-5	L	14-31-8	Vernon	**Thibault**	19	28	0-5	3-7	Murphy	Korolyuk	Houlder
2/12	Det	1-2	L	14-32-8	Osgood	**Thibault**	26	25	0-4	2-5	Osgood	Murphy	**Chelios**
2/13	@Tor	6-2	W	15-32-8	**Thibault**	Joseph	27	26	1-5	1-5	**Simpson**	**Gilmour**	Sullivan

2/15	@Ott	2-6	L	15-33-8	Rhodes	**Thibault**	24	30	1-6	1-4	Prospal	Redden	Yashin
2/17	Van	4-**0**	W	16-33-8	**Thibault**	Snow	14	29	1-3	0-3	**Thibault**	**Kilger**	**Brown**
2/19	@Dal	1-5	L	16-34-8	Belfour	**Thibault**	17	31	0-1	2-4	Modano	Zubov	Verbeek
2/21	Bos	3-6	L	16-35-8	Tallas	**Thibault**	31	28	1-3	1-5	Khristich	Samsonov	Allison
2/24	@StL	3-1	W	17-35-8	**Fitzpatrick**	McLennan	16	26	0-2	0-3	**Gilmour**	**Chelios**	MacInnis
2/26	LA	1-2	L	17-36-8	Storr	**Fitzpatrick**	34	**17**	0-4	1-2	Storr	R.Blake	**Emerson**
2/28	StL	1-3	L	17-37-8	Johnson	**Thibault**	27	27	0-5	2-4	Turgeon	Young	Johnson
3/06	@SJ	4-**0**	W	18-37-8	**Thibault**	Shields	27	23	1-5	0-7	**Dumont**	**Daze**	**Thibault**
3/07	@Van	2-2*	T	18-37-9	**Thibault**	Snow	23	29	0-4	1-6	**Gilmour**	Holden	Mogilny
3/10	Nsh	5-2	W	19-37-9	**Thibault**	Dunham	**38**	21	1-4	0-**1**	**Daze**	**Chelios**	**Zhamnov**
3/12	@Nsh	3-5	L	19-38-9	Dunham	**Thibault**	34	30	1-7	2-7	Bordeleau	Walker	**Amonte**
3/14	StL	2-5	L	19-39-9	Carey	**Thibault**	24	25	0-3	1-3	Demitra	MacInnis	**Fitzpatrick**
3/17	Cgy	3-1	W	20-39-9	**Thibault**	Brathwaite	34	25	0-4	0-3	**Amonte**	Brathwaite	**Olczyk**
3/20	@Col	5-5*	T	20-39-10	**Fitzpatrick**	Roy	33	28	0-4	3-8	Sakic	**Zhamnov**	Lemieux
3/21	Col	4-3	W	21-39-10	**Thibault**	Roy	35	25	1-6	1-4	**Zhamnov**	Sakic	**Mironov**
3/23	@Pit	2-5	L	21-40-10	Skudra	**Thibault**	29	29	1-3	2-6	Jagr	Straka	Titov
3/25	@Bos	3-3*	T	21-40-11	**Thibault**	Dafoe	22	26	1-3	3-7	Bourque	Heinze	**Mironov**
3/27	@NJ	4-4*	T	21-40-12	**Fitzpatrick**	Terreri	26	35	1-2	0-5	Sykora	**Olczyk**	**Zhamnov**
3/28	StL	3-1	W	22-40-12	**Fitzpatrick**	Fuhr	16	37	1-7	1-7	**Amonte**	**Mironov**	**Eriksson**
3/31	Buf	2-1	W	23-40-12	**Thibault**	Hasek	25	20	0-5	0-5	**Thibault**	**Manson**	**Dumont**
4/02	@Det	3-5	L	23-41-12	Ranford	**Fitzpatrick**	30	31	1-4	2-9	Kozlov	Murphy	Clark
4/03	Car	2-1	W	24-41-12	**Thibault**	Irbe	26	25	1-6	0-5	**Thibault**	Irbe	**Leroux**
4/05	Van	2-1	W	25-41-12	**Thibault**	Weekes	33	25	0-5	0-5	**Daze**	**Mironov**	Weekes
4/08	NYR	6-2	W	26-41-12	**Thibault**	Richter	34	24	1-2	1-**1**	**Dumont**	**Mironov**	**Leroux**
4/12	@Was	4-2	W	27-41-12	**Fitzpatrick**	Tabaracci	31	26	1-4	0-2	Reekie	Black	Witt
4/15	Nsh	4-2	W	28-41-12	**Thibault**	Vokoun	25	23	1-5	0-3	**Zhamnov**	**Olczyk**	Timonen
4/17	Det	3-2	W	29-41-12	**Thibault**	Osgood	19	24	0-3	0-3	**Amonte**	**Zhamnov**	**Manson**

Chicago Blackhawks 1998-99 Player Statistics

Skater	Ps	Regular Season GP	G	A	Pts	+/–	PIM	PP	SH	GW	GT	S	SPct	P/G
Tony Amonte	R	**82**	**44**	31	**75**	0	60	**14**	**3**	**8**	0	**256**	**17.2**	**.91**
Alexei Zhamnov	C	76	20	**41**	61	-10	50	8	1	2	1	200	10.0	.80
Doug Gilmour	C	72	16	40	56	-16	56	7	1	4	0	110	14.5	.78
Eric Daze	L	72	22	20	42	-13	22	8	0	2	**3**	189	11.6	.58
Chris Chelios†	D	65	8	26	34	-4	89	2	1	0	1	172	4.7	.52
Chad Kilger†	C	64	14	11	25	-1	30	2	1	1	1	68	20.6	.39
Ed Olczyk	C	61	10	15	25	-3	29	2	1	2	0	88	11.4	.41
Bob Probert	L	78	7	14	21	-11	**206**	0	0	3	0	87	8.0	.27
Dave Manson†	D	64	6	15	21	**4**	107	2	0	0	0	134	4.5	.33
* Jean-Pierre Dumont	R	25	9	6	15	7	10	0	0	2	0	42	21.4	.60
Ethan Moreau†	L	66	9	6	15	-5	84	0	0	1	0	80	11.3	.23
Nelson Emerson†	R	27	4	10	14	8	13	0	0	1	1	94	4.3	.52
Doug Zmolek	D	62	0	14	14	1	102	0	0	0	0	33	0.0	.23
* Todd White	C	35	5	8	13	-1	20	2	0	0	0	43	11.6	.37
Christian Laflamme†	D	62	2	11	13	0	70	0	0	0	0	53	3.8	.21
Reid Simpson	L	53	5	4	9	2	145	1	0	0	0	23	21.7	.17
* Daniel Cleary	L	35	4	5	9	-1	24	0	0	0	0	49	8.2	.26
Boris Mironov†	D	12	0	9	9	7	27	0	0	0	0	35	0.0	.75
Jean-Yves Leroux	L	40	3	5	8	-7	21	0	0	0	0	47	6.4	.20
* Brad Brown†	D	61	1	7	8	-4	184	0	0	0	1	26	3.8	.13
Anders Eriksson†	D	11	0	8	8	6	0	0	0	0	0	12	0.0	.73
* Mike Maneluk†	R	28	4	3	7	2	8	1	0	1	0	29	13.8	.25
Josef Marha†	C	22	2	5	7	5	4	1	0	1	0	32	6.3	.32
Dean McAmmond†	C	12	1	4	5	3	2	0	0	1	0	16	6.3	.42
* Bryan Muir†	D	53	1	4	5	1	50	0	0	0	0	78	1.3	.09
Jamie Allison	D	39	2	2	4	0	62	0	0	0	0	24	8.3	.10
Eric Weinrich†	D	14	1	3	4	-13	12	0	0	0	0	24	4.2	.29
Paul Coffey†	D	10	0	4	4	-6	0	0	0	0	0	8	0.0	.40
Jeff Shantz†	C	7	1	0	1	-1	4	0	0	0	0	5	20.0	.14
Mark Janssens	C	60	1	0	1	-11	65	0	0	0	0	27	3.7	.02
Mark Fitzpatrick	G	27	0	1	1	—	8	0	0	0	0	0	—	.04
Jocelyn Thibault†	G	52	0	1	1	—	2	0	0	0	0	0	—	.02
Andrei Trefilov†	G	1	0	0	0	—	0	0	0	0	0	0	—	.00
Steve Dubinsky†	C	2	0	0	0	0	0	0	0	0	0	1	0.0	.00
Roman Vopat†	C	3	0	0	0	-4	4	0	0	0	0	0	—	.00
Chris Murray†	R	4	0	0	0	0	14	0	0	0	0	4	0.0	.00
R. VandenBussche	R	6	0	0	0	0	17	0	0	0	0	3	0.0	.00
Radim Bicanek†	D	7	0	0	0	-3	6	0	0	0	0	7	0.0	.00
* Sylvain Cloutier	C	7	0	0	0	-1	0	0	0	0	0	3	0.0	.00
* Craig Mills	R	7	0	0	0	-2	2	0	0	0	0	1	0.0	.00
* Alain Nasreddine†	D	7	0	0	0	-2	19	0	0	0	0	2	0.0	.00
Cam Russell†	D	7	0	0	0	1	10	0	0	0	0	1	0.0	.00
* Ty Jones	R	8	0	0	0	-1	12	0	0	0	0	3	0.0	.00
Jeff Hackett†	G	10	0	0	0	—	6	0	0	0	0	0	—	.00
* Dennis Bonvie	R	11	0	0	0	-4	44	0	0	0	0	1	0.0	.00
* Remi Royer	D	18	0	0	0	-10	67	0	0	0	0	24	0.0	.00
Trent Yawney	D	20	0	0	0	-6	32	0	0	0	0	11	0.0	.00
Bench		—	—	—	—	—	0	—	—	—	—	—	—	—
TEAM TOTALS		82	202	333	535	-93	1799	50	8	29	8	2145	9.4	6.52

Postseason GP	G	A	Pts	+/–	PIM	PP	SH	GW	OT	S	SPct	P/G

Team Did Not Qualify for Postseason Play

Goaltender	Regular Season G	Min	GAA	W	L	T	ENG	ShO	GA	SA	SvPct
Jocelyn Thibault†	**52**	**3014**	**2.71**	**21**	**26**	5	**6**	**4**	**136**	**1435**	.905
Mark Fitzpatrick	27	1403	2.74	6	8	**6**	2	0	64	682	**.906**
Jeff Hackett†	10	524	3.78	2	6	1	3	0	33	256	.871
Andrei Trefilov†	1	25	9.60	0	1	0	0	0	4	20	.800
TEAM TOTALS	82	4989	2.98	29	41	12	11	4	248	2404	.897

Postseason G	Min	GAA	W	L	ENG	ShO	GA	SA	SvPct

1998-99 Chicago Blackhawks

Record When:

Overtime games	1-2-12
In second game of back-to-back games	6-5-3
Vs playoff teams	15-30-7
Leading after two periods	20-2-2
Tied after two periods	6-6-5
Losing after two periods	3-33-5
Scoring first	22-11-3
More shots than opponents	14-13-5
Fewer shots than opponents	15-25-7
Team had at least one fighting major	17-23-7
Team had more PIM	12-24-9
Team had fewer PIM	12-10-0
Team had even PIM	5-7-3

Team

Longest winning streak	6	Apr. 3 — Apr. 17
Longest unbeaten streak	6	Apr. 3 — Apr. 17
Longest losing streak	7	Jan. 30 — Feb. 12
Longest winless streak	10	Oct. 28 — Nov. 15
Most shots, game	38	vs. Nsh, Mar. 10
Most shots, period	17	2nd, @Det, Dec. 8
Fewest shots, game	14	3 times
Fewest shots, period	0	1st, vs. NJ, Oct. 10

Individual

Longest goal streak	6	Tony Amonte
Longest point streak	6	6 times
Most goals, game	3	3 times
Most assists, game	3	4 times
Most points, game	4	3 times
Highest +/–, game	4	Boris Mironov
Lowest +/–, game	-4	4 times
Most shots, game	10	2 times

Did You Know?

The Blackhawks had the league's best record after the trading deadline last year, posting a mark of 8-1-2 (.818).

Miscellaneous

		NHL Rank
PP Pct.	14.9 (50-335)	14
SH goals allowed	10	18t
PK Pct.	80.2 (325-405)	25
SH goals scored	8	8t
Special Team Index	94.2	26
Shots on goal	2,145 (26.2/G)	21
Shots against	2,404 (29.3/G)	19
Unassisted goals	16	5
Unassisted goals allowed	21	26
Team Average Weight	204.6	6
Game Star Points	290	24

Game Star Breakdown

Player	1st	2nd	3rd	Pts
Jocelyn Thibault	7	3	4	48
Tony Amonte	6	2	6	42
Doug Gilmour	3	5	4	34
Alexei Zhamnov	4	2	4	30
Chris Chelios	2	3	4	23
Eric Daze	3	2	0	21
Mark Fitzpatrick	2	1	3	16
Chad Kilger	0	4	1	13
Jean-Pierre Dumont	2	0	1	11
Boris Mironov	0	3	2	11
Jeff Hackett	2	0	0	10
Ed Olczyk	0	2	1	7
Brad Brown	1	0	1	6
Reid Simpson	1	0	0	5
Dave Manson	0	1	2	5
Mike Maneluk	0	1	0	3
Jean-Yves Leroux	0	0	2	2
Nelson Emerson	0	0	1	1
Anders Eriksson	0	0	1	1
Ethan Moreau	0	0	1	1

Colorado Avalanche 1998-99 Game Log (44-28-10)

					Goalies		Shots		Power Plays		Game Stars		
Date	Opp	Score	W/L/T	Record	W/T	L/T	Col	Opp	Col	Opp	1st	2nd	3rd
10/10	Ott	3-4	L	0-1-0	Rhodes	**Roy**	20	34	1-5	2-7	**Sakic**	Phillips	Redden
10/12	Buf	0-3	L	0-2-0	Hasek	**Roy**	32	27	0-8	2-10	Peca	Ward	Hasek
10/14	Bos	0-3	L	0-3-0	Dafoe	**Roy**	34	23	0-6	2-6	Dafoe	Bourque	Allison
10/15	@Pho	2-5	L	0-4-0	Khabibulin	**Billington**	24	28	1-4	1-5	Tverdovsky	Ronning	**Forsberg**
10/18	@LA	5-5*	T	0-4-1	**Roy**	Storr	34	23	0-5	1-3	**Lemieux**	Perreault	**Forsberg**
10/24	Edm	6-4	W	1-4-1	**Roy**	Essensa	27	35	3-5	1-9	**Lemieux**	**Sakic**	**Deadmarsh**
10/26	Pho	1-5	L	1-5-1	Waite	**Roy**	20	27	1-7	2-4	Tkachuk	Roenick	Tocchet
10/29	SJ	4-2	W	2-5-1	**Billington**	Vernon	30	23	1-6	1-7	**Sakic**	**Hejduk**	**Corbet**
10/31	@Nsh	2-3	L	2-6-1	Dunham	**Roy**	43	27	1-5	1-8	Dunham	Brunette	**Forsberg**
11/02	@Car	3-2	W	3-6-1	**Billington**	Irbe	23	21	0-3	0-3	**Forsberg**	**Billington**	**Kamensky**
11/04	@Tor	0-3	L	3-7-1	Joseph	**Roy**	24	28	0-3	0-4	Joseph	Thomas	Sundin
11/06	@Edm	5-2	W	4-7-1	**Roy**	Essensa	32	21	2-6	0-5	**Kamensky**	**Forsberg**	**Lemieux**
11/08	@Cgy	1-3	L	4-8-1	Giguere	**Roy**	40	20	1-7	0-2	Giguere	Smith	**Sakic**
11/10	@Pho	1-1*	T	4-8-2	**Roy**	Waite	21	25	0-5	0-3	Tkachuk	Corkum	**Forsberg**
11/13	TB	**8**-1	W	5-8-2	**Roy**	Puppa	45	18	**4**-7	0-4	**Sakic**	**Forsberg**	**Gusarov**
11/15	@Van	2-1	W	6-8-2	**Roy**	Snow	31	20	1-**9**	0-7	**Deadmarsh**	**Sakic**	Snow
11/17	NYI	5-2	W	7-8-2	**Roy**	Salo	28	22	2-5	1-8	**Kamensky**	**Miller**	Czerkawski
11/19	Van	0-5	L	7-9-2	Snow	**Billington**	35	27	0-8	2-5	Ohlund	Aucoin	Messier
11/21	@Mon	3-2	W	8-9-2	**Roy**	Hackett	26	22	0-4	1-5	**Forsberg**	Brunet	**DeVries**
11/25	@Edm	0-3	L	8-10-2	Shtalenkov	**Roy**	26	41	0-3	0-4	Shtalenkov	**Roy**	Grier
11/28	NJ	2-3	L	8-11-2	Brodeur	**Roy**	26	32	1-3	1-4	Holik	Brodeur	Elias
12/02	Det	4-2	W	9-11-2	**Roy**	Maracle	30	29	0-5	2-5	**Roy**	**Sakic**	**Hejduk**
12/04	StL	2-**0**	W	10-11-2	**Roy**	McLennan	16	25	0-1	0-4	**Roy**	**Forsberg**	**Miller**
12/05	@StL	3-1	W	11-11-2	**Billington**	McLennan	22	30	2-4	0-4	**Forsberg**	**Billington**	Eastwood
12/08	@NYI	2-1	W	12-11-2	**Roy**	Salo	22	32	0-2	0-5	**Forsberg**	**Sakic**	Linden
12/09	@NYR	2-1	W	13-11-2	**Roy**	Richter	29	20	0-2	0-2	**Sakic**	Richter	**Forsberg**
12/12	@NJ	3-5	L	13-12-2	Brodeur	**Billington**	19	31	0-3	2-2	Holik	**Corbet**	Rolston
12/14	StL	0-**0***	T	13-12-3	**Roy**	Fuhr	22	32	0-6	0-3	**Roy**	Fuhr	**Forsberg**
12/17	@Van	1-2	L	13-13-3	Snow	**Roy**	24	21	0-6	2-8	Naslund	**Corbet**	Baron
12/19	@SJ	1-2	L	13-14-3	Vernon	**Billington**	18	32	0-8	0-4	Murphy	Lowry	Marchment
12/21	@Anh	4-2	W	14-14-3	**Billington**	Hebert	33	29	1-4	1-6	**Kamensky**	Olausson	**Drury**
12/22	Anh	0-1	L	14-15-3	Roussel	**Roy**	45	20	0-5	0-6	Roussel	**Foote**	Nielsen
12/26	Dal	2-4	L	14-16-3	Turek	**Roy**	19	23	1-3	3-4	Hull	Lehtinen	Modano
12/27	@Cgy	2-1	W	15-16-3	**Billington**	Giguere	28	31	1-2	0-4	**Billington**	**Foote**	Cassels
12/29	@Van	4-2	W	16-16-3	**Billington**	Snow	27	**16**	2-6	1-4	**Forsberg**	**Deadmarsh**	**Foote**
12/31	NYR	3-6	L	16-17-3	Richter	**Billington**	34	24	1-5	3-4	Gretzky	Nedved	**Lemieux**
1/02	@LA	2-4	L	16-18-3	Storr	**Billington**	26	27	1-4	1-3	Ferraro	Robitaille	**Drury**
1/04	Mon	4-3	W	17-18-3	**Denis**	Theodore	28	34	2-5	0-5	**Lemieux**	**Sakic**	**Drury**
1/06	Fla	2-2*	T	17-18-4	**Denis**	McLean	35	35	1-6	0-5	**Sakic**	Mellanby	**Foote**
1/09	@Det	2-3	L	17-19-4	Osgood	**Denis**	29	31	0-5	2-7	Lidstrom	Lapointe	**Lemieux**
1/10	@Chi	3-2*	W	18-19-4	**Billington**	Thibault	37	26	1-3	0-5	**Sakic**	Thibault	**Lemieux**
1/12	Chi	4-1	W	19-19-4	**Roy**	Thibault	30	24	0-3	1-5	**Forsberg**	**Sakic**	**Roy**
1/16	StL	2-**0**	W	20-19-4	**Roy**	Fuhr	19	28	0-5	0-3	**Roy**	**Miller**	Pronger
1/19	@LA	5-4	W	21-19-4	**Roy**	Fiset	33	31	0-1	1-2	**Sakic**	**Forsberg**	Courtnall
1/21	Cgy	4-2	W	22-19-4	**Roy**	Brathwaite	30	24	2-**9**	0-7	**Corbet**	**Sakic**	**Forsberg**
1/27	@Anh	4-3	W	23-19-4	**Roy**	Hebert	22	34	1-3	1-5	**Roy**	Selanne	**Sakic**
1/28	Anh	6-2	W	24-19-4	**Roy**	Hebert	38	34	2-4	1-5	**Yelle**	**Lemieux**	**Sakic**
1/30	SJ	5-**0**	W	25-19-4	**Roy**	Vernon	28	22	1-4	0-4	**Roy**	**Deadmarsh**	**Sakic**
2/02	@Bos	3-2	W	26-19-4	**Roy**	Dafoe	22	25	1-5	1-7	**Drury**	Allison	**Forsberg**
2/03	@Buf	5-3	W	27-19-4	**Roy**	Hasek	35	40	2-6	1-3	**Corbet**	Satan	**Kamensky**
2/05	@Det	3-1	W	28-19-4	**Roy**	Osgood	30	28	1-2	0-3	**Roy**	**Foote**	Draper
2/07	@Dal	3-**0**	W	29-19-4	**Roy**	Belfour	12	27	1-4	0-7	**Roy**	**Lemieux**	**Foote**
2/09	Cgy	1-2	L	29-20-4	Wregget	**Roy**	29	29	0-5	0-5	Wregget	Nazarov	Fleury
2/13	Pho	1-4	L	29-21-4	Khabibulin	**Roy**	26	21	1-5	1-4	Tkachuk	Adams	**Sakic**
2/14	Phi	4-4*	T	29-21-5	**Roy**	Vanbiesbrouck	31	25	1-6	0-4	**Kamensky**	**Forsberg**	Desjardins

2/19	@Nsh	4-4*	T	29-21-6	**Roy**	Dunham	43	36	2-5	3-8	Krivokrasov	**Sakic**	Ronning
2/21	@Dal	1-1*	T	29-21-7	**Roy**	Belfour	18	24	0-4	1-7	Hatcher	**Forsberg**	Hull
2/23	Van	4-4*	T	29-21-8	**Billington**	Snow	43	27	**4**-8	1-5	**Deadmarsh**	Naslund	**Ozolinsh**
2/25	Pit	2-3	L	29-22-8	Barrasso	**Billington**	24	30	0-4	0-2	Straka	Jagr	**Billington**
2/27	Nsh	3-1	W	30-22-8	**Roy**	Dunham	32	22	2-5	0-**0**	**Deadmarsh**	**Messier**	**Lemieux**
3/01	Edm	3-4	L	30-23-8	Essensa	**Roy**	**50**	29	0-6	2-5	Essensa	**Fleury**	Mironov
3/03	@Fla	7-5	W	31-23-8	**Billington**	Burke	34	28	2-5	3-5	**Forsberg**	Bure	**Sakic**
3/04	@TB	1-2	L	31-24-8	Schwab	**Roy**	18	26	1-3	0-5	Hogue	Gratton	**Roy**
3/07	@Pit	3-1	W	32-24-8	**Billington**	Skudra	22	24	0-3	0-4	**Hejduk**	**Billington**	Straka
3/09	@Was	3-2*	W	33-24-8	**Billington**	Kolzig	20	37	1-5	0-4	**Ozolinsh**	**Deadmarsh**	Bondra
3/11	@Phi	5-3	W	34-24-8	**Roy**	Vanbiesbrouck	27	36	0-1	1-4	**Forsberg**	**Drury**	Lindros
3/14	Det	1-3	L	34-25-8	Maracle	**Roy**	22	28	0-4	1-7	Larionov	Murphy	**Foote**
3/18	Car	3-2	W	35-25-8	**Roy**	Kidd	34	29	1-6	1-6	**Sakic**	**Foote**	Primeau
3/20	Chi	5-5*	T	35-25-9	**Roy**	Fitzpatrick	28	33	3-8	0-4	**Sakic**	Zhamnov	**Lemieux**
3/21	@Chi	3-4	L	35-26-9	Thibault	**Roy**	25	35	1-4	1-6	Zhamnov	**Sakic**	Mironov
3/24	Van	5-2	W	36-26-9	**Roy**	Weekes	25	34	3-6	0-3	**Fleury**	**Forsberg**	**Sakic**
3/26	Was	3-1	W	37-26-9	**Roy**	Kolzig	25	20	0-4	0-2	**Miller**	**Lemieux**	**Yelle**
3/28	LA	7-2	W	38-26-9	**Roy**	Fiset	33	28	0-2	0-2	**Fleury**	**Sakic**	**Hejduk**
3/30	Cgy	3-3*	T	38-26-10	**Roy**	Wregget	24	34	1-4	2-4	Morris	**Fleury**	Bure
3/31	@SJ	3-2	W	39-26-10	**Billington**	Vernon	23	27	0-2	0-4	**Billington**	Norton	**Forsberg**
4/03	Edm	5-2	W	40-26-10	**Roy**	Essensa	24	32	1-4	2-8	**Fleury**	**Ozolinsh**	**Sakic**
4/05	LA	4-1	W	41-26-10	**Roy**	Fiset	35	27	2-3	0-3	**Forsberg**	**Foote**	**Roy**
4/07	Nsh	4-1	W	42-26-10	**Roy**	Vokoun	29	28	2-4	1-4	**Drury**	**Roy**	**Foote**
4/11	@StL	4-2	W	43-26-10	**Roy**	Fuhr	20	36	0-4	0-5	**Roy**	**Forsberg**	Demitra
4/15	@Cgy	1-5	L	43-27-10	Wregget	**Roy**	25	24	0-2	1-2	Stillman	Wilm	Domenichelli
4/16	@Edm	1-5	L	43-28-10	Salo	**Billington**	18	31	0-7	0-6	Poti	Devereaux	Murray
4/18	Dal	2-1	W	44-28-10	**Roy**	Fernandez	29	31	0-4	1-5	**Roy**	**Fleury**	Fernandez

Postseason

4/24	@SJ	3-1	W	1-0	**Roy**	Vernon	31	43	**2**-8	1-7	**Sakic**	**Roy**	Friesen
4/26	@SJ	2-1*	W	2-0	**Roy**	Vernon	36	**24**	1-7	0-4	**Hejduk**	Vernon	**Foote**
4/28	SJ	2-4	L	2-1	Vernon	**Roy**	36	33	1-7	1-7	Ricci	Sturm	Vernon
4/30	SJ	3-7	L	2-2	Vernon	**Roy**	36	31	0-7	2-7	Korolyuk	Damphousse	Marleau
5/01	SJ	6-2	W	3-2	**Roy**	Shields	36	31	**2-10**	2-9	**Fleury**	**Roy**	**Lemieux**
5/03	@SJ	3-2*	W	4-2	**Roy**	Vernon	33	29	1-3	1-7	Vernon	**Roy**	**Hejduk**
5/07	Det	2-3*	L	0-1	Ranford	**Roy**	39	34	1-7	2-7	Maltby	**Deadmarsh**	Ranford
5/09	Det	0-4	L	0-2	Ranford	**Roy**	28	37	0-5	2-8	Yzerman	Ranford	Lidstrom
5/11	@Det	5-3	W	1-2	**Roy**	Ranford	36	47	1-4	1-6	**Roy**	**Fleury**	**Miller**
5/13	@Det	6-2	W	2-2	**Roy**	Ranford	24	33	**2**-4	1-5	**Forsberg**	**Deadmarsh**	**Roy**
5/16	Det	3-**0**	W	3-2	**Roy**	Osgood	26	36	1-6	0-6	**Roy**	**Forsberg**	**Deadmarsh**
5/18	@Det	5-2	W	4-2	**Roy**	Osgood	31	37	0-4	1-4	**Forsberg**	**Kamensky**	**Roy**
5/22	@Dal	2-1	W	1-0	**Roy**	Belfour	28	31	0-3	0-**2**	**Forsberg**	**Roy**	**Kamensky**
5/24	@Dal	2-4	L	1-1	Belfour	**Roy**	19	45	1-4	1-7	Modano	Zubov	Nieuwendyk
5/26	Dal	0-3	L	1-2	Belfour	**Roy**	34	26	0-3	0-4	Belfour	Nieuwendyk	Hatcher
5/28	Dal	3-2*	W	2-2	**Roy**	Belfour	**45**	45	0-5	1-5	**Drury**	**Foote**	Langenbrunner
5/30	@Dal	**7**-5	W	3-2	**Roy**	Belfour	26	30	1-4	2-5	**Drury**	**Forsberg**	Verbeek
6/01	Dal	1-4	L	3-3	Belfour	**Roy**	27	40	0-3	1-3	Langenbrunner	Nieuwendyk	Belfour
6/04	@Dal	1-4	L	3-4	Belfour	**Roy**	19	25	0-2	0-3	Keane	Verbeek	Matvichuk

Colorado Avalanche 1998-99 Player Statistics

Skater	Ps	Regular Season GP	G	A	Pts	+/–	PIM	PP	SH	GW	GT	S	SPct	P/G	Postseason GP	G	A	Pts	+/–	PIM	PP	SH	GW	OT	S	SPct	P/G
Peter Forsberg	C	78	30	**67**	**97**	**27**	108	9	2	7	0	217	13.8	1.24	**19**	**8**	**16**	**24**	7	31	1	**1**	0	0	54	14.8	**1.26**
Joe Sakic	C	73	**41**	55	96	23	29	**12**	**5**	6	**1**	255	**16.1**	**1.32**	**19**	6	13	19	-2	8	1	**1**	1	0	56	10.7	1.00
Claude Lemieux	R	**82**	27	24	51	0	102	11	0	**8**	**1**	**292**	9.2	.62	**19**	3	11	14	5	26	1	0	0	0	**69**	4.3	.74
Adam Deadmarsh	R	66	22	27	49	-2	99	10	0	3	**1**	152	14.5	.74	**19**	**8**	4	12	2	20	**3**	0	0	0	44	**18.2**	.63
* Milan Hejduk	R	**82**	14	34	48	8	26	4	0	5	0	178	7.9	.59	16	6	6	12	3	4	1	0	3	**2**	38	15.8	.75
* Chris Drury	C	79	20	24	44	9	62	6	0	3	**1**	138	14.5	.56	**19**	6	2	8	2	4	0	0	**4**	1	40	15.0	.42
Valeri Kamensky	L	65	14	30	44	1	28	2	0	2	0	123	11.4	.68	10	4	5	9	5	4	1	0	1	0	18	22.2	.90
Sandis Ozolinsh	D	39	7	25	32	10	22	4	0	3	0	81	8.6	.82	**19**	4	8	12	-5	22	**3**	0	1	0	56	7.1	.63
Theo Fleury†	R	15	10	14	24	8	18	1	0	2	**1**	51	19.6	1.60	18	5	12	17	-2	20	2	0	0	0	56	8.9	.94
Rene Corbet†	L	53	8	14	22	3	58	2	0	1	0	82	9.8	.42	—	—	—	—	—	—	—	—	—	—	—	—	—
Adam Foote	D	64	5	16	21	20	92	3	0	0	0	83	6.0	.33	**19**	2	3	5	3	24	1	0	0	0	28	7.1	.26
Sylvain Lefebvre	D	76	2	18	20	18	48	0	0	0	0	64	3.1	.26	**19**	0	1	1	6	12	0	0	0	0	16	0.0	.05
Shean Donovan	R	68	7	12	19	4	37	1	0	1	0	81	8.6	.28	5	0	0	0	0	2	0	0	0	0	1	0.0	.00
Aaron Miller	D	76	5	13	18	3	42	1	0	2	0	87	5.7	.24	**19**	1	5	6	**8**	10	0	0	0	0	22	4.5	.32
Stephane Yelle	C	72	8	7	15	-8	40	1	0	0	0	99	8.1	.21	10	0	1	1	-1	6	0	0	0	0	18	0.0	.10
Alexei Gusarov	D	54	3	10	13	12	24	1	0	0	0	28	10.7	.24	5	0	0	0	1	2	0	0	0	0	2	0.0	.00
Shjon Podein†	L	41	2	6	8	-3	24	0	0	0	0	49	4.1	.20	**19**	1	1	2	-1	12	0	0	0	0	33	3.0	.11
Eric Messier	D	31	4	2	6	0	14	1	0	1	0	30	13.3	.19	3	0	0	0	-1	0	0	0	0	0	1	0.0	.00
Dale Hunter†	C	12	2	4	6	0	17	0	0	0	0	6	33.3	.50	**19**	1	3	4	0	**38**	0	0	0	0	10	10.0	.21
Jeff Odgers	R	75	2	3	5	-3	**259**	1	0	0	0	39	5.1	.07	15	1	0	1	0	14	0	0	1	0	3	33.3	.07
Keith Jones†	R	12	2	2	4	-6	20	1	0	0	0	11	18.2	.33	—	—	—	—	—	—	—	—	—	—	—	—	—
Greg DeVries†	D	67	1	3	4	-3	60	0	0	0	0	56	1.8	.06	**19**	0	2	2	3	22	0	0	0	0	7	0.0	.11
Cam Russell†	D	35	1	2	3	-5	84	0	0	0	0	14	7.1	.09	—	—	—	—	—	—	—	—	—	—	—	—	—
Jon Klemm	D	39	1	2	3	4	31	0	0	0	0	28	3.6	.08	**19**	0	1	1	1	10	0	0	0	0	11	0.0	.05
* Christian Matte	R	7	1	1	2	-2	0	0	0	0	0	9	11.1	.29	—	—	—	—	—	—	—	—	—	—	—	—	—
Warren Rychel	L	28	0	2	2	3	63	0	0	0	0	15	0.0	.07	12	0	1	1	-1	14	0	0	0	0	6	0.0	.08
Patrick Roy	G	61	0	2	2	—	28	0	0	0	0	0	—	.03	**19**	0	2	2	—	4	0	0	0	0	1	0.0	.11
Ted Crowley†	D	7	0	1	1	-1	2	0	0	0	0	10	0.0	.14	—	—	—	—	—	—	—	—	—	—	—	—	—
* Serge Aubin	C	1	0	0	0	0	0	0	0	0	0	1	0.0	.00	—	—	—	—	—	—	—	—	—	—	—	—	—
Chris Dingman†	L	1	0	0	0	0	7	0	0	0	0	0	—	.00	—	—	—	—	—	—	—	—	—	—	—	—	—
* Mike Gaul	D	1	0	0	0	0	0	0	0	0	0	1	0.0	.00	—	—	—	—	—	—	—	—	—	—	—	—	—
* Brian White	D	2	0	0	0	0	0	0	0	0	0	0	—	.00	—	—	—	—	—	—	—	—	—	—	—	—	—
* Marc Denis	G	4	0	0	0	—	0	0	0	0	0	0	—	.00	—	—	—	—	—	—	—	—	—	—	—	—	—
* Jeff Buchanan	D	6	0	0	0	1	6	0	0	0	0	1	0.0	.00	—	—	—	—	—	—	—	—	—	—	—	—	—
Eric Lacroix†	L	7	0	0	0	-2	2	0	0	0	0	4	0.0	.00	—	—	—	—	—	—	—	—	—	—	—	—	—
* Dan Smith	D	12	0	0	0	5	9	0	0	0	0	6	0.0	.00	—	—	—	—	—	—	—	—	—	—	—	—	—
Craig Billington	G	21	0	0	0	—	2	0	0	0	0	0	—	.00	1	0	0	0	—	0	0	0	0	0	0	—	.00
* Wade Belak†	D	22	0	0	0	-2	71	0	0	0	0	5	0.0	.00	—	—	—	—	—	—	—	—	—	—	—	—	—
* Scott Parker	R	27	0	0	0	-3	71	0	0	0	0	3	0.0	.00	0	0	0	0	0	0	0	0	0	0	0	—	—
Bench		—	—	—	—	—	0	—	—	—	—	—	—	—	—	—	—	—	—	0	—	—	—	—	—	—	—
TEAM TOTALS		82	239	420	659	119	1605	71	7	44	5	2299	10.4	8.04	19	56	97	153	33	309	14	2	11	3	590	9.5	8.05

Goaltender	Regular Season G	Min	GAA	W	L	T	ENG	ShO	GA	SA	SvPct	Postseason G	Min	GAA	W	L	ENG	ShO	GA	SA	SvPct
Patrick Roy	**61**	**3648**	**2.29**	**32**	**19**	**8**	**4**	**5**	**139**	**1673**	**.917**	**19**	**1173**	**2.66**	**11**	**8**	**1**	**1**	**52**	**650**	**.920**
* Marc Denis	4	217	2.49	1	1	1	0	0	9	110	.918	—	—	—	—	—	—	—	—	—	—
Craig Billington	21	1086	2.87	11	8	1	1	0	52	492	.894	1	9	6.67	0	0	0	0	1	6	.833
TEAM TOTALS	82	4974	2.47	44	28	10	5	5	205	2280	.910	19	1185	2.73	11	8	1	1	54	657	.918

1998-99 Colorado Avalanche

Record When:

Overtime games	2-0-10
In second game of back-to-back games	7-5-1
Vs playoff teams	23-18-4
Leading after two periods	27-2-1
Tied after two periods	12-5-7
Losing after two periods	5-21-2
Scoring first	28-8-5
More shots than opponents	25-11-4
Fewer shots than opponents	19-16-5
Team had at least one fighting major	25-15-5
Team had more PIM	23-16-1
Team had fewer PIM	12-8-8
Team had even PIM	9-4-1

Team

Longest winning streak	12	Jan. 10 — Feb. 7
Longest unbeaten streak	12	Jan. 10 — Feb. 7
Longest losing streak	4	Oct. 10 — Oct. 15
Longest winless streak	7	Feb. 9 — Feb. 25
Most shots, game	50	vs. Edm, Mar. 1
Most shots, period	22	2 times
Fewest shots, game	12	@Dal, Feb. 7
Fewest shots, period	2	2 times

Individual

Longest goal streak	5	Adam Deadmarsh
Longest point streak	15	Peter Forsberg
Most goals, game	3	4 times
Most assists, game	4	4 times
Most points, game	6	Peter Forsberg
Highest +/–, game	5	Peter Forsberg
Lowest +/–, game	-4	Milan Hejduk
Most shots, game	10	Claude Lemieux

Did You Know?

In their first 40 games last season—all without Sandis Ozolinsh in the lineup—the Avalanche averaged 2.40 goals per game. In their last 42 games—of which Ozolinsh played all but three—the Av's improved their output by one goal per game, averaging 3.40 tallies per contest.

Miscellaneous

		NHL Rank
PP Pct.	18.9 (71-375)	5
SH goals allowed	12	25
PK Pct.	83.7 (323-386)	17
SH goals scored	7	15t
Special Team Index	101.2	9
Shots on goal	2,299 (28.0/G)	14
Shots against	2,280 (27.8/G)	14
Unassisted goals	10	21t
Unassisted goals allowed	15	17t
Team Average Weight	198.0	20
Game Star Points	436	3

Game Star Breakdown

Player	1st	2nd	3rd	Pts
Joe Sakic	9	10	8	83
Peter Forsberg	9	8	9	78
Patrick Roy	10	2	3	59
Claude Lemieux	3	3	6	30
Adam Deadmarsh	3	3	1	25
Theo Fleury	3	3	0	24
Valeri Kamensky	4	0	2	22
Craig Billington	2	3	1	20
Adam Foote	0	5	5	20
Rene Corbet	2	2	1	17
Chris Drury	2	1	3	16
Aaron Miller	1	2	1	12
Milan Hejduk	1	1	2	10
Sandis Ozolinsh	1	1	1	9
Stephane Yelle	1	0	1	6
Eric Messier	0	1	0	3
Greg DeVries	0	0	1	1
Alexei Gusarov	0	0	1	1

Dallas Stars 1998-99 Game Log (51-19-12)

					Goalies		Shots		Power Plays		Game Stars		
Date	Opp	Score	W/L/T	Record	W/T	L/T	Dal	Opp	Dal	Opp	1st	2nd	3rd
10/10	Buf	4-1	W	1-0-0	**Belfour**	Hasek	26	28	3-8	1-6	**Modano**	**Zubov**	**Sydor**
10/13	Chi	3-1	W	2-0-0	**Belfour**	Hackett	31	14	1-9	0-5	Hackett	**Modano**	**Belfour**
10/15	@Car	2-2*	T	2-0-1	**Belfour**	Irbe	38	22	0-3	0-3	Roberts	Irbe	**Modano**
10/17	@Chi	3-4	L	2-1-1	Hackett	**Belfour**	29	36	3-7	1-5	Chelios	**Hull**	Moreau
10/20	Cgy	3-1	W	3-1-1	**Turek**	Wregget	37	14	2-11	0-6	**Sydor**	**Zubov**	**Carbonneau**
10/22	Pho	2-1	W	4-1-1	**Belfour**	Khabibulin	32	21	2-6	1-5	**Nieuwendyk**	**Verbeek**	**Reid**
10/24	SJ	2-1	W	5-1-1	**Belfour**	Vernon	24	17	2-4	1-4	**Langenbrunner**	**Marshall**	Vernon
10/30	Anh	3-3*	T	5-1-2	**Turek**	Hebert	27	34	1-3	0-5	Rucchin	**Nieuwendyk**	Kariya
10/31	Det	3-2	W	6-1-2	**Belfour**	Osgood	33	24	0-8	1-9	**Hull**	**Lehtinen**	**Modano**
11/04	@SJ	0-4	L	6-2-2	Vernon	**Belfour**	21	9	0-7	1-3	Ricci	Vernon	Rathje
11/07	@LA	4-3	W	7-2-2	**Belfour**	LeGace	25	23	2-6	1-6	**Hatcher**	Robitaille	**Hrkac**
11/11	Pho	0-2	L	7-3-2	Waite	**Belfour**	38	18	0-4	0-3	Waite	Tkachuk	Numminen
11/13	@Det	5-1	W	8-3-2	**Belfour**	Osgood	28	35	1-7	1-7	**Nieuwendyk**	**Hatcher**	**Modano**
11/14	@Bos	3-1	W	9-3-2	**Turek**	Dafoe	29	28	0-4	0-4	**Hull**	**Turek**	Dafoe
11/20	NYI	4-2	W	10-3-2	**Belfour**	Flaherty	26	17	2-6	0-4	**Gusev**	**Sydor**	**Hatcher**
11/21	@StL	3-3*	T	10-3-3	**Turek**	Parent	18	34	2-8	1-4	Demitra	Chase	**Marshall**
11/23	SJ	3-2	W	11-3-3	**Belfour**	Vernon	21	18	0-5	2-8	**Matvichuk**	Houlder	**Nieuwendyk**
11/25	NJ	2-5	L	11-4-3	Brodeur	**Belfour**	18	25	2-5	0-4	Rolston	Pandolfo	**Chambers**
11/27	Was	4-0	W	12-4-3	**Belfour**	Kolzig	15	15	1-6	0-4	**Modano**	**Hatcher**	**Langenbrunner**
12/02	@SJ	3-0	W	13-4-3	**Belfour**	Vernon	23	26	0-6	0-2	**Hrkac**	**Keane**	**Belfour**
12/04	@Van	1-4	L	13-5-3	Snow	**Belfour**	37	18	0-5	1-3	Naslund	Snow	Messier
12/06	@Edm	6-2	W	14-5-3	**Belfour**	Essensa	24	25	1-5	0-5	**Lehtinen**	**Modano**	**Zubov**
12/07	@Cgy	3-2	W	15-5-3	**Turek**	Moss	32	25	2-6	0-6	**Modano**	Morris	**Carbonneau**
12/09	SJ	3-3*	T	15-5-4	**Belfour**	Vernon	28	17	3-5	1-5	**Sydor**	Marleau	**Nieuwendyk**
12/11	Mon	3-2	W	16-5-4	**Belfour**	Theodore	30	23	0-6	1-4	**Langenbrunner**	**Marshall**	**Carbonneau**
12/13	@Chi	2-2*	T	16-5-5	**Belfour**	Fitzpatrick	32	30	1-2	1-2	**Belfour**	Fitzpatrick	Amonte
12/15	StL	7-3	W	17-5-5	**Belfour**	McLennan	23	24	2-5	1-2	**Hull**	**Hatcher**	**Nieuwendyk**
12/18	@Det	3-1	W	18-5-5	**Belfour**	Osgood	26	25	1-5	0-5	**Verbeek**	**Keane**	**Ludwig**
12/20	@Ott	3-2	W	19-5-5	**Turek**	Tugnutt	30	29	1-4	2-3	**Turek**	**Nieuwendyk**	Alfredsson
12/21	@Mon	2-2*	T	19-5-6	**Belfour**	Hackett	37	29	0-1	0-0	Hackett	**Sydor**	Ulanov
12/23	@Tor	5-1	W	20-5-6	**Belfour**	Joseph	24	22	1-1	0-5	**Modano**	**Lehtinen**	**Ludwig**
12/26	@Col	4-2	W	21-5-6	**Turek**	Roy	23	19	3-4	1-3	**Hull**	**Lehtinen**	**Modano**
12/28	Nsh	1-0	W	22-5-6	**Belfour**	Fichaud	21	14	0-5	0-1	**Chambers**	**Matvichuk**	**Belfour**
12/31	Bos	6-1	W	23-5-6	**Belfour**	Tallas	26	31	1-3	1-2	**Verbeek**	**Zubov**	**Belfour**
1/01	@Pho	2-1*	W	24-5-6	**Turek**	Khabibulin	31	27	1-3	0-6	**Hull**	**Turek**	Quint
1/06	Van	6-4	W	25-5-6	**Belfour**	Snow	28	20	3-6	2-2	**Carbonneau**	**Sydor**	Naslund
1/08	@Cgy	0-1	L	25-6-6	Brathwaite	**Belfour**	21	27	0-3	0-2	Brathwaite	Shantz	Bassen
1/10	@Van	0-2	L	25-7-6	Hirsch	**Turek**	13	20	0-5	0-1	Scatchard	Hirsch	Mogilny
1/12	@Edm	2-2*	T	25-7-7	**Belfour**	Essensa	23	20	1-4	0-4	Smyth	**Keane**	Marchant
1/13	@SJ	2-1	W	26-7-7	**Turek**	Vernon	20	32	0-4	0-3	**Turek**	Korolyuk	**Zubov**
1/15	@Anh	3-1	W	27-7-7	**Belfour**	Hebert	29	28	1-2	1-2	**Modano**	Trepanier	**Lehtinen**
1/18	Van	3-5	L	27-8-7	Snow	**Belfour**	21	23	2-7	2-6	Naslund	Messier	Gagner
1/20	Tor	4-6	L	27-9-7	Joseph	**Belfour**	34	24	2-5	2-4	Joseph	**Sydor**	Berard
1/27	LA	3-2	W	28-9-7	**Turek**	Fiset	28	24	0-4	1-6	**Turek**	Robitaille	**Skrudland**
1/29	@TB	4-1	W	29-9-7	**Belfour**	Schwab	32	32	0-5	1-5	**Modano**	**Belfour**	Richer
1/30	@Fla	5-2	W	30-9-7	**Belfour**	Burke	30	28	1-5	1-5	**Hrkac**	**Belfour**	**Modano**
2/01	Cgy	2-2*	T	30-9-8	**Belfour**	Brathwaite	33	29	1-5	0-3	Brathwaite	**Belfour**	Fleury
2/07	Col	0-3	L	30-10-8	Roy	**Belfour**	27	12	0-7	1-4	Roy	Lemieux	Foote
2/12	@Anh	3-2	W	31-10-8	**Belfour**	Hebert	29	28	1-7	1-5	**Belfour**	**Hatcher**	Selanne
2/13	@LA	3-2	W	32-10-8	**Turek**	Fiset	22	26	0-3	0-3	**Hull**	**Severyn**	Laperriere
2/15	Edm	4-1	W	33-10-8	**Belfour**	Essensa	27	13	2-6	0-5	**Hull**	**Langenbrunner**	**Marshall**
2/17	Fla	2-1	W	34-10-8	**Turek**	Burke	29	16	1-6	0-2	**Nieuwendyk**	**Langenbrunner**	Burke
2/19	Chi	5-1	W	35-10-8	**Belfour**	Thibault	31	17	2-4	0-1	**Modano**	**Zubov**	**Verbeek**
2/21	Col	1-1*	T	35-10-9	**Belfour**	Roy	24	18	1-7	0-4	**Hatcher**	Forsberg	**Hull**
2/23	@Nsh	4-3	W	36-10-9	**Belfour**	Dunham	45	32	0-3	0-3	**Modano**	Dunham	Walker

2/24	Nsh	1-2	L	36-11-9	Vokoun	**Turek**	18	25	0-2	1-3	Krivokrasov	Ronning	Vokoun
2/26	Pit	6-4	W	37-11-9	**Belfour**	Barrasso	35	18	0-2	0-4	**Verbeek**	Straka	**Langenbrunner**
2/28	LA	1-**0**	W	38-11-9	**Belfour**	Fiset	35	18	0-3	0-3	**Nieuwendyk**	Fiset	**Belfour**
3/02	@NYR	2-2*	T	38-11-10	**Belfour**	Richter	30	26	0-7	0-3	Graves	Leetch	**Nieuwendyk**
3/04	@NYI	3-2*	W	39-11-10	**Turek**	Salo	32	30	0-2	1-1	**Nieuwendyk**	Palffy	**Modano**
3/05	@Buf	1-2	L	39-12-10	Biron	**Belfour**	27	28	0-3	1-6	Biron	Peca	**Belfour**
3/07	StL	4-3	W	40-12-10	**Turek**	Carey	22	34	1-5	1-5	**Modano**	MacInnis	**Turek**
3/10	Edm	**7**-4	W	41-12-10	**Belfour**	Shtalenkov	21	25	2-7	1-8	**Nieuwendyk**	**Modano**	**Chambers**
3/12	Anh	4-**0**	W	42-12-10	**Belfour**	Hebert	34	27	0-5	0-6	**Nieuwendyk**	**Belfour**	**Modano**
3/14	@Phi	1-1*	T	42-12-11	**Belfour**	Vanbiesbrouck	23	27	0-6	0-6	Hull	**Modano**	Brind'Amour
3/16	@Pit	2-2*	T	42-12-12	**Turek**	Aubin	31	15	1-3	0-4	Jagr	Straka	**Hrkac**
3/17	@Was	1-2*	L	42-13-12	Tabaracci	**Belfour**	27	23	0-6	1-3	Bellows	Tabaracci	Nikolishin
3/19	Ott	1-2	L	42-14-12	Rhodes	**Belfour**	32	14	1-4	0-2	Rhodes	**Modano**	Hossa
3/21	Car	3-2*	W	43-14-12	**Belfour**	Irbe	17	28	0-3	0-4	**Modano**	**Hatcher**	Kapanen
3/23	@Pho	3-2	W	44-14-12	**Belfour**	Khabibulin	23	28	1-3	0-5	Tocchet	**Langenbrunner**	Tkachuk
3/25	@LA	2-1	W	45-14-12	**Turek**	Fiset	26	32	0-2	0-4	**Turek**	**Hull**	Fiset
3/26	@Anh	1-5	L	45-15-12	Hebert	**Belfour**	26	32	1-4	2-2	Selanne	Kariya	Hebert
3/28	@Nsh	3-**0**	W	46-15-12	**Turek**	Vokoun	34	21	0-2	0-4	**Nieuwendyk**	**Turek**	Vokoun
3/31	TB	6-4	W	47-15-12	**Turek**	Schwab	39	27	0-2	0-2	**Nieuwendyk**	Richer	**Marshall**
4/03	@StL	2-5	L	47-16-12	Fuhr	**Turek**	21	21	0-5	1-1	Demitra	Pronger	Fuhr
4/04	Det	0-3	L	47-17-12	Osgood	**Belfour**	27	26	0-5	0-6	Osgood	Clark	Chelios
4/07	Anh	5-1	W	48-17-12	**Belfour**	Hebert	26	23	2-5	1-2	**Zubov**	**Hull**	**Belfour**
4/09	NYR	3-1	W	49-17-12	**Belfour**	Cloutier	34	22	1-1	0-1	**Keane**	**Belfour**	**Nieuwendyk**
4/11	LA	6-2	W	50-17-12	**Turek**	Fiset	36	23	**3**-6	0-**0**	**Zubov**	**Keane**	**Sydor**
4/14	Pho	4-2	W	51-17-12	**Belfour**	Shtalenkov	23	35	1-7	0-6	**Modano**	**Zubov**	**Nieuwendyk**
4/17	@Pho	0-2	L	51-18-12	Khabibulin	**Belfour**	27	23	0-7	1-5	Ylonen	Reichel	Leach
4/18	@Col	1-2	L	51-19-12	Roy	**Fernandez**	31	29	1-5	0-4	Roy	Fleury	**Fernandez**

Postseason

4/21	Edm	2-1	W	1-0	**Belfour**	Salo	31	13	0-4	0-**2**	**Carbonneau**	**Lehtinen**	Salo
4/23	Edm	3-2	W	2-0	**Belfour**	Salo	34	19	0-6	0-3	**Belfour**	**Lehtinen**	Salo
4/25	@Edm	3-2	W	3-0	**Belfour**	Salo	28	22	0-6	2-7	**Modano**	Smyth	**Nieuwendyk**
4/27	@Edm	3-2*	W	4-0	**Belfour**	Salo	**56**	39	**2**-6	0-5	**Nieuwendyk**	**Belfour**	Salo
5/06	StL	3-**0**	W	1-0	**Belfour**	Fuhr	25	23	0-7	0-5	**Verbeek**	**Belfour**	**Matvichuk**
5/08	StL	**5**-4*	W	2-0	**Belfour**	Fuhr	25	34	0-4	1-3	**Nieuwendyk**	Turgeon	Demitra
5/10	@StL	2-3*	L	2-1	Fuhr	**Belfour**	18	28	1-5	0-6	Demitra	Hecht	**Hull**
5/12	@StL	2-3*	L	2-2	Fuhr	**Belfour**	25	30	0-5	1-7	Turgeon	**Belfour**	MacInnis
5/15	StL	3-1	W	3-2	**Belfour**	Fuhr	16	31	**2**-5	0-4	**Belfour**	**Lehtinen**	**Hatcher**
5/17	@StL	2-1*	W	4-2	**Belfour**	Fuhr	29	29	0-4	0-3	**Modano**	MacInnis	**Hull**
5/22	Col	1-2	L	0-1	Roy	**Belfour**	31	28	0-2	0-3	Forsberg	Roy	Kamensky
5/24	Col	4-2	W	1-1	**Belfour**	Roy	45	19	1-7	1-4	**Modano**	**Zubov**	**Nieuwendyk**
5/26	@Col	3-**0**	W	2-1	**Belfour**	Roy	26	34	0-4	0-3	**Belfour**	**Nieuwendyk**	**Hatcher**
5/28	@Col	2-3*	L	2-2	Roy	**Belfour**	45	45	1-5	0-5	Drury	Foote	**Langenbrunner**
5/30	Col	**5**-7	L	2-3	Roy	**Belfour**	30	26	**2**-5	1-4	Drury	Forsberg	**Verbeek**
6/01	@Col	4-1	W	3-3	**Belfour**	Roy	40	27	1-3	0-3	**Langenbrunner**	**Nieuwendyk**	**Belfour**
6/04	Col	4-1	W	4-3	**Belfour**	Roy	25	19	0-3	0-**2**	**Keane**	**Verbeek**	**Matvichuk**
6/08	Buf	2-3*	L	0-1	Hasek	**Belfour**	37	24	1-**10**	1-4	Woolley	Hasek	**Lehtinen**
6/10	Buf	4-2	W	1-1	**Belfour**	Hasek	31	21	0-6	2-4	**Hull**	**Nieuwendyk**	Primeau
6/12	@Buf	2-1	W	2-1	**Belfour**	Hasek	29	**12**	0-2	0-8	**Nieuwendyk**	**Langenbrunner**	Barnes
6/15	@Buf	1-2	L	2-2	Hasek	**Belfour**	31	18	1-3	0-5	Hasek	Ward	**Belfour**
6/17	Buf	2-**0**	W	3-2	**Belfour**	Hasek	21	23	1-3	0-3	**Belfour**	**Hatcher**	**Verbeek**
6/19	@Buf	2-1*	W	4-2	**Belfour**	Hasek	50	54	0-2	0-**2**	**Hull**	**Belfour**	Barnes

Dallas Stars 1998-99 Player Statistics

Skater	Ps	Regular Season GP	G	A	Pts	+/–	PIM	PP	SH	GW	GT	S	SPct	P/G	Postseason GP	G	A	Pts	+/–	PIM	PP	SH	GW	OT	S	SPct	P/G
Mike Modano	C	77	**34**	**47**	**81**	**29**	44	6	**4**	7	1	**224**	15.2	**1.05**	**23**	5	**18**	**23**	6	16	1	**1**	1	1	83	6.0	**1.00**
Brett Hull	R	60	32	26	58	19	30	**15**	0	**11**	0	192	16.7	.97	22	8	7	15	3	4	3	0	2	1	**86**	9.3	.68
Joe Nieuwendyk	C	67	28	27	55	11	34	8	0	8	1	157	**17.8**	.82	**23**	**11**	10	21	7	19	3	0	**6**	**2**	72	15.3	.91
Jere Lehtinen	R	74	20	32	52	**29**	18	7	1	2	0	173	11.6	.70	**23**	10	3	13	8	2	1	**1**	0	0	55	18.2	.57
Sergei Zubov	D	81	10	41	51	9	20	5	0	3	0	155	6.5	.63	**23**	1	12	13	**13**	4	0	0	0	0	46	2.2	.57
Darryl Sydor	D	74	14	34	48	-1	50	9	0	2	1	163	8.6	.65	**23**	3	9	12	8	16	1	0	1	0	49	6.1	.52
Jamie Langenbrunner	C	75	12	33	45	10	62	4	0	1	0	145	8.3	.60	**23**	10	7	17	7	16	**4**	0	3	0	46	**21.7**	.74
Pat Verbeek	R	78	17	17	34	11	**133**	8	0	2	1	134	12.7	.44	18	3	4	7	4	14	0	0	1	0	33	9.1	.39
Grant Marshall	R	**82**	13	18	31	1	85	2	0	4	0	112	11.6	.38	14	0	3	3	1	20	0	0	0	0	23	0.0	.21
Derian Hatcher	D	80	9	21	30	21	102	3	0	2	0	125	7.2	.38	18	1	6	7	4	**24**	0	0	0	0	28	3.6	.39
Mike Keane	R	81	6	23	29	-2	62	1	1	1	0	106	5.7	.36	**23**	5	2	7	-1	6	0	**1**	1	0	41	12.2	.30
Tony Hrkac	C	69	13	14	27	2	26	2	0	2	**2**	67	19.4	.39	5	0	2	2	3	4	0	0	0	0	3	0.0	.40
Dave Reid	L	73	6	11	17	0	16	1	0	1	0	81	7.4	.23	**23**	2	8	10	4	14	0	0	0	0	30	6.7	.43
Guy Carbonneau	C	74	4	12	16	-3	31	0	0	2	0	60	6.7	.22	17	2	4	6	0	6	0	0	1	0	29	6.9	.35
Richard Matvichuk	D	64	3	9	12	23	51	1	0	0	0	54	5.6	.19	22	1	5	6	4	20	0	0	0	0	26	3.8	.27
Shawn Chambers	D	61	2	9	11	6	18	1	0	1	0	82	2.4	.18	17	0	2	2	-1	18	0	0	0	0	19	0.0	.12
Craig Ludwig	D	80	2	6	8	5	87	0	0	0	0	39	5.1	.10	**23**	1	4	5	2	20	0	0	0	0	6	16.7	.22
Brian Skrudland	C	40	4	1	5	2	33	0	0	1	0	33	12.1	.13	19	0	2	2	0	16	0	0	0	0	10	0.0	.11
Derek Plante†	C	10	2	3	5	1	4	1	0	0	0	24	8.3	.50	6	1	0	1	0	4	0	0	0	0	8	12.5	.17
* Sergey Gusev†	D	22	1	4	5	5	6	0	0	1	0	30	3.3	.23	—	—	—	—	—	—	—	—	—	—	—	—	—
Benoit Hogue†	C	12	1	3	4	2	4	0	0	0	0	20	5.0	.33	14	0	2	2	-1	16	0	0	0	0	20	0.0	.14
* Brad Lukowich	D	14	1	2	3	3	19	0	0	0	0	8	12.5	.21	8	0	1	1	3	4	0	0	0	0	6	0.0	.13
Brent Severyn	L	30	1	2	3	-2	50	0	0	0	0	22	4.5	.10	—	—	—	—	—	—	—	—	—	—	—	—	—
* Jon Sim	C	7	1	0	1	1	12	0	0	0	0	8	12.5	.14	4	0	0	0	-1	0	0	0	0	0	1	0.0	.00
Dan Keczmer†	D	22	0	1	1	-2	22	0	0	0	0	12	0.0	.05	—	—	—	—	—	—	—	—	—	—	—	—	—
* Kelly Fairchild	C	1	0	0	0	0	0	0	0	0	0	4	0.0	.00	—	—	—	—	—	—	—	—	—	—	—	—	—
Manny Fernandez	G	1	0	0	0	—	0	0	0	0	0	0	—	.00	—	—	—	—	—	—	—	—	—	—	—	—	—
* Petr Buzek	D	2	0	0	0	0	2	0	0	0	0	0	—	.00	—	—	—	—	—	—	—	—	—	—	—	—	—
Aaron Gavey	C	7	0	0	0	-1	10	0	0	0	0	4	0.0	.00	—	—	—	—	—	—	—	—	—	—	—	—	—
* Jamie Wright	L	11	0	0	0	-3	0	0	0	0	0	10	0.0	.00	—	—	—	—	—	—	—	—	—	—	—	—	—
* Blake Sloan	R	14	0	0	0	-1	10	0	0	0	0	7	0.0	.00	19	0	2	2	-1	8	0	0	0	0	7	0.0	.11
* Jason Botterill	L	17	0	0	0	-2	23	0	0	0	0	8	0.0	.00	—	—	—	—	—	—	—	—	—	—	—	—	—
Doug Lidster	D	17	0	0	0	0	10	0	0	0	0	7	0.0	.00	4	0	0	0	0	2	0	0	0	0	1	0.0	.00
Roman Turek	G	26	0	0	0	—	0	0	0	0	0	0	—	.00	—	—	—	—	—	—	—	—	—	—	—	—	—
Ed Belfour	G	61	0	0	0	—	26	0	0	0	0	0	—	.00	**23**	0	0	0	—	4	0	0	0	0	0	—	.00
Bench		—	—	—	—	—	0	—	—	—	—	—	—	—	—	—	—	—	—	0	—	—	—	—	—	—	—
TEAM TOTALS		82	236	396	632	173	1100	74	6	51	6	2266	10.4	7.71	23	64	113	177	72	277	13	3	16	4	728	8.8	7.70

Goaltender	Regular Season G	Min	GAA	W	L	T	ENG	ShO	GA	SA	SvPct	Postseason G	Min	GAA	W	L	ENG	ShO	GA	SA	SvPct
Ed Belfour	**61**	**3536**	**1.99**	**35**	**15**	**9**	0	**5**	**117**	**1373**	**.915**	**23**	**1544**	**1.67**	**16**	**7**	**1**	**3**	**43**	**617**	**.930**
Manny Fernandez	1	60	2.00	0	1	0	0	0	2	29	.931	—	—	—	—	—	—	—	—	—	—
Roman Turek	26	1382	2.08	16	3	3	**1**	1	48	562	.915	—	—	—	—	—	—	—	—	—	—
TEAM TOTALS	82	4986	2.02	51	19	12	1	6	168	1965	.915	23	1547	1.71	16	7	1	3	44	618	.929

1998-99 Dallas Stars

Record When:

Overtime games	3-1-12
In second game of back-to-back games	7-6-2
Vs playoff teams	28-12-8
Leading after two periods	38-2-5
Tied after two periods	12-3-5
Losing after two periods	1-14-2
Scoring first	40-7-7
More shots than opponents	35-10-9
Fewer shots than opponents	14-8-3
Team had at least one fighting major	18-4-3
Team had more PIM	12-3-2
Team had fewer PIM	29-16-5
Team had even PIM	10-0-5

Team

Longest winning streak	6	Dec. 23 — Jan. 6
Longest unbeaten streak	15	Dec. 6 — Jan. 6
Longest losing streak	2	5 times
Longest winless streak	4	Mar. 14 — Mar. 19
Most shots, game	45	@Nsh, Feb. 23
Most shots, period	19	1st, vs. Pit, Feb. 26
Fewest shots, game	13	@Van, Jan. 10
Fewest shots, period	1	1st, vs. Car, Mar. 21

Individual

Longest goal streak	5	Brett Hull
Longest point streak	9	2 times
Most goals, game	3	Mike Modano [3]
Most assists, game	3	Sergei Zubov
Most points, game	3	22 times
Highest +/–, game	4	3 times
Lowest +/–, game	-4	Derian Hatcher
Most shots, game	8	Brett Hull

Did You Know?

The Stars led the NHL in points by defensemen in 1998-99, with 169.

Miscellaneous

		NHL Rank
PP Pct.	18.8 (74-393)	6
SH goals allowed	4	1t
PK Pct.	86.5 (276-319)	6
SH goals scored	6	21t
Special Team Index	106.2	2
Shots on goal	2,266 (27.6/G)	16
Shots against	1,965 (24.0/G)	3
Unassisted goals	14	8t
Unassisted goals allowed	10	9t
Team Average Weight	198.4	19
Game Star Points	447	1

Game Star Breakdown

Player	1st	2nd	3rd	Pts
Mike Modano	11	5	7	77
Joe Nieuwendyk	9	2	6	57
Brett Hull	7	3	1	45
Ed Belfour	2	5	7	32
Roman Turek	4	3	1	30
Sergei Zubov	2	5	2	27
Derian Hatcher	2	5	1	26
Darryl Sydor	2	4	2	24
Jamie Langenbrunner	2	3	2	21
Pat Verbeek	3	1	1	19
Mike Keane	1	4	0	17
Jere Lehtinen	1	3	1	15
Tony Hrkac	2	0	2	12
Grant Marshall	0	2	3	9
Richard Matvichuk	1	1	0	8
Guy Carbonneau	1	0	3	8
Shawn Chambers	1	0	2	7
Sergey Gusev	1	0	0	5
Brent Severyn	0	1	0	3
Craig Ludwig	0	0	2	2
Manny Fernandez	0	0	1	1
Dave Reid	0	0	1	1
Brian Skrudland	0	0	1	1

Detroit Red Wings 1998-99 Game Log (43-32-7)

Date	Opp	Score	W/L/T	Record	Goalies W/T	Goalies L/T	Shots Det	Shots Opp	Power Plays Det	Power Plays Opp	Game Stars 1st	Game Stars 2nd	Game Stars 3rd
10/10	@Tor	1-2	L	0-1-0	Joseph	**Osgood**	39	27	1-7	1-7	Joseph	McCauley	**Yzerman**
10/13	@Was	3-2	W	1-1-0	**Osgood**	Kolzig	25	30	1-3	0-3	**McCarty**	**Brown**	Mironov
10/16	StL	4-1	W	2-1-0	**Osgood**	Fuhr	25	25	1-4	0-5	**Shanahan**	**Yzerman**	**McCarty**
10/18	Cgy	2-**0**	W	3-1-0	**Osgood**	Wregget	28	32	0-4	0-8	**Osgood**	**Shanahan**	Fleury
10/21	Nsh	5-2	W	4-1-0	**Osgood**	Dunham	**57**	15	2-9	0-3	**McCarty**	Dunham	**Roest**
10/23	Tor	3-5	L	4-2-0	Joseph	**Hodson**	37	27	1-6	0-4	Berezin	Joseph	**Larionov**
10/24	@Mon	3-**0**	W	5-2-0	**Osgood**	Thibault	29	18	1-4	0-3	**Yzerman**	**Osgood**	**Lidstrom**
10/28	@Fla	**7**-2	W	6-2-0	**Osgood**	Burke	29	18	2-5	1-5	**Holmstrom**	**Yzerman**	**Lidstrom**
10/29	@StL	1-3	L	6-3-0	Fuhr	**Osgood**	26	25	1-5	1-6	Courtnall	Conroy	**Brown**
10/31	@Dal	2-3	L	6-4-0	Belfour	**Osgood**	24	33	1-9	0-8	Hull	Lehtinen	Modano
11/03	Cgy	2-5	L	6-5-0	Moss	**Osgood**	47	26	1-**10**	3-5	Fleury	Housley	Moss
11/06	@Pho	1-3	L	6-6-0	Khabibulin	**Osgood**	31	25	1-6	0-5	Khabibulin	Numminen	Corkum
11/08	@Anh	3-2	W	7-6-0	**Osgood**	Hebert	34	39	1-6	2-7	**Osgood**	**Shanahan**	McInnis
11/11	StL	6-2	W	8-6-0	**Osgood**	McLennan	31	28	1-4	0-2	**Kocur**	**Yzerman**	**Draper**
11/13	Dal	1-5	L	8-7-0	Belfour	**Osgood**	35	28	1-7	1-7	Nieuwendyk	Hatcher	Modano
11/16	@Cgy	3-5	L	8-8-0	Moss	**Osgood**	34	34	0-3	1-3	Morris	Moss	**Krupp**
11/18	@Edm	6-2	W	9-8-0	**Osgood**	Essensa	26	22	1-4	1-5	**Yzerman**	**Murphy**	**Lidstrom**
11/21	@Van	4-2	W	10-8-0	**Maracle**	Snow	30	31	0-6	0-2	**Shanahan**	Scatchard	**Lidstrom**
11/25	Anh	5-2	W	11-8-0	**Maracle**	Hebert	35	28	2-3	1-5	**Fedorov**	**Murphy**	**Maracle**
11/27	Van	**7**-1	W	12-8-0	**Maracle**	Snow	39	20	2-9	1-4	**Shanahan**	**Larionov**	**Kozlov**
11/29	SJ	4-1	W	13-8-0	**Maracle**	Vernon	28	20	2-8	0-4	**Maracle**	**Holmstrom**	**McCarty**
12/02	@Col	2-4	L	13-9-0	Roy	**Maracle**	29	30	2-5	0-5	Roy	Sakic	Hejduk
12/04	@SJ	2-2*	T	13-9-1	**Maracle**	Shields	25	37	0-4	0-3	Ricci	**Maracle**	Stern
12/05	@LA	4-3	W	14-9-1	**Osgood**	Fiset	45	27	0-3	1-6	**Yzerman**	Murray	**Brown**
12/08	Chi	3-2	W	15-9-1	**Osgood**	Fitzpatrick	45	33	0-3	0-2	**Yzerman**	**Osgood**	Fitzpatrick
12/11	Edm	3-2	W	16-9-1	**Osgood**	Essensa	26	30	2-6	0-5	**Fedorov**	**Yzerman**	Kovalenko
12/12	@Car	0-3	L	16-10-1	Irbe	**Osgood**	35	26	0-6	0-9	Primeau	Irbe	Wesley
12/16	Bos	5-3	W	17-10-1	**Osgood**	Dafoe	25	26	2-3	0-6	**Fedorov**	Allison	**Holmstrom**
12/18	Dal	1-3	L	17-11-1	Belfour	**Osgood**	25	26	0-5	1-5	Verbeek	Keane	Ludwig
12/19	@Bos	1-4	L	17-12-1	Dafoe	**Maracle**	24	32	0-5	2-5	Dafoe	Gill	Bourque
12/22	Pho	2-6	L	17-13-1	Khabibulin	**Osgood**	38	29	1-4	1-3	Drake	Numminen	Corkum
12/23	@Nsh	3-5	L	17-14-1	Vokoun	**Osgood**	53	34	0-3	0-5	Vokoun	Ronning	Walker
12/26	@StL	3-4	L	17-15-1	Fuhr	**Osgood**	32	22	0-8	2-5	Pellerin	Fuhr	**Dandenault**
12/28	StL	4-4*	T	17-15-2	**Maracle**	Fuhr	20	32	1-6	1-4	**Kozlov**	Pronger	**Lidstrom**
12/31	Tor	2-4	L	17-16-2	Joseph	**Osgood**	40	27	0-6	1-6	Joseph	Sundin	**Maltby**
1/02	Chi	5-2	W	18-16-2	**Osgood**	Thibault	35	35	0-6	2-5	**Yzerman**	**Murphy**	**McCarty**
1/03	@Chi	3-1	W	19-16-2	**Osgood**	Thibault	26	27	2-6	0-3	**Lidstrom**	**Osgood**	**Murphy**
1/06	Ott	0-2	L	19-17-2	Tugnutt	**Osgood**	24	30	0-6	1-5	Yashin	Tugnutt	Kravchuk
1/09	Col	3-2	W	20-17-2	**Osgood**	Denis	31	29	2-7	0-5	**Lidstrom**	**Lapointe**	Lemieux
1/10	@Ott	1-4	L	20-18-2	Tugnutt	**Osgood**	21	33	1-3	1-4	Gardiner	Tugnutt	York
1/12	Mon	5-1	W	21-18-2	**Osgood**	Hackett	39	18	0-3	0-2	**Fedorov**	**Yzerman**	**Gill**
1/14	Nsh	2-1*	W	22-18-2	**Osgood**	Vokoun	41	16	0-3	0-4	Vokoun	**Maltby**	**Kozlov**
1/16	@Van	2-2*	T	22-18-3	**Osgood**	Snow	37	16	0-8	0-2	Snow	**Yzerman**	**Lidstrom**
1/17	@Edm	1-4	L	22-19-3	Essensa	**Osgood**	26	26	0-2	1-5	Devereaux	Murray	Poti
1/19	@Cgy	1-3	L	22-20-3	Brathwaite	**Maracle**	37	33	1-4	1-3	Brathwaite	Iginla	**Yzerman**
1/21	Car	4-1	W	23-20-3	**Osgood**	Irbe	26	26	1-4	0-5	**Osgood**	**Lidstrom**	Primeau
1/26	@Nsh	4-1	W	24-20-3	**Osgood**	Dunham	33	26	1-5	1-7	**Fedorov**	**Larionov**	Atcheynum
1/30	NYR	2-3	L	24-21-3	Richter	**Osgood**	40	**14**	1-3	0-1	Richter	Sundstrom	**Brown**
2/01	@NJ	2-2*	T	24-21-4	**Osgood**	Brodeur	32	34	0-4	0-5	Odelein	**Kozlov**	Sykora
2/03	NYI	5-1	W	25-21-4	**Maracle**	Salo	44	28	2-6	0-7	**McCarty**	**Lidstrom**	**Yzerman**
2/05	Col	1-3	L	25-22-4	Roy	**Osgood**	28	30	0-3	1-2	Roy	Foote	**Draper**
2/07	@Pit	1-2	L	25-23-4	Barrasso	**Osgood**	36	21	1-3	0-4	Barrasso	Kovalev	Miller
2/09	@Nsh	5-2	W	26-23-4	**Osgood**	Dunham	50	21	0-4	0-**1**	**Shanahan**	**Fedorov**	Johnson
2/11	Edm	4-2	W	27-23-4	**Osgood**	Essensa	37	31	2-7	1-5	**Fedorov**	Weight	**Dandenault**
2/12	@Chi	2-1	W	28-23-4	**Osgood**	Thibault	25	26	2-5	0-4	**Osgood**	**Murphy**	Chelios

2/14	@NYR	4-2	W	29-23-4	**Osgood**	Richter	30	31	0-7	0-4	**Yzerman**	Fedyk	**Fedorov**
2/17	SJ	3-1	W	30-23-4	**Osgood**	Vernon	23	31	0-5	0-5	**Larionov**	**Osgood**	**Dandenault**
2/19	NJ	3-1	W	31-23-4	**Osgood**	Terreri	27	22	1-4	0-3	**Yzerman**	**Larionov**	Brylin
2/21	@Buf	4-4*	T	31-23-5	**Osgood**	Roloson	38	25	1-2	1-**1**	**Kozlov**	Satan	Grosek
2/24	LA	2-3*	L	31-24-5	Fiset	**Osgood**	26	40	0-2	1-2	Robitaille	R.Blake	**Fedorov**
2/26	Fla	5-5*	T	31-24-6	**Osgood**	McLean	36	17	**3**-9	1-6	**Larionov**	Bure	**Maltby**
2/27	@NYI	1-3	L	31-25-6	Salo	**Hodson**	36	30	0-5	2-6	Salo	Reichel	Lapointe
3/05	@Pho	**7**-2	W	32-25-6	**Osgood**	Waite	27	38	2-5	2-4	**Shanahan**	**Osgood**	**Larionov**
3/07	@Anh	1-3	L	32-26-6	Hebert	**Osgood**	34	25	1-8	1-9	Hebert	**Yzerman**	Haller
3/09	@LA	2-4	L	32-27-6	Fiset	**Osgood**	40	24	0-7	0-2	Laperriere	**Larionov**	Fiset
3/12	@SJ	0-2	L	32-28-6	Shields	**Maracle**	26	34	0-5	0-6	Shields	Murphy	Rathje
3/14	@Col	3-1	W	33-28-6	**Maracle**	Roy	28	22	1-7	0-4	**Larionov**	**Murphy**	Foote
3/17	Pho	3-4	L	33-29-6	Shtalenkov	**Maracle**	31	27	1-3	0-3	Tkachuk	**Larionov**	Corkum
3/19	@TB	5-3	W	34-29-6	**Osgood**	Schwab	34	39	1-4	1-2	**Fedorov**	Clark	**Osgood**
3/21	@Phi	4-5	L	34-30-6	Vanbiesbrouck	**Osgood**	21	31	2-4	0-4	Lindros	**Shanahan**	Recchi
3/24	Buf	2-1	W	35-30-6	**Osgood**	Roloson	30	25	0-3	0-3	**Fedorov**	**Yzerman**	**Brown**
3/26	TB	6-1	W	36-30-6	**Osgood**	Schwab	40	24	1-4	0-2	**Chelios**	**Fedorov**	**Lidstrom**
3/28	Phi	3-2*	W	37-30-6	**Osgood**	Vanbiesbrouck	30	25	1-3	1-5	**Clark**	**Kozlov**	Brind'Amour
3/31	LA	2-1	W	38-30-6	**Osgood**	Fiset	37	28	0-4	0-2	**Osgood**	**Fedorov**	Fiset
4/02	Chi	5-3	W	39-30-6	**Ranford**	Fitzpatrick	31	30	2-9	1-4	**Kozlov**	**Murphy**	**Clark**
4/04	@Dal	3-**0**	W	40-30-6	**Osgood**	Belfour	26	27	0-6	0-5	**Osgood**	**Clark**	**Chelios**
4/05	Anh	3-2	W	41-30-6	**Ranford**	Hebert	33	18	0-6	1-2	**Yzerman**	**Lidstrom**	**Dandenault**
4/07	Van	6-1	W	42-30-6	**Osgood**	Weekes	26	28	2-8	0-6	**Yzerman**	**Larionov**	**Shanahan**
4/09	@StL	1-1*	T	42-30-7	**Ranford**	Fuhr	22	26	1-6	1-4	Fuhr	MacInnis	**Ranford**
4/11	Pit	0-3	L	42-31-7	Barrasso	**Osgood**	20	23	0-1	0-4	Hrdina	Slegr	Barrasso
4/14	Nsh	4-2	W	43-31-7	**Ranford**	Dunham	27	24	0-4	1-4	**Murphy**	**Fedorov**	**Gilchrist**
4/17	@Chi	2-3	L	43-32-7	Thibault	**Osgood**	24	19	0-3	0-3	Amonte	Zhamnov	Manson

Postseason

4/21	Anh	**5**-3	W	1-0	**Osgood**	Askey	37	29	1-6	1-5	**Yzerman**	Kariya	**Clark**
4/23	Anh	**5**-1	W	2-0	**Osgood**	Hebert	36	31	**3-9**	1-5	**Shanahan**	**Fedorov**	**Chelios**
4/25	@Anh	4-2	W	3-0	**Osgood**	Hebert	24	**24**	2-6	2-6	**Lidstrom**	Marshall	**Fedorov**
4/27	@Anh	3-**0**	W	4-0	**Osgood**	Hebert	38	31	1-2	0-**4**	**Osgood**	**Shanahan**	**Yzerman**
5/07	@Col	3-2*	W	1-0	**Ranford**	Roy	34	39	2-7	1-7	**Maltby**	Deadmarsh	**Ranford**
5/09	@Col	4-**0**	W	2-0	**Ranford**	Roy	37	28	2-8	0-5	**Yzerman**	**Ranford**	**Lidstrom**
5/11	Col	3-5	L	2-1	Roy	**Ranford**	**47**	36	1-6	1-**4**	Roy	Fleury	Miller
5/13	Col	2-6	L	2-2	Roy	**Ranford**	33	**24**	1-5	2-**4**	Forsberg	Deadmarsh	Roy
5/16	@Col	0-3	L	2-3	Roy	**Osgood**	36	26	0-6	1-6	Roy	Forsberg	Deadmarsh
5/18	Col	2-5	L	2-4	Roy	**Osgood**	37	31	1-4	0-**4**	Forsberg	Kamensky	Roy

Detroit Red Wings 1998-99 Player Statistics

		Regular Season													Postseason												
Skater	**Ps**	**GP**	**G**	**A**	**Pts**	**+/–**	**PIM**	**PP**	**SH**	**GW**	**GT**	**S**	**SPct**	**P/G**	**GP**	**G**	**A**	**Pts**	**+/–**	**PIM**	**PP**	**SH**	**GW**	**OT**	**S**	**SPct**	**P/G**
Steve Yzerman	C	80	29	45	**74**	8	42	**13**	**2**	4	0	231	12.6	**.93**	**10**	**9**	4	**13**	2	0	**4**	0	**2**	0	**41**	**22.0**	**1.30**
Sergei Fedorov	C	77	26	37	63	9	66	6	**2**	3	0	224	11.6	.82	**10**	1	8	9	**3**	8	0	0	0	0	38	2.6	.90
Igor Larionov	C	75	14	**49**	63	13	48	4	**2**	2	1	83	**16.9**	.84	7	0	2	2	-1	0	0	0	0	0	3	0.0	.29
Brendan Shanahan	L	81	**31**	27	58	2	123	5	0	**5**	0	**288**	10.8	.72	**10**	3	7	10	2	6	1	0	1	0	31	9.7	1.00
Slava Kozlov	C	79	29	29	58	10	45	6	1	4	**2**	209	13.9	.73	**10**	6	1	7	-3	4	3	0	0	0	28	21.4	.70
Nicklas Lidstrom	D	81	14	43	57	14	14	6	**2**	3	0	205	6.8	.70	**10**	2	**9**	11	0	4	2	0	0	0	29	6.9	1.10
Larry Murphy	D	80	10	42	52	**21**	42	5	1	2	0	168	6.0	.65	**10**	0	2	2	2	8	0	0	0	0	14	0.0	.20
Darren McCarty	R	69	14	26	40	10	108	6	0	1	1	140	10.0	.58	**10**	1	1	2	-1	**23**	0	0	0	0	15	6.7	.20
Tomas Holmstrom	L	**82**	13	21	34	-11	69	5	0	4	0	100	13.0	.41	**10**	4	3	7	2	4	2	0	1	0	26	15.4	.70
Martin Lapointe	R	77	16	13	29	7	**141**	7	1	4	0	153	10.5	.38	**10**	0	2	2	0	20	0	0	0	0	14	0.0	.20
Doug Brown	R	80	9	19	28	5	42	3	1	1	0	180	5.0	.35	**10**	2	2	4	0	4	1	0	1	0	15	13.3	.40
Kris Draper	C	80	4	14	18	2	79	0	1	1	0	78	5.1	.23	**10**	0	1	1	-1	6	0	0	0	0	9	0.0	.10
Kirk Maltby	R	53	8	6	14	-6	34	0	1	2	0	76	10.5	.26	**10**	1	0	1	-2	8	0	0	1	**1**	13	7.7	.10
Mathieu Dandenault	R	75	4	10	14	17	59	0	0	0	0	94	4.3	.19	**10**	0	1	1	0	0	0	0	0	0	15	0.0	.10
* Stacy Roest	C	59	4	8	12	-7	14	0	0	1	0	50	8.0	.20	—	—	—	—	—	—	—	—	—	—	—	—	—
Anders Eriksson†	D	61	2	10	12	5	34	0	0	1	0	67	3.0	.20	—	—	—	—	—	—	—	—	—	—	—	—	—
Aaron Ward	D	60	3	8	11	-5	52	0	0	0	0	46	6.5	.18	8	0	1	1	2	8	0	0	0	0	6	0.0	.13
Jamie Macoun	D	69	1	10	11	-1	36	0	0	0	0	62	1.6	.16	1	0	0	0	-1	0	0	0	0	0	1	0.0	.00
Joey Kocur	R	39	2	5	7	0	87	0	0	0	0	20	10.0	.18	—	—	—	—	—	—	—	—	—	—	—	—	—
Wendel Clark†	L	12	4	2	6	1	2	0	0	1	0	44	9.1	.50	**10**	2	3	5	-1	10	1	0	0	0	29	6.9	.50
Uwe Krupp	D	22	3	2	5	0	6	0	0	0	0	32	9.4	.23	—	—	—	—	—	—	—	—	—	—	—	—	—
Todd Gill†	D	23	2	2	4	-4	11	0	0	1	0	25	8.0	.17	2	0	1	1	0	0	0	0	0	0	3	0.0	.50
Chris Osgood	G	63	0	3	3	—	8	0	0	0	0	0	—	.05	6	0	0	0	—	0	0	0	0	0	0	—	.00
Chris Chelios†	D	10	1	1	2	5	4	1	0	1	0	15	6.7	.20	**10**	0	4	4	-6	14	0	0	0	0	21	0.0	.40
Brent Gilchrist	L	5	1	0	1	-1	0	0	0	1	0	4	25.0	.20	3	0	0	0	-2	0	0	0	0	0	2	0.0	.00
Petr Klima	L	13	1	0	1	-3	4	0	0	1	0	12	8.3	.08	—	—	—	—	—	—	—	—	—	—	—	—	—
Doug Houda	D	3	0	1	1	-2	0	0	0	0	0	1	0.0	.33	—	—	—	—	—	—	—	—	—	—	—	—	—
* Yan Golubovsky	D	17	0	1	1	4	16	0	0	0	0	10	0.0	.06	—	—	—	—	—	—	—	—	—	—	—	—	—
* Darryl Laplante	C	3	0	0	0	0	0	0	0	0	0	0	—	.00	—	—	—	—	—	—	—	—	—	—	—	—	—
* Phillipe Audet	L	4	0	0	0	-2	0	0	0	0	0	3	0.0	.00	—	—	—	—	—	—	—	—	—	—	—	—	—
Kevin Hodson†	G	4	0	0	0	—	0	0	0	0	0	0	—	.00	—	—	—	—	—	—	—	—	—	—	—	—	—
Bill Ranford†	G	4	0	0	0	—	0	0	0	0	0	0	—	.00	4	0	0	0	—	0	0	0	0	0	0	—	.00
Ulf Samuelsson†	D	4	0	0	0	-1	6	0	0	0	0	2	0.0	.00	9	0	3	3	1	10	0	0	0	0	6	0.0	.33
* Norm Maracle	G	16	0	0	0	—	0	0	0	0	0	0	—	.00	2	0	0	0	—	0	0	0	0	0	0	—	.00
Bench		—	—	—	—	—	0	—	—	—	—	—	—	—	—	—	—	—	—	0	—	—	—	—	—	—	—
TEAM TOTALS		82	245	434	679	90	1192	67	14	43	4	2622	9.3	8.28	10	31	55	86	-4	137	14	0	6	1	359	8.6	8.60

	Regular Season											Postseason									
Goaltender	**G**	**Min**	**GAA**	**W**	**L**	**T**	**ENG**	**ShO**	**GA**	**SA**	**SvPct**	**G**	**Min**	**GAA**	**W**	**L**	**ENG**	**ShO**	**GA**	**SA**	**SvPct**
Bill Ranford†	4	244	1.97	3	0	1	0	0	8	98	.918	4	183	3.28	2	**2**	0	**1**	10	105	.905
* Norm Maracle	16	821	2.27	6	5	2	1	0	31	379	.918	2	58	3.10	0	0	0	0	3	22	.864
Chris Osgood	**63**	**3691**	**2.42**	**34**	**25**	**4**	**4**	**3**	**149**	**1654**	**.910**	**6**	**358**	**2.35**	**4**	**2**	0	**1**	**14**	**172**	**.919**
Kevin Hodson†	4	175	3.09	0	2	0	0	0	9	79	.886	—	—	—	—	—	—	—	—	—	—
TEAM TOTALS	82	4962	2.44	43	32	7	5	3	202	2215	.909	10	604	2.68	6	4	0	2	27	299	.910

1998-99 Detroit Red Wings

Record When:

Overtime games	2-1-7
In second game of back-to-back games	5-7-0
Vs playoff teams	19-23-5
Leading after two periods	34-3-2
Tied after two periods	7-6-3
Losing after two periods	2-23-2
Scoring first	34-10-5
More shots than opponents	26-19-3
Fewer shots than opponents	14-11-4
Team had at least one fighting major	11-11-0
Team had more PIM	12-13-1
Team had fewer PIM	27-10-6
Team had even PIM	4-9-0

Team

Longest winning streak	8	Mar. 24 — Apr. 7
Longest unbeaten streak	9	Mar. 24 — Apr. 9
Longest losing streak	5	Dec. 18 — Dec. 26
Longest winless streak	7	Dec. 18 — Dec. 31
Most shots, game	57	vs. Nsh, Oct. 21
Most shots, period	27	2nd, vs. Nsh, Oct. 21
Fewest shots, game	20	2 times
Fewest shots, period	2	2 times

Individual

Longest goal streak	5	Brendan Shanahan
Longest point streak	11	Sergei Fedorov
Most goals, game	3	3 times
Most assists, game	3	6 times
Most points, game	3	27 times
Highest +/–, game	3	22 times
Lowest +/–, game	-4	3 times
Most shots, game	8	5 times

Did You Know?

Over the last 12 seasons, the Red Wings are 167 games over .500, easily the best mark in the NHL. Over the previous 12 seasons, from 1975-76 through 1986-87, Detroit was 234 games under .500, second-worst in the league.

Miscellaneous

		NHL Rank
PP Pct.	16.1 (67-415)	11
SH goals allowed	7	9t
PK Pct.	87.3 (310-355)	3
SH goals scored	14	2
Special Team Index	105.7	5
Shots on goal	2,622 (32.0/G)	1
Shots against	2,215 (27.0/G)	9
Unassisted goals	10	21t
Unassisted goals allowed	17	21t
Team Average Weight	200.9	13
Game Star Points	397	11

Game Star Breakdown

Player	1st	2nd	3rd	Pts
Steve Yzerman	9	8	3	72
Sergei Fedorov	8	4	2	54
Chris Osgood	6	5	1	46
Brendan Shanahan	5	3	1	35
Igor Larionov	3	6	2	35
Nicklas Lidstrom	2	3	7	26
Larry Murphy	1	6	1	24
Slava Kozlov	3	2	2	23
Darren McCarty	3	0	3	18
Wendel Clark	1	1	1	9
Tomas Holmstrom	1	1	1	9
Norm Maracle	1	1	1	9
Doug Brown	0	1	4	7
Chris Chelios	1	0	1	6
Joey Kocur	1	0	0	5
Kirk Maltby	0	1	2	5
Mathieu Dandenault	0	0	4	4
Martin Lapointe	0	1	0	3
Kris Draper	0	0	2	2
Brent Gilchrist	0	0	1	1
Todd Gill	0	0	1	1
Uwe Krupp	0	0	1	1
Bill Ranford	0	0	1	1
Stacy Roest	0	0	1	1

Edmonton Oilers 1998-99 Game Log (33-37-12)

					Goalies		Shots		Power Plays		Game Stars		
Date	Opp	Score	W/L/T	Record	W/T	L/T	Edm	Opp	Edm	Opp	1st	2nd	3rd
10/10	LA	1-2	L	0-1-0	Fiset	**Shtalenkov**	24	32	0-4	1-6	Fiset	Robitaille	**Shtalenkov**
10/13	Tor	2-3	L	0-2-0	Joseph	**Shtalenkov**	30	29	0-4	2-6	Sundin	Joseph	**Guerin**
10/14	@Van	4-1	W	1-2-0	**Shtalenkov**	Snow	24	**13**	**3**-7	1-6	**Mironov**	**K.Brown**	Muckalt
10/17	@NJ	4-2	W	2-2-0	**Shtalenkov**	Brodeur	23	34	1-5	1-2	**Guerin**	**Shtalenkov**	**Kovalenko**
10/20	@NYR	2-3	L	2-3-0	Richter	**Essensa**	26	28	2-6	2-9	**Beranek**	Schneider	Leetch
10/21	@NYI	4-2	W	3-3-0	**Shtalenkov**	Salo	30	30	2-9	1-7	**Devereaux**	**Weight**	**Buchberger**
10/24	@Col	4-6	L	3-4-0	Roy	**Essensa**	35	27	1-9	3-5	Lemieux	Sakic	Deadmarsh
10/28	Was	**8**-2	W	4-4-0	**Essensa**	Kolzig	33	24	**3**-9	1-4	**Guerin**	**Mironov**	**Niinimaa**
10/31	Pit	4-1	W	5-4-0	**Essensa**	Aubin	15	22	1-7	1-7	**Mironov**	**Essensa**	Barnes
11/02	Van	5-3	W	6-4-0	**Essensa**	Hirsch	**49**	16	**3-10**	1-3	**Beranek**	**Guerin**	Hirsch
11/04	Nsh	3-2	W	7-4-0	**Essensa**	Dunham	29	28	0-4	0-6	**Beranek**	**Essensa**	Ronning
11/06	Col	2-5	L	7-5-0	Roy	**Essensa**	21	32	0-5	2-6	Kamensky	Forsberg	Lemieux
11/08	@Chi	3-2*	W	8-5-0	**Shtalenkov**	Fitzpatrick	32	24	1-5	0-4	**Beranek**	**Shtalenkov**	Chelios
11/11	@Tor	2-3	L	8-6-0	Joseph	**Shtalenkov**	34	21	0-5	1-3	Joseph	**Lindgren**	Cote
11/12	@Ott	1-1*	T	8-6-1	**Essensa**	Tugnutt	27	34	0-3	0-6	Tugnutt	**Essensa**	Prospal
11/14	@Mon	4-1	W	9-6-1	**Shtalenkov**	Theodore	27	26	1-7	0-8	**Guerin**	**Murray**	**Shtalenkov**
11/18	Det	2-6	L	9-7-1	Osgood	**Essensa**	22	26	1-5	1-4	Yzerman	Murphy	Lidstrom
11/20	@Anh	3-2*	W	10-7-1	**Shtalenkov**	Hebert	23	21	1-5	1-5	**Kovalenko**	Aalto	**Hamrlik**
11/21	@Pho	2-3*	L	10-8-1	Khabibulin	**Shtalenkov**	15	39	0-5	0-7	Tocchet	Isbister	Adams
11/25	Col	3-**0**	W	11-8-1	**Shtalenkov**	Roy	41	26	0-4	0-3	**Shtalenkov**	Roy	**Grier**
11/27	@Cgy	3-2	W	12-8-1	**Shtalenkov**	Moss	36	31	0-3	0-2	**Kovalenko**	Moss	**Hamrlik**
11/29	Chi	2-3	L	12-9-1	Thibault	**Shtalenkov**	38	18	2-8	1-**1**	Chelios	Thibault	**Smyth**
12/02	Pho	4-3	W	13-9-1	**Shtalenkov**	Khabibulin	22	48	1-3	1-5	**Shtalenkov**	**Falloon**	Lumme
12/04	TB	1-2	L	13-10-1	Schwab	**Shtalenkov**	35	23	0-5	1-2	Schwab	Renberg	**Shtalenkov**
12/06	Dal	2-6	L	13-11-1	Belfour	**Essensa**	25	24	0-5	1-5	Lehtinen	Modano	Zubov
12/08	@Nsh	3-3*	T	13-11-2	**Shtalenkov**	Vokoun	40	27	2-6	0-4	Ronning	**Guerin**	Kjellberg
12/09	@Chi	1-3	L	13-12-2	Thibault	**Shtalenkov**	25	18	0-4	0-5	Daze	Thibault	Chelios
12/11	@Det	2-3	L	13-13-2	Osgood	**Essensa**	30	26	0-5	2-6	Fedorov	Yzerman	**Kovalenko**
12/13	@Phi	2-2*	T	13-13-3	**Shtalenkov**	Vanbiesbrouck	24	19	0-7	0-3	Desjardins	**Shtalenkov**	Vanbiesbrouck
12/15	@Car	0-3	L	13-14-3	Irbe	**Shtalenkov**	29	24	0-2	0-3	Irbe	Wesley	Roberts
12/18	@TB	4-1	W	14-14-3	**Essensa**	Schwab	38	23	0-6	0-2	**Marchant**	**Guerin**	**Hamrlik**
12/19	@Fla	1-3	L	14-15-3	Burke	**Shtalenkov**	30	26	0-4	0-3	Garpenlov	Burke	Whitney
12/23	SJ	3-5	L	14-16-3	Vernon	**Shtalenkov**	23	20	0-3	0-4	Sturm	Korolyuk	**Falloon**
12/27	Van	3-**0**	W	15-16-3	**Shtalenkov**	Snow	34	25	1-6	0-5	**Shtalenkov**	**Poti**	**Buchberger**
12/29	Mon	2-5	L	15-17-3	Hackett	**Shtalenkov**	22	34	0-4	1-5	Recchi	Koivu	Weinrich
1/03	Phi	3-3*	T	15-17-4	**Shtalenkov**	Vanbiesbrouck	29	26	1-5	0-4	Brind'Amour	**Smyth**	LeClair
1/05	LA	3-4*	L	15-18-4	Storr	**Shtalenkov**	36	23	1-4	1-4	**Mironov**	Stumpel	**Smyth**
1/07	@Pho	7-1	W	16-18-4	**Essensa**	Waite	35	45	0-7	0-6	**Essensa**	**Devereaux**	**Falloon**
1/09	@LA	1-1*	T	16-18-5	**Essensa**	Fiset	33	30	1-5	1-5	Fiset	R.Blake	**Smyth**
1/10	@Anh	4-6	L	16-19-5	Hebert	**Shtalenkov**	**49**	29	2-8	3-9	Selanne	Olausson	Trepanier
1/12	Dal	2-2*	T	16-19-6	**Essensa**	Belfour	20	23	0-4	1-4	**Smyth**	Keane	**Marchant**
1/14	@Van	3-1	W	17-19-6	**Essensa**	Hirsch	29	17	0-8	1-5	**Niinimaa**	Messier	**Beranek**
1/17	Det	4-1	W	18-19-6	**Essensa**	Osgood	26	26	1-5	0-2	**Devereaux**	**Murray**	**Poti**
1/21	@SJ	3-3*	T	18-19-7	**Essensa**	Vernon	31	22	1-5	0-2	Marleau	**Guerin**	Nolan
1/27	Chi	3-4*	L	18-20-7	Thibault	**Essensa**	38	33	2-6	0-2	**Niinimaa**	Gilmour	Amonte
1/30	Anh	1-**0**	W	19-20-7	**Shtalenkov**	Hebert	27	22	0-6	0-5	**Niinimaa**	**Shtalenkov**	Salei
2/01	StL	3-4*	L	19-21-7	Parent	**Shtalenkov**	30	21	0-6	2-3	Pronger	**Smyth**	Turgeon
2/03	Ott	2-2*	T	19-21-8	**Essensa**	Tugnutt	23	34	1-3	1-6	**Essensa**	Tugnutt	**Marchant**
2/05	Nsh	4-2	W	20-21-8	**Essensa**	Vokoun	32	23	1-6	2-4	**Guerin**	Ronning	**Selivanov**
2/08	@Cgy	1-2	L	20-22-8	Brathwaite	**Essensa**	36	26	0-8	1-5	Brathwaite	**Essensa**	Housley
2/09	Bos	0-2	L	20-23-8	Dafoe	**Shtalenkov**	31	27	0-7	1-5	Dafoe	Gill	**Grier**
2/11	@Det	2-4	L	20-24-8	Osgood	**Essensa**	31	37	1-5	2-7	Fedorov	**Weight**	Dandenault
2/13	@StL	3-2	W	21-24-8	**Essensa**	McLennan	22	33	1-6	0-5	**Smyth**	**Essensa**	**Mironov**
2/15	@Dal	1-4	L	21-25-8	Belfour	**Essensa**	13	27	0-5	2-6	Hull	Langenbrunner	Marshall
2/17	@Anh	6-2	W	22-25-8	**Shtalenkov**	Hebert	31	32	0-3	1-7	**Selivanov**	**Guerin**	**Shtalenkov**

2/18	@LA	2-3	L	22-26-8	Fiset	**Shtalenkov**	19	27	0-2	1-4	Boucher	**Selivanov**	Robitaille
2/21	NYR	1-2*	L	22-27-8	Richter	**Essensa**	40	28	0-2	0-2	Richter	**Essensa**	Lacroix
2/24	Anh	1-2	L	22-28-8	Roussel	**Passmore**	33	24	0-5	0-2	Kariya	**Falloon**	Salei
2/26	Buf	6-3	W	23-28-8	**Essensa**	Biron	39	30	**3**-7	0-3	**Marchant**	**McAmmond**	**Grier**
2/27	Car	2-2*	T	23-28-9	**Passmore**	Irbe	32	36	1-5	0-5	**Passmore**	**McAmmond**	Primeau
3/01	@Col	4-3	W	24-28-9	**Essensa**	Roy	29	50	2-5	0-6	**Essensa**	Fleury	**Mironov**
3/03	@Buf	5-3	W	25-28-9	**Passmore**	Roloson	26	32	1-4	0-5	**Mironov**	Peca	**Passmore**
3/05	@Pit	2-2*	T	25-28-10	**Essensa**	Skudra	21	36	1-5	1-7	**Essensa**	Lang	Kovalev
3/06	@Was	3-4	L	25-29-10	Kolzig	**Passmore**	25	36	1-4	1-4	Oates	Bondra	Gonchar
3/10	@Dal	4-7	L	25-30-10	Belfour	**Shtalenkov**	25	21	1-8	2-7	Nieuwendyk	Modano	Chambers
3/13	@StL	4-6	L	25-31-10	Fuhr	**Essensa**	28	31	1-8	1-3	Conroy	Bartecko	**Hamrlik**
3/14	@Nsh	1-3	L	25-32-10	Dunham	**Passmore**	25	20	0-5	1-5	Bordeleau	Ronning	Dunham
3/17	NJ	1-4	L	25-33-10	Brodeur	**Passmore**	22	36	0-2	2-5	Niedermayer	Arnott	**Passmore**
3/20	Van	4-3	W	26-33-10	**Salo**	Snow	37	26	1-7	2-6	**Grier**	Aucoin	**Moreau**
3/22	Cgy	2-2*	T	26-33-11	**Salo**	Wregget	32	31	1-7	2-5	Housley	**Hamrlik**	Wregget
3/24	Mon	0-2	L	26-34-11	Hackett	**Salo**	32	26	0-2	0-3	Hackett	Koivu	**Beranek**
3/26	StL	2-1	W	27-34-11	**Salo**	Fuhr	25	22	1-4	0-2	**Murray**	**Salo**	Fuhr
3/28	SJ	5-2	W	28-34-11	**Salo**	Vernon	24	18	1-6	2-6	**Guerin**	**Smith**	Damphousse
3/30	Pho	4-7	L	28-35-11	Khabibulin	**Essensa**	35	25	1-3	1-3	Tkachuk	Roenick	Doan
4/01	Tor	1-5	L	28-36-11	Joseph	**Salo**	31	23	0-6	3-6	Berezin	D.King	Yushkevich
4/03	@Col	2-5	L	28-37-11	Roy	**Essensa**	32	24	2-8	1-4	Fleury	Ozolinsh	Sakic
4/07	Cgy	4-2	W	29-37-11	**Salo**	Wregget	30	25	2-4	0-2	**Weight**	**Marchant**	**Poti**
4/09	@Cgy	4-1	W	30-37-11	**Salo**	Wregget	25	27	2-6	0-4	**Niinimaa**	Cassels	**Guerin**
4/10	@Van	1-1*	T	30-37-12	**Salo**	Snow	24	24	0-5	1-3	**Salo**	Snow	**Weight**
4/12	@SJ	5-4*	W	31-37-12	**Salo**	Shields	34	20	1-7	0-3	Korolyuk	**Marchant**	Ricci
4/16	Col	5-1	W	32-37-12	**Salo**	Billington	31	18	0-6	0-7	**Poti**	**Devereaux**	**Murray**
4/17	Cgy	3-2	W	33-37-12	**Salo**	Brathwaite	27	33	1-4	1-4	**Grier**	Wilm	**Weight**

Postseason

4/21	@Dal	1-**2**	L	0-1	Belfour	**Salo**	13	31	0-2	0-**4**	Carbonneau	Lehtinen	**Salo**
4/23	@Dal	**2**-3	L	0-2	Belfour	**Salo**	19	34	0-3	0-6	Belfour	Lehtinen	**Salo**
4/25	Dal	**2**-3	L	0-3	Belfour	**Salo**	22	**28**	**2-7**	0-6	Modano	**Smyth**	Nieuwendyk
4/27	Dal	**2**-3*	L	0-4	Belfour	**Salo**	**39**	56	0-5	2-6	Nieuwendyk	Belfour	**Salo**

Edmonton Oilers 1998-99 Player Statistics

		Regular Season													Postseason												
Skater	**Ps**	**GP**	**G**	**A**	**Pts**	**+/–**	**PIM**	**PP**	**SH**	**GW**	**GT**	**S**	**SPct**	**P/G**	**GP**	**G**	**A**	**Pts**	**+/–**	**PIM**	**PP**	**SH**	**GW**	**OT**	**S**	**SPct**	**P/G**
Bill Guerin	R	80	**30**	**34**	**64**	7	133	**13**	0	2	1	**261**	11.5	**.80**	3	0	2	2	-4	2	0	0	0	0	8	0.0	.67
Josef Beranek	L	66	19	30	49	6	23	7	0	2	0	160	11.9	.74	2	0	0	0	-1	4	0	0	0	0	0	—	.00
Mike Grier	R	**82**	20	24	44	5	54	3	**2**	1	0	143	14.0	.54	**4**	1	1	2	**3**	6	0	0	0	0	9	11.1	.50
Pat Falloon	R	**82**	17	23	40	-4	20	8	0	2	0	152	11.2	.49	**4**	0	1	1	0	4	0	0	0	0	6	0.0	.25
Boris Mironov†	D	63	11	29	40	6	104	5	0	**4**	1	138	8.0	.63	—	—	—	—	—	—	—	—	—	—	—	—	—
Rem Murray	L	78	21	18	39	4	20	4	1	**4**	1	116	**18.1**	.50	**4**	1	1	2	-1	2	0	0	0	0	6	16.7	.50
Doug Weight	C	43	6	31	37	-8	12	1	0	0	1	79	7.6	.86	**4**	1	1	2	-3	**15**	0	0	0	0	4	25.0	.50
Todd Marchant	C	**82**	14	22	36	3	65	3	1	2	0	183	7.7	.44	**4**	1	1	2	2	12	0	0	0	0	**10**	10.0	.50
Roman Hamrlik	D	75	8	24	32	9	70	3	0	0	0	172	4.7	.43	3	0	0	0	1	2	0	0	0	0	1	0.0	.00
Ryan Smyth	L	71	13	18	31	0	62	6	0	2	**2**	161	8.1	.44	3	**3**	0	**3**	-1	0	**2**	0	0	0	7	**42.9**	**1.00**
Janne Niinimaa	D	81	4	24	28	7	88	2	0	1	0	142	2.8	.35	**4**	0	0	0	-2	2	0	0	0	0	5	0.0	.00
Andrei Kovalenko†	R	43	13	14	27	-4	30	2	0	3	1	75	17.3	.63	—	—	—	—	—	—	—	—	—	—	—	—	—
Dean McAmmond†	C	65	9	16	25	5	36	1	0	0	0	122	7.4	.38	—	—	—	—	—	—	—	—	—	—	—	—	—
* Tom Poti	D	73	5	16	21	**10**	42	2	0	3	0	94	5.3	.29	**4**	0	1	1	-3	2	0	0	0	0	9	0.0	.25
Mats Lindgren†	C	48	5	12	17	4	22	0	1	0	0	53	9.4	.35	—	—	—	—	—	—	—	—	—	—	—	—	—
Alexander Selivanov†	R	29	8	6	14	0	24	1	0	1	0	57	14.0	.48	2	0	1	1	0	2	0	0	0	0	3	0.0	.50
Boyd Devereaux	C	61	6	8	14	2	23	0	1	**4**	1	39	15.4	.23	1	0	0	0	0	0	0	0	0	0	3	0.0	.00
Kelly Buchberger	R	52	4	4	8	-6	68	0	**2**	1	0	29	13.8	.15	**4**	0	0	0	-4	0	0	0	0	0	2	0.0	.00
* Sean Brown	D	51	0	7	7	1	**188**	0	0	0	0	27	0.0	.14	1	0	0	0	0	10	0	0	0	0	0	—	.00
Kevin Brown	R	12	4	2	6	-2	0	2	0	0	0	13	30.8	.50	—	—	—	—	—	—	—	—	—	—	—	—	—
Ethan Moreau†	L	14	1	5	6	2	8	0	0	1	0	16	6.3	.43	**4**	0	**3**	**3**	**3**	6	0	0	0	0	6	0.0	.75
* Georges Laraque	R	39	3	2	5	-1	57	0	0	0	0	17	17.6	.13	**4**	0	0	0	-2	2	0	0	0	0	1	0.0	.00
* Todd Reirden	D	17	2	3	5	-1	20	0	0	0	0	26	7.7	.29	—	—	—	—	—	—	—	—	—	—	—	—	—
Marty McSorley	D	46	2	3	5	-5	101	0	0	0	0	29	6.9	.11	3	0	0	0	1	2	0	0	0	0	3	0.0	.00
Frank Musil	D	39	0	3	3	0	34	0	0	0	0	9	0.0	.08	1	0	0	0	-1	2	0	0	0	0	2	0.0	.00
Vladimir Vorobiev	R	2	2	0	2	1	2	0	0	0	0	5	40.0	1.00	1	0	0	0	-1	0	0	0	0	0	1	0.0	.00
Jason Smith†	D	12	1	1	2	0	11	0	0	0	0	15	6.7	.17	**4**	0	1	1	0	4	0	0	0	0	1	0.0	.25
Chad Kilger†	C	13	1	1	2	-3	4	0	0	0	0	13	7.7	.15	**4**	0	0	0	-2	4	0	0	0	0	1	0.0	.00
* Craig Millar	D	24	0	2	2	-6	19	0	0	0	0	18	0.0	.08	—	—	—	—	—	—	—	—	—	—	—	—	—
Chris Ferraro	R	2	1	0	1	1	0	0	0	0	0	1	100.0	.50	—	—	—	—	—	—	—	—	—	—	—	—	—
* Steve Passmore	G	6	0	1	1	—	2	0	0	0	0	0	—	.17	—	—	—	—	—	—	—	—	—	—	—	—	—
Christian Laflamme†	D	11	0	1	1	-3	0	0	0	0	0	15	0.0	.09	**4**	0	1	1	-4	2	0	0	0	0	5	0.0	.25
Bob Essensa	G	39	0	1	1	—	0	0	0	0	0	0	—	.03	—	—	—	—	—	—	—	—	—	—	—	—	—
Jim Dowd	C	1	0	0	0	0	0	0	0	0	0	1	0.0	.00	—	—	—	—	—	—	—	—	—	—	—	—	—
Joe Hulbig	L	1	0	0	0	1	2	0	0	0	0	2	0.0	.00	—	—	—	—	—	—	—	—	—	—	—	—	—
Bill Huard	L	3	0	0	0	0	0	0	0	0	0	2	0.0	.00	—	—	—	—	—	—	—	—	—	—	—	—	—
* Dan LaCouture	L	3	0	0	0	1	0	0	0	0	0	0	—	.00	—	—	—	—	—	—	—	—	—	—	—	—	—
Daniel Lacroix	L	4	0	0	0	0	13	0	0	0	0	5	0.0	.00	—	—	—	—	—	—	—	—	—	—	—	—	—
* Fredrik Lindquist	C	8	0	0	0	-2	2	0	0	0	0	6	0.0	.00	—	—	—	—	—	—	—	—	—	—	—	—	—
Tommy Salo†	G	13	0	0	0	—	0	0	0	0	0	0	—	.00	**4**	0	0	0	—	0	0	0	0	0	0	—	.00
Mikhail Shtalenkov†	G	34	0	0	0	—	2	0	0	0	0	0	—	.00	—	—	—	—	—	—	—	—	—	—	—	—	—
Bench		—	—	—	—	—	0	—	—	—	—	—	—	—	—	—	—	—	—	0	—	—	—	—	—	—	—
TEAM TOTALS		82	230	385	615	30	1361	63	8	33	8	2396	9.6	7.50	4	7	14	21	-19	85	2	0	0	0	93	7.5	5.25

	Regular Season											Postseason									
Goaltender	**G**	**Min**	**GAA**	**W**	**L**	**T**	**ENG**	**ShO**	**GA**	**SA**	**SvPct**	**G**	**Min**	**GAA**	**W**	**L**	**ENG**	**ShO**	**GA**	**SA**	**SvPct**
Tommy Salo†	13	700	2.31	8	2	2	0	0	27	279	.903	**4**	**296**	**2.23**	0	**4**	0	0	**11**	**149**	**.926**
Mikhail Shtalenkov†	34	1819	**2.67**	**12**	**17**	3	**2**	**3**	81	782	.896	—	—	—	—	—	—	—	—	—	—
Bob Essensa	**39**	**2091**	2.75	**12**	14	**6**	**2**	0	**96**	**974**	**.901**	—	—	—	—	—	—	—	—	—	—
* Steve Passmore	6	362	2.82	1	4	1	1	0	17	183	.907	—	—	—	—	—	—	—	—	—	—
TEAM TOTALS	82	4997	2.71	33	37	12	5	3	226	2223	.898	4	298	2.21	0	4	0	0	11	149	.926

1998-99 Edmonton Oilers

Record When:

Overtime games	3-5-12
In second game of back-to-back games	3-8-3
Vs playoff teams	17-22-8
Leading after two periods	24-4-2
Tied after two periods	7-4-5
Losing after two periods	2-29-5
Scoring first	27-9-1
More shots than opponents	21-25-6
Fewer shots than opponents	10-12-5
Team had at least one fighting major	14-17-1
Team had more PIM	10-13-3
Team had fewer PIM	19-17-9
Team had even PIM	4-7-0

Team

Longest winning streak	4	Oct. 28 — Nov. 4
Longest unbeaten streak	6	Apr. 7 — Apr. 17
Longest losing streak	5	Mar. 6 — Mar. 17
Longest winless streak	7	Dec. 4 — Dec. 15
Most shots, game	49	2 times
Most shots, period	23	3rd, @Anh, Jan. 10
Fewest shots, game	13	@Dal, Feb. 15
Fewest shots, period	2	2 times

Individual

Longest goal streak	5	Bill Guerin
Longest point streak	7	3 times
Most goals, game	3	2 times
Most assists, game	4	Janne Niinimaa
Most points, game	4	2 times
Highest +/–, game	4	3 times
Lowest +/–, game	-5	2 times
Most shots, game	11	Ryan Smyth

Did You Know?

Only seven of the 41 players used by Edmonton last year were Oilers draft picks. Excluding the expansion Predators, no NHL team used fewer of its own draft picks in 1998-99.

Miscellaneous

		NHL Rank
PP Pct.	14.4 (63-438)	18
SH goals allowed	10	18t
PK Pct.	82.1 (307-374)	21
SH goals scored	8	8t
Special Team Index	96.3	20
Shots on goal	2,396 (29.2/G)	7
Shots against	2,223 (27.1/G)	11
Unassisted goals	14	8t
Unassisted goals allowed	9	4t
Team Average Weight	204.7	5
Game Star Points	349	17

Game Star Breakdown

Player	1st	2nd	3rd	Pts
Bill Guerin	5	5	2	42
Bob Essensa	4	6	0	38
Mikhail Shtalenkov	3	4	4	31
Boris Mironov	4	1	2	25
Josef Beranek	4	0	2	22
Janne Niinimaa	4	0	1	21
Ryan Smyth	2	2	3	19
Todd Marchant	2	2	2	18
Boyd Devereaux	2	2	0	16
Mike Grier	2	0	3	13
Doug Weight	1	2	2	13
Andrei Kovalenko	2	0	2	12
Rem Murray	1	2	1	12
Tom Poti	1	1	2	10
Alexander Selivanov	1	1	1	9
Tommy Salo	1	1	0	8
Pat Falloon	0	2	2	8
Steve Passmore	1	0	2	7
Roman Hamrlik	0	1	4	7
Dean McAmmond	0	2	0	6
Kevin Brown	0	1	0	3
Mats Lindgren	0	1	0	3
Jason Smith	0	1	0	3
Kelly Buchberger	0	0	2	2
Ethan Moreau	0	0	1	1

Florida Panthers 1998-99 Game Log (30-34-18)

Date	Opp	Score	W/L/T	Record	Goalies W/T	Goalies L/T	Shots Fla	Shots Opp	Power Plays Fla	Power Plays Opp	Game Stars 1st	Game Stars 2nd	Game Stars 3rd
10/09	TB	4-1	W	1-0-0	**Burke**	Ranford	36	29	0-3	0-6	**Parrish**	**Kozlov**	**Burke**
10/10	@Nsh	1-**0**	W	2-0-0	**McLean**	Dunham	26	26	1-9	0-6	**Whitney**	**McLean**	Dunham
10/16	@Buf	2-2*	T	2-0-1	**Burke**	Hasek	34	25	1-5	1-6	**Kvasha**	Hasek	Sanderson
10/21	LA	1-1*	T	2-0-2	**Burke**	LeGace	**50**	19	0-8	0-8	LeGace	**Gagner**	Robitaille
10/23	Van	0-5	L	2-1-2	Snow	**McLean**	35	27	0-5	1-3	Messier	Bertuzzi	Snow
10/24	@Was	2-2*	T	2-1-3	**Burke**	Tabaracci	33	20	1-7	0-4	Tabaracci	**Dvorak**	Witt
10/28	Det	2-7	L	2-2-3	Osgood	**Burke**	18	29	1-5	2-5	Holmstrom	Yzerman	Lidstrom
10/30	@Chi	**7**-3	W	3-2-3	**Burke**	Hackett	25	33	3-**11**	1-8	**Parrish**	**Niedermayer**	**Whitney**
10/31	@NJ	1-3	L	3-3-3	Terreri	**McLean**	17	28	0-3	2-5	Andreychuk	Pederson	Terreri
11/02	@NYI	2-6	L	3-4-3	Salo	**Burke**	20	29	1-7	3-7	Reichel	Smolinski	Linden
11/04	Chi	2-1	W	4-4-3	**Burke**	Fitzpatrick	32	34	1-6	0-5	**Ciccarelli**	**Lindsay**	**Burke**
11/07	NJ	3-4	L	4-5-3	Brodeur	**Burke**	26	38	0-5	0-**1**	Pandolfo	**Niedermayer**	Andreychuk
11/11	NYR	4-1	W	5-5-3	**Burke**	Richter	35	26	0-4	0-**1**	**Worrell**	**Kvasha**	**Burke**
11/12	@Phi	2-1	W	6-5-3	**McLean**	Vanbiesbrouck	15	40	1-3	0-4	**Parrish**	**Murphy**	Svoboda
11/14	@Pit	0-4	L	6-6-3	Barrasso	**Burke**	23	32	0-3	2-6	Barrasso	Barnes	Werenka
11/19	@Bos	5-5*	T	6-6-4	**Burke**	Dafoe	44	29	1-5	1-3	**Laus**	Van Impe	**Kvasha**
11/21	@NJ	3-3*	T	6-6-5	**McLean**	Brodeur	25	27	1-7	1-4	Pandolfo	Niedermayer	**Whitney**
11/22	Phi	1-2*	L	6-7-5	Vanbiesbrouck	**McLean**	26	16	0-3	0-2	Vanbiesbrouck	Jones	**Jovanovski**
11/25	Bos	0-1	L	6-8-5	Dafoe	**McLean**	23	19	0-3	1-**1**	Samsonov	Dafoe	**McLean**
11/27	@TB	2-1	W	7-8-5	**Burke**	Ranford	28	24	0-3	1-6	**Mellanby**	**Burke**	Ranford
11/28	Buf	6-2	W	8-8-5	**McLean**	Roloson	47	23	3-9	1-5	**Whitney**	**Svehla**	**McLean**
12/01	@NYR	4-5*	L	8-9-5	Richter	**Burke**	23	29	1-4	3-6	Graves	Gretzky	Leetch
12/02	@Buf	1-2	L	8-10-5	Hasek	**McLean**	28	28	0-4	0-4	Hasek	Ward	**Whitney**
12/05	Car	3-3*	T	8-10-6	**Burke**	Kidd	26	27	2-5	1-5	**Ciccarelli**	Sheppard	**Parrish**
12/09	Ott	6-5	W	9-10-6	**Burke**	Tugnutt	27	30	**5**-10	2-6	**Whitney**	**Kozlov**	Bonk
12/12	Cgy	2-4	L	9-11-6	Giguere	**McLean**	38	35	0-2	1-3	Fleury	**Kozlov**	Giguere
12/16	Pit	4-1	W	10-11-6	**Burke**	Barrasso	36	30	1-4	0-4	**Burke**	Barrasso	**Mellanby**
12/19	Edm	3-1	W	11-11-6	**Burke**	Shtalenkov	26	30	0-3	0-4	**Garpenlov**	**Burke**	**Whitney**
12/23	Was	0-4	L	11-12-6	Kolzig	**Burke**	29	20	0-5	2-4	Kolzig	Bondra	Reekie
12/26	@TB	3-1	W	12-12-6	**Burke**	Ranford	35	24	1-3	0-5	**Burke**	Selivanov	**Svehla**
12/28	NYI	5-1	W	13-12-6	**Burke**	Flaherty	36	27	1-2	0-4	**Burke**	**Whitney**	**Carkner**
12/30	@Pit	4-7	L	13-13-6	Skudra	**McLean**	30	37	1-5	1-5	Straka	Miller	Lang
1/01	Car	3-3*	T	13-13-7	**Burke**	Irbe	33	28	1-4	0-4	**Niedermayer**	Primeau	Ranheim
1/02	Pit	2-4	L	13-14-7	Barrasso	**Burke**	17	34	1-3	2-6	Kovalev	Jagr	**Kvasha**
1/05	@Pho	2-2*	T	13-14-8	**Burke**	Khabibulin	26	28	0-3	0-5	Roenick	Adams	**Svehla**
1/06	@Col	2-2*	T	13-14-9	**McLean**	Denis	35	35	0-5	1-6	Sakic	**Mellanby**	Foote
1/08	@Van	1-1*	T	13-14-10	**Burke**	Hirsch	27	24	1-3	0-4	Messier	**Svehla**	Hirsch
1/10	@Cgy	2-1	W	14-14-10	**Burke**	Brathwaite	35	25	0-5	0-6	**Whitney**	**Jovanovski**	Brathwaite
1/13	Tor	3-3*	T	14-14-11	**Burke**	Joseph	33	37	1-6	1-3	**Mellanby**	Sullivan	**Niedermayer**
1/14	@Car	2-3	L	14-15-11	Irbe	**Burke**	16	23	0-3	1-5	Francis	Wesley	**Ratchuk**
1/16	NYI	1-**0**	W	15-15-11	**Burke**	Potvin	19	27	1-4	0-4	**Burke**	**Ciccarelli**	Brewer
1/18	Buf	0-4	L	15-16-11	Hasek	**Burke**	33	39	0-5	1-4	Zhitnik	Hasek	Peca
1/20	@NYI	5-2	W	16-16-11	**McLean**	Potvin	20	19	1-5	1-5	**Bure**	Reichel	**Spacek**
1/21	@NYR	2-1	W	17-16-11	**Burke**	Richter	26	28	0-7	0-7	**Hedican**	**Burke**	Richter
1/26	@Phi	3-3*	T	17-16-12	**Burke**	Vanbiesbrouck	19	30	1-4	0-3	**Bure**	Langkow	Desjardins
1/27	Mon	2-1	W	18-16-12	**Burke**	Hackett	32	30	0-4	0-5	**Burke**	Brisebois	**Bure**
1/30	Dal	2-5	L	18-17-12	Belfour	**Burke**	28	30	1-5	1-5	Hrkac	Belfour	Modano
2/03	Tor	5-2	W	19-17-12	**Burke**	Joseph	38	36	0-4	0-6	**Burke**	**Dvorak**	**Parrish**
2/05	@Pit	0-3	L	19-18-12	Barrasso	**McLean**	29	26	0-1	0-4	Jagr	Barrasso	Sonnenberg
2/06	@Car	3-3*	T	19-18-13	**Burke**	Irbe	33	41	0-3	0-5	**Parrish**	Sheppard	Primeau
2/08	StL	4-5	L	19-19-13	Parent	**Burke**	25	29	0-6	1-5	Demitra	Yake	**Lindsay**
2/11	@Ott	3-1	W	20-19-13	**McLean**	Tugnutt	17	25	1-5	0-4	**Kozlov**	**Worrell**	Hossa
2/13	@Mon	0-4	L	20-20-13	Hackett	**Burke**	16	35	0-6	2-6	Koivu	Corson	Dawe
2/15	SJ	2-2*	T	20-20-14	**Burke**	Shields	33	27	0-1	0-3	**Whitney**	Shields	Friesen
2/17	@Dal	1-2	L	20-21-14	Turek	**Burke**	16	29	0-2	1-6	Nieuwendyk	Langenbrunner	**Burke**

2/18	@StL	0-**0***	T	20-21-15	**Burke**	McLennan	21	27	0-3	0-3	**Burke**	McLennan	MacInnis
2/20	Pho	**7**-1	W	21-21-15	**Burke**	Khabibulin	30	35	1-4	1-4	**Dvorak**	**Lindsay**	**Burke**
2/24	Phi	5-3	W	22-21-15	**Burke**	Vanbiesbrouck	24	27	2-5	1-7	**Kvasha**	Lindros	**Parrish**
2/26	@Det	5-5*	T	22-21-16	**McLean**	Osgood	17	36	1-6	3-9	Larionov	**Bure**	Maltby
2/27	@Tor	1-4	L	22-22-16	Joseph	**Burke**	23	30	0-4	1-3	Johnson	McCauley	Sundin
3/03	Col	5-7	L	22-23-16	Billington	**Burke**	28	34	3-5	2-5	Forsberg	**Bure**	Sakic
3/06	Car	2-2*	T	22-23-17	**McLean**	Irbe	35	**15**	1-6	2-3	Irbe	**Mellanby**	Primeau
3/08	@Mon	5-2	W	23-23-17	**McLean**	Hackett	27	33	1-5	0-3	**Whitney**	**Lindsay**	**Worrell**
3/09	@Bos	0-2	L	23-24-17	Dafoe	**Burke**	19	41	0-5	1-5	Bourque	Khristich	Dafoe
3/11	@Was	2-1	W	24-24-17	**Burke**	Kolzig	20	27	0-6	0-4	**Burke**	**Kozlov**	Reekie
3/13	TB	1-**0**	W	25-24-17	**Burke**	Schwab	33	24	0-6	0-4	**Burke**	**Niedermayer**	Schwab
3/17	@SJ	2-4	L	25-25-17	Shields	**Burke**	34	22	0-5	0-3	Marleau	Korolyuk	Ragnarsson
3/20	@LA	3-4	L	25-26-17	Fiset	**Burke**	32	20	2-6	2-5	Norstrom	Robitaille	**Mellanby**
3/21	@Anh	5-2	W	26-26-17	**Burke**	Hebert	41	27	1-4	1-2	**Whitney**	**Kozlov**	**Lindsay**
3/24	NYR	1-2	L	26-27-17	Richter	**Burke**	35	24	0-5	1-2	Richter	Nedved	**Whitney**
3/26	Nsh	4-1	W	27-27-17	**Burke**	Vokoun	36	28	2-3	1-4	**Dvorak**	**Boyle**	**Burke**
3/28	NJ	2-2*	T	27-27-18	**Burke**	Brodeur	19	39	0-6	1-4	**Parrish**	**Burke**	**Niedermayer**
3/31	NYI	3-5	L	27-28-18	Flaherty	**Burke**	36	19	0-6	1-**1**	Lawrence	**Parrish**	Czerkawski
4/01	@Was	3-5	L	27-29-18	Kolzig	**Burke**	35	37	0-6	1-4	Kolzig	Gonchar	Bellows
4/03	Ott	4-6	L	27-30-18	Rhodes	**Burke**	26	36	0-2	1-4	Yashin	**Garpenlov**	Dackell
4/05	Was	0-3	L	27-31-18	Kolzig	**McLean**	28	30	0-5	1-5	Gonchar	Oates	**McLean**
4/07	Bos	2-5	L	27-32-18	Dafoe	**McLean**	18	26	1-4	2-6	Carter	DiMaio	**Johnson**
4/09	@Buf	1-3	L	27-33-18	Hasek	**Burke**	29	22	0-5	1-6	Woolley	Hasek	Satan
4/10	@Tor	1-9	L	27-34-18	Healy	**Burke**	26	32	0-4	2-3	Sullivan	Thomas	Valk
4/12	@Ott	2-**0**	W	28-34-18	**McLean**	Tugnutt	11	39	0-4	0-7	**McLean**	Yashin	Prospal
4/14	Mon	3-2*	W	29-34-18	**McLean**	Chabot	31	21	0-2	0-2	**Nilson**	**Parrish**	**Dvorak**
4/17	TB	6-2	W	30-34-18	**McLean**	Wilkinson	35	29	0-2	2-5	**Muller**	**Whitney**	**Mellanby**

Florida Panthers 1998-99 Player Statistics

Regular Season

Skater	Ps	GP	G	A	Pts	+/–	PIM	PP	SH	GW	GT	S	SPct	P/G
Ray Whitney	C	81	**26**	**38**	**64**	-3	18	**7**	0	**6**	1	193	13.5	**.79**
Rob Niedermayer	C	**82**	18	33	51	-13	50	6	1	3	2	142	12.7	.62
Viktor Kozlov	C	65	16	35	51	13	24	5	1	1	0	**209**	7.7	.78
Scott Mellanby	R	67	18	27	45	5	85	4	0	3	**3**	136	13.2	.67
Radek Dvorak	R	**82**	19	24	43	7	29	0	**4**	0	0	182	10.4	.52
* Mark Parrish	L	73	24	13	37	-6	25	5	0	5	1	129	**18.6**	.51
Robert Svehla	D	80	8	29	37	-13	83	4	0	0	1	157	5.1	.46
Bill Lindsay	L	75	12	15	27	-1	92	0	1	2	0	135	8.9	.36
* Oleg Kvasha	L	68	12	13	25	5	45	4	0	2	1	138	8.7	.37
Johan Garpenlov	L	64	8	9	17	-9	42	0	1	0	1	71	11.3	.27
Pavel Bure	R	11	13	3	16	3	4	5	1	0	1	44	29.5	1.45
Ed Jovanovski†	D	41	3	13	16	-4	82	1	0	1	0	68	4.4	.39
Kirk Muller	L	**82**	4	11	15	-11	49	0	0	1	0	107	3.7	.18
* Jaroslav Spacek	D	63	3	12	15	**15**	28	2	1	0	0	92	3.3	.24
Dave Gagner†	C	36	4	10	14	-7	39	2	0	0	1	50	8.0	.39
Terry Carkner	D	62	2	9	11	0	54	0	0	0	0	25	8.0	.18
Bret Hedican†	D	25	3	7	10	-2	17	0	0	1	0	38	7.9	.40
Paul Laus	D	75	1	9	10	-1	218	0	0	0	0	54	1.9	.13
* Peter Worrell	L	62	4	5	9	0	**258**	0	0	2	0	50	8.0	.15
* Dan Boyle	D	22	3	5	8	0	6	1	0	1	0	31	9.7	.36
Dino Ciccarelli	R	14	6	1	7	-1	27	5	0	1	0	23	26.1	.50
Rhett Warrener†	D	48	0	7	7	-1	64	0	0	0	0	33	0.0	.15
Gord Murphy	D	51	0	7	7	4	16	0	0	0	0	56	0.0	.14
Alex Hicks†	L	51	0	6	6	-4	58	0	0	0	0	47	0.0	.12
Sean Burke	G	59	0	4	4	—	27	0	0	0	0	0	—	.07
* Marcus Nilson	R	8	1	1	2	2	5	0	0	1	0	7	14.3	.25
* Peter Ratchuk	D	24	1	1	2	-1	10	0	0	0	0	34	2.9	.08
Chris Wells	C	20	0	2	2	-4	31	0	0	0	0	28	0.0	.10
* Ryan Johnson	C	1	1	0	1	0	0	0	0	0	0	1	100.0	1.00
David Nemirovsky	R	2	0	1	1	1	0	0	0	0	0	2	0.0	.50
* Filip Kuba	D	5	0	1	1	2	0	0	0	0	0	5	0.0	.20
* Jeff Ware	D	6	0	1	1	-6	6	0	0	0	0	1	0.0	.17
* Chris Allen	D	1	0	0	0	1	0	0	0	0	0	0	—	.00
Slava Butsayev†	C	1	0	0	0	-1	2	0	0	0	0	0	—	.00
* John Jakopin	D	3	0	0	0	-1	0	0	0	0	0	0	—	.00
Jeff Norton†	D	3	0	0	0	0	2	0	0	0	0	2	0.0	.00
Steve Washburn†	C	4	0	0	0	-1	4	0	0	0	0	0	—	.00
Mike Wilson†	D	4	0	0	0	2	0	0	0	0	0	8	0.0	.00
* Herbert Vasiljevs	C	5	0	0	0	-1	2	0	0	0	0	6	0.0	.00
* Dwayne Hay	L	9	0	0	0	-1	0	0	0	0	0	3	0.0	.00
Kirk McLean	G	30	0	0	0	—	2	0	0	0	0	0	—	.00
Bench		—	—	—	—	—	0	—	—	—	—	—	—	—
TEAM TOTALS		82	210	352	562	-32	1504	51	10	30	12	2307	9.1	6.85

Postseason

GP	G	A	Pts	+/–	PIM	PP	SH	GW	OT	S	SPct	P/G

Team Did Not Qualify for Postseason Play

Regular Season

Goaltender	G	Min	GAA	W	L	T	ENG	ShO	GA	SA	SvPct
Sean Burke	**59**	**3402**	**2.66**	**21**	**24**	**14**	**3**	**3**	**151**	**1624**	**.907**
Kirk McLean	30	1597	2.74	9	10	4	1	2	73	727	.900
TEAM TOTALS	82	5017	2.73	30	34	18	4	5	228	2355	.903

Postseason

G	Min	GAA	W	L	ENG	ShO	GA	SA	SvPct

1998-99 Florida Panthers

Record When:

Overtime games	1-2-18
In second game of back-to-back games	6-9-4
Vs playoff teams	11-23-15
Leading after two periods	23-3-2
Tied after two periods	5-4-8
Losing after two periods	2-27-8
Scoring first	23-8-7
More shots than opponents	16-11-8
Fewer shots than opponents	13-22-9
Team had at least one fighting major	16-20-9
Team had more PIM	13-14-7
Team had fewer PIM	14-14-8
Team had even PIM	3-6-3

Team

Longest winning streak	3	Apr. 12 — Apr. 17
Longest unbeaten streak	5	Jan. 5 — Jan. 13
Longest losing streak	7	Mar. 31 — Apr. 10
Longest winless streak	8	Mar. 28 — Apr. 10
Most shots, game	50	vs. LA, Oct. 21
Most shots, period	21	3rd, @Anh, Mar. 21
Fewest shots, game	11	@Ott, Apr. 12
Fewest shots, period	2	2 times

Individual

Longest goal streak	4	2 times
Longest point streak	6	Pavel Bure
Most goals, game	4	Mark Parrish
Most assists, game	3	7 times
Most points, game	4	3 times
Highest +/–, game	4	4 times
Lowest +/–, game	-4	4 times
Most shots, game	8	3 times

Did You Know?

Paul Laus' 110 fights over the past four years are the most in the NHL. Laus has been responsible for 36.6 percent of the fighting majors (133 of 363) in Panther history.

Miscellaneous

		NHL Rank
PP Pct.	13.4 (51-380)	22
SH goals allowed	11	23t
PK Pct.	81.9 (303-370)	22
SH goals scored	10	6t
Special Team Index	95.1	25
Shots on goal	2,307 (28.1/G)	13
Shots against	2,355 (28.7/G)	16
Unassisted goals	14	8t
Unassisted goals allowed	12	13t
Team Average Weight	198.8	18
Game Star Points	344	18

Game Star Breakdown

Player	1st	2nd	3rd	Pts
Sean Burke	9	4	6	63
Ray Whitney	7	2	5	46
Mark Parrish	5	2	3	34
Viktor Kozlov	1	5	0	20
Scott Mellanby	2	2	3	19
Pavel Bure	2	2	1	17
Radek Dvorak	2	2	1	17
Rob Niedermayer	1	3	2	16
Oleg Kvasha	2	1	2	15
Dino Ciccarelli	2	1	0	13
Kirk McLean	1	1	3	11
Bill Lindsay	0	3	2	11
Peter Worrell	1	1	1	9
Johan Garpenlov	1	1	0	8
Robert Svehla	0	2	2	8
Bret Hedican	1	0	0	5
Paul Laus	1	0	0	5
Kirk Muller	1	0	0	5
Marcus Nilson	1	0	0	5
Ed Jovanovski	0	1	1	4
Dan Boyle	0	1	0	3
Dave Gagner	0	1	0	3
Gord Murphy	0	1	0	3
Terry Carkner	0	0	1	1
Ryan Johnson	0	0	1	1
Peter Ratchuk	0	0	1	1
Jaroslav Spacek	0	0	1	1

Los Angeles Kings 1998-99 Game Log (32-45-5)

Date	Opp	Score	W/L/T	Record	Goalies W/T	L/T	Shots LA	Opp	Power Plays LA	Opp	Game Stars 1st	2nd	3rd
10/10	@Edm	2-1	W	1-0-0	**Fiset**	Shtalenkov	32	24	1-6	0-4	**Fiset**	**Robitaille**	Shtalenkov
10/12	@Van	2-4	L	1-1-0	Snow	**Storr**	25	24	0-6	1-8	Zezel	**Perreault**	Aucoin
10/16	Bos	2-1*	W	2-1-0	**Fiset**	Dafoe	27	23	1-2	0-4	**Robitaille**	**Fiset**	Dafoe
10/18	Col	5-5*	T	2-1-1	**Storr**	Roy	23	34	1-3	0-5	Lemieux	**Perreault**	Forsberg
10/21	@Fla	1-1*	T	2-1-2	**LeGace**	Burke	19	50	0-8	0-8	**LeGace**	Gagner	**Robitaille**
10/23	@TB	2-3	L	2-2-2	Ranford	**Bach**	39	38	0-4	0-6	Tucker	Ranford	Renberg
10/25	@Car	3-2	W	3-2-2	**LeGace**	Kidd	25	31	0-1	0-4	**Robitaille**	Primeau	**LeGace**
10/27	@NYI	0-1	L	3-3-2	Salo	**LeGace**	20	34	0-4	0-2	Salo	**LeGace**	Sacco
10/28	@NJ	4-0	W	4-3-2	**Fiset**	Brodeur	18	40	1-1	0-5	**Fiset**	**R.Blake**	**Perreault**
10/30	TB	0-3	L	4-4-2	Puppa	**LeGace**	27	28	0-4	0-4	Puppa	Langkow	**LeGace**
11/01	Pho	0-3	L	4-5-2	Khabibulin	**LeGace**	31	28	0-5	0-4	Khabibulin	Lumme	Ylonen
11/05	StL	2-2*	T	4-5-3	**LeGace**	McLennan	33	28	0-6	2-7	**Robitaille**	**Murray**	McLennan
11/07	Dal	3-4	L	4-6-3	Belfour	**LeGace**	23	25	1-6	2-6	Hatcher	**Robitaille**	Hrkac
11/09	@Van	4-3	W	5-6-3	**LeGace**	Hirsch	23	19	0-5	0-2	**Robitaille**	Mogilny	**Murray**
11/10	@Cgy	4-5*	L	5-7-3	Giguere	**Bach**	26	37	0-4	0-2	Cassels	**Murray**	**Jokinen**
11/12	Nsh	1-3	L	5-8-3	Dunham	**LeGace**	36	18	0-3	0-2	Dunham	Peltonen	**Stumpel**
11/14	Car	3-5	L	5-9-3	Irbe	**LeGace**	40	29	0-7	2-7	Primeau	Sheppard	**Robitaille**
11/16	@Anh	1-3	L	5-10-3	Hebert	**LeGace**	39	28	1-6	1-3	Hebert	Green	Davidsson
11/18	@SJ	4-5	L	5-11-3	Vernon	**LeGace**	30	40	1-5	1-7	Granato	Friesen	Vernon
11/19	NYR	1-5	L	5-12-3	Cloutier	**LeGace**	29	25	0-2	2-4	Cloutier	Malhotra	**Visheau**
11/21	Chi	5-0	W	6-12-3	**Storr**	Thibault	32	21	2-7	0-2	**Storr**	**LaFayette**	**Duchesne**
11/28	Pho	0-4	L	6-13-3	Khabibulin	**Storr**	20	31	0-4	2-7	Doan	Ylonen	Khabibulin
11/30	@Mon	1-3	L	6-14-3	Hackett	**Fiset**	19	30	0-2	1-4	Koivu	Savage	Hackett
12/02	@Tor	1-3	L	6-15-3	Joseph	**Storr**	28	27	0-4	3-5	Joseph	Berezin	**Tsyplakov**
12/03	@Ott	1-3	L	6-16-3	Tugnutt	**Fiset**	32	18	0-5	0-5	Tugnutt	Bonk	**Norstrom**
12/05	Det	3-4	L	6-17-3	Osgood	**Fiset**	27	45	1-6	0-3	Yzerman	**Murray**	Brown
12/09	Was	2-1	W	7-17-3	**Fiset**	Kolzig	22	33	0-6	0-2	**Robitaille**	**Murray**	**Fiset**
12/12	Van	3-0	W	8-17-3	**Fiset**	Snow	38	25	1-7	0-6	**Fiset**	**Robitaille**	**Norstrom**
12/13	@Anh	0-3	L	8-18-3	Hebert	**Fiset**	35	34	0-4	1-2	Hebert	Selanne	Kariya
12/17	NYI	4-5*	L	8-19-3	Salo	**Storr**	25	25	1-3	1-4	Berard	**Rosa**	Richter
12/19	@StL	2-5	L	8-20-3	Fuhr	**Storr**	25	27	1-4	0-1	Demitra	Conroy	Bartecko
12/20	@Chi	4-1	W	9-20-3	**Storr**	Thibault	34	25	1-4	0-2	**Murray**	**Storr**	Zhamnov
12/22	@Pit	3-0	W	10-20-3	**Storr**	Skudra	31	25	0-2	0-1	**Murray**	**Storr**	**Audette**
12/26	Pho	1-2	L	10-21-3	Khabibulin	**Storr**	27	31	0-5	0-2	Adams	Roenick	**Rosa**
12/28	@Pho	4-2	W	11-21-3	**Storr**	Khabibulin	26	34	1-2	0-3	**Robitaille**	**Storr**	**Stumpel**
12/30	SJ	5-1	W	12-21-3	**Storr**	Vernon	23	32	1-3	0-5	**Murray**	**R.Blake**	**M.Johnson**
1/02	Col	4-2	W	13-21-3	**Storr**	Billington	27	26	1-3	1-4	**Ferraro**	**Robitaille**	Drury
1/05	@Edm	4-3*	W	14-21-3	**Storr**	Shtalenkov	23	36	1-4	1-4	Mironov	**Stumpel**	Smyth
1/07	Buf	4-2	W	15-21-3	**Storr**	Roloson	24	23	1-2	1-5	**Robitaille**	**R.Blake**	**Storr**
1/09	Edm	1-1*	T	15-21-4	**Fiset**	Essensa	30	33	1-5	1-5	**Fiset**	**R.Blake**	Smyth
1/11	@SJ	0-4	L	15-22-4	Vernon	**Fiset**	30	33	0-6	2-6	Houlder	Murphy	Vernon
1/14	Cgy	3-0	W	16-22-4	**Storr**	Brathwaite	30	22	1-5	0-6	**Audette**	**Robitaille**	**Storr**
1/16	Pit	1-5	L	16-23-4	Barrasso	**Storr**	17	18	1-3	2-3	Jagr	Lang	Moran
1/19	Col	4-5	L	16-24-4	Roy	**Fiset**	31	33	1-2	0-1	Sakic	Forsberg	**Courtnall**
1/21	NJ	2-3	L	16-25-4	Brodeur	**Storr**	26	40	0-5	1-7	Holik	**Stumpel**	McKay
1/27	@Dal	2-3	L	16-26-4	Turek	**Fiset**	24	28	1-6	0-4	Turek	**Robitaille**	Skrudland
1/29	@Was	6-3	W	17-26-4	**Fiset**	Kolzig	27	41	2-4	2-7	**Ferraro**	**R.Blake**	**Fiset**
1/30	@Buf	1-4	L	17-27-4	Hasek	**Storr**	26	31	0-5	0-2	Sanderson	Peca	Zhitnik
2/01	@Phi	2-4	L	17-28-4	Vanbiesbrouck	**Fiset**	25	25	0-3	1-3	Vanbiesbrouck	Jones	Desjardins
2/04	Chi	3-2	W	18-28-4	**Fiset**	Thibault	33	37	0-4	1-6	**Audette**	**Duchesne**	Kilger
2/06	SJ	2-0	W	19-28-4	**Storr**	Vernon	18	27	1-7	0-7	**Robitaille**	**Storr**	**Norstrom**
2/10	@Pho	0-3	L	19-29-4	Khabibulin	**Storr**	26	40	0-5	0-5	Adams	Khabibulin	Diduck
2/11	Phi	4-3	W	20-29-4	**Fiset**	Hextall	25	31	0-6	0-5	**Stumpel**	**Robitaille**	**Rosa**
2/13	Dal	2-3	L	20-30-4	Turek	**Fiset**	26	22	0-3	0-3	Hull	Severyn	**Laperriere**
2/15	Anh	1-3	L	20-31-4	Hebert	**Fiset**	24	29	0-3	1-4	Sandstrom	Hebert	**Jokinen**

2/18	Edm	3-2	W	21-31-4	**Fiset**	Shtalenkov	27	19	1-4	0-2	**Boucher**	Selivanov	**Robitaille**
2/20	@Cgy	2-2*	T	21-31-5	**Storr**	Brathwaite	33	27	1-5	0-3	**R.Blake**	Brathwaite	Fleury
2/22	@StL	1-5	L	21-32-5	McLennan	**Fiset**	23	40	0-3	1-4	Demitra	McLennan	Turgeon
2/24	@Det	3-2*	W	22-32-5	**Fiset**	Osgood	40	26	1-2	0-2	**Robitaille**	**R.Blake**	Fedorov
2/26	@Chi	2-1	W	23-32-5	**Storr**	Fitzpatrick	17	34	1-2	0-4	**Storr**	**R.Blake**	Emerson
2/28	@Dal	0-1	L	23-33-5	Belfour	**Fiset**	18	35	0-3	0-3	Nieuwendyk	**Fiset**	Belfour
3/03	@Anh	1-2	L	23-34-5	Hebert	**Fiset**	34	**14**	0-5	1-4	Hebert	**Robitaille**	Selanne
3/04	Nsh	3-4	L	23-35-5	Dunham	**Storr**	35	22	**2**-4	0-2	**Audette**	Bordeleau	Slaney
3/06	Cgy	1-4	L	23-36-5	Brathwaite	**Fiset**	28	28	0-6	1-6	Brathwaite	Stillman	**Norstrom**
3/09	Det	4-2	W	24-36-5	**Fiset**	Osgood	24	40	0-2	0-7	**Laperriere**	Larionov	**Fiset**
3/13	Van	3-1	W	25-36-5	**Fiset**	Weekes	40	20	1-5	0-4	**Audette**	**Stumpel**	Weekes
3/15	Ott	4-**0**	W	26-36-5	**Fiset**	Tugnutt	30	29	1-4	0-3	**Fiset**	**R.Blake**	**Audette**
3/18	Anh	2-4	L	26-37-5	Hebert	**Fiset**	39	24	1-6	2-3	Kariya	Selanne	Hebert
3/20	Fla	4-3	W	27-37-5	**Fiset**	Burke	20	32	**2**-5	2-6	**Norstrom**	**Robitaille**	Mellanby
3/21	@Pho	1-4	L	27-38-5	Khabibulin	**Storr**	38	43	0-2	1-3	Khabibulin	Reichel	Quint
3/25	Dal	1-2	L	27-39-5	Turek	**Fiset**	32	26	0-4	0-2	Turek	Hull	**Fiset**
3/28	@Col	2-7	L	27-40-5	Roy	**Fiset**	28	33	0-2	0-2	Fleury	Sakic	Hejduk
3/30	@Bos	2-1*	W	28-40-5	**Storr**	Dafoe	27	25	0-1	0-2	**Jokinen**	Dafoe	**R.Blake**
3/31	@Det	1-2	L	28-41-5	Osgood	**Fiset**	28	37	0-2	0-4	Osgood	Fedorov	**Fiset**
4/03	@Nsh	2-3	L	28-42-5	Vokoun	**Fiset**	36	29	0-1	0-2	Walker	Valicevic	Vokoun
4/05	@Col	1-4	L	28-43-5	Roy	**Fiset**	27	35	0-3	2-3	Forsberg	Foote	Roy
4/08	SJ	3-2	W	29-43-5	**Fiset**	Vernon	25	34	0-1	1-4	**Tsyplakov**	**Ferraro**	**Fiset**
4/11	@Dal	2-6	L	29-44-5	Turek	**Fiset**	23	36	0-0	3-6	Zubov	Keane	Sydor
4/12	@Nsh	4-3	W	30-44-5	**Fiset**	Dunham	28	42	**2**-3	0-4	**Robitaille**	Walker	**Jokinen**
4/15	Anh	4-3*	W	31-44-5	**Fiset**	Roussel	**44**	25	**2**-5	0-3	**Ferraro**	Selanne	**Robitaille**
4/16	@SJ	2-**0**	W	32-44-5	**Fiset**	Vernon	34	33	1-6	0-4	**Fiset**	**Ferraro**	Nolan
4/18	StL	2-3	L	32-45-5	McLennan	**Bach**	38	27	0-4	0-3	Atcheynum	McLennan	**J.Blake**

Los Angeles Kings 1998-99 Player Statistics

Regular Season

Skater	Ps	GP	G	A	Pts	+/–	PIM	PP	SH	GW	GT	S	SPct	P/G
Luc Robitaille	L	82	39	35	74	-1	54	11	0	7	0	292	13.4	.90
Donald Audette	R	49	18	18	36	7	51	6	0	2	0	152	11.8	.73
Rob Blake	D	62	12	23	35	-7	128	5	1	2	0	216	5.6	.56
Jozef Stumpel	C	64	13	21	34	-18	10	1	0	1	0	131	9.9	.53
Glen Murray	R	61	16	15	31	-14	36	3	3	3	0	173	9.2	.51
Ray Ferraro	C	65	13	18	31	0	59	4	0	4	0	84	15.5	.48
Yanic Perreault†	C	64	10	17	27	-3	30	2	2	1	0	113	8.8	.42
Vladimir Tsyplakov	L	69	11	12	23	-7	32	0	2	2	0	111	9.9	.33
Steve Duchesne†	D	60	4	19	23	-6	22	1	0	1	0	99	4.0	.38
* Olli Jokinen	C	66	9	12	21	-10	44	3	1	1	0	87	10.3	.32
Craig Johnson	L	69	7	12	19	-12	32	2	0	2	0	94	7.4	.28
Russ Courtnall	R	57	6	13	19	-9	19	0	1	1	0	77	7.8	.33
* Pavel Rosa	R	29	4	12	16	0	6	0	0	0	0	61	6.6	.55
Garry Galley	D	60	4	12	16	-9	30	3	0	0	0	77	5.2	.27
Doug Bodger	D	65	3	11	14	1	34	0	0	0	0	67	4.5	.22
Sean O'Donnell	D	80	1	13	14	1	186	0	0	0	0	64	1.6	.18
Ian Laperriere	C	72	3	10	13	-5	138	0	0	1	0	62	4.8	.18
Philippe Boucher	D	45	2	6	8	-12	32	1	0	0	0	87	2.3	.18
Mattias Norstrom	D	78	2	5	7	-10	36	0	1	0	0	61	3.3	.09
Sandy Moger	C	42	3	2	5	-9	26	0	0	2	0	28	10.7	.12
Nathan LaFayette	R	33	2	2	4	0	35	0	1	1	0	42	4.8	.12
* Josh Green	L	27	1	3	4	-5	8	1	0	0	0	35	2.9	.15
* Mark Visheau	D	28	1	3	4	-7	107	0	0	0	0	10	10.0	.14
Matt Johnson	L	49	2	1	3	-5	131	0	0	0	0	14	14.3	.06
Dave Babych†	D	8	0	2	2	-2	2	0	0	0	0	5	0.0	.25
* Jason Blake	C	1	1	0	1	1	0	0	0	0	0	5	20.0	1.00
* Jan Nemecek	D	6	1	0	1	-1	4	0	0	1	0	8	12.5	.17
Steve McKenna	L	20	1	0	1	-3	36	0	0	0	0	12	8.3	.05
Jaroslav Modry	D	5	0	1	1	1	0	0	0	0	0	11	0.0	.20
Sean Pronger†	C	13	0	1	1	2	4	0	0	0	0	8	0.0	.08
* Manny LeGace	G	17	0	1	1	—	0	0	0	0	0	0	—	.06
Eric Lacroix†	L	27	0	1	1	-5	12	0	0	0	0	17	0.0	.04
* Jamie Storr	G	28	0	1	1	—	6	0	0	0	0	0	—	.04
* Ryan Bach	G	3	0	0	0	—	0	0	0	0	0	0	—	.00
Brandon Convery†	C	3	0	0	0	-1	4	0	0	0	0	2	0.0	.00
Roman Vopat†	C	3	0	0	0	0	6	0	0	0	0	2	0.0	.00
Jason Podollan†	R	6	0	0	0	-3	5	0	0	0	0	7	0.0	.00
Dan Bylsma	R	8	0	0	0	-1	2	0	0	0	0	3	0.0	.00
Stephane Fiset	G	42	0	0	0	—	2	0	0	0	0	0	—	.00
Bench		—	—	—	—	—	0	—	—	—	—	—	—	—
TEAM TOTALS		82	189	302	491	-152	1369	43	12	32	0	2317	8.2	5.99

Postseason

GP	G	A	Pts	+/–	PIM	PP	SH	GW	OT	S	SPct	P/G

Team Did Not Qualify for Postseason Play

Regular Season

Goaltender	G	Min	GAA	W	L	T	ENG	ShO	GA	SA	SvPct
* Jamie Storr	28	1525	2.40	12	12	2	3	4	61	724	.916
Stephane Fiset	42	2403	2.60	18	21	1	2	3	104	1217	.915
* Manny LeGace	17	899	2.60	2	9	2	5	0	39	439	.911
* Ryan Bach	3	108	4.44	0	3	0	0	0	8	66	.879
TEAM TOTALS	82	4960	2.69	32	45	5	10	8	222	2456	.910

Postseason

G	Min	GAA	W	L	ENG	ShO	GA	SA	SvPct

1998-99 Los Angeles Kings

Record When:

Overtime games	5-2-5
In second game of back-to-back games	5-8-0
Vs playoff teams	20-33-3
Leading after two periods	23-4-1
Tied after two periods	6-11-4
Losing after two periods	3-30-0
Scoring first	25-9-4
More shots than opponents	17-17-2
Fewer shots than opponents	15-25-3
Team had at least one fighting major	18-26-4
Team had more PIM	13-19-3
Team had fewer PIM	16-18-2
Team had even PIM	3-8-0

Team

Longest winning streak	5	Dec. 28 — Jan. 7
Longest unbeaten streak	6	Dec. 28 — Jan. 9
Longest losing streak	6	Nov. 10 — Nov. 19
Longest winless streak	6	Nov. 10 — Nov. 19
Most shots, game	44	vs. Anh, Apr. 15
Most shots, period	19	2nd, vs. Van, Mar. 13
Fewest shots, game	17	2 times
Fewest shots, period	2	3rd, vs. Pit, Jan. 16

Individual

Longest goal streak	4	5 times
Longest point streak	5	2 times
Most goals, game	3	Luc Robitaille
Most assists, game	3	3 times
Most points, game	3	13 times
Highest +/–, game	3	4 times
Lowest +/–, game	-5	Russ Courtnall
Most shots, game	9	3 times

Did You Know?

The Kings are 0-12-6 in their last 18 games against the Dallas Stars, dating back to the start of the 1995-96 season. The 18-game winless streak is the longest current streak for any NHL team against a single opponent.

Miscellaneous

		NHL Rank
PP Pct.	13.1 (43-327)	24
SH goals allowed	11	23t
PK Pct.	85.8 (283-330)	9
SH goals scored	12	3t
Special Team Index	99.2	18
Shots on goal	2,317 (28.3/G)	12
Shots against	2,456 (30.0/G)	22
Unassisted goals	11	19t
Unassisted goals allowed	16	19t
Team Average Weight	207.4	3
Game Star Points	331	21

Game Star Breakdown

Player	1st	2nd	3rd	Pts
Luc Robitaille	10	9	4	81
Stephane Fiset	6	2	6	42
Rob Blake	1	8	1	30
Glen Murray	3	4	1	28
Jamie Storr	2	4	2	24
Donald Audette	4	0	2	22
Ray Ferraro	3	2	0	21
Jozef Stumpel	1	3	2	16
Manny LeGace	1	1	2	10
Mattias Norstrom	1	0	4	9
Olli Jokinen	1	0	3	8
Yanic Perreault	0	2	1	7
Ian Laperriere	1	0	1	6
Vladimir Tsyplakov	1	0	1	6
Philippe Boucher	1	0	0	5
Pavel Rosa	0	1	2	5
Steve Duchesne	0	1	1	4
Nathan LaFayette	0	1	0	3
Jason Blake	0	0	1	1
Russ Courtnall	0	0	1	1
Matt Johnson	0	0	1	1
Mark Visheau	0	0	1	1

Montreal Canadiens 1998-99 Game Log (32-39-11)

Date	Opp	Score	W/L/T	Record	Goalies W/T	Goalies L/T	Shots Mon	Shots Opp	Power Plays Mon	Power Plays Opp	Game Stars 1st	Game Stars 2nd	Game Stars 3rd
10/10	NYR	7-1	W	1-0-0	**Thibault**	Richter	30	21	1-6	1-5	**Recchi**	**Brunet**	**Thibault**
10/13	Anh	1-0	W	2-0-0	**Thibault**	Hebert	24	30	1-3	0-3	**Thibault**	**Malakhov**	Hebert
10/16	@Was	2-2*	T	2-0-1	**Thibault**	Kolzig	27	36	0-2	1-3	**Thibault**	**Thornton**	Oates
10/17	Buf	3-4	L	2-1-1	Hasek	**Thibault**	35	27	0-3	2-11	Ward	**Damphousse**	**Brunet**
10/19	Chi	1-2	L	2-2-1	Fitzpatrick	**Theodore**	27	20	1-6	0-3	Fitzpatrick	Daze	**Damphousse**
10/21	Ott	3-2	W	3-2-1	**Thibault**	Rhodes	18	28	1-5	0-3	**Thibault**	**Recchi**	Dackell
10/24	Det	0-3	L	3-3-1	Osgood	**Thibault**	18	29	0-3	1-4	Yzerman	Osgood	Lidstrom
10/28	Bos	2-9	L	3-4-1	Dafoe	**Theodore**	35	34	0-5	5-9	Dafoe	Ferraro	Thornton
10/29	@Bos	1-1*	T	3-4-2	**Thibault**	Dafoe	23	31	1-5	1-9	**Recchi**	**Thibault**	Dafoe
10/31	@Ott	1-5	L	3-5-2	Tugnutt	**Thibault**	28	28	0-5	1-2	Tugnutt	Yashin	McEachern
11/04	@NYR	4-1	W	4-5-2	**Theodore**	Richter	32	20	1-4	0-4	**Recchi**	**Theodore**	MacLean
11/07	NYI	4-2	W	5-5-2	**Theodore**	Salo	23	30	4-7	0-6	**Recchi**	**Theodore**	Lapointe
11/09	Phi	5-1	W	6-5-2	**Theodore**	Vanbiesbrouck	19	31	1-5	0-7	**Savage**	**Theodore**	**Rucinsky**
11/11	@NJ	0-3	L	6-6-2	Brodeur	**Theodore**	24	32	0-8	1-6	Niedermayer	Brodeur	Brylin
11/12	@NYI	0-4	L	6-7-2	Salo	**Thibault**	21	25	0-4	1-6	Czerkawski	Salo	Richter
11/14	Edm	1-4	L	6-8-2	Shtalenkov	**Theodore**	26	27	0-8	1-7	Guerin	Murray	Shtalenkov
11/17	@Car	4-5	L	6-9-2	Irbe	**Theodore**	31	26	3-7	1-4	Dineen	Sheppard	Roberts
11/19	Cgy	4-3	W	7-9-2	**Hackett**	Giguere	36	19	1-6	1-5	**Stevenson**	**Damphousse**	Giguere
11/21	Col	2-3	L	7-10-2	Roy	**Hackett**	22	26	1-5	0-4	Forsberg	**Brunet**	DeVries
11/27	@Bos	1-5	L	7-11-2	Dafoe	**Hackett**	25	26	0-5	0-3	Bourque	DiMaio	Samsonov
11/28	Pit	3-4	L	7-12-2	Barrasso	**Theodore**	31	18	1-4	1-3	Straka	**Poulin**	Morozov
11/30	LA	3-1	W	8-12-2	**Hackett**	Fiset	30	19	1-4	0-2	**Koivu**	**Savage**	**Hackett**
12/02	@Car	1-4	L	8-13-2	Kidd	**Hackett**	25	20	0-2	1-2	Sheppard	Wesley	Kidd
12/04	@NJ	1-1*	T	8-13-3	**Hackett**	Brodeur	22	38	0-2	0-3	Andreychuk	**Corson**	Odelein
12/05	Tor	3-4*	L	8-14-3	Joseph	**Hackett**	28	26	1-4	1-6	Kaberle	**Rucinsky**	Yushkevich
12/09	@Pho	2-4	L	8-15-3	Waite	**Hackett**	21	23	0-6	1-4	Tkachuk	Numminen	Sullivan
12/11	@Dal	2-3	L	8-16-3	Belfour	**Theodore**	23	30	1-4	0-6	Langenbrunner	Marshall	Carbonneau
12/12	@Nsh	2-2*	T	8-16-4	**Hackett**	Vokoun	27	43	0-2	1-3	Walker	**Hoglund**	Brunette
12/14	Pho	2-2*	T	8-16-5	**Hackett**	Khabibulin	35	31	0-5	0-4	**Corson**	**Hoglund**	Tverdovsky
12/18	@Buf	2-4	L	8-17-5	Hasek	**Theodore**	38	21	0-7	0-5	Ward	Hasek	Brown
12/19	NJ	1-1*	T	8-17-6	**Hackett**	Brodeur	23	31	0-7	0-6	**Hackett**	**Weinrich**	Brodeur
12/21	Dal	2-2*	T	8-17-7	**Hackett**	Belfour	29	37	0-0	0-1	**Hackett**	Sydor	**Ulanov**
12/23	@Ott	1-3	L	8-18-7	Tugnutt	**Hackett**	25	30	1-4	0-4	Phillips	Arvedson	Tugnutt
12/26	@Tor	2-1	W	9-18-7	**Hackett**	Joseph	27	30	0-4	0-5	**Hackett**	Sundin	**Quintal**
12/29	@Edm	5-2	W	10-18-7	**Hackett**	Shtalenkov	34	22	1-5	0-4	**Recchi**	**Koivu**	**Weinrich**
12/31	@Cgy	2-1	W	11-18-7	**Hackett**	Trefilov	24	26	2-3	0-4	**Hackett**	Trefilov	**Koivu**
1/02	@Van	2-1	W	12-18-7	**Hackett**	Hirsch	22	17	0-2	1-6	**Hackett**	**Rucinsky**	Hirsch
1/04	@Col	3-4	L	12-19-7	Denis	**Theodore**	34	28	0-5	2-5	Lemieux	Sakic	Drury
1/07	TB	4-1	W	13-19-7	**Hackett**	Ranford	33	20	2-6	0-4	**Malakhov**	**Corson**	Ranford
1/09	NYI	3-2	W	14-19-7	**Hackett**	Cousineau	23	23	1-4	0-3	**Quintal**	**Poulin**	Nemchinov
1/11	StL	3-1	W	15-19-7	**Hackett**	McLennan	25	23	1-4	0-2	McLennan	**Damphousse**	**Recchi**
1/12	@Det	1-5	L	15-20-7	Osgood	**Hackett**	18	39	0-2	0-3	Fedorov	Yzerman	Gill
1/15	@Was	3-0	W	16-20-7	**Hackett**	Kolzig	25	23	0-3	0-2	**Recchi**	**Malakhov**	**Hackett**
1/16	NYR	3-0	W	17-20-7	**Hackett**	Cloutier	32	17	2-4	0-3	**Malakhov**	**Hackett**	**Koivu**
1/18	Was	4-4*	T	17-20-8	**Hackett**	Tabaracci	30	28	1-3	2-3	**Malakhov**	Bondra	**Savage**
1/21	@Chi	0-3	L	17-21-8	Thibault	**Hackett**	33	37	0-2	1-4	Thibault	**Hackett**	Gilmour
1/26	@TB	2-1	W	18-21-8	**Hackett**	Schwab	29	29	0-3	0-2	**Hackett**	**Rucinsky**	Hogue
1/27	@Fla	1-2	L	18-22-8	Burke	**Hackett**	30	32	0-5	0-4	Burke	**Brisebois**	Bure
1/30	Car	1-3	L	18-23-8	Irbe	**Hackett**	45	10	1-7	2-5	Irbe	Kron	**Rucinsky**
1/31	Pit	3-5	L	18-24-8	Skudra	**Hackett**	26	24	2-5	1-4	Jagr	Slegr	Titov
2/03	Van	2-1	W	19-24-8	**Hackett**	Hirsch	34	22	0-4	1-5	**Stevenson**	**Poulin**	Hirsch
2/04	@Phi	2-5	L	19-25-8	Vanbiesbrouck	**Hackett**	21	24	0-5	1-4	LeClair	McGillis	Lindros
2/06	Buf	3-2	W	20-25-8	**Hackett**	Roloson	19	29	1-2	1-7	**Weinrich**	Peca	**Chabot**
2/09	@Pit	2-3*	L	20-26-8	Barrasso	**Chabot**	29	32	1-7	0-5	Jagr	Kovalev	Barrasso
2/11	@Buf	2-5	L	20-27-8	Hasek	**Theodore**	37	17	0-6	0-4	Cunneyworth	Hasek	Kruse

2/13	Fla	4-**0**	W	21-27-8	**Hackett**	Burke	35	16	2-6	0-6	**Koivu**	**Corson**	**Dawe**
2/17	@NYR	6-3	W	22-27-8	**Hackett**	Cloutier	**46**	38	0-3	2-9	**Brunet**	Knuble	**Recchi**
2/18	@Phi	3-1	W	23-27-8	**Hackett**	Vanbiesbrouck	21	22	1-3	0-3	**Brunet**	**Recchi**	Lindros
2/20	@Tor	2-3*	L	23-28-8	Joseph	**Hackett**	30	24	1-5	0-5	Sundin	**Recchi**	Joseph
2/25	@Ott	1-3	L	23-29-8	Rhodes	**Hackett**	25	28	0-5	0-2	Johansson	Rhodes	Yashin
2/27	Ott	4-1	W	24-29-8	**Hackett**	Rhodes	29	26	0-2	0-3	**Malakhov**	**Hackett**	**Koivu**
3/02	Phi	4-1	W	25-29-8	**Hackett**	Vanbiesbrouck	17	38	0-2	1-4	**Hackett**	**Quintal**	**Malakhov**
3/03	@Pit	4-4*	T	25-29-9	**Hackett**	Skudra	37	18	1-4	1-3	Jagr	**Malakhov**	Kasparaitis
3/06	TB	1-6	L	25-30-9	Schwab	**Hackett**	30	26	0-5	1-2	Clark	Richer	Schwab
3/08	Fla	2-5	L	25-31-9	McLean	**Hackett**	33	27	0-3	1-5	Whitney	Lindsay	Worrell
3/11	@StL	3-**0**	W	26-31-9	**Hackett**	Johnson	25	41	0-4	0-3	**Hackett**	**Koivu**	**Zubrus**
3/13	Tor	2-1	W	27-31-9	**Hackett**	Joseph	31	28	2-5	0-4	**Damphousse**	Joseph	**Hackett**
3/18	Nsh	3-2	W	28-31-9	**Hackett**	Dunham	33	31	1-2	0-**1**	**Poulin**	Dunham	**Stevenson**
3/20	Was	0-1	L	28-32-9	Tabaracci	**Hackett**	29	21	0-4	0-3	Tabaracci	**Quintal**	**Hackett**
3/22	SJ	1-1*	T	28-32-10	**Hackett**	Shields	44	17	1-5	0-4	Shields	**Weinrich**	**Corson**
3/24	@Edm	2-**0**	W	29-32-10	**Hackett**	Salo	26	32	0-3	0-2	**Hackett**	**Koivu**	Beranek
3/25	@Cgy	1-2	L	29-33-10	Wregget	**Hackett**	28	36	1-5	0-5	Wregget	**Hackett**	Bure
3/27	@Van	1-5	L	29-34-10	Snow	**Hackett**	22	24	0-7	2-8	Ohlund	Messier	Aucoin
4/01	Bos	2-3	L	29-35-10	Dafoe	**Hackett**	24	24	0-2	1-4	Carter	Bourque	Thornton
4/03	Buf	2-1	W	30-35-10	**Chabot**	Hasek	24	32	1-5	0-3	**Chabot**	**Koivu**	Peca
4/05	@Bos	0-3	L	30-36-10	Dafoe	**Chabot**	25	26	0-1	1-3	Carter	Sweeney	Dafoe
4/07	Car	2-**0**	W	31-36-10	**Theodore**	Irbe	31	27	0-2	0-3	**Theodore**	**Thornton**	**Rivet**
4/08	@NYI	1-3	L	31-37-10	Flaherty	**Theodore**	21	29	1-3	0-3	Czerkawski	Palffy	Linden
4/10	NJ	2-6	L	31-38-10	Brodeur	**Theodore**	28	31	1-4	0-2	Elias	Rolston	Sykora
4/13	@TB	2-2*	T	31-38-11	**Hackett**	Wilkinson	27	22	0-5	0-5	Kubina	Gratton	**Savage**
4/14	@Fla	2-3*	L	31-39-11	McLean	**Chabot**	21	31	0-2	0-2	Nilson	Parrish	Dvorak
4/17	Tor	3-2	W	32-39-11	**Hackett**	Joseph	16	27	1-3	0-6	**Quintal**	Cote	**Weinrich**

Montreal Canadiens 1998-99 Player Statistics

Regular Season

Skater	Ps	GP	G	A	Pts	+/–	PIM	PP	SH	GW	GT	S	SPct	P/G
Mark Recchi†	R	61	12	**35**	**47**	-4	28	3	0	2	0	152	7.9	**.77**
Saku Koivu	C	65	14	30	44	-7	38	4	**2**	0	0	145	9.7	.68
V. Damphousse†	C	65	12	24	36	-7	46	3	**2**	2	0	147	8.2	.55
Martin Rucinsky	L	73	**17**	17	34	-25	50	5	0	1	0	**180**	9.4	.47
Vladimir Malakhov	D	62	13	21	34	-7	77	**8**	0	3	0	143	9.1	.55
Shayne Corson	L	63	12	20	32	-10	**147**	7	0	**4**	0	142	8.5	.51
Benoit Brunet	L	60	14	17	31	-1	31	4	**2**	0	0	115	12.2	.52
Turner Stevenson	R	69	10	17	27	**6**	88	0	0	2	**1**	102	9.8	.39
Stephane Quintal	D	**82**	8	19	27	-23	84	1	1	**4**	0	159	5.0	.33
Brian Savage	L	54	16	10	26	-14	20	5	0	**4**	**1**	124	**12.9**	.48
Patrick Poulin	L	81	8	17	25	**6**	21	0	1	1	0	87	9.2	.31
Sergei Zholtok	C	70	7	15	22	-12	6	2	0	3	0	102	6.9	.31
Jonas Hoglund	R	74	8	10	18	-5	16	1	0	0	**1**	122	6.6	.24
Eric Weinrich†	D	66	6	12	18	-12	77	4	0	1	**1**	95	6.3	.27
Patrice Brisebois	D	54	3	9	12	-8	28	1	0	1	0	90	3.3	.22
Igor Ulanov	D	76	3	9	12	-3	109	0	0	0	0	55	5.5	.16
Scott Thornton	C	47	7	4	11	-2	87	1	0	1	**1**	56	12.5	.23
Craig Rivet	D	66	2	8	10	-3	66	0	0	0	0	39	5.1	.15
Jason Dawe†	R	37	4	5	9	0	14	1	0	1	0	52	7.7	.24
Dainius Zubrus†	R	17	3	5	8	-3	4	0	0	1	0	31	9.7	.47
Brett Clark	D	61	2	2	4	-3	16	0	0	0	0	36	5.6	.07
Eric Houde	C	8	1	1	2	-2	2	0	0	1	0	4	25.0	.25
Scott Lachance†	D	17	1	1	2	-2	11	0	0	0	0	22	4.5	.12
Dave Manson†	D	11	0	2	2	-3	48	0	0	0	0	11	0.0	.18
* Matt Higgins	C	25	1	0	1	-2	0	0	0	0	0	12	8.3	.04
* Miloslav Guren	D	12	0	1	1	-1	4	0	0	0	0	11	0.0	.08
Jeff Hackett†	G	53	0	1	1	—	6	0	0	0	0	0	—	.02
* Jonathan Delisle	R	1	0	0	0	0	0	0	0	0	0	0	—	.00
* Terry Ryan	L	1	0	0	0	0	5	0	0	0	0	0	—	.00
* Sylvain Blouin	L	5	0	0	0	0	19	0	0	0	0	1	0.0	.00
* Brad Brown†	D	5	0	0	0	0	21	0	0	0	0	0	—	.00
J.F. Jomphe†	C	6	0	0	0	0	0	0	0	0	0	4	0.0	.00
* Arron Asham	R	7	0	0	0	-4	0	0	0	0	0	5	0.0	.00
* Alain Nasreddine†	D	8	0	0	0	1	33	0	0	0	0	1	0.0	.00
* Andrei Bashkirov	L	10	0	0	0	-3	0	0	0	0	0	4	0.0	.00
* Dave Morrisette	L	10	0	0	0	1	52	0	0	0	0	2	0.0	.00
Jocelyn Thibault†	G	10	0	0	0	—	0	0	0	0	0	0	—	.00
Frederic Chabot	G	11	0	0	0	—	2	0	0	0	0	0	—	.00
* Jose Theodore	G	18	0	0	0	—	0	0	0	0	0	0	—	.00
Trent McCleary	R	46	0	0	0	-1	29	0	0	0	0	18	0.0	.00
Bench		—	—	—	—	—	0	—	—	—	—	—	—	—
TEAM TOTALS		82	184	312	496	-153	1285	50	8	32	5	2269	8.1	6.05

Postseason

GP	G	A	Pts	+/–	PIM	PP	SH	GW	OT	S	SPct	P/G

Team Did Not Qualify for Postseason Play

Regular Season

Goaltender	G	Min	GAA	W	L	T	ENG	ShO	GA	SA	SvPct
Frederic Chabot	11	430	2.23	1	3	0	0	0	16	188	.915
Jeff Hackett†	**53**	**3091**	**2.27**	**24**	**20**	**9**	**2**	**5**	**117**	**1360**	**.914**
Jocelyn Thibault†	10	529	2.61	3	4	2	0	1	23	250	.908
* Jose Theodore	18	913	3.29	4	12	0	1	1	50	406	.877
TEAM TOTALS	82	4988	2.51	32	39	11	3	7	209	2207	.905

Postseason

G	Min	GAA	W	L	ENG	ShO	GA	SA	SvPct

1998-99 Montreal Canadiens

Record When:

Overtime games	0-4-11
In second game of back-to-back games	2-11-4
Vs playoff teams	16-28-7
Leading after two periods	25-4-5
Tied after two periods	6-12-4
Losing after two periods	1-23-2
Scoring first	27-11-5
More shots than opponents	17-16-5
Fewer shots than opponents	13-21-6
Team had at least one fighting major	9-16-3
Team had more PIM	13-17-5
Team had fewer PIM	16-19-5
Team had even PIM	3-3-1

Team

Longest winning streak	4	Dec. 26 — Jan. 2
Longest unbeaten streak	4	Dec. 26 — Jan. 2
Longest losing streak	4	Nov. 11 — Nov. 17
Longest winless streak	11	Dec. 2 — Dec. 23
Most shots, game	46	@NYR, Feb. 17
Most shots, period	21	1st, @NYR, Feb. 17
Fewest shots, game	16	vs. Tor, Apr. 17
Fewest shots, period	2	3rd, @NJ, Dec. 4

Individual

Longest goal streak	4	2 times
Longest point streak	6	2 times
Most goals, game	2	9 times
Most assists, game	4	2 times
Most points, game	4	3 times
Highest +/–, game	4	2 times
Lowest +/–, game	-4	3 times
Most shots, game	7	2 times

Did You Know?

Excluding the lockout-shortened 1994-95 campaign, last year marked the first season in 50 years in which no Montreal player scored at least 50 points. Mark Recchi, who was traded to Philadelphia in March, led the Canadiens with 47 points in '98-99.

Miscellaneous

		NHL Rank
PP Pct.	14.5 (50-344)	16
SH goals allowed	10	18t
PK Pct.	87.2 (300-344)	4
SH goals scored	8	8t
Special Team Index	101.2	10
Shots on goal	2,269 (27.7/G)	15
Shots against	2,207 (26.9/G)	8
Unassisted goals	12	16t
Unassisted goals allowed	19	24t
Team Average Weight	202.2	11
Game Star Points	338	19

Game Star Breakdown

Player	1st	2nd	3rd	Pts
Jeff Hackett	9	4	4	61
Mark Recchi	6	3	2	41
Vladimir Malakhov	4	3	1	30
Saku Koivu	2	4	3	25
Jocelyn Thibault	3	1	1	19
Benoit Brunet	2	2	1	17
Stephane Quintal	2	2	1	17
Shayne Corson	1	3	1	15
Vincent Damphousse	1	3	1	15
Patrick Poulin	1	3	0	14
Jose Theodore	1	3	0	14
Eric Weinrich	1	2	2	13
Turner Stevenson	2	0	1	11
Martin Rucinsky	0	3	2	11
Brian Savage	1	1	2	10
Frederic Chabot	1	0	1	6
Jonas Hoglund	0	2	0	6
Scott Thornton	0	2	0	6
Patrice Brisebois	0	1	0	3
Jason Dawe	0	0	1	1
Craig Rivet	0	0	1	1
Igor Ulanov	0	0	1	1
Dainius Zubrus	0	0	1	1

Nashville Predators 1998-99 Game Log (28-47-7)

					Goalies		Shots		Power Plays		Game Stars		
Date	Opp	Score	W/L/T	Record	W/T	L/T	Nsh	Opp	Nsh	Opp	1st	2nd	3rd
10/10	Fla	0-1	L	0-1-0	McLean	**Dunham**	26	26	0-6	1-9	Whitney	McLean	**Dunham**
10/13	Car	3-2	W	1-1-0	**Dunham**	Kidd	30	36	1-3	0-8	**Dunham**	**Brunette**	**Johnson**
10/17	@Ott	1-3	L	1-2-0	Tugnutt	**Dunham**	22	34	0-6	1-6	Tugnutt	**Dunham**	Johansson
10/19	@Tor	2-2*	T	1-2-1	**Dunham**	Joseph	25	32	1-5	0-5	**Dunham**	McCauley	Sullivan
10/21	@Det	2-5	L	1-3-1	Osgood	**Dunham**	15	57	0-3	2-9	McCarty	**Dunham**	Roest
10/23	Cgy	3-4	L	1-4-1	Wregget	**Dunham**	27	24	1-**8**	2-6	Iginla	**Johnson**	Housley
10/24	@Chi	4-5	L	1-5-1	Fitzpatrick	**Fichaud**	23	25	1-3	1-4	Amonte	Kilger	Zhamnov
10/27	Van	5-4	W	2-5-1	**Dunham**	Snow	30	31	1-5	2-6	**Krivokrasov**	**Fitzgerald**	Mogilny
10/31	Col	3-2	W	3-5-1	**Dunham**	Roy	27	43	1-**8**	1-5	**Dunham**	**Brunette**	Forsberg
11/04	@Edm	2-3	L	3-6-1	Essensa	**Dunham**	28	29	0-6	0-4	Beranek	Essensa	**Ronning**
11/06	@Cgy	2-1	W	4-6-1	**Dunham**	Moss	27	32	1-3	1-5	**Dunham**	Iginla	**Fitzgerald**
11/07	@Van	3-5	L	4-7-1	Hirsch	**Vokoun**	30	21	0-5	1-4	Ohlund	Hirsch	**Johnson**
11/10	@SJ	4-2	W	5-7-1	**Dunham**	Vernon	20	35	0-5	1-6	**Krivokrasov**	**Dunham**	Nolan
11/12	@LA	3-1	W	6-7-1	**Dunham**	LeGace	18	36	0-2	0-3	**Dunham**	**Peltonen**	Stumpel
11/14	@StL	1-5	L	6-8-1	McLennan	**Dunham**	17	39	0-4	1-2	Conroy	Young	Pronger
11/17	Chi	1-2	L	6-9-1	Fitzpatrick	**Dunham**	38	32	1-6	1-4	Amonte	Gilmour	**Ronning**
11/19	StL	3-2	W	7-9-1	**Dunham**	McLennan	32	31	0-5	0-4	**Ronning**	**Dunham**	**Lambert**
11/21	NYI	3-6	L	7-10-1	Salo	**Dunham**	42	40	1-4	3-6	Watt	Reichel	**Turcotte**
11/24	@StL	0-4	L	7-11-1	McLennan	**Fichaud**	19	41	0-3	2-3	Demitra	MacInnis	McLennan
11/25	Cgy	4-3	W	8-11-1	**Dunham**	Giguere	33	22	1-6	0-3	**Yachmenev**	**Bouchard**	Iginla
11/27	Anh	3-1	W	9-11-1	**Dunham**	Roussel	31	27	1-4	1-8	**Kjellberg**	**Dunham**	**Bouchard**
11/29	@NYR	1-5	L	9-12-1	Richter	**Dunham**	25	35	0-3	2-3	Gretzky	MacLean	Stevens
12/01	Ott	1-3	L	9-13-1	Tugnutt	**Fichaud**	28	35	0-3	1-3	Tugnutt	Alfredsson	Redden
12/05	Buf	1-3	L	9-14-1	Hasek	**Fichaud**	37	28	1-7	0-3	Hasek	**Fichaud**	Holzinger
12/08	Edm	3-3*	T	9-14-2	**Vokoun**	Shtalenkov	27	40	0-4	2-6	**Ronning**	Guerin	**Kjellberg**
12/10	SJ	2-1	W	10-14-2	**Vokoun**	Shields	26	35	1-3	0-5	**Bordeleau**	**Vokoun**	**Krivokrasov**
12/12	Mon	2-2*	T	10-14-3	**Vokoun**	Hackett	**43**	27	1-3	0-2	**Walker**	Hoglund	**Brunette**
12/16	@Anh	1-6	L	10-15-3	Hebert	**Vokoun**	39	37	0-4	4-7	Hebert	Selanne	Green
12/17	@SJ	1-3	L	10-16-3	Vernon	**Vokoun**	31	27	0-4	1-3	Sturm	Korolyuk	Vernon
12/19	@Van	**6**-4	W	11-16-3	**Vokoun**	Snow	24	24	**3**-4	2-4	**Bordeleau**	**Krivokrasov**	Naslund
12/23	Det	5-3	W	12-16-3	**Vokoun**	Osgood	34	53	0-5	0-3	**Vokoun**	**Ronning**	**Walker**
12/26	Was	3-1	W	13-16-3	**Vokoun**	Kolzig	28	27	0-5	0-3	**Vokoun**	**Boughner**	**Johnson**
12/28	@Dal	0-1	L	13-17-3	Belfour	**Fichaud**	14	21	0-1	0-5	Chambers	Matvichuk	Belfour
12/30	Bos	2-5	L	13-18-3	Tallas	**Vokoun**	29	38	0-3	1-4	Carter	Heinze	**Bordeleau**
1/01	StL	5-6	L	13-19-3	McLennan	**Fichaud**	29	37	1-2	2-3	Demitra	**Johnson**	Yake
1/02	@Car	1-4	L	13-20-3	Kidd	**Vokoun**	27	22	0-4	2-7	Kapanen	Kidd	Wesley
1/04	Anh	2-1	W	14-20-3	**Vokoun**	Hebert	20	29	1-4	1-4	**Ronning**	**Vokoun**	Kariya
1/07	SJ	3-4	L	14-21-3	Vernon	**Vokoun**	33	30	1-6	0-2	Granato	**Ronning**	Murphy
1/09	Chi	3-3*	T	14-21-4	**Vokoun**	Fitzpatrick	27	34	0-4	0-3	**Johnson**	**Yachmenev**	**Berehowsky**
1/11	@Phi	0-8	L	14-22-4	Vanbiesbrouck	**Vokoun**	24	41	0-5	4-6	Lindros	McGillis	Vanbiesbrouck
1/14	@Det	1-2*	L	14-23-4	Osgood	**Vokoun**	16	41	0-4	0-3	**Vokoun**	Maltby	Kozlov
1/15	Pho	2-**0**	W	15-23-4	**Vokoun**	Khabibulin	31	31	1-4	0-5	**Vokoun**	**Ronning**	Khabibulin
1/18	@Bos	1-8	L	15-24-4	Dafoe	**Vokoun**	17	37	0-3	1-5	Heinze	Ferraro	Sweeney
1/19	Van	4-1	W	16-24-4	**Dunham**	Snow	40	19	0-3	0-4	**Atcheynum**	**Krivokrasov**	**Johnson**
1/21	TB	2-3	L	16-25-4	Ranford	**Dunham**	36	26	0-5	1-4	Ranford	**Krivokrasov**	Cross
1/26	Det	1-4	L	16-26-4	Osgood	**Dunham**	26	33	1-7	1-5	Fedorov	Larionov	**Atcheynum**
1/28	@Buf	4-2	W	17-26-4	**Vokoun**	Hasek	31	32	1-5	0-2	**Atcheynum**	**Ronning**	Peca
1/30	@NJ	3-2*	W	18-26-4	**Dunham**	Brodeur	23	29	0-3	1-3	**Bordeleau**	**Dunham**	Pederson
1/31	Pho	1-5	L	18-27-4	Khabibulin	**Vokoun**	20	33	0-3	0-2	Tkachuk	Khabibulin	**Johnson**
2/04	@Cgy	2-2*	T	18-27-5	**Dunham**	Brathwaite	27	36	1-4	0-4	Albelin	**Fitzgerald**	Nazarov
2/05	@Edm	2-4	L	18-28-5	Essensa	**Vokoun**	23	32	2-4	1-6	Guerin	**Ronning**	Selivanov
2/09	Det	2-5	L	18-29-5	Osgood	**Dunham**	21	50	0-1	0-4	Shanahan	Fedorov	**Johnson**
2/12	@NYI	2-1	W	19-29-5	**Dunham**	Potvin	23	41	0-2	1-6	**Dunham**	**Ronning**	**Krivokrasov**
2/13	Pit	2-3*	L	19-30-5	Skudra	**Vokoun**	34	34	0-6	0-6	**Vokoun**	Skudra	Miller
2/15	NYR	4-7	L	19-31-5	Cloutier	**Vokoun**	33	28	0-5	3-6	Gretzky	**Walker**	Harvey

2/19	Col	4-4*	T	19-31-6	**Dunham**	Roy	36	43	**3-8**	2-5	**Krivokrasov**	Sakic	**Ronning**
2/20	@StL	4-3	W	20-31-6	**Vokoun**	McLennan	22	37	1-5	0-2	**Vokoun**	**Heward**	**Slaney**
2/23	Dal	3-4	L	20-32-6	Belfour	**Dunham**	32	45	0-3	0-3	Modano	**Dunham**	**Walker**
2/24	@Dal	2-1	W	21-32-6	**Vokoun**	Turek	25	**18**	1-3	0-2	**Krivokrasov**	**Ronning**	**Vokoun**
2/27	@Col	1-3	L	21-33-6	Roy	**Dunham**	22	32	0-0	2-5	Deadmarsh	Messier	Lemieux
3/02	StL	1-5	L	21-34-6	Johnson	**Dunham**	31	35	0-3	0-3	Chase	Conroy	Eastwood
3/04	@LA	4-3	W	22-34-6	**Dunham**	Storr	22	35	0-2	2-4	Audette	**Bordeleau**	**Slaney**
3/05	@Anh	2-3	L	22-35-6	Roussel	**Dunham**	24	34	1-4	1-4	Nielsen	Drury	Salei
3/07	@Pho	3-4	L	22-36-6	Khabibulin	**Dunham**	26	35	0-1	0-3	Tkachuk	Drake	**Walker**
3/10	@Chi	2-5	L	22-37-6	Thibault	**Dunham**	21	38	0-1	1-4	Daze	Chelios	Zhamnov
3/12	Chi	5-3	W	23-37-6	**Dunham**	Thibault	30	34	2-7	1-7	**Bordeleau**	**Walker**	Amonte
3/14	Edm	3-1	W	24-37-6	**Dunham**	Passmore	20	25	1-5	0-5	**Bordeleau**	**Ronning**	**Dunham**
3/16	Cgy	2-4	L	24-38-6	Wregget	**Dunham**	34	34	2-4	1-2	Bure	Stillman	**Keczmer**
3/18	@Mon	2-3	L	24-39-6	Hackett	**Dunham**	31	33	0-1	1-2	Poulin	**Dunham**	Stevenson
3/20	@Pit	1-1*	T	24-39-7	**Vokoun**	Aubin	23	30	0-7	1-6	Lang	**Vokoun**	Aubin
3/24	@TB	3-**0**	W	25-39-7	**Dunham**	Schwab	24	27	0-3	0-4	**Krivokrasov**	**Johnson**	**Dunham**
3/26	@Fla	1-4	L	25-40-7	Burke	**Vokoun**	28	36	1-4	2-3	Dvorak	Boyle	Burke
3/28	Dal	0-3	L	25-41-7	Turek	**Vokoun**	21	34	0-4	0-2	Nieuwendyk	Turek	**Vokoun**
3/30	@Was	3-2	W	26-41-7	**Vokoun**	Tabaracci	23	36	0-3	1-6	**Walker**	**Boughner**	Gonchar
4/01	Phi	1-2	L	26-42-7	Vanbiesbrouck	**Vokoun**	23	39	0-1	0-4	Renberg	Brind'Amour	**Vokoun**
4/03	LA	3-2	W	27-42-7	**Vokoun**	Fiset	29	36	0-2	0-**1**	**Walker**	**Valicevic**	**Vokoun**
4/07	@Col	1-4	L	27-43-7	Roy	**Vokoun**	28	29	1-4	2-4	Drury	Roy	Foote
4/09	@Pho	4-3	W	28-43-7	**Vokoun**	Khabibulin	21	29	0-2	1-7	**Valicevic**	Adams	**Ronning**
4/12	LA	3-4	L	28-44-7	Fiset	**Dunham**	42	28	0-4	2-3	Robitaille	**Walker**	Jokinen
4/14	@Det	2-4	L	28-45-7	Ranford	**Dunham**	24	27	1-4	0-4	Murphy	Fedorov	Gilchrist
4/15	@Chi	2-4	L	28-46-7	Thibault	**Vokoun**	23	25	0-3	1-5	Zhamnov	Olczyk	**Timonen**
4/17	NJ	1-4	L	28-47-7	Brodeur	**Dunham**	28	40	0-5	2-4	Sykora	Morrison	Brodeur

Nashville Predators 1998-99 Player Statistics

Skater	Ps	Regular Season GP	G	A	Pts	+/–	PIM	PP	SH	GW	GT	S	SPct	P/G
Cliff Ronning†	C	72	18	**35**	**53**	-6	40	8	0	3	0	**239**	7.5	**.74**
Greg Johnson	C	68	16	34	50	-8	24	2	**3**	0	0	120	13.3	.74
Sergei Krivokrasov	R	70	**25**	23	48	-5	42	**10**	0	**6**	**1**	208	12.0	.69
Sebastien Bordeleau	C	72	16	24	40	-14	26	1	2	3	0	168	9.5	.56
Scott Walker	R	71	15	25	40	**0**	103	0	1	2	0	96	**15.6**	.56
Tom Fitzgerald	R	**80**	13	19	32	-18	48	0	0	1	0	180	7.2	.40
Patrik Kjellberg	R	71	11	20	31	-13	24	2	0	2	0	103	10.7	.44
Andrew Brunette	L	77	11	20	31	-10	26	7	0	1	0	65	16.9	.40
Jamie Heward	R	63	6	12	18	-24	44	4	0	1	0	124	4.8	.29
Vitali Yachmenev	R	55	7	10	17	-10	10	0	1	2	0	83	8.4	.31
Drake Berehowsky	D	74	2	15	17	-9	140	0	0	0	0	79	2.5	.23
Denny Lambert	L	76	5	11	16	-3	218	1	0	0	0	66	7.6	.21
Joel Bouchard	D	64	4	11	15	-10	60	0	0	0	0	78	5.1	.23
Blair Atcheynum†	R	53	8	6	14	-10	16	2	0	1	0	70	11.4	.26
John Slaney	D	46	2	12	14	-12	14	0	0	1	0	84	2.4	.30
Bob Boughner	D	79	3	10	13	-6	137	0	0	1	0	59	5.1	.16
* Kimmo Timonen	D	50	4	8	12	-4	30	1	0	0	0	75	5.3	.24
Jan Vopat	D	55	5	6	11	**0**	28	0	0	0	0	46	10.9	.20
Ville Peltonen	L	14	5	5	10	1	2	1	0	0	0	31	16.1	.71
Darren Turcotte	C	40	4	5	9	-11	16	0	0	1	0	73	5.5	.23
* Robert Valicevic	R	19	4	2	6	4	2	0	0	2	0	23	17.4	.32
* Mark Mowers	C	30	0	6	6	-4	4	0	0	0	0	24	0.0	.20
J.J. Daigneault†	D	35	2	2	4	-4	38	1	0	1	0	38	5.3	.11
Jeff Daniels	L	9	1	3	4	-1	2	0	0	0	0	8	12.5	.44
Jeff Nelson	C	9	2	1	3	-1	2	0	0	0	0	8	25.0	.33
* Patrick Cote	L	70	1	2	3	-7	**242**	0	0	0	0	21	4.8	.04
Jay More	D	18	0	2	2	2	18	0	0	0	0	24	0.0	.11
Doug Friedman	L	2	0	1	1	0	14	0	0	0	0	3	0.0	.50
* Karlis Skrastinsh	D	2	0	1	1	0	0	0	0	0	0	0	—	.50
Tomas Vokoun	G	37	0	1	1	—	6	0	0	0	0	1	0.0	.03
* David Legwand	C	1	0	0	0	0	0	0	0	0	0	2	0.0	.00
* Matt Henderson	R	2	0	0	0	-1	2	0	0	0	0	0	—	.00
* Petr Sykora	C	2	0	0	0	-1	0	0	0	0	0	2	0.0	.00
Rob Zettler	D	2	0	0	0	-2	2	0	0	0	0	0	—	.00
* Chris Mason	G	3	0	0	0	—	0	0	0	0	0	0	—	.00
Brad Smyth	R	3	0	0	0	-1	6	0	0	0	0	5	0.0	.00
Greg DeVries†	D	6	0	0	0	-4	4	0	0	0	0	1	0.0	.00
Eric Fichaud	G	9	0	0	0	—	0	0	0	0	0	0	—	.00
Dan Keczmer†	D	16	0	0	0	-3	12	0	0	0	0	12	0.0	.00
Mike Dunham	G	44	0	0	0	—	4	0	0	0	0	0	—	.00
Bench		—	—	—	—	—	0	—	—	—	—	—	—	—
TEAM TOTALS		82	190	332	522	-195	1406	40	7	28	1	2219	8.6	6.37

Postseason — GP G A Pts +/– PIM PP SH GW OT S SPct P/G

Team Did Not Qualify for Postseason Play

Goaltender	Regular Season G	Min	GAA	W	L	T	ENG	ShO	GA	SA	SvPct
Tomas Vokoun	37	1954	**2.95**	12	18	**4**	**4**	**1**	96	1041	.908
Mike Dunham	**44**	**2472**	3.08	**16**	**23**	3	3	**1**	**127**	**1387**	**.908**
Eric Fichaud	9	447	3.22	0	6	0	1	0	24	229	.895
* Chris Mason	3	69	5.22	0	0	0	0	0	6	44	.864
TEAM TOTALS	82	4964	3.15	28	47	7	8	2	261	2709	.904

Postseason — G Min GAA W L ENG ShO GA SA SvPct

1998-99 Nashville Predators

Record When:

Overtime games	1-2-7
In second game of back-to-back games	5-9-0
Vs playoff teams	15-32-4
Leading after two periods	17-2-5
Tied after two periods	6-6-2
Losing after two periods	5-39-0
Scoring first	16-7-3
More shots than opponents	6-12-1
Fewer shots than opponents	20-32-6
Team had at least one fighting major	17-27-4
Team had more PIM	14-20-3
Team had fewer PIM	10-18-3
Team had even PIM	4-9-1

Team

Longest winning streak	3	Dec. 19 — Dec. 26
Longest unbeaten streak	3	2 times
Longest losing streak	4	2 times
Longest winless streak	5	Oct. 17 — Oct. 24
Most shots, game	43	vs. Mon, Dec. 12
Most shots, period	20	2nd, vs. Mon, Dec. 12
Fewest shots, game	14	@Dal, Dec. 28
Fewest shots, period	2	4 times

Individual

Longest goal streak	5	2 times
Longest point streak	7	Greg Johnson
Most goals, game	2	16 times
Most assists, game	3	Sebastien Bordeleau
Most points, game	4	2 times
Highest +/–, game	3	8 times
Lowest +/–, game	-3	14 times
Most shots, game	9	Sebastien Bordeleau

Did You Know?

Last year Predators defensemen scored only 89 points, the fewest of any team, and tied for the fewest by a team in the last 23 seasons. Since 1976-77, only the 1997-98 Tampa Bay Lightning recorded as few as 89 points by their defense.

Miscellaneous

		NHL Rank
PP Pct.	12.3 (40-324)	25
SH goals allowed	10	18t
PK Pct.	79.0 (282-357)	27
SH goals scored	7	15t
Special Team Index	90.2	27
Shots on goal	2,219 (27.1/G)	18
Shots against	2,709 (33.0/G)	27
Unassisted goals	10	21t
Unassisted goals allowed	17	21t
Team Average Weight	194.1	27
Game Star Points	328	22

Game Star Breakdown

Player	1st	2nd	3rd	Pts
Mike Dunham	6	8	3	57
Tomas Vokoun	6	3	4	43
Cliff Ronning	3	8	4	43
Sergei Krivokrasov	5	3	2	36
Sebastien Bordeleau	5	1	1	29
Scott Walker	3	3	3	27
Greg Johnson	1	3	6	20
Blair Atcheynum	2	0	1	11
Robert Valicevic	1	1	0	8
Vitali Yachmenev	1	1	0	8
Andrew Brunette	0	2	1	7
Tom Fitzgerald	0	2	1	7
Patrik Kjellberg	1	0	1	6
Bob Boughner	0	2	0	6
Joel Bouchard	0	1	1	4
Eric Fichaud	0	1	0	3
Jamie Heward	0	1	0	3
Ville Peltonen	0	1	0	3
John Slaney	0	0	2	2
Drake Berehowsky	0	0	1	1
Dan Keczmer	0	0	1	1
Denny Lambert	0	0	1	1
Kimmo Timonen	0	0	1	1
Darren Turcotte	0	0	1	1

New Jersey Devils 1998-99 Game Log (47-24-11)

Date	Opp	Score	W/L/T	Record	Goalies W/T	Goalies L/T	Shots NJ	Shots Opp	Power Plays NJ	Power Plays Opp	Game Stars 1st	Game Stars 2nd	Game Stars 3rd
10/10	@Chi	1-2	L	0-1-0	Hackett	**Brodeur**	36	15	0-3	1-5	Hackett	Gilmour	Amonte
10/14	Pit	1-3	L	0-2-0	Barrasso	**Brodeur**	23	25	0-2	1-6	Titov	Barrasso	Jagr
10/16	@NYR	2-1	W	1-2-0	**Brodeur**	Cloutier	30	25	0-2	0-7	**Elias**	Harvey	**Brodeur**
10/17	Edm	2-4	L	1-3-0	Shtalenkov	**Brodeur**	34	23	1-2	1-5	Guerin	Shtalenkov	Kovalenko
10/22	@Phi	3-2	W	2-3-0	**Brodeur**	Vanbiesbrouck	18	22	1-3	1-4	**Rolston**	**McKay**	Lindros
10/24	Bos	3-1	W	3-3-0	**Terreri**	Tallas	31	21	1-3	1-4	**Pandolfo**	**Terreri**	**Stevens**
10/28	LA	0-4	L	3-4-0	Fiset	**Brodeur**	40	18	0-5	1-1	Fiset	R.Blake	Perreault
10/29	@NYI	2-1	W	4-4-0	**Brodeur**	Salo	21	23	0-5	0-3	**Holik**	**Andreychuk**	**Brodeur**
10/31	Fla	3-1	W	5-4-0	**Terreri**	McLean	28	17	2-5	0-3	**Andreychuk**	**Pederson**	**Terreri**
11/03	NYR	3-1	W	6-4-0	**Brodeur**	Richter	29	25	1-2	0-2	**Niedermayer**	**Stevens**	Stevens
11/07	@Fla	4-3	W	7-4-0	**Brodeur**	Burke	38	26	0-1	0-5	**Pandolfo**	Niedermayer	**Andreychuk**
11/08	@TB	1-3	L	7-5-0	Puppa	**Brodeur**	35	27	1-3	0-2	Clark	Puppa	Sykora
11/11	Mon	3-0	W	8-5-0	**Brodeur**	Theodore	32	24	1-6	0-8	**Niedermayer**	**Brodeur**	**Brylin**
11/13	Pit	4-3	W	9-5-0	**Terreri**	Barrasso	28	20	1-3	0-2	**McKay**	**Holik**	Straka
11/14	@Phi	1-6	L	9-6-0	Hextall	**Brodeur**	18	40	0-4	1-6	Lindros	Hextall	Jones
11/19	Car	3-2*	W	10-6-0	**Brodeur**	Irbe	41	20	0-7	2-4	**Pandolfo**	Irbe	Sheppard
11/21	Fla	3-3*	T	10-6-1	**Brodeur**	McLean	27	25	1-4	1-7	**Pandolfo**	**Niedermayer**	Whitney
11/22	@Car	5-2	W	11-6-1	**Brodeur**	Irbe	40	28	0-4	0-4	**McKay**	**Pederson**	**Pandolfo**
11/25	@Dal	5-2	W	12-6-1	**Brodeur**	Belfour	25	18	0-4	2-5	**Rolston**	**Pandolfo**	Chambers
11/26	@Pho	2-3	L	12-7-1	Waite	**Brodeur**	29	24	1-7	0-1	Adams	Tocchet	**Sykora**
11/28	@Col	3-2	W	13-7-1	**Brodeur**	Roy	32	26	1-4	1-3	**Holik**	**Brodeur**	**Elias**
12/01	@Was	4-0	W	14-7-1	**Brodeur**	Kolzig	26	22	2-5	0-3	**Niedermayer**	**Brodeur**	**Sykora**
12/04	Mon	1-1*	T	14-7-2	**Brodeur**	Hackett	38	22	0-3	0-2	**Andreychuk**	Corson	**Odelein**
12/05	@NYI	7-5	W	15-7-2	**Terreri**	Flaherty	40	25	2-3	2-2	**Oliwa**	**Andreychuk**	Donato
12/08	Phi	5-5*	T	15-7-3	**Brodeur**	Hextall	20	25	1-4	2-5	**Arnott**	Lindros	**Daneyko**
12/10	@Phi	5-4*	W	16-7-3	**Brodeur**	Hextall	34	30	2-4	1-5	**Andreychuk**	Lindros	**McKay**
12/12	Col	5-3	W	17-7-3	**Brodeur**	Billington	31	19	2-2	0-3	**Holik**	Corbet	**Rolston**
12/16	NYR	6-3	W	18-7-3	**Brodeur**	Richter	27	26	0-3	2-6	**Arnott**	**Sykora**	Gretzky
12/18	Cgy	2-5	L	18-8-3	Giguere	**Terreri**	38	25	1-5	1-6	Giguere	Wilm	Fleury
12/19	@Mon	1-1*	T	18-8-4	**Brodeur**	Hackett	31	23	0-6	0-7	Hackett	Weinrich	**Brodeur**
12/23	StL	4-2	W	19-8-4	**Brodeur**	Fuhr	25	25	2-5	1-3	**Holik**	**Sharifijanov**	**Niedermayer**
12/26	Buf	0-2	L	19-9-4	Hasek	**Brodeur**	34	24	0-4	0-3	Hasek	**Brodeur**	Satan
12/28	@Buf	7-4	W	20-9-4	**Brodeur**	Roloson	18	40	2-5	2-6	**Morrison**	Peca	**Lakovic**
12/30	@Was	3-2	W	21-9-4	**Brodeur**	Tabaracci	26	20	0-2	1-7	**Holik**	**Sharifijanov**	Konowalchuk
1/02	@Ott	0-6	L	21-10-4	Rhodes	**Brodeur**	30	32	0-4	1-5	Rhodes	Arvedson	Hossa
1/05	SJ	3-3*	T	21-10-5	**Brodeur**	Vernon	33	23	1-2	1-3	**Holik**	**McKay**	Friesen
1/06	@NYR	5-2	W	22-10-5	**Brodeur**	Richter	29	32	1-5	2-6	**McKay**	**Brodeur**	**Niedermayer**
1/09	Was	2-3	L	22-11-5	Kolzig	**Terreri**	41	25	0-3	0-3	Kolzig	Juneau	Bellows
1/11	Ott	2-4	L	22-12-5	Rhodes	**Brodeur**	22	28	0-2	0-5	Yashin	Alfredsson	Hossa
1/14	@Ott	2-3	L	22-13-5	Rhodes	**Brodeur**	32	24	0-4	1-8	Johansson	Prospal	Redden
1/15	TB	3-1	W	23-13-5	**Brodeur**	Schwab	33	20	3-5	1-3	**Rolston**	**Sykora**	**Daneyko**
1/18	@SJ	1-3	L	23-14-5	Vernon	**Brodeur**	34	24	1-3	1-3	Friesen	Vernon	Ricci
1/20	@Anh	4-3	W	24-14-5	**Brodeur**	Roussel	28	35	1-5	0-5	**Stevens**	Rucchin	**Sharifijanov**
1/21	@LA	3-2	W	25-14-5	**Brodeur**	Storr	40	26	1-7	0-5	**Holik**	Stumpel	**McKay**
1/26	Ott	4-1	W	26-14-5	**Terreri**	Rhodes	34	25	0-2	0-3	**Terreri**	**Morrison**	**Rolston**
1/28	@Bos	2-0	W	27-14-5	**Brodeur**	Dafoe	30	40	0-1	0-3	**Brodeur**	**Arnott**	Thornton
1/30	Nsh	2-3*	L	27-15-5	Dunham	**Brodeur**	29	23	1-3	0-3	Bordeleau	Dunham	**Pederson**
2/01	Det	2-2*	T	27-15-6	**Brodeur**	Osgood	34	32	0-5	0-4	**Odelein**	Kozlov	**Sykora**
2/03	@Car	4-1	W	28-15-6	**Brodeur**	Irbe	35	30	1-5	1-6	**Sykora**	Primeau	**Brodeur**
2/04	@StL	2-0	W	29-15-6	**Terreri**	Parent	22	36	0-2	0-2	**Terreri**	**Rolston**	**Stevens**
2/06	Tor	2-3	L	29-16-6	Joseph	**Brodeur**	41	20	0-5	0-3	Sullivan	Joseph	**Souray**
2/09	Van	3-4	L	29-17-6	Snow	**Brodeur**	41	33	0-2	0-1	Bertuzzi	**Stevens**	Jovanovski
2/12	Was	2-3	L	29-18-6	Kolzig	**Brodeur**	28	21	0-5	2-5	Konowalchuk	Bulis	Bondra
2/13	Car	6-4	W	30-18-6	**Brodeur**	Kidd	30	30	1-6	0-5	**Morrison**	**Sykora**	**Daneyko**
2/15	Tor	3-3*	T	30-18-7	**Brodeur**	Joseph	22	31	1-3	0-4	**Niedermayer**	**Brylin**	**Pandolfo**

2/17	TB	**7**-1	W	31-18-7	**Brodeur**	Schwab	37	25	1-4	0-2	**Brylin**	**Niedermayer**	**Sykora**
2/19	@Det	1-3	L	31-19-7	Osgood	**Terreri**	22	27	0-3	1-4	Yzerman	Larionov	**Brylin**
2/20	NYI	2-3	L	31-20-7	Salo	**Brodeur**	26	19	0-4	1-4	Smolinski	**Sykora**	**Elias**
2/22	@TB	3-2	W	32-20-7	**Brodeur**	Wilkinson	28	28	1-4	0-2	**Rolston**	Lecavalier	**Brodeur**
2/25	@Bos	3-3*	T	32-20-8	**Brodeur**	Dafoe	39	28	0-2	0-2	**Arnott**	Thornton	**Sykora**
2/28	Pho	4-1	W	33-20-8	**Brodeur**	Khabibulin	25	27	1-3	0-6	**Sykora**	**Brodeur**	**Arnott**
3/03	@Tor	5-2	W	34-20-8	**Brodeur**	Joseph	28	25	0-0	1-4	**Arnott**	**Brodeur**	Berezin
3/05	Bos	1-4	L	34-21-8	Dafoe	**Brodeur**	25	21	1-2	0-4	Thornton	Dafoe	McLaren
3/07	@NYI	4-2	W	35-21-8	**Brodeur**	Salo	29	21	1-5	1-4	**Sykora**	**Morrison**	**Pederson**
3/09	@Pit	3-2	W	36-21-8	**Brodeur**	Skudra	23	23	0-3	0-2	Jagr	**Arnott**	**Sykora**
3/15	@Van	2-1	W	37-21-8	**Brodeur**	Snow	27	26	1-3	1-2	**Brodeur**	**Niedermayer**	Scatchard
3/17	@Edm	4-1	W	38-21-8	**Brodeur**	Passmore	36	22	2-5	0-2	**Niedermayer**	**Arnott**	Passmore
3/20	@Tor	1-3	L	38-22-8	Joseph	**Brodeur**	31	28	1-4	0-2	Sundin	Joseph	Sullivan
3/23	Buf	1-1*	T	38-22-9	**Brodeur**	Hasek	32	19	0-2	0-2	Satan	**Nemchinov**	Hasek
3/25	Pit	5-3	W	39-22-9	**Brodeur**	Skudra	39	**14**	2-3	1-4	**Sykora**	**Bombardir**	**Niedermayer**
3/27	Chi	4-4*	T	39-22-10	**Terreri**	Fitzpatrick	35	26	0-5	1-2	**Sykora**	Olczyk	Zhamnov
3/28	@Fla	2-2*	T	39-22-11	**Brodeur**	Burke	39	19	1-4	0-6	Parrish	Burke	Niedermayer
3/31	Anh	**7**-1	W	40-22-11	**Brodeur**	Hebert	36	**14**	2-3	1-3	**Sharifijanov**	**Andreychuk**	**McKay**
4/03	@Pit	4-2	W	41-22-11	**Terreri**	Aubin	40	18	0-4	1-2	**Andreychuk**	Aubin	**Arnott**
4/04	NYR	4-1	W	42-22-11	**Brodeur**	Cloutier	29	20	2-6	0-4	**Sykora**	**Niedermayer**	**Elias**
4/06	@Car	2-4	L	42-23-11	Irbe	**Brodeur**	32	15	1-4	1-6	Irbe	Primeau	Hill
4/08	Was	1-**0**	W	43-23-11	**Brodeur**	Kolzig	25	15	0-4	0-**1**	**Rolston**	**Brodeur**	**Dean**
4/10	@Mon	6-2	W	44-23-11	**Brodeur**	Theodore	31	28	0-2	1-4	**Elias**	**Rolston**	**Sykora**
4/12	NYI	2-4	L	44-24-11	Potvin	**Brodeur**	**57**	23	1-5	1-3	Potvin	Nabokov	**Arnott**
4/14	@Buf	2-1	W	45-24-11	**Brodeur**	Roloson	34	30	1-3	0-5	Roloson	**Brodeur**	**Niedermayer**
4/16	Phi	3-2*	W	46-24-11	**Terreri**	Vanbiesbrouck	29	29	1-2	0-3	**Holik**	**Terreri**	Brind'Amour
4/17	@Nsh	4-1	W	47-24-11	**Brodeur**	Dunham	40	28	2-4	0-5	**Sykora**	**Morrison**	**Brodeur**

Postseason

4/22	Pit	3-**1**	W	1-0	**Brodeur**	Barrasso	22	25	0-4	0-3	**Sykora**	**Niedermayer**	**Brodeur**
4/24	Pit	1-4	L	1-1	Barrasso	**Brodeur**	29	17	0-5	0-6	Barrasso	Andrusak	Straka
4/25	@Pit	2-4	L	1-2	Barrasso	**Brodeur**	33	22	**2-7**	1-6	Straka	Barrasso	Kovalev
4/27	@Pit	**4**-2	W	2-2	**Brodeur**	Barrasso	**39**	18	1-2	2-4	**McKay**	**Holik**	**Stevens**
4/30	Pit	**4**-3	W	3-2	**Brodeur**	Barrasso	27	17	1-3	1-3	**Sykora**	**McKay**	Kovalev
5/02	@Pit	2-3*	L	3-3	Barrasso	**Brodeur**	27	28	1-3	0-3	Jagr	Straka	**Brodeur**
5/04	Pit	2-4	L	3-4	Barrasso	**Brodeur**	20	**13**	0-3	0-**1**	Straka	Jagr	Kovalev

New Jersey Devils 1998-99 Player Statistics

		Regular Season													Postseason												
Skater	**Ps**	**GP**	**G**	**A**	**Pts**	**+/–**	**PIM**	**PP**	**SH**	**GW**	**GT**	**S**	**SPct**	**P/G**	**GP**	**G**	**A**	**Pts**	**+/–**	**PIM**	**PP**	**SH**	**GW**	**OT**	**S**	**SPct**	**P/G**
Petr Sykora	C	80	**29**	**43**	**72**	16	22	**15**	0	7	0	222	13.1	**.90**	**7**	**3**	3	6	-3	4	0	0	**1**	0	12	25.0	.86
Bobby Holik	L	78	27	37	64	16	119	5	0	**8**	0	**253**	10.7	.82	**7**	0	**7**	**7**	-1	6	0	0	0	0	**21**	0.0	**1.00**
Brian Rolston	C	**82**	24	33	57	11	14	5	**5**	3	0	210	11.4	.70	**7**	1	0	1	-1	2	0	**1**	0	0	15	6.7	.14
Jason Arnott	C	74	27	27	54	10	79	8	0	3	**1**	200	13.5	.73	**7**	2	2	4	-3	4	1	0	0	0	12	16.7	.57
Patrik Elias	L	74	17	33	50	19	34	3	0	2	0	157	10.8	.68	**7**	0	5	5	0	6	0	0	0	0	14	0.0	.71
* Brendan Morrison	C	76	13	33	46	-4	18	5	0	2	0	111	11.7	.61	**7**	0	2	2	-1	0	0	0	0	0	10	0.0	.29
Scott Niedermayer	D	72	11	35	46	16	26	1	1	3	0	161	6.8	.64	**7**	1	3	4	-5	**18**	1	0	0	0	13	7.7	.57
Randy McKay	R	70	17	20	37	10	143	3	0	5	0	136	12.5	.53	**7**	**3**	2	5	1	2	0	0	**1**	0	16	18.8	.71
Lyle Odelein	D	70	5	26	31	6	114	1	0	0	**1**	101	5.0	.44	**7**	0	3	3	-1	10	0	0	0	0	12	0.0	.43
Dave Andreychuk	L	52	15	13	28	1	20	4	0	3	**1**	110	13.6	.54	4	2	0	2	0	4	0	0	0	0	7	**28.6**	.50
Jay Pandolfo	L	70	14	13	27	3	10	1	1	4	0	100	**14.0**	.39	**7**	1	0	1	-5	0	0	0	0	0	10	10.0	.14
* Vadim Sharifijanov	R	53	11	16	27	11	28	1	0	2	0	71	15.5	.51	4	0	0	0	0	0	0	0	0	0	3	0.0	.00
Scott Stevens	D	75	5	22	27	**29**	64	0	0	1	0	111	4.5	.36	**7**	2	1	3	-2	10	**2**	0	0	0	14	14.3	.43
Denis Pederson	C	76	11	12	23	-10	66	3	0	1	0	145	7.6	.30	3	0	1	1	0	0	0	0	0	0	3	0.0	.33
Sergei Brylin	C	47	5	10	15	8	28	3	0	1	0	51	9.8	.32	5	**3**	1	4	2	4	1	0	**1**	0	12	25.0	.80
Krzysztof Oliwa	L	64	5	7	12	4	**240**	0	0	1	0	59	8.5	.19	1	0	0	0	0	2	0	0	0	0	0	—	.00
Ken Daneyko	D	**82**	2	9	11	27	63	0	0	0	0	63	3.2	.13	**7**	0	0	0	**3**	8	0	0	0	0	5	0.0	.00
Kevin Dean	D	62	1	10	11	4	22	1	0	0	0	51	2.0	.18	**7**	0	0	0	-4	0	0	0	0	0	7	0.0	.00
Bob Carpenter	C	56	2	8	10	-3	36	0	0	0	0	69	2.9	.18	**7**	0	0	0	-1	2	0	0	0	0	7	0.0	.00
Brad Bombardir	D	56	1	7	8	-4	16	0	0	0	0	47	2.1	.14	5	0	0	0	0	0	0	0	0	0	2	0.0	.00
Sheldon Souray	D	70	1	7	8	5	110	0	0	0	0	101	1.0	.11	2	0	1	1	1	0	0	0	0	0	0	—	.50
Sergei Nemchinov†	C	10	4	0	4	4	6	1	0	1	0	13	30.8	.40	4	0	0	0	-2	0	0	0	0	0	2	0.0	.00
Martin Brodeur	G	70	0	4	4	—	4	0	0	0	0	0	—	.06	**7**	0	2	2	—	2	0	0	0	0	0	—	.29
Sasha Lakovic	L	16	0	3	3	0	59	0	0	0	0	10	0.0	.19	—	—	—	—	—	—	—	—	—	—	—	—	—
Ken Sutton	D	5	1	0	1	1	0	0	0	0	0	5	20.0	.20	—	—	—	—	—	—	—	—	—	—	—	—	—
* John Madden	L	4	0	1	1	-2	0	0	0	0	0	4	0.0	.25	—	—	—	—	—	—	—	—	—	—	—	—	—
Chris Terreri	G	12	0	1	1	—	0	0	0	0	0	0	—	.08	—	—	—	—	—	—	—	—	—	—	—	—	—
Scott Daniels	L	1	0	0	0	0	0	0	0	0	0	0	—	.00	—	—	—	—	—	—	—	—	—	—	—	—	—
* Bryan Muir†	D	1	0	0	0	0	0	0	0	0	0	4	0.0	.00	—	—	—	—	—	—	—	—	—	—	—	—	—
Bench		—	—	—	—	—	0	—	—	—	—	—	—	—	—	—	—	—	—	0	—	—	—	—	—	—	—
TEAM TOTALS		82	248	430	678	178	1341	60	7	47	3	2565	9.7	8.27	7	18	33	51	-22	84	5	1	3	0	197	9.1	7.29

	Regular Season											Postseason									
Goaltender	**G**	**Min**	**GAA**	**W**	**L**	**T**	**ENG**	**ShO**	**GA**	**SA**	**SvPct**	**G**	**Min**	**GAA**	**W**	**L**	**ENG**	**ShO**	**GA**	**SA**	**SvPct**
Martin Brodeur	**70**	**4239**	**2.29**	**39**	**21**	**10**	**4**	**4**	**162**	**1728**	**.906**	**7**	**425**	**2.82**	**3**	**4**	**1**	0	**20**	**139**	**.856**
Chris Terreri	12	726	2.48	8	3	1	0	1	30	294	.898	—	—	—	—	—	—	—	—	—	—
TEAM TOTALS	82	4986	2.36	47	24	11	4	5	196	2026	.903	7	429	2.94	3	4	1	0	21	140	.850

1998-99 New Jersey Devils

Record When:

Overtime games	3-1-11
In second game of back-to-back games	10-5-2
Vs playoff teams	26-14-6
Leading after two periods	37-3-4
Tied after two periods	7-6-5
Losing after two periods	3-15-2
Scoring first	36-7-6
More shots than opponents	34-19-9
Fewer shots than opponents	8-5-2
Team had at least one fighting major	21-13-4
Team had more PIM	21-12-6
Team had fewer PIM	21-7-3
Team had even PIM	5-5-2

Team

Longest winning streak	4	3 times
Longest unbeaten streak	8	Nov. 28 — Dec. 16
Longest losing streak	3	2 times
Longest winless streak	3	2 times
Most shots, game	57	vs. NYI, Apr. 12
Most shots, period	23	1st, @LA, Jan. 21
Fewest shots, game	18	3 times
Fewest shots, period	2	2 times

Individual

Longest goal streak	6	Bobby Holik
Longest point streak	9	Brian Rolston
Most goals, game	3	Bobby Holik
Most assists, game	3	7 times
Most points, game	3	24 times
Highest +/–, game	4	5 times
Lowest +/–, game	-4	3 times
Most shots, game	8	2 times

Did You Know?

Last season, Scott Stevens' 17th in the NHL, marked the 17th consecutive campaign in which Stevens played at least 40 games and recorded a plus/minus of even or better. No other player currently has a streak as long as 12 straight seasons.

Miscellaneous

		NHL Rank
PP Pct.	19.7 (60-304)	4
SH goals allowed	5	4t
PK Pct.	85.5 (278-325)	11
SH goals scored	7	15t
Special Team Index	105.8	4
Shots on goal	2,565 (31.3/G)	2
Shots against	2,026 (24.7/G)	4
Unassisted goals	12	16t
Unassisted goals allowed	18	23
Team Average Weight	207.4	2
Game Star Points	440	2

Game Star Breakdown

Player	1st	2nd	3rd	Pts
Petr Sykora	7	4	7	54
Bobby Holik	8	1	0	43
Martin Brodeur	2	9	6	43
Scott Niedermayer	5	4	4	41
Brian Rolston	5	2	2	33
Jason Arnott	4	3	3	32
Dave Andreychuk	4	3	1	30
Jay Pandolfo	4	1	2	25
Randy McKay	3	2	3	24
Brendan Morrison	2	3	0	19
Chris Terreri	2	2	1	17
Patrik Elias	2	0	3	13
Scott Stevens	1	2	2	13
Vadim Sharifijanov	1	2	1	12
Sergei Brylin	1	1	2	10
Denis Pederson	0	2	2	8
Lyle Odelein	1	0	1	6
Krzysztof Oliwa	1	0	0	5
Brad Bombardir	0	1	0	3
Sergei Nemchinov	0	1	0	3
Ken Daneyko	0	0	3	3
Kevin Dean	0	0	1	1
Sasha Lakovic	0	0	1	1
Sheldon Souray	0	0	1	1

New York Islanders 1998-99 Game Log (24-48-10)

					Goalies		Shots		Power Plays		Game Stars		
Date	Opp	Score	W/L/T	Record	W/T	L/T	NYI	Opp	NYI	Opp	1st	2nd	3rd
10/10	Pit	3-4	L	0-1-0	Barrasso	**Salo**	25	21	2-4	1-4	**Linden**	Werenka	Jagr
10/12	@Bos	0-3	L	0-2-0	Dafoe	**Salo**	28	17	0-4	1-5	Dafoe	**Lapointe**	Samsonov
10/14	@TB	2-**0**	W	1-2-0	**Salo**	Puppa	23	22	0-5	0-4	**Reichel**	**Salo**	Samuelsson
10/17	@StL	1-**0**	W	2-2-0	**Salo**	McLennan	12	23	1-6	0-3	**Salo**	**Berard**	Rivers
10/21	Edm	2-4	L	2-3-0	Shtalenkov	**Salo**	30	30	1-7	2-9	Devereaux	Weight	Buchberger
10/22	@NYR	2-3	L	2-4-0	Richter	**Salo**	30	29	0-3	0-4	Stevens	Knuble	**Salo**
10/24	Buf	5-4	W	3-4-0	**Salo**	Hasek	28	36	1-4	1-6	**Lapointe**	**Smolinski**	Sanderson
10/27	LA	1-**0**	W	4-4-0	**Salo**	LeGace	34	20	0-2	0-4	**Salo**	LeGace	**Sacco**
10/29	NJ	1-2	L	4-5-0	Brodeur	**Salo**	23	21	0-3	0-5	Holik	Andreychuk	Brodeur
10/31	Phi	3-2	W	5-5-0	**Salo**	Vanbiesbrouck	17	30	0-3	0-4	**Smolinski**	**Watt**	Zelepukin
11/02	Fla	6-2	W	6-5-0	**Salo**	Burke	29	20	**3**-7	1-7	**Reichel**	**Smolinski**	**Linden**
11/05	Car	3-6	L	6-6-0	Kidd	**Salo**	19	31	1-3	0-4	O'Neill	Manderville	Ranheim
11/07	@Mon	2-4	L	6-7-0	Theodore	**Salo**	30	23	0-6	4-7	Recchi	Theodore	**Lapointe**
11/09	@Tor	3-1	W	7-7-0	**Salo**	Joseph	19	39	0-0	0-3	**Salo**	Sundin	**Lapointe**
11/10	@Pit	2-3	L	7-8-0	Aubin	**Salo**	31	20	1-2	0-3	Straka	Aubin	Werenka
11/12	Mon	4-**0**	W	8-8-0	**Salo**	Thibault	25	21	1-6	0-4	**Czerkawski**	**Salo**	**Richter**
11/14	Was	3-5	L	8-9-0	Kolzig	**Salo**	24	34	2-4	1-2	Black	Oates	Tinordi
11/17	@Col	2-5	L	8-10-0	Roy	**Salo**	22	28	1-**8**	2-5	Kamensky	Miller	**Czerkawski**
11/20	@Dal	2-4	L	8-11-0	Belfour	**Flaherty**	17	26	0-4	2-6	Gusev	Sydor	Hatcher
11/21	@Nsh	6-3	W	9-11-0	**Salo**	Dunham	40	42	**3**-6	1-4	**Watt**	**Reichel**	Turcotte
11/25	Phi	4-2	W	10-11-0	**Salo**	Vanbiesbrouck	14	46	**3**-5	1-6	**Salo**	**Berard**	LeClair
11/26	@Ott	1-4	L	10-12-0	Rhodes	**Flaherty**	28	33	1-1	1-4	Rhodes	Yashin	McEachern
11/28	Car	1-3	L	10-13-0	Kidd	**Salo**	22	23	0-3	1-5	Primeau	Kapanen	Dineen
12/02	NYR	2-3	L	10-14-0	Richter	**Salo**	27	17	2-4	0-5	Nedved	Richter	Gretzky
12/04	@Was	1-5	L	10-15-0	Tabaracci	**Salo**	23	28	0-5	0-4	Tabaracci	Johansson	Juneau
12/05	NJ	5-7	L	10-16-0	Terreri	**Flaherty**	25	40	2-2	2-3	Oliwa	Andreychuk	**Donato**
12/08	Col	1-2	L	10-17-0	Roy	**Salo**	32	22	0-5	0-2	Forsberg	Sakic	**Linden**
12/12	TB	1-2*	L	10-18-0	Schwab	**Salo**	35	26	0-3	0-3	Hogue	**Linden**	Gratton
12/15	@SJ	1-**0**	W	11-18-0	**Salo**	Vernon	26	**13**	0-4	0-6	**Watt**	**Jonsson**	**Salo**
12/17	@LA	5-4*	W	12-18-0	**Salo**	Storr	25	25	1-4	1-3	**Berard**	Rosa	**Richter**
12/18	@Anh	2-2*	T	12-18-1	**Salo**	Hebert	32	41	0-4	1-3	Olausson	**Linden**	Salei
12/20	@Pho	2-4	L	12-19-1	Khabibulin	**Salo**	22	34	0-5	2-6	Adams	Tkachuk	Roenick
12/22	StL	3-3*	T	12-19-2	**Flaherty**	Fuhr	17	28	1-4	0-**1**	**Czerkawski**	Gill	**Palffy**
12/26	Bos	4-2	W	13-19-2	**Flaherty**	Dafoe	21	27	1-5	0-3	**Linden**	**Watt**	**Chara**
12/28	@Fla	1-5	L	13-20-2	Burke	**Flaherty**	27	36	0-4	1-2	Burke	Whitney	Carkner
12/29	@TB	0-3	L	13-21-2	Ranford	**Cousineau**	35	17	0-4	2-4	Ranford	Lecavalier	Cross
12/31	@Chi	0-1	L	13-22-2	Thibault	**Cousineau**	28	21	0-3	0-2	Thibault	**Cousineau**	**Palffy**
1/02	SJ	3-4*	L	13-23-2	Shields	**Cousineau**	21	29	2-4	1-5	Sturm	**Palffy**	Ricci
1/05	Chi	1-1*	T	13-23-3	**Salo**	Thibault	41	23	0-**8**	0-4	Thibault	**Salo**	**Reichel**
1/07	@Phi	0-5	L	13-24-3	Vanbiesbrouck	**Salo**	27	26	0-4	1-3	Vanbiesbrouck	Lindros	Greig
1/09	@Mon	2-3	L	13-25-3	Hackett	**Cousineau**	23	23	0-3	1-4	Quintal	Poulin	**Nemchinov**
1/11	@Was	3-4	L	13-26-3	Kolzig	**Potvin**	25	35	1-3	1-4	Gonchar	Reekie	Eagles
1/13	@NYR	3-4*	L	13-27-3	Richter	**Potvin**	21	27	1-7	0-7	Graves	MacLean	Sundstrom
1/16	@Fla	0-1	L	13-28-3	Burke	**Potvin**	27	19	0-4	1-4	Burke	Ciccarelli	**Brewer**
1/20	Fla	2-5	L	13-29-3	McLean	**Potvin**	19	20	1-5	1-5	Bure	**Reichel**	Spacek
1/21	@Pit	5-2	W	14-29-3	**Salo**	Barrasso	24	28	0-3	1-7	**Lapointe**	**Salo**	**Sacco**
1/26	Bos	4-1	W	15-29-3	**Salo**	Dafoe	20	26	0-4	0-4	**Reichel**	**Palffy**	**Richter**
1/29	Pho	4-4*	T	15-29-4	**Salo**	Waite	33	35	0-3	0-2	**Reichel**	Corkum	**Chara**
1/30	@Ott	2-9	L	15-30-4	Tugnutt	**Potvin**	22	43	1-6	3-13	Yashin	Dackell	McEachern
2/03	@Det	1-5	L	15-31-4	Maracle	**Salo**	28	44	0-7	2-6	McCarty	Lidstrom	Yzerman
2/04	@Bos	5-4	W	16-31-4	**Potvin**	Dafoe	38	41	0-2	0-4	Allison	**Linden**	**Pilon**
2/07	Van	3-3*	T	16-31-5	**Potvin**	Hirsch	32	37	0-6	1-4	**Reichel**	**Palffy**	Ohlund
2/09	Was	1-2	L	16-32-5	Kolzig	**Salo**	22	25	0-5	1-5	Kolzig	Oates	Tinordi
2/12	Nsh	1-2	L	16-33-5	Dunham	**Potvin**	41	23	1-6	0-2	Dunham	Ronning	Krivokrasov
2/13	@Buf	2-2*	T	16-33-6	**Salo**	Hasek	18	26	0-3	0-4	**Czerkawski**	Kruse	Satan

2/15	TB	3-3*	T	16-33-7	**Salo**	Schwab	31	23	0-5	0-**1**	**Palffy**	**Czerkawski**	Lecavalier
2/17	Pit	3-1	W	17-33-7	**Salo**	Skudra	31	21	1-7	0-4	**Pilon**	**Salo**	**Reichel**
2/20	@NJ	3-2	W	18-33-7	**Salo**	Brodeur	19	26	1-4	0-4	**Smolinski**	Sykora	Elias
2/21	@Car	1-4	L	18-34-7	Irbe	**Salo**	29	37	0-3	1-3	O'Neill	Irbe	Primeau
2/25	Tor	1-4	L	18-35-7	Healy	**Salo**	28	22	1-5	0-4	Berezin	Healy	Kaberle
2/27	Det	3-1	W	19-35-7	**Salo**	Hodson	30	36	2-6	0-5	**Salo**	**Reichel**	**Lapointe**
3/02	Ott	2-4	L	19-36-7	Tugnutt	**Salo**	37	29	1-7	0-**1**	Arvedson	Tugnutt	**Lawrence**
3/04	Dal	2-3*	L	19-37-7	Turek	**Salo**	30	32	1-1	0-2	Nieuwendyk	**Palffy**	Modano
3/06	@Phi	3-3*	T	19-37-8	**Salo**	Vanbiesbrouck	25	28	1-4	1-6	**Palffy**	Lindros	**Pilon**
3/07	NJ	2-4	L	19-38-8	Brodeur	**Salo**	21	29	1-4	1-5	Sykora	Morrison	Pederson
3/09	Phi	2-2*	T	19-38-9	**Salo**	Vanbiesbrouck	22	35	1-2	2-8	**Lawrence**	**Palffy**	Langkow
3/11	Tor	1-2	L	19-39-9	Joseph	**Salo**	**42**	22	0-3	0-4	Joseph	D.King	**Czerkawski**
3/14	NYR	2-3*	L	19-40-9	Cloutier	**Salo**	33	21	0-3	2-5	Graves	Cloutier	Savard
3/15	@Buf	1-2	L	19-41-9	Roloson	**Flaherty**	24	22	1-**8**	1-5	Satan	Barnes	Roloson
3/19	@Van	3-1	W	20-41-9	**Flaherty**	Weekes	28	22	1-3	1-4	**Jonsson**	**Lapointe**	Naslund
3/21	@Cgy	1-2	L	20-42-9	Wregget	**Flaherty**	12	34	0-5	1-7	Bure	**Flaherty**	Cassels
3/24	@Car	1-2	L	20-43-9	Irbe	**Flaherty**	25	29	0-4	0-6	Kovalenko	Irbe	Kron
3/27	Ott	3-7	L	20-44-9	Tugnutt	**Flaherty**	23	36	0-5	2-8	Hossa	Yashin	York
3/29	@NYR	1-3	L	20-45-9	Richter	**Flaherty**	22	35	0-3	0-5	Gretzky	Leetch	**Flaherty**
3/31	@Fla	5-3	W	21-45-9	**Flaherty**	Burke	19	36	1-1	0-6	**Lawrence**	Parrish	**Czerkawski**
4/03	Anh	2-2*	T	21-45-10	**Flaherty**	Roussel	33	26	0-2	1-4	Cullen	**Lindgren**	**Flaherty**
4/06	Buf	3-4	L	21-46-10	Roloson	**Flaherty**	41	21	2-5	2-3	Woolley	Peca	**Brewer**
4/08	Mon	3-1	W	22-46-10	**Flaherty**	Theodore	29	21	0-3	1-3	**Czerkawski**	**Palffy**	**Linden**
4/10	Car	1-6	L	22-47-10	Kidd	**Flaherty**	25	24	0-3	0-3	Kapanen	Roberts	Kidd
4/12	@NJ	4-2	W	23-47-10	**Potvin**	Brodeur	23	57	1-3	1-5	**Potvin**	**Nabokov**	Arnott
4/14	@Tor	2-3*	L	23-48-10	Joseph	**Potvin**	24	38	1-4	0-3	**Potvin**	Berezin	Berard
4/17	@Pit	**7**-2	W	24-48-10	**Flaherty**	Barrasso	24	29	2-3	1-6	**Palffy**	**Linden**	**Flaherty**

New York Islanders 1998-99 Player Statistics

Skater	Ps	GP	G	A	Pts	+/–	PIM	PP	SH	GW	GT	S	SPct	P/G
		Regular Season												
Robert Reichel†	C	70	19	**37**	**56**	-15	50	5	1	1	1	186	10.2	.80
Zigmund Palffy	R	50	**22**	28	50	-6	34	5	**2**	1	0	168	13.1	**1.00**
Trevor Linden	C	**82**	18	29	47	-14	32	**8**	1	1	0	167	10.8	.57
Bryan Smolinski	C	**82**	16	24	40	-7	49	7	0	3	0	**223**	7.2	.49
Mariusz Czerkawski	R	78	21	17	38	-10	14	4	0	1	**2**	205	10.2	.49
Claude Lapointe	C	**82**	14	23	37	-19	62	2	**2**	1	0	134	10.4	.45
Mark Lawrence	R	60	14	16	30	-8	38	4	0	2	1	88	**15.9**	.50
Kenny Jonsson	D	63	8	18	26	-18	34	6	0	0	0	91	8.8	.41
* Mike Watt	L	75	8	17	25	**-2**	12	0	0	**4**	0	75	10.7	.33
Barry Richter	D	72	6	18	24	-4	34	0	0	2	0	111	5.4	.33
Ted Donato†	L	55	7	11	18	-10	27	2	0	0	0	68	10.3	.33
Sergei Nemchinov†	C	67	8	8	16	-17	22	1	0	0	0	61	13.1	.24
Bryan Berard†	D	31	4	11	15	-6	26	2	0	3	0	72	5.6	.48
* Eric Brewer	D	63	5	6	11	-14	32	2	0	0	0	63	7.9	.17
Scott Lachance†	D	59	1	8	9	-19	30	1	0	0	0	37	2.7	.15
Mats Lindgren†	C	12	5	3	8	2	2	3	0	1	0	30	16.7	.67
* Zdeno Chara	D	59	2	6	8	-8	83	0	1	0	0	56	3.6	.14
David Harlock	D	70	2	6	8	-16	68	0	0	0	0	35	5.7	.11
Gino Odjick	L	23	4	3	7	-2	**133**	1	0	2	0	28	14.3	.30
Kevin Miller	C	33	1	5	6	-5	13	0	0	0	0	37	2.7	.18
Jason Dawe†	R	22	2	3	5	0	8	0	0	0	0	29	6.9	.23
Craig Janney†	C	18	1	4	5	-2	4	0	0	0	0	9	11.1	.28
Rich Pilon	D	52	0	4	4	-8	88	0	0	0	0	27	0.0	.08
Joe Sacco	R	73	3	0	3	-24	45	0	1	2	0	84	3.6	.04
Eric Cairns	D	9	0	3	3	1	23	0	0	0	0	2	0.0	.33
Ted Crowley†	D	6	1	1	2	0	0	1	0	0	0	10	10.0	.33
Ken Belanger†	L	9	1	1	2	1	30	0	0	0	0	3	33.3	.22
* Dmitri Nabokov	C	4	0	2	2	4	2	0	0	0	0	4	0.0	.50
* Vladimir Orszagh	R	12	1	0	1	2	6	0	0	0	0	5	20.0	.08
Tom Chorske†	L	2	0	1	1	1	2	0	0	0	0	9	0.0	.50
Dean Malkoc	D	2	0	1	1	3	7	0	0	0	0	1	0.0	.50
Mike Kennedy	C	1	0	0	0	0	2	0	0	0	0	0	—	.00
* Ray Schultz	D	4	0	0	0	-2	7	0	0	0	0	2	0.0	.00
* Marcel Cousineau	G	6	0	0	0	—	0	0	0	0	0	0	—	.00
* Vladimir Chebaturkin	D	8	0	0	0	6	12	0	0	0	0	4	0.0	.00
Mike Hough	L	11	0	0	0	-2	2	0	0	0	0	4	0.0	.00
* Warren Luhning	R	11	0	0	0	-4	8	0	0	0	0	11	0.0	.00
Felix Potvin†	G	11	0	0	0	—	0	0	0	0	0	0	—	.00
Wade Flaherty	G	20	0	0	0	—	4	0	0	0	0	0	—	.00
Steve Webb	R	45	0	0	0	-10	32	0	0	0	0	18	0.0	.00
Tommy Salo†	G	51	0	0	0	—	12	0	0	0	0	0	—	.00
Bench		—	—	—	—	—	0	—	—	—	—	—	—	—
TEAM TOTALS		82	194	314	508	-232	1089	54	8	24	4	2157	9.0	6.20

Postseason

GP	G	A	Pts	+/–	PIM	PP	SH	GW	OT	S	SPct	P/G

Team Did Not Qualify for Postseason Play

Goaltender	G	Min	GAA	W	L	T	ENG	ShO	GA	SA	SvPct
	Regular Season										
Tommy Salo†	**51**	**3018**	**2.62**	**17**	**26**	**7**	**5**	**5**	**132**	**1368**	**.904**
* Marcel Cousineau	6	293	2.87	0	4	0	0	0	14	119	.882
Wade Flaherty	20	1048	3.03	5	11	2	3	0	53	491	.892
Felix Potvin†	11	606	3.66	2	7	1	0	0	37	345	.893
TEAM TOTALS	82	4990	2.93	24	48	10	8	5	244	2331	.895

Postseason

G	Min	GAA	W	L	ENG	ShO	GA	SA	SvPct

1998-99 New York Islanders

Record When:

Overtime games	1-6-10
In second game of back-to-back games	3-9-2
Vs playoff teams	15-29-7
Leading after two periods	19-3-4
Tied after two periods	3-10-4
Losing after two periods	2-35-2
Scoring first	21-12-5
More shots than opponents	8-21-3
Fewer shots than opponents	15-25-7
Team had at least one fighting major	4-14-2
Team had more PIM	12-25-3
Team had fewer PIM	10-14-7
Team had even PIM	2-9-0

Team

Longest winning streak	2	7 times
Longest unbeaten streak	4	Feb. 13 — Feb. 20
Longest losing streak	7	Nov. 26 — Dec. 12
Longest winless streak	11	Dec. 28 — Jan. 20
Most shots, game	42	vs. Tor, Mar. 11
Most shots, period	18	3 times
Fewest shots, game	12	2 times
Fewest shots, period	1	2 times

Individual

Longest goal streak	4	Robert Reichel
Longest point streak	7	2 times
Most goals, game	3	Zigmund Palffy
Most assists, game	3	4 times
Most points, game	5	Zigmund Palffy
Highest +/–, game	4	4 times
Lowest +/–, game	-4	Eric Brewer
Most shots, game	8	3 times

Did You Know?

In the last 16 seasons, no Islander goaltender has played as many as 20 games in a season and recorded a save percentage as high as .910. Rollie Melanson's .910 save percentage in 1982-83—the first year the NHL recorded the statistic—stands as the best single-season mark in Islander history.

Miscellaneous

		NHL Rank
PP Pct.	15.8 (54-341)	13
SH goals allowed	7	9t
PK Pct.	83.5 (303-363)	18
SH goals scored	8	8t
Special Team Index	99.5	15
Shots on goal	2,157 (26.3/G)	19
Shots against	2,331 (28.4/G)	15
Unassisted goals	18	2t
Unassisted goals allowed	19	24t
Team Average Weight	199.2	17
Game Star Points	288	25

Game Star Breakdown

Player	1st	2nd	3rd	Pts
Tommy Salo	5	5	2	42
Robert Reichel	5	3	2	36
Zigmund Palffy	3	6	2	35
Mariusz Czerkawski	4	1	3	26
Trevor Linden	2	4	3	25
Claude Lapointe	2	2	3	19
Bryan Smolinski	2	2	0	16
Mike Watt	2	2	0	16
Mark Lawrence	2	0	1	11
Bryan Berard	1	2	0	11
Felix Potvin	2	0	0	10
Kenny Jonsson	1	1	0	8
Rich Pilon	1	0	2	7
Wade Flaherty	0	1	3	6
Marcel Cousineau	0	1	0	3
Mats Lindgren	0	1	0	3
Dmitri Nabokov	0	1	0	3
Barry Richter	0	0	3	3
Eric Brewer	0	0	2	2
Zdeno Chara	0	0	2	2
Joe Sacco	0	0	2	2
Ted Donato	0	0	1	1
Sergei Nemchinov	0	0	1	1

New York Rangers 1998-99 Game Log (33-38-11)

Date	Opp	Score	W/L/T	Record	Goalies		Shots		Power Plays		Game Stars		
					W/T	L/T	NYR	Opp	NYR	Opp	1st	2nd	3rd
10/09	Phi	0-1	L	0-1-0	Vanbiesbrouck	**Richter**	20	30	0-6	1-5	Vanbiesbrouck	**Richter**	Daigle
10/10	@Mon	1-7	L	0-2-0	Thibault	**Richter**	21	30	1-5	1-6	Recchi	Brunet	Thibault
10/12	StL	2-4	L	0-3-0	Fuhr	**Richter**	18	42	0-3	1-4	MacInnis	Turgeon	Pronger
10/16	NJ	1-2	L	0-4-0	Brodeur	**Cloutier**	25	30	0-7	0-2	Elias	**Harvey**	Brodeur
10/17	@Pit	3-3*	T	0-4-1	**Richter**	Skudra	26	30	2-6	1-7	Jagr	**Harvey**	Hatcher
10/20	Edm	3-2	W	1-4-1	**Richter**	Essensa	28	26	2-**9**	2-6	Beranek	**Schneider**	**Leetch**
10/22	NYI	3-2	W	2-4-1	**Richter**	Salo	29	30	0-4	0-3	**Stevens**	**Knuble**	Salo
10/24	@Phi	2-2*	T	2-4-2	**Richter**	Vanbiesbrouck	13	37	1-3	1-4	**Richter**	LeClair	**Gretzky**
10/27	Buf	0-**0***	T	2-4-3	**Richter**	Hasek	16	24	0-6	0-5	**Richter**	Hasek	**Samuelsson**
10/30	Car	1-**0**	W	3-4-3	**Richter**	Irbe	24	30	1-5	0-7	**Richter**	**Harvey**	**Gretzky**
11/03	@NJ	1-3	L	3-5-3	Brodeur	**Richter**	25	29	0-2	1-2	Niedermayer	Stevens	**Stevens**
11/04	Mon	1-4	L	3-6-3	Theodore	**Richter**	20	32	0-4	1-4	Recchi	Theodore	**MacLean**
11/07	@Tor	6-6*	T	3-6-4	**Cloutier**	Joseph	32	32	1-2	0-**1**	**Harvey**	Korolev	**Savard**
11/10	@TB	**10**-2	W	4-6-4	**Cloutier**	Ranford	30	28	2-6	1-3	**Stevens**	**Leetch**	**Samuelsson**
11/11	@Fla	1-4	L	4-7-4	Burke	**Richter**	26	35	0-1	0-4	Worrell	Kvasha	Burke
11/13	Bos	3-3*	T	4-7-5	**Richter**	Dafoe	25	27	2-4	1-5	**MacLean**	**Kovalev**	Khristich
11/18	@Anh	1-3	L	4-8-5	Hebert	**Richter**	30	**16**	0-**9**	1-7	Rucchin	Hebert	Haller
11/19	@LA	5-1	W	5-8-5	**Cloutier**	LeGace	25	29	2-4	0-2	**Cloutier**	**Malhotra**	Visheau
11/21	@SJ	2-2*	T	5-8-6	**Cloutier**	Vernon	23	40	1-6	0-5	Stern	**Cloutier**	Vernon
11/25	@Buf	2-4	L	5-9-6	Hasek	**Cloutier**	26	30	1-3	1-2	Ward	Peca	Varada
11/27	@Pit	2-2*	T	5-9-7	**Richter**	Barrasso	21	31	1-3	0-4	Kovalev	**Leetch**	Morozov
11/29	Nsh	5-1	W	6-9-7	**Richter**	Dunham	35	25	2-3	0-3	**Gretzky**	**MacLean**	**Stevens**
12/01	Fla	5-4*	W	7-9-7	**Richter**	Burke	29	23	3-6	1-4	**Graves**	**Gretzky**	**Leetch**
12/02	@NYI	3-2	W	8-9-7	**Richter**	Salo	17	27	0-5	2-4	**Nedved**	**Richter**	**Gretzky**
12/05	@Ott	2-1	W	9-9-7	**Richter**	Rhodes	17	30	1-1	0-4	**Richter**	Arvedson	**Nedved**
12/07	Tor	6-2	W	10-9-7	**Richter**	Joseph	29	26	0-2	0-4	**Sundstrom**	**Nedved**	**Leetch**
12/09	Col	1-2	L	10-10-7	Roy	**Richter**	20	29	0-2	0-2	Sakic	**Richter**	Forsberg
12/11	@Buf	0-2	L	10-11-7	Hasek	**Richter**	16	32	0-4	1-6	Peca	Hasek	**Richter**
12/14	Cgy	5-2	W	11-11-7	**Richter**	Giguere	29	37	3-5	0-6	**Richter**	**Savard**	**Knuble**
12/16	@NJ	3-6	L	11-12-7	Brodeur	**Richter**	26	27	2-6	0-3	Arnott	Sykora	**Gretzky**
12/19	@Tor	4-7	L	11-13-7	Healy	**Richter**	26	31	3-5	1-5	McCauley	D.King	Johnson
12/23	Car	0-1	L	11-14-7	Irbe	**Richter**	29	25	0-3	0-5	Sheppard	Irbe	**Richter**
12/26	@Car	6-3	W	12-14-7	**Richter**	Kidd	20	22	0-2	1-5	**Nedved**	**Graves**	**Pronger**
12/30	@Pho	1-3	L	12-15-7	Khabibulin	**Cloutier**	30	26	0-2	0-3	Briere	Isbister	Corkum
12/31	@Col	6-3	W	13-15-7	**Richter**	Billington	24	34	3-4	1-5	**Gretzky**	**Nedved**	Lemieux
1/02	@StL	1-**0**	W	14-15-7	**Richter**	McLennan	10	24	1-4	0-2	**Richter**	**MacLean**	MacInnis
1/04	SJ	4-3	W	15-15-7	**Richter**	Shields	27	27	1-4	0-4	**Harvey**	**Graves**	**Stevens**
1/06	NJ	2-5	L	15-16-7	Brodeur	**Richter**	32	29	2-6	1-5	McKay	Brodeur	Niedermayer
1/07	@Was	1-5	L	15-17-7	Kolzig	**Richter**	18	33	0-2	1-2	Bulis	Konowalchuk	Hunter
1/10	TB	5-2	W	16-17-7	**Cloutier**	Ranford	27	24	2-6	1-**8**	**MacLean**	**Leetch**	**Cloutier**
1/13	NYI	4-3*	W	17-17-7	**Richter**	Potvin	27	21	0-7	1-7	**Graves**	**MacLean**	**Sundstrom**
1/15	Chi	1-3	L	17-18-7	Thibault	**Richter**	33	26	0-4	0-2	Thibault	Maneluk	**Sundstrom**
1/16	@Mon	0-3	L	17-19-7	Hackett	**Cloutier**	17	32	0-3	2-4	Malakhov	Hackett	Koivu
1/19	Ott	1-2	L	17-20-7	Tugnutt	**Richter**	22	28	1-3	0-2	Bonk	Tugnutt	**Richter**
1/21	Fla	1-2	L	17-21-7	Burke	**Richter**	28	26	0-7	0-7	Hedican	Burke	**Richter**
1/26	@Was	4-1	W	18-21-7	**Richter**	Kolzig	23	35	1-2	0-3	**Gretzky**	**Richter**	**Graves**
1/28	@Car	2-3*	L	18-22-7	Irbe	**Richter**	26	30	1-5	0-3	Roberts	Manderville	**Schneider**
1/30	@Det	3-2	W	19-22-7	**Richter**	Osgood	14	40	0-1	1-3	**Richter**	**Sundstrom**	Brown
2/01	Was	1-3	L	19-23-7	Kolzig	**Richter**	25	38	0-4	0-2	Juneau	Kolzig	Bondra
2/04	Van	8-4	W	20-23-7	**Richter**	Snow	36	31	2-7	1-4	**Graves**	**Gretzky**	**MacLean**
2/07	@Bos	2-3	L	20-24-7	Dafoe	**Richter**	27	23	0-4	1-5	Thornton	**Leetch**	Allison
2/12	Car	1-3	L	20-25-7	Irbe	**Richter**	31	26	0-5	0-4	Irbe	Kapanen	**Leetch**
2/14	Det	2-4	L	20-26-7	Osgood	**Richter**	31	30	0-4	0-7	Yzerman	**Fedyk**	Fedorov
2/15	@Nsh	7-4	W	21-26-7	**Cloutier**	Vokoun	28	33	3-6	0-5	**Gretzky**	Walker	**Harvey**
2/17	Mon	3-6	L	21-27-7	Hackett	**Cloutier**	38	46	2-**9**	0-3	Brunet	**Knuble**	Recchi

2/19	Pit	6-1	W	22-27-7	**Cloutier**	Barrasso	20	33	1-2	0-6	**Cloutier**	**Stevens**	**MacLean**
2/21	@Edm	2-1*	W	23-27-7	**Richter**	Essensa	28	40	0-2	0-2	**Richter**	Essensa	**Lacroix**
2/22	@Cgy	2-6	L	23-28-7	Brathwaite	**Richter**	31	38	1-6	1-2	Fleury	Stillman	Housley
2/26	Pho	3-**0**	W	24-28-7	**Richter**	Khabibulin	21	25	1-4	0-4	**Richter**	**MacLean**	**Malhotra**
2/28	Phi	6-5	W	25-28-7	**Richter**	Vanbiesbrouck	26	26	**4**-7	2-7	**Nedved**	**Graves**	Lindros
3/02	Dal	2-2*	T	25-28-8	**Richter**	Belfour	26	30	0-3	0-7	**Graves**	**Leetch**	Nieuwendyk
3/04	@Was	4-2	W	26-28-8	**Richter**	Kolzig	34	36	0-4	2-5	**Knuble**	**Richter**	**Sundstrom**
3/07	@Bos	3-1	W	27-28-8	**Richter**	Dafoe	18	38	0-6	0-6	**Richter**	**Schneider**	Bourque
3/08	Tor	3-2*	W	28-28-8	**Richter**	Healy	35	26	2-6	0-3	**Nedved**	**Leetch**	D.King
3/10	Ott	0-3	L	28-29-8	Rhodes	**Richter**	29	33	0-4	1-5	Yashin	Rhodes	Bonk
3/12	Bos	4-5	L	28-30-8	Dafoe	**Richter**	**44**	38	0-4	1-4	Carter	**MacLean**	**Graves**
3/14	@NYI	3-2*	W	29-30-8	**Cloutier**	Salo	21	33	2-5	0-3	**Graves**	**Cloutier**	**Savard**
3/15	Was	1-1*	T	29-30-9	**Richter**	Kolzig	23	34	0-4	0-4	**Richter**	**Ndur**	Hunter
3/19	Buf	2-3*	L	29-31-9	Hasek	**Richter**	29	24	2-7	2-4	Satan	Hasek	**Schneider**
3/21	Pit	2-2*	T	29-31-10	**Richter**	Aubin	24	32	1-2	1-4	**Richter**	Jagr	**Nedved**
3/22	@TB	3-6	L	29-32-10	Schwab	**Cloutier**	30	27	1-4	1-3	Forbes	Sillinger	Gratton
3/24	@Fla	2-1	W	30-32-10	**Richter**	Burke	24	35	1-2	0-5	**Richter**	**Nedved**	Whitney
3/27	@Phi	1-3	L	30-33-10	Vanbiesbrouck	**Richter**	22	29	0-5	1-3	Zelepukin	Renberg	**Richter**
3/29	NYI	3-1	W	31-33-10	**Richter**	Flaherty	35	22	0-5	0-3	**Gretzky**	**Leetch**	Flaherty
4/02	Anh	1-4	L	31-34-10	Hebert	**Richter**	13	28	0-5	1-5	Selanne	Kariya	Green
4/04	@NJ	1-4	L	31-35-10	Brodeur	**Cloutier**	20	29	0-4	2-6	Sykora	Niedermayer	Elias
4/05	@Phi	5-1	W	32-35-10	**Richter**	Hextall	27	37	2-4	1-4	**Richter**	**Gretzky**	**Stevens**
4/08	@Chi	2-6	L	32-36-10	Thibault	**Richter**	24	34	1-1	1-2	Dumont	Mironov	Leroux
4/09	@Dal	1-3	L	32-37-10	Belfour	**Cloutier**	22	34	0-1	1-**1**	Keane	Belfour	Nieuwendyk
4/12	TB	2-1	W	33-37-10	**Richter**	Schwab	28	25	1-5	0-3	**Schneider**	**Langdon**	**MacLean**
4/15	@Ott	2-2*	T	33-37-11	**Cloutier**	Rhodes	23	33	0-4	1-6	**Gretzky**		
4/18	Pit	1-2*	L	33-38-11	Barrasso	**Richter**	38	23	1-2	0-**1**	**Gretzky**		

New York Rangers 1998-99 Player Statistics

Regular Season

Skater	Ps	GP	G	A	Pts	+/–	PIM	PP	SH	GW	GT	S	SPct	P/G
Wayne Gretzky	C	70	9	**53**	**62**	-23	14	3	0	3	**1**	132	6.8	**.89**
John MacLean	R	**82**	28	27	55	5	46	11	1	2	0	231	12.1	.67
Brian Leetch	D	**82**	13	42	55	-7	42	4	0	1	0	184	7.1	.67
Adam Graves	L	**82**	**38**	15	53	-12	47	**14**	**2**	**7**	0	**239**	15.9	.65
Petr Nedved	C	56	20	27	47	-6	50	9	1	3	0	153	13.1	.84
Marc Savard	C	70	9	36	45	-7	38	4	0	1	0	116	7.8	.64
Kevin Stevens	L	81	23	20	43	-10	64	8	0	3	0	136	**16.9**	.53
Niklas Sundstrom	L	81	13	30	43	-2	20	1	**2**	3	0	89	14.6	.53
Michael Knuble	R	**82**	15	20	35	-7	26	3	0	1	0	113	13.3	.43
Mathieu Schneider	D	75	10	24	34	-19	71	5	0	2	0	159	6.3	.45
Todd Harvey	R	37	11	17	28	-1	72	6	0	2	**1**	58	19.0	.76
* Manny Malhotra	C	73	8	8	16	-2	13	1	0	2	0	61	13.1	.22
Ulf Samuelsson†	D	67	4	8	12	**6**	**93**	0	0	0	0	37	10.8	.18
Brent Fedyk	L	67	4	6	10	-11	30	0	1	0	0	47	8.5	.15
Jeff Beukeboom	D	45	0	9	9	-2	60	0	0	0	0	8	0.0	.20
Alexei Kovalev†	R	14	3	4	7	-6	12	1	0	1	0	35	8.6	.50
Scott Fraser	R	28	2	4	6	-12	14	1	0	0	0	35	5.7	.21
Chris Tamer†	D	52	1	5	6	-12	92	0	0	1	0	46	2.2	.12
Peter Popovic	D	68	1	4	5	-12	40	0	0	0	0	64	1.6	.07
* Richard Brennan	D	24	1	3	4	-4	23	0	0	0	0	36	2.8	.17
* Rumun Ndur†	D	31	1	3	4	-2	46	0	0	0	0	21	4.8	.13
Eric Lacroix†	L	30	2	1	3	-5	4	0	0	1	0	17	11.8	.10
Sean Pronger†	C	14	0	3	3	-3	4	0	0	0	0	3	0.0	.21
Esa Tikkanen	L	32	0	3	3	-5	38	0	0	0	0	25	0.0	.09
* Jan Mertzig	D	23	0	2	2	-5	8	0	0	0	0	10	0.0	.09
A. Karpovtsev†	D	2	1	0	1	1	0	0	0	0	0	4	25.0	.50
Jeff Finley†	D	2	0	0	0	-1	0	0	0	0	0	0	—	.00
Derek Armstrong	C	3	0	0	0	0	0	0	0	0	0	1	0.0	.00
* Mike Maneluk†	R	4	0	0	0	-1	4	0	0	0	0	3	0.0	.00
Geoff Smith	D	4	0	0	0	-5	2	0	0	0	0	0	—	.00
* Johan Witehall	L	4	0	0	0	0	0	0	0	0	0	1	0.0	.00
P.J. Stock	L	5	0	0	0	-1	6	0	0	0	0	0	—	.00
Harry York†	C	5	0	0	0	-1	4	0	0	0	0	5	0.0	.00
Christian Dube	C	6	0	0	0	0	0	0	0	0	0	0	—	.00
Stanislav Neckar†	D	18	0	0	0	-1	8	0	0	0	0	8	0.0	.00
* Dan Cloutier	G	22	0	0	0	—	2	0	0	0	0	0	—	.00
Darren Langdon	L	45	0	0	0	-3	80	0	0	0	0	8	0.0	.00
Mike Richter	G	68	0	0	0	—	0	0	0	0	0	0	—	.00
Bench		—	—	—	—	—	0	—	—	—	—	—	—	—
TEAM TOTALS		82	217	374	591	-176	1073	71	7	33	2	2085	10.4	7.21

Postseason

GP	G	A	Pts	+/–	PIM	PP	SH	GW	OT	S	SPct	P/G

Team Did Not Qualify for Postseason Play

Regular Season

Goaltender	G	Min	GAA	W	L	T	ENG	ShO	GA	SA	SvPct
Mike Richter	**68**	**3878**	**2.63**	**27**	**30**	**8**	**6**	**4**	**170**	**1898**	**.910**
* Dan Cloutier	22	1097	2.68	6	8	3	2	0	49	570	.914
TEAM TOTALS	82	4996	2.73	33	38	11	8	4	227	2476	.908

Postseason

G	Min	GAA	W	L	ENG	ShO	GA	SA	SvPct

1998-99 New York Rangers

Record When:

Overtime games	5-3-11
In second game of back-to-back games	6-8-2
Vs playoff teams	16-26-10
Leading after two periods	21-2-5
Tied after two periods	5-9-5
Losing after two periods	7-27-1
Scoring first	18-5-7
More shots than opponents	11-13-0
Fewer shots than opponents	20-25-10
Team had at least one fighting major	14-10-2
Team had more PIM	12-14-6
Team had fewer PIM	13-16-3
Team had even PIM	8-8-2

Team

Longest winning streak	5	Nov. 29 — Dec. 7
Longest unbeaten streak	6	3 times
Longest losing streak	4	2 times
Longest winless streak	5	Oct. 9 — Oct. 17
Most shots, game	44	vs. Bos, Mar. 12
Most shots, period	18	2 times
Fewest shots, game	10	@StL, Jan. 2
Fewest shots, period	1	3 times

Individual

Longest goal streak	3	5 times
Longest point streak	9	John MacLean
Most goals, game	3	2 times
Most assists, game	5	Wayne Gretzky
Most points, game	5	2 times
Highest +/–, game	5	2 times
Lowest +/–, game	-4	7 times
Most shots, game	11	Petr Nedved

Did You Know?

In his final NHL season in 1998-99, Wayne Gretzky tallied nine goals in 70 games. As an Edmonton Oiler in 1981, Gretzky once scored nine goals in a *two*-game span.

Miscellaneous

		NHL Rank
PP Pct.	20.4 (71-348)	2
SH goals allowed	9	15t
PK Pct.	85.7 (288-336)	10
SH goals scored	7	15t
Special Team Index	105.6	6
Shots on goal	2,085 (25.4/G)	26
Shots against	2,476 (30.2/G)	24
Unassisted goals	10	21t
Unassisted goals allowed	16	19t
Team Average Weight	204.4	7
Game Star Points	374	16

Game Star Breakdown

Player	1st	2nd	3rd	Pts
Mike Richter	14	5	5	90
Wayne Gretzky	7	3	4	48
Adam Graves	5	3	2	36
Petr Nedved	4	3	2	31
John MacLean	2	5	4	29
Brian Leetch	0	7	4	25
Todd Harvey	2	3	1	20
Dan Cloutier	2	2	1	17
Kevin Stevens	2	1	4	17
Mathieu Schneider	1	2	2	13
Michael Knuble	1	2	1	12
Niklas Sundstrom	1	1	3	11
Marc Savard	0	1	2	5
Manny Malhotra	0	1	1	4
Brent Fedyk	0	1	0	3
Alexei Kovalev	0	1	0	3
Darren Langdon	0	1	0	3
Rumun Ndur	0	1	0	3
Ulf Samuelsson	0	0	2	2
Eric Lacroix	0	0	1	1
Sean Pronger	0	0	1	1

Ottawa Senators 1998-99 Game Log (44-23-15)

Date	Opp	Score	W/L/T	Record	Goalies W/T	Goalies L/T	Shots Ott	Shots Opp	Power Plays Ott	Power Plays Opp	Game Stars 1st	Game Stars 2nd	Game Stars 3rd
10/10	@Col	4-3	W	1-0-0	**Rhodes**	Roy	34	20	2-7	1-5	Sakic	**Phillips**	**Redden**
10/11	@Pho	4-1	W	2-0-0	**Rhodes**	Khabibulin	25	23	0-3	0-4	**Rhodes**	**Gardiner**	Roenick
10/17	Nsh	3-1	W	3-0-0	**Tugnutt**	Dunham	34	22	1-6	0-6	**Tugnutt**	Dunham	**Johansson**
10/21	@Mon	2-3	L	3-1-0	Thibault	**Rhodes**	28	18	0-3	1-5	Thibault	Recchi	**Dackell**
10/22	StL	3-5	L	3-2-0	McLennan	**Tugnutt**	28	32	1-10	0-5	Picard	Reasoner	**Johansson**
10/24	Car	1-3	L	3-3-0	Irbe	**Rhodes**	28	26	1-8	1-5	Primeau	**Prospal**	Irbe
10/29	Phi	3-1	W	4-3-0	**Rhodes**	Hextall	22	29	1-6	0-5	**Johansson**	**Rhodes**	Lindros
10/31	Mon	5-1	W	5-3-0	**Tugnutt**	Thibault	28	28	1-2	0-5	**Tugnutt**	**Yashin**	**McEachern**
11/01	@Phi	5-4	W	6-3-0	**Rhodes**	Hextall	20	29	1-3	0-2	**Prospal**	**York**	Maneluk
11/05	Pit	2-4	L	6-4-0	Aubin	**Rhodes**	26	22	1-2	1-4	Titov	Jagr	Hatcher
11/07	Was	5-8	L	6-5-0	Rosati	**Rhodes**	28	35	0-5	2-3	Bondra	Juneau	**Oliver**
11/10	@Buf	2-2*	T	6-5-1	**Rhodes**	Hasek	40	23	1-8	0-5	Hasek	**Rhodes**	Brown
11/12	Edm	1-1*	T	6-5-2	**Tugnutt**	Essensa	34	27	0-6	0-3	**Tugnutt**	Essensa	**Prospal**
11/14	@Tor	1-2	L	6-6-2	Joseph	**Rhodes**	28	29	0-4	0-4	Joseph	K.King	**Redden**
11/15	@Chi	2-2*	T	6-6-3	**Rhodes**	Fitzpatrick	31	25	0-7	2-4	Fitzpatrick	**Rhodes**	Amonte
11/20	@Was	4-1	W	7-6-3	**Rhodes**	Tabaracci	29	34	1-5	0-3	**Yashin**	**Dackell**	**Rhodes**
11/21	Cgy	4-1	W	8-6-3	**Rhodes**	Moss	27	24	2-7	0-5	**Yashin**	**York**	**Van Allen**
11/23	Van	4-3	W	9-6-3	**Tugnutt**	Snow	31	43	2-8	2-6	**Tugnutt**	**Johansson**	Muckalt
11/26	NYI	4-1	W	10-6-3	**Rhodes**	Flaherty	33	28	1-4	1-1	**Rhodes**	**Yashin**	**McEachern**
11/28	@Tor	2-3*	L	10-7-3	Joseph	**Rhodes**	24	27	0-1	1-4	Joseph	**Yashin**	D.King
12/01	@Nsh	3-1	W	11-7-3	**Tugnutt**	Fichaud	35	28	1-3	0-3	**Tugnutt**	**Alfredsson**	**Redden**
12/03	LA	3-1	W	12-7-3	**Tugnutt**	Fiset	18	32	0-5	0-5	**Tugnutt**	**Bonk**	Norstrom
12/05	NYR	1-2	L	12-8-3	Richter	**Rhodes**	30	17	0-4	1-1	Richter	**Arvedson**	Nedved
12/08	@TB	4-2	W	13-8-3	**Tugnutt**	Schwab	**44**	19	0-8	1-4	**McEachern**	**Yashin**	Hogue
12/09	@Fla	5-6	L	13-9-3	Burke	**Tugnutt**	30	27	2-6	5-10	Whitney	Kozlov	**Bonk**
12/12	Pho	0-2	L	13-10-3	Khabibulin	**Tugnutt**	42	25	0-3	0-2	Khabibulin	**Kravchuk**	**Tugnutt**
12/17	@Bos	2-5	L	13-11-3	Dafoe	**Rhodes**	31	27	0-4	2-3	Bourque	DiMaio	Axelsson
12/18	Car	5-1	W	14-11-3	**Tugnutt**	Irbe	34	24	2-4	1-4	**Yashin**	**McEachern**	**Tugnutt**
12/20	Dal	2-3	L	14-12-3	Turek	**Tugnutt**	29	30	2-3	1-4	Turek	Nieuwendyk	**Alfredsson**
12/23	Mon	3-1	W	15-12-3	**Tugnutt**	Hackett	30	25	0-4	1-4	**Phillips**	**Arvedson**	**Tugnutt**
12/26	@Pit	1-2*	L	15-13-3	Skudra	**Tugnutt**	31	17	0-5	0-3	Skudra	Jagr	Moran
12/28	Anh	2-2*	T	15-13-4	**Tugnutt**	Roussel	39	16	0-6	0-3	Roussel	**McEachern**	Salei
12/30	@Buf	3-2*	W	16-13-4	**Rhodes**	Hasek	**44**	23	1-4	0-3	**Dackell**	**McEachern**	Hasek
1/01	@Was	4-3	W	17-13-4	**Rhodes**	Kolzig	23	27	1-4	1-4	**Yashin**	**McEachern**	Black
1/02	NJ	6-**0**	W	18-13-4	**Rhodes**	Brodeur	32	30	1-5	0-4	**Rhodes**	**Arvedson**	**Hossa**
1/04	@Car	4-4*	T	18-13-5	**Tugnutt**	Irbe	35	24	0-2	0-1	Ranheim	Manderville	**York**
1/06	@Det	2-**0**	W	19-13-5	**Tugnutt**	Osgood	30	24	1-5	0-6	**Yashin**	**Tugnutt**	**Kravchuk**
1/08	TB	5-1	W	20-13-5	**Tugnutt**	Schwab	35	20	2-7	0-2	**Yashin**	**McEachern**	**Alfredsson**
1/10	Det	4-1	W	21-13-5	**Tugnutt**	Osgood	33	21	1-4	1-3	**Gardiner**	**Tugnutt**	**York**
1/11	@NJ	4-2	W	22-13-5	**Rhodes**	Brodeur	28	22	0-5	0-2	**Yashin**	**Alfredsson**	**Hossa**
1/14	NJ	3-2	W	23-13-5	**Rhodes**	Brodeur	24	32	1-8	0-4	**Johansson**	**Prospal**	**Redden**
1/16	Buf	1-1*	T	23-13-6	**Tugnutt**	Hasek	39	15	0-4	1-7	Hasek	**Arvedson**	**Laukkanen**
1/18	Phi	0-5	L	23-14-6	Vanbiesbrouck	**Rhodes**	36	28	0-7	1-4	Vanbiesbrouck	Desjardins	Lindros
1/19	@NYR	2-1	W	24-14-6	**Tugnutt**	Richter	28	22	0-2	1-3	**Bonk**	**Tugnutt**	Richter
1/21	@Bos	3-1	W	25-14-6	**Tugnutt**	Dafoe	28	26	0-4	0-6	**Salo**	**Tugnutt**	Dafoe
1/26	@NJ	1-4	L	25-15-6	Terreri	**Rhodes**	25	34	0-3	0-2	Terreri	Morrison	Rolston
1/30	NYI	**9**-2	W	26-15-6	**Tugnutt**	Potvin	43	22	**3-13**	1-6	**Yashin**	**Dackell**	**McEachern**
2/01	@Van	1-**0**	W	27-15-6	**Tugnutt**	Snow	29	14	1-6	0-6	Snow	**Tugnutt**	**York**
2/03	@Edm	2-2*	T	27-15-7	**Tugnutt**	Essensa	34	23	1-6	1-3	Essensa	**Tugnutt**	Marchant
2/06	@Cgy	2-1	W	28-15-7	**Rhodes**	Brathwaite	18	20	1-3	1-5	**Arvedson**	Brathwaite	**Yashin**
2/09	Buf	1-1*	T	28-15-8	**Rhodes**	Hasek	37	32	1-5	0-7	**Martins**	Hasek	**Rhodes**
2/11	Fla	1-3	L	28-16-8	McLean	**Tugnutt**	25	17	0-4	1-5	Kozlov	Worrell	**Hossa**
2/13	Was	2-1	W	29-16-8	**Rhodes**	Kolzig	24	32	0-2	0-3	**Rhodes**	**Laukkanen**	Bondra
2/15	Chi	6-2	W	30-16-8	**Rhodes**	Thibault	30	24	1-4	1-6	**Prospal**	**Redden**	**Yashin**
2/18	Bos	2-**0**	W	31-16-8	**Tugnutt**	Dafoe	28	30	1-3	0-5	**Tugnutt**	**Bonk**	**Prospal**

2/20	Phi	4-1	W	32-16-8	**Tugnutt**	Vanbiesbrouck	19	34	1-3	0-6	**Tugnutt**	**Bonk**	Desjardins
2/23	@Bos	2-5	L	32-17-8	Dafoe	**Tugnutt**	28	32	0-4	1-2	Mann	Dafoe	**McEachern**
2/25	Mon	3-1	W	33-17-8	**Rhodes**	Hackett	28	25	0-2	0-5	**Johansson**	**Rhodes**	**Yashin**
2/27	@Mon	1-4	L	33-18-8	Hackett	**Rhodes**	26	29	0-3	0-2	Malakhov	Hackett	Koivu
3/02	@NYI	4-2	W	34-18-8	**Tugnutt**	Salo	29	37	0-1	1-7	**Arvedson**	**Tugnutt**	Lawrence
3/04	@Phi	5-**0**	W	35-18-8	**Rhodes**	Pelletier	29	24	1-2	0-4	**Yashin**	**Alfredsson**	**Rhodes**
3/06	Tor	3-1	W	36-18-8	**Tugnutt**	Joseph	30	26	1-6	1-5	**Tugnutt**	**Bonk**	**Hossa**
3/08	TB	**9**-3	W	37-18-8	**Rhodes**	Schwab	38	19	**3**-6	0-**1**	**Arvedson**	**Yashin**	**Hossa**
3/10	@NYR	3-**0**	W	38-18-8	**Rhodes**	Richter	33	29	1-5	0-4	**Yashin**	**Rhodes**	**Bonk**
3/13	@SJ	2-3	L	38-19-8	Shields	**Rhodes**	36	20	1-5	0-2	Stern	Shields	**Dackell**
3/15	@LA	0-4	L	38-20-8	Fiset	**Tugnutt**	29	30	0-3	1-4	Fiset	R.Blake	Audette
3/17	@Anh	2-2*	T	38-20-9	**Rhodes**	Hebert	43	21	1-3	0-**1**	**Hossa**	Hebert	**Yashin**
3/19	@Dal	2-1	W	39-20-9	**Rhodes**	Belfour	14	32	0-2	1-4	**Rhodes**	Modano	**Hossa**
3/20	@StL	3-2	W	40-20-9	**Tugnutt**	Fuhr	15	22	0-4	0-**1**	Demitra	**McEachern**	**Tugnutt**
3/24	Bos	0-3	L	40-21-9	Dafoe	**Tugnutt**	28	17	0-5	1-2	Dafoe	Gill	Bourque
3/26	SJ	1-1*	T	40-21-10	**Rhodes**	Vernon	41	26	0-5	0-4	Vernon	**Redden**	**Yashin**
3/27	@NYI	7-3	W	41-21-10	**Tugnutt**	Flaherty	36	23	2-8	0-5	**Hossa**	**Yashin**	**York**
3/30	@Pit	6-4	W	42-21-10	**Rhodes**	Skudra	27	25	0-1	1-3	**Salo**	**Arvedson**	Jagr
4/01	Pit	3-3*	T	42-21-11	**Tugnutt**	Aubin	34	21	0-5	1-3	**Bonk**	Jagr	**Hossa**
4/03	@Fla	6-4	W	43-21-11	**Rhodes**	Burke	36	26	1-4	0-2	**Yashin**	Garpenlov	**Dackell**
4/05	@TB	4-4*	T	43-21-12	**Tugnutt**	Schwab	39	24	2-6	1-4	Zamuner	**Arvedson**	Daigle
4/07	@Tor	2-4	L	43-22-12	Joseph	**Rhodes**	29	31	1-8	1-5	Perreault	Yushkevich	**Hossa**
4/08	Tor	3-1	W	44-22-12	**Tugnutt**	Joseph	36	31	1-6	0-5	**Prospal**	**Arvedson**	Berezin
4/10	Buf	1-1*	T	44-22-13	**Rhodes**	Hasek	18	12	1-8	0-5	Hasek	**Yashin**	Woolley
4/12	Fla	0-2	L	44-23-13	McLean	**Tugnutt**	39	**11**	0-7	0-4	McLean	**Yashin**	**Prospal**
4/15	NYR	2-2*	T	44-23-14	**Rhodes**	Cloutier	33	23	1-6	0-4	Gretzky		
4/17	@Car	1-1*	T	44-23-15	**Tugnutt**	Irbe	31	25	1-4	0-2	Battaglia	**Tugnutt**	Irbe
						Postseason							
4/21	Buf	1-**2**	L	0-1	Hasek	**Tugnutt**	41	**15**	1-**9**	1-**3**	Hasek	Peca	**Emerson**
4/23	Buf	2-3*	L	0-2	Hasek	**Rhodes**	**47**	39	**2-9**	1-7	Satan	Hasek	**McEachern**
4/25	@Buf	0-3	L	0-3	Hasek	**Rhodes**	31	26	0-4	1-5	Hasek	Holzinger	Varada
4/27	@Buf	**3**-4	L	0-4	Hasek	**Tugnutt**	43	26	0-5	1-**3**	Varada	Hasek	**Alfredsson**

Ottawa Senators 1998-99 Player Statistics

Skater	Ps	Regular Season GP	G	A	Pts	+/–	PIM	PP	SH	GW	GT	S	SPct	P/G	Postseason GP	G	A	Pts	+/–	PIM	PP	SH	GW	OT	S	SPct	P/G
Alexei Yashin	C	**82**	**44**	**50**	**94**	16	54	**19**	0	5	1	**337**	13.1	**1.15**	**4**	0	0	0	-4	**10**	0	0	0	0	**24**	0.0	.00
Shawn McEachern	L	77	31	25	56	8	46	7	0	4	1	223	13.9	.73	**4**	**2**	0	2	**1**	6	**1**	0	0	0	11	**18.2**	.50
Andreas Dackell	R	77	15	35	50	9	30	6	0	3	0	107	14.0	.65	**4**	0	1	1	-3	0	0	0	0	0	3	0.0	.25
Magnus Arvedson	L	80	21	26	47	**33**	50	0	**4**	**6**	0	136	**15.4**	.59	3	0	1	1	-1	2	0	0	0	0	8	0.0	.33
Andreas Johansson	C	69	21	16	37	1	34	7	0	**6**	0	144	14.6	.54	2	0	0	0	-3	0	0	0	0	0	4	0.0	.00
Vaclav Prospal	C	79	10	26	36	8	58	2	0	3	0	114	8.8	.46	**4**	0	0	0	-2	0	0	0	0	0	6	0.0	.00
Jason York	D	79	4	31	35	17	48	2	0	0	1	177	2.3	.44	**4**	1	1	2	-1	4	0	0	0	0	12	8.3	.50
Daniel Alfredsson	R	58	11	22	33	8	14	3	0	5	0	163	6.7	.57	**4**	1	2	3	-1	4	**1**	0	0	0	13	7.7	.75
Radek Bonk	C	81	16	16	32	15	48	0	1	**6**	0	110	14.5	.40	**4**	0	0	0	-1	6	0	0	0	0	8	0.0	.00
* Marian Hossa	L	60	15	15	30	18	37	1	0	2	**2**	124	12.1	.50	**4**	0	2	2	**1**	4	0	0	0	0	11	0.0	.50
Wade Redden	D	72	8	21	29	7	54	3	0	1	1	127	6.3	.40	**4**	1	2	3	-1	2	**1**	0	0	0	11	9.1	.75
Igor Kravchuk	D	79	4	21	25	14	32	3	0	0	0	171	2.3	.32	**4**	0	0	0	-5	0	0	0	0	0	12	0.0	.00
* Sami Salo	D	61	7	12	19	20	24	2	0	1	0	106	6.6	.31	**4**	0	0	0	-3	0	0	0	0	0	10	0.0	.00
Shaun Van Allen	C	79	6	11	17	3	30	0	1	0	0	47	12.8	.22	**4**	0	0	0	-1	0	0	0	0	0	2	0.0	.00
Bruce Gardiner	C	59	4	8	12	6	43	0	0	1	0	70	5.7	.20	3	0	0	0	0	4	0	0	0	0	4	0.0	.00
Janne Laukkanen	D	50	1	11	12	18	40	0	0	0	0	46	2.2	.24	**4**	0	0	0	**1**	4	0	0	0	0	8	0.0	.00
* Patrick Traverse	D	46	1	9	10	12	22	0	0	0	0	35	2.9	.22	—	—	—	—	—	—	—	—	—	—	—	—	—
Lance Pitlick	D	50	3	6	9	7	33	0	0	0	0	34	8.8	.18	2	0	0	0	-1	0	0	0	0	0	2	0.0	.00
Steve Martins	C	36	4	3	7	4	10	1	0	1	0	27	14.8	.19	—	—	—	—	—	—	—	—	—	—	—	—	—
David Oliver	R	17	2	5	7	1	4	0	0	0	0	18	11.1	.41	—	—	—	—	—	—	—	—	—	—	—	—	—
Chris Murray†	R	38	1	6	7	-2	**65**	0	0	0	0	33	3.0	.18	—	—	—	—	—	—	—	—	—	—	—	—	—
Chris Phillips	D	34	3	3	6	-5	32	2	0	0	0	51	5.9	.18	3	0	0	0	-1	0	0	0	0	0	1	0.0	.00
Ted Donato†	L	13	3	2	5	2	10	1	0	0	0	16	18.8	.38	1	0	0	0	0	0	0	0	0	0	0	—	.00
Bill Berg	L	44	2	2	4	4	28	0	0	0	1	40	5.0	.09	2	0	0	0	0	0	0	0	0	0	0	—	.00
Nelson Emerson†	R	3	1	1	2	-1	2	0	0	0	0	10	10.0	.67	**4**	1	**3**	**4**	0	0	0	0	0	0	12	8.3	**1.00**
Damian Rhodes	G	45	1	1	2	—	4	0	0	0	0	1	100.0	.04	2	0	0	0	—	0	0	0	0	0	0	—	.00
Stanislav Neckar†	D	3	0	2	2	-1	0	0	0	0	0	2	0.0	.67	—	—	—	—	—	—	—	—	—	—	—	—	—
Steve Leach†	R	9	0	2	2	-1	6	0	0	0	0	4	0.0	.22	—	—	—	—	—	—	—	—	—	—	—	—	—
Slava Butsayev†	C	2	0	1	1	0	2	0	0	0	0	5	0.0	.50	—	—	—	—	—	—	—	—	—	—	—	—	—
Philip Crowe	L	8	0	1	1	1	4	0	0	0	0	2	0.0	.13	—	—	—	—	—	—	—	—	—	—	—	—	—
Yves Sarault	L	11	0	1	1	1	4	0	0	0	0	7	0.0	.09	—	—	—	—	—	—	—	—	—	—	—	—	—
John Gruden	D	13	0	1	1	0	8	0	0	0	0	10	0.0	.08	—	—	—	—	—	—	—	—	—	—	—	—	—
Radim Bicanek†	D	7	0	0	0	-1	4	0	0	0	0	6	0.0	.00	—	—	—	—	—	—	—	—	—	—	—	—	—
Ron Tugnutt	G	43	0	0	0	—	0	0	0	0	0	0	—	.00	2	0	0	0	—	0	0	0	0	0	0	—	.00
Bench		—	—	—	—	—	0	—	—	—	—	—	—	—	—	—	—	—	—	0	—	—	—	—	—	—	—
TEAM TOTALS		82	239	392	631	222	880	59	6	44	7	2503	9.5	7.70	4	6	12	18	-25	46	3	0	0	0	162	3.7	4.50

Goaltender	Regular Season G	Min	GAA	W	L	T	ENG	ShO	GA	SA	SvPct	Postseason G	Min	GAA	W	L	ENG	ShO	GA	SA	SvPct
Ron Tugnutt	43	**2508**	**1.79**	**22**	10	**8**	**2**	**3**	75	1005	**.925**	**2**	118	3.05	0	**2**	0	0	**6**	41	.854
Damian Rhodes	**45**	2480	2.44	**22**	**13**	7	1	**3**	**101**	**1060**	.905	**2**	**150**	**2.40**	0	**2**	0	0	**6**	**65**	**.908**
TEAM TOTALS	82	4999	2.15	44	23	15	3	6	179	2068	.913	4	271	2.66	0	4	0	0	12	106	.887

1998-99 Ottawa Senators

Record When:

Overtime games	1-2-15
In second game of back-to-back games	10-2-1
Vs playoff teams	20-15-12
Leading after two periods	32-2-2
Tied after two periods	11-3-10
Losing after two periods	1-18-3
Scoring first	33-6-9
More shots than opponents	29-13-15
Fewer shots than opponents	14-10-0
Team had at least one fighting major	9-3-1
Team had more PIM	12-7-2
Team had fewer PIM	26-14-13
Team had even PIM	6-2-0

Team

Longest winning streak	5	2 times
Longest unbeaten streak	11	Dec. 28 — Jan. 16
Longest losing streak	3	2 times
Longest winless streak	6	Nov. 5 — Nov. 15
Most shots, game	44	2 times
Most shots, period	20	2nd, vs. TB, Mar. 8
Fewest shots, game	14	@Dal, Mar. 19
Fewest shots, period	1	2 times

Individual

Longest goal streak	5	Alexei Yashin [2]
Longest point streak	11	Alexei Yashin
Most goals, game	3	3 times
Most assists, game	3	7 times
Most points, game	5	Alexei Yashin
Highest +/–, game	4	Magnus Arvedson
Lowest +/–, game	-3	5 times
Most shots, game	12	Jason York

Did You Know?

The 1998-99 Senators, with a winning percentage of .628, were just the third team in the last 15 years to post a regular-season winning percentage of .600 or better, then fail to win a playoff game. Only the 1992-93 Boston Bruins (.649) and '92-93 Chicago Blackhawks (.631) also managed this dubious feat.

Miscellaneous

		NHL Rank
PP Pct.	14.9 (59-397)	15
SH goals allowed	13	26
PK Pct.	86.1 (273-317)	8
SH goals scored	6	21t
Special Team Index	99.6	14
Shots on goal	2,503 (30.5/G)	3
Shots against	2,068 (25.2/G)	5
Unassisted goals	24	1
Unassisted goals allowed	8	2t
Team Average Weight	200.8	14
Game Star Points	435	4

Game Star Breakdown

Player	1st	2nd	3rd	Pts
Alexei Yashin	11	8	5	84
Ron Tugnutt	9	8	4	73
Damian Rhodes	5	5	3	43
Magnus Arvedson	3	7	0	36
Shawn McEachern	1	6	4	27
Vaclav Prospal	3	2	3	24
Radek Bonk	2	4	2	24
Andreas Johansson	3	1	2	20
Marian Hossa	2	0	8	18
Andreas Dackell	1	2	3	14
Daniel Alfredsson	0	3	2	11
Sami Salo	2	0	0	10
Wade Redden	0	2	4	10
Jason York	0	2	4	10
Bruce Gardiner	1	1	0	8
Chris Phillips	1	1	0	8
Steve Martins	1	0	0	5
Igor Kravchuk	0	1	1	4
Janne Laukkanen	0	1	1	4
David Oliver	0	0	1	1
Shaun Van Allen	0	0	1	1

Philadelphia Flyers 1998-99 Game Log (37-26-19)

					Goalies		Shots		Power Plays		Game Stars		
Date	Opp	Score	W/L/T	Record	W/T	L/T	Phi	Opp	Phi	Opp	1st	2nd	3rd
10/09	@NYR	1-0	W	1-0-0	**Vanbiesbrouck**	Richter	30	20	1-5	0-6	**Vanbiesbrouck**	Richter	**Daigle**
10/11	Anh	4-1	W	2-0-0	**Vanbiesbrouck**	Hebert	32	22	2-8	1-7	**Lindros**	**LeClair**	**McGillis**
10/16	@TB	5-2	W	3-0-0	**Hextall**	Puppa	36	26	2-5	0-5	**LeClair**	**Lindros**	**Brind'Amour**
10/17	@Car	1-1*	T	3-0-1	**Vanbiesbrouck**	Irbe	19	19	0-5	1-6	Wesley	**Lindros**	Irbe
10/20	SJ	3-1	W	4-0-1	**Vanbiesbrouck**	Vernon	37	18	1-5	1-4	**Brind'Amour**	**Forbes**	Vernon
10/22	NJ	2-3	L	4-1-1	Brodeur	**Vanbiesbrouck**	22	18	1-4	1-3	Rolston	McKay	**Lindros**
10/24	NYR	2-2*	T	4-1-2	**Vanbiesbrouck**	Richter	37	13	1-4	1-3	Richter	**LeClair**	Gretzky
10/27	StL	2-1	W	5-1-2	**Vanbiesbrouck**	McLennan	20	30	1-9	0-4	**McGillis**	**Forbes**	Turgeon
10/29	@Ott	1-3	L	5-2-2	Rhodes	**Hextall**	29	22	0-5	1-6	Johansson	Rhodes	**Lindros**
10/31	@NYI	2-3	L	5-3-2	Salo	**Vanbiesbrouck**	30	17	0-4	0-3	Smolinski	Watt	**Zelepukin**
11/01	Ott	4-5	L	5-4-2	Rhodes	**Hextall**	29	20	0-2	1-3	Prospal	York	**Maneluk**
11/03	@Pit	4-4*	T	5-4-3	**Vanbiesbrouck**	Skudra	24	22	2-6	1-7	Galanov	**Lindros**	Jagr
11/07	Buf	2-2*	T	5-4-4	**Vanbiesbrouck**	Hasek	37	19	1-4	0-2	Hasek	**Brind'Amour**	Sanderson
11/09	@Mon	1-5	L	5-5-4	Theodore	**Vanbiesbrouck**	31	19	0-7	1-5	Savage	Theodore	Rucinsky
11/12	Fla	1-2	L	5-6-4	McLean	**Vanbiesbrouck**	40	15	0-4	1-3	Parrish	Murphy	**Svoboda**
11/14	NJ	6-1	W	6-6-4	**Hextall**	Brodeur	40	18	1-6	0-4	**Lindros**	**Hextall**	**Jones**
11/17	@Pit	4-1	W	7-6-4	**Vanbiesbrouck**	Barrasso	20	26	1-6	0-7	**Vanbiesbrouck**	**Brind'Amour**	Lang
11/20	@Car	3-1	W	8-6-4	**Hextall**	Irbe	27	19	1-5	0-5	**Hextall**	Sheppard	**Lindros**
11/22	@Fla	2-1*	W	9-6-4	**Vanbiesbrouck**	McLean	16	26	0-2	0-3	**Vanbiesbrouck**	**Jones**	Jovanovski
11/25	@NYI	2-4	L	9-7-4	Salo	**Vanbiesbrouck**	46	14	1-6	3-5	Salo	Berard	**LeClair**
11/27	Tor	4-3	W	10-7-4	**Vanbiesbrouck**	Joseph	23	22	0-2	0-3	**Lindros**	Warriner	**LeClair**
11/29	Van	6-2	W	11-7-4	**Hextall**	Snow	35	22	1-5	0-3	**LeClair**	**Jones**	**Lindros**
12/04	@Buf	0-3	L	11-8-4	Hasek	**Vanbiesbrouck**	31	15	0-7	1-5	Hasek	Shannon	Sanderson
12/05	Was	2-1	W	12-8-4	**Hextall**	Tabaracci	28	23	2-4	1-3	**Brind'Amour**	**Hextall**	**Lindros**
12/08	@NJ	5-5*	T	12-8-5	**Hextall**	Brodeur	25	20	2-5	1-4	Arnott	**Lindros**	Daneyko
12/10	NJ	4-5*	L	12-9-5	Brodeur	**Hextall**	30	34	1-5	2-4	Andreychuk	**Lindros**	McKay
12/12	@Tor	3-0	W	13-9-5	**Vanbiesbrouck**	Joseph	27	23	0-4	0-7	**Lindros**	**LeClair**	**Vanbiesbrouck**
12/13	Edm	2-2*	T	13-9-6	**Vanbiesbrouck**	Shtalenkov	19	24	0-3	0-7	**Desjardins**	Shtalenkov	**Vanbiesbrouck**
12/17	Cgy	3-3*	T	13-9-7	**Vanbiesbrouck**	Giguere	42	35	1-3	1-7	Fleury	**Renberg**	Giguere
12/19	Chi	3-1	W	14-9-7	**Vanbiesbrouck**	Fitzpatrick	40	24	1-6	0-4	**Bureau**	**Vanbiesbrouck**	**McGillis**
12/20	TB	2-2*	T	14-9-8	**Hextall**	Ranford	32	30	1-5	0-2	**Brind'Amour**	Ranford	**Hextall**
12/23	@Bos	2-1	W	15-9-8	**Vanbiesbrouck**	Dafoe	32	29	0-3	0-4	**LeClair**	Thornton	**Lindros**
12/26	@Chi	3-2	W	16-9-8	**Vanbiesbrouck**	Thibault	28	20	1-8	1-5	**Lindros**	**Desjardins**	Gilmour
12/28	@SJ	1-1*	T	16-9-9	**Vanbiesbrouck**	Vernon	23	23	1-4	0-4	Vernon	**Lindros**	Marchment
12/29	@Cgy	4-3*	W	17-9-9	**Hextall**	Trefilov	37	27	0-5	1-4	Trefilov	**Zubrus**	**Zelepukin**
12/31	@Van	6-2	W	18-9-9	**Vanbiesbrouck**	Snow	24	25	0-4	1-4	**Brind'Amour**	**Desjardins**	**LeClair**
1/03	@Edm	3-3*	T	18-9-10	**Vanbiesbrouck**	Shtalenkov	26	29	0-4	1-5	**Brind'Amour**	Smyth	**LeClair**
1/07	NYI	5-0	W	19-9-10	**Vanbiesbrouck**	Salo	26	27	1-3	0-4	**Vanbiesbrouck**	**Lindros**	**Greig**
1/09	Car	2-0	W	20-9-10	**Hextall**	Irbe	30	20	0-4	0-4	**Lindros**	**Brind'Amour**	**Hextall**
1/11	Nsh	8-0	W	21-9-10	**Vanbiesbrouck**	Vokoun	41	24	4-6	0-5	**Lindros**	**McGillis**	**Vanbiesbrouck**
1/13	@Was	3-0	W	22-9-10	**Vanbiesbrouck**	Kolzig	28	25	0-4	0-3	**Desjardins**	**Vanbiesbrouck**	**Lindros**
1/16	Tor	3-4	L	22-10-10	Joseph	**Vanbiesbrouck**	28	32	1-4	1-4	D.King	Sullivan	**LeClair**
1/18	@Ott	5-0	W	23-10-10	**Vanbiesbrouck**	Rhodes	28	36	1-4	0-7	**Vanbiesbrouck**	**Desjardins**	**Lindros**
1/21	Was	4-1	W	24-10-10	**Hextall**	Kolzig	26	18	1-3	0-1	**Jones**	**Lindros**	**Dykhuis**
1/26	Fla	3-3*	T	24-10-11	**Vanbiesbrouck**	Burke	30	19	0-3	1-4	Bure	**Langkow**	**Desjardins**
1/28	Pho	4-2	W	25-10-11	**Vanbiesbrouck**	Khabibulin	25	25	0-4	0-5	**LeClair**	**Jones**	**Zelepukin**
1/30	TB	6-2	W	26-10-11	**Hextall**	Schwab	44	21	2-7	0-4	**Brind'Amour**	**McGillis**	**LeClair**
2/01	LA	4-2	W	27-10-11	**Vanbiesbrouck**	Fiset	25	25	1-3	0-3	**Vanbiesbrouck**	**Jones**	**Desjardins**
2/04	Mon	5-2	W	28-10-11	**Vanbiesbrouck**	Hackett	24	21	1-4	0-5	**LeClair**	**McGillis**	**Lindros**
2/06	Bos	2-2*	T	28-10-12	**Hextall**	Tallas	27	29	1-8	0-3	Samsonov	**Lindros**	Bourque
2/10	@Anh	4-5	L	28-11-12	Hebert	**Vanbiesbrouck**	32	24	3-9	3-6	Selanne	**Lindros**	Olausson
2/11	@LA	3-4	L	28-12-12	Fiset	**Hextall**	31	25	0-5	0-6	Stumpel	Robitaille	Rosa
2/14	@Col	4-4*	T	28-12-13	**Vanbiesbrouck**	Roy	25	31	0-4	1-6	Kamensky	Forsberg	**Desjardins**
2/16	@Pho	4-1	W	29-12-13	**Vanbiesbrouck**	Khabibulin	41	33	0-1	0-3	**LeClair**	**Jones**	**Lindros**
2/18	Mon	1-3	L	29-13-13	Hackett	**Vanbiesbrouck**	22	21	0-3	1-3	Brunet	Recchi	**Lindros**

2/20 @Ott	1-4	L	29-14-13	Tugnutt	**Vanbiesbrouck**	34	19	0-6	1-3	Tugnutt	Bonk	**Desjardins**
2/21 Pit	2-1	W	30-14-13	**Hextall**	Barrasso	26	19	1-5	1-4	**Lindros**	**Langkow**	Straka
2/24 @Fla	3-5	L	30-15-13	Burke	**Vanbiesbrouck**	27	24	1-7	2-5	Kvasha	**Lindros**	Parrish
2/26 @TB	1-4	L	30-16-13	Schwab	**Hextall**	37	20	1-5	1-5	Schwab	Lecavalier	Gratton
2/28 @NYR	5-6	L	30-17-13	Richter	**Vanbiesbrouck**	26	26	2-7	4-7	Nedved	Graves	**Lindros**
3/02 @Mon	1-4	L	30-18-13	Hackett	**Vanbiesbrouck**	38	17	1-4	0-2	Hackett	Quintal	Malakhov
3/04 Ott	0-5	L	30-19-13	Rhodes	**Pelletier**	24	29	0-4	1-2	Yashin	Alfredsson	Rhodes
3/06 NYI	3-3*	T	30-19-14	**Vanbiesbrouck**	Salo	28	25	1-6	1-4	Palffy	**Lindros**	Pilon
3/07 @Buf	1-1*	T	30-19-15	**Vanbiesbrouck**	Biron	31	22	0-3	0-5	Biron	Shannon	**Zelepukin**
3/09 @NYI	2-2*	T	30-19-16	**Vanbiesbrouck**	Salo	35	22	2-8	1-2	Lawrence	Palffy	**Langkow**
3/11 Col	3-5	L	30-20-16	Roy	**Vanbiesbrouck**	36	27	1-4	0-**1**	Forsberg	Drury	**Lindros**
3/13 @Pit	0-4	L	30-21-16	Skudra	**Hextall**	24	19	0-4	1-4	Jagr	Straka	Skudra
3/14 Dal	1-1*	T	30-21-17	**Vanbiesbrouck**	Belfour	27	23	0-6	0-6	**Hull**	Modano	**Brind'Amour**
3/16 @StL	2-5	L	30-22-17	Fuhr	**Vanbiesbrouck**	28	27	0-4	2-4	MacInnis	Pronger	Young
3/21 Det	5-4	W	31-22-17	**Vanbiesbrouck**	Osgood	31	21	0-4	2-4	**Lindros**	Shanahan	**Recchi**
3/22 @Tor	3-1	W	32-22-17	**Vanbiesbrouck**	Joseph	28	20	2-5	0-6	**Lindros**	**Babych**	Markov
3/27 NYR	3-1	W	33-22-17	**Vanbiesbrouck**	Richter	29	22	1-3	0-5	**Zelepukin**	**Renberg**	Richter
3/28 @Det	2-3*	L	33-23-17	Osgood	**Vanbiesbrouck**	25	30	1-5	1-3	Clark	Kozlov	**Brind'Amour**
3/30 Car	3-3*	T	33-23-18	**Hextall**	Kidd	31	21	3-6	1-4	**Brind'Amour**	Halko	**Renberg**
4/01 @Nsh	2-1	W	34-23-18	**Vanbiesbrouck**	Vokoun	39	23	0-4	0-**1**	**Renberg**	**Brind'Amour**	Vokoun
4/03 @Bos	0-3	L	34-24-18	Dafoe	**Vanbiesbrouck**	24	20	0-3	0-3	Bates	Samsonov	Dafoe
4/05 NYR	1-5	L	34-25-18	Richter	**Hextall**	37	27	1-4	2-4	Richter	Gretzky	Stevens
4/08 Pit	3-1	W	35-25-18	**Vanbiesbrouck**	Skudra	33	17	1-3	1-3	**Brind'Amour**	**Vanbiesbrouck**	**Desjardins**
4/10 @Was	2-1	W	36-25-18	**Vanbiesbrouck**	Kolzig	32	18	0-2	0-**1**	**Jones**	Gratton	**Desjardins**
4/13 Buf	2-2*	T	36-25-19	**Vanbiesbrouck**	Hasek	33	15	1-5	0-3	**LeClair**	Hasek	**Desjardins**
4/16 @NJ	2-3*	L	36-26-19	Terreri	**Vanbiesbrouck**	29	29	0-3	1-2	Holik	Terreri	**Brind'Amour**
4/18 Bos	3-1	W	37-26-19	**Vanbiesbrouck**	Tallas	22	**11**	2-5	0-**1**	**LeClair**	**Greig**	**Desjardins**

Postseason

4/22 @Tor	3-**0**	W	1-0	**Vanbiesbrouck**	Joseph	24	25	1-5	0-6	**Vanbiesbrouck**	Berezin	**LeClair**
4/24 @Tor	1-2	L	1-1	Joseph	**Vanbiesbrouck**	25	21	0-4	0-7	Sundin	Joseph	**Brind'Amour**
4/26 Tor	1-2	L	1-2	Joseph	**Vanbiesbrouck**	**41**	21	0-5	1-**4**	Joseph	**Dykhuis**	Thomas
4/28 Tor	**5**-2	W	2-2	**Vanbiesbrouck**	Joseph	**41**	25	**2**-5	2-8	**LeClair**	**Desjardins**	**Vanbiesbrouck**
4/30 @Tor	1-2*	L	2-3	Joseph	**Vanbiesbrouck**	34	34	0-2	1-**4**	Perreault	D.King	**Brind'Amour**
5/02 Tor	0-1	L	2-4	Joseph	**Vanbiesbrouck**	26	**20**	0-**6**	1-5	Berezin	Joseph	**Vanbiesbrouck**

Philadelphia Flyers 1998-99 Player Statistics

Skater	Ps	GP	G	A	Pts	+/–	PIM	PP	SH	GW	GT	S	SPct	P/G	GP	G	A	Pts	+/–	PIM	PP	SH	GW	OT	S	SPct	P/G
		Regular Season													Postseason												
Eric Lindros	C	71	40	53	93	35	120	10	1	2	3	242	16.5	1.31	—	—	—	—	—	—	—	—	—	—	—	—	—
John LeClair	L	76	43	47	90	36	30	16	0	7	3	246	17.5	1.18	6	3	0	3	0	12	2	0	0	0	15	20.0	.50
Rod Brind'Amour	C	82	24	50	74	3	47	10	0	3	2	191	12.6	.90	6	1	3	4	1	0	0	0	0	0	19	5.3	.67
Eric Desjardins	D	68	15	36	51	18	38	6	0	2	0	190	7.9	.75	6	2	2	4	1	4	1	0	1	0	21	9.5	.67
Keith Jones†	R	66	18	31	49	29	78	2	0	3	0	124	14.5	.74	6	2	1	3	4	14	0	0	0	0	11	18.2	.50
Daniel McGillis	D	78	8	37	45	16	61	6	0	4	0	164	4.9	.58	6	0	1	1	2	12	0	0	0	0	15	0.0	.17
Mikael Renberg†	R	46	11	15	26	7	14	4	0	2	0	112	9.8	.57	6	0	1	1	-1	0	0	0	0	0	18	0.0	.17
Valeri Zelepukin	L	74	16	9	25	0	48	0	0	5	0	129	12.4	.34	4	1	0	1	1	4	0	0	1	0	5	20.0	.25
Daymond Langkow†	C	56	10	13	23	-8	24	3	1	1	0	109	9.2	.41	6	0	2	2	3	2	0	0	0	0	4	0.0	.33
Chris Therien	D	74	3	15	18	16	48	1	0	0	0	115	2.6	.24	6	0	0	0	1	6	0	0	0	0	6	0.0	.00
Colin Forbes†	L	66	9	7	16	0	51	0	0	4	0	92	9.8	.24	—	—	—	—	—	—	—	—	—	—	—	—	—
Jody Hull	R	72	3	11	14	-2	12	0	0	1	1	73	4.1	.19	6	0	0	0	-1	4	0	0	0	0	6	0.0	.00
Marc Bureau	C	71	4	6	10	-2	10	0	0	0	0	52	7.7	.14	6	0	2	2	2	2	0	0	0	0	3	0.0	.33
* Dmitri Tertyshny	D	62	2	8	10	-1	30	1	0	0	0	68	2.9	.16	1	0	0	0	0	2	0	0	0	0	1	0.0	.00
Dainius Zubrus†	R	63	3	5	8	-5	25	0	1	0	0	49	6.1	.13	—	—	—	—	—	—	—	—	—	—	—	—	—
* Mike Maneluk†	R	13	2	6	8	4	8	0	0	0	0	23	8.7	.62	—	—	—	—	—	—	—	—	—	—	—	—	—
Chris Gratton†	C	26	1	7	8	-8	41	0	0	0	0	54	1.9	.31	—	—	—	—	—	—	—	—	—	—	—	—	—
Steve Duchesne†	D	11	2	5	7	0	2	1	0	1	0	19	10.5	.64	6	0	2	2	2	2	0	0	0	0	10	0.0	.33
Mark Recchi†	R	10	4	2	6	-3	6	0	0	0	0	19	21.1	.60	6	0	1	1	-1	2	0	0	0	0	18	0.0	.17
Petr Svoboda†	D	25	4	2	6	5	28	1	1	1	0	37	10.8	.24	—	—	—	—	—	—	—	—	—	—	—	—	—
Dave Babych†	D	33	2	4	6	0	20	2	0	0	0	44	4.5	.18	—	—	—	—	—	—	—	—	—	—	—	—	—
Karl Dykhuis†	D	45	2	4	6	-2	32	1	0	0	0	61	3.3	.13	5	1	0	1	1	4	0	0	0	0	12	8.3	.20
Luke Richardson	D	78	0	6	6	-3	106	0	0	0	0	49	0.0	.08	—	—	—	—	—	—	—	—	—	—	—	—	—
Alexandre Daigle†	C	31	3	2	5	-1	2	1	0	1	0	26	11.5	.16	—	—	—	—	—	—	—	—	—	—	—	—	—
Mark Greig	R	7	1	3	4	1	2	0	0	0	0	9	11.1	.57	2	0	1	1	1	0	0	0	0	0	3	0.0	.50
Mike Sillinger†	C	25	0	3	3	-9	8	0	0	0	0	23	0.0	.12	—	—	—	—	—	—	—	—	—	—	—	—	—
Roman Vopat†	C	48	0	3	3	-3	80	0	0	0	0	25	0.0	.06	—	—	—	—	—	—	—	—	—	—	—	—	—
Ron Hextall	G	23	0	2	2	—	2	0	0	0	0	0	—	.09	—	—	—	—	—	—	—	—	—	—	—	—	—
Shjon Podein†	L	14	1	0	1	-2	0	0	0	0	0	26	3.8	.07	—	—	—	—	—	—	—	—	—	—	—	—	—
* Ryan Bast	D	2	0	1	1	0	0	0	0	0	0	1	0.0	.50	—	—	—	—	—	—	—	—	—	—	—	—	—
* Andy Delmore	D	2	0	1	1	-1	0	0	0	0	0	2	0.0	.50	—	—	—	—	—	—	—	—	—	—	—	—	—
Mikael Andersson†	R	7	0	1	1	1	0	0	0	0	0	11	0.0	.14	6	0	1	1	1	2	0	0	0	0	7	0.0	.17
Andrei Kovalenko†	R	13	0	1	1	-5	2	0	0	0	0	8	0.0	.08	—	—	—	—	—	—	—	—	—	—	—	—	—
Sandy McCarthy†	R	13	0	1	1	-2	25	0	0	0	0	18	0.0	.08	6	0	1	1	1	0	0	0	0	0	7	0.0	.17
Adam Burt†	D	17	0	1	1	1	14	0	0	0	0	24	0.0	.06	6	0	0	0	1	4	0	0	0	0	3	0.0	.00
John Vanbiesbrouck	G	62	0	1	1	—	12	0	0	0	0	0	—	.02	6	0	0	0	—	2	0	0	0	0	0	—	.00
* Jean-Marc Pelletier	G	1	0	0	0	—	0	0	0	0	0	0	—	.00	—	—	—	—	—	—	—	—	—	—	—	—	—
* Brian Wesenberg	R	1	0	0	0	1	5	0	0	0	0	0	—	.00	—	—	—	—	—	—	—	—	—	—	—	—	—
Chris Joseph	D	2	0	0	0	0	2	0	0	0	0	1	0.0	.00	—	—	—	—	—	—	—	—	—	—	—	—	—
Trent Klatt†	R	2	0	0	0	0	0	0	0	0	0	2	0.0	.00	—	—	—	—	—	—	—	—	—	—	—	—	—
Dan Kordic	L	2	0	0	0	-1	2	0	0	0	0	0	—	.00	—	—	—	—	—	—	—	—	—	—	—	—	—
Jason Zent	L	2	0	0	0	0	0	0	0	0	0	1	0.0	.00	—	—	—	—	—	—	—	—	—	—	—	—	—
Peter White	C	3	0	0	0	0	0	0	0	0	0	0	—	.00	—	—	—	—	—	—	—	—	—	—	—	—	—
Richard Park	C	7	0	0	0	-1	0	0	0	0	0	5	0.0	.00	—	—	—	—	—	—	—	—	—	—	—	—	—
Craig Berube†	L	11	0	0	0	-3	28	0	0	0	0	7	0.0	.00	6	1	0	1	1	4	0	0	0	0	7	14.3	.17
Bench		—	—	—	—	—	0	—	—	—	—	—	—	—	—	—	—	—	—	0	—	—	—	—	—	—	—
TEAM TOTALS		82	231	399	630	111	1063	65	4	37	9	2451	9.4	7.68	6	11	18	29	20	82	3	0	2	0	191	5.8	4.83

Goaltender	G	Min	GAA	W	L	T	ENG	ShO	GA	SA	SvPct	G	Min	GAA	W	L	ENG	ShO	GA	SA	SvPct
	Regular Season											Postseason									
John Vanbiesbrouck	62	3712	2.18	27	18	15	4	6	135	1380	.902	6	369	1.46	2	4	0	1	9	146	.938
Ron Hextall	23	1235	2.53	10	7	4	0	0	52	464	.888	—	—	—	—	—	—	—	—	—	—
* Jean-Marc Pelletier	1	60	5.00	0	1	0	0	0	5	29	.828	—	—	—	—	—	—	—	—	—	—
TEAM TOTALS	82	5025	2.34	37	26	19	4	7	196	1877	.896	6	372	1.45	2	4	0	1	9	146	.938

1998-99 Philadelphia Flyers

Record When:

Overtime games	2-3-19
In second game of back-to-back games	4-3-5
Vs playoff teams	18-15-13
Leading after two periods	29-2-8
Tied after two periods	5-5-6
Losing after two periods	3-19-5
Scoring first	27-7-13
More shots than opponents	29-20-13
Fewer shots than opponents	6-4-4
Team had at least one fighting major	19-6-4
Team had more PIM	12-6-6
Team had fewer PIM	17-15-11
Team had even PIM	8-5-2

Team

Longest winning streak	4	3 times
Longest unbeaten streak	15	Dec. 12 — Jan. 13
Longest losing streak	5	Feb. 24 — Mar. 4
Longest winless streak	12	Feb. 24 — Mar. 16
Most shots, game	46	@NYI, Nov. 25
Most shots, period	20	2 times
Fewest shots, game	16	@Fla, Nov. 22
Fewest shots, period	2	2nd, @Fla, Nov. 22

Individual

Longest goal streak	7	Eric Lindros
Longest point streak	18	Eric Lindros
Most goals, game	4	John LeClair
Most assists, game	5	Eric Lindros
Most points, game	5	Eric Lindros [2]
Highest +/–, game	4	5 times
Lowest +/–, game	-4	Daniel McGillis
Most shots, game	8	2 times

Did You Know?

On April 22, 1999, the Flyers' John Vanbiesbrouck became just the fifth goaltender in NHL history to stop a penalty shot en route to a postseason shutout. Vanbiesbrouck stopped Toronto's Mats Sundin as Philadelphia won the opening-round contest, 3-0.

Miscellaneous

		NHL Rank
PP Pct.	16.8 (65-386)	10
SH goals allowed	7	9t
PK Pct.	84.1 (280-333)	16
SH goals scored	4	26
Special Team Index	100.3	11
Shots on goal	2,451 (29.9/G)	5
Shots against	1,877 (22.9/G)	2
Unassisted goals	8	25t
Unassisted goals allowed	9	4t
Team Average Weight	208.4	1
Game Star Points	393	12

Game Star Breakdown

Player	1st	2nd	3rd	Pts
Eric Lindros	10	12	13	99
Rod Brind'Amour	8	4	4	56
John LeClair	8	3	6	55
John Vanbiesbrouck	6	3	3	42
Eric Desjardins	2	3	8	27
Keith Jones	2	5	1	26
Daniel McGillis	1	3	2	16
Ron Hextall	1	2	2	13
Mikael Renberg	1	2	1	12
Valeri Zelepukin	1	0	4	9
Daymond Langkow	0	2	1	7
Colin Forbes	0	2	0	6
Marc Bureau	1	0	0	5
Jody Hull	1	0	0	5
Mark Greig	0	1	1	4
Dave Babych	0	1	0	3
Dainius Zubrus	0	1	0	3
Alexandre Daigle	0	0	1	1
Karl Dykhuis	0	0	1	1
Mike Maneluk	0	0	1	1
Mark Recchi	0	0	1	1
Petr Svoboda	0	0	1	1

Phoenix Coyotes 1998-99 Game Log (39-31-12)

Date	Opp	Score	W/L/T	Record	Goalies W/T	Goalies L/T	Shots Pho	Shots Opp	Power Plays Pho	Power Plays Opp	Game Stars 1st	Game Stars 2nd	Game Stars 3rd
10/11	Ott	1-4	L	0-1-0	Rhodes	**Khabibulin**	23	25	0-4	0-3	Rhodes	Gardiner	**Roenick**
10/15	Col	5-2	W	1-1-0	**Khabibulin**	Billington	28	24	1-5	1-4	**Tverdovsky**	**Ronning**	Forsberg
10/19	Bos	3-1	W	2-1-0	**Khabibulin**	Dafoe	26	**14**	1-6	0-5	**Roenick**	**Corkum**	**Ylonen**
10/22	@Dal	1-2	L	2-2-0	Belfour	**Khabibulin**	21	32	1-5	2-6	Nieuwendyk	Verbeek	Reid
10/25	@Anh	2-2*	T	2-2-1	**Khabibulin**	Hebert	36	34	0-5	0-5	Hebert	**Khabibulin**	Kariya
10/26	@Col	5-1	W	3-2-1	**Waite**	Roy	27	20	2-4	1-7	**Tkachuk**	**Roenick**	**Tocchet**
10/28	@SJ	4-2	W	4-2-1	**Khabibulin**	Shields	23	26	0-5	1-5	**Tkachuk**	Nolan	**Carney**
11/01	@LA	3-**0**	W	5-2-1	**Khabibulin**	LeGace	28	31	0-4	0-5	**Khabibulin**	**Lumme**	**Ylonen**
11/06	Det	3-1	W	6-2-1	**Khabibulin**	Osgood	25	31	0-5	1-6	**Khabibulin**	**Numminen**	**Corkum**
11/10	Col	1-1*	T	6-2-2	**Waite**	Roy	25	21	0-3	0-5	**Tkachuk**	**Corkum**	Forsberg
11/11	@Dal	2-**0**	W	7-2-2	**Waite**	Belfour	18	38	0-3	0-4	**Waite**	**Tkachuk**	**Numminen**
11/14	TB	4-1	W	8-2-2	**Waite**	Puppa	39	21	0-6	0-4	**Roenick**	**Tkachuk**	**Briere**
11/18	Van	4-2	W	9-2-2	**Waite**	Snow	27	30	1-7	0-4	**Tocchet**	**Roenick**	**Waite**
11/20	@SJ	2-1*	W	10-2-2	**Khabibulin**	Shields	17	21	1-4	0-4	**Drake**	Ragnarsson	**Carney**
11/21	Edm	3-2*	W	11-2-2	**Khabibulin**	Shtalenkov	39	15	0-7	0-5	**Tocchet**	**Isbister**	**Adams**
11/24	Chi	3-2	W	12-2-2	**Khabibulin**	Thibault	23	32	1-2	0-3	**Tkachuk**	**Roenick**	**Drake**
11/26	NJ	3-2	W	13-2-2	**Waite**	Brodeur	24	29	0-1	1-7	**Adams**	**Tocchet**	Sykora
11/28	@LA	4-**0**	W	14-2-2	**Khabibulin**	Storr	31	20	2-7	0-4	**Doan**	**Ylonen**	**Khabibulin**
12/02	@Edm	3-4	L	14-3-2	Shtalenkov	**Khabibulin**	**48**	22	1-5	1-3	Shtalenkov	Falloon	**Lumme**
12/05	@Cgy	3-2	W	15-3-2	**Khabibulin**	Moss	37	18	1-3	0-3	**Carney**	**Isbister**	Moss
12/06	@Van	3-3*	T	15-3-3	**Waite**	Snow	46	24	1-6	1-4	Snow	**Roenick**	**Tkachuk**
12/09	Mon	4-2	W	16-3-3	**Waite**	Hackett	23	21	1-4	0-6	**Tkachuk**	**Numminen**	**Sullivan**
12/12	@Ott	2-**0**	W	17-3-3	**Khabibulin**	Tugnutt	25	42	0-2	0-3	**Khabibulin**	Kravchuk	Tugnutt
12/14	@Mon	2-2*	T	17-3-4	**Khabibulin**	Hackett	31	35	0-4	0-5	Corson	Hoglund	**Tverdovsky**
12/16	@Tor	2-5	L	17-4-4	Joseph	**Khabibulin**	34	32	0-2	1-3	Korolev	Joseph	Hendrickson
12/17	@StL	2-3	L	17-5-4	Fuhr	**Waite**	22	29	0-5	1-6	Demitra	Handzus	**Numminen**
12/20	NYI	4-2	W	18-5-4	**Khabibulin**	Salo	34	22	2-6	0-5	**Adams**	**Tkachuk**	**Roenick**
12/22	@Det	6-2	W	19-5-4	**Khabibulin**	Osgood	29	38	1-3	1-4	**Drake**	**Numminen**	**Corkum**
12/23	@Chi	3-4	L	19-6-4	Thibault	**Waite**	35	17	**3-8**	2-5	Gilmour	**Roenick**	Thibault
12/26	@LA	2-1	W	20-6-4	**Khabibulin**	Storr	31	27	0-2	0-5	**Adams**	**Roenick**	Rosa
12/28	LA	2-4	L	20-7-4	Storr	**Khabibulin**	34	26	0-3	1-2	Robitaille	Storr	Stumpel
12/30	NYR	3-1	W	21-7-4	**Khabibulin**	Cloutier	26	30	0-3	0-2	**Briere**	**Isbister**	**Corkum**
1/01	Dal	1-2*	L	21-8-4	Turek	**Khabibulin**	27	31	0-6	1-3	Hull	Turek	**Quint**
1/05	Fla	2-2*	T	21-8-5	**Khabibulin**	Burke	28	26	0-5	0-3	**Roenick**	**Adams**	Svehla
1/07	Edm	1-7	L	21-9-5	Essensa	**Waite**	45	35	0-6	0-7	Essensa	Devereaux	Falloon
1/08	@Anh	1-4	L	21-10-5	Roussel	**Khabibulin**	22	30	0-4	1-3	Kariya	Cullen	Salei
1/11	Buf	1-**0**	W	22-10-5	**Khabibulin**	Hasek	22	23	0-3	0-3	**Khabibulin**	**Drake**	Hasek
1/13	Pit	5-3	W	23-10-5	**Khabibulin**	Barrasso	28	25	1-4	3-6	**Roenick**	**Carney**	**Murray**
1/15	@Nsh	0-2	L	23-11-5	Vokoun	**Khabibulin**	31	31	0-5	1-4	Vokoun	Ronning	**Khabibulin**
1/17	@Chi	1-1*	T	23-11-6	**Waite**	Thibault	21	22	1-5	0-6	Brown	**Waite**	Thibault
1/19	StL	4-2	W	24-11-6	**Khabibulin**	McLennan	23	28	0-3	1-3	**Tocchet**	**Adams**	MacInnis
1/21	Anh	3-3*	T	24-11-7	**Khabibulin**	Roussel	44	24	1-6	1-6	**Numminen**	Kariya	**Stapleton**
1/26	@Buf	1-1*	T	24-11-8	**Khabibulin**	Hasek	25	27	1-4	1-4	**Khabibulin**	Hasek	Brown
1/28	@Phi	2-4	L	24-12-8	Vanbiesbrouck	**Khabibulin**	25	25	0-5	0-4	LeClair	Jones	Zelepukin
1/29	@NYI	4-4*	T	24-12-9	**Waite**	Salo	35	33	0-2	0-3	Reichel	**Corkum**	Chara
1/31	@Nsh	5-1	W	25-12-9	**Khabibulin**	Vokoun	33	20	0-2	0-3	**Tkachuk**	**Khabibulin**	Johnson
2/02	Cgy	2-2*	T	25-12-10	**Khabibulin**	Brathwaite	28	36	1-4	0-5	**Tkachuk**	Simpson	**Khabibulin**
2/04	SJ	3-1	W	26-12-10	**Khabibulin**	Shields	30	34	1-4	0-5	**Tocchet**	**Khabibulin**	**Ylonen**
2/06	Chi	3-**0**	W	27-12-10	**Khabibulin**	Thibault	35	28	1-7	0-2	**Khabibulin**	**Lumme**	**Ylonen**
2/08	SJ	0-3	L	27-13-10	Vernon	**Khabibulin**	27	27	0-4	1-6	Vernon	Ricci	**Carney**
2/10	LA	3-**0**	W	28-13-10	**Khabibulin**	Storr	40	26	0-5	0-5	**Adams**	**Khabibulin**	**Diduck**
2/13	@Col	4-1	W	29-13-10	**Khabibulin**	Roy	21	26	1-4	1-5	**Tkachuk**	**Adams**	Sakic
2/14	Anh	1-5	L	29-14-10	Hebert	**Waite**	38	28	0-3	0-5	Rucchin	Hebert	**Corkum**
2/16	Phi	1-4	L	29-15-10	Vanbiesbrouck	**Khabibulin**	33	41	0-3	0-1	LeClair	Jones	Lindros
2/19	@TB	2-4	L	29-16-10	Wilkinson	**Khabibulin**	38	25	0-5	1-2	Wilkinson	Gratton	Hogue

2/20	@Fla	1-7	L	29-17-10	Burke	**Khabibulin**	35	30	1-4	1-4	Dvorak	Lindsay	Burke
2/22	@Pit	1-4	L	29-18-10	Skudra	**Khabibulin**	20	25	0-2	1-3	Barnes	Lang	Morozov
2/24	@Was	2-1	W	30-18-10	**Khabibulin**	Kolzig	16	20	1-1	0-**1**	**Tkachuk**	**Carney**	Gonchar
2/26	@NYR	0-3	L	30-19-10	Richter	**Khabibulin**	25	21	0-4	1-4	Richter	MacLean	Malhotra
2/28	@NJ	1-4	L	30-20-10	Brodeur	**Khabibulin**	27	25	0-6	1-3	Sykora	Brodeur	Arnott
3/02	@Bos	2-3	L	30-21-10	Dafoe	**Esche**	30	22	0-3	0-4	McLaren	**Roenick**	Axelsson
3/05	Det	2-7	L	30-22-10	Osgood	**Waite**	38	27	2-4	2-5	Shanahan	Osgood	Larionov
3/07	Nsh	4-3	W	31-22-10	**Khabibulin**	Dunham	35	26	0-3	0-**1**	**Tkachuk**	**Drake**	Walker
3/09	@SJ	2-4	L	31-23-10	Shields	**Khabibulin**	15	30	1-4	1-6	Marleau	Korolyuk	Marchment
3/11	Van	0-3	L	31-24-10	Snow	**Khabibulin**	33	22	0-4	0-4	Snow	Jovanovski	McCabe
3/13	Anh	1-**0**	W	32-24-10	**Khabibulin**	Hebert	22	27	0-4	0-5	**Khabibulin**	Selanne	**Stapleton**
3/15	Car	5-5*	T	32-24-11	**Khabibulin**	Kidd	42	29	1-2	1-5	**Tkachuk**	Francis	**Roenick**
3/17	@Det	4-3	W	33-24-11	**Shtalenkov**	Maracle	27	31	0-3	1-3	**Tkachuk**	Larionov	**Corkum**
3/18	@StL	2-2*	T	33-24-12	**Shtalenkov**	Fuhr	22	31	1-4	0-4	MacInnis	Demitra	Eastwood
3/21	LA	4-1	W	34-24-12	**Khabibulin**	Storr	43	38	1-3	0-2	**Khabibulin**	**Reichel**	**Quint**
3/23	Dal	2-3	L	34-25-12	Belfour	**Khabibulin**	28	23	0-5	1-3	**Tocchet**	Langenbrunner	**Tkachuk**
3/25	Was	4-2	W	35-25-12	**Khabibulin**	Tabaracci	25	38	0-2	0-6	**Reichel**	**Khabibulin**	**Tkachuk**
3/27	Cgy	2-1	W	36-25-12	**Khabibulin**	Wregget	25	35	0-2	1-2	**Khabibulin**	**Tverdovsky**	**Reichel**
3/29	@Van	0-1	L	36-26-12	Snow	**Shtalenkov**	22	20	0-3	0-3	Snow	Schaefer	Jovanovski
3/30	@Edm	**7**-4	W	37-26-12	**Khabibulin**	Essensa	25	35	1-3	1-3	**Tkachuk**	**Roenick**	**Doan**
4/01	@Cgy	4-1	W	38-26-12	**Khabibulin**	Wregget	23	34	0-3	0-6	**Tkachuk**	**Adams**	**Tocchet**
4/06	SJ	0-1	L	38-27-12	Shields	**Khabibulin**	33	25	0-6	1-4	Shields	Houlder	**Khabibulin**
4/09	Nsh	3-4	L	38-28-12	Vokoun	**Khabibulin**	29	21	1-7	0-2	Valicevic	**Adams**	Ronning
4/11	@Anh	0-3	L	38-29-12	Hebert	**Khabibulin**	40	31	0-6	0-7	Hebert	Kariya	Nielsen
4/14	@Dal	2-4	L	38-30-12	Belfour	**Shtalenkov**	35	23	0-6	1-7	Modano	Zubov	Nieuwendyk
4/15	StL	4-6	L	38-31-12	Fuhr	**Khabibulin**	26	35	2-5	4-7	Pronger	**Doan**	Yake
4/17	Dal	2-**0**	W	39-31-12	**Khabibulin**	Belfour	23	27	1-5	0-7	**Ylonen**	**Reichel**	**Leach**

Postseason

4/22	StL	1-3	L	0-1	Fuhr	**Khabibulin**	27	**25**	0-6	1-**3**	MacInnis	**Reichel**	Fuhr
4/24	StL	4-3*	W	1-1	**Khabibulin**	Fuhr	28	34	**1**-6	2-4	**Doan**	MacInnis	**Drake**
4/25	@StL	**5**-4	W	2-1	**Khabibulin**	McLennan	18	38	**1-12**	3-7	**DeBrusk**	MacInnis	Courtnall
4/27	@StL	2-**1**	W	3-1	**Khabibulin**	Fuhr	20	28	**1**-3	0-4	**Numminen**	**Khabibulin**	Rheaume
4/30	StL	1-2*	L	3-2	Fuhr	**Khabibulin**	27	43	**1**-6	1-6	MacInnis	Handzus	**Tkachuk**
5/02	@StL	3-5	L	3-3	Fuhr	**Khabibulin**	21	34	**1**-4	2-5	Turgeon	Finley	Conroy
5/04	StL	0-**1***	L	3-4	Fuhr	**Khabibulin**	**35**	35	0-4	0-4	Turgeon	Fuhr	**Khabibulin**

Phoenix Coyotes 1998-99 Player Statistics

		Regular Season													Postseason												
Skater	**Ps**	**GP**	**G**	**A**	**Pts**	**+/–**	**PIM**	**PP**	**SH**	**GW**	**GT**	**S**	**SPct**	**P/G**	**GP**	**G**	**A**	**Pts**	**+/–**	**PIM**	**PP**	**SH**	**GW**	**OT**	**S**	**SPct**	**P/G**
Jeremy Roenick	C	78	24	**48**	**72**	7	130	4	0	3	0	203	11.8	.92	1	0	0	0	-1	0	0	0	0	0	2	0.0	.00
Keith Tkachuk	L	68	**36**	32	68	**22**	151	**11**	**2**	**7**	1	**258**	14.0	**1.00**	**7**	1	**3**	4	-4	**13**	1	0	0	0	**22**	4.5	.57
Rick Tocchet	R	81	26	30	56	5	147	6	1	5	0	178	**14.6**	.69	**7**	0	**3**	3	-3	8	0	0	0	0	14	0.0	.43
Greg Adams	L	75	19	24	43	-1	26	5	0	3	0	176	10.8	.57	3	1	0	1	1	0	0	0	0	0	9	11.1	.33
Teppo Numminen	D	**82**	10	30	40	3	30	1	0	0	**2**	156	6.4	.49	**7**	2	1	3	-5	4	**2**	0	0	0	18	11.1	.43
Dallas Drake	R	53	9	22	31	17	65	0	0	3	0	105	8.6	.58	**7**	**4**	**3**	**7**	3	4	**2**	0	1	0	18	**22.2**	**1.00**
Jyrki Lumme	D	60	7	21	28	5	34	1	0	4	0	121	5.8	.47	**7**	0	1	1	-2	6	0	0	0	0	8	0.0	.14
Oleg Tverdovsky	D	**82**	7	18	25	11	32	2	0	2	0	117	6.0	.30	6	0	2	2	3	6	0	0	0	0	6	0.0	.33
Juha Ylonen	C	59	6	17	23	18	20	2	0	1	0	66	9.1	.39	2	0	2	2	2	2	0	0	0	0	2	0.0	1.00
* Daniel Briere	C	64	8	14	22	-3	30	2	0	2	0	90	8.9	.34	—	—	—	—	—	—	—	—	—	—	—	—	—
Shane Doan	R	79	6	16	22	-5	54	0	0	0	0	156	3.8	.28	**7**	2	2	4	4	6	0	0	**2**	**1**	17	11.8	.57
Bob Corkum	C	77	9	10	19	-9	17	0	0	0	0	146	6.2	.25	**7**	0	1	1	1	4	0	0	0	0	6	0.0	.14
Mike Stapleton	C	76	9	9	18	-6	34	0	**2**	2	0	106	8.5	.24	**7**	1	0	1	-1	0	0	0	0	0	3	33.3	.14
Keith Carney	D	**82**	2	14	16	15	62	0	**2**	0	0	62	3.2	.20	**7**	1	2	3	**5**	10	0	0	0	0	5	20.0	.43
Robert Reichel†	C	13	7	6	13	2	4	3	0	3	0	50	14.0	1.00	**7**	1	**3**	4	-2	2	0	0	0	0	16	6.3	.57
Deron Quint	D	60	5	8	13	-10	20	2	0	0	0	94	5.3	.22	—	—	—	—	—	—	—	—	—	—	—	—	—
Brad Isbister	R	32	4	4	8	1	46	0	0	2	0	48	8.3	.25	—	—	—	—	—	—	—	—	—	—	—	—	—
Jim Cummins	R	55	1	7	8	3	**190**	0	0	0	0	26	3.8	.15	3	0	1	1	1	0	0	0	0	0	0	—	.33
Cliff Ronning†	C	7	2	5	7	3	2	2	0	1	0	18	11.1	1.00	—	—	—	—	—	—	—	—	—	—	—	—	—
J.J. Daigneault†	D	35	0	7	7	-8	32	0	0	0	0	27	0.0	.20	6	0	0	0	-1	8	0	0	0	0	4	0.0	.00
Mike Sullivan	C	63	2	4	6	-11	24	0	1	1	0	66	3.0	.10	5	0	0	0	0	2	0	0	0	0	2	0.0	.00
* Trevor Letowski	C	14	2	2	4	1	2	0	0	0	0	8	25.0	.29	—	—	—	—	—	—	—	—	—	—	—	—	—
* Tavis Hansen	C	20	2	1	3	-4	12	0	0	0	0	14	14.3	.15	2	0	0	0	1	0	0	0	0	0	1	0.0	.00
Rob Murray	R	13	1	2	3	2	4	0	0	0	0	11	9.1	.23	—	—	—	—	—	—	—	—	—	—	—	—	—
Steve Leach†	R	22	1	1	2	-6	37	0	0	0	0	23	4.3	.09	**7**	1	1	2	0	2	0	0	0	0	4	25.0	.29
Gerald Diduck	D	44	0	2	2	9	72	0	0	0	0	39	0.0	.05	3	0	0	0	-1	2	0	0	0	0	4	0.0	.00
* Jason Doig	D	9	0	1	1	2	10	0	0	0	0	0	—	.11	—	—	—	—	—	—	—	—	—	—	—	—	—
Jamie Huscroft†	D	11	0	1	1	-1	27	0	0	0	0	7	0.0	.09	—	—	—	—	—	—	—	—	—	—	—	—	—
Stanislav Neckar†	D	11	0	1	1	3	10	0	0	0	0	6	0.0	.09	6	0	1	1	3	4	0	0	0	0	0	—	.17
J.F. Jomphe†	C	1	0	0	0	0	2	0	0	0	0	0	—	.00	—	—	—	—	—	—	—	—	—	—	—	—	—
* Scott Langkow	G	1	0	0	0	—	0	0	0	0	0	0	—	.00	—	—	—	—	—	—	—	—	—	—	—	—	—
Andrey Vasilyev	L	1	0	0	0	-2	0	0	0	0	0	0	—	.00	—	—	—	—	—	—	—	—	—	—	—	—	—
Joe Dziedzic	L	2	0	0	0	-2	0	0	0	0	0	1	0.0	.00	—	—	—	—	—	—	—	—	—	—	—	—	—
* Sean Gagnon	D	2	0	0	0	-2	7	0	0	0	0	1	0.0	.00	—	—	—	—	—	—	—	—	—	—	—	—	—
* Robert Esche	G	3	0	0	0	—	0	0	0	0	0	0	—	.00	—	—	—	—	—	—	—	—	—	—	—	—	—
Mikhail Shtalenkov†	G	4	0	0	0	—	0	0	0	0	0	0	—	.00	—	—	—	—	—	—	—	—	—	—	—	—	—
Brian Noonan	R	7	0	0	0	-3	0	0	0	0	0	1	0.0	.00	5	0	2	2	2	4	0	0	0	0	10	0.0	.40
Brad Tiley	D	8	0	0	0	-1	0	0	0	0	0	1	0.0	.00	1	0	0	0	0	0	0	0	0	0	0	—	.00
* Bryan Helmer†	D	11	0	0	0	2	23	0	0	0	0	11	0.0	.00	—	—	—	—	—	—	—	—	—	—	—	—	—
Louie DeBrusk	L	15	0	0	0	-2	34	0	0	0	0	6	0.0	.00	6	2	0	2	-1	6	0	0	0	0	5	40.0	.33
Jimmy Waite	G	16	0	0	0	—	2	0	0	0	0	0	—	.00	—	—	—	—	—	—	—	—	—	—	—	—	—
Nikolai Khabibulin	G	63	0	0	0	—	8	0	0	0	0	0	—	.00	**7**	0	0	0	—	2	0	0	0	0	0	—	.00
Bench		—	—	—	—	—	0	—	—	—	—	—	—	—	—	—	—	—	—	0	—	—	—	—	—	—	—
TEAM TOTALS		82	205	357	562	55	1400	41	8	39	3	2398	8.5	6.85	7	16	28	44	5	95	5	0	3	1	176	9.1	6.29

	Regular Season											Postseason									
Goaltender	**G**	**Min**	**GAA**	**W**	**L**	**T**	**ENG**	**ShO**	**GA**	**SA**	**SvPct**	**G**	**Min**	**GAA**	**W**	**L**	**ENG**	**ShO**	**GA**	**SA**	**SvPct**
Nikolai Khabibulin	**63**	**3657**	**2.13**	**32**	**23**	**7**	**6**	**8**	**130**	**1681**	**.923**	**7**	**449**	**2.41**	**3**	**4**	**1**	0	**18**	**236**	**.924**
Mikhail Shtalenkov†	4	243	2.22	1	2	1	1	0	9	104	.913	—	—	—	—	—	—	—	—	—	—
Jimmy Waite	16	898	2.74	6	5	4	0	1	41	390	.895	—	—	—	—	—	—	—	—	—	—
* Robert Esche	3	130	3.23	0	1	0	0	0	7	50	.860	—	—	—	—	—	—	—	—	—	—
* Scott Langkow	1	35	5.14	0	0	0	0	0	3	17	.824	—	—	—	—	—	—	—	—	—	—
TEAM TOTALS	82	4985	2.37	39	31	12	7	9	197	2249	.912	7	453	2.52	3	4	1	0	19	237	.920

1998-99 Phoenix Coyotes

Record When:

Overtime games	2-1-12
In second game of back-to-back games	4-6-3
Vs playoff teams	20-22-6
Leading after two periods	28-2-8
Tied after two periods	8-8-1
Losing after two periods	3-21-3
Scoring first	27-7-7
More shots than opponents	16-19-7
Fewer shots than opponents	23-9-5
Team had at least one fighting major	19-15-6
Team had more PIM	19-15-5
Team had fewer PIM	12-14-3
Team had even PIM	8-2-4

Team

Longest winning streak	8	Nov. 11 — Nov. 28
Longest unbeaten streak	14	Oct. 25 — Nov. 28
Longest losing streak	5	2 times
Longest winless streak	5	2 times
Most shots, game	48	@Edm, Dec. 2
Most shots, period	22	1st, @Van, Dec. 6
Fewest shots, game	15	@SJ, Mar. 9
Fewest shots, period	2	2 times

Individual

Longest goal streak	4	Keith Tkachuk
Longest point streak	10	Keith Tkachuk
Most goals, game	3	Keith Tkachuk
Most assists, game	4	Keith Tkachuk
Most points, game	4	Keith Tkachuk [2]
Highest +/–, game	4	4 times
Lowest +/–, game	-4	3 times
Most shots, game	11	Keith Tkachuk

Did You Know?

Last year Rick Tocchet became the first player in NHL history to play in Game 7 overtime losses with three different teams. Prior to last year's Coyotes' loss to St. Louis, Tocchet was on the losing end of Game 7 OTs with Philadelphia in 1988 (vs. Washington) and Pittsburgh in 1993 (vs. the Islanders).

Miscellaneous

		NHL Rank
PP Pct.	12.0 (41-342)	26
SH goals allowed	5	4t
PK Pct.	87.1 (303-348)	5
SH goals scored	8	8t
Special Team Index	99.9	13
Shots on goal	2,398 (29.2/G)	6
Shots against	2,249 (27.4/G)	13
Unassisted goals	8	25t
Unassisted goals allowed	7	1
Team Average Weight	195.4	26
Game Star Points	404	9

Game Star Breakdown

Player	1st	2nd	3rd	Pts
Keith Tkachuk	14	3	3	82
Nikolai Khabibulin	9	5	4	64
Jeremy Roenick	4	8	3	47
Greg Adams	4	5	1	36
Rick Tocchet	5	1	2	30
Dallas Drake	2	2	1	17
Teppo Numminen	1	3	2	16
Keith Carney	1	2	3	14
Bob Corkum	0	3	5	14
Robert Reichel	1	2	1	12
Juha Ylonen	1	1	4	12
Shane Doan	1	1	1	9
Oleg Tverdovsky	1	1	1	9
Jimmy Waite	1	1	1	9
Brad Isbister	0	3	0	9
Jyrki Lumme	0	2	1	7
Daniel Briere	1	0	1	6
Cliff Ronning	0	1	0	3
Deron Quint	0	0	2	2
Mike Stapleton	0	0	2	2
Gerald Diduck	0	0	1	1
Steve Leach	0	0	1	1
Rob Murray	0	0	1	1
Mike Sullivan	0	0	1	1

Pittsburgh Penguins 1998-99 Game Log (38-30-14)

Date	Opp	Score	W/L/T	Record	Goalies W/T	Goalies L/T	Shots Pit	Shots Opp	Power Plays Pit	Power Plays Opp	Game Stars 1st	Game Stars 2nd	Game Stars 3rd
10/10	@NYI	4-3	W	1-0-0	**Barrasso**	Salo	21	25	1-4	2-4	Linden	**Werenka**	**Jagr**
10/14	@NJ	3-1	W	2-0-0	**Barrasso**	Brodeur	25	23	1-6	0-2	**Titov**	**Barrasso**	**Jagr**
10/17	NYR	3-3*	T	2-0-1	**Skudra**	Richter	30	26	1-7	2-6	**Jagr**	Harvey	**Hatcher**
10/21	@TB	0-5	L	2-1-1	Puppa	**Skudra**	28	18	0-5	2-4	Tucker	Puppa	Clark
10/24	Tor	4-6	L	2-2-1	Potvin	**Skudra**	34	27	1-4	1-2	Sundin	**Jagr**	Modin
10/26	@Tor	2-**0**	W	3-2-1	**Skudra**	Joseph	19	27	2-4	0-8	**Skudra**	**Jagr**	Thomas
10/28	@Cgy	5-2	W	4-2-1	**Skudra**	Wregget	21	16	**5-9**	1-6	**Jagr**	**Barnes**	Iginla
10/30	@Van	2-2*	T	4-2-2	**Skudra**	Snow	25	20	2-6	0-4	Snow	**Jagr**	Mogilny
10/31	@Edm	1-4	L	4-3-2	Essensa	**Aubin**	22	15	1-7	1-7	Mironov	Essensa	**Barnes**
11/03	Phi	4-4*	T	4-3-3	**Skudra**	Vanbiesbrouck	22	24	1-7	2-6	**Galanov**	Lindros	**Jagr**
11/05	@Ott	4-2	W	5-3-3	**Aubin**	Rhodes	22	26	1-4	1-2	**Titov**	**Jagr**	**Hatcher**
11/07	Bos	0-**0***	T	5-3-4	**Aubin**	Dafoe	26	18	0-2	0-3	Dafoe	**Aubin**	**Jagr**
11/10	NYI	3-2	W	6-3-4	**Aubin**	Salo	20	31	0-3	1-2	**Straka**	**Aubin**	**Werenka**
11/13	@NJ	3-4	L	6-4-4	Terreri	**Barrasso**	20	28	0-2	1-3	McKay	Holik	**Straka**
11/14	Fla	4-**0**	W	7-4-4	**Barrasso**	Burke	32	23	2-6	0-3	**Barrasso**	**Barnes**	**Werenka**
11/17	Phi	1-4	L	7-5-4	Vanbiesbrouck	**Barrasso**	26	20	0-7	1-6	Vanbiesbrouck	Brind'Amour	**Lang**
11/19	@TB	5-1	W	8-5-4	**Barrasso**	Ranford	35	23	0-4	0-2	**Straka**	**Barnes**	**Hatcher**
11/21	TB	5-2	W	9-5-4	**Aubin**	Puppa	22	21	2-7	0-**1**	**Straka**	**Jagr**	**Werenka**
11/25	@Was	4-5	L	9-6-4	Kolzig	**Barrasso**	22	31	2-4	0-4	**Barnes**	Bondra	Black
11/27	NYR	2-2*	T	9-6-5	**Barrasso**	Richter	31	21	0-4	1-3	**Kovalev**	Leetch	**Morozov**
11/28	@Mon	4-3	W	10-6-5	**Barrasso**	Theodore	18	31	1-3	1-4	**Straka**	Poulin	**Morozov**
12/01	Anh	4-4*	T	10-6-6	**Barrasso**	Hebert	36	35	1-4	2-2	**Jagr**	**Straka**	Selanne
12/04	@Car	3-3*	T	10-6-7	**Barrasso**	Irbe	25	**14**	0-3	1-2	Kron	**Kesa**	Emerson
12/05	@Bos	1-2	L	10-7-7	Dafoe	**Barrasso**	34	22	0-2	0-2	Dafoe	**Kovalev**	**Jagr**
12/12	@StL	4-3	W	11-7-7	**Barrasso**	Fuhr	14	34	1-4	1-3	**Kovalev**	**Jagr**	Yake
12/15	TB	3-2*	W	12-7-7	**Barrasso**	Schwab	32	20	0-3	1-2	**Hatcher**	**Lang**	**Straka**
12/16	@Fla	1-4	L	12-8-7	Burke	**Barrasso**	30	36	0-4	1-4	Burke	**Barrasso**	Mellanby
12/19	Was	3-**0**	W	13-8-7	**Barrasso**	Kolzig	24	24	1-6	0-3	**Barrasso**	**Kovalev**	**Jagr**
12/21	@Tor	1-7	L	13-9-7	Joseph	**Barrasso**	31	27	0-5	2-5	McCauley	Sundin	Karpovtsev
12/22	LA	0-3	L	13-10-7	Storr	**Skudra**	25	31	0-1	0-2	Murray	Storr	Audette
12/26	Ott	2-1*	W	14-10-7	**Skudra**	Tugnutt	17	31	0-3	0-5	**Skudra**	**Jagr**	**Moran**
12/30	Fla	**7**-4	W	15-10-7	**Skudra**	McLean	37	30	1-5	1-5	**Straka**	**Miller**	**Lang**
1/02	@Fla	4-2	W	16-10-7	**Barrasso**	Burke	34	17	2-6	1-3	**Kovalev**	**Jagr**	Kvasha
1/05	Cgy	5-1	W	17-10-7	**Barrasso**	Garner	25	29	1-6	0-7	**Barrasso**	**Hatcher**	**Straka**
1/07	Car	4-2	W	18-10-7	**Barrasso**	Kidd	24	25	3-5	1-3	**Jagr**	**Barrasso**	**Straka**
1/09	StL	2-1	W	19-10-7	**Barrasso**	Fuhr	14	30	0-5	0-4	**Barrasso**	**Lang**	**Titov**
1/13	@Pho	3-5	L	19-11-7	Khabibulin	**Barrasso**	25	28	3-6	1-4	Roenick	Carney	Murray
1/15	@SJ	2-3	L	19-12-7	Shields	**Barrasso**	19	23	0-5	0-2	Nolan	Lowry	Marleau
1/16	@LA	5-1	W	20-12-7	**Barrasso**	Storr	18	17	2-3	1-3	**Jagr**	**Lang**	**Moran**
1/18	@Anh	3-5	L	20-13-7	Hebert	**Barrasso**	**47**	29	1-7	2-7	McInnis	**Straka**	Selanne
1/21	NYI	2-5	L	20-14-7	Salo	**Barrasso**	28	24	1-7	0-3	Lapointe	Salo	Sacco
1/26	Car	3-5	L	20-15-7	Irbe	**Skudra**	35	22	0-3	0-2	Sheppard	Kron	Irbe
1/28	Tor	6-**0**	W	21-15-7	**Skudra**	Reese	33	21	0-2	0-5	**Jagr**	**Skudra**	**Miller**
1/30	Bos	5-2	W	22-15-7	**Skudra**	Tallas	28	27	0-4	0-6	**Kovalev**	**Titov**	**Hatcher**
1/31	@Mon	5-3	W	23-15-7	**Skudra**	Hackett	24	26	1-4	2-5	**Jagr**	**Slegr**	**Titov**
2/02	Buf	5-3	W	24-15-7	**Skudra**	Hasek	29	34	2-6	1-3	**Jagr**	**Miller**	**Hrdina**
2/05	Fla	3-**0**	W	25-15-7	**Barrasso**	McLean	26	29	0-4	0-**1**	**Jagr**	**Barrasso**	**Sonnenberg**
2/07	Det	2-1	W	26-15-7	**Barrasso**	Osgood	21	36	0-4	1-3	**Barrasso**	**Kovalev**	**Miller**
2/09	Mon	3-2*	W	27-15-7	**Barrasso**	Chabot	32	29	0-5	1-7	**Jagr**	**Kovalev**	**Barrasso**
2/11	Van	6-5*	W	28-15-7	**Skudra**	Hirsch	40	18	0-6	0-3	**Jagr**	Naslund	**Straka**
2/13	@Nsh	3-2*	W	29-15-7	**Skudra**	Vokoun	34	34	0-6	0-6	Vokoun	**Skudra**	**Miller**
2/15	Was	**7**-3	W	30-15-7	**Skudra**	Kolzig	21	32	2-5	0-3	**Titov**	**Morozov**	**Jagr**
2/17	@NYI	1-3	L	30-16-7	Salo	**Skudra**	21	31	0-4	1-7	Pilon	Salo	Reichel
2/19	@NYR	1-6	L	30-17-7	Cloutier	**Barrasso**	33	20	0-6	1-2	Cloutier	Stevens	MacLean
2/21	@Phi	1-2	L	30-18-7	Hextall	**Barrasso**	19	26	1-4	1-5	Lindros	Langkow	**Straka**

2/22	Pho	4-1	W	31-18-7	**Skudra**	Khabibulin	25	20	1-3	0-2	**Barnes**	**Lang**	**Morozov**
2/25	@Col	3-2	W	32-18-7	**Barrasso**	Billington	30	24	0-2	0-4	**Straka**	**Jagr**	Billington
2/26	@Dal	4-6	L	32-19-7	Belfour	**Barrasso**	18	35	0-4	0-2	Verbeek	**Straka**	Langenbrunner
2/28	@Was	3-4	L	32-20-7	Kolzig	**Barrasso**	25	26	1-2	2-3	Nikolishin	**Titov**	Svejkovsky
3/03	Mon	4-4*	T	32-20-8	**Skudra**	Hackett	18	37	1-3	1-4	**Jagr**	Malakhov	**Kasparaitis**
3/05	Edm	2-2*	T	32-20-9	**Skudra**	Essensa	36	21	1-7	1-5	Essensa	**Lang**	**Kovalev**
3/07	Col	1-3	L	32-21-9	Billington	**Skudra**	24	22	0-4	0-3	Hejduk	Billington	**Straka**
3/09	NJ	2-3	L	32-22-9	Brodeur	**Skudra**	23	23	0-2	0-3	**Jagr**	Arnott	Sykora
3/10	@Car	3-2*	W	33-22-9	**Skudra**	Irbe	26	21	0-1	0-3	**Miller**	Kapanen	**Straka**
3/13	Phi	4-**0**	W	34-22-9	**Skudra**	Hextall	19	24	1-4	0-4	**Jagr**	**Straka**	**Skudra**
3/16	Dal	2-2*	T	34-22-10	**Aubin**	Turek	15	31	0-4	1-3	**Jagr**	**Straka**	Hrkac
3/17	@TB	2-**0**	W	35-22-10	**Aubin**	Schwab	18	16	0-6	0-4	**Aubin**	McCarthy	**Jagr**
3/20	Nsh	1-1*	T	35-22-11	**Aubin**	Vokoun	30	23	1-6	0-7	**Lang**	Vokoun	**Aubin**
3/21	@NYR	2-2*	T	35-22-12	**Aubin**	Richter	32	24	1-4	1-2	Richter	**Jagr**	Nedved
3/23	Chi	5-2	W	36-22-12	**Skudra**	Thibault	29	29	2-6	1-3	**Jagr**	**Straka**	**Titov**
3/25	@NJ	3-5	L	36-23-12	Brodeur	**Skudra**	14	39	1-4	2-3	Sykora	Bombardir	Niedermayer
3/27	Buf	1-1*	T	36-23-13	**Aubin**	Hasek	32	25	0-8	0-6	**Aubin**	Hasek	**Barnaby**
3/28	@Buf	3-4*	L	36-24-13	Hasek	**Aubin**	22	21	3-7	2-5	Ward	**Jagr**	Satan
3/30	Ott	4-6	L	36-25-13	Rhodes	**Skudra**	25	27	1-3	0-**1**	Salo	Arvedson	**Jagr**
4/01	@Ott	3-3*	T	36-25-14	**Aubin**	Tugnutt	21	34	1-3	0-5	Bonk	**Jagr**	Hossa
4/03	NJ	2-4	L	36-26-14	Terreri	**Aubin**	18	40	1-2	0-4	Andreychuk	**Aubin**	Arnott
4/05	@Buf	1-3	L	36-27-14	Hasek	**Skudra**	26	22	0-4	0-4	Hasek	Woolley	**Brown**
4/08	@Phi	1-3	L	36-28-14	Vanbiesbrouck	**Skudra**	17	33	1-3	1-3	Brind'Amour	Vanbiesbrouck	Desjardins
4/11	@Det	3-**0**	W	37-28-14	**Barrasso**	Osgood	23	20	0-4	0-**1**	**Hrdina**	**Slegr**	**Barrasso**
4/15	@Bos	2-4	L	37-29-14	Dafoe	**Barrasso**	15	25	1-2	1-2	Allison	Gill	**Kovalev**
4/17	NYI	2-7	L	37-30-14	Flaherty	**Barrasso**	29	24	1-6	2-3	Palffy	Linden	Flaherty
4/18	@NYR	2-1*	W	38-30-14	**Barrasso**	Richter	23	38	0-1	1-2	Gretzky		

Postseason

4/22	@NJ	1-3	L	0-1	Brodeur	**Barrasso**	25	22	0-3	0-4	Sykora	Niedermayer	Brodeur
4/24	@NJ	**4**-1	W	1-1	**Barrasso**	Brodeur	17	29	0-**6**	0-5	**Barrasso**	**Andrusak**	**Straka**
4/25	NJ	**4**-2	W	2-1	**Barrasso**	Brodeur	22	33	1-**6**	2-7	**Straka**	**Barrasso**	**Kovalev**
4/27	NJ	2-4	L	2-2	Brodeur	**Barrasso**	18	39	**2**-4	1-**2**	McKay	Holik	Stevens
4/30	@NJ	3-4	L	2-3	Brodeur	**Barrasso**	17	27	1-3	1-3	Sykora	McKay	**Kovalev**
5/02	NJ	3-2*	W	3-3	**Barrasso**	Brodeur	**28**	27	0-3	1-3	**Jagr**	**Straka**	Brodeur
5/04	@NJ	**4**-2	W	4-3	**Barrasso**	Brodeur	13	**20**	0-1	0-3	**Straka**	**Jagr**	**Kovalev**
5/07	@Tor	2-**0**	W	1-0	**Barrasso**	Joseph	19	**20**	1-3	0-4	**Barrasso**	Warriner	**Straka**
5/09	@Tor	2-4	L	1-1	Joseph	**Barrasso**	27	25	0-5	1-3	Sundin	Joseph	Bohonos
5/11	Tor	**4**-3	W	2-1	**Barrasso**	Joseph	21	29	**2**-4	0-4	**Jagr**	**Barrasso**	**Brown**
5/13	Tor	2-3*	L	2-2	Joseph	**Barrasso**	14	30	0-3	0-3	Berezin	Sundin	**Barrasso**
5/15	@Tor	1-4	L	2-3	Joseph	**Barrasso**	16	**20**	0-2	0-5	Yushkevich	Thomas	Valk
5/17	Tor	3-4*	L	2-4	Joseph	**Barrasso**	**28**	30	1-2	0-4	Valk	Joseph	**Jagr**

Pittsburgh Penguins 1998-99 Player Statistics

		Regular Season													Postseason												
Skater	**Ps**	**GP**	**G**	**A**	**Pts**	**+/–**	**PIM**	**PP**	**SH**	**GW**	**GT**	**S**	**SPct**	**P/G**	**GP**	**G**	**A**	**Pts**	**+/–**	**PIM**	**PP**	**SH**	**GW**	**OT**	**S**	**SPct**	**P/G**
Jaromir Jagr	R	81	**44**	**83**	**127**	17	66	10	1	**7**	2	**343**	12.8	**1.57**	9	5	7	12	1	16	1	0	**1**	**1**	**32**	15.6	**1.33**
Martin Straka	C	80	35	48	83	12	26	5	**4**	4	1	177	**19.8**	1.04	**13**	**6**	**9**	**15**	0	6	1	0	0	0	27	22.2	1.15
German Titov	C	72	11	45	56	**18**	34	3	1	3	1	113	9.7	.78	11	3	5	8	**4**	4	0	0	0	0	15	20.0	.73
Alexei Kovalev†	R	63	20	26	46	8	37	5	1	4	0	156	12.8	.73	10	5	7	12	0	14	0	0	**1**	0	24	20.8	1.20
Robert Lang	C	72	21	23	44	-10	24	7	0	3	**3**	137	15.3	.61	12	0	2	2	-3	0	0	0	0	0	9	0.0	.17
Kip Miller	C	77	19	23	42	1	22	1	0	4	0	125	15.2	.55	**13**	2	7	9	-1	19	1	0	0	0	18	11.1	.69
* Jan Hrdina	C	**82**	13	29	42	-2	40	3	0	2	0	94	13.8	.51	**13**	4	1	5	-1	12	1	0	**1**	0	14	**28.6**	.38
Kevin Hatcher	D	66	11	27	38	11	24	4	2	3	0	131	8.4	.58	**13**	2	3	5	1	4	1	0	0	0	22	9.1	.38
Stu Barnes†	C	64	20	12	32	-12	20	**13**	0	3	0	155	12.9	.50	—	—	—	—	—	—	—	—	—	—	—	—	—
Rob Brown	R	58	13	11	24	-15	16	9	0	1	0	78	16.7	.41	**13**	2	5	7	-2	8	**2**	0	0	0	14	14.3	.54
Brad Werenka	D	81	6	18	24	17	**93**	1	0	4	0	77	7.8	.30	**13**	1	1	2	0	6	0	0	0	0	10	10.0	.15
Jiri Slegr	D	63	3	20	23	13	86	1	0	0	0	91	3.3	.37	**13**	1	3	4	1	12	0	0	**1**	0	17	5.9	.31
Alexei Morozov	R	67	9	10	19	5	14	0	0	0	0	75	12.0	.28	10	1	1	2	1	0	0	0	0	0	13	7.7	.20
Dan Kesa	R	67	2	8	10	-9	27	0	0	0	1	33	6.1	.15	**13**	1	0	1	-2	0	1	0	**1**	0	5	20.0	.08
Bobby Dollas	D	70	2	8	10	-3	60	0	0	0	0	34	5.9	.14	**13**	1	0	1	-4	6	0	0	0	0	6	16.7	.08
Ian Moran	R	62	4	5	9	1	37	0	1	0	0	65	6.2	.15	**13**	0	2	2	-3	8	0	0	0	0	12	0.0	.15
* Maxim Galanov	D	51	4	3	7	-8	14	2	0	0	1	44	9.1	.14	1	0	0	0	0	0	0	0	0	0	0	—	.00
Jeff Serowik	D	26	0	6	6	-4	16	0	0	0	0	26	0.0	.23	—	—	—	—	—	—	—	—	—	—	—	—	—
Darius Kasparaitis	D	48	1	4	5	12	70	0	0	0	0	32	3.1	.10	—	—	—	—	—	—	—	—	—	—	—	—	—
Matthew Barnaby†	R	18	2	2	4	-10	34	1	0	0	0	27	7.4	.22	**13**	0	0	0	-2	**35**	0	0	0	0	10	0.0	.00
Tom Barrasso	G	43	0	3	3	—	20	0	0	0	0	0	—	.07	**13**	0	0	0	—	4	0	0	0	0	0	—	.00
* Martin Sonnenberg	L	44	1	1	2	-2	19	0	0	0	0	12	8.3	.05	7	0	0	0	-2	0	0	0	0	0	0	—	.00
Patrick Lebeau	L	8	1	0	1	-2	2	0	0	0	0	4	25.0	.13	—	—	—	—	—	—	—	—	—	—	—	—	—
* Greg Andrusak	D	7	0	1	1	4	4	0	0	0	0	2	0.0	.14	12	1	0	1	-1	6	0	0	**1**	0	9	11.1	.08
* Victor Ignatjev	D	11	0	1	1	-3	6	0	0	0	0	15	0.0	.09	1	0	0	0	0	2	0	0	0	0	0	—	.00
Todd Hlushko	L	—	—	—	—	—	—	—	—	—	—	—	—	—	2	0	0	0	0	0	0	0	0	0	1	0.0	.00
* Chris Kelleher	D	1	0	0	0	0	0	0	0	0	0	0	—	.00	—	—	—	—	—	—	—	—	—	—	—	—	—
Sean Pronger†	C	2	0	0	0	0	0	0	0	0	0	3	0.0	.00	—	—	—	—	—	—	—	—	—	—	—	—	—
Harry York†	C	2	0	0	0	0	0	0	0	0	0	0	—	.00	—	—	—	—	—	—	—	—	—	—	—	—	—
* Ryan Savoia	C	3	0	0	0	-1	0	0	0	0	0	0	—	.00	—	—	—	—	—	—	—	—	—	—	—	—	—
* Pavel Skrbek	D	4	0	0	0	2	2	0	0	0	0	1	0.0	.00	—	—	—	—	—	—	—	—	—	—	—	—	—
Brian Bonin	C	5	0	0	0	-2	0	0	0	0	0	2	0.0	.00	3	0	0	0	-1	0	0	0	0	0	4	0.0	.00
Chris Tamer†	D	11	0	0	0	-2	32	0	0	0	0	2	0.0	.00	—	—	—	—	—	—	—	—	—	—	—	—	—
* J. Aubin	G	17	0	0	0	—	0	0	0	0	0	0	—	.00	—	—	—	—	—	—	—	—	—	—	—	—	—
* Sven Butenschon	D	17	0	0	0	-7	6	0	0	0	0	8	0.0	.00	—	—	—	—	—	—	—	—	—	—	—	—	—
Neil Wilkinson	D	24	0	0	0	-2	22	0	0	0	0	11	0.0	.00	—	—	—	—	—	—	—	—	—	—	—	—	—
* Peter Skudra	G	37	0	0	0	—	2	0	0	0	0	0	—	.00	—	—	—	—	—	—	—	—	—	—	—	—	—
Tyler Wright	C	61	0	0	0	-2	90	0	0	0	0	16	0.0	.00	**13**	0	0	0	-2	19	0	0	0	0	3	0.0	.00
Bench		—	—	—	—	—	0	—	—	—	—	—	—	—	—	—	—	—	—	0	—	—	—	—	—	—	—
TEAM TOTALS		82	242	417	659	25	965	65	10	38	9	2089	11.6	8.04	13	35	53	88	-16	181	8	0	6	1	265	13.2	6.77

	Regular Season											Postseason									
Goaltender	**G**	**Min**	**GAA**	**W**	**L**	**T**	**ENG**	**ShO**	**GA**	**SA**	**SvPct**	**G**	**Min**	**GAA**	**W**	**L**	**ENG**	**ShO**	**GA**	**SA**	**SvPct**
* J. Aubin	17	756	2.22	4	3	**6**	0	2	28	304	.908	—	—	—	—	—	—	—	—	—	—
Tom Barrasso	**43**	**2306**	**2.55**	**19**	**16**	3	4	**4**	**98**	**993**	**.901**	**13**	**787**	**2.67**	**6**	**7**	**1**	**1**	**35**	**350**	**.900**
* Peter Skudra	37	1914	2.79	15	11	5	**6**	3	89	822	.892	—	—	—	—	—	—	—	—	—	—
TEAM TOTALS	82	5011	2.69	38	30	14	10	9	225	2129	.894	13	793	2.72	6	7	1	1	36	351	.897

1998-99 Pittsburgh Penguins

Record When:

Overtime games	7-1-14
In second game of back-to-back games	8-6-1
Vs playoff teams	16-21-8
Leading after two periods	27-5-3
Tied after two periods	5-2-4
Losing after two periods	6-23-7
Scoring first	27-10-5
More shots than opponents	18-14-10
Fewer shots than opponents	17-15-4
Team had at least one fighting major	12-2-2
Team had more PIM	13-9-4
Team had fewer PIM	20-14-6
Team had even PIM	5-7-4

Team

Longest winning streak	10	Jan. 28 — Feb. 15
Longest unbeaten streak	10	Jan. 28 — Feb. 15
Longest losing streak	3	3 times
Longest winless streak	8	Mar. 25 — Apr. 8
Most shots, game	47	@Anh, Jan. 18
Most shots, period	19	3rd, @Anh, Jan. 18
Fewest shots, game	14	3 times
Fewest shots, period	1	2 times

Individual

Longest goal streak	6	2 times
Longest point streak	13	Jaromir Jagr
Most goals, game	3	2 times
Most assists, game	4	Jaromir Jagr
Most points, game	5	Jaromir Jagr
Highest +/–, game	4	9 times
Lowest +/–, game	-4	2 times
Most shots, game	10	2 times

Did You Know?

Jaromir Jagr scored or assisted on 52.5 percent of Pittsburgh's goals last year. He was the first NHL player to be involved in more than half of his team's goals since 1988-89, when Mario Lemieux scored or assisted on 57.3 percent of the Penguins' goals.

Miscellaneous

		NHL Rank
PP Pct.	17.9 (65-363)	7
SH goals allowed	14	27
PK Pct.	81.5 (246-302)	23
SH goals scored	10	6t
Special Team Index	98.8	19
Shots on goal	2,089 (25.5/G)	25
Shots against	2,129 (26.0/G)	6
Unassisted goals	13	14t
Unassisted goals allowed	22	27
Team Average Weight	201.3	12
Game Star Points	421	5

Game Star Breakdown

Player	1st	2nd	3rd	Pts
Jaromir Jagr	16	12	9	125
Martin Straka	6	6	8	56
Tom Barrasso	5	4	2	39
Alexei Kovalev	4	4	2	34
German Titov	3	2	3	24
Robert Lang	1	5	2	22
Jean-Sebastian Aubin	2	3	1	20
Stu Barnes	2	3	1	20
Peter Skudra	2	2	1	17
Kip Miller	1	2	3	14
Kevin Hatcher	1	1	4	12
Jan Hrdina	1	0	1	6
Jiri Slegr	0	2	0	6
Alexei Morozov	0	1	3	6
Brad Werenka	0	1	3	6
Maxim Galanov	1	0	0	5
Dan Kesa	0	1	0	3
Ian Moran	0	0	2	2
Matthew Barnaby	0	0	1	1
Rob Brown	0	0	1	1
Darius Kasparaitis	0	0	1	1
Martin Sonnenberg	0	0	1	1

San Jose Sharks 1998-99 Game Log (31-33-18)

Date	Opp	Score	W/L/T	Record	Goalies W/T	Goalies L/T	Shots SJ	Shots Opp	Power Plays SJ	Power Plays Opp	Game Stars 1st	Game Stars 2nd	Game Stars 3rd
10/09	@Cgy†	3-3*	T	0-0-1	**Vernon**	Wregget	25	30	1-7	0-4	Wregget	**Ricci**	**Murphy**
10/10	Cgy†	3-5	L	0-1-1	Wregget	**Vernon**	26	32	1-8	2-8	Fleury	**Marleau**	Morris
10/18	Bos	0-3	L	0-2-1	Tallas	**Vernon**	22	17	0-4	1-6	Tallas	**Nolan**	Khristich
10/20	@Phi	1-3	L	0-3-1	Vanbiesbrouck	**Vernon**	18	37	1-4	1-5	Brind'Amour	Forbes	**Vernon**
10/22	@Chi	2-2*	T	0-3-2	**Shields**	Hackett	25	33	0-7	1-8	Amonte	**Nolan**	Chelios
10/24	@Dal	1-2	L	0-4-2	Belfour	**Vernon**	17	24	1-4	2-4	Langenbrunner	Marshall	**Vernon**
10/28	Pho	2-4	L	0-5-2	Khabibulin	**Shields**	26	23	1-5	0-5	Tkachuk	**Nolan**	Carney
10/29	@Col	2-4	L	0-6-2	Billington	**Vernon**	23	30	1-7	1-6	Sakic	Hejduk	Corbet
10/31	TB	6-1	W	1-6-2	**Vernon**	Ranford	31	21	1-5	1-8	**Sutter**	**Craven**	**Friesen**
11/04	Dal	4-**0**	W	2-6-2	**Vernon**	Belfour	9	21	1-3	0-7	**Ricci**	**Vernon**	**Rathje**
11/06	@Anh	2-2*	T	2-6-3	**Shields**	Hebert	30	47	0-6	2-9	Sandstrom	**Shields**	Salei
11/07	StL	2-2*	T	2-6-4	**Vernon**	McLennan	17	25	0-6	0-3	**Sturm**	Turgeon	**Vernon**
11/10	Nsh	2-4	L	2-7-4	Dunham	**Vernon**	35	20	1-6	0-5	Krivokrasov	Dunham	**Nolan**
11/12	Car	3-**0**	W	3-7-4	**Vernon**	Irbe	18	20	1-4	0-5	**Vernon**	**Friesen**	**Ricci**
11/18	LA	5-4	W	4-7-4	**Vernon**	LeGace	**40**	30	1-7	1-5	**Granato**	**Friesen**	**Vernon**
11/20	Pho	1-2*	L	4-8-4	Khabibulin	**Shields**	21	17	0-4	1-4	Drake	**Ragnarsson**	Carney
11/21	NYR	2-2*	T	4-8-5	**Vernon**	Cloutier	**40**	23	0-5	1-6	**Stern**	Cloutier	**Vernon**
11/23	@Dal	2-3	L	4-9-5	Belfour	**Vernon**	18	21	2-8	0-5	Matvichuk	**Houlder**	Nieuwendyk
11/25	@Car	0-3	L	4-10-5	Kidd	**Vernon**	36	24	0-4	0-3	Primeau	Kidd	Sheppard
11/27	@StL	4-2	W	5-10-5	**Shields**	McLennan	21	21	1-6	1-5	**Sturm**	**Guolla**	Demitra
11/29	@Det	1-4	L	5-11-5	Maracle	**Vernon**	20	28	0-4	2-8	Maracle	Holmstrom	McCarty
12/02	Dal	0-3	L	5-12-5	Belfour	**Vernon**	26	23	0-2	0-6	Hrkac	Keane	Belfour
12/04	Det	2-2*	T	5-12-6	**Shields**	Maracle	37	25	0-3	0-4	**Ricci**	Maracle	**Stern**
12/06	Anh	1-2	L	5-13-6	Hebert	**Shields**	24	23	1-6	2-6	Kariya	**Nolan**	Haller
12/09	@Dal	3-3*	T	5-13-7	**Vernon**	Belfour	17	28	1-5	3-5	Sydor	**Marleau**	Nieuwendyk
12/10	@Nsh	1-2	L	5-14-7	Vokoun	**Shields**	35	26	0-5	1-3	Bordeleau	Vokoun	Krivokrasov
12/12	Was	2-1	W	6-14-7	**Vernon**	Tabaracci	36	26	2-7	1-7	**Friesen**	**Nolan**	Tabaracci
12/15	NYI	0-1	L	6-15-7	Salo	**Vernon**	13	26	0-6	0-4	Watt	Jonsson	Salo
12/17	Nsh	3-1	W	7-15-7	**Vernon**	Vokoun	27	31	1-3	0-4	**Sturm**	**Korolyuk**	**Vernon**
12/19	Col	2-1	W	8-15-7	**Vernon**	Billington	32	18	0-4	0-8	**Murphy**	**Lowry**	**Marchment**
12/23	@Edm	5-3	W	9-15-7	**Vernon**	Shtalenkov	20	23	0-4	0-3	**Sturm**	**Korolyuk**	Falloon
12/26	Van	2-**0**	W	10-15-7	**Shields**	Snow	27	25	1-7	0-9	**Shields**	**Marleau**	**Nolan**
12/28	Phi	1-1*	T	10-15-8	**Vernon**	Vanbiesbrouck	23	23	0-4	1-4	**Vernon**	Lindros	**Marchment**
12/30	@LA	1-5	L	10-16-8	Storr	**Vernon**	32	23	0-5	1-3	Murray	R.Blake	M.Johnson
1/02	@NYI	4-3*	W	11-16-8	**Shields**	Cousineau	29	21	1-5	2-4	**Sturm**	Palffy	**Ricci**
1/04	@NYR	3-4	L	11-17-8	Richter	**Shields**	27	27	0-4	1-4	Harvey	Graves	Stevens
1/05	@NJ	3-3*	T	11-17-9	**Vernon**	Brodeur	23	33	1-3	1-2	Holik	McKay	**Friesen**
1/07	@Nsh	4-3	W	12-17-9	**Vernon**	Vokoun	30	33	0-2	1-6	**Granato**	Ronning	**Murphy**
1/09	Buf	2-2*	T	12-17-10	**Shields**	Hasek	26	31	1-5	2-7	**Nolan**	Woolley	**Friesen**
1/11	LA	4-**0**	W	13-17-10	**Vernon**	Fiset	33	30	2-6	0-6	**Houlder**	**Murphy**	**Vernon**
1/13	Dal	1-2	L	13-18-10	Turek	**Vernon**	32	20	0-3	0-4	Turek	**Korolyuk**	Zubov
1/15	Pit	3-2	W	14-18-10	**Shields**	Barrasso	23	19	0-2	0-5	**Nolan**	**Lowry**	**Marleau**
1/16	Cgy	3-3*	T	14-18-11	**Vernon**	Brathwaite	33	22	1-6	1-5	**Nolan**	**Marleau**	Fleury
1/18	NJ	3-1	W	15-18-11	**Vernon**	Brodeur	24	34	1-3	1-3	**Friesen**	**Vernon**	**Ricci**
1/21	Edm	3-3*	T	15-18-12	**Vernon**	Essensa	22	31	0-2	1-5	**Marleau**	Guerin	**Nolan**
1/26	StL	0-3	L	15-19-12	Parent	**Shields**	20	36	0-5	1-5	Parent	Pronger	**Shields**
1/30	@Col	0-5	L	15-20-12	Roy	**Vernon**	22	28	0-4	1-4	Roy	Deadmarsh	Sakic
2/01	Chi	5-1	W	16-20-12	**Vernon**	Thibault	33	23	1-5	0-3	**Friesen**	**Nolan**	**Ragnarsson**
2/04	@Pho	1-3	L	16-21-12	Khabibulin	**Shields**	34	30	0-5	1-4	Tocchet	Khabibulin	Ylonen
2/06	@LA	0-2	L	16-22-12	Storr	**Vernon**	27	18	0-7	1-7	Robitaille	Storr	Norstrom
2/08	@Pho	3-**0**	W	17-22-12	**Vernon**	Khabibulin	27	27	1-6	0-4	**Vernon**	**Ricci**	Carney
2/10	@Chi	5-2	W	18-22-12	**Vernon**	Thibault	28	19	**3**-7	0-5	**Murphy**	**Korolyuk**	**Houlder**
2/11	@StL	5-1	W	19-22-12	**Shields**	Parent	25	30	1-5	1-5	**Korolyuk**	**Shields**	**Nolan**
2/13	@TB	3-1	W	20-22-12	**Vernon**	Ranford	36	31	1-6	0-5	**Vernon**	Cullimore	**Craven**
2/15	@Fla	2-2*	T	20-22-13	**Shields**	Burke	27	33	0-3	0-1	Whitney	**Shields**	**Friesen**

2/17	@Det	1-3	L	20-23-13	Osgood	**Vernon**	31	23	0-5	0-5	Larionov	Osgood	Dandenault
2/19	@Buf	2-4	L	20-24-13	Roloson	**Shields**	32	28	1-5	0-6	Brown	Satan	Roloson
2/20	@Was	1-3	L	20-25-13	Kolzig	**Vernon**	15	21	1-7	2-4	Gonchar	**Friesen**	Johansson
2/24	Van	1-1*	T	20-25-14	**Vernon**	Snow	**40**	**13**	1-**9**	0-3	**Korolyuk**	Snow	**Ricci**
2/26	@Anh	1-3	L	20-26-14	Hebert	**Vernon**	31	30	0-4	2-4	Selanne	Hebert	Green
2/27	Anh	1-4	L	20-27-14	Hebert	**Shields**	29	30	1-**9**	1-6	Selanne	Kariya	Haller
3/01	@Cgy	2-1	W	21-27-14	**Vernon**	Wregget	14	30	1-3	0-4	**Houlder**	**Vernon**	Stillman
3/03	@Van	4-3	W	22-27-14	**Shields**	Weekes	15	31	1-4	0-5	**Marleau**	Schaefer	**Houlder**
3/06	Chi	0-4	L	22-28-14	Thibault	**Shields**	23	27	0-7	1-5	Dumont	Daze	Thibault
3/09	Pho	4-2	W	23-28-14	**Shields**	Khabibulin	30	15	1-6	1-4	**Marleau**	**Korolyuk**	**Marchment**
3/12	Det	2-**0**	W	24-28-14	**Shields**	Maracle	34	26	0-6	0-5	**Shields**	**Murphy**	**Rathje**
3/13	Ott	3-2	W	25-28-14	**Shields**	Rhodes	20	36	0-2	1-5	**Stern**	**Shields**	Dackell
3/17	Fla	4-2	W	26-28-14	**Shields**	Burke	22	34	0-3	0-5	**Marleau**	**Korolyuk**	**Ragnarsson**
3/20	@Bos	2-2*	T	26-28-15	**Shields**	Dafoe	20	31	0-3	1-3	Allison	**Sturm**	Heinze
3/22	@Mon	1-1*	T	26-28-16	**Shields**	Hackett	17	44	0-4	1-5	**Shields**	Weinrich	Corson
3/24	@Tor	**8**-5	W	27-28-16	**Shields**	Healy	27	35	**3**-5	2-6	**Damphousse**	**Nolan**	D.King
3/26	@Ott	1-1*	T	27-28-17	**Vernon**	Rhodes	26	41	0-4	0-5	**Vernon**	Redden	Yashin
3/28	@Edm	2-5	L	27-29-17	Salo	**Vernon**	18	24	2-6	1-6	Guerin	Smith	**Damphousse**
3/31	Col	2-3	L	27-30-17	Billington	**Vernon**	27	23	0-4	0-2	Billington	**Norton**	Forsberg
4/02	@Van	7-**0**	W	28-30-17	**Shields**	Snow	24	18	2-5	0-4	**Murphy**	**Friesen**	**Damphousse**
4/03	Van	5-2	W	29-30-17	**Shields**	Snow	28	32	2-6	2-6	**Damphousse**	**Shields**	**Murphy**
4/06	@Pho	1-**0**	W	30-30-17	**Shields**	Khabibulin	25	33	1-4	0-6	**Shields**	**Houlder**	Khabibulin
4/08	@LA	2-3	L	30-31-17	Fiset	**Vernon**	34	25	1-4	0-**1**	Tsyplakov	Ferraro	Fiset
4/09	@Anh	4-1	W	31-31-17	**Shields**	Hebert	31	29	1-4	1-6	**Shields**	**Murphy**	**Ragnarsson**
4/12	Edm	4-5*	L	31-32-17	Salo	**Shields**	20	34	0-3	1-7	**Korolyuk**	Marchant	**Ricci**
4/16	LA	0-2	L	31-33-17	Fiset	**Vernon**	33	34	0-4	1-6	Fiset	Ferraro	**Nolan**
4/17	Anh	3-3*	T	31-33-18	**Shields**	Roussel	29	30	0-5	2-7	**Nolan**	**Korolyuk**	Kariya

Postseason

4/24	Col	1-3	L	0-1	Roy	**Vernon**	**43**	**31**	1-7	2-8	Sakic	Roy	**Friesen**
4/26	Col	1-**2***	L	0-2	Roy	**Vernon**	24	36	0-4	1-7	Hejduk	**Vernon**	Foote
4/28	@Col	4-**2**	W	1-2	**Vernon**	Roy	33	36	1-7	1-7	**Ricci**	**Sturm**	**Vernon**
4/30	@Col	**7**-3	W	2-2	**Vernon**	Roy	31	36	**2**-7	0-7	**Korolyuk**	**Damphousse**	**Marleau**
5/01	@Col	2-6	L	2-3	Roy	**Shields**	31	36	**2-9**	2-10	Fleury	Roy	Lemieux
5/03	Col	2-3*	L	2-4	Roy	**Vernon**	29	33	1-7	1-**3**	**Vernon**	Roy	Hejduk

† game played in Japan

San Jose Sharks 1998-99 Player Statistics

		Regular Season													Postseason												
Skater	**Ps**	**GP**	**G**	**A**	**Pts**	**+/–**	**PIM**	**PP**	**SH**	**GW**	**GT**	**S**	**SPct**	**P/G**	**GP**	**G**	**A**	**Pts**	**+/–**	**PIM**	**PP**	**SH**	**GW**	**OT**	**S**	**SPct**	**P/G**
Jeff Friesen	L	78	22	**35**	**57**	3	42	**10**	1	3	1	**215**	10.2	**.73**	**6**	2	2	4	-1	**14**	1	0	0	0	20	10.0	.67
Joe Murphy	R	76	**25**	23	48	10	73	7	0	2	1	176	14.2	.63	**6**	0	3	3	0	4	0	0	0	0	21	0.0	.50
Patrick Marleau	C	81	21	24	45	10	24	4	0	4	1	134	**15.7**	.56	**6**	2	1	3	-1	4	2	0	0	0	7	28.6	.50
Owen Nolan	R	78	19	26	45	**16**	129	6	**2**	3	1	207	9.2	.58	**6**	1	1	2	0	6	0	0	0	0	**26**	3.8	.33
Mike Ricci	C	**82**	13	26	39	1	68	2	1	2	1	98	13.3	.48	**6**	2	3	5	1	10	1	0	0	0	9	22.2	.83
Marco Sturm	C	78	16	22	38	7	52	3	**2**	3	**2**	140	11.4	.49	**6**	2	2	4	1	4	0	0	**1**	0	15	13.3	.67
Bill Houlder	D	76	9	23	32	8	40	7	0	**5**	0	115	7.8	.42	**6**	**3**	0	3	2	4	**3**	0	0	0	8	**37.5**	.50
* Alexander Korolyuk	R	55	12	18	30	3	26	2	0	0	1	96	12.5	.55	**6**	1	3	4	-3	2	0	0	**1**	0	7	14.3	.67
Stephane Matteau	L	68	8	15	23	2	73	0	0	0	0	72	11.1	.34	5	0	0	0	-3	6	0	0	0	0	4	0.0	.00
Jeff Norton†	D	69	4	18	22	2	42	2	0	1	0	68	5.9	.32	**6**	0	**7**	**7**	**5**	10	0	0	0	0	3	0.0	**1.17**
Ronnie Stern	R	78	7	9	16	-3	**158**	1	0	2	0	94	7.4	.21	**6**	0	0	0	-1	6	0	0	0	0	10	0.0	.00
Dave Lowry	L	61	6	9	15	-5	24	2	0	0	1	58	10.3	.25	1	0	0	0	0	0	0	0	0	0	0	—	.00
Mike Rathje	D	**82**	5	9	14	15	36	2	0	1	0	67	7.5	.17	**6**	0	0	0	-6	4	0	0	0	0	4	0.0	.00
Murray Craven	L	43	4	10	14	-3	18	0	1	1	0	55	7.3	.33	—	—	—	—	—	—	—	—	—	—	—	—	—
V. Damphousse†	C	12	7	6	13	3	4	3	0	1	0	43	16.3	1.08	**6**	**3**	2	5	1	6	0	**2**	0	0	22	13.6	.83
Marcus Ragnarsson	D	74	0	13	13	7	66	0	0	0	0	87	0.0	.18	**6**	0	1	1	-4	6	0	0	0	0	9	0.0	.17
Tony Granato	R	35	6	6	12	4	54	0	1	1	1	65	9.2	.34	**6**	1	1	2	-1	2	0	0	0	0	5	20.0	.33
Bob Rouse	D	70	0	11	11	0	44	0	0	0	0	75	0.0	.16	**6**	0	0	0	-1	6	0	0	0	0	4	0.0	.00
Ron Sutter	C	59	3	6	9	-8	40	0	0	1	0	67	4.5	.15	**6**	0	0	0	-1	4	0	0	0	0	10	0.0	.00
Bryan Marchment	D	59	2	6	8	-7	101	0	0	0	0	49	4.1	.14	**6**	0	0	0	0	4	0	0	0	0	7	0.0	.00
Andrei Zyuzin	D	25	3	1	4	5	38	2	0	0	0	44	6.8	.16	—	—	—	—	—	—	—	—	—	—	—	—	—
Steve Guolla	C	14	2	2	4	3	6	0	0	1	0	22	9.1	.29	—	—	—	—	—	—	—	—	—	—	—	—	—
* Andy Sutton	D	31	0	3	3	-4	65	0	0	0	0	24	0.0	.10	—	—	—	—	—	—	—	—	—	—	—	—	—
Jarrod Skalde	C	17	1	1	2	-6	4	0	0	0	1	17	5.9	.12	—	—	—	—	—	—	—	—	—	—	—	—	—
* Scott Hannan	D	5	0	2	2	0	6	0	0	0	0	4	0.0	.40	—	—	—	—	—	—	—	—	—	—	—	—	—
Bernie Nicholls	C	10	0	2	2	-4	4	0	0	0	0	11	0.0	.20	—	—	—	—	—	—	—	—	—	—	—	—	—
Brantt Myhres	R	30	1	0	1	-2	116	0	0	0	0	7	14.3	.03	—	—	—	—	—	—	—	—	—	—	—	—	—
Jamie Baker	C	1	0	1	1	1	0	0	0	0	0	1	0.0	1.00	—	—	—	—	—	—	—	—	—	—	—	—	—
Alex Hicks†	L	4	0	1	1	-1	4	0	0	0	0	4	0.0	.25	—	—	—	—	—	—	—	—	—	—	—	—	—
Shawn Burr	L	18	0	1	1	-3	29	0	0	0	0	22	0.0	.06	—	—	—	—	—	—	—	—	—	—	—	—	—
Steve Shields	G	37	0	1	1	—	6	0	0	0	0	0	—	.03	1	0	0	0	—	0	0	0	0	0	0	—	.00
Mike Craig	R	1	0	0	0	-1	0	0	0	0	0	1	0.0	.00	—	—	—	—	—	—	—	—	—	—	—	—	—
* Sean Gauthier	G	1	0	0	0	—	0	0	0	0	0	0	—	.00	—	—	—	—	—	—	—	—	—	—	—	—	—
Gary Suter	D	1	0	0	0	0	0	0	0	0	0	1	0.0	.00	—	—	—	—	—	—	—	—	—	—	—	—	—
* Shawn Heins	D	5	0	0	0	0	13	0	0	0	0	4	0.0	.00	—	—	—	—	—	—	—	—	—	—	—	—	—
Mike Vernon	G	49	0	0	0	—	8	0	0	0	0	0	—	.00	5	0	1	1	—	0	0	0	0	0	0	—	.20
Bench		—	—	—	—	—	0	—	—	—	—	—	—	—	—	—	—	—	—	0	—	—	—	—	—	—	—
TEAM TOTALS		82	196	330	526	53	1413	53	8	31	11	2143	9.1	6.41	6	17	27	44	-12	102	7	2	2	0	191	8.9	7.33

	Regular Season											Postseason									
Goaltender	**G**	**Min**	**GAA**	**W**	**L**	**T**	**ENG**	**ShO**	**GA**	**SA**	**SvPct**	**G**	**Min**	**GAA**	**W**	**L**	**ENG**	**ShO**	**GA**	**SA**	**SvPct**
* Sean Gauthier	1	3	.00	0	0	0	0	0	0	2	1.000	—	—	—	—	—	—	—	—	—	—
Steve Shields	37	2162	**2.22**	15	11	8	1	**4**	80	1011	**.921**	1	60	6.00	0	1	0	0	6	36	.833
Mike Vernon	**49**	**2831**	2.27	**16**	**22**	**10**	**3**	**4**	**107**	**1200**	.911	**5**	**321**	**2.43**	**2**	**3**	0	0	**13**	**172**	**.924**
TEAM TOTALS	82	5016	2.28	31	33	18	4	8	191	2217	.914	6	381	2.99	2	4	0	0	19	208	.909

1998-99 San Jose Sharks

Record When:

Overtime games	1-2-18
In second game of back-to-back games	4-5-5
Vs playoff teams	15-22-11
Leading after two periods	23-3-3
Tied after two periods	7-5-9
Losing after two periods	1-25-6
Scoring first	28-9-10
More shots than opponents	15-17-4
Fewer shots than opponents	14-15-13
Team had at least one fighting major	15-9-5
Team had more PIM	16-10-9
Team had fewer PIM	13-15-8
Team had even PIM	2-8-1

Team

Longest winning streak	4	3 times
Longest unbeaten streak	8	Mar. 9 — Mar. 26
Longest losing streak	3	3 times
Longest winless streak	8	Oct. 9 — Oct. 29
Most shots, game	40	3 times
Most shots, period	17	3 times
Fewest shots, game	9	vs. Dal, Nov. 4
Fewest shots, period	1	3rd, vs. NYI, Dec. 15

Individual

Longest goal streak	3	2 times
Longest point streak	8	Jeff Friesen
Most goals, game	3	2 times
Most assists, game	3	3 times
Most points, game	5	Marco Sturm
Highest +/–, game	5	Marco Sturm
Lowest +/–, game	-3	13 times
Most shots, game	9	2 times

Did You Know?

With zero goals on 87 shots last year, the Sharks' Marcus Ragnarsson took the most shots of any player who failed to score.

Miscellaneous

		NHL Rank
PP Pct.	13.3 (53-399)	23
SH goals allowed	4	1t
PK Pct.	85.0 (346-407)	13
SH goals scored	8	8t
Special Team Index	99.3	17
Shots on goal	2,143 (26.1/G)	22
Shots against	2,217 (27.0/G)	10
Unassisted goals	12	16t
Unassisted goals allowed	9	4t
Team Average Weight	203.6	8
Game Star Points	387	13t

Game Star Breakdown

Player	1st	2nd	3rd	Pts
Owen Nolan	4	7	5	46
Steve Shields	5	5	1	41
Mike Vernon	5	3	7	41
Alexander Korolyuk	3	7	0	36
Patrick Marleau	4	4	1	33
Jeff Friesen	3	4	4	31
Marco Sturm	5	1	0	28
Joe Murphy	3	3	3	27
Mike Ricci	2	2	5	21
Bill Houlder	2	2	2	18
Vincent Damphousse	2	0	2	12
Ronnie Stern	2	0	1	11
Tony Granato	2	0	0	10
Dave Lowry	0	2	0	6
Marcus Ragnarsson	0	1	3	6
Ron Sutter	1	0	0	5
Murray Craven	0	1	1	4
Steve Guolla	0	1	0	3
Jeff Norton	0	1	0	3
Bryan Marchment	0	0	3	3
Mike Rathje	0	0	2	2

St. Louis Blues 1998-99 Game Log (37-32-13)

Date	Opp	Score	W/L/T	Record	Goalies W/T	Goalies L/T	Shots StL	Shots Opp	Power Plays StL	Power Plays Opp	Game Stars 1st	Game Stars 2nd	Game Stars 3rd
10/10	@Bos	3-3*	T	0-0-1	**Fuhr**	Dafoe	32	24	1-3	2-8	Baumgartner	**Demitra**	Samsonov
10/12	@NYR	4-2	W	1-0-1	**Fuhr**	Richter	42	18	1-4	0-3	**MacInnis**	**Turgeon**	**Pronger**
10/16	@Det	1-4	L	1-1-1	Osgood	**Fuhr**	25	25	0-5	1-4	Shanahan	Yzerman	McCarty
10/17	NYI	0-1	L	1-2-1	Salo	**McLennan**	23	12	0-3	1-6	Salo	Berard	**Rivers**
10/22	@Ott	5-3	W	2-2-1	**McLennan**	Tugnutt	32	28	0-5	1-10	**Picard**	**Reasoner**	Johansson
10/24	Cgy	4-3	W	3-2-1	**McLennan**	Wregget	36	19	2-**8**	0-4	**MacInnis**	**Pronger**	Fleury
10/27	@Phi	1-2	L	3-3-1	Vanbiesbrouck	**McLennan**	30	20	0-4	1-9	McGillis	Forbes	**Turgeon**
10/29	Det	3-1	W	4-3-1	**Fuhr**	Osgood	25	26	1-6	1-5	**Courtnall**	**Conroy**	Brown
10/31	Anh	2-2*	T	4-3-2	**Fuhr**	Hebert	**45**	27	1-5	0-5	Hebert	**MacInnis**	**Young**
11/04	@Anh	3-1	W	5-3-2	**Fuhr**	Hebert	36	29	0-2	1-5	**Picard**	Davidsson	**Demitra**
11/05	@LA	2-2*	T	5-3-3	**McLennan**	LeGace	28	33	2-7	0-6	Robitaille	Murray	**McLennan**
11/07	@SJ	2-2*	T	5-3-4	**McLennan**	Vernon	25	17	0-3	0-6	Sturm	**Turgeon**	Vernon
11/10	Chi	5-2	W	6-3-4	**McLennan**	Hackett	41	14	3-6	0-3	**Turgeon**	**Demitra**	**Twist**
11/11	@Det	2-6	L	6-4-4	Osgood	**McLennan**	28	31	0-2	1-4	Kocur	Yzerman	Draper
11/14	Nsh	5-1	W	7-4-4	**McLennan**	Dunham	39	17	1-2	0-4	**Conroy**	**Young**	**Pronger**
11/19	@Nsh	2-3	L	7-5-4	Dunham	**McLennan**	31	32	0-4	0-5	Ronning	Dunham	Lambert
11/21	Dal	3-3*	T	7-5-5	**Parent**	Turek	34	18	1-4	2-8	**Demitra**	**Chase**	Marshall
11/24	Nsh	4-**0**	W	8-5-5	**McLennan**	Fichaud	41	19	2-3	0-3	**Demitra**	**MacInnis**	**McLennan**
11/27	SJ	2-4	L	8-6-5	Shields	**McLennan**	21	21	1-5	1-6	Sturm	Guolla	**Demitra**
11/28	Was	4-2	W	9-6-5	**McLennan**	Kolzig	25	34	1-4	1-6	**McLennan**	**Conroy**	**Handzus**
12/04	@Col	0-2	L	9-7-5	Roy	**McLennan**	25	16	0-4	0-1	Roy	Forsberg	Miller
12/05	Col	1-3	L	9-8-5	Billington	**McLennan**	30	22	0-4	2-4	Forsberg	Billington	**Eastwood**
12/08	Buf	2-2*	T	9-8-6	**McLennan**	Hasek	43	16	1-**8**	1-6	Hasek	**Demitra**	Brown
12/12	Pit	3-4	L	9-9-6	Barrasso	**Fuhr**	34	14	1-3	1-4	Kovalev	Jagr	**Yake**
12/14	@Col	0-**0***	T	9-9-7	**Fuhr**	Roy	32	22	0-3	0-6	Roy	**Fuhr**	Forsberg
12/15	@Dal	3-7	L	9-10-7	Belfour	**McLennan**	24	23	1-2	2-5	Hull	Hatcher	Nieuwendyk
12/17	Pho	3-2	W	10-10-7	**Fuhr**	Waite	29	22	1-6	0-5	**Demitra**	**Handzus**	Numminen
12/19	LA	5-2	W	11-10-7	**Fuhr**	Storr	27	25	0-1	1-4	**Demitra**	**Conroy**	**Bartecko**
12/22	@NYI	3-3*	T	11-10-8	**Fuhr**	Flaherty	28	17	0-1	1-4	Czerkawski	**Gill**	Palffy
12/23	@NJ	2-4	L	11-11-8	Brodeur	**Fuhr**	25	25	1-3	2-5	Holik	Sharifijanov	Niedermayer
12/26	Det	4-3	W	12-11-8	**Fuhr**	Osgood	22	32	2-5	0-8	**Pellerin**	**Fuhr**	Dandenault
12/28	@Det	4-4*	T	12-11-9	**Fuhr**	Maracle	32	20	1-4	1-6	Kozlov	**Pronger**	Lidstrom
1/01	@Nsh	6-5	W	13-11-9	**McLennan**	Fichaud	37	29	2-3	1-2	**Demitra**	Johnson	**Yake**
1/02	NYR	0-1	L	13-12-9	Richter	**McLennan**	24	10	0-2	1-4	Richter	MacLean	**MacInnis**
1/04	Van	4-**0**	W	14-12-9	**McLennan**	Hirsch	34	20	1-5	0-3	**McLennan**	**Rheaume**	**Yake**
1/07	Chi	4-2	W	15-12-9	**McLennan**	Thibault	32	15	1-5	0-5	**Pronger**	**Demitra**	Gilmour
1/09	@Pit	1-2	L	15-13-9	Barrasso	**Fuhr**	30	14	0-4	0-5	Barrasso	Lang	Titov
1/11	@Mon	1-3	L	15-14-9	Hackett	**McLennan**	23	25	0-2	1-4	**McLennan**	Damphousse	Recchi
1/13	@Buf	4-2	W	16-14-9	**Fuhr**	Hasek	30	25	3-7	1-10	**Pronger**	**MacInnis**	**Fuhr**
1/16	@Col	0-2	L	16-15-9	Roy	**Fuhr**	28	19	0-3	0-5	Roy	Miller	**Pronger**
1/19	@Pho	2-4	L	16-16-9	Khabibulin	**McLennan**	28	23	1-3	0-3	Tocchet	Adams	**MacInnis**
1/21	Tor	2-4	L	16-17-9	Reese	**Fuhr**	24	21	1-3	2-6	Warriner	Thomas	Reese
1/26	@SJ	3-**0**	W	17-17-9	**Parent**	Shields	36	20	1-5	0-5	**Parent**	**Pronger**	Shields
1/28	@Van	4-2	W	18-17-9	**Parent**	Snow	25	19	1-2	1-4	**Young**	**Pronger**	Klatt
1/30	@Cgy	3-4*	L	18-18-9	Brathwaite	**Parent**	23	19	1-2	0-6	**Pronger**	Fleury	Shantz
2/01	@Edm	4-3*	W	19-18-9	**Parent**	Shtalenkov	21	30	2-3	0-6	**Pronger**	Smyth	**Turgeon**
2/04	NJ	0-2	L	19-19-9	Terreri	**Parent**	36	22	0-2	0-2	Terreri	Rolston	Stevens
2/06	Anh	3-4	L	19-20-9	Hebert	**Fuhr**	26	19	2-4	1-5	**MacInnis**	Cullen	Selanne
2/08	@Fla	5-4	W	20-20-9	**Parent**	Burke	29	25	1-5	0-6	**Demitra**	**Yake**	Lindsay
2/10	@TB	5-4	W	21-20-9	**McLennan**	Schwab	38	22	0-2	1-3	**Demitra**	Tucker	**Yake**
2/11	SJ	1-5	L	21-21-9	Shields	**Parent**	30	25	1-5	1-5	Korolyuk	Shields	Nolan
2/13	Edm	2-3	L	21-22-9	Essensa	**McLennan**	33	22	0-5	1-6	Smyth	Essensa	Mironov
2/15	Van	**8**-1	W	22-22-9	**McLennan**	Snow	27	21	0-0	1-4	**MacInnis**	**Turgeon**	**Demitra**
2/18	Fla	0-**0***	T	22-22-10	**McLennan**	Burke	27	21	0-3	0-3	Burke	**McLennan**	**MacInnis**
2/20	Nsh	3-4	L	22-23-10	Vokoun	**McLennan**	37	22	0-2	1-5	Vokoun	Heward	Slaney

2/22	LA	5-1	W	23-23-10	**McLennan**	Fiset	40	23	1-4	0-3	**Demitra**	**McLennan**	**Turgeon**
2/24	Chi	1-3	L	23-24-10	Fitzpatrick	**McLennan**	26	16	0-3	0-2	Gilmour	Chelios	**MacInnis**
2/26	@Cgy	4-2	W	24-24-10	**Johnson**	Brathwaite	34	29	0-3	0-4	**Conroy**	Hulse	**MacInnis**
2/28	@Chi	3-1	W	25-24-10	**Johnson**	Thibault	27	27	2-4	0-5	**Turgeon**	**Young**	**Johnson**
3/02	@Nsh	5-1	W	26-24-10	**Johnson**	Dunham	35	31	0-3	0-3	**Chase**	**Conroy**	**Eastwood**
3/04	Tor	0-4	L	26-25-10	Joseph	**Johnson**	28	**9**	0-2	0-2	Joseph	Sullivan	Cote
3/07	@Dal	3-4	L	26-26-10	Turek	**Carey**	34	22	1-5	1-5	Modano	**MacInnis**	Turek
3/09	Cgy	4-7	L	26-27-10	Wregget	**Carey**	33	34	2-5	1-8	Iginla	Corbet	Stillman
3/11	Mon	0-3	L	26-28-10	Hackett	**Johnson**	41	25	0-3	0-4	Hackett	Koivu	Zubrus
3/13	Edm	6-4	W	27-28-10	**Fuhr**	Essensa	31	28	1-3	1-8	**Conroy**	**Bartecko**	Hamrlik
3/14	@Chi	5-2	W	28-28-10	**Carey**	Thibault	25	24	1-3	0-3	**Demitra**	**MacInnis**	Fitzpatrick
3/16	Phi	5-2	W	29-28-10	**Fuhr**	Vanbiesbrouck	27	28	2-4	0-4	**MacInnis**	**Pronger**	**Young**
3/18	Pho	2-2*	T	29-28-11	**Fuhr**	Shtalenkov	31	22	0-4	1-4	**MacInnis**	**Demitra**	**Eastwood**
3/20	Ott	2-3	L	29-29-11	Tugnutt	**Fuhr**	22	15	0-1	0-4	**Demitra**	McEachern	Tugnutt
3/22	Car	5-2	W	30-29-11	**Fuhr**	Irbe	27	22	1-5	1-6	**Picard**	**Demitra**	**Turgeon**
3/25	@Van	4-1	W	31-29-11	**Fuhr**	Weekes	28	20	0-6	0-2	**Turgeon**	**Pellerin**	McCabe
3/26	@Edm	1-2	L	31-30-11	Salo	**Fuhr**	22	25	0-2	1-4	Murray	Salo	**Fuhr**
3/28	@Chi	1-3	L	31-31-11	Fitzpatrick	**Fuhr**	37	16	1-7	1-7	Amonte	Mironov	Eriksson
4/01	TB	3-**0**	W	32-31-11	**Fuhr**	Hodson	24	27	0-2	0-4	**Fuhr**	**Pellerin**	**Mayers**
4/03	Dal	5-2	W	33-31-11	**Fuhr**	Turek	21	21	1-1	0-5	**Demitra**	**Pronger**	**Fuhr**
4/05	@Tor	2-2*	T	33-31-12	**Fuhr**	Joseph	28	31	0-2	0-**1**	Joseph	**Fuhr**	Berard
4/07	@Was	4-2	W	34-31-12	**Fuhr**	Tabaracci	32	29	0-3	0-**1**	**Young**	Gratton	**MacInnis**
4/09	Det	1-1*	T	34-31-13	**Fuhr**	Ranford	26	22	1-4	1-6	**Fuhr**	**MacInnis**	Ranford
4/11	Col	2-4	L	34-32-13	Roy	**Fuhr**	36	20	0-5	0-4	Roy	Forsberg	**Demitra**
4/14	@Anh	3-1	W	35-32-13	**Fuhr**	Hebert	24	32	0-1	0-3	**Fuhr**	**MacInnis**	Kariya
4/15	@Pho	6-4	W	36-32-13	**Fuhr**	Khabibulin	35	26	**4**-7	2-5	**Pronger**	Doan	**Yake**
4/18	@LA	3-2	W	37-32-13	**McLennan**	Bach	27	38	0-3	0-4	**Atcheynum**	**McLennan**	J.Blake

Postseason

4/22	@Pho	3-1	W	1-0	**Fuhr**	Khabibulin	25	27	1-3	0-6	**MacInnis**	Reichel	**Fuhr**
4/24	@Pho	3-4*	L	1-1	Khabibulin	**Fuhr**	34	28	2-4	1-6	Doan	**MacInnis**	Drake
4/25	Pho	4-5	L	1-2	Khabibulin	**McLennan**	38	18	**3-7**	1-12	DeBrusk	**MacInnis**	**Courtnall**
4/27	Pho	1-2	L	1-3	Khabibulin	**Fuhr**	28	20	0-4	1-**3**	Numminen	Khabibulin	**Rheaume**
4/30	@Pho	2-1*	W	2-3	**Fuhr**	Khabibulin	**43**	27	1-6	1-6	**MacInnis**	**Handzus**	Tkachuk
5/02	Pho	**5**-3	W	3-3	**Fuhr**	Khabibulin	34	21	2-5	1-4	**Turgeon**	**Finley**	**Conroy**
5/04	@Pho	1-**0***	W	4-3	**Fuhr**	Khabibulin	35	35	0-4	0-4	**Turgeon**	**Fuhr**	Khabibulin
5/06	@Dal	0-3	L	0-1	Belfour	**Fuhr**	23	25	0-5	0-7	Verbeek	Belfour	Matvichuk
5/08	@Dal	4-5*	L	0-2	Belfour	**Fuhr**	34	25	1-3	0-4	Nieuwendyk	**Turgeon**	**Demitra**
5/10	Dal	3-2*	W	1-2	**Fuhr**	Belfour	28	18	0-6	1-5	**Demitra**	**Hecht**	Hull
5/12	Dal	3-2*	W	2-2	**Fuhr**	Belfour	30	25	1-**7**	0-5	**Turgeon**	Belfour	**MacInnis**
5/15	@Dal	1-3	L	2-3	Belfour	**Fuhr**	31	**16**	0-4	2-5	Belfour	Lehtinen	Hatcher
5/17	Dal	1-2*	L	2-4	Belfour	**Fuhr**	29	29	0-3	0-4	Modano	**MacInnis**	Hull

St. Louis Blues 1998-99 Player Statistics

		Regular Season													Postseason												
Skater	**Ps**	**GP**	**G**	**A**	**Pts**	**+/–**	**PIM**	**PP**	**SH**	**GW**	**GT**	**S**	**SPct**	**P/G**	**GP**	**G**	**A**	**Pts**	**+/–**	**PIM**	**PP**	**SH**	**GW**	**OT**	**S**	**SPct**	**P/G**
Pavol Demitra	L	**82**	**37**	**52**	**89**	13	16	**14**	0	**10**	1	259	14.3	**1.09**	**13**	**5**	4	9	-5	4	**3**	0	1	1	31	**16.1**	.69
Pierre Turgeon	C	67	31	34	65	4	36	10	0	5	**2**	193	**16.1**	.97	**13**	4	**9**	**13**	3	6	0	0	**2**	**2**	42	9.5	**1.00**
Al MacInnis	D	**82**	20	42	62	**33**	70	11	1	2	**2**	**314**	6.4	.76	**13**	4	8	12	-2	20	2	0	0	0	**66**	6.1	.92
Scott Young	R	75	24	28	52	8	27	8	0	4	0	205	11.7	.69	**13**	4	7	11	2	10	1	0	1	1	40	10.0	.85
Chris Pronger	D	67	13	33	46	3	113	8	0	0	0	172	7.6	.69	**13**	1	4	5	-2	**28**	1	0	0	0	43	2.3	.38
Scott Pellerin	L	80	20	21	41	1	42	0	**5**	4	0	138	14.5	.51	8	1	0	1	-2	4	0	0	0	0	11	9.1	.13
Craig Conroy	C	69	14	25	39	14	38	0	1	1	0	134	10.4	.57	**13**	2	1	3	-3	6	0	0	0	0	20	10.0	.23
Mike Eastwood	C	**82**	9	21	30	6	36	0	0	0	0	76	11.8	.37	**13**	1	1	2	2	6	0	0	0	0	8	12.5	.15
Pascal Rheaume	C	60	9	18	27	10	24	2	0	0	0	85	10.6	.45	5	1	0	1	1	4	0	0	0	0	10	10.0	.20
Terry Yake	R	60	9	18	27	-9	34	3	0	4	0	59	15.3	.45	**13**	1	2	3	-3	14	1	0	0	0	13	7.7	.23
Jim Campbell	R	55	4	21	25	-8	41	1	0	0	0	99	4.0	.45	—	—	—	—	—	—	—	—	—	—	—	—	—
Michel Picard	L	45	11	11	22	5	16	0	0	2	0	69	15.9	.49	5	0	0	0	-3	2	0	0	0	0	7	0.0	.00
* Lubos Bartecko	L	32	5	11	16	4	6	0	0	1	0	37	13.5	.50	5	0	0	0	-3	2	0	0	0	0	8	0.0	.00
* Michal Handzus	C	66	4	12	16	-9	30	0	0	0	0	78	5.1	.24	11	0	2	2	0	8	0	0	0	0	16	0.0	.18
Ricard Persson	D	54	1	12	13	4	94	0	0	0	0	52	1.9	.24	**13**	0	3	3	-1	17	0	0	0	0	12	0.0	.23
Geoff Courtnall	L	24	5	7	12	2	28	1	0	2	0	60	8.3	.50	**13**	2	4	6	-4	10	2	0	0	0	18	11.1	.46
* Marty Reasoner	C	22	3	7	10	2	8	1	0	0	0	33	9.1	.45	—	—	—	—	—	—	—	—	—	—	—	—	—
Kelly Chase	R	45	3	7	10	2	143	0	0	1	0	25	12.0	.22	—	—	—	—	—	—	—	—	—	—	—	—	—
* Jamal Mayers	C	34	4	5	9	-3	40	0	0	0	0	48	8.3	.26	11	0	1	1	-2	8	0	0	0	0	9	0.0	.09
Tony Twist	L	63	2	6	8	0	**149**	0	0	0	0	23	8.7	.13	1	0	0	0	-1	0	0	0	0	0	0	—	.00
Jamie Rivers	D	76	2	5	7	-3	47	1	0	0	0	78	2.6	.09	9	1	1	2	-2	2	1	0	1	0	4	25.0	.22
Todd Gill†	D	28	2	3	5	-6	16	1	0	0	1	36	5.6	.18	—	—	—	—	—	—	—	—	—	—	—	—	—
Blair Atcheynum†	R	12	2	2	4	2	2	0	0	1	0	23	8.7	.33	**13**	1	3	4	2	6	0	0	0	0	19	5.3	.31
* Bryan Helmer†	D	29	0	4	4	3	19	0	0	0	0	38	0.0	.14	—	—	—	—	—	—	—	—	—	—	—	—	—
Jeff Finley†	D	30	1	2	3	12	20	0	0	0	0	16	6.3	.10	**13**	1	2	3	-4	8	0	0	1	0	5	20.0	.23
Chris McAlpine	D	51	1	1	2	-10	50	0	0	0	0	56	1.8	.04	**13**	0	0	0	0	2	0	0	0	0	7	0.0	.00
Marc Bergevin	D	52	1	1	2	-14	99	0	0	0	0	40	2.5	.04	—	—	—	—	—	—	—	—	—	—	—	—	—
Rory Fitzpatrick	D	1	0	0	0	-3	2	0	0	0	0	0	—	.00	—	—	—	—	—	—	—	—	—	—	—	—	—
* Tyson Nash	L	2	0	0	0	-1	5	0	0	0	0	1	0.0	.00	1	0	0	0	-3	2	0	0	0	0	0	—	.00
* Jochen Hecht	C	3	0	0	0	-2	0	0	0	0	0	4	0.0	.00	5	2	0	2	**4**	0	0	0	0	0	20	10.0	.40
Jim Carey	G	4	0	0	0	—	0	0	0	0	0	0	—	.00	—	—	—	—	—	—	—	—	—	—	—	—	—
* Brent Johnson	G	6	0	0	0	—	0	0	0	0	0	0	—	.00	—	—	—	—	—	—	—	—	—	—	—	—	—
* Rich Parent	G	10	0	0	0	—	2	0	0	0	0	0	—	.00	—	—	—	—	—	—	—	—	—	—	—	—	—
Brad Shaw†	D	12	0	0	0	0	4	0	0	0	0	10	0.0	.00	4	0	0	0	2	0	0	0	0	0	3	0.0	.00
Rudy Poeschek	D	16	0	0	0	0	33	0	0	0	0	8	0.0	.00	—	—	—	—	—	—	—	—	—	—	—	—	—
Jamie McLennan	G	33	0	0	0	—	0	0	0	0	0	0	—	.00	1	0	0	0	—	6	0	0	0	0	0	—	.00
Grant Fuhr	G	39	0	0	0	—	12	0	0	0	0	0	—	.00	**13**	0	1	1	—	2	0	0	0	0	0	—	.08
Bench		—	—	—	—	—	0	—	—	—	—	—	—	—	—	—	—	—	—	0	—	—	—	—	—	—	—
TEAM TOTALS		82	237	409	646	60	1302	61	7	37	6	2469	9.6	7.88	13	31	53	84	-24	177	11	0	6	4	412	7.5	6.46

	Regular Season											Postseason									
Goaltender	**G**	**Min**	**GAA**	**W**	**L**	**T**	**ENG**	**ShO**	**GA**	**SA**	**SvPct**	**G**	**Min**	**GAA**	**W**	**L**	**ENG**	**ShO**	**GA**	**SA**	**SvPct**
* Brent Johnson	6	286	2.10	3	2	0	0	0	10	127	.921	—	—	—	—	—	—	—	—	—	—
Jamie McLennan	33	1763	**2.38**	13	**14**	4	**3**	**3**	70	640	.891	1	37	.00	0	1	**1**	0	0	7	1.000
Grant Fuhr	**39**	**2193**	2.44	**16**	11	**8**	1	2	**89**	**827**	**.892**	**13**	**790**	**2.35**	**6**	**6**	**1**	**1**	**31**	**305**	**.898**
* Rich Parent	10	519	2.54	4	3	1	1	1	22	193	.886	—	—	—	—	—	—	—	—	—	—
Jim Carey	4	202	3.86	1	2	0	0	0	13	76	.829	—	—	—	—	—	—	—	—	—	—
TEAM TOTALS	82	4989	2.51	37	32	13	5	6	209	1868	.888	13	832	2.38	6	7	2	1	33	314	.895

1998-99 St. Louis Blues

Record When:

Overtime games	1-1-13
In second game of back-to-back games	3-8-1
Vs playoff teams	14-22-10
Leading after two periods	26-3-6
Tied after two periods	6-3-5
Losing after two periods	5-26-2
Scoring first	29-9-6
More shots than opponents	27-24-11
Fewer shots than opponents	8-5-2
Team had at least one fighting major	19-12-3
Team had more PIM	23-21-7
Team had fewer PIM	10-6-3
Team had even PIM	4-5-3

Team

Longest winning streak	3	3 times
Longest unbeaten streak	6	Oct. 29 — Nov. 10
Longest losing streak	4	Mar. 4 — Mar. 11
Longest winless streak	6	Dec. 4 — Dec. 15
Most shots, game	45	vs. Anh, Oct. 31
Most shots, period	19	2nd, @Nsh, Jan. 1
Fewest shots, game	21	3 times
Fewest shots, period	1	3rd, vs. Det, Dec. 26

Individual

Longest goal streak	5	Pavol Demitra
Longest point streak	9	Scott Young
Most goals, game	3	3 times
Most assists, game	3	9 times
Most points, game	5	Pavol Demitra
Highest +/–, game	4	3 times
Lowest +/–, game	-4	Pierre Turgeon
Most shots, game	11	Al MacInnis

Did You Know?

The Blues outshot their opponents in 1998-99 by an NHL-best differential of 7.3 shots per game. However, the Blues had the league's worst save percentage, .888.

Miscellaneous

		NHL Rank
PP Pct.	20.3 (61-301)	3
SH goals allowed	4	1t
PK Pct.	87.9 (340-387)	2
SH goals scored	7	15t
Special Team Index	108.6	1
Shots on goal	2,469 (30.1/G)	4
Shots against	1,868 (22.8/G)	1
Unassisted goals	8	25t
Unassisted goals allowed	9	4t
Team Average Weight	199.3	16
Game Star Points	387	13t

Game Star Breakdown

Player	1st	2nd	3rd	Pts
Pavol Demitra	11	6	4	77
Al MacInnis	6	7	6	57
Chris Pronger	5	6	3	46
Pierre Turgeon	3	3	4	28
Craig Conroy	3	4	0	27
Grant Fuhr	3	3	3	27
Jamie McLennan	3	3	2	26
Scott Young	2	2	2	18
Michel Picard	3	0	0	15
Scott Pellerin	1	2	0	11
Kelly Chase	1	1	0	8
Terry Yake	0	1	5	8
Blair Atcheynum	1	0	0	5
Geoff Courtnall	1	0	0	5
Rich Parent	1	0	0	5
Lubos Bartecko	0	1	1	4
Michal Handzus	0	1	1	4
Todd Gill	0	1	0	3
Marty Reasoner	0	1	0	3
Pascal Rheaume	0	1	0	3
Mike Eastwood	0	0	3	3
Brent Johnson	0	0	1	1
Jamal Mayers	0	0	1	1
Jamie Rivers	0	0	1	1
Tony Twist	0	0	1	1

Tampa Bay Lightning 1998-99 Game Log (19-54-9)

					Goalies		Shots		Power Plays		Game Stars		
Date	Opp	Score	W/L/T	Record	W/T	L/T	TB	Opp	TB	Opp	1st	2nd	3rd
10/09	@Fla	1-4	L	0-1-0	Burke	**Ranford**	29	36	0-6	0-3	Parrish	Kozlov	Burke
10/10	@Car	4-4*	T	0-1-1	**Puppa**	Kidd	25	34	1-5	3-9	Francis	**Janney**	Chiasson
10/14	NYI	0-2	L	0-2-1	Salo	**Puppa**	22	23	0-4	0-5	Reichel	Salo	**Samuelsson**
10/16	Phi	2-5	L	0-3-1	Hextall	**Puppa**	26	36	0-5	2-5	LeClair	Lindros	Brind'Amour
10/18	Was	1-4	L	0-4-1	Kolzig	**Ranford**	32	32	0-6	0-3	Mironov	Herr	**Andersson**
10/21	Pit	5-**0**	W	1-4-1	**Puppa**	Skudra	18	28	**2**-4	0-5	**Tucker**	**Puppa**	**Clark**
10/23	LA	3-2	W	2-4-1	**Ranford**	Bach	38	39	0-6	0-4	**Tucker**	**Ranford**	**Renberg**
10/25	Van	3-2	W	3-4-1	**Puppa**	Snow	26	17	1-4	0-5	Ohlund	**Langkow**	**Lecavalier**
10/28	@Anh	3-5	L	3-5-1	Hebert	**Puppa**	**45**	31	**2-9**	1-5	Grimson	Hebert	Sandstrom
10/30	@LA	3-**0**	W	4-5-1	**Puppa**	LeGace	28	27	0-4	0-4	**Puppa**	**Langkow**	LeGace
10/31	@SJ	1-6	L	4-6-1	Vernon	**Ranford**	21	31	1-8	1-5	Sutter	Craven	Friesen
11/04	@Was	5-2	W	5-6-1	**Puppa**	Kolzig	18	36	1-5	1-4	**Puppa**	**Clark**	Oates
11/06	Chi	2-2*	T	5-6-2	**Ranford**	Fitzpatrick	24	37	1-5	2-4	**Ranford**	Chelios	**Kubina**
11/08	NJ	3-1	W	6-6-2	**Puppa**	Brodeur	27	35	0-2	1-3	**Clark**	**Puppa**	**Sykora**
11/10	NYR	2-10	L	6-7-2	Cloutier	**Ranford**	28	30	1-3	2-6	Stevens	Leetch	Samuelsson
11/13	@Col	1-8	L	6-8-2	Roy	**Puppa**	18	45	0-4	4-7	Sakic	Forsberg	Gusarov
11/14	@Pho	1-4	L	6-9-2	Waite	**Puppa**	21	39	0-4	0-6	Roenick	Tkachuk	Briere
11/19	Pit	1-5	L	6-10-2	Barrasso	**Ranford**	23	35	0-2	0-4	Straka	Barnes	Hatcher
11/21	@Pit	2-5	L	6-11-2	Aubin	**Puppa**	21	22	0-1	2-7	Straka	Jagr	Werenka
11/24	Bos	1-4	L	6-12-2	Tallas	**Ranford**	16	33	0-4	1-4	Khristich	Bourque	Heinze
11/27	Fla	1-2	L	6-13-2	Burke	**Ranford**	24	28	1-6	0-3	Mellanby	Burke	**Ranford**
11/29	Buf	3-6	L	6-14-2	Hasek	**Schwab**	33	33	1-3	0-3	Peca	**Tucker**	Brown
12/03	@Cgy	1-4	L	6-15-2	Moss	**Schwab**	30	24	1-4	1-5	Moss	Morris	Fleury
12/04	@Edm	2-1	W	7-15-2	**Schwab**	Shtalenkov	23	35	1-2	0-5	**Schwab**	**Renberg**	Shtalenkov
12/06	@Chi	5-7	L	7-16-2	Thibault	**Schwab**	36	30	0-3	1-3	Zhamnov	Kilger	Amonte
12/08	Ott	2-4	L	7-17-2	Tugnutt	**Schwab**	19	44	1-4	0-8	McEachern	Yashin	**Hogue**
12/11	Cgy	1-2	L	7-18-2	Giguere	**Bierk**	25	21	0-3	1-1	Stillman	Cassels	**Renberg**
12/12	@NYI	2-1*	W	8-18-2	**Schwab**	Salo	26	35	0-3	0-3	**Hogue**	Linden	**Gratton**
12/15	@Pit	2-3*	L	8-19-2	Barrasso	**Schwab**	20	32	1-2	0-3	Hatcher	Lang	Straka
12/18	Edm	1-4	L	8-20-2	Essensa	**Schwab**	23	38	0-2	0-6	Marchant	Guerin	Hamrlik
12/20	@Phi	2-2*	T	8-20-3	**Ranford**	Hextall	30	32	0-2	1-5	Brind'Amour	**Ranford**	Hextall
12/21	@Bos	2-3	L	8-21-3	Tallas	**Ranford**	26	34	1-4	1-6	McLaren	Allison	**Gratton**
12/23	@Buf	0-2	L	8-22-3	Hasek	**Ranford**	38	22	0-7	1-5	Hasek	Holzinger	Satan
12/26	Fla	1-3	L	8-23-3	Burke	**Ranford**	24	35	0-5	1-3	Burke	**Selivanov**	Svehla
12/29	NYI	3-**0**	W	9-23-3	**Ranford**	Cousineau	17	35	**2**-4	0-4	**Ranford**	**Lecavalier**	**Cross**
12/30	@Car	3-4	L	9-24-3	Irbe	**Ranford**	27	38	**2**-5	2-5	Roberts	**Clark**	Dineen
1/04	@Tor	4-5*	L	9-25-3	Joseph	**Ranford**	29	37	0-2	0-5	Thomas	**Clark**	Yushkevich
1/07	@Mon	1-4	L	9-26-3	Hackett	**Ranford**	20	33	0-4	2-6	Malakhov	Corson	**Ranford**
1/08	@Ott	1-5	L	9-27-3	Tugnutt	**Schwab**	20	35	0-2	2-7	Yashin	McEachern	Alfredsson
1/10	@NYR	2-5	L	9-28-3	Cloutier	**Ranford**	24	27	1-8	2-6	MacLean	Leetch	Cloutier
1/12	Tor	3-4	L	9-29-3	Joseph	**Ranford**	29	24	1-4	2-5	Johnson	Sundin	**Tucker**
1/15	@NJ	1-3	L	9-30-3	Brodeur	**Schwab**	20	33	1-3	3-5	Rolston	Sykora	Daneyko
1/16	@Bos	2-2*	T	9-30-4	**Ranford**	Tallas	39	29	0-6	0-4	Tallas	**Kubina**	**Ranford**
1/19	Buf	2-1	W	10-30-4	**Schwab**	Hasek	32	**15**	0-6	0-3	**Zamuner**	**Wilkie**	**Kubina**
1/21	@Nsh	3-2	W	11-30-4	**Ranford**	Dunham	26	36	1-4	0-5	**Ranford**	Krivokrasov	**Cross**
1/26	Mon	1-2	L	11-31-4	Hackett	**Schwab**	29	29	0-2	0-3	Hackett	Rucinsky	**Hogue**
1/29	Dal	1-4	L	11-32-4	Belfour	**Schwab**	32	32	1-5	0-5	Modano	Belfour	**Richer**
1/30	@Phi	2-6	L	11-33-4	Hextall	**Schwab**	21	44	0-4	2-7	Brind'Amour	McGillis	LeClair
2/02	Tor	0-3	L	11-34-4	Joseph	**Schwab**	23	29	0-3	2-5	Berezin	Joseph	**Schwab**
2/03	@Was	1-10	L	11-35-4	Kolzig	**Schwab**	22	46	0-3	2-6	Bondra	Bellows	Johansson
2/05	Anh	3-5	L	11-36-4	Hebert	**Ranford**	31	33	1-4	2-4	Kariya	Selanne	**Kubina**
2/10	StL	4-5	L	11-37-4	McLennan	**Schwab**	22	38	1-3	0-2	Demitra	**Tucker**	Yake
2/13	SJ	1-3	L	11-38-4	Vernon	**Ranford**	31	36	0-5	1-6	Vernon	**Cullimore**	Craven
2/15	@NYI	3-3*	T	11-38-5	**Schwab**	Salo	23	31	0-1	0-5	Palffy	Czerkawski	**Lecavalier**
2/17	@NJ	1-7	L	11-39-5	Brodeur	**Schwab**	25	37	0-2	1-4	Brylin	Niedermayer	Sykora

2/19	Pho	4-2	W	12-39-5	**Wilkinson**	Khabibulin	25	38	1-2	0-5	**Wilkinson**	**Gratton**	**Hogue**
2/20	Car	2-3	L	12-40-5	Irbe	**Schwab**	30	30	1-5	0-6	Kapanen	**Samuelsson**	Roberts
2/22	NJ	2-3	L	12-41-5	Brodeur	**Wilkinson**	28	28	0-2	1-4	Rolston	**Lecavalier**	Brodeur
2/26	Phi	4-1	W	13-41-5	**Schwab**	Hextall	20	37	1-5	1-5	**Schwab**	**Lecavalier**	**Gratton**
3/02	Was	2-8	L	13-42-5	Kolzig	**Wilkinson**	26	26	1-5	3-4	Bondra	Johansson	**Daigle**
3/04	Col	2-1	W	14-42-5	**Schwab**	Roy	26	18	0-5	1-3	**Hogue**	**Gratton**	Roy
3/06	@Mon	**6**-1	W	15-42-5	**Schwab**	Hackett	26	30	1-2	0-5	**Clark**	**Richer**	**Schwab**
3/08	@Ott	3-9	L	15-43-5	Rhodes	**Schwab**	19	38	0-1	3-6	Arvedson	Yashin	Hossa
3/09	@Tor	1-6	L	15-44-5	Joseph	**Ranford**	40	41	0-2	0-2	Sundin	Joseph	Berezin
3/11	@Buf	5-2	W	16-44-5	**Schwab**	Biron	21	37	1-4	0-6	**Schwab**	**Petrovicky**	Grosek
3/13	@Fla	0-1	L	16-45-5	Burke	**Schwab**	24	33	0-4	0-6	Burke	Niedermayer	**Schwab**
3/17	Pit	0-2	L	16-46-5	Aubin	**Schwab**	16	18	0-4	0-6	Aubin	**McCarthy**	Jagr
3/19	Det	3-5	L	16-47-5	Osgood	**Schwab**	39	34	1-2	1-4	Fedorov	**Clark**	Osgood
3/22	NYR	**6**-3	W	17-47-5	**Schwab**	Cloutier	27	30	1-3	1-4	**Forbes**	**Sillinger**	**Gratton**
3/24	Nsh	0-3	L	17-48-5	Dunham	**Schwab**	27	24	0-4	0-3	Krivokrasov	Johnson	Dunham
3/26	@Det	1-6	L	17-49-5	Osgood	**Schwab**	24	40	0-2	1-4	Chelios	Fedorov	Lidstrom
3/28	@Car	3-3*	T	17-49-6	**Hodson**	Irbe	34	33	1-2	0-3	Francis	Kapanen	**Daigle**
3/31	@Dal	4-6	L	17-50-6	Turek	**Schwab**	27	39	0-2	0-2	Nieuwendyk	**Richer**	Marshall
4/01	@StL	0-3	L	17-51-6	Fuhr	**Hodson**	27	24	0-4	0-2	Fuhr	Pellerin	Mayers
4/03	Was	4-3	W	18-51-6	**Hodson**	Tabaracci	25	34	**2**-3	1-4	**Gratton**	Nikolishin	**Tucker**
4/05	Ott	4-4*	T	18-51-7	**Schwab**	Tugnutt	24	39	1-4	2-6	**Zamuner**	Arvedson	**Daigle**
4/08	Bos	3-**0**	W	19-51-7	**Hodson**	Tallas	21	27	0-4	0-9	**Richer**	Tallas	**Schwab**
4/10	@Bos	2-3	L	19-52-7	Tallas	**Schwab**	21	33	0-4	2-8	Thornton	Heinze	**Svoboda**
4/12	@NYR	1-2	L	19-53-7	Richter	**Schwab**	25	28	0-3	1-5	Schneider	Langdon	MacLean
4/13	Mon	2-2*	T	19-53-8	**Wilkinson**	Hackett	22	27	0-5	0-5	**Kubina**	**Gratton**	Savage
4/16	Car	2-2*	T	19-53-9	**Schwab**	Kidd	32	26	1-3	1-4	Kidd	**Richer**	**Samuelsson**
4/17	@Fla	2-6	L	19-54-9	McLean	**Wilkinson**	29	35	**2**-5	0-2	Muller	Whitney	Mellanby

Tampa Bay Lightning 1998-99 Player Statistics

Skater	Ps	Regular Season GP	G	A	Pts	+/–	PIM	PP	SH	GW	GT	S	SPct	P/G
Darcy Tucker	C	**82**	21	**22**	**43**	-34	**176**	8	**2**	**3**	0	**178**	11.8	.52
Wendel Clark†	L	65	**28**	14	42	-25	35	**11**	0	2	1	171	**16.4**	**.65**
Stephane Richer	R	64	12	21	33	-10	22	3	**2**	1	0	139	8.6	.52
* Vincent Lecavalier	C	**82**	13	15	28	-19	23	2	0	2	1	125	10.4	.34
Chris Gratton†	C	52	7	19	26	-20	102	1	0	1	1	127	5.5	.50
Benoit Hogue†	C	62	11	14	25	-12	50	2	0	**3**	0	101	10.9	.40
Craig Janney†	C	38	4	18	22	-13	10	2	0	0	1	36	11.1	.58
* Pavel Kubina	D	68	9	12	21	-33	80	3	1	1	1	119	7.6	.31
Rob Zamuner	L	58	8	11	19	-15	24	1	1	2	0	89	9.0	.33
Alexander Selivanov†	R	43	6	13	19	-8	18	1	0	0	0	120	5.0	.44
Cory Cross	D	67	2	16	18	-25	92	0	0	0	0	96	2.1	.27
Jassen Cullimore	D	78	5	12	17	-22	81	1	1	1	0	73	6.8	.22
Petr Svoboda†	D	34	1	16	17	-4	53	0	0	0	0	46	2.2	.50
Alexandre Daigle†	C	32	6	6	12	-12	2	3	0	0	**2**	56	10.7	.38
Sandy McCarthy†	R	67	5	7	12	-22	135	1	0	0	0	89	5.6	.18
Mikael Renberg†	R	20	4	8	12	-2	4	2	0	0	0	42	9.5	.60
Mike Sillinger†	C	54	8	2	10	-20	28	0	**2**	0	0	69	11.6	.19
Daymond Langkow†	C	22	4	6	10	0	15	1	0	1	0	40	10.0	.45
Michael Nylander†	C	24	2	7	9	-10	6	0	0	0	0	26	7.7	.38
David Wilkie	D	46	1	7	8	-19	69	0	0	0	0	35	2.9	.17
Robert Petrovicky	C	28	3	4	7	-8	6	0	0	0	0	32	9.4	.25
Mike McBain	D	37	0	6	6	-11	14	0	0	0	0	22	0.0	.16
Mikael Andersson†	R	40	2	3	5	-8	4	0	0	0	0	40	5.0	.13
Kjell Samuelsson	D	46	1	4	5	**-6**	38	0	0	0	0	22	4.5	.11
Colin Forbes†	L	14	3	1	4	-5	10	0	1	0	0	25	12.0	.29
Steve Kelly	C	34	1	3	4	-15	27	0	0	1	0	15	6.7	.12
Corey Schwab	G	40	0	4	4	—	4	0	0	0	0	0	—	.10
Brent Peterson	L	20	2	1	3	-2	0	0	0	0	0	16	12.5	.15
Karl Dykhuis†	D	33	2	1	3	-21	18	0	0	0	0	27	7.4	.09
Michal Sykora	D	10	1	2	3	-7	0	0	0	1	0	24	4.2	.30
Drew Bannister	D	21	1	2	3	-4	24	0	0	0	0	29	3.4	.14
* Sergey Gusev†	D	14	0	3	3	-8	10	0	0	0	0	16	0.0	.21
Jason Bonsignore	C	23	0	3	3	-4	8	0	0	0	0	12	0.0	.13
Andrei Nazarov†	L	26	2	0	2	-5	43	0	0	0	0	18	11.1	.08
* Paul Mara	D	1	1	1	2	-3	0	1	0	0	0	1	100.0	2.00
Enrico Ciccone†	D	16	1	1	2	-1	24	0	0	0	0	9	11.1	.13
* Andrei Skopintsev	D	19	1	1	2	1	10	0	0	0	0	17	5.9	.11
* Karel Betik	D	3	0	2	2	-3	2	0	0	0	0	2	0.0	.67
* Sami Helenius†	D	4	1	0	1	-3	15	0	1	0	0	3	33.3	.25
* Corey Spring	R	8	0	1	1	0	2	0	0	0	0	6	0.0	.13
Paul Ysebaert	C	10	0	1	1	-5	2	0	0	0	0	10	0.0	.10
Daren Puppa	G	13	0	1	1	—	0	0	0	0	0	0	—	.08
* Zac Bierk	G	1	0	0	0	—	0	0	0	0	0	0	—	.00
* Xavier Delisle	C	2	0	0	0	0	0	0	0	0	0	1	0.0	.00
John Cullen	C	4	0	0	0	-2	2	0	0	0	0	3	0.0	.00
Kevin Hodson†	G	5	0	0	0	—	0	0	0	0	0	0	—	.00
* Mario Larocque	D	5	0	0	0	-4	16	0	0	0	0	3	0.0	.00
* Derek Wilkinson	G	5	0	0	0	—	0	0	0	0	0	0	—	.00
Bill Ranford†	G	32	0	0	0	—	2	0	0	0	0	0	—	.00
Bench		—	—	—	—	—	0	—	—	—	—	—	—	—
TEAM TOTALS		82	179	291	470	-449	1306	43	11	19	7	2130	8.4	5.73

Postseason GP	G	A	Pts	+/–	PIM	PP	SH	GW	OT	S	SPct	P/G

Team Did Not Qualify for Postseason Play

Goaltender	Regular Season G	Min	GAA	W	L	T	ENG	ShO	GA	SA	SvPct
* Zac Bierk	1	59	2.03	0	1	0	0	0	2	21	.905
Kevin Hodson†	5	238	2.77	2	1	1	0	0	11	118	.907
Daren Puppa	13	691	2.87	5	6	1	1	**2**	33	350	.906
* Derek Wilkinson	5	253	3.08	1	3	1	0	0	13	128	.898
Corey Schwab	**40**	**2146**	**3.52**	**8**	**25**	**3**	**2**	0	**126**	**1153**	**.891**
Bill Ranford†	32	1568	3.90	3	18	**3**	**2**	1	102	858	.881
TEAM TOTALS	82	4974	3.52	19	54	9	5	4	292	2633	.889

Postseason G	Min	GAA	W	L	ENG	ShO	GA	SA	SvPct

1998-99 Tampa Bay Lightning

Record When:

Overtime games	1-2-9
In second game of back-to-back games	2-11-3
Vs playoff teams	9-36-6
Leading after two periods	12-8-1
Tied after two periods	6-5-4
Losing after two periods	1-41-4
Scoring first	14-15-7
More shots than opponents	4-9-3
Fewer shots than opponents	15-38-6
Team had at least one fighting major	5-24-3
Team had more PIM	9-33-5
Team had fewer PIM	6-13-4
Team had even PIM	4-8-0

Team

Longest winning streak	3	Oct. 21 — Oct. 25
Longest unbeaten streak	3	4 times
Longest losing streak	9	Nov. 10 — Dec. 3
Longest winless streak	10	Jan. 26 — Feb. 17
Most shots, game	45	@Anh, Oct. 28
Most shots, period	17	4 times
Fewest shots, game	16	2 times
Fewest shots, period	2	1st, @Phi, Jan. 30

Individual

Longest goal streak	4	Wendel Clark
Longest point streak	6	Petr Svoboda
Most goals, game	3	Wendel Clark [3]
Most assists, game	3	2 times
Most points, game	3	5 times
Highest +/–, game	3	15 times
Lowest +/–, game	-4	9 times
Most shots, game	8	2 times

Did You Know?

Darcy Tucker led the Lightning in scoring last year. His 43 points ranked tied for 118th in the league's scoring race.

Miscellaneous

		NHL Rank
PP Pct.	13.9 (43-310)	20
SH goals allowed	10	18t
PK Pct.	82.4 (319-387)	20
SH goals scored	11	5
Special Team Index	95.9	22
Shots on goal	2,130 (26.0/G)	24
Shots against	2,633 (32.1/G)	26
Unassisted goals	11	19t
Unassisted goals allowed	10	9t
Team Average Weight	205.4	4
Game Star Points	233	27

Game Star Breakdown

Player	1st	2nd	3rd	Pts
Bill Ranford	3	2	3	24
Wendel Clark	2	4	1	23
Corey Schwab	3	0	4	19
Darcy Tucker	2	2	2	18
Chris Gratton	1	3	4	18
Daren Puppa	2	2	0	16
Stephane Richer	1	3	1	15
Benoit Hogue	2	0	3	13
Pavel Kubina	1	1	3	11
Vincent Lecavalier	0	3	2	11
Rob Zamuner	2	0	0	10
Daymond Langkow	0	2	0	6
Colin Forbes	1	0	0	5
Derek Wilkinson	1	0	0	5
Mikael Renberg	0	1	2	5
Kjell Samuelsson	0	1	2	5
Jassen Cullimore	0	1	0	3
Craig Janney	0	1	0	3
Sandy McCarthy	0	1	0	3
Robert Petrovicky	0	1	0	3
Alexander Selivanov	0	1	0	3
Mike Sillinger	0	1	0	3
David Wilkie	0	1	0	3
Alexandre Daigle	0	0	3	3
Cory Cross	0	0	2	2
Mikael Andersson	0	0	1	1
Petr Svoboda	0	0	1	1
Michal Sykora	0	0	1	1

Toronto Maple Leafs 1998-99 Game Log (45-30-7)

					Goalies		Shots		Power Plays		Game Stars		
Date	Opp	Score	W/L/T	Record	W/T	L/T	Tor	Opp	Tor	Opp	1st	2nd	3rd
10/10	Det	2-1	W	1-0-0	**Joseph**	Osgood	27	39	1-7	1-7	**Joseph**	**McCauley**	Yzerman
10/13	@Edm	3-2	W	2-0-0	**Joseph**	Shtalenkov	29	30	2-6	0-4	**Sundin**	**Joseph**	Guerin
10/16	@Cgy	7-3	W	3-0-0	**Potvin**	Wregget	31	33	0-6	1-5	**Sundin**	**McCauley**	Iginla
10/17	@Van	1-4	L	3-1-0	Snow	**Joseph**	40	17	0-7	3-4	Snow	Messier	May
10/19	Nsh	2-2*	T	3-1-1	**Joseph**	Dunham	32	25	0-5	1-5	Dunham	**McCauley**	**Sullivan**
10/23	@Det	5-3	W	4-1-1	**Joseph**	Hodson	27	37	0-4	1-6	**Berezin**	**Joseph**	Larionov
10/24	@Pit	6-4	W	5-1-1	**Potvin**	Skudra	27	34	1-2	1-4	**Sundin**	Jagr	**Modin**
10/26	Pit	0-2	L	5-2-1	Skudra	**Joseph**	27	19	0-**8**	2-4	Skudra	Jagr	**Thomas**
10/30	@Buf	1-4	L	5-3-1	Hasek	**Joseph**	37	23	0-6	1-3	Plante	Hasek	Smehlik
10/31	Buf	3-6	L	5-4-1	Hasek	**Potvin**	33	25	0-5	1-3	Sanderson	Peca	**K.King**
11/04	Col	3-**0**	W	6-4-1	**Joseph**	Roy	28	24	0-4	0-3	**Joseph**	**Thomas**	**Sundin**
11/05	@Bos	1-4	L	6-5-1	Dafoe	**Joseph**	35	30	1-7	2-6	Samsonov	Khristich	Dafoe
11/07	NYR	6-6*	T	6-5-2	**Joseph**	Cloutier	32	32	0-1	1-2	Harvey	**Korolev**	Savard
11/09	NYI	1-3	L	6-6-2	Salo	**Joseph**	39	19	0-3	0-**0**	Salo	**Sundin**	Lapointe
11/11	Edm	3-2	W	7-6-2	**Joseph**	Shtalenkov	21	34	1-3	0-5	**Joseph**	Lindgren	**Cote**
11/12	@Chi	**10**-3	W	8-6-2	**Potvin**	Hackett	30	25	2-**8**	1-7	**Sundin**	**Yushkevich**	**D.King**
11/14	Ott	2-1	W	9-6-2	**Joseph**	Rhodes	29	28	0-4	0-4	**Joseph**	**K.King**	Redden
11/18	@Was	1-4	L	9-7-2	Kolzig	**Joseph**	27	30	1-7	0-3	Bulis	Zednik	Kolzig
11/20	@Buf	1-4	L	9-8-2	Hasek	**Potvin**	33	26	0-5	0-4	Brown	Ward	Holzinger
11/21	Buf	2-1	W	10-8-2	**Joseph**	Hasek	31	18	0-3	0-5	**Domi**	**Sullivan**	Brown
11/23	Cgy	3-2	W	11-8-2	**Joseph**	Giguere	33	29	2-6	2-3	**Korolev**	**Joseph**	Morris
11/25	Van	5-1	W	12-8-2	**Joseph**	Snow	25	34	2-7	1-5	**Joseph**	**Modin**	**Johnson**
11/27	@Phi	3-4	L	12-9-2	Vanbiesbrouck	**Joseph**	22	23	0-3	0-2	Lindros	**Warriner**	LeClair
11/28	Ott	3-2*	W	13-9-2	**Joseph**	Rhodes	27	24	1-4	0-1	**Joseph**	Yashin	**D.King**
12/02	LA	3-1	W	14-9-2	**Joseph**	Storr	27	28	**3**-5	0-4	**Joseph**	**Berezin**	Tsyplakov
12/05	@Mon	4-3*	W	15-9-2	**Joseph**	Hackett	26	28	1-6	1-4	**Kaberle**	Rucinsky	**Yushkevich**
12/07	@NYR	2-6	L	15-10-2	Richter	**Joseph**	26	29	0-4	0-2	Sundstrom	Nedved	Leetch
12/11	@Chi	3-2	W	16-10-2	**Healy**	Thibault	19	30	0-4	1-4	**Healy**	**Yushkevich**	**Johnson**
12/12	Phi	0-3	L	16-11-2	Vanbiesbrouck	**Joseph**	23	27	0-7	0-4	Lindros	LeClair	Vanbiesbrouck
12/16	Pho	5-2	W	17-11-2	**Joseph**	Khabibulin	32	34	1-3	0-2	**Korolev**	**Joseph**	**Hendrickson**
12/19	NYR	7-4	W	18-11-2	**Healy**	Richter	31	26	1-5	3-5	**McCauley**	**D.King**	**Johnson**
12/21	Pit	7-1	W	19-11-2	**Joseph**	Barrasso	27	31	2-5	0-5	**McCauley**	**Sundin**	**Karpovtsev**
12/23	Dal	1-5	L	19-12-2	Belfour	**Joseph**	22	24	0-5	1-1	Modano	Lehtinen	Ludwig
12/26	Mon	1-2	L	19-13-2	Hackett	**Joseph**	30	27	0-5	0-4	Hackett	**Sundin**	Quintal
12/30	Anh	4-1	W	20-13-2	**Joseph**	Hebert	39	31	0-3	0-3	**Modin**	**Smith**	**Joseph**
12/31	@Det	4-2	W	21-13-2	**Joseph**	Osgood	27	40	1-6	0-6	**Joseph**	**Sundin**	Maltby
1/02	Was	2-5	L	21-14-2	Kolzig	**Joseph**	31	28	0-5	2-4	Bellows	Kolzig	**Modin**
1/04	TB	5-4*	W	22-14-2	**Joseph**	Ranford	37	29	0-5	0-2	**Thomas**	Clark	**Yushkevich**
1/07	@Bos	1-2	L	22-15-2	Dafoe	**Healy**	28	27	0-3	0-3	Dafoe	Allison	**Korolev**
1/09	Bos	6-3	W	23-15-2	**Joseph**	Dafoe	23	32	1-4	2-6	**Johnson**	**Joseph**	**Valk**
1/12	@TB	4-3	W	24-15-2	**Joseph**	Ranford	24	29	2-5	1-4	**Johnson**	**Sundin**	Tucker
1/13	@Fla	3-3*	T	24-15-3	**Joseph**	Burke	37	33	1-3	1-6	Mellanby	**Sullivan**	Niedermayer
1/16	@Phi	4-3	W	25-15-3	**Joseph**	Vanbiesbrouck	32	28	1-4	1-4	**D.King**	**Sullivan**	LeClair
1/18	@Car	2-4	L	25-16-3	Irbe	**Joseph**	31	26	1-4	0-2	Roberts	Francis	Irbe
1/20	@Dal	6-4	W	26-16-3	**Joseph**	Belfour	24	34	2-4	2-5	**Joseph**	Sydor	**Berard**
1/21	@StL	4-2	W	27-16-3	**Reese**	Fuhr	21	24	2-6	1-3	**Warriner**	**Thomas**	**Reese**
1/28	@Pit	0-6	L	27-17-3	Skudra	**Reese**	21	33	0-5	0-2	Jagr	Skudra	Miller
1/30	Was	5-3	W	28-17-3	**Joseph**	Tabaracci	23	30	2-4	2-5	**Thomas**	Nikolishin	**Joseph**
2/02	@TB	3-**0**	W	29-17-3	**Joseph**	Schwab	29	23	2-5	0-3	**Berezin**	**Joseph**	Schwab
2/03	@Fla	2-5	L	29-18-3	Burke	**Joseph**	36	38	0-6	0-4	Burke	Dvorak	Parrish
2/06	@NJ	3-2	W	30-18-3	**Joseph**	Brodeur	20	41	0-3	0-5	**Sullivan**	**Joseph**	Souray
2/10	Car	5-6	L	30-19-3	Irbe	**Joseph**	29	25	0-2	1-4	Francis	**Berezin**	Roberts
2/13	Chi	2-6	L	30-20-3	Thibault	**Joseph**	26	27	1-5	1-5	Simpson	Gilmour	**Sullivan**
2/15	@NJ	3-3*	T	30-20-4	**Joseph**	Brodeur	31	22	0-4	1-3	Niedermayer	Brylin	Pandolfo
2/17	@Buf	3-2*	W	31-20-4	**Healy**	Hasek	29	27	1-4	0-3	**Sundin**	Satan	**Sullivan**

2/20	Mon	3-2*	W	32-20-4	**Joseph**	Hackett	24	30	0-5	1-5	**Sundin**	Recchi	**Joseph**
2/22	@Was	3-4	L	32-21-4	Kolzig	**Joseph**	25	28	0-2	1-3	Eagles	Oates	Klee
2/24	Car	2-2*	T	32-21-5	**Joseph**	Irbe	31	31	0-4	1-3	Primeau	**McCauley**	**Sundin**
2/25	@NYI	4-1	W	33-21-5	**Healy**	Salo	22	28	0-4	1-5	**Berezin**	**Healy**	**Kaberle**
2/27	Fla	4-1	W	34-21-5	**Joseph**	Burke	30	23	1-3	0-4	**Johnson**	**McCauley**	**Sundin**
3/03	NJ	2-5	L	34-22-5	Brodeur	**Joseph**	25	28	1-4	0-**0**	Arnott	Brodeur	**Berezin**
3/04	@StL	4-**0**	W	35-22-5	**Joseph**	Johnson	9	28	0-2	0-2	**Joseph**	**Sullivan**	**Cote**
3/06	@Ott	1-3	L	35-23-5	Tugnutt	**Joseph**	26	30	1-5	1-6	Tugnutt	Bonk	Hossa
3/08	@NYR	2-3*	L	35-24-5	Richter	**Healy**	26	35	0-3	2-6	Nedved	Leetch	**D.King**
3/09	TB	6-1	W	36-24-5	**Joseph**	Ranford	**41**	40	0-2	0-2	**Sundin**	**Joseph**	**Berezin**
3/11	@NYI	2-1	W	37-24-5	**Joseph**	Salo	22	42	0-4	0-3	**Joseph**	**D.King**	Czerkawski
3/13	@Mon	1-2	L	37-25-5	Hackett	**Joseph**	28	31	0-4	2-5	Damphousse	**Joseph**	Hackett
3/17	Bos	1-4	L	37-26-5	Dafoe	**Joseph**	26	29	0-4	2-6	Dafoe	**Korolev**	McLaren
3/20	NJ	3-1	W	38-26-5	**Joseph**	Brodeur	28	31	0-2	1-4	**Sundin**	**Joseph**	**Sullivan**
3/22	Phi	1-3	L	38-27-5	Vanbiesbrouck	**Joseph**	20	28	0-6	2-5	Lindros	Babych	**Markov**
3/24	SJ	5-8	L	38-28-5	Shields	**Healy**	35	27	2-6	3-5	Damphousse	Nolan	**D.King**
3/26	@Car	7-2	W	39-28-5	**Joseph**	Irbe	27	25	1-6	0-7	**Thomas**	**Modin**	**Sundin**
3/27	Bos	2-2*	T	39-28-6	**Joseph**	Dafoe	27	26	0-4	1-5	**Markov**	McLaren	**Joseph**
3/31	@Van	6-5	W	40-28-6	**Healy**	Weekes	27	32	2-5	1-2	**Perreault**	**Thomas**	Mogilny
4/01	@Edm	5-1	W	41-28-6	**Joseph**	Salo	23	31	**3**-6	0-6	**Berezin**	**D.King**	**Yushkevich**
4/03	@Cgy	5-1	W	42-28-6	**Joseph**	Wregget	23	28	0-4	1-2	**Sundin**	**Karpovtsev**	Cassels
4/05	StL	2-2*	T	42-28-7	**Joseph**	Fuhr	31	28	0-1	0-2	**Joseph**	Fuhr	**Berard**
4/07	Ott	4-2	W	43-28-7	**Joseph**	Rhodes	31	29	1-5	1-8	**Perreault**	**Yushkevich**	Hossa
4/08	@Ott	1-3	L	43-29-7	Tugnutt	**Joseph**	31	36	0-5	1-6	Prospal	Arvedson	**Berezin**
4/10	Fla	9-1	W	44-29-7	**Healy**	Burke	32	26	2-3	0-4	**Sullivan**	**Thomas**	**Valk**
4/14	NYI	3-2*	W	45-29-7	**Joseph**	Potvin	38	24	0-3	1-4	Potvin	**Berezin**	**Berard**
4/17	@Mon	2-3	L	45-30-7	Hackett	**Joseph**	27	**16**	0-6	1-3	Quintal	**Cote**	Weinrich

Postseason

4/22	Phi	0-3	L	0-1	Vanbiesbrouck	**Joseph**	25	24	0-6	1-5	Vanbiesbrouck	**Berezin**	LeClair
4/24	Phi	2-1	W	1-1	**Joseph**	Vanbiesbrouck	21	25	0-7	0-4	**Sundin**	**Joseph**	Brind'Amour
4/26	@Phi	2-1	W	2-1	**Joseph**	Vanbiesbrouck	21	41	1-4	0-5	**Joseph**	Dykhuis	**Thomas**
4/28	@Phi	2-5	L	2-2	Vanbiesbrouck	**Joseph**	25	41	2-8	2-5	LeClair	Desjardins	Vanbiesbrouck
4/30	Phi	2-1*	W	3-2	**Joseph**	Vanbiesbrouck	**34**	34	1-4	0-**2**	**Perreault**	**D.King**	Brind'Amour
5/02	@Phi	1-**0**	W	4-2	**Joseph**	Vanbiesbrouck	20	26	1-5	0-6	**Berezin**	**Joseph**	Vanbiesbrouck
5/07	Pit	0-2	L	0-1	Barrasso	**Joseph**	20	19	0-4	1-3	Barrasso	**Warriner**	Straka
5/09	Pit	4-2	W	1-1	**Joseph**	Barrasso	25	27	1-3	0-5	**Sundin**	**Joseph**	**Bohonos**
5/11	@Pit	3-4	L	1-2	Barrasso	**Joseph**	29	21	0-4	2-4	Jagr	Barrasso	Brown
5/13	@Pit	3-2*	W	2-2	**Joseph**	Barrasso	30	**14**	0-3	0-3	**Berezin**	**Sundin**	Barrasso
5/15	Pit	4-1	W	3-2	**Joseph**	Barrasso	20	16	0-5	0-**2**	**Yushkevich**	**Thomas**	**Valk**
5/17	@Pit	4-3*	W	4-2	**Joseph**	Barrasso	30	28	0-4	1-**2**	**Valk**	**Joseph**	Jagr
5/23	Buf	4-5	L	0-1	Roloson	**Joseph**	32	21	**3-9**	1-4	Sanderson	**Sundin**	Rasmussen
5/25	Buf	**6**-3	W	1-1	**Joseph**	Roloson	28	33	0-5	3-5	**Joseph**	Barnes	**Perreault**
5/27	@Buf	2-4	L	1-2	Hasek	**Joseph**	26	24	1-4	1-8	Satan	Hasek	**Sullivan**
5/29	@Buf	2-5	L	1-3	Hasek	**Joseph**	33	32	1-5	0-4	Sanderson	Satan	Ray
5/31	Buf	2-4	L	1-4	Hasek	**Joseph**	22	24	1-7	1-4	Rasmussen	**K.King**	Varada

Toronto Maple Leafs 1998-99 Player Statistics

Skater	Ps	Regular Season GP	G	A	Pts	+/–	PIM	PP	SH	GW	GT	S	SPct	P/G	Postseason GP	G	A	Pts	+/–	PIM	PP	SH	GW	OT	S	SPct	P/G
Mats Sundin	C	**82**	31	**52**	**83**	22	58	4	0	6	0	209	14.8	**1.01**	**17**	**8**	**8**	**16**	2	16	**3**	0	**2**	0	44	**18.2**	.94
Steve Thomas	L	78	28	45	73	26	33	**11**	0	**7**	0	209	13.4	.94	**17**	6	3	9	-1	12	2	0	1	0	41	14.6	.53
Sergei Berezin	R	76	**37**	22	59	16	12	9	1	4	0	**263**	14.1	.78	**17**	6	6	12	0	4	2	0	**2**	**1**	**65**	9.2	.71
Derek King	L	81	24	28	52	15	20	8	0	4	0	150	16.0	.64	16	1	3	4	0	4	0	0	0	0	26	3.8	.25
Igor Korolev	R	66	13	34	47	11	46	1	0	2	0	99	13.1	.71	1	0	0	0	0	0	0	0	0	0	0	—	.00
Mike Johnson	R	79	20	24	44	13	35	5	**3**	2	0	149	13.4	.56	**17**	3	2	5	-1	4	0	0	1	0	26	11.5	.29
Steve Sullivan	C	63	20	20	40	12	28	4	0	5	0	110	**18.2**	.63	13	3	3	6	-3	14	2	0	0	0	21	14.3	.46
Fredrik Modin	L	67	16	15	31	14	35	1	0	3	**1**	108	14.8	.46	8	0	0	0	-2	6	0	0	0	0	11	0.0	.00
Garry Valk	L	77	8	21	20	8	53	1	0	0	**1**	93	8.6	.38	**17**	3	4	7	-1	22	0	0	1	**1**	14	21.4	.41
Sylvain Cote	D	79	5	24	29	22	28	0	0	1	0	119	4.2	.37	**17**	2	1	3	-3	10	0	0	0	0	19	10.5	.18
Dimitri Yushkevich	D	78	6	22	28	25	88	2	1	0	0	95	6.3	.36	**17**	1	5	6	7	22	1	0	0	0	17	5.9	.35
A. Karpovtsev†	D	56	2	25	27	**38**	52	1	0	1	0	61	3.3	.48	14	1	3	4	-7	12	1	0	0	0	13	7.7	.29
Alyn McCauley	C	39	9	15	24	7	2	1	0	1	**1**	76	11.8	.62	—	—	—	—	—	—	—	—	—	—	—	—	—
Tie Domi	R	72	8	14	22	5	**198**	0	0	1	0	65	12.3	.31	14	0	2	2	-1	24	0	0	0	0	7	0.0	.14
* Tomas Kaberle	D	57	4	18	22	3	12	0	0	2	0	71	5.6	.39	14	0	3	3	0	2	0	0	0	0	14	0.0	.21
Todd Warriner	L	53	9	10	19	-6	28	1	0	1	0	96	9.4	.36	9	0	0	0	0	2	0	0	0	0	12	0.0	.00
Bryan Berard†	D	38	5	14	19	7	22	2	0	2	**1**	63	7.9	.50	**17**	1	**8**	9	-10	8	1	0	0	0	29	3.4	.53
Yanic Perreault†	C	12	7	8	15	10	12	2	1	2	0	28	25.0	1.25	**17**	3	6	9	-6	6	0	0	**2**	**1**	15	20.0	.53
Jason Smith†	D	60	2	11	13	-9	40	0	0	0	0	53	3.8	.22	—	—	—	—	—	—	—	—	—	—	—	—	—
* Daniil Markov	D	57	4	8	12	5	47	0	0	0	**1**	34	11.8	.21	**17**	0	6	6	**9**	18	0	0	0	0	11	0.0	.35
Yanick Tremblay	D	35	2	7	9	0	16	0	0	0	0	37	5.4	.26	—	—	—	—	—	—	—	—	—	—	—	—	—
Darby Hendrickson†	C	35	2	3	5	-4	30	0	0	0	0	34	5.9	.14	—	—	—	—	—	—	—	—	—	—	—	—	—
Curtis Joseph	G	67	0	5	5	—	6	0	0	0	0	0	—	.07	**17**	0	0	0	—	2	0	0	0	0	1	0.0	.00
Kris King	L	67	2	2	4	-16	105	0	1	1	0	34	5.9	.06	**17**	1	1	2	-1	**25**	0	0	0	0	15	6.7	.12
* Ladislav Kohn	R	16	1	3	4	1	4	0	0	0	0	23	4.3	.25	2	0	0	0	0	5	0	0	0	0	0	—	.00
Lonny Bohonos	R	7	3	0	3	3	4	0	0	0	0	13	23.1	.43	9	3	6	9	3	2	0	0	0	0	26	11.5	**1.00**
Dallas Eakins	D	18	0	2	2	3	24	0	0	0	0	11	0.0	.11	1	0	0	0	0	0	0	0	0	0	0	—	.00
Chris McAllister†	D	20	0	2	2	4	39	0	0	0	0	12	0.0	.10	6	0	1	1	-1	4	0	0	0	0	2	0.0	.17
* Adam Mair	C	—	—	—	—	—	—	—	—	—	—	—	—	—	5	1	0	1	-1	14	0	0	0	0	3	33.3	.20
* Kevyn Adams	C	1	0	0	0	0	0	0	0	0	0	1	0.0	.00	7	0	2	2	-2	14	0	0	0	0	9	0.0	.29
Jeff Reese	G	2	0	0	0	—	0	0	0	0	0	0	—	.00	—	—	—	—	—	—	—	—	—	—	—	—	—
Kevin Dahl	D	3	0	0	0	0	2	0	0	0	0	0	—	.00	—	—	—	—	—	—	—	—	—	—	—	—	—
Jason Podollan†	R	4	0	0	0	0	0	0	0	0	0	2	0.0	.00	—	—	—	—	—	—	—	—	—	—	—	—	—
Felix Potvin†	G	5	0	0	0	—	0	0	0	0	0	0	—	.00	—	—	—	—	—	—	—	—	—	—	—	—	—
Glenn Healy	G	9	0	0	0	—	0	0	0	0	0	0	—	.00	1	0	0	0	—	0	0	0	0	0	0	—	.00
Bench		—	—	—	—	—	0	—	—	—	—	—	—	—	—	—	—	—	—	0	—	—	—	—	—	—	—
TEAM TOTALS		82	268	454	722	235	1079	53	7	45	5	2318	11.6	8.80	17	43	73	116	-19	252	12	0	9	3	441	9.8	6.82

Goaltender	Regular Season G	Min	GAA	W	L	T	ENG	ShO	GA	SA	SvPct	Postseason G	Min	GAA	W	L	ENG	ShO	GA	SA	SvPct
Curtis Joseph	**67**	**4001**	**2.56**	**35**	**24**	**7**	**4**	**3**	**171**	**1903**	**.910**	**17**	**1011**	**2.43**	**9**	**8**	**5**	**1**	**41**	**440**	**.907**
Glenn Healy	9	546	2.97	6	3	0	1	0	27	257	.895	1	20	.00	0	0	0	0	0	5	1.000
Felix Potvin†	5	299	3.81	3	2	0	1	0	19	142	.866	—	—	—	—	—	—	—	—	—	—
Jeff Reese	2	106	4.53	1	1	0	0	0	8	51	.843	—	—	—	—	—	—	—	—	—	—
TEAM TOTALS	82	4972	2.79	45	30	7	6	3	231	2359	.902	17	1036	2.66	9	8	5	1	46	450	.898

1998-99 Toronto Maple Leafs

Record When:

Overtime games	6-1-7
In second game of back-to-back games	10-6-2
Vs playoff teams	24-18-4
Leading after two periods	37-1-2
Tied after two periods	4-6-2
Losing after two periods	4-23-3
Scoring first	31-12-4
More shots than opponents	18-14-5
Fewer shots than opponents	27-16-0
Team had at least one fighting major	18-11-1
Team had more PIM	13-8-4
Team had fewer PIM	22-20-3
Team had even PIM	10-2-0

Team

Longest winning streak	3	6 times
Longest unbeaten streak	7	Mar. 26 — Apr. 7
Longest losing streak	3	Oct. 26 — Oct. 31
Longest winless streak	3	3 times
Most shots, game	41	vs. TB, Mar. 9
Most shots, period	18	2 times
Fewest shots, game	9	@StL, Mar. 4
Fewest shots, period	2	2 times

Individual

Longest goal streak	4	Fredrik Modin
Longest point streak	10	Steve Thomas
Most goals, game	4	2 times
Most assists, game	4	Steve Thomas
Most points, game	5	Steve Thomas
Highest +/–, game	4	9 times
Lowest +/–, game	-5	Dimitri Yushkevich
Most shots, game	9	Sergei Berezin

Did You Know?

Curtis Joseph has faced 14,360 shots over the last eight seasons, the most of any goaltender in the league over that span.

Miscellaneous

		NHL Rank
PP Pct.	14.4 (53-367)	17
SH goals allowed	6	6t
PK Pct.	80.3 (261-325)	24
SH goals scored	7	15t
Special Team Index	95.3	24
Shots on goal	2,318 (28.3/G)	11
Shots against	2,359 (28.8/G)	17
Unassisted goals	17	4
Unassisted goals allowed	10	9t
Team Average Weight	198.0	21
Game Star Points	413	6

Game Star Breakdown

Player	1st	2nd	3rd	Pts
Curtis Joseph	12	10	4	94
Mats Sundin	9	5	4	64
Sergei Berezin	4	3	3	32
Steve Thomas	3	4	1	28
Steve Sullivan	2	4	4	26
Alyn McCauley	2	5	0	25
Mike Johnson	3	0	3	18
Derek King	1	3	4	18
Igor Korolev	2	2	1	17
Fredrik Modin	1	2	2	13
Dimitri Yushkevich	0	3	3	12
Yanic Perreault	2	0	0	10
Glenn Healy	1	1	0	8
Todd Warriner	1	1	0	8
Tomas Kaberle	1	0	1	6
Daniil Markov	1	0	1	6
Tie Domi	1	0	0	5
Sylvain Cote	0	1	2	5
Alexander Karpovtsev	0	1	1	4
Kris King	0	1	1	4
Jason Smith	0	1	0	3
Bryan Berard	0	0	3	3
Garry Valk	0	0	2	2
Darby Hendrickson	0	0	1	1
Jeff Reese	0	0	1	1

Vancouver Canucks 1998-99 Game Log (23-47-12)

					Goalies		Shots		Power Plays		Game Stars		
Date	Opp	Score	W/L/T	Record	W/T	L/T	Van	Opp	Van	Opp	1st	2nd	3rd
10/12	LA	4-2	W	1-0-0	**Snow**	Storr	24	25	1-8	0-6	**Zezel**	Perreault	**Aucoin**
10/14	Edm	1-4	L	1-1-0	Shtalenkov	**Snow**	13	24	1-6	3-7	Mironov	K.Brown	**Muckalt**
10/17	Tor	4-1	W	2-1-0	**Snow**	Joseph	17	40	**3**-4	0-7	**Snow**	**Messier**	**May**
10/20	@Car	1-3	L	2-2-0	Irbe	**Snow**	17	27	0-4	1-8	Primeau	Irbe	Roberts
10/21	@Was	2-1	W	3-2-0	**Snow**	Kolzig	29	35	1-5	0-6	**Snow**	**Aucoin**	Juneau
10/23	@Fla	**5-0**	W	4-2-0	**Snow**	McLean	27	35	1-3	0-5	**Messier**	**Bertuzzi**	**Snow**
10/25	@TB	2-3	L	4-3-0	Puppa	**Snow**	17	26	0-5	1-4	**Ohlund**	Langkow	Lecavalier
10/27	@Nsh	4-5	L	4-4-0	Dunham	**Snow**	31	30	2-6	1-5	Krivokrasov	Fitzgerald	**Mogilny**
10/30	Pit	2-2*	T	4-4-1	**Snow**	Skudra	20	25	0-4	2-6	**Snow**	Jagr	**Mogilny**
11/01	Was	4-1	W	5-4-1	**Hirsch**	Kolzig	22	26	0-6	1-5	**Muckalt**	**Convery**	**Hirsch**
11/02	@Edm	3-5	L	5-5-1	Essensa	**Hirsch**	16	49	1-3	3-10	Beranek	Guerin	**Hirsch**
11/07	Nsh	**5**-3	W	6-5-1	**Hirsch**	Vokoun	21	30	1-4	0-5	**Ohlund**	**Hirsch**	Johnson
11/09	LA	3-4	L	6-6-1	LeGace	**Hirsch**	19	23	0-2	0-5	Robitaille	**Mogilny**	Murray
11/12	@Cgy	4-3	W	7-6-1	**Snow**	Moss	24	29	2-4	1-5	**Ohlund**	Shantz	**Messier**
11/13	Anh	**5**-2	W	8-6-1	**Snow**	Roussel	25	26	0-4	0-5	**Snow**	**McCabe**	Kariya
11/15	Col	1-2	L	8-7-1	Roy	**Snow**	20	31	0-7	1-9	Deadmarsh	Sakic	**Snow**
11/18	@Pho	2-4	L	8-8-1	Waite	**Snow**	30	27	0-4	1-7	Tocchet	Roenick	Waite
11/19	@Col	**5-0**	W	9-8-1	**Snow**	Billington	27	35	2-5	0-8	**Ohlund**	**Aucoin**	**Messier**
11/21	Det	2-4	L	9-9-1	Maracle	**Snow**	31	30	0-2	0-6	Shanahan	**Scatchard**	Lidstrom
11/23	@Ott	3-4	L	9-10-1	Tugnutt	**Snow**	**43**	31	2-6	2-8	Tugnutt	Johansson	**Muckalt**
11/25	@Tor	1-5	L	9-11-1	Joseph	**Snow**	34	25	1-5	2-7	Joseph	Modin	Johnson
11/27	@Det	1-7	L	9-12-1	Maracle	**Snow**	20	39	1-4	2-9	Shanahan	Larionov	Kozlov
11/29	@Phi	2-6	L	9-13-1	Hextall	**Snow**	22	35	0-3	1-5	LeClair	Jones	Lindros
12/01	@Bos	1-1*	T	9-13-2	**Snow**	Dafoe	21	27	0-2	0-6	Samsonov	**Ohlund**	Carter
12/04	Dal	4-1	W	10-13-2	**Snow**	Belfour	18	37	1-3	0-5	**Naslund**	**Snow**	**Messier**
12/06	Pho	3-3*	T	10-13-3	**Snow**	Waite	24	46	1-4	1-6	**Snow**	Roenick	Tkachuk
12/09	@Anh	4-4*	T	10-13-4	**Hirsch**	Hebert	41	34	0-2	1-5	Davidsson	**Messier**	Cullen
12/12	@LA	0-3	L	10-14-4	Fiset	**Snow**	25	38	0-6	1-7	Fiset	Robitaille	Norstrom
12/17	Col	2-1	W	11-14-4	**Snow**	Roy	21	24	2-8	0-6	**Naslund**	Corbet	**Baron**
12/19	Nsh	4-6	L	11-15-4	Vokoun	**Snow**	24	24	2-4	3-4	Bordeleau	Krivokrasov	**Naslund**
12/22	@Cgy	**5**-3	W	12-15-4	**Snow**	Giguere	27	26	1-5	2-7	**York**	**Scatchard**	Gauthier
12/23	Cgy	**5**-2	W	13-15-4	**Snow**	Giguere	25	20	0-1	1-4	**Naslund**	**Zezel**	**Muckalt**
12/26	@SJ	0-2	L	13-16-4	Shields	**Snow**	25	27	0-**9**	1-7	Shields	Marleau	Nolan
12/27	@Edm	0-3	L	13-17-4	Shtalenkov	**Snow**	25	34	0-5	1-6	Shtalenkov	Poti	Buchberger
12/29	Col	2-4	L	13-18-4	Billington	**Snow**	16	27	1-4	2-6	Forsberg	Deadmarsh	Foote
12/31	Phi	2-6	L	13-19-4	Vanbiesbrouck	**Snow**	25	24	1-4	0-4	Brind'Amour	Desjardins	LeClair
1/02	Mon	1-2	L	13-20-4	Hackett	**Hirsch**	17	22	1-6	0-2	Hackett	Rucinsky	**Hirsch**
1/04	@StL	0-4	L	13-21-4	McLennan	**Hirsch**	20	34	0-3	1-5	McLennan	Rheaume	Yake
1/06	@Dal	4-6	L	13-22-4	Belfour	**Snow**	20	28	2-2	3-6	Carbonneau	Sydor	**Naslund**
1/08	Fla	1-1*	T	13-22-5	**Hirsch**	Burke	24	27	0-4	1-3	**Messier**	Svehla	**Hirsch**
1/10	Dal	2-**0**	W	14-22-5	**Hirsch**	Turek	20	**13**	0-1	0-5	**Scatchard**	**Hirsch**	**Mogilny**
1/14	Edm	1-3	L	14-23-5	Essensa	**Hirsch**	17	29	1-5	0-8	Niinimaa	**Messier**	Beranek
1/16	Det	2-2*	T	14-23-6	**Snow**	Osgood	16	37	0-2	0-8	**Snow**	Yzerman	Lidstrom
1/18	@Dal	**5**-3	W	15-23-6	**Snow**	Belfour	23	21	2-6	2-7	**Naslund**	**Messier**	**Gagner**
1/19	@Nsh	1-4	L	15-24-6	Dunham	**Snow**	19	40	0-4	0-3	Atcheynum	Krivokrasov	Johnson
1/28	StL	2-4	L	15-25-6	Parent	**Snow**	19	25	1-4	1-2	Young	Pronger	**Klatt**
1/30	Chi	3-2	W	16-25-6	**Snow**	Thibault	26	20	1-6	0-6	**Naslund**	Amonte	**Mogilny**
2/01	Ott	0-1	L	16-26-6	Tugnutt	**Snow**	14	29	0-6	1-6	**Snow**	Tugnutt	York
2/03	@Mon	1-2	L	16-27-6	Hackett	**Hirsch**	22	34	1-5	0-4	Stevenson	Poulin	**Hirsch**
2/04	@NYR	4-8	L	16-28-6	Richter	**Snow**	31	36	1-4	2-7	Graves	Gretzky	MacLean
2/07	@NYI	3-3*	T	16-28-7	**Hirsch**	Potvin	37	32	1-4	0-6	Reichel	Palffy	**Ohlund**
2/09	@NJ	4-3	W	17-28-7	**Snow**	Brodeur	33	41	0-1	0-2	**Bertuzzi**	Stevens	**Jovanovski**
2/11	@Pit	**5**-6*	L	17-29-7	Skudra	**Hirsch**	18	40	0-3	0-6	Jagr	**Naslund**	Straka
2/13	Bos	3-1	W	18-29-7	**Snow**	Tallas	24	15	0-3	1-4	**Bertuzzi**	**Mogilny**	Carter
2/15	@StL	1-8	L	18-30-7	McLennan	**Snow**	21	27	1-4	0-**0**	MacInnis	Turgeon	Demitra

2/17	@Chi	0-4	L	18-31-7	Thibault	**Snow**	29	14	0-3	1-3	Thibault	Kilger	Brown
2/20	Anh	1-5	L	18-32-7	Hebert	**Hirsch**	26	22	1-6	3-4	McInnis	Selanne	Kariya
2/23	@Col	4-4*	T	18-32-8	**Snow**	Billington	27	43	1-5	4-8	Deadmarsh	**Naslund**	Ozolinsh
2/24	@SJ	1-1*	T	18-32-9	**Snow**	Vernon	13	40	0-3	1-9	Korolyuk	**Snow**	Ricci
2/26	Car	1-**0**	W	19-32-9	**Snow**	Irbe	16	23	0-**9**	0-10	**Snow**	Primeau	**Aucoin**
2/28	Buf	0-2	L	19-33-9	Roloson	**Snow**	15	18	0-4	0-3	Shannon	Zhitnik	**Strudwick**
3/03	SJ	3-4	L	19-34-9	Shields	**Weekes**	31	15	0-5	1-4	Marleau	**Schaefer**	Houlder
3/05	Cgy	1-5	L	19-35-9	Brathwaite	**Snow**	23	30	1-6	2-6	Stillman	Iginla	Brathwaite
3/07	Chi	2-2*	T	19-35-10	**Snow**	Thibault	29	23	1-6	0-4	Gilmour	**Holden**	**Mogilny**
3/10	@Anh	4-4*	T	19-35-11	**Weekes**	Hebert	28	45	2-6	3-5	Kariya	**Naslund**	McInnis
3/11	@Pho	3-**0**	W	20-35-11	**Snow**	Khabibulin	22	33	0-4	0-4	**Snow**	**Jovanovski**	**McCabe**
3/13	@LA	1-3	L	20-36-11	Fiset	**Weekes**	20	40	0-4	1-5	Audette	Stumpel	**Weekes**
3/15	NJ	1-2	L	20-37-11	Brodeur	**Snow**	26	27	1-2	1-3	Brodeur	Niedermayer	**Scatchard**
3/19	NYI	1-3	L	20-38-11	Flaherty	**Weekes**	22	28	1-4	1-3	Jonsson	Lapointe	**Naslund**
3/20	@Edm	3-4	L	20-39-11	Salo	**Snow**	26	37	2-6	1-7	Grier	**Aucoin**	Moreau
3/24	@Col	2-5	L	20-40-11	Roy	**Weekes**	34	25	0-3	3-6	Fleury	Forsberg	Sakic
3/25	StL	1-4	L	20-41-11	Fuhr	**Weekes**	20	28	0-2	0-6	Turgeon	Pellerin	**McCabe**
3/27	Mon	**5**-1	W	21-41-11	**Snow**	Hackett	24	22	2-8	0-7	**Ohlund**	**Messier**	**Aucoin**
3/29	Pho	1-**0**	W	22-41-11	**Snow**	Shtalenkov	20	22	0-3	0-3	**Snow**	**Schaefer**	**Jovanovski**
3/31	Tor	**5**-6	L	22-42-11	Healy	**Weekes**	32	27	1-2	2-5	Perreault	Thomas	**Mogilny**
4/02	SJ	0-7	L	22-43-11	Shields	**Snow**	18	24	0-4	2-5	Murphy	Friesen	Damphousse
4/03	@SJ	2-5	L	22-44-11	Shields	**Snow**	32	28	2-6	2-6	Damphousse	Shields	Murphy
4/05	@Chi	1-2	L	22-45-11	Thibault	**Weekes**	25	33	0-5	0-5	Daze	Mironov	**Weekes**
4/07	@Det	1-6	L	22-46-11	Osgood	**Weekes**	28	26	0-6	2-8	Yzerman	Larionov	Shanahan
4/10	Edm	1-1*	T	22-46-12	**Snow**	Salo	24	24	1-3	0-5	Salo	**Snow**	Weight
4/12	@Cgy	2-**0**	W	23-46-12	**Snow**	Brathwaite	23	41	0-1	0-4	**Snow**	Brathwaite	**Aucoin**
4/14	Cgy	4-5	L	23-47-12	Brathwaite	**Snow**	25	33	1-3	0-2	**Naslund**	Iginla	**Scatchard**

Vancouver Canucks 1998-99 Player Statistics

Regular Season

Skater	Ps	GP	G	A	Pts	+/–	PIM	PP	SH	GW	GT	S	SPct	P/G
Markus Naslund	R	80	**36**	30	**66**	-13	74	15	**2**	**3**	**1**	**205**	**17.6**	**.83**
Mark Messier	C	59	13	**35**	48	-12	33	4	**2**	2	0	97	13.4	.81
Alexander Mogilny	R	59	14	31	45	0	58	3	**2**	1	**1**	110	12.7	.76
* Bill Muckalt	R	73	16	20	36	-9	98	4	**2**	1	0	119	13.4	.49
Mattias Ohlund	D	74	9	26	35	-19	83	2	1	1	0	129	7.0	.47
Adrian Aucoin	D	**82**	23	11	34	-14	77	**18**	**2**	**3**	**1**	174	13.2	.41
Dave Scatchard	C	**82**	13	13	26	-12	140	0	**2**	2	0	130	10.0	.32
Bryan McCabe	D	69	7	14	21	-11	120	1	**2**	0	0	98	7.1	.30
Donald Brashear	L	**82**	8	10	18	-25	**209**	2	0	1	0	112	7.1	.22
Brad May	L	66	6	11	17	-14	102	1	0	1	0	91	6.6	.26
Todd Bertuzzi	C	32	8	8	16	-6	44	1	0	**3**	0	72	11.1	.50
Harry York†	C	49	7	9	16	-2	20	1	0	0	**1**	55	12.7	.33
Peter Zezel	C	41	6	8	14	5	16	1	0	2	0	45	13.3	.34
Trent Klatt†	R	73	4	10	14	-3	12	0	0	0	0	58	6.9	.19
Dave Gagner†	C	33	2	12	14	-9	24	0	0	1	0	50	4.0	.42
Bret Hedican†	D	42	2	11	13	**7**	34	0	**2**	0	**1**	52	3.8	.31
Ed Jovanovski†	D	31	2	9	11	-5	44	0	0	0	0	41	4.9	.35
Brandon Convery†	C	12	2	7	9	5	8	0	0	1	0	12	16.7	.75
* Peter Schaefer	L	25	4	4	8	-1	8	1	0	1	0	24	16.7	.32
Murray Baron	D	81	2	6	8	-23	115	0	0	0	0	53	3.8	.10
* Josh Holden	C	30	2	4	6	-10	10	1	0	0	0	44	4.5	.20
Darby Hendrickson†	C	27	2	2	4	-15	22	1	0	0	0	36	5.6	.15
Bert Robertsson	D	39	2	2	4	-7	13	0	0	0	0	13	15.4	.10
Jason Strudwick	D	65	0	3	3	-19	114	0	0	0	0	25	0.0	.05
Chris McAllister†	D	28	1	1	2	-7	63	0	0	0	**1**	6	16.7	.07
Dana Murzyn	D	12	0	2	2	1	21	0	0	0	0	7	0.0	.17
* Matt Cooke	L	30	0	2	2	-12	27	0	0	0	0	22	0.0	.07
Steve Staios	R	57	0	2	2	-12	54	0	0	0	0	33	0.0	.04
* Brent Sopel	D	5	1	0	1	-1	4	1	0	0	0	5	20.0	.20
Jamie Huscroft†	D	26	0	1	1	-3	63	0	0	0	0	20	0.0	.04
Garth Snow	G	65	0	1	1	—	34	0	0	0	0	0	—	.02
* Robb Gordon	C	4	0	0	0	0	2	0	0	0	0	1	0.0	.00
Steve Washburn†	C	8	0	0	0	0	2	0	0	0	0	6	0.0	.00
* Kevin Weekes	G	11	0	0	0	—	0	0	0	0	0	0	—	.00
Corey Hirsch	G	20	0	0	0	—	0	0	0	0	0	0	—	.00
Bench		—	—	—	—	—	0	—	—	—	—	—	—	—
TEAM TOTALS		82	192	305	497	-246	1748	57	17	23	6	1945	9.9	6.06

Postseason

GP	G	A	Pts	+/–	PIM	PP	SH	GW	OT	S	SPct	P/G

Team Did Not Qualify for Postseason Play

Regular Season

Goaltender	G	Min	GAA	W	L	T	ENG	ShO	GA	SA	SvPct
Garth Snow	**65**	**3501**	**2.93**	**20**	**31**	**8**	**5**	**6**	**171**	**1715**	**.900**
Corey Hirsch	20	919	3.13	3	8	3	0	1	48	435	.890
* Kevin Weekes	11	532	3.83	0	8	1	0	0	34	257	.868
TEAM TOTALS	82	4981	3.11	23	47	12	5	7	258	2412	.893

Postseason

G	Min	GAA	W	L	ENG	ShO	GA	SA	SvPct

1998-99 Vancouver Canucks

Record When:

Overtime games	0-1-12
In second game of back-to-back games	5-7-1
Vs playoff teams	12-32-9
Leading after two periods	17-5-0
Tied after two periods	4-4-6
Losing after two periods	2-38-6
Scoring first	16-13-6
More shots than opponents	7-13-3
Fewer shots than opponents	16-33-8
Team had at least one fighting major	10-27-3
Team had more PIM	15-24-9
Team had fewer PIM	6-20-3
Team had even PIM	2-3-0

Team

Longest winning streak	2	4 times
Longest unbeaten streak	4	Dec. 1 — Dec. 9
Longest losing streak	7	Dec. 26 — Jan. 6
Longest winless streak	8	Dec. 26 — Jan. 8
Most shots, game	43	@Ott, Nov. 23
Most shots, period	19	2 times
Fewest shots, game	13	2 times
Fewest shots, period	0	2 times

Individual

Longest goal streak	3	5 times
Longest point streak	6	4 times
Most goals, game	3	Markus Naslund
Most assists, game	3	3 times
Most points, game	4	Alexander Mogilny
Highest +/–, game	3	14 times
Lowest +/–, game	-4	4 times
Most shots, game	9	Bryan McCabe

Did You Know?

Vancouver led the NHL with 17 shorthanded goals last year, yet no Canuck registered more than two shorthanded tallies. Eight players scored two SHG apiece for Vancouver. No previous NHL team had as many as eight players score multiple shorthanded goals.

Miscellaneous

		NHL Rank
PP Pct.	15.9 (57-358)	12
SH goals allowed	9	15t
PK Pct.	82.9 (373-450)	19
SH goals scored	17	1
Special Team Index	100.1	12
Shots on goal	1,945 (23.7/G)	27
Shots against	2,412 (29.4/G)	20
Unassisted goals	14	8t
Unassisted goals allowed	13	15
Team Average Weight	203.1	9
Game Star Points	277	26

Game Star Breakdown

Player	1st	2nd	3rd	Pts
Garth Snow	11	3	2	66
Markus Naslund	6	3	3	42
Mattias Ohlund	5	1	1	29
Mark Messier	2	5	3	28
Todd Bertuzzi	2	1	0	13
Dave Scatchard	1	2	2	13
Adrian Aucoin	0	3	4	13
Alexander Mogilny	0	2	6	12
Corey Hirsch	0	2	5	11
Peter Zezel	1	1	0	8
Bill Muckalt	1	0	3	8
Peter Schaefer	0	2	0	6
Harry York	1	0	0	5
Ed Jovanovski	0	1	2	5
Bryan McCabe	0	1	2	5
Brandon Convery	0	1	0	3
Josh Holden	0	1	0	3
Kevin Weekes	0	0	2	2
Murray Baron	0	0	1	1
Dave Gagner	0	0	1	1
Trent Klatt	0	0	1	1
Brad May	0	0	1	1
Jason Strudwick	0	0	1	1

Washington Capitals 1998-99 Game Log (31-45-6)

					Goalies		Shots		Power Plays		Game Stars		
Date	**Opp**	**Score**	**W/L/T**	**Record**	**W/T**	**L/T**	**Was**	**Opp**	**Was**	**Opp**	**1st**	**2nd**	**3rd**
10/10	Anh	1-**0**	W	1-0-0	**Kolzig**	Roussel	34	29	1-6	0-6	**Juneau**	**Kolzig**	Roussel
10/13	Det	2-3	L	1-1-0	Osgood	**Kolzig**	30	25	0-3	1-3	McCarty	Brown	**Mironov**
10/16	Mon	2-2*	T	1-1-1	**Kolzig**	Thibault	36	27	1-3	0-2	Thibault	Thornton	**Oates**
10/18	@TB	4-1	W	2-1-1	**Kolzig**	Ranford	32	32	0-3	0-6	**Mironov**	**Herr**	Andersson
10/21	Van	1-2	L	2-2-1	Snow	**Kolzig**	35	29	0-6	1-5	Snow	Aucoin	**Juneau**
10/23	@Buf	1-**0**	W	3-2-1	**Kolzig**	Hasek	36	30	0-5	0-7	**Kolzig**	Hasek	**Bondra**
10/24	Fla	2-2*	T	3-2-2	**Tabaracci**	Burke	20	33	0-4	1-7	**Tabaracci**	Dvorak	**Witt**
10/28	@Edm	2-8	L	3-3-2	Essensa	**Kolzig**	24	33	1-4	3-9	Guerin	Mironov	Niinimaa
10/30	@Cgy	0-**0***	T	3-3-3	**Tabaracci**	Wregget	27	20	0-2	0-3	Wregget	**Tabaracci**	Housley
11/01	@Van	1-4	L	3-4-3	Hirsch	**Kolzig**	26	22	1-5	0-6	Muckalt	Convery	Hirsch
11/04	TB	2-5	L	3-5-3	Puppa	**Kolzig**	36	18	1-4	1-5	Puppa	Clark	**Oates**
11/06	Car	2-3	L	3-6-3	Irbe	**Kolzig**	34	31	1-6	0-3	O'Neill	**Juneau**	Manderville
11/07	@Ott	8-5	W	4-6-3	**Rosati**	Rhodes	35	28	2-3	0-5	**Bondra**	**Juneau**	Oliver
11/12	Buf	0-2	L	4-7-3	Hasek	**Kolzig**	23	25	0-6	0-2	Hasek	Peca	**Reekie**
11/14	@NYI	5-3	W	5-7-3	**Kolzig**	Salo	34	24	1-2	2-4	**Black**	**Oates**	**Tinordi**
11/18	Tor	4-1	W	6-7-3	**Kolzig**	Joseph	30	27	0-3	1-7	**Bulis**	**Zednik**	**Kolzig**
11/20	Ott	1-4	L	6-8-3	Rhodes	**Tabaracci**	34	29	0-3	1-5	Yashin	Dackell	Rhodes
11/21	@Bos	4-5*	L	6-9-3	Tallas	**Tabaracci**	35	45	0-3	2-6	Allison	Khristich	**Gonchar**
11/25	Pit	5-4	W	7-9-3	**Kolzig**	Barrasso	31	22	0-4	2-4	Barnes	**Bondra**	**Black**
11/27	@Dal	0-4	L	7-10-3	Belfour	**Kolzig**	15	**15**	0-4	1-6	Modano	Hatcher	Langenbrunner
11/28	@StL	2-4	L	7-11-3	McLennan	**Kolzig**	34	25	1-6	1-4	McLennan	Conroy	Handzus
12/01	NJ	0-4	L	7-12-3	Brodeur	**Kolzig**	22	26	0-3	2-5	Niedermayer	Brodeur	Sykora
12/04	NYI	5-1	W	8-12-3	**Tabaracci**	Salo	28	23	0-4	0-5	**Tabaracci**	**Johansson**	**Juneau**
12/05	@Phi	1-2	L	8-13-3	Hextall	**Tabaracci**	23	28	1-3	2-4	Brind'Amour	Hextall	Lindros
12/09	@LA	1-2	L	8-14-3	Fiset	**Kolzig**	33	22	0-2	0-6	Robitaille	Murray	Fiset
12/11	@Anh	0-1	L	8-15-3	Hebert	**Kolzig**	31	24	0-2	1-4	Hebert	**Nikolishin**	McInnis
12/12	@SJ	1-2	L	8-16-3	Vernon	**Tabaracci**	26	36	1-7	2-7	Friesen	Nolan	**Tabaracci**
12/17	@Chi	3-1	W	9-16-3	**Kolzig**	Thibault	29	19	2-**8**	1-3	**Konowalchuk**	**Johansson**	Manson
12/19	@Pit	0-3	L	9-17-3	Barrasso	**Kolzig**	24	24	0-3	1-6	Barrasso	Kovalev	Jagr
12/23	@Fla	4-**0**	W	10-17-3	**Kolzig**	Burke	20	29	2-4	0-5	**Kolzig**	**Bondra**	**Reekie**
12/26	@Nsh	1-3	L	10-18-3	Vokoun	**Kolzig**	27	28	0-3	0-5	Vokoun	Boughner	Johnson
12/28	Bos	5-1	W	11-18-3	**Tabaracci**	Dafoe	37	22	0-3	0-4	**Konowalchuk**	**Bondra**	**Gonchar**
12/30	NJ	2-3	L	11-19-3	Brodeur	**Tabaracci**	20	26	1-7	0-2	Holik	Sharifijanov	**Konowalchuk**
1/01	Ott	3-4	L	11-20-3	Rhodes	**Kolzig**	27	23	1-4	1-4	Yashin	McEachern	**Black**
1/02	@Tor	5-2	W	12-20-3	**Kolzig**	Joseph	28	31	2-4	0-5	**Bellows**	**Kolzig**	Modin
1/07	NYR	5-1	W	13-20-3	**Kolzig**	Richter	33	18	1-2	0-2	**Bulis**	**Konowalchuk**	**Hunter**
1/09	@NJ	3-2	W	14-20-3	**Kolzig**	Terreri	25	41	0-3	0-3	**Kolzig**	**Juneau**	**Bellows**
1/11	NYI	4-3	W	15-20-3	**Kolzig**	Potvin	35	25	1-4	1-3	**Gonchar**	**Reekie**	**Eagles**
1/13	Phi	0-3	L	15-21-3	Vanbiesbrouck	**Kolzig**	25	28	0-3	0-4	Desjardins	Vanbiesbrouck	Lindros
1/15	Mon	0-3	L	15-22-3	Hackett	**Kolzig**	23	25	0-2	0-3	Recchi	Malakhov	Hackett
1/16	@Car	3-2*	W	16-22-3	**Kolzig**	Irbe	38	21	0-2	1-7	**Miller**	Primeau	Irbe
1/18	@Mon	4-4*	T	16-22-4	**Tabaracci**	Hackett	28	30	2-3	1-3	Malakhov	**Bondra**	Savage
1/21	@Phi	1-4	L	16-23-4	Hextall	**Kolzig**	18	26	0-1	1-3	Jones	Lindros	Dykhuis
1/26	NYR	1-4	L	16-24-4	Richter	**Kolzig**	35	23	0-3	1-2	Gretzky	Richter	Graves
1/29	LA	3-6	L	16-25-4	Fiset	**Kolzig**	41	27	2-7	2-4	Ferraro	R.Blake	Fiset
1/30	@Tor	3-5	L	16-26-4	Joseph	**Tabaracci**	30	23	2-5	2-4	Thomas	**Nikolishin**	Joseph
2/01	@NYR	3-1	W	17-26-4	**Kolzig**	Richter	38	25	0-2	0-4	**Juneau**	**Kolzig**	**Bondra**
2/03	TB	**10**-1	W	18-26-4	**Kolzig**	Schwab	**46**	22	2-6	0-3	**Bondra**	**Bellows**	**Johansson**
2/05	Car	4-1	W	19-26-4	**Kolzig**	Kidd	28	24	1-4	0-6	**Bondra**	**Kolzig**	**Tinordi**
2/07	Buf	3-1	W	20-26-4	**Kolzig**	Hasek	34	20	0-4	0-4	**Konowalchuk**	**Kolzig**	**Johansson**
2/09	@NYI	2-1	W	21-26-4	**Kolzig**	Salo	25	22	1-5	0-5	**Kolzig**	**Oates**	**Tinordi**
2/12	@NJ	3-2	W	22-26-4	**Kolzig**	Brodeur	21	28	2-5	0-5	**Konowalchuk**	**Bulis**	**Bondra**
2/13	@Ott	1-2	L	22-27-4	Rhodes	**Kolzig**	32	24	0-3	0-2	Rhodes	Laukkanen	**Bondra**
2/15	@Pit	3-7	L	22-28-4	Skudra	**Kolzig**	32	21	0-3	2-5	Titov	Morozov	Jagr
2/18	@Car	2-2*	T	22-28-5	**Kolzig**	Irbe	22	39	1-4	0-8	Battaglia	**Kolzig**	**Juneau**

2/20	SJ	3-1	W	23-28-5	**Kolzig**	Vernon	21	**15**	2-4	1-7	**Gonchar**	Friesen	**Johansson**
2/22	Tor	4-3	W	24-28-5	**Kolzig**	Joseph	28	25	1-3	0-2	**Eagles**	**Oates**	**Klee**
2/24	Pho	1-2	L	24-29-5	Khabibulin	**Kolzig**	20	16	0-1	1-**1**	Tkachuk	Carney	**Gonchar**
2/27	@Bos	3-4	L	24-30-5	Dafoe	**Kolzig**	36	19	1-4	3-5	Dafoe	**Klee**	Khristich
2/28	Pit	4-3	W	25-30-5	**Kolzig**	Barrasso	26	25	2-3	1-2	**Nikolishin**	Titov	**Svejkovsky**
3/02	@TB	8-2	W	26-30-5	**Kolzig**	Wilkinson	26	26	**3**-4	1-5	**Bondra**	**Johansson**	Daigle
3/04	NYR	2-4	L	26-31-5	Richter	**Kolzig**	36	34	2-5	0-4	Knuble	Richter	Sundstrom
3/06	Edm	4-3	W	27-31-5	**Kolzig**	Passmore	36	25	1-4	1-4	**Oates**	**Bondra**	**Gonchar**
3/09	Col	2-3*	L	27-32-5	Billington	**Kolzig**	37	20	0-4	1-5	Ozolinsh	Deadmarsh	**Bondra**
3/11	Fla	1-2	L	27-33-5	Burke	**Kolzig**	27	20	0-4	0-6	Burke	Kozlov	**Reekie**
3/13	Cgy	4-5*	L	27-34-5	Brathwaite	**Tabaracci**	35	27	0-1	1-2	Bure	Housley	**Oates**
3/15	@NYR	1-1*	T	27-34-6	**Kolzig**	Richter	34	23	0-4	0-4	Richter	Ndur	**Hunter**
3/17	Dal	2-1*	W	28-34-6	**Tabaracci**	Belfour	23	27	1-3	0-6	**Bellows**	**Tabaracci**	**Nikolishin**
3/20	@Mon	1-**0**	W	29-34-6	**Tabaracci**	Hackett	21	29	0-3	0-4	**Tabaracci**	Quintal	Hackett
3/21	Bos	1-4	L	29-35-6	Dafoe	**Kolzig**	19	34	0-1	1-6	Allison	McLaren	Bourque
3/25	@Pho	2-4	L	29-36-6	Khabibulin	**Tabaracci**	38	25	0-6	0-2	Reichel	Khabibulin	Tkachuk
3/26	@Col	1-3	L	29-37-6	Roy	**Kolzig**	20	25	0-2	0-4	Miller	Lemieux	Yelle
3/30	Nsh	2-3	L	29-38-6	Vokoun	**Tabaracci**	36	23	1-6	0-3	Walker	Boughner	**Gonchar**
4/01	Fla	5-3	W	30-38-6	**Kolzig**	Burke	37	35	1-4	0-6	**Kolzig**	**Gonchar**	**Bellows**
4/03	@TB	3-4	L	30-39-6	Hodson	**Tabaracci**	34	25	1-4	2-3	Gratton	**Nikolishin**	Tucker
4/05	@Fla	3-**0**	W	31-39-6	**Kolzig**	McLean	30	28	1-5	0-5	**Gonchar**	**Oates**	McLean
4/07	StL	2-4	L	31-40-6	Fuhr	**Tabaracci**	29	32	0-1	0-3	Young	**Gratton**	MacInnis
4/08	@NJ	0-1	L	31-41-6	Brodeur	**Kolzig**	15	25	0-1	0-4	Rolston	Brodeur	Dean
4/10	Phi	1-2	L	31-42-6	Vanbiesbrouck	**Kolzig**	18	32	0-1	0-2	Jones	**Gratton**	Desjardins
4/12	Chi	2-4	L	31-43-6	Fitzpatrick	**Tabaracci**	26	31	0-2	1-4	**Reekie**	**Black**	**Witt**
4/14	@Car	0-3	L	31-44-6	Irbe	**Brochu**	19	26	0-5	2-5	Francis	Irbe	Kron
4/18	@Buf	0-3	L	31-45-6	Hasek	**Brochu**	25	29	0-2	1-3	Hasek	Satan	Warrener

Washington Capitals 1998-99 Player Statistics

Regular Season

Skater	Ps	GP	G	A	Pts	+/–	PIM	PP	SH	GW	GT	S	SPct	P/G
Peter Bondra	R	66	**31**	24	**55**	-1	56	6	**3**	**5**	**1**	**284**	10.9	.83
Adam Oates	C	59	12	**41**	53	-1	22	3	0	0	0	79	15.2	**.90**
Joe Juneau†	L	63	14	27	41	-3	20	2	1	3	0	142	9.9	.65
Brian Bellows	L	76	17	19	36	-12	26	8	0	3	0	166	10.2	.47
Andrei Nikolishin	L	73	8	27	35	0	28	0	1	1	0	121	6.6	.48
Sergei Gonchar	D	53	21	10	31	1	57	**13**	1	3	0	180	11.7	.58
James Black	C	75	16	14	30	5	14	1	1	3	0	135	11.9	.40
Calle Johansson	D	67	8	21	29	10	22	2	0	2	**1**	145	5.5	.43
Steve Konowalchuk	C	45	12	12	24	0	26	4	1	2	0	98	**12.2**	.53
Jan Bulis	C	38	7	16	23	3	6	3	0	3	0	57	12.3	.61
Ken Klee	R	**78**	7	13	20	-9	80	0	0	1	0	132	5.3	.26
Richard Zednik	L	49	9	8	17	-6	50	1	0	2	0	115	7.8	.35
Dmitri Mironov	D	46	2	14	16	-5	80	2	0	0	0	86	2.3	.35
Jaroslav Svejkovsky	R	25	6	8	14	-2	12	4	0	2	0	50	12.0	.56
Michal Pivonka	C	36	5	6	11	-6	12	2	0	0	0	30	16.7	.31
Chris Simon	L	23	3	7	10	-4	48	0	0	0	0	29	10.3	.43
Joe Reekie	D	73	0	10	10	**12**	68	0	0	0	0	81	0.0	.14
Craig Berube†	L	66	5	4	9	-7	**166**	0	0	0	0	45	11.1	.14
* Benoit Gratton	L	16	4	3	7	-1	16	0	0	0	0	24	16.7	.44
Brendan Witt	D	54	2	5	7	-6	87	0	0	0	0	51	3.9	.13
Kelly Miller	L	62	2	5	7	-5	29	0	0	1	0	49	4.1	.11
Mike Eagles	C	52	4	2	6	-5	50	0	0	0	0	41	9.8	.12
Jeff Toms	L	21	1	5	6	0	2	0	0	0	0	30	3.3	.29
Mark Tinordi	D	48	0	6	6	-6	108	0	0	0	0	32	0.0	.13
Dale Hunter†	C	50	0	5	5	-7	102	0	0	0	0	18	0.0	.10
* Matt Herr	C	30	2	2	4	-7	8	1	0	0	0	40	5.0	.13
* Trevor Halverson	L	17	0	4	4	-5	28	0	0	0	0	16	0.0	.24
Enrico Ciccone†	D	43	2	0	2	-7	103	0	0	0	**1**	43	4.7	.05
Tom Chorske†	L	17	0	2	2	-4	4	0	0	0	0	22	0.0	.12
Olaf Kolzig	G	64	0	2	2	—	19	0	0	0	0	0	—	.03
* Patrick Boileau	D	4	0	1	1	-4	2	0	0	0	0	7	0.0	.25
* Mike Rosati	G	1	0	0	0	—	0	0	0	0	0	0	—	.00
Patrik Augusta	R	2	0	0	0	0	0	0	0	0	0	4	0.0	.00
* Martin Brochu	G	2	0	0	0	—	2	0	0	0	0	0	—	.00
* Patrice Lefebvre	R	3	0	0	0	-2	2	0	0	0	0	2	0.0	.00
Brad Shaw†	D	4	0	0	0	0	4	0	0	0	0	5	0.0	.00
* Nolan Baumgartner	D	5	0	0	0	-3	0	0	0	0	0	1	0.0	.00
* Alexei Tezikov	D	5	0	0	0	-1	0	0	0	0	0	4	0.0	.00
Stewart Malgunas	D	10	0	0	0	-5	6	0	0	0	0	2	0.0	.00
Steve Poapst	D	22	0	0	0	-8	8	0	0	0	0	11	0.0	.00
Rick Tabaracci	G	23	0	0	0	—	2	0	0	0	0	0	—	.00
Bench		—	—	—	—	—	0	—	—	—	—	—	—	—
TEAM TOTALS		82	200	323	523	-101	1375	52	8	31	3	2377	8.4	6.38

Postseason

GP	G	A	Pts	+/–	PIM	PP	SH	GW	OT	S	SPct	P/G

Team Did Not Qualify for Postseason Play

Regular Season

Goaltender	G	Min	GAA	W	L	T	ENG	ShO	GA	SA	SvPct
* Mike Rosati	1	28	.00	1	0	0	0	0	0	12	1.000
Rick Tabaracci	23	1193	2.51	4	12	**3**	3	2	50	530	.906
Olaf Kolzig	**64**	**3586**	**2.58**	**26**	**31**	**3**	**5**	**4**	**154**	**1538**	**.900**
* Martin Brochu	2	120	3.00	0	2	0	0	0	6	55	.891
TEAM TOTALS	82	4959	2.64	31	45	6	8	6	218	2143	.898

Postseason

G	Min	GAA	W	L	ENG	ShO	GA	SA	SvPct

1998-99 Washington Capitals

Record When:

Overtime games	2-3-6
In second game of back-to-back games	4-9-1
Vs playoff teams	17-31-1
Leading after two periods	23-1-2
Tied after two periods	7-10-2
Losing after two periods	1-34-2
Scoring first	22-9-2
More shots than opponents	23-24-3
Fewer shots than opponents	6-19-3
Team had at least one fighting major	9-19-0
Team had more PIM	18-30-3
Team had fewer PIM	4-11-1
Team had even PIM	9-4-2

Team

Longest winning streak	6	Feb. 1 — Feb. 12
Longest unbeaten streak	6	Feb. 1 — Feb. 12
Longest losing streak	6	Apr. 7 — Apr. 18
Longest winless streak	6	2 times
Most shots, game	46	vs. TB, Feb. 3
Most shots, period	25	2nd, vs. TB, Feb. 3
Fewest shots, game	15	2 times
Fewest shots, period	2	3 times

Individual

Longest goal streak	4	Sergei Gonchar [2]
Longest point streak	7	2 times
Most goals, game	4	Peter Bondra
Most assists, game	3	6 times
Most points, game	5	Peter Bondra
Highest +/–, game	5	2 times
Lowest +/–, game	-3	14 times
Most shots, game	12	Peter Bondra

Did You Know?

Olaf Kolzig's winning percentage fell from .623 in 1997-98 to .458 last year. The dropoff of .165 was the largest among goaltenders who played at least 40 games in both seasons. Klozig also posted the second-largest drop in save percentage (.020) and the third-largest increase in GAA (0.38).

Miscellaneous

		NHL Rank
PP Pct.	17.3 (52-301)	9
SH goals allowed	7	9t
PK Pct.	84.4 (298-353)	15
SH goals scored	8	8t
Special Team Index	101.6	8
Shots on goal	2,377 (29.0/G)	8
Shots against	2,143 (26.1/G)	7
Unassisted goals	14	8t
Unassisted goals allowed	15	17t
Team Average Weight	202.2	10
Game Star Points	312	23

Game Star Breakdown

Player	1st	2nd	3rd	Pts
Olaf Kolzig	5	6	1	44
Peter Bondra	4	5	5	40
Steve Konowalchuk	4	1	1	24
Sergei Gonchar	3	1	5	23
Rick Tabaracci	3	2	1	22
Joe Juneau	2	3	3	22
Adam Oates	1	4	3	20
Brian Bellows	2	1	2	15
Andrei Nikolishin	1	3	1	15
Jan Bulis	2	1	0	13
Calle Johansson	0	3	3	12
Joe Reekie	1	1	3	11
James Black	1	1	2	10
Mike Eagles	1	0	1	6
Dmitri Mironov	1	0	1	6
Benoit Gratton	0	2	0	6
Kelly Miller	1	0	0	5
Ken Klee	0	1	1	4
Matt Herr	0	1	0	3
Richard Zednik	0	1	0	3
Mark Tinordi	0	0	3	3
Dale Hunter	0	0	2	2
Brendan Witt	0	0	2	2
Jaroslav Svejkovsky	0	0	1	1

Final 1998-99
NHL Regular Season Standings

EASTERN CONFERENCE

NORTHEAST	W-L-T	Pts	Pct
Ottawa	44-23-15	103	.628
Toronto	45-30-7	97	.591
Boston	39-30-13	91	.555
Buffalo	37-28-17	91	.555
Montreal	32-39-11	75	.457

ATLANTIC	W-L-T	Pts	Pct
New Jersey	47-24-11	105	.640
Philadelphia	37-26-19	93	.567
Pittsburgh	38-30-14	90	.549
NY Rangers	33-38-11	77	.470
NY Islanders	24-48-10	58	.354

SOUTHEAST	W-L-T	Pts	Pct
Carolina	34-30-18	86	.524
Florida	30-34-18	78	.476
Washington	31-45-6	68	.415
Tampa Bay	19-54-9	47	.287

WESTERN CONFERENCE

CENTRAL	W-L-T	Pts	Pct
Detroit	43-32-7	93	.567
St. Louis	37-32-13	87	.530
Chicago	29-41-12	70	.427
Nashville	28-47-7	63	.384

PACIFIC	W-L-T	Pts	Pct
Dallas	51-19-12	114	.695
Phoenix	39-31-12	90	.549
Anaheim	35-34-13	83	.506
San Jose	31-33-18	80	.488
Los Angeles	32-45-5	69	.421

NORTHWEST	W-L-T	Pts	Pct
Colorado	44-28-10	98	.598
Edmonton	33-37-12	78	.476
Calgary	30-40-12	72	.439
Vancouver	23-47-12	58	.354

1999 Postseason Results

(team in italics had home-ice advantage)

Eastern First Round
Pittsburgh 4—*New Jersey 3*
Buffalo 4—*Ottawa 0*
Boston 4—*Carolina 2*
Toronto 4—Philadelphia 2

Western First Round
Dallas 4—Edmonton 0
Colorado 4—San Jose 2
Detroit 4—Anaheim 0
St. Louis 4—*Phoenix 3*

Eastern Semifinals
Toronto 4—Pittsburgh 2
Buffalo 4—*Boston 2*

Western Semifinals
Dallas 4—St. Louis 2
Colorado 4—Detroit 2

Eastern Conference Finals
Buffalo 4—*Toronto 1*

Western Conference Finals
Dallas 4—Colorado 3

Stanley Cup Finals
Dallas 4—Buffalo 2

1999 NHL Postseason Team Totals

	Overall							Power Play			Short Hand			Penalty							Misc	
Tm	GP	G	A	Pts	+/–	S	SPct	G	A	Pts	G	A	Pts	Num	PIM	Maj	Mnr	Fgt	Rgh	HHT	Hat	OT
Bos	12	30	46	76	8	337	8.9	9	18	27	0	0	0	63	126	0	63	0	16	15	0	1
Buf	21	59	95	154	40	559	10.6	19	35	54	4	6	10	153	349	1	147	1	30	44	0	2
Car	6	10	19	29	–20	164	6.1	2	4	6	0	0	0	31	62	0	31	0	9	8	0	1
NJ	7	18	33	51	–22	197	9.1	5	10	15	1	1	2	39	86	0	38	0	10	9	0	0
Ott	4	6	12	18	–25	162	3.7	3	6	9	0	0	0	23	46	0	23	0	4	5	0	0
Phi	6	11	18	29	20	191	5.8	3	6	9	0	0	0	41	82	0	41	0	14	7	0	0
Pit	13	35	53	88	–16	265	13.2	8	14	22	0	0	0	71	183	3	64	2	11	20	1	1
Tor	17	43	73	116	–19	441	9.8	12	22	34	0	0	0	99	252	2	91	2	24	25	0	3
Anh	4	6	12	18	–40	115	5.2	4	8	12	0	0	0	32	80	0	30	0	9	5	0	0
Col	19	56	97	153	33	590	9.5	14	28	42	2	2	4	137	309	1	132	0	25	28	0	3
Dal	23	64	113	177	72	728	8.8	13	26	39	3	3	6	126	279	1	122	1	29	31	0	4
Det	10	31	55	86	–4	359	8.6	14	23	37	0	0	0	67	137	1	66	0	18	15	1	1
Edm	4	7	14	21	–19	93	7.5	2	4	6	0	0	0	29	85	1	25	0	7	4	0	0
Pho	7	16	28	44	5	176	9.1	5	10	15	0	0	0	46	95	1	45	1	8	13	0	1
SJ	6	17	27	44	–12	191	8.9	7	14	21	2	0	2	51	102	0	51	0	12	9	0	0
StL	13	31	53	84	–24	412	7.5	11	21	32	0	0	0	88	179	1	87	1	12	25	0	4
Tot		440	748	1188	–23	4980	8.8	131	249	380	12	12	24	1096	2452	12	1056	8	238	263	2	21

1999 NHL Postseason Opponent Totals

	Overall							Power Play			Short Hand			Penalty							Misc	
Tm	GP	G	A	Pts	+/–	S	SPct	G	A	Pts	G	A	Pts	Num	PIM	Maj	Mnr	Fgt	Rgh	HHT	Hat	OT
Bos	12	27	47	74	–11	331	8.2	8	15	23	1	2	3	75	150	0	75	0	18	21	0	1
Buf	21	49	86	135	–46	657	7.5	17	32	49	0	0	0	133	309	1	127	1	37	32	0	1
Car	6	16	24	40	19	182	8.8	4	8	12	0	0	0	28	56	0	28	0	7	7	0	1
NJ	7	21	34	55	19	140	15.0	4	8	12	0	0	0	37	74	0	37	0	8	11	1	1
Ott	4	12	24	36	25	106	11.3	4	8	12	0	0	0	31	62	0	31	0	7	11	0	1
Phi	6	9	16	25	–22	146	6.2	5	10	15	0	0	0	34	68	0	34	0	10	10	0	1
Pit	13	36	63	99	12	351	10.3	6	12	18	1	1	2	66	154	2	62	2	14	15	0	2
Tor	17	46	69	115	11	450	10.2	13	24	37	3	4	7	115	311	3	103	2	21	30	0	0
Anh	4	17	30	47	40	135	12.6	7	12	19	0	0	0	28	56	0	28	0	5	5	1	0
Col	19	54	91	145	–40	657	8.2	19	35	54	3	2	5	121	245	1	120	0	30	27	0	1
Dal	23	44	69	113	–76	618	7.1	9	16	25	0	0	0	138	306	2	133	1	22	31	0	4
Det	10	27	46	73	3	299	9.0	9	18	27	1	1	2	79	193	1	74	0	16	13	0	0
Edm	4	11	19	30	19	149	7.4	2	4	6	0	0	0	24	72	0	21	0	5	6	0	1
Pho	7	19	36	55	–5	237	8.0	9	17	26	0	0	0	53	109	1	52	1	9	16	0	2
SJ	6	19	36	55	8	208	9.1	7	14	21	1	1	2	54	124	0	52	0	16	8	0	2
StL	13	33	58	91	21	314	10.5	8	16	24	2	1	3	80	163	1	79	1	13	20	0	3
Tot		440	748	1188	–23	4980	8.8	131	249	380	12	12	24	1096	2452	12	1056	8	238	263	2	21

1998-99 NHL Regular Season Team Totals

	Overall							Power Play			Short Hand			Penalty							Misc	
Tm	**GP**	**G**	**A**	**Pts**	**+/–**	**S**	**SPct**	**G**	**A**	**Pts**	**G**	**A**	**Pts**	**Num**	**PIM**	**Maj**	**Mnr**	**Fgt**	**Rgh**	**HHT**	**Hat**	**OT**
Bos	82	214	366	580	–10	2262	9.5	65	125	190	3	4	7	430	1182	46	361	40	60	121	3	2
Buf	82	207	348	555	184	2150	9.6	49	91	140	6	5	11	565	1561	53	478	51	90	**175**	2	3
Car	82	210	348	558	78	2142	9.8	42	72	114	5	2	7	464	1158	34	414	31	51	133	0	1
Fla	82	210	352	562	–32	2307	9.1	51	92	143	10	11	21	563	1522	76	466	72	91	150	3	1
Mon	82	184	312	496	–153	2269	8.1	50	95	145	8	8	16	475	1299	47	402	45	60	140	0	0
NJ	82	248	430	678	178	2565	9.7	60	117	177	7	7	14	495	1353	65	409	64	91	95	1	3
NYI	82	194	314	508	–232	2157	9.0	54	102	156	8	5	13	458	1111	25	418	23	46	151	1	1
NYR	82	217	374	591	–174	2085	10.4	71	135	206	7	6	13	458	1087	33	416	33	67	151	2	5
Ott	82	239	392	631	222	2503	9.5	59	115	174	6	7	13	394	892	16	371	14	46	145	3	1
Phi	82	231	399	630	111	2451	9.4	65	120	185	4	4	8	456	1075	41	410	39	75	138	2	2
Pit	82	242	417	659	25	2089	**11.6**	65	119	184	10	9	19	399	977	25	361	25	52	126	2	**7**
TB	82	179	291	470	–449	2130	8.4	43	81	124	11	15	26	513	1316	45	448	42	71	168	3	1
Tor	82	**268**	**454**	**722**	**235**	2318	11.6	53	102	155	7	6	13	437	1095	47	380	46	62	146	**5**	6
Was	82	200	323	523	–101	2377	8.4	52	96	148	8	12	20	509	1381	49	433	49	68	153	3	2
Anh	82	215	350	565	–73	2331	9.2	**83**	**157**	**240**	6	4	10	533	1323	43	474	43	78	154	1	1
Cgy	82	211	348	559	4	2344	9.0	51	97	148	12	12	24	552	1389	55	482	54	89	121	2	3
Chi	82	202	333	535	–93	2145	9.4	50	94	144	8	4	12	632	**1807**	**93**	506	**92**	**132**	108	3	1
Col	82	239	420	659	119	2299	10.4	71	137	208	7	8	15	590	1619	77	487	77	87	146	4	2
Dal	82	236	396	632	173	2266	10.4	74	135	209	6	7	13	452	1108	36	404	34	67	149	3	3
Det	82	245	434	679	90	**2622**	9.3	67	131	198	14	**18**	32	484	1202	30	436	26	85	152	3	2
Edm	82	230	385	615	30	2396	9.6	63	122	185	8	4	12	534	1371	53	463	51	79	150	2	3
LA	82	189	302	491	–152	2317	8.2	43	80	123	12	15	27	497	1383	71	404	68	57	144	1	5
Nsh	82	190	332	522	–195	2219	8.6	40	78	118	7	10	17	525	1420	70	435	68	74	166	0	1
Pho	82	205	357	562	55	2398	8.5	41	81	122	8	11	19	503	1412	58	416	54	58	121	1	2
SJ	82	196	330	526	53	2143	9.1	53	99	152	8	10	18	556	1423	45	489	41	77	141	2	1
StL	82	237	409	646	60	2469	9.6	61	115	176	7	7	14	515	1308	50	449	50	56	161	3	1
Van	82	192	305	497	–246	1945	9.9	57	99	156	**17**	16	**33**	**653**	1764	78	**547**	77	110	158	1	0
Tot		5830	9821	15651	–293	61699	9.4	1533	2887	4420	220	227	447	13642	35538	1361	11759	1309	1979	3863	56	60
Avg	82	216	364	580	–11	2285	9.4	57	107	164	8	8	17	505	1316	50	436	48	73	143	2	2

1998-99 NHL Regular Season Opponent Totals

	Overall							Power Play			Short Hand			Penalty							Misc	
Tm	**GP**	**G**	**A**	**Pts**	**+/–**	**S**	**SPct**	**G**	**A**	**Pts**	**G**	**A**	**Pts**	**Num**	**PIM**	**Maj**	**Mnr**	**Fgt**	**Rgh**	**HHT**	**Hat**	**OT**
Bos	82	181	294	475	–7	2226	8.1	**33**	**61**	**94**	9	9	18	499	1308	42	434	39	59	161	**0**	2
Buf	82	175	**289**	464	–207	2461	**7.1**	55	102	157	7	4	11	518	1409	55	437	52	79	135	2	3
Car	82	202	355	557	–94	2399	8.4	51	97	148	6	8	14	515	1299	31	462	31	77	139	3	5
Fla	82	228	386	614	7	2355	9.7	67	127	194	11	13	24	575	1574	72	477	71	84	175	3	2
Mon	82	209	339	548	130	2207	9.5	44	85	129	10	12	22	478	1278	46	409	45	65	148	2	4
NJ	82	196	315	511	–197	2026	9.7	47	87	134	5	5	10	456	1222	66	376	65	60	143	**0**	1
NYI	82	244	407	651	211	2331	10.5	60	114	174	7	8	15	432	**1040**	24	395	23	**41**	155	1	6
NYR	82	227	376	603	157	2476	9.2	48	93	141	9	9	18	468	1118	34	424	31	80	134	3	3
Ott	82	179	302	481	–248	2068	8.7	44	82	126	13	12	25	494	1179	**21**	457	**16**	74	156	2	2
Phi	82	196	336	532	–121	1877	10.4	53	99	152	7	9	16	512	1235	41	460	39	87	146	3	3
Pit	82	225	359	584	–55	2129	10.6	56	108	164	14	7	21	459	1109	29	417	25	85	129	2	1
TB	82	292	505	797	425	2633	11.1	68	133	201	10	12	22	431	1085	45	375	42	53	131	4	2
Tor	82	231	398	629	**–252**	2359	9.8	64	120	184	6	9	15	494	1345	47	420	46	56	149	2	1
Was	82	218	371	589	82	2143	10.2	55	103	158	7	7	14	437	1125	49	375	48	65	117	1	3
Anh	82	206	353	559	59	2596	7.9	60	111	171	7	8	15	528	1367	45	461	43	66	133	1	3
Cgy	82	234	399	633	–30	2415	9.7	78	148	226	6	4	10	521	1341	57	448	55	90	116	2	1
Chi	82	248	409	657	61	2404	10.3	80	148	228	10	7	17	549	1537	93	436	91	77	147	6	2
Col	82	205	332	537	–143	2280	9.0	63	121	184	12	10	22	577	1578	79	474	77	89	165	1	**0**
Dal	82	**168**	**289**	**457**	–181	1965	8.5	43	85	128	**4**	**2**	**6**	529	1324	38	472	35	87	139	1	1
Det	82	202	322	524	–119	2215	9.1	45	82	127	7	8	15	543	1287	27	501	26	88	161	1	1
Edm	82	226	402	628	–49	2223	10.2	67	127	194	10	11	21	613	1598	52	534	52	87	165	3	5
LA	82	222	365	587	124	2456	9.0	47	78	125	11	17	28	494	1438	70	394	68	54	129	1	2
Nsh	82	261	447	708	170	2709	9.6	75	139	214	10	11	21	490	1326	70	403	68	71	136	4	2
Pho	82	197	343	540	–75	2249	8.8	45	82	127	5	4	9	493	1330	56	415	54	60	156	1	1
SJ	82	191	322	513	–71	2217	8.6	61	116	177	**4**	5	9	560	1465	43	490	42	98	145	1	2
StL	82	209	364	573	–84	**1868**	11.2	47	91	138	**4**	6	10	**418**	1053	51	**359**	50	57	**111**	3	1
Van	82	258	442	700	214	2412	10.7	77	148	225	9	10	19	559	1568	78	454	75	90	142	3	1
Tot		5830	9821	15651	–293	61699	9.4	1533	2887	4420	220	227	447	13642	35538	1361	11759	1309	1979	3863	56	60
Avg	82	216	364	580	–11	2285	9.4	57	107	164	8	8	17	505	1316	50	436	48	73	143	2	2

Leader Boards

The following pages list both the 1998-99 and active career NHL leaders in an array of statistical categories. For all "percentage" categories, the minimum requirement to qualify for each Leader Board is listed in parentheses.

For questions on the definitions of particular categories, please consult the Glossary.

1998-99 NHL Leader Boards (Skaters)

Goals

Player, Team	Goals
Teemu Selanne, Anh	**47**
Tony Amonte, Chi	44
Jaromir Jagr, Pit	44
Alexei Yashin, Ott	44
John LeClair, Phi	43
Joe Sakic, Col	41
Theo Fleury, Cgy-Col	40
Eric Lindros, Phi	40
Miroslav Satan, Buf	40
2 tied with	39

Assists

Player, Team	Assists
Jaromir Jagr, Pit	**83**
Peter Forsberg, Col	67
Paul Kariya, Anh	62
Teemu Selanne, Anh	60
Joe Sakic, Col	55
Jason Allison, Bos	53
Theo Fleury, Cgy-Col	53
Wayne Gretzky, NYR	53
Eric Lindros, Phi	53
2 tied with	52

Points

Player, Team	Points
Jaromir Jagr, Pit	**127**
Teemu Selanne, Anh	107
Paul Kariya, Anh	101
Peter Forsberg, Col	97
Joe Sakic, Col	96
Alexei Yashin, Ott	94
Theo Fleury, Cgy-Col	93
Eric Lindros, Phi	93
John LeClair, Phi	90
Pavol Demitra, StL	89

Goals Per Game

(minimum 30 goals)

Player, Team	Goals/G
Teemu Selanne, Anh	**.63**
John LeClair, Phi	.57
Eric Lindros, Phi	.56
Joe Sakic, Col	.56
Jaromir Jagr, Pit	.54
Tony Amonte, Chi	.54
Alexei Yashin, Ott	.54
Theo Fleury, Cgy-Col	.53
Brett Hull, Dal	.53
Keith Tkachuk, Pho	.53

Assists Per Game

(minimum 41 assists)

Player, Team	Ast/G
Jaromir Jagr, Pit	**1.02**
Peter Forsberg, Col	.86
Teemu Selanne, Anh	.80
Wayne Gretzky, NYR	.76
Paul Kariya, Anh	.76
Joe Sakic, Col	.75
Eric Lindros, Phi	.75
Theo Fleury, Cgy-Col	.71
Adam Oates, Was	.69
Igor Larionov, Det	.65

Points Per Game

(minimum 41 points)

Player, Team	Points/G
Jaromir Jagr, Pit	**1.57**
Teemu Selanne, Anh	1.43
Joe Sakic, Col	1.32
Eric Lindros, Phi	1.31
Peter Forsberg, Col	1.24
Theo Fleury, Cgy-Col	1.24
Paul Kariya, Anh	1.23
John LeClair, Phi	1.18
Alexei Yashin, Ott	1.15
Pavol Demitra, StL	1.09

Games Played

Player, Team	Games
Robert Reichel, NYI-Pho	**83**
46 tied with	82

Shots

Player, Team	Shots
Paul Kariya, Anh	**429**
Jaromir Jagr, Pit	343
Alexei Yashin, Ott	337
Al MacInnis, StL	314
Theo Fleury, Cgy-Col	301
Claude Lemieux, Col	292
Luc Robitaille, LA	292
Brendan Shanahan, Det	288
Peter Bondra, Was	284
Teemu Selanne, Anh	281

Penalty Minutes

Player, Team	Minutes
Rob Ray, Buf	**261**
Jeff Odgers, Col	259
Peter Worrell, Fla	258
Patrick Cote, Nsh	242
Krzysztof Oliwa, NJ	240
Denny Lambert, Nsh	218
Paul Laus, Fla	218
Donald Brashear, Van	209
Bob Probert, Chi	206
Brad Brown, Mon-Chi	205

Plus/Minus

Player, Team	+/–
Alexander Karpovtsev, NYR-Tor	**39**
John LeClair, Phi	36
Eric Lindros, Phi	35
Magnus Arvedson, Ott	33
Al MacInnis, StL	33
Jere Lehtinen, Dal	29
Mike Modano, Dal	29
Scott Stevens, NJ	29
Darryl Shannon, Buf	28
2 tied with	27

Shooting Percentage

(minimum 82 shots)

Player, Team	Pct
Dimitri Khristich, Bos	**20.1**
Dixon Ward, Buf	19.8
Martin Straka, Pit	19.8
Anson Carter, Bos	19.5
Miroslav Satan, Buf	19.2
Mark Parrish, Fla	18.6
Andrei Kovalenko, Edm-Phi-Car	18.3
Steve Sullivan, Tor	18.2
Rem Murray, Edm	18.1
Joe Nieuwendyk, Dal	17.8

Fights

Player, Team	Fights
Patrick Cote, Nsh	**30**
Jeff Odgers, Col	29
Krzysztof Oliwa, NJ	28
Peter Worrell, Fla	21
Tie Domi, Tor	20
Stu Grimson, Anh	20
Paul Laus, Fla	20
Bob Probert, Chi	20
Rob Ray, Buf	19
Denny Lambert, Nsh	18

1998-99 NHL Leader Boards (Skaters)

Power Play Goals

Player, Team	Goals
Teemu Selanne, Anh	**25**
Alexei Yashin, Ott	19
Adrian Aucoin, Van	18
John LeClair, Phi	16
Brett Hull, Dal	15
Markus Naslund, Van	15
Petr Sykora, NJ	15
Tony Amonte, Chi	14
Pavol Demitra, StL	14
Adam Graves, NYR	14

Power Play Assists

Player, Team	Assists
Jaromir Jagr, Pit	**34**
Fredrik Olausson, Anh	33
Paul Kariya, Anh	32
Ray Bourque, Bos	31
Teemu Selanne, Anh	29
Peter Forsberg, Col	28
Wayne Gretzky, NYR	27
Al MacInnis, StL	26
Darryl Sydor, Dal	26
2 tied with	25

Power Play Points

Player, Team	Points
Teemu Selanne, Anh	**54**
Jaromir Jagr, Pit	44
Paul Kariya, Anh	43
Fredrik Olausson, Anh	43
Alexei Yashin, Ott	42
Ray Bourque, Bos	39
Peter Forsberg, Col	37
Al MacInnis, StL	37
Darryl Sydor, Dal	35
Joe Sakic, Col	34

Shorthanded Goals

Player, Team	Goals
Scott Pellerin, StL	**5**
Brian Rolston, NJ	**5**
Joe Sakic, Col	**5**
Magnus Arvedson, Ott	4
Radek Dvorak, Fla	4
Mike Modano, Dal	4
Martin Straka, Pit	4
9 tied with	3

Shorthanded Assists

Player, Team	Assists
Mark Messier, Van	**5**
Peter Forsberg, Col	4
Andrew Cassels, Cgy	3
Kris Draper, Det	3
Benoit Hogue, TB-Dal	3
Alexander Mogilny, Van	3
Adam Oates, Was	3
Dave Scatchard, Van	3
Scott Stevens, NJ	3
Robert Svehla, Fla	3

Shorthanded Points

Player, Team	Points
Mark Messier, Van	**7**
Peter Forsberg, Col	6
Scott Pellerin, StL	6
Joe Sakic, Col	6
Martin Straka, Pit	6
7 tied with	5

Even Strength Goals

Player, Team	Goals
Jaromir Jagr, Pit	**33**
Theo Fleury, Cgy-Col	29
Eric Lindros, Phi	29
Luc Robitaille, LA	28
Tony Amonte, Chi	27
Sergei Berezin, Tor	27
John LeClair, Phi	27
Mats Sundin, Tor	27
3 tied with	26

Even Strength Assists

Player, Team	Assists
Jaromir Jagr, Pit	**49**
Mats Sundin, Tor	40
John LeClair, Phi	38
Steve Thomas, Tor	38
Pavol Demitra, StL	37
Eric Lindros, Phi	36
Peter Forsberg, Col	35
Dimitri Khristich, Bos	35
Theo Fleury, Cgy-Col	34
Steve Yzerman, Det	33

Even Strength Points

Player, Team	Points
Jaromir Jagr, Pit	**82**
Mats Sundin, Tor	67
John LeClair, Phi	65
Eric Lindros, Phi	65
Theo Fleury, Cgy-Col	63
Pavol Demitra, StL	60
Joe Sakic, Col	56
Paul Kariya, Anh	55
Martin Straka, Pit	55
Steve Thomas, Tor	55

Clutch Goals

Player, Team	Goals
Tony Amonte, Chi	**9**
Paul Kariya, Anh	8
Pavol Demitra, StL	6
Peter Forsberg, Col	6
Adam Graves, NYR	6
Luc Robitaille, LA	6
12 tied with	5

Clutch Assists

Player, Team	Assists
Peter Forsberg, Col	**10**
Jaromir Jagr, Pit	9
Valeri Kamensky, Col	9
Mike Modano, Dal	8
12 tied with	7

Clutch Points

Player, Team	Points
Peter Forsberg, Col	**16**
Paul Kariya, Anh	15
Jaromir Jagr, Pit	14
Tony Amonte, Chi	12
Mats Sundin, Tor	12
Theo Fleury, Cgy-Col	11
John MacLean, NYR	11
Mike Modano, Dal	11
Teemu Selanne, Anh	11
4 tied with	10

1998-99 NHL Leader Boards (Skaters)

Game-Winning Goals

Player, Team	Goals
Brett Hull, Dal	**11**
Pavol Demitra, StL	10
Tony Amonte, Chi	8
Bobby Holik, NJ	8
Claude Lemieux, Col	8
Joe Nieuwendyk, Dal	8
Mike Peca, Buf	8
Sergei Samsonov, Bos	8
11 tied with	7

Game-Tying Goals

Player, Team	Goals
Curtis Brown, Buf	**3**
Eric Daze, Chi	**3**
Robert Lang, Pit	**3**
John LeClair, Phi	**3**
Eric Lindros, Phi	**3**
Scott Mellanby, Fla	**3**
18 tied with	2

Overtime Goals

Player, Team	Goals
Adam Graves, NYR	**3**
Jaromir Jagr, Pit	**3**
Bryan Berard, NYI-Tor	2
Kip Miller, Pit	2
Luc Robitaille, LA	2
48 tied with	1

Unassisted Goals

Player, Team	Goals
Paul Kariya, Anh	**8**
Anson Carter, Bos	6
Markus Naslund, Van	6
Magnus Arvedson, Ott	5
Alexei Kovalev, NYR-Pit	5
Zigmund Palffy, NYI	5
5 tied with	4

Empty Net Goals

Player, Team	Goals
Tony Amonte, Chi	**4**
Anson Carter, Bos	**4**
Paul Kariya, Anh	**4**
Vincent Damphousse, Mon-SJ	3
Patrik Elias, NJ	3
Marco Sturm, SJ	3
25 tied with	2

Blowout Goals

Player, Team	Goals
Adam Graves, NYR	**5**
Mike Johnson, Tor	**5**
Peter Bondra, Was	4
17 tied with	3

Goals by Defenseman

Player, Team	Goals
Adrian Aucoin, Van	**23**
Sergei Gonchar, Was	21
Al MacInnis, StL	20
Fredrik Olausson, Anh	16
Eric Desjardins, Phi	15
Nicklas Lidstrom, Det	14
Darryl Sydor, Dal	14
Brian Leetch, NYR	13
Vladimir Malakhov, Mon	13
Chris Pronger, StL	13

Assists by Defenseman

Player, Team	Assists
Ray Bourque, Bos	**47**
Phil Housley, Cgy	43
Nicklas Lidstrom, Det	43
Brian Leetch, NYR	42
Al MacInnis, StL	42
Larry Murphy, Det	42
Sergei Zubov, Dal	41
Fredrik Olausson, Anh	40
Boris Mironov, Edm-Chi	38
Daniel McGillis, Phi	37

Points by Defenseman

Player, Team	Points
Al MacInnis, StL	**62**
Ray Bourque, Bos	57
Nicklas Lidstrom, Det	57
Fredrik Olausson, Anh	56
Brian Leetch, NYR	55
Phil Housley, Cgy	54
Larry Murphy, Det	52
Eric Desjardins, Phi	51
Sergei Zubov, Dal	51
Boris Mironov, Edm-Chi	49

Goals by Rookie

Player, Team	Goals
Mark Parrish, Fla	**24**
Chris Drury, Col	20
Bill Muckalt, Van	16
Marian Hossa, Ott	15
Milan Hejduk, Col	14
Jan Hrdina, Pit	13
Vincent Lecavalier, TB	13
Brendan Morrison, NJ	13
Alexander Korolyuk, SJ	12
Oleg Kvasha, Fla	12

Assists by Rookie

Player, Team	Assists
Milan Hejduk, Col	**34**
Brendan Morrison, NJ	33
Jan Hrdina, Pit	29
Chris Drury, Col	24
Bill Muckalt, Van	20
Tomas Kaberle, Tor	18
Alexander Korolyuk, SJ	18
Mike Watt, NYI	17
Tom Poti, Edm	16
Vadim Sharifijanov, NJ	16

Points by Rookie

Player, Team	Points
Milan Hejduk, Col	**48**
Brendan Morrison, NJ	46
Chris Drury, Col	44
Jan Hrdina, Pit	42
Mark Parrish, Fla	37
Bill Muckalt, Van	36
Marian Hossa, Ott	30
Alexander Korolyuk, SJ	30
Vincent Lecavalier, TB	28
Vadim Sharifijanov, NJ	27

1998-99 NHL Leader Boards (Goaltenders)

Games Played

Player, Team	Games
Martin Brodeur, NJ	**70**
Guy Hebert, Anh	69
Byron Dafoe, Bos	68
Mike Richter, NYR	68
Curtis Joseph, Tor	67
Garth Snow, Van	65
Dominik Hasck, Buf	64
Olaf Kolzig, Was	64
Tommy Salo, NYI-Edm	64
3 tied with	63

Minutes Played

Player, Team	Minutes
Martin Brodeur, NJ	**4239**
Guy Hebert, Anh	4083
Byron Dafoe, Bos	4001
Curtis Joseph, Tor	4001
Mike Richter, NYR	3878
Dominik Hasek, Buf	3817
Tommy Salo, NYI-Edm	3718
John Vanbiesbrouck, Phi	3712
Chris Osgood, Det	3691
Nikolai Khabibulin, Pho	3657

Goals Allowed

Player, Team	Goals
Curtis Joseph, Tor	**171**
Garth Snow, Van	**171**
Mike Richter, NYR	170
Guy Hebert, Anh	165
Martin Brodeur, NJ	162
Tommy Salo, NYI-Edm	159
Jocelyn Thibault, Mon-Chi	159
Olaf Kolzig, Was	154
Sean Burke, Fla	151
Jeff Hackett, Chi-Mon	150

Wins

Player, Team	Wins
Martin Brodeur, NJ	**39**
Ed Belfour, Dal	35
Curtis Joseph, Tor	35
Chris Osgood, Det	34
Byron Dafoe, Bos	32
Nikolai Khabibulin, Pho	32
Patrick Roy, Col	32
Guy Hebert, Anh	31
Dominik Hasek, Buf	30
3 tied with	27

Losses

Player, Team	Losses
Olaf Kolzig, Was	**31**
Garth Snow, Van	**31**
Mike Richter, NYR	30
Jocelyn Thibault, Mon-Chi	30
Guy Hebert, Anh	29
Tommy Salo, NYI-Edm	28
Jeff Hackett, Chi-Mon	26
Chris Osgood, Det	25
Corey Schwab, TB	25
2 tied with	24

Goals Against Average

(minimum 27 games)

Player, Team	Average
Ron Tugnutt, Ott	**1.79**
Dominik Hasek, Buf	1.87
Ed Belfour, Dal	1.99
Byron Dafoe, Bos	1.99
Nikolai Khabibulin, Pho	2.13
John Vanbiesbrouck, Phi	2.18
Steve Shields, SJ	2.22
Arturs Irbe, Car	2.22
Mike Vernon, SJ	2.27
Patrick Roy, Col	2.29

Shots Faced

Player, Team	Shots
Guy Hebert, Anh	**2114**
Curtis Joseph, Tor	1903
Mike Richter, NYR	1898
Dominik Hasek, Buf	1877
Byron Dafoe, Bos	1800
Arturs Irbe, Car	1753
Martin Brodeur, NJ	1728
Garth Snow, Van	1715
Jocelyn Thibault, Mon-Chi	1685
Nikolai Khabibulin, Pho	1681

Saves

Player, Team	Saves
Guy Hebert, Anh	**1949**
Dominik Hasek, Buf	1758
Curtis Joseph, Tor	1732
Mike Richter, NYR	1728
Byron Dafoe, Bos	1667
Arturs Irbe, Car	1618
Martin Brodeur, NJ	1566
Nikolai Khabibulin, Pho	1551
Garth Snow, Van	1544
Patrick Roy, Col	1534

Save Percentage

(minimum 27 games)

Player, Team	Pct
Dominik Hasek, Buf	**.937**
Byron Dafoe, Bos	.926
Ron Tugnutt, Ott	.925
Arturs Irbe, Car	.923
Nikolai Khabibulin, Pho	.923
Guy Hebert, Anh	.922
Steve Shields, SJ	.921
Patrick Roy, Col	.917
Jamie Storr, LA	.916
Ed Belfour, Dal	.915

Shutouts

Player, Team	Shutouts
Byron Dafoe, Bos	**10**
Dominik Hasek, Buf	9
Nikolai Khabibulin, Pho	8
Guy Hebert, Anh	6
Arturs Irbe, Car	6
Garth Snow, Van	6
John Vanbiesbrouck, Phi	6
5 tied with	5

Times Pulled

Player, Team	Pulled
Garth Snow, Van	**13**
Tom Barrasso, Pit	10
Jeff Hackett, Chi-Mon	8
Olaf Kolzig, Was	8
Corey Schwab, TB	7
Jean-Sebastian Aubin, Pit	6
Sean Burke, Fla	6
Mike Richter, NYR	6
6 tied with	5

Penalty Minutes

Player, Team	Minutes
Garth Snow, Van	**34**
Patrick Roy, Col	28
Sean Burke, Fla	27
Ed Belfour, Dal	26
Byron Dafoe, Bos	25
Tom Barrasso, Pit	20
Olaf Kolzig, Was	19
Dominik Hasek, Buf	14
4 tied with	12

1998-99 Streaks/Individual Game Performances

Goal Scoring Streaks

Player, Team	Dates	Strk
M.Satan, Buf	**12/19-01/02**	**8**
T.Selanne, Anh	**02/17-03/05**	**8**
E.Lindros, Phi	01/07-01/21	7
R.Sheppard, Car	11/14-11/25	6
B.Holik, NJ	12/05-12/18	6
K.Miller, Pit	02/07-02/17	6
M.Satan, Buf	02/11-02/21	6
T.Amonte, Chi	03/10-03/21	6
R.Brown, Pit	03/28-04/08	6
14 tied with		5

Hat Tricks

Player, Team	Number
Peter Bondra, Was	**3**
Wendel Clark, TB-Det	**3**
Theo Fleury, Cgy-Col	**3**
Mike Modano, Dal	**3**
Tony Amonte, Chi	2
Sergei Berezin, Tor	2
Pavel Bure, Fla	2
John LeClair, Phi	2
Brendan Shanahan, Det	2
34 tied with	1

Consecutive Wins

Player, Team	Dates	Wins
P.Roy, Col	**01/12-02/07**	**11**
N.Khabibulin, Pho	10/28-11/28	7
J.Hackett, Mon	12/26-01/11	7
P.Skudra, Pit	01/28-02/15	7
7 tied with		6

Consecutive Losses

Player, Team	Dates	Loss
J.Theodore, Mon	**11/11-02/11**	**8**
J.Thibault, Chi	01/30-02/12	7
K.Weekes, Van	03/13-04/07	7
E.Fichaud, Nsh	10/24-01/01	6
F.Potvin, Tor-NYI	11/20-01/30	6
C.Schwab, TB	01/26-02/10	6
14 tied with		5

Point Scoring Streaks

Player, Team	Dates	Strk
E.Lindros, Phi	**01/07-02/18**	**18**
T.Selanne, Anh	02/03-03/10	17
T.Fleury, Cgy-Col	02/08-03/30	15
P.Forsberg, Col	02/14-03/24	15
J.Jagr, Pit	12/26-01/28	13
P.Kariya, Anh	11/06-11/27	11
R.Sheppard, Car	12/18-01/18	11
A.Yashin, Ott	12/28-01/16	11
S.Fedorov, Det	03/19-04/09	11
5 tied with		10

Five-Point Games

Player, Team	Number
Eric Lindros, Phi	**2**
15 tied with	1

Undefeated Streak

Player, Team	Dates	Strk
Vanbiesbrouck, Phi	**12/12-01/13**	**8-0-4**
P.Roy, Col	01/12-02/07	11-0-0
S.Shields, SJ	03/09-04/09	9-0-2
E.Belfour, Dal	12/06-01/06	8-0-3
R.Tugnutt, Ott	12/28-02/03	7-0-4
D.Hasek, Buf	11/25-12/18	8-0-1
D.Hasek, Buf	10/27-11/20	6-0-3
M.Brodeur, NJ	11/28-12/23	6-0-3
J.Aubin, Pit	11/05-03/27	4-0-5
5 tied with		8

Winless Streak

Player, Team	Dates	Strk
Vanbiesbrouck, Phi	**02/18-03/16**	**0-7-4**
B.Ranford, TB	10/31-12/26	0-8-2
C.Schwab, TB	01/26-02/20	0-8-1
K.Weekes, Van	03/03-04/07	0-8-1
J.Hackett, Mon	12/02-12/23	0-4-5
J.Theodore, Mon	11/11-02/11	0-8-0
J.Thibault, Chi	01/28-02/12	0-7-1
19 tied with		7

Points in a Game

Player, Team	Date Opp	Pts
P.Forsberg, Col	**03/03 @Fla**	**6**
16 tied with		5

Shots in a Game

Player, Team	Date Opp	S
P.Kariya, Anh	**11/08 Det**	**12**
J.York, Ott	**01/30 NYI**	**12**
P.Bondra, Was	**03/04 NYR**	**12**
P.Kariya, Anh	**03/10 Van**	**12**
7 tied with		11

Shots Faced in a Game

Player, Team	Date Opp	S-GA
F.Potvin, NYI	**04/12 @NJ**	**57-2**
M.Dunham, Nsh	**10/21 @Det**	**57-5**
T.Vokoun, Nsh	12/23 Det	53-3
M.LeGace, LA	10/21 @Fla	50-1
B.Essensa, Edm	03/01 @Col	50-3
C.Hirsch, Van	11/02 @Edm	49-5
M.Shtalenkov, Edm	12/02 Pho	48-3
S.Shields, SJ	11/06 @Anh	47-2
G.Hebert, Anh	01/18 Pit	47-3
2 tied with		46-2

Shots Faced in a Shutout

Player, Team	Date Opp	S
D.Roussel, Anh	**12/22 @Col**	**45**
N.Khabibulin, Pho	12/12 @Ott	42
J.Hackett, Mon	03/11 @StL	41
G.Snow, Van	04/12 @Cgy	41
M.Brodeur, NJ	01/28 @Bos	40
G.Hebert, Anh	04/11 Pho	40
K.McLean, Fla	04/12 @Ott	39
J.Waite, Pho	11/11 @Dal	38
D.Hasek, Buf	12/23 TB	38
4 tied with		36

1998-99 Miscellaneous

Total Penalties

Player, Team	Penalties
Peter Worrell, Fla	**69**
Paul Laus, Fla	67
Gary Roberts, Car	65
Donald Brashear, Van	63
Denny Lambert, Nsh	62
Jeff Odgers, Col	62
Krzysztof Oliwa, NJ	62
Brad Brown, Mon-Chi	60
Sean Brown, Edm	60
Ronnie Stern, SJ	60

HHT Penalties

Player, Team	Penalties
Drake Berehowsky, Nsh	**25**
Alexei Zhitnik, Buf	23
Igor Ulanov, Mon	22
Jassen Cullimore, TB	20
Igor Larionov, Det	19
Ricard Persson, StL	19
Dimitri Yushkevich, Tor	19
Kevin Haller, Anh	18
Ken Klee, Was	18
Petr Svoboda, Phi-TB	18

Penalty Min. in a Game

Player, Team	Date	Opp	Min
G.Odjick, NYI	**11/07**	**@Mon**	**39**
T.Wright, Pit	12/21	@Tor	34
S.Brown, Edm	02/26	Buf	32
T.Domi, Tor	03/22	Phi	32
M.Lapointe, Det	12/12	@Car	32
M.Ohlund, Van	11/27	@Det	29
7 tied with			27

Times as First Star

Player, Team	Number
Jaromir Jagr, Pit	**16**
Dominik Hasek, Buf	14
Mike Richter, NYR	14
Keith Tkachuk, Pho	14
Curtis Joseph, Tor	12
7 tied with	11

Times as Star

Player, Team	Number
Jaromir Jagr, Pit	**37**
Eric Lindros, Phi	35
Dominik Hasek, Buf	34
Paul Kariya, Anh	27
Joe Sakic, Col	27
Peter Forsberg, Col	26
Curtis Joseph, Tor	26
Theo Fleury, Cgy-Col	25
Arturs Irbe, Car	25
2 tied with	24

Penalty Minutes/Game

(minimum 27 games)

Player, Team	Min/G
Peter Worrell, Fla	**4.2**
Brantt Myhres, SJ	3.9
Mark Visheau, LA	3.8
Krzysztof Oliwa, NJ	3.8
Sean Brown, Edm	3.7
Patrick Cote, Nsh	3.5
Jim Cummins, Pho	3.5
Jeff Odgers, Col	3.5
Rob Ray, Buf	3.4
Ken Belanger, NYI-Bos	3.4

Assists by Goaltender

Player, Team	Assists
Curtis Joseph, Tor	**5**
Martin Brodeur, NJ	4
Sean Burke, Fla	4
Corey Schwab, TB	4
Tom Barrasso, Pit	3
Chris Osgood, Det	3
5 tied with	2

Shots Faced/60 Minutes

(minimum 27 games)

Player, Team	S/60
Mike Dunham, Nsh	**33.7**
Corey Schwab, TB	32.2
Tomas Vokoun, Nsh	32.0
Bill Ranford, TB-Det	31.7
Guy Hebert, Anh	31.1
Stephane Fiset, LA	30.4
Dominik Hasek, Buf	29.5
Garth Snow, Van	29.4
Mike Richter, NYR	29.4
Mark Fitzpatrick, Chi	29.2

Goals Allowed in a Game

Player, Team	Date	Opp	GA
B.Ranford, TB	**11/10**	**NYR**	**10**
G.Snow, Van	02/04	@NYR	8
12 tied with			7

Worst Plus/Minus

Player, Team	+/–
Darcy Tucker, TB	**-34**
Pavel Kubina, TB	-33
Mike Sillinger, Phi-TB	-29
Chris Gratton, Phi-TB	-28
Donald Brashear, Van	-25
Cory Cross, TB	-25
Martin Rucinsky, Mon	-25
Eric Weinrich, Chi-Mon	-25
4 tied with	-24

Fewest Points/Game

(minimum 27 games)

Player, Team	Points/G
Tyler Wright, Pit	**.00**
Trent McCleary, Mon	**.00**
Darren Langdon, NYR	**.00**
Steve Webb, NYI	**.00**
Scott Parker, Col	**.00**
Mark Janssens, Chi	.02
Dan Keczmer, Dal-Nsh	.03
Wade Belak, Col-Cgy	.03
Brantt Myhres, SJ	.03
Steve Staios, Van	.04

Worst Save Percentage

(minimum 27 games)

Player, Team	Pct
Bill Ranford, TB-Det	**.885**
Jamie McLennan, StL	.891
Corey Schwab, TB	.891
Peter Skudra, Pit	.892
Grant Fuhr, StL	.892
Mikhail Shtalenkov, Edm-Pho	.898
Kirk McLean, Fla	.900
Olaf Kolzig, Was	.900
Garth Snow, Van	.900
Tom Barrasso, Pit	.901

Career NHL Leader Boards—1998-99 Active Skaters

Games Played

Player	Games
Wayne Gretzky	**1487**
Larry Murphy	1477
Ray Bourque	1453
Mark Messier	1413
Dale Hunter	1407
Ron Francis	1329
Paul Coffey	1322
Scott Stevens	1275
Craig Ludwig	1256
Guy Carbonneau	1249

Goals

Player	Goals
Wayne Gretzky	**894**
Mark Messier	610
Dino Ciccarelli	608
Steve Yzerman	592
Brett Hull	586
Dave Andreychuk	532
Luc Robitaille	517
Brian Bellows	485
Pat Verbeek	478
Bernie Nicholls	475

Assists

Player	Assists
Wayne Gretzky	**1963**
Paul Coffey	1102
Ray Bourque	1083
Mark Messier	1050
Ron Francis	1037
Steve Yzerman	891
Larry Murphy	880
Adam Oates	837
Doug Gilmour	835
Al MacInnis	775

Points

Player	Points
Wayne Gretzky	**2857**
Mark Messier	1660
Paul Coffey	1487
Ron Francis	1486
Steve Yzerman	1483
Ray Bourque	1468
Doug Gilmour	1232
Bernie Nicholls	1209
Dino Ciccarelli	1200
Larry Murphy	1155

Plus/Minus

Player	+/–
Wayne Gretzky	**518**
Ray Bourque	505
Al MacInnis	307
Paul Coffey	306
Scott Stevens	287
Mark Messier	250
Gary Roberts	230
Sergei Fedorov	221
Petr Svoboda	221
Larry Murphy	202

Power Play Goals

Player	Goals
Dino Ciccarelli	**233**
Dave Andreychuk	220
Brett Hull	214
Wayne Gretzky	204
Brian Bellows	198
Luc Robitaille	187
Pat Verbeek	169
Joe Nieuwendyk	168
Steve Yzerman	165
Ray Bourque	158

Game-Winning Goals

Player	Goals
Wayne Gretzky	**91**
Brett Hull	85
Mark Messier	76
Dino Ciccarelli	73
Stephane Richer	69
Pierre Turgeon	69
Steve Yzerman	69
Joe Nieuwendyk	67
Luc Robitaille	67
2 tied with	63

Points Per Game

(minimum 100 points)

Player	Points/G
Wayne Gretzky	**1.92**
Eric Lindros	1.39
Teemu Selanne	1.33
Jaromir Jagr	1.30
Peter Forsberg	1.28
Steve Yzerman	1.26
Paul Kariya	1.25
Joe Sakic	1.24
Brett Hull	1.21
Mark Messier	1.17

Penalty Minutes

Player	Minutes
Dale Hunter	**3565**
Marty McSorley	3319
Bob Probert	2907
Rick Tocchet	2773
Pat Verbeek	2665
Craig Berube	2651
Dave Manson	2604
Rob Ray	2529
Joey Kocur	2519
Scott Stevens	2504

Shorthanded Goals

Player	Goals
Wayne Gretzky	**73**
Mark Messier	57
Steve Yzerman	47
Guy Carbonneau	31
Russ Courtnall	29
Esa Tikkanen	29
Theo Fleury	28
Bernie Nicholls	28
Dave Reid	28
Joe Sakic	26

Hat Tricks

Player	Number
Wayne Gretzky	**50**
Brett Hull	28
Dino Ciccarelli	19
Mark Messier	19
Bernie Nicholls	18
Steve Yzerman	18
Teemu Selanne	15
Theo Fleury	14
Alexander Mogilny	14
Rick Tocchet	14

Shots

Player	Shots
Ray Bourque	**5730**
Wayne Gretzky	5089
Paul Coffey	4202
Al MacInnis	4155
Steve Yzerman	3869
Brett Hull	3717
Dino Ciccarelli	3706
Mark Messier	3667
Dave Andreychuk	3625
Brian Bellows	3588

Career NHL Leader Boards—1998-99 Active Goaltenders

Games Played

Player	Games
Grant Fuhr	**845**
John Vanbiesbrouck	779
Patrick Roy	778
Tom Barrasso	708
Mike Vernon	673
Bill Ranford	631
Ron Hextall	608
Kirk McLean	567
Ed Belfour	550
Ken Wregget	546

Minutes Played

Player	Minutes
Grant Fuhr	**47,740**
Patrick Roy	45,404
John Vanbiesbrouck	44,595
Tom Barrasso	40,472
Mike Vernon	38,587
Bill Ranford	35,151
Ron Hextall	34,750
Kirk McLean	32,664
Ed Belfour	31,553
Curtis Joseph	30,156

Goals Against Average

(minimum 100 games)

Player	Average
Martin Brodeur	**2.19**
Dominik Hasek	2.26
Chris Osgood	2.35
Ed Belfour	2.51
Damian Rhodes	2.58
Jim Carey	2.58
Olaf Kolzig	2.58
Patrick Roy	2.66
Byron Dafoe	2.68
Trevor Kidd	2.69

Wins

Player	Wins
Patrick Roy	**412**
Grant Fuhr	398
Mike Vernon	347
Tom Barrasso	345
John Vanbiesbrouck	333
Ron Hextall	296
Ed Belfour	276
Curtis Joseph	248
Bill Ranford	236
2 tied with	230

Losses

Player	Losses
John Vanbiesbrouck	**303**
Grant Fuhr	282
Bill Ranford	273
Tom Barrasso	248
Kirk McLean	244
Patrick Roy	243
Ken Wregget	238
Sean Burke	233
Mike Vernon	223
Ron Hextall	214

Winning Percentage

(minimum 100 games)

Player	Pct
Chris Osgood	**.661**
Martin Brodeur	.632
Patrick Roy	.613
Ed Belfour	.597
Mike Vernon	.595
Grant Fuhr	.573
Tom Barrasso	.572
Ron Hextall	.571
Dominik Hasek	.571
Mike Richter	.561

Shots Faced

(since 1982-83)

Player	Shots
Grant Fuhr	**22,311**
John Vanbiesbrouck	22,148
Patrick Roy	21,848
Tom Barrasso	20,394
Bill Ranford	17,862
Mike Vernon	17,178
Ron Hextall	16,366
Ken Wregget	15,975
Kirk McLean	15,684
Curtis Joseph	15,677

Goals Allowed

Player	Goals
Grant Fuhr	**2679**
John Vanbiesbrouck	2259
Tom Barrasso	2208
Patrick Roy	2014
Bill Ranford	1995
Mike Vernon	1932
Ken Wregget	1847
Kirk McLean	1775
Ron Hextall	1723
Sean Burke	1598

Save Percentage

(minimum 100 games)

Player	Pct
Dominik Hasek	**.926**
Martin Brodeur	.913
Guy Hebert	.911
Chris Osgood	.909
Byron Dafoe	.908
Nikolai Khabibulin	.908
Patrick Roy	.908
Felix Potvin	.907
Curtis Joseph	.906
Jocelyn Thibault	.905

Shutouts

Player	Shutouts
Patrick Roy	**46**
Ed Belfour	45
Dominik Hasek	42
Martin Brodeur	36
John Vanbiesbrouck	35
Tom Barrasso	34
Grant Fuhr	25
Ron Hextall	23
Chris Osgood	23
5 tied with	22

Assists

Player	Assists
Tom Barrasso	**48**
Grant Fuhr	46
Patrick Roy	34
John Vanbiesbrouck	34
Ron Hextall	32
Mike Vernon	32
Curtis Joseph	27
Bill Ranford	24
Ken Wregget	23
2 tied with	22

Penalty Minutes

Player	Minutes
Ron Hextall	**584**
Tom Barrasso	427
Ed Belfour	292
John Vanbiesbrouck	292
Mike Vernon	253
Sean Burke	242
Patrick Roy	196
Ken Wregget	182
Grant Fuhr	118
Garth Snow	106

Game Stars

This section lists all 578 players who earned star mention during the 1998-99 regular season and the 123 who were named as stars during the postseason. In all cases, the players listed here were the stars chosen at the game, as reported to the league office.

The points are weighted on a 5-3-1 basis—a No. 1 Star earns five points, a No. 2 Star three, and a No. 3 Star one. As in the team statistics, an asterisk (*) indicates a rookie.

In two regular-season games last year, no No. 2 or No. 3 Star was selected. The Rangers' Wayne Gretzky was honored in his last two NHL games—April 15 at Ottawa and April 18 at home vs. Pittsburgh—as the only star of each contest. The slight modifications to league tradition hardly seemed inappropriate for The Great One.

NHL Stars Summary

	Player, Team	1st	2nd	3rd	Points
1.	Jaromir Jagr, Pit	16	12	9	125
2.	Dominik Hasek, Buf	14	15	5	120
3.	Eric Lindros, Phi	10	12	13	99
4.	Curtis Joseph, Tor	12	10	4	94
5.	Mike Richter, NYR	14	5	5	90
6.	Alexei Yashin, Ott	11	8	5	84
7.	Joe Sakic, Col	9	10	8	83
8.	Keith Tkachuk, Pho	14	3	3	82
9.	Luc Robitaille, LA	10	9	4	81
10.	Guy Hebert, Anh	11	7	4	80
11.	Peter Forsberg, Col	9	8	9	78
12.	Pavol Demitra, StL	11	6	4	77
	Mike Modano, Dal	11	5	7	77
14.	Byron Dafoe, Bos	11	4	8	75
	Theo Fleury, Cgy-Col	10	5	10	75
16.	Ron Tugnutt, Ott	9	8	4	73
	Paul Kariya, Anh	7	9	11	73
	Arturs Irbe, Car	6	12	7	73
19.	Steve Yzerman, Det	9	8	3	72
	Teemu Selanne, Anh	8	9	5	72
21.	Jeff Hackett, Chi-Mon	11	4	4	71
22.	Jocelyn Thibault, Mon-Chi	10	4	5	67
23.	Garth Snow, Van	11	3	2	66
24.	Keith Primeau, Car	7	8	6	65
25.	Nikolai Khabibulin, Pho	9	5	4	64
	Mats Sundin, Tor	9	5	4	64
27.	Sean Burke, Fla	9	4	6	63
28.	Patrick Roy, Col	10	2	3	59
29.	Joe Nieuwendyk, Dal	9	2	6	57
	Mike Dunham, Nsh	6	8	3	57
	Al MacInnis, StL	6	7	6	57
32.	Rod Brind'Amour, Phi	8	4	4	56
	Martin Straka, Pit	6	6	8	56
34.	John LeClair, Phi	8	3	6	55
35.	Sergei Fedorov, Det	8	4	2	54
	Petr Sykora, NJ	7	4	7	54
37.	Miroslav Satan, Buf	5	7	7	53
38.	Mike Peca, Buf	4	9	5	52
39.	Tommy Salo, NYI-Edm	6	6	2	50
40.	Wayne Gretzky, NYR	7	3	4	48
	Robert Reichel, NYI-Pho	6	5	3	48
42.	Jeremy Roenick, Pho	4	8	3	47
43.	Ray Whitney, Fla	7	2	5	46
	Chris Osgood, Det	6	5	1	46
	Chris Pronger, StL	5	6	3	46
	Ray Bourque, Bos	5	5	6	46
	Owen Nolan, SJ	4	7	5	46
	Cliff Ronning, Pho-Nsh	3	9	4	46
49.	Brett Hull, Dal	7	3	1	45
	Fred Brathwaite, Cgy	6	4	3	45
51.	Olaf Kolzig, Was	5	6	1	44
52.	Bobby Holik, NJ	8	1	0	43
	Tomas Vokoun, Nsh	6	3	4	43
	Damian Rhodes, Ott	5	5	3	43
	Martin Brodeur, NJ	2	9	6	43
56.	Markus Naslund, Van	6	3	3	42
	Mark Recchi, Mon-Phi	6	3	3	42
	John Vanbiesbrouck, Phi	6	3	3	42
	Tony Amonte, Chi	6	2	6	42
	Stephane Fiset, LA	6	2	6	42
	Bill Guerin, Edm	5	5	2	42
62.	Steve Shields, SJ	5	5	1	41
	Scott Niedermayer, NJ	5	4	4	41
	Mike Vernon, SJ	5	3	7	41
65.	Jason Allison, Bos	5	4	3	40
	Peter Bondra, Was	4	5	5	40
67.	Tom Barrasso, Pit	5	4	2	39
68.	Bob Essensa, Edm	4	6	0	38
69.	Sergei Samsonov, Bos	5	3	3	37
	Alexei Kovalev, NYR-Pit	4	5	2	37
71.	Adam Graves, NYR	5	3	2	36
	Sergei Krivokrasov, Nsh	5	3	2	36
	Greg Adams, Pho	4	5	1	36
	Boris Mironov, Edm-Chi	4	4	4	36
	Magnus Arvedson, Ott	3	7	0	36
	* Alexander Korolyuk, SJ	3	7	0	36
77.	Brendan Shanahan, Det	5	3	1	35
	Igor Larionov, Det	3	6	2	35
	Zigmund Palffy, NYI	3	6	2	35
80.	Dixon Ward, Buf	5	3	0	34
	* Mark Parrish, Fla	5	2	3	34
	Doug Gilmour, Chi	3	5	4	34
83.	Brian Rolston, NJ	5	2	2	33
	Sami Kapanen, Car	4	4	1	33
	Patrick Marleau, SJ	4	4	1	33
86.	Ron Francis, Car	5	2	1	32
	Jason Arnott, NJ	4	3	3	32
	Sergei Berezin, Tor	4	3	3	32
	Wendel Clark, TB-Det	3	5	2	32
	Ray Sheppard, Car	3	5	2	32
	Ed Belfour, Dal	2	5	7	32
92.	Petr Nedved, NYR	4	3	2	31
	Cory Stillman, Cgy	4	3	2	31
	Jeff Friesen, SJ	3	4	4	31
	Mikhail Shtalenkov, Edm-Pho	3	4	4	31
96.	Rick Tocchet, Pho	5	1	2	30
	Dave Andreychuk, NJ	4	3	1	30
	Vladimir Malakhov, Mon	4	3	1	30
	Roman Turek, Dal	4	3	1	30
	Alexei Zhamnov, Chi	4	2	4	30
	Claude Lemieux, Col	3	3	6	30
	Rob Blake, LA	1	8	1	30
103.	Sebastien Bordeleau, Nsh	5	1	1	29
	Mattias Ohlund, Van	5	1	1	29

	Player, Team	1st	2nd	3rd	Points
	Steve Rucchin, Anh	4	3	0	29
	Chris Chelios, Chi-Det	3	3	5	29
	John MacLean, NYR	2	5	4	29
108.	Marco Sturm, SJ	5	1	0	28
	Gary Roberts, Car	4	1	5	28
	Glen Murray, LA	3	4	1	28
	Steve Thomas, Tor	3	4	1	28
	Dimitri Khristich, Bos	3	3	4	28
	Pierre Turgeon, StL	3	3	4	28
	Mark Messier, Van	2	5	3	28
115.	Anson Carter, Bos	5	0	2	27
	Andrei Kovalenko, Edm-Phi-Car	5	0	2	27
	Craig Conroy, StL	3	4	0	27
	Vincent Damphousse, Mon-SJ	3	3	3	27
	Grant Fuhr, StL	3	3	3	27
	Joe Murphy, SJ	3	3	3	27
	Scott Walker, Nsh	3	3	3	27
	Sergei Zubov, Dal	2	5	2	27
	Eric Desjardins, Phi	2	3	8	27
	Shawn McEachern, Ott	1	6	4	27
125.	Ken Wregget, Cgy	5	0	1	26
	Mariusz Czerkawski, NYI	4	1	3	26
	Jamie McLennan, StL	3	3	2	26
	Derian Hatcher, Dal	2	5	1	26
	Keith Jones, Col-Phi	2	5	1	26
	Steve Sullivan, Tor	2	4	4	26
	Nicklas Lidstrom, Det	2	3	7	26
132.	Jay Pandolfo, NJ	4	1	2	25
	Adam Deadmarsh, Col	3	3	1	25
	Bill Ranford, TB-Det	3	2	4	25
	Alyn McCauley, Tor	2	5	0	25
	Jarome Iginla, Cgy	2	4	3	25
	Saku Koivu, Mon	2	4	3	25
	Trevor Linden, NYI	2	4	3	25
	Brian Leetch, NYR	0	7	4	25
140.	Steve Konowalchuk, Was	4	1	1	24
	Randy McKay, NJ	3	2	3	24
	Vaclav Prospal, Ott	3	2	3	24
	Joe Thornton, Bos	3	2	3	24
	German Titov, Pit	3	2	3	24
	Radek Bonk, Ott	2	4	2	24
	* Jamie Storr, LA	2	4	2	24
	Darryl Sydor, Dal	2	4	2	24
	Larry Murphy, Det	1	6	1	24
149.	Slava Kozlov, Det	3	2	2	23
	Sergei Gonchar, Was	3	1	5	23
	Stu Barnes, Pit-Buf	2	4	1	23
152.	Donald Audette, LA	4	0	2	22
	Josef Beranek, Edm	4	0	2	22
	Valeri Kamensky, Col	4	0	2	22
	Rick Tabaracci, Was	3	2	1	22
	Jason Woolley, Buf	3	2	1	22
	Joe Juneau, Was-Buf	2	3	3	22
	Robert Lang, Pit	1	5	2	22
159.	Janne Niinimaa, Edm	4	0	1	21

	Player, Team	1st	2nd	3rd	Points
	Eric Daze, Chi	3	2	0	21
	Ray Ferraro, LA	3	2	0	21
	Jamie Langenbrunner, Dal	2	3	2	21
	Mike Ricci, SJ	2	2	5	21
164.	Andreas Johansson, Ott	3	1	2	20
	* Jean-Sebastian Aubin, Pit	2	3	1	20
	Craig Billington, Col	2	3	1	20
	Rene Corbet, Col-Cgy	2	3	1	20
	Todd Harvey, NYR	2	3	1	20
	Kyle McLaren, Bos	2	2	4	20
	Viktor Kozlov, Fla	1	5	0	20
	Adam Oates, Was	1	4	3	20
	Greg Johnson, Nsh	1	3	6	20
	Adam Foote, Col	0	5	5	20
174.	Pat Verbeek, Dal	3	1	1	19
	Corey Schwab, TB	3	0	4	19
	* Brendan Morrison, NJ	2	3	0	19
	Andrew Cassels, Cgy	2	2	3	19
	Claude Lapointe, NYI	2	2	3	19
	Scott Mellanby, Fla	2	2	3	19
	Ryan Smyth, Edm	2	2	3	19
	Glen Wesley, Car	1	4	2	19
182.	Mike Johnson, Tor	3	0	3	18
	Darren McCarty, Det	3	0	3	18
	Marty McInnis, Cgy-Anh	3	0	3	18
	Bill Houlder, SJ	2	2	2	18
	Trevor Kidd, Car	2	2	2	18
	Todd Marchant, Edm	2	2	2	18
	Derek Morris, Cgy	2	2	2	18
	Darcy Tucker, TB	2	2	2	18
	Scott Young, StL	2	2	2	18
	* Marian Hossa, Ott	2	0	8	18
	Chris Gratton, Phi-TB	1	3	4	18
	Derek King, Tor	1	3	4	18
194.	Valeri Bure, Cgy	3	0	2	17
	Benoit Brunet, Mon	2	2	1	17
	Pavel Bure, Fla	2	2	1	17
	* Dan Cloutier, NYR	2	2	1	17
	Dallas Drake, Pho	2	2	1	17
	Radek Dvorak, Fla	2	2	1	17
	Igor Korolev, Tor	2	2	1	17
	Yanic Perreault, LA-Tor	2	2	1	17
	Stephane Quintal, Mon	2	2	1	17
	* Peter Skudra, Pit	2	2	1	17
	Chris Terreri, NJ	2	2	1	17
	Kevin Stevens, NYR	2	1	4	17
	Curtis Brown, Buf	2	0	7	17
	Hal Gill, Bos	1	4	0	17
	Mike Keane, Dal	1	4	0	17
	Steve Heinze, Bos	1	3	3	17
	Mikael Renberg, TB-Phi	1	3	3	17
211.	Blair Atcheynum, Nsh-StL	3	0	1	16
	Boyd Devereaux, Edm	2	2	0	16
	Daren Puppa, TB	2	2	0	16
	Bryan Smolinski, NYI	2	2	0	16

	Player, Team	1st	2nd	3rd	Points
	Robbie Tallas, Bos	2	2	0	16
	* Mike Watt, NYI	2	2	0	16
	* Chris Drury, Col	2	1	3	16
	Mark Fitzpatrick, Chi	2	1	3	16
	Dwayne Roloson, Buf	2	1	3	16
	Daniel McGillis, Phi	1	3	2	16
	* Tyler Moss, Cgy	1	3	2	16
	Rob Niedermayer, Fla	1	3	2	16
	Teppo Numminen, Pho	1	3	2	16
	Jozef Stumpel, LA	1	3	2	16
	Phil Housley, Cgy	1	2	5	16
226.	Jeff O'Neill, Car	3	0	0	15
	Michel Picard, StL	3	0	0	15
	Brian Bellows, Was	2	1	2	15
	* Oleg Kvasha, Fla	2	1	2	15
	Geoff Sanderson, Buf	2	0	5	15
	Shayne Corson, Mon	1	3	1	15
	Matt Cullen, Anh	1	3	1	15
	Jere Lehtinen, Dal	1	3	1	15
	Andrei Nikolishin, Was	1	3	1	15
	Fredrik Olausson, Anh	1	3	1	15
	Stephane Richer, TB	1	3	1	15
237.	Patrick Poulin, Mon	1	3	0	14
	* Jose Theodore, Mon	1	3	0	14
	Bryan Berard, NYI-Tor	1	2	3	14
	Keith Carney, Pho	1	2	3	14
	Andreas Dackell, Ott	1	2	3	14
	Michal Grosek, Buf	1	2	3	14
	Kip Miller, Pit	1	2	3	14
	Bob Corkum, Pho	0	3	5	14
245.	Bates Battaglia, Car	2	1	0	13
	Todd Bertuzzi, Van	2	1	0	13
	Jan Bulis, Was	2	1	0	13
	Dino Ciccarelli, Fla	2	1	0	13
	Patrik Elias, NJ	2	0	3	13
	* Jean-Sebastian Giguere, Cgy	2	0	3	13
	Mike Grier, Edm	2	0	3	13
	Benoit Hogue, TB-Dal	2	0	3	13
	Ron Hextall, Phi	1	2	2	13
	Brian Holzinger, Buf	1	2	2	13
	Robert Kron, Car	1	2	2	13
	Fredrik Modin, Tor	1	2	2	13
	Dave Scatchard, Van	1	2	2	13
	Mathieu Schneider, NYR	1	2	2	13
	Scott Stevens, NJ	1	2	2	13
	Doug Weight, Edm	1	2	2	13
	Eric Weinrich, Chi-Mon	1	2	2	13
	Chad Kilger, Chi-Edm	0	4	1	13
	Daymond Langkow, TB-Phi	0	4	1	13
	Kent Manderville, Car	0	4	1	13
	Adrian Aucoin, Van	0	3	4	13
266.	Tony Hrkac, Dal	2	0	2	12
	Michael Knuble, NYR	1	2	1	12
	Aaron Miller, Col	1	2	1	12
	Rem Murray, Edm	1	2	1	12

	Player, Team	1st	2nd	3rd	Points
	Alexander Selivanov, TB-Edm	1	2	1	12
	* Vadim Sharifijanov, NJ	1	2	1	12
	Kevin Hatcher, Pit	1	1	4	12
	Juha Ylonen, Pho	1	1	4	12
	Rob DiMaio, Bos	0	4	0	12
	Calle Johansson, Was	0	3	3	12
	Dimitri Yushkevich, Tor	0	3	3	12
	Alexander Mogilny, Van	0	2	6	12
278.	* Jean-Pierre Dumont, Chi	2	0	1	11
	Mark Lawrence, NYI	2	0	1	11
	Dominic Roussel, Anh	2	0	1	11
	Tomas Sandstrom, Anh	2	0	1	11
	Ronnie Stern, SJ	2	0	1	11
	Turner Stevenson, Mon	2	0	1	11
	Colin Forbes, Phi-TB	1	2	0	11
	Martin Gelinas, Car	1	2	0	11
	Scott Pellerin, StL	1	2	0	11
	Darryl Shannon, Buf	1	2	0	11
	* Pavel Kubina, TB	1	1	3	11
	Kirk McLean, Fla	1	1	3	11
	Joe Reekie, Was	1	1	3	11
	Niklas Sundstrom, NYR	1	1	3	11
	Daniel Alfredsson, Ott	0	3	2	11
	* Vincent Lecavalier, TB	0	3	2	11
	Bill Lindsay, Fla	0	3	2	11
	Martin Rucinsky, Mon	0	3	2	11
	Corey Hirsch, Van	0	2	5	11
297.	* Martin Biron, Buf	2	0	0	10
	Tony Granato, SJ	2	0	0	10
	Felix Potvin, Tor-NYI	2	0	0	10
	* Sami Salo, Ott	2	0	0	10
	Rob Zamuner, TB	2	0	0	10
	James Black, Was	1	1	2	10
	Sergei Brylin, NJ	1	1	2	10
	* Milan Hejduk, Col	1	1	2	10
	* Manny LeGace, LA	1	1	2	10
	* Tom Poti, Edm	1	1	2	10
	Brian Savage, Mon	1	1	2	10
	Wade Redden, Ott	0	2	4	10
	Jason York, Ott	0	2	4	10
310.	* Johan Davidsson, Anh	1	1	1	9
	Shane Doan, Pho	1	1	1	9
	Tomas Holmstrom, Det	1	1	1	9
	* Norm Maracle, Det	1	1	1	9
	Sandis Ozolinsh, Col	1	1	1	9
	Don Sweeney, Bos	1	1	1	9
	Oleg Tverdovsky, Pho	1	1	1	9
	Jimmy Waite, Pho	1	1	1	9
	* Peter Worrell, Fla	1	1	1	9
	Alexei Zhitnik, Buf	1	1	1	9
	Mattias Norstrom, LA	1	0	4	9
	Valeri Zelepukin, Phi	1	0	4	9
	Brad Isbister, Pho	0	3	0	9
	* Clarke Wilm, Cgy	0	3	0	9
	Ed Jovanovski, Fla-Van	0	2	3	9

	Player, Team	1st	2nd	3rd	Points
	Grant Marshall, Dal	0	2	3	9
	Ruslan Salei, Anh	0	0	9	9
327.	Kelly Chase, StL	1	1	0	8
	Bruce Gardiner, Ott	1	1	0	8
	Johan Garpenlov, Fla	1	1	0	8
	Glenn Healy, Tor	1	1	0	8
	Kenny Jonsson, NYI	1	1	0	8
	Richard Matvichuk, Dal	1	1	0	8
	Chris Phillips, Ott	1	1	0	8
	Andrei Trefilov, Chi-Cgy	1	1	0	8
	* Robert Valicevic, Nsh	1	1	0	8
	Todd Warriner, Tor	1	1	0	8
	Jason Wiemer, Cgy	1	1	0	8
	Vitali Yachmenev, Nsh	1	1	0	8
	Peter Zezel, Van	1	1	0	8
	Guy Carbonneau, Dal	1	0	3	8
	* Olli Jokinen, LA	1	0	3	8
	* Bill Muckalt, Van	1	0	3	8
	Pat Falloon, Edm	0	2	2	8
	Denis Pederson, NJ	0	2	2	8
	Robert Svehla, Fla	0	2	2	8
	Terry Yake, StL	0	1	5	8
347.	Shawn Chambers, Dal	1	0	2	7
	Kevin Dineen, Car	1	0	2	7
	Jeff Nielsen, Anh	1	0	2	7
	* Steve Passmore, Edm	1	0	2	7
	Rich Pilon, NYI	1	0	2	7
	Paul Ranheim, Car	1	0	2	7
	Andrew Brunette, Nsh	0	2	1	7
	Tom Fitzgerald, Nsh	0	2	1	7
	Jyrki Lumme, Pho	0	2	1	7
	Ed Olczyk, Chi	0	2	1	7
	Jeff Shantz, Chi-Cgy	0	2	1	7
	Doug Brown, Det	0	1	4	7
	Roman Hamrlik, Edm	0	1	4	7
360.	* Daniel Briere, Pho	1	0	1	6
	* Brad Brown, Mon-Chi	1	0	1	6
	Frederic Chabot, Mon	1	0	1	6
	* Mike Crowley, Anh	1	0	1	6
	Mike Eagles, Was	1	0	1	6
	* Jan Hrdina, Pit	1	0	1	6
	* Tomas Kaberle, Tor	1	0	1	6
	Patrik Kjellberg, Nsh	1	0	1	6
	Ian Laperriere, LA	1	0	1	6
	* Daniil Markov, Tor	1	0	1	6
	Dmitri Mironov, Was	1	0	1	6
	Lyle Odelein, NJ	1	0	1	6
	Vladimir Tsyplakov, LA	1	0	1	6
	Stephane Yelle, Col	1	0	1	6
	Bob Boughner, Nsh	0	2	0	6
	Peter Ferraro, Bos	0	2	0	6
	* Benoit Gratton, Was	0	2	0	6
	Jonas Hoglund, Mon	0	2	0	6
	Mats Lindgren, Edm-NYI	0	2	0	6
	Dave Lowry, SJ	0	2	0	6

	Player, Team	1st	2nd	3rd	Points
	Dean McAmmond, Edm-Chi	0	2	0	6
	* Peter Schaefer, Van	0	2	0	6
	Jiri Slegr, Pit	0	2	0	6
	Jason Smith, Tor-Edm	0	2	0	6
	Scott Thornton, Mon	0	2	0	6
	Wade Flaherty, NYI	0	1	3	6
	Travis Green, Anh	0	1	3	6
	Alexei Morozov, Pit	0	1	3	6
	Marcus Ragnarsson, SJ	0	1	3	6
	Brad Werenka, Pit	0	1	3	6
390.	Tommy Albelin, Cgy	1	0	0	5
	* Shawn Bates, Bos	1	0	0	5
	Ken Baumgartner, Bos	1	0	0	5
	Philippe Boucher, LA	1	0	0	5
	Marc Bureau, Phi	1	0	0	5
	Geoff Courtnall, StL	1	0	0	5
	Randy Cunneyworth, Buf	1	0	0	5
	Tie Domi, Tor	1	0	0	5
	* Maxim Galanov, Pit	1	0	0	5
	Stu Grimson, Anh	1	0	0	5
	* Sergey Gusev, Dal-TB	1	0	0	5
	Bret Hedican, Van-Fla	1	0	0	5
	Jody Hull, Phi	1	0	0	5
	Joey Kocur, Det	1	0	0	5
	Paul Laus, Fla	1	0	0	5
	* Cameron Mann, Bos	1	0	0	5
	Steve Martins, Ott	1	0	0	5
	Kelly Miller, Was	1	0	0	5
	Kirk Muller, Fla	1	0	0	5
	* Marcus Nilson, Fla	1	0	0	5
	Krzysztof Oliwa, NJ	1	0	0	5
	* Rich Parent, StL	1	0	0	5
	Derek Plante, Buf-Dal	1	0	0	5
	Nolan Pratt, Car	1	0	0	5
	Reid Simpson, Chi	1	0	0	5
	Ron Sutter, SJ	1	0	0	5
	Tim Taylor, Bos	1	0	0	5
	* Derek Wilkinson, TB	1	0	0	5
	Harry York, NYR-Pit-Van	1	0	0	5
	Sylvain Cote, Tor	0	1	2	5
	Kirk Maltby, Det	0	1	2	5
	Dave Manson, Mon-Chi	0	1	2	5
	Bryan McCabe, Van	0	1	2	5
	* Pavel Rosa, LA	0	1	2	5
	Kjell Samuelsson, TB	0	1	2	5
	Marc Savard, NYR	0	1	2	5
426.	* Lubos Bartecko, StL	0	1	1	4
	Joel Bouchard, Nsh	0	1	1	4
	Murray Craven, SJ	0	1	1	4
	Steve Duchesne, LA-Phi	0	1	1	4
	Dave Gagner, Fla-Van	0	1	1	4
	Todd Gill, StL-Det	0	1	1	4
	Mark Greig, Phi	0	1	1	4
	* Michal Handzus, StL	0	1	1	4
	Alexander Karpovtsev, NYR-Tor	0	1	1	4

Rank	Player, Team	1st	2nd	3rd	Points
	Kris King, Tor	0	1	1	4
	Ken Klee, Was	0	1	1	4
	Igor Kravchuk, Ott	0	1	1	4
	Paul Kruse, Buf	0	1	1	4
	Janne Laukkanen, Ott	0	1	1	4
	* Manny Malhotra, NYR	0	1	1	4
	* Mike Maneluk, Phi-Chi-NYR	0	1	1	4
	Andrei Nazarov, TB-Cgy	0	1	1	4
	Sergei Nemchinov, NYI-NJ	0	1	1	4
	Todd Simpson, Cgy	0	1	1	4
	* Pascal Trepanier, Anh	0	1	1	4
	Darren Van Impe, Bos	0	1	1	4
	Dainius Zubrus, Phi-Mon	0	1	1	4
	Alexandre Daigle, Phi-TB	0	0	4	4
	Mathieu Dandenault, Det	0	0	4	4
	Kevin Haller, Anh	0	0	4	4
451.	* Antti Aalto, Anh	0	1	0	3
	Dave Babych, Phi-LA	0	1	0	3
	Brad Bombardir, NJ	0	1	0	3
	* Dan Boyle, Fla	0	1	0	3
	Patrice Brisebois, Mon	0	1	0	3
	Kevin Brown, Edm	0	1	0	3
	Brandon Convery, Van-LA	0	1	0	3
	* Marcel Cousineau, NYI	0	1	0	3
	Jassen Cullimore, TB	0	1	0	3
	Ted Drury, Anh	0	1	0	3
	Brent Fedyk, NYR	0	1	0	3
	Eric Fichaud, Nsh	0	1	0	3
	Steve Guolla, SJ	0	1	0	3
	* Steve Halko, Car	0	1	0	3
	* Matt Herr, Was	0	1	0	3
	Jamie Heward, Nsh	0	1	0	3
	* Josh Holden, Van	0	1	0	3
	Cale Hulse, Cgy	0	1	0	3
	Craig Janney, TB-NYI	0	1	0	3
	Dan Kesa, Pit	0	1	0	3
	Nathan LaFayette, LA	0	1	0	3
	Darren Langdon, NYR	0	1	0	3
	Martin Lapointe, Det	0	1	0	3
	Sandy McCarthy, TB-Phi	0	1	0	3
	Eric Messier, Col	0	1	0	3
	Gord Murphy, Fla	0	1	0	3
	* Dmitri Nabokov, NYI	0	1	0	3
	* Rumun Ndur, Buf-NYR	0	1	0	3
	Jeff Norton, Fla-SJ	0	1	0	3
	Ville Peltonen, Nsh	0	1	0	3
	Robert Petrovicky, TB	0	1	0	3
	* Marty Reasoner, StL	0	1	0	3
	Pascal Rheaume, StL	0	1	0	3
	Brent Severyn, Dal	0	1	0	3
	Mike Sillinger, Phi-TB	0	1	0	3
	Steve Smith, Cgy	0	1	0	3
	David Wilkie, TB	0	1	0	3
	Richard Zednik, Was	0	1	0	3
	Ken Daneyko, NJ	0	0	3	3
	Mike Eastwood, StL	0	0	3	3
	Nelson Emerson, Car-Chi-Ott	0	0	3	3
	Sean Hill, Car	0	0	3	3
	Bryan Marchment, SJ	0	0	3	3
	Barry Richter, NYI	0	0	3	3
	Mark Tinordi, Was	0	0	3	3
496.	Per Axelsson, Bos	0	0	2	2
	Bob Bassen, Cgy	0	0	2	2
	* Eric Brewer, NYI	0	0	2	2
	Kelly Buchberger, Edm	0	0	2	2
	* Zdeno Chara, NYI	0	0	2	2
	Steve Chiasson, Car	0	0	2	2
	Cory Cross, TB	0	0	2	2
	Kris Draper, Det	0	0	2	2
	Dale Hunter, Was-Col	0	0	2	2
	Jean-Yves Leroux, Chi	0	0	2	2
	Craig Ludwig, Dal	0	0	2	2
	Ian Moran, Pit	0	0	2	2
	Ethan Moreau, Chi-Edm	0	0	2	2
	Deron Quint, Pho	0	0	2	2
	Mike Rathje, SJ	0	0	2	2
	Joe Sacco, NYI	0	0	2	2
	Ulf Samuelsson, NYR-Det	0	0	2	2
	John Slaney, Nsh	0	0	2	2
	Mike Stapleton, Pho	0	0	2	2
	Petr Svoboda, Phi-TB	0	0	2	2
	Garry Valk, Tor	0	0	2	2
	Vaclav Varada, Buf	0	0	2	2
	* Kevin Weekes, Van	0	0	2	2
	Brendan Witt, Was	0	0	2	2
520.	Mikael Andersson, TB-Phi	0	0	1	1
	Matthew Barnaby, Buf-Pit	0	0	1	1
	Murray Baron, Van	0	0	1	1
	Drake Berehowsky, Nsh	0	0	1	1
	* Jason Blake, LA	0	0	1	1
	Rob Brown, Pit	0	0	1	1
	Terry Carkner, Fla	0	0	1	1
	Russ Courtnall, LA	0	0	1	1
	Jason Dawe, NYI-Mon	0	0	1	1
	Kevin Dean, NJ	0	0	1	1
	Greg DeVries, Nsh-Col	0	0	1	1
	Gerald Diduck, Pho	0	0	1	1
	Hnat Domenichelli, Cgy	0	0	1	1
	Ted Donato, Bos-NYI-Ott	0	0	1	1
	Karl Dykhuis, TB-Phi	0	0	1	1
	Anders Eriksson, Det-Chi	0	0	1	1
	Manny Fernandez, Dal	0	0	1	1
	* Denis Gauthier, Cgy	0	0	1	1
	Brent Gilchrist, Det	0	0	1	1
	Alexel Gusarov, Col	0	0	1	1
	Darby Hendrickson, Tor-Van	0	0	1	1
	* Brent Johnson, StL	0	0	1	1
	Matt Johnson, LA	0	0	1	1
	* Ryan Johnson, Fla	0	0	1	1
	Darius Kasparaitis, Pit	0	0	1	1

Player, Team	1st	2nd	3rd	Points
Dan Keczmer, Dal-Nsh	0	0	1	1
Trent Klatt, Phi-Van	0	0	1	1
Uwe Krupp, Det	0	0	1	1
Eric Lacroix, Col-LA-NYR	0	0	1	1
Sasha Lakovic, NJ	0	0	1	1
Denny Lambert, Nsh	0	0	1	1
Steve Leach, Ott-Pho	0	0	1	1
Brad May, Van	0	0	1	1
* Jamal Mayers, StL	0	0	1	1
Rob Murray, Pho	0	0	1	1
David Oliver, Ott	0	0	1	1
Sean Pronger, Pit-NYR-LA	0	0	1	1
* Peter Ratchuk, Fla	0	0	1	1
Jeff Reese, Tor	0	0	1	1
Dave Reid, Dal	0	0	1	1
Jamie Rivers, StL	0	0	1	1
Craig Rivet, Mon	0	0	1	1
* Stacy Roest, Det	0	0	1	1
Brian Skrudland, Dal	0	0	1	1
Richard Smehlik, Buf	0	0	1	1
* Martin Sonnenberg, Pit	0	0	1	1
Sheldon Souray, NJ	0	0	1	1
* Jaroslav Spacek, Fla	0	0	1	1
Jason Strudwick, Van	0	0	1	1
Mike Sullivan, Pho	0	0	1	1
Jaroslav Svejkovsky, Was	0	0	1	1
Michal Sykora, TB	0	0	1	1
* Kimmo Timonen, Nsh	0	0	1	1
Darren Turcotte, Nsh	0	0	1	1
Tony Twist, StL	0	0	1	1
Igor Ulanov, Mon	0	0	1	1
Shaun Van Allen, Ott	0	0	1	1
* Mark Visheau, LA	0	0	1	1
Rhett Warrener, Fla-Buf	0	0	1	1

Postseason

	Player, Team	1st	2nd	3rd	Points
1.	Ed Belfour, Dal	4	4	1	33
2.	Dominik Hasek, Buf	3	4	0	27
3.	Patrick Roy, Col	2	4	2	24
4.	Curtis Joseph, Tor	2	4	0	22
5.	Peter Forsberg, Col	3	2	0	21
	Joe Nieuwendyk, Dal	2	3	2	21
7.	Al MacInnis, StL	2	3	1	20
8.	Pierre Turgeon, StL	3	1	0	18
9.	Tom Barrasso, Pit	2	2	1	17
10.	Mats Sundin, Tor	2	2	0	16
11.	Mike Modano, Dal	3	0	0	15
	Geoff Sanderson, Buf	3	0	0	15
	Martin Straka, Pit	2	1	2	15
14.	Jaromir Jagr, Pit	2	1	1	14
15.	Sergei Berezin, Tor	2	1	0	13
	Miroslav Satan, Buf	2	1	0	13
17.	Brett Hull, Dal	2	0	2	12
18.	Steve Yzerman, Det	2	0	1	11
19.	* Chris Drury, Col	2	0	0	10
	Petr Sykora, NJ	2	0	0	10
	Pat Verbeek, Dal	1	1	2	10
	Jere Lehtinen, Dal	0	3	1	10
23.	Anson Carter, Bos	1	1	1	9
	Mike Vernon, SJ	1	1	1	9
25.	Jason Allison, Bos	1	1	0	8
	Byron Dafoe, Bos	1	1	0	8
	Theo Fleury, Col	1	1	0	8
	Randy McKay, NJ	1	1	0	8
	Brendan Shanahan, Det	1	1	0	8
	Jason Woolley, Buf	1	1	0	8
	Mike Peca, Buf	0	2	2	8
32.	John Vanbiesbrouck, Phi	1	0	2	7
	Vaclav Varada, Buf	1	0	2	7
	Adam Deadmarsh, Col	0	2	1	7
35.	Pavol Demitra, StL	1	0	1	6
	* Milan Hejduk, Col	1	0	1	6
	Jamie Langenbrunner, Dal	1	0	1	6
	John LeClair, Phi	1	0	1	6
	Nicklas Lidstrom, Det	1	0	1	6
	Yanic Perreault, Tor	1	0	1	6
	* Erik Rasmussen, Buf	1	0	1	6
	Don Sweeney, Bos	1	0	1	6
	Garry Valk, Tor	1	0	1	6
44.	Curtis Brown, Buf	1	0	0	5
	Guy Carbonneau, Dal	1	0	0	5
	Louie DeBrusk, Pho	1	0	0	5
	Rob DiMaio, Bos	1	0	0	5
	Shane Doan, Pho	1	0	0	5
	Mike Keane, Dal	1	0	0	5
	* Alexander Korolyuk, SJ	1	0	0	5
	Kirk Maltby, Det	1	0	0	5
	Teppo Numminen, Pho	1	0	0	5
	Chris Osgood, Det	1	0	0	5
	Mike Ricci, SJ	1	0	0	5
	Gary Roberts, Car	1	0	0	5
	Joe Sakic, Col	1	0	0	5
	Sergei Samsonov, Bos	1	0	0	5
	Ray Sheppard, Car	1	0	0	5
	Dixon Ward, Buf	1	0	0	5
	Dimitri Yushkevich, Tor	1	0	0	5
	Derian Hatcher, Dal	0	1	2	5
	Wayne Primeau, Buf	0	1	2	5
63.	Per Axelsson, Bos	0	1	1	4
	Stu Barnes, Buf	0	1	1	4
	Sergei Fedorov, Det	0	1	1	4
	Adam Foote, Col	0	1	1	4
	Grant Fuhr, StL	0	1	1	4
	Valeri Kamensky, Col	0	1	1	4
	Nikolai Khabibulin, Pho	0	1	1	4

	Player, Team	1st	2nd	3rd	Points
	Bill Ranford, Det	0	1	1	4
	Steve Thomas, Tor	0	1	1	4
	Joe Thornton, Bos	0	1	1	4
73.	* Greg Andrusak, Pit	0	1	0	3
	Vincent Damphousse, SJ	0	1	0	3
	Eric Desjardins, Phi	0	1	0	3
	Karl Dykhuis, Phi	0	1	0	3
	Jeff Finley, StL	0	1	0	3
	Martin Gelinas, Car	0	1	0	3
	* Michal Handzus, StL	0	1	0	3
	* Jochen Hecht, StL	0	1	0	3
	Bobby Holik, NJ	0	1	0	3
	Brian Holzinger, Buf	0	1	0	3
	Paul Kariya, Anh	0	1	0	3
	Derek King, Tor	0	1	0	3
	Kris King, Tor	0	1	0	3
	Jason Marshall, Anh	0	1	0	3
	Scott Niedermayer, NJ	0	1	0	3
	Robert Reichel, Pho	0	1	0	3
	Ryan Smyth, Edm	0	1	0	3
	Marco Sturm, SJ	0	1	0	3
	Tim Taylor, Bos	0	1	0	3
	Rhett Warrener, Buf	0	1	0	3
	Todd Warriner, Tor	0	1	0	3
	Alexei Zhitnik, Buf	0	1	0	3
	Sergei Zubov, Dal	0	1	0	3
	Alexei Kovalev, Pit	0	0	3	3

	Player, Team	1st	2nd	3rd	Points
	Tommy Salo, Edm	0	0	3	3
98.	Rod Brind'Amour, Phi	0	0	2	2
	Martin Brodeur, NJ	0	0	2	2
	Steve Heinze, Bos	0	0	2	2
	Richard Matvichuk, Dal	0	0	2	2
102.	Daniel Alfredsson, Ott	0	0	1	1
	Bates Battaglia, Car	0	0	1	1
	Ken Belanger, Bos	0	0	1	1
	Lonny Bohonos, Tor	0	0	1	1
	Ray Bourque, Bos	0	0	1	1
	Rob Brown, Pit	0	0	1	1
	Chris Chelios, Det	0	0	1	1
	Wendel Clark, Det	0	0	1	1
	Craig Conroy, StL	0	0	1	1
	Geoff Courtnall, StL	0	0	1	1
	Dallas Drake, Pho	0	0	1	1
	Nelson Emerson, Ott	0	0	1	1
	Jeff Friesen, SJ	0	0	1	1
	Claude Lemieux, Col	0	0	1	1
	Patrick Marleau, SJ	0	0	1	1
	Shawn McEachern, Ott	0	0	1	1
	Aaron Miller, Col	0	0	1	1
	Rob Ray, Buf	0	0	1	1
	Pascal Rheaume, StL	0	0	1	1
	Scott Stevens, NJ	0	0	1	1
	Steve Sullivan, Tor	0	0	1	1
	Keith Tkachuk, Pho	0	0	1	1

1998-99 Debuts, First Goals, First Wins

Player	Team	First Career Game	First Career Goal	First Career Win
Antti Aalto	Anh	—	November 20 vs. Edmonton (Mikhail Shtalenkov)	—
Arron Asham	Mon	November 28 vs. Pittsburgh	—	—
Jean-Sebastian Aubin	Pit	October 21 at Tampa Bay	—	November 5 at Ottawa
Serge Aubin	Col	December 31 vs. NY Rangers	—	—
Phillipe Audet	Det	December 23 at Nashville	—	—
Ryan Bach	LA	October 23 at Tampa Bay	—	—
Lubos Bartecko	StL	November 28 vs. Washington	December 19 vs. Los Angeles (Jamie Storr)	—
Andrei Bashkirov	Mon	November 21 vs. Colorado	—	—
Ryan Bast	Phi	November 1 vs. Ottawa	—	—
Karel Betik	TB	February 15 at NY Islanders	—	—
Martin Biron	Buf	—	—	March 5 vs. Dallas
Jason Blake	LA	April 18 vs. St. Louis	April 18 vs. St. Louis (Jamie McLennan)	—
Brian Bonin	Pit	April 8 at Philadelphia	—	—
Dan Boyle	Fla	February 18 at St. Louis	February 24 vs. Philadelphia (John Vanbiesbrouck)	—
Eric Brewer	NYI	October 10 vs. Pittsburgh	November 5 vs. Carolina (Trevor Kidd)	—
Martin Brochu	Was	April 14 at Carolina	—	—
Brad Brown	Chi	—	January 17 vs. Phoenix (Jimmy Waite)	—
Jeff Buchanan	Col	November 6 at Edmonton	—	—
Zdeno Chara	NYI	—	January 29 vs. Phoenix (Jimmy Waite)	—
Daniel Cleary	Chi	—	October 19 at Montreal (Jose Theodore)	—
Sylvain Cloutier	Chi	March 10 vs. Nashville	—	—
Matt Cooke	Van	October 14 vs. Edmonton	—	—
Patrick Cote	Nsh	—	March 24 at Tampa Bay (Corey Schwab)	—
Johan Davidsson	Anh	October 10 at Washington	November 16 vs. Los Angeles (Manny LeGace)	—
Jonathan Delisle	Mon	October 21 vs. Ottawa	—	—
Xavier Delisle	TB	February 13 vs. San Jose	—	—
Andy Delmore	Phi	November 1 vs. Ottawa	—	—
Marc Denis	Col	—	—	January 4 vs. Montreal
Chris Drury	Col	October 10 vs. Ottawa	October 18 at Los Angeles (Stephane Fiset)	—
Jean-Pierre Dumont	Chi	November 12 vs. Toronto	March 6 at San Jose (Steve Shields)	—
Robert Esche	Pho	February 20 at Florida	—	—
Rico Fata	Cgy	October 9 vs. San Jose *	—	—
Maxim Galanov	Pit	—	November 3 vs. Philadelphia (John Vanbiesbrouck)	—
Tyrone Garner	Cgy	January 2 at Buffalo	—	—
Mike Gaul	Col	December 19 at San Jose	—	—
Denis Gauthier	Cgy	—	February 12 vs. Boston (Byron Dafoe)	—
Sean Gauthier	SJ	March 6 vs. Chicago	—	—
Jonathan Girard	Bos	October 18 at San Jose	—	—
Robb Gordon	Van	April 3 at San Jose	—	—
Jean-Luc Grand Pierre	Buf	February 19 vs. San Jose	—	—
Benoit Gratton	Was	—	April 7 vs. St. Louis (Grant Fuhr)	—
Josh Green	LA	October 10 at Edmonton	October 16 vs. Boston (Byron Dafoe)	—
Miloslav Guren	Mon	October 10 vs. NY Rangers	—	—
Sergey Gusev	Dal	—	November 20 vs. NY Islanders (Wade Flaherty)	—
Trevor Halverson	Was	October 13 vs. Detroit	—	—
Michal Handzus	StL	October 10 at Boston	November 28 vs. Washington (Olaf Kolzig)	—
Scott Hannan	SJ	October 9 at Calgary *	—	—
Tavis Hansen	Pho	—	February 2 vs. Calgary (Fred Brathwaite)	—
David Harlock	NYI	—	November 20 at Dallas (Ed Belfour)	—
Jochen Hecht	StL	January 13 at Buffalo	—	—
Shawn Heins	SJ	February 19 at Buffalo	—	—
Milan Hejduk	Col	October 10 vs. Ottawa	October 10 vs. Ottawa (Damian Rhodes)	—

Sami Helenius	TB	—	January 30 at Philadelphia (Ron Hextall)	—
Bryan Helmer	Pho	October 11 vs. Ottawa	—	—
Jay Henderson	Bos	October 28 at Montreal	—	—
Matt Henderson	Nsh	April 14 at Detroit	—	—
Matt Herr	Was	October 10 vs. Anaheim	October 18 at Tampa Bay (Bill Ranford)	—
Matt Higgins	Mon	—	October 28 vs. Boston (Byron Dafoe)	—
Josh Holden	Van	November 1 vs. Washington	March 10 at Anaheim (Guy Hebert)	—
Marian Hossa	Ott	—	December 9 at Florida (Sean Burke)	—
Jan Hrdina	Pit	October 10 at NY Islanders	November 5 at Ottawa (Damian Rhodes)	—
Victor Ignatjev	Pit	October 10 at NY Islanders	—	—
Brent Johnson	StL	February 15 vs. Vancouver	—	February 26 at Calgary
Ryan Johnson	Fla	—	April 7 vs. Boston (Byron Dafoe)	—
Olli Jokinen	LA	—	November 10 at Calgary (Jean-Sebastian Giguere)	—
Ty Jones	Chi	October 10 vs. New Jersey	—	—
Tomas Kaberle	Tor	October 10 vs. Detroit	October 23 at Detroit (Kevin Hodson)	—
Chris Kelleher	Pit	March 28 at Buffalo	—	—
Patrik Kjellberg	Nsh	—	October 24 at Chicago (Jeff Hackett)	—
Filip Kuba	Fla	April 9 at Buffalo	—	—
Oleg Kvasha	Fla	October 9 vs. Tampa Bay	October 16 at Buffalo (Dominik Hasek)	—
Antti Laaksonen	Bos	October 10 vs. St. Louis	October 16 at Los Angeles (Stephane Fiset)	—
Dan LaCouture	Edm	February 24 vs. Anaheim	—	—
Christian Laflamme	Chi	—	October 24 vs. Nashville (Eric Fichaud)	—
Georges Laraque	Edm	—	January 7 at Phoenix (Jimmy Waite)	—
Mario Larocque	TB	January 7 at Montreal	—	—
Mark Lawrence	NYI	—	December 20 at Phoenix (Nikolai Khabibulin)	—
Vincent Lecavalier	TB	October 9 at Florida	October 25 vs. Vancouver (Garth Snow)	—
Patrice Lefebvre	Was	December 19 at Pittsburgh	—	—
Manny LeGace	LA	October 21 at Florida	—	October 25 at Carolina
David Legwand	Nsh	April 17 vs. New Jersey	—	—
Trevor Letowski	Pho	January 1 vs. Dallas	January 13 vs. Pittsburgh (Tom Barrasso)	—
Fredrik Lindquist	Edm	October 10 vs. Los Angeles	—	—
Brad Lukowich	Dal	—	March 31 vs. Tampa Bay (Corey Schwab)	—
Craig MacDonald	Car	January 7 at Pittsburgh	—	—
John Madden	NJ	January 6 at NY Rangers	—	—
Manny Malhotra	NYR	October 10 at Montreal	October 20 vs. Edmonton (Bob Essensa)	—
Mike Maneluk	Phi	October 9 at NY Rangers	October 31 at NY Islanders (Tommy Salo)	—
Cameron Mann	Bos	—	February 21 at Chicago (Jocelyn Thibault)	—
Paul Mara	TB	April 17 at Florida	April 17 at Florida (Kirk McLean)	—
Chris Mason	Nsh	December 16 at Anaheim	—	—
Marquis Mathieu	Bos	October 28 at Montreal	—	—
Jamal Mayers	StL	—	February 8 at Florida (Sean Burke)	—
Jan Mertzig	NYR	October 9 vs. Philadelphia	—	—
Dave Morrisette	Mon	October 16 at Washington	—	—
Mark Mowers	Nsh	January 15 vs. Phoenix	—	—
Bill Muckalt	Van	October 12 vs. Los Angeles	October 20 at Carolina (Arturs Irbe)	—
Bryan Muir	Chi	—	January 30 at Vancouver (Garth Snow)	—
Tyson Nash	StL	April 3 vs. Dallas	—	—
Alain Nasreddine	Chi	October 10 vs. New Jersey	—	—
Rumun Ndur	NYR	—	March 15 vs. Washington (Olaf Kolzig)	—
Jan Nemecek	LA	November 7 vs. Dallas	April 12 at Nashville (Mike Dunham)	—
Eric Nickulas	Bos	January 7 vs. Toronto	—	—
Marcus Nilson	Fla	January 6 at Colorado	April 14 vs. Montreal (Frederic Chabot)	—
Peter Nordstrom	Bos	October 10 vs. St. Louis	—	—
Vladimir Orszagh	NYI	—	April 12 at New Jersey (Martin Brodeur)	—
Rich Parent	StL	—	—	January 26 at San Jose

Scott Parker	Col	November 28 vs. New Jersey	—	—
Mark Parrish	Fla	October 9 vs. Tampa Bay	October 9 vs. Tampa Bay (Bill Ranford)	—
Steve Passmore	Edm	February 24 vs. Anaheim	—	March 3 at Buffalo
Jean-Marc Pelletier	Phi	March 4 vs. Ottawa	—	—
Tom Poti	Edm	October 10 vs. Los Angeles	November 18 vs. Detroit (Chris Osgood)	—
Nolan Pratt	Car	—	November 29 vs. Anaheim (Guy Hebert)	—
Peter Ratchuk	Fla	December 16 vs. Pittsburgh	January 14 at Carolina (Arturs Irbe)	—
Marty Reasoner	StL	October 10 at Boston	October 16 at Detroit (Chris Osgood)	—
Todd Reirden	Edm	January 7 at Phoenix	January 10 at Anaheim (Dominic Roussel)	—
Damian Rhodes	Ott	—	January 2 vs. New Jersey (Martin Brodeur)	—
Byron Ritchie	Car	December 21 vs. Buffalo	—	—
Stacy Roest	Det	October 21 vs. Nashville	November 29 vs. San Jose (Mike Vernon)	—
Pavel Rosa	LA	December 17 vs. NY Islanders	December 17 vs. NY Islanders (Tommy Salo)	—
Mike Rosati	Was	November 7 at Ottawa	—	November 7 at Ottawa
Remi Royer	Chi	October 10 vs. New Jersey	—	—
Sami Salo	Ott	October 10 at Colorado	January 21 at Boston (Byron Dafoe)	—
Cory Sarich	Buf	February 9 at Ottawa	—	—
Andre Savage	Bos	January 7 vs. Toronto	January 18 vs. Nashville (Chris Mason)	—
Ryan Savoia	Pit	March 27 vs. Buffalo	—	—
Peter Schaefer	Van	November 7 vs. Nashville	November 12 at Calgary (Jean-Sebastian Giguere)	—
Vadim Sharifijanov	NJ	—	November 14 at Philadelphia (Ron Hextall)	—
Jon Sim	Dal	March 28 at Nashville	March 31 vs. Tampa Bay (Corey Schwab)	—
Andrei Skopintsev	TB	November 19 vs. Pittsburgh	February 5 vs. Anaheim (Guy Hebert)	—
Karlis Skrastinsh	Nsh	February 9 vs. Detroit	—	—
Pavel Skrbek	Pit	March 28 at Buffalo	—	—
Blake Sloan	Dal	March 12 vs. Anaheim	—	—
Brandon Smith	Bos	January 9 at Toronto	—	—
Dan Smith	Col	October 12 vs. Buffalo	—	—
Martin Sonnenberg	Pit	November 21 vs. Tampa Bay	February 5 vs. Florida (Kirk McLean)	—
Brent Sopel	Van	April 5 at Chicago	April 10 vs. Edmonton (Tommy Salo)	—
Lee Sorochan	Cgy	March 27 at Phoenix	—	—
Jaroslav Spacek	Fla	October 9 vs. Tampa Bay	October 24 at Washington (Rick Tabaracci)	—
Martin St. Louis	Cgy	October 9 vs. San Jose *	October 20 at Dallas (Roman Turek)	—
Andy Sutton	SJ	October 20 at Philadelphia	—	—
Petr Sykora	Nsh	April 14 at Detroit	—	—
Dean Sylvester	Buf	April 14 vs. New Jersey	—	—
Chris Taylor	Bos	—	October 28 at Montreal (Jose Theodore)	—
Dmitri Tertyshny	Phi	October 11 vs. Anaheim	February 16 at Phoenix (Nikolai Khabibulin)	—
Alexei Tezikov	Was	April 8 at New Jersey	—	—
Kimmo Timonen	Nsh	December 16 at Anaheim	March 26 at Florida (Sean Burke)	—
Patrick Traverse	Ott	—	January 2 vs. New Jersey (Martin Brodeur)	—
Pascal Trepanier	Anh	—	February 6 at St. Louis (Grant Fuhr)	—
Robert Valicevic	Nsh	December 8 vs. Edmonton	March 30 at Washington (Rick Tabaracci)	—
Herbert Vasiljevs	Fla	April 9 at Buffalo	—	—
Terry Virtue	Bos	January 16 vs. Tampa Bay	—	—
Mark Visheau	LA	—	November 19 vs. NY Rangers (Dan Cloutier)	—
Tomas Vokoun	Nsh	—	—	December 10 vs. San Jose
Brian Wesenberg	Phi	April 10 at Washington	—	—
Brian White	Col	November 21 at Montreal	—	—
Shane Willis	Car	February 5 at Washington	—	—
Clarke Wilm	Cgy	October 9 vs. San Jose *	November 19 at Montreal (Jeff Hackett)	—
Johan Witehall	NYR	January 30 at Detroit	—	—
Peter Worrell	Fla	—	February 8 vs. St. Louis (Rich Parent)	—

* game played in Japan

Glossary

Age

Listed through 12/31/99, or how old the player will be about midway through the 1999-2000 season.

Blowouts

Performance any time the score difference is five goals or greater.

Clutch

Performance in OT, and in the last 10 minutes of the 3rd period when the score difference is zero or one goal.

Days Rest

Number of days off between games.

Fights

Number of fighting majors.

Game Stars

At the conclusion of every NHL contest, the game's top three players are chosen (generally by the media). The game's best player is named the No. 1 Star, the second-best the No. 2 Star and the third-best the No. 3 Star.

Game Star Points

This is the sum total of all the Game Stars a player receives during a season, weighted by five points for a No. 1 Star, three for a No. 2 Star and one for a No. 3 Star.

Game-Tying Goal

The last goal scored in a tie game.

Game-Winning Goal

The goal that gives the winning team one more goal than its opponent eventually scores.

Goals Against Average

The number of non-empty net goals allowed by a goalie per 60 minutes. The formula is (Goals Allowed x 60)/Minutes.

Hat Trick

If a player scores three or more goals in a game, he is credited with a hat trick.

HHT Penalties

Number of Holding, Hooking or Tripping penalties. These are the penalties generally called when a player gets burned and is forced to use illegal measures to impede an opposing skater's progress.

Last 5 Min

Performance in last five minutes of any period, excluding overtime.

Losing

Performance while a player's team is losing.

National TV

Games broadcast on CBC, ESPN, ESPN2 or Fox.

Outstanding Effort

To be credited with an OE, a player must be his team's only goalie in the game and also fulfill at least one of the following two criteria:

a) Make 30 or more saves and allow 3 or fewer goals;

b) allow 0 goals.

A goalie *can* get a loss and an OE in the same game.

+/–(Plus/Minus)

A statistic to measure a player's overall contribution to his team. A skater gets a +1 if he is on the ice when his team scores an even strength or shorthanded goal. He gets a –1 if he is on the ice when his team allows an even strength or shorthanded goal. His overall +/– is a sum total of all his "plusses" and "minuses." Plus/minus is not figured in for power play goals, nor is it applied to goalies.

Points

The sum of goals and assists.

Special Team Index

This is a way of looking at a team's overall special teams performance. It takes a team's power play stats but factors in SH goals allowed, then looks at the team's penalty killing stats and factors in the number of SH goals scored. Those two numbers are then added together and multiplied by 100. The league average will always be 100.0. The formulas:

$$A = \frac{\text{PP Goals} - \text{SH Goals allowed}}{\text{PP Opportunities}}$$

$$B = \frac{\text{Times shorthanded} - \text{Opponent PP goals} + \text{Own SH Goals}}{\text{Times Shorthanded}}$$

Special Teams Index = (A + B) x 100

Start/Non Start

Goalie's performance based on whether or not he was the starting netminder.

Team Average Weight

This is the average weight of the team's non-goalies, factored by the number of games each player appears in.

Tied

Stats while the game is tied.

Times Pulled

This is the number of times a goalie is removed from a game and replaced by a different netminder. A goalie can only get a maximum of one TP per game.

Winning

Performance while a player's team is winning.

Winning Percentage

The formula for winning percentage is as follows:

$$\frac{(2 \times \text{wins}) + \text{ties}}{2\,(\text{wins} + \text{losses} + \text{ties})}$$

Abbreviations

Assists	A	Penalty Shot Situations	PenShot
Fighting Penalties	Fgt	Total Penalty Minutes	PIM
Goals	G	Penalty Killing	PK
Goals Against	GA	Plus/Minus	+/–
Goals Against Average	GAA	Power Play	PP
Games Played	GP	Power Play Goals Allowed	PPGA
Games Started	GS	Points	Pts
Game Tying Goals	GT	Roughing Penalties	Rgh
Game Winning Goals	GW	Shots on Goal	S
Hat Tricks	Hat	Shots Against	SA
Holding/Hooking/Tripping Penalties	HHT	Shorthanded Goals Allowed	SHGA
Losses	L	Shutouts	ShO
Major Penalties	Maj	Shots Faced by Goalie	Shots
Minutes Played	Min	Shooting Percentage	SPct
Minor Penalties	Mnr	Save Percentage	SvPct
Number of Penalties	Num	Ties	T
Outstanding Efforts	OE	Times Pulled	TP
Overtime Goals	OT	Wins	W
Points per Game	P/G		

Team Abbreviations

Mighty Ducks of Anaheim	Anh	New Jersey Devils	NJ
Boston Bruins	Bos	New York Islanders	NYI
Buffalo Sabres	Buf	New York Rangers	NYR
Calgary Flames	Cgy	Ottawa Senators	Ott
Carolina Hurricanes	Car	Philadelphia Flyers	Phi
Chicago Blackhawks	Chi	Phoenix Coyotes	Pho
Colorado Avalanche	Col	Pittsburgh Penguins	Pit
Dallas Stars	Dal	Quebec Nordiques	Que
Detroit Red Wings	Det	San Jose Sharks	SJ
Edmonton Oilers	Edm	St. Louis Blues	StL
Florida Panthers	Fla	Tampa Bay Lightning	TB
Hartford Whalers	Har	Toronto Maple Leafs	Tor
Los Angeles Kings	LA	Vancouver Canucks	Van
Minnesota North Stars	Min	Washington Capitals	Was
Montreal Canadiens	Mon	Winnipeg Jets	Wpg
Nashville Predators	Nsh		

About STATS, Inc.

STATS, Inc. is the nation's leading independent sports information and statistical analysis company, providing detailed sports services for a wide array of commercial clients.

As one of the fastest growing companies in sports, STATS provides the most up-to-the-minute sports information to professional teams, print and broadcast media, software developers and interactive service providers around the country. STATS was recently recognized as "One of Chicago's 100 most influential technology players" by *Crain's Chicago Business* and was one of 16 finalists for KPMG/Peat Marwick's Illinois High Tech Award. Some of our major clients are ESPN, the Associated Press, America Online, *The Sporting News*, Fox Sports, Electronic Arts, MSNBC, SONY and Topps. Much of the information we provide is available to the public via STATS On-Line. With a computer and a modem, you can follow action in the four major professional sports, as well as NCAA football and basketball. . . as it happens!

STATS Publishing, a division of STATS, Inc., produces 12 annual books, including the *Major League Handbook*, *The Scouting Notebook*, the *Pro Football Handbook*, the *Pro Basketball Handbook* and the *Hockey Handbook*. In 1998, we introduced two baseball encyclopedias, *The All-Time Major League Handbook* and *The All-Time Baseball Sourcebook*. Together they combine for over 5,000 pages of baseball history. We also published *Ballpark Sourcebook: Diamond Diagrams*, an authoritative look at major and minor league ballparks of today and yesterday. Also available is *From Abba Dabba to Zorro: The World of Baseball Nicknames*, a wacky look at monikers and their origins. These publications deliver STATS' expertise to fans, scouts, general managers and media around the country.

In addition, STATS offers the most innovative—and fun—fantasy sports games around, from *Bill James Fantasy Baseball* and *Bill James Classic Baseball* to *STATS Fantasy Football* and our newest game, *Diamond Legends Internet Baseball*. Check out our immensely popular Fantasy Portfolios and our great new web-based product, STATS Fantasy Advantage.

Information technology has grown by leaps and bounds in the last decade, and STATS will continue to be at the forefront as both a vendor and supplier of the most up-to-date, in-depth sports information available. For those of you on the information superhighway, you can always catch STATS in our area on America Online or at our Internet site.

For more information on our products, or on joining our reporter network, contact us on:

America Online — (Keyword: STATS)

Internet — www.stats.com

Toll Free in the USA at 1-800-63-STATS (1-800-637-8287)

Outside the USA at 1-847-470-8798

Or write to:

STATS, Inc.
8130 Lehigh Ave.
Morton Grove, IL 60053

Rookies of the Year!

(New titles from STATS)

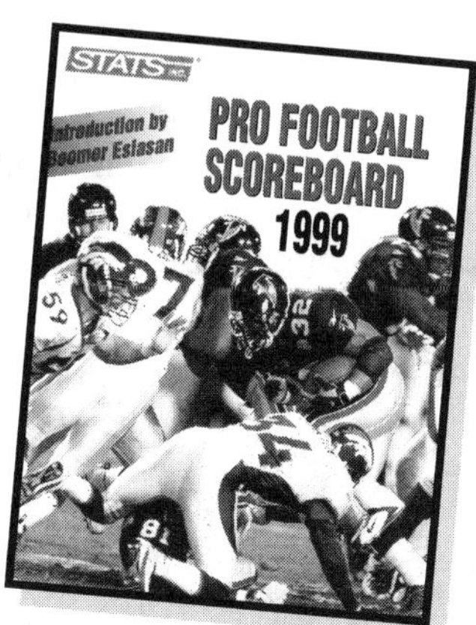

STATS Pro Football Scoreboard 1999

New from STATS, the *Pro Football Scoreboard* follows the lead of the popular *Baseball Scoreboard* and takes an insightful look into the NFL. Like the baseball edition, the *Pro Football Scoreboard* features creative articles and essays about every team that provide fans a greater understanding of all their favorite teams and players. General questions about the game and the league are asked and answered as well.

Actual questions include:

- Is Dan Marino the best player never to win a title?
- Which defenses say "No way" to the big play?
- Was Randy Moss' rookie season the best ever?

This unique book is a must have for all football fans. Become pigskin-smart!

Item #SF99, $19.95, Available Now!

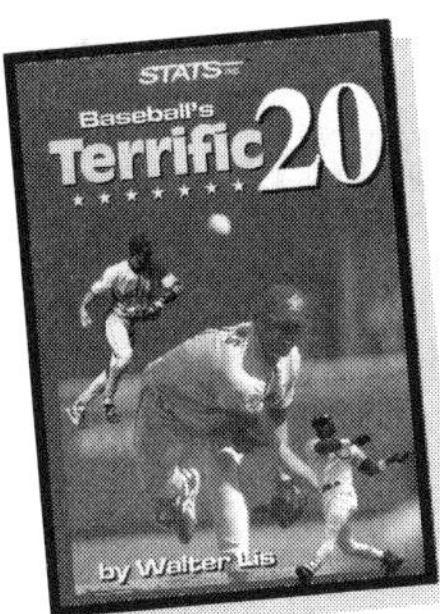

STATS Baseball's Terrific 20

- Perfect for baseball fans ages 7-12
- Featuring Mark McGwire, Ken Griffey Jr., Sammy Sosa and more
- Awesome color action photos of kids' favorite players
- Children will love the Triple Play Trivia Game

Item #KID1, $9.95, Available Now!

From Abba-Dabba To Zorro: The World of Baseball Nicknames

- STATS reveals the unusual and funny stories behind player nicknames
- Who are "Skoonj," "Big Six" and "The Tabasco Kid"?
- The All-Food Team, All-Body Parts Team and many more
- Baseball celebrities including Bob Costas, Ernie Harwell, and Jim Palmer pick their favorite baseball nicknames

Item #ABBA, $9.95, Available Now!

Order From STATS INC. Today!

SPORTS TEAM ANALYSIS & TRACKING SYSTEMS

1-800-63-STATS 847-470-8798 www.stats.com

Free First-Class Shipping for Books over $10

(Order Form in Back of This Book)

More of STATS' Baseball Lineup

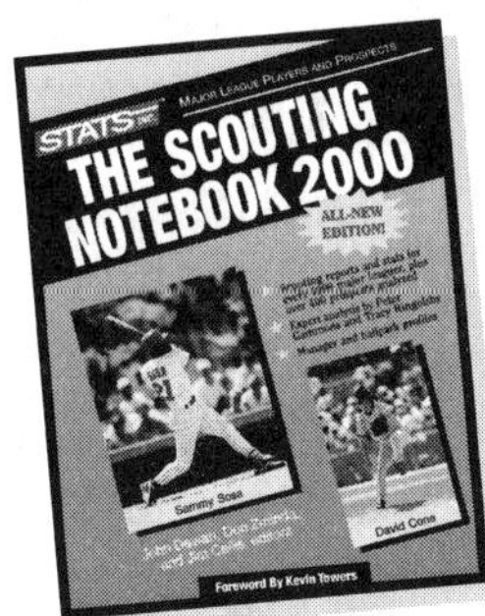

The Scouting Notebook 2000

- Extensive scouting reports on nearly 700 major league players
- Evaluations of more than 400 minor league prospects
- Expert analysis from nationally known writers
- Manager and ballpark profiles

"A phenomenal resource!"
—Jayson Stark, *Philadelphia Inquirer/Baseball America/ESPN*

Item #SN00, $19.95, Available January 2000!

Comb-bound #SC00, $24.95, Available January 2000!

STATS Minor League Scouting Notebook 2000

- Evaluation of every organization's top prospects
- Essays, stat lines and grades for more than 1,200 prospects
- Author John Sickels' exclusive list of baseball's top 50 prospects
- Recap of the 1999 amateur draft

"*STATS Minor League Scouting Notebook* is a valuable tool that serves as an excellent complement to our scouting reports."
—Greg Smith, Director of Scouting, Detroit Tigers

Item #MN00, $19.95, Available February 2000!

Bill James Presents:

STATS Batter Versus Pitcher Match-Ups! 2000

- Career stats for pitchers vs. batters (5+ career matchups)
- Leader boards and stats for all 1999 major league players
- Batter and pitcher performances for each major league ballpark

"No other book delivers as much info that's so easy to use."
—Peter Gammons, *Boston Globe/ESPN*

Item #BP00, $24.95, Available February 2000!

Order From STATS INC. Today!

SPORTS TEAM ANALYSIS & TRACKING SYSTEMS

1-800-63-STATS 847-470-8798 www.stats.com

Free First-Class Shipping for Books over $10

(Order Form in Back of This Book)

Clearing the Bases!

STATS Ballpark Sourcebook: Diamond Diagrams

- Analytical essays and historical summaries for more than 100 major and minor league parks
- Extensive playing characteristics, anecdotes and accounts of memorable players and events at each playing field
- Photos, charts and diagrams detail every featured ballpark

As Featured on the History Channel!

Item #BSDD, $24.95, Available Now!

STATS Baseball Scoreboard 2000

- STATS answers baseball's hottest questions
- Easy-to-understand charts help to answer the questions fans ask
- Intriguing questions on each and every team and the game in general
- Informative, entertaining and fun to read
- Leader boards and fielding stats

"A perfect companion to the baseball season."
—Alan Schwarz, *Baseball America*

Item #SB00, $19.95, Available March 2000!

STATS Diamond Chronicles 2000

- Essays, debates and discussions from the 1999 season and offseason
- In-depth, often-heated dialogue between well-known baseball analysts
- Learn what experts think of trades, managerial strategies, etc.
- Featuring commentary by Bill James, Don Zminda, John Dewan and others

Item #CH00, $19.95, Available March 2000!

Order From STATS INC. Today!
SPORTS TEAM ANALYSIS & TRACKING SYSTEMS

1-800-63-STATS 847-470-8798 www.stats.com

Free First-Class Shipping for Books over $10

(Order Form in Back of This Book)

Books (Free first-class shipping for books over $10)				
Qty	**Product Name**	**Item Number**	**Price**	**Total**
	STATS Major League Handbook 2000	HB00	$19.95	
	STATS Major League Handbook 2000 (Comb-bound)	HC00	$24.95	
	The Scouting Notebook 2000	SN00	$19.95	
	The Scouting Notebook 2000 (Comb-bound)	SC00	$24.95	
	STATS Minor League Handbook 2000	MH00	$19.95	
	STATS Minor League Handbook 2000 (Comb-bound)	MC00	$24.95	
	STATS Player Profiles 2000	PP00	$19.95	
	STATS Player Profiles 2000 (Comb-bound)	PC00	$24.95	
	STATS Minor League Scouting Notebook 2000	MN00	$19.95	
	STATS Batter Vs. Pitcher Match-Ups! 2000	BP00	$24.95	
	STATS Ballpark Sourcebook: Diamond Diagrams	BSDD	$24.95	
	STATS Baseball Scoreboard 2000	SB00	$19.95	
	STATS Diamond Chronicles 2000	CH00	$19.95	
	STATS Pro Football Handbook 1999	FH99	$19.95	
	STATS Pro Football Handbook 1999 (Comb-bound)	FC99	$24.95	
	STATS Pro Football Scoreboard 1999	SF99	$19.95	
	STATS Hockey Handbook 1999-2000	HH00	$19.95	
	STATS Pro Basketball Handbook 1999-2000	BH00	$19.95	
			Total	

Books Under $10 *(Please include $2.00 S&H for each book)*				
	From Abba-Dabba to Zorro: The World of Baseball Nicknames	ABBA	$ 9.95	
	STATS Baseball's Terrific 20	KID1	$ 9.95	
	STATS Player Projections Update 2000	PJUP	$ 9.95	
			Total	

Previous Editions *(Please circle appropriate years and include $2.00 S&H for each book)*				
	STATS Major League Handbook	'91 '92 '93 '94 '95 '96 '97 '98 '99	$ 9.95	
	The Scouting Notebook/Report	'94 '95 '96 '97 '98 '99	$ 9.95	
	STATS Player Profiles	'93 '94 '95 '96 '97 '98 '99	$ 9.95	
	STATS Minor League Handbook	'92 '93 '94 '95 '96 '97 '98 '99	$ 9.95	
	STATS Minor League Scouting Notebook	'95 '96 '97 '98 '99	$ 9.95	
	STATS Batter Vs. Pitcher Match-Ups!	'94 '95 '96 '97 '98 '99	$ 9.95	
	STATS Diamond Chronicles	'97 '98 '99	$ 9.95	
	STATS Baseball Scoreboard	'92 '93 '94 '95 '96 '97 '98 '99	$ 9.95	
	Pro Football Revealed: The100-Yard War	'94 '95 '96 '97 '98	$ 9.95	
	STATS Pro Football Handbook	'95 '96 '97 '98	$ 9.95	
	STATS Hockey Handbook	'96-97 '97-98 '98-99	$ 9.95	
	STATS Pro Basketball Handbook	'93-94 '94-95 '95-96 '96-97 '97-98 '98-99	$ 9.95	
			Total	

Fantasy Games				
	Bill James Classic Baseball	BJCB	$129.95	
	Bill James Fantasy Baseball	PJUP	$ 89.95	
	STATS Fantasy Football	SFF	$ 49.95	
			Total	

1st Fantasy Team Name (ex. Colt 45's):____________________
Which Fantasy Game is the team for?____________________

2nd Fantasy Team Name (ex. Colt 45's):____________________
Which Fantasy Game is the team for?____________________

Note: $1.00/player is charged for all roster moves and transactions.

Mail:
STATS, Inc.
8130 Lehigh Avenue
Morton Grove, IL 60053

Phone:
1-800-63-STATS
(847) 677-3322

Fax:
(847) 470-9140

Bill To:
Company____
Name____
Address____
City____________________ State____________ Zip____________
Phone (   )____________________ Ext.____ Fax (   )____________________
E-mail Address____

Ship To: *(Fill in this section if shipping address differs from billing address)*
Company____
Name____
Address____
City____________________ State____________ Zip____________
Phone (   )____________________ Ext.____ Fax (   )____________________
E-mail Address____

Method of payment:
All prices stated in U.S. Dollars

❑ Charge to my *(circle one)*
Visa
MasterCard
American Express
Discover

❑ Check or Money Order
(U.S. funds only)

Please include credit card number and expiration date with charge orders!

Exp. Date [/]
Month Year

X________________________________
Signature *(as shown on credit card)*

Totals for STATS Products:	
Books	
Books Under $10 *	
Prior Book Editions *	
order 2 or more books/subtract: $1.00/book *(Does not include prior editions)*	
Illinois residents add 8.5% sales tax	
Sub Total	

Shipping Costs		
Canada	**Add $3.50/book**	
*** All books under $10**	**Add $2.00/book**	
Fantasy Games		
Grand Total		

(No other discounts apply)

(Orders subject to availability)

Free First-Class Shipping for Books over $10